A COMPREHENSIVE GUIDE TO TOXICOLOGY IN NONCLINICAL DRUG DEVELOPMENT

Dedication

The book is dedicated to my Mom and Dad, to my siblings, my kids (Hani, Abdullahi, Suad and Issra) and to my dear Yasmine Allas

A COMPREHENSIVE GUIDE TO TOXICOLOGY IN NONCLINICAL DRUG DEVELOPMENT

SECOND EDITION

Edited by

ALI SAID FAQI, DVM, PhD, DABT
Fellow ATS Senior Director MPI Research, Mattawan, Michigan, United States
Wayne State University, Detroit, Michigan, United States

AMSTERDAM • BOSTON • HEIDELBERG • LONDON
NEW YORK • OXFORD • PARIS • SAN DIEGO
SAN FRANCISCO • SINGAPORE • SYDNEY • TOKYO
Academic Press is an imprint of Elsevier

Academic Press is an imprint of Elsevier
125 London Wall, London EC2Y 5AS, United Kingdom
525 B Street, Suite 1800, San Diego, CA 92101-4495, United States
50 Hampshire Street, 5th Floor, Cambridge, MA 02139, United States
The Boulevard, Langford Lane, Kidlington, Oxford OX5 1GB, United Kingdom

Notices
Knowledge and best practice in this field are constantly changing. As new research and experience broaden our understanding, changes in research methods, professional practices, or medical treatment may become necessary.

Practitioners and researchers must always rely on their own experience and knowledge in evaluating and using any information, methods, compounds, or experiments described herein. In using such information or methods they should be mindful of their own safety and the safety of others, including parties for whom they have a professional responsibility.

To the fullest extent of the law, neither the Publisher nor the authors, contributors, or editors, assume any liability for any injury and/or damage to persons or property as a matter of products liability, negligence or otherwise, or from any use or operation of any methods, products, instructions, or ideas contained in the material herein.

Library of Congress Cataloging-in-Publication Data
A catalog record for this book is available from the Library of Congress

British Library Cataloguing-in-Publication Data
A catalogue record for this book is available from the British Library

ISBN: 978-0-12-803620-4

For information on all Academic Press publications
visit our website at http://www.elsevier.com/

Working together
to grow libraries in
developing countries

www.elsevier.com • www.bookaid.org

Publisher: Mica Haley
Acquisition Editor: Kristine Jones
Editorial Project Manager: Molly McLaughlin
Production Project Manager: Laura Jackson
Designer: Victoria Pearson

Typeset by TNQ Books and Journals

Transferred to Digital Printing in 2017

Contents

1. Introduction
A.S. FAQI

I
DRUG DISCOVERY, METABOLISM, AND PHARMACOKINETICS

2. Critical Aspects of Integrated Nonclinical Drug Development: Concepts, Strategies, and Potential Pitfalls
E. KOCH AND S. PLASSMANN

3. ADME in Drug Discovery
J. VRBANAC AND R. SLAUTER

4. Pharmacokinetics and Toxicokinetics
M. SCHRAG AND K. REGAL

II
TOXICOLOGICAL STUDIES AND IND APPLICATION, AND FIRST IN-HUMAN CLINICAL TRIAL

5. Acute, Subacute, Subchronic, and Chronic General Toxicity Testing for Preclinical Drug Development
K.H. DENNY AND C.W. STEWART

6. Genetic Toxicology Testing
J. NICOLETTE

III

CLINICAL PATHOLOGY, HISTOPATHOLOGY, AND BIOMARKERS

VI

NONCLINICAL DEVELOPMENT OF MONOCLONAL ANTIBODIES, STEM CELLS, ONCOGENIC AND NON-ONCOGENIC DRUGS, OLIGONUCLEOTIDES, AND VACCINES

VII

SAFETY EVALUATION OF OCULAR DRUGS, BOTANICAL PRODUCTS, AND MEDICINAL DEVICES

VIII

PREDICTIVE TOXICOLOGY, TOXICOMETABOLOMICS, TOXICOGENOMICS, AND IMAGING

List of Contributors

M.M. Abdi   GlaxoSmithKline, Ware, Hertfordshire, United Kingdom

N.H. Al-Humadi   Food and Drug Administration (FDA), Silver Spring, MD, United States

C.J. Amuzie[1]   Janssen Pharmaceutical Research and Development, Spring House, PA, United States

S.M. Arnold   The Dow Chemical Company, Midland, MI, United States

M. Attar   Allergan, plc., Irvine, CA, United States

A.D. Aulbach   MPI Research, Mattawan, MI, United States

T.J. Baird   MPI Research, Mattawan, MI, United States

J.A. Brassard   Tustin, CA, United States

T.T.A. Chang   Van Andel Research Institute, Grand Rapids, MI, United States

D.B. Colagiovanni   Verde Research, Lakewood, CO, United States

J.B. Colerangle   Sanofi U.S. Inc., Bridgewater, NJ, United States

R. Collins   Biostat Consultants, Portage, MI, United States

J.A. Dalton   MPI Research, Mattawan, MI, United States

K.H. Denny   Teva Pharmaceuticals, West Chester, PA, United States

R.R. Dietert   Cornell University College of Veterinary Medicine, Ithaca, NY, United States

J.N. Duncan   Pfizer Inc., Groton, CT, United States

A.S. Faqi   MPI Research, Mattawan, MI, United States; Wayne State University, Detroit, MI, United States

J.T. Farmer   ICON Development Solutions, Whitesboro, NY, United States

M. Ferrell Ramos   AbbVie Inc., North Chicago, IL, United States

P.D. Forbes   Toxarus, Inc., Malvern, PA, United States

S. Frantz   MPI Research, Mattawan, MI, United States

L. Freshwater   Biostat Consultants, Portage, MI, United States

T.C. Fuchs   Merck KGaA, Darmstadt, Germany

D.V. Gauvin   MPI Research, Mattawan, MI, United States

N.S. Goud   Cook Medical, Bloomington, IN, United States

M.D. Green   Food and Drug Administration (FDA), Silver Spring, MD, United States

L. Guo   Metabolon Inc., Durham, NC, United States

S.P. Henry   Ionis Pharmaceuticals Inc., Carlsbad, CA, United States

P.G. Hewitt   Merck KGaA, Darmstadt, Germany

A. Hoberman   Charles River Laboratories, Horsham, PA, United States

J.Y. Hui   Celgene Corporation, Summit, NJ, United States

C. Johnson   Toxicology Consultant, Hamilton, VA, United States

J.W. Kille   J.W. Kille Associates, Stanton, NJ, United States

A.S. Kim   Theravance Biopharma, South San Francisco, CA, United States

T.W. Kim   Ionis Pharmaceuticals Inc., Carlsbad, CA, United States

E. Koch   NonClinical Safety Consulting LLC, Denver, CO, United States

D. Kornbrust   Preclinsight, Reno, NV, United States

D.B. Learn   Charles River Laboratories, Horsham, PA, United States

E. Lewis   Charles River Laboratories, Horsham, PA, United States

S. Matsumoto   Allergan, plc., Irvine, CA, United States

D.L. McCormick   IIT Research Institute, Chicago, IL, United States

O.R. Mendes   Eurofins US, Dayton, OH, United States

K.B. Meyer-Tamaki   Sangamo BioSciences Inc., Richmond, CA, United States

I. Mikaelian   Hoffmann-La Roche, Inc., Nutley, NJ, United States

M.V. Milburn   Metabolon Inc., Durham, NC, United States

J. Nicolette   AbbVie, Inc., North Chicago, IL, United States

P. Nugent   Pfizer Inc., Groton, CT, United States

H.H. Oh   Boehringer Ingelheim Pharmaceuticals, Inc., Ridgefield, CT, United States

L. Oyejide   Regeneron Pharmaceuticals, Inc., Tarrytown, NY, United States

S. Plassmann   PreClinical Safety (PCS) Consultants Ltd, Basel, Switzerland

K. Regal   ProPharma Services, LLC, Westminster, CO, United States

D. Rehagen   MPI Research, Mattawan, MI, United States

J.C. Resendez   Charles River Laboratories, Ashland, OH, United States

[1]The author transitioned from MPI Research, Mattawan, MI, United States during the publication process.

J.C. Rowlands   The Dow Chemical Company, Midland, MI, United States

J.A. Ryals   Metabolon Inc., Durham, NC, United States

C.P. Sambuco   Charles River Laboratories (Retired), Horsham, PA, United States

M. Schrag   ProPharma Services, LLC, Westminster, CO, United States

R.S. Settivari   The Dow Chemical Company, Midland, MI, United States

R. Slauter   MPI Research, Mattawan, MI, United States

P.J. Spencer   The Dow Chemical Company, Midland, MI, United States

M.E. Stern   ImmunEyeZ LLC, Mission Viejo, CA, United States

C.W. Stewart   MPI Research, Mattawan, MI, United States

D. Stump   WIL Research Laboratories, LLC, Ashland, OH, United States

S. Surapaneni   Celgene Corporation, Summit, NJ, United States

M. Templin   Preclinical, SNBL USA, Everett, WA, United States

G.L. Truisi   Merck KGaA, Darmstadt, Germany

C. Vangyi   Glaukos, Laguna Hills, CA, United States

T. Vidmar   Biostat Consultants, Portage, MI, United States

J. Vrbanac   MPI Research, Mattawan, MI, United States

Z.J. Wang   Advance Medical Systems Limited and MITRO Biotech., China

L.O. Whiteley   Pfizer Inc., Cambridge, MA, United States

D.M. Wilson   The Dow Chemical Company, Midland, MI, United States

J.S. Yan   Hutchison MediPharma Ltd., Shanghai, China

M.J. York   Bedfordshire, United Kingdom

H.S. Younis   NGM Biopharmaceuticals, South San Francisco, CA, United States

Foreword

When the initial edition of *A Comprehensive Guide to Toxicology in Preclinical Drug Development* was published in 2013, I identified the relevance of this new text for those involved in the many different areas of the drug and device development process designed to bring new products into the marketplace, and I indicated that it should become almost mandatory as a resource for those professionals involved in those areas of development. Based on the acceptance of that text by those professionals and with the speed and pace of the science involved in drug and device development, it is not surprising that a second edition is needed so soon after the first. The world we live in seems to change by the minute and we can find ourselves suddenly involved with dangers that we had not contemplated, such as the spread of the deadly Ebola virus in Africa and the nearly worldwide spread of the Zika virus, which has shown to cause severe fetal brain defects such as microcephaly in newborn infants. In response to the Ebola outbreak, we saw a sudden surge by pharmaceutical companies to initiate drug development programs to create vaccines and treatment therapies against this deadly disease. Although the threat of the Zika virus is more recent, we should expect to see the same amount of resources and energy being spent by those in the drug development industry in response to this threat. In each of these cases and in those unknown cases that will occur at some time in the future, the information and guidance of the scientific experts contributing their experience and expertise to the second edition will allow those in the development of new drugs and devices to chart a more predictable and less risky course.

In my opinion, the initial edition of *A Comprehensive Guide to Toxicology in Preclinical Drug Development* quickly became a signal scientific text within the drug development community and remains one of the best, if not the best, comprehensive text currently published dealing with preclinical testing. Its strength lies in its broad yet detailed inclusion of the numerous issues involved with bringing a new drug or device to the marketplace, which includes chapters on toxicogenomics, predictive toxicology, and imaging as new tools to understanding toxicity, and its comprehensiveness in discussing issues associated with both small- and large-molecule compounds. As compared to the 36 chapters in the initial edition, this edition has 35 chapters. Several chapters have either been combined or were identified as being covered in other existing chapters, and most chapters have been revised and updated to reflect the most current state of that particular area of discussion, which is specifically seen in the chapter on juvenile toxicity testing. Four new chapters have been added and I believe that each of these new chapters add relevant and significant completeness to the text. These chapters deal with concepts, strategies, and pitfalls of nonclinical drug development; biomarkers; nonclinical safety assessment of cell-based therapies; and medical devices. Furthermore, the organization of the text has been reordered with a more orderly presentation of the different topics, leading to a better flow among the chapters than in the original edition.

I remain honored that my colleague, Dr. Ali Faqi, has again asked me to write the foreword to this impressive scientific text. Having worked together for over 13 years, I remain fully impressed with his scientific knowledge and personal and professional qualities, and I consider it a rare gift that I can call him my friend.

David G. Serota, Ph.D., D.A.B.T.
Senior Vice President and Director of Research
MPI Research
President, American College of Toxicology - 2012

1

Introduction

A.S. Faqi

Drug development is defined as the entire process of bringing a new drug or device to the market. It involves discovery and synthesis, nonclinical development (chemical testing, biological testing, pharmacology, toxicology, safety, etc.), clinical development (Phase I–III), regulatory review, marketing approval, market launch, and postmarketing development (Fig. 1.1).

The process of drug discovery comprises research on (1) target identification, (2) target prioritization/validation, (3) lead identification, and (4) lead optimization.

A range of techniques is used to identify and isolate individual drug targets. The target identification process isolates drugs that have various interactions with the disease targets and might be beneficial in the treatment of a specific disease. A poor understanding of the molecular mechanisms underlying both disease progression and drug action is one of the major challenges of drug discovery as insufficient drug specificity and side effects are often discovered during the late stages of drug development or even after marketing approval [1]. A "target" can be either proteins physically binding to the drug or to proteins that are only functionally related. A decent target needs to be efficacious, safe, meet clinical and commercial needs, and, above all, be "druggable" [2]. On binding, a druggable target elicits a biological response that may be measured both in vitro and in vivo as the putative drug molecule, be that of a small molecule, or biologicals is accessible to the target [2].

Identification of drug target is followed by a target prioritization/validation phase, during which experimental tests are conducted to confirm that interactions with the drug target are associated with the desired change in the behavior of diseased cells. It is the process by which the predicted molecular target of a drug is verified. The following criteria serve as decision-making tools prior to advancement beyond target validation [3]:

1. Known molecules modulating target
2. The target has a history of success
3. Genetic confirmation
4. Availability of known animal models
5. Availability of low-throughput target validation assay that represents biology
6. Intellectual property of the target
7. Determination of the marketability of the target

The next phase following target validation is obviously the lead identification. Identification of lead compounds are sometimes developed as collections, or libraries, of individual molecules that possess the properties required in a new drug. Once the lead is identified, experimental testing is then performed on each of the molecules to confirm their effect on the drug target. This progresses further to lead optimization. Lead optimization studies are conducted on *animals* or in vitro or modulation of a desired target in disease patients [2] to compare various lead compounds, to determine how they are metabolized, and what affect they might induce in the body. The information obtained from lead optimization studies helps scientists in the pharmaceutical industry sort out the compounds with the greatest potential to be developed into a safe and effective drug [2].

Toxicology studies in the drug discovery process are conducted to evaluate the safety of potential drug candidates. This is accomplished using relevant animal models and validated procedures. The ultimate goal is to translate the animal responses into an understanding of the risk for human subjects. This demands additional studies and investment earlier in the candidate evaluation, coupled with an arduous selection process for drug candidates and a speedy kill to avoid spending money and time on compounds that would likely fail in development.

Even after a successful drug candidate for a disease target is identified, drug development still faces enormous challenges, which many drugs fail because of their unacceptable toxicity. The new paradigm in drug discovery should consider a vigorous means of identifying issues related to toxicity early in the discovery process

A Comprehensive Guide to Toxicology in Nonclinical Drug Development, Second Edition
http://dx.doi.org/10.1016/B978-0-12-803620-4.00001-3

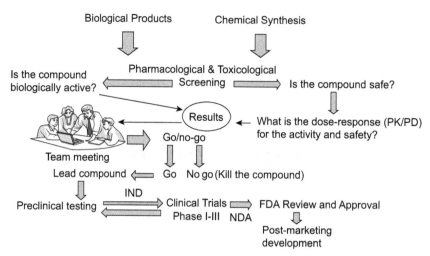

FIGURE 1.1 Drug development and nonclinical testing process.

where the cost of a failed drug is far less than in late drug development stages [4].

The successful drug candidate undergoes a nonclinical safety-testing program. Key factors affecting the type of nonclinical testing include the chemical structure, nature of the compound (small molecules or biologics), proposed human indication, target population, method of administration, and duration of administration (acute, chronic). During nonclinical drug testing, the toxicity and pharmacologic effects of the new chemical entity (NCE) are evaluated by in vitro and in vivo laboratory animal testing. An investigations on drug absorption and metabolism, toxicity of the drug's metabolites, and the speed with which the drug and its metabolites are excreted from the body. Investigational new drug application (IND)-enabling safety studies include acute toxicity of the drug in at least two species of animals, and short-term toxicity studies ranging from 2 weeks to 1 month, genotoxicity, safety pharmacology, and bioanalytical. Furthermore, post-IND nonclinical testing may include subchronic, chronic toxicity, developmental, and reproductive toxicology and carcinogenicity.

It is estimated that it takes 10–12 years to develop and test a new drug before it can be approved for clinical use. This estimate includes early laboratory and animal testing as well as later clinical trials using human subjects. A new study by the Tufts Center for the Study of Drug Development estimates the cost of developing a new drug that gains marketing approval to be around $2.6 billion [5]. Safety issues are the leading cause of attrition at all stages of the drug development process. It is important, however, to understand that the majority of safety-related attrition occurs preclinically, suggesting that approaches that could

identify "predictable" nonclinical safety liabilities earlier in the drug development process could lead to the design and/or selection of better drug candidates with increased chances of succeeding for marketing approval [6]. An overview of drug discovery screening assay is shown in Fig. 1.2 [2].

Toxicology testing in animals traditionally focus on phenotypic changes in an organism that result from exposure to the drug; therefore efficient and accurate approaches to assess toxicological effects of drugs on living systems are still less developed. One of the key factors used for a go/no-go decision-making for an NCE relies on the early knowledge of any potential toxic effect. Thus the traditional approach based on the determination of the No-observed-adverse-effect-level (NOAEL) is far from accurate. One of the limitations of this approach is that it may fail to detect adverse effects that manifest at low frequencies.

Indeed, in the past quarter of a century new technologies have emerged that have improved current approaches and are leading to novel predictive approaches for studying disease risk. Increased understanding of the mode of action and the use of scientific tools to predict toxicity is expected to reduce the attrition rate of NCE and thus decrease the cost of developing new drugs. In fact, most big pharmaceutical companies are now using improved model systems for predicting potential drug toxicity, both to decrease the rate of drug-related adverse reactions and to reduce attrition rates. A wide range of biological assay platforms, including toxicogenomics and metabolomics employed in constructing predictive toxicity, are included as separate chapters in this book. The discipline of toxicogenomics is defined as the application of global mRNA, protein and metabolite analysis-related technologies to study the effects of

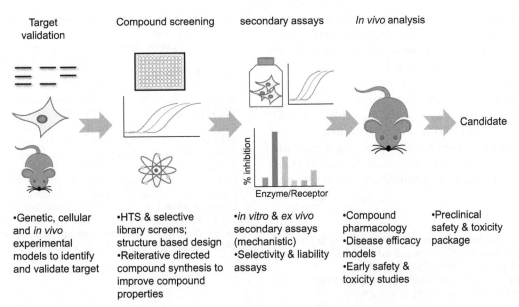

Target
validation

Compound screening

secondary assays

In vivo analysis

Candidate

% inhibition

Enzyme/Receptor

•Genetic, cellular
and *in vivo*
experimental
models to identify
and validate target

•HTS & selective
library screens;
structure based design
•Reiterative directed
compound synthesis to
improve compound
properties

•*in vitro* & *ex vivo*
secondary assays
(mechanistic)
•Selectivity & liability
assays

•Compound
pharmacology
•Disease efficacy
models
•Early safety &
toxicity studies

•Preclinical
safety & toxicity
package

FIGURE 1.2 Overview of drug discovery screening assay. *Hughes JP, Rees S, Kalindjian SB, Philpott KL. Principles of early drug discovery. Br J Pharmacol 2011;162(6):1239–49.*

hazards on organisms [7]. Examining the patterns of altered molecular expression caused by specific exposures can reveal how toxicants act and cause their effect. Identification of toxicity pathways and development of targeted assays to systematically assess potential mode of actions allow for a more thorough understanding of safety issues. Indeed, there is high expectation that toxicogenomics in drug development will predict/better assess potential drug toxicity, and hence reduce failure rates.

In addition metabolomics, a more recent discipline related to proteomics and genomics, uses metabolic signatures to determine the molecular mechanisms of drug actions and predict physiological toxicity. The technology involves rapid and high throughput characterization of the small molecule metabolites found in an organism, and is increasingly gaining attention in nonclinical safety testing. Moreover, the introduction of pharmacogenetics assays has also brought success in drug development in terms of predictability of safety and efficacy. There is a need felt for pharmacogenomics studies, where the effects of multiple genes are assessed with the study of entire genome [8].

Nonclinical safety data are used to select doses in Phase I clinical trial, to provide information on potential side effects, and thus minimize the risk of serious side effects in clinical trials. It also identifies potential target organs and determines toxicity endpoints not amenable to evaluation in clinical trials, such as genetic toxicity, developmental toxicity, and carcinogenicity.

This second edition of the book *Comprehensive Guide to Toxicology in Nonclinical Drug Development* has been reorganized and chapters updated and expanded to include pitfalls in drug development, medical devices, safety assessment of stem cells, and more. Each chapter is carefully crafted to reflect current knowledge and latest research reports/breakthroughs in the field of drug development. The book encompasses series of chapters regrouped into eight units, namely (1) drug discovery, metabolism, and pharmacokinetics, (2) toxicological studies and IND application and first in-human clinical trial, (3) clinical pathology, histopathology, and biomarkers, (4) biostatistics, regulatory toxicology and role of study directors, (5) specialty route of administration, (6) nonclinical development of monoclonal antibodies, stem cells, oncogenic, and nononcogenic drugs, oligonucleotides, and vaccines, (7) safety evaluation of ocular drugs, botanical products, and medicinal devices, and (8) predictive toxicology, toxicometabolomics, toxicogenomics, and imaging.

The book is considered to be a comprehensive guide for toxicologists, regulatory scientists, students, and academics interested in the drug development process and safety testing. It provides a wealth of knowledge of the complex and highly interlinked disciplines of drug development especially in areas of nonclinical safety assessments, absorption, distribution, metabolism, and excretion, regulatory guidelines and submissions, potential pitfalls, biomarkers, predictive toxicology tools, and imaging, which are keys to planning and executing successful drug development projects.

Last but not least, we want to emphasize that one of the biggest strengths of this book comes from the contributors, who are considered to be leading experts in their respective field. In essence, scientific knowledge gained through experience in the field truly shapes personal lives, hence reinforcing the individual intellect, and wisdom. My expectation is that the second edition will be equally successful as the previous edition if not more.

In conclusion, I would like to thank the contributors for their commitment, hard work, and on time delivery of a high-quality product. Likewise, my deepest gratitude and appreciations goes to Kristine Jones, Molly M. McLaughlin, and Laura Jackson and all the production team at Elsevier.

References

[1] Sivachenko AY, Yuryev A. Pathway analysis software as a tool for drug target selection, prioritization and validation of drug mechanism. Expert Opin Ther Targets 2007;11(3):411–21.

[2] Hughes JP, Rees S, Kalindjian SB, Philpott KL. Principles of early drug discovery. Br J Pharmacol 2011;162(6):1239–49.

[3] Hughes M, Inglese J, Kurtz A, Andalibi A, Patton L, Austin C, et al. Early drug discovery and development guidelines: for academic researchers, collaborators, and start-up companies. In: Sittampalam GS, Coussens NP, Nelson H, et al., editors. A assay guidance manual. 2004. [Bethesda (MD)].

[4] McKim JM. Building a tiered approach to in vitro predictive toxicity screening: a focus on assays with in vivo relevance. Comb Chem High Throughput Screen 2010;13(2):188–206.

[5] http://csdd.tufts.edu/news/complete_story/pr_tufts_csdd_2014_cost_study [accessed 26.02.16].

[6] Kramer JA, Sagartz JE, Morris DL. The application of discovery toxicology and pathology towards the design of safer pharmaceutical lead candidates. Nat Rev Drug Discov 2007;6(8):636–49.

[7] Hamadeh HK, Amin RP, Paules RS, Afshari CA. An overview of toxicogenomics. Curr Issues Mol Biol 2002;4:45–56.

[8] Surendiran A, Pradhan SC, Adithan C. Role of pharmacogenomics in drug discovery and development. Indian J Pharmacol 2008;40(4):137–43.

DRUG DISCOVERY, METABOLISM, AND PHARMACOKINETICS

Critical Aspects of Integrated Nonclinical Drug Development: Concepts, Strategies, and Potential Pitfalls

E. Koch, S. Plassmann

A Comprehensive Guide to Toxicology in Nonclinical Drug Development, Second Edition
http://dx.doi.org/10.1016/B978-0-12-803620-4.00002-5

INTRODUCTION

The development of a new drug is a complicated, long, and expensive process and confronts the experts in all disciplines involved with unexpected challenges during the complex process it takes to bring new medicines in a variety of indications to the market. These challenges require integration into what proves to be a demanding journey through often unknown territories that need to be explored as the route unfolds itself on the way.

From understanding a disease and identifying a "druggable" target to bringing a safe and effective new treatment to patients take on average 10–15 years. According to DiMasi et al. [39] the cost to develop and get marketing approval for a new drug is $2.6 billion. This figure includes the price of failure and opportunity costs. The costs have more than tripled from the $800 million estimated for the year 2000 [38]. Of every 5000 to 10,000 compounds entering the research and development pipeline only one may receive approval.

The goal of nonclinical (or preclinical) development is to build a bridge from "bench to bedside," ie, to characterize molecules—small or large—in a step-wise process to support specific phases of clinical development, ie, to generate knowledge providing the basis for the conduct of defined clinical studies of a given scope and duration as well as the marketing authorization for pharmaceuticals. The master guideline describing this process is ICH M3(R2) [90].

However, potential obstacles hindering drug development at any stage are numerous and during each step the unexpected has to be expected. Critical questions need to be addressed along the way, such as what do we understand at a specific moment in time when we are facing an issue? Will this issue be a "show stopper" or only make us take a more complicated but still potentially successful route? How can we mitigate potential risks in humans? How reliably can we translate data from animals or clinical studies to the patient target population? How can we responsibly balance potential risks against essential benefits? How certain can we be as to whether we have asked the right questions along the way? Are we sure we really understand the answers to those questions?

In this chapter, we present historical examples from medicines during different phases of drug development highlighting general or specific issues, that, in turn, may have led either to modifications of general requirements for the nonclinical characterization of investigational medicinal products [IMPs—this term is used in the European Union (EU)]/investigational new drugs (INDs—this term is used in the United States) or to modifications of the requirements for risk management and mitigation in humans or to a combination of both. Certain issues are

recognized by the scientific community as unresolved at present, and we must understand ourselves to be inquirers that often will not understand the full picture at a given moment in time as is the intrinsic nature of medicine as an empiric discipline. We will also provide context as to how predictive nonclinical studies for human risk assessment are in certain areas, discuss typical issues that may arise during nonclinical development, and how such issues may be addressed. However, given the complexity of this area, this chapter will only be able to highlight selected aspects that may serve as examples to help understand how the main objectives of nonclinical development can be achieved, the final aim of which is to arrive at a robust risk–benefit assessment to either support the registration of new medications often with a high unmet medical need or to provide the basis for a decision to discontinue programs with an unfavorable safety profile.

TARGET IDENTIFICATION AND VALIDATION

The healthcare community is asking for novel approaches to treat patients, with special emphasis on indications with a high unmet medical need, such as oncology or diseases affecting the central nervous system (CNS) as well as highly complex metabolic or autoimmune diseases. In recent decades, a number of medicines have been successfully developed for many serious conditions, but further improvement has been difficult to achieve and treatment often remains unsatisfactory. Substantial progress often requires truly novel approaches, which includes the need for the identification of new targets to arrive at genuine innovations. In identifying those novel targets the pharmaceutical industry also relies on basic research conducted in academia and published in the literature. The scientific community assumes that results published in a peer-reviewed journal can be taken for granted. However, Prinz et al. [158] reported that validation projects that were started in-house based on published data often could not reproduce published key results. The authors collected data from 67 projects (47 oncology, 12 women's health, and 8 cardiovascular). In only ~20–25% of the projects relevant published data were in line with in-house findings. In almost two-thirds of the projects, there were inconsistencies between published data and in-house data that either considerably prolonged the duration of the target validation process or, in most cases, resulted in termination of the projects because the evidence generated for the therapeutic hypothesis was insufficient to justify further investment into these projects. Similarly, Begley and Ellis [8] were not able to reproduce 47 of 53 landmark publications on basic cancer research published in top journals from reputable laboratories. Prinz et al. [158] concluded that data on potential drug targets should be viewed with caution, and underline the importance of confirmatory validation studies for pharmaceutical companies and academia before larger investments are made in assay development, high-throughput screening campaigns, lead optimization, and animal testing.

Another important consideration regarding the selection of suitable targets is their specificity in relation to binding molecules, and vice versa. Lounkine et al. [126] have reported on the application of an in silico computational strategy to assess the potential of several 100 marketed drugs regarding their liability to bind to previously unrecognized targets and their possible relevance to the development of known adverse clinical side effects. The aim was to discover unintended secondary ("off") targets through which these drugs may exert adverse drug reactions and to propose tools that may supplement empirical data. Indeed, they identified COX-1 as an off-target for chlorotrianisene, a synthetic estrogen associated with abdominal pain as a side effect. The clinical relevance of this inhibition was demonstrated in whole-human blood platelet aggregation assays. The authors proposed, as a conclusion, that their approach may be useful to predict toxicological liability at the stage of drug discovery. Classical examples for medications that were withdrawn from the market due to off-target toxicity include fen-phen and terfenadine. The former was found to be associated with valvular heart disease (VHD). Rothman et al. [168] concluded that "serotonic medications, which do not activate 5-HT$_{2B}$ receptors, are unlikely to produce VHD." It appears that this liability is brought about by the established role of serotonin as a mitogen [168,177,201], but the specific binding receptor, not surprisingly, mediates the critical effect. In the case of terfenadine, the well-known liability to prolong the QT interval [169] is mediated through its binding to the hERG (human ether-à-go-go related gene) encoded protein K$_v$11.1, which is the alpha subunit of a potassium ion channel [170] and is also referred to as an hERG channel. In addition, the active metabolite of terfenadine, terfenadine carboxylate, does not show this liability. The case of terfenadine (marketed eg, as Seldane in the United States) led to the development of applicable guidelines (see later) to characterize and manage risk associated with this type of cardiotoxicity. With this molecule, two factors were involved in its cardiotoxicity, ie, binding of the prodrug terfenadine only to the hERG channel as well as an alteration of the metabolic state to increase systemic exposures to the parent drug, terfenadine itself, rather than the active metabolite that does not have this liability [169]. Since then, screening for hERG channel binding has become an integral part of early drug safety assessment, and the field of safety pharmacology has developed into a mature discipline.

Molecules with high target promiscuity or targets with high binding promiscuity or a combination of both intrinsically increase the risk of off-target toxicity at concentrations that may be clinically relevant. Therefore an integrated approach from discovery to the development of new medicines on the market will aid in the selection of new molecules and targets that a priori have a lower liability and therefore may result in more favorable safety profiles.

Biopharmaceuticals, in general, have lower intrinsic liability than small molecules to exert off-target effects and experience to-date indicates that their safety profile will often be dominated by on-target effects also referred to as "exaggerated pharmacology." The intrinsic advantage of this propensity is obvious, as it will allow predicting the occurrence of side effects from exposures at the target, which can be achieved by pharmacodynamic–pharmacokinetic modeling (PK/PD). However, with increasing knowledge about the design of protein scaffolds, there have also been reports about the potential for off-target toxicities for biopharmaceuticals [15,79,82,172], and given the diversity and nature of this class of compounds, it is increasingly acknowledged that biopharmaceuticals need to be carefully evaluated for their potential to cause adverse effects that are not a function of their primary mode of action.

PRINCIPAL ASPECTS OF PRECLINICAL TOXICOLOGY TESTING

Before a new compound can enter clinical trials for the first time the side-effect profile has to be characterized in initial nonclinical safety studies in vitro and in vivo. Those studies are aimed at identifying potential target organs of toxicity, contributing to determining the starting dose in first in human (FIH) trials, and guiding the monitoring program in clinical studies. To support longer clinical studies, the duration of the preclinical studies has to be extended. Nonclinical and clinical development remain closely intertwined from the early beginning until application for a marketing authorization.

Dose Selection for Toxicity Studies with Small Molecules

The first in vivo studies are preliminary dose-range-finding studies in a small number of animals. Based on the results generated applicable doses are selected for the first GLP (good laboratory practice) studies, usually 4-week toxicity studies in rodents and nonrodents. These first studies are intended to characterize the general safety profile including the identification of potential target organs of toxicity and thereby to contribute to setting the starting dose in the first human trial.

A common challenge during this early stage of preclinical development is the availability of sufficient drug substance at the required quality. Limitations in this regard may lead to the conduct of inadequate dose-range finding studies and the selection of doses that fail to show an MTD (maximum tolerated dose) in the subsequent GLP studies. For small molecules, however, it is mandatory to characterize the dose range in its entirety, comprising the no observed adverse effect level (NOAEL) up to the MTD over the duration of the study tested [90]. This principle is key to the characterization of the safety profile of small molecules, although it is not essential to demonstrate the MTD in every study. If no MTD can be demonstrated, a limit dose of 1000 mg/kg/day is usually considered an acceptable high dose in all species provided a mean exposure margin of 10-fold the clinical exposure is achieved. It is of note, however, that suitable high doses are not necessarily based on the same considerations depending on the study type, and specific recommendations are laid out for reproductive and carcinogenicity studies. Limit doses also vary depending on the dose in humans. The various concepts regarding limit doses in the absence of an MTD are summarized in Table 2.1. For biopharmaceuticals, 10-fold multiples compared to human exposures should generally be aimed for ICHS6(R1) [102].

As can be seen from Table 2.1 above, an exposure margin of 50-fold the clinical exposure is considered acceptable as the maximum dose in toxicology studies under the provisions detailed for the US. The obvious limitation is, however, that the estimate of the required clinical exposure may not be correct, particularly during earlier stages of development, and is likely to change once the first pharmacodynamic investigations in humans have been conducted and even later in development, with increasing knowledge regarding the required systemic exposures in humans to achieve efficacy. Actually, maximum recommended human doses (MRHDs) and associated clinical exposures may be a moving target until advanced stages of clinical development. Consequently, safety margins keep changing that complicates dose selection for toxicology studies based on exposures.

In order to avoid repeating toxicity studies and thus wasting cost, time, resources, and animals; doses for the toxicity studies need to be high enough to fulfill regulatory requirements as outlined in the ICH M3(R2) guideline. Clearly, the MTD concept is the most robust approach to guide dose selection and shield against

TABLE 2.1 Overview on Limit Doses Laid Out in ICH Guidance Documents

Guideline	Limit Dose (Human) (mg/person/day)	Limit Dose (Rodent and Nonrodent) (mg/kg/day)	Systemic Exposure Multiples -Fold	Other	Comments
ICH M3(R2)	≤1000	1000	≥10	n/a[a]	
	≥1000	Up to 2000	10	MFD[b]	Whichever is lower
	n/a	2000	<Human exposure	Up to MFD	
	n/a	n/a	50[c]	n/a	To support Phase III clinical trials in the United States, dose-limiting toxicity to be identified in at least one species when using the 50-fold margin as a limit dose.[d]
ICH S1C(R2) carcinogenicity	≤500	1500	≥10	n/a	
	>500	n/a	≥25	Up to MFD	
ICH S5(R2) reproduction	n/a	1000	n/a	n/a	

Note: If genotoxicity endpoints are to be incorporated into a general toxicity study, then an appropriate maximum dose should be selected based on an MFD, MTD or limit dose of 1000 mg/kg/day.

[a]n/a = not applicable.

[b]MFD = maximum feasible dose.

[c]According to ICH M3(R2) usually based on group mean AUC values [see Note 1] of the parent drug or the pharmacologically active molecule of a prodrug. [...] Note 1: [...] "exposure" generally means group mean AUC. In some circumstances (eg, if the compound or compound class is known to produce acute functional cardiovascular changes or central nervous system-related clinical signs) it might be appropriate to base the exposure margin on group mean C_{max} values rather than AUC.

[d]If this is not the case, a study of one-month or longer duration in one species that is conducted at the 1000 mg/kg limit dose, MFD or MTD, whichever is lowest, is recommended. However, on a case-by-case basis this study might not be warranted if a study of a shorter duration identifies dose-limiting toxicity at doses higher than those resulting in a 50-fold exposure margin.

TABLE 2.2   Dose and Duration of General Toxicology Studies to Support Clinical Trials in Nononcology and Oncology Indications

Nononcology [90]	Oncology [104][a]
Nonclinical studies of equal or longer duration are needed to support clinical trials of respective length.	Treatment can continue according to the patient's response and can continue beyond the duration of the completed toxicology studies.
Maximal exposure in clinical trials usually limited by exposure in animals.	Highest dose or exposure tested in the nonclinical studies does not limit exposures in cancer patients.
Longer-term toxicology studies (often 3 months) are required to support phase II clinical trials.	Nonclinical data to support Phase I clinical trials are sufficient for moving into Phase II clinical trials.
For clinical trials of >6 months, chronic studies are needed (usually prior to phase III trials).	3-month toxicology studies are needed prior to phase III clinical trials. Further characterization may be done postmarketing.

[a]Applicable to trials in patients with advanced disease and limited therapeutic options.

unexpected outcomes later in development, although indeed, for compounds with a benign safety profile, alternative approaches as presented in Table 2.1 may need to be considered. The concept behind dosing up to an MTD is based on the understanding that this approach is most likely to identify all potential target organs of toxicity, but will not result in unspecific toxicity related to excessive systemic exposures. Mortality usually indicates that the MTD has been exceeded, although this may be difficult to establish and is always subject to an integrated assessment of the overall pattern of observations. Dosing below the MTD may not allow for full characterization of all aspects of the safety profile and the results generated therefore may not be suitable to fully support the required clinical monitoring program and consequently may expose patients to unnecessary risks. Failure to establish suitable high-dose levels may thus lead to a hold of clinical programs called for by regulatory authorities until the pivotal preclinical safety studies have been repeated at appropriate exposures.

Another important aspect is the dosing schedule. If the drug is supposed to be given twice or more often/day in the clinic, preclinical dosing schemes should generally mimic the clinical situation, unless exposures in animals can be demonstrated to be adequate following less frequent dosing. Multiple dosing is usually required for drugs with a short half-life. Therefore prior to planning the GLP toxicity studies the pharmacokinetic profile in the respective animal species has to be characterized.

In oncology, special approaches to select doses and treatment schemes in the toxicology studies apply if the first trials are to be conducted in patients with advanced disease and limited therapeutic options [104]. This approach does not relate to drugs that may be tested in healthy volunteers, in which case the same principles have to be followed as laid out above for any drug in development. In oncology, in the clinical setting, a drug may not be given daily, but in cycles. The intended schedule in patients also has to be adopted in the toxicology studies. There is some flexibility in that animals in the toxicology studies can be treated more frequently

than patients in the clinical trials. However, in doing so one has to keep in mind that more frequent dosing in toxicology studies may cause more severe toxicity and the drug substance may only be tolerated at lower doses. This will have an impact on the starting dose in the FIH study, which may be lower and hence prolong the dose escalation phase of the clinical trial and unnecessarily expose patients to subtherapeutic doses. As opposed to nonlife-threatening indications, neither the duration nor the dose in advanced stage cancer patients is limited by the duration of the nonclinical studies or the maximal systemic exposures achieved in animals. To illustrate the difference between nononcology and oncology programs, refer to Table 2.2. Subchronic studies are sufficient to support marketing of anticancer medications with the aim to provide access to efficacious treatments in the shortest possible time. However, many oncology drugs are characterized more extensively following marketing, and even carcinogenicity studies may be conducted.

Dose Selection for Toxicity Studies with Biopharmaceuticals

The same general principles as outlined for small molecules also apply to the selection of dose levels investigating the toxicology profile of biopharmaceuticals in nonclinical studies [102]. However, due to their high specificity to the human target, biopharmaceuticals may show little or no toxicity in the animal species used for safety testing and it may not be possible to define a maximum tolerated dose. In these cases, scientific justification of the rationale for the dose selection and projected multiples of human exposure have to be provided [102]. Rather than focusing on the dose-selection aspect of a toxicity study the main focus for biopharmaceuticals is to identify a species in which the molecule is biologically active, ie, a pharmacologically relevant species. The toxicity of most biopharmaceuticals is related to their targeted mechanism of action and typically becomes evident as exaggerated pharmacology, also referred to as "on-target toxicity," whereas the side-effect profile of small molecules typically is mediated through "off-target toxicity," ie, via binding to other than the intended primary pharmacodynamic target.

As for small molecules, doses selected for biopharmaceuticals need to be justified. The rationale should take the dose–response relationship into account. ICH S6(R1) specifies that PK/PD (pharmacokinetic–pharmacodynamic) approaches (eg, simple exposure–response relationships or more complex modeling and simulation approaches) can assist in high-dose selection by identifying (1) a dose that provides the maximum intended pharmacological effect in the preclinical species; and (2) a dose that provides an approximately 10-fold exposure multiple over the maximum exposure to be achieved in the clinic. The higher of these two doses should be chosen for the high-dose group in preclinical toxicity studies unless there is justification for using a lower dose (eg, maximum feasible dose). In addition, differences in target binding and pharmacological activity should be taken into account to adjust the exposure margin over the highest clinical exposure. However, should no toxicity be evident at the doses selected adopting this approach then higher exposures are considered unlikely to provide any additional useful information.

In practice, many biopharmaceuticals show a benign safety profile even at high multiples of clinical exposure. In general, since many of them are proteins, too high exposures may lead to unspecific effects related to protein overload that does not aid in characterizing the intrinsic safety profile of a biopharmaceutical in development. Furthermore, foreign proteins are prone to elicit an immune response in the host, which can lead to a loss of pharmacological activity through the formation of neutralizing antibodies. Generally, many biopharmaceuticals intended for humans are immunogenic in animals and measurement of antidrug antibodies (ADAs) should be performed in order to aid in the interpretation of these studies both from a toxicological as well as from a pharmacological point of view. The pharmacological response in the toxicological species should preferably be measurable through a pharmacodynamic endpoint that also allows monitoring the strength of the signal in the presence of ADAs to provide information about whether these may be neutralizing the response and if so, to what extent. There is little sense in running toxicity studies longer than until pharmacological activity may have been lost due to the formation of neutralizing antibodies in a large proportion of animals, but typically, the immune response is variable, as in humans. On the other hand, ADAs may not be neutralizing in which case pharmacodynamic endpoints help demonstrate the maintenance of the pharmacological activity and relevance of the species studied. It is of note, however,

that the formation of ADAs in preclinical species is species-specific and is not predictive of a potential for antibody formation in humans.

Species Selection for Small Molecules

For small molecules nonclinical toxicity testing has to be conducted in two species, ie, a rodent and a nonrodent [90]. The rodent species is usually the rat and for nonrodents usually dogs, mini-pigs, or monkeys are utilized. For ethical reasons nonhuman primates are only the last resort and whenever possible the dog or increasingly the mini-pig are selected as nonrodent species. In reproductive toxicity studies, typically the rabbit is selected as nonrodent, unless in very special circumstances rendering this model irrelevant.

The preclinical toxicology species should be predictive for humans. This requires that the drug metabolism and pharmacokinetic (DMPK) profiles of a compound are similar in animals and humans. Metabolites that are not formed in the nonclinical test species or are formed in humans at disproportionately higher levels than in any of the animal species during standard toxicology testing may require additional testing in toxicological studies. A major metabolite is considered to be formed in humans at >10% of parent systemic exposure [based on the area under the concentration curve (AUC)] [65]. Therefore it is prudent to conduct a thorough cross-species metabolism profile and select the preclinical species based on their metabolic pathways. The rush into toxicity studies using the default species rat and dog without this knowledge can later be proven to have been the wrong choice resulting in the need to basically start a nonclinical testing program de novo in more appropriate animal models.

Species Selection for Biopharmaceuticals

The development of biopharmaceuticals adds a new layer of complexity. Those compounds have to be tested in at least one pharmacologically active species [102]. Initially, biotechnology-derived pharmaceuticals were developed in the early 1980s, and since then advances in bioengineering have enabled the development of novel efficacious biopharmaceuticals, particularly in areas with a high unmet medical need, such as oncology; the function of these molecules is brought about by the very specific targeting of molecular pathways in humans that cause a particular disease (eg, Ref. [122]). This specificity has great advantages as it can eliminate the potential for toxicity that is not related to the primary mode of action. Consequently, the toxicity of biopharmaceuticals is usually rather more consistent with exaggerated pharmacology than with the off-target toxicity that is typical for small molecules and can often be predicted based on the understanding of the intended function. However, this specificity to the human target comes with the challenge of identifying a preclinical species for toxicology testing that is pharmacologically relevant. In cases where no pharmacologically active species can be identified the use of homologous proteins can also be used for hazard detection and identification of potential adverse effects. However, such studies are usually not useful in quantitative risk assessment [102]. Another challenge are all those situations where specific targets are only expressed in aberrant tissues that are not present in healthy animals, which are used in nonclinical safety studies.

If the pharmacological effects of a new biopharmaceutical are not similar between the toxicological species and humans the results of the studies conducted can lead to wrong or even dangerous conclusions. An alarming example is TGN1412, a humanized antibody binding to the CD28 protein located on T cells inducing activation of those immune cells.

There are several subtypes of T cells, one being the T effector memory (T_{EM}) cells, another one being the T regulatory (T_{reg}) cells, among others. Activation of T_{EM} cells causes proinflammatory cytokine release, whereas the activation of T_{reg} cells induces antiinflammatory cytokine release, thus suppressing and regulating potential side effects of T_{EM} cells. Imbalances of T_{reg} cells have been related to human autoimmune and vascular inflammatory diseases [35,124] and activation of T_{reg} cells has been shown to be effective in the treatment of autoimmune diseases preclinically [10]. Administration of TGN1412 caused a life-threatening cytokine release syndrome in six healthy male volunteers at the initial dose in the FIH trial. This was not predicted from in vivo preclinical studies in cynomolgus monkeys with TGN1412 and in rats with the homologous antibody (JJ316), and from ex vivo studies exposing human peripheral blood mononuclear cells (PBMC) or diluted blood to TGN1412 [192]. Following the outcome of the first clinical trial with TGN1412 a lot of new knowledge has been gained explaining why the preclinical experiments failed to predict the toxic effects in humans.

Why TGN1412 is bound to human and macaque CD28 with equal affinity but only causes a cytokine release syndrome in humans was investigated by Eastwood et al. [41]. The authors provided convincing evidence that the T_{EM} cells, the cell type that responds with the release of proinflammatory cytokines in humans, does not express the target molecule CD28 in cynomolgus monkeys. During differentiation into T_{EM} cells CD28 expression gets lost only in monkeys, but not in humans. Therefore the cynomolgus monkey was not a biologically active species to establish the safety profile for TGN1412.

The functional equivalent JJ316 did not induce a cytokine release syndrome in rats. Laboratory rats are bred and housed under clean conditions and therefore do not have the chance to accumulate large numbers of T_{EM} cells that can release proinflammatory cytokines [88]. In addition, Mueller et al. [138] found that the activation pattern in rats occurs in two waves. First, there is fast and transient activation of both conventional T_{EM} and T_{reg} cells, followed by a second wave that exclusively activates T_{reg} cells. It is believed that in rats the activation and expansion of T_{reg} cells is so fast that they suppress proinflammatory cytokine release from T_{EM} cells before they reach levels causing clinical symptoms.

Neither the ex vivo cytokine release assays using human peripheral blood mononuclear cells (PBMCs) nor diluted human blood showed cytokine release when exposed to an aqueous solution of TGN1412 [61]. In the meantime it has been discovered that immobilization of the antibody was able to induce the release of proinflammatory cytokines in human PBMCs [184]. Roemer et al. [167] found that when human PBMCs are cultured at high cell density, soluble TGN1412 can subsequently activate the cells. The authors hypothesized that both monocytes and T-cells upregulate functional activity, possibly by acquiring tissue-like properties during high-density culture. Eastwood et al. [42] demonstrated that the severity of the adverse response to TGN1412 correlated with the level of IL-2 release in a solid phase assay.

The experimental conduct of cytokine release assays remains a matter of ongoing debate [74]. There is no formal agreement on assay formats, validation protocols, or appropriate standard procedures on how a cytokine release assay should be conducted and due to the inherent variety of molecule types, a case-by-case approach is needed [108]. A negative in vitro cytokine release assay is still a challenge since the results cannot be exclusively relied on to predict the definitive absence of a respective risk in humans. Unfortunately, in this as well as in many other contexts, absence of evidence is not evidence of absence. Recently issued guidelines on immunogenicity [53,71] address, among other aspects, the need to predict a cytokine response in humans from preclinical in vitro and in vivo animal data, and discuss strategies for testing.

This example emphasizes that knowledge of the nature and comparability of the pharmacological effects in animals and human are of paramount importance in the development of novel biopharmaceuticals.

A general overview of the different aspects that need to be considered when selecting the species and doses for preclinical toxicity studies with either small molecules or biopharmaceuticals is given in Table 2.3.

TABLE 2.3 Criteria for the Selection of Species and Dose for Small Molecules and Biopharmaceuticals

Small molecules	Biopharmaceuticals
SPECIES REQUIRED	
One rodent and one nonrodent species	Pharmacologically relevant species
Selected based on • Comparative in vitro cross-species metabolism data incl. humans	Selected based on • Homology of the target compared to humans • Target-binding affinity • Receptor ligand occupancy • Functional activity (CAVEAT: Binding is not = function!)
HIGH-DOSE SELECTION	
According to ICH M3(R2), S1C(R2) and S5(R2) • MTD[c] (preferred) • Limit dose • Maximum feasible dose • Human systemic exposures and sufficient multiples thereof	Highest dose of either of the two below: • A dose that provides the maximum intended pharmacological effect in the preclinical species • A dose that provides approximately 10-fold exposure multiples over the maximum systemic exposure to be achieved in the clinic
Toxicity driven by unknown endpoints	Pharmacology driven by known endpoints
CONCEPTS TO DERIVE STARTING DOSE IN FIH[A] TRIALS	
NOAEL[d]-driven	MABEL[b] or PAD[e] driven
Maximum recommended starting dose • Based on toxicity • Determination of human equivalent dose based on body surface area • Application of safety factor	• Based on pharmacology • Need of pharmacologically relevant assays in humans and animals (in vitro and in vivo) • Pharmacokinetic/pharmacodynamic modeling • Adjustment for interspecies differences in affinity and potency
Highest dose thought to be safe	Lowest dose thought to be active

[a]FIH = First in human.
[b]MABEL = Minimal anticipated biological effect level [48].
[c]MTD = Maximum tolerated dose [90].
[d]NOAEL = No observed adverse effect level [63,90].
[e]PAD = Pharmacologically active dose [63].

PHASE I

Following years of nonclinical work during drug discovery, lead optimization, animal testing, pharmacokinetic characterization, and toxicology investigations the administration of the first dose of a novel compound in humans is an exciting step. The entry into clinical development is designated as Phase I. It is the first step to determine if the predictions made from preclinical models will also translate into the clinic. In most cases, healthy volunteers are tested. In some instances, the FIH study may be conducted in patients, such as in oncology. Historically, drugs to treat cancer patients have been very toxic themselves, prohibiting the administration of those test materials to healthy volunteers, and in this disease area FIH studies are regularly conducted in patients. Newer anticancer medicines have fewer side effects, opening the possibility to also include healthy volunteers in the clinical development process. The dose in the FIH study is well below a dose that caused toxicity in animals and the first dose is usually uneventful. However, this cannot be taken for granted.

TGN1412

Sometimes the unexpected can happen and the events on March 13, 2006 resulting from the administration of TGN1412 to six healthy volunteers are a warning example. TGN1412 is a humanized IgG4 agonistic anti-CD28 monoclonal antibody designed to stimulate T cells by activating CD28 signaling without the need for prior activation of the T-cell antigen receptor. Due to this ability TGN1412 was also called a "superagonist" [192]. It was intended for the treatment of hematological malignancies, such as B-cell chronic lymphatic leukaemia (B-CLL) and autoimmune/inflammatory diseases, such as rheumathoid arthritis (RA).

In the FIH trial, all six healthy male volunteers developed a cytokine release syndrome with multiorgan failure requiring intensive treatment and supportive care by the intensive care unit [61]. FIH trials until then had a very good safety record and, as far as the Expert Scientific Group could determine, the TGN1412 trial outcome was unprecedented. TGN1412 underwent preclinical testing according to current regulatory requirements. TGN1412 cross-reacted with CD28 expressed on T cells from humans and cynomolgus and rhesus monkeys, thus establishing the cynomolgus monkey as an appropriate species for toxicological testing. The compound was well tolerated in cynomolgus monkeys at doses up to 50 mg/kg/week for 4 consecutive weeks, and this dose level was designated to be the NOAEL. Moderate elevations of IL-2, IL-5, and IL-6 serum levels were observed in individual animals, but no clinical signs of a cytokine release syndrome were observed. The FIH dose was derived using the FDA guidance [63] to calculate a human-equivalent dose. After applying a default factor of 10 the maximum recommended starting dose in healthy volunteers was estimated to be 1.6 mg/kg. The company then applied an additional safety margin and proposed a starting dose of 0.1 mg/kg [192]. This dose was 500-fold below the NOAEL established in cynomolgus monkeys. Despite meeting all regulatory requirements this approach failed to establish a safe starting dose in the FIH trial with TGN1412. However, it should be noted that when calculating the human starting dose for TGN1412 no consideration had been given to the pharmacologically active dose (PAD). In step 5 of the FDA guidance document it is noted that for certain classes of drugs or biopharmaceuticals like monoclonal antibodies toxicity may arise from exaggerated pharmacologic effects. In such a case, the PAD may be a more sensitive indicator of potential toxicity than the NOAEL. However, the FDA guidance document focuses on the NOAEL approach and does not give much detail on the PAD because "selection of a PAD depends on many factors and differs markedly among pharmacologically drug classes and clinical indications; therefore, selection of a PAD is beyond the scope of this guidance."

Regulatory requirements laid out in applicable guidelines are only guidance documents that assist in the general principles and scientific standards that should be met. They cannot cover all possibilities and in no way can they be used as a check box system. Sponsors are the experts on their investigational medicinal products and have the responsibility to conduct a thorough preclinical evaluation and a critical review of the available data. Of course, "hindsight is 20/20" and with all we know today the decision to treat six healthy volunteers with 0.1 mg/kg TGN1412 within 10 min would not have been made. But could the disaster have been avoided based on the knowledge available prior to trial initiation?

Based on pharmacological effects in healthy and arthritic rats using the rat CD28-specific homologous antibody JJ316 and pharmacological effects of TGN1412 in rhesus and cynomolgus monkeys the minimal anticipated biological effect level (MABEL) could be considered to be between 0.1 and 1 mg/kg [61]. The ESG calculated a safe starting dose in humans of 5 μg/kg, considering the MABEL dose to be 0.5 mg/kg and applying a safety factor of 1/100th as proposed for microdosing in

the respective European Medicines Agency (EMA) [44] position paper. The association of the British Pharmaceutical Industry and the BioIndustry Association [139] calculated that the initial FIH dose of 0.1 mg/kg resulted in >90% receptor occupancy and hence was likely to achieve the maximum pharmacological effect. For a drug like TGN1412 with a novel agonistic mode of action, an initial receptor occupancy of below 10% may be more appropriate. This level of occupancy was predicted to be achieved with a dose of 1 μg/kg, ie, a dose by a factor of 100 lower than the actual starting dose, whereas a dose of 5 μg/kg would have resulted in approximately 33% receptor occupancy [87,127,140].

TGN1412 is an excellent example of how the dose makes the poison, an observation originally made more than 500 years ago by Paracelsus. TGN1412 is now called TAB08 and has been safely administered to healthy volunteers at doses of 0.1–7 μg/kg [190]. The starting dose was 1000-fold less than applied in the 2006 clinical trial. At 5 and 7 μg/kg (15–20 times less than the dose used in the 2006 trial) evidence showed that TAB08 had stimulated an antiinflammatory response in the absence of cytokine release. Clinical development of TAB08 continues in RA patients [193].

PHASE II

During this phase of clinical development the drug is given to patients to further assess efficacy and safety with the aim to establish the basis for the pivotal phase III trials. In the nonclinical arena additional toxicity studies, mostly repeated dose toxicity studies of longer duration and reproductive toxicity studies are conducted. The CMC (chemistry, manufacturing, and control) aspects of drug development are equally complex and closely intertwined with the nonclinical and clinical fields, and changes affecting CMC often have a knock-on effect on the latter areas.

Introduction of Salt or Change of Salt Form

A "new drug substance" is defined as follows in ICH Q3A(R2) [93]: "The designated therapeutic moiety that has not been previously registered in a region or member state (also referred to as a new molecular entity or new chemical entity). It can be a complex, simple ester, or salt of a previously approved substance." This implies that a change in salt form may render the available results from earlier safety studies with another form of the drug substance at least partly invalid to support registration, if the new salt form is considered to represent a new drug substance.

Salts are used to alter the physical or chemical properties of a drug, but are not intended to change the intrinsic properties of the therapeutic moiety. Changing the salt form can improve solubility and thereby enhance absorption and increase systemic bioavailability. Salts can also improve stability and therefore prolong the shelf life of a drug; furthermore, the formulation of the final product is influenced by the salt form. It is estimated that about 50% of the drugs on the market are administered as salts [7]. A formal salt selection program takes time and requires compound. In the race to bring new compounds early into clinical development the toxicology and FIH studies may be conducted with a suboptimal salt or with the free acid or base of the drug. The later in development the final salt form is introduced the more studies may need to be repeated. Ideally a change in salt form should only take place prior to initiating long-term toxicity studies.

Since a new salt form can change the bioavailability of a drug pharmacokinetic bridging studies need to be conducted in order to show either bioequivalence, ie, comparable systemic exposures and DMPK profiles, or get information on how to adjust doses for future human or toxicology studies. For drugs with a narrow therapeutic window, the change in salt form can have a significant influence on the dose required to achieve bioequivalence. In some cases, toxicological bridging studies may be needed in addition prior to the conduct of longer term studies.

Impurities

During drug development the compound manufacturing process continues to be optimized and until final procedures are definitively established the impurity profile of an active pharmaceutical ingredient (API, also referred to as drug substance or therapeutic moiety) or of the final formulation of the API (referred to as drug product) can change. Modifications of the impurity profile can, for example, be caused by changes in the route of synthesis, in starting materials or intermediates or it could be a degradation product developing over time. Changes can still occur postmarketing, in the event of further CMC modifications, such as for generic products.

A number of guidelines has been issued to regulate maximum amounts of impurities allowed in drug substances and drug products, and also to specifically address genotoxic impurities, including:

- ICH Q3A(R2) Impurities in New Drug Substances [93]
- ICH Q3B(R2) Impurities in New Drug Products [94]
- ICH Q3C(R5) Guideline for Residual Solvents [95]
- ICH Q3D Guideline for elemental impurities [96]
- ICH M7, Assessment and Control of DNA Reactive (Mutagenic) Impurities in Pharmaceuticals to Limit Potential Carcinogenic Risk [91]
- ICH M7(R1) Draft Addendum – Assessment and Control of DNA Reactive (Mutagenic) Impurities

in Pharmaceuticals to Limit Potential Carcinogenic Risk. Application of the Principles of the ICH M7 Guideline to Calculation of Compound-Specific Acceptable Intakes [92]
- EMA, Guideline on the Limits of Genotoxic Impurities [47]
- EMA, Questions and Answers on the CHMP Guideline on the limits of genotoxic impurities [51]
- FDA Draft Guidance for Industry: Genotoxic and Carcinogenic Impurities in Drug Substances and Products: Recommended Approaches [66]

These regulations are unfortunately not fully consistent with each other and are not always clear with respect to their specific recommendations. Importantly, in general only selected aspects are considered and addressed. The impurity limits laid out in the ICH Q3x guidelines issued several years before ICH M7 may be well above those laid out in the recent ICH M7 guideline, regardless of any genotoxic potential (Note 1 in ICH M7). On the other hand, the focus of ICH M7 is on mutagenic (but not clastogenic or aneugenic) genotoxic mechanisms, which can be tested in the bacterial reverse mutation assay. In contrast to ICH Q3x, ICH M7 does not take daily doses into consideration, whereas the duration of dosing is an integral part of concepts laid out in both ICH Q3x as well as in ICH M7. ICH Q3A(R2) and ICH Q3B(R2) define so-called reporting, identification, and qualification thresholds for impurities in the drug substance and drug product, which reflect quantitative (relative or absolute) limits of respective impurity in the drug substance or product above which applicable action has to be taken. If the qualification threshold is exceeded, a toxicological assessment must be made based on either published information or on available or even new safety studies. Any impurity that was adequately tested in safety studies or an impurity that is a significant metabolite in animal studies can be considered qualified. However, if new impurities arise after the toxicology program has been finalized additional studies may be needed. If no information is available, as a minimum, in vitro genotoxicity studies (a study investigating point mutations and a chromosomal aberration test) and a repeated dose toxicity study in one species are required for qualification. The duration of the repeated dose toxicity study can vary from 14 to 90 days to support short to chronic treatment, respectively. Furthermore, ICH Q3x guidelines suggest evaluating "other specific toxicity endpoints, as appropriate," which implies that a scientific judgment is required to review the extent of the investigations considered mandatory. This implies a case-by-case approach and no fixed limits are proposed for such event, but it is implied that an integrated toxicological assessment be made to deduce an applicable safe level based on specific aspects and not using a default approach.

The most problematic impurities are those that are mutagenic, since there is increased concern regarding potential carcinogenicity without a threshold level, although this is a matter of debate and currently under review [92]. Other types of genotoxicants typically have a threshold mechanism and usually do not pose a carcinogenic risk in humans at the levels present as impurities [92]. ICH M7 defines five classes of impurities with respect to their mutagenic and carcinogenic potential; chemicals in class 1 are those that are classified as known mutagenic carcinogens. The general principles described in ICH M7 adopt a threshold of toxicological concern (TTC) concept that was developed to define an acceptable intake for any unstudied chemical that poses a negligible risk of carcinogenicity or other toxic effects. The methods on which the TTC is based are generally considered to be very conservative since they involve a simple linear extrapolation from the dose giving a 50% tumor incidence (TD_{50}) to a 1 in 10^6 incidence, using TD_{50} data for the most sensitive species and most sensitive site of tumor induction. For application of a TTC in the assessment of acceptable limits of mutagenic impurities in drug substances and drug products, a value of 1.5 µg/day corresponding to a theoretical 10^{-5} excess lifetime risk of cancer, can be justified. Some structural groups were identified to be of such high potency that intakes even below the TTC would theoretically be associated with potential for significant carcinogenic risk. This group of high-potency mutagenic carcinogens, referred to as the "cohort of concern," comprises aflatoxin-like-, N-nitroso-, and alkyl-azoxy compounds.

ICH M7 also provides specific guidance for applicable higher limits during clinical development, where the duration of treatment is shorter. The concept of ICH M7 is taken further in the recently issued draft addendum ICH M7(R1) that describes appropriate approaches for selected chemicals that are considered to be carcinogens with a likely mutagenic mode of action and gives insight into the applicability of setting threshold levels rather than adopting a linear extrapolation approach for some class 1 chemicals, ie, mutagenic carcinogens.

For some areas of toxicology, there is no specific recommendation in any of these guidelines, such as with respect to the need (or lack) of addressing a potential for reproductive toxicity.

Taken together, all guidelines have to be considered in context and with respect to the target population, dose, and duration of clinical use. The most stringent approach should be chosen for chronic treatment.

In essence, changes in CMC processes during drug development require an integrated approach between disciplines to proactively address potential issues, but still here, unexpected situations may result in challenging situations. Such situations could be those where the formation of a toxic impurity may not have been expected and the impurity has to be reduced to levels that are not technically achievable. In turn, such outcomes my trigger the need for altering the CMC process and/or require additional toxicology studies, which obviously has an impact on the resources needed and may well delay approval of new drug substances at a stage where the majority of studies has been completed.

PHASE III

During this phase of clinical development the drug is given to a sufficient number of patients to gather pivotal information on efficacy and safety; in many indications this may involve several 100 or even 1000 volunteers. Those trials are usually randomized and double-blinded where neither the investigator nor the patient knows if the new therapy or a comparator (ie, placebo or another therapy) is given. These pivotal phase III trials provide the basis for the definitive risk–benefit assessment prior to marketing application and support the registration of a new therapeutic. In the nonclinical arena usually the reproductive toxicology package is completed and the carcinogenicity studies conducted. As in all stages of development, further mechanistic toxicity studies may be performed to support hypotheses about the relevance of nonclinical findings for human safety.

Clinical Hold

Once a compound has entered clinical development testing in animals continues in parallel. In most therapeutic indications the treatment duration in clinical trials must not exceed the treatment duration in nonclinical toxicology studies. There are both predefined points in time at which data are typically compiled by sponsors for discussion with regulators to approve the next phase of development, such as before entering first clinical studies, or at the end of phase II of clinical development, ie, prior to starting the big and expensive pivotal clinical studies, as well as situations where the sponsor has to notify regulators of side effects in specific situations in a predefined short timeframe. In the United States, for example, the sponsor is required to notify the FDA and all participating investigators in an IND (investigational new drug) safety report (ie, 7- or 15-day expedited report) of *potentially serious risks* from clinical trials or *any other source* as soon as possible, but no later than 15 calendar days after the sponsor receives the safety information and determines that the information qualifies for reporting [70]. This definition also embraces findings from toxicology studies and implies that the responsibility of judgment lies with the sponsor. The shorter timeline relates to unexpected fatal or life-threatening adverse reactions.

The agency can order a clinical hold following a review of data at predefined time-points as well as after reporting potentially serious risks, in which case all or some of the investigations conducted under an IND application may be suspended and subjects enrolled in clinical trials may no longer be given the investigational drug. The agency may ask for additional studies to investigate the issue identified. The clinical hold may be lifted if additional animal data can be provided that demonstrate the safe use in the proposed clinical trial. Similar processes and timelines are in place in other regions, such as the EU and are established to ensure patient safety.

Generally, the earlier the stage of development the more weight that is attributed to nonclinical observations. In view of the impact of a clinical hold on the one hand, but unexpected side effects in humans even at advanced stages of development or during postmarketing, which were not anticipated from nonclinical results, the question arises as to how predictive in general preclinical data are for humans. Classical observations that present challenges in development and specific fields of particular concern are discussed in the following.

PREDICTIVITY OF TOXICOLOGICAL FINDINGS FOR HUMAN SAFETY

Typical Issues and How to Deal with Them: Clinical Intolerance, Liver Toxicity, Nervous System and Retinal Toxicity, Endocrine Disorders, Phospholipidosis

Typical issues encountered in preclinical studies include clinical and target organ toxicity in the toxicological species often associated with low safety ratios (SRs), although in general, a safety margin of at least 10 is a minimum requirement (see Table 2.1). SRs are derived from a comparison of systemic drug exposures in patients at therapeutic doses and animals at the NOAEL. For small molecules, SRs would be preferred to be >20, and greater margins are certainly a safeguard particularly in situations where there is a steep dose–response, but for some classes including CNS drugs, SRs often can be <10 and may even be <1. In the latter class, dose-limiting clinical intolerance in animals and healthy volunteers at doses below those tolerated in patients is not uncommon. Typical features may include the lack of a histopathological correlate, reversibility on cessation of dosing, and not infrequently, an amelioration with continued dosing. CNS toxicity generally presents as signs consistent with exaggerated pharmacology, such as tremors, increased or decreased activity/sedation, recumbency, loss of balance/ataxia, hypothermia (rats), seizures/convulsions, and death. Examples include clozapine, haloperidol, bupropion, tricyclic antidepressants

(eg, trimiparmin, nortriptyline), benzodiazapines (eg, diazepam) (NIH–TOXNET [142–147]), risperidone [166], and AChE (acetylcholine esterase inhibitors) inhibitors (eg, rivastigmine) [45,60].

Target organs of toxicity for a variety of drugs may include the liver, CNS/PNS (peripheral nervous system), endocrine system, lung or retina, or may feature as phospholipidosis across a number of organs. Hepatotoxicity can be present in one or more preclinical species and generally is predictive for humans. Characteristics may include elevated serum enzymes, increased liver weight, and morphological alterations (such as hepatocyte hypertrophy, vacuolation, lipid deposition, degeneration, and necrosis or hepatobiliary changes). Hepatocyte hypertrophy is often adaptive due to stimulation of drug metabolism and nonadverse, but this change could lead to potentially severe toxicity at higher doses or on prolonged treatment. In contrast, idiosyncratic liver toxicity in man is not predicted from animal studies and often due to metabolic differences in (individual) humans or may be immunologically mediated, which results in higher susceptibility of the individual affected. In general, animal species are poor predictors of adverse human immunological issues [54,130,136,154,156].

Morphological changes of the nervous system are variable and can include findings, such as vacuoles in the neurones, in their axons, in glial cells, and/or in the myelin sheath, as neuronal pigmentation and as necrosis, reflecting neuronal damage. They may be the result of direct neurotoxic action of a drug and/or result from vascular injury. Such alterations may or may not be reversible and/or be associated with a functional deficit. Examples from animal studies include a number of drugs, eg, interacting with the NMDA receptor, such as phencyclidine, MK-801, or memantine [5,29,148,182]. Morphological findings in the CNS are nonmonitorable in the clinic unless they were reliably identifiable by a biomarker indicating a fully reversible functional stage well preceding any changes at the histopathological level. For obvious reasons, such monitoring is severely hampered by medical and technical limitations, and mostly, compounds with such findings are not developed further.

Endocrine disorders can for instance be caused by dopamine D_2 antagonists through elevated circulating prolactin levels, possibly associated with pituitary and mammary proliferative changes or disruption of male and female reproductive function, or dopamine D_2 agonists that may reduce prolactin levels. Examples for compounds associated with such hormonal alterations include risperidone [165,166], aripiprazole [1,2], and bromocriptine [153]. In the rat, pregnancy loss due to systemic (maternal) hypoprolactinemia is a known effect since pregnancy is established and maintained by prolactin rather than progesterone in this species unlike in rabbits and humans. The early phase of pregnancy in rats is dominated by surges of prolactin produced by the maternal anterior pituitary. Therefore any effects on early pregnancy due to reduced maternal systemic prolactin levels are not predictive for humans but could hamper the validity of reproductive studies in the rat depending on the type and severity of effects secondary to a potential hypoprolactinemia. Furthermore, such effects could potentially confound the interpretation of animal studies [69,181].

Retinal atrophy particularly in the albino rat may feature as a loss of nuclei of the outer nuclear layer with thinning of the photoreceptor layer and progress to the loss of all layers with disruption of the pigment epithelial layer. This alteration has been described for a number of drugs, eg, pregabalin [128], pramipexole [135], aripiprazole [1,2], and citalopram [19], none of which has been associated with retinal changes in humans, suggesting a limitation regarding the predictive value of this type of toxicological finding in albino rats for human safety, although this cannot be taken for granted, and respective measures for each project have to be taken to address this issue in the event of similar observations.

Phospholipidosis caused by cationic amphiphilic drugs for many different indications is characterized by excessive accumulation of phospholipids in cells, usually within lysosomes, and presents with a lamellar structure often in lungs and liver but possibly also in lymphoid and other tissues (eg, kidney). Different species and even strains within species and also different age groups may not react similarly to the same agent, and overall, the response to a specific cationic amphiphilic drug in a particular species is considered unpredictable [137]. The severity (extent of accumulation) varies between drugs. Phospholipidosis may reflect an adaptive rather than toxic response and does not usually disrupt organ function. There are no validated biomarkers available for clinical use as yet. Examples include amiodarone, imipramine, and fluoxetine [137,141,152,161,171]. The significance of phospholipidosis in preclinical animal studies for human risk assessment is a matter of ongoing debate [68,162].

If issues are identified during nonclinical development, the following steps are recommended:

1. Do not stop development immediately but:
2. Review the finding in detail first to answer the following questions:
   a. Is it a real observation or could it be an artifact?
   b. What is its nature?
   c. Is it an exacerbation of a spontaneous finding?
   d. Is it a known class finding?
   e. Was the finding statistically significant or does it only affect individual animals; if so are these individuals representative for the group, specifically susceptible or outliers?
   f. Could it be a chance finding?
   g. May the finding be species-specific?
   h. Is the observation reversible?
   i. Does the observation deteriorate with ongoing treatment—perhaps to an irreversible stage?
   j. What is the degree of severity?
   k. Can the observation be reliably monitored in the clinic?
   l. Is the finding considered predictive or relevant for man?
   m. Can this question be answered at all at the respective stage of development?
   n. What are the predicted safety ratios?
   o. Is the sensitivity comparable between species?
   p. Can this question be answered at all?
   q. If not, are the safety ratios a reliable tool to estimate human risk, or do additional factors need to be taken into account?
3. The answers to these questions will inform on the overall risk for further development of the project and, if deemed appropriate, provide a sound basis for working out an appropriate action plan. It is recommended to proactively enter into a dialogue for scientific advice with governmental regulators at an early stage to establish whether the action plan is deemed appropriate and/or how it might need to be modified for a successful testing strategy.

Preclinical issues and low SRs are not necessarily impediments to successful drug development. Many issues would be "stoppers" for new drugs in "soft" indications but not necessarily for indications with a high unmet medical need. Some preclinical issues do not appear to be predictive for patients. Others are predictive but are monitorable clinically and safety can be ensured, whereas nonmonitorable and severe toxicities may indeed require discontinuation of further development of the drug concerned.

Cardiotoxicity

The heart is a remarkable organ. With about 100,000 beats a day it pumps approximately 7000 L of blood through a network of vessels that when laid out end-to-end would circle more than twice the planet Earth (97,000 km). It is not a surprise that this vital organ is also prone to toxic insults. There are two major classes of myocardial injury, ie, structural and nonstructural injuries. Cardiotoxicity can be caused by alterations in biochemical pathways, energy metabolism, cellular structures, electrophysiology, and contractility leading to decreased cardiac output and peripheral tissue hypoperfusion. In vitro (eg, ion-channel function, Purkinje fiber assay) and in vivo studies (eg, telemetry, electrocardiography, histopathology) are conducted during the nonclinical development to investigate potential side effects on the heart. Any finding is of concern and requires an appropriate risk assessment and possibly follow-up studies.

QT Prolongation

During the 1990s several drugs from different therapeutic indications were removed from the market due to drug-induced cardiac arrhythmias (eg, terfenadine (antihistamine), grepafloxacine (antibiotic), sertindole (antipsychotic), cisapride (heartburn)). The overall frequency of those serious adverse events leading eventually to market withdrawal can be extremely low (eg, less than 1 in 100,000 patients experienced TdP with terfenadine) [121]. It was found that those arrhythmias were associated with prolongation of the QTc interval, which may lead to polymorphic ventricular tachycardia, also known as torsade de pointes (TdP), which can be fatal. This led to the development of preclinical [103] and clinical [89] guidance documents requiring drug developers to test for drug-induced QT prolongation prior to seeking drug approval. Since the most common mechanism for QT-interval prolongation by pharmaceuticals is inhibition of the delayed rectifier potassium channel pharmaceutical companies have started early screening for hERG channel-blocking properties. However, not every compound that blocks the hERG channel also induces QT prolongation and possibly the feared TdP. A screening solely toward unwanted hERG effects may sort out promising candidates for drug development. Drugs that block the hERG channel may not cause QT prolongation if they counteract the potential hERG channel block by simultaneous blockage of L-type Ca^{2+} channels, eg, Verapamil [14]. For a new compound that blocks the hERG channel but does not induce QT prolongation in the in vivo telemetry study mixed channel activities may be suspected that does not always preclude further drug development. CIPA (comprehensive in vitro proarrhythmia assay) is a new ILSI (International Life Sciences Institute) initiative that is evaluating the current paradigm of testing and is in the process of proposing a suite of preclinical in vitro and in vivo studies that may sufficiently support clinical development and eliminate the need for a thorough QT/QTc study in the clinic (ICH E14).

Cardiomyopathy

This is a common background lesion in rat toxicology studies [20]. If a dose-dependent increase in incidence and severity is seen in toxicology studies its relevance to humans has to be evaluated. This finding is frequently observed with immunosuppressive compounds. In a study investigating the mechanism of sirolimus-induced myocardial degeneration the finding could be attributed to the activation of latent parvovirus in the hearts of immunosuppressed rats. Subsequently, this effect was not considered to be adverse [46]. In the sirolimus scientific discussion it is also noted that cyclosporin A and tacrolimus have also been reported to induce myocardial degeneration in rats.

The Cardiovascular Safety of Anticancer Therapies

The cardiotoxic potential of cytotoxic chemotherapeutics (eg, anthracyclines) is well known. The so-called "targeted" therapies, which interact with targets that are overexpressed and/or mutated in tumor cells, specifically the protein kinase inhibitors (eg, Gleevec/Glivec, imatinib), have revolutionized the treatment of certain cancers with better tolerability than conventional chemotherapies. However, these kinases are also expressed in cardiac tissue and play a crucial role in normal homeostasis. Consequently, a number of protein kinase inhibitors has been associated with cardiotoxicity in humans [21,151]. There are, however, distinct mechanistic differences in the manifestation of chemotherapy-induced cardiotoxicity. Type I cardiotoxicity causes myocardial damage that is characterized by direct myocyte injury (eg, vacuolation, myofibril disarray, necrosis) resulting in dose-dependent permanent toxicity [57,59,205]. Examples of type I agents are anthracyclines (eg, doxorubicin, daunorubicin, epirubicin), mitoxantrone, and cyclophosphamide [58,59], which are classical cytotoxic anticancer therapies. Type II cardiotoxicity is characterized by myocyte dysfunction that is not dose-related or associated with structural damage and often reversible and therefore has a more favorable prognosis [57]. Examples of type II agents are trastuzumab, sunitinib, imatinib, and lapatinib [58,59], which belong to the new "targeted" cancer therapies.

Cardiovascular side effects have been seen with both small molecules and biopharmaceuticals. Cancer is often treated with a combination of medicines to improve efficacy, but this approach comes with the risk of additive or synergistic side effects. Trastuzumab (Herceptin [85]), a humanized monoclonal antibody approved for the treatment of HER2-overexpressing breast cancer and HER2-overexpressing metastatic gastric or gastroesophageal junction adenocarcinoma, has a boxed warning for cardiomyopathy (Herceptin prescribing information). Congestive heart failure (CHF) occurred in 7% of patients treated with either Herceptin alone or with a combination of anthracycline and cyclophosphamide. However, when all three agents were coadministered the incidence of CHF increased to 28%. A less pronounced synergistic effect (11%) was seen when Herceptin was combined with paclitaxel (Herceptin prescribing information). Although the exact mechanism of Herceptin-induced cardiotoxicity is not fully understood there is evidence that the ErbB2 receptor (synonym for HER2/neu) is involved in growth and survival pathways of adult cardiomyocytes that are probably essential for cell repair [30,36,75,111].

Force and Kolaja [76] reviewed the cardiotoxicity of kinase inhibitors, which can be associated both with the primary ("on-target") as well as with unintended ("off") targets, and the predictivity and translation of preclinical models to clinical outcomes, which had limited success to date. Therefore in clinical practice patient monitoring is crucial in the management of side effects of targeted anticancer therapies [40]. Cancer patients in many indications today have prolonged life expectancy and improved survival rates and the long-term safety of anticancer therapies has to be revealed. Cardiovascular side effects in this medical field have given birth to the emerging clinical discipline of cardio-oncology.

Genotoxicity

Genotoxicity tests are designed to detect compounds that induce genetic damage and are mainly used for the prediction of carcinogenicity [100]. Carcinogenicity is a complicated multistep process, and in experimental animal testing the "gold standard" for human risk assessment still is the 2-year carcinogenicity bioassay in rodents, although ICH is currently reviewing the need and extent of requirements for carcinogenicity testing. The available genotoxicity tests are fairly simple, short-term in vitro and in vivo tests and it is not surprising that their predictivity toward the gold standard is far from perfect. In order to develop safe compounds those tests should show high sensitivity (ie, correctly predict a positive response in the 2-year carcinogenicity assay). But on the other hand, those tests have also been shown to have low specificity (to correctly identify a negative response in the 2-year carcinogenicity assay). This leads to a high number of false-positive assays that need to be evaluated further. This problem has been described in several review articles [34,114–116,196,197] and has led to the development of a revised guideline on genotoxicity testing [100].

Positive Ames Test—What Next?

The false-positive rate of the Ames mutagenicity test is very low. Extensive reviews have shown that many compounds that are mutagenic in the bacterial reverse mutation (Ames) test are indeed rodent carcinogens [132,209]. Due to the established strong correlation between a positive Ames test and a positive rodent carcinogenicity study a positive Ames test requires extensive follow-up testing to assess the mutagenic and carcinogenic potential of the compound. However, there are situations where the Ames test can be false-positive. Compounds that can release amino acids (histidine or tryptophan) into the culture medium can create a false-positive effect [3]. This mode of action has to be kept in mind when testing compounds that are derived from biological material (eg, proteins,

peptides, food additives, cosmetics, herbal extracts). Bacterial-specific metabolic activation, such as nitroreductases has been linked to the creation of genotoxic impurities. Therefore positive Ames tests with aromatic nitro compounds may not be predictive for genotoxicity using mammalian assays [117]. AMP397, a novel antiepileptic drug with an aromatic nitro group, was positive in the Ames test, but negative in nitroreductase-deficient Ames tester strains [185]. In addition, no genotoxic activity was determined with AMP397 in several in vivo assays, including a comet assay in the jejunum a tissue where nitroreductases would be present. This example shows the kind of scrutiny and follow-up investigations that may be needed to successfully continue development of an Ames-positive compound even in a nonlife-threatening indication.

Positive In Vitro Mammalian Cell Assay—What Next?

The false-positive rate of the in vitro mammalian cell assay is quite high. Therefore the ICH S2(R1) [100] gives guidance on evaluation of test results and on follow-up test strategies. Those include but are not limited to the assessment of reproducibility, biological significance (statistically significant findings that are still within the historical control range), nonphysiological conditions (pH, osmolality, precipitates), and the concentration-effect relationship (positive only at the highest, most toxic concentration). A positive in vitro genotoxicity test has to be followed by mechanistic information that contributes to the weight of evidence for a lack of relevant genotoxicity. This can include in vitro or in vivo assays, depending on the kind of findings observed. Aneugens affect cell division by interaction with the spindle apparatus and not directly by interacting with DNA. For this mechanism, it might be possible to determine a threshold exposure below which the loss of chromosomes does not occur. Such a compound could be safely given to humans if an appropriate safety margin exists. Clastogens damage chromosomes and if an in vitro test is positive, two negative assays measuring the same endpoints are required in vivo to demonstrate the lack of relevance of the in vitro assay.

Carcinogenicity

Drugs that are indended to be used continuously for at least 6 months have to be tested for their potential to induce tumors. For pharmaceuticals used frequently in an intermittent manner in the treatment of chronic or recurrent conditions, carcinogenicity studies are generally needed. Examples include drugs for the treatment of allergic rhinitis, depression, or anxiety [98]. Carcinogenicity studies are conducted in two rodent species, usually the rat and the mouse [99], although ICH is currently reviewing the need and extent of requirements for carcinogenicity testing [97].

The 2-year bioassay conducted in either species or a combination of a 2-year bioassay in rats with a 6-month transgenic mouse assay in mice are common strategies.

Given the high cost and extensive use of animals those studies are among the last to be conducted during preclinical testing prior to applying for marketing approval. In certain cases, eg, indications of high medical needs, carcinogenicity studies may also be conducted postapproval. Only in exceptional situations, ie, in case of significant cause for concern, carcinogenicity studies may need to be submitted to support clinical trials [90].

Positive Results in Rodent Carcinogenicity Study—What Next?

A positive carcinogenicity study does not necessarily mean the end of development. Contrera et al. [27] reviewed 282 (229 marketed) human pharmaceuticals in the FDA database and found that 44.3% of the compounds had positive carcinogenicity findings. Similarly, Van Oosterhout et al. [202] reported that for nearly 50% of the compounds for which a marketing authorization was applied in Germany and the Netherlands a positive carcinogenicity study was submitted, with the rat being more sensitive than the mouse. Once a positive finding is discovered its relevance to humans has to be determined. Genotoxic compounds are usually sorted out early in development and will not make it to the stage of carcinogenicity testing. One exception is the development of drugs to treat cancer or other life-threatening conditions where the benefit outweighs the risk of possibly developing a drug-induced tumor. Several authors have critically reviewed the relevance of the 2-year carcinogenicity assay for human risk assessment and some also proposed alternative testing strategies [6,163,180]. A review of these alternative testing strategies is outside the scope of this chapter, which focuses on how to deal with a positive finding in carcinogenicity studies for nongenotoxic compounds and how to assess the human risk.

In the event of a positive carcinogenicity study, the principal initial approach is to first evaluate a mode of action (MOA) of tumorigenesis in animals and then to assess its relevance for humans. A framework for analyzing the MOA by which chemicals induce tumors in laboratory animals has been developed by the International Programme on Chemical Safety (IPCS) and was published by Sonich-Mullin et al. [183]. According to these authors, the MOA analysis includes the following steps:

1. Introduction: The description of the cancer endpoint/endpoints.
2. Postulated mode of action (theory of the case): The description of the sequence of events on the path to cancer.
3. Key events: Measurable events that are critical to the induction of tumors.

4. Dose–response relationship: A discussion of whether the dose–response of the key events parallels the dose–response relationship of the tumor.
5. Temporal association: The key events should be observed before the tumor appearance.
6. Strength, consistency, and specificity of association of tumor response with key events: The weight of evidence linking the key events, precursor lesions, and the tumor response.
7. Biological plausibility and coherence: Consideration of whether the mode of action is consistent with what is known about carcinogenesis in general (biological plausibility) and in relation to what is known specifically for the substance (coherence).
8. Other modes of action: Discussion of alternative modes of action.
9. Assessment of postulated modes of action: Statement of the level of confidence in the postulated mode of action.
10. Uncertainties, inconsistencies, and data gaps: Uncertainties should include both those related to the biology of tumor development and those related to the database on the compound of interest. Inconsistencies should be flagged and data gaps be identified; gaps should be judged as to whether they are critical as support for the postulated MoA or just serve to increase confidence therein.

In order to provide guidance in determining the relevance of the MOA in animals for human risk assessment a human relevance framework concept (HRF) was developed by the International Life Sciences Institute/Risk Science Institute (ILSI/RSI) working group [25,26,134]. The HRF is based on the following four questions:

1. Is the weight of evidence sufficient to establish an MOA in animals?
2. Are key events in the animal MOA plausible in humans?
3. Taking into account kinetic and dynamic factors, is the animal MOA plausible in humans?
4. Conclusion: Statement of confidence, analysis, and implications.

The above process has been applied to several types of tumors and classes of compounds [25,86] and is a useful tool in conducting a human risk assessment based on a positive carcinogenicity study.

Examples of Rodent Tumors of Questionable Relevance to Humans

Mononuclear cell leukemia (MNCL) in F-344 rat: This tumor type is unique to the rat and is only common in the F-344 strain. King-Herbert and Thayer [113] reported a frequency in untreated F-344 rats in studies conducted by the National Toxicology Program of 48.2% and 23.7% in males and females, respectively. Tumor development occurs only after an apparent threshold is exceeded. Some genotoxic carcinogens did not increase the incidence of MNCL, whereas several noncarcinogens did induce an increase. Therefore an increase in MNCL in F-344 rats is not considered relevant to humans [16].

α2μm-globulin associated renal tumors: These are male-rat-specific tumors occurring as a result of accumulation of a male-rat-specific protein, α2μm-globulin, in phagolysosomes of renal proximal tubular cells. As an analogous protein is not produced in humans those rodent tumors are not considered relevant for human risk assessment. The International Agency for Research on Cancer (IARC) has published a list of criteria that have to be met in order to support this mechanism of action [186].

Thyroid tumors rats: In rats, thyroid carcinogenesis can be induced by agents interfering with the pituitary-thyroid feedback mechanism. Hepatic enzyme inducers can increase thyroid hormone metabolism leading via a positive feedback mechanism to a stimulation of the thyroid gland. The same pathways also exist in humans, but there are some differences making the human more resistant to developing thyroid tumors. Species differences in thyroid physiology between rodent and human can explain the formation of thyroid tumors. Thyroxine-binding globulin (TBG) is the main human plasma protein that binds and transports thyroid hormone in the blood. Rodents are lacking this protein. In addition, the half-life of thyroxine is 16h in rats versus 5–9days in humans and serum levels are about 25 times higher in rodents than in humans, indicating higher activity of the rodent thyroid gland [194].

Urinary bladder tumors in mice and rats: Urinary bladder tumors can be induced through chronic irritation and subsequent increased cell proliferation followed by malignant transformation caused by precipitates. The same mechanism can also occur in humans if the chemical causing the formation of irritating objects is present in sufficient amounts. However, there are some physiological and anatomical differences between rodents and humans that make humans less susceptible. Rodent urine has high osmolality and a high concentration of protein compared to humans [24]. Calculi can more easily remain in the horizontal quadruped rodents compared to the upright walking humans [37]. Rodent bladder tumors are not relevant for humans if they only occur above a threshold concentration at which precipitation occurs.

Liver tumors in mice and rats: Many nongenotoxic chemicals produce liver tumors in rodents, especially in mice [81]. Proposed MOAs include cytotoxicity followed by persistent regenerative growth, enzyme induction, hormonal perturbation, immunosuppression, and porphyria [11,86,134]. A compound that causes liver tumors in mice only is frequently regarded as being of limited relevance to humans [17].

Hormonal disturbance: Disturbance of the hormonal balance is a common cause for induction of tumors in rodents, which is often due to the specific endocrine physiology of rodents and, therefore, without relevance to humans.

Leydic cell tumors: Various agents interfering with the hypothalamic–pituitary–testicular (HPT) axis and ultimately causing increased concentrations of serum LH (luteinizing hormone) have been shown to increase Leydic cell tumors especially in rats, but also in mice and beagle dogs (eg, androgen receptor agonists, 5α-reductase inhibitors, testosterone biosynthesis inhibitors, aromatase inhibitors dopamine agonists, gonadotropin-release hormone agonists, estrogen agonists/antagonists). The regulatory mechanisms of the HPT axis in rats and humans are similar, but humans seem to be less sensitive in their response to increased LH levels. Based on the fact that Leydig cell adenomas and carcinomas in the general population are very low and surveillance databases have detected no increased incidence it was concluded that human males are generally less sensitive than rodents. However, each situation has to be evaluated on a case-by-case basis [22,157].

Uterine tumors: Dopaminergic alkaloids have significant endocrine effects in rodents, particularly in rats, through their inhibitory effect on prolactin secretion [55]. Bromocriptin caused squamous cell metaplasia of the uterine endometrium in a chronic 53-week study in rats that progressed to uterine adenocarcinomas in the 2-year bioassay [56]. Normally older rats remain in diestrus with high prolactin and low LH levels. Lowering prolactin bromocriptine treatment initiated cyclic activity. However, a normal estrus cycle was not achieved and a higher estrogen/progesterone ratio led to the development of squamous endometrial metaplasia, which facilitated endometritis and pyometra and through irritation resulted in increased cell proliferation and finally to neoplasia. No such findings were detected in a 52-week dog study or in a carcinogenicity study in mice [56,153]. Endometrial biopsies of patients did not show any drug-related changes [164]. Therefore, the uterine changes in rats are without relevance for women and considered an exaggerated pharmacodynamic effect specific for aging female rats.

Target Organ Concordance Between Test Species and Human

Harderian gland (eye), Zymbal's gland (ear), preputial gland, clitoral gland, and forestomach are rodent specific organs that do not have a human equivalent, and hence, tumors in those organs are often regarded as not relevant to humans. However, target organ concordance is not a prerequisite for the relevance of animal study results to human risk assessment. Physiological growth control mechanisms at the cellular level are similar among mammalian species, but these mechanisms are not necessarily site concordant. Specific considerations, however, may apply occasionally. For example, the rodent forestomach resembles the epithelium of the esophagus. Locally irritating substances may be rodent forestomach carcinogens through prolonged contact with the epithelium causing chronic irritation and inflammation. A carcinogenic risk for humans is considered unlikely, since exposure of the epithelium in the mouth, pharynx, and esophagus in patients swallowing a pill is short-lived. By contrast, the local exposure of the stomach of rodents treated by oral gavage is prolonged. Therefore exposure to nongenotoxic compounds at concentrations far below those having irritating potential is not a risk to human [208]. For other rodent-specific tumors a mode of action may not be easy to establish and a full weight of evidence approach has to be used in order to assess the risk to man, as described above [183].

The cases described above are only examples of tumors observed in animal studies that may not be relevant to humans. However, for new developmental compounds the hypothesis of a possible mode of action and the relevance to humans need to be supported by a weight of evidence approach for each case specifically.

Reproductive Toxicity Testing

Reproductive toxicity testing is a special area in preclinical safety because there are no dedicated follow-up studies in humans, ie, the aim of this part of the program is not to establish appropriate monitoring in humans but to identify potential hazards to reproduction based on which an integrated risk assessment is made to assess the possible impact of the observations in animal studies for humans. Based on this assessment, appropriate measures are to be implemented to manage and mitigate respective risks in humans with the ultimate aim to prevent adverse effects on all stages of human reproduction. These concepts are laid out in a number of guidelines across regions, some of which were issued recently including:

- ICH S5(R2). Detection of toxicity to reproduction for medicinal products and toxicity to male fertility [101].
- ICH M3(R2). Conduct of human clinical trials and marketing authorization for pharmaceuticals [90].
- FDA Guidance for industry. Reproductive and developmental toxicities—Integrating study results to assess concerns [69].
- EMA Guideline on risk assessment of medicinal products on human reproduction and lactation: From data to labeling [50].

- FDA Content and format for human prescription drug and biological products; requirements for pregnancy and lactation labeling [72].
- CTFG (Clinical Trial Facilitation Group) in Europe. Recommendations related to contraception and pregnancy testing in clinical trials [52].
- FDA Guidance for industry: Assessment of male-mediated developmental risk for pharmaceuticals (draft guidance) [73].

It is outside the scope of this chapter to explain the experimental methods used as to how the range of studies is being conducted, but detailed descriptions are laid out in the ICH S5-R2 guideline on the Detection of Toxicity to Reproduction for Medicinal Products and Toxicity to Male Fertility, 2005 and are discussed in chapter 9 of this book. The principal testing strategy should ensure exposure of all mature adults and all stages of development from conception to sexual maturity. To allow for detection of immediate and latent effects of exposure, observations should be continued through one complete lifecycle, ie, from conception in one generation through conception in the following generation. Exposures from weaning through puberty are not fully covered in the reproductive toxicity studies, and additional studies in juvenile animals should be considered, where appropriate; juvenile studies are also outside the scope of this chapter but are described in chapter 11 of this book. If several reproductive toxicity studies are conducted, it is mandatory to assure that no gaps in treatment occur, which can be determined by an overlap of at least one day in the exposure period of related studies.

The history of drug development shows how this field has developed in recent decades, and how we are still on a learning curve as to the predictivity of animal findings for humans in certain cases.

Thalidomide

Unfortunately, long before standard methods for the evaluation of developmental and reproductive toxicity (DART) were established and used routinely in the pharmaceutical industry as is the case today, and before the knowledge of experts in this field was well developed, thalidomide was discovered, received marketing approval in Germany in 1957, and was available over the counter from the beginning. The legal framework for the regulation of new medications was not comparable to our today's global standards, and these have also greatly developed since. Based on nerve damage in hands and feet, reported in elderly patients in 1959, Grünenthal applied step-wise for prescription-only status in selected German federal states in May 1961 [84]. In November 1961, the appearance of the very severe and typical malformations in humans was associated with this highly potent human teratogen by two physicians, Dr. Widukind Lenz (in Germany) and Dr. William BcBride (Australia) and within 10 days, Grünenthal decided to withdraw thalidomide from the market [84].

Since then, reproductive toxicity testing became an integral part of preclinical safety testing. It is worth reviewing the thalidomide case to provide some insight as to how this tragedy has happened and to ask the question of how well we may or may not be protected today against a similar situation. James Schardein has described the history of thalidomide on the background of the general scientific understanding and attitude in the 1950–1960s in his chapter: "Thalidomide: The Prototype Teratogen" in *Chemically Induced Birth Defects*, 3rd edition, 2000 and highlights the fact that in these early days, reproductive toxicity testing was not an integral part of the safety assessment of medicines in development at all, and, moreover, that testing of fetal endpoints was generally missing from the testing paradigm. In addition, the knowledge about teratogenesis was not yet well developed then, and only 9 years before thalidomide had been identified as the cause of the human malformations in West Germany, it was known that drugs (ie, aminopterin) can cause human malformations when given during pregnancy. Dally [32] published an article in *The Lancet* about thalidomide to ask the question of whether the tragedy was preventable. This article highlights the fact that in spite of the available evidence demonstrating that fetal damage could occur through environmental influences, such as alcohol—already established in nineteenth century—this knowledge simply was largely forgotten by the mid-twentieth century. Medical students learned that the placenta was a barrier that protected the fetus up to doses that would kill the mother. Schardein highlights in his article that even leading teratologists at the time were skeptical about the association of thalidomide with human malformations [77,207].

Originally, thalidomide was studied for its anxiolytic, mild hypnotic, antiemetic, and adjuvant analgesic properties. Later it was found to be efficacious in the treatment of the cutaneous forms of leprosy (erythema nodosum leprosum) and since has been approved for the treatment of multiple myeloma; actually, it is considered to be potentially efficacious for the treatment of many more severe clinical conditions [49,155]. Its pharmacological mechanism of action is characterized by antiangiogenic and immunomodulatory properties. A number of mechanisms has been proposed for the former, including a downregulation of TNF-α, of vascular endothelial growth factor (VGEF) expression, the inhibition of response to basic fibroblastic growth factor (bFGF), and VEGF potentially through the modulation of integrin expression and impairment of migration, the inhibition of endothelial cell proliferation, and even blocking of cyclooxygenase-2 (COX-2). More mechanisms, however, are being evaluated, and thalidomide appears to influence many biological activities [49,109]. Many of these mechanisms play a fundamental role in physiology, but other drugs that interact with the same molecular pathways were not found to show comparable potential to cause a similar pattern of adverse effects on human embryo–fetal development.

The developmental toxicity of thalidomide in humans is characterized by typical congenital malformations, most prominently presenting as phocomelia, ie, stunted limbs, or the complete absence of limbs (amelia). Malformations may also affect the digits and hips or the ears, lips, palate, eyes, heart, spine, respiratory or gastrointestinal tract, and the urogenital system, ie, the kidneys or reproductive organs. Tragically, even a single dose of 50 mg was sufficient to cause the characteristic pattern of malformations, when taken during the critical phase of development of the limbs and the major organ systems, ie, during days 21–35 after conception [49,109,155]. This implies that a pregnant woman may not even have been aware of her pregnancy and/or could have been suffering from morning sickness against which the strong antiemetic properties of thalidomide were highly effective.

Since then, thalidomide has been extensively characterized in numerous species, strains and breeds ([175] and references cited within) including rats, mice, rabbits, dogs, hamsters, primates, cats, armadillos, guinea pigs, swine and ferrets. However, the pattern of adverse effects is greatly variable across species and a number of studies was negative, even for different strains of the same species. Thalidomide was found to be mostly embryo-toxic in the rat whereas rabbits and primates showed the best concordance with the typical human phocomelia. In addition, thalidomide is a much more potent teratogen in humans than in any of the animal species studied except the hamster and is much more toxic to the embryo than to the mother. Until today, the mechanism of developmental toxicity remains a mystery [175].

This example highlights the tragic combination of issues that together led to the most dramatic unexpected and adverse outcome in humans affecting such a high number of individuals:

- the misleading medical understanding of the nature of the placenta at the time that was considered to be an impermeable barrier to environmental influences;
- the testing paradigm of medicine in development at the time;
- the antiemetic efficacy of thalidomide in particular;

- the treatment of morning sickness, a common condition in pregnant women during the early and most vulnerable phase of gestation;
- the free availability over the counter due to much less restrictive legal regulations of new medicines entering the market;
- the fact that low and even single doses were sufficient to adversely affect embryo–fetal development;
- the much greater human sensitivity compared to most animals;
- the greater toxicity to the developing conceptus compared to the mother;
- and finally, the variable, often negative response in animals that hardly reflected the pattern in humans even after full knowledge of the human adverse effects.

It is of note that in rats, the prevailing outcome was characterized by embryotoxicity rather than teratogenicity, which highlights that the response in a biological system A may differ significantly from the response in a biological system B and yet still reflect a similar reaction to a common insult. Today, we do understand that *any* adverse effect on reproduction and development in animals may signify potential toxicity to these systems at unknown doses in humans, the development of which could have a very different phenotypic appearance. Therefore, a weight of evidence approach of all nonclinical safety studies is pursued to arrive at an integrated assessment of a potential reproductive or developmental risk for humans [50,69]. Based on the current understanding of thalidomide, a rabbit fertility and early embryonic development study was conducted by the applicant to support approval of thalidomide in multiple myeloma. This study demonstrated adverse effects on a number of parameters including an increase in resorptions. However, in prospective programs, such a study would not be conducted in rabbits but in rats instead and it is unclear whether the rat would have shown similar observations. It is not uncommon to see drugs in development with fairly unspecific, variable, and often mild outcomes in different species, as was the case for thalidomide and also for other compounds for which some more examples are discussed in the following.

For the new indications, treatment with thalidomide is highly regulated through a specifically developed risk evaluation and mitigation strategy (REMS), called Thalomid REMS [18]. The only purpose of an REMS managing a drug with a safety profile, such as of thalidomide is to prevent unintended exposure of a developing conceptus to a medication that is known or suspected to be developmentally toxic in humans. However, very strict measures have to be implemented and followed to achieve this goal and even under an effective REMS there remains a residual risk to expose pregnant women to thalidomide. Only in serious or even fatal conditions with little or no therapeutic alternatives may such risks be considered acceptable and the risk–benefit ratio still positive in spite of severe side effects, provided that effective measures can be implemented to minimize the associated risks.

Angiotensin-Converting Enzyme (ACE) Inhibitors

This class of compounds is indicated for the treatment of hypertension and congestive heart failure, with the first in class being captopril (Capoten approved in the United States in 1981) and the second in class being enalapril [203]. Enalapril may serve as an example here to illustrate the findings in humans and how they were missed in the toxicological studies.

Enalapril much in contrast to thalidomide was characterized in a full set of reproductive toxicity studies [203, 204], some of which used a modified design compared to the routine since the implementation of ICH in 1993 [101], particularly for the study for fertility and early embryonic development. That is, this study included a fetal evaluation and a lactation phase and was called "study of fertility and general reproductive performance." Since the implementation of ICH, in this type of study, usually, mated females are sacrificed around mid-pregnancy, which allows for evaluation of embryo toxicity but not teratogenicity or postnatal development.

In the rat embryo–fetal development study, maternal and fetal body weight development were reduced that could be prevented with the supplementation of pregnant dams with physiological saline, pointing to an underlying pharmacological effect. Enalapril was found to be neither teratogenic nor embryo-lethal. The rabbit study on embryo–fetal development showed no teratogenic effects either but maternal and embryo–fetal toxicity across the dose range tested, which could be prevented with the supplementation of physiological saline in the low-to-mid dose range but not at higher dose levels.

The rat study on peri- and postnatal development with treatment from day 15 of gestation to day 20 of lactation revealed reduced maternal and pup weight gain and an associated developmental delay for righting reflex, negative geotaxis, and landmarks of sexual developmental but no malformations. Behavioral assessments (open field and swimming maze) were unaffected. The reproductive phase showed no adverse effects on the F1 generation including their offspring, ie, litter size, the number of live and dead pups, or pup weight. The F2 pups revealed no external abnormalities. The ICH standard study design nowadays requires treatment from around implantation (ie, day 6 of gestation) to day 20 of lactation, which covers the major organogenesis in that study in addition.

In the rat study on fertility and general reproductive performance, males were treated from 70 days before mating, throughout mating and until termination of gestation of the corresponding female. Females were treated for 2 weeks prior to mating, throughout mating and gestation. One half was sacrificed on day 20 of gestation; their fetuses were subjected to skeletal (and assumed visceral) evaluation. Offspring allocated to this phase of the study showed reduced fetal weight. The other half of the dams was allowed to litter down and rear their offspring that underwent extensive postweaning examinations including sexual development and behavioral assessments; pup mortality was increased during the lactation phase and body weight gains in male pups were reduced after weaning. The F1 generation was allowed to mate and deliver; F2 litters were evaluated for litter size, numbers of live and dead pups, pup weight, and external abnormalities; these investigations revealed no effects on either the F1 of F2 generation. Fetal skeletal evaluations showed variations, ie, incomplete ossification of sternebrae and lumbar ribs. The description states that skeletal variations were not seen in F1 pups born normally, which implies a skeletal examination phase for delivered offspring, but in this respect, the details given are insufficient to confirm this aspect. In the F1 offspring, there were delays in the development of the surface righting reflex, auditory startle, and vaginal opening but no behavioral changes.

The overall pattern of observations therefore revealed unspecific and fairly mild observations that are not uncommon in this type of study, but with confounding maternal toxicity. Saline supplementation was preventive, which seems to point to a pharmacologically mediated effect. The signal was most evident in the F1 generation from the study on fertility and general reproductive performance. Overall, the combination of findings could be interpreted to indicate a pattern of "developmental delay secondary to maternal toxicity and/or pharmacological effects" that was not deemed too concerning. There was no indication of a primary dysmorphogenic mode of action; the findings are more likely secondary effects mediated through the primary mode of action on the dams and/or the offspring.

Unfortunately, human data demonstrated unexpected and serious concerns, particularly becoming evident during the second and third trimester as intrauterine growth retardation and an increased risk of fetopathy, presenting as renal dysplasia, renal failure, anuria and death, oligohydramnios, and specific adverse outcomes secondary to amniotic fluid volume, ie, limb deformities, cranial ossification deficits, and lung hypoplasia. In addition, neonatal renal failure was observed. Fetal urine production in humans starts toward the end of the first trimester [13,28,188].

This adverse human outcome was totally unexpected from the comprehensive preclinical studies, and it is worth reviewing the designs that were used. Human risk was most evident when treating women with hypertension—a common complication in pregnancy—during the second and third trimester of pregnancy, but not during the first. In the study on peri- and postnatal development, treatment started on day 15 of pregnancy, which is slightly before the end of organogenesis and best reflects the clinical treatment conditions leading to adverse human outcomes. However, there was no indication for such a severe adverse effect in this study. The question therefore is how the difference can be explained and why the animal studies failed to predict the risk in humans.

Tabacova and Kimmel [187] reviewed the typical ACE-inhibitor induced adverse fetal outcome termed ACEI fetopathy. In humans, the target system of enalapril, ie, the kidney and the renin–angiotensin system, develops at the end of the first trimester and prior to skeletal ossification. In most of the animal species studied, the enalapril target systems are comparably less mature, and consequently, enalapril cannot work on them until they are functional. Only shortly before term are these systems developed, at which point the fetus is more mature and less vulnerable. In particular, the rat shows greatest disparity with respect to the relative development of the kidney and skeletal ossification compared to humans, which explains why effects similar to humans were not detected in the rat reproductive toxicity program, in spite of some apparent pharmacological effects. Rhesus monkeys show the best concordance of the prenatal development of these systems with humans, but this species is not routinely used in embryo–fetal development studies unless there is a specific justification. For the testing of ACE inhibitors, indeed, the use of the rhesus may have been the better choice, but this was not evident at the time of prospective testing of this new class of compounds. Tabacova also pointed out that it is unclear whether a similar pathology would be seen in this animal model. It appears that exposure to enalapril after the first trimester was strongly associated with oligohydramnios and the specific adverse outcomes were considered secondary to the reduced amniotic fluid volume, as well as with neonatal renal failure [188]. Tabacova [189] concluded that "animal studies that follow standard protocols and evaluate developmental toxicity only for exposures during embryogenesis will miss developmental effects arising secondary to disruption of target systems that develop after the period of major organogenesis. Thus, although the animal mode of action (MOA) for enalapril and other ACEI is plausible in humans, differences in the timing of development of critical target organ systems, particularly the renal system and renin–angiotensin system (RAS), explain the absence of definitive structural abnormalities in test animals." This example highlights again how the absence of evidence is not evidence of absence, and that a profound understanding of the test system is key for the interpretation of results.

Since the discovery of the adverse effects brought about by the ACE inhibitors when treating pregnant women during the second and third trimester of pregnancy, it also became a matter of debate whether ACE inhibitors could be potential teratogens when given during the first trimester. Angiotensin II receptors are widely expressed in fetal tissue [4] and Cooper et al. [28] suggested an increased risk of major congenital malformations, particularly of the heart and CNS. This hypothesis has stimulated a dialogue, but the answer to this question remains unresolved at present due to conflicting evidence [123,206]. There are confounding factors that complicate the assessment in a clinical setting, including obesity, diabetes, the hypertension itself, or other antihypertensive medications [123,159,173]. Sealey and Itskovitz-Eldor [176] commented that it is unknown whether the postulated effects are specific to ACEI or could be applicable to other drugs that block the RAS (eg, betablockers, ACE receptor blockers, renin inhibitors) [120], given that the oocyte, embryo, and developing fetus are continuously "bathed" in "prorenin, the precursor of renin, from just before ovulation until parturition" [80,106,107]. This aspect is particularly interesting in view of the more pronounced but still unspecific findings in the study on fertility and general reproductive performance as opposed to the peri- and postnatal study and in view of the complete absence of evidence for teratogenicity in the reproductive toxicity studies, which is not readily explicable if prorenin is a key determinant in embryo–fetal development. Since 2012, enalapril and other drugs, such as aliskiren [191], which fall into this category, have received a boxed warning in the United States indicating that "Drugs that act directly on the renin-angiotensin system can cause injury and death to the developing fetus." This statement is, notably, based on a hypothesis that yet needs to be confirmed, but is the current basis to aid in human risk management.

Endothelin Receptor Antagonists

The endothelin receptor antagonists were discovered in the late 1980s, with the first in class being bosentan (Tracleer), a mixed antagonist of endothelin receptors (ET_A and ET_B), which entered clinical development in 1993 and was approved as orphan drug for the treatment of pulmonary arterial hypertension in 2001 [23,195]. Generally, from its pharmacology, bosentan was believed to be a promising candidate for the management of clinical disorders associated with vasoconstriction. Among these, migraine was also evaluated clinically but bosentan was reported not to be effective [129].

In the course of development, bosentan was found to be teratogenic and embryo-toxic in the rat when given orally at doses as low as two times the MRHD based on body surface area [198,199]. The findings encountered included craniofacial abnormalities, such as agenesis of the palate, shortened/misshapen mandibles, fusion of the pterygoid process with the tympanic annulus, abnormal zygomatic arch, shortened tongues, anophthalmia, and microphthalmia. Blood-vessel findings were also observed. Similar observations could be demonstrated in a mouse knockout model, and these effects were more pronounced when pregnant dams were treated with other agents antagonizing endothelin or the ET_A receptor in addition [118,119]. Regulatory studies with bosentan in the rabbit, however, failed to show evidence of teratogenicity [198]. The only findings observed in this species were an impaired fetal body weight in the presence of maternal toxicity only and a higher incidence of some skeletal variations in the high-dose group. Hence, the rabbit is less sensitive than the rat in this case, and testing in the rabbit only would have resulted in a false-negative outcome, although it was noted that systemic exposures in the rabbit were lower than in the rat. It is of note that the high dose was 1500 mg/kg/day, which exceeds the limit dose in the ICH S5 guideline (see Table 2.1) [198,199]. The difference in exposures may explain the variable response between the animal species, since the pattern of findings in rats and knock-out mice strongly suggests a class effect associated with the mode of action. Indeed, other endothelin antagonists in development were published to cause a concordant pattern of malformations in rats and rabbits and the authors concluded that teratogenicity is a likely class effect of endothelin receptor antagonists [200].

In general, variable outcomes between species may be a matter of specificity or of different levels of sensitivity—also in a broader sense, ie, encompassing not only lower species sensitivity but also reduced sensitivity of the testing conditions—particularly in cases like this one where it would be difficult to understand why such a fundamental physiological target, which is involved in embryo–fetal development, does not result in a similar phenotypic outcome when inhibited. Again, macitentan (Opsumit), another endothelin antagonist approved for pulmonary arterial hypertension in the United States in 2013 [149,150], was demonstrated to show similar effects as bosentan in the rat, and was also teratogenic in the rabbit at all doses tested with both species showing a similar pattern, evidenced as cardiovascular and mandibular arch fusion abnormalities. Administration of macitentan to female rats from late pregnancy through lactation caused reduced pup survival and impairment of male fertility of the offspring at all dose levels tested [150]. Therefore lactating women should either discontinue macitentan or nursing. The same precaution is also recommended for bosentan [199].

The example of the endothelin antagonists demonstrates the importance and obligation to manage potential human risks in the most responsible manner, ie, it must be postulated that the adverse effects established in the DART studies are predictive for humans, even in cases where only one species seems to show adverse effects. Potential risks need to be mitigated accordingly. Therefore in this case, again, unintended exposure of pregnant women must be avoided. In practical terms, the Tracleer [bosentan] label contains a boxed warning indicating the following: "Based on animal data, Tracleer is likely to cause major birth defects if used during pregnancy." Tracleer is only available through a restricted distribution program called the Tracleer Access Program (T.A.P.) because of this risk (and the risk of liver failure). Macitentan is handled accordingly. The applied risk management strategy is—notably—based on clear evidence of developmental risk to the unborn from regulatory animal studies and—thankfully—not on clinical evidence from epidemiological data, and this shows how the sound nonclinical characterization allowed for a meaningful risk–benefit evaluation based on which the risk can be managed effectively. However, it also is evident that bosentan or other endothelin antagonists are not approvable for "soft(er)" indications where alternative medications are available and/or where the risk of exposure of pregnant women is much greater, such as migraine, and therefore the risks outweigh potential benefits. By contrast, pulmonary arterial hypertension is a fatal condition and a very rare disease for which bosentan was originally granted an orphan designation. The potential benefit for this condition therefore was deemed to outweigh potential risks, when successfully managed. To the best of our knowledge, indeed, clinically, no case of congenital malformations associated with the use of endothelin antagonists has been reported to date.

Triptanes

In 1995, the first triptane, sumatriptan, received approval in the United States. This new class of compounds targeting serotonin receptors was developed for the treatment of migraine.

This indication affects all populations, including children, peaks around the age of 40, and then declines (data from the US). Females are more frequently affected than males. The age and gender distribution demonstrate that in this indication women of childbearing potential represent a great proportion of the target patient population, which makes reproductive toxicity assessment a key determinant in the safety assessment of new drugs in this field [125].

Sumatriptan, the first triptane in class, may serve as an example to tell the history of success of this innovative class of medicines with respect to the characterization of its developmental toxicity profile.

Sumatriptan was evaluated in a full range of regulatory studies using different routes of exposure, including intravenous (i.v.) and oral and was found to be embryolethal in rabbits when given daily i.v. at doses approximating the maximum recommended single human subcutaneous dose of 6 mg on a body surface area basis (MRHD). The doses were at or close to those producing maternal toxicity. Fetuses of pregnant rabbits administered oral sumatriptan (at doses greater than 50 times the MRHD) during organogenesis had an increased incidence of cervicothoracic vascular and skeletal anomalies. In contrast, embryo–fetal lethality was not observed in pregnant rats treated throughout organogenesis with i.v. doses approximately 20 times the MRHD. Moreover, no rat embryo–fetal lethality or teratogenicity was observed with daily subcutaneous doses before and throughout gestation [105]. Shepard [178] described a study in which no fetal adverse effects were observed in rats given up to 1000 mg/kg orally during organogenesis.

Following approval, the Sumatriptan/Naratriptan/Treximet Pregnancy Registry was established to monitor pregnancy outcomes following treatment with these medications. The interim report summarizing data from the 1st of January 1996 through the 31st of October 2011 was issued in May 2012 and concluded for sumatriptan that the "data do no indicate a signal for major teratogenicity." Data on Naratriptan and Treximet were too limited for the registry to meet its primary objective.

This example highlights several important aspects in the prospective risk assessment of new drugs—particularly for new classes of compounds. From the preclinical data set, clearly there was concern as to whether the data might signify an adverse effect of sumatriptan on embryo–fetal development in a particularly vulnerable target patient population. The findings were—as for thalidomide (rat), the ACE inhibitors, and many drugs in development (personal experience)—fairly unspecific and did not demonstrate a defined pattern as for the endothelin antagonists. In addition, maternal toxicity was a confounding factor. Obviously, however, there is a clear need to distinguish the hazardous compounds from those that are benign. In this case, a new class of compounds with major benefit for the patients affected was approved but at the same time, any potential risks were prospectively, carefully, and successfully managed, which is an important element in the development of innovative and beneficial drugs.

Overall, the field of reproductive toxicology has developed into a mature discipline since the occurrence of the thalidomide tragedy. Schardein et al. [174] have reviewed species sensitivities and the prediction of teratogenic potential based on the observation that many xenobiotics shown to be teratogenic in animals are not known to be teratogenic in humans. The reasons for this apparent difference remain to be established and could involve a number of factors, including, indeed, lower species sensitivity of humans, but also subteratogenic exposure levels or a lack of appropriate methods to identify human teratogens. By contrast, with the exception of the coumarin anticoagulant drugs, all well-accepted human teratogens were also demonstrated to be teratogenic in at least one laboratory animal species. However, there is no single species that in general is giving a more reliable response than another; in fact, rats and mice showed the best concordance for findings observed in humans but in other cases also produced the most nonconcordant responses, whereas rabbits were more unlikely to give a false-positive response. Primates in general are showing higher predictivity levels but are less commonly used. In essence, the authors concluded that neither a single species nor a single study will be sufficient to detect a potential reproductive hazard but all endpoints must be taken into account, including results from other toxicology studies, pharmacokinetic and metabolic data as well as the pharmacological mode of action to arrive at an integrated assessment of human risk.

Maternal toxicity as a confounding factor is a matter of ongoing debate in the scientific community. Khera [112] has proposed this concept to put adverse developmental findings occurring at maternally toxic dose levels into context. While maternal toxicity is an important consideration and may well be a contributory factor to the development of unspecific effects in the offspring—such as a reduction of fetal weight at dose levels that simultaneously significantly impair maternal body weight development—specific patterns of malformations are highly unlikely to be secondary to maternal toxicity [9,33]. On the other hand, typical but rare malformations may be observed in a given strain due to genetic liability. In such a case, the actual incidence in a given study as compared to background data and aspects, such as the distribution across groups and a potential association with dose levels—for example, if malformations typical for this strain become evident only at a maternally toxic doses—are critical aspects and, depending on the outcome, may or may not increase concern with regards to potential developmental toxicity of a given test item. It is therefore critical to have a robust set of background data to be able to put findings in context on a case-by-case basis. The more limited a set of background data and the higher the incidence of background observations the lower is the sensitivity of a test system in a given laboratory. As a basic principle, it is important to assess whether adverse effects on the conceptus—be they specific or not—are observed in the presence of maternal toxicity only or whether the conceptus appears to be more vulnerable than the dam, which is an especially hazardous situation. Obviously, this correlation may not be the same in another species.

The current nonclinical tools to assess a developmental and reproductive hazard can be considered to be fairly effective but, inevitably, an intrinsic residual risk of failure remains given the biological complexity of reproduction, involving the closely intertwined maternal and embryo–fetal systems and their manifold interactions, which also show species-specific features. For the purpose of human risk assessment, the most challenging situations are those where the experimental data are inconclusive, eg, due to unspecific findings associated with confounding factors, such as maternal toxicity, a lack of concordance between species, or a lack of biological plausibility. Human evidence may either increase concern, such as in the case of the ACE inhibitors, or, alternatively, decrease concern, such as in the case of the triptanes. In some cases, projects with such inconclusive profiles will be terminated and not developed further.

It is virtually impossible to definitively confirm the absence of an adverse potential on embryo–fetal development in humans. Approximately 3% of newborns have congenital malformations requiring medical intervention, with about one-third being life-threatening. More than twice as many are detected later in life [179]. This demonstrates that any human teratogen would likely have to occur at a distinctly higher incidence, perhaps in a cluster or to be of a very unusual type, to be identified. History shows that this was the case indeed, eg, for the detection of thalidomide or diethylstilbestrol (DES) as human teratogens [174].

With regards to human safety, specific patterns of adverse developmental effects in animal studies must be considered to be predictive a priori and potential risks be managed appropriately to prevent harmful human outcomes, such as with the REMS in place for thalidomide or bosentan. In such cases, the severity of the human condition and the unmet medical need for treatment will determine whether potential benefits still outweigh potential risks in the target patient population.

POSTMARKETING

After years of comprehensive nonclinical and clinical characterization, finally, a new therapeutic made it all the way and got marketing approval. The launch was successful and large patient populations treated. The development costs can be recuperated und money can be made to support new research and development. However, in spite of well-conducted nonclinical and clinical studies, the unexpected can still occur at this stage and may even result in the withdrawal of prescription drugs from the market. Such situations are not rare events.

Qureshi et al. [160] evaluated the reason for withdrawal of new molecular entities (NMEs) approved by the Food and Drug Administration (FDA) from 1980 to 2009. Out of 740 approved NMEs the number of drugs discontinued was 118 (15.9%). The authors found that 3.5% of market withdrawals were due to safety reasons and the average time from approval to safety withdrawal was 5.9 years, with a range of 0.3–18.2 years. Major reasons were severe hepatotoxicity, cardiovascular effects, and gastrointestinal issues. Fung et al. [78] conducted an analysis to evaluate prescription drugs withdrawn from worldwide markets for the time period from 1960 to 1999. The authors identified 121 drugs that were withdrawn for the following top five safety reasons: hepatic (26.2%), hematologic (10.5%), cardiovascular (8.7%), dermatologic (6.3%), and carcinogenic (6.3%) issues. A more recent study investigating the withdrawal throughout the European Union between 2002 and 2011 identified 19 drugs that were withdrawn due to safety reasons [133]. Cardiovascular events or disorders were the main reason (9/19), followed by hepatic and neurological or psychiatric disorders (each 4/19). Daggumalli and Irwin [31] evaluated 15 drugs withdrawn between 2001 and 2010 from the US marked. Cardiovascular side effects were noted for 7 and hepatotoxicity for 1 of the 15 discontinued drugs. Hence, the top two main reasons for market withdrawal are hepatotoxicity and cardiovascular toxicity. While hepatotoxicity was the main reason in the past, cardiovascular side effects seem to be the leading reason for prescription drug withdrawals in recent years.

The general paradigm of preclinical animal studies is to dose a smaller number of healthy animals at high(er) doses in order to predict possible side effects in a much more heterogeneous population of patients that are treated at significantly lower doses, although it is appreciated that in special cases, clinical doses may actually be higher than those used in animals (see above). Clinical development of a new drug can only be done in a limited number of patients. Rare adverse events, treatment of very sick and particularly sensitive patients with comorbidities and cotreatments, off-label use, or use not according to the labeling instructions may result in adverse events not previously observed in the closely selected patient population in the pivotal Phase III studies. Therefore the complete safety profile of a new prescription drug will only become evident once larger patient populations are exposed under marketing conditions. The following discusses some examples for drugs that successfully completed preclinical and clinical development without any indication for the serious side effects that were discovered later when the drug was administered to larger patient populations.

Drug Withdrawal Due to Hepatotoxicity

Drug induced liver injury (DILI) falls into two categories, ie, intrinsic or idiosyncratic types. Drugs that are intrinsic hepatotoxic cause similar effects across species and the effect in humans can be predicted from animal data when sufficiently high doses are administered. A good example of intrinsic DILI is acetaminophen, the effects of which can be demonstrated in preclinical animal studies and are clearly dose-related. Idiosyncratic DILI is less common, unpredictable from animal studies, does not have a clear dose response and has a variable latency period. The effects in humans are severe and may result in the need of liver transplantation. The incidence of idiosyncratic liver injury in humans is low (<1 in 10,000) and is usually not discovered in clinical trials that usually study 1000–3000 subjects within the registration package [67]. This type of DILI is called idiosyncratic as it is dependent on a person's susceptibility and not predicted from nonhuman systems including animals. Elevations of serum aminotransferases are often seen during drug development in preclinical animal studies as well as in clinical trials. In humans those effects can also be generated by drugs that have low potential for causing idiosyncratic DILI (eg, aspirin, statins, tacrine, heparin) [67], but in turn, aminotransferase increases are not suitable to predict idiosyncratic DILI.

Bromfenac (Duract)

This peripherally acting nonnarcotic analgesic nonsteroidal antiinflammatory drug (NSAID) was approved in the United States in 1997 for short-term management of acute pain (use for 10 days or less). The duration of treatment was limited to 10 days as a higher incidence of liver enzyme elevations was noted in patients treated in long-term clinical trials. With respect to the severity of findings, preclinical animal species (rat and monkey) were not predictive for what happened in humans. The liver was identified in rats and mice as a possible target organ of toxicity in the 2-year carcinogenicity studies only and merely mild liver enzyme elevations were noted in the 12-month toxicity study in rhesus monkeys [154]. However, glutathione depletion was found in the liver and kidney of rats. Postmarketing reports of severe hepatitis and liver failure (some requiring transplantation) in patients taking the drug for longer than 10 days' duration were received. In 1998 the label was strengthened with a special black box warning, and a "Dear Doctor" letter was issued by the manufacturer. Despite those actions patients continued to have severe liver injuries and even death following long-term use of bromfenac; overall, a total of four deaths occurred and eight patients received liver transplants. One patient with preexisting significant liver disease used the drug within the specified duration. All other patients used the drug for longer than 10 days [62]. In total an estimated 200,000–400,000 patients took bromfenac longer than the 10-day maximum for which it should be prescribed. The company voluntarily withdrew the drug from the market in 1998.

It is obvious that bromfenac was not used as described in the label. However, it has to be noted that other drugs in this class (NSAIDs) do not have limited treatment duration and are usually used for weeks or months at a time. Preclinical animal studies did not predict the severity of the problem. Liver enzyme elevations were seen in clinical studies, leading to the decision to limit the duration of use in patients to a maximum of 10 days. None of these measures, however, predicted the severity of liver toxicity becoming evident following marketing, and mostly observed following treatment for longer than the approved duration. Noncompliance issues are an important consideration in the safety of marketed drugs. In this context, the risk–benefit evaluation also has to take into account that alternatives may exist. For short-term management of pain many medicines with more favorable safety profiles are available.

Troglitazone (Rezulin)

Troglitazone, the first in class peroxisome proliferator-activated receptor gamma (PPAR gamma) agonist, was approved in the United States in 1997 for the treatment of type 2 diabetes mellitus. No case of liver failure occurred among the 2510 subjects exposed to drug during clinical development. However, a larger percentage of troglitazone-treated patients had elevated alanine aminotransferase (ALT) levels, including five patients with ALT>30xULN (upper limit of normal) out of which two developed jaundice [67]. After reports of acute liver failure following troglitazone treatment surfaced four "Dear Doctor Letters" were sent to healthcare providers between 1997 and 1999 recommending monthly liver function monitoring. In addition, the label received a hepatotoxicity black box warning recommending ALT level measurements prior to the start of therapy and at least monthly during the first year on therapy. Graham et al. [83] found that less than 5% of the patients received all recommended liver enzyme tests by the third month of continuous use. An analysis of 94 cases of liver failure reported to the FDA showed that the progression from normal hepatic tests to irreversible liver injury can occur in less than one month [67]. This demonstrated that even if serum ALT levels were monitored as recommended those measurements would not have been sufficiently effective in preventing severe liver injuries.

Troglitazone was withdrawn from the US market in 2000 when other drugs from this class without evidence of hepatotoxicity became available.

Drug Withdrawal Due to Cardiotoxicity

During the 1990s several drugs were withdrawn due to fatal arrhythmias caused by QT/QTc prolongation. Following the implementation of extensive screening for this possible side-effect market withdrawal due to QT/QTc prolongation has not occurred in recent years. However, despite the absence of cardiotoxicity in animals cardiovascular side effects remain one of the major causes for postmarketing withdrawal. Two examples follow. The overall low incidence and the higher susceptibility of patients with preexisting conditions complicate the prediction of those serious adverse events during nonclinical and clinical development.

Tegaserod (Zelnorm)

Tegaserod was approved in 2002 for the short-term treatment of women with irritable bowel syndrome with constipation and for patients younger than 65 with chronic constipation. In 2007 the drug was withdrawn from the US market when a new safety analysis of 29 clinical studies became available. In this analysis, 11,614 patients on tegaserod were compared with 7031 patients on placebo. Thirteen patients (0.1%) treated with tegaserod suffered from heart attack, stroke, or severe heart chest pain that can turn into a heart attack compared to one patient (0.01%) on placebo [64]. Although the number of patients having serious and life-threatening side effects was small it was clear that patients on tegaserod had a higher risk than those who were treated with placebo.

Sibutramine (Meridia)

Sibutramine, a norepinephrine and serotonin reuptake inhibitor, was approved by the FDA in 1997 for weight loss and maintenance of weight loss in obese people. In the EU, it was approved in Germany in January 1999 and subsequently applications were submitted to Member States through the mutual recognition procedure. Already in October 1999 Belgium drew attention to sibutramine-induced increased blood pressure and heart rate and requested a reassessment of the risk–benefit balance. The Committee for Proprietary Medicinal Products (CPMP) recommended the maintenance of the marketing authorizations provided that the marketing authorization holder (MAH) performs a clinical study to evaluate the cardiovascular risk and submits six monthly periodic safety update reports [43]. In March 2002, sibutramine was temporarily withdrawn from the Italian market on the basis of cardiac adverse event reports and two deaths form cardiovascular disease [12,43]. This time Italy asked the CPMP for a reassessment of the risk–benefit balance. The calculated incidence of fatal events was 2.4–2.86 in 100,000 treatment years with sibutramine. This was then compared to the best-available control population, ie, a body mass index-matched cohort from the large Nurse's Health Study [131], ie, 390 deaths per 100,000 treatment years. Based on available data CPMP confirmed a favorable risk–benefit balance and maintained the marketing authorization for sibutramine [43].

Overweight and obese people have a higher risk of cardiac complications masking the identification of an increased drug induced risk in this target population. Therefore the path from early adverse event case reports to the proof of sibutramine-induced cardiovascular side effects was long. The MAH further studied the long-term effects of sibutramine treatment on the rates of cardiovascular events and cardiovascular death in overweight or obese subjects with preexisting cardiovascular disease, type 2 diabetes mellitus, or both. This study, also known as the SCOUT trial, lasted 6 years. All subjects received sibutramine in addition to participating in a weight-management program during a 6-week, single-blind, lead-in period. Thereafter subjects were randomly assigned to sibutramine (4902 subjects) or placebo (4898 subjects). The mean duration of treatment was 3.4 years. Subjects with preexisting cardiovascular conditions receiving sibutramine had an increased risk of nonfatal myocardial infarction and nonfatal stroke (11.4% on sibutramine compared to 10.0% on placebo) but not of cardiovascular death or death from any cause [110]. Based on the results of this study the MAH voluntarily withdraw sibutramine from the market in 2010.

CONCLUDING REMARKS

What do thalidomide, the ACE inhibitors, terfenadine, and TGN1412 as well as many of the examples discussed above have in common? All of them caused severe and/or fatal side effects that were totally unexpected at the time and not revealed before they had adversely and irrevocably affected humans that received these drugs either after marketing according to the label or under controlled conditions in a clinical trial. How could this happen in spite of extensive testing during the drug development process and measures in place that were believed to effectively manage potential risks?

Basically, in all of these cases, it comes down to the same basic underlying reason: the medical and/or scientific concepts at the time were fundamentally wrong or at least were characterized by incomplete medical and/or scientific knowledge, that in turn, led to deficient testing strategies then in force. Inevitably, at some point, these deficits became evident when the adverse human outcomes were discovered and finally attributed to the drugs involved.

The question is, however, whether and how such disasters can be prevented in the future. Certainly, the process of drug development has greatly evolved in recent decades and is now one of the most complex areas involving experts from numerous disciplines. However, as the requirements to develop effective medications continue to advance in evermore complex disease areas with unmet medical needs the experts involved are facing situations that they cannot fully comprehend at a given moment in time. Medicine is an empiric discipline and, hence, progress made is often rather descriptive and needs to be undertaken in a step-wise approach, due to the extremely complex interaction of countless aspects involved. Therefore unfortunately, while we are now successfully managing many risks after they were recognized based on adverse outcomes in the past, inevitably, if medical progress is to be made, unknown territories continue to be discovered and our concepts and strategies in exploring them may be wrong or deficient again. Indeed, our apparent knowledge of today might be revealed to be our errors of tomorrow, and we will remain on a learning curve. Therefore we should understand ourselves as researchers and ensure we take every possible measure to ascertain successful drug development—with the knowledge that we are never sure when we are going to face an issue that is challenging us. Therefore we should expect the unexpected at all times as we go ahead to accomplish our mission to build the bridge from "bench to bedside." Medical progress, however, has been extremely successful and today many severe diseases can be safely and effectively treated for which no medicines were available only 100 years ago. Alongside with this extremely rewarding process we should keep challenging our beliefs and convictions with the aim to critically assess our concepts, which, in turn, will hopefully continue to provide the basis for robust testing strategies supporting successful development of new medications in the future.

References

[1] Abilify® (aripiprazole) pharmacology review, Drugs@FDA; 2002.

[2] Abilify® (aripiprazole) prescribing information, Drugs@FDA; 2014.

[3] Aeschbacher HU, Finot PA, Wolleb U. Interactions of histidine-containing test substances and extraction methods with the Ames mutagenicity test. Mutat Res 1983;113(2):103–16.

[4] Archivist. Teratogenicity of first trimester ACE inhibitors. Arch Dis Child 2006;91(10):840.

[5] Auer RN. Effect of age and sex on N-Methyl-d-Aspartate antagonist-induced neuronal necrosis in rats. Stroke 1996;27:743–6.

[6] Alden CL, Lynn A, Bourdeau A, Morton D, Sistare FD, Kadambi VJ, et al. A critical review of the effectiveness of rodent pharmaceutical carcinogenesis testing in predicting for human risk. Vet Pathol 2011;48(3):772–84.

[7] Bansal AK, Kumar L, Amin A. Salt selection in drug development. Pharm Technol 2008;3(32).

[8] Begley CG, Ellis LM. Drug development: raise standards for preclinical cancer research. Nature 2012;483:531–3.

[9] Beyer B, Chernoff N, Danielsson BR, Davis-Bruno K, Harrouk W, Hood RD, et al. ILSI/HESI maternal toxicity workshop summary: maternal toxicity and its impact on study design and data interpretation. Birth Defects Res B Dev Reprod Toxicol 2011;92(1):36–51.

[10] Beyersdort N, Hanke T, Kerkau T, Huenig T. Superagonistc anti-CD28 antibodies: potent activators of regulatory T cells for the therapy of autoimmune diseases. Ann Rheum Dis 2005;64:iv91–5.

[11] Boobis AR, Cohen SM, Nancy G, Doerrer NG, Galloway SM, Haley PJ, et al. A data-based assessment of alternative strategies for identification of potential human cancer hazards. Toxicol Pathol 2009;37(6):714–32.

[12] Bosello O, Carruba MO, Ferrannini E, Rotella CM. Sibutramine lost and found. Eat Weight Disord 2002;7(3):161–7.

[13] Briggs GG. Drug effects on the fetus and breast-fed infant. Clin Obstetrics Gynecol 2002;45(1):6–21.

[14] Bril A, Gout B, Bonhomme M, Landais L, Faivre J-F, Linee P, et al. Combined potassium and calcium channel blocking activities as a basis for antiarrhythmic efficacy with low proarrhythmic risk: experimental profile of BRL-3272. J Pharmacol Exp Ther 1996;276(2):637–46.

[15] Bumbaca D, Wong A, Drake E, Reyes 2nd AE, Lin BC, Stephan JP, et al. Highly specific off-target binding identified and eliminated during the humanization of an antibody against FGF receptor 4. MAbs 2011;3(4):376–86.

[16] Caldwell DJ. Review of mononuclear cell leukemia in F-344 rat bioassays and its significance to human cancer risk: a case study using alkyl phthalates. Regul Toxicol Pharmacol 1999;30(1):45–53.

[17] Carmichael NG, Enzmann H, Pate I, Waechter F. The significance of mouse liver tumor formation for carcinogenic risk assessment: results and conclusions from a survey of ten years of testing by the agrochemical industry. Environ Health Perspect 1997;105(11):1196–203.

[18] Ceglene. Welcome to the THALOMID REMS™ program. 2014. http://www.thalomidrems.com.

[19] Celexa® (citalopram) prescribing information, Drugs@FDA; 1998.

[20] Chanut F, Kimbrough C, Hailey R, Berridge B, Hughes-Earle A, Davies R, et al. Spontaneous cardiomyopathy in young Sprague-Dawley rats: evaluation of biological and environmental variability. Toxicologic Pathol 2013;41(8):1126–36.

[21] Cheng H, Force T. Molecular mechanisms of cardiovascular toxicity of targeted cancer therapeutics. Circ Res 2010;106(1):21–34.

[22] Clegg ED, Cook JC, Chapin RE, Foster PMD, Daston GP. Leydic cell hyperplasia and adenoma formation: mechanisms and relevance to humans. Reprod Toxicol 1997;11(1):107–21.

[23] Clozel M, Breu V, Gray GA, Kalina B, Löffler BM, Burri K, et al. Pharmacological characterization of bosentan, a new potent orally active nonpeptide endothelin receptor antagonist. J Pharmacol Exp Ther 1994;270(1):228–35.

[24] Cohen SM. Urinary bladder carcinogenesis. Toxicol Pathol 1998;26(1):121–7.

[25] Cohen SM, Meek ME, Klaunig JE, Patton DE, Fenner-Crisp P. The human relevance of information on carcinogenic mode of action: overview. Crit Rev Toxicol 2003;33(6):581–9.

[26] Cohen SM, Klaunig J, Meek ME, Hill RN, Pastoor R, Lehman-McKeeman L, et al. Evaluating the human relevance of chemically induced animal tumors. Toxicol Sci 2004;78(2):181–6.

[27] Contrera JF, Jacobs AC, DeGeorge JJ. Carcinogenicity testing and the evaluation of regulatory requirements for pharmaceuticals. Regul Toxicol Pharmacol 1997;25(2):130–45.

[28] Cooper WO, Hernandes-Diaz S, Arbogast PG, Dudley JA, Dyer S, Gideon PS, et al. Major congenital malformations after first-trimester exposure to ACE inhibitors. New Engl J Med 2006;354(23):2443–51.

[29] Creely CE, Wozniak DF, Nardi A, Farber NB, Olney JW. Donepezil markedly potentiates memantine neurotoxicity in the adult rat brain. Neurobiol Aging 2008;29(2):153–67.

[30] Crone SA, Zhao YY, Fan L, Gu Y, Minamisawa S, Liu Y, et al. ErbB2 is essential in the prevention of dilated cardiomyopathy. Nat Med 2002;8(5):459–65.

[31] Daggumalli JSV, Martin IG. Are pharmaceutical market withdrawals preventable? A preliminary analysis. Drug Inform J 2012;46(6):694–700.

[32] Dally A. Thalidomide: was the tragedy preventable? The Lancet 1998;351(9110):1197–9.

[33] Danielsson BR. Maternal toxicity. In: Barrow PC, editor. Teratogenicity testing: methods and protocols. Methods in molecular biology, vol. 947. Springer Science + Business Media, LLC; 2013. p. 311–25.

[34] Dearfield KL, Thybaud V, Cimino MC, Custer L, Czich A, Harvew JS, et al. Follow-up actions from positive results of in vitro genetic toxicity testing. Environ Mol Mutagen 2011; 52(3):177–204.

[35] Dejaco C, Duftner C, Grubeck-Loebenstein B, Schirmer M. Imbalance of regulatory T cells in human autoimmune diseases. Immunology 2006;117(3):289–300.

[36] de Korte MA, de Vries EG, Lub-de Hooge MN, Jager PL, Gietema JA, van der Graff WT, et al. [111]Indium-trastuzumab visualizes myocardial human epidermal growth factor receptor 2 expression shortly after anthracycline treatment but not during heart failure: a clue to uncover the mechanism of trastuzumab-related cardiotoxicity. Eur J Cancer 2007;43(13):2046–51.

[37] DeSecco JM. Anatomical relationships of urinary bladders compared: their potential role in the development of bladder tumours in humans and rats. Food Chem Toxicol 1995;33(9):705–14.

[38] DiMasi JA, Hansen RW, Grabowski HG. The price of innovation: new estimates of drug development costs. J Health Econ 2003;22(2):151–85.

[39] DiMasi JA, Grabowski HG, Hansen RW. Cost of developing a new drug. Tufts Center for the Study of Drug Development; 2014. http://csdd.tufts.edu/news/complete_story/pr_tufts_csdd_2014_cost_study.

[40] Dy GK, Adjei AA. Understanding, recognizing, and managing toxicities of targeted anticancer therapies. CA Cancer J Clin 2013;63:249–79.

[41] Eastwood D, Findlay L, Poole S, Bird C, Wadhwa M, Moore M, et al. Monoglonal antibody TGN1412 trial failure explained by species differences in CD28 expression on CD4[+] effector memory T-cells. Br J Pharmacol 2010;161(3):512–26.

[42] Eastwood D, Bird C, Dilger P, Hockley J, Findlay L, Poole S, et al. Severity of the TGN1412 trial disaster cytokine storm correlated with IL-2-release. Br J Clin Pharmacol 2013;76(2):299–315.

[43] EMA. Sibutramine – post-authorisation evaluation of medicines for human use. Committee for Proprietary Medicinal Products; 2002. CPMP/4514/02.

[44] EMA. Position paper on non-clinical safety studies to support clinical trials with a single microdose. Committee for Medicinal Products for Human Use; 2003a. CPMP/SWP/2599/02.

[45] EMA. Scientific discussion. Exelon® (rivastigmine). 2003b. http://www.ema.europa.eu/docs/en_GB/document_library/EPAR_-_Scientific_Discussion/human/000169/WC500032592.pdf.

[46] EMA. Scientific discussion. Rapamune® (sirolimus). 2004. http://www.ema.europa.eu/docs/en_GB/document_library/EPAR_-_Scientific_Discussion/human/000273/WC500046434.pdf.

[47] EMA. Guideline on the limits of genotoxic impurities. Committee for Medicinal Products for Human Use; 2006. Doc. Ref.: EMEA/CHMP/QWP/251344/2006.

[48] EMA. Guideline on strategies to identify and mitigate risks for first-in-human clinical trials with investigational medicinal products. Committee for Medicinal Products for Human Use; 2007. Doc. Ref.: EMEA/CHMP/SWP/28367/07.

[49] EMA. European assessment report for thalidomide pharmion. 2008a. Doc. Ref.: EMEA/176582/2008.

[50] EMA. Guideline on risk assessment of medicinal products on human reproduction and lactation: from data to labelling. Committee for Medicinal Products for Human Use; 2008b. Doc Ref: EMEA/CHMP/203927/2005.

[51] EMA. Questions and answers on the guideline on the limits of genotoxic impurities. Committee for Medicinal Products for Human Use; 2010. Doc. Ref.: EMA/CHMP/SWP/431994/2007 Rev. 3.

[52] EMA. CTFG (Clinical Trial Facilitation Group) in Europe. Recommendations related to contraception and pregnancy testing in clinical trials. 2014.

[53] EMA. Guidance on immunogenicity assessment of biotechnology-derived therapeutic proteins. Committee for Medicinal Products for Human Use (draft); 2015. Doc. Ref.: EMEA/CHMP/BMWP/14327/2006 Rev. 1.

[54] Ennulat D, Walker D, Clemo F, Magid-Slav M, Ledieu D, Graham M, et al. Effects of hepatic drug-metabolizing enzyme induction on clinical pathology parameters in animals and man. Toxicol Pathol 2010;38(5):810–28.

[55] Ettlin RA, Junker U, Prentice DE. Dopomine agonists. In: Karbe K, Drommer W, Germann PG, Morawietz G, Kellner R, editors. Classic examples in toxicologic pathology. 3rd ed. Hannover: European Society of Toxicologic Pathology; 2009. CD-ROM.

[56] Ettlin RA, Kuroda J, Plassmann S, Hayashi M, Prentice DE. Successful drug development despite adverse preclinical findings part 2: examples. J Toxicol Pathol 2010;23(4):213–34.

[57] Ewer MS, Lippman SM. Type II chemotherapy-related cardiac dysfunction: time to recognize a new entity. J Clin Oncol 2005;23(13):2900–2.

[58] Ewer MS, Ewer SM. Cardiotoxicity of anticancer treatments: what the cardiologist needs to know. Nat Rev Cardiol 2010;7(10):564–75.

[59] Ewer MS, Ewer SM. Cardiotoxicity of anticancer treatments. Nat Rev Cardiol 2015;12(11):620. http://dx.doi.org/10.1038/nrcardio.2015.133.

[60] Exelon® (rivastigmine) pharmacology review, Drugs@FDA; 2000.

[61] Expert Scientific Group on phase one clinical trials. The Stationery Office, http://webarchive.nationalarchives.gov.uk/20130107105354/http://www.dh.gov.uk/prod_consum_dh/groups/dh_digitalassets/@dh/@en/documents/digitalasset/dh_073165.pdf; 2006.

[62] FDA: Talk paper. Wyeth-Ayerst Laboratories announces the withdrawal of Duract from the market. 1998. http://www.fda.gov/ohrms/dockets/ac/98/briefingbook/1998-3454B1_03_WL06.pdf.

[63] FDA. Guidance for industry. Estimating the maximum safe starting dose in initial clinical trials for therapeutics in adult and healthy volunteers. Center for Drug Evaluation and Research (CDER) and Center for Biologics Evaluation and Research (CBER); 2005.

[64] FDA: Drug safety podcast. Tegaserod maleate (marketed as Zelnorm) – Full Version, http://www.fda.gov/Drugs/DrugSafety/DrugSafetyPodcasts/ucm078972.htm; 2007.

[65] FDA. Guidance for industry. Safety testing of drug metabolites, 2008. Center for Drug Evaluation and Research (CDER); 2008a.

[66] FDA. Guidance for industry. Genotoxic and carcinogenic impurities in drug substances and products: recommended approaches (draft guidance). Center for Drug Evaluation and Research (CDER) and Center for Biologics Evaluation and Research (CBER); 2008b.

[67] FDA. Guidance for industry. Drug-induced liver injury: premarketing clinical evaluation. Center for Drug Evaluation and Research (CDER) and Center for Biologics Evaluation and Research (CBER); 2009.

[68] FDA. Advisory committee for pharmaceutical science and clinical pharmacology. Center for Drug Evaluation and Research (CDER); 2010.

[69] FDA. Guidance for industry. Reproductive and developmental toxicities – Integrating study results to assess concerns. Center for Drug Evaluation and Research (CDER); 2011.

[70] FDA. Guidance for industry and investigators. Safety reporting requirements for INDs and BA/be studies. Center for Drug Evaluation and Research (CDER) and Center for Biologics Evaluation and Research (CBER); 2012.

[71] FDA. Guidance for industry. Immunogenicity assessment for therapeutic protein products. Center for Drug Evaluation and Research (CDER) and Center for Biologics Evaluation and Research (CBER); 2014.

[72] FDA. Guidance for industry. Pregnancy, lactation, and reproductive potential: labeling for human prescription drugs and biological products – content and formal. Center for Drug Evaluation and Research (CDER) and Center for Biologics Evaluation and Research (CBER); 2015a.

[73] FDA. Guidance for industry: assessment of male-mediated developmental risk for pharmaceuticals (draft guidance). Center for Drug Evaluation and Research (CDER); 2015b.

[74] Finco D, Grimaldi C, Fort M, Walker M, Kiessling A, Wolf B, et al. Cytokine release assays: current practices and future directions. Cytokine 2014;66(2):143–55.

[75] Force T, Kerkelä R. Cardiotoxicity of the new cancer therapeutics – mechanisms of, and approaches to, the problem. Drug Discov Today 2008;13(17–18):778–84.

[76] Force T, Kolaja KL. Cardiotoxicity of kinase inhibitors: the prediction and translation of preclinical models to clinical outcomes. Nat Rev 2011;10:111–26.

[77] Fraser FC. Thalidomide perspective: what did we learn? Teratology 1998;38(3):201–2.

[78] Fung M, Thornton A, Mybeck K, Hui JH-H, Hornbuckle K, Muniz E. Evaluation of the characteristics of safety withdrawal of prescription drugs from worldwide pharmaceutical markets – 1960–1999. Drug Inform J 2001;35:293–317.

[79] Gienzen TJ, Mantel-Teeuwisse AK, Straus SMJM, Schellekens H, Schellekens H, Leufkens HGM, et al. Safety-related regulatory actions for biologicals approved in the United States and the European Union. J Am Med Assoc 2008;300(16):1887–96.

[80] Glorioso N, Atlas SA, Laragh JH, Jewelewisz T, Sealey JE. Prorenin in high concentrations in human ovarian follicular fluid. Science 1986;233(4771):1422–4.

[81] Gold LS, Manley NB, Slone TH, Ward JM. Compendium of chemical carcinogens by target organ: results of chronic bioassay in rats, mice, hamster, dogs, and monkeys. Toxicol Pathol 2001;29(6):639–52.

[82] Gorovits B, Krinos-Fiorotti C. Proposed mechanism of off-target toxicity for antibody–drug conjugates driven by mannose receptor uptake. Cancer Immunol Immunother 2013;62(2):217–23.

[83] Graham DJ, Drinkard CR, Shatin D, Tsong Y, Burgers MJ. Liver enzyme monitoring in patients treated with troglitazone. JAMA 2001;286(7):831–3.

[84] Grünenthal. Thalidomide chronology. 2015. http://www.contergan.grunenthal.info/grt-ctg/GRT-CTG/Die_Fakten/Chronologie/152700079.jsp.

[85] Herceptin® (trastuzumab) prescribing information, Drugs@FDA; 2015.

[86] Holsapple MP, Pitot HC, Cohen SH, Boobis AR, Klaunig JE, Pastoor T, et al. Mode of action in relevance of rodent liver tumors to human cancer risk. Toxicol Sci 2006;89(1):51–6.

[87] Horvath CJ, Milton MN. The Tegenero incident and the Duff report conclusions: a series of unfortunate events or an avoidable event? Toxicol Pathol 2009;37(3):372–83.

[88] Huenig T. The storm has cleared: lessons from the CD28 superagonist TGN1412 trial. Nat Rev Immunol 2012;12(5):317–8.

[89] ICH E14. The clinical evaluation of QT/QTc interval prolongation and proarrhythmic potential for non-antiarrhythmic drugs. 2005.

[90] ICH M3(R2). Guidance on nonclinical safety studies for the conduct of human clinical trials and marketing authorization for pharmaceuticals. 2009.

[91] ICH M7. Assessment and control of DNA reactive (mutagenic) impurities in pharmaceuticals to limit potential carcinogenic risk. 2014.

[92] ICH M7 Addendum. Assessment and control of DNA reactive (mutagenic) impurities in pharmaceuticals to limit potential carcinogenic risk. Application of the principles of the ICH M7 guideline to calculation of compound-specific acceptable intakes M7(R1) current step 2. 2015.

[93] ICH Q3A(R2). Impurities in new drug substances. 2006.

[94] ICH Q3B(R2). Impurities in new drug products. 2006.

[95] ICH Q3C(R5). Impurities: guideline for residual Solvents. 2011.

[96] ICH Q3D. Impurities: guideline for elemental impurities. 2014.

[97] ICH S1. Proposed change to rodent carcinogenicity testing of pharmaceuticals – regulatory notice document. 2015.

[98] ICH S1A. Guideline on the need for carcinogenicity studies of pharmaceuticals. 1995.

[99] ICH S1B. Testing for carcinogenicity of pharmaceuticals. 1997.

[100] ICH S2(R1). Guidance on genotoxicity testing and data interpretation for pharmaceuticals intended for human use. 2011.

[101] ICH S5(R2). Detection of toxicity to reproduction for medicinal products and toxicity to male fertility. 2005.

[102] ICH S6(R1). Preclinical safety evaluation of biotechnology-derived pharmaceuticals. 2011.

[103] ICH S7B. The non-clinical evaluation of the potential for delayed ventricular repolarization (QT interval prolongation) by human pharmaceuticals. 2005.

[104] ICH S9. Nonclinical evaluation for anticancer pharmaceuticals. 2009.

[105] Imitrex® (sumitriptan) pharmacology review, Drugs@FDA; 2003.

[106] Itskovitz J, Rubattu S, Rosenwaks Z, Liu HC, Sealey JE. Relationship of follicular fluid prorenin to oocyte maturation, steroid levels, and outcome of in vitro fertilization. J Clin Endocrinol Metab 1991;72(1):165–71.

[107] Itskovitz J, Rubattu S, Levron J, Sealey JE. Highest concentrations of prorenin and human chorionic gonadotropin in gestational sacs during early human pregnancy. J Clin Endocrinol Metab 1992;75(3):906–10.

[108] ILSI Workshop on Cytokine Release. State of science, current challenges and future directions. 2013. ILSI Health and Environmental Sciences Institute Immunotoxicology Technical Committee 22 October 2013 http://www.hesiglobal.org/i4a/pages/Index.cfm?pageID=3621.html.

[109] Jacobson JM. Thalidomide: a remarkable comeback. Expert Opin Pharmacother 2000;1(4):849–63.

[110] James WPT, Caterson ID, Coutinho W, Finer N, Van Gaal LF, Maggioni AP, et al. Effect of sibutramine on cardiovascular outcomes in overweight and obese sujects. New Engl J Med 2010;363(10):905–17.

[111] Jiang Z, Zhou M. Neuregulin signaling and heart failure. Curr Heart Fail Rep 2010;7(1):42–7.

[112] Khera KS. Maternal Toxicity: a possible etiological factor in embryo-fetal deaths and fetal malformations of rodent-rabbit species. Teratology 1985;31:129–53.

[113] King-Herbert A, Thayer KNTP. Workshop: animal models for the NTP rodent cancer bioassay: stocks and strains – should be switch? Toxicologic Pathol 2006;34(6):802–5.

[114] Kirkland D, Aardema M, Henderson L, Mueller L. Evaluation of the ability of a battery of three in vitro genotoxicity tests to discriminate rodent carcinogens and non-carcinogens I. Sensitivity, specificity and relative predictivity. Mutat Res 2005;584(1–2):1–256.

[115] Kirkland D, Aardema M, Mueller L, Makoto H. Evaluation of the ability of a battery of three in vitro genotoxicity tests to discriminate rodent carcinogens and non-carcinogens II. Further analysis of mammalian cell results, relative predictivity and tumour profiles. Mutat Res 2006;608(1):29–42.

[116] Kirkland D, Pfuhler S, Tweats D, Aardema M, Corvi R, Darroudi F, et al. How to reduce false positive results when undertaking in vitro genotoxicity testing and thus avoid unnecessary follow-up animal tests: report of an ECVAM workshop. Mutat Res 2007a;628(1):31–55.

[117] Kirkland DJ, Aardema M, Banduhn N, Carmichael P, Fautz R, Meunier J-R, et al. In vitro approaches to develop weight of evidence (WoE) and mode of action (MoA) discussions with positive in vitro genotoxicity results. Mutagenesis 2007b;22(3):161–75.

[118] Kurihara Y, Kurihara H, Suzuki H, Kodama T, Maemura K, Nagai R, et al. Elevated blood pressure and craniofacial abnormalities in mice deficient in endothelin-1. Nature 1994;368(6473):703–10.

[119] Kurihara Y, Kurihara H, Oda H, Maemura K, Nagai R, Ishikawa T, et al. Aortic arch malformations and ventricular septal defect in mice deficient in endothelin-1. J Clin Invest 1995;96(1):293–300.

[120] Laragh J. Laragh's lessons in pathophysiology and clinical pearls for treating hypertension. Am J Hypertens 2001;14(3):296–304.

[121] Laverty HG, Benson C, Cartwright EJ, Cross MJ, Garland C, Hammond T, et al. How can we improve our understanding of cardiovascular safety liabilities to develop safer medicines? Br J Pharmacol 2011;163:675–93.

[122] Lee CS, Cragg M, Glennie M, Johnson P. Novel antibodies targeting immune regulatory checkpoints for cancer therapy. Br J Clin Pharmacol 2013;76(2):233–47.

[123] Li D-K, Yang C, Andrade S, Tavares V, Ferber JR. Maternal exposure to angiotensin converting enzyme inhibitors in the first trimester and risk of malformations in offspring: a retrospective cohort study. BMJ 2011;343:d5931. http://dx.doi.org/10.1136/bmj.d5931.

[124] Lintermans LL, Stegeman CA, Heeringa P, Abdulahad WH. T-cells in vascular inflammatory disease. Front Immunol 2014;5:504. 1–12.

[125] Lipton RB, Stewart WF, Diamond S, Diamond ML, Reed M. Prevalence and burden of migraine in the United States: data from the American migraine study II. Headache 2001;41(7):646–57.

[126] Lounkine E, Keiser MJ, Whitebread S, Mikhailov D, Hamon J, Jenkins J, et al. Large scale prediction and testing of drug activity on side-effect targets. Nature 2012;486(7406):361–7.

[127] Lowe PJ, Hijazi Y, Luttringer O, Yin H, Sarangapani R, Howard D. On the anticipation of the human dose in first-in-man trials from preclinical and prior clinical information in early drug development. Xenobiotica 2007;37(10–11):1331–54.

[128] Lyrica® (pregabalin) pharmacology review, Drugs@FDA; 2004.

[129] May A, Gijsman HJ, Wallnöfer A, Jones R, Diener HC, Ferrari MD. Endothelin antagonist bosentan blocks neurogenic inflammation, but is not effective in aborting migraine attacks. Pain 1996;67(2–3):375–8.

[130] Maronpot R, Yoshizawa K, Nyxka A, Harada T, Flake G, Mueller G, et al. Hepatic enzyme induction: histopathology. Toxicol Pathol 2010;38(5):776–95.

[131] Manson JE, Willett WC, Stampfer MJ, Colditz GA, Hunter DJ, Hankinosn SE, et al. Body weight and mortality among women. N Engl J Med 1995;333(11):677–85.

[132] McCann J, Choi E, Yamasaki E, Ames BN. Detection of carcinogens as mutagens in the Salmonella/microsome test: assay of 300 chemicals. Proc Natl Acad Sci USA 1975;72(12):5135–9.

[133] McNaughton R, Huet G, Shakir S. An investigation into drug products withdrawn from the EU market between 2002 and 2011 for safety reasons and the evidence used to support the decision-making. BMJ Open 2014;4:e004221. http://dx.doi.org/10.1136/bmjopen-2013-004221.

[134] Meek ME, Bucher JR, Cohen SM, Dellarco V, Hill RN, Lehman-McKeeman LD, et al. A framework for human relevance analysis of information on carcinogenic modes of action. Crit Rev Toxicol 2003;33(6):591–653.

[135] Mirapex® (pramipexole) pharmacology review, Drugs@FDA; 1997.

[136] Mohutsky MA, Romeike A, Meador V, Lee WM, Fowler J, Franke-Carroll S. Hepatic drug-metabolizing enzyme induction and implications for preclinical and clinical risk assessment. Toxicol Pathol 2010;38(5):799–809.

[137] Muehlbacher M, Tripal P, Roas F, Kornhuber J. Identificatin of drugs inducing phospholipidosis by novel in vitro data. ChemMedChem 2012;7(11):1925–34.

[138] Mueller N, van den Brandt J, Odoardi F, Tischner D, Herath J, Fluegel A, et al. A CD28 superagonistic antibody elicits 2 functionally distinct waves of T cell activation in rat. J Clin Invest 2008;118(4):1405–16.

[139] Muller PY, Brennan FR. Safety assessment and dose selection for first-in-human clinical trials with immunomodulatory monoclonal antibodies. Clin Pharmacol Ther 2009;85(3):247–58.

[140] Muller PY, Milton M, Lloyd P, Sims J, Brennan FR. The minimum anticipated biological effect level (MABEL) for selection of first human dose in clinical trials with monoclonal Antibodies. Curr Opin Biotechnol 2009;20(6):722–9.

[141] Muster W, Breidenbach A, Fischer H, Kirchner S, Müller L. Computational toxicology in drug development. Drug Discov Today 2008;13(7–8):303–10.

[142] NIH Bupropion. National Institute of Health, US National Library of Medicine, TOXNET, Toxicology Data Network, http://chem.sis.nlm.nih.gov/chemidplus/rn/31677-93-7.

[143] NIH Clozapine. National Institute of Health, US National Library of Medicine, TOXNET, Toxicology Data Network, http://chem.sis.nlm.nih.gov/chemidplus/rn/5786-21-0.

[144] NIH Diazepam. National Institute of Health, US National Library of Medicine, TOXNET, Toxicology Data Network, http://chem.sis.nlm.nih.gov/chemidplus/name/diazepam.

[145] NIH Haloreridol. National Institute of Health, US National Library of Medicine, TOXNET, Toxicology Data Network, http://chem.sis.nlm.nih.gov/chemidplus/rn/52-86-8.

[146] NIH Trimipramine. National Institute of Health, US National Library of Medicine, TOXNET, Toxicology Data Network, http://chem.sis.nlm.nih.gov/chemidplus/name/trimipramine.

[147] NIH Nortriptyline. National Institute of Health, US National Library of Medicine, TOXNET, Toxicology Data Network, http://chem.sis.nlm.nih.gov/chemidplus/rn/72-69-5.

[148] Olney JW, Labruyere J, Price MT. Pathological changes induces in cerebrocortical neurons by phencyclidine and related drugs. Science 1989;244(4910):1360–2.

[149] Opsumit® (micitentan) pharmacology review, Drugs@FDA; 2013.

[150] Opsumit® (micitentan) prescribing information, Drugs@FDA; 2015.

[151] Orphanos GS, Ioannidis GN, Ardavanis AG. Cardiotoxicity induced by tyrosine kinase inhibitors. Acta Oncol 2009;48:964–70.

[152] Parkinson A. Lysosomal trapping of lipophilic amines and its relationship to drug transporters and phospholipidosis. Presentation ISE-ETS (early toxicity screening). 2011.

[153] Parlodel® (bromocriptine) prescribing information, Drugs@FDA; 2012.

[154] Peters TS. Do testing strategies help predict human hepatotoxic potentials? Toxicol Pathol 2005;33:146–54.

[155] Peuckmann V, Fisch M, Bruera E. Potential novel uses of thalidomide: focus on palliative care. Drugs 2000;60(2):273–92.

[156] Plassmann S. Impact of the ICH M3 guidelines on the early development of biologics. In: Joint conference of European human pharmacological societies and 20th anniversary of AGAH. 2011.

[157] Prentice DE, Meikle AW. A review of drug-induced Leydig cell hyperplasia and neoplasia in rats and some comparisons with man. Hum Exp Toxicol 1995;14(7):562–72.

[158] Prinz F, Schlange T, Asadullah K. Believe it or not: how much can we rely on published data on potential drug targets? Nat Rev Drug Discov 2011;10(9):712.

[159] Pucci M, Sarween N, Knox E, Lipkin G, Martin U. Angiotensin-converting enzyme inhibitors and angiotensin receptor blockers in women of childbearing age: risk versus benefits. Expert Rev Clin Pharmacol 2015;8(2):221–31.

[160] Qureshi ZP, Seoane-Vasquez E, Rodriguez-Monguio R, Stevenxon KB, Szeinbach SL. Market withdrawal of new molecular entities approved in the United States from 1980 to 2009. Pharmacoepidemiol Drug Saf 2011;20(7):772–7.

[161] Reasor MR, Kecew S. Drug-induced phospholipidosis: are there functional consequences? Exp Biol Med 2001;226(9):825–30.

[162] Reasor MJ, Hastings KL, Ulrich RG. Drug-induced phospholipidosis: issues and future directions. Expert Opin Drug Saf 2006;5(4):567–83.

[163] Reddy MV, Sistare FD, Christensen JS, DeLuca JG, Wollenberg GK, DeGeorge JJ. An evaluation of chronic 6- and 12-month rat toxicity studies as predictors of 2-year tumor outcome. Vet Pathol 2010;47(4):614–29.

[164] Richardson BP, Turkalj I, Flückiger E. Bromocriptine. In: Laurence DR, McLean AEM, Weatherall M, editors. Safety testing of new drugs: laboratory predictions and clinical performance. London, Orlando: Academic Press; 1984. p. 19–63.

[165] Risperdal® (risperidone) prescribing information, Drugs@FDA; 2014.

[166] Risperdal® (risperidone) Monograph, http://www.janssen.com/canada/sites/www_janssen_com_canada/files/product/pdf/ris06112014cpm2_snds_0.pdf; 2014.

[167] Roemer PS, Berr S, Avota E, Na S-Y, Battaglia M, ten Berge I, et al. Preculture of PBMCs at high cell density increases sensitivity of T-cell responses, revealing cytokine release by CD28 superagonist TGN1412. Blood 2011;118(26):6772–82.

[168] Rothman RB, Baumann MH, Savage JE, Rauser L, McBride A, Hufeisen SJ, et al. Evidence for possible involvement of 5-HT$_{2B}$ receptors in the cardiac valvulopathy associated with fenfluramine and other serotonergic medications. Circulation 2000;102(23):2836–41.

[169] Roy M-L, Dumaine R, Brown AM. HERG, a primary human ventricular target of the nonsedating antihistamine terfenadine. Circulation 1996;94(4):817–23.

[170] Sanguinetti MC, Jiang C, Curran ME, Keating MT. A mechanistic link between an inherited and an acquired cardiac arrhythmia: hERG encodes the I$_{Kr}$ potassium channel. Cell 1995;81:299–307.

[171] Sadrieh N. The regulatory challenges of drug-induced phospholipidosis. 2010. ACPS Meeting http://www.fda.gov/downloads/AdvisoryCommittees/CommitteesMeetingMaterials/Drugs/AdvisoryCommitteeforPharmaceuticalScienceandClinicalPharmacology/UCM210798.pdf.

[172] Santostefano MJ, Kirchner J, Vissinga C, Fort M, Lear S, Pan WJ, et al. Off-target platelet activation in macaques unique to a therapeutic monoclonal antibody. Toxicol Pathol 2012;40(6):899–917.

[173] Scialli AR, Lione A. ACE inhibitors and major congenital malformations, comments to the editor. N Engl J Med 2006;355(12):1280.

[174] Schardein JL, Schwetz BA, Kenel MF. Species sensitivities and prediction of teratogenic potential. Environ Health Perspect 1985;61:55–67.

[175] Schardein JL. Thalidomide: the protoype teratogen. In: Chemically induced birth defects. 3rd ed. New York: Marcel Dekker; 2000. p. 89–119.

[176] Sealey JE, Itskovitz-Eldor J. ACE inhibitors and major congenital malformations. Comments to the editor. N Engl J Med 2006;355(12):1280–1.

[177] Seuwen K, Magnaldo I, Pouysségur J. Serotonin stimulates DNA synthesis in fibroblasts through 5-HT1B receptors couples to a Gi-protein. Nature 1988;335(6187):254–6.

[178] Shepard TH. Catalog of teratogenic agents. 8th ed. Baltimore, MD: Johns Hopkins University Press; 1995. p. 397.

[179] Shepard TH, Lemire RJ. Catalog of teratogenic agents. 11th ed. 2004.

[180] Sistare FD, Morton D, Alden C, Christensen J, Keller D, DeJonghe S, et al. An analysis of pharmaceutical experience with decades of rat carcinogenicity testing: support for a proposal to modify current regulatory guidelines. Toxicol Pathol 2011;39(4):716–44.

[181] Soares MJ. The prolactin and growth hormone families: pregnancy-specific hormones/cytokines at the maternal-fetal interface. Reprod Biol Endocrinol 2004;2(51).

[182] Song S-W, Sun Y, Su B-L, Liu C, Yang C, Godfraind T, et al. Risperidone enhances the vulnerability to stroke in hypertensive rats. Neurosci Ther 2012;18:343–9.

[183] Sonich-Mullin C, Fielder R, Wiltse J, Baetcke K, Dempsey J, Fenner-Crisp P, et al. Conceptual framework for evaluating a mode of action for chemical carcinogenesis. Regul Toxicol Pharmacol 2001;34(2):146–52.

[184] Stebbings R, Findlay L, Edwards CE, Eastwood D, Bird C, North D, et al. "Cytokine storm" in the phase I trial of monoclonal antibody TGN1412: better understanding the causes to improve preclinical testing of immunotherapeutics. J Immunol 2007;179(5):3325–31.

[185] Suter W, Hartmann A, Poetter F, Sagelsdorff P, Hoffmann P, Martus H-J. Genotoxicity assessment of the antiepileptic drug AMP397, an Ames-positive aromatic nitro compound. Mutat Res 2002;518(2):181–94.

[186] Swenberg JA, Lehman-McKeeman LD. α2-urinary globulin-associated nephropathy as a mechanism of renal tubule cell carcinogenesis in male rats. In: Capen CC, Dybing E, Rice JM, Wilbourn JD, editors. Species differences in thyroid, kidney and urinary bladder carcinogenesis. Lyon, France: IARC Scientific Publications; 1999. No. 147.

[187] Tabacova SA, Kimmel CA. Enalapril: pharmacokinetic/dynamic inferences for comparative developmental toxicity. A review. Reprod Toxicol 2001;15(5):467–78.

[188] Tabacova S, Little R, Tsong Y, Vega A, Kimmel CA. Adverse pregnancy outcomes associated with maternal enalapril antihypertensive treatment. Pharmacoepidemiol Drug Saf 2003;12(8):633–46.

[189] Tabacova S. Mode of action: angiotensin-converting enzyme inhibition-developmental effects associated with exposure to ACE inhibitors. Crit Rev Toxicol 2005;35(8–9):747–55.

[190] Tabares P, Berr S, Roemer PS, Chuvpilo S, Matskevich AA, Tyrsin D, et al. Human regulatory T cells are selectively activated by low-dose application of the CD28 superagonist TGN1412/TAB08. Eur J Immunol 2014;44(4):1225–36.

[191] Tekturna® (aliskiren) prescribing information, Drugs@FDA; 2015.

[192] TGN1412 Investigator's Brochure, http://www.circare.org/foia5/tgn1412investigatorbrochure.pdf; 2005.

[193] TheraMAB GmbH press release. TheraMAB LLC announces initiation of phase II clinical trial of mAb TAB08 for the treatment of rheumatoid arthritis. 2014. http://www.theramab.ru/en/news/phase_II.

[194] Thomas GA, Williams ED. Thyroid stimulating hormone (TSH)-associated follicular hypertrophy and hyperplasia as a mechanism of thyroid carcinogenesis in mice and rats. In: Capen CC, Dybing E, Rice JM, Wilbourn JD, editors. Species differences in thyroid, kidney and urinary bladder carcinogenesis. IARC Scientific Publications 147; 1999. p. 45–59.

[195] Thorin E, Clozel M. The cardiovascular physiology and pharmacology of endothelin-1. Adv Pharmacol 2010;60:1–26.

[196] Thybaud V, Aardema M, Clements J, Dearfield K, Galloway S, Hayashi M, et al. Expert working group on hazard identification and risk assessment in relation to in vitro testing. Strategy for genotoxicity testing: hazard identification and risk assessment in relation to in vitro testing. Mutat Res 2007a;627(1):41–58.

[197] Thybaud V, Aardema M, Casciano D, Dellarco V, Embry MR, Gollapudi BB, et al. Relevance and follow-up of positive results in in vitro genetic toxicity assays: an ILSI-HESI initiative. Mutat Res 2007b;633(2):67–79.

[198] Tracleer® (bosentan) pharmacology review, Drugs@FDA; 2001.

[199] Tracleer® (bosentan) prescribing information, Drugs@FDA; 2013.

[200] Treinen KA, Louden C, Dennis MJ, Wier PJ. Developmental toxicity and toxicokinetics of two endothelin receptor antagonists in rats and rabbits. Teratology 1999;59(1):51–9.

[201] Tzirogiannis KN, Kourentzi KT, Zyga S, Papalimneou V, Tsironi M, Grypioti AD, et al. Effect of 5-HT7 receptor blockade on liver regeneration after 60-70% partial hepatectomy. BMC Gastroenterol 2014;14(201). http://dx.doi.org/10.1186/s12876-014-0201-2.

[202] Van Oosterhout JP, Van der Laan JW, De Waal EJ, Olejniczak K, Hilgenfeld M, Schmidt V, et al. The utility of two rodent species in carcinogenic risk assessment of pharmaceuticals in Europe. Regul Toxicol Pharmacol 1997;25(1):6–17.

[203] Vasotec® (enalapril) pharmacology review, Drugs@FDA; 1985.

[204] Vasotec® (enalapril) prescribing information, Drugs@FDA; 2015.

[205] Volkova M, Russell R. Anthracycline cardiotoxicity: prevalence, pathogenesis and treatment. Curr Cardiol Rev 2011;7:214–20.

[206] Walfisch A, Al-maawali A, Moretti ME, Nickel C, Koren G. Teratogenicity of angiotensin converting enzyme inhibitors or receptor blockers. J Obstetrics Gynaecol 2011;6:465–72.

[207] Warkany J. Why I doubted that thalidomide was the cause of the epidemic of limb defects of 1959 to 1961. Teratology 1988;38(3):217–9.

[208] Wester PW, Kroes R. Forestomach carcinogens: pathology and relevance to man. Toxicologic Pathol 1988;16(2):165–71.

[209] Zeiger E. Identification of rodent carcinogens and noncarcinogens using genetic toxicity tests: premises, promises, and performance. Regul Toxicol Pharmacol 1998;28(2):85–95.

3

ADME in Drug Discovery

J. Vrbanac, R. Slauter

INTRODUCTION

Overview of ADME Science

The drug discovery and development process represents an overlapping continuum of research activities designed to address specific scientific questions. These questions include by what mechanism(s) is a drug eliminated from the body, what concentrations are necessary to produce therapeutic and toxic effects, does the drug have long-term actions related to changes in gene expression, and what are the kinetics of movement of a drug in the body. The scientific discipline of preclinical drug discovery and development can be described as a risk assessment process, whereby data are used to estimate the usefulness of some agent in preventing, curing, or slowing the progression of human disease. In a very real sense, all of the development of therapeutics represents a risk–benefit assessment. For drug therapies, the preclinical phase of research allows subsequent clinical studies to be initiated and proceed with some knowledge of risk–benefit. It is an iterative process that varies in form between different programs at any one time. This process is constantly evolving, as new knowledge and technologies are introduced: The research plan of today has both many general similarities and significant differences from 25 years ago.

The constants in this process are drug efficacy and drug safety evaluation, which together represent the science of pharmacology, which is the science of drugs. Toxicokinetic data, pharmacokinetics in a toxicology study, or the study of the relationship of exposure to toxicity, are important for the design of definitive safety studies (general toxicology, safety pharmacology, developmental and reproductive toxicology, etc.). Toxicokinetic data allow for estimation (calculation) of a safety margin in preclinical studies and ultimately the early estimation of a *therapeutic index* in humans. In parallel, the study of absorption, distribution, metabolism, and excretion are central to finding new, safe, and effective drugs. The central message of this chapter is that early characterization of PK (pharmacokinetics; ADME) properties is critical to the development of successful drug discovery programs [1–7].

ADME scientists have two "customers" in the preclinical setting: The *drug discovery* scientists, who provide new chemical entities for evaluation in various pharmacology and toxicology screens, and the preclinical *drug development* scientists who perform more refined evaluations of safety and efficacy for preparation of the IND (Investigational New Drug Application). ADME studies supply the toxicologist with critical measurements of drug exposure that can be correlated with observed toxicity, which in turn directly relates to the therapeutic index (TI). The clinical TI is calculated by dividing the dose that causes toxicity in 50% of subjects (eg, cardiac arrhythmia) by the dose that causes a desired therapeutic effect in 50% of subjects (eg, increase in cardiac output). Early on in the drug discovery and development process, ADME scientists are interested in estimating clearance (CL), bioavailability (F), and pharmacokinetic/pharmacodynamic (PK/PD) data for entry into compound libraries. In addition, ADME scientists are charged with providing to their toxicology colleagues an understanding of exposure (dose) and toxicity. Considerations include the PK/PD (or TK/TD; toxicokinetic/toxicodynamic) relationship, the role of metabolism and transporters, induction of specific drug-metabolizing enzymes, and drug accumulation. This chapter will address ADME in discovery research, or ADME at

the interface of drug discovery and drug development, which as stated above is commonly now referred to as *early ADME (eADME)*. Not all *eADME* topics will be covered. For example, plasma protein binding (PPB) has been omitted, since it is arguably less important to *eADME* than critical concepts such as stability and clearance [8].

The characterization of ADME properties of compounds early in the drug discovery process has well-characterized value for the selection of better drug candidates, and has become more important as technologies impacting this process have developed and matured [9–11]. The cytochrome P450 (CYPs) enzymes are intimately involved in ADME. The catalytic cycle of the P450-dependent monooxygenase system is shown in Fig. 3.1 (showing the second electron insertion step from cytochrome b_5). Over the past 20 years, an understanding of the biochemistry of the cytochrome P-450 system and the role that CYP inhibition, CYP phenotype, and CYP induction play in the identification of better drug therapies has impacted how preclinical ADME research is conducted [12–14]. Consider that 20 years ago approximately 40% of clinical drug failures could be tied to PK and ADME drug characteristics, and today this failure rate is 10% or less for companies with comprehensive, state-of-the-art preclinical discovery/development programs addressing these issues [15]. The drug discovery process continues to evolve and early ADME evaluation has become a routine part of the "big picture" process to examine the utility of drug templates in the discovery of novel therapeutics. The FDA has released the "Industry, Drug Interaction Studies, Study Design, Data Analysis, Implications for Dosing, and Labeling Recommendations" guidance, which provides much needed regulatory guidance for many of the ADME investigations discussed in this chapter [16].

Definitions. As already stated, the two constants in the drug discovery process are an assessment of drug efficacy and drug safety. Pharmacology is divided into two distinct domains, the separate but interactive domains of *dynamics* and *kinetics. Pharmacodynamics (toxicodynamics)* or PD (TD) is the study of the effects of *xenobiotics* (drugs; foreign substances; opposite of *endobiotics*) on the body. *Pharmacokinetics (toxicokinetics)* or PK (TK) is the study of the effects of the body on the xenobiotic, or the study of the journey of the drug molecules (the atoms) within the body and excretion from the body. Pharmacokinetics, in the broad sense of the term as defined by Leslie Benet [17], includes concentration-time (C-T) kinetic relationships, chemical reaction kinetics, and the formation of new chemical structures (biotransformation; formation of drug metabolites). As stated in *Goodman and Gilman's The Pharmacological Basis of Therapeutics* (2006):

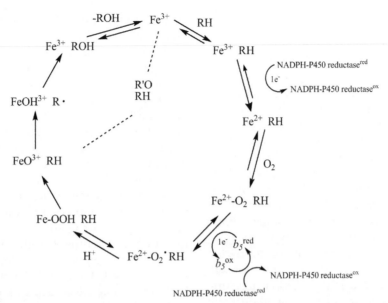

FIGURE 3.1 The catalytic cycle of the P450-dependent monooxygenase system, with the second electron insertion step from cytochrome b_5 (alternatively, NADPH may serve this function).

"When a drug enters the body, the body begins immediately to work on the drug: absorption, distribution, metabolism (biotransformation), and elimination. These are the processes of pharmacokinetics. The drug also acts on the body, an interaction to which the concept of a drug receptor is central, since the receptor is responsible for the selectivity of drug action and for the quantitative relationship between drug and effect. The mechanisms of drug action are the processes of pharmacodynamics." [18].

It is now common practice to segregate pharmacokinetics into: (1) The study of the *ADME* of a drug, and in particular the ADME determined by following the distribution of radioactivity, from the narrower definition of (2) PK as the sojourn of the parent drug into, through and out of the blood, and in particular C-T plasma/blood data. For nonbiologics (small molecules) these C-T data are determined by highly selective and sensitive quantitative methods developed for the parent drug and at times metabolites, now almost exclusively performed using liquid chromatography-mass spectrometry analysis (LC-MS). Another popular acronym in common usage is DM&PK, ie, drug metabolism and pharmacokinetics, which encompasses the broad definition of PK. Pharmacokinetics of the parent drug and active or toxic metabolites in plasma/blood is covered in a separate chapter.

Absorption, distribution, metabolism, and excretion of a xenobiotic is related to the intrinsic properties of the chemical structure, including its molecular weight, the shape of the molecule ("chemical space"), the ionization properties, the degree of lipophilicity and water solubility of the various forms (charged and uncharged sites), and associations with macromolecules (eg, a tissue protein-binding drug). Some properties are of obvious relevance:

Compounds that are rapidly metabolized in the liver have poor oral bioavailability. The common barrier to drug distribution is the cell membrane, which is why in the absence of other mechanisms such as active transport (transport of nutrients, for example), substances moving into and out of the cell can pass across the plasma membrane as a result of their lipophilic properties. Other properties determining ADME are not as obvious. For example, redistribution is the mechanism responsible for termination of action of thiopental, a highly lipophilic drug that rapidly partitions into the brain to act rapidly and briefly and then redistributes into other tissues, eventually concentrating in adipose tissue [19]. In this example, a physicochemical property of a drug dramatically affects drug kinetics and therefore dynamics.

Drugs are administered by various routes of administration:

1. Starting outside the body including oral and topical (skin, nasal mucosa, ocular topical), or having an intermediate starting location, such as rectal, vaginal, and inhalation

2. Parenteral routes: Intravenous (IV), intramuscular (IM), intraperitoneal (IP), subcutaneous (SC), and depositions (DEPOT)

There are also special parenteral routes, such as intraarticular and various ocular parenteral routes (intravitreal and retrobulbar, for example). The oral route is by far the most important route when discussing ADME and drug discovery. We will focus on this route in this chapter, and will not specifically discuss any unique kinetics and ADME associated with other routes of administration.

ADME in Drug Discovery

The drug discovery process is complicated and interdisciplinary. Scientists must work with drug discovery teams for a significant period of time to gain the experience and clarity of scientific vision to lead drug discovery programs. The overall process is usually described as consisting of drug discovery and drug development "phases," with considerable overlap between these phases [17]. The process (Fig. 3.2) can also be described in terms of preclinical and clinical phases, where there is a clear demarcation of activities (the term *commercialization phase* for late stage activities has also been used). In the modern setting, the pharmacological basis of therapeutics is a highly interactive, dynamic process that includes several iterations of the following processes: The identification of a drug target that will produce the desired effect (decreasing blood pressure, for example); the development of some methodology to evaluate the effect(s) of compounds on this target (*assay* development); the use of this assay to evaluate a large number of compounds (to *screen* a *drug library*); and more refined testing of the pharmacological and toxicological properties of the chemical template and/

or lead compounds. The process eventually transitions into a drug development phase, in which a small group of "lead compounds" are evaluated in a more stringent manner, including in vivo testing using preclinical species including but not limited to mouse, rat, dog, and monkey. When successful, this process leads to selection of a few (1–2) compounds as successful IND candidates and entry into Phase I Clinical Trials [20–25]. The target ID stage has changed with the sequencing of the human genome and the introduction of the "omics" technologies of genomics, proteomics, and metabolomics. Although the anticipated revolutionary impact of the "omics" and combinatorial chemistry is greatly improving the drug discovery process has not come to fruition, continued technological advances have improved the process of evaluating and testing drug targets. New, safer, and more effective drug therapies, both small molecule and large molecule (predominately biologics), will be a part of our future [26–28].

Technological advances impacting the ADME part of pharmacology research include:

1. The ability to follow drug-related material in fluids and tissues without radioactive studies
2. The early application of PET/SPECT imaging of biologics for early drug disposition studies
3. The successful identification of "biomarkers" useful in characterizing PK/PD (TK/TD) relationships
4. The increased role of in silico in making predictions of certain ADME properties for chemical templates and individual compounds

Technological advances will continue to dramatically impact the *eADME* research process. It is indeed an exciting time for scientists active in the field of drug discovery and development.

One of the most important aspects in determining the "what and when" for studying ADME properties is cost effectiveness, since cost per compound and the cost of each step increases exponentially at each stage of the drug discovery/development process. The vast majority of compounds do not have the necessary intrinsic properties to constitute effective and safe therapeutics in man, and thus the real job of the drug development scientist is to identify compounds with "losing" properties, which is a process of elimination, or as drug discovery/development scientists are fond of saying, "finding and killing the losers." Thus the actual job of the drug development scientist is to "kill" compounds/programs that can be shown to represent future clinical failures. Compounds that survive this process will have a far better chance of success in the clinic and become marketed drugs. *eADME* is a critical part of this evaluation process.

So where are "ADME data" first gathered in the drug discovery process? The answer is that, with the exception of the very earliest stages of new compound

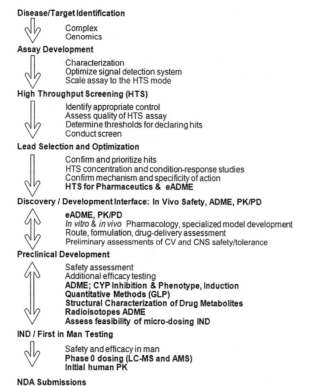

FIGURE 3.2 The *traditional* drug discovery and development process, ADME focus in bold. Different individuals will draw this differently. This is a highly complex and constantly evolving research process.

characterization, research protocols designed in part to assess ADME properties occur at all stages of the drug discovery/development process, including very early characterizations as part of the first chemical properties listed in "Drug Chemical Libraries." For example, an assessment of CYP3A4 inhibition liability (covered below) may be determined along with water solubility and plasma stability, which represents one of the early data points determined for new compounds.

The interest in ADME is easy to understand since failure of drugs in the clinic is due to any of three distinct reasons: (1) Efficacy, (2) Safety, and (3) ADME (PK).

Confusing, isn't it? This is why the authors prefer the older, all-encompassing term "kinetics"/"pharmacokinetics." However, ADME is used in this chapter by default to common usage.

Effective ADME programs can greatly impact success in the clinic and early assessment of ADME characteristics has real merit in improving the drug discovery and development process [15]. This chapter has been divided up into:

1. Absorption
2. Distribution and Elimination
3. Metabolism

Distribution and elimination are considered together, since they are often characterized together (eg, MS analysis of tissues and excreta) and elimination can be considered to be *distribution out of the body*. Some subjects are considered in more than one section. For example, stability and metabolism rates are part of the characterization of absorption. Large molecules and biologics will not be considered in this chapter. The chapter "Use of Imaging for Preclinical Evaluation" (eg, PET and SPECT) discusses large molecules.

DRUG ABSORPTION

In order for a xenobiotic (drug) to reach the blood, the "central compartment," when ingested orally (Fig. 3.3), it must first pass out of the gastrointestinal tract and be delivered to the liver via the hepatic portal vein (the portal vein conducts blood from the digestive system, spleen, pancreas, and gallbladder to the liver). The drug and its metabolites are then available to move into the liver and from the liver to the blood, where they are then distributed throughout the body by the arterial circulation [29]. There are two major anatomical and biochemical barriers to movement of drug from the intestinal lumen to the blood:

1. The tissues between the intestinal lumen and the portal blood
2. The liver tissues

The liver is the most important site of the metabolism of xenobiotics, and in this capacity serves as a protection system for the body from chemical insults. Over

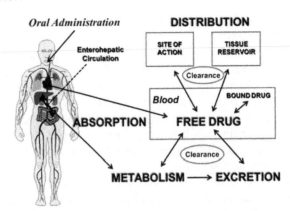

FIGURE 3.3 Scheme for movement of drugs through the body following oral administration.

half of the small molecule drugs on the market are primarily cleared by metabolism. It is not surprising that experimental protocols designed to approximate the oral absorption process use tissues and enzymes associated with this process. The important role of GIT transporters and metabolic enzymes in drug absorption is a subject of considerable past and present scientific interest.

The above points concerning movement of drug from the GIT to the blood are very important, since most drugs are administered orally (PO). Physicochemical properties (eg, solubility), cell membrane permeabilities, specificities for transporters, and drug-metabolizing enzyme substrate specificities are important in oral absorption, and thus also in the characterization of compounds under evaluation.

Physicochemical Properties and Permeability

Scientists experienced with the drug discovery and development process have coined the phrase "does it look like a drug" by which they mean do the physicochemical properties of the drug candidate fit the typical drug profile (fall within some characteristic range of properties observed for small molecules)?

One of the more useful observations concerning physicochemical properties of drugs is the "Lipinski rule of 5" which states that poor absorption or permeation is more likely when there are more than 5 H-bond donors, 10 H-bond acceptors, the molecular weight (MW) is greater than 500, and the calculated log P (ClogP) is greater than 5 [30,31]. Small-molecule compounds (drug candidates) with atypically large molecular weights and a large number of heteroatoms do not "look" like orally available drugs. One good example of a drug that successfully entered clinical development but that does not "look" like it would exhibit significant oral bioavailability (F) is tirilazad (Freedox). Tirilazad has a molar mass of 624.9 g/mole, a logP>5.0, and 6 basic nitrogen atoms (Fig. 3.4). The alicyclic tertiary amines in tirilazad represent good candidates for CYP metabolism. It is not surprising that the oral bioavailability (F) for tirilazad is zero to extremely low. This compound did enter clinical trials as an IV drug. Not surprisingly, these physicochemical properties complicated preclinical development of this drug. Tirilazad also exhibited a species-specific metabolic toxicity in the dog, with a predominant pathway being *N*-dealkylation between the two chemical domains, forming a metabolite that was cardio-toxic in the dog. This metabolic characteristic eliminated the dog from consideration as the nonrodent toxicology species.

In Silico. The use of software to predict chemical, pharmaceutical, and biological properties of compounds from chemical structures is an area of intense interest. This subject matter lies outside the scope of this chapter and will only be mentioned briefly. Several recent overviews have been published [32–36]. In silico prediction of physicochemical properties has developed to the point of being relatively useful for log P, log D, pKa, and lipophilicity, but prediction of water solubilities has proven to be far more difficult. One reason for this is that predicting the various *forms* a solid can take (such as crystalline vs. amorphous solid) is difficult for novel compounds. Prediction of ADME properties by in silico methods is highly variable and is less effective for novel compound templates.

Physicochemical properties (water solubility, log D, CHI, stability). Physicochemical properties of compounds, such as molecular weight, charge state, water solubility, and lipophilicity, in part result in the observed in vivo ADME properties. As for their influence on what is called the "drug-ability" of compounds (a slang term referring to certain properties of a compound or template as relative to overall "ideal" drug properties), exhibiting *poor* physicochemical properties (pharmaceutical properties) is not always a "show stopper," but can make drug development very difficult. Water solubility and lipophilicity influence the dissolution of drugs in the GIT and the ultimate free drug concentration, since they determine the ability of the drug to dissolve in and move through cell membranes and distribute throughout the body. Since water solubility, lipophilicity, and permeability are important parameters in estimating drug absorption properties in vivo, they are discussed in this section.

Solubility. The solubility of a compound in water is measured at thermodynamic equilibrium in a saturated solution. The concentration at saturation is determined by LC-UV (LC-ultraviolet) or another appropriate analytical procedure. This is usually done in both water and/or in phosphate buffered saline, pH 7.4, and at physiological osmolality. Water solubility is commonly estimated in a high-throughput screening (HTS) setup by adding the compound dissolved in dimethyl sulfoxide (DMSO) into buffer or water at a wide final concentration range and noting the turbidity of the solution (if cloudy, then the drug is assumed not to be completely in solution).

Log D. A partition coefficient is the ratio of the amount of compound existing in a nonionized state in two immiscible solvents, usually n-octanol and water. The pH is adjusted so that the predominant form is the nonionized form. This is expressed as log P:

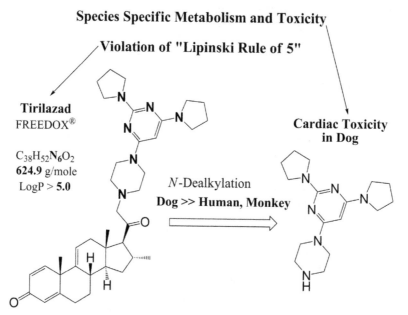

Species Specific Metabolism and Toxicity

Violation of "Lipinski Rule of 5"

Tirilazad
FREEDOX®

$C_{38}H_{52}N_6O_2$
624.9 g/mole
LogP > 5.0

N-Dealkylation
Dog >> Human, Monkey

Cardiac Toxicity in Dog

FIGURE 3.4 The structure of tirilazad, Freedox. This compound is a good example of a drug that does not follow the *Lipinski Rule of 5*. The molecular weight of tirilazad is 624.9 g/mole, the logP is greater than five, and there are six basic nitrogen atoms. These physicochemical properties complicated preclinical development of this drug. In addition, tirilazad exhibited a species-specific metabolic toxicity in the dog, with a predominant pathway being *N*-dealkylation between the two chemical domains, forming a metabolite that was cardio-toxic in the dog. This metabolic characteristic led to the monkey being the nonrodent toxicology species in drug development.

$$\text{Log P}_{\text{octanol/water}} = \log \left(\frac{[\text{unionized solute}]_{\text{octanol}}}{[\text{unionized solute}]_{\text{neutral water}}} \right).$$

A more physiologically relevant measure is log D, which is the ratio of nonionized form in octanol (or all forms) to the nonionized plus ionized forms in water:

$$\text{Log D}_{\text{(octanol/water)}} = \text{Log} \left(\frac{[\text{unionized solute}]_{\text{octanol}}}{[\text{unionized solute}]_{\text{water}} + [\text{ionized solute}]_{\text{water}}} \right)$$

For drug research, these values are typically measured at pH 7.4, with the aqueous phase being buffered such that the drug does not alter the pH.

Chromatographic hydrophobicity index (CHI) [37,38]. As with log D, the chromatographic hydrophobicity index (CHI) is a measurement of the lipophilicity of a drug. The elution properties of compounds are evaluated using a rapid gradient, reversed-phase, liquid chromatography (RP-LC), typically with UV or MS detection. The analysis is carried out under acidic, neutral, and basic conditions (pH = 2.0, 7.4, and 10.5). CHI was originally calculated by determining the isocratic retention factor (log k″) at various acetonitrile concentrations and plotting log k′ as a function of that concentration. From this relationship, the slope (S) and the intercept (log k′(w)) values were obtained, and the hydrophobicity phi(0) calculated as −log k′(w)/S. There is a linear correlation between the gradient retention time values, t(R), and the isocratically determined phi(0) values. In practice, a plot of CHI vs. retention times for standards is used to determine CHI for the test compound.

Parallel artificial membrane permeability assay (PAMPA). PAMPA is a screening technique to estimate passive diffusion permeability (transcellular permeation). PAMPA estimates passive diffusion alone with no consideration of active transport. It is desirable to consider a large pH range when considering absorption from the GIT. The apparatus consists of a donor compartment and an acceptor compartment. The movement from donor to acceptor compartments through an artificial membrane containing lipid is determined. Multiwell plate "sandwiches" have been devised for high-throughput operation. Data obtained in this manner correlates well with Caco2 (a cell line used to study drug transport) data, passive movement from the GIT, movement through the skin, and distribution into the brain. Caco2 and MDCK permeability are discussed in the next section.

Membrane-Bound Drug Transporters

It has become clear that drug transporters play a key role in the absorption, distribution, and elimination of drugs into and out of organisms, including man. Recognition of this fact is critical in the discovery and development of new therapeutic agents. This section will focus on those transporters that have been well characterized, and for which in vitro methods exist that can be used as screening tools for the rank ordering of drug candidates in the lead optimization activities leading up to selection of a lead candidate(s) for further development. Because this is an active area of research and an area where regulatory guidance is still being formulated, this section is expanded somewhat relative to other topics. Fig. 3.5 displays important transporters effecting ADME and their intracellular locations in the most important cell types (quantitatively). Specific transporters are discussed below. Fig. 3.5 was adapted from the recent CDER (Center for Drug Evaluation and Research) guidance [16]. The expression of transporters in the GIT, the liver, and in renal tubules is displayed. Drug transporters are membrane-bound, or in most cases, trans-membrane, proteins that are present in all organisms. These proteins work to pump a myriad of nutrients, cofactors, and ions into the cell and mediate the efflux of cellular waste, environmental toxins, and xenobiotics out of the cell. Transport using these proteins is of two general types: active or passive. The actions of these membrane-transport proteins may be passive in nature, facilitating the passage of molecules down concentration gradients into or out of the cell via a process that does not require

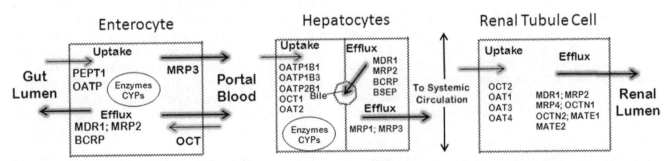

FIGURE 3.5   Location of efflux and uptake transporters in the GIT, liver, and kidney thought to be important in drug ADME. *MRP*, multidrug resistance associated protein; *PEPT1*, peptide transporter one; *OATP*, organic anion transporting polypeptide; *OAT*, organic anion transporter; *OCT*, organic cation transporter; *BCRP*, breast cancer resistance protein; *MDR1*, multidrug resistance 1(P-glycoprotein (P-gp)); *MATE*, multidrug and toxic compound extrusion protein.

energy (ATP or reducing equivalents). Conversely, many transporters actively pump molecules and ions against their concentration gradients in an active transport process that requires energy [39–41].

In considering the transport of drugs in the discovery and development process, the most attention has been focused on transporters from two major superfamilies due to their roles in the uptake into and elimination of drugs out of the cell, respectively. By virtue of these activities, these membrane-transport proteins can cause drug resistance and significant drug–drug interactions. As a comprehensive review of this area is beyond the scope of this chapter, we focus on the most well-characterized transporters from the two major genetic superfamilies: the ABC (ATP *b*inding *c*assette) transporter family and the SLC (solute carrier) transporter family.

Most ABC proteins are active transporters that hydrolyze ATP to actively pump their substrates across membranes. There are 49 known genes for ABC proteins, which can be grouped into seven subclasses or families (ABCA to ABCG) [39]. The most commonly studied transporters in the ABC superfamily are P-glycoprotein (P-gp, *MDR1*) and the cystic fibrosis transmembrane regulator (CFTR).

The SLC superfamily includes facilitated transporters and ion-coupled secondary active transporters that reside in various cell membranes. Forty-three SLC families with approximately 300 transporters have been identified in the human genome [40–42]. In view of the fact that membrane drug transporter activity can have a major influence on the pharmacokinetic, safety, and efficacy profiles of drugs, several key questions become critically important for drug development. These questions include which transporters are of clinical importance in drug absorption and disposition, and what in vitro methods exist that represent viable methods for screening development candidates for interactions with these transporters. These and other important factors in the discovery and development process are discussed below.

ATP Binding Cassette (ABC) Transport Proteins: P-glycoprotein (P-gp, MDR1, ABCB1)

P-gp (MDR1, ABCB1) mediates the ATP-dependent export of drugs from cells. As with all ABC-transport proteins, the ABC region of P-gp binds and hydrolyzes ATP, and the protein uses the energy for transport of its substrates across the membrane. It is expressed in the luminal membrane of the brush-border cells in the small intestine, in the epithelial and other cells that comprise the blood–brain barrier (BBB), in the apical membranes of hepatocytes, and in kidney proximal tubular epithelia.

P-gp plays an important role in the intestinal absorption and in the biliary and urinary excretion of drugs, while in the cells of the BBB it helps limit entry of various drugs into the central nervous system. The level of expression and functionality of P-gp can be modulated by inhibition and induction, which can affect the pharmacokinetics, efficacy, safety, or tissue levels of P-gp substrates [43–45]. Initially discovered as a result of its interaction with multiple anticancer drugs, P-gp is responsible for the efflux across biological membranes of a broad range of therapeutic drugs. P-gp substrates tend to share a hydrophobic planar structure with positively charged or neutral moieties. These include structurally and pharmacologically unrelated compounds, many of which are also substrates for CYP3A4, a major drug-metabolizing enzyme in the human liver and GI tract. Alteration of MDR1 activity by inhibitors (drug–drug interactions) affects oral absorption and renal clearance. Drugs with narrow therapeutic windows (such as the cardiac glycoside digoxin and the immunosuppressants cyclosporine and *tacrolimus*) should be used with great care if MDR1-based drug–drug interactions are likely.

Cell lines that express P-gp, as well as polarized, inside-out membrane vesicles prepared from these cell lines, can be used to determine whether a drug is a P-gp substrate or inhibitor. In these polarized cell monolayer preparations, P-gp is located in the apical plasma membrane. When efflux across the cell membrane is measured in these cell monolayers, the ratio of basal-to-apical to apical-to-basal flux is used to evaluate whether P-gp may play a significant role in transporting drugs across these cell monolayers. Transport across cells is not always related to excretion; P-gp may also have a role in drug penetration into the central nervous system [46–48]. Likewise, a high efflux ratio does not always translate into poor oral absorption. The involvement of P-gp in absorption of a drug is more pronounced in cases in which there is an apparent balance between metabolism and efflux.

BCRP (MXR, ABCG2)

The human membrane transport protein known as the breast cancer resistance protein (BCRP) has been shown to be responsible for resistance to a number of therapeutics. The BCRP transporter is encoded by the ABCG2 gene. As with other members of the ABC superfamily of transporters, BCRP uses energy derived from ATP hydrolysis to pump drugs and xenobiotics across the plasma membrane. It serves to limit the absorption of substrates, prevent them from entering the brain, and also to mediate their hepatic elimination. The drugs to which BCRP can confer resistance in tumor cell lines include mitoxantrone, methotrexate, topotecan derivatives, bisantrene, etoposide, SN-38, and flavopiridol [49–51].

BCRP is present in many normal tissues, for instance, in the apical membrane of placental cells, in the bile canalicular membrane of hepatocytes, in the luminal membranes of brush border epithelial cells in the small intestine and colon, and in the venous and capillary endothelial cells of almost all tissues [52]. The localization of BCRP in those tissues with barrier or elimination functions results in the BCRP transporter having a significant pharmacological role in the disposition of drugs and xenobiotics.

BSEP (SPGP, ABCB11)

The ABC superfamily transport protein known as the bile salt export pump (BSEP) is encoded by the ABCB11 gene. BSEP is expressed in hepatocytes on the apical side of the bile canalicular membrane. It serves to pump bile salts from the liver into bile and as such is the predominant facilitator of bile acid efflux in hepatocytes.

BSEP activity in the liver canalicular membrane is inhibited by a number of drugs or drug metabolites. This is potentially a significant mechanism for drug-induced cholestasis. Dysfunction of individual bile salt transporters such as BSEP is an important cause of cholestatic liver disease. This can occur due to genetic mutation, suppression of gene expression, disturbed signaling, or steric inhibition.

In addition to bile salts, BSEP mRNA has been shown to be induced by classical liver enzyme inducers. There is, however, a limited amount of information on whether atypical BSEP inducers such as 3-methylcholanthrene (3MC) are also substrates of the export pump. BSEP mediates the transport of taurocholic acid (TC) very efficiently. The rate and amount of transport into polarized membrane vesicles can be quantified using methods such as LC/MS/MS, and also by labeling with fluorescent or radioactive (^{3}H-TC) tags. Compounds that interact with the transporter can modulate the rate of TC transport. If a substance is a transported substrate, it might compete with TC, thus reducing the rate of TC transport. If a compound is an inhibitor of the transporter, it will block the transport of TC into polarized membrane vesicles. Some compounds can be cotransported with TC, increasing its rate of transport compared to the control level [39,40].

Solute Carrier (SLC) Transport Proteins: Organic Anion Transporting Proteins (OATPs)

The organic anion transporting proteins (OATPs) belong to the *SLC* gene superfamily of transporters and are 12 trans-membrane domain glycoproteins expressed in various epithelial cells. Some OATPs are expressed in a single organ, while others occur ubiquitously. The functionally characterized members of the OATPs mediate sodium-independent transport of a variety of structurally independent, mainly amphipathic organic compounds, including bile salts, hormones and their conjugates, toxins, and various drugs. Uptake transporters (OATPs, NTCP, OCT1, and OAT2) are localized in the basolateral membrane. These transporters mediate the uptake of substrates into the liver from the

circulation. OATP1B1 and OATP1B3 are liver specific and show broad substrate specificity (statins, rifampicin, and telmisartan). Inhibition of OATP-mediated uptake of several statins by cyclosporin A and rifampicin causes clinically significant DDIs [39,40,53–55].

OTC1

For the elimination of environmental toxins and metabolic waste products, the body is equipped with a range of broad-specificity transporters that are present in the liver, kidney, and intestine. The polyspecific organic cation transporters OCT1, 2, and 3 (SLC22A1–3) mediate the facilitated transport of a variety of structurally diverse organic cations, including many drugs, toxins, and endogenous compounds. OCT1 and OCT2 are found in the basolateral membrane of hepatocytes, enterocytes, and renal proximal tubular cells. OCT3 has more widespread tissue distribution and is considered to be the major component of the extra-neuronal monoamine transport system (or uptake-2), which is responsible for the peripheral elimination of monoamine neurotransmitters. Studies with knockout mouse models have directly demonstrated that these transporters can have a major impact on the pharmacological behavior of various substrate organic cations. The recent identification of polymorphic genetic variants of human OCT1 and OCT2 that severely affect transport activity thus suggests that some of the interpatient differences in response and sensitivity to cationic drugs may be caused by variable activity of these transporters [39,40].

SLC Transport Proteins

Among the SLC superfamily, two families (SLC21 and 22) with polyspecific members have been identified, which together mediate the transport of a variety of structurally diverse organic anions, cations, and uncharged compounds. The SLC21 family of organic anion transporting polypeptides is currently known to consist of nine members in humans, transporting a range of relatively large (usually >450 Da), mostly anionic amphipathic compounds (compounds with both hydrophobic and hydrophilic domains), including bile salts, eicosanoids, steroid hormones, and their conjugates. The SLC22 family currently consists of 12 members in humans and rats, encompassing organic cation transporters (OCTs), the carnitine transporter (OCTN2/SLC22A5), the urate anion-exchanger (URAT1/SLC22A12), and several organic anion transporters [39,40].

Role of Membrane Transporters on ADME Characteristics of Drugs

The body is continuously exposed to a variety of environmental toxins and metabolic waste products. To rid itself of these compounds, it is equipped with various detoxification mechanisms such as metabolizing enzymes and transport proteins mediating their inactivation and excretion. For excretion, a plethora of trans-membrane-transport proteins is present in the major excretory organs (liver, kidney, and intestine). The solute carrier (SLC) superfamily is by far the largest superfamily of transporters, consisting of about 225 members in humans.

While most of these transporters are highly specialized, mediating facilitated transport of essential nutrients (eg, glucose, amino acids, nucleosides, and fatty acids), some members are more generalized. Due to their broad substrate specificity, the latter are also termed polyspecific transporters. They play a major role in the elimination of, and protection against, noxious compounds.

P-gp can export an astonishing variety (chemically diverse) of amphipathic drugs, natural products, and peptides from mammalian cells, powered by the energy of ATP hydrolysis. The transporter consists of two homologous halves, each with six membrane-spanning helices and a cytosolic nucleotide binding domain. P-gp has been purified and studied extensively, but its mechanism of action is still not well understood. X-ray crystal structures of P-gp bound to two cyclic peptide substrates has shown that the protein has a large, flexible, drug-binding cavity located within the membrane-bound domain. Drugs can bind to several subsites within this pocket, via different sets of interactions, helping to explain the unusual polyspecificity of the transporter. P-gp substrates are generally lipid-soluble and interact with the protein within the membrane before being either expelled into the extracellular aqueous phase or moved to the extracellular aspect of the membrane.

P-gp substrates include many drugs that are used clinically, and the protein plays an important role in drug absorption and disposition in vivo. It is a key determinant in the pharmacokinetic profile of many drugs, and, ultimately, the clinical response. The protein is located at the luminal surface of the intestine, and limits absorption of drugs from the gut. Its presence in the luminal membrane of brain capillary endothelial cells also makes a major contribution to the BBB and strongly reduces accumulation of many different drugs in the brain. The physiological role of P-gp is thought to involve protection against toxic xenobiotics and endogenous metabolites by efflux or secretion of these compounds following absorption by other mechanisms. The transporter also plays an important role in the multidrug resistance (MDR) displayed by many human tumors, and it is an important factor in predicting the outcome of chemotherapy treatment [39,40,43–45].

If a drug interacts strongly with P-gp, the compound will likely have reduced absorption in the gut, very limited entry into the brain, and be unable to enter drug-resistant tumors. Screening drugs for their ability to compete with P-gp-mediated transport of a probe compound can give quantitative information on their affinity for the transporter, and provide an indicator of their behavior in vivo. The availability of this type of information for a specific drug can be useful in anticipating potential problems with its use in a clinical setting.

Transporter Mediated Drug–Drug Interactions: P-glycoprotein

Drug–drug interactions involving membrane transport can be classified into two categories. One is caused by competition for the substrate binding sites of the transporters, and the other by a change in the expression level of the transporters. As mentioned previously, P-gp has a very broad range of substrate specificity; hence drug–drug interactions involving it are very likely. P-gp inhibitors, such as quinidine and verapamil, are known to increase plasma concentrations of digoxin, a cardiac glycoside, because they block its biliary and/or urinary excretion via P-gp inhibition. Since the therapeutic range of digoxin is small, changes in its plasma concentration are potentially very serious.

Organic Anion (OATs) and Organic Cation Transporters (OCTs)

OCTs transport a number of drugs including cimetidine, metformin, procainamide, and triamterene from the plasma into hepatocytes and renal tubular cells. As with the cytochromes P450, a variety of different OAT and OCT transporters exist. It is well known that probenecid inhibits the renal secretion of many anionic drugs via organic anion transport systems. The renal clearance of furosemide, ciprofloxacin, and benzylpenicillin is reduced by coadministration of probenecid. OAT1 is a candidate for the transporter responsible for these interactions on the renal basolateral membrane because probenecid has been found to be able to inhibit OAT1 [39,40,53–55].

Metformin's uptake into the liver, where it exerts its pharmacologic effect, is mediated by OCT1, while its elimination via the kidney is primarily due to OCT2 activity. The capacity of OCT2 to transport metformin is at least 10 times greater than OCT1. Thus OTC2 in combination with the renal elimination of metformin is primarily responsible for its pharmacological properties. Cimetidine is also known to be a substrate for OCT and can compete with metformin for both OCT1 and OCT2. Because OCT2 is primarily responsible for metformin's elimination, competition from cimetidine will result in reduced renal clearance of metformin and elevated plasma concentrations. Procainamide is another known OCT substrate. Its renal clearance has been reduced following coadministration with several drugs, including amiodarone, levofloxacin, and cimetidine [53–55].

The clinical outcome of drug–drug interactions based on OAT or OCT inhibition will depend on the pharmacological properties of the drug in question. For example, inhibiting the hepatic uptake of a drug may reduce its metabolism, leading to higher plasma concentrations. If the site of action of the drug is intrahepatic, however, a reduction in the desired pharmacological effect also may occur, despite increased plasma concentrations. Nevertheless, the resulting increase in the drug's plasma concentration may lead to an increase in side effects unrelated to the drug's therapeutic effect. An example would be that patients taking statins might have an increased risk of myopathy, whereas those on metformin could have a greater risk of developing lactic acidosis. The effect of inhibited renal clearance will depend on the percent of drug eliminated via the kidney and its therapeutic window. In general, clinically significant effects will occur with drugs having at least 50% of their elimination via renal secretion and that also have a narrow therapeutic window [39,40,53–55].

Transporter-Mediated Drug Resistance

The multidrug-resistance protein (MRP) has been recognized as being correlated with drug resistance in cancer chemotherapy for some time. MRP is a trans-membrane protein that is, in part, responsible for the resistance of human tumor cells to cytotoxic drugs. Stably transfected, MRP-overexpressing cells have been shown to be resistant to doxorubicin, daunorubicin, vincristine, VP-16, colchicine, and rhodamine 123, but not to 4′-(9-acridinyl-amino) methanesulfon-m-anisidide or taxol. Intracellular accumulation of antineoplastic drugs (daunorubicin, vincristine, and VP-16) is decreased and the efflux of drug (daunorubicin) is increased in these cells [39,40]. Accumulation of daunorubicin has been shown to be reversed when the plasma membrane of these cells is permeabilized using nonionic detergent. This would seem to demonstrate conclusively that MRP lowers the intracellular daunorubicin level by pumping the drug out of the cells against a concentration gradient, thereby identifying it as a transmembrane efflux pump [56].

Pancreatic cancers are among the tumor types that have proven to be most chemoresistant to a variety of chemotherapy agents. Chemoresistance of this nature can be mediated by various cellular mechanisms, including reduced uptake of the drugs into the target cells; alterations within the cells, such as changes in the metabolism of the drugs; changes in the cellular capacity for DNA repair; and an increased efflux of the drugs from the cells. In studies of human pancreatic carcinoma cells, Hagmann et al. showed that in cells stably transfected with human transporter cDNAs, or in cells in which a specific transporter was knocked down by RNA interference, 5-fluorouracil treatment affects the expression profile of relevant cellular transporters including MRPs, and that MRP5 (ABCC5) influences the chemoresistance of these tumor cells [57]. Similarly, cell treatment with the nucleoside drug gemcitabine or a combination of chemotherapeutic drugs can variably influence the expression pattern and relative amount of uptake and export transporters in pancreatic carcinoma cells. In addition, cytotoxicity studies with MRP5-overexpressing or MRP5-silenced cells additionally demonstrated a contribution of MRP5 to gemcitabine resistance [57].

Chemotherapy is a major form of treatment for cancers. Unfortunately, the majority of cancers are either resistant to chemotherapy or acquire resistance during treatment. One of the mechanisms by which human cancers develop multidrug resistance is the overexpression of efflux transport proteins on the plasma membrane of cancer cells. P-gp and MRP1 have been shown to confer resistance to a broad spectrum of chemotherapeutic agents. Several other human ATP-binding cassette (ABC) transporters with a potential role in drug resistance have been described as having a role in multidrug resistance. Among them, a novel protein, now known as the breast cancer resistance protein (BCRP), mitoxantrone-resistance protein (MXR) [58], or placenta-specific ABC protein (ABCP), were shown to be present in the plasma membrane of the drug-resistant cells overexpressing the transporter [59]. Such studies provide strong evidence that BCRP is a cause of drug resistance for certain types of chemotherapeutic agents, including mitoxantrone and topotecan, in tissue culture models. BCRP is prominently expressed in organs important for absorption (the small intestine), distribution (the placenta and BBB), and elimination (the liver and small intestine) of drugs, and an increasing amount of evidence is now emerging to support the conclusion that BCRP also plays an important role in drug disposition [39,40].

Methodologies for Evaluating Drug Interactions With Transporters

Drug–drug interaction involving hepatic membrane transporters can occur as a result of competition for the same substrate-binding site of the transporter, very tight binding, by binding that interferes with the transporter allosterically leading to inhibition of transporter activity, or by a change in expression level of transporters. This has the potential to alter the blood concentration time profiles of drugs, leading to elevated levels of a coadministered compound. Evaluating the substrate potential of a drug candidate for the hepatic uptake transporters in vitro is particularly beneficial when the liver is the drug target. For example, the hepatitis C drugs alpha-interferon and S-acyl-2-thioethyl esters or the HMGCoA inhibitors (statins) must achieve adequate concentrations in the liver for pharmacological activity.

In addition to drug–drug interactions, hepatic transporters also play a role in toxicities including cholestasis and hyperbilirubinemia. Drug-induced hepatotoxicity is a major problem in drug development and there is growing evidence that inhibition of bile acid transporters is a contributing mechanism.

Hepatocytes in suspension, attached to tissue culture dishes or in primary sandwich culture, are all good models of hepatic transport. The contribution of transporter-mediated uptake to hepatic clearance (CLH) was recognized when CLH was consistently underpredicted for many series of chemotypes using just metabolic stability for the calculations. Factoring in transporter-mediated hepatic uptake, along with metabolic clearance using hepatocytes in suspension, improved these predictions [39,40].

ABC transporter assays including epithelial cell barrier systems using Caco-2 or LLC-PK1 cells are widely accepted in vitro models used to rank the absorption of drug candidates. In addition to these standard models, we may specifically measure human P-gp-mediated drug transport using cDNA-transfected LLCPK porcine cell lines. These human P-gp expressing cell lines allow the study of this important efflux transporter without interference from other expressed transporters.

Alternatively, a less specific but faster ATPase assay in membranes or membrane vesicles allows determination of whether the compounds of interest interact with ABC transporters. ATP hydrolysis is required for in vivo drug efflux by ABC transporters. The membrane ATPase assay measures the phosphate liberated from drug-stimulated ATP hydrolysis in ABC transporter membranes [42–47].

Caco-2 cells are the most popular cellular model in studies on passage and transport. They were derived from a human colorectal adenocarcinoma. In culture, they differentiate spontaneously into polarized intestinal cells possessing an apical brush border and tight junctions between adjacent cells, and they express hydrolases and typical microvillar transporters. This cell line was first used as a model for studying differentiation in the intestinal epithelium and later for estimating the relative contributions of paracellular and transcellular passage in drug absorption.

Caco-2 cells, despite their colonic origin, express in culture the majority of the morphological and functional characteristics of small intestinal absorptive cells, including phase I and phase II enzymes, which can be detected either by measurement of their activities toward specific substrates, or by immunological techniques. CYP3A, which is present in almost all intestinal cells, is very weakly expressed in Caco-2 cells, but expression levels can be increased by treatment with 1α,25-dihydroxyvitamin D3, an inducer of CYP3A4, or transfection of CYP3A4 cDNA. But the resulting expression levels do not reach the levels observed in vivo. With regard to phase II enzymes, Caco-2 cells do express N-acetyl transferase and glutathione transferase. In summary, the Caco-2 cell transport assay appears to be a good and predictive approach to understanding transport across the intestinal absorptive barrier [39,40].

Drug-transport assays in polarized cell monolayers can be used to screen for P-gp involvement in transport. P-gp, encoded by MDR1, is expressed in the human intestine, liver, brain, and other tissues. Localized to the cell membrane, P-gp functions as an ATP-dependent efflux pump capable of transporting many structurally unrelated xenobiotics out of cells. Intestinal expression of P-gp may affect the oral bioavailability of drug molecules that are substrates for this transporter. P-gp substrates can be identified by a direct measure of transport across polarized cell monolayers. Bidirectional transport (apical to basolateral and basolateral to apical) is measured in Caco-2 cells, or in LLC-PK1 cells expressing P-gp cDNA and corresponding control cells. Quantitation of the rate of transport and total mass transported can be achieved by a variety of methods including LC/MS/MS, fluorescence, or by using a radio-labeled substrate [39,40,47]. Evaluation of drug candidates as a substrate and inhibitor of P-gp should be performed according to FDA guidance [16].

As a means of studying the transport of drugs and xenobiotics into and out of the brain, capillaries can be isolated from brain and digested to separate out brain capillary endothelial cells for growth in cell culture. The endothelial monolayer can be grown on porous membranes, which can be placed in side-by-side diffusion chambers for measurement of drug transport across the monolayer in vitro. The problem with this approach is that BBB-specific gene expression is severely downregulated in vitro. For example, the expression of the GLUT1 glucose transporter or the LAT1 large neutral amino acid transporter is downregulated >100-fold in cultured endothelium compared to freshly isolated brain capillaries. For example, L-DOPA for Parkinson's disease is effective, because this drug crosses the BBB on the LAT1 endogenous transporter [39,40].

Alternatively, these transport systems can be studied in vivo. Drug transport from blood to cerebrospinal fluid (CSF) is a function of drug transport across the choroid plexus epithelium, which forms the blood-CSF barrier in vivo. This epithelial barrier is anatomically separate from the BBB, which limits drug transport from the brain into brain interstitial fluid (ISF) across the capillary endothelium. The capillary endothelium (the BBB) and the choroid plexus (the blood-CSF barrier) have different transporter gene expression profiles. Drugs may readily enter CSF, due to rapid transport across the choroid plexus, but do *not* undergo significant transport into brain tissue, due to limited BBB transport. This is illustrated with azidothymidine (AZT), a treatment for neuro-AIDS. AZT is readily transported into CSF, but is not transported across the BBB.

BBB active efflux transporters (AET) such as p-glycoprotein actively transport drugs from brain to blood. There are many other BBB efflux systems for both small and large molecules. The efflux transporters can be measured using the brain efflux index (BEI) method, which involves direct injection of the drug into the brain under stereotaxic guidance. The kinetics of drug loss from the brain compartment (which is a function only of BBB efflux transport) can then be quantified [39,40].

Metabolism in the GIT and Liver: Stability Testing

Clearly, metabolism is important in determining the amount of drug absorbed from the GIT into the bloodstream. The absorption and distribution of a drug following PO administration leading to some desired pharmacological effect occurring at a target organ, such as the brain, requires that the metabolism of the drug is not extensive, either in the gut or the liver. Following oral administration, the metabolism of drugs in the gut tissues and/or the liver upon absorption from the intestinal lumen is termed "first-pass metabolism."

Stability Testing: Plasma and Microsomal Stability

Several simple stability tests allow the assessment of the "drug-ability" of a compound or chemical template. For example, if a compound is highly unstable in a tissue (liver, for example) or fluid (blood, for example) that is likely to be encountered during the sojourn from the intestinal lumen to interaction with the drug receptor (brain, for example), then activity following oral administration will by definition be low. For drug library screening stability testing, typically a one data-point determination (with a zero time-point control) is made, in which the time and other parameters (such as protein concentration) are such that a certain percentage of loss of a compound can be used as a screening data point (information about whether to keep or eliminate a compound, or information to consider in the context of additional compound data) [1,2,4,5].

Plasma Stability

Drugs must have sufficient stability in the body to exert a pharmacological effect over a reasonable period of time. A wide variety of compounds are unstable (are degraded) when incubated in blood or plasma at rates that are inconsistent with the PK properties necessary for drug therapeutics. Plasma (blood) stability determination is a widely used, simple test that can eliminate compounds in drug discovery screens. As already stated above, the drug discovery/development process involves not only the identification of drug targets and demonstration of desirable activities in model systems, but also the elimination of compounds that must, by definition, fail in the clinic and poor plasma stability usually represents one such characteristic. For determination of

stability in plasma, typically a compound is incubated in plasma (blood) at approximately 10 μM at 37°C for 30–60 min and its stability determined by an appropriate analytical method, such as LC-UV or LC-MS. Viable drug candidates should be "relatively" stable under these conditions.

Microsomal Stability

Common in vitro metabolism systems include cells (hepatocytes), the S9 fraction, microsomes, and the soluble fraction. The preparation of S9 fraction, soluble fraction, and microsomes is shown in Fig. 3.6. Microsomes are artificial structures derived from pieces of endoplasmic reticulum (ER) formed during tissue homogenization. As shown in Fig. 3.6 microsomes are prepared by differential centrifugation at 10,000 and 100,000 × g and contain cytochrome P450 enzymes (CYPs), but do not contain soluble enzymes. The family of CYP enzymes contained in microsomes are responsible for most of the Phase I biotransformations of xenobiotics, and incubation of test material with hepatic microsomal preparations in various species is the primary means by which the Phase I biotransformations of xenobiotics (drugs) are determined. For microsomal stability determination, the compound is typically incubated in approximately 1.0 mg/ml microsomal protein, phosphate buffer, pH 7.4 at 37°C for 30 min. Compound stability is then determined by an appropriate analytical method such as LC-UV or LC-MS. Viable drug candidates should have a species-specific, predetermined percentage remaining under these conditions. Early in the drug discovery process, microsomal stability testing is often undertaken in an HTS format using microsomes from rodent [60].

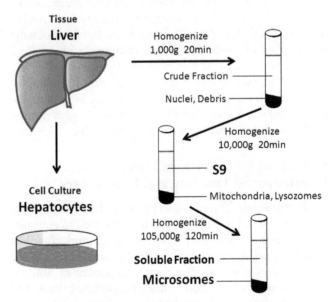

FIGURE 3.6 Preparation of microsomal, S9, and soluble fractions commonly used in drug metabolism studies.

DRUG DISTRIBUTION AND EXCRETION

For simplicity, we have combined drug distribution and drug excretion in this section. Modern eADME studies that evaluate drug-related material distribution by MS usually analyze specific tissues, blood/plasma, and excreta. For example, when a drug is administered by IV or PO, samples of blood (plasma), tissues (brain, for example), and excreta (urine and feces) are taken at specific time intervals and are analyzed for drug-related material by LC-MS, giving both distribution and excretion data. This has been made possible by the revolutionary changes in MS technology over the last 20–25 years, allowing for rapid development of sensitive and specific methods for the quantitative analysis of drugs in tissues and fluids by LC-MS (expanded below). In addition, another tool available to the ADME scientist is the direct determination of xenobiotics (and endogenous compounds) in tissue slices by desorption of compounds for analysis by MS imaging (MSI). In this technique, compounds are desorbed into the gaseous phase for analysis using either matrix-assisted laser desorption ionization (MALDI) or secondary ion mass spectrometry (SIMS) [61]. To summarize, MS allows for the qualitative and quantitative analysis of small and large molecules in tissues and fluids without the use of radiotracers. The evolving technologies surrounding the use of radioactive tags to study the disposition of biologics early in drug discovery using PET and SPECT are discussed in a separate chapter.

The study of the distribution of a xenobiotic is the study of its movement into, through, and out of body compartments. Data are expressed in terms of C-T for the parent drug and its metabolites. Kinetic analysis can afford insight into drug properties and PK/PD relationships. A concept central to any discussion of distribution is the *volume of distribution*. The (apparent) volume of distribution (V_D) is a pharmacokinetic "parameter" used to quantify the distribution of a medication between plasma and the rest of the body. Certain changes in physiological function(s) and certain disease states may alter V_D. This is discussed in detail in the chapter on PK (Chapter 4). The reader should consider Chapter 4 as part of the ADME material and refer to this chapter to gain a more in-depth understanding of blood-plasma PK.

Kinetics of Metabolism in Microsomes, Hepatocyte S9 Fraction, and Hepatocytes

Over the past 25 years or so there has been an increase in the use of in vitro systems as models used to estimate the in vivo ADME properties of drugs and chemical templates under evaluation for *drug-ability* [62,63]. These systems represent an important component of allometric scaling for estimation of drug properties in man. For example, the rate of metabolism (and metabolic clearance) observed in vitro for hepatic preparations can be used as an estimate of what to expect in vivo. To some extent, the popularity of in vitro systems has been driven by their use by numerous research groups and the eventual commercialization of in vitro test products that are economical and effective. However, there is a lot of "bang for the buck" in using in vitro systems in drug discovery research, especially in identifying drugs that will fail in the clinic, as previously noted. In vitro systems include intact cells such as perfused liver preparations, liver slices, freshly prepared, or frozen hepatocytes and other cell lines. Cell fractions include S9 fraction, soluble fraction (cytosol), and microsomes (Fig. 3.6).

Rate of Drug Disappearance in Liver Microsomes or Hepatocytes [64]

A typical experiment for *stability screening* purposes using microsomes involves incubation of drug at approximately 3 μM. Typical conditions would be incubation of the drug at 37°C with 100 mM phosphate buffer pH=7.4, 1.0 mM nicotinamide adenine dinucleotide phosphate (NADPH) and approximately 1.0 mg/ml microsomal protein. Reaction starts with the addition of NADPH (time zero). Typically, 5 to 7 time points are taken (0, 2, 5, 10, 20, 30, and 60 min, for example) and the reaction is stopped by the addition of methanol or acetonitrile. The drug is analyzed using LC-MS and the kinetics of disappearance data are entered into drug (chemical) libraries. Determination of the rate of disappearance of the drug using plated hepatocytes and hepatocytes in suspension has become more popular recently. Although hepatocyte preparations represent a more complicated and more expensive experiment, all hepatic enzymes are available to act on parent compound and metabolites, including Phase II enzymes. This represents a significant advantage over microsome and S9 preparations. However, a disadvantage with using this approach to kinetic analysis is that the kinetics of movement of the drug across membranes becomes a complicating factor, although it can be argued that this is a situation closer to that encountered in vivo. In summary, there are advantages and disadvantages of using whole cells, microsomes, or S9 fractions and often when choosing drugs to enter development, all these data are available for consideration, or should be available.

In Vivo eADME Disposition and Balance Studies

The impact of new analytical techniques and instrumentation, and improvements in existing technologies on the way we conduct biochemical studies, cannot be overstated [65]. For example, the ability of MS to obtain high-quality spectra or quantify molecules in biological matrices has increased by several orders of magnitude; 10^4–10^7 times, depending upon the application, between the late 1960s and today. The impact of electrospray (ESI) and other MS techniques on the ability to detect, quantify, and identify molecules in biological matrices has been profound (a Nobel Prize was awarded for the invention of ESI) [66]. The biochemists and pharmacologists of 50 years ago relied heavily on the use of spectroscopy and isotopes such as ^{14}C, or ^{13}C in the elucidation of metabolic pathways. Multistep purifications, spectral absorbance, mass spectral, and nuclear magnetic resonance spectroscopy (NMR) analysis were used, which involved a considerable investment in time. Today, modern instrumentation techniques have allowed the determination of xenobiotic metabolites in a fraction of the time with online combinations of MS, NMR, and radioactivity detection.

Continued advances in analytical instrumentation have even allowed the rapid estimation of the disposition of drug-related materials without the use of isotopes. The introduction of tandem quadrupole MS and advancements in LC-MS interfaces (ESI; atmospheric pressure chemical ionization, APCI) have greatly improved the practicability of studying absorption in vivo [2,6,67–70]. In fact, modern MS technology has allowed for early PK data (in vivo) to be obtained in drug discovery programs for tens to a few hundreds of candidate compounds. Generic LC-MS-MS methods, or methods needing little development, can be used to quantitatively analyze a drug in plasma with high sensitivity and selectivity. Provided that sufficient amounts of compound are available (tens of mg), drugs can be dosed to mice or rats by PO and IV and blood samples taken at appropriate intervals to obtain early PK data. For a typical study, 10–12 samples are taken by each route of administration with the last time point at 12 or 24 h postdose. More abbreviated protocols are also useful if less accuracy is considered acceptable for ranking drug candidates. Typically, tissue and fluid samples are homogenized and then extracted using a generic method for extraction of drug-related material. This could be as simple as addition of one volume of water to urine and analysis by LC-MS or as complicated as homogenization of feces in buffer using glass beads and sonication, followed by one or two extractions. For LC-MS-MS analysis using tandem quadrupole MS, methods are developed by first evaluating the relative response factors using the four combinations of ±ESI and ±APCI (+/−; positive and negative ions detected) and then examining the appearance of the product-ion mass spectrum for determination of selected reaction monitoring (SRM) precursor-product ions that impart the greatest selectivity and specificity. LC conditions are quickly evaluated and then quantitative analysis can be performed for selected fluid/tissue samples. In addition, gradient LC-MS analysis using repetitive scanning MS can be performed to examine the drug metabolite profile in a semi-quantitative manner. Results of these analyses are used to determine how additional samples are best analyzed. One additional technique is to metabolize the radio-labeled drug,

if available, and determine relative response factors for drug metabolites by LC-MS-RAM (radioactivity monitoring) analysis. The RAM analysis is quantitative since the specific activity is known and thus relative response factors can be estimated and subsequent experiments can be normalized in a quantitative manner [71].

Cassette Dosing. As detailed above, modern MS instrumentation is more sensitive and easier to use than older techniques and also exhibits reasonable analyte selectivity and sensitivity. Modern ± ESI and ± APCI coupled with tandem quadrupole instruments has allowed PK studies in which drugs are administered concomitantly, a technique commonly known as "cassette dosing" or "n-in-1" dosing (5-in-1; a mixture of five compounds in the same formulation, for example). In these studies, drug mixtures are dosed IV and PO and LC-MS analysis methods are used to quantitatively analyze samples taken at appropriate time points. Either selected ion monitoring (SIM) or selected reaction monitoring (SRM) can be used for the MS analysis. Although caution must be applied in the use of this approach, the screening value of cassette dosing can be high when applied to compounds within a specific chemical template [72,73].

Drug Distribution Using Molecular Imaging

Over 80% of investigational new drugs fail during drug development because of unsatisfactory absorption, distribution, metabolism, excretion, and toxicity (ADME and toxicity; ADME) characteristics. Tools that help to predict the ADME responses early in development present an advantage as they avoid wasting valuable resources on compounds that are bound to fail. A multitude of noninvasive, high-resolution imaging technologies are now used regularly in ADME studies. Drug companies currently have hundreds of thousands of potential drug compounds; however, very few (<1:10,000) will eventually enter the market as an FDA-approved treatment. The techniques available today for real-time molecular imaging of the disposition of drugs in the body provide a unique, early opportunity to identify which drugs will fail in the later stages of drug development, thereby improving the quality of the molecules ultimately selected to move forward. These technologies have particular, fundamental advantages in the study of large molecules (biologics). Again, this area is so important that a separate chapter is dedicated to it (see Chapter 35).

DRUG METABOLISM

Biotransformation: Drug Metabolite Profile

Mammals have evolved mechanisms to rapidly metabolize and eliminate potentially harmful substances from biological sources (xenobiotics) that have been ingested. Examples include the plethora of toxins associated with the kingdoms of fungi (mushrooms, for example) and plants. Mammals must be able to metabolize and eliminate toxins present in plants or the plant cannot be consumed as food. The same mechanisms for handling plant toxins, both enzymatic and transport systems, are involved in the metabolism of drugs. It is worth noting here that many of the compounds used as drugs are found in plants or were derived from plant chemical templates (eg, morphine from the opium poppy and digitalis from foxglove [18,19]). These metabolism systems for dealing with xenobiotics are critical, since many ingested xenobiotics are lipophilic and would accumulate in the body without metabolism with subsequent elimination. Drugs are also usually lipophilic, an intrinsic property that allows them to pass through cell and intracellular membranes to reach drug receptors. The same property that allows drugs to reach receptors, however, also allows them to accumulate in the absence of some clearance mechanism involving metabolism or active transport.

The metabolism of xenobiotics hence represents a doubled-edged sword: It allows their elimination from the body, but may also convert the drugs to toxic substances, including highly reactive carcinogenic, mutagenic, or teratogenic molecules. Electrophilic metabolites can react with nucleophilic macromolecules such as nucleic acids and proteins leading to cell damage [1,2,4,7].

The most common enzyme types and biotransformation reactions are listed in Tables 3.1 and 3.2. In general, reactions that aid in the elimination of xenobiotics (drugs) involve oxidative, reductive, hydrolysis, and transferase reactions that increase the water solubility of the compound (decrease the lipophilicity). Xenobiotic-metabolizing enzymes are grouped into two classes: Phase I and Phase II reactions. Phase I reactions include oxidation, reduction, and hydrolysis reactions, and Phase II reactions refer to conjugations of xenobiotics with glucuronic acid, sulfuric acid, specific amino acids, and other groups, this conjugation occurring at functional groups containing oxygen, sulfur and nitrogen (-OH, -NH-, -COOH, -SH, for example). Hydrolysis reactions, such as cleavage of an

TABLE 3.1　Table of Enzymes, Subcellular Fraction Localizations, and Reactions for Drug-Metabolizing Enzymes

Enzyme Types	Subcellular Fraction; Reaction
PHASE I	
Cytochrome P450s (CYP)	ER[a]; C and O oxidation, dealkylation, and other oxidations
Flavin-containing monooxygenases (FMO)	ER; N, S, and P oxidation
Epoxide hydrolases (EH)	ER, cytosol; hydration of epoxides
Reductases	Cytosol, reduction reactions
Monoamine oxidase	Oxidative deamination of monoamines
HYDROLASES	
Esterases	ER, cytosol; hydrolyzes ester bonds
Amidases	ER, cytosol; hydrolyzes amide bonds
PHASE II TRANSFERASES (COFACTOR)	
UDP-glucuronosyltransferases (UGT) (*uridine diphosphate glucuronic acid*)	ER; addition of glucuronic acid
Sulfotransferases (SULT) (*3″-phosphoadenosine-5″-phosphosulfate*)	Cytosol: Addition of sulfate
Glutathione-S-transferases (GST) (*glutathione*)	ER, cytosol; addition of glutathione
Miscellaneous transferases[b]	
MISCELLANEOUS ENZYMES	
Alcohol dehydrogenase	Cytosol; oxidation of alcohols
Aldehyde dehydrogenase	Cytosol; oxidation of aldehydes
NADPH-quinone oxidoreductase (NQO)	ER; reduction of quinones

[a]*Endoplasmic reticulum (ER).*
[b]*Amino acid transferases, methyltransferases, and N-acetyltransferases (NACT) are found in the soluble fraction and the ER. Conjugation reactions vary across species. The cofactor for methyltransferases is S-adenosyl methionine and the cofactor for N-acetyltransferases is acetyl CoA. Methylation and acetylation generally do not lead to more polar products with increased water solubility.*

TABLE 3.2 Table of Schematics of General Reaction Types Involved in Drug Metabolism

Reaction Type	Chemistry

OXIDATIVE REACTIONS

Aromatic Hydroxylation

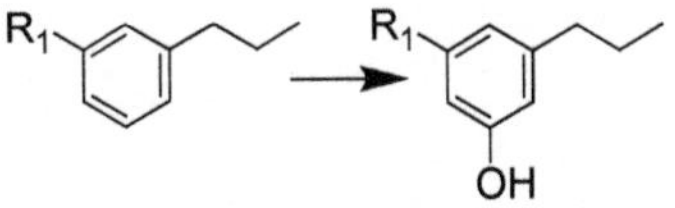

Aliphatic Hydroxylation

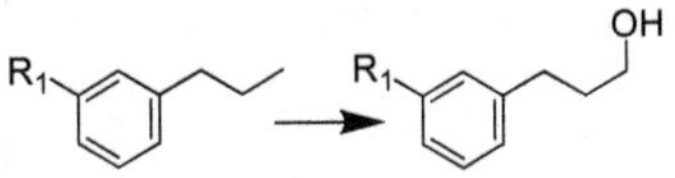

N-Dealkyation

O-Dealkyation

N-Oxidation

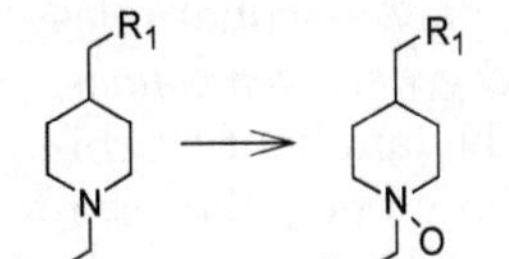

S-oxidation

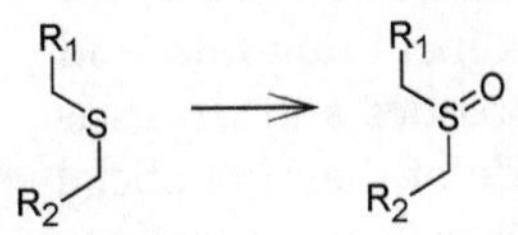

Deamination

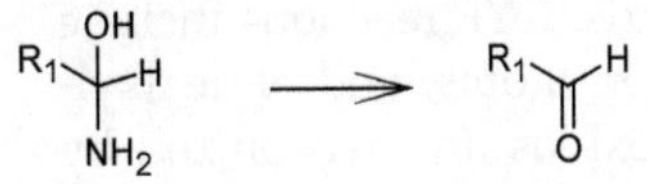

HYDROLYSIS REACTIONS

Ester hydrolysis

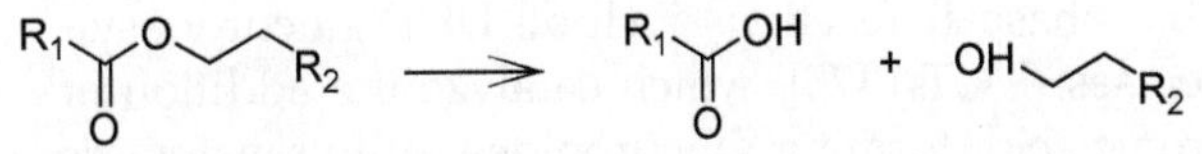

Amide hydrolysis

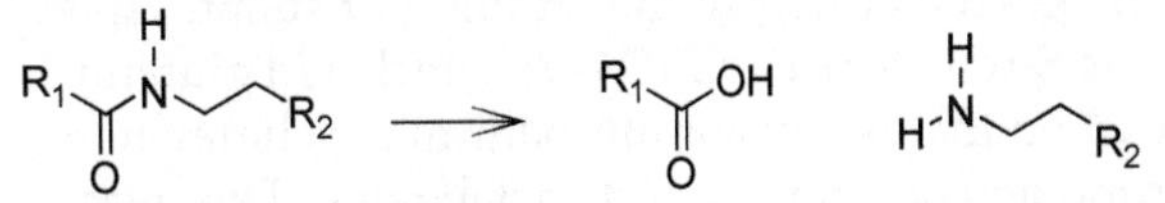

Epoxide hydrolysis

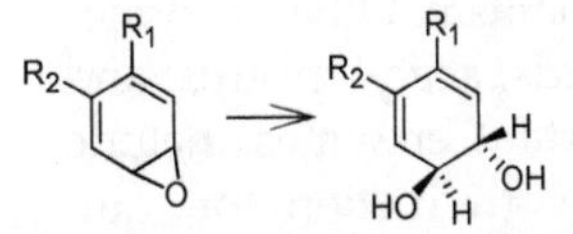

CONJUGATION REACTIONS

Glucuronidation

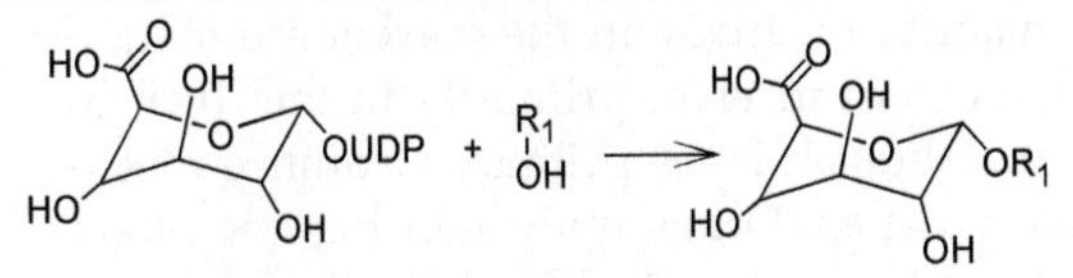

Continued

I. DRUG DISCOVERY, METABOLISM, AND PHARMACOKINETICS

TABLE 3.2   Table of Schematics of General Reaction Types Involved in Drug Metabolism—cont'd

Reaction Type	Chemistry
Sulfation	$R_1{-}OH + PAPS \longrightarrow R_1{-}O{-}\overset{O}{\underset{O}{\overset{\|}{\underset{\|}{S}}}}{-}OH + PAP$
Amino acid conjugation	$R_1\overset{O}{\overset{\|}{C}}{-}OH \longrightarrow R_1\overset{O}{\overset{\|}{C}}{-}N\underset{H}{-}\overset{CO_2H}{\underset{R_2}{\overset{\|}{C}{-}H}}$
Glutathione conjugation	$R + GSH \longrightarrow R\text{-}GSH$

ester, amide, or phospho-amide bond can result in loss of drug activity; however, in specific situations prodrugs are activated in this manner. Phase I oxidation reactions are primarily carried out by cytochrome P450 enzymes (P450; CYP) and flavin-monooxygenases (FMO) [74].

The importance of cytochrome P450 in metabolism cannot be overstated. CYP enzymes play essential roles in the biosynthesis of important *endogenous compounds*, *endobiotics*, such as steroids/sterols, the family of arachidonic acid derived, locally acting hormones, the eicosanoids, and other physiologically important compounds and intermediates. They also play important roles in the metabolism of lipophilic compounds including fats, and their role in the elimination of xenobiotics and drugs is critical. As already noted, the flip side of their beneficial effects in eliminating toxins is that these same reactions can produce reactive compounds. CYP reactions include oxidation of carbon and oxygen atoms, and *N*-dealkylation and *O*-dealkylation. Epoxides are hydrolyzed by soluble and microsomal expoxide hydrolase and FMO is involved in the oxidation of nitrogen, sulfur, and phosphorous. Phase II reactions include UDP-glucuronosyltransferases (UGTs) [75], which catalyze the addition of glucuronic acid, forming glucuronides, sulfotransferases (SULTs) [76], which catalyze the addition of sulfate, and glutathione-S-transferases (GST) [77], which add glutathione, a reaction that is a major mechanism for elimination of electrophilic compounds and metabolites. This reaction is a critical detoxification mechanism. Other enzymes catalyze the addition of amino acids, acetyl groups, and methyl groups. Additional important enzymes include NADPH-quinone oxidoreductase (reduction of quinones), alcohol dehydrogenases, and aldehyde dehydrogenases (shown in Table 3.1).

The vast majority of drugs on the market are metabolized to some extent in vivo, primarily in the liver. In fact, hepatic metabolism is the primary clearance mechanism for many drugs. Drugs with high hepatic blood clearance (the product of hepatic blood flow and hepatic extraction ratio ($Q_H \cdot E_H$)) include desipramine, lidocaine, morphine, propranolol, and verapamil [78]. It should be noted that the liver is also the primary metabolic clearing mechanism for a wide range of endogenous chemicals, including cholesterol, steroid hormones, and vitamins. Important sites of metabolism of drugs other than the liver, ie, the extrahepatic sites of metabolism, include the GIT, lung, and kidney. For example, extrahepatic metabolism of propofol by glucuronidation has been observed during liver transplantation [79].

As a result of dramatic improvements in analytical instrumentation, the ADME properties of an NCE (new chemical entity) can be studied with some degree of confidence by administering the unlabeled drug (without a radioactive tag) to a preclinical species and collecting excreta, blood, and tissues and using modern LC-MS instrumentation to determine the amount of parent drug (unchanged drug) present and the approximate amounts and structures of metabolites. (Note: A popular term is "drug-related material" since this is an all-encompassing term that covers nonenzymatic processes.)

Traditional ADME studies require the synthesis of a radio-labeled standard with the radio-isotope in a position that is metabolically stable. The drug is then administered by PO or IV, or by the route under study, and the journey of the radio-labeled atoms through the body is tracked by collecting samples and determining the amount of radioactivity present, a quantitative exercise since the specific activity is known and the quench can be determined. LC-RAM (radioactivity monitoring) is also usually performed, resulting in a *quantitative metabolic profile*. When protocols include collection of all excreta, these studies are usually termed *balance studies* or *radioactive balance studies*. The following discusses what can now be accomplished without the use of radio-isotopes [2,6].

Role of Mass Spectrometry in Drug Development [61,67–71,80]

In the middle of the twentieth century, the use of both stable and radio-isotopes in biochemical studies coupled with analysis by MS, NMR, and photon spectroscopy made it possible to understand in great detail the important metabolism/catabolism reactions occurring in living systems and in addition how living systems interact with xenobiotics biochemically. More recent advances in MS have made it possible to quantitatively and qualitatively follow the path of xenobiotics through the body in the absence of radio-labeled tags. Prior to the widespread use of ESI and APCI, analysis of biological samples by MS was limited to GC–MS with chemical derivatization, LC-MS techniques with serious limitations (thermospray, particle beam, moving belt, continuous flow FAB (fast atom bombardment)), and off-line desorption techniques (FAB, SIMS, and MALDI (matrix-assisted laser desorption/ionization)). ESI and APCI drastically changed this situation, since large or polar small molecules can be analyzed online with LC elution and without the need for chemical derivatization.

The pairing of ESI and APCI with another revolutionary technique, the tandem quadrupole analyzer, changed how drug research has been conducted over the last 25 years [67–71]. Quantitative methods, with or without stable-isotope-labeled internal standards (termed *stable-isotope dilution mass spectrometry* when stable isotopes are employed), that are sensitive, highly selective, and rugged could be developed rapidly using these combined technologies. Drug metabolites, especially Phase II conjugates, could be detected with a high degree of confidence by sifting through LC-MS repetitive scanning data and searching for logical mass additions and losses and then obtaining product-ion mass spectra of the pseudo-molecular ions (MH+, [M−1]−, for example).

Each product ion observed in a tandem mass spectrometer product-ion mass spectrum conveys two types of information: 1) the mass of the ion and 2) the neutral loss producing this ion, and the tandem mass spectrometer can scan for product ions or neutral losses characteristic of a given structure or substructure [61,67–71,80–82]. Thus metabolites of xenobiotics could also be "screened" for and specifically detected using parent and neutral loss scans [68–70]. As an example, glucuronide, glutathione, or sulfate conjugates of drugs exhibit characteristic neutral losses (positive ion) of 176, 129 (272 in negative ion), and 80 Da in their product-ion mass spectra, and this information can be used to screen for these conjugates. Specific neutral losses and product ions can also be used to screen for Phase I drug metabolites and this approach can at times be quite selective [69,70]. However, this approach could also miss metabolites where these fundamental characteristics of the product-ion mass spectrum have changed (specific ions or neutral losses not observed).

More recently, there has been an increased interest in the use of high-resolution analyzers for both qualitative and quantitative analysis of biological samples [81,82]. This approach has the advantage that MS data obtained at sufficiently high resolution can be searched

for metabolites by computer, since only a limited number of biotransformations are possible. This means that a finite number of exact masses can be derived from the elemental composition of the parent drug. Since the elemental composition of a drug is often dissimilar to that of endogenous compounds (number of heteroatoms relative to carbon atoms, presence of halogens, etc.), this approach can usually rule out endogenous compounds simply from their elemental composition. The use of proper control samples and the skillful interpretation of product-ion mass spectra enhances the interpretative value of these techniques.

Currently, there is also significant interest in using HR-MS in quantitative analysis. This has the distinct advantage that MS–MS tuning is eliminated (collision cell gas pressure and collision energy) and all the mass data can be collected all of the time, allowing for reversed searches of data for metabolites that are not part of the original analysis scheme. Expect to see rapid advances in quantitative analysis by LC-MS, as the technology continues to evolve rapidly [61,67–71,80,81].

With modern MS instrumentation it is possible to detect drug-related material, usually at nM concentrations, and to estimate the absorption, distribution, metabolism, and excretion of a compound over the timespan of the in-life protocol, plus a day or two to process and then analyze samples. However, when the analysis employs a nonradiolabeled drug and MS, there is always the possibility that the molar relative response factor has decreased significantly. The relative molar response factor, or RF, is the response observed for a known quantity of a molecule in isolation and is an intrinsic property of the molecule. Another problem in conducting studies without the use of radioactivity is the frequently encountered phenomenon of "suppression of ionization." This can occur when coeluting material interferes with the ionization of drug-related material. However, this problem can be overcome for the most part by analyzing one to two samples containing high concentrations of drug-related material by all four typically-used ionization modes (±ESI and ±APCI), and by employing additional techniques such as derivatization chemistry, an underutilized technology in the opinion of the authors. Also, avoidance of short columns and attention to possible formation of parent drug from *N*-oxides, *N*-glucuronides, and acyl glucuronides are important considerations, with or without a radio-labeled drug standard.

In the absence of a radio-labeled standard, knowledgeable attention to detail greatly reduces the chances of missing important metabolites due to a fundamental change in the properties of the molecule (altered RF) or because of other issues. For example, repeating analyses using a fundamentally different stationary phase or separation chemistry will expose most problems with suppression of ionization. For situations in which this is a known problem (eg, analysis of feces), a more comprehensive approach would be to fractionate the sample using normal phase LC and then to repeat the analysis (reversed phase-LC), analyzing specific fractions using a range of ionization techniques. This process can be automated in the modern laboratory setting. Finally, another pitfall of not using radioactive labeling is that some compounds exhibit low recoveries from various fluids and tissues [2,6,61,67–70,80].

Feces and Other "Problem" Tissues

As noted above, one situation where matrix effects are always a problem is in the extraction and analysis of drug-related material from feces. If a radio-labeled compound has been administered, it is a simple exercise to count the sample before and after extraction and thus determine recovery. Recoveries from this matrix are usually between 70 and 90% but can often be less than 50%. There are techniques to address this problem. For most tissues and fluids, using one to two extraction techniques on selected samples is recommended, such as solid-phase extraction and dilute-and-shoot. For "problem" tissues, such as feces or certain tough tissues like ocular sclera, sonicating with glass beads such that nanoparticle-sized material remains at the time of extraction seems to cover most of the situations encountered. The above techniques having been noted, and as a cautionary note, there will always be some degree of uncertainty when using nonradiolabeled compounds. A comprehensive review of the literature dealing with approaches that take full advantage of modern MS instrumentation for this application is beyond the present overview; however, a skilled analyst familiar with these issues can devise an analytical scheme that will result in an ADME report that can make broad statements (eg, "low excretion of drug-related material was observed in urine") with a high degree of confidence without the use of radio-isotopes [83].

Drug Disposition Studies Using MS Without Isotopic Labeling

Disposition Using Radioactivity. A typical drug disposition study using radioactive standards would employ a ^{14}C-labeled drug standard. The position of the ^{14}C-label must have been demonstrated to be metabolically stable in vitro and in vivo (for ^{14}C-labeled drugs, carbon dioxide would be trapped and counted in this experiment). A radioactivity license from the NRC must be in place, and all procedures for safe handling and disposal of radioactive materials must be followed throughout the study. Drug administration is usually oral, but other routes can be indicated by the discovery program (IV, DEPOT, topical, etc.). Following dosing, samples of tissues, fluids, and excreta (urine and feces) are taken at various time points, and the samples are analyzed by scintillation counting and by LC-RAM. The data obtained indicates the distribution and kinetics of movement of the drug-related material [2,6,61,67–70,80].

Disposition Without Radioactivity. As with plasma PK and metabolism studies, and as already noted, one way to estimate the results obtained in the disposition study just described is to use modern MS without radio-labeled drug. The unlabeled drug is administered, and samples are taken in the same manner. Then each sample is analyzed by MS using both ESI and APCI ionization techniques and positive and negative ion detection. Although standards are not available for drug metabolites, the metabolic profile of the species under study can be estimated qualitatively using the combined data obtained from plated hepatocytes and microsomes and LC-UV analysis.

In man, the vast majority of enzymes responsible for the biotransformations important in drug clearance are expressed in the liver. Other tissues may contribute to the observed metabolite profile; however, the qualitative nature of the profile is contained in the combined hepatocyte and microsomal metabolism data set, which can be used to search for metabolites in the unknown samples collected from the nonradioisotope disposition in vivo study. Collection of product-ion mass spectra (MS–MS data) with spectral interpretation leads to structural information for metabolites generated in the hepatocyte and microsomal metabolism studies. As previously mentioned, the power of repetitive scanning high-resolution MS applied to the analysis of complex mixture has been discussed as a simpler and more general method to qualitatively and quantitatively analyze drugs in biological matrices in support of early ADME studies [81].

Metabolism can be a direct cause of toxicity. The biotransformation (metabolism) of drugs is a major determinant of the pharmacological and toxicological responses observed in vivo in mammalian systems [84]. The enzymes involved in detoxification of xenobiotics are for the most part the same enzymes responsible for the metabolism of xenobiotics to reactive (toxic) species. A fundamental knowledge of these detoxification systems is therefore required for broad appreciation of toxicology, and the reader should familiarize themselves with this subject, which is described in detail in general toxicology and pharmacology texts [85–87]. An example of species-specific metabolic toxicity has already been given in Fig. 3.4. During preclinical development, tirilazad exhibited a species-specific metabolic toxicity in the dog. This was the direct result of a predominant metabolic pathway being N-dealkylation between the two chemical domains, forming a metabolite that was cardio-toxic in the dog. The dog was thus eliminated as the nonrodent toxicology species.

Bioactivation

Metabolism and the effects of xenobiotics, both wanted and unwanted, are closely linked. Most commonly, metabolism results in a decrease in the effects of a xenobiotic on the body, both desired and undesired. Bioactivation to more toxic metabolites may also happen. Often the more toxic metabolites are electrophiles, which bind covalently to cellular macromolecules, such as proteins and nucleic acids, resulting in a disruption of normal cellular processes. Fig. 3.7 (top) displays a general scheme of the role metabolism plays in *toxicodynamics* (toxic effects of the drug on the body), and Table 3.2 illustrates the reactions undergone by typical biochemical compounds. Metabolism can be responsible for the bioactivation of prodrugs to the active moiety, often via hydrolysis of an ester or amide bond. Drugs may be metabolized in one or more steps to compounds that cause toxicity. Frequently, these species cause toxicity in the organ where they were produced, so it is not surprising that the liver is often affected. (Note: Reactive species can circulate, so the expression of toxicity may occur separate from reactive metabolite formation [2,3,88–90].)

Drug-induced liver toxicity is a significant cause of morbidity and mortality. In fact, drug-induced liver toxicity is the leading reason for drug-marketing withdrawals [91]. In the example shown in Fig. 3.7 (bottom), acetaminophen is metabolized to the electrophile *N*-acetyl-benzoquinoneimine. Normally, this species is rapidly removed by detoxification with glutathione. However, glutathione can be depleted at high doses of acetaminophen, in which case, *N*-acetyl-benzoquinoneimine reacts with the electron-rich heteroatoms of proteins and nucleic acids, resulting in toxicity. Similar examples

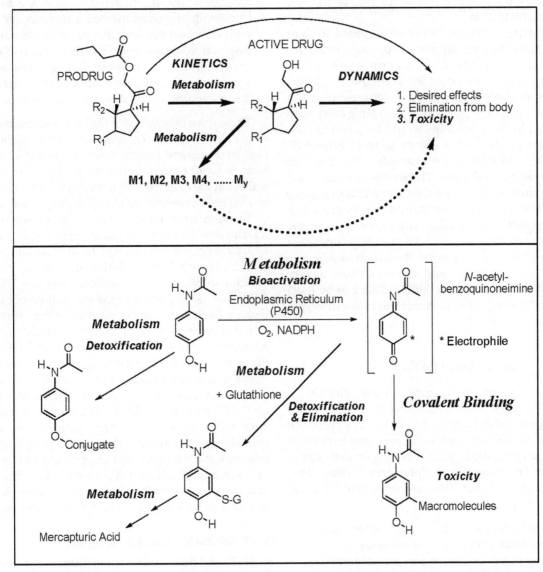

FIGURE 3.7   General scheme for the role metabolism plays in *toxicodynamics* (the study of the toxic effects a xenobiotic has on a living system).

abound in the literature [1–6]. A comprehensive review is beyond the scope this chapter, but an excellent review of metabolism and toxicity can be found in *Principles and Methods of Toxicology* by A. Wallace Hayes, fourth or fifth editions.

Kinetics of Metabolism

Kinetic protocols measure the rate of disappearance of a parent drug in various systems, usually by LC MS. Besides the quantitative data, qualitative analysis of the samples (hepatocytes, microsomes) may also be performed allowing for estimation of the drug metabolite profile. Kinetic experiments differ from stability experiments, primarily in the number of C-T samples collected. Such determinations can be used in determining early "drug-able" properties for chemical libraries, since compounds that are very unstable in liver microsomal preparations will have high first-pass metabolism, and hence are not suitable for oral administration.

Hepatic microsomes can be either prepared fresh or purchased from various suppliers. Suppliers of microsomes typically provide CYP isoform characterization and suggested protocols for their use. Typically, the drug is incubated at a range of concentrations in microsomal protein (approximately 1.0 mg/ml) with NADPH and buffers. Samples would be taken at time zero, plus four to five other points up to 45–60 min (0, 5, 10, 20, 30, and 45 min, for example). The data are useful in three general ways. The first is as a screening data point early in the drug discovery process, since compounds with very poor stability in microsomes would be expected to be eliminated rapidly from the body by liver metabolism or have very high first-pass metabolism. This is analogous to the situation whereby stability in plasma can be used as a compound library screening tool. Second, these kinetic data can be used to estimate the drug's PK, and third to make interspecies comparisons [2,16].

Drug–Drug Interactions (DDIs)

The deleterious effects of drugs can arise directly, or, as already discussed, from metabolites produced by biotransformation. A third way in which drugs can produce unwanted side effects is via their interactions with other drugs through their direct actions on drug-metabolizing enzymes, ie, "inhibition" and "phenotype" drug–drug interactions (DDIs) [1,92]. The most important DDIs fall into three general types:

1. A drug may interfere by inhibiting CYP enzymes, either reversibly (competitive inhibition) or irreversibly (time- or mechanism-based inhibition). This can happen in two general ways:

   a. The drug (or a metabolite of the drug) may interfere with the metabolism of another drug by inhibiting the enzyme(s) responsible for the clearance of this second drug (the drug being studied is termed a *perpetrator*);
   b. The metabolic clearance of a drug may be significantly decreased (the drug being studied is termed a *victim*) by the action of a second drug inhibiting the enzyme(s) responsible for the clearance of the first drug (the reverse of the first situation). In the situation of irreversible enzyme inhibition, days may pass before the enzyme is fully resynthesized (assuming nonchronic administration).

2. The drug (or a metabolite of the drug) may induce production of more drug-metabolizing enzyme protein via induction at the transcription level, and thus influence its own clearance or the clearance of a concomitantly administered drug(s); and finally

3. Concomitantly administered drugs can interfere with transport proteins that are important in drug disposition, thus altering the disposition of one of or both of the coadministered drugs. However, the (quantitative) clinical relevance of this mechanism is low compared to metabolism interactions.

These three categories are the best characterized mechanisms for DDIs, and clear quantitative and qualitative data exist in the clinical literature demonstrating some effect in man. In order to characterize the likelihood of these interactions in the clinic (the *DDI liability*), various in vitro and in vivo tests have been validated in the preclinical setting.

To summarize, a drug of type 1a above is referred to as a DDI *perpetrator* new chemical entity (NCE), and 1b is a DDI *victim* characterization of an NCE (assumes competitive inhibition). CYP Inhibition studies (1a; perpetrator) attempt to address the question: Does the NCE inhibit CYPs that are important to the elimination of other drugs that are likely to be coadministered in the course of effective therapeutics? CYP phenotyping studies (1b; victim) attempt to address the question: Which CYP(s) are capable of significantly metabolizing the NCE, and are thus relevant to drug clearance, and what is the likelihood that coadministration of a drug that inhibits this particular CYP will result in a DDI [93]? The relevance of either situation will depend on the target disease state and likely comedications. Finally, induction of drug-metabolizing enzymes at the level of transcription can also be an effect of a xenobiotic, which is discussed below (the reader is also referred to CDER guidance for an extended discussion of the characterization of this phenomenon) [16].

CYP Inhibition and Phenotyping

CYP inhibition studies using human liver enzymes are important screens in drug development. The major human

CYPs are available as cloned, expressed purified enzyme preparations, and a number of highly specific substrates have been identified and characterized. It is therefore possible to examine the test compound's ability to inhibit a CYP enzyme in isolation, or in crude preparations such as microsomes or S9 fraction. The preferred method is to use human liver microsomal preparations pooled from a range of donors. Pools can be from mixed sex donors or from males and females separately. Various marker substrates for specific CYPs have been identified in the scientific literature [16,94–96]. Inhibition liability is determined by noting the effect of the test species on the metabolism of these CYP-selective marker substrates in human liver microsomes. The appearance of the metabolite is noted with and without the test compound. Analysis of these metabolites is typically performed by stable-isotope dilution MS, which is rapid and cost-effective in volume [13]. The phenotyping experiment asks the question "what CYP(s) are responsible for the metabolism of the test compound?" by determining the kinetics of disappearance of the test compound in human liver microsomes and determining the effects of various marker inhibitors to specific CYPs on the disappearance of test article. Table 3.3 lists representative marker substrates and inhibitors, sourced from the CDER website. The investigation of the acceptability of old and novel compounds as specific inhibitors

and specific substrates still represents an active area of inquiry. (Table 3.3 is representative of the most important CYPs but is still an incomplete list.)

A typical inhibition study involves incubating the test compound at selected screening concentrations (0.3–30 μM, for example) and determining its effect on the kinetics of formation of the marker substrate metabolite. The resulting data are expressed as a percent inhibition at a test concentration. If inhibition is noted at the lower test concentrations, then a more exhaustive study is undertaken to determine an IC_{50}, which is the concentration of drug required for 50% inhibition in vitro. Another term commonly encountered is the K_i.

$$K_i = IC_{50} / (1 + [S] / K_m)$$

A typical phenotype determination study would examine the metabolism of the test species at two concentrations (1.0 and 10 μM, for example) that were representative of observed or projected human plasma concentrations, and incubate each CYP-specific inhibitor at these concentrations. Care must be taken to use appropriate concentrations of inhibitor to maintain the inhibition selectivity, eg, quinidine is a selective inhibitor of CYP2D6 at 1 μM but will also inhibit CYP3A4 at higher concentrations. The phenotyping experiment identifies which CYPs are

TABLE 3.3 Representative "CYP Chemical Probes"

CYP	Representative Substrate[a]	Reaction	Representative Inhibitor[a]	Representative Inducer[c]
1A2	Phenacetin	Phenacetin O-deethylation	Furafylline	Omeprazoleβ-Naphthoflavone(2)3-Methylcholanthrene
2A6	Coumarin	Coumarin 7-hydroxylation	Tranylcypromine	Dexamethasone
2B6	Bupropion	Bupropion hydroxylation	Phencyclidine[b]	Phenobarbital
2C8	Paclitaxel	Paclitaxel 6α-hydroxylation	Montelukast	Rifampin
2C9	Diclofenac	Diclofenac 4′-hydroxylation	Sulfaphenazole	Rifampin
2C19	S-Mephenytoin	S-Mephenytoin 4′-hydroxylation	Ticlopidine[b]	Rifampin
2D6	Dextromethorphan	Dextromethorphan O-demethylation	Quinidine	None identified
2E1	Chlorzoxazone	Chlorzoxazone 6-hydroxylation	Diethyldithiocarbamate[b]	None identified
3A4/5	Midazolam	Midazolam 1′-hydroxylation	Ketoconazole	Rifampin
3A4/5	Testosterone	Testosterone 6β-hydroxylation		

[a]Representative marker substrates and inhibitors from CDER guidelines (incomplete). http://www.fda.gov/Drugs/DevelopmentApprovalProcess/DevelopmentResources/DrugInteractionsLabeling/ucm093664.htm. Other substrates include nicotine (2A6), efavirenz (CYP2B6), amodiaquine (CYP2C8), tolbutamide and S-warfarin (2C9), bufuralol (CYP2D6), chlorzoxazone (CYP2E1), nifedipine and atorvastatin (CYP3A4/5), and lauric acid (CYP4A11).

[b]Acceptable inhibitor (not listed as a preferred inhibitor).

[c]Reference [16].

capable of metabolizing the NCE. This helps to work out the likelihood that concomitant administration of another marketed drug with the test species would result in a DDI in which the metabolic clearance of the new drug could decrease, leading to drug accumulation and increased pharmacological effect. It should always be kept in mind that both inhibition and phenotyping studies are estimates used to indicate whether specific clinical studies looking for DDIs are warranted.

It should also be noted that if the in vivo clearance mechanism is excretion of an unchanged drug or significant Phase II conjugation, we only need to be concerned about the NCE being a perpetrator of DDIs, not a victim. Also, clinical tests must eventually be performed to more accurately determine the actual clinical liability. In addition, the relevance of a DDI is also related to the therapeutic area. Drugs with a narrow therapeutic index represent one important situation. Treatment of life-threatening conditions, such as infectious diseases or cancer, may represent situations where potential DDIs need to be clinically managed with drug plasma concentration monitoring and dose modification. Clearly, clinical management of potential DDIs is irrational for DDIs that could occur for over-the-counter (OTC) drugs, such as nonsedating antihistamines, and therefore the potential DDI liability for OCTs is kept very low.

CYP Induction Studies

The first type of DDI we discussed was the inhibition of one or more CYPs by concomitantly administered drugs, either a marketed drug (victim) or the test article (perpetrator). Another type can occur if the test agent induces one or more of these drug-metabolizing enzymes, and thus changes the metabolic clearance of a drug (either concomitantly administered drugs or the test agent). The human hepatocyte induction assay (HIAA) has become a standard preclinical test to estimate this liability in the clinic [16]. Typically, human hepatocytes are plated and incubated with the test article, and as a control also incubated with drugs known to induce the synthesis of CYP proteins, such as phenobarbital, rifampin, dexamethasone, or omeprazole (Table 3.3). The test drug concentration should be based upon clinical data, if available, or expected human plasma concentrations. Three concentrations spanning the targeted therapeutic concentrations should be employed. If clinical estimates are not available, then concentrations covering a range of at least two orders of magnitude should be used, with the maximum being 10 times greater than the highest concentration anticipated in man. At least three donors should be used to account for intersubject variability, and the study should be performed in triplicate.

Three endpoints have been used as a determination of induction: mRNA, enzyme protein concentration, and CYP enzyme activities. For IND-enabling studies, phenotype measurements (activities) are preferred.

CYP activities are determined using marker substrates in an analogous manner to hepatic microsomes, and the inducing activities of test drug and control drug(s), ie, known inducers are compared. A test drug change in CYP activity equal to or greater than 40% of the control inducer is considered enough to warrant further study. In addition to changes in the expression of genes encoding CYP enzymes, the effect on UGT enzymes such as UGT1A1, UGT1A4, UGT1A6, UGT1A9, UGT1B7, and transporters such as P-glycoprotein may be determined.

SUMMARY AND TRENDS

Use of Preclinical ADME Data

The process of interpreting all of the data generated in a drug discovery program is highly complex. Assessment of eADME data is a critical component of this assessment. If a drug cannot be delivered to the drug target receptor at therapeutic concentrations for the needed time period, then the drug will not be an effective therapeutic in humans. Drug candidates that will be very rapidly metabolized in the liver or are delivered poorly to the target organ are eliminated by a robust eADME program early in the evaluation process. The first job of the ADME drug discovery scientist is to find and eliminate the "losers." The second job of the ADME scientist is to evaluate groups of compounds with regard to their likely performance relative to one another in the clinic. If a long half-life is very important, then preclinical studies are used to estimate this property. The process of estimating PK properties (ADME properties) in man from the data obtained in preclinical species is termed *allometric scaling*. In this exercise, in vitro human data are also taken into consideration. Allometric scaling is a valuable part of the drug discovery and development process [97–99]. A third job of the ADME scientist is to help the toxicologist and clinical scientist estimate clinical doses and derive a *therapeutic index* based solely on animal data. Finally, a fourth job of the ADME scientist is to identify drug metabolites that humans will be exposed to that preclinical toxicology species were not exposed to in the same relative amounts (discussed in Chapter 4, "Pharmacokinetics/Toxicokinetics").

One very important situation occurs when a drug metabolite is absent or present at low concentrations in the circulation of rodents and the nonrodent toxicology species (dog, monkey), but represents significant exposure in man. Significant exposure has been arbitrarily defined as a plasma concentration (exposure as quantified by AUC or C_{max}) that is greater than or equal 10% of the parent drug. CDER has issued guidance for addressing this situation as *Metabolites in Safety Testing, or* MIST [100–104]. Modern NMR and MS technologies are critical tools in identifying problems early so that the appropriate testing of metabolites can be done prior to introduction into humans [105]. One technique uses microdoses of the ^{14}C-labeled drug and analysis by accelerator mass spectrometry (AMS). The drug is administered to humans in very low absolute doses (weight, moles) and spiked with very low amounts of ^{14}C-labeled drug, both of which are low enough not to be of significant toxicological concern (abbreviated safety evaluations are performed, in any case). LC separation is performed on plasma samples and fractions are collected approximately every 30 s. The ratio of ^{14}C/^{13}C is determined by AMS in each sample and is used to quantify the amount of parent drug or metabolite present. Another approach involves the metabolism of radiolabeled and stable-isotope labeled compounds, thus providing standards for determination of the amounts of metabolites produced in a biological system (from the radiolabeled standards) and stable-isotope labeled internal standards for performing stable-isotope dilution MS. In this approach, high-resolution MS analysis is used instead of MS–MS [71].

Technologies Impacting ADME in Drug Discovery

The evolution of molecular imaging technologies, especially PET and SPETC, are important enough to have been covered in a separate chapter (see Chapter 35, "Use of Imaging for Preclinical Evaluation").

Mass spectrometry has always been an important technology impacting drug research.

More recently, the power of repetitive scanning at high resolution has been "rediscovered" as a powerful technique for the quantitative and qualitative analysis of complex mixtures, a trend encouraged by the introduction of high-resolution analyzers better adapted to ESI, primarily time-of-flight (TOF) [106–108] and Orbitrap [109,110] mass analyzers.

Resolution is the ability of a mass analyzer to distinguish one distinct mass-to-charge ratio (m/z) from another, and is usually defined as M/ΔM, where ΔM is a defined resolving power such as peak width at ½ peak height for a mass vs. intensity peak. Figs. 3.8 and 3.9 display mass spectral data obtained at R = 300 and at R = 30,000, respectively. The data in Fig. 3.8 were obtained at *unit resolution* using a quadrupole mass analyzer, which operates at approximately unit resolution across the mass range (the resolution at m/z 300 is R = 300 and the resolution at m/z 700 is R = 700). Mass m/z 300 can clearly be distinguished from mass m/z 301. However, the mass m/z 300.25 cannot be distinguished from m/z 300.27 at *unit resolution*, and thus their signal intensities cannot be recorded separately. The unit resolution displayed in Fig. 3.8 stands in sharp contrast with Fig. 3.9 (R = 30,000). This is an important distinction (unit vs. high resolution) since many endogenous compounds represent interferences when using nominal

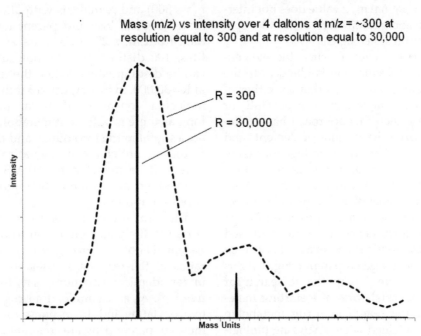

Mass (m/z) vs intensity over 4 daltons at m/z = ~300 at
resolution equal to 300 and at resolution equal to 30,000

R = 300

R = 30,000

Intensity

Mass Units

FIGURE 3.8   LC-MS spectra obtained using a quadrupole instrument (dashed line, nominal resolution) and an Orbitrap high-resolution analyzer (solid line). Resolution (mass-resolving power) is M/ΔM, where ΔM is a defined resolving power. Nominal resolution data: Displayed is MH$^+$ (m/z 289; quadrupole instrument) and the isotopic cluster observed for testosterone, the so-called A + 1 (m/z 290) and A + 2 (m/z 291) ions. Resolution that can distinguish one nominal mass from another is also called *unit resolution*. A simple way to define and calculate is to define ΔM as the peak width at ½ height and calculate directly from a *profile* mass spectrum. High-resolution data: Displayed is MH$^+$ (m/z 260) and the isotopic cluster observed for propranolol for the A + 1 (m/z 261) and A + 2 (m/z 262) ions. This mass spectrum was obtained at a resolution of 30,000.

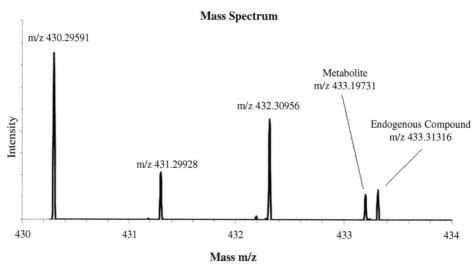

FIGURE 3.9   Mass spectrum from LC-MS data obtained at high resolution (Orbitrap mass analyzer). These data were obtained for an in vivo, radiolabeled ADME study for a biological sample. Both endogenous (naturally found in the body) and xenobiotic (drug) materials are easily distinguished by the differences in mass defect for the different empirical formula. In this example, a drug metabolite at m/z 433.19,731 is clearly differentiated from an endogenous compound (or possibly another xenobiotic) at m/z 433.31,316. This mass spectrum was obtained at a resolution of 30,000. The determination of mass at *high resolution* allowing for the determination of empirical formulas greatly aids in the elucidation of structures of drug metabolites and in selectivity of an assay for quantitative analysis studies. High-resolution MS coupled with LC will continue to greatly impacting *eADME* research.

mass analysis. However, when operated at high resolution, the *mass defect* (the mass difference from nominal mass) differences between drugs, drug metabolites, and endogenous compounds can be resolved and observed (detected) separately. The appearance of more than one species at a particular nominal m/z value does not interfere with the detection and quantitation of the other species since they represent distinct signals.

Limitations can occur, however, when the elemental composition of the molecular ion is identical to the endogenous contaminants. For drugs that are either of endogenous origin (a prostaglandin such as PGE_2 or estradiol, for example), then this approach has limitations. However, most drugs have ratios of elements and ring structures that are uncommon in endogenous compounds, such as high number of hetero atoms relative to carbon, or halogen atoms attached to carbons. Also, there are also a limited number of additions and subtractions of masses (exact masses) that are possible through biotransformaton reactions, hence there are a limited number of m/z values (nominal and exact) that can be assigned to metabolites of a given parent drug. All this lends itself perfectly to using computers to search for distinct m/z values for metabolites of a starting material, thus automating the search for drug metabolite masses in the spectra obtained when analyzing biological materials [61,67–71,80,81]. (Note: When using HRMS for structure ID, it is incorrect to use the term *empirical formula* determination; *elemental composition* should be used instead.)

In a typical low-resolution (nominal resolution) mass analysis experiment, previous metabolism data is considered, and various scanning experiments are performed, involving repetitive scanning of the data (say from m/z 100 to m/z 600 every 0.5 s for a drug of mass 300) and reanalysis with SIM, SRM, and MS–MS scans (neutral loss and parent ion scans). When the data from m/z 250 to 350 are examined for metabolites, 100 distinct pseudo-molecular ion m/z values can be distinguished. When the mass analysis occurs at R = 30,000, in theory, up to 3 million distinct pseudo-molecular ion m/z values can be distinguished. As long as there is sufficient metabolite present to generate a signal in the ion source, and the relative response factor has not changed dramatically, then the metabolite will be detected by HRMS, provided that the elemental composition is distinguishable from endogenous compounds.

The term *relative response* is important, since this is currently the major limitation to quantitative analysis. As stated above, *relative response factors* (RF) are arbitrary ratios of the responses observed for two compounds under identical situations, say for LC-ESI-MS (positive ion). As an example, if a drug undergoes aromatic hydroxylation and the response for the same number of moles of parent drug are compared to the same number of moles for the metabolite, this response will differ by some factor, RF, either an increase or a decrease relative to the parent drug. If the response observed was 110% that of the parent drug, then the *relative response factor* is 1.1, and so forth. Sometimes RFs can be very small for drug metabolites compared to the parent drug, which may create problems, as the metabolite may not be observed. As already stated, the traditional way of circumventing this problem is to obtain a ^{14}C-labeled drug standard (labeled in a metabolically stable position) and analyze the drug metabolic profile quantitatively by LC-MS-RAM, since the specific activity of the metabolites will be the same as that of the parent drug [61,67–71,80,81]. However, MS has impacted ADME so dramatically that a reevaluation discussion as to when *radioactivity mass balance* studies are to be conducted has started [111].

Continued advances in MS and other technologies will impact the way drug discovery research is conducted, although we should be careful in making statements about the future, especially when technology is involved. That being duly noted eADME studies are likely to become easier and more cost-effective to conduct, and will likely be conducted on more compounds. Mass spectrometry will impact small and large molecule research and PET and SPECT will continue supply early ADME data for large biologics. All of this means earlier assessment of the toxicodynamics of new drug candidates, a welcome trend for the professional toxicologist.

References

[1] Rodrigues DA. Drug-drug interactions. 2nd ed. Drugs and the pharmaceutical sciences, vol. 179. New York: Informa Healthcare; 2007.

[2] Pearson PG, Wienkers LC. Handbook of drug metabolism. 2nd ed. Drugs and the pharmaceutical sciences, vol. 186. New York: Informa Healthcare; 2009.

[3] Renwick AG. Toxicokinetics: pharmacokinetics in toxicology. In: Hayes AW, editor. Principles and methods of toxicology. 4th ed. New York: Raven Press; 2001. p. 137–92.

[4] Rogge MC, Taft DR. Preclinical drug development. 2nd ed. Drugs and the pharmaceutical sciences, vol. 187. New York: Informa Healthcare; 2010.

[5] Tsaioun K, Kates SA. ADMET for medicinal chemists: a practical guide. Hoboken, New Jersey: Wiley; 2011.

[6] Nassar AF. Biotransformation and metabolite elucidation of xenobiotics. Hoboken, New Jersey: Wiley; 2010.

[7] Beck BD, Slayton TM, Calabrese EJ, Baldwin L, Rudel R. Metabolism: a determinant of toxicity. In: Hayes AW, editor. Principles and methods of toxicology. 4th ed. New York: Raven Press; 2001. p. 23–76.

[8] Smith DA, Di L, Kerns EH. The effect of plasma protein binding on in vivo efficacy: misconceptions in drug discovery. Nat Rev Drug Discov 2010;9:929–39.

[9] Lin JH, Lu AY. Role of pharmacokinetics and metabolism in drug discovery and development. Pharmacol Rev 1997;49:403–49.

[10] White RE. Short and long term projections about the use of drug metabolism in drug discovery and development. Drug Metab Dispos 1998;26:1213–6.

[11] Eddershaw PJ, Beresford AP, Bayliss MK. ADME/PK as part of a rational approach to drug discovery. Drug Discov Today 2000;5:409–14.

[12] Kosugi Y, Hirabayashi H, Igari T. Evaluation of cytochrome P450-mediated drug-drug interactions based on the strategies recommended by regulatory authorities. Xenobiotica 2012;42:127–38.

[13] Walsky RL, Obach RS. Validated assays for human cytochrome P450 activities. Drug Metab Dispos 2004;32:647–60.

[14] Wienkers LC, Heath TG. Predicting in vivo drug interactions from in vitro drug discovery data. Nat Rev Drug Discov 2005;4:825–33.

[15] Kola I, Landis J. Can the pharmaceutical industry reduce attrition rates? Nat Rev Drug Discov 2004;3:711–6.

[16] Guidance for Industry, Drug Interaction Studies, Study Design, Data Analysis, Implications for Dosing, and Labeling Recommendations, DRAFT GUIDANCE, US Department of Health and Human Services Food and Drug Administration Center for Drug Evaluation and Research (CDER). Pharmacology and Toxicology, February 2012, and the earlier Draft Guidance, Guidance for Industry, Drug Interaction Studies, Study Design, Data Analysis, Implications for Dosing, and Labeling Recommendations, DRAFT GUIDANCE, US Department of Health and Human Services Food and Drug Administration Center for Drug Evaluation and Research (CDER). Clinical Pharmacology, September 2006.

[17] Guarino RA. New drug approval process. 5th ed. Drugs and the pharmaceutical sciences, vol. 190. New York: Informa Healthcare; 2009.

[18] Goodman and Gilman's the pharmacological basis of therapeutics. 11th ed. New York: McGraw-Hill.

[19] Benet LZ, Kroetz DL, Sheiner LB. The dynamics of drug absorption, distribution and elimination. In: Hardman JG, Limbird LE, Molinoff PB, Ruddon RW, Gilman AG, editors. Goodman and Gillman's the pharmacological basis of therapeutics. New York: The McGraw-Hill Companies, Inc.; 1996. p. 3–27.

[20] Knowles J, Gromo G. Target selection in drug discovery. Nat Rev Drug Discov 2003;2:63–9.

[21] Seethala R, Fernandes PB. Handbook of drug screening. 2nd ed. Drugs and the pharmaceutical sciences, vol. 114. New York: Informa Healthcare; 2001.

[22] Lombardino JG, Lowe JA. The role of the medicinal chemist in drug discovery – then and now. Nat Rev Drug Discov 2004;3:853–62.

[23] Bleicher KH, Böhm H-J, Müller K, Alanine AI. Hit and lead generation: beyond high-throughput screening. Nat Rev Drug Discov 2003;2:369–78.

[24] Kenakin T. Predicting therapeutic value in the lead optimization phase of drug discovery. Nat Rev Drug Discov 2003;2:429–38.

[25] Walters QP, Namchuk M. Designing screens: how to make your hits a hit. Nat Rev Drug Discov 2003;2:259–66.

[26] Pritchard JF, Jurima-Romet M, Reimer MLJ, Mortimer E, Rolfe B, Cayen MN. Making better drugs: decision gates in non-clinical drug development. Nat Rev Drug Discov 2003;2:542–53.

[27] Geysen MH, Schoenen F, Wagner D, Wagner R. Combinatorial compound libraries for drug discovery: an ongoing challenge. Nat Rev Drug Discov 2003;2:222–30.

[28] Reichert JM. Trends in development and approval times for new therapeutics in the United States. Nat Rev Drug Discov 2003;2:695–702.

[29] Dressman JB, Reppas C. Oral drug absorption. 2nd ed. Drugs and the pharmaceutical sciences, vol. 193. New York: Informa Healthcare; 2010.

[30] Lipinski CA, Lombardo F, Dominy BW, Feeney PJ. Experimental and computational approaches to estimate solubility and permeability in drug discovery and development settings. Adv Drug Deliv Rev 2001;46:3–26.

[31] Lipinski CA. Lead- and drug-like compounds: the rule-of-five revolution. Drug Discov Today Technol 2004;1(4):337–41.

[32] Hop CECA, Cole MJ, Davidson RE, Duignan DB, Federico J, Janiszewski JS, et al. High throughput ADME screening: practical considerations, impact on the portfolio and enabler of in silico ADME models. Curr Drug Metab 2008;9:847–53.

[33] Singh B, Dhake AS, Sethi D, Paul Y. In silico ADME predictions using quantitative structure pharmacokinetic relationships. Part I: fundamental aspects. Pharm Rev 2007;5:93–100.

[34] Singh B, Parle M, Paul Y, Khurana L. In silico ADME predictions using quantitative structure pharmacokinetic relationships. Part II: descriptors. Pharm Rev 2007;5:63–8.

[35] Moda TL, Torres LG, Carrara AE, Andricopulo AD. PK/DB: database for pharmacokinetic properties and predictive in silico ADME models. Bioinformatics 2008;24:2270–1.

[36] Caldwell GW, Yan Z, Tang W, Daspugta M, Becki H. ADME optimization and toxicity assessment in early- and late-phase drug discovery. Curr Top Med Chem 2009;9:965–80.

[37] Camurri G, Zaramella A. High-throughput liquid chromatography/mass spectrometry method for the determination of the chromatographic hydrophobicity index. Anal Chem 2001;73:3716–22.

[38] Valkó K, Bevan C, Reynolds D. Chromatographic hydrophobicity index by fast-gradient RP-HPLC: a high-throughput alternative to log P/log D. Anal Chem 1997;69:2022–9.

[39] Borst P, Elferink RO. Mammalian ABC transporters in health and disease. Ann Rev Biochem 2002;71:537–92.

[40] Hediger MA, editor. Special issue: the ABCs of solute carriers: physiological, pathological and therapeutic implications of human membrane transport proteins. Berlin: Springer-Verlag; 2004.

[41] Giacomini KM, Sugiyama Y. In: Brunton LL, Lazo JS, Parker RL, editors. Goodman and Gilman's the pharmacological basis of therapeutics. New York: McGraw-Hill; 2006. p. 41–70.

[42] Schinkel AH, Jonker JW. Mammalian drug efflux transporters of the ATP binding cassette (ABC) family: an overview. Adv Drug Deliv Rev 2003;55:3–29.

[43] Cascorbi I. Role of pharmacogenetics of ATP-binding cassette transporters in the pharmacokinetics of drugs. Pharmacol Ther 2006;112:457–73.

[44] Hediger MA, Romero MF, Peng JB, Rolfs A, Takanaga H, Bruford EA. The ABCs of solute carriers: physiological, pathological and therapeutic implications of human membrane transport proteins. Pflugers Arch 2004;447:465–8.

[45] Choudhuri S, Klaassen CD. Structure, function, expression, genomic organization, and single nucleotide polymorphisms of human ABCB1 (MDR1), ABCC (MRP), and ABCG2 (BCRP) efflux transporters. Int J Toxicol 2006;25:231–59.

[46] Feng B, Mills JB, Davidson RE, Mireles RJ, Janiszewski JS, Troutman MD, et al. In vitro P-glycoprotein assays to predict the in vivo interactions of P-glycoprotein with drugs in the central nervous system. Drug Metab Dispos 2008;36:268–75.

[47] Yamazaki M, Neway WE, Ohe T, Chen I, Rowe JF, Hochman JH, et al. In vitro substrate identification studies for P-glycoprotein-mediated transport: species difference and predictability of in vivo results. J Pharmacol Exp Ther 2001;296:723–35.

[48] Sasongko L, Link JM, Muzi M, Mankoff DA, Yang X, Collier AC, et al. Imaging P-glycoprotein transport activity at the human blood–brain barrier with positron emission tomography. Clin Pharmacol Ther 2005;77:503–14.

[49] Cisternino S, Mercier C, Bourasset F, Roux F, Scherrmann JM. Expression, upregulation, and transport activity of multidrug-resistance protein Abcg2 at the mouse blood–brain barrier. Cancer Res 2004;64:3296–301.

[50] Doyle LA, Ross DD. Multidrug resistance mediated by the breast cancer resistance protein BCRP (ABCG2). Oncogene 2003;22:7340–58.

[51] Maliepaard M, Scheffer GL, Faneyte IF, van Gastelen MA, Pijnenborg AC, Schinkel A, et al. Subcellular localization and distribution of the breast cancer resistance protein transporter in normal human tissues. Cancer Res 2001;61:3458–64.

[52] Maliepaard M, van Gastelen MA, Tohgo A, Hausheer FH, van Waardenburg RC, de Jong LA, et al. Circumvention of breast cancer resistance protein (BCRP)-mediated resistance to camptothecins in vitro using nonsubstrate drugs or the BCRP inhibitor GF120918. Clin Cancer Res 2001;7:935–41.

[53] Kimura N, Masuda S, Tanihara Y, et al. Metformin is a superior substrate for renal organic cation transporter OCT2 rather than hepatic OCT1. Drug Metab Pharmacokinet 2005;20:379–86.

[54] Somogyi A, Stockley C, Keal J, Rolan P, Bochner F. Reduction of metformin renal tubular secretion by cimetidine in man. Br J Clin Pharmacol 1987;23:545–51.

[55] Wang ZJ, Yin OQ, Tomlinson B, Chow MS. OCT2 polymorphisms and in-vivo renal functional consequence: studies with metformin and cimetidine. Pharmacogenet Genomics 2008;18(7):637–45.

[56] Zaman GJR, Flens MJ, Van Leusden MR, De Haas M, Mulder HS, Lankelma J, et al. The human multidrug resistance-associated protein MRP is a plasma membrane drug-efflux pump. Proc Nat Acad Sci USA 1994;91:8822–6.

[57] Hagmann W, Faissner R, Schnölzer M, Löhr M, Jesnowski R. Membrane drug transporters and chemoresistance in human pancreatic carcinoma. Cancers 2011;3:106–25.

[58] Miyake K, Mickley L, Litman T, et al. Molecular cloning of cDNAs which are highly overexpressed in mitoxantrone-resistant cells: demonstration of homology to ABC transport genes. Cancer Res 1999;59:8–13.

[59] Rocchi E, Khodjakov A, Volk EL, et al. The product of the ABC half-transporter gene ABCG2 (BCRP/MXR/ABCP) is expressed in the plasma membrane. Biochem Biophys Res Comm 2000;271:42–6.

[60] Sarawek S, Li L, Yu XQ, Rooney S, Nouraldeen A, Moran L, et al. Examination of the utility of the high throughput in vitro metabolic stability assay to estimate in vivo clearance in the mouse. Open Drug Metab J 2009;3:31–42.

[61] Lee MS, Kerns EH. LC/MS applications in drug development. Mass Spectrom Rev 1999;18:187–279.

[62] Lin JH, Rodrigues AD. In vitro models for early studies of drug metabolism. In: Testa B, van de Waterbeemd H, Folkers G, Guy R, editors. Pharmacokinetic optimization in drug research: biological, physiochemical, and computational strategies. New York: Wiley VCH; 2001. p. 217–43.

[63] van de Kerkhof EG, de Graaf IA, Groothuis GM. In vitro methods to study intestinal drug metabolism. Curr Drug Metab 2007;8:658–75.

[64] Soars MG, McGinnity DF, Grime K, Riley RJ. The pivotal role of hepatocytes in drug discovery. Chem Biol Interact 2007;168:2–15.

[65] Francis L-ST. Preclinical drug disposition. 2nd ed. Drugs and the pharmaceutical Sciences, vol. 46. New York: Informa Healthcare; 1991.

[66] Fenn JB, Mann M, Meng CK, Wong SF, Whitehouse CM. Electrospray ionization for mass spectrometry of large biomolecules. Science 1989;246:64–71.

[67] Yost RA, Enke CG. Selected ion fragmentation with a tandem quadrupole mass spectrometer. J Am Chem Soc 1978;100:2274–5.

[68] Lee MS, Yost YA. Rapid identification of drug metabolites with tandem mass spectrometry. Biol Mass Spectrom 1998;15:193–204.

[69] Yost RA, Brotherton HO, Perchalski RJ. Tandem mass spectrometry for studies of drug action and metabolism. Int J Mass Spectrom Ion Phys 1983;48:77–80.

[70] Vrbanac JJ, O"Leary IA, Baczynskyj. Utility of the parent-neutral loss scan screening technique: partial characterization of urinary metabolites of U-78875 in monkey urine. Biol Mass Spectrom 1992;21:517–22.

[71] Vrbanac JJ, Hilgers A, Dubnicka T, Shilliday FB, Humphries D, Hayes RN. High-resolution isotope-dilution mass spectrometry using metabolism of isotope-labeled compounds: application to drug metabolites. Rapid Comm Mass Spectrom 2012;26:2569–76.

[72] Smith, N.F., Raynauld, F.L., and Workman, P.. The application of cassette dosing for pharmacokinetic screening in small-molecule cancer drug discovery. Mol Cancer Ther. 6:428–440.

[73] White RE, Manitpisitkul P. Pharmacokinetic theory of cassette dosing in drug discovery screening. Drug Met Disp 2001;29:957–66.

[74] Nelson DR, Koymans L, Kamataki T, Stegeman JJ, Feyereisen R, Waxman DJ, et al. P450 superfamily: update on new sequences, gene mapping, accession numbers and nomenclature. Pharmacogenetics 1996;6:1–42.

[75] Mackenzie PI, Bock KW, Burchell B, Guillemette C, Ikushiro S, Iyanagi T, et al. Nomenclature update for the mammalian UDP glycosyltransferase (UGT) gene superfamily. Pharmacogenet Genomics 2005;15:677–85.

[76] Gamage N, Barnett A, Hempel N, Duggleby RG, Kelly F, Windmill KF, et al. Review: human sulfotransferases and their role in chemical metabolism. Toxicol Sci 2006;90:5–22.

[77] Tukey RH, Strassburg CP. Human UDP-glucuronosyl-transferases: metabolism, expression, and disease. Ann Rev Pharmacol Toxicol 2000;40:581–616.

[78] Roland M, Tozer TN. Clinical pharmacokinetics: concepts and applications, chapter 11, elimination. 3rd ed. Media, PA: Williams and Wilkins; 1995.

[79] Veroli P, O"Kelly B, Bertrand F, Trouvin JH, Farinotti R, Ecoffey C. Extrahepatic metabolism of propofol in man during the anhepatic phase of orthotopic liver transplantation. Br J Anaesth 1992;68:183–6.

[80] Hsieh Y, Korfmacher WA. Increasing speed and throughput when using hplc-ms/ms systems for drug metabolism and pharmacokinetic screening. Curr Drug Metab 2006;7:479–89.

[81] Zhu M, Zhang H, Humphreys WG. Drug metabolite profiling and identification by high-resolution mass spectrometry. J Biol Chem 2011;286:25419–25.

[82] Perry RH, Cooks RG, Noll RJ. Orbitrap mass spectrometry: instrumentation, ion motion and applications. Mass Spectrom Rev 2008;27:661–99.

[83] Obach RS, Nedderman AN, Smith DA. Radiolabelled mass-balance excretion and metabolism studies in laboratory animals: are they still necessary? Xenobiotica 2012;42:46–56.

[84] Baillie TA. Metabolism and toxicity of drugs. Two decades of progress in industrial drug metabolism. Chem Res Toxicol 2008;21:129–37.

[85] deBethizy JD, Hayes JR. Metabolism: a determinant of toxicity. In: Hayes AW, editor. Principles and methods of toxicology. 4th ed. New York: Raven Press; 2001. p. 77–136.

[86] Gonzalez FJ, Tukey RH. Drug metabolism. The pharmacological basis of therapeutics. 11th ed. New York: McGraw-Hill Companies; 2006. p. 71–91.

[87] Klaassen CED, Casarett LJ. Casarett and Doull's toxicology: the basic science of poisons. New York: McGraw-Hill Companies; 2007.

[88] Leung L, Kalgutkar AS, Obach RS. Metabolic activation in drug-induced liver injury. Drug Metab Rev 2012;44:18–33.

[89] Pessayre D, Fromenty B, Berson A, Robin M-A, Lettéron P, Moreau R, et al. Central role of mitochondria in drug-induced liver injury. Drug Metab Rev 2012;44:34–87.

[90] Jaeschke H, McGill MR, Ramachandran A. Oxidant stress, mitochondria, and cell death mechanisms in drug-induced liver injury: lessons learned from acetaminophen hepatotoxicity. Drug Metab Rev 2012;44:88–106.

[91] Ju C. Preface to the drug-induced liver injury special issue. Drug Metab Rev 2012;44:1–4.

[92] Rodriques DA. Drug-drug interaction. Drugs and the pharmaceutical Sciences, vol. 116. NY: Marcel Dekker; 2002.

[93] Bjornsson TD, Callaghan JT, Einolf HJ, Fischer V, Gan L, Grimm S, et al. The conduct of *in vitro* and *in vivo* drug-drug interaction studies: a Pharmaceutical Research and Manufacturers of America (PhRMA) perspective. Drug Metab Dispos 2003;31:815–32.

[94] Yu J, Ritchie TK, Mulgaonkar A, Rugueneau-Majlessi I. Minireview. Drug disposition and drug-drug interaction data in 2013 FDA new drug applications: a systematic review. Drug Met Dis 2014;2014(39):2219–32.

[95] Tucker GT, Houston JB, Huang SM. Optimizing drug development: strategies to assess drug metabolism/transporter interaction potential – toward a consensus. Pharm Res 2001; 18:1071–80.

[96] Chen Y, Liu L, Monshouwer M, Fretland AJ. Determination of time-dependent inactivation of CYP3A4 in cryopreserved human hepatocytes and assessment of human drug-drug interactions. Drug Met Disp 2011;39:2219–32.

[97] Mahmood I. Allometric issues in drug development. J Pharm Sci 2000;88:1101–6.

[98] Houston JB, Galetin A. Progress towards prediction of human pharmacokinetic parameters from *in vitro* technologies. Drug Metab Rev 2003;35:393–415.

[99] Shiran MR, Proctor NJ, Howgate EM, Rowland-Yeo K, Tucker GT, Rostami-Hodjegan A. Prediction of metabolic drug clearance in humans: in vitro in vivo extrapolation vs. allometric scaling. Xenobiotica 2006;36:567–80.

[100] Slatter GJ, Nassar AF. Safety testing of drug metabolites: MIST guidance impact on the practice of industrial drug metabolism. Biotransformation and metabolite elucidation of xenobiotics: characterization and identification. 2010. p. 295–312.

[101] Guidance for Industry: Safety Testing of Drug Metabolites. Pharmacology and Toxicology. US Department of Health and Human Services Food and Drug Administration Center for Drug Evaluation and Research (CDER); February 2008.

[102] Smith DA, Obach RS. Metabolites in safety testing (MIST): considerations of mechanisms of toxicity with dose, abundance, and duration of treatment. Chem Res Toxicol 2009;22:267–79.

[103] Gao H, Jacobs A, White R, Booth BP, Obach RS. Meeting report: metabolites in safety testing (MIST) symposium—safety assessment of human metabolites: what's REALLY necessary to ascertain exposure coverage in safety tests? AAPS J 2013:970–3.

[104] Baillie TA, Cayen MN, Fouda H, Gerson RJ, Green JD, Grossman SJ, et al. Metabolites in safety testing. Tox Appl Pharmacol 2002;182:188–96.

[105] Schadt S, Chen L-A, Bischoff D. Evaluation of relative LC-MS response of metabolites to parent drug in LC/nanospray ionization mass spectrometry: potential implication in MIST assessment. J Mass Spectrom 2011;46:1281–6.

[106] Mamyrin BA, Karataev VI, Shmikk DV, Zagulin VA. The mass-reflectron, a new nonmagnetic time-of-flight mass spectrometer with high resolution. Sov Phys JETP 1973;37:45.

[107] Stephens WE. A pulsed mass spectrometer with time dispersion. Phys Rev 1946;69:691.

[108] Doroshenko VM, Cotter RJ. Ideal velocity focusing in a reflectron time-of-flight mass spectrometer. J Am Soc Mass Spectrom 1999;10:992–9.

[109] Makarov A. Electrostatic axially harmonic orbital trapping: a high-performance technique of mass analysis. Anal Chem 2000;72:1156–62.

[110] Hu Q, Noll RJ, Li H, Makarov A, Hardmanc M, Cooks RG. The orbitrap: a new mass spectrometer. J Mass Spectrom 2005;40:430–43. Makarov A. Mass spectrometer. US Patent 5,886,346 w1999.

[111] Roffey SJ, Obach RS, Gedge JI, Smith DA. What is the objective of the mass balance study? A retrospective analysis of data in animal and human excretion studies employing radiolabeled drugs. Drug Metab Rev 2007;39:17–43.

Pharmacokinetics and Toxicokinetics

M. Schrag, K. Regal

INTRODUCTION

Drugs are administered for many indications, both chronic and acute. Patients who are potentially at risk of a stroke, or who have had a stroke, may be on a chronic or once-a-day dosing regimen to control blood clotting. They may be taking a blood thinner, such as aspirin, Coumadin, or Plavix. On the other hand, drugs also are used for acute indications, such as a headache or fever, in which case the patient may be dosed with one or a few doses of acetaminophen or ibuprofen. Whether a drug is taken chronically or acutely, pharmacokineticists concern themselves with how much and how often the drug can be administered to achieve the desired therapeutic effect. Variables or considerations, such as body weight, age, renal function, and concomitant medications are a few of the important variables involved in determining an efficacious dose and dose regimen. Decades ago, it was presumed that the in vivo response to a drug was related only to its intrinsic pharmacological activity, and potency was defined in terms of a milligram per kilogram dose [1]. Factors, such as drug concentration in plasma, individual differences in metabolism, and drug half-life were not part of the tool set used to ensure efficacy.

In addition to systemic absorption, a balance of drug distribution and elimination achieves and maintains appropriate drug concentrations at the targeted site. While drug distribution can directly affect onset and the intensity of the desired in vivo response, drug elimination affects the duration of this response. The most common routes of elimination or excretion include renal or hepatic elimination, as well as biotransformation (metabolism) in the liver and other organs. Thus, absorption, distribution, metabolism, and elimination (ADME) all affect the in vivo concentrations of a drug, as well as the in vivo effects of the drug. Because toxicology can be viewed as the undesired complement to the pharmacological response, ADME also plays a role in the toxicology.

The field of TK, which is an extension of PK, relates in vivo drug concentrations to observable toxicological effects. In addition to having a different focus, the two approaches differ in the doses that are analyzed. TK studies are generally carried out at higher doses than those used in PK studies. In preclinical toxicology studies, the higher doses push both drug absorption and elimination processes to the limit, and sometimes past it, to evaluate the toxicity of the drug. TK describes the drug concentrations required to induce undesirable side effects. The resulting TK parameters may differ in magnitude from the PK parameters of the same drug at lower, safer doses. However, the basics of PK and TK analyses are the same.

This chapter will present some of the basic PK concepts and describe how they are applied to TK evaluations in preclinical safety studies. A second objective of this chapter is to compare and contrast the toxicological assessment of both small and large molecules and the issues that are applicable to each modality.

Table 4.1 compares some of the characteristics of small molecules versus biologics. In many cases, the PK behavior of biologics is not only different but involves complexities unique to this modality [2]. For example, the potential immunogenicity of protein therapeutics may influence the PK parameters as well as their pharmacodynamics (PD) and toxicity. This chapter will briefly discuss some of the issues that confront both modalities during drug development. The term biologic can apply to many agents (eg, viruses, toxins, small peptides, large proteins, or monoclonal antibodies), but the focus of this chapter will be on the PK characteristics of monoclonal antibodies unless otherwise stated.

DRUG ADMINISTRATION AND DELIVERY

Delivery of small molecules can involve almost any route into the body, eg, oral (PO), intravenous (IV), and inhalation. Many small molecules enjoy the advantages of PO administration, ie, they are easy to administer with reasonable patient compliance, although the PK of poorly absorbed small molecules can be somewhat problematic. Variables that influence solubility and permeability of a poorly absorbed compound can have profound effects on the PK of the molecule, sometimes leading to unpredictable and variable exposure. In a review of a set of structurally diverse drugs, Hellriegel et al. noted that the inter-subject variability in bioavailability or the relative amount of unchanged drug in systemic circulation was highest with poorly absorbed drugs, ie, the control of drug delivery is more difficult in this situation [3].

In contrast to small molecules, biologic drugs are protein- or peptide-based, and they generally cannot be administered PO due to poor intestinal absorption and/or degradation in the stomach. It is quite common for biologics to have extremely low PO bioavailability (<1–2%). As a result, these drugs are often administered via parenteral routes, such as subcutaneous (SC), intramuscular (IM), or IV administration [4,5]. For all methods of parenteral delivery, patient compliance issues can often challenge the therapeutic value of the drug (eg, insulin injections for the treatment of diabetes).

INTRAVENOUS ADMINISTRATION

Toxicological studies are generally conducted using the targeted route of drug administration in humans, and quite frequently this is PO administration for small

TABLE 4.1 Comparison of Aspects Critical to PK and TK Analyses for Small Molecules Versus Biologics [2,4]

Small Molecules	Biologics
Molecular weight generally below 500 Da	Molecular weight of proteins tend to be very high, eg, denosumab MW ~147 kDa. Molecular weight of peptides is intermediate, eg, atrial natriuretic peptide, MW ~3 kDa
Generally chemically synthesized	Produced from cell lines expressing the biologic of interest (eg, CHO cells, *E. coli*)
Physicochemical properties (molecular weight, melting point, etc.) are well defined	Physicochemical properties are complex and can vary. For example, molecular weight can vary with changes in the extent of glycosylation
Relatively stable shelf life	Sensitive to both heat and shear stress. For toxicology studies, stability testing is critical
Oral administration once daily is common but any route is possible	Generally administered through parenteral routes. Small proteins, eg, EPO or GCSF, may be dosed daily, while monoclonal antibodies may be dosed once weekly or once monthly
Wide range of dosing vehicles are possible. Clinical studies can involve capsules, tablets, dose in bottle, etc. Marketed drugs are generally delivered as suspensions, solutions, or in solid dosage form(s)	Generally injectable. Sheer stress, adsorption, aggregation, and stability are significant concerns in selecting and optimizing the formulation. Marketed drugs are delivered as lyophilized material (requiring reconstitution) or as solutions
Compounds with good solubility and permeability generally enter systemic circulation rapidly via absorption across membranes or paracellular spaces. Metabolism in the GI and liver during absorption may attenuate bioavailability	Biologics do not absorb across cell membranes readily. When the MW is >15–20 kDa, the lymphatic system becomes an increasingly important mechanism to reach circulation after extravascular administration. These molecules are subject to proteolysis at the site of injection as well as during interstitial and lymphatic transit
Wide range of clearance values and half-lives are possible. Clearance frequently occurs in the liver and kidneys	Clearances are generally low, and half-lives are generally long for monoclonal antibodies and fusion proteins. Clearance can occur in blood, liver, kidneys, at the site of injection, or by receptor-mediated clearance
Wide range of distribution volumes possible	Volume of distribution is usually small, and limited to plasma and/or extracellular fluids for monoclonal antibodies. The smaller the protein, the larger the volume of distribution
Partitioning into blood cells is possible but not particularly common	Partitioning into blood cells is not a concern
Metabolism can be quite complex, and because both active and non-active metabolites can be formed, they must be characterized for investigational new drug/new drug application work. Safety assessment of metabolites may be critical, ie, see MIST guidance from the FDA	Limited "metabolism," eg, catabolism, to endogenous amino acids. Safety assessment of metabolites not required
Both target and non-target related toxicities are possible	Toxicity often related to an exaggerated pharmacologic effect or antigenicity (immune response)
Generally not antigenic unless reactive intermediates bind to protein (hapten hypothesis; rare). Idiosyncratic toxicity can be particularly challenging for small molecules	Can potentially be antigenic with MW > 10 kDa. Extent of antigenicity can vary with site of injection (SC > IM > IV)
Generally one bioanalytical method for preclinical studies and similar validated methods for GLP toxicology and human PK. LC-MS/MS assays are very common	In many cases, biologics may require several bioanalytical assays, eg, mass assays, bioassay, anti-drug antibody assays, etc., for PK/TK studies. Validated assays required for GLP toxicology studies as well as clinical studies

molecules and IV administration for biologics. Intravenous administration facilitates a more accurate assessment of clearance values, distribution volumes, and half-lives because the availability of the dose is not complicated by the factors limiting absorption (see the section Absorption After Extravascular Dosing). Intravenous injection can occur within a few seconds or over time, ie, an IV bolus versus an IV infusion. When the duration of injection lasts more than 1–2 min, the delivery is considered to be an infusion. In patients, as well as in larger preclinical species, it is not uncommon for the infusion of a biologic to take 15–30 min. The following sections will cover some of the basic PK parameters generally associated with an IV dose. These include clearance (CL), volume of distribution (V_d), half-life ($t_{1/2}$), and exposure [C_{max} and area under the curve (AUC)]. An extensive discussion of mean residence time (MRT) is also included. In the authors' experience, MRT is a useful parameter, but it can be a difficult concept to grasp. As a consequence, additional attention will be given to the introduction of this parameter.

The majority of both preclinical PK and TK studies use a noncompartmental approach for data analysis. Noncompartmental analysis (NCA) allows the evaluation of various PK parameters, including but not limited to CL, V_d, $t_{1/2}$, and AUC, without assuming or understanding the mechanistic properties of the drug within the body [6,7]. NCA is versatile and rugged, and it is the most common method of analysis used within the pharmaceutical industry. As a consequence, this method of PK analysis will be the primary emphasis throughout the rest of this chapter. Discussion of compartmental PK analysis is beyond the scope of this chapter, and the interested reader is referred to some of the excellent references that have preceded this writing [7].

Clearance

A definition of clearance is the rate of removal or elimination of a drug from an apparent volume of fluid [8]. To illustrate this concept, Fig. 4.1 shows a beaker with a U-shaped tube that runs from the bottom to the top of a beaker. This tube contains a pump that facilitates mixing the contents of the beaker. To mimic an IV injection, a compound has been introduced into the top of the beaker with a single injection. After a short amount of time, the pump mixes the contents, and the solution becomes homogeneous. Assuming the volume of fluid in the beaker was not initially measured, all that is currently known is the amount of compound that was initially injected. When samples are taken with a syringe from the sampling port (on the lower right side), this is analogous to taking blood samples from a subject at specified PK or TK time points. The concentration in the collected samples can be determined. Using the concentration data and the amount injected, we can now determine the volume in the beaker, eg,

$$\text{volume} = \frac{\text{amount of compound injected}}{\text{sample concentration}} \quad (4.1)$$

This volume is analogous to the volume of distribution or V_d, which will be discussed in greater detail in the section Volume of Distribution.

In Fig. 4.2, a similar beaker is shown, but in this case a filter has been inserted in front of the pump. This filter removes some of the molecules as the fluid passes through. Sampling soon after injection would result in a concentration similar to that achieved in Fig. 4.1 where no filter was in place. However, sampling at a later time (eg, minutes or hours) will result in a lower concentration as the filter has reduced the amount of compound in the beaker. The filter in this example is analogous to the liver, which frequently removes a drug from circulation, and it is a site of both drug excretion (via the bile) and metabolism. Fig. 4.3 depicts the collection of seven

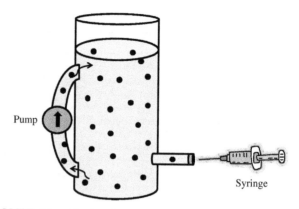

FIGURE 4.1 A beaker that contains water that is continuously circulated and mixed by a pump. Compound is introduced into the top of the beaker and the syringe at the bottom is used to withdraw samples from the portal for concentration analysis (similar to withdrawing blood from a vein for drug concentration analysis).

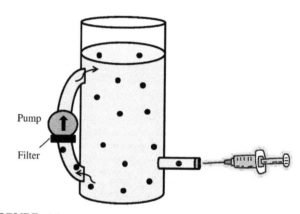

FIGURE 4.2 A beaker that contains water that is continuously circulated and mixed by a pump. In this diagram, a filter has been introduced just before the pump. The filter removes compound from the water as it flows past. This is analogous to the liver (for example), which removes drug from hepatic blood flow. The syringe withdraws samples for concentration analysis and mimics blood sampling from a vein. Since there is only one beaker in this diagram, this is called a "one compartment" system.

samples at varying sequential time points and the resulting plot of concentration versus time data. This plot is analogous to a plot of plasma concentration versus time after an IV injection.

If we define the beaker elimination rate as the amount of compound lost to the filter at any given point in time, then this is directly related to the concentration of compound in the beaker at a specific time, multiplied by the filter clearance rate, as shown in Eq. (4.2).

$$\text{beaker elimination rate} = \text{filter clearance rate} \\ \cdot \text{concentration} \quad (4.2)$$

It should be noted that the concentration is always changing with time, and consequently, so does the beaker elimination rate. Considering the units involved, if

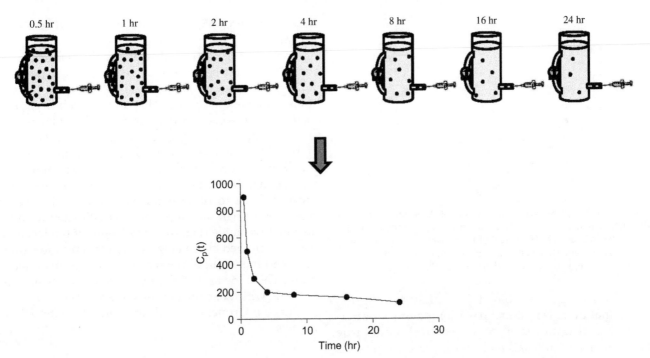

FIGURE 4.3 Sequential points in time shown after introduction of compound into the beaker (at time = 0) and the continuous removal of the compound via the filter. Also shown, on the bottom of the figure, is an extrapolation to a "plasma" concentration [$C_p(t)$] versus time plot, with the corresponding progressive decline in compound concentration over time.

the dose delivered to the beaker was in milligrams (mg), the time measurement was in hours (h), and the volume was measured in milliliters (mL), the beaker elimination rate in mg/h is equivalent to the product of the filter clearance rate in mL/h and the compound concentration in mg/mL, eg, mg/mL × mL/h = mg/h. The filter clearance rate does not change with time, and this parameter is analogous to the clearance (CL) parameter used to describe the PK of a molecule after an IV injection. This is not surprising because in our example, the filter equals the liver, and the liver is a site of drug elimination. At this point, however, it is not clear how to estimate CL from the concentration curve data shown in Fig. 4.3. To do this, a few additional mathematical steps are necessary. If we consider the amount of compound eliminated from the beaker in a small time interval, then CL can be estimated by the following Eq. (4.3):

$$\frac{\text{amount elimination from beaker}}{\Delta t} = \text{clearance} \cdot \text{Conc} \quad (4.3)$$

or

$$\text{amount elimination from beaker} = \text{clearance} \cdot \text{Conc} \cdot \Delta t \quad (4.4)$$

where Conc is the average concentration during a short duration of time, Δt is the time interval, and clearance is equivalent to the filter clearance rate. Eq. (4.4) is related to the data in Fig. 4.4 because the product of

Conc·Δt is the area of a rectangle with a width that corresponds to a time interval (x-axis) and a height that corresponds to the average concentration in this interval (y-axis). For example, if we consider the time interval between 2 and 4h, then Δt is equal to 2h. The average concentration between 2 and 4h can be estimated from the plasma concentrations measured at these time points: (200 + 300)/2 = 250 mg/mL. Thus, in Fig. 4.4 the area of the rectangle that estimates the AUC between 2 and 4h is 250 mg/mL × 2h = 500 mg h/mL. The total amount of drug that is eliminated after an IV dose is related to the sum of all of the rectangles under the concentration versus time curve. If we sum or integrate both sides of Eq. (4.4), the resultant equation links the total amount of drug eliminated to the product of CL and total AUC. The sum of all of the amounts of compound eliminated during all time intervals [left-hand side of Eq. (4.4)] is simply equivalent to the dose administered. On the right hand side of the equation, a sum of all possible rectangles under the curve estimates the AUC. Thus, summing or integrating both sides of Eq. (4.4) results in the following:

$$\text{Dose} = CL \cdot AUC \quad (4.5)$$

Therefore, CL can be estimated from both the dose and AUC using the relationship in Eq. (4.5).

For small molecules, CL is most frequently estimated from plasma concentrations, and plasma CL

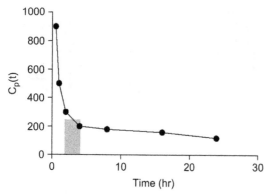

FIGURE 4.4 Plasma concentration versus time curve after IV administration with a *gray rectangle* representing an estimate of the AUC between 2 and 4h. The height of the rectangle is approximately the average concentration between 2 and 4h, and the width is 2h. The area of the rectangle is therefore ~250mg/mL × 2h = 500mg h/mL.

acts as a surrogate for blood CL. A key assumption here is that there is minimal partitioning or sequestering of the drug in red blood cells, which holds true for the majority of small molecules. For biologics, CL is often estimated from plasma or serum, with serum being the preferred or "cleaner" matrix. Since a number of physiological fluids can be sampled, it is important to recognize that CL values can vary depending on the matrix sampled. For example, for a compound targeting a central nervous system (CNS) receptor, it is not uncommon to track drug concentrations in cerebral spinal fluid (CSF) or total brain homogenate. Depending on the properties of the compound and disposition within the CNS, the compound CL from the CNS may be slower, faster, or equivalent to the systemic or plasma CL.

In addition, a compound may be cleared by more than one mechanism, pathway, or "pump." Quite commonly, elimination of small molecules occurs in several organs, such as the liver and the kidneys, although one may predominate. Because blood flow is fractionally distributed between the various potential organs of elimination, clearance from these organs is a parallel process. Thus, the CL from each organ is additive [9], which is summarized by the following:

$$\text{Total } CL = \text{hepatic } CL + \text{renal } CL + \text{other } CL \quad (4.6)$$

One exception to this relationship occurs when there is significant elimination by the lung, for which blood flow is in series rather than in parallel with all of the other organs.

Obviously, organ-specific pathology may impact organ-specific CL, which in turn will affect the total observed CL. For example, if renal tubule toxicity is identified in a multiple dose toxicology study, and these tubules contribute to the overall CL of the drug, then the observed CL may change as a function of the pathology.

Based upon Eq. (4.5), a decrease in CL would be also be accompanied by an increase in AUC.

Since drug measurements are normally made from fluids, CL generally has units that are the same as a flow rate [6] (eg, mL/min, mL/h, and L/h) are frequently used. It also is common to normalize CL for body weight to facilitate cross-species comparisons, so the units become mL/min/kg, mL/h/kg, or L/h/kg. For example, in Eq. (4.5), if dose units are expressed in mg/kg, and the units for CL as mL/min/kg, then AUC units are in min · mg/mL. Upon initial inspection, the units for AUC are sometimes difficult to understand; however, recall that the AUC (for a small time interval) was estimated from the area of a rectangle (Fig. 4.4). The height of the rectangle was determined by average drug concentration (mg/mL), and the width of the rectangle was a time interval (min). Thus, the area of the rectangle has units of min · mg/mL, which of course is the same as AUC.

Noncompartmental analysis will estimate CL as follows:

$$CL = \frac{D_{IV}}{AUC_{0-\infty}} \quad (4.7)$$

where D_{IV} is the amount administered as an IV dose, and $AUC_{0-\infty}$ is the AUC extrapolated out to infinity. This is simply a rearrangement of Eq. (4.5).

Finally, note that CL is considered to be an independent PK parameter [10]. This implies that CL can be determined independently of other PK parameters, and it directly reflects in vivo physiological (elimination) mechanisms. Perturbation of the elimination mechanism(s) typically has a direct effect on the reported CL value, independent of other PK parameters. The equations above, ie, $CL = D/AUC$ [Eqs. (4.5) and (4.7)], are those typically used to calculate CL but are not meant to imply CL is solely dependent on or determined by dose and AUC.

Volume of Distribution

Volume of distribution (V_d) is a proportionality factor that relates the amount of drug in the body to the drug concentration in the measured matrix [11], as shown in Eq. (4.8). Quite frequently, the matrix of choice is plasma.

$$V_{d,t} = \frac{\text{Amount in the body}}{C_p(t)} \quad (4.8)$$

The term $V_{d,t}$ is the volume of distribution at a particular point in time, and $C_p(t)$ is the concentration of drug in plasma. In Fig. 4.1, recall that the volume of distribution was quite simple. An injection of a given amount of drug was made into a beaker. Then, a concentration was quantitated from a sample withdrawn from the beaker, and this value was used to calculate a volume. Eq. (4.1) was used [similar to Eq. (4.8)], and the volume calculated was the actual physical volume of the beaker. In Fig. 4.2, the situation became more complex because drug was withdrawn from the beaker by the filter attached to the pump. However, at any given time, Eq. (4.8) applies because as the measured concentration decreases, the total amount of drug in the beaker also decreases. Thus, the ratio(s) from Eq. (4.1) or (4.8) remain the same, and consequently, the volume of distribution also remains the same.

Fig. 4.5 presents a situation with yet another layer of complexity. In this instance, an elliptical sponge is introduced into the beaker, and the molecules of the compound adhere to it. The amount of free or unbound compound in solution is therefore decreased. Eqs. (4.1) and (4.8) can still be used to calculate a volume; however, the volume calculated will now be larger than the actual volume of the beaker. This is because a sample withdrawn from the beaker for concentration analysis will yield a lower concentration, and thus, the ratio in Eqs. (4.1) and (4.8) becomes larger. This analogy is similar to what one encounters in vivo. After an IV infusion, a drug distributes from the blood compartment to different tissues and organs in the body with different affinities. The relative concentration in the plasma may be quite low, or it may be higher if distribution is limited. For a small molecule, the volume of distribution may have no physical meaning for the reasons mentioned earlier, and thus, the resulting volume is sometimes called an apparent volume of distribution. For example, the apparent volume of distribution for Sensipar, which is used in the treatment of secondary hyperparathyroidism, is approximately 1000–1200 L [12,13]. Obviously, this large volume significantly exceeds any physiological volume in humans (see Table 4.2). When the volume of distribution is high and the corresponding plasma concentration is therefore low, the compound is said to be widely distributed. However, one must be careful with this designation and recognize that the drug could be sequestered predominantly into just one tissue, eg, adipose tissue.

In contrast to the potentially high apparent volumes of distribution sometimes observed for small molecules, the distribution of monoclonal antibodies outside of the blood compartment is often limited [4,5]. The volume of distribution for biologics varies but is usually within two- to threefold of the plasma volume.

The reported units for volume of distribution are typically mL or L, unless they are normalized for body weight, in which case the units are mL/kg or L/kg.

More Than One Volume Term: V_c, V_{ss}, and $V\beta$

After IV injection, plasma concentration versus time profiles can exhibit various shapes. The simplest IV

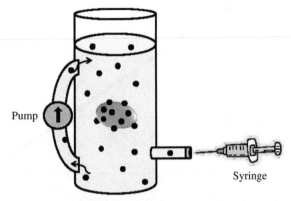

FIGURE 4.5 A beaker containing water that is continuously circulated by a pump. An elliptical sponge has been introduced into the beaker, and compound molecules adhere to the surface, reducing the "free" concentration of compound in solution. After withdrawal of a sample for concentration analysis, the measured compound concentration is lower relative to the measurement in Fig. 4.1. Thus, the calculated volume of distribution from the current sampling (V = amount added/concentration measured) will be greater than that in Fig. 4.1, and it will no longer reflect the actual volume of the water in the beaker. In an analogous fashion, drug tissue binding outside the blood or central compartment reduces the amount drug measured in plasma, and it increases the apparent volume of distribution.

TABLE 4.2 Physiological Volumes of Body Fluids and Tissues in an Average 70-kg Human [14,15]

Fluid	Volume (L)
Total body water	42
Plasma	3.0
Blood	5.5
Extravascular fluid	39
Interstitial fluid	11
Intracellular fluid	28
Body solids and fat	20

profile is characterized by a decline in concentration that is monophasic on a semi-log plot as shown in Fig. 4.6A, and it implies that the compound is primarily located in the central compartment, eg, blood, plasma, serum, or well-perfused organs like the liver and kidneys [15]. This is often called a one compartment model and is conceptually similar to the illustrations in Fig 4.1–4.3 and 4.5. If the profile is characterized by a decline in concentration that appears to be biphasic or bi-exponential, as shown in Fig. 4.6B, then it is likely that the compound is distributing between central and peripheral compartment(s) (see Fig. 4.7). At this point, the reader should be cautioned that it is also possible for a compound to distribute into a peripheral compartment, as illustrated by Fig. 4.7, but have a plasma concentration profile that is similar to Fig. 4.6A. In this latter case, the rate of distribution is very fast such that a multicompartment system looks like a

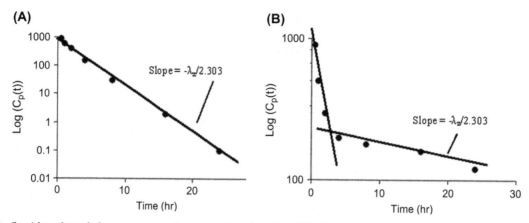

FIGURE 4.6 Semi-log plots of plasma concentration versus time data after IV bolus administration of compound: concentrations decrease in either a monoexponential/monophasic (A) or multiexponential/biphasic (B) decline. The PK profile illustrated in panel (A) is consistent with drug distribution into a single compartment similar to that illustrated in Fig. 4.2. In panel (B), the PK profile is consistent with tissue binding and drug distributed in more than one compartment (see also Fig. 4.7). Special note: the concentration of drug in plasma is commonly plotted on a semi-log plot, ie, the x-axis is linear and y-axis is logarithmic. Typically, there are two possibilities for a log-based scale, either the natural log (ln) or the more common log with base 10 ($\log_{10}$). It is generally assumed after an IV dose that plasma concentrations decline as described by a mono-exponential equation ($C_p(t) = A \cdot e^{-\alpha \cdot t}$) or by a multiexponential equation. In the specific example illustrated in panel (B), this is a bi-exponential decline ($C_p(t) = A \cdot e^{-\alpha \cdot t} + B \cdot e^{-\beta \cdot t}$). The slopes are calculated by taking the ln or $\log_{10}$ of either equation. Specifically for panel (A), the transformed equation(s) would be $\ln C_p(t) = \ln C_p(0) - \alpha \cdot t$, or $\log_{10} C_P(t) = \log_{10} C_P(0) - \dfrac{\alpha}{2.303} \cdot t$. Thus, the slope of the log transformed data is either $-\alpha$ or $-\alpha/2.303$ depending on which logarithm is used. In panel (B), the analogous slope is either $-\beta$ or $-\beta/2.303$. In Eq. (4.20), the half-life is calculated from λ_z, which is equal to either α or β depending on the drug concentration profile.

single compartment in the plasma concentration versus time profile.

In the many instances where the PK profile presents as a biphasic plot (Fig. 4.6B), there are three separate volumes to consider, and these volumes are functions of time as implied in Eq. (4.8). The first is the volume of the central compartment (V_c). Immediately after an IV injection, the compound distributes into the plasma, or by analogy, into the first beaker (see Fig. 4.7). The following equation shows that the central compartment volume may be calculated from the total dose divided by the concentration in the beaker (or plasma) at time 0, eg, C(0):

$$V_c = \frac{D_{IV}}{C(0)} \quad (4.9)$$

There are several assumptions that must be met for this equation to be applicable. First, the drug must distribute instantly in the plasma and the highly perfused tissue(s) that constitute the central compartment. Second, it is assumed that very little drug has distributed into peripheral compartments or tissue (Fig. 4.7, top). In practice, one never truly obtains a zero plasma concentration [$C_p(0)$] because it is logistically difficult to inject and draw a blood sample at the same time, and even if this were possible, there would be some question as to whether complete mixing had occurred. As a

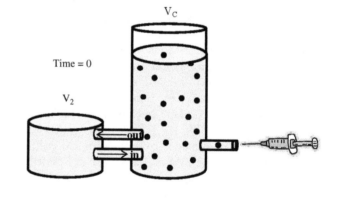

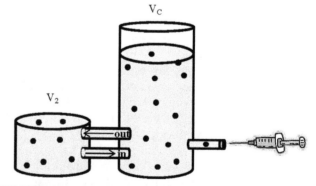

FIGURE 4.7 A beaker with distribution of water and compound to a second compartment, representing a two compartment system. If a pump and filter are included in this system as shown earlier, then the resulting decline in compound concentration may appear biphasic or bi-exponential, as seen in Fig. 4.6B.

consequence, $C_p(0)$ is estimated by back extrapolation from the first few plasma concentration time points to the y-axis (see Fig. 4.8). From the amount injected and an estimated value of $C_p(0)$, the value of V_c can be calculated. Generally, V_c is similar to the plasma volume and cannot realistically be smaller. If the initial V_c estimates are smaller, then factors, such as a dosing error should be considered.

Once a compound has been introduced to the central compartment, it begins to distribute into peripheral tissue(s). This, of course, means that the plasma concentration is declining, and from Eq. (4.8) the volume is therefore increasing with time, as shown in Fig. 4.9. At some point in time, the rate "out" of the central compartment is equal to the rate "in," and when this occurs, the system has reached steady state. At this point, the volume is said to be the volume of distribution at steady state (V_{ss}). Theoretically, when V_{ss} has been reached, the highest concentration in the peripheral tissue has also been reached. If additional volume measurements are made, subsequent to achieving V_{ss}, then it will be observed that the apparent volume continues to increase until a plateau is observed (see Fig. 4.9). Once a volume plateau is reached, the ratio between the amount of drug in the peripheral tissue and the amount in the central compartment remains constant. When this condition has been met, then the apparent volume of distribution is called $V\beta$ or V_z. V_z, which can be estimated from the following:

$$V_z = \frac{CL}{\lambda_z} = \frac{Dose_{IV}}{AUC_{IV} \cdot \lambda_z} \quad (4.10)$$

where λ_z is the first-order elimination rate constant and can be calculated from the slope of the terminal phase of the IV plasma concentration versus time curve (see Fig. 4.6).

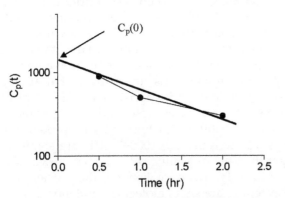

FIGURE 4.8 Semi-log plot of plasma concentration data within the first 2.5 min after IV bolus administration of compound. The initial concentration at time 0 is calculated by back extrapolation from a regression line fit to the first few concentrations. Many commercially available software programs use the first two points only for the back extrapolation.

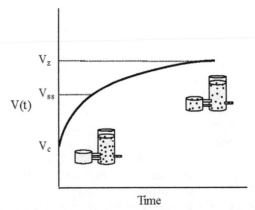

FIGURE 4.9 Changes in compound distribution in a two compartment model. Shortly after an IV bolus administration of compound, $V(t)$ is equivalent to V_c or the volume of the central compartment. When the rates in and out of the central compartment are equal, ie, the distributional equilibrium between the central and peripheral compartments has been achieved, then the observed $V(t)$ is equal to the volume of distribution at steady state (V_{ss}). After sufficient time, the ratio of compound in the central and peripheral compartment(s) remains constant, in which case pseudo-distribution equilibrium has been achieved, and the observed $V(t)$ is equal to V_z.

Volume of Distribution at Steady State

After introduction of a drug into the central compartment and as equilibrium is approached, the extent of distribution is affected by many factors, such as plasma volume, total body water (including the intra- and extracellular fluid), plasma protein binding, and partitioning into red blood cells and tissue depots (eg, adipose tissue) [15]. The most common method of estimating a value for V_{ss} is as follows:

$$V_{ss} = MRT_{IV} \cdot CL \quad (4.11)$$

In this equation, V_{ss} is calculated from mean residence time after an IV dose (MRT_{IV}). In the section Mean Residence Time (MRT), the concept of MRT will be discussed in detail. Eq. (4.11) is presented here for completeness.

At steady state, the amount of drug in the body is related to the amount of drug in the plasma, tissue (or total extravascular space), and red blood cells, as shown by the following relationship:

$$C_{p,ss} \cdot V_{ss} = C_{p,ss} \cdot V_p + C_{t,ss} \cdot V_{tiss} + C_{rb,ss} \cdot V_{rb} \quad (4.12)$$

$C_{p,ss}$, $C_{t,ss}$, and $C_{rb,ss}$ are the concentrations of drug in plasma, tissue, and red blood cells at steady state, respectively. The terms V_p, V_{tiss}, and V_{rb} are volumes of plasma, tissue, and red blood cells, respectively. Dividing each side of the equation by $C_{p,ss}$ yields the following:

$$V_{ss} = V_p + \frac{C_{t,ss}}{C_{p,ss}} \cdot V_{tiss} + \frac{C_{rb,ss}}{C_{p,ss}} \cdot V_{rb} \quad (4.13)$$

In general, drug candidates have a package of in vitro data that has been generated for the compound prior to nomination for clinical studies. The assessment of blood-to-plasma partitioning for preclinical species as well as humans is routinely performed and is part of this package of information.

The concentration of the compound in the blood cells divided by the concentration in plasma ($C_{rb,ss}/C_{p,ss}$) is proportional to the blood-to-plasma partitioning ratio. Thus, compounds that are sequestered into red blood cells may have very high blood cell concentrations relative to plasma concentrations. Examples of drugs with significant red blood cell partitioning include the antimalarials like chloroquine, immunosuppressive agents like rapamycin and tacrolimus, and diuretics like methazolamide and chlorthalidone [16]. Under such circumstances, V_{ss} in Eq. (4.13) can potentially increase due to the blood partitioning due to an increase in the $C_{rb,ss}/C_{p,ss}$ ratio. In a similar fashion, compounds that partition into tissue by receptor binding or sequestration in adipose tissue would also result in an increase in the $C_{t,ss}/C_{p,ss}$ ratio, consequently increasing V_{ss}. However, tissue partition ratios are not routinely available. Eq. (4.13) is a mathematical statement of what was illustrated and discussed earlier. Remember that if a compound is significantly bound to the sponge introduced into the beaker (Fig. 4.5), then the apparent volume increases. By analogy, if the compound is sequestered in any tissue, or distributes significantly outside of the central compartment, this will lead to a higher apparent V_{ss}.

An additional variable to consider is the effect of protein binding on the extent of drug distribution [17]. Only a free or unbound drug can move freely across membranes to distribute between plasma and tissue. It is generally thought that free concentrations in plasma should be equivalent to free concentrations in tissue at steady state, as shown by Eq. (4.14):

$$f_{u,p} \cdot C_{p,ss} = f_{u,t} \cdot C_{t,ss} \qquad (4.14)$$

The term $f_{u,p}$ is the free fraction in plasma, and $f_{u,t}$ is the free fraction in tissue. When a compound is tightly bound to plasma proteins, eg, 99%, then the free fraction is small (1%). Rearranging Eq. (4.14) results in the following relationship:

$$\frac{C_{t,ss}}{C_{p,ss}} = \frac{f_{u,p}}{f_{u,t}} \qquad (4.15)$$

For the purpose of illustrating the effects of plasma protein binding on volume of distribution, assume that the compound does not sequester into red blood cells significantly, and that the red blood cell compartment can be ignored, or combined with the tissue compartment(s). Eq. (4.13) then simplifies to the following:

$$V_{ss} = V_p + \frac{C_{t,ss}}{C_{p,ss}} \cdot V_{tiss} \qquad (4.16)$$

Next, incorporating Eq. (4.15) into Eq. (4.16) results in the following relationship:

$$V_{ss} = V_p + \frac{f_{u,p}}{f_{u,t}} \cdot V_{tiss} \qquad (4.17)$$

Thus, this relationship demonstrates that extensive plasma or tissue protein binding can affect the apparent volume of distribution. As noted earlier, a drug that is tightly bound to plasma proteins ($\geq 99\%$), ie, the value for $f_{u,p}$ is low ($\leq 1\%$), may not be available to freely distribute into tissue, resulting in small apparent volumes of distribution. Conversely, it would be expected that a compound with tighter binding in tissue, ie, small $f_{u,t}$, would have an enlarged volume of distribution. Eq. (4.17) is consistent with these concepts.

As an example of one extreme, antipyrine is a drug that essentially exhibits no plasma or tissue protein binding [14]. For this compound the free fraction is approximately equal to the total concentration, as follows:

$$\frac{C_{t,ss}}{C_{p,ss}} = \frac{f_{u,p}}{f_{u,t}} \cong 1 \qquad (4.18)$$

Thus, Eq. (4.13) reduces to the following:

$$V_{ss} = V_p + V_{tiss} + V_{rb} \qquad (4.19)$$

The volume of distribution for antipyrine is equal to the aqueous volume of plasma, tissue, and red blood cells. As shown in Table 4.2, total human body water is estimated at 42 L. The reported volume for antipyrine is ~42 L or essentially body water, as predicted by Eq. (4.19). In contrast, a drug that is highly protein bound and does not penetrate tissue outside the central compartment would have a volume of ~3–4 L, similar to the plasma volume. Thus, the apparent volumes of distribution of drugs that have no affinity for plasma protein or tissue, or drugs that are highly plasma protein bound, approximate the true physical volumes. Moreover, as described, the apparent volumes of distribution of highly tissue protein bound drugs, eg, Sensipar at ~1000–1200 L, are significantly larger than the physiological volumes shown in Table 4.2 [12,13]. However, in general, these examples are the exception for small molecules, and most drugs distribute to varying degrees across body water, plasma, and tissue [18,19].

In the case of monoclonal antibodies, tissue distribution is limited. The volume of distribution after IV injection is typically similar or slightly larger than the plasma volume ($\geq$43 mL/kg or $\geq$3 L for a 70 kg human), while V_{ss} tends to be no more than twice the initial ~V_c observation [4]. However, there is at least one example where active tissue uptake and binding to intra- and extravascular proteins substantially increases the apparent volumes of distribution. This example is atrial natriuretic peptide, which has a reported V_{ss} of ~12 L and a V_z of 32 L [20].

Finally, it should be noted that V_{ss} is also considered to be an independent PK parameter [10]. Similar to the discussion for CL, this implies that V_{ss} can be determined independently of other PK parameters, and it directly reflects in vivo physiological (steady-state distribution) mechanisms. Perturbation of the distribution mechanism(s) typically has a direct effect on the reported V_{ss} value, independent of other PK parameters. While the equation $V_{ss}=MRT_{IV}\cdot CL$ [Eq. (4.11)] is often used to calculate V_{ss}, it should not be assumed that V_{ss} is dependent on or solely determined by these parameters. Thus, both CL and V_d are independent PK parameters. By analogy with the beaker example presented in Fig. 4.2, the volume of the beaker (V_d) and the filtration rate (CL) are independent variables and are not dependent on dose or AUC. Although this concept may seem obvious, it is often overlooked or forgotten during routine PK/TK analysis.

Half-Life

Half-life ($t_{1/2}$) is defined as the amount of time required for the drug concentration measured in plasma (or other biological matrices) to be reduced to exactly half of its starting concentration or amount. After IV dosing, the drug concentrations in plasma decline due to both elimination and distribution [15]. In Fig. 4.6B, a plasma profile is shown that is characterized by an initial rapid decline, followed by a slower decline at later time points. The first phase or rapid decline is assumed to be primarily due to distribution, while the later phase of decline is slower and assumed to be primarily due to elimination. It is important to note that both processes are occurring in both phases, but the dominant process differs between the two phases. Eventually, after sufficient time has passed, distribution is assumed to be complete. Consequently, the elimination half-life is generally determined from the terminal or elimination (dominant) phase of the plasma concentration versus time curve (Fig. 4.6B). While the most accurate half-life is determined after IV administration, it is not unusual to evaluate oral half-lives in a multidose toxicology study. Changes in oral $t_{1/2}$ (across time and/or increasing doses) can be an indication of an alteration in the CL mechanism(s) or an indication of the type of toxicology, eg, reduced renal or liver function.

The following equation is used to calculate the half-life:

$$t_{1/2} = \frac{0.693}{\lambda_z} \qquad (4.20)$$

where λ_z is the elimination rate constant, presented in Eq. (4.10) (also see Fig. 4.6). Because $t_{1/2}$ and λ_z are inversely proportional, a compound with a long half-life will have a long, flat terminal phase, corresponding to a small λ_z or terminal slope value, similar to the profile shown in Fig. 4.6B. In contrast, a compound with a shorter half-life will have a steeper slope and a larger λ_z value. See Practical Considerations in the section Data Evaluation: Look at a Visual Representation of the Data (eg, Graphs) for further discussions on determining half-life.

The parameters of CL and V_d are closely related to half-life, ie, half-life is a "dependent" parameter [10,19]. After a simple rearrangement of Eq. (4.10), Eq. (4.21) shows the relationship between clearance, volume of distribution, and the elimination rate constant, λ_z:

$$CL = \lambda_z \cdot V_z \qquad (4.21)$$

Considering Eq. (4.20), solving for λ_z and substituting into Eq. (4.21) yields the following equation, which reflects the dependence of half-life on clearance and volume of distribution:

$$t_{1/2} = \frac{0.693}{CL} \cdot V_z \qquad (4.22)$$

Thus, $t_{1/2}$ will increase as CL decreases or V_d increases (V_z in this case). Eq. (4.22) is written specifically to highlight that CL and V_d, two independent parameters, both control $t_{1/2}$ which is a dependent parameter. Inulin, which is used to assess kidney function, has a clearance of 7.2 L/h [19]. Because the volume of distribution is limited to extracellular water (~16 L), the resulting and observed half-life is 1.5 h. The example of Sensipar is not as clear [12,13]. Estimates of V_{ss} range from 1000 to 1200 L (for a 70 kg human), while the CL estimate after a single 0.29 mg/kg IV dose is 1.1 L/h/kg (~87% of hepatic blood flow; see the section Practical Considerations, section Normalization of Clearance Values to Liver Blood Flow). These data suggest that the $t_{1/2}$ of Sensipar should be 11.1 h. The $t_{1/2}$ reported in the IV study was 19.9 h, while a PO study suggested a $t_{1/2}$ of 10.3 h. Independent of the variability in the reported $t_{1/2}$ for Sensipar, it is interesting to note that despite high CL, the large V_{ss} facilitates a long $t_{1/2}$ [consistent with Eq. (4.22)] as well as desirable efficacy in patients. Thus, it is not always true that a drug with high CL will have a short $t_{1/2}$.

Mean Residence Time (MRT)

Previously, MRT was presented as a parameter used to calculate V_{ss} [Eq. (4.11)]. A definition of MRT

is the average time that molecules of a dosed drug spend in the body [21]. As noted, this is one of the more difficult concepts to grasp in PK. To understand the basis of *MRT*, let us start with a simple example. If three molecules of drug A are injected into an animal, each of these molecules would spend differing amounts of time in the system before being excreted. Let us assume that the time spent is 1, 2, and 3 h for the first, second, and third molecules, respectively. Each of these time intervals represents a residence time for each molecule. The resulting MRT would be 2 h, as shown in Eq. (4.23).

$$MRT = \frac{1}{3} + \frac{2}{3} + \frac{3}{3} = 2 \qquad (4.23)$$

In the lab, of course, it is physically impossible to track just one molecule at a time. Using Avagadro's number, eg, $1\,\text{mol} = 6.023 \times 10^{23}$ molecules, and assuming a molecular weight of ~300 mg/mmol, a 0.5-mg dose represents ~10.2×10^{17} molecules, ie, too many molecules to track individually. Thus, Eq. (4.23) is limited in the sense that it represents an infinitesimal fraction of a normal dose. In the laboratory, subsequent to an IV dose, molecules are collected in samples of urine and/or bile at specific time points or intervals. Each sample represents a collection of molecules (*m*). The total residence time for this particular collection of molecules can be estimated as time (Δ*t*), eg, the time interval for which the sample was collected after the dose, multiplied by the number of molecules in that sample, or Δ*t·m*. The *MRT* for this group of molecules is (Δ*t·m*)/*m*. To calculate an *MRT* for the dose, however, additional groups of molecules also need to be considered across additional time intervals. To accomplish this, the following equation describes the summing of residence times for multiple groups:

$$MRT = \frac{\sum_1^n \Delta t_i \cdot m_i}{\sum_1^n m_i} = \frac{\sum_1^n \Delta t_i \cdot m_i}{\text{Dose}} \qquad (4.24)$$

where m_i is the number of molecules in group i, and Δt_i is the time for that particular group or time interval. The term *n* is the total number of groups. If many groups are considered, then the denominator is equivalent to the total number of molecules administered, which can be rewritten as the dose. Thus, Eq. (4.24) is really the same as Eq. (4.23), except that it has been rewritten to accommodate many molecules so the *MRT* of the whole dose may be determined. Additional modification of Eq. (4.24) is necessary because the concentration (eg, mass/volume or mg/mL) is reported in the PK samples, not the number of molecules. The mass of drug is directly proportional to the number of

molecules in each group (m_i) multiplied by the molecular weight and normalized by Avagadro's number, as shown in Eq. (4.25).

$$\text{mass}_i = \frac{m_i \cdot \text{MW}}{6.023 \times 10^{23}} \qquad (4.25)$$

Thus, *MRT* can be rewritten as follows in terms of the mass of compound eliminated:

$$MRT = \frac{\sum_1^n \Delta t_i \cdot m_i}{\sum_1^n m_i} = \frac{\sum_1^n \Delta t_i \cdot \text{mass}_i}{\sum_1^n \text{mass}_i} \qquad (4.26)$$

The terms for Avagadro's number and *MW* cancel out, which simplifies Eq. (4.26). Although Eq. (4.26) is nearly a useful equation, additional derivation is required to achieve a relationship that relates *MRT* with parameters measured routinely in PK experiments. In the beginning of this chapter, Eq. (4.3) was used to describe the elimination of compound from a beaker with a clearance "filter." Rearrangement of this equation gives the following:

$$\text{filter clearance} = \frac{\left(\dfrac{\text{amount elimination from beaker}}{\Delta t} \right)}{\begin{array}{c}\text{average drug concentration in}\\\text{beaker during time interval } t\end{array}}$$

$$(4.27)$$

Another way to write this equation (relating it to plasma concentration) is as follows:

$$CL = (\Delta\,\text{mass}/\Delta\,\text{time}) / (C_p\,(\text{average})) \qquad (4.28)$$

Rearranging Eq. (4.28) gives Eqs. (4.29) and (4.30):

$$\frac{\Delta\,\text{mass}}{\Delta\,\text{time}} = CL \cdot C_p\,(\text{average}) \qquad (4.29)$$

$$\Delta\,\text{mass} = CL \cdot C_p\,(\text{average}) \cdot \Delta\,\text{time} \qquad (4.30)$$

The term Δmass represents an amount of mass eliminated during a time period, eg, Δtime or Δ*t*. From Eq. (4.26), mass$_i$ represents a mass of compound eliminated during a small time segment, Δt_i. Therefore, Eq. (4.26) can be rewritten as follows:

$$MRT = \frac{CL \cdot \sum_1^n \Delta t_i \cdot C_{pi}\,(\text{average}) \cdot \Delta t_i}{CL \cdot \sum_1^n C_{pi}\,(\text{average}) \cdot \Delta t_i} \qquad (4.31)$$

The term C_{pi}(average) is the average concentration during a short span of time, Δt_i. In Fig. 4.4, the area of the small rectangle shown was equivalent to the average plasma concentration during the specified time interval multiplied by the increment of time. In Eq. (4.31), the term $C_p(\text{average}) \times \Delta t$ is the area of a rectangle. As previously discussed, when all of these rectangles are summed, the resulting value is an estimate of the AUC for the plasma concentration curve. Hence, MRT can be calculated from the following:

$$MRT = \frac{CL \cdot t \cdot AUC}{CL \cdot AUC} = \frac{AUMC}{AUC} \qquad (4.32)$$

The numerator in Eq. (4.32) is referred to as the area under the first moment curve ($AUMC$) because AUC is multiplied by time, which is raised to the first power or 1. Because Eq. (4.32) is the summation of all molecules introduced into the body or the total dose, MRT expressed in this manner is the average time that a single molecule of the dose will spend in the body.

Exposure: C_{max} and AUC

The parameters C_{max} and AUC are both measures of a compound's in vivo exposure [22]. In TK, an important endpoint is the estimation of exposure, and AUC is routinely used to estimate safety margins that are critical to projecting the starting human dose in Phase I clinical studies. Exposure margins based upon C_{max} may also be considered; however, AUC is the parameter that is generally most relevant.

The definition of C_{max} is simply the observed maximal concentration in whatever biological matrix is being evaluated. Thus, C_{max} concentrations can be measured in any matrix, ie, C_{max} can be determined in blood, plasma, serum, CSF, liver homogenate, etc. As previously discussed, the determination of AUC is more complex, involving the summation of the area of many rectangles under the plasma concentration versus time curve (Fig. 4.4). Conceptually, this is correct, but mathematically, the area is estimated by the summation of many trapezoids [7]. To further clarify this statement, the area under a portion of the curve can be estimated from a trapezoid as follows:

$$\begin{aligned} AUC_{t_2-t_1} &= \text{area between sampling points} \\ &\quad t_1 \text{ and } t_2 \text{ (estimated by a trapezoid)} \\ &= (t_2 - t_1) \cdot \frac{C_2 + C_1}{2} \end{aligned} \qquad (4.33)$$

The term $(t_2 - t_1)$ is just the time interval or Δt, and the concentration term $[(C_2 + C_1)/2)]$ is the average concentration during the time interval. Thus, mathematically, we are estimating the AUC using the formula for the area of a trapezoid; however, this is equivalent to

the area of a rectangle (see Fig. 4.4) where the width of the rectangle is Δt and the length of the rectangle is the average concentration in the time interval. As discussed previously, to estimate the AUC over a period of time, eg, the dosing interval, all of the trapezoids (or rectangles) under the curve should be summed, as shown in Eq. (4.34).

$$AUC_{0-t_{last}} = \sum_1^n \frac{C_i + C_{i+1}}{2} \cdot \Delta t \qquad (4.34)$$

Fig. 4.10 visually demonstrates that a series of trapezoids can estimate the area under a smooth curve reasonably well (in this case a curve after PO administration). By analogy, $AUMC$ can also be estimated from the sum of the area of each trapezoid multiplied by time, as shown in Eq. (4.35).

$$AUMC_{0-t_{last}} = \sum_1^n \frac{t_i(C_i + C_{i+1})}{2} \cdot \Delta t \qquad (4.35)$$

When the last concentration in the plasma concentration time curve is nonzero, or significantly greater than zero, then $AUC_{0-t_{last}}$ does not fully reflect the exposure associated with the entire dose. There is some AUC past the last sampled time point that is not incorporated (Fig. 4.10B). In this case, it is desirable to calculate the AUC extrapolated to infinity ($AUC_{0-\infty}$) from the last plasma concentration. However, since there is no data beyond this point in the curve, an assumption must be made about the decline of plasma concentrations after the last time point. In general, it is assumed that drug concentrations decline or are eliminated in a manner that is approximated by the following:

$$C(t) = C_0 e^{-\lambda_z \cdot t} \qquad (4.36)$$

The portion of the curve that we are seeking to estimate is the decline in plasma concentration after t_{last}:

$$C(t) = C_{last} e^{-\lambda_z \cdot (t - t_{last})} \qquad (4.37)$$

where C_{last} is the concentration of the last data point, and t_{last} is the time at which this data point was collected [19]. Next, if we start at the last time point (t_{last}) and integrate, ie, calculate the AUC from t_{last} to infinity, then the area past the last data point can be estimated. Recalling integration rules from calculus, the following equations apply:

$$AUC_{t_{last}-\infty} = \int_{t_{last}}^{\infty} C_p(\text{last}) \cdot e^{-\lambda_z \cdot (t - t_{last})} dt; \qquad (4.38)$$

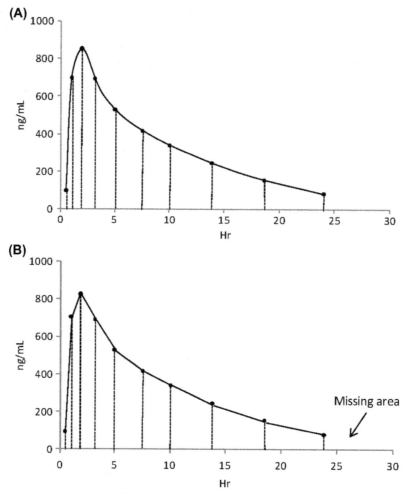

FIGURE 4.10 In panel (A), a smooth PK curve consistent with oral administration is presented. In panel (B), the same data points are used to define trapezoids under the curve for each small time interval between blood sampling time points. Qualitatively, the *AUC* is estimated well by a series of trapezoids. Also shown is a truncation of the full PK curve because the plasma collection time points did not extend past 24 h post-dose. In this case, the remaining *AUC* after the last data point is estimated using Eq. (4.40).

$$= C_{p}\,(\text{last}) \left[\frac{e^{-\lambda_z \cdot (t - t_{\text{last}})}}{-\lambda_z} \right]_{t_{\text{last}}}^{\infty} = C_{p}\,(\text{last}) \left[0 - \frac{1}{-\lambda_z} \right] \quad (4.39)$$

$$AUC_{t_{\text{last}} - \infty} = \frac{C_{p}\,(\text{last})}{\lambda_z} \quad (4.40)$$

Thus, we can now derive a formula for *AUC* from time zero to infinity ($AUC_{0-\infty}$) as follows:

$$AUC_{0-\infty} = \left[\sum_1^n \frac{C_i + C_{i+1}}{2} \cdot \Delta t \right] + \frac{C_{p}\,(\text{last})}{\lambda_z} \quad (4.41)$$

Thus, the trapezoidal rule is used to calculate *AUC* in the portion of the curve where data have been collected, and the assumption of exponential decay [Eq. (4.36)] is used in the final extrapolation to infinity where data

have not been collected. By analogy, *AUMC* from time zero to infinity is given by the following analogous:

$$AUCM_{0-\infty} = \left[\sum_1^n \frac{C_i + C_{i+1}}{2} \cdot \Delta t \right] + \frac{C_{p}\,(\text{last}) \cdot t_{\text{last}}}{\lambda_z}$$
$$+ \frac{C_{p}\,(\text{last})}{\lambda_z^2}$$

$$(4.42)$$

In practice, *AUC* is routinely calculated with commercial PK software, and several variants of the trapezoidal rule are possible [7,15]. The first is the linear trapezoidal rule, already described (eg, see Fig. 4.10), which connects adjacent plasma concentration data points with a linear line, and the *AUC* is then approximated by the area of a trapezoid. This method is well known and widely used;

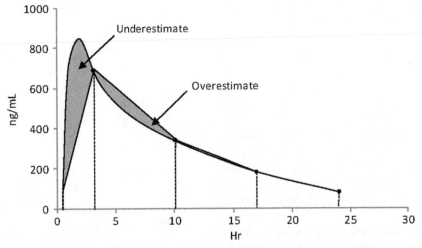

FIGURE 4.11 When plasma concentrations of compound rise quickly, and there is inadequate sampling such that the interval between plasma collection time points is large, then the trapezoid under the curve may underestimate the true *AUC* for that interval. Conversely, a rapid decline in combination with insufficient plasma sampling can yield an overestimate of area compared to the true *AUC*.

however, the reader should be aware that there are several conditions under which it is prone to error. The first occurs when the width of the trapezoid is large, or when inadequate sampling has resulted in PK time points that are spaced too far apart. The second source of error relates to the fit of the PK profile curvature. In some cases, the linear trapezoidal rule can overestimate the *AUC* when drug concentrations are declining (Fig. 4.11). In contrast, when drug concentrations are increasing, eg, in the absorption phase after a PO dose, the area under the true PK curve can be underestimated. The extent to which the linear trapezoidal rule is in error depends on the curvature of the PK profile as well as the frequency of sampling time points. In general, this linear trapezoidal method produces a reasonable estimate of *AUC*. The key to reducing the error associated with this method is to use more PK sampling time points, realizing that there are limitations on the number of nonterminal blood draws that can be withdrawn within a given time frame (see Practical Considerations, in particular Sampling Time Points and Blood Sampling Limitations).

The second trapezoidal method that may be used for PK analysis is the log trapezoidal rule. In contrast to the linear trapezoidal rule, this method assumes that plasma concentrations between adjacent data points decline in a monoexponential or curved manner. As a result, this method closely estimates declining plasma concentrations when those concentrations are decaying exponentially. The area between two plasma concentration data points is given by a modification of Eq. (4.33) as follows:

$$AUC_{t_2 - t_1} = (t_2 - t_1) \cdot \frac{C_2 + C_1}{\ln\left(\frac{C_2}{C_1}\right)} \qquad (4.43)$$

It is important to note that this method only applies to descending data, and fails when one of the concentrations

is zero, or when there are two consecutive concentrations in the profile that are equivalent.

Finally, the best solution may be to use a combination of both approaches. In other words, when the plasma concentration versus time curve is flat or ascending, the linear trapezoidal rule is applied, and when the curve is descending, the log trapezoidal rule is applied.

ABSORPTION AFTER EXTRAVASCULAR DOSING

For a drug designed to influence a systemic target, the first requirement is that the compound gains access or exposure within systemic circulation. All methods of drug delivery requiring absorption, independent of modality (small molecules or biologics), can result in lower or variable systemic exposure relative to IV administration [23]. Both small and large molecule drugs that are subject to absorption processes tend to have delayed and reduced C_{max} values in plasma/serum in contrast to the C_{max} values achieved after IV (bolus) dosing. There are a several reasons for this. For small molecules, there are physiological barriers that limit absorption. Oral dosing requires a compound to pass through the stomach prior to arriving at the main site of absorption, which is the upper gastrointestinal tract (GI). Gastric pH, gastric (acid) output, and gastric emptying time potentially influence the timing of the arrival of the dosed compound into the GI. Once in the GI, the mucosal lining of enterocytes, ie, mature absorptive columnar epithelial cells, forms a diffusional and/or a permeability (absorption) barrier. In addition to a physical diffusion barrier, there are drug metabolizing enzymes as well as uptake and efflux transporters in these enterocytes [24]. Moreover, the innate physicochemical properties of the intestinal fluids, eg, pH, the presence of bile salts, etc., may also play a role in compound dissolution and availability for absorption [23]. Next, the orally dosed compound that has been absorbed from the GI has to pass through additional "first-pass" organs (liver, lungs; the upper GI is also considered a first-pass organ), where it is subject to additional metabolism and/or transport prior to reaching the systemic circulation. Blood flow from the GI flows through the liver to the heart, into the lungs, and back to the heart prior to carrying the remaining dosed compound to the rest of the body. The collective drug metabolism/elimination by the GI, liver, and lungs is generally referred to as first-pass metabolism or the first-pass effect.

Factors limiting the absorption of biologic drugs after PO administration differ from those for small molecules, and they include enzymatic and pH-dependent degradation as well as low epithelial permeability due to the higher molecular weight. In addition to IV dosing, biologics are frequently delivered via other routes, eg, SC, IM, or intraperitoneal (IP) administration [4,5]. Parenteral routes of administration bypass the limitations associated with the GI. However, IM, SC, or IP administration is subject to other absorption limitations. For example, all molecules are influenced by compound-independent or physiological variables including but not limited to the depth of injection, the speed of injection, the vascularity or extent of blood flow at the injection site, and factors affecting blood flow, such as exercise and temperature. Absorption of biologics is specifically influenced by their large inherent molecular weight, which can also determine the pathway by which a biologic enters systemic circulation, ie, via blood capillaries or via the lymphatic system. The significance of the lymphatic system becomes more important as molecular weight increases (>16 kDa). Lymphatic flow is quite slow, and therefore significant drug delivery into circulation via the lymphatic system can result in a delayed time at which maximal drug concentrations are achieved (T_{max}), eg, T_{max} can be as long as 36–49 h for Aranesp [25].

Considering this long list of variables, it should come as no surprise that the site of parenteral administration can influence the resulting PK of a compound. Subsequent to extravascular (PO, SC, etc.) administration, the rate of drug absorption is commonly described by first-order or linear kinetics that depend primarily on drug concentration. Pharmacokineticists characterize first-order absorption with an absorption rate constant or k_a, ie, rate of absorption $= k_a \times$ drug concentration [26,27]. It is important to recognize that all of the processes discussed here can be involved in the absorption phase, and thus k_a often represents a composite of many rate constants. It is not unusual to have T_{max} values that occur at 0.25–1 h post-dose for small molecules, implying that

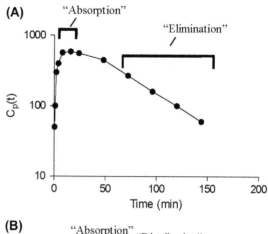

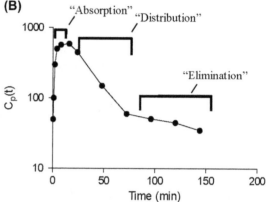

FIGURE 4.12 Time course(s) of plasma concentrations of compound after administration to a site that requires absorption: concentrations decrease in either a monoexponential (A) or multiexponential (B) decline. Although the processes of absorption, distribution, and elimination are all occurring simultaneously in much of the PK curve, the labels of "absorption," "distribution," and "elimination" are those typically used for descriptive purposes.

the absorption processes or rates can be quite rapid. As mentioned earlier, the T_{max} for biological molecules can be quite variable, and it is influenced by factors, such as molecular weight and posttranslational modifications (eg, glycosylation).

Occasionally, a compound is absorbed with zero-order kinetics; that is, at a constant rate independent of drug concentration, ie, rate of absorption $= k_a$. In the current context, toxicology studies rarely use or estimate absorption rates, and consequently, this topic is only briefly discussed here.

Fig. 4.12 shows two typical PK curves from a dosing route that requires absorption. The characteristics of both curves include an initial time interval where plasma concentrations are rising, which is commonly referred to as the absorption phase. This is followed in both cases by declining plasma concentrations. Similar to the previous discussion for IV plasma concentration profiles, when plasma concentration appears to decline at two rates after a PO dose, the earlier faster decline is called the distribution phase, and the later slower decline is referred to as the elimination phase (Fig. 4.12B). In some cases the declining concentrations appear to be monophasic, as illustrated in Fig. 4.12A. In practice, it may be difficult to tell if one or more phases of decline exist, and it may be necessary to replot the data on a semi-log scale to better visualize the rates of decline.

It should be pointed out that the labels in Fig. 4.12 are descriptive only because absorption, distribution, and elimination can occur throughout the entire plasma concentration versus time profile. For example, in Fig. 4.12A, if we assume single compartment kinetics once the drug has been delivered to the site of absorption, eg, time 0 for SC, IM, or IP injections (or slightly later after PO dosing), the rate of absorption is maximal, and the rate of elimination is zero. As time increases and the concentration of drug available for absorption decreases, the rate of absorption also decreases. At the same time, increasing plasma drug concentrations in systemic circulation translate to increases in the rate(s) of elimination. When plasma/serum concentrations increase after time 0, the rate of absorption exceeds the rate of elimination. At any given point in time, the following equation describes how drug concentrations change:

Rate of change of drug in plasma = rate in − rate out
$$= \text{rate of absorption} - \text{rate of}$$
$$\text{elimination} - \text{rate of distribution}$$

$$(4.44)$$

Toward the end of the absorption phase, there exists a point in time, eg, T_{max}, when the plasma concentrations reach their highest level. This corresponds to the point in time when the rate of absorption is equivalent to the rate of elimination. The concentration at which this happens is C_{max}. After extravascular dosing, both T_{max} and C_{max} are important descriptors of a TK curve and should be reported in TK studies. In addition to AUC, C_{max} is also considered a measure of exposure.

To expand on this further, Fig. 4.13 depicts another PK curve, showing the administration of a compound with an apparent absorption phase. Also depicted in this figure is the rate of absorption (straight line) from the

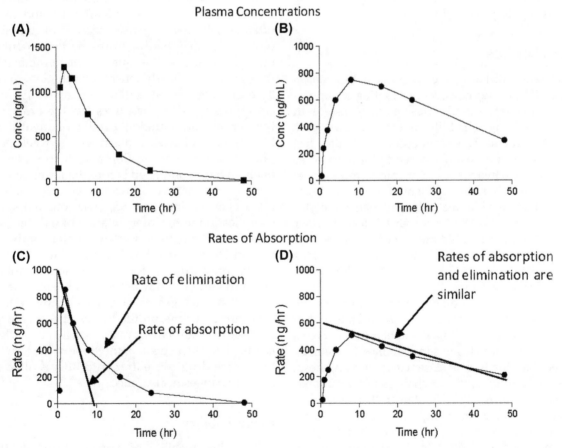

FIGURE 4.13 Linear plots of plasma concentration versus time after compound administration that requires absorption, panels (A) and (B). Panels (C) and (D) depict the rate of absorption (*straight line*) and the rate of elimination. The rate of absorption is faster than elimination in panels (A) and (C), while the rate of elimination is faster than the rate of absorption in panels (B) and (D). In the latter panels, the rate of elimination is limited or determined by the absorption rate.

site of administration and the rate of elimination (curved line). When the absorption rate is faster (steeper) than the elimination rate (left panel), the rate of input, ie, the slope of the straight line, is greater than the apparent rate of elimination. In this case, absorption is essentially complete during the later time points of the curve. In contrast, the right panel of Fig. 4.13 depicts a rate of absorption that is rate limiting, ie, the rate of absorption is slower than the rate of elimination, and the slope of the elimination phase parallels or estimates the rate of absorption (right panels). Going from left to right in Fig. 4.13, plasma C_{max} decreases, and T_{max} is delayed as the rate of absorption slows down or decreases.

When absorption is the rate limiting process, the terminal slope of the PK curve is relatively insensitive to changes in elimination, and it can therefore mask important changes in half-life that may occur with repeat dosing. Moreover, it may not be possible to establish a true half-life from later points on the curve. In toxicology studies, it is not unusual to see T_{max} increasingly delayed across a large dose range ($\leq 1000\,mg/kg$). When this occurs, it is entirely possible that the process of absorption may not be complete at the later time points. Under such circumstances, changes in half-life with increasing dose should be interpreted with caution.

Apparent Half-Life

The inherent half-life of a compound is best determined after IV dosing; however, estimating an apparent half-life after extravascular dosing can be useful. In practice, determining a half-life from a PO curve may be somewhat difficult. This often occurs when data has not been collected for a sufficient length of time, or as discussed earlier, when there are ongoing processes, ie, absorption or distribution. In general, the observed oral half-life for a small molecule is longer than the corresponding half-life calculated from an IV dose. Further details on estimating half-life are discussed at the end of this chapter [see the section Practical Considerations particularly Data Evaluation: Look at a Visual Representation of the Data (eg, Graphs)].

In small molecule toxicology studies, although the oral half-life will most likely not be an accurate reflection of the true IV half-life, this parameter may serve as an early litmus test for changes in clearance. Sometimes the apparent half-life will increase with increasing dose, potentially indicating nonlinear changes in the elimination rate or clearance. These nonlinear changes reflect the fact that with increasing drug concentrations, nearly every elimination mechanism (especially if it is enzymatically mediated) will saturate at some point, or the rate no longer increases with increasing drug concentration. For monoclonal antibodies, the interaction of the drug with the intended biological target is a significant

contributor to both antibody distribution and elimination (via endocytosis). This target mediated elimination is generally saturable at lower doses as compared to small molecules. After a clearance mechanism is saturated, and as the drug dose is increased, the apparent CL will decrease, the apparent half-life will increase, and the AUC will increase disproportionately. For example, AUC may be observed to increase fivefold with only a twofold increase in dose (see the section Practical Considerations particularly Dose Linearity Versus Dose Proportionality). Saturation of small molecule clearance is commonly observed with the high doses employed in toxicology studies, and it is easily recognized by inspection of the TK profiles at different dose levels and a visual comparison of the slope (half-life) of each terminal phase. In addition to changes in the apparent half-life that can occur with increasing dose, change may also occur with respect to time, ie, changes after repeat dosing. The Practical Considerations section Evaluate Potential Changes in TK Parameters on the Last Study Day Versus Day 1 discusses some of the reasons why it is important to compare TK parameters on the first day of dosing with those at the end if the study.

In contrast to small molecules, the half-life of monoclonal antibodies estimated after IV and SC dosing often closely match. A reasonable explanation for this observation may be due to the limited distribution of biologics, and as a consequence, the terminal portion of the curve more clearly reflects elimination. In addition, because monoclonal antibodies generally have low clearances and long half-lives (on the order of days), the serum concentration profile frequently includes time points collected more than one week post-dose. The processes of absorption and distribution are very likely to have completed before the terminal portion of the curve is reached. However, because biologics can often elicit an immune response, this adds a further complication to the interpretation of half-life [see Practical Considerations section Evaluation for the Presence of Anti-Drug Antibodies (ADAs)]. Since concentration versus time profiles for a monoclonal antibody can be on the order of days, it is possible to observe time-dependent changes in clearance within one plasma concentration time profile, rather than comparing TK profiles on different days for small molecules. Once again, visual inspection of the slope of the terminal portion of the drug concentration profile is often an early test for changes in clearance.

Bioavailability

The bioavailability of a drug (F) is the fractional amount of the dose that reaches the systemic circulation unchanged after an extravascular dose (PO, SC, etc.), relative to the amount of drug delivered after an IV dose [28]. Assuming the same dose was administered by IV and PO routes, ie, $xD_{IV} = D_{PO}$, Eq. (4.5) becomes the following:

$$D_{IV} = D_{PO} = CL_{IV} \cdot AUC_{IV,0-\infty} \qquad (4.45)$$

and

$$CL_{PO} = \frac{D_{PO}}{AUC_{PO,0-\infty}} = \frac{CL_{IV} \cdot AUC_{IV,0-\infty}}{AUC_{PO,0-\infty}} = \frac{CL_{IV}}{F} \qquad (4.46)$$

The term F is the bioavailability of the drug. Recall that the exposure of the drug in systemic circulation is given by AUC. If one assumes that 100% of the drug reaches systemic circulation after the IV dose, then the fraction of the drug reaching circulation after a PO dose is given by the following equation [see also Eqs. (4.46)]:

$$F = \frac{AUC_{PO,0-\infty}}{AUC_{IV,0-\infty}} \qquad (4.47)$$

when the same dose was delivered. It is important to note that if different IV and PO dose levels are compared, then the AUC values must first be dose normalized. Bioavailability is often expressed as a percentage, as shown in Eq. (4.48).

$$F\% = F \cdot 100\% \qquad (4.48)$$

A key assumption with these equations is that the other PK parameters remain unchanged, ie, if CL changes between the IV dose and the PO dose, the estimated bioavailability may be artificially elevated (in the case where $CL_{PO} < CL_{IV}$). This situation commonly occurs when clearance is not constant with dose, and elimination pathways become saturated at higher dose levels (as discussed earlier).

In toxicology studies, especially due to the high dose levels used, the estimation of $AUC_{PO,0-\infty}$ can sometimes involve significant extrapolation (>20–25%) due to inadequate terminal plasma sampling, and therefore, there may be some uncertainty for the estimate of this parameter [see Eq. (4.40) and Practical Considerations section Data Evaluation: Look at a Visual Representation of the Data (eg, Graphs)].

The following relationship may be useful at steady state:

$$AUC_{PO,ss} = AUC_{PO,0-\infty} \qquad (4.49)$$

where $AUC_{PO,ss}$ is equal to the area under the curve within the dosing interval at steady state, eg, the dosing interval would be 24h for once a day dosing [15]. Thus,

if the duration of the toxicology study is long enough to achieve steady state after multiple doses, then the AUC during the last dosing interval may be used to estimate the value of $AUC_{PO,0-\infty}$ and vice versa. This again assumes that CL has not changed with time and dosing.

Finally, after SC dosing (for example), when apparent parameters, such as CL and V_{ss} are reported in association with a toxicology study (for either a small molecule or a biologic), they should be reported as CL/F or V_{ss}/F. In the case of an IV study where bioavailability is 1, eg, 100% of the drug is delivered directly into the systemic circulation, the parameters are simply reported as CL and V_{ss}.

Accumulation

A common question after multiple dosing is whether the dosed compound will accumulate in the body, especially when the half-life is long. This is particularly important for toxicology studies because it is the exposure at the end of the study that will be used to calculate exposure- or AUC-based safety margins, ie, the estimated boundaries between safe and toxic doses.

The basic question regarding accumulation can be divided into two parts. Given preexisting experimental PK data, the first part is predicting when steady state would be expected to occur, thus estimating when and after how many doses the maximal exposure will be achieved. Although there is certainly error in this type of projection, it is useful to have some idea of when steady state will occur when considering study design and dose selection. There are several approaches to this question. The first is a "back of the envelope" calculation that can be used to estimate when steady state is achieved. Regardless of the route of administration, it generally will take four to five half-lives to reach steady state drug concentrations after multiple dosing, assuming that the drug exhibits "one compartment" kinetics and that there are no changes in CL and V_{ss} with increasing dose. For example, if a drug has a half-life of 12h, it will take approximately 60h to achieve steady state.

In addition to time, the extent of accumulation, or the final concentration at steady state, depends on the $t_{1/2}$ and the dosing interval [7]. The following equation illustrates this concept:

$$R = \frac{1}{1 - e^{(0.698/t_{1/2}) \cdot \tau}} \qquad (4.50)$$

R is known as the accumulation ratio. Eq. (4.50) defines the dependence of the accumulation ratio on the $t_{1/2}$ and the dosing interval (τ). The relationship between R and AUC will be discussed subsequently. It should be noted that this equation assumes monoexponential decline in the plasma concentration versus time curve, ie, single compartment PK [see Practical Considerations section Data Evaluation: Look at a Visual Representation of the Data (eg, Graphs)]. The term R can also be estimated from the following:

$$R = \frac{AUC_{ss}}{AUC_{0-\tau}} \qquad (4.51)$$

or

$$R = \frac{AUC_{0-\infty}}{AUC_{0-\tau}} \qquad (4.52)$$

where $AUC_{0-\infty}$ is substituted for AUC_{ss} based on Eq. (4.49). The term in the denominator, $AUC_{0-\tau}$, is the AUC in the first dosing interval. Thus, if single-dose data exist for a compound and the PK parameters have been calculated (ie, $AUC_{0-\infty}$ and $t_{1/2}$), then R can be estimated from Eqs. (4.50) and (4.52), and the extent of accumulation as well as final exposure at the end of the toxicology study can be predicted.

Several other methods can be used to estimate exposure at the end of the study. These include nonparametric superposition and PK model fitting to existing PK data. Although nonparametric superposition does not assume any type of model (eg, one vs. two compartment PK), this method does assume that each dose of a drug acts independently of every other dose. Moreover, the rate and extent of absorption, along with systemic clearance, are assumed to be the same for each dosing interval. The method of superposition can be set up using a spreadsheet, but it is most conveniently done in one of the popular PK analysis programs that are currently available. Complete discussion of this method is beyond the intended scope of the current chapter, but the interested reader is directed to other references [28]. Finally, some modeling software allows the plasma concentration data to be fit to compartmental PK models (one or two compartment, etc.), and once a good fit is obtained, the model can be scaled to other dose levels and/or used to predict multiple dosing profiles over time. There are many considerations for developing a model that fits PK data well, and this also is well beyond the scope of the current chapter (see Ref. [29] for more information).

CALCULATION OF EXPOSURE-BASED SAFETY MARGINS

Drug or drug candidate safety is always a primary concern for the toxicologist. In some cases, a toxicologist may be faced with the potential development or progression of more than one preclinical candidate, and as a consequence, the primary concern will be to take forward the safest candidate (although the overall decision may be significantly more complex). The safety of a drug can be assessed by a safety margin based upon exposure (AUC). The input required to estimate exposure-based safety margins, and facilitate selection of the starting dose in humans, includes the following: (1) predicted human PK parameters including CL, V_{ss}, and $\%F$ (assuming extravascular administration); and (2) the AUC associated with the no adverse effect level (NOAEL) in the preclinical toxicology studies. In some cases, the pharmacokineticist may be requested to estimate an efficacious dose for humans (and the associated AUC) to project a potential therapeutic window between the estimated safe drug levels and those associated with undesirable effects. This involves establishing a pharmacokinetic–pharmacodynamic (PK–PD) relationship in preclinical models and then extrapolating that relationship to humans. The details involved in PK–PD study design and modeling will not be covered here; however, additional information can be readily found elsewhere [29,30].

Predicting Human PK

The two main approaches that industrial pharmacokineticists use to predict human PK parameters are allometry and a physiologically based approach [31–35]. Allometry is based upon the similarity of anatomical, physiological, and biochemical variables in mammals as well as the empirical observation of a mathematical relationship that relates variables from one species to another as a function of body weight [31,34]. The practice of correlating human body weight with the preclinical animal weights and PK parameters, to predict human PK parameters, has become a widely used approach. It appears to be particularly useful for compounds that are eliminated unchanged by physical transport or passive processes, including biliary and renal excretion.

Interspecies allometric scaling uses a power function, and the relationship is evaluated with the body weight of each species plotted against the PK parameter of interest [31,34,36]. Using the following equation, clearance, volume of distribution, and elimination half-life are the three most frequently extrapolated PK parameters:

$$y = a \cdot [\text{body weight}]^b \qquad (4.53)$$

In Eq. (4.53), y is the PK parameter to be scaled, and body weight (BW) is the average body weight of the preclinical species used in the prediction. The term a is called the allometric coefficient and b is the allometric exponent. Both the a and b terms are estimated by plotting the log of the body weights across species on an x-axis and the log of parameter y (eg, clearance) across

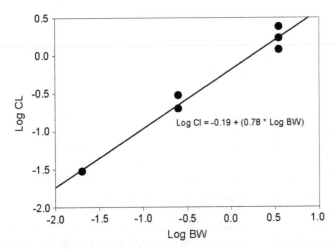

FIGURE 4.14 An example of clearance and body weight data from mouse, rat, and monkey used for allometric scaling. Note that the units for the y-axis should not be normalized to body weight, ie, they should be volume per time (L/h, mL/min, etc.).

species on the y-axis. Converting Eq. (4.53) into a log-based equation gives the following:

$$\log(y) = \log(a) + b \cdot \log(BW) \tag{4.54}$$

where the slope of the plot is b and the Y-intercept is $\log(a)$. Fig. 4.14 presents a representative plot of log (BW) versus log (CL).

Allometric Scaling of Volume of Distribution

For small molecules, allometric scaling of the volume of distribution across species is generally a successful method. This is not surprising because, as discussed earlier, the volume of distribution is determined largely by the affinity of the compound for tissue (binding) as well as the physiochemical properties of the compound. Since body tissues do not dramatically differ across species, the allometric relationship quite frequently has an allometric exponent (or slope) of approximately one. The following equation describes simple allometry for scaling of volume of distribution:

$$V_d = a \cdot [BW]^d \tag{4.55}$$

One important point to remember is that only free drug in circulation, eg, $f_{u,p} \times C_p$, is available to distribute to tissue. While tissue binding tends to be similar across species [37], simple allometric scaling of the volume of distribution works best when plasma protein binding is also similar across species. Thus, if plasma protein binding is species-specific, then the allometric scaling of the volume of distribution should be based on free concentrations and the corrected free V_d values. To correct for unbound drug or free fraction, Obach et al. [32]

used values of unbound plasma for each species to calculate adjusted unbound volumes of distribution with the following:

$$V_{d,unbound} = \frac{V_{d,total}}{f_u} \tag{4.56}$$

Then, values of $V_{d,unbound}$ for each species were plotted using the simple allometric relationship in Eqs. (4.54) and (4.55). In addition, as an example of another type of approach, Obach et al. estimated human volume of distribution from $V_{d,dog}$ (volume of distribution in dog), $f_{u,dog}$ (fraction unbound in dog plasma), and $f_{u,human}$ (fraction unbound in human plasma) using the following:

$$V_{d,human} = \frac{f_{u,human} \cdot V_{d,dog}}{f_{u,dog}} \tag{4.57}$$

Eq. (4.57) assumes that the tissue binding of the drug is similar between dogs and humans and that extracellular fluid volumes are also similar between the two species. It is important to note that Eq. (4.57) yields a projected value for the human V_d in terms of volume per kg of body weight, eg, L/kg.

In the group of compounds that were examined ($n \leq 16$), Obach et al. [32] found that simple allometry [Eq. (4.55)] predicted volumes for 53% of compounds within twofold of actual values, whereas use of unbound drug–corrected allometry [Eq. (4.56)] predicted the volumes of distribution within twofold for 77% of the compounds. Finally, the approach that did not use allometery, ie, Eq. (4.57), predicted volumes of distribution within twofold for 81% of the compounds.

In contrast to small molecules, when considering biologics, the large size of these molecules tends to preclude extensive distribution to tissue, and generally a volume of distribution within one- to twofold of the volume of the central compartment can be assumed [4,5]. Projection of human V_{ss} from preclinical data utilizes Eq. (4.55), and exponent $b = 1$ is often assumed. Alternatively, human V_{ss} can be estimated as being slightly greater than the expected human plasma volume. The degree to which this value is greater can be estimated from a comparison of preclinical species V_{ss} values with the corresponding species-specific plasma volumes.

Allometric Scaling of Clearance

As discussed previously, allometric scaling appears to be particularly useful for compounds that are eliminated unchanged by physical transport or passive processes. Allometric scaling often fails when there are species differences in the (hepatic) metabolism and/or the excretion of compounds. Moreover, when the rate of hepatic (metabolism-based) clearance is moderate or low (see Practical Considerations section Normalization of Clearance Values to Liver Blood Flow), allometry often overpredicts the observed rate of clearance [7,31,32]. This is due to the fact that other processes determine the overall rate of elimination. Some of these factors include the activities of drug metabolizing enzymes and/or transporter proteins. Enzymatic activity can vary from species to species, and these differences do not scale directly as a function of body weight. For such compounds, there are alternate ways to predict clearance, and these will be discussed below. When hepatic clearance is high and the rate of hepatic elimination is determined or limited by the rate of blood flow to the liver, allometric scaling can be successful in predicting human CL. Blood flow is a physiological parameter that scales relatively well across species using the relationships presented in Eqs. (4.53) and (4.54).

Eq. (4.53) is entirely empirical, ie, based upon observational evidence only. As such, remember that there is nothing inherently true or fundamental about it. For a given set of preclinical CL data, there are several similar equations that could potentially be used that may be more predictive of clearance (see later). It is incumbent upon the PK scientist to try a variety of allometric approaches to identify which method achieves good predictions of the existing preclinical CL data. An allometric method that predicts preclinical data well strengthens the case for its use in predicting human CL. However, as is often the case, limited preclinical data may not allow this exercise.

As noted earlier, for some drugs that are eliminated primarily through hepatic (metabolism) mechanisms, it has been observed that allometry produces an overestimate of clearance. Consequently, Boxenbaum and D'Souza [38] suggested that maximum lifetime span potential (MLP) could be incorporated into the allometric equation as a corrective factor. This was based upon the observation that life span is frequently inversely correlated with hepatic cytochrome P450 (CYP)-mediated drug oxidation rates. CYPs are the most common group of enzymes responsible for small molecule biotransformation or metabolism. The modified equation is as follows:

$$CL \cdot MLP = a \cdot [\text{body weight}]^b \qquad (4.58)$$

In addition, because brain weight (BrW) correlates with MLP, Boxenbaum and D'Souza [38] also explored the following relationship:

$$CL \cdot BrW = a \cdot [\text{body weight}]^b \qquad (4.59)$$

Both equations establish methods to correct the potential overestimation of CL by simple allometry.

Additional work from Mahmood and Balian [34] suggested the use of the "rule of exponents" (ROE). In this case, data are first fit by the simple allometric approach [Eq. (4.53)], and then the resulting allometric exponent b is evaluated. If b is found to be 0.71–1.0, then the suggested method is clearance adjusted by MLP [Eq. (4.58)]. If the exponent is greater than 1.0, then clearance should be adjusted by BrW [Eq. (4.59)]. Finally, if the exponent is between 0.55 and 0.71, then simple allometry will suffice. Tang and Mayersohn [39] have noted some limitations to this approach, depending on the species that have been used for allometry, and the interested reader is directed to this paper for additional information. These authors also published an equation that was established after the analysis of more than 60 different small molecules [40]. It was concluded that CL could be estimated by the following:

$$CL = 33.35 \text{ mL/min} \cdot \left(\frac{a}{Rf_u}\right)^{0.77} \qquad (4.60)$$

where Rf_u is the ratio of unbound drug in human versus rat plasma, and a is the coefficient obtained from allometric scaling.

It has been the authors' experience that with small molecules, when PK is obtained from at least three species, a better allometric relationship is established. However, some investigators have published results suggesting that only two species may be necessary, and predictions from only one preclinical species have also been proposed [41]. Unfortunately, the literature in this area has a number of novel methods of allometric analysis and data sets that do or do not support the use of one method versus another. In additional, some of the data sets are quite small.

In summary, there appears to be no "one size fits all" method for the prediction of small molecule CL. As a consequence, and in the absence of a compelling reason to use one approach versus others, it is suggested that the scientist applying allometry to predict human PK should construct a spreadsheet with some of the representative equations from the literature, ie, some of those listed earlier. Then, the clearance data specific to the project is used to populate the spreadsheet, and a range of human clearance projections is obtained. It is important to remember that a good fit of the data does not necessarily guarantee a good prediction. The projected human clearance can then be described as potentially falling within a prediction range determined by the various methods. Drug development project teams are more comfortable with a single number for human PK predictions. However, reporting a range is important (in the authors' experience) because it imparts some idea of the inherent error associated with human PK projections, and it attempts to prevent a false sense of certainty that is sometimes attached to a single estimate.

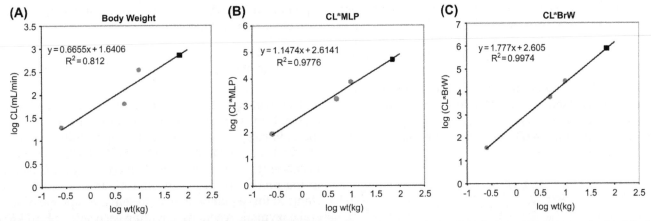

FIGURE 4.15 Allometric scaling of clearance for midazolam. *Circles* represent clearance in preclinical species (rat, dog, monkey), while the *square* represents the extrapolation to humans [49,71–73]. The following allometric methods were used: simple allometry, panel (A); allometry corrected by MLP, panel (B); and allometry corrected by brain weight, panel (C). Also shown in each panel is the regression line and fit (r^2) from which the allometric exponent may be obtained.

Finally, Fig. 4.15 presents some preclinical CL data for midazolam (*circles*) as well as the prediction for human CL (*square*). Simple allometry as well as allometry adjusted for MLP or BrW were applied and are shown in the three panels in addition to the regression line from which the allometric exponent may be obtained. Midazolam is eliminated primarily from liver metabolism, and the rate of elimination is 4.8–8.4 mL/min/kg, ie, moderate clearance ([18]; see Practical Considerations section Normalization of Clearance Values to Liver Blood Flow). Thus, midazolam falls into the category of compounds that are cleared via hepatic metabolism at a moderate rate of elimination. Recall that the CL of such compounds is often over-predicted by simple allometry, and thus, Eqs. (4.58) and (4.59) (Fig. 4.15B and C, respectively) may be used to compensate for the potential over-prediction. From the allometric fits in Fig. 4.15, going from left to right, the human CL estimates are 10.6, 8.7, and 7.8 mL/min/kg using simple allometry, allometry adjusted by MLP, and allometry adjusted for BrW, respectively. Although all of the CL predictions are reasonably close, the methods that incorporate MLP and BrW fall very close to or within the range of observed human CL values for midazolam. In addition, the corresponding allometric plots (Fig. 4.15B and C, respectively) show that the linear regression provides a better fit of the data ($r^2 > 0.97$) relative to the linear regression for the simple allometric scaling ($r^2 > 0.8$; Fig. 4.15A). Interestingly, the simple allometry in panel (A) of Fig. 4.15 reports an allometric exponent of 0.66. According to the ROE, the allometric exponent would fall in a range where simple allometry should be used for the prediction [34]. This illustrates the point that practical use of allometry may require the investigator to rely upon experience gained from similar molecules, or to simply make a judgment call. The authors suggested reporting a range of estimated CL values. In the case of midazolam, the predicted range reported would be 7.8–10.6 mL/min/kg (depending on the methods used), which happens to closely estimate the actual observed human CL range.

For biologics, allometric scaling of clearance appears to be more straightforward. In general, it is reported that good human CL estimates may be obtained using a fixed exponent method [42]. Recently, Wang and Prueksaritanont [43] have published a paper evaluating the use of allometric scaling to retrospectively predict human CL for 34 therapeutic proteins. It was concluded that human CL could be approximated with a simple allometric scaling approach that featured a fixed exponent of 0.8, as shown in Eq. (4.61).

$$CL_{\text{human}} = CL_{\text{animal}} \cdot \left(\frac{BW_{\text{human}}}{BW_{\text{animal}}} \right)^{0.8} \qquad (4.61)$$

Roughly 95% of the predictions resulted in human CL values within twofold of the observed values when the CL data from multiple species were used or 90% of the predictions when using CL only from monkeys.

Estimating CL Using a Physiologically Based Approach

While allometry determines an empirical relationship between PK parameters and body weight, the general methods discussed subsequently are termed "physiological," because they are developed from rational modeling of the underlying biological processes. These processes or factors include organ blood flow rates, organ size, activities of drug metabolizing enzymes, body fluid volumes, plasma protein binding, and the blood-to-plasma ratio. On the surface, this approach may seem more complicated, but it allows the use of in vitro data to predict in vivo PK parameters. It is therefore quicker and less resource intensive when compared to time-consuming in vivo experiments prior to the availability of human PK data. To be clear, this methodology is applied to small molecules and assumes that the mechanism of clearance is mediated primarily by metabolism.

The next two equations present the two most common models used to describe in vivo hepatic drug clearance (CL_h). Eq. (4.62) describes the well-stirred model, while Eq. (4.63) describes the parallel tube model [44–46].

$$CL_h = \frac{Q_h \cdot f_u \cdot CL_{i,h}}{Q_h + f_u \cdot CL_{i,h}} \qquad (4.62)$$

$$CL_h = Q_h \cdot \left(1 - e^{-f_u \cdot CL_{i,h}/Q_h}\right) \qquad (4.63)$$

The terms Q_h and $CL_{i,h}$ correspond to hepatic blood flow and the in vivo intrinsic hepatic clearance, respectively, while f_u is the unbound fraction of drug in plasma described earlier. From these equations, the hepatic clearance of a small molecule can be calculated from three parameters. A value of hepatic blood flow can be obtained from the literature, and the compound- and species-specific f_u can be derived from plasma protein binding experiments. That leaves one parameter to be determined, which is the term $CL_{i,h}$.

In vitro intrinsic clearance (CL_i) is the rate at which an in vitro system, specifically hepatic microsomes or S9 fraction, or hepatocytes, can metabolize a given molecule at a specific concentration [31]. Care should be taken not to confuse this term with the in vivo intrinsic hepatic clearance ($CL_{i,h}$) mentioned earlier. To avoid confusion for the reader, a general outline of the process to be discussed is to first estimate the in vitro intrinsic clearance (CL_i), which is next scaled to an in vivo intrinsic hepatic clearance ($CL_{i,h}$), which is finally used to calculate the predicted in vivo hepatic clearance (CL_h). The relationship between these parameters will be shown presently. CL_i can be written mathematically as follows:

$$CL_i = \frac{\text{rate of drug disappearance}}{\text{drug concentration in the in vitro system}} \qquad (4.64)$$

The rate of drug disappearance in Eq. (4.64), or metabolism of the drug, is measured in a test tube on a laboratory bench for a given in vitro system (eg, liver microsomes, S9, or hepatocytes). The rates of drug disappearance in the in vitro incubation can be modeled by equations that describe enzyme kinetics because, at this level, it is generally enzymatic activity that is responsible for the elimination. The most common and basic equation that describes enzyme kinetics is the Michaelis-Menten

equation that describes the rate of drug disappearance or metabolism, as follows:

$$\text{rate of drug disappearance} = \frac{V_{max} \cdot C}{K_m + C} \qquad (4.65)$$

The term V_{max} is the maximal rate or velocity of drug metabolism, C is the concentration of drug added to the in vitro system, and K_m is the concentration of drug at which the metabolism rate is 50% of V_{max}. In many instances, there will be more than one enzyme involved in the process of drug metabolism, and thus, the constants in this equation may represent a composite of several enzymatic reactions. Dividing each side of Eq. (4.65) by C, the following equation is obtained:

$$\frac{\text{rate of drug disappearance}}{C} = \frac{V_{max}}{K_m + C} \qquad (4.66)$$

Because C is the concentration of drug in the in vitro system, and the rate of disappearance was previously equated to the rate of elimination by Eq. (4.3), then Eq. (4.66) becomes the following:

$$CL_{\text{in vitro}} = \frac{V_{max}}{K_m + C} \qquad (4.67)$$

$CL_{\text{in vitro}}$ is the same as CL_i, or the in vitro intrinsic clearance. Furthermore, when C is very small, Eq. (4.67) simplifies to the following:

$$CL_i \approx \frac{V_{max}}{K_m} \qquad (4.68)$$

The terms V_{max} and K_m are both constants that can be readily determined from a set of in vitro incubations across a range of concentrations.

Once CL_i has been calculated, there are still a few more steps involved in estimating an intrinsic in vivo hepatic clearance, as mentioned earlier. The value for CL_i only reports the ability of an in vitro system to metabolize a drug. The next step is to scale this up to the actual organ, eg, the liver, to provide an estimate of the intrinsic clearance from it. This latter value is still intrinsic because liver blood flow has not yet been incorporated. From Table 4.3, two variables are used to scale an in vitro intrinsic clearance (in liver microsomes) to a hepatic intrinsic clearance, and note that the values vary across species. The value $CL_{i,h}$ for human liver microsomes can be estimated by the following equation:

$$CL_{i,h} = Cl_i \cdot 52.5 \frac{\text{mg protein}}{\text{gram liver}} \cdot 25.7 \frac{\text{gram liver}}{\text{kg body weight}} \qquad (4.69)$$

TABLE 4.3 Average Liver Microsome Protein Concentrations, Liver Weight, and Liver Blood Flows for Routine Preclinical Species and Humans[a] [31]

Species	Protein Concentration (mg/g Liver)	Liver Weight (g/kg BW)	Q_H (mL/min/kg)
Mouse	50	88	90
Rat	45	40	55
Dog	78	32	31
Cynomolgus	49	30	44
Human	52.5	26	21

[a]Houston [74].

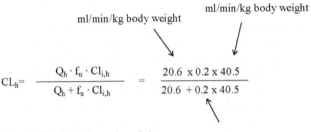

$$CL_h = \frac{Q_h \cdot f_u \cdot Cl_{i,h}}{Q_h + f_u \cdot Cl_{i,h}} = \frac{20.6 \times 0.2 \times 40.5}{20.6 + 0.2 \times 40.5}$$

ml/min/kg body weight

ml/min/kg body weight

$CL_h = 5.81$ ml/min/kg body weight

Fraction unbound
No units

FIGURE 4.16 Demonstration of the calculation of in vivo human hepatic clearance (CL_h) using the well-stirred model. It is assumed that the f_u in plasma is 0.2, ie, 20%, and the in vivo intrinsic hepatic clearance ($CL_{i,h}$) is 40.5 mL/min/kg. The value for human liver blood flow (Q_h) is listed in Table 4.3.

The units for CL_i are mL/min/mg protein, and thus, the units for $CL_{i,h}$ are mL/min/kg body weight. Once $CL_{i,h}$ is obtained, then application of either Eq. (4.62) [or Eq. (4.63)] provides an estimate for human hepatic clearance, as shown in Fig. 4.16. It is important to evaluate how well this physiologically based approach works for the preclinical species, and once a good preclinical correlation is established, there is more confidence that the clearance mechanism is likely to be similar across species and the human CL prediction by this method is more relevant (see Practical Considerations section Evaluation of Preclinical In Vitro–In Vivo Correlations for CL).

The inherent assumption in Fig. 4.16 is that there is minimal partitioning of the compound into red blood cells. If there is notable red blood cell partitioning, Yang et al. [47] provide the following updated equation for the prediction of in vivo hepatic clearance:

$$CL_h = \frac{Q_h \cdot f_u \cdot CL_{i,h}}{Q_h + f_u \cdot CL_{i,h} / \left(\frac{C_B}{C_P}\right)} \quad (4.70)$$

where C_B/C_P is equivalent to the blood-to-plasma ratio based on Eq. (4.13).

Prediction of Bioavailability

In predicting human PK parameters, bioavailability is another important parameter to assess, especially when the compound is destined for extravascular (PO, SC) administration in the clinic. As mentioned earlier, oral bioavailability is the amount of drug that reaches systemic circulation unchanged after passing through a number of hurdles that can potentially deplete the drug. As an example, recalling midazolam with the moderate IV clearance in humans, the bioavailability after PO administration can be as low as 31%, while the bioavailability after IM administration is 85–91%, implying that there is significant first-pass metabolism of midazolam [48,49]. Helmann et al. [49] noted that oral bioavailability for midazolam in humans ranges from 31% to 70%. Midazolam is primarily metabolized by CYP3A in the GI and liver, and human CYP3A4 protein concentrations can vary 17-fold in the GI and over 100-fold in the liver [24,50], directly impacting the oral bioavailability of midazolam in humans. Consequently, predicting the effects of first-pass metabolism, or having an understanding of the mechanism of elimination (and potential variability) involved, can be very important in the process of estimating F.

While an orally absorbed compound also has to pass through the lungs prior to reaching the systemic circulation, lung effects on bioavailability need not be considered. Oral and IV administered compounds both pass through the lungs prior to blood sampling at a peripheral venous site. Thus, theoretically, the metabolic effects of the lung are cancelled out as long as clearance is independent of dose.

First-pass metabolism is often subject to species differences; however, despite this complication, it is often observed that bioavailability in human is similar to the preclinical species. If a compound has a %F of 10, 15, and 25% in rats, dogs, and monkeys, respectively, it would be highly unusual to obtain 90% F for humans. Thus, unless there is metabolism or transporter data suggesting that human is an outlier relative to the preclinical species, in many cases the human estimate of F is based simply on an average of the data available for the preclinical species.

Another method of estimating small molecule %F is the following:

$$\%F = 100\% \cdot \left(1 - \frac{CL_h}{Q_h} - \frac{CL_g}{Q_g}\right) \quad (4.71)$$

where CL_h/Q_h is the hepatic extraction ratio (see the Practical Considerations section Normalization of Clearance Values to Liver Blood Flow), and CL_g/Q_g is the analogous GI extraction ratio [26]. The terms CL_h and Q_h are hepatic clearance and hepatic blood flow (as defined earlier); CL_g and Q_g are intestinal clearance and intestinal blood flow, respectively. This equation assumes that bioavailability is only limited by first-pass metabolism in the liver and the GI. If the first-pass metabolism occurs predominantly in the liver, then the bioavailability is primarily dependent on the hepatic extraction ratio, and vice versa. In practice, the data available for Eq. (4.71) is often limited to estimates for hepatic CL. Thus, if a compound is a substrate for an enzyme known to be expressed in both the liver and GI (eg, midazolam is a substrate for CYP3A4), then additional experiments to estimate the intestinal extraction ratio may be necessary.

Using Preclinical Data to Set a Safe Human Starting Dose

In both drug discovery and development, the ability to predict human PK from preclinical data is critical to activities, such as selecting a drug candidate or projecting an efficacious dose [51,52]. The preceding sections reviewed various methods of estimating human PK parameters from preclinical data. In this section, several approaches to generating a safe Phase I human starting dose will be reviewed. Some of these methods rely on the scaling of the NOAEL dose and exposure, while others depend on the prediction of a human PK profile. In general, there is no universal method for predicting human starting doses in the clinic. However, one common method is to use a pharmacokinetically guided approach.

Pharmacokinetically Guided Dose Extrapolation/ Selection

The use of this approach is quite simple. From the toxicology studies that are done to support the filing of an investigational new drug, the species that yields the lowest NOAEL is selected, and the corresponding AUC from this particular species is used as one parameter in the human dose calculation. The second step is to use any of the previously discussed methods to estimate a predicted human CL. Then, Eq. (4.5) is used to calculate a predicted NOAEL human dose, and a safety factor is applied to obtain the safe starting dose for humans [35,53].

Example: A 4-week toxicology study was performed in rats, and the NOAEL dose for the study was found to be 50 mg/kg, which was associated with an AUC of 22.1 µg h/mL. An additional toxicology study was performed in monkeys; however, the NOAEL dose for this study was 100 mg/kg. Thus, the lowest NOAEL dose was 50 mg/kg in rats, and the exposure from this study was used to set a safe human dose. Human clearance was predicted from allometry to be 800 mL/h.

NOAEL dose in human = AUC of NOAEL(rat) × human CL = (22.1 µg h/mL) × (800 mL/h) = 17,680 µg = ~18 mg. In general, a safety factor of ~10 is applied to the NOAEL human dose (this will be discussed in more detail subsequently), and thus, the final starting dose in man would be 1.8 mg. Note that bioavailability (F) was not considered in this example.

The Dose Conversion Approach

Drug development occurs in companies of all sizes, and correspondingly, companies vary in the resources and expertise that can be applied to preclinical studies. In some instances, there is inadequate preclinical PK data to facilitate reliable human PK projections. For example, a small molecule may be developed by a company, and although numerous oral PK and PK/PD studies were performed, insufficient IV studies were completed to facilitate a clearance projection to humans. Let us further suppose that the compound in question was relatively stable, ie, there was no quantifiable disappearance of parent drug in the in vitro CL assays, so projections from the in vitro data could not be made. In response to such cases, the FDA has released a guidance document with the aim of establishing a maximum recommended starting dose (MRSD) [54]. In agreement with what has been stated earlier, the guidance notes the following:

> In the majority of investigational new drug applications (INDs), animal data are not available in sufficient detail to construct a scientifically valid, PK model whose aim is to accurately project an MRSD.

In this case, when preclinical data do not allow for human PK parameter extrapolation, the FDA guidance recommends identifying the dose from the most sensitive species, ie, the lowest NOAEL dose from preclinical toxicology testing. This preclinical dose is then scaled to humans based upon the relative body surface area(s) (BSA) of the most sensitive species versus humans, and a safety factor is applied to yield a final maximum safe starting dose in the clinic. The following steps are given by the guidance:

Step 1. Review and evaluate all preclinical safety (toxicology) data so a NOAEL can be determined for each study in each species.

Step 2. For each safety study, determine the dose (eg, mg/kg) associated with each NOAEL. Once this has been determined, each NOAEL dose is converted to a human equivalent dose (HED). This conversion is based upon normalization of dose by BSA. BW has been shown to be related to BSA as described by the following [54].

$$BSA = BW^{0.67} \qquad (4.72)$$

Thus, when converting a rat NOAEL dose to an HED, the following equations and values would be used:

$$\frac{\text{Dose in human (mg)}}{\text{Dose in rat (mg)}} = \frac{BW_{human}^{0.67}}{BW_{rat}^{0.67}}$$

$$= \frac{\text{Dose in human} \left(\frac{mg}{kg}\right) \cdot 60 \, kg}{\text{Dose in rat} \left(\frac{mg}{kg}\right) \cdot 0.25 \, kg}$$

$$= \frac{60^{0.67}}{0.25^{0.67}}$$

$$(4.73)$$

In Eq. (4.73), the human and rat body weights in kg are 60 and 0.25 kg, respectively. Of course, when calculating an HED from other species, the appropriate values for body weight may be substituted into the previous equation.

$$\text{Dose in human} \left(\frac{mg}{kg}\right) = \left(\frac{60}{0.25}\right)^{0.67}$$

$$\cdot \, \text{Dose in rat} \left(\frac{mg}{kg}\right) \cdot \frac{0.25}{60}$$

$$(4.74)$$

$$\text{Dose in human} \left(\frac{mg}{kg}\right) = \text{Dose in rat} \left(\frac{mg}{kg}\right) \cdot 0.16$$

$$(4.75)$$

The conversion factor in Eq. (4.75)–(0.16) has no units, and it matches with the unit-less conversion factor for rats listed in the guidance document ([54]; see Table 1 in this reference). Thus, Eq. (4.75) converts, based upon body surface area, an animal mg/kg dose to the equivalent human mg/kg dose.

Step 3. After the HEDs have been determined from the NOAEL doses in each toxicology species, the species that has the lowest HED is chosen. In some cases, there may be a specific or mechanistic reason why the toxicology observed in one particular species may be more predictive of human toxicity. It can, therefore, be rationalized that the NOAEL from this species can be used to calculate a maximum starting dose. However, in the absence of such information, the default is to use the NOAEL dose level from the most sensitive species.

Step 4. Once the HED of the NOAEL in the most appropriate (sensitive) species has been determined, an additional safety factor is applied to arrive at the MRSD. The safety factor provides a margin of safety to protect the human subjects receiving the initial clinical dose. There is a "gray area" around what an appropriate safety factor is. For example, if an oncology drug is being tested immediately in cancer patients, then the risk to benefit ratio may be such that a safety factor of ~1 can be applied. In pediatric populations, or for a chronic, non-life threatening disease, the safety factor may be higher than 10. The FDA states that it "…is incumbent on the evaluator to clearly explain the reasoning behind the applied safety factor when it differs from the default value of 10, particularly if it is less than 10."

Example: An 8-week toxicology study was performed in dogs, and the NOAEL for the study was found to be 20 mg/kg.

$$HED = 20 \, mg/kg \times 0.541 = 10.82 \, mg/kg$$

The body weights for dog and human are assumed to be 10 and 60 kg, respectively. Eq. (4.74) can be used to calculate a conversion factor, or tables within the FDA guidance can be consulted (see Table 1 in Ref. [54]). Finally, a safety factor of ~10 is applied to the human NOAEL dose, resulting in a human starting dose of ~1.08 mg/kg, or ~65 mg for a 60-kg human.

The FDA guidance states that the linear mg/kg approach should be used for "proteins administered intravascularly with $M_r > 100,000 \, Da$" [54]. It is important to note that there are additional considerations for protein biologics that will be discussed later [55].

Example: An 8-week toxicology study was performed for a protein biologic in dogs and the NOAEL for the study was found to be 20 mg/kg.

$$HED = 20 \, mg/kg$$

A safety factor of ~10 is applied to the dose, resulting in a human starting dose of 2, or 120 mg for a 60-kg human.

Because monoclonal antibodies are designed to interact with human specific targets, they may not interact, or interact strongly, with similar biological targets in the preclinical (nonhuman) safety species. This can be a challenge in biologic development because the toxicity of monoclonal antibodies is often an exaggeration of the targeted pharmacological response. Thus, adequate preclinical toxicology assessment may not be possible due to a lack of cross-reactivity in the preclinical species. The example next underscores the importance of considering all pertinent data when setting the first dose for human studies.

Example: On March 13, 2006, the monoclonal antibody TGN1412 had just entered Phase I clinical trials and was administered to humans for the very first time [56]. The starting dose was low, ie, 0.1 mg/kg. Immediately after administration, there was rapid T-cell activation and cytokine release, followed by depletion of circulating T-cells. Symptoms were consistent with what is known as a "cytokine storm." Patients exhibited severe and life threatening toxicities, and by midnight after the first dose, all six patients (who started the day as normal healthy volunteers) were transferred to the intensive care unit. The patients received exhaustive cardiopulmonary support (including dialysis), a high dose of methylprednisolone, and an anti-interleukin-2 receptor antagonist antibody. For some time, the survival of all six patients was questionable.

What went wrong in this study? If we analyze the starting dose based upon the approach outlined in the FDA's guidance (MRSD; 54), the NOAEL from the cynomolgus monkey toxicology study was 50 mg/kg. The molecular weight of TGN1412 was approximately 150,000 Da, and thus the FDA guidance recommends that the scaling of dose between monkeys and humans be based upon the mg/kg approach. A 50 mg/kg dose in human would have been predicted to have been equivalent to 50 mg/kg dose in monkey. Using a safety factor of 10 would yield a safe starting dose of 5 mg/kg, or about 50-fold higher than the actual dose given to patients. At the time, a 0.1 mg/kg dose must have appeared to be a safe and conservative dose. However, one critical factor was not considered, and that factor was the targeted pharmacology.

As mentioned earlier, the toxicology of monoclonal antibodies is often due to exaggerated pharmacology. In addition to high receptor affinity, the rates of the antibody binding and unbinding, ie, on and off the target, are much slower than small molecules. As a consequence, pharmacological effects can be long in duration. This, in combination with the long $t_{1/2}$ of monoclonal antibodies, can result in toxicity associated with an exaggerated pharmacological response that may last dramatically longer than small molecules. After a single dose of TGN1412, two patients required intensive organ support for 8 and 16 days.

The Minimum Anticipated Biological Effect Level

An important lesson learned from the "TeGenero incident" (aforementioned) is that in addition to the NOAEL considerations, a safe human starting dose also must consider the pharmacological response. This is the concept of using a dose known as the minimal anticipated biological effect level or MABEL [57,58]. Retrospective analysis has demonstrated that, had a potential pharmacological response been taken into consideration for TGN1412, then the first dose in humans would have been lower [56]. The dose would have been lowered to a starting dose of 0.001–0.005 mg/kg or 20–100-fold lower. A discussion of the methods used to assess a pharmacologically active dose will not be presented here; however, an assessment must be made on a case-by-case basis, and no set methods will apply for all molecules. It is now recognized that, particularly for monoclonal antibodies, predicting a safe human dose is a process that

integrates all of the knowledge gained from toxicology studies (NOAEL), preclinical studies (to estimate human CL), the pharmacology, and the PK/PD studies.

Predicting a Human PK Profile

Once human PK parameters (CL, V_{ss}, $t_{1/2}$, F) have been estimated, it is possible to generate a plasma profile. While this can be particularly challenging depending on the preclinical data available, one of the advantages to modeling a human PK profile is that AUC and C_{max} can be estimated from the concentration versus time plot. When a profile is constructed, then the corresponding AUC and C_{max} values from the lowest preclinical NOAEL study can be compared and safety margins can be evaluated for each parameter, facilitating the selection of the safe starting dose in humans. In addition to safety margins, the estimated human PK profile provides an educated guess as to when efficacy may initially be observed in clinical trials. While safety assessment of the drug in people is the primary goal of Phase I clinical studies, it is highly desirable to see hints of efficacy or biomarker effects as early as possible.

Depending on the therapeutic indication, varying PK parameters can be targeted in the assessment of PD or efficacy. For example, clinical trials in oncology patients sometimes target the maintenance of baseline drug concentrations or C_{min}. In addition, clinical trials for a CNS indication, eg, Parkinson, Alzheimer, etc., may also target maintenance of a specified C_{min} in the brain or CSF. The estimated human PK profile can yield some idea of whether a C_{min} can be maintained such that receptor occupancy is significant with a specified dose and dosing interval. Specifically, if a drug has a high target receptor occupancy at 500 nM (eg, determined by in vitro or in vivo experiments), then the dose and the estimated human profile can be scaled up or down to assess which dose will yield a C_{min} equal to or greater than 500 nM (over the dosing interval). Thus, by modeling a human PK profile, estimates of C_{max} and AUC (and in some cases C_{min}) allow safety margin comparisons, selection of the safe starting clinical dose, and projection of an efficacious dose. As a general statement, it is advantageous to have an adequate safety margin (eg, 10×) between the projected C_{max} and AUC of the proposed starting dose and the lowest preclinical NOAEL, although this will vary with the targeted therapeutic indication.

Wajima et al. have published a method of predicting a human PK profile, eg, a C_{vss}-MRT method, that is simple and can be applied to PK profiles that exhibit one or multi-compartment kinetics [59]. Fura et al. extended this work and successfully used this approach to model oral human plasma PK curves [51]. Work also has been done with numerous monoclonal antibodies, and in general, human IV PK curves can be constructed with estimates of human V_{ss} and CL, in conjunction with an IV PK model fit to monkey plasma concentration data [60].

PRACTICAL CONSIDERATIONS

Formulations

The ideal dosing vehicle for IV administration of both small molecules and biologics is an isotonic saline solution (0.9% NaCl). However, it is not unusual for additional excipients to be needed (eg, due to poor solubility) [23], and the selections can be different for small molecules versus biologics. Additional complications to be considered in formulating biologics include but are not limited to sheer stress, aggregation, stability, adsorption to dosing syringe, and limited dosing volume (particularly for IV administration).

Small molecules have great diversity in physical properties, and their lipophilicity and solubility can vary significantly, ie, ClogP values range from <0 to >5, and solubilities range from <10 μg/mL to >10 mg/mL. As a consequence, it is not uncommon for small molecule IV or PO dosing solutions to contain nonaqueous cosolvents/excipients, such as dimethyl sulfoxide (DMSO), ethanol, Cremophor, propylene glycol, polyethylene glycol (PEG), cyclodextrins, or detergents, such as Tween 80 or sodium dodecyl sulfate (SDS; 23). Sometimes the oral vehicle of choice is a suspension, using one of the many available forms of modified cellulose.

It should also be noted that excipients or vehicles may have their own in vivo effects, including but not limited to hemolysis and effects on transporters and enzymes responsible for clearing drugs, as well as effects on the immune system. Most importantly, these agents can have their own toxicological profiles, and their effects may be species-dependent. For example Tween 80 can cause anaphylactic shock and death after IV administration to dogs. Thus, in toxicological and pharmacological studies, it is very important to distinguish the toxicological effects of the experimental drug from those of the vehicle alone. This underscores the importance of using the simplest vehicles possible so as not to confound the findings of the safety study.

Dosing Volumes

Intravascular (IV) dosing. Generally, IV doses are delivered in the smallest volumes possible: 1 mL/kg is not unusual for rats, dogs, and monkeys. However, mice require larger dosing volumes (5 or 10 mL/kg) to have a reasonable volume to dose, eg, 5 mL/kg for a 20-g mouse equates to dosing a volume of ~100 μL. Dosing volume affects dosing concentrations, and thus, a 10-mg/kg dose for a mouse may require a dose solution concentration of 1–2 mg/mL, while the same dose in a dog (at 1 mL/kg) would require a dose solution concentration of 10 mg/mL. This type of discrepancy in dosing solution concentration potentially affects vehicle selection

TABLE 4.4 Administration Volumes Considered to be Good Practice [61]

Species	Routes and Volumes (mL/kg)				
	PO	IV (Bolus)	SC	IP	IM
Mouse	10	5	10	20	0.05
Rat	10	5	5	10	0.1
Rabbit	10	2	1	5	0.25
Mini-pig	10	2.5	1	1	0.25
Marmoset	10	2.5	2	<20[a]	0.25
Macaque	5	2	2	<10[a]	0.25
Dog	5	2.5	1	1	0.25

[a]Volume given in mL per site.

for small molecules, depending on the physicochemical properties of the particular compound to be dosed.

Extravascular dosing. In addition to IV dosing, the volumes used for PO or SC administration are also affected by the physiochemical properties of the compound to be dosed. Low aqueous solubility may necessitate larger dose volumes, while the need for repeat dosing may limit the volume that can be delivered on a daily basis. Dose ranging studies, eg, 10–1000 mg/kg, may require larger dose volumes to facilitate delivery of the doses on the high end of the range. It has been shown that large dose volumes (eg, 40 mL/kg) may exceed stomach volume, depending on the species, resulting in immediate passage into the small intestine [61]. Larger volumes may also result in reflux or emesis, although rats are incapable of emesis. Table 4.4 lists some examples of desired target volumes along with maximal values. The lower limit of volume administration is determined by compound solubility and the ability to accurately measure the volume administered.

Fed or Fasted State

The simultaneous presence of both food and drug in the GI tract can alter compound solubility and availability, affecting the rate and extent to which the drug is absorbed into systemic circulation. In some instances, food improves absorption, while in others, absorption is inhibited. It is not unusual for the early single dose PK studies to be performed in fasted animals, with the exception of mice (due to the high metabolism rate for this species, fasting overnight is considered by many to be unethical, as it induces a state of starvation). In general, toxicology and repeat dose studies are often performed with fed animals, and thus, it is useful to evaluate food effects in pilot PK studies, so that the potential impact of food is known. In addition, it is important to have some early expectations of the potential for food effects in the clinic. Moreover, the absence of food effects in preclinical PK may obviate the need to evaluate food effects in the clinic, depending on the targeted patient population.

Sampling Time Points

The minimum number of blood time points to collect within a 24-h window should be approximately seven. To adequately define an oral plasma concentration versus time curve, at least two points should be collected to define the absorption phase, an additional time point at or near T_{max}, and at least three time points are needed in the declining or terminal phase of the curve. Some commercial PK analysis software will not calculate λ_z from the declining portion of the profile unless there are at least three consecutive declining concentration time points. In addition, some software stipulates that the three points cannot include C_{max}. The suggestion of seven time points for an oral concentration versus time profile is somewhat oversimplified, and the number is actually dependent on several variables, including the shape of the PK or TK curve; the half-life of the compound; the number of animals in the study; and the amount of volume that can reasonably be taken from any given animal. The time points required for an IV profile can be less, eg, ~5 time points minimum, and this too is highly dependent on how well these data points reflect the shape of the plasma concentration versus time profile. If adequate PK data is not available, it may be helpful to initially run a small pilot study to determine the best sampling times.

Blood Sampling Limitations

Table 4.5 lists some practical blood volumes that may be withdrawn from a single animal. The sensitivity of the bioanalytical assay used to measure drug concentrations, eg, the lower limit of quantitation, may play a role in determining the blood sampling volumes. The toxicologist will likely collect additional (non-TK) blood samples to look at clinical chemistries. Generally, total blood draws target ~10% of the total blood volume in an

TABLE 4.5 Blood Draw Volume Limits and Necessary Recovery Times [61]

Single PK/TK Sample		Multiple TK Sampling	
% Total Blood Volume Removed	Recovery Time	% Total Blood Volume Removed[a]	Recovery Time
7.5	7 days	7.5	7 days
10	14 days	10–15	14 days
15	28 days	20	21 days

[a]Within 24-h period.

TABLE 4.6 Typical Body Weights, Total Blood Volumes, and Blood Sampling Volumes Across Preclinical Species [61]

Species	Typical Weights (kg)	Blood Volume[a] (mL/kg)	Total Blood Volume[b] (mL)	10% Blood Volume (mL)
Mouse	0.025	63–80	1.8	0.18
Rat	0.25	58–70	16	1.6
Marmoset	0.350	58–82	25	2.5
Rabbit	4	44–70	224	~22
Monkey (Rhesus)	5	44–67	280	28
Monkey (Cynomolgus)	5	55–75	325	~32
Dog (Beagle)	10	79–90	850	85
Mini-pig	15	61–68	975	~98

[a]Range of means.
[b]Calculated by multiplying the typical weight by the mid-range blood volume.

animal within a 7-day period. Table 4.6 presents typical body weights and blood volumes across the preclinical species.

Alternate study designs are often employed to mitigate the conflict between blood requirements for PK or TK data versus the blood sampling limitations from an animal health standpoint, particularly for rodents. One scenario occasionally employed in rat toxicology studies is to create subsets of animals in each dose group, with each subset only providing two to three of the desired blood time points. The collective data set from all subsets is then used to construct a composite PK curve for analysis. This can facilitate the evaluation of both toxicology and TK from the same animals. Another scenario is to use satellite groups of animals, separate from the toxicology animals but dosed in an identical fashion, to mitigate blood sampling limitations. It is quite common to use a single mouse for each blood sampling time point, ie, terminal non-serial blood sampling. If the bioanalytical assay is particularly sensitive, it may be possible to collect two time points per mouse. Thus, a seven-point TK curve with data points in duplicate may require 7–14 mice, and if there is sampling at the beginning and end of the toxicology study to evaluate changes in the TK with repeat dosing, the number of required animals would double. The number of time points in any given study is a balance between animal resources, the sensitivity of the bioanalytical assay, the compound-specific half-life, and the number of points that a pharmacokineticist decides is necessary for adequate TK profiling.

Site of Blood Sampling

It is important that blood sampling occurs at a different site (or portal) as compared to the dosing site, particularly for IV administration. Compounds that are lipophilic or prone to nonspecific binding, eg, preferential binding to plastic, can linger in the tubing or at the dose site. This potentially results in artificially elevated drug concentrations, particularly at the early sampling time points, and skewed PK parameter estimation.

Normalization of Clearance Values to Liver Blood Flow

While small molecule drugs are cleared or eliminated predominantly by the liver and kidneys, a high percentage are cleared primarily by biotransformation, eg, metabolism, in the liver. Since one of the primary considerations determining the extent of hepatic clearance (CL_H) is liver blood flow (Q_H), it is quite common in the pharmaceutical industry to compare the IV clearances of small molecules to liver blood flow. This leads to the concept of an extraction ratio (ER; [9]) which is defined as follows for the liver:

$$ER = CL_H / Q_H \qquad (4.76)$$

The value of ER can range from 0 to 1, with an ER > 0.7 corresponding to a high clearance compound, and ER < 0.3 generally considered to describe a low clearance compound. When the clearance exceeds liver blood flow, this is an indication that other organs may be involved in the clearance of that particular molecule.

Biologics can also be eliminated in the liver and kidney, as well as other organs capable of catabolism of proteins, eg, muscle, skin, blood, and the site of administration. In addition, the biological target itself may contribute to elimination (via receptor endocytosis). When the analogous ERs are calculated for biologics, they almost always fall into the low clearance category, particularly for monoclonal antibodies. Note that for biologics, clearance is generally inversely related to molecular weight, ie, CL can be high for small proteins.

Evaluation for the Presence of Anti-Drug Antibodies (ADAs)

It is not uncommon for a therapeutic human-based biologic to stimulate an immune response in the preclinical species used for PK, pharmacology, and toxicology studies, especially subsequent to multiple dose administration [4,5]. ADAs are more likely to be observed after SC dosing relative to IM or IV dosing. Other reasons for immunogenicity may relate to the manufacturing process, the storage conditions, or the formulation, eg, aggregate formation over time.

Often, an observed preclinical immune response does not translate to the clinic, so these observations do not necessarily impact development of the biologic drug candidate. However, an immune response may affect the ability to fully test the toxicology of the biologic and to establish safety margins prior to dosing in the clinic. In certain cases, preclinical safety species can develop ADAs that increase the clearance of the biological agent being tested [62]. In these cases, the ADA is said to be a "clearing" ADA. Thus, at the end of the toxicology study, when clearing ADAs are present, the increased drug clearance may reduce exposure over time, eg, day 28 versus day 1, eroding the *AUC*-based safety margins.

In addition to clearing ADAs, the following are also possible: (1) sustaining ADAs; and (2) neutralizing ADAs [63,64]. A sustaining ADA decreases the drug clearance by binding to the drug and keeping it in circulation longer, ie, protecting it from or slowing the processes of elimination. The implication for a toxicology study is that when sustaining ADAs are present, the recovery assessment period at the end of the study may have to be lengthened to see the true reversibility of the toxological effect(s). Moreover, increased levels of drug may lead to an exaggerated pharmacological effect. As a consequence, the dose levels may need to be altered to account for greater accumulation or increased exposure.

Neutralizing ADAs bind the drug and reduce its ability to elicit a pharmacological effect. They can be either clearing or sustaining, but in either case, the pharmacological activity of the biologic can be reduced. This may be problematic because the toxicology of biologics (as noted previously) is often due to exaggerated pharmacology. Thus, the inability to see a pharmacological response in preclinical species reduces the effectiveness of the safety testing of the drug candidate. In some cases, this is a moot point because the high specificity of the biologics for the human target may preclude interaction with the analogous target in preclinical species.

The detection of ADAs can be compromised when high concentrations of the biologic are present in the serum or plasma samples. One method to avoid this complication is to analyze the samples after cessation of dosing, ie, after a recovery period. If dosing stops on the last week of a 4-week toxicology study, then ADAs may be more detectable in the subsequent weeks. The timing of the blood sampling during a recovery period would be highly dependent on the expected half-life of the biologic, eg, it takes three half-lives to eliminate 92.5% of the dosed compound. Given the long half-lives of many monoclonal antibodies, this consideration may be especially important in the study design.

In summary, alterations in the PK profile of biologics due to immune-mediated clearance mechanisms may affect the TK concentration versus time profiles, exposure, pharmacology, and consequently, the interpretation of the preclinical toxicity data.

Data Evaluation: Look at a Visual Representation of the Data (eg, Graphs)

Determination of λ_z

Whether estimating the slope of the terminal phase (λ_z) by hand, in a spreadsheet, or within PK software, it is important to visually examine the data in the terminal phase. Several points need to be discussed in this regard. The first point involves the estimation of the true terminal phase, ie, the phase where elimination is the primary contributor to the decline in plasma concentration versus time profile. To estimate this phase, it is sometimes easier to plot the data on a semi-log scale. Fig. 4.6 shows two plots of plasma concentration versus time data. In Fig. 4.6A, the data points used to determine λ_z are easy to identify. However, the profile in Fig. 4.6B is biphasic, ie, there are two phases that are apparent. In this latter plot, the last four data points were used to calculate λ_z, and the first three data points were ascribed to distribution into a second compartment.

Often there is a judgment call required to determine which data points best define λ_z. Some PK software iteratively estimates the λ_z value by fitting a regression line through increasing numbers of terminal data points and selecting for the best data fit. In other words, the regression line is fit to the last three points, then the last four points, etc., and the resulting r^2 values are compared. The linear regression with the highest r^2 value is the one that is associated with the reported λ_z value. The advantage to this automated approach is the convenience when evaluating large data sets with multiple subjects and multiple days of PK or TK data. However, there are instances when anomalous data in the terminal phase can bias λ_z estimates. In these cases, it is better to manually select the data points used to estimate λ_z. Under circumstances where the reported r^2 value is less than 0.8, it is important to highlight parameters that depend on λ_z, eg, $t_{1/2}$, V_d, and $AUC_{0-\infty}$, and/or to urge caution when interpreting the values of these parameters.

Finally, visual inspection of the last few data points in the terminal phase of the IV curve in Fig. 4.17A suggests that the final concentration may be anomalously high. Thus, calculation of the $AUC_{t_{last}-\infty}$, based upon this anomalous data point, would generate an artificially elevated value. One approach to avoid these potential inaccuracies would be to use the last *predicted* (vs. observed) values to estimate $AUC_{t_{last}-\infty}$. In Fig. 4.17B, the regression line through three of the last four points predicts a final concentration that is more consistent with the rest of the data in the terminal phase, thereby providing what may be a more accurate estimate of $AUC_{t_{last}-\infty}$ and therefore $AUC_{0-\infty}$. When a predicted final concentration is used, parameters, such as AUC and V_z are sometimes called $AUC_{0-\infty}$ or V_z "predicted." Generally, it is advisable to use "$AUC_{0-\infty}$ predicted" when the terminal phase

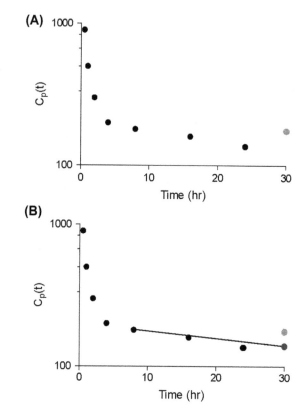

FIGURE 4.17 Plasma concentration versus time plot on a semi-log scale with a potential anomalous terminal concentration.

of the PK/TK curve appears to contain anomalous data. However, there are always exceptions, and one possible exception involves a compound that is subject to enterohepatic recirculation, eg, biliary excretion of compound into the intestine followed by reabsorption. In this case, it is possible that the rise in the final plasma concentration in the last data point is real, as the compound reabsorbs and then reappears in the systemic circulation at a later time point. In contrast, the presence of clearing ADAs may decrease monoclonal antibody half-life measured from the terminal portion of the PK/TK curve. In this instance the later time point concentration values will be lower than expected or the terminal slope may be steeper than expected. In either example, once anomalous data have been identified, the PK/TK investigator will have to make a judgment call; again, it is emphasized that plotting the data for visual examination is a critical first step to recognizing when additional data interpretation is necessary.

Monitor the "AUC Percent (%) Extrapolated"

In general, when reporting $AUC_{0-\infty}$, the contribution of the extrapolated area, eg, $AUC_{t_{last}-\infty}$, to the overall area should not contribute significant error. The amount of $AUC_{0-\infty}$ that is extrapolated is frequently referred to as the "AUC % extrapolated." It is often accepted that when the AUC % extrapolated exceeds 20–25%, there may be significant error associated with $AUC_{0-\infty}$ estimation. To expand on this further, if significant error is associated with the reported $AUC_{0-\infty}$ value, then other PK parameters that depend on $AUC_{0-\infty}$, including CL and V_{ss}, may also be in error. In PK and TK reports, the "AUC % extrapolated" should be included in the reported parameters. Again, if visual inspection of the plasma concentration versus time profile suggests that the terminal phase of elimination has not been adequately sampled, it will be particularly important to closely inspect the percent of extrapolated area as well as the impact on estimates of $AUC_{0-\infty}$, and CL, and V_{ss}.

Examine Outliers

As discussed earlier for biologics, it is possible for preclinical species to develop an immune response to the test compound. This may happen in one study animal or in all animals. Regardless, it is important to visualize the data so that subjects with confirmed ADAs can be correlated with unusual PK profiles and parameter estimates. These comparisons may be the justification for PK reanalysis of subpopulations, eg, subjects with or without ADAs, within the overall study.

Evaluate Potential Changes in TK Parameters on the Last Study Day Versus Day 1

For a biologic, when the TK parameters change between day 1 and the last study day, it is quite often due to ADAs, as discussed earlier. If exposure has decreased by the last day, this may be due to increased CL over the course of the study. Conversely, increased exposure may be the result of decreasing CL with time. Clearing or sustaining ADAs may be responsible for changes in CL over time.

For a small molecule, drug exposure may decrease substantially over time, possibly due to induction (or upregulation) of the associated clearance pathways. As mentioned earlier, small molecules are frequently eliminated by metabolism in the liver, and thus induction of liver drug metabolizing enzyme(s) would be a reasonable first explanation for decreased exposure over time. Some small molecules bind to nuclear receptors, which in turn influence the expression, and consequently, the amount of phase I (eg, CYPs) and phase II (eg, glucronlytransferases) drug metabolizing enzymes. There are several consequences to this phenomenon. First, this decrease in exposure at the end of the study will reduce the human safety margin determined from the TK studies, which as discussed will affect the starting dose in the clinic. A low clinical starting dose can significantly affect the time required to dose up to drug levels that correspond with early signs of efficacy in the clinic.

Second, many patients take multiple concurrent medications, also known as "polypharmacy." If one medication causes induction of a clearance pathway(s)

for another drug (or itself), this may result in decreased exposure for that drug, and thus decreased or compromised efficacy. When drug exposure decreases over time in a multiple dose toxicology study, this often leads to additional in vitro studies aimed at enhancing the understanding of whether this liability could potentially translate to human enzyme induction in the clinic. Moreover, decreased TK exposure over time may lead to greater regulatory agency scrutiny as the drug is progressed in clinical trials (eg, drug–drug interaction studies may be required earlier in development).

In contrast, drug exposure for a small molecule may increase substantially across the time course of a TK study. Depending on the estimated half-life and dosing interval, this increase may have been expected [see Eq. (4.50)]. However, in some cases, the increase in exposure is unexpected. In such instances, it is important to rule out a mechanism, such as time-dependent inhibition of a drug metabolizing enzyme(s), and this is particularly relevant for CYP-mediated elimination pathways. Such enzymatic inhibition is generally irreversible, meaning that recovery of enzymatic activity occurs only after new protein synthesis by the body (days). Thus, when the activity of a drug metabolizing enzyme is significantly inhibited, a critical clearance pathway may be affected, resulting in slower clearance and therefore greater exposure. Again, similar to induction, the effect on the PK parameters of both the drug itself and those drugs that may be concurrently administered are of concern.

Mibefradil (Posicor; for the treatment of hypertension) is an example of a potent mechanism-based inhibitor of CYP3A4. Mibefradil administration in patients resulted in CYP3A4-mediated drug–drug interactions, some of them severe, and ultimately the drug was withdrawn from the market in 1998 [65]. Similarly, L-754,934 was a compound developed as a highly selective inhibitor of HIV-1 protease. Preclinical in vivo experiments with this compound demonstrated a decrease in clearance from 87 mL/min/kg after the first dose to 25 mL/min/kg after the last dose (7-day IV study; [66]). Subsequent in vitro experiments showed that this compound was an extremely potent mechanism-based inhibitor of CYP3A4, and further development of the compound was discontinued [67].

Dose Linearity Versus Dose Proportionality

When PK is "well behaved" or dose proportional, the parameters CL, V_{ss}, $t_{1/2}$, and %F are constant across a large dose range, so a 10- or 100-fold increase in dose will correspond to a 10- or 100-fold increase in exposure, eg, C_{max} and AUC. When this condition is met, then it is valid to state that "exposure increases in a dose proportional manner." As a specific example, doses of 30, 100, and 300 mg/kg would be expected to result in dose proportional *AUC* increases of ~100, 333, and 1000 µg h/mL, respectively. Dose proportional PK should not be confused with linear PK, which is characterized by linear increases in C_{max} and *AUC* with increasing dose, but the changes are not necessarily dose proportional. For example, if doses of 30, 100, and 300 mg/kg resulted in the *AUC*s of 40, 70, and 150 µg h/mL, respectively, the PK for this drug is linear but not dose proportional.

To determine whether PK is dose proportional, the investigator must examine the increases in exposure with dose, and they must also take into consideration the variability of the data. One graphical method that can be used is to plot dose on the *x*-axis versus a dose-normalized exposure parameter on the *y*-axis (eg, *AUC*/dose). The resulting data points should approximate a flat line if the *AUC* increases in a dose-proportional manner (slope=0). In Fig. 4.18A and B, plots of dose versus dose-normalized *AUC* values are shown. Also displayed in both panels is a solid regression line, dotted lines representing a 90% confidence interval, and vertical bars that illustrate the standard deviation around each data point. In Fig. 4.18A, the regression line is not flat, ie, the slope is nonzero even with the error taken into account, and therefore, *AUC* is said to increase in a greater than dose-proportional manner. The regression line shown in Fig. 4.18B is also not flat. However, due to variability of the data, it cannot be stated whether the line is flat or not (note: more rigorous statistical analyses can be used to test whether the slope of the regression line deviates significantly from 0). Thus, the conclusion from Fig. 4.18B would be that the increases in *AUC* are dose proportional within the variability of the data.

Plasma and Urine Metabolite Identification

The standards for testing the safety of metabolites (MIST) have changed over time for small molecules. Originally, if a major circulating metabolite was detected in humans, the safety of this metabolite was considered adequately tested as long as the preclinical safety (toxicology) species also had the same metabolite in circulation, independent of the relative concentration of the metabolite. A quantitative comparison of metabolite exposure in human versus the preclinical safety species was not officially part of the safety assessment consideration. In a seminal Pharma position paper by Baille et al., it was proposed that safety assessment of metabolites should be more rigorously defined [68]. This paper argued that major metabolites should potentially be monitored in select toxicological studies. Not only should the major metabolites be monitored, but PK exposure parameters should be used to quantitatively estimate how much these metabolites may or may not have contributed to the observed toxicology. Three years

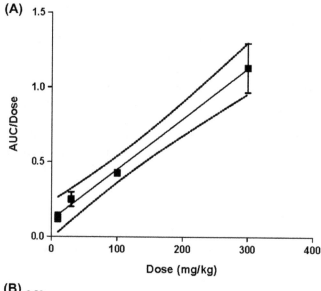

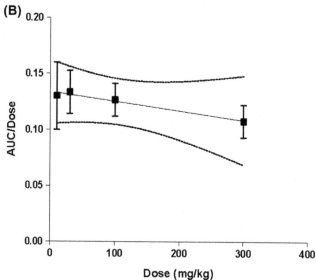

FIGURE 4.18 **Plots of dose-normalized *AUC* versus dose.** Shown in each plot is *AUC/D* versus dose data, a regression line, and the 90% confidence intervals. Panel (A) presents exposure data that increase in a greater than dose proportional fashion. Panel (B) presents exposure data that appear to increase in a dose proportional fashion, within the variability of the data.

later, the FDA responded with a draft guidance on safety testing of drug metabolites, followed by a full guidance in 2008 [69]. In this guidance, independent safety studies were recommended for major human metabolites that were unique (disproportionately produced in human vs. animals) or when safety had not been adequately assessed in the standard toxicology studies. This recommendation applied to "major" metabolites in human circulation that accounted for greater than 10% of total systemic exposure of parent drug at steady state. Thus, if the *AUC* of a metabolite measured in human (>10% of parent drug *AUC*) is 1200 µg h/mL, then the safety of the metabolite is considered to have been tested in preclinical species if the exposure was found to be 1200 µg h/mL or greater. To avoid confusion for the reader, this guidance was intended for small molecules and does not consider biologics.

In response to this paradigm shift in metabolite safety assessment, both pilot and good laboratory practice (GLP) TK studies are an excellent opportunity (one may strongly argue a necessity) to perform exploratory metabolite profiling and identification studies. Profiling of preclinical plasma and urine provides a first look at in vivo metabolites. These data, in combination with in vitro metabolism studies, provide an initial assessment of the strength of an in vitro–in vivo correlation for metabolite formation. For example, if in vitro studies indicated that metabolite A was the major metabolite formed in liver microsome incubations for rat, dog, and humans, and metabolite A was a prominent metabolite in rat and dog plasma (and urine) profiles, this would strongly support the monitoring of metabolite A (in addition to parent compound) in the clinic as well as in preclinical safety or toxicology studies. The correct decision for metabolite monitoring for each individual project will require the experience and judgment of the investigator as well as agreement from the development team and management. However, there is little doubt that monitoring of significant preclinical metabolites in circulation during toxicology testing is almost an obligatory function.

Determination of Intrinsic Clearance (CL_i) by the Half-Life Method

As noted previously, this method is the most widely used procedure in the pharmaceutical industry to estimate CL_i. The in vitro half-life method uses a single concentration of compound (small molecule), and consequently the ease of automation for the incubations is much simpler, allowing for the screening of hundreds of compounds in the "discovery" stage of drug development. Buffer, compound, and enzyme are added to a single tube or well, the metabolism is started, usually by the addition of NADPH, and aliquots are taken over the course of time. With each aliquot, the enzymatic reaction is stopped (generally by diluting the aliquot into organic solvent), and the amount of drug remaining is then typically measured by LC-MS/MS. Next, the data are plotted as the log of the percent drug remaining versus time. From this graph, the half-life of compound disappearance is determined, which is subsequently inserted into the following:

$$CL_{\text{in vitro}} = \frac{0.693}{t_{1/2} \cdot \text{mic protein conc}} \qquad (4.77)$$

where $t_{1/2}$ is the half-life of drug disappearance and "mic protein conc" is simply the concentration of microsomal protein (typically liver) used in the in vitro incubation.

This equation is not derived here, and the interested reader is referred to alternate references [32,70].

Two key points must be made:

1. The single concentration used in the incubations must be ~1/10 of the K_m value or lower for Eq. (4.77) to be applicable. Thus, low concentrations should be used for this type of experiment. In general, most reactions catalyzed by CYP proteins have K_m values in the 5–100-μM range, consequently making a concentration of 0.5–1 μM useful for screening. However, the reader is warned that there are exceptions, and some compounds may have lower K_m values.
2. In the case where the plot of drug remaining (log) versus time yields data that are best described by a curved plot, the first time points (which are hopefully linear) should be used to calculate the $t_{1/2}$. In such instances, this curvature may be due to in vitro artifacts, such as product inhibition, and it is more accurate to use the initial linear rate.

Evaluation of Preclinical In Vitro–In Vivo Correlations for CL

In addition to the discussion in the Estimating CL Using a Physiologically Based Approach section, it is suggested that the scientist evaluate whether the preclinical in vitro–in vivo correlations are better with or without the incorporation of plasma protein binding data. In some instances, the equilibrium between bound and free drug may be so rapid that the protein binding data are not a critical part of the preclinical or human CL prediction. In the authors' experience, the observed in vivo preclinical CL values generally fall somewhere between the predicted CL_h values obtained with and without the incorporation of the f_u data. If the in vitro–in vivo correlation is poor, ie, the differences in CL observed versus CL_h are at least threefold, or the predicted CL_h values are inconsistently higher or lower than the observed preclinical CL values, additional factors may need to be considered prior to accepting the predicted human CL_h. A partial list of confounding factors are clearance by non-hepatic organs (GI, lung, kidney), microsomal protein binding, nonspecific binding, instability of enzyme during the in vitro preparation, or inhibition of drug metabolizing enzymes. The scope of the discussion surrounding this issue is extensive with a correspondingly large body of literature. The interested reader should be aware that the discussion in this chapter only serves as an introduction.

What is a Good Projection of Human Clearance?

Generally, when a pharmacokineticist can produce a clearance projection within twofold of the observed value, this is acceptable. It may not be ideal, but it is realistic in light of the significant error that is inherently involved in human clearance projections.

CONCLUSIONS

This chapter has presented some introductory concepts in PK/TK with the inclusion of basic PK equations. In addition to an introduction to PK/TK, another chapter objective was to make the reader aware of some of the differences between small and large molecules. Moreover, it was also intended that the presentation of some of the practical considerations (at the end of the chapter) would hopefully stimulate the reader to think more broadly, beyond the basics of PK. The practical considerations are also some of the issues that the authors of this chapter have faced during their career in the pharmaceutical industry.

As a matter of practicality, the pharmaceutical industry setting is highly collaborative because it requires the concerted effort of many fields of expertise to successfully discover and develop a drug. It is probable that the readers of this book will spend at least some part of their career in an industrial setting. In drug development, toxicologists, pharmacologists, and pharmacokineticists have to work in parallel, and it is therefore incumbent on the professionals within each area to become more familiar with the process as a whole. In addition, investigators must become modality independent, that is, a desirable target may be approached with either a small molecule drug, a monoclonal antibody, or both. Consequently, it is important that the successful project representative have some knowledge of either drug development approach.

When setting safe doses in the clinic, for monoclonal antibodies in particular, the TeGenero incident [56] has demonstrated the need to integrate knowledge of pharmacology, toxicology and PK into one cohesive method. In addition, the FDA (and the pharmaceutical industry) has advocated the increased use of biomarkers in the clinical setting to establish efficacy sooner rather than later. In response to these changes, the field of PK and PK/PD has grown in importance in recent years. One deficiency of the current chapter was that PK/PD was not a subject that was introduced. As a consequence, the reader in encouraged to investigate this topic on their own and become at least somewhat familiar with the basic concepts [30]. In the past, it was possible to be somewhat specialized within a pharmaceutical organization; however, the age of the specialist has been over for some time now. In the future it will be important for young investigators to be broadly based in knowledge and skill to meet the demands of an increasingly complex development and regulatory environment.

References

[1] Gibaldi M. Preface. 4th ed. Biopharmaceutics and clinical pharmacokineticsMalvern, PA: Lea and Febiger; 1991. p. vii–i.

[2] Baumann A. Early development of therapeutic biologics – pharmacokinetics. Curr Drug Met 2006;7:15–21.

[3] Hellriegel E, Bjornsson T, Hauck W. Interpatient variability in bioavailability is related to the extent of absorption: implications for bioavailability and bioequivalence studies. Clin Pharmacol Ther 1996;60:601–7.

[4] Tang L, Meibohm B. Pharmacokinetics of peptides and proteins. In: Meibohm B, editor. Pharmacokinetics and pharmacodynamics of biotech drugs: principles and case studies in drug development. Weinheim, Germany: Wiley-VCH; 2006. p. 17–43.

[5] Kuester K, Kloft C. Pharmacokinetics of monoclonal antibodies. In: Meibohm B, editor. Pharmacokinetics and pharmacodynamics of biotech drugs: principles and case studies in drug development. Weinheim, Germany: Wiley-VCH; 2006. p. 45–91.

[6] Gibaldi M, Perrier D. One-compartment model. In: Swarbrick J, editor. Pharmacokinetics, revised and expanded. 2nd ed. New York: Marcel Dekker, Inc.; 1982. p. 409–17.

[7] Gabrielsson J, Weiner D. Pharmacokinetic concepts. 4th ed. Pharmacokinetic and pharmacodynamic data analysis: concepts and applicationsStockholm, Sweden: Swedish Pharmaceutical Press; 2000. p. 11–224.

[8] Gibaldi M, Perrier D. Clearance concepts. In: Swarbrick J, editor. Pharmacokinetics, revised and expanded. 2nd ed. New York: Marcel Dekker, Inc.; 1982. p. 319–53.

[9] Rowland M, Towzer T. Elimination. 3rd ed. Clinical pharmacokinetics: concepts and applicationsMedia, PA: Lippincott, Williams, and Wilkins; 1995. p. 156–83.

[10] Jusko W. Guidelines for collection and analysis of pharmacokinetic data. In: Burton M, Shaw L, Schentag J, Evans W, editors. Applied pharmacokinetics and pharmacodynamics: principles of therapeutic drug monitoring. 4th ed. Baltimore, MD: Lippincott, Williams, and Wilkins; 2006. p. 8–29.

[11] Toutain PL, Bousquet-Mélou A. Volumes of distribution. J Vet Pharmacol Therap 2004;27:441–535.

[12] Package insert for Sensipar®. Available online at: http://pi.amgen.com/united_states/sensipar/sensipar_pi_hcp_english.pdf.

[13] Sensipar Pharmacology and Toxicology Review of NDA (NDA # 21-688; p. 31). 2004. Available online at: http://www.accessdata.fda.gov/drugsatfda_docs/nda/2004/21-688.pdf_Sensipar_Pharmr_P1.pdf.

[14] Belpaire F, Bogaert M. The fate of xenobiotics in living organisms. In: Wermuth CG, editor. The practice of medicinal chemistry. 3rd ed. San Diego, CA: Elsevier/Academic Press; 2003. p. 501–16.

[15] Kwon Y. Pharmacokinetic study design and data interpretation. In: Handbook of essential pharmacokinetics, pharmacodynamics, and drug metabolism for industrial scientists. New York: Kluwer Academic/Plenum Publishers; 2001. p. 3–28.

[16] Hinderling P. Red blood cells: a neglected compartment in pharmacokinetics and pharmacodynamics. Pharmacol Rev 1997; 49:279–95.

[17] Jusko WJ, Chiang ST. Distribution volume related to body weight and protein binding. J Pharm Sci 1982;71:469–70.

[18] Pharmacokinetic data. In: Goodman Gilman A, Rall T, Nies A, Taylor P, editors. The pharmacological basis of therapeutics. 8th ed. Elmsford, NY: Pergamon Press; 2000. p. 1655–735.

[19] Rowland M, Towzer T. Intravenous dose. 3rd ed. Clinical pharmacokinetics: concepts and applicationsMedia, PA: Lippincott, Williams, and Wilkins; 1995. p. 18–33.

[20] Nakao K, Sugawara A, Morii N, Sakamoto M, Yamada T, Itoh H, et al. The pharmacokinetics of alpha-human atrial natriuretic polypeptide in healthy subjects. Eur J Clin Pharmacol 1986; 31:101–3.

[21] Rowland M, Towzer T. Mean residence time (appendix I–D). 3rd ed. Clinical pharmacokinetics: concepts and applicationsMedia, PA: Lippincott, Williams, and Wilkins; 1995. p. 485–7.

[22] Rowland M, Towzer T. Extravascular dose. 3rd ed. Clinical pharmacokinetics: concepts and applicationsMedia, PA: Lippincott, Williams, and Wilkins; 1995. p. 34–50.

[23] Neervannan S. Preclinical formulations for discovery and toxicology: physicochemical challenges. Expert Opin Drug Metab Toxicol 2006;2(5):715–31.

[24] Paine MF, Hart HL, Ludington SS, Haining RL, Rettie AE, Zeldin DC. The human intestinal cytochrome P450 'Pie.'. Drug Metab Disp 2006;34:880–6.

[25] MacDougall IC, Gray SJ, Elston O, Breen C, Jenkins B, Browne J, et al. Pharmacokinetics of novel Erythropoiesis stimulating protein compared with Epoetin Alfa in dialysis patients. J Am Soc Nephrol 1999;10:2392–5.

[26] Rowland M, Towzer T. Absorption. 3rd ed. Clinical pharmacokinetics: concepts and applicationsMedia, PA: Lippincott, Williams, and Wilkins; 1995. p. 119–36.

[27] Kwon Y. Absorption. Handbook of essential pharmacokinetics, pharmacodynamics, and drug metabolism for industrial scientistsNew York: Kluwer Academic/Plenum Publishers; 2001. p. 35–72.

[28] Thron CD. Linearity and superposition in pharmacokinetics. Pharmacol Rev 1974;26:3–31.

[29] Bonate PL. The art of modeling. Pharmacokinetic-pharmacodynamic modeling and simulationNew York: Springer; 2005. p. 1–56.

[30] Gabrielsson J, Weiner D. Pharmacodynamic concepts. 4th ed. Pharmacokinetic and pharmacodynamic data analysis: concepts and applicationsStockholm, Sweden: Swedish Pharmaceutical Press; 2000. p. 225–360.

[31] Kwon Y. Predicting pharmacokinetics in humans. Handbook of essential pharmacokinetics, pharmacodynamics, and drug metabolism for industrial scientistsNew York: Kluwer Academic/Plenum Publishers; 2001. p. 207–28.

[32] Obach R, Baxter J, Liston T, Silber M, Jones B, MacIntyre F, et al. The prediction of human pharmacokinetic parameters from preclinical and in vitro metabolism data. J Pharmacol Exp Ther 1997;283:46–58.

[33] De Buck SS, Sinha VK, Fenu LA, Nijsen MJ, Mackie CE, Gilissen RAHJ. Prediction of human pharmacokinetics using physiologically based modeling: a retrospective analysis of 26 clinically tested drugs. Drug Metab Disp 2007;35:1766–80.

[34] Mahmood I, Balian J. Interspecies scaling: predicting clearance of drugs in humans. Three different approaches. Xenobiotica 1996;26:887–95.

[35] Sharma V, McNeill JH. To scale or not to scale: the principles of dose extrapolation. Br J Pharmacol 2009;157:907–21.

[36] Mahmood I. Prediction of clearance, volume of distribution and half-life by allometric scaling and by use of plasma concentrations predicted from pharmacokinetic constants: a comparative study. J Pharm Pharmacol 1999;51:905–10.

[37] Mahmood I, Balian J. A comparative study for the prediction of clearance and volume using two or more than two species. Life Sci 1996;59:579–85.

[38] Boxenbaum H, D'Souza R. Interspecies pharmacokinetic scaling, biological design, and neoteny. Adv Drug Res 1990;19:139–96.

[39] Tang H, Mayersohn M. Accuracy of allometrically predicted pharmacokinetic parameters in humans: role of species selection. Drug Metab Disp 2005;33:1288–93.

[40] Tang H, Mayersohn M. A novel model for prediction of human drug clearance by allometric scaling. Drug Metab Disp 2005;33:1297–303.

[41] Tang H, Hussain A, Leal M, Mayersohn M, Fluhler E. Interspecies prediction of human drug clearance based on scaling data from one or two animal species. Drug Metab Disp 2007;35:1886–93.

[42] Ling J, Zhou H, Jiao Q, Davis HM. Interspecies scaling of therapeutic monoclonal antibodies: initial look. J Clin Pharm 2009;49:1382–402.

[43] Wang W, Prueksaritanont T. Prediction of human clearance of therapeutic proteins: simple allometric scaling method revisited. Biopharm Drug Disp 2010;31:253–63.

[44] Rowland M, Benet L, Graham G. Clearance concepts in pharmacokinetics. J Pharmacokinet Biopharm 1973;1:123–36.

[45] Gillette J. Other aspects of pharmacokinetics. In: Gillette JR, Mitchell JR, editors. Concepts in biochemical pharmacology, vol. 3. New York: Springer-Verlag; 1975. p. 35–85.

[46] Wilkinson GR, Shand DG. A physiologic approach to hepatic drug clearance. Clin Pharmacol Ther 1975;18:377–90.

[47] Yang J, Jamei M, Yeo K, Rostami-Hodjegan A, Tucker G. Misuse of the well-stirred model of hepatic drug clearance. Drug Metab Disp 2007;35:501–2.

[48] Crevoisier C, Eckert M, Helzmann P, Thurneysen D, Ziegler W. Relation between the clinical effect and the pharmacokinetics of midazolam following IM and IV administration/2nd communication: pharmacokinetic aspects. Arzneimittelforschung 1981;31:2211–5.

[49] Helzmann P, Eckert M, Ziegler W. Pharmacokinetics and bioavailability of midazolam in man. Br J Clin Pharmacol 1983;16(Suppl. 1): 43S–9S.

[50] Lin YS, Dowling ALS, Quigley SD, Farin FM, Zhang J, Lamba J, et al. Co-regulation of CYP3A4 and CYP3A5 and contribution to hepatic and intestinal midazolam metabolism. Mol Pharmacol 2002;62:162–72.

[51] Fura A, Vyas V, Humphreys W, Chimalokonda A, Rodrigues D. Prediction of human oral pharmacokinetics using nonclinical data: examples involving four proprietary compounds. Biopharm Drug Disp 2008;29:455–68.

[52] Deng R, Iyer S, Theil F-P, Mortensen D, Fielder P, Prabhu S. Projecting human pharmacokinetics of therapeutic antibodies from nonclinical data: what have we learned? MAbs 2011;3:61–6.

[53] Mahmood I. Pharmacokinetic allometric scaling of antibodies: application to the first-in-human dose estimation. J Pharm Sci 2008;98:3850–61.

[54] FDA guidance on maximum safe starting dose. Available online at: http://www.fda.gov/downloads/Drugs/GuidanceComplianceRegulatoryInformation/Guidances/ucm078932.pdf.

[55] Agoram B. Use of pharmacokinetic/pharmacodynamic modeling for starting dose selection in first-in-human trials of high-risk biologics. Br J Clin Pharmacol 2008;67:153–60.

[56] Horvath C, Milton M. The TeGenero incident and the duff report conclusions: a series of unfortunate events or an avoidable event? Toxicol Pathol 2009;37:372–83.

[57] Milton MN, Horvath CJ. The EMEA guideline on first-in-human clinical trials and its impact on pharmaceutical development. Toxicol Pathol 2009;37:363–71.

[58] Guideline on requirements for first-in-man clinical trials for potential high-risk medicinal products. Available online at: http://www.fda.gov/downloads/Drugs/GuidanceComplianceRegulatoryInformation/Guidances/ucm078932.pdf.

[59] Wajima T, Yano Y, Fukumura K, Oguma T. Prediction of human pharmacokinetic profile in animal scale up based on normalizing time course profiles. J Pharm Sci 2004;93:1890–900.

[60] Dong QD, Salinger DH, Endres CJ, Gibbs JP, Hsu C-P, Stouch BJ, et al. Quantitative prediction of human pharmacokinetics for monoclonal antibodies. Clin Pharmacokinet 2011;50:131–42.

[61] Diehl K-H, Hull R, Morton D, Pfister R, Rabemampianina Y, Smith D, et al. A good practice guide to the administration of substances and removal of blood, including routes and volumes. J Appl Toxicol 2001;21:15–23.

[62] Richter WF, Gallati H, Schiller C-D. Animal pharmacokinetics of the tumor necrosis factor-immunoglobulin fusion protein lenercept and their extrapolation to human. Drug Metab Disp 1999;27:21–5.

[63] Jones AT, Ziltener HJ. Enhancement of the biologic effects of interleukin-3 *in vivo* by anti-interleukin-3 antibodies. Blood 1993;82:1133–41.

[64] Finkelman FD, Madden KB, Morris SC, Holmes JM, Boiani N, Katona IM, et al. Anti-cytokine antibodies as carrier proteins. Prolongation of *in vivo* effects of exogenous cytokines by injection of cytokine-anti-cytokine antibody complexes. J Immunol 1993;151:1235–44.

[65] Announcement of Posicor® withdrawal from Roche Laboratories can be found online at: http://www.hdcn.com/8/806fdpos.htm.

[66] Lin JH, Chiba M, Chen I-W, Vastag KG, Nishime JA, Dorsey BD, et al. Time- and dose-dependent pharmacokinetics of L-754,394, an HIV protease inhibitor in rats, dogs and monkeys. J Pharmacol Exp Ther 1995;274:264–9.

[67] Chiba M, Nishime JA, Lin JH. Potent and selective inactivation of human liver microsomal cytochrome P-450 isoforms by L-754,394, an investigational human immune deficiency virus protease inhibitor. J Pharm Exp Ther 1995;275:1527–34.

[68] Baillie TA, Cayen MN, Fouda H, Gerson RJ, Green JD, Grossman SJ, et al. Drug metabolites in safety testing. Toxicol Appl Pharmacol 2002;182:188–96.

[69] FDA Guidance on safety testing of drug metabolites can be found online at: http://www.fda.gov/downloads/Drugs/Guidance-ComplianceRegulatoryInformation/Guidances/ucm079266.pdf.

[70] Segel IH. Kinetics of unireactant enzymes. In: Enzyme kinetics: behavior and analysis of rapid equilibrium and steady state enzyme systems (Wiley Classics Library). New York: John Wiley and Sons, Inc.; 1993. p. 18–99.

[71] Kotegawa T, Laurijssens BE, Von Moltke LL, Cotreau MM, Perloff MD, Venkatakrishnan K, et al. *In vitro*, pharmacokinetic, and pharmacodynamic interactions of ketoconazole and midazolam in the rat. J Pharmacol Exp Ther 2002;302:1228–37.

[72] Kuroha M, Azumano A, Kuze Y, Shimoda M, Kokue E. Effect of multiple dosing of ketoconazole on the pharmacokinetics of midazolam, a cytochrome P-450 3A substrate, in beagle dogs. Drug Metab Disp 2002;30:63–8.

[73] Akabane T, Tabata K, Kadono K, Sakuda S, Terashita S, Teramura T. A comparison of pharmacokinetics between humans and monkeys. Drug Metab Disp 2010;38:308–16.

[74] Houston J. Utility of *in vitro* drug metabolism data in predicting *in vivo* metabolic clearance. Biochem Pharmacol 1994; 47:1469–79.

SECTION II

TOXICOLOGICAL STUDIES AND IND APPLICATION, AND FIRST IN-HUMAN CLINICAL TRIAL

5

Acute, Subacute, Subchronic, and Chronic General Toxicity Testing for Preclinical Drug Development

K.H. Denny, C.W. Stewart

INTRODUCTION

Pharmaceutical products must undergo a battery of preclinical general toxicology studies to provide information regarding the safety of a new drug candidate prior to initiation of clinical trials in humans, and prior to the approval of the drug in the market. Toxicology studies are generally required by regulatory agencies worldwide before testing in humans can commence or progress for a potential new drug candidate, but the specific criteria for conduct of the preclinical studies vary by region. The three largest regions (United States, Europe, and Japan) for drug development have worked together in a continuing effort to unify many regulatory expectations for preclinical studies, which have been published through the International Conference for Harmonization (ICH) compendium of guidance. Prior to the ICH and modern general toxicology planning, it was not uncommon for a drug developer to conduct acute to chronic Good Laboratory Practice (GLP) studies before entry into the clinical phase [1]. This approach was reasonable

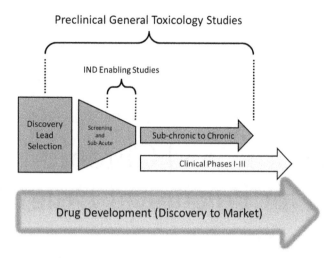

FIGURE 5.1   Preclinical general toxicology studies.

TABLE 5.1   Comparison of Preclinical General Toxicology Program Considerations for NCEs and NBEs

NCE	NBE
MTD-DRF (rodent and nonrodent)	MFD-DRF (relevant species)
Subacute toxicology (rodent and nonrodent)	Subacute toxicology (relevant species)
Safety pharmacology (integrated, if feasible)[a]	Safety pharmacology (integrated)[a]
(Central nervous system, cardiovascular, and pulmonary)	(Central nervous system, cardiovascular, and pulmonary)
Subchronic toxicology (rodent and nonrodent)	Subchronic toxicology (relevant species)
Chronic toxicology (rodent and nonrodent)	Chronic toxicology (relevant species)
Subchronic DRF (mouse or rat)	May not be needed
Carcinogenicity (mouse and rat)	May not be needed

[a]*Safety Pharmacology is included in this table because these in vivo parameter assessments may be integrated into the general toxicology studies.*

because prudent preclinical planning would consider the most stringent regional regulatory submission criteria, but would also slow the development process. Fortunately, the ICH has modernized the development process to stagger the clinical study phases in association with the availability of general toxicology data from studies of sufficient duration (see Fig. 5.1). In addition to providing data for the rigorous assessment of safety during the clinical trials, the preclinical toxicology studies also inform the labeling of an approved pharmaceutical product.

This chapter reviews the current regulatory requirements and guidance used in the conduct of preclinical general toxicity studies for small molecules (new chemical entities; NCEs) and for biotechnology-derived pharmaceuticals (new biological entities; NBEs). However, less detail is provided on special considerations for the many classes of NCE and NBE. This is purposeful, because an understanding of the types of general toxicology studies needed in drug development will easily facilitate a transition into understanding class considerations in study design. Table 5.1 gives a basic comparative view of the general toxicology program plans for NCEs and NBEs. These studies are categorized based on duration of exposure, as follows:

- Acute (single dose)
- Subacute (14–28 days)
- Subchronic (90 days)
- Chronic (180 days, rodent; 270 days, nonrodent)

These exposure durations are standard study periods often addressed in regulatory requirements and guidance(s), along with categorization of the length of the studies into somewhat arbitrary subsets based on the length of dosing or number of potential exposures

to the molecule under investigation. However, the practical length of a general toxicology study, along with the number of doses administered to animals, is based on specific characteristics of the drug as well as on the expected human exposure(s) during each phase of human clinical trials.

In the United States, the preclinical studies used to support the initiation of human clinical trials are referred to as Investigative New Drug (IND)-enabling studies. Once the IND is submitted to the USFDA, the Sponsor must wait 30 calendar days before initiating any clinical trials. During this time, the USFDA has an opportunity to review the IND submission for safety as a means to ensure that human volunteers will not be subjected to unreasonable risk. The Phase I clinical trial (generally considered as the dose range-finding and initial safety evaluation in humans) can be initiated after the 30-day waiting period. However, additional preclinical studies of longer duration are required to support subsequent clinical phases. The Phase II human clinical trial (generally considered the first evaluation of efficacy in humans) is supported by preclinical general toxicology studies of up to 13 weeks in duration, which are typically conducted during the Phase I trial(s) as human data are generated. The information from the Phase I trial(s) is then used to refine the preclinical program, with the possible addition of key biomarkers, metabolites, study conditions, etc., for the sole purpose of enhancing patient safety. For molecules that provide evidence of safety and efficacy through Phase II, additional preclinical safety evaluations are conducted to support the Phase III human clinical trial (generally considered as the definitive determination of efficacy and safety in the risk/benefit assessment).

A basic principle of general toxicology evaluations is that toxicity is categorized as either acute or chronic depending on the effects resulting from exposure to a molecule. Acute effects are defined as those that occur rapidly—usually after a single or only a few exposures to a toxicant. Chronic effects are defined as those that occur after repeated (multiple) exposures and are further delineated into two distinct categories: noncarcinogenic and carcinogenic effects [2]. Because carcinogenic potential is a specialized evaluation in toxicology, which covers a lifetime exposure protocol, that topic has been covered in a separate chapter and will not be discussed here.

The stepwise preclinical toxicological evaluation process in pharmaceutical development has the primary goal of characterizing potential dose-related adverse effects with respect to tissues, organs, organ systems, and, when appropriate, their potential reversibility [3]. Thus data from preclinical studies are useful for estimating an initial safe starting dose for human trials, and to identify parameters for clinical monitoring of the potential adverse effects that may occur in humans [4]. Each preclinical toxicology program, although limited in scope at the beginning of drug development, is designed to be adequate for characterization of potential adverse effects that might occur under the conditions of the clinical trial [2,4].

The nature of the toxicology assessment implies that the doses used for preclinical exposure will be multiple factors higher than the doses in humans [5,6]. Thus characterization of side effects is the intent of the preclinical study. Due to this fact, regulatory documents are written to inform about the general "stepwise" process of safety assessments, while also alluding to the concept of the case-by-case approach. Simply stated, the case-by-case approach is a process of scientific considerations and justifications that should be used to modify the preclinical program in an effort to facilitate an improved human safety assessment. Thus the case-by-case concept by its nature requires additional discussion in order to determine the importance of adverse data in the overall toxicological evaluation. For small molecules, the case-by-case consideration may be associated with a combination of side effects and pharmacodynamics effects, but for biologically derived molecules, most case-by-case considerations are associated with pharmacodynamics effect (also known as exaggerated pharmacology) [7].

The global effort to standardize preclinical toxicology programs began in the 1990s and resulted in a compendium of harmonized guidance produced by the International Conference on Harmonization (ICH), which now serves as a framework for preclinical safety evaluations for pharmaceutical products [5,8–14]. There were six original ICH sponsors, including the European Commission, the European Federation of Pharmaceutical Industries Association, the Japanese Ministry of Health and Human Welfare, the Japanese Pharmaceuticals Manufacturers Association, the US FDA [the Center for Drug Evaluation and Research (CDER) and the Center for Biological Evaluation and Research (CBER)], and the Pharmaceutical Research and Manufacturers of America. In addition, the ICH Steering Committee includes representatives from each of the six ICH sponsors and the International Federation of Pharmaceutical Manufacturers Associations (IFPMA), as well as observers from the World Health Organization, the Canadian Health Protection Branch, and the European Free Trade area. The applicable guidelines regarding the conduct of safety and efficacy studies are available on several websites including the US FDA website, the EMA website, and the ICH website.

The consensus reached among the signatories to the ICH as presented in M3(R2) "Nonclinical Safety Studies for the Conduct of Human Clinical Trials and Marketing Authorization for Pharmaceuticals" [2] is guidance for pharmaceutical manufacturers or sponsors of potential pharmaceutical products. The legal requirements for the registration and approval of a pharmaceutical product can and do differ in individual countries. The ICH guidelines recommend international standards and promote harmonization of preclinical safety studies to support human clinical trials. This harmonization is an effort to provide consistency for both regulatory authorities and the pharmaceutical industry, with beneficial impact on the protection of public health. It is also intended to enhance the safety and effectiveness of the regulatory assessment process for new drug applications and make this more streamlined; hence reducing the development times and resources needed for drug development [2]. However, it is ultimately the responsibility of the sponsor of the potential drug candidate to determine any specific regional registration or marketing requirements.

REGULATORY CONSIDERATIONS FOR CONDUCTING PRECLINICAL TOXICOLOGY STUDIES

International minimum expectations for preclinical toxicology studies to support clinical trials are best summarized in ICH M3(R2). The basic tenet of this guidance is that preclinical studies should identify potential toxicities that may be associated with multiples of the anticipated clinical dose, formulation concentration, dosing schedule, route of administration, and duration of the proposed clinical studies. In addition to ICH M3(R2), local and regional regulatory agencies tend to adopt guidance documents that more clearly delineate specific expectations for a given region. An example of this can be seen with the EMA, where guidance on repeated toxicity was adopted by the European Committee for Human Medicinal Products (CHMP) in March 2010 [3]. In addition, the guidance assembled by CHMP entitled "Strategies to Identify and Mitigate Risks for First-in-Human Clinical Trials with Investigational Medicinal Products" is a joint effort by European regulators and scientists from various disciplines. This guideline is applicable to any new molecular entity, chemical and biotechnological, and/or biologically derived molecules. Its main principle, which is widely applied by regulators assessing clinical trial applications in Europe, is an approach of risk identification and risk mitigation. The EMA evaluates risk identification and mitigation by assessing the mode of action, the nature of the pharmacological target, and the relevance of the animal species used for preclinical safety and toxicity evaluation. These issues are particularly pertinent to the design of first-in-human clinical trials of products that have a potentially higher risk in the first administration to humans than do iterations/reformulations of an established product. Thus the most important consideration is to commence testing with a conservatively calculated safe starting dose and sequential inclusion of subjects in the trial to limit human risk following exposure [15]. Europe is a unique regulatory region, because multiple countries participate to unify the drug application process. Therefore the CHMP routinely prepares scientific guidelines in consultation with regulatory authorities in the European Union (EU) Member States in order to help applicants prepare marketing-authorization applications for human medicines. These guidelines apply to the situations usually encountered during the conventional development of pharmaceuticals and are viewed as providing general guidance for drug development.

The following is an abbreviated list of international regulatory and guidance documents that address the need for preclinical toxicology studies:

- ICH S6(R1) Addendum (Step 4) Guideline: Safety Studies for Biotechnological Products; 2011 [8]
- ICH M3 Guideline: Guidance on Nonclinical Safety Studies for the Conduct of Human Clinical Trials and Marketing Authorization for Pharmaceuticals; June 2009 [5]
- ICH S3A Toxicokinetics: the Assessment of Systemic Exposure Studies in Toxicity Studies (ICH S3A); 1995 [9]

- ICH S4 Duration of Chronic Toxicity Testing in Animals (Rodent and Nonrodent Toxicity Testing) (ICH S4); 1998 [10]
- ICH S7A: Safety Pharmacology Studies for Human Pharmaceuticals (ICH S7A); 2000 [11]
- ICH S7B The Preclinical Evaluation of the Potential for Delayed Ventricular Repolarization (QT Interval Prolongation) by Human Pharmaceuticals (ICH S7B); 2000 [12]
- ICH S5(R2) ICH Harmonized Tripartite Guideline Detection of Toxicity to Reproduction for Medicinal Products and Toxicity to Male Fertility; ICH S5(R2); 2005 [13]
- ICH M4 Organization of the Common Technical Document for the Registration of Pharmaceuticals for Human Use; 2003 [14]
- FDA Points to Consider: Points to Consider in the Manufacture and Testing of Monoclonal Antibody Products for Human Use; 1997 [16]
- Code of Federal Regulations: 21CFR58: Good Laboratory Practice for Nonclinical Laboratory Studies; 2004
- FDA: Estimating the Maximum Safe Starting Dose in Initial Clinical Trials for Therapeutics in Adult Healthy Volunteers; 1998 [4]
- EMEA Guideline Strategies to Identify and Mitigate Risks for First-In-Human Clinical Trials with Investigational Medicinal Products; 2007 [15]
- EMEA Position Paper on the Preclinical Safety Studies to Support Clinical Trials with a Single Microdose; 2002 [17]

Preclinical toxicology studies from single dose to lifetime exposure studies (with few exceptions) must be conducted under the Good Laboratory Practice (GLP) regulations, as promulgated by the laws of the region in which a submission is planned. For example, in the EU, two directives address the requirements for conducting preclinical studies under GLPs (directive 2004/10/EC [18] and directive 2004/09/EC [19]). These directives lay down the obligation of the Member States to designate the authorities responsible for GLP inspections in their territory. It also comprises requirements for reporting and for the internal market (ie, mutual acceptance of data). GLP directive 2004/9/EC covers the OECD revised guidelines for Compliance Monitoring Procedures for GLP, and the OECD guidance for the Conduct of Test Facility Inspections and Study Audits covers laboratory inspections and study audits for laboratories certified to conduct GLP studies in the European Union member countries [19]. There are also "product-oriented directives" referring to GLP obligations:

1. REACH Regulation of 18 December 2006 and Directive 2006/121/EC [20,21]
2. Medicinal products Directive 2001/83/EC on the community code relating to medicinal products for

human use of November 6, 2001 as amended by Commission Directive 2003/63/EC [22]

The development of the various local regulations and local and global guidance provides the substantives framework for data generation and scientific interpretation by which regulatory safety can be evaluated. These two document categories (regulations and guidance) are distinctly different, in that GLP regulations ensure data quality and integrity while guidance documents ensure the scientific validity. Without the guidance documents issued by regulators, it would be daunting for any regulatory body to solely depend on the interpretations of drug sponsors for the meaning of a quality study as is promulgated by GLPs. In effect, the GLPs help to assure regulatory authorities that the data submitted are an accurate and trustworthy reflection of the results obtained during the preclinical safety studies and can therefore be relied on for making decisions about human exposure (ie, risk/safety assessments).

GLP requirements typically include specifications for the following:

1. Organization and Personnel
   - Management Responsibilities
   - Sponsor Responsibilities
   - Study Director Responsibilities
   - Principal Investigator Responsibilities
   - Study Personnel Responsibilities
2. Quality Assurance Program
   - Quality Assurance Personnel
3. Facilities
   - Test System Facilities
   - Facilities for Test and Reference Items
4. Equipment, Reagents and Materials
5. Test Systems
   - Physical/Chemical
   - Biological
6. Test and Reference Items
7. Standard Operating Procedures
8. Performance of Study
   - Study Plan
   - Conduct of Study
9. Reporting of Results
10. Storage of Records and Reports

GENERAL CONSIDERATIONS FOR THE CONDUCT OF PRECLINICAL TOXICOLOGY STUDIES

Preclinical Safety Testing for Phases I–III and Registration Product Label for Marketing Basic Components

The duration of the animal toxicity studies conducted in two mammalian species (generally one rodent and one nonrodent) should be equal to or exceed the anticipated duration of the human clinical trials. In support of an initial Phase I trial, a single- and/or multiple-dose toxicity study may be conducted depending on the patient population, disease indication, intended number of cycles of treatment in humans, and risk–benefit relationship. A period of 1–3 months is a typical duration for subacute to subchronic repeated-dose toxicity studies, while shorter duration studies or acute single-dose toxicity studies may be adequate to support a short duration Phase I trial for life-threatening illnesses, such as cancer. In such life-threatening cases, when evidence of clinical benefit is observed in oncology patients, additional doses may be administered to those patients during the Phase I trial without the immediate need for additional preclinical testing. However, this is an exception to the standard practice. In fact, the regulatory expectation is that an amendment to the initial clinical dosing schedule should be preceded by preclinical studies of sufficient duration and dosage levels to assure human safety [4].

Preclinical general toxicity studies of any duration conducted to support human clinical trials and marketing authorizations share common components, regardless of the therapeutic indication for the potential pharmaceutical product. Decisions on strategies for development of a new pharmaceutical and the experimental approaches used to assemble information relevant to the safety of first-in-human clinical trials must be scientifically based, and should be made and justified on a case-by-case basis. Each protocol must be developed within a standardized framework dictated in part by regulatory requirements, guidance documents, and the GLPs. Notwithstanding, each protocol is also unique because the properties of the molecule under development must be used to design each successive study, as data obtained in prior studies are used to define dose, biomarkers, target organs, etc.

One caveat in the development of a new molecule not intended for intravenous administration is that the intravenous route, along with systemic toxicity assessments, may be required to establish bioavailability parameters. These exploratory studies are often acute studies, and are among the first animal studies to be conducted. Thus potential adverse effects are unknown. When this acute toxicity information is available, additional single-dose general toxicity studies with the nonclinical route are not necessary. Thus further studies providing acute toxicity information can generally be limited to the clinical route only, and such data can be obtained from non-GLP studies because clinical administration will be supported by the appropriate GLP repeated-dose general toxicity studies [2]. Although it is generally correct that a new molecule intended for oral exposure does not require repeated intravenous administration, we have experienced cases where regulators required repeated intravenous administration because the new molecule had abnormal characteristics of low, but variable, oral absorption, prolonged systemic pharmacokinetics, and no observable side effects. In these cases, the regulators were interested to know more about the potential for side effects if a patient happened to be on the high side of the absorption spectrum. It should also be understood that in some specific situations, acute general toxicity studies may be the primary support for single-dose studies in humans. If that is the case, then these studies should be performed in compliance with GLPs and lethality should not be an intended endpoint. Lethality is mentioned here because information on severe acute toxicity of pharmaceutical agents could be useful in predicting the consequences of human overdose situations, and should be available prior to Phase III [2]. Thus an earlier assessment of severe acute toxicity could also be important for therapeutic indications for which patient populations are at higher risk of overdosing.

It is important to note that the preclinical testing and experimental approaches for first-in-human studies might identify potential factors influencing risk for investigational pharmaceutical products. The ability of preclinical studies to predict safety issues in humans may be limited, because the target could be more specific to humans, or there may be species differences that affect the preclinical development program. Thus pharmaceutical development programs for a potential drug candidate rely on the integrated data from many sources and are an iterative process [15].

Selection of Animal Models (Advantages and Disadvantages)

Depending on the type of drug candidate under development, safety regulations require definitive toxicity studies in at least one animal species. However, the use of only one animal species is considered to be the exception. In fact, it is more common to use as many as four different animal species in a preclinical toxicity program. This is not readily apparent in the scope of a general toxicology assessment alone, but becomes clear when planning the conduct of developmental and reproductive toxicity studies and the conduct of carcinogenicity studies. For example, the rat and dog may be selected as the species of choice during the early phases of a drug development program, but the rabbit is typically added to assess teratology parameters. In addition, the mouse is usually utilized in the final stages of program development because two rodent species are commonly used for the evaluation of carcinogenic potential. This is important to keep in mind as we discuss the selection of animal models.

Regional and harmonized guidance documents specify that definitive toxicity studies should be conducted in at least one and possibly two laboratory animal species (one rodent, eg, rat or mouse, and one nonrodent, eg, rabbit, dog, pig, monkey, or other suitable species). However, there are many cases where only one species (rodent) may be acceptable, and a nonrodent species is not used or limited to the use of the rabbit (vaccines) or the monkey (antibodies) [7,23]. The criteria for species selection are typically based on metabolic profiles, pharmacokinetic profiles, species tolerance, and pharmacological activity of the molecule in the species under consideration for safety evaluation. In order to obtain such information during the discovery phases of drug development, in vitro and in silico models can be used, as well as to assess structure–activity relationships. Later on in development, in vitro testing may continue to be used, and programs may start to conduct screening evaluations in the in vivo systems as well. Within these in vivo systems, more predictive data for species selection can be generated for determination of metabolic profiles and for determination of systemic bioavailability, pharmacokinetics, and toxicity, which will allow the preclinical development team to make informed decisions regarding the species to be used in the definitive toxicology studies. Some advantages and disadvantages of laboratory animals for use in preclinical safety testing are listed in Table 5.2.

Even though species are selected prudently prior to human exposure, it may still be necessary to reconsider one or more of the selected preclinical species following the first clinical trials, because new data may emerge that favors one species over another. Thus the ultimate decision for species selection is based on the relative comparability of the previously mentioned animal screening data to the data collected in the human studies. However, there are exceptions to this rule because there are some cases where the drug under investigation is not directed at a human target, such as certain vaccines or other pathogen programs involving biopharmaceuticals. In these circumstances, there may be no physiological basis for the selection of a relevant species, and a selection may be based on assurance of systemic exposure and an evaluation of local tolerance.

As an example for the species-selection process consider the following case:

- Exploratory toxicity screening was done in the mouse, rat, and dog. All species had similar tolerability to dose based on a surface area (mg/m^2) conversion [4].
- Exploratory pharmacokinetic screening was done in the mouse, rat, dog, and monkey. The data shows dose proportionality as rat > mouse = dog >> monkey.

TABLE 5.2 Common Species Selection Considerations in General Toxicology Studies

Species	Advantages	Disadvantages
Mouse	Small size minimizes use of test article Relatively easy to handle Multiple routes of exposure are possible Several transgenic models available Easy to group house	Limited blood volume Requires use of cohorts for toxicokinetic evaluations
Rat	Small size decreases use of test article Easy to handle Multiple routes of exposure are possible Easy to group house	Limited blood volume Requires use of cohorts for toxicokinetic evaluations
Dog (beagle)	Easy to handle Multiple routes of exposure are possible Easy to group house	Size requires use of large quantities of test article Prone to emesis
Monkey	Size will decrease use of test article Multiple routes of exposure are possible Relatively high homology to human	Requires highly specialized handling techniques Requires specialized group housing considerations Target species for animal-rights groups
Swine	Most clinically relevant dermal model Gaining acceptance for use in oral administration	Size requires use of large quantities of test article Requires highly specialized handling techniques Limited routes of exposure due to vascular access Limited group housing potential based on dermal routes of exposure
Rabbit	Sensitivity of dermal model is greater than human	Prone to stress-induced mortality

- In vitro metabolism was done in liver microsomes from the mouse, rat, dog, monkey, and human. The data show that all preclinical species produced similar major metabolites to humans, but the dog had one identified major metabolite that was approximately 30% higher than the other species.

Given this information, the mouse, rat, and dog would be the reasonable species for use in the toxicology studies. For the rodent, the rat would likely be the best choice, due to the higher blood volume requirements of toxicology studies. For the nonrodent, the dog would be selected over the monkey because systemic exposure in the monkey was quite low. The difference in the major metabolite level for the dog was of less concern, because the metabolite had the same identity as that found in other preclinical species and in humans. If the metabolite were different, then the monkey would have been the better selection for the toxicology studies.

Dose Selection and Routes of Administration

The regulatory expectation for general toxicology studies is that the dose selected for the high dose will produce observable toxicity, as defined by decrements either in weight gain or food consumption and/or alterations in clinical observations, clinical chemistry, and hematology parameters as well as organ-related alterations. The five general criteria for defining the high dose are maximum tolerated dose (MTD), maximum feasible dose (MFD), 50-fold margin dose, limit dose, and saturation of exposure [2,24]. The MTD is considered to be a dose where target-organ toxicity is expected to occur but should not cause mortality. Conversely, the MFD is based on the fact that a dose cannot be given at a high enough level to demonstrate a definitive dose-limiting toxicity profile. This MFD determination is influenced by the technical capability to deliver the dose and/or by the physiochemical properties of the drug candidate. The 50-fold margin dose and the limit dose are similar, in practical application, to the MFD. High doses that are determined based on these two criteria are not influenced by technical or physiochemical issues but are based on the opinion that any higher dose would not provide any additional relevance for the assessment of clinical safety.

The presumption within the explanations of the four criteria mentioned thus far is that systemic exposure increases with dose. However, the last criterion for high-dose selection evaluates this presumption by direct comparison. Saturation of exposure describes the systemic exposure achieved in animals and correlates that exposure to the dose, sex, species, and the time course of the toxicity study. The data obtained can indicate the absorption limitation of exposure to the drug candidate. In such a case, the lowest dose that achieves the maximum systemic exposure should be used as the high dose (in the absence of any other dose-limiting constraints).

The process of dose selection for general toxicology studies involves generating and compiling data from early in vitro and in vivo (non-GLP studies) studies to derive the doses proposed in the initial GLP animal studies. The selection of doses for definitive general toxicity studies should cover the dose–response continuum from pharmacologically relevant doses through the MTD. By following such a plan, the doses selected will cover exposures that form relevant multiples of the proposed human therapeutic doses. The clinical indication(s) and the expected route of human exposure should also be considered. As an example, dose selection for a short-term use oncology drug will differ from a long-term use pharmaceutical, such as cholesterol-lowering medication.

Regulatory positions regarding high-dose selection in toxicity studies include:

- ICH S1C (R2) Predicted to produce a minimum toxic effect over the course of the toxicity study…may be predicted from a 90-day range-finding study in which minimal toxicity is observed…factors to consider include: ≤10% decrease in body weight gain relative to controls; target organ toxicity; significant alterations in clinical pathology. Maximum doses for general toxicity studies may be based on margins of exposure or limit doses [25].
- US IGS Highest dose in chronic study just high enough to elicit signs of minimal toxicity without significantly altering normal lifespan due to effects other than carcinogenicity. Determined in a 90-day study. Considers alteration in body and organ weight, clinical pathology and more definitive toxic, pathologic, or histopathologic endpoints [25].
- CHMP (2008) Should enable identification of target organ toxicity or other nonspecific toxicity, or until limited by volume of dose…Ideally, systemic exposure to the drug and/or principal metabolites should be a significant multiple of the anticipated clinical systemic exposure…Need for adjustment if unexpected toxicity or lack thereof [25].

These studies are generally designed to maximize the potential for identifying adverse effects, whether "on-target" (associated with the intended pharmacology) or "off-target" (other than the intended biologic target). Employing high doses is part of the strategy for fully maximizing that potential [26]. Typically, use of the term "high dose" reflects a consideration of an MTD or an MFD, when applied to the design of general toxicology studies conducted to support human clinical trials for new potential pharmaceuticals.

In some cases, the pharmacological properties of the investigational drug can limit the number of doses that can be administered, or can alter the dosing frequency in a particular species. For example, cytotoxic oncogenic compounds often have severe effects on the hematopoietic system, resulting from the compound's selective activity on rapidly dividing cells. For these small molecule anticancer pharmaceuticals, hematology changes may be used in conjunction with clinical observations and body weight changes to define the MTD in early studies. It is also reasonable to determine a severely toxic dose (STD; ie, dose that causes death or irreversible severe toxicity) in 10% of rodents. Similar studies are also conducted in nonrodents as a precaution because the target patient population is highly susceptible to unanticipated adverse events. Thus it becomes quite important to test the upper levels of toxicity and potential recovery from those toxicities.

For other pharmaceutical targets, it may be reasonable and justifiable to choose a high dose in the range of the lowest-observed-effect-level (LOEL) or lowest-observed-adverse-effect-level (LOAEL) based on the premise that such doses would be more applicable to human exposure [25]. For example, the development of recombinant proteins as a replacement therapy for blood disorders should be evaluated within normal physiological constraints or maximum intended pharmacology [8]. Practically, this approach should be used to avoid excessive findings of exaggerated pharmacology, which could impede the generation of useful data. Nevertheless, the basic principles of toxicology indicate that the dose selection in shorter-term studies should be on the higher side, maximizing the potential for identification of "system failure" using an MTD. As exposure duration increases and additional perspectives are gained from clinical trials, the high dose in the preclinical general toxicology study could correctly move toward the more clinically relevant LOEL/LOAEL. Doses in the range of LOEL/LOAEL allow for development (progression) of potential toxicity over longer exposure duration, which is an important part of a toxicology profile [25].

The low dose in a general toxicology study should ideally demonstrate a no-observable-effect-level (NOEL) while maintaining at least a 1X equivalent of the anticipated human therapeutic dose. However, depending on the level of target engagement, it is not uncommon to find effects at the low dose that are related to the pharmacology of the drug candidate, but which are deemed to be nonadverse. This would be an example of a dose that can be considered as the no-observable-adverse-effect-level (NOAEL), because the effects are either considered not to be a side effect, not biologically relevant, and/or are within estimations of background historical data. Recognition of the differences between adverse and nonadverse effects is key in toxicity evaluations. Adverse is generally considered to be a side effect (or unintended effect) of the drug candidate, but not all side effects are biologically or physiologically relevant. Additional consideration must be given to the fact that many therapeutic effects (or intended effects) can be considered adverse because the effect can negatively impact biological or physiological process. Thus the trained toxicologist needs to understand and utilize a number of contributing factors in the toxicological evaluation process. The intermediate dose(s) in a general toxicology study are needed to demonstrate a dose–response relationship, which is critical in defining the optimum pharmacological dose and important in establishing the margins of safety.

Study designs and dose-selection criteria for biopharmaceuticals may differ from those for small molecules due to the fact that these molecules generally do not produce adverse effects even at high levels of exposure. This is because they tend to have highly targeted mechanisms of action and have differences in the biological nature of their metabolic/catabolic end products (eg, amino acids and sugars) [25]. With biopharmaceuticals, there is low potential for "off-target" toxicity, and the addendum to the ICH S6 guidance states that a high dose that is at least 10 times the intended high dose in humans, and which is expected to result in saturation of the target (with possible demonstration of maximum pharmacological effect), may be considered an adequate high dose [8]. Alternatively, an MFD approach for protein therapeutics (100 mg/kg) may be considered based on 20 mg/mL formulated dose concentration and a 5 mL/kg dose volume [8].

One additional point to consider for dose selection is that dose levels almost always change over the course of the general toxicology program. This is because as studies become longer in duration the generation of more data is likely to necessitate adjustments. Acute studies generally are conducted to find the MTD, but this MTD level cannot be administered repeatedly. Thus the duration of administration will continuously influence the high-dose selection. As the highest dose level is necessarily decreased, the intermediate doses are also decreased to maintain an extrapolation for dose response. For example, we have observed cases where the acute MTD might have been ≥1000 mg/kg, but repeated dosing up to 28 days in duration may only allow for a high dose of ≤100 mg/kg because of toxicity. Because such situations can occur, it is prudent to always consider conducting short duration repeated-dose studies (eg, 5–14 days) to evaluate tolerance under subacute conditions before conducting the definitive IND enabling repeated-dose studies.

Unlike the selection of dose levels, the selection of the route of administration is more straightforward. Table 5.3 gives a summary of those commonly used. The most common routes of clinical exposure are oral, parenteral, and dermal. Thus the historical delivery route for a given class of compound will dictate the route used in the preclinical studies. When multiple routes of

TABLE 5.3 Common Routes of Administration in General Toxicology Studies

Route	Advantages	Disadvantages
P.O. (gavage)	Easily used in all common species (including swine) Flexibility with various formulation vehicles Well tolerated from acute to chronic exposure	Limitations on systemic bioavailability
P.O. (capsule)	Most common in dogs Formulation not typically needed Well tolerated following an acclimation period	Limitations on systemic bioavailability
I.V.	Easily used in common species (excluding swine) Complete systemic bioavailability Relatively flexible with various formulation vehicles	Requires sterile preparations and administration techniques Formulations must be hemocompatible
S.C.	Easily used in all common species (including swine) Relatively high systemic bioavailability Relatively flexible with various formulation vehicles	Requires sterile preparations and administration techniques Local tolerance issues
I.M.	Easily used in all common species (including swine) Relatively high systemic bioavailability Relatively flexible with various formulation vehicles	Requires sterile preparations and administration techniques Relative limitation of administration volume per injection site Local tolerance issues
Dermal	Preferred route of exposure in swine Minimum systemic exposure	Requires specialized administration procedures to prevent oral ingestion Local tolerance issues

TABLE 5.4 Practical Volumes for Common Routes of Administration in General Toxicology Studies

Species	Route of Administration Good Practice (Possible Maximum) (mL/kg)				
	P.O.-Gavage	I.V.-Bolus	I.V.-Slow Injection	S.C.	I.M.-per Site
Mouse	10 (50)	5	(25)	10 (40)	0.05 (0.1)
Rat	10 (40)	5	(20)	5 (10)	0.1 (0.2)
Rabbit	10 (15)	2	(10)	1 (2)	0.25 (0.5)
Dog	5 (15)	2.5	(5)	1 (2)	0.25 (0.5)
Macaque	5 (15)	2	Not available	2 (5)	0.25 (0.5)
Swine	10 (15)	2.5	(5)	1 (2)	0.25 (0.5)

Adapted from Diehl K-H, Hull R, Morton D, Pfister R, Rabemampianina Y, Smith D, et al. A good practice guide to the administration of substances and removal of blood, including routes and volumes. J Appl Toxicol 2001;21:15–23.

exposure are used clinically for a particular drug class, then the preclinical administration plan for a drug candidate will still be based on the planned clinical route for the specific drug candidate. An additional consideration for the route of exposure is the volume to be delivered by that route. Table 5.4 summarizes the practical volumes by various common routes.

STUDY TYPES USED IN THE ASSESSMENT OF GENERAL TOXICOLOGY

Acute/Dose-Range Finding Toxicity Studies

Acute toxicology evaluations are some of the more basic types of in vivo safety assessments required for regulatory submission. Although basic in their nature, the specificity of the data obtained from such a study has specialized utility in regulatory safety assessments. The objective of these studies is to determine an MTD/MFD in the initial toxicity characterization. The data obtained from these studies are the foundation for dose selection in the safety pharmacology studies (ie, cardiovascular, central nervous system, and pulmonary assessments) and in the definitive IND enabling general toxicity studies. Before we discuss an acute study that would be part of a regulatory submission, we will cover those used for screening purposes. These early phase acute studies are used to select candidate compounds for potential further development, sometimes together with an abbreviated multiple-dose phase. In the following, we discuss these designs in more detail. It should be noted that for any acute study to provide quality information, some knowledge of bioavailability and systemic exposure must be available depending on route of exposure and clinical indication.

Acute/Repeated-Dose Screening Studies

The screening acute study can have many formats, but the primary purpose is the same, ie, to determine whether the drug candidate is tolerable at multiples of a potential clinically relevant dose. The added benefit of the screening study is that the scientist can compare multiple drug candidates in the same study. When this is done, tolerability indicators, such as alterations in body weight and/or food consumption, as well as observations of abnormal clinical signs, can provide some perspective on which species may be the better lead candidate. At this stage, species selection is typically not complete. However, at least a rodent and possibly a nonrodent species should be evaluated. With drug candidates that are intended for daily use, it is also reasonable to assess repeated exposure over a period of 5–7 days' duration. This can facilitate the initial assessment of potential alterations in clinical pathology endpoints, and can be useful in the selection of dose levels in a regulatory program, but should not be used as a replacement for any of the acute studies that are intended for submission. This is because the study conditions may lack certain quality standards (eg, drug-batch purity, environmental controls, certified food source, etc.) necessary to minimize confounding factors in the interpretation of the data.

Acute Preclinical Studies for Regulatory Submission

Exploratory IND: The exploratory IND is a guidance offered by the US FDA [27]. The content of the guidance and provisions are similar to that available from other regulatory bodies in other regions. The provisions permit an applicant with an opportunity to take a first step into a regulatory testing environment and capitalize on a screening approach in humans. Multiple potential drug candidates and/or multiple formulations of potential drug candidates can be tested in humans after limited safety data are collected in a rodent and nonrodent species. Acute studies with this type of submission can be used to support microdosing in humans, which can be useful in gathering preliminary pharmacokinetic, biodistribution, pharmacodynamics, and mechanism of action data. As mentioned previously, most acute study designs include a repeated-dose phase, and the same is true for the exploratory IND (see Fig. 5.2). Even though the exploratory IND is intended to allow for more clinical screening of potential drug candidates, it has not been utilized much. This is because the maximum allowable clinical dose is usually below pharmacologically relevant levels, but in some cases a pharmacologically relevant may be possible, depending on the amount of preclinical data for each candidate. Due to these complexities and limitations on dose, investigators tend to

Addition of Exploratory IND Component

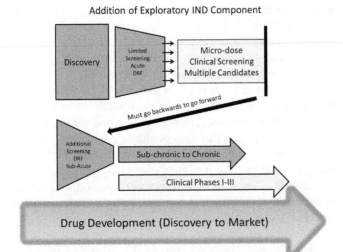

FIGURE 5.2 Addition of exploratory IND component.

utilize the lead candidate screening process in preclinical toxicology studies and choose the traditional IND for human safety testing.

Traditional IND: The primary difference between acute and DRF studies for the traditional IND is that only one potentially new pharmaceutical product is under investigation. However, the traditional IND will include other definitive toxicity studies that allow human trials to progress into safety assessment as mentioned previously. (Note: The study design considerations for parameter evaluations are discussed in the section "Common Protocol Components for General Toxicity Assessments in GLP Studies" in this chapter.)

The basic design for an acute study includes a relatively small number of animals per dose evaluated. For rodent studies, five animals of each sex per dose group are considered adequate. The second species evaluated typically employs two to three animals. A vehicle control group and at least three dose levels of the test article under evaluation should be included. Additional dose levels may be added, especially if little is known of the toxicological profile at the time of the acute study. Body weights, food consumption, and clinical observations are critical data, informing about the toxicological effects following a single dose of the test article. Surviving animals are euthanized at a specified number of days after the dose administration (14 days is the most common timeframe). A gross necropsy is then conducted to evaluate tissues and organ systems for gross changes. However, in most cases further histological evaluation of these tissues is not conducted. Assessment is generally limited to observation of overt toxicity as evidenced by the aforementioned weight changes, reduced food consumption, and/or clinical observation of mortality, morbidity, and pharmacological effects of the test article. Data from the acute study are used to plan appropriate doses for subsequent repeated dose studies.

REPEATED-DOSE TOXICITY STUDIES

Although there is much harmony in the requirements of repeated-dose general toxicity studies intended to support human clinical trials, some regional differences in the suggested minimum duration of repeated-dose general toxicity studies do exist [2]. For example, in the United States and European Union, 2-week rodent and nonrodent studies can support a single-dose or short-term repeated dose human clinical trial, while in Japan a 4-week rodent and 2-week nonrodent study may be needed to support the Phase I clinical trials. As discussed in the introduction, each clinical trial phase is typically started as soon as permissible, which is just after the respective supporting preclinical investigations are completed. In the repeated-dose preclinical studies, the objective shifts to establishing an NOAEL. Due to the fact that limited preclinical data are available, it is important to understand some basic "milestones" that can allow the investigator to make decisions about the progression or termination of the development of a species. Some key checkpoints are listed below; it is worth noting that at any one of these checkpoints, even if some concerns would seem to call for terminating the project, it might be advisable to contemplate conducting further investigative studies.

- The earliest checkpoint is connected to understanding the primary pharmacodynamic data obtained in the research phase of the project. The objective is to determine which candidate has the better specificity profile. For synthetic chemicals, it is common to test a number of substances that are derived from a "lead compound," with the objective of deciding which show the most promising properties.
- A next checkpoint will be reached when the results of the early toxicology studies are available. If an assessment of these results demonstrates the presence of unacceptable toxic hazards, the project may be terminated, or the compound replaced by another from the investigated series of substances. Due to the nature of the preclinical toxicity studies, most adverse events are characterized there and may never be observed in a clinical trial.
- As the drug development process moves further along the path to submission and to marketing, the clinical data and concerns become the prominent information used as decision criteria. Lack of adequate efficacy, or the emergence of intolerable side effects (intolerable in terms of either frequency or seriousness), may at least curtail, if not terminate, the development and marketing potential of an investigational drug.

TABLE 5.5 Duration of Repeated Dose Toxicity Studies to Support Clinical Trials in the US, EU, and Japan[a]

Duration of Clinical Trials	Minimum Duration of Repeated Dose Toxicity Studies: Rodents	Minimum Duration of Repeated Dose Toxicity Studies: Nonrodents
Single dose	2–4 weeks[b]	2 weeks
Up to 2 weeks	2–4 weeks[b]	2 weeks
Up to 1 month	1 month	1 month
Up to 3 months	3 months	3 months
Up to 6 months	6 months	6 months[c]
>6 months	6 months	Chronic[c]

[a]In Japan, if there are no Phase II clinical trials of equivalent duration to the planned Phase III trials, conduct of longer duration toxicity studies should be considered.

[b]In EU and US, 2-week studies are the minimum duration. In Japan, 2-week nonrodent and 4-week rodent studies are needed. In the US, as an alternative to 2-week studies, single-dose toxicity studies with extended examinations can support single-dose human trials.

[c]Data from 6 months of administration in nonrodents should be available before the initiation of clinical trials longer than 3 months. Alternatively, if applicable, data from a 9-month nonrodent study should be available before the treatment duration exceeds that which is supported by the available toxicity studies.

Recommendations for the dose duration of preclinical safety studies used to support human dosing in clinical trials are summarized in ICH M3, ICH S4A, and ICH S6(R1). A repeated-dose toxicity study in two species (one nonrodent) for a minimum duration of 2–4 weeks (Table 5.5) would support Phase I (Human Pharmacology) and Phase II (Therapeutic Exploratory) studies up to 2 weeks in duration. Beyond this, 1-, 3-, or 6-month toxicity studies would support these types of human clinical trials for up to 1, 3, or 6 months, respectively. Six-month rodent and chronic nonrodent studies would support clinical trials of longer duration than 6 months [2,3].

Subacute Toxicity Studies (2–4 Weeks)

The duration of the repeated-dose toxicity studies is usually related to the duration, therapeutic indication, and proposed dose period of the Phase I clinical trial. For some clinical indications, a 2-week study may be sufficient to support the Phase I clinical trial. However, for most products, a 4-week study is necessary to provide sufficient safety information for trials where more than single doses are planned. The duration of the animal toxicity studies should equal, or exceed, the duration of the human clinical trials, up to the maximum recommended duration of the preclinical repeated-dose toxicity studies. The 4-week repeated-dose toxicity study is usually conducted as a "follow-on" study after the acute (single-dose) and 1- to 2-week (dose-range finding) studies have been conducted. Thus the 4-week study is conducted to strengthen the toxicity data for the potential pharmaceutical product. These studies should further develop the toxicity profile by elucidating the MTD and by establishing the first NOAEL when the test article is administered over the longer dose period.

Repeated-dose studies evaluate additional parameters in the toxicokinetic profile because the number of doses (ie, the dose period) is extended. Two-week and 4-week studies generally identify toxicity as evidenced by alterations in clinical observations, body weight, and food consumption, but also evaluate clinical pathology, hematology, and histopathology parameters (including the potential for target organs of toxicity), and these are the first studies in which a recovery period should be considered to evaluate the reversibility of any adverse effects [28].

As noted in previous sections, the route of administration should be the same as the intended route of human dosing, and the dosing regimen will depend on the pharmacodynamic properties of the product under development. (Note: There are separate guidelines to consider for chemical, biological, and vaccine preclinical safety studies.) In general, the 4-week rodent study utilizes the standard study design information given in previous sections, and the number of animals for the main toxicity evaluation is typically 10 animals per sex, per group, with additional animals included for toxicokinetic evaluations. If toxicokinetic assessments are included, then the number of additional animals will depend on the acceptable collection volumes attainable from the rodent species of choice, the number of blood collections planned, and the timing of sample collections for analysis. There are guidelines covering blood volumes that can be safely collected over a 24-h period, which should be considered to prevent physiological complications that can potentially distort the bioanalytical data [29]. To provide adequate statistical power for the bioanalytical analysis, at least three individual animal samples per time point are needed. There is guidance to assist in determining appropriate timing and sampling for rodents in "The FELASA Guidelines: Pain and distress in laboratory rodents and lagomorphs (1994) 28:97–112" and "Laboratory Animal Management: Rodents. 1996, National Research Council (Adopted September 1998)" [30,31].

At the time of protocol development, the following should be determined:

- Species to be bled
- Size of the animal to be bled
- Type of the sample required (eg, serum, plasma, whole cells, etc.)
- Quality of the sample required (sterility, tissue fluid contamination, etc.)
- Quantity of blood required
- Frequency of sampling

- Health status of the animal being bled
- Training and experience of the technician

Both the quantity and frequency of blood sampling depend on the circulating blood volume of the animal. The approximate blood volume of a mouse is 80 mL/kg and 70 mL/kg for a rat [29].

If the mouse is the rodent species, then more animals may be required for the toxicokinetic analyses because the blood volume available from each mouse is limited by physiological constraints, and at this early stage of development, the bioanalytical method typically requires a volume of serum or plasma that only allows a single collection time point in the mouse. As a result, individual mice are required for blood collections.

For studies that include a recovery period, additional animals should be included in the main study groups and subjected to the same doses and conditions as the other study animals. If potential target-organ toxicities or evidence of other toxicities as evidenced by body weight changes or clinical observations are identified in previous studies, the inclusion of a recovery period is recommended to evaluate whether observed toxicities are partially to completely reversible over the designated recovery interval.

Subchronic Toxicity Studies (13 Weeks)

For rodent studies, 20–25 animals per sex, per group, are commonly assigned to the 13-week toxicology study. Most studies also include additional animals for toxicokinetic evaluation because of the size constraints previously discussed. Toxicokinetic sampling (at a minimum) is done at the initiation, midway point, and end of the dosing period. Additional animals may be included for assignment to a recovery period to evaluate the reversibility of any adverse finding. A common study design is to assign 25 animals per sex per group, necropsy 20 animals at the completion of the dose period, and place surviving animals into the recovery phase. In rodents, the 13-week study has one additional caveat. During the final stages of the preclinical program, it may be necessary to conduct carcinogenicity evaluations in a second rodent species. This is normally the case for small molecules. Because either the rat or the mouse was the primary species used in support of toxicology characterization, data will need to be collected on the second rodent species in preparation for the carcinogenicity evaluation. This necessitates an additional 13-week study (now termed DRF) exclusively for selection of doses to be used in the carcinogenicity evaluation. The data collected are the same as those in a standard repeated-dose general toxicity study, but the objective is not to fully characterize toxicity, but to find a high dose that is clinically relevant and that does not produce more than a 10% weight change (in comparison to respective controls) over the 13-week exposure period.

For nonrodents, the canine and nonhuman primate are the two most commonly used species in 13-week general toxicology studies. The study design of the 13-week nonrodent study differs from the rodent study primarily in the number of animals assigned per group and the toxicokinetic sampling. Nonrodent 13-week studies typically have four to five animals per sex, per group. If a recovery phase is planned, then one to two animals per sex, per group are generally carried into the recovery phase of the study. In the event that mortality occurs in any group, the number of animals assigned to the recovery group is reduced and the animal will be evaluated with the main study animals.

The 13-week studies are not only used to support extended dosing in human clinical trials but also to establish dose levels in chronic studies. These studies build on the toxicology data established so far and provide important toxicological and toxicokinetic data from longer exposure periods. They are therefore critical in assessing potential human toxicities from increased dose periods.

Chronic Toxicity Studies (6–12 Months)

Prior to the formation of the ICH, regulatory expectations for chronic toxicity testing differed between the three regions (USA, Japan, and the EU). The USA and Japan required 12-month and the European agencies 6-month studies to cover the interim period between the 3-month and 2-year carcinogenicity studies. This resulted in many pharmaceutical companies conducting two chronic repeated-dose studies in rodents and in nonrodents, one of 6 months' duration in each species to support clinical trials, and one of 12 months' duration to support marketing in the USA and Japan.

After lengthy evaluation of the databases of these duplicative studies, ICH S4 recommended that the maximum duration of long-term repeated-dose toxicity studies should be reduced from 12 months to 6 months in rodents and from 12 months to 9 months in nonrodents [10]. The USFDA agreed to this change because the data showed that any late-emerging toxicity in the rat would be identified in the 2-year carcinogenicity study, which was required anyway. The situation with regard to the nonrodent was less straightforward, as the chronic study is the longest test in this species (ie, there is no requirement for a nonrodent carcinogenicity study). The European and Japanese regulatory agencies agreed that nonrodent studies should be limited to a maximum of 6 months, based on the findings of the Center for Medicines Research and JPMA databases [32]. However, the US FDA continued to require a 12-month nonrodent study. Following reevaluation by US FDA, it was determined that 9 months may be sufficient to capture most of the new toxicity findings that emerged after 6 months. Thus, the 9-month study in nonrodents was proposed as the basis for harmonization within all ICH regions [10]. This conclusion was arrived at by an expert working group, which was assembled to evaluate the data from several chronic studies. Of the 18 cases evaluated, 11 supported a study-duration of 9–12 months, 4 supported a duration of 12 months, and the 3 remaining cases indicated that a 6-month study would be adequate. The expert working group recommended that there was sufficient evidence to support a harmonized 9-month duration for nonrodent toxicity studies, which would be applicable for most categories of pharmaceuticals [10].

In rodent and nonrodent studies, the number of animals used is generally the same as the number used in the 13-week studies, and the same toxicological parameters are evaluated. These extended repeated-dose studies area conducted for the following reasons:

- Six-month studies may be acceptable for indications of human exposure in chronic conditions with short-term or intermittent human exposure.
- Six-month studies are also acceptable for pharmaceuticals intended to treat life-threatening diseases (eg, cancer or HIV).
- Twelve-month studies are more appropriate for chronically used drugs for which human clinical trial data are limited to short-term exposure.
- Twelve-month studies may also be more applicable for new molecular entities acting on new molecular targets where there is limited human data, especially for longer-term exposure.

Since there are differences between the US FDA and the other ICH signatories regarding the appropriate length of repeated-dose studies greater than 13 weeks, the sponsor must assess the appropriate length of the studies to be conducted. These decisions must take into consideration the regulatory requirements for both the conduct of clinical trials and marketing applications based on regional differences [32].

SPECIAL CONSIDERATIONS FOR BIOPHARMACEUTICAL SAFETY EVALUATIONS

Preclinical toxicology studies, especially the duration of the chronic studies, are complicated when the molecule is a large, biotechnology-derived molecule, or the therapeutic agent is a human protein. This is due to the specificity of these molecules to its human target. Potential issues for evaluation are:

1. the human protein or target may not be pharmacologically active in rodents or dogs; and
2. the therapeutic agent may be so immunogenic in these species that longer-duration studies are not possible due to the formation of neutralizing antibodies.

Thus preclinical safety testing of biopharmaceuticals poses a particular challenge in selecting a relevant animal species for use in toxicology studies. However, many of the components of toxicity studies conducted on small molecules can be applied to testing of large molecules. The most important consideration in species selection in these instances is that the drug be pharmacologically active in the species used for the study. This is a key consideration because biopharmaceuticals are designed with specificity to target certain functional groups and rarely demonstrate off-target toxicity. Nonhuman primates are frequently the only relevant species that can be used to assess the safety of a biopharmaceutical, but it is not uncommon to include a rodent species based on a reasonable target homology [26].

As for any pharmaceutical, it is normal for a biological drug to undergo toxicity testing to support entry into the clinic, further clinical development, and marketing approval. Such testing is in agreement with international regulatory guidance given by the International Conference on Harmonization [8,26]. Repeated-dose general toxicology studies in rodents and nonrodents follow a standard design, with assessment of clinical signs, body weight, food consumption, toxicokinetics, ophthalmology, clinical pathology (hematology, clinical chemistry, and urinalysis), organ weights, macroscopic examination, and histopathology, along with electrocardiogram (ECG) when the nonrodent is used. Assessment in studies to support early clinical trials generally involves one vehicle-treated control group and three drug-treated (low, mid, and high) groups as shown in a recent evaluation. Toxicology studies of biologics may also include an assessment of the presence of antidrug antibodies. As discussed previously, the antidrug antibody assessment is primarily necessary for determining whether systemic exposure to the biopharmaceutical is maintained at clinically relevant levels throughout the duration of the dosing periods.

Since biopharmaceuticals are usually designed to target human epitopes, it should be understood that qualitative and quantitative differences might exist in biological responses in animals other than humans. Differences in affinity for molecular targets, tissue distribution of the molecular target, cellular consequences of target binding, cellular regulatory mechanisms, metabolic pathways, and/or compensatory responses to an initial physiological perturbation must be considered in the interpretation process. It should be noted that a similar response in human and animal cells in vitro is not necessarily a guarantee that the in vivo response will be similar. In practice, this means that animal studies with highly species-specific pharmaceutical products may:

- not reproduce the intended pharmacological effect in humans;
- give rise to misinterpretation of pharmacokinetic and pharmacodynamic results;
- not identify relevant toxic effects [2,5].

For development of biopharmaceuticals (unlike small molecules), the mechanism of action together with numerous other physiochemical specificities must be considered in every case, and knowledge of receptor/epitope distribution can provide greater understanding of potential in vivo toxicity. Relevant animal species testing is critical because toxicity studies in nonrelevant species may be misleading and are therefore discouraged.

The exception to this rule occurs when no relevant species exists. In those instances, the use of relevant transgenic animals expressing the human receptor, or the use of homologous proteins should be considered, but these are not ideal [3,8]. In the end, the complexities of biopharmaceuticals provide the investigator with the opportunity to use the case-by-case approach to drug development.

COMMON PROTOCOL COMPONENTS OF GENERAL TOXICITY ASSESSMENTS IN GLP STUDIES

1. **Statement of GLP Compliance**: All definitive general toxicity studies carried out to assess safety of a drug should be performed according to Good Laboratory Practices [14,15]. Regardless of the study length, there are components of any study intended to be submitted for regulatory approval that incorporate GLP-driven specifications for the conduct of the study.
2. **Computerized Systems**: Computerized systems that are used in the generation, measurement, or assessment of data should be developed, validated, operated, and maintained in ways that are compliant with Good Laboratory Practice principles.
3. **Study objectives:**
   - To establish a "no observable adverse effect level" (NOAEL)
   - To characterize dose–response relationships following repeated doses
   - To identify and characterize specific organs affected after repeated administration
   - To predict a reasonable and appropriate dose for chronic exposure studies (maximum tolerated dose or MTD)

4. **Test Substance**: The test substance used in toxicity studies should be the same substance that the petitioner/notifier intends to use in human clinical trials and ultimately obtain an approval for marketing. If possible, a single lot of test substance should be used throughout the study. If a single lot will not allow completion of the study, lots that are similar in purity and composition should be used.
5. **Identity, Composition, and Purity**: The composition identity and purity of the test substance should be characterized, including the name and quantities of all major components, known contaminants and impurities, and the percentage of unidentifiable materials.
6. **Conditions of Storage and Expiration Date**: The test sample should be stored under conditions that maintain its stability, quality, and purity until the studies are complete. The expiration date of the test material should be known and easily available. Test materials should not be used past their expiration date.
7. **Test Systems and Husbandry**: Two species are required for most pharmaceutical products: rodents and nonrodents. There are recommendations and legal requirements in most countries for the care, maintenance, and housing of animals, and these are specified as a requirement in all GLPs. An abbreviated list of international governmental regulations/guidance regarding the use of animals in research is as follows:
   - NIH publication 85–23, "Guide for the Care and Use of Laboratory Animals"
   - 8th Edition of the Guide for the Care and Use of Laboratory Animals (NRC 2011)
   - European Convention for the Protection of Vertebrate Animals used for Experimental and Other Scientific Purposes: Appendix A of the ETS 123; Directive 2010/63/EU on the protection of animals used for scientific purposes
   - Guidelines for Proper Conduct of Animal Experiments June 1, 2006 (Science Council of Japan)
   - Animal Welfare Act 7 Usc 2131 et seq. (PL 89-544, August 24, 1966; amended PL 91-579, December 24, 1970; amended PL 94-279, April 22, 1976; amended PL 99-198, December 23, 1985)
8. **Selection of Species, Strains, Gender, and Number**: Rationale for selection of the species, strain, gender, and animal numbers should be given. If only one sex is to be used in the study, then this should be justified based on the intended clinical use, or prior data. For the vast majority of toxicology studies, both male and female test animals should be used. All animals must be healthy and have not been subject to previous experimental procedures. Scientists should also consider the test animals' general sensitivity and

the responsiveness of particular organs and tissues of test animals to toxic chemicals when selecting rodent species, strains, and substrains for toxicity studies. The selection of inbred, out-bred, or hybrid rodent strains for toxicity studies should be based upon the scientific questions to be answered.

9. **Animal Age and Identification**: In rodents, toxicity testing generally initiates at 6–8 weeks of age. In nonrodents, toxicity testing generally initiates as the animals approach sexual maturity. Depending on the objective of the study, the ages at initiation may vary appropriately. Thus the most important point is to verify the age of the animals at study initiation. Test animals should be individually identified by a permanent mechanism and their housing should also be identified with their species, strain (and substrain), sex, age, and unique identification number (eg, ear tag, implanted identification chip, tattoo animal identification).

10. **Randomization of Animals**: Animals should be assigned to control and dose groups in a stratified random manner to minimize bias and assure comparability of pertinent variables across compound treated and control groups (eg, mean body weights and body weight ranges). If other characteristics are used as the basis for randomization, then this should be described and justified. Animals should be placed on study on the same day, if possible. If the number of animals prohibits one-day assignment, animals may be placed on study over several days but equal portions of the control and experimental animals should be placed on the study each day in order to maintain concurrence.

11. **Basal Diet**: Feed and water should be provided ad libitum to animals in toxicity studies, and the diets for these studies should meet the nutritional requirements of the species for normal growth and reproduction. Unless special circumstances apply that justify otherwise, care should be taken to ensure that the diets of the compound treated groups of animals are isocaloric (equivalent in caloric density) with and contain the same levels of nutrients (eg, fiber, micronutrients) as the diets of the control group.

12. **Controls and Treatment Groups**: A concurrent control group of test animals is required. A carrier or vehicle for the test substance should be given to control animals at a volume equal to the maximum volume of carrier or vehicle given to any dosed group of animals. Sufficient toxicology information should be available on the carrier or vehicle to ensure that its use will not compromise the results of the study. If there is insufficient information about

the toxic properties of the vehicle used to administer the test substance, an additional control group that is not exposed to the carrier or vehicle should be included. In all other respects, animals in the control group should be treated the same as animals in dosed groups. At least three dose levels (plus the concurrent control) given by the same route as the intended route of human exposure, the lowest dose producing no apparent toxicity and the highest producing overt toxicity as demonstrated by:

- Mortality or morbidity (not recommended end-points but can be used)
- Food consumption change
- Weight change
- Signs of toxicity
- Clinical pathology
- Pathology and histopathology

13. **Recovery Groups**: The assessment of recovery is generally required in at least one toxicology study and implies that a nonexposure period be added at the end of the dosing phase for the exclusive purpose of determining the potential reversibility of any test article-related finding. However, the assessment of recovery as defined by the duration of the recovery period, the selection of dose levels for evaluation of recovery, and the determination of when to include recovery groups in a study plan should be justified on a case-by-case basis.

14. **Route and Duration of Administration**: The route of administration of the test substance should approximate that of normal human exposure, if possible. A justification should be provided when other routes are used. The same method of administration should be used for all test animals throughout the study. Animals should be exposed to the test substance daily unless there is pharmacological evidence that daily dosing is not necessary or this is not the intended-dose regimen for humans (eg, many biologics and large molecules have pharmacokinetic profiles that warrant modified-dose schedules). Dose regimens must take into consideration the pK profiles, species differences, and the clinical exposure regimen for humans when developing the preclinical dose schedule and other regimens must be justified.

15. **Body Weight and Feed Intake Data**: Test animals should be weighed at least once a week. Feed consumption (or water consumption if the test substance is administered in the drinking water) should be measured every week during the subchronic toxicity study.

16. **Clinical Observations**: Ophthalmological examination, hematology profiles, clinical chemistry tests, and urinalyses should be performed.

17. **Toxicokinetics:** Systemic exposure assessments should be conducted to confirm the relationship of the administered dose to plasma levels, to evaluation-dose proportionality, to evaluate any potential differences between acute and repeated exposure, to evaluate accumulation/saturation dynamics, and to determine if there are gender differences.

18. **Immunogenicity:** Evaluations for antidrug antibodies are exclusive to biopharmaceutical molecules (chemically synthesized or biologically derived) that are of sufficient size to potentially evoke an immune response. Regional criteria for when to conduct these studies can be diverse. However, the primary purpose of these evaluations in preclinical general toxicology studies is to determine whether the generation of antibodies to the biopharmaceutical molecule (if present) has any potential to alter its exposure profile, which could alter systemic exposure criteria in the general toxicity determination.

19. **Immunotoxicology:** Evaluation of immunotoxicological parameters is conducted in a tiered approach. Initial assessments are done in the standard clinical pathology and microscopic pathology evaluations. If further evaluations are needed, then more elaborate techniques (ie, immunophenotype and functional assays) can be used to determine whether the immune system has been compromised following exposure to the pharmaceutical under development.

20. **Hematology:**

The following determinations are recommended for evaluation of hematological changes:
- hematocrit
- hemoglobin concentration
- erythrocyte count
- total and differential leukocyte counts
- mean corpuscular hemoglobin
- mean corpuscular volume
- mean corpuscular hemoglobin concentration
- measure of clotting potential (such as clotting time, prothrombin time, thromboplastin time, or platelet count).

(Note: Test compounds may have an effect on the hematopoietic system and therefore appropriate measures should be employed to ensure that evaluations of reticulocyte counts and bone-marrow cytology may be performed if warranted. Reticulocyte counts should be obtained for each animal using automated reticulocyte counting capabilities, or from air-dried blood smears. Bone-marrow slides should be prepared from each animal for evaluating bone-marrow cytology. These slides would only need to be examined microscopically if effects on the hematopoietic system were noted.)

21. **Clinical Chemistry:** Blood samples should be obtained for the determination of clinical chemistry tests, including measurements of electrolyte balance, carbohydrate metabolism, and liver and kidney function. Specific determinations should include:
- Hepatocellular evaluation; select at least three of the following five:
  - alanine aminotransferase (SGPT, ALT)
  - aspartate aminotransferase (SGOT, AST)
  - sorbitol dehydrogenase
  - glutamate dehydrogenase
  - total bile acids
- Hepatobiliary evaluation; select at least three of the following five:
  - alkaline phosphatase
  - bilirubin (total)
  - gamma-glutamyl transpeptidase (GG transferase)
  - 5′ nucleotidase
  - total bile acids
- Other markers of cell changes or cellular function:
  - albumin
  - calcium
  - chloride
  - cholesterol (total)
  - cholinesterase
  - creatinine
  - globulin (calculated)
  - glucose (in fasted animals)
  - phosphorous
  - potassium
  - protein (total)
  - sodium
  - triglycerides (fasting)
  - urea nitrogen

However, when adequate volumes of blood cannot be obtained from test animals, the following determinations should generally be given priority. Appropriate justification for alternative tests should be presented in study reports.
- alanine aminotransferase
- alkaline phosphatase
- chloride
- creatinine
- gamma-glutamyl transpeptidase (GG transferase)
- glucose (in fasted animals)
- potassium
- protein (total)
- sodium
- urea nitrogen

22. **Urinalyses:** (typically conducted beginning with the 28-day toxicity studies) Timed urine volume collection during the last week of the study on at least 10 animals of each sex in each group.

The volume of urine collected, specific gravity, pH, glucose, and protein should be determined as well as conducting a microscopic evaluation of urine for sediment and presence of blood–blood cells.

23. **Necropsy and Microscopic Examination:**
Gross Necropsy: All test animals should be subjected to complete gross necropsy, including examination of external surfaces, orifices, cranial, thoracic and abdominal cavities, carcass, and all organs.
Organ Weight: Organ weights should be obtained from adrenals, brain, epididymides, heart, kidneys, liver, spleen, testes, thyroid/parathyroid, thymus, ovaries, and uterus. Organs should be carefully dissected and trimmed to remove fat and other contiguous tissue and then be weighed immediately to minimize the effects of drying on organ weight.
Preparation of Tissues for Microscopic Examination: Tissues should be fixed in 10% buffered formalin (or another generally recognized fixative) and sections prepared and stained with hematoxylin and eosin (or another appropriate stain) in preparation for microscopic examination. Lungs should be inflated with fixative prior to immersion in fixative.
Microscopic Evaluation: All gross lesions should be examined microscopically. All tissues from the control and high-dose groups should be examined histopathologically. If treatment-related effects are observed in certain tissues, the next lower-dose level tested of those specific tissues should be examined. Successive examination of the next lower-dose level continues until no effects are noted. In addition, all tissues from animals dying prematurely or sacrificed during the study should be examined microscopically to assess any potential toxic effects.

- adrenals
- aorta
- bone (femur)
- bone marrow (sternum)
- brain (at least three different levels)
- cecum
- colon
- corpus and cervix uteri
- duodenum
- epididymis
- esophagus
- eyes
- gall bladder (if present)
- harderian gland (if present)
- heart
- ileum
- jejunum
- kidneys

- liver
- lung (with main-stem bronchi)
- lymph nodes (one related to route of administration and one from a distant location)
- mammary glands
- nasal turbinates
- ovaries and fallopian tubes
- pancreas
- pituitary
- prostate
- rectum
- salivary gland
- sciatic nerve
- seminal vesicle (if present)
- skeletal muscle
- skin
- spinal cord (three locations: cervical, midthoracic, lumbar)
- spleen
- stomach
- testes
- thymus (or thymic region)
- thyroid/parathyroid
- trachea
- urinary bladder
- vagina
- all tissues showing abnormality

FINAL THOUGHTS

As we did in the previous edition, this chapter was written to provide a view of general toxicology testing from the point of view of the toxicologist conducting various studies in the laboratory. Toxicologists working in the preclinical drug development need to understand the entire drug development process to better design and conduct preclinical safety studies. Acute toxicity evaluations are among the first preclinical tests to be performed on a drug candidate that may progress to IND. Thus prudent characterization of the acute toxicity is critical, because the data obtained are the basis for dose-level selection on other studies included in the IND application. We have discussed important aspects of general toxicology testing in the drug development process (acute, subacute, subchronic, and chronic testing). Relevant knowledge needed by the toxicologist includes selection of the appropriate species, advantages and disadvantages of each species, concepts employed to select dose levels from acute to chronic toxicity testing, applicable guidelines, the GLP requirements, and appropriate endpoints. Finally, if they understand the intricacies of the general toxicology plan, the toxicologist will be able to progress smoothly as the potential pharmaceutical moves forward in development.

References

[1] Morton DM. Importance of species selection in drug toxicity testing. Toxicol Lett 1998;102–103:545–50.

[2] M3(R2) nonclinical safety studies for the conduct of human clinical trials and marketing authorization for pharmaceuticals. International Conference on Harmonization (ICH).

[3] Guideline on repeated dose toxicity, Committee for Human Medicinal. CPMP/SWP/1042/99 Rev 1 Corr products (CHMP).

[4] Estimating the maximum safe starting dose in initial clinical trials for therapeutics in adult healthy volunteers. Federal register of January 16, 2003 (68 FR 2340).

[5] ICH M3 author. Nonclinical Safety Studies for the conduct of human clinical trials for pharmaceuticals, www.fda.gov/cder/Guidance/1855fnl.pdf.

[6] Dorato MA, McMillian CL, Vodicnik MJ. The toxicological assessment of pharmaceutical and biotechnology products. In: Wallace Hayes A, editor. Principles and methods of toxicology. 5th ed. CRC Press; 2008. p. 325–67.

[7] Bussiere JL, Martin P, Horner M, Couch J, Flaherty M, Andrews L, et al. Alternative strategies for toxicity testing of species-specific biopharmaceuticals. Int J Toxicol 2009;28(3):230–53.

[8] ICH S6(R1) Addendum (Step 4) Guideline: Safety Studies for biotechnological products, www.fda.gov/cder/Guidance/1859fnl.pdf.

[9] ICH S3A author. Toxicokinetics the assessment of systemic exposure in toxicity studies, www.fda.gov/CDER/GUIDANCE/ichs3a.pdf.

[10] ICH S4 author. Duration of chronic toxicity testing in animals (rodent and nonrodent toxicity testing), www.ich.org/LOB/media/MEDIA497.pdf.

[11] ICH S7A author. Safety pharmacology studies for human pharmaceuticals, www.ich.org/LOB/media/MEDIA504.pdf.

[12] ICH S7B author. The preclinical evaluation of the potential for delayed ventricular repolarisation (QT interval prolongation) by human pharmaceuticals, www.ich.org/LOB/media/MEDIA2192.pdf.

[13] ICH S5(R2) author. Detection of toxicity to reproduction for medicinal products and toxicity to male fertility, www.ich.org/LOB/media/MEDIA498.pdf.

[14] ICH M4 author. Organisation of the common technical document for the registration of pharmaceuticals for human use, www.ich.org/LOB/media/MEDIA554.pdf.

[15] Guideline on strategies to identify and mitigate risks for first-in-human clinical trials with investigational medicinal products; strategies to identify and mitigate risks for first-in-human clinical trials with investigational medicinal products. London: Committee for Medicinal Products for Human Use (CHMP); European Medicines Agency; July 19, 2007. Doc. Ref.EMEA/CHMP/SWP/294648/2007.

[16] FDA PTC author. Points to consider in the manufacture and testing of monoclonal antibody products for human use, www.fda.gov/CBER/gdlns/ptc_mab.pdf.

[17] Position paper on the preclinical safety studies to support clinical trials with a single micro dose, www.emea.europa.eu/pdfs/human/swp/259902en.pdf.

[18] OECD series on principles of good laboratory practice and compliance monitoring; number 13, consensus document of the working group on good laboratory practice, the application of the OECD principles of GLP to the Organisation and Management of MultiSite studies, JT00128856. Directive 2004/10 of the European Parliament and of the Council of 11 February 2004 on the application of the principles of good laboratory practice and their verification of their application for tests on chemical substances.

[19] Directive 2004/9/EC of the European Parliament and of the Council of 11 February 2004 on the inspection and verification of good laboratory practice (GLP) (codified version).

[20] Regulation (EC) No 1907/2006 of the European Parliament and of the Council of 18 December 2006 concerning the registration, evaluation, authorization and Restriction of chemicals (REACH), establishing a European chemicals agency, amending directive 1999/45/EC and repealing Council regulation (EEC) No 793/93 and Commission regulation (EC) No 1488/94 as well as Council directive 76/769/EEC and Commission directives 91/155/EEC, 93/67/EEC, 93/105/EC and 2000/21/EC.

[21] Reach regulation of 18 December 2006 and directive 2006/121/EC of 18 December 2006.

[22] Medicinal products; Directive 2001/83/EC on the Community code relating to medicinal products for human use of 6 November 2001 as amended by Commission Directive 2003/63/EC.

[23] Preclinical safety evaluation of biopharmaceuticals. In: Cavagnaro JA, editor. A science-based approach to facilitating clinical trials. John Wiley and Sons; 2008.

[24] Guidance on dose level selection for regulatory general toxicology studies for pharmaceuticals, Laboratory Animal Science Association and National Center for the replacement. Refinement and Reduction of animals in research.

[25] Buckley LA, Benson K, Davis-Bruno K, Dempster M, Finch GL, Harlow P, et al. Nonclinical aspects of biopharmaceutical development: discussion of case studies at a PhRMA-FDA workshop. Int J Toxicol 2008;27(4):303–12.

[26] Shankar G, Shores E, Wagner C, Mire-Sluis A. Scientific and regulatory considerations on the immunogenicity of biologics. Trends Biotechnol 2006;24(6):274–80.

[27] Guidance for Industry. Investigators and reviewer. 2006. Exploratory IND Studies. http://www.fda.gov/downloads/Drugs/GuidanceComplianceRegulatoryInformation/Guidance/ucm078933.pdf. For AU26 to AU28.

[28] Pandher K, Leach MW, Burns-Naas LA. Appropriate use of recovery groups in nonclinical toxicity studies: value in a science-driven case-by-case approach. Vet Pathol 2012;49(2):357–61.

[29] Diehl K-H, Hull R, Morton D, Pfister R, Rabemampianina Y, Smith D, et al. A good practice guide to the administration of substances and removal of blood, including routes and volumes. J Appl Toxicol 2001;21:15–23.

[30] FELASA Guidelines, 1994. Pain and distress in laboratory rodents and lagomorphs 28, 97–112. http://la.rsmjournals.com/cgi/reprint/28/2/97.pdf.

[31] Laboratory Animal Management: Rodents. National Research Council, http://www.nap.edu/books/0309049369/html/index.html; 1996 [Adopted September 1998].

[32] Lumley CE, Neil JA, McAuslane CMR. Centre for Medicines Research: assessment of pharmaceuticals for potential human carcinogenic risk. [CMR Workshop, CMR International]. July 1999.

6

Genetic Toxicology Testing

J. Nicolette

INTRODUCTION

Genetic toxicology testing assesses a compound's ability to cause DNA damage that can lead to heritable defects and possibly cancer [1]. While testing the safety of a drug candidate, all organ systems are evaluated for macro- and microscopic changes that could translate to toxic effects in humans. Most toxicities of drug candidates are evident in animal studies of 2-, 4- or 13-week duration. However, the ability of compounds to cause genetic damage is most often not evident in these safety tests. Carcinogenesis is a long, complex process that does not manifest itself for years after exposure to a carcinogen. Carcinogenicity testing in rodents takes up to 24 months of dosing and is expensive. In addition to lengthy delays in providing medicines urgently needed by patients, it is impractical for drug companies to conduct such studies prior to clinical trials without knowing whether a drug candidate produces any efficacy signals or is tolerated in patients.

Many carcinogens directly impact DNA (ie, genotoxic carcinogens), causing mutations as initiating events that are promoted and progress until tumors form. It is these initiating events that are most concerning, theoretically, as such events would not be expected to display a no-effect level (ie, no threshold). In other words, one hit from a mutagen could lead to one mutation, and this mutation could lead to one tumor. The resulting change in the structure of the DNA can be elucidated by genetic toxicity testing, identifying potentially carcinogenic drug candidates early in development.

Genetic toxicology gives a rapid, early, and inexpensive way of determining a compound's ability to interact with DNA and cause mutations, chromosome damage, or altered DNA repair, leading to permanent structural abnormalities, all of which are hallmarks of carcinogenesis. Utilizing both in vitro and in vivo tests, a compound's genotoxic profile can be ascertained prior to initial dosing in humans. These tests are required for drugs being developed at various stages of the drug development process and prior to specific clinical trials [2].

In addition to testing the drug itself (the active pharmaceutical ingredient, or API), genetic toxicology testing is critical for protecting clinical trial volunteers and patients from the adverse effects of impurities that may be created in synthesis, or from potentially genotoxic metabolites of the parent compound. While often found at trace levels, these potentially reactive materials can have detrimental effects on patients if they are exposed to them over long periods of time. Finally, the simplicity of the genetic toxicology endpoints has made it easy to create many versions and variations of testing to determine the genotoxic potential of compounds in higher throughput and/or miniaturized assays, allowing companies to prescreen many potential candidates at once, helping to deemphasize those that have a propensity to cause DNA damage and focus resources on the compounds with the best safety profile.

The objective of this chapter is to briefly describe the most commonly used core tests that support clinical development, provide an overview of how genetic toxicity testing can be used to identify genotoxic compounds early to reduce candidate attrition, characterize hazards, and how genetic toxicology is used to qualify metabolites and impurities that may also represent a hazard to human health.

THE CONCEPT OF THRESHOLDS

For most toxicities a certain exposure level of the xenobiotic is needed in the target organ to elicit the toxic response. This level may be elucidated in short or longer duration dosing studies, or may only appear in one highly sensitive species. An effect is considered thresholded when doses can be administered (ie, the test system is exposed to the xenobiotic) and no toxicity is seen at low doses, but at higher dosages toxic effects of the drug are observed. Thresholds are important for drug development because almost all compounds are toxic at sufficiently high exposures (lowest observed effect level or LOEL), but may be therapeutic at exposure levels well below the toxic level (no-effect level or NOEL). This allows clinicians to safely administer drugs at the therapeutic or supratherapeutic level, knowing that the dosages are well below those expected to cause adverse effects. This is referred to as a margin of safety or the ratio of the dose or exposure at the LOEL compared to the NOEL.

Genetic toxicity testing identifies compounds that have the ability to cause mutations or other DNA damage. The prevailing view on genotoxic compounds is that a single interaction with DNA can lead to a mutation and that these mutations ultimately could lead to tumor formation. Since mutation events are typically considered to have no threshold (Fig. 6.1), regulatory agencies treat mutagenic compounds as determined in genotoxicity tests with a great deal of caution before allowing human clinical trial subjects to be exposed to them.

Despite the long-held dogma that no safe level exists for genotoxicants, a growing body of evidence shows that low-dose exposures to genotoxic agents do display thresholds [3,4]. Hence, drugs that induce genotoxicity through indirect mechanisms (eg, damaging the mitotic spindle, inhibition of topoisomerase, or inhibiting DNA synthesis) can be administered at doses where the mechanism for such damage does not occur [5–7]. In 2008, the mutagenic contaminant ethyl methansulfonate (EMS) found in some lots of the AIDS medication

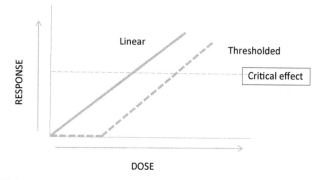

FIGURE 6.1 Linear dose effect (solid) versus thresholded response (dotted). The critical effect (such as an adverse toxic response) occurs at a lower dose and a dose response theoretically occurs at all doses when the dose response is linear. With a thresholded effect, no response is seen at the low end of the dose range until a dose is reached where homeostasis is lost. Drug development tries to take advantage of the low-dose non-linear portion of the dose response curves to avoid adverse toxic events at doses that are efficacious to treat disease.

Viracept was shown to have a NOEL in a series of experiments, ensuring that patients exposed were not harmed and eventually leading to a determination of a tolerable daily intake for this mutagenic impurity [3,6]. Finally, for genotoxic or potentially genotoxic impurities (GTI) in the API, a threshold of toxicological concern (TTC) has been established, below which no significant detrimental effect from lifetime exposure is expected [8,9].

It is important to keep in mind that without additional evidence, a mutagenic result in a test would be considered a signal for potential carcinogenicity in most cases. But as discussed above, there is increasing evidence showing that genotoxic agents can show thresholds at low doses, illustrating the growing use of genetic toxicology tests not only as hazard identification tools but as an integral part of the risk assessment process.

GENETIC TOXICITY TESTING TO SUPPORT CLINICAL TRIALS

Guidelines ICHS2(R1) and ICHM3

Prior to clinical trial in humans, drug candidates must go through a number of rigorous assays and studies to evaluate their safety. Assessments for carcinogenicity induction at this early stage of development are too costly and time-consuming, and could delay getting new medications to patients in need. To protect clinical trial subjects, a series of genetic toxicity tests are therefore conducted to assess mutagenic potential in vitro, as well as chromosome damaging capability both in vitro and in vivo. The core battery of tests is well defined by the regulatory guideline International Conference on Harmonization (ICH) S2R1, and is expected to support various stages of clinical development (Fig. 6.2) [2]. These tests are expected to follow good laboratory practices (GLPs), are protocol-driven, and are usually conducted following an established study design as outlined by the Organization for Economic Co-operation and Development (OECD). Table 6.1 highlights the most frequently used tests and the timing in relation to clinical trial phases [10]. In addition to the core battery, additional studies can be useful to understand the mechanisms of a genotoxic response and the relevance of the finding to the risk to humans. Some of these tests are given in Table 6.2.

The core battery of genetic toxicity endpoints is a required part of the regulatory submissions for most small molecule therapeutics [10]. No single genetic toxicity test covers the array of possible genetic damage that could be induced by exposure to a xenobiotic; therefore multiple tests evaluating several in vitro and in vivo endpoints are required. The battery may be modified, based on characteristics of the small molecule evaluated. For example, a mammalian cell mutation test may be included in a safety package when a candidate's mode of action may have preferential cytotoxic effects on bacteria that are used in the bacterial reverse mutation assay.

There are two options for conducting an appropriate genetic toxicology battery for support of drug development [2]:

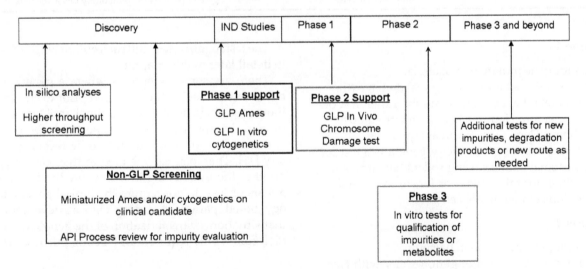

FIGURE 6.2 **Genetic toxicity usage through compound lifecycle.** Genetic toxicity evaluation through the drug lifecycle. Early discovery can utilize in silico evaluations to prioritize compounds for high throughput tests. More robust non-good laboratory practice (GLP) testing can be done late in discovery prior to candidate nomination. At this time, the synthetic route should be evaluated for potentially genotoxic impurities. Regulatory required GLP testing supports the various clinical trial phases and is performed prior to these trials with adequate time to provide data and reports for filing. Genetic toxicity tests can still be employed late in the lifecycle if the synthetic route changes, for impurity qualification prior to Phase III trials, or if new impurities/degradation products need qualification.

TABLE 6.1　Standard Genetic Toxicity Tests [2,10]

Tests	Endpoint	Clinical Trial Phase[a]	Guideline
Bacterial reverse mutation test (Ames assay)	Gene mutations	Required prior to Phase I, single-dose trials, impurity qualification	OECD 471
In vitro cytogenetics Chromosome aberrations Micronucleus Mouse lymphoma	Chromosome breakage or loss. Mouse lymphoma assay also detects gene mutations	Required prior to Phase I, repeated-dose trials, impurity qualifications	OECD 473 (aberrations) OECD 487 (MNvit) OECD 476 (MLA)
In vivo chromosome damage Micronucleus Chromosome aberrations	Chromosome breakage or loss	Required prior to Phase II trials	OECD 474 (MN) OECD 475 (aberrations)

[a]Biopharmaceuticals and pharmaceuticals for life-threatening indications may not need genotoxicity tests at the stages indicated.

TABLE 6.2　Additional Tests for Genetic Toxicology

Test	Endpoint	Typical Usage
IN VITRO TESTS		
In vitro comet or alkaline elution	DNA strand breaks and alkali labile sites	Early screening, many cell types, mechanistic evaluations
GreenScreen	DNA repair (green fluorescent protein activated by GADD45)	High-throughput screening, human TK6 cells
Cell transformation	Morphologic transformation	Follow-up for carcinogenic compounds with no genotoxicity; suspected nongenotoxic carcinogenic series
IN VIVO RODENT TESTS		
In vivo comet (OECD 489)	DNA strand breaks and alkali labile sites	Follow-up/clarification for positive in vitro test in battery
Transgenic rodent gene mutation (OECD 488)	Mutation in vivo in bacterial transgenes	Follow-up/clarification of in vitro gene mutation results
Unscheduled DNA synthesis (OECD 486)	Increased DNA repair activity in ex vivo rodent hepatocytes	Follow-up/clarification of in vitro (Ames) positive; compounds forming bulky DNA adducts

Option 1

1. A test for gene mutation in bacteria.
2. A cytogenetic test for chromosomal damage (the in vitro metaphase chromosome aberration test or in vitro micronucleus test), or an in vitro mouse lymphoma Tk gene mutation assay.
3. An in vivo test for genotoxicity, generally a test for chromosomal damage using rodent hematopoietic cells, either for micronuclei or for chromosomal aberrations in metaphase cells.

Option 2

1. A test for gene mutation in bacteria.
2. An in vivo assessment of genotoxicity with two different tissues, usually an assay for micronuclei using rodent hematopoietic cells and a second in vivo assay. Typically, this would be a DNA strand breakage assay in liver, unless otherwise justified.

The test required to fulfill each option will be described in detail later in this chapter.

There are some exceptions where a genetic toxicology safety package is not required prior to clinical trials. Biotherapeutics, such as monoclonal antibodies or large protein therapeutics, are not expected to be genotoxic, and therefore are not required to be tested in the battery [11]. Therapeutics intended to treat cancer patients or other life-threatening illness where life expectancy is 5 years or less do not require the typical genetic toxicology tiered paradigm during clinical development. In that situation, characterization of the genotoxicity of the molecule is only required for labeling purposes [12].

Bacterial Reverse Mutation Assays

- Guideline: OECD471
- In vitro test for gene mutations in bacteria
- Required prior to Phase I clinical trials

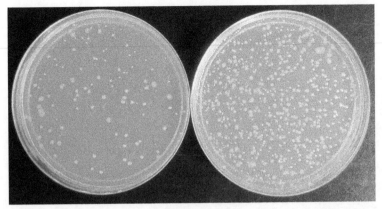

FIGURE 6.3   Ames plates. Plates from bacterial reverse mutation (Ames) assay. On the left is a negative control showing few revertant colonies. On the right is a positive control plate showing many colonies, indicative of a mutagenic response. *Photos courtesy of BioReliance, Rockville, MD.*

The cornerstone of genetic toxicology testing is the bacterial reverse mutation assay. The assay is based on the work of Bruce Ames and colleagues on *Salmonella typhimurium* strains and is often referred to as the Ames assay [13,14]. This simple assay detects compounds that are capable of causing mutations using minimal test material [15]. Because of its simplicity, the bacterial reverse mutation test is often used throughout the early stages of drug development, from determining mutagenic potential in early discovery through regulatory testing in early development (see Fig. 6.2).

The bacteria are engineered with mutations at either the histidine or tryptophan locus. In the presence of a mutagen, the bacteria can be back-mutated such that they are able to synthesize their own amino acids and no longer need exogenously supplied amino acids to survive. In the assay, the test article is mixed with the bacterial strains, molten overlay agar, small quantities of the amino acids, and either an exogenously supplied metabolic activation system (rat-liver microsomes with a mix of cofactors) or a sham mix that does not contain liver microsomes. This mixture is poured onto a Petri plate containing a minimal glucose agar and the overlay agar is allowed to solidify. The amino acids allow the bacteria to go through one or two divisions, then, once exhausted, only back-mutated bacteria can survive. The mutations are fixed in the DNA when the bacteria divide and these continue to divide and eventually form colonies that are easily countable 48–72h later.

The metabolic activation, usually in a form of an induced rat-liver microsome mixture, helps to provide some metabolic capability (primarily mixed function oxidase enzymes), in the activated arm of the test such that promutagens can be identified in addition to direct effects of the test article in the nonactivated arm [16]. Spontaneous reversion occurs, so to determine if the bacteria were exposed to a mutagen, colony counts from plates where bacteria have been exposed to the test article are compared to counts from control plates (see Fig. 6.3) [14,15].

Numerous tester strains of *Salmonella* with mutations in the histidine locus in GC-rich regions have been characterized. These strains have a number of characteristics that distinguish them from each other and from their parent auxotrophic strains. Each has a deep rough mutation (rfa-) such that the lipopolysaccharide cell wall is "leaky," allowing larger molecules to penetrate, therefore making them available to interact with the bacterial DNA. Many of the strains have no meaningful repair capability, and can be identified as such by their sensitivity to ultraviolet light (uvrB-) and to ampicillin. To enhance the sensitivity to mutagens, some of the strains contain plasmids with many copies of the mutated gene [17].

In addition to the *Salmonella* strains routinely employed in the assay, a number of *Escherichia coli* strains have been engineered. These typically do not have defects in the cell wall, are TRP⁻, and have mutations through AT sequences. Some of the strains of *E. coli* have plasmids to enhance sensitivity and are uvrA sensitive [18].

In order to detect a broad range of mutagens, five strains of bacteria are typically utilized in regulatory assays [2,15,19]. The combination of strains detects frameshift and point mutagens as well as those that act on either GC or AT sites. The addition of strains with repair capabilities improves sensitivity to mutagens that would only be detected during repair of DNA damage. A list of strains and characteristics that are suggested for use appear in Table 6.3.

In Vitro Mammalian Cell Assays

A second in vitro assay, performed in mammalian cells, is typically required to support drug development. Several types of tests are considered acceptable for regulatory submissions, although each looks at the potential of the test article to cause chromosome breakage and are considered to be chromosome damage assays.

TABLE 6.3　Bacterial Reverse Mutation Assay: Standard Strains [14,15,18,135]

Indicator Strain	Mutation	Mutation Detected	LPS	UV Repair	Plasmids
SALMONELLA TYPHIMURIUM					
TA98	hisD3052	Frameshift	rfa	ΔuvrB	pKM101
TA1535	hisG46	Frameshift	rfa	ΔuvrB	–
TA100	hisG46	Frameshift/basepair	rfa	ΔuvrB	pKM101
TA1537	hisD6610	Frameshift	rfa	ΔuvrB	–
TA97	hisD6610	Frameshift	rfa	ΔuvrB	pKM101
TA102	hisG428	Base-pair, oxidative damage, cross-linking agents	rfa	+	pKM101pAQ1
TA97a	hisD6610his 01242	Frameshift	rfa	+	pKM101
ESCHERICHIA COLI					
WP2	trpE	Basepair	+	+	–
WP2 *uvrA*	trpE	Basepair	+	ΔuvrA	–
WP2 *uvrA* pKM101	trpE	Basepair	+	ΔuvrA	pKM101

In Vitro Chromosome Aberration Test

- Guideline: OECD473
- In vitro mammalian cells testing for chromosome damage
- Conducted prior to Phase I clinical trials

The in vitro chromosome aberration test is a cell-culture assay that looks at individual chromosomes from cells arrested in mitosis for clastogenic events (chromosome breakage) [20–22]. Numerous cell types can be employed but cell lines of Chinese hamster origin or primary human lymphocytes are often used in drug development. For human lymphocytes, the population can be enriched from whole blood or used as collected; cells are induced to divide by culturing with agents like phytohemmaglutanin. After cells go through an initial culture period, the test compound is added to the culture, either in a formulation or dissolved in media. Several exposure conditions are used (Table 6.4).

After the exposure period, the exposure medium is replaced with fresh medium for the conditions requiring a recovery period. Since rat-liver microsomes can be cytotoxic over long periods of time, recovery is done without microsomes after initial exposure conditions with metabolic activation. In order to evaluate individual chromosomes, a chemical that arrests cells in mitosis (eg, colchicine) is added to the cultures approximately 2 h prior to harvest. At harvest the cells are fixed using three parts methanol to one part acetic acid, slides are prepared, and cells stained with dyes, such as Giemsa. This staining allows for small gaps or breaks or rearrangements to be visible under light microscopy (Fig. 6.4).

Cultures are evaluated for the frequency of mitoses (mitotic index), and this value is compared back to the frequency seen in the vehicle control cultures. Reductions in the relative mitotic index indicate a cytostatic impact on the cells, and this is often referred to as cytotoxicity. Other parameters for measuring cytotoxicity can be used, such as relative cell counts and population doubling [23]. Ideally, compound concentrations exhibiting 50% cytotoxicity are used as the high end of the concentration range to be evaluated for chromosome aberrations. The percentage of cells in each culture with aberrations is calculated and comparisons made between compound-exposed culture and negative controls. Abnormal segregation events, such as polyploidy (multiple copies of the set of chromosomes) or endoreduplication (aberrant separation of replicated chromosomes) are also scored as these may be an indication of concerns on the replicative machinery and possible aneugenicity (alteration in chromosome number) induced by the compound. However, it is beyond the scope of this assay to be used in the interpretation of a possible aneugenic response.

The in vitro chromosome aberration assay is evaluated microscopically. Slides are coded to prevent bias by the evaluator, and each chromosome in 300 or more cells is inspected for damage. In addition, the evaluator looks at several 100–1000 cells to determine a mitotic index. This makes the in vitro chromosome aberration test one of the more labor-intensive assays in genetic toxicity evaluation.

Because of the nature of the evaluation, little progress has been made on improving or automating methods for the assessment. For determining mitotic index, some alternative methods are available. Imaging systems can

TABLE 6.4 Common Exposure Conditions for In Vitro Cytogenetics

Exposure Duration	Metabolic Activation	Recovery	Colchicine
CHROMOSOME ABERRATIONS[A]			
3–6h	With and without	1.5 to 2.0 cell cycles	2h prior to harvest
1.5–2.0 cell cycles (20–24h)	Without	0h	2h prior to harvest
	Without	24h	2h prior to harvest
	Without	48h	2h prior to harvest

Exposure Duration	Metabolic Activation	CYB	Recovery
MICRONUCLEUS ASSAY[B]			
3–6h	With and without	At wash	1.5 to 2.0 cell cycles
1.5–2.0 cell cycles	Without	At initiation of exposure	None
	Without	At wash	1.5 to 2.0 cell cycles

Exposure Duration	Expression Period
MOUSE LYMPHOMA ASSAY[C]	
3–6h (with and without S9)	48h

[a]*Positive controls: Mitomycin C, methyl- or ethyl-methanesulfonate, ethylnitrosourea (without S9); cyclophosphamide or benzo(a) pyrene (with S9).*
[b]*CYB, cytochalasin B. Positive controls: Mitomycin C or cytosine arabinoside for clastogenicity, vinblastine, or colchicine for aneugenicity (without S9); cyclophosmamide, benzo(a) pyrene (with S9).*
[c]*Positive controls: Methylmethanesulfonate (without S9); cyclophosphamide, benzo(a) pyrene or 3-methylcholanthrene (with S9).*

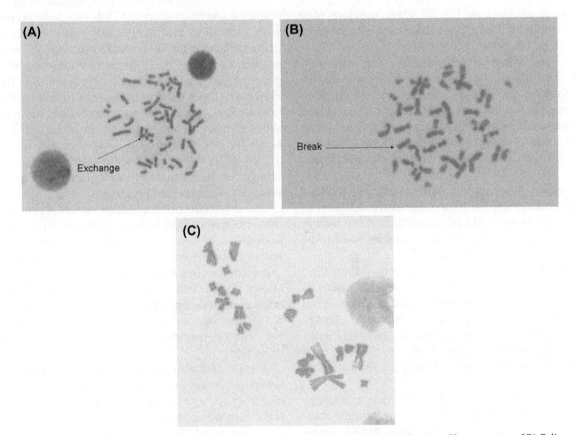

FIGURE 6.4 Chromosome aberrations. (A) Exchange, (B) chromosome break, (C) endoreduplication. *Photos courtesy of BioReliance, Rockville, MD and Midwest Bioresearch, Skokie, IL.*

TABLE 6.5 Reported Range of Sensitivity and Specificity of In Vitro Genetox Tests for Rodent Carcinogens [29]

Test	Sensitivity (%)	Specificity (%)	Size of Db
Ames	52–59	72–74	541–3711 chemicals
In vitro micronucleus	79–88	23–31	89–182 chemicals
In vitro chromosome aberrations	55–66	45–63	352–1391 chemicals
Mouse lymphoma	71–73	39–44	245–827 chemicals
COMBINATION OF TESTS			
Ames + micronucleus	94	12	372 chemicals
Ames + mouse lymphoma + chromosome aberrations	84	23	202 chemicals

Table adapted from Committee on Mutagenicity of Chemicals in Food Consumer Products and the Environment (COM). Guidance on a strategy for genotoxicity testing of chemical substances; 2011, referencing database analyses by Kirkland (2005) and Matthews (2006).

scan slides and determine the frequency of mitoses; flow cytometry can also be used [24,25]. These methods may offer more consistent and less subjective evaluations of cytotoxicity in this assay.

Toxicity and compound insolubility are important considerations in cell-culture cytogenetic assays. Excessive cytotoxicity can lead to the appearance of chromosome damage that is not necessarily a sign of direct DNA interaction. Insolubility of the compound in media can lead to extended exposures if the compound cannot be removed for the designated recovery period, and cells may take up compound particulates via endocytosis, leading to effects that are not representative of the true risk of exposure to the compound. Similarly, extremes of culture conditions (low pH, high osmolarity) can lead to chromosome aberrations, so that conditions need to be monitored during the study [22,26,27].

Positive results in the in vitro chromosome aberration test indicate the compound has the potential for interacting with the DNA and is a potential hazard. This test has a high degree of sensitivity and is thus able to identify true chromosome damaging agents with great efficiency [28]. However, historically specificity (ie, nongenotoxicants identified as negative) has been poor for this assay (Table 6.5).

Looking at a comparison with rodent noncarcinogens or nongenotoxicants, specificity for the chromosome aberration assay is around 45–63% [29]. Some of this can be attributed to the high concentrations used in culture (up to 10 mM), exposing dividing cells to conditions that may not be attainable in the in vivo situation. A recent revision

of the ICH guideline S2 on conducting genotoxicity testing for human pharmaceuticals lowered this top exposure condition to 1 mM or 500 µg/mL, in an effort to keep exposures closer to worst-case physiological conditions and to reduce the number of false positive findings [2].

In Vitro Micronucleus Assay

- Guideline: OECD 487
- In vitro mammalian cell test for chromosome damage or loss
- Conducted prior to Phase I clinical trials

The in vitro micronucleus assay (MNvit) also identifies chromosome damage, but rather than investigating metaphases for individual chromosomes, cells are evaluated for the presence of small, DNA-staining bodies outside of their main nucleus (hence, a micronucleus, or MN). MN can arise from two pathways: pieces of chromosomes can be broken off during clastogenic events, or whole chromosomes can become dislodged from the mitotic spindle (see Fig. 6.5). As the nucleus divides into two daughter nuclei, these entities cannot be repackaged into the main nucleus and thus reside in the cytoplasm.

Conduct of the MNvit is very similar to the in vitro chromosome aberration test [30]. The assay is conducted with both short and continuous exposures, conditions using metabolic activation and those without, and recovery times of 1.5–2.0 cell cycles to ensure the cells have gone through nuclear division before scoring (Table 6.4). However, rather than arresting cells in mitosis this assay is evaluated on cells in interphase. Cells are harvested; slides are prepared and stained. Since the fine detail that is needed for chromosome assessments is unnecessary for the MNvit test, fluorescent stains, such as acridine orange can be employed in addition to light microscopy stains like Giemsa (see Fig. 6.6).

There are two cell types in which MN are measured: mononuclear cells or binucleated cells. To obtain a large population of binucleated cells, cytochalasin B (CYB) is added to the recovery media or the media at the outset of exposure for continuous exposure conditions [31]. CYB allows the nucleus to divide, but does not allow cytokinesis (cell division) to proceed. Thus the resulting cell is binucleated, and having gone through nuclear division, is an appropriate cell to evaluate for micronucleus induction.

A ratio of the mononucleated to binucleated population gives an indication of the proliferation index of the culture, allowing for assessment of the cytostatic/cytotoxic state of the culture after exposure to the compound. Evaluation of mononucleate cells is performed in a similar manner, but CYB is not added to the cultures. Twice as many cells must be evaluated as resulting MN will reside in only one of the

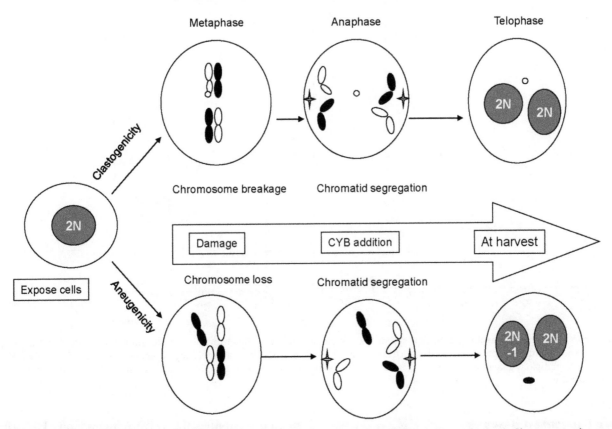

FIGURE 6.5 Formation of micronuclei (MN) by clastogenic pathway (top) and aneugenic pathway (bottom). Chromosome fragments or whole chromosome cannot segregate and be packaged into the nucleus. Cytochalasin B (CYB) treatment leads to binucleate formation for easy scoring of cells that have gone through the requisite division for possible MN identification.

two daughter cells. Imaging systems or flow cytometry can be employed to score more cells objectively without issues of scorer fatigue [32–37]. Cytotoxicity can be evaluated by a number of methods, and should be limited to approximately 55% toxicity [30]. The same concerns about excessive toxicity and culture conditions in the in vitro chromosome aberration assay apply to the in vitro micronucleus test as both are looking at chromosome damage [27,30]. Statistical methods or fold increase in MN over controls can be used to set criteria for a positive response.

The MNvit test as described with standard DNA stains does not discriminate between direct DNA interaction and indirect damage. Alternative staining methods can be employed to do this. Clastogenesis, where chromosomes break, is an indication of direct DNA interaction. Aneugenicity, on the other hand, is an interaction between the test article and the mitotic spindle. Because of the redundancy within the spindle apparatus, damage can occur without manifesting in chromosome loss until a certain concentration overwhelms the system and a chromosome falls off the spindle, ie, the response can often be thresholded (see Fig. 6.5). Identifying aneugenic events can distinguish a test article from one that causes chromosome breakage,

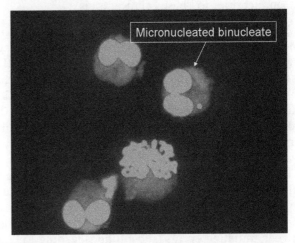

FIGURE 6.6 Binucleated cells in the MNvit assay. Binucleated V79 cells, stained with acridine orange, from MNvit assay.

and provides a possible development opportunity by demonstrating a safety margin. Special staining techniques can identify the presence of whole chromosomes [38,39]. New, higher throughput techniques, such as flow cytometry can also help in making this important determination from the same basic laboratory assay (see Fig. 6.7) [36,37,40].

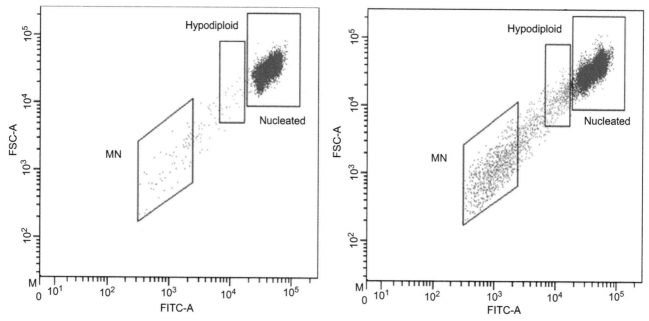

FIGURE 6.7 **Micronucleus evaluation by flow cytometry.** Dot plots from flow cytometric analysis of cultures exposed to DMSO as a negative control (left) and mitomycin C positive control (right). Events in the MN gate are counted against a total number of nuclei in the "nucleated" gate. Events in the hypodiploid gate represent nuclei that have less than the full complement of DNA, which may help identify compounds that are aneugenic in nature.

Mouse Lymphoma Assay

- Guideline: OECD 476
- In vitro mammalian cell test (mouse lymphoma cells) for gene mutation and chromosome damage
- Conduct prior to Phase I clinical trials

Another regulatory option for determining a drug candidate's potential to cause chromosome damage in vitro is the mouse lymphoma assay (MLA). The MLA assay is a gene mutation test using L5178Y tk±cells that looks for DNA damage evidenced by forward mutation at the thymidine kinase (TK) locus [41,42]. Because of the ability to detect chromosome damage as well as mutations in mammalian cells, the mouse lymphoma assay is a valuable tool to identify genotoxic hazards. Mutation to $TK^{-/-}$ results in resistance to the cytotoxic effects of trifluorothymidine. Mutant cells are able to divide and proliferate in contrast to those that do not mutate [41]. By sizing the resulting colonies, one can distinguish between mutation events (substitutions leading to large colony formation) or chromosome damage events (deletions leading to the formation of small colonies). Mutant frequency is determined by counting the number of colonies among the number of viable cells as determined in a parallel culture without the selection agent trifluorothymidine.

Relative cloning efficiency, determined from the parallel test-article culture viability as compared to the controls, should be >20%; otherwise cytotoxicity may influence the findings by increasing mutation frequency not representative of true DNA interactions. Historically, the rate of positive findings only at cytotoxic conditions was a problem when interpreting the results of this assay. Reanalysis of the acceptance criteria, along with routine use of the Global Evaluation Factor, and a reevaluation of a number of tested compounds based on the newer criteria have improved its specificity [43].

Like the chromosome aberration test and the MNvit, short treatments (with and without metabolic activation) and continuous exposure (typically 24 h) are required for a regulatory-acceptable MLA test (Table 6.4). Depending on the extent of damage, the growth rate of the cells can differ, thus leading to various-sized colonies after the expression period. Small colonies result from large-scale deletions to chromosomes, representing chromosome aberrations, stemming from longer doubling times. In contrast, mutations through the TK locus lead to less overall damage (but not less meaningful) and the cells show a relatively higher rate of doubling, leading to large colonies [41].

THE SENSITIVITY AND SPECIFICITY OF IN VITRO ASSAYS

An important consideration for any in vitro test is its ability to accurately predict results of in vivo testing. In vitro studies should be predictive of appropriate in vivo endpoints to save on compound usage early in development as well as eliminating, when appropriate, the need for further animal testing on drug candidates that should no longer be considered for development. For the in vitro genetic toxicity tests, comparisons are typically made against carcinogenicity or in vivo genotoxic endpoints (Table 6.5).

The Ames test has a sensitivity (positive results when testing rodent carcinogens) of 52–59% against rodent carcinogenicity and 72–74% specificity for rodent noncarcinogens [29].

In vitro cytogenetic and gene mutation tests have higher sensitivity than the Ames test (55–88% depending on the data set evaluated), but the specificity is much lower (23–63%) [29]. As previously noted, it is this lower specificity that can lead to additional in vivo testing to prove that the in vitro positive compound does not have the potential to cause in vivo genotoxicity and thus the compound would be considered nongenotoxic by virtue of the weight of evidence [44]. A combination of an Ames test for mutations and any of the in vitro tests for chromosome damage leads to an overall increase in sensitivity of the battery, with a concomitant decrease in specificity [29]. The low specificity of the battery of in vitro tests has led to the suggestion that for certain chemical classes of drug candidates, the in vitro cytogenetic tests should be replaced by a pair of in vivo endpoints in either individual studies or, preferably, a single study where multiple tissues are evaluated [2].

In the in vitro cytogenetic tests there are several sources of apparent DNA damage not related to genotoxicity, which can lead to positive findings that would not be seen when the compound is tested in vivo. Toxicity, in the form of cell death, inhibition of DNA synthesis, and reduction in cell growth compared to control have been shown to increase the number of damaged chromosomes or the mutation frequency [26,27]. Testing to concentrations well beyond the solubility limits presents several problems. Insolubility represents difficulty in following exposure guidelines as outlined in the appropriate OECD protocols. Removal of the test material from the cells through wash steps may be impossible when exceeding the solubility limits, leading to continuous exposure rather than recovery from exposure. Extremes of culture conditions, such as low pH or high osmolarity can also lead to increases in chromosome damage [27]. Finally, differences in sensitivity and specificity can be seen between cells from different species or even different cell types from the same species [45–47].

All of these factors can contribute to varying responses but also, more importantly, the potential for in vitro false-positive results. In addition, many marketed pharmaceuticals have a positive finding in cytogenetics assays [28,48], which has led to use of the term "false-positive" findings associated with the use of in vitro cytogenetics tests. However, it is important to note that a well-conducted, OECD-compliant cytogenetic test will provide the researcher with an identification of a potential hazard. Results cannot be dismissed when developing a compound as a potential drug, especially with no additional information that can refute the in vitro finding. To conclude that a positive result is "false" or "misleading," additional testing must be conducted prior to advancing further in the clinic [44].

The low specificity of individual cytogenetics tests has led to discussion about the utility of these assays as part of the standard battery for pharmaceutical development [28,49,50]. In the revision of the ICH guideline for genotoxicity testing, in addition to the traditional battery of bacterial mutation tests, in vitro cytogenetics, and a single in vivo cytogenetic endpoint, sponsors could consider a second option in which instead of conducting the in vitro cytogenetics test, two in vivo endpoints, derived from two different tissues, could be substituted [2]. This second option effectively treats the test compound as "positive" in the in vitro cytogenetics test, and sponsors go straight to the typical course of action as if they had conducted the in vitro study. The revision to the ICHS2 guideline begins to focus the genetic toxicology battery on risk, noting that the potential risk may be more appropriately defined by in vivo studies where the test compound is administered repeatedly, and the compound has to be absorbed, metabolized, and distributed to target tissues, and resulting damage sufficient to overcome DNA repair mechanisms represents a true genotoxic risk.

IN VIVO CORE TESTS

In addition to the highly sensitive in vitro tests, an in vivo genetox test is required for small molecules. This test is required for development prior to initiating Phase II clinical trials [10]. Additional in vivo testing can be done to help ensure patient safety when a positive result is seen in the in vitro mutagenicity or chromosome damage assays [44]. These tests have limited sensitivity but good specificity so positive in vivo genotoxicity tests carry considerable weight for concern for human health [51].

The test typically required for routine drug development is an in vivo study in rodents for chromosome damage in blood cells, either an in vivo micronucleus or chromosome aberration test. Other tests may be employed as required [2].

In Vivo Micronucleus

- Guideline: OECD 474, ICHS2R1
- Test species: rats or mice, using peripheral blood or bone marrow
- Conduct in support of Phase II clinical trials

The in vivo rodent micronucleus test is the one most often used to support the clinical development of small molecules [2]. The target cells are bone-marrow erythrocytes or peripheral blood cells, and either rats or mice can be used. The test has been conducted as a standalone study, ie, a specific in vivo test is conducted just for identification of genotoxicity in vivo [52,53]. Mouse peripheral blood reticulocytes have also been used historically to evaluate micronucleus formation [54]. Since the rat spleen efficiently removes abnormal circulating erythrocytes, use of peripheral blood in the rat had been discouraged [55]. With the development of new staining techniques and new technologies, such as the flow cytometric method or image analysis, it is possible to identify the early circulating reticulocytes for evaluation of the presence of micronuclei and to score millions of cells to give appropriate sensitivity to the assay [56,57]. With such capabilities, it is possible to include the micronucleus endpoint as an integrated endpoint within general toxicology studies of 2–4 weeks' duration. This can eliminate the need for a separate standalone micronucleus in vivo study and reduce the animal usage associated with such a test. ICHS2R1, the guidance for genotoxicity testing for human-use pharmaceuticals, provides information and requirements when selecting these different testing designs [2].

The micronucleus test was first described in the early 1970s, and testing protocols have been further refined [52,53,55]. The test article can cause chromosome breakage or loss during division of erythrocyte precursors. When the cells expel their nuclei, the MN cannot be eliminated, leaving a DNA staining body in the cell with no nucleus. The process takes about 24–48h to manifest the damage.

In the standalone assay, rats or mice are dosed with the test article under one of two testing regimens. A single-dose study design requires two harvests, typically 24 and 48h after dosing, and thus two groups of animals at each dose group are used. When using a two or three daily dose design, a single harvest time point 24h after dosing is needed. It is important to note that the micronuclei present are a result of damage that had occurred in the last 24–48h and that these events are not cumulative. DNA replication is a requirement to see the damage and thus cells from the erythropoietic compartment are highly suited for this assay.

High doses are used, since only one to three doses are given, and the animals should be exposed to as high a dose as possible as long as lethality is not expected or to a dosage where the test item saturates toxicokinetic properties [55]. Typically a range-finding assay is conducted prior to the definitive micronucleus test to establish a maximum tolerated dose (MTD). The limit dose for the assay is 2000mg/kg body weight per day [55]. Five animals per sex per dose group are used, and in addition to

TABLE 6.6　In Vivo MN Dosing Designs [2]

Duration of Dosing	Uses	Highest Dose Requirements
Short-duration (1–3 daily dosages)	Option 1 (routine clinical support)	Highest dose that does not produce lethality (OECD474)
Integrated design (add-on endpoint in general toxicity study or multiweek genetox study)	Option 1	Highest dosage for general toxicity study acceptable
	Option 2 or follow-up to in vitro positive study	Must meet one of the following: • maximum feasible dose • 1000mg/kg/day (limit dose for 14+-day study) • maximum exposure • top dose ≥50% acute near-lethal dosage

the high-dose group, two lower dosing groups (usually one-half and one-fourth of the high dose) are used along with a positive control group (Table 6.6). Male animals have been shown to be more sensitive to micronucleus induction, and so, when there is no significant difference in toxicity, exposure, or if the drug candidate being studied is expected to treat disease in both men and women, male rodents only can be used for the test [2].

Animals are observed for signs of toxicity after dosing. At the appropriate time points, target cells are harvested and slides prepared. Cells are stained with Giemsa or acridine orange to identify polychromatic erythrocytes (PCE) containing RNA and normochromatic erythrocytes (NCE) devoid of nuclear material. These preparations can be evaluated by microscopy. The proportion of PCE to NCE can indicate bone-marrow toxicity if greatly decreased in the dosing groups compared to untreated or vehicle-treated control animals. Micronuclei are scored in the PCE population, typically 4000cells per animal. The stains used distinguish DNA material (dark red/purple with Giemsa; yellow with acridine orange) from the RNA in the cytoplasm (blue with Giemsa; red/orange with acridine orange) (Fig. 6.8).

This makes evaluation of the cells by microscopy a relatively simple task. Following the original criteria for identifying MN, defined by Schmid, MN are enumerated in all groups and statistical significance determined, including evaluation for dose dependency [52].

Additional methods for evaluating micronuclei have been established to allow automation or investigation of circulating erythrocytes [57]. These methods can evaluate more cells in an objective manner without scorer fatigue. Since the early reticulocyte population averages 2–4% of the blood cell population in a sample, manual evaluation of enough cells for statistical evaluation represents a substantial task. Image analysis methods or evaluation by flow cytometry can evaluate millions of

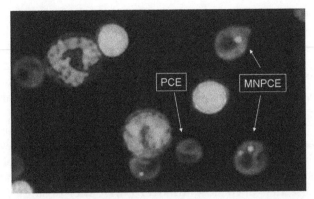

FIGURE 6.8 In vivo MN. Micronucleated erythrocytes (MNPCE) stained with acridine orange from bone-marrow sample.

cells without the limitations inherent in manual evaluations [57,58]. The evaluation system must identify young reticulocytes, such that elimination of MN cells by the spleen would be minimized. Another advantage of evaluating circulating erythrocytes is the ability to sample during the course of a repeated-dose toxicity study without the need to euthanize the animals. This minimizes animal usage for routine toxicity evaluation and can be an acceptable approach when in vitro tests are negative.

A positive result often means that there is a likelihood of DNA damage to whole organisms exposed to the compound. The damage could be direct, causing DNA breakage, or indirect due to damage to the mitotic apparatus. Many cancer therapies, such as cyclophosphamide or methotrexate, are positive in this assay because of their mechanism of action. A positive finding in vivo with a concurrent positive in vitro, without mechanistic explanation to the contrary, usually means that the compound is genotoxic and appropriate evaluation of the risk to clinical trial subjects is necessary. For nononcology drug candidates, such a profile typically results in termination of clinical development.

It is unusual to have a positive in vivo study with a negative in vitro test. Differing metabolite production in the intact animal from what can be accomplished with liver microsomes in vitro is thought to be the case with urethane, while folate depletion by salicylazosulfapyridine is thought to be the cause of MN formation in vivo not seen in vitro [59]. Induction of MN in vivo can occur by non-DNA damaging mechanisms as well. Examples are drugs that induce hypothermia (morphine, chlorpromazine), hyperthermia, or increased erythropoiesis following prior bone-marrow toxicity or direct stimulation of precursor cells to divide (erythropoietins, phenylhydrazine) [59].

In addition to assessing micronuclei in blood cells, methods have been developed for MN evaluation in other tissues, such as liver and gut [60–63]. The rapid turnover of the gut tissue makes it a reasonable tissue to investigate site of contact DNA damage by the MN test [63]. Methods using young or partially hepatectomized rats can allow for damage to be investigated where cellular division is not as rapid but where the drug may accumulate or where metabolites may exert genotoxic effects [60–62]. These alternative tissues are typically used in a weight-of-evidence approach, when in vitro DNA damage is seen but in vivo results are negative. When drug candidates are not bioavailable or when they accumulate in the liver, these alternative tissue MN tests can be helpful in determining the true risk of DNA damage from exposure to the compound.

In Vivo Chromosome Aberration Assay

- Guideline: OECD 475
- In vivo evaluation of peripheral blood lymphocytes in rodents
- Acute or repeated dosing; can be used in support of Phase II or as additional mechanistic follow-up to in vitro positive findings

Like the in vivo MN test, the in vivo chromosome aberration assay can be routinely used to support Phase II clinical trials and the overall genetic toxicology package for a drug candidate [2]. The typical protocol requirements are outlined in OECD 475 [64]. As the name implies, the assay is an in vivo version of the chromosome aberration test. The test article can be administered in similar study designs as the in vivo MN test. To evaluate metaphases, colchicine is administered 3–5h prior to harvest. Cells are collected from bone marrow, fixed with a methanol and acetic-acid fixative, and slides are prepared. The slides are then stained with Giemsa to show the individual chromosomes and allow the reader to evaluate each metaphase microscopically for chromosome/chromatid breaks or rearrangements, similar to what is done in vitro. By identifying clastogenicity, direct DNA damage can be established. This can also clarify concerns from in vivo MN positive findings when mechanisms, such as hypothermia or induction of erythropoiesis are suspected [59]. Unlike the MN test, the chromosome aberration test requires a greater degree of training and experience for proper evaluation, and is much more time consuming. The resource and data turnaround concerns are the main reasons sponsors do not routinely conduct in vivo chromosome aberration tests.

OTHER IN VIVO TESTS FOR GENOTOXICITY

While the chromosome damage tests in vivo are the prescribed tests for development of small molecules in drug development, there are other tests that are typically employed to evaluate in vivo potential for genotoxicity.

These tests are usually performed when a positive result occurs in one of the in vitro tests. Some are indicator tests, which imply the potential for genotoxicity in vivo, adding to the weight of evidence that the compound being developed is a genotoxicant. Some of these tests are listed in Table 6.2 and will be described below.

DNA Strand-Break Assays: Comet and Alkaline Elution Assays

- Guideline OECD 489
- DNA strand breaks (multiple tissues)
- Can be used as part of test battery option 2 or for mechanistic follow-up after in vitro positive results

Both the comet and the alkaline elution assays are DNA damage indicator assays (ie, they do not directly determine a compound's ability to cause mutation or direct DNA interaction). These assays detect increases in DNA single- and double-strand breaks (under neutral conditions). They can also detect repair induced breaks, a basic site, DNA cross-linking agents, and alkali labile sites [29].

The compound can be given in single administrations or two to three daily doses, with organ harvests at appropriate times to capture breaks before they are repaired. In the alkaline elution assay, cells pass through a micropore filter membrane with the elution rate proportional to the number of DNA strand breaks. This assay historically required a greater initial investment and training, and also required large numbers of cells, which limited the number of tissues that could be evaluated [65]. However, recent advances in automation have enabled the analysis to be done in many more tissues without compromising its sensitivity [66]. In the comet assay, the tissues from target organs of interest (typically liver and stomach) are processed to obtain single cells and embedded in agarose, subjected to alkaline conditions and electrophoresis. Smaller DNA fragments migrate further away from the "head" of the "comet," the tightly coiled nuclear DNA (see Fig. 6.9). Because single cells are analyzed, the potential for direct damage under toxic conditions can be evaluated [65].

An advantage of these assays is that any target tissue can be used for analysis, even those that do not routinely divide [67]. Thus different harvest times allow for collection of rapidly dividing cells (2–5h postdosing) and those that have slow turnover (~24h after dosing). In using the comet assay, different parameters can be measured, and the percentage of DNA in the tail is considered most widely used and accepted [68,69].

Because any tissue can be evaluated, the in vivo comet assessment can look at both direct effect of the compound at site of contact, such as the stomach, intestine, or duodenum, and those caused by metabolic products of the compound in hepatocytes [29]. Increases in comet tails or elution slope factors due to potential genotoxicity must be differentiated from damage that occurs due to necrosis or apoptosis.

A new OECD guidance was adopted in 2014 for the in vivo comet or alkaline elution assays [70]. These assays have been used more frequently by pharmaceutical sponsors as follow-up tests to elucidate the in vivo potential for genotoxicity after an in vitro positive result, since regulatory authorities require either mechanistic or weight of evidence clarity to avoid placing clinical trial patients at risk. More often, the comet test is used to follow up on compounds that have tested positive in the in vitro regulatory genetic toxicology test battery [76]. These strand-break tests use normal rodents and can be used to evaluate multiple target tissues. Therefore, this

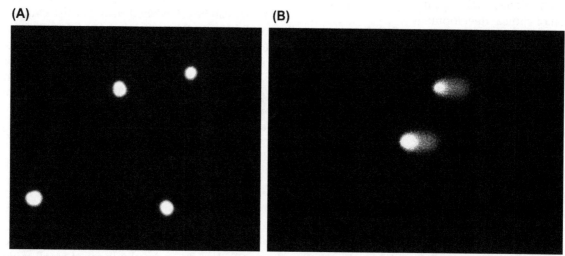

FIGURE 6.9 Comet formation. Images of nuclei from an in vivo comet assay. Negative controls (left) show tightly coiled, undamaged nuclei; cells treated with positive controls (right) show DNA fragments from strand breaks migrating during electrophoresis, giving the classic "comet" appearance. *Images courtesy of BioReliance, Rockville, MD.*

endpoint can be integrated with an in vivo bone-marrow or peripheral blood MN assessment [77–79]. The animals are dosed for 3 days to allow the MN endpoint to be evident with a single harvest and appropriate target tissues for the comet evaluation harvested, usually at T_{max} after the third dosage to ensure that rapidly dividing tissues can be assessed for DNA strand breaks. Such a design allows genotoxicity assessments in multiple tissues and endpoints in the same animals, thereby reducing the number of animals used.

Because the analysis can be conducted in any tissue, the comet and alkaline elution assays are also considered a favored assay in the alternative test battery in the revision of ICH guideline S2 as previously described [2]. The second option for a test battery eliminates routine use of the in vitro cytogenetics tests and instead requires genotoxicity assessment of at least two endpoints in two different tissues. The combined test of MN and comet, for example, utilizing multiple tissues in one set of study animals, would satisfy such a battery.

Since the endpoint of both assay designs is DNA strand breaks, they are often used to follow up on DNA damage tests, such as chromosome aberrations or MNvit. However, it has been shown that the comet test has very high sensitivity for detecting in vitro (Ames) mutagenic carcinogens [80]. The sensitivity for rodent carcinogens is very high, and it can detect nearly 90% of rodent carcinogens not detected by the rodent MN test [81]. Therefore the comet test can be an appropriate follow-up in vivo assay to evaluate in vitro gene mutation positives. There is less research demonstrating the sensitivity of the alkaline elution assay with mutagenic carcinogens, but demonstration of comparable sensitivity to the comet test would indicate that the alkaline elution assay could be an appropriate follow-up in vivo study as well [66].

Transgenic Gene Mutation Test

- Guideline: OECD 488
- Gene mutation evaluation in multiple tissues
- Can be used as part of test battery option 2 or as mechanistic follow-up to in vitro positive results

Transgenic rodent gene mutation tests (TGR) evaluate potential mutations in all tissues of transgenic rodents exposed to the compound. Rats (Big Blue, gpt Delta) and mice (Big Blue, Muta Mouse, gpt delta, lac z plasmid) are most commonly used, and the target gene is bacterial in nature [82,83]. The bacterial genes are incorporated in a lambda bacteriophage or shuttle vector. The test article is typically administered for 28 days (although alternate protocols can be used with appropriate scientific justification) up to a limit dose of 1000 mg/kg/day, and tissue of interest collected 3 days after dosing to allow unrepaired DNA lesions to

become fixed or expressed. The extracted DNA is packaged into a lambda phage, and the phage is grown in suitable conditions to determine whether the bacterial gene has been mutated [83,84]. The mutant frequency in 125,000–300,000 plaques is calculated and compared to control values [82]. The assay has demonstrated reliable results for identifying carcinogens (79% sensitivity, 78% specificity) and has the advantage of not only being applicable to all tissues, but also the tissues can be stored frozen for years and subsequently analyzed without impacting the analysis [82,84]. The effects of repeated dosing can be additive, thus longer dosing duration protocols can yield more mutated genes. The recommended dosing of 28 days for routine studies should be sufficient to detect even weak mutagens [84]. Expression times can range from 3 days after cessation of dosing to 28 days depending on target tissue turnover. For example, the liver is often a tissue considered for evaluation for potential toxicity, due to exposure to the compound prior to metabolism. With the slow turnover of hepatocytes, 28-day postdose collection times are warranted [84]. Suggested tissues for evaluation are rapidly dividing tissues (glandular stomach or bone marrow) and the liver; however, information regarding such factors as site of first contact, pharmacokinetic data on tissue distribution/accumulation, or organs of toxicity should be considered [82]. The lack of response at the locus under evaluation does not mean that there is not a mutation at another locus; however, typically two or three tissues examined can be sufficient to determine the in vivo mutation potential of the test item [83].

The genes being studied are surrogates for endogenous genes. While some differences in responses of transgenic and endogenous genes have been reported, in general, the weight of evidence in cases where direct comparisons can be made indicates that for the most part, transgenes and endogenous genes respond similarly [82,83,85]. Sequencing mutants can be an additional aid in understanding mechanisms, clarifying equivocal results or interindividual variability in a weak response; however, this is a labor-intensive and costly addition to the experimental design [85].

OECD guideline, TG488, was recently published for the conduct of transgenic gene mutation assays [82]. The test is most often used by drug developers as a follow-on test when an in vitro positive result is seen. An Ames-positive compound might be investigated further in the 28-day dosing TGR assay as part of a weight-of-evidence approach for getting approval to move the drug candidate into the clinic. An important aspect to consider is that the TGR assay would need to be done as a dedicated test since transgenic animals are required and not as an integrated mutation endpoint in a general toxicity study. Duration of the test is an important consideration as well. If faced with a positive Ames test, to mitigate the finding in the in vitro bacterial system, the TGR protocol used might need as long as 2 months just for dosing and expression time (worst case if looking at the liver as a target organ, for example). Additional time would be needed to extract DNA, package, plate, score, and potentially sequence the mutants.

Pig-a Gene Mutation Test

- Gene mutations in rodent circulating blood cells

The Pig-a gene mutation test is a relatively new assay being investigated as a rapid, simple gene mutation test that can be incorporated into repeated-dose testing regimens. The endpoint is based on the phenotype of red blood cells from a disease condition, paroxysmal nocturnal hematoglobinuria (PNH), where genes coding for the GPI anchor proteins are mutated, leading to a lack of certain cell-surface markers. The phosphatidyl inosital glycan A gene (Pig-a) is an X-linked gene and its product is the first in the GPI anchor assembly [86]. Mutations in this gene mean that the cell-surface markers, such as CD-59 on rat RBCs, will not be present. In addition, only one mutation is needed to knock out the gene product since it is an X-linked gene. Utilizing flow cytometry, cells can be gated for the presence or absence of these surface markers in rodents treated with the test article. Test article-induced damage seems to impact stem cells, thus the mutant cell phenotype can be detected months after cessation of dose administration [87,88]. Manifestation of the effect in RBCs can take several weeks as mature RBCs already in circulation are slowly replaced by newer mutant cells. To get an earlier read, the reticulocyte population can be gated and similarly subgated for mutant and normal phenotypes. A key feature of this assay system is the ability to assess a true mutation event within a repeated-dose toxicology study with wild-type strains, with only a small amount of blood (<100 μL) being needed for the analysis. In addition, the mutation events accumulate, so low doses that are needed for animal tolerability in 28-day toxicity studies can still show significant increases in number of mutant cells over time [78,79,89,90]. Validation of this assay is ongoing and additional questions remain; however, the assay holds much promise as a potential follow-up assay that could be done either as a standalone or integrated test [91]. Studies need to be conducted to assess the impact of alterations in hematopoiesis on the gene, and currently the assay can only be conducted in the hematopoietic compartment.

In Vivo Unscheduled DNA Synthesis Assay

- Guideline: OECD 486
- DNA repair in hepatocytes

The in vivo unscheduled DNA synthesis assay (UDS) is a validated assay and is listed in the ICH guidelines as a useful follow-up test to a positive result in the standard genetic toxicity battery [92]. The assay is conducted in rodents, and, after dosing, the liver is perfused and single cells isolated. The cells are then cultured in the presence of tritiated thymidine. Slides are then prepared and dipped in autoradiographic emulsion, exposed refrigerated in the dark for 7–14 days, developed, and stained. The exposed silver grains are then counted, comparing the number of grains in the nuclei of cells from animals exposed to the test article to those of the controls. Increase in grains indicates DNA lesions that were repaired as these cells would not be expected to be dividing, hence the name unscheduled DNA synthesis [93]. The assay has been shown to detect genotoxic carcinogens with few false-positive findings and was frequently used to investigate positive results from in vitro tests in conjunction with an in vivo micronucleus assay to determine if a drug candidate could be considered viable [94,95]. However, concerns about the sensitivity of the in vivo UDS assay for general drug candidate assessment have led to decreased confidence in this assay for routine use [29]. The UDS assay can provide useful mechanistic understanding of genotoxic compounds in the liver or substances that induce bulky adducts [2].

ADDITIONAL TESTS INDICATING GENOTOXICITY

In Silico Tools

Compounds can contain substructures within them that are highly associated with positive results in mutagenicity or other genotoxicity tests [96]. Computer software has allowed the creation of quantitative structure–activity relationships, or Q(SAR), which are programs that can predict whether an unknown compound may be genotoxic when run against its algorithm, or can identify structurally alerting moieties based on expert knowledge. These programs are useful tools to help identify chemical series that may possess genotoxic liabilities. In addition, these programs are essential for the assessment of impurities in the synthetic route of drug substance production, which will be described below [9]. It is important to understand that these are predictive tools and not definitive identifiers of genotoxicity. Each has assets and liabilities. For example, the knowledge-based system DEREK (Deductive Estimation of Risk based on Existing Knowledge) is updated at least once a year with additional information to modify, add, or exclude alerts as the experts review data. This can keep this program current and reflective of what is being seen in real-world testing. However, such appropriate modifications depend on the data being provided and contributed by users of the system.

Two general categories of in silico systems are available: rule-based expert knowledge systems, where structural alerts are created based on biological data typically captured in the literature or from large donated databases (eg, DEREK, ToxTree) and Q(SAR) modeling systems that utilize training and validation sets, molecular descriptors, and algorithms to build models (MultiCase, Leadscope Model Applier). No one system predicts all genotoxic compounds with 100% accuracy, and, as seen when combining test systems in a battery approach, the more systems used, the more sensitivity can be increased at the expense of specificity.

In Vitro Comet and In Vitro Alkaline Elution Assays

Like the in vivo version of the assay, the in vitro single-cell gel or comet test looks at DNA strand breakage in cells by exposing cultured cells to the test compound and creating slides that are subjected to electrophoresis under alkaline conditions [65]. Most cell lines or primary cell cultures used for standard in vitro cytogenetic tests can be used, as can the exposure condition (with and without the addition of exogenous metabolic activation, short and long duration exposures), with similar caveats around interpreting data from cultures with high cytotoxicity [65].

Similarly, the alkaline elution assay detects DNA strand breaks in primary rat hepatocyte cultures exposed to genotoxicants. An advantage of this assay is the utilization of metabolically competent cells and high sensitivity as a screening test for genotoxicants [75,97]. A difference is the ability to look at single cells in the comet assay whereas the alkaline elution assay requires large quantities of cells to elicit a result [65].

Syrian Hamster Embryo Cell Transformation Assay

The Syrian hamster embryo (SHE) cell transformation assay is not a genetic toxicity assay, but rather a test that can assess the potential of a drug candidate to cause morphologic changes in cells that might be indicative of nongenotoxic carcinogenic damage. This assay can be used as an adjunct to a genotoxicity battery if nongenotoxic carcinogenicity may be of concern. While the genotoxicity test battery is designed to help sponsors avoid drug candidates that may be carcinogenic, it does not identify carcinogens that act via nongenotoxic mechanisms. The SHE assay can help to show the nongenotoxic mechanisms of carcinogenicity, especially for drug candidates that produce tumors at relevant concentrations [98]. The assay relies on identifying primary hamster embryo cells that have undergone transformation. This endpoint is typically identified through microscopy and is subjectively determined, leading to reproducibility issues. The SHE assay is not routinely used but can serve as an adjunct assay when nongenotoxic mechanisms are suspected as a concern for the drug candidate.

Green Screen

Another indicator assay frequently used in high-throughput laboratories is the GADD45 assay or the GreenScreen test [99,100]. This assay looks at a reporter gene in the GADD45a promoter and a gene encoding for green fluorescence protein (GFP) that has been transfected into the human TK6 cell line. The competent p53 gene in the TK6 cell is involved in DNA repair, and generation of the marker protein is indicative of repair of DNA damage. The assay can be utilized as a part of a high-throughput screening paradigm in a microplate testing format where negative results in the GreenScreen assay are highly predictive of a lack of DNA damaging capability [101,102]. Positive results, indicating DNA damage, may be further investigated for the relevance to standard genotoxicity endpoints [101]. An important aspect of the GreenScreen assay is that it shows how the cell responds to DNA damage [103].

Yeast Deletion Assay

The yeast deletion assay is an assay in higher organisms that primarily looks at clastogenic damage as evidenced by intrachromosomal rearrangements of engineered mutant alleles in the HIS3 gene [104,105]. This assay is capable of detecting large chromosomal deletions from homologous recombination. The yeast cell wall has been engineered to allow larger molecules to penetrate and reach the genome. A high-throughput (384-well plate) assay has been developed and is another alternative for higher throughput clastogenesis evaluation, showing good correlation with more standard in vitro cytogenetic tests [106,107].

DNA Adducts

DNA adduct identification through P^{32} postlabeling has been used extensively to quantify adduct formation [108]. Carcinogens can form DNA adducts detectable by the method at a level as sensitive as 1 per 10^{10} base pairs [109]. The technique can identify an array of different adduct types. The assay is not a direct detection of mutation events; rather it provides an indication of the damage from exposure to a genotoxic agent, which can be useful as a follow-up assessment when a positive result is seen in a standard assay [110]. Some of the drawbacks to routine use include:

1. the need for radiation
2. specific conditions unique to the specific drug are required for adduct resolution,
3. further analytical techniques by mass spectrometry are needed to identify the adducts [111].

Toxicogenomics

The integration of toxicogenomic approaches into the mechanistic understanding of genotoxic data is relatively new. Transcriptional evaluations could identify signatures from chemicals that might reduce the need for more expensive follow-up animal tests. These techniques can probe genomic responses to chemicals correlating to in vivo perturbations, with gene expression profiles potentially used to screen for mode of action of genotoxicants [112]. For example, compounds identified as positive in vitro in standard tests may be shown to act in a nondirect manner by inhibiting mitotic spindles by evaluating gene expression profiles [113]. Such approaches could be incorporated into a screening strategy or mechanistic follow-up evaluation. Establishing biomarkers through toxicogenomics of known carcinogens can identify those biomarkers that have greater relevance to human health concerns. The ability to identify nongenotoxic mechanisms of carcinogenicity (and the relevance to human health), not detectable through conventional genetic toxicity testing and predicting long-term carcinogenicity results, would be added benefits for understanding the potential of drug candidates to fall into such a classification before a large investment in resources occurs [112,114].

GENETOX TESTING STRATEGY: DISCOVERY THROUGH DEVELOPMENT

Identifying drug candidates that may be carcinogenic with a rapid, low-cost highly predictive testing battery is the goal of regulatory genetic toxicity testing for pharmaceuticals (see Fig. 6.2). The safety of clinical trial subjects is of the utmost importance during the early phases of clinical development. Thus the highly sensitive in vitro battery of mutation and chromosome damage tests are required before the initiation of most clinical trials [2,10,115].

Positive (genotoxic) findings during preclinical testing typically require follow-up testing to assure subject safety. In some cases, a positive finding may lead to termination of development of a molecule, as a relatively small investment has been made and more elaborate and expensive testing would be required to conduct repeated

dosing in the clinic. Often backup molecules are available and can be advanced while the first or lead molecule is further characterized. However, a look at the Physician's Desk Reference (PDR) shows that a number of marketed pharmaceuticals not intended to treat cancer have at least one positive result in genetic toxicology testing [48,116]. This illustrates the fact that a well-characterized drug candidate can survive attrition due to genotoxicity when that hazard is thoroughly evaluated for its risk to patient safety.

Even though these required tests are typically conducted well in advance of regulatory submissions for initiation of clinical trials [Investigational New Drug (IND) or Clinical Trial Applications (CTA)], bringing drug candidates to preclinical regulatory GLP testing and finding out that these are truly genotoxic is costly. Therefore identifying potentially genotoxic compounds in the discovery phase can save precious time and resources and enables the selection of more appropriate candidates (Fig. 6.2) [117].

Early Discovery: Evaluating Chemical Series and Core Structures

As early as the identification of core structures that show promise for interaction with the biological target of interest (so-called "hits"), a structure–activity analysis using in silico software and expert knowledge can be used to identify moieties on the core with potential genotoxic liabilities. Core chemical structures and representatives of good chemical series for the target can then be prioritized for testing for genotoxicity from such assessments. It is important not to eliminate a chemical series solely on the basis of in silico structural alerts. At early discovery stages, the in silico tools should have high specificity, having a low false-positive rate (ie, the tool predicts true negative results accurately) so discovery teams do not discard potentially good chemical series. Since the negative predictivity in these programs is very high, series that do not show a tendency to have structural concerns could move further with a high degree of confidence. Series with structural alerts can be evaluated for actual genotoxicity in lab tests and reprioritized depending on the results.

Early in discovery, the amount of chemical matter available to test is very small, and usually not sufficient for the standard, OECD-compliant in vitro tests. Furthermore, these discovery lots are usually not adequately characterized, and often contain high levels of irrelevant impurities. In addition, since mutagenicity testing has the highest predictivity for rodent carcinogenicity, mutagenicity testing may be sufficient to answer a discovery project team's concern. There are a number of modifications to the standard bacterial reverse mutation (Ames) test that can be used to provide mutation data with much less material in a non-GLP environment. The assay can be miniaturized into 6-well or 24-well multiwell plates [118,119]. A liquid-based assay, the Ames II test, can be used in a higher throughput design with a 384-well plate format [120]. These tests use much less compound (on the scale of mg) and provide the same type of simple endpoint (either colony counts or media color change in the case of the Ames II test) such that testing can be done rapidly and provide meaningful answers to inform decision-making and guide early chemistry on the chemical series.

Lead Optimization

With additional test material, more data can be generated by a number of modifications of standard testing or indicator tests designed for high-throughput evaluation. The standard in vitro chromosome aberration, micronucleus, or mouse lymphoma test can be scaled back to give indications of chromosome damage with fewer cells scored and less test article needed. Reduction in the number of conditions assayed can reduce the amount of compound required and increase the speed of the evaluation. Imaging systems or flow cytometric evaluations can greatly enhance the speed and objectivity of the evaluation and be tools for high-throughput evaluations [33,35,37,121]. In addition, these systems as well as differential staining techniques in manual microscopy evaluations can provide insights into the type of damage seen in the cytogenetic assay, identifying compounds that are inherently aneugenic vs. those that are clastogenic [36,37]. Aneugenic compounds identified through modification of the in vitro micronucleus test to identify the presence of kinetochores in the micronucleus or by whole chromosome painting or fluorescent in situ hybridization techniques do not act by direct interaction with DNA [38,39,122]. These compounds may have a threshold above which they cause the formation of MN by interacting with the mitotic spindle apparatus, causing enough damage for chromosomes to fall off the spindle-forming MN. Such compounds may be considered for further development due to their lack of direct DNA interaction, assuming they are negative in other genotoxicity evaluations [123,124]. Other high-throughput tests can be employed in early discovery to give a profile for the potential for genotoxic damage the compounds or the chemical series may cause.

Candidate Selection

As a development candidate is identified, lower-throughput but high-fidelity assays can be employed for greater confidence that the candidate has no true genotoxic issues. At this point, the assays used should have a low false-negative rate (ie, good sensitivity); testing here

is done at the compound level, and a large investment in animal testing and pharmaceutical manufacture may be forthcoming, so true genotoxicants must be identified at this stage and eliminated from further development. Unexpected positive results may be seen either at this stage or in the ensuing GLP studies. Understanding the predictivity and shortcomings of these high-throughput and modified assays based on the chemical matter being tested is important to identifying the true predictive value and liabilities of a particular screening strategy. For example, if a sponsor typically screens discovery compounds with a bacterial mutation test and MNvit test, positive results in the MNvit test could be further investigated to better determine the liabilities of continuing to develop such a compound. The sponsor may decide to include staining for kinetochores for elucidation of the mechanism of action (aneugenicity or clastogenicity). Additional tests can also be conducted, which may further show that the proposed candidate has been adequately characterized before initiating early GLP studies.

Good Laboratory Practice Studies

The regulatory genetic toxicity battery is performed under GLP conditions to support regulatory submission. If the traditional battery (ICHS2R1 option 1) is used, the inclusion of the in vivo MN test is optional prior to first-in-human clinical trials, as it is not required until support is needed for Phase II clinical trials. The decision to conduct the required in vivo genetic toxicity test at this time with no other evidence of genotoxicity is at the discretion of the sponsor. The in vivo evaluation can be integrated into the general toxicity rodent study design to minimize animal usage [2]. In addition, should an unexpected in vitro positive result occur, a combination study looking at both MN in the hematopoietic system and DNA strand breaks in other tissues could be performed again, combining the two endpoints into one study, reducing costs and animal usage. Alternatively, the second battery option can be employed, where only a bacterial mutation test and a two-tissue, two-endpoint in vivo study is conducted [2].

Negative results in the in vitro battery allow the sponsor to apply for clinical trials in healthy volunteers, as the risk for genotoxicity is extremely low. When a positive finding in the in vitro cytogenetic evaluation is seen, a sponsor may be able to conduct single-administration trials even in healthy volunteers [115]. However, to proceed to repeat dosing in the clinic, two negative in vivo endpoints need to be shown, or a clear mechanistic understanding needs to be developed to demonstrate that the risk from exposure to the candidate is low. For example, a positive result in the bacterial reverse mutation test can be investigated in a comet test or a transgenic gene mutation test to help mitigate the finding along with the required in vivo cytogenetic assessment. Overall, the decisions for appropriate follow-up testing for candidates that have in vitro genotoxicity must be based on sound scientific judgment. A thorough understanding of the attributes of the compound is needed in order to establish a weight-of-evidence or mode of action rationale to avoid putting trial subjects at risk [125].

As previously noted, biological drugs are not subject to genotoxicity testing [11]. For compounds designed for treating life-threatening illness, such as cancer, which are often evaluated only in patients, genotoxicity testing may not be needed until marketing [12].

Exploratory Investigational New Drugs

For an exploratory IND (eIND), a small clinical trial is conducted in which no therapeutic benefit is expected. These early clinical trials are designed to investigate translation of mechanism of action from preclinical species to human (eg, enzyme inhibition), distribution of the compound in the body, or pharmacokinetic properties of the compound in humans. Doses are low and duration of the trials is short, usually less than 7 days, and a limited number of subjects are exposed to the compound [126]. Under these conditions, regulatory authorities allow alterations to the typically required genetic toxicity testing battery prior to the first dose in humans. For single-dose pharmacokinetic evaluations (ie, microdose trials), either on one or multiple drug candidates, only micrograms of compound are given to trial subjects, and genetic toxicology tests are not required. When testing for pharmacological activity, the in vitro battery is needed (eg, bacterial mutation test and cytogenetics or mouse lymphoma assay) [126]. These studies are expected to comply with GLPs and to be conducted in accordance with appropriate OECD and ICH guidelines.

Metabolite Qualification

The US FDA has produced a guideline for safety testing of drug metabolites [127]. Generally, metabolites of concern (ie, major metabolites) are those formed in humans at greater than 10% of the parent drug exposure at steady state [127]. While exogenously supplied S9 may form some of the metabolites in vitro, the quantity formed is often insufficient for qualification. For genetic toxicity testing, therefore, the neat metabolite should be tested when possible. The tests required are the Ames assay and an in vitro assay that detects chromosome damage; these tests should be conducted in accordance with ICH and OECD guidelines [127]. Toxicological qualification, including genotoxicity testing, must follow GLPs and is typically carried out prior to the Phase III clinical trials (see Fig. 6.2) [10].

Genotoxic Impurities

The prevailing viewpoint is that exposure to genotoxic agents represents a potential health hazard at any dosage, since genotoxic compounds are viewed to have no threshold for toxicity. As discussed previously, this view has been changing, as more evidence indicates that genotoxic compounds can also have exposures where no toxicity may be seen. In addition, the duration of exposure to genotoxicants can play a role in understanding the risk of possible cancer formation from genotoxic agents.

The API is required to go through the test battery before large groups of healthy volunteers or patients are given the potential new drug in a clinical setting. The API should be of sufficient purity that effects (either efficacious or safety related) are due to the compound and not to toxic impurities. To manufacture a drug candidate, reactive starting materials, solvents, and other components are part of the synthetic route. During this process, various intermediates and process impurities can form. During storage of the final material, degradation products can also start to form. All of these nonbeneficial materials must be controlled in order to be sure the compound of interest is adequately characterized in the clinical setting.

A set of guidelines has been established to inform when sponsors are required to identify by analytical methods an impurity in either the drug substance (API) or the drug product (the actual pill or medicine). In addition, if the identified impurity is sufficiently abundant, a sponsor is required to "qualify" the impurity through a set of toxicology tests. Qualification studies usually consist of the in vitro battery of genotoxicity tests and a 2–13-week repeated-dose toxicity study in one rodent species, usually rats [128,129]. These quality guidelines are applicable to the marketed product, and testing by sponsors usually occurs prior to or during Phase III clinical trials, when the final route is well worked out and the impurity and degradation product profile is well characterized.

However, until recently there were no guidelines for identification or qualification of impurities during clinical development. Most sponsors will utilize the identification threshold throughout the development process. Thus an early candidate may be given to healthy volunteers in a Phase I trial at a dosage of 1 g per day, and impurities in the API may be as high as 0.1% (1000 parts per million) before being identified. In other words, the volunteer would receive dosages of the impurity up to 1 mg per day and the impurity would not require qualification in genotoxicity tests.

In order to provide guidance on controlling genotoxic impurities (GTI) and to protect clinical trial subjects, a guideline was drafted and eventually approved by the European Medicines Agency (EMEA) [9]. This guideline considered an assessment conducted for exposure to genotoxic carcinogens in food, using some of the most potent carcinogens from the Carcinogenicity Potency Database (CPDB), applying linear back-extrapolation using a number of conservative safety factors [8,130]. The result of this analysis for food led to a "threshold of toxicological concern," or TTC for genotoxic carcinogens of 0.15 μg per day that would lead to one additional cancer in one million over a 70-year period. That is, a person could ingest 0.15 μg of known genotoxic carcinogens for a lifetime and the risk for getting cancer from this intake is one in one million, which is typically considered a *de minimus* risk level. The EMEA considered that a pharmaceutical product with genotoxic impurities would have a beneficial impact from the drug that outweighs the exposure to the genotoxic material. Thus the pharmaceutical TTC is 1.5 μg per day, for a lifetime, with an associated increase in cancer incidence risk of 1×10^{-5} [9]. Since most people are not on a pharmaceutical for 70 years, and they receive benefit from the drug, this risk level is considered acceptable. Many of these original concepts were kept as part of an ICH guideline on identifying and controlling DNA reactive (mutagenic) impurities, ICH M7, published in 2014 [136]. A cohort of problematic chemical classes has been identified, which may be required to be controlled at lower levels, and also certain disease indications, such as cancer may allow sponsors to have more genotoxic impurities than the TTC level [9]. Because clinical trials are much shorter than lifetime exposures and some therapies are expected to be administered for a limited duration, a step-wise or less-than-lifetime approach has been accepted based on the duration of trial (or therapeutic duration), including an additional 10-fold safety factor, where more GTIs could be in the drug candidate during the trial (see Table 6.7) [8,131]. Importantly, GTI that clearly demonstrate thresholds (ie, they do not act directly on DNA) can be controlled at levels based on a permissible daily exposure calculation rather than the TTC [9,132].

Sponsors are expected to assess their route of chemical synthesis for components that may be genotoxic. Some are obvious, such as those having been tested previously and identified as genotoxic in the literature. Others have unknown genotoxic potential, and it would be impractical to test all for mutagenicity. The Ames test is typically employed at this stage for early GTI qualification, in accordance with OECD471 and ICHS2(R1)

recommendations. Since manufacture of impurities in sufficient quantities for a standard Ames test can often be challenging, modifications to the testing can be made if justified [136]. Sponsors are expected to evaluate potential impurities in the API (be it an intermediate, starting material, residual solvent, degradation product, or API impurity) for structural alerts using two methodologies: rules-based knowledge systems (such as DEREK) and a statistical-based QSAR mode (such as Leadscope Model Applier, or CASE Ultra) [131]. Additional expertise and experience can also be applied. The results can then be classified as:

- concerning with either mutagenic carcinogenicity (class 1) or genotoxicity (class 2) being known for the specific compound;
- alerting with no genotoxicity data available (class 3); or
- not concerning because alerts that are in the API (or structurally similar molecule to the unknown impurity) and considered qualified through testing (class four) or no alerts noted in the structure (class 5) [8,134].

Some impurities can be controlled based on data already generated through a compound-specific risk assessment. Alerting impurities that require further consideration, typically with no genetic toxicity data available, are thus identified. From there, sponsors have several options, such as:

1. altering the route to avoid the impurity,
2. reducing the level to as low as reasonably possible or below the appropriate TTC level, or
3. toxicology testing (Fig. 6.10).

Mutagenicity testing in an Ames-based test would qualify the alerting structure as either genotoxic or not. Genotoxic materials then should be controlled by the appropriate TTC level for use of the clinical lot of the drug. Alternatively, an analytical method can be developed where control of the appropriate TTC is assured, and genetic toxicology testing would not be needed. Finally, a sound scientific rationale for why the offending impurity would not be at a level of concern in the API could be included in the data submission package for review by the appropriate regulatory agency.

CONCLUDING REMARKS AND FUTURE DIRECTIONS

Genotoxicity testing offers a simple, relatively inexpensive way to identify compounds that may interact with DNA or cause chromosome loss. These tests are required by regulatory agencies for small molecules prior to clinical trials and for impurity qualifications.

TABLE 6.7 Acceptable Intakes for Individual Impurities [9,131]

	Duration of Exposure			
	≤1 month	>1–12 months	1–10 years	>10 years to Life-Time
Allowable intake	120 μg	20 μg	10 μg	1.5 μg

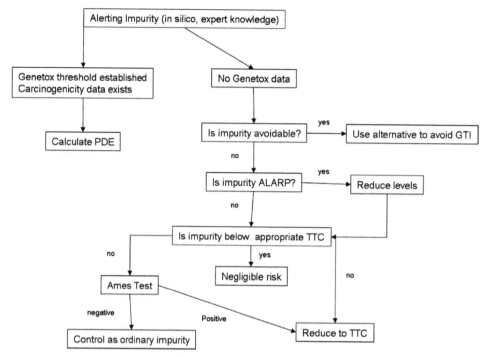

FIGURE 6.10 **Decision tree for assessing alerting impurities in API [9].** *ALARP,* as low as reasonably practicable; *GTI,* genotoxic impurity; *PDE,* permissible daily exposure; *(Q)SAR,* (quantitative) structure–activity relationship; *TTC,* threshold of toxicological concern.

Pharmaceutical companies often use these tests, modified versions, or other indicator tests throughout the drug discovery and development process to eliminate potentially genotoxic chemical series, in order to ensure that development candidates have insignificant genotoxic liability, and to clarify the risk to human health after a positive finding in one or more assay. Individual genotoxicity tests identify hazards, and a weight-of-evidence approach can be used as part of a comprehensive risk assessment. While most routinely used genetic toxicity tests are decades old, the discipline will most likely benefit from additional mechanistic clarity that novel technology, like toxicogenomics, can provide.

Acknowledgments

The author would like to thank Dr. Eric Blomme, Dr. Brinda Mahadevan, Dr. Ronnie Yeager, Mr. Paul Sonders, and Mr. Joel Murray for their diligent review of this chapter. In addition, the author would like to acknowledge the contribution of BioReliance, Rockville, MD and MidWest BioResearch, Skokie, IL for providing some of the images used in this chapter.

References

[1] Friedberg EC. A brief history of the DNA repair field. Cell Res 2008;18:3–7.

[2] International Conference on Harmonization (ICH). S2(R1) Step 4: guidance on genotoxicity testing and data interpretation for pharmaceuticals intended for human use. 2011.

[3] Gocke E, Mueller L. *In vivo* studies in the mouse to define a threshold for the genotoxicity of EMS and ENU. Mutat Res 2009;678:101–7.

[4] Pottenger L, Schisler M, Zhang F, Bartels M, Fontaine D, McFadden L, et al. Dose-response and operational thresholds/NOAELs for *in vitro* mutagenic effects from DNA-reactive mutagens, MMS and MNU. Mutat Res 2009;678:138–47.

[5] Elhajouji A, Van Hummelen P, Kirsch-Volders M. Indications for a threshold of chemically-induced aneuploidy *in vitro* in human lymphocytes. Environ Mol Mutagen 1995;26:292–304.

[6] European Medicines Agency (EMEA). Studies assessed by the EMEA indicate no increased risk of developing cancer for patients who have taken Viracept contaminated with ethyl mesilate. [London]. 2008.

[7] Mueller L, Kasper P. Human biological relevance and the use of threshold-arguments in regulatory genotoxicity assessment: experience with pharmaceuticals. Mutat Res 2000;464:19–34.

[8] Müller L, Mauthe RJ, Riley CM, Andino MM, Antonis DD, Beels C, et al. A rationale for determining, testing, and controlling specific impurities in pharmaceuticals that possess potential for genotoxicity. Regul Toxicol Pharmacol 2006;44:198–211.

[9] European Medicines Agency (EMEA). Guideline on the limits of genotoxic impurities. [London]. 2006.

[10] International Conference on Harmonization (ICH). M3(R2): guidance on nonclinical safety studies for the conduct of human clinical trials and marketing authorization for pharmaceuticals. 2009.

[11] International Conference on Harmonization (ICH). S6(R1): preclinical safety evaluation of biotechnology-derived pharmaceuticals. 2011.

[12] International Conference on Harmonization (ICH). S9: nonclinical evaluation for anticancer pharmaceuticals. 2010.

[13] Ames BN, McCann J, Yamasaki E. Methods for detecting carcinogens and mutagens with the *Salmonella*/mammalian-microsome mutagenicity test. Mutat Res 1975;31:347–64.

[14] Maron D, Ames B. Revised methods for the *Salmonella* mutagenicity test. Mutat Res 1983;113:173–215.

[15] Organization for Economic Co-operation and Development (OECD). Guideline 471: bacterial reverse mutation test. 1997.

[16] Mortelmans K, Zeiger E. The Ames *Salmonella*/microsome mutagenicity assay. Mutat Res/Fundam Mol Mech Mutagen 2000;455:29–60.

[17] Mortelmans K. Isolation of plasmid pKM101 in the Stocker laboratory. Mutat Res 2006;612:151–64.

[18] Green M, Muriel W. Mutagen testing using TRP+ reversion in *Escherichia coli*. Mutat Res 1976;38:3–32.

[19] Gatehouse D, Haworth S, Cebula T, Gocke E, Kier L, Matsushima T, et al. Recommendations for the performance of bacterial mutation assays. Mutat Res 1994;312:217–33.

[20] Evans HJ, O'Riordan ML. Human peripheral blood lymphocytes for the analysis of chromosome aberrations in mutagen tests. Mutat Res/Environ Mutagen Relat Subj 1975;31:135–48.

[21] Galloway SM, Aardema MJ, Ishidate M, Ivett JL, Kirkland DJ, Morita T, et al. Report from working group on *in vitro* tests for chromosomal aberrations. Mutat Res/Environ Mutagen Relat Subj 1994;312:241–61.

[22] Organization for Economic Co-operation and Development (OECD). Guideline 473: *in vitro* mammalian chromosome aberration test. 2014.

[23] Galloway S, Lorge E, Aardema MJ, Eastmond D, Fellows M, Heflich R, et al. Workshop summary: top concentration for *in vitro* mammalian cell genotoxicity assays; and report from working group on toxicity measures and top concentration for *in vitro* cytogenetics assays (chromosome aberrations and micronucleus). Mutat Res/Genet Toxicol Environ Mutagen 2011;723:77–83.

[24] Huber R, Kulka U, Lörch T, Braselmann H, Bauchinger M. Automated metaphase finding: an assessment of the efficiency of the METAFER2 system in a routine mutagenicity assay. Mutat Res/Environ Mutagen Relat Subj 1995;334:97–102.

[25] Muehlbauer PA, Schuler MJ. Measuring the mitotic index in chemically-treated human lymphocyte cultures by flow cytometry. Mutat Res/Genet Toxicol Environ Mutagen 2003;537:117–30.

[26] Morita T, Nagaki T, Fukuda I, Okumura K. Clastogenicity of low pH to various cultured mammalian cells. Mutat Res 1992;268:297–305.

[27] Scott D, Galloway SM, Marshall RR, Ishidate Jr M, Brusick D, Ashby J, et al. International Commission for Protection Against Environmental Mutagens and Carcinogens. Genotoxicity under extreme culture conditions. A report from ICPEMC Task Group 9. Mutat Res 1991;257:147–205.

[28] Kirkland D, Aardema M, Henderson L, Müller L. Evaluation of the ability of a battery of three *in vitro* genotoxicity tests to discriminate rodent carcinogens and noncarcinogens: I. Sensitivity, specificity and relative predictivity. Mutat Res 2005;584:1–256.

[29] Committee on Mutagenicity of Chemicals in Food Consumer Products and the Environment (COM). Guidance on a strategy for genotoxicity testing of chemical substances. 2011.

[30] Organization for Economic Co-operation and Development (OECD). Guideline 487: *in vitro* mammalian cell micronucleus test. 2014.

[31] Fenech M. The *in vitro* micronucleus technique. Mutat Res 2000;455:81–95.

[32] Decordier I, Papine A, Plas G, Roesems S, Vande Loock K, Moreno-Palomo J, et al. Automated image analysis of cytokinesis-blocked micronuclei: an adapted protocol and a validated scoring procedure for biomonitoring. Mutagenesis 2009;24:85–93.

[33] Decordier I, Papine A, Vande Loock K, Plas G, Soussaline F, Kirsch-Volders M. Automated image analysis of micronuclei by IMSTAR for biomonitoring. Mutagenesis 2011;26:163–8.

[34] Rossnerova A, Spatova M, Schunck C, Sram RJ. Automated scoring of lymphocyte micronuclei by the MetaSystems Metafer image cytometry system and its application in studies of human mutagen sensitivity and biodosimetry of genotoxin exposure. Mutagenesis 2011;26:169–75.

[35] Avlasevich SL, Bryce SM, Cairns SE, Dertinger SD. *In vitro* micronucleus scoring by flow cytometry: differential staining of micronuclei versus apoptotic and necrotic chromatin enhances assay reliability. Environ Mol Mutagen 2006;47:56–66.

[36] Bryce SM, Bemis JC, Avlasevich S, Dertinger SD. *In vitro* micronucleus assay scored by flow cytometry provides a comprehensive evaluation of cytogenetic damage and cytotoxicity. Mutat Res 2007;630:78–91.

[37] Nicolette J, Diehl M, Sonders P, Bryce S, Blomme E. *In vitro* micronucleus screening of pharmaceutical candidates by flow cytometry in Chinese hamster V79 cells. Environ Mol Mutagen 2010;52:355–362.

[38] Eastmond D, Tucker J. Kinetochore localization in micronucleated cytokinesis-blocked Chinese hamster ovary cells: a new and rapid assay for identifying aneuploidy-inducing agents. Mutat Res 1989;224:517–25.

[39] Schuler M, Rupa DS, Eastmond DA. A critical evaluation of centromeric labeling to distinguish micronuclei induced by chromosomal loss and breakage *in vitro*. Mutat Res/Genet Toxicol Environ Mutagen 1997;392:81–95.

[40] Shi J, Bezabhie R, Szkudlinska A. Further evaluation of a flow cytometric *in vitro* micronucleus assay in CHO–K1 cells: a reliable platform that detects micronuclei and discriminates apoptotic bodies. Mutagenesis 2010;25:33–40.

[41] Organization for Economic Co-operation and Development (OECD). Guideline 476: *in vitro* mammalian cell gene mutation test. [Paris]. 1997.

[42] Clive D, Spector JF. Laboratory procedure for assessing specific locus mutations at the TK locus in cultured L5178Y mouse lymphoma cells. Mutat Res 1975;31:17–29.

[43] Moore MM, Honma M, Clements J, Bolcsfoldi G, Burlinson B, Cifone M, et al. Mouse lymphoma thymidine kinase gene mutation assay: follow-up meeting of the International Workshop on Genotoxicity Testing – Aberdeen, Scotland, 2003 – assay acceptance criteria, positive controls, and data evaluation. Environ Mol Mutagen 2006;47:1–5.

[44] US Food and Drug Administration (USFDA). Recommended approaches to integration of genetic toxicology study results. 2006.

[45] Hilliard C, Hill R, Armstrong M, Fleckenstein C, Freeland E, Duffy D, et al. Chromosome aberrations in Chinese hamster and human cells: a comparison using compounds with various genotoxicity profiles. Mutat Res 2007;616:103–18.

[46] Erexson G, Periago MV, Spicer C. Differential sensitivity of Chinese hamster V79 and Chinese hamster ovary (CHO) cells in the *in vitro* micronucleus screening assay. Mutat Res 2001;495:75–80.

[47] Honma M, Hayashi M. Comparison of *in vitro* micronucleus and gene mutation assay results for p53-competent versus p53-deficient human lymphoblastoid cells. Environ Mol Mutagen 2011;52:373–84.

[48] Snyder R, Green J. A review of the genotoxicity of marketed pharmaceuticals. Mutat Res 2001;488:151–69.

[49] Kirkland DJ. Improvements in the reliability of *in vitro* genotoxicity testing. Expert Opin Drug Metab Toxicol 2011;7:1513–20.

[50] Elespuru R, Agarwal R, Atrakchi A, Bigger CA, Heflich RH, Jagannath D, et al. Current and future application of genetic toxicity assay: the role and value of *in vitro* mammalian cell assays. Toxicol Sci 2009;109:172–9.

[51] Tweats DJ, Blakey DH, Heflich RH, Jacobs A, Jacobsen SD, Morita T, et al. Report of the IWGT working group on strategy/interpretation for regulatory *in vivo* tests II. Identification of *in vivo*-only positive compounds in the bone marrow micronucleus test. Mutat Res 2007;627:92–105.

[52] Schmid W. The micronucleus test. Mutat Res 1975;31.

[53] Heddle JA, Fenech M, Hayashi M, MacGregor JT. Reflections on the development of micronucleus assays. Mutagenesis 2011;26:3–10.

II. TOXICOLOGICAL STUDIES AND IND APPLICATION, AND FIRST IN-HUMAN CLINICAL TRIAL

[54] MacGregor JT, Wehr CM, Gould DH. Clastogen-induced micronuclei in peripheral blood erythrocytes: the basis for an improved micronucleus test. Environ Mutagen 1980;2:509–14.

[55] Organization for Economic Co-operation and Development (OECD). Mammalian erythrocyte micronucleus test. 2014.

[56] Hayashi M, Tice RR, MacGregor JT, Anderson D, Blakey DH, Kirsh-Volders M, et al. In vivo rodent erythrocyte micronucleus assay. Mutat Res/Environ Mutagen Relat Subj 1994;312:293–304.

[57] Torous DK, Hall NE, Illi-Love AH, Diehl MS, Cederbrant K, Sandelin K, et al. Interlaboratory validation of a CD71-based flow cytometric method (Microflow®) for the scoring of micronucleated reticulocytes in mouse peripheral blood. Environ Mol Mutagen 2005;45:44–55.

[58] Parton JW, Hoffman WP, Garriott ML. Validation of an automated image analysis micronucleus scoring system. Mutat Res/Genet Toxicol 1996;370:65–73.

[59] Tweats DJ, Blakey DH, Heflich RH, Jacobs A, Jacobsen SD, Morita T, et al. Report of the IWGT working group on strategies and interpretation of regulatory in vivo tests. I. Increases in micronucleated bone marrow cells in rodents that do not indicate genotoxic hazards. Mutat Res 2007;627:78–91.

[60] Cliet I, Fournier E, Melcion C, Cordier A. In vivo micronucleus test using mouse hepatocytes. Mutat Res/Environ Mutagen Relat Subj 1989;216:321–6.

[61] Tates AD, Neuteboom I, Hofker M, den Engelse L. A micronucleus technique for detecting clastogenic effects of mutagens/carcinogens (DEN, DMN) in hepatocytes of rat liver in vivo. Mutat Res/Environ Mutagen Relat Subj 1980;74:11–20.

[62] Takasawa H, Suzuki H, Ogawa I, Shimada Y, Kobayashi K, Terashima Y, et al. Evaluation of a liver micronucleus assay in young rats (III): a study using nine hepatotoxicants by the Collaborative Study Group for the Micronucleus Test (CSGMT)/Japanese Environmental Mutagen Society (JEMS) – Mammalian Mutagenicity Study Group (MMS). Mutat Res 2010;698:30–7.

[63] Coffing S, Engel M, Dickinson D, Thiffeault C, Spellman R, Shutsky T, et al. The rat gut micronucleus assay: a good choice for alternative in vivo genetic toxicology testing strategies. Environ Mol Mutagen 2011;52:269–79.

[64] Organization for Economic Co-operation and Development (OECD). Mammalian bone marrow chromosome aberration test. 2014.

[65] Tice RR, Agurell E, Anderson D, Burlinson B, Hartmann A, Kobayashi H, et al. Single cell gel/comet assay: guidelines for in vitro and in vivo genetic toxicology testing. Environ Mol Mutagen 2000;35:206–21.

[66] Kraynak AR, Gealy R, Cunningham C, Ng A, Gill S, Barnum JE, et al. A semi-automated in vivo alkaline elution DNA damage assay has equivalent sensitivity and specificity to the single cell gel electrophoresis (comet) assay and is more efficient. In: Genetic toxicology association annual meeting, Newark, DE. 2010.

[67] Hartmann A, Schumacher M, Plappert-Helbig U, Lowe P, Suter W, Mueller L. Use of the alkaline in vivo comet assay for mechanistic genotoxicity investigations. Mutagenesis 2004;19:51–9.

[68] Olive PL, Banáth JP, Durand RE. Heterogeneity in radiation-induced DNA damage and repair in tumor and normal cells measured using the 'comet' assay. Radiat Res 1990;122:86–94.

[69] Kumaravel T, Vilhar B, Faux S, Jha A. comet assay measurements: a perspective. Cell Biol Toxicol 2009;25:53–64.

[70] Organization for Economic Co-operation and Development (OECD). In vivo mammalian alkaline comet assay. 2014.

[71] Deleted in review.

[72] Deleted in review.

[73] Deleted in review.

[74] Deleted in review.

[75] Gealy R, Wright-Bourque J, Kraynak AR, McKelvey TW, Barnum JE, Storer RD. Validation of a high-throughput in vitro alkaline elution/rat hepatocyte assay for DNA damage. Mutat Res 2007;629:49–63.

[76] Gollapudi B, Thybaud V, Kim J, Holsapple M. Strategies for the follow-up of positive results in the in vitro genotoxicity assays – an international collaborative initiative. Environ Mol Mutagen 2011;52:174–6.

[77] Rothfuss A, Honma M, Czich A, Aardema MJ, Burlinson B, Galloway S, et al. Improvement of in vivo genotoxicity assessment: combination of acute tests and integration into standard toxicity testing. Mutat Res/Genet Toxicol Environ Mutagen 2011;723:108–20.

[78] Shi J, Krsmanovic L, Bruce S, Kelly T, Paranjpe M, Szabo K, et al. Assessment of genotoxicity induced by 7,12-dimethylbenz(a)anthracene or diethylnitrosamine in the Pig-a, micronucleus and comet assays integrated into 28-day repeat dose studies. Environ Mol Mutagen 2011;52:711–20.

[79] Stankowski LF, Roberts DJ, Chen H, Lawlor T, McKeon M, Murli H, et al. Integration of Pig-a, micronucleus, chromosome aberration, and comet assay endpoints in a 28-day rodent toxicity study with 4-nitroquinoline-1-oxide. Environ Mol Mutagen 2011;52:738–47.

[80] Sasaki YF, Sekihashi K, Izumiyama F, Nishidate E, Saga A, Ishida K, et al. The comet assay with multiple mouse organs: comparison of comet assay results and carcinogenicity with 208 chemicals selected from the IARC monographs and US NTP carcinogenicity database. Crit Rev Toxicol 2000;30:629–799.

[81] Kirkland D, Speit G. Evaluation of the ability of a battery of three in vitro genotoxicity tests to discriminate rodent carcinogens and noncarcinogens: III. Appropriate follow-up testing in vivo. Mutat Res/Genet Toxicol Environ Mutagen 2008;654:114–32.

[82] Organization for Economic Co-operation and Development (OECD). Guideline 488: transgenic rodent somatic and germ cell gene mutation assays. 2011.

[83] Heddle JA, Dean S, Nohmi T, Boerrigter M, Casciano D, Douglas GR, et al. In vivo transgenic mutation assays. Environ Mol Mutagen 2000;35:253–9.

[84] Thybaud V, Dean S, Nohmi T, de Boer J, Douglas GR, Glickman BW, et al. In vivo transgenic mutation assays. Mutat Res 2003;540:141–51.

[85] Lambert I, Singer T, Boucher S, Douglas G. Detailed review of transgenic rodent mutation assays. Mutat Res 2005;590:1–280.

[86] Dertinger SD, Heflich RH. In vivo assessment of Pig-a gene mutation – recent developments and assay validation. Environ Mol Mutagen 2011;52:681–4.

[87] Miura D, Dobrovolsky VN, Kasahara Y, Katsuura Y, Heflich RH. Development of an in vivo gene mutation assay using the endogenous Pig-a gene: I. Flow cytometric detection of CD59-negative peripheral red blood cells and CD48-negative spleen T-cells from the rat. Environ Mol Mutagen 2008;49:614–21.

[88] Miura D, Dobrovolsky VN, Kimoto T, Kasahara Y, Heflich RH. Accumulation and persistence of Pig-A mutant peripheral red blood cells following treatment of rats with single and split doses of N-ethyl-N-nitrosourea. Mutat Res/Genet Toxicol Environ Mutagen 2009;677:86–92.

[89] Dertinger SD, Phonethepswath S, Weller P, Avlasevich S, Torous DK, Mereness JA, et al. Interlaboratory Pig-a gene mutation assay trial: studies of 1,3-propane sultone with immunomagnetic enrichment of mutant erythrocytes. Environ Mol Mutagen 2011;52:748–55.

[90] Lynch AM, Giddings A, Custer L, Gleason C, Henwood A, Aylott M, et al. International Pig-a gene mutation assay trial (Stage III): results with N-methyl-N-nitrosourea. Environ Mol Mutagen 2011;52:699–710.

[91] Schuler M, Gollapudi BB, Thybaud V, Kim JH. Need and potential value of the Pig-a *in vivo* mutation assay – A HESI perspective. Environ Mol Mutagen 2011;52:685–9.

[92] International Organization for Harmonization (ICH). S2B genotoxicity: a standard battery for genotoxicity testing of pharmaceuticals. 1997.

[93] Organization for Economic Co-operation and Development (OECD). Test guideline 486: unscheduled DNA synthesis (UDS) test with mammalian liver cells in vivo. 1997.

[94] Mirsalis JC, Tyson K, Butterworth BE. Detection of genotoxic carcinogens in the *in vivo-in vitro* hepatocyte DNA repair assay. Environ Mutagen 1982;4:553–62.

[95] Tweats DJ. The predictive value of batteries of short-term tests for carcinogens. Food Addit Contam 1984;1:189–97.

[96] Ashby J, Tennant RW. Definitive relationships among chemical structure, carcinogenicity and mutagenicity for 301 chemicals tested by the US NTP. Mutat Res 1991;257:229–306.

[97] Storer RD, McKelvey TW, Kraynak AR, Elia MC, Barnum JE, Harmon LS, et al. Revalidation of the *in vitro* alkaline elution/rat hepatocyte assay for DNA damage: improved criteria for assessment of cytotoxicity and genotoxicity and results for 81 compounds. Mutat Res 1996;368:59–101.

[98] Oshiro Y, Balwierz P, Morris D, Alden C, Bunch RT. Morphological transformation of Syrian hamster embryo cells at pH 6.7 by bemitradine, a nongenotoxic carcinogen. In Vitro Mol Toxicol 2001;14:121–7.

[99] Billinton N, Hastwell PW, Beerens D, Birrell L, Ellis P, Maskell S, et al. Interlaboratory assessment of the GreenScreen HC GADD45a-GFP genotoxicity screening assay: an enabling study for independent validation as an alternative method. Mutat Res 2008;653:23–33.

[100] Walmsley RM. GADD45a-GFP GreenScreen HC genotoxicity screening assay. Expert Opin Drug Metab Toxicol 2008;4:827–35.

[101] Olaharski AJ, Albertini S, Mueller L, Zeller A, Struwe M, Gocke E, et al. GADD45alpha induction in the GreenScreen HC indicator assay does not occur independently of cytotoxicity. Environ Mol Mutagen 2009;52:28–34.

[102] Knight AW, Birrell L, Walmsley RM. Development and validation of higher throughput screening approach to genotoxicity testing using the GADD45a-GFP GreenScreen HC assay. J Biomol Screen 2009;14:16–30.

[103] Hastwell PW, Chai LL, Roberts KJ, Webster TW, Harvey JS, Rees RW, et al. High-specificity and high-sensitivity genotoxicity assessment in a human cell line: validation of the GreenScreen HC GADD45a-GFP genotoxicity assay. Mutat Res 2006;607:160–75.

[104] Schiestl RH. Nonmutagenic carcinogens induce intrachromosomal recombination in yeast. Nature 1989;337:285–8.

[105] Schiestl RH, Gietz RD, Mehta RD, Hastings PJ. Carcinogens induce intrachromosomal recombination in yeast. Carcinogenesis 1989;10:1445–55.

[106] Brennan RJ, Schiestl RH. Detecting carcinogens with the yeast DEL assay. Methods Mol Biol 2004;262:111–24.

[107] Kirpnick Z, Homiski ML, Rubitski E, Repnevskaya M, Howlett N, Aubrecht J, et al. Yeast DEL assay detects clastogens. Mutat Res 2005;582:116–34.

[108] Randerath K, Reddy MV, Gupta R. 32P-labeling test for DNA damage. Proc Natl Acad Sci 1981;78:6126–9.

[109] Reddy MV, Blackburn G, Bleicher W, Irwin S, Mehlman M, Mackerer C. 32P-postlabeling assay of DNA adducts formed *in vitro* and *in vivo* with benzene and its meabolites: new assays to measure adducts as 5'-32P labeled dinucleotides and nucleoside monophosphates. In: Garner RC, Farmer PB, Steel GT, Wright AS, editors. Human carcinogen exposure: biomonitoring and risk assessment. New York: IRL Press; 1992. p. 369–80.

[110] Pottenger LH, Carmichael N, Banton MI, Boogaard PJ, Kim J, Kirkland D, et al. ECETOC workshop on the biological significance of DNA adducts: summary of follow-up from an expert panel meeting. Mutat Res/Genet Toxicol Environ Mutagen 2009;678:152–7.

[111] Guzzie-Peck P, Sakaki J, Weiner S. Genetic toxicology. In: Lodola A, Stadler J, editors. Pharmaceutical toxicology in practice – a guide to non-clinical development. Hoboken: Wiley – A John Wiley and Sons, Inc. Publication; 2011.

[112] Mahadevan B, Snyder R, Waters MD, Benz RD, Kemper RA, Tice RR, et al. Genetic toxicology in the 21st century: reflections and future directions. Environ Mol Mutagen 2011;52:339–354.

[113] Ellinger-Ziegelbauer H, Aubrecht J, Kleinjans JC, Ahr HJ. Application of toxicogenomics to study mechanisms of genotoxicity and carcinogenicity. Toxicol Lett 2009;186:36–44.

[114] Blomme E. Application to *in vivo* toxicology. In: Semizarov D, Blomme E, editors. Genomics in drug discovery and development. Hoboken: Toxicogenomics John Wiley & Sons; 2009. p. 219–91.

[115] Jacobson-Kram D, Jacobs A. Use of genotoxicity data to support clinical trials or positive genetox findings on a candidate pharmaceutical or impurity. Now what? Int J Toxicol 2005;24:129–34.

[116] Brambilla G, Martelli A. Update on genotoxicity and carcinogenicity testing of 472 marketed pharmaceuticals. Mutat Res 2009;681:209–29.

[117] Martus H-J. Devising predictive genotoxicity test strategies for pharmaceuticals in light of changing regulatory requirements. Int Drug Discov 2010:73–6.

[118] Diehl MS, Willaby SL, Snyder RD. Comparison of the results of a modified miniscreen and the standard bacterial reverse mutation assays. Environ Mol Mutagen 2000;36:72–7.

[119] Aubrecht J, Osowski JJ, Persaud P, Cheung JR, Ackerman J, Lopes SH, et al. Bioluminescent *Salmonella* reverse mutation assay: a screen for detecting mutagenicity with high throughput attributes. Mutagenesis 2007;22:335–42.

[120] Flückiger-Isler S, Baumeister M, Braun K, Gervais V, Hasler-Nguyen N, Reimann R, et al. Assessment of the performance of the Ames II(TM) assay: a collaborative study with 19 coded compounds. Mutat Res/Genet Toxicol Environ Mutagen 2004;558:181–97.

[121] Lukamowicz M, Woodward K, Kirsch-Volders M, Suter W, Elhajouji A. A flow cytometry based *in vitro* micronucleus assay in TK6 cells – validation using early stage pharmaceutical development compounds. Environ Mol Mutagen 2011;52:363–72.

[122] Elhajouji A, Tibaldi F, Kirsch-Volders M. Indication for thresholds of chromosome nondisjunction versus chromosome lagging induced by spindle inhibitors *in vitro* in human lymphocytes. Mutagenesis 1997;12:133–40.

[123] Kirsch-Volders M, Vanhauwaert A, Eichenlaub-Ritter U, Decordier I. Indirect mechanisms of genotoxicity. Toxicol Lett 2003;140–141:63–74.

[124] Kirsch-Volders M, Vanhauwaert A, De Boeck M, Decordier I. Importance of detecting numerical versus structural chromosome aberrations. Mutat Res/Fundam Mol Mech Mutagen 2002;504:137–48.

[125] Thybaud V, Aardema MJ, Clements J, Dearfield K, Galloway SM, Hayashi M, et al. Strategy for genotoxicity testing: hazard identification and risk assessment in relation to *in vitro* testing. Mutat Res 2007;627:41–58.

[126] US Food and Drug Administration (USFDA). Exploratory IND studies. 2006.

[127] US Food and Drug Administration (USFDA). Safety testing of drug metabolites. 2008.

[128] International Conference on Harmonization (ICH). Q3A(R2): impurities in new drug substances (revised guideline). 2006.

[129] International Conference on Harmonization (ICH). Q3B(R2): impurities in new drug products (revised guideline). 2006.

[130] Kroes R, Renwick AG, Cheeseman M, Kleiner J, Mangelsdorf I, Piersma A, et al. Structure-based thresholds of toxicological concern (TTC): guidance for application to substances present at low levels in the diet. Food Chem Toxicol 2004;42:65–83.

[131] European Medicines Agency (EMEA). Questions and answers on the 'Guideline on the limits of genotoxic impurities'. [London]. 2010.

[132] International Conference on Harmonization (ICH). Q3C(R5): guideline for residual solvents. 2007.

[133] Deleted in review.

[134] Dobo KL, Greene N, Cyr M, Caron S, Ku WW. The application of structure-base assessment to support safety and chemistry diligence to manage genotoxic impurities in active pharmaceutical ingredients during drug development. Regul Toxicol Pharmacol 2006;44.

[135] Levin D, Marnett L, Ames BN. Spontaneous and mutagen-induced deletions: mechanistic studies in *Salmonella* tester strain TA102. Proc Natl Acad Sci USA 1984;81:4457–61.

[136] International Conference on Harmonization (ICH). M7: assessment and control of DNA reactive (mutagenic) impurities in pharmaceuticals to limit potential carcinogenic risk. 2014.

7

Contemporary Practices in Core Safety Pharmacology Assessments

T.J. Baird, D.V. Gauvin, J.A. Dalton

BACKGROUND AND OVERVIEW

The origins of safety pharmacology are grounded upon observations that organ functions (like organ structures) can be toxicological targets in humans exposed to novel therapeutic agents and that drug effects on organ functions (unlike organ structures) are not readily detected by standard toxicological testing [1].

Safety pharmacology is an investigative, regulatory science grounded in disciplines including, perhaps most importantly, physiology, pharmacology, and toxicology. Due to early recognition of the fundamental importance of off-target drug activity, especially functional "side effects," the practice of safety pharmacology dates back decades. It has long been an integral part of drug development programs as conducted within institutions supporting drug-safety research. In this chapter, we will examine elements of the history and development of safety pharmacology as a discipline, with particular focus on how contemporary practice of this specialty science has evolved in the past 10 years, and the nature of models enjoying current acceptance by today's safety pharmacologists. Although many of the essential experimental questions and some basic dependent measures addressing potential adverse functional effects of drugs in development on physiological systems have changed surprisingly little over time (eg, isolated tissue/organ preparations to assess pharmacological activity, in vivo behavioral and physiological assays to evaluate integrative drug responses), the context in which these questions are posed, particularly in the case of whole-animal safety studies, has changed dramatically in just the past 15 years [2,3]. These contextual factors, which determine how safety pharmacology is practiced contemporarily, and will be in the future, have significant impact on the quality of data derived from research investigations, as well as on the appropriateness of decision-making at key steps in drug development.

As suggested above, safety pharmacology investigations attempt to assess the potential for off-target drug activity, particularly as this relates to adversity, and the potential to influence multiple physiological systems critical for the sustenance of life. Beyond the minimum expectation of basic, or "first tier," dose–response hazard identification in support of first-in-human clinical trials, it is also within the mandate of safety pharmacology to elucidate the potential reversibility of any characterized effects, as well as the mechanism(s) of action involved. Safety pharmacology studies are most typically conducted preclinically, but may also be employed at any stage of clinical development or in postmarketing surveillance in order to model potential effects of concern that might be observed in human populations exposed to a given therapeutic. Because of the sensitive and labile nature of many variables of interest, whether these represent the behavioral or physiological manifestations of drug action, it is often the case that safety pharmacology investigations are conducted within rigorously controlled testing environments to promote assay sensitivity, reliability, and predictive validity. This represents another distinguishing feature of the discipline, which often contrasts sharply with research environments supporting regulatory investigative toxicology testing. Indeed, a significant challenge and opportunity in contemporary safety pharmacology is related to the development of strategies appropriate for integrating functional safety and traditional toxicological approaches. This is especially true as pharmacotherapy incorporates the latest developments in molecular biology, allowing selective molecular activity with a targeted substrate as never before possible with traditional small-molecule therapeutics.

As with any scientific discipline, including particularly those concerned with safety evaluation, our expectations of safety pharmacology must necessarily be defined, and these definitions refined over time. Although there is an almost limitless set of assays from which we may draw, the scope of potential application of safety pharmacology study data in pursuit of comprehensively defining safety concerns must necessarily be more limited. Indeed, in relation to the overall consideration of industry-defined categories of adverse drug reactions (ADRs), it is arguably optimistic to think that the traditional definition of (acute) safety pharmacology study designs are amenable to characterizing such reactions beyond those "Type A" ADRs evidencing clear dose–response expression (see Table 7.1). Nevertheless, even this small subset of ADRs is of major concern, as off-target functional effects, particularly those impacting the central nervous and cardiovascular systems, continue to represent a significant cause of drug withdrawals [4,5]. Since the inception of the Safety Pharmacology Society (SPS)—the nonprofit organization that promotes knowledge, development, application, and training in Safety Pharmacology [1]—the continued refinement and redefinition of the discipline has been reflected in the scientific content presented by members at its annual meetings, as well as in the peer-reviewed manuscripts published within the *Journal of Pharmacological and Toxicological Methods* and other peer-reviewed journals [3,6–13]. This necessary refinement in our definition of safety pharmacology in terms of its routine practices and application to drug development will be considered in detail in later sections of this chapter and discussed as it relates to the future of the discipline amid an ever-changing scientific and regulatory environment.

SAFETY PHARMACOLOGY AS A REGULATORY SCIENCE

It seems obvious that comprehensive characterization of the constellation of all off-target and potentially adverse effects associated with a putative therapeutic molecule is a more daunting undertaking than the

TABLE 7.1 Categories of Adverse Drug Reaction Amenable to Preclinical Safety Pharmacology Study Detection and Characterization

ADR Type	Features	Predictable by Acute Pharmacology Studies
A	Dose-dependent	Yes[a]
B	Idiosyncratic response, not dose-related	Not genearlly[b]
C	Long-term, adaptive, common	Not generally[c]
D	Delayed effect, low incidence	Not generally[d]
E	Rebound or discontinuation effect	Yes[e]

[a]*Primary, Secondary Pharmacodynamic, or Safety Pharmacology.*
[b]*Identified in postmarketing surveillance by exposure in large populations.*
[c]*May be identified by appropriate measures in repeat-dosing designs.*
[d]*May be identified by appropriate designs for carcinogenicity/teratogenicity assessment.*
[e]*Primary, Secondary Pharmacodynamic or Safety Pharmacology (Abuse/Dependence).*

Adapted from Breckenridge A. A clinical pharmacologist's view of drug toxicity. Br J Pharmacol 1996;42:53–58. Lazarou J, Pomeranz BH, Corey PN. Incidence of adverse drug reactions in hospitalized patients: a meta-analysis of prospective studies. J Am Med Assoc 1998;279:1200–1205.Redfern WS, Wakefield ID, Prior H, Pollard CE, Hammond TG, Valentin J-P. Safety pharmacology – a progressive approach. Fund Clin Pharmacol 2002;16:161–173. Gad SC. Safety pharmacology in pharmaceutical development and approval. Boca Raton: LLCCRC Press, LLC; 2004.

relatively narrower focus of understanding that entity's mechanism of therapeutic efficacy. This notion seems particularly true when considered within the historical context in which safety pharmacology as a regulatory science was born. In many respects, the litany of notable failures directly related to issues that clearly fall into the category of safety pharmacology concerns [4,5,18], and in particular the issue of drug-induced change in cardiac electrophysiology as it particularly presents as a predisposing factor to proarrhythmia [19,20], inevitably has led to a transition in the practice of safety pharmacology from a relatively unregimented process supporting general pharmacological characterization of a new molecular entity to the much more formalized and regulated endeavor we recognize today [16]. Accordingly, regulatory status now represents another distinguishing feature impacting the practice of secondary pharmacodynamic (safety pharmacology) studies, versus those pharmacodynamic studies designed to assess therapeutic effects and mechanism(s). Although the continued focus of the discipline is to adequately address potential threats to core physiological systems, albeit with appropriate enhancements related to technical and scientific developments over time [3,21,22], there is now a significantly enhanced regulatory framework detailing the manner in which these functions should ideally be performed. This regulatory framework has its roots in early efforts to more formally define safety pharmacology disciplinary practice. It has had a fundamental impact on developments within the past decade, and continues to be elaborated, with the effect of influencing contemporary industry practices for years to come [23].

Among the earliest references to experimental designs consistent with what we now understand as safety pharmacology investigations are those contained within Japanese regulatory history, including in 1975, the "Notes on Applications for Approval to Manufacture (Import) New Drugs, Japan MHW" [24], and in 1995, the "Japanese Guidelines for Nonclinical Studies of Drugs Manual Tokyo, Japan" [25]. This history, with the 1998 "Guideline for Safety Pharmacology Study, Japan" [26], were major bases, which ultimately led to the inception of the ICH S7A harmonized tripartite guidance, "Safety Pharmacology Studies for Human Pharmaceuticals" [27]. This harmonized guidance made formal recommendations for the design, execution, and interpretive elements of safety pharmacology investigations [1,28]. The related, later-emerging, ICH S7B "Guidance on Safety Pharmacology Studies for Assessing the Potential for Delayed Ventricular Repolarization (QT-Interval Prolongation) by Human Pharmaceuticals" [29] has provided additional and specific recommendations on the techniques considered appropriate for determining the liability of a new chemical entity to produce alterations in patterns of cardiac conduction, especially as it relates to shifts in repolarization status that may precipitate the emergence of potentially fatal arrhythmia(s). The logic of testing strategies continues to be elaborated in this, and other areas, as we gain deeper perspective on how to identify and approach the specific variables of interest in predicting human safety concerns. The development and promulgation of internationally harmonized guidance documents has been conducted with the goal of enhancing the reliability and predictive validity of the preclinical models employed in developing risk data to protect the health and well-being of early human clinical trial participants. Although a full review of the regulatory history and content of the contemporary harmonized guidelines for safety pharmacology is beyond the scope of this chapter, much of the material to follow is naturally very closely aligned with the sentiments articulated in these documents, as their influence on current practice has been profound.

It is notable that issued expert guidance on safety pharmacology, from the earliest indications to those reflecting present understanding and experience (see Bass et al., 2004 [1]; for a comprehensive review), and which lend specific expert opinion-based recommendations for model selection, study design, experimental conduct, and data interpretation, are quite steeped in the milieu of small-molecule drug development. A review of the specific language and recommendations contained within these documents clearly conveys the ubiquity of this "small-molecule" perspective. In consideration of the explosive growth of molecularly targeted therapies over the past 15 years, which are often considerably different from small molecules in terms of their relative promiscuity for off-target interactions, among other factors, this historical orientation represents a potential liability and a gap that must be addressed to elucidate the most appropriate strategies for functional (safety pharmacology) assessment of these newer, novel agents.

Although there has been some recent work in this direction [30,31], and some relevant regulatory guidance [32] does exist, questions often present regarding the contextual features surrounding execution of the specific safety pharmacology support plan for biopharmaceuticals. Likewise, the situation with cancer therapeutics, including either small-molecule or targeted biological therapeutic approaches, often deviates from the standard strategy for small-molecule safety pharmacology program development [33]. Vaccine development also exists within a similar, less-defined context in terms of safety pharmacology, and individual situations must be considered carefully in terms of what assays are required, and in what context these will be performed to satisfy needs for key functional endpoint data while maintaining requisite levels of assay sensitivity [32,34]. Strategies for effectively addressing the needs of new pharmacotherapies, including special therapeutic and drug class considerations, currently may not be indicated clearly by guidance documents, but are, like other core issues in safety pharmacology practice, being resolved by ongoing basic research and technical innovations. With time, consensus should begin to emerge regarding preferred or "best" practices.

TEMPORAL APPLICATION OF CURRENT EXPERIMENTAL PARADIGMS

As highlighted previously, core safety pharmacology programs are designed to address specific functional safety issues that may be expressed within any of several key physiological systems critical to the maintenance of life. Translation of this concept into terms of the minimum expectations for routine safety pharmacology assessment has been articulated in the harmonized ICH S7A and S7B guidelines and generally includes the conduct of integrated screening studies to evaluate central nervous (CNS) and cardiorespiratory systems, including specific tests for cardiac ion-channel interaction, as well as directed evaluations of any supplemental tissues or organ systems, consistent with existing knowledge regarding the pharmacology and/or toxicity of the molecular class of interest. These studies are generally required to be performed in accordance with good laboratory practice (GLP) regulations when feasible, with the so-called "core battery" of assays (cardiovascular, respiratory, CNS) conducted prior to the first application of the new chemical entity in human clinical trials (21 Code of Federal Regulations (CFR) Part 58). The diagram below (Fig. 7.1) indicates a general organizational scheme suitable for appreciating the temporal context of selected cardiovascular and CNS preclinical safety pharmacology assays in relation to the continuum from discovery through clinical development efforts, with perhaps a particular emphasis on small molecules.

As illustrated in Fig. 7.1, it is clear that there exist a number of choices regarding how and when to implement variably scaled safety pharmacology testing in order to enhance program development. In general, the GLP core battery of safety pharmacology is conducted at the same time as other pivotal safety (toxicology) investigations that permit a reasonably full appreciation of the essential risks that must be understood and managed prior to progression of any one of perhaps several clinical candidates to human clinical trials. An exception to this general guideline is the abuse and dependence liability assessment, for which there is no firm requirement for performance prior to first-in-human clinical trials. There is simply an acknowledgment that these assays must be completed for the relevant classes of molecules, especially those with novel mechanisms of action, at some point prior to the marketing application. However, in general it is prudent to at least begin to understand

the need for, and plan the likely scope of, such studies in anticipation of clinical trials. Indeed, the timing of availability of safety data that inform on and enable critical elements of the abuse/dependence liability program is very much tied to the results of IND-enabling studies (detailed clinical observations on MTD and repeat-dose designs, especially those including recovery periods, behavioral profiles of effect on Tier I safety pharmacology studies), which makes planning for these programs very convenient in this general timeframe.

Some contemporary arguments have highlighted the utility of "front-loading" safety pharmacology endpoints early in preclinical development, with the goal of maximizing early knowledge of the potential relative pharmacological liabilities of molecular variants [9,35]. It has further been suggested that possession of this kind of information at an early stage should facilitate the capacity to modify development parameters to "engineer" molecules toward those characteristics that enhance therapeutic efficacy while reducing liabilities leading to unacceptable risk profiles [36]. Front-loading strategies have been exemplified contemporarily in routine industry practices that have been adopted over time, such as the use of high-throughput screening for potential cardiac ion-channel interactions, or the use of receptor panel screens to characterize nervous system ligand–receptor interactions and predict potential electrocardiographic and functional CNS liabilities, respectively [37]. Additional opportunities exist in incorporating key safety endpoints (CNS, respiratory, cardiovascular) into early in vivo toxicity studies with the aim of characterizing potential activity of interest at this integrative level. Such data would theoretically provide key insights contributing to the design of, and correspondingly enhancing the value of data elicited by, subsequent definitive safety pharmacology investigations.

With continued refinement, the concept of "front-loading" safety pharmacology may be more suitably appreciated within a proposed elaboration of the definition of the discipline into two distinct subdisciplines with different mandates: exploratory safety pharmacology and regulatory safety pharmacology [36]. According to this proposed structure, exploratory safety pharmacology represents practice of a refining set of (non-GLP) in silico, in vitro, ex vivo, and/or in vivo assays within the theater of early discovery research toward:

1. identifying drug candidates carrying specific "vital organ" system liabilities of concern,
2. using mechanism-of-action based information early in the discovery process to categorize molecules with regard to relative risks and mitigate these by programmatic adjustments, and thereby allowing
3. screening out compounds ultimately possessing clinically unmanageable adverse effect profiles [36].

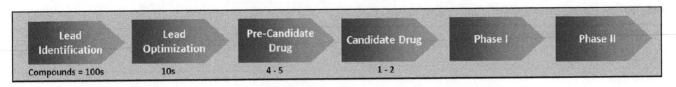

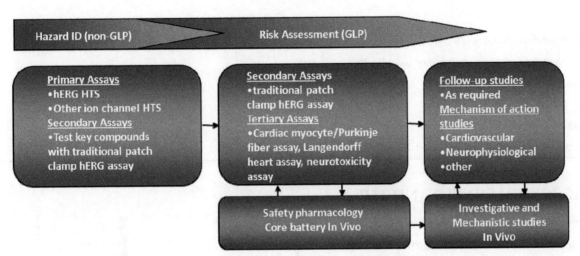

FIGURE 7.1 Temporal context of key safety pharmacology assessments in early drug development.

This process is distinguished from regulatory safety pharmacology in that the goal is to (prospectively) evaluate drug candidates for potentially undesirable *mechanisms of action*, as opposed to (reactively) characterizing a constrained set of potential adverse pharmacodynamic *effects*.

The sections that follow largely describe some of the possible experimental and technical iterations comprising current practice in regulatory safety pharmacology, drawing examples that reflect upon the contemporary application of essential assays and use of a tiered approach to such testing, as initially suggested by Kinter and Dixon [28,38]. The examples used and topics covered are not meant to be exhaustive, but to provide a clear picture of the essentials of contemporary practice of the core, IND-enabling, GLP assays in safety pharmacology, and to explain key components of study designs presently in widespread use, highlighting rationales behind these that may be more or less obvious, but also that may be seldom elaborated.

CARDIOVASCULAR SYSTEM AND MODELS OF SAFETY ASSESSMENT

By its very nature, the cardiovascular system is complex, with varied and diverse intrinsic properties of constituent tissues and multiple regulatory feedback loops, including integrated systems for ascending and descending nervous system communication and control. A comprehensive overview of cardiovascular anatomy and physiology and the many models applicable to cardiovascular safety

assessment are beyond the scope of this chapter, but are available in various sources [2,39,40]. Relevant features of the cardiovascular system may be examined at many different levels, from the subcellular to the unified organism, and using a variety of techniques (electrophysiology, mechanical properties, etc.) to evaluate different aspects of coordinated functions. While many diverse assays are potentially informative toward characterizing potential drug effects on essential functions of this system, contemporary practice has focused on a limited set of essential evaluations to be employed at a minimum: assessment of the potential for interaction with cardiac ion channels, and particularly potassium channels, and evaluation of basic cardiovascular status variables (blood pressure, heart rate, qualitative and quantitative electrophysiological features) in vivo in a suitable test system [27,29]. Additional variables of interest based on drug class or existing safety data may be incorporated using these or other model systems, as necessary. Alternatively, and again in relation to consideration of these variables as well as the context of therapy, the exclusion of some elements of these core assessments may be indicated, depending on the specific development program under review. Table 7.2 depicts representative examples of "core battery" or first tier and supplemental (designated Tier II) cardiovascular safety variables. For even the limited subset of variables intrinsic to the "core battery" cardiovascular safety studies, there are numerous methods that may be utilized for data collection and analysis; choices regarding these have implications for the quality of data collected, and accordingly, to the nature of decisions ultimately made in program development.

TABLE 7.2　Core and Supplemental Cardiovascular Measures

Safety Pharmacology Measure	Core Battery (Tier I)	Supplemental (Tier II)
CARDIOVASCULAR		
hERG interaction	X	
Heart rate and (qualitative) rhythm	X	
Blood pressure	X	
Quantitative ECG Parameters (PR, QRS, QT, QTc)	X	
Ventricular pressure and derivatives (ie, contractility and relaxation estimates)		X
Vascular Compliance/Resistance		X
Cardiac output		X
Estimates of Myocardial work (CI, SI, LVW, etc.)		X
Biomarkers for cardiotoxicity (CK-MB Isoforms, cTnl, BNP, CRP, IL-6, TNFα)		X

CARDIAC ION CHANNELS AND THE HERG ASSAY

Potential interactions of drugs with cardiac ion channels are important because the operation of these channels permits the gating of sodium, potassium, and calcium ions, which in turn govern contractile/refractory status of cardiomyocytes and ultimately form the basis of the electromechanical cardiac cycling that sustains the normal circulatory function of the heart. Several subtypes of these three ion channels have been described, with relatively high (with some notable exceptions) conservation across species. This allows a number of variations in methodological scale to evaluate functional aspects of drug ion-channel interactions, particularly as these could engender an arrhythmogenic substrate [20]. Such methods may range from the microscopic to macroscopic, and include, for example, isolated channel systems in various expression vectors, evaluations of monophasic action potentials in native cells (eg, Purkinje fibers, cardiomyocytes, etc.), isolated tissue (eg, cardiac wedge) preparations, whole-organ (eg, Langendorff isolated, perfused heart) models, or even whole-organism (eg, open-chest, anesthetized) preparations [20,41–43]. The differential analysis afforded at each of these levels permits either more granular (ion-channel expression systems) or more global (evaluation of monophasic action potential or electrocardiogram (ECG), as in wedge, whole-heart, or whole-organism models) determinations of the nature and/or consequences of ion-channel interactions.

In general, evaluation of ion-channel activity is something done relatively early in the progression from discovery through early safety characterization, as noted previously in the discussion of "front-loading" of functional safety endpoints [37]. The evaluation of cardiac ion-channel interactions, and specifically the capacity of molecules to interfere with cardiac potassium channels,

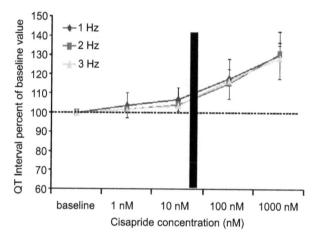

Effects of cisapride on rabbit QT Interval at various stimulation frequencies, Shaded rectangle marks hERG IC$_{50}$ value for cisapride.

FIGURE 7.2　Relationship between a measure of hERG potassium channel interaction and change in the QT interval assessed in an isolated perfused (Langendorff) heart model.

is routinely performed because of the reasonably strong proclivity of drugs with such action to also produce functional cardiovascular changes of concern, including potential alterations in quantitative (repolarization delay) and qualitative (arrhythmia) indicators [44] of heart electrical/mechanical cycling, particularly in the range of therapeutically efficacious levels (see Figs. 7.2 and 7.3 for an illustration of the relationships that may exist between hERG channel interaction (inhibition), quantitative increase in cardiac ventricular repolarization as reflected in the QT interval of the ECG, and the emergence of qualitative alterations in cardiac cycling in the form of ventricular arrhythmia). The preferred methods for evaluating ion-channel interactions tend to be based on functional electrophysiological assays [37,41], either high-throughput or manual patch clamp

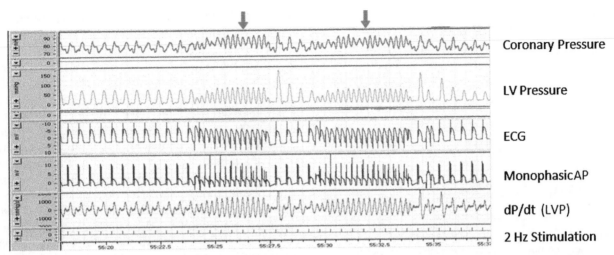

FIGURE 7.3 Emergence of ventricular arrhythmia (arrows) consequent to cisapride treatment (>100 nM) in an isolated perfused (Langendorff) heart model.

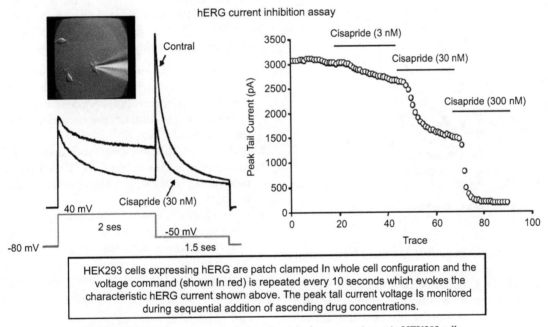

FIGURE 7.4 Illustration of whole-cell patch clamp experiment in HEK293 cells.

techniques. These are often employed prior to exploratory non-GLP cardiovascular studies, and certainly before definitive, GLP regulatory safety pharmacology investigations.

One standard approach to examine the ability of a compound to inhibit the *trans*-membrane current associated with the gating of potassium ions is commonly known as an hERG assay. One of the most common variations on the technique is conducted in human kidney cells (designated HEK293), transfected with a protein that encodes hERG subunits comprising the potassium ion channel, using manual patch clamp electrophysiology techniques [41]. Its advantages are several, including:

1. it represents a functional assay, as opposed to merely demonstrating binding without functional change,
2. it offers the ability to directly control voltage conditions and evaluate real-time changes in potassium current, and accordingly,
3. the technique tends to yield the highest quality data [20,41].

Although alternative high-throughput techniques are available, manual patch clamp techniques still represent the "gold standard" since they can accurately and precisely determine the nature of functional channel interactions. In addition, this is done in an environment conducive to the ready incorporation of important good laboratory

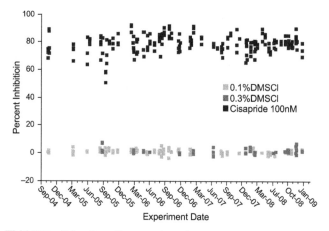

FIGURE 7.5 Compilation of within-experiment positive and vehicle (negative) control data across approximately 4 years of testing within the same electrophysiology laboratory.

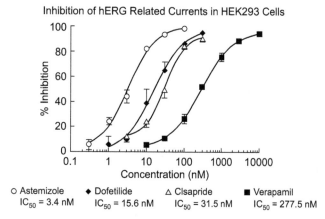

FIGURE 7.6 Relative potency of several classes of molecules active at hERG channels expressed in HEK 293 cells.

practice (GLP) elements, including test-item formulations analyses. Figs. 7.4 and 7.5 illustrate some key elements of the assay and the importance of application of positive and negative control conditions within experiment. Multiple environmental factors (eg, temperature, stimulation parameters, vehicle components, etc.) can influence any one individual experiment, and may tend to promote heterogeneity from study to study, either within or across experimental laboratories. Fig. 7.5 also illustrates the relative stability of the procedure across numerous experiments when these factors are well controlled.

Interactions with hERG channels may be ranked according to potency for various compounds including positive control in-class comparators. This is particularly relevant for those drugs for which repolarization and/or conductance liabilities have also been defined across complementary cardiovascular safety assays, against which new molecular entities may be evaluated for a preliminary assessment of potential relative risk. An example of this is depicted in Fig. 7.6, which shows several representative classes of molecules having differing degrees of activity in the assay. Although potency (as defined by an IC_{50} or other suitable

marker derived from the concentration–response function [eg, IC_{20}]) is an important consideration in determining relative concern for potential QT-interval prolongation and/or arrhythmia expression in vivo, multichannel pharmacology is also appreciated as a factor that may potentially mitigate or exacerbate this liability. For example, in Fig. 7.6, it may be observed that the relative potency of verapamil is less than the comparator compounds depicted. However, if one describes the potential hERG liability of verapamil in terms of a ratio of the drug's hERG IC_{50} to its therapeutic concentration in vivo (half maximally effective unbound drug concentration or similar estimate), the ratio of approximately 1.7 would fall far short of the 30-fold difference proposed to represent an adequate cardiac safety index, or provisional safety margin [20,44]. Multichannel pharmacology is thought to be responsible ultimately for the relative clinical safety of verapamil [44], as electrophysiological activity conferred via calcium-channel activity tends to offset hERG-mediated actions promoting increased ventricular refractoriness [45,46]. As a general rule, evaluations for hERG (and other ion-channel activity) should be conducted for the following reasons:

1. to ensure an adequate range of formulations has been tested in order to develop, to the extent possible, a concentration response function, including evaluation of concentrations up to the limits of solubility;
2. to derive useful indicators, such as IC_{50}/IC_{20} values;
3. to compare such measures (IC50/IC20) to some measure of the effective therapeutic concentration in vivo;
4. to consider these data in relation to other risk factors, other sources of cardiovascular safety data, and the proposed clinical indication of the molecule, to guide decisions regarding relative risk and mitigating circumstances (eg, lack of effective existing therapies, life-threatening disease, etc.) [44].

Ultimately, due to the heterogeneity of drug action and lack of adequate predictive validity of any one model in characterizing functional cardiotoxicity [47], the sampling of a variety of surrogate markers, including hERG activity or data derived from other in vitro/ex vivo model(s) predictive of cardiac ion-channel activity, as well as in vivo evaluations of biomarkers associated with arrhythmia (eg, QT/QTc or other markers of repolarization delay or increased heterogeneity of repolarization) is indicated, and will lead to a more complete understanding of relative risk and clinical management of such risk.

IN VIVO CARDIOVASCULAR SAFETY STUDY

It has become generally accepted practice to utilize canines for in vivo cardiovascular safety studies.

TABLE 7.3 A General Design Tier I (Core Battery) Cardiovascular Safety Study

In Vivo Cardiovasular Safety Study							
Sample Design			Latin Square Sequencing				
Treatment	Dose (mg/kg, p.o.)	Number of Animals	Animal ID	Dose Order			
1	0 (vehicle)	4	1	0	3	30	300
2	3	4	2	3	300	0	30
3	30	4	3	30	0	300	3
4	300	4	4	300	30	3	0

In addition, when appropriate, nonhuman primates (NHPs) are used as the standard in vivo test system, as a preponderance of data supports the validity and reliability of these species for characterizing potential drug effects of concern on the essential (Tier I) endpoints indicated in Table 7.3 [3,22,27,29,48–51]. The mini-pig has also recently been considered as a model with potential application in cardiovascular safety evaluation [52–57]. Other models, such as the marmoset and ferret have also been proposed as suitable for these purposes [58,59], but like the mini-pig, such models have enjoyed relatively less experimental scrutiny in defining key cardiovascular baselines and responses to pharmacological challenge, and accordingly significantly less use than the canine and NHP as a cardiovascular safety model [3]. As well as species selection, there are several features of experimental design that have become commonplace within the industry for cardiovascular safety studies. These are illustrated in Table 7.2.

For the majority of small molecules for which an evaluation of acute cardiovascular effects is the goal, repeat-dosing designs with appropriate "washout" or recovery periods between several discrete dose administrations at different dose levels is a common model. The reasons for this are:

1. the long effective duration of surgically implanted telemetry instrumentation, allowing colonies of telemetry animals to be set up within individual laboratories;
2. the general validity of the assumption of independence of treatments utilizing a within-subjects design, particularly for small molecules, provided that a suitable recovery period is instituted between treatments on a given experiment, and between use of animals on independent experiments;
3. the need to reduce, reuse, and refine (3Rs) as these relate to the employment of animal experimental models. Goals oriented toward experimental design and institutional efficiencies are actually very often supportive of 3R principles, particularly as this relates to evolving best practices promoting the reliable instrumentation, maintenance, and use of telemetry stock colonies.

There are a number of advantages to the use of remote telemetry monitoring in preclinical safety pharmacology:

1. telemetry-enabled observation provides the most humane method of monitoring physiologic endpoints in conscious, freely moving laboratory animals, eliminating the stress and artifactual changes related to the use of physical or chemical restraint;
2. in the intervening decades since its inception, remote telemetry has become more affordable and reliable, and now easy-to-use commercial products are readily available for monitoring a variety of physiological signals, including all Tier I and several Tier II cardiovascular endpoints;
3. indwelling sensors for monitoring variables of interest, such as blood pressure, are more accurate, precise, and reliable than alternate noninvasive methods, including transcutaneous laser-Doppler devices, tail-cuff blood pressure monitors, etc.;
4. biotelemetry allows for automated, high temporal resolution, continuous, and long-term data collection via computer, for days, weeks, or months, without any special demands in relation to animal care or maintenance.

When used in tandem with remote video monitoring, radiotelemetry can be used to the exclusion of any direct human contact for prolonged periods of time, which minimizes this additional source of interference with physiologically normal baselines. The minimization of human contact during recording intervals can greatly augment the readability, as well as the reliability, of the data derived from emotional animals, whose physiological parameters demonstrate significant synchronous changes with such contact. This is a major influence on resulting assay sensitivity, which is always an issue when extrapolating from the preclinical model to the clinic. However, one of the most important features of telemetry is the reduction of animal use. This is estimated at 60–70% in single-dose studies [60] and more than 90% in multiple-dose or repeat studies [61,62], and impacts both study efficiency and 3Rs concerns.

Due to the above concerns, as well as the relative economic competitiveness of reutilizing experimentally

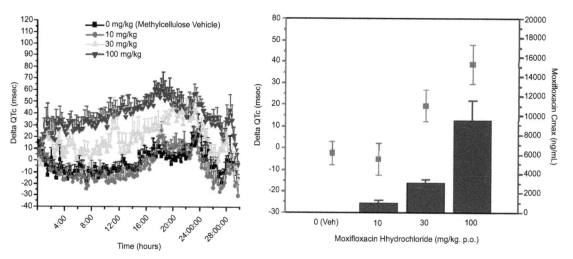

FIGURE 7.7 Dose- and time-response for heart rate corrected (QTc) interval prolongation with moxifloxacin administration in the mini-pig (left panel). Derivation of dose- and time-series data to illustrate basic pharmacodynamic/pharmacokinetic (PK/PD) modeling of the relationship between a measure of systemic exposure (Cmax) and average QTc interval duration increase over 24 h (right panel). Individual animal data may also be modeled, although summary data are depicted.

nonnaïve animals for cardiovascular safety evaluations, the establishment of stock colonies of test animals within pharmaceutical and contract research laboratories is likely to be a lasting industry trend. Accordingly, an understanding of requisite animal care and experimental qualification procedures has commensurately evolved over time. In this context, periodic assessments of the health status of individual animals using a number of key procedures (eg, clinical and physical examinations, ECG and clinical pathology evaluations), as well as confirmations of device functionality are needed. This ensures healthy animals, with high-quality physiological telemetry signals, are studied. These concepts are illustrated in more detail in the following sections.

Dose-level selection is a key consideration of the cardiovascular safety study design. In general, dose selection proceeds in the cardiovascular safety study design in the same manner as for other core battery (respiratory and CNS function) studies. A negative (most often vehicle) control condition is required, in addition to an adequate number and range of doses to evaluate the dose–response pharmacology, taking into consideration any practical issues (eg, drug solubility, required route of administration, etc.). A positive control condition is generally not needed in every individual experiment; however, having historical control data characterizing normal baseline and corresponding experimental power characteristics, as well as possession of archived positive control data illustrating effects of interest in relevant test systems in use in any given laboratory, is considered contemporary industry best practice [22]. The dose levels should approximate the predicted therapeutic exposure level at the low end of the selected range, and approach a maximum tolerated dose at the high end of the selected range, ideally without engendering potentially

confounding toxicity-related effects, interpolating intermediate dose(s) as required [27,29]. Appropriate dose selection will afford a definitive test for the elicitation of potential adverse pharmacology, and in the event this is detected, allow for dose-response characterization, and with appropriate pharmacokinetic evaluations incorporated into the study design, permit pharmacodynamic/pharmacokinetic (PK/PD) modeling (Fig. 7.7). This kind of analysis is often useful to compare sensitivity of different preclinical models as well as to predict clinical exposures of concern and accordingly may promote appropriate adjustments in clinical trials study designs.

Another important element of the study design is the inclusion of multiple continuous and high temporal fidelity baseline recordings. These may be used for several purposes, including the evaluation of overall signal quality and animal health prior to assignment to study (Figs. 7.8 and 7.9). Baseline recordings may also be used to establish the relationship between heart rate and the QT-interval duration of the ECG (or other important relationships between time-series telemetry data collected, such as QTc and core body temperature (Fig. 7.10), dP/dt$_{max}$ and heart rate, etc.), and to aid in the interpretation of test item- related effects from one treatment period to the next [63–66]. Baseline heart rate, blood pressure, ECG, and body temperature data are important indicators of the health status of the animal, and may also be used to diagnose technical issues affecting data-sensing components of the telemetry device. For example, elevated white blood cell counts that may be determined from prestudy clinical pathology screening, in the presence of sustained hyperthermia detected by telemetry, may serve as a basis for excluding an animal from study because of possible systemic infection, perhaps related to implanted instrumentation, surgical complication, or undetermined cause.

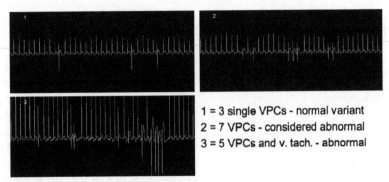

1 = 3 single VPCs - normal variant
2 = 7 VPCs - considered abnormal
3 = 5 VPCs and v. tach. - abnormal

FIGURE 7.8 Representative ECGs collected in three different study animals (cynomolgus monkeys) prior to assignment to study with implications to study eligibility. Panel 1 represents the expression of an arrhythmia that may be considered a "normal" variant in that single, periodic ventricular premature contractions (VPCs) may be observed in a small percentage of otherwise healthy animals of this species. Panel 2 depicts a potentially abnormal arrhythmia in that the expression of the observed VPCs is not just singlet occurrences, but couplets and triplets, which are of relatively greater concern inasmuch as these may represent a more serious underlying (congenital or experiential-induced) conduction disturbance. Panel 3 represents a clearly abnormal condition, characterized by five VPCs (including groupings of VPCs) and ventricular tachycardia; this is clearly indicative of a preexisting conduction disturbance in this animal. Any of the three circumstances depicted would be of concern in terms of placing an animal on study, as the underlying conduction disturbance(s) may have potential to interact with ongoing drug treatments in a manner that complicates dissociation of the preexisting conduction abnormality from potential test item related effects. In such circumstances, 24-h baseline data may be used to characterize the magnitude of expressed arrhythmia(s) so as to facilitate quantitative analysis of rhythm variants and clearly dissociate those that are drug related from those that exist as background in any individual animal. Used a priori, such data may be instrumental in decision-making regarding subject assignment.

Establishing the relationship between heart rate and the QT interval, based on adequate data sampling over diurnal and nocturnal phases, is important for in vivo cardiovascular safety studies. Sampling this relationship over a period of 24h enables high-fidelity modeling of the HR/QT relationship over a significant range of variation, and is essential for individual QT-correction procedures. These procedures have become industry standard due to repeated demonstrations of comparably sound performance across multiple species (Fig. 7.11), which are ultimately translatable to the human clinical situation [67].

Finally, the inclusion of several baselines is a valuable tool for discrimination of test item-related effects because of the inherent interval-to-interval variability in various quantitative and qualitative cardiovascular study parameters. The inclusion of predose study baselines with each treatment allows another basis for judging potential dose- and time-related effects, and accordingly strengthens the overall study design and the potential generalizability of conclusions drawn from study data. Long periods of high-quality data may be collected by telemetry, making this methodology an incredibly powerful tool for estimating true baseline incidence rates of qualitative ECG variants (eg, compare Gauvin et al. [68] and Cools et al. [69] for the beagle dog), and also for discriminating treatment-related findings (Leishman et al. [22]). In addition, long-term shifts in blood pressure regulation, which may reflect a pattern of change characteristic of cardiovascular toxicity associated with certain molecular classes or drug therapy within the context of ongoing cardiovascular disease, may be more easily characterized by telemetric techniques amenable

to definitive baseline construction and long-term, repetitive monitoring [70].

Experimental designs must reflect the general goals of cardiovascular safety pharmacology studies to be considered useful in program development. Since the inception of the ICH S7A and S7B guidance documents [27,29], the minimum expectation for safety pharmacology investigations has been understood to be detection and characterization of catastrophic effects, in order to protect clinical trials participants from potentially life-threatening situations. Beyond this minimum expectation, some additional goals of cardiovascular safety testing recently have been articulated, as shown in Table 7.4. It is worth noting that, regardless of the particular dependent measure, as the intended goal of the safety evaluation becomes more refined, the sensitivity and specificity of the preclinical model used in prediction must be correspondingly enhanced [22]. Comparing the intended goal to the corresponding magnitude of effect in Table 7.4 clearly indicates that as the goal of cardiovascular safety pharmacology studies moves beyond the rudimentary exclusion of catastrophic effects, the sensitivity of the preclinical model that is required to deliver these enhanced goals is increased.

Enhanced sensitivity (and ideally specificity) may be gained in different ways, including either improving techniques to augment experimental control, or substituting an entirely different model that has increased capacity to detect and characterize the specific effect(s) of interest. In the first case, a particular study design can be improved, such as in the manner of data collection and/or analysis, or by including environmental controls to improve data quality. The second case goes beyond, and may involve

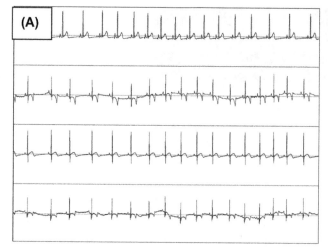

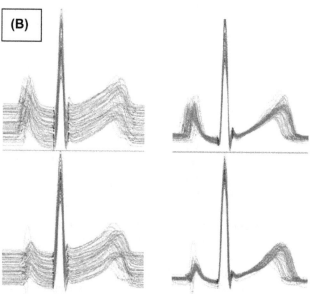

FIGURE 7.9 (A) Depicts ECG signal quality variations collected simultaneously from four different lead arrangements: Intravascular (positive electrode within superior vena cava)/diaphragmatic (negative electrode sutured near the diaphragm and the ventricular apex) lead array (top panel), jacketed external telemetry system with approximate Lead II derived from surface electrode array (second panel from top), Epicardial base-apex array (third panel from top), and Lead II subcutaneous array (bottom panel). The bottom three traces were derived from the same animal simultaneously via use of several internal and external telemetry lead arrangements. Tracings illustrate the differential morphology, susceptibility to movement and respiratory artifact, and consistency of tracings collected by different lead arrangements; these differences hold important implications with regard to the proportion of raw signal amenable to quantitative and qualitative analysis. Assessment of the variability in ECG and blood pressure signal waveforms and derived parameters also may be used to establish the functionality and operating characteristics of the transmitter device prior to study assignment. (B) Illustrates ultradian/circadian variation in ECG signal morphology in beagle dogs. Within each individual panel, prototypical ECG waveforms were constructed from individual waveform morphologies characterizing single cardiac cycles (P-QRS-T wave sequence) contained within 10s samplings conducted every 15min for approximately 22–24h.

more fundamental and significant changes to the whole experimental approach. For example, in practical experience, it is difficult to produce the arrhythmia, *torsades de pointes*, in normal, healthy animals in the preclinical research setting, at doses that reasonably approximate the range of therapeutic efficacy, with a variety of different drugs that have clearly demonstrated this liability in (often genetically or pharmacologically predisposed) humans [42,73–77]. Assessment of the liability of a drug to produce this rarely observed arrhythmia within the context of preclinical testing may be much more easily accomplished by forgoing the standard core battery cardiovascular safety study paradigm (eg, normal healthy canine) in favor of an alternative model with greater relative sensitivity engaged by specific manipulations leading to decreased cardiac repolarization reserve and/or increased heterogeneity of repolarization. Two examples of such specific models that manipulate the repolarization substrate are the beagle dog with chronic AV block [56] and the methoxamine-sensitized rabbit model [78]. A variety of alternative, specific models of proarrhythmia have also been reviewed [20,42,43,73].

Either of the methods used to increase model sensitivity may be judged as acceptable, depending on the primary goals of the research investigation. For example, if the main goal is to simply assess the potential for QT-interval change as the preclinical in vivo (surrogate) biomarker for arrhythmia that will inform on the potential liability of ECG-indicated repolarization change in humans, then the standard cardiovascular core battery study may be entirely adequate. Refinements that do not fundamentally change the model, but that instead enhance its sensitivity to QT change may be employed as needed and depending on the degree of extrapolation expected of the preclinical model. However, if there is a need to go beyond this, and specifically assess potential proarrhythmic liability, then a more radical refinement to the experimental approach may be required. In these circumstances, no refinements to the essential elements of the standard, core battery study design are likely to produce the level of sensitivity to proarrhythmia required, and so the model may alternately use a test system with altered repolarization characteristics. In the sections to follow, some additional examples of the relationships between experimental design, data-sampling techniques, and resulting model sensitivity are presented, using the convenient context of qualitative and quantitative ECG analysis.

ECG assessment is a core component of cardiovascular safety evaluation that, in various forms, has been successfully integrated into both safety pharmacology studies and repeat-dose toxicity investigations (Table 7.5). However, it is now considered that historically accepted procedures for evaluating quantitative changes in ECG intervals by means of temporally limited collections of strip-chart recordings

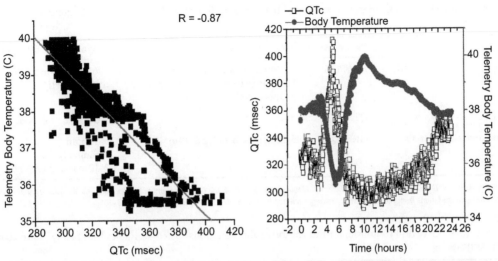

FIGURE 7.10 Depiction of the relationship between core body temperature and the heart rate corrected QT interval (QTc) in the mini-pig. The increase in QTc occurs in response to a shift in core body temperature towards mild hypothermia, secondary to an acute systemic administration of anesthetic agent. This relationship has also been demonstrated using other agents similarly inert with respect to direct mechanisms of QT interval prolongation, within the range of normal biological variation in QTc and core body temperature, and in other species, including common preclinical cardiovascular models, such as the canine, and also in humans. High-density and temporally correlated sampling of such variables by telemetry allows for accurate modeling of such relationships for potential application in delineating direct versus indirect mechanisms of action. In the mini-pig, similar to other species [65], variability of just 1°C in body temperature may account for a 5–7% shift in the heart rate corrected QT interval (QTc).

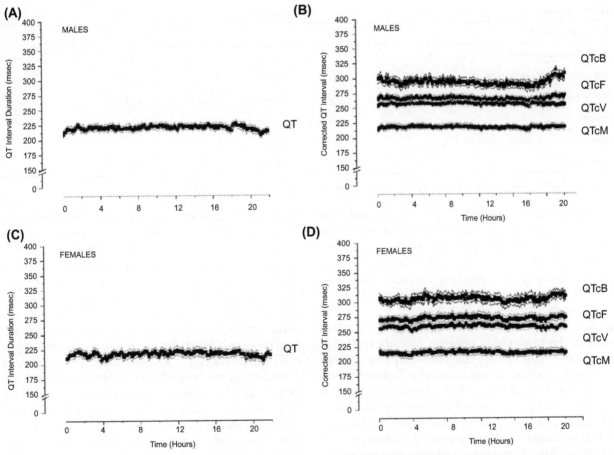

FIGURE 7.11 Relative performance of individual, probabilistic versus fixed factor population-based QT correction formulae. Uncorrected QT values (panels a and b derived from ECGs collected over 22h in male and female beagle dogs. Corrected QT-interval values in male and female beagle dogs (panels c and d) following application of either individual, probabilistic correction methodology (*QTcM*, QTc$_{Miyazaki\ and\ Tagawa}$), or fixed factor, population-based correction methodology (*QTcV*, QTc$_{van\ de\ Water}$; *QTcF*, QTc$_{Fridericia}$; *QTcB*, QTc$_{Bazzet}$). Application of fixed-factor correction formulae in other species results in similar overestimation of QTc intervals [71,72]. *Reproduced with permission from Gauvin DV, Tilley LP, Smith Jr FWK, Baird TJ. Electrocardiogram, hemodynamics, and core body temperatures of the normal freely moving laboratory beagle dog by remote radiotelemetry. J Pharmacol Toxicol Methods 2006;53:128–39.*

TABLE 7.4　Some Potential Goals of Cardiovascular Safety Pharmacology Testing and Corresponding Requirements for Preclinical Animal Model Sensitivity

Intended Goal	Parameter	Magnitude of Effect in Human	Magnitude of Effect in Animal Model
Exclude "Catastrophic" Effect (ICH S7A)	HRBPQTc	>110 bpm or 40 bpm ↑ (supine) > 30 mm Hg change (static posture)↑ 60 ms or 500 ms ab Val	≥40 bpm ≥ 30 mm Hg ≥ 30–60 ms (canine/NHP)
Predict outcome of TQT study	QTc	5 ms	2–5 ms (canine/NHP)
Predict outcome in Large clinical trials in Patients	HRBPQTc	5–10 bpm2-5 mm Hg 5–10 ms	5–10 bpm 2–5 mm Hg 2–10 ms (canine/NHP)

Adapted from Leishman DJ, Beck TW, Dybdal N, Gallacher DJ, Guth BD, Holbrook M. et al. Best practice in the conduct of key nonclinical cardiovascular safety assessments in drug development: current recommendations from the safety pharmacology society. J Pharmacol Toxicol Methods 2011;65(3):93–101.

TABLE 7.5　Current Perspective on Possibilities for Integration of Key Functional Safety Variables Into Safety Pharmacology and Repeat-Dose Toxicology Investigations

Parameter	Safety Pharmacology	Rodent Toxicology	Nonrodent Toxicology
CNS SAFETY			
Functional observational battery	+++	++/+++	+/++
CARDIOVASCULAR SAFETY			
EKG	+++	+/++	+++
Blood pressure	+++	+/++	+/++
Ventricular pressure	+++	+/++	+/++
RESPIRATORY SAFETY			
Inspiratory/expiratory time	+++	+/++	+/++
Peak Inspiratory/expiratory flow	+++	+/++	+/++
Respiratory rate	+++	+/++	+/++
Tidal volume	+++	+/++	+/++
Pulmonary resistance and compliance	+	−/+	−/+
Hyperreactivity	+	−/+	−/+

Adapted from Gad SC. Safety pharmacology in pharmaceutical development and approval. Boca Raton: LLC CRC Press; 2004.

may have inadequate sensitivity [79,80]. Recent data from our laboratory have indicated that the sensitivity of preclinical telemetric models to changes of a magnitude of interest according to the intended goals for data application may be more or less adequate, depending on specific features of the employed technology, the study context in which the recording occurs, and data analysis routines.

Fig. 7.12 illustrates the results of an experiment that investigated the relationship between different modes of application of telemetry data collection, employing either internally implanted devices or an external, jacketed telemetry system for ECG collection. The lead array was manipulated to derive raw ECG signals that were then suitable for postcollection processing, to generate signal quality estimates and electrocardiogram intervals of interest (eg, RR, QRS, PR, QT, QTc). The effect of different lead configurations on raw ECG signal visual characteristics is illustrated in Fig. 7.9A. This experiment explored whether variations

in raw-signal characteristics based on artifactual and other sources of signal distortion [79] could translate to a convenient marker of signal quality (Fig. 7.12A), and whether this quantitative measure of signal quality held any particular relation to the capacity to characterize a given magnitude of effect on a quantitative ECG interval parameter of interest (Fig. 7.12B). As may be seen in Fig. 7.12A, the quantitative estimate of signal quality, designated "good wave (percent),e as defined by the ability to identify important ECG landmarks (eg, P, R, T waves), did vary primarily as a function of the type of lead solution employed for collection. Based on analysis of continuously collected signals over 24h, the relative quality of signals by solution was Epicardial > Subcutaneous > Skin Surface. Based on the variable exposure of each lead type to potential disruption based on factors, such as muscle/movement artifact, this result is not altogether unexpected. What is interesting is the correlation between this variable and the magnitude of

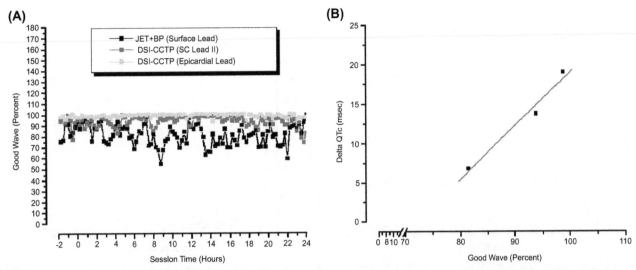

FIGURE 7.12 Signal quality estimates as a function of lead configuration and the resulting relation to average ($n=4$/point) magnitude of change characterized for QTc with sotalol hydrochloride (17.8 mg/kg, p.o.) administration. Signals were recorded from three different lead arrays within the same animal, simultaneously, by means of either fully implanted telemetry (subcutaneous and epicardial leads), or external jacketed telemetry (surface lead). (A) Depicts absolute values for the quantitative signal quality estimate according to the type of lead. (B) Illustrates the relationship between differential signal quality and the magnitude of effect engendered within the same animal to an oral administration of sotalol.

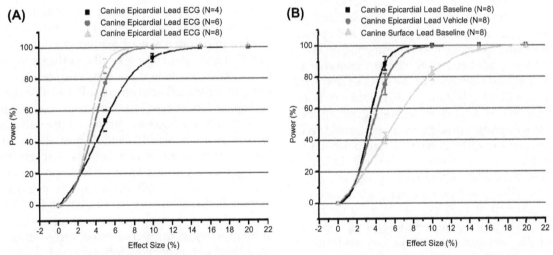

FIGURE 7.13 Power analyses conducted on individual probabilistic QTc(Miyazaki) data collected in different numbers of male beagle dogs instrumented identically with epicardial leads for cardiovascular telemetry (A), and in the same number of beagle dogs under different recording conditions (B). Jacketed external telemetry demonstrates the lowest sensitivity in relation to two alternative epicardial collections.

change in 24-h averaged QTc values engendered following administration of sotalol hydrochloride (17.8 mg/kg, p.o.). Within the limited range of variation in average good-wave proportion and average delta QTc values, a significant positive relationship was observed.

Many factors might account for such covariation in signal quality and magnitude of change in this quantitative ECG endpoint of interest, including, for example, characteristics of signal quality as a function of lead solution, as well as temporal variations in signal (eg, t-wave polarity, morphology, etc.). These and other potential contributing factors remain to be investigated in terms of their relative contribution to the observed relationship. Regardless of the

specific source of variation, a related observation of interest in this discussion of the contribution of technique to raw-signal variability and sensitivity to detect change of interest is indicated in Fig. 7.13. The influence of the number of independent observations is well understood in terms of the power to detect difference within any given model. Fig. 7.13A illustrates this relationship specifically in the context of power to detect a given magnitude of change in the QTc interval in beagle dogs. Fig. 7.13B also shows the impact of the measurement technique on experimental power. Note the correspondence of the power analysis data depicted in Fig. 7.13B to the objective analysis of the relationship between lead array and capacity to detect a magnitude of

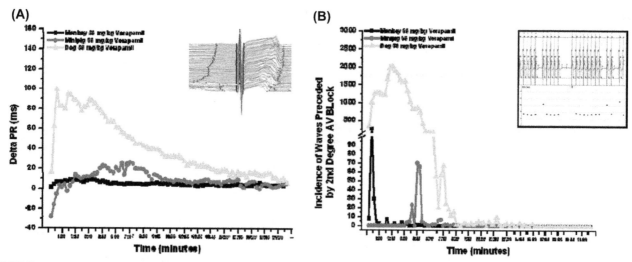

FIGURE 7.14   Illustration of the relationship between the emergence of quantitative (left panel) and qualitative (right panel) evidence of first degree and higher order AV block, respectively. Data were derived from integration of the ECG interval by setting appropriate validation marks to define the PR interval duration and by utilizing a pattern matching feature to quantify higher order (2°) AV block in beagle dogs, cynomolgus monkeys, and Gottingen mini-pigs.

change related to positive control (sotalol) administration in the same subject illustrated in Fig. 7.12B. These data highlight the significant contribution of the manner of application of data-sensing technology to experimental power in the context of assessment of cardiac repolarization change.

Effective qualitative analysis of the ECG to characterize potential rhythm variants is similarly subject to the above considerations related to technological application and data sampling. As suggested previously, qualitative analysis of the ECG to characterize potential for test item-induced conductance and/or repolarization abnormalities (ICH S7B) is afforded by the utilization of multiple baselines, and may be conducted based on the full complement of ECG signal collected by telemetry (see Fig. 7.14), or by using a subsampling approach whereby smaller segments of the ECG waveform are evaluated for arrhythmias at discrete, selected intervals. The difference in the range of possible solutions to this issue of qualitative analysis is vast, and is represented on one end of the continuum by a comprehensive evaluation wherein all beats in a 24-h period, or in several 24-h periods prior to dose initiation, and at least one, but perhaps also several 24 h periods following various test-item dose administrations at different levels, are analyzed. On the other end of the continuum, a qualitative analysis may be based on a subsampling routine whereby either a designated number of minutes per hour of ECG data are fully analyzed from predose and posttreatment 24-h recordings, or selected intervals (perhaps 5–10 min, for example) of data are analyzed at discrete points prior to, and at several selected intervals following a given drug treatment. In either case, comprehensive or subsampling routines, rhythm variants may be quantitatively analyzed either manually, or by computer-assisted detection.

Until recently, largely automated qualitative analysis for rhythm variants (arrhythmias) of clinical concern were elusive in preclinical cardiovascular safety strategies; to some degree, depending on the software analysis program utilized, manual analysis and/or overreading of computer-assisted analysis is still a reality that must be addressed. However, strategies for computer-assisted arrhythmia detection are under intense discussion and development presently, with expectations for technical and procedural enhancements that are anticipated to significantly mitigate the labor-intensiveness of this endeavor, while ideally enhancing sensitivity and prediction [22] (see also Figs. 7.14A,B and 7.15A,B for an illustration of examples of arrhythmias of interest and strategies for computer-assisted arrhythmia detection with resultant impact on detection probabilities).

In summary, as with the quantitative interval data that may be derived from the ECG (RR, QRS, PR, QT, QTc intervals, etc.), signal quality and sampling frequency are two factors that dramatically impact qualitative (arrhythmia) analysis. The optimization of qualitative ECG analyses relies on several important factors including:

1. utilization of high-quality signals as afforded by epicardial ECG,
2. use of a sampling routine adequate to detect rhythm variants according to their expected or actual (if known) relative frequency,
3. recording of an adequate baseline period of data to establish background rhythm characteristics and any potential existing variants a priori, and
4. corresponding collection of an adequate period of postdose data that is compatible for analysis relative to predose sampling.

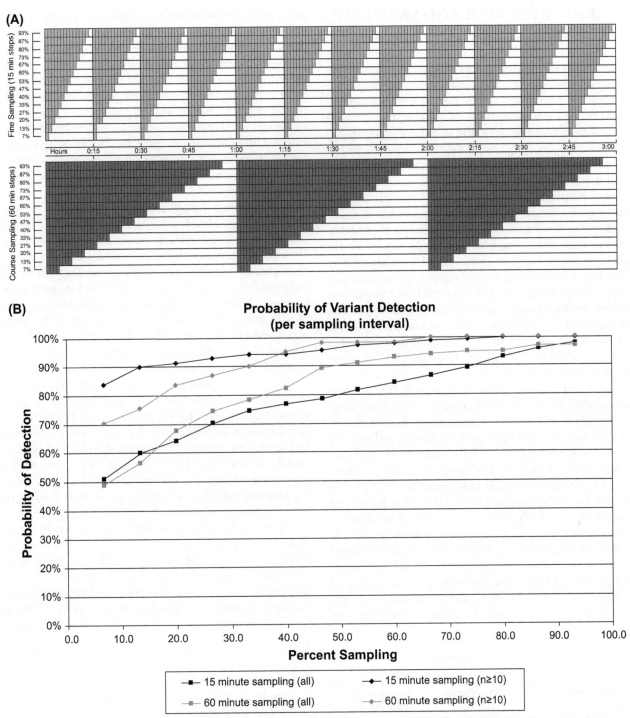

FIGURE 7.15 Influence of different sampling methodologies and arrhythmia incidence rates on the probability of detection of ECG qualitative (rhythm) variants. Detection curves (B) illustrate that the probability of correctly identifying a rhythm variant, when present for any given sampling period, is enhanced with increases in the overall number of rhythm variants (compare either 15-or 60-min sampling methods when the number of variants is greater than [$n \geq 10$] or less than [all] 10 events per interval evaluated). The probability of variant detection is best when number of variants present exceeds 10 per epoch evaluated, and with increased temporal granularity of analysis (utilization of the 15-min sampling approach—see (A). Sampling schemes for any individual experiment may be selected based on the desired level of sensitivity in consideration of overall (baseline) qualitative variant incidence rate and anticipated or actual expression of drug-induced rhythm variants.

Application of these principles with an understanding of baseline expression of rhythm variants in relevant test systems will allow a heretofore qualitative evaluation yielding nominal to ordinal level data to be conducted using quantitative scales of measurement and potentially permitting commensurate application of more powerful parametric statistical analyses to the question of arrhythmia detection in preclinical cardiovascular safety studies.

RESPIRATORY SYSTEM AND MODELS OF SAFETY ASSESSMENT

Assessment of the respiratory system in safety pharmacology investigations evaluates the operating characteristics of two main components: the mechanical conduction system comprised of conducting airways and neuromuscular control of the ventilatory (pumping) apparatus, and the lung mechanics (resistance/compliance) and gas-exchange functions mediated by deeper (alveolar-vascular) networks [81]. A comprehensive review of respiratory system anatomy and physiology is well beyond the scope of this discussion, but is available in various sources [2,82,83]. Although there have been divergent ideas concerning which particular assays might be representative of Tier I, Tier II, or higher order endpoints, unless there is specific concern for a particular molecule based on therapeutic class and/or mechanism of action, contemporary practice involves, at minimum, an assessment of respiratory rate and volume, or some combination of rate and another index of functional gas exchange, such as blood gas analyses for Tier I respiratory safety studies (Table 7.6).

Assessment by either type of approach yields a reasonable initial indication of whether or not a given drug, by whatever mechanism, has propensity to change any vital parameters correlated with primary pulmonary functions supporting life. In the case of respiratory rate and volume monitoring, minute volume values derived from rate and tidal volume estimates may be monitored to determine whether a drug has produced a change in this stable measure of relative ventilatory capacity over time; significant decrement in minute volume, for example, may ultimately lead to impaired gas exchange and any number of resultant secondary complications. In the case where respiratory rate and a convenient alternative functional measure (eg, gas exchange parameters as may be reflected by blood-gas

TABLE 7.6 Core and Supplemental Respiratory Function Measures

Safety Pharmacology Measure	Core Battery (Tier I)	Supplemental (Tier II)
RESPIRATORY		
Respiratory rate	X	
Tidal volume	X	
Minute volume	X	
Resistance/compliance		X
Pulmonary hemodynamics		X
Gas exchange (blood gas, pH, cooximetry)		X

analyses) are selected for monitoring, the primary endpoints of interest are partial pressures of oxygen, carbon dioxide, hemoglobin oxygen saturation, etc.; changes in these measures should correlate in some meaningful way with respiratory rate, and ultimately inform directly on the primary gas exchange function of the respiratory system. Supplemental studies with more refined experimental focus and methods may be utilized thereafter to more fully elucidate the mechanisms, duration of action and dose–response, potential reversibility, and clinical relevance of primary (Tier I) study findings.

A ubiquitous assay currently utilized to evaluate respiratory mechanics is plethysmography, whether whole-body, head out, or some alternative variation. Various plethysmography techniques are amenable to characterization of respiratory mechanics in both small (rodents) and large (canines, NHP, swine, etc.) animal species. However, current plethysmography techniques are, and will tend to be, used more frequently in rodent species [84], while the application of newer methodologies including telemetric respiratory inductance plethysmography (RIP) will be primarily focused on large animal test systems [57,85–88]. Regardless of the particular technique or species employed, certain elements of study design are essential for addressing key concerns in respiratory function safety evaluation. Using the example of whole-body plethysmography (WBP) in the rat, Fig. 7.16 illustrates some of these experimental design features, in addition to highlighting some of the relative advantages of the unrestrained, WBP technique.

There are a number of different plethysmography techniques, employing whole body plethysmograph (WBP), head-out plethysmograph (HOP), and/or dual chamber plethysmograph (DCP) devices. Fig. 7.17 illustrates two of these, the WBP and HOP, utilized to facilitate recordings collected in rats. WBP, HOP, and DCP plethysmographs differ in the following ways:

1. the relative need for prestudy device acclimation sessions,
2. the manner in which nasal and/or thoracic pressure signals are utilized and/or integrated to produce a respiratory waveform,
3. theoretical assumptions and corresponding parameters that may be derived from the generated respiratory waveform, and
4. the relative ease of application to animals of various species [84,89–91].

As may be seen by comparison of Figs. 7.17 and 7.18, the WBP and HOP devices are associated with differential levels of restraint stress-induced baseline elevation in respiratory rate and minute volume values, as well as a differential temporal pattern of habituation toward a

Treatment	Dose (mg/kg, p.o.)	Number of animals
1	0 (vehicle)	8
2	3	8
3	30	8
4	300	8

•Animals experimentally naïve

•Oral gavage dosing, Independent (between subjects) group design

•Monitoring of unrestrained animal via plethysmography for at least 30 minutes prior to dose (with sufficient within-session acclimation period), and for up to X hours post-dose
> •Respiratory Rate
> •Tidal Volume
> •Minute Volume

•Clinical Observations (baseline, selected intervals approximating critical times of exposure, recovery)

•Formulations Analyzed (uniformity, concentration, stability)

•Descriptive and inferential statistics (RMANOVA)

•PK Sampling: Separate group(s) of animals, if required (PK/PD modeling)

•Supplemental variables defining more specific elements of breath architecture may be employed (inspiratory/expiratory time, peak flow, etc.)

FIGURE 7.16 A general design of a Tier I (core battery) respiratory safety study. Some important elements of the experimental design include (1) the utilization of predose baseline data recording, (2) unrestrained monitoring of study animals in order to mitigate effects of chemical or physical restraint that may be necessitated by use of alternative models, (3) group-counterbalanced sequencing of dosing and other salient experimental manipulations to control for potential order effects and maintain integrity of between-subjects experimental design assumptions, (4) incorporation of postdose recording interval(s) to characterize onset and resolution of potential drug and/or metabolite effects, (5) PK sampling arranged in a separate group of designated satellite animals so as not to interfere with continuously collected physiological parameters or clinical behavioral observations, and (6) utilization of repeated measures analysis of variance/covariance procedures appropriate for independent groups design and time-series data.

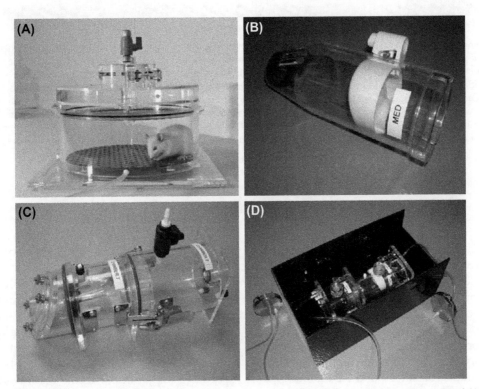

FIGURE 7.17 Alternative methods and equipment utilized for evaluation of respiratory mechanics in rodents. Panel (A) depicts the whole-body plethysmograph (WBP); panel (B) illustrates a modified cone restraint used to secure a rat within a head-out or two-chamber plethysmograph apparatus, minimizing movement artifact and allowing the animal a more comfortable resting position; panel (C) illustrates a common configuration of the head-out plethysmograph chamber, without modified cone restraint insert (B); panel (D) depicts an alternative model head-out/dual-chamber plethysmograph, employed with modified cone restraint insert and an environmental enclosure designed to mitigate the influence of external stimuli on respiratory parameters and promote baseline stability in this assay. Note also the articulation of differential pressure transducer(s) with the device via intermediary tubing connections.

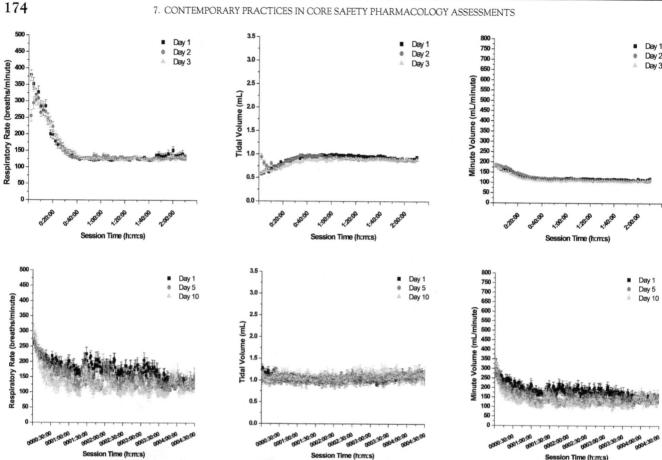

FIGURE 7.18 Some representative respiratory habituation data from Sprague–Dawley rats, collected by means of either whole body plethysmography (WBP; top series) or head-out plethysmography (HOP; bottom series) utilizing a restraint system as illustrated in Fig. 7.17D. Clear differences in the pattern of habituation may be observed with animals in the WBP apparatus demonstrating very rapid within-session changes in respiratory rate, tidal volume, and minute volume values, and no demonstrable change in this pattern over three days of habituation in the WBP environment. The HOP environment is also conducive to habituation learning, as indicated by the within- and between-session patterns of change in these same variables. Note the effect of restraint on overall initial and acclimated values in comparison to WBP data. Clearly, habituation learning is differentially engaged by each method. This has implications for the experimental design in terms of necessary periods of time to allow adequate within-session acclimation, as well as for prestudy habituation to the testing environment, with HOP procedures requiring additional episodes to engender stable respiratory function that is comparable to that observed in the WBP.

stable baseline, both within and between independent, successive recording sessions.

Although baseline respiratory rate and volume measurements may vary with the device employed, the data from Fig. 7.18 also indicate that, with the institution of appropriate within- and between-session acclimation protocols, very comparable baseline data ultimately may be achieved. Accordingly, the sensitivity of WBP and HOP methods for detecting changes in essential Tier I respiratory function parameters theoretically should be comparable. Figs. 7.19 and 7.20 demonstrate this for two positive control compounds with differential pharmacologically mediated activity on minute volume: amphetamine and fentanyl. Also included for comparison are minute volume values for the same active treatments in a different group of experimental animals that were evaluated using DCP devices.

Observed dose-dependent magnitudes of change and general temporal patterns of variation in values for this general measure of ventilatory capacity over time demonstrate reasonable concordance.

Although a range of plethysmography techniques are theoretically available for use in large animal species, the most frequently implemented have tended to be head-only (or similar procedures utilizing a mask apparatus instead of head-dome) or head-out plethysmography, described in primarily canine and NHP large-animal species [85–88]. Similar to the rodent plethysmography procedures described previously, these large-animal methodologies rely on capture of either nasal or thoracic flow/pressure signals correlated with breathing via a differential pressure transducer. Such techniques have been valuable for enabling basic respiratory function data collections, but share the issue of restraint-induced

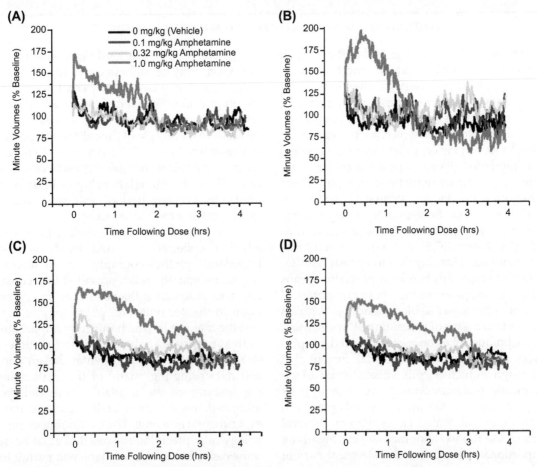

FIGURE 7.19 Effects of amphetamine hydrochloride administration (0, 0.1, 0.32, 1.0 mg/kg, IV) on minute volume values in male Sprague–Dawley rats tested in WBP (A), HOP, (B) and DCP simultaneously capturing nasal flow, and (C) and thoracic pressure (D) signals.

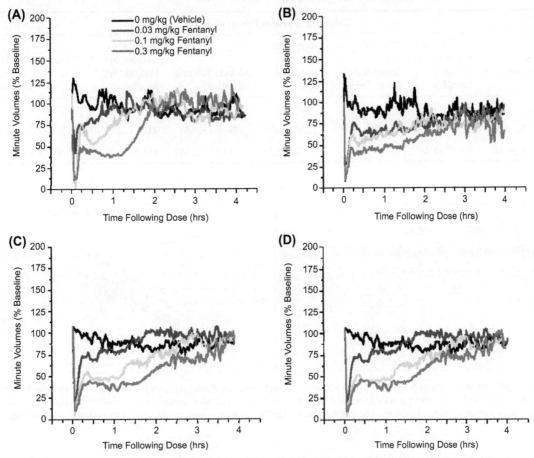

FIGURE 7.20 Effects of fentanyl citrate administration (0, 0.03, 0.1, 0.3 mg/kg, IV) on minute volume values in male Sprague–Dawley rats tested in WBP (A), HOP (B), and DCP simultaneously capturing nasal flow (C), and thoracic pressure (D) signals.

deviation from normal physiological baselines with HOP and DCP devices used in rodents, and because of the physical restraint, are necessarily limited in terms of the duration of data collections that may be performed.

Alternative methodologies to monitor respiratory parameters in large animals have recently become available including those relying on either externally applied or surgically implanted devices operating on the principle of respiratory inductance plethysmography. These techniques may be applied to any standard large-animal test system utilized for cardiorespiratory safety testing, yielding quantitative respiratory rate values as well as calibrated tidal volumes [57,85–88]. Used in combination with techniques allowing simultaneous cardiovascular data collection, this can be a powerful means of understanding interrelationships between potential cardiorespiratory effects (see Table 7.7 and Fig. 7.22), as well as an important means of promoting 3Rs principles. In brief, the technique relies on systematic and proportional changes in a low-voltage electrical current that is passed through inductive coils affixed either externally or surgically (subcutaneously placed array). As the relative positioning of the inductive coils placed in relation to the thorax/abdomen varies with mechanical deformations of the thorax/abdomen during breathing activity, proportional variations in the electrical current

are generated. The temporal expression of these current deviations may be calibrated to a stable measure of tidal volume, and may be similarly continuously recorded by means of traditional plethysmography, allowing quantitative data characterizing this parameter to be generated on study. An example of the calibration procedure (data) is presented in Fig. 7.21. An important consideration when using this technique is growth of the animal over time. The changing relationship of body dimensions to tidal volume means periodic calibration data are needed to support any individual study.

Data from large- and small-animal test systems, whether collected via traditional plethysmography, impedance plethysmography, or an alternative technique, are equally valid, provided that consideration is given to potential influence of the experimental paradigm to the behavior and physiology of the organism, and the manner in which this may impact study design. With appropriate application of acclimation procedures, structuring of key experimental design contingencies, and data sampling, many of the challenging or limiting features of the available methodologies may be mitigated toward the overall success of the individual experimental outcome. The continuing evolution of technology may precipitate issues that must be overcome in some cases, but in many others, will permit increasingly

TABLE 7.7 Cardiorespiratory Parameters Collected by Telemetry in Three Species

				20-h Data Averages (Mean ± S.D.)				
Species	Temperature (°C)	Mean Arterial Pressure (mmHg)	Heart Rate (beats/minute)	Respiratory Rate (breaths/min)	Minute Volume (ml/min)	Minute Volume by Weight (ml/min/kg)	Tidal Volume (ml)	Tidal Volume by Weight (ml/kg)
Macaques	37.08 ± 0.89	97.39 ± 14.28	133.65 ± 21.58	24.19 ± 5.92	352.20 ± 267.40	77.92 ± 40.84	15.36 ± 6.07	5.11 ± 3.23
Swine	38.76 ± 0.57	121.13 ± 17.82	104.53 ± 15.89	21.54 ± 8.92	1329.10 ± 519.54	93.11 ± 34.42	90.31 ± 21.31	6.37 ± 1.59
Canine	37.98 ± 0.26	109.97 ± 6.66	100.55 ± 14.70	23.72 ± 11.20	4133.16 ± 3747.44	448.01 ± 373.11	123.13 ± 39.06	13.56 ± 3.65

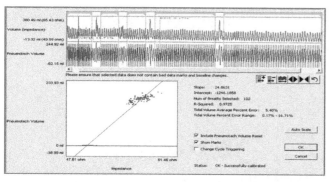 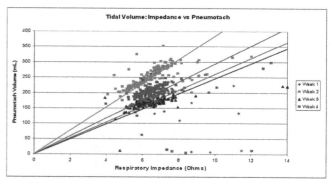

FIGURE 7.21 Calibration of impedance-derived tidal volume. A temporally correlated sampling of data (left panel) collected from two signal sources (impedance and plethysmography) is utilized to define the relationship between incremental variation in impedance units (ohms) and absolute volume measures determined by plethysmography (right panel) to allow continuous respiratory function data recording via telemetry.

sophisticated, sensitive, and ultimately predictive models to characterize potential clinical cardiorespiratory safety issues.

CENTRAL NERVOUS SYSTEM AND MODELS OF SAFETY ASSESSMENT

As detailed in the sections above, the purpose of the safety pharmacology core battery is to investigate the effects of the test substance on vital functions, which are acutely critical for life, such as the cardiovascular, respiratory, and central nervous systems. The effects of a test substance on these functions should be investigated prior to first administration in humans. The CNS safety evaluation is primarily observational in nature, at least as practiced during early screening procedures, and measured outputs range from categorical discriminations (eg, present/absent) to continuous scaled numerical values (eg, body temperature, open-field rearing counts) that can be used to determine effects of concern, from the idiosyncratic to those constellations of findings indicating more systematic change according to a broad functional domain of behavior and/or physiology (see Fig. 7.23).

In general, safety pharmacology studies are performed by single-dose administration, ideally after completion of appropriate exposure (PK) studies, standard dose-range finding (DRF), and some reasonable term (2 week, 1 month) of repeat-dose toxicity testing

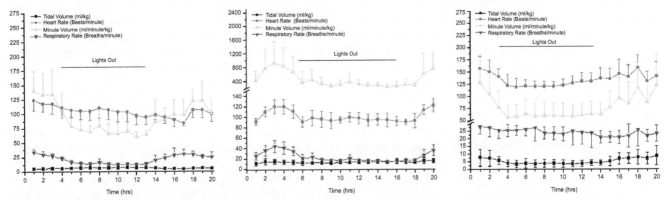

FIGURE 7.22 Respiratory function values in relation to heart rates collected simultaneously via respiratory inductance plethysmography and telemetry.

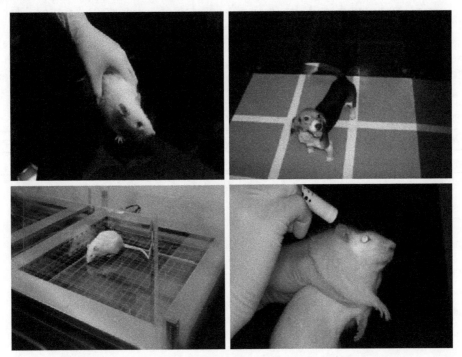

FIGURE 7.23 Examples of observational measures in CNS safety evaluation.

has been completed. The doses used in safety assessments are usually selected to approximate the lower end of a dose range that may reasonably be expected to elicit an adverse or dose-limiting effect at one end of the continuum (high dose) and compared to the doses eliciting the primary pharmacodynamic effect in the test species or the proposed therapeutic effect in humans, if feasible. Intermediate dose levels may be interpolated, as needed to best characterize dose–response pharmacology. It is recognized that there are species differences in pharmacodynamic sensitivity. Therefore the ICH guidelines (S7A) [27] recommend dose selections that should include and exceed the primary pharmacodynamic or therapeutic range of the test compound. In the absence of an adverse effect on the safety pharmacology parameter(s) evaluated in the study, the highest tested dose should approximate a dose that produces moderate adverse effects in this or in other studies of similar route and duration. These adverse effects can include dose-limiting pharmacodynamic effects or other toxicity. In practice, some effects in the toxic range (eg, tremors or fasciculation during ECG recording) may confound the interpretation of the results and may also limit dose levels. Testing of a single group at the limiting dose as described within the guidelines may be sufficient in the absence of an adverse effect on safety pharmacology endpoints in the test species.

APPROACHES TO TIER I CNS SAFETY EVALUATION

Generally, any parent compound and its major metabolite(s) that achieve, or are expected to achieve, systemic exposure in humans should be evaluated in safety pharmacology studies. Evaluation of major metabolites is often accomplished through studies of the parent compound in animals. If the major human metabolite(s) is (are) found to be absent or present only at relatively low concentrations in animals, assessment of the effects of such metabolite(s) on safety pharmacology endpoints should be considered. For CNS safety assessments the current "best practices" include, at a minimum, the quantitative assessments of motor activity, behavioral changes, coordination, sensory/motor reflex responses, and body temperature. For example, a functional observational battery (FOB) [92,93], modified Irwin test [94,95], or other appropriate tests [96] should be used to characterize the essential Tier I evaluations indicated in Table 7.8.

The "Irwin screen" is a detailed behavioral assessment battery developed in mice by Dr. Samuel Irwin in 1968. The battery included approximately 60 dependent measures, which combined, required 20–30 min per animal to conduct. Many of these assays were redundant (ie, three to four measures of analgesia and/or locomotor assessments in the original assay). In common contemporary practice, almost all testing utilizing the "Irwin screen" is in fact a modified procedure, comprised of a more limited set of essential observations from the original publication that is comparable to standard FOB procedures described in the literature in terms of capacity to characterize general domains of CNS activity and guide the development of any requisite follow-up testing.

In 1986, the International Program on Chemical Safety (IPCS) within the World Health Organization (WHO) recommended the inclusion of a neurobehavioral approach for the first-tier assessment of new chemical entities. In 1988 a steering committee was formed to develop an experimental protocol for the collaborative study. The steering committee constructed a subset of the dependent measures reported in the original Irwin screen with the intent of setting forth a common set of nonredundant behavioral assays that could be used

TABLE 7.8 Core and Supplemental Central Nervous System Evaluations

Safety Pharmacology Measure	Core Battery (Tier I)	Supplemental (Tier II)
CNS		
FOB/Irwin	X	
Motor activity	X	
Ligand binding		X
Neurochemistry		X
Behavioral pharmacology		X
Learning and memory		X
Abuse/Dependence liability		X
Proconvulsant properties		X
Special senses		X

within and across laboratories. Since that time, many authors have suggested the use of a unified neurobehavioral assessment tool for both drug and chemical CNS safety assessments [96–101]. The US Interagency Committee on Neurotoxicity (ICON) consisting of members of the US Food and Drug Administration, US Department of Agriculture, US National Institute on Drug Abuse (NIDA), and the National Institutes of Health have adopted the US Environmental Protection Agency's OPPTS 6200 CNS toxicity requirements [102] as the "standard" neurobehavioral assessment tool to be used for preclinical safety assessment screening of both food and drugs [103–106].

The CNS regulates and maintains diverse biological processes that are essential not only for survival but also for maintaining an acceptable quality of life. The proper functioning of the CNS enables an organism to receive information from its internal and external environments and to orchestrate appropriate adaptive physiological and behavioral responses. An extensive body of evidence has clearly demonstrated that diverse chemical and pharmaceutical substances can alter the structure and function of the nervous system, with notable human health consequences [107]. As previously highlighted by Mattsson (1994) [108], after discovery of treatment-related changes in nervous system function, it is essential to determine whether the changes are adverse. All treatment-related changes are not necessarily adverse. According to the FDA, any alterations that significantly compromise an organism's ability to function appropriately in its environment are considered *adverse*. Adverse effects diminish the ability of an organism to perform a function. A diminished ability would always be deleterious. According to Mattsson [108], the utility of this definition is that it focuses attention on a specific ability, such as strength, coordinated movement, hearing, attention, or memory. Ability is inferred from measures of behavior. Weiss [109] has pointed out that behavioral changes are frequently among the first to be detected following chemical or drug exposure in humans and may precede more obvious signs of neurotoxicity. Under the appropriate testing conditions, it is clear that behavioral tests can be used to characterize specific neurological or behavioral deficits in sensory, motor, and cognitive functions [110,111].

The term *neurotoxicity* has been defined as "any adverse effects of exposure to chemical, biological, or physical agents on the structure or functional integrity of the developing or adult nervous system" [105]. Neurotoxic effects may involve a spectrum of biochemical, morphological, behavioral, and physiological abnormalities whose onset can vary from immediate to delayed following exposure to a toxic substance, and whose duration may be transient or persistent. Depending on their severity, some of these abnormalities may have life-threatening consequences; more commonly, they result in diminished quality of life. Neurotoxicity may result from effects of the toxic substance acting directly on the elements of the nervous system, or acting on other biological systems, which then adversely affect the nervous system. From a safety standpoint, neurotoxic effects resulting from either a direct or indirect action of a chemical on the nervous system are important components of a chemical's toxicological profile. However, in those instances where neurotoxicity is elicited secondary to some nonnervous system toxicity, the latter would typically represent the more sensitive endpoint.

In terms of the focus of CNS safety assessments, it is critical to clearly distinguish test materials that produce frank, irreversible CNS damage from those that produce acute, reversible effects. An example of a representative reversible effect is CNS depression, or narcosis, following acute high-dose exposure to a barbiturate prescribed for sleep induction, excessive voluntary alcohol intake, or opiate administration for pain control. Typically, the effect is reversible on cessation of treatment and recovery of function is complete, unless complicated by accidental hypoxia. In contrast to such reversible functional CNS effects are those neurologic effects that are deemed irreversible or only slowly reversible, and which are often associated with neuropathological lesions. An example is 1-methyl-4-phenyl-1,2,3,6-tetrahydropyridine (MPTP) exposure [112]. For purposes of safety assessment one would certainly want to distinguish compounds in the former category (reversible CNS depression) from those in the latter category (irreversible or slowly reversible neurotoxicity).

A second major issue to be considered in safety assessments is that of direct versus indirect effects on the CNS. This issue is closely associated with the problem that at sufficiently high doses nearly all pharmaceutical and chemical agents will produce changes in an animal's behavior. These behavioral changes are typically assumed to be a consequence of generalized systemic toxicity or other target-organ toxicity and not a direct effect of the new chemical entity on the nervous system. For example, a peripheral acting drug that stimulates insulin secretion by the pancreas may result in overt seizure activity that may be interpreted as direct CNS toxicity. This example demonstrates the importance of assessing systemic toxicity (eg, DRF, 2-week toxicity studies) before initiating CNS safety assessment protocols that have the potential to contraindicate continued development of a compound at an early stage.

In 1982, the FDA issued guidelines for toxicological testing of food ingredients. Although neurotoxicity and CNS safety were neither explicitly discussed nor defined in these guidelines, there were certain elements included in the conventional toxicity studies that have traditionally been used to assess nervous system toxicity. In general, these included a routine pathological evaluation of neuronal tissue and cage-side observations for clinical signs of toxicity. In 1985, the FDA commissioned the Federation of American Societies for Experimental Biology (FASEB) to assess the utility of these current FDA guidelines for detecting neurotoxic hazards [113,114]. One conclusion of the FASEB report was that the current guidelines are too broad and nonspecific with respect to the nature and extent of information that needs to be provided to the FDA for an evaluation of a chemical's neurotoxic potential. The limited information derived from conventional toxicity screening studies, as currently conducted and reported, enables little more than the detection of clearly evident nervous system toxicity associated with general neuropathology and overt neurological dysfunction. Little consistent or systematically documented information is typically available about other possibly less severe, but equally important, types of neurotoxic effects including, for example, behavioral and physiological dysfunction and developmental neurotoxicity. Incomplete documentation about the range of adverse effects to the structural and functional integrity of the nervous system limits the effective evaluation of the full spectrum of neurotoxic hazards [115,116]. The present FDA guidelines are intended to explicate more clearly the nature and extent of information deemed necessary for the assessment of neurotoxic potential and to suggest a strategy for obtaining this information as part of the safety evaluation process.

Until recently, neurotoxicity was equated with neuropathy involving frank neuropathological lesions or overt neurological dysfunctions, such as seizure, paralysis, or tremor. Although neuropathy is appropriately recognized as a manifestation of neurotoxicity, it is now clear that there are numerous other endpoints that may signal nervous system toxicity [104]. Ongoing research continues to reveal the diversity of biochemical, structural, and functional abnormalities that toxicants can elicit, both directly and indirectly [114]. Neurotoxic entities invariably initiate their effects at the molecular level, altering cellular neurochemical processes. The qualitative nature of these alterations or their magnitude may result in cytoarchitectural changes and neuropathological effects accompanied by nervous system dysfunction expressed as physiological or behavioral abnormalities [107,114]. Motor incoordination, sensory deficits, learning and memory impairment, changes in emotion, and altered states of arousal in the adult and the developing organism are examples of deficits recognized as functional indices of possible neurotoxicity. Notably, physiological or behavioral dysfunctions may occur prior to, or even in the absence of, evident neuropathology or other signs of toxicity [113,114,117,118]. This is exemplified by the behavioral dysfunctions associated with exposure to such neuroactive chemicals as barbiturates, amphetamines, ethanol, lead, and carbon monoxide at exposure levels that elicit little or no apparent signs of neuropathy [119]. This dissociation of neuropathology and functional changes may involve a number of factors, including the intrinsic toxicity of a chemical and, particularly, the dose and regimen of exposure. Continued reliance on neuropathy as the primary criterion of neurotoxicity is overly simplistic and does not adequately reflect contemporary "best practices" on evaluation of the broader spectrum of potential neurotoxic effects on the adult and developing organism.

Among the various approaches that can be used for assessing neurotoxicity, behavioral testing in conjunction with neuropathological evaluation represent a practical means of obtaining a relatively comprehensive assessment of the functional development and integrity of the nervous system within the context of a standard toxicity study, but the postmortem histopathology is not required for acute safety assessments. Behavior is an adaptive response of an organism, orchestrated by the nervous system, to changing constellations of internal and external stimuli. A behavioral response represents the integrated end product of multiple neuronal subsystems including sensory, motor, cognitive, attentional, and integrative components, as well as an array of physiological functions [120–124]. As such, behavior can serve as a measurable index of the status of multiple functional components of the nervous system. Since behavioral testing is noninvasive, it can be applied acutely following a single dose in safety assessment programs, or repeatedly for longitudinal assessment of the neurotoxicity of a test compound, including persistent or delayed treatment-related effects [114]. Furthermore, since neuronal function can be influenced by the status of other organ systems in the body (eg, cardiovascular, endocrine, and immunologic systems), certain types of behavioral changes may indirectly reflect significant primary toxicity in other organ systems. For this reason it is important to emphasize that the assessment of neurotoxicity necessitates an integrated interpretation of all toxicological and safety data.

Because of the impact that nervous system toxicity can have on human health, assessing the neurotoxic potential of a new chemical entity proposed for use as a drug or food additive should be an essential element in that chemical's preclinical assessment prior to its first delivery in man (ICH S7A) [27]. Behavioral testing has been established as a reliable toxicological index in safety assessment. Considerable progress has been made in the standardization and validation of neurobehavioral and neurodevelopmental testing procedures [93]. As a result, a variety of behavioral methodologies are available for use in determining the potential of new chemical entities to affect adversely the functional integrity of the nervous system in adult animals during preclinical safety assessments.

To effectively minimize the risk of potential damage or irrecoverable adverse functional changes to the CNS in humans, it is important that the best available science be used to develop the necessary information. It should be clear that neurobehavioral effects identified in experimental animal models may not always compare exactly with what may occur in humans. Nonetheless, these effects are still interpreted as being indicative of treatment-related effects on the nervous system and predictive of possible adverse health effects in humans. As advances in the neurosciences continue to evolve, our understanding of the processes underlying neurotoxicity will become increasingly clear. This will enhance our ability to assess the impact of a new chemical entity on CNS function in a manner that is more predictive of potential human risk and to apply the available neurobehavioral information more reliably in support of regulatory decisions.

EVALUATING CNS SAFETY

CNS safety screening, or first-tier testing using the FOB or Irwin test, is recommended by the International Commission on Harmonisation (ICH S7A) and is common "best practice" in contemporary drug and chemical safety evaluation. Second-tier testing involves more complex assessments that provide a more complete description of compound-related effects and dose–response relationship [9]. Lindgren et al. (2008) has reported survey results of more than 100 testing laboratories conducting safety pharmacology studies and revealed that approximately 64% of responding laboratories utilize some form of an FOB and 75% referred to an "Irwin protocol" [9]. Although it is not clear from the survey whether respondents were referring to these procedures interchangeably, or whether both procedures were in effect, the former seems more likely. There often appears to be a preference of pharmaceutical companies for using the Irwin test, and chemical testing laboratories for using the FOB or, as often referred to as, expanded clinical observations [125]. Upon review, these batteries overlap significantly, and to some extent are interchangeable [93]. Unlike the Irwin screen, which was originally developed as an assay to be conducted in mice and has been less amenable to cross-species utilization, the rodent FOB approach has been extended to nonrodent laboratory species, including the dog [126,127], guinea pig [128], and NHP [129–131].

In the Irwin screen and/or FOB, a range of simple to complex behaviors (eg, locomotor activity, sensory function, and gait) provides a broad assessment of neurological function [93]. The behavioral assessments vary in the degree of specificity, are not definitive for any particular variable being evaluated, may be mediated

independently of CNS activity, and are subject to learning phenomena with repeated evaluations. Accordingly, these measures often are subject to considerable variability, and therefore it may be difficult to interpret when conducted with small sample sizes. The OPPTS 6200 US EPA neurotoxicity guidelines have recommended at least 10 animals per gender per group included as a standard experimental design for the conduct of FOB evaluations. In adopting these same EPA guidelines the Interagency Committee on Neurotoxicity has also adopted this requirement.

One goal of using the FOB is to "cast a wide net" to detect any potential nervous system effects, especially when dealing with new chemical entities for which little or no such information exists. For regulatory safety testing, the FOB provides information on effects of even low doses. Such data are needed to help determine the most sensitive endpoint across a range of other tests including systemic, developmental, respiratory, immune, and carcinogenicity endpoints [93].

In brief, observations take place in the home cage and within an "open-field" arena during which time the subject's gait, stance, movements, physical appearance, and reflexive reactions to various stimuli are evaluated. For most laboratories, this evaluation includes assessment of grip strength [132], landing foot splay [133], some type of assessment of antinociception (eg, rat tail flick, hot plate [paw-lick latency], etc.). Behavioral domains are evaluated in terms of general activity and coordinated movements and abnormal and unusual behaviors, including tremors, muscle fasciculations, and convulsions. Additional endpoints of general activity, reactivity, and responses may be considered motor-affective domain, while other responses, such as corneal reflex and visual placing are categorized within the sensorimotor domain. Neurologic function, such as gait, stance, equilibrium or balance, and righting-reflex are considered as a separate domain. Autonomic and general physiological measures include pupil response, salivation, lacrimation, urination/defecation, body temperature, respiration rates or respiratory pattern, and others. This observational approach allows for the detection of low-, moderate-, and high-dose treatment effects and provides a profile of CNS function that subsequently may be used to chart a course for more specific/definitive follow-up preclinical investigations of CNS activity that will generally predict potential adverse effects in the first clinical population that may receive the test article in Phase I clinical trials. A summary of the measurements in a standard FOB is given in Table 7.9.

To permit valid and reliable performance of these CNS safety-screening batteries, a clearly defined protocol and well-trained technicians/observers are critical. Subjective evaluations that are specified as distinct rating scales provide a semiquantitative aspect to the data and a more descriptive array of changes across the dose continuum. Detailed descriptions of behaviors are often documented as nonstandard comments to assist in *post hoc* determinations of the full scope of the CNS-related changes induced by the new chemical entity. It is imperative that the technicians conducting the observational battery remain "blinded" to experimental groups, or unaware of each animal's treatment, so as not to introduce bias, however unintentional, into the dataset. Detailed training of the observers is essential and must include basic principles of experimental design, good laboratory techniques, as well as experience with, and an understanding of, "normal" behavioral repertoire of the animal subject being tested. These training aspects are prerequisite to experience with rating animals that have been administered active (positive control) compounds selected from pharmacological classes to induce specific changes in FOB/Irwin parameters. The technician must be at ease in handling the experimental subject and be alert and cognizant of the effects of such handling on the behavior of the animal being evaluated. Most critical in the evaluation and summarization of the data collected in the FOB is an assessment of "interrater" reliability of the pattern of data individually derived from the subjective and objective rating scales and procedures used in the study protocol. A key factor that promotes consistency in execution of the battery and therefore enhances reliability, aside from adequate training and experience, is allowing the same individual to rate a given subject on all aspects of the test battery, in the required sequence. This tends to promote a holistic appreciation of the subject's status, with multiple correlated measures offering

corroborative feedback. Retaining different observers to conduct different aspects of the behavioral battery (eg, home-cage assessments or open-field assessments) within the same subject leads unacceptably to decreases in the internal consistency of data and does nothing to enhance reliability and validity of the procedure.

Automated locomotor activity (photobeam) chambers (LMA) have been widely used in conjunction with the standard FOB or Irwin screen as a functional test of integrated and coordinated neurological motor control, which includes cortical, subcortical, cerebellar, and vestibular functions of the CNS. The specific type of LMA system utilized does not appear to matter, as most devices are capable of a similar generalized set of evaluative endpoints describing motor activity. Crofton, Howard, Moser, Gill, Reiter, and Tilson [134] previously reported high interlaboratory reliability across a diverse set of chemicals using several different LMA systems. While overall levels of activity during a test session can help to dissociate dose-related effects of a given compound, other specific features, such as "habituation,a a general decline in activity levels within a session, or spatial distribution, the general pattern of within-chamber activity, such as wall-walking or center area exposure, may expose more subtle behavioral differences between treatment groups that may be engendered by other nonspecific attributes of the compound of interest. For example, rats often demonstrate thigmotaxis, ambulating close to the walls of an open arena. Benzodiazepines will generally induce a state of relaxation or reduced anxiety in rats that increases the likelihood that rats will walk in the center of the open arena away from close proximity

TABLE 7.9 Illustration of Endpoints and Statistical Analyses for Continuous (Ratio Level Data) and Categorical (Nominal/Ordinal Level Data) Contained Within a Functional Observational Battery (FOB)

FOB (Continuous Endpoints)[a]	FOB (Categorical Endpoints)[b]	
• Thermal response	• Posture	• Arousal
• Men forelimb grip strength	• Ease of removal	• Vocalizations
• Mean hind-limb grip strength	• Handling reactivity	• respiration
• Body weight	• Lacrimation	• Stereotypy
• Body temperature	• Palpebral closure	• Bizarre behavior
• Rearing	• Piloerection	• Approach response
• Defecation	• Exophthalmus	• Touch response
• Urination	• Salivation	• Click response
• Mean hind-limb splay	• Clonic Movements	• Tail Pinch response
	• Tonic Movements	• Pupil response
	• Gait	• Righting reflex
	• Mobility	

[a]*Parametric Statistical Analysis (ANOVA).*
[b]*Nonparametric Statistical Analysis (Cochran Mantel Haenszel Test).*

to the walls. Despite the variety of objective and quantitative data generated by the LMA system, changes in motor activity cannot be attributed to any one specific CNS substrate.

Integrative analysis of FOB data requires a diagnostic scheme that needs to include a range of confidences. No one finding is demonstrative evidence of CNS adverse effects or neurotoxicity. Changes in gait, ambulation, and rearing in the open arena may be suggestive of general muscle weaknesses, but not be supported by objective measures of intact fore- and hind-limb grip strength or hind-limb splay measurements. In our laboratory, the neurotoxicant acrylamide was used as part of a "proof of concept" validation study required for GLP compliance. Acrylamide induces a "dying back" sensory axonopathy resulting in loss of neural control of the limbs [135]. While many laboratories have concluded that acrylamide produces "muscle weakness" our comparative data of fore- and hind-limb grip strength and hind-limb splay data clearly identified a dose and treatment strategy that easily differentiated acrylamide's effects on motor strength and sensory loss (see Table 7.10). Four groups of 10 rats per gender per group were orally dosed once daily with vehicle (distilled water) or 5.6, 10, or 32 mg/kg acrylamide for 14 days. FOB evaluations were conducted prior to dose initiation and following treatment on days 7 and 14. Summary grip strength and hind-limb splay measurements for each group quantified on day 14 show the group-dependent changes from daily exposure to the neurotoxicant.

As is clearly demonstrated by these data, the well-characterized sensory axonopathy associated with acrylamide treatments is associated with an increase in hind-limb splay measurements in both male and female rats and is dissociated from any change in muscular performance as measured in grip strength. In fact, female rats receiving the 5.6 and 10 mg/kg daily dose of acrylamide demonstrated greater forelimb grip strengths compared to vehicle control group and their high dose acrylamide treated cohorts. The hind-limb splay changes were confirmed by postmortem histopathology of peripheral limb nerves. The increase in hind-limb splay values in these rats are more likely due to the loss of sensory input to the CNS that helps to identify where the limbs are in three-dimensional space (cerebellar function) rather than some general loss of muscle tone or muscle weakness.

As described by Tilson and MacPhail [136] there are inherent difficulties in CNS safety assessments where multiple behavioral measures are taken (eg, many different effects are observed and sometimes there is little consistent pattern in statistically significant effects). The endpoints used in the FOB produce qualitatively different types of data (eg, continuous [ratio scale], dichotomous [nominal scale], and categorical [ordinal scale]), requiring multiple statistical comparisons. Muller [137] highlighted three specific problems that tend to inflate Type I error rates in FOBs:

1. the existence of many dependent variables (up to 20),
2. the existence of many tests on a variable, and
3. data "snooping".

The first problem arises because it is less resource-intensive to perform multiple tests on each subject than to perform each test on a separate group of subjects. Depending on the analysis, many tests may be conducted for a single variable and yield the same problem. According to Muller, data "snooping" tends to inflate Type I error rate in a less obvious way. First, exploratory analysis usually includes many different tests of the same hypothesis. Second, exploratory analysis tends

TABLE 7.10 End of Study FOB Data for Grip Strength and Hind-Limb Splay Measurements in Rats Treated Daily With Various Doses of Acrylamide

Measurements	Acrylamide Treatment (mg/kg) Dosed Once Daily per os			
	0	5.6	10.0	32.0
MALES				
Mean fore-limb grip strength (kg)	0.82 ± 0.15	0.86 ± 0.14	0.72 ± 0.16	0.81 ± 0.16
Mean hind-limb grip strength (kg)	0.44 ± 0.08	0.45 ± 0.09	0.40 ± 0.05	0.38 ± 0.09
Mean hind-limb splay (mm)	115.2 ± 11.7	106.9 ± 14.9	114.07 ± 24.0	151.9 ± 9.8[b]
FEMALES				
Mean fore-limb grip strength (kg)	0.64 ± 0.11	0.70 ± 0.08	0.70 ± 0.18	0.61 ± 0.14
Mean fore-limb grip strength (kg)	0.27 ± 0.05	0.34 ± 0.07[a]	0.36 ± 0.05[a]	0.24 ± 0.07
Mean hind-limb splay	96.3 ± 16.4	85.9 ± 14.8	101.93 ± 9.7	132.3 ± 11.2[b]

[a]$p < .05$.
[b]$p < .01$.

to capitalize on chance by searching for the maximum group differences. Any time a choice is made based on the smallest p value by:

1. comparing different transformations of the independent or dependent variables,
2. comparing subsets of many dependent measures, or
3. selecting a subset of many independent variables, then exploratory analysis has occurred.

The inflation of α increases as the amount of exploratory analysis increases.

A second set of design problems lead to inflated β, Type II error rate, which results in lack of power. The most obvious reason for the lack of power is too small a sample size. As described above, regulatory agencies have suggested that because of the inherent variability in behavior at least 10 rats per sex per group should be used in CNS safety and neurotoxicity FOB studies. In attempts to save costs and reduce animal use in these assays, it may seem tempting to take such measures as conducting the CNS safety in animals of only one sex and with sample sizes of less than 5. Consideration should be given to how these kinds of choices in study design may influence power, increasing Type II error. Even a conscientious researcher who attempts to control α through the use of a Bonferroni correction while testing many hypotheses may also inadvertently inflate β. Interests in small effects, choosing the wrong dependent measures, and choosing a low-power testing method can inflate Type II error rates.

In summary, the same general study design features that are important for other core safety pharmacology studies also apply to the CNS safety evaluation. Testing is similarly arranged in a tiered structure where the initial screening evaluations are designed to elicit, in a dose–response manner, adverse pharmacology that may be associated with off-target or unexpected activity of a new chemical entity. Results of these initial studies are utilized to guide follow-up preclinical investigations designed to elicit more specific information concerning effects of interest and to guide the design of clinical trials inasmuch as the particular biomarkers identified are translatable to the clinical situation. Specialized behavioral testing strategies require relatively more intensive and recurring training, compared to cardiovascular and respiratory function testing procedures that rely on the application of specialized instrumentation to derive necessary biological endpoints. Objective, critical, and integrative analysis of factors influencing study design, as well as a strong foundation in neurological functions and the knowledge of the normal behavioral repertoire of the specific animal subjects employed in any FOB by the study director or researcher will help to ensure reliability and validity of the data set that will accurately predict that a safe and effective dose of compound can be selected for Phase I clinical trials.

References

[1] Bass A, Kinter L, Williams P. Origins, practices, and future of safety pharmacology. J Pharmacol Toxicol Methods 2004;49:145–51.

[2] Vogel HG, editor. Drug discovery and evaluation: pharmacological assays. 2nd ed. Berlin: Springer-Verlag; 2002.

[3] Redfern WS, Valentin J-P. Trends in safety pharmacology: posters presented at the annual meetings of the Safety Pharmacology Society 2001–2010. J Pharmacol Toxicol Methods 2011;64:102–10.

[4] Fung M, Thorton A, Mybeck K, Hsaio-Hui Wu J, Hornbuckle I, Muniz E. Evaluation of the characteristics of safety withdrawal of prescription drugs from the worldwide pharmaceutical markets – 1960 to 1999. Drug Inform J 2001;35:293–317.

[5] Schuster D, Laggner C, Langer T. Why drugs fail – a study on the side effects in new chemical entities. Curr Pharm Des 2005;11:3545–59.

[6] Pugsley MK. Safety pharmacology matures into a unique pharmacological discipline. J Pharmacol Toxicol Methods 2004;49:137–9.

[7] Pugsley MK. Methodology used in safety pharmacology: appraisal of the state-of-the-art, the regulatory issues and new directions. J Pharmacol Toxicol Methods 2005;52:1–5.

[8] Pugsley MK, Curtis MJ. Safety pharmacology in focus: new methods developed in the light of the ICH S7B guidance document. J Pharmacol Toxicol Methods 2006;54:94–8.

[9] Lindgren S, Bass AS, Briscoe R, Burse K, Friedrich GS, Kallman MJ, et al. Benchmarking safety pharmacology regulatory packages and best practice. J Pharmacol Toxicol Methods 2008;58:99–109.

[10] Pugsley MK, Gallacher DJ, Towart R, Authier S, Curtis MJ. Methods in safety pharmacology in focus. J Pharmacol Toxicol Methods 2008;58:69–71.

[11] Pugsley MK, Authier S, Towart R, Gallacher DJ. Beyond the safety assessment of drug-mediated changes in the QT interval…what's next? J Pharmacol Toxicol Methods 2009;60:24–7.

[12] Pugsley MK, Towart R, Authier S, Gallacher DJ. Nonclinical models: validation, study design and statistical consideration in safety pharmacology. J Pharmacol Toxicol Methods 2010;62:1–3.

[13] Pugsley MK, Towart R, Authier S, Gallacher DJ, Curtis MJ. Innovation in safety pharmacology testing. J Pharmacol Toxicol Methods 2011;64:1–6.

[14] Breckenridge A. A clinical pharmacologist's view of drug toxicity. Br J Pharmacol 1996;42:53–8.

[15] Lazarou J, Pomeranz BH, Corey PN. Incidence of adverse drug reactions in hospitalized patients: a meta-analysis of prospective studies. J Am Med Assoc 1998;279:1200–5.

[16] Redfern WS, Wakefield ID, Prior H, Pollard CE, Hammond TG, Valentin J-P. Safety pharmacology – a progressive approach. Fund Clin Pharmacol 2002;16:161–73.

[17] Gad SC. Safety pharmacology in pharmaceutical development and approval. Boca Raton: LLC CRC Press; 2004.

[18] Arrigoni C. Cardiovascular liabilities of drugs. Regulatory aspects. In: Minotti G, editor. Cardiotoxicity of non-cardiovascular drugs. West Sussex, United Kingdom: John Wiley & Sons, Ltd; 2010.

[19] Roden DM, Anderson ME. Proarrhythmia. Handbook Exp Pharmacol 2006;171:73–97.

[20] Farkas AS, Nattel S. Minimizing repolarization-related proarrhythmic risk in drug development and clinical practice. Drugs 2010;70:573–603.

[21] Cavero I. Cardiovascular system assessment best practices: a safety pharmacology society meeting. Expert Opin Drug Saf 2010;9:855–66.

[22] Leishman DJ, Beck TW, Dybdal N, Gallacher DJ, Guth BD, Holbrook M, et al. Best practice in the conduct of key nonclinical cardiovascular safety assessments in drug development: current recommendations from the safety pharmacology society. J Pharmacol Toxicol Methods 2011;65(3):93–101.

[23] Bass AS, Vargas HM, Valentin J-P, Kinter LB, Hammond T, Wallis R, et al. Safety pharmacology in 2010 and beyond: survey of significant events of the past 10 years and roadmap to the immediate-, intermediate-, and long-term future in recognition of the tenth anniversary of the safety pharmacology society. J Pharmacol Toxicol Methods 2011;64:7–15.

[24] Anon. Notes on applications for approval to manufacture (import) new drugs. Tokyo, Japan: MHW; 1975.

[25] Anon. Japanese guidelines for nonclinical studies of drugs manual. Tokyo, Japan: Yakuji Nippo Limited; 1995.

[26] Anon. Guideline for safety pharmacology study. 1998. [Tokyo, Japan].

[27] Anon. US Department of Health and Human Services, Food and Drug Administration. Center for Drug Evaluation and Research (CDER), Center for Biologics Evaluation and Research (CBER), Guidance for Industry; 2001. S7A: Safety Pharmacology Studies for Human Pharmaceuticals (ICH S7A).

[28] Kinter LB, Valentin J-P. Safety pharmacology and risk assessment. Fund Clin Pharmacol 2002;16:175–82.

[29] Anon. US Department of Health and Human Services, Food and Drug Administration. Center for Drug Evaluation and Research (CDER), Center for Biologics Evaluation and Research (CBER), Guidance for Industry; 2005. S7B: The Non-clinical Evaluation of the Potential for Delayed Ventricular Repolarization (QT Interval Prolongation) by Human Pharmaceuticals (ICH S7B).

[30] Vargas HM, Bass A, Breidenbach A, Feldman HS, Gintant GA, Harmer AR, et al. Scientific review and recommendations on preclinical cardiovascular safety evaluation of biologics. J Pharmacol Toxicol Methods 2008;58:72–6.

[31] Bernton EW. Safety pharmacology: similarities and differences between small molecules and novel biopharmaceuticals. In: Cavagnaro JA, editor. Preclinical safety evaluation of biopharmaceuticals: a science-based approach to facilitating clinical trials. Hoboken, NJ: John Wiley & Sons, Inc.; 2008.

[32] Anon. US Department of Health and Human Services, Food and Drug Administration. Center for Drug Evaluation and Research (CDER), Center for Biologics Evaluation and Research (CBER), Guidance for Industry; 2011. S6(R1): Preclinical Safety Evaluation of Biotechnology Derived Pharmaceuticals. ICH S6(R1).

[33] Anon. US Department of Health and Human Services, Food and Drug Administration. Center for Drug Evaluation and Research (CDER), Center for Biologics Evaluation and Research (CBER), Guidance for Industry; 2010. S9: Nonclinical Evaluation for Anticancer Pharmaceuticals (ICH S9).

[34] Sun Y, Gruber M, Matsumoto M. Overview of global regulatory toxicology requirements for vaccines and adjuvants. J Pharmacol Toxicol Methods 2012;65(2):49–57.

[35] Valentin J-P, Bialecki R, Ewart L, Hammond T, Leishman D, Lindgren S, et al. A framework to assess the translation of safety pharmacology data to humans. J Pharmacol Toxicol Methods 2009;60:152–8.

[36] Cavero I. Exploratory safety pharmacology: a new safety paradigm to de-risk drug candidates prior to selection for regulatory science investigations. Expert Opin Drug Saf 2009;8:627–47.

[37] Kaczorowski GJ, Garcia ML, Bode J, Hess SD, Patel UA. The importance of being profiled: improving drug candidate safety and efficacy using ion channel profiling. Front Pharmacol 2011;2:1–11.

[38] Kinter LB, Dixon LW. Safety pharmacology program for pharmaceuticals. Drug Dev Res 1995;35:179–82.

[39] Ramos KS, Chacon E, Acosta Jr D. Toxic responses of the heart and vascular systems. In: Klassen CD, editor. Casarett and Doull's toxicology: The basic science of poisons. 5th ed. 1996.

[40] Fuster V, Alexander RW, O'Rourke RA, Roberts R, King SB, Wellens H,JJ. Hurst's the heart. 10th ed. New York: McGraw-Hill Medical Publishing Division; 2001.

[41] Polak S, Wisniowska B, Brandys J. Collation, assessment and analysis of literature *in vitro* data on hERG receptor blocking potency for subsequent modeling of drugs' cardiotoxic properties. J Appl Toxicol 2009;29:183–206.

[42] Lee N, Authier S, Pugsley MK, Curtis MJ. The continuing evolution of *torsades de pointes* liability testing methods: is there an end in sight? Toxicol Appl Pharmacol 2010;243:146–53.

[43] Picard S, Goineau S, Guillaume P, Henry J, Hanouz J-L, Rouet R. Supplemental studies for cardiovascular risk assessment in safety pharmacology: a critical overview. Cardiovasc Toxicol 2011;11:285–307.

[44] Redfern WS, Carlsson L, Davis AS, Lynch WG, MacKenzie I, Palethorpe S, et al. Relationships between preclinical cardiac electrophysiology, clinical QT interval prolongation, and torsade de pointes for a broad range of drugs: evidence for a provisional safety margin in drug development. Cardiovasc Res 2003;58:32–45.

[45] Yang T, Snyders D, Roden DM. Drug block of I(kr): model systems and relevance to human arrhythmias. J Cardiovasc Pharmacol 2001;38:737–44.

[46] Milberg P, Reinsch N, Osada N, Wasmer K, Monnig G, Stypmann J, et al. Verapamil prevents torsade de pointes by reduction of transmural dispersion of repolarization and suppression of early after-depolarizations in an intact heart model of LQT3. Basic Res Cardiol 2005;100:365–71.

[47] Pugsley MK, Hancox JC, Curtis MJ. Perception of validity of clinical and preclinical methods for assessment of *torsades de pointes* liability. Pharmacol Ther 2008;119:115–7.

[48] Greaves P. Patterns of drug-induced cardiovascular pathology in the beagle dog: relevance for humans. Exp Toxicol Pathol 1998;50:289–93.

[49] Eckardt L, Haverkamp W, Borggrefe M, Breithardt G. Experimental models of torsade de pointes. Cardiovasc Res 1998;39:178–93.

[50] Gralinski MR. The dog's role in the preclinical assessment of QT interval prolongation. Toxicol Pathol 2003;31:11–6.

[51] Nattel S, Duker G, Carlsson L. Model systems for the discovery and development of antiarrhythmic drugs. Prog Biophys Mol Biol 2008;98:328–39.

[52] Stubhan M, Markert M, Mayer K, Trautmann T, Klumpp A, Henke J, et al. Evaluation of cardiovascular and ECG parameters in the normal, freely moving Göttingen Mini-Pig. J Pharmacol Toxicol Methods 2008;57:202–11.

[53] Markert M, Stubhan M, Mayer K, Trautmann T, Klumpp A, Schuler-Metz A, et al. Validation of the normal, freely moving Gottingen mini-pig for pharmacological safety testing. J Pharmacol Toxicol Methods 2009;60:79–87.

[54] van der Laan JW, Brightwell J, McAnulty P, Ratky J, Stark C. Regulatory acceptability of the mini-pig in the development of pharaceuticals, chemicals, and other products. J Pharmacol Toxicol Methods 2010;62:184–95.

[55] Bode G, Clausing P, Gervais F, Loegsted J, Luft J, Nogues V, et al. The utility of the mini-pig as an animal model in regulatory toxicology. J Pharmacol Toxicol Methods 2010;62:196–220.

[56] Sugiyama A. Sensitive and reliable proarrhythmia in vivo animal models for predicting drug-induced *torsades de pointes* in patients with remodeled hearts. Br J Pharmacol 2008;154:1528–37.

[57] Authier S, Gervais J, Fournier S, Gauvin D, Maghezzi S, Troncy E. Cardiovascular and respiratory safety pharmacology in Göttingen mini-pigs: pharmacological characterization. J Pharmacol Toxicol Methods 2011;64:53–9.

[58] Baryla UM, Fleming JS, Stanton HC. The anesthetized ferret, an *in vivo* model for evaluating inotropic activity: effects of milrinone and anagrelide. J Pharmacol Methods 1988;20:299–306.

[59] Komatsu R, Honda M, Holzgrefe HH, Kubo J, Yamada Y, Isobe T, et al. Sensitivity of common marmosets to detect drug induced QT interval prolongation: moxifloxacin case study. J Pharmacol Toxicol Methods 2010;61:271–6.

[60] van Acker SA, Kramer K, Voest EE, Grimbergen JA, Zhang J, van der Vijgh WJF, et al. Doxorubicin-induced cardiotoxicity monitored by ECG in freely moving mice. A new model to test potential protectors. Cancer Chemother Pharmacol 1996;38:95–101.

[61] Kinter LB. Cardiovascular telemetry and laboratory animal welfare: new reduction and refinement alternatives (Abstract). In: General pharmacology/safety pharmacology meeting, Philadelphia, PA. 1996.

[62] Kramer K, Kinter LB. Evaluation and application of radiotelemetry in small laboratory animals. Physiol Genom 2003;13:197–205.

[63] Miyazaki H, Tagawa M. Rate-correction technique for QT interval in long-term telemetry ECG recording in beagle dogs. Exp Anim 2002;51:465–75.

[64] Holzgrefe HH, Cavero I, Gleason CR, Warner WA, Buchanan LV, Gill MW, et al. Novel probabilistic method for precisely correcting the QT interval for heart rate in telemetered dogs and cynomolgus monkeys. J Pharmacol Toxicol Methods 2007;55:159–75.

[65] van der Linde HJ, Van Deuren B, Tiesman A, Towart R, Gallacher DJ. The effect of changes in core body temperature on the QT interval in beagle dogs: a previously ignored phenomenon, with method for correction. Br J Pharmacol 2008;154:1474–81.

[66] Hamlin RL, del Rio C. dP/dtmax – a measure of baroinometry. J Pharmacol Toxicol Methods 2012;66(2):63–5.

[67] Holzgrefe Jr HH, Ferber G, Morrison R, Meyer O, Greiter-Wilke A, Singer T. Characterization of the human QT interval: novel distribution-based assessment of the repolarization effects of moxifloxacin. J Clin Pharmacol 2011;52(8):1222–39.

[68] Gauvin DV, Tilley LP, Smith Jr FWK, Baird TJ. Spontaneous cardiac arrhythmias recorded in three experimentally- and drug-naïve laboratory species (canine, primate, swine) during standard prestudy screening. J Pharmacol Toxicol Methods 2009;59:57–61.

[69] Cools F, Janssens S, Vanlommel A, Teisman A, Towart R, Gallacher DJ. ECG arrhythmias in nonimplanted vs. telemetry-implanted dogs: need for screening before and sufficient recovery time after implantation. Pharmacol Toxicol Methods 2011;64:60–7.

[70] Minotti G, editor. Cardiotoxicity of non-cardiovascular drugs. West Sussex, United Kingdom: John Wiley & Sons, Ltd; 2010.

[71] Gauvin DV, Tilley LP, Smith Jr FWK, Baird TJ. Electrocardiogram, hemodynamics, and core body temperatures of the normal freely moving laboratory beagle dog by remote radiotelemetry. J Pharmacol Toxicol Methods 2006;53:128–39.

[72] Gauvin DV, Tilley LP, Smith Jr FWK, Baird TJ. Electrocardiogram, hemodynamics, and core body temperatures of the normal freely moving cynomolgus monkey by remote radiotelemetry. J Pharmacol Toxicol Methods 2006;53:140–51.

[73] Lawrence CL, Pollard CE, Hammond TG, Valentin J-P. Nonclinical proarrhythmia models: predicting *torsades de pointes*. J Pharmacol Toxicol Methods 2005;52:46–59.

[74] Ando K, Hombo T, Kanno A, Ikeda H, Imaizumi M, Shimizu N, et al. QT PRODACT: In vivo QT assay with a conscious monkey for assessment of the potential for drug-induced QT interval prolongation. J Pharmacol Sci 2005;99:487–500.

[75] Toyoshima S, Kanno A, Kitayama T, Sekiya K, Nakai K, Haruna M, et al. QT PRODACT: In vivo QT assay in the conscious dog for assessing the potential for QT interval prolongation by human pharmaceuticals. J Pharmacol Sci 2005;99:459–71.

[76] Schmitt MW, Von Landenberg F, Poth H, Wimmer E, Goddemeier T, Cavero I. Simple-to-use, reference criteria for revealing drug-induced QT interval prolongation in conscious dogs. Eur J Pharmacol 2007;554:46–52.

[77] Haushalter TM, Friedrichs GS, Reynolds DL, Barecki-Roach M, Pastino G, Hayes R, et al. The cardiovascular and pharmacokinetic profile of dofetilide in conscious telemetered beagle dogs and cynomolgus monkeys. Br J Pharmacol 2008;154:1457–64.

[78] Carlsson L, Amos GJ, Andersson B, Drews L, Duker G, Wadstedt G. Electrophysiological characterization of the prokinetic agents cisapride and mosapride in vivo and in vitro: implications for proarrhythmic potential? JPET 1997;282:220–7.

[79] Hamlin RL. Nondrug-related electrocardiographic features in animal models in safety pharmacology. J Pharmacol Toxicol Methods 2005;52:60–76.

[80] Guth BD, Bass AS, Briscoe R, Chivers S, Markert M, Siegl PKS, et al. Comparison of electrocardiographic analysis for risk of QT interval prolongation using safety pharmacology and toxicological studies. J Pharmacol Toxicol Methods 2009;60:107–16.

[81] Murphy DJ. Respiratory function assessment in safety pharmacology. Curr Protoc Pharmcol 2003:10.9.1–1.

[82] Parent RA. Treatise on pulmonary toxicology: comparative biology of the normal lung. vol. 1. Boca Raton: CRC Press; 1992.

[83] Levitzky MG. Pulmonary physiology. 6th ed. New York: McGraw Hill; 2003.

[84] Hoymann HG. Invasive and noninvasive lung function measurements in rodents. J Pharmacol Toxicol Methods 2007;55:16–26.

[85] Kearney K, Metea M, Gleason T, Edwards T, Atterson P. Evaluation of respiratory function in freely moving beagle dogs using implanted impedance technology. J Pharmacol Toxicol Methods 2010;62:119–26.

[86] Murphy DJ, Renninger JP, Schramek D. Respiratory inductive plethysmography as a method for measuring ventilatory parameters in conscious, nonrestrained dogs. J Pharmacol Toxicol Methods 2010;62:47–53.

[87] Authier S, Haefner P, Fournier S, Troncy E, Moon B. Combined cardiopulmonary assessments with implantable telemetry device in conscious freely moving cynomolgus monkeys. J Pharmacol Toxicol Methods 2010;62:6–11.

[88] Ingram-Ross JL, Curran AK, Miyamoto M, Sheehan J, Thomas G, Verbeeck J, et al. Cardiorespiratory safety evaluation in nonhuman primates. J Pharmacol Toxicol Methods 2012;66(2):114–24.

[89] DeLorme MP, Moss OR. Pulmonary function assessment by whole-body plethysmography in restrained versus unrestrained mice. J Appl Physiol 2002;94:1129–36.

[90] Harris D, Graham M, Price J, Munro F, Templeton A, Young R, et al. Respiratory function in rats restrained for extended periods: assessment of the effects of bethanecol. J Pharmacol Toxicol Methods 2005;52:83–9.

[91] Ewart LC, Haley M, Bickerton S, Bright J, Elliott K, McCarthy A, et al. Pharmacological validation of a telemetric model for the measurement of bronchoconstriction in conscious rats. J Pharmacol Toxicol Methods 2010;61:219–29.

[92] Moser VC. Applications of a neurobehavioral screening battery. Intern J Toxicol 1991;10:661–9.

[93] Moser VC. Functional assays for neurotoxicity testing. Toxicol Pathol 2010;39:36–45.

[94] Irwin S. Drug screening and evaluative procedures. Science 1962;136:123–8.

[95] Irwin S. Comprehensive observational assessments: Ia. A systematic, quantitative procedure for assessing the behavioral and physiologica state of the mouse. Psychopharmacologia (Berlin) 1968;13:222–57.

[96] Haggerty GC. Strategy for and experience with neurotoxicity testing of new pharmaceuticals. Intern J Toxicol 1991;10:677–88.

[97] Middaugh LD, Dow-Edwards D, Li AA, Sandler JD, Seed J, Sheets LP, et al. Neurobehavioral assessment: a survey of use and value in safety assessment studies. Toxicol Sci 2003;76:250–61.

[98] Tilson HA. Neurobehavioral methods used in neurotoxicological research. Toxicol Lett 1993;68:231–40.

[99] Tilson HA, Hong JS, Gerhart JM, Walsh TJ. Animal models of neurotoxicology: the neurobehavioral effects of chlordecone (Kepone). In: Thompson T, Dews PB, Barrett EJ, editors. Neurobehavioral pharmacology. Hillsdale, NJ: Lawrence Erlbaum Assoc; 1987. p. 49–73.

[100] Tilson HA, Moser VC. Comparison of screening approaches. Neurotoxicol 1992;13:1–13.

[101] MacPhail RC. International validation of a neurobehavioral screening battery: the IPCS/WHO collaborative study. Toxicol Lett 1992;64/65:217–23.

[102] Anon US. Environmental protection agency. Guidelines for neurotoxicity risk assessment. Fed Regist May 14, 1998;63(93):26926–54.

[103] Slikker W, Acuff K, Boyes WK, Chelonis J, Crofton KM, Dearlove GE, et al. Behavioral test methods workshop. Neurotox Teratol 1985;27:417–27.

[104] Tilson HA. Behavioral indices of neurotoxicity: what can be measured? Neurotox Teratol 1987;9:427–43.

[105] Tilson HA. Neurotoxicology in the 1990s. Neurotox Teratol 1990;12:293–300.

[106] Miya TS, Gibson JE, Hok JB, McClellan RO. Preparing for the twenty-first century: report of the Tox-90's commission. Toxicol Appl Pharmacol 1988;96:1–6.

[107] Anger WK, Johnson BL. Chemicals affecting behavior. In: O'Donoghue JL, editor. Neurotoxicity of industrial and chemical chemicals, vol. 1. Boca Raton, FL: CRC Press; 1985. p. 51–148.

[108] Mattsson JL. A neurotoxicologic definition of adverse. In: Weiss B, O'Donoghue J, editors. Neurobehavioral toxicity analysis and interpretation. NY: Raven Press; 1994. p. 41–5.

[109] Weiss B. Quantitative perspectives on behavioral toxicology. Toxicol Lett 1988;43:285–93.

[110] Weiss B, Laities V. Behavioral toxicology. NY: Plenum Press; 1975.

[111] Cory-Slechta DA. Behavioral measures of neurotoxicity. Neurotox 1989;10:271–96.

[112] Fox SH, Brotchie JM. The MPTP-lesioned nonhuman primate models of Parkinson's disease. Past, present, and future. Prog Brain Res 2010;184:133–57.

[113] Federation of American Societies for Experimental Biology (FASEB). Predicting neurotoxicity and behavioral dysfunction from preclinical toxicological data. In: Final Report: Task Order #3, Contract No. FDA 223-83-2020. Food and Drug Adminstration (FDA). Washington, DC.

[114] Leukoth RW. Predicting neurotoxicity and behavioral dysfunction from preclinical toxicological data. Symposium Introduction. Neurotox Teratol 1987;9:397–401.

[115] McMillan DE. Risk assessment for neurobehavioral toxicity. Environ Health Perspect 1987;76:155–61.

[116] Vorhees CV. Reliability, sensitivity, and validity of behavioral indices of neurotoxicity. Neurotox Teratol 1987;9:445–64.

[117] Reiter LW. Neurotoxicology in regulation and risk assessment. Dev Pharmacol Ther 1987;10:354–68.

[118] Riley EP, Vorhees DV. Handbook of behavioral Teratology. NY: Plenum Press; 1986.

[119] Hutchings DE, Callaway CW, Sobotka TJ. Symposium introduction: predicting neurotoxicity and behavioral dysfunction from preclinical toxicologic data. Neurotox Teratol 1987;9:397–401.

[120] Mitchel CL, Tilson HA. Behavioral toxicology in risk assessment: problems and research needs. Crit Rev Toxicol 1982;10:265–74.

[121] Russell RW, Flattau PE, Pope AM. Behavioral measures of neurotoxicity: report of a symposium. Washington, DC: National Research Council. National Academy Press; 1990.

[122] Jacobson-Kram D, Keller KA. Toxicology testing Handbook: principles, applications, and data interpretation. NY: Marcel Dekker, Inc.; 2001.

[123] Annau Z. Neurobehavioral toxicology. Baltimore: The Johns Hopkins University Press; 1986.

[124] Chang LW. Principles of neurotoxicology. NY: Marcel Dekker, Inc.; 1994.

[125] Ross JF, Mattsson JL, Fix AS. Expanded clinical observations in toxicity studies: historical perspectives and contemporary issues. Regul Toxicol Pharmacol 1988;28:17–26.

[126] Wasielewski JA, White JC, Newton PE, Briscoe RJ, Baird TJ. Development and validation of a canine functional observational battery (FOB) for use in toxicity studies. J Soc Toxicol 2002;66(1–S):1286.

[127] Gad SC, Gad SE. A functional observational battery for use in canine toxicity studies: development and validation. Int J Toxicol 2003;22:415–22.

[128] Hulet SW, McDonough JH, Shih TM. The dose-response effects of repeated subacute sarin exposure on guinea pigs. Pharmacol Biochem Behav 2002;72:835–45.

[129] Gauvin DV, Baird TJ. A functional observational battery in nonhuman primates for regulatory-required neurobehavioral assessments. J Pharmacol Toxicol Methods 2008;58:88–93.

[130] O'Keefe RT, Lifshitz K. Nonhuman primates in neurotoxicity screening and neurobehavioral toxicity studies. J Am Coll Toxicol 1989;8:127–40.

[131] Smith JJ, Hadzic V, Li X, Liu P, Day T, Utter A, et al. Objective measures of health and well-being in laboratory rhesus monkeys (Macaca mulatta). J Med Primatol 2006;35:388–96.

[132] Meyer OA, Tilson HA, Byrd WC, Riley MT. A method for the routine assessment of fore- and hind-limb grip strength of rats and mice. Neurobehav Toxicol 1979;1:233–6.

[133] Edwards PM, Parker VH. A simple, sensitive, and objective method for early assessment of acrylamide neuropathy in rats. Toxicol Appl Pharmacol 1977;40:589–91.

[134] Crofton KM, Howard JL, Moser VC, Gill MW, Reiter LW, Tilson HA, et al. Interlaboratory comparison of motor activity experiments: implications for neurotoxicological assessments. Neurotoxicol Teratol 1991;13:599–609.

[135] Weisenburger WP. Neurotoxicology. In: Jacobson-Kram D, Keller KA, editors. Toxicology testing handbook: principles, applications, and data interpretation. NY: Marcel Deckker Inc; 2001. p. 255–89.

[136] Tilson HA, MacPhail RC. Interpretation of neurobehavioral data in toxicological studies. In: Weiss B, O'Donoghue J, editors. Neurobehavioral toxicity analysis and interpretation. NY: Raven Press; 1994. p. 345–56.

[137] Muller KE. Design and analytical methods. In: Annau Z, editor. Neurobehavioral toxicology. Baltimore: The Johns Hopkins University Press; 1986. p. 404–23.

8

Preparation of a Preclinical Dossier to Support an Investigational New Drug (IND) Application and First-In-Human Clinical Trial

P. Nugent, J.N. Duncan, D.B. Colagiovanni

INTRODUCTION

Overview of the Nonclinical Toxicology Support for Clinical Trials

Nonclinical studies in pharmacology, pharmacokinetics, and toxicology [termed First-in-Human (FIH)-enabling or, in the United States, Investigational New Drug (IND)-enabling] studies are required to support the introduction of a new drug candidate to human subjects in the setting of a controlled clinical trial. This initial human testing, considered to be Phase I in the drug development pipeline and usually conducted in healthy volunteers, is designed to determine the pharmacokinetic (PK) relationship to dose (eg, to confirm animal or in silico projections), identify a maximum tolerated dose (MTD), and perform an initial identification of adverse events. Efficacy is not often a Phase I endpoint, but some information may be garnered from results of initial clinical trials. It is therefore critical that the toxicity profile of the drug candidate has been evaluated in animals, at least to the extent that the safe dosing of humans in the

A Comprehensive Guide to Toxicology in Nonclinical Drug Development, Second Edition
http://dx.doi.org/10.1016/B978-0-12-803620-4.00008-6

initial clinical program is supported. The toxicity profile should, at a minimum, include identification of the types of toxicities and target organs, the associated systemic concentrations and exposures, the maximum tolerated dose, and NOAEL dose and associated exposures for the various toxicities manifest. Other information, such as the reversibility of toxicity and identification of prodromal signs valuable in monitoring in the clinic, is also useful in designing an appropriate strategy to support the proposed clinical program. These data should then contribute to a rational evaluation of the initial dose and subsequent dose escalation to be used in humans, as well as the identification of potential human risks and incorporation of appropriate safety biomarkers, if available, in the clinical plan.

In preparation for clinical studies, certain documents must be submitted to the appropriate regulatory agencies to support human dosing. The International Conference on Harmonization of Technical Requirements for Registration of Pharmaceuticals for Human Use (ICH) has developed a process that, over the past 22 years, has harmonized the criteria and documents necessary for submission of an application to conduct clinical trials in the United States, Europe, and Japan [1]. A major benefit of the ICH process has been the harmonization of both the content and format of the submission dossier such that the work of sponsors and reviewers has been greatly facilitated, and medicines have been brought to patients more quickly. Harmonization of format has been achieved to a large extent through development of the Common Technical Document (CTD). This "global tool" has been readily adopted by regulatory agencies and pharmaceutical companies, and has contributed to the development of an electronic process that has greatly enhanced the speed of dossier submission and review [2]. The CTD is composed of five modules (see details later), with the nonclinical safety assessment described in Modules 2 and 4.

Through the Center for Drug Evaluation and Research (CDER) and the Center for Biologics Evaluation and Research (CBER), the Food and Drug Administration (FDA) publishes guidance documents specific to the regulatory requirements for initiating FIH studies in the United States. These studies are conducted under an IND application, which is submitted to, and reviewed by, the FDA in advance of initial dosing of human subjects. The requirements for content and format of the IND are outlined in the Code of Federal Regulations, Title 21, Part 312 (21 CFR 312), found at http://www.fda.gov. These requirements include a commitment that the sponsor will not begin clinical investigations "until an IND covering the investigations is in effect." The regulation 21 CFR 312.40 specifies that an IND automatically goes into effect 30 days after the FDA receives the application, unless the Agency notifies the sponsor that

the investigations described in the IND are subject to a clinical hold because of deficiencies in the application. An important aspect of the IND going into effect is the legal authorization for the sponsor to ship the investigative drug candidate into the United States and/or across state borders to the clinical trial center(s), and the authorization for the clinical investigators to administer the drug candidate to the human subjects.

Initial clinical trials are increasingly being conducted outside the United States, with attendant need for sponsors to become familiar with the requirements of regional regulatory authorities [3]. By the nature of it being composed of 28 individual countries, initiating clinical trials in the European Union (EU) is more complicated than in the United States. The European Medicines Agency (EMA) is the overall regulatory body; it is responsible for evaluating applications for marketing of medicines in the EU. The Committee for Medicinal Products and Human Use (CHMP) of the EMA provides advice on drug development strategies, including nonclinical aspects. However, the local (national) regulatory agencies and ethics committees are responsible for authorizing clinical trials in their respective countries, and may have specific requirements that must be addressed by consultation before a clinical trial is started. A Clinical Trial Application (CTA) must be submitted to the regulatory authority in the EU country in which the clinical trial will be conducted [4]. The CTA will include an Investigational Medicinal Product Dossier (IMPD), which should contain the nonclinical information supporting the clinical plan. The format and content of the IMPD follows that of the CTD as described in the ICH guideline M4SR(2), **"The Common Technical Document for the Registration of Pharmaceuticals for Human Use: Safety – M4S(R2). The Nonclinical Overview and Nonclinical Summaries of Module 2 Organization of Module 4"** ([5], see details below). The EU guideline *"Detailed guidance for the request for authorization of a clinical trial on a medicinal product for human use to the competent authorities, notification of substantial amendments and declaration of the end of the trial"* [6,7] provides information on the nonclinical pharmacology and toxicology data that should be included in the IMPD. Furthermore, details are provided on the use of a simplified IMPD if the nonclinical information can be made available by referring to other submissions, including previously submitted IMPDs or cross-referencing to the Investigator's Brochure (IB). Cross-referencing to the IB is a very convenient option in the case of a drug candidate for which an IND application has already been submitted in the United States, and hence an IB is already prepared. However, it is important to include in an IMPD template any additional information generated since the IB was last updated. To conduct an FIH trial in Japan, a sponsor must submit a Clinical Trial Protocol Notification to the Pharmaceuticals and Medical Devices Agency (PMDA), the appropriate Japanese regulatory agency. The nonclinical components of the submission should adhere to the ICH M3 guideline *"Guidance on Nonclinical Safety Studies for the Conduct of Human Clinical Trials and Marketing Authorization for Pharmaceuticals M3(R2),"* especially with respect to the differences in expectations between Japanese and American regulatory authorities [8,9]. In addition to those differences documented in that guideline, there are also differences in expectations regarding a number of study-related issues, including interpretation of study findings, identification of NOAELs, and demonstration of reversibility of toxicities [4]. A CTA is also required for Phase I clinical studies in Canada, the majority submitted to the Therapeutics Products Directorate of Health Canada [10]. Pre-CTA consultations with the appropriate department in the agency are encouraged. Health Canada has formally endorsed the ICH M4 guidance (see later) for submission of information in the CTA, with summaries of the nonclinical information being provided in the IB. Health Canada contributes to the ICH process in an observer capacity, and, in general, adherence to ICH guidance is expected by the agency.

The Common Technical Document (CTD)

The documents that comprise the IND dossier conform to the harmonized CTD format, the preparation of which is covered by the ICH M4 guidance for industry entitled *"The Organization of the CTD"* [11]. The administrative guidance describes a CTD that is organized into five modules, four of which (Modules 2, 3, 4, and 5) are intended to be common for all regions, and Module 1, which is region-specific and not actually part of the CTD. The organization of the CTD can be represented as a pyramid (Fig. 8.1), with the information being increasingly summarized as one ascends toward the apex. For example, the information in the individual nonclinical study reports in Module 4 (Nonclinical Study Reports) at the base of the pyramid is summarized in the Nonclinical Written and Tabulated Summaries Section 2.6 at the next level up, and in turn is further summarized and integrated in the Nonclinical Overview Section 2.4.

Table 8.1 provides an outline of the various Modules, with Sections 2.4 and 2.6 (to be discussed further in Section 3) shown in some detail.

From the perspective of the nonclinical information, the CTD format identifies an important component—the **Nonclinical Overview (NCO)** —of Module 2 (Section 2.4) that summarizes and, importantly, integrates the nonclinical pharmacology, pharmacokinetics, and toxicology information on the drug candidate. Details on the content and structural format of the NCO are provided in the separate M4S(R2) ICH guideline *Pharmaceuticals for Human Use: Safety – M4S(R2). The Nonclinical Overview and Nonclinical Summaries of Module 2 Organization of Module 4* [5] and are discussed in detail later. Although the guidance was created with a focus on marketing applications, it is commonly also used to describe the more limited extent of studies conducted in support of the FIH clinical trial. Headings for nonclinical studies not yet conducted are retained and a note indicating that data are not yet available is also included. As noted in the guideline, *the Nonclinical Overview should present an integrated and critical assessment of the pharmacologic, pharmacokinetic, and toxicologic evaluation of the pharmaceutical.* The guideline outlines the general presentation of information within the various subsections of Sections 2.4 and 2.6, noting that some flexibility in format is permissible to

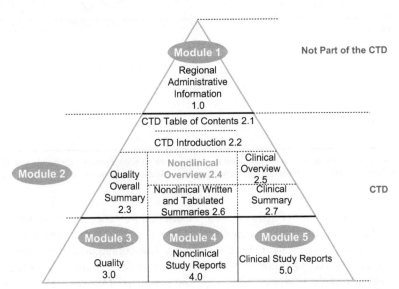

FIGURE 8.1 Representation of the components of the CTD. The nonclinical components required for an IND dossier are highlighted in **bold**.

TABLE 8.1   Organization of the Common Technical Document (CTD), with Emphasis on the Subsections Containing Nonclinical Information (Highlighted)

Module		Topic
MODULE 1:		
1.1.	Table of contents of the submission including Module 1	*Administrative information and*
1.2.	Documents specific to each region (for example, application forms, prescribing information)	*prescribing information*
MODULE 2:		
2.1.	CTD table of contents	*Common technical document*
2.2.	CTD introduction	*summaries in tabular and narrative*
2.3.	Quality overall summary	*form*
2.4.	**Nonclinical overview**	
	2.4.1. **Overview of nonclinical testing strategy**	
	2.4.2. **Pharmacology**	
	2.4.3. **Pharmacokinetics**	
	2.4.4. **Toxicology**	
	2.4.5. **Integrated overview and conclusions**	
	2.4.6. **List of literature references**	
2.5.	Clinical overview	
2.6.	**Nonclinical written and tabulated summary**	
	2.6.1. **Introduction**	
	2.6.2. **Pharmacology written summary**	
	2.6.3. **Pharmacology tabulated summary (series of tabulated summaries of pharmacology studies)**	
	2.6.4. **Pharmacokinetics written summary**	
	2.6.5. **Pharmacokinetic tabulated summary (series of tabulated summaries of pharmacokinetic studies)**	
	2.6.6. **Toxicology written summary**	
	2.6.7. **Toxicology tabulated summary (series of tabulated summaries of toxicology studies)**	
2.7.	Clinical summary	
	Biopharmaceutics and associated analytical methods	
	Clinical pharmacology studies	
	Clinical efficacy	
	Clinical safety	
	Synopses of individual studies	
MODULE 3:		
3.1.	Module 3 table of contents	*Quality [chemistry, manufacturing,*
3.2.	Body of data	*and controls (CMC)]*
3.3.	Literature references	
MODULE 4:		
4.1.	**Module 4 table of contents**	*Nonclinical study reports*
4.2.	**Full study reports**	
4.3.	**Literature references**	
MODULE 5:		
5.1.	Module 5 table of contents	*Clinical study reports*
5.2.	Tabular listing of all clinical studies	
5.3.	Clinical study reports	
5.4.	Literature references	

Note: The NCO may have sections without any information since nonclinical studies have not yet been conducted for these areas. This may be acceptable as the full complement of studies is not normally needed to support the initial clinical trial (eg, embryo-fetal development studies) but will be completed before submission of a New Drug Application (NDA).

allow for the best presentation of the data. Furthermore, as noted in the guidance, "*the interpretation of the data, the clinical relevance of the findings, cross-linking with the quality aspects of the pharmaceutical, and the implications of the nonclinical findings for the safe use of the pharmaceutical … should be addressed in the Overview.*" The final subsection of the NCO—subsection 2.4.5 **Integrated Overview and**

Conclusion—constitutes a summary of the preceding subsections, providing an opportunity for an integrated summary and conclusion that supports the safety of the drug candidate for the intended clinical use, and specifically the proposed FIH clinical trial. ICH M4S(R2) also offers guidance on the organization of the Nonclinical Written and Tabulated Summaries that provide a comprehensive factual synopsis of the data in the nonclinical studies, and contain information that is further summarized in the NCO. Again, it is recommended that the Discussion and Conclusion subsections of the pharmacology, pharmacokinetics, and toxicology Nonclinical Written Summaries (Subsections 2.6.2, 2.6.4, and 2.6.6) provide information in a form integrated across studies and species, and with discussion of exposures related to those projected for the maximum intended clinical dose. Finally, the guideline also presents an agreed format for the organization of the nonclinical study reports. Data tables that summarize study findings should be prepared for each study to be included in Subsection 2.6.6.1, thus enabling quick referral to any adverse effects.

It is important to understand that ICH M4S(R2) does not indicate which study types are required; this is covered in the ICH M3 guidance, *"Guidance on Nonclinical Safety Studies for the Conduct of Human Clinical Trials and Marketing Authorization for Pharmaceuticals M3(R2),"* most recently updated in a major revision in 2010 [8,9]. However, what M4 and M4S(R2) do provide are critical guidance for a sponsor preparing an FIH-enabling application for submission to the three ICH regions and most other regulatory authorities. There are several advantages to following these recommendations: the increased likelihood of a more speedy review by regulatory agencies expecting to see the submission in this standard ICH-recommended format; a reduction in the time needed to prepare simultaneous global marketing applications in an electronic format (e-CTD); the preparation of a core nonclinical summary in the form of the NCO that can be utilized for other drug development-related activities (eg, the preparation of the IB (detailed in Section 3); and the availability of a convenient summary for providing nonclinical information to company management or for in-/out-licensing due-diligence purposes).

In addition to the ICH guidelines mentioned earlier, there are also documents produced by regional regulatory authorities that provide guidance on specific study types and more general aspects of predicting human safety from nonclinical toxicology studies. For example, the FDA's CDER and CBER divisions have produced guidance dealing with specific issues, eg, *Guidance for Industry: Single Dose Acute Toxicity Testing for Pharmaceuticals* [12]. In addition, the European Medicines Agency (EMA) issued a guideline in 2007 entitled *"Guideline on Strategies to Identify and Mitigate Risks for First-in-Human Clinical Trials with Investigational Medicinal Products"* (EMEA/CHMP/SWP/28367/07) [13] that covers both biologics and new chemical entities, and has been described as being very much influenced by the TeGenero monoclonal antibody incident in 2006 [14]. Regional variation in regulatory expectations is also reflected in the slight differences between the ICH regions in terms of recommendations in the M3 guideline, eg, in the United States, an extended single-dose toxicity study (rather than a 2-week study) can support single-dose human trials, and clinical studies of less than 14 days may be supported with toxicity studies of the same duration as the proposed clinical study [8].

The FDA has initiated a process to require sponsors to submit documents by electronic format, beginning no earlier than 24 months after the FDA issues final guidance specifying an electronic submission format (*Providing Regulatory Submissions in Electronic Format – Submissions Under Section 745A(a) of the Federal Food, Drug and Cosmetics Act, 2014*) [15]. As part of this process, recent guidance, *Providing Regulatory Submissions in Electronic Format – Standardized Study Data, 2014* [16] informs organizations of the requested standards for presentation of nonclinical data. The intent of this guidance is to allow FDA reviewers to improve the data review of submissions by ensuring that all sponsors conform to data and terminology standards. This will permit cohesive assessment of data across programs from different submissions and potentially allow for the pooling of data to aid in high-level safety and efficacy assessments. The data standards adopted in the guidance document are the Clinical Data Interchange Standards Consortium (CDISC), which has developed data domain-specific standards or platforms, including the Standard Exchange of Nonclinical Data (SEND), which is, of course, particularly pertinent to this chapter. Each platform allows for individual studies, down to discrete animal data, to be evaluated in a standardized format. There are several vendors offering SEND-compatible software for purchase or the ability to utilize their services for submissions. The CDISC provides excellent resources online (http://www.cdisc.org/CDISC-Vision-and-Mission) with more information. General toxicology studies and carcinogenicity studies that initiate after December 17, 2016 will be required to be submitted in these formats for NDA submissions. For new INDs this format will be required for studies that initiate after December 17, 2017. Other types of pharmacology and toxicology studies will be required to meet these standards in the future. It is suggested that an End of Phase II meeting with the FDA is an appropriate time to discuss the study data standardization plan for NDA submissions. The Japanese regulatory authority, the Pharmaceutical and Medical Devices Agency (PMDA), does not have a current mandate for submission of nonclinical data in the SEND format, but will likely follow a similar procedure in the near future.

With regard to the compliance expectations for the nonclinical safety data to be used in regulatory submissions, the Organization for Economic Cooperation and Development (OECD) has adopted a procedure [Mutual Acceptance of Data (MAD)] for monitoring GLP compliance through government inspection and study audits, as well as a framework for international liaison among monitoring and data-receiving authorities (http://www.oecd.org/env/ehs/mutualacceptanceofdata mad.htm). The OECD Principles of Good Laboratory Practice, created in the context of harmonizing the testing procedures for MAD, set out managerial concepts covering the organization of test facilities and the conditions under which preclinical safety studies are conducted. In addition to OECD member states, nonmember-adherent states that have verified compliance of their laboratories with GLP requirements, using OECD-agreed procedures, may benefit from the agreement. Adherence to these requirements results in the confident interchange of study data generated in different countries, with associated economic and regulatory benefits.

Finally, several recent reviews and book chapters that outline the requirements for preclinical toxicology studies may also be of use in interpreting regulatory guidelines and expectations. These documents include discussion of biotherapeutics [17], oncology drugs [18,19], exploratory INDs/CTAs [20], and IND-enabling programs in general [21], with a 2008 multiauthor volume being an excellent resource on preclinical safety evaluation of biopharmaceuticals [22]. The recently published *Nonclinical Safety Assessment. A Guide to International Pharmaceutical Regulations* (2013) provides information on regulatory requirements for clinical trials and approval of drug candidates in a broad range of countries, as well as details on study designs [10].

Preparation of the IND Submission

The preparation of an IND submission requires the close collaboration of a team comprising scientists, individuals familiar with regulatory affairs, and project managers charged with authoring and compiling the various components of the dossier in accordance with a strategy designed to achieve regulatory approval with minimum delay. In the case of small or virtual companies, it is possible to contract out the various pieces to experienced contract research organizations (CROs).

Prior to starting to write the technical sections, a thorough review of all study reports and laboratory notebooks that have been generated for the program is valuable. Organizing reports into pharmacology, pharmacokinetic, and toxicology files helps to shape the outlines for the various sections in the IND dossier. All reports documenting nonclinical findings, potentially keys to understanding human safety, should be included in the submission, regardless of GLP compliance. These documents would include results of in vitro screening assays and in vivo exploratory toxicology studies, but in the case of the latter, only those studies that produced findings different than those seen in the GLP-compliant definitive toxicology studies need be included.

When crafting the discussion of in vivo studies, there is an order recommended by the FDA for animal species:

mouse, rat, hamster, other rodents, rabbit, dog, monkey, other nonrodent mammals, and nonmammals with discussion of findings in males preceding those in females [5]. Information on adult animals should precede that on juvenile or geriatric animals (if available). The routes of administration also have a standard order of presentation: oral, intravenous (IV), intramuscular (IM), intraperitoneal (IP), subcutaneous, inhalation, topical, and other in vivo and in vitro. In terms of order of studies discussed, pilot or exploratory studies should precede the definitive GLP-compliant studies and single-dose study results should come before multiple-dose studies with data presented as mg/kg doses (rather than for body surface area). The detail presented in each summary section is determined by the depth or duration of the study. For example, a brief summary can accompany an exploratory study with few endpoints, whereas a GLP-compliant study with numerous endpoints including clinical pathology and histology data would be more comprehensive [5].

Traditionally, INDs and other FIH-enabling dossiers have been submitted to the FDA and other regulatory agencies, respectively, as very large paper compendia, often requiring transport in large vehicles to the offices of the regulatory agency. In recent years, companies have chosen to file the submission electronically as an electronic or eIND, but this is becoming a mandatory mode of submission as the FDA's 2014 initiative is implemented (see earlier) with the paper submission becoming obsolete. If you choose not to file electronically, the sponsor can now provide the "paper" filing on CD format, rather than printing out the materials. There are CROs that can assist with paper or electronic filings if the expertise is lacking at the sponsor company. The mode of the submission will not change the content of what is included.

Responsibility within the sponsor company for preparation of the components of the IND dossier depends, to some extent, on the resources of the company, but can generally be allocated as in Table 8.2.

Ideally, the primary NCO author is a scientist with experience in toxicology and/or toxicokinetics/ADME (absorption, distribution, metabolism, elimination), and knowledge of the regulatory strategy around the nonclinical components of an IND dossier. Of course, in a smaller-sized company, the entire nonclinical strategy may be handled by a single individual familiar with the pharmacology, pharmacokinetics, and toxicology of the candidate compounds, and, indeed, he or she may also be called on to manage everything from the production of study reports at CROs to the formatting of the documents in the dossier. A close working relationship between the nonclinical and clinical teams will ensure the appropriate clinical starting dose (see Section 4), the dose-escalation strategy, and the projected clinically efficacious dose are supported by the nonclinical toxicology

TABLE 8.2 Components of, and Responsibilities for, Authoring the IND (With Toxicology-Related Components Highlighted)

Table of Contents	Purpose	Author Responsibility
Executive summary	Target validation (for targeted therapy)	Project team leader/scientific officer
Nonclinical overview	**Scientific rationale and summary of all nonclinical data**	**Designated nonclinical scientist(s) (primarily a toxicologist, with support from pharmacologist and ADME expert)**
Clinical overview	Synthesis of clinical program and any available study data	Clinical Operations
Chemistry	Physicochemical data Synthesis and Scale-up	Chemist
Chemistry, manufacturing and controls (CMC)	Quality profile (impurity profile) Formulations and Accelerated stability Analytical methodology	CMC specialist
Pharmacology	In vitro Biochemical Activity In vivo efficacy Safety pharmacology	Pharmacologist/**toxicologist**
Pharmacokinetics and drug metabolism	PK, ADME, preliminary metabolite identification, clinical dosing	Drug metabolism/PK scientist
Toxicology	**In vitro cytotoxicity** **In vivo exploratory studies** **In vivo GLP-compliant single and repeat-dose studies** **Genetic toxicology** **Safety margin calculations**	**Toxicologist**
Clinical plan	Overview of proposed program	Clinical operations
Investigator's brochure	A compilation of all relevant information clinical sites/Directors need for the trial	Clinical operations

program. This collaboration should also extend to experts in regulatory affairs to ensure that nonclinical and clinical programs are consistent with regulatory expectations in the region where the FIH studies will be conducted. In addition to ensuring that the toxicology studies are of appropriate design and duration, it is important that the nonclinical toxicologist confirm that the appropriate coverage for the projected clinical exposure is established in the animal studies. To ensure a speedy path to IND submission, this communication between the nonclinical scientists and the clinical scientists on the project team should start well in advance of the planned date for finalizing the IND submission and should continue throughout the later stages of the pre-IND phase of drug development up to completion of the nonclinical components of the IND dossier. This collaboration should include the generation of a timeline of critical activities from planning of the definitive toxicology studies that will support the clinical plan to the finalization of the NCO (see later), and its incorporation into the IND dossier and submission of the IND application. A formal "IND/NCO Kick-off Meeting," convened at the start of the rate-limiting toxicology/nonclinical study, is a useful forum for the project team to establish agreement on expectations about the content of the various nonclinical sections of the NCO, identification of individual responsibilities of project team members and/or those representing CROs conducting work in support of the program, and the overall timeline to completion of the NCO and the whole IND dossier. Attendance at this meeting can be limited to a subset of the overall project team, eg, the individuals responsible for coordinating the pharmacology, pharmacokinetic, and toxicology studies (essentially, the project team representatives for these disciplines), the regulatory affairs representative, the project team leader, and project manager; depending on the size of the company, this can be as few as three or four individuals. The timeline to IND submission will be driven by several factors specific to the sponsor company, at least some of which include the date when the last toxicology study to be included in the IND (the "rate-limiting toxicology study") is completed, where this and other nonclinical studies are to be conducted (in-house vs. outsourced to a CRO), the preferred date for starting the FIH clinical trial, the level of resources available for the project, etc. However, once identified at the NCO kick-off meeting, every effort should be made by team members to comply with agreed-on deadlines and deliverables. Such advance planning and diligent execution will greatly increase the likelihood of timely delivery of a cogent and complete nonclinical dossier that successfully supports the FIH clinical trial.

II. TOXICOLOGICAL STUDIES AND IND APPLICATION, AND FIRST IN-HUMAN CLINICAL TRIAL

In summary, the nonclinical toxicology, pharmacology, and pharmacokinetic information supporting the initial clinical dosing is presented in the IND/CTA dossier as an integrated NCO (Section 2.4) of the CTD, the format and content of which is clearly outlined in the ICH M4S(R2) guideline. In drafting the NCO, sponsors should also consider other ICH and regional guidance produced by local regulatory authorities. While the generation of suitable data to ensure the safety of clinical subjects is of prime importance in the planning and conduct of nonclinical toxicology studies, the presentation of these data as a coherent, well-argued case, conforming to local regulatory expectations, will likely ensure regulatory approval in a timely manner.

THE DRUG DEVELOPMENT PIPELINE

In the drug discovery process, numerous chemical series are often assessed prior to the identification of "hits" against a desired target. The same process is true with development of biologic drugs, as modified proteins and antibodies are screened to find the optimal candidate. This selection process often takes months to years to identify the lead series for drug development, followed by selection of the clinical candidate. A thorough review of the process can be found in Chapter 2 of this book.

Once the lead series is selected, the work of the toxicologist begins in earnest. Selection of the optimal drug candidate is often determined by the least toxic compound with substantial efficacy demonstrated in in vitro and in vivo studies; thus the evaluation of the toxicity of early candidates is important in allocation of resources for further drug development. It is often at the stage of lead selection that a project team is formed to determine the characteristics for an optimal compound, and input from the toxicologist, pharmacologist, and pharmacokineticist, as well as early clinical input, should shape the decisions leading to selection of the optimal candidate. A thorough review of the lead molecules for the desired drug properties will be based on the particular therapeutic indication(s) and medical needs, with the selection of the best compound from the standpoint of safety and efficacy being the ultimate goal.

Early Discovery Studies and Their Presentation in the NCO

In the screening stage for small molecule leads, numerous in vitro assays will be conducted. These include assessments of cytotoxicity [23], off-target screens that may include receptors and enzymes, specific screens related to the target (ie, evaluating the effects of exaggerated pharmacology), and an examination of metabolic stability and potential interactions with CYP450 isozymes. Other screens can be included as warranted by the individual program. In the case of biotherapeutics, toxicity is often an extension of the pharmacology, making selection of an appropriate species key to the in vivo toxicity testing strategy. As outlined in ICH S6(R1), a relevant species is one in which the test material is pharmacologically active. Standard rodent and nonrodent general toxicity studies must be completed if both species are pharmacologically relevant. In the case of some monoclonal antibody candidates, only nonhuman primates may be pharmacologically relevant, with target expression and binding similar to human cells or tissue. In such cases the toxicity program may feature only the nonhuman primate.

Once a compound is selected, in vivo exploratory studies may begin. These may encompass short-term evaluations (5–7 days) in a rodent with escalating or fixed doses of the drug. Study endpoints typically include effects on body weight, clinical pathology, necropsy findings, and histopathology on a limited panel of tissues. The compound should be administered by the intended clinical route, although the formulation administered may be different from that which will be used for the marketed drug product. Early formulations are designed to be as simple as possible, consistent with the need to provide adequate solubility allowing robust examination of the safety profile in vivo. Gad and colleagues have compiled useful information about acceptable vehicles and their potential toxicities [24]. In the case of some biologics where nonhuman primates are the only relevant species, it may be impractical to conduct exploratory toxicity studies. In such cases toxicity endpoints could be added to pharmacology studies.

A dose-escalation study in a nonrodent species is often conducted on the most promising candidates. Such a study requires a small number of (usually) non-naïve animals (1 or 2/sex) and involves increasing doses of the test compound in the same animals following a washout period. After each dose, clinical pathology and pharmacokinetic data can be collected, with the animals being returned to the colony at the end of the study. These initial exploratory studies provide important safety information for a series of compounds and can help triage leads for further examination. Although the primary purpose of these studies is to help select doses for future pivotal toxicology studies, findings may need to be reported in the NCO if they differ from those in the subsequent pivotal studies. In that case, reports for these exploratory studies will need to be prepared for possible inclusion in the IND submission.

IND/FIH-enabling Studies

The type of clinical trial planned for the initial administration of human subjects with a drug candidate will impact the nature of the pivotal nonclinical toxicology program. Collaboration with clinical colleagues and/or external consultants is critical to determine the program goals, and therefore the nonclinical toxicology strategy for FIH studies. Some important questions that the project team should discuss include: Is this a new class of drugs with completely unknown human toxicity, or is class-specific toxicity expected and generally understood? Will healthy volunteers or patients be used for the Phase I program? What are the durations of the trials for Phase I development? Will the trials involve single and multiple doses? Is there an acceptable product formulation or will it be concurrently developed with the nonclinical studies? Will subjects be fed or fasted with drug administration? Are there concomitant medications that could impact the PK? All these questions will help shape the design of the nonclinical program.

The FIH programs supported by the ICH guidance documents M3(R2) and M4 include traditional INDs and exploratory INDs. The entire suite of studies described later is required for most traditional IND applications. For an exploratory IND, however, the content can be more limited. Exploratory INDs involve limited human exposure, have no therapeutic intent, and are not intended to examine clinical tolerability [8,20]. The nonclinical supporting data that are appropriate in these situations will be dependent on the extent of proposed human exposure, both with respect to the maximum clinical dose used and the duration of dosing. In this situation, a pre-IND meeting with the FDA is recommended to discuss the proposed plans and studies.

Advancement of the FIH Candidate—The Core IND-enabling Studies

Once the "trigger is pulled" for a new clinical program, the project team enters a very busy phase in preparation for the IND submission. The analytical scientists and chemists will commence manufacture of the active pharmaceutical ingredient (API) for the nonclinical safety pharmacology and toxicology studies. There is a regulatory expectation that the core battery of safety pharmacology and toxicity studies conducted to support clinical trials will be conducted to GLP standards (as specified by US federal regulations 21 CFR 58.105). The test article may be manufactured to GMP standards, and the API used in toxicology studies should be representative of that anticipated for use in clinical trials. In general, it is preferable to have a higher level of impurities in the API used in the general toxicology studies, provided that the purity of the API is greater than 95%. If the material to be used in the clinical studies has a higher impurity profile than that used in the toxicology studies, a bridging study may be required to qualify impurities present at higher levels than in the lot used for

the core nonclinical studies. Such qualification studies are normally performed on rodents, and may require a dosing period of 2 weeks to 3 months, depending on the intended duration of clinical treatment [25].

All material used in the safety pharmacology and toxicology studies must be evaluated for stability and potency under the conditions of use. The stability data can be generated in an on-going manner to cover the final day of the in-life phase of animal studies. This stability information would then be included in all final study reports. In addition, the potency of the test article must be verified in all studies. The actual dose formulation samples are analyzed to confirm the potency and stability of the compound, thus verifying that the animals received the intended dose in the study.

Safety Pharmacology Section

As a component of the pharmacology section of the NCO, the safety pharmacology data are presented following those covering primary pharmacology, per the ICH M4 guideline. Safety Pharmacology evaluates the critical organ systems of the body, including the central nervous, cardiovascular, and the respiratory systems. Secondary pharmacodynamic assessments are included at the start of this section. These assays are most often conducted in an in vitro fashion and comprise receptor-binding assays studying inhibition of a panel of biologically significant targets (Table 8.3). While details of the panels may vary depending on the therapeutic target, a standard baseline panel is available commercially. Example data from a screening battery assessing binding of a candidate drug to a number of CNS receptors are shown in the following, with the degree to which binding of control substrates to a series of key "off-target" CNS receptors is inhibited by the presence of the drug candidate was determined. Further study of the interaction of the candidate drug with particular targets, such as determination of IC50 or K_i values, is warranted if screening data indicate that presence of the drug candidate results

TABLE 8.3   Example of an Off-Target Receptor Screen

Receptor	Specific Binding (% Inhibition of Control)	IC_{50} (μM)	K_i (μM)
Dopamine D_1 (antagonist)	7	–	–
Dopamine D_2 (agonist)	23	–	–
Dopamine D_3 (antagonist)	39	–	–
Monoamine oxidase-A	0	–	–
5-HT$_{1A}$ (agonist)	33	–	–
5-HT$_{2B}$ (agonist)	59[a]	3.6	3.2
5-HT$_3$ (antagonist)	−3	–	–

The drug candidate was tested at a concentration of 10 μM in all screens.
[a]>50% inhibition with test compound.

in ≥50% inhibition of binding of the control substrate to the target. In the following example, the K_i for the drug candidate at the 5-HT$_{2B}$ receptor was about 600-fold higher than the K_i of the drug against its intended target and about 30-fold higher than the projected efficacious drug concentration in human. This information can be utilized within the NCO to provide a perspective on the risk of secondary or off-target pharmacodynamic effects being observed at clinically relevant concentrations of the drug candidate.

There is a core battery of GLP-compliant studies that is required to evaluate the critical organ systems of the nervous, cardiovascular, and pulmonary systems, and these should generally be conducted before initiation of clinical studies. Safety pharmacology and pharmacodynamic studies are defined in the ICH S7A and S7B guidance [26,27]. While these studies may be conducted in a toxicology department, it is important to note that doses used are in the pharmacological rather than potentially toxicological range. A comprehensive review of safety pharmacology studies is provided by Baird, Gauvin, and Dalton in Chapter 7 of this book.

Adverse findings in the safety pharmacology studies may slow or halt a development program, so it is wise to initiate these studies in a timely fashion. When warranted, supplemental and follow-up safety pharmacology studies can be conducted on an as-needed basis later in clinical development, with the caveat that, if substantial adverse effects to a critical organ system are observed during the initial safety assessment, additional safety pharmacology studies should be included in the nonclinical dossier. Consideration should be given to inclusion of in vivo evaluations as add-ons to general toxicity studies, to the extent feasible, in order to reduce animal use [8]. In the case of evaluation of biologics, standalone safety pharmacology studies are not conducted routinely unless there are potential cardiovascular or CNS risks associated with the pharmacological target, per the ICH S6 guidance [28]. Any add-on safety pharmacology assessments should be performed to the same rigor as would be expected in standalone safety pharmacology studies. In addition, primary pharmacodynamic studies (in vivo and/or in vitro) intended to investigate the mode of action and/or effects of a drug candidate in relation to its desired therapeutic target are included, but are not required to be GLP-compliant [8]. In the case of biologics, species selection is critical to confirm effects of exaggerated pharmacology [28]. The results will be included in the NCO for the overall safety evaluation of the new molecular entity, as well as in Section 2.6.2 (Pharmacology Written Summary) of the dossier.

The CNS is evaluated in a functional observation battery (FOB) or modified Irwin's assay in the mouse or rat [29]. These screening assays are a series of tests in rodents that include home-cage and open-field observations, neuromuscular and sensorimotor tests, and physiologic measures. They evaluate arousal, rearing, reactivity, gait, posture, responses, foot splay, grip strength, and excretions [30,31]. The ICH S7A guidance outlines particulars for the experiments [26]. A positive outcome in any of these experiments would necessitate determination of the safety margin and may warrant follow-up studies to further evaluate the results.

The cardiovascular system is assessed in two ways: in vitro in a hERG screen and in vivo in a conscious, telemeterized nonrodent species, usually dog [26,27]. The hERG (human ether-à-go-go-related gene) screen evaluates the potassium-channel current in a single-cell patch clamp assay. The S7B guidance outlines requirements for this assay [27]. The in vivo assessment of the cardiovascular system includes arterial blood pressure and electrocardiogram monitored by telemetry, often in beagle dogs. Occasionally other nonrodent species, such as the mini-pig are used for these investigations due to similarities with human cardiac and respiratory architecture. In some facilities, the assessment of respiratory function can also be conducted concurrently in dogs, with endpoints including respiratory rate, tidal volume, and minute volume in conscious animals.

The findings from the safety pharmacology studies are integrated in the NCO, and may, with results of the general toxicity studies, aid in the defining any adverse events. For example, emesis noted in a dog's general toxicity study may correlate with central nervous system toxicity and this could be noted in the rodent CNS battery. These results often add information that may not be garnered in traditional toxicology studies and can provide insight into target organs for toxicity.

Pharmacokinetics

Demonstration of exposure of animals to the test article is a critical component of toxicology studies. It is important to gain information on the relationships between dose and exposure and the impact of repeated dosing on exposure. In general, only a limited blood-sampling schedule is employed to assess drug exposure in toxicology studies, and the usual toxicokinetic (TK) parameters reported include C_{max}, T_{max}, and AUC. The pharmacokinetics of the drug candidate following single-dose administration to the intended toxicology species should be assessed before initiation of the in vivo toxicology program. Although such studies are usually conducted following a single-dose paradigm at doses assumed to be subtoxicological, information from the pharmacokinetic studies is important for the selection of dose levels for future toxicology studies. In addition, these studies provide information on the design of the TK sampling schedule to be employed and the justification for the species selected for the toxicology program. Assessment of the degree of binding of the drug candidate to plasma proteins, and of its metabolism during incubation in vitro with hepatic microsomes or hepatocytes from nonclinical species and human, are expected for nonbiologic drugs prior to the initial clinical study [32]. For biotherapeutic drug candidates, an assessment of antidrug antibodies (ADA) is also performed since many such candidates are "humanized" or human in origin, and may appear foreign to the test species, thus eliciting an immunological response and neutralizing the activity of the molecule. The presence of ADA can impact target exposure to the candidate drug; understanding of this is important to the interpretation of the studies. A pharmacokineticist or drug metabolism expert will normally serve as the project team resource for generating TK and ADA data. In the absence of in-house expertise, CROs have personnel to assist in designing appropriate studies. These data can be used to compare projected metabolites in humans and animals and for determining if any additional testing is warranted [5]. If substantial differences in the routes of metabolism are observed across species in vitro, especially if potential human metabolites are not generated by the proposed toxicology species, alternate species should be considered.

Recognition of the importance of drug metabolites in the assessment of safety of drug candidates has evolved through much scientific discussion over the past 10 years or so, leading to a number of publications from industry, academia, and regulators. Metabolites in Safety Testing (MIST), as the topic has become known, evolved from an initial concept paper in 2002 [33], with the FDA issuing a guidance on the subject in 2008 [34]; most recently, the ICH M3(R2) guidance of 2010 addressed the topic [8]. The ability to identify metabolites and then demonstrate that their potential risk to humans has been adequately characterized, either through their exposure in toxicology species or, if this does not occur, by direct safety assessment of a metabolite molecule, remains the central theme of this work. MIST has shown itself to be a complex issue with no simple solutions to providing absolute assurance of drug safety. FDA guidance on Safety Testing of Drug Metabolites [34] states that, in general, equal circulating concentrations of major metabolites (10% or greater of parent) is sufficient to qualify a metabolite for safety if it is found in one of the standard species administered the parent drug during the course of standard toxicology studies to support clinical trials as outlined in the ICH M3 guidance. Following much debate around the practical considerations associated with the definition of "10% or greater of parent," this point has been clarified in the ICH M3 (R2) guidance [8]. This document states that *"nonclinical characterization of a human metabolite(s) is only warranted when that metabolite(s) is observed at exposures greater than 10 percent of total drug-related exposure and at significantly greater levels in humans than the maximum exposure seen in the toxicity studies."*

The first question to consider is whether a given metabolite is likely to be present at a significant level in man and, if so, is it likely to be present at sufficient levels within the toxicology species to support the human exposure? In addition to assessing the abundance of metabolites to determine if human safety is adequately supported, structural considerations can provide other important information. The structure of a metabolite will indicate if it is likely to contribute to the desired or primary pharmacological response and is therefore important for PK/PD considerations. Structural alerts for known reactive moieties or toxicophores may flag a specific safety concern for the compound. Definitive data on the total metabolite profile of a novel drug candidate in humans can only be gained from an in vivo study in which radiolabeled compound is administered and blood/plasma and excreta samples are collected to profile and quantitate radioactive components. In advance of this, data can be obtained from in vitro human and animal studies, and this level of information would normally be expected prior to entry of the candidate drug into clinical trials. Example decision trees for assessment of metabolite safety through drug discovery and development have been proposed [35].

Toxicology

The overarching purpose of toxicology studies conducted in animals is to provide an assessment or prediction of likely toxicities in humans, as well as to establish adequate safety margins supporting the safety of the proposed clinical trial. The overall design and composition of a safety program appropriate to support entry of a small molecule drug candidate into clinical trials is generally agreed and understood and is outlined in some detail in the recent ICH M3 guidance [8]. The situation is more complicated for biological drug candidates where considerations of species differences in physiological processes and pathways and target expression become critical. The increased target specificity, effector function, and (generally) half-life associated with biological candidates influence the design and timing of toxicology studies. The recent ICH S6 guidance *Preclinical Safety Evaluation of Biotechnology-Derived Pharmaceuticals* provides greater insight and reflects the different considerations for toxicology study design for such candidates versus small molecules [28]. Pre-IND/scientific advice discussions with regulatory authorities may be advisable, especially in cases where pertinent epitopes are present only in a single species (such as primate). In some biologic cases, animal models of disease can replace a second toxicology species. In addition, the reader is referred to a recent excellent review on the challenges of general safety evaluations of biologics compared to small molecules [22].

The toxicology package for an IND dossier will include repeat-dose studies usually of 14–28 days duration, though not necessarily single-dose studies, in compliance with the recent update of the ICH M3 guidance on study duration. Acute toxicity may be evaluated after the initial dose(s). The study types are partially determined by the indication. In addition to the general toxicology studies, evaluation of genotoxicity and, with some routes of administration, local tolerance studies are included for small-molecule drug development. In the case of biotherapeutics, some form of immunotoxicity assessment may be required (over and above measurement of ADA discussed earlier). This is particularly important in the case of agents intended to have an immunomodulatory mechanism of action; studies may include a cytokine release assay, Fc receptor binding, and complement binding assays. More comprehensive evaluations of reproductive and developmental toxicity, immunotoxicity, and carcinogenicity are included in the final NDA submission.

Limit doses for acute, subchronic, and chronic toxicity studies of 1000 mg/kg/day for rodents and nonrodents are considered appropriate in all cases, except when a dose of 1000 mg/kg/day does not result in a mean exposure margin of 10-fold greater than the clinical exposure, or the clinical dose exceeds 1 g per day. In these cases, the doses in the toxicity studies should be limited by a 10-fold exposure margin or a dose of 2000 mg/kg/day or the maximum feasible dose (MFD), whichever is lower [8]. In those rare situations in which the dose of 2000 mg/kg/day results in an exposure that is less than the projected clinical dose, a higher dose up to the MFD can be considered [8].

Single-Dose Acute Studies

These GLP-compliant studies should adhere to applicable ICH and regional authority guidelines. The rat and dog are often selected as the rodent and nonrodent toxicology species, respectively. They are the historical species of choice for small-molecule drug development, assuming no findings from exploratory studies preclude their use. Evaluation of the in vitro metabolism of the drug candidate in these species and the plasma-protein binding in comparison to human samples should give an indication of their relevance for toxicology studies. If the PK or other ADME parameter warrants a different species, the mouse, monkey, and pig are suitable alternatives. In the case of biologics, there is often species specificity for drug pharmacological activity, and antidrug antibodies can prevent a true assessment of an agent's activity in nonrelevant species. Primates are often the species of choice for evaluation of biologics. Considerations of metabolism are not relevant for species selection in the case of biologic agents; however, assessment of TK is as essential as for small molecules.

In the single-dose acute toxicity studies, effects that may be clinically relevant can be adequately characterized using doses up to the maximum tolerated dose (MTD) [8]. It is not essential to demonstrate the MTD in every study. Other equally appropriate limiting doses include those that achieve large exposure multiples or saturation of exposure or use the maximum feasible dose (MFD) [8]. For a drug candidate intended for clinical administration via the intravenous route, no additional routes of administration need to be tested in nonclinical studies. However, for any other route, the intravenous route must also be evaluated in MTD studies to allow for maximal exposure potential.

The objectives of these studies are to determine the acute toxicity, the TK profile, and the MTD of the test article following a single administration to the nonclinical species. The reversibility of any observed changes can be assessed following a 14-day recovery period. During the study, animals are routinely evaluated for effects on clinical condition, body weight, food consumption, and clinical pathology parameters. Additional endpoints can be added to standard panels depending on target organs of toxicity. The main study animals are euthanized at the end of the dosing period, while animals in the recovery group are sacrificed following a 14-day observation period and subjected to a complete necropsy examination, including collection of tissues for histological evaluation.

As noted in the recent update to the ICH M3 guidance, while acute toxicity information has historically been obtained from specific single-dose studies, it may also be obtained from appropriately conducted dose-escalation studies or short-duration dose range-finding studies that define a maximum tolerated dose, and do not have lethality as a required endpoint [8,9]. Such data can be obtained from non GLP-compliant studies if clinical administration is supported by the appropriate GLP-compliant repeat-dose studies.

Repeat-Dose Studies

The objectives of these studies are to determine the subchronic toxicity and any differences in the TK profile following 14–28 days of daily administration compared to single administration. The reversibility of any observed changes can be assessed, or indications of reversibility detected, following a recovery period of appropriate duration. These studies are critical for establishing the NOAEL doses used in the maximum recommended starting dose (MRSD) calculations for clinical studies. The maximum exposure achieved should be at least 10-fold greater than that which is predicted to be efficacious in humans. During the study conduct, animals are routinely evaluated for effects on clinical condition, body weight, food consumption, and clinical pathology. Additional endpoints can be added to standard panels depending on target organs of toxicity previously identified or considered likely. The main study animals are euthanized at the end of the dosing period, while recovery animals are sacrificed following an appropriate observation period (based on the half-life of the drug candidate) and subjected to a complete necropsy examination. If target organs are identified, those tissues can be examined in the lower-dose groups to determine the NOAEL dose. The rodent and non-rodent NOAELs are determined relative to significant drug-related study findings at the lowest-observed-adverse-effect-level (LOAEL).

Genotoxicity Studies

The genotoxicity of a novel compound should be assessed in the standard battery of assays recommended by the FDA guidelines and the ICH S2 guidance for a small molecule [25]. The newly revised ICH guidance document has streamlined the testing requirements for registration. Biologics do not routinely require assessment of genotoxicity [22]. The bacterial mutagenicity assay, with an assessment of clastogenicity, such as the mouse lymphoma assay or chromosomal aberration assays with human peripheral blood lymphocytes (PBLs), may comprise the in vitro assessment. If genotoxicity endpoints are to be incorporated into a general toxicity study, an appropriate maximum dose should be selected based on an MFD, MTD, or the limit dose [8]. A more comprehensive review of genotoxicity studies is provided in Chapter 5.

In addition to evaluation of the parent molecule for genotoxicity, a thorough assessment of any impurity that may be genotoxic is also required, based on the ICH M7 guidance *Assessment and Control of DNA Reactive (Mutagenic) Impurities in Pharmaceuticals to Limit Potential Carcinogenic Risk* [36]. Major degradant products of chemical synthesis/impurities must be evaluated. Known mutagenic impurities require derivation of an acceptable intake (AI) value. The M7(R1) document provides examples of major impurities for which sufficient data exist to warrant compound specific risk assessments, rather than a threshold of toxicological concern approach. The general methods for deriving the AIs are provided in the M7(R1) document, with additional information in the ICHQ3A(R2) and Q3B(R2) documents [37,38]. This guidance provides limits for the qualification and control of the majority of impurities in drug substances (Q3A) and drug product (Q3B). DNA reactive impurities are excluded from this guidance but covered in the M7(R1) guidance.

Local Tolerance

Included in the submission of an IND application for a parenteral drug candidate is information as to any adverse effects seen at the site of injection or on dermal application. A brief summary of all noted effects should be included in a standalone section of the NCO.

Immunotoxicity

Often at the stage of IND submission, no specific studies have been conducted to assess the immunotoxic potential of a new candidate drug. As components of the routine subchronic toxicology studies, the organs of the immune system including lymph nodes, spleen, and thymus should be grossly evaluated and weighed. Assuming no findings are noted in these tissues, no additional studies are required, but if routine toxicity studies yield immunotoxicity findings additional studies should be conducted. These could include a more comprehensive assessment of cell-mediated immunity, humoral immunity, or delayed-type hypersensitivity [39]. Biologics, which often act to modulate the immune system, should be assessed for antidrug antibodies. In addition, new guidance from the EMA [13] discusses assessment of the potential for cytokine storms and unanticipated greater receptor affinity/activation in human studies compared to primates.

Juvenile Animals

The increased focus on the use of pediatric patients in clinical trials requires the inclusion of juvenile toxicity endpoints at an earlier stage of the nonclinical development strategy. Therefore a plan for conducting juvenile animal studies, or including juvenile animals in standard general toxicology studies, should be developed early in the drug development program. While most NMEs will require studies in juvenile animals to be completed by the time of registration, there are certain circumstances when you may ask for an exemption. This would include, for example, drugs granted orphan drug status, or drugs being developed only for geriatric diseases. A Pediatric Study Plan in the United States [40], or a Pediatric Investigation Plan (PIP) in the EU, is developed and provided to the regulatory authorities following an End of Phase 2 Meeting.

Summary

The ICH M3 and S6 guidance provide the outline for study designs that will generate the appropriate data to form the basis of a risk assessment (the NCO) to support the initial clinical trials. As such, we should pay particular attention to several key subsections in the design of the toxicity studies supporting a particular clinical plan. For example, selection of the high dose to be used in the toxicity studies, the recommended duration of repeated-dose toxicity studies, and the appropriate pharmacology and toxicology programs required to support a variety of exploratory clinical trials are particularly important elements of the M3(R2) guidance updated in 2010 [8]. In addition, the reader may find the ICH Q&A guidance useful, which can found on the ICH website (http://www.ich.org/fileadmin/Public_Web_Site/ICH_Products/Guidelines/Multidisciplinary/M3_R2/Q_As/M3_R2_Q_AStep4.pdf), on implementation of the various components of M3 in the form of questions and answers on key issues identified by the various contributors to ICH.

PRESENTATION OF THE NONCLINICAL PACKAGE

As discussed earlier, overviews of nonclinical data are included in several locations in the IND. The most comprehensive of these is the NCO, followed by the Investigator's Brochure (IB) and the clinical protocol. Once the NCO is complete, select text can be used to compile specific sections of the initial IB. For example, the toxicology section of the NCO (Section 2.4.4) can be used to populate the toxicology section of the IB (Section 5.3), with the majority of the content transferred directly. The Integrated Overview and Conclusions section of the NCO (Section 2.4.5) can be utilized as source material for generation of the IB summary section (Section 2) and for completion of the nonclinical summary section of the initial clinical protocol. Using the NCO as a source document ensures consistency of terminology and interpretation of nonclinical data across the NCO, IB, and Clinical Protocol—a clear advantage since, depending on the sponsor organization, different reviewers may be involved in review and approval of these documents. For these reasons, completion of at least a draft NCO may be wise even when the initial clinical study is planned to be conducted in Europe where an NCO is not a component of the CTA.

The Nonclinical Overview

As outlined in earlier parts of this chapter, the main function of the NCO is to clearly define the characteristics of the drug candidate as demonstrated in the nonclinical studies. The pharmacology, pharmacokinetics, and toxicology results should support the safety of the product, at least for the intended initial clinical studies. In order to meet this objective, sufficient detail must be presented around the biology/pharmacology of the candidate, its disposition and metabolism, and its safety in relevant nonclinical species at appropriate multiples of projected clinical therapeutic exposures. This necessitates presentation of not only the scope and outcomes of studies conducted in each of the nonclinical disciplines but also, and most importantly, integration of data and findings across studies and disciplines. Since study

reports will be included elsewhere in an IND submission (Module 4), or will be available to the regulatory authority reviewer (eg, the FDA Pharm/Tox reviewer) on request, details around the design and conduct of studies should be minimized in the NCO. Study results, where key to the overall study conclusion, should be presented within the text but, in general, the use of summary tables within the NCO is more appropriate for an overview document. The study design details can also be found in the individual study tabulated summaries.

When compiling the NCO it is important to keep in mind the main needs of the FDA pharm/tox reviewer, a key "customer" for your work. Fundamentally, the available data should permit a rigorous assessment of risk to the volunteers or patients enrolled in the initial clinical studies with the new drug candidate. Implicit in this goal is the understanding that the package submitted will contain all the component elements outlined by relevant regulatory guidelines. Questions to be kept in mind when compiling the NCO include, but are not necessarily limited to, the following: Do the nonclinical data support the proposed clinical trial in terms of dose/exposure duration via the intended clinical route of administration, and are the safety margins (calculated on the basis of achieved exposure in animal studies) reasonable, bearing in mind the adverse events identified in the toxicology species? Do such toxicities exhibit prodromal signs and/or could they be readily monitored in the clinic? To what extent is it understood whether potential toxicity is the result of interaction with the intended target (excessive pharmacology) or of interactions at off-target sites? To what extent are the PK and disposition of the drug candidate in the species used in toxicology studies believed to be predictive of human responses? Is the extent of exposure highly variable between animals and between species? Are there significant species differences in systemic protein binding? Are humans likely to be exposed to metabolites not produced in the toxicology species? Are there any particular concerns associated with the proposed clinical formulation or with drug substance impurities and/or degradants?

To achieve the objectives outlined earlier, it is important that the NCO should not just be a catalog of study summaries. Although information is broadly grouped into scientific subsections, such as pharmacology, pharmacokinetics, and toxicology, findings reported in one section should reference related findings in other subsections whenever reasonable to produce an *integrated overview* of the findings. This concept is routinely followed in toxicology study summaries where clinical signs may be related to biomarker changes and, finally, correlated with histological observations. A simple example of the extension of this principle into the NCO is provided by an observation of microscopic changes in the heart in rats in the high-dose group of a toxicology study. In this case it would clearly be useful and appropriate to relate these findings to results from broad-screen in vitro pharmacology studies (potential off-target pharmacology), with data from cardiovascular safety pharmacology studies (potential impact on blood pressure and/or heart rate) and, finally, to the apparent clinical safety margin based on exposure assessments and projected pharmacologically active dose in humans. In the case of the main findings defining the NOAEL doses in the toxicology studies (HNSTD/STD10—highest nonseverely toxic dose/ severely toxic dose in 10% of animals tested—generally used for oncology therapeutics), all information related to these findings or targets should be presented in the NCO in the form of a summary table. A separate section may provide a more detailed summary of information on identified target organs. However, not all findings or scientific linkages may be covered by findings defining the NOAEL doses, hence the importance of linkage to other sections of the NCO.

As indicated previously, the ICH M4S guidance indicates that the NCO should be organized into five main sections, namely: overview of the nonclinical testing strategy, pharmacology, pharmacokinetics, toxicology, integrated overview, and conclusions and, finally, list of literature references. To address all the areas of potential toxicological concern indicated in the guidance, it is reasonable, but not essential, to insert further subdivisions into an NCO template. A suggested example outline of a typical NCO for a small-molecule drug candidate is shown in the following. Several of the subsections included are topics specifically alluded to in the guidance text on content and structural format. Others are included in the suggested template as they can help to organize the text into a logical flow that tells a story and provides adequate details to satisfy regulatory expectations with respect to science and content.

The rest of this section will focus on a discussion of selected sections of the NCO that, in the opinion of the authors, provide clear examples of where integration of the range of nonclinical studies and findings is needed. Example text for these sections is provided. It is important to state that *these examples are included for illustration purposes only*, ie, to show how data from different sections or nonclinical disciplines may be integrated into the NCO; there is no intention to imply that the descriptions of actual findings and the arguments outlined in these examples represent best practices. Numbering of the sections is as it would be in the NCO.

Overview of Nonclinical Testing Strategy

As the title implies, this section should serve as the introduction to the NCO, encompassing contributions from the three major nonclinical disciplines

(pharmacology, pharmacokinetics, and toxicology), and outline the nonclinical testing strategy employed. It is important that the scope of the nonclinical studies performed be presented, including any deviations from normally anticipated standard assessments and study design, such as, for example, if specific safety pharmacology and genetic toxicology studies have not been performed (eg, the candidate is a monoclonal antibody). Generally, study data and conclusions should not be provided in this section. A description of the test article should be included and care should be taken to ensure consistency with the chemical name and form used in the appropriate section of Module 3 (Chemistry Manufacturing and Controls) within the submission and in the Investigator's Brochure.

The Overview section should be ordered to correspond to the presentation sequence of the NCO. Thus a high-level summary of the studies conducted to assess primary and secondary pharmacology, including a rationale for their performance, should be followed by an outline of the safety pharmacology studies and the program to evaluate the pharmacokinetics and metabolism of the candidate. The species, route, and duration of dosing in the toxicology studies should be justified briefly, in addition to an introduction to other toxicology assessments made, such as genetic toxicology. In addition, a comment on the GLP status of the studies submitted should be provided. For biotherapeutics the species selection should be justified by referring to data presented in the subsequent sections, such as general species-specific protein sequence, homology, and binding data, as compared to comparable human data. Reference should be made to data in subsequent sections that supports the pharmacological relevance/activity of the selected nonclinical toxicity species (ie, in vitro, ex vivo, and/or in vivo data). If a single species is used for toxicity testing (eg, cynomolgus monkey), provide the rationale and refer to the data presented in later sections that eliminated the possibility of a second relevant species.

In the case of an initial IND submission, the range of studies conducted will be limited. It is highly unlikely that, for example, reproductive or carcinogenicity studies will have been initiated or completed. It is reasonable to simply acknowledge this, either in the overview or within the toxicology section of the NCO. In some circumstances it may be useful to indicate within the overview that the sponsor is aware that, in accordance with the recommendations in the ICH M3 guideline, such studies will be required either before conducting larger clinical trials or before final approval of the drug. Situations in which such a course of action might be warranted are cases where known class-effect toxicities have been documented, or where the mechanism of action of the candidate may suggest increased cause for concern (eg, for carcinogenicity in the case of a drug targeting a component of the endocrine system, or phototoxicity in the case of a compound displaying high absorbance of UV light).

The following is an example of text that may be appropriate for the Overview section:

<The candidate> is <a potent and selective inverse agonist/competitive antagonist of the X receptor> under development for the treatment of <disease>. To support early clinical trials, in vitro and in vivo studies have been performed in animal models to evaluate the therapeutic and safety profiles of <the candidate>. All nonclinical studies were conducted using <the free base active moiety> as the test article.

To evaluate primary pharmacodynamics of <the candidate>, the following studies were conducted in vitro and in vivo. Secondary pharmacology was assessed by evaluating the binding potency of <the candidate> against a broad panel of receptors, transporters, enzymes, and ion channels in vitro. Safety pharmacology studies were conducted in vitro and in rats and dogs to assess potential effects on cardiovascular, respiratory, and neurological endpoints. An in vitro study was conducted to assess <the compound's> electrophysiological effects on human ether-à-go-go related gene (hERG) current.

The nonclinical pharmacokinetics and metabolism program was designed to characterize the in vivo and in vitro absorption, distribution, metabolism, and excretion (ADME) properties, and the pharmacokinetic/pharmacodynamic (PK/PD) relationship of <the candidate> to support the nonclinical safety evaluation and to assess their potential relevance to humans. The single-dose pharmacokinetics of <the candidate> following intravenous (IV) and oral administration was assessed in the toxicology species (rats and dogs). Data were obtained using a <validated liquid chromatography—mass spectrometry/mass spectrometry (LC–MS/MS) assay> to evaluate the toxicokinetics of the candidate following repeated-dose administration. Protein binding of <the candidate> was determined in rat, dog, and human plasma using equilibrium dialysis. Preliminary evaluation of the in vitro metabolism of <the candidate> was assessed following incubation in rat, dog, monkey, and human liver microsomes and hepatocytes. Although no pharmacokinetic drug interaction studies have been conducted in animals, <the candidate> was examined for effects on several drug-metabolizing enzyme activities in pooled human liver microsomes.

Due to species differences in protein binding, exposure multiples between animals and projected human values are calculated based on unbound drug concentrations. It is believed for this compound that unbound concentrations in plasma are in equilibrium with the available compound at the location of the intended drug target and that unbound plasma concentrations will drive interaction with biological targets, leading to pharmacological and possibly toxicological effects.

General toxicology was evaluated in studies up to <1 month> in duration following <oral> administration of the candidate to rats and dogs. The <oral route> of administration was selected for toxicology studies, and for the majority of safety pharmacology studies, since it is the intended route of clinical exposure. Rats and dogs were chosen as the nonclinical species based on the standard acceptance of these species in nonclinical toxicology studies and the demonstrated drug exposure in these species following <oral> drug administration. Nonpivotal (exploratory) studies used to support dose selection for the pivotal <1-month> studies included a dose-range-finding single-dose escalation study in <dogs> and <14-day repeat-dose studies in rats and dogs>. Genetic toxicity studies included the standard battery of bacterial mutagenicity and structural chromosome aberration assays in vitro, and evaluation of formation of micronuclei in bone marrow of rats in vivo. In the UV spectral analysis, <the candidate showed absorbance in the range of interest (290–700nm)>, suggesting that in vivo phototoxicity testing and/or appropriate precautions <may be> warranted prior to outpatient clinical trials.

Pharmacology

The objectives of this section are to outline the data that demonstrate the interaction of the candidate with the intended pharmacological target, to provide evidence of the specificity of this interaction, and to define the pharmacodynamic response. The section may be broken down into a description of studies performed in vitro and in vivo, the latter possibly having been conducted in animal models of the target disease (therapeutic indication). Details of the study methodology employed are not necessary if study reports are included with the submission. The section should summarize the primary pharmacology of the candidate, as well as its off-target or secondary pharmacology effects. Any such interactions may provide a rationale for observations made in the toxicology program and may provide insight as to potential risks in future clinical trials. It is important that a discussion of the pharmacodynamics of the candidate indicates which studies/models were used to derive projections for therapeutic concentrations in future clinical trials, especially if the discussion of safety margins in the toxicology section makes reference to projected therapeutic exposure in humans. Authors might consider the inclusion of a brief table summarizing the key pharmacological properties of the candidate, as shown in the following table.

In Vitro Assays

Receptor Binding Studies	Human K_i (nM)	Rat K_i (nM)	
μ Opioid Receptor	0.8	15.1	
κ Opioid Receptor	1.4	2.8	
δ Opioid Receptor	20	94	

Receptor Functional Studies

GTPγS Antagonism

μOpioid Receptor	0.34	0.13	
κ Opioid Receptor	0.3	0.2	
δ Opioid Receptor	6.6	6.1	

Schild Analysis	Slope	K_B	K_B/K_i
μOpioid Receptor	0.8	0.7	2
κ Opioid Receptor	0.96	0.4	1
δ Opioid Receptor	0.93	17	3

In Vivo Assays

Food Intake	Oral Dose (mg/kg)	% Decrease in 2-h Cumulative Food Intake Relative to Vehicle
Spontaneous Food Intake in Lean Rats	3	42
	10	69

Studies performed to assess the safety pharmacology of the candidate should follow this section. Where possible, results of in vivo studies should be considered in light of the in vitro data, especially where the latter might provide a mechanistic explanation for the former. For biotherapeutic programs (eg, mAbs) without an identified or known safety pharmacology signal or liability, safety pharmacology endpoints are typically incorporated into the design of the toxicity studies and the findings interpreted and discussed in an integrated fashion within the repeat-dose and target organ sections of Section 2.4.4. A short summary of the safety pharmacology endpoints measured, and findings obtained, should be provided in the safety pharmacology section.

Pharmacokinetics

In addition to a description of the main pharmacokinetic parameters determined for the candidate across the species used in toxicology studies, normally following IV and the proposed clinical route of drug administration, the section should contain an assessment of the distribution and metabolism of the compound; this may provide a context for the relevance of the toxicology species to humans and a means of extrapolating nonclinical safety endpoints to human safety. For a small molecule, topics of particular note in the context of relevance to other components of the NCO include plasma-protein binding, metabolite profiling across species (including human), and an assessment of the

potential for drug–drug interactions (DDI). Information from protein-binding studies will provide a means for comparing exposures associated with signs of toxicity across animal species in a relevant fashion. Metabolite profiling will provide assurance that at least one of the toxicology species has been exposed to metabolites of the drug predicted to be formed in human. Information from in vitro DDI studies will be utilized mainly in the clinical section of the IND, particularly in relation to justification of doses for the initial clinical studies in cases where the subjects are patients who are maintained on prescribed medications. Studies performed as part of the DDI assessment to investigate the potential for the candidate to act as an inducer of key CYP450 isozymes may be relevant to other sections of the NCO, such as data from animal safety studies possibly indicating hepatic enzyme induction (eg, reduction of exposure with duration of dosing, elevated AST, ALT, and/or increased liver weights or histopathological findings). For biological drug candidates, assessment of antidrug antibodies (ADA) is expected as well as tissue cross-reactivity studies. Whether this latter topic is addressed in the pharmacokinetics section of the NCO is, to some extent, a matter for individual sponsor preference. Information on the formation of ADA is clearly essential to an understanding of the relationships between dose levels and drug exposures achieved in animal safety studies. Although antibody development against a human protein in animals is generally not considered to be predictive of antibody development in humans [41], some consequences of immune responses may be relevant to humans [28,42].

Toxicology

As already indicated, the recent ICH M3(R2) guidance outlines the anticipated program of safety studies to be performed in support of an application to initiate studies in human [8]. The toxicology section is likely to be the largest component of the NCO and, for an initial IND, will comprise results of exploratory and pivotal (GLP) studies in two species (possibly one in the case of a biologic drug candidate), as well as the results of genotoxicity studies and any other specialized study performed, such as local toleration and developmental and reproductive toxicology (DART). ICH M4S(R2) does not recommend any specific method of subdivision of the toxicology section, although some further breakdown of the section is implicit in this guidance document. One potential way of organizing this section was presented in the outline given earlier in this section. The main aim of Section 2.4.4 is to provide an outline of the toxicology program and a summary of the main findings in the exploratory and pivotal studies. This is then followed by a discussion of the relationship between findings and drug exposure. Finally, as discussed previously, an integrated cross-species interpretation and risk assessment of the target-organ toxicities noted in the repeat-dose toxicology program is provided. More details on these points follows:

Example Text Outlining the Toxicology Program (Section 2.4.4):

<Compound> was administered to rats and dogs in oral studies up to 1 month in duration. The no-observed-adverse-effect level (NOAEL) in rats was 100/50 mg/kg/day (male/female) with free C_{max} and $AUC_{(0-24)}$ values of 1130/987 ng/mL and 6500/6600 ng h/mL (male/female), respectively. These exposures provide margins of ≥37-fold and ≥13-fold compared to the projected C_{max} and $AUC_{(0-24)}$, respectively, associated with a predicted pharmacological exposure in human. In dogs, the NOAEL was 30 mg/kg/day with associated free C_{max} and $AUC_{(0-24)}$ values of 1670 ng/mL and 21,000 ng h/mL, respectively. These exposures provide margins of 62-fold and 41-fold compared to the projected C_{max} and $AUC_{(0-24)}$, respectively, associated with predicted therapeutic exposure in human.

Based on the nonclinical studies conducted, the cardiovascular and central nervous systems have been identified as the major potential targets. Other findings related to administration of <Compound> to rat and dog included effects on the adrenal glands and, at higher doses, on liver, thyroid gland, and the gastrointestinal system. Changes in lung noted in rat were considered to be secondary to cardiac dysfunction related to the cardiac findings. <Compound> was negative in genetic toxicology testing.

It is useful to provide an in-text table summarizing the studies conducted, including study number and the doses evaluated. Studies should be listed in order by species, by route, and by duration [5]. Screening and/or preliminary in vitro/in vivo toxicology studies should be included in the table, along with definitive toxicology studies/assays. Use of study titles in the in-text table that are consistent with those of the individual study reports and/or protocols (without abbreviation) makes it easy to link to the actual study reports located in Module 4 within the electronic CTD. Key protocol information need not be included in the toxicology summary, as experimental details (eg, species/strain, method of administration, doses, gender and number per group, observed maximum nonlethal dose, approximate lethal dose, and noteworthy findings) will be provided in the CTD tabulated summary that will be submitted as part of Module 2.6 of the IND.

In general, it may be preferable not to present just a series of summaries of studies performed (especially not a series of study abstracts excerpted from the individual study reports), except where there are few studies to review. Rather, the text should provide a high-level and brief interpretive summary of relevant findings of studies arranged by species, as well as high-level conclusions. The potential relevance of these findings to human safety may also be discussed at this point. In general, exploratory studies should be summarized in much less detail, just taking care to highlight any unique findings in these studies that are important for target-organ characterization, particularly those not observed in subsequent studies.

Relationship of Findings to Pharmacokinetics

The focus of this section of the NCO is to briefly describe the exposures of the candidate drug achieved in toxicology studies and to relate these to toxicology findings. This paragraph should provide a rationale for the choice of the exposure metric, for example C_{max}, AUC, C_{av} (average concentration), or dose (mg/kg or mg/m^2), and address (1) sex differences in exposure, (2) dose-exposure relationships, (3) accumulation or reduction of exposure following repeated dosing, and (4) significant metabolites (if relevant). For biotherapeutics, any impact on exposure due to immunogenicity should be discussed, and exposures and exposure margins explained, as appropriate. This may be followed by a table detailing all toxicological findings, which are, or may be, relevant for human safety, detailing drug exposures determined at the doses that resulted in these findings in the study animals. Priority should be given to potentially important clinical signs or measures that are readily translated to human (eg, changes in cardiovascular parameters, convulsions, and/or significant deviations from normal levels of clinical chemistry analytes). Test article-related or unexplained deaths should always be included. This table should contain all relevant findings listed in the study-specific CTD tables (CTD Module 2.6.7) prepared for the individual studies. Exposures determined in toxicology studies are quoted in associated toxicokinetic reports in terms of total drug concentration in the matrix analyzed (commonly plasma). Total drug in the analytical matrix comprises unbound drug and drug bound to components of the matrix, usually proteins. The calculated unbound drug concentrations may be shown in this table.

An example of text outlining the toxicokinetic findings is shown as follows:

Toxicokinetic data from nonpivotal and pivotal (4-week) toxicology studies in rat and monkey were evaluated for gender-related differences in exposure, dose–exposure relationship, and time-dependent changes in systemic exposure to the drug candidate. In both rat and monkey, mean AUC and C_{max} values were similar between male and female animals indicating lack of gender-related differences in systemic exposure. Data from males and females were combined for the purpose of reporting and discussion. In rats and monkeys, exposures increased between day 1 and day 28. The increase was more pronounced in monkeys than in rats. In rats, mean drug candidate AUC and C_{max} values increased with increasing dose. The increase in systemic exposures was approximately proportional to dose between 10 and 100 mg/kg/day. In general, exposure was higher on day 28 than on day 1. In monkeys, systemic exposures increased with dose between 4 and 100 mg/kg/day. The increase in systemic exposures was approximately proportional to dose between 4 and 25 mg/kg and less than proportional to dose between 25 and 100 mg/kg/day.

The table with all toxicological findings (the "key responses") that are considered relevant for humans should follow, and should identify the MTD and the NOAEL/LOAEL doses (HNSTD/STD10 doses in the case of oncology candidates); where such identifications were made in the original study reports; associated exposure information should also be included. For single-dose toxicity studies, the MTD may not be identified in the study report and may be estimated (for the purpose of this document) based on study results. The NOAEL for a particular study will be identified in the associated CTD tabulated summary (Module 2.6.7) and study report (Module 4). The LOAEL will be considered to be the next higher dose above the NOAEL at which toxicological (or adverse pharmacological) findings were noted. In the last column of the table, calculated exposure margins for both NOAEL and LOAEL doses are reported. Exposure margins may be calculated by either an exposure-based method (eg, AUC at the NOAEL or at the LOAEL/AUC projected human therapeutic dose) or an applied-dose method (eg, NOAEL or LOAEL/clinical starting dose). In the case of applied-dose methods, the NOAEL or LOAEL may need to be converted to mg/m^2 units if the clinical starting dose is expressed on a body surface area (mg/m^2) basis.

Data presented in the "key response" table should be consistent with that included in the study summary tables (CTD table) included in Module 2.6.7 of the IND, although the purpose of each table is different, with the key response table relating effects to exposure and the CTD tables being a summary of the study findings (with exposure data included). As an example of differences in data presentation in the two tables, a portion of the key response table for a 1-month rat study and the relevant part of the 2.6.7 tabulated summary CTD table for that study are shown in the forthcoming table.

Target Organs

As noted at the start of this discussion, although there is no formal requirement to include a specific section describing target organs identified in the animal toxicology studies, such a section does provide a convenient method of summarizing key data across species and duration of exposure, and the opportunity to present an integrated interpretation across species and risk assessment of the target-organ toxicities. Such toxicities may be best described in terms of overall effect rather than in a specific organ-related fashion. Targets most important/relevant to humans may be discussed first, with a brief description of each of the changes and any relationships between the affected organ systems among species, along with the relevance for humans. Data or conclusions from studies presented in other sections of the NCO (eg, safety pharmacology) can be brought to bear to provide a more comprehensive discussion. Where known, the consequences for overall health of the animals, as well as evidence of reversibility following drug withdrawal, can also be discussed here. An explanation of how exposure margins were derived from NOAEL margins can be a useful inclusion to the section. The risk and relevance of these toxicities for humans can be discussed. Such considerations and arguments will be further developed in terms of potential clinical relevance within Section 7 of the IB (guidance for investigators) and a high-level summary will likely also be included in the integrated overview of the NCO and in the nonclinical summary section of the clinical protocol for the intended first clinical study with the drug candidate.

The following represents an example of suitable text describing the target organs:

Two single-dose safety pharmacology studies were conducted in dogs to evaluate the cardiovascular effects of oral administration of <Compound> at doses up to 150 mg/kg. A dose of 10 mg/kg did not result in any

Key Response(s)	Dose (mg/kg)	AUC$_{(0\text{-}last)}$[a] Total/unbound (ng•h/mL)	C$_{max}$[a] Total/unbound (ng/mL)	Exposure Margin[b] Total AUC/C$_{max}$	Exposure Margin[b] unbound AUC/C$_{max}$
1-month toxicity study in rats (10/sex/dose)					
NOAEL, ↓ White blood cells, ↓ lymphocytes, ↓ basophils, ↓ eosinophils, ↓ large unstained cells, ↓ hemoglobin, ↓ hematocrit, ↓ red blood cell count, ↑ red cell distribution width, ↑ reticulocyte count, ↓ spleen weight, Thymus - ↑ lymphocyte cellularity in medulla, ↓ thickness of the cortex, Spleen -↓ lymphocytes in marginal zone/periarteriolar lymphatic sheath, ↑ lymphocyte cellularity of lymphatic follicles, Mesenteric lymph node - ↓ lymphocyte cellularity in subcapsular/medulla sinusoids	10	20600/412	1530/30.6	8.3/12	17/23
Same as above plus, ↓ body weight, ↓ food consumption, ↑ platelet count, Glandular Stomach - depletion/atrophy of parietal cells	100	213000/4260	12100/242	86/92	172/185
1000 mg/kg/day: Same as above plus, sacrificed moribund (1F plus 2F from TK group), dose-limiting significant ↓ body weight 300 mg/kg/day: ↓ Body weight, Spleen – ↓ cellularity, mononuclear cells, red pulp	1000→300	365000/7300[c]	19200/384[c]	148/147	296/293

NOAEL = No-Observed Adverse Effect Level; F = Female; TK = Toxicokinetic.

[a] In repeat-dose studies, AUC and C$_{max}$ values indicate mean serum concentrations. Reported values were obtained near termination, or as specified. In the Safety Pharmacology study, C$_{max}$ values represent those obtained 4 hours postdose.

[b] Predicted total human C$_{max}$ and AUC expected from a projected efficacious dose of 12 mg are 131 ng/mL and 2470 ng•h/mL, respectively, and predicted unbound C$_{max}$ and AUC are 1.31 ng/mL and 24.7 ng•h/mL, respectively. Additional exposure margins were calculated using unbound values because of the difference in protein binding between human (Fu 0.01) and rat and monkey (Fu 0.02).

[c] Values are from Day 28 at a dose of 300 mg/kg/day.

effects on the cardiovascular system. C_{max} at this dose was not determined in this study but the mean plasma concentration at 6 h postdose was 335 ng/mL (unbound), representing a margin of approximately 1.4-fold the projected steady state unbound drug exposure in human at a dose of 125 mg. Doses ≤50 mg/kg were associated with increases in heart rate of up to 21 bpm. Heart rate remained elevated throughout the data-collection period and maximum increases appeared to be associated with T_{max}. In general, cardiovascular findings correlated with measured exposure to <Compound>. Interanimal variability in exposure to <Compound> was high within dose groups and increases in dose were not reflected by proportional increases in exposure, especially between 50 and 150 mg/kg doses. The mean C_{max} at a dose of 50 mg/kg in the two studies expressed in terms of unbound drug ranged from 3400 to 6360 ng/mL representing a margin of 15–27-fold to the projected unbound drug exposure in human at steady state following a single dose of 125 mg. A 20 ms increase in QTc was observed 1.5–3 h postdose in one dog dosed at 50 mg/kg. At 6 h postdose the plasma concentration of <Compound>

Repeat-Dose Toxicity	Report Title: 1-Month Oral Gavage Toxicity	Test Article:
Species/Strain: Rat/Sprague-Dawley	Duration of Dosing: 1 Month	Study Number: -
Initial Age: ~ 7 Weeks	Duration of Postdose: None	Location in Module
Date of First Dose: -	Method of Administration: Oral gavage, QD, 10 mL/kg	GLP Compliance: Yes
		Lot Number:

Vehicle/Formulation: -

No Observed Adverse Effect Level: 10 mg/kg/day

2.6.7.7A Repeat-Dose Toxicity

Dose[a] (mg/kg/day)	0 (Control)		10		100		1000→300[b]	
Sex	M	F	M	F	M	F	M	F
Spleen								
Decreased cellularity, mononuclear cells, red pulp								
Minimal	0	0	0	0	0	0	2	0
Slight	0	0	0	0	0	0	8	8
Thymus								
Increased cellularity, lymphocytes, medulla								
Minimal	0	0	0	0	0	0	0	1
Slight	0	0	5	0	1	0	1	2
Moderate	0	0	5	10	9	10	9	6
Decreased thickness, cortex								
Minimal	0	0	1	0	1	0	2	2
Slight	0	0	8	10	9	9	8	1
Moderate	0	0	0	0	0	1	0	6
Mesenteric lymph node								
Decreased cellularity, lymphocytes, medulla/subcapsular sinusoid								
Minimal	0	0	6	5	6	1	1	3
Slight	0	0	1	5	3	9	9	5
Moderate	0	0	0	0	0	0	0	1
Glandular stomach								
Depletion/atrophy, parietal cells								
Minimal	0	0	0	0	3	0	0	0
Slight	0	0	0	0	7	4	0	0
Moderate	0	0	0	0	0	6	10	9
Additional Examination								
Micronucleus Assessment	-	-	-	-	-	-	-	-

M = Male; F = Female; - = No noteworthy findings.

[a] All dose levels are expressed as mg of active drug moiety per kg of body weight per day.

[b] Animals received 1000 mg/kg/day on Days 1 through 8 and 300 mg/kg/day on Days 12 through 29 (dosing suspended on Days 9 through 11 due to significant reductions in body weight).

in this animal was 14,600 ng/mL (unbound) and was higher than seen in any other animal, even those dosed at 150 mg/kg. This animal displayed a C_{max} of 14,400 ng/mL (free) at 2 h postdose representing a margin of >60-fold the projected steady state unbound C_{max} in human at a dose of 125 mg. Given that monitoring of cardiovascular events may be performed readily in the clinic, and the large margin of exposure anticipated, the risk to human is considered to below.

Integrated Overview and Conclusions

The purpose of this final section of the NCO is clearly laid out in the ICH M4 guidance [5], and is described in the following text from the guidance: *The Integrated Overview and Conclusions should clearly define the characteristics of the human pharmaceutical as demonstrated by the nonclinical studies and arrive at logical, well-argued conclusions supporting the safety of the product for the intended clinical use. Taking the pharmacology, pharmacokinetics and toxicology results into account, the implications of the nonclinical findings for the safe human use of the pharmaceutical should be discussed.*

Key data and conclusions from the pharmacology, pharmacokinetic, and toxicology sections of the NCO should be included, with linkage of findings and conclusions where possible. For an NCO supporting the first administration of the candidate to humans, the Integrated Overview and Conclusion section is likely to run to one to two pages in length.

ESTABLISHING THE CLINICAL SAFETY OF A NEW DRUG CANDIDATE

Determine if Proposed Clinical Trial is safe to Proceed

Once the core nonclinical studies, including efficacy, safety pharmacology, toxicology, and ADME studies, are completed for the IND submission, the maximum recommended starting dose (MRSD) must be established for small-molecule candidates, while the minimal anticipated biological effect level (MABEL) should be established for biologics. The MRSD will be the proposed starting dose for the initial clinical trial and should be set conservatively. As the FDA suggests, *"Toxicity should be avoided at the initial clinical dose. However, doses should be chosen that allow reasonably rapid attainment of the Phase 1 trial objectives"* [43]. In the Phase I trials for most indications, healthy volunteers will be dosed. Oncology is an exception due to the cytotoxic nature of most oncology agents and the fact that patients, instead of healthy subjects, are routinely included in Phase I studies. Setting the MRSD is a multistep process: first, the human equivalent dose (HED) must be derived for each species;

next, the safety factor must be determined prior to the MRSD calculations. For the MABEL determination, a pharmacological assessment is made that incorporates in vitro target-cell information with concentration-effect data [44]. The calculations should account for differences between human and animal affinity and potency at the target cell/receptor. This requirement was driven by the adverse findings noted in TeGenero's TGN1412 anti-CD-28 agonist clinical trial [45]. The European Medicines Agency's Committee for Medicinal Products crafted guidance that emphasizes the determination of the pharmacological dose rather than the NOAEL [13]. The pharmacological dose may be derived from doses at which biological effects, such as ligand suppression or receptor occupancy have been observed.

Human Equivalent Dose (HED) Calculations

To determine the HED, the toxicology studies are reviewed for the established NOAEL doses. Each study may have identified a different NOAEL, depending on study duration and species used. These are examined with respect to the proposed clinical trial-dosing regimen. In general, NOAELs from 2- to 4-week repeated-dose toxicity studies will be used to establish the HEDs, as these values will build in a conservative safety margin *if* the clinical trial is of a shorter duration. There are cases where nonclinical data on bioavailability, metabolite profile, and plasma drug levels associated with toxicity may influence use of the NOAEL [43]. For example, when saturation of drug absorption occurs at a dose that produces no toxicity, the lowest saturating dose, not the highest (nontoxic) dose, should be used for calculating the HED.

Whether using the NOAEL or the lowest saturating dose, the next step in the MRSD determination is to convert the NOAEL to the HED using appropriate scaling factors (see Table 8.4). For most systemically administered therapeutics, this conversion should be based on the normalization of doses to body surface area [43]. The body surface area normalization should be done by dividing the NOAEL in the animal species by the appropriate body surface area conversion factor. This conversion factor (k_m) converts the animal mg/kg dose to a mg/m^2 unit. There are exceptions to using the body surface area versus mg/kg dose, including therapeutics administered by routes for which the dose is limited by local toxicities, such as topical, intranasal, subcutaneous, or intramuscular, or for local delivery whereby there will be limited distribution (ie, intrathecal). Such therapeutics should be normalized to concentration (eg, mg/area of application) or amount of drug (mg) at the application site [43]. The HED can be calculated directly from the animal dose by dividing the animal dose by the ratio of the human/animal k_m factor (third column in Table 8.4) or by multiplying by the ratio of the animal/human k_m factor (fourth column in Table 8.4).

TABLE 8.4 Conversion of Animal Doses to Human Equivalent Doses Based on Body Surface Area

Species	To Convert Animal Dose in mg/kg to Dose in mg/m², Multiply by k_m	To Convert Animal Dose in mg/kg to HED in mg/kg, Either:	
		Divide Animal Dose By	Multiply Animal Dose By
Human	37	–	–
Child (20 kg)b	25	–	–
Mouse	3	12.3	0.08
Hamster	5	7.4	0.13
Rat	6	6.2	0.16
Ferret	7	5.3	0.19
Guinea pig	8	4.6	0.22
Rabbit	12	3.1	0.32
Dog	20	1.8	0.54
Primates:			
Monkey	12	3.1	0.32
Marmoset	6	6.2	0.16
Squirrel monkey	7	5.3	0.19
Baboon	20	1.8	0.54
Micro-pig	27	1.4	0.73
Mini-pig	35	1.1	0.95

Used with permission from the Food and Drug Administration. Estimating the maximum safe starting doses in initial clinical trials for therapeutics in adult healthy volunteers. Washington, D.C.: Government Printing Office; 2005.

Establishing the MRSD or MABEL

After the HEDs have been determined from the NOAELs of the toxicology studies relevant to the proposed human trial, the next step is to pick one HED for subsequent derivation of the MRSD. This HED should be chosen from the most appropriate species. In the absence of data on species relevance, a default position is that the most appropriate species for deriving the MRSD for a trial in adult healthy volunteers is the most sensitive species (ie, the species in which the lowest HED can be identified). Factors that could influence the choice of the most appropriate species rather than the default to the most sensitive species include: (1) differences between the species in the absorption, distribution, metabolism, and excretion of the drug candidate, and (2) class experience that may indicate a particular animal model is more predictive of human toxicity. Factors, such as whether an animal species expresses relevant target receptors or epitopes may affect species selection [28].

A safety factor should then be applied to the HED to account for the possibility that humans may be more sensitive to the toxic effects of a therapeutic agent than is predicted by the animal models, that bioavailability may vary across species, and that the models tested do not evaluate all possible human toxicities [43]. The MRSD is obtained by dividing the HED by the safety factor. In general, a safety factor of at least 10 is common practice. A safety factor smaller than 10 could be justified when the NOAEL is determined based on toxicity studies of longer duration compared to the proposed clinical schedule in healthy volunteers. In this case, a greater margin of safety should be built into the NOAEL. This assumes that toxicities are cumulative, are not associated with acute peaks in drug concentration (eg, hypotension), and did not occur early in the repeat-dose study [43].

Safety Factor Considerations

Safety concerns or design shortcomings noted in animal studies may increase the safety factor, and thus reduce the MRSD further. An increase in the safety factor may be required if multiple concerns are identified. As recommended by the FDA [43], items that warrant an upward adjustment of the safety factor include:

- *Steep-dose response curve.* A steep-dose response curve for significant toxicities in the most appropriate species or in multiple species may indicate a greater risk to humans.
- *Severe toxicities.* Qualitatively severe toxicities or damage to an organ system (eg, central nervous system (CNS)) indicate increased risk to humans.
- *Nonmonitorable toxicity.* Nonmonitorable toxicities may include histopathologic changes in animals that are not readily monitored by clinical pathology markers. *Toxicities without premonitory signs.* If the onset of significant toxicities is not reliably associated with premonitory signs in animals, it may be difficult to know when toxic doses are approached in human trials. *Variable bioavailability.* Widely divergent or poor bioavailability in several animal species, or poor bioavailability in the test species used to derive the HED, suggest a greater possibility for underestimating the toxicity in humans.
- *Irreversible toxicity.* Irreversible toxicities in animals suggest the possibility of permanent injury in human trial participants.
- *Unexplained mortality.* Mortality that is not predicted by other parameters raises the level of concern.
- *Large variability in doses or plasma drug levels eliciting effect.* When doses or exposure levels that produce a toxic effect differ greatly across species or among individual animals of a species, the ability to predict a toxic dose in humans is reduced.

- **Nonlinear pharmacokinetics.** *When plasma drug levels do not increase in a dose-related manner, the ability to predict toxicity in humans in relation to dose is reduced and a greater safety factor may be needed.*
  Inadequate dose–response data. *Poor study design (eg, few dose levels, wide dosing intervals) or large differences in responses among animals within dosing groups may make it difficult to characterize the dose–response curve.*
- **Novel therapeutic targets.** *Therapeutic targets that have not been previously clinically evaluated may increase the uncertainty of relying on the nonclinical data to support a safe starting dose in humans.*

Having accounted for the appropriate safety factor, the MRSD is determined and included in the clinical section of the IND dossier and in the IB.

SUMMARY AND CONCLUSIONS

The content of the IND dossier represents the culmination of years of work on the part of the nonclinical and clinical teams. The product, the IND application, should have all the pertinent information about the new molecular entity integrated into a cogently argued proposal supporting the clinical program. When considering what material should be included in the document, it is better to err on the side of caution and be more inclusive with data. Providing more information is always beneficial to FDA reviewers, as opposed to a document lacking the depth and details required for a thorough review. Providing information in tabular format, in addition to the text, can serve as a quick summary reference for study information. As detailed earlier, the NCO constitutes the most important component of the nonclinical dossier in that it comprises an integrated summary of the nonclinical data that supports the safe dosing of human subjects in the FIH Phase I clinical trial.

When submitting the IND application, it is a requirement that reports be at least in a draft format, with all data adequately summarized. An additional 120 days after IND submission are allowed for submission of the final reports. A well-argued and thorough nonclinical section will greatly reduce the chance of a clinical hold. As the program progresses in the clinic, it is the toxicologist's responsibility to initiate any follow-on studies to support longer duration of trials, inclusion of women of childbearing potential, and any specialty studies warranted based on the indication and target organs of toxicity.

References

[1] Kuhnert BR. ICH at 20: an overview. Glob Forum 2011;3:17–8.
[2] Juillet Y. The CTD: a tool for global development and assessment. Glob Forum 2011;3:25–6.
[3] Finkle CD, Atkins J. Project management and international regulatory requirements and strategies for first-in-human trials. In: Cayen MN, editor. Early drug development: strategies and routes to first-in-human trials. Hoboken, NJ: Wiley; 2010. p. 513–41.
[4] Sommer MR, Ammann M, Hillgren UB, Kovacs KK, Wilner K. First-in-human regulatory submissions. In: Cayen MN, editor. Early drug development: strategies and routes to first-in-human trials. Hoboken, NJ: Wiley & Sons, Inc; 2010. p. 543–93.
[5] International Conference on Harmonization of Technical Requirements for Registration of Pharmaceuticals for Human Use ICH Harmonized Tripartite Guideline. The common technical document for the registration of pharmaceuticals for human Use: safety-M4S(R2) – nonclinical overview and nonclinical summaries of module 2. Organisation of module 4, Geneva, Switzerland. 2002.
[6] European Commission. Revision 2. Detailed guidance for the request for authorization of a clinical trial on a medicinal product for human use to the competent authorities, notification of substantial amendments and declaration of the end of the trial. Brussels, Belgium: Enterprise Directorate General; 2005.
[7] European Commission. Draft Revision 3. Detailed guidance for the request for authorization of a clinical trial on a medicinal product for human use to the competent authorities, notification of substantial amendments and declaration of the end of the trial. Brussels, Belgium: Enterprise Directorate General; 2009.
[8] International Conference on Harmonization of Technical Requirements for Registration of Pharmaceuticals for Human Use ICH Harmonized Tripartite Guideline. Guidance on nonclinical safety studies for the conduct of human clinical trials and marketing authorization for pharmaceuticals M3(R2). Geneva (Switzerland). 2010.
[9] Wang T, Jacobson-Kram D, Pilaro AM, Lapadula D, Jacobs A, Brown P, et al. ICH guidelines: inception, revision, and implications for drug development. Toxicol Sci 2010;118:356–67.
[10] Brock WJ, Hastings K, McGowan KM. Nonclinical safety assessment. A Guide to international pharmaceutical regulations. Chichester (UK): Wiley and Sons, Ltd.; 2013.
[11] Food and Drug Administration, CDER Division. Guidance for industry M4: organization of the CTD. Washington, D.C.: Government Printing Office; 2001.
[12] Food and Drug Administration, CDER Division. Guidance for industry: single dose acute toxicity for pharmaceuticals. Washington, D.C.: Government Printing Office; 1996.
[13] European Medicines Agency. Committee for medicinal products for human use (CHMP). Guideline on strategies to identify and mitigate risks for first-in-human clinical trials with investigational medicinal products. London (England). 2007.
[14] Milton MN, Horvath CJ. The EMEA guideline on first-in-human clinical trials and its impact on pharmaceutical development. Toxicol Pathol 2009;37:363–71.
[15] Food and Drug Administration, CDER Division. Providing regulatory submissions in electronic format – submissions under section 745A(a) of the Federal food, drug and Cosmetics act, 2014. Washington, D.C.: Government Printing Office; 2014.
[16] Food and Drug Administration, CDER Division. Guidance for industry: providing regulatory submissions in electronic format-standardized study data. Washington, D.C.: Government Printing Office; 2014.
[17] Buckley LA, Chapman K, Burns-Naas LA, Todd MD, Martin PL, Lansita JA. Considerations regarding nonhuman primate use in safety assessment of biopharmaceuticals. Int J Toxicol 2011;30:583–90.
[18] DeGeorge JJ, Ahn C-H, Andrews PA, Brower ME, Giogio DW, Goheer MA, et al. Regulatory considerations for preclinical development of anticancer drugs. Cancer Chemother Pharmacol 1998;41:173–85.

[19] Ponce R. ICH S9: developing anticancer drugs, one year later. Toxicol Pathol 2011;39:913–5.

[20] Muller PY. Comparative requirements for exploratory clinical trials – eIND, eCTA, and microdosing. Adv Drug Deliv Rev 2011;63:511–7.

[21] Black HE, Montgomery SB, Moch RW. Toxicology program to support initiation of a clinical phase 1 program for a new medicine. In: Cayen MN, editor. Early drug development: strategies and routes to first-in-human trials. Hoboken, NJ: Wiley & Sons, Inc.; 2010. p. 283–307.

[22] Cavagnaro JA, editor. Preclinical safety evaluation of biopharmaceuticals. Hoboken, NJ: Wiley; 2008.

[23] Benbow JW, Aubrecht J, Banker MJ, Nettleton D, Aleo MD. Predicting safety toleration of pharmaceutical chemical leads: cytotoxicity correlations to exploratory toxicity studies. Toxicol Lett 2011;197:175–82.

[24] Gad SC, Cassidy CD, Aubert N, Spainhour B, Robbe H. Nonclinical vehicle use in studies by multiple routes in multiple species. Int J Toxicol 2006;25:499–521.

[25] International Conference on Harmonization of Technical Requirements for Registration of Pharmaceuticals for Human Use ICH Harmonized Tripartite Guideline. Guidance on genotoxicity testing and data interpretation for pharmaceuticals intended for human use S2(R1). Geneva (Switzerland). 2011.

[26] International Conference on Harmonization of Technical Requirements for Registration of Pharmaceuticals for Human Use ICH Harmonized Tripartite Guideline. Safety pharmacology studies for human pharmaceuticals. S7A. Geneva. CPMP/ICH/539/00-ICH S7A. Geneva (Switzerland). 2000.

[27] International Conference on Harmonization of Technical Requirements for Registration of Pharmaceuticals for Human Use ICH Harmonized Tripartite Guideline. The nonclinical evaluation of the potential for safety pharmacology studies for delayed ventricular repolarization (QT interval polarization) by human pharmaceuticals S7B. Geneva (Switzerland). 2005.

[28] International Conference on Harmonization of Technical Requirements for Registration of Pharmaceuticals for Human Use ICH Harmonized Tripartite Guideline. Preclinical safety evaluation of biotechnology-derived pharmaceuticals. S6(R1). Geneva (Switzerland). 1997 and Addendum 2011.

[29] Irwin S. Comprehensive observational assessment: Ia. A systematic, quantitative procedure for assessing the behavioral and physiologic state of the mouse. Psychopharmacologia (Berl) 1968;13:222–57.

[30] Moser VC. Screening approaches to neurotoxicity: a functional observational battery. Int J Toxicol 1989;8:85–93.

[31] Moser VC. Functional assays for neurotoxicity testing. Toxicol Pathol 2011;39:36–45.

[32] Pellegatti M, Pagliarusco S, Solazzo L, Colato D. Plasma protein binding and blood-free concentrations: which studies are needed to develop a drug? Expert Opin Drug Metab Toxicol 2011;7:1009–20.

[33] Baillie TA, Cayen MN, Fouda H, Gerson RJ, Green JD, Grossman SJ, et al. Contemporary issues in toxicology: drug metabolites in safety testing. Toxicol Appl Pharmacol 2002;182:188–96.

[34] Food and Drug Administration, CDER Division. Testing of drug metabolites. Washington, D.C.: Government Printing Office; 2008.

[35] Walker D, Brady JT, Dalvie D, Davis JW, Dowty M, Duncan JN, et al. A holistic strategy for characterizing the safety of metabolites through drug discovery and development. Chem Res Toxicol 2002;22:1653–62.

[36] International Conference on Harmonization of Technical Requirements for Registration of Pharmaceuticals for Human Use ICH Harmonized Tripartite Guideline. Assessment and control of DNA reactive (mutagenic) impurities in pharmaceuticals to limit potential carcinogenic risk M7. Geneva (Switzerland). 2014.

[37] International Conference on Harmonization of Technical Requirements for Registration of Pharmaceuticals for Human Use ICH Harmonized Tripartite Guideline. Impurities in pharmaceuticals new drug substances (Q3A(R2)) Geneva (Switzerland). 2006.

[38] International Conference on Harmonization of Technical Requirements for Registration of Pharmaceuticals for Human Use ICH Harmonized Tripartite Guideline. Impurities in new drug products (Q3B(R2)) Geneva (Switzerland). 2006.

[39] International Conference on Harmonization of Technical Requirements for Registration of Pharmaceuticals for Human Use ICH Harmonized Tripartite Guideline. S8. Immunotoxicity studies for human pharmaceuticals. Geneva (Switzerland). 2006.

[40] Food and Drug Administration, CDER Division. Guidance for industry: pediatric study plans: content of and process of submitting initial pediatric study plans and amended pediatric study plans. Washington, D.C.: Government Printing Office; 2013.

[41] Bugelski PJ, Treacy G. Predictive power of preclinical studies in animals for the immunogenicity of recombinant therapeutic proteins in humans. Curr Opin Mol Ther 2004;6:10–6.

[42] Ponce R, Abad L, Amaravadi L, Gelzleichter T, Gore E, Green J, et al. Immunogenicity of biologically-derived therapeutics: assessment and interpretation of nonclinical safety studies. Regul Toxicol Pharmacol 2009;54:164–82.

[43] Food and Drug Administration. Estimating the maximum safe starting doses in initial clinical trials for therapeutics in adult healthy volunteers. Washington, D.C.: Government Printing Office; 2005.

[44] Muller PY, Milton M, Lloyd P, Sims J, Brennan FR. The minimum anticipated biological effect level (MABEL) for selection of first human dose in clinical trials with monoclonal antibodies. Curr Opin Biotechnol December 2009;20(6):722–9.

[45] Suntharalingam G, Perry R, Ward S, Brett SJ, Castello-Cortes A, Brunner MD, et al. Cytokine storm in phase 1 trial of the antiCD28 monoclonal antibody. N Engl J Med 2006;355:1018–28.

Developmental and Reproductive Toxicology

A.S. Faqi, A. Hoberman, E. Lewis, D. Stump

A Comprehensive Guide to Toxicology in Nonclinical Drug Development, Second Edition
http://dx.doi.org/10.1016/B978-0-12-803620-4.00009-8

OVERVIEW AND HISTORY OF REPRODUCTIVE TESTING GUIDELINES

Background

In October of 1957, thalidomide was marketed under the name Contergen by Chemie Grünenthal, a German pharmaceutical company, as a potent and apparently safe nonbarbiturate sedative hypnotic, which was prescribed to women during pregnancy for treatment of the symptoms of morning sickness [1]. It was approved and sold in a number of countries across the world including Australia. In the United States, Dr. Frances Kelsey, a medical officer of the FDA, rejected the drug firm Richardson Merrell's application to market Kevadon (thalidomide) there, because she was not convinced that the drug would be safe to be taken during pregnancy. Soon after launching Contergan (thalidomide) in West Germany, German medical practitioners began to see children with gross malformations of a most unusual pattern including malformations of the limbs and ears, often accompanied by malformations of the internal organs. In 1961, Dr. William McBride suspected that thalidomide was the cause of limb and bowel malformations in three children he had seen at his hospital in Sydney, Australia. In the same year, Dr. Widukind Lenz in Germany suggested that these deformities resulted from the mothers being exposed to thalidomide during pregnancy [2]. On November 27, 1961, Grünenthal withdrew its product from the market.

Many scientists believe that if there had been more extensive testing on laboratory animals before the drug was launched, the disaster could have been avoided. After several years of abandonment because of its teratogenic effects, thalidomide has reemerged as an alternative treatment in many dermatological diseases, especially in South America. In 1998, the FDA approved the use of thalidomide for the acute treatment and suppression of the cutaneous manifestations of erythema nodosum leprosum (ENL) [3].

The thalidomide tragedy was the beginning and the rise of regulatory bodies, such as the United Kingdom's Committee on the Safety of Drugs and the strengthening of the regulatory authority of the US FDA [4]. The Kefauver–Harris drug amendment, signed into law by President John F. Kennedy, was passed in 1962 to ensure drug efficacy and greater drug safety. The two key provisions of the amendment imposed drug companies to show a proof-of-efficacy for the first time and introduced new safety testing procedures. The law requires that no new drug can be marketed until the FDA has determined that it is both safe and effective for its intended use [5].

The Forthcoming Revision of ICH S5 (R2) [6]

Final concept paper ICH S5(R3), "Detection of Toxicity to Reproduction for Medicinal Products and Toxicity to Male Fertility" dated February 9, 2015 and endorsed by the ICH Steering Committee on March 27, 2015 [7] addresses the forthcoming revision of ICH S5 (R2) [6]. Over 20 years ago, the ICH S5 (R2) *Guideline on Reproductive Toxicity* was implemented. Since then, tremendous experience has been gained through the testing of pharmaceuticals using current and novel testing paradigms, and at the same time, the field has encountered significant advancement in science, technology, and regulatory experience. These advancements have provided opportunities for modernizing the testing paradigms to enhance human risk assessment. In addition, there may be areas in which the guideline requires a revision or amendment for greater clarity or usefulness as well as to align more fully with other guidelines including ICH M3(R2), ICH S6(R1), and ICH S9.

According to the proposed action of harmonization, final concept paper [7]; the expert working group for ICH S5(R3) will revise the guideline and conduct the necessary data analysis consistent with the identified areas. Some of the topics expected to be addressed are as follows:

1. Alignment of the existing ICH S5(R2) guideline with the revised ICH S6(R1) and ICH M3 (R2), and the ICH S9 guidelines.
2. Use of human-exposure data to determine appropriate dose levels for mammalian reproductive toxicity studies with the aim of optimizing testing strategies for human risk assessment, and to provide more clarity to Section 3.1 (Dosage) of the ICH S5(R2) guideline. Prospects for improvement of the current guideline might include providing guidance on appropriate exposure multiples or other endpoints for high-dose setting in reproductive toxicity studies, as do other ICH guidelines (eg, ICH M3 (R2)). In addition, as the current ICH S5(R2) suggests providing dose–response data and establishing a no observed adverse effect level (NOAEL), ICH S5(R3) could clarify expectations when such a dose response and NOAEL would be in the anticipated subtherapeutic exposure range.
3. Expand the options of combining reproductive toxicity studies and their designs as appropriate for specific purposes. The description of these options could enhance human risk assessment (eg, for compounds with long half-lives) and at the same time contribute substantially to reduction in animal usage.
4. Under limited circumstances, yet to be defined, ICH S5(R3) will note that in vitro, ex vivo, and nonmammalian in vivo assays might be considered for regulatory purposes. Specific in vitro, ex vivo, and nonmammalian in vivo assays will not be recommended in the guideline. The guidelines may include basic principles, possibly as appended information that would assist in the development and potential regulatory use of in vitro, ex vivo, and nonmammalian assays.
5. Describe the circumstances under which the outcome of "preliminary EFD studies" could obviate the need for more comprehensive evaluation in a definitive EFD study. The preliminary EFD will determine the ultimate risk assessment for EFD, thereby providing more clarity on the application of Section 11.3 and Note 4 of ICH M3(R2).

Early Guidelines

Guidelines for *Reproductive Studies for Safety Evaluation of Drugs for Human Use* were finalized in 1966 [8]. They consisted of a series of studies divided into three segments, each of which pertained to a specific phase of the reproductive process. The Segment I design addresses fertility and general reproductive performance; the Segment II design entails classic teratology testing; and the Segment III design extends treatment to the peri- and postnatal period. Testing requirements for food additives, color additives, and animal drugs administered to food producing animals were extended to include multigeneration reproduction studies with a teratology phase incorporated into the design [9,10]. Similar guidelines were then adopted by other regulatory agencies in the United States and the western world including Japan, which were applied not only to pharmaceutical drugs, but also to all classes of chemicals with significant human exposure potential.

In the 1960s and 1970s, there was a rapid increase in laws, regulations, and guidelines for reporting and evaluating the data on safety, quality, and efficacy of new drugs. A major issue emerged as the pharmaceutical industry became more international and began seeking new global markets. The discrepancy in technical requirements from country to country was such that the industry found itself obliged to duplicate many time-consuming and expensive test procedures. To attain international conformity of guidelines, a joint initiative involving both regulators and research-based industry representatives of the European Union, Japan, and the United States in scientific and technical discussions of the testing procedures required to assess and ensure the safety, quality, and efficacy of medicines was then established in 1990.

ICH Established

The International Conference on Harmonization (ICH) of Technical Requirements for Registration of Pharmaceuticals for Human Use brought together the regulatory authorities of Europe, Japan, and the United States and included experts in the pharmaceutical industry from these three regions [4]. The main objective of the ICH was to develop a process aimed at reducing or preventing the need to duplicate the testing conducted during the research and development of new drugs by recommending ways to achieve greater harmonization in the application of technical guidelines and requirements for product registration. This harmonization has led to a more economical use of human, animal, and material resources and the elimination of unnecessary delay in the global development and availability of quality, safety, and efficacy of new drugs, and in the meantime enforcing regulatory obligations to protect public health. Terms of reference were agreed on at the first ICH Steering Committee (SC) meeting, and it was decided that the topics selected for harmonization should be divided into safety, quality, and efficacy to reflect the three criteria, which are the basis for approving and authorizing new medicinal products.

The ICH made it easier for drugs developed in Europe and the United States to be marketed in Japan.

In 1993, a draft of the tripartite harmonized ICH guidelines for reproductive testing was completed. They were then finalized (Step 4) in June 1993, and an addendum to the core ICH guideline with respect to male fertility studies was finalized (Step 4) in November 1995. This was later amended on November 9, 2000, under the Maintenance Process. These guidelines, known as ICH 4.1.1, ICH 4.1.2, and ICH 4.1.3, are similar to the original FDA guidelines with some minor exceptions. The ICH guidelines allow for flexibility in developing the testing strategy rather than following a standard checklist approach. As the objective of these tests is to assess all stages of reproduction, the total exposure period includes mature adults and all stages of development of the offspring from conception to weaning.

Reproductive Lifecycle

Harmonization of the testing guidelines provided an opportunity for reproductive toxicologists to step back and recognize that reproductive toxicology has a level of complexity that makes it different from general toxicity studies. One way to look at this complexity is through the reproductive lifecycle (Fig. 9.1). While the importance of dose and exposure are key to all toxicity studies, reproductive toxicity studies introduce the concept of timing of exposure in addition to the dose attained during that exposure.

An insult or exposure to a drug that occurs to a cycling F_0 generation female can have a consequence later in the lifecycle of that female or in subsequent generations. For example, an antiviral compound administered to a female can produce direct toxicity on various target organs and systems. If the female is pregnant when the exposure occurs, gametes developing in utero can also be affected, with the result of this insult not being manifested until the next generation (F_1 generation females) is mated. A reduction in fertility to the F_1 generation may occur as the result of an insult to the developing eggs, up to the last meiotic division, in the ova of the F_1 generation fetus in utero.

From the thalidomide tragedy, we learned that exposure of a pregnant woman during a critical period of development at a dose of a drug that was therapeutic resulted in malformations in the offspring. Subsequent to the thalidomide tragedy we learned that in utero exposure of fetuses to methyl mercury results in functional deficits, such as mental retardation. More recently we have come to recognize that exposure of a child (preterm births to adolescents) to a drug or chemical may not produce the same effect as exposure of an adult to the same dose. Pediatric or juvenile toxicity testing has

become an entirely separate area of the nonclinical safety assessment of a new drug and is addressed in a separate chapter. Reproductive toxicologists are now beginning to elucidate how epigenetic changes that can affect sperm, ova, and the developing embryo can lead to effects later in the reproductive lifecycle. How research in this area will affect safety testing in the future has yet to be determined.

ICH Approach

The International Conference on Harmonization (ICH) approach to studying the reproductive lifecycle has been to divide the cycle into various stages [11–13]. These six stages, A to F, as defined later, allow the effect of an insult that might occur during one stage to be studied. Separate studies allow data to be collected on various doses of a pharmaceutical that enter the cycle at various times. While appropriate for a pharmaceutical from which exposure to the father or mother should be intentional, exposure to a chemical, such as pesticides on food, is usually unintentional and may occur throughout the reproductive lifecycle. Therefore, for unintentional exposures single-study or multigenerational designs that cover all parts of the reproductive lifecycle are appropriate. Understanding that the exposure of the embryo is almost always unintentional makes focused studies for evaluating developmental toxicity a practical way to test the potential hazard of a pharmaceutical to the developing conceptus. ICH study designs are presented in Figs. 9.2–9.5.

ICH Stages of Development

The ICH stages A to F are defined as follows:

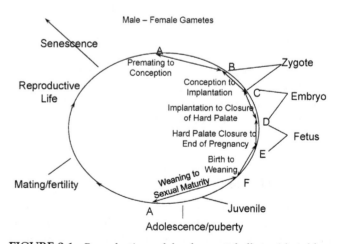

FIGURE 9.1   Reproductive and developmental effects. *Adapted from Christian MS. Test methods for assessing female reproductive and developmental toxicology. In: Hayes AW, editor. Principles and methods of toxicology. Philadelphia: Taylor and Francis; p. 1301–82.*

Measures effects on fertility and early establishment of pregnancy

FIGURE 9.2   ICH 4.1.1 Fertility and early embryonic development to implantation.

Rat and rabbit embryo-fetal toxicity study

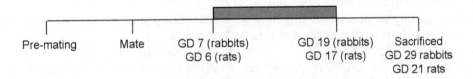

- Also known as teratology or organogenesis studies

- Assesses effects of compound on development of offspring from implantation through closure of the hard palate, i.e., the period of organogenesis

FIGURE 9.3   ICH 4.1.3 Embryo-fetal development toxicity study.

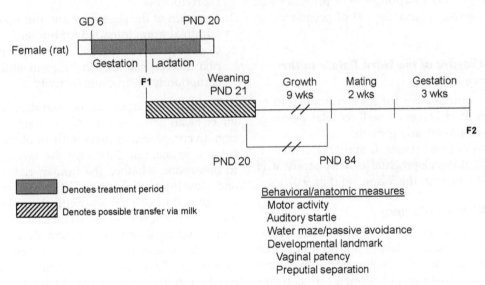

FIGURE 9.4   ICH 4.1.2 Peri-postnatal study including behavioral/anatomic parameters.

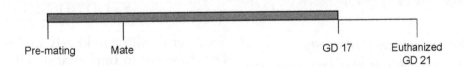

Measures effect on fertility, early establishment of pregnancy and organogenesis

FIGURE 9.5   ICH 4.1.1./4.1.3 Combined fertility and early embryo-fetal development.

II. TOXICOLOGICAL STUDIES AND IND APPLICATION, AND FIRST IN-HUMAN CLINICAL TRIAL

ICH Stage A—Premating to Conception

This ICH stage evaluates reproductive functions in adult males and females, including development and maturation of gametes, mating behavior, and fertilization. By convention, it was agreed that pregnancy would be timed on the basis of when spermatozoa are identified in a vaginal smear or a copulatory plug is observed, and that these events would identify gestation day (GD) 0, even if mating occurs overnight.

ICH Stage B—Conception to Implantation

This ICH stage examines reproductive functions in the adult female and preimplantation and implantation stages of the conceptus. Implantation occurs in rats, mice, and rabbits on days 6–7 of pregnancy.

The evaluation of these stages, A and B, are covered in the male and female fertility study ICH 4.1.1 as described earlier (Fig. 9.2).

ICH Stage C—Implantation to Closure of the Hard Palate

This ICH stage evaluates adult female reproductive functions, embryonic development, and major organ formation. The period of embryogenesis is completed at closure of the hard palate, which by convention is considered to occur on days 15 through 18 of pregnancy in rats, mice, and hamsters (and day 30 of pregnancy in guinea pigs).

ICH Stage D—Closure of the Hard Palate to the End of Pregnancy

Adult female reproductive function continues to be examined in this ICH stage, as well as fetal development, organ development, and growth.

The evaluation of these stages, C and D, are covered in the embryo-fetal developmental toxicity study ICH 4.1.3 design as described in the following (Fig. 9.3).

ICH Stage E—Birth to Weaning

Again, adult female reproductive function is examined; this ICH stage also evaluates adaptation of the neonate to extrauterine life, including preweaning development and growth of the neonate. By convention, the day of birth is considered postnatal day (PND) 0, unless specified otherwise. It is also noted that when there are delays or accelerations of pregnancy, postnatal age may be optimally based on postcoital age.

ICH Stage F—Weaning to Sexual Maturity

This ICH stage is generally treated only when the intended use of the pharmaceutical product is in children. The ICH guideline recognizes that it may sometimes be appropriate to also treat the neonate during this ICH stage, in addition to the required evaluations of the offspring. This ICH stage provides observations of postweaning development and growth, adaptation to independent life, and attainment of full sexual development.

The evaluation of these stages, E and F, are covered in the peripostnatal study ICH 4.1.2 design described earlier (Fig. 9.4).

As noted by Christian [14], the ICH guidelines cite recommendations that were often not identified in earlier reproductive and developmental toxicity guidelines, including use of:

1. Scientific justification of flexible study designs
2. Kinetics
3. Expanded male reproductive toxicity evaluations
4. A requirement for mechanistic studies
5. Essentially equal emphasis on all endpoints of developmental toxicity (death, malformation, reduced weight, functional/behavioral alterations), rather than emphasizing malformation as the most important outcome

Based on the harmonized ICH guideline, flexible testing strategies are to be based on:

1. Anticipated drug use, especially in relation to reproduction
2. The form of the substance and route(s) of administration intended for humans
3. Consideration of existing data on toxicity, pharmacodynamics, kinetics, and similarity to other compounds in structure/activity

In total, the purpose of these studies is to identify any effect of an active substance on mammalian reproduction, to compare this effect with all other pharmacological and toxicological data for the agent, and ultimately to determine whether the human risk of reproductive and developmental effects is the same as, increased, or reduced in comparison with the risks of other toxic effects of the agent. As for all toxicological observations, additional pertinent information should be considered before the results of the animal studies are extrapolated to humans. This information includes human exposure considerations, comparative kinetics, and the mechanism of the toxic effect.

STUDY DESIGNS

Study of Fertility and Early Embryonic Development to Implantation (ICH 4.1.1)

We only need to look at the history of the various male and female fertility designs as promulgated by the United States, Great Britain, and Japan and the resulting

ICH S5 (R2) guideline [6] to understand that the focus of the male and female fertility study has changed significantly over time.

As outlined by Lerman et al. [15], prior to the ICH initiative, the various study designs for evaluating male and female fertility resulted in multiple studies being conducted to meet the various guidelines and redundant evaluations of developmental toxicity. Initially defined as an evaluation of fertility and general reproductive performance, including examination of potential adverse effects on gonadal function and mating behavior in male and female animals, conception rates, early and late stages of gestation, parturition, lactation, and development of the offspring, the initial study design was an abbreviated multigeneration study, usually ending at weaning of the second generation.

Each of the various designs involved administration of a test material to mature male rodents for approximately 70 days (10 weeks) prior to mating, covering a full spermatogenic cycle (spermatogenesis plus capacitation in the epididymis) and administration to the female rodents for 14 days prior to mating. The US FDA version continued dosing through gestation with one-half of the females being terminated midgestation and the other one-half being allowed to deliver, with the offspring going out to weaning. The British version had half of the females Caesarean-sectioned at the end of gestation and the other half of the females allowed to deliver, with the offspring carried to weaning. The Japanese version ended dosing at implantation, and the females were terminated at the end of gestation.

The ICH S5 guidance [6] was amended on the basis of information from a review by Ulbrich and Palmer [16], and a collaborative study [17] that revealed effects on testicular weight and adverse histopathology were generally detected following 2–4 weeks of exposure. The resultant amendment to the ICH S5 guidance [6] noted that if there is no evidence of impaired male reproductive performance from other studies, based on adequate microscopic examination [eg, by using appropriate fixatives (Bouin's or Davidson's)], paraffin embedding, transverse section of testes, longitudinal section for epididymis, and periodic Acid-Schiff's or hematoxylin staining, males may be treated for 28- or 14-day intervals before mating with cohort females.

Pregnancy and Lactation Labeling

The preclinical studies of reproductive and developmental toxicity described in this chapter have principally been conducted to assess the hazard of a pharmaceutical to the conceptus (embryo/fetus) and assess any effects on reproductive performance in adult males and females. These assessments are reflected or communicated to the doctor and patient in the label or package insert that accompanies each drug. Since 1979, in the United States, the risk to the conceptus has been characterized with a letter, A, B, C, D, or X [18].

On June 30, 2015, the new labeling rules [19] became effective, and will affect all new labels and eventually result in the revision of all drug labels in the United States. In addition, label updates for all marketed products will be a continual process as new information becomes available to ensure that meaningful data are consistently communicated to the physician and patient.

The new rules remove the pregnancy categories the FDA determined were often "confusing and did not accurately or consistently communicate differences in degrees of fetal risk" [18]. The letters have been replaced by narrative summaries of the risk a drug may pose during pregnancy and/or lactation with the intent of providing the clinician with more meaningful information. The use of a drug in men and women of reproductive potential or continued use during pregnancy or lactation needs to be evaluated in the context of the disease state to be treated and known hazards as presented in the package insert.

Labeling changes mandated by the new law will combine information on pregnancy, labor, and delivery into the pregnancy section (8.1) of the label. Information for nursing mothers will be summarized in the lactation section (8.2) and a new section has been added (Section 8.3) to address males and females of reproductive potential.

Each section, 8.1, 8.2, and 8.3 will have a specific structure. Section 8.1 will first list the name and contact information for any pregnancy registry established to monitor pregnancies once the product is marketed. This section will be updated as new information is added to the registry. The second subsection will contain the risk summary, which is a succinct presentation of the known risks in view of the background risk information in the general population, and if known, the disease population. Human risk data or the lack thereof will always be presented first, followed by risk based on animal data and the pharmacology of the drug. At marketing, the animal data will usually be the only information available. The third subsection will consist of the clinical considerations or any medical/disease factors that should be considered. Information on the value of controlling a disease state (eg, asthma) during pregnancy versus the lack of control should be discussed. Any dose adjustments that might be relevant during pregnancy will also be presented in the third subsection. The fourth and final subsection is the data section in which all known data from humans (if any) and animals will be summarized to support the statements made in the previous subsections. The types of studies conducted, species used, animal doses in relation to human exposure or timing and duration of exposure, study findings including the presence or absence of maternal toxicity, and any limitations of the data will be included in this subsection.

Section 8.2, Lactation, will follow a similar format as previously described for Section 8.1, with a risk statement, followed by a clinical considerations paragraph and data paragraph. When human data are not available animal data will be presented. So the presence of the drug in milk and effects on milk production will be presented. Based on the known benefits of breastfeeding, any information on drug in the milk becomes important to support breastfeeding after childbirth.

Section 8.3, Females and Males of Reproductive Potential, will only be included when there is a need to recommend a pregnancy test and/or contraception especially when the animal data suggests there is the potential to affect fertility. This section will have three subsections, including Pregnancy Testing, Contraception, and Infertility. The details on animal studies will be cross-referenced to Section 13, Nonclincal Toxicology.

Species Selection

Most studies are performed using rats, mice, rabbits, or hamsters; however, the same principles described here can be applied to ferrets, guinea pigs, mini-pigs, dogs, and nonhuman primates (NHPs), using species-specific considerations. One caveat is that the selection of the species for study should be based on evidence that the agent is pharmacologically/toxicologically active in the species, absorbed (if administered orally or topically), and, if possible, similarly handled metabolically by the test species and humans. As described by Chellman et al. [20], reproductive toxicology endpoints can be evaluated in NHPs in conjunction with chronic toxicology studies, unless cause for concern exists. Incorporation of the reproductive endpoints into the chronic toxicology study design: (1) minimizes the use of animals by reducing the total number of studies required; and (2) optimizes the use of NHPs since the supply of sexually mature animals is limited. This trend to incorporate the reproductive endpoints into the chronic toxicology study design is a good example of how reductions in animal usage and refinements to study designs continue to meet the needs of drug development programs while aligning with the principles of the 3Rs (reduce, refine, replace).

Common Fertility Protocol Design

A common fertility protocol design is outlined in Fig. 9.2. Refinements of the test include:

1. A combined design of treated females mated with untreated males and then using the same males (after treatment) to mate with untreated females.

This allows evaluation of any potential reproductive effects in a separate population of males or females within the same study design.

2. Double-sized control and high-dose groups during the premating period, with cross-mating of one-half of the animals in these two groups. This is done to determine whether administration of the test material to animals of only one sex causes different effects from those observed when both sexes are treated.

3. Extension of the female treatment period through the remainder of gestation (eg, for rats, until GD 17 or 19, with Caesarean-sectioning on GD 20 or 21), and evaluation of the fetuses for viability and gross external, soft tissue, and skeletal alterations. This design addresses both male and female fertility, reproductive performance, and developmental toxicity.

4. Extension of the female treatment period through the remainder of gestation and then through parturition and lactation (eg, for rats until lactation day 21). This design facilitates an evaluation of both male and female fertility, reproductive performance, and F_1 generation evaluations (pup growth and development, sexual maturation, postnatal behavior and function, behavioral changes, and fertility).

Dose Selection

In general, regulatory studies require that the high dose be maternally and/or developmentally toxic, and that the low dose should be a NOAEL. In the past, no more than 10% mortality and/or 10% reduction in body weight was considered sufficient evidence of toxicity at the high dose. The ICH guidelines indicate that the high dose should produce minimal maternal (adult) toxicity and be selected on the basis of data from all available studies, including pharmacological, acute, and subchronic toxicity and kinetic studies. Timing for conduct of the fertility studies is typical during late Phase II or Phase III clinical trials when most nonclinical toxicity studies have been completed and exposure levels from both animal studies and human trials are known. Therefore the need for dose-range studies prior to the fertility study is minimal. Doses for the fertility study should be selected based on previous evidence of maternal toxicity including reduced or increased weight gain, target organ toxicity, or based on a biomarker, such as a change in clinical pathology. An exaggerated pharmacological response, which may or may not be reflected as marked clinical reactions (eg, sedation, convulsions), can also be used to justify a high dose. Additional justification for high-dose selection include physicochemical properties of the test substance or dose formulation, which, in combination with the route of administration, can be justification for limiting the administered amount (generally 1–1.5 g/kg/day provides an adequate limit dose) [14].

Number of Animals per Group

The number of animals per dose group is usually twice that used in general toxicity studies, with 20–25 rodents/sex/group, 3 dose groups, and a control group. The increased number of animals per group increases the power of the tests performed and is deemed important for reproductive studies when parameters are evaluated only once. This is in contrast to general toxicity studies in which the group sizes are smaller, but in general, a series of studies differing in length and dose are conducted. With the general toxicity studies, we can look across these studies for dose-dependent trends and effects.

EVALUATING FERTILITY AND REPRODUCTION

Parameters evaluated in a fertility study include those typically evaluated in general toxicity studies, including clinical observations, body weight, and food consumption. Evaluation of female reproductive toxicity relies on data generated from estrous cycle evaluations, mating and fertility assessments, and ovarian and uterine evaluations, including the number and distribution of corpora lutea and implantation sites and embryonic viability. In addition, organ weights (ovaries, uterus with cervix, and/or vagina) and histopathology are often required by the regulatory guidelines [21–24] to fully elucidate reproductive findings in females and/or to aid in the proper identification of a reproductive toxicant. Similar to females, evaluation of male reproductive toxicity can be determined by mating and fertility assessments and reproductive organ weights [testes, epididymides, cauda epididymal weight, seminal vesicles with coagulating glands (with and without fluids), and prostate]. Additional endpoints in males, although not mandated, include histopathology of the testes and epididymides and an evaluation of sperm for count, concentration, and morphology. Such analyses may also be appropriate if previous histopathology suggested a change to testicular epithelium, keeping in mind the large sperm reserve in the rodent compared to man.

Parameters unique to the fertility assessment are summarized in the following.

EVALUATION OF ESTROUS CYCLING

Estrous cycling in rodent species, specifically the rat and mouse, is evaluated by obtaining a sample of cells from the vagina by lavage, followed by an examination of the cytology. Cycling changes are staged as estrus, metestrus, diestrus, and proestrus. The stage of the estrous cycle is determined by the predominant cell type observed microscopically. The duration of the stage varies among the species, with diestrus representing the longest stage in rats (60–70 h) and mice (22–33 h). Estrus (10–15 h in rats and up to 21 h in mice) is the only stage in the cycle when the female will copulate with the male. Proestrus denotes the beginning of the next cycle. The duration of an estrous cycle is calculated for each animal based on the number of days between estrus stages per interval observed. In a typical fertility study, estrous cycling is evaluated for 14 days before dose administration, for the first 14 days of dose administration before cohabitation, and until mating occurs. Pretreatment estrous evaluations facilitate exclusion of abnormally cycling females prior to the initiation of dose administration. It is important to continue to monitor estrous cycling during the dose and cohabitation periods to identify potential perturbations, which may predict reduced female receptivity and fertility.

Similar to rats and mice, the length of the estrous cycle in hamsters is 4 days and the stages are the same (ie, proestrus, metestrus, estrus, and diestrus). However, the technique for evaluating the estrous cycle varies, in that the signs are manifested externally and the stage is determined by an examination of the vaginal opening/perivaginal area and the presence or absence of a discharge. For guinea pigs, the duration of the estrous cycle is up to 18 days, and staging of the estrous cycle is impractical because the vaginal orifice is closed by a membrane until the animal is in estrus [25].

Mating Behavior and Fertilization

In general, the mating ratio for rodents is one to one, which allows for easy identification of the sire and dam, and excludes potential reductions in performance associated with excess use of the same male. The same applies to most other species. However, based on published fertility study designs for guinea pigs, it is possible to successfully harem mate guinea pigs such that one untreated breeder male is paired with two or more treated females.

Mating (copulation) in rats, mice, and hamsters is confirmed by the presence of spermatozoa in the contents of the vaginal smear and/or the observation of a copulatory plug in situ; these findings designate GD 0. For mice, the presence of an expelled copulatory plug in the pan is often considered adequate proof of mating, although only approximately 85% of the mice identified in this fashion actually become pregnant. In fertility designs using guinea pigs, presumed pregnant females have been successfully utilized because it facilitates synchronization of mating and gestation, delivery, and postpartum estrus/mating. Pregnancy rates in the guinea pig are notably much higher when pregnant guinea pigs are allowed to mate just following delivery (postpartum mating).

Female mating performance in rats, mice, and hamsters can be measured by several endpoints. These include identifying:

1. The number of days in cohabitation before mating
2. The number of mated (inseminated) female animals per group
3. Pregnancy incidence based on the total population per group (percentage of pregnant/number cohabited) and on the inseminated population per group (percentage of pregnant/number inseminated)

The number of females assigned to an alternate male and the duration of cohabitation with the second male should always be identified.

Rats and mice generally have multiple intromissions in one copulatory interval. Mating in rats and mice generally occurs during offpeak hours (ie, the dark period) when aberrant copulatory behavior cannot be readily observed. In the event that aberrant copulatory behavior needs to be further evaluated, the animals can be videotaped and graded for the number of copulations, the number of intromissions, the duration of intromission, and receptive behavior in females as evidenced by the occurrence of lordosis. Mating behavior in mice may be altered by environmental conditions, such as overcrowding, same sex cohousing prior to mating, or introduction of strange males after mating. Confounding factors that may affect mating behavior in rats include the photoperiod, nutrition, stress, lactation, and endocrine disruptors.

Preimplantation Loss, Impaired Implantation, and Uterine Contents

Calculation of preimplantation loss is accomplished by counting the number of corpora lutea and comparing this number to the total number of implantation sites identified at terminal euthanasia of the dams. The animals are euthanized near the beginning of the fetal period, between GD 13 and 15 for rats and mice and GD 30 for guinea pigs, to facilitate viability assessments of the developing offspring, based on a beating heart.

Follicle Number and Size

Ovarian histopathology is an optional assessment for evaluating the potential effects of a test agent on the female reproductive system that can result in loss of oogonia, oocytes, or supportive somatic cells. Knowledge of normal ovarian morphology, estrous cycling, and age-related changes is essential to adequately interpret microscopic findings and/or subsequent reproductive effects. The stage at which a test agent depletes or destroys ovarian follicles ultimately determines the impact on fertility. For instance, agents damaging large-growing and antral follicles interrupt the reproduction temporarily; however, xenobiotics damaging oocytes in primordial or primary follicles may lead to infertility that is permanent [26].

Several researchers have outlined methods pertaining to processing and microscopic evaluation of the ovaries [27–30]. The procedure described by Smith et al. [27] is laborious and expensive, requiring 30–60 sections per ovary for mice and rats, which results in 300 and 600 sections per group of 10 animals, respectively. Conversely, the method described by Plowchalk et al. [28] is a shorter screening method for potential use when indicated by observations in companion studies (eg, pharmacological action or reduced ovarian weight or atresia) [14]. In the latter method, the ovaries are fixed in Bouin's solution, standard histological techniques are used to prepare 6.0-μm serial sections, and five random sections are evaluated for primordial, growing, and antral follicles [14]. It is noteworthy to mention that the method described by Plowchalk et al. [28] reduces the statistical power of the assay, but allows assessment of loss of specific follicle types and changes in component volumes. Based on a Society of Toxicological Pathology (STP) position paper [31], there is insufficient evidence to warrant the use of ovarian follicle counting as a first-tier screening method in rodent toxicity studies; however, qualitative microscopic examination has merit as a first-tier screening tool for reproductive toxicity.

Sperm Evaluations

Based on the addendum to the ICH S5 guidelines, sperm analyses are optional; however, these analyses remain a relevant endpoint for evaluating male reproductive toxicity, specifically spermatogenesis and sperm maturation. In both animals and man, fertility is dependent on the number of sperm and the quality of the sperm produced. Perreault et al. [32] surmised that:

> If sperm quality is high, sperm number must be reduced substantially before fertility by natural mating is affected. If sperm number is normal in rodents, a relatively large effect on sperm motility is required before fertility is affected.

In rats, approximately 95% of the sperm produced are normal, and sperm production in rodents can, in theory, be reduced by 50% without impacting fertility.

Sperm count and sperm concentration may be derived from ejaculates, epididymidal or testicular samples [29]. Although subject to variability, sperm count is a good measure of sperm output and storage. Rabbits are considered the smallest laboratory animal from which semen samples can be readily obtained by serial sampling techniques; however, sperm number from ejaculated samples may be confounded by sexual immaturity and abstinence. For rabbits, a regular sampling schedule often resolves intra- and interanimal variability observed in ejaculated semen samples. In rats, epididymidal samples are obtained from the cauda epididymis at terminal euthanasia.

As previously described, sperm motility is an important aspect of normal fertilization. Sperm motility is a good measure of sperm function, and samples may be obtained from ejaculates, the vas deferens, or the cauda epididymis. Other optional sperm assessments include:

1. Sperm morphology to identify abnormalities associated with the sperm head (affects penetration) or sperm flagellum (affects motility)
2. Spermatid counts to measure survivability and sperm production from the stem cells
3. Histopathology ("sperm staging") to detect alterations in spermatogenesis or provide mechanistic information

Spermatogenesis is a self-renewing cellular system within the body that is characterized by distinct cellular associations among germ cells at each differentiation cycle [33]. Staging of the seminiferous tubules is a qualitative process that allows an experienced pathologist to identify stage-specific cellular changes and to recognize the presence or absence of germ cells. The length of the spermatogenesis cycle is species-dependent, with the shortest cycle occurring in the mouse (45–54 days) and the longest cycle in an animal model is that of the dog (68–82 days). In contrast to man, rabbits and rodents (rats and mice) produce the highest amount of sperm per gram testis on a daily basis, demonstrating the efficiency of spermatogenesis in animal models used to evaluate reproductive toxicity.

HORMONAL REGULATION

Direct measurements of hormone levels (eg, luteinizing hormone, follicle-stimulating hormone, estradiol, progesterone, prolactin, and testosterone) are also optional assessments for evaluating the reproductive system. Changes in hormone levels during the course of the estrous cycle result in distinct morphological changes in the female reproductive organs (ie, ovary, uterus, and vagina) [26]. Hormones (ie, LH and FSH) released by the pituitary act on the ovaries to stimulate production of reproductive steroids, progesterone and estradiol. Prolactin is another hormone that is secreted

primarily by the pituitary gland, and has many physiological functions.

In rats, but not in humans, prolactin is *luteotropic* and it may act in conjunction with LH or FSH on *luteal* function to stimulate progesterone biosynthesis and secretion. Progesterone, secreted by the corpus luteum, plays a fundamental role in influencing the length of the estrous cycle in rodents, induction of sexual receptivity, and stimulating ovulation and uterine implantation. Estradiol, which is secreted by ovarian follicles, influences the growth and development of the female reproductive tract.

The level of sex hormones in female rats varies depending on the estrous cycle stage, the length of the cycle, reproductive status, and the age of the rat. Estradiol levels are at their lowest during estrus and metestrus, but gradually rise during diestrus and peak during proestrus in normally cycling female rats. The rise in estradiol levels leads to a surge in prolactin and LH levels during proestus. Estradiol, prolactin, and LH levels eventually decline during the transition from proestrus to estrus. Progesterone levels typically peak twice during the estrous cycle. The first surge is minimal and coincides with the formation of new corpora lutea during metestrus. Overall, the highest levels of progesterone occur during late proestrus and the early stage of estrus, with the lowest levels being observed during diestrus. FSH mimics the pattern of LH, with the highest levels peaking during late proestrus, and again early in estrus.

In rats, corticosterone is the primary glucocorticoid produced by the adrenal glands. In normal cycling female rats, corticosterone demonstrates a sex-cycle-associated biorhythm and is synchronized with the normal biological rhythm. When compared to the estrous cycle, the highest levels of corticosterone are observed late in proestrus and the lowest levels during estrus and early diestrus. When compared to the photoperiod, the highest levels of corticosterone are often at the end of the light phase and the lowest levels are at the end of the dark phase.

Several sites in the hypothalamic-pituitary-gonadal axis can be perturbed by different chemicals.

EMBRYO-FETAL DEVELOPMENT

Timing and Exposure

Hazard identification of the developing conceptus (embryo/fetus) from exposure to a test agent has always been considered one of the critical endpoints in developmental testing because:

1. Pregnant women are rarely purposely exposed to a new test agent during clinical trials since it is

generally considered unethical. The fetus can never give consent to participation in the trial.

2. The sensitive time of fetal exposure leading to production of a fetal malformation is during the first few weeks of pregnancy, often before a woman realizes she is pregnant.

Therefore the identification of any agent that is a selective developmental toxicant is the major reason for conducting embryo-fetal developmental toxicity studies [6]. A selective developmental toxicant is any agent that causes developmental effects (structural malformations, growth retardations, functional impairment, and/or embryo-fetal death) at doses that are within the therapeutic range or not paternally or maternally toxic.

Wilson's Principles

Even today, Wilson's basic principles remain valid, and continue to serve as the basic premise for training up-and-coming investigators in the field of developmental and reproductive toxicology [34]. The terminology in the principles [34] outlined in the following was previously updated [14] to align with current terminology (eg, developmental toxicity used in place of teratogenesis).

1. Susceptibility to developmental toxicity depends on the genotype of the conceptus and the manner in which this interacts with adverse environmental factors.
2. Susceptibility to developmental toxicity varies with the developmental stage at the time of exposure to an adverse influence.
3. Developmental toxins act in specific ways (mechanisms) on developing cells and tissues to initiate sequences of abnormal developmental events (pathogenesis).
4. The access of adverse influences to developing tissues depends on the nature of the influence (agent).
5. The four manifestations of deviant development are death, malformation, growth retardation, and functional deficit. Only the first three are evaluated in the developmental toxicity study. Functional deficits are evaluated in the peripostnatal study as discussed later in this chapter.
6. Manifestations of deviant development increase in frequency and degree as dosage increases, from the no effect to the totally lethal level.

Wilson [35] also proposed potential mechanisms of developmental toxicity, and we can assume that any alterations in these mechanisms will ultimately affect normal development of an offspring. These mechanisms include mitotic interference, altered membrane function/signal transduction, altered energy sources, enzyme inhibition, altered nucleic acid synthesis, and mutations. Based on the current understanding of the molecular mechanisms associated with normal development [36], the mechanisms initially proposed by Wilson can be expanded to include perturbations in gene or protein expression and programmed cell death.

Based on these definitions, developmental toxicology can be considered a study of the entire reproductive process, with special emphasis on the developing conceptus, but including the development and function of that conceptus throughout its entire lifespan.

In the ICH 4.1.3 study design (embryo-fetal development, EFD) two species are traditionally tested when evaluating pharmaceuticals (small molecules) because: (1) selective developmental toxicants remain the most sensitive regulatory concern; and (2) thalidomide did not cause phocomelia in the rat, although it can produce phocomelia in the rabbit [37]. Developmental and reproductive toxicology (DART) testing guidelines [6,21–24,38] emphasize the importance of testing in two species, one rodent and one nonrodent. In addition, the ICH guidelines recommend testing the species and strain of animal that was tested in preceding general toxicology studies or kinetic studies.

The increased consideration of the metabolism of test agents has resulted in the animal species whose metabolism of an agent is most like that of humans generally being considered the most appropriate species. Historically, the rat and rabbit have been regarded as the most "relevant" animal models for evaluating pharmaceuticals. However, due to species-specificity issues, developmental and reproductive toxicology testing for biologics is limited to a pharmacologically relevant animal model, which in most cases is the NHP. As noted in the ICH S6 guideline:

> The use of one species is justified when the biological activity of the biopharmaceutical is well understood or the clinical candidate is pharmacologically active in only one species [39].

When rodents are deemed the most relevant species, investigators are encouraged to select species and strains that are outbred with good fertility and adequate historical control data.

Prior to the full embryo-fetal developmental toxicity study, dose-range finding studies are commonly conducted to aid in selection of dose levels. The concept of the dose-range-finding study is to evaluate a minimum number of pregnant animals/litters to identify dose levels that may be too toxic for evaluation of reproductive or developmental toxicity and to identify a selective reproductive or developmental toxicant.

Beginning in 2009, the ICH M3 guideline [40] specified the inclusion of dose-range-finding studies in the drug development program to allow a limited number of women of child-bearing age (WOCB) to be evaluated in clinical trials following conduct of two developmental toxicity studies with a limited number of pregnant animals ($n = 6$) per group and limited fetal evaluations (gross external, sex, weight, and visceral examinations).

Study Design Requirements

There are a number of publications available that provide a detailed review of the embryo-fetal developmental study design [14,37,41,42]. However, for the purposes of this chapter a concise overview of the embryo-fetal developmental study design is provided in the following.

Species

One rodent and one nonrodent.

Number per Group

The ICH S5 [6] guideline recommends 16–20 animals per dose group, with a control and at least 3 dose groups administered the test agent. Generally, 20 rodents and 16 nonrodents per dose group have been considered appropriately sized populations for testing. The FDA Redbook [22], OECD 414 [21], and US EPA [23] guidelines, however, recommend 20 pregnant animals per group, regardless of species.

Treatment Period

GD 0 is generally recognized as the day sperm, a vaginal or copulatory plug, or insemination is observed. Pregnant females are administered the test agent throughout the period of major organogenesis, generally between implantation and palate closure. This period was extended from that in the guidelines [8] to include sexual differentiation and initial renal development.

In-life Observations

Pregnant females are evaluated for maternal function and/or toxicity, including mortality, clinical observations, body weights and body weight gains, food consumption, and/or water consumption.

Maternal Evaluations

Females are examined for gross lesions shortly before expected parturition (usually on GD 15, 18, 21, 29, or 65 in hamsters, mice, rats, rabbits, and guinea pigs, respectively). Ovarian and uterine contents are recorded, including the number and distribution of corpora lutea, implantation sites, and embryo-fetal viability (live and dead fetuses and early and late resorptions). In addition, each placenta is examined for any abnormalities (changes in size, shape, or color).

Fetal Examinations

Each fetus is weighed and examined for sex and external abnormalities (malformations and variations). In rodent studies, approximately one-half of the fetuses in each litter are examined for soft-tissue abnormalities by fresh dissections [43,44] or following adequate fixation [44]. The remaining fetuses are examined for skeletal abnormalities following staining with alizarin red S [45–47]. In nonrodent studies, all fetuses are examined for soft-tissue and skeletal abnormalities.

Optional Assessments

Crown-rump lengths, anogenital distance, organ weights, double-staining of the fetuses with alizarin red S and alcian blue to facilitate a thorough examination of the skeleton and the cartilage, and maternal and/or fetal toxicokinetics (eg, blood samples, amniotic fluid, placentas) are all fetal assessments that can be performed if deemed appropriate based on the nature of the test article under investigation.

It should be recognized that a complete assessment of developmental toxicity includes an evaluation of functional deficits that can be more appropriately performed in the F_1-generation offspring naturally delivered from F_0-generation animals exposed to a test agent during pregnancy. This study design is the ICH 4.1.2, which is fully described elsewhere in this chapter.

Modifications to the embryo-fetal developmental study design are based on the test agent and can include, but are not limited to, initiation of dose administration prior to implantation, continuation of dosing after the closure of the hard palate, or "pulse" dosing through the period of major organogenesis. In addition, in cases where the test agent is not expected to pose any reproductive or developmental issues then the embryo-fetal developmental study can be incorporated into the fertility study design to address both male and female fertility, reproductive performance, and developmental toxicity, as previously described.

Terminal Procedures

Maternal Examinations

As mentioned previously, there are a number of publications available that provide a detailed review of the embryo-fetal developmental study design [14,41,42]. However, for the purposes of this chapter a concise overview of the terminal procedures included in an embryo-fetal developmental study design is provided in the following. The general practice is to euthanize hamsters, mice, rats, rabbits, and guinea pigs on GD 15, 18, 20, or 21, 29, and 65, respectively.

Following maternal euthanasia, each female is subject to an ovarian and uterine evaluation consisting of:

1. An examination of each ovary for the number of corpora lutea
2. A count of the number of implantation sites in each uterine horn
3. A determination of fetal viability (live or dead)
4. Staging (early or late) and counting the number of resorptions
5. An examination of each placenta for macroscopic changes

Prior to examination, the intact uterus of each pregnant female may be excised and weighed (with ovaries/oviducts attached). Measurement of the gravid uterine weight is required by the US EPA [23], US FDA Redbook [22], and OECD [21,38] embryo-fetal developmental toxicity guidelines. Incorporation of this endpoint into the study design facilitates calculation of corrected maternal body weights and maternal body weight gains and interpretation of the maternal body weight data without contribution of the offspring. Where necessary, each placenta may be weighed. However, as noted by Christian [14], placental weights may be highly variable because of fetal size and blood status at the time of maternal death.

Females that are visibly not pregnant should be further evaluated by either pressing the uterus between glass plates and examining it for the presence of implantation sites or staining the uterus with 10% ammonium sulfide [48]. However, this procedure renders this tissue useless for histological processing and microscopic examination. Alternative staining methods have been described by Tyl and Marr [49].

Fetal Examinations

Following the maternal examination, each conceptus (live or dead fetus and late resorption) is placed in a compartmentalized container for the litter, and the litter is evaluated for fetal body weight and sex and gross, soft-tissue and/or skeletal abnormalities depending on the study type (ie, dose-range finding or definitive). In a typical dose-range-finding study, all fetuses are examined for gross abnormalities, fetal body weights, and sex. However, the ICH M3 [40] guidelines note that the assessments in a dose-range-finding study ("preliminary embryo-fetal study") should also include an examination of the fetal soft-tissue morphology. With this preliminary information and adequate precautions to prevent pregnancy, up to 150 women of childbearing age may be enrolled in clinical trials of short duration prior to the initiation of the definitive embryo-fetal developmental toxicity study.

In the definitive embryo-fetal developmental toxicity study, all rodent and nonrodent fetuses are examined for gross abnormalities. Approximately one-half of all rodent fetuses in each litter are evaluated for soft-tissue or skeletal abnormalities, while all nonrodent fetuses are examined for both soft-tissue and skeletal abnormalities. Dead fetuses are generally examined to the extent possible, unless otherwise precluded by autolysis.

There are a variety of published methods pertaining to examination of soft-tissue morphology, including a fresh soft-tissue examination [43,44], free-hand sectioning following adequate fixation [50,51], or a combination of both techniques. The method selected should be based on the resources, training, historical experience, and scheduling requirements. Skeletal examinations require evisceration, skinning (where appropriate), clearing, and staining of the fetal specimens prior to evaluation of the ossified bone and/or cartilage. Alizarin red S is the stain used for single-staining techniques [46,47], while double-staining techniques require the use of both alizarin red S and alcian blue [52–55]. As noted by Christian [14], calculation of ossification site averages for each litter of various bony structures, including the hyoid, vertebrae, ribs, sternum, forepaws, and hindpaws, aids in identifying delays in ossification.

In 2009, Makris et al. published an update to the *Terminology of Developmental Abnormalities in Common Laboratory Mammals*. This publication expanded on the work published by Wise et al. [56], which was a valiant effort to assemble and harmonize to common nomenclature used to describe fetal and neonatal morphology. The latest publication [57] included nomenclature for common laboratory animals (rats, mice, and rabbits), and was centrally focused on descriptive terminology rather than diagnostic terminology. The publication was also organized in a manner that aligns with standard fetal-evaluation processes conducted in a laboratory setting (gross external, soft tissue, and skeletal). The reader is encouraged to refer to the aforementioned articles published by Wise et al. [56] and Makris et al. [57] to gain awareness of the internationally accepted fetal/neonatal morphological terminology and to understand the uses and misuses of the glossary.

PRE- AND POSTNATAL DEVELOPMENT STUDIES

The objective of the pre- and postnatal development (PPND) study, including maternal function, is to detect adverse effects on the pregnant/lactating female and on development of the conceptus and the offspring following exposure of the female from implantation through weaning. Since manifestations of effect induced during this period may be delayed, observations should be continued through sexual maturity [6].

This study is typically the last developmental and reproductive toxicity study performed. In all ICH regions (United States, European Union, and Japan), the pre- and postnatal development study should be submitted for marketing approval of a pharmaceutical [40]. These studies are often performed concurrently with 2-year carcinogenicity studies. However, because the PPND study is the only reproductive toxicity study design that has dose administration during the period of parturition, the preweaning postnatal period, and assesses potential functional deficits during the postweaning period, this study may be conducted earlier in drug development if the pharmaceutical is suspected of affecting this period. An example of a pharmaceutical that affected postnatal survival only when administered after the end of major organogenesis is the AT_1-selective angiotensin II receptor antagonist, Losartan [58,59]. For this pharmaceutical, no developmental toxicity was evident in rats treated from GD 6–17. However, when rats were treated from GD 15 through lactation day (LD) 20, lower pup weights and pre- and postweaning deaths were observed.

Selection of Species

According to ICH S5 R2 guidelines, a single species, preferably the rat, is used for PPND studies. Reasons for this preference include, but are not limited to, availability of data from other studies in this species with the same pharmaceutical and accessibility of historical control data in the rat. Alternative species can be used. However, justification for the selection of an alternate species is required (eg, the rat produces neutralizing antibodies to the pharmaceutical, lack of bioavailability in the rat, or lack of pharmacological response in the rat). Alternative models for the PPND study include the mouse, rabbit, hamster, and NHP. All study endpoints that are evaluated for the rat can also be evaluated for the mouse. However, the amount of historical control data for the mouse in PPND designs is usually much less than for the rat, and behavioral data is often more variable than in the rat.

On rare occasions, the rabbit has been used for PPND designs. The use of the rabbit in PPND designs can be very challenging because postnatal survival is lower than in rodents, there is a lack of validated behavioral assessments in this species, and only a limited amount of historical control data is available. The use of NHPs for PPND studies has grown in the past decade as a result of the increased development of biopharmaceuticals. The use of the NHP in PPND study designs is described elsewhere in this chapter.

Treatment Regimen

Fig. 9.4 presents a schematic that shows the basic study design of a rat PPND study. The endpoints contained in the PPND study design have been listed in detail previously [60]. The treatment regimen is from implantation until the end of lactation [6]. In the rat, a dosing regimen of GD 6 through LD 20 is generally accepted as complying with the ICH guideline. Dosing is typically performed once daily but should be based on toxicokinetic data. For pharmaceuticals with short half-lives, dosing more than once per day may be required in order to increase systemic exposure. Conversely, for pharmaceuticals with long half-lives, less frequent dose administration can be used if systemic exposure can be demonstrated on days the animals are not dosed. There is no guideline requirement for direct dosing of the offspring. While not specifically required by the ICH guidelines, fetal and pup exposure levels are often assessed to determine whether placental or lactational transfer occurs. This toxicokinetic assessment can be performed by blood collection from fetuses and pups and may also include collection of milk during lactation. In order to obtain a sufficient quantity of fetal or pup plasma for analysis, it is often necessary to pool blood from multiple fetuses or pups from the same litter. The route of administration should mimic the clinical route of administration.

Group Size and Animal Source

The standard study design has four groups, a control group plus three groups receiving the pharmaceutical. Group sizes of 20–25 dams are employed. The ICH guidelines recommend 16–20 L for rodents to provide a degree of consistency between studies. At the time of weaning on PND 21, one pup/sex/litter will be selected to comprise the F_1 postweaning phase of the study. The guidelines further state that 16–20 L are required for not just the parental generation, but also the F_1 generation. In cases of high preweaning pup death, it is not appropriate to select more than one pup/sex/litter as pups from the same litter will respond more similarly than pups from different litters. The litter should always be considered the experimental unit even after weaning. Because all bred F_0 females will not maintain litters until weaning, it is advisable to start with more than 20 dams per group.

The dams used in the study should be nulliparous and sexually mature. The most common strains of rat used for these studies are Sprague–Dawley and Wistar. Fertility rates and litter size are most stable when the females are 12–18 weeks of age at the time of breeding. The dams can be bred at the testing facility or mated animals can be purchased from the animal supplier. If time-mated females are used, it is advisable to receive the animals from the supplier as soon as possible after mating to allow sufficient time to acclimatize to the testing facility prior to the start of dosing on GD 6. If the females are bred at the testing facility, the males used for breeding should be sexually mature and of the same strain and source as the females.

Dose-Selection Criteria

Criteria for dose-level selection include using a high dose that will produce minimal maternal toxicity. Minimal maternal toxicity can be defined as producing a reduction in body weight gain, increased body weight gain, specific target organ toxicity, effects on hematology or serum chemistry parameters, or exaggerated pharmacological response. In most cases a limit dose of 1 g/kg/day is sufficient for a pharmaceutical that has low toxicity [6]. The high dose should avoid excessive maternal toxicity that can result in secondary effects on the offspring, which are the result of poor maternal condition instead of direct developmental toxicity. The dose levels should also be selected to avoid excessive offspring lethality because this could lead to the inability to have a sufficient number of pups available to assess the F_1 postweaning period.

Dose levels are often selected on the basis of results of an embryo-fetal development (EFD) study in rats. As described elsewhere in this chapter, the EFD study has a treatment regimen from implantation until closure of the hard palate. This design covers the majority of the PPND gestation treatment period. Data from the EFD study, such as maternal clinical signs and body weight data are generally very predictive for determining a dose that will produce minimal maternal toxicity in the PPND study. The data from the EFD design are also predictive of the extent of effect expected to be observed on intrauterine growth and survival and fetal morphology. An understanding of the significance of fetal malformations observed in the EFD study is critical. For example, a fetus with the cardiac malformation interventricular septal defect can survive in utero but will not be able to survive after birth. If the incidence of this malformation is high at a particular dose in the EFD study, this dose may not allow a sufficient number of pups to survive until weaning in a PPND study.

While the EFD study is usually very useful for selection of dose levels for the PPND study, it does not provide information regarding the potential of the pharmaceutical to produce effects on late gestational development, parturition, or lactation. As described previously, the EFD study for the AT_1-selective angiotensin II receptor antagonist Losartan [58,59] did not predict the effects observed on postnatal survival. In an EFD study performed in the laboratory of one

of the authors, no effects were observed on intrauterine growth and survival. However, in the PPND study using the same dose levels, the pharmaceutical produced severe dystocia, such that no dams in the high-dose group were able to complete parturition. Subsequent information provided by the company sponsoring the project identified the pharmaceutical as an inhibitor of smooth muscle contraction. For this compound, the dams in the high-dose group were unable to produce sufficient uterine contractions to allow parturition to occur.

The dose volume delivered is calculated in a standard way, based on the most recent body weight to maintain a consistent mg/kg dose. However, because maternal weight gain during the fetal period (GD 17 until parturition) is almost entirely the result of the growth of the contents of the uterus, some researchers will base all doses during the fetal period on the GD 15, 16, or 17 body weights to avoid overdosing the dams during this period.

If the pharmacology or class of the pharmaceutical indicates the potential to affect parturition or postnatal growth and survival, then a pilot PPND study should be performed to select dose levels for the PPND study. The treatment regimen should be from GD 6 through LD 6 or LD 20. Group sizes of 8–10 are recommended. In addition to maternal clinical signs, body weights and intrauterine survival data that can also be obtained from EFD studies, this pilot PPND study will provide data on gestation length, parturition (including dystocia), postnatal survival, birth weights, and preweaning growth. While performance of a pilot study will delay the start of the PPND study by 1–2 months, the information obtained in this pilot study can be valuable for pharmaceuticals suspected of affecting parturition or postnatal development.

Maternal Endpoints

The minimum F_0 maternal endpoints for a PPND study include daily clinical signs (should include postdosing observations based on T_{max}), twice weekly body weight and body weight change evaluation, weekly feed consumption until parturition, and duration of pregnancy and parturition. Assessment of feed consumption is often continued during at least the first 2 weeks of lactation. Feed consumption during LD 14–21 is difficult to interpret because during the last week of the preweaning period, pups will begin to directly consume the diets. It is therefore difficult to determine if lower feed consumption in a pharmaceutical group relative to the control group during LD 14–21 is due to lower maternal feed consumption, lower pup feed consumption, or a combination of both. While not specifically listed in the ICH S5 R2 [6] guideline, assessment of maternal nesting and nursing behavior is highly recommended to obtain evidence if effects on pup growth and survival are related to poor maternal care.

If a target organ has been identified in previous studies with the pharmaceutical, it is advisable to include an assessment of this endpoint in the PPND design. Endpoints that can be added include target-organ weight and histopathology, hematology, and serum chemistry. A necropsy is performed of all F_0 dams at weaning. Gross lesions are preserved, and the numbers of former implantation sites are recorded. Postimplantation loss is determined by subtracting the number of pups born from the number of former implantation sites.

Preweaning Litter Parameters

Litter parameters that are required to be assessed are the number of live and dead offspring at birth, survival following birth, and pup weights at birth and following birth. While the ICH guidelines do not specify the frequency of assessment of survival after birth, standard convention is to examine each litter on a daily basis for pup viability. Pup body weights are normally assessed at least once weekly. Many laboratories cull litters on PND 4 to four pups/sex or five pups/sex to reduce variability across litters. While culling is not required, it should be done consistently within a laboratory because this will allow for the best comparison with historical control data. When culling is done, the selection process should be performed in a random manner so as not to bias the results following culling. The ICH S5 R2 [6] guidelines also recommend assessment of physical development. However, attainment of preweaning developmental landmarks, such as surface righting, eye opening, pinna detachment, incisor eruption, and presence of hair coat are highly correlated with body weight. Therefore these endpoints are of little value for assessment of offspring development, and some laboratories do not assess these landmarks in the PPND study.

Postweaning Offspring Parameters

As previously mentioned, one pup/sex/litter is selected at the time of weaning to comprise the F_1 postweaning phase of the PPND study. This selection should be performed in a random manner with the following exception. If a pup is not expected to survive following weaning, this animal should be excluded from the selection process for the F_1 postweaning phase. During the postweaning period, clinical signs and body weights are monitored, typically on a weekly basis. Two landmarks of physical development should

be assessed, balanopreputial separation for males and vaginal patency in females. These two parameters indicate the onset of sexual maturity. Body weights on the day of attainment of these two landmarks should be recorded because body weight can affect the day of attainment of vaginal patency [61] and balanopreputial separation [61–63]. The most common pharmaceutical-related effects are earlier attainment of vaginal patency (estrogenic compounds) and delay in attainment of balanopreputial separation (antiandrogenic compounds). Examination of vaginal patency in the rat should be performed daily beginning on PND 25. Examination of balanopreputial separation in the rat should be performed daily beginning on PND 35.

Once the animals reach approximately 12 weeks of age, the F_1 animals are bred. In order to avoid sibling mating, the identification of the litter each animal came from needs to be maintained. Following positive evidence of mating, the females can be examined at midpregnancy or can be allowed to deliver. While allowing the females to deliver will slightly extend the duration of the study, it allows the option of rebreeding the F_1 generation if the outcome of the mating is equivocal. Endpoints evaluated include precoital interval, mating and fertility indices, number of corpora lutea, implantation sites and viable fetuses or pups, preimplantation loss and postimplantation loss. While not required by the ICH S5 R2 [6] guidelines, assessment of the estrous cyclicity of F_1 females prior to the start of the mating period is often included in the PPND study design. If fertility is reduced, disruption of estrous cyclicity will help to identify that the female is contributing to the reduced fertility.

Behavioral Assessment

The ICH S5 R2 [6] guideline recommends functional tests to assess the behavior of the F_1 animals. Investigators are encouraged to find methods to assess sensory function, motor activity, and learning and memory. No clear guidance is provided on the type of assays or the age of testing. Testing is typically performed around the time of weaning and when the animals are young adults. There are numerous commercially available motor activity systems for performing these tests. In these systems, animals are placed into an enclosure and motor activity is quantitated by the number of photobeams broken during the session. For sensory assessment, automated auditory startle response systems are available. In these systems, rodents are placed on a platform, a sound burst is presented causing the animal to jump, and the force the animal applies to the platform is measured. For assessment of learning and memory, the most common assessments used are passive avoidance or a water maze. In the passive avoidance test, the rodent learns to enter the correct compartment to avoid an electrical shock. The water maze requires the rodent to solve the maze to be able to escape the water.

While there are many different assays that can be used for assessment of sensory function, motor activity, and learning and memory, there are several criteria that each assay should meet.

1. Quantitative assessments are preferred over subjective assessments because of problems with variability between observers.
2. The laboratory should demonstrate proficiency with the assay. This requires validating the assay using positive control agents. As part of the validation, sensitivity of the assay to detect a change is critical. If the laboratory can only detect a change at a dose level that is an order of magnitude higher than that reported in the literature, then the laboratory has not demonstrated proficiency with the assay. An example of assay sensitivity is that complex water mazes have been shown to be much more sensitive at detecting changes in learning and memory than passive avoidance.
3. The laboratory must have an acceptable amount of variability. Behavioral test data can be quite variable. It is critical that the laboratory does everything possible to control this variability. Otherwise, the assay will not be able to detect a change. Time of day of testing can have a big impact on data variability. If testing is performed during the light portion of the light:dark cycle, remember that rodents are most active during the morning and late afternoon. Consistency of time-of-day for testing will limit the amount of variability between animals. External stimuli should be kept to a minimum. White noise is often used to provide a consistent background.
4. For subjective observational assessments, demonstration of interobserver reliability is required. Because testing will often occur over several days, it is unlikely that the same observer can perform all of the assessments. Therefore the laboratory must demonstrate that two different observers will describe the same behaviors in a similar manner.

Immune Function Assessment

While not required by the ICH guidelines, consideration should be given to assessment of the developing immune system in the F_1 animals. The decision as to whether to include immune system function should be based on the pharmacological action of the test compound and results of previous studies that indicate the potential of the compound to modulate immune system function. This assessment is typically performed by maintaining additional F_1 weanlings during the postweaning period and can include evaluation of humeral, cell-mediated, and/or innate immunity. A basic approach to assess developmental immune function was described by Holsapple et al. [64].

Data Presentation and Statistical Analysis

Similar to EFD studies, the litter, not the pup, should be considered to be the experimental unit for evaluation of preweaning litter parameters. In order to accomplish this, mean values for each litter need to be determined for percentages of preimplantation loss, postimplantation loss, postnatal survival, and sex ratio. This same approach should be used for pup weights. Group mean values for these parameters can then be calculated from the litter means. Although the number of pups within each litter will vary, each litter is weighted evenly when this approach is used. In addition, a standard deviation and standard error can be calculated to measure the variability between litters in the same group. As long as only one pup/sex/litter is selected for the F_1 postweaning phase of the study, litter does not need to be taken into account when summarizing the data during this portion of the study.

For statistical analysis, parametric analyses are typically performed for body weight (adult and pup), feed consumption, litter size, gestation length, precoital intervals, and day of attainment of developmental landmarks. Nonparametric analyses are typically used for percentage data, such as preimplantation loss, postimplantation loss, postnatal survival, and sex ratios.

Because behavioral data are often variable, use of repeated measure analyses is encouraged to increase the power of the analyses to detect a change. This can be performed within a session or across sessions. For example, within a session repeated measures assessment of motor activity will examine activity across subintervals during the session. Across session repeated measures analysis examines the activity across the age of testing.

TOXICOKINETICS

In alignment with the ICH S3A guideline [65], it is advisable to have supporting "pharmacokinetic" data prior to conducting any reproductive or developmental toxicology studies to ensure appropriate species selection, dose selection, and dosing frequency. This preliminary data may be derived from nonpregnant animals, and, in most cases, sufficient data on the kinetics of a test agent are available from repeat-dose toxicity studies conducted in rats. It is noteworthy to mention that kinetics may differ between pregnant and nonpregnant animals, thus necessitating an evaluation under both conditions. These differences in pregnant animals include plasma volume expansion, increases in extracellular fluid space, and total body water as well as increased renal blood flow.

During the conduct of the fertility, embryo-fetal, or peripostnatal assessment, pharmacokinetic (toxicokinetic) evaluations may be particularly useful when administering test agents of low toxicity. Depending on the study design, toxicokinetic data may be derived from main study animals or a separate group of satellite animals, and concentrations of the test agent may be found in plasma/serum samples, blood (eg, dried blood spot analysis), urine samples, or milk (in the case of lactating animals) depending on the method of detection. Sampling criteria are based on the nature of the test article and can be derived from previous studies, as well as the technical feasibility of the sampling procedure. Maternal samples are generally collected on the first and last days of dose administration at multiple time points (up to six or seven at each collection interval). The volume of matrix required for analysis and the number of time points included at each sampling interval dictates the number of animals that will be needed for these evaluations.

As noted by Wangikar et al. [26], evaluation of maternal plasma concentrations is important to assess the NOAEL and safety margins. Inclusion of fetal or pup toxicokinetic evaluations in an embryo-fetal study design or a peripostnatal is usually case-by-case, but can provide valuable information as to whether the fetus/pup was exposed to appreciable amounts of the test agent in utero (placental transfer) or through secretions in the milk.

DEVELOPMENTAL TOXICITY TESTING OF BIOPHARMACEUTICALS IN RODENTS AND RABBITS

Developmental and reproductive toxicity studies should be conducted only in pharmacologically relevant species and when the clinical candidate is pharmacologically active in rodents and rabbits; these species should be used unless there is a scientific reason to use NHPs [66]. Safety studies in nonrelevant species may be misleading and are discouraged. As discussed earlier in this chapter the developmental and reproductive toxicity testing should entail the following assessments:

1. Study of fertility and early embryonic developmental to implantation (ICH 4.1.1)
2. Study for effects on pre and postnatal development, including maternal function (ICH 4.1.2)

3. Study for effects on embryo-fetal development (ICH 4.1.3)

The pharmaceutical industries are in the process of designing monoclonal antibodies (mAbs) that are pharmacologically active in rodents and rabbits to avoid conducting safety studies in NHPs or use homologous proteins, transgenic models, knockouts, and/or disease models. With the exception of the route of administration, which is usually parenteral for biopharmaceuticals, the developmental and reproductive toxicity study designs for biopharmaceuticals are similar to that of small molecules. Biopharmaceuticals or large molecules do not diffuse across the maternal placenta to the fetus to the same extent as small molecules, resulting in lower fetal exposure. This means that potential developmental toxicity for nonantibody biopharmaceuticals is likely to be low; nevertheless, effects due to maternal or placental toxicity cannot be excluded. In contrast to many of the other large-molecular-weight proteins and peptides, antibodies are actively transferred across the placenta from mother to fetus.

IgG-type antibodies cross the yolk sac in rodents/rabbits by a neonatal Rc receptor (FcRn) transport mechanism and exposure will occur during late organogenesis if exposed during pregnancy [67]. Similarly, offspring of rat/mouse dams dosed during lactation will be exposed via the milk. In rats only, fewer IgGs are transferred in late gestation, and most of the transfer is postnatal. In rabbits, the majority of the IgG transfer takes place between GD 15 and delivery, and as a result the conventional dosing period (GD 6–17 in rats and GD 6 to 18 in rabbits) may not be adequate to assess the human exposure scenario and may not be suitable for detecting abnormalities. This leads us to think that conventional EFD study designs in rodents and rabbits are not adequate to assess the safety of mAbs during pregnancy. A study design that extends from GD 6 to weaning in rats with 50% of the litters examined on GD 20 and offspring evaluation performed on PND 21 or 28 seems to be more appropriate.

An argument supporting this design that warrants consideration includes the shorter late gestation period following organogenesis in rodents, which provides no space for further dosing if treatment has to be limited during pregnancy. In contrast we may argue about the longer half-life of mAbs leading to further exposure even after cessation of treatment. However, it is important to note that the duration of the late gestation period in humans is longer than that of rodents, which means that human fetuses will be exposed to mAbs for longer than rodents, resulting in inadequate prediction of human exposure when using the traditional dosing period (GD 6–GD 17). Martin et al. [68] noted that in order to mimic human exposure of mAbs during the fetal period (ie, the second and third trimesters), it would be necessary to treat the pregnant rodents starting at the end of organogenesis and to continue dosing during the postnatal lactation period. Although the authors did not mention specific days of dosing duration, their concept is consistent with the proposed designs.

Contrary to rats, rabbits have a longer gestation period following organogenesis allowing further treatment with the mAbs during pregnancy. Therefore we propose dosing of pregnant rabbits be extended to GD 28 and C-section performed on GD 29. This exposure scenario better mimics the human exposure scenario. In mice, although the information regarding IgG maternal transfer is limited, for an EFD study, the rat design just presented may be appropriate. These proposed study designs should be supplemented with exposure assessments in dams/does and fetuses during pregnancy and in dams/pups during lactation.

REPRODUCTIVE AND DEVELOPMENTAL ASSESSMENTS IN NONHUMAN PRIMATES

Biopharmaceuticals

Nonhuman primates (NHPs) are commonly used in developmental and reproductive toxicity testing (DART) for biopharmaceuticals as these are often the only species that express pharmacological responses similar to humans. Following the thalidomide tragedy in the late 1950s, the NHP was recognized as an animal model for the study of developmental toxicity. Since then NHPs have played important roles in both testing biopharmaceuticals for human safety, and as models for studying specific malformations commonly observed in children. Note 1 of ICH S6 (R1) [39] states that when considering the choice of species for testing embryo-fetal/pre- and postnatal development studies, the type of molecule and potential differences in placental transfer should be considered. Tissue cross-reactivity is no longer considered to be appropriate for the species selection. It is recommended, however, to study comparisons of target-sequence homology between species, followed by cell-based assays enabling qualitative and quantitative cross-species comparisons of relative target-binding affinities and receptor/ligand occupancy and kinetics [39]. Cynomolgus monkeys have several physiological similarities to humans, including ovarian endocrine function, menstrual length, endocrinology of early pregnancy, similar ovulation period [69], and placental function [70] and are reported to exhibit similar response to known human teratogens (eg, thalidomide and

vitamin A) [71,72]. Although safety testing in preclinical studies represents one of the major uses of NHPs, in reality, only a few compounds are tested in these animals. They are not commonly used as a second species for safety testing, but used only in circumstances where no alternative methods are available and when testing is considered essential for safety assessment. It is important to note, however, that when designing DART studies for biopharmaceuticals, consideration should be given to product characteristics, clinical indication, patient population, and the availability of a relevant animal model [68].

ICH, NHPs, and DART Studies

DART studies are designed to identify the effects of drugs on mammalian reproduction and include exposure of mature adults, as well as all stages of development from conception to sexual maturity. Consequently, the ICH S5 (R2) [6] divides the reproductive cycle into stages A to F. The ICH stages were discussed at the beginning of this chapter.

In NHPs the potential adverse effects of a drug product on different segments of the reproductive cycle, defined as stages A–F, cannot be fully assessed [73]. Stage A involves evaluation of reproductive functions in adult male and female animals including mating and fertilization. Full assessment of stage A is impractical and is not evaluated as part of the study design for any NHP DART study. Similarly, ICH stage B is not assessed in any NHP DART studies; it involves the evaluation from conception to implantation. The earliest dosing of pregnant NHPs is on GD 20 with the implantation window for cynomolgus monkeys ranging between GD 9 and GD 15. In contrast, stage C assessment is evaluated in NHP DART studies with the exception that the evaluation of this stage begins postimplantation. The e-PPND (enhanced) study involves the evaluation of stage D. Stage E, which involves birth to weaning, is evaluated in the enhanced e-PPND study; however, the examination of the neonate does not extend to weaning. It is limited to the evaluation of adaptation of the neonate to extrauterine life and may include preweaning development and growth of the neonate. The neonates of NHPs are generally weaned at 1 year of age.

ICH stage F, which involves the evaluation of the neonates from weaning to sexual maturation, is logistically and financially impractical as sexual maturity is achieved between 3 and 4 years of age in cynomolgus monkeys [73].

According to the International Conference for Harmonization (ICH S5 R2) [6] guideline for the detection of toxicity to reproduction for medicinal products the developmental and reproductive toxicity testing should entail the following assessments:

1. Study of fertility and early embryonic development to implantation (ICH 4.1.1)
2. Study of effects on pre and postnatal development, including maternal function (ICH 4.1.2)
3. Study of effects on embryo-fetal development (ICH 4.1.3)

Study of Fertility and Early Embryonic Development to Implantation (ICH 4.1.1)

Fertility testing comprises evaluation of adverse effects on libido, sexual behavior, spermatogenesis, oogenesis, fertilization, and implantation. In contrast to rodent fertility studies, it is recognized that mating is not practical in NHPs. This is because the spontaneous conception rate is low (approximately 45%), the litter size is usually one, and assessing implantation sites is impossible; as a result fertility assessment in NHPs focuses on reproductive potential rather than fertility per se.

Evaluation of the number of successful pregnancies as a measurable parameter in NHPs is evidently impractical or unethical, as this would require approximately 90 females per group to attain an 80% power to detect a 20% change in fertility [68]. In fact, ICH S6 (R1) [39], addressing this particular limitation, stated that if there is a specific concern from the pharmacological activity of the biopharmaceutical regarding the potential effects on conception/implantation, and the NHP is the only relevant species, the concern should be addressed experimentally.

In NHPs, a fertility study can be conducted as a standalone study, or fertility endpoints can be incorporated into a less than 3-month repeated-dose toxicity study (Figs. 9.6–9.7). Due to the small group sizes used and the difficulties of assessing pubertal status at the start of the study, only sexually mature animals should be employed in the study. In repeat-dose toxicity testing, the potential for effects on male and/or female fertility can be assessed by evaluation of the reproductive tract at necropsy (organ weights and histopathology). Five animals per group with two groups (a control and a dose group) are considered to be appropriate.

Age and body weight are used to determine sexual maturity in male and female monkeys. To be sexually mature, males must be at least 4 years old and weigh approximately 5 kg [74]. The males should be dosed for at least 60 days to cover the entire spermatogenic cycle, which is calculated to be approximately 40–46 days [75].

Sexual maturity in female monkeys can adequately be determined by confirming regular menstrual cycles of normal duration. Females are considered to be sexually mature if the individual animal is older than 3 years, weighs at least 2.5 kg, and has had at least three consecutive regular menstrual cycles [20]. Assessment of vaginal swabs is minimally invasive and provides a convenient and reliable approach to monitoring the menstrual cycle. Vaginal swabs are collected daily using a cotton swab. The cotton swab is then evaluated and recorded as showing (0) no, (1) light, (2) moderate, or (3) heavy bleeding.

In NHPs the potential for effects on male and female fertility can be assessed by standard histopathological evaluation and assessment of menstrual cyclicity in

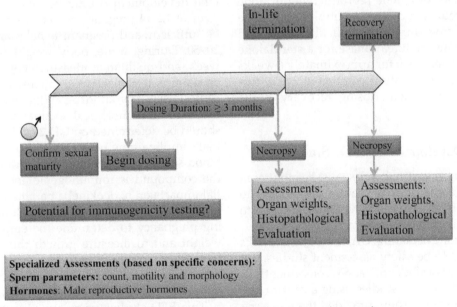

FIGURE 9.6 Study design for male fertility in cynomolgus monkeys.

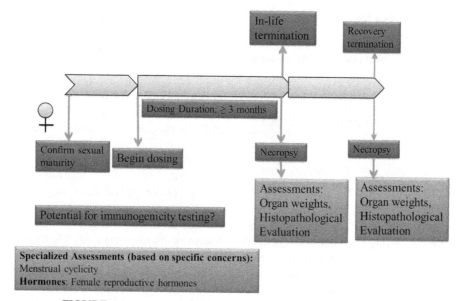

FIGURE 9.7　Study design for female fertility in cynomolgus monkeys.

repeat-dose toxicity studies. However, if there is a specific cause for concern, sperm assessments including motility, morphology, sperm count, testicular volume, and male or female reproductive hormone levels should be evaluated as well [41].

When designing female fertility testing it is very important that the study is scheduled with respect to the stage of the menstrual cycle (eg, dosing, blood sampling for hormone analysis, and/or necropsy). Starting dosing on day 1 of the menstrual cycle provides more comprehensive data and makes it easier to interpret the data [20], particularly when the design includes assessment of female reproductive hormone levels. In this circumstance blood samples should be collected every 2 days during the follicular phase and every 3 days during the luteal phase for a standalone study and 3 times per week for approximately 6 weeks to cover longer cycle duration conducted once during each phase (pretreatment, dosing, recovery) of the study [20].

Embryo-Fetal Development (EFD) Study

In the EFD study, menstrual cycles must be monitored for at least 2–3 months prior to mating the females to ensure that the animals are cycling regularly, and also to estimate the ovulation period, which is critical to determine the optimal time of mating. DART studies in NHPs are not considered to be safety assessment studies, but are regarded as a hazard identification; consequently, it is possible to conduct these studies using a control animal group and one dose group, provided there is a scientific justification for the dose level selected [39]. Dose

selection is usually derived from general toxicity studies or from a range-finding study. For low-toxicity biopharmaceuticals, the dose should be based on the kinetics. Prior to breeding the females, ultrasound is performed as a part of prescreening to examine reproductive organs and ensure normal anatomy. Females are bred midcycle to proven male breeders 1–8 h/day for 3 consecutive days with the second day of mating considered to be GD 0. The pregnancy is confirmed on GD 18–20 using ultrasound (see Fig. 9.8).

The use of ultrasound provides an efficient method of pregnancy detection, and of monitoring of the embryo-fetal development during gestation. In general, group sizes of 12–14 pregnancies per group are considered to be sufficient, and pregnant females are dosed from GD 20–50. During in-life, body weight is collected once a week, and qualitative measurements are made of feed consumption, clinical observations, TK, hematology and clinical chemistry, antidrug antibody determination, and maternal immunological evaluation. Exposure levels should be determined on GD 20, 50, or 100 using minimal sampling time points. It is also important to obtain blood samples for analysis of neutralizing antibodies if the compound is immunogenic and may have potential impacts on toxicokinetic parameters [20]. Moreover, ultrasound is performed at least once a month during pregnancy to determine the embryo-fetal size and weight and to measure growth thus making sure the fetus is developing.

C-section is performed on GD 100, and fetuses are evaluated for external, visceral, and skeletal abnormalities.

This EFD study design can identify maternal-mediated effects that can have indirect adverse effects on

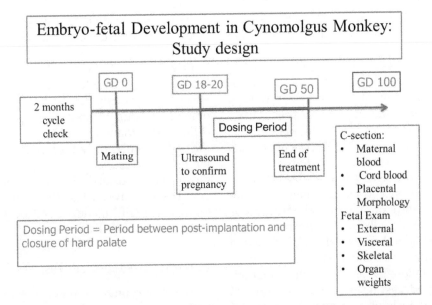

FIGURE 9.8 Embryo-fetal development in cynomolgus monkeys: study design.

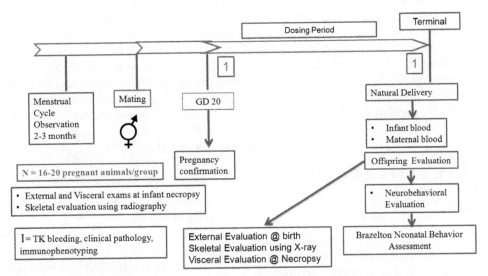

FIGURE 9.9 Enhanced pre- and postnatal development study design.

development [68], but provides limited information for potential developmental effects of monoclonal antibodies (mAbs).

Enhanced Pre- and Postnatal Development (e-PPND)

Monoclonal antibodies (mAbs) of IgG nature are actively transferred across the placenta from mother to fetus by FcRn receptors expressed on syncytiotrophoblast cells [67]. The Fc-receptor appears to protect IgG from degradation and allows the long half-life of this class of antibody in the blood. The transfer of antibodies in the NHP occurs at the end of organogenesis, therefore, the sensitivity period of antibodies that produce little or no maternal toxicity will be during fetal development and not during organogenesis.

Stewart [76] postulated that the appropriate study design (Fig. 9.9) for developmental toxicity of mAbs should allow the detection of both the indirect effects in early gestation, and the effects of the direct fetal exposure in mid and late gestation based on the pattern of placental IgG transfer. This study design, baptized as the enhanced pre- and postnatal development (e-PPND), is particularly relevant for mAbs where fetal exposure to maternal IgG is known to increase as pregnancy progresses. The conventional EFD study, which limits the dosing period from GD 20–50, does not adequately mimic the human exposure scenario and consequently may not be suitable to detect fetal abnormalities.

Sixteen to 20 pregnancies per group are considered to be sufficient for the study. The goal is to have sufficient numbers of confirmed pregnant cynomolgus monkeys per group to detect three-fold increase in pregnancy/parturition-associated losses in order to obtain 80% power with 95% confidence interval [77]. Dosing begins usually on GD 20 and continues through delivery.

The e-PPND study is designed to evaluate offspring viability, growth, and survival as well as infant exposure data (if available). In addition external abnormality is assessed at birth, skeletal evaluation performed using X-ray, and ultimately visceral abnormalities are assessed at necropsy. The duration of postnatal assessment is variable, and is generally tailored to assess specific functionality in the offspring addressing particular concerns of the test compound (eg, including immune function and neurobehavior). The Brazelton Newborn Assessment Scale [78], primarily used for assessing human neonates, is also used as the behavioral assessment panel for the neonatal NHPs. In the cynomolgus monkey, infants are assessed for clasp support, dorsireflex, grasp support, glabellar tap, rooting and the suckling reflex, moro reflex, visual following, and papillary reflex on PNDs 1 and 7. In case of negative results on PNDs 1 and 7, the test for papillary reflex is repeated on PND 14 and grip strength is performed on PND 28 [79].

ALTERNATIVE METHODS USED IN REPRODUCTIVE AND DEVELOPMENTAL TOXICITY TESTING

Alternatives to animal testing in developmental toxicology have been a subject of research for about half a century. These test methods are intended to reduce, refine, or replace (3Rs) animal use in toxicity testing. The 3Rs concept was first introduced in 1959 by British scientists William M. S. Russell and Rex L. Burch in their book *The Principles of Humane Experimental Technique*, in which they wrote that scientific excellence and humane use of laboratory animals are inextricably linked. Laws that mandate replacement, reduction, and refinement alternatives (the 3Rs) in scientific research were passed in the United Kingdom, Germany, the Netherlands, the United States, and the European Union in the 1980s [80]. The debate over alternative developmental toxicity testing has recently increased, and is being driven by the massive number of chemicals subject to REACH legislation. There is a general desire to develop more predictive tools for toxicity testing that include more in vitro assays and computational models. The new regulations require a toxicological evaluation with strong emphasis on reproductive toxicity, using in vitro methods, especially for those chemicals marketed at more than 1 ton per year [81].

Over the past three decades, many methods have been proposed as alternative systems for testing toxic effects on various processes of reproduction and development. A large number exist, including the micromass (MM) assay, the whole embryo culture assay, zebrafish, the embryonic stem-cell test (EST), and the frog embryo teratogenesis assay Xenopus (FETAX) assay. The three most widely studied alternative assays are the mouse embryonic stem-cell test (EST), the zebrafish embryotoxicity test (ZET), and the rat postimplantation whole embryo culture (WEC).

Embryonic Stem-Cell Test (EST)

The embryonic stem-cell test (EST) is an in vitro system developed to assess the possible embryotoxic potential of chemicals and drug candidates [82]. It examines the cytotoxicity of chemical compounds on embryonic stem (ES) cells and 3T3-A31 fibroblasts and measures the ability of ES cells to differentiate into contracting cardiomyocytes following drug exposure [83]. Stem cells can be continuously cultured in the undifferentiated stage and are capable of renewal, giving rise to more specialized cells, such as heart, liver, bone marrow, blood vessels, pancreatic islets, and nerve cells on addition of or removal of growth factors [84] (Fig. 9.10).

The embryotoxic potential of a test substance is predicted assessing three endpoints:

1. The inhibition of differentiation into beating cardiomyocytes
2. Outgrowths compared to cytotoxic effects on stem cells
3. Differentiated NIH-3T3 fibroblasts [85]

A particular aspect of the EST is that it is exclusively based on permanent cell lines, meaning that primary embryonic cells and tissues from pregnant animals are not required. The classical EST has been modified to include scalable production of embryonic stem cell-derived cardiomyocytes [86], molecular endpoints, and molecular marker [87,88], and assessment of extracellular matrices as endpoints [89], to broaden its applicability and improve its accuracy [84] (Fig. 9.10).

Using a set of 20 reference compounds with different embryotoxic potencies (nonembryotoxic, weakly embryotoxic, and strongly embryotoxic), the EST was found to provide a predictive index of 78% of all tests. However, for strong embryotoxicants, the predictive performance increased to 100% [90]. Since early 2000, the EST has attracted substantial interest in the pharmaceutical industry, and has been used as a tool for testing the

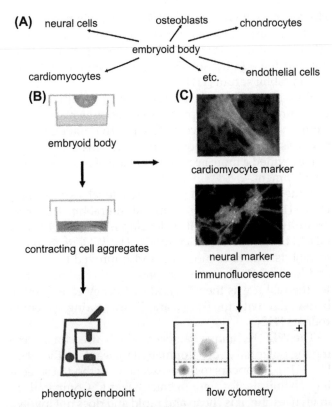

FIGURE 9.10 Diagram illustrating embryonic stem cells for embryotoxicity testing. (A) Embryonic stem cells have the potency to differentiate into all cell types of the body. (B) Schematic representation of the validated embryonic stem cell test (EST) for embryotoxicity testing. (C) Modification of the EST to broaden its applicability domain using molecular endpoints. *From Liebsch M, Grune B, Seiler A, Butzke D, Oelgeschläger M, Pirow R, et al. Alternatives to animal testing: current status and future perspectives. Arch Toxicol 2011;85(8):841–58 with permission.*

developmental toxicity of lead compounds at an early stage in the research and development of new drug candidates [91]. "Hanging drop" cultures and seeding embryonic bodies (EBs) to tissue culture plates are major time-consuming steps in the experimental procedures [92]. The key weakness of classical EST is its reliance on a morphological endpoint (beating cardiomyocytes) and the need for experienced personnel to ensure reliable assessments of this endpoint [93].

Paquette et al. [94] used the European Center for the Validation of Alternative Methods' (ECVAM) EST protocol, but employed a different mouse embryonic stem cell (ESC) line and an alternative differentiation medium. They used a subset of the compounds to validate the EST assay along with a number of Pfizer pharmaceutical compounds plus marketed pharmaceutical compounds to assess the EST performance with receptor-mediated compounds. Their conclusion was that the EST has a significant false-positive rate (approximately 40%), but a very low false-negative rate (approximately 7%).

Recently, de Jong et al. [95] compared the mouse embryonic stem-cell test, the rat whole embryo, and the zebrafish embryotoxicity test using as test six 1,2,4-triazole antifungals (flusilazole, hexaconazole, cyproconazole, triadimefon, myclobutanil, and triticonazole) and found that WEC exhibited a general pattern of teratogenic effects, typical of exposure to triazoles. In the EST, all triazole compounds inhibited cardiomyocyte differentiation in a concentration-dependent manner. However, the ZET gave the best correlation with the relative in vivo developmental toxicities of the tested compounds, closely followed by the EST. The authors concluded that differences in the efficacy between the test systems might be due to differences in compound kinetics, in developmental stages represented, and in the relative complexity of the alternative assays [95].

West et al. [96] developed a method using human embryonic stem cells (hES) and metabolomics. In this study, hES were dosed with several drugs with known developmental toxicity, then were analyzed by LC-MS to measure changes in abundance levels of small molecules in response to drug exposure. They showed a correlation between developmental toxicants and changes of greater than 10% in the ratio of arginine to asymmetric dimethylarginine levels. The model was then tested for its predictive accuracy in two blinded studies using eight drugs with known developmental toxicity, where it correctly predicted the developmental toxicity for seven of the eight drugs. They concluded that their platform is a robust alternative to animal and other in vitro models for the prediction of the developmental toxicity of chemicals that may also provide invaluable information about the underlying biochemical pathways [96].

Zebrafish Embryotoxicity Test (ZET)

The zebrafish (*Danio rerio*) has high developmental similarities to mammals in most aspects of embryo development [97]. The embryogenesis of zebrafish is rapid, requiring only 24 h postfertilization to establish its entire body plan, and with most of the internal organs including the heart, liver, intestine, and kidney developing in less than 1 week. Because of its small size, the zebrafish model necessitates smaller amounts of compounds per assay. It has the ability to absorb compounds through the water, and its transparent chorion makes observation of embryonic development easy [98].

The ZET is based on a 48 h exposure of newly fertilized eggs in a static or semistatic system followed by evaluating toxicological endpoints including coagulation of eggs and embryos, failure to develop somites, lack of heart beat as well as nondetachment of the tail from the yolk. These are recorded after 24 and 48 h and used for the calculation of an LC50 value. In an effort to use zebrafish as a predictive model for teratogenicity, 34 compounds with adequate in vivo developmental toxicity data were evaluated by Brannen et al. [99]. The model successfully predicted 87% of the compounds as teratogens or nonteratogens, with only two false-positives and two false-negatives, concluding that the assay is promising for screening compounds for teratogenic potential. In contrast, Van den Bulck et al. [100] found that although the majority of drugs testing positive (75%) in mammals were also positive in zebrafish, they found a relative high number of false positives (43%) following the evaluation of different concentrations of 15 compounds of which 8 were teratogenic and 7 nonteratogenic.

A zebrafish morphological score system was recently devised by Panzica-Kelly et al. [101]. The score system allows the evaluation of most structures and organ systems and grades relative severity of abnormalities. The system provides information on tissue-specific teratogenicity, which has been found to have good concordance with structures found to be affected in in vivo animal testing and it can also be used to rank compounds based on the severity of malformations.

Hermsen et al. [102] studied the developmental toxicity of eight glycol ethers and six 1,2,4-triazole antifungals in the ZET model based on general morphology score (GMS) system and compared the results with in vivo developmental toxicity potencies. Growth retardation and malformations were induced by glycol ether metabolites (methoxyacetic acid and ethoxyacetic acid). For the 1,2,4-triazole compounds, flusilazole appeared the most potent followed by hexaconazole, cyproconazole, triadimefon, myclobutanil, and triticonazole, respectively. It was concluded that the ZET with the GMS system is an efficient and useful test system for screening the embryotoxic properties of chemicals within the classes of compounds tested.

Whole Embryo Culture (WEC)

The whole embryo culture (WEC) technique was developed in the 1950s by New and his collaborators [103]. It allows the culture of the ex vivo condition of mouse and rat embryos during limited periods corresponding to midgestation stages during embryonic day (E) 6.5–12.5 in the mouse or E 8.5–14.5 in the rat [104]. The fundamental concept of the WEC system is to culture early organogenesis-stage rodent embryos (late headfold – early somite stage) in rotated culture bottles, over a 48 h period, which can be extended to up to 72 h. The culture medium is supplemented with serum and the culture bottles are constantly supplied with specific percentages of oxygen over the culture period. At the beginning of the culture, test compounds are added to the culture medium. At the end of the culture, the embryos are examined and evaluated for developmental abnormalities and overall embryonic growth [105]. The most commonly used medium for the culture of postimplantation embryos was rat or mouse serum [106].

However, in the last two decades, the medium has been modified and embryos are cultured in human serum [107], in monkey serum [108], in bovine serum with or without the addition of 15% tyrodes solution [109,110], and in rabbit serum [111].

Brown and Fabro [112] developed a scoring system consisting of six developmental stages, which are scored from 0 to 5. The total score for an individual embryo is taken as a total morphological score. This scoring system provided a more accurate measure of morphological development.

A method for WEC in rabbits was developed by Naya et al. [113] using Japanese white strain rabbit. They successfully reported in vitro development of GD 9 and GD 10 of normal rabbit embryos. The WEC technology in rabbits was later modified and improved by Carney and Tornesi [114] and a morphological scoring system for the rabbit was then devised by Carney et al. [115] to better align with the Brown and Fabro scoring system in rodents [112].

The WEC technique had been widely used for screening the potential of developmental toxicants in the 1980s [116–118]. It appears to be an excellent method of screening chemicals for teratogenic hazard. Compared to in vivo testing, it is cheap and rapid and does not involve experimentation on live adult animals [119]. The system showed a high predictability for the compounds tested and suggested that the postimplantation embryo culture system may also be useful in the prospective testing of new drugs and environmental chemicals [118]. Similarly, following a formal validation study on the performance of the postimplantation rat whole embryo culture (WEC) test in the European Center for the Validation of Alternative Methods (ECVAM), it was concluded that the WEC test can be considered as a scientifically validated test, and is ready for consideration for use in assessing the embryotoxic potentials of chemicals for regulatory purposes [120].

The main advantage of the WEC assay is that it is a model system that represents a whole organism of the test species most routinely used in vivo for embryo-fetal development toxicity studies; however, the short timespan (2–3 days) of organogenesis during which the whole rodent embryos can be cultured, and the lack of maternal–fetal interactions or maternal influences during drug testing are the major limitations of the WEC assay.

A workshop on the state-of-the-art in developmental toxicity screening methods laid out the advantages and the limitations of WEC, EST, and ZET [121]. It has been recognized that none of these assays is ready to replace the in vivo developmental toxicity design at the present time; however, several tasks were identified that if completed might lead to significant improvements in the conduct and performance of these assays.

The evaluation of embryonic development is a continuous process of a precisely orchestrated sequence of events, and any alternative assay in the field of developmental toxicity represents only part of the complexity of the whole developing conceptus and its maternal environment; therefore the design of in vitro alternatives with good predictivity of in vivo effects is a daunting task [122]. There is little likelihood that these tests will ever replace in vivo mammalian testing [123]. Because of the complexity of the manifestations in the assessments of developmental toxicity, the establishment of a test battery in combination with human embryonic stem cell technology and the microarray techniques may provide a unique opportunity, leading to a deeper understanding of the toxicological mechanisms of developmental toxicants in humans [124].

CONCLUDING REMARKS AND FUTURE DIRECTIONS

Since the thalidomide tragedy, the assessment of developmental and reproductive toxicity has become an integral part of the safety evaluation for pharmaceuticals and chemicals.

Although fundamental understanding of embryonic development, molecular targets, and mechanisms of developmental toxicity has greatly advanced, study designs, endpoints, data evaluation and analyses, and the interpretation of developmental and reproductive toxicity studies for regulatory safety assessment have remained unchanged [125]. The current testing strategy for developmental and reproductive toxicity testing is comprehensive and effective in preventing false-negatives, but the limitations include low throughput, slow turnaround, and are costly both in terms of finance and animal resources [126].

Toxicity Testing in the 21st Century: A Vision and a Strategy [127] has called for renewed examination to improve the current approach for better assessment of potential risk to human health.

Over the past three decades, many alternative methods have been proposed as test systems for testing toxic effects on the various processes involved in reproduction and development. However, the design of in vitro alternatives with good predictivity of in vivo effects is a daunting task. Embryonic development is a continuous process of a precisely orchestrated sequence of events, and any alternative assay used so far represents only part of the complexity of the whole developing conceptus and its maternal environment [122], and there is less likelihood for these tests to ever replace in vivo mammalian testing [123]. Due to the complexity of the manifestations in the assessments of developmental toxicity, the establishment of a test battery in combination with

human embryonic stem-cell technology and the microarray techniques may provide a unique opportunity, leading to a deeper understanding of the toxicological mechanisms of developmental toxicants in humans [124]. Moreover, genomics, proteomics, and metabolomics are new frontiers with major initiatives in developmental and reproductive toxicology [128]. The application of new automated technologies and the use of in silico models have been widely discussed as new tools to enhance developmental toxicity testing [129–131]. Automated high-throughput screening (HTS), high-content screening (HCS), and computational in silico methods will inspire a paradigm shift for testing developmental toxicity studies that highlights drug or chemical interactions with sensitive molecular targets and the identification of the relevant biological pathways that lead to the endpoints of toxicity observed in traditional in vivo testing [127]. The implementation and the success the *Toxicity Testing in the 21st Century: A Vision and a Strategy* will require better coordination of the ongoing efforts at national and international levels including education, training, and dissemination of the technologies.

Nevertheless, the future of developmental toxicity safety assessments using new automated technologies will depend on the accuracy and predictive values of these models as reduced accuracy and predictivity could be obstacles for a broader regulatory acceptance and thus minimize their value of these assays in safety assessments.

Acknowledgment

The authors would like to thank Ms. Marj Vargo for her technical support.

References

[1] Diggle G. Thalidomide: 40 years on. Int J Clin Pract 2001;55(9): 627–31.

[2] Smithells RW, Newman CG. Recognition of thalidomide defects. J Med Genet 1992;29:716–23.

[3] Perri 3rd AJ, Hsu S. A review of thalidomide's history and current dermatological applications. Dermatol Online J 2003;9(3):5.

[4] Speid LH, Lumley CE, Walker SR. Harmonization of guidelines for toxicity testing of pharmaceuticals by 1992. Regul Toxicol Pharmacol 1990;12:179–211.

[5] Peltzman S. An evaluation of consumer protection legislation: the 1962 drug amendments. J Polit Econ September–October, 1973;81(5):1051.

[6] ICH S5 (R2). Guidance on reproductive toxicology and male fertility: detection of toxicity to reproduction for medicinal products; 2005. http://www.ich.org/products/guidelines/safety/article/safety-guidelines.html.

[7] ICH S5 (R3). Final concept paper S5(R3): detection of toxicity to reproduction for medicinal products & toxicity to male fertility dated 9 February 2015. Endorsed by the ICH Steering Committee on 27 March 2015a. http://www.ich.org/fileadmin/Public_Web_Site/ICH_Products/Guid.

[8] Goldenthal E. Current view on safety evaluation of drugs FDA paper; May 13–18, 1966.

[9] Frankos V. FDA perspectives on the use of teratology data for human risk assessment. Fundam Appl Toxicol 1985;5:615–25.

[10] Hoar R. Reproduction/teratology. Fundam Appl Toxicol 1984;4:S335–40.

[11] ICH. Harmonized tripartite guideline. Detection of toxicity to reproduction for medicinal products. (Proposed rule Endorsed by the ICH Steering Committee at step 4 of the ICH process, 24 June 1993.). In: D'Arcy PF, Harron DWG, editors. Proceedings of the second international conference on harmonization, 1994. Greystone Books, Ltd., Antrim, N. Ireland OIFPMA, Orlando, Florida; 1993. p. 5567–86.

[12] ICH. Harmonized tripartite guideline. Male fertility studies in reproductive toxicology. In: D'Arcy PF, Harron DWG, editors. Proceedings of the third international conference on harmonization, 1996. Greystone Books, Ltd., Antrim, N. Ireland IFPMA; 1995. p. 245–52.

[13] Barrow PC. Reproductive toxicity for pharmaceuticals under ICH. Reprod Toxicol 2009;28:172–6.

[14] Christian MS. Test methods for assessing female reproductive and developmental toxicology. In: Hayes AW, editor. Principles and methods of toxicology. Philadelphia: Taylor and Francis; 2001. p. 1301–82.

[15] Lerman SA, Hew KW, Stewart J, Stump DG, Wise DL. The clinical fertility study design for pharmaceuticals. Birth Defects Res (Part B) 2009;86(6):429–36.

[16] Ulbrich B, Palmer AK. Detection of effects on male reproduction – a literature survey. Int J Toxicol 1995;14(4):293–327.

[17] Takayama S, Akaike M, Kawashima K, Takahashi M, Kurokawa Y. A collaborative study in Japan on optimal treatment period and parameters for detection of male fertility disorders induced by drugs in rats. Intl J Toxicol 1995;14(4):266–92.

[18] Pregnancy, lactation, and reproductive potential: labeling for human prescription drug and biological products – content and format, guidance for industry, draft guidance, December 2014, Labeling.

[19] Federal Register, rules and regulations, Thursday December 4, 2014, Vol 79, No, 233, 21 CFR Part 201 content and format of labeling for human Prescription drug and biological products; requirement for pregnancy and lactation labeling.

[20] Chellman G, Bussiere JL, Makori N, Martin PL, Ooshima Y, Weinbauer G. Developmental and reproductive toxicology studies in nonhuman primates. Birth Defects Res (Part B) 2009;86:446–62.

[21] OECD 414: Organization for economic cooperation and development (OECD). Guidelines for testing of chemicals. Section 4, No. 414: teratogenicity, adopted 22 January, 2001(a).

[22] US Food and Drug Administration. Toxicological principles and procedures for priority based assessment of food additives (red book 2000), guidelines for reproductive studies, center for food safety and applied nutrition; 2000.

[23] US EPA 870.3800. Us environmental protection agency (EPA-OPPTS). Health effects test guidelines; reproduction and fertility effects. Office of prevention, pesticides and toxic substances (OPPTS) 870.3800; 1998.

[24] US EPA 870.3550. Us environmental protection agency. Design for the environment program alternatives assessment criteria for hazard evaluation (version 2.0) 870.3550; 2011.

[25] Rocca MS, Wehner NG. The guinea pig as an animal model for developmental and reproductive toxicology studies. Birth Defects Res (Part B) 2009;86:92–7.

[26] Wangikar P, Ahmed T, Vangala S. Toxicologic pathology of the reproductive system. In: Gupta RC, editor. Reproductive and developmental toxicology. London: Elsevier; 2011. p. 1003–26.

[27] Smith BJ, Plowchalk DR, Sipes IG, Mattison DR. Comparison of random and serial sections in assessment of ovarian toxicity. Reprod Toxicol 1991;5:379–83.

[28] Plowchalk DR, Smith BJ, Mattison DR. Assessment of toxicity to the ovary using follicle quantitation and morphometrics. In: Heindel JJ, Chapin RE, editors. Methods in toxicology. San Diego: Academic Press; 1993. p. 57–68.

[29] Bolon B, Bucci TJ, Warbritton AR, Chen JJ, Mattison DR, Heindel JJ. Differential follicle counts as a screen for chemically induced ovarian toxicity in mice: results from continuous breeding bioassays. Fundam Appl Toxicol 1997;39(1):1–10.

[30] Bucci TJ, Bolon B, Warbritton AR, Chen JJ, Heindel JJ. Influence of sampling on the reproducibility of ovarian follicle counts in mouse toxicity studies. Reprod Toxicol 1997;11(5):689–96.

[31] Reagen KS, Cline JM, Creasy D, Davis B, Foley GL, Lanning L, et al. STP position: ovarian follicular counting in the assessment of rodent reproductive toxicity. Toxicol Pathol 2005;33:409–12.

[32] Perreault SD, Klinefelter GR, Clegg E. Assessment of male reproductive toxicity. In: Hayes AW, editor. Principles and methods of toxicology. Florida: CRC Press; 2008. p. 1605–40.

[33] França LR, Ogawa T, Avarbock MR, Brinster RL, Russel LD. Germ cell genotype controls cell cycle during spermatogenesis in the rat. Biol Reprod 1998;59:1371–7.

[34] Wilson JG. Principles of teratology. Environment and birth defects. New York: Academic Press; 1973.

[35] Wilson JG. Handbook of teratology. New York: Plenum Press; 1977.

[36] Faustman EM, Gohlke JM, Ponce RA, Lewandowski TA, Seeley MR, Whittaker SG, et al. In: Hood RD, editor. Experimental approaches to evaluate mechanisms of developmental toxicity in developmental and reproductive toxicology: a practical approach. Hoboken, N.J: CRC Press, Taylor and Francis Group; 2006.

[37] Garg RC, Bracken WM, Hoberman AM. Reproductive and developmental safety evaluation of new pharmaceutical compounds. In: Gupta R, editor. Reproductive and developmental toxicology. United Kingdom: Academic Press; 2011. p. 89–109.

[38] OECD 416: Organization for economic cooperation and development (OECD). OECD guidelines for testing of chemicals. Section 4, No. 416: two-generation reproduction toxicity, adopted 22 January, 2001(b).

[39] ICH S6 (R1). Addendum to ICH S6: preclinical safety evaluation of biotechnology-derived pharmaceuticals; 2009. http://www.ich.org/products/guidelines/safety/article/safety-guidelines.html.

[40] ICH M3 (R2). Nonclinical studies for the conduct of human clinical trials and marketing authorization for pharmaceuticals, CPMP/ICH/286/95; 2009.

[41] Hood RD. Developmental and reproductive toxicology. Boca Raton, FL: CRC Press; 2006.

[42] Wise LD, Buschmann J, Feuston MH, Fisher JE, Hew KW, Hoberman AM, et al. Embryo-fetal developmental toxicity study design for pharmaceuticals. Birth Defects Res (Part B) 2009;86(6):418–28.

[43] Staples RE. Detection of visceral alterations in mammalian fetuses. Teratology 1974;9(3):A37–8.

[44] Stuckhardt JL, Poppe SM. Fresh visceral examination of rat and rabbit fetuses used in teratogenicity testing. Teratogen Carcinog Mutag 1984;4:181.

[45] Redfern BG, Wise LD. High-throughput staining for the evaluation of fetal skeletal development in rats and rabbits. Birth Defects Res (Part B) 2007;80(3):177–82.

[46] Staples RE, Schnell VL. Refinement in rapid clearing technic in the KOH-Alizarin red S method for fetal bone. Stain Technol 1964;29:61–3.

[47] Dawson HB. A note on the staining of the skeleton of cleared specimens with Alizarin red S. Department of Biology, New York University; 1926. p. 123–4.

[48] Salewski E. Färbemethode zum makroskopischen Nachweis von Implantationsstellen am Uterus der Ratte. Arch Pathol Exp Pharmakol 1964;247:367.

[49] Tyl RW, Marr MC. Developmental toxicity testing – methodology. In: Hood R, editor. Handbook of developmental toxicology. New York: CRC Press; 2006. p. 201–61.

[50] Wilson JG. Methods for administering agents and detecting malformations in experimental animals. Teratology, Principles and Techniques. Chicago: University of Chicago Press; 1965. p. 262.

[51] Barrow MV, Taylor WJ. A rapid method for detecting malformations in rat fetuses. J Morph 1969;127:291–306.

[52] Inouye M. Differential staining of cartilage and bone in fetal mouse skeleton by alcian blue and alizarin red S. Cong Anom 1976;16:171–3.

[53] Kimmel CA, Trammell C. A rapid procedure for routine double staining of cartilage and bone in fetal and adult animals. Stain Technol 1981;56(5):271–3.

[54] Marr MC, Myers CB, George JD, Price CJ. Comparison of single and double staining for evaluation of skeletal development: the effects of ethylene glycol (EG) in CD rats. Teratology 1988;37:476.

[55] Marr MC, Price CJ, Myers CB, Morrissey E. Developmental states of the CD® (Sprague-Dawley) rat skeleton after maternal exposure to ethylene glycol. Teratology 1992;46:169–81.

[56] Wise DL, Beck SL, Beltrame D, Beyer BK, Chajhouid I, Clark RL, et al. Terminology of developmental abnormalities in common laboratory mammals (version 1). Teratology 1997;55:249–92.

[57] Makris SL, Solomon HM, Clark R, Shiota K, Barbellion S, Buschmann J, et al. Terminology of developmental abnormalities in common laboratory mammals (version 2). Birth Defects Res (Part B) 2009;46:179–81.

[58] Spence SG, Allen HL, Cukierski MA, Manson JM, Robertson RT, Eydelloth RS. Defining the susceptible period of developmental toxicity for the AT₁-selective angiotensin II receptor antagonist Losartan in rats. Teratology 1995;51:367–82.

[59] Spence SG, Cukierski MA, Manson JM, Robertson RT, Eydelloth RS. Evaluation of the reproductive and developmental toxicity of the AT₁-selective angiotensin II receptor antagonist Losartan in rats. Teratology 1995;51:383–97.

[60] Bailey GP, Wise LD, Buschmann J, Hurtt M, Fisher JE. Pre and postnatal developmental toxicity study designs for pharmaceuticals. Birth Defects Res (Part B) 2009;86:437–45.

[61] Carney EW, Zablotny CL, Marty MS, Crissman JW, Anderson P, Woolhiser W, et al. The effects of feed restriction during in utero and postnatal development in rats. Toxicol Sci 2004;82:237–49.

[62] Ashby J, Lefevre PA. The peripubertal male rat assay as an alternative to the Hershberger castrated male rat assay for the detection of antiandrogens, oestrogens and metabolic modulators. J Appl Toxicol 2000;20:35–47.

[63] Clark RL. Endpoints of reproductive system development. In: Daston G, Kimmel CA, editors. An evaluation and interpretation of reproductive endpoints for human health risk assessment, chapter IV. International Life Sciences Institute; 1998.

[64] Holsapple MP, Burns-Naas LA, Hastings KL, Ladics GS, Lavin AL, Makris SL, et al. A proposed testing framework for developmental immunotoxicology (DIT). Toxicol Sci 2005;83:18–24.

[65] ICH S3A. Guideline for industry toxicokinetics: the assessment of systemic exposure in toxicity studies; 1995.

[66] ICH S6. Preclinical safety evaluation of biotechnology-derived pharmaceuticals; 1997. http://www.ich.org/products/guidelines/safety/article/safety-guidelines.html.

[67] Pentsuk N, Van der Laan JW. An interspecies comparison of placental antibody transfer: new insights into developmental toxicity testing of monoclonal antibodies. Birth Defects Res (Part B) 2009;86:328–44.

[68] Martin PL, Breslin W, Rocca M, Wright D, Cavagnaro J. Considerations in assessing the developmental and reproductive toxicity potential of biopharmaceuticals. Birth Defects Res (Part B) 2009;86:176–203.

[69] Van Esch E, Buse E, Weinbauer GF, Cline JM. The macaque endometrium, with special reference to the cynomolgus monkey (Macaca fascicularis). Toxicol Pathol 2008;36:67S–100S.

[70] De Rijk E, Van Esch E. The Macaque placenta – a mini-review. Toxicol Pathol 2008;36:108S–18S.

[71] Hendrickx AG, Binkerd PE, Rowland JM. Developmental toxicity and nonhuman primates – interspecies comparison. In: Kalter H, editor. Issues and reviews in teratology, vol. 1. London: Plenum Press; 1983. p. 149–80.

[72] Hummler H, Korte R, Hendrickx AG. Induction of malformations in the cynomolgus monkey with 13-cis retinoic acid. Teratology 1990;42(3):263–72.

[73] Faqi AS. A critical evaluation of the developmental and reproductive toxicity in nonhuman primates. Syst Biol Reprod Med 2012;58(1):23–32.

[74] Meyer JK, Fitzsimmons D, Hastings TF, Chellman GJ. Methods for the prediction of breeding success in male cynomolgus monkeys (Macaca fasciculararis) used for reproductive toxicology studies. J Am Assoc Lab Anim Sci 2006;45:31–6.

[75] Aslam H, Rosiepen G, Krishnamurthy H, Arslan M, Clemen G, Nielschlag E, et al. The cycle duration of the seminiferous epithelium remains unaltered during GnRH antagonist induced testicular involution in rats and monkeys. J Endocrinol 1999;161:281–8.

[76] Stewart J. Developmental toxicity testing of monoclonal antibodies: an enhanced pre and postnatal study design option. Reprod Toxicol 2009;28(2):220–5.

[77] Jarvis P, Srivastav S, Vogelwedde E, Stewart J, Mitchard T, Weinbauer G. The cynomolgus monkey as a model for developmental toxicity studies: variability of pregnancy losses, statistical power estimates, and group size considerations. Birth Defects Res (Part B) 2010;89:175–87.

[78] Brazelton TB. Neonatal behavioral assessment Scale. 2nd ed. Philadelphia: Lippincott; 1984.

[79] Weinbauer GF, Frings W, Fuchs A, Niehaus M, Osterburg I. Reproductive/developmental toxicity assessment of biopharmaceuticals in nonhuman primates. In: Cavagnaro J, editor. Preclinical safety evaluation of biopharmaceuticals: a science-based approach to facilitating clinical trials. New York: Wiley & Sons, Inc.; 2008.

[80] Zurlo J, Rudacille D, Goldberg AM. The three Rs: the way forward. Environ. Health Perspect 1996;104(8):878–80.

[81] Louekari K, Sihvonen K, Kuittinen M, Sømnes V. In vitro tests within the REACH information strategies. Altern Lab Anim 2006;34(4):377–86.

[82] Spielmann H, Pohl I, Doring B, Liebsch M, Moldenhauer F. The embryonic stem cell test (EST), an in vitro embryotoxicity test using two permanent mouse cell lines; 3t3 fibroblasts and embryonic stem cells. Toxicol Vitro 1997;10:119–27.

[83] zur Nieden NI, Kempka G, Ahr HJ. Molecular multiple endpoint embryonic stem cell test – a possible approach to test for the teratogenic potential of compounds. Toxicol Appl Pharmacol 2004;194(3):257–69.

[84] Liebsch M, Grune B, Seiler A, Butzke D, Oelgeschläger M, Pirow R, et al. Alternatives to animal testing: current status and future perspectives. Arch Toxicol 2011;85(8):841–58.

[85] Seiler AE, Spielmann H. The validated embryonic stem cell test to predict embryotoxicity in vitro. Nat Protoc 2011;6(7):961–78.

[86] Zandstra PW, Bauwens C, Yin T, Liu Q, Schiller H, Zweigerdt R, et al. Scalable production of embryonic stem cell-derived cardiomyocytes. Tissue Eng 2003;9:767–78.

[87] Seiler A, Visan A, Buesen R, Genschow E, Spielmann H. Improvement of an in vitro stem cell assay for developmental toxicity: the use of molecular endpoints in the embryonic stem cell test. Reprod Toxicol 2004;18:231–40.

[88] Honda M, Kurisaki A, Ohnuma K, Okochi H, Hamazaki TS, Asashima M. N-cadherin is a useful marker for the progenitor of cardiomyocytes differentiated from mouse ES cells in serum-free condition. Biochem Biophys Res Commun 2006;351:877–82.

[89] Baharvand H, Azarnia M, Parivar K, Ashtiani SK. The effect of extracellular matrix on embryonic stem cell-derived cardiomyocytes. J Mol Cell Cardiol 2005;38:495–503.

[90] Genschow E, Spielmann H, Scholz G, Pohl I, Seiler A, Clemann N, et al. Validation of the embryonic stem cell test in the international ECVAM validation study on three in vitro embryotoxicity tests. Altern Lab Anim 2004;32(3):209–44.

[91] Whitlow S, Burgin H, Clemann N. The embryonic stem cell test for the early selection of pharmaceutical compounds. ALTEX 2007;24:3–7.

[92] Peters AK, Steemans M, Mesens N, Hansen E, Verheyen GR, Spanhaak S, et al. A higher throughput method to the Embryonic Stem cell Test (EST), to detect embryotoxicity in early development. AATEX 2007;14:673–7. [special issue].

[93] Buesen R, Genschow E, Slawik B, Visan A, Spielmann H, Luch A, et al. Embryonic stem cell test remastered: comparison between the validated EST and the new molecular FACS-EST for assessing developmental toxicity in vitro. Toxicol Sci 2009;108(2):389–400.

[94] Paquette JA, Kumpf SW, Streck RD, Thomson JJ, Chapin RE, Stedman DB. Assessment of the embryonic stem cell test and application and use in the pharmaceutical industry. Birth Defects Res (Part B) 2008;83(2):104–11.

[95] de Jong E, Barenys M, Hermsen SA, Verhoef A, Ossendorp BC, Bessems JG, et al. Comparison of the mouse embryonic stem cell test, the rat whole embryo culture and the zebrafish embryotoxicity test as alternative methods for developmental toxicity testing of six 1,2,4-triazoles. Toxicol Appl Pharmacol 2011;253(2):103–11.

[96] West PR, Weir AM, Smith AM, Donley EL, Cezar GG. Predicting human developmental toxicity of pharmaceuticals using human embryonic stem cells and metabolomics. Toxicol Appl Pharmacol 2010;247(1):18–27.

[97] McCollum CW, Ducharme NA, Bondesson M, Gustafsson JA. Developmental toxicity screening in zebrafish. Birth Defects Res (Part C) 2011;93:67–114.

[98] Rubinstein AL. Zebrafish assays for drug toxicity screening. Expert opinion. Drug Metab Toxicol 2006;2(2):231–40.

[99] Brannen KC, Panzica-Kelly JM, Danberry TL, Augustine-Rauch KA. Development of a zebrafish embryo teratogenicity assay and quantitative prediction model. Birth Defects Res (Part B) 2010;89(1):66–77.

[100] Van den Bulck K, Hill A, Mesens N, Diekman H, De Schaepdrijver L, Lammens L. Zebrafish developmental toxicity assay: a fishy solution to reproductive toxicity screening, or just a red herring? Reprod Toxicol 2011;32(2):213–9.

[101] Panzica-Kelly JM, Zhang C, Danberry TL, Flood A, DeLan JW, Brannen KC, et al. Morphological score assignment guidelines for the dechorionated zebrafish teratogenicity assay. Birth Defects Res (Part B) 2010;89(5):382–95.

[102] Hermsen SA, van den Brandhof EJ, van der Ven LT, Piersma AH. Relative embryotoxicity of two classes of chemicals in a modified zebrafish embryotoxicity test and comparison with their in vivo potencies. Toxicol Vitro 2011;25(3):745–53.

[103] New DAT. Whole-embryo culture and the study of mammalian embryos during organogenesis. Biol Rev 1978;53:81–122.

[104] Takahashi M, Osumi N. The method of rodent whole embryo culture using the rotator-type bottle culture system. Vis Exp 2010;28(42):2170.

[105] Flynn TY. Teratological research using in vitro systems. Mammalian whole embryo culture. Environ Health Perspect 1987;72:203–10.

[106] New DAT. Development of rat embryos cultured in blood sera. J Reprod Fertil 1966;12:509–22.

[107] Chatot CA, Klein NW, Piatek J, Pierro LI. Successful culture of rat embryos on human serum: use in the detection of teratogens. Science 1980;207:1471–3.

[108] Klein NW, Plenefisch JD, Carey SW, Fredrickson WT, Sackett GP, Burbacher TM, et al. Serum from monkeys with histories of fetal wastage causes abnormalities in cultured rat embryos. Science 1982;215:66–9.

[109] Klug S, Lewandowski C, Neubert D. Modification and standardization of the culture of postimplantation embryos for toxicological studies. Arch Toxicol 1985;58:84–8.

[110] Klug S, Lewandowski C, Neubert D. Bovine serum: an alternative to serum as a culture medium for the rat whole embryo culture. Toxicol Vitro 1990;4:598–601.

[111] Nakajima M, Sasaki M, Kobayashi Y, Ohno Y, Usami M. Rat embryo culture using rabbit serum as a medium for developmental toxicity studies. J Appl Toxicol 1997;17(3):185–8.

[112] Brown NA, Fabro S. Quantitation of rat embryonic development in-vitro: a morphological scoring system. Teratology 1981;24:65–78.

[113] Naya M, Kito Y, Eto K, Deguchi T. Development of rabbit whole embryo culture during organogenesis. Cong Anomal 1991;31(3):153–6.

[114] Carney EW, Tornesi B. Culture of postimplantation rabbit embryo sans placenta. Birth Defect Res (Part A) 2003;68:262.

[115] Carney EW, Tornesi B, Keller C, Findlay HA, Nowland WS, Marshall VA, et al. Refinement of a morphological scoring system for postimplantation rabbit conceptuses. Birth Defects Res B Dev Reprod Toxciol 2007;80(3):213–22.

[116] Schmid BP, Goulding E, Kitchin K, Sanyal MK. Assessment of the teratogenic potential of acrolein and cyclophosphamide in a rat embryo culture system. Toxicology 1981;22:235–43.

[117] Sadler TW, Horton WE, Warner CW. Whole embryo culture: a screening technique for teratogens. Teratog Carcinog Mutagen 1982;2:243–53.

[118] Cicurel L, Schmid BP. Postimplantation embryo culture: validation with selected compounds for teratogenicity testing. Xenobiotic 1988;18(6):617–24.

[119] Webster WS, Brown-Woodman PD, Ritchie HE. A review of the contribution of whole embryo the determination of hazard and risk in teratogenicity testing. Int J Dev Biol 1997;41:329–35.

[120] Piersma AH, Genschow E, Verhoef A, Spanjersberg MQ, Brown NA, Brady M, et al. Validation of the postimplantation rat whole-embryo culture test in the international ECVAM validation study on three in vitro embryotoxicity tests. Altern Lab Anim ATLA 2004;32(3):275–307.

[121] Chapin R, Augustine-Rauch K, Beyer B, Daston G, Finnell R, Flynn T, et al. State of the art in development toxicity screening methods and a way forward: a meeting report addressing embryonic stem cells, whole embryo-culture and zebrafish. Birth Defect Res (Part B) 2008;83:446–56.

[122] Piersma AH. Alternative methods for developmental toxicity testing. Basic Clin Pharmacol Toxicol 2006;98(5):427–31.

[123] Daston PG. The theoretical and empirical case for in vitro developmental toxicity screens, and potential applications. Teratology 1996;53:339–44.

[124] Bremer S, Hartung T. The use of embryonic stem cells for regulatory developmental toxicity testing in vitro – the current status of test development. Curr Pharm Des 2004;10(22):2733–47.

[125] Shuey D, Kim JH. Overview: developmental toxicology – new directions. Birth Defects Res (Part B) 2011;92(5):381–3.

[126] Hartung T. Toxicology for the twenty first century. Nature 2009;469:208–12.

[127] National Research Council (NRC). Toxicity testing in the 21st century. Washington, DC: The National Academic Press; 2007.

[128] Makris SL, Kim JH, Ellis A, Faber W, Harrouk W, Lewis JM, et al. Current and future needs for developmental toxicity testing. Birth Defects Res (Part B) 2011;92:384–94.

[129] Kleinstreuer NC, Judson RS, Reif DM, Sipes NS, Singh AV, Chandler KJ, et al. Environmental impact on vascular development predicted by high throughput screening. Environ Health Perspect 2011;119(11):1596–603.

[130] Martin MT, Reif DM, Houck KA, Judson RS, Kavlock RJ, Dix DJ. Predictive model of rat reproductive toxicity from Tox Cast high throughput screening. Biol Reprod 2011;85(2):327–39.

[131] Sipes NS, Martin MT, Reif DM, Kleinstreuer NC, Judson RS, Singh AV, et al. Predictive models of prenatal developmental toxicity from ToxCast high-throughput screening data. Toxicol Sci 2011;124(1):109–27.

Immunotoxicology Assessment in Drug Development

J.T. Farmer, R.R. Dietert

HISTORY AND CURRENT REGULATORY FRAMEWORK FOR IMMUNOTOXICOLOGY TESTING

Immunotoxicology, defined formally in 1987 [1], is a new discipline that began in the mid-1970s through the interest of industry and academic scientists in efforts to identify methods and standardize assessment of new chemical entities that showed immunomodulatory activity [2]. Early working definitions of immunotoxicology primarily addressed unintended immunosuppression, potential hypersensitivity, and allergic responses [3], but the current definition in the International Conference on Harmonization S8 guideline, which applies to new human pharmaceuticals (ICH S8), defines immunotoxicity as "unintended immunosuppression or enhancement" [4]. The ICH S8 guideline specifically excludes assessment of allergenicity and drug specific autoimmunity [4]. In practice immunotoxicology is a discipline that requires the synthesis of immunology, immunopharmacology, and toxicology to evaluate the range of potentially adverse effects of pharmaceuticals on the immune system.

A Comprehensive Guide to Toxicology in Nonclinical Drug Development, Second Edition
http://dx.doi.org/10.1016/B978-0-12-803620-4.00010-4

The ICH S6 guideline [5], which delineates preclinical evaluation of biotechnology-derived pharmaceuticals, does not explicitly require immunotoxicological testing for biotechnology-derived pharmaceuticals, but does acknowledge that immunotoxicology testing may be required, which when combined with the ICH S8 guidance, indicates that biotechnology-derived pharmaceuticals should undergo immunotoxicity testing if the weight of evidence review indicates that testing would be appropriate. This chapter will focus primarily on immunotoxicity testing derived from the ICH S8 guideline for testing of new human pharmaceuticals, as this guideline is being inculcated by the regulatory bodies of the European Union, Japan, and the United States. The key factors for determining whether immunotoxicity testing is required include the pharmacological properties of the drug, drug disposition, structural similarities to extant immunomodulators, the intended indication and patient population, preliminary toxicology findings indicating immunomodulation, and clinical observations if the drug is currently in clinical trial.

Currently approved drugs that may be submitted for use in a secondary indication, specifically the treatment of immunological or inflammatory diseases, may require immunotoxicology testing. It is the preponderance of findings and the weight of each finding that determines whether a pharmaceutical will require immunotoxicity testing and if so what evaluations are most appropriate. In addition, immunotoxicity testing for new pharmaceuticals if required should be completed before Phase III clinical trials [4]. Immunotoxicity evaluation is generally performed using a tiered approach based in part on preclinical study findings indicating potential immunotoxicity. These must be carefully weighed against the drug's mechanism of action, potential differences in interspecies potency, physiological stress response of the species, lymphoid organ anatomy, indirect pharmacological or pathological processes that can alter immune system function, and the immunological reserve of the species. The constellation of findings typically indicating immunotoxicity provided the aforementioned parameters have been accounted for include:

Increased incidence of infection or repeated infection with normally commensal microbes;
Abnormal stress leukogram in the absence of direct causal pathology;
Pronounced changes in proinflammatory biomarkers;
Marked change in globulin or albumin/globulin ratio;
Histopathological changes in primary and secondary lymphoid organs, eg, unusual patterns of leukocytic infiltration in normal tissues.

DEVELOPMENTAL IMMUNOTOXICOLOGY

Drug therapies provide a significant component of healthcare management for adults and children alike. However, with increasing reliance on drug therapies for health management there has been elevated concern regarding the safety and unintended adverse outcomes of drug administration. Part of this concern is linked to what has been a striking increase in the prevalence of noncommunicable diseases (NCDs) (ie, chronic diseases) on a global scale based largely on shifting environmental factors. In fact, the Harvard School of Public Health and World Economic Forum recently estimated that NCDs account for a majority of deaths worldwide and over the next 20 years will grow to represent 48% of the global gross domestic product [6].

The connection of epidemic in chronic diseases and developmental immunotoxicity (DIT) safety testing concerns the recently recognized connection of inflammatory dysregulation as a root of many, if not most, chronic diseases. The diseases not only affect a significant proportion of the adult population but are increasing in prevalence at an alarming rate among the pediatric population [7–9], resulting in increased focus on early-life drug and chemical safety. Immune-inflammatory dysfunction appears to be at the epicenter of chronic diseases and conditions as diverse as asthma, psoriasis, Alzheimer's disease, frailty, depression, atherosclerosis, diabetes, and rheumatoid arthritis [10]. With this in mind, the National Institutes of Health recently devoted its multiinstitute Fall 2011 STEP Symposium Program to this same topic (November 15, 2011).

The lengthy duration of some drug therapies, and the multiple therapies that may be needed to combat comorbid chronic diseases, have contributed to the concern regarding adequate safety testing. This is particularly true when it comes to the safety of children. As many as a quarter of all children in developed countries are estimated to have at least one immune dysfunction-based chronic disease [11]. In addition, many adult onset immune dysfunction-based chronic diseases are thought to have their origins in early life. Table 10.1 lists some examples of immune-inflammatory dysfunction-based chronic diseases where risk of disease is affected by early-life environmental conditions.

When it comes to unintended adverse reactions to drugs, an emerging challenge for DIT testing is to ensure that exposure of nonadults to drugs (directly and/or via pregnant women) does not unnecessarily contribute to the risk of these chronic diseases and conditions. This

TABLE 10.1 Major Targets of Developmental Immunotoxicity (DIT) Testing: Examples of Chronic Disease and Conditions Dependent Upon Immune-Inflammation Dysregulation and Affected by Early-Life Environmental Risk Factors

Alopecia Areata	Colon Cancer	Myalgic Encepholomyelitis	Rheumatoid Arthritis
Alkylosing spondilitis	Crohn's disease	Myasthenia gravis	Restless legs syndrome
Alzheimer's disease	Depression	Multiple sclerosis	Sarcoidosis
Allergic rhinitis	Endometriosis	Narcolepsy	Scleroderma
Asthma		Nonalcoholic hepatic steatosis	Sjogren's syndrome
Atherosclerosis	Food allergies	Obesity	
Atopic dermatitis	Fraility		Sleep disorders
Autism	Grave's disease	Parkinson's disease	Systemic lupus erythematosus (SLE)
Autoimmune myocarditis		Pemphigus	Type 1 diabetes
Behavioral disorders	Hashimoto's thyroiditis	Peripheral neuropathy	Type 2 diabetes
Behcet's disease			Vasculitis
Celiac disease			Vitiligo
Chagas disease	Insulin resistance	Psoriasis	Ulcerative colitis
Chronic kidney disease	Juvenile idiopathic arthritis	Recurrent otitis media	Uveitis
Chronic obstructive pulmonary disease (COPD)	Kawasaki disease	Reiter's syndrome	

Information adapted from Dietert RR, Luebke RW, editors. Immunotoxicity, immune dysfunction, and chronic disease. NY, USA: Springer (Science + Business Media); 2011.

includes the potential for epigenetic fetal programming of adult disease [12].

Not surprisingly, chronic diseases, such as the approximately 100 different autoimmune conditions are a major growth area for new drug development. A recent survey of 851 new drugs in development by the Pharmaceutical Research and Manufacturers of America (PhRMA) underscored the fact that a majority of new drugs were directed toward chronic diseases with an emphasis on cytokine imbalance-driven autoimmune and inflammatory conditions that disproportionately affect women [13,14]. Yet ironically, currently required safety testing provides little to no direct information on the potential for pediatric drugs to increase the risk of these immune-based chronic diseases. This lack of disease-relevant information is a glaring gap in current drug safety evaluation.

Current regulatory guidelines for preclinical drug safety do not specifically address the expectations for DIT testing. There are two pertinent guidance documents. The ICH S8 guidelines for immunotoxicity addresses immunotoxicity and has a "cause for concern" trigger that would lead agencies to specifically request immunotoxicity information should routine toxicological assessment suggest a potential unintended immune effect [5]. That guidance is directed toward adults and lacks provisions for pediatric/juvenile immune assessment. In addition, it does not inherently require immune functional testing [15].

The Guidance Addressing Nonclinical Safety Evaluation of Pediatric Drug Products covers the issue of assessment during the nonadult period but lacks any consideration of immune assessment [16]. Therefore DIT safety testing of drugs is a significant gap in the current US FDA Guidance.

This section will consider:

1. The need to close the gap on DIT testing;
2. Options for DIT testing; and
3. Potential cost–benefits in obtaining the most child-relevant immune assessment information.

Specialized Developmental Considerations

Early-life development represents a specialized challenge when it comes to preclinical drug safety evaluation. Many physiological systems, such as the neurological, respiratory, and immune systems are not fully developed in children and some development continues in specialized systems into the young adult. For this reason, safety predictions based on what are irrelevant age-specific exposures have the risk of providing misleading information concerning the potential impact of exposure of the nonadult. The issue goes beyond only the labeling of drugs for use in children, since the exposure of women during pregnancy is an added risk based on potential prenatal vulnerabilities. Fig. 10.1 provides a sample inverted pyramid

Distinct Critical Developmental Periods of Human Immune Vulnerability

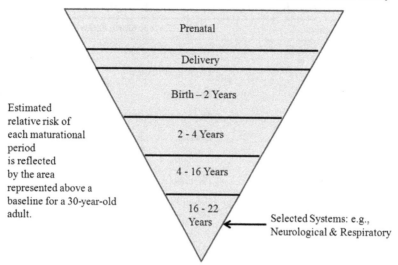

FIGURE 10.1   The inverted pyramid provides one example of estimated relative risk (above that for a 30-year-old adult) for drug-induced developmental immunotoxicity (DIT). Estimations are based on: (1) the number of unique maturation processes that occur at these developmental stages (but are not prominent in the adult) and (2) the present literature on relative environmental sensitivity of the prenatal, neonatal, and adolescent immune system. This is presented as a sample guide but does illustrate the need to perform age-relevant preclinical immune safety testing.

estimation of relative increased immunological risk (vs. the baseline for a 30-year-old adult) for distinct maturational periods.

Each developmental period or window is characterized by different maturational processes (eg, T-cell repertoire selection in the prenatal thymus, maturation of toll-like receptors on neonatal innate immune cells, interaction of infant innate immune cells with the gut microbiome). These maturational processes can serve as major targets for drug- and/or chemical-induced disruption, subsequent immune dysfunction, and elevated risk of later-life chronic disease [17–19].

The risk to the developing immune system from adverse drug reactions is varied and requires both a sensitive and a comprehensive assessment plan. While the historic goal of immune safety testing was detection of loss of immune-cell populations, lymphoid organ alterations, and reduced immune function (ie, immunosuppression), this is not the type of adverse reactions that are linked with the most prevalent immune dysfunction-driven diseases of today. For this reason alone, immune safety assessment including DIT testing that is unable to detect the full spectrum of unintended immune functional alterations (not just immunosuppression) is unlikely to provide information that is relevant to risk of human disease.

A majority of drugs have been developed specifically for adult use based on adult-specific preclinical safety testing. But there is increasing pressure to have therapeutic tools for the treatment of juvenile-adolescent onset chronic diseases (eg, pediatric celiac disease, juvenile idiopathic arthritis, Kawasaki disease). In fact, there is evidence to suggest that what used to be largely adult-onset diseases are being seen in an increasing percentage of juvenile and adolescents [20,21]. In addition, the exposures most relevant for risk of chronic diseases are known to occur before adulthood [22]. This is reflected in the fact that biomarkers of largely adult-onset diseases, such as atherosclerosis are detectable in children [23,24].

Preclinical Developmental Immunotoxicity Testing Strategies

Preclinical assessment of developmental immunotoxicity should be based on several criteria including: (1) appropriate species selection for the drug or biologic and (2) life-stage relevant exposure and assessment with relevance to the human target population(s) (eg, newborns, infants, juveniles, adolescents, across all periods of the nonadult, pregnant women). It is important to include and separately assess both sexes in a DIT evaluation. A high percentage of developmental immunotoxicants have been found to exhibit sex-specific differences in dose–response sensitivity for DIT and/or the nature of the adverse immunological outcomes. As shown in Fig. 10.2 and previously reviewed in [25], once species selection and developmental windows for exposure assessment have been determined, there are decisions to be made concerning criteria for challenge and assessment.

Example of a Flow Chart for Preclinical DIT Testing

Males and Females Assessed Separately Regardless of Species Used and the Specific Challenge Protocol Selected

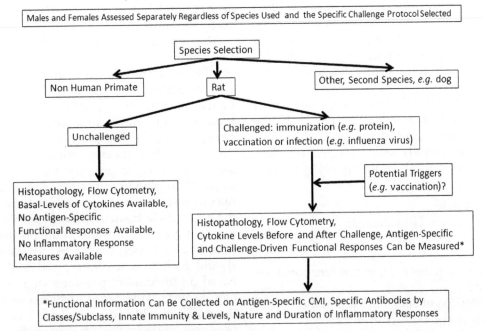

FIGURE 10.2 The diagram illustrates the options available for preclinical developmental immunotoxicity (DIT) testing. Both males and females should be included in the testing and separately analyzed regardless of the species utilized in testing. Examples of protocol decisions following species selection are shown only for the rat. Similar decisions would be made when testing is performed using other species. The benefits of employing challenge-assessment protocols that permit a full assessment of multiple immune functions as well as inflammatory regulation are stressed.

The diagram illustrates the options available for preclinical developmental immunotoxicity (DIT) testing. Both males and females should be included in the testing and separately analyzed regardless of the species utilized in testing. Examples of protocol decisions following species selection are shown only for the rat. Similar decisions would be made when testing is performed using other species. The benefits of employing challenge-assessment protocols that permit a full assessment of multiple immune functions as well as inflammatory regulation are stressed.

Historical approaches to the collection of data often involved a histological assessment of immune organs [26], usually taken from animals in a resting state (unchallenged by robust immunizations or infections) as well as cell-population enumerations often using flow cytometry [27]. While these procedures provide important confirmation of potential drug-induced DIT, as routinely practiced they provide little direct information on the potential for immune-inflammatory dysfunction. Direct functional assessment in challenged animals has been recommended for DIT testing [28,29]. Detection of early-life immune-inflammatory dysfunction is a critical factor for reducing the prevalence of immune-based chronic diseases [30].

Recent reviews have suggested that the rat would be the default preferred species for preclinical DIT drug testing [31], although a pharmacologically responsive

species would be needed in the case of certain biologics [32,33]. Other species (eg, mouse, dog) have been examined as potential second test species [34,35]. In addition, protocols combining DIT, developmental, and reproductive assessment have been suggested as a way forward as they offer potential efficiencies in animal use [31,36,37]. This is a similar strategy to what has been recommended for DIT evaluation of chemicals [28,38].

Choices of challenge and functional assessment protocols should best mimic the conditions associated with immune dysfunction-based promotion of disease occurring in children if the testing is to have relevance for priority adverse outcomes. By challenging the animals with a robust and relevant immunization-vaccination and/or infection protocol, it is possible to collect a wide range of functional information that is not available in the unchallenged animal. As shown in Fig. 10.2, this can facilitate the collection of information not only on the full range of adaptive and innate immune functions but also on the potential for disease-promoting inflammatory dysregulation.

Use of unchallenged animals does not facilitate an examination of dysfunction as an adverse outcome of test drug exposure. Of course, children invariably have immunizations/vaccinations and at least some infections (eg, respiratory) as part of their early life. Making DIT assessment relevant to this childhood reality is not a trivial consideration. Infections are known to serve as triggers of immune-based chronic diseases when immune dysfunction is already in place [39]. For this reason it can be desirable to include relevant triggers or some infectious agent components as part of the challenge-assessment protocol. This enables preclinical DIT testing to better simulate the actual risk in humans.

In summary, preclinical DIT testing is needed and is readily feasible to conduct. In light of the risk of chronic diseases caused by developmental immunotoxicity, four immunotoxicologists recently called for required DIT testing of drugs and chemicals [40]. Suggested protocols should:

1. Use animals efficiently;
2. Allow for both sexes to be evaluated;
3. Have maximum relevance to the experience of children;
4. Facilitate a broad spectrum of immune functional assessment; and
5. Include the collection of data that support the identification of immune and inflammatory dysfunction (eg, histopathology, flow cytometry, and cytokine analysis).

EVALUATION OF HUMORAL IMMUNITY

The first-line toxicological evaluation of antigen-specific humoral immunity in small animal toxicology models currently endorsed by regulatory bodies is the T-cell-dependent antibody response (TDAR) assay [4,41,42]. The assay requires successful protein antigen presentation via the T-cell receptor, T-cell and antigen presenting cell (APC) cytokine production, and cell contact-dependent costimulatory signaling to produce antigen-specific antibodies. Each component of the humoral immune system must be anatomically intact and functional to produce a response, which is why the TDAR assay is considered a primary first-line functional assessment of immunity.

The TDAR assay as originally developed by Jerne and Nordin was a modified hemolytic plague assay that was conducted by immunizing mice with sheep erythrocytes (SRBC) followed by splenectomy at the peak of IgM production, typically 4–5 days postimmunization, and preparation of a single-cell suspension that was subsequently suspended in SRBC-infused agar containing complement [43]. Single B-cell colonies producing sufficient quantities of anti-SRBC IgM induce IgM-mediated complement lysis of SRBC via the classical pathway, which forms a clear or opaque plaque and the total numbers of plaques were enumerated. The SRBC plaque-forming assay is typically incorporated into a mouse or rat 28-day repeat-dose toxicology study, in which SRBC are administered intravenously after administration of test article, 4–5 days prior to study termination.

The standard TDAR study design consists of five treatment groups of 8–10 animals/sex/group, the first of which is the SRBC control group; the purpose of this is to calculate the magnitude of the anti-SRBC response in the absence of test article. The second group is typically an immunosuppressant control, often cyclophosphamide, cyclosporine A, or dexamethasone, the dose of which has been previously determined during assay validation to produce a statistically significant decrease in plaque formation. The SRBC and immunosuppressant control groups are the comparators for the test article-treated groups and the immunosuppressant group is considered the positive control. The dose-level selection for the test article-treated groups should include a low, mid, and high dose selected based on the data of previous well-designed toxicology studies of sufficient statistical power to determine the no observable adverse effect level (NOAEL) that produces measureable toxicity, such as reduction in peripheral blood leukocytes, altered lymphoid tissue morphology, or general indication of systemic toxicity, such as loss of ≤10% of body weight or reduced food consumption. A mid-dose is necessary in combination with a low dose to determine a dose–response relationship, and the dose route and administration scheme should match that of the toxicology studies. Vehicles with suspected or known immunomodulatory activity should be tested as a separate group within the TDAR assay. The SRBC TDAR plaque assay has been shown to be a more sensitive indicator of immunotoxicity in rodents compared with conventional toxicology endpoints including hematology, lymphoid organ weights, and histopathology [44]. The SRBC TDAR plaque assay is limited in that it is a terminal endpoint, it is time and labor intensive, it is sensitive to antigenic variability of SRBC between donors, variations in complement activity, and it represents primarily the response of the spleen resident immune-cell populations.

The majority of laboratories have adopted a ligand-binding SRBC TDAR enzyme-linked immunosorbent assay (ELISA) for testing serum samples. This method offers the advantages of similar sensitivity to the plaque assay, serial sampling and sample batching, greater potential for interlaboratory standardization, and measurement of total serum antigen-specific antibody including IgG. The SRBC TDAR ELISA is conducted similarly to the plaque assay for immunization of SRBC, the required number of experimental groups, and sample collection timing. The SRBC ELISA assay is performed using high-binding ELISA plates coated with SRBC membranes that capture anti-SRBC antibodies in the serum sample. The anti-SRBC antibodies are detected as antiisotype or polyclonal antibodies specific to the species or strain in the study, conjugated to an enzyme that produces color upon addition of a development reagent. The color intensity of the unknown sample is compared with that of a standard curve spanning multiple concentrations of anti-SRBC antibody and a concentration result for the tested sample is generated by regression analysis. Key variables in the performance of the SRBC ELISA are the variability of SRBC antigen from the donor, consistency in preparation of the SRBC membrane, and plate coating. In addition, the concentration, purification, and avidity of the detection antibody and the standard curve model will affect assay robustness. The SRBC plaque assay and ELISA have been shown to have comparable sensitivity for detection of immunotoxicity in rodents [45].

The keyhole limpet hemocyanin (KLH) ELISA is a more recent method that is increasingly being utilized for TDAR assessment in both rodent and large animal models, but the method has not been inculcated by regulatory bodies to date [46,47]. Keyhole limpet hemocyanin is a high molecular weight, heavily glycosylated oxygen carrying metalloprotein isolated from *Megathura crenulata* that is highly immunogenic due to its structure and phylogenetic distance from mammalian proteins [48]. The KLH antigen was adopted as an immunogen in the TDAR assay due to its potent immunogenicity across multiple species, evidence of minimal toxicity at typical immunization dosages, and the ability to standardize KLH preparations that facilitate interlaboratory assay validation.

The KLH TDAR assay can provide reliable quantitative assessment of anti-KLH IgM and IgG in both rodent and non-human primates (NHP) (*Cynomolgus macaque*) following a single immunization, provided the assay is properly validated. Key factors to assess in any TDAR assay can be divided into two functional areas: assay and statistical. A rigorous TDAR assay validation for a semiquantitative assay should encompass testing of the standard curve model, assay range, upper and lower limits of quantitation, dilutional linearity, inter- and intraassay precision and accuracy, plate stability, critical reagent stability, and should be routinely reevaluated if lots of critical reagents change and to detect assay drift due to changes in assay performance or changes in the animal population being tested. In addition, a priori defined statistical criteria should be applied to both the in-life and assay phases of TDAR validation to assure rigor in powering, defining, and detecting positive responses, in the context of biological and assay variability. The application of a priori defined statistics can ameliorate commonly observed phenomenon including the presence of preexisting antibodies in unimmunized animals and the

variability of response to immunization within a species. *Meta*-analysis of SRBC and KLH rodent TDAR responses show acceptable correlation between ELISA SRBC and KLH TDAR methods despite differences in assay protocols, and the TDAR assay has been shown to correlate with immunotoxicity in humans, which confirm the utility of this test [49,50].

A key publication in the assessment of the TDAR assay in NHP was the collaborative work systematically assessing NHP TDAR assays under the aegis of the Health and Environmental Sciences (HESI) Immunotoxicology Technical Committee [51]. This work retrospectively assessed TDAR data from 178 NHP, both male and female of differing geographical origins. The study showed that sex or geographic origin were not substantial sources of variation in NHP TDAR assays, and that the percentage of responders was similar using SRBC, Tetanus Toxoid, or KLH antigens. The work showed that in NHP mean peak secondary TDAR responses were of greater magnitude than mean peak primary responses. A key finding in this paper was that standard toxicology studies, which often use less than four animals/sex/group, may only detect changes of large magnitude. The authors suggested using pooled data from both sexes to enhance the ability of the TDAR assay to detect low-magnitude changes in NHP.

The canine model is often used for toxicity assessment of biopharmaceuticals, but due to the lack of basic immunological knowledge in this species and the paucity of publications specifically investigating TDAR assays more research is clearly needed before routine TDAR assessment in canines is feasible.

EVALUATION OF INNATE IMMUNITY

The innate immune system consists of the combination of in-born anatomical, physiological, and immune system responses that serve as the organism's first line of defense upon encountering pathogens. The evaluation of innate immunity in immunotoxicology is limited in scope and consists of evaluation of complement activity, granulocyte phagocytosis, granulocyte respiratory burst, natural killer-cell activity, immune-cell phenotyping, and lymphocyte proliferation. Cytokine evaluation is included in this section, although it is not strictly an innate or acquired immune endpoint but links both arms of the immune system.

Evaluation of Complement

The complement system is an evolutionarily ancient system of proteins produced in zymogen form in vertebrates. They are found in plasma and other body fluids, and are activated upon contact with microbial surface structures, foreign molecular structures, or upon contact with the constant regions of specific immunoglobulins [52]. Activated complement binds to the surface of the initiating structure where it functions to opsonize or directly lyse the target. The complement system of inactive precursor proteins produced primarily by the liver, and to lesser degrees by monocytes, macrophages, and adipocytes, can be activated by three different pathways: the classical, alternative, and mannose binding lectin pathways [53]. A diagram of the complement pathways is shown in Fig. 10.3.

As shown in the figure, the initiating event for each complement pathway is different but all pathways converge to activate C3, liberating the anaphylatoxin C3a. Following activation C3b covalently binds to the target surface and combines with other factors to form the C5 convertase. This cleaves C5, producing the second anaphylatoxin C5a. The C5b component remains bound to the initiating surface, where it forms the central point of assembly for components C6–C9. The entire C5b–C9 protein complex is designated the membrane attack complex (MAC) and it is MAC formation that lyses the target. Anaphylatoxins C3a and C5a bind to G protein-coupled receptors on the surface of target cells after diffusing from the immediate site of complement activation to exert physiological or pathological effects.

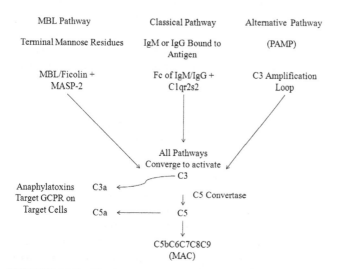

FIGURE 10.3 The figure shows that the initiating event for each complement pathway is different, but all pathways converge to activate C3 liberating the anaphylatoxin C3a. Following activation C3b covalently binds to the target surface and combines with other factors to form the C5 convertase. C5 convertase cleaves C5, producing the second anaphylatoxin C5a. The C5b component remains bound to the initiating surface where it forms the central point of assembly for components C6-C9. The entire C5b-C9 protein complex is designated the membrane attack complex (MAC) and it is MAC formation that lyses the target. Anaphylatoxins C3a and C5a bind to G protein-coupled receptors on the surface of target T cells after diffusing from the immediate site of complement activation to exert physiological or pathological effects.

A detailed review of the complement system is beyond the scope of this chapter; refer to the following reference for detailed discussion of the complement system and its regulation [54].

The standard screening tests to detect alterations in the activity of the classical and alternative pathways are the total complement hemolytic assay for the classical pathway (CH50) and alternative pathway (AH50). In the CH50 assay, erythrocytes that have been previously incubated with antibody or sensitized are incubated with dilutions of the test subject's sera where the presence of antibody induces lysis of the erythrocyte by the classical complement pathway. The activity of serum samples is expressed as the reciprocal of the dilution that lyses 50% of the erythrocytes. The AH50 assay is performed in a similar manner, but utilizes erythrocytes that have not been previously exposed to antibody. The AH50 assay relies upon the functional activity of properdin, Factor B and Factor D in the animal's serum to initiate the alternative pathway. These assays were originally developed to screen for genetic complement component deficiencies in human patients [55]. In immunotoxicology studies, they are employed to detect deleterious activation of the complement pathway or changes in complement activity due to test-article administration. In many cases increased complement activation will produce decreases in CH50 and AH50 activity, because the activated complement factors are consumed in vivo more rapidly than nonactivated factors. This pattern of response may not be observed in acute-phase reactions as hepatocyte production of complement components is upregulated during the acute phase response, which masks the increase in consumption of activated complement components [56]. The CH50 and AH50 assays do not measure MBL complement activity.

Recent work has established an ELISA that provides quantitative measurement of the activity of each pathway by utilizing precoated assay wells that contain specific inhibitors for each pathway [57]. Modified versions of the CH50 and AH50 assays can be performed for the majority of preclinical models, but assay qualification procedures and historical control data specific to the species being tested and the laboratory performing the assay are key elements for quality data. A recently developed, commercially available, quantitative ELISA testing the activity of all three pathways represents a significant improvement in complement activity screening in immunotoxicology as pathway-specific activity can be measured with minimal sample volume with less inter-assay and interlaboratory variability. The enumeration of specific complement components can be performed by radial immunodiffusion (RID), radio-immunoassay (RIA), and homogeneous, time-resolved fluorescence (HTRF), but these investigations are rarely indicated and require the expertise of an experienced investigator who routinely performs these types of assessments. An additional area of complement testing of interest to immunotoxicologists is the detection and quantification of the anaphylatoxins, C3a and C5a. The anaphylatoxins are fragments of the precursor C3 and C5 proteins that initiate several of the proinflammatory responses at the site of complement activation and in the surrounding microenvironment including neutrophil and macrophage recruitment, endothelium activation, platelet activation, cytokine release, and increase production of peptidoleukotrienes [58]. Commercially available kits for several different assay platforms are available to assess plasma and serum concentrations of anaphlytoxins. Anaphlytoxin measurements are useful in determining complement-mediated immunotoxicity arising directly from test article-mediated complement activation or complement activation via immune complex formation.

In summary, complement assessment via CH50, AH50, or quantitative ELISA screening with assessment of anaphylatoxins are useful methods to assess potentially test article-mediated effects on complement activity, and, in combination with clinical observations and clinical/histopathology evaluations, provide valuable information to guide the investigation of toxicities that may be caused by alterations in complement pathway activity.

Evaluation of Phagocyte Function

Phagocytes are bone marrow-derived cells of myeloid origin, including neutrophils, eosinophils, basophils, monocytes, and the mature form of the monocyte. They are pivotal cells for controlling the initial response to infection, and initiating, sustaining, or resolving inflammation, and their responses must be tightly coordinated and highly regulated to prevent infection while not damaging host tissues. Professional phagocytes, namely neutrophils, monocytes, and macrophages, are the primary cell populations that have been historically investigated by immunotoxicologists, as their mechanisms of response to infection and roles in the inflammatory process have been most closely studied in humans, and in the standard preclinical toxicology models. Phagocytosis is a process initiated by the binding of opsonized microbes or particles to opsonic receptors on the surface of the phagocyte. These include receptors for the constant regions of immunoglobulins, as well as receptors for components of the complement cascade. The engagement of opsonic receptors activates the phagocyte to rearrange cytoskeletal elements, thus altering plasma-membrane folding, allowing invagination and allowing cytoplasmic granules to fuse with the internalized target forming a phagosome. Inside the phagosome a variety of microbicidal and microbiostatic proteins are activated by changes in pH and ion concentration. Activation of NADPH oxidase generates antimicrobial concentrations of hydrogen peroxide, superoxide anion, hypochlorous acid, and other reactive species through the rapid metabolism of oxygen, the respiratory burst. A great body of literature is available concerning the processes of phagocyte transmigration, chemotaxis, phagocytosis, and oxygen-dependent and independent killing mechanisms briefly described above; the reader is referred to the following selected references on these subjects [59,60].

Immunotoxological investigation of phagocyte phenotype or function primarily involves assessment of phenotype, phagocytosis, and respiratory burst. Microscopic methods including direct staining, immunohistochemistry, and confocal microscopy are available [61]. In addition, assessment of peripheral blood phagocyte population phenotype and number, as well as spleen resident phagocyte populations, is routinely performed by flow cytometry [62]. Phenotypic assessment of phagocyte populations should be accompanied by functional assessment, as indicated by the test-article mechanism of action and the weight of evidence.

Assessment of phagocytosis can be performed by flow cytometry utilizing an array of fluorescently labeled targets including beads, bacteria, and fungi using a semiquantitative assay format [63]. A typical flow cytometric assay to measure phagocytosis would utilize whole blood, peripheral blood mononuclear cells, or isolated phagocytes incubated with fluorescently labeled targets for a period to time followed by appropriate gating by forward and side scatter or using combination gating to separate monocytes and neutrophils from lymphocytes. Typically, results would be presented as the fluorescent intensity of the internalized target normalized to unstained control and compensated with appropriate staining controls. An additional aspect of testing that provides useful information is the use of opsonized and unopsonized targets to determine the pathway by which phagocytosis is occurring. Assessment of respiratory burst activity can be assessed by multiple methods including plate-based luminescent and colorimetric methods and flow cytometry.

Evaluation of Natural Killer Cell Activity

Natural killer (NK) cells are lymphocytes of bone-marrow origin with a distinct phenotype. These cells function to recognize and lyse host cells showing aberrant expression of activating and inhibiting cell-surface receptors recognized by NK cells as signals indicating active infection or cellular dysregulation [64]. The classical evaluation of NK-cell function is the chromium-release assay originally developed by Brunner [65]. The assay is typically conducted using chromium 51-labeled tumor cells previously established to be sensitive to lysis (targets). These are incubated with lymphoid cells from the animal exposed to the drug (effectors) at different effector to target ratios in media within a 96-well tissue-culture plate. Assay controls include spontaneous release, which consists of labeled target cells alone, and total release, which consists of label target cells treated with a detergent to elicit maximum chromium 51 release into the culture media. Assay results are presented as the mean counts per minute (CPM) of the replicate wells that represent the degree of lysis for each effector:target ratio corrected for spontaneous release compared to total release. Appropriate target-cell lines are available to conduct this assay in rodents, canine, and nonhuman primate species. The assay has disadvantages including the use of radioisotopes, variability in spontaneous release, and in rodents it is usually a terminal endpoint due to the necessity to use spleen-cell suspension to achieve the number of cells required to conduct the assay. More recent developments in measuring NK-cell activity include several variations of flow cytometric methods utilizing propidium iodide or carboxy-fluorescein succinimidyl ester (CFSE) [66]. The flow cytometric methods appear comparable in sensitivity to the chromium 51-release assay but lack the large body of accumulated data and historical acceptance of the release assay, which has hindered complete adoption of these methods [67].

Evaluation of Immune-Cell Phenotypes

Flow cytometric evaluation of peripheral blood and lymphoid tissue-cell populations in preclinical models including mice, rats, canines, and primates has greatly improved in the last decade, as reagents have become available to monitor mature lymphoid and myeloid populations correlating to human-cell populations. In addition, the rapid pace of research in human immunology is generating reagents for identification and enumeration of specialized populations, including T regulatory subpopulations, Th9, Th17, effector, and memory T-cell subpopulations, NK-cell subpopulations, and progenitor and precursor populations of many immune cell types. Assessment of the corresponding populations in preclinical models may provide valuable data that may be directly indicative of population-specific effects in human patients. The standard immunophenotyping panel for preclinical testing typically includes enumeration of total leukocytes or lymphocytes, mature CD4+ and CD8+ T lymphocytes, mature B-cells, mature NK cells, and monocytes. Past work has shown concordance between changes in peripheral blood immune-cell populations and detection of immunotoxicity in rodents, specifically immunosuppression, and this concordance, approximately 83% was increased when both immunophenotyping and NK cell assessments were performed to approximately 90% [44].

Immunophenotyping analysis should be conducted using validated assays that have assessed intra- and interassay and animal variability, pre- and postfixation sample stability, reagent stability, and sample dilution effect and should include a minimum number of events for each population. In addition, properly designed validations should include power analysis and minimum detectable difference statistics for the tested populations. If lymphoid-tissue immunophenotyping is included in the validation, these cell-population numbers and relative percentages should be normalized by weight. In addition, following validation, accrual of historical control data is valuable as it tracks population variability over time and can be organized by sex and age to account for population changes that occur due to these factors.

Key factors for incorporation of immunophenotyping analysis into preclinical studies are drug mechanism of action, pharmacokinetics, group size and number, study length, and practical limitations regarding sample collection and stability. Ideally, immunophenotyping time points should be selected accounting for the above factors to correlate changes in peripheral or lymphoid-tissue cell populations and should be assessed across multiple dose levels at least once. Data from immunophenotyping assessment includes both the absolute number and relative percentage for each population and should be analyzed using the appropriate statistical technique to account for treatment, time, and sex effects. If recovery or return to baseline is being evaluated, these criteria should be selected prior to the study and be based on the validation study. Complete evaluation of immunophenotyping data requires knowledge of pathological or toxicological effects on bone marrow and primary and secondary lymphoid organs, in order to differentiate an indirect or direct immunotoxicity from changes secondary to nonimmunotoxic toxicological or pathological changes.

Evaluation of Lymphocyte Proliferation and Cytokine Production

The ability of lymphocytes to proliferate in response to the appropriate stimuli including antigen presentation, cell contact-dependent signaling from antigen presenting cells, and cytokines is a fundamental requirement for successful immunity. Although cell proliferation is not a specific indicator of the type of immunotoxicity nor as sensitive as TDAR, immunophenotyping, or NK-cell assessment it does provide direct assessment of a xenobiotic's or pharmaceutical's ability to suppress the metabolic events required for proliferation [68]. The original method of assessing in vitro or ex vivo lymphocyte proliferation used tritiated thymidine, which was measured by scintillation counts with the mean counts of replicate wells from stimulated lymphocytes representing dividing cells compared against unstimulated controls [69].

Lymphocyte proliferation assays can now be performed using a plethora of techniques, including colorimetric, luminescent, and flow cytometric approaches, with lymphocytes isolated from peripheral blood, spleen, or lymphoid organs, provided sufficient numbers of lymphocytes can be obtained. In addition, a pharmaceutical's effect on proliferation can be assessed globally using the aforementioned populations or a cell population-specific effect can be tested following isolation of the desired population. These techniques are in many cases as sensitive as tritiated thymidine incorporation, but care should be taken to ensure the method is specific for cell proliferation and not a general increase in metabolic activity and that a sufficient increase above background is achievable, eg, those reagents relying on a change in redox status to induce color change. Lymphocyte proliferation assays do require good sterile technique, knowledge of culture conditions and cell-growth kinetics, and knowledge of the pharmacological properties of the different agents commonly used to stimulate lymphocyte proliferation.

The choice of agent to induce proliferation is important, as plant lectins including phytohemagglutinin (PHA), concanavilin A (Con A), and pokeweed mitogen (PWM) bind to multiple cell-surface proteins and exhibit more or less potent mitogenic effects on T- and B-cells, respectively [70]. Additional pharmacological agents are available, such as phorbol myristate acetate, which when used with ionomycin bypass cell-surface receptor-induced signaling [70]. Isolated T lymphocytes can be stimulated with anti-CD3 and anti-CD28 antibodies.

Evaluation of Cytokines

Cytokines are proteins produced by cells of the immune system that act by intracrine, paracrine, autocrine, and at times systemically to coordinate, regulate, and resolve the immune response [71]. Cytokines should be viewed not as discrete entities with singular actions, but as integrated biological networks with compensatory capabilities and innate redundancy of action. Toxicity produced by cytokines is the result of alteration of these networks, and typically arises from over- or underproduction due to pharmacological or toxic effects on target cells or organs [72]. The implementation of multiplex platforms including electrochemiluminescence and bead-based luminex technologies allows the measurement of multiple cytokines in the same sample, typically in serum, plasma, and cell supernatants [73].

Assessment of cytokines relies on knowledge of the test article's mechanism of action, potential of target effects, pharmacokinetics, and an intimate understanding of basic cytokine biology. Typically, assessment of cytokine concentrations in serum and plasma collected from the treated animals over a period of time do not correlate well with systemic toxicity. An approach more likely to produce results that correlate with or predict cytokine-related toxicity is assessment of whole blood, isolated PBMC, or isolated immune-cell populations exposed to the test article and compared against appropriate pharmacological controls. Implementation of cytokine assessment should be designed to answer a specific question related to drug toxicity, should measure the cytokines most relevant to the predicted or observed toxicity, and the data should be viewed as complementary to other immunotoxicology investigations.

Key issues to consider in interpreting cytokine data are the assay sensitivity, range, and variance, confounding physiological conditions, and biological variability as reference ranges and historical control data are not available or practical to construct for the majority of cytokines.

EVALUATION OF CELL-MEDIATED IMMUNITY

Evaluation of antigen specific cell-mediated immunity in preclinical immunotoxicity testing is performed using the cytotoxic T-lymphocyte (CTL) assay or the delayed type hypersensitivity (DTH) assay. CTL and DTH assays measure the ability of antigen-specific CD8+ T lymphocytes to lyse or induce an inflammatory response against a previously encountered antigen [74]. Cell-mediated immunity as measured by either the CTL or DTH assay requires successful antigen presentation, with attendant cytokine and cell contact-dependent signaling to generate T-cell memory that results in a functional T-cell response [74]. Key differences between these methods is that effective CTL response requires antigen presentation by both mean corpuscular hemoglobin (MCH) Class I and II proteins and the result is produced by in vitro measurement of CD8+ T-cell lytic activity. The DTH method involves sensitization with the antigen typically via skin exposure followed by challenge or reexposure at an anatomically distant site at which erythema, induration, or inflammation develops. It can be argued that the DTH assay is a broader assessment of cell-mediated immunity, as a measurable response requires not only antigen presentation and CD8+ T-cell memory but also production of inflammatory mediators, intact cell trafficking, and involves other components of the inflammatory cascade [75]. Historically both the CTL and DTH assays have been conducted in mice or rats and the greatest body of data and publications is available for these models. There are CTL and

DTH assays being conducted in large animal models as well, although standardized protocols for preclinical testing have not been adopted.

The preferred method for CTL analysis in mice or rats utilizes live influenza virus of various strains. The mature animal is infected intranasally with the selected virus strain. MCH Class I matched target cells are cultured with a known quantity of virus overnight or for a predetermined timeframe before labeling with chromium 51. Following infection and after viral replication (typically several days to a week), spleen, lungs, lymph nodes, or bone marrow are collected and processed to single-cell suspensions. The effector cells from the lymphoid tissue are cultured with the MHC Class I-matched targets at different ratios or a single ratio previously determined. The percentage of lysis is calculated for each ratio or the single ratio by comparing the counts per minute from the replicate wells minus spontaneous release control divided by the total release control minus the spontaneous release control. The total release control is chromium 51-labeled targets exposed to a detergent to obtain maximum release into culture media.

The DTH assay is typically performed by administration of SRBC to mice or KLH to rats subcutaneously without adjuvant, although other antigens can be used, eg, ovalalbumin. Following sensitization the animal is challenged, usually one to two weeks later, by injection of SRBC or KLH into the hind footpad. A sham injection control is administered in the opposite footpad, usually sterile saline. Usually 24–72–h post–challenge, the thickness of the footpad that received the antigen is compared with that of the sham injection control using spring-loaded or electronic calipers. Obviously, conduct of the DTH assay requires establishment of the optimal sensitization and challenge antigen concentrations and timing of response. In addition it is critical that personnel performing the assay are experienced with performing the sensitization and challenge injections as well as use of the calipers to ensure consistent measurements and reduce artifacts due to technical error or interanalyst variability. There is considerable interest in assessment of DTH responses in NHP, as many biopharmaceuticals are active only in these species, but currently there is no consensus regarding the method and there may be significant differences in the conduct of this method between laboratories.

INTERPRETATION OF IMMUNOTOXICOLOGY DATA

This section is specifically written for the general toxicologist to provide an overview of immunotoxicity data interpretation from the viewpoint of a single study or a small series of studies, and presents suggestions for interpretation in the order in which they will most likely be encountered during the course of safety investigation. Interpretation of immunotoxicology data should be viewed within the context of the test-article mechanism of action, pharmacokinetics, the bioequivalent potency of the test article in the model used, and the inherent assumptions underlying the methods used, as historically immunotoxicology assays are heavily biased toward detection of immunosuppression. In addition, knowledge of the compensatory mechanisms of the immune system and species-specific differences in immunity are necessary for evaluation of immunotoxicology data.

In general, the first step in framing the interpretation is a review of the toxicology findings with particular emphasis being placed on correlation of changes in bone-marrow cellularity, clinical pathology changes including the leukogram, acute-phase proteins, globulin levels, and a detailed review of histopathological findings of primary and secondary lymphoid organs, if available, in consultation with the study pathologist. A review of clinical findings and the associated veterinary records can also be beneficial, as constitutional symptoms and signs requiring veterinary consult including recurring signs of infection, hypersensitivity reactions, chronic diarrhea, and recurrent skin lesions particularly pyogenic lesions can be clues indicating alteration of immunity.

Evaluation of TDAR Data

The tier I assessment is TDAR, and evaluation of TDAR data is performed by comparing high-, mid-, and low-dose groups with the immunosuppressive control. Ligand-binding TDAR assays produce quantitative concentration values, eg, ng/mL or U/mL. A positive TDAR result is a test article-related decrease in antigen-specific IgM or IgG antibody in treated groups compared with immunosuppressive control at predefined statistical significance levels. A positive TDAR result indicates impaired antigen-specific humoral immunity and indicates further immunological assessment is warranted based on the factors mentioned at the start of this section. In many cases, tier two assessments including immunophenotyping and NK-cell assay are the next tests to be performed with or without assessment of complement, spleen-cell proliferation, CTL, or DTH.

Evaluation of Immunophenotyping Data

Immunophenotyping data analysis is performed using standard parametric or nonparametric statistics that assign statistical significance to values, but assigning biological significance is slightly more complex. The primary focus in interpretation should be assigning significance to changes in absolute cell number as opposed to percentage. Assessment of changes in absolute cell number has the greatest relevance as every species has a range of immune-cell numbers required for adequate defense, above or below which an effective response cannot be mounted. Currently there is no formulaic method for the interpretation of immunophenotyping data. The interpretation relies on the comparison of the statistically significant values to establish historical normal ranges, when viewing time, dose-dependence, and time–treatment interactions. The incorporation of recovery intervals is particularly useful in immunophenotyping, as most study designs use a limited number of collection intervals, which may provide a skewed view of population changes occurring over a limited timeframe. In addition, a thorough interpretation synthesizes changes in cell number with bone-marrow cellularity, hematology values, and histological changes in primary and secondary lymphoid organs. Although immunophenotyping provides much useful information, it is a technique that is best used to examine specific cell populations, complement broad assessments, such as TDAR, or point the investigator toward effects on a specific population.

Evaluation of Proliferation, Natural Killer Cell, and Cell-Mediated Immunity Data

Interpretation of spleen-cell proliferation, NK-cell assay, and CTL is straightforward and standard statistical techniques are employed to compare the proliferative index or lytic index of treated versus untreated animals in the proliferation, NK, or CTL assay regardless of the specific method used. It is important that the method employed has a large stimulation or lytic index between the means of stimulated or total lysis control cells from untreated animals and nonstimulated background or spontaneous release controls to detect significant impairment in proliferative or lytic response. Immunosuppression is indicated by a decrease in proliferative index or target-cell lysis in the respective assays. DTH assay data are analyzed by comparing the caliper readings from the sham-injected footpad with that of the footpad that received the challenge when using a protein antigen. Treated and control group means can be compared using standard statistical techniques. Decreases or increases in-group mean caliper readings in treated animals when compared with sham-injection control indicate suppression or enhancement of the antigen-specific cell-mediated immune response. In addition, erythema and induration can be assigned numerical grades for semiquantitative assessment.

Evaluation of Complement Data

Interpretation of complement data generated by the CH50 or AH50 assay is completely dependent on the specific assay procedure, the quality of sample received, the positive serum control if used, and the establishment of a reference range produced at the laboratory conducting the testing. In the CH50 and AH50 assays, serial dilutions of test and control sera are incubated with sensitized or unsensitized erythrocytes, respectively, for a specified period of time followed by reagent addition to stop the lytic reaction. Spontaneous and total lysis controls are also included, and if calibrated positive control sera are available, they may be used to construct a dilutional activity curve and normalize the data across runs. The assay result is calculated by spectrophotometry with the optical density of the total lysis control serving as the maximum value in the absence of positive control sera. Increasing optical density reflects increased hemolysis. The result is reported as the reciprocal of the dilution that lyses 50% of the RBC per mL of serum (CH50 U/mL or AH50 U/mL) calculated from a probability plot, linear regression, or Kabat–Mayer plot [76]. Animals that fall within the established reference range are considered to have normal activity while those falling below the range may have decreased complement synthesis or in vivo consumption of complement mediated by immune-complex activation or fixation at the initiating surface. Conversely, increases in CH50 or AH50 may indicate systemic inflammation without activation.

It is important to compare both pathways in assessing pharmaceuticals as vehicles, adjuvants, excipients, or direct test-article activity may preferentially activate a specific pathway. Evaluation of complement activity data produced by the more recent EIA plate-based method is similar, in that the sample produces a percent activity value compared to kit positive and negative controls. However, it has the advantage of testing all three complement pathways simultaneously, is less labor intensive, and does not require the level of technical expertise compared to conventional CH50 and AH50 assays. Plate-based methods to determine the concentration of C3a and C5a run concurrently with complement screening assays provide quantitative data that can be used to link altered pathway activity with toxicity, as C3a and C5a are central mediators of toxicity due to complement activation. Evaluation of the concentrations of specific complement components via the RID assay or ELISA methods should be pursued only after screening results have been received, and in consultation with an experienced complement scientist, as ascribing biological significance to changes in specific factor concentrations can be difficult in the absence of a specific mechanistic-based hypothesis.

Evaluation of Cytokine Data

Interpretation of cytokine data can be challenging in the context of preclinical testing, as reference ranges are not available for the majority of cytokines in preclinical species, inherent limitations in serial sampling in preclinical studies limit time-course study, and species-specific differences in cytokine networks are not fully understood. The majority of methods used to generate such data provide concentration data extrapolated from a standard curve. Cytokine data are best used to explore phenomena that have the highest concordance across species, eg, the acute phase response, acute and chronic inflammation, T- and B-cell activation, and changes in key regulatory cytokines. As a general rule it is best to limit cytokine analysis to the fewest number of cytokines involved that may be relevant to the toxicological question at hand and have the greatest degree of functional homology across species. The current trend introduced by multiplexing technology is to analyze an ever-expanding number of cytokines over a limited number of time points. This can produce massive amounts of data, well beyond the limited number of questions a safety study design is capable of answering.

Evaluation of Phagocytosis Data

Assessment of phagocytosis data produced by flow cytometry or plate-based methods is performed by comparing the ability of cells to induce phagocytosis or induce respiratory burst after pharmacological stimulation versus unstimulated control cells from treated and untreated animals. For flow cytometric methods, cell and staining controls serve to determine background fluorescence, and spontaneous phagocytosis, and labeled fluorescent targets per unit volume in the absence of cells determine maximum signal. A typical flow cytometric phagocytosis assay would involve stimulated and unstimulated PBMC or spleen cells from control and treated animals in suspension, incubated with a predetermined concentration of fluorescently labeled target for a predetermined period of time, followed by addition of an agent inhibiting phagocytosis or cold incubation. The cells are then washed to remove free or cell surface-bound targets followed by flow cytometric analysis.

Flow cytometry data for phagocytosis assays is routinely presented as mean fluorescent intensity (MFI) of the internalized target corrected for background but can also be represented ratiometrically or by fold increase compared to control. Statistical comparison between groups can be conducted using standard techniques, and many assays will have predefined confidence intervals based on the MFI scale of the assay. Plate-based enzymatic assays measure oxidative burst by measuring the enzymatic rate of conversion of a substrate to one or more

of the free radicals or ions generated during oxidative burst, or the interaction of these metabolites with assay indicators in colorimetric, fluorometric, or luminescent assays. These assays generally require pharmacological or chemical activation of cells and preparation of cell extracts. They provide quantitative data usually derived from Michaelis–Menten or Lineweaver–Burk equations or modified forms thereof. Data from these assays are usually kinetic and may be analyzed by a variety of statistical methods but in the majority of cases, a simple comparison of V_{max} and Michaelis–Menten constant (K_M) interpreted by comparing replicate assessments between treated and untreated animals with the inclusion of positive control cells from an animal not exposed to test article but pharmacologically treated to induce respiratory burst provides satisfactory data. Decreased respiratory burst activity will be readily apparent from V_{max} and K_M values.

CONCLUDING REMARKS AND FUTURE DIRECTIONS

The need for predictive immunotoxicity testing that can directly correlate with human immunotoxicity will continue to grow over the next decade, as the development of immunomodulatory biopharmaceuticals and small molecules outpaces that of conventional small-molecule pharmaceuticals. There is a clear need to identify alternative methods to test for antidrug antibodies, hypersensitivity, immunosuppression, immunostimulation, and auto-immunity [77]. Despite the large body of literature for different animal models and immunotoxicology assays that are predictive for immunosuppression and the increasing degree of sophistication of immunological assessment in preclinical studies, preclinical animal models and assays are not sufficiently predictive of specific immunotoxicity in humans.

This body of literature may suggest that we approach the problem from a patient-centered medical perspective, and implement the principles of refinement, reduction, and replacement to remove unnecessary testing. Prediction of specific immunotoxicity in humans will require the use of human immune cells and tissue. The modular immune system in vitro construct (MIMIC®) system produced by VaxDesign (a subsidiary of Sanofi Pastuer), if recognized by regulatory authorities, could make animal immunotoxicity testing obsolete or substantially reduce the amount of such testing required [78]. This system uses harvested human lymphocytes and lymphoid tissue to build matrices that mimic the microenvironments and types of tissues that would normally encounter a pathogen or receive an immunization. The different system constructs, including peripheral and lymphoid tissue, can, along with harvested lymphocytes, test immunogenicity, response to vaccination, T-cell-dependent antibody response, cytokine production, hypersensitivity, immunostimulation, and immunosuppression [78]. This system has not been thoroughly vetted or rigorously compared with existing immunotoxicology assays, but offers many theoretical advantages including incorporation of population diversity through donor selection, ability to conduct functional immunotoxicity studies including challenge models in a closed system, high throughput, increased ability to perform interlaboratory validation if the technology is freely available, and increased safety for laboratory personnel. In vitro immunotoxicity assessments, particularly the human PBMC cytokine release assay, have been tested by numerous investigators but currently are accepted by regulatory authorities as only complementary assessments to preclinical animal studies [79].

References

[1] Berlin A, Dean J, Draper M, Smith EMB, Spreafico F. Synopsis, conclusions, and recommendations. In: Berlin A, Dean J, Draper M, Smith EMB, Spreafico F, editors. Immunotoxicology. Dordrecht: Martinus Nijhoff; 1987. p. xi–xvii.

[2] Herzyk DJ, Bussiere JL, editors. Immunotoxicology strategies for pharmaceutical safety assessment. Hoboken NJ, USA: John Wiley & Sons Inc.; 2008. p. 3–10. [chapter 1].

[3] Vos JG. Immune suppression as related to toxicology. CRC Crit Rev Toxicol 1977;5:67–101.

[4] ICH Harmonized Tripartite Guideline. Immunotoxicity studies for human pharmaceuticals (S8). 2006. Available at: http://www.ich.org.

[5] ICH Harmonized Tripartite Guideline. Preclinical safety evaluation of biotechnology-derived (S6). 1997. Available at: http://www.ich.org1997.

[6] Bloom DE, Cafiero ET, Jané-Llopis E, Abrahams-Gessel S, Bloom LR, Fathima S, et al. The global economic burden of non-communicable diseases. Switzerland, Geneva: World Economic Forum; 2011.

[7] Forlenza GP, Rewers M. The epidemic of type 1 diabetes: what is it telling us? Curr Opin Endocrinol Diabetes Obes 2011;18:248–51.

[8] Prescott S, Allen KJ. Food allergy: riding the second wave of the allergy epidemic. Pediatr Allergy Immunol 2011;22:155–60.

[9] Codoñer-Franch P, Valls-Bellés V, Arilla-Codoñer A, Alonso-Iglesias E. Oxidant mechanisms in childhood obesity: the link between inflammation and oxidative stress. Transl Res 2011;158:369–84.

[10] Dietert RR, Luebke RW, editors. Immunotoxicity, immune dysfunction, and chronic disease. NY, USA: Springer (Science + Business Media); 2011.

[11] Dietert RR, Zelikoff JT. Pediatric immune dysfunction and health risks following early-life immune insult. Curr Pediatr Rev 2009;5:36–51.

[12] Chen M, Zhang L. Epigenetic mechanisms in developmental programming of adult disease. Drug Discov Today 2011;16:1007–18.

[13] PhRMA. Medicines in development for women. 2011. http://www.phrma.org/research/medicines-development-women.

[14] PhRMA. More than 850 medicines in development for diseases that disproportionately strike women. 2011. http://www.phrma.org/media/releases/more-850-medicines-development-diseases-disproportionately-strike-women.

[15] Spanhaak S. The ICH S8 immunotoxicity guidance. Immune function assessment and toxicological pathology: autonomous or synergistic methods to predict immunotoxicity? Exp Toxicol Pathol 2006;57:373–6.

[16] CDER. Guidance for industry nonclinical safety evaluation of pediatric drug products. US Food and Drug Administration; 2006. http://www.fda.gov/ohrms/dockets/98fr/03d-0001-gdl002.pdf.

[17] Dietert RR, Piepenbrink MS. Perinatal immunotoxicity: why adult exposure assessment fails to predict risk. Environ Health Perspect 2006;114:477–83.

[18] Dietert RR, Dietert JM. Potential for early-life immune insult including developmental immunotoxicity in autism and autism spectrum disorders: focus on critical windows of immune vulnerability. J Toxicol Environ Health B Crit Rev 2008;11:660–80.

[19] Dietert RR. Role of developmental immunotoxicity and immune dysfunction in chronic disease and cancer. Reprod Toxicol 2011;31:319–26.

[20] Hong YM. Atherosclerotic cardiovascular disease beginning in childhood. Korean Circ J 2011;40:1–9.

[21] Napoli C. Developmental mechanisms involved in the primary prevention of atherosclerosis and cardiovascular disease. Curr Atheroscler Rep 2011;13:170–5.

[22] Dietert RR. Developmental immunotoxicology: focus on health risks. Chem Res Toxicol 2009;22:17–23.

[23] McNeal CJ, Wilson DP, Christou D, Bush RL, Shepherd LG, Santiago J, et al. The use of surrogate vascular markers in youth at risk for premature cardiovascular disease. J Pediatr Endocrinol Metab 2009;22:195–211.

[24] Kelishadi R. Inflammation-induced atherosclerosis as a target for prevention of cardiovascular diseases from early life. Open Cardiovasc Med J 2010;4:24–9.

[25] Dietert RR. Developmental immunotoxicity (DIT) in drug safety testing: matching DIT testing to adverse outcomes and childhood disease risk. Curr Drug Saf 2008;3:216–26.

[26] Elmore SA. Enhanced histopathology evaluation of lymphoid organs. Methods Mol Biol 2010;598:323–39.

[27] Lappin PB. Flow cytometry in preclinical drug development. Methods Mol Biol 2010;598:303–21.

[28] Dietert RR, Holsapple MP. Methodologies for developmental immunotoxicity (DIT) testing. Methods 2007;41:123–31.

[29] Dietert RR, DeWitt JC, Germolec DR, Zelikoff JT. Breaking patterns of environmentally influenced disease for health risk reduction: immune perspectives. Environ Health Perspect 2010;118:1091–9.

[30] Dietert RR, DeWitt JC, Luebke RW. Reducing the prevalence of immune-based chronic disease. In: Dietert RR, Luebke RW, editors. Immunotoxicity, immune dysfunction, and chronic disease. NY, USA: Springer (Science + Business Media); 2012, pp. 419–440. [chapter 17].

[31] Weinstock D, Lewis DB, Parker GA, Beyer J, Collinge M, Brown TP, et al. Toxicopathology of the developing immune system: investigative and development strategies. Toxicol Pathol 2010;38:1111–7.

[32] Grote-Wessels S, Frings W, Smith CA, Weinbauer GF. Immunotoxicity testing in nonhuman primates. Methods Mol Biol 2010;598:341–59.

[33] Buckley LA, Chapman K, Burns-Naas LA, Todd MD, Martin PL, et al. Considerations regarding nonhuman primate use in safety assessment of biopharmaceuticals. Int J Toxicol 2011;30:583–90.

[34] Holladay SD, Blaylock BL. The mouse as a model for developmental immunotoxicology. Hum Exp Toxicol 2002;21:525–31.

[35] Lebrec H, O'Lone R, Freebern W, Komocsar W, Moore P. Survey: immune function and immunotoxicity assessment in dogs. J Immunotoxicol 2012, 1–14.

[36] Burns-Naas LA, Hastings KL, Ladics GS, Makris SL, Parker GA, Holsapple MP. What's so special about the developing immune system? Int J Toxicol 2008;27:223–54.

[37] Barrow PC. Reproductive toxicity testing for pharmaceuticals under ICH. Reprod Toxicol 2009;28:172–9.

[38] Dewitt JC, Peden-Adams MM, Keil DE, Dietert RR. Current status of developmental immunotoxicity: early-life patterns and testing. Toxicol Pathol 2011, 1–7.

[39] Dietert RR. Distinguishing environmental causes of immune dysfunction from pediatric triggers of disease. The Open Pediatr Med J 2009;3:38–44.

[40] Dietert RR, Dewitt J. Developmental immunotoxicity (DIT): the why, when, and how of DIT testing. Methods Mol Biol 2010;598:17–25.

[41] CPMP (Committee for Proprietary Medicinal Products). Note for guidance on repeated dose toxicity. CPMP/SWP/1042/99. 2000.

[42] FDA (Food & Drug Administration, Center for Drug Evaluation and Research). Guidance for industry. Immunotoxicology evaluation of investigational new drugs. 2002.

[43] Jerne NK, Nordin AA. Plaque formation in agar by single antibody producing cells. Science 1963;140:405.

[44] Luster MI, Portier C, Pait DG, White KL, Gennings C, Munson AE, et al. Risk assessment in immunotoxicology. I. Sensitivity and predictability of immune tests. Fundam Appl Toxicol 1992;18:200–10.

[45] Temple L, Kawabata TT, Munson AE, White KL. Comparison of ELISA and plaque-forming cell assays for measuring the humoral immune response to SRBC in rats and mice treated with benzo[a]pyrene or cyclophosphamide. Fundam Appl Toxicol 1993;21:412–9.

[46] Gore ER, Gower J, Kurali E, Sui J-L, Bynum J, Ennulat D, et al. Primary antibody response to keyhole limpet hemocyanin in rat as a model for immunotoxicity evaluation. Toxicology 2004;197:23–35.

[47] Piccotti JR, Alvey JD, Reindel JF, Gusman RE. T-cell-dependent antibody response: assay development in cynomolgus monkeys. J Immunotoxicol 2005;2:191–6.

[48] Harris JR, Markl J. Keyhole limpet hemocyanin: a biomedical review. Micron 1999;30:597–623.

[49] Kim CJ, Berlin JA, Bugelski PJ, Haley P, Herzyk DJ. Comparison of immune functional tests using T dependent antigens in immunotoxicology studies: a meta analysis. Per Exp Clin Immunotox 2007;1:60–73.

[50] Vos JG, Van Loveren H. Experimental studies of immunosuppression: how do they predict for man? Toxicology 1998;129:13–26.

[51] Lebrec H, Cowan L, Lagrou M, Kresja C, Nreadilek MB, Polissar NL, et al. An inter-laboratory retrospective analysis of immunotoxicological endpoints in nonhuman primates: T-cell dependent antibody responses. J Immunotoxicol July–September 2011;8(23):238–50.

[52] Murphy K. JaneWay's immunobiology. 8th ed. NY, USA: Garland Science, Taylor & Francis Group. LLC; 2012. p. 37–73. [chapter 2].

[53] Paul WE. Paul's fundamental immunology. 5th ed. Philadelphia, PA, USA: Lippincott Williams & Wilkins; 2003. p. 1077–105. [chapter 34].

[54] Zipfel PF, Skerka C. Complement regulators and inhibitory proteins. Nat Rev Immunol October 2009;9(10):729–40.

[55] Detrick B, Hamilton RG, Folds JD, editors. Manual of molecular and clinical laboratory immunology. 7th ed. Washington, DC, USA: ASM Press. American Society for Microbiology; 2006. p. 115–7. [chapter 12].

[56] Nijkamp FP, Parnham MJ, editors. Principles of immunopharmacology. 2nd ed. The Netherlands: Birkhauser Verlag; 2005. p. 63–79. [chapter A5].

[57] Detrick B, Hamilton RG, Folds JD, editors. Manual of molecular and clinical laboratory immunology. 7th ed. Washington, DC, USA: ASM Press. American Society for Microbiology; 2006. p. 124–7. [chapter 14].

[58] Peng Q, Li K, Sacks SH, Zhou W. The role of anaphyltoxins C3a and C5a in regulating innate and adaptive immune responses. Inflamm Allergy Drug Targets July 2009;8(3):236–46.

[59] Beutler B. Microbe sensing, positive feedback loops, and the pathogenesis of inflammatory disease. Immunol Rev 2009;227:248–63.

[60] Aderem A, Underhill DM. Mechanisms of phagocytosis in macrophages. Annu Rev Immunol 1999;17:593–623.

[61] Dietert RR, editor. Immunotoxicity testing: methods and protocols. Methods in molecular biology, vol. 598. Humana Press; 2010. p. 75–94. [chapter 6].

[62] Lehmann AK, Sornes S, Halstensen A. Phagocytosis: measurement by flow cytometry. J Immunol Methods 2000;243:229–42.

[63] Herzyk DJ, Bussiere JL, editors. Immunotoxicology strategies for pharmaceutical safety assessment. Hoboken, NJ, USA: John Wiley & Sons Inc.; 2008. p. 81. [chapter 3.1.2].

[64] Yokoyama WM, Plougastel BF. Immune functions encoded by the natural killer gene complex. Nat Rev Immunol 2003;2003(3):304–16.

[65] Brunner K, Mauel J, Cerottini JC, Chapus B. Quantitative assay of the lytic action of immune lymphoid cells on 51Cr-labelled allogenic targeT-cells in vitro; inhibition by isoantibody and by drugs. Immunology 1968;14:181–96.

[66] Lee-MacAry AE, Ross EL, Davies D, Laylor R, Honeychurch J, Glennie MJ, et al. Development of a novel flow-cytometric cell mediated cytotoxicity assay using the fluorophores PKH-26 and TO-PRO3 idodide. J Immunol Methods 2001;252:83–92.

[67] Marcusson-Stahl M, Cederbrant K. A flow cytometric NK-cytotoxicity assay adapted for use in rat repeated dose toxicity studies. Toxicology 2003;193:269–79.

[68] Vial T, Descotes J. Immunosuppressive drugs and cancer. Toxicology 2003;185:229–40.

[69] Anderson J, Moller G, Sjoberg O. Selective induction of DNA synthesis in T and B lymphocytes. Cell Immunol 1972;4:381–93.

[70] Herzyk DJ, Bussiere JL, editors. Immunotoxicology Strategies for pharmaceutical safety assessment. Hoboken, NJ, USA: John Wiley & Sons Inc.; 2008. p. 130. [chapter 4.1].

[71] Murphy K. JaneWay's immunobiology. 8th ed. NY, USA: Garland Science, Taylor & Francis Group. LLC; 2012. p. 264–74. [chapter 7].

[72] Descotes J. Methods of evaluating immunotoxicity. Expert Opin Drug Metab Toxicol 2006;2:249–59.

[73] De Jager W, Rijkers GT. Solid-phase and bead based cytokine immunoassay: a comparison. Methods 2006;38:294–303.

[74] Dietert RR, editor. Immunotoxicity testing: methods and protocols. Methods in molecular biology, vol. 598. Humana Press; 2010. [chapters 13 & 14].

[75] Herzyk DJ, Bussiere JL, editors. Immunotoxicology strategies for pharmaceutical safety assessment. Hoboken, NJ, USA: John Wiley & Sons Inc.; 2008. p. 87–101. [chapter 3.1.3].

[76] Coligan JE, Bierer BE, Margulies DH, Shevach EM, Strober W. Editorial board current protocols in immunology, vol. 4. Hoboken, NJ, USA: John Wiley & Sons Inc.; 1994-2009. [section 13].

[77] Descotes J. Immunotox Monoclonal Antibodies MABS 2009;1(2):104–11.

[78] S. Pasteur, VaxDesign, Campus 2501, Discovery Drive Suite 300, Orlando, FL 32826. http://www.vaxdesign.com/mimic-technology.

[79] Corsini E, Roggen EL. Immunotoxicology: opportunities for non-animal test development. ATLA 2009;37:387–97.

11

Juvenile Testing to Support Clinical Trials in Pediatric Population

A.S. Faqi

INTRODUCTION

Just few decades ago, over 70% of drugs marketed worldwide and used in pediatric patients lacked adequate information in the labeling for use in pediatrics. However, pediatric drug development has evolved in the past two decades due to regulatory shifts in the United States and European Union. It is important to recognize that children are not simply miniature adults; thus off-label use of drugs for children is a major health concern. It must be reiterated that there are profound anatomical, physiological, and developmental differences between children and adults, leading to differences in the metabolism, renal clearance, drug–drug interactions, and overall response to medications [1,2]. The first 2–3 years of postnatal life is a period of particularly rapid growth and development. Inherent differences with immature systems may lead to drug toxicity or resistance to toxicity that is not seen in mature systems [3].

Differences in drug distribution between immature and mature systems include dissimilarity in membrane permeability, plasma-protein binding, and total body water [4]. Also, differences in gastric pH and renal blood flow in the pediatric population may also affect drug absorption and excretion. Gastric pH is practically neutral (pH 6–8) at birth, then falls to approximately 1–3 within the first 24h following birth, and later on gradually returns to neutrality by day 10, which then declines again slowly to reach adult values (pH 1.5–3.5) [5].

Renal blood flow at birth is only 5–6% of cardiac output; it increases from 15% to 25% by 1 year of age and reaches adult values after 2 years of age [6].

Developmental changes in renal function can dramatically alter the plasma clearance of compounds with extensive renal elimination and thus can enhance renal and systemic toxicity of these drugs. Thus pharmacokinetics parameters in neonates differ from adults due to functional immaturity of the kidney. Comparison of toxicokinetics values on day 27 with day-1 parameters in a 28-day repeated dose juvenile toxicity with Faropenem (FPM) in dogs showed a change in FPM pharmacokinetic behavior over time with an apparent increase in the rate of clearance characterized by a decrease in AUC (0–6) and T_{max} values on day 27 with little to no change in C_{max} values [7]. The apparent increase in clearance was consistent with expected changes in physiologic renal development in beagle dogs between 3 and 7 weeks of age.

Furthermore, differences in immaturity of glomerular filtration, renal tubular secretion, and tubular reabsorption at birth and their maturation may lead to the differences in excretion of drugs in the pediatric population compared to adults [8]. In young mice and rats the concentration of urine and secretion of organic compounds is reduced and renal expression of organic anion transporters (OATs) increases substantially [9]. Due to the immature nature of drug transporter system, the kidney and other organ systems are vulnerable to drug injury at birth [10].

Significant differences exist in Phase I and Phase II metabolic enzymes between the pediatric population and adults. Approximately 75% of drugs that are primarily cleared via metabolism are biotransformed by members of the cytochrome P450 (P450) superfamily.

Human drug-metabolizing P450 genes have been categorized into three developmental patterns based on hepatic ontogenic gene expression patterns [11]. The first group of enzymes represented by CYP3A7 is expressed at their highest level during the first trimester and either remains at high concentrations or decreases during gestation and are silenced or expressed at low levels within 1–2 years after birth. A second group of enzymes including CYP3A5 and CYP2C19 are expressed at relatively constant levels throughout gestation, but only CYP2C19 are expressed postnatally within the first year. The third group of enzymes including CYP2C9, 2E1, and 3A4 are not expressed or are expressed at low levels in the fetus with the onset of expression generally in either the second or third trimester [11]. In addition, substantial increases in expression are observed within the first 1–2 years after birth; however, considerable interindividual variability is observed in the immediate postnatal (1–6 months) onset or increase in expression of these enzymes, often resulting in a window of hypervariability [11].

Significant changes in Phase II drug-metabolizing enzyme expression occurring during development have a profound impact on drug disposition and clinical outcome. Nevertheless, the dynamic balance between Phase I and II metabolizing enzymes regulates the final disposition of many drugs and toxicants and since our understanding of these changes remains scant, the ability to predict adverse effects and develop effective therapeutic doses for the pediatric population remains a challenge [12].

Additionally, significant differences in the ontogenic gene expression contribute to variations in drug metabolism between children and adults. These differences result in children being less responsive to drug therapy and higher risks for adverse reactions for some drugs metabolized by P450 enzymes [13].

By the same token differences in drug efficacy by age group have been observed; a regimen of two daily doses of nelfinavir (Viracept), an HIV drug, was pharmacologically superior to three daily doses, particularly in smaller, younger children [2].

In regards to the anatomical, physiological, and metabolical differences discussed so far, preclinical studies using adult animals, or safety information from adult humans, cannot always adequately predict the differences in safety profiles for all pediatric age groups, especially effects on immature systems, such as the developing brain, the pulmonary system, the kidneys, the reproductive system, the immune system, and the skeletal system [3]. A literature review of the postnatal organ system maturation in humans shows that kidneys reach adult function at approximately 1 year of age [14], whereas neural development continues throughout adolescence [15], reproductive organ system maturation is achieved at adolescence, and skeletal system maturation continues well into adulthood [16].

EU AND FDA PEDIATRIC REGULATORY INITIATIVES

The introduction of regulation (EC) 1901/2006, *Medicinal Products for Pediatric Use*, which became went into force on January 26, 2007, has generated a massive paradigm shift in European drug development. It is now mandatory for pharmaceutical companies to submit a Pediatric Investigational Plan (PIP) to the Pediatric Committee (PDCO) at the European Medicines Agency (EMA) around the end of the first phase of testing a new drug in adults [17,18].

A PIP is intended to outline the development of the medicinal product, defining the design and timing of nonclinical and clinical measures needed to support the application of marketing authorization for pediatric use. It is reviewed and approved or refused by the PDCO of the European medicines [19]. The PDCO is a committee of experts with competence in development and assessment of all aspects of pediatric drugs [20]. In late 2008, a nonclinical working group (NcWG) was established by the PDCO to support it in the review process of the nonclinical section of pediatric investigation plans (PIPs).

A PIP contains "key legally binding elements" that must be adhered to. It is expected to include:

1. A description of the studies and measures made to adapt a drug formulation (aiding acceptable use in children, eg, use of a liquid formulation versus large tablets)
2. All age groups of children, from birth to adolescence
3. Clearly defined timing of studies in children compared to adults

Following the submission of PIP, the EMA will automatically assign unique product identifier (UPI) numbers, which are sent by email to the applicants to facilitate future communication between the applicants and the agency.

Once approved, a PIP can be modified as knowledge of the drug increases. Modifications can also be made if the applicant encounters difficulties implementing the plan, such that it is impractical or no longer appropriate [20].

A PIP waiver is warranted when there are no known pediatric indications for the drug, or when the intended use of the drug does not apply to children (eg, Parkinson's disease). Nevertheless, a waiver must be approved prior to submission of a Marketing Authorization Application (MAA). In certain other cases, however, it may not be safe to test drugs in children (or subsets of children) until preclinical studies have completed, or studies in adult and/or specific pediatric subsets. In such cases, pediatric studies can be deferred until there is confirmation that it is safe and ethical to initiate studies in pediatrics or specific age subsets.

In 2008, PDCO published a list of 42 class waivers that was then revised in 2009 and 2010 that provide exemption from the obligation to submit a PIP or specific waiver request. These waiver classes included drugs for 25 illnesses that were believed to not occur in children. European pediatric oncologists and parents opposed the waiver list and called for the implementation of PIPs on the basis of the mechanism of action of drugs and revocation of the class waiver list [21]. To address some of the concerns raised, in July 2015, the PDCO further published a revised class waiver list, which will come into effect in 2018, revoking eight class waivers because the diseases may occur in children, including two for cancer (liver or intrahepatic bile duct carcinoma and kidney or renal pelvis carcinoma). This is aimed to better balance the need to support pediatric drug development with the goal of avoiding exposing children to unnecessary drugs and encouraging companies to develop new drugs for use in children.

Although this move from the PDCO is considered as a step in the right direction, there is still concern that it might not substantially reduce the number of relevant drugs unjustifiably class waived [22].

In the United States, Congress enacted two laws to address this situation: the Best Pharmaceuticals for Children Act (BPCA) and the Pediatric Research Equity Act (PREA). The PREA of 2007 stipulates that all new drug applications (NDAs) as well as biologics licensing applications (BLAs) for a new active ingredient, indication, dosage form, dosing regimen, or route of administration must contain a pediatric assessment unless the applicant has obtained either a waiver or a deferral of the assessment until after approval has been granted in adults [23]. The BPCA offers pharmaceutical companies a 6-month exclusivity term in return for their agreement to conduct pediatric tests on drugs. It also provides public funding and organizes private funding to help conduct pediatric research on those drugs that pharmaceutical companies determine do not need tested in children [24].

The Pediatric Review Committee (PeRC) of the FDA, which is the equivalent of the PDCO in EU, reviews all aspects of waivers and deferrals before the approval of an application that triggers the PREA. Complying with the PREA is an essential part of any drug development plan, and pharmaceutical companies are encouraged to start considering their pediatric assessments and appropriate study plan early in development.

Under PREA, the FDA can waive studies in children if (1) studies would be impossible or highly impractical to conduct; (2) the disease for which the drug is being used in adults does not exist in children, such as prostate cancer; (3) there is a strong evidence suggesting that the product would be ineffective or unsafe in all pediatric age groups; and (4) the drug does not provide a meaningful therapeutic benefit over existing therapies for pediatric patients [25]. A deferral is issued when a pediatric assessment is required but has not been completed at the time the NDA, BLA, or supplemental NDA or BLA is ready for approval.

The FDA can issue written requests to pharmaceutical companies to request pediatric studies prior to approval of a new drug or to holders of an approved application if the FDA has determined that information related to the use of the drug in the pediatric population may produce health benefits [26].

On July 9, 2012 President Obama signed into law the Food and Drug Administration Safety and Innovation Act (FDASIA), reauthorizing, strengthening, and making both legislations (PREA and BPCA) permanent [27]. The FDASIA aims to ensure that pediatric evaluation under the PREA are conducted earlier in the drug development process to improve quality and accountability for completion of such studies and to advance the neonatal drug studies under the BPCA and PREA. It expands market incentives for conducting pediatric trials and extending exclusivity for products studied further to support pediatric labeling.

Under the FDASIA, for the first time, the PREA includes a provision that mandates pharmaceutical companies submitting an NDA/BLA that is subject to the PREA to submit a Pediatric Study Plan (PSP) at the End of Phase II clinical trials and no later than 60 calendar days after the date of the End of Phase II meeting [28]. The initial PSP should include (1) an outline of the pediatric study plan including objectives, study design, age group, relevant endpoints; and (2) any request for a deferral, partial waiver, or waiver. For nonclinical safety studies, the plan should include the species to be studied, the age of animals at the start of dosing, duration of dosing, endpoints, and target organ of concern. Review division and PeRC will review the initial PSP within 90 days of submission and meets with the sponsor by day 90 to discuss the initial PSP or the sponsor may receive written comments from the FDA. The sponsor is expected

II. TOXICOLOGICAL STUDIES AND IND APPLICATION, AND FIRST IN-HUMAN CLINICAL TRIAL

to incorporate the FDA recommendation and submit "AGREED INITIAL PSP" within 90 days from the date of the FDA meeting or receiving the written FDA comments. The PeRC then reviews the "AGREED INITIAL PSP" within 30 days and formally sends a letter to confirm agreement within the same 30-day window [28].

Both the European and US pediatric regulations work form a carrot and stick perspective. The "carrot" is the prospect of a 6-month extension to the Supplementary Protection Certificate (SPC) of products tested in children. The stick is the requirement that pharmaceutical companies filing for approval submit data on the product's use in children, unless they can demonstrate that such studies would not be appropriate. Together, the BPCA and PREA have been instrumental in adding information to drug labels and reducing the off-label use of drugs in children in the United States to about 50% [25]. In essence the BPCA is the carrot, while the PREA is the stick of the legislator.

There are differences and similarities between the PREA and BPCA. The PREA is triggered by an application for a new indication, dosage form, dosing regimen, route of administration, or a new active ingredient. It mandates the FDA to require a pediatric assessment of some approved drugs (small and large molecules) for certain indications. A minimum assessment may typically include pharmacokinetic or pharmacodynamic data and safety studies. The FDA may sometimes allow the extrapolation of efficacy, or require full safety and efficacy studies. In rare cases the FDA may accept literature review for a drug that has been in the marketplace for a long time. Under the PREA pediatric studies for orphan indications are exempt.

The BPCA demands voluntary pediatric drug assessments via a written request, including clinical and nonclinical studies for both small and large molecules. It also authorizes the FDA to request studies of approved and/or unapproved pediatric indications. The BPCA echoes a public health need for pediatric studies and establishes the requirement that an internal committee review all written requests prior to their issuance.

The FDA and EMA have agreed in principle to network and share information on pediatric issues to encourage the global endeavor of developing high-quality medicines for children. Likewise, collaborations with other regulators such as in Japan and Canada and with the World Health Organization (WHO) also exist.

THE NONCLINICAL SAFETY GUIDELINES

The increased interest and/or need to perform pediatric clinical trials for marketing and safe use of a wider range of medicines in children have raised the necessity to conduct juvenile animal studies [29]. In order to design a clinical trial in a pediatric population, preclinical safety assessment, drug metabolism, and toxicokinetics in juvenile animals are essential. The main objective of testing pharmaceuticals in juvenile animals is to obtain safety data, including information on the potential for adverse effects on postnatal growth and development.

Guidance documents have been issued for the nonclinical safety testing of juvenile animals. The first one, *Guidance for Industry Nonclinical Safety Evaluation of Pediatric Drug Products*, was issued by the US FDA in 2006 [3]. Only 2 years later in 2008, the EMEA issued the second guidance document, *Guideline on the Need for Nonclinical Testing in Juvenile Animals of Pharmaceuticals for Pediatric Indications* [30]. But it was not until October 2012 that has the ministry of health, labor, and welfare in Japan finalized its *Nonclinical Safety Study in Juvenile Animals for Pediatric drugs* [31]. Studies on juvenile animals may assist in identifying postnatal developmental toxicities or other adverse effects that are not adequately assessed in the routine toxicity evaluations and cannot be safely or adequately measured in pediatric clinical trials [32]. Studies on juvenile animals might be warranted in order to address a specific concern or to study reversibility or possible worsening of the expected findings, as well as to establish safety factors [30]. However, safety data generated from juvenile animals are useful only if obtained from the most appropriate species at the most relevant age considering the comparability of a specific human organ system in question [33].

Efforts to harmonize these guidelines and conform to the current state of science are ongoing. A new ICH guideline (ICH S11) [34] on nonclinical safety studies to support a pediatric development program is in progress and is expected to result in a clear, consistent, and harmonized guideline across all the ICH regions. The final concept note of the ICH S11 states that juvenile animal study design considerations including dose-selection considerations, species selection, developmental stage of animals in relation to pediatric population, route of administration, dosing duration, reversibility, toxicokinetics, and the utility of the safety data from young animals and its impact and specific assessment endpoints will be addressed in the guideline. The guideline will also include recommendations for drugs used for pediatric-only indications.

The regional (FDA, EMA, and Japanese) guidelines recommend that the study design for juvenile safety testing take a case-by-case approach. The proposed guideline (ICH S11) [34] stipulates that the design be appropriate and scientifically justified, and options are described for both a targeted design and modification of a repeat general toxicity study or a pre- and postnatal development toxicity study. The objective is to streamline drug development with high scientific rigor while minimizing the unnecessary use of animals.

It is anticipated that a Step 2b (adoption of draft guideline by regulatory parties) will be completed in 2016 and that Step 5 (implementation) will be reached in 2018.

STUDY DESIGN CONSIDERATION, SPECIES, AGE, AND ENDPOINTS

The development of drugs including pediatric drugs for children is a stepwise process involving evaluation of both human efficacy and safety testing in animals.

Safety assessment in juvenile animals is an integral part of drug development in children. According to the FDA and EMA guidance principles, juvenile animal studies should be conducted when (1) findings in nonclinical adult studies indicate target-organ toxicities relevant to developing systems; (2) mechanisms of action of the medicinal product showing concern that the compound might affect a developing organ system; (3) there are insufficient human and animal data for safety evaluation in the intended pediatric population; (4) or special concern predicted in adult animals requiring further evaluation, such as study of reversibility or a need to establish safety factors.

The juvenile toxicity study design is based on scientific rationale and should mimic the pediatric clinical trial on a case-by-case basis. Critical points relevant to juvenile animals studies include the need to design studies focused on addressing specific questions pertinent to children, rather than adapting standard toxicology designs into juvenile studies (see Fig. 11.1), and the desire for consistent dialog between investigators and regulatory authorities [35].

The principles of preclinical study conduct in pediatric drug development for small molecules are similar to those of biopharmaceuticals. They both follow the same regulatory guidance outlined by the FDA and EMA. However, many biopharmaceuticals are also inherently different, with limited species specificity or immunogenic potential, which may impact the study design and species-selection approach taken [36].

Species/Age: Rats and dogs have been the rodent and nonrodent species of choice in preclinical studies for most therapeutics. In some circumstances, for example, when drug metabolism in a particular species differs significantly from humans, an alternative species (eg, mini-pigs, pigs, monkeys) may be more appropriate for testing. In juvenile toxicity testing, considerations should be given to certain factors such as pharmacology, pharmacokinetics, and toxicology of the therapeutic agent; comparative developmental status of the major organs of concern between juvenile animals and pediatric patients; and the sensitivity of the selected species to a particular toxicity [3].

The US FDA guideline (2006) [3] reiterates that one species may be sufficient to evaluate toxicity endpoints for therapeutics that are well characterized in both adult humans and animals, whereas the EMA guideline considers safety testing in one appropriate species sufficient [30].

A compilation of 39 juvenile toxicity studies from 10 pharmaceutical companies showed that the rat is by far the most preferred species and mini-pigs are generally used only when the rat is not an appropriate species [37].

When performing nonclinical safety testing in juvenile animals, it is important that the stage of development in the animals being studied is comparable to that in the intended pediatric population. In pediatrics, age groups are categorized as shown in Table 11.1 [3,34,38]. These age groups are somewhat subjective because of the wide variability in body weight within the age category and the prospect for considerable maturational or developmental overlap. Consequently, caution must be exercised and a flexible approach adopted to ensure the study design reflects current knowledge of developmental biology and pediatric pharmacology [20].

In industry it has become standard to use the guidelines for comparative age categories between different animal species and humans based on the central nervous system and reproductive organ development (Fig. 11.2). It is important, however, to note that this does not account for postnatal organ maturations.

Dose Selection: For dose selection in juvenile animal studies, the FDA guidance document calls for establishment of a clear dose–response relationship when possible. The high dose should produce identifiable toxicity (either developmental or general). The intermediate dose should produce some toxicity so that a dose–response relationship can be demonstrated if one exists. The low dose should produce little or no toxicity, and a no observed adverse effect level should be identified, if possible. As doses that produce toxicity in adults may be different and juvenile animals may be more sensitive or less sensitive to a pharmaceutical product compared to adult animals, a pilot study will help identify doses that produce toxicity that will not confound evaluations in a definitive study. Overt toxicity in juvenile animal studies may lead to growth retardation with secondary effects on organ systems, which may further lead to maternal neglect/rejection of offspring, thus giving rise to uninterruptible results.

Routes of Administration/TK Bleeding: The intended human route of administration should be used; if not, justification should be provided to why an alternative route is chosen. In addition to scientific considerations, the feasibility of dosing should be considered when designing a juvenile toxicity study, especially in rodents at neonatal age and prior to weaning. The most common route of administration for dosing in children is oral, but pediatric medications are available

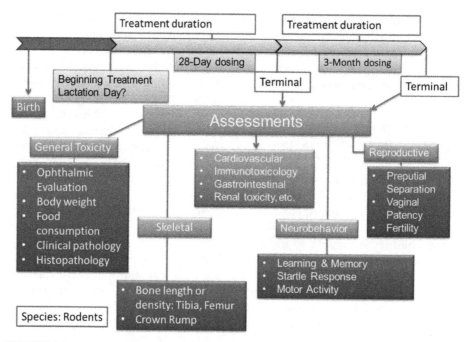

FIGURE 11.1   A study design for a 28-day or 3-month repeat dose in neonatal/juvenile animals.

both in liquid or solid form. Liquid formulation is often appropriate for toddlers who are unable to swallow capsules or tablets, whereas parental formulations are often used in neonates [20]. The general recommendation for the earliest age at which to start oral dosing in rodents is PND 4 or PND 7. If treatment is required right after birth, the use of intraperitoneal injection or subcuatneous is a reasonable alternative for dosing rodents (including mice) at this early age. Moreover, administration of the test article by inhalation is technically feasible in preweaning pups, but it could introduce multiple concurrent exposures via dermal and oral routes in addition to inhalation exposure. Additionally, intravenous dosing of a pup-tail vein is practical when the tail has developed and the vein can be viewed and accessed [39]. However, available data in the literature show that daily IV dosing is possible beginning as early as PND 4 [40]. But it must be stressed that not all labs are able to perform IV dosing in PND 4 rats.

It should be noted that neonatal pups do not have their own independent thermoregulation and may encounter thermal challenges when temporarily removed from their mother during dosing. This may cause cold body temperature and impaired lactation and modulation of the toxic potency of the substance administered, making it increasingly difficult to differentiate specific from nonrelated drug effects.

When designing a juvenile toxicity study, technical and logistical limitations associated with the feasibility of the dosing procedure, dosing volume, group assignments (such cross-fostering), and collection of blood samples for toxicokinetics and clinical pathology

TABLE 11.1   Classification of Pediatric Age Categories

Age Groups	Position Paper 2007	FDA	ICH E11
Newborn	>38 gestational weeks	–	–
Neonate/ newborn infants	0–30 days	Birth–1 month	0–27 days
Infants	1 month–3 years	1 month–2 years	
Children	6–12 years	2–12 years	2–11 years
Adolescents	12–18 years	12 to <16 years	12 to 16–18 years[a]

[a]Depending on the region.

evaluations particularly in neonatal animals need to be carefully weighed. Toxicokinetic (TK) evaluation provides explanation on age-related differences in sensitivity to the compound; it assists in the extrapolation of animal data to humans and reduces uncertainty in risk assessment. Satellite groups are traditionally used for TK blood collections and pups are bled on the first day and last of day of treatment. On day 1 of TK, blood is pooled per litter basis and pups discarded following bleeding. Advances in bioanalytical techniques have created the potential to use microsamples to assess exposure levels in blood, plasma, and/or serum. Microsampling provides the opportunity to refine blood-sampling procedures, enhance scientific and business capabilities, and significantly reduce animal use in safety assessment studies [41].

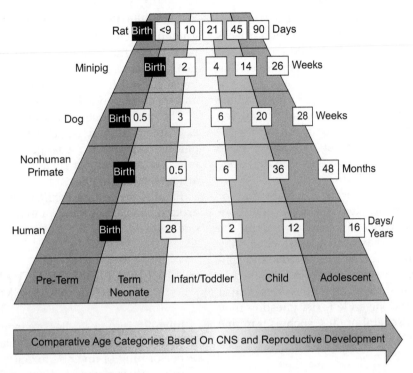

FIGURE 11.2 Comparative age categories based on CNS and reproductive development.

Group Assignments: Several approaches to group assignments can be employed in juvenile animal studies. These may include, but are not limited to, split-litter, whole-litter design, cross-fostering, and one pup per sex per litter design. In split-litter design, all dose levels should be equally represented within a litter. In this procedure no two same-sex siblings are assigned to the same dose group. In the split-litter design there is risk of technical errors and cross-contamination.

In whole-litter design, all pups from the same litter get the same dose. This approach reduces the chance for cross-contamination, but it has a risk of inducing litter effect and genetic bias. Cross-fostering is used to minimize the effect of litter and genetic bias, but true fostering replaces the original litter of a dam with one offspring from each of several litters of other dams and requires the birth of a sufficient number of litters on the same day. The one pup per sex per litter design is primarily used in pre- and postnatal development studies. It eliminates cross-contamination [42].

Endpoints: In general, juvenile toxicity studies should be designed to determine the drug reactions on the overall growth of the organ systems that develop postnatally (eg, skeletal, renal, lung, neurological, immunologic, and reproductive systems). Studies should include, at a minimum, measurement of growth (eg, serial measurements of crown-rump length, femur and tibia length, or other appropriate indices), external indices of sexual maturation, body weight, physical signs, clinical pathology, organ weights, and gross and microscopic examinations [3]. In contrast, the endpoints for juvenile toxicity testing may be limited to developmental landmarks, exposure assessment, hematology, clinical pathology, histopathology, and general growth and development. This is particularly true for 28-day juvenile toxicity testing with treatment beginning in the first week of birth.

Endpoints may be a limiting factor in species selection. The rat is considered to be the species of choice for reproductive endpoint assessments. Estrus cycle determination in females, mating, sperm assessment in males, and determination of hormone levels in both males and female can easily be evaluated in rats or rodents. Very young rats lack adult-like locomotion; thus parameters like gait and rearing that are generally included in functional observational batteries (FOB) for CNS evaluations would not be relevant in rats. Male dogs achieve sexual maturation at 1 year of age, which corresponds to about 21 years of age in human. On average the first estrus cycle in the female dog will occur between 6 and 12 months and prolonged estrus cycle (6–7 months) in beagles, which renders estrus cycle measurement less valuable. Sexual maturation in nonhuman primates is about 4–6 years, making reproductive assessment in juvenile primate impractical.

Rat, dog, and nonhuman primates can all be used to study the effects of drugs on bone growth and development; however, the following limitations should be considered.

Epiphyseal plate closure in dogs is 0.6–0.9 years; 5.5–6.5 years in Cynomolgus monkey; and the rat lacks complete epiphyseal closure. It should be emphasized that much of the skeletal development can be covered in standard chronic toxicity studies.

Bone-length measurements including femur and tibia length can be easily evaluated immediately following necropsy; measurements of bone length during the in-life portion of the study are cumbersome and may be unreliable. Bone-density measurements can be done using DEXA scan, CT scan, and MRI.

If histopathological effects occur in male and/or female reproductive organs, then the functional consequences including fertility assessment should be performed [30]. Neurobehavioral assessments may be performed in juvenile studies of 3 months and longer. The assessment of these parameters is described in Chapter 9. Furthermore, depending on the target-organ toxicity of the compound, juvenile toxicity testing may include assessments of several organs, such as immune system, cardiovascular, kidney, liver, GI tract, etc.

TESTING FACILITY

Outsourcing a juvenile toxicity study requires careful selection of a contract laboratory organization (CRO). In industry, juvenile toxicity testing is typically conducted by scientists and technical staff from the developmental and reproductive toxicology group because of the group's background in handling neonatal/juvenile animals from pre- and postnatal developmental studies, and their obvious experience in interpreting data generated from common endpoints with juvenile animal studies. The testing facility should have the technical and logistical capabilities of managing and conducting juvenile toxicity studies in various species. Administration of drugs to laboratory animals requires careful consideration and planning to optimize adequate delivery of the drug to the animal while minimizing potential dosing errors. Issues such as volume of administration, site of delivery, pH of the substance, and other factors must be considered to refine the technique of dosing route [43]. The technical staff should receive adequate training in handling, dosing, and/or bleeding neonatal/juvenile animals and be familiar with the in-life study functions.

IV dosing is very challenging, particularly in neonatal rodents because of the difficulties of accessing the tail vein as well as other veins at this age. Hence, labs must have well-trained IV technicians for neonatal studies requiring IV route of exposure. Consideration should be given to use of the smallest needle to enhance animal comfort and minimize inflammation of the injection sites.

The study director must be familiar with the regulatory guidelines, be able to design studies on a case-by-case basis, have the knowledge and experience to interpret neonatal/juvenile studies, and should be mindful of the logistical and technical challenges essential to planning and executing juvenile animal studies.

The pathologists performing the histopathological assessment should be able to differentiate congenital defects, microscopic changes related to growth, and microscopic changes related to physiology from test article-related changes.

Finally, the testing facilities must also develop background clinical pathology and microscopic data on juvenile animals.

APPLICATION OF JUVENILE DATA IN RISK ASSESSMENT

Juvenile animal studies are increasingly requested by US and European legislators [44] and the planning and/or performing of juvenile toxicity studies in the EU has significantly increased because of the need for early consideration of pediatric investigation plans (PIP) to support an indication in pediatric populations [45]. Similarly, pharmaceutical companies are now required to submit a pediatric study plan early in the drug development in the United States. According to the FDA guidance for industry on the nonclinical safety evaluation of pediatric drug products [3], juvenile animal data are used in (1) clinical trials and (2) in product approval and labeling.

1. In clinical trials: juvenile studies can provide information useful in limiting the risk of experiencing adverse events and identify appropriate clinical monitoring. This can be attained by identifying biomarkers of adverse effects in nonclinical juvenile studies which could be useful in monitoring pediatric clinical trials. When biomarkers cannot be identified or safely used in clinical studies, nonclinical PK/TK data could be useful because a given adverse effect could be associated with a particular level of systemic exposure. To reduce the probability of the adverse effect(s), blood level monitoring can be employed in clinical trial.

2. In product approval and labeling: juvenile animal studies could identify potential adverse effects that could impact its use in a particular pediatric population [3]. In order to obtain a value-added juvenile study that will identify potential safety and add new information to the product label, appropriate strategy and design is required and prior to the inclusion in the study design, each endpoint should be carefully considered in terms of practicality and interpretability [46]. Likewise, only with appropriate juvenile toxicity study designs is it possible to

adequately identify safety or pharmacokinetic issues, suggest clinical endpoints, and contribute to the product label [37]. A retrospective review of products with pediatric information in their labels using publically available product listings as well as internal FDA records revealed regular use of the juvenile animal toxicity data to better characterize safety [47].

There is no doubt the safety data from juvenile animals has played a significant role in the increased number of approved and labeled drugs in children in recent years. In 2009, 46% of the drugs used in the United States were labeled for use in children [48], and between July 1998 and September 2011, the FDA approved 500 labeling changes [25,35,49].

References

[1] Kearns GL, Abdel-Rahman SM, Alander SW, Blowey DL, Leeder JS, Kauffman RE. Development pharmacology-drug disposition, action and therapy in infants and children. N Engl J Med 2003;349:1157–62.

[2] Mckinney Jr HE. Congress, the FDA, and the fair development of new medications for children. Pediatrics 2003;112:669–70.

[3] Food and Drug Administration (FDA). Guidance for industry non clinical testing of pediatric drug products. 2006.

[4] Fernandez E, Perez R, Hernandez A, Tejada P, Arteta M, Ramos JT. Factors and mechanisms for pharmacokinetic differences between pediatric population and adults. Pharmaceutics 2011;3(1):53–72. Review.

[5] Bartelink IH, Rademaker CM, Schobben AF, van den Anker JN. Guidelines on paediatric dosing on the basis of developmental physiology and pharmacokinetic considerations. Clin Pharmacokinet 2006;45:1077–97.

[6] Alcorn J, McNamara PJ. Ontogeny of hepatic and renal systemic clearance pathways in infants: part II. Clin Pharmacokinet 2002;41:1077–94.

[7] Faqi A, Lanphear C, Gill S, Collagiovanni D. Juvenile Toxicity study of faropenem medoxomil in beagle puppies. Reprod Toxicol 2010;20:619–24.

[8] Benedetti SM, Baltes EL. Drug metabolism and disposition in children. Fundam Clin Pharmacol 2003;17:281–99.

[9] Buist SC, Klaassen CD. Rat and mouse differences in gender-predominant expression of organic anion transporter (Oat1–3; Slc22a6–8) mRNA levels. Drug Metab Dispos 2004;32:620–5.

[10] Sweeney DE, Vallon V, Rieg T, Wu W, Gallegos TF, Nigam SK. Functional maturation of drug transporters in the developing, neonatal, and postnatal kidney. Mol Pharmacol 2011;80(1):147–54.

[11] Hines RN. Ontogeny of human hepatic cytochromes P450. J Biochem Mol Toxicol 2007;21:169–75.

[12] McCarver DG, Hines RN. The ontogeny of human drug-metabolizing enzymes: phase II conjugation enzymes and regulatory mechanisms. J Pharmacol Exp Ther 2002;300(2):361–6.

[13] Hart SN, Cui Y, Klaassen CD, Zhong XB. Three patterns of cytochrome p450 gene expression during liver maturation in mice. Drug Metab Dispos 2009;37:116–21.

[14] Radde IC. Mechanism of drug absorption and their development. In: Macleod SM, Radde IC, editors. Textbook of pediatric clinical pharmacology. Littleton, MA: PSG publishing Co.; 1985. p. 17–45.

[15] Rice D, Barone S. Critical periods of vulnerability for the developing nervous system: evidence from humans and animal models. Environ Health Perspect 2000;108(Suppl. 3):511–33.

[16] Zoetis T, Walls I. Principles and practices for direct dosing of pre-weaning mammals in toxicity testing and research. Washington DC: ILSI Press; 2003. p. 11 and 13.

[17] European Union. Regulation (EC) no. 1902/2006 of the European Parliament and of the Council of 20 December 2006 amending Regulation1901/2006 on medicinal products for pediatric use. Official J Eur Union L378/20 2006a, 1–2.

[18] European Union. Regulation (EC) no. 1902/2006 of the European Parliament and of the Council of 12 December 2006 on medicinal products for pediatric use and amending regulation (EEC) 1768/92 directive 2001/20/EC, directive 2001/83/EC and regulation (EC) No. 76/2004. Official J Eur Union 378/L 2006b.

[19] Carleer J, Karres J. Juvenile animal studies and pediatric drug development: a European regulatory perspective. Birth Defects Res B Dev Reprod Toxicol 2011;92:254–60.

[20] Zisowsky J, Krause A, Dingemanse J. Drug development for pediatric populations: regulatory aspects. Pharmaceutics 2010;2(4):364–88.

[21] Vassal G, Blanc P, Pearson A. Need for change in implementation of pediatric regulation. Lancet Oncol 2013;14:1156–7.

[22] Vassal G, Blanc P, Copland C, Pearson. Will the revised class waiver list make it? Lancet Oncol 2015;16(9):425–6.

[23] http://www.fda.gov/downloads/Drugs/DevelopmentApprovalProcess/DevelopmentResources/UCM049870.pdf.

[24] Breslow LH. The best pharmaceuticals for children act of 2002: the rise of the voluntary incentive structure and congressional refusal to require pediatric testing. Harv J Legis 2003;40:134–92.

[25] Yao L. FDA takes step to encourage pediatric drug studies. Posted on August 26, 2013 by FDA Voice.

[26] http://www.fda.gov/RegulatoryInformation/Legislation/SignificantAmendmentstotheFDCAct/FDAMA/ucm089179.htm.

[27] Food and Drug Administration Safety and Innovation Act (FDA-SIA). Pub L. No. 2012; 112–144.

[28] FDA. Guidance for industry pediatric study plans: content of and process for submitting initial pediatric study plans and amended pediatric study plans. U.S. Department of Health and Human Services Food and Drug Administration; 2013.

[29] Baldrick P. Developing drugs for pediatric use. A role for juvenile animal studies. Regul Toxicol Pharmacol 2004;39:381–9.

[30] European Medicines Agency (EMA) Committee for Human Medicinal Products (CHMP). Guideline on the need for non-clinical testing in juvenile animals on human pharmaceuticals for pediatric indications. 2008.

[31] Japanese Ministry of Health Labor and Welfare, Pharmaceutical and Food Safety Bureau. Guideline on the nonclinical safety study in juvenile animals for pediatric drugs. 2012.

[32] Cappon GD, Bailey G, Buschmann J, Feuston MH, Fischer JE, Hew KW, et al. Juvenile animal toxicity study designs to support pediatric drug development. Birth Defects Res B Dev Reprod Toxicol 2009;86(6):463–9.

[33] Anderson T, Khan NK, Tassinari MS, Hurtt ME. Comparative juvenile safety testing of new therapeutic candidates: relevance of laboratory animal data to children. J.Toxicol Sci 2009;34(Suppl. 2). SP209-2015.

[34] http://www.ich.org/fileadmin/Public_Web_Site/ICH_Products/Guidelines/Safety/S11/S11_Final_Concept_Paper_10_November_2014.pdf.

[35] Turner MA, Catapano M, Hirschfeld S, Giaquinto C. Pediatric drug development: the impact of evolving regulations. Adv Drug Deliv Rev 2014;73:2–13.

[36] Morford LL, Bowman CJ, Blanset DL, Bøgh IB, Chellman GJ, Halpern WG, et al. Preclinical safety evaluations supporting pediatric drug development with biopharmaceuticals: strategy, challenges, and current practices. Birth Defects Res B Dev Reprod Toxicol 2011;92(4):359–80.

[37] Bailey GP, Mariën D. The value of juvenile animal studies "What have we learned from preclinical juvenile toxicity studies? Birth Defects Res B Dev Reprod Toxicol 2011;92(4):273–91.

[38] http://archives.who.int/eml/expcom/children/Items/PositionPaperAgeGroups.pdf Pediatric age categories to be used in differentiating between listing on a model essential medicines list for children (2007).

[39] Moser VC, Walls I, Zoetis T. Direct dosing of preweaning rodents in toxicity testing and research; deliberations of an ILSI/HESI expert working group. Int J Toxicol 2005;24(2):87–94.

[40] Ciaravino V, Hanover J, Lin L, Sullivan T, Corash L. Assessment of safety in neonates for transfusion of platelets and plasma prepared with amotosalen photochemical pathogen inactivation treatment by a one-month intravenous toxicity study in neonatal rats. Transfusion 2009;49(5):985–94.

[41] Chapman K, Chivers S, Gliddon D, Mitchell D, Robinson S, Sangster T, et al. Overcoming the barriers to the uptake of nonclinical microsampling in regulatory safety studies. Drug Discov Today 2014;19(5):528–32.

[42] Beck M, Padget EL, Bowman Ch, Wilson D, Kaufman L, Varsho B, et al. Nonclinical juvenile toxicity testing. In: Hood R, editor. Developmental and reproductive toxicology – a practical approach. Boca Raton, FL: Taylor and Francis; 2007. p. 263–327.

[43] Turner PV, Brabb TH, Pekow C, Vasbinder MA. Administration of substances to laboratory animals: routes of administration and factors to consider. J Am Assoc Lab Anim Sci 2011;50(5):600–13.

[44] Rose K. The value of juvenile animal studies: a pediatric clinical perspective. Birth Defects Res B Dev Reprod Toxicol 2011;92(4):252–3.

[45] Duarte DM, Silva-Lima B. Juvenile animal studies in the development of pediatric medicines: experience from European medicines and pediatric investigation plans. Birth Defects Res B Dev Reprod Toxicol 2011;92(4):353–8.

[46] De Schaepdrijver L, Rouan MC, Raoof A, Bailey GP, De Zawrt L, Monbaliu J, et al. Real life Juvenile toxicity case studies: the good, the bad and the ugly. Reprod Toxicol 2008;26:54–5.

[47] Tassinari MS, Benson K, Elayan I, Espandiari P, Davis-Bruno K. Juvenile animal studies and pediatric drug development retrospective review: use in regulatory decisions and labeling. Birth Defects Res B Dev Reprod Toxicol 2011;92(4):261–5.

[48] Sachs AN, Avant D, Lee CS, Rodriguez W, Murphy MD. Pediatric information in drug product labeling. JAMA 2012;307(18):1914–5.

[49] Committee on Drugs. Off-label use of drugs in children. Pediatrics 2014;133(3):1–9.

12

Preclinical Evaluation of Carcinogenicity Using Standard-Bred and Genetically Engineered Rodent Models

D.L. McCormick

A Comprehensive Guide to Toxicology in Nonclinical Drug Development, Second Edition
http://dx.doi.org/10.1016/B978-0-12-803620-4.00012-8

INTRODUCTION

Assessment of potential carcinogenicity is an essential component of the preclinical development of small-molecule therapeutics whose anticipated human-use profile involves chronic administration, or for which a signal suggesting possible carcinogenicity has been identified on the basis of chemical class, in vitro activity, or the results of genetic toxicology or other short-term in vivo toxicology studies.

For several decades, the 2-year bioassay in standard-bred rats and mice has been considered to be the "gold standard" for preclinical evaluations of carcinogenicity. This study design has been used widely to evaluate the potential carcinogenicity of new drugs, agricultural chemicals, occupational chemicals, environmental contaminants, and a wide range of other agents, and has been demonstrated to be a useful predictor of human cancer responses [2,22]. In independent analyses, the International Agency for Research on Cancer (IARC) and US National Toxicology Program (NTP) have both concluded that the results of 2-year carcinogenicity bioassays in rodents demonstrate a high degree of concordance with human cancer responses [20,44]. Some important limitations to the chronic rodent bioassay as a predictor of human carcinogenicity have been identified [8,11], and the value of performing parallel assays in both rats and mice has been questioned [49]. However, in view of the demonstrated concordance between carcinogenicity in chronic rodent bioassays and evidence of carcinogenicity in humans, and as a result of the acceptance of chronic rodent bioassay data by the US Food and Drug Administration (FDA), the US Environmental Protection Agency (EPA) and other regulatory agencies around the world, it is generally agreed among toxicologists that the chronic rodent bioassay provides the best available experimental approach to identify agents that may be carcinogenic in humans.

In consideration of their extended duration and substantial cost, chronic carcinogenicity studies of nongenotoxic therapeutics are most often performed following the completion of Phase I and Phase II clinical trials. However, in situations where a positive or equivocal result has been obtained in genetic toxicology bioassays, studies to assess potential carcinogenic activity using a 6-month oncogenicity bioassay in genetically engineered mice may be required by regulatory agencies prior to the start of Phase I clinical trials. Strains of genetically engineered mice used in 6-month bioassays demonstrate a predisposition to neoplasia as the result of the insertion of an oncogene or deletion of a tumor suppressor gene from the germ line; the increased sensitivity of these animals to neoplastic development permits the completion of a predictive oncogenicity bioassay with a much shorter period of test article exposure.

This chapter focuses on technical procedures and scientific considerations for the conduct and evaluation of carcinogenicity data generated in (1) chronic (18 or 24 months) bioassays performed in standard-bred rodents and (2) 6-month bioassays performed in genetically engineered mice.

CHRONIC CARCINOGENICITY BIOASSAYS IN STANDARD-BRED RODENTS

Overview

Preclinical evaluations of the carcinogenicity of a new molecular entity (NME) are most often performed by conducting parallel studies in which rats and mice receive graded doses of a test agent for a period that encompasses the majority of their normal lifespan (2 years in most studies; some studies in mice are conducted for 18 months). In most studies, the test agent is administered daily by a route that simulates human exposure. Dose levels of the test agent are selected to induce (at most) minimal evidence of toxicity in treated animals, as demonstrated by comparable patterns of survival and body weight gain in treated and control groups, and by normal clinical observations in treated animals.

Although the design of the chronic carcinogenicity bioassay includes a battery of in-life toxicology observations and health-status evaluations, the key experimental endpoints in these studies are the incidences of site-specific malignant and benign neoplasms in treated and control animals, as determined through a comprehensive microscopic evaluation of tissues.

Regulatory Compliance

Most carcinogenicity bioassays are performed to meet regulatory requirements. For this reason, minimum standard protocols for chronic rodent bioassays have been developed to meet the requirements of US-based regulatory agencies such as the FDA and EPA; over the past 20 years, extensive effort has been put forth to harmonize US and international regulatory requirements so that the same study design will meet the requirements of American, European, Japanese, and other regulatory agencies. Design considerations for carcinogenicity bioassays are discussed in the International Conference on Harmonisation (ICH) Guideline S1B [23]; an extensive presentation and discussion of technical approaches for the design and conduct of bioassays to determine the possible carcinogenicity of food additives and ingredients is provided in draft form in the FDA Redbook [59]. However, note that the study designs discussed in the FDA Redbook are considered to be minimum designs;

final designs of carcinogenicity bioassays often include additional groups, larger group sizes, and/or additional experimental endpoints to address specific scientific or regulatory questions.

It is essential that carcinogenicity bioassays that are intended for submission to regulatory agencies be performed in strict compliance with applicable Good Laboratory Practice (GLP) regulations. GLP regulations for submissions to the FDA are presented in the Code of Federal Regulations (CFR) and published in the Federal Register (21 CFR Part 58). EPA GLP standards are defined in two sites in the CFR; GLP standards applicable to studies performed in response to the testing requirements of the Toxic Substances Control Act (TSCA) are defined in 40 CFR Part 793, whereas GLP standards applicable to safety and toxicology studies performed in response to the testing requirements of the Federal Insecticide, Fungicide, and Rodenticide Act (FIFRA) are defined in 40 CFR Part 160. GLP regulations and requirements set forth by regulatory agencies from countries other than the United States are often available on the websites of the agency or agencies to which studies are being designed for submission.

Design of 2-Year Carcinogenicity Studies in Standard-Bred Rodents

A protocol summary for a 2-year carcinogenicity evaluation in standard-bred rats or mice is presented in Table 12.1. This protocol summary is designed to address current ICH and FDA requirements for carcinogenicity bioassays in standard-bred rodents. However, it is important to note that the study design presented in Table 12.1 is necessarily generic, and will require customization to address relevant scientific and regulatory considerations for specific NMEs undergoing assessment for possible carcinogenicity. Individual elements of study design are discussed in subsequent subsections.

Experimental Animals

In consideration of the importance of subchronic toxicology data in the selection of doses to be used in chronic bioassays, carcinogenicity studies in rats and mice are most often performed using animal strains in which toxicology studies of shorter duration have been performed with the test agent. The availability of historical tumor pathology data is also an important consideration in animal model selection; in addition to comparisons of tumor incidences in treated groups versus contemporaneous controls, analysis of carcinogenicity bioassay data often includes comparisons of tumor incidences in treated groups versus historical controls. The importance of historical control data increases in studies in which any pattern of unusual or rare tumors is seen [19]. Comparisons with both contemporaneous and historical

TABLE 12.1 Protocol Summary for Carcinogenicity Evaluation in Standard-Bred Rats or Mice

Group	Sex[a]	Minimum Number of Animals per Sex[b]	Agent	Dose Level
1	Male and female	50	Vehicle control	0 (Control)
2	Male and female	50	Test article	Low
3	Male and female	50	Test article	Middle
4	Male and female	50	Test article	High
5[c]	Male and female	50	Vehicle control #2	0 (Control)

[a]Both sexes included unless agent is being developed for a sex-specific disease endpoint.
[b]Minimum number to satisfy regulatory requirements. Group size may be increased to increase assay sensitivity and/or to ensure adequate number of surviving animals at study termination.
[c]Control group #2 is optional (see text); tissues may not be evaluated histopathologically.

Experimental Animals: viral antibody-free rodents (rats: usually Sprague–Dawley, Wistar, or F344 strains; mice: usually CD-1, Swiss, or B6C3F1 strains) from an approved commercial supplier. Animals are received from the supplier at 5–6 weeks of age.

Quarantine: minimum of 1 week prior to initiation of test or control article administration. Viral antibody-free status is confirmed in a minimum of five sentinel animals per sex.

Diet and Drinking Water: certified laboratory animal chow from an approved commercial supplier is provided ad libitum to all animals (except for scheduled fasts prior to clinical pathology evaluations). City drinking water is provided ad libitum to all animals. Analytical records for experimental diet and drinking water are maintained with the study records.

Test and Control Articles: administered by a route that simulates human exposure [most commonly oral (gavage or diet), inhalation (nose-only or whole body), or topical (direct application to skin)]. Control animals in gavage or topical administration studies receive a comparable volume of vehicle without test article. Control animals in inhalation studies are most commonly exposed to filtered air.

Duration of Exposure: 24 months (some studies in mice are performed for 18 months only).

In-Life Observations: survival, clinical observations, physical observations (including palpation for masses), body weight, food consumption (optional), clinical pathology (optional), and pharmacokinetics (optional).

Postmortem Observations: gross pathology at necropsy (complete necropsy with tissue collection), organ weights, histopathologic evaluation of tissues (all gross lesions identified at necropsy + approximately 45–50 tissues per animal).

controls may also reduce the likelihood of false-positive or false-negative results in bioassays in which incidence comparisons with contemporaneous controls suggest a possible weak carcinogenic effect [27].

Rat strains that are commonly used in carcinogenicity bioassays include Sprague–Dawley rats and derivative strains such as the CD rat, the F344 (Fischer) rat, and several substrains of the Wistar rat. Commonly used mouse strains include various strains of Swiss or Swiss-derived mice (such as ICR and CD-1 mice) and the B6C3F1 hybrid mouse.

Sprague–Dawley Rats

Sprague–Dawley and Sprague–Dawley-derived rats are outbred strains that have been used extensively in carcinogenicity bioassays. The availability of large historical databases for control or background tumor incidences in the Sprague–Dawley rat is a major factor supporting its use as a model. Negative considerations for the use of Sprague–Dawley rats include their large body size and the relatively high incidences of spontaneous tumors in several organ sites, notably the pituitary, thyroid, and mammary glands. Both factors may underlie the relatively low survival (35–55%) at 2 years that is often seen in Sprague–Dawley-derived strains [15].

The large mass of Sprague–Dawley rats has a number of potential negative implications that should be considered in model selection. Assuming that animals will be dosed on a mg/kg basis (by gavage or other route) rather than by dietary supplementation, more test agent will be required for study conduct than would be required in studies using rat strains with lower mean body weights. If the test agent is inexpensive to produce, this difference in drug requirement may have no substantive effect on total study costs. However, the increased drug requirement may become an important factor in rat strain selection if the test agent is difficult and/or expensive to synthesize.

Body weights in Sprague–Dawley rats in chronic studies may approach (and sometimes exceed) 1 kg; this large body size may complicate animal handling and observation, and may also make in-life toxicology endpoint evaluations more difficult or less sensitive. In particular, the presence of extensive body fat may reduce the ability of technical personnel to identify small masses during palpation examinations that are performed as part of physical examinations.

Perhaps more important from a scientific perspective is the relatively high incidence of "spontaneous" tumors that appear in otherwise untreated or vehicle-treated Sprague–Dawley rats and Sprague–Dawley-derived strains such as the CD rat. In an overview of tumor pathology in control groups from 20 chronic bioassays performed in CD rats [15], tumor incidences of >10% were reported in male CD rats in the adrenal (pheochromocytomas); pancreas (islet cell adenomas); pituitary (adenomas); skin and subcutis (several tumor types); testis (interstitial cell adenomas); and thyroid (C-cell and F-cell adenomas and carcinomas). Spontaneous tumors were also identified in high incidences in control female CD rats: tumor incidences of greater than 10% were reported in control female CD rats in the adrenal (cortical adenomas, cortical carcinomas, and pheochromocytomas); mammary gland (fibroadenomas/fibromas, adenomas, adenocarcinomas); pancreas (islet cell adenomas and carcinomas); pituitary (adenomas and carcinomas); skin (multiple tumor types); thyroid (C-cell and F-cell adenomas and carcinomas); and uterus (polyps, adenomas, and carcinomas).

As a likely result of their high incidences of spontaneous tumors, Sprague–Dawley-derived rats demonstrate

poor survival at 104 weeks in many chronic bioassays. Regulatory agencies commonly require that a minimum of 25 animals/sex/group survive to the scheduled termination of a carcinogenicity bioassay. Because 2-year survival rates below 50% are commonly reported in chronic bioassays in Sprague–Dawley-derived strains [15], increasing group sizes beyond the default minimum 50 animals per sex has often been required to meet regulatory requirements for survival at 2 years. Group sizes of 60 or 70 per sex per group are common, and group sizes of up to 100 rats per sex per group have been reported.

F344 (Fischer) Rats

Although used less commonly for preclinical toxicology studies than are Sprague–Dawley rats, the F344 (Fischer) rat also has an extensive history of use in carcinogenicity evaluations. The F344 rat is an inbred strain that was for many years the primary rat strain used by the NTP in its testing program. The NTP website [41] includes study reports (including pathology summary tables) for more than 500 testing projects, the vast majority of which include carcinogenicity assessments in F344 rats.

The F344 rat offers several advantages over the Sprague–Dawley rat for use in chronic carcinogenicity bioassays. From a technical perspective, the smaller body size of the F344 rat may reduce drug requirements and facilitate animal handling and observation. Importantly, the reported incidences of spontaneous tumors in several organ sites in control F344 rats are lower than in control Sprague–Dawley rats, and survival at 2 years is generally higher. Although F344 rats in NTP studies demonstrate higher incidences of mononuclear cell leukemia than do Sprague–Dawley-derived animals, lower incidences of spontaneous tumors in the pituitary and mammary glands of female F344 rats are particularly notable [9,18]. Finally, the very large, publicly available NTP database for pathology findings in F344 rats [41] supports their use as a model system.

However, there are also several disadvantages to the use of the F344 rat in chronic rodent bioassays. Importantly, carcinogenicity evaluations performed for the NTP have been conducted using either NIH-07 or NTP-2000 as basal diets; neither of these diets is commonly used in chronic rodent bioassays performed for sponsors other than the NTP. The use of different basal diets introduces a possible response variable that may complicate the application of historical control data from NTP studies to studies being performed for other sponsors. Secondly, in the personal experience of this investigator, diet avoidance due to taste aversion is more common in F344 rats than in Sprague–Dawley rats; this diet avoidance could result in suppression of body weight gain, and thereby have a negative impact on toxicology bioassays in which the test agent is administered by dietary admixture. Finally, and perhaps most importantly, the NTP has discontinued the use of the F344 rat as a standard test system for carcinogenicity evaluations, and is now using the Sprague–Dawley rat in these studies. As a result, publicly available databases for clinical pathology and microscopic pathology findings in historical controls from chronic bioassays in Sprague–Dawley rats are likely to expand rapidly, while historical control databases for chronic bioassays in the F344 strain will not.

Wistar Rats

Wistar rats encompass a number of rat substrains that have been derived from a common lineage over the past 50+ years. The Wistar rat, Wistar Hannover (Wistar HAN) rat, and Wistar Unilever (WU) rat are outbred rat strains, while the Wistar Kyoto and Wistar Furth rats are inbred strains. The outbred Wistar and Wistar HAN strains have been used widely in Europe for preclinical safety assessments, including 2-year carcinogenicity bioassays. Although other Wistar substrains are commonly used in specialized carcinogenesis and safety studies, these strains offer neither a substantial history of use in chronic carcinogenicity bioassays nor a significant publicly available database of historical control pathology and clinical pathology data.

As with F344 rats, Wistar rats have a smaller body size than do Sprague–Dawley rats, offering the potential for easy handling. The publicly available database for spontaneous tumors in control Wistar rats is substantially smaller than for either Sprague–Dawley rats or F344 rats; however, it does appear that the total incidence of spontaneous tumors in aged control animals in various Wistar strains is lower than has been reported for Sprague–Dawley and Sprague–Dawley-derived rats [6,43].

Swiss-Derived Mice (Including ICR and CD-1 Strains)

Strains of outbred Swiss and Swiss-derived mice (including ICR mice, Swiss Webster mice, NIH Swiss mice, and CD-1 mice) are commonly used as model systems for preclinical toxicology studies. Swiss-derived mice are widely available from commercial suppliers, and a substantial body of historical control data is available for several Swiss strains. Two-year survival rates ranging from approximately 25% to more than 80% have been reported in both sexes of control CD-1 mice in chronic bioassays [3,14]. Although survival in most chronic bioassays has been well above 50%, the lower 2-year survival reported in some studies may influence decisions regarding group sizes to be used for carcinogenicity testing.

A major factor supporting the use of these strains as models for murine carcinogenicity bioassays is their broad use as model systems for acute and subchronic toxicity studies. Because a large fraction of murine preclinical studies are performed in mouse strains of Swiss origin, data from subchronic studies can be used to support dose selection for the carcinogenicity bioassays. On this basis, the use of Swiss mice and Swiss-derived mice in murine carcinogenicity bioassays is a logical extension of the toxicology database used to support preclinical drug development.

Background tumor incidences have been extensively characterized for several strains of Swiss mice. In a recent tabulation of tumor data from 14 published carcinogenicity studies [14], substantially lower incidences of spontaneous tumors were seen in CD-1(ICR) mice than have been reported in various strains of rats (discussed above). In male CD-1 mice, the most common sites of neoplastic development in control animals were the lung (bronchiolar-alveolar adenoma and carcinoma), liver (hepatocellular adenomas and carcinomas), and skin (multiple tumor types). Individual tumor incidences at all other sites in male controls were less than 3%. In female CD-1 mice, malignant lymphoma, lung tumors (adenomas and carcinomas), and skin tumors (several histologic types) were common spontaneous lesions. Individual tumor incidences in all other individual organs (including the mammary gland) were less than 4%.

B6C3F1 Mice

The B6C3F1 mouse is a hybrid strain that is produced as a cross between a male C3H mouse and a female C57BL/6 mouse. B6C3F1 mice are available from a variety of commercial sources, and have been used extensive in carcinogenicity bioassays. B6C3F1 mice are relatively large; mean body weights ranging from 50 to 60 g are commonly reported in both sexes in control groups in later months of 2-year bioassays. In our laboratory, survival of control B6C3F1 mice at 2 years has been very high (70–80%); survival at 2 years in our most recent study was 74% in male mice and 73% in female mice (unpublished). Comparably high survivals in this strain have also been reported in other laboratories [61].

The B6C3F1 mouse has been used for many years in murine carcinogenicity evaluations performed for the NTP bioassay program; these studies have generated a very large historical control database for background incidences of spontaneous tumors in this mouse model [41]. In addition, a tabulation of spontaneous lesions in B6C3F1 mice from 20 chronic bioassays that were performed for sponsors other than the NTP is available [29]. The key difference in the studies performed for the NTP versus studies performed for other sponsors is that the studies performed for the NTP used either NIH-07 or NTP-2000 open formula diets as a basal ration; the NTP-2000 diet has been used exclusively by the NTP for approximately 20 years. By contrast, studies performed for sponsors other than the NTP have most commonly been performed using commercial chow diets based on proprietary (rather than open) formulas.

Experimental Groups

As indicated in Table 12.1, a chronic carcinogenicity bioassay in standard-bred rodents includes a minimum of four experimental groups for each species (one vehicle or sham control group and three treatment groups that receive graded doses of the test agent). Occasionally, study designs will include a fourth treatment group; addition of the fourth group may support better definition of dose–response curves for any observed effects, and may also support the more accurate definition of a no observed adverse effect level (NOAEL).

A more common addition to the study design is a second vehicle control group (identified as Group 5 in Table 12.1). In most studies that include a second vehicle control group, procedures for vehicle dosing, in-life toxicology evaluations, and necropsy in the second vehicle control group are identical to those used in the first vehicle control group. However, unlike the approach used with the first vehicle control group, tissues collected at necropsy from animals in the second vehicle control group are held for possible processing and histopathologic evaluation rather than processed immediately for histopathology.

The purpose of the second control group is to ensure that tumor incidence comparisons in control and treated groups are not skewed by an unusual tumor incidence pattern in the first vehicle control group. In most cases, tumor incidences in the first vehicle control group will fall within an expected range that has been established on the basis of historical control data from studies in the species and strain being used as an experimental model. In such studies, tumor incidence patterns in the first vehicle control group will provide a suitable baseline against which tumor incidences in treatment groups may be assessed. However, tumor incidences in the first vehicle control group may occasionally fall outside of the historical control range. For example, if the incidence of mammary gland tumors in female rats is below the range of tumor incidences that have been seen in previous studies, comparisons with treatment groups may suggest that the test agent is a mammary gland carcinogen. In such cases, tissues from the second vehicle control group may be evaluated microscopically to confirm the differential response.

Group Size

Although carcinogenicity bioassays are often performed using the minimum group size of 50 animals per sex, group sizes are commonly increased beyond 50 animals per sex to ensure that survival at study termination meets regulatory agency requirements. A decision to increase group size is based on the historical survival rates of the species and strain being used as an experimental model. In order to ensure the survival of a minimum of 25 animals per sex per group at 2 years, group sizes in many carcinogenicity bioassays performed using rat models (particularly studies performed in Sprague–Dawley and Sprague–Dawley-derived strains) are often increased to 60 or 70 animals per sex.

Although a less common approach in carcinogenicity bioassays performed as part of preclinical development packages, group sizes in carcinogenicity studies may also be increased to increase the statistical power of the bioassay and its ability to identify quantitatively small effects. In our laboratory, rodent carcinogenicity bioassays involving as many as 100 animals per sex per group have been performed in order to maximize the sensitivity of bioassays to identify carcinogenic effects (eg, see Refs. [5,34]). These substantial increases in group size were implemented to maximize the power of the study to detect weak carcinogenic activity, thereby reducing the possibility of false negative responses.

Increasing group sizes will increase both (1) the quantity of test agent that is required for study performance and (2) study costs; as a result, test agent availability and program budget may ultimately become key determinants of the final study design. However, it should be noted that it is ultimately less expensive to perform a single study with increased group sizes than to repeat a carcinogenicity study because animal survival at study termination is insufficient to meet regulatory requirements.

Dose Levels of Test Agent

Selection of dose levels for the chronic carcinogenicity bioassay is a complex process, and a number of approaches to dose selection have been proposed [17,23,45]. The overarching criterion for proper study design is that the selected dose levels should maximize the likelihood of inducing a positive response. Using this approach, dose levels should be as high as possible, and should induce demonstrable (but not limiting) toxicity in the high-dose group. The high dose of the test agent (1) should not induce a substantial number of early deaths that are unrelated to neoplastic development, and (2) should not induce reductions in body weight or suppressions of body weight gain that are large enough to suppress tumorigenesis.

In most cases, the high dose selected for carcinogenicity bioassays is the maximum tolerated dose (MTD) for the test agent, as determined in subchronic toxicology studies performed in the species and strains to be used in carcinogenicity bioassays. The FDA Redbook specifically mandates that the MTD be used as the high dose in carcinogenicity bioassays [59]; by contrast, European and Japanese regulatory agencies also accept the selection of the high dose as a large multiple (generally ≥100×) of the maximum anticipated human dose [23].

Although in many cases the MTD will provide the maximum likelihood of producing a positive response, its use as the basis for selection of the high dose for carcinogenicity studies has been strongly criticized. The primary criticism of the use of the MTD to establish the high dose for carcinogenicity bioassays relates to its potential to induce artifactual responses due to disruption of normal homeostatic regulatory mechanisms that would not be impacted by administration of the test agent at lower levels. The specific concern is that positive responses may be seen at very high doses that disrupt normal homeostasis, but not at lower doses that are (1) more closely comparable to those to which humans may reasonably be exposed and (2) do not alter normal homeostatic control mechanisms.

Some researchers have suggested a more broadly based approach and identified a number of parameters that may provide appropriate bases for dose selection for carcinogenicity bioassays [23]. Criteria on which a high dose could be selected may include:

- Toxicity endpoints, which could include (but are not limited to) the MTD. Such endpoints have provided the basis for dose selection in the overwhelming majority of past bioassays of agents for carcinogenic activity.
- Pharmacodynamic factors that could identify a practical maximum dose level for the agent being investigated. This approach could be used with agents for which escalation of doses above a certain level may be difficult or impossible due to their pharmacologic activity. Specific examples of such pharmacodynamic activities identified by [23] include induction of hypotension and inhibition of hemostasis.
- Pharmacokinetic endpoints, through which the high dose is selected on the basis of (1) its generation of maximum plasma levels of the test agent (or key metabolite(s)), and/or (2) the generation of a large multiple (≥25×) of presumed human plasma levels. Relative exposure levels are determined by comparisons of area under the curve (AUC) values for the test agent and/or metabolites in humans with AUC values for the rodent

species and strains to be used in carcinogenicity bioassays. In this regard, it is important to note that carcinogenicity bioassays for therapeutic agents are commonly performed after Phase I and/or Phase II clinical trials have been initiated; as such, human pharmacokinetic data should be available to support interspecies comparisons of pharmacokinetic parameters for both the test agent and major metabolites.

- Saturation of absorption or excretion, based on demonstrations that dose levels in excess of a specific maximum (1) do not increase the quantity of agent entering the systemic circulation or (2) saturate clearance mechanisms, thereby resulting in local accumulation of the test agent or metabolites. Saturation of absorption may occur as a result of physical or solubility factors, and will result in a plateau in plasma and tissue levels of the test agent and/or metabolites. In such cases, substantial quantities of the test agent may be excreted without systemic absorption. Conversely, saturation of excretion pathways could result in local accumulation of the test agent as a result of, for example, impaired transit through the gastrointestinal tract (due to impaction in the stomach), or reduced pulmonary clearance due to saturation of normal clearance mechanisms.
- Limit dose. In cases where the anticipated maximum human dose will not exceed 500 mg/kg/day, it has been proposed that a maximum limit dose of 1500 mg/kg/day be used for carcinogenicity bioassays in rodent models [23]. However, it should be noted that this limit dose is based on the assumption that it will exceed the anticipated maximum human dose by at least a factor of 10. In cases where this dose multiple cannot be achieved, the high dose selected for carcinogenicity studies may be increased above the limit dose, and may ultimately be selected as the maximum dose of the test agent that is feasible to administer.
- Maximum feasible dose. The ability to identify an MTD or induce observable toxicity may be limited for some agents as a result of low toxicity and/or limited solubility. Although the maximum feasible dietary dose level is currently being re-evaluated, it is generally accepted that administration of a test agent at 5% of the diet (w/w) represents a reasonable upper bound [59]. In studies involving gavage administration, the quantity of test agent that may be delivered is limited by the volume of dosing formulation that can be administered to the test species; similar logistic and other considerations may limit the high dose in carcinogenicity studies in which the test agent is administered by inhalation.

II. TOXICOLOGICAL STUDIES AND IND APPLICATION, AND FIRST IN-HUMAN CLINICAL TRIAL

In the ideal case, the high dose of the test article selected for the carcinogenesis bioassay will induce identifiable evidence of toxicity in treated animals, but will not (1) induce mortality that is unrelated to carcinogenic action; (2) suppress group mean body weights by more than 10% in comparison to sex-matched vehicle controls; or (3) induce significant, limiting toxicity that has a substantive negative impact on animal health.

Under optimal circumstances, survival curves in treated groups will be comparable to those in sex-matched vehicle controls throughout the study. Intercurrent mortality that is unrelated to neoplastic development is clearly not desirable; such mortality reduces the number of animals at risk for neoplasia over the scheduled period of agent administration, and also raises critical issues in data interpretation. Importantly, early mortality at the high dose or in other dose groups suggests that this dose is above the MTD for the test agent in the species and strain being used in the bioassay. Increases in cancer incidence in experimental groups receiving the test agent at dose levels that exceed the MTD are most often considered to be irrelevant to human risk assessment; in general, such findings are only considered as adequate to support a finding of potential human risk if neoplasms or precancerous lesions are also identified in the same site at doses that are at or below the MTD [47].

The reduced incidence of cancers in animals demonstrating reduced food intake has been known for more than 75 years [26,54]. For this reason, suppression of body weight gain as a result of decreased food intake or generalized toxicity is also not a desirable outcome in chronic bioassays. Dietary restriction and resulting suppression of body weight have been demonstrated to suppress tumorigenesis in both 2-year carcinogenesis bioassays [26] and in several (but not all) organ-specific cancer models [28,35].

Absent significant effects on animal survival and body weight, toxicity may be identified through clinical observations, clinical pathology, organ weights, gross pathology, or microscopic pathology. The goal of such endpoint evaluations is to demonstrate that the high dose used in the study did, in fact, induce toxicity. Evidence of toxicity at the high dose suggests that further dose escalation may induce limiting toxicity and therefore be above the MTD; this supports the argument that the high dose used maximizes the likelihood of inducing a positive response.

Selection of the middle and low doses of test agents for carcinogenicity bioassays has been much less contentious than selection of the high dose. In the best case, the middle and low doses of the agent should induce either no toxicity or very limited toxicity, and should provide the opportunity to characterize dose–response relationships for any observed tumors. The low dose is often selected as a multiple of the presumed human dose,

while the middle dose is selected to be logarithmically between the low and high doses.

SIX-MONTH CARCINOGENICITY BIOASSAYS IN GENETICALLY ENGINEERED MICE

Overview

Our expanding understanding of the role of specific genetic alterations in the etiology of human cancer provides the scientific rationale for the use of genetically engineered animals in carcinogenicity evaluations and hazard identification. When compared to standard-bred mouse strains used for carcinogenicity testing, genetically engineered mouse models that are in current use for carcinogenicity evaluation demonstrate increased incidences of spontaneous tumors in several sites [10,48]; sites of increased spontaneous tumorigenesis vary by mouse strain. In addition, these animal models demonstrate greater responses (defined as higher incidences of induced tumors and decreased latency of those tumors) to known chemical carcinogens [7,62]. The greater sensitivity of genetically engineered mice to carcinogenesis permits definitive carcinogenicity evaluations to be performed with a much shorter in-life period (6 months) than is possible in studies using standard-bred mice (18–24 months).

The use of genetically engineered mice for carcinogen identification lacks the long historical precedent of the 2-year carcinogenicity bioassay in standard-bred mice or rats. As a result, historical databases for tumor pathology in genetically engineered mouse models are smaller than are the historical databases available to support the analysis of carcinogenesis data from studies in standard-bred rodent models. However, substantial effort has been put forth to evaluate the suitability of several strains of genetically engineered mice for carcinogenicity testing, with specific emphasis on the ability of these models to predict responses seen in the 2-year rodent bioassay and in humans. The largest of these validation efforts was performed by a consortium of US pharmaceutical companies and the US National Institute of Environmental Health Sciences/National Toxicology program to evaluate the utility of the p53 knockout and rasH2 models as short-term bioassays [46]. A similar program to evaluate the utility of the rasH2 mouse model was performed by a consortium of Japanese pharmaceutical companies [63]. Assay validation data from these programs were deemed sufficient by the FDA and the ICH to support the regulatory review and acceptance of carcinogenicity data from the rasH2 mouse and the hemizygous p53 knockout mouse in place of data generated in 2-year bioassays in mice [25].

As a result of this regulatory acceptance, carcinogenicity testing in genetically engineered mouse models has increased greatly over the past two decades. This increased use has supported the expansion of pathology databases for incidences of both spontaneous and induced tumors in several strains of genetically engineered mice, has improved our understanding of the strengths and limitations of specific transgenic and knockout mouse models for use in carcinogenicity assessments, and has provided greater insight into the predictive nature of these models and their suitability for use in safety assessments and hazard identification.

At the present time, no genetically engineered rat strains have been sufficiently validated for use in carcinogenicity evaluations. Several genetically engineered rat models are currently in development or are being validated for use in carcinogenicity testing; however, these models are not currently accepted by regulatory agencies for this purpose.

Regulatory Compliance

As discussed above, it is essential that carcinogenicity bioassays that are intended for submission to regulatory agencies be performed in strict compliance with applicable GLP regulations. GLP regulations for submissions to the FDA are presented in the CFR, and published in the Federal Register (21 CFR Part 58). GLP regulations and requirements set forth by regulatory agencies from countries other than the United States are often available on the websites of the agency or agencies to which studies are being designed for submission.

It should be noted that the EPA does not currently view the results of carcinogenicity bioassays in genetically engineered mice to be sufficient to support a comprehensive assessment of carcinogenic potential. The EPA Guidelines for Carcinogen Risk Assessment state that "assays in genetically engineered rodents may provide insight into the chemical and gene interactions involved in carcinogenesis", but that "on the basis of currently available information, it is unlikely that any of these assays…will replace all chronic bioassays for hazard identification" [57]. Because carcinogenicity studies in genetically engineered mice are not currently considered by the EPA as sufficient to serve as standalone evaluations of carcinogenicity in mice, these studies are more commonly performed for submission to the FDA or international regulatory agencies.

Design of 6-Month Bioassays in Genetically Engineered Mice

As discussed previously in this chapter, evaluations of the potential carcinogenicity of an NME commonly include studies in both rats and mice. In view of its acceptability to the FDA, a 6-month bioassay in an appropriate strain of genetically engineered mice may

replace a chronic bioassay in standard-bred mice. Using this approach, preclinical assessment of carcinogenicity may include the conduct of a 2-year bioassay in standard-bred rats and a 6-month bioassay in genetically engineered mice. In both studies, the key experimental endpoints are comparisons of the incidences of site-specific benign and malignant tumors in animals exposed to the test article in comparison to the incidences of those tumors in negative control animals receiving vehicle-only or sham exposure for the same period. The sensitivity of the genetically engineered model to carcinogenesis is demonstrated by a robust cancer response in a positive control group exposed to a known carcinogen.

A protocol summary for a 6-month carcinogenicity study in genetically engineered mice is provided in Table 12.2; the details of this experimental design have

TABLE 12.2 Protocol Summary for Carcinogenicity Evaluation in Genetically Engineered Mice

Group	Sex[a]	Minimum Number of Animals per Sex[b]	Agent	Dose Level
1	Male and female	25	Vehicle control	0 (Control)
2	Male and female	25	Test article	Low
3	Male and female	25	Test article	Middle
4	Male and female	25	Test article	High
5	Male and female	25	Positive control[c]	Model-specific[c]

[a]Both sexes included unless agent is being developed for a sex-specific disease endpoint.
[b]Minimum number to satisfy regulatory requirements.
[c]Positive control article and dose level are model-specific (see text).

Experimental Animals: viral antibody-free rasH2 mice or TSG-p53$^{(+/-)}$ mice obtained from an approved commercial supplier. Mice are received from the supplier at 5–6 weeks of age.

Animal Genotyping: GLP-compliant genotyping report confirming the presence of the relevant molecular alteration in each study animal is provided by the animal supplier.

Quarantine: minimum of 1 week prior to initiation of test or control article administration.

Diet and Drinking Water: certified laboratory animal chow from an approved commercial supplier is provided ad libitum to all animals. City drinking water is provided ad libitum to all animals. Analytical records for diet and drinking water are maintained with the study records.

Test Article: administered by a route that simulates human exposure [most commonly oral (gavage or diet), inhalation (nose-only or whole body), or topical (direct application to skin)].

Negative Control Article: vehicle control animals in gavage or topical administration studies receive a comparable volume of vehicle without test article. Control animals in inhalation studies are most commonly exposed to filtered air.

Positive Control Article: positive control article and dose are determined on the basis of the specific genetically engineered animal model being used (see text).

Duration of Exposure: 6 months.

In-Life Observations: survival, clinical observations, physical observations (including palpation for masses), body weight, food consumption (mandatory for diet studies; optional for others), clinical pathology (optional).

Postmortem Observations: gross pathology at necropsy (complete necropsy with tissue collection), organ weights, histopathologic evaluation of tissues (all gross lesions identified at necropsy + approximately 45–50 tissues per animal).

been formulated for a 6-month study with either *ras*H2 mice [36,63] or hemizygous p53 knockout mice [12,16]. Although this protocol summary is designed to address current regulatory requirements for carcinogenicity bioassays in genetically engineered mice, the study design in Table 12.2 is necessarily generic, and will require customization to address relevant scientific and regulatory considerations for each agent being evaluated for possible carcinogenicity.

Key Differences in the Design of Carcinogenicity Studies in Standard-Bred and Genetically Engineered Mice

The design and conduct of carcinogenicity bioassays in transgenic and knockout animals demonstrate many similarities to the performance of 2-year carcinogenicity bioassays in standard-bred rodents. However, carcinogenicity bioassays in genetically engineered mice do demonstrate several important differences from the 2-year bioassay. Key differences in study design are discussed in the following subsections.

Study Duration

Carcinogenicity evaluations in genetically engineered animals generally involve an exposure period of 6 months, versus exposure periods of 18–24 months for carcinogenicity evaluations in standard-bred mice. The shorter duration of carcinogenicity studies in genetically engineered mice reflects the shorter latency of neoplastic development and provides substantial benefits in terms of both calendar time and study cost.

The primary determinant of the duration of carcinogenicity evaluations in transgenic or knockout mice is the kinetics of spontaneous and chemically induced oncogenesis in the animal model being used in the bioassay. As indicated above, most carcinogenicity studies in transgenic or knockout mice are designed for completion using an in-life period of 6 months; however, the in-life period in certain models (most commonly used for research purposes) may require longer periods of exposure. The standard protocol for carcinogenicity bioassays in *ras*H2 transgenic and hemizygous p53 knockout mice involves 26 weeks of agent exposure, followed by complete histopathologic evaluation of tissues. These protocols are used widely in safety assessments of novel drugs and natural products being submitted for FDA approval.

Group Size

Carcinogenicity studies in genetically engineered mice that are performed for regulatory submission ordinarily include group sizes of 25 mice per sex per group. This group size compares to a minimum of 50 animals per sex per group in 2-year bioassays

in standard-bred rodents; as discussed earlier in this chapter, group size in 2-year rodent bioassays is commonly increased above 50, and experimental groups in carcinogenicity bioassays in standard-bred rodents may include as many as 100 animals per sex to increase assay sensitivity.

The smaller group size in carcinogenicity studies performed in genetically engineered mice reflects the greater sensitivity of these mice to neoplastic development in response to known carcinogens and statistical considerations that permit adequate assessment of potential carcinogenic activity with this smaller number of animals. Although the acquisition costs of commercially available transgenic and knockout mice used for carcinogenicity testing are far greater than the costs of nontransgenic rodents, the smaller group sizes used in carcinogenicity studies in genetically engineered mice provide substantial decreases in study costs associated with animal husbandry and with histopathologic evaluation of tissues.

Inclusion of a Positive Control Group

A positive control group is commonly included in the design of oncogenicity studies in genetically engineered mice, but is very uncommon in the design of a 2-year carcinogenicity bioassay. The presence of a robust cancer response in the positive control group provides clear evidence of the sensitivity of the animal model to carcinogenesis over the period of agent administration. Inclusion of a positive control group is especially important in studies in which the test article is found to be without carcinogenic activity. Evidence of increased cancer incidence in animals exposed to a positive control article is necessary to demonstrate that the test animal is, in fact, sensitive to carcinogenesis within the relatively short period of exposure specified in the study protocol.

Genotyping of Study Animals

The increased sensitivity to carcinogenesis observed in strains of transgenic and knockout mice used in carcinogenicity evaluations results from a specific molecular alteration in the germ line of these animals (insertion of a transgene in *ras*H2 mice or deletion of a tumor suppressor gene in p53 knockout mice). Similar to the inclusion of a positive control group in the study design, demonstration that study animals do, in fact, demonstrate the predisposing genetic alteration is essential to the analysis of study data. This demonstration is particularly important in "negative" studies in which tumor incidences are comparable in control and test article-treated groups. Absent evidence that study animals demonstrate the predisposing genetic alteration (presence of the transgene or absence of the tumor suppressor gene), it cannot be concluded that the animals were actually at risk of neoplastic development over the relatively short (6-month) period of exposure. Restated, adequate demonstration of a negative result (lack of carcinogenicity) in a 6-month carcinogenicity bioassay in genetically engineered mice requires clear evidence that the predisposing genetic alteration was present in all study animals, and that these animals were therefore at risk of neoplasia during the study period.

Genotyping of study animals (usually by southern blot or polymerase chain reaction) is essential to confirm that each animal does, in fact, demonstrate the molecular alteration that is responsible for increased sensitivity to cancer induction. Absent this molecular alteration, the animal may be a nontransgenic littermate of the transgenic animal, and as such, may not be at risk for carcinogenesis during the 6-month period of exposure that is specified in the study protocol. Alternatively, the animal may have undergone a spontaneous mutation or genetic rearrangement that has resulted in alteration or loss of expression of the transgene. The critical importance of genotyping study animals was clearly demonstrated by the identification of a nonresponder phenotype in Tg.AC mice [60], a ras transgenic mouse strain that was studied extensively in the 1990s as a model for carcinogenicity bioassays [56]. This nonresponder phenotype occurred as the result of a rearrangement of the transgene [60] in some Tg.AC mice; lack of reproducibility of tumorigenic responses as a result of this genetic rearrangement provided the basis for a decision that the Tg.AC mouse was not an appropriate model system for carcinogenicity bioassays.

Experimental Animals

The scientific rationale supporting the use of genetically engineered mice for evaluations of agent carcinogenicity began with studies reported in 1990, in which two research groups working independently with different strains of genetically engineered mice demonstrated that cancer incidence is increased and tumor latency is decreased in mice into whose germ line the Ha-ras oncogene has been inserted [30,48]. In 1992, studies by a third group of investigators demonstrated that deletion of the p53 tumor suppressor gene from the germ line also accelerates neoplastic development [10]. These and an extensive series of follow-on studies clearly demonstrated that, in comparison to standard-bred mice, selected strains of genetically engineered (transgenic and knockout) mice demonstrate both increased incidences of spontaneous tumors and accelerated neoplastic responses to a broad range of chemical carcinogens. The predisposition to neoplastic development in genetically engineered mice has been applied to the process of carcinogen testing, with the goal of decreasing the time and costs of such bioassays, while potentially increasing assay sensitivity.

rasH2 Transgenic Mice

The scientific rationale underlying the use of ras transgenics for carcinogenicity testing is based on the frequent presence of activated ras genes in human cancers and well-documented alterations in ras signaling that appear to underlie aberrant growth in neoplasms [30]. A large number of genetically engineered mouse strains that carry ras genes have been developed; many of these models were developed in university laboratories and have been used primarily as research tools in studies of molecular mechanisms of carcinogenesis.

Over the past 20 years, the overwhelming majority of oncogenicity studies performed using a ras transgenic strain of mouse have been performed using the rasH2 model. The rasH2 mouse was developed by Saitoh et al. [48] at the Central Institute for Experimental Animals (CIEA) in Japan, and is widely used for carcinogenicity testing of both genotoxic and nongenotoxic agents. This transgenic mouse carries five to six copies of the human c-Ha-ras gene (with its own promoter) in the germ line; mutation of the transgene is not required for increased sensitivity to carcinogenic insult. As a result of the integration of multiple copies of a functional transgene, the Ha-ras gene product, p21, is present in rasH2 mice at 2 to 3 times the levels that are measured in nontransgenic mice of the same background [63].

rasH2 mice used for carcinogen testing are generated by crossing a transgenic male (on a C57BL/6J background) with a nontransgenic BALB/c female [63]. Bioassays are performed using transgenic F1 animals from this cross; nontransgenic littermates have been used in some studies to confirm the increased sensitivity of the transgenic mouse to neoplastic development, and to investigate the role of the c-Ha-ras transgene in increasing susceptibility to spontaneous and agent-induced carcinogenesis [53].

After 6 months on test, spontaneous tumors in untreated rasH2 mice have been reported in several tissues [37,52], including the lung (adenoma and adenocarcinoma; ~7% incidence); hematopoietic system and vasculature (lymphoma and hemangiosarcoma; 4–8% incidence); forestomach (papilloma and squamous cell carcinoma; 2–3% incidence); and skin and subcutis (papilloma and sarcoma, ~1% incidence). At 20 months, the most common neoplasms in untreated rasH2 mice are seen in the vasculature (hemangiomas and hemangiosarcomas; 30% incidence) and lung (adenomas and adenocarcinomas; 20% incidence) [63]. The incidence of spontaneous tumors in nontransgenic littermates of rasH2 mice is low [52,63].

*ras*H2 mice are susceptible to the induction of malignancies in several sites (notably the lung, forestomach, skin, and hematopoietic system) by a broad range of genotoxic carcinogens [31,52,63]. Data from validation studies performed by a consortium of Japanese pharmaceutical companies demonstrated that the *ras*H2 mouse can identify carcinogens that induce neoplasms by either genotoxic or nongenotoxic mechanisms [52]. Tumors were seen in a wide range of sites in *ras*H2 mice in response to carcinogen treatment, but the sites of tumor induction in *ras*H2 mice were not necessarily the same as seen in studies with the same test agents in B6C3F1 mice and other standard-bred mouse strains used for carcinogenicity evaluations [63]. *ras*H2 mice appear to demonstrate a predilection for tumorigenesis in the lung, forestomach, and vasculature (spleen), and these organ sites have been suggested as likely sites of tumorigenesis in response to carcinogenic agents [63].

Carcinogenicity bioassays in the *ras*H2 mouse can be performed using the standard protocol provided in Table 12.2, followed by complete histopathologic evaluation of tissues. The most common positive control article used in studies in this transgenic mouse model is the synthetic nitrosamide carcinogen, *N*-methyl-*N*-nitrosourea (MNU). MNU is a potent direct-acting genotoxic carcinogen that induces tumors in numerous sites in both standard-bred and transgenic animals; the agent is commonly used as a model carcinogen for organ-specific carcinogenesis and cancer chemoprevention studies in animal models for cancer of the breast, prostate, urinary bladder, colon, and skin, among other tissues [32,33].

When used as a positive control article, MNU is administered as a single intraperitoneal injection at a dose of 75 mg/kg body weight [52,63]; effective systemic delivery of this agent can also be achieved by intravenous or subcutaneous injection. Administration of MNU to *ras*H2 mice induces a >75% incidence of neoplasms in the hematopoietic system (malignant lymphoma), forestomach (papilloma and squamous cell carcinoma), and skin (papilloma); lower incidences of tumors are observed in several other sites [31,52,63].

An important consideration with the use of MNU as a positive control article is its stability in solution; MNU is light sensitive and degrades rapidly in solutions that have a neutral or basic pH. As a result, preparation of MNU solutions should be performed in subdued light, and must include protection of the dosing formulation from visible light through the use of amber glass or foil-wrapped glassware. In addition, the pH of the dosing formulation should be <5.0; this can be performed by adding acidified saline to crystalline MNU prior to the addition of sterile physiologic saline. To ensure their integrity, MNU solutions should be used within 1 h after the completion of dose formulation.

Hemizygous p53 Knockout Mice

Loss or inactivation of the p53 tumor suppressor gene is the most common genetic alteration in human cancers. p53 is mutated in more than 50% of sporadic (nonfamilial) human cancers; in cancers where p53 is not mutated, its function is often inactivated or reduced [50]. In humans, germline transmission of a mutated p53 allele causes Li-Fraumeni syndrome, a syndrome characterized by increased cancer risk and the early onset of neoplasms in any of several sites [42].

The inverse relationship between p53 function and cancer risk in humans appears to be accurately recapitulated in mice. Deletion of one allele of the p53 tumor suppressor gene from the germline predisposes mice to spontaneous neoplastic development [10,16], and also increases animal sensitivity to cancer induction by chemical carcinogens [16]. Spontaneous tumorigenesis is further accelerated in mice in which both alleles of the p53 gene have been deleted [10,16]. The importance of p53 function in the regulation of neoplastic development in humans, and its apparent parallel role in mice, suggest that mice with defective p53 function may provide useful tools for the rapid identification of carcinogens.

Genetically engineered mice in which one p53 allele has been deleted from the germline (p53$^{(+/-)}$ mice) are commonly referred to as hemizygous (or heterozygous) p53 knockout mice. In 1992, Donehower et al. at Baylor University reported the development of a line of hemizygous p53 knockout mice on a mixed genetic background (75% C57BL/6, 25% 129/Sv). Since this initial report, this line of p53$^{(+/-)}$ mice has been backcrossed with C57BL/6 mice over multiple generations. As a result of this backcrossing, the genetic background of commercially available mice hemizygous p53 knockout mice of this lineage can be considered to be C57BL/6.

In comparison to nongenetically engineered control mice (with intact p53 function) of the same genetic background, hemizygous p53 knockout mice demonstrate increased incidences of spontaneous neoplasms, primarily malignant lymphoma [10]. Importantly, the incidence of spontaneous tumors in hemizygous p53 knockout mice at 6 months is relatively low (<5%), but increases with age beyond 6 months. These animals also develop tumors rapidly in response to genotoxic carcinogens [12,16].

On the basis of the demonstrated sensitivity of p53$^{(+/-)}$ mice to carcinogenesis, and the results of a multilaboratory validation effort that demonstrated the value of this animal model in identifying carcinogenic agents [51], p53$^{(+/-)}$ mice are accepted by the FDA as a suitable model for the identification of genotoxic carcinogens. 6-month oncogenicity studies in p53$^{(+/-)}$ mice are often required by the FDA prior to the initiation of Phase I clinical trials for any nononcology agent that demonstrates a positive or equivocal result in a genetic toxicology assay (most commonly the mouse lymphoma assay). The p53$^{(+/-)}$ mouse is also accepted by European regulatory agencies for the identification of nongenotoxic carcinogens [13].

One quarter of the offspring generated through crosses of male p53$^{(+/-)}$ mice with female p53$^{(+/-)}$ mice have a nullizygous (or homozygous null) phenotype (p53$^{(-/-)}$); in these animals, both alleles of p53 are deleted from the germline. The nullizygous p53 knockout demonstrates even greater sensitivity to neoplastic development than does the hemizygous p53 knockout [10]. For this reason, the nullizygous p53 knockout mouse has been used extensively in mechanistic studies of the role of p53 in cancer. However, the very short latency and high incidence of spontaneous tumors in the nullizygous mouse make it relatively insensitive for use in carcinogen identification, as tumors that may be induced by a test agent are often impossible to differentiate from those that occur spontaneously. For this reason, carcinogenicity testing in p53 knockout mice is performed almost exclusively in the hemizygous p53 knockout (p53$^{(+/-)}$) animal model.

It should be noted that researchers at the Center for Cancer Research at MIT independently developed a p53-deficient mouse that has been used extensively as a model for studies of p53 function [24]. Although this p53-deficient model has been used in numerous academic laboratories, it has not undergone extensive testing and validation for possible use as a model system for carcinogenicity evaluations. As a result, the Donehower p53 knockout mouse (p53$^{(+/-)}$) that is currently sold by Taconic is the p53 knockout model of choice for carcinogenicity testing.

Carcinogenicity bioassays in the p53$^{(+/-)}$ mouse are performed using the standard protocol provided in Table 12.2. The test article can be administered by any of several routes [gavage, dosed feed, dosed water, inhalation, topical application, or whole-body exposure (eg, ionizing or nonionizing radiation)] that simulate the anticipated route of human exposure. Animals are exposed to the test article daily for 6 months, followed by necropsy and complete histopathologic evaluation of tissues from all study animals.

The positive control article used in most studies in this model system is *p*-cresidine (400 mg/kg/day, administered by gavage). Tumors induced in p53$^{(+/-)}$ mice by *p*-cresidine are most commonly seen in the urinary bladder, ureter, and kidney [21]; tumors in the liver have also been reported. As an alternative to *p*-cresidine, MNU (75 mg/kg) has been used as a positive control article; when administered to p53$^{(+/-)}$ mice, MNU induces a >75% incidence of malignant lymphoma and lower incidences of cancers in several regions of the intestinal tract [40].

Experimental Groups

As indicated in Table 12.2, a 6-month carcinogenicity bioassay in genetically engineered mice generally includes a minimum of five experimental groups (one vehicle or sham control group, three treatment groups that receive graded doses of the test agent, and a positive control group that receives exposure to a known carcinogen).

The inclusion of a positive control group differs from the design used in chronic bioassays in standard-bred rats, and is included to demonstrate the sensitivity of the test system to carcinogenic insult. Absent a statistically significant response in the positive control group, the sensitivity of the experimental design to detect a true carcinogen must be questioned. The positive control material used in these studies varies with animal strain; specific positive control articles used in specific mouse models were discussed in the description of each model.

Group Size

For several years following the initial regulatory acceptance of carcinogenicity studies in genetically engineered mouse models, studies were commonly performed using 15 mice per sex per group. More recently, a group size of 25 mice per sex per group has become standard; this larger group size improves the statistical power of the assay to detect a weak effect and thereby increases its sensitivity.

Dose Levels of Test Agent

As discussed previously, selection of appropriate dose levels of the test article for carcinogenicity bioassays is a complex process, and numerous approaches have been proposed. As a general rule, dose levels of a test article for use in a carcinogenicity bioassay in genetically engineered mice are selected on the basis of a preliminary subchronic toxicity study (generally 28 or 90 days in duration) that is performed in the parental (nontransgenic) strain of the mouse to be used in the carcinogenicity study.

As is the case with 2-year bioassays in standard-bred animals, the most important single criterion for proper study design is that the dose levels selected for use should maximize the likelihood of inducing a positive response. As such, dose levels should be as high as possible, and should induce at least some degree of toxicity (generally a modest suppression of body weight gain) in the high-dose group. The high dose of the test article should not induce early deaths or suppress body weight to the extent that it may interfere with tumorigenesis.

In general, the high dose used in carcinogenicity bioassays is MTD, as determined in preliminary studies performed in the parental (nongenetically modified) strain of the transgenic or knockout animal that will be used in the carcinogenicity bioassay. The FDA Redbook specifically mandates that the MTD be used as the high dose in carcinogenicity bioassays [59]; by contrast, ICH guidelines also accept the selection of the high dose as a large multiple (generally >100×) of the maximum anticipated human dose [23]. Issues associated with the use of the MTD as the high dose in carcinogenicity bioassays, and possible alternative strategies for selection of the high dose, were discussed previously.

Ideally, the high dose of the test article will induce at least some evidence of toxicity in treated animals, thereby demonstrating that this dose approximates the maximum dose that can be administered. However, the high dose should not induce mortality that is unrelated to agent carcinogenicity; survival curves in treated groups should be comparable to those in sex-matched vehicle controls throughout the study. Furthermore, any suppression of body-weight gain should not exceed 10% in comparison to sex-matched vehicle controls, as greater alterations in body weight may impact tumor response.

The middle and low doses of the test article are generally selected as fractions of the high doses. The doses of the test agent should induce either no overt toxicity or very limited toxicity, and should provide the opportunity to characterize dose–response relationships for any observed tumors. The low dose is often selected as a multiple of the presumed human dose, while the middle dose is selected to be logarithmically between the low and high doses.

GENERAL EXPERIMENTAL PROCEDURES FOR THE CONDUCT OF CARCINOGENICITY BIOASSAYS

The procedures outlined below for the conduct of carcinogenicity bioassays are generic, but identify major technical components of the study designs. Procedures used to conduct carcinogenicity bioassays in different laboratories will necessarily be customized to comply with (1) standard operating procedures (SOPs) that have been established in the performing laboratory, (2) regulatory requirements of the agency or agencies to which the study data are intended for submission, and (3) sponsor requirements.

Laboratory Animal Receipt and Quarantine

Animals are purchased from commercial colonies that are viral antibody-free. At the time of animal receipt, the entire shipment is inspected by the study veterinarian to determine its suitability for use in the study. On the basis of this inspection, a decision is made concerning

the suitability of the entire animal shipment; acceptable shipments are then placed into quarantine.

The viral antibody status of the specific barrier facility from which animals are sourced is provided by the animal vendor, and is generally confirmed independently by the performing laboratory through analysis of blood samples collected from sentinel animals during quarantine. In addition to the collection of blood samples for viral antibody analysis, blood samples for clinical pathology are collected and gross necropsies are performed on selected sentinel animals (generally a minimum of five animals per sex per study) to identify possible evidence of microbial, parasitic, or other infestation. Gross pathology and clinical pathology data are evaluated to identify any pattern of findings that suggest organ dysfunction, disease, or other health issues in the colony that could interfere with the conduct of the study or the interpretation of study data.

Several days prior to the initiation of dosing, each animal in the shipment is weighed and undergoes a hand-held clinical and physical examination to determine its suitability for use as a test animal. The study veterinarian reviews the sentinel animal data and the results of clinical and physical observations performed during the quarantine period. On the basis of this review, a decision is made concerning the suitability of the entire shipment of animals for use in the study, as well as the suitability of individual animals as a study subject. Assuming that the shipment of animals meets laboratory requirements for viral antibody status and overall health, the shipment is released from quarantine.

After release from quarantine, animals are assorted into experimental groups; most commonly, animals are assigned to experimental groups on the basis of body weight, with a goal of establishing comparable mean body weights in all study groups. Animals whose physical examination data suggested possible abnormalities are excluded from the randomization process, and are not used as study animals. In addition, animals whose body weight deviates by more than 20% from group mean body weights are generally not entered into the study.

Animal Age

In most carcinogenicity bioassays, test agent administration is initiated when rodents are 6–8 weeks of age (young adults). To support this study schedule, animals are approximately 5–7 weeks of age at the time of receipt, and are held in quarantine for 1 to 2 weeks prior to the start of test agent administration.

In some study designs, exposure to the test agent includes the perinatal period; in these studies, exposure to the test article begins in utero. To support this study design, adult male and female rodents from a viral antibody-free barrier facility are received from the vendor, held in quarantine for 1 to 2 weeks, and mated in the performing laboratory. As an alternative, timed-pregnant females can be obtained from the vendor, but this approach limits the quarantine period to no more than approximately 3 days, depending on dosing schedule.

In chronic studies that include perinatal exposure, the test article is most commonly administered to pregnant dams beginning on gestation day (GD) 6. Pregnant dams are dosed from GD 6 throughout gestation and parturition, and continuing until pups are weaned at 21–28 days of age. At postnatal day 4, litters are culled to equivalent sizes (usually four pups per litter) and numbers of male and female pups (ideally, two per sex). Between parturition and weaning, exposure of juvenile rodents to the test agent is via milk transmission; direct administration of the test agent to pups begins at the time of weaning. At weaning, dams are removed from the study.

Sentinel Animals

As discussed above, evaluations of the health status of sentinel animals during the quarantine period are important elements of the overall assessment of the health of study animals. After the dosing period has been initiated, sentinel animals (generally selected from animals that have been randomized out of the study) are maintained in the animal room in which the study is housed, and are used to monitor the overall health status of the animal colony. At selected intervals during the dosing period (most commonly at 6-month intervals), cohorts of five sentinel animals per sex are bled for clinical pathology and serology evaluations, and undergo a complete gross necropsy to identify any pattern of gross lesions that could suggest infection or other disease.

Animal Housing

Unless otherwise specified by the sponsor, animals in most carcinogenicity studies are housed individually; either in suspended wire mesh cages made of stainless steel or in suspended shoebox (solid bottom) cages made of polycarbonate. Absorbent cage boards or papers are placed underneath suspended stainless-steel cages to contain liquid and solid waste; certified hardwood bedding is used in shoebox cages to absorb wastes. Cages are cleaned and sanitized on a schedule that is determined by the study veterinarian and facility SOPs, and which is designed to optimize animal health.

Some sponsors prefer that study animals be group-housed whenever possible, with the goal of optimizing animal welfare by permitting socialization. Although group housing of study animals may provide animal welfare benefits in some cases, housing animals in groups has a number of important disadvantages; these are particularly important in male mice. First, group housing of animals introduces the possibility of cannibalism of tissues from animals that die during the study; such cannibalism cannot occur if animals are singly housed. Although loss of study data as a result of cannibalism often cannot be avoided completely in a 2-year study, a proactive policy of euthanasia in extremis may reduce the number of animals that die between observation periods, and are therefore subject to possible cannibalism by cage mates.

An often more challenging problem in group-housing animals involves fighting among male mice. Group-housed male mice will commonly establish a hierarchy within the cage, and the dominant male may inflict physical injury on weaker males and/or prevent them from eating. For this reason, it is considered inadvisable to group-house male mice, even in preclinical programs in which female mice and both sexes of rats are group-housed.

Diet and Drinking Water

With the exception of fasts prior to scheduled bleeds for clinical pathology, all animals are permitted free access to a certified chow diet at all times during the study. Certified rodent diets are available through several commercial vendors; each lot of certified diet is analyzed to ensure that it contains no contaminants at levels that could interfere with the study. Analytical data from each lot of diet used in the study are maintained with the study records.

It should be noted that feeding animals on a restricted basis, rather than permitting ad libitum access to diet, has been recommended by some investigators as an approach to improve overall animal health, reduce intercurrent mortality during chronic bioassays, and reduce the incidence of spontaneous tumors. Although the effects of food restriction regimens on animal survival, body weight, and tumorigenesis are clear, this approach to study conduct is highly labor intensive, and is technically possible only in animals that are individually housed. Furthermore, the NTP has concluded that dietary restriction *decreases* the sensitivity of rodent carcinogenicity bioassays [1]. For these reasons, the conduct of carcinogenesis bioassays using dietary restriction protocols has not been adopted by most laboratories.

Animals are permitted free access to drinking water throughout the study. In most cases, coarse-filtered city water is provided; in some cases, water that has undergone additional purification by reverse-osmosis filtration or distillation may be used. The use of acidified water is specifically not recommended for chronic bioassays. Drinking water is most commonly provided to study animals using automatic watering systems, but may also be provided by water bottles.

Water samples are collected from the animal room on a regular schedule throughout the study, and are analyzed for both microbial contamination and possible chemical contamination. The records of microbial and chemical analyses of water samples are maintained with the study records.

Administration of Test and Control Articles

Test and control articles are administered to study animals by a route that simulates the expected route of human exposure. The most common routes of compound administration in carcinogenicity bioassays include oral administration by gavage or dietary admixture, topical application, and inhalation. In carcinogenicity bioassays in standard-bred rodents, test and control articles are most commonly administered for 24 months; some murine carcinogenicity bioassays are performed using an exposure period of 18 months. Carcinogenicity bioassays in either rasH2 or p53 knockout mice involve an exposure period of 6 months.

Carcinogenicity bioassays of occupational chemicals that are designed to simulate workplace exposures may involve administration of test and control articles for 5 days per week. By contrast, carcinogenesis bioassays of therapeutic agents are commonly performed using daily exposures, 7 days per week.

The selection of a vehicle for gavage studies is primarily dependent on agent solubility. Agents that are lipid soluble are administered in a vehicle of corn oil, trioctanoin, or other lipid-based liquid. Water-soluble test agents are commonly administered in a vehicle of distilled or other purified water. Insoluble test agents are most often administered as a suspension in a vehicle of aqueous carboxymethylcellulose (CMC). Dosing is performed on a mg/kg basis; within each dose group, the concentration of test agent in the dosing formulation is held constant. Using this approach, the volume of dosing formulation that is administered to each study animal is linearly related to body weight. Gavage dosing volumes in rats are ideally 5 mL/kg/day or less, and should not exceed 10 mL/kg/day; dosing volumes in mice should not exceed 1 mL/kg/day. Assuming adequate solubility of the test agent in the vehicle selected for use, use of a smaller dosing volume is desirable. Animals in the vehicle control group in each species receive a comparable volume of vehicle only by the same route and schedule by which the test agent is administered.

Assuming that the test agent is stable under ambient animal room conditions, dietary admixtures can be prepared by direct addition of the test agent to the diet. If dose levels being tested are low, diet homogeneity may be improved by the preparation of a premix of the test agent in a small quantity of sucrose or other carrier (generally ≤10 g/kg diet), followed by blending of the premix

into the test diet. The use of sucrose or other carrier may also be required in cases where the taste of the test agent in a diet may result in food aversion in test animals. If a carrier is used in diet formulation, the same quantity of carrier (without test agent) is added to diets administered to animals in the control groups.

The selection of vehicles for carcinogenicity bioassays involving topical administration of the test agent may be more complex, in consideration of issues such as dermal penetration of the dosing formulation and the possibility of oral ingestion of the test substance by rodents as a result of grooming. In the best case, topical application studies can be performed using a vehicle such as acetone that will rapidly carry lipid-soluble materials through the stratum corneum and into the epithelium, thereby limiting the quantity of unabsorbed material on the skin surface. If solubility or stability issues prevent the use of a vehicle that will result in rapid absorption of the test agent, efficient topical delivery may require that (1) after application, the dosing formulation be rubbed into a shaved area of the dorsal surface of the skin with a gloved finger (eg, with agents being administered in a cream or gel vehicle); or (2) an occlusive dressing be applied to the dosing site for several hours each day after compound administration. The use of an occlusive dressing is followed by washing unabsorbed material from the skin surface after removal of the dressing at the end of the exposure period. Both approaches can substantially increase the absorption of a topical formulation, while reducing the likelihood of oral exposure to the test agent as a result of animal grooming behavior.

Analytical Chemistry Support

GLP require that study records include complete documentation of the identity, strength, purity, and composition of test agents being used in the study. The identity of the bulk test agent is generally provided in a certificate of analysis provided by the sponsor; the identity of the test agent is independently confirmed by the performing laboratory. The stability of both bulk test agent and dosing formulations containing the test agent must be demonstrated under storage conditions comparable to those that will be used during the study. In addition, documentation of the homogeneity of dosing formulations is required, as is a regular schedule of analyses to confirm the concentration of dosing formulations. Characterization of vehicles used in the study is also required by regulatory agencies.

The schedule for the preparation of dosing formulations or test diets is determined by the stability of these formulations under the conditions to be used in the study. The concentration of the test agent in representative dosing formulations must be confirmed to demonstrate that the dose levels specified in the protocol are actually being delivered. Although schedules for analytical verification of dose formulation concentration will vary, a common approach is to verify dose concentrations weekly for the first 3 months of the study and monthly thereafter. A less labor-intensive and less costly approach is to verify dose formulation concentrations monthly for the first 3 months of the study and quarterly thereafter. These schedules may be modified in consideration of both the stability of dosing formulations and the frequency of dose formulation preparation.

In-Life Toxicology Endpoint Evaluations

Although the most critical body of study data generated in carcinogenicity bioassays comes from the histopathologic evaluation of tissues, a series of in-life toxicology evaluations is commonly included in the study design.

Clinical Observations

Mortality/Moribundity Observations

Observations to identify dead or moribund study animals are performed twice daily (am and pm) throughout the quarantine and dosing periods. Mortality/moribundity observations include (1) the identification and removal of intercurrent deaths for necropsy; and (2) the identification of moribund animals or other animals that should be considered for removal from the study and euthanasia in extremis. Identification of moribund animals and other animals that appear unlikely to survive until the next observation period is appropriate in terms of animal welfare, and can optimize study data by reducing the possible loss of tissues from intercurrent deaths as a result of cannibalism (in group-housed animals) or autolysis. The decision to euthanize moribund animals is made by the Study Director or designate (commonly the Study Veterinarian or the Study Pathologist).

Cage-Side Clinical Observations

Cage-side clinical observations are performed daily, at approximately 1 h after dosing. These observations are performed to identify any evidence of agent toxicity that is present shortly after dosing, and will identify study animals that should be closely monitored for possible adverse effects of agent exposure.

Handheld Clinical and Physical Examinations

Handheld examinations are performed weekly; in some study designs, these observations are performed weekly for the first 3 or 6 months of the study, and monthly thereafter. These observations provide the opportunity to perform a detailed evaluation of the clinical health of each study animal, and are particularly valuable in later months of the study when palpation for masses may identify tumors.

Body Weight

In most studies, body-weight measurements are performed weekly throughout the experimental period; in some studies, collection of body-weight data is performed weekly for the first 3 or 6 months of the dosing period, and monthly thereafter. Body-weight data are essential not only as a means to evaluate the systemic toxicity of a test agent, but also to support the accurate calculation of doses of the test agent that are delivered on a mg/kg basis.

Food Consumption

Food consumption is commonly performed using the same schedule as collection of body weights. Food consumption is a particularly important parameter in studies involving administration of the test agent by dietary admixture, as it permits a calculation of actual agent exposure levels. Food consumption data can also be important in understanding the mechanisms responsible for body weight changes and mortality in animals receiving the test agent by gavage, by topical application, or by inhalation. However, this endpoint is not always included in the design of studies that do not involve dietary administration of the test agent.

Clinical Pathology

Although clinical pathology evaluations are sometimes included to identify possible late-appearing toxicities, it is expected that a comprehensive battery of clinical pathology evaluations will have been performed as part of subchronic (generally 90-day) toxicity studies that were completed prior to the start of a chronic carcinogenicity study. On this basis, and in consideration of the fact that clinical pathology evaluations are considered unlikely to provide mechanistic or other insights into the carcinogenicity of a test agent, these evaluations are not generally considered to be essential to interpreting the results of the 2-year carcinogenicity bioassay. However, clinical pathology data can be used to provide evidence of agent toxicity; as such, alterations in clinical pathology parameters can be used to support the validity of dose selection for the study. If included in the design of murine toxicity studies, clinical pathology evaluations are most commonly performed in samples collected from satellite animals designated for clinical pathology studies only. Blood samples for clinical pathology evaluations can generally be collected from rats in the main study.

Pharmacokinetics

The situation with pharmacokinetics evaluations in the 2-year bioassay is directly comparable to that of clinical pathology. In most cases, detailed pharmacokinetics studies will have been performed as part of earlier stages of test agent development. Absent a compelling reason (such as potent induction of drug-metabolizing enzymes) to include these evaluations in the chronic bioassay, pharmacokinetics studies are not generally included. However, should pharmacokinetics endpoints be included in the study design, the number of timed bleeds required for a pharmacokinetic evaluation may mandate the inclusion of satellite rats and mice in the study design.

Necropsy, Gross Pathology, and Microscopic Pathology

All study animals, whether dying during the dosing period, euthanized in extremis, or surviving until the scheduled terminal necropsy, undergo a complete necropsy with tissue collection. Animals found dead during the study are necropsied as soon as possible after they are discovered. Study animals that are euthanized in extremis and animals surviving until the terminal necropsy are necropsied immediately after euthanasia.

The necropsy procedure includes examination of the external surface of the body, all orifices, the cranial, thoracic, and abdominal cavities, and their contents. Gross lesions are identified by the prosector, and all gross lesions and approximately 50 additional tissues are collected from all study animals. A representative list of tissues (from the FDA Redbook [59]) designated for collection from study animals in carcinogenicity bioassays is provided in Table 12.3.

After completion of the necropsy, the study pathologist confirms gross lesions that were identified by the prosector and reviews protocol-specified tissues to ensure they were collected appropriately. Most tissues collected at the terminal necropsy are fixed in 10% neutral buffered formalin. As required by the study protocol, specialized fixatives may be used for selected tissues (eg, Davidson's fixative for the eyes and Bouin's solution for the testes).

Following fixation, tissues are processed by routine histologic methods, embedded in paraffin, cut at 5 µm, and stained with hematoxylin and eosin for histopathologic evaluation. In specialized cases, other histologic techniques (eg, embedding in plastic, thin sectioning for electron microscopy) may be included in the study design. However, these specialized approaches are not included in standard study designs, and are performed only if in-life observations or other toxicology data suggest that specialized histopathologic evaluations may be required.

The most important endpoint evaluation in a carcinogenicity bioassay is the site-specific incidence of benign and malignant tumors; total incidences of benign and malignant tumors are generally considered to be less informative. Tumor incidences are determined through the microscopic evaluation of all gross lesions identified at necropsy, as well as the list of tissues that was specified in the study protocol. Currently, regulatory agencies commonly require that all tissues from all study animals be evaluated by the study pathologist. This approach to pathology differs from that used previously, in which all tissues were evaluated only from animals in the high-dose and vehicle-control groups; in this earlier approach, evaluations of tissues from animals in intermediate dose groups were limited to identified target tissues only.

Statistical Analysis

The statistical analysis of tumor incidence data is a critical element of the interpretation of the results of carcinogenicity bioassays. Unfortunately, the complexity of the statistical analyses required, when considered with

TABLE 12.3 Tissues Designated for Histopathologic Evaluation in Carcinogenicity Bioassays in Standard-Bred Rodents and Genetically Engineered Mice

Adrenals	Nasal Turbinates
Aorta	Ovaries and fallopian tubes
Bone (femur)	Pancreas
Bone marrow (sternum)	Pituitary
Brain (evaluate ≥3 levels)	Prostate
Cecum	Rectum
Colon	Salivary gland
Corpus and cervix uteri	Sciatic nerve
Duodenum	Seminal vesicle (if present)
Epididymides	Skeletal muscle
Esophagus	Skin
Eyes	Spinal cord (cervical, midthoracic, lumbar)
Gall bladder (mice only)	Spleen
Harderian gland	Stomach
Heart	Testes
Ileum	Thymus (if present)
Jejunum	Thyroid/parathyroid
Kidneys	Trachea
Liver	Urinary bladder
Lung (with main-stem bronchi)	Vagina
Lymph node (related to route of administration)	Zymbal's gland
Lymph node (distant)	All gross lesions
Mammary glands	

Tissue list for animals in the positive control group (bioassays in genetically engineered mice only) may be limited to known target tissues for the positive control article.
Source: FDA Redbook (9).

the number of different statistical approaches that may be used to evaluate carcinogenicity data, suggest that a comprehensive analysis and discussion of these analyses is beyond the scope of the current chapter.

Numerous approaches to the statistical analysis of carcinogenicity data have been proposed (eg, see Refs. [4,38,55]), and the Center for Drug Evaluation and Research at the FDA has issued a draft guidance document in which statistical approaches to the analysis and interpretation of carcinogenicity data are discussed [58]. However, there is relatively little overall consensus on what constitutes the "optimal" approach to statistical analysis of tumor data from carcinogenesis bioassays, and no single approach to the analysis of these data has received broad support from the scientific community. As an example, a white paper in which members of the Society of Toxicologic Pathology [38] discussed approaches to statistical analysis of carcinogenicity data generated seven commentaries in which alternate approaches to this analysis were proposed [39].

In consideration of the complexity of the statistical analysis of carcinogenicity data, it is strongly recommended that the practicing toxicologist enlist the support of a statistician who is experienced in the analyses of such data.

References

[1] Abdo KM, Kari FW. The sensitivity of the NTP bioassay for carcinogen hazard evaluation can be modulated by dietary restriction. Exp Toxicol Pathol 1996;48:129–37.

[2] Allen BC, Crump KS, Shipp AM. Correlation between carcinogenic potency of chemicals in animals and humans. Risk Anal 1988;8:531–44.

[3] Baldrick P, Reeve L. Carcinogenicity evaluation: comparison of tumor data from dual control groups in the CD-1 mouse. Toxicol Pathol 2007;35:562–9.

[4] Bickis M, Krewski D. Statistical issues in the analysis of the long-term carcinogenicity bioassay in small rodents: an empirical evaluation of statistical decision rules. Fund Appl Toxicol 1989;12:202–21.

[5] Boorman GA, McCormick DL, Findlay JC, Hailey JR, Gauger JR, Johnson TR, et al. Chronic toxicity/oncogenicity evaluation of 60Hz (power frequency) magnetic fields in F344/N rats. Toxicol Pathol 1999;27:267–78.

[6] Carlus M, Elies L, Fouque MC, Maliver P, Schorsch F. Historical control data of neoplastic lesions in the Wistar Hannover rat among eight 2-year carcinogenicity studies. Exp Toxicol Pathol 2011;65:243–53.

[7] Cohen SM. Alternative models for carcinogenicity testing: weight of evidence evaluations across models. Toxicol Pathol 2001;29(Suppl.):183–90.

[8] Cohen SM. Human carcinogenic risk evaluation: an alternative approach to the 2-year rodent bioassay. Toxicol Sci 2004;80:225–9.

[9] Dinse GE, Peddada SD, Harris SF, Elmore SA. Comparison of NTP historical control tumor incidence rates in female Harlan Sprague Dawley and Fischer 344/N rats. Toxicol Pathol 2010;38:765–75.

[10] Donehower LA, Harvey M, Slagle BL, McArthur MJ, Montgomery CAJ, Butel JS, et al. Mice deficient for p53 are developmentally normal but susceptible to spontaneous tumors. Nature 1992;356:215–21.

[11] Fourcier T, McGovern T, Stavitskaya L, Kruhlak N, Jocobson-Kram D. Improving prediction of carcinogenicity to reduce, refine, and replace the use of experimental animals. J Am Assoc Lab Anim Sci 2015;54:163–9.

[12] French JE, Storer RD, Donehower LA. The nature of the heterozygous Trp53 knockout model for identification of mutagenic carcinogens. Toxicol Pathol 2001;29(Suppl.):24–9.

[13] French JE, Leblanc C, Long GG, Morton D, Storer R, Leighton J, et al. Panel discussion: alternative mouse models for carcinogenicity assessment. Toxicol Pathol 2010;38:72–5.

[14] Giknis MLA, Clifford CB. Spontaneous neoplastic lesions in the Crl:CD1 (ICR mouse in control groups from 18month to 2year studies. 2010. http://www.criver.com/files/pdfs/rms/cd1/rm_rm_r_cd1_mouse_tox_data_2010.aspx.

[15] Giknis MLA, Clifford CB. Compilation of spontaneous neoplastic lesions and survival in Crl:CD (SD) rats from control groups. 2013. http://www.criver.com/files/pdfs/rms/cd/rm_rm_r_cd_rat_tox_data_2013.aspx.

[16] Harvey M, McArthur MJ, Montgomery CAJ, Butel JS, Bradley A, Donehower LA. Spontaneous and carcinogen-induced tumorigenesis in p53-deficient mice. Nat Genet 1993;5:225–9.

[17] Haseman JK. Issues in carcinogenicity testing: dose selection. Fund Appl Toxicol 1985;5:66–78.

[18] Haseman JK, Rao GN. Effects of corn oil, time-related changes, and inter-laboratory variability on tumor occurrence in control Fischer 344 (F344/N) rats. Toxicol Pathol 1992;20:52–60.

[19] Haseman JK, Boorman GA, Huff J. Value of historical control data and other issues related to the evaluation of long-term rodent carcinogenicity studies. Toxicol Pathol 1997;25:524–7.

[20] Haseman J, Melnick R, Tomatis L, Huff J. Carcinogenesis bioassays: study duration and biological relevance. Food Chem Toxicol 2001;39:739–44.

[21] Horn TL, Cwik MJ, Morrissey RL, Kapetanovic I, Crowell JA, Booth TD, et al. Oncogenicity evaluation of resveratrol in p53$^{(+/-)}$ (p53 knockout) mice. Food Chem Toxicol 2007;45:55–63.

[22] Huff J. Long-term chemical carcinogenesis bioassays predict human cancer hazards. Issues, controversies, and uncertainties. Ann NY Acad Sci 1999;895:56–79.

[23] International Conference on Harmonisation of Technical Requirements for Registration of Pharmaceuticals for Human Use. ICH harmonised tripartite guideline S1B, testing for carcinogenicity of pharmaceuticals. 1997. Step 4 version http://www.ich.org/fileadmin/Public_Web_Site/ICH_Products/Guidelines/Safety/S1B/Step4/S1B_Guideline.pdf.

[24] Jacks T, Remington L, Williams BO, Schmitt EM, Hatachmi S, Bronson RT, et al. Tumor spectrum analysis in p53-mutant mice. Curr Biol 1994;4:1–7.

[25] Jacobson-Kram D. Cancer risk assessment approaches at the FDA/CDER: is the era of the 2-year bioassay drawing to a close? Toxicol Pathol 2010;38:169–70.

[26] Keenan KP, Laroque P, Ballam GC, Soper KA, Dixit R, Mattson BA, et al. The effects of diet, ad libitum overfeeding, and moderate dietary restriction on the rodent bioassay: the uncontrolled variable in safety assessment. Toxicol Pathol 1996;24:757–68.

[27] Kobayashi K, Inoue H. Statistical analytical methods for comparing the incidence of tumors to the historical control data. J Toxicol Sci 1994;19:1–6.

[28] Kritchevsky D. Caloric restriction and experimental carcinogenesis. Toxicol Sci 1999;52(Suppl.):13–6.

[29] Lang PL. Spontaneous neoplastic lesions in the B6C3F1/CrlBR mouse. 1989. http://www.criver.com/SiteCollectionDocuments/rm_rm_r_lesions_b6c3f1_crlbr_mouse.pdf.

[30] Leder A, Kuo A, Cardiff R, Sinn E, Leder P. v-Ha-*ras* transgene abrogates the initiation step in mouse skin tumorigenesis: effects of phorbol esters and retinoic acid. Proc Natl Acad Sci USA 1990;87:91789–9182.

[31] Machida K, Urano K, Yoshimura M, Tsutsumi H, Nomura T, Usui T. Carcinogenic comparative study on rasH2 mice produced by two breeding facilities. J Toxicol Sci 2008;33:493–501.

[32] McCormick DL, Adamowski CB, Fiks A, Moon RC. Lifetime dose-response relationships for mammary tumor induction by a single administration of N-methyl-N-nitrosourea. Cancer Res 1981;41:1690–4.

[33] McCormick DL, Rao KVN, Dooley L, Steele VE, Lubet RA, Kelloff GJ, et al. Influence of N-methyl-N-nitrosourea, testosterone, and N-(4-hydroxyphenyl)-all-trans retinamide on prostate cancer induction in Wistar-Unilever rats. Cancer Res 1998;58:3282–8.

[34] McCormick DL, Boorman GA, Findlay JC, Hailey JR, Johnson TR, Gauger JR, et al. Chronic toxicity/oncogenicity evaluation of 60 Hz (power frequency) magnetic fields in B6C3F1 mice. Toxicol Pathol 1999;27:279–85.

[35] McCormick DL, Johnson WD, Haryu TM, Bosland MC, Lubet RA, Steele VE. Null effect of dietary restriction on prostate carcinogenesis in the Wistar-Unilever rat. Nutr Cancer 2007;57:194–200.

[36] Mitsumori K, Koizumi H, Nomura T, Yamamoto S. Pathological features of spontaneous and induced tumors in transgenic mice carrying a human prototype c-Ha-ras gene used for six-month carcinogenicity studies. Toxicol Pathol 1998;26:520–31.

[37] Morton D, Alden DL, Roth AJ, Usui T. The Tg rasH2 mouse in cancer hazard identification. Toxicol Pathol 2002;30:139–46.

[38] Morton D, Elwell M, Fairweather W, Fouillet X, Keenan K, Lin K, et al. The Society of Toxicologic Pathology's recommendations on statistical analysis of rodent carcinogenicity studies. Toxicol Pathol 2002;30:415–8.

[39] Morton D, Lee PN, Fry JS, Fairweather WR, Haseman JK, Kodell RL, et al. Commentaries re: statistical methods for carcinogenicity studies. Toxicol Pathol 2002;30:403–14.

[40] Morton D, Bailey KL, Stout CL, Weaver RJ, White KA, Lorenzen MJ, et al. N-methyl-N-nitrosourea: a positive control chemical for p53+/− mouse carcinogenicity studies. Toxicol Pathol 2008;36:926–31.

[41] National Toxicology Program. Abstracts & reports on test articles. 2015. http://ntp.niehs.nih.gov/results/pubs/index.html#Abstracts-Reports-on-Test-Articles.

[42] Nichols KE, Malkin D, Garber JE, Fraumeni Jr JF, Li FP. Germ-line p53 mutations predispose to a wide spectrum of early-onset cancers. Cancer Epidemiol Biomarkers Prev 2001;10:83–7.

[43] Poteracki J, Walsh KM. Spontaneous neoplasms in control Wistar rats: a comparison of reviews. Toxicol Sci 1998;45:1–8.

[44] Rall DP. Laboratory animal tests and human cancer. Drug Metab Rev 2000;32:119–28.

[45] Rhomberg LR, Baetcke K, Blancato J, Bus J, Cohen S, Conolly R, et al. Issues in the design and interpretation of chronic toxicity and carcinogenicity studies in rodents: approaches to dose selection. Crit Rev Toxicol 2007;37:729–837.

[46] Robinson DE, MacDonald JS. Background and framework for ILSI's collaborative evaluation program on alternative models for carcinogenicity assessment. Toxicol Pathol 2001;29(Suppl.):13–9.

[47] Roth A, Kadyszewski E, Geffray B, Paulissen J, Weaver RJ. Excess mortality in 2-year rodent carcinogenicity studies. Toxicol Pathol 2007;35:1040–3.

[48] Saitoh A, Kimura M, Takahashi R, Yokoyama M, Nomura T, Izawa M, et al. Most tumors in transgenic mice with human c-Ha-ras gene contained somatically activated transgenes. Oncogene 1990;5:1195–200.

[49] Sistare FD, Morton D, Alden C, Christensen J, Keller D, Jonghe SD, et al. An analysis of pharmaceutical experience with decades of rat carcinogenicity testing: support for a proposal to modify current regulatory guidelines. Toxicol Pathol 2011;39:716–44.

[50] Spike BT, Wahl GM. p53, stem cells, and reprogramming: tumor suppression beyond guarding the genome. Genes & Cancer 2011;2:404–19.

[51] Storer RD, French JE, Haseman J, Hajian G, LeGrand EK, Long GG, et al. p53(+/−) hemizygous knockout mouse: overview of available data. Toxicol Pathol 2001;29(Suppl.):30–50.

[52] Takaoka M, Sehata S, Maejima T, Imai T, Torii M, Satoh H, et al. Interlaboratory comparison of short-term carcinogenicity studies using CB6F1-rasH2 transgenic mice. Toxicol Pathol 2003;31:191–9.

[53] Tamaoki N. The rasH2 transgenic mouse: nature of the model and mechanistic studies on tumorigenesis. Toxicol Pathol 2001;29(Suppl.):81–9.

[54] Tannenbaum A. The genesis and growth of tumors. II. Effects of caloric restriction per se. Cancer Res 1940;2:673–7.

[55] Ten Berge WF. Kaplan-Meier tumor probability as a starting point for dose-response modeling provides accurate lifetime risk estimates from rodent carcinogenicity studies. Ann NY Acad Sci 1999;895:112–24.

[56] Thompson KL, Rosenzweig BA, Sistare FD. An evaluation of the hemizygous transgenic Tg.AC mouse for carcinogenicity testing of pharmaceuticals. II. A genotypic marker that predicts tumorigenic responsiveness. Toxicol Pathol 1998;26:548–55.

[57] United States Environmental Protection Agency. Guidelines for carcinogen risk assessment. 2005. http://www2.epa.gov/risk/guidelines-carcinogen-risk-assessment.

[58] United States Food and Drug Administration. Draft guidance for industry: statistical aspects of the design, analysis, and interpretation of chronic rodent carcinogenicity studies of pharmaceuticals. 2001. http://www.fda.gov/downloads/drugs/guidancecompliance regulatoryinformation/guidances/ucm079272.pdf.

[59] United States Food and Drug Administration. Carcinogenicity studies with rodents. In: Redbook 2000: toxicological principles for the safety assessment of food ingredients. 2007. http://www.fda.gov/food/guidanceregulation/guidancedocumentsregulatoryinformation/ingredientsadditivesgraspackaging/ucm078388.htm.

[60] Weaver JL, Contrera JF, Rosenzweig BA, Thompson KL, Fausting PJ, Strong JM, et al. An evaluation of the hemizygous transgenic Tg.AC mouse for carcinogenicity testing of pharmaceuticals. I. Evidence for a confounding nonresponder phenotype. Toxicol Pathol 1998;26:532–40.

[61] Yamamoto T, Kakamu S, Nukata H, Inoue H. Mortality, body weight, food and water consumption, and clinical signs in Slc:B6C3F1 (C53BL/6 x C3H) mice utilized in chronic toxicity and carcinogenicity studies. Jikken Dobutsu 1993;42:397–404.

[62] Yamamoto S, Mitsumori K, Kodama Y, Matsunuma N, Manabe S, Okamiya H, et al. Rapid induction of more malignant tumors by various genotoxic carcinogens in transgenic mice harboring a human prototype c-Ha-ras gene than in control nontransgenic mice. Carcinogenesis 1996;17:2455–61.

[63] Yamamoto S, Urano K, Koizumi H, Wakana S, Hioki K, Mitsumori K, et al. Validation of transgenic mice carrying the human prototype c-Ha-ras gene as a bioassay model for rapid carcinogenicity testing. Environ Health Perspect 1998;106(Suppl. 1):57–69.

Current Strategies for Abuse Liability Assessment of New Chemical Entities

D.V. Gauvin, J.A. Dalton, T.J. Baird

INTRODUCTION

Guidelines for regulatory review of all new psychoactive substances for both human and veterinary approval have been disseminated by the European Monitoring Centre for Drug and Chemical Addiction [1], the committee for medicinal products for human use (CHMP) of the European Medicines Agency [2], the International Conference on Harmonisation [ICH, M3, R2] [3], and the United States Food and Drug Administration (FDA)[4]. These guidelines are intended to (1) help define the scope of the term "psychoactive substances" and (2) put in place a sound methodological and procedural basis for carrying out risk assessments in regard to health and social risks of the use of, manufacture of, and traffic in these new psychoactive substances that involve member

states of both the 1961 United Nations (UN) Single Convention on Narcotic Drugs [5] and the 1971 United Nations Convention on Psychotropic Substances [6].

As a party to both drug control treaties, the Congress of the United States adopted the Comprehensive Drug Abuse Prevention and Control Act, commonly referred to as the Controlled Substances Act (CSA) [7]. In ratifying the Single Convention [4] and the UN Psychotropic Convention [5], Congress clearly declared that many drugs have a useful and legitimate medical purpose and are necessary to maintain the health and general welfare of citizens, and accepted the requirements of both international treaties to establish control over international and domestic traffic of controlled substances. While the FDA is charged with the responsibility and duty to establish, control, and ensure the manufacture and distribution of safe and effective new drugs into the U.S. marketplace, the U.S. Drug Enforcement Administration (DEA) has been charged with the ominous duty to *prevent* the diversion and abuse of those legitimate drug products that are approved for medical use. In total, the U.S. Congress has set forth a balanced, coordinated, multifaceted strategy for both promoting research and development of new drug entities (FDA) while attempting to predict and prevent the unlawful diversion of these new chemical entities from their intended supply chain (DEA). Under the initial drug control treaties, the World Health Organization (WHO) has established a tiered schedule of drug control. The purpose of scheduling new drug substances under the CSA is to minimize the potential for abuse and diversion while affording appropriate medical and research access to those same drug substances. The enforcement approach set forth by Congress, the FDA, and the DEA is twofold: (1) to prevent diversion of drugs with a potential for abuse from the legitimate market by regulating drug manufacture and distribution, and (2) to suppress clandestine trafficking of the drug substances outside the closed free-market system of drugs that have been approved as safe and effective for medical use in both human and veterinary patients.

Before a drug with a potential for abuse is controlled under the CSA, the Secretary of the Department of Health and Human Services (HHS) must provide a scientific and medical evaluation and scheduling recommendation under the CSA to the Administrator of the DEA. The statutory responsibilities for this process are described in the CSA under 21 US C. §811 and 812, as well as regulatory controls set forth in 21 CFR (Code of Federal Regulations) parts 1300–1316.

Under the CSA, if at the time a new drug application (NDA) is submitted to the FDA for any new drug having a "stimulant, depressant, or hallucinogenic effect" on the central nervous system, it appears that such drug has an abuse potential, such information shall be forwarded to the Secretary of HHS by the Controlled Substances Staff (CSS) of the Center for Drug Evaluation and Research (CDER) of the FDA, who will then review the evaluation and either reject or accept its findings and forward this evaluation to the Administrator of the DEA for schedule control review. Upon receiving the notice of schedule control action of the NDA by the DEA Administrator, the Office of Diversion Control of the Operational Division of the DEA will conduct a separate and independent evaluation for scheduling action based on (1) the existing published scientific literature of abuse liability of drugs from within similar functional pharmacological or therapeutic targets, and similar chemical structure activity relationships; (2) the data supplied by the FDA in regards to the specific new drug entity; as well as (3) the known current and past patterns of abuse documented by national and international law enforcement and health care agencies

for similar licit and illicit stimulant, depressant, or hallucinogenic substances. While the DEA is legally bound to the scientific evaluation of the CSS staff at CDER in regards to the pharmacology, structure, and efficacy of the new drug entity, these are only minimal elements of the multifactorial evidence that is considered by the DEA in its drug control decision-making process.

Under the CSA, the Secretary of the HHS is required to consider, in a scientific and medical evaluation, eight factors determinative of scheduled control of the new chemical entity. Following the consideration of the eight factors, the Secretary of HHS must determine if (1) there is legitimate medical use of the new drug compound, (2) the new compound has demonstrated relative safety with regards to standard preclinical toxicology programs applicable to all NDA applications, and (3) the new compound demonstrates a relative abuse/dependence potential similar to any other known CNS stimulant, depressant, or hallucinogen currently scheduled under the CSA. The eight factors that have to be addressed for all new drug applications are as follows:

1. Its actual or relative potential for abuse.
   a. A new drug may have limited actual abuse data; however, data related to any other compounds with similar stimulant, depressant, and/or hallucinogenic effects need to be addressed. Data derived from behavioral assays described in this chapter may be applied here.
2. Scientific evidence of the drug's pharmacological effects.
   a. This is generally based on the data supplied to the FDA by the pharmaceutical company; however, pharmacological data extracted from peer-reviewed scientific journals of structurally or functionally similar drug elements need to be addressed. Data derived from behavioral assays described in this chapter may be applied here.
3. The state of current scientific knowledge regarding the drug or other substances.
   a. This is generally based on the preclinical or clinical data supplied to the FDA by the drug company; however, if it is a new chemical entity with novel mechanisms of action, the general knowledge of the functional pharmacology of similar therapeutically based compounds may be used for the judgment of the relative abuse liability of the new chemical entity. Data derived from behavioral assays described in this chapter may be applied here.
4. Its history and pattern of abuse.
   a. Again, with new chemical entities, this data may be sparse; however, the history and pattern of abuse of similar drugs within the same pharmacological class may be used to judge

relative abuse liability. For example, a new pain-control medication with a novel mechanism of action may be judged against similar efficacious opiate-based pain medications to assess the relative potential for misuse or abuse within that population of potential users.

5. The scope, duration, and significance of abuse.
    a. New chemical entities may have no demonstrative evidence of abuse within the clinical trials milieu; however, the relative scope, duration, and significance of actual abuse may be estimated or judged based on other controlled substances with the same functional or structural pharmacology.
6. What, if any, risk there is to the public health.
    a. This refers to relative risk: cost to human life, work performance, treatment-related costs associated with potential abuse or misuse, and financial and psychological costs to the "general health and welfare." This can be addressed by the data from behavioral assays described in this chapter.
7. Its psychic or physiological dependence liability.
    a. This may be addressed by comparative analysis of drugs with functionally similar pharmacology or from the behavioral assays described in this chapter.
8. Whether the substance is an immediate precursor of a substance already controlled.
    a. This is usually a simple determination by a qualified medicinal or structural chemist.

When a Sponsor submits a new drug application to the FDA for review, the sponsor must include "a description and analysis of studies or information related to abuse of the drug," including a "proposal for scheduling under the CSA" (21 CFR 314.50(d)(5)(vii)). One factor to note here is that the CSA, and thus the DEA, requires this information to be provided to them by the Secretary of HHS for any new drug with stimulant, depressant, or hallucinogenic effects on the CNS.

That is, under the original CSA, the documentation is required by statute for new drug applications related to only three distinct CNS-mediated effects. In contrast, the current draft Guidance for Industry from the CSS staff at the FDA has interpreted FDA's regulatory statutes (21 CFR 314.50(d)(5)(vii)) to expand these requirements to include whether the drug:

1. Affects the CNS.
2. Is chemically or pharmacologically similar to other drugs with known abuse potential.
3. Produces psychoactive effects such as *sedation, euphoria, and mood changes*; or
4. Has any *direct or indirect* actions and effects on other neurotransmitter systems associated with abuse potential:
    a. Dopamine
    b. Norepinephrine
    c. Serotonin
    d. GABA
    e. Acetylcholine
    f. Opioid
    g. N-methyl-D-aspartate (NMDA)
    h. Cannabinoid

Under the DEA's CSA requirements, not all drugs affecting the CNS are required by statute to be assessed for relative abuse liability—only those with CNS-mediated stimulant, depressant, or hallucinogenic effects. Under the FDA's Guidance for Industry, an overly expansive umbrella for the abuse liability assessment requirements appears to include ALL CNS-mediated effects including those that may be described as sedating, euphorigenic, or inducing "mood changes." An applicant may wonder, "What's the difference?"

For example, let's assume that a new chemical entity has demonstrated pharmacological activity as a dopamine antagonist, which is being targeted as an antiemetic, antidepressant, or novel neuroleptic, such as a variation of haloperidol, thorazine, or olanzapine. The history of all currently used dopamine antagonists would tend to support the conclusion that they lack abuse potential. However, this new chemical entity may require abuse potential studies under the FDA's guidance document because of its sedating or mood-changing effects, but assessment would not be expected by the statutory requirements of the CSA. Similarly, a new chemical entity developed for the treatment of the mania associated with bipolar affective disorders may be required to include abuse liability testing by the FDA's guidelines based on CNS-mediated and mood-change effects, but not required under the CSA since the drug does not produce stimulant, depressant, or hallucinogenic effects or specifically target any one specific neurotransmitter system associated with abuse liability.

Because of these noted differences in regulatory data sets for drug schedule control decisions required by the FDA and DEA, it is highly recommended that ALL preclinical screening protocols for abuse liability assessment be reviewed by CSS staff prior to initiation of these studies. An additional suggestion would be to open a dialogue with the Office of Diversion Control at the DEA early in the process of drug development to help ensure that a complete data set is available at the time of NDA application. As a regulatory agency intimately involved in the process of schedule control actions of the new chemical entity, positioning the study design team with both CSS staff at the FDA and the Drug Diversion Team at the DEA may significantly improve the review process early in development of the molecule and set the direction for the progress of preclinical to clinical trial advancement. While it is clear that prereview of preclinical protocols by the regulatory agencies is not legally binding on the agency's final review, it is highly recommended that such protocols be openly discussed prior to initiation of Phase II clinical trials, and that discussion should include members of both the FDA and DEA.

Experimental Protocols

A critical cornerstone that must be kept in mind when discussing the experimental analysis of behavior regarding abuse liability in both animals and humans is that what is being sought by the agencies in these tests is the abuse or dependence potential of a new drug entity when the drug is used nonmedically, rather than when it is used medically under a doctor's auspices [12]. Therefore when thinking about the procedural variables required in these studies, it is imperative to think outside the box. These are NOT general toxicology studies. In these study designs we desire to uncover the potential for abuse when the drug is administered outside the scope of medical practice. Based on the hundreds of years of experience of humans abusing drugs, these assays may require the use of dose strategies that are not part of standardized toxicology or safety study plans and are designed specifically to unmask or highlight aspects of the new drug entity with the intention of operating outside the range of the known therapeutic window. International and national drug control policies rarely identify or mention anything regarding a therapeutic dose. By definition, drug abuse is assumed to involve doses and dosing strategies outside the scope of standard medical practice.

A tripartite evidence-based preclinical risk assessment plan requires standardized behavioral assays of at least self-administration, drug discrimination, and dependence potential to be conducted in either rodents (the primary model) or nonhuman primates (NHPs) prior to health agency approval of any new chemical entity. Other behavioral tests may be used to support the three basic core battery tests for abuse liability.

Psychoactive drugs have the capacity to modify ongoing behavior and to enter into important behavioral processes [13]. Over the last six decades of experimental analysis, it has been repeatedly demonstrated that drugs and drug-produced states are capable of serving the same stimulus functions as exteroceptive stimuli; that is, drugs can function as unconditioned stimulus, discriminative stimulus, and reinforcing stimulus. The notion that a drug can serve to maintain consequences for instrumental or operant responding has been well documented, and convincing evidence now exists of an extremely high concordance between the range of CNS-acting drugs self-administered in the context of preclinical drug abuse liability assessment and those drugs abused by humans [13–15]. The recognition of cross-species and cross-substance generalities has changed the

regulatory conceptualization of drug and alcohol abuse from a reactive to a more active process and has been the foundation for regulatory requirements for the functional analysis of drug-seeking and drug-taking behaviors in animal models during the preclinical evaluation of all new chemical entities.

A series of open public meetings between the Pharmaceutical Research and Manufacturers of America (PhRMA) and members of the CSS staff was conducted over the last few years. PhRMA represents a consortium of the country's leading pharmaceutical research and biotechnology companies. PhRMA's mission is to conduct effective advocacy for public policies that encourage discovery of important new medicines for patients by biopharmaceutical research companies. The public meetings between PhRMA and the CSS staff of the CDER at the FDA were the basis for the draft Guidelines for Industry detailing the behavioral operant conditioning assays now required for all new CNS-acting drugs.

The description of these assays in this chapter represents the current best-practices approach adopted by PhRMA and the FDA in addressing the abuse liability of all new chemical entities during product development. A wide and expansive range of investigational approaches to the solution of abuse liability assessment has been reported in the peer-reviewed scientific literature. There are significant between- and within-laboratory operant conditioning procedures used in the preclinical laboratory analysis of the functional stimulus properties of drugs [16]. A large number of differences in training procedures, session duration, and schedules of drug delivery exist across laboratories that have been conducting these types of analysis over the last six decades. In spite of the differences in experimental approaches used in the analysis of abuse liability between laboratories, there remains a striking similarity in the conclusions drawn from their data. The CSS staff at the FDA and members of PhRMA have reviewed the vast expanse of operant and classical conditioning assays used over the last six to seven decades of reports published in peer-reviewed scientific journals, and have consolidated a tripartite core battery of risk-assessment strategies that represent the most reliable, methodologically sound, relatively simple procedures or methods that will address the current regulatory requirements for abuse liability assessments. Guidance documents from government regulatory agencies represent the agencies current thinking on the topic. Guidance documents are not legally binding on the agency and do not establish legally enforceable responsibilities. While the FDA acknowledges that there are always differences in the specific procedures a laboratory can use in predicting a new drug entity's abuse liability, the current guidelines represent the agencies opinion on the industry's best-practices approach to conduct these study designs that will provide the most sound and reliable risk assessment for drug scheduling control actions by both the FDA and DEA.

Regulatory Guidelines

The specific study designs described in this chapter are based on generally accepted procedures for the testing of pharmaceutical compounds for abuse liability [17–21]. They are designed to comply with the requirements of the Drug Abuse Prevention and Control Act (Amended 1996; Title 21, U.S.C.A., Chapter 13 § 811(c) and §812); the three international drug control treaties that govern the Schedule Control review of new drug applications [5,6,23]; and the *Guideline on the Non-Clinical Investigation of the Dependence Potential of Medicinal Products* of the European Medicines Agency [2]. The study designs are also in compliance with the Food and Drug Administration's draft document titled "Guidance for Industry: Assessment of Abuse Potential of Drugs" released on January 26, 2010 [4]. It should be clear that all of these study protocols and the current industry standard equipment used to conduct these study designs are amenable to good laboratory practice (GLP) compliance in both rodent and NHP assays.

First and foremost in addressing regulatory submission for NDA approval is the question of compliance with GLP guidelines (FDA) Good Laboratory Practice Regulations, 21 CFR Part 58; OECD Principles of Good Laboratory Practice, ENV/MC/CHEM(98)17; and OECD Consensus Document no. 13, Management of Multi-site Studies: publication ENV/JM/MONO [23]. With reference to the FDA's position on GLP compliance, when asked in 1981 if abuse liability testing needed to be conducted under the GLPs, the FDA response was, "Yes they do, but only when the studies are required to be submitted to the agency as part of an application for a research or marketing permit" [Guidelines for Industry: Good Laboratory Practices Questions and Answers" (http://www.fda.gov/ora/compliance_ref/bimo/GLP/81GLP-qanda.pdf)]. As cited by Balster and Bigelow (2003), the FDA's position has been "regardless of whether abuse liability testing is designated as pharmacology or toxicology, the purpose of applying GLP regulations is to ensure application of top quality procedures and data quality control. FDA's experience in this area has been that laboratories must be handled equitably and that application of the GLP regulations must apply across the board in order to ensure maintenance of the high standards." Standard operant chambers used in these assays and the commercially available computer software packages used to control and collect the temporally stamped behavioral data are also amenable for full systems validation under the GLPs. The recommendation of all current EMEA, ICH, and FDA guidance documents (listed earlier) are to conduct these studies, as much as possible, under the GLP guidelines.

Self-Administration

One of the specific aims of abuse liability testing is to accurately predict whether a new chemical entity will maintain patterns of nonmedical use that could result in the disruption of the activities of normal daily living or produce undesirable consequences in the patient given access to the compound through legitimate means. One role served by psychoactive drugs is that of a "reinforcer," defined as an event whose presentation, contingent upon a response, increases the future likelihood of that response. The demonstration that drugs can reinforce behavior, that is, can increase the likelihood that lever-press responses have no consequence other than drug delivery, has supported the view that drugs themselves can act to shape the development of drug-seeking and drug-taking behaviors [13]. Operant drug self-administration is considered the gold standard of preclinical abuse liability testing because of its high face validity and predictive validity. There is a relatively high correspondence between drugs that are self-administered by NHP subjects and those that function as reinforcers in humans [14,24–26].

On important factor that must be kept in mind in understanding the dynamics of the self-administration paradigm is this:

> To say that a drug is "self-administered" says as much about the current and past behavioral and drug contingencies in effect at the time of self-administration as it does about the physical chemical structure of the entity itself.

Drug self-administration studies have increased since those initial reports almost 45 years ago, and the current guideline recommendation is to use intravenous self-administration in *rodents* as the standard model to assess the reinforcing properties of new chemical entities. The standard equipment setup and design we use for this assay are shown in Fig. 13.1.

Surgical techniques have been developed in concert with operant conditioning procedures that allows for the long-term placement of indwelling catheters in both NHP primates and rats to allow for the experimental analysis of the reinforcing properties of new chemical entities. Deneau et al. [27], Schuster and Thompson [24], and Woods [28] helped to develop the surgical procedures and operant conditioning techniques in rhesus monkeys that have since established the behavioral and drug contingencies to show that a number of psychoactive drugs will initiate and maintain lever-press responding (work) for the delivery of a single bolus of drug. Weeks and Davis [29] authored the first published methodology for chronic intravenous cannulation in

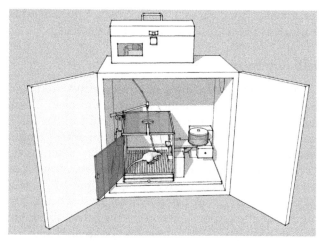

FIGURE 13.1 Schematic diagram of standard rodent self-administration operant chamber located within a sound-attenuating cubicle. The animal is placed into the operant chamber and connected through a catheter swivel system to a drug syringe drive infusion system located in a lock-box secured to the top of the cubicle. Both the lock-box and cubicle are permanently mounted on the supportive cabinets, below. Sixteen separate chambers are located in an isolated laboratory space equipped with key card lock access from a common hallway under constant remote security video monitoring. The system thus allows for a two-lock barrier between controlled substances used in the assay and the general laboratory population in the secure and monitored adjacent hallways. *Drawing by Joshua Yoder, MPI Research.*

laboratory rats for self-administration. The rat catheters are relatively smaller than those used in NHPs, and the rat catheter is generally placed in the jugular vein and advanced down into the right atrium of the heart, while NHPs are generally instrumented in the femoral arteries. While improvements in both material and procedures have been published since the early investigational reports, the issues of catheter patency remains a significant experimental confound in these study plans. Loss of catheter patencies in rats as high as 50% at 2 weeks [30] and 50% at 28 days [31] have been reported.

In a report from this laboratory [32], we have developed procedures and methods to maintain greater than 80% catheter patency for up to 90 days following surgical implantation of the jugular catheters in rats. Catheter patency life approximating 50% reported by other laboratories at 14 [30] and 28 days [31] are extended to 180 days patency life here at MPI Research. The rodent self-administration model has an "in-life" expectancy sufficient to complete any abuse liability assessment for FDA submission.

Tomoji Yanagita [12] was one of the first authors to detail the current FDA-guideline-suggested testing procedures in self-administration protocols. In the original report, Yanagita referred to the design as a cross–self-administration test, but it is most often simply referred to as a drug substitution procedure. In the current procedure suggested by the FDA, animals are first trained to lever-press at fixed ratios of 1 to 10 (FR10) for the

delivery of a single bolus of a known exemplar of drug abuse, such as cocaine, through the indwelling venous catheter connected to the syringe drive system and the animal. The recommended lever-press requirements have been set at FR10, that is, 10 consecutive responses on the lever are required for the delivery of a single bolus of the positive control article, cocaine. Cocaine has been suggested as the standard maintenance/training drug for the self-administration assay. Cocaine provides a rather robust stimulus that has repeatedly been shown to maintain stable day-to-day patterns of responding in both rodents and monkeys. The observation that behaviors originally reinforced by one drug (cocaine) may be maintained readily by a different drug has encouraged the development of substitution procedures as the standard procedure for the assessment of the reinforcing effects of novel compounds [13,28,33–35]. It is also important to note that, to date, the particular history used to establish a drug as a reinforcer has not been shown to control the later behavior maintained by a novel test compound [13].

Daily sessions are conducted in which an animal can receive (1) an unlimited number of injections of the drug during the session or (2) the daily compliment of total drug available is set at some predetermined limit (for example, 10 injections). Session duration can be varied, but generally 1–2 h sessions are sufficient to initiate and maintain consistent patterns of lever-press contingent drug deliveries. To avoid toxicity and to promote a rapid expression of day-to-day stability, most maintenance/training sessions are limited to 10 to 20 injections per session. This allows for a clear and distinct behavioral baseline to distinguish the maintenance of the lever-press response being reinforced by the cocaine injections, but prevents the possibility of overdose or toxicity during the initial training phases of the study. Once stable day-to-day operant lever-press responding has been established, usually defined as less than 15–20% day-to-day variability over three consecutive sessions, the animal can be tested. During test sessions, animals are given unlimited access to the drug unless there is evidence of a significant toxic or lethal dose that will set the upper limit for the total number of injections that can be earned during the session. Typically, lever press responding is self-limiting in that as toxicity is induced by drug delivered in the self-administration procedure, the animals tend to reduce their behavior and discontinue lever-press responding to autoregulate the total dose consumed within a session.

Members of the CSS staff at CDER have repeatedly voiced their concerns regarding the use of equivalent volumes and infusion durations for all vehicles, positive control (maintenance drug), and test article doses. Previous published reports have demonstrated that the rate of intravenous infusion (ie, infusion pump speed) may be varied from immediate to up to 100 s without any significant effects on the acquisition of self-administration [36] or the assessment of the reinforcing properties of intravenously administered drugs in animals already maintained to self-administer drugs [37–39]. In contrast, a potentially important procedural consideration in these types of operant procedures, whether using conventional food [40] or drug reinforcement schedules [41,42], is the delay in the onset of reinforcer deliveries. In the present study design this refers to the time interval between completion of the FR component and the onset of the infusion pump delivery of the drug. To comply with the FDA's current thinking on the subject, all infusions should be initiated at the registration of the completion of the fixed ratio component by the computer software and be less than 10 s in full duration or, in case of solubility issues with the test article, not more than 30 s.

These operant-conditioning procedures make explicit use of the fact that drug-reinforced responding undergoes extinction and eventually decreases in probability when a reinforcing drug dose is replaced with vehicle (saline) or an ineffective drug or drug dose. In trained animals exhibiting day-to-day stability for drug deliveries, the substitution of the normal drug dose with saline will produce an initial increase of lever-press responding during day 1 of substitution, as if the animal is searching for his normal compliment of cocaine. This increase in responding is commonly referred to as an extinction burst. Generally, days 2 and 3 of a substitution test will show a day-to-day decline in a downward staircase fashion, demonstrating the vehicle lacks the reinforcing properties that have been established by the known drug of abuse, cocaine. Failure to observe such extinction behavior when a new drug, drug dose, or novel test condition is substituted for cocaine suggests that the test condition is reinforcing the continued responding. Fig. 13.2 shows the typical differential pattern of responding in rats conditioned to self-administer doses of 0.56 mg/kg/injection of cocaine in daily 1-h sessions. Day-to-day stability is maintained by the maintenance dose of cocaine, with each animal delivering approximately 10 injections per day, resulting in a total delivered daily dose of 5.6 mg/kg intravenous cocaine. In contrast, an extinction burst is seen on day 1 of substitution tests with access to saline. Lower numbers of injections are delivered on days 2 and 2, resulting in a downward staircase pattern typical of a nonreinforcer in this assay. In our laboratory, a distinct day-to-day differential pattern of responding is demonstrated in standard tests conducted with saline and the maintenance dose of cocaine with a 3-day substitution testing strategy (Fig. 13.3). The substitution test sessions can easily be extended to 5, 7, or more days if a clear identifiably distinct pattern is not demonstrated between the maintenance dose of cocaine and the vehicle.

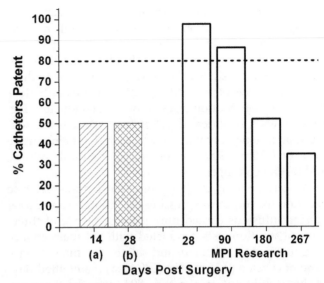

FIGURE 13.2 Catheter patency life established for rat jugular catheters for use in self-administration abuse liability testing assays. Published reports of approximately 50% catheter loss at (A) 14 days *(Yoburn BC, Morales R, Inturrisi CE. Chronic vascular catheterization in the rat: comparison of three techniques. Physiol Behav 1984;33(1):89–94.)* and (B) 28 days *(Peternel L, Skrajnar S, Cerne M. A comparative study of four permanent cannulation procedures in rats. J Pharmacol Toxicol Methods 2010;61(1):20–6.)* have been improved by strict adherence to standardized procedures and methods imposed under GLP compliance. Less than 20% catheter loss has been achieved for as much as 90 days following surgical implantation of the catheters.

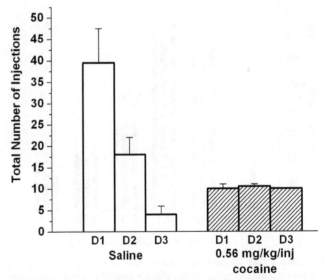

FIGURE 13.3 Group mean total number of injections earned during 1-h substitution test sessions in 32 rats trained to initiate and maintain self-administration of 0.56 mg/kg/injection cocaine (expressed as the salt) in daily 1-h sessions. During substitution test sessions animals had unlimited access to the drug stimulus provided through the syringe drive system attached to the chronic indwelling jugular catheters. Ten lever presses initiated a single bolus of less than 1 mL of cocaine or saline. A 10-s time-out was initiated following the completion of 10 responses on the lever during the period of drug deliveries. Each bar represents the group mean for each day of the substitution period, and error bars represent ± 1 SEM.

Complete dose–effect functions can be generated by repeated substitution tests conducted with a novel cocaine dose. Daily maintenance sessions are interspersed between three-day substitution test sessions. Once an animal shows day-to-day stability over three contiguous days of responding for the maintenance dose of cocaine, substitution test sessions are conducted. Fig. 13.4 shows a historical data set from another rat self-administration study that utilized a similar maintenance dose of 0.56 mg/kg/infusion under identical training and testing contingencies.

As can be seen in this prototypical dose–response function for cocaine, expressing the group mean of total session infusions earned during the sequence of three-day substitution tests conducted with the maintenance or training drug, cocaine, and saline. The maintenance dose of cocaine (0.56 mg/kg/infusion) maintained day-to-day stability of greater than 80% over the three-day test period. When a nonreinforcer such as saline was tested, the total number of injections earned over the three-day substitution tests declined. This downward staircase response pattern represents the typical within- and between-session *extinction* patterns of lever-press responding usually seen with both drug, and more traditional nondrug, reinforcers (ie, food and water).

Historically, this low level of responding represents "sampling" behavior within the session.

When a known drug of abuse from outside the pharmacological class of psychomotor stimulant is tested in this protocol, a similar day-to-day pattern of self-administration is maintained. Fig. 13.5 represents sessions conducted with oxycodone, a nonstimulant, Schedule II narcotic with a long history of abuse in the general population.

As previously described, the observation that behaviors originally reinforced by one drug (cocaine) may be maintained readily by a different drug (oxycodone) has encouraged the development of substitution procedures as the standard procedure for the assessment of the reinforcing effects of novel compounds [13,28,33–35]. Under these conditions, the opioid, oxycodone, would be considered to be self-administered by rats previously conditioned to self-administer the psychomotor stimulant, cocaine.

As previously shown, saline engendered a typical pattern of extinction in this assay: a high number of infusions on day 1, with subsequent day-to-day decline on days 2 and 3 of substitution. When a weak noncontrolled stimulant, caffeine, is tested in animals that have been conditioned to initiate and maintain 0.56 mg/kg/

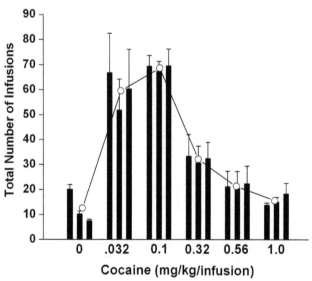

FIGURE 13.4 Group mean total number of injections earned during 1-h substitution test sessions in 32 rats trained to initiate and maintain self-administration of 0.56 mg/kg/injection cocaine (expressed as the salt) in daily 1-h sessions. Each bar represents the mean of six rats tested with various doses of cocaine over three consecutive substitution test sessions. Each error bar represents ±1 SEM. The open circles represent the three-day grand mean for each tested dose of cocaine. During substitution test sessions animals had unlimited access to the drug stimulus provided through the syringe drive system attached to the chronic indwelling jugular catheters. Ten lever presses initiated a single bolus of less than 1 mL of cocaine or saline. A 10-s time-out was initiated following the completion of 10 responses on the lever during the period of drug deliveries.

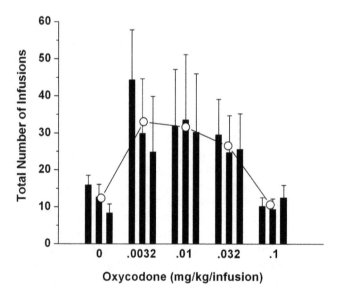

FIGURE 13.5 Group mean total number of injections earned during 1-h substitution test sessions in 32 rats initially trained maintain self-administration of 0.56 mg/kg/injection cocaine (expressed as the salt) in daily 1-h sessions. Each bar represents the mean of six rats tested with various doses of oxycodone over three consecutive substitution test sessions. Each error bar represents ±1 SEM. The open circles represent the three-day grand mean for each tested dose of oxycodone. During substitution test sessions animals had unlimited access to the drug stimulus provided through the syringe drive system attached to the chronic indwelling jugular catheters. Ten lever presses initiated a single bolus of less than 1 mL of oxycodone or saline. A 10-s time-out was initiated following the completion of 10 responses on the lever during the period of drug deliveries.

infusion of cocaine, a slightly different pattern emerges. This is shown in Fig. 13.6.

All four doses of caffeine tested engendered a group mean total number of injections higher than saline on day 1 of substitution; however, on days 2wo and 3 all doses of caffeine engendered a general decline in the total number of injections earned in the 1-h sessions. While a downward staircase pattern of responding was engendered by each tested dose of caffeine, in regards to the FDA's abuse liability risk-assessment guidance document, the conclusion drawn from these data would be that caffeine produced a *weak positive signal* for abuse liability in this assay. These results suggest an acute reinforcing effect elicited by caffeine on day 1 of substitution for each of the tested doses of caffeine. While caffeine might *initiate* self-administration in rats conditioned to self-administer cocaine, it did not maintain such behavior over the course of the three-day substitution period. In regards to risk assessment, these results suggest that under the current behavioral and drug contingencies of this study design, caffeine may function as a weak positive acute reinforcing stimulus in rats.

When a novel test article was assessed for abuse liability in this assay a different pattern of responding emerged (Fig. 13.7).

The new chemical entity engendered responding equivalent to or less than the nonreinforcer vehicle used in the study. In this scenario, the risk assessment for abuse is minimal. A downward staircase pattern of responding was engendered across all tested doses of the novel compound. In fact, the highest tested dose of 1.0 mg/kg/infusion appeared to show some signs of toxicity or aversion. On day 1, rats engendered significantly less than vehicle or low doses of the new chemical entity, and by day 3 showed complete extinction of the lever-press response, such that not a single dose was administered by the animals in the 1-h session. Additionally, recapturing stimulus control by cocaine following the test of 1.0 mg/kg of the test article took an average of 6 days in contrast to almost an immediate recovery under all previous testing conditions (data not shown). In regards to abuse liability, the new chemical entity engendered a negative signal for abuse and supports the conclusion that the new chemical entity engenders a pattern of behavior consistent with a nonreinforcing stimulus.

It should be noted that maintained or sustained lever-press responding during substitution self-administration tests in animal subjects in which saline or other nonreinforcers are substituted for the training or maintenance dose is common and similar to the extinction

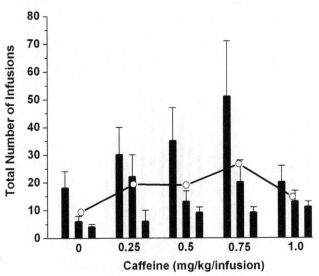

FIGURE 13.6 Group mean total number of injections earned during 1-h substitution test sessions in 32 rats initially trained maintain self-administration of 0.56 mg/kg/injection cocaine (expressed as the salt) in daily 1-h sessions. Each bar represents the mean of six rats tested with various doses of caffeine over three consecutive substitution test sessions. Each error bar represents ± 1 SEM. The open circles represent the three-day grand mean for each tested dose of caffeine. During substitution test sessions animals had unlimited access to the drug stimulus provided through the syringe drive system attached to the chronic indwelling jugular catheters. Ten lever presses initiated a single bolus of less than 1 mL of caffeine or saline. A 10-s time-out was initiated following the completion of 10 responses on the lever during the period of drug deliveries.

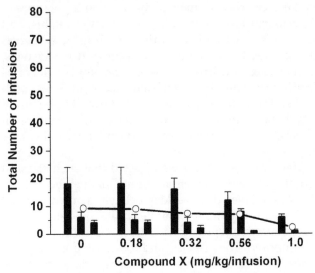

FIGURE 13.7 Group mean total number of injections earned during 1-h substitution test sessions in 32 rats initially trained to maintain self-administration of 0.56 mg/kg/injection cocaine (expressed as the salt) in daily 1-h sessions. Each bar represents the mean of six rats tested with various doses of a new chemical entity over three consecutive substitution test sessions. Each error bar represents ± 1 SEM. The open circles represent the three-day grand mean for each tested dose of the new chemical entity. During substitution test sessions animals had unlimited access to the drug stimulus provided through the syringe drive system attached to the chronic indwelling jugular catheters. Ten lever presses initiated a single bolus of less than 1 mL of the new chemical entity or its vehicle. A 10-s time-out was initiated following the completion of 10 responses on the lever during the period of drug deliveries.

bursts described with more traditional food reinforcers. The response to cocaine during initial training and testing is greatly affected by environmental stimuli (such as the retractable levers, stimulus lamps, and white noise) Both internal and external stimuli repeatedly paired with cocaine self-administration during the initial training and maintenance sessions on this study become classically conditioned to the subjective effects of cocaine. After some number of drug administrations during the training phase, each administration session reliably signaled by a conditioned stimulus (lever, stimulus lamp, etc.), pharmacological conditioned lever-press responding can be observed in response to the controlled substance (CS; [43]).

Subsequently, when a nonreinforcer, such as saline or another vehicle, is substituted for cocaine, environmental stimuli serve to cue the presence of cocaine, based on the prior experimental and drug history of the animal. Such classical conditioned environmental stimuli serve as conditioned secondary reinforcers, which serve to drive or motivate the animals to maintain lever-press responding in the absence of the drug reinforcer. The maintained responding does not necessarily represent "acute reinforcing" properties of these nonreinforcers, but rather classical conditioned environmental stimuli that serve to cue the presence of drug availability [44]. It has been clearly documented that even in the absence of explicit conditioned stimuli (such as levers, lights, and white noise), naturally occurring pre-drug cues (such as opening the box containing the syringe drive systems, or changing out drug supply containers) can serve as conditioned stimuli for sustained lever-press responding [44] throughout an extinction test trial. These stimuli may have contributed to the intermediate patterns of responding for caffeine (described earlier) over the three days of test substitutions.

Many researchers have suggested that such classical conditioned environmental stimuli define the robustness of sustained drug-seeking behaviors in both animal subjects in self-administration studies and in human drug abusers in spite of long drug-free extinction periods imposed. The presence and robust reinforcing properties of these conditioned stimuli associated with the self-administration environment require time to extinguish. Historical data here at MPI Research have demonstrated that rats trained to self-administer cocaine required 18 days of saline substitution prior to complete extinguishing of "sampling" or conditioned lever-press responding. This delay in extinction has been used as a measure of reinforcing efficacy, and is why the current study protocol established three days of substitution test cycles to assess the relative acute reinforcing properties of test compounds to compare to conditioned responding due to environmental stimuli. Saline or other vehicles used and tested in this assay do not maintain stable

responding over the three consecutive days of substitution testing. Sampling behaviors consistent with conditioned responding elicited by environmental stimuli were demonstrated with all of these behaviorally inactive stimuli.

The most commonly used measure in drug self-administration studies is the rate of responding (Fig. 13.8). The use of response rate reflects the importance of this measure in the area of operant conditioning [45]. However, absolute response rate can be a misleading indicator of reinforcing effects [33]. As can be seen by comparing Figs 13.4 and 13.8, in self-administration studies, response rates are similar to the distribution of the total number of injections earned in the session, presenting as an inverted U-shaped function of drug dose [34,46,47]. Differences among drug classes in the temporal pattern of drug-maintained responding and drug intake under limited access conditions, as are typically used in this assay, have been observed consistently in different laboratories and different species. One factor that may modulate the pattern of drug intake shown in the cumulative records (described later) across experimental sessions is the change in blood levels produced by successive drug deliveries. As drug levels rise, the direct effects of the drug on ongoing rates of responding are exposed. The relative ability of factors such as drug

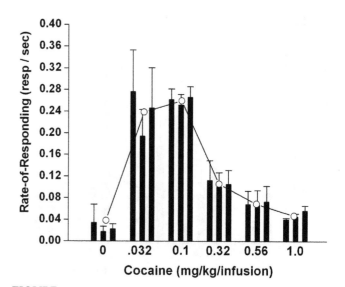

FIGURE 13.8 Group mean rates-of-responding maintained during 1-h substitution test sessions in 32 rats trained to initiate and maintain self-administration of 0.56 mg/kg/injection cocaine (expressed as the salt) in daily 1-h sessions. Each bar represents the mean of six rats tested with various doses of cocaine over three consecutive substitution test sessions. Each error bar represents ± 1 SEM. The open circles represent the 3-day grand mean for each tested dose of cocaine. During substitution test sessions animals had unlimited access to the drug stimulus provided through the syringe drive system attached to the chronic indwelling jugular catheters. Ten lever presses initiated a single bolus of less than 1 mL of cocaine or saline. A 10-s time-out was initiated following the completion of 10 responses on the lever during the period of drug deliveries.

class (psychomotor stimulant), duration of access (1h), schedule of access (FR10), and the direct action of the drug on the rate of ongoing behavior are set to modulate the characteristics of drug-reinforced behavior within and between experimental sessions. As already stated, it should be noted that analysis of raw response rates can be an unreliable marker for the reinforcing properties of drugs [48]. The individual animal's rates of lever-press responding can be influenced by a number of factors including drug and experimental history, present and past behavioral contingencies, the specific schedule of reinforcer delivery used during the test session, direct motor effects of the drug on ongoing behaviors (toxicity), drug aversion, the induction of other behaviors not consistent with lever press responding (ie, expression of stereotypy), or the lack of reinforcing properties of the stimulus itself [44,49].

"Local" rates of responding typically recorded with the use of another standard staple of operant conditioning laboratories can assist in identifying the drug class of the test article of interest. A typical cumulative record generated by a rat conditioned to maintain lever-press responding for a dose of 0.56 mg/kg/infusion of cocaine in 1-h sessions (as described above) is shown in Fig. 13.9.

Cumulative records plotting the moment-to-moment patterns of reinforced responding are typically a series of closely spaced infusions (bursts) early in the test session followed by periods of pauses during which no infusions are taken. Records from these and other cocaine

sessions show the typical pattern of responding that has been described in other published reports of cocaine self-administration [13,33]. In our experience under the current behavioral and drug contingencies described here, cocaine will generally be administered in a cluster at the beginning of the session as if the animal "ramps up" to some preferred level of intoxication. During the rest of the session, cocaine is generally administered in a regularly spaced pattern, the time between infusions being increased as a function of increasing dose. In contrast, a CNS depressant, methohexital, typically shows a "burst and pause" pattern across the test sessions [50]. Patterns of responding maintained by intravenous infusions of ethanol or morphine differ from the barbiturate-type or cocaine-type response topographies in that alcohol- and morphine-reinforced responding is rapid in the beginning of a session and slows as the session progresses [51–53].

In contrast to cocaine and shown in Fig. 13.10, saline, a nonreinforce, shows a typical extinction burst pattern at the beginning of the day 1 substitution test session and then episodic sampling lever presses occur throughout the rest of the session as if testing to see if their normal compliment of cocaine is available. Within-session learning is evident—the animals learn that cocaine is no longer available. Sporadic sampling behaviors may be seen, motivated by the animal's behavioral and drug history, which has been that cocaine has always been available to the animal. The duration of the operant response in the

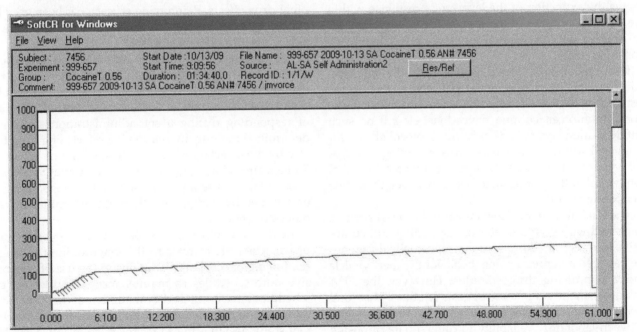

FIGURE 13.9 Cumulative record of responding maintained under an FR10 schedule of intravenous injections of 0.56 mg/kg/infusion of cocaine in a single rat. The record represents one test session. The cumulative number of lever presses are plotted as a function of time. The "pen" resets at the end of session (+60 min). Downward diagonal strokes of the pen indicate injections earned. Each upward movement of the pen represents a lever-press response. The interval between diagonal strokes represents the temporal pauses between individually earned injections during the session.

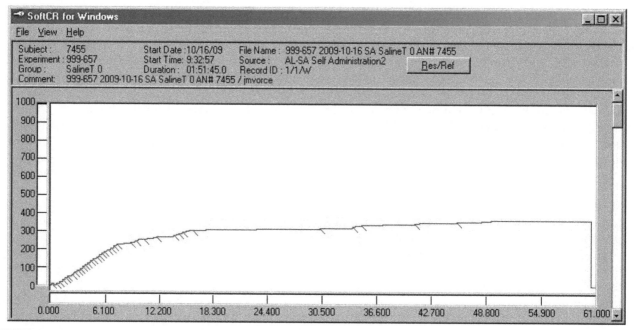

FIGURE 13.10   Extinction burst of responding when tested with saline. The cumulative record of responding for a rat maintained under an FR10 schedule of intravenous injections of 0.56 mg/kg/infusion of cocaine and tested with saline available in the syringe. The record represents the first day of saline substitution. The cumulative number of lever presses are plotted as a function of time. The "pen" resets at the end of session (+60 min). Downward diagonal strokes of the pen indicate injections earned. Each upward movement of the pen represents a lever-press response. The interval between diagonal strokes represents the temporal pauses between individually earned injections during the session.

presence of a nonreinforcer, or the resilience to extinction, may be used as a measure of reinforce efficacy for the training or maintenance drug in this assay.

By day 3, the typical pattern of lever-press responding shows the extinction of the lever-press response within the first few minutes of the session. Very few responses are emitted once the animal receives a few saline injections (Fig. 13.11).

In our laboratory, three days of substitution has typically demonstrated differential patterns of lever-press responding that clearly separate a nonreinforcer (saline) from a reinforcer (cocaine, oxycodone, etc.). If no such differentiation occurs in a study, our protocol allows for longer substitution intervals, such as extending to 3, 5, or 7-day substitution intervals, to ensure that a differential behavioral pattern of behavior exists between these two competing stimuli.

The total number of infusions earned in a test session, combined with both the rates of responding and cumulative records from those sessions, can usually differentiate between a nonreinforcing, behaviorally inert vehicle and a reinforcing drug stimulus. However, the FDA risk-assessment guidelines suggests another behavioral measure that has demonstrated remarkable within- and between-laboratory reliability to differentiate opposing stimulus functions by quantifying the relative reinforcing efficacy of the test stimuli.

As described above, the rate of self-administration is determined not only by reinforcing effects of a drug but

also by the direct effects of the drug on motor behavior. To measure reinforcing effects in a quantitative way, it is necessary to use a procedure in which responding is determined by reinforcing effects uncontaminated with other drug effects. Reinforcing efficacy has been used by behavioral pharmacologists to refer to the magnitude of a drug's reinforcing effects [13].

A progressive ratio (PR) procedure is used to measure a drug's relative reinforcing efficacy by determining the maximum amount of responding (ie, work) that can be maintained by a specific dose of a compound. The rate of responding during a self-administration session is determined not only by reinforcing effects of a drug but also by the direct effects of the drug on motor behavior. To measure reinforcing effects in a quantitative way, it is necessary to use a procedure in which responding is determined by reinforcing effects uncontaminated with other drug effects.

Reinforcing efficacy has been used by behavioral pharmacologists to refer to the magnitude of a drug's reinforcing effects [48]. Variations in the use of progressive ratio schedules as maintenance schedules or test schedules have been used by a number of different laboratories. The intended use of the PR schedule in the current study design is to test for the relative abuse liability among a number of test compounds for regulatory risk assessment as suggested by the FDA's guidance document. As described by Brady et al. [49], standard abuse liability PR experiments involve first introducing a drug

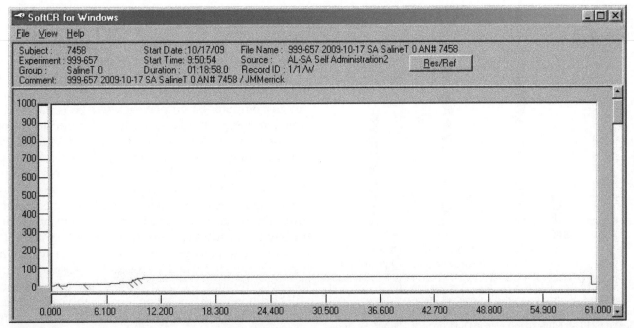

FIGURE 13.11 Extinction of the lever-press response engendered on the third day of saline substitution tests in a rat maintained under an FR10 schedule of intravenous injections of 0.56 mg/kg/infusion of cocaine. For the third day, only saline was available in the syringe. The record represents day 3 of saline substitution. The last injection earned during the session occurred approximately 10 min into the 60-min session.

on a baseline of low-response requirement (FR10 for this protocol) to obtain a consistently stable drug self-injection performance in the animal. Once the animals demonstrate a day-to-day stability of self-administration of the maintenance drug (cocaine) under the fixed ratio schedule of drug deliveries, a unique test session is initiated. The response requirement is then systematically increased until the rate of drug self-injection is diminished to some preset criterion or ceases completely, which then defines the breakpoint. After the breaking point is quantified for a given dose of drug, the original response requirements on the drug lever is lowered back to the original response requirement (FR10) and another baseline performance recovers prior to replication of the experiment or substitution of another dose of the drug [54–56].

Under the progressive ratio schedule of drug reinforcer delivery, the animal responded on the lever for a delivery of the drug of interest. For each subsequent drug delivery, the total number of responses emitted on the lever required for drug delivery was incremented upward using a logarithmic (base e) scale using the following equation:

$$\text{Response requirement} = 5 * e^{(\text{response increment} * 0.2)} - 5$$

The progressive "break point" is defined as the highest number of responses emitted by the animal to earn a single reinforcer delivery of drug or vehicle. The break point may reflect motivational variables, as it varies

systematically with increases in food deprivation and the volume and concentration of a liquid reinforcer. In drug-abuse research, the progressive ratio schedules have been used to assess the reinforcing value of self-administered substances. The amount of work expended to earn a single reinforcer is used to compare the efficacy of drug deliveries with respect to the hedonic valence induced by the drug injection with the assumption that the subjective hedonic valence of a reinforcer determines its abuse liability.

For a given situation (eg, saline), the progressive ratio may vary over time due to the relative idiosyncratic, subject-specific changes in motivational factors impinging on each separate PR test session. For this reason, we refer to the breaking point as a measure of *relative* reinforcing efficacy—relative to the recent past behavioral and drug contingencies, experimental history, and idiosyncratic motivation to respond to the drug on a given day.

When the averaged or group mean breakpoints are plotted as a function of drug dose, the results generally show a typical inverted U-shaped dose–response function [49]. The shape and distribution of the breakpoint dose–response function is similar to the dose–response function plotted for standard substitution test sessions, when the group mean total number of injections earned during a test session is plotted as a function of drug dose.

Fig. 13.12 shows the progressive ratio breakpoints for the maintenance drug, cocaine, and other tested controlled substances that have shown to initiate and maintain self-administration under the current protocol. Once performance in daily 1-h operant sessions

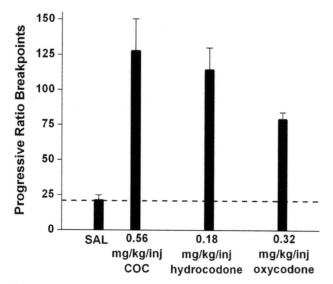

FIGURE 13.12 Progressive ratio breakpoints for saline and selected doses of three controlled substances that have demonstrated initiation and maintenance of self-administration in rats maintained under an FR10 schedule of intravenous injections of 0.56 mg/kg/infusion of cocaine. The breakpoint represents the highest ratio requirement completed during a single test session in which the total number of lever presses required for the delivery of a single dose of drug was increased exponentially throughout the session. The PR breakpoint is used to quantify the relative reinforcing efficacy of drugs in this standardized self-administration study design for regulatory submission.

under unlimited access conditions to cocaine had demonstrated day-to-day stability, defined as less than 20% variability for three contiguous cocaine maintenance sessions, a single PR test was conducted with various doses of three known controlled substances with a long history of abuse in the clinical population—cocaine, hydrocodone, and oxycodone.

Finally, for a complete risk-assessment protocol, the self-administration study should include an assessment of the plasma/serum test article concentrations achieved during test sessions. One factor that has been proposed to modulate the pattern of drug intake across an experimental session is the change in test article blood levels produced by successive drug deliveries [13]. The intake patterns observed during limited-access conditions, as described in the above sections, may function to maintain a constant blood level of drug [57,58]. Due to the limitations of the self-administration study design, the blood sampling cannot be conducted during the initial exposure to the test article since the rate of ongoing behavior would be seriously compromised by the blood-sampling procedure. The actual blood-sampling design, as regards the specific doses and sampling times, may be adapted to behavioral markers obtained during the operant substitution phase of the self-administration study. After the completion of the last test (substitution and/or PR breakpoint tests), the animals can be submitted to a special blood-sampling test session.

As shown in Figs. 13.3–13.7, the first day of substitution testing usually has the largest number of injections earned over the three days of substitution. Either as an extinction burst or by the reinforcing properties of the drug dose itself, day 1 usually provides for the most robust response rate over the remaining sessions. A unique computer-based playback session is imposed in which the computer plays back the exact infusion record recorded on day 1 of substitution and delivers pulses of noncontingent drug injections to the animal as it sits tethered in the operant chamber. No lever-press responding by the animal is required in this unique test session. The computer is programmed to deliver noncontingent drug at the exact same time frame as was recorded during day 1's substitution session for each rat on study. The inter-injection intervals will be different for each animal tested on the study, and therefore the plasma test article concentrations sampled during or after the session will be different. By collecting blood samples for plasma analysis of the test article and/or its active metabolites, the laboratory can determine if a psychoactive dose of drug or therapeutic dose levels were achieved during the free-choice self-administration portion of the study plan. Generally we collect blood samples prior to the session start, and then at 1/2 h and 1 h (completion of the study session). The risk-assessment monitoring team would like to have the information as to the relevant test article concentrations achieved during the substitution tests. If the drug achieves plasma concentrations several-fold higher than targeted therapeutic doses AND is not avidly self-administered in this assay, the conclusion of safety and risk can be confirmed.

SAMPLE SIZE DETERMINATIONS (POWER)

A Generalized Linear Mixed Model power analysis was conducted assuming a negative binomial distribution with a Treatment × Day repeated measures design. Separate Cholesky factored unstructured variance-covariance matrixes were fitted for tests conducted with saline and maintenance dose of cocaine in 302 Sprague–Dawley rats conditioned to self-administer 0.56 mg/kg/injection of cocaine. Ten-thousand bootstrap samples were generated from the database, with samples ranging from four rats per test to 17 rats. Power for the various tests was calculated as the proportion of samples that were significant at the 5% level out of the samples that converged (roughly 91% of all samples converged). A sample size of four rats per test was required to provide a power of 90.0% for the Treatment × Day interaction. A sample size of five rats provided a power of >80% for significant differences between treatments on day 3 of the three-day substitution protocol. With this in mind, we generally use six rats per test randomly selected from our standard of conditioning 32 rats for the study. In this way five test article doses may be tested in six rats per dose to generate the full dose–response function without repeat. This allows for an independent group Treatment × Day ANOVA to be conducted for comparative analysis.

In summary, the self-administration study design that represents the industry's and the FDA's current thinking on the best-practices approach for risk assessment is as follows.

1. Rat is the preferred species; NHPs can be used, if justified.
2. Keep it simple; use cocaine as the maintenance drug.
3. A standard A-B-A substitution test study design should be employed.

Conditions for Self-Administration of Cocaine

Once stable performance is achieved, test novel doses or novel test articles established against the stable cocaine baseline. Multiple substitution test sessions should be employed. Regardless of the number of substitution test sessions required for stable performance, data from ALL substitution sessions should be reported so that the FDA can assess the relative acute reinforcing effects demonstrated during these sessions.

1. Cocaine self-administration under a FR10 schedule of drug deliveries.
2. Session lengths of 1 to 2h duration.
3. All infusion volumes and durations should be equivalent for all vehicle, positive control, and test article doses to be tested in the study.
4. Supplemental progressive ratio test sessions should be used to assess relative reinforcing efficacy of any and all novel doses or test compounds that initiate and maintain self-administration under the standard FR10 substitution tests.
5. Blood samples should be collected to quantify the systemic exposures achieved during test article substitution test sessions to confirm the levels relative to the targeted therapeutic plasma levels.

Drug Discrimination

It seems intuitive that how a drug makes you feel is an important factor in the acquisition and continued use of a drug. The drug discrimination (DD) assay is an operant conditioning assay that establishes the interoceptive effects of a drug as a discriminative stimulus to a behavioral response [16]. The internal events that are elicited by drug administration are by definition subjective in the sense that no objective measure of their reality can be identified. There is no way of ever knowing if the color

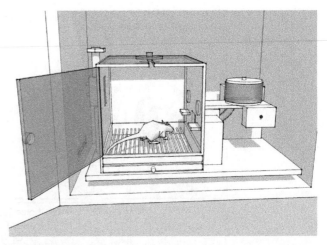

FIGURE 13.13 Standard two-lever operant chamber used for rat drug discrimination assays. Food pellets are delivered automatically by a computer-based program interfaces with the operant chamber. Lever, stimulus lamps, house lamps, and white noise can be monitored and controlled by the computer system to establish drug discriminative control. *Drawing by Joshua Yoder, MPI Research.*

red perceived by one observer is identical to the subjective experience of another observer witnessing the same physical light stimulus. The same holds true of drug effects. The actual internal changes and/or psychological experience induced by administration of morphine in human or animal, is a subjective experience. The dimensions of the internal experience may differ between subjects (human or animal), and therefore the interoceptive stimulus properties of drugs that gain control of behavior are simply defined by the change in that observable behavior.

Drug discrimination usually involves appetitively or aversively motivated instrumental conditioning. The procedure is analogous to procedures used to establish sensory discriminations (eg, stop when the light is red, go when the light is green) except in the DD assay differential sensory learning is replaced with the internal, subjective effects induced by drug administration.

The FDA's current guideline recommends a simple two-choice drug discrimination assay in which the standard species (rats) is trained to discriminate a given dose (training dose) of a particular controlled or legend drug (training drug) from its vehicle. Food pellets are delivered to food-deprived rats after pressing one of the two levers (drug lever, DL) in sessions preceded by training drug injection, and after pressing the other lever (saline lever, SL) in saline sessions (see Fig. 13.13).

On an alternating presentation schedule, the rat is administered vehicle and, following a brief pretreatment interval, is placed into the operant chamber located within a sound-attenuating cubicle (Fig. 13.14). The insertion of the levers, onset of the stimulus lamps located above each lever, the onset of the house lamp, and the presentation of white noise through an

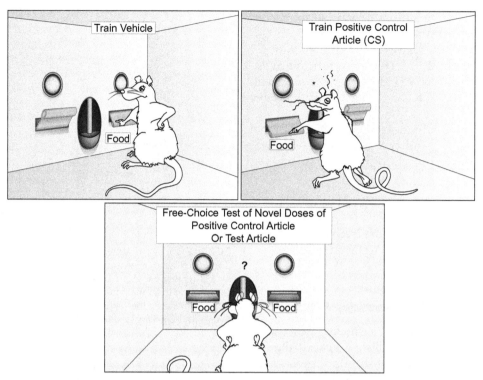

FIGURE 13.14 Schematic depiction of training and testing in the standard two-choice drug discrimination task in rats. *Drawing by Kelly Dormer, University of Oklahoma Health Sciences Center.*

external speaker system signals the beginning of a conditioning session. Responding on one lever (right lever) will produce a food pellet delivery controlled by the computer. On the next day, animals are pretreated with a dose of the training drug. Following a brief pretreatment interval the animal is placed into the chamber and when initiated, the rat will be reinforced with a food pellet for each lever press response emitted on the opposite lever (left lever). Initially, each lever press is reinforced by the delivery of a single food pellet. Over successive sessions the number of lever presses required for a food delivery is increased from one (FR1) to the final requirement of ten consecutive responses (FR10). Once the response requirements are raised above the initial single response requirement, any response on the alternate lever will reset the response counter on the "correct" lever. The correct lever to earn food deliveries is determined by the injection administered to the animal before the session start. The two responses are mutually exclusive. The only available and reliable stimulus that determines which lever will produce food is the internal, subjective effects induced by drug administration. The training days are alternated throughout the training phase, ensuring an equal number of presentations of vehicle and the training dose of the positive control articles to avoid a response bias to any one lever. Training is generally continued until each rat emits greater

than 80–90% of the total session responses on the "injection"-appropriate lever. Asymptotic behavioral choice is usually demonstrated within 40–60 training sessions. Once stimulus control has been demonstrated, test sessions can be conducted. On a test day, a novel dose of the training drug, or a dose of test article, is administered before the session. In test sessions both levers are active and will initiate food deliveries when 10 consecutive responses are emitted by the rat. Once the session is initiated, the animal is given a *free choice* between both levers. Test sessions are interspersed between continued training sessions in the original training states, which serves to demonstrate and maintain response control by the training stimuli.

Complete dose–response functions can be generated over repeated test/train session cycles. Typical dose–response functions for the most typical drugs used in the drug discrimination assay in our laboratory under the current FDA guidance document are shown in Fig. 13.15.

The "TD" in Fig. 13.15 identifies the training dose used in each study design. In tests conducted in this assay, the novel dose of novel treatment is said to produce generalization with the training drug if it makes the animal respond on the drug-appropriate lever; the treatment is said not to do so if it yields saline-lever responding. The dose–response functions shown demonstrate the quantitative specificity of the learned

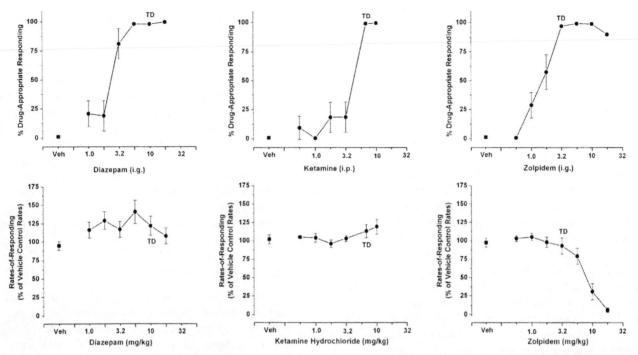

FIGURE 13.15 Representative dose–response functions generated in rats trained to discriminate between vehicle and 10 mg/kg (ip) cocaine (upper left panel), 5.6 mg/kg (sc) morphine (upper middle panels), 5.6 mg/kg (ip) chlordiazepoxide (upper right panels), 10 mg/kg (ip) diazepam, 7.5 mg/kg (ip) ketamine, or 3.2 mg/kg (ip) zolpidem. Top panels of each pair represents the percentage of total session responses emitted on the drug-appropriate lever expressed as a function of the tested dose. The bottom panel of each pair shows the response rates (responses/second) expressed as a percentage of saline response rates, used as a second measure of behavioral activity in this assay.

discriminations. Once a dose of drug is judged to be "training dose like," all higher doses generally produce exclusive drug-lever responding. The effective dose producing 50% drug-appropriate responding is similar to a classic "limen" or "threshold" sensitivity level in this assay. A second measure of the rates of responding on the lever (lower panels) is used to identify that a full behaviorally active range of doses has been used to assess the pharmacological effects in this assay.

The subjective or interoceptive stimulus effects produced by the training dose of a drug do not appear to be limited by the route of administration in this assay. Animals trained to discriminate the presence and absence of an opiate, 1.8 mg/kg oxycodone, administered subcutaneously 20 min before training sessions, show similar pharmacological generalization profiles to oxycodone following subcutaneous, oral, or intraperitoneally administered compound (Fig. 13.16).

The shape of the dose–response functions are similar. The differential threshold doses of drug that engendered complete generalization to the 1.8 mg/kg sc-based training dose of oxycodone are attributed to the differential pharmacokinetics of oxycodone, that is, by either the first-pass metabolism of intraperitoneal injections or the slower absorption profile of orally administered oxycodone. Regardless of the route of administration, oxycodone's subjective effects in rats are similar.

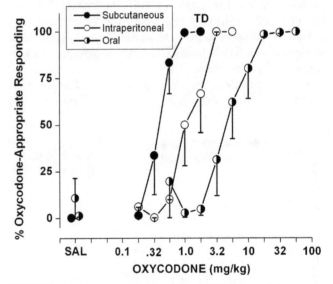

FIGURE 13.16 Dose–response functions for oxycodone administered via three routes of administration in rats trained to discriminate the presence and absence of 1.0 mg/kg (sc) oxycodone in a standard two-choice drug discrimination task. "Drug-like" responding was engendered by doses of oxycodone regardless of route of administration.

Similarly, rats trained to discriminate the presence versus absence of 0.32 mg/kg subcutaneously administered nicotine engendered complete generalization with doses of orally administered nicotine (Fig. 13.17).

In a number of presentations, the CSS staff at the FDA has admonished using the new chemical entity or test article as the training stimulus in the DD assay. They recommend using an "appropriate" training stimulus selected from the published peer-reviewed scientific literature that is functionally or pharmacologically similar to the therapeutic target for the NCE. The guidance document suggests the use of a simple two-choice discrimination assay in rat subjects. There is an abundance of published reports using this strategy and species to select the target for investigation. In some cases there may be a need to train two different groups of rats to discriminate the presence and absence of two distinct pharmacological stimuli. For example, a new chemical entity is being examined for the treatment of anxiety disorders. When compared to standard benzodiazepine treatments, the new chemical entity has a novel mechanism of action through the N-methyl-D-aspartic acid (NMDA), excitatory amino acid receptor (EEA) neurotransmitter system. Like the $GABA_A$ receptor–benzodiazepine interaction, the NMDA receptor is a complex molecular entity endowed with a number of distinct recognition sites for endogenous and exogenous ligands. In this case two groups of rats were used for FDA submission. One group was trained to discriminate the presence and absence of 5.6 mg/kg chloridiazepoxide and another group was trained to discriminate the presence and absence of 7.5 mg/kg ketamine. Following successful training of the rats, complete dose–response functions were generated using the test article in both chlordiazepoxide and ketamine trained animals.

The preponderance of available published data generated using this behavioral assay has shown remarkable pharmacological specificity with the training drug. For example, as described by Colpaert [59], most of the evidence obtained in rats trained to discriminate relatively moderate to high doses of an opiate have shown that generalizations to the training dose of the opiate have occurred with only other opiate test drugs but not other centrally acting drugs or nonopiate analgesics; the ability to produce the "opiate discriminative stimulus" thus appears to be a property of opiate compounds and of opiates only. These types of data have led researchers to conclude that one of the best predictors of future abuse of a novel analgesic is to show complete generalization to a morphine training stimulus in an animal drug discrimination assay.

There are three possible outcomes from a drug discrimination assay (see Fig. 13.18).

1. The test article may engender greater than 80% of the total session responses emitted on the drug-appropriate lever. We would conclude that the test article (Compound X) completely generalizes to the controlled substance serving as the positive control/training drug. This would be considered a positive signal in risk assessment for abuse liability.
2. The test article may engender less than 20% of the total session responses emitted on the drug-appropriate lever during similar test sessions. We would conclude that the test article (Compound Z) does not produce stimulus events that are similar to the training drug and thus does not generalize to the training drug. This would be considered a negative signal suggesting minimal abuse liability of the new compound.

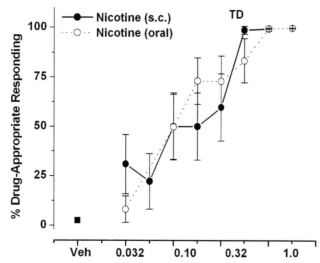

FIGURE 13.17 Dose–response function for nicotine administered subcutaneously or orally in rats trained to discriminate the presence and absence of 0.32 mg/kg (sc) nicotine.

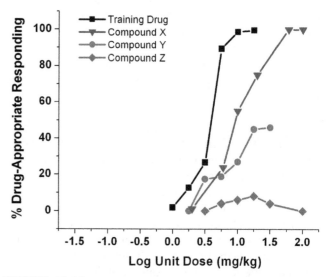

FIGURE 13.18 Comparative theoretical dose–response functions showing the results of a standard two-choice drug discrimination task. Complete, partial, and nongeneralization functions are compared against the training drug dose–response function.

3. The test article may engender intermediate levels of responding on the drug lever resulting in greater than 20%, but less than 80%, of the total session responses emitted on the drug-appropriate lever (Compound Y). This is commonly referred to as "partial generalization." In regards to risk assessment, this would be considered a weak positive signal for abuse liability screening.

The interpretation give to "partial generalization" remains open to debate:

1. Colpeart [60] has concluded that partial generalization reflects random responding or responding at the chance level. Under this model, no clear interpretation can be given for partial generalization.
2. Woods et al. [61] have suggested that partial generalization accurately reflects the predicted outcome based on basic receptor theory of agonism, partial agonism, and antagonism. Woods et al. have suggested that partial generalization reflects partial agonist effects of the test compound at the receptor complex mediating the effects of the training dose of the training drug (for example, the mu opioid receptor).
3. Gauvin and Baird [62] and Gauvin et al. [63] have suggested that, as with exteroceptive stimuli, training drug stimuli in drug discrimination studies are based on multiple dimensions of the drug that may reflect multiple neural substrates from a number of interactive receptor systems. Partial generalization functions accurately reflect the subjective similarity of stimulus elements shared by the test article (Compound Y) and training drug stimulus. Under this model, similarity is not identity of effects. The degree of generalization under this model serves as a "behavioral barometer" of subjective similarities between drugs along one or more commonly shared subjective effects produced by the training drug and the test article.

With respect to risk assessment, partial generalization would be conservatively considered as a positive signal for a potential for abuse.

In summary, then, with respect to drug discrimination studies, the guidance documents on abuse liability screening call for the following:

1. Rat subjects are the preferred species, NHPs can be used if justified
2. Use a simple two-choice drug discrimination assay with an FR10 schedule of reinforcer deliveries.
3. The training drug and test article should be administered using the same route of administration, with intraperitoneal injections cited by the CSS staff as the norm.

4. NCE should NOT be used as the training stimulus. Choose a drug and a moderate to high dose of a known controlled substance as a comparator. The specific drug and dose may be selected from the published peer-reviewed literature targeting a drug from the same functional or structural pharmacology as the test article.
5. Use a sufficient number of animals to ensure reliable data sets; commonly, 4 to 10 rats have been used for each test article dose (typically four monkeys have been used in comparison).
6. Test a full behaviorally active range of positive control and test article doses in ascending order for comparisons. The test and control articles should be tested up to the maximal tolerable dose (>50% reduction in the rates of responding, expressed as a percentage of vehicle control rates) or to the maximal soluble dose.

Drug Dependence Liability

A key component in abuse liability testing is the appropriate evaluation of an objectively verified potential withdrawal or discontinuation syndrome induced by high-dose chronic administration of the test article. This has importance, because one of the most significant motivating factors of continued abuse of a drug is based on the fear of withdrawal if the drug is abruptly discontinued. Physical dependence does not by itself predict the drug-seeking and drug self-administration that are essential features of abuse. It is consequences of drug administration, both acute and chronic, that define a pharmacological agent's physical dependence potential.

In 1993, the WHO's 28th Expert Committee on Drug Dependence [64] recommended against the use of the term "physical (physiological) dependence" because the distinction between physical dependence and psychological dependence was difficult to make clinically and because such a distinction would also be inconsistent with the modern view that all drug effects are potentially understandable in biological terms. At that time, the committee defined "dependence" as:

> a cluster of physiological, behavioural and cognitive phenomena of variable intensity, in which the use of a psychoactive drug (or drugs) takes on high priority. The necessary descriptive characteristics are preoccupation with a desire to obtain and take the drug and persistent drug-taking behaviour. Determinants and the problematic consequence of drug dependence may be biological, psychological, or social, and usually interact.

Ten years later, the WHO's 33rd Expert Committee on Drug Dependence [65] gave the simplest explanation of drug dependence, as "a state in which the individual has a need for repeated doses of the drug to feel good or to avoid feeling bad." The same committee concluded at that time that:

1. It is clear that acceptable medical use of a drug, whether or not it results in drug dependence, is not drug abuse.
2. Drug dependence may be reported as an adverse drug reaction, but not as drug abuse.
3. It is useful to stress that dependence liability alone is not sufficient reason for proposing the international control of a psychoactive drug.

To avoid confusion over terminology that can affect proper reporting, interpretation, and communication of adverse drug reactions related to dependence, an increasing number of researchers have used a different term, "discontinuation syndrome," instead of "withdrawal syndrome." Nielsen et al. [66] concluded that "discontinuation syndrome" is the preferred term among those with vested interests who do not wish to regard their test article as "addictive," while other researchers perceive this term as misleading. In many people's minds, "withdrawal syndrome" is synonymous with dependence while "discontinuation syndrome" is more neutral (cf. Haddad, [67]).

There are multiple phases to the classic drug withdrawal phenomena in humans; at least three distinct phases of withdrawal have been identified for most of the prototypic drugs of abuse (Fig. 13.19).

As delineated in Tables 13.1–13.4, three distinct phases of the withdrawal syndrome have been identified for morphine, alcohol, benzodiazepines, and cocaine.

Multiple factors are involved in selecting the doses for dependence liability studies. Okamoto [68] and Hollister [69] have suggested that the severity of withdrawal reaction is related to the rate of disappearance of drugs from plasma. Drugs that have short half-lives have little potential for producing physical dependence because their residual CNS concentrations at the time of successive doses are small. There is insufficient drug to produce and maintain functional dependence. According to Okamoto [68] and Hollister [69], drugs that have long half-lives are less likely to result in severe withdrawal signs and symptoms despite the fact that they produce severe physical dependence. That is, the CNS can gradually readapt, when the drug is no longer administered, due to the slow elimination of the drug from the CNS. Additionally, the dose of drugs must be selected so as to insure that the CNS is chronically exposed to the drug during the dosing interval. As drug plasma concentrations approach zero, withdrawal reactions will be expressed. If the half-life of the compound is short, then the animal will be exposed to many small episodes of withdrawal over the course of dosing. It is well known that small withdrawal symptoms have the potential

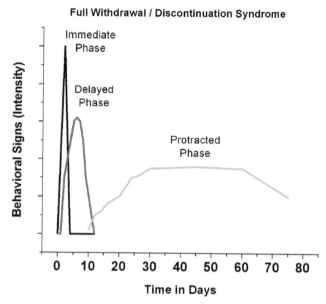

FIGURE 13.19 Theoretical schematic of the intensity and duration of the three distinct phases of drug withdrawal syndrome.

TABLE 13.1 Phases and Symptoms of Classic Opiate Withdrawal

Immediate Phase	Delayed Withdrawal	Protracted Withdrawal
Appears 6–10h after last dose	Appears 2–5 days following last dose and last for several weeks	Evident for as long as four months of observation Complete recovery not evident for at least 6months of total abstinence
SYMPTOMS		
Restlessness	Restlessness	Exaggerated cardiovascular response to cold pressor tests
Lacrimation, rhinorrhea	Insomnia	Instability in blood pressure, heart rates, pupil size, sensitivity of respiratory centers to CO_2
Perspiration, piloerection	Weakness	Hyperalgesia to cold pressor test for at least 5months
Muscle twitches	Muscle aches and pain	
Nausea		
Vomiting		
[97–99]	[99]	[101–103]

to serve as subthreshold chemical stimuli in a process called chemical kindling. Both clinical and experimental evidence support the existence of a kindling mechanism during withdrawal. Withdrawal symptoms result from neurochemical imbalances in the brain when drug

TABLE 13.2 Phases and Symptoms of Classic Alcohol Withdrawal

Immediate Phase	Delayed Withdrawal	Protracted Withdrawal
Appears within hours after last dose peaks at 24 h	Appears 2–6 days following last dose and last for several weeks	Evident for as long as 6 months of observation Complete recovery not evident for years of total abstinence
SYMPTOMS		
Weakness	Weakness	Diminished cortisol response to cold pressor tests
Restlessness, tremulousness	Insomnia	Instability in blood pressure and heart rates
Lacrimation, rhinorrhea	Restlessness	Conditioned withdrawal elicited by alcohol-related cues
Irritability	Disordered sense perception/frank hallucinations	Seizure thresholds may be diminished
Nausea	Convulsions	
Vomiting		
[104,105,110]	[110–112]	[106–109]

TABLE 13.3 Phases and Symptoms of Classic Sedative/Hypnotic (Benzodiazepine) Withdrawal

Immediate Phase	Delayed Withdrawal	Protracted Withdrawal
Appears 1–7 days after last dose	Appears 2–6 weeks following last dose	Evident for as long 10 months to 3.5 years of observation
SYMPTOMS		
Tachycardia	Tremor	Perceptual disorders
Hypertension	Anorexia	Paresthesias
Clouding of consciousness	Sweating	Hypersensitivity to light and sound
Hallucinations	Anxiety	Muscular and abdominal Pain
	Agitation	Depersonalization
	Insomnia	Seizure threshold shifts
	Myoclonus	
[113,114]	[113,114]	[115–117]

TABLE 13.4 Phases and Symptoms of Classic Stimulant (Cocaine) Withdrawal

Immediate Phase	Delayed Withdrawal	Protracted Withdrawal
Appears 9 h to 4 days after last dose	Appears 1–10 weeks following last dose	Indefinite
SYMPTOMS		
Agitation	Sleep normalized	Episodic craving
Depression	Euthymic mood	Slow normalization of hedonic responses
Anorexia	Anxiety	Euthymic mood
Fatigue	Anhedonia	Conditioned stimuli elicit craving
Depression	Anergia	
Hypersomnolence	High craving	
[118,119]		

administration is discontinued. These imbalances may be exacerbated after repeated withdrawal experiences [70–72]. If over the weeks of drug exposure an animal is exposed to subthreshold withdrawal symptoms, the degree and magnitude of the withdrawal symptoms will be potentiated due to chemical kindling of CNS effects.

The current FDA guidance document recommends that a fixed-dosing strategy be used in dependence liability assays. The highest dose is recommended to be "several fold higher" than the relative equivalent therapeutic dose. Generally, CSS staff prestudy reviews of protocols have suggested that the high dose provide two to three fold higher than therapeutic plasma concentrations.

It should be noted that dependence liability studies using fixed-dose procedures recommended by the FDA for abuse risk assessment may not meet the basic requirements for scheduling actions by the U.S. DEA or the WHO [22]. As described in the Introduction, the assessment of a new chemical entity's dependence potential is driven, in part, by the regulatory requirements set forth by the CSA and in the international treaties described earlier.

In Title 21, Chapter 13, §811(c)[7], the U.S. Congress has required that both the psychic and physical dependence liability of new chemical entities must be fully assessed relative to drugs listed in the Schedule targeted for placement of the new chemical entity. Similarly, the WHO Technical Report (#903), titled "WHO Expert Committee on Drug Dependence" [65], has defined the criteria for control under international treaties to include:

> the *substance* has the capacity to produce (a) a state of dependence, and (b) central nervous system stimulation or depression, resulting in hallucinations or disturbances in motor function, thinking, behaviour, perception, or mood; or the substance has the capacity to produce similar abuse and similar ill effects to a substance in Schedule I, II, III, or IV…

Note here that there is *no mention of drug dose* by either the CSA or international treaties governing dependence potential assessments. The focus of both U.S.

and international drug control policy on new chemical entities is based on the *ability of the substance to produce dependence* and NOT a specific dose or dose range of the substance as implied in the current FDA guidance document.

One significant finding that must be addressed for scheduling actions by the U.S. DEA is whether or not the dependence syndrome (withdrawal) produced by a new chemical entity is equivalent to or less than the dependence syndrome of other drugs schedule within one of the five classes of compounds listed in the Controlled Substances Act. In spite of these requirements, the draft guidance document of the FDA has recommended the use of a fixed-dose strategy of repeated dose administrations "several fold higher" than the therapeutic dose to assess a drug's dependence liability with respect to "*safety*" assessments. As admonished by Tatum et al. over 80 years ago, "abstinence phenomena are more marked after progressive rise in dosage than on a constant small or moderate dosage [73]."

With the knowledge that the well-characterized withdrawal syndromes established by morphine, alcohol, barbiturates, and benzodiazepines were established using the "escalating dose" strategies [74], the conduct of a study suggested by the FDA using a fixed-dose procedure to the exclusion of the escalating dose strategy may fail to provide the data required by the CSA for scheduling actions by the DEA and by the international treaties governing drug control. Documentation of the degree, magnitude or intensity, and duration of the potential withdrawal syndrome from the new chemical entity or substance, as it compares to those of other schedule controlled substances such as the hallucinogens, stimulants, CNS depressants, or opiates, may not be fully addressed under the fixed-dose dependence liability model. With this cautionary note in mind, the current chapter is guided by the stated requirements set forth in the draft guidance documents of the FDA relative to "safety risk assessment" of a health agency and NOT by the requirements set forth in the CSA by the law enforcement agency setting the schedule control actions for the new chemical entity.

DEPENDENCE LIABILITY METHODOLOGIES

The selection of drug-dosing strategies is critically linked to the test article's pharmacokinetic profile. The intent of this assay is to keep the plasma test article concentrations above zero for the full length of the exposure periods. This may require once a day or twice a day dosing or even more depending on the test article half-life in the test animals. We have generally administered twice-daily administrations in the studies we have conducted.

The duration of dosing is generally two to four weeks; our general outline is for four continuous weeks of administration based on our historical data and systems validation studies.

The FDA recommends a series of diverse behavioral and physiological endpoints to assess animals during and following the subchronic dosing regimens. We have elected to use the standard modified Irwin screen, also referred to as the functional observational battery (FOB) required under the ICH S7A guidelines for general CNS safety assessment as the core battery in this assay [75]. It allows for a series of behavioral and physiological measures to be conducted that spans multiple domains (eg, physiology, activity/arousal, sensorimotor, neurobehavioral functions, etc.).

SAMPLE SIZE DETERMINATIONS FOR DEPENDENCE LIABILITY STUDIES (POWER)

In 1986, K.E. Muller [76] concluded that a significant design problem often found in neurotoxicity screening batteries leads to an inflated β, type II error rate, which results from a lack of power. The best-known reasons for a lack of power are too small a sample size and inadequate control of error in the laboratory [76]. The functional observational battery or Modified Irwin screen represents a series of multiple dependent measures. These batteries provide for a higher coefficient of variation, making it less likely that subtle effects (like the ones representing acute neurological changes to be assessed in this study) will be detected. Thus the logistics of testing in tier I negatively affect the scientific power of the safety assessments [77].

More recently, the CSS staff at the FDA has been requesting that sponsors address sample size determinations based on power analyses. In 1990, the U.S. Congressional Office of Technology Assessment published a report that identified the need for more formal coordination among federal agencies in addressing neurotoxicological issues and concerns. To address this need, neuroscientists from the U.S. FDA, EPA, Department of Agriculture, and National Institutes of Health formed the Interagency Committee on Neurotoxicity (ICON). The ICON [78] has adopted the requirements of the harmonized test guidelines requiring at least 10 animals per gender per dose group described in both the EPA's Neurotoxicity Guidelines *and* the FDA's Redbook to be applied to *all* neurotoxicity studies regardless of the new chemical entity of interest (40 CFR, 798.6050, of the U.S. Environmental Protection Agency (EPA), titled, "Health Effects Test Guidelines, Office of Prevention, Pesticide, and Toxic Substances" (OPPTS) 870-6200) [79]. Both the FDA's Redbook and the EPA's Neurotoxicity Guidelines delineate the requisite use of 10 animals per gender per treatment group as standard design requirements. Further, the IPCS Collaborative Study on Neurobehavioral Screening Methods [80–84] has also conducted detailed within and between laboratory power analyses on available data published in peer-reviewed scientific journals and has recommended the use of at least 10 animals per gender per group for these study designs. These group size requirements are consistent, and in full agreement, with standard statistical models for behavioral research [85].

The U.S. Department of Agriculture has provided guidance documents for the design of experimental paradigms for the most commonly used species and models in the context of U.S. national regulatory requirements for animal welfare and to be used in the context of the Animal Welfare Act, the Public Health Service Policy on Humane Care and Use of Laboratory Animals, or other relevant regulations and guidelines [86]. This document further cites the Institute for Laboratory Animal Research (ILAR) document, titled, "Guidelines for the Care and Use of Mammals in Neuroscience and Behavioral Research" [87]. This document contains an appendix that addresses important issues related to sample size determinations in animal research. These power functions were utilized on standard behavioral assays in the promulgation of the FDA's Redbook, the EPA's Neurotoxicology Batteries [78], and the IPCS validation studies [80–84] that confer the sample size in standard behavioral assays as 10 animals per gender per group.

For European studies, the OECD guidelines for rodent neurotoxicity may apply (OECD 424, July 21, 1997). The draft proposal for this Test Guideline resulted from an OECD ad hoc meeting on neurotoxicity testing held in Washington, D.C. in March 1990, and a subsequent consultation meeting of an ad hoc Working Group of Experts on Systemic Short-term and (Delayed) Neurotoxicity held in Paris in February 1992. It is based on both a proposal developed as a result of these meetings and a U.S. EPA Neurotoxicity Guideline [78]. The final proposal was prepared by an OECD ad hoc Working Group on Neurotoxicity that met in Ottawa, Canada in March 1995. The Working Group took into account comments from the National Coordinators to the OECD Test Guideline Programme as well as a Canadian Proposal for Neurotoxicity Testing Guidelines and set the policy as:

> When the study is conducted as a separate study, at least 20 animals (10 females and 10 males) should be used in each dose and control group for the evaluation of detailed clinical and functional observations.

Generally, doses of 1×, 2×, and 3× the species-relevant therapeutic dose are selected. Based on the known

variability, four groups of 10 animals per gender are usually preferred in behavioral testing models (Table 13.5).

The FOB is conducted prior to dose administrations (day −1) to show no baseline differences between groups or gender. On day 1, the dosing schedule is initiated and at approximately T_{max}, an FOB is conducted to assess the acute functional effects of the test article dose. The FDA recommends an assessment for tolerance development as a part of the dependence liability assays. Therefore, FOBs are conducted on days 7, 15, 21, and 30 at approximately (T_{max}) to compare against day 1 and all subsequent days of dosing (day 7 vs. day 1, day 15 vs. day 7 vs. day 1, etc.). These data are used to assess the degree of tolerance developed over the course of the four weeks of dosing. The duration of the dosing regimen may be varied from 14 to 30 depending on the pharmacokinetics of the compound. (Here we describe the 30-day model.)

On the evening of day 30, the animals receive their last test article dose of the study—no further drug treatment is administered. On day 31 at the standard time of dosing, all animals are given an injection of inert vehicle (saline) instead of their test article treatments. Sham injections of vehicle are administered on the same daily schedule as test article for the first week of the "withdrawal" phase of the study. This series of control/sham injections is conducted to avoid any classically (Pavlovian) conditioned responses that may have been acquired by the presence of technicians, dosing procedures, or other environmental stimuli during the previous 30 days of dosing.

Depending on the metabolic half-life of the new chemical entity, symptoms of a discontinuation syndrome should be initiated as plasma test article concentrations approach the nadir. With short or moderate half-life drugs that might occur during the nighttime hours following the administration of day 30 doses. Direct observations are limited during the lights-out period (ie, 1800 to 0600h), so we generally propose to put the rats into a photobeam locomotor activity monitoring chamber for the 12h of lights out over the first drug-free night (1800h day 30–0600h day 31).

A series of FOBs are conducted daily from days 31 through 37 to assess the presentation of any symptoms during the acute phase of the expected withdrawal

TABLE 13.5 Study Design Table for Dependence Liability

Dosing Group	Animals	
	Male	Female
1 (vehicle)	10	10
2 (1× therapeutic dose)	10	10
3 (2× therapeutic dose)	10	10
4 (3× therapeutic dose)	10	10

syndrome. If there are between-group differences in the expressed behavior/physiology of the animals on day 37, FOBs are conducted on days 40 and 45. If there are no between group differences on day 37, the study is terminated.

The pragmatic use of the FOB for dependence liability studies allows for additional dependent measures to be easily added to the standard study design. For example, radiotelemetry can be easily added to the study design to measure core body temperatures and general activity during the dosing and postdosing intervals without affecting the quality or integrity of the standard FOB assessments [76]. If the test article is suspected to involve seizure thresholds, a simple auditory evoked seizure assessment can be added to each FOB during the withdrawal phase of the study. The current study design is open for a multitude of simple behavioral and physiological monitoring probes to be added, as needed.

Identification of Discontinuation Syndrome

Any physiologic, biologic, or statistically significant difference between any measure of FOB, clinical examination, or nonschedule clinical finding in the vehicle control group data (Group 1) and test article treated animals (Groups 2 and 3) will be considered signs of a spontaneous withdrawal syndrome. The syndrome should show both dose and time dependency upon abrupt withdrawal of the drug on day 30.

As summarized by Eddy et al. [74], drug dependence is defined as a state of psychic or physical dependence on a drug, arising in the animal following administration of that drug on a periodic or continuous basis. The characteristics of such a state will vary with the agent involved, and these characteristics must always be made clear by designating the particular type of drug dependence in each specific case: The specification of the type of dependence is essential and should form an integral part of the study conclusion.

Drug Dependence of the Morphine Type

The characteristics of the morphine type of dependence is that it represents changes in all major areas of the nervous system, including alterations in behavior, excitation of both divisions of the autonomic nervous system (sympathetic and parasympathetic), and dysfunction of the somatic nervous system. The complex of symptoms includes anxiety, restlessness, generalized reaction to touch (body aches), insomnia, yawning, lacrimation, rhinorrhea, perspiration, mydriasis, piloerection, hot flashes (reddening of facial, chest, or sexual skin), nausea, vomiting, diarrhea, elevation of body temperature, elevation of respiration

rates, abdominal and other muscle cramps (abdominal writhing), dehydration, anorexia, and loss of body weight.

Drug Dependence of the Barbiturate–Alcohol Type

While dependence on drugs of the barbiturate type presents certain similarities to the dependence on drugs of the morphine type, there is a characteristically different picture both during the course of intoxication and during withdrawal. During the intoxication phase there may be some persistence of sedating effects, ataxia, etc. through the development of tolerance that will be assessed during the FOBs conducted on days 1 through 30. During the intoxication phase the subjects may show mental impairment, confusion, and increased emotional instability when approached by technical staff.

The abstinence syndrome usually appears with the first 24 h of cessation of drug treatment, reaches a peak within two or three days, and subsides slowly. The characteristics of the dependence syndrome of the barbiturate–alcohol type are anxiety, involuntary twitching of muscles, tremor of hands and fingers, progressive weakness, dizziness (gait instability), distortion of visual perception, nausea, vomiting, insomnia, weight loss, drop in blood pressure when standing or walking, convulsions of the grand-mal type, delirium resembling alcoholic delirium tremens, and hallucinogenic behaviors (reaching for objects in air, phantom limb behavior, facial grimacing to no specific threat, etc.).

Drug Dependence of the Benzodiazepine Type

The withdrawal from chronic low- or high-dose benzodiazepines has been described to be similar to that appearing following repeat dose administrations of alcohol and/or barbiturates. Reported signs include tremors, muscle twitches, excessive anxiety, muscle cramps, weight loss, appetite loss, excessive perspiration, gastrointestinal distress, and in severe cases, delirium and convulsions.

Drug Dependence of the Cocaine-Amphetamine Type

No physical dependence syndrome from cocaine or amphetamine is noted upon abrupt withdrawal of the drug. Anhedonia is usually considered in human subjects, but this is a difficult subjective experience to assess in animal subjects [96]. Irritability and heightened response to noise or human contact can suggest a syndrome of the amphetamine type, but is not characteristic of same.

Drug Dependence of the Khat Type

Similar to the other prototypic stimulants, no physical dependence syndrome from khat-like (cathinone, metcathinone) substances is noted upon abrupt withdrawal of the drug(s). As with the other stimulants, anhedonia is usually considered in human subjects, but this is a difficult subjective experience to assess in animal subjects. Irritability and heightened response to noise or human contact can suggest a syndrome of all of the "stimulant-type," but is not characteristic of same.

Drug Dependence of the Cannabis (Marijuana) Type

There is an absence of an overt discontinuation syndrome for this type of dependence. However, lethargy, self-neglect (poor grooming and maintenance), irritability, increases in gross motor movements, exaggerated eye movements and eye contact with technicians, teeth barring, and tachycardia have been reported in rhesus monkeys after abrupt discontinuation of THC.

As can be seen by these descriptions of the typical withdrawal syndromes from classic drugs of abuse, the selected use of just radiotelemetry, or just simple home-cage observations, may not objectively discriminate the complex set of physiological and behavioral changes that help to identify and classify the withdrawal syndrome and supports the use of a series of diverse measures like the standard FOB for these study designs.

ANCILLARY PARALLEL BEHAVIORAL ASSAYS SENSITIVE TO WITHDRAWAL

Among withdrawal signs, locomotor activity in the rat is widely considered the most sensitive and reliable index of withdrawal intensity and is the most commonly used [88–94].

As described above, the termination of the dependence liability study design usually occurs once the last dose of the day is administered on day 30 of the repeat dose phase. To avoid any experimental confound induced by disruption of circadian rhythms associated with standard 12h lights-on/lights-out environmental controls in this study design, our laboratory uses 0700 and 1700h for b.i.d. dosing to allow for the normal ambient light circadian timing of 1800 to 0600h lights-out periods. With lights out in the room following the administration of the last dose on study, it is difficult to directly observe any changes in behavior that might be expressed as plasma concentrations approach the nadir over the first 12h of the withdrawal period. The industry-standard infrared automated photobeam locomotor activity chambers provide an excellent ancillary behavioral assay to combine with the standard FOBs that serve to objectively measure changes in basic movements, fine movements, rearing, and total area traversed during that first 12h lights-out period. The infrared photobeam arrays are contained within light- and sound-attenuating, ventilated chambers that reside in a standard vivarium room. The last dose of the study may be administered immediately prior to placement of the rat into the locomotor activity chambers without compromising circadian rhythms. The data are automatically recorded through the electronic interface with an IBM-based computer system in the dark. Recordings can be conducted uninterrupted for 12h without human contact or transient lighting changes.

Fig. 13.20 shows the onset of locomotor activity changes recorded overnight. Rats were incrementally dosed up from 40mg/kg/day to 300mg/kg/day. On the evening of day 30 each rat received only a 50-mg/kg dose to abate any withdrawal from the AM dose as we moved the animal cage racks up to the locomotor activity chamber monitoring room.

The escalating dose strategy has been reported to change the pharmacokinetic profile of morphine in rats. Under this dosing regimen, the elimination half-life of morphine is reported to be approximately 19min [95]. The onset of the discontinuation syndrome of the morphine type would be predicted to occur approximately five half-lives following the 50-mg/kg low dose administered 1h before placement into the chamber. As can be seen in Fig. 13.20, there is a sudden shift from declining activity counts for the first portion of the recording period in all four measures of the LMA software (basic, fine, rearing, and total distance) to a sudden and dramatic shift to hyperactivity appearing approximately 30–35min from the start of the recording session (see arrow on top panel). This corresponds to 90–95min from the rat's last low-dose injection; five half-lives of 19-min duration are equal to 95min. The LMA activity data appear to be sensitive enough to identify the period in which the rats shifted from dependence to withdrawal.

In summary, abuse liability assessments of all new chemical entities that involve the CNS need to be conducted [100]. The health and drug control agencies have repeatedly voiced a strong encouragement for GLP compliance of all of these assays. The current zeitgeist is to conduct these studies following completion of Phase I clinical trials when a targeted therapeutic dose is determined. This allows for the studies to be conducted in tandem with Phase II clinical trials and can be completed within 90–120 days of study initiation. The exact design of the self-administration, drug discrimination, and dependence liability studies can be tailored for the known pharmacology of each test article based on preclinical toxicology and safety studies required to be conducted prior to Phase I clinical trials.

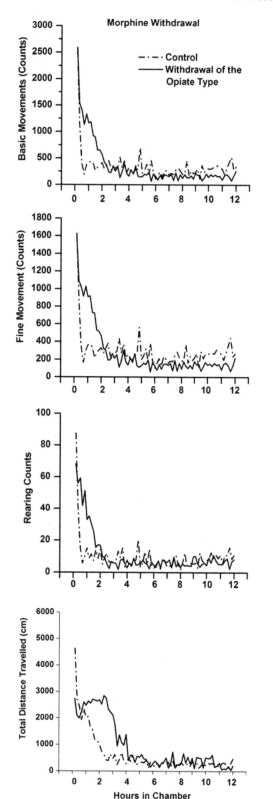

FIGURE 13.20 Changes in locomotor activity in rats (10 per group) during the first 12h of withdrawal. Basic movements (top panel), fine movements (second panel), rearing counts (third panel) and total distance traversed (cm) were recorded at night following the last dose of a 30-day treatment regimen of morphine. The shift from morphine dependence to morphine withdrawal is indicated by a shift from hypoactivity to hyperactivity (see arrow top panel) that occurred as morphine plasma concentrations were expected to approach the nadir.

References

[1] EMCDDA. Guidelines for the risk assessment of new synthetic drugs. European monitoring centre for drugs and drug addiction. Lisbon: The Publication Office of the European Union; 1999. ISBN: 978-92-9168-402-1.

[2] EMEA. Guideline on the non-clinical investigation of the dependence potential of medicinal products. London: Committee for Medicinal Products for Human Use (CHMP); 2006. http://www.ema.europa.eu/docs/mailto:en_GB/document_library/Scientific_guideline/2009/09/WC500003360.pdf.

[3] International Conference on Harmonisation of Technical Requirements for Registration of Pharmaceuticals for Human Use. ICH harmonised tripartite guideline, guidance on nonclinical safety studies for the conduct of human clinical trials and marketing authorization for pharmaceuticals, M3(R2). June 2009. http://www.ich.org/fileadmin/Public_Web_Site/ICH_Products/Guidelines/Multidisciplinary/M3_R2/Step4/M3_R2__Guideline.pdf.

[4] U.S. Department of Health and Human Services, Food and Drug Administration. Guidance for industry. Assessment of abuse potential of drugs. 2010. http://www.fda.gov/cder/guidance/index.htm.

[5] United Nations International Narcotic Control Board [INCB]. Single convention on narcotic drugs. As amended by the 1972 protocol amending the single convention on narcotic drugs (1961). 1961. http://www.incb.org/pdf/e/conv/convention_1961_en.pdf.

[6] United Nations, the Economic and Social Council. Convention on psychotropic substances, 1971. 1971. http://www.unodc.org/pdf/convention_1971_en.pdf.

[7] Title 21, USCA, food and drugs, Chapter 1, Drug abuse prevention and control, as amendmended to February 15, 1996. U.S. Department of Justice; 1970. http://uscode.house.gov/download/pls/21C13.txt.

[8] Deleted in review.

[9] Deleted in review.

[10] Deleted in review.

[11] Deleted in review.

[12] Yanagita T. Methodological considerations in testing physical dependence potential of sedative-hypnotics in animals. In: Thompson T, Unna KR, editors. Predicting dependence liability of stimulant and depressant drugs. Baltimore: University Park Press; 1977. p. 47–56.

[13] Young AM, Herling S. Drugs as reinforcers: studies in laboratory animals. In: Goldberg SR, Stolerman IP, editors. Behavioral analysis of drug dependence. New York: Academic Press; 1986. p. 9–67.

[14] Carter LP, Griffiths RR. Principles of laboratory assessment of drug abuse liability and implications for clinical development. Drug Alcohol Depend 2009;105(Suppl. 1):S14–25.

[15] Brady JV. Animal models for assessing drugs of abuse. Neurosci Biobehav Rev 1991;15(1):35–43.

[16] Thompson T, Pickens R. Interoceptive stimulus control of behavior. In: Thompson T, Pickens R, editors. Stimulus properties of drugs. New York: Appleton-Century-Crofts 1971; p. 3–11.

[17] Sapienza FL. Abuse deterrent formulations and the controlled substances act (CSA). Drug Alcohol Depend 2006;83(Suppl.):S23–30.

[18] Wright CIV, Kramer ED, Zalman M-A, Smith MY, Haddox D. Risk identification, risk assessment, and risk management of abusable drug formulations. Drug Alcohol Depend 2006;3(Suppl.):S68–76.

[19] McCormick CG. Regulatory challenges for new formulations of controlled substances in today's environment. Drug Alcohol Depend 2006;83(Suppl.):S63–7.

[20] Balster RL, Bigelow GE. Guidelines and methodological reviews concerning drug abuse liability assessment. Drug Alcohol Depend 2003;70(Suppl. 3):S13–40.

[21] Ator NA, Griffiths RR. Principles of drug abuse liability assessment in laboratory animals. Drug Alcohol Depend 2003;70(Suppl.):S55–72.

[22] United Nations. Commission on narcotic drugs. United Nations convention against illicit traffic in narcotic drugs and psychotropic substances. 1988. http://www.unodc.org/pdf/convention_1988_en.pdf.

[23] Organisation for Economic Co-operation and Development. Environment directorate, joint meeting of the chemicals committee and the working party on chemicals, pesticides, and biotechnology. OECD series principles of good laboratory practice and compliance monitoring, number 13. The application of the OECD principles of GLP to the organization and management of multi-site studies. 2002. http://www.oecd.org/officialdocuments/publicdisplaydocumentpdf/?cote=ENV/JM/MONO(2002)9&docLanguage=En.

[24] Schuster CR, Thompson T. Self administration of and behavioral dependence on drugs. Annu Rev Pharmacol 1969;9:483–502.

[25] Haney M, Spealman R. Controversies in translational research: drug self-administration. Psychopharmacology (Berl) 2008;199(3):403–19.

[26] Griffiths RR, Bigelow GE, Henningfield JE. Similarities in animal and human drug-taking behavior. In: Mello NK, editor. Advances in substance abuse, vol. 1. Greenwich, CT: JAI Press; 1980. p. 1–90.

[27] Deneau G, Yanagita T, Seevers MH. Self-administration of psychoactive substances by the monkey. Psychopharmacologia 1969;16(1):30–48.

[28] Woods JH. Narcotic-reinforced responding: a rapid evaluation procedure. Drug Alcohol Depend 1980;5:223–30.

[29] Weeks JR, Davis JD. Chronic intravenous cannulas for rats. J Appl Physiol 1964;19:540–1.

[30] Yoburn BC, Morales R, Inturrisi CE. Chronic vascular catheterization in the rat: comparison of three techniques. Physiol Behav 1984;33(1):89–94.

[31] Peternel L, Skrajnar S, Cerne M. A comparative study of four permanent cannulation procedures in rats. J Pharmacol Toxicol Methods 2010;61(1):20–6.

[32] McComb MM, Code RA, Selent CD, Gauvin DV. Long-term maintenance of chronic catheterized rats used in standard self-administration study designs. In: Poster presented at the American association of laboratory animal science (AALAS) national meeting, San Diego, CA. 2011.

[33] Griffiths RR, Brady JV, Bradford LD. Predicting abuse liability of drugs with animal drug self-administration procedures: psychomotor stimulants and hallucinogens. In: Thompson T, Dews PB, editors. Advances in behavioral pharmacology, vol. 2. New York: Plenum Press; 1979. p. 163–208.

[34] Johanson CE, Balster RL. A summary of the results of a drug self-administration study using substitution procedures in rhesus monkeys. Bull Narcotics 1979;30:43–50.

[35] Thompson T, Unna KR, editors. Predicting dependence liability of stimulant and depressant drugs. Baltimore: University Park Press; 1977.

[36] Crombag HS, Ferrario CR, Robinson TE. The rate of intravenous cocaine or amphetamine delivery does not influence drug-taking and drug-seeking behavior in rats. Pharmacol Biochem Behav 2008;90:797–804.

[37] Balster RL, Schuster CR. Fixed interval schedule of cocaine reinforcement: effect of dose and infusion duration. J Exper Anal Behav 1973;20:119–29.

[38] Panlilio LV, Goldberg SR, Gilman JP, Jufer R, Cone EJ, Schindler CW. Effects of delivery rate and non-contingent infusion of cocaine on cocaine self-administration in rhesus monkeys. Psychopharmacology 1998;137(3):253–8.

[39] Thompson T, Pickens R. Behavioral variables influencing drug self-administration. In: Harris RT, McIsaac WM, Schuster CR, editors. Drug dependence. Austin: University of Texas Press; 1970. p. 143–57.

[40] Green L, Snyderman. Choice between rewards differing in amount and delay: toward a choice model of self-control. J Exp Anal Behav 1980;34:135–47.

[41] Johanson CE. Pharmacological and environmental variables affecting drug preference in rhesus monkeys. Pharmacol Rev 1976;27:343–55.

[42] Johanson CE, Schuster CR. A choice procedure for drug reinforcers: cocaine and methylphenidate in the rhesus monkey. J Pharmacol Exp Ther 1975;193:676–88.

[43] Siegel S. Pharmacological conditioning and drug effects. In: Goudi AJ, Emmett-Oglesby MW, editors. Psychoactive drugs: tolerance and sensitization. Clifton, NJ: Humana Press; 1989. p. 115–80.

[44] Gold LH, Balster RL. Evaluation of the cocaine-like discriminative stimulus effects and reinforcing effects of modafinil. Psychopharmacology (Berl) 1996;126(4):286–92.

[45] Katz JL. Drugs as reinforcers: pharmacological and behavioral factors. In: Liebman JM, Coopers SJ, editors. The neuropharmacological basis of reward. Oxford: Oxford University Press; 1989. p. 164–213.

[46] Wise RA. Intravenous drug self-administration: a special case of positive reinforcement. In: Bozarth MA, editor. Methods of assessing the reinforcing properties of abused drugs. New York: Springer Verlag; 1987. p. 117–41.

[47] Woolverton WL, Nader MA. Methods for studying the reinforcing effects of drugs. In: Adler WM, editor. Testing and evaluation of drugs of abuse. New York: Liss; 1990. p. 165–92.

[48] Meisch R, Lemaire GA. Drug self-administration. In: Van Haaren F, editor. Methods in behavioral pharmacology. New York: Elsevier Press; 1993. p. 257–300.

[49] Brady JV, Griffiths RR, Heinz RD, Ator NA, Lukas SE, Lamb RJ. Assessing drugs for abuse liability and dependence potential in laboratory primates. In: Bozarth MA, editor. Methods of assessing the reinforcing properties of abused drugs. New York: Springer-Verlag; 1987. p. 45–85.

[50] Winger G, Stitzer ML, Woods JH. Barbiturate-reinforced responding in rhesus monkeys: comparisons of drugs with different durations of action. J Pharmacol Exp Ther 1975;195:505–14.

[51] Schlichting UU, Goldberg SR, Wuttke W, Hoffmeister F. D-Amphetamine self-administration by rhesus monkeys with different self-administration histories. Proc Eur Soc Study Drug Toxic Excerpta Med Int Congr Ser 1970;220:62–9.

[52] Woods JH, Ikomi F, Winger G. The reinforcing property of ethanol. In: Roach MK, McIsaac WM, Creaven PJ, editors. Biological aspects of alcohol. Austin TX: University of Texas Press; 1971. p. 371–88.

[53] Woods JH, Villareal JE. Patterns of cocaine, codeine, and pentazocine-reinforced responding in the rhesus monkey. Pharmacologist 1970;12:230.

[54] Winger G, Galuska CM, Hursh SR, Woods JH. Relative reinforcing effects of cocaine, remifentanil, and their combination in rhesus monkeys. J Pharmacol Exp Ther 2006;318(1):223–9.

[55] Ko MC, Terner J, Hursh S, Woods JH, Winger G. Relative reinforcing effects of three opioids with different durations of action. J Pharmacol Exp Ther 2002;301(2):698–704.

[56] Winger G, Hursh SR, Casey KL, Woods JH. Relative reinforcing strength of three N-methyl-D-aspartate antagonists with different onsets of action. J Pharmacol Exp Ther 2002;301(2):690–7.

[57] Karoly AJ, Winger G, Ikomi F, Woods JH. The reinforcing property of ethanol in the rhesus monkey II. Some variables related to the maintenance of intravenous ethanol-reinforced responding. Psychopharmacology (Berl) 1978;58(1):19–25.

[58] Yokel RA, Pickens R. Drug level of D- and L-amphetamine during intravenous self-administration. Pscychopharmacologia 1974;34(3):255–64.

[59] Colpaert FC. Drug discrimination: behavioral, pharmacological, and molecular mechanisms of discriminative drug effects. In: Goldberg SR, Stolerman IP, editors. Behavioral analysis and drug dependence. New York: Academic Press; 1986. p. 161–93.

[60] Colpaert FC. Drug-induced cues and states. Some theoretical and methodological inferences. In: Lal H, editor. Discriminative stimulus properties of drugs. New York: Plenum Press; 1977. p. 5–22.

[61] Woods JH, Bertalmio AJ, Young AM, Essman WD, Winger G. Receptor mechanisms of opioid drug discrimination. In: Colpaert FC, Balster RL, editors. Transduction mechanisms of drug stimuli. New York: Springer-Verlag; 1988. p. 95–106.

[62] Gauvin DV, Baird TJ. Discriminative effects of compound drug stimuli: a focus on attention. Pharmacol Biochem Behav 1999;64:229–35.

[63] Gauvin DV, Harland RD, Holloway FA. Drug discrimination procedures: a method to analyze adaptation levels of affective states. Drug Develop Res 1989;16:183–94.

[64] WHO expert committee on drug dependence, 28th report, WHO technical report series no. 836. Geneva: World Health Organization; 1993.

[65] WHO expert committee on drug dependence, 33rd report, WHO technical report series no. 915. Geneva: World Health Organization; 2003.

[66] Nielsen M, Hansen EH, Gotzsche PC. What is the difference between dependence and withdrawal reactions? A comparison of benzodiazepine and selective serotonin reuptake inhibitors. Addiction 2012. http://dx.doi.org/10.1111/j.1360-0443.2011.03686.x.

[67] Haddad P. Do antidepressants cause dependence? Epidemiol Psichiatr Soc 2005;14:58–62.

[68] Okamoto M. Barbiturate tolerance and physical dependence: contribution of pharmacological factors. In: Sharp CW, editor. Mechanisms of tolerance and dependence. NIDA research monograph, vol. 54. 1984. p. 333–47.

[69] Hollister LE. Dependence on benzodiazepines. In: Szara EI, Ludford JP, editors. Benzodiazepines: a review of research results. NIDA research monograph, ;33. 1981. p. 70–82.

[70] Becker HC. Kindling in alcohol withdrawal. Alcohol Health Res World 1998;22:25–33.

[71] Vgontzas AN, Kales A, Bixler EO. Benzodiazepine side effects: role of pharmacokinetics and pharmacodynamics. Pharmacology 1995;51:205–23.

[72] Allison C, Pratt JA. Neuroadaptive processes in GABAergic and glutamatergic systems in benzodiazepine dependence. Pharmacol Ther 2003;98:71–95.

[73] Tatum AL, Seevers MH, Collins KH. Morphine addiction and its physiological interpretation based on experimental evidences. J Pharmacol Exp Ther 1930;33(3):447–75.

[74] Eddy NB, Halbach H, Isbell H, Seevers MH. Drug dependence: its significance and characteristics. Bull WHO 1965;32:721–33.

[75] International Conference on Harmonisation of Technical Requirements for Registration of Pharmaceuticals for Human Use. Safety pharmacology studies for human pharmaceuticals, S7A. 2000. http://www.ich.org/fileadmin/Public_Web_Site/ICH_Products/Guidelines/Safety/S7A/Step4/S7A_Guideline.pdf.

[76] Muller KE. Design and analytical methods. In: Annau Z, editor. Neurobehavioral toxicology. Baltimroe: Johns Hopkins University Press; 1986. p. 404–23.

[77] Sette WF. The role of scheduled-controlled operant behavior in the identification of toxic effects of environmental chemicals. In: Weiss B, O'Donoghue J, editors. Neurobehavioral toxicity: analysis and interpretation. New York: Raven Press; 1994. p. 231–97.

[78] U.S. Environmental Protection Agency. Guidelines for neurotoxicity risk assessment. Fed Regist May 14, 1998;63(933):26926–54.

[79] Slikker W, Acuff K, Boyes WK, Chelonis J, Crofton M, Dearlove GE, et al. Behavioral test methods workshop. Neurotoxicol Teratol 2005;27:417–27.

[80] Moser VC, Tilson HA, MacPhail RC, Becking GC, Cuomo V, Frantik E, et al. The IPCS collaborative study on neurobehavioral screening methods. II. Protocol design and testing procedures. Neurotoxicology 1970a;18:939–46.

[81] Moser VC, Becking GC, Cuomo V, Frantik E, Kulig BM, MacPhail RC, et al. The IPCS collaborative study on neurobehavioral screening methods. Iii. Results of proficiency studies. Neurotoxicology 1997b;18:939–46.

[82] Moser VC, Becking GC, Cuomo V, Frantik E, Kulig BM, MacPhail RC, et al. The IPCS collaborative study on neurobehavioral screening methods. IV. Control data. Neurotoxicology 1997c;18:947–68.

[83] Moser VC, Becking GC, Cuomo V, Frantik E, Kulig BM, MacPhail RC, et al. The IPCS collaborative study on neurobehavioral screening methods: V. Results of chemical testing. Neurotoxicology 1997d;18:969–1056.

[84] Catalano PJ, McDaniel KL, Moser VC. The IPCS collaborative study on neurobehavioral screening methods: VI. Agreement and reliability of the data. Neurotoxicology 1997;18:1057–64.

[85] Cohen J. Statistical power analysis for the behavioral Sciences. 2nd ed. Hillsdale, NJ: Lawrence Erlbaum Assoc.; 1988.

[86] U.S. Department of Agriculture (Online). http://awic.nal.usda.gov/nal_display/index.php? info_center=3&tax_level=3&tax_subject=169&topic_id=1078&level3_id=5326&level4_id=0&level5_id=0&placement_default=0, http://www.the aps.org/pa/action/exercise/book.pdf.

[87] Committee on Guidelines for the Use of Animals in Neuroscience and Behavioral Research, Institute for Laboratory Animal Research, Division on Earth and Life Sciences, National Research Council of the National Academies. 2001. Appendix A & B, p. 175–90.

[88] Blasig J, Herz A, Reinhold K, Zieglgansberger S. Development of physical dependence on morphine in respect to time and dosage and quantification of the precipitated withdrawal syndrome in rats. Psychopharmacologia 1973;33:19–38.

[89] Mucha RF, Kalant H, Linseman MA. Quantitative relationship among measures of morphine tolerance and physical dependence in the rat. Pharmacol Biochem Behav 1979;10:397–405.

[90] Fuentes VO, Hunt WH, Crossland J. The production of morphine tolerance and physical dependence by the oral route in the rat. A comparative study. Pscyhopharmacology (Berl) 1978;59:65–9.

[91] Schulteis G, Markou A, Gold LH, Stinus L, Koob GF. Relative sensitivity to naloxone of multiple indices of opiate withdrawal: a quantitative dose response analysis. J Pharmacol Exp Ther 1994;271:1391–8.

[92] Beach HD. Morphine addiction in rats. Can J Psychol 1957;11:104–12.

[93] van der Laan JW, de Groot G. Changes in locomotor activity patterns as a measure of spontaneous morphine withdrawal: no effect of clonidine. Drug Alcohol Dependence 1988;22:133–40.

[94] Stinus S, Robert C, Karasinski P, Limoge A. Continuous quantitative monitoring of spontaneous opiate withdrawal: locomotor activity and sleep disorders. Pharmacol Biochem Behav 1998;59:83–9.

[95] Vetulani J, Melzacka M, Adamus A, Danek L. Changes in morphine pharmacokinetics in nervous and peripheral tissues following different schedules of administration. Arch Int Pharamcodyn Ther 1983;265:180–91.

[96] Gauvin DV, Briscoe RJ, Baird TJ, Vallett M, Carl KL, Holloway FA. Physiological and subjective effects of acute cocaine withdrawal (crash) in rats. Pharmacol Biochem Behav 1997;57(4):923–34.

[97] Kolb L, DuMez AG. Experimental addiction of animals to opiates. Public Health Rep 1931;46(13):698–726.

[98] Seevers MH, Pfeiffer CC. A study of the analgesia, subjective, depression, and euphoria produced by morphine, heroine, dilaudid, and codeine in the normal human subject. J Pharmacol Exp Ther 1936;56:166–87.

[99] Seevers MH, Deneau GA. A critique of the "dual action" hypothesis of morphine physical dependence. Res Publ Assoc Res Nerv Ment Dis 1968;46:199–205.

[100] Himmelsbach CK. Studies on the relation of drug addiction to the autonomic nervous system: results of cold pressor tests. J Pharmacol Exp Ther 1941;73:91–8.

[101] Himmelsbach CK. Studies of the addiction liability of "demerol" (D-140). J Pharmacol Exp Ther 1942;75:64–8.

[102] Ren Z-Y, Shi J, Epstein DH, Wang J. Abnormal pain response in pain-sensitive opiate addicts after prolonged abstinence predicts increased drug craving. Psychopharmacology (Berl) 2009;204:423–9.

[103] Martin JE, Inglis J. Pain tolerance and narcotic addiction. Br J Soc Clin Psychol 1965;4(3):224–9.

[104] Goldstein DB. Pharmacology of alcohol. London: Oxford University Press; 1983.

[105] Majchrowicz E. Induction of physical dependence upon ethanol and the associated behavioral changes in rats. Psychopharmacologia 1975;43(3):245–54.

[106] Errico AL, Parsons OA, Kling OR, King AC. Investigation of the role of sex hormones in alcoholics' visualspatial deficits. Neuropsychologia 1992;30:417–26.

[107] Errico AL, Parsons OA, King AC, Lovallo WR. Attenuated cortisol response to biobehavioral stressors in sober alcoholics. J Stud Alcohol 1993;54:392–8.

[108] Errico AL, King AC, Lovallo WR, Parsons OA. Cortisol dysregulation and cognitive impairment in abstinent male alcoholics. Alcohol Clin Exp Res 2002;26(8):1198–204.

[109] King AC, Errico AL, Parsons OA, Lovallo WR. Blood pressure dysregulation associated with alcohol withdrawal. Alcohol Clin Exp Res 1991;15(3):478–82.

[110] Victor M, Adams RD. The effect of alcohol on the nervous system. Res Publ Assoc Res Nerv Ment Dis 1953;32:526–73.

[111] Victor M, Hope JM, Adams RD. Auditory hallucinations in the alcoholic patient. Trans Am Neurol Assoc 1953;3(78th meeting):273–5.

[112] Victor M, Brausch C. The role of abstinence in the genesis of alcoholic epilepsy. Epilepsia 1967;8(1):1–20.

[113] Hollister LE, Bennett JL, Kimbell Jr I, Savage C, Overall JE. Diazepam in newly admitted schizophrenics. Dis Nerv Syst 1963;24:746–50.

[114] Mellor CS, Jain VK. Diazepam withdrawal syndrome: its prolonged changing nature. Can Med Assoc J 1982;127(11):1093–6.

[115] Ashton H. Benzodiazepine withdrawal: outcome in 50 patients. Br J Addict 1987;82(6):665–71.

[116] Golombock S, Higgitt A, Fonagy P, Dodds S, Saper J, Lader M. A follow-up study of patients treated for benzodiazepine dependence. Br J Med Psychol 1987;60(2):141–9.

[117] Holton A, Tyrer P. Five year outcome in patients withdrawn from long term treatment with diazepam. BMJ 1990;300(6734):1241–2.

[118] Gawin FH, Ellinwood Jr EH. Cocaine dependence. Annu Rev Med 1989;40:149–61.

[119] Gawin FH, Ellinwood Jr EH. Cocaine and other stimulants. Actions, abuse, and treatment. N Engl J Med 1988;318(18):1173–82.

CLINICAL PATHOLOGY, HISTOPATHOLOGY, AND BIOMARKERS

14

Clinical Pathology

M.J. York

A Comprehensive Guide to Toxicology in Nonclinical Drug Development, Second Edition
http://dx.doi.org/10.1016/B978-0-12-803620-4.00014-1

INTRODUCTION

Clinical pathology, traditionally comprising clinical chemistry, coagulation, hematology, and urinalysis evaluations, is established as an integral part of the preclinical safety assessment of test articles (new chemical entities, exploratory novel medicines, xenobiotics), especially in short- and medium-term toxicity studies. Measurements of conventional clinical pathology biomarkers, historically translated from clinical diagnostics, performed on biological fluids (typically whole blood, serum, plasma, and urine), cells, or tissues may inform on homeostatic balance and movement between cells, endocrine control, cellular synthesis and release from body tissue and synthesis, metabolism and excretion of biochemical components. Alterations of activity, concentration, or appearance within body fluid(s) outside of normal biological variation may indicate an ongoing toxicological/pathophysiological process (eg, disruption of endogenous control or synthetic processes, cellular or tissue damage or functional impairment, inflammatory responses, physiological adaptation to drug treatment) or may reflect exogenous factors or report preanalytic or analytic variation. Therefore clinical pathology testing may help to support safety margins and to indicate and influence decision-making during the course of a study or design of future studies.

To strengthen the role of clinical pathology in the preclinical safety assessment of new chemical entities, interpretation and integration of clinical pathology findings with clinical observations, body and organ weights, toxicokinetics, and anatomic pathology data is considered to be paramount [1,2]. This chapter indicates the application of clinical pathology testing in preclinical safety assessment, considerations for quality assurance (QA) in the generation and interpretation of clinical pathology data, and the strengths and limitations of the conventional clinical pathology biomarkers. It also discusses current areas of development for novel biomarker implementation within the laboratory, intended to expand testing capability, and to improve contribution to the identification of more sensitive, early signals of drug-induced target organ toxicity or pathophysiology.

CORE CLINICAL PATHOLOGY TESTING

The core clinical pathology panel recommends standardized lists for clinical chemistry, coagulation, hematology, and urinalysis (Fig. 14.1), conducted in repeat-dose (subchronic and chronic) studies in rodents and nonrodents [3]. These represent the minimum tests required and may be supplemented to meet various regulatory agency requirements and the type of compound being tested [4]. These panels have recently been reviewed by the Regulatory Affairs Committee (RAC) of the American Society for Veterinary Clinical Pathology (ASVCP) [5], referencing the current FDA and OECD guidelines as well as the previously published recommendations of a joint international scientific committee [3]. Although mainly in agreement with the current standardized lists, the ASVCP RAC recommended some adjustments to the core panels. For example, reporting absolute counts for reticulocytes (recommended for core measurement) and white blood cell differential counts rather percentages was emphasized. Also measurement of glutamate dehydrogenase and/or sorbitol dehydrogenase activity was recommended for measurement with minipigs. Newer tests available with updated hematology analyzers, supporting characterization of red blood cell and platelet abnormalities, were proposed on an investigative basis but recommended for standard testing. The ASVCP RAC supported the inclusion of additional tests to the core on a case-by-case basis, as influenced by the nature and/or potential toxicity of the test article. The core and nonstandard clinical pathology testing panels will be discussed further in subsequent sections.

Incorporation of Clinical Pathology Into Multidose General Toxicology Studies

Preclinical toxicity evaluation of test articles must usually include evaluation of a rodent and nonrodent species. Clinical pathology is typically incorporated into designs of subacute (≤28 days duration), subchronic (up to 13 weeks), and chronic (up to 26, 39, and 52 weeks duration) general toxicology repeat-dose studies. The minimum recommendation is for sampling to occur at study termination in rodents. Interim study testing may not be necessary on subchronic or chronic studies, provided that it has been conducted in subacute studies using dose levels not substantially lower than those used in the earlier studies [3]. However, interim sampling may be included for studies of 13, 26, and 39 weeks duration, particularly if they are conducted in different laboratories to the location of the subacute studies or in different strains of the animal. In nonrodent species (typically dog and nonhuman primates), pretreatment clinical pathology measurements (one to two occasions) and interim sampling are conducted on subchronic and chronic studies. For subacute studies, interim blood sampling may be included on a case-by-case basis. For studies of 7 days duration that may reflect dose range finding

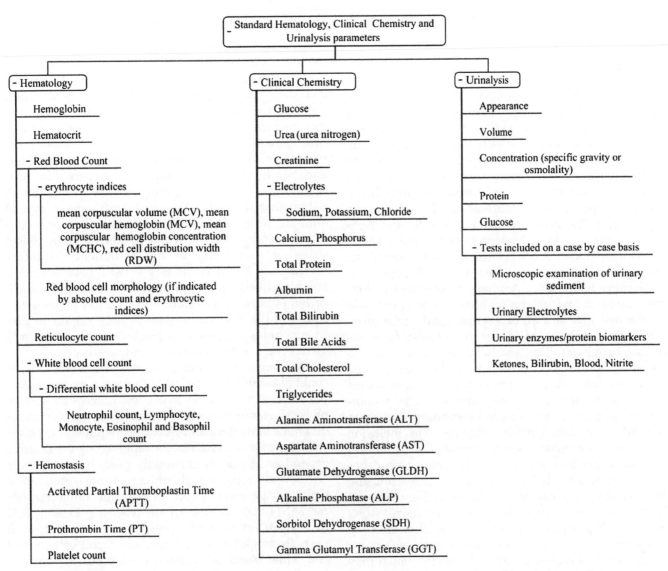

FIGURE 14.1 Standard hematology, clinical chemistry, and urinalysis parameters performed in toxicology studies.

or candidate selection objectives, clinical pathology testing may be restricted to a core clinical chemistry and hematology screen. If additional measurements are indicated by either previous experience or effects of the same compound class suggesting toxicity, and hence could be potentially informative for dose selection for studies of longer duration, then these should be included. For the studies of longer duration, the full scope of core testing will be applied, particularly if regulatory toxicology studies are being conducted to good laboratory practice (GLP) [4]. Urinalysis requiring overnight urine collection in rodents (up to 16 h) and overnight fasting is usually scheduled the day before termination.

Guidance documents addressing carcinogenicity studies provide limited reference to the inclusion of clinical pathology testing in two-year rodent studies.

Recently the Society of Toxicological Pathology (STP) and ASVCP convened a Clinical Pathology in Carcinogenicity Studies Working Group to recommend best practices for inclusion of clinical pathology testing in carcinogenicity studies [6]. The working group recommended that clinical pathology testing be limited to collection of blood smears at scheduled and unscheduled sacrifices, to be examined only if indicated to aid in the diagnosis of possible hematopoietic neoplasia following histopathological evaluation. This recommendation was supported by the ASVCP RAC [5], highlighting that determination of the clinical pathology profile should be restricted to general toxicity studies where age-related changes were not confounding to interpretation [5]. Additional clinical pathology testing could be included to address specific issues arising from prior toxicity studies or known test-article-related class effects. These recommendations were consistent with previous recommendations [3].

Study Protocol Design

In a regulated environment, the study protocol dictates the objectives of the study, test article, dose and dosing routes, test species strain and age, environmental conditions and period of acclimatization, nutrition, and observation and procedures, including biological sample collection (blood, urine, tissues, and others as required), dates and timings of procedures, measurements to be performed, and analysis and reporting of the generated data. Scientific and technical expertise, under the control of the Study Director, will facilitate the conduct of the study towards its main objectives in the spirit of, or to, GLP, dependent on the aims of the study. Animal stress can be an inherent feature of toxicity studies attributable to the dose of the test article and/or experimental procedures. Study designs should minimize the potential for stress during toxicity studies, and hence the impact of possible stress-induced effects on clinical pathology data interpretation where the primary dose-proportionate effects of the test article may also result in proportionate secondary stress-related responses, leading to difficulties in differentiating changes. The inclusion of appropriate control groups (treated with vehicle and subjected to the same experimental procedures as the subjects treated with the test article), housing that minimizes isolation, environmental enrichment, and experimental procedures that minimize stress and sampling and analytical bias are advocated [7]. The clinical pathologist must have a good awareness of the protocol requirements and therefore must play a QA role in assessing study design prior to its start, to ensure optimal conditions for the generation of biological samples submitted to the laboratory for clinical pathology analysis.

Historically, knowledge has grown regarding the scope of preanalytical variation in the generation of samples for conventional clinical pathology biomarker measurements which could lead to compromised analysis and/or lead to misinterpretation of clinical pathology data. There are a number of excellent reviews which have drawn attention to preanalytical variation [8–10], and key sources of preanalytical variables are reemphasized here, to ensure these foundation principles are applied not only to core regulatory clinical pathology testing, but also are considered and examined at a very early stage in the analytical validation and biological characterization of novel biomarkers introduced into the clinical pathology laboratory (Fig. 14.2).

Environment and Acclimatization

All species require a period of acclimatization prior to blood sampling, to minimize the influences of transportation from the supplier to the test facility and the changes in housing conditions, handling procedures, and diet. In nonrodent species (particularly dogs, nonhuman primates, and minipigs), two prestudy baseline hematology and clinical chemistry screens are preferable, with the second screen acting as the reference baseline for comparison with data generated during the study. It is not uncommon to see pretreatment values that are higher than post-treatment in control animals, reflecting adjustment to handling or study-related procedures. Particular parameters may reflect stress or excitability in the nonrodent, including increases in blood levels of glucose, creatine kinase, red blood cells, leukocyte counts (neutrophils and/or lymphocytes), and hormones such as cortisol and prolactin [7]. Rodents are not usually subject to pretreatment bleeds, given the greater numbers per study group, but similar effects are known to occur.

The nature and timing of other study procedures could also influence clinical pathology data. For example, the use of anesthesia to perform procedures such as physical examinations, eye examinations, or electrocardiograms in nonhuman primates is required. Intramuscular injection of ketamine, a rapid-acting dissociative general anesthetic, is commonly used; however, there are several reports highlighting changes in clinical pathology parameters such as aspartate aminotransferase (AST) and creatine kinase reflecting local muscle irritancy of ketamine plus possible decreases in red cell mass (hemoglobin, hematocrit, red blood cell counts) and white blood cell counts (predominantly lymphocytes), suggesting fluid influx into the vascular space [11–13]. Sufficient time should therefore be allowed for the animals to recover (≥3 days) from the intramuscular ketamine injection to minimize compromise of interpretation of potential test article-related effects of skeletal muscle toxicity [14].

Blood Sampling

Clinical pathology tests are subject to influence by the conditions under which the blood is collected such as feeding or fasting, anesthesia, and the site of blood collection. For this reason it is critical that the blood be collected in the same manner from concurrent controls and test-article-treated animals [3]. Fasting (defined as food deprivation but with access to water) is a common procedure in animals in toxicity studies prior to bleeding for clinical pathology testing and will influence blood sample quality, and carbohydrate and lipid

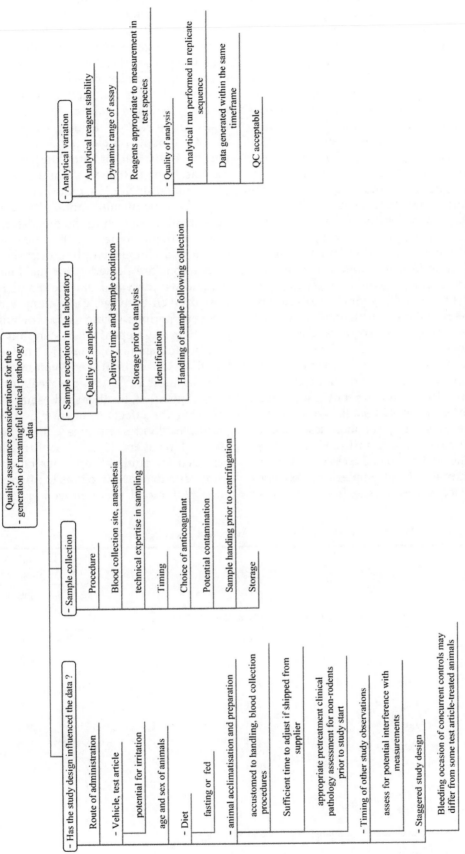

FIGURE 14.2 Quality assurance considerations for the generation of meaningful clinical pathology data.

metabolism, with a greater impact on rodents. Awareness of differences in clinical pathology parameters influenced by the fed and fasted states is important [15], including the duration of the fasting period [16]. In a review of fasting of mice [17], changes in hormone balance, body weight, carbohydrate and lipid metabolism, hepatic enzymes, cardiovascular parameters, body temperature, and toxicological responses reflected the fasting state. For example, the increase in stress-responsive corticosterone levels with increasing duration of fasting, up to 48 h, was highlighted. The author noted that overnight fasting of mice is not comparable with overnight fasting in humans because the mouse has a nocturnal circadian rhythm and a higher metabolic rate. Since many physiological parameters are regulated by circadian rhythms, fasting initiated at different points in the circadian rhythm has different impacts and produces different results [17]. In the conduct of postprandial metabolic studies in the dog [18], the authors noted that controlling for stressors (identified by measurement of the stress biomarkers adreno-corticotrophic hormone and cortisol) as well as factors that may alter digestion is critical, and the development of optimized protocols can reduce experimental variability and improving animal care and comfort.

The frequency of blood volume removal for clinical pathology testing in general toxicity studies will be dependent on study objectives, study duration, test material, animal species, the need to allow animal survival, and regulatory requirements. Optimal blood collection is crucial for achieving the study aim. Blood samples can be obtained by a wide variety of techniques and sites from live animals and at necropsy, but removal of blood can be stressful for laboratory animals because of the handling, restraint, anesthesia, or discomfort associated with a particular technique. Technical expertise in handling and sampling the chosen species is therefore paramount in obtaining both good samples and keeping stress to a minimum.

When blood is collected, a number of factors need to be considered, particularly in the smaller animals. These factors include sample volume relative to total blood volume, frequency of sampling during the study, site of sampling, and agents used for anesthesia or euthanasia. Guidance for the removal of the blood, including routes and volumes, are provided by several publications [19–21], and practitioners are also referred to the blood-sampling microsite of the national center for the three Rs (http://www.nc3rs.org.uk/bloodsamplingmicrosite/page). Recommendations are provided for maximal sample blood volume withdrawal from the circulation of test species of given body weights, along with approximate recovery periods (Table 14.1). For animals weighing more than 1 kg, repeat blood sampling is rarely a problem, but for smaller animals the guidance of collecting less than 15% of total blood volume for a single sampling and less than 7.5% per week for repetitive sampling is justified. Further studies have been conducted assessing the effects of acute blood volume removal (multiple blood samplings over a 24-h period) and assessed recovery [22,23], confirming the guidance provided for minimal repetitive blood sampling. In a study with design analogous to pharmacokinetic sampling [23], blood was removed six times during 24h

TABLE 14.1 Optimum Blood Volume Removal From Laboratory Animals in Toxicology Studies

Species	Nominal Animal Weight	Total Blood Volume (mL)	Circulating Blood Volume Removed in Single Sampling*		
			7.5%	10%	15%
			mL	mL	mL
Mouse	25 g	1.8	0.1	0.2	0.3
Rat	250 g	16	1.2	1.6	2.4
Marmoset	350 g	25	2.0	2.5	3.5
Rabbit	4 kg	224	17	22	34
Macaque (rhesus)	5 kg	280	21	28	42
Macaque (cynomolgus)	5 kg	325	24	32	49
Dog	10 kg	850	64	85	127
Minipig	15 kg	975	73	98	146
Approximate recovery period (weeks)			1	2	4
Circulating blood volume removed in multiple sampling** (eg, toxicokinetic study)			7.5	10–15	20
Approximate recovery period (weeks)			1	2	3

*Indicates single sampling; **Indicates double sampling.*

from nonfasted animals. Total blood volume removal equating to approximately 22% of the total blood volume resulted in a decrease in red blood cell parameters by up to 30%. Changes in total white blood cell counts, reflecting both decreases and increases in lymphocyte and neutrophil counts, respectively, were also accompanied by reductions in body weight and food consumption.

Numerous sites of blood collection, particularly in rodents, have been/are utilized [24] (Fig. 14.3). In rodents, investigative studies have been conducted to assess the influence of blood sampling collection from central sites (heart, abdominal aorta, vena cava), with comparison against peripheral sites (retro-orbital venous plexus, sublingual veins, or tail vein) [25–29]. Additionally, repeated blood sampling in mice by automated blood sampling from the carotid artery and from the tail vein was found to be less stressful (as measured by reductions in body weights, elevations of plasma corticosterone and fecal corticosterone metabolites, and anxious behavior) than cheek blood sampling [30]. The most favored methods in rodents for collection of blood

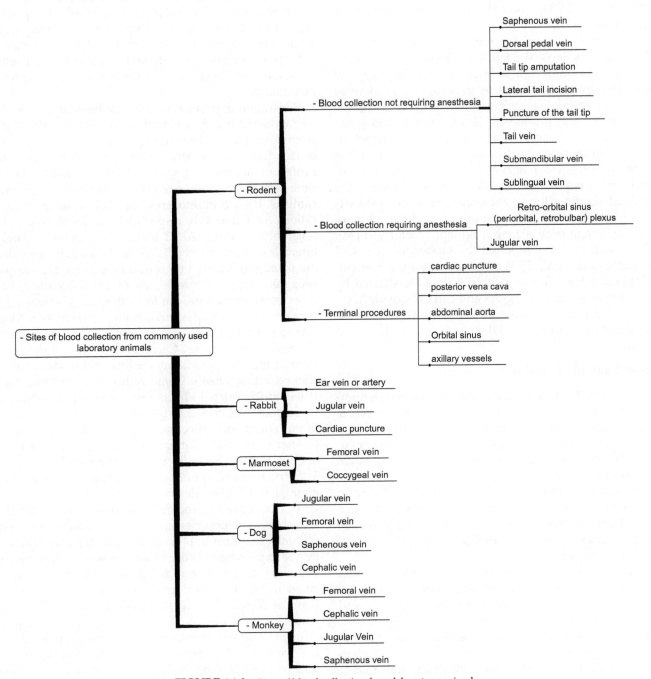

FIGURE 14.3   Sites of blood collection from laboratory animals.

in life are from the retro-orbital venous plexus, tail vein, and the sublingual vein. Orbital sinus blood sampling is considered controversial since it can cause clinically visible alterations and tissue damage and when performed as an in-life procedure, and requires good reproducible technique and expertise [31]. Additionally, the requirement for use of anesthesia is not favored for an in-life procedure, inducing stress and influencing changes in clinical pathology parameters [23]. Hence a number of investigative studies have directly compared retro-orbital bleeding in rodents against other peripheral blood collection sites and not requiring anesthesia, including sublingual vein [23], tail vein [32], submandibular vein [33,34], and tail tip amputation, puncture, and incision [35].

Collective observations from these studies indicated that a clean sample (ie, free from hemolysis) could be obtained from retro-orbital bleeding, but the procedure was stressful to the rodent, as indicated by an increase in glucose and endocrine measurements (prolactin, corticosterone), and produced a level of tissue damage as indicated by increases in creatine kinase. Nevertheless, in one study assessing the impact of blood-sampling technique on blood quality and animal welfare in hemophilic mice, retro-orbital bleeding was concluded as the optimal technique for coagulation, since excessive bleedings were observed following puncture of the submandibular vein in mice lacking coagulation factor VIII [34]. Other workers have reported the saphenous vein [36] or sublingual vein [37] as preferred sites for blood collection in mice. Clinical pathology data are affected by anesthesia to varying degrees and carbon dioxide/oxygen (80%/20%) and isoflurane are considered to be the most suitable anesthetics [38].

Blood Sample Handling

For a profile of clinical pathology parameters, a number of sample types may be required, which increases the total blood volume requirements. For routine hematological measurements, which require whole, uncoagulated blood, the anticoagulant of choice is the potassium salt of EDTA, available as powder or liquid, which prevents coagulation by binding calcium ions. Owing to the influence of the volume requirements of modern hematology instrumentation, a routine blood count can be performed on volumes of 0.5 mL (including repeat analysis if required).

Volumes of blood transferred into the collection device should be optimal to the level of anticoagulant present; underfilling or overfilling the tubes may lead to compromised results. Sodium citrate is the preferred anticoagulant for coagulation measurements and prevents coagulation by forming a complex with calcium ions. Immediately following collection, the EDTA,

citrate-anticoagulated blood tubes and/or lithium heparinized blood should be mixed by inversion and then placed on a roller mixer. Transfer of blood to the tube should be done without excessive force to avoid potential erythrocyte fragmentation and potential for hemolysis. Timely processing of these samples is recommended, preferably within 1 h of collection for all laboratory animal species [39]. If delays in analysis are unavoidable, storage of the blood samples at 4°C will produce increases in mean cell volume (MCV), red blood cell distribution width (RDW), and mean platelet volume and decreases in monocyte counts and mean corpuscular hemoglobin concentration (MCHC), but these changes are regarded as analytically acceptable and clinically negligible. Preparation of peripheral blood films should be conducted within 2 h of blood collection. Samples are allowed to air dry, fixed with methanol, and then stained for possible microscopic evaluation.

Separation of plasma for coagulation analysis should be conducted in a timely manner (usually less than 2 h). In an investigation determining the effect of storage conditions (room temperature, refrigerated, and frozen) on prothrombin time (PT), activated partial thromboplastin time (APTT), and fibrinogen concentration in rat plasma samples, PT and fibrinogen were stable at all three conditions for 6 and 48 h, respectively, although to ensure reliability of results APTT should be run immediately after plasma collection [40]. Clinical chemistry analyses are usually conducted on serum or plasma, the sample type reflecting the preference of the laboratory. For most parameters, there are few differences between the respective sample types, but certain parameters (in addition to fibrinogen), eg, specific enzymes and potassium, show clear differences. Consideration should be given to reducing the opportunity for this preanalytical variation reflecting release from erythrocytes and platelets, if test-article-related effects are suspected to influence these data. The choice of the blood collection device is important. Blood collection devices interact with blood to alter blood composition, serum, or plasma fractions and in some cases may be a source of preanalytical error. The structure and various chemical constituents used in a range of collection devices (stopper lubricants, surfactants, clot activators, separator gels) may add materials, adsorb blood components, or interact with protein and cellular components [41]. In an internal investigation evaluating a range of core clinical chemistry parameters including cardiac troponin I in serum harvested from either minicollect Z serum gel sep/clot activator tubes (Greiner Bio-One Ltd, Gloucestershire, UK) or BD microtainer serum tubes (BD, Oxford, UK), no meaningful differences in the measured clinical chemistry parameters were identified between the tubes, with the exception of identification of higher activities of aspartate aminotransferase (AST), creatine kinase (CK), and lactate dehydrogenase (LD) in the clot activator tubes when compared against the BD serum tubes. The source of this increased recovery was considered to reflect rapid disruption of platelets during the clotting process. New blood collection devices should be validated prior to introduction into the laboratory to assess their potential for causing changes in measured values of clinical pathology parameters.

Urine Collection

The essential features of urine collection in toxicology studies are:

1. Obtaining clean urine without fecal or food contamination.
2. Collecting urine without any direct intervention.
3. Ease, convenience, and efficiency of collection [42].

Additionally, stress to the laboratory animal during the urine collection procedure should be kept to a minimum. The preferred method for urine collection is metabolism cages. This is a straightforward noninvasive technique that requires the animals to be transferred to special cages in which urine is separated from feces and collected over a specified time period. This time period may be during the working day (0–8 h) or involve an overnight collection over 12–16 h. The approach to the collection period may be influenced by the test article under investigation or by clinical observations made during the study (eg, repeated bed wetting) prior to the scheduled day for urine collection. In situations where urine volumes collected are typically low, eg, from mice, then pooling of the urine collected from animals within the same dose group may be considered. An alternative approach in mice is to extend the acclimatization period in the metabolism cage prior to urine collection. A period of 3–4 days' confinement in metabolism cages has been reported to establish equilibrium in mice, as assessed by stability of dietary intake, body weight, and urinary output [43]. In the dog, urine can also be collected via metabolism cage assuming avoidance of fecal contamination can be clearly controlled. Acclimatization of the dogs (and other larger laboratory animals) to the metabolism cages prior to the scheduled collection is recommended to minimize potential stress on the animals. Other approaches to obtaining urine from the dog involve direct sampling of the urine from the live animal by cystocentesis or catheterization. Both procedures require good aseptic technique to avoid the potential for bacterial infection and procedural induced injury, which may influence the composition of the urine and compromise interpretation of clinical pathology findings. Urine may also be directly sampled from the bladder at necropsy, but the information gained from this sample is limited. Sampling from the bladder indicates urinary composition at that time and may be less meaningful. Additionally, increased sampling via catheterization over time increases the potential for procedural induced injury and increased appearance of some biomarkers in the urine that may reflect the procedure rather than actual test-article-induced renal injury. Urine collection from metabolism cages allows collection from the animal over a longer time period and gives a more representative sample from the urinary system (emphasizing that fecal contamination should be avoided). For extended periods, urine samples may be kept chilled (ie, collected over wet ice) to avoid bacterial growth or analyte degradation, possibly resulting in crystal precipitation reflecting the cooling of the urine [5]. The effects of duration of urine collection periods (6 vs. 18 h) have been examined in dosed and control animals in the evaluation of novel urinary renal biomarkers with a cisplatin model of kidney injury [44]. The authors concluded that although there are minor differences in the concentration of some urinary biomarkers that are dependent upon the time and duration of collection, shorter, more welfare friendly, collection protocols do not influence subsequent interpretation of normalized urinary biomarkers data for most biomarkers. The possible interference on some urine tests precludes recommendation of the use of urine preservatives [5].

Analytical Variation and Quality Control

Minimizing variability in the analytical procedure is central to generating quality results from which meaningful conclusions can be drawn. Analytical variation is minimized by a robust quality control (QC) system within the clinical pathology laboratory. Detailed discussion of laboratory QC systems, although outside the scope of this chapter, can be found in a number of sources [45–47]. At a minimum, the QC system should include initial verification that the methodology employed satisfies the goals of the laboratory for accuracy and precision in terms of the analyte being measured. In the regulatory environment, adherence to defined standards should be met. These include generating and maintaining standard operating procedures (SOPs) for all laboratory functions necessary for the analysis and reporting of test results; documentation of routine and nonroutine instrument maintenance; documentation of appropriate personnel training; proper labeling of all reagents controls, standards, calibrators, and other chemicals in the laboratory; routine analysis of QC specimens and review of QC data for systematic errors; routine review of subject data for detection of random errors and appropriate commentary on the raw data to explain further actions if taken; and standard procedures for responding to and documenting out-of-control situations [48]. Additionally, it is considered important that the operator demonstrates a sound understanding of the calibration data, including monitoring of the reagent magnitude of response to the calibration material. This can help in identifying issues in reagent preparation, changes of reagent batches or calibrator preparation errors, if they occur. In a regulatory environment, the acceptable degree of variation must be defined, monitored, and controlled.

A QA program must be implemented that specifies the procedures used to produce the data of known variability (precision) and bias (accuracy). This set of operating principles serves as a means of monitoring analytical variability to ensure the validity of results. In a laboratory's QA program, analytical variation must be defined by means of equipment qualification and method validation. Variability and bias are monitored and managed by way of specified equipment maintenance, as directed in the SOPs and analytical QC. A systematic approach to the use of QC facilitates the measurement of assay variability and bias over time and comparison against set criteria. This is typically accomplished by using commercially available QC material that is analyzed at the same time as the test sample. The recovered concentration of the control material is evaluated against specified acceptance criteria. In addition, external QC or proficiency programs determine the quality of the data produced by the laboratory by comparing laboratory results for an unknown (laboratory intercomparison samples and performance evaluation samples) using the same methods and equipment and participation in these programs is recommended by the ASVCP RAC [5]. Proper implementation of these robust internal and external QA programs provides reasonable confidence regarding suitable instrument performance and accurate, precise, and reproducible data generation, as prescribed within regulatory environments [49].

Clinical pathology laboratories that analyze animal samples frequently use tests that are optimized for accuracy using human samples. It is likely that many of these tests have small systematic biases. When used for animal specimens, in most cases, however, the excellent precision provided by using standardized commercial reagent kits, standards, and calibrators is preferable to time-consuming, costly efforts to optimize the accuracy of a test for different animal species by using home brew material that undermines precision [48]. The use of species-specific controls is encouraged to potentially detect changes in commercial reagents that have been further optimized for clinical use. It is not unknown for an immunoassay supplier to change an assay formulation to improve performance in the clinical setting, but fail to adequately communicate this change to the customer. If this assay had been previously validated for use with a selected animal species, the change in assay formulation (eg, employment of different antibodies) may lead to consequential loss of analytical response. Uses of species-specific controls can, at a minimum, identify the loss of response at an early stage. For regulatory studies, it is good practice to ensure the inclusion of QC samples within each of the studies and the results maintained with each study dataset. If results from a control sample are found to exceed the allowable limits for one or more analytes, then actions should be taken to resolve the problem. Consideration should also be made of the possibility of analytical interference in a test where there is no other supporting evidence for results (high, low, and exposure related) and the results are unexpected and not biologically plausible.

Hematology

Blood and hematopoietic tissue rank with liver and kidney as target organs worthy of careful scrutiny in preclinical and clinical safety evaluations. The importance of blood examination of toxicity studies is a direct consequence of the intimate exposure of experimental compounds to the cellular and humoral components of the blood, and a range of toxic agents have been identified to exert hematotoxic effects by differing actions and mechanisms [50]. Factors contributing to this include the high mitotic rate of hematopoietic tissue, the exposure of blood cells to agents administered systemically, and the consequences of blood cell damage and bone marrow impairment. The complete blood count (CBC) is the foundation of the evaluation of the hematopoietic system in preclinical toxicity studies, and the key parameters measured are red blood cell count (RBC), hematocrit, hemoglobin concentration, white blood cell (WBC) and differential count, and platelet count. Evaluation of the bone marrow is also conducted if warranted following analysis of the CBC and morphological examination of bone marrow tissue.

Instrumentation

The availability of highly sophisticated hematology instrumentation (eg, ADVIA 120/2120, Siemens medical solutions; CELL-DYN 3500, Abbot Laboratories; Sysmex XT-2000iV; Sysmex Europe), using a combination of light scatter, impedance, conductivity, or cytochemistry principles, now provides the capability to generate comprehensive information from the EDTA-anticoagulated blood sample, from a volume of <300 μL, for laboratory and veterinary animals using multispecies software [51]. For example, the ADVIA 120/2120 hematology systems are commonly found in toxicological clinical pathology laboratories. These flow cytometry-based systems use low- and high-angle laser light scatter, differential WBC lysis and myeloperoxidase,

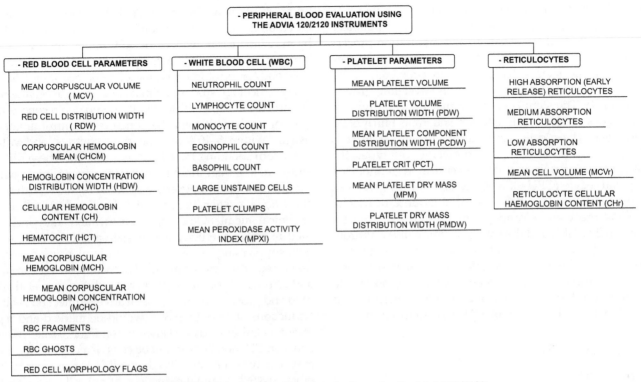

FIGURE 14.4 Peripheral blood evaluation using the Advia120/2120.

and oxazine 750 staining to determine cell number (RBC, WBC, platelet, and reticulocyte counts), cell type (WBC differential count and reticulocyte count), cell size and distribution [MCV, RDW, and mean platelet volume (MPV)], and hemoglobin concentration (by two methods). RBC and platelet indices are calculated and RBC morphology flags are also presented (Fig. 14.4). The automated generation and reporting of absolute differential counts (neutrophils, lymphocytes, monocytes, eosinophils, and basophils) provide more accurate data and enable the detection of reductions in minor leukocyte counts, eg, eosinophils. Automated instruments have virtually replaced manually performed differential WBC counts. Given the comprehensive information available from these instruments, also including the generation of reticulocyte absolute counts and subpopulations, some laboratories adopt the process of only preparing and staining peripheral blood films at the time of sample receipt but do not routinely examine them, unless this is required to support or clarify abnormal findings in the absolute data and/or scatter cytogram(s) appearance. However, when performed, the peripheral blood film may show variation in cell shape, degree of staining, cellular inclusions, and other features, and can be highly informative as to the cause of toxicological change [52]. Automated determination of absolute reticulocyte counts and subpopulations can give useful information of the temporal responses of the bone marrow to RBC changes. Increases in the ratio of high absorption (early maturation) reticulocyte counts

to the medium and low absorption populations can be observed within 24 h, eg, following small blood volume withdrawal from rats (≤7%) and preceding changes in the total absolute counts. Analytical interference with automated hematology measurements may sometimes occur. Recently rat-strain-specific intermittent analytical interference producing atypical RBC channel cytograms has been observed with Crl: Wistar Han rat EDTA-blood samples in internal studies and also externally [53]. The atypical RBC channel cytogram appears as a tail-shaped cloud on top of the usual RBC population, indicating the presence of normocytic to macrocytic, normochromic to hyperchromic RBCs. This interference reflected RBC agglutination, caused by the presence of glutaraldehyde in the RBC reagent on the Advia 2120 hematology analyzer. As a consequence, some RBC agglutinates are counted by the Advia 2120 analyzer as single large red cells, thereby increasing the RDW. This effect had not been previously noted in the Crl: CD (Sprague Dawley) rat. Given the incidence of the analytical interference in the Wistar Han, our laboratory decided to report the gated RDW, RBC, and MCV parameters measured by the gated reticulocyte channel from the Advia 2120 analyzer as an alternative as the reticulocyte reagent contains no glutaraldehyde.

Hematopoiesis

The bone marrow is the major hematopoietic organ and primary lymphoid organ responsible for the production of erythrocytes, granulocytes (neutrophils, eosinophils, and basophils), lymphocytes, monocytes, and platelets. The production, differentiation, and maturation process of blood cells depends on a complex interplay between hematopoietic stem cells, committed progenitor cells, the bone marrow, and both local and systemic growth factors [54]. The stem cells in the marrow can give rise to all types of blood cells, and are known as pluripotent stem cells. These cells can differentiate into stem cells that are capable of giving rise to myeloid cell types, the colony-forming unit granulocyte/erythroid/monocyte/ megakaryocyte (CFU-GEMM), which in turn gives rise to progenitor cells, whose potential is more restricted, such as the colony-forming unit granulocyte/macrophage (CFU-GM) and the colony-forming unit erythroid (CFU-E) [52]. A basic understanding of this process that leads to hematopoietic cellular differentiation and release of these cells into the circulation is important to accurately interpret the changes in bone marrow and blood that may be seen in preclinical toxicity studies.

Assessment of Hematotoxicity

Erythrocytes

The function of erythrocytes is to transport oxygen to the tissues. The principal promoter of red cell production is erythropoietin (EPO), a glycoprotein hormone that is secreted in response to variation in circulating oxygen tension by renal cortical interstitial cells [55]. The erythroid series of cells is derived from the stem cell and then the CFU-GEMM. The earliest progenitor restricted to the red cell lineage is the burst-forming unit-erythroid (BFU-E), from which is derived the CFU-E. This gives rise to the precursor cell, the rubriblast, which matures to a prorubricyte, rubricyte, and then to a metarubricyte. The last stage in maturation to the non-nucleated biconcave erythrocyte is to the reticulocyte. This maturation process from rubriblast to reticulocyte within the bone marrow takes on the order of 8 days. The reticulocyte lifespan in laboratory animals is less than 2 days before it becomes a mature red blood cell. The reticulocyte reflects the number of circulating erythrocytes that are removed by the macrophages of the reticuloendothelial system, as the production and destruction of the erythrocytes are normally balanced. Normally the reticulocyte numbers will vary inversely with the red cell lifespan, which is shorter in most laboratory animal species than in humans (120 days) [56]. Lifespan of erythrocytes in the circulation generally increases with size of the laboratory animal, and estimated lifespans for mouse, rat, monkey, and dog are 20–45, 45–68, 85–100, and 100–120 days, respectively [57].

Reductions in Red Cell Mass

Anemia is broadly defined as a decrease in the oxygen-carrying capacity of the blood due to a reduction in numbers of circulating red cells. Laboratory diagnosis is based on detecting a reduction in red cell mass (evaluated by measurement of hematocrit, RBC count, and hemoglobin concentration) [58], in comparison to concurrent controls and/or prestudy baseline or reference intervals. In many toxicology studies, animals in a group receiving the test article have lower RBC counts, hemoglobin concentration, or hematocrit than the concurrent control animals, usually within 5–10% of concurrent controls, and without a corresponding increase in reticulocyte. These differences are less than those necessary to cause clinical signs (eg, pallor, weakness, exercise intolerance, tachycardia) or affect tissue oxygenation, and are therefore not indicative of clinical anemia. Other study observations may include mild reductions in body weight gain and food consumption, suppressing hematopoiesis and influencing a reduction in reticulocytes and minimal reductions in total protein and albumin. These decreases in red cell mass are relatively mild and probably do not have an adverse effect on health. Reductions of more than 30% would be marked and represent a clinically adverse anemic condition, while values between 10% and 30% would be considered moderate and may or may not be clinically adverse [59]. In agreement with others [48,59], minimal reductions of red cell mass should first be discussed in terms of magnitude of change, and the clinical term "anemia" should be used only after careful consideration, unless a marked reduction is observed and it is important to emphasize the effect.

Reductions in red cell mass may be caused by decreased circulating lifespan, blood loss (hemorrhage), accelerated erythrocyte destruction (hemolysis), or decreased bone marrow production, and can be broadly classified as regenerative or nonregenerative, according to the presence or absence of reticulocytosis. Additionally, cell size (ie, normocytic, macrocytic, microcytic) and hemoglobin content (normochromic, hypochromic) can classify the reduction in red cell mass. The reporting of absolute reticulocyte counts (and, if available, the high, medium, and low absorption reticulocyte subpopulation counts) is considered essential for interpretation of the bone marrow and extramedullary erythropoietic response.

Regenerative responses, reflecting a compensatory increase in erythropoiesis in the bone marrow or extramedullary hematopoiesis in the spleen, occur in response to hemorrhage or hemolysis, and changes associated with the erythrocytic response are detectable in the peripheral blood after a lapse of 3–5 days. Magnitude of response may vary across species, with the rodent more responsive than the dog. Examination of the peripheral blood film may show marked anisocytosis (variation in cell size), polychromasia (variation in color), and if the demand is extensive, nucleated RBCs. These findings accompany increased MCV, increased RDW, bone marrow erythroid hyperplasia, and reticulocytosis. Earlier indications of a bone marrow response (from 24 h) can be seen if the high-absorption reticulocyte (most immature) subpopulation is evaluated. The regenerative response (as reflected in the increase of the absolute reticulocyte count) is generally more pronounced in hemolytic than in hemorrhagic red cell mass reductions because iron is conserved for erythropoiesis following hemolysis [58].

Hemolytic anemia is characterized by a shortened RBC lifespan. RBCs are either lysed within the circulation (intravascular hemolysis) or phagocytosed by the mononuclear macrophages of the reticuloendothelial system in the bone marrow, spleen, or liver (extravascular hemolysis). Intravascular hemolysis is characterized by the presence of free hemoglobin in the plasma or urine. Haptoglobin, an α_2-glycoprotein in human and animals, binds free hemoglobin, forming a stable complex. During episodes of intravascular hemolysis, haptoglobin acts to prevent excretion of hemoglobin from the body and prevent the kidneys from tissue damage due to the destructive effect of free iron.

Extravascular hemolysis is characterized by splenomegaly, bone marrow hypercellularity, and/or extramedullary hematopoiesis. Histologically an increase in hemosiderin is generally observed in the spleen and sometimes other organs, indicating increased red cell turnover and processing of hemoglobin. The mechanisms for acquired hemolytic anemias may be subdivided into those due to oxidation, immune responses, and red cell fragmentation and those that are secondary to other disorders, eg, hepatic and renal injury.

There are two main mechanisms for xenobiotically induced hemolytic anemia; namely oxidative stress and immune mechanisms [56]. Oxidative stress may manifest through inhibition of erythrocytic enzymes primarily by the pentose–phosphate and Embden–Meyerhof pathways or exhaustion of the glutathione redox-dependent cycle resulting in oxidation of hemoglobin methemoglobin, or sulfhemoglobin with or without the formation of Heinz bodies. Heinz bodies are particles of irreversibly denatured hemoglobin attached to the inner surface of the RBC membrane, which result from disulfide bond formation from oxidation of the sulfhydryl groups of hemoglobin.

Many oxidant drugs (eg, aniline), when given in sufficient concentrations either in vivo or in vitro, will overcome the erythrocyte's reducing potential. In an example of the changes observed in extravascular hemolysis, the hematoxicity of aniline was demonstrated by the inhaled route [60]. The predominant manifestation of toxicity was methemoglobin formation (approximately 15% of total hemoglobin concentration in the high-dose animals; concurrent controls 0–1%) and associated erythrocytoxicity. In those animals receiving the highest inhaled doses (96.5 and 274.9 mg aniline/m^3), changes observed included anemia (up to a 20% reduction in red cell mass parameters from concurrent controls at day 4), RBC morphological alterations including observations

of Heinz bodies, and reticulocytosis (up to two- and six-fold increases from concurrent controls at days 4 and 11, respectively). Effects on the spleen were also evident, including splenomegaly, hemosiderin accumulation, and extramedullary hematopoiesis. Accumulation of iron within the spleen was proportionate to dose, and time-dependent and iron accumulation was also demonstrated in the liver. The primary toxicity of aniline is characterized by methemoglobinemia. The increase in production of methemoglobin (MetHb) in erythrocytes results from the oxidation of heme iron from the ferrous (Fe^{2+}) to the ferric (Fe^{3+}) states. Methemoglobin is incapable of carrying oxygen reversibly in the way that hemoglobin does, with the result that methemoglobinemia represents a loss of oxygen carrying power of the blood and very high levels (>50% of total hemoglobin concentration) are potentially lethal [42]. The measurement of methemoglobin (by spectrophotometry using instruments called cooximeters) requires careful sampling and measurement; the assay needs to be conducted within a short space of time of the sample being drawn (ideally within 30 min) and typically the analysis occurs in or very close to the animals' room. Methemoglobin levels in normal samples are very low (0–4%, varying with species and with analytical methodology), but since hemoglobin in a sample tube oxidizes slowly to methemoglobin, time from sampling to analysis is critical. Methemoglobin can be rapidly reversible in vivo, so timing of the sample relative to administration of the test article must be considered. Interspecies differences in methemoglobinemias appear to be mainly due to the ability of the erythrocytes to reduce red cell methemoglobin concentrations. Rats and mice appear to have greater ability to reduce erythrocytic methemoglobin (and hence recover more quickly) than dogs or humans, with nonhuman primates having a lower capacity. Dogs are considered to be the best model for humans in assessing potential risk of methemoglobinemia [52].

Decreased red cell mass is an uncommon adverse response to biotherapeutics and can be caused by effects on circulating erythrocytes (hemolysis) or erythropoiesis in the bone marrow [61]. Destruction of erythrocytes may occur as a result of immune activation. In immune red cell destruction (autoimmune hemolytic anemia), antibodies to drugs may coincidentally possess the same specificity for red cell membrane proteins. In the case of immune complex formation, complement may be bound to the erythrocyte, leading to intravascular destruction of the cell, or alternatively the biconcave shape of the erythrocyte is lost and it becomes spherical, smaller, round, and lacking central pallor (spherocyte formation). The test article may bind to the erythrocyte membrane, and drug antibody complexes may form (eg, penicillin). In these examples involving the erythrocyte, antibody can be demonstrated on the cells by the direct antiglobulin (direct Coombs) test [50]. Animals with test-article-induced immune-mediated hemolytic anemia become severely anemic with repeated test article administration; however, they will usually exhibit a strong regenerative response and will always recover if test administration is stopped [48].

Alterations of RBC structure that are subsequently recognized as abnormal by the mononuclear phagocyte system can also trigger extravascular hemolysis. In a published example, SCH900875, a selective CXCR3 (chemokine) receptor antagonist, induced a severe hemolytic anemia in rats (decrease in RBC count of 35% compared to concurrent controls in females given 100 mg/kg/day) and thrombocytopenia with acanthocytosis at 75, 100, and 150 mg/kg/day, over a 13/14-week time period [62]. Acanthocytes are smaller red cells with spicules of varied length that are irregularly distributed over the cell surface. Their formation is generally associated with alterations in lipid composition and fluidity of the red cell membrane. These abnormal red cells were the trigger for increases in phagocytosis and massively enlarged spleens and corresponded histologically to extramedullary hematopoiesis, macrophages, and hemosiderin pigment and sinus congestion. Alterations of the lipid profile of the RBC plasma membrane was identified and considered the trigger for the increased cell destruction.

Blood Loss (Hemorrhagic Anemia)

Hemorrhagic anemia may be acute (2 to 3 days), subchronic (3–12 days), or chronic (>10 days) in duration. Acute hemorrhage is characterized by consistent reductions in hematocrit, inconsistent decreases in platelet counts and plasma protein concentrations, and the absence of a regenerative response. In subchronic hemorrhage, there is evidence of a regenerative response, namely anisocytosis, polychromasia, reticulocytosis, and bone marrow erythroid hyperplasia. Increases in platelet count and decreases in plasma protein concentration are inconsistently observed. With continued hemorrhage, particularly external hemorrhage, excessive iron loss may occur, bone marrow reserves may become depleted, and the marrow fails to respond adequately. Hence chronic hemorrhage is variable in presentation, and depending on duration and severity it may present as a regenerative, nonregenerative, or iron-deficiency anemia. It may require additional tests (eg, fecal occult blood or blood in urine) to help identify the cause, in addition to clinical observations [56,57].

Nonregenerative Reductions in Red Cell Mass

Reductions in red cell mass caused by decreased bone marrow production will be nonregenerative due to the lack of immature red cell production. Nonregenerative conditions may reflect either reduced or defective erythropoiesis in the bone marrow. Impairment of bone marrow erythropoiesis takes longer to cause anemia due to the comparatively long red cell lifespan. Erythrocytes will generally appear normocytic and normochromic; the MCV is unchanged or decreased and the absolute reticulocyte is unchanged or decreased. Recovery following removal of the test article will start to be observed in peripheral blood within a week, because the time of development from a committed stem cell to a reticulocyte is about 4–5 days. However, recovery to circulating red cell numbers approximating pretest values or concurrent values may take several weeks, dependent on the degree of anemia caused by the test article.

Since hypoxia stimulates the bone marrow to respond, a rapid response may not occur in cases of mild anemia. Decreased erythropoiesis may be secondary to inanition associated with inappetance, reduced activity, lack of activity, and other systemic toxicological effects of the administered test article. Additionally, reductions in erythropoiesis may be observed in the presence of a marked acute-phase response, reflecting the release of proinflammatory cytokines including interleukin-6. Depending on the magnitude of the release, partial to complete suppression of erythrocyte production may be observed. Other secondary causes include decreased availability of iron or as a consequence of chronic inflammatory disease. Small reductions in circulating red-cell mass may be associated with hypothyroidism. Indirect effects on erythropoiesis tend to be relatively mild and are not as important as the direct effects of the primary target tissue.

Compounds that have direct toxic effects on proliferating bone marrow cells or stromal cells of the bone marrow may produce nonregenerative (hypoproliferative) anemia [63]. Examples are antineoplastic drugs that target DNA and drugs that interfere with hemoglobin synthesis. Abnormal maturation of red blood cell, such as in folate or B_{12} deficiency, may result in a megaloblastic anemia. The timing of sample collection following administration of a test article that temporarily interrupts hematopoiesis (eg, cytotoxic chemotherapeutics) will dictate the findings in peripheral blood and can impact interpretation [64]. Reductions in reticulocytes, neutrophils, eosinophils, platelets, and often lymphocytes are decreased in number at the peak effect. Recovery is identified characteristically as increased counts for reticulocytes and platelets above concurrent controls (rebound effect). Following cessation of dosing, the time taken for bone marrow recovery may vary between different treatments [65] and it is advantageous to perform hematology measurements at multiple time intervals to characterize the recovery response [48,64,65].

Erythrocytosis

Erythrocytosis is a relative or absolute increase in the number of circulating RBCs, resulting in increases in hematocrit and hemoglobin above control levels. Primary erythrocytosis describes a condition where there is proliferation of erythroid cells in the absence of increased erythropoietin, producing increases in total red blood cell mass. If the erythrocytosis is concurrent with a neoplastic proliferation of leukocytes and megakaryocytes, then polycythemia vera is present [66]. Secondary erythrocytosis represents the stimulation of erythropoiesis following increased EPO activity, producing erythroid hyperplasia and increased red blood cell mass. The increased EPO activity may be in response to generalized tissue hypoxia as a result of hypoxia or pulmonary damage or by inappropriate and excessive production of EPO or EPO-like substance in an animal with normal blood oxygen levels. Transient erythrocytosis is caused by splenic contraction, which injects concentrated RBCs into the circulation in a momentary response to epinephrine, the hormone that reacts to stress, anger, and fear. Erythrocytosis of hemoconcentration is more common in toxicity studies and describes conditions where the red blood cell mass is elevated, but the change is caused by reductions in plasma volume resulting from either dehydration or following severe fluid loss from the gastrointestinal tract, stress perturbations of fluid balance, and with diuretics [56]. Administration of erythropoiesis stimulating agents (ESAs) is associated with sporadic mortality and prothrombotic events in rats, beagle dogs, and cynomolgus monkeys in the presence of a high hematocrit [67]. Investigative studies conducted with a hyperglycosylated analog of recombinant human EPO (AMG 114) identified prothrombotic risk factors in the presence of a sustained hematocrit. These factors were higher numbers of circulating immature reticulocytes and nucleated red blood cells, severe functional iron deficiency and increased intravascular destruction of iron-deficient reticulocyte/red cells [68], and pleiotropic cytokine production [69]. The dose, dose frequency, and dosing duration of AMG114 was identified as important, as similar prothrombotic risk factors were not observed in the low-dose group, even though a similar hematocrit was observed.

Leukocytes

Collectively the neutrophils, eosinophils, and basophils are termed granulocytes because of their granular contents. Granulocytes are also known as polymorphonuclear leukocytes, or polymorphs, having segmented nuclei and cytoplasmic granules. These cells have a short half-life within the circulation before migrating into tissues. Granulocytopoiesis (the production of neutrophils, eosinophils, and basophils) and monocyte production occur in the bone marrow and have two main phases: proliferation and maturation. The mitotic pool of cells—the myeloblasts, promyelocytes, and myelocytes—undergo three to five divisions before yielding the postmitotic pool of metamyelocytes, band cells, and mature segmented cells. The postmitotic cells are distributed into four compartments: the maturation, storage, circulating, and tissue pools. The maturation pool contains metamyelocytes and band cells that mature but do not proliferate. In the storage pool, the cells include segmented neutrophils that act as a reservoir of mature cells; these cells can be released into the circulation at short notice, eg, as a response to stress [70–72]. Within the circulating pool, the granulocytes can be located either in a freely circulating pool or within the marginated cell pool temporarily adhered to endothelial cells primarily within small capillaries and veins. After adhesion, the granulocytes may migrate into tissues or reenter the circulation. Mature cells enter the circulation usually for a short period before migrating to the tissues and body cavities, and many cells stay for only a short time within the tissue pool, limited by their active function and before consumption by the tissue. The spleen, liver, and lymph nodes in most species are able to produce granulocytes when there is increased demand (extramedullary granulocytopoiesis).

Alterations in Leukocyte Counts

Neutrophils and lymphocytes principally influence the WBC count; however, there are noticeable differences in the ratios of the various cell types of the blood in different laboratory animals. Thus in the rat, mouse, and minipig, the most frequent WBC in the circulation is the lymphocyte (accounting for approximately 75% (rodent) and 60% (minipig) of the cells), while in the dog, the neutrophil is the dominant cell type. In nonhuman primates, the ratio between the neutrophil and lymphocyte is more variable and a bias between neutrophils and lymphocytes is less evident. Alterations in the concentrations of the leukocyte populations may occur for a number of reasons depending on the cell lineage involved. Leukocyte cell numbers may be increased and termed cytosis or philia; reduction in cell numbers is termed penia.

Neutrophils

In healthy individuals, neutrophils have a blood half-life of 5–10h before they enter tissues. Influences on circulating levels of neutrophils reflect:

1. Production in the bone marrow.
2. Release from the marrow.
3. Distribution between the circulation and marginated neutrophil pools.
4. Migration from blood to tissues (mature neutrophils have greater potential to migrate than immature neutrophils).

Neutrophilia may be caused by bacterial infections, hemorrhage and hemolysis, increased production from the bone marrow, exercise or stress, impaired exit from the peripheral blood, and decreases in the marginated pool and concomitant increases in the circulating pool. Fear, excitement, and stress may lead to a physiological neutrophilia, reflecting catecholamine-mediated mobilization of neutrophils from the marginal pool to the circulating pool; this is a mild (up to twofold increase) and short lived (10–20 min) event [71–73]. This may be observed in some laboratory animals (eg, dog, nonhuman primate) in the pretreatment hematology bleed where animals are not sufficiently acclimatized (to environment or study procedures). Some facilities prefer the option of performing two pretreatment bleeds to reduce the biological variation, using the second bleed as a baseline. Endogenous or exogenous glucocorticoids may also trigger neutrophilia [73].

In the author's experience, neutrophilia is less apparent with chronic administration of glucocorticoids (in the presence of lymphopenia and eosinopenia reflecting pharmacology of the glucocorticoid), unless opportunistic infection is present following long-term immunosuppression. The neutrophilia observed generally reflects a release of mature neutrophils from the bone marrow and marginal pools. When demand exceeds the normal homeostatic rate of production, such as in a severe inflammatory response or acute infection with increased tissue requirements, the release of more immature forms of cells (so-called left shift) may be required to maintain the marginal, circulating, and tissue neutrophil levels [72,73]. In a severe or sustained inflammatory response, increases in the neutrophil count would be accompanied by monocytosis, increased serum/plasma globulin concentration reflecting acute- phase protein response and reductions in serum/plasma albumin. Neutrophilia may also be observed following increased production of marrow progenitors after administration of biotechnology-derived growth factors. Neutropenia may occur as a result of reduced or ineffective proliferation of the bone marrow, reflecting destruction of proliferating precursor cells, suppression of multipotent stem cells, or alteration of the hematopoietic microenvironment [74]. Hematopoietic stem cell destruction resulting in suppression of all cell lines (resulting in decreased numbers of neutrophils, monocytes, eosinophils, lymphocytes, reticulocytes, and platelets) is termed aplastic anemia, and is induced by chemotherapeutic agents such as busulfan and cyclophosphamide [64]. Given the reserve capacity of the bone marrow (approximately a 5-day supply of mature neutrophils is present in the marrow storage pool), suppression of granulopoiesis results in a rapid drop in circulating neutrophils within 5–7 days. The time period for recovery following withdrawal of the agent will be dose dependent and may vary between differing chemotherapeutic agents [64], and detection and duration of the neutropenia and subsequent recovery will be dependent on the frequency of hematology testing and bone marrow assessment.

Neutropenia may also result from increased tissue consumption (in excess of bone marrow production), cellular shifting from the circulating to the marginal pools, and immune-mediated mechanisms leading to increased removal of neutrophils from the circulation. Example compounds causing neutropenia include chloramphenicol, rifampicin, ristocetin, estrogens, phenylbutazone, sulfonamides, indomethacin, and procainamide [70].

Eosinophils

Eosinopoiesis is stimulated by specific mediators within the bone marrow. Marginated and circulating blood eosinophils remain in the blood from minutes to hours. Eosinophils have phagocytic and bactericidal properties, inactivate mediators from mast cells, and attack larval and adult stages of a few parasites. Eosinophilia may indicate parasitic infection and can occur secondary to some hypersensitivity reactions. Eosinopenia may be observed following acute administration of glucocorticoids, and is one of the early clinical pathology signals (along with reductions in lymphocyte counts) to indicate glucocorticoid exposure [75]. The decreased eosinophil counts are maintained for the duration of the dosing period and recover within a few days following glucocorticoid withdrawal. Eosinopenia occurs because of inhibition of eosinophil release from the bone marrow and sequestration of eosinophils within tissues. Additionally, eosinopenia may be a reflection of stress due to excess endogenous glucocorticoid and catecholamine production [7,73].

Basophils

The production and differentiation of basophils is controlled by interleukin-3 and other cytokines. The marrow transit time of basophils is at least 2.5 days, their circulating half-life is about 6 h, and they may survive for as long as two weeks in tissue [57]. Basophil migration to tissues is promoted by IL-1, TNFα, and endotoxin and is similar to the process used by neutrophils. Basophil granules contain substances that promote hypersensitivity inflammation reactions and attract eosinophils. Their numbers within the circulation are low and effects on basophils are very rare.

Monocytes

Monocytes and neutrophils share a common bipotential stem cell (CFU-GEMM) that is stimulated to differentiate by inflammatory cytokines and develop from monoblasts and promonocytes [57]. When released from the bone marrow, monocytes distribute between marginated and circulating pools and circulate for around 24 h. Like other leukocytes, monocytes emigrate to tissues after binding to endothelial cells. Once in tissues, monocytes may differentiate into cells of the mononuclear phagocyte system: macrophages (including Kupffer cells, alveolar macrophages, and type A synoviocytes), micoglial cells, or dendritic cells. The resting macrophage is also called a histocyte or fixed macrophage [71,72]. Increased monocyte counts (monocytosis) are observed with protozoal or bacterial infections and chronic and widespread inflammatory conditions, and monocytosis is often seen in association with neutrophilia. Decreases in monocytes counts may be seen following severe bone marrow toxicity, eg, after the administration of cytotoxic chemotherapeutic agents [64].

Lymphocytes

Mature lymphocytes are small mononuclear cells derived from hemopoietic stem cells; a common lymphoid stem cell undergoes differentiation and proliferation to give rise to major subpopulations: the B-cells and the T-cells. B-cell lymphocyte maturation occurs primarily in the bone marrow, and T-cell lymphocytes mature primarily in the thymus. At these sites, two functionally and phenotypically different populations of lymphocyte precursors develop for involvement in antibody mediated immunity (B-cells) and cell mediated immunity (T-cells). These then migrate to the peripheral organs (lymph nodes, spleen, and gut-associated lymphoid tissue) where they become immune-competent T- and B-cells in response to the appropriate antigenic stimulation. In comparison with the granulocytes, lymphocytes are distributed into circulating and margin-ated pools and may enter lymphoid or nonlymphoid tissues. Lymphocytes are unique in that they are continually recirculating within the vascular system, and their lifespan varies from hours to years [71,72]. Increases in lymphocyte counts (lymphocytosis) may be observed in chronic infections, inflammatory conditions, especially in rodents, lymphocytic malignancy, or with administration of test articles that are antigenic and elicit an immune response by the test animals [38]. Short-term stress (within minutes) can result in increases in circulating lymphocytes [7]. Additionally, agents that inhibit lymphocyte trafficking and recircula-tion through different organs, and hence migration from the circulating pool into tissues, by antagonism of adhesion molecules (eg, alpha$_4$ beta$_1$ and alpha$_4$ beta$_7$ integrins) can produce lymphocytosis [76]. Physiological lymphocytosis may also be observed following excitement or stress.

Reductions in lymphocyte counts (lymphopenia) may reflect direct cytotoxic chemotherapeutic effects on bone marrow production, with the response in rodents easier to detect than nonrodents due to the higher number of lymphocytes in comparison to neutrophils. With com-pounds producing experimental aplastic anemia in mice, lymphocyte decline and recovery following withdrawal of the test agent parallels other WBC types [64].

Lymphopenia may be observed following acute administration of glucocorticoids, and is one of the early clinical pathology signals indicating glucocorticoid expo-sure and concomitant pharmacology [75]. The decreased lymphocytes counts are maintained for the dosing period and recover within a few days following gluco-corticoid withdrawal. The lymphopenia is attributed to redistribution of circulating lymphocytes. Long-term administration of glucocorticoids may produce lym-pholysis associated with thymic atrophy. Excess endog-enous corticosteroid effects, reflecting chronic stress, will also produce lymphopenia [7]. Lymphopenia has also been reported with novel immunosuppressant thera-pies following demonstration of acceleration of lympho-cyte migration into lymphoid tissue (peripheral lymph nodes, mesenteric lymph nodes, and Peyer's patches) coupled with inhibition of lymphocyte egress from the lymph nodes into the lymph and from the thymus into the blood [77]. Additionally, alteration of peripheral blood lymphocyte morphology reflecting the inclusion of cytoplasmic vacuoles consistent with phospholipid accumulation has been observed with cationic amphilic drugs [78]. The vacuolated lymphocyte observed with systemic phospholipidosis serves as a useful screen for detection of this drug-induced disorder.

Hemostasis

Hemostasis is the term used to describe the arrest of bleeding or the interruption of blood flow through a ves-sel. Hemostasis represents an intricate, highly balanced interaction between blood vessels, platelets, plasma coag-ulation factors, and fibrinolytic proteins in the formation and dissolution of blood clots. Under normal conditions these balanced physiological processes maintain blood in a free-flowing state. Hemostasis may be categorized into primary (platelet plug formation), secondary (formation of a stabilized fibrin clot through the coagulation cascade), and tertiary (formation of plasmin for breakdown of fibrin via fibrinolysis) concurrent processes. Disorders of hemo-stasis or unbalanced hemostasis may lead to hypocoagula-tion (hemorrhage) or hypercoagulation (thromboembolic disorders) [79,80]. Evaluation of hemostasis in preclinical toxicology studies includes an assessment of both plasma coagulation factors and platelets. Fibrinogen is also recom-mended where blood volume is not limiting [5]. A recent survey of the laboratory assessment of hemostasis was con-ducted amongst discovery, preclinical and clinical research scientists by the Health and Environmental Sciences Insti-tute Cardiac Biomarkers Working Group [81]. Inconsisten-cies in approach were identified and the need for a broader utilization of translatable biomarkers to detect alterations in hemostasis, including prothrombotic states, to improve preclinical safety assessment of test articles early in the development process was identified.

Platelets

Platelets are the second most numerous circulating cells in blood and are essential for coagulation, maintenance of vascular integrity, and control of hemostasis. Megakaryocytes give rise to circulating platelets (thrombocytes) though commitment of the multipotent stem cell to megakaryocyte lineage, proliferation of the progenitors, and terminal differentiation of megakaryocytes. This process is characterized by DNA endoreduplication, cytoplasmic maturation and expansion, and release of cytoplasmic fragments as platelets, producing thousands of platelets per megakaryocyte [82]. Thrombopoietin (TPO), also known as c-Mpl ligand, is the primary physiological growth factor regulating the process of megakaryocytopoiesis and thrombopoiesis within the complex bone marrow microenvironment. TPO is primarily produced by hepatocytes, stromal cells in the bone marrow, and renal epithelial cells. TPO is produced constitutively and its circulating levels are regulated by the extent of binding to c-Mpl receptors on circulating platelets and marrow megakaryocytes, with the TPO blood concentration being inversely related to the platelet mass. When circulating platelet mass is decreased, the concentration of unbound TPO available to stimulate megakaryocytopoiesis and thrombopoiesis is increased, and vice versa. Platelet concentration in the blood reflects a balance between platelet production and consumption, destruction, or redistribution to the vasculature of the organs. Aged platelets are removed by macrophages and the spleen plays a major role in determining platelet survival. The circulating lifespan of platelets in healthy animals ranges from 5 to 10 days (eg, 5 days in mice, rats; 7 days in dogs). Measurement of reticulated platelets in rats, analogous to assessing reticulocyte responses as a marker of erythropoiesis, has been advocated to assess thrombopoiesis [83].

Thrombocytosis

Increased platelet count in peripheral blood is defined as thrombocytosis, which may reflect a direct test-article-related effect (primary thrombocytosis) or may reflect an indirect effect (reactive or secondary thrombocytosis). Primary thrombocytosis, an unusual finding, is an anticipated effect when the test article is a hematopoietic growth factor such as TPO. Additionally, administration of interleukin-6 (IL-6) has been demonstrated to induce thrombopoiesis, along with acute-phase protein synthesis [84]. Reactive or secondary thrombosis may occur secondary to catecholamine-induced splenic contraction or to generalized bone marrow response as in hemolytic anemia, blood loss, or inflammation. One report noted that in dogs, thrombocytosis occurred most frequently secondary to neoplastic and inflammatory diseases and was commonly associated with glucocorticoid and vincristine administration [85]. Also, a rebound thrombocytosis may follow thrombocytopenia due to reversible inhibition by chemotherapeutic agents.

Thrombocytopenia

Thrombocytopenia is defined as a decrease in circulating platelets and results from one or a combination of the following basic mechanisms: generalized bone marrow suppression (decreased or defective platelet production), increased peripheral platelet loss or consumption, increased platelet destruction, or abnormal distribution (sequestration) [63]. Additionally artifactual or spurious thrombocytopenia, associated with difficulties with venipuncture or inadequate anticoagulation and subsequent in vitro platelet aggregation, can be observed in toxicology studies.

Alterations of platelet kinetics (reductions in platelet counts, survival time, and platelet half-life) associated with rapid and selective sequestration in the spleen have been reported in dogs given a glycoprotein IIb/IIIa peptide antagonist orally for 4 days [86]. Abnormal platelet sequestration is almost invariably due to hypersplenism and can be suspected in the presence of significant splenic enlargement. In contrast, it may be difficult to distinguish between hyperplastic and hyperdestructive forms of thrombocytopenia. Clinically significant thrombocytopenia has been observed in cynomolgus monkeys induced by a therapeutic human antibody [87]. This unexpected event was considered to reflect antibody-induced direct/indirect activation of monocytes/macrophages and phagocytosis of platelets. The presence of normal or increased numbers of megakaryocytes in the bone marrow essentially excludes the diagnoses of hypoplastic thrombocytopenia, such as aplastic anemia and amegakaryocytic thrombocytopenia. Selective megakaryocytic toxicity, either through toxicity or an immune-mediated mechanism, is associated with paucity of megakaryocytes in bone marrow. Conversely, with platelet destruction or consumption, the marrow will show a marked increase in megakaryocytic numbers. Any signal in the data from preclinical studies that suggest platelets are a target should be carefully and fully evaluated. Automated assessment of platelet morphology [eg, MPV, platelet distribution width (PDW), mean platelet component (MPC), mean platelet component distribution width, mean platelet mass (MPM), platelet mass distribution width (PMDW), and large platelets] assessing size, density, granularity, and distribution is possibly underutilized in the preclinical laboratory. These parameters can help characterize changes in thrombocytopenia and the bone marrow response in platelet production, whether caused by decreased bone marrow platelet production or increased peripheral destruction [88]. Internal studies have demonstrated marked increases in MPV, MPDW, MPM, and MPDW in response to pronounced test-article-induced thrombocytopenia in the dog. The collection of MPV data when measuring the platelet count is of proven clinical value, and a number of studies have shown that patients with higher MPV with thrombocytosis are at an increased risk for a thrombotic event, reflecting immaturity and probably reactivity of the platelets in comparison to mature normal platelets [88]. In the utilization of platelet parameters in a recent investigation, associated increases in platelets and MPV with increased functional iron deficiency were observed [67].

Coagulation

The coagulation factors are mostly serine proteases, which are proenzymes and procofactors. These act in a sequential manner termed the coagulation cascade. This cascade begins with the activation of the extrinsic (or tissue factor) or the intrinsic (or contact) pathways, both of which, through an interconnected series of enzyme-activating steps, result in the formation of factor IIa and the conversion of soluble fibrinogen (factor I) into an insoluble fibrin plug through the common pathway [89,90]. A majority of the proteins involved in the coagulation pathways are synthesized by the liver. Factors II, VII, IX, and X require vitamin K for their conversion from inactive to active factors. Activities of the coagulation factors, when compared to humans, vary across laboratory animal species [90]. The extrinsic system involves the reactions of the tissue factor and factor VII that result in the conversion of factor X to factor Xa. The intrinsic system is composed of factors VIII, IX, XI, and XI, prekallikrein, and kininogen. The common pathway includes factors V, X, and XIII, prothrombin, and fibrinogen. The reactions of the blood coagulant system are carefully controlled by several anticoagulant mechanisms and under normal conditions they prevail over the procoagulant forces [91].

The PT and APTT assays are routinely incorporated into study protocols, to assess the function of the plasma coagulation factors, with the exception of factor XIII. The thrombin time (TT) assay is utilized to assess the presence of functional fibrinogen. Plasma coagulation assays are divided into the assessment of the extrinsic, intrinsic, and common pathways. The PT assay is a nonspecific test that measures the functional ability of the extrinsic coagulation system. The PT assay measures plasma clotting time in seconds after the addition of tissue thromboplastin (factor III) and calcium chloride to the specimen. A prolonged PT is indicative of abnormalities of factor VII or X, prothrombin, or fibrinogen. It may also be prolonged due to the presence of an inhibitor. The APTT assay is a nonspecific test that measures the functional ability of the intrinsic and common coagulation pathways. The assay measures plasma clotting time in seconds after the specimen is incubated with a surface-activating agent (factor VII activator), partial thromboplastin, and calcium chloride. A prolonged APTT may be due to abnormalities of factor V, VII, IX, X, XI, or XII. It may also be due to the presence of an inhibitor. Coagulation assays require the use of whole blood collected using trisodium citrate as the anticoagulant. The ratio of anticoagulant to whole blood is critical since excessive sodium citrate anticoagulant in the plasma sample can artifactually prolong PT and APTT [92].

The TT assay is an alternative, specific test that estimates the quantity of functionally active fibrinogen. The assay measures plasma clotting time in seconds after the specimen is incubated with thrombin and calcium chloride. TT prolongation may be due to reduced functional fibrinogen (dysfibrinogenemia), reduced fibrinogen (hypofibrinogenemia), the presence of fibrinogen degradation products, heparin, and antibody to thrombin or amyloidosis.

The APTT and PT assays are considered to be relatively insensitive and nonspecific, as the activity of single clotting factor must be reduced to about 30% of normal before meaningful prolongation of clotting times occurs. Normal clotting times for the APTT and PT tests vary considerably between species. For example, normal PTs in the dog and marmoset are considerably shorter than in the human. Given this variation, the generation of species-specific reference intervals is considered important in coagulation testing. Factor VII deficiency is occasionally observed in the laboratory beagle, as reflected in an increased PT during prestudy screening. These animals are, as a default, excluded from the study. Despite the differences in normal times these screening tests appear to work well—ie, they can detect inhibitory effects on coagulation factors in laboratory animals and small statistically significant differences between group mean values for controls and test-article-treated animals can be observed in toxicology studies. Similarly to platelet count, coagulation times can be spuriously prolonged by difficult blood collection or poor collection technique. The combination of low platelet count and prolonged coagulation times, in an otherwise healthy animal, is an indication of poor sample quality [48].

Test-article-induced prolongation of clotting times may reflect an effect on vitamin-K-dependent proteins (factors II, VII, IX, and X). Vitamin K is a fat-soluble vitamin that is either consumed in the diet or synthesized by bacterial microflora in the ileum and colon. Prolongation of clotting times are more likely to manifest in subacute studies and longer (≥ 2 weeks), because the liver stores of vitamin K are adequate for several days. Compound-related vitamin K deficiencies are most frequently associated with vitamin K antagonists (eg, warfarin); impairment of fat absorption (including fat-soluble vitamins) through targeted pharmacology or as a secondary effect due to gastrointestinal, hepatic, renal, or pancreatic toxicity; and use of antibiotics with resultant decreases in bacterial flora in the intestines [93]. Prolongation of clotting times is observed with profibrinolytic agents, eg, recombinant staphylokinase [94]. Prolongation of APTT times has also been observed following the administration of antisense oligodeoxynucleotides (AS ODN) in primates [95]. The effect is dose related, correlates with plasma ODN levels, and has been noted as a class effect and occurring in other laboratory animals. It is due to inhibition of the tenase complex (factors IXa, VIIIa, phospholipid, and calcium) of the intrinsic clotting pathway.

The prolongation of APTT in primates is transient due to the short plasma half-life of AS ODN and shows reversibility with drug clearance. No clinical manifestations of this transient inhibition have been observed. In this situation the APTT signal acts as a surrogate biomarker of exposure to AS ODNs.

Measurement of plasma fibrinogen is often included in an assessment of compound-related effects on hemostasis. Decreases in fibrinogen, especially when accompanied by decreased platelet count, and increases in APTT and PT, can be indicative of consumption of coagulation factor and intravascular formation of fibrin associated with disseminated intravascular coagulopathy (DIC). The underlying initiators of test article-related DIC can be diverse including systemic inflammation, uncontrolled immune-mediated cellular destruction (eg, hemolysis), metabolic acidosis, and hepatosplenic disease. In a recent example of a monoclonal antibody (RN6G) -induced immune complex disease, thrombocytopenia and coagulopathy (prolongation of PT and APTT times with decreased fibrinogen), and increased serum levels of activated complement products (C3a, C4d, and SC5b-9), associated with a nephrotic syndrome profile (decreased albumin and increased triglycerides and urea), were observed in cynomolgus monkeys [96]. Identification of antidrug antibodies (ADA) and lowering of exposure of RN6G preceded the clinical pathology changes. Immunohistochemical localization of RNG was associated with monkey immunoglobulin and complement components in glomeruli and other tissues.

Additional tests to assess this condition include antithrombin III quantification and fibrin degradation products (FDPs), so that effects on accelerated coagulation and fibrinolysis are evaluated [93]. Marked decreases in fibrinogen in studies with test articles with pharmacological activity targeted towards thrombin inhibition, and associated with marked prolongation of clotting times, are considered to reflect interference with the assay, since fibrinogen is routinely determined by measuring the conversion of fibrinogen to fibrin, a process requiring thrombin activity. An increase in fibrinogen levels (eg, observed with infectious or inflammatory conditions) may reflect an acute-phase reaction more often than coagulation dysfunction. Although effects on PT, APTT, platelet count, and fibrinogen are valuable in screening for test-article-induced alterations of hemostasis, they are usually inadequate to provide a mechanistic explanation.

It should be noted that APTT and PT are considered insensitive measures of liver function. Although the liver synthesizes most clotting factors, the large liver functional reserve means that severe liver pathology (accompanied by alterations of clinical chemistry parameters of hepatic integrity and/or function) is generally required before coagulation times are affected.

CYTOLOGICAL EVALUATION OF BONE MARROW

Various techniques have been described for the preparation and examination of bone marrow smears, and success using these techniques depends on the procedures for collection, smear preparation, staining, and careful microscopic evaluation. Histopathological examination of bone marrow is generally performed in most toxicity studies (generally subchronic and chronic). While it is common practice to sample and prepare bone marrow smears, many laboratories elect to examine bone marrow smears only when there is evidence suggesting hematopoietic effects from either the hematology profile, including peripheral blood film, or histological evidence from the bone marrow sections and examination of the spleen and other tissues [54]. More detailed information on the preparation and evaluation of quality bone marrow smear preparations and the use of flow cytometric analysis for bone marrow evaluations can be found elsewhere [54,97–99].

The main indications for bone marrow smear evaluation toxicology studies are moderate to marked nonregenerative anemia, leukopenia, or thrombocytopenia with no apparent etiology or significant morphological abnormalities of peripheral blood cells [48]. Recommendations from the Bone Marrow Working Group of the American Society for Veterinary Clinical Pathology and the Society of Toxicological Pathology on when to perform bone marrow cytological examination have recently been published [99]. The need for cytological evaluation of bone marrow smears on a case-by-case basis was emphasized. If the evaluation of the combined study data indicated that characterization of the hematopoietic system was, or will be, inadequate using hematology and histopathology, then cytological evaluation of the bone marrow should be considered.

The group considered the following situations would warrant additional information collection from bone marrow cytological examination to support hematology and histopathology findings:

1. Differentiation of early hematopoietic precursors.
2. Additional characterization of effects on hematopoietic cell lines.
3. Determining whether changes in the bone marrow cellularity result from changes in the erythroid versus lymphoid populations.
4. Changes in erythrocyte indices or red cell morphology, eg, if changes in indices such as MCV and MCHC suggest abnormal erythropoiesis or neoplasia and accompanied by large or megalocytic erythroid cells in the blood.

5. Atypical changes in leukocyte morphology in the peripheral blood unrelated to inflammation (eg, "toxic changes"), antigenic stimulation (eg, lymphoid reactivity), or known effects of the drug (eg, vaculoation caused by phospholipidosis).

Additional situations where cytological evaluation of the bone marrow may not be necessary were also identified. These included decreased food intake in study animals, changes in peripheral blood lymphocyte numbers, where evidence is already present of a regenerative change in the bone marrow or blood, and in situations of platelet or granulocyte dysfunction where other methods could be used to assess functional deficiencies [99]. Qualitative and quantitative approaches to bone marrow smear evaluation can be performed, all of which should be interpreted in conjunction with the peripheral blood cell counts. Cytological evaluation should assess the quality and cellularity of the smear, the presence and relative proportions of precursors for each of the three major cell lines (erythrocytes, granulocytes, and platelets), and the maturation and progression of each of the cell lines.

EMERGING BIOMARKERS AND APPLICATION WITHIN THE CLINICAL PATHOLOGY LABORATORY

Over the last decade there has been increased activity in the identification of novel biomarkers to improve the preclinical and clinical safety assessment of exploratory new medicines, with the objective of reducing compound attrition during the drug development process. Significant progress in biomarker discovery, validation, and qualification has increased drug-development decision-making and regulatory applications [100]. Strategic paths for biomarker qualification, involving various consortia and working groups composed of regulatory, academic, and industry professionals, have been actively pursued in order to reach consensus around biomarker context-independent and context-dependent qualification, and the qualification of biomarkers is considered to be an incremental process [101]. For example, the Innovative Medicines Initiative (IMI) Safer and Faster Evidence based Translation (SAFE-T) consortium has published a generic scientific and operational strategy for qualification of translational safety biomarkers to link biomarkers to clinical processes and clinical endpoints [102]. This biomarker qualification process defined criteria for biomarker selection (identity of biomarkers with strong preclinical and clinical evidence); an exploratory phase identifying proof of translation; and a confirmatory phase assessing proof of performance

(sensitivity, specificity) in clinical populations prior to any recommendations to regulatory agencies for approval. During the exploratory phase, a key element of the qualification process is the generation of preclinical data encompassing insight into molecular mechanisms of toxicity, tissue specificity, and reversibility, characterization of the biomarker signal (onset of change, magnitude, duration, recovery, half-life, and stability), and concordance with histological findings. Concurrent measurement of appropriate established clinical pathology parameters relevant to the target organ or process should be conducted [102].

A biomarker is defined as any measurable biological characteristic encompassing the detection of physiological, pharmacological, and pathogenic processes [103]. Safety or toxicity biomarkers will directly report or predict susceptibility to a structural and/or functional consequence of exposure to a chemical or biological therapeutic. Toxicity biomarkers that are not directly related to the desired pharmacological activity of the drug constitute off-target activity or a secondary (indirect) pathological process. In this circumstance, the biomarker is purely a signal of toxicity. When the indirect toxicity depends on the complex biological iterations between organ systems in vivo, the marker may behave differently across species and be contingent on other study design variables [104]. Desirable characteristics, reflecting analytical validation and qualification, for cardiac [105], hepatic [106], and renal [107] biomarkers and blood cytokines [104] as biomarkers of toxicity have been defined. Generally these toxicity biomarker characteristics are comparable (and are summarized in Table 14.2). Analytical validation may be considered as the process of assessing the assay or measurement performance characteristics, whereas qualification is the evidentiary process linking a biomarker with biological processes and clinical endpoints [101]. The rigor of the analytical validation and scope of assay development will be influenced by the intended use of the assay, and a "fit-for-purpose" approach is advocated [108]. Basics of method development and analytical validation, specific for clinical pathology in nonclinical studies [5], the adaptation and validation of commercial immunoassay kits, [109] and general concepts of study design and assay conduction for hormone measurement [110] highlight the current structured approach to biomarker quantification required in drug development.

Particular attention has been paid to the assessment of emerging safety biomarkers in the early identification of cardiotoxicity, nephrotoxicity, hepatotoxicity, and vascular toxicity. This has created opportunities for the clinical pathology laboratory to expand assay portfolios, mainly through use of single- and multiplex protein biomarker immunoassays, and thereby potentially increase

TABLE 14.2　Criteria for the Analytical Validation and Biological Qualification of a New Biomarker

Biomarker Analytical Validation (Process of Assessing the Assay and Its Measurement Performance Characteristics)	Biomarker Qualification (Evidentiary Process of Linking a Biomarker With Biological Processes and Clinical Endpoints)
Analytical sensitivity Lower limits of detection Lower limits of quantification at acceptable coefficient of variation	Biomarker sensitivity (potential for false negatives)
Analytical specificity Immunoreactivity defined Potential for assay interference assessed	Biomarker specificity (potential for false positives)
Accuracy and dynamic range of assay Dilutional linearity Spike recovery	High ratio in tissue to biological fluid. Not expressed in nontarget tissues
Assay imprecision reproducibility with commercial and species-specific QC controls multiday precision studies	Sufficiently long and characterized half-life (diagnostic time window) in biological fluid
Potential sources or preanalytical variation evaluated	The toxicity-induced biomarker signal is of sufficient magnitude to clearly distinguish from biological variation, precedes manifestation of structural and/or function injury, is proportionate to the magnitude of the structural or functional injury, tracks progression of injury and recovery from damage/functional impairment, is characterized in experimental animal models, and displays similar reliability across multiple species, translating to humans
In vitro stability of biomarker investigated	Context of use of the biomarker is clearly defined
Robustness of assay technology between lots reagent variability	Helps to better define safety margins and risk-benefit characterization

its contribution to the safety assessment process in drug development. The use of multiplexing platforms, such as the Luminex xMAP or the MesoscaleDiscovery (MSD) technology, is now becoming well established in most testing facilities. The Luminex xMap technology (www.luminexcorp.com) is based on two proven, existing technologies: flow cytometry of color-coded, tiny microspheres in combination with a detection system that is characterized by its flexibility and open-architecture design (immunoassay in the case of nephrotoxicity biomarkers). Specific antibodies to an analyte are coated on one microsphere bead type. The beads float freely around, enhancing the sensitivity of this technology. After incubation with a streptavidin–phycoerythrin-labeled secondary antibody against the analyte, the bead–analyte–fluorophore complex is detected within the Luminex compact analyzer. In this way the xMAP technology in theory allows the multiplexing of up to 100 unique assays within a single sample [111].

The MSD technology (www.mesoscale.com) is a combination of electrochemiluminescence detection and patterned arrays. In contrast to the liquid array of the Luminex-based technology, detection is performed on a solid phase. On a carbon surface in single spots, on the bottom of a multiwell plate (maximum 10 spots per well in a 96-well plate, 4 spots per well in a 384-well plate, and 100 spots per well in a 24-well plate), antibodies against specific analytes are coated. During measurement, sensitive photodetectors are used to collect and quantitatively measure light emitted from the microplates [111]. Novel preclinical safety biomarkers

are qualified by correlation to an established toxicity endpoint, eg, histopathology, traditional clinical pathology parameters, and/or functional test in animal toxicity studies. Unbiased histopathology results are important in order to establish the correlation between histopathology and the new biomarker measurements [101]. Generation of receiver operator characteristic (ROC) curves are performed to correlate biomarker data to histopathology observations and assess the sensitivity and specificity of the biomarker(s). The y-axis of a graph plots the sensitivity of a biomarker value against the x-axis, where 1 minus the specificity value is plotted to test for the degree of correlation. In general, the applicability of a novel toxicity biomarker to clinical trials will center on a comparable biological response between nonclinical species and humans, invasiveness of the procedure, and availability of the technology and expertise.

In the following sections, appropriate emerging protein biomarkers are considered, along with traditional clinical pathology parameters in the assessment of specific target organ toxicities or pathophysiologies. Additionally, reference will be made to circulating microRNAs as emerging preclinical safety biomarkers for target organ toxicity. MicroRNAs are short, noncoding RNA molecules of approximately 18–23 nucleotides in length. They regulate gene expression either by translational expression or affecting messenger RNA (mRNA) stability. These genomic biomarkers often display tissue-specific expression, may be released from the tissues into the plasma during toxic events, change early and with high magnitude in tissues and in the blood during specific organ toxicities, and can be measured using multiplex formats [112]. A number of investigative studies assessing the specific microRNAs have been conducted, and performance compared against conventional clinical pathology tests and novel protein biomarkers and examples will be discussed in the relevant sections.

CLINICAL PATHOLOGY INDICATORS OF TARGET ORGAN TOXICITY

Assessment of Hepatotoxicity

The liver performs many vital physiological functions involving protein, carbohydrate, and lipid metabolism; storage of glycogen, triglyceride, vitamins, and elements including copper and iron; detoxification/biotransformation of endogenous and exogenous compounds; immune function through action of the mononuclear phagocytic system; and excretory functions by conversion of compounds to water-soluble forms for excretion by the biliary system, urinary system, or intestines. Hepatocytes metabolize cholesterol to bile acids for excretion in bile [113].

The marked vulnerability of the liver to drug-induced liver injury (DILI) is a function of its anatomical proximity to the portal blood supply from the digestive tract, its ability to concentrate and biotransform foreign chemicals, and its role in the excretion of xenobiotics or their metabolites into the bile. Preclinical and/or clinical DILI is the most frequent cause of discontinuation of new chemical entities during development. This can be intrinsic/predictable or an idiosyncratic type, which contrast in their manifestation and diagnosis [114]. Detection of potential human hepatic injury is a major challenge in the preclinical safety assessment phase of drug development. Identification of hepatic injury in preclinical studies results in termination of the candidate test compound or further development with substantial patient monitoring if there are safety margins identified. The multiple functions and diseases of the liver make it best to use multiple tests for assessing hepatic injury and changes to function.

Updated recommendations for the measurement of appropriate clinical pathology parameters for the detection of drug-induced hepatic injury in preclinical studies were provided by the Regulatory Affairs Committee of the American Society for Veterinary Clinical Pathology [115]. All the recommended parameters were included in previous published recommendations [3]. Indicators of hepatocellular injury were confirmed as alanine aminotransferase (ALT) and aspartate aminotransferase (AST), with sorbitol dehydrogenase (SDH) and glutamate dehydrogenase (GLDH) as supplemental indicators of hepatocellular injury. Indicators of hepatobiliary injury

were confirmed as alkaline phosphatase (ALP) and total bilirubin (TBIL) with gamma-glutamyl transferase (GGT) as a supplemental indicator of hepatobiliary injury. Total protein, albumin, triglycerides, cholesterol, glucose, urea, activated partial thromboplastin time, and prothrombin time were considered as supplemental indicators of hepatic synthetic function. Evaluation of these parameters in DILI may be helpful in identifying effects on glucose metabolism and hepatic synthesis of proteins, lipids, and coagulation factors [115].

The use of diagnostic enzymology to assess the integrity of the liver has long been established in the clinical environment, and has influenced testing in the preclinical environment. Alterations in serum hepatic enzyme activity provide a sensitive means to evaluate DILI. Increased appearance of enzymes within the circulation will be a reflection of:

1. Hepatocellular leakage and necrosis.
2. Induction of synthesis by the test article.
3. Cell proliferation (hyperplastic or neoplastic).
4. Decreased enzyme clearance.

Hepatocellular leakage enzymes are soluble cytosolic enzymes [eg, ALT, AST, GLDH, SDH, LDH, and alpha glutathione S-transferase (α-GST)] that have a high activity in hepatocytes (and often in other tissues), being released on damage to the hepatocyte membranes in association with sublethal injury (reversible) or hepatocellular necrosis (irreversible injury). Their appearance in the blood does not necessarily indicate cell death [116,117]. This view is influenced by the lack of histological evidence of necrosis in spite of enzyme activity or a lack of sensitivity of histological techniques when necrosis is patchy or involves a small number of cells. The mechanism proposed to explain the appearance of cytosolic enzymes in blood with reversible damage is by the formation of membrane blebs that detach and allow the membrane to reseal without cell death. Ultrastructural changes of reversible cell death confirm plasma membrane blebbing. Large increases of enzyme releases represent cell death, while small increases may represent membrane blebbing [118].

Enzymes vary in their concentration in liver tissue, and specificity for liver disease in different species varies. Tissue enzyme distribution studies show that to accurately assess hepatic injury, a panel of markers should be used rather than a single marker in isolation. Although a single enzyme may exist in more than one tissue, it is typically distributed more abundantly within a particular tissue. Therefore, its elevation within the circulation may reflect damage to this main organ but may additionally reflect damage to tissues that express the same enzyme to a lesser degree, as can be observed with the measurement of AST [119]. The concentration of an enzyme within a tissue and the overall mass of each organ can have a substantial effect on the degree to which serum enzyme activity may change following its release from cells [120]. The magnitude of the increase in serum enzymes depends on the number of hepatocytes affected, the severity of the injury, and the serum half-life of the enzyme, and following hepatocellular injury increased serum enzyme activity is evident within hours.

Several enzymes that originate from the hepatocytes and biliary epithelial cells are typically membrane bound and are not released into the serum with increased membrane permeability. These inducible enzymes, eg, ALP and GGT, are increased in the serum as a result of increased synthesis or release following intrahepatic or extrahepatic cholestasis or in conjunction with biliary hyperplasia or drug or hormonal effects. The increased appearance of cholestatic enzymes in the circulation reflects the redistribution from the apical to the basolateral surfaces of the hepatocytes and subsequent release into the sinusoids [117]. Discrepancies between clinical chemistry findings and liver histopathology can be seen in nonclinical toxicology studies, where marked changes in plasma or serum markers of hepatocellular or hepatobiliary injury can occur in the absence of morphological evidence of drug-induced liver injury, and vice versa. During liver injury, differences in the magnitude of biochemical signals and morphological changes may arise because of differences in the temporal onset and duration of these effects [117].

Hepatocellular Enzymes

Alanine Aminotransferase

Alanine aminotransferase (ALT) is generally the most useful enzyme for identifying the presence of hepatocellular damage. It is found in many tissues but its greatest activity is in the liver [119,120]. The enzyme is primarily cytosolic, with an isoenzyme (ALT2) also found in mitochondria, and is predominantly found in the periportal zone of the liver with a hepatocyte concentration up to 10,000 times that found in serum/plasma. It has a primary role in gluconeogenesis and amino acid metabolism. The magnitude of serum activity elevation is proportional to the number of affected hepatocytes, and marked increases will reflect irreversible cell damage and necrosis, while mild increases may indicate mostly membrane blebbing and reversible cell damage [94,118]. Following an acute hepatotoxic episode, plasma ALT activity will rise within 6–12 h, depending on severity of injury; the activity will peak within 1–2 days and then decline. Estimated half-lives of plasma ALT in different species range from 3 to 10 h in the rat, to 50 h in the dog and human [121]. Prolonged elevations of ALT in the circulation may reflect increased production of ALT in regenerative liver tissue or continued release from hepatocytes. Cholestatic lesions, reflecting impairment of bile flow, can also increase ALT activity. The proposed mechanism is that retained bile salts physically damage the membranes of surrounding hepatocytes. Drugs such as corticosteroids and anticonvulsants appear to induce ALT production [122]. However, in cases such as subchronic or chronic corticosteroid administration, ALT release into the circulation may represent pharmacological modulation of gluconeogenesis and increase of hepatic ALT, and perturbation of hepatocyte integrity due to concomitant glycogen accumulation.

Aspartate Aminotransferase

Aspartate aminotransferase (AST) has a ubiquitous distribution within tissues [120] with significant concentrations in the heart, liver, kidney, and skeletal muscle. It therefore should not be solely used as an indicator of liver damage unless other supporting enzymes are measured [119]. In most species, elevations of AST may not be as marked as increases in ALT with minimal to mild liver injury. This may be a reflection of both its cytosolic and mitochondrial location within the hepatocyte and differing serum half-life. Internal observations have noted that 5- to 10-fold increases in AST activity at 6–8 h after a single dose of hepatotoxic drug candidates to the dog can be cleared from the circulation within 24 h. Comparable changes noted in ALT after 6–8 h remain elevated at 24 h. With marked hepatocellular damage (centrilobular necrosis), following twice-weekly repeat dosing of an experimental hepatotoxin (carbon tetrachloride) to the rat over a 6 week time period, magnitude of dose-related plasma ALT and AST increases were comparable [123]. Marked increases in AST activity in the presence of a minimal to mild change in ALT activity is indicative of increased release from nonhepatic sources such as skeletal muscle. Reflex measurement of markers such as creatine kinase (dog, nonhuman primate) and aldolase (rat) may confirm the changes from skeletal muscle origin.

Reductions of ALT and AST may be observed with inhibition of its cofactor (vitamin B_6), following losses of total protein resulting from gastrointestinal injury, and reductions in hepatic synthesis in the presence of reduced nutrition.

Glutamate Dehydrogenase

Glutamate dehydrogenase (GLDH) measurement has been established in Europe for decades due to ease of availability of commercial diagnostic kits, which has only recently been addressed globally. This enzyme is highly liver-specific and is located mainly in the mitochondria. GLDH may become a more effective biomarker of acute hepatic injury than ALT, AST, SDH, or ALP in the rat, based primarily on the large increase and prolonged persistence following hepatocellular injury [119,120,124], high sensitivity for detection of injury and low baseline levels, high tissue specificity, and lower susceptibility to inhibition or induction [124]. Plasma GLDH values also correlate with increases in ALT (and ALP) activity observed in biliary obstruction in the dog. However, it is noted that biological variation of GLDH increases with aging in rats (>12 weeks), reducing the diagnostic sensitivity of this test in chronic toxicology rat studies. In an investigation in human subjects with acetaminophen-induced liver injury, GLDH (and malate dehydrogenase; MDH) strongly associated with elevations of ALT and possessed a high predictive power for liver injury, as determined by ROC analysis [125]. Commenting on this investigation, other workers suggested that GLDH is more than a general hepatocyte cell death marker and may be a specific biomarker of mitochondrial dysfunction [126].

Sorbitol Dehydrogenase

Sorbitol dehydrogenase (SDH) is relatively specific to the liver [120], and studies have shown that it can outperform other hepatocellular enzyme markers in magnitude of change following experimentally induced liver injury. However, the sample needs to be analyzed fresh since activity can be lost following freezing [95,119], and there is uncertainty about stability of this enzyme [127].

Alpha-Glutathione S-Transferase

The measurement of alpha-glutathione S-transferase (α-GST), an enzyme involved in phase II metabolism of xenobiotics, is also a good marker of hepatocellular injury. It is distributed predominantly in the liver and kidney, comprises 5–10% of the soluble hepatic protein, is rapidly released following experimentally induced acute hepatotoxicity, and the magnitude of change is proportionate to the severity of injury [119]. However, the temporal kinetic profile of this enzyme following hepatic injury is not considered superior to other hepatocellular enzymes. In an evaluation of α-GST, along with arginase and 4-hydroxy-phenol-pyruvate dioxygenase in 34 rat toxicity studies, the performance of each biomarker to accurately detect hepatocellular injury singularly or in combination with ALT was demonstrated [128]. A multibiomarker approach to confirm ALT elevations continues to be advocated. These include historically established (GLDH, SDH, α-GST) enzymes used to varying degrees with the pharmaceutical industry, and those parameters where more data are required: paraoxonase-1 (PON-1), malate dehydrogenase, purine-nucleoside phosphorylase (PNP), arginase, regucalcin, and ALT2 [129]. Histopathology was emphasized as the reference standard for historical biomarkers and qualification of new biomarkers with the generation of ROC curves to assess specificity and sensitivity of the new assays. Improvement of the specificity of the ALT assay by measuring the isoforms (ALT1 or ALT2) and

distinguishing nonhepatic potential causes for elevation of ALT are also a consideration [114,129].

Alkaline Phosphatase

Alkaline phosphatase (ALP) and TBIL, and GGT as a supplementary indicator, are recommended for identification of hepatobiliary injury [115]. ALP and GGT are considered cholestatic-induction enzymes. ALP plays a crucial role in bone formation and in the dephosphorylation of various substrates. Following drug-induced impairment of bile flow (cholestasis), the increased synthesis (induction) of these enzymes occurs within hours and they are released into the circulation. Although ALP is present in a variety of tissues in both the dog and rat, hepatobiliary and bone isoforms in the dog and intestinal and bone isoforms in the rat are the major contributors to circulating ALP activity. With increasing age of the animals, the bone isoforms decrease under normal conditions [115]. The plasma half-lives of ALP in rat, dog, and human are up to 72, 140, and 180 h, respectively [121]. Increase in ALP activity is also associated with corticosteroids, hyperadrenocorticism, and anticonvulsant therapy. The corticosteroid induced isoform in the dog is a unique pharmacologically mediated event that is not related to cholestasis or induction of hepatic drug metabolizing enzyme activity [122,130]. In mature rats, the predominant circulating form of ALP comes from the intestine. This isoform is very responsive to food intake and is generally considered to be a better indicator of reduced food intake (decreased total ALP activity) than as a marker of hepatobiliary injury [131]. Internally, increases in ALP activity have been noted in dogs and rats in the presence of marked evidence of an acute-phase response. These changes are considered to reflect proinflammatory cytokine release including IL-6, which has been demonstrated to induce ALP synthesis [132].

Increases in ALP activity associated with hepatic microsomal enzyme induction, in the absence of accompanying degenerative histopathological findings, have been reported in the dog by a number of workers [133–135]. These studies correlated an increase in ALP activity with increased microsomal enzyme activity, and demonstrated that the source of the ALP increase was of hepatic origin in the absence of histologically detectable hepatobiliary injury. Recovery of ALP levels to baseline after an 8-day treatment-free period was in concordance with a reduction in hepatic microsomal enzyme activity [133]. Additionally, the ALP change reported was not associated with any other changes in clinical pathology parameters [134]. Internal examples highlighting increases in circulating ALP activity in the dog, but in the absence of changes of other markers of hepatic injury, with associated increased liver weight and histological evidence of hepatocellular hypertrophy but without hepatocellular degeneration, are interpreted as an adaptive, rather than an adverse response to xenobiotic exposure [135].

Gamma-Glutamyl Transferase

The highest concentrations of gamma-glutamyl transferase (GGT) are found in the kidney, pancreas, and liver where it is mostly located within the epithelial cells of the bile ducts. In the rat kidney, the level of GGT is approximately 200 times higher than the level found in hepatic tissue. Circulating activity of GGT is virtually undetectable in healthy rats and is very low in the dog, but substantially greater in the nonhuman primate. Observations support the use of serum GGT in the rat as diagnostic of bile duct necrosis when increases are detected shortly after insult, and as a marker of bile duct hypertrophy in the marmoset. In the marmoset, the enzyme is located in the peribiliary arterial plexus and consequently it may also reflect capillary damage in the liver. Induction of hepatocyte GGT has also been reported with several compounds, including sodium phenobarbitone, which is known to cause liver weight increases and induce hepatic metabolism as well as various cytochrome P450s (CYPs) [136]. Internal studies, which have incorporated hepatic gene expression profiling, have shown induction of hepatic GGT mRNA in a number of repeat-dose (7 days) oral toxicity studies in the rat where centrilobular hypertrophy, increased liver weights, increased CYPs (predominantly 2B2 and 3A3), and phase 2 metabolic enzymes activities [predominantly GSTA3 and uridine diphosphate glucuronyl transferase (GT1A6)] were observed. However, this only translated into increases in circulating GGT activity where marked induction (>50-fold) of hepatic GGT mRNA was observed. In a reported study where kava kava was administered to rats for 14 weeks, statistically significant increases in serum GGT were observed in both males and particularly so in females, which accompanied hepatocellular hypertrophy, liver weight increases, and significant induction of CYPs [137]. The authors concluded that the changes seen in the liver, including the increases in serum GGT, were adaptive in nature.

Total Bilirubin

Bilirubin is an oxidative end-product of heme catabolism. A significant amount is produced daily, primarily from the breakdown of hemoglobin. Erythrocytic destruction within macrophages of the spleen, liver, or bone marrow is followed by the degradation of heme and its conversion to unconjugated bilirubin, accounting for around 80% of bilirubin production. A small percentage (20%) is derived from the catabolism of various heme-containing molecules (catalase, peroxidase, myoglobin, cytochrome P450) and heme degradation associated with ineffective erythropoiesis. As unconjugated bilirubin leaves a macrophage, it forms a noncovalent

association with albumin, being transported in the blood bound to albumin. Unconjugated bilirubin is dissociated from albumin at the sinusoidal surface of the hepatocyte membrane and is taken into the hepatocyte by plasma membrane transporters. It is conjugated with glucuronide in the endoplasmic reticulum by a specific bilirubin UDP-glucuronyltransferase (UGT1A1), rendering the molecule water soluble. Conjugated bilirubin is secreted across the bile-canalicular membrane by specific ATP-dependent transporters into the bile canaliculi and flows to the intestine via the biliary system, where it is degraded to urobilinogen. Urobilinogen can be passively absorbed in the intestine and then enter hepatocytes for excretion in the bile, or bypass the liver and be excreted in the urine. It can also be degraded to stercobilinogen and excreted in the feces [113,116,138]. Conjugated bilirubin is freely filtered through the glomerulus. In most species, this is completely reabsorbed by renal tubular epithelial cells unless the amount of filtered bilirubin is excessive. In the dog, the renal threshold is low and traces of bilirubin are normal in concentrated urine [48]. Overproduction (reflecting accelerated red blood cell destruction or hemolysis), reduced uptake, and low or partial inhibition of glucuronidation capacity [139] can cause increased plasma unconjugated bilirubin levels, while impairment of intra- or extra-hepatic bile flow (cholestasis) can lead to increased conjugated bilirubin in the serum/plasma. However, the individual bilirubin fractions are rarely measured, unless a significant increase in total bilirubin concentration in laboratory animals is noted (eg, >10 μmol/L), and both components are measured in the total bilirubin concentration.

Decreased serum total bilirubin concentration is occasionally noted with test articles that increase bilirubin clearance by upregulation of the constitutive androstane receptor [140]. In rodents this observation can usually be associated with hepatocellular hypertrophy, liver weight, increased clearance of thyroxine associated with elevation of thyroid-stimulating hormone (TSH), and microscopic evidence of thyroid follicular cell hypertrophy.

Total Bile Acids

Total serum bile acids (SBAs) are synthesized from cholesterol by hepatocytes, conjugated to an amino acid, and secreted into the intestine, where they facilitate fat absorption. They are therefore a measure of hepatic function [48]. Metabolism of the primary bile acids by bacterial flora to secondary bile acids occurs in the intestine, and this can be disrupted by antibiotics, leading to a lowering of total bile acid levels. Measurement of total bile acids is influenced by feeding, and increases of up to two- to threefold can be observed in dogs 2 h postprandially. Total bile acid measurement is more variable in rats and is less commonly used. Measurement of individual bile acid measurements (eg, cholic acid, glycocholic acid, and taurocholic acid) may be more informative and are reported to differentiate specific forms of liver injury in rodent toxicology studies [141]. Additionally, measurement of serum glycodeoxycholic acid levels has been proposed as a prognostic biomarker in acetaminophen-induced acute liver failure patients [142].

Other liver parameters reflective of the metabolic functions of the liver can provide meaningful information in severe hepatic disease. Marked decreases in serum urea, glucose, cholesterol, and protein (especially albumin) and prolonged coagulation times can reflect impairment of synthetic functions in hepatocellular dysfunction. Serum cholesterol can be increased in cholestasis. Minimal to mild increases in serum cholesterol concentration may also be observed in hepatic induction, reflecting metabolic adaptation.

A recent study, seeking to characterize the relationship between biochemical and morphological changes during subacute liver injury in the rat, compared the diagnostic performance of hepatocellular and hepatobiliary markers for specific manifestations of drug-induced liver injury. Specificity and comparable diagnostic utility of ALT, AST, TBIL, and SBA for prediction of manifestations of hepatocellular necrosis/degeneration and biliary pathology was demonstrated [143]. In the absence of hepatocellular necrosis, ALT increases were observed with biochemical or morphological evidence of cholestasis. The diagnostic utility of ALP and GGT for biliary injury was limited; however, ALP had modest diagnostic value for peroxisome proliferation, and ALT, AST, and CHOL had moderate diagnostic utility for phospholipidosis. None of the eight markers evaluated had diagnostic value for manifestations of hypertrophy, cytoplasmic rarefaction, inflammation, or lipidosis [143].

A liver-specific microRNA species, microRNA-122 (mir-122), has shown potential for predicting liver injury in addition to standard hepatic injury biomarkers [144]. The increases in circulating mir-122 were shown to parallel conventional biomarker changes following exposure of rats to acetaminophen, allyl alcohol, or α-napthyl isothiocyanate, and were consistent with histopathological identification of hepatic injury. Increases were detected earlier than standard liver markers and exhibited a wide dynamic range. Additionally, mir-122 detection in hepatocyte-enriched homogeneous and heterogeneous cultures provides the potential for the marker to bridge in-vitro experiments to in-vivo models and human samples and to link findings from clinical studies in determining the relevance of in vitro models being developed for the study of drug-induced toxicity [145].

Assessment of Nephrotoxicity

The kidney normally performs a variety of functions essential for the regulation of a constant extracellular environment and the maintenance of metabolic homeostasis. In order to sustain glomerular filtration and renal metabolism, the renal vascular bed receives a large blood flow, averaging 20–25% of resting cardiac output (up to 150–180 L of blood per day in humans and 5 L in the rat). The functional units of the kidney, the nephrons, process the plasma filtrate to regulate fluid, electrolyte, and acid–base balance while eliminating waste products. Additionally, the kidney also produces hormones important for cardiovascular, hematological, and skeletal muscle homeostasis [107]. The functional reserve capacity of the kidney is high, and between 50% and 75% loss of nephron mass is required before renal function is impaired. As a result of the high blood flow, cells of the renal vasculature, glomerulus, tubules, and interstitium are exposed to high volumes of blood-borne toxicants [111]. The proximal tubule is particularly susceptible to injury, as these cells express a variety of transporters, which enable active uptake and intracellular accumulation of toxic xenobiotics or metabolites. In addition, tubular epithelial cells are highly metabolically active and can bioactivate relatively nontoxic compounds into reactive intermediates, which may cause damage to cellular macromolecules.

The varying balance of transporters, metabolic characteristics, blood flow characteristics, and oxygen tension along the nephron is a likely explanation for drugs with different mechanisms of toxicity frequently affecting different parts of the kidney [107]. Assessment of nephrotoxicity is therefore important for the determination of the safety of drug candidates, since drug-induced kidney injury (DIKI), defined as rapid damage to the cells of the kidney that results in loss of function, is one of the main adverse events seen during drug development. However, only 7% of new drug candidates fail in preclinical trials because of nephrotoxicity, while the incidence in intensive care units of acute kidney injury is about 30–50%. This discrepancy may help to explain the underestimation of nephrotoxicity in preclinical toxicity testing. To minimize the risk of subclinical DIKI or the initiation of chronic kidney disease, the data generated during preclinical toxicity testing and provided to the clinicians for the different phases have to be as detailed and informative as possible [138]. Histopathological changes in the kidney are associated with drug toxicity. These changes have been well characterized in commonly used experimental animals and they currently remain as the "gold standards" against which biomarkers from body fluids are measured [107,147].

Conventional Assessment of Renal Function

In preclinical toxicity studies, potential for nephrotoxicity is routinely assessed by serum biochemistry and urinalysis [3]. The most widely used and accepted indicators of kidney injury include plasma/serum markers (principally urea, creatinine) and urinary markers such as urinary volume, urine concentration (specific gravity or osmolality), glucose, protein, fractional electrolyte excretion, and sediment examination. Although many of these measurements are valid indicators of renal function, generally encompassing glomerular filtration, tubular function, and urine formation and excretion, they lack sensitivity and/or specificity in detecting the early stages of injury or disease, and in some cases may be influenced by prerenal changes, which can make interpretation difficult [148].

Serum urea (also referred to as urea nitrogen) and creatinine concentration are the traditional indicators of glomerular filtration rate (GFR) in humans and laboratory animals, being both freely filtered at the glomerulus and excreted into the urine with minimal secretion and reabsorption. Reductions in the functional nephron mass can be reflected in GFR. Increases in serum urea and creatinine above concurrent control levels and reference intervals (azotemia) indicate that GFR is decreased [49], but only when significant functional nephron mass has been lost. Urea is synthesized in the liver from ammonia, released by deamination of amino acids from endogenous protein catabolism or from ammonia that is absorbed from the intestine. It is reabsorbed passively with water in the proximal tubule (between 40% and 70%) with the amount reabsorbed being inversely related to the rate of urine flow through the tubule. Serum urea concentration is therefore affected by the rate of urea production, glomerular filtrate rate, and the flow rate of urine through the kidneys, and increases can be categorized as prerenal, renal, or postrenal [48].

Prerenal causes of increased serum urea are increased urea synthesis and decreased renal blood volume. The former results from consumption of high-protein diets, or conditions that increase protein catabolism, such as starvation, fever, infection, tissue necrosis, or gastrointestinal hemorrhage. Decreased renal blood flow decreases GFR and may be caused by conditions such as dehydration, cardiovascular dysfunction, or shock. When increased urea nitrogen is due to prerenal causes, renal concentrating ability is typically maintained. If the prerenal condition is dehydration, urine volume will be reduced and urine concentration will be increased as the kidneys attempt to conserve water. Increased urea due to renal causes results from diseases or toxicity of the renal parenchyma. Increases will be observed with a substantial loss of functional capacity of the kidney (>75%). When the cause of the increased urea nitrogen is primary renal disease, renal concentrating ability may be impaired, and urine specific gravity may be isothenuric (ie, the same as glomerular filtrate; approximately 1.008–1.012). Increased urea nitrogen due to renal causes will generally accompany histopathological evidence of renal damage and clinical observations of poor health.

Postrenal causes of increased urea nitrogen and reduced GFR reflect obstruction of the outflow of urine. Obstruction by naturally occurring urinary calculi is occasionally observed as an incidental finding in rodent studies, but test articles that promote urinary calculi formation can also be responsible for this condition.

Creatinine is a nonprotein nitrogenous waste product formed by the nonenzymatic breakdown of muscle creatine metabolism. Serum creatinine concentration is therefore influenced by, and reflective of, muscle mass and conditioning, but is relatively independent of dietary influences (with the exception of high-meat diets) and protein catabolism. Following alterations in renal blood flow, renal function, or urine outflow, changes in serum creatinine tend to parallel those of serum urea concentration. The timing and magnitude of the changes in serum creatinine may lag behind those of serum urea. This usually occurs as a result of the tubular reabsorption of urea, especially when there is increased formation of urea. Serum creatinine is a better marker of glomerular filtration than serum urea because it is influenced by fewer secondary factors.

Unfortunately, the most commonly used method for determining creatinine, the Jaffe reaction, is nonspecific, and interfering compounds called noncreatinine chromagens affect its accuracy. The enzymatic creatinine assay is considered more specific, being free of interference. Reference intervals in the rat are approximately 30% lower when measured by the enzymatic assay than with the Jaffe reaction. It should be noted that if serum creatinine concentrations are increased in the absence of correlative effects on serum urea or histopathology, the possibility of drug-related analytical interference should be investigated using a combination of different methodology (enzymatic creatinine assay) and control serum samples with spiked levels of the test article or metabolites. Endogenous creatinine clearance is sometimes used as a noninvasive measure of GFR because blood levels of creatinine are relatively stable over short intervals; creatinine is freely filtered and is not significantly secreted or stored. Other clinical chemistry findings observed when renal function is significantly impaired include increased serum phosphate, representing decreased filtration, and decreased serum sodium and chloride concentration resulting from loss of tubular function and reabsorption [48].

Urinalysis

Urinalysis, usually consisting of the evaluation of the physicochemical properties of the urine and sediment examination, has the potential to provide a specific evaluation of the urogenital tract, as well as information concerning systemic changes. For standard toxicology studies in laboratory animals, visual assessment (color, clarity), volume, specific gravity or osmolality, pH, and quantitative or semiquantitative determination of protein, glucose, and creatinine, are recommended [3]. A semiquantitative approach may be used by the toxicology facility using commercially available dipstix tests, and this will provide additional information on ketone, bilirubin, urobilinogen, hemoglobin, nitrite, and leukocyte esterase. The inclusion of microscopic examination of the sediment is performed on a case-by-case basis. Difficulties surrounding sample collection from laboratory animals may mean that the sample is not optimal, for example from a single time-point. Timed urine collection is preferable but may be more susceptible to bacterial, fecal, or food contamination. The concentrating ability of the kidney is usually assessed by measuring either the specific gravity or urine osmolality.

Urine volume, combined with the assessment of urine concentration, can also serve as an index to renal function; with severe loss of functional nephron mass, urine output is decreased (oliguria) or absent (anuria), while loss of the ability of the kidney to adequately concentrate urine results in the excretion of large volumes of dilute urine. These findings should be interpreted with knowledge of factors such as hydration state, water consumption, diet, and the presence of other factors that reflect the role of the kidney in water and electrolyte homeostasis [148]. Quantitative analysis of the urine may be restricted to measurement of urine creatinine, protein, and glucose concentration. Urine creatinine concentration will provide additional supporting information for the concentration of the urine and is inversely proportional to the urine volume collected. When timed urine collections are performed, the calculation of creatinine excretion can be performed. Assuming that there are no effects on glomerular filtrate rate, creatinine excretion will show a positive association with muscle mass and hence body weight of the animal. This allows a quality check on the urine collected to help identify incomplete or water-contaminated samples. Measurement of urine creatinine also allows for normalization of other urine analytes measured quantitatively, assuming the test article has not induced effects on muscle mass (increased with β_2-adrenergic agonists or decreased with corticosteroids, dependent on dose).

Other quantitative analytes, eg, electrolytes, may be included to support Japanese regulatory authority requirements. Additional information may need to be collected on compounds showing potential nephrotoxicity in previous studies (increased proteinuria; microscopic evidence of renal lesions), and to explain changes observed in the serum/plasma (eg, reductions in circulating electrolytes) or marked increases in urine volumes.

Microscopic examination of the urine sediment allows for the detection of epithelial cells, bacteria, casts, RBCs, WBCs, and crystals. It should be remembered that some bacteria will grow in the urine during the collection period,

unless minimized by collection over ice. Casts in the sediment are indicative of renal tubular damage. Crystals are often precursors to renal and/or bladder stones, or could reflect test-article precipitation within the tubular lumen. RBCs are typically seen in conjunction with urinary bladder or urethral mucosal damage. The presence of WBCs is indicative of infectious changes in the kidney, urinary bladder, ureter, and/or urethra [92].

Emerging Urinary Renal Protein Biomarkers in Preclinical Toxicity Testing

Recently, regulatory authorities in Europe, the United States, and Japan endorsed the use of a number of renal-specific biomarkers [urinary kidney injury molecule-1 (KIM-1), clusterin, albumin, β_2-microglobulin, renal papillary antigen, total protein, trefoil factor 3 and serum cystatin C] for the detection of nephrotoxic injury to either the renal tubules or the glomeruli in preclinical safety studies [146,147,149–151], thereby marking advances in the application of biomarkers to drug development. These biomarkers for the detection of acute drug-induced renal toxicity were judged to be qualified for limited use in nonclinical and clinical drug development in order to help guide safety assessments [149]. A range of nephrotoxicants were used by the Predictive Safety Testing Consortiums (PSTC) in generating the experimental data. Biomarker performance was assessed by the generation of ROCs in which the sensitivity and specificity of the biomarker response was correlated with histopathological assessment of the kidneys. Superiority of the biomarkers over the insensitive serum creatinine and urea measures was clearly demonstrated. In reaching this level of regulatory acceptance, these biomarkers met defined qualification criteria [149]. A range of urinary biomarkers as candidates for the detection of acute kidney injury, reflecting their preclinical and clinical application and location within nephron, have been identified in several publications [107,111,152–156].

Some of the urinary biomarkers assessed as part of the PTSC submission and in other investigative studies with other nephrotoxicants have demonstrated the strengths and limitations and indicated the context of use. As part of these investigations, immunoassay multiplex technology (Luminex, MSD) facilitated panels of urinary biomarkers are utilized to assess renal injury, inflammation, and regeneration, recognizing that biomarkers for one type of kidney toxicity may not be useful in another type. For example, a good biomarker of injury may not reliably indicate delayed repair; a biomarker that detects inflammation effectively may not be as sensitive in detecting early proximal tubule injury in the absence of inflammation. A biomarker of injury might not detect a functional defect. Both the Luminex and MSD technologies have a range of renal biomarker panels targeting identification of glomerular, proximal tubular, distal tubular, and collecting injury [111].

Using a model of hexachloro-1:3-butadiene (HCBD)-induced acute kidney injury in the female Hanover Wistar rat, a nephrotoxin that causes segment-specific injury to the proximal tubule, multiplexed renal biomarker measurements on urine collected 24h after dosing were performed using both the Luminex and MSD platforms [157]. When comparing the protein biomarker levels, the absolute values reported differed between the two platforms, but more importantly, fold changes of the protein biomarker levels in animals with kidney injury from concurrent controls were very comparable across the two platforms. A more detailed investigation assessing gender differences and variability in control Sprague Dawley rats also noted marked differences between the two platforms [158] and recommended that absolute values should not be compared across the analytical platforms. In a second study assessing the acute nephrotoxicity of HCBD, correlation of minimal histopathological changes with biomarkers of renal injury (measured using the MSD platform) were assessed 24h after a single dose [159]. In both these studies, the most sensitive biomarkers of HCBD renal injury were urinary α-GST (a proximal tubular cell marker of cytoplasmic leakage), and KIM-1 (a marker of tubular regeneration), together with albumin (a marker of both proximal tubular function and glomerular integrity). When a time course study was conducted, up to 28 days following a single intraperitoneal dose of HCBD (45 mg/kg) [160], peak excretion of α-GST and albumin occurred at 24h (day 1) postdose while KIM-1 peaked on days 3/4, reflecting its role both as a marker of tubular injury and regeneration, correlating with histopathologic evidence of tubular degeneration (days 1–3) followed by tubular regeneration from day 2 onwards. Concurrent assessment of kidney gene expression reflected changes in xenobiotic metabolism, oxidative stress, inflammation, and regeneration and repair. The use of the urinary renal toxicity biomarker panel enables injury monitoring for a broad context of study designs and potential sampling timepoints. No single biomarker is likely to be applied universally across the many possible renal injury contexts. For example, α-GST appears to be an excellent early toxicity marker of epithelial cell necrosis. In contrast, KIM-1 and clusterin levels persist during regeneration and appear to reflect the triggering and continuation of the repair process. Elevations in levels of albumin correlate strictly with early loss of function seen after tubular epithelial necrosis and degeneration. Measurement of all the renal injury markers measured in parallel enables the investigator to capture critical information with regard to renal toxicity, repair, and function, from study start to finish [150].

Urinary KIM-1 seems to be the most effective molecule of this new generation of protein biomarkers, being able to report both early minimal kidney injury and indicate tubular regeneration, and thus has a broader diagnostic window than renal biomarkers of pure cellular damage or function.

Additionally, KIM-1 has clearly shown that it is a sensitive quantitative biomarker for early detection of kidney tubular injury [161,162], it is specific for the kidney, and it outperforms traditional biomarkers of kidney injury in preclinical qualification studies [163]. Limited data for the application of novel renal biomarkers is available in nonrodent species; however, urinary neutrophil gelatinase-associated lipocalin (NGAL: LCN-2) and clusterin have been demonstrated to be potential biomarkers for the early assessment of drug-induced renal damage in a model of acute kidney injury induced by gentamicin [164]. While Urinary NGAL is a promising biomarker of renal toxicity for the early identification of acute kidney injury, it is not as specific for kidney injury as generally assumed. Upregulation of NGAL at other sites or organs may also occur as part of an acute phase response to systemic inflammation or tissue damage, followed by renal filtration and urinary excretion [123,152,165]. Additionally as NGAL is a neutrophil-related protein, the important potential interference of leukocyturia in confounding the interpretation of NGAL in the diagnosis of AKI has been demonstrated [166]. The potential of urinary microRNAs as specific biomarkers for kidney injury has been investigated and possible utility has been demonstrated in the identification of acute kidney injury [167] and glomerulonephritis [168]. Levels of 25miRNAs were significantly increased in the urine of cisplatin-treated rats, while decreases of these miRNAs in either the cortex or outer medulla of the kidney, or both, were observed. The levels of the miRNAs were increased in urine in a time- and dose-dependent manner and correlated with both urine protein biomarker increases (KIM-1; clusterin) and severity of necrosis in the proximal tubule [167]. In an antiglomerular basement membrane glomerulonephritis (GN) model in rats, five microRNAs (-miR-10a, -10b, -100, -211, and -486) were found to be increased by nephrotoxic serum-induced GN but not in cisplatin –induced proximal tubular injury and detected by day 8. Urinary protein biomarkers in situ hybridization of the kidney showed that mir-10b and -100 were primarily expressed in the distal nephron and thus were not site specific glomerular markers [167].

Assessment of Cardiotoxicity and Myotoxicity

The types of drug-induced cardiac injury may be categorized according to structural damage or functional deficits that may or may not be associated with histopathological changes, and altered cell or tissue homeostasis in the absence of obvious structural or functional deficits [105]. Specific examples of drug classes with known cardiotoxic liability range from anticancer drugs, antiretroviral compounds and antipsychotics to sympathomimetic and peroxisome proliferator receptor agonists [105,169]. Historically, identification of cardiac injury has mainly focused on enzymes and proteins that report damage to the cardiomyocyte. Enzymes such as aspartate aminotransferase, lactate dehydrogenase, and isoenzymes, creatine kinase, and isoenzymes and proteins such as myoglobin have been utilized as markers of cardiomyocyte damage. These biomarkers lacked specificity and sensitivity (although diagnostic performance improved with specific isoenzymes measurement), and their inclusion in study protocols for preclinical testing has now become more limited following the introduction of serum/plasma cardiac troponin measurements.

Cardiac Troponins

Cardiac Troponins (cTn) are globular proteins and structural components of the contractile regulatory complex in cardiac myocytes. Three cardiac troponin proteins have been identified (C, I, and T), and cardiac and skeletal muscle isoforms (fast-twitch and slow-twitch) of TnI and TnT are encoded by their respective and distinct genes [105]. The majority of cTnI and cTnT is found in the contractile apparatus, myofibril bound and released into the circulation via proteolytic degradation. Cardiac troponin has also been reported to occur as a free cytosolic component of cTnT (6–8%) and cTnI (2–8%) [170]. Clinically cardiac troponins (cTn) are well-established, important biomarkers of ischemic cardiac injury in patients with acute coronary syndrome. In conjunction with clinical criteria, electrocardiogram (ECG) changes and imaging, cTn(I and T) are the preferred cardiac biomarkers for diagnosis of myocardial infarction [171,172], reflecting their near-absolute myocardial tissue specificity and high clinical sensitivity, and with magnitude of cardiac troponin increases providing good correlation of infarct size, as determined by cardiac magnetic resonance imaging [173]. Additionally, cardiotoxicity is a major limitation of chemotherapy, strongly affecting the quality of life and the overall survival of cancer patients; cardiac biomarker (notably cardiac troponins and natriuretic peptides) monitoring is emerging as a potential strategy for identifying patients more prone to developing cardiotoxicity and in whom a preventative pharmacological strategy and closer cardiac monitoring are pivotal [174].

In preclinical safety assessment, cTn has become more commonly utilized as a sensitive and specific tool for assessing acute active/ongoing ischemic and nonischemic myocardial injury in a variety of animal safety models including the rat, mouse, dog, and monkey [175]. There are six potential major pathobiological mechanisms of troponin release: myocyte necrosis, apoptosis, normal myocyte cell turnover, cellular release of proteolytic troponin degradation, increased cellular wall permeability without necrosis, and formation of membranous blebs [176]. In this latter mechanism, large cytoplasmic molecules can pass from the intracellular to the extracellular space without cellular necrosis occurring. This occurs by the formation of membranous blebs that bud off from the plasma membrane of the cell. Blebs develop during cellular ischemia which, if limited and allowing reoxygenation to occur,

results in release into the circulation without rupture of the plasma membrane [177]. Evidence from cardiac studies supporting the presence of membranous blebs in cardiac myocytes and enabling troponin to be released due to ischemia alone, without necrosis, has been presented [177]. Increased concentration of these specific cardiac troponin isoforms (cTnI and cTnT) within the circulation signals release of these contractile proteins from the cardiomyocyte, indicating an ongoing injury or perturbation of the cardiomyocyte. Once in circulation, the cardiac troponins are cleared rapidly, with reported half-lives of 2h in humans [178], 0.8h in rat, and 0.5h in dog [179]. However, the half-life or clearance rate is variable according to the distribution of injury and degree of plasma flow rate, with fast cTnT clearance from the circulation a reflection of high flow rate through the heart [180]. Duration of sustained circulating cTn increase after myocardial infarction is influenced by slow washout from myocardial tissue, a reflection of damage volume and the local plasma flow through the damaged myocardium [180]. Drugs that induce acute and short-duration cardiomyocellular injury (eg, isoproterenol) have been associated with transient (24–48h) increases in cTn with magnitudes that reflect the severity of injury. Drugs that induce chronic and/or progressive cardiomyocellular injury are more likely to cause small but persistent increases in cTn and differences in the pathogenesis of the lesion (eg, doxorubicin) [175].

The use of cTn for preclinical application has been extensively reviewed [105,169,181,182], and the number of published experimental toxicology studies in rats and dogs that have characterized the response of cTn to chemically induced acute myocardial injury has risen dramatically [169]. A number of these investigative studies in the rat have focused on inducing acute cardiomyocyte injury and following the temporal relationship of cTn elevation, duration, and recovery with concurrent morphological identification of injury, severity, and repair processes (eg, Refs. [181,183,184]). In a study conducted on behalf of the ILSI HESI cardiac troponin biomarker working group [184], the temporal progression of morphological changes (as assessed by light microscopy, cTnI immunohistochemistry, and transmission electron microscopy) was characterized in the myocardium of rats given either single doses of 100 or 4000 µg/kg isoproterenol and compared with the kinetics of cTnI and cTnT release into the circulation. Dose-dependent increases of comparable magnitude in cTnI and cTnT occurred early (0.5h), peaking at 2–3h, and declined to baseline after 48–72h, from concurrent controls. Myocardial injury was detected morphologically after 0.5h (although no ultrastructural evidence of cardiomyocyte death was seen), correlating well with loss of cTnI immunoreactivity in the myocardium, and serum cTn elevation at early time points. However, a clear temporal disconnect occurred after 3 h, with morphological lesion score increase in the presence of declining cTn values for the remainder of the time period of assessment. Thus cTn maximal elevations will typically precede maximal severity of cardiac myonecrosis/degeneration seen histologically in acute injury. The early loss of cTn from myocardial tissue and appearance within the circulation and rapid clearance from the circulation was interpreted to reflect high plasma flow rate and washout of cTn around the damaged area [180]. Transient increases in serum cTnI concentrations that did not have a consistent microscopic correlate have also been reported in rats given rosiglitazone [185] and hydralazine [186]. Additionally, microscopic detection of myocardial steatosis and necrosis in atria and ventricles of rats given pyruvate dehydrogenase kinase inhibitors could not be supported by evidence of plasma cardiac biomarker (cTnI, cTnT) changes. However, the investigators demonstrated multifocal or diffuse loss of myocardial troponin I staining in the atria, suggesting that the timing of sampling for the plasma cardiac biomarkers measurements was not optimal [187].

Thus a not uncommon finding in studies in which the test article may induce an acute cardiomyocyte injury is the lack of good correlation between the cTn value and morphological assessment. Morphological evidence of cardiomyocyte injury (degeneration, necrosis, and fibrosis) and a negative cTn value may suggest myocardial insult at a time earlier than information collection.

The strength of cardiac troponin I as a sensitive biomarker of progressive cardiac structural injury was demonstrated in an example of drug (casopitant)-induced progressive cardiac toxicity in the dog [188]. At the earliest time point of an integrated assessment of casopitant-induced cardiac toxicity (week 6), minimal increases of serum cTnI concentration, up to 0.15 µg/L, correlated with ultrastructural evidence of scattered sarcoplasmic bodies within the cardiomyocyte and accumulation of casopitant metabolite within heart tissue, increases in heart rate (of up to 65 beats per minute from pretreatment baseline), two- to threefold elevations of serum NT-proBNP, but no light-microscopic (hematoxylin and eosin) signal was identified. Progressive increases in cTnI concentration, severity of ultrastructural findings, and further metabolite accumulation within heart tissue were demonstrated at weeks 13, 20, and 26 with reproducible light microscopic findings of myofiber degeneration and necrosis in all casopitant-treated dogs evident at week 20 (with one animal showing a light microscopic signal at week 13, but following extensive sampling of the heart). The investigators noted that correlations between cTnI values and light microscopic evaluations were observed only when cTnI values reached approximately 1 µg/L

(approximately 15 times above the cut-off point of 0.07 µg/L). This key study clearly demonstrated the power of cTnI as a sensitive, specific, and early marker of active, progressive structural myocardial injury in the dog, showing enhanced sensitivity when correlated with electron microscopy, and with low level progressive elevations of cTnI observed in the absence of a light microscopic signal. The progressive cardiotoxicity of anthracyclines (eg, doxorubicin, daunorubicin), chemotherapeutic agents indicated for the treatment of a variety of cancer types, has also been extensively studied [105]. Recent studies have demonstrated that plasma cTns progressively increase with the rising number of chemotherapy cycles. The cTn diagnostic window was systematically described during the development of chronic daunorubicin toxicity in the rabbit [189] and in the rat, where cTn responses and histologic changes were evident at the higher total exposures of doxorubicin but the magnitude of cTn response did not match closely with the histologic grade of vaculoation of the cardiomyocytes of the atria/ventricles [190]. A rat model of progressive doxorubicin-induced cardiomyopathy was utilized to assess the time course of serological, pathological, and functional events characterizing the cardiotoxicity [191]. Subcellular cardiomyocyte degeneration was the earliest marker, followed by progressive functional decline and histopathological manifestations. Myocardial contract enhancement and elevations of cTnI occurred later, but all these markers preceded clinical left ventricular function. Cardiac troponins (I and T) have also been demonstrated to provide effective linkage between in vitro and in vivo preclinical experiments of anthracycline-induced cardiotoxicity [192].

Cardiac troponin data should be interpreted like data from other routine clinical chemistry and hematology tests and should consider individual animal variability, change over time, differences in group means, dose response, concurrent conditions, histological correlates, thresholds of concern, and the establishment of appropriate reference intervals for relevant animal species and assays. Comparisons with control animals matched for species, strain, collection methods (including bleeding site and anesthesia), age, and sex are particularly important with cTn testing [169,193,194].

The FDA Biomarker Qualification Review Team (BQRT) completed a review of a submission from veterinary and pharmaceutical industry representatives [195] advocating the use of circulating cardiac troponins T (cTnT) and I (cTnI) in nonclinical drug development studies in rats, dogs, and monkeys (http://www.fda.gov/downloads/Drugs/DevelopmentApprovalProcess/DrugDevelopmentToolsQualificationProgram/UCM294644.pdf). Concurring with the scope of the proposal, the BQRT concluded that serum/plasma cardiac troponin measurements were qualified biomarkers in safety assessment studies in dogs and rats for the following context of use:

1. When there is previous indication of cardiac structural damage with a particular drug.
2. When there is known cardiac structural damage with a particular pharmacological class of a drug and histopathological analyses do not reveal structural damage, circulating cardiac troponins may be used to support or refute the inference of low cardiotoxic potential.
3. When unexpected cardiac structural toxicity study is found in a nonclinical study, the retroactive ("reflex") examination of serum or plasma from that study for cardiac troponins (which has been appropriately stored) can be used to help determine a no observed adverse effect level (NOAEL) or lowest observed adverse effect level (LOAEL).

The results of this testing may support inclusion of cardiac troponin testing in subsequent safety assessment studies.

Additionally, the BQRT concluded that effective implementation of cardiac troponins in nonclinical drug development studies, including gaining confidence in the validity of negative troponin data, required validation of the assay for the species and laboratory conditions of use, knowledge of the time course of damage by the drug to allow for sampling that will accurately capture troponin elevations resulting from ongoing or active damage, and understanding of the relevance of the nonclinical metabolite profile to humans.

Measurement of Cardiac Troponins

There are numerous immunoassays available for the measurement of cTnI and cTnT in which improved analytical sensitivity and antibody selectivity have been key goals. There are fewer cTnT assays available due to historical commercial restrictions [181]. The majority of the published literature in preclinical or veterinary studies reports the values collected from first-, second-, and third-generation assays using commercially available tests designed for human cTn testing, many of which can be effectively used because of the high degree of cross-species conservation of the protein [169,181,182]. Levels of cTn in healthy animals (mice, rats, dogs, rabbits, and nonhuman primates), in concordance with humans, tend to be at or below the limit of quantification of these assays. Precision of the assay at the lower limit of quantification is especially important to be able to reproducibly detect a limited cTn release that may occur in response to a mild toxicant or early in the kinetic response to a more potent toxicant. Overall these common commercial assays can detect cardiac injury at low levels before significant histological damage occurs. They also have a large dynamic range, capable of assessing significant troponin increases.

However, not all of these assays will provide comparative cTn responses, and unacceptable immunoreactivity in specific preclinical species (eg, rat) has been demonstrated in a number of investigations [181,183,196,197]. In a study conducted on behalf of the ILSI HESI cardiac biomarkers working group [197], which evaluated analytical characteristics of cTn assays used in preclinical studies (commercial automated human assays and species-specific ELISAs), different responses (in terms of immunoreactive response and imprecision) were found for each assay and each species tested. Not all cTn assays were found to be suitable for cTn measurement in each animal species or strain, and the study clearly demonstrated that individual assay characterization is needed for each animal species to prevent misinterpretation of myocardial injury based on cardiac troponin findings. The clinical pathologist also needs to be aware that, as new generations of cTn assays are introduced commercially (particularly those that are optimized for clinical use) [198], analytical validation of the new-generation assays must be conducted to ensure continuity of diagnostic specificity and sensitivity. Loss of cross-species reactivity in the cTnT assay has been observed for new generations of the assay. This may be a consequence of assay refinement over successive generations to be more "cardiac" rather than "skeletal" muscle-specific and to have a higher sensitivity for use in humans [199]. When establishing capability for cardiac troponin measurements or adopting latest-generation cTn assays, the laboratory should conduct or revisit analytical validation of the assay including specificity, sensitivity, precision at low levels of cTn concentration, and sample stability, and conduct a correlation experiment between previous-generation and latest-generation versions of the assay with species-specific samples with varying levels of cTn to obtain a level of confidence with the assay [197].

High-Sensitivity Cardiac Troponin Assays

The threshold for detecting cardiomyocyte injury has been continuously lowered and a new generation of highly sensitive (hs) assays with improved analytical sensitivity and precision is already being evaluated for clinical application [198] and preclinical evaluation [186,200]. With these assays, measurable levels of circulating troponins are found in all healthy subjects in the general population (human and animal). In one investigation [201], surgically cannulated rats (femoral artery) were bled to quantify hourly concentrations of cTnI using the Erenna Singulex hs assay, to establish biological variation under three different standard laboratory conditions. Transient changes in serum cTnI concentration could be accurately quantified and respective mean values and ranges of 4.94 pg/mL and 1–15 pg/mL were reported. Minimal biological variability was identified in the cannulated rats, and doubling of cTnI concentration was considered to be above biological variability. These data suggest an approximate 5- to 10-fold improvement in analytical sensitivity. The clinical pathologist will need to fully explore the impact and implications of incorporating the improved analytical sensitivity of these assays within the laboratory.

Other Cardiac Biomarkers

Heart-Type Fatty Acid-Binding Protein

Heart-type fatty acid-binding protein (H-FABP) is a low-molecular-weight cytosolic protein that is involved in the intracellular uptake and buffering of fatty acids in the myocardium. It is expressed primarily in heart, but it is not 100% cardiospecific since it is expressed to a lesser extent in skeletal muscle, brain, and kidneys [202]. During myocardial injury, the H-FABP level in serum is elevated rapidly, making it an ideal marker for myocardial infarction, and it is a useful prognostic marker in patients with proven acute coronary syndrome [203]. However, in renal failure and skeletal muscle disease, it has limited diagnostic value for AMI [202]. It is released early into the circulation following isoproterenol-induced cardiomyocyte damage in the rat [184] and additionally in drug-induced skeletal muscle necrosis in the rat [204]. Short-term increases of serum cTnI and heart fatty acid-binding protein have been demonstrated in dogs following administration of formoterol [205]. The utility of H-FABP was highlighted in a single-dose study, but the biomarker was not considered superior to cTnI with regard to sensitivity in the identification of myocardial injury. However, its use as a cardiac biomarker would require exclusion of muscle injury and renal disease. Given its low molecular weight, H-FABP is filtered into the urine following release into the circulation. An immunoreactive, detectable signal can be identified in rat urine following myocardial injury, which is proportionate to the level of injury induced [206]. Urine H-FABP offers a possible additional marker of cardiotoxicity in the absence of renal and skeletal muscle injury.

Natriuretic Peptides

Natriuretic peptides (NPs) are produced and stored in the heart, both in the atria and ventricles, and released from the heart due to abnormal stretch in response to pressure changes and volume overload in the heart. They have proven to be reliable, noninvasive clinical biomarkers for diagnostic, prognostic, and therapeutic monitoring of heart failure. There are three major NPs: atrial natriuretic peptide (ANP), B-type natriuretic peptide (BNP), and C-type NP, all of which share a common 17-amino-acid ring structure and have actions that are targeted to protecting the cardiovascular system from the effects of volume overload [207]. ANP and BNP have

very short half-lives, of the order of minutes. Due to their important physiological role, they are rapidly cleared from circulation through receptor-mediated clearance and proteolytic degradation. Amino-terminal pro-atrial natriuretic peptide (NT-proANP) and amino-terminal pro-brain natriuretic peptide (NT-proBNP) have no known physiological function or receptor, leading to longer half-lives in blood. ANP and BNP are released primarily from the heart, but circulate as hormones to act in various tissues in the body and induce natriuresis, diuresis, smooth muscle relaxation, and vasodilation through the inhibition of vasoconstrictive mediators such as aldosterone and renin [208]. Although ANP is preferentially synthesized and secreted from the atria and BNP from the ventricles, both can be synthesized in either chamber. Unlike ANP, which is stored in granules and thus released with even minor triggers such as exercise, BNP has minimal storage in granules; rather it is synthesized and secreted in bursts [207]. In an investigation of the time course of myocardial ANP and BNP mRNA expression following surgical induction of myocardial infarction in rats, substantial increases in the mRNA levels of BNP and ANP in the infarcted and noninfarcted regions of the heart were observed [209]. These increases were paralleled by elevated circulating concentrations of ANP, BNP, and NT-proANP 2 days postsurgery, which persisted to the end of the study (day 28).

The usefulness of these functional biomarkers in preclinical safety assessment is being explored. Measurement of circulating NT-proBNP as a biomarker for the assessment of a potential cardiovascular drug-induced liability in beagle dogs demonstrated that NT-proBNP acts as an early biomarker for detection of changes related to heart hypertrophy. Additionally, increases in NT-proBNP preceded anatomical and functional changes associated with cardiotoxicity [210]. However, it is necessary to consider potential effects of impairment of renal function, as reduced GFR can be associated with increased circulating NT-proBNP that is not reflective of myocardial injury or disease [211]. However, a high degree of variability in circulating NT-proBNP concentrations in healthy dogs [212] has been reported, indicating emphasis on consideration of individual variability in the interpretation of NT-proBNP results in dogs and the identification of possible test-article-related effects. Limitations of first-generation assays for NT-proBNP in the dog (eg, limited dynamic range, need for protease inhibitors to maintain sample and storage stability) have reportedly been addressed with the introduction of a second-generation immunoassay [213,214]. Other studies in the dog have shown that NT-proBNP may be a helpful diagnostic indicator of acute and subacute myocardial injury [215] and that plasma ANP is a useful, noninvasive parameter for measuring rapid hemodynamic changes [216]. Analytical validation of an enzyme immunoassay for NT-proANP and subsequent biological characterization using samples with and without pressure-induced cardiac hypertrophy has been successfully conducted in the rat [217]. Additionally, cross-laboratory analytical validation of a commercial assay for NT-proANP in the rat showed acceptable inter-laboratory precision, accuracy, recovery, and stability when frozen at −70°C for up to 12 months [218]. Early detection of left ventricular hypertrophy in rats induced by suprapharmacologic doses of a peroxisome proliferator was indicated by increased concentrations of serum NT-proANP [219]. The use of NT-proBNP and NT-proANP in dog and rat studies, respectively, should be considered if the test article has a potential cardiovascular liability, preferably being used in conjunction with cardiac troponin measurements. Circulating myocardial-derived microRNAs might be useful as potential biomarkers for myocardial injury, and candidate microRNAs have been identified in investigation of acute myocardial infarction in humans and mice [220] and isoproterenol-induced myocardial injury in rats and mice [221,222]. Plasma concentrations of cTnI and mir-208 were highly correlated and exhibited similar time courses as markers of isoproterenol (ISO)-induced myocardial injury in the rat [221], but mir-208a may be a better indicator of later-stage cardiomyocyte damage (≥24 h) after iso-induced injury in mice than that of cTnI [221]. Further parallel investigations of mir-208 and cTnI are required to determine which is the superior biomarker of cardiac damage.

Assessment of Myotoxicity

Drug-induced myopathy is produced by lipid-lowering drugs such as ezetimibe, niacin, fibrates (PPAR agonists), and statins, and clinical myopathy occurs in more than 5% of human patients given these drugs [219]. Given the potential for skeletal muscle toxicity as a serious adverse event, the monitoring of skeletal muscle injury is of particular interest during preclinical testing of new drug candidates targeted for the treatment of hyperlipidemia [223]. Laboratory measurements may utilize conventional biomarkers (creatine kinase, AST, aldolase) as a Tier 1 screen and emerging biomarkers [skeletal troponin I (skTnI)]; heart fatty acid-binding protein (Fabp3; H-FABP) as a follow-up Tier 2 screen, if further information is required.

Increases in plasma creatine kinase (CK) and lactate dehydrogenase (LDH) occur with degenerative or necrotic muscle injury. Most CK in the circulation originates from skeletal muscle, with the main contribution coming from the MM isoenzymes. Platelets are a source of CK and LDH activity, and hence plasma is a preferable sample type to serum for analysis, since both enzymes can be released during the clotting process, increasing sample background variation. Although CK has a high tissue concentration in the rat, up to 110-fold greater than AST in some muscle types, it is a comparatively

insensitive biomarker due to a short half-life (0.5–1 h) within the circulation [224]. Timing of blood sampling is therefore critical for CK measurement in rat toxicology studies if meaningful information is to be collected. The author prefers to add aldolase (assessed in combination with AST) to the clinical pathology core screen if skeletal muscle toxicity is a potential test-article-related effect in the rat and liver injury is excluded. Both AST and aldolase have longer half-lives in the rat. The half-lives of creatine kinase in the dog and the nonhuman primate are comparable to the human and therefore there is no additional requirement for aldolase inclusion in these species. Variability of CK and AST associated with physiological and mechanical stress due to handling or exercise adds another layer of difficulty in interpretation. Monitoring of serum/plasma electrolytes is also considered useful in the possible identification of myotoxicity, since intracellular calcium, potassium, and sodium concentrations are all vital in the functioning muscle fiber [49].

New biomarkers of skeletal muscle injury are being introduced into the laboratory. Skeletal muscle troponin I (skTnI) is considered to have similar characteristics to cardiac troponin I and potentially should be a superior biomarker. It has already been noted as a more sensitive, persistent, and specific biomarker than CK, myosin, or myoglobin [223]. In a comprehensive range of short-duration toxicology studies in the rat, the diagnostic performance of Fabp3 as a biomarker of skeletal muscle toxicity was compared with conventional biomarkers. Its superiority was demonstrated in terms of sensitivity, concordance with histology, positive and negative predictive values, and false-negative rates [224]. Parvalbumin, a small (12 kDa) cytoplasmic, calcium-binding protein found in striated muscle, was noted to be excreted in the urine of rats following acute doses of an experimental skeletal muscle toxicant, 2,3,5,6-tetramethylphenylene diamine (TMPD). The magnitude of change was associated with increases in plasma aldolase and AST activity, indicating skeletal muscle injury in the absence of liver injury [225].

Multiplexed panels comprising Fabp3, cTnI, cTnT, skTnI, and myosin light chains (Myl3) are available using the Meso Scale Discovery MULTI-ARRAY technology (Gaithersburg, Maryland, USA) to screen for potential cardiac and skeletal muscle injury. The biomarkers on the panel were selected to collectively distinguish myocardial damage from damage to skeletal muscle and other tissues. The usefulness of these biomarkers was investigated in rat models treated with myotoxic and nonmyotoxic compounds and compared against the conventional biomarkers AST, LDH, and CK [226]. The biomarkers cTnI, cTnT, Fabp3, Myl3, and sTnI were found to be superior to the conventional biomarkers for the detection of cardiac and skeletal myotoxicity, as they had specific and abundant distribution within the heart and/or skeletal muscles; exhibited a positive correlation between the amplitude of increases and the degree of pathological alterations; and had higher diagnostic accuracy for detecting pathological alterations.

Fluid and Electrolyte Balance

Depending on their electrical charge, electrolytes exist as anions or cations, and electrical neutrality requires an equal number of both. In the body, electrolytes fulfill a number of vital roles in maintaining fluid balance and pH, membrane potentials, muscular functions, and nervous conduction, and they serve as cofactors in many enzyme-mediated reactions [227]. For most animals, total body water comprises approximately 60% of body weight, and it can be separated into two interlinked fluidic compartments: intracellular (ICF) and extracellular (ECF). These two compartments are in an osmotic equilibrium governed by the osmotically active molecules in each compartment, and water diffuses freely between them. Osmotically active solutes (sodium, chloride, potassium, glucose, bicarbonate, and urea) determine water distribution in body compartments. Potassium, magnesium, phosphate, and proteins predominate within the ICF, while sodium, calcium, chloride, and bicarbonate are the major ECF solutes [49]. Endocrine and transmembrane regulatory mechanisms work to maintain plasma electrolyte concentrations tightly controlled within a narrow range. Changes in electrolyte concentrations result from altered hydration and electrolyte intake, transmembrane shifts, altered renal handling, or loss via alimentary tract, skin, or airways. Unexplained alteration in plasma electrolyte concentrations should be supported by urinary electrolyte analysis.

Endocrine Control of Electrolyte and Fluid Balance

Regulatory mechanisms involve several hormones, including aldosterone and the renin–angiotensin axis, arginine vasopressin (AVP), the natriuretic peptides, and parathyroid hormone. These hormones have differing sites of synthesis and actions. Renal handling of electrolyte balance is controlled at two levels. First, systemic regulatory loops with their effector hormones like renin–angiotensin–aldosterone, natriuretic peptides, arginine vasopressin, or parathyroid hormone, ensure the balance of body salt and water metabolism. Second, cellular feedback loops and glomerulo-tubular balance adjust tubular function and single-cell homeostasis [228]. Arginine vasopressin (AVP), also called antidiuretic hormone, is released from the posterior pituitary in response to changes of osmolality and plasma sodium.

The renin–angiotensin–aldosterone axis plays a key role in sodium and potassium homeostasis. Renin is synthesized in the juxta-glomerular apparatus of glomerular afferent arterioles and is secreted in response to reduced renal perfusion and excessive loss of sodium. It cleaves angiotensinogen, an α_2-globulin produced by the liver, to release angiotensin I. The production of angiotensin I occurs within blood vessels and the nephron. Angiotensin-converting enzyme (ACE), which is present in pulmonary circulation, kidney, and vascular beds in several organs, converts angiotensin I to angiotensin II. This octapeptide enhances aldosterone secretion and increases glomerular filtration via its vasoconstrictive actions. It promotes reabsorption of sodium and water in the proximal tubules and stimulates production of AVP.

In an internal study, exaggerated pharmacology of an angiotensin II antagonist (antihypertensive agent) in dogs resulted in marked sodium and water loss from the body, coupled with potassium retention. This resulted in reductions of plasma volume and glomerular filtration rate, and consequential increases in plasma urea and creatinine, reduced plasma sodium and chloride and increased plasma potassium, marked hemoconcentration, and markedly raised plasma aldosterone concentrations. Aldosterone is synthesized and secreted from the zona glomerulosa of the adrenal cortex. Aldosterone stimulates sodium reabsorption in exchange for potassium and hydrogen ion secretion in the renal collecting tubules. Several feedback mechanisms acting on aldosterone exist, and these include plasma, adrenal, and electrolyte concentrations and the renin–angiotensin axis [229]. The natriuretic peptides (discussed earlier) act to inhibit renal tubular sodium reabsorption and the renin–angiotensin–aldosterone axis, thereby promoting sodium loss from the body. Parathyroid hormone (PTH) regulates calcium homeostasis and therefore indirectly affects phosphate metabolism. PTH secretion is increased in response to hypocalcemia, and it promotes both the renal reabsorption of calcium and the excretion of phosphate.

Electrolytes

Sodium is the major extracellular cation in plasma, and its concentration is closely related to osmotic homeostasis, maintenance of body fluid volumes, and neuromuscular excitability. Plasma sodium is freely filtered via the renal glomeruli, but about 70% is reabsorbed in the proximal tubules and 25% in the loop of Henle together with chloride ions and water. Plasma chloride is the major extracellular anion, and in most instances, changes in plasma sodium and chloride concentrations tend to parallel each other. Decreases in the plasma concentration of sodium and chloride can occur with gastrointestinal losses (vomiting or diarrhea in nonrodents), and renal losses through alteration of electrolyte handling (diuretics and decreased aldosterone production). Decreases in plasma chloride may also be reflected in changes in acid–base balance and alterations of plasma bicarbonate.

In a series of subacute studies (7 days duration) conducted internally with a specific class of compounds, a lowering of plasma chloride of ≥4% from concurrent controls was a reproducible and unexpected finding. This was demonstrated, through investigation, to be a signal of acute primary electrolyte changes (increased urinary sodium and electrolyte excretion and hemoconcentration within 4h). Ion-channel gene expression analysis in the kidney identified reduced transcription of most genes examined (mainly involving sodium, potassium, and chloride transport). Compensatory mechanisms reflected by increases in plasma bicarbonate and aldosterone were evident after 12h [230]. Increased plasma sodium concentration, which is a less common finding in toxicology studies, can reflect increased sodium intake, sodium retention, reductions in ECF volume, or increased mineralocorticoid and glucocorticoid administration. Potassium is the major intracellular cation, with plasma values approximately 20-fold less than the intracellular concentrations. The intracellular potassium gradient is maintained by an ATP-dependent active extrusion of sodium, which is balanced by the pumping of potassium and hydrogen ions into cells. Investigations into potassium balance within the circulation should primarily be based on plasma rather than serum (since potassium is released from platelets and red cells during the clotting process and can influence artifactual increases in serum).

Increases in plasma potassium concentration may reflect increased intake, reduced excretion due to hormonal effects, renal effects, metabolic and respiratory acidosis, cellular necrosis, intravascular hemolysis, and artifactual increases from hemolysis, release from leucocytes and platelets (eg, thrombocytosis) or difficult blood collections, and potassium-containing anticoagulant, commonly EDTA. Decreases in plasma potassium may reflect decreased intake, extra-renal loss (vomiting, diarrhea), increased fecal loss, compounds that increase GI loss, hyperaldosteronism, renal tubular injury, drugs, and alteration of renal excretion. Pharmaceutical compounds such as aldosterone agonists, aminoglycosides, diuretics, and antineoplastic agents can cause hypokalemia [231]. At high doses, the β_2-adrenergic agonist salmeterol produces an acute and rapid hypokalemia (within 1h) in healthy human subjects. This is considered to be due to increased intracellular uptake by both liver and skeletal muscle secondary to an activation of cell membrane sodium potassium ATPase [232]. In toxicology studies where blood sampling is routinely performed 24h post dosing, plasma potassium concentrations were observed to be mildly increased following β_2-adrenergic agonist administration [233]. This is considered to reflect overcompensation in reestablishing osmotic equilibrium between the ECF and ICF.

Calcium is involved in neuromuscular transmission, cardiac and skeletal muscle contraction and relaxation, bone formation, coagulation, cell growth, membrane transport mechanisms, and enzymatic reactions. Approximately 40–50% is free or ionized and the remainder is bound to proteins, principally albumin. Consideration of total protein, albumin levels (and by inference globulin) should be made when interpreting plasma/serum total calcium levels. Higher levels are observed in younger animals. Increases in serum calcium concentration may result from hyperparathyroidism, hyperthyroidism, increased total protein (increased albumin and/or gamma globulin levels), poor venipuncture technique ,and exposure to drugs such as thiazides, lithium, and calciferol. Decreases in serum calcium may occur with renal failure, fasting or inadequate intake of calcium, protein loss, hypoparathyroidism, acute pancreatitis, and increased calcitonin or drug/toxin exposure (diuretics, anticonvulsants, fluoride, ethylene glycol) [227].

Phosphate is the major intracellular anion. Serum/plasma phosphate concentration is primarily inorganic orthophosphate and is protein bound, free anion, or complexed to sodium, calcium, or magnesium. Concentrations of serum phosphate are affected by diurnal cycle and pH. Phosphate is more sensitive than calcium to dietary intake and renal excretion and higher levels are normally observed in younger animals [49]. Increased serum phosphate is observed with reductions of GFR, and increased concentrations parallel changes in serum urea and creatinine concentration. Other increases in serum phosphate may reflect increased dietary intake, tissue necrosis, acidosis, altered bone metabolism, decreased renal excretion, artifactually delayed sample separation, or hemolysis. Compounds that increase plasma inorganic phosphate include anabolic steroids, furosemide, and thiazides. Causes of decreased serum phosphate may reflect redistribution of phosphate between ECF and ICF, decreased nutritional intake, hepatic disease, hyperparathyroidism, infection, and increased excretion. Examples of compounds that lower serum phosphate include antacids, renal tubular toxins, ethanol, intravenous glucose, and insulin.

Magnesium is an important structural component of bone and muscle that predominates in the ICF and is found free, complexed, or protein-bound in blood. This cation is essential for many enzyme reactions, neuromuscular activity, and bone formation; however, it is not well characterized or routinely assessed in preclinical studies [49]. Increases in serum magnesium may reflect decreased excretion in acute and chronic renal failure, increased intake, cellular necrosis, and adrenal hypofunction. Decreased serum magnesium levels may reflect reduced nutritional intake, malabsorption, increased gastrointestinal loss, pancreatitis, increased renal excretion, hypoparathyroidism, hyperthyroidism, hypocalcemia, and hypokalemia. Examples of compounds that lower plasma magnesium include aminoglycosides, cisplatin, cyclosporine, and loop diuretics [231].

Proteins, Lipids, and Carbohydrates

Plasma proteins are primarily synthesized in the liver (albumin and globulins) and the immune system (namely immunoglobulins, produced by B-lymphocytes and plasma cells). Additionally, endocrine organs such as the pituitary are the sites for protein hormone production. Individual proteins can be classified according to their actions as enzymes, coagulation factors, complement factors, hormones, acute-phase reactants, and transport proteins. Collectively the proteins provide nutritional support, determine colloid osmotic pressure, and are involved in the maintenance of acid–base balance. Serum contains all of the plasma proteins with the exception of those consumed during the clotting process, namely fibrinogen, factor V, and factor VIII. Catabolism of plasma proteins occurs primarily in the liver, with the turnover rate being specific to each plasma protein. Additionally, a direct correlation exists between body size and turnover of the major plasma protein, albumin, with half-lives ranging from 1 to 2 days in rodents, 5 days in monkeys, 8 days in dogs, and 15–19 days in humans. Albumin is synthesized in the liver, accounts for approximately 40–60% of the total plasma protein in laboratory animals, and is the major determinant of colloid osmotic pressure. It binds and transports large organic ions (eg, bilirubin), vitamins, and hormones (eg, steroids) that are normally insoluble or poorly soluble in aqueous fluids. Other major transport proteins include transferrin, which transports iron and the thyroid hormone binding proteins.

Subtraction of the albumin concentration from the total protein concentration provides calculation of the total globulin concentration. In toxicology studies, increases in total protein concentration (hyperproteinemia), including albumin, mainly reflect dehydration of the animals. This may be associated with fluid losses from the gastrointestinal tract (vomiting, diarrhea, and excessive salivation), loss via the kidney (polyuria), and decreased water consumption. Decreases in food consumption leading to decreases in water consumption in rodents cause relative dehydration. Hyperproteinemia may also be associated in inflammatory responses leading to the production of acute-phase proteins, immunoglobulins, a resultant hyperglobulinemia, and decrease in the albumin:globulin ratio. Hypoproteinemia reflects decreased total protein synthesis or increased protein loss. Concomitant decreases in albumin and globulin occur with malnutrition, hemorrhage, intestinal malabsorption, protein-losing enteropathy, severe exudative skin lesions/burns, and overzealous administration of

fluids. Hypoalbuminemia can be the result of significant hepatocellular damage/insufficiency leading to reductions in protein synthesis, increased catabolism (tissue damage), impaired nutritional status, glomerulopathy with proteinuria, or altered distribution (ascites).

In toxicity studies, small decreases in albumin are frequently observed in animals administered high doses of test article. This may correlate with effects on other parameters (eg, hematocrit, glucose, cholesterol, and body weight), and is usually an indication of the overall poor condition of the animals rather than evidence of a specific toxic mechanism [48].

Acute-Phase Proteins

The varied reactions of the host to infection, inflammation, or trauma are collectively known as the acute-phase response, and encompass a wide range of pathophysiological responses such as pyrexia, leukocytosis, hormone alterations, and muscle protein depletion combining to minimize tissue damage while enhancing the repair process. The mechanism for stimulation of hepatic production of acute-phase proteins (APPs) is by release of proinflammatory cytokines interleukin-1 (IL-1), interleukin-6 (IL-6), and tumor necrosis factor, which induce both local and systemic responses [234]. These APPs have a wide range of activities that contribute to host defense mechanisms by directly neutralizing inflammatory agents, helping to minimize the extent of local tissue damage, and participating in tissue repair and regeneration [235]. By definition these proteins change their serum concentrations by >25% in response to proinflammatory cytokines stimulated during the disease process.

As quantitative biomarkers of disease, APPs can be used in diagnosis, prognosis, and in monitoring response to therapy, as well as in general health screening [236]. Similarly in an acute-phase response elicited by drug-induced toxicity, the onset, magnitude, progression, and recovery of APPs can be useful in characterizing animal response to the test article and in relation to onset of the causative injury. These biomarkers are highly sensitive indicators of inflammation, but lack specificity. Major interspecies differences exist in the APP response, which must be taken into account in preclinical studies [236]. In any given species, particular APPs demonstrate "major," "moderate," or "minor" responses. For example, a major APP responder (eg, C-reactive protein in dog and nonhuman primate) has a low serum concentration in healthy animals that rises dramatically by 100- to 1000-fold on stimulation, peaking at 24–48 h and then declining rapidly during the recovery phase. Moderate and minor responders will demonstrate lower magnitudes of change in comparison to major APPs but they may persist in the circulation for longer time periods. "Negative" APP biomarkers, which fall in concentration during the inflammatory response, have also been identified. Their concentrations decrease because of decreased production by hepatocytes due to the actions of cytokines such as IL-6 and IL-1. The major negative APPs are albumin and transferrin, which is a major transport protein for iron [235]. The major acute-phase proteins for humans, dogs, and monkeys are C-reactive protein (CRP) and serum amyloid A (SAA) [236–238]. Haptoglobin, an alpha 2 globulin and a moderate acute-phase protein in human, dog, and rat, has been shown to be elevated in the dog following treatment with corticosteroids and during naturally occurring hyperadrenocorticism [239]. This markedly reduces the specificity of this APP as a marker of inflammation in animals receiving steroid treatment. Exogenous glucocorticoids do not affect the concentrations of other APPs such as CRP and SAA [240]. Thus a panel of APPs that included CRP and SAA could be used to assess concurrent inflammatory conditions in the presence of exogenous or endogenous corticosteroids [241].

In the rat, α_2-macroglobulin and thiostatin are considered to be major APPs [235,237]. Moderate APPs in the dog and rat are α_1-acid glycoprotein, haptoglobin, and fibrinogen [235]. Serum CRP is a poor marker of acute inflammation in the rat in comparison with serum haptoglobin and plasma fibrinogen [237,242]. Lipocalin-2 (LCN-2), a 25-kDa secretory protein, currently used as a biomarker for renal injury and inflammation, has been identified as a major APP in the rat and mouse [243]. In a model of turpentine oil-induced sterile abscess, serum LCN-2 concentrations were increased 200-fold after 48 h. Marked elevations in hepatic LCN-2 mRNA expression at 24 h after injection were approximately eightfold greater than α_2-macroglobulin hepatic mRNA expression. In the mouse, LCN-2 gene expression data were generated with SAA, a major APP in the mouse. In rats, the production of acute-phase proteins (α_2-macroglobulin and α_1-acid glycoprotein) has upper limits even with increased strength of turpentine oil-induced inflammatory stimulation [244]. Data generated in our laboratories also support LCN-2 as a major APP in the rat. In an acute model of carbon tetrachloride (CCl_4)-induced hepatotoxicity, LCN-2 hepatic mRNA expression increased 1000-fold after 24 h, associated with a 275-fold increase in LCN-2 in serum in female Wistar Han rats given 1.6 CCl_4 mL/kg body weight. LCN-2 was found to clearly outperform other APP biomarkers [α_2-macroglobulin, α_1-acid glycoprotein, haptoglobin, tissue inhibitor of metalloproteinase (TIMP-1), and monocyte chemo-attractant protein-1(MCP-1)].

Multiplex assays (Luminex, MSD) are available to measure these acute-phase proteins in rats and mice. The inclusion of APPs in toxicology protocols is usually as a Tier 2 testing strategy determined by appropriate changes in clinical pathology and/or histopathology. Consideration for inclusion of species-specific APPs as a part of the toxicology study protocol should be made on a case-by-case basis if indicated by the nature or intended pharmacology of the test article or observations made in previous studies.

Lipids

The two major and most frequently measured lipids are cholesterol and triglycerides. They are derived from dietary intake and endogenous synthesis, primarily by the liver. They are components of lipoproteins and can be eliminated via the hepatobiliary system. Cholesterol is required for the synthesis of cellular membranes, bile acids, corticosteroids, and sex steroids. Triglycerides are an important source of energy. Cholesterol (CHOL) and triglycerides (TG) circulate as components of chylomicrons and lipoprotein particles: high-density lipoprotein (HDL), low-density lipoprotein (LDL), and very-low-density lipoprotein (VLDL). The general composition of lipoproteins is similar in animals and humans. The outside surfaces of the lipoprotein particles contain phospholipids, nonesterified cholesterol molecules, and apolipoproteins (which are specific protein and polypeptide components of lipopoproteins). The hydrophilic aspects of the molecules are on the plasma surface; the hydrophobic aspects are adjacent to the core of mostly TG and cholesterol ester molecules. Fatty acids may be in the core but also circulate outside of lipoproteins bound to albumin. The major lipid content alters, and the lipid-to-protein ratio decreases, in the lipoprotein molecules moving from chylomicrons to VLDL to LDL and HDL. Chylomicrons, formed in the small intestine, mainly contain dietary TG, while LDL and HDL lipoproteins mainly contain phospholipid and cholesterol ester [244]. Nearly all cholesterol within a fasting serum sample is within lipoproteins, mostly produced in hepatocytes.

In contrast to humans, HDL is responsible for a significant majority of cholesterol transport in most laboratory animal species, and there are marked species differences generally between the species and strains for plasma cholesterol, triglycerides, and lipoproteins, and some of the lipoprotein-metabolizing enzymes [245]. Species differences in lipid metabolism cause difficulties in correlating lipid effects in animal models with potential effects in humans. Changes in cholesterol and triglycerides are typically reflective of general metabolic events, rather than as serving as indicators of specific target organ toxicity, although cholesterol may be the pharmacological target of hypolipidemic agents leading to extremely low serum cholesterol levels at dose levels used in toxicology studies. Small changes in serum CHOL and TG concentrations, both increases and decreases, are relatively frequent findings in toxicology studies. The changes are generally believed to represent minor alterations in lipid metabolism that do not adversely affect the animals' health. For example, internal observation of minimal to mild increases in serum CHOL in rats associated with hepatocellular hypertrophy and evidence of hepatic enzyme induction has been noted in rat candidate selection studies. Young rats (eg, 7–20 weeks of age) usually exhibit less interanimal variability than dogs or monkeys, making it easier to identify small effects in short-term rat studies. Other factors to consider include alterations in food consumption, body weight and composition, liver function, and hormones [246].

Serum TG concentration is elevated postprandially, while serum cholesterol is relatively stable. Corticosteroid administration can produce increases in CHOL concentration in rats and dogs due to alteration in lipid metabolism. While animals are usually fasted before clinical pathology bleeds, different approaches may be adopted to assess the effects of potential lipid-lowering agents. When fat is mobilized to meet energy requirements because of starvation, malabsorption, or impaired digestion, serum TG are usually increased [48]. Liver disorders, including cholestasis, are frequently accompanied by alterations of serum and tissue lipids. In nephrotic syndrome, hypercholesterolemia (and sometimes hypertriglyceridemia) is secondary to enhanced synthesis of CHOL-containing lipoproteins. Lipoprotein synthesis is thought to be stimulated by hypoalbuminemia, and decreased plasma oncotic pressure [49]. Decreases in plasma TG concentrations may also be associated with increased fat vaculoation in the liver.

Glucose

Several hormones influence glucose homeostasis, most importantly the glucose-lowering action of insulin and the glucose-elevating action of glucagon. The maintenance of blood glucose concentrations occurs via hepatic glycogenolysis, glycolysis, and gluconeogenesis. In addition, corticosteroids, catecholamines, and growth hormones are insulin antagonists and interfere with cellular actions of insulin. Common causes of increased glucose concentrations in toxicology studies include nonfasting samples, samples from moribund animals, catecholamine release, and stress. Administration of β_2-adrenergic agonists can produce acute and rapid increases in glucose concentration, reflecting glycogenolysis in the muscle and liver. However, opposite changes (reductions in glucose) to those observed acutely may be noted at 24 h after dosing in toxicology studies [233]. Corticosteroid administration promotes gluconeogenesis and inhibits glycogenolysis, leading to increase of glycogen stores in the liver, and additionally produces antagonistic effects to the actions of insulin. All these factors combine to increase serum glucose concentrations. Additionally, test-article-induced pancreatic islet β-cell toxicity leading to absolute insulin deficiency will lead to markedly elevated serum glucose concentrations, glucosuria, reductions in plasma volume, loss of body weight, and other secondary changes related to the

animals' inability to utilize glucose within tissues. Use of anesthesia increases blood glucose concentrations in rats in comparison to live blood collection (and no anesthesia). In contrast, artifactual in vitro sample glycolysis, decreased food consumption, malabsorption, and hepatic disease may lead to decreased blood glucose concentrations.

INTERPRETATION OF CLINICAL PATHOLOGY DATA IN PRECLINICAL SAFETY STUDIES

An awareness of the factors that may influence artifactual changes in the test of interest will increase its diagnostic value. In addition, analytical performance of the assay and biological variation are key information in the association with possible toxicity or physiological change. In general, the biological component is higher than the analytical component. Components of biological variation can be used to assess the usefulness of reference intervals, to evaluate the significance of changes in serial results from an individual, and to define objective analytical goals. These components are increasingly evaluated in new biomarkers being introduced for clinical laboratory diagnosis [247]. It is important to recognize the factors that contribute to biological variation and to minimize these variables. Failure to control such factors reduces the predictive value of the data and can obscure real toxic or pathological effects. The tools of sensitivity (ie, the proportion of the treated animals showing specific disease or pathology with test result(s) at above/below certain cut-off values) and specificity (ie, the proportion of clinically healthy or control animals with a test result that does not exceed the chosen cut-off value) may be used, but their application has been limited in preclinical safety assessment. This is generally a reflection of the clinical pathologists' reliance on concurrent control animal information and/or individual animal prestudy baseline data to assist in the assessment of meaningful treatment-related changes in clinical pathology. However, with the implementation of new biomarkers within the clinical pathology laboratory, increased attention has been paid to the assessment of sensitivity and specificity.

Statistical Analysis, Use of Concurrent Control, and Historical Reference Range Data

Appropriate statistical methods should be used to analyze clinical pathology data. Regardless of the outcome of the statistical analysis, scientific interpretation is necessary for the ultimate determination of test material treatment effects. Statistical significance alone should not be used to infer toxicological or biological relevance of clinical pathology findings. Additionally the absence of statistical significance should not exclude the possibility that test article effects exist. Both parametric and nonparametric statistical models are used in preclinical studies. Most parametric statistical models are suitable for data that are normally distributed and exhibit homogeneous variance. Nonparametric procedures are used when data are not normally distributed [248]. The power of a statistical test is proportional to the number of animals per group. As the number of animals increases, more differences of small magnitude become statistically significant, although they may not be toxicologically relevant. Conversely, with small groups of animals, the numbers of statistically significant values tend to be low. When evaluating group mean clinical pathology data, careful assessment of the standard deviation values as indicators of variability should be made [59].

Given the number of parameters or conditions that may be unique to the study, the most appropriate method of interpreting clinical pathology data in treated animals is to compare against concurrent control animals and/or prestudy baseline levels, particularly in nonrodent studies or rat candidate selection studies where treatment group numbers may be small. The purpose of a concurrent control group is to represent the normal spectrum of untreated values. Inevitably, the selection process used in assigning animals to experimental groups and the group size in toxicity studies will result in the concurrent control group representing only an approximation of the entire control population [249]. If historical reference intervals are used exclusively to interpret clinical pathology data, many drug-related changes in analytes would not be considered meaningful because the group mean value is often within the limits of historical reference ranges [250]. The use of historical reference data should be viewed as a tool for better understanding the events or apparent differences observed within a study. They should not be seen as a convenient device for discounting unwanted or difficult findings [249].

There may be occasions in which it is good practice to compare study data against reference intervals. If the concurrent control group mean value and many individual values clearly fall outside the reference range (which is known to be of good quality), other variables in the study should be investigated. This may be helpful in detecting drifts of analyte values due to analytical problems or changing animal populations, evaluating data in studies with small numbers of animals per dose group, and in helping animal selection from prestudy health screens [251].

Interpretation of Clinical Pathology Data

Compound-related effects on clinical pathology values in preclinical trials in rats, dogs, and nonhuman primates are determined by comparison with mean and individual animal data from concurrent controls. In dogs and nonhuman primates, additional comparison of interim, terminal, or reversibility data with pretreatment data is recommended for determining test-article-related effects and their reversibility. Review of reference intervals developed from historic control data (within that laboratory) will also be made, where appropriate. In order to identify if a clinical pathology effect is adverse, it should be quantified (a multiplier, or % change vs. controls or in some cases pretest values), qualified (minimal to severe), and corroborated with clinical observations, body weights, food consumption, water consumption, morphologic pathology findings, test article exposure, and/or any other clinical pathology findings. A change that is readily and completely reversible on cessation of treatment would suggest a lower level of concern. The change is more likely to be adverse if the effect is inconsistent with class effects, mode of action/pharmacology, or what is otherwise known or expected of the test article. Judgments are required as to whether or not any observed intergroup differences merely represent chance events or actual responses to exposure to the test material. The biological significance and toxicological importance of any changes that result from administration of the test material has then to be placed into perspective [1].

In order to correctly interpret the clinical pathology data generated during the course of toxicity investigations [1,252], the reviewer should identify if any effects in the data are apparent in the light of:

- The diagnostic and pathological significance of values that differ from concurrent controls or fall outside expected ranges.
- The potential impact of study conditions/design/procedure on the diagnostic utility of tests. These conditions include timing and/or site of sample collection, formulation of test material including vehicle and pH, pharmacology of the compound, route of administration, and possible sources of preanalytical and analytical variation not apparent at the time of study design.
- How biological variation may affect results (normal inter- and intra-animal variability) and species differences for each test.
- How changes in the physiological status of the animals as a result of the intended biological/pharmacological activity of the test material, or alterations in food and water consumption as a result of the administration of the test material, can affect intergroup distribution of values.
- Patterns of changes in linked parameters that are related to specific organs/systems or other relevant study observations.
- The association between the time course of changes in clinical pathology parameters and associated pathological events in the target organs or tissues.

TABLE 14.3 Assessment and Scientific Interpretation of Clinical Pathology Data

Are Effects in the Data Apparent? (Data Analysis)	Scientific Interpretation and Integration of Test-Article-Related Clinical Pathology Changes
Quality of analysis confirmed and accepted	Are there changes in other life study observation: body weight, food consumption, water intake, clinical observations?
Any changes to study design? Staggered dosing (no concurrent control information) Opportunity for potential sources of preanalytical variation assessed	Do data reflect altered physiology or metabolism?
Are differences between concurrent control and test article-treated animals apparent?	Are there linked changes in parameters that relate to specific organs, systems, or physiology? Do data associate with histological correlates, if present? Do data reflect pharmacology or exaggerated pharmacology of the test article? Previous experience with class of compound.
Individual animal variation apparent?	Do data indicate toxicity of the test article? Dose related? Exposure data confirmed.
Differences from pretreatment baseline?	Are data considered adverse in the absence of correlating microscopic lesions? Is magnitude of change of clinical pathology parameter(s) sufficient to warrant concern? Is the change adaptive? Do data indicate functional change? Is a temporal relationship observed? Do data indicate structural injury?
For nonrodents with concurrent controls: Are changes post treatment in agreement with reference to both pretreatment baseline and concurrent controls?	Are data considered adverse in the presence of correlating microscopic lesions? Do the magnitude of change of parameter concur with severity of the histological correlate?
Are both sexes affected?	
Dose related?	
Magnitude and direction of change of affected clinical pathology parameters: Single parameter or multiple parameters affected?	
Do values in control animals fall within reference intervals (no effect from vehicle or procedure influencing data)?	
Are statistically significant differences evident between control and treated animals?	
Are the changes biologically significant?	

A structured approach to assessing whether the changes in the clinical pathology data are meaningful could require answers to several questions from several disciplines involved in the study (Table 14.3). The identification of the no observed adverse effect level (NOAEL) can be a challenging process and should be determined for each toxicity study as a whole, rather than for individual findings. The initial opinions on where harmful and nonharmful effects occur may change as additional information related to the molecule is generated over the course of developing a test material. Data from longer-term studies may give the toxicologist a new, or additional, perspective on whether or not an observation thought to be subtle or minor in a short-term study is an early indicator of a harmful effect.

A framework to facilitate the consistent interpretation of toxicity studies has also been proposed [249]. This structured process involves two main steps. In the first, a decision must be made as to whether differences from concurrent control values are treatment related or if they are chance deviations. A difference is less likely to be an effect of treatment if there is no obvious dose response, it is due to findings(s) in one or more animals that could be considered outliers, the measurement of the endpoint under evaluation is inherently imprecise, it is within normal biological variation (within range of historical control values or other reference intervals), or there is a lack of biological plausibility (the difference is inconsistent with class effects, mode of action of the test substance, or the measured value for the parameter exceeds the biological or physiological range).

In the second stage, only those differences judged to be effects are further evaluated in order to discriminate between those that are adverse and those that are not. An adverse effect and a biologically significant finding are defined as follows.

Adverse Effect: A biochemical, morphological, or physiological change (in response to a stimulus) that either singly or in combination adversely affects the performance of the whole organism, or reduces the organism's ability to respond to an additional environmental challenge. Adverse toxicologic effects are categorized as chemical-based, on-target, or off-target effects. Chemical-based toxicity is defined as toxicity that is related to the physicochemical characteristics of a compound and its effects on cellular organelles, membranes, and/ or metabolic pathways. On-target refers to exaggerated and adverse pharmacologic effects at the target of interest in the test system. Off-target refers to adverse effects as a result of modulation of other targets; these may be related biologically or totally unrelated to the target of interest [253] Contrasted to adverse effects, nonadverse effects can be defined as those biological effects that do not cause biochemical, morphological, or physiological changes that affect the general well-being, growth, development, or lifespan of an animal.

Biologically Significant Effect: A response (to a stimulus) in an organism or other biological system that is considered to have substantial or noteworthy effect (positive or negative) on the well-being of the biological system. The concept is to be distinguished from statistically significant effects or changes that may or may not be meaningful to the general state of health of the system.

An effect is less likely to be adverse if:

- There is no alteration in the general function of the test species or the organ/tissue affected, it is an adaptive response, transient, and severity is limited and below thresholds of concern, and/or the effect is isolated or independent.
- Changes in other parameters usually associated with the effect of concern are not observed, the effect is not part of a continuum of changes known to progress with time to an established adverse effect, and it is secondary to other adverse effects and/or it is a consequence of the experimental model [249].

In conclusion, the interpretation of clinical pathology data from preclinical studies can be affected by the low numbers of animals tested (particularly in dog and non-human primate studies), the normal variability between and within individual animals, and the effects of other study-related procedures. Effective review of all available study data and structured interpretation of associated changes in clinical pathology parameters should be performed to support identification of test-article-related effects.

References

[1] James RW. The relevance of clinical pathology to toxicology studies. Comp Haem Int 1993;3:190–5.

[2] Popp JA. Need for integrative assessment of toxicology data. Toxicol Pathol 2009;37:833–4.

[3] Weingand K, Brown G, Hall R, Davies D, Gossett K, Neptun D, et al. Harmonization of animal clinical pathology testing in toxicity and safety studies. The joint scientific committee for international harmonization of clinical pathology testing. Fundam Appl Toxicol 1996;29:198–201.

[4] Evans GO. General introduction. In: Evans GO, editor. Animal clinical chemistry, a practical handbook for toxicologists and biomedical researchers. 2nd ed. Boca Raton (FL): CRC Press, Taylor & Francis; 2009. p. 1–13.

[5] Tomlinson L, Boone L, Ramiah L, Penraat K, Von Beust BR, Ameri M, et al. Best practices for veterinary toxicologic clinical pathology, with emphasis on the pharmaceutical and biotechnology industries. Vet Clin Pathol 2013;42:252–69.

[6] Young JK, Hall RL, O'Brien P, Strauss V, Vahle J. Best practices for clinical pathology testing in carcinogenicity studies. Toxicol Pathol 2011;39:429–34.

[7] Everds NE, Snyder PW, Bailey KW, Bolon B, Creasy DM, Foley GL, et al. Interpreting stress responses during routine toxicity studies; a review of the biology, impact and assessment. Toxicol Pathol 2013;41:560–614.

[8] Evans GO. Preanalytical variables. In: Evans GO, editor. Animal clinical chemistry, a practical handbook for toxicologists and biomedical researchers. 2nd ed. Boca Raton (FL): CRC Press, Taylor & Francis; 2009. p. 255–75.

[9] Evans GO. Preanalytical variables. In: Evans GO, editor. Animal hematotoxicology, a practical handbook for toxicologists and biomedical researchers. Boca Raton (FL): CRC Press, Taylor & Francis; 2009. p. 125–38.

[10] Sanford KW, Mcpherson RA. Preanalysis. In: McPherson RA, Pincus MR, editors. Henry's clinical diagnosis and management by laboratory methods. 22nd ed. Philadelphia (PA): Elsevier Saunders; 2011. p. 24–36.

[11] Davy CW, Trennery PN, Edmunds JG, Altman JFB, Eichler DA. Local muscle irritancy of ketamine hydrochloride in the marmoset. Lab Anim 1987;21:60–7.

[12] Bennett JS, Gossett KA, McCarthy MP, Simpson ED. Effects of ketamine hydrochloride on serum biochemical and hematologic variables in rhesus monkeys (Macaca mulatta). Vet Clin Pathol 1992;21:15–8.

[13] Lugo-Roman LA, Rico PJ, Sturdivant R, Burks R, Settle TL. Effects of serial anesthesia using ketamine or ketamine/medetomidine on hematology and serum biochemistry values in rhesus macaques (Macaca mulatta). J Med Primatol 2010;39:41–9.

[14] Hall RL, Everds NE. Factors affecting the interpretation of canine and nonhuman primate clinical pathology. Toxicol Pathol 2003;31:6–10.

[15] Matsuzawa T, Sakazume M. Effects of fasting on haematology and clinical chemistry values in the rat and dog. Comp Haematol Int 1994;4:152–6.

[16] Nowland MH, Hugunin MS, Rogers KL. Effects of short term fasting in male Sprague Dawley rats. Comp Med 2011;61:138–44.

[17] Jensen TL, Kiersgaard MK, Sorensen DB, Mikkelsen LF. Fasting of mice: a review. Lab Anim 2013;47:225–40.

[18] Bellanger S, Benrezzak O, Battista MC, Naimi F, Labbé SM, Frisch F. Experimental dog model for assessment of fasting and postprandial fatty acid metabolism: pitfalls and feasibility. Lab Anim 2015;49:228–40.

[19] McGuill MW, Rowan AN. Biological effects of blood loss: implications for sampling volumes and techniques. ILAR News 1989;31:5–18.

[20] Morton DB, Abbot D, Barclay R, Close BS, Ewbank R, Gask D, et al. Removal of blood from laboratory mammals. First report of the BVA/FRAME/RSPCA/UFAW joint working group on refinement. Lab Anim 1993;27:1–22.

[21] Diehl K-H, Hull R, Morton D, Pfister R, Rabemampianina Y, Smith D, et al. A good practice guide to the administration of substances and removal of blood, including routes and volumes. J Appl Toxicol 2001;21:15–23. van de Vorstenbosh.

[22] Nahas K, Provost JP, Baneux PH, Rabemampianina Y. Effects of acute blood removal via the sublingual vein on haematological and clinical parameters in Sprague-Dawley rats. Lab Anim 2000;34:362–71.

[23] Mahl A, Heining P, Ulrich P, Jakubowski J, Bobadilla M, Zeller W, et al. Comparison of clinical pathology parameters with two different blood sampling techniques in rats: retrobular plexus versus sublingual vein. Lab Anim 2000;34:351–61.

[24] Hoff J. Methods of blood collection in the mouse. Lab Anim 2000;29:47–53.

[25] Dameron GW, Weingand KW, Didersadt JM, Odioso LW, Dierckmann TA, Schwecke W, et al. Effect of bleeding site on clinical laboratory testing of rats: orbital venous plexus versus posterior vena cava. Lab Anim Sci 1992;42:299–301.

[26] Neptun DA, Smith N, Irons RD. Effect of sampling site and collection method on variations in baseline clinical pathology parameters in Fischer-344 rats. I. Clinical chemistry. Fundam Appl Toxicol 1985;5:1180–5.

[27] Smith CN, Neptun DA, Irons RD. Effect of sampling site and collection method on variations in baseline clinical pathology parameters in Fischer-344 rats. II. Clinical hematology. Fundam Appl Toxicol 1986;7:658–63.

[28] Bernardi C, Monet D, Brughera M, Di Salvo M, Lamparelli D, Mazue G, et al. Hematology and clinical chemistry in rats: comparison of different blood collection sites. Comp Haematol Int 1996;6:160–6.

[29] Siebel J, Bodie K, Weber S, Bury D, Kron M, Blaich G. Comparison of haematology, coagulation and clinical chemistry parameters in blood samples from the sublingual vein and vena cava in Sprague-Dawley rats. Lab Anim 2010;44:344–51.

[30] Teilmann AC, Kalliokoski O, Sorenson DB, Hau J, Abelson KSP. Manual versus automated blood sampling: impact of repeated blood sampling on stress parameters and behaviour in male NMRI mice. Lab Anim 2014;48:278–91.

[31] Van Herck H, Baumans V, Brandt CJWM, Hesp APM, Sturkenboom JH, van Lith HA, et al. Orbital sinus blood sampling in rats as performed by different animal technicians: the influence of technique and expertise. Lab Anim 1998;32:377–86.

[32] Goicoechea M, Cia F, San Jose C, Asensio A, Emparanza JI, Gil AG, et al. Minimising creatine kinase variability in rats for neuromuscular research purposes. Lab Anim 2008;42:19–25.

[33] Fernández I, Peña A, Del Teso N, Pérez V, Rodrígez-Cuesta J. Clinical biochemistry parameters in C57BL/6J mice after blood collection from the submandibular vein and retroorbital plexus. J Am Assoc Lab Anim Sci 2010;49:202–6.

[34] Holmberg H, Kiersgaard MK, Mikkelsen LF, Tanholm M. Impact of blood sampling technique on blood quality and animal welfare in haemophilic mice. Lab Anim 2011;45:114–20.

[35] Christensen SD, Mikkelsen LF, Fels JJ, Bodvarsdottir TB, Hansen AK. Quality of blood sampling by different methods for multiple blood sampling in mice. Lab Anim 2009;43:65–71.

[36] Aasland KE, Skjerve E, Smith AJ. Quality of blood samples from the saphenous vein compared with the tail vein during multiple blood sampling of mice. Lab Anim 2010;44:25–9.

[37] Heimann M, Roth DR, Ledieu D, Pfister R, Classen W. Sublingual and submandibular blood collection in mice: a comparison of effects on body weight, food consumption and tissue damage. Lab Anim 2010;44:352–8.

[38] Deckardt K, Weber I, Kaspers U, Hellwig J, Tennekes H, van Ravenzwaay B. The effects of inhalation anaesthetics on common clinical pathology parameters in laboratory rats. Food Chem Toxicol 2007;45:1709–18.

[39] Ameri M, Schnaars HA, Sibley JR, Honor J. Stability of haematologic analytes in monkey, rabbit, rat and mouse blood stored at 4°C in EDTA using the ADVIA 120 hematology analyser. Vet Clin Pathol 2011;40:188–93.

[40] Goyal VK, Kakade S, Pandey SK, Gothi AK, Nirogi R. Determining the effect of storage conditions on prothrombin time, activated partial thromboplastin time and fibrinogen concentration in rat plasma samples. Lab Anim 2015;49:311–8.

[41] Bowen RAR, Hortin GL, Csako G, Otañez OH, Remaley AT. Impact of blood collection devices on clinical chemistry assays. Clin Biochem 2010;43:4–25.

[42] Kurien BT, Everds NE, Scofield RH. Experimental animal urine collection: a review. Lab Anim 2004;38:333–61.

[43] Stechman MJ, Ahmad BN, Loh NY, Reed AC, Stewart M, Wells S, et al. Establishing normal plasma and 24-hour urinary biochemistry ranges in C3H, BALB/c and C57BL/6J mice following acclimitization in metabolic cages. Lab Anim 2010;44:218–25.

[44] Pinches MD, Betts CJ, Bickerton SJ, Beattie L, Burdett LD, Thomas HT, et al. Evaluation of novel urinary renal biomarkers with cisplatin model of kidney injury: effects of collection period. Toxicol Pathol 2012;40:534–40.

[45] Kjelgaard-Hansen M, Lundorff Jensen A. Quality control. In: Weiss DJ, Wardrop KJ, editors. Schlam's veterinary hematology. 6th ed. Iowa: Blackwell Publishing Limited; 2010. p. 1021–6.

[46] Stockham SL, Scott MA. Introductory concepts. In: Stockham SL, Scott MA, editors. Fundamentals of veterinary clinical pathology. 2nd ed. Iowa: Blackwell Publishing Limited; 2008. p. 4–51.

[47] Miller G. Quality control. In: McPherson RA, Pincus MR, editors. Henry's clinical diagnosis and management: by laboratory methods. 22nd ed. Philadelphia (PA): Elsevier Saunders; 2011. p. 119–34.

[48] Hall RL, Everds NE. Principles of clinical pathology for toxicology studies. In: Hayes AW, editor. Principles and methods of toxicology. Boca Raton: CRC Press; 2007. p. 1318–58.

[49] Gosselin S, Ramaiah L, Earl L. Clinical chemistry in toxicity testing: scope and methods. General, applied and systems toxicology. West Sussex, UK: John Wiley & Sons, Ltd; 2009. p. 2–35.

[50] Andrews CM. The haematopoietic system. In: Turton J, Hoosen J, editors. Target organ pathology, a basic text. London: Taylor & Francis Ltd; 1998. p. 177–205.

[51] Moritz A, Becker M. Automated haematology systems. In: Weiss DJ, Wardrop KJ, editors. Schlam's veterinary hematology. 6th ed. Iowa: Blackwell Publishing Limited; 2010.

[52] Marrs TC, Warren S. Hematology and toxicology. In: Ballantyne B, Marrs TC, Syversen T, editors. General, applied and systems toxicology. 3rd ed. West Sussex, UK: John Wiley & Sons Ltd; 2009.

[53] Poitout F, Lourdel D, Zelmanovic D. Atypical Wistar rat red blood cell channel cytograms of the Advia Hematology System (Abstract 20). Vet Clin Pathol 2009;38. Suppl, s1 E10.

[54] Travlos GS. Normal structure, function and histology of the bone marrow. Toxicol Pathol 2006;34:548–65.

[55] Fried W. Erythropoietin and erythropoiesis. Exp Hematol 2009;37:1007–15.

[56] Evans GO. Erythrocytes, anemias, and polycythemias. In: Evans GO, editor. Animal hematotoxicology, a practical handbook for toxicologists and biomedical researchers. Boca Raton (FL): CRC Press, Taylor & Francis; 2009. p. 23–42.

[57] Haschek WM, Rousseaux CG, Wallig MA. Clinical pathology. In: Haschek WM, Rousseaux CG, Wallig MA, editors. Fundamentals of toxicological pathology. 2nd ed. London: Academic Press (Elsevier); 2010.

[58] McGrath JP. Assessment of hemolytic and hemorrhagic anemias in preclinical safety assessment studies. Toxicol Pathol 1993;21:158–63.

[59] Poitout-Belissent FM, McCartney JE. Interpretation of hematology data in preclinical toxicological studies. In: Weiss DJ, Wardrop KJ, editors. Schlam's veterinary hematology. 6th ed. Iowa Blackwell Publishing Limited; 2010. p. 78–84.

[60] Pauluhn J. Subacute inhalation toxicity study of aniline in rats: analysis of time-dependence and concentration dependence of hematotoxic and splenic effects. Toxicol Sci 2004;81:198–215.

[61] Everds NE, Tarrant JM. Unexpected hematologic effects of biotherapeutics in nonclinical species and in humans. Toxicol Pathol 2013;41:280–302.

[62] Poulet FM, Penraat K, Collins N, Evans E, Thackaberry E, Manfra D, et al. Drug-induced hemolytic anemia and thrombocytopenia associated with alterations of cell membrane lipids and acanthocyte formation. Toxicol Pathol 2010;38:907–22.

[63] O'Rourke LG. Preclinical evaluation of compound-related cytopenias. In: Weiss DJ, Wardrop KJ, editors. Schlam's veterinary hematology. 6th ed. Iowa: Blackwell Publishing Limited; 2010. p. 85–91.

[64] Molyneux G, Andrews M, Sones W, York M, Barnett A, Quirk E, et al. Haemotoxicity of busulphan, doxorubicin, cisplatin and cyclophosphamide in the female BALB/c mouse using a brief regimen of drug administration. Cell Biol Toxicol 2011;27:13–40.

[65] Turton JA, Fagg R, Sones WR, Williams TC, Andrews CM. Characterization of the myelotoxicity of chloramphenicol succinate in the B6C3F1 mouse. Int J Exp Pathol 2006;87:101–12.

[66] Stockham SL, Scott MA. Erythrocytes. In: Stockham SL, Scott MA, editors. Fundamentals of veterinary clinical pathology. 2nd ed. Iowa: Blackwell Publishing Limited; 2008. p. 107–221.

[67] Andrews DA, Pyrah ITG, Boren BM, Tannehill-Gregg SH, Lightfoot-Dunn RM. High hematocrit resulting from administration of erythropoiesis-stimulating agents is not fully predictive of mortality or toxicities in preclinical species. Toxicol Pathol 2014;42:510–23.

[68] Andrews DA, Boren BM, Turk JR, Boyce RW, He YD, Hamadeh HK, et al. Dose-related differences in the pharmacodynamic and toxicologic response to a novel hyperglycosylated analog of recombinant human erythropoietin in sprague-dawley rats with similarly high hematocrit. Toxicol Pathol 2013;42:524–39.

[69] Andrews DA, Hamadeh HK, He YK, Boren BM, Turk JR, Boyce RW, et al. Cytokines associated with increased erythropoiesis in Sprague-Dawley rats administered a novel hyperglycosylated analog of recombinant human erythropoietin. Toxicol Pathol 2013:540–4.

[70] Evans GO. Leukocytes. In: Evans GO, editor. Animal hematotoxicology, a practical handbook for toxicologists and biomedical researchers. Boca Raton (FL): CRC Press, Taylor & Francis; 2009. p. 65–83.

[71] Webb JL, Latimer KS. Leukocytes. In: Latimer KS, editor. Duncan & Prasse's veterinary laboratory medicine: clinical Pathology. 5th ed. West Sussex, UK: John Wiley & Sons, Ltd; 2011. p. 45–82.

[72] Stockham SL, Scott MA. Leukocytes. In: Stockham SL, Scott MA, editors. Fundamentals of veterinary clinical pathology. 2nd ed. Iowa: Blackwell Publishing Limited; 2008. p. 53–106.

[73] Schultze AE. Interpretation of canine leukocyte responses. In: Weiss DJ, Wardrop KJ, editors. Schlam's veterinary hematology. 6th ed. Iowa: Blackwell Publishing Limited; 2010. p. 321–34.

[74] Weiss DJ. Leukocyte response to toxic injury. Toxicol Pathol 1993;21:135–40.

[75] Moore GE, Mahaffey EA, Hoenig M. Hematological and serum biochemical effects of long term administration of anti-inflammatory doses of prednisone. Am J Vet Res 1992;53:1034–7.

[76] Leone D, Giza K, Gill A, Dolinski B. An assessment of the mechanistic differences between two integrin $\alpha_4\beta_1$ inhibitors, the monoclonal antibody TA-2 and the small molecule BI05192, in rat experimental encephalomyelitis. J Pharmcol Exp Ther 2003;305:1150–62.

[77] Fujii Y, Hirayama T, Ohtake H, Ono N, Inoue T, Sakurai T, et al. Amelioration of collagen-induced arthritis by a novel $S1P_1$ antagonist with immunomodulatory activities. J Immunol 2012;188:206–15.

[78] Rudmann DG, McNerney ME, Vandereide SL, Schemmer JK, Eversole RR, et al. Epididymal and systemic phospholipidosis in rats and dogs treated with the dopamine D3 selective antagonist PNU–17786. Toxicol Pathol 2004;32:326–32.

[79] Boudreaux MK, Spangler EA, Wells EG. Hemostasis. In: Latimer KS, editor. Duncan & Prasse's veterinary laboratory medicine: clinical pathology. 5th ed. West Sussex, UK: John Wiley & Sons, Ltd; 2011. p. 107–44.

[80] Boon GD. An overview of hemostasis. Toxicol Pathol 1993;21: 170–9.

[81] Schultze AE, Walker DB, Turk JR, Tarrant JM, Brooks MB, Pettit SD. Current practices in preclinical drug development: gaps in hemostasis testing to assess risk of thromboembolic injury. Toxicol Pathol 2013;41:445–53.

[82] Deutsch VR, Tomer A. Megakaryocyte development and platelet production. Br J Haematol 2006;134:453–66.

[83] Pankraz A, Ledieu D, Pralet D, Provencher-Bolliger A. Detection of reticulated platelets in whole blood of rats using flow cytometry. Exp Toxicol Pathol 2008;60:443–8.

[84] Ryffel B, Car G, Woerly M, Weber F, DiPadova F, Kammuller M, et al. Long term interleukin-6 administration stimulates sustained thrombopoiesis and acute phase protein synthesis in a small primate-the marmoset. Blood 1994;83:2093–102.

[85] Neel JA, Synder L, Grindem CB. Thrombocytosis: a retrospective study of 165 dogs. Vet Clin Pathol 2012;41. Published online March 2012.

[86] Weiss DJ, Mirsky ML, Evanson OA, Fagliari J, McClenahan D, McCullough B. Platelet kinetics in dogs treated with a glycoprotein IIb/IIIA peptide antagonist. Toxicol Pathol 2000;28:310–6.

[87] Everds NE, Li N, Bailey K, Fort M, Stevenson R, Jawando R, et al. Unexpected thrombocytopenia and anaemia in cynomolgus monkeys induced by a therapeutic human monoclonal antibody. Toxicol Pathol 2013;41:951–69.

[88] Chaves F. Platelet morphology: reliable technology doesn't require duplication. Med Lab Obs 2012;44:28–34.

[89] Stockham SL, Scott MA. Hemostasis. In: Stockham SL, Scott MA, editors. Fundamentals of veterinary clinical pathology. 2nd ed. Iowa: Blackwell Publishing Limited; 2008. p. 259–321.

[90] Evans GO. Hemostasis. In: Evans GO, editor. Animal hematotoxicology, a practical handbook for toxicologists and biomedical researchers. Boca Raton (FL): CRC Press, Taylor & Francis; 2009.

[91] Dahlback B. Blood coagulation and its regulation by anticoagulant pathways; genetic pathogenesis of bleeding and thrombotic diseases. J Int Med 2005;257:209–23.

[92] Lanning LL. Toxicological pathology assessment. In: Jacobsen-Kram D, Keller KA, editors. Toxicological testing handbook: principles, application and data interpretation. 2nd ed. New York: Informa Healthcare; 2006. p. 109–33.

[93] Criswell KA. Preclinical evaluation of compound-related alterations in hemostasis. In: Weiss DJ, Wardrop KJ, editors. Schlam's veterinary hematology. 6th ed. Iowa: Blackwell Publishing Limited; 2010. p. 92–7.

[94] Lu Q, Li L, We L, Guo S, Chen Y, Lu W, et al. Safety evaluation of recombinant staphylokinase in rhesus monkeys. Toxicol Pathol 2003;31:14–21.

[95] Farman CA, Kornbrust DJ. Oligodeoxynucleotide studies in primates: antisense and immune stimulatory indications. Toxicol Pathol 2003;31:119–22.

III. CLINICAL PATHOLOGY, HISTOPATHOLOGY, AND BIOMARKERS

[96] Heyen JR, Rojko J, Evans M, Brown TP, Bobrowski WF, Vitsky A, et al. Characterization, biomarkers and reversibility of a monoclonal antibody induced immune complex disease in cynomolgus monkeys (Macaca fascicularis). Toxicol Pathol 2014;42:765–73.

[97] Provencher Bolliger A. Cytological evaluation of bone marrow in rats: indications, methods, and normal morphology. Vet Clin Pathol 2004;33:58–67.

[98] Moritz A, Bauer NB, Weiss DJ, Laneveschi A, Saad A. Evaluation of bone marrow. In: Weiss DJ, Wardrop KJ, editors. Schlam's veterinary hematology. 6th ed. Iowa: Blackwell Publishing Limited; 2010. p. 1054–66.

[99] Reagan WJ, Irizarry-Rovira A, Poitout-Belissent F, Provencher Bollinger A, Ramiah SK, Travlos G, et al. Bone marrow working group of ASVCP/STP. Best practices for evaluation of bone marrow in nonclinical studies. Vet Clin Pathol 2011;40:119–35.

[100] Wagner JA. Strategic approach to fit-for-purpose biomarkers in drug development. Annu Rev Pharmacol Toxicol 2008;48:631–51.

[101] Goodsaid FM, Frueh FW, Mattes W. Strategic paths for biomarker qualification. Toxicology 2008;245:219–23.

[102] Matheis K, Laurie D, Andramandroso C, Arber N, Badimon L, Benain X, et al. A generic operational strategy to qualify translational safety biomarkers. Drug Discov Today 2011;16:600–8.

[103] Biomarkers Definitions Working Group. Biomarkers and surrogate endpoints: preferred definitions and conceptual framework. Clin Pharmacol Ther 2001;69:89–95.

[104] Tarrant JM. Blood cytokines as biomarkers of in vivo toxicity in preclinical safety assessment: considerations for their use. Toxicol Sci 2010;117:4–16.

[105] Wallace KB, Hausner E, Herman E, Holt G, Macgregor JT, Metz AL, et al. Serum troponins as biomarkers of drug-induced cardiac toxicity. Toxicol Pathol 2004;32:106–21.

[106] Ramiah SK. Preclinical safety assessment: current gaps, challenges, and approaches in identifying translatable biomarkers of drug-induced liver injury. Clin Lab Med 2011;31:161–72.

[107] Bonventre JR, Vaidya VS, Schmouder RS, Feig P, Dieterle F. Next generation biomarkers for detecting kidney toxicity. Nat Biotechnol 2010;28:436–40.

[108] Lee JW, Devanarayan V, Chen Barrett Y, Weiner R, Allinson J, Fountain S. Fit- for-purpose method development and validation for successful biomarker measurement. Pharm Res 2006;23:312–28.

[109] Khan M, Bowsher R, Cameron M, Devanarayan V, Keller S, King L, et al. Recommendations for adaptation and validation of commercial kits for biomarker quantification in drug development. Bioanalysis 2015;7:229–42.

[110] Stanislaus D, Andersson H, Chapin R, Creasy D, Ferguson D, Gilbert M. Assessment of circulating hormones in nonclinical toxicity studies: general concepts and considerations. Toxicol Pathol 2012;40:943–50.

[111] Fuchs TC, Hewitt P. Biomarkers for drug-induced renal damage and nephrotoxicity – an overview for applied toxicology. AAPS J 2011;13:615–31.

[112] Mikaelian I, Scicchitano M, Mendes O, Thomas R, Leroy BE. Frontiers in preclinical safety biomarkers: microRNAs and messenger RNAs. Toxicol Pathol 2013;41:18–31.

[113] Stockham SL, Scott MA. Liver function. In: Stockham SL, Scott MA, editors. Fundamentals of veterinary clinical pathology. 2nd ed. Iowa: Blackwell Publishing Limited; 2008. p. 675–706.

[114] Ozer JS, Chetty R, Kenna G, Palandra J, Zhang Y, Lanevschi A, et al. Enhancing the utility of alanine aminotransferase as a reference standard biomarker for drug-induced liver injury. Regul Toxicol Pharmacol 2010;56:237–46.

[115] Boone L, Meyer D, Cusick P, Ennulat D, Provencher Bolliger A, Everds N, et al. For the Regulatory Affairs Committee of the American Society for Veterinary Clinical Pathology. Selection and interpretation of clinical pathology indicators of hepatic injury in preclinical studies. Vet Clin Pathol 2005;34:182–7.

[116] Bain PJ. Liver. In: Latimer KS, editor. Duncan & Prasse's veterinary laboratory medicine: clinical pathology. 5th ed. West Sussex, UK: John Wiley & Sons, Ltd; 2011.

[117] Solter PF. Clinical pathology approaches to hepatic injury. Toxicol Pathol 2005;33:9–16.

[118] Stockham SL, Scott MA. Enzymes. In: Stockham SL, Scott MA, editors. Fundamentals of veterinary clinical pathology. 2nd ed. Iowa: Blackwell Publishing Limited; 2008. p. 639–74.

[119] Giffen PS, Pick CR, Price MA, Williams A, York MJ. Alpha-glutathione S-transferase in the assessment of hepatotoxicity – its diagnostic utility in comparison with other recognized markers in the Wistar Han rat. Toxicol Pathol 2002;30:365–72.

[120] Boyd JW. The mechanisms relating to increases in plasma enzymes and isoenzymes in diseases of animals. Vet Clin Pathol 1983;12:9–24.

[121] Evans GO. General enzymology. In: Evans GO, editor. Animal clinical chemistry, a practical handbook for toxicologists and biomedical researchers. 2nd ed. Boca Raton (FL): CRC Press, Taylor & Francis; 2009. p. 17–36.

[122] Ennulat D, Walker D, Clemo F, Magid-Slav M, Ledieu D, Graham M, et al. Effects of hepatic drug-metabolizing enzyme induction on clinical pathology parameters in animals and man. Toxicol Pathol 2010;38:810–28.

[123] Smyth R, Munday M, York MJ, Clarke CJ, Dare T, Turton JA. Comprehensive characterization of serum clinical chemistry parameters and the identification of urinary superoxide dismutase in a carbon tetrachloride-induced model of hepatic fibrosis in the female Hanover Wistar rat. Int J Pathol 2007;88: 361–76.

[124] O'Brien PJ, Slaughter MR, Polley SR, Kramer K. Advantages of glutamate dehydrogenase as a blood biomarker of acute hepatic injury in rats. Lab Anim 2002;36:313–21.

[125] Schomaker S, Warner R, Bick J, Johnson K, Potter D, Van Winkle J, et al. Assessment of emerging biomarkers of liver injury in human subjects. Toxicol Sci 2012;132:276–83.

[126] Jaeschke H, McGill MR. Serum glutamate dehydrogenase – biomarker for liver cell death or mitochondrial dysfunction. Toxicol Sci 2013;134:221–2.

[127] Ozer J, Ratner M, Shaw M, Bailey W, Schomaker S. The current state of serum biomarkers of hepatotoxicity. Toxicology 2008;245:194–205.

[128] Bailey W, Holder D, Patel H, Devlin P, Gonzalez RJ, Hamilton V, et al. A performance evaluation of three drug-induced liver injury biomarkers in the rat: alpha-glutathione S-transferase, arginase-1 and 4-hydroxyphenyl-pyruvate dioxygenase. Toxicol Sci 2012;130:229–44.

[129] Ozer JS, Cheety R, Kenna G, Koppiker N, Karamjeet P, Li D, et al. Recommendations to qualify biomarker candidates of drug-induced liver injury. Biomark Med 2010;4:475–83.

[130] Ramaiah SK. A toxicologist guide to the diagnostic interpretation of hepatic biochemical parameters. Food Chem Toxicol 2007;45:1551–7.

[131] Travlos GS, Morris RW, Elwell MR, Duke S, Rosenblum S, Thompson MB. Frequency and relationships of clinical chemistry and liver and kidney histopathology findings in 13 week toxicity studies in rats. Toxicology 1996;107:17–29.

[132] Kapojos JJ, Poelstra K, Borghus T, Van Den Berg A, Baelde HJ, Klok PA, et al. Induction of glomerular alkaline phosphatase after challenge with lipopolysaccharide. Int J Pathol 2003;84: 135–44.

[133] Litchfield MH, Conning DM. Effect of phenobarbitone on plasma and hepatic alkaline phosphatase activity in the dog. Naunyn Schmiedebergs Arch Pharmacol 1972;272:358–62.

[134] Robertson DG, Loewen G, Walsh KM, Dethloff LA, Sigler RS, Dominick MA, et al. Subacute and subchronic toxicology studies of Cl-986, a novel anti-inflammatory compound. Fundam Appl Toxicol 1993;20:446–55.

[135] Hall AP, Elcombe CR, Foster JR, Harada T, Kaufmann W, Knippel A. Liver hypertrophy: a review of adaptive (adverse and non-adverse) changes – conclusions from the 3rd International ESTP Workshop. Toxicol Pathol 2012;40:971–94.

[136] Ratanasavanh D, Tazi A, Galteau MM, Siest G. Localization of gamma-glutamyltransferase in subcellular fractions of rat and rabbit liver: effect of phenobarbital. Biochem Pharmacol 1979;28:1363–5.

[137] Clayton NP, Yoshizawa K, Kissling GE, Burka LT, Chan P-C, Nyaska A. Immunohistochemical analysis of expressions of hepatic cytochrome P450 in F344 rats following treatment with kava extract. Exp Toxicol Pathol 2007;58:223–36.

[138] Wang X, Chowdhury JR, Chowdhury NR. Bilirubin metabolism: applied physiology. Curr Paediatr 2006;16:70–4.

[139] Zhang D, Chando TJ, Everett DW, Everett DW, Patten CJ, Dehal SS, et al. In vitro inhibition of UDP glucuronosyltransferases by atazanavir and other HIV protease inhibitors and the relationship of this property to in vivo bilirubin glucuronidation. Drug Metab Dispos 2005;33:1729–39.

[140] Huang W, Zhang J, Chua SS, Qatanani M, Han Y, Granata R, et al. Induction of bilirubin clearance by the constitutive androstane receptor (CAR). Proc Natl Acad Sci USA 2003;100:4156–61.

[141] Luo L, Schomaker S, Houle C, Aubrecht J, Colangelo JL. Evaluation of serum bile acid profiles as biomarkers of liver injury on rodents. Toxicol Sci 2014;137:12–25.

[142] Woolbright BL, McGill MR, Staggs VS, Winefield RD, Gholami P, Olyaee M, et al. Glycodeoxycholic acid levels as prognostic biomarker in acetaminophen-induced acute liver failure. Toxicol Sci 2014;142:436–44.

[143] Ennulat D, Magid-Slav M, Rhem S, Tatsuoka KS. Diagnostic performance of traditional hepatobiliary biomarkers of drug-induced injury in the rat. Toxicol Sci 2010;116:397–412.

[144] Starckx S, Batheja A, Verheyn GR, De Jonghe S, Steemans K, Van Dijk B, et al. Evaluation of miR-122 and other biomarkers in distinct acute liver injury in rats. Toxicol Pathol 2012;41:795–804.

[145] Kia R, Kelly L, Sison-Young RLC, Zhang F, Pridgeon CS, Heslop JA, et al. MicroRNA-122: a novel hepatocyte-enriched in vitro marker of drug-induced cellular toxicity. Toxicol Sci 2015:173–85.

[146] Ferguson MA, Vaidya VS, Bonventre JV. Biomarkers of nephrotoxic acute kidney injury. Toxicology 2008;245:182–93.

[147] Harpur E, Ennulat D, Hoffman D, Betton G, Gautier J-C, Riefke B, et al. On behalf of the HESI Committee on Biomarkers of Nephrotoxicity. Biological qualification of biomarkers of chemical induced renal toxicity in two strains of male rat. Toxicol Sci 2011;122:235–52.

[148] Emeigh Hart SG. Assessment of renal injury in vivo. J Pharmacol Toxicol Methods 2005;52:30–45.

[149] Dieterle F, Sistare F, Goodsaid F, Papaluca M, Ozer J, Webb CP, et al. Renal biomarker qualification submission: a dialog between the FDA-EMEA and predictive safety testing consortium. Nat Biotechnol 2010;28:455–62.

[150] Ozer JS, Dieterle F, Troth S, Perentes E, Cordier A, Verdes P, et al. A panel of urinary biomarkers to monitor reversibility of renal injury and a serum marker with improved potential to assess renal function. Nat Biotechnol 2010;28:486–94.

[151] Yu Y, Jin H, Molder D, Ozer S, Villareal JS, Shughhrue P, et al. Urinary biomarkers trefoil factor 3 and albumin enable early detection of kidney tubular injury. Nat Biotechnol 2010;28:470–7.

[152] Vlasakova K, Erdos Z, Troth SP, McNulty K, Chapeu-Campredon V, Mokrzycki N. Evaluation of the relative performance of 12 urinary biomarkers for renal safety across 22 rat sensitivity and specificity studies. Toxicol Sci 2014;138:3–20.

[153] Wadey R, Pinches MG, Jones HW, Riccardi D, Price SA. Tissue expression and correlation of a panel of urinary biomarkers following cisplatin-induced kidney injury. Toxicol Pathol 2014;42:591–602.

[154] Vinken P, Starckx S, Barale-Thomas E, Looszova A, Sonee M, Goeminne N, et al. Tissue Kim-1 and urinary clusterin as early indicators of cisplatin-induced acute kidney injury in rats. Toxicol Pathol 2012;40:1049–62.

[155] Zhang Q, Gamboa da Costa G, Von Tungeln LS, Jacob CC, Brown RP, Goering PL. Urinary biomarker detection of melamine- and cyanuric acid-induced kidney injury in rats. Toxicol Sci 2012;129:1–8.

[156] Fuchs TC, Frick K, Emde B, Czasch S, Von Landebergh F, Hewitt P. Evaluation of novel acute urinary rat kidney toxicity biomarker for subacute toxicity studies in preclinical trials. Toxicol Pathol 2012;40:1031–48.

[157] Swain A, Turton J, Scudamore C, Pereira I, Viswanathan N, Smyth R, et al. Urinary biomarkers in hexchloro-1:3 butadiene-induced acute kidney injury in the female Hanover Wistar rat; correlation of α-glutathione S-transferase, albumin and kidney injury molecule-1 with histopathology and gene expression. J Appl Toxicol 2011;31:366–77.

[158] Gautier J-C, Gury T, Guffroy M, Khan-Malek R, Hoffman D, Pettit S, et al. Normal ranges and variability of novel urinary renal biomarkers in sprague-dawley rats: comparison of constitutive values between males and females and across assay platforms. Toxicol Pathol 2014;42:1092–104.

[159] Swain A, Turton J, Scudamore C, Maguire D, Periera I, Freitas S, et al. Nephrotoxicity of hexachlorobutadiene in the male Hanover Wistar rat; correlation of minimal histopathological changes with biomarkers of renal injury. J Appl Toxicol 2012;32:417–28.

[160] Maguire DP, Turton JA, Scudamore CL, Swain AJ, MClure FM, Smyth R. Correlation of histopathology, urinary biomarkers, and gene expression responses following hexachlor-1:3-butadiene-induced acute nephrotoxicity in male Hanover Wistar rats: a 28-day time course study. Toxicol Pathol 2013;41: 779–94.

[161] Vaidya VS, Ramirez V, Ichimura T, Bobadilla NA, Bonventre JV. Urinary kidney injury molecule-1: a sensitive quantitative biomarker for early detection of kidney tubular injury. Am J Physiol Renal Physiol 2005;290:F517–29.

[162] Sabbisenti VS, Ito K, Wang C, Yang L, Meffers SC, Bonventre JV. Novel assays for detection of urinary KIM-1 in mouse models of kidney injury. Toxicol Sci 2013;131:13–25.

[163] Vaidya VS, Ozer JS, Dieterle F, Collings FB, Ramirez V, Troth S, et al. Kidney injury molecule-1 outperforms traditional biomarkers of kidney injury in preclinical biomarker qualification studies. Nat Biotechnol 2010;28:478–85.

[164] Zhou X, Ma B, Lin Z, Qu Z, Huo Y, Wang J, et al. Evaluation of the usefulness of novel biomarkers for drug-induced acute kidney injury in beagle dogs. Toxicol Appl Pharmacol 2014;280:30–5.

[165] Hoffmann D, Adler M, Vaidya VS, Rached E, Mulrane L, Gallagher WM, et al. Performance of novel kidney biomarkers in preclinical toxicity studies. Toxicol Sci 2010;116:8–22.

[166] Cullen RC, Murray PT, Fitzgibbon MC. Establishment of a reference interval for urinary neutrophil gelatinase-associated lipocalin. Ann Clin Biochem 2012;2102(49):190–3.

[167] Kanki M, Moriguchi A, Sasaki D, Mitori H, Yamada A, Unami A, et al. Identification or urinary miRNA bioamrkers for detecting cisplatin-induced proximal tubular injury in rats. Toxicology 2014;324:158–68.

[168] Pavkovic M, Riefke B, Frisk A-L, Groticke I, Ellinger-Ziegelbauer H. Glomerulonephritis-induced changes in urinary and kidney microRNA profiles in rats. Toxicol Sci 2015: 348–59.

[169] O'Brien PJ. Cardiac troponin is the most effective translational safety biomarker for myocardial injury in cardiotoxicity. Toxicology 2008;245:206–18.

[170] Voss EM, Sharkey SW, Gernert AE, Murikami MM, Johnston RB, Hsieh CC, et al. Human and canine cardiac troponin T and creatine kinase-MB distribution in normal and diseased myocardium. Infarct size using serum profiles. Arch Pathol Lab Med 1995;119:799–806.

[171] Thygesen K, Alpert JS, White HD. Jaffe on behalf of the Joint ESC/ACCF/AHA/WHF Task Force for the redefinition of myocardial infarction. Universal definition of myocardial infarction. J Am Coll Cardiol 2007;50:2173–95.

[172] Thygesen K, Alpert JS, Jaffe AS, Simoons L, Chaitman BR, White HD, et al. Third universal definition of myocardial infarction. Eur Heart J 2012;33:2551–67.

[173] Giannitsis E, Steen H, Kurz K, Ivandic B, Simon AC, Futterer S, et al. Cardiac magnetic resonance imaging study for quantification of infarct size comparing directly serial versus single time-point measurements of cardiac troponin T. J Am Coll Cardiol 2008;51:307–14.

[174] Cardinale D, Cipolla CM. Assessment of cardiotoxicity with cardiac biomarkers in cancer patients. Herz 2011;36:325–32.

[175] Newby KL, Rodriguez I, Finkle J, Becker RC, Kicks KA, Hausner E, et al. Troponin measurements during drug development-considerations for monitoring and management of potential cardiotoxicity: an educational collaboration among the cardiac safety research consortium, the Duke Clinical Research Institute, and the US Food and Drug Administration. Am Heart J 2011;162:64–73.

[176] White HD. Pathobiology of troponin elevations. J Am Coll Cardiol 2011;24:2406–8.

[177] Hickman PE, Potter J, Aroney C, Koerbin G, Southcott E, Wu AH, et al. Cardiac troponin may be released by ischemia alone, without necrosis. Clin Chim Acta 2010;411:318–23.

[178] Gerhardt W, Katus H, Ravkilde J, Hamm C, Jorgensen PJ, Peheim E, et al. S-Troponin T in suspected ischemic myocardial injury compared with mass and catalytic concentrations of S-creatine kinase isoenzyme MB. Clin Chem 1991;37:1405–11.

[179] Dunn M, Coluccio D, Hirkaler G, Mikaelian I, Nicklaus R, Lipshultz SE, et al. The complete pharmacokinetic profile of serum cardiac troponin I in the rat and dog. Toxicol Sci 2011;123:368–73.

[180] Starnberg K, Jeppsson A, Lindahl B, Hammarsten O. Revision of the troponin T release mechanism from damaged human myocardium. Clin Chem 2014;60:1098–104.

[181] O'Brien PJ, Smith DE, Knechtel TJ, Marchak MA, Pruimboom-Brees I, Brees DJ, et al. Cardiac troponin I is a sensitive, specific biomarker of cardiac injury in laboratory animals. Lab Anim 2006;40:153–71.

[182] Walker DB. Serum chemical biomarkers of cardiac injury for nonclinical safety testing. Toxicol Pathol 2006;34:94–104.

[183] York M, Scudamore C, Brady S, Chen C, Wilson S, Curtis M, et al. Characterization of troponin responses in isoproterenol-induced cardiac injury in the Hanover Wistar rat. Toxicol Pathol 2007;35:606–17.

[184] Clements P, Brady S, York M, Berridge B, Mikaelian I, Nicklaus R, et al. Time course characterization of serum cardiac troponins, heart fatty acid binding protein, and morphological findings with isoproterenol-induced myocardial injury in the rat. Toxicol Pathol 2010;38:703–14.

[185] Mikaelian I, Buness A, Hirkaler G, Fernandes R, Coluccio D, Geng W, et al. Serum cardiac troponin I concentrations transiently increases in rats given rosiglitazone. Toxicol Lett 2011;201:110–5.

[186] Mikaelian I, Coluccio D, Hirkaler GM, Downing JC, Rasmussen E, Todd J. Assessment of the toxicity of hydralazine in the rat using an ultrasensitive flow-based cardiac troponin I immunoassay. Toxicol Pathol 2009;37:878–81.

[187] Bowen Jones H, Reens J, Johnson E, Brocklehurst S, Slater I. Myocardial steatosis and necrosis in atria and ventricles of rats given pyruvate dehydrogenase kinase inhibitors. Toxicol Pathol 2014;42:1250–66.

[188] Casartelli A, Lanzoni A, Comelli R, Crivellente F, Defazio R, Dorigatti R, et al. A novel and integrated approach for the identification and characterization of drug-induced cardiac toxicity in the dog. Toxicol Pathol 2011;39:361–71.

[189] Adamcova M, Lencova-Popelova O, Jirkovsky E, Mazurova Y, Palicka V, Simko F, et al. Experimental determination of diagnostic window of cardiac troponins in the development of chronic anthracycline cardiotoxicity and estimation of its predictive value. Int J Cardiol 2015;201:358–67.

[190] Reagen WJ, York MJ, Berridge B, Schultze E, Walker D, Pettit S. Comparison of cardiac troponin I and T, including the evaluation of an ultrasensitive assay, indicators of doxorubicin-induced cardiotoxicity. Toxicol Pathol 2013;41:1146–58.

[191] Cove-Smith L, Woodhouse N, Hargreaves A, Kirk J, Smith S, Price SA, et al. An integrated characterization of serological, pathological and functional events in doxorubicin cardiotoxicity. Toxicol Sci 2014;140:3–15.

[192] Adamcova M, Simunek T, Kaiserova H, Popelova O, Sterba M, Potacova A. In vitro and in vivo examination of cardiac troponins as biochemical markers of drug-induced cardiotoxicity. Toxicology 2007:218–28.

[193] Berridge BR, Pettit S, Walker DB, Jaffe AS, Schulze AE, Herman E, et al. A translational approach to detecting drug-induced cardiac injury with cardiac troponins: consensus and recommendations from the Cardiac Troponins Biomarkers Working Group of the Health and Environmental Sciences Institute. Am Heart J 2009;158:21–9.

[194] Herman EH, Knapton A, Liu Y, Lipschultz SE, Estis J, Todd J. The influence of age on serum concentrations of cardiac troponin I: results in rats, monkeys and commercial sera. Toxicol Pathol 2014;42:888–96.

[195] Reagan WJ. Troponin as a biomarker of cardiac toxicity: past, present and future. Toxicol Pathol 2010;38:1134–7.

[196] O'Brien PJ, Landt Y, Ladenson JH. Differential reactivity of cardiac and skeletal muscle from various species in a cardiac troponin I immunoassay. Clin Chem 1997;43:2333–8.

[197] Apple FS, Murikami MM, Ler R, Walker D, York M. Analytical characteristics of commercial cardiac troponin I and T immunoassays in serum from rats, dogs and monkeys with acute myocardial injury. Clin Chem 2008;54:1982–9.

[198] Apple FS, Collinson PO. Analytical characteristics of high-sensitivity cardiac troponin assays. Clin Chem 2012;58:54–61.

[199] Serra M, Papakonstantinou S, Adamcova M, O'Brien PJ. Veterinary and toxicological applications for the detection of cardiac injury using cardiac troponin. Vet J 2010;185:50–7.

[200] Schultze AE, Konrad RJ, Cedille KM, Lu QA, Todd J. Ultrasensitive cross-species measurement of cardiac troponin I using the Erenna immunoassay system. Toxicol Pathol 2008;36:777–82.

[201] Schultze AE, Carpenter KH, Wians FH, Agee SJ, Minyard J, Lu QA, et al. Longitudinal studies of cardiac troponin I concentrations in serum from male Sprague Dawley rats: baseline reference ranges and effects of handling and placebo dosing on biological variability. Toxicol Pathol 2009;37:754–60.

[202] Alhadi HA, Fox KAA. Do we need additional markers of myocyte necrosis: the potential value of heart fatty-acid-binding protein. QJM 2004;97:187–98.

[203] Viswanathan K, Kilcullen N, Morrell C, Thistlethwaite SJ, Sivanathan MU, Hassan TB, et al. Heart-type fatty acid-binding protein predicts long-term mortality and re-infarction in consecutive patients with suspected acute coronary syndrome who are troponin-negative. J Am Coll Cardiol 2010;55:2590–8.

[204] Zhen EY, Berna MJ, Jin Z, Pritt ML, Watson DE, Ackermann BL, et al. Quantification of heart fatty acid binding protein as a biomarker for drug-induced cardiac and musculoskeletal necroses. Proteomics Clin Appl 2007;1:661–71.

[205] Strauss V, Wohrmann T, Frank I, Hübel U, Luft J, Bode G, et al. Short term increase of serum troponin I and serum heart-type fatty acid-binding protein (H-FABP) in dogs following administration of formoterol. Exp Toxicol Pathol 2010;62:343–52.

[206] Brady S. The assessment of cardiac biomarkers in rat models of cardiotoxicity. University of London; 2008. [Ph.D. thesis].

[207] Daniels LB, Maisel AS. Natriuretic peptides. J Am Coll Cardiol 2007;25:2357–67.

[208] Ruskoaho H. Atrial natriuretic peptide: synthesis, release and metabolism. Pharmacol Rev 1992;44:479–602.

[209] Hystad ME, Øie E, Grøgaard HK, Kuusnemi K, Vuolteenaho O, Vuolteenaho O, et al. Gene expression of natriuretic peptides and their receptors type-A and -C after myocardial infarction in rats. Scand J Clin Lab Invest 2001;61:139–50.

[210] Crivellente F, Tontodonati M, Fasdelli N, Casartelli A, Dorigatti R, Faustinelli I, et al. NT-proBNP as a biomarker for the assessment of a potential cardiovascular drug-induced liability in beagle dogs. Toxicol Pathol 2011;27:425–38.

[211] Miyagawa Y, Tominaga Y, Toda N, Takemura N. Relationship between glomerular filtration rate and plasm N-terminal pro B-type natriuretic peptide concentrations in dogs with chronic kidney disease. Vet J 2013;197:445–50.

[212] Kellihan HB, Oyama MA, Reynolds CA, Stepien RL. Weekly variability of plasma and serum NT-proBNP measurements in normal dogs. J Vet Cardiol 2009;11:593–7.

[213] Cahill RJ, Pigeon K, Strong-Townsend MI, Drexel JP, Clark GH, Buch JS. Analytical validation of a second-generation immunoassay for the quantification of N-terminal pro-B-type natriuretic peptide in canine blood. J Vet Diagn Invest 2015;27:61–7.

[214] Hezzell MJ, Boswood A, Lotter N, Elliott J. The effects of storage conditions on measurements of canine N-terminal pro-B-type natriuretic peptide. J Vet Cardiol 2015;17:34–41.

[215] Hori Y, Oshima N, Chikazwa S, Kanai K, Hoshi F, Itoh N, et al. Myocardial injury-related changes in plasma NT-proBNP and ANP concentrations in a canine model of ischemic myocardial injury. Vet J 2011;191:46–51.

[216] Hori Y, Sano N, Kanai K, Hoshi F, Itoh N, Higuchi S-I. Acute cardiac volume load-related changes in plasma atrial natriuretic peptide and N-terminal pro-B-type natriuretic peptide concentrations in healthy dogs. Vet J 2010;185:317–21.

[217] Colton HM, Stokes AH, Yoon LW, Qualie MP, Novak PJ, Falls JG, et al. An initial characterization of N-terminal proatrial natriuretic peptide in serum of Sprague Dawley rats. Toxicol Sci 2011;120:262–8.

[218] Vinken P, Reagan WJ, Rodriguez LA, Buck WR, Lai-Zhang J, Goeminne N, et al. Cross-laboratory analytical validation of the cardiac biomarker NT-proANP in rat. J Pharmacol Toxicol Methods 2016;77:58–65.

[219] Engle SK, Solter PF, Credille KM, Bull CM, Adams S, Berna MJ, et al. Detection of left ventricular hypertrophy in rats administered a peroxisome proliferator-activated receptor α/γ dual agonist using natriuretic peptides and imaging. Toxicol Sci 2010;114:183–92.

[220] D'Alessandra Y, Devann P, Limana F, Straino S, Di Carlo A, Brambilla PG. Circulating microRNAs are new and sensitive biomarkers of myocardial infarction. Eur Heart J 2010;31:2765–73.

[221] Ji X, Takahashi R, Hiura Y, Hirokawa G, Fukushima Y, Iwai N. Plasma mir-208 as a biomarker of myocardial injury. Clin Chem 2009;55:1944–9.

[222] Liu L, Aguirre SA, Evering WEN, Hirakawa BP, May JR, Palacio K. miR-208a as a biomarker of isoproterenol-induced cardiac injury in Sod2+/− and C57BL/6J wild-type mice. Toxicol Pathol 2014;42:1117–29.

[223] O'Brien PJ. Assessment of cardiotoxicity and myotoxicity. In: Evans GO, editor. Animal clinical chemistry, a practical handbook for toxicologists and biomedical researchers. 2nd ed. Boca Raton (FL): CRC Press, Taylor & Francis; 2009. p. 145–57.

[224] Pritt ML, Hall DG, Recknor J, Credille KM, Brown DD, Ymumibe NP, et al. Fabp3 as a biomarker of skeletal muscle toxicity in the rat: comparison with conventional biomarkers. Toxicol Sci 2008;103:382–96.

[225] Dare TO, Davies HA, Turton JA, Lomas L, Williams TC, York MJ. Application of surface-enhanced laser desorption/ionization technology to the detection and identification of urinary parvalbumin-α: a biomarker of compound-induced skeletal muscle toxicity in the rat. Electrophoresis 2002;23:3241–51.

[226] Tonomura Y, Matsushima S, Kashiwaga E, Fujisawa K, Takagi S, Nishimura Y. Biomarker panel of cardiac and skeletal troponins, fatty acid binding protein 3 and myosin light chain 3 for the accurate diagnosis of cardiotoxicity and musculoskeletal toxicity in rats. Toxicology 2012;302:179–89.

[227] Evans GO. Fluid balance, electrolytes and mineral metabolism. In: Evans GO, editor. Animal clinical chemistry, a practical handbook for toxicologists and biomedical researchers. 2nd ed. Boca Raton (FL): CRC Press, Taylor & Francis; 2009. p. 115–44.

[228] Bleich M, Greger R. Mechanism of action of diuretics. Kidney Int 1997;51:S11–5.

[229] White PC. Disorders of aldosterone biosynthesis and action. N Engl J Med 1994;331:250–8.

[230] Clements P, York M, Simecek N, Polley S, Billings H, McFarlane M, et al. Morphological, clinical pathological, and gene expression changes indicative of xenobiotic-associated effects on renal ion transporters in the rat. Toxicol Pathol 2009;37:151 (abstract p. 91).

[231] York MJ, Evans GO. Electrolyte and fluid balance. In: Evans GO, editor. Animal clinical chemistry, a primer for toxicologists. London: Taylor & Francis; 1996. p. 163–76.

[232] Maconochie JG, Forster JK. Dose-response study with high-dose inhaled salmeterol in healthy subjects. Br J Clin Pharmacol 1992;33:342–5.

[233] Owen K, Beck SL, Damment SJP. The preclinical toxicology of salmeterol hydroxynapthoate. Hum Exp Toxicol 2010;29:393–406.

[234] Jain S, Gautam V, Naseem S. Acute-phase proteins: as diagnostic tool. J Pharm Bioallied Sci 2011;3:118–27.

[235] Waterson CL. Proteins. In: Evans GO, editor. Animal clinical chemistry, a practical handbook for toxicologists and biomedical researchers. 2nd ed. Boca Raton (FL): CRC Press, Taylor & Francis; 2009. p. 159–81.

[236] Eckersall PD, Bell R. Acute phase proteins; biomarkers of infection and inflammation. Vet J 2010;185:23–7.

[237] Waterson C, Lanevschi A, Horner J, Louden C. A comparative analysis of acute-phase proteins as inflammatory biomarkers in preclinical toxicology studies: implications for preclinical to clinical translation. Toxicol Pathol 2009;37:28–33.

[238] Gabay C, Kushner I. Acute-phase proteins and other systemic responses to inflammation. N Engl J Med 1999;340:448–54.

[239] Harvey JW, West CL. Prednisone-induced increases in serum alpha-2 globulin and haptoglobin concentrations in dogs. Vet Pathol 1987;24:90–2.

[240] Thomson D, Milford-Ward A, Whicher J. The value of acute phase protein measurements in clinical practice. Ann Clin Biochem 1992;29:123–31.

[241] Caldin M, Tasca S, Carli E, Bianchini S, Furlanello T, Martinez-Subiela S, et al. Serum acute phase protein concentrations in dogs with hyperadrenocorticism with and without concurrent inflammatory conditions. Vet Clin Pathol 2009;38:63–8.

[242] Giffen PS, Turton J, Andrews CM, Barrett P, Clarke CJ, Fung KW, et al. Markers of experimental acute inflammation in the Wistar Han rat with particular reference to haptoglobin and C-reactive protein. Arch Toxicol 2002;77:392–402.

[243] Sultan S, Pascucci M, Ahmad S, Malik IA, Ramadori P, Ahmad G, et al. Lipocalin-2 is a major acute-phase protein in a rat and mouse model of sterile abscess. Shock 2012;37:191–6.

[244] Kuribayashi T, Tomizawa M, Seita T, Tagata K, Yamamoto S. Relationship between production of acute-phase proteins and strength of inflammatory stimulation in rats. Lab Anim 2011;25:215–8.

[245] Stockham SL, Scott MA. Lipids. In: Stockham SL, Scott MA, editors. Fundamentals of veterinary clinical pathology. 2nd ed. Iowa: Blackwell Publishing Limited; 2008. p. 763–82.

[246] Evans GO. Lipids. In: Evans GO, editor. Animal clinical chemistry, a practical handbook for toxicologists and biomedical researchers. 2nd ed. Boca Raton (FL): CRC Press, Taylor & Francis; 2009. p. 183–200.

[247] Fraser CG. Biological variation: from principles to practice. Washington, DC: AACC Press; 2001.

[248] Dickens A, Robinson J, Evans GO. Statistical approaches. Animal clinical chemistry, a primer for toxicologists. London: Taylor & Francis; 1996. p. 45–58.

[249] Lewis RW, Billington R, Debryune E, Gamer A, Lang B, Carpanini F. Recognition of adverse and nonadverse effects in toxicity studies. Toxicol Pathol 2002;30:66–74.

[250] Hall RL. Lies, damn lies and reference intervals (or hysterical control values for clinical pathology data). Toxicol Pathol 1997;25:647–9.

[251] Clemo FAS. Response to the utility of clinical pathology reference ranges in preclinical safety studies. Toxicol Pathol 1997;650:25.

[252] Everds NE. Evaluation of clinical pathology data: correlating changes with other study data. Toxicol Pathol 2015;43:90–7.

[253] Rudmann DG. On-target and off-target-based toxicologic effects. Toxicol Pathol 2013;41:310–4. http://www.fda.gov/downloads/Drugs/DevelopmentApprovalProcess/Drug-DevelopmentToolsQualificationProgram/UCM294644.pdf. Cardiac.

15

Best Practice in Toxicological Pathology

M.M. Abdi

INTRODUCTION

In recent years, a number of drugs have been withdrawn from the market on safety grounds due to severe toxicity in patients [1–3]. The toxicities include major organ system injuries such as hepatotoxicity and cardiovascular changes, which were not seen in preclinical animal toxicity studies or in human subjects during clinical trials. In order to maximize the value of preclinical studies, it is vital they are robust in their design, conduct, and interpretation of the data. This chapter is intended to give the reader a summary of the processes and procedures in toxicological pathology that helps the generation of complete histology and histopathology data, which are communicated in an integrated pathology report. The aim is not to write a comprehensive chapter about the science of toxicological pathology—there are excellent textbooks on this subject, some of which will be given in the references section for further reading. However, some of the common spontaneous lesions seen in routine toxicity studies will be highlighted.

The main general toxicology studies that are conducted to assess the safety of new chemical or biological entities are repeat-dose studies of up to 52 weeks. The studies are conducted in a rodent (mainly rat and mouse and occasionally hamster) and nonrodent (beagle dog) species. In certain circumstances where the dog is deemed to be unsuitable, the nonhuman primate (mainly cynomolgus macaque) or, more recently, the minipig is used as an alternative nonrodent species. Carcinogenicity studies are normally conducted in two rodent species. In some cases it is acceptable to use transgenic mouse models as alternatives to the two-year mouse study; this saves animal usage, time, and money. The p53±model is considered appropriate for the testing of genotoxic and nongenotoxic compounds and is accepted by regulatory agencies. Other transgenic models, such as the Tg.AC and rasH2, may be used as appropriate [4,5]. Because of their short durations, these alternative models are also sometimes used to address a regulatory or mechanistic question. Other

A Comprehensive Guide to Toxicology in Nonclinical Drug Development, Second Edition
http://dx.doi.org/10.1016/B978-0-12-803620-4.00015-3

specialized studies are conducted in appropriate species or in vitro assays to address specific safety issues such as cardiovascular function or developmental abnormalities. Study animals generally have a single source, are similar in age, and are maintained under the same feed and housing conditions. The animals have a health certificate from the breeder that also covers the microbiological status of the stock from which they came (not the individual animal), and when they reach the test facility, their health is assessed by visual and physical examination by a qualified veterinarian, and there will be a period of acclimatization. However, the animals could remain asymptomatic and show no overt signs of any underlying pathological condition such as changes in hematology or blood chemistry; any histopathological change would only be shown when the animals are killed and histopathological examination is performed. It is not always easy to distinguish between lesions that were present in the animals prior to being placed in a study or have developed spontaneously during the study, and those that were caused by the test article. Toxicology studies are regulated by guidelines issued by international bodies such as the Organization of Economic Cooperation and Development (OECD) and regulatory agencies such as the U.S. Food and Drug Administration (FDA) and the European Medicines Agency. These studies also adhere to defined protocols and applicable Standard Operating Procedures (SOPs) at the testing laboratory.

HISTOPATHOLOGY PROCESSES AND PROCEDURES

Toxicological pathology is the study of the injurious effects of chemical, physical, or biological entities on the body. In their article on "Best Practice Guideline: Toxicological Histopathology," James Crissman and others summarized the best practice in histopathology as the process elements and procedural considerations necessary for high-quality histopathological evaluation of toxicology studies and the production of valid study results [6]. The science of toxicological pathology is mainly concerned with the interpretation of primary study results and secondary mechanistic considerations to understand the biological basis of the pathological findings. Except for some specialized studies, all regulatory-required toxicity studies have pathology endpoints that are aimed at identifying and characterizing morphological changes attributable to treatment with a test article. Such changes must be distinguished from common background lesions of unknown etiology and the morphological variations caused by the normal physiology of the tissue or organ, particularly those under hormonal influence. Both types of changes must

be distinguished from artifacts that can appear during the processing of the tissue specimen. The background pathology and natural diseases in these animal species are factors that could impact on the interpretation of the changes caused by test articles. Therefore, during the evaluation of drug-induced pathological changes, it is important that the pathologist is aware of the natural diseases and the background lesions that are prevalent in the different species of laboratory animals. It may be necessary to collect additional tissues to address the disease status of the animals. In order to make sure that the correct tissues are collected and examined, the study pathologist must be involved, where possible, in the study design and contribute to the generation of the study protocol.

The drive to identify early on those development molecules that could potentially fail later due to animal toxicity (reduce attrition) makes a huge demand on the time and expertise of the pathologists beyond their conventional role in general drug safety evaluation. In addition to general toxicity studies, toxicological pathologists also contribute to specialized studies such as phototoxicity, dermal toxicity, and tissue cross-reactivity; the latter has become more common as the development of biological entities as medicine has increased. The role of the toxicological pathologist is not limited to the safety assessment of a drug candidate in development. They play an important role in establishing disease models, the identification, characterization, and investigation of mechanisms of drug-related injuries in toxicology studies, and monitoring the clinical occurrence, progression, and reversibility of adverse events [7]. Their expertise is also used in the field of regenerative medicine and the use of tissue regeneration technologies [8].

In order to carry out these activities, the toxicological pathologist must have the qualifications, training, and experience in the evaluation, description, interpretation, and reporting of histopathological changes. The majority of toxicological pathologists are educated in veterinary science and are trained in diagnostic pathology, the aim of which is to make a disease-oriented diagnosis using specific and appropriate diagnostic terms. In toxicological pathology, animals that are given a test article, usually at different doses, are compared with control animals that are given only the vehicle in which the test article is formulated, in order to determine whether a test article elicits pathological changes. In this discipline, descriptive rather than diagnostic terms are used. The pathologist must have a good understanding of the necropsy procedures and tissue processing. The critical importance of the training of the pathologists engaged in drug safety evaluation was recognized, and the need for consistent training was addressed by the recommendation of the

International Federation of Toxicological Pathologists (IFTP) [9].

The following areas of histopathology will be covered in this chapter:

- Necropsy, histology, electron microscopy, histochemistry, and immunohistochemistry.
- Primary histopathology evaluation and peer review of tissues.
- Data collation, interpretation, and reporting.
- Examples of spontaneous and drug-induced histopathological changes.

Necropsy: At the end of the in-life phase of the study, the animals are euthanized and prepared for necropsy. The necropsy of the animals at the end of a toxicity study is a critical procedure. It is a one-off event that cannot be repeated or reproduced, and mistakes that occur at this stage cannot be rectified at a later date. Gross abnormalities that are missed or tissues that are not collected during necropsy will be lost forever. In order for this important step of the study to run smoothly, it must be conducted systematically and by technical staff who are trained to a high standard in necropsy procedures and in the identification of abnormalities in tissues. A senior technician or a pathologist supervises the process and is responsible for the quality of the descriptions and the integrity of the recording of gross abnormalities. The data are generally recorded in a validated computer system.

The necropsy staff are required to strictly adhere to the relevant SOPs. Before the necropsy procedure starts, the prosectors should be familiar with the necropsy section of the study protocol and understand the specific requirements regarding tissue collection and fixation; a copy of the study protocol is available or accessible in the necropsy room. The prosectors should also be aware of all the relevant clinical observation including ophthalmoscopy comments that have been generated during the in-life phase, and should pay particular attention to the tissues and organs that are relevant to the clinical observations and collect additional samples where necessary. The necropsy room is equipped with the instruments necessary to conduct the necropsy procedure correctly and safely. The containers for blood and tissue samples are appropriately labeled with the correct animal identifications to avoid mixing up of samples.

The necropsy is a standardized procedure that is carried out in a consistent manner in order to gain the maximum information and at the same time avoid damage to or loss of tissues. The tissues and organs are examined thoroughly under good light, and all gross abnormalities are described accurately in terms of size, color, consistency, location, and distribution, using recognizable descriptive terms and avoiding the use of specific diagnostic terms. The procedure must be conducted at a reasonable pace that minimizes the effects of autolysis but makes sure that all the tissues are thoroughly examined and any abnormality is correctly identified. Subtle gross abnormalities could be missed if the procedure is conducted in haste. Accurate and consistent identification and description of gross abnormalities depends on the training and experience of the prosector in recognizing the normal appearance of organs and tissues in terms of color, consistency, and the general appearance of the organs and the cross-section of solid organs. Prosectors must be aware of differences in the topography of some tissues in different species. For example, in the minipig most of the thymus is located in the cervical region and the thyroid is located on the ventral part of the trachea. The parathyroids are not embedded or attached to the thyroids but located in the cranial part of the thymus [10]. In dermal studies, it is recommended the location of gross abnormalities are marked with ink to help in their identification during processing, as it is possible some subtle changes could disappear when the tissue is immersed in the fixative. Tissue damage such as tears or excessive pressure with the hand or instruments could introduce artifacts that could mask potential test-article-related changes, and therefore must be avoided. For example, care must be taken when handling the testes, as excessive pressure could cause sloughing of germ cells into the lumen of seminiferous tubules, which could be interpreted incorrectly. The tissues to be collected at necropsy depend on the objective of the study and are specified in the study protocol. In some tissues, such as skin and mammary gland, the protocol specifies the area of the body from which the samples are collected. The tissues must be promptly immersed in a fixative to avoid the onset of postmortem changes that could mask potential test-article-related changes. There should be a high ratio of fixative-to-tissue sample (at least 10:1 ratio), and small samples of large tissues (eg, liver) may need to be selected at necropsy to ensure good penetration of fixative. Animals that are killed moribund or found dead must be stored at 4°C and necropsied as soon as possible after death to avoid tissue autolysis, which could impact the quality of histopathology data. It is important that the control and dosed groups are necropsied and processed by the same team and that animals from all groups are randomly allocated to each necropsy technician.

Organ Weight: The following organs are weighed in a Good Laboratory Practice (GLP)-compliant study. Before weighing, the organs are dissected free from fat and other contiguous tissue; paired organs are weighed together. Other organs and tissues may be weighed on a case-by-case basis.

Adrenal glands	Liver	Spleen
Brain	Ovaries	Testes
Heart	Prostate gland	Thymus
Kidneys	Pituitary gland	Thyroid/parathyroid glands

Histology: The study protocol identifies a standard list of tissues to be retained at necropsy from single and repeat dose toxicity or carcinogenicity studies regardless of the objective or duration of these studies. The tissues that should be examined microscopically are also identified in the protocol. Depending on the type or objective of the study, these could range from a short list of the major organs to a full list of most of the tissues collected at necropsy. A typical tissue list is shown next.

Adrenals	Larynx	Salivary glands: Parotid, Sublingual, Submandibular
Aorta (thoracic)	Liver	Seminal vesicle
Brain	Lungs	Skeletal muscle
Cecum	Mammary gland	Skin
Cervix	Mandibular lymph node	Spinal cord
Colon	Mesenteric lymph node	Spleen
Duodenum	Nasal cavity	Sternum with bone marrow
Epididymides	Optic nerves	Stomach
Esophagus	Ovaries	Testes
Eyes	Pancreas	Thymus
Femur	Parathyroid	Thyroids
Gallbladder	Peripheral nerve (sciatic)	Tongue
Heart	Pituitary	Trachea
Ileum	Rectum	Urinary bladder
Jejunum	Popliteal lymph node	Uterus
Kidneys	Prostate	Vagina

Additional tissues may be examined, depending on the route of administration or the mode of action and/ or known toxicity profile of the drug under investigation. These include the injection and application sites for intravenous and subcutaneous administration and dermal application, and the upper respiratory tract for nasally administered or inhaled material. In some laboratories, the nasal cavity may be routinely examined in oral studies in rodents due to lesions frequently observed in the posterior area of the nasal cavity caused by reflux of the administered material [11]. For an oral rodent study with potential for lesions in the intestine, the Swiss roll process may be used to increase the surface area available for examination [12]. This technique allows the processing and examination of the entire intestine in one block. The intestine is divided into various segments, opened longitudinally, and rolled with the mucosa outwards (Fig. 15.1).

Fixation: The standard fixative for primary histopathology is 10% neutral buffered formaldehyde solution; it fixes all the tissues well and is cost-effective. During necropsy, the tissues that are required for weighing are trimmed of the surrounding fat and connective tissues and weighed. The tissues are immersed in the fixative as soon as possible. Prompt fixation is essential for the maintenance of tissue morphology and the avoidance of postmortem changes. Delayed or inadequate fixation would result in the tissues undergoing postmortem changes that could mask potential test-article-related morphological changes. Bony tissues such as sternum, femur, or nasal turbinate are further treated with appropriate acidic solution (eg, organic acid) for decalcification to soften the tissue for trimming and sectioning. The tissues may be X-rayed to ensure complete decalcification has been achieved.

The testes and eyes are fixed in modified Davidson's solution, although some laboratories may still use Bouin's solution. Davidson's solution (and the modified version) is a combination of formaldehyde, ethanol, and glacial acetic acid in various proportions. This fixative is considered better than Bouin's both in terms of fixation and its reduced health and environmental effects. There has been a gradual move away from Bouin's as the picric acid it contains is a health hazard and stains everything with which it comes into contact bright yellow. In addition, testes fixed in Bouin's were also found to show shrinkage of the seminiferous tubules, creating artificially exaggerated distension of the interstitial spaces, which could mask interstitial edema [13].

The lungs are a major target of toxicity in inhalation as well as noninhalation studies. Proper fixation of the lung can be achieved with intratracheal infusion of a fixative. Care should be taken not to use excessive force, as this can result in overstretching and rupture of alveolar walls, creating spaces that resemble emphysema; this procedure can also create clear perivascular and peribronchiolar spaces that could mask test-article-related edema. However, the disadvantage is outweighed by the advantage of having properly inflated tissue with structures that can be examined clearly [14]. When the lung is immersion-fixed without inflation, it remains collapsed, and the detailed structure of the alveoli cannot be seen, making it difficult to examine the organ thoroughly (Fig. 15.2). Clamping the airway before removing the lung would keep the lung inflated and avoid potential artifacts created by the intratracheal

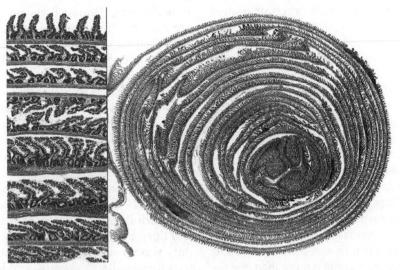

FIGURE 15.1 **Rat—intestine.** Swiss roll technique. The panel on the left shows well-preserved layers of villi of the various segments of the intestinal mucosa.

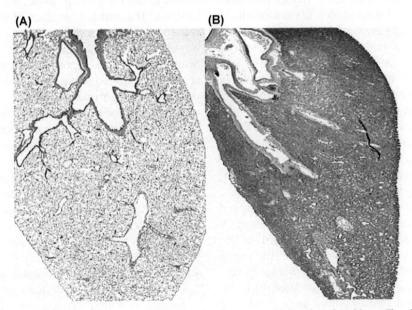

FIGURE 15.2 **Rat—lung.** (A) Properly inflated lung showing the alveolar spaces. (B) Poorly inflated lung. The alveolar spaces are collapsed and difficult to examine.

infusion of fixative. However, this method is only used on a case-by-case basis.

In rodents, the pituitary is fixed in situ in the base of the skull (with nasal turbinates) to avoid damage, and removed during trimming. The thyroids are also fixed in situ with the trachea and larynx. In all species, the contents of the gastrointestinal tract, gall bladder, and urinary bladder may be gently washed away to improve fixation. During the trimming of the fixed tissues, if the histologist identifies any additional gross abnormalities, these will be recorded and an extra block may be required if the abnormality is not observed in the standard sample for the tissue. Abnormalities identified at necropsy that are not identified at trimming are recorded as such in the

histology data. A comprehensive guide for organ sampling and trimming in rats and mice is now available [15–17].

Embedding: After keeping the samples in fixative for an appropriate and standardized length of time, the tissues are trimmed to smaller sizes in order to select blocks that are cut consistently throughout the study; for most tissues this is achievable. The brain needs extreme care when trimming, due to its heterogeneous morphology. The rodent brain may be trimmed using a special brain-trimming matrix for consistent sample thickness across the study, which is difficult to achieve when the trimming is done by free hand [17]. During tissue trimming, the brain sections are carefully examined for gross abnormalities such as areas of discoloration or dilated ventricles which could not have been observed when the tissue was fresh as the tissue is fixed intact. The tissues are then passed through increasing concentrations of alcohol (70%, 90%, and 100%) on an automated processing machine to remove the water. The dehydration is followed by a clearing process that uses clearing agents such as xylene to remove the alcohol, and then impregnated with molten wax. The tissue is then placed in a metal mold base to a standard orientation, and filled with molten paraffin wax, which on hardening is ready for sectioning. Each block is identified with the study, animal, and block numbers.

The number of blocks prepared from each tissue varies according to tissue and animal species. For most, one block is sufficient, but for some tissues more than one is prepared, and some blocks may contain more than one tissue. The brain is a complex and structurally heterogeneous organ. In a standard rodent toxicity study with a nonneuroactive substance, two blocks (4 sections) may be prepared. In a study with a neuroactive substance, up to four blocks (9 sections) are prepared to examine all the possible areas of the brain. Similarly, in an oral toxicity study, two sections of the lung are sufficient for the assessment of test-article-related changes; but in inhalation studies, the number could be four sections or more. In the dog, the number of the areas of the heart that need to be examined cannot be accommodated in one block, and four to six blocks are needed for a comprehensive assessment. With cardioactive drugs, additional blocks may be required.

In rodents, the heart is normally sectioned longitudinally, or a combination of longitudinal and transverse sectioning for comprehensive examination. The heart valves may not be assessed comprehensively in routine histopathology due to the difficulty of sampling; a standard heart section may contain one or two valves. Assessment of all the valves would require serial sections of the heart, a process which, in standard toxicity studies, would be considered impractical, particularly in rodent studies with a large number of animals per group. However, in studies with test articles that are known or suspected to cause valvular changes, eg, activin-like kinase 5 (ALK5) [18], it is important to include the valves in the sections.

The nasal cavity is sectioned at various levels. After decalcification, the tissue is cut at multiple standard points representing the various tissue types in the cavity. The processing of the blocks follows the standard procedure in the laboratory [19]. In inhalation studies, multiple blocks of the nasal cavity are prepared to cover the squamous, respiratory, transitional, and olfactory regions, whereas in an oral study, only one block of the olfactory region may be prepared to assess the effect of potential reflux of the dose of the test article and/or gastric content into the posterior region of the nasal cavity.

Sectioning: Thin sections of three to five μm thickness are cut from the paraffin-embedded blocks and stained with hematoxylin and eosin (H&E). Slides for light microscopic examination must be of high quality, have consistent thickness, be properly stained, and have minimum artifacts. Tissues with multiple structures must be sectioned with care so that every anatomical part is represented in the section. Tissue samples from large organs such as the liver, lung, or heart are easy to orientate and section. In rodent studies, great care is taken when sectioning smaller tissues, such as the adrenal or pituitary, in order to make sure that the various anatomical features of the organs are represented in the section. The medulla of the adrenal is as important as the cortex and must be examined. Similarly, the section of the pituitary should contain the pars distalis, pars nervosa, and pars intermedia. Transverse and longitudinal sections of the testes are generally used in routine toxicity studies. The section of the femur must contain the cartilage of the femur head, the growth plate, the bone shaft, and bone marrow. The cartilage surface of the femur must be sectioned carefully for the assessment of compounds that affect the joint cartilage, such as quinolone antibiotics. Similarly, it is also important that the growth plate in the femur is sectioned adequately in order to establish effect on chondrocyte turnover [20,21].

When a tissue is not identified on a slide, an additional section is cut from the same block, or, should that fail, the specimen is either reembedded or an additional wet sample may be processed. This is a very important part of the process of accounting for protocol-required tissues in a study. When all efforts fail, the pathologist marks the tissue as "inadequate" or "missing." During processing, if the histologist cannot identify a tissue, he or she records the tissue as missing and the pathologist confirms only if there is no evidence of it on the section provided. An occasional missing tissue would not impact the study, but if a tissue is recorded as inadequate or missing in a number of animals that are given the test article, the completeness of the study could be questioned. It is imperative that the tissue trimming and sectioning are done with due care, as mistakes at this stage might not be rectifiable and might have serious consequences. Like the blocks, the slides are identified with the study, animal, and block numbers.

Histochemistry: In addition to hematoxylin and eosin, other staining methods are used to further characterize lesions that are identified in the primary histopathological examination. Histochemistry and immunohistochemistry are used frequently in toxicological pathology, and a large number of stains and antibodies are used to identify the various tissue components that may be associated with a lesion and that may increase the understanding of the pathogenesis of the lesion. Some of the more commonly used histochemical stains are listed next.

Stain	What Is Stained	Color
Alcian blue periodic acid Schiff (PAS)	Mucin	Magenta, blue, or purple depending on the type of mucin
Oil-red-O	Neutral lipid	Red
Perl's Prussian blue	Ferric iron	Dark blue
Schmorl's	Lipofuscin, melanin	Dark blue
Von Kossa	Mineral deposits	Black
Masson's trichrome	Collagen	Bright green
Phosphotungstic acid hematoxylin (PTAH)	Skeletal muscle striation	Dark blue
Martius scarlet blue (MSB)	Muscle, fibrin, collagen	Pale red, bright red, blue, respectively
Congo red	Amyloid deposits	Pink-green (under polarized light)

Immunohistochemistry: Immunohistochemistry is used to identify specific cell types using antibodies raised against specific proteins (markers) on the surfaces of the cells or protein products in the cytoplasm. This technique is regularly used in the immune system when a test-article-related change is suspected during the primary histopathology evaluation. Hematoxylin and eosin stain would show changes in the total lymphoid cell population, but cannot distinguish between B- and T-lymphocytes. The cell-surface markers that are commonly used to distinguish between the different types of lymphocyte population include CD3 and CD79a (T-cell); CD4, CD8, and CD45R (B-cell); and CD68 for tissue macrophages [22]. Immunohistochemistry can also be used to identify cells by their protein products such as hormones (eg, hormone-producing cells in the anterior pituitary or in the adrenal medulla) or $\alpha2\mu m$ globulin in the kidney of male rats. In situ hybridization can also be used to identify specific RNA involved in protein synthesis. Immuno-histochemical detection using a monoclonal antibody to administered bromodeoxyuridine (BrdU) can be used to evaluate cell proliferation, but has been replaced in many cases by use of Ki-67 or proliferating cell nuclear antigen (PCNA) IHC. Apoptosis, or programmed cell death, is a normal biological process that may be altered by exposure to toxicants. Apoptosis may be detected and quantified using light microscopy, DNA fragmentation, and detection of caspases using immunocytochemistry or DNA polymerase chain reaction (PCR) and microarray technology [23]. Cell proliferation and apoptosis have long been recognized as key factors in carcinogenesis, but are also useful tools to detect and quantify cellular

changes in short-term toxicology studies. Immunohisto-chemistry is also used to distinguish between different types of lipids such as phospholipids and neutral lipid using adipophilin and lysosome-associated membrane protein (LAMP-2) as biomarkers [24].

Electron Microscopy: Transmission electron microscopy (TEM) is used frequently in preclinical histopathology to identify and characterize ultrastructural changes in cell organelles such as mitochondria, endoplasmic reticulum, or cell membrane. In toxicological pathology, TEM is used to further characterize changes that are identified under light microscopy, such as hepatocellular hypertrophy (increased rough and smooth endoplasmic reticulum) and phospholipidosis (lamellar bodies); it is not used as a primary diagnostic tool or to define effect or no-effect doses. Routine formalin fixation can usually be adequate for retrospective TEM, but generally prospective sampling and fixation is required. Tissues for electron microscopy are cut into small pieces of 1mm in thickness and fixed by immersion in a primary fixative, which is normally 4% formaldehyde/1% glutaraldehyde. The tissues are then postfixed in osmium tetroxide and then follow a process similar to routine histology of gradual dehydration and then infiltration with epoxy resin. The processed samples are polymerized at 60°C overnight. Semi-thin sections (1.0 μm) of the specimen are stained with toluidine blue for an initial quality assessment, before ultrathin sections (0.1 μm) are prepared and stained with gold. The gold-stained specimen is examined with a transmission electron microscope using a resolution that is optimal for the target. For example, the resolution to identify lamellar bodies in an alveolar macrophage would be different from the resolution needed for the identification of viral particles. Other techniques that are occasionally used in toxicological pathology include scanning electron microscopy (SEM).

Imaging in Pathology: Recent advances in imaging technology have greatly enhanced the use of digital imaging for evaluating histological samples by light microscopy. Although this technology is not currently used in primary histopathological evaluation, its use in remote peer reviewing of non-GLP studies is gaining acceptance. Some of the available technologies provide high-quality images that would satisfy most situations. In addition, the ability to annotate the images helps pathologists to resolve differences in diagnoses or description of lesions. It would also save companies valuable time and financial resources in travel and transport costs. Digital microscopy overcomes all the limitations inherent in traditional microscopy. It eliminates the movement of slides and the need for a microscope to view one slide at a time and instead uses a computer monitor that permits viewing multiple slides and remote viewing by several users at the same time. In addition, the software used in digital microscopy allows morphometric analysis, which gives accurate measurement of cell and nuclear sizes, thus adding a degree of certainty in some of the difficult diagnoses such as hepatocellular hypertrophy. However, scanned images do not allow the pathologist to focus through the depth of the tissue section, which in some cases can be a useful technique applied to the traditional glass slide. Digital microscopy also simplifies the archiving and retrieval of digitalized slide images [25]. An imaging system that is gaining increased application in preclinical studies is MRI. This powerful tool is used in studies in which it is important to track lesions over time or to show evidence of recovery of a drug-induced lesion or the regression of a tumor. This tool also helps in reducing animal usage in the study of the time course of the development of lesions. Such study is normally done by sacrificing animals at regular intervals and examining them. With MRI that objective could be achieved with the live animal.

Artifacts: Both the study pathologist and peer review pathologist must be aware of the artifacts that could be present on the slides submitted for histopathological evaluation, particularly those that mimic real pathological changes in a particular tissue. Artifacts can be introduced into histology sections at any stage in the processing of tissue sections from necropsy to coverslipping. During necropsy, inappropriate use of necropsy instruments such as forceps could result in pinch artifacts that could persist throughout the processing phase. Inadequate fixation of the tissue could result in autolysis due to poor penetration of the fixative into the tissue caused by either inadequate amount of fixative in relation to the size of the tissue (the recommended fixative to tissue ratio is 10:1) or insufficient time in the fixative. Poor fixation also causes the formation of formalin pigment (hematin). Other types of artifact include compression, streaks, cracks, and tracks caused by vibration of the specimen or blunt microtome knife during cutting or entrapped air during mounting of the specimen on glass [26,27]. These artifacts need to be removed or minimized where possible, as they could interfere with the evaluation of the specimen and confound potential test-article-related changes. Staff training in tissue processing and strict adherence to SOPs should reduce artifacts.

HISTOPATHOLOGICAL EXAMINATION

Histopathological assessment of tissues is considered an important endpoint in preclinical toxicity studies. It is conducted by experienced pathologists who evaluate the slides and produces an interpretative report of the findings. In a standard GLP-compliant study, over 40 tissues are examined from each animal. Prior to the assessment, the study pathologist should have access to the study protocol and protocol amendments and all

the data on clinical signs, body weight and food consumption, clinical pathology, organ weight, necropsy observations, toxicokinetics, the relevant biology of the target molecule (eg, expression and tissue distribution and function of the target molecule, if known), and any known toxicity of the test article. When a study is conducted at a contract research organization (CRO), the sponsor should provide the study pathologist with a summary of all the target tissues identified in previous studies, in order to maintain consistency of the descriptive and grading terminologies. It is also desirable for the study pathologist to have information on the biology, pharmacology, and metabolic profile of the new drug candidate to aid in the generation of a comprehensive integrated pathology report.

The study pathologist must review the clinical pathology and organ weight data. The biochemical and hematological parameters could show changes indicative of cell injury, even if there is no evidence of correlating injury in the tissue during the microscopic examination. For example, increased activity of serum alanine aminotransferase (ALT) and bilirubin are considered clear indications of hepatocellular injury, which is normally confirmed by histopathological evidence of liver cell damage. The correlation between these parameters and liver injury is so consistent that increases above a certain magnitude are considered a manifestation of liver injury even when there is no obvious morphological evidence of tissue injury. Similarly, an increase in serum troponin or KIM-1 (kidney injury molecule-1) are indicators of myocardial and kidney injury, respectively. These biomarkers appear in the circulation when the integrity of the cell is compromised. Some lesions are reversible if the stimulus is removed, depending on the extent of the damage and the involvement of cells that are necessary for regeneration. However, the availability of a validated biomarker helps the detection, monitoring, and reversibility of cell injury in an animal or patient.

Similarly, hematological parameters such as reduced red blood cell count, hemoglobin concentration, or increased circulating reticulocytes give a clue to potential toxicity. In general, a decrease in red blood cell count indicates destruction of red cells and their removal from the circulation; or the failure of the bone marrow to produce red cells. If the decreased red blood count is accompanied by an increase in reticulocytes in circulation, it indicates that the bone marrow still has the capacity to produce red cells to replace those that are destroyed. This regenerative ability would not be present if the change is due to a failure in hematopoiesis. The histopathological examination of the bone marrow would confirm whether the change is central (bone marrow related) or peripheral; examination of bone marrow smears could identify the cell types that are affected. Histopathology of the spleen and liver could also show evidence of red blood cell destruction by showing excessive iron pigment (hemosiderin), which could be confirmed by staining with Perl's stain.

The review of the organ weight data also draws attention to tissues that show an increase or decrease in their weight. Increased weight would indicate increased cell size (hypertrophy), cell number (hyperplasia), fluid accumulation (edema), etc.; whereas decreased weight indicates decreased cell size (atrophy) or cell number (hypoplasia). These changes give the pathologist a pointer to the tissues that need particular attention. Taken together, by the time the available data are reviewed, the pathologist would have clues of the toxicity of the test article and the type of cells that might be affected.

The histopathological examination of the slides is normally conducted by one pathologist. In carcinogenicity studies, one pathologist could evaluate the neoplastic lesions and a second pathologist examines the nonneoplastic lesions [28]; however, the practice is rare.

Histopathological examination is conducted in a systematic way that allows a thorough evaluation of all the tissues. There is no specific method for slide evaluation or regulations on the magnifications to be used. However, the study pathologist must make sure that the evaluation of the tissues is accurate, consistent, and complete, and that the pathology report reflects the pathology data. In rodent studies, due to the large number of animals involved, the protocol-required tissues from control and high-dose animals are examined initially; the examination of the lower-dose animals depends on identifying test-article-related changes at the high dose. In nonrodent studies, due to the small number of animals involved, all the tissues are examined from all the animals on the study. The examination of the tissues is an open process, which means that the study pathologist knows the identity of the animals and all the relevant in-life data associated with each animal. Blind-reading of slides is not considered appropriate for primary slide evaluation, but is useful only when it is targeted to assess subtle changes in treated animals [6,29]. In toxicological pathology, the use of internationally agreed descriptive terminology is preferred over specific diagnostic terms; the latter is a legacy from the early days of toxicological pathology when diagnostic terms from veterinary or medical pathology were used. Standardized nomenclature and diagnostic criteria for histopathology, intended to enhance the consistency of the pathology data and interpretation, have been published by various organizations including the Society of Toxicological Pathology (STP) and International Harmonization of Nomenclature and Diagnostic Criteria (INHAND) [30,31].

The order in which the slides are examined is the choice of the pathologist. Some examine the slides by animal, ie, they examine all the tissues from one animal before moving to the next. This method helps the early identification of potential target tissues. In rodent studies, in which only the control and high-dose animals are initially examined, this method would allow the processing of the target organ(s) from the lower-dose groups early on in the process, thus potentially reducing the reporting timeframe. The disadvantage of this method is that it runs the risk of inconsistency in the diagnosis or the grading of the severity of a lesion, as the evaluation of a single tissue is spread over a number of days. This inconsistency would be more serious in rodent studies in which the number of animals per group is typically 10–12 animals per sex per group. Rereading affected tissue(s) from all animals at the end of the evaluation would rectify any inconsistency in diagnosis or grading. Reading slides by animal is appropriate in a two-year rodent carcinogenicity bioassay in which multiple lesions in single animals, many of which die prior to the scheduled kill, may require this approach.

The carcinogenic potential of a new chemical entity is assessed in 2-year rodent bioassays, usually in rats and mice, with group sizes of 50–60 animals. The tumors identified in the study are assessed in terms of incidence, tumor type, the number of tumors in an animal (tumor burden), the first time the tumor was noted (mainly palpable masses), and the part a tumor played in the demise of the animal (factors contributing to death). Because of the long duration of the study, some of the animals die or are killed during the study for various reasons and the tissues are processed in batches at certain timepoints in the study and examined for an early indication of test-article-related changes. Increased tumors in treated animals that die during the study compared to controls could indicate a shift in the latency period of tumors. The tumor data are then subjected to statistical analysis for evidence of potential carcinogenic effect [32,33]. Although the toxicity profile of the molecule has been characterized in short-term studies prior to a carcinogenicity study being conducted, test-article-related nonneoplastic changes are also assessed in carcinogenicity studies, but generally not subjected to statistical analysis. Considering all these issues associated with a carcinogenicity study, the examination of the slides by animal makes more sense than examining them by tissue. Carcinogenicity assays are also performed in genetically modified animal mouse models, such as the p53 knockout, as these could identify the tumorigenic potential of a new drug more quickly than the conventional two-year study [4,5].

Some pathologists prefer examining the slides by tissue across the groups, particularly in studies other than two-year bioassays. The advantage of this method is that a single tissue is examined within a short period of time, when the characteristics of the lesion and the grades are still fresh in the mind. This makes the recognition of subtle changes in a tissue easier and there is less chance for inconsistency in terminology or grading across the study. The disadvantage of this method is that a target organ might be identified towards the end of the slide-evaluation phase, thus losing significant time while waiting for the processing of late identified target tissues from the lower-dose groups. The time lost could impact on timelines if there is a large number of animals per group or if a bony tissue that needs decalcification is one of the target organs. This risk is often minimized by processing all protocolled tissues from all groups to blocking stage in the first instance, but only cutting, staining, and examining from lower-dose animals only the target tissues identified in the high dose. Whatever the method of slide evaluation, the pathology data must be accurate and consistent in description and interpretation.

The severity of a lesion, which indicates the extent of the tissue damage or reaction to an injury, is graded semiquantitatively using terms such as minimal, mild (slight), moderate, and marked. It is mainly used in non-neoplastic findings; neoplastic lesions are not graded in this way, but only described as benign and malignant; the latter could show evidence of spread into the adjacent tissues or metastasize to distant organs and tissues (Fig. 15.3).

The grade a pathologist assigns to a severity of a lesion is subjective, but the margin of variability decreases through experience; however, it is important that the grading is applied consistently across the study. A lesion may be graded quantitatively using image analysis, which would remove the subjectivity and increase the accuracy and consistency of the use of a grade; this in turn facilitates interpretation [34,35]. However, quantitative image analysis is not performed as part of standard toxicity studies.

The distribution of a lesion indicates its spread within a tissue, and terms such as focal, multifocal, diffuse, lobular, acinar, and segmental are used to describe it. It is also important to record whether a lesion is unilateral or bilateral in paired organs. For example, a bilateral change in a paired organ in a number of animals in a study is considered more likely to be test-article-related than a unilateral lesion, even if the two are of similar severity. Similarly, the location of the lesion could give a clue to its pathogenesis. Because of the location in which the lesion develops, drug-induced myocardial necrosis in the papillary muscle of the heart in a short-term dog study with a hypotensive drug may indicate a pathogenesis that is different from myocardial necrosis in the right atrium of the heart caused by a noncardioactive drug. The distribution and location of a lesion are less subjective than the severity and could contribute to the clarity of the description of the lesion. The severity and distribution of a lesion contribute to the weight of evidence that is used to determine the adversity of the lesion.

There are specific requirements for the evaluation of the testes in a GLP-compliant study that is intended to support the administration of a new drug to humans for the first time. In this type of study, in addition to the assessment of general overt testicular toxicity, the stages of the spermatogenic cycle are also examined. Similar to other tissue in a study, the testicular evaluation is initially carried out in the control and high-dose groups; lower doses are assessed based on the outcome of the initial examination. Pathologists must be trained in the recognition of the various stages of the spermatogenic cycle and the types of germ cell associated with each stage. The testes, prostate, and seminal vesicles are weighed in regulatory studies, and the first indication of potential testicular effect may come from changes in the weight of these organs. The presence of cell debris, immature germ cells, or reduced sperm content in the epididymides would also indicate an effect on the germ cells upstream. Without this detailed knowledge and experience, it would be difficult for the pathologist to identify subtle changes in the germ cell population and their associations.

The detailed assessment of the spermatogenic cycle in the general toxicology study does not obviate the need to conduct a male fertility study, which is normally conducted at a later stage in the development of a new drug, but it helps to mitigate the risk for the short-term administration of the new drug in human male subjects. The

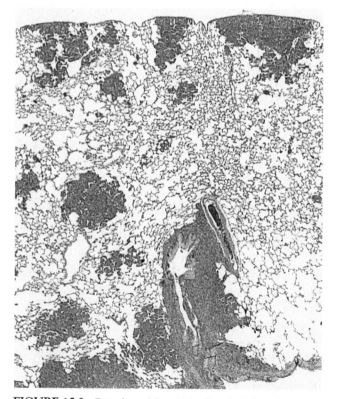

FIGURE 15.3 **Rat—lung.** Metastasis of uterine adenocarcinoma.

pathology report specifically states that stage-dependent evaluation of spermatogenesis in the testes was performed and, if no test article-related changes are identified, the report concludes that the testes revealed normal progression of the spermatogenic cycle and the presence of the expected cell associations. The study pathologist records his or her findings in an appropriate and validated computer system that allows the tabulation of the data for ease of interpretation.

Peer Review: Histopathological evaluation of tissue samples is of paramount importance in preclinical toxicity studies. Once the study pathologist completes the primary assessment of the slides and writes a draft report (depending on the practice at the test facility), an experienced pathologist conducts a peer review of the slides, the data generated, and the draft report. The role of the peer review pathologist is to ascertain the accuracy of the histopathological changes identified by the study pathologist in terms of consistency of terminology and grading of severity of lesions, accuracy of interpretation of the changes, and the quality of the report.

Normally, peer review of pathology data and the report is conducted for GLP-compliant studies; other study types may be peer reviewed depending on their objectives. The peer review is conducted by a qualified and experienced pathologist, and it facilitates the delivery of a high-quality and consistent final pathology data set and interpretative report [36–38]. There is no regulatory requirement for pathology peer review, but both regulators and sponsors understand that this enhances the quality of the pathology report and gives the regulators extra confidence in the quality and integrity of the data. Normally, the peer review is contemporaneous in that it is planned for, and the location and peer review pathologist are named in the study protocol; the process is also covered by an SOP at the site of peer review or provided by the sponsor. However, on occasions, a peer review may be conducted retrospectively on a study for which a peer review was not previously required, in order to address an issue that arose subsequently. The peer review is normally conducted by a sponsor pathologist for both internal as well as CRO studies; however, in a study conducted at a CRO, a pathologist employed at the test facility may conduct the review. Occasionally, when there are specific reasons pertaining to the nature of a study or a finding, a sponsor may request an external pathologist with recognized expertise to carry out the peer review. The peer review pathologist receives the slides and all the pathology data, including the individual animal pathology data, the incidence table of all the histopathological findings, a draft pathology report, and any other relevant study data that are deemed necessary for the review. The peer review is an abridged version of the primary evaluation of the slides. As with primary examination, there is no specific procedure for

peer reviewing; however, best practice guidance is available [37,38]. In general, after reviewing the pathology data and the draft pathology report, the peer review pathologist examines the slides from all the target tissues for accuracy and consistency of diagnosis, grading, and interpretation of all test-article-related findings and confirmation of effect and no-effect doses.

The peer review pathologist also examines the slides from all protocol-required tissues from a number of control and high-dose animals. A minimum number of high-dose animals per sex may be examined. In a carcinogenicity study, all the tumors may be examined, and given the large number of animals involved, all tissues from a proportion of the animals are examined from the high-dose and controls. However, the peer review pathologist has the discretion to extend the review to more tissues or animals as deemed necessary. At the end of the peer review, the peer review pathologist and study pathologist discuss the findings and resolve any differences between their respective views in order to reach a consensus on the outcome of the review. Differences could arise in the diagnosis of lesions, appropriate use of diagnostic terms, and grading, as well as in the interpretation of the lesions. In recent years, the standardization of diagnostic terminology and criteria in toxicological pathology have reduced the potential for differences in terminology to arise. But it is possible to have differences in opinion on lesions that do not fit the standardized lexicon. With regards to the grading of the severity of a lesion, a difference of one grade point does not constitute a major difference. Slight increases in the incidence of common background lesions or their severities could pose difficulty in interpretation as they could indicate potential exacerbation of these lesions by the test article. The background historic control data in the test facility usually helps to put the change in the general context of the species and strain/breed used in the study. The opinion of a third pathologist may be sought on rare occasions to help settle any unresolved differences. The process is similar in studies conducted in CROs, where the peer review is conducted by a sponsor pathologist. In these studies, an independent pathologist may occasionally be involved to resolve differences, should the CRO and sponsor pathologists fail to reach an agreement. At the end of the peer review process, a peer review statement is issued that details the process and the conclusion.

Once the peer review is complete, the study pathologist makes all the necessary amendments to the data and the report. The study pathologist then locks the pathology data and generates the final incidence tables and individual animal data. There have been discussions on the need to lock the histopathology data prior to the start of the peer review. Since only the signed and dated final pathology report is considered to represent the histopathology raw data, the general consensus is that the pathology data need not be locked before the contemporaneous peer review [38,39]. The report is then submitted to the study director for incorporation into the main toxicology report. The study pathologist is often a signatory to the main toxicology report, and as such must review the final report and make sure that the pathology report and conclusion are correctly integrated in the report. In studies conducted at a CRO, the study pathologist is not a signatory to the toxicology report.

The Pathology Working Group: The pathology working group (PWG) is an independent ad hoc committee of experienced toxicological pathologists that is convened at the request of a sponsor to retrospectively review the pathology data of a study, including the examination of slides, to resolve issues of diagnosis or interpretation of histopathology findings around which there are regulatory questions or concern [6,40]. The members of the PWG are selected for their experience and expertise in toxicological pathology. The meeting may be attended by a representative of the sponsor, whose role is limited to supply information and answer questions but not take part in either the evaluation of the slides or the interpretation of the data. At the end of the review, the PWG prepares a formal report on the conclusion of their deliberations for the sponsor. Regulatory agencies consider the view of the PWG on an issue, but they are not bound by its conclusion.

INTERPRETATION OF PATHOLOGY DATA AND PATHOLOGY REPORT

A pathology report must be complete, accurate, and communicate the relative importance of the lesions identified in a study. The lesions are interpreted in conjunction with clinical pathology and organ weight data. The report also states the effect and no-effect doses as well as the findings that are considered to be adverse to the animal. The overall no-observed-adverse-effect-level (NOAEL) for the study is determined from all the changes in the study on a weight-of-evidence basis, but the histopathology data are often central to establishing adversity [6,41]. The pathology report is a signed, standalone document that is appended to the main study report. The study pathologist is responsible for the integrity and reliability of the contents of the report. In order to be able to correctly interpret test results, particularly those with numerical data, the pathologist must understand basic statistical tests and know the limit of their application [28].

In general, a pathology report comprises sections on study design (methods), results, discussion, and conclusion. Some laboratories might add a summary at the beginning of the report.

Summary: This is a succinct statement on test article-related histopathological changes and the no-effect dose.

Study Design: The study design defines the purpose of the study with regards to the identity and nature of the test article under investigation, the species, strain/breed of animal used in the study, the dose levels and the number of animals per dose group, the route of administration, and the duration of dosing. This section also lists all the standard and nonstandard histopathological procedures that are used in the study.

Results: The results section describes in detail the nature, incidence, and severity of all test-article-related macroscopic and microscopic findings in the study and the doses affected. The findings of any animal that dies during the study (decedent) are normally described separately. The results of any special histochemical and immunohistochemical stains, electron microscopy, or other specialized techniques are also detailed in this section. Text tables are not mandatory, but may be added if they contribute to the clarity of the report. Spontaneous lesions that are within the limit of the concurrent controls are recorded in the raw data but are not reported; however, spontaneous changes that show increased incidences and/or severity in treated group(s) compared to the concurrent controls are described and discussed. Findings with increased incidence but which are not considered to be test-article related may be put into context in the results section with suitable scientific justification, including citation of literature references. The organ weight assessment is done both as absolute and relative to body or brain weight and interpreted with gross necropsy observation, clinical pathology, and histopathology findings; the mechanism of action of the compound is also taken into consideration in the assessment [42]. Organ weight changes without macroscopic or microscopic correlation should be interpreted with caution. Equally, the weight of female reproductive tract must be interpreted with caution as it can be influenced by age, sexual maturity, and stage of estrus cycle. In histopathology, it is often not enough to present a lesion in terms of a diagnostic term and numeric incidence and an indication of severity and distribution. It is very important that all the morphological features of a lesion are adequately described, even when a common descriptive term is assigned to it. A detailed description, mostly as free text, could highlight certain distinguishing features that would be pivotal to proper interpretation. For example, the coexistence of inflammatory cell infiltrate and transitional cell hyperplasia in the urinary bladder is more likely to be a response to chronic inflammation rather than a pre-neoplastic proliferative change. But if the additional inflammatory cell infiltrate is not recorded, a different conclusion could be drawn.

Discussion: The main objective of the discussion in a report is to bring together all the relevant information in the study, and beyond, to put the histopathology findings into context. This section incorporates clinical observations, food and water consumption, organ weight, clinical pathology, systemic exposure, and histopathology into a clear and coherent discussion that gives the reader an understanding of the relationship between apparently disparate events. The findings of decedent animals are discussed in conjunction with other data to establish where possible the cause of death. Data from discovery biology on the molecule and published literature are used, where available, to elucidate potential mechanism of toxicity. Similarly, the results of special stains, immunohistochemical stains, electron microscopy, and other specialized techniques are incorporated into the discussion. The discussion of potential mechanism of test-article-related changes must avoid unsupported speculations. In cases where there is an increase in a spontaneous lesion in treated groups compared to concurrent controls, historical control data from the test laboratory are used to determine whether such lesion is within the normal range of the general control population of the species of the animals used. Historical control data must be from recent studies that were conducted in the same laboratory with the same strain, age, and sex as the animals in the study under review, and ideally not be more than five years old. In the absence of control data from the testing laboratory, data from other laboratories fulfilling these criteria may be used. The result of any statistical analysis may be incorporated in this section.

Conclusion: The conclusion of the report is a summary of the main drug-induced changes highlighting the ones that are adverse.

ADVERSE AND NONADVERSE FINDINGS

The principle objective of the evaluation of the chemicals in animal studies is the protection of humans against the adverse effects of these chemicals. The interpretation of the pathology data requires an understanding of the spontaneous background pathology of the species and strains used in the study, the drug disposition and the pharmacology of the test article. In most tissues the adversity of a test-article-related lesion depends to a great extent on the severity of the lesion. But lesions in the brain or retina of the eye are considered adverse even if they are of low severity; this may be due to the lack of reversibility of lesions in the nervous system due to its limited regenerative capacity. The determination of a NOAEL in a study is based on a weight-of-evidence approach taking all the data in the study into consideration. It is generally recognized that evaluating the outcome of complex multi-endpoint toxicology studies is not easy. A comprehensive assessment of toxicological data requires experience to integrate

complex and diverse information into a coherent report. Adverse effect is defined as a biochemical, morphological, or physiological change (in response to a stimulus) that either singly or in combination adversely affects the performance of the whole organism or reduces the organism's ability to respond to an additional environmental challenge [43,44]. Although the endpoints that might be considered adverse in a study are specific to the study, they are generally used in human risk assessment to help clinicians set the starting and/or stopping doses and be aware of potentially serious test-article-related changes. Although the nature of the lesion and its severity play a significant part in reaching that conclusion, there are certain determining factors that are taken into consideration in distinguishing between adverse and nonadverse effects. These factors include whether the effect is an adaptive response, a transient effect, a precursor to a more significant effect, an effect secondary to an adverse effect, or of a severity below threshold of concern. For example, phenobarbital-induced hepatocyte hypertrophy [45], or myocardial hypertrophy due to overwork in response to demand for increased output [46], are considered to be adaptive responses. The NOAEL, which is defined as the highest dose or exposure without adverse effect, is derived from all the data in the study and not only from the pathology report, although the latter is very important. With the increased use of molecular biology in preclinical toxicity studies, transcript data are also taken into consideration in building a weight of evidence to determine the NOAEL [47]. The NOAEL is used to help the clinician to set the initial dose in Phase I clinical trials, if the change is considered relevant in human risk assessment. If the adverse effect is not relevant to humans, then the NOAEL in the animal study is not used in the risk assessment.

Adverse Outcome Pathway

A new concept that has a great potential in risk assessment is the adverse outcome pathways (AOPs). While the NOAEL in preclinical or clinical is assessed at specific time points in a study without much consideration to the process by which such an outcome is reached, the AOPs span the whole spectrum of preclinical and clinical activities. The pathway starts with a molecular initiating event and follows a series of key events before an adverse outcome is determined [48]. In the preclinical phase, considerations are given to the properties of the test article, its mode of action, the species difference in the metabolism of the test article, the histopathological findings in chronic repeat dose studies and carcinogenicity bioassays, and the relevance of the identified changes for the humans. This concept could give a more reliable assessment of adversity outcome and a more robust determination of the NOAEL.

Toxicokinetics: Toxicokinetics (TK) is an integral part of toxicology. It is important for the toxicological pathologists to have an understanding of the basic principles of TK in order to be able to interpret the histopathological findings in the context of systemic exposure. The concepts of C_{max}, the highest concentration of a drug in the blood after a dose, and AUC (area under the concentration curve), which is the overall amount of drug in the bloodstream over time after a dose, are always used to relate toxicity and exposures. For example, acute onset of clinical signs is often thought to be related to C_{max} rather than to AUC. In addition, the pathologist needs to understand the other concepts of TK such as half-life ($T\frac{1}{2}$), volume of distribution, and clearance as they influence systemic exposure and are also impacted by diseases and organic injuries such as liver and kidney injuries [49,50].

Test-article-related histopathological findings are often attributed to systemic exposure to the drug, even if such a relationship cannot be immediately appreciable from the conventional interpretative paradigm, ie, a direct correlation between the incidence and/or severity of the lesion and the exposure achieved. The absence of an association between the lesion and the dose of the drug administered is sometimes interpreted as an absence of causative relationship, especially if the lesion in question is occasionally seen as a background change in the test animal species. A difficult situation arises from time to time, when the animals given the high dose of the test article show an adverse systemic effect that is not present in the lower-dose groups, although the systemic exposures are similar across the groups. In this case, the debate would be whether the lower doses could be considered safe for clinical use, or that the absence of a lesion at the lower doses in the presence of drug concentration that was capable of causing an effect is chance occurrence and therefore risky to be used in the clinic. It could be concluded that there is a no-effect dose but there is no no-effect exposure. Therefore, it is vital that histopathological changes are interpreted in conjunction with all the parameters in the study, including TK data.

SPONTANEOUS AND INDUCED HISTOPATHOLOGICAL LESIONS IN PRECLINICAL STUDIES

Principles of General Pathology

The interpretation of drug-induced histopathological findings in preclinical toxicity studies requires a clear understanding of the basic structural and functional changes that occur in the body as a general response to an injury. These changes could be manifested in the whole animal in the form of overt clinical signs, or in the organ and tissues as morphological changes that can be seen at the light microscopic level or, in the case of subtle changes, at the ultrastructural or molecular levels; in severe cases, drug-induced changes could be fatal to the experimental animal. In conventional preclinical studies, drug-induced changes could be identified at any of these levels. The cell homeostasis is maintained in narrow range of physicochemical conditions, the departure from which results in cell damage.

The structure and function of cells and organs depends on an unimpeded flow of blood circulation that provides and uninterrupted delivery of oxygen and nutrients and the removal of byproducts. The smooth running of the circulation depends on the integrity of the blood vessel walls, sufficient hydrostatic and osmotic pressures, and the maintenance of the blood in a fluid and clot-free status. The perturbation of these elements of blood circulation would lead to hemodynamic disorders such as hyperemia/congestion, edema, hemorrhage, thrombosis, embolism, and infarction. The following is a brief description of these disorders, which are encountered in disease conditions as well as in preclinical toxicity studies.

Hyperemia and congestion refer to the pooling of the blood in the vasculature in a tissue. The first is an active process, normally associated with conditions that demand excess blood in a particular area, such as inflammation; whereas the second, also called passive congestion, is mainly due to impaired outflow of blood, either locally due to obstruction or systemically as a consequence of heart failure.

Edema, which is increased fluid in interstitial tissues, can be the consequence of increased hydrostatic pressure, decreased intravascular osmotic pressure, or obstruction of the flow of lymph. Edema is also a consistent feature of inflammation. It is, therefore, important for the pathologist to distinguish between edema and artifactual expansion of the interstitium caused by nonpathological reasons such as the clear space that is seen around blood vessels in a lung that is inflated by intratracheal infusion of a fixative (Fig. 15.4).

Hemorrhage or extravasation of blood, of low severity and focal distribution, is a common histopathological finding. The lesion, which is generally the result of vascular rupture, can be seen in any tissue or organ, but some tissues are more prone to it. While it is commonly seen in the subcutis of the skin, it is rare in major organs such as the brain or heart. The lungs of animals that are euthanized may show focal areas of fresh hemorrhage, referred to as agonal. In areas of hemorrhage of longer duration, pigment-laden macrophages and inflammatory cell infiltrate are seen. The pigment is from the breakdown of hemoglobin and is positive with Perl's stain for iron. Hyperemia, edema, and hemorrhage can coexist in an inflammatory process.

Thrombus forms when an injury to the endothelial lining of a blood vessel causes the release of tissue coagulation factors and initiates the adhesion of platelets and

(A)   **(B)**

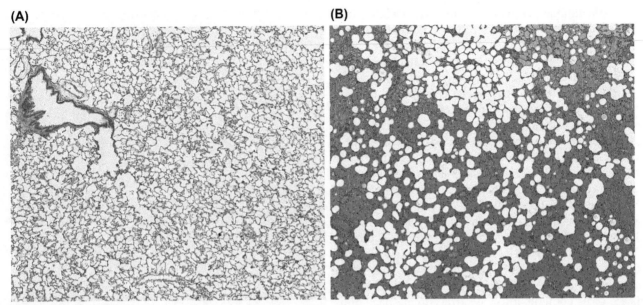

FIGURE 15.4 Rat—lungs. (A) Normal with clear air-filled alveolar spaces. (B) Pulmonary edema, with homogenous pink fluid-filled alveolar space.

fibrin deposition. Over time, a thrombus builds up that can partially or completely occlude a blood vessel; the circulatory crisis it precipitates depends on the size of the artery involved and the presence of collateral blood supply. A thrombus in a coronary artery of the heart could result in myocardial infarction and possible death. Parts of a thrombus could detach and form emboli, which could occlude small-diameter arteries and cause infarction and death of tissues. The clinical consequence depends on the tissue or organ affected. Emboli of liquid or gas nature could have the same adverse effect as solid ones. These hemodynamic disorders are described in detail in Robinson's *Pathologic Basis of Disease* and *Pathologic Basis of Veterinary disease* (see Suggested Further Reading).

Cells can adapt to external stimuli or altered demand by establishing new levels of metabolic or functional activity without impairing their ability to survive. This cellular adaptation, which often correlates with morphological changes, is seen as a response to altered workload. For example, when the workload is reduced, the cell reduces its metabolism and functions and, over time, the cell becomes atrophic. An example of atrophy is seen in an immobilized muscle in which the muscle fibers become reduced in size as the demand for its function is reduced. Cells undergoing atrophy due to reduced demand lose components such as mitochondria, myofilaments, and endoplasmic reticulum. However, these cells are alive and could return to normal morphological and functional status if subjected to increased workload. On the other hand, an increased workload would increase metabolic and functional activity of the cell, and as a result the whole organ becomes larger in size. Cells under this kind of stress increase the size of their

components and would cause the cell to increase in size and become hypertrophic. A good example of cellular hypertrophy through increased workload is seen in the myocardium of patients with valvular stenosis [51]. Hepatocellular hypertrophy is a particular type of hypertrophy with a major impact on drug development, as it could impact the rate at which the test article is metabolized, thus affecting systemic exposure [45]. It is also important in drug–drug interactions, as it could increase the toxicity of a drug through the inhibition of its metabolism by another drug that shares a metabolizing enzyme. The interaction could also result in the reduction of the efficacy of a drug by its rapid elimination through an enhanced metabolism caused by a coadministered drug. Induction of drug metabolizing enzymes in the liver can also lead to thyroid follicular cell hypertrophy, particularly in the rat, through the rapid clearance of thyroxine by the induced enzymes and the subsequent increased attempt of the gland to raise and maintain the level of thyroxine to a physiological level [52].

Two other important adaptive cellular responses are hyperplasia and metaplasia. These are common features in the nasal cavities and larynx in inhalation toxicity studies, due to the irritant effect of administered formulation [53]. The cells of these tissues change into related but more resilient cell types in order to withstand the deleterious effects of the inhaled substance. The respiratory or transitional epithelium of the nasal cavity or larynx changes into squamous epithelia under the influence of an irritant material; squamous epithelium is more resistant to irritation than the other cell types in the upper respiratory tract.

Tissue injury is manifested in a limited number of morphological changes, regardless of the cause.

Nonneoplastic changes generally start with cell degeneration and cell death when the cell can no longer adapt to the altered demand and reaches a "point of no return." The causes of cell death vary, but occur either by necrosis or by apoptosis. Necrosis is an acute process that causes metabolic disruption resulting in changes in the cell membrane, mitochondria, or endoplasmic reticulum. The typical histological features of necrosis include loss of cell architecture, vacuolation, increased eosinophilia, and the dissolution of the cell (karyolysis) (Fig. 15.5). The rupture of the cell elicits an inflammatory response that tries to contain and subsequently eliminate the cause of the injury by diluting it with fluid (edema) and destroying it by phagocytic cells such as polymorphonuclear leukocytes (PMN) and macrophages [54,55] (Fig. 15.6).

The other form of cell death is apoptosis, in which the cell does not swell or undergo abrupt lysis but rather undergoes a slow, orderly resorption, with minimal leakage of its contents into the extracellular space, thus eliciting little or no inflammatory reaction [23]. While necrosis represents an acute, unplanned, and undesired damage to a physiologically normal cell, apoptosis is the physiological deletion of a cell that is no longer fulfilling its role in homeostasis and can be exacerbated by test article. Drug-induced cell damage occurs mainly by necrosis, as the body is subjected to a stimulus that could overwhelm the normal cell processes and result in derangement of the defense mechanism. New drug candidates could also cause an increase in the rate of apoptosis in a tissue that could be interpreted as undesirable. The body attempts to repair the damage by a complicated process that involves inflammation, cell proliferation, formation of granulation tissue, and angiogenesis (new blood vessel growth) [56]. Certain types of drug-induced morphological changes are only a reflection of an interference with the normal movement of cells, as is the case with compounds that interfere with the migration of lymphocytes from the lymphoid system to the hemolymphatic circulation [57,58]. Drug-induced morphological changes could also be due to an interference with the metabolism of nutrients such as fat or glucose. For example, hypoglycemia could cause central as well as peripheral neuropathy [59,60].

The pathogenesis of a lesion is a complicated process that involves various cell types and cell products. A lesion is a dynamic process that is a product of an interaction between an injurious stimulus and the body's reaction to the injury. The study pathologist examines a two-dimensional (5 μm) section of a tissue in order to assess this dynamic process and, depending on the time of onset of the initial injury, various stages of a lesion process, ranging from acute necrosis to fibrosis, may be identified in a specimen. For example, drug-induced myocardial injury initially appears as focal myofiber necrosis within 4h of administration of a cardiac toxicant [61]. Within a few hours, inflammation

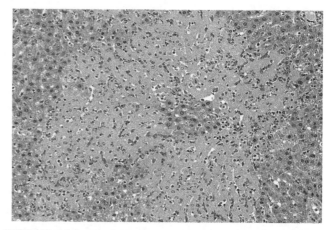

FIGURE 15.5 **Rat–liver.** Acute necrosis, following carbon tetrachloride administration, showing loss of architecture and cells with pale homogeneous cytoplasm.

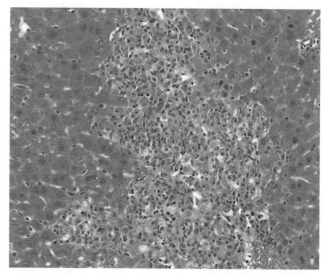

FIGURE 15.6 **Rat—liver.** Necrosis with inflammation, following carbon tetrachloride administration. The inflammatory cells completely replaced the initial injury.

is the predominant feature at the site of injury, and by 72h the damaged area could be completely resolved by fibrosis. The various stages of the lesion process may be evident in the same specimen, especially in a repeat-dose study in which myofiber damage may be initiated after each dose. Whatever the final morphological diagnosis, the pathologist should understand the various stages the development of a lesion goes through to its final state, which may be a return to normal or to a new steady state. The histological appearance of a lesion is often a manifestation of the body's reaction to the injury rather than the injury itself. It is therefore important not only to identify a drug-induced injury but also to distinguish the primary injury (necrosis) from the reaction to it (inflammation, fibrosis, etc.).

Preclinical toxicity studies are designed to induce morphological and/or functional changes, at least at the high dose in one or both sexes of the test species in order to determine the maximum tolerated dose (MTD), as required by regulatory agencies. Subsequent studies use the MTD to ensure maximum sensitivity of the species to the test article. Hazard identification is the recognition and qualitative assessment of test-article-related adverse findings in terms of incidence, severity, and time of onset in treated animals compared with controls. The pathologist must distinguish these findings from artifacts and from spontaneously occurring lesions. Toxicity could also be seen as an increase in the incidence of tumors in a two-year carcinogenicity study or as developmental abnormalities in reproductive toxicity studies.

Spontaneous and Drug-Induced Changes

Spontaneous lesions, many of which are age-related, are commonly seen in laboratory animals used in safety assessment of new drugs [62–66]. A number of factors contribute to their appearance, including age, diet, housing, husbandry, asymptomatic infection, and transport. For example, ad libitum feeding of rats increases the incidence of chronic progressive nephropathy and/or mammary tumors, while restricted or reduced food intake increases longevity and reduces tumor incidences [67]. However, reducing food intake below certain critical levels could cause body weight loss, decreased organ weight, and decreased resistance to infection. Increased light intensity in the room could cause retinal degeneration [68]. The pathologist must bear in mind the housing conditions of the animals when assessing the tissues. It is not easy to distinguish between spontaneous and drug-induced morphological changes, and the study pathologist should be given all the information pertinent to the study. In this section, the general pathology of some of the commonly seen spontaneous and drug-induced lesions will be highlighted. Detailed description of histopathological changes can be found in the literature, some of which is cited here.

Gastrointestinal Tract, Liver, and Pancreas: The digestive system, like the respiratory system, is exposed to the external environmental condition, and as such is exposed to noxious chemical and biological products. The oral cavity is not usually a site of histopathological changes in short-term toxicity studies. The tongue is the only tissue in the oral cavity that is routinely examined in preclinical studies; other tissues are examined as necessary based on clinical or gross abnormalities that become evident during the study. Drug-induced lesions are not common in the tongue. Spontaneous lesions observed in toxicity studies include focal erosion/ulceration and inflammatory cell infiltrate associated with myofiber degeneration. In minipigs, tongue lesions are often seen in oral administration due to mechanical damage caused by biting the tongue during dosing. The teeth

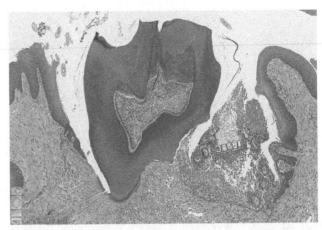

FIGURE 15.7 **Teeth.** Degeneration and inflammation of the teeth and surrounding tissue caused by trauma. Plant material visible.

are not routinely examined histologically in standard toxicity studies unless there are clinical observations or gross abnormalities identified during necropsy. Physical injuries in the oral cavity caused by food particles can become infected and spread to surrounding tissues and cause gross as well as histological changes in the teeth (Fig. 15.7). Therefore it is vital that the teeth are assessed thoroughly during the in-life phase of the study as well as at necropsy. Spontaneous and induced dental lesions have been described in detail by Weber [69]. Gingival lesions are not common in toxicity studies. Histopathological changes such as gingival hyperplasia have been reported in dogs given high doses of immunosuppressant compounds [70].

The salivary gland is adequately sampled and examined in routine toxicity studies. It is worth noting that there is a sex-related dimorphism of the submandibular salivary gland in rats. In the males, the number of mucous cells increases at sexual maturation, whereas in females the number decreases [71]. The most common spontaneous findings in the salivary glands are focal mononuclear inflammatory cell infiltrate, acinar atrophy, and squamous metaplasia. Drug-induced changes have been reported in the salivary glands in rats given antimuscarinic drugs, which affect the secretion of saliva.

The stomach is a common site of pathological changes in oral administration toxicity studies. Spontaneous and induced epithelial changes ranging from minimal focal degeneration and necrosis to erosions and ulcerations are seen in the stomach of laboratory animals. The changes, which are visible grossly as focal areas of dark discoloration on the mucosa, are often seen in animals given high doses of irritant substances (Fig. 15.8). Hyperplasia of the squamous epithelium of the nonglandular mucosa of the forestomach, which could develop into a papilloma, is seen in rodents as a consequence of dosing with irritant chemical products (Fig. 15.9). Treatment of rodents with high doses of selective histamine

FIGURE 15.8   Rat—glandular stomach. Erosion/ulcer. The superficial epithelial cells are necrotic and the underlying cells are showing regenerative hyperplasia.

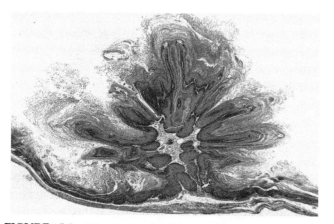

FIGURE 15.9   Mouse—nonglandular stomach. Papilloma. Marked hyperplasia of the squamous epithelium due to persistent irritation.

H-2 receptor blocking agents causes epithelial hyperplasia of the glandular mucosa, which could progress to a neoplastic lesion such as carcinoid or adenocarcinoma [72]. Villus atrophy, hypertrophy, and hyperplasia of the mucosa of the small intestine are seen in laboratory animals. Erosion and ulceration of the intestinal epithelium is seen with certain compounds such as cyclooxygenase 2 (Cox-2) inhibitors. When a compound is suspected of causing intestinal lesions, the tissue is processed by the Swiss roll method, which allows the examination of large areas of the intestine and thus increases the chance of seeing a lesion [12]. The large intestine is not a common site for drug-induced lesions.

The liver is prone to drug-induced injury because of its central role in xenobiotic metabolism, its anatomical structure, and its location within the circulatory system [73]. It is divided into lobules, each one of which is centered on a central vein. Hepatocytes close to the portal area are less susceptible to injury, as they receive blood rich in oxygen and nutrients, while those around the central vein receive the least oxygenated blood and are more susceptible to injury as they constitute the major site of metabolism. Most drugs are not intrinsically toxic to the liver, but it can be injured by a toxic intermediate of the metabolism of the parent compound, or by reactive oxygen species that could also be generated during metabolism. For example, liver injury from acetaminophen ingestion is due to the toxic metabolite N-acetyl-p-benzoquinone imine (NAPQI) [74].

Drug-induced hepatotoxicity is generally associated with changes in clinical chemistry parameters, such as alanine aminotransferase (ALT), aspartate aminotransferase (AST), glutamate dehydrogenase (GLDH), bilirubin, and other biomarkers of injury. Drug-induced liver injury is generally reversible, but sometimes could be fatal to animals as well as humans. However, idiosyncratic liver injury is difficult to predict as it is not dose related or exposure related. Not all liver injuries seen in the toxicity studies are drug induced; spontaneous histopathological changes are commonly seen in short- as well as long-term toxicity studies. These include foci of hepatocellular degeneration/necrosis with inflammatory cell infiltrate. This might not be surprising, as some of the multitude of chemical and biological products absorbed from the gastrointestinal tract as well as those that reach the organ through the systemic route could cause cell injury. Some of the changes seen in the liver could be due to changes in the nutritional status of the animals.

Cytoplasmic rarefaction is an intracytoplasmic vacuolation of hepatocytes, which is seen in most routine preclinical toxicity studies. The change is mainly due to increased glycogen content and is indicative of the nutritional status of the animal; it is more conspicuous in animals that are not fasted prior to necropsy. However, it could be exacerbated by treatment with certain chemicals such as cyclosporine A. Another type of cytoplasmic vacuolation of hepatocytes or bile ducts caused by excessive accumulation of lipid is not uncommon in the liver. This could be due to excessive mobilization of fat from nutritional or other extrahepatic sources, metabolic disorder, or toxic injury. The identification of the type of lipid that accumulates in the cells is not always easy. Phospholipid and nonphosphorylated lipid are usually distinguished histochemically using Oil-red-O or Sudan Black, which identify nonphosphorylated neutral lipid. These methods require nonparaffin-embedded tissue samples, which are normally not available in a standard toxicology study. Fixed frozen samples may be used, but the result is not as good as with nonformalin-fixed samples. Immunohistochemical methods are available that use formalin-fixed paraffin-embedded tissue samples and that label the lysosome-associated membrane protein (LAMP-2), which is indicative of phospholipid accumulation and adipophilin protein for neutral lipid. These methods are used as first-line discrimination between the two types of lipid [24]. If the vacuoles are

(A)   **(B)**

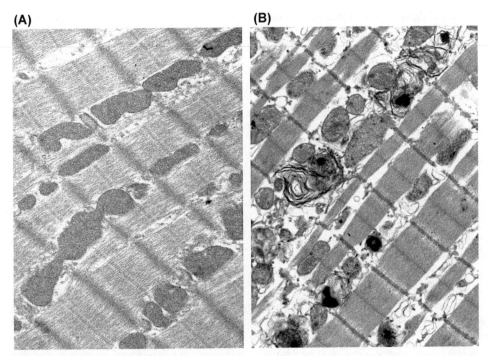

FIGURE 15.10   **Rat heart TEM.** (A) Control showing normal myocardial structure. (B) Lamellar bodies due to phospholipid accumulation.

negative for LAMP-2, it means that it is unlikely that the vacuolation is due to phospholipid accumulation, and there is no need to carry out an electron microscopic examination to show the typical lamellar bodies that are identified with phospholipid accumulation, thus saving time and resources (Fig. 15.10).

Focal areas of coagulative necrosis of hepatocytes, with or without inflammatory cell reaction, are commonly seen in the liver of rodents. Single-cell necrosis is not uncommon in the liver. These changes can confound test-article-related hepatocellular necrosis, which is frequently seen in routine toxicity studies. For example, carbon tetrachloride causes liver injury that starts as focal hepatocellular necrosis which elicits an inflammatory cell response. If the injurious stimulus is removed, the lesion resolves over time by fibrosis; persistence of the stimulus could lead to the exacerbation of the lesions and possible failure of the organ. A common, but mostly test-article-related, lesion in the liver is hepatocellular hypertrophy, which is often associated with increased liver weight. Microscopically, the cells look larger, are pale, and contain granular cytoplasm (ground glass appearance). Electron microscopy of affected cells would show proliferation of the smooth endoplasmic reticulum. The change is mainly associated with chemicals that induce drug-metabolizing enzymes. Spontaneous lesions of the bile ducts are rarely seen in laboratory animals. Bile duct hyperplasia and oval cell proliferation are induced by some chemicals such as D-galactosamine [75]. The gall bladder is infrequently a target tissue for drug-induced morphological changes. The most common spontaneous lesions in the gall bladder are inflammatory cell infiltrate, predominantly lymphocytic, and epithelial vacuolation due to lipid accumulation.

The exocrine part of the pancreas produces digestive enzymes such as trypsinogen, amylase, lipase, and protease. In the exocrine pancreas, acinar atrophy and acinar and peri-islet inflammatory cell infiltrate are seen in control animals; degeneration/necrosis, and inflammation of the pancreas with interlobular edema can also be induced by xenobiotics [76]. The endocrine part of the pancreas is represented by the islets of Langerhans, which secrete hormones such as insulin and glucagon and other polypeptides. Spontaneous lesions seen in the pancreatic islets include inflammatory cell infiltrate, predominantly lymphocytic, and hyperplasia. In both exocrine and endocrine components of the pancreas, neoplastic changes are seen in aging animals.

Cardiovascular: The adverse effects of drugs on the cardiovascular system have been recognized as one of the major causes of drug withdrawal from the market; therefore, the identification of substances that could adversely affect this system is critical in preclinical drug development. Cardiotoxicity manifests itself as functional changes, such as changes in blood pressure, heart rate, or arrhythmia without overt cell injury; or morphological changes where there is cell damage. In the assessment of potential cardiovascular toxicity, it is important to carefully examine the early short-term studies for evidence of subtle heart lesions that could easily be missed. Identifying subtle changes could also help in understanding the pathogenesis of the lesion. Drug candidates can exert their toxicity via a direct effect on cardiomyocytes, such as in the case with anthracycline-induced toxicity, or indirectly as a consequence of functional changes. The anthracyclines, such as doxorubicin, are potent cytotoxic drugs but have serious cardiotoxic side effects. The mechanism of anthracycline-induced cardiotoxicity is not known, but is thought to involve the formation of free radicals, leading to oxidative stress, which may cause apoptosis of cardiac cells or immunological reactions [77,78].

The pattern of injury varies with the pharmacological action of the causative agent. For example, minoxidil causes myocardial injury in the atrium, whereas a β2 adrenoceptor agonist mainly affects the papillary muscles [79–81]. The myocardial injury caused by β2 adrenoceptor agonists and coronary stenosis are the consequences of hypoxia. In the dog, β2 adrenoceptor agonists, when given in sufficiently high doses, cause myocardial necrosis mainly in the papillary muscles as a consequence of tachycardia-induced hypoxia; this could be seen grossly as a focal area of discoloration. The papillary muscles are metabolically more active and therefore more prone to hypoxic injury. On the other hand, phosphodiesterase (PDE) inhibitors cause vasodilation and vascular wall distension that could lead to vascular wall necrosis. Drug-induced vascular injury is difficult to distinguish from spontaneous change; however, there are some morphological features that could help distinguish between the two types of lesions, especially if the drug-induced injury is identified early on before the change becomes part of the general biological response to injury [82,83].

Spontaneous lesions of the cardiovascular system are frequently seen in the laboratory animals used in safety assessment studies; they are among the most commonly encountered findings in nonhuman primates. In the heart, the most commonly observed change is focal myocardial degeneration/necrosis with or without inflammatory cell infiltrate, predominantly mononuclear. This type of lesion, which is still referred to as "cardiomyopathy" in the literature, is seen more frequently in long-term toxicity studies. In rats, cardiomyopathy is more frequent in the Sprague Dawley than in the Wistar Hannover strain. Less common are focal areas of myocardial fibrosis, which appears to be a sequel of myofiber degeneration and can occur more frequently in aged rodents in carcinogenicity studies. Spontaneous lesions of the blood vessels are not uncommon. In the dog, necrotizing arteritis, a particular type of vascular injury involving the external coronary arteries, is occasionally seen [84]. The lesion, which affects all the different layers of the blood vessel wall, is characterized by proliferation of the intima and degeneration and necrosis and inflammatory cells in the media and adventitia of the affected blood vessels (Fig. 15.11). Although the lesion is thought to be part of the spectrum of the beagle pain syndrome, it is sporadic, mainly asymptomatic, and is mostly seen as an incidental finding. The occurrence of the lesion is low, but can occur in a high-dose group and might obscure a potential drug-related change. Once a cardiovascular lesion is identified, there are a limited number of avenues open for further investigation. A time course study might be conducted to establish the time of onset of the lesion and to measure biomarkers for cardiac injury, such as cardiac troponin, which is widely used to detect subclinical myocardial injury. In aging mice, atrial thrombus is frequently seen in long-term studies, which is often considered a factor contributing to the death of the animal.

In the past, histopathological changes involving the heart valves were rarely reported in preclinical studies. However, since the discovery of cardiac valve injury associated with the antiobesity drug combination fenfluramine–phentermine and ALK5 inhibitor, the need to assess valvular changes has been accentuated [85–87].

Urinary: The kidney is a major organ of drug metabolism and excretion of drugs from the body and a common site of spontaneous and drug-induced changes. Although histological examination of tissue samples detects morphological evidence of kidney injury in preclinical animal studies, it is important to detect any injury as early as possible both for the safety of the patient and for drug attrition. Biomarkers that are used to detect and help locate sites of renal injury in toxicity studies include KIM-1 (kidney injury molecule-1), albumin, TFF3 (trefoil factor 3), clusterin, total protein, cystatin C, and β2-microglobulin [88,89]. There are a number of common spontaneous lesions in the kidney that can be exacerbated by treatment. These include nephropathy, which shows cortical tubular basophilia; tubular degeneration and/or dilation; cast formation; and in some cases, inflammatory cell infiltration (Fig. 15.12). Other changes include pelvic dilation (also referred to as hydronephrosis) which could be a developmental malformation or the result of obstruction in the lower part of the renal system, such as the renal pelvis or ureters. Tubular basophilia is a common spontaneous change in the kidney in routine toxicity studies. This change, which represents regenerating tubules following mild tubular degeneration/necrosis, could be exacerbated by treatment. Papillary necrosis is seen with some drugs such as NSAIDs [90–92]. The microscopic appearance of the change can range from focal necrosis limited to the tip of the papilla to extensive necrosis involving the whole of the renal papilla. The papillary necrosis could cause obstruction and the development of cortical tubular changes. Changes in the cortical and papillary tubules are often associated with changes in routine kidney function test parameters, such as urine specific gravity, plasma blood urea nitrogen (BUN), and serum creatinine. If the morphological changes involve the glomeruli, protein will be detected in the urine.

Chronic progressive nephropathy (CPN) is a syndrome of pathological lesions seen in older rats. The

(A) **(B)**

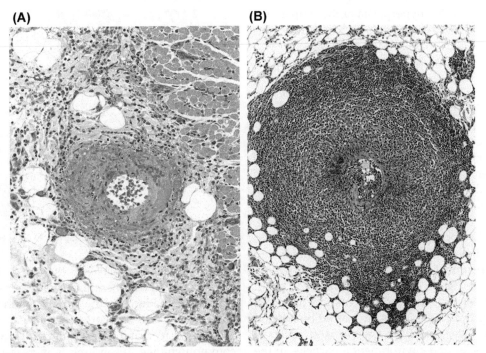

FIGURE 15.11   **Dog heart.** (A) Drug-induced acute vascular necrosis and inflammation with areas of hemorrhage. (B) Spontaneous juvenile arteritis involving a coronary artery.

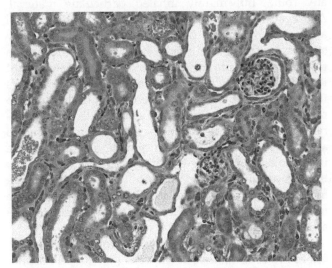

FIGURE 15.12   **Rat—kidney.** Chronic nephropathy with cortical tubule changes.

change is characterized by renal tubular degeneration/regeneration with associated tubular dilation, inflammatory cell infiltrate, eosinophilic cellular casts, and fibrosis [93–95]. It is only encountered in chronic toxicity studies and carcinogenicity bioassays. Another type of nephropathy recognized in male rats is caused by an abnormal accumulation of α2μm-microglobulin in kidney lysosomes. The protein is normally present in renal tubular epithelium and is seen histologically as hyaline droplets of various sizes; but exposure to a variety

of chemicals such as unleaded gasoline, decalin, and the antihelminthic agent levamisole is known to exacerbate the condition by increasing its concentration in lysosomes principally through impaired decrease in its breakdown and clearance [96]. The accumulation of the protein results in cell damage and the development of nephropathy. Female rats do not normally show hyaline droplets, as they do not excrete this protein. The hyaline droplet accumulation is also associated with renal tumorigenesis in this species [97–99]. The protein can be stained immunohistochemically using poly- or monoclonal antibodies. The excretion of this protein has no functional impact on the animals.

There are various mechanisms of drug-induced renal injury. Drugs such as the anthracycline antibiotic doxorubicin cause direct effects on cellular constituents. A variety of other drugs, including penicillin, ampicillin, and sulfonamides, cause renal injury through an immune-mediated mechanism. Hemodynamic perturbation result in renal injury due to ischemia. Pelvic dilation, also referred to as hydronephrosis, is seen as a spontaneous change in laboratory animals that could be developmental or the result of an obstruction. In the former, the dilation is usually unilateral and not associated with morphological changes in the tubules or transitional epithelium lining the pelvis. Obstructive pelvic dilation due to precipitation of crystals is often accompanied by tubular dilation and degeneration and necrosis [100]. The dilated tubules may contain eosinophilic and granular casts.

In the urinary bladder, hyperplasia of the transitional epithelial cells is occasionally seen in toxicity studies due to persistent irritation from excreted chemicals or naturally formed uroliths. Neoplastic lesions of the urinary system are rare. However, prolonged irritation by irritant substances or uroliths could result in transitional-cell tumors. Similar tumors were induced by prolonged treatments with dual agonists of peroxisome proliferator-activated receptors (PPARgamma + alpha) agonists [101]. In male mice, a change referred to as urological syndrome is seen in male mice; this is often a factor contributing to death in these animals. Macroscopically, the bladder is distended with fluid, and histologically there are eosinophilic inclusions that block the flow of urine. A detailed description of neoplastic and nonneoplastic lesions of the kidney and urinary bladder is available in the INHAND document of the urinary system [102].

Respiratory: Drugs reach the respiratory system through inhalation or via the blood circulation; however, most of the drug-induced injuries are caused by inhaled xenobiotics. The nasal cavity is the point of entry of inhaled test particles and environmental particles in the body. The cavity has a complicated structure, the proper assessment of which needs knowledge of the histological features of the different areas. The histotechnologists must generate good quality and consistent sections for the pathologist to carry out this assessment. The nasal cavity contains a number of different epithelial structures that react to exogenous materials. These are the squamous epithelium; the respiratory epithelium, which contains goblet cells and cilia; the transitional epithelium; and the olfactory epithelium. These epithelial structures are affected by and react to inhaled particulate material. The changes that are observed in the nasal cavity depend on the epithelial type affected.

The various epithelia, bones, and cartilages in the nasal cavity react to irritation in a number of ways. Mild irritation may cause degeneration and necrosis of the epithelium with hyperplasia, metaplasia, and inflammatory cell infiltrate. Severe irritation might cause erosion and ulceration and loss of the epithelium, which in cases may be superimposed with infections that could lead the nasal turbinates to be filled with inflammatory cells and cell debris. Similar to the nasal cavity, the larynx may also show a number of changes in the different parts of the tissue in response to the irritation of inhaled substances. These include degeneration and necrosis, with or without inflammatory cell infiltrate, of the respiratory epithelium of the ventrolateral areas, the ventral pouch, and the squamous epithelium of the arytenoid projections. Squamous metaplasia, and in some cases degeneration and necrosis of the ventral cartilage, are common changes induced by inhaled substances.

The trachea and the tracheal bifurcation (carina) are also important areas for irritation by inhaled substances.

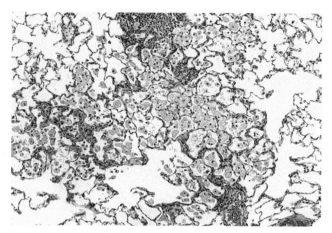

FIGURE 15.13 **Rat—lung.** Aggregates of alveolar macrophage.

Common changes seen in these tissues include loss of cilia, epithelial degeneration, and metaplasia. The bronchiolar epithelium in the lung contains mucin-secreting cells that become prominent when the epithelium is exposed to irritating substances. However, the most common change in the lung is increased aggregates of alveolar macrophages, which may be foamy in appearance (Fig. 15.13). The function of macrophages is to ingest and remove substances that reach the lung by any route, but mainly inhaled particulate material. Aggregates of macrophages are seen in treated as well as in control animals, particularly rats, used in toxicity studies, but more commonly in inhalation studies as a response to the administered test article. It is important to distinguish between increased alveolar macrophages that are part of the adaptive mechanism of the lungs to maintain normal function, and a change that could significantly modify the function of the organ and lead to an adverse outcome. The interpretation of an increase in alveolar macrophages becomes problematic when there is an inflammatory process in which the change in the macrophages could be considered as part of the inflammatory process rather than an independent test-article-related change [103].

A common cause of foamy macrophages is phospholipid accumulation in the cells [104,105]. Phospholipidosis is a systemic condition that is seen in animals following treatment with cationic amphiphilic drugs (CAD). Confirmation of the diagnosis of phospholipid accumulation is conventionally done by identification of ultrastructural lamellar bodies using transmission electron microscopy. The lung is also a site for inflammatory reaction due to inhaled noxious substances. The degree of inflammation ranges from the minimal focal and clinically inconsequential to a fulminant life-threatening reaction that the animal manifests clinically. Another common spontaneous lesion in the dog lung is alveolar fibrosis, which is usually subpleural and with little or no inflammatory cell infiltrate. Foreign-body granulomas of varying sizes are seen in the lungs of laboratory animals as incidental findings. In intravenous route studies, this type of lesion is commonly seen, with most of them containing hair shafts. These are emboli of fragments of hair that were introduced into the bloodstream through the needle.

The lung is also a common site for proliferative lesions. Primary benign and malignant neoplastic lesions of bronchial/bronchiolar (bronchial and alveolar origin) are commonly seen in two-year rodent carcinogenicity bioassays. In addition, the lungs are a common site for metastatic tumors.

Endocrine: The organs and glands of the endocrine system comprise a number of different cell types that produce many different hormones and must be assessed thoroughly. Hormones control normal physiological processes, maintaining the body's homeostasis. Compounds that are toxic to the endocrine system may result in hypothyroidism, diabetes mellitus, hypoglycemia, reproductive disorders, and cancer. Exposure to endocrine-disrupting chemicals such as polychlorinated biphenyls (PCBs) and DDT have caused a host of toxic effects in wildlife, including impaired reproduction and development. Other endocrine toxicants, such as persistent organochlorine pesticides and dioxins, are being studied for their possible role in promoting hormone-induced cancers (such as breast cancer) and in lowering sperm counts and male fertility. The evaluation of the endocrine system for evidence of hormone imbalance requires an understanding of the normal structure and function of the organs and tissues of the system. This helps the pathologist to distinguish between normal physiological variations and histopathological changes indicative of endocrine disruption. This can be more evident in the reproductive tracts, which normally undergo cyclical in morphological appearance that can be disrupted by endocrine toxicants.

Spontaneous and drug-induced neoplastic and nonneoplastic lesions are commonly seen in the endocrine glands in routine toxicity studies; some of these changes are the result of perturbation of the hormonal balance. The various organs of the endocrine system are functionally interdependent and are regulated by feedback mechanisms [106]; for example, drug-induced testicular atrophy caused by inhibition of testosterone secretion causes hypertrophy of pituitary gonadotrophs [107]. Endocrine-disrupting substances can affect the hypothalamus–pituitary–ovarian axis and produce morphological changes in the female reproductive tract in laboratory animals. Potent synthetic estrogenic compounds such ethinyl estradiol cause ovarian atrophy, uterine hypertrophy, and keratinization of the vaginal epithelium in rats, while weaker estrogenic compounds, such as genistein, may cause slight mucification of the vaginal epithelium. Persistent stimulation by estrogen could result in polycystic ovaries and endometrium gland hyperplasia [108]. Similarly, the effects of changes in an endocrine gland can be seen in a non-endocrine gland, as is the case with the effects of changes in the prolactin cells of the pituitary gland being detected in the mammary gland.

Endocrine tumors are common in laboratory animals, but deciding whether an increase in such tumors is a chance occurrence or the consequence of treatment is not easy. As tumors are age-related, a large proportion of control and treated animals will develop tumors at some point before their death. Therefore, the number of animals needed to determine whether a difference in the incidence of a tumor is statistically significant must be large [109]. When test-article-related changes are identified in an endocrine gland, immunohistochemical stains may be used to identify the cell type involved. In the pituitary, there are various cell types that are under the influence of different hormones. Similarly, in the pancreatic islets, IHC is used to identify insulin and glucagon-secreting cells.

Adrenal Gland: The adrenal glands are paired organs that are located above the kidney. The gland has an outer cortex and an inner medulla. The cortex is further divided into three zones, which secrete different hormones: zona glomerulosa, zona fasciculate, and zona reticularis, which secrete mineralcorticoids, glucocorticoids, and androgen hormones, respectively. The inner medulla secretes the catecholamines adrenalin and noradrenalin. Morphological changes in any of these regions could lead to a perturbation of the hormone it secretes, which could result in clinical or biochemical changes in the body. For example, the zona glomerulosa of the adrenal gland produces mineralcorticoids, the most important of which is aldosterone, which maintains normal blood pressure by facilitating the reabsorption of sodium and water. If the animals on treatment exhibit test-article-related changes in cardiovascular parameters and/or changes in blood electrolytes, the pathologist would consider the zona glomerulosa of the adrenal gland as a potential target tissue.

Thyroid/Parathyroid: In laboratory animals used in toxicology studies, the thyroid gland is located ventrolaterally and on either side of the trachea; or ventrally as in minipigs. The thyroid is under the trophic influence of follicular stimulating hormone (FSH), a pituitary-secreted hormone. There are two cell types in the thyroid: (1) follicular epithelial cells, which produce triiodothyronine (T3) and thyroxine (T4); and (2) C-cells, which produce calcitonin. T3 and T4 regulate basic metabolic processes, and calcitonin regulates calcium and phosphorus homeostasis. Thyroid follicular cell hypertrophy is seen in rats as an adaptive response to compounds that cause induction of drug-metabolizing enzymes that cause rapid clearance of thyroid hormone

[52]; in carcinogenicity studies this could result in increased follicular cell tumors. Spontaneous nonneoplastic changes are not frequently seen in laboratory animals, but include cysts of the ultimobranchial bodies or thyroglossal duct and inflammatory cell infiltrate, predominantly mononuclear cell; an immune-mediated inflammation called Hashimoto's disease is occasionally diagnosed in dogs.

Pituitary: The pituitary gland is divided into adenohypophysis (anterior lobe) and neurophypophysis (posterior lobe); the intermediate lobe is considered part of the anterior lobe. The anterior lobe contains five different cell types that produce different hormones with different functions in the body. These cells and the hormones they secrete are somatotrophs (growth hormone); lactotrophs (prolactin); corticotrophs (adenocorticotrophic hormone, or ACTH); thyrotrophs (thyroid stimulating hormone, or TSH); and gonadotrophs follicular stimulating hormone (FSH and luteinizing hormone, or LH). Spontaneous nonproliferative lesions are not common in the pituitary gland. Cysts of varying sizes are frequently seen in rats and dogs in short- as well as long-term studies. Drug-induced hypertrophy of the cells of the pars distalis is not uncommon, and proliferative lesions are common in old rats and mice. Pituitary adenomas have a high incidence in rodent carcinogenicity studies; immunohistochemistry can be used to identify the cell of origin of the tumors. Carcinomas are not common in the pituitary; this may be due to the fact that a definitive diagnosis of carcinomas is based on the spread of the tumor dorsally to the brain rather than on cell morphology, such as cellular pleomorphism or atypia, and that ventrolateral spread to the base of the skull and surrounding tissues may not be routinely sampled. Drug-induced changes are often associated with changes in the endocrine system that affect the various trophic cells in the organ. Dopaminergic substances can affect the prolactin homeostasis and cause an increased demand for prolactin, thus causing hypertrophy of the prolactin-producing cells in the pituitary.

Immune System: The immune system is a highly regulated network of lymphoid cells that requires continued renewal, activation, and differentiation for full immunological competence. The immune cells are either circulating cells such as leukocytes and monocytes or resident in tissues such as macrophages. Single or repeat-dose administration of novel compounds could result in changes in the immune system such as decreased or increased immune function, autoimmunity, and allergic reaction. Cell depletion, dysregulation, and functional deficits within this cellular network can result in a pathological process marked by altered responses to antigens or increased susceptibility to infectious agents and tumor cells. Immunosuppression occurs following exposure of humans or animals to a wide range of chemicals. Standardized protocols using animal models for immunotoxicological investigations may permit prediction of potential human toxicity [110].

A two-tier testing system is employed in rodents, in which the first tier is general toxicity screening, including enhanced histopathology of lymphoid organs [111]. The second tier consists of more specific studies of immune function including host resistance tests or mechanistic studies. The general screening of the immune system is assessed in all toxicity studies. In short-term studies such as dose-range-finding studies, the assessment may be limited to one or two lymphoid tissues such as the spleen and thymus. In GLP-compliant studies, which may be considered as Tier 1, the lymph nodes and hematopoietic tissues of the bone marrow are evaluated in addition to the spleen and thymus. The first tier will detect hematological changes such as increased or decreased circulating leukocytes, changes in the immune system organ weights and/or histology, and changes in serum globulins that occur without a plausible explanation. These changes can be viewed as a sign of immunosuppression in the absence of other plausible causes such as genotoxicity, hormonal effects, or liver enzyme induction. This weight-of-evidence approach would be sufficient to demonstrate the immunotoxic potential of a drug.

The thymus undergoes involution with age. It is therefore difficult to distinguish between an involution that is a physiological phenomenon and a pathological condition. The thymus is also an organ that is affected by nonspecific stress often associated with the adverse clinical condition, or by the test article. Acute stress caused by rapid deterioration of the clinical condition of the animal could result in lymphocytolysis in the thymus and must be distinguished from drug-induced immunotoxicity.

Compounds that modulate hematopoiesis and migration of the lymphoid cells cause effects in the immune system. The two functional zones of the spleen—the hematogenous red pulp and the lymphoid white pulp—are examined; the latter for changes in the lymphoid population in the periarterial lymphoid sheath (PALS), the follicles, and in the marginal zone. Drug-induced increased or decreased cellularity may be seen in the spleen, thymus, lymph nodes, and bone marrow. Immunohistochemistry and flow cytometry can be used to evaluate changes in lymphocyte subsets in peripheral blood and lymphocyte trafficking in lymphoid tissues including T-cells, B-cells, and NK cells using CD marker specific to the various cell types. Flow cytometry is not routinely used in Tier 1 toxicity studies; however, where there is evidence of real or potential effect on the immune system, its inclusion in Tier 1 and 2 studies is warranted.

Spontaneous lesions in the immune system are not common, with the exception of the thymic atrophy/involution described earlier.

Skin, Bone, and Muscle: The skin is the largest barrier in the body against external injurious stimuli; it is also one of routes of drug administration in the body. In a standard oral toxicity study, a sample of the skin is taken from a small area of the body, usually abdominal, whereas in a topical dermal study, samples from the areas of application are examined. The skin is a complex structure consisting of the epidermis, hair follicles, and associated sweat and sebaceous glands; and the dermis; all of which are susceptible to injury. The epidermis is made of thick keratinized squamous epithelium that can withstand mild trauma or irritation. Damage to the epidermal layer caused by physical, chemical or biological agents elicits reactions that range from epithelial hyperplasia and hyperkeratosis in injuries limited to the epidermis, to severe inflammation in the case epidermal necrosis, which breaches the basement membrane and brings the injurious elements into contact with blood vessels in the underlying dermis. The reaction may involve the hair follicles and adnexa and could extend to the deep dermis and affect the muscles and fat. Knowledge of the hair follicle cycle is important for a proper assessment of the changes in this tissue. The skin is also a common site for all types of neoplastic lesions affecting epithelial as well as mesenchymal tissues. A comprehensive list and description of neoplastic and nonneoplastic lesions of the skin in rat and mouse can be found in the INHAND publication [112].

In routine toxicity studies, a limited number of muscles are examined, usually the quadriceps femoris or gastrocnemius. Other muscles are examined as needed, and some skeletal muscles are processed as part of other tissues. These include the intercostal muscles, which are processed with the sternum, the periorbial muscle around the eye, and the muscle around the esophagus. Although they are not submitted for examination, sometimes they provide valuable information. The predominant cell type of the skeletal muscle is the myofiber or myocyte. The myofibers are generally classified into two types: Type I (slow twitch), which is rich in myoglobin and mitochondria and energy production is by oxidation; and Type II (fast twitch), which is low in myoglobin and mitochondria and in which energy production is by glycolysis.

Spontaneous lesions of the skeletal muscles in short-term toxicity studies comprise myofiber degeneration with associated inflammatory cell infiltrates, which are predominantly macrophages. Atrophy of skeletal muscles frequently affecting hind limbs is seen in aging rats and mice in carcinogenicity studies. This change is often associated with neuropathy of the sciatic nerve [113].

Careful examination of the sciatic nerve and the spinal root ganglions of affected animals would normally show degenerative changes. Drug-induced skeletal muscle injury is rare in toxicology studies. Glucocorticoids are known to cause muscle injury when given at high doses; but in animals given low doses of the drug, such as in inhalation toxicity studies, muscle injury is not a significant feature. Lesions of the skeletal muscle occur with lipid-lowering compound of the hydroxymethylglutaryl-coenzyme A (HMG-CoA) reductase inhibitor class.

Bone remodeling is a dynamic complex process that is regulated by the interplay between circulating hormones and locally produced factors that act to regulate osteoblast and osteoclast activity [114]. Spontaneous lesions of the bone are not frequently seen in toxicity studies. Healed fractures, of unknown cause, but probably due to traumatic injury, are sometimes seen in animals on a study. In aging animals in long-term toxicity studies, cartilage and synovial changes are frequently seen in the joints of the feet and legs. Drug-induced cartilage changes are seen animals dosed with quinolone antibiotics, with juvenile dogs showing increased susceptibility to the arthropathy, which appears grossly as vesicles on the cartilage surface. Histologically, the lesion is characterized by erosions of cartilage surfaces of varying degree of severity with chondrocyte degeneration and necrosis and thinning of the cartilage matrix [115]. Treatment with corticosteroids cause thinning of the bone through increased bone resorption during remodeling [114].

Male Reproductive Tract: In all species, the testis is a dynamic organ that goes through various stages in a defined period. The initiation of the spermatogenic cycle is under the influence of testosterone, which is produced by the interstitial cells under the influence of luteinizing hormone (LH). The number of stages in the spermatogenic cycle varies between species, with the rat having 14 stages, the mouse 16, the dog 8, the nonhuman primate 12 [116], and the minipig 8 [117]. It is a complicated tissue that comprises tubules in various stages of development and maturation starting from spermatogonia (types A and B) through spermatoytes (primary and secondary) and spermatids (round and elongated) and ending in spermatozoa, which are shed into the lumen of the tubules. There are also the supporting Sertoli cells in the seminiferous tubules and the testosterone-producing interstitial (Leydig) cells. The germinal cells in the tubules are associated with each other in a specific ways in the various stages. It is important that the pathologist is familiar with the general structure of the seminiferous tubules and morphologies of the germ cells at the various stages of the cycle in order to be able to identify subtle test-article-related changes. All the different organs and tissues of the male reproductive tract are susceptible to spontaneous and induced changes. These tissues are under hormonal influence, and as such, changes that occur here might be secondary to a primary effect on an endocrine gland. The study pathologist must be familiar with the normal morphology of the testes in the different animal species used in preclinical studies and the various stages of spermatogenesis. Only with good understanding of the stages would the pathologist be able to identify stage-specific changes. Compared to other species, minipigs have extensive interstitial cells that could be misdiagnosed as hyperplasia (Fig. 15.14). Nonneoplastic changes in the testes is problematic in the dog, in which hypospermatogenesis, characterized by loss of one or more germ cell layers, is commonly seen in animals used in toxicity studies [118,119]. Given the low number of animals used in a dog studies, it is difficult to determine if this type of change is test-article-related or preexisting.

Testicular change could be due to a primary effect on the germ or Sertoli cells, or it could be due to changes in hormones of the hypothalamus–pituitary–testes axis, which results in reduced testosterone production by Leydig cells; the hormone is essential for spermatogenesis. In either case, there is depletion of the germ cells, which could result in decreased male fertility. The first indication of testicular change is normally seen at necropsy, when a change in the size of the organ in treated animals is noted. Changes in organ weight (absolute and relative to body weight) in treated animals compared to controls are important indicators of test-article effect. Both the macroscopic and organ weight changes alert the pathologist to potential microscopic changes. Spontaneous changes in the testes include hypoplasia and

atrophy of the seminiferous epithelium, which may be unilateral or bilateral, and is frequently seen in control as well as in animals treated with xenobiotics [120]. In nonrodent animals, hypospermatogenesis is preferred over atrophy as a diagnostic term. The change could affect a few tubules or an entire testis. Segmental hypoplasia, which normally affects a group of tubules, is considered a developmental abnormality and should be distinguished from spontaneous or test-article-related atrophy. In affected tubules, only Sertoli cells are visible. As a dynamic organ, the testis is a target organ for any substance that affects cells undergoing cell division. For example, synthetic nucleoside analogs, which mimic their physiological counterparts, cause a testicular effect presumably through inhibition of cell division by incorporation into DNA and RNA, which is the same mechanism by which they inhibit tumor cell division and viral replication [121,122]. Proliferative changes are commonly seen in long-term rodent studies. In two-year carcinogenicity studies in rodents, interstitial cell tumors are commonly observed; however, seminomas, which are tumors of the germinal cells, are rare. Spontaneous background changes seen in the epididymides include foci of inflammatory cell infiltrate, predominantly lymphocytic; and sperm granulomas of varying sizes, some of which could cause obstruction of the tubule, which could result in dilatation of the seminiferous tubules of the testis. Decreased sperm content in the epididymides and/or sloughed degenerating germ cells is seen when the testes show atrophy/hypospermatogenesis.

Accessory sex organs such as the prostate and seminal vesicles are not commonly targets for drug-induced

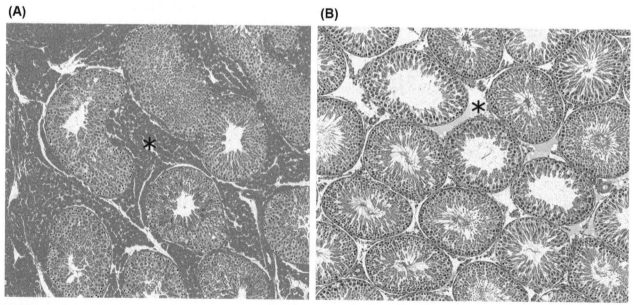

(A)   **(B)**

FIGURE 15.14 **Testes.** (A) Minipig—extensive interstitial (Leydig) cells, which is a normal feature in this species. (B) Rat—showing scant interstitial cells.

changes. Spontaneous histopathological changes in the prostate gland include acinar and lobular atrophy, inflammatory cell infiltrate, and abscesses. In long-term studies, neoplastic lesions, mainly adenoma and adenocarcinoma, are seen. Drug-induced changes in the prostate gland are not frequently encountered. However, hormone modulating particularly prolactin and testosterone could cause pathological changes such as hypertrophy, hyperplasia, and neoplasia given that the gland is under the influence of both hormones [123] Increased testosterone administration causes marked increase in prostate weight, which is due to hypertrophy of the gland [124].

Female Reproductive Tract: Similar to the male reproductive organs, the female reproductive organs are under the influence of hormones, and any perturbation of the hormonal balance could be manifested in morphological changes. The female reproductive system also goes through cyclic changes that are under hormonal control. It is important that the pathologist understands the structure of the various parts of the system at the various stages of the cycle, particularly in rodents in which the cycle is more uniform and short in duration. For nonrodent species, staging of the estrus cycle is not easy given the lengthy duration of some of its phases. In rodents, the ovary, uterus, and vagina morphologies are used to determine the estrus cycle. These organs and tissues undergo distinct changes that correspond to each of the four stages of the cycle (proestrus, estrus, metaestrus, and diestrus). Pathologists need to be familiar with these changes and the stages they represent.

Nonneoplastic spontaneous lesions are not frequently seen in the female reproductive tract in laboratory animals [125]. Cystic endometrial hyperplasia is commonly seen in aged rats and mice. Neoplastic lesions frequently seen in the uterus include endometrial polyp, adenocarcinoma, leiomyoma, leiomyosarcoma, and histiocytic sarcoma. In addition to smooth muscle tumors, granular cell tumor is occasionally seen in the vagina. In nonhuman primates, cysts in and around the ovary are common incidental findings in all ages. The most common tumor of the ovary in the macaque is the granulosa cell tumor. Drug-induced lesions of the female reproductive tract are generally the consequence of hormonal perturbation. An early indication of such changes is an effect on the estrus cycle in rodents in repeat-dose toxicity studies.

Mammary Gland: There is sexual dimorphism in the morphology of the mammary gland in the rat. The male mammary gland is mainly acinar whereas in the females it is tubular. Knowledge of this dimorphism is essential, as drug-induced feminization of the male mammary gland is not uncommon. The normal physiology of the mammary gland is under the influence of hormones and the histopathological changes commonly seen in this tissue are reflective of hormonal status of the animal. Therefore, the tissue must be examined in conjunction with the reproductive tract. Familiarity with the normal morphology of the mammary gland in the different phases of the estrus cycle is very important for the identification of treatment-related changes. Spontaneous and induced nonneoplastic lesions are not common in the mammary gland but mammary gland tumors are common in rodent bioassays [126]. They are presented as palpable masses that can grow in size to a degree that makes movement difficult for the animal; the overlying skin can also become ulcerated. These masses are often one of the main reasons the animals are killed prematurely in carcinogenicity studies. A detailed description of the common neoplastic and nonneoplastic lesions in the mammary gland is given in the INHAND document for this tissue [127].

Nervous System: Neurotoxicity is not commonly seen in laboratory animals. Drug-induced neurotoxicity has been reported with various compounds [128]. Potential neurotoxicity in the animals may be reflected in their behavior after dosing. Signs such as tremor, ataxia, head shaking, and splayed legs or similar gaits are recognized as reflecting CNS disturbances. Spontaneous nonneoplastic lesions of the central and peripheral nervous system are occasionally seen in laboratory animals used in preclinical toxicity studies [129]. These changes include dilation of the ventricles in the brain, focal inflammatory cell infiltrate (mainly around blood vessels), and degeneration of neurons or nerve fibers. The latter is predominantly seen in aging rats in long-term toxicity studies [130].

Histopathological changes such as vacuolation of the neurons in the white matter, which could be due to demyelination, must be distinguished from vacuolation that is the result of processing artifact [131]. Similarly, focal mineralization of various sizes in the brain and spinal cord needs to be distinguished from artifacts caused by small fragment of bone or bone sawdust embedded in the tissue during necropsy.

Spontaneous tumors of the central nervous system are seen in rodent carcinogenicity studies; they are seen more frequently in rats than in mice [132]. It is beyond the scope of this chapter to list the types of tumors and the reader is advised to consult reference books that describe these lesions in detail [133–135]. Drug-induced lesions of the nervous system are rare and are always considered adverse regardless of the severity of the lesion, given the limited potential of this organ for recovery upon cessation of treatment.

Eye: The main parts of the eye that normally show morphological changes are the cornea, the lens, and the retina. Every anatomic part of the eye is susceptible to drug-induced injury. Spontaneous ocular lesions seen in preclinical studies are of variable incidence and are age dependent. Since these lesions cannot be distinguished from drug-induced changes on morphological basis, it makes the interpretation of the latter difficult. Pathological changes are seen in any of the structures of the eye. Because of its anatomical position, the cornea is the most susceptible to external injuries and infectious diseases. Among the spontaneous ocular changes observed in toxicity studies are focal corneal ulceration with epithelial hyperplasia and revascularization, lenticular degeneration (cataract), anterior uveitis, and retinal degeneration. In long-term studies, the most predominant change observed in the eye is posterior subcapsular cataract and retinal atrophy [136,137]. Retinal toxicity is a special type of neural toxicity and needs to be distinguished from light-induced retinopathy in albino rodents [63]. Drug-induced retinal changes are always considered as adverse in drug development, and often lead to the termination of the drug. Diagnosing drug-induced early retinal changes may be challenging even for an experienced pathologist. With prolonged treatment, entire layers of the retina might disappear. Some drugs that bind to melanin could accumulate in the eye of pigmented test species and cause toxicity. However, the binding of drugs to the melanin in the eye is not predictive of ocular toxicity [138].

RISK ASSESSMENT

The toxicological pathologist's role in drug development goes beyond tissue assessment and the generation of a report. It extends to the risk assessment of new drug candidates. Risk assessment is a multidisciplinary exercise that evaluates all the preclinical data generated from the various disciplines. The objective is to highlight the hazards that have been identified in terms of their nature and severity and their potential impact on human health. The hazard is put into the context of its relevance to humans, exposure–response relationship, reversibility, and whether the mechanism of toxicity is known. Other factors taken into consideration in risk assessment include the indication for which the drug is being developed, its safety margin, and comparison of its toxicity profile with those of existing similar therapies. Except for drugs that cause exclusively functional changes such as cardiovascular or neurological, most of the risk assessment is based on the results from general toxicity and carcinogenicity studies. The toxicological pathologist's contribution in these studies, in terms of data generation and interpretation, is very important.

In summary, histopathology is a subjective evaluation of tissues and organs. In preclinical safety evaluation of potential medicinal drugs, accurate diagnosis of test-article-related injuries and their proper interpretation

are the cornerstone of human safety. The training and experience of the pathologist and the consistent use of the internationally agreed standardized nomenclature and diagnostic criteria will reduce the subjectivity of the diagnosis and increase the quality of the data and report and increase the value of the risk assessment of the hazard identified in these studies.

References

[1] Lexchin J. Drug withdrawals from the Canadian market for safety reasons, 1963–2004. Can Med Assoc J 2005;172(6):765–7.

[2] Bakke OM, Manocchia M, de Abajo F, Kaitin KI, Lasagna L. Drug safety discontinuations in the United Kingdom, the United States, and Spain from 1974 through 1993: a regulatory perspective. Clin Pharmacol Ther 1995;58:108–17.

[3] Abraham J, Davis C. A comparative analysis of drug safety withdrawals in the UK and the US (1971–1992): implications for current regulatory thinking and policy. Social Sci Med 2005;61(5):881–92.

[4] Jacobs AC, Hatfield KP. History of chronic toxicity and animal carcinogenicity studies for pharmaceuticals. Vet Pathol 2012;50(2):324–33.

[5] Morton D, Sistare FD, Nambiar P, Turner OC, Radi Z, Bower N. Regulatory forum commentary: alternative mouse models for future cancer risk assessment. Toxicol Pathol 2014;42:799–806.

[6] Crismann JW, Goodman DG, Hildebrandt PK, Robert R, Maronpot RR, Prater DA, et al. Best practices guideline: toxicological histopathology. Toxicol Pathol 2004;32:126–31.

[7] Burkhardt E, Ryan AM, Germann P-G. Practical aspects of discovery pathology. Toxicol Pathol 2002;30(1):8–10.

[8] Jayo MJ, Watson DD, Wagner BJ, Bertram TA. Tissue engineering and regenerative medicine: role of toxicological pathologists for an emerging medical technology. Toxicol Pathol 2008;36:92–6.

[9] Bolon B, Barle-Thomas E, Bradley A, Ettlin RA, Franchi CAS, George C. International recommendations for training future toxicological pathologists participating in regulatory-type, nonclinical toxicity studies. Toxicol Pathol 2010;38:984–92.

[10] Svendsen O. The minipig in toxicology. Exp Toxicol Pathol 2006;57:335–9.

[11] Damsch S, Eichenbaum G, Tonelli A, Lammens L, Van den Bulck K, Feyen B. Gavage-related reflux in rats: identification, pathogenesis, and toxicological implications (review). Toxicol Pathol 2011;39:348–60.

[12] Moolenbeek C, Ruitenberg EJ. The 'Swiss roll': a simple technique for histological studies of rodent intestine. Lab Anim 1981;15:57–9.

[13] Latendresse JR, Warbritton AR, Jonassen H, Creasy DM. Fixation of testes and eyes using a modified Davidson's fluid: comparison with Bouin's fluid and conventional Davidson's fluid. Toxicol Pathol 2002;30(4):524–33.

[14] Renne R, Fouillet X, Maurer J, Assaad A, Morgan K, Hahn F. Recommendation of optimal method for formalin fixation of rodent lungs in routine toxicology studies. Toxicol Pathol 2001;29(5):587–9.

[15] Ruehl-Fehlert C, Kittel B, Morawietz G, Deslex P, Keenan C, Mahrt CR. Revised guides for organ sampling and trimming in rats and mice – part 1: a joint publication of the RITA and NACAD groups. Exp Toxicol Pathol 2003;55(2–3):91–106.

[16] Kittel B, Ruehl-Fehlert C, Morawietz G, Klapwijk J, Elwell MR, Lenz B. Revised guides for organ sampling and trimming in rats and mice – part 2: a joint publication of the RITA and NACAD groups. Exp Toxicol Pathol 2004;55(6):413–31.

[17] Morawietz G, Ruehl-Fehlert C, Kittel B, Bube A, Keane K, Halm S. Revised guides for organ sampling and trimming in rats and mice – part 3: a joint publication of the RITA and NACAD groups. Exp Toxicol Pathol 2004;55(6):433–49.

[18] Engebretsen KVT, Skårdal K, Bjørnstad S, Marstein HS, Skrbic B, Sjaastad I, et al. Attenuated development of cardiac fibrosis in left ventricular pressure overload by SM16, an orally active inhibitor of ALK5. J Mol Cell Cardiol 2014;76:148–57.

[19] Young JF. Histopathological examination of the rat nasal cavity. Fundam Appl Toxicol 1981;1:309–12.

[20] Emons J, Chagin AS, Malmlöf T, Lekman M, Tivesten Å, Ohlsson C. Expression of vascular endothelial growth factor in the growth plate is stimulated by estradiol and increases during pubertal development. J Endocrinol 2010;205:61–8.

[21] Evans KD, Oberbauer AM. Alendronate inhibits VEGF expression in growth plate chondrocytes by acting on the mevalonate pathway. Open Orthop J 2009;3:83–8.

[22] Suzuki M, Teruya S, Fujii E, Misawa Y, Sugimoto T. Immunohistochemical identification of T- and B-lymphocytes in formalin-fixed, paraffin-embedded rat sections. J Toxicol Pathol 2002;15:167–70.

[23] Elmore S. Apoptosis: a review of programmed cell death. Toxicol Pathol 2007;35(4):495–516.

[24] Obert LA, Sobocinski GP, Bobrowski WF, Metz AL, Rolsma MD, Altrogge DM. An immunohistochemical approach to differentiate hepatic lipidosis from hepatic phospholipidosis in rats. Toxicol Pathol 2007;35:728–34.

[25] Potts SJ. Digital pathology in drug discovery and development: multisite integration. Drug Discov Today 2009;14(19/20):935–41.

[26] Thompson SW, Luna LG. An atlas of artifacts encountered in the preparation of microscopic tissue sections. Springfield (Illinois): Charles Thomas Publisher; 1978.

[27] McInness E. Artifacts in histopathology. Comp Clin Pathol 2005;13:100–8.

[28] Ettlin RA, Kuroda J, Plassmann S, Prentice DE. Successful drug development despite adverse preclinical findings part 1: processes to address issues and most important findings. J Toxicol Pathol 2010;23(4):189–211.

[29] McInnes EF, Scudamore CL. Review of approaches to the recording of background lesions in toxicologic pathology studies in rats. Toxicol Lett 2014;229(2014):134–43.

[30] http://www.toxpath.org/inhand.asp.

[31] http://goreni.item.fraunhofer.de/back_standard.php.

[32] Morton D. The Society of Toxicological Pathology's position on statistical methods for rodent carcinogenicity. Toxicol Pathol 2001;29:670–2.

[33] Peto R, Pike MC, Day NE, Gray RG, Lee PN, Parish S. Guidelines for simple, sensitive significance tests for carcinogenic effects in long-term animal experiments. In: IARC monographs on the evaluation of the carcinogenic risk of chemicals to humans, supplement 2, long-term and short-term screening assays for carcinogens: a critical appraisal. Lyon: IARC Press; 1980. p. 311–426.

[34] Shackelford C. Qualitative and quantitative analysis of non-neoplastic lesions in toxicology studies: quantitative toxicological pathology. Toxicol Pathol 2002;30(1):93–6.

[35] Ward JM, Thoolen B. Grading of lesions. Toxicol Pathol 2011;39:745–6.

[36] McKay JS, Barale-Thomas E, Bolon B, George C, Hardisty J, Manabe SW. A commentary on the process of peer review and pathology data locking. Exp Toxicol Pathol 2010;63(2011):197–8.

[37] Boorman GA, Wolf DC, Francke-Carroll S, Maronpot RR. Pathology peer review. Toxicol Pathol 2010;38:1009–10.

[38] Morton D, Sellers RS, Barale-Thomas E, Bolon B, George C, Hardisty JF. Recommendations for pathology peer review. Toxicol Pathol 2010;38:1118–27.

[39] Japanese Society of Toxcologic Pathology. Panel discussion: regulatory perspective for pathology data. J Toxicol Pathol 2009;22:209–27.

[40] Hardisty JF, Willson GA, Brown WR, McConnell EE, Frame SR, Gaylor DW. Pathology Working Group review and evaluation of proliferative lesions of mammary gland tissues in female rats fed ammonium perfluorooctanoate (APFO) in the diet for 2 years. Drug Chem Toxicol 2010;33(2):131–7.

[41] Morton D, Kemp RK, Francke-Carroll S, Jensen K, McCartney J, Monticello TM. Best practice for reporting pathology interpretations within GLP toxicology studies. Toxicol Pathol 2006;34:806–9.

[42] Sellers RS, Morton D, Michael B, Roome N, Johnson JK, Yano BL, et al. Society of toxicologic pathology position paper: organ weight recommendations for toxicology studies. Toxicol Pathol 2007;35:751.

[43] Lewis RW, Billington R, Derbyune E, Gamer A, Land B, Carpanini F. Recognition of adverse and nonadverse effects in toxicity studies. Toxicol Pathol 2002;30(1):66–74.

[44] Karbe E, Williams GM, Lewis RW, Kimber I, Foster PMD. Distinguishing between adverse and non-adverse effects. J Toxicol Pathol 2001;14:321–5.

[45] Greaves P. Histopathology of preclinical toxicity studies – interpretation and relevance in drug safety evaluation. 3rd ed. San Diego: Academic Press; 2007. p. 470–2.

[46] Matsuo T, Carabello BA, Nagatomo Y, Koide M, Hamawaki M, Zile MR. Mechanisms of cardiac hypertrophy in canine volume overload. Am J Physiol 1998;275(Heart Circ Physiol 44):H65–74.

[47] Rouquie D, Friry-Santini C, Schorsch F, Tinwell H, Bars R. Standard and molecular NOAELs for rat testicular toxicity induced by flutamide. Toxicol Sci 2009;109(1):59–65.

[48] Vinken M. The adverse outcome pathway concept: a pragmatic tool in toxicology. Toxicology 2013;312:158–65.

[49] Benet LZ, Zia-Amirhosseini P. Basic principles of pharmacokinetics. Toxicol Pathol 1995;23(2):115–23.

[50] Caldwell J, Gardner I, Swales N. An introduction to drug disposition: the basic principles of absorption, distribution, metabolism and excretion. Toxicol Pathol 1995;23,102–14.

[51] Landesburg G, Zhou W, Aversano T. Tachycardia-induced subendocardial necrosis in acutely instrumented dogs with fixed coronary stenosis. Anesth Analg 1999;88:973–9.

[52] Hood A, Hashmi R, Klaassen CD. Effects of microsomal enzyme inducers on thyroid-follicular cell proliferation, hyperplasia, and hypertrophy. Toxicol Appl Pharmacol 1999;160:163–70.

[53] Morgan DL, Price HC, O'Connor RW, Seely JC, Ward SM, Wilson RE. Upper respiratory tract toxicity of inhaled methylvinyl ketone in F344 rats and B6C3F1 mice. Toxicol Sci 2000;58(1):182–94.

[54] Slauson DO, Cooper BJ. Mechanisms of disease: a textbook of comparative general pathology. 3rd ed. Mosby; 2001.

[55] Golstein P, Kroemer G. Cell death by necrosis: towards a molecular definition. Trend Biochem Sci 2006;32(1):37–43.

[56] Wallace JL. Prostaglandins, NSAIDs, and gastric mucosal protection: why doesn't the stomach digest itself? Physiol Rev 2008;88:1547–65.

[57] Schwab SR, Cyster JG. Finding a way out: lymphocyte egress from lymphoid organs. Nat Immunol 2007;8(12):1295–301.

[58] Laird DJ, von Andrian UH, Wagers AJ. Stem cell trafficking in tissue development, growth, and disease. Cell 2008;132:612–30.

[59] Mohseni S. Hypoglycemic neuropathy. Acta Neuropathol 2001;102:413–21.

[60] Ohshima J, Nukada H. Hypoglycaemic neuropathy: microvascular changes due to recurrent hypoglycaemic episodes in rat sciatic nerve. Hypoglycaemic neuropathy: microvascular changes due to recurrent hypoglycaemic episodes in rat sciatic nerve. Brain Res 2002;947:84–9.

[61] Clements P, Brady S, York M, Berridge B, Mikaellan I, Nicklaus R. Time course characterization of serum cardiac troponins, heart fatty acid-binding protein, and morphologic findings with isoproterenol-induced myocardial injury in the rat. Toxicol Pathol 2010;38:703–14.

[62] Peter CP, Burek JD, van Zwieten MJ. Spontaneous nephropathies in rats. Toxicol Pathol 1986;14:91–100.

[63] Robertson J. Spontaneous renal disease in dogs. Toxicol Pathol 1986;14:101–8.

[64] Suwa T, Nyska A, Haseman JK, Mahler JF, Maronpot RR. Spontaneous lesions in control B6C3F1 mice and recommended sectioning of male accessory sex organs. Toxicol Pathol 2002;30:228–34.

[65] Chamanza R, Parry NMA, Rogerson P, Nicol JR, Bradley AE. Spontaneous lesions of the cardiovascular system in purpose-bred laboratory non-human primates. Toxicol Pathol 2006;34:357–63.

[66] Foster JR. Spontaneous and drug-induced hepatic pathology of the laboratory beagle dog, the cynomolgus macaque and the marmoset. Toxicol Pathol 2005;33:63–74.

[67] Keenan KP, Ballam GC, Dixit R, Soper KA, Laroque P, Mattson BA. The effects of diet, overfeeding and moderate dietary restriction on Sprague-Dawley rat survival, disease and toxicology. J Nutr 1997;127:851S–6S.

[68] Pérez J, Perentes E. Light-induced retinopathy in the albino rat in long-term studies: an immunohistochemical and quantitative approach. Exp Toxicol Pathol 1994;46(3):229–35.

[69] Klaus Weber J. Induced and spontaneous lesions in teeth of laboratory animals. J Toxicol Pathol 2007;20:203–13.

[70] Nyska A, Waner T, Zlotogorski A, Pirak M, Scolnik M, Nyska M. Oxodipine-induced gingival hyperplasia in beagle dogs. Am J Pathol 1990;137(3):737–9.

[71] Hatakeyama D, Sashima M, Suzuki A. A sexual dimorphism of mucous cells in the submandibular salivary gland of rat. Arch Oral Biol 1987;32(10):689–93.

[72] Brittain RT, Jack D, Reeves JJ, Stables R. Pharmacological basis for the induction of gastric carcinoid tumors in the rat by loxtidine, an unsurmountable histamine H2-receptor blocking drug. Br J Pharmacol 1985;85:843–7.

[73] Sturgill MG, Lambert GH. Xenobiotic-induced hepatotoxicity: mechanisms of liver injury and methods of monitoring hepatic function. Clin Chem 1997;43(8):1512–26.

[74] Rowden AK, Norvell J, Eldridge DL, Kirk MA. Updates on acetaminophen toxicity. Med Clin North Am 2005;89:1145–59.

[75] Taye A, El-Moselhy MA, Hassan MKA, Ibrahim HM, Mohammed AF. Hepatoprotective effect of pentoxifylline against D-galactosamine-induced hepatotoxicity in rats. Ann Hepatol 2009;8(4):364–70.

[76] Chadwick KD, Fletcher AM, Parrula MC, Bonner-Weir S, Mangipudy RS, Janovitz E, et al. Occurrence of spontaneous pancreatic lesions in normal and diabetic rats – a potential confounding factor in the nonclinical assessment of GLP-1-based therapies. Diabetes 2014;63:1303–14.

[77] Arola OJ, Saraste A, Pulkki K, Kallajoki M, Parvinen M, Voipio-Pulkki L. Acute doxorubicin cardiotoxicity involves cardiomyocyte apoptosis. Cancer Res 2000;60:1789–92.

[78] Schimmel KJM, Richel DJ, van den Brinkc RBA, Guchelaard H-J. Cardiotoxicity of cytotoxic drugs. Cancer Treat Rev 2004;30:181–91.

[79] Mesfin GM, Robinson FG, Higgins MJ, Zhong W-Z, Ducharme DW. The pharmacological basis of the cardiovascular toxicity of minoxidil in the dog. Toxicol Pathol 1995;23(4):498–506.

[80] Sandusky GE, Mean JR, Todd GC. Comparative cardiotoxicity in dogs given inotropic agents by continuous intravenous infusion. Toxicol Pathol 1990;18:268–78.

[81] Balazs T, Earl FL, Bierbower GW, Weinberger MA. The cardiotoxic effects of pressurized aerosol isoproterenol in the dog. Toxicol Appl Pharmacol 1973;26:407–17.

[82] Clemo FA, Evering WE, Snyder WP, Albassam MA. Differentiating spontaneous from drug-induced vascular injury in the dog. Toxicol Pathol 2003;31(Suppl.):25–31.

[83] Louden C, Morgan DG. Pathology and pathophysiology of drug-induced arterial injury in laboratory animals and its implications on the evaluation of novel chemical entities for human clinical trials. Pharmacol Toxicol 2001;89,158–70.

[84] Kemi M, Usui T, Narama I, Takahashi R. Histopathology of spontaneous panarteritis in beagle dogs. Jpn J Vet Sci 1990;52(1):55–61.

[85] Elangbam C. Drug-induced valvulopathy: an update. Toxicol Pathol 2010;38:837–48.

[86] Droogmans S, Franken PR, Garbar C, Weytjens C, Cosyns B, Lahoutte T. In vivo model of drug-induced valvular heart disease in rats: pergolide-induced valvular heart disease demonstrated with echocardiography and correlation with pathology. Eur Heart J 2007;28:2156–62.

[87] Donnelly KB. Cardiac valvular pathology: comparative pathology and animal models of acquired cardiac valvular diseases. Toxicol Pathol 2008;36:204–17.

[88] Dieterle F, Sistare F, Goodsaid F, Papaluca M, Ozer JS, Webb CP. Renal biomarker qualification submission: a dialog between the FDA-EMEA and Predictive Safety Testing Consortium. Nat Biotechnol 2010;28(5):455–62.

[89] Stern AW, Ritchey JW, Hall B, Ketz-Riley CJ, Genova SDG. Nonsteroidal anti-inflammatory drug-associated renal papillary necrosis in a white-tailed deer (Odocoileus virginianus). J Vet Diagn Invest 2010;22:476–8.

[90] Brix AE. Renal papillary necrosis. Toxicol Pathol 2002;30(6):672–4.

[91] Tsuchiya Y, Takahashi Y, Jindo T, Furuhama K, Suzuki KT. Comprehensive evaluation of canine renal papillary necrosis induced by nefiracetam, a neurotransmission enhancer. Eur J Pharmacol 2003;475:119–28.

[92] Hard GC, Khan KN. A contemporary overview of chronic progressive nephropathy in the laboratory rat, and its significance for human risk assessment. Toxicol Pathol 2004;32:171–80.

[93] Hard GC, Seely JC. Histological investigation of diagnostically challenging tubule profiles in advanced chronic progressive nephropathy (CPN) in the Fischer 344 RaT. Toxicol Pathol 2006;34:941–8.

[94] Seely JC, Hard GC. Chronic progressive nephropathy in the rat: review of pathology and relationship to tumorigensis. J Toxicol Pathol 2008;21:199–205.

[95] Cuervo AM, Hildebrand H, Bomhard EM, Dice JF. Direct lysosomal uptake of alpha 2-microglobulin contributes to chemically induced nephropathy. Kidney Int 1999;55(2):529–45.

[96] Swenberg JA. α2u-Globulin nephropathy: review of the cellular and molecular mechanisms involved and their implications for human risk assessment. Environ Health Perspect 1993;101(Suppl. 6):39–44.

[97] Kurata Y, Diwan BA, Lehman-McKeeman L, Rice JM, Ward JM. Comparative hyaline droplet nephropathy in male F344/NCr rats induced by sodium barbital and diethylacetylurea, a breakdown product of sodium barbital. Toxicol Appl Pharmacol 1994;126(2):224–32.

[98] Hard GC. Some aids to histological recognition of hyaline droplet nephropathy in ninety-day toxicity studies. Toxicol Pathol 2008;36:1014–7.

[99] Doi AM, Hill G, Seely J, Hailey JR, Kissling G, Bucher JR. α2u-Globulin nephropathy and renal tumors in national toxicology program studies. Toxicol Pathol 2007;35(4):533–40.

[100] Perazella MA. Crystal-induced acute renal failure. Am J Med 1999;106:459–65.

[101] Cohen SM. Effects of PPARγ and combined agonists on the urinary tract of rats and other species. Toxicol Sci 2005;87(2):322–7.

[102] Frazier KS, Seely JC, Hard GC, Betton G, Burnett R, Nakatsuji S, et al. Proliferative and nonproliferative lesions of the rat and mouse urinary system. Toxicol Pathol 2012;40:14S–86S.

[103] Lewis DJ, Williams TC, Beck SL. Foamy macrophage responses in the rat lung following exposure to inhaled pharmaceuticals: a simple, pragmatic approach for inhaled drug development. J Appl Toxicol 2014;34:319–31.

[104] Nonoyama T, Fukuda R. Drug-induced phospholipidosis – pathological aspects and its prediction. J Toxicol Pathol 2008;21(1):9–24.

[105] Halliwell WH. Cationic amphiphilic drug-induced phospholipidosis. Toxicol Pathol 1997;25(1):53–60.

[106] Harvey PW, Rush KC, Cockburn A. Endocrine and hormonal toxicology. Chichester: John Wiley & Sons Ltd.; 1999. p. 15–6.

[107] Harvey PW, Rush KC, Cockburn A. Endocrine and hormonal toxicology. Chichester: John Wiley & Sons Ltd.; 1999. p. 3–5.

[108] Arifin E, Shively CA, Register TC, Cline JM. Polycystic ovary syndrome with endometrial hyperplasia in a cynomolgus monkey (Macaca fascicularis). Vet Pathol 2008;45:512–5.

[109] Capen CC. Pathogenic mechanism of endocrine disease in domestic and laboratory animals. J Toxicol Pathol 2002;15:1–6.

[110] Dean JH, Thurmond L. Immunotoxicology: an overview. Toxicol Pathol 1987;15(3):265–71.

[111] Elmore SA. Enhanced histopathology of the immune system: a review and update. Toxicol Pathol 2012;40(2):148–56.

[112] Mecklenburg L, Kusewitt D, Kolly C, Treumann S, Adams ET, Diegel K, et al. Proliferative and non-proliferative lesions of the rat and mouse integument. J Toxicol Pathol 2013;26(Suppl. 3):27S–57S.

[113] Gopinath C, Mowat V. The musculoskeletal system and skin. In: Atlas of toxicological pathology. 2014. p. 233.

[114] Samir SM, Malek HA. Effect of cannabinoid receptors 1 modulation on osteoporosis in a rat model of different ages. J Physiol Pharmacol 2014;65(5):687–94.

[115] Nagai A, Nayazaki M, Morita T, Furubo S, Kizawa K, Fukumoto H, et al. Comparative articular toxicity of garenoxacin, a novel quinolone antimicrobial agent in juvenile beagle dogs. J Toxicol Sci 2002;27(3):219–28.

[116] Dreef HC, Van Esch E, De Rijk EP. Spermatogenesis in the cynomolgus monkey (Macaca fascicularis): a practical guide for routine morphological staging. Toxicol Pathol 2007;35(3):395–404.

[117] McAnulty PA, Barrow P, Marsden E. Reproductive system including studies in juvenile minipig. In: McAnulty PA, Dayan AD, Ganderup N-C, Hastings KL, editors. The minipig in biomedical research. Boca Raton (USA): CRC Press Taylor & Francis Group; 2012.

[118] Rehm S. Spontaneous testicular lesions in purpose-bred beagle dogs. Toxicol Pathol 2000;28(6):782–7.

[119] Sato J, Doi T, Wako Y, Hamamura M, Kanno T, Tsuchitani M, et al. Histopathology of incidental findings in beagles used in toxicity studies. J Toxicol Pathol 2012;25:103.

[120] Goedken MJ, Kerlin RL, Morton D. Spontaneous and age-related testicular findings in beagle dogs. Toxicol Pathol 2008;36:465–71.

[121] Jordheim LP, Durantel D, Zoulim F, Dumontet C. Advances in the development of nucleoside and nucleotide analogues for cancer and viral diseases. Nat Rev Drug Discov 2013;12:447–64.

[122] Movahed E, Nejati V, Sadrkhanlou R, Ahmadi A. Toxic effect of acyclovir on testicular tissue in rats. Iran J Reprod Med 2013;11(2):111–8.

[123] Herrera-Covarrubias D, Coria-Avila GA, Chavarría Xicoténcatl P, Fernández-Pomares C, Manzo J, Aranda-Abreu GE, et al. Long-term administration of prolactin or testosterone induced similar precancerous prostate lesions in rats. Exp Oncol 2015;37(1):13–8.

[124] Auger-Pourmarin L, Roubert P, Chabrier PE. Endothelin receptors in testosterone-induced prostatic hypertrophy in rats. Jpn J Pharmacol 1998;77(4):307–10.

[125] Cline M, Wood CE, Vidal JD, Tarara RP, Buse E, Weinbauer GF. Selected background findings and interpretation of common lesions in the female reproductive system in macaques. Toxicol Pathol 2008;36:142S–63S.

[126] Russo IH, Russo J. Mammary gland neoplasia in long-term rodent studies. Environ Health Perspect 1996;104:938–67.

[127] Rudmann D, Cardiff R, Chouinard L, Goodman D, Kuttler K, Marxfeld H, et al. Proliferative and nonproliferative lesions of the rat and mouse mammary, Zymbal's, preputial, and clitoral glands. Toxicol Pathol 2012;40:7S–39S.

[128] James SE, Burden H, Burgess R, Xie Y, Yang T, Massa SM, et al. Anti-cancer drug induced neurotoxicity and identification of Rho pathway signaling modulators as potential neuroprotectants. Neurotoxicology 2008;29:605–12.

[129] McMartin DN, O'Donoghue JL, Morrissey R, Fix AS. Nonproliferative lesions of the nervous system in rats, NS-1. Washington, DC. In: Maronpot R, editor. Guides for toxicologic pathology STP/ARP/AFIP, pathology of the mouse: reference and atlas (1999). Vienna (USA): Cache River Press; 1997. p. 452–70.

[130] Greaves P. Histopathology of preclinical toxicity studies – interpretation and relevance in drug safety evaluation. 3rd ed. San Diego: Academic Press; 2007. p. 874.

[131] Krinke GJ, Zurbriggen A. Spontaneous demyelinating myelopathy in aging laboratory mice. Exp Toxicol Pathol 1997;49:501–3.

[132] Krinke GJ, Kaufmann W, Mahrous AT, Schaette P. Morphologic characterization of spontaneous nervous system tumors in mice and rats. Toxicol Pathol 2000;28(1):178–92.

[133] Jones TC, Mohr U, Hunt RD. Nervous system: monograph on pathology of laboratory animals. New York: International Life Sciences Institute, Springer-Verlag Berlin Heidelberg; 1988.

[134] Turusov V, Mohr U. Pathology of tumors in laboratory animals. Volume 1 – tumours of the rat. International Agency for Research and Cancer; 1990.

[135] Turusov V, Mohr U. Pathology of tumors in laboratory animals. Volume 2 – tumours of the mouse. Lyon (France): International Agency for Research and Cancer; 1994.

[136] Wegener A, Kaegler M, Stinn W. Frequency and nature of spontaneous age-related eye lesions observed in a 2-year inhalation toxicity study in rats. Ophthalmic Res 2002;34:281–7.

[137] Mukaratirwa S, Petterino C, Naylor SW, Bradley A. Incidence and range of spontaneous lesions in the eye of Crl:CD-1(ICR)BR mice used in toxicity studies. Toxicol Pathol 2015;43(4):530–5.

[138] Leblanc B, Jezequel S, Davies T, Hanton G, Taradach C. Binding of drugs to eye melanin is not predictive of ocular toxicity. Regul Toxicol Pharmacol 1998;28:124–32.

Suggested Further Reading for Comprehensive Toxicological Pathology

[1] Vinay Kumar V, Abbas AK, Aster JC. Robbins & Cotran pathologic basis of disease. 9th ed. Saunders; 2014.

[2] Zachary J, McGavin MD. Pathologic basis of veterinary disease. 5th ed. Mosby; 2011.

[3] Greaves P. Histopathology of preclinical toxicity studies – interpretation and relevance in drug safety evaluation. 4th ed. San Diego: Academic Press; 2012.

[4] Haschek WM, Rousseaux CG, Wallig MA. Fundamentals of toxicologic pathology. 3rd ed. San Diego: Academic Press; 2013.

[5] Gopinath C, Prentice DE, Lewis DJ. Atlas of experimental toxicological pathology. Lancaster (England): MTP Press Limited; 1987.

[6] Gopinath C, Mowat V. The atlas of toxicological pathology. Human Press; 2014.

[7] McInnes EF. Background lesions in laboratory animals – a color atlas. Saunders Elsevier; 2012.

[8] Mohr U, Dungworth DL, Capen CC, editors. Pathobiology of the aging rat, volume 1. Washington (DC): ILSI Press; 1992.

[9] Mohr U, Dungworth DL, Capen CC. In: Pathobiology of the aging rat, volume 2. Washington (DC): ILSI Press; 1994.

[10] Mohr U, Dungworth DL, Capen CC, Carlton WW, Sundberg JP, Ward JM. Pathobiology of the aging mouse, volume 1 and 2. Washington (DC): ILSI Press; 1996.

[11] Sahota PS, Popp JA, Hardisty JF, Gopinath C, editors. Toxicologic pathology, preclinical safety assessment. CRC Press, Taylor and Francis Group; 2013.

16

Molecular Pathology: Applications in Nonclinical Drug Development

L. Oyejide, O.R. Mendes, I. Mikaelian

A Comprehensive Guide to Toxicology in Nonclinical Drug Development, Second Edition
http://dx.doi.org/10.1016/B978-0-12-803620-4.00016-5

INTRODUCTION

The purpose of molecular pathology is to elucidate the mechanisms of disease by identifying molecular and pathway alterations. At the core of this still-evolving discipline is the application of classical and novel techniques developed in biochemistry, cell biology, molecular biology, proteomics, and genetics, to the evaluation of pathological processes. Within the pharmaceutical industry, the effectiveness of molecular pathology as an adjunct to histopathology in nonclinical drug development is well recognized [1]. Many of the techniques of molecular pathology rely on the use of labeled antibodies and nucleic acid probes and are either slide-or fluid-based. In this chapter, we provide brief descriptions of the basic principles underlying the slide-based techniques and emphasize their applications in the nonclinical phase of drug development. Specifically, we will discuss the nonclinical applications of immunohistochemistry (IHC), immunofluorescence (IF), in situ hybridization (ISH), microRNA (miRNA) analysis, digital pathology imaging, and toxicogenomic evaluation. This chapter will focus less on technical aspects, which are readily available in many excellent texts and journal reviews, but more on the utility of these techniques in facilitating various aspects of the drug discovery and development processes.

The basis of IHC is the binding of labeled antibodies to epitopes in tissue sections on a slide and the detection of the colored reaction product or fluorescence in tissue sections [2]. Here, we elaborate on the basic methodologies of IHC and IF, the challenges associated with the laboratory practice of these techniques, and the utility of IHC or IF as a tool to identify and monitor the expression of target epitopes in tissues in nonclinical studies. Applications of IHC as a tool to monitor efficacy, identify tissue-based biomarkers (BMs), assess toxicity, and evaluate possible unexpected cross-reactivity of biotherapeutics with human and animal tissues will be examined.

In situ hybridization is the process of establishing a noncovalent sequence-specific interaction between a labeled complementary DNA or RNA strand (ie, probe) and a specific DNA or RNA sequence of interest in a section of tissue [3]. The approach of slide-based ISH lends itself well as a complementary tool to histopathology. This chapter examines the various ways by which the application of ISH may contribute to the resolution of drug-discovery problems in the nonclinical space.

Biomarkers are characteristic biological properties that can be detected and measured in fluids or tissues. In this chapter, we discuss BMs of tissue injury that can be readily detected in histopathology tissue sections, or other biological specimens, using IHC, IF, ISH, or other techniques. Additionally we describe the relevance of

molecular imaging tools for the analysis and interpretation of data for the monitoring of drug efficacy and hazard assessment. We also touch briefly on the use of toxicogenomic analysis to investigate mechanisms of xenobiotic-induced injury.

Toxicogenomics (TGX) is a scientific tool based on the acquisition, interpretation, and storage of information about gene expression and associated protein activity within particular cells or tissue(s) of an organism in response to toxic substances. Here we review and discuss the available evidence indicating that judicious nonclinical application of TGX can potentially detect toxicity of candidate compounds earlier and at lower drug doses than current gold-standard techniques, including histopathology. In addition, we examine TGX signatures that have been found useful for the prediction of long-term toxicities, including carcinogenicity as well as those for the characterization of novel BMs. We present data to show that TGX may be more sensitive than gold-standard hematology parameters to identify hemolytic anemia or than histopathology to identify focal/multifocal lesions.

Finally, we briefly examine the biology and nonclinical utility of microRNAs (miRNAs). MicroRNAs are 19–23 nucleotide-long, noncoding, ribonucleic acid (RNA) molecules that are highly conserved across species. By binding to complementary sequences on target messenger RNA (mRNA), miRNAs can cause degradation of target mRNAs. Because circulating miRNAs are stable and detectable by quantitative real-time PCR (qRTPCR), which eliminates the need to develop specific enzyme-linked immunosorbent assay (ELISA)-based methods for each marker, they represent a unique opportunity to develop BMs of diseases that may overcome some of the technological limitations of current BMs. Here, we discuss the various applications of miRNAs in nonclinical investigations of pharmaceutical compounds.

In conclusion, this chapter aims to provide a better understanding of various molecular pathology tissue-based assays available to drug development scientists by discussing their specific applications in the nonclinical space.

IMMUNOHISTOCHEMISTRY

Immunohistochemistry (IHC) has arguably advanced the discipline of diagnostic pathology in the last 20 years more than any other histological technologies. Less well acknowledged but just as important is the tremendous and increasing contribution of IHC to the successful investigation of a wide range of pathophysiological mechanisms encountered routinely in nonclinical drug discovery and toxicology. The primary utility of IHC is the direct visualization of the cellular distribution of a molecule (or molecules) using labeled antibodies or other ligands. The label can be enzymatic for light microscopy, fluorescent for fluorescence microscopy, radioactive for autoradiography, or electron-dense for electron microscopy. The pivotal reagent common to all IHC techniques is the antibody, which may also be replaced by an aptamer [4,5]. The availability of immunoglobulin fractions and monoclonal antibodies to an ever-increasing number of clinically relevant antigen epitopes has enormously expanded the utility of IHC for candidate selection and lead optimization in the drug-development cycle. Several novel technologies including Biacore (http://www.biacore.com/lifesciences/company/index.html) can help select antibodies that are adequate for IHC or that perform well on the automated IHC stainers [6]. The technical aspects of IHC are well described elsewhere [2,7–14]. In our experience, nonclinical toxicological pathology laboratories tend to adopt simple, straightforward IHC protocols, such as are described below. This is because, traditionally, the majority of histopathology units within drug-safety departments of pharmaceutical companies have primarily supported diagnostic pathology work. However, more recently many drug-safety departments have been folded together with discovery operations. This organizational shift has resulted in drug-safety histopathology units that also provide direct investigative and discovery support, with implications for more involved IHC protocols. With this in mind, the goal of this chapter is to provide some background on the general principles and challenges of IHC, while focusing on the nonclinical applications of the technique.

Methodology

Starting with 4–6 µm-thick tissue sections mounted on positively charged slides, the basic IHC protocol can be summarized as shown in Fig. 16.1.

Tissue sections cut from paraffin bocks have to be deparaffinized and rehydrated to bring the tissues to conditions permissive of epitope–antibody reactions. Next, facultative antigen unmasking is accomplished using heat, chemical, or enzyme-based target-retrieval solutions. This is followed by quenching of endogenous peroxidase activity using hydrogen peroxide. To eliminate cross-reactivity of nonspecific tissue proteins with labeled antibody, it is customary to apply nonspecific protein block at this stage. The sections are finally incubated with primary antibody. After a predetermined incubation period, horseradish peroxidase-labeled polymer (as in Fig. 16.1) or other suitable detection system (described below) is applied. Color development is achieved using 3,3′-diaminobenzidine (DAB) or another chromogen.

The integrity of tissues used in IHC runs may be validated by including parallel staining for β2-microglobulin (B2M), a component of MHC class I molecules, which are present on all nucleated cells (excluding red blood cells). Poor or negative staining for B2M suggests compromised tissue integrity, rendering the tissue unsuitable for IHC analysis.

Tissue Fixation

Immunohistochemistry is routinely performed on formalin-fixed paraffin-embedded (FFPE), frozen, or Epon-embedded tissues depending on antigen type.

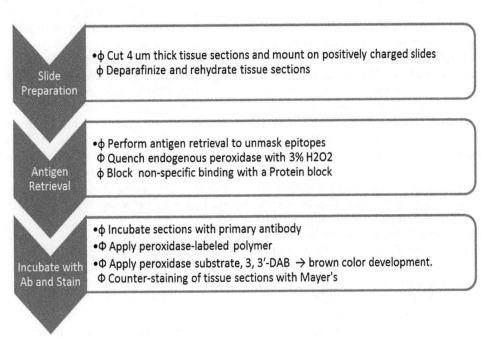

Slide Preparation
- φ Cut 4 um thick tissue sections and mount on positively charged slides
- φ Deparafinize and rehydrate tissue sections

Antigen Retrieval
- φ Perform antigen retrieval to unmask epitopes
- Φ Quench endogenous peroxidase with 3% H2O2
- φ Block non-specific binding with a Protein block

Incubate with Ab and Stain
- φ Incubate sections with primary antibody
- Φ Apply peroxidase-labeled polymer
- Φ Apply peroxidase substrate, 3, 3′-DAB → brown color development.
- Φ Counter-staining of tissue sections with Mayer's

FIGURE 16.1 Basic steps for polymer immunohistochemistry.

The preferred fixative is 10% neutral buffered formalin (NBF), but other fixatives that may be used, depending on antigen type, including Bouin's solution and 3% paraformaldehyde. Alternatively, so-called "zinc fixatives" may be used for epitopes degraded by cross-linking fixatives [15–17]. Prolonged fixation with cross-linking fixatives may cause tissue shrinkage, hardening, and, most importantly, reduced immunoreactivity [7,8,16]. For embedding, paraffin wax with a melting temperature of not more than 56°C is preferred. It is often recommended that tissue sections be mounted on precoated or positively charged slides to prevent detachment during the many wash cycles. Poly-L-lysine and chrome alum gelatin are two commonly used adhesive agents for coating IHC slides. One simple technique to create coated slides involves immersion of clean glass slides in 0.01% polylysine for 15–45 min, followed by thorough rinsing in distilled water. The slides are then dried and stored in boxes [18]. Mounted sections are dried at 37°C to aid tissue adhesion, but some sections should be dried at room temperature to preserve target epitopes. Some surface epitopes of cell membranes or nuclear receptors cannot be detected in conventionally fixed tissues. Many other antigens, such as leukocyte surface markers, survive neither paraffin processing nor fixation with additive (in which the fixing agent attaches to the protein molecule) fixatives. For these, alcohol, methanol, or acetone fixation is preferred. Cryostat sections of tissues embedded in optical coherence tomography (OCT) medium and fixed in cold acetone ensure better antigen preservation than paraffin sections, but the morphological detail and resolution of such frozen sections are inferior to those of FFPE tissues.

Epitope Retrieval

It has been 20 years since the first article on antigen retrieval (AR) was published by Shi and colleagues [19]. The simple technique of boiling FFPE tissue sections in water has since played a significant role in extending the reach and use of IHC in coaxing molecular information out of archival FFPE tissues further than anyone could have imagined [20]. The demonstration of many epitopes can be significantly improved by pretreatment with epitope retrieval (ER) reagents that break the protein cross-links formed by formalin fixation and thereby uncover epitopes [19–22]. To determine the most suitable ER agent for a particular antigen, tissue sections are exposed to one of the following commonly used ER reagents: trypsin, proteinase K, urea, or citrate buffer [20–22]. Application of heat with or without ER reagent [ie, heat-induced epitope retrieval (HIER)] has further significantly improved the process of antigen unmasking, enabling more widespread detection of antigens from FFPE tissues [2,8,14]. Microwave oven, pressure cooker, steamer, and water baths are commonly used

heating devices that aid the ER process. Heating lengths of up to 20 min appear to be generally satisfactory, and it is important to follow each heat cycle with appropriate cooling time [7–9].

Detection Systems

Immunohistochemistry detection systems are either direct or indirect. Direct labeling of primary antibody is a one-step technique that involves an enzyme- or fluorochrome-labeled antibody binding directly with the antigen in tissue sections. Because the technique utilizes only one antibody, the procedure is short, quick, and circumvents the problems of cross-over and nonspecific binding of secondary reagents. Another advantage is that it permits the study of multiple protein complexes using antibodies generated from either the same or different species. The main disadvantage of the direct labeling technique is that it lacks signal amplification and thus has limited usefulness unless the target epitope is abundantly expressed in the tissue.

In the indirect IHC method, a target epitope is identified by the unlabeled primary antibody, and the resulting epitope/antibody complex is subsequently detected by a labeled secondary antibody developed in a different species (two-step indirect technique). A three-step indirect IHC configuration involves the addition of a third layer of labeled tertiary antibody specific for the secondary antibody. The labeled secondary antibody binds to many epitopes on the unlabeled primary immunoglobulin, resulting in considerable signal amplification compared to the direct method. Similarly, signal amplification and assay sensitivity are exponentially increased in the three-step indirect technique. Thus indirect IHC techniques are recommended for procedures where low-level expression of the epitope of interest is anticipated.

Soluble enzyme immune complex methods were developed to increase the stability as well as sensitivity of the indirect IHC assay. In the typical protocol, unlabeled primary antibody is combined with excess of secondary antibody. Preformed immune complexes of peroxidase and antiperoxidase antibody (PAP method) or alkaline phosphatase-antialkaline phosphatase complexes (APAAP) are then added. Since the secondary antibody is in excess, one of its Fab sites is available to bind to the antibody of the stable enzyme immune complex [11].

Streptavidin/Avidin–Biotin Methods

The techniques described above have been mostly supplanted in nonclinical laboratories by the more sensitive and specific streptavidin/avidin–biotin methods. Streptavidin (from *Streptomyces avidinii*) and avidin (from egg white) have high-binding affinity for biotin ($K = 10{-}15 M$). Exploiting this property, an unlabeled primary antibody that reacts specifically with an epitope in a tissue section is detected using a biotinylated secondary antibody; the signal is amplified by adding either preformed (Strept) avidin–biotin–enzyme complex (ABC technique) or by the enzyme-labeled streptavidin (LAB or LSAB technique). The enzyme substrate is then added to develop the desired staining intensity.

Catalyzed Signal Amplification

An enhanced version of the ABC system, the catalyzed signal amplification (CSA) system, incorporates a signal amplification reagent, biotinyl-tyramide [23]. This reagent is catalyzed by the bound peroxidase to form insoluble biotinylated phenols that react further with labeled streptavidin, resulting in additional signal amplification, increasing the signal by up to 200-fold when compared to the noncatalyzed configuration [23]. Various groups or vendors have referred to this as "catalyzed reporter deposition," "catalyzed signal amplification," or "ImmunoMax" [24,25].

Polymeric Immunohistochemistry Methods

More recently, detection systems employing link antibodies and marker enzymes attached to a polymer backbone have been introduced into IHC technology [11,26]. The commercial versions of these include EnVision (Dako, Carpinteria, CA) and Power Vision (Immuno-Vision Technologies, Daly City, CA). These technologies utilize a synthetic polymer carrier to conjugate the secondary antibody to the enzyme. This approach increases the enzyme density at the antigenic binding site, consequently amplifying total reactivity to chromogen. Because the system is biotin-free, it eliminates nonspecific binding due to endogenous biotin. Additional advantages include increased sensitivity, improved detection efficiency, and a simpler protocol that is easier to standardize. In a more advanced iteration of the polymer-staining technology, a polymer detection helper is added to the polymeric horse radish peroxidase-linked or AP-linked secondary antibody conjugates, constituting a two-step polymer system that achieves a significantly higher amplification and sensitivity than the first-generation polymer systems. This enhanced system permits the use of much higher dilution of the primary antibodies resulting in reduced false-positive signals. Finally, double-stain polymer-enzyme conjugate kits are now commercially available for the detection of two antigens simultaneously or sequentially. Polymer-detection systems for animal tissue are particularly useful in solving difficult tasks, such as using mouse antibodies on mouse tissues. The disadvantages of the polymeric methods include high cost and difficulty adapting to the automated immunohistochemical stainers that use proprietary reagents [26].

Multiplex Immunostaining Chip Method

A novel technology, the multiplex immunostaining chip (MI chip) method, is intended to examine multiple antigens in the same tissue section [27]. MI chip technology differs from tissue microarray in that it permits analysis of the expression of as many as 50 antigens in a single specimen, while the microarray only permits the analysis of a single antigen in many specimens simultaneously. The chip is a panel of antibodies contained in a silicon rubber plate with 50 2mm-diameter wells. A tissue section on a slide is placed on the plate and is fastened tightly with a specially designed clamp. The plate is then turned upside down, which applies 50 different antibodies discreetly to the one section. In addition to enabling direct comparison of the expression of multiple epitopes on a tissue section simply by changing microscopic fields on a single slide, the MI chip technology does not require expensive instrumentation and is highly cost-effective. This device can be used in various applications in investigative molecular pathology and in the differential diagnosis of tumors [27].

The Challenges of Laboratory Immunohistochemistry Practice

Several pitfalls must be overcome for the successful routine practice of laboratory IHC [2,7,8,28]; these pitfalls may differ depending on the equipment, reagents, and technical skills of each laboratory [29]. Many of these challenges relate to the prevention of false positive or background staining. Table 16.1 lists the common challenges encountered in IHC laboratories and offers suggestions for their resolution.

Immunofluorescence

Immunofluorescence (IF) is typically performed on frozen rather than on paraffin-embedded sections [39,40]. Immunofluorescence represents one of pathology's most versatile tools, enabling the visualization of very small antigen imprints in cells or tissues with the aid of fluorochromes and ultraviolet light. In the nonclinical drug-development space, IF is used to analyze the distribution of proteins, glycans, and small biological and nonbiological molecules. Immunofluorescence is also used to screen hybridomas. Commonly used fluorochromes include fluorescein (yellow green) and tetramethyl-rhodamine (red), both of which are readily conjugated to immunoglobulins [10]. Others include acridine orange, rhodamine, lissamine, and calcofluor white. IF is often used in combination with other, nonantibody methods of fluorescent staining. For example, 4',6-diamidino-2-phenylindole (DAPI), is a popular nuclear counterstain for use in multicolor fluorescent techniques [41,42]. Its blue fluorescence stands out in

TABLE 16.1 Causes and Prevention of Background Staining in IHC

Cause	Mechanism	Solution
Endogenous peroxidase	Pseudoperoxidase in RBC or myeloperoxidase in granulocytes react with DAB→brown product like specific immunostaining [2,28]	Treat sections with 3% H_2O_2 in methanol (10% if hemorrhage and hematin present)
Hydrophobicity of proteins	Hydrophobicity of proteins during fixation increases background staining [8]	Limit fixation in formalin; postfix in Bouin's, Zenker's, or B5
Ionic and electrostatic charge	Nonimmune binding of tissues/cells with negative charge such as endothelium and collagen	Abolish by using buffers with high ionic strength
Nonspecific Fc receptor binding	Nonspecific adherence of 1 degree antibody to Fc receptors of mononuclear cells in lightly fixed, frozen sections of lymphoid tissue	Block with buffer containing sodium borohydride, lysine, ammonium chloride, or glycine
Attachment of antibodies to free aldehyde groups	Use of glutaraldehyde or prolonged fixation in formaldehyde→free aldehydes	Limit aldehyde fixation time; use nonaldehyde fixative; perform IF instead of IHC
Avidin	Avidin has high affinity for oppositely charged molecules: Nucleic acids, phospholipids, and glycosaminoglycans in the cytoplasm of mast cells→nonspecific binding [30]	Substitute with streptavidin
EB	EB is widely dispersed in tissues→strong background [31]	Use polymeric method
Endogenous AP	Intestinal and nonintestinal forms of AP can produce background	Inhibit nonintestinal form with 1 mM levamisole [32], and block intestinal isoforms with 1% acetic acid [33,34]
Nonspecific Ag diffusion (sequestration)	Ag diffusion out of one cell type can lead to nonspecific sequestration by other cells or interstitium, example: As seen in tissues with a high concentration of Igs in blood plasma	Cautious interpretation of IHC slides
Pigments	Presence of black/brown pigments (melanin or hemosiderin) may complicate the reading of IHC reactions [8]	Use detection system producing a different colored precipitate. Counterstain with Giemsa or Azure B dyes – melanin stains blue-green, DAB product remains brown; use permanganate-oxalate or 10% H_2O_2 to bleach melanin [35,36]
Excessive fixation	Prolonged storage in formalin may result in tissues falsely negative for the marker of interest or unreliable results with nonspecific staining	Use B2M, CD31, or vimentin as a marker to check for loss of signal due to long-term fixation [37]; apply HIER to unmask epitope(s)
Nonspecific antibody (Ab) binding (background staining)	Overapplication of HIER, improper Ab dilution, using Ab raised in the same species as the tissues being investigated, and general errors in technique [2]	Monitor HIER parameters; titrate out 1 degree Ab; apply background blockers; co-incubate 1 degree Ab with thiol-reactive compounds such as reduced GSH [38]
Use of antihuman Abs in animal studies	There's wide variability in results obtained with different animal species	Investigate species cross-reactivity of human research antibodies prior to use on study sections

AP, alkaline phosphatase; *DAB*, 3,3′-diaminobenzidine; *EB*, endogenous biotin; *HIER*, heat-induced epitope retrieval; *IHC*, immunohistochemistry.

vivid contrast to green, yellow, or red fluorescent probes of other structures. Immunofluorescence techniques are powered by the epifluorescence or the more complex confocal microscope system. The basic function of a fluorescence microscope is to irradiate the specimen with a desired and specific band of wavelengths and to separate the much weaker emitted fluorescence from the excitation light. In a properly configured microscope, only the emission light reaches the eye or so that the resulting fluorescent structures are superimposed with high contrast against a very dark background.

As with standard IHC, primary or direct IF uses a single Ab that is chemically linked to a fluorophore. Direct conjugation to fluorophore reduces the number of steps in the staining procedure making the process faster and reducing background signal by avoiding issues with Ab cross-reactivity or nonspecificity. However, direct IF lacks amplification and is less sensitive than indirect IF. Secondary or indirect IF uses two antibodies, the unlabeled primary Ab binds the target molecule, and the secondary Ab, which carries the fluorophore, recognizes the primary antibody and binds to it. Multiple secondary antibodies can bind a single primary antibody. This provides signal amplification by increasing the number of fluorophore molecules per antigen. This protocol is more complex and time-consuming than the direct protocol, but the payoff is significant, in the form of a marked increase in signal amplification, and more flexibility because a variety of different secondary antibodies and detection techniques can be used for a given primary antibody.

A common complication of IF is the phenomenon of auto-fluorescence observed with a variety of animal tissues and pathogens when illuminated by ultraviolet excitation in the absence of fluorochromes. Collagen and elastic fibers and natural substances in brain sections often auto-fluoresce [43]. This "natural" fluorescence is due to the presence of substances like flavins and porphyrins. These substances are generally extracted by solvents and therefore are not problematic in fixed and dehydrated sections. However, they may persist (and be redistributed) in frozen sections that have passed through various aqueous reagents. Lipofuscin is a native auto-fluorescent material that persists even in paraffin sections, especially in certain large neurons in the CNS, producing a green-yellow-orange emission under UV blue-light excitation. With age, lipofuscin accumulates in the cytoplasm of neurons, glial cells, and cardiac muscle cells [44,45]. The spectra of lipofuscin overlap those of all commonly used fluorophores, making distinctions between specific labeling and nonspecific auto-fluorescence difficult or impossible [46]. Aldehyde fixatives may also react with amines and proteins to generate fluorescent products; glutaraldehyde is worse than formaldehyde in this regard. Several procedures for chemically blocking auto-fluorescence have been described [44,45,47,48]. For example, immersion of the sections in dilute osmium tetroxide (0.2% for 5 min) followed by 12 h or so in running water effectively auto-fluorescence. Furthermore, 1–10 mM $CuSO_4$ in 50 mM ammonium acetate buffer (pH 5) or 1% Sudan Black B (SB) in 70% ethanol reduced or eliminated lipofuscin auto-fluorescence in neural tissues [44]. However, auto-fluorescence may also be titered out during image acquisition.

Nonclinical Applications of Immunohistochemistry

Immunohistochemistry and immunofluorescence are widely used in basic research to understand the distribution and localization of target proteins expressed at specific tissue locations. Since specific molecular markers are characteristic of certain cellular events such as cell cycling, the techniques of IHC represent powerful assays for probing the effects of test articles on proteins that regulate central pathophysiological processes. In spite of the well-recognized clarity that IHC can bring to the resolution of problematic diagnostic pathology, there has been widespread reluctance to adopt these techniques as full-fledged adjuncts to histopathology in the morphological evaluation of regulatory toxicology studies. For one thing, standard histopathological evaluation (H&E)

is considered sufficient for the vast majority of routine toxicology studies. Secondly, there are currently no regulatory requirements to involve IHC or IF in any aspect of H&E, other than tissue cross-reactivity (TCR) studies. Still, IHC remains a potentially useful tool to determine the role of specific proteins associated with toxicological findings. For example, because proteins expressed during drug-related liver toxicity may serve as surrogate biomarkers of associated morphological alterations, a pilot IHC study was deployed to study the relationship between drug-induced hepatocellular hypertrophy and the expression of cytochrome P450 (CYP) enzymes in rats exposed to known CYP inducers: 3-methyl-cholanthrene (3-MC), phenobarbital (PB), pregnenolone-16-a-carbonitrile (PCN), and isoniazid (ISN). In comparison to controls, the chemicals-induced variable centrilobular hepatocellular hypertrophy, which correlated well with increased IHC expression of CYP1A (3-MC), CYP 2B, 3A, and 2E (PB) and CYP 2E (PCN and ISN) (see Fig. 16.2). Microsomal assay data confirmed significant induction of CYP1A by 3-MC and CYP2B, 3A, and 2E by PB. The data suggested that CYP IHC represents a potentially useful adjunct to H&E histopathology for comprehensive evaluation of drug-induced morphological alterations in the liver [49].

Analysis of Rodent Carcinogenicity Studies

Immunohistochemistry has demonstrated significant added value as an adjunct to the routine H&E of rodent carcinogenicity studies. In these studies, the H&E classifications of epithelial and mesenchymal tumors based on morphological criteria may occasionally be problematic. This can potentially allow a compound to be incorrectly labeled as a suspect carcinogen, or incorrectly cleared of carcinogenic potential. The IHC technique is especially suited to tackle this problem since it can be used effectively to more accurately identify the lineage of a poorly differentiated neoplasm than the H&E light microscopy histopathology [37,50,51]. For example, an initial screen of undifferentiated tumors with a "pancytokeratin" antibody blend, such as cytokeratin (CK) AE1/AE3 (a mixture of two different clones of anticytokeratin monoclonal antibodies), generally helps identify an epithelial lineage. Individual cytokeratins such as CK7 and CK20 can be used to further characterize the epithelial components of the tumor [37,50,51]. When data from the CK screen are underwhelming, the tumor may be screened for vimentin, an intermediate filament that is present in most mesenchymal cells and is found in almost all sarcomas and melanomas but is variable in lymphomas and even some carcinomas [50]. Because vimentin may be coexpressed with CK in a wide range of carcinomas and other tumors, it has high sensitivity but poor specificity. If the tumor tissue section has stained poorly with antibodies to pancytokeratin and

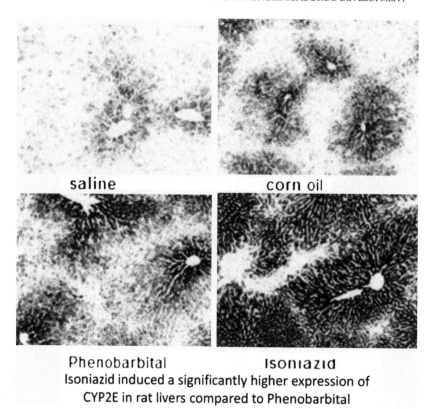

saline   corn oil

Phenobarbital   Isoniazid
Isoniazid induced a significantly higher expression of
CYP2E in rat livers compared to Phenobarbital

FIGURE 16.2   Comparison of CYP 2E induction in rat liver following exposure to different chemicals.

vimentin, broad-spectrum marker for hematopoietic neoplasms like CD45 may be applied. The CD45 molecule is specific for (but not restricted to) tumors of a lymphoid lineage. As with vimentin and other screening markers, there may be variable staining results in individual anaplastic and early-stage neoplasms. If the tumor is positive for CD45, a lymphoid lineage is established; additional stains such as CD3 (T-cell), CD79a (B-cell), and/or PAX-5 (B-cell) may then be used to further characterize specific lymphoid cell types. CD3-positive neoplastic tumors can be characterized further using CD4 or CD8 markers, or functional markers, such as CXCL13, PD1, and BCL6 that are associated with follicular T-helper cells [T(FH)] [52]. Histiocytic sarcoma, a systemic neoplasm of histiocytes/macrophages, can be diagnosed using lysozyme, vimentin, CD68, ED1/ED2, or F4/80.

Applications of Immunohistochemistry to Study Mechanisms of Carcinogenesis

Immunohistochemistry has been effectively used to predict the potential carcinogenic risk of compounds by demonstrating increased proliferative activity of treated cells through the expression of the Ki67 protein (also known as MKI67) and/or proliferating cell nuclear antigen (PCNA). For example, PPARα agonists including fenofibrate (FF) and clofibrate (CF) are known to induce

liver tumors in mice [53]. However, their carcinogenic potential in rats and man is not well understood. Yet, FF, a member of the fibrate class of hypolipidemic drugs, has been extensively used for a long time to treat hypertriglyceridemia and mixed hyperlipidemia [54]. In one study, the incidence of preneoplastic foci in FF-treated rasH2 mice was evaluated using IHC for PCNA and cytokeratin 8/18 [55]. Preneoplastic foci and PCNA-positive cells were significantly increased in mice from the FF-treated groups. In addition, the transgene and several downstream molecules such as c-myc, c-Jun, activating transcription factor 3 (ATF3), and cyclin D1 were overexpressed following FF treatment. The model demonstrated direct hepatocarcinogenic activity of FF in rasH2 mice, and showed that upregulation of genes for the ras/MAPK pathway and cell cycle was probably involved in the hepatocarcinogenic mechanism of rasH2 mice [55]. PCNA and Ki67 IHC staining may be applied to further explore the carcinogenic potential of drug compounds that cause certain generally recognized "preneoplastic" lesions. For example, while some chemicals that induce α2-macroglobulin (α2M) nephropathy in male rats ultimately cause renal neoplasms [56–58], others, including gabapentin and lindane, induce α2M nephropathy but not tumors [58–60]. Thus the observation of α2M nephropathy in a rat toxicity study should not automatically trigger program cancellation. Rather, supplemental

PCNA/Ki67 IHC studies should be considered to determine if an increased proliferation index is present, suggesting test article-related carcinogenic potential.

Immunohistochemistry offers practically unlimited possibilities to study any target molecules against which a monoclonal or polyclonal antibody can be raised. For this reason, it has been a highly effective technique for implementing translational studies to compare the mechanisms of carcinogenesis in animal models and humans. For example, the phenotype and cellular origin of dimethylbenzanthracene (DMBA)-induced pancreatic tumors in rats and the natural disease in humans were compared using IHC [61]. Pancreatic adenocarcinomas induced by DMBA in rats express markers consistent with a ductal phenotype, as observed in human tumors [62]. Importantly, the data provided evidence that the DMBA-induced carcinogenesis model could serve as an excellent nonclinical model for anticancer drug efficacy studies. In another example of the application of IHC in translational cancer studies, the role of regulatory T-cells (Tregs) was investigated in the tumor progression seen with human glioblastoma (GBM) [63]. Elimination of CD25+ T lymphocytes (Tregs) caused tumor regression and improved long-term survival in almost 50% of mice [63].

Finally, in another example, the risk of drug-induced foci of altered hepatocytes (FAH) progressing to hepatocellular carcinomas was assessed using the polychlorinated biphenyl (PCB) model in female F344 rats. Data from this study showed that a subset of glutathione-S-transferase pi-positive FAHs possessed a competitive growth advantage over surrounding hepatic tissue due to increased expression of the growth-stimulatory transforming growth factor alpha and decreased expression of the growth-inhibitory transforming growth factor beta receptor II [51].

Applications of Immunohistochemistry in Cancer Drug Development

The development of the next generation of molecularly targeted therapeutics is guided by multiple principles, supported by the availability of appropriate investigative molecular tools, including IHC, ISH, miRNA, and tissue microarrays. Indeed, the standard techniques in cancer-drug development involve hypothesis testing and demonstration of efficacy in appropriate in vitro and in vivo systems. For example, the hypothesis that the Chinese herb Patrinia heterophylla contained polysaccharides with potent anticancer activity was investigated first by demonstrating significant inhibitory effects of Patrinia polysaccharides on the growth of human cervical cancer HeLa cells in culture using the 3-(4,5-dimethylthiazol-2-yl)-2,5-diphenyltetrazolium bromide (MTT) assay [64,65]. The mechanisms of this growth-inhibition were investigated using DNA fragmentation and TdT-mediated dUTP nick-end labeling (TUNEL) staining assays to detect apoptosis. These apoptotic events were characterized by performing IHC to demonstrate the expression of the apoptosis-associated proteins p53, Bcl-2, and Bax genes in HeLa cells. Meanwhile, the distribution of cell-cycle proteins was analyzed by flow cytometry. Compared with the control group, Patrinia polysaccharide-treated HeLa cells accumulated apoptosis in the G0/G1 phase, which was associated with downregulation of the Bcl-2 gene and upregulation of the p53 and Bax genes. The data suggested that Patrinia polysaccharides might act as inhibitors of cell proliferation in vitro and might be a potential, natural apoptosis-inducing anticancer agent [64,65]. Following on the standard principles articulated earlier, the next step in the development of these polysaccharides would be to evaluate their efficacy in vivo using animal tumor models.

In tumor types such as oncogenic human papillomavirus (HPV)-associated cervical cancer where the molecular interactions are mediated by proteins [66], the molecular pathways are readily analyzed by studying the functions of these proteins using the capabilities of IHC and other molecular techniques. After demonstrating that modulation of the candidate target has significant anticancer effects, a robust and reliable companion diagnostic assay is often required to measure the expression of the target in the nonclinical species and in human tumors. Such companion diagnostics may be tissue or blood biomarkers (BMs) detectable by molecular assays based on IHC or other companion molecular technologies. For example, when the novel targeted therapy Gefitinib [an anti-EGFR (epidermal growth factor receptor) tyrosine kinase inhibitor] was developed for nonsmall-cell lung cancer, it was shown that response to Gefitinib was restricted to those patients with activating EGFR mutations developed against a growth factor receptor that could be readily identified by IHC or fluorescence ISH (FISH) assays [67–69]. Similarly, in colorectal cancer, the presence of activating downstream kirsten rat sarcoma gene (KRAS) mutations is associated with resistance to the anti-EGFR mAb cetuximab. Thus testing for this mutation is now recommended, and only those with wild-type KRAS are treated with cetuximab [69,70].

This is consistent with the assumption that overexpression of a given oncogene may identify the best group of patients to treat with a novel targeted therapeutic. Clearly then, molecular assays, or companion diagnostics based on IHC, IF, or other molecular pathology technologies, currently offer the best chance to identify the subpopulation of certain tumor patients that will likely gain benefit from therapy. For this reason, molecular profiling of tumors has become central to all clinical development programs for novel targeted therapies [69], resulting in the development of companion diagnostic assays for several FDA-approved biotherapeutics, including trastuzumab, vemurafenib, and crizotenib and small molecules [71–78].

In conclusion, the development of a molecular assay that reproducibly identifies patients that would benefit from a new drug is often an important prerequisite for a successful targeted anticancer therapy. These assays are often initiated in the nonclinical phase and perfected for drug trials. For example, VYSIS' PathVysion FISH test or DAKO's HercepTest are FDA-approved assays for identifying patients that could benefit from treatment with Trastuzumab.

Tissue Microarrays

Definition

Tissue microarrays (TMAs) and cell microarrays are high-throughput technologies allowing comprehensive assessment of the expression of a single antigen across many tissues and cells, respectively, in a single experiment [27,79–95]. Tissue microarrays are used to analyze the expression of proteins simultaneously in multiple individual tissue samples on one slide.

Tissue microarrays are composed of small-tissue cores as small as 0.6mm in diameter, from regions of interest in paraffin-embedded tissues. These tissue cores are obtained using hollow needles of set diameters inserted into paraffin blocks. The cores are then transferred into slots in a recipient paraffin block in a precisely spaced array pattern. Sections from the array block are cut using a microtome, mounted on a microscope slide, and analyzed by a variety of assay and staining techniques including IHC, ISH, FISH, TUNEL analysis, in situ PCR, and cDNA hybridization aided by laser-capture microdissection (LCM). Each microarray block can be cut into 50–1000 sections that can be subjected to independent tests.

Clinical TMAs include multitumor microarrays (samples from multiple histological tumor types), progression microarrays (samples of different stages of tumor progression within a given organ), prognosis microarray (samples from which clinical follow-up data are available), and cryomicroarrays (frozen samples that might be more suitable than formalin fixed tissues for the detection of mRNA). Tissue microarrays for discovery and nonclinical work are less stringently classified; they are usually either formalin fixed paraffin-embedded or frozen TMAs.

The advantages of TMAs are the same as those usually obtained with high-throughput conversion: there are significant savings in the amount of work to prepare and read IHC/ISH slides and in reagents. In addition, there is rapid data accumulation since the readout and data can be automated. However, building tissue microarrays is laborious, and heterogeneous tissues such as tumors may require multiple punches to ensure adequate representations of the samples examined.

Nonclinical Applications of Microarrays

The primary use of TMAs in nonclinical development is to assess target distribution in a wide variety of tissues across species. This broad mapping of target distribution provides guidance as to which tissues to collect in the first efficacy and toxicity studies to identify potential effects beyond those anticipated based on the literature. Once differentially expressed genes have been identified from database screening, the expression level is confirmed by qRTPCR, and the cell source and incidence are determined in TMAs by ISH [89,91]. When relevant antibodies are available, comprehensive protein-expression analysis is also completed in TMAs.

Frozen TMAs are especially useful for IHC, particularly when the antibodies are not suitable for use in formalin-fixed tissues. The use of an adhesive-coated slide system (eg, Instrumedics) facilitates the transfer of TMA sections on the slide and minimizes tissue loss, thereby increasing the number of sections that can be taken from each TMA block.

Tissue microarrays have proven robust to support established associations between the expression of specific tumor receptors and their known tissue alterations. For example, TMAs were used to verify the association between the estrogen receptor and progesterone receptor, and separately ERBB2 (also known as HER2/neu) alterations, and survival in breast cancer; and between Ki67 labeling index and prognosis in urinary bladder cancer [96], and soft-tissue sarcoma [82,97]. Similarly, an association was made between IGFBP2 protein expression and local recurrence of prostatic tumors [89].

Tissue Cross-Reactivity Studies

Regulatory Position

Regulatory agencies have stipulated that monoclonal antibody (mAb) test-article binding to target and possible binding to nontarget tissue should be considered in their nonclinical safety evaluation [98–101]. One of the methods recommended to achieve this goal is the IHC-based TCR study [98–101]. A TCR study is defined as the binding of a candidate mAb to an epitope different from the directed target (ie, an off-target structure) [98]. In reality, the study measures binding mAb complementarity determining region (CDR) to an epitope different from the directed target. Tissue cross-reactivity studies are therefore inappropriate for biotherapeutics that do not have CDRs, such as those composed only of peptide fragments. From a practical perspective, TCR studies provide ex vivo information regarding the range and intensity of distribution of potential epitopes reactive with a mAb test article prior to its administration to humans. As suggested by Hall et al. [98], the predictive value of the assay lies in incorporating the characteristics of the mAb (isotype, subtype, and other molecular modifications) with its biological activity and potential in vivo distribution. According to the FDA's "Points to Consider in the Manufacture and Testing of Monoclonal Antibody Products for Human Use" [102], TCR studies should be conducted prior to Phase I human studies, and it is recommended that the actual clinical material be tested, not a surrogate product. Regulatory agencies have sanctioned the use of TCR studies in the selection of relevant animal species for toxicity testing [99,102]. According to ICH S6, a relevant species is one in which the test material is pharmacologically active due to the expression of the receptor or an epitope (in the case of monoclonal antibodies) [102]. In its "Guideline on Strategies to Identify and Mitigate Risks for First-In-Human Clinical Trials with Investigational Medicinal Products" the European Medicines Agency (EMEA) also stated that TCR data may be considered in the selection of relevant animal species for toxicity testing [99].

At minimum, data from TCR studies should provide:

1. Nonclinical indication of possible target-organ toxicity based on the presence of staining in tissues; and
2. Comparison of the ex vivo patterns of staining between human and animal tissue panels to support the relevance of species evaluated in nonclinical toxicity studies.

Tissues for Tissue Cross-Reactivity Studies

The regulatory agencies have suggested a list of human tissues (Table 16.2) to be used for TCR studies. By default, TCR studies in monkeys (and in rodents, to a large extent) tend to be configured to include a similar tissue set.

The source of the tissues used in TCR studies is important because of its possible impact on the study outcome. Human tissues obtained from surgical biopsies are considered superior to cadaveric (autopsy) tissues. Certain tissues (such as brain and eye) are invariably obtained from cadaveric (autopsy) sources; they should be harvested as soon as possible after death to provide optimal materials. As described in earlier sections, anti-CD31, antitransferrin receptor, or anti-B2M staining may be useful as a control to assess overall tissue and cell integrity. The CD31 adhesion molecule, also known as PECAM-1, is expressed in large amounts on endothelial cells at intercellular junctions, on T-cell subsets, and to a lesser extent on platelets and most leukocytes. Transferrin receptor (TfR) is a carrier protein for transferrin and is ubiquitous in cells. B2M is a component of MHC class I molecules, which are present on all nucleated cells. Each of these molecules should be abundant in any tissue section; loss of staining for any one of these would therefore suggest unacceptable tissue quality. A standard indirect immunoperoxidase IHC

procedure may be employed to demonstrate the presence of CD31, TfR, or B2M. For human TCR studies, samples should be obtained from at least three unrelated adult (>18 years) donors. For primary pediatric indications, juvenile tissue samples must be obtained. For nonhuman primate studies, samples are required from at least two separate animals.

In addition to the tissue list in Table 16.2, other tissues typically included in the study are positive, negative, and ancillary control tissues. Positive control tissue may be recombinant human target (candidate) protein in UV-resin spot slides. Negative control tissue may be recombinant human protein unrelated to the candidate protein in UV-resin spot slides. Ancillary control may include cryosections of relevant human embryonic cells expressing the human candidate proteins. Fresh, unfixed tissue samples are placed into molds, filled with Tissue-Tek OCT compound, and frozen. Sections are cut at 4–6 μm and fixed in acetone at room temperature. Just prior to staining, the slides are fixed with 10% NBF.

The Tissue Cross-Reactivity Immunohistochemistry Configuration

A variety of IHC methods can be used for TCR studies. Here we discuss the example of a TCR study based on the precomplexing indirect immunoperoxidase staining method. Control tissues known to express the epitope of interest (positive control tissues) and those known to lack the epitope of interest (negative controls) are included in the assay. The potential ancillary control clinical/diseased tissue expected to express the epitope

TABLE 16.2 Recommended Human Tissue List for Good Laboratory Practice Tissue Cross-Reactivity Studies

Adrenal	Lung	Spinal cord
Blood cells[a]	Lymph node	Spleen
Blood vessels (endothelium)[b]	Ovary	Striated (skeletal) muscle
Bone marrow	Fallopian tube (oviduct)	Testis
Brain – cerebrum (cortex)	Pancreas	Thymus
Brain – cerebellum	Parathyroid	Thyroid
Breast (mammary gland)	Peripheral nerve	Tonsil
Eye	Pituitary	Ureter
Gastrointestinal tract[c]	Placenta	Urinary bladder
Heart	Prostate	Uterus – body (endometrium)
Kidney (glomerulus, tubule)	Salivary gland	Uterus – cervix
Liver	Skin	

[a]Blood cells included granulocytes, lymphocytes, monocytes, and platelets.
[b]Examined in all tissues.
[c]Gastrointestinal tract to include esophagus, stomach, small intestine, and colon.

of interest (eg, skin samples from patients with moderate to severe psoriasis when assessing a mAb with a psoriasis indication) should be included whenever possible. The test article is titrated over a range of concentrations (eg, 50, 30, 20, 10, 2, and 1 μg/mL). The selection of staining concentrations should take into account the following observations:

1. Comparison of test-article staining of the positive control UV-resin spot at all concentrations examined;
2. Lack of test-article staining of unrelated UV-resin spot slides (negative control);
3. Adequate test-article staining of expressing cells at the concentrations examined (50, 30, 20, 10, 2, and 1 μg/mL), characterized by decreased staining at decreasing test-article concentrations; and
4. Lack of test-article staining of negative cells at all concentrations examined.

Pathology Evaluation of Tissue Cross-Reactivity Studies

The initial pathology review is typically conducted to ensure that tissue sections contain sufficient amounts of required tissue for evaluation and that the morphology of the tissue section permits meaningful evaluation. When detached, deformed, or insufficient tissues are found, additional sample(s) of the tissue are requested and evaluated to obtain the required three samples of each tissue. Slides are initially examined by the pathologist for adequacy and completeness of tissue elements and staining. The pathologist may then proceed to evaluate tissue sections to identify the tissue or cell type stained and the intensity of staining; IHC staining is typically scored on an intensity scale of 0–4+ where 0 = negative, 1+ = weak/minimal, 2+ = mild, 3+ = moderate, and 4+ = intense/marked reactivity. Frequency of cell-type staining may be identified as follows: very rare (<1% of cells of a particular cell type); rare (1–5% of cells of a particular cell type); rare to occasional (>5–25% of cells of a particular cell type); occasional (>25–50% of cells of a particular cell type); occasional to frequent (>50–75% of cells of a particular cell type); and frequent (>75–100% of cells of a particular cell type). Tissues are listed as missing (M) if not present on the slide. A tissue that is judged inadequate for evaluation (eg, missing tissue elements, suboptimal morphology) may be listed as not evaluated (NE). Tissue comments are provided for individual tissues in the form of a table. All slides stained with CD31, TfR, or anti-B2M antibody may be interpreted as being negative (Neg) or positive (Pos) for staining.

Nonclinical Implications of Tissue Cross-Reactivity Studies

The purpose of the TCR study is to assure that the experimental antibody does not bind to epitopes other than the target site, since such off-target binding could lead to treatment-related toxicity in human subjects. While binding to the expected target is generally confirmatory of the specificity of a therapeutic protein for the test epitope, specific binding does not always translate to functional pharmacology. Hall et al. [98] described the potential hierarchy of cross-reactivity findings according to site of test-article staining. More toxicological significance (and highest regulatory concern) is ascribed to membrane staining because access of test articles to the cell membrane is generally greatest in vivo. Test-article binding to high-density epitopes on membranes likely has a greater probability to trigger events such as complement fixation, antibody-dependent cell mediated cytotoxicity (ADCC), and cell destruction than antibody binding to other cellular locations. Positive cytoplasmic staining, on the other hand, is of lower regulatory concern because the probability of direct test-article access to the cytoplasmic milieu in vivo is likely limited. The significance of binding of test article to nuclei is not fully understood, but may suggest the probability of immune mediated disease [98]. Similarly, there is a wide gap in our understanding of the significance of test-article binding and staining in the serum, interstitial fluid, cerebrospinal fluid, and even extracellular structures. In general, cross-reactivity at unexpected sites may be due to the presence of the target antigen at such tissue sites, a potential toxicologically significant finding when real, or it may be due to the presence of unrelated cross-reactive epitopes. Leach et al. [99] presented an example of a TCR study where off-target staining did not result in off-target toxicity. The test article was a humanized mAb to a receptor on T cells and macrophages. TCR studies of the test article in humans and monkeys showed widespread staining of blood vessels in both species. Despite this widespread endothelial staining, there was no evidence of vascular toxicity in a 3-month study in monkeys. The TCR findings may have resulted from the presence of unrelated cross-reactive epitope(s) on vascular endothelial cells. Sometimes, the cross-reactivity observed is due to assay artifact. Additional analyses are thus needed to further characterize the nature and/or specificity of any unexpected staining.

In early TCR studies, the mouse origin and intact structure of mouse-derived mAbs made detection of targets in human, nonhuman primate, and rat tissues relatively easy because a specific secondary antimouse antibody could be used to detect binding of the test article to the target or cross-reactive epitopes without interference by reactivity with endogenous human, nonhuman primate, or rat IgG. However, due to the high frequency of immunogenicity complications, mouse mAbs have been systematically replaced by chimeric, humanized, and most recently, fully human mAbs. This has had the effect of making detection of the test article progressively more difficult, because the antihuman secondary antibodies do not readily distinguish between the humanized or human antibody product used in relatively low concentrations in an IHC assay and the endogenous antibodies naturally present in much higher concentrations in human tissues [99]. One approach to this problem is to use the direct IHC method where target tissue is reacted directly with biotinylated human mAb. In the special case where the TCR study needs to be configured for cocktail biotherapeutics made up of two human mAbs, both antibodies in the cocktail may be biotinylated (careful to make sure the labeling ratio is similar and mAbs are in the same ratios that they would be used in their drug cocktail); staining is then compared to what is seen when one or the other member of the cocktail is biotinylated and run independently (Shari A. Price-Schiavi, Personal Communication, 2012). In summary, regulatory documents from the FDA and EMEA have highlighted the relevance of TCR data as part of the overall submission for the qualification of a biotherapeutic to advance into Phase I (FIH) studies. Data from TCR studies can potentially be used to argue against the need to conduct any nonclinical in vivo toxicity studies in certain circumstances [102]. However, the TCR assay by itself has variable correlation with toxicity or efficacy. Therefore any findings of interest should be further evaluated and interpreted in the context of the overall pharmacology and safety assessment data package. Overall, the design, implementation, and interpretation of TCR studies should follow a case-by-case approach.

Biodistribution Studies: Nonclinical Applications Based on Immunohistochemistry Configuration

Biodistribution studies are in vivo test-article distribution or localization studies performed in selected nonclinical species to support early biotherapeutic drug development. Currently marketed biotherapeutic mAbs target a diverse array of epitopes distributed in a variety of tissues including tumors, lungs, synovial fluid, psoriatic plaques, and lymph nodes. Since drug concentration at the biological receptor site determines the magnitude of the pharmacological response, a significant consideration in effective therapeutic application of mAbs is a thorough understanding of the processes that regulate antibody biodistribution [103–106]. Temporal biodistribution profiles may be used to address kinetics and reversibility of target- and/or off-target-mediated accumulation. The biodistribution of biotherapeutic with a short half-life because of antiproduct antibodies may be best assessed by TCR studies. Comparison of temporal biodistribution profiles between the genetically engineered and wild-type mouse strains or between the disease models and healthy animals may provide useful insight on sites and kinetics of target-mediated elimination. Biodistribution studies are often performed using radioactive tracers. However, tissue biodistribution studies have become more frequent due largely to improvements in IHC reagents that permit staining of human IgG (ie, test article) in the presence of endogenous monkey, rabbit, rat, or mouse IgG [107]. Thus inappropriate tissue targeting by a mAb test article and ensuing toxicities in nonclinical species may be studied using IHC or IF configurations. Much like TCR studies, the interpretation of biodistribution studies takes into account the species of origin, the isotype, the format of the mAb (intact immunoglobulin, fragment, immunoconjugate, bispecific), the method of labeling, the stability of the immunoconjugate, the level of epitope expression in animal model and in patients, the binding to serum proteins, the route of administration, and vascular leakiness at the site of therapeutic activity [103–105]. For all these reasons, CBER guidelines suggest that mAb biodistribution studies be carried out in animal model species that share a cross-reactive or identical target epitope with humans [100]. The default animal model species is the nonhuman primate.

Immunohistochemistry biodistribution studies help identify differences between the animal model species and humans in epitope level of expression, the affinity of a mAb for the epitope, or the cellular response to mAb binding. These data may be leveraged to estimate the safety margins and to extrapolate safe human starting doses. It is important to remember that therapeutic antibodies may bind the specific target with different affinity in man compared to nonclinical species. In particular, mice often develop strong humoral immune responses against human immunoglobulins, resulting in rapid clearance of the candidate therapeutic antibodies and immune complex deposition in the glomeruli. Data from pharmacokinetic studies in animal models that do not express the target epitope(s) provide important information on the relative importance of epitope-mediated disposition of the candidate therapeutic antibody and immune-mediated disposition.

Differences in biodistribution between antibody-based therapeutics to the same target can result in a competitive advantage for one drug versus another and therefore next-generation leads often are centered on leveraging such improvements to gain market penetration. For example, the many marketed anti-TNF agents may be differentiated by their individual biodistribution-related properties [103,108]. While full-length immunoglobulin G (IgG) anti-TNF agents are primarily distributed within the bloodstream (30–80 mL/kg) [103,104,108], smaller IgG-derived competitors, namely Etanercept, a dimeric fusion protein consisting of the extracellular ligand-binding protein of p75 TNF receptor linked to human IgG1 Fc, distributes within tissues to a greater extent (0.1–0.2 L/kg) [108]. Thus nonclinical scientists have a vested interest in coming up with even more innovative IHC and

IF configurations capable of specifically ferreting out tissue location of humanized biotherapeutic proteins and protein-conjugates to support claims of superiority over competitors.

Immunohistochemistry technology has been applied to great effect in the nonclinical assessment of the biodistribution and safety of vectors in gene therapy [109–111]. For example, the biodistribution of recombinant adeno-associated virus (AAV) expressing glutamic acid decarboxylase (AAV2-GAD) was shown to be confined within the brain and mostly restricted to the ipsilateral subthalamic nucleus (STN), following intrasubthalamic injection in the rat [109]. AAV genomes were not detected in blood or cerebrospinal fluid, and did not disseminate to organs outside of the brain in the majority of animals. This study met FDA requirements, in addition to efficacy and toxicity studies in rodents and nonhuman primates, to support and supplement a Phase II clinical trial for gene transfer of AAV2-GAD to the human STN for the potential therapy of Parkinson's disease [109]. Gene delivery to other tissues outside the brain may also benefit from biodistribution studies to verify localization and assess efficacy. For example, the airway epithelium is a major goal for lung gene therapy, but success depends on overcoming the biological and physicochemical barriers the vector encounters in the tracheobronchial tree. Intravenous and intratracheal delivery of DNA complexes have been envisioned as two strategies to obtain gene transfer to the lungs. In a direct comparison between two routes of administration, considering lipid and polymeric classes of nonviral vectors, transgene expression in mouse lung was detected by performing IHC with an antibody directed against green fluorescent protein (GFP) [110]. Data showed that complexes with the same charge ratio behaved differently according to the route of administration [110]. Finally, IHC biodistribution studies have become quite common in the nonclinical safety evaluation of cancer gene therapy formulations. The concern, as always, is whether these gene vectors might migrate to nontarget tissues following chronic exposure. For example, the safety and biodistribution of Ad-EGFP-MDR1, an adenovirus encoding human multidrug resistance gene (human MDR1), was assessed in a mouse-colon carcinoma model [111]. Bone-marrow cells infected with Ad-EGFP-MDR1 were administered by intrabone marrow–bone marrow transplantation (IBM-BMT). Total adenovirus antibody and serum adenovirus neutralizing factor (SNF) were determined. Biodistribution of Ad-EGFP-MDR1 was subsequently detected by ISH and IHC. Neither total adenovirus antibody nor SNF increased weeks after BMT. ISH and IHC demonstrated concordant expression of human MDR-1/P-gp found in lung, intestine, kidney, and bone-marrow cells after BMT, but not detected in liver, spleen, brain, and tumor [111].

Other Methodologies for Tissue-Based Assays

Autostainers

The value of IHC and ISH is to both characterize the distribution and to provide slides to semiquantify the abundance of proteins and RNA species. Until a few years ago, IHC and ISH were performed manually, which limited the usefulness of these methods to adequately quantify proteins/RNAs in tissues. The need for better reliability and quantification has led to the gradual use of autostainers.

Multiple automated platforms are available and have been compared [112–114]. First and foremost a platform should produce reproducible and reliable results, which depends on several factors. These include factors related to the platform itself, such as the openness of the system to use reagents not provided by the manufacturer of the autostainer, the use of air vortex mixers, liquid coverslips, and heated pads. They also include the familiarity of the technician with the platform, the physical and immunological properties of the antibody used, the target of interest, the possibility to run simultaneous or staggered runs, the connectivity of the autostainer to the laboratory information system, the number of robotic arms, the number of slides accommodated, and the amount of reagents used.

Histochemistry

Histochemistry combines the techniques of biochemistry and histology in the study of the chemical constitution of cells and tissues. The importance of histochemistry has decreased as IHC methods have developed. However, the breadth of knowledge for many histochemical methods is such that they are still used in decision-making [115], including in our laboratories (Table 16.3). The availability of commercial staining kits for many established histochemical methods is a draw to continue using these methods. However, some complex stains may require contracting out the staining to specialized laboratories [116–119]. Finally, histochemical stains often provide high contrast, which allows for image analysis [120].

Laser-Capture Microdissection

Laser-capture microdissection (LCM) consists of using a laser to isolate specific cells on a section in order to increase the specific signal compared to the signal from the whole tissue. The laser energy may be infrared (810 nm) or ultraviolet (355 nm) or used in combination [121]. The isolated cells may then be subjected to DNA, RNA, or protein analysis. The major hurdle of using tissues that have undergone LCM is target degradation. However, LCM recently was successfully performed on immunolabeled slides followed by microRNA profiling [122].

TABLE 16.3 Specificity of Common Histochemical Stains

Stain name	Results
Acid fast blue – Kinyoun's method	Lipofuscin: Yellowish-redTubercle bacilli: bright redBackground: Light blue
Acid fast blue – Ziehl Neelsen	Lipofuscin: Yellow to bright redTubercle bacilli: bright redRed blood cells: Yellowish-orangeBackground: Light blue
Alcian blue pH 2.5	Acid mucopolysaccharides: blueSialomucins and weakly acid sulfomucins: blueStrongly acidic sulfomucins: Weak blue or no staining
Alcian blue pH 2.5/Periodic acid-Schiff	Same as Alcian blue pH 2.5 plus:Basement membranes, glycogen and neutral mucosubstances: pink to red
Amyloid – Congo red	Amyloid: pink to dark salmon; "apple-green birefringence" with polarized light
Bielschowsky silver	Axons, neurofibrillary tangles and senile plaques: blackBackground: Yellow to brown
Cupric silver	Degenerating neuron cell bodies, dendrites, synaptic terminals and axons: Black
Fluoro-Jade B	Degenerating neurons: Fluoresce (FITC filter)
Giemsa	Bacteria: deep blueNuclei: blueMast cell granules: purpleCytoplasm: pink
Gomori's iron stain	Iron pigments: bright blueNuclei: redCytoplasm: Light pink
Grocott's methenamine silver	Fungi, Nocardia, *actinomyces*: blackMucin: Taupe to dark greyBackground: pale green
Hall's method	Bile pigment: greenMuscle and cell cytoplasm: yellowCollagen: red
Jones' methenamine silver	Basement membranes and reticulin fibers: blackNuclei: red
Luxol fast blue	Myelin, including phospholipids: Blue to greenNeuron: pink to violet
Mallory's phosphotungstic acid hematoxylin	Dendrites, nuclei, fibrin, platelets and muscle: blueRed blood cells and collagen: red
Martius/Scarlet/Blue	Nuclei: Brown/blackCollagen: blueRed blood cells: yellowMuscle and fibrin: red
Mayer's mucicarmine	Mucin, cryptococci capsulae: deep rose to redNuclei: blackOther tissue elements: Yellow
Oil red O (frozen sections)	Lipid: redNuclei: Blue
PAS/Diastase	Nuclei: Blue
p-dimethylaminobenzylidene rhodamine	Copper deposits: bright red to orangeNuclei: Blue
Periodic acid-Schiff's	Glycogen: redNuclei: Blue
Perl's method for iron	Ferric iron: bright blueNuclei: redCytoplasm: Light pink
Picrosirius red	Collagen: red (orange/red in polarized light)Other tissue elements: Yellow
Trichrome	Muscle, red blood cells, keratin: redCollagen: blueFibrin: pinkNuclei: Blue/black
Twort's Gram	Gram + organisms: Blue/blackGram – organisms: Red/pinkNuclei: redCollagen, red blood cells, cytoplasm: Shades of green
Verhoeff–Van Gieson	Elastic fibers, nuclei: Blue/blackCollagen: redOther tissue elements: Yellow
Von Kossa	Calcium salts: blackNuclei: redCytoplasm: pink

The major application of LCM is the assessment of molecular events in cancer, especially in metastases [123–125]. LCM is also used in toxicological pathology (eg, in BM development [126]) to obtain cell-specific transcriptomic signatures of toxicity [127] and for the identification of the mechanisms of toxicity [128]. An alternative method to LCM includes "nondestructive molecular extraction" (NDME), which consists of using ultrasound and microwave to release macromolecules from the histological section into an overlying buffer. Imaging mass spectrometry (IMS) using matrix-assisted laser desorption/ionization is another alternative to LCM [129–131]. These latter methods are in the early phases of development and have yet to gain the acceptance of LCM.

BIOMARKERS: BEST PRACTICES FOR PATHOLOGY EVALUATION

A biomarker (BM) is a substance that is measured in a biological system as an indicator of exposure, effect, susceptibility, or clinical disease [132,133]. There are several types of BMs (Table 16.4).

TABLE 16.4 Types of Biomarker

Type	Definition
Surrogate	Intended to be a substitute for a clinical endpoint
Exposure	Exogenous substance or its metabolite or the product of an interaction between a drug agent and a target molecule or cell that is measured in a compartment within an organism
Effect	Change that is predictive, qualitatively or quantitatively, of a health impairment or potential impairment resulting from exposure
Efficacy	Correlates with the desired effect of a treatment
Mechanism	Provides evidence the drug affects a targeted pathway
Translational	Performs translationally across common laboratory species and to humans
Toxicity	Indicates potential adverse effects in vitro and in vivo
Type 0	Reflects genotype or phenotype
Type 1	Reflects concentration of drug and or metabolite in blood/tissue
Type 2	Reflects molecular target occupancy
Type 3	Indicates molecular target activation
Type 4	Physiological measurements of laboratory tests
Type 5	Measures disease process
Type 6	Reflects the natural history of a disease over time with known clinical indicators

TABLE 16.5 Methods of Candidate Biomarker Identification

Transcriptomics	Assesses gene expression changes in in vitro and in vivo toxicity studies to identify pathway modulation and correlates these with histopathological findings. The power of transcriptomics is illustrated by their contribution to the identification of novel kidney BMs in nonclinical species.
Proteinomics	Assesses protein changes using antibodies, lectins, two-dimension electrophoresis, PROTOMAP, matrix-assisted laser desorption/ionization, mass spectrometry, etc. The complexity of posttranslational modifications and the absence of knowledge of the half-life of each protein species have made it difficult to incorporate proteinomics in routine discovery pathology and BM identification studies.
Metabonomics	Relies on ^{1}H-nmr spectra of body fluids to quantitatively measure the dynamic multiparametric metabolic response of living systems to pathophysiological stimuli.

simultaneously. These new markers facilitate the monitoring of functional disturbance, molecular and cellular damage, and damage response. Improved imaging technologies have made it feasible to image some of these molecular events noninvasively and have contributed to a better understanding of the kinetics of toxicity events and the subsequent release of BMs [135].

Characterization and Validation of Biomarkers

Biomarkers are commonly used to support drug submissions for regulatory approval. The FDA has guidance on both genetic and translational BMs. Genomic BMs are usually entered as clinical and nonclinical markers for efficacy or safety for the purpose of selecting patients for clinical trials. Translational BMs are used to monitor a response and can be seen as early indicators of toxicity or adverse events. One way to evaluate exploratory BMs is through a voluntary exploratory data submission to the regulatory agencies.

On a case-by-case basis, the FDA may allow possible applications of BMs to Phase I clinical trials. When reviewing NDAs (new drug applications) or BLAs (biological license applications) regulatory agencies may consider other test results in addition to traditional BMs such as blood urea nitrogen [136].

The process of BM validation for use in clinical protocols takes into consideration a number of parameters, including the study design, sample processing, storage protocols, analytical platform, analysis algorithms, statistical methods, biological pathway interpretation, and electronic data submission format.

Several consortia and working groups, composed of professionals from industry, academia, and government

Biomarkers are extensively used in nonclinical studies as a means of characterizing the toxicity and efficacy of drugs prior to the initiation of human clinical trials. Additionally, knowledge of toxicity mechanisms may lead to the development of translational pharmacodynamic BMs [134]. Comparative analyses of dose-dependent BM responses between rodents and humans are critical to assessing risk relevance at human exposure levels.

Efficacy markers, which represent a specific type of pharmacodynamic markers, are used to monitor endpoints of desired clinical significance in in vitro or in vivo systems. An example of surrogate marker of target engagement is the level of pERK in circulating leukocytes, which is used as a marker of MEK inhibition in cancer cells.

Investigative approaches to identify novel BMs incorporate large-scale technologies, including transcriptomics, proteinomics, and metabonomics (Table 16.5). The combination of transcriptomics has made markers available that facilitate the correlation of genetic variation with biological outcomes. These new technologies permit efficient monitoring of gene transcripts, proteins, and intermediary metabolites, making it possible to monitor a large number of key cellular pathways institutions, have undertaken nonclinical studies to qualify safety BMs of tissue injury and function. As this work has developed and voluntary data have been submitted to regulatory authorities, study practices have come under close scrutiny in an attempt to ensure scientific rigor [137].

Several points must be addressed when considering best practices for BM qualification. The study results are frequently summarized by receiver operating characteristic (ROC) curves, which are plots of true positive rate (sensitivity) against the rate of false positives (specificity) for a continuous variable against a specific reference standard. The corresponding area under the curve (AUC) is a measure of the diagnostic performance of a BM. It is important, in the early assessment of a BM, that correlation with histopathological injury is performed. When performing histopathology evaluation a specific, predetermined lexicon should be used to both maximize reproducibility and comparability between different studies and sites and streamline communication of results with the regulatory agencies. When evaluating BM in body fluids such as urine, there needs to be normalization of urinary BM values to urinary creatinine concentrations in the same sample, which is also standard in clinical practice. All analytical methods need to be reliable and reproducible for the intended use [138]. The data generated by toxicity studies (standard clinical chemistry parameters, in vivo data, etc.) should be submitted not only as part of study reports but electronically as well. Adequate statistical analysis is also very important. Exclusion from data analyses of animals that could yield false-positive results will need two types of statistical performance analyses, deemed the inclusion analysis and the exclusion analysis.

In order to qualify BMs for regulatory submission, all prospective measurements of these BMs implemented in good laboratory practice (GLP) studies and clinical pharmacogenomics in support of a medicinal product's development must be reported to the health authorities [139].

The validation of nonclinical BMs to be used in clinical settings also requires observational longitudinal assessment of the intrasubject and intersubject variability in baseline BM levels across well-characterized age- and gender-matched normal patients with underlying conditions known to be related to that specific BM. These data will provide baseline values and natural longitudinal variance [140].

Best Practices for Histopathology Evaluation in Biomarker Qualification Studies

In nonclinical development, pathologists are involved in the H&E of toxicology data from animal studies and its correlation to parameters and endpoints that are associated with BM development.

Histopathology studies can be used to evaluate relationships between drug-induced organ injury and the expression of urinary or blood BMs. Furthermore, pathologists may use molecular tools such as IHC and ISH to evaluate molecular endpoints in tissues. However, there are many limiting factors for microscopic evaluation of BM qualifying studies. There is also an increasing need for additional molecular pathology tools that correlate to more in-depth knowledge of molecular pathways of disease.

The presence of a microscopic lesion can be used as positive reference of given cellular processes and therefore may be used to assess diagnostic performance of new BM candidates using methods such as ROC analyses. The read of adjacent slides from animals with negative histopathology, but positive BM readout, may demonstrate that, on a molecular level, considerable changes have already occurred that are not visible by standard light microscopy. The determination of the contribution of focal lesions in increased BM values can be evaluated by stepwise sectioning of the target organ for histopathology assessment in animals.

One of the most pressing issues associated with standard histopathology evaluation is the concern from the regulatory agencies over potential study bias involving H&E. The knowledge of additional data, such as comparator BM results or treatment, may influence histopathology assessment and potentially confound the diagnostic performance of a candidate BM in safety BM qualification studies [141].

Histopathological diagnostic outcome may be affected by the availability of clinical history data during statistical evaluation in observational studies. Knowledge of control animal identity may also affect the pathology readout [141]. To help reduce this concern, guidelines to decrease bias during H&E have been proposed, including the use of clear objective criteria for lesion diagnosis and grading. Guidelines published by the Society of Toxicological Pathology (STP) state that the knowledge of dose-group assignment, gross observations at necropsy, organ weight changes, in-life data, and results from clinical chemistry are important pieces of information to have at the time of pathology evaluation. Current best practices for histopathology evaluation were endorsed by the STP [142]. They indicate that study pathologists should:

1. Have knowledge of the treatment group from which the sample was obtained;
2. Have complete knowledge of all available study-related data that are associated with the animal from which the tissue was obtained; and
3. Be blinded to the data that is specific to the novel BM undergoing qualification.

However, study pathologists should be involved in the attendant *meta*-analyses of these data.

Sampling bias in tissue selection and sectioning is inherent in histopathology evaluation and must be managed appropriately. Best practices also include conducting peer review for quality assurance. This may involve a second (or even a third) pathologist corroborating the interpretations of the study pathologist. The use of "targeted masked" evaluation is also widely used and can contribute to an unbiased evaluation of BM data. "Targeted masked evaluation" entails reexamination of selected or all treated dose groups, randomly combined with controls and without knowledge of animal or group identity, to determine whether a subtle or equivocal finding can be identified consistently from control tissues.

In specific cases, where bias can be a confounder, blinded histopathology evaluation can be used as an experimental tool in BM qualification studies under conditions in which well-defined criteria for specific desired endpoints have been achieved prior to the blinded review of the said endpoint.

A blinded pathology evaluation is relevant when a specific question has to be answered based on promising preliminary data, such as late-stage clinical development. A blinded histopathology evaluation is often used when microscopic features can be quantified and compared across treatment groups as endpoints on a continuous scale. Blinded histopathology evaluation may be appropriate in cases where the toxicity model is well characterized and accepted scoring criteria were determined from previous studies, and where these requirements are established prior to the conduct of the BM qualification study. To maximize the use of blinded pathology evaluation in BM studies, data should be appropriately characterized and specific treatment, exposure, and time-course response should be categorized to yield maximum unbiased results. Qualitative and quantitative tissue responses should be well documented or defined and detailed criteria for characterizing and scoring tissue findings should be specified and broadly accepted.

Renal Biomarkers

The number of renal BMs has considerably increased in recent years, expanding from BMs or renal function such as blood urea nitrogen and creatinine, to Bristol Myers Squibb (BMS) of tubular health. These BMs may be assessed in the urine or in the blood.

Urinary Biomarkers of Renal Function

Urinary samples are typically collected overnight on Nalgene mini chiller blocks from animals in metabolism cages and stored frozen at −80°C. Parameters that are frequently evaluated in the urine include α-glutathione S transferase (aGST), kidney injury molecule 1 (KIM1), lipocalin-2 (Lcn2; also named neutrophil gelatinase-associated lipocalin), micro-albumin, osteopontin (Spp1), clusterin (Clu), trefoil factor 3 (TFF3), and renal papillary

TABLE 16.6 Urine Biomarkers for Renal Injury and Disease [141]

Biomarker	Performance	Lesions Monitored
KIM1, Clu, albumin	May individually outperform and add information to blood urea nitrogen (BUN) and SCr	Acute kidney tubular alterations in rat
Total protein, B2M, cystatin C	May individually outperform SCr assay and add information to BUN and SCr assays	Early diagnostic biomarkers in rat of acute drug-induced glomerular alterations or damage resulting in impairment of kidney tubular reabsorption
TFF3	Adds information to BUN and SCr assays in rat	Drug-induced acute kidney tubular alterations

antigen (Table 16.6). These can be detected with electrochemiluminescent assays. Other parameters used as urinary BMs include phenylacetylglycine (PAG) and Bis (monoacyglycerol) phosphate (BMP) (metabonomic markers for phospholipidosis) that can be detected in the urine using UPLC-TOF-MS (ultraperformance liquid chromatography-time of flight-mass spectrometer) [143]. These urinary BMs are assessed in parallel to blood urea nitrogen (BUN) and serum creatinine (SCr).

Urinary KIM-1, CLU, albumin, and TFF3 have demonstrated that drug-induced acute kidney tubular alterations can be monitored in rat GLP studies used to support the safe conduct of early-phase clinical trials.

Total urinary protein, cystatin C, or β_2 microglobulin (B2M) have demonstrated that drug-induced acute glomerular alterations or damage resulting in impairment of kidney tubular reabsorption are monitorable in rat GLP studies used to support the safe conduct of early-phase clinical trials.

Urinary KIM-1, albumin, total protein, cystatin C, and B2M have been used on a voluntary basis in Phase I and II clinical trials for monitoring kidney safety when animal toxicology findings generated a concern for tubular injury or glomerular alterations. In support of their value in early-phase clinical trials, these markers are gradually gaining acceptance as BMs of efficacy in clinical trials [144].

The current recommendations from regulatory authorities are to use the novel renal BMs in conjunction with the traditional BMs BUN and SCr and with histopathology. These novel BMs may be used in clinical trials on a case-by-case basis with the prerequisites of nonclinical demonstration of reversibility of both BM levels and histopathology and the establishment of prespecified cutoff values (thresholds). However, until further data become available that demonstrate the correlation of these BMs with the evolution of drug-induced lesions and their reversibility, the general use of these BMs for monitoring nephrotoxicity in the clinical setting is not recommended. Additional data to address the temporal relationship between BM levels and the emergence and recovery of histopathological lesions are needed.

Blood Biomarker of Renal Function

There are several parameters classically used to evaluate kidney function that are measured in the blood. These include BUN, SCr, protein (albumin and globulin and albumin/globulin ratios), and a number of electrolytes. Another BM that can be used to evaluate renal function, specifically the glomerular filtration rate (GFR), is the small molecular weight protein cystatin C (cys-C). Cys-C is at least equal if not superior to SCr as a marker of GFR [145].

Genomic Biomarker of Renal Function

The analysis of RNA extracted from the kidney using microarray tools and confirmatory qRT-PCR can be used to evaluate expression profiles of genes involved in renal toxicity. Among the genes examined in such studies, signature genes have been confirmed to be highly induced or repressed in rats treated with nephrotoxicants. Further investigation identified that a few of these genes were also altered by hepatotoxicants. These data led to the identification of a set of genomic BM candidates whose expression in kidney is selectively regulated only by nephrotoxicants. Among those genes displaying the highest expression changes specifically in nephrotoxicant-treated rats were Kim1, Lcn2, and Spp1 [146]. These transcriptomic findings resulted in these proteins being identified as specific BMs of renal toxicity.

Hepatic Biomarkers

The evaluation of the liver function can be done using panels of BM evaluated in the serum (Table 16.7) [147].

Evaluation for specific types of liver histopathology by ROC analysis led to the identification of parameters considered as relevant markers of hepatic injury. Alanine aminotransferase (ALT), aspartate aminotransferase (AST), total bilirubin (Tbili), and serum bile acids (SBA) have the greatest diagnostic utility for manifestations of hepatocellular necrosis and biliary injury, with comparable magnitude of area under the ROC curve and serum hepatobiliary marker changes for both. In the absence of hepatocellular necrosis, ALT increases were observed with biochemical or morphological evidence of cholestasis. After the challenge by hepato-toxicants ($CHCl_3$ and CCl_4) the activities of AST and ALT, marker enzymes for liver damage, were elevated remarkably [148]. The diagnostic utility of alkaline phosphatase (ALP) and gamma glutamyl transferase (GGT) for biliary injury was limited. Alkaline phosphatase had modest diagnostic value for peroxisome proliferation. Alanine aminotransferase, aspartate aminotransferase, and total Chol had moderate diagnostic utility for phospholipidosis.

TABLE 16.7 Serum Biomarkers of Liver Effects

Alanine aminotransferase
Aspartate aminotransferase
Total bilirubin
Serum bile acids
Alkaline phosphatase
Gamma glutamyl transferase
Total cholesterol
Triglycerides
Paraoxonase
Purine nucleoside phosphorylase
Glutamate dehydrogenase
Malate dehydrogenase
miR-122

None of these markers had diagnostic value for manifestations of hypertrophy, cytoplasmic rarefaction, inflammation, or steatosis [149].

Additionally, enzymatic activity can also be used to evaluate the effect of specific toxicants on the liver. For example, in dietary restriction-induced hepatotoxicity, increases in hepatic cytochrome P450 2E1 (CYP2E1) enzymes were observed. The hepatic glutathione (GSH) content, which protects the liver from hepatotoxic agents, was depleted.

Cardiac Biomarkers

Major steps forward have been made in the field of cardiac BMs in the past few years, and these have revolved primarily around identifying BMs of myocardial necrosis. This rapid progress in part is the result of the development of ultrasensitive assays for cardiac troponins I (cTnI) and T (cTnT) [150–158]. Cardiac troponins are parts of the contractile apparatus proteins, are specific to the heart, and increases in their serum concentrations were traditionally equated to myocardial necrosis. The ultrasensitive cTn assays have enabled the identification of baseline serum cTnI and cTnT concentrations that may be increased as a result of strenuous physical effort, birth, central nervous system damage, and respiratory diseases in man [159–162] or in the absence of detectable myocardial necrosis in a wide variety of rat models of cardiac hypertrophy [163], necrosis [164,165], and routine handling procedures. Marginal increases of cTnT have also been shown to be a long-term predictor of cardiovascular events in man [166]. The fact that serum cTn may be increased in the absence of histomorphological evidence of myocardial necrosis in rat and as a long-term predictor of cardiovascular events in man suggests that cTn may be released as a result of sublethal cardiomyocyte injury such as would be induced by focal disturbances of cardiomyocyte metabolism or increased cardiomyocytes stretching. Alternatively, the mediocre sensitivity of histopathology to identify minimal focal lesions may account for the absence of serum cTn increases in the rat models. The occurrence of marginal increases of serum cTn concentrations prior to irreversible myocardial damage also supports their use as ideal translational BMs in clinical drug development. For example, knowledge of serum cTn concentrations in clinical trials would help to better balance the benefit/risk ratio and to adjust the dosing regimen for compounds that cause increased heart weight, affect lipid metabolism, or target angiogenesis.

Another important element contributing to progress in the field of BMs of cardiac necrosis is the acknowledgment that each cardiac BM has specific kinetics. For example, the short half-life of 1–2h for cTnI [167], combined with the fact that acute cardiotoxicants cause cardiomyocyte necrosis at or within a few hours after C_{max}, indicates that the current strategy of collecting clinical pathology parameters 24h after the last dose is inappropriate to measure cardiac effects using cTnI [165,168,169]. For those late time points, serum myosin light-chain 3 (Myl3) concentrations may be more appropriate because of a longer serum half-life for Myl3 than for cTn, with high serum Myl3 concentrations 48h after an acute episode of myocardial necrosis [165,170]. However, because Myl3 is also expressed in slow-twitch muscle fibers, it cannot be used as a standalone marker of cardiomyocyte necrosis. All other markers of cardiomyocyte necrosis are less sensitive and/or specific than cTn and Myl3, including creatine kinase isoforms, fatty acid-binding protein 3, lactate dehydrogenase, alanine aminotransferase, aspartate aminotransferase, and aldolase [165,169,171]. Similarly, serum concentrations of several microRNAs have been proposed as biomarkers of cardiomyocyte necrosis in man [172–174] and rat [175]. These include miR-1, miR-30c, miR-133a, miR-145, miR-208a, miR-208b, and miR-499-5p. The value of these microRNAs as potential BMs of cardiomyocyte necrosis is limited because of the body of literature around cTn, the sensitivity of the cTn assays, and because of indications that microRNAs might be less sensitive than cTn for this specific endpoint [173].

Myocardial necrosis certainly is an important toxicity endpoint. However, findings other than cardiomyocyte necrosis are often identified in safety studies. The most concerning of these findings include increased heart weight [163,176–181], valve lesions [182,183], interstitial cell damage, heart failure [184], and fibrosis. These findings may have functional effects, which may be monitored by measuring serum N-terminal-proatrial natriuretic peptide (NT-proANP) and/or N-terminal-probrain natriuretic peptide (NT-proBNP) [185–190]. Based on studies conducted in man, serum BMs may exist for these endpoints and include myostatin [184],

microRNAs [172], and transforming growth factor β receptor 1 [191]. However, there is a gradual transition from histopathology and serum BMs as gold standards to the highly relevant electrophysiology and cardiac function and structure endpoints [192–196]. In particular, the role of in vivo imaging using echocardiography is anticipated to increase in the coming years, because this permits the monitoring of cardiac structure and function in individual animals over time, thereby reducing the number of animals used in safety studies and refining the selection of the time points for serum BM collection. In addition, echocardiography is highly translational.

Skeletal Muscle Biomarkers

A variety of drugs, including statins, PPAR-α agonists, steroids, and β-adrenergic receptor agonists, may cause muscle toxicity [197–201]. Such drug-induced skeletal muscle toxicity may result in serious liability, as illustrated by the withdrawal from the market of cerivastatin (Baycol), the 3-hydroxy-3-methylglutaryl-coenzyme A (HMG-CoA) reductase inhibitor, after it was associated with 100 rhabdomyolysis-related deaths [202]. Nonclinical detection of skeletal muscle toxicity typically hinges on standard histopathological evaluation, supplemented by the assessment of serological BMs, including creatine kinase (CK), and AST.

Although CK is the most common serum marker for skeletal muscle injury, it is not ideal for several reasons, including lack of tissue specificity, inability to reveal damage to specific skeletal fiber types (fast or slow), and inappropriately low values when glutathione concentrations are decreased because of liver or multiple-organ failure [203]. There is now consensus that the commonly used BMs lack sensitivity and specificity, particularly in rats [199]. Recently, fatty-acid binding protein 3 (Fabp3), a sensitive BM of myocardial injury in humans, was shown to be useful for assessing skeletal muscle toxicity in rats [204]. The use of cardiac troponins [cardiac troponin I (cTnI) and/or cTnT] for diagnosis of myocardial infarction (MI), as well as for diagnosis and management of unstable angina, is based on their superior tissue specificity over such conventional BMs as CK [205]. Skeletal troponin I (sTnI), with its two distinct isoforms [fast (fsTnI) and slow (ssTnI)], like cTnI and cTnT, has been shown to have a similar advantage over conventional markers for detecting skeletal muscle injury. Recently, it was observed that fsTnI in conjunction with standard clinical assays may comprise a useful diagnostic panel for assessing drug-induced myopathy in rats [199].

Vascular Injury Biomarkers

Drug-induced vascular injury is a toxic endpoint for which there currently is no validated BM. Biomarkers are needed to monitor vascular injury because the translational significance of this finding in nonclinical species is questionable as compounds such as minoxidil cause vascular injury in dog and rat but not in man [206], or the development of phosphodiesterase III and IV inhibitors that cause vasculitis in animal species has been hampered by the absence of reliable biomarker to initiate clinical studies [207–216]. Common etiologies for vascular injury include localized hemodynamics effects such as vasospasms and vasodilation and direct endothelial toxicity. It is assumed that intense vasospasm or vasoconstriction may cause collapse of blood supply provided by the *vasa vasorum* system of the large blood vessels, resulting in ischemic conditions that may culminate in medial necrosis. Endothelial damage may also be a primary process such as caused by bacterial lipopolysaccharides, or secondary to a massive efflux of inflammatory cells into the tissues such as is caused by administration of interleukin 2. Finally, it is important to differentiate drug-induced vascular injury from "beagle pain syndrome" which is a common spontaneous vascular disease in laboratory beagle dogs [217].

The Critical Path Institute's Predictive Safety Testing Consortium (C-Path's PSTC) and International Life Science Institute's Health and Environmental Sciences Institute (ILSI-HESI) coordinate the pharmaceutical industry's efforts to identify BMs of vascular injury. These BMs broadly fall in three categories:

1. BMs of endothelial damage
2. BMs of smooth muscle cell damage
3. BMs of vascular inflammation

Candidate BMs of endothelial damage include caveolin-1(Cav1), thrombospondin 1 (Thbs1), von Willebrand propetide, E-selectin (Sele), angiopoietin 2 (Angpt2), nitric oxide (NO), asymmetric dimethyl arginine, vascular endothelial growth factor (VEGF), endothelin 1 (Edn1), tyrosine kinase with immunoglobulin-like and EGF-like domains 1 (Tie1), endothelial-specific receptor tyrosine kinase (Tek), endothelial-specific molecule 1 (Esm1), and microRNAs [218,219]. The most promising candidate BM microRNAs for vascular damage are miR-126, mirR-134, miR-409-3p, and miR-511. In addition, markers of endothelial damage include circulating endothelial cells microparticles and circulating endothelial progenitor cells [220–223]. The validation of protein BMs is hampered by antibody availability. The efforts to identify circulating endothelial cell microparticles has been hampered by the low dynamic range in the studies presented thus far, which may be related to their rapid uptake by reticuloendothelial cells and healthy endothelial cells [224].

Candidate BMs of mural smooth-muscle cell damage currently include smooth-muscle alpha actin (Acta2), calponin 1 (Cnn1), smoothelin (Smtn), H-caldesmon 1 (Cald1), transgelin (Tagln), smooth-muscle myosin-heavy polypeptide 11 (Myh11), and miR-145. The last category of candidate BMs of vascular injury are markers of inflammation, which by their nature are not specific and have mediocre sensitivity. These include complement component 3a (C3a), lipocalin 2 (Lcn2, NGAL), Lcn2: matrix metallopeptidase 9 (Mmp9) heterodimer, chemokine (C-X-C motif) ligand (Cxcl1), orosomucoid 1 (Orm1), C-reactive protein (CRP), and a variety of cytokines. Of note, CRP is not a good marker of inflammation in rodents. Validated assays are also not available for all of these endpoints.

Digital Pathology Imaging

Digital imaging has become fundamental for the evaluation and quantification of molecular pathology parameters. The establishment of protocols for the evaluation of pathology specimens contributes in many ways to decrease subjectivity in the pathology evaluation. At the same time it easily translates data into numeric outputs increasing the ability to perform detailed statistical analyses and allowing for an increase in reproducibility and more thorough approach to pathology data interpretation.

The use of image analysis as a tool for histopathology evaluation may be used to provide:

1. Cell quantification by measuring membrane and/ or nuclear counts. Counts of negative and positive nuclei or membrane stained cells can be categorized based on their stain intensity (0, 1+, 2+, 3+). Digital evaluation of pathology specimens can also categorize and segregate nuclei as to size and shape;
2. Area quantification by color deconvolution that can separate and quantitate up to three different stains on one given image (the data output is percent of area stained and the stain intensity) and colocalization [how stains overlap with one another (data output is percent of area stained and percent area of stain overlap)];
3. Objective identification such as microvessel analysis or rare events; and
4. Pattern-recognition systems [eg, Los Alamos National Laboratory: Genetic Imagery Exploration (Genie Pro) image-pattern recognition technology in digital pathology].

Image analysis may include several phases of image preprocessing. These may include color definition, thresholding, clustering, and pixel/shape expansion or shrinkage. The resulting images may then be quantified for surface area or shape.

Quality image analysis is dependent on several factors that will ultimately define the scientific relevance of the data obtained. Factors to consider are:

1. Standardization of the upstream processes (fixation, staining, mounting, cover slipping, tissue section thickness) to reduce variability;

2. Antibody optimization for IHC applications;
3. Processing of slides to be evaluated for the same marker within the same batch to decrease/avoid side-to-side variability and allow for side-to-side spot comparative analysis;
4. Inclusion of appropriate controls with each run batch (positive control, negative control); and
5. Background and staining thresholds established by adding staining and negative controls.

One of the most recent applications of digital imaging is the evaluation, assessment, and/or quantification of IHC specimens in the development of nonclinical BMs. The use of tissue microarrays allows systematic analysis of BM expression using IHC in tissues with side-to-side comparison. The same sample may be used with serial sections to assess multiple BMs. Digital spot view allows rapid stain comparison and easy access of image data. Each individual spot may also be analyzed in regards to membrane staining (intensity and completeness) and/or nuclear staining (intensity) and provide discrete data for each spot in an accurate and consistent manner. Additionally, the stain separation into different components can be done for each spot (eg, in case of DAB with a fast-green counter stain) and the intensity of staining can also be measured by area. Additional analysis may include pattern recognition based on features such as percent of positivity for a certain parameter, the intensity score, and total percent of feature present in the section [225,226].

Imaging in Nonclinical Development

There are multiple imaging techniques/modalities that can be used as research tools in nonclinical development and can serve as tools to identify, assess, and/or quantify directly or indirectly molecular pathology parameters. These include, but are not limited to, the following:

1. Magnetic resonance imaging (MRI) obtains quantitative morphometric (volume and surface area) data and can visualize the site and location of a lesion. MRI delineates tissue structure based on proton stains. Applications of MRI include the evaluation of stroke (morphometric measurements of cerebral ischemia); the diagnosis of chemically induced renal lesions (loss of cortical vs. medullary zonation); and evaluation of kidney vasculature [227–229].
2. Magnetic resonance microscopy (MRM) may be used to conduct image analysis studies on the heart in mouse models. MRM has good image contrast with the ability to easily distinguish one tissue from another [228].
3. Cardiac microCT may also be used as an image analysis method for the heart of the mouse. It has 25-µm spatial resolution but cannot be used in vivo due to noise associated with small voxel and motion. It also it has low soft-tissue resolution [228].
4. Luciferase imaging may procure measurements in transgenic mice coupled with a CCD camera. Luciferase imaging is used to visualize and quantify the presence of a molecular endpoint within an organ/tissue/organism [230].
5. PET scanning uses drugs labeled with 11C or 18F to monitor their distribution [231,232]. Nanoparticles are used as contrast agents in vivo (near infrared) fluorescence (NIRF) and also for PET and MRI [233].
6. Imaging signaling pathways is performed using fluorescence resonance energy transfer (FRET) microscopy. However, the use of FRET microscopy with direct targeting of ligands has two issues: lack of efficient clearance of the unbound or nonspecific bound fraction of reporter molecules, and signal amplification for inhibitor-based probes [231].

Good Laboratory Practice Validation and Regulatory Considerations

In nonclinical research and development it is important that there is GLP validation of imaging processes that will allow for data submission to the FDA and other regulatory agencies. The FDA has provided guidelines for the techniques related to the generation, acquisition, and interpretation of image data (http://www.accessdata.fda.gov/scripts/cdrh/cfdocs/cfPMN/pmn.cfm).

This process of validation is substantially equivalent to manual microscopy, in which slides are scored in the traditional way using a light microscope by a group of pathology peers scoring individually. The same slides are then scanned into a digital database and evaluated independently by pathologists using image analysis. The College of American Pathologists expressed concerns regarding the test conditions in terms of representative slide; sample size, which can affect performance differences; type of specimen; diagnostic spectrum; and evaluating criteria that can vary with pathologists. However, digital image evaluation may contribute to the implementation of quantitative image analysis, slide-quality control (folds, rips, etc.), and automated flagging of test article-induced abnormalities.

Regulatory compliance with 21 CRF part 11 requires integration with image acquisition and analysis, configurable administration, comprehensive audit, project archive/restore, image versioning and validated tissue stamps, electronic long-time-archive and electronic signatures. The 21CFR11 GLP compliance functionality requires system logins and passwords, access control and user privileges, autodetection of data tampering, comprehensive audit log and electronic signature records. A validation system that verifies the following is needed to ensure that all:

1. System components have been properly installed (IQ)
2. System components operate correctly (OQ)
3. System performs as expected (PQ)

Standard operating procedures (SOPs) for pattern recognition with appropriate training records are also needed. Tissue variability and error rates should be evaluated on image-analysis projects and should be included in the SOPs. Slide storage is important because the slide is the raw data. However, the digital slide may also be considered raw data if it is permanently archived and securely managed.

Image Storage and Retrieval

Digital imaging can be used by the pathologist to produce, store, and easily retrieve pathology data (Table 16.8) [234,235].

Cameras used to capture images should have large color dynamic range to ensure true color fidelity, high spatial resolution to match optical microscopic resolution, high image acquisition rate (real-time view), high-speed data transfer, and connection to a light microscope.

Multiple slide-scanning technologies include:

1. Automated area scan microimaging (CCD camera) with tile-by-tile acquisition;
2. Automated ID line-scan microimaging with linear scanning of small tissues from images;
3. Array microscopy images with lens-array parallel scanning of an entire slide.

These image-acquisition systems need to be in compliance with the code of Federal Regulation (CFR) vol. 21, part 58 (GLP) and part 11 in order to be used in GLP nonclinical studies.

TABLE 16.8 Advantages and Disadvantages of Image Storage and Retrieval

Advantages	Disadvantages
• Identical digital format reproduction • Transfer • Storage • Image printing • Image management • Computer analysis • Increase microphotograph quality • Image documentation	• Nonuniform illumination • Display of image: Multimega pixel true color may be difficult to obtain on flat screen LCD monitor • Obsolescence of image and data management software • Cost of bioinformatics resources to store large image banks

Whole-Slide Image Analysis

There is an emerging preference in nonclinical research to use image analysis to supplement historical semiquantitative scoring with computer-assisted quantitation and morphometry, especially for immunolabeled tissues. Whole-slide analysis uses image pattern-recognition algorithms paired with engineering and image analysis to target solutions that are highly optimized and provide quantitative endpoints to pathological evaluations. It uses scaled to multiread architecture to ensure linear improvement of the throughput and spatially invariant vector quantification that allows for spatial pattern recognition [236]. The digitalization of tissue sections allows the capture of the histopathology image that can then be processed in order to perform digital analysis of that image. One of the most frequent endpoints achieved by digitalization includes digital quantification of histopathological features.

The advantages of digital quantification include:

1. Decreased subjectivity
2. Increased reproducibility
3. Increased intra- and interobserver reliability
4. Increased precision in lesion quantification
5. The ability to improve and enhance statistical data treatment

The technical aspects taken into consideration when optimizing the IHC technique include:

1. Consistency of fixation
2. Epitope retrieval method
3. The presence of standardized internal and external controls

Digital analysis of IHC specimens allows numeric quantification of the data. The visual results obtained can be treated with Levy–Jennings and Westgard rules. These generate a chart system that may be used for extensive quality assurance of the data. Computerized algorithms may be used to perform colorimetry and morphometry measurements that contribute to distinguish and localize different cellular components such as cytoplasm and nucleus and perform calibration tests.

The American College of Pathology has issued guidance for IHC testing for Her2. It notes that the level of prediction should have 5% concordance and that there should be review of negative and positive controls, biannual validation, external proficiency testing, and ongoing QA assessment. There should be special attention given to tissue fixation, automated antigen retrieval, and automated staining systems. For example, the optimal ICH testing requirements for Her2 includes fixation for more that 6h and less that 48h, slices of 5–10mm for optimal fixation, the use of appropriate controls, consideration of sample artifacts, homogeneous staining, and normal membrane staining of breast ducts that act as internal controls. Additionally, the interpreters need to maintain consistency during the evaluation [237].

Computer-Aided Diagnosis

Image analysis can be used for detection of "abnormalities" in histology sections of a tissue or organ, including for the diagnosis of cancer lesions. Computer-aided diagnosis (CAD) allows biopsy specimen analysis by creating a quantitative image composed of metrics against tissue patterns that can be compared, reducing diagnostic time and enabling the pathologist to analyze data with more detail. This system performs a multihierarchical multiscale analysis that uses a large set of texture features to describe each pixel in the image. Based on these features a classifier is trained to distinguish between nonneoplastic and cancerous patterns. Images can be scanned at 40× magnification to high-resolution whole slides, which are decomposed into constituent scales. Each scale has a number of image features extracted. Each feature in the set is assessed for its performance and subsequently used to discriminate between "cancer" and "noncancer" [238].

This same principle can be applied to the detection of other (or any) pathological lesions or even certain histological features. The validation of the features in the set is time- and resource-intensive and requires constant QA by an experienced pathologist.

Histochemical Measurements

Whole-slide image analysis can also be used for quantification of structures or features that are evaluated by histochemical special staining techniques. Histochemical staining aims to highlight a particular histological characteristic, structure, or molecule with a specific color. Image analysis algorithms can be developed to quantify the abundance/amount of a particular color within the histological section. This quantification can then be translated into the relative expression of that particular endpoint. As with all previously described parameters, there are many limitations and aspects that need to be taken into consideration when analyzing data provided by this type of data acquisition. One commonly used endpoint in research is collagen quantification in multiple tissue/organs [239]. For example, collagen quantification in the liver requires the removal of artifacts such as staining of sinusoids or other nonspecific staining. To minimize such artifacts careful consideration should be given to the staining technique. Technical aspects of histochemical staining that can be limiting to the quality of digital image analysis include, but are not limited to, stain intensity, color contrast, stain uniformity,

presence of off-target, or nonspecific staining. Only after optimization of all these aspects should the digital image be obtained. The presence of cell debris and tissue fragmentation and other processing and microtomy artifacts can also be confounders during image analysis. White space, such as seen in distended blood vessels, and edge artifacts should be addressed prior to endpoint quantification.

Pattern Analysis: Skeletonization

One of the major challenges of whole-slide imaging is the limited ability to generate pattern-recognition algorithms. Pattern recognition is the basis of most semiqualitative histopathological evaluations. Skeletonization (ie, skeleton extraction from a digital binary picture) provides region-based shape features. It is a common preprocessing operation in raster-to-vector conversion or in pattern recognition. Pattern-recognition analysis can be useful in the evaluation of endpoints such as angiogenesis, bone trabecular density, neuronal tracing, and hepatic portal-to-portal lesions, allowing computer-assisted digital analysis of morphometry parameters [240].

Quantification of angiogenesis can be done using a fluorescent microscope with optronics (TEC470) with a single chip-cooled camera with metamorph image analysis software (Westchester PA). This will allow count of positive blood vessels at 200× magnification. The image can be inverted to obtain skeletonization of the image (Adobe command: filter; IP* morphology: Skeletonize). This reduces the microvessels to a black line with a single pixel width and two additional gray levels for pixels that occur at branch points/nodes and at endpoints. These are scored together for a total vessel count. The objective is to record vessel architecture instead of vessel density. This analysis can also be done by grid intersection and fractal dimension analysis [241].

In the evaluation of bone microstructure, 2D stereological techniques-based histological sections have been supplanted by 3D morphological analyses that allow determination of trabecular bone connectivity in addition to the classical thickness, number, and spacing parameters. The process of skeletonization extracts node and branch network information, generating data that improves the reliability of trabecular bone assessment [242].

Stereology in Image Analysis

Traditional pathology slide evaluation is based on 2D examination of tissues. This approach is usually based on subjective examination of one representative section of a tissue or organ. While this approach is sufficient for most pathology endpoints, such as lesion diagnosis, it has many limitations when experimental pathology endpoints are assessed. Stereology is a subset of morphometry that relates 3D parameters defining structures to 2D measurements obtained on sections of the structure. It allows evaluation of structural parameters such as volume, surface, length, and number of cells.

Stereological methods are precise tools used to quantify and evaluate structures in a tri-dimensional level. These methods are based on observations made on 2D or 3D subsamples of tissues with applied test probes and counting interactions of these probes with the structures that are evaluated [211]. Stereology methodology allows the estimation of density using the Delesse principle according to which relative volumes can be estimated from relative lengths and hence from ratios from intersection points. The Delesse principle established the basis for several important concepts underlying the stereological analysis of biological objects by relating the area of an object in 2D planes to its corresponding volume in 3D. Additionally, it shows that single-plane sections do not provide a good base for quantification of particles. This principle advocates indirectly the need to perform stereology analysis as an accurate method for quantification of pathology endpoints.

Stereology is also a technique that permits estimation of relative numbers of particles. This is computed from fractions of particle-profile counts made using unbiased counting frames and volume probes. A known fraction of an object sample, the structural quantity (usually number), is estimated. The total structural quantity is estimated by multiplying the inverse sampling fraction by the number in the final sample. The evaluation of number of particles is based on counting frames. In 2D the counting depends on whether the particle intersects the counting frame. Each and every particle is counted only once. In stereology the reference volume is sliced. The number of profiles is different from the number of particles and cannot be used to evaluate particle number.

In pathology evaluation, stereology serves as the gold standard to validate image-quantification methods. Usually software generates a grid system. Within this grid system a selected number of random areas are selected from the tissue slides. The number of intersections between the desired histological feature (eg, collagen fiber) and the grid within the reference area is noted and the relative area occupied by the histological feature is calculated [243]. Stereology data are then assessed by statistical analysis.

Several aspects need to be taken into consideration when preparing tissues for stereology analysis. All sections that originate for either vibratome or cryostat sectioning should be kept in the sequential order they are obtained. If volumetric analysis is intended, tissue shrinkage must be minimized with adequate fixation using perfusion techniques and optimal tissue-freezing

TABLE 16.9 Types of Sampling for Stereology

Type of Sampling	Characteristics of Sampling Technique
Uniform random sample	Every particle in the whole population has an equal chance of being selected
Systematic uniform random sample	Systematically takes every nth particle. Reduces the variance when compared to random sampling
Isotropic uniform random sample	Sampling is uniform in any orientation (often used in evaluating liver and kidney)
Vertical uniform random sample	Sampling is nonuniform, follows an axis (used in sampling heart and lung)

protocols. Different types of stereology sampling are summarized in Table 16.9.

Stereology has been extensively applied to the kidney and has proven superior to classical 2D analysis for multiple endpoints. These include the measurement of total kidney volume, total nephron number, total numbers and volume of glomeruli, and length/number of renal tubules [244].

Estimation of tubule-length density relies on the fact that test planes intersect curve length. Isotropic sections (completely spherical) use vertical sections (cycloids) or central sections that are rotated in different degrees. These can be used for surface estimation. Finally, stereology may be used to assess glomerular capillaries. The intersections counted between the stereological grid lines and the surface area can be used to count test points. The number of test points by intersection areas between test lines and capillary membranes can then be determined, providing a numerical endpoint to the glomerular capillary evaluation.

TOXICOGENOMICS

Toxicogenomics (TGX) are a scientific tool based on the acquisition, interpretation, and storage of information about gene expression and associated protein activity within particular cells or tissue of an organism in response to toxic substances. The promises of TGX were many and chiefly included the ability to predict toxicity at lower doses and earlier than the current gold standards such as histopathology [245]. There are multiple publications that support the association between specific patterns of gene expression and specific pharmacological effects and mechanisms of toxicity [246–255]. In addition, TGX signatures have been used to identify novel BMs [248,252], to predict long-term toxicities, including carcinogenicity, to identify interspecies differences in the toxic or pharmacological response [248], to detect a toxic signal in a surrogate tissue, and to identify toxicity in in vitro systems

[253,254]. Finally, TGX may be more sensitive than the classical gold standards, for example, than hematology to identify hemolytic anemia [256] or than histopathology to identify focal/multifocal lesions [247] and may be more time efficient, for example, to screen for phospholipidosis in vitro [254,257].

There are a number of data analysis platforms that can be used to interpret TGX data. These include:

1. Go-Quant, which combines gene ontology (GO) and pathway mapping to extract quantitative gene-expression values and to calculate the average intensity or ratio for those significantly altered by functional gene category based on MAPPFinder results, enabling the user to calculate the corresponding 50% effective dose (ED50) for each specific function.
2. Array Track developed by the National Center for Toxicological Research of the US Food and Drug administration (FDA), probably the best-known free bioinformatics resource to manage, analyze, and interpret "omics" data. It contains a large collection of functional information about genes, proteins, and pathways for biological interpretation.
3. Commercial packages of Ingenuity (Ingenuity Systems, Redwood City, CA) and Pathway Studio [Ariadne Genomics and Metacore (GeneGo, Carlsbad, CA)].
4. Freely available software packages such as DAVID (National Cancer Institute at Frederick, Frederick, MD; http://david.abcc.ncifcrf.gov/) and Onto-Express (Wayne State University, Detroit, MI; http://vortex.cs.wayne.edu/ontoexpress/) can be easily accessed.

Additionally, there are publicly available datasets in data repositories that play a key role in the interpretation of transcriptomic findings. These data repositories include:

1. Gene Expression Omnibus (GEO; http://www.ncbi.nlm.nih.gov/gds), a rich resource for TGX data that lacks toxicology-specific controlled vocabulary and chemical indexing [257,258].
2. The Comparative Toxicogenomics Database (CTD; http://ctd.mdibl.org/) [259], a useful comparator for toxicology experiments, although it does not store raw genomics data.
3. The Toxicogenomics Project–Genomics Assisted Toxicity Evaluation system (TG-GATEs; http://thedatahub.org/dataset/open-tggates [260]).
4. Transcriptomics data analysis is also aided by commercial resources such as ToxFX (Entelos, San Mateo, CA), a TGX analysis suite utilizing Iconix's Drug Signatures database, specially curated biochemical pathways and other relevant data.
5. Iconix's reference database provides information on more than 630 reference compounds, more than

4500 dose–time–tissue combinations, and more than 15,000 microarray experiments. The application generates a TGX report, providing information about a compound's predictive safety profile.
6. GeneLogic's ToxExpress Program (Gaithersburg, MD) contains a database comprised of more than 14,000 drug-treated animal tissues and controls. Their predictive TGX models employ primary rat hepatocytes in vitro to provide quantitative information of a test compound's potential to induce hepatotoxicity in vivo. This can enable the elucidation of mechanisms of toxicity and the identification of BMs.

The pathologist has an important role in the design of TGX studies because of his understanding of the whole animal biology, which includes knowledge of the feeding patterns, light, circadian rhythms, age, species, strains, sexual maturity and cycles, background tissue changes, heterogeneity within organs, etc. [261,262]. For example, each chamber of the heart has a distinct transcriptomic profile [263] and each liver lobe has a specific transcriptomic response to hepatotoxicants [264,265]. Finally, the pathologist will also be indispensable when correlating TGX findings with clinical pathology and histopathology findings and in designing subsequent experiments and applying and analyzing ISH/IHC results.

Consultation with the pathologist is relevant especially to perform additional tissue-based confirmation assays and to assess the relevance of the findings. The pathologist also provides important contributions in data interpretation based on specialized knowledge of the tissue morphology, composition of the controls and treated tissues, the impact of morphological alterations on biological pathways, and the kinetics of tissue changes.

Considerations for the Design of Nonclinical Toxicogenomics Studies

Samples for TGX analysis generally are collected as part of routine toxicology studies. This may be a shortcoming because samples for routine toxicology studies typically are collected 24–28 h after the last dose and may not be optimal to fully evaluate the pharmacokinetic and pharmacodynamics characteristics of the test article. Therefore just as for BM studies, TGX studies may have to be specifically designed to capture the transcriptomic changes at more appropriate time points. The time points used as default often include 6 h after the first dose to identify effects occurring a few hours after the first Cmax (maximum concentration); 24 h after the first dose to evaluate gene changes prior to the establishment of morphological changes the magnitude of which may obscure changes directly related to the mechanism of toxicity; and after 5–14 days of dosing at a regimen similar to that in routine toxicity studies to evaluate a time point where morphological changes are present.

In addition to a vehicle-treated dose group, the doses used for TGX studies generally include a low dose aimed at causing pharmacodynamics effects and a high dose aimed at causing toxic effects. The use of an intermediate dose may help in assessing the transition from a pharmacodynamics dose to a toxic dose.

Most TGX studies are conducted in rats. They are generally not conducted in large animal species for ethical reasons and to reduce the use of the test article. Therefore the information on the transcriptomic profile in response to toxicants is essentially based on rat studies. Most TGX studies are also performed in mature young (7–10-week-old) male rats because of estrous cycle-related fluctuations in females. The rats generally are fasted overnight to reduce variability associated with the feeding status. The number of animals assessed typically is a minimum of five per group to achieve statistical and biological significance.

A complete clinical pathology and histopathology evaluation must be carried out, and is essential to identify the cause of outliers, which may be incidental background changes such as the early stages of hydronephrosis, spontaneous cardiomyopathy, and incidental liver necrosis and inflammation. Samples for toxicokinetics are generally not collected from animals intended to be used for TGX assessment because the repeated bleeds required for toxicokinetics would confound the TGX assessment. However, when warranted, a parallel group of animals used for toxicokinetic evaluation may be added.

Tissue Collection

It is generally recommended that large portions of organs be homogenized for transcriptomic evaluation because small samples may not be representative [168,266,267]. The rapid degradation of messenger RNA in tissues imposes prioritization of the collection of samples for TGX over those for histopathology. The tissues may be snap-frozen in liquid nitrogen and stored at −65°C to −85°C for TGX analysis. Alternatively, they may be stored, immersed in RNAlater (Life Technology, Carlsbad, CA) for up to 24h prior to transfer to −65°C to −85°C.

RNA Labeling and Hybridization

There are a number of options available for performing RNA labeling and hybridization. These technologies are in constant upgrade; therefore we will provide information for one of the most currently used platforms. The Affymetrix platform (Affymetrix, Santa Clara, CA) has been shown to produce highly reproducible results at multiple test sites (MAQC Consortium, 2006). Quality-control testing is performed on all reagents prior to use on experimental samples. Total RNA (1 µg) is converted to double-stranded cDNA by priming with an oligo-dT primer containing a T7 RNA polymerase promoter at the 5′ end and using Superscript II reverse transcriptase and T4 DNA polymerase (Invitrogen, Carlsbad, CA). The cDNA is used as the template for in vitro transcription using a BioArray HighYield Transcript Labeling Kit containing biotinylated CTP and UTP (Enzo, Farmingdale, NY). Labeled cRNA is fragmented in 40mM Tris-acetate pH 8.1, 100mM KOAc, and 30mM MgOAc for 35min at 94°C in a final volume of 40µL. Labeled probes are denatured at 99°C for 5min and then 45°C for 5min and hybridized to Affymetrix 230 2.0 GeneChip arrays. Arrays are generally hybridized for 16h at 45°C with rotation at 60rpm. After hybridization, probes are removed and the gene-array cartridges washed extensively and stained with phycoerythrin coupled to streptavidin. GeneChip image files are generated using the Affymetrix GeneChip Operating Software version 1.1.1052 using the manufacturer's default settings.

RNAScope

RNAScope technology is a novel in situ hybridization technique for applying unique probe design strategies for the simultaneous signal amplification and background suppression to achieve single-molecule visualization while preserving tissue morphology. Importantly, RNAscope is compatible with routine FFPE tissue specimens and can use either conventional chromogenic dyes for bright-field microscopy or fluorescent dyes for multiplex analysis. Compared to the loss of structural integrity associated with the tissue-grinding method of standard ISH, the RNAScope ISH method represents a robust method for the detection of the morphologic expression of RNA in FFPE tissues. Thus, the technique represents a powerful new platform for the application of molecular pathology to the elucidation of the effects of drugs on the tissue distribution of specific RNA molecules, including, for example, diagnostic biomarker RNAs.

Toxicogenomics Data Analysis Workflow

The data provided to the pathologist by the molecular laboratory and the statistician generally consists of large Excel spreadsheets that include data for individual rats and for the groups, with information on the statistically significant probes. The success of data interpretation (Table 16.10) relies on the familiarity of the pathologist with the test article and its pharmacological effects, the physiology of the target organ, and the molecular pathways associated with the toxicity mechanism. Multiple public and commercial databases are helpful in reviewing transcriptomic datasets. These include BioGPS (http://biogps.org/), Gene Ontology (GO; http://www.geneontology.org), Gene Map Annotator and Pathway Profiler (http://www.genmapp.org), the Science Signaling Connections Map (http://stke.sciencemag.org/cm/), BioCarta (http://www.biocarta.com/genes/index.asp), Reactome (http://www.genomeknowledge.org), KEGG (http://www.genome.jp/kegg/pathway.

TABLE 16.10   TGX Data Interpretation Matrix as a Multitiered Approach

TGX Analysis Technique	Relevance to TGX Data Interpretation
High density array technology	Microarray platforms use mRNA extracted from tissues and then reversed transcribed to cDNA, fluorescently labeled and hybridized to a cDNA or oligonucleotide microarray. The data are represented as a matrix of fluorescent intensity such as Affymetrix gene chips (Affymetrix Inc., Santa Clara, CA)
Validation of microarray data	qRT-PCR, TaqMan probe method, ISH
Bioinformatics	Algorithms comparing data between genes and samples will sort out nonspecific variations from actual signal. Example: Gene Spring (silicon genetics, Redwood, CA). Rosetta Inpharmatics, Inc. (Kirland, WA) computational tool that allows interrogation and queries in large microarray data sets by similar expression profiles
Clustering	Statistical-based data organization and ordering to help generate hypothesis, confirm status of vehicle-treated rats, identify a dose–response, etc.; similar levels of expression are usually related to similar or related biological functions
Statistical analysis	Fold increase may not be representative of biological significance because a large gene change may not be representative of a biological function and a small change in gene expression may have a dramatic biological effect. Statistical analysis is more likely to represent experimental relevance. Log-intensity ratios may allow the calculation of confidence intervals and ANOVA-based analyses may also contribute to determine statistical significance of data
Correlation with cell pathways	Statistical methods for associating cellular pathways and annotations with gene expression changes such as (1) GOMiner, (2) Significance analysis of functional categories, (3) Onto-tools

ISH, in situ hybridization; *TGX*, toxicogenomics.

html), Ingenuity System Pathway Analysis (Redwood City, CA), and GeneGo (Carlsbad, CA).

Pathway Analysis

Determination of the regulation of responses can be complex because they are controlled by multiple genes, proteins, and metabolites. Therefore accurate identification of gene–gene interactions and regulation is essential for determining well-defined pathways that could serve as potential targets in therapeutic development or intervention. Transcriptional pathway-level analysis may prove essential for determining molecular perturbations that are associated with subclinical pathologies because alterations in gene expression are likely to be a more sensitive endpoint than the clinically observed toxicity.

There are multiple public databases available for the annotation and interpretation of gene expression data in terms of cellular process, functions, and pathways [268].

Regulatory Aspects of Toxicogenomics Submission

The US FDA Center for Drug Evaluation and Research (CDER) formed the Nonclinical Pharmacogenomics Subcommittee (NPSC) in 2004. The NPSC has reviewed data from several "mock submissions" of nonclinical studies that were voluntarily submitted to the committee or to review divisions. The term "mock submissions" is used

in this report as opposed to "voluntary submission." Similar guidelines have been provided by the European Medicines Agency (EMEA) [269].

The NPSC evaluated the content of the mock submissions using the framework for reporting microarray data outlined by the Microarray Gene Expression Data (MGED) Society in their proposals of the minimum information about a microarray experiment (MIAME). The fields specified in MIAME present a foundation for the content necessary for review of pharmacogenomics data. More recently, a framework for reporting biological investigations across "omics" technologies has been initiated through the MGED Society that includes an investigational design description checklist, a discipline-specific checklist (eg, MINTox—minimum information needed for a toxicology experiment), and a technology-based checklist (eg, MIAME).

There are multiple points to consider in toxicogenic submissions to the FDA. Information on laboratory and informatics infrastructure should be well documented and available on request, possibly as part of a device master file or SOPs. The electronic files need to be consistent with regulatory guidance [268,269]. It is important to present data for QC metrics and to provide graphical presentation of all relevant metrics. Electronic data sets are an integral part of the submission, even for subsets of genes. The utility and suitability of particular electronic formats will depend on whether these files are used to populate a database with data-mining capabilities or as a data repository. User-friendly software tools to analyze and visualize data are preferred. Protocols for the in-life portion of toxicogenomics studies should follow practices used for standard toxicity studies and can be submitted in the format of a standard GLP toxicology study. These include the use of both sexes (unless there is scientific justification to limit the study to one sex) and using appropriate doses of drug. The number of replicates and power needed will vary depending on the sponsor's intended claim and the experimental objectives. However, in order to perform some minimal statistical analysis, there needs to be at least three animals per sex per time point. Gene expression changes that are critical to the sponsor's argument may be confirmed with qPCR on a limited number of genes. Toxicological findings relevant to the genomic data interpretation should be discussed as per any general toxicology study and appropriate correlations should be made.

The regulatory authorities may perform their own independent data analysis; mock submissions should therefore include electronic files for independent analysis of the sponsor's results. The NPSC have used Spotfire software (Spotfire Inc., Somerville, MA) to analyze the microarray data from 4- and 15-day experiments.

It is important to ensure that mRNA is of good biological quality and that replicates (including control) are processed on the same day. The arrays for the controls and treated groups for each day should be processed together. Thus the results for the treated groups can be compared separately with the results for the appropriate control. Principal component analysis (PCA) analysis should be performed to evaluate sample clustering. Although PCA is a valuable method to inspect sample homogeneity and general treatment-related changes in gene expression data, it is a subjective and relative method of analysis. Additional analyses of the data (eg, using heat maps, pathway analysis) can also be useful to provide more support for the conclusions.

Use of a contextual database containing genomics data annotated with toxicity data is important for the interpretation of the potential toxicity of a drug. Gene signatures would require additional experiments for confirmation. Potential toxicities suggested by gene signatures would be addressed in different sections of full investigational new drug/NDA submissions (eg, safety pharmacology and histopathology in a longer toxicology study).

In conclusion, TGX are a very valuable tool of paramount importance to evaluate system toxicity. To use TGX to its full potential requires an integrated approach of biologists (mainly toxicologists), geneticists, and statisticians. To the skeptics of TGX one can only reaffirm that it is an extremely powerful tool that when applied with scientific rigor provides true insight on the biology of in vivo toxicological response.

MICRORNAS

The Biology of MicroRNAs

MicroRNAs (miRNAs) are 19–23 nucleotide-long, noncoding, ribonucleic acid (RNA) molecules that are highly conserved across species. miRNAs bind to complementary sequences on target messenger RNA (mRNA), which results in withholding mRNAs from translation or, in the context of the RNA-induced silencing complex (RISC), degradation of the target mRNAs. Several factors influence the affinity of miRNAs for mRNAs, including their degree of complementarity and the relative abundance of the target mRNAs [270]. The ability of an miRNA to bind to tens to hundreds of target mRNAs with different affinity depending on the relative concentration of the target mRNAs limits our current understanding of the functions of miRNAs.

From a BM perspective, miRNAs circulate in the plasma bound to Argonaute 2 [271], high-density lipoproteins [272], exosomes, and microvesicles. Exosomes are 30–110-nm diameter RNA- and protein-containing vesicles secreted by mammalian cells [273]. Exosomal miRNA is protected from nucleases and can be shuttled from cell to cell, which results in silencing specific mRNAs in recipient cells. Microvesicles are larger than exosomes with a diameter of up to 1 μm [274,275]. Therefore consistent centrifugation methods are needed to ensure reproducible miRNA yields.

MicroRNAs in Mechanistic Toxicity

The use of miRNAs to investigate the mechanisms of toxicity of compounds in development is in its infancy, because of the paucity of information regarding events occurring downstream of the engagement of an miRNA with its target mRNAs. Therefore most papers reporting miRNA profiles in animals that have been administered pharmaceutical compounds are descriptive in nature and lack the fine mechanistic interpretation afforded by mRNA transcriptomic data [276]. In particular, there is already a significant collection of references describing miRNA profiles in the liver and lung of rodents exposed to carcinogens [277–279].

More promisingly, specific miRNAs have been mechanistically involved in the effects of pharmaceutical compounds. For example, downregulation of let-7c by peroxisome proliferator-activated receptor (PPAR) alpha-agonists results in longer stability of c-myc mRNA, thereby resulting in cell proliferation culminating in hepatic carcinogenesis [280]. It was also proposed that the hepatic toxicity of 2,3,7,8-tetrachlorodibenzo-p-dioxin (TCDD) in mouse is secondary to upregulation of cyclooxygenase-2 (COX-2) as a result of downregulation of miR-101a by TCDD [281].

TABLE 16.11   Candidate Biomarkers miRNA in Rodent Species Administered Toxicants

Species	Target Organ	Matrix	miRNAs	Compound	Type of Damage	References
Mouse	Liver	Plasma	34a, 122, and 192	Methyl-deficient diet	Nonalcoholic fatty liver	[282]
Mouse	Pancreas	Serum	217	Caerulein	Apoptosis/necrosis	[283]
Rat	Brain	Plasma	124	Stroke (surgical)	Necrosis	[284]
Rat	Stomach, intestine	Feces	194	p21-activated kinase 4 (PAK4) inhibitor	Necrosis/degeneration	[285]
Rat	Heart	Plasma	208a	Isoproterenol	Degeneration/necrosis	[175]
Rat	Kidney	Urine	192	Cisplatin	Tubular necrosis	[286]
Rat	Liver	Plasma	122	Methapyrilene	"Hepatotoxicity"	[286]
Rat	Liver	Plasma	21, 29a, 29c, 31, 34a, 101a, 122, 192, 211, 194, 365, Let-7f	Acetaminophen	Necrosis	[287]
Rat	Liver	Plasma	122	$CBrCl_3$	Degeneration/necrosis	[284]
Rat	Liver	Plasma	122	CCl_4	Degeneration/necrosis	[284]
Rat	Liver	Serum	122	Multiple	Liver changes (hypertrophy, hepatocellular vacuolation, necrosis, single cell necrosis, biliary injury, inflammation)	[288]
Rat	Liver	Urine	Panel of 72	Acetaminophen, CCl_4	Necrosis	[289]
Rat	Mesenteric vasculature	Serum	1, 98, 127, 135a, 302, 376c, 409-3p, 494, 511, 872, U87	Dopamine	Vascular injury (arterial)	[290]
Rat	Mesenteric vasculature	Serum	1, 134, 205, 218, 409-3p, 434-3p, 511, 872	Fenoldopam	Vascular injury (arterial)	[290]
Rat	Mesenteric vasculature	Serum	135a, 302a, 494, U87	Midodrine	Vascular injury (arterial)	[290]
Rat	Pancreas	Serum	217	Caerulein	Apoptosis/necrosis	[283]
Rat	Skeletal muscle	Plasma	133a	2,3,5,6-Tetramethyl-*p*-phenylenediamine	Degeneration/necrosis	[284]
Rat	Skeletal muscle	Plasma	133a	Hydroxymethylglutaryl-CoA	Degeneration/necrosis	[284]

MicroRNAs as Biomarkers of Organ-Specific Toxicity

Circulating miRNAs represent an opportunity to overcome some of the technological limitations of current BMs (Table 16.11). MicroRNAs are stable and are detected by quantitative real-time PCR (qRTPCR), which eliminates the need to develop specific ELISA-based methods for each marker, and are conserved throughout species, which suggests that they may be used as translational BMs. However, miRNAs may compare unfavorably in terms of sensitivity when excellent BMs such as for cTnI are already available [172–174]. In contrast, miRNAs may add considerable value where the current assays lack sensitivity, such as for serum creatinine and blood urea nitrogen as renal BMs [132] or when BMs are not available such as with gastrointestinal [285] or pancreatic toxicity [283].

MicroRNAs may be obtained from a variety of body fluids and from the feces [289,291–299]. In this early stage of the evaluation of miRNAs as candidate BMs, the material and method section of each publication should be carefully evaluated prior to trying to replicate published data. The organs/tissues for which data are currently available on miRNAs as BMs of toxicity are the liver, the kidney, the heart, the gastrointestinal tract, and the vasculature. The translational value of these markers in the toxicity setting is supported by their concurrent identification as markers of organ disease in the clinic.

CONCLUSION

In this chapter we discussed current molecular pathology approaches to the identification and localization of test article-related molecular events in tissues that might be encountered in the course of nonclinical drug development. Specifically, we presented information showing IHC and ISH as useful tools for the analysis of molecular events in pathophysiological processes characterizing pharmacodynamic parameters during drug therapy. We described the particularly relevant role of IHC in the development of monoclonal antibodies as biotherapeutics. Immunohistochemistry forms the technical basis for tissue cross-reactivity assays that are routinely performed to determine potential sites of binding of monoclonal antibodies in both human tissues and animal models. Consequently, the nonclinical applications of IHC have the potential to enhance overall drug safety through rapid, sensitive, and specific detection of drug-associated changes in biomacromolecules at the cellular level [103,104,300,301].

We described a variety of molecular pathology approaches to the identification of novel BMs of disease and tissue toxicity. We also discussed the need for more specific and sensitive drug-related BMs of tissue injury, with specific reference to their application for safe candidate selection during the nonclinical phase. For example, we discussed the urgent need for BMs to monitor vascular injury because the progression in the clinics of compounds such as phosphodiesterase inhibitors has been hampered by the absence of reliable BMs of vascular injury. More sensitive and specific BMs could also be applied, for example, to monitor skeletal muscle injury because serum CK, the historic BM of muscle damage, is not specific and sensitive enough. Alternatively, when more sensitive BMs or assays are identified, such as cTns measured with ultrasensitive assays, a considerable amount of work is needed to validate these biomarkers and achieve scientific and regulatory acceptance.

We discussed the growing value of pathology conferred by the use of imaging technologies, which include image analysis and stereology. Similarly, the ability to measure gene and mRNA responses to toxicants (toxicogenomics) is of paramount importance in the investigation of mechanisms of toxicity and the establishment of novel BMs.

Finally, the new biotechnology-derived drug candidates, including oligonucleotides, gene therapy products, engineered antibodies, etc., clearly depend on the specialized molecular pathology techniques discussed here to meet the expectations of the scientific community and become marketed drugs to the benefit of the public.

References

[1] Gillett NA, Chan CM. Molecular pathology in the preclinical development of biopharmaceuticals. Toxicol Pathol 1999;27:48–52.

[2] Ramos-Vara JA. Technical aspects of immunohistochemistry. Vet Pathol 2005;42:405–26.

[3] Jin L, Lloyd RV. In situ hybridization: methods and applications. J Clin Lab Anal 1997;11:2–9.

[4] Gupta S, Thirstrup D, Jarvis TC, Schneider DJ, Wilcox SK, Carter J, et al. Rapid histochemistry using slow off-rate modified aptamers with anionic competition. Appl Immunohistochem Mol Morphol 2011;19:273–8.

[5] Zeng Z, Zhang P, Zhao N, Sheehan AM, Tung CH, Chang CC, et al. Using oligonucleotide aptamer probes for immunostaining of formalin-fixed and paraffin-embedded tissues. Mod Pathol 2010;23:1553–8.

[6] Malmborg AC, Borrebaeck CA. BIAcore as a tool in antibody engineering. J Immunol Methods 1995;183:7–13.

[7] Shi SR, Shi Y, Taylor CR. Antigen retrieval immunohistochemistry: review and future prospects in research and diagnosis over two decades. J Histochem Cytochem 2011;59:13–32.

[8] Shi SR, Liu C, Taylor CR. Standardization of immunohistochemistry for formalin-fixed, paraffin-embedded tissue sections based on the antigen-retrieval technique: from experiments to hypothesis. J Histochem Cytochem 2007;55:105–9.

[9] Shi SR, Cote RJ, Taylor CR. Antigen retrieval techniques: current perspectives. J Histochem Cytochem 2001;49:931–7.

[10] Johnstone AP, Thorpe R. Immunochemistry in practice. 3rd ed. London (England): Wiley-Blackwell; 1996.

[11] Kumar GL, Rudbeck L. Immunohistochemical (IHC) staining methods. 5th ed. Carpinteria (CA): Dako North America; 2009.

[12] Renshaw S. Immunohistochemistry. In: Hames BD, editor. The methods express series. 1st ed. Bloxham Mill (UK): Scion Publishing Ltd; 2005.

[13] Burry RW. Specificity controls for immunocytochemical methods. J Histochem Cytochem 2000;48:163–6.

[14] Syrbu SI, Cohen MB. An enhanced antigen-retrieval protocol for immunohistochemical staining of formalin-fixed, paraffin-embedded tissues. Methods Mol Biol 2011;717:101–10.

[15] Beckstead JH. A simple technique for preservation of fixation-sensitive antigens in paraffin-embedded tissues. J Histochem Cytochem 1994;42:1127–34.

[16] Tome Y, Hirohashi S, Noguchi M, Shimosato Y. Preservation of cluster 1 small cell lung cancer antigen in zinc-formalin fixative and its application to immunohistological diagnosis. Histopathology 1990;16:469–74.

[17] Vince DG, Tbakhi A, Gaddipati A, Cothren RM, Cornhill JF, Tubbs RR. Quantitative comparison of immunohistochemical staining intensity in tissues fixed in formalin and Histochoice. Anal Cell Pathol 1997;15:119–29.

[18] Thibodeau TR, Shah IA, Mukherjee R, Hosking MB. Economical spray-coating of histologic slides with poly-L-lysine. J Histotechnol 1997;20:369–70.

[19] Shi SR, Key ME, Kalra KL. Antigen retrieval in formalin-fixed, paraffin-embedded tissues: an enhancement method for immunohistochemical staining based on microwave oven heating of tissue sections. J Histochem Cytochem 1991;39:741–8.

[20] Taylor CR, Cote MD. Immunomicroscopy: A diagnostic tool for the surgical pathologist. 3rd ed. Philadelphia (PA): Immunomicroscopy. W B Saunders Co.; 2006.

[21] Pileri SA, Roncador G, Ceccarelli C, Piccioli M, Briskomatis A, Sabattini E, et al. Antigen retrieval techniques in immunohistochemistry: comparison of different methods. J Pathol 1997;183:116–23.

[22] Cattoretti G, Fei Q. Application of the antigen retrieval technique in experimental pathology: from human to mouse. In: Shi SR, Gu J, Taylor CR, editors. Antigen retrieval techniques: immunohistochemistry and molecular morphology. Natick (MA): Eaton Publishing; 2000. p. 165–79.

[23] Bobrow MN, Shaughnessy KJ, Litt GJ. Catalyzed reporter deposition, a novel method of signal amplification. II. Application to membrane immunoassays. J Immunol Methods 1991;137:103–12.

[24] Merz H, Ottesen K, Meyer W, Mueller A, Zhang Y, Feller AC. Combination of antigen retrieval techniques and signal amplification of immunohistochemistry in situ hybridization and FISH techniques. In: Shi SR, Gu J, Taylor CR, editors. Antigen retrieval techniques: Immunohistochemistry and molecular morphology. Natick (MA): Eaton Publishing; 2000. p. 219–48.

[25] Merz H, Malisius R, Mannweiler S, Zhou R, Hartmann W, Orscheschek K, et al. ImmunoMax. A maximized immunohistochemical method for the retrieval and enhancement of hidden antigens. Lab Invest 1995;73:149–56.

[26] Ramos-Vara JA, Miller MA. Comparison of two polymer-based immunohistochemical detection systems: ENVISION+ and ImmPRESS. J Microsc 2006;224:135–9.

[27] Furuya T, Ikemoto K, Kawauchi S, Oga A, Tsunoda S, Hirano T, et al. A novel technology allowing immunohistochemical staining of a tissue section with 50 different antibodies in a single experiment. J Histochem Cytochem 2004;52:205–10.

[28] Key M. In: Kumar GL, Rudbeck L, editors. In immunohistochemical staining methods. Carpinteria (CA): Dako North America; 2009. p. 57–60.

[29] Buchwalow I, Samoilova V, Boecker W, Tiemann M. Nonspecific binding of antibodies in immunohistochemistry: fallacies and facts. Sci Rep 2011;1:28.

[30] Simson JA, Hintz DS, Munster AM, Spicer SS. Immunocytochemical evidence for antibody binding to mast cell granules. Exp Mol Pathol 1977;26:85–91.

[31] Wang H, Pevsner J. Detection of endogenous biotin in various tissues: novel functions in the hippocampus and implications for its use in avidin-biotin technology. Cell Tissue Res 1999;296:511–6.

[32] Swanson NR, Bartholomaeus WN, Reed WD, Joske RA. An enzyme-linked immunosorbent assay for the detection of hepatocyte plasma membrane antibodies. J Immunol Methods 1985;85:203–16.

[33] Yam LT, Janckila AJ, Epremian BE, Li CY. Diagnostic significance of levamisole-resistant alkaline phosphatase in cytochemistry and immunocytochemistry. Am J Clin Pathol 1989;91:31–6.

[34] Ponder BA, Wilkinson MM. Inhibition of endogenous tissue alkaline phosphatase with the use of alkaline phosphatase conjugates in immunohistochemistry. J Histochem Cytochem 1981;29:981–4.

[35] Li LX, Crotty KA, Kril JJ, Palmer AA, McCarthy SW. Method of melanin bleaching in MIB1-Ki67 immunostaining of pigmented lesions: a quantitative evaluation in malignant melanomas. Histochem J 1999;31:237–40.

[36] Alexander RA, Cree IA, Foss AJ. The immunoalkaline phosphatase technique in immunohistochemistry: the effect of permanganate–oxalate melanin bleaching upon four final reaction products. Br J Biomed Sci 1996;53:170–1.

[37] Dabbs DJ. Diagnostic immunohistochemistry. 1st ed. Philadelphia (PA): Churchill Livingstone; 2002.

[38] Rogers AB, Cormier KS, Fox JG. Thiol-reactive compounds prevent nonspecific antibody binding in immunohistochemistry. Lab Invest 2006;86:526–33.

[39] Coons AH, Kaplan MH. Localization of antigen in tissue cells; improvements in a method for the detection of antigen by means of fluorescent antibody. J Exp Med 1950;91:1–13.

[40] Coons AH, Leduc EH, Kaplan MH. Localization of antigen in tissue cells. VI. The fate of injected foreign proteins in the mouse. J Exp Med 1951;93:173–88.

[41] Tarnowski BI, Spinale FG, Nicholson JH. DAPI as a useful stain for nuclear quantitation. Biotech Histochem 1991;66:297–302.

[42] Coleman AW, Goff LJ. Applications of fluorochromes to pollen biology. I. Mithramycin and 4′,6-diamidino-2-phenylindole (DAPI) as vital stains and for quantitation of nuclear DNA. Stain Technol 1985;60:145–54.

[43] Deyl Z, Macek K, Adam M, Vancikova O. Studies on the chemical nature of elastin fluorescence. Biochim Biophys Acta 1980;625:248–54.

[44] Schnell SA, Staines WA, Wessendorf MW. Reduction of lipofuscin-like autofluorescence in fluorescently labeled tissue. J Histochem Cytochem 1999;47:719–30.

[45] Billinton N, Knight AW. Seeing the wood through the trees: a review of techniques for distinguishing green fluorescent protein from endogenous autofluorescence. Anal Biochem 2001;291:175–97.

[46] Correa FM, Innis RB, Rouot B, Pasternak GW, Snyder SH. Fluorescent probes of alpha- and beta-adrenergic and opiate receptors: biochemical and histochemical evaluation. Neurosci Lett 1980;16:47–53.

[47] Neumann M, Gabel D. Simple method for reduction of autofluorescence in fluorescence microscopy. J Histochem Cytochem 2002;50:437–9.

[48] Cowen T, Haven AJ, Burnstock G. Pontamine sky blue: a counterstain for background autofluorescence in fluorescence and immunofluorescence histochemistry. Histochemistry 1985;82:205–8.

[49] Oyejide A, Ling J, Rosacia W, Attar M, Linke N. Correlation of drug-induced hepatocellular hypertrophy with cytochrome P450 expression using immunohistochemistry. Toxicol Pathol 2008;36(1):160.

[50] Bahrami A, Folpe AL. Adult-type fibrosarcoma: a reevaluation of 163 putative cases diagnosed at a single institution over a 48-year period. Am J Surg Pathol 2010;34:1504–13.

[51] Painter JT, Clayton NP, Herbert RA. Useful immunohistochemical markers of tumor differentiation. Toxicol Pathol 2010;38:131–41.

[52] Gaulard P, de Leval L. Follicular helper T-cells: implications in neoplastic hematopathology. Semin Diagn Pathol 2011;28:202–13.

[53] Nesfield SR, Clarke CJ, Hoivik DJ, Miller RT, Allen JS, Selinger K, et al. Evaluation of the carcinogenic potential of clofibrate in the rasH2 mouse. Int J Toxicol 2005;24:301–11.

[54] Staels B, Dallongeville J, Auwerx J, Schoonjans K, Leitersdorf E, Fruchart JC. Mechanism of action of fibrates on lipid and lipoprotein metabolism. Circulation 1998;98:2088–93.

[55] Kawai M, Jin M, Nishimura J, Dewa Y, Saegusa Y, Matsumoto S, et al. Hepatocarcinogenic susceptibility of fenofibrate and its possible mechanism of carcinogenicity in a two-stage hepatocarcinogenesis model of rasH2 mice. Toxicol Pathol 2008;36:950–7.

[56] Hard GC, Whysner J. Risk assessment of d-limonene: an example of male rat-specific renal tumorigens. Crit Rev Toxicol 1994;24:231–54.

[57] Swenberg JA, Lehman-McKeeman LD. Alpha 2-urinary globulin-associated nephropathy as a mechanism of renal tubule cell carcinogenesis in male rats. IARC Sci Publ 1999:95–118.

[58] Williams KD, Dunnick J, Horton J, Greenwell A, Eldridge SR, Elwell M, et al. p-Nitrobenzoic acid alpha2u nephropathy in 13-week studies is not associated with renal carcinogenesis in 2-year feed studies. Toxicol Pathol 2001;29:507–13.

[59] Dominick MA, Robertson DG, Bleavins MR, Sigler RE, Bobrowski WF, Gough AW. Alpha 2u-globulin nephropathy without nephrocarcinogenesis in male Wistar rats administered 1-(aminomethyl) cyclohexaneacetic acid. Toxicol Appl Pharmacol 1991;111:375–87.

[60] Dietrich DR, Swenberg JA. The presence of alpha 2u-globulin is necessary for d-limonene promotion of male rat kidney tumors. Cancer Res 1991;51:3512–21.

[61] Jimenez RE, Z'Graggen K, Hartwig W, Graeme-Cook F, Warshaw AL, Fernandez-del Castillo C. Immunohistochemical characterization of pancreatic tumors induced by dimethylbenzanthracene in rats. Am J Pathol 1999;154:1223–9.

[62] Jimenez RE, Warshaw AL, Z'Graggen K, Hartwig W, Taylor DZ, Compton CC, et al. Sequential accumulation of K-ras mutations and p53 overexpression in the progression of pancreatic mucinous cystic neoplasms to malignancy. Ann Surg 1999;230:501–9. discussion 509–11.

[63] Curtin JF, Candolfi M, Fakhouri TM, Liu C, Alden A, Edwards M, et al. Treg depletion inhibits efficacy of cancer immunotherapy: implications for clinical trials. PLoS One 2008;3:e1983.

[64] Lu WZ, Geng GX, Li QW, Li J, Liu FZ, Han ZS. Antitumor activity of polysaccharides isolated from *Patrinia heterophylla*. Pharm Biol 2010;48:1012–7.

[65] Lu W, Li Q, Li J, Liu F, Yang X. Polysaccharide from *Patrinia heterophylla* Bunge inhibits HeLa cell proliferation through induction of apoptosis and cell cycle arrest. Lab Med 2009;40:161–6.

[66] Syrjanen KJ. Immunohistochemistry in assessment of molecular pathogenesis of cervical carcinogenesis. Eur J Gynaecol Oncol 2005;26:5–19.

[67] Paez JG, Janne PA, Lee JC, Tracy S, Greulich H, Gabriel S, et al. EGFR mutations in lung cancer: correlation with clinical response to gefitinib therapy. Science 2004;304:1497–500.

[68] Takano T, Ohe Y, Sakamoto H, Tsuta K, Matsuno Y, Tateishi U, et al. Epidermal growth factor receptor gene mutations and increased copy numbers predict gefitinib sensitivity in patients with recurrent nonsmall-cell lung cancer. J Clin Oncol 2005;23:6829–37.

[69] Johnston SR. Are current drug development programs realising the full potential of new agents? the scenario. Breast Cancer Res 2009;11(Suppl. 3):S21.

[70] Allegra CJ, Jessup JM, Somerfield MR, Hamilton SR, Hammond EH, Hayes DF, et al. American Society of Clinical Oncology provisional clinical opinion: testing for KRAS gene mutations in patients with metastatic colorectal carcinoma to predict response to antiepidermal growth factor receptor monoclonal antibody therapy. J Clin Oncol 2009;27:2091–6.

[71] Schmidt C. Challenges ahead for companion diagnostics. J Natl Cancer Inst 2012;104:14–5.

[72] Philip R, Carrington L, Chan M. US FDA perspective on challenges in co-developing in vitro companion diagnostics and targeted cancer therapeutics. Bioanalysis 2011;3:383–9.

[73] Hinman LM, Carl KM, Spear BB, Salerno RA, Becker RL, Abbott BM, et al. Development and regulatory strategies for drug and diagnostic co-development. Pharmacogenomics 2010;11:1669–75.

[74] Dimou A, Harrington K, Syrigos KN. From the bench to bedside: biological and methodology considerations for the future of companion diagnostics in nonsmall cell lung cancer. Pathol Res Int 2011;2011:312346.

[75] Halait H, Demartin K, Shah S, Soviero S, Langland R, Cheng S, et al. Analytical performance of a real-time PCR-based assay for V600 mutations in the BRAF gene, used as the companion diagnostic test for the novel BRAF inhibitor vemurafenib in metastatic melanoma. Diagn Mol Pathol 2012;21:1–8.

[76] Anderson S, Bloom KJ, Vallera DU, Rueschoff J, Meldrum C, Schilling R, et al. Multisite analytic performance studies of a real-time polymerase chain reaction assay for the detection of BRAF V600E mutations in formalin-fixed paraffin-embedded tissue specimens of malignant melanoma. Arch Pathol Lab Med 2012;136.

[77] Giltnane JM, Molinaro A, Cheng H, Robinson A, Turbin D, Gelmon K, et al. Comparison of quantitative immunofluorescence with conventional methods for HER2/neu testing with respect to response to trastuzumab therapy in metastatic breast cancer. Arch Pathol Lab Med 2008;132:1635–47.

[78] Shaw AT, Solomon B, Kenudson MM. Crizotinib and testing for ALK. J Natl Compr Cancer Netw 2011;9:1335–41.

[79] Battifora H. The multitumor (sausage) tissue block: novel method for immunohistochemical antibody testing. Lab Invest 1986;55:244–8.

[80] Kononen J, Bubendorf L, Kallioniemi A, Barlund M, Schraml P, Leighton S, et al. Tissue microarrays for high-throughput molecular profiling of tumor specimens. Nat Med 1998;4:844–7.

[81] Hierck BP, Iperen LV, Gittenberger-DeGroot AC, Poelmann RE. Modified indirect immunodetection allows study of murine tissue with mouse monoclonal antibodies. J Histochem Cytochem 1994;42:1499–502.

[82] Hoos A, Nissan A, Stojadinovic A, Shia J, Hedvat CV, Leung DH, et al. Tissue microarray molecular profiling of early, node-negative adenocarcinoma of the rectum: a comprehensive analysis. Clin Cancer Res 2002;8:3841–9.

[83] Jensen TA. Tissue microarray: advanced techniques. J Histotechnol 2003;26:101–4.

[84] Jensen TA, Hammond MEH. The tissue microarray. A technical guide for histologists. J Histotechnol 2001;24:283–7.

[85] McKay JS, Bigley A, Bell A, Jenkins R, Somers R, Brocklehurst S, et al. A pilot evaluation of the use of tissue microarrays for quantitation of target distribution in drug discovery pathology. Exp Toxicol Pathol 2006;57:181–93.

[86] Mehta N, Wolujczyk A. Agarose tissue strips microarrays for rapid assembly of tissue microarrays. In: 34th Annual National Society of Histotechnology Symposium/Convention, Pittsburgh, PA. September 12–18, 2008.

[87] Miller RT, Groothuis CL. Multitumor 'sausage' blocks in immunohistochemistry. Simplified method of preparation, practical uses, and roles in quality assurance. Am J Clin Pathol 1991;96:228–32.

[88] Rubin MA, Dunn R, Strawderman M, Pienta KJ. Tissue microarray sampling strategy for prostate cancer biomarker analysis. Am J Surg Pathol 2002;26:312–9.

[89] Russo G, Zegar C, Giordano A. Advantages and limitations of microarray technology in human cancer. Oncogene 2003;22:6497–507.

[90] Takahashi M, Yang XJ, Sugimura J, Backdahl J, Tretiakova M, Qian CN, et al. Molecular subclassification of kidney tumors and the discovery of new diagnostic markers. Oncogene 2003;22:6810–8.

[91] Torhorst J, Bucher C, Kononen J, Haas P, Zuber M, Kochli OR, et al. Tissue microarrays for rapid linking of molecular changes to clinical endpoints. Am J Pathol 2001;159:2249–56.

[92] Wan WH, Fortuna MB, Furmanski P. A rapid and efficient method for testing immunohistochemical reactivity of monoclonal antibodies against multiple tissue samples simultaneously. J Immunol Methods 1987;103:121–9.

[93] Xie W, Mertens JC, Reiss DJ, Rimm DL, Camp RL, Haffty BG, et al. Alterations of Smad signaling in human breast carcinoma are associated with poor outcome: a tissue microarray study. Cancer Res 2002;62:497–505.

[94] Yan P, Seelentag W, Bachmann A, Bosman FT. An agarose matrix facilitates sectioning of tissue microarray blocks. J Histochem Cytochem 2007;55:21–4.

[95] Simon R, Sauter G. Tissue microarrays for miniaturized high-throughput molecular profiling of tumors. Exp Hematol 2002;30:1365–72.

[96] Nocito A, Bubendorf L, Tinner EM, Suess K, Wagner U, Forster T. Microarrays of bladder cancer tissue are highly representative of proliferation index and histological grade. J Pathol 2001;194:349–57.

[97] Hoos A, Stojadinovic A, Mastorides S, Urist MJ, Polsky D, Di Como CJ, et al. High Ki-67 proliferative index predicts disease specific survival in patients with high-risk soft tissue sarcomas. Cancer 2001;92:869–74.

[98] Hall WC, Price-Schiavi SA, Wicks J, Rojko JL. Tissue cross-reactivity studies for monoclonal antibodies: predictive value and use for selection of relevant animal species for toxicity testing. In: Cavagnaro JA, editor. Nonclinical safety evaluation of biopharmaceuticals: a science-based approach to facilitating clinical trials. Hoboken (NJ): John Wiley; 2010. p. 207–40.

[99] Leach MW, Halpern WG, Johnson CW, Rojko JL, MacLachlan TK, Chan CM, et al. Use of tissue cross-reactivity studies in the development of antibody-based biopharmaceuticals: history, experience, methodology, and future directions. Toxicol Pathol 2010;38:1138–66.

[100] Anon. In: PTC F, editor. Points to consider in the manufacture and testing of monoclonal antibody products for human use. 1997. Washington (DC) http://www.fda.gov/downloads/Biologics BloodVaccines/GuidanceComplianceRegulatoryInformation/ OtherRecommendationsforManufacturers/UCM153182.pdf.

[101] Lynch CM, Hart BW, Grewal IS. Practical considerations for nonclinical safety evaluation of therapeutic monoclonal antibodies. mAbs 2009;1:2–11.

[102] ICH S6 guidance for industry: preclinical safety evaluation of biotechnology-derived pharmaceuticals. FDA, http://www. emea.europa.eu/docs/en_GB/document_library/Scientific_ guideline/2009/09/WC500002828.pdf.

[103] Tabrizi M, Bornstein GG, Suria H. Biodistribution mechanisms of therapeutic monoclonal antibodies in health and disease. AAPS J 2010;12:33–43.

[104] Mascelli MA, Zhou H, Sweet R, Getsy J, Davis HM, Graham M, et al. Molecular, biologic, and pharmacokinetic properties of monoclonal antibodies: impact of these parameters on early clinical development. J Clin Pharmacol 2007;47:553–65.

[105] Tomlinson IM. Next-generation protein drugs. Nat Biotechnol 2004;22:521–2.

[106] Wolf E, Hofmeister R, Kufer P, Schlereth B, Baeuerle PA. BiTEs: bispecific antibody constructs with unique antitumor activity. Drug Discov Today 2005;10:1237–44.

[107] Rojko JL, Price-Schiavi SA. Physiologic IgG biodistribution, transport and clearance: implications for monoclonal antibody products. In: Cavagnaro JA, editor. Nonclinical safety evaluation of biopharmaceuticals: a science-based approach to facilitating clinical trials. Hoboken (NJ): John Wiley; 2010. p. 241–76.

[108] Nestorov I, Zitnik R, DeVries T, Nakanishi AM, Wang A, Banfield C. Pharmacokinetics of subcutaneously administered etanercept in subjects with psoriasis. Br J Clin Pharmacol 2006;62:435–45.

[109] Fitzsimons HL, Riban V, Bland RJ, Wendelken JL, Sapan CV, During MJ. Biodistribution and safety assessment of AAV2-GAD following intrasubthalamic injection in the rat. J Gene Med 2010;12:385–98.

[110] Bragonzi A, Dina G, Villa A, Calori G, Biffi A, Bordignon C, et al. Biodistribution and transgene expression with nonviral cationic vector/DNA complexes in the lungs. Gene Ther 2000;7:1753–60.

[111] Zhao Z, Liu W, Su Y, Zhu J, Zheng G, Luo Q, et al. Evaluation of biodistribution and safety of adenovirus vector containing MDR1 in mice. J Exp Clin Cancer Res 2010;29:1.

[112] Baszler TV, Kiupel M, Williams ES, Thomsen BV, Gidlewski T, Montgomery DL, et al. Comparison of two automated immunohistochemical procedures for the diagnosis of scrapie in domestic sheep and chronic wasting disease in North American white-tailed deer (Odocoileus virginianus) and mule deer (Odocoileus hemionus). J Vet Diagn Invest 2006;18:147–55.

[113] Arihiro K, Umemura S, Kurosumi M, Moriya T, Oyama T, Yamashita H, et al. Comparison of evaluations for hormone receptors in breast carcinoma using two manual and three automated immunohistochemical assays. Am J Clin Pathol 2007;127:356–65.

[114] Bankfalvi A, Boecker W, Reiner A. Comparison of automated and manual determination of HER2 status in breast cancer for diagnostic use: a comparative methodological study using the Ventana BenchMark automated staining system and manual tests. Int J Oncol 2004;25:929–35.

[115] Luna LG. Manual of histologic staining methods of the Armed Forces Institute of Pathology. 3rd ed. New York (NY): McGraw-Hill Book Company; 1968.

[116] Switzer 3rd RC, Lowry-Franssen C, Benkovic SA. Recommended neuroanatomical sampling practices for comprehensive brain evaluation in nonclinical safety studies. Toxicol Pathol 2011;39:73–84.

[117] Switzer 3rd RC. Application of silver degeneration stains for neurotoxicity testing. Toxicol Pathol 2000;28:70–83.

[118] Fix AS, Stitzel SR, Ridder GM, Switzer RC. MK-801 neurotoxicity in cupric silver-stained sections: lesion reconstruction by 3-dimensional computer image analysis. Toxicol Pathol 2000;28:84–90.

[119] Fix AS, Ross JF, Stitzel SR, Switzer RC. Integrated evaluation of central nervous system lesions: stains for neurons, astrocytes, and microglia reveal the spatial and temporal features of MK-801-induced neuronal necrosis in the rat cerebral cortex. Toxicol Pathol 1996;24:291–304.

[120] Bacci S, DeFraia B, Romagnoli P, Bonelli A. Advantage of affinity histochemistry combined with histology to investigate death causes: indications from sample cases. J Forensic Sci 2011;56:1620–5.

[121] Gallagher RI, Blakely SR, Liotta LA, Espina V. Laser capture microdissection: Arcturus(XT) infrared capture and UV cutting methods. Methods Mol Biol 2012;823:157–78.

[122] Schuster C, Budczies J, Faber C, Kirchner T, Hlubek F. MicroRNA expression profiling of specific cells in complex archival tissue stained by immunohistochemistry. Lab Invest 2010;91:157–65.

[123] Specht K, Richter T, Muller U, Walch A, Werner M, Hofler H. Quantitative gene expression analysis in microdissected archival formalin-fixed and paraffin-embedded tumor tissue. Am J Pathol 2001;158:419–29.

[124] Wang W, Wyckoff JB, Frohlich VC, Oleynikov Y, Huttelmaier S, Zavadil J, et al. Single cell behavior in metastatic primary mammary tumors correlated with gene expression patterns revealed by molecular profiling. Cancer Res 2002;62:6278–88.

[125] Zhu G, Reynolds L, Crnogorac-Jurcevic T, Gillett CE, Dublin EA, Marshall JF, et al. Combination of microdissection and microarray analysis to identify gene expression changes between differentially located tumor cells in breast cancer. Oncogene 2003;22:3742–8.

[126] Dalmas DA, Scicchitano MS, Mullins D, Hughes-Earle A, Tatsuoka K, Magid-Slav M, et al. Potential candidate genomic biomarkers of drug induced vascular injury in the rat. Toxicol Appl Pharmacol 2011;257:284–300.

[127] Roberts ES, Thomas RS, Dorman DC. Gene expression changes following acute hydrogen sulfide (H_2S)-induced nasal respiratory epithelial injury. Toxicol Pathol 2008;36:560–7.

[128] Saturno G, Pesenti M, Cavazzoli C, Rossi A, Giusti AM, Gierke B, et al. Expression of serine/threonine protein-kinases and related factors in normal monkey and human retinas: the mechanistic understanding of a CDK2 inhibitor induced retinal toxicity. Toxicol Pathol 2007;35:592–83.

[129] Khatib-Shahidi S, Andersson M, Herman JL, Gillespie TA, Caprioli RM. Direct molecular analysis of whole-body animal tissue sections by imaging MALDI mass spectrometry. Anal Chem 2006;78:6448–56.

[130] Schwamborn K, Caprioli RM. Molecular imaging by mass spectrometry – looking beyond classical histology. Nat Rev Cancer 2010;10:639–46.

[131] Meistermann H, Norris JL, Aerni HR, Cornett DS, Friedlein A, Erskine AR, et al. Biomarker discovery by imaging mass spectrometry: transthyretin is a biomarker for gentamicin-induced nephrotoxicity in rat. Mol Cell Proteomics 2006;5:1876–86.

[132] Sistare FD, Degeorge JJ. Promise of new translational safety biomarkers in drug development and challenges to regulatory qualification. Biomark Med 2011;5:497–514.

[133] Wang F. In: Kang YJ, editor. Biomarker methods in drug discovery and development methods in pharmacology and toxicology. New York (NY): Humana Press; 2008.

[134] Sarker D, Workman P. Pharmacodynamic biomarkers for molecular cancer therapeutics. Adv Cancer Res 2007;96:213–68.

III. CLINICAL PATHOLOGY, HISTOPATHOLOGY, AND BIOMARKERS

[135] Bloom JC. Biomarkers in clinical drug development: definitions and disciplines. In: Bloom JC, Dean RA, editors. Biomarkers in clinical drug development. New York (NY): Marcel Dekker Inc.; 2003. p. 1–10.

[136] Bleavins MR, Carini C, Jurima-Romet M, Rahbari R. Biomarkers in drug development: a handbook of practice, application, and strategy. Hoboken (NJ): Wiley; 2010.

[137] Burkhardt JE, Ennulat D, Pandher K, Solter PF, Troth SP, Boyce RW, et al. Topic of histopathology blinding in nonclinical safety biomarker qualification studies. Toxicol Pathol 2010;38:666–7.

[138] Anon. Guidance for industry: bioanalytical method validation. US department of health and human services. Rockville (MD): Food and Drug Administration. Center for Drug Evaluation and Research (CDER). Center for Veterinary Medicine (CVM); May 2001. http://www.fda.gov/downloads/drugs/guidancecomplianceregulatoryinformation/guidances/ucm070107.pdf.

[139] Anon. Guidance for industry: pharmacogenomic data submissions. Rockville (MD): US Department of Health and Human Services, F. a. D. A. Center for Drug Evaluation and Research (CDER), Center for Biologics Evaluation and Research (CBER), Center for Devices and Radiological Health (CDRH), Food and Drug Administration; 2005.

[140] Anon. In: Agency EM, editor. Qualification of novel methodologies for drug development: guidance to applicants. January 22, 2009. http://www.emea.europa.eu/docs/en_GB/document_library/Regulatory_and_procedural_guideline/2009/10/WC500004201.pdf. London (UK).

[141] Dieterle F, Sistare F, Goodsaid F, Papaluca M, Ozer JS, Webb CP, et al. Renal biomarker qualification submission: a dialog between the FDA-EMEA and Predictive Safety Testing Consortium. Nat Biotechnol 2010;28:455–62.

[142] Crissman JW, Goodman DG, Hildebrandt PK, Maronpot RR, Prater DA, Riley JH, et al. Best practices guideline: toxicologic histopathology. Toxicol Pathol 2004;32:126–31.

[143] Tengstrand EA, Miwa GT, Hsieh FY. Bis(monoacylglycerol) phosphate as a noninvasive biomarker to monitor the onset and time-course of phospholipidosis with drug-induced toxicities. Expert Opin Drug Metab Toxicol 2010;6:555–70.

[144] Nielsen SE, Schjoedt KJ, Astrup AS, Tarnow L, Lajer M, Hansen PR, et al. Neutrophil Gelatinase-Associated Lipocalin (NGAL) and Kidney Injury Molecule 1 (KIM1) in patients with diabetic nephropathy: a cross-sectional study and the effects of lisinopril. Diabet Med 2010;27:1144–50.

[145] Filler G, Bokenkamp A, Hofmann W, Le Bricon T, Martinez-Bru C, Grubb A. Cystatin C as a marker of GFR – history, indications, and future research. Clin Biochem 2005;38:1–8.

[146] Wang EJ, Snyder RD, Fielden MR, Smith RJ, Gu YZ. Validation of putative genomic biomarkers of nephrotoxicity in rats. Toxicology 2008;246:91–100.

[147] Ennulat D, Magid-Slav M, Rehm S, Tatsuoka KS. Diagnostic performance of traditional hepatobiliary biomarkers of drug-induced liver injury in the rat. Toxicol Sci 2010;116:397–412.

[148] Qin LQ, Wang Y, Xu JY, Kaneko T, Sato A, Wang PY. One-day dietary restriction changes hepatic metabolism and potentiates the hepatotoxicity of carbon tetrachloride and chloroform in rats. Tohoku J Exp Med 2007;212:379–87.

[149] Amacher DE. Strategies for the early detection of drug-induced hepatic steatosis in preclinical drug safety evaluation studies. Toxicology 2011;279:10–8.

[150] Schultze AE, Carpenter KH, Wians FH, Agee SJ, Minyard J, Lu QA, et al. Longitudinal studies of cardiac troponin-I concentrations in serum from male Sprague Dawley rats: baseline reference ranges and effects of handling and placebo dosing on biological variability. Toxicol Pathol 2009;37:754–60.

[151] Giannitsis E, Becker M, Kurz K, Hess G, Zdunek D, Katus HA. High-sensitivity cardiac troponin T for early prediction of evolving non-ST-segment elevation myocardial infarction in patients with suspected acute coronary syndrome and negative troponin results on admission. Clin Chem 2010;56:642–50.

[152] Januzzi Jr JL. Use of biomarkers to predict cardiac risk from medications: getting to the heart of the matter. Clin Chem 2008;54:1107–9.

[153] Januzzi Jr JL, Bamberg F, Lee H, Truong QA, Nichols JH, Karakas M, et al. High-sensitivity troponin T concentrations in acute chest pain patients evaluated with cardiac computed tomography. Circulation 2010;121:1227–34.

[154] Kavsak PA, Wang X, Ko DT, MacRae AR, Jaffe AS. Short- and long-term risk stratification using a next-generation, high-sensitivity research cardiac troponin I (hs-cTnI) assay in an emergency department chest pain population. Clin Chem 2009;55:1809–15.

[155] Schultze AE, Konrad RJ, Credille KM, Lu QA, Todd J. Ultrasensitive cross-species measurement of cardiac troponin-I using the Erenna immunoassay system. Toxicol Pathol 2008;36:777–82.

[156] Todd J, Freese B, Lu A, Held D, Morey J, Livingston R, et al. Ultrasensitive flow-based immunoassays using single-molecule counting. Clin Chem 2007;53:1990–5.

[157] Wu AH, Agee SJ, Lu QA, Todd J, Jaffe AS. Specificity of a high-sensitivity cardiac troponin I assay using single-molecule-counting technology. Clin Chem 2009;55:196–8.

[158] Wu AH, Lu QA, Todd J, Moecks J, Wians F. Short- and long-term biological variation in cardiac troponin I measured with a high-sensitivity assay: implications for clinical practice. Clin Chem 2009;55:52–8.

[159] Mingels A, Jacobs L, Michielsen E, Swaanenburg J, Wodzig W, van Dieijen-Visser M. Reference population and marathon runner sera assessed by highly sensitive cardiac troponin T and commercial cardiac troponin T and I assays. Clin Chem 2009;55:101–8.

[160] Regwan S, Hulten EA, Martinho S, Slim J, Villines TC, Mitchell J, et al. Marathon running as a cause of troponin elevation: a systematic review and meta-analysis. J Interv Cardiol 2010;23:443–50.

[161] Kelley WE, Januzzi JL, Christenson RH. Increases of cardiac troponin in conditions other than acute coronary syndrome and heart failure. Clin Chem 2009;55:2098–112.

[162] Lipshultz SE, Simbre 2nd VC, Hart S, Rifai N, Lipsitz SR, Reubens L, et al. Frequency of elevations in markers of cardiomyocyte damage in otherwise healthy newborns. Am J Cardiol 2008;102:761–6.

[163] Mikaelian I, Buness A, Hirkaler G, Fernandes R, Coluccio D, Geng W, et al. Serum cardiac troponin I concentrations transiently increase in rats given rosiglitazone. Toxicol Lett 2011;201:110–5.

[164] Mikaelian I, Coluccio D, Hirkaler GM, Downing JC, Rasmussen E, Todd J, et al. Assessment of the toxicity of hydralazine in the rat using an ultrasensitive flow-based cardiac troponin I immunoassay. Toxicol Pathol 2009;37:878–81.

[165] Schultze AE, Main BW, Hall DG, Hoffman WP, Lee HY, Ackermann BL, et al. A comparison of mortality and cardiac biomarker response between three outbred stocks of Sprague Dawley rats treated with isoproterenol. Toxicol Pathol 2011;39.

[166] deFilippi CR, de Lemos JA, Christenson RH, Gottdiener JS, Kop WJ, Zhan M, et al. Association of serial measures of cardiac troponin T using a sensitive assay with incident heart failure and cardiovascular mortality in older adults. JAMA 2010;304:2494–502.

[167] Dunn M, Abrams R, Coluccio D, Hirkaleri G, Babiarz J, Nicklaus R, et al. Serum cardiac troponin in rats given rosiglitazone. Washington (DC): Society of Toxicology; 2011.

[168] Mikaelian I, Coluccio D, Morgan KT, Johnson T, Ryan AL, Rasmussen E, et al. Temporal gene expression profiling indicates early up-regulation of interleukin-6 in isoproterenol-induced myocardial necrosis in rat. Toxicol Pathol 2008;36:256–64.

[169] Clements P, Brady S, York M, Berridge B, Mikaelian I, Nicklaus R, et al. Time course characterization of serum cardiac troponins, heart fatty acid-binding protein, and morphologic findings with isoproterenol-induced myocardial injury in the rat. Toxicol Pathol 2010;38:703–14.

[170] Berna MJ, Zhen Y, Watson DE, Hale JE, Ackermann BL. Strategic use of immunoprecipitation and LC/MS/MS for trace-level protein quantification: myosin light chain 1, a biomarker of cardiac necrosis. Anal Chem 2007;79:4199–205.

[171] York M, Scudamore C, Brady S, Chen C, Wilson S, Curtis M, et al. Characterization of troponin responses in isoproterenol-induced cardiac injury in the Hanover Wistar rat. Toxicol Pathol 2007;35:606–17.

[172] Meder B, Keller A, Vogel B, Haas J, Sedaghat-Hamedani F, Kayvanpour E, et al. MicroRNA signatures in total peripheral blood as novel biomarkers for acute myocardial infarction. Basic Res Cardiol 2011;106:13–23.

[173] Widera C, Gupta SK, Lorenzen JM, Bang C, Bauersachs J, Bethmann K, et al. Diagnostic and prognostic impact of six circulating microRNAs in acute coronary syndrome. J Mol Cell Cardiol 2011;51:872–5.

[174] Gidlof O, Andersson P, van der Pals J, Gotberg M, Erlinge D. Cardiospecific microRNA plasma levels correlate with troponin and cardiac function in patients with ST elevation myocardial infarction, are selectively dependent on renal elimination, and can be detected in urine samples. Cardiology 2011;118:217–26.

[175] Ji X, Takahashi R, Hiura Y, Hirokawa G, Fukushima Y, Iwai N. Plasma miR-208 as a biomarker of myocardial injury. Clin Chem 2009;55:1944–9.

[176] Ajjan RA, Grant PJ. The cardiovascular safety of rosiglitazone. Expert Opin Drug Saf 2008;7:367–76.

[177] Arakawa K, Ishihara T, Aoto M, Inamasu M, Kitamura K, Saito A. An antidiabetic thiazolidinedione induces eccentric cardiac hypertrophy by cardiac volume overload in rats. Clin Exp Pharmacol Physiol 2004;31:8–13.

[178] Edgley AJ, Thalen PG, Dahllof B, Lanne B, Ljung B, Oakes ND. PPARgamma agonist induced cardiac enlargement is associated with reduced fatty acid and increased glucose utilization in myocardium of Wistar rats. Eur J Pharmacol 2006;538:195–206.

[179] FDA. Muraglitazar. El-Hage. G. NDA 21–865. 2005.

[180] Sena S, Rasmussen IR, Wende AR, McQueen AP, Theobald HA, Wilde N, et al. Cardiac hypertrophy caused by peroxisome proliferator-activated receptor-gamma agonist treatment occurs independently of changes in myocardial insulin signaling. Endocrinology 2007;148:6047–53.

[181] Shah P, Mudaliar S. Pioglitazone: side effect and safety profile. Expert Opin Drug Saf 2010;9:347–54.

[182] Anderton MJ, Mellor HR, Bell A, Sadler C, Pass M, Powell S, et al. Induction of heart valve lesions by small-molecule ALK5 inhibitors. Toxicol Pathol 2011;39:916–24.

[183] Elangbam CS. Drug-induced valvulopathy: an update. Toxicol Pathol 2010;38:837–48.

[184] Gruson D, Ahn SA, Ketelslegers JM, Rousseau MF. Increased plasma myostatin in heart failure. Eur J Heart Fail 2011;13:734–6.

[185] Engle SK, Solter PF, Credille KM, Bull CM, Adams S, Berna MJ, et al. Detection of left ventricular hypertrophy in rats administered a peroxisome proliferator-activated receptor alpha/gamma dual agonist using natriuretic peptides and imaging. Toxicol Sci 2010;114:183–92.

[186] Colton HM, Stokes AH, Yoon LW, Quaile MP, Novak PJ, Falls JG, et al. An initial characterization of N-terminal-proatrial natriuretic peptide in serum of Sprague Dawley rats. Toxicol Sci April 2011;120(2):262–8. Epub 2011 January 17.

[187] Partanen N, Husso M, Vuolteenaho O, Sipola P, Ruskoaho H, Peuhkurinen K, et al. N-terminal proatrial natriuretic peptide reflects cardiac remodelling in stage 1 hypertension. J Hum Hypertens December 2011;25(12):746–51. Epub 2011 January 20.

[188] Crivellente F, Tontodonati M, Fasdelli N, Casartelli A, Dorigatti R, Faustinelli I, et al. NT-proBNP as a biomarker for the assessment of a potential cardiovascular drug-induced liability in beagle dogs. Cell Biol Toxicol December 2011;27(6):425–38. Epub 2011 August 08.

[189] Januzzi L. Fibrosis and heart failure: the use of cardiac biomarkers to gauge therapeutic success. In Case Report. 2011.

[190] Felker GM, Zannad F. The role of biomarkers in heart failure management. Focus on fibrosis. 2011. webpage http://www.medscape.org/viewarticle/741550.

[191] Devaux Y, Bousquenaud M, Rodius S, Marie PY, Maskali F, Zhang L, et al. Transforming growth factor beta receptor 1 is a new candidate prognostic biomarker after acute myocardial infarction. BMC Med Genomics 2011;4:83.

[192] Herman EH, Knapton A, Rosen E, Thompson K, Rosenzweig B, Estis J, et al. A multifaceted evaluation of imatinib-induced cardiotoxicity in the rat. Toxicol Pathol 2011;39:1091–106.

[193] Bryson HM, Palmer KJ, Langtry HD, Fitton A. Propafenone. A reappraisal of its pharmacology, pharmacokinetics and therapeutic use in cardiac arrhythmias. Drugs 1993;45:85–130.

[194] Shah SJ, Fonarow GC, Gheorghiade M, Lang RM. Phase II trials in heart failure: the role of cardiovascular imaging. Am Heart J 2011;162:3–15e3.

[195] Tontodonati M, Fasdelli N, Repeto P, Dorigatti R. Characterisation of rodent dobutamine echocardiography for preclinical safety pharmacology assessment. J Pharmacol Toxicol Methods 2011;64.

[196] McAdams RM, McPherson RJ, Dabestani NM, Gleason CA, Juul SE. Left ventricular hypertrophy is prevalent in Sprague-Dawley rats. Comp Med 2010;60:357–63.

[197] Braunstein Jr PW, DeGirolami U. Experimental corticosteroid myopathy. Acta Neuropathol 1981;55:167–72.

[198] De Souza AT, Cornwell PD, Dai X, Caguyong MJ, Ulrich RG. Agonists of the peroxisome proliferator-activated receptor alpha induce a fiber-type-selective transcriptional response in rat skeletal muscle. Toxicol Sci August 2006;92(2):578–86. Epub 2006 May 17.

[199] Vassallo JD, Janovitz EB, Wescott DM, Chadwick C, Lowe-Krentz LJ, Lehman-McKeeman LD. Biomarkers of drug-induced skeletal muscle injury in the rat: troponin I and myoglobin. Toxicol Sci 2009;111:402–12.

[200] Schaefer WH, Lawrence JW, Loughlin AF, Stoffregen DA, Mixson LA, Dean DC, et al. Evaluation of ubiquinone concentration and mitochondrial function relative to cerivastatin-induced skeletal myopathy in rats. Toxicol Appl Pharmacol 2004;194:10–23.

[201] Ng Y, Goldspink DF, Burniston JG, Clark WA, Colyer J, Tan LB. Characterisation of isoprenaline myotoxicity on slow-twitch skeletal versus cardiac muscle. Int J Cardiol 2002;86:299–309.

[202] Thompson PD, Clarkson P, Karas RH. Statin-associated myopathy. JAMA 2003;289:1681–90.

[203] Gunst JJ, Langlois MR, Delanghe JR, De Buyzere ML, Leroux-Roels GG. Serum creatine kinase activity is not a reliable marker for muscle damage in conditions associated with low extracellular glutathione concentration. Clin Chem 1998;44:939–43.

[204] Pritt ML, Hall DG, Recknor J, Credille KM, Brown DD, Yumibe NP, et al. Fabp3 as a biomarker of skeletal muscle toxicity in the rat: comparison with conventional biomarkers. Toxicol Sci 2008;103:382–96.

[205] Alpert JS, Thygesen K, Antman E, Bassand JP. Myocardial infarction redefined – a consensus document of the Joint European Society of Cardiology/American College of Cardiology Committee for the redefinition of myocardial infarction. J Am Coll Cardiol 2000;36:959–69.

[206] Sobota JT. Review of cardiovascular findings in humans treated with minoxidil. Toxicol Pathol 1989;17:193–202.

[207] Mecklenburg L, Heuser A, Juengling T, Kohler M, Foell R, Ockert D, et al. Mesenteritis precedes vasculitis in the rat mesentery after subacute administration of a phosphodiesterase type 4 inhibitor. Toxicol Lett 2006;163:54–64.

[208] Slim RM, Robertson DG, Albassam M, Reily MD, Robosky L, Dethloff LA. Effect of dexamethasone on the metabonomics profile associated with phosphodiesterase inhibitor-induced vascular lesions in rats. Toxicol Appl Pharmacol 2002;183:108–9.

[209] Zhang J, Snyder RD, Herman EH, Knapton A, Honchel R, Miller T, et al. Histopathology of vascular injury in Sprague-Dawley rats treated with phosphodiesterase IV inhibitor SCH 351591 or SCH 534385. Toxicol Pathol 2008;36:827–39.

[210] Zhang J, Herman EH, Robertson DG, Reily MD, Knapton A, Ratajczak HV, et al. Mechanisms and biomarkers of cardiovascular injury induced by phosphodiesterase inhibitor III SK&F 95654 in the spontaneously hypertensive rat. Toxicol Pathol 2006;34:152–63.

[211] Dietsch GN, Dipalma CR, Eyre RJ, Pham TQ, Poole KM, Pefaur NB, et al. Characterization of the inflammatory response to a highly selective PDE4 inhibitor in the rat and the identification of biomarkers that correlate with toxicity. Toxicol Pathol 2006;34:39–51.

[212] Guionaud S, Cacoub P, Lawton M, Bendjama K, Firat H, and the other members of SafeT Workpackage 4. Histological comparisons of clinical and non-clinical of drug-induced vascular injury to support qualification of translational biomarkers. In: 30th Annual Symposium of Society of Toxicologic Pathology, Denver, USA; June 19–23, 2011.

[213] Weaver JL, Snyder R, Knapton A, Herman EH, Honchel R, Miller T, et al. Biomarkers in peripheral blood associated with vascular injury in Sprague-Dawley rats treated with the phosphodiesterase IV inhibitors SCH 351591 or SCH 534385. Toxicol Pathol 2008;36:840–9.

[214] Sheth CM, Enerson BE, Peters D, Lawton MP, Weaver JL. Effects of modulating in vivo nitric oxide production on the incidence and severity of PDE4 inhibitor-induced vascular injury in Sprague-Dawley rats. Toxicol Sci 2011;122:7–15.

[215] Bian H, Zhang J, Wu PE, Varty LA, Jia Y, Mayhood T, et al. Differential type 4 cAMP-specific phosphodiesterase (PDE4) expression and functional sensitivity to PDE4 inhibitors among rats, monkeys and humans. Biochem Pharmacol December 01, 2004;68(11):2229–36.

[216] Losco PE, Evans EW, Barat SA, Blackshear PE, Reyderman L, Fine JS, et al. The toxicity of SCH 351591, a novel phosphodiesterase-4 inhibitor, in cynomolgus monkeys. Toxicol Pathol 2004;32:295–308.

[217] Clemo FA, Evering WE, Snyder PW, Albassam MA. Differentiating spontaneous from drug-induced vascular injury in the dog. Toxicol Pathol 2003;31(Suppl.):25–31.

[218] Yang J, Huang J, Zhang YZ, Chen L. Tie2 mRNA in peripheral blood: a new marker to assess damage of endothelial cells in a rat model of sepsis. Chin J Traumatol 2010;13:308–12.

[219] Louden C, Brott D, Katein A, Kelly T, Gould S, Jones H, et al. Biomarkers and mechanisms of drug-induced vascular injury in nonrodents. Toxicol Pathol 2006;34:19–26.

[220] Dignat-George F, Boulanger CM. The many faces of endothelial microparticles. Arterioscler Thromb Vasc Biol 2011;31:27–33.

[221] Challah M, Nadaud S, Philippe M, Battle T, Soubrier F, Corman B, et al. Circulating and cellular markers of endothelial dysfunction with aging in rats. Am J Physiol 1997;273:H1941–8.

[222] Thomas RA, Pietrzak DC, Scicchitano MS, Thomas HC, McFarland DC, Frazier KS. Detection and characterization of circulating endothelial progenitor cells in normal rat blood. J Pharmacol Toxicol Methods 2009;60:263–74.

[223] Shaked Y, Bertolini F, Emmenegger U, Lee CR, Kerbel RS. On the origin and nature of elevated levels of circulating endothelial cells after treatment with a vascular disrupting agent. J Clin Oncol 2006;24:4040. author reply 4040–1.

[224] Dini L, Lentini A, Diez GD, Rocha M, Falasca L, Serafino L, et al. Phagocytosis of apoptotic bodies by liver endothelial cells. J Cell Sci 1995;108(Pt 3):967–73.

[225] Lloyd MC, Allam-Nandyala P, Purohit CN, Burke N, Coppola D, Bui MM. Using image analysis as a tool for assessment of prognostic and predictive biomarkers for breast cancer: how reliable is it? J Pathol Inform 2010;1:29.

[226] Baatz M, Arini N, Schape A, Binnig G, Linssen B. Object-oriented image analysis for high content screening: detailed quantification of cells and sub cellular structures with the Cellenger software. Cytometry A 2006;69:652–8.

[227] Badea A, Johnson GA, Jankowsky JL. Remote sites of structural atrophy predict later amyloid formation in a mouse model of Alzheimer's disease. Neuroimage 2010;50:416–27.

[228] Badea CT, Bucholz E, Hedlund LW, Rockman HA, Johnson GA. Imaging methods for morphological and functional phenotyping of the rodent heart. Toxicol Pathol 2006;34:111–7.

[229] Delnomdedieu M, Hedlund LW, Johnson GA, Maronpot RR. Magnetic resonance microscopy – a new tool for the toxicologic pathologist. Toxicol Pathol 1996;24:36–44.

[230] Carlsen H, Moskaug JO, Fromm SH, Blomhoff R. In vivo imaging of NF-kappa B activity. J Immunol 2002;168:1441–6.

[231] Rudin M. Noninvasive imaging of receptor function: signal transduction pathways and physiological readouts. Curr Opin Drug Discov Devel 2008;11:606–15.

[232] Rudin M, Weissleder R. Molecular imaging in drug discovery and development. Nat Rev Drug Discov 2003;2:123–31.

[233] Hahn MA, Singh AK, Sharma P, Brown SC, Moudgil BM. Nanoparticles as contrast agents for in vivo bioimaging: current status and future perspectives. Anal Bioanal Chem 2011;399:3–27.

[234] Ying X, Monticello TM. Modern imaging technologies in toxicologic pathology: an overview. Toxicol Pathol 2006;34:815–26.

[235] Leong FJ, Leong AS. Digital imaging in pathology: theoretical and practical considerations, and applications. Pathology 2004;36:234–41.

[236] Hipp JD, Cheng JY, Toner M, Tompkins RG, Balis UJ. Spatially Invariant Vector Quantization: a pattern matching algorithm for multiple classes of image subject matter including pathology. J Pathol Inform 2011;2:13.

[237] Minot DM, Kipp BR, Root RM, Meyer RG, Reynolds CA, Nassar A, et al. Automated cellular imaging system III for assessing HER2 status in breast cancer specimens: development of a standardized scoring method that correlates with FISH. Am J Clin Pathol 2009;132:133–8.

[238] Lexe G, Monaco J, Doyle S, Basavanhally A, Reddy A, Seiler M, et al. Towards improved cancer diagnosis and prognosis using analysis of gene expression data and computer aided imaging. Exp Biol Med (Maywood) 2009;234:860–79.

[239] Rawlins SR, El-Zammar O, Zinkievich JM, Newman N, Levine RA. Digital quantification is more precise than traditional semi-quantitation of hepatic steatosis: correlation with fibrosis in 220 treatment-naive patients with chronic hepatitis C. Dig Dis Sci 2010;55:2049–57.

[240] Al-Kofahi Y, Dowell-Mesfin N, Pace C, Shain W, Turner JN, Roysam B. Improved detection of branching points in algorithms for automated neuron tracing from 3D confocal images. Cytometry A 2008;73:36–43.

[241] Wild R, Ramakrishnan S, Sedgewick J, Griffioen AW. Quantitative assessment of angiogenesis and tumor vessel architecture by computer-assisted digital image analysis: effects of VEGF-toxin conjugate on tumor microvessel density. Microvasc Res 2000;59:368–76.

[242] Liu XS, Sajda P, Saha PK, Wehrli FW, Guo XE. Quantification of the roles of trabecular microarchitecture and trabecular type in determining the elastic modulus of human trabecular bone. J Bone Miner Res 2006;21:1608–17.

[243] Hadi AM, Mouchaers KT, Schalij I, Grunberg K, Meijer GA, Vonk-Noordegraaf A, et al. Rapid quantification of myocardial fibrosis: a new macro-based automated analysis. Cell Oncol (Dordr) 2011;34:343–54.

[244] David FS, Cullen-McEwen L, Wu XS, Zins SR, Lin J, Bertram JF, et al. Regulation of kidney development by Shp2: an unbiased stereological analysis. Anat Rec (Hoboken) 2010;293:2147–53.

[245] Van Hummelen P, Sasaki J. State-of-the-art genomics approaches in toxicology. Mutat Res 2010;705:165–71.

[246] Aardema MJ, MacGregor JT. Toxicology and genetic toxicology in the new era of 'toxicogenomics': impact of '-omics' technologies. Mutat Res 2002;499:13–25.

[247] Foster WR, Chen SJ, He A, Truong A, Bhaskaran V, Nelson DM, et al. A retrospective analysis of toxicogenomics in the safety assessment of drug candidates. Toxicol Pathol 2007;35:621–35.

[248] Pettit S, des Etages SA, Mylecraine L, Snyder R, Fostel J, et al. Current and future applications of toxicogenomics: results summary of a survey from the HESI Genomics State of Science Subcommittee. Environ Health Perspect 2010;118:992–7.

[249] Kramer JA, Curtiss SW, Kolaja KL, Alden CL, Blomme EA, Curtiss WC, et al. Acute molecular markers of rodent hepatic carcinogenesis identified by transcription profiling. Chem Res Toxicol 2004;17:463–70.

[250] Blomme EA, Yang Y, Waring JF. Use of toxicogenomics to understand mechanisms of drug-induced hepatotoxicity during drug discovery and development. Toxicol Lett 2009;186:22–31.

[251] Guerreiro N, Staedtler F, Grenet O, Kehren J, Chibout SD. Toxicogenomics in drug development. Toxicol Pathol 2003;31:471–9.

[252] Kondo C, Minowa Y, Uehara T, Okuno Y, Nakatsu N, Ono A, et al. Identification of genomic biomarkers for concurrent diagnosis of drug-induced renal tubular injury using a large-scale toxicogenomics database. Toxicology 2009;265:15–26.

[253] Cheng F, Theodorescu D, Schulman IG, Lee JK. In vitro transcriptomic prediction of hepatotoxicity for early drug discovery. J Theor Biol 2011;290:27–36.

[254] Sawada H, Takami K, Asahi S. A toxicogenomic approach to drug-induced phospholipidosis: analysis of its induction mechanism and establishment of a novel in vitro screening system. Toxicol Sci 2005;83:282–92.

[255] Tugendreich S, Pearson CI, Sagartz J, Jarnagin K, Kolaja K. NSAID-induced acute phase response is due to increased intestinal permeability and characterized by early and consistent alterations in hepatic gene expression. Toxicol Pathol 2006;34:168–79.

[256] Rokushima M, Omi K, Imura K, Araki A, Furukawa N, Itoh F, et al. Toxicogenomics of drug-induced hemolytic anemia by analyzing gene expression profiles in the spleen. Toxicol Sci 2007;100:290–302.

[257] Sayers EW, Barrett T, Benson DA, Bolton E, Bryant SH, Canese K, et al. Database resources of the National Center for Biotechnology Information. Nucleic Acids Res 2012;40:D13–25.

[258] Wilhite SE, Barrett T. Strategies to explore functional genomics data sets in NCBI's GEO database. Methods Mol Biol 2012;802:41–53.

[259] Davis AP, Wiegers TC, Murphy CG, Mattingly CJ. The curation paradigm and application tool used for manual curation of the scientific literature at the Comparative Toxicogenomics Database. Database, 2011, bar034Oxford, 2011, bar034. 2011.

[260] Kiyosawa N, Ando Y, Watanabe K, Niino N, Manabe S, Yamoto T. Scoring multiple toxicological endpoints using a toxicogenomic database. Toxicol Lett 2009;188:91–7.

[261] Morgan KT, Jayyosi Z, Hower MA, Pino MV, Connolly TM, Kotlenga K, et al. The hepatic transcriptome as a window on whole-body physiology and pathophysiology. Toxicol Pathol 2005;33:136–45.

[262] Bates S. The role of gene expression profiling in drug discovery. Curr Opin Pharmacol 2011;11:549–56.

[263] Tabibiazar R, Wagner RA, Liao A, Quertermous T. Transcriptional profiling of the heart reveals chamber-specific gene expression patterns. Circ Res 2003;93:1193–201.

[264] Irwin RD, Parker JS, Lobenhofer EK, Burka LT, Blackshear PE, Vallant MK, et al. Transcriptional profiling of the left and median liver lobes of male f344/n rats following exposure to acetaminophen. Toxicol Pathol 2005;33:111–7.

[265] Hamadeh HK, Jayadev S, Gaillard ET, Huang Q, Stoll R, Blanchard K, et al. Integration of clinical and gene expression endpoints to explore furan-mediated hepatotoxicity. Mutat Res 2004;549:169–83.

[266] Mikaelian I, Buness A, de Vera-Mudry MC, Kanwal C, Coluccio D, et al. Primary endothelial damage is the mechanism of cardiotoxicity of tubulin-binding drugs. Toxicol Sci 2010;117:144–51.

[267] Foley JF, Collins JB, Umbach DM, Grissom S, Boorman GA, Heinloth AN. Optimal sampling of rat liver tissue for toxicogenomic studies. Toxicol Pathol 2006;34:795–801.

[268] Harrill AH, Rusyn I. Systems biology and functional genomics approaches for the identification of cellular responses to drug toxicity. Expert Opin Drug Metab Toxicol 2008;4:1379–89.

[269] Corvi R, Ahr HJ, Albertini S, Blakey DH, Clerici L, Coecke S, et al. Meeting report: validation of toxicogenomics-based test systems: ECVAM-ICCVAM/NICEATM considerations for regulatory use. Environ Health Perspect 2006;114:420–9.

[270] Bartel DP. MicroRNAs: target recognition and regulatory functions. Cell 2009;136:215–33.

[271] Arroyo JD, Chevillet JR, Kroh EM, Ruf IK, Pritchard CC, Gibson DF, et al. Argonaute2 complexes carry a population of circulating microRNAs independent of vesicles in human plasma. Proc Natl Acad Sci USA 2011;108:5003–8.

[272] Vickers KC, Palmisano BT, Shoucri BM, Shamburek RD, Remaley AT. MicroRNAs are transported in plasma and delivered to recipient cells by high-density lipoproteins. Nat Cell Biol 2011;13:423–33.

[273] Chen C, Skog J, Hsu CH, Lessard RT, Balaj L, Wurdinger T, et al. Microfluidic isolation and transcriptome analysis of serum microvesicles. Lab Chip 2010;10:505–11.

[274] Cocucci E, Racchetti G, Meldolesi J. Shedding microvesicles: artefacts no more. Trends Cell Biol 2009;19:43–51.

[275] Wang K, Zhang S, Weber J, Baxter D, Galas DJ. Export of microRNAs and microRNA-protective protein by mammalian cells. Nucleic Acids Res 2010;38:7248–59.

[276] Cui W, Ma J, Wang Y, Biswal S. Plasma miRNA as biomarkers for assessment of total-body radiation exposure dosimetry. PLoS One 2011;6:e22988.

[277] Chen T, Li Z, Yan J, Yang X, Salminen W. MicroRNA expression profiles distinguish the carcinogenic effects of riddelliine in rat liver. Mutagenesis 2012;27:59–66.

[278] Melkamu T, Zhang X, Tan J, Zeng Y, Kassie F. Alteration of microRNA expression in vinyl carbamate-induced mouse lung tumors and modulation by the chemopreventive agent indole-3-carbinol. Carcinogenesis 2010;31:252–8.

[279] Ross JA, Blackman CF, Thai SF, Li Z, Kohan M, Jones CP, et al. A potential microRNA signature for tumorigenic conazoles in mouse liver. Mol Carcinog 2010;49:320–3.

[280] Gonzalez FJ, Shah YM. PPARalpha: mechanism of species differences and hepatocarcinogenesis of peroxisome proliferators. Toxicology 2008;246:2–8.

[281] Yoshioka W, Higashiyama W, Tohyama C. Involvement of microRNAs in dioxin-induced liver damage in the mouse. Toxicol Sci 2011;122:457–65.

[282] Latendresse JR, Beland FA, Porgibny IP. Plasma microRNAs as sensitive indicators of liver injury. San Francisco (CA): Society of Toxicology; 2012.

[283] Rouse RL, Rosenzweig BA, Thompson KL. Comparative profile of urinary biomarkers. San Francisco (CA): Society of Toxicology; 2012.

III. CLINICAL PATHOLOGY, HISTOPATHOLOGY, AND BIOMARKERS

[284] Laterza OF, Lim L, Garrett-Engele PW, Vlasakova K, Muniappa N, Tanaka WK, et al. Plasma microRNAs as sensitive and specific biomarkers of tissue injury. Clin Chem 2009;55:1977–83.

[285] John-Baptiste A, Huang W, Kindt E, Wu A, Vitsky A, Scott W, et al. Evaluation of potential gastrointestinal biomarkers in a PAK4 inhibitor-treated preclinical toxicity model to address unmonitorable gastrointestinal toxicity. Toxicol Pathol April 2012;40(3):482–90.

[286] Pavkovic M, Riefke B, Ellinger-Ziegelbauer H. Poster #551. San Francisco (CA): Society of Toxicology; 2012.

[287] Bertinetti-Lapatki C, Mikaelian I, Fischer S, Eichinger-Chapelon A, Zabka TS, Weiser T, et al. Poster #1714. San Francisco (CA): Society of Toxicology; 2012.

[288] Maher J, Sharapova T, Devanarayan V. Poster # 1712. San Francisco (CA): Society of Toxicology; 2012.

[289] Yang X, Greenhaw J, Shi Q, Su Z, Qian F, Davis K, et al. Identification of urinary microRNA profiles in rats that may diagnose hepatotoxicity. Toxicol Sci 2012;125:335–44.

[290] Scicchitano M, Thomas R. Poster #1656. San Francisco (CA): Society of Toxicology; 2012.

[291] de Planell-Saguer M, Rodicio MC. Analytical aspects of microRNA in diagnostics: a review. Anal Chim Acta August 2011;699(2):134–52. Epub 2011 May 20. Review.

[292] Etheridge A, Lee I, Hood L, Galas D, Wang K. Extracellular microRNA: a new source of biomarkers. Mutat Res 2011;717.

[293] Jang JS, Simon VA, Feddersen RM, Rakhshan F, Schultz DA, Zschunke MA, et al. Quantitative miRNA expression analysis using fluidigm microfluidics dynamic arrays. BMC Genomics 2011;12:144.

[294] Keller S, Ridinger J, Rupp AK, Janssen JW, Altevogt P. Body fluid derived exosomes as a novel template for clinical diagnostics. J Transl Med 2011;9:86.

[295] Kosaka N, Iguchi H, Ochiya T. Circulating microRNA in body fluid: a new potential biomarker for cancer diagnosis and prognosis. Cancer Sci 2010;101:2087–92.

[296] Wang G, Tam LS, Li EK, Kwan BC, Chow KM, Luk CC, et al. Serum and urinary free microRNA level in patients with systemic lupus erythematosus. Lupus 2011;20:493–500.

[297] Weber DG, Casjens S, Rozynek P, Lehnert M, Zilch-Schoneweis S, Bryk O, et al. Assessment of mRNA and microRNA stabilization in peripheral human blood for multicenter studies and biobanks. Biomark Insights 2010;5:95–102.

[298] Weber JA, Baxter DH, Zhang S, Huang DY, Huang KH, Lee MJ, et al. The microRNA spectrum in 12 body fluids. Clin Chem 2010;56:1733–41.

[299] Zen K, Zhang CY. Circulating microRNAs: a novel class of biomarkers to diagnose and monitor human cancers. Med Res Rev March 2012;32(2):326–48. Epub 2010 November 09. Review.

[300] Ferrara C, Brunker P, Suter T, Moser S, Puntener U, Umana P. Modulation of therapeutic antibody effector functions by glycosylation engineering: influence of Golgi enzyme localization domain and co-expression of heterologous beta1, 4-N-acetylglucosaminyltransferase III and Golgi alpha-mannosidase II. Biotechnol Bioeng 2006;93:851–61.

[301] Mossner E, Brunker P, Moser S, Puntener U, Schmidt C, Herter S, et al. Increasing the efficacy of CD20 antibody therapy through the engineering of a new type II antiCD20 antibody with enhanced direct and immune effector cell-mediated B-cell cytotoxicity. Blood 2010;115:4393–402.

CHAPTER

17

Biomarkers in Nonclinical Drug Development

A.D. Aulbach, C.J. Amuzie

BIOMARKERS IN NONCLINICAL SAFETY ASSESSMENT

The use of biomarkers in nonclinical drug development covers a broad range of disciplines, modalities, and development stages that extend from the identification and assessment of drug targets to issue resolution during the clinical trial of investigative drugs. Biomarkers became more applicable in drug development after the complete sequencing of the human genome and the expansion of omics technologies that followed. The National Institutes of Health (USA) has defined biomarkers as a characteristic that is objectively measured as an indicator of biological processes or pharmacological responses [1]. When adapted to the context of nonclinical drug development, a biomarker may be defined as any specific parameter that is objectively measured and evaluated as an indicator of normal biological processes, pathologic processes, or pharmacologic responses to a drug or test article, which helps to diagnose or monitor a disease and/or the outcome of therapeutic intervention [2,3].

In safety assessment, biomarkers are most commonly used for monitoring early signs of toxicity; as such they are often called "safety" biomarkers in nonclinical and clinical environments. However, scientists in drug discovery are aware that biomarkers are used in a broader context than "safety" and can sometimes be selected as a molecular index to evaluate the efficacy of new therapeutic entities. For example, the human epidermal growth factor receptor (HER2) is a protein in 20% of breast cancers and its presence is associated with very aggressive tumor behavior, yet it is a target for several effective drugs targeting breast cancer [4]. This example illustrates that a discussion on the utility of biomarkers should be broad to include their physiology, expose the range of possible applications, and also keep the applicable details to their most common uses.

There are three broad categories of biomarkers in nonclinical drug development based on the drug exposure–effect continuum. They are biomarkers of exposure, susceptibility, and effect. Most of the discussion in this chapter will be focused on biomarkers of effect, but the other categories will be discussed briefly. A biomarker of exposure is the administered test article or a metabolite that is measured in a specific tissue or body fluid as evidence that the animal or human biological system was exposed to the test article. For example, acetaminophen is an oral analgesic that is metabolized to a reactive intermediate N-acetyl-p-benzoquinone imine (NAPQI). Both acetaminophen and NAPQI can be measured as biomarkers of exposure to help investigators understand acetaminophen exposure and toxicity. Note that in acetaminophen overdose, NAPQI levels are used more like a biomarker of effect to monitor the magnitude of acetaminophen toxicity or the effectiveness of acetaminophen antidote, N-acetyl cysteine. This NAPQI example illustrates that a single biomarker can provide a picture of both exposure and effect of the test article, highlighting that biomarker categories can overlap and should be contextually understood in order to be meaningfully applied.

Biomarkers of susceptibility are specific genotypes in animals or people that make them more prone to a particular disease or more likely to be affected by a particular therapy. Warfarin (Coumadin) is an anticoagulant used to manage thrombotic disorders and acts by inhibiting vitamin K-dependent clotting factors. Specific alleles of the gene that encode the metabolizing cytochrome P-450 enzyme (CYP2C9*2 and CYP2C9*3) are associated with reduced metabolism of Warfarin, a higher circulating drug concentration, and an increased risk for bleeding disorders in patients that are taking Warfarin [5]. The genotyping of patients provides information from these alleles, from which patients are ranked according to their susceptibility to bleeding disorders while taking Warfarin. Therefore patients with thrombotic disorders who also have these alleles are given lower doses of Warfarin to mitigate this risk. The understanding of biomarkers of susceptibility and their application to a particular drug or target is useful in selecting the correct animal model of disease and/or safety in drug discovery and development, understanding toxicokinetics in the appropriate haplotype, and selecting the right patient population for early clinical trials.

Pharmacodynamic (efficacy) or toxicity (safety) biomarkers are essentially biomarkers of effect. They indicate that a specific alteration or injury has occurred in a receptor, tissue compartment, or body fluid after a test article has been administered. The ideal biomarker of effect is a characteristic that can be objectively measured as an index of test article-related alterations in a minimally invasive way. Therefore biomarkers that can be obtained in body fluids (saliva, urine, blood, and plasma) or imaging are generally preferred to those that can be obtained by biopsies or other invasive techniques. The identification of biomarkers of effect requires a thorough understanding of the effect pathway in a specific tissue or the signaling pathway and their interaction(s) with other systems within the whole organism. For example, growth hormone is released from the anterior pituitary and binds to growth hormone receptors in the liver to produce an elevation of insulin-like growth factor-1 (IGF-1) and its acid-labile binding subunit (IGFALS) in the plasma. Therefore molecules that alter growth or growth hormone signaling, such as the toxin deoxynivalenol, are also expected to change the levels of IGF-1 or IGFALS in plasma, and these circulating proteins can be used as biomarkers to determine the effect of a xenobiotic on growth hormone signaling [6]. In general, a good understanding of the circulating kinetics of the test article and the biomarker is absolutely necessary to properly understand and interpret any biomarker of effect data.

BIOMARKER VALIDATION, QUALIFICATION, AND APPLICATION IN NONCLINICAL STUDIES

It is clear that biomarkers are playing an increasingly important role in pharmaceutical development and are receiving increased attention from both regulators and industry. Although there are many biomarkers that would be considered "traditional," in the sense that they have been in use for many years and utilize standardized methodologies, most of the newly emerging biomarkers discussed in this section are quantified by relatively novel immunoassay methodologies, often using proprietary commercially available assay kits. Many of these kits and their associated reagents are not consistently regulated, monitored, or standardized across industry. These factors result in inconsistent and sometimes improper use and application of biomarkers across different organizations/laboratories and emphasize the importance of stringent validation and assay characterization practices. In this section some of the challenges in biomarker validation and their application in nonclinical toxicology studies are reviewed.

Biomarker Qualification

The need for high-quality biomarkers that are robust, predictive, and cost effective has been thoroughly discussed by a variety of industry and regulatory groups for a number of years [7–11]. Regulatory organizations like the Food and Drug Administration (FDA), the Organisation for Economic Co-operation and Development (OECD), and the European Medicines Agency (EMEA) have engaged in a dialogue with the pharmaceutical industry on what they deem necessary to develop a qualified biomarker. The term "qualification" should not be confused with the term "validation," since the latter represents the performance characterization of a method or assay. In a regulatory context, qualification represents the endorsement of a particular biomarker by a regulatory body under a very specific set of conditions (eg, "…may be used for the characterization of renal effects in rats…"). The FDA has established a Biomarker Qualification Review Team (BRQT) that provides evaluations of qualification data for biomarkers submitted as part of IND (investigational new drug)/NDA (new drug application) applications to the FDA [12]. The BRQT aims to ensure that biomarkers are integrated in the review process and to encourage development of biomarkers that add value to the development program of a given drug

candidate. Submission of qualification data is largely driven by international consortiums such as the Predictive Safety Testing Consortium (PSTC), the International Life Sciences Institute—Health and Environmental Sciences Institute (ILSI-HESI), whose work ultimately leads to the discovery, critical evaluation, and application of promising new biomarker candidates. Once qualified, results from specific biomarkers are then officially "considered" by the endorsing regulatory body as part of nonclinical data submission packages under a very specific set of circumstances as outlined by the agency. That said, biomarkers that have not been officially qualified by the FDA, but have demonstrated repeated utility in nonclinical settings, are still routinely applied to nonclinical safety data packages to provide additional perspective.

Biomarker Assay Kits

Unlike traditional clinical pathology, clinical chemistry, and other well-established testing methods, commercially available first-to-market biomarker kits often use ligand-based (immunoassay) testing methods and reagents that vary greatly in their quality, performance, and overall value. Despite the availability of a multitude of commercial kits from numerous vendors, the extent of assay characterization and critical reagent performance of these assays is often insufficient to support their use. Because these products are distributed as "research use only," there is essentially no oversight over the manufacture, distribution, or marketing of such products. These kits are often marketed for the broadest possible use and are often not designed for specific applications in which they are used (ie, cross-species, multiple matrices, insufficient stability). Additionally, the specific techniques and performance assessment procedures used by the end-users prior to undertaking sample testing varies greatly. These factors can negatively impact the quality of biomarker data used in making key decisions during drug development. Hence when using novel biomarkers to generate nonclinical data, it is critical to obtain assay kits from reputable vendors, execute a robust site-specific fit-for-purpose performance characterization, and maintain consistency of the materials and methods used throughout a nonclinical program.

Two main categories of commercial biomarker kits are used in drug development and research purposes: in vitro diagnostic assays (IVD) and research use only (RUO) assays. An understanding of these categories and their inherent differences is important to gain insight into whether or not a given assay may be suitable for the intended use. IVD assays make up a large majority of the traditional clinical pathology assays as well as a number of the newer biomarker kits. These assays have been approved by the FDA (defined in 21 CFR 809.33) for intended use in human clinical diagnosis or patient care and undergo intense screening/monitoring, and regulation as to how these materials are manufactured, distributed, and used in laboratories [13]. For these reasons, traditional clinical pathology assays and IVD biomarker tests have been better characterized, standardized from lab-to-lab, and generally have better performance characteristics than novel first-to-market biomarker assays. Conversely, the large majority of commercially available novel biomarker kits used in nonclinical laboratories to which most of this chapter is devoted fall under the RUO category. Assays that are labeled RUO are exempt from the regulatory requirements and approvals needed for clinical diagnosis or patient management. They are intended for use only in research and discovery work and since there are no rigorous requirements or guidelines for the RUO label, the extent of manufacturing quality compliance, assay characterization, and documentation varies considerably across different vendors and from assay to assay. Hence most novel biomarker assays are not standardized between laboratories and need to have a robust performance characterization/validation prior to use.

Fit-for-Purpose (Analytical) Validation

The term validation is used in a multitude of different contexts, sometimes inappropriately, and often interchangeably with the term qualification. Generally the term validation represents the actual analytical performance characterization of a method or assay by executing various experiments (eg, spike and recovery, dilutional linearity, stability, etc.) to gain an understanding of the ability of the assay to accurately quantitate the analyte of interest. For many years industry investigators went without a consistent approach to this process, which led to disharmony and confusion between laboratories, particularly when attempting to compare results between different labs. Eventually leading ligand-binding scientists began to harmonize this process by promoting the fit-for-purpose validation model.

The fit-for-purpose paradigm has been in use for over a decade now and was initially described in 2006 with an intention to provide a framework for the validation and performance characterization of ligand-binding (immunoassay) biomarker kits [8]. The core principle of the fit-for-purpose approach surrounds the notion of executing a performance characterization/validation equal in robustness to the intended use of the data being generated. For example, the level of robustness of a validation for a renal biomarker assay being used during an early non-GLP discovery phase would not be as great as the validation of a cardiac biomarker being used during a 13-week GLP study for a compound

in which there was a known cardiac liability. Briefly, the key elements included in a fit-for-purpose validation include preparation of a validation plan, testing of dynamic range, intra- and interassay precision and accuracy, dilutional linearity, parallelism, establishment of quality control (QC) samples in species-specific matrix, normal baseline ranges from species of interest in matrix, and short/long-term stability in matrix. In accordance with the fit-for-purpose approach, the overall level of rigor (ie, number of runs, length of stability testing, standard curve points, lot-to-lot variability testing, etc.) is determined by the level of confidence one puts into the data being generated. For a more detailed and comprehensive discussion of an analytical fit-for-purpose validation readers are directed to the references discussed in this section.

Recommendations for fit-for-purpose biomarker assay development and validation have been described for immunoassays developed de novo at pharmaceutical companies and contract research laboratories [7,8]. However, specific regulatory guidance has been sparse and incomplete, which does not help the pharmaceutical end user determine the appropriate practices to select, adapt, validate, and ensure long-term supplies of reliable commercial biomarker assay kits for drug development purposes. The most comprehensive of the *nonbinding* recommendations on the subject are found in the 2013 Bioanalytical Method Validation, which that states the following points regarding commercial biomarker assay validation [14]:

- The performance of diagnostic kits should be assessed in the facility conducting (site-specific) the sample analysis.
- Diagnostic kit validation data provided by the manufacturer may not ensure reliability of the kit for drug development purposes.
- Specificity, accuracy, precision, and stability should be demonstrated under actual conditions of use.
- Quality control (QC) samples with known concentrations should be prepared and used, independent of the kit-supplied materials.
- Standards and QCs should be prepared in the same matrix as the subject samples.
- If multiple kit lots are used within a study, lot-to-lot variability and comparability should be addressed for critical reagents.

Although these guidelines remain somewhat vague, they are consistent with most published fit-for-purpose documents as well as those inherent to bioanalytical method validation practices, which share many features of immunoassay biomarker methodologies. Currently, most laboratories conducting biomarker analysis have adopted some form of the fit-for-purpose validation model when establishing new methods.

Biomarker Application in Nonclinical Studies

Inherent to the use of biomarker assays in toxicology studies is an understanding of the identification and interpretation of a positive biomarker signal. We have discussed the relative diversity of assays, levels of performance, and lack of standardized methods for biomarker assays. All of these factors contribute to the difficulty in identifying a positive signal, which must be distinguished not only from background biologic variability, but also from the analytical "noise" that is generally much higher than traditional clinical pathology tests. Thus it remains crucial for the interpreting scientist to understand the inherent variation of the specific assay/reagent set based on the analytical validation data, as well as the biologic variation, which can be determined by establishing historical control data sets for the intended reference population. Once a positive signal has been identified, a thorough understanding of what a positive signal represents is fundamental to accurate drug hazard identification. For example, for cardiac biomarkers, some markers are indicators of direct cardiac myocyte injury (troponins) while others are indicators of a functional defect (natriuretic peptides). The renal biomarker NGAL (neutrophil gelatinase-associated lipocalin) is an indicator of renal tubular injury, but can also be seen in cases of systemic and urinary tract inflammation [15].

A key feature to interpreting data from novel biomarkers is to have an appreciation for the heterogeneity of positive biomarker response signals in timing, magnitude, and by species. Every individual biomarker will have its own unique signature in response to a specific compound and pathophysiologic mechanism. For example, in the dog, compound A may induce a 10-fold increase in cardiac troponin I (cTnI) within 24h, but with compound B the response is twofold and isn't seen until 72h postdose. If this same example is used, replacing cTnI with another commonly used cardiac biomarker like proBNP, the magnitudes and timing would be completely different that those observed with cTnI. These differences are related to the specific pathology induced by the compounds both in timing and severity, and what each biomarker actually represents pathologically. In addition, some species may show different magnitudes or even nonexistent responses to injury when using certain biomarkers. The best examples of this phenomenon are seen with the acute-phase proteins (eg, CRP, α2-macroglobulin, serum amyloid A, etc.). These biomarkers show a large degree of species-specific diversity among their individual responses to the same inflammatory stimuli [16]. All of these factors emphasize the importance of correlating biomarker data with study data generated from more traditional endpoints (eg, pathology, clinical pathology).

Another important concept is to have an understanding of the specific timing of individual biomarker signals.

For example, in the case of inflammation, IL-6 (6–24h), CRP (1–2days), and fibrinogen (2–3days) are all positive acute phase reactants that will increase in response to the same inflammatory stimulus. However, each will have a different window in which you can capture their increases (listed in parentheses). Attempting to draw blood at 3days postdose for a cytokine like IL-6 will generally result in no positive signal, which can lead to mischaracterization of the safety profile for the compound.

Lab-to-Lab and Method-to-Method Diversity

One final important feature in the application and interpretation of biomarkers in nonclinical studies is related to the lack of standardization between laboratories and methods. For any given biomarker, the methods and reagents used for quantification will vary by laboratory and by kit or platform. This results in a number of different methods being used by different laboratories to measure the same biomarker. Objective comparisons between methods/kits from different laboratories have been made for a number of routinely used biomarker assays, and have generally demonstrated the lack of concordance between them. A recent study comparing renal biomarkers across different platforms revealed differences in individual biomarkers that ranged up to 15-fold and showed that these differences were probably due to the use of different antibodies with varying degrees of affinity and specificity [17]. This phenomenon is not uncommon and emphasizes the importance of establishing laboratory/method-specific reference ranges.

BIOMARKERS OF LIVER INJURY

The liver is a critical organ because of its broad role in nutrient homeostasis, as well as metabolism/detoxification and excretion of xenobiotics or endogenous compounds. Examples of liver function are synthesis of albumin and blood clotting factors, synthesis and storage of glucose, use and recycling of bilirubin and cholesterol, metabolism of hormones, and detoxification of various drugs. In order to accomplish these functions the liver is organized into lobular units that comprise cords of hepatocytes that are separated by sinusoidal spaces. The sinusoids contain spaced-out (fenestrated) endothelial cells and resident macrophages (Kupffer cells) as well as stellate cells that reside in small spaces (Space of Disse) between the hepatocyte cords and sinusoidal basement membrane. Within each lobular cord, individual hepatocytes are separated by bile canaliculi, which are useful for bile transport and recycling. Each liver lobule has a portal (periportal) blood input that supplies the periportal hepatocytes with the most oxygenated blood within the lobule, hence the periportal area has been referred to as Zone 1—the highest oxygen tension within a hepatic lobule. A central (centrilobular) vein with least oxygenated blood (Zone 3) is at the opposite end of the periportal blood supply within a liver lobule, while the midzone (Zone 2) is an intermediate zone of oxygenation that resides between Zones 1 and 3. The gradient of metabolizing enzymes such as cytochrome p450 is opposite to that of oxygenation, so hepatocytes around the central vein (Zone 3) have the most metabolizing enzymes, while those around the periportal area usually have the least metabolizing enzymes. This simplified understanding of the liver architecture, oxygen, and metabolizing enzyme gradients is frequently used to understand and interpret patterns of liver injury in toxicology. For example, the liver injury related to acetaminophen overdose is often driven by the reactive intermediate N-acetyl-p-quinone imine and is predominately centrilobular because of the high concentration of metabolizing enzymes that create the reactive intermediate around the central vein. On the other hand, injury related to iron toxicity/overdose is predominately periportal because iron toxicity involves redox cycling of ferrous and ferric iron, which occurs more in the zone with higher oxygen tension. The zoning of injury within the liver is a useful and relatively common practice in safety assessment because it can help identify potential mechanism(s) of injury and is useful for investigative toxicologists who design experiments to further understand toxicity or characterize the injury.

Drug-induced liver injury (DILI) is among the leading causes of pharmaceutical withdrawals from the market in the last three decades [18,19], and these withdrawals are impactful for the patients who need/rely on the drug and the drug maker who often has large economic loses and liabilities. Efforts to use biomarkers for improved prediction of DILI in nonclinical safety assessment are increasing in scope and complexity. In order to appreciate the scope of biomarkers of liver injury, we need to remember that xenobiotic-related liver injury may take several forms and involve different cell types depending on the chemical stimuli, dose, and/or duration of exposure. Examples of key biological events in different types of toxic liver injury are cell death, alteration of canalicular patency and function, disruption of cytoskeleton, increased accumulation of lipid molecules, alteration of sinusoidal patency and function, activation of Kupffer cells and inflammation, hapten-mediated liver injury, and increased fibrosis/collagen deposition.

Several traditional markers indicate liver injury in both clinical and nonclinical species. Some of these markers may be occasionally and often incorrectly termed "liver function tests," or LFTs. The concepts of liver injury and liver function need to be carefully delineated in order to understand and communicate toxic responses of the liver to injury. The details of such delineation during nonclinical safety data acquisition and

interpretation is outside the scope of this chapter and has been addressed elsewhere [19–21]. It is important to remember that there may be a biologically and/or statistically significant alteration in markers of liver injury without a corresponding effect on the indices of liver function, and vice-versa.

There are increasing numbers of in vitro systems that are useful for prioritizing chemical and biological entities in development. These in vitro systems use alterations in several molecular markers to predict toxicity. They are predominately used in non-GLP discovery settings and will not be discussed specifically in this chapter. The discussion of biomarkers in this section will be largely focused on liver injury that occurs in vivo in integrated animal systems. Currently there are two broad classes of liver injury biomarkers, called traditional and novel/emerging biomarkers. The traditional markers are most often routine clinical chemistry markers, most of which are part of a standard drug development program and will be described in detail below. Most of the emerging biomarkers and their associated methods have not been standardized or fully qualified but are currently being used on a case-by-case basis to understand or further characterize xenobiotic-related liver injury.

Traditional Biomarkers

The current best practice recommendation for nonclinical safety assessment is that a minimum of four serum parameters should be used to assess hepatocellular (minimum of two markers) and hepatobiliary (minimum of two markers) injury [19]. Any two markers from alanine transaminase (ALT) activity, aspartate transaminase (AST) activity, sorbitol Dehydrogenase (SDH) activity, and glutamate dehydrogenase (GLDH) will assess hepatocellular injury, while any two from alkaline phosphatase (ALP) activity, gamma-glutamyltransferase (GGT) activity, total bilirubin (TBILI), total bile acids (TBA), and 5′-nucleotidase will assess hepatobiliary injury. Among these serum parameters, ALT, AST, ALP, and TBILI are also used clinically to identify liver injury in humans, so they tend to be used relatively more frequently. It is important to note that these markers vary in their utility among nonclinical species. Therefore the proper selection of liver injury markers for each program is a thoughtful deliberation that often involves consultation with a qualified and experienced pathologist.

Biomarkers of Hepatocellular Injury

Alanine Transaminase

Alanine transaminase (ALT), which may be referred to in other literature as alanine aminotransferase (ALAT) or serum glutamate-pyruvate transaminase (SGPT), is found in blood and many tissues. ALT catalyzes the transfer of an amino group from alanine to alpha-keto-glutarate to yield glutamate and pyruvate as a part of amino acid metabolism and gluconeogenesis. Damaged hepatocytes leak their ALT into the extracellular space and ultimately plasma, so that ALT activity and/or amount will be increased in animals with damaged hepatocytes when compared to those with normal hepatocytes. Among the traditional markers of hepatocellular injury, ALT is considered to be a sensitive and translatable indicator of hepatocellular in the common preclinical species. Serum ALT activity is the most frequently relied upon indicator of hepatotoxic effects of drugs [22], although it does not always correlate well with histopathology data [23]. Increases in ALT activity may be observed with enzyme induction in rats and dogs [24,25] or muscle injury [19]. Furthermore, there may be instances of hepatic injury where ALT activity is not elevated due to inhibitory factors such as Vitamin B12 deficiency [26], or interference by the presence of pyridoxal-5′-phosphate inhibitors such as isoniazid or lead [23]. Due to the nonspecificity of ALT to hepatocellular injury, ancillary clinical chemistry and/or histopathology tests are often used to help interpret ALT values. In human clinical trials, it is an acceptable and recommended practice to interpret a greater than 3× elevation of ALT above the upper limit of normal (ULN) combined with TBILI elevation of greater than 2× above ULN as indicative of severe injury with/without any other evidence. This practice in human clinical medicine is called Hy's Law. A related recommendation for ALT interpretation in the absence of correlative histopathology in a nonclinical setting is the biomarker of two rule, which considers an ALT elevation of 3× ULN combined with a significant alteration in another liver injury biomarker as a sign of liver injury [27]. In general, caution should be exercised when applying human clinical recommendations to preclinical species because enzymes such as TBILI that reflect biliary function in humans do not accurately reflect liver function in all preclinical species [26]. ALT may also have reduced sensitivity and specificity to liver injury in some species such as swine, guinea pigs, and in some strains of rats [19]. The interpretation of ALT response in short-term nonclinical studies, especially in the absence of other indices of hepatic injury, needs to consider the so-called "adapter" phenomenon where transient, nonclinically relevant ALT elevations occur after the introduction of new drugs, but return to normal following continuous exposure [28]. Due to the challenges associated with using ALT, some have suggested an inclusion of immunoassay for ALT1, an ALT isozyme that is more specific for the liver, as a measure of hepatocellular injury, although these tests have not yet reached widespread acceptance on routine nonclinical studies [23]. Since ALT has not always been predictive of DILI in the clinical setting another marker(s) is

necessary for nonclinical predictive testing, hence the need for emerging biomarkers, discussed below.

Aspartate Transaminase

Aspartate transaminase (AST), which may also be referred to as aspartate aminotransferase or serum glutamic-oxaloacetic transaminase (SGOT) in other literature, catalyzes the reversible transfer of amino group between aspartate and glutamate. Like ALT, AST is found in the cytoplasm of hepatocytes and other tissues, including skeletal muscle. Injury to hepatocytes causes leakage of AST into the extracellular compartment with subsequent elevation in serum AST activity. AST activity may also be elevated in times of skeletal muscle injury in preclinical species. The magnitude of ALT elevation is usually greater than AST when both are elevated due to hepatocellular injury because of the longer half-life of ALT and the greater fraction of AST that is bound to the mitochondria [29]. The practice of considering a high ratio of AST/ALT to be more indicative of skeletal muscle injury [23] has been suggested and may aid in distinguishing muscle versus liver injury. Animal restraint procedures leading to mild muscle trauma may also elevate AST activity in nonclinical studies [30]. Given the nuances associated with interpreting leakage enzymes in the liver, careful integration of enzyme kinetics, enzyme half-lives, and all other data by well-qualified personnel is very important in the practice of safety assessment.

Glutamate Dehydrogenase

Glutamate dehydrogenase (GLDH) is a mitochondrial enzyme that reversibly converts glutamate to alpha-ketoglutarate as part of the urea cycle. GLDH activity increases with liver injury and the magnitude of elevation may be higher and longer lasting when compared to ALT [31]. Unlike ALT and AST, compounds that interfere with pyridoxal-5′-phosphate are less likely to alter the GLDH activity assay [23]. Unlike ALT, serum GLDH activity is neither affected by skeletal muscle damage nor induced by corticosteroids. GLDH is not currently used routinely in nonclinical settings often due to the limited availability of reliable reagents, but there may be instances where GLDH is an appropriate adjunct to help delineate liver injury in preclinical species. Interest in GLDH as a more specific nonclinical biomarker of hepatocellular injury in some species when compared to ALT or AST is increasing and will be discussed further in the section "Emerging Biomarkers."

Sorbitol Dehydrogenase

Sorbitol dehydrogenase (SDH) is present in several tissues where it catalyzes the reversible oxidation reduction of sorbitol, fructose, and NADPH (nicotinamide adenine dinucleotide phosphate). SDH is a sensitive and specific indicator of acute hepatocellular injury in rodents, dogs, and nonhuman primates and has been reported as valuable in humans [23]. However, SDH has a short half-life (4h in canine) and has limited stability compared to most other clinical chemistry analytes requiring it to be analyzed as soon as possible after necropsy [27]. To our knowledge, no large study has determined whether SDH adds any additional value to ALT quantitation.

Total Bile Acids

Total bile acids are important in the hepatic metabolism of cholesterol and absorption of fat and fat-soluble vitamins. The levels of circulating bile acids are influenced by diet and fasting but their elevation may also be a sign of hepatocellular injury and/or functional change in the liver [32]. TBA is a useful adjunct to assess the extent and consequence of liver injury because it is an index of hepatocellular function in preclinical species.

BIOMARKERS OF HEPATOBILIARY INJURY

Alkaline Phosphatase

Alkaline phosphatase (ALP) is a hydrolase that removes the phosphate group from various proteins and nucleotides. ALP is a leading biomarker of hepatobiliary injury in common preclinical species. Serum ALP levels increase when the patency of the bile duct is reduced, so ALP is widely used in nonclinical and human clinical settings as a marker of cholestatic liver injury. Like ALT, ALP is not specific for hepatobiliary injury as increased activity of ALP may be seen in conditions of bone growth and disease, glucocorticoid treatment, and microsomal enzyme induction [25,33]. Fluctuations of ALP need to be interpreted cautiously in nonclinical settings because there is an intestinal isoform of ALP that drives a decrease in ALP activity, particularly in rodents, during fasting or anorexia and a transient increase postprandially [19]. Specific ALP isoforms may be assessed to separate liver from bone and intestinal sources, but isoform measurement does not offer any additional diagnostic information in preclinical species compared to total ALP [19].

Total Bilirubin

Total bilirubin is a yellowish-green breakdown product of hemoglobin from aging red blood cells. TBILI is made of hepatic/conjugated and extrahepatic/unconjugated sources. Elevations in TBILI are usually indicative of cholestasis, but may be a reflection of increased

bilirubin production from erythrocyte destruction, altered bilirubin metabolism from drug-related inhibition of metabolizing enzymes such as uridine diphosphate glucuronosyltransferase, or faltering liver function [34]. A careful and integrated assessment of all study data associated with hyperbilirubinemia is often needed to identify a specific cause of TBILI elevations.

γ-Glutamyl Transferase and Other Hepatobiliary Markers

γ-glutamyl transferase (GGT) is a liver canalicular enzyme responsible for the transfer of glutamyl moiety to other acceptors as part of gluthathione recycling, and is present in other tissues. GGT is elevated through induction in conditions of cholestasis and may be used to confirm ALP activity elevations that are associated with cholestasis. In dogs and cats GGT is a less sensitive marker of cholestasis than ALP, but is more specific [19].

Two other hepatobiliary markers, 5'-nucleotidase (5'NT) and total bile acids (TBA), may be used to assess biliary function in nonclinical studies. However, they do not offer additional information when compared to ALP and TBILI and will not be discussed further.

Emerging Biomarkers

Due to the specificity issues with existing liver injury biomarkers such as ALT efforts are being made to identify additional biomarkers that are more specific and those that may provide additional information about the zone of injury and/or affected cell types. Within the last decade, proteomic approaches were used by investigators to identify a group of 19 putative liver injury biomarkers from a mechanistically diverse group of hepatototoxins based on early onset of biomarker alteration relative to time of liver [35]. The Hepatototoxcity Working Group of the Predictive Safety Testing Consortium (PSTC) has listed some promising classic and newly identified markers of injury for further qualification. The first set of biomarkers for qualification includes glutamate dehydrogenase (GLDH), malate dehydrogenase (MDH), paraoxonase-1 (PON1), and purine nucleoside phosphorylase (PNP). PSTC also listed a second set of biomarkers sorbitol dehydrogenase (SDH), arginase 1 (ARG-1), and gluthathione-s-transferase alpha (GSTα) for qualification while a circulating microRNA marker (miR-122) is being considered for qualification under the third set. This decision is based, in part, on published evidence in specific liver injury situations indicating that these biomarkers are likely to provide additional value in predicting liver injury. A robust qualification process is currently ongoing and some of these markers may become more routine in nonclinical testing panels after the qualification process.

Glutamate Dehydrogenase

Glutamate dehydrogenase (GLDH) is a mitochondrial enzyme that is predominantly located in the centrilobular (Zone 3) region of the liver lobule [36]. GLDH is a classic serum enzyme like ALT and AST. Unlike ALT, serum GLDH activity is neither affected by skeletal muscle damage nor induced by corticosteroids, and is not sensitive to interference by pyridoxal phosphate inhibitors. GLDH activity increases with liver injury and the magnitude of elevation may be higher and longer lasting when compared to ALT [31]. However, in the past there has been limited availability of reliable GLDH reagents in the United States. Recently, GLDH was reported as a specific biomarker of liver injury in a cohort of human clinical cases of drug-induced liver injury [37]. Furthermore, a human reference interval has been established for GLDH from a relatively large cohort. GLDH is emerging from a less commonly used classic biomarker to one that may be used more routinely to detect acute liver injury based on possible increases in sensitivity compared to ALT, and transnational use in humans.

Malate Dehydrogenase

Malate dehydrogenase (MDH) is a predominately periportal enzyme that is expressed highly in the extramitochondrial cytoplasm of the liver, although 10% of MDH has been reported in the mitochondria [23]. It is an enzyme in the citric acid cycle that catalyzes the reversible conversion of malate into oxaloacetate. Serum MDH activity is correlated with liver injury, although cardiac injury can cause an elevation in activity. Like GLDH, MDH levels are stable in healthy patients across gender and age groups, but are elevated with liver injury [37]. Due to the predominantly periportal location of MDH and possible translation to human clinical setting, MDH is among the first set of biomarkers undergoing qualification through the PSTC.

Paraoxonase-1

Paraoxonase-1 (PON1) is an esterase that protects low-density lipoproteins from oxidation and detoxifies organophosphates. PON1 is predominantly produced in the liver, although enzyme activity has been detected in the kidney and brain. Unlike MDH and GDH, PON1 decreases during liver injury, probably due to decreased synthesis and/or secretion. Initial baseline data suggests that PON1 varies among healthy people based on their ethnicity [37]; therefore it is not clear how PON1 will translate from nonclinical to clinical settings. However, since all other liver injury biomarkers are elevated in times of injury, PON1 is an attractive biomarker candidate because it decreases with injury. PON1 is currently undergoing qualification as a liver injury biomarker.

Purine Nucleoside Phosphorylase

Purine nucleoside phosphorylase (PNP) is an enzyme that catalyzes phosphorolysis of nucleosides in the purine salvage pathway. It is located in the cytoplasm of hepatocytes, Kupffer cells, and endothelial cells and is released into the sinusoids in times of hepatocellular necrosis [23]. PNP has also been shown to be relevant in clinical settings. PNP is a good biomarker candidate because it also has the possibility to detect nonparenchymal hepatic injury [26]. PNP is among the first set of markers that are currently being qualified for liver injury.

Other Emerging Biomarkers of Liver Injury

Arginase 1 (Arg-1) is a liver-specific hydrolase that catalyzes the breakdown of arginine to urea and ornithine. In a limited number of investigative studies ARG-1 has been shown to be an early onset marker of liver injury [23]. Arginase is not commonly measured in routine nonclinical safety assessment.

Gluthathione-s-transferase (GST) is a phase II detoxifying enzyme with four isozymes (alpha, pi, mu, and theta) expressed in mammals. The alpha isozyme, GSTα, is found in high concentrations in centrilobular hepatocytes; as such, it is a good biomarker candidate to identify injuries that occur in the metabolic zone of the liver. The occurrence of GSTα within the metabolic zone of the liver makes it a good candidate for qualification.

miR-122 is a single-stranded noncoding (micro) RNA with about 22 nucleotides that is involved in posttranscriptional control of protein synthesis within the eukaryotic genome. miR-122 is predominately expressed in the liver and has been shown to be elevated in circulation during conditions of drug overdose [26]. Although, the evidence for miR-122 association with DILI is limited, qualification of a microRNA biomarker is potentially useful because of its stability and the availability of more sensitive PCR-based assays compared to colorimetric and ligand-based assays for current biomarkers.

In conclusion, there are several markers currently available to assess liver injury, and these markers offer a lot of useful information about liver injury when interpreted properly. However, the occurrence of DILI after drug approval indicates that more predictive biomarkers are necessary in nonclinical safety assessment. PSTC has taken the lead in qualifying new markers. As the new markers become qualified and adapted, further understanding of their comparative relevance in different preclinical species should be an integral part of improving nonclinical safety assessment.

RENAL INJURY BIOMARKERS

Nephrotoxicity and acute kidney injury (AKI) is a common occurrence in nonclinical safety studies and continues to rank among the top reasons for drug attrition of promising new drug candidates. The kidneys are uniquely susceptible to a wide array of xenobiotics due to their receiving a large proportion of circulating blood volume (up to 25% of cardiac output) resulting in high exposure to compounds and/or their metabolites in circulation. The nephrons are also involved in the urine formation process, which further serves to concentrate toxicants in renal tubular fluid. Some of the most common nephrotoxins include heavy metals (eg, chromium, lead, mercury), nonsteroidal antiinflammatories therapeutics (eg, acetaminophen), aminoglycoside antibiotics (eg, gentamicin), and immunosuppressive and chemotherapeutic agents (eg, cyclosporine, cisplatin) [38].

The use of traditional clinical pathology endpoints such as blood urea nitrogen (BUN), serum creatinine (sCr), phosphorus, and urine-specific gravity as indicators of renal function have long been established; however, these parameters are relatively insensitive indicators of renal injury and will not demonstrate discernible alterations until a functional deficit of up to 65–75% has occurred [39]. Clearly, the performance of these markers is not sufficient for monitoring kidney injury in many nonclinical settings. The need for renal biomarkers with improved sensitivity has led to more recent efforts, largely driven by collaborative groups like the Predictive Safety Testing Consortium (PSTC) and the International Life Sciences Institute—Health and Environmental Sciences Institute (ILSI–HESI), resulting in the discovery of a number of promising next-generation renal injury biomarkers that provide earlier and more specific detection of renal injury for use in drug development.

Initially, a set of seven urinary biomarkers was qualified by the FDA for use in the rat for monitoring drug-induced kidney injury in conjunction with BUN and SCr [40]. These seven biomarkers include kidney injury molecule-1 (Kim-1), albumin, total protein, β2-microglobulin (B2M), cystatin C, clusterin, and trefoil factor-3. Additional data for four more biomarkers were later submitted to the FDA and EMA for nonclinical qualification and two of them, clusterin and renal papillary antigen-1 (RPA-1), were accepted for use in detecting acute drug-induced renal tubule alterations in rat. In addition to this list, a fair number of other renal biomarkers have been described (eg, osteopontin, NGAL, GST-α, calbindin) and are being used in drug development settings [17,41]. It is worth noting that qualification of a biomarker by a regulatory body represents their endorsement of its use under very specific circumstances, in a specific species, and does not discount the utility or prevent the inclusion of data from other biomarkers for informational purposes, or to provide additional perspective.

When measuring urinary biomarkers it is important to utilize metabolism cages to collect urine and institute efforts to minimize urine sample contamination by environmental materials such as food, bedding, feces, and other debris, which can introduce undesired preanalytical variation resulting in poor datasets. When quantifying any urinary-based analyte it is also critical to normalize analyte concentration to urine concentration or volume by performing either a creatinine ratio or an analyte over timed urine volume ratio (eg, analyte/16 h) to correct for fluctuations in urine output. Although the release kinetics of each biomarker into the urine will be compound-dependent and vary slightly, collecting urine for 12–16 h at least 2–3 days following anticipated renal injury is a standard approach in nonclinical toxicology studies. Some biomarkers have been shown to be released into the urine within hours following an acute insult [42].

Renal biomarkers generally are classified into several groups indicating their association with injury to a specific part of the nephron (eg, proximal tubule, glomerulus, collecting duct). However, recent work suggests that there is a fair amount of overlap and redundancy among individual biomarkers in regards to their specific nephron segment, hence classifying biomarker effects to either the glomerulus or the tubules appears to be the most appropriate approach in most cases [41]. The magnitude, timing, and sensitivity of positive signals among specific biomarkers will differ between test compounds, and between assay methodologies and laboratories, hence the selection of specific biomarkers should be made with consideration of assay availability, species, anticipated pathophysiology, and analyte stability [17,43]. Lastly, it is important to have an understanding of the relationship between positive biomarker signals and microscopic pathology as histologic effects on the kidney as assessed by light microscopy continues to be the reference standard used to assess the overall performance and sensitivity of the emerging renal biomarkers.

Tubular Injury Biomarkers

Kidney Injury Molecule-1 (Kim-1/TIM-1/HAVCR-1)

Kidney injury molecule-1 (Kim-1/TIM-1/HAVCR-1) is probably the most popular and commonly utilized of next-generation or novel renal biomarkers for detecting acute kidney injury (see Table 17.1). It is an 85-kDa type I cell membrane glycoprotein conserved across many species including, rodents, dogs, primates, and humans and is classically considered a proximal tubular marker [44]. Kim-1 is shed from tubular epithelial cells into the urine in response to injury (eg, toxic, ischemic, septic,

TABLE 17.1 Summary of Renal Injury Biomarkers

Biomarker	Sources	Interpretation
Kidney injury molecule 1 (KIM-1, TIM-1, HAVCR-1)	Proximal tubules	Toxic, ischemic, septic renal tubular injury
Neutrophil gelatinase-associated lipocalin (NGAL, lipocalin-2)	Proximal and distal tubules, neutrophils, bone marrow	Renal tubular injury (urinary), inflammatory (blood)
Clusterin	Proximal and distal tubules	Toxic, ischemic, septic renal tubular injury
Cystatin C	All nucleated cells, renal tubules	Plasma levels inversely related to GFR; renal tubular injury (urine)
Alkaline phosphatase (ALP)	Renal tubules	Renal tubular injury
N-acetyl-β-glucosaminidase (NAG)	Renal tubules	Renal tubular injury
Gamma glutamyltransferase (GGT)	Renal tubules	Renal tubular injury
Total protein	Plasma protein	Glomerular injury
Albumin (micro albumin)	Plasma protein	Glomerular injury
α1/β2-microglobulin	Plasma protein	Glomerular injury

GFR, glomerular filtration rate.

and transplant), and has been shown to be a sensitive and early diagnostic indicator of renal injury in a variety of animal models and human disease states [42,45–47]. In humans, increased levels have also been shown to be predictive of adverse disease outcomes [48]. Kim-1 is routinely used in rat and nonhuman primate studies; however, anecdotal evidence suggests Kim-1 may not be a useful indicator of renal effects in dog. Kim-1 assays are widely available and are often included in species-specific renal injury panels on multiplex platforms [43].

Neutrophil Gelatinase-Associated Lipocalin or Lipocalin-2

Neutrophil gelatinase-associated lipocalin (NGAL) (lipocalin-2) is a 25-kDa protein originally observed within specific granules of the neutrophil produced during granulocyte maturation in bone marrow [49]. However, more recently it has been shown to be unregulated in the proximal and distal tubules in response to a variety of renal injury conditions including ischemia and chemical toxicity [41,50,51]. Although it has not specifically been qualified for use by regulatory agencies, NGAL has generated much interest as a biomarker for the early detection of acute proximal tubular injury and is routinely used in nonclinical studies. In healthy individuals NGAL is expressed at low levels in various tissues, filtered at the glomerulus, and reabsorbed by the proximal tubule [52]. In addition to increasing renal production of NGAL following injury, damage to the nephron may enhance NGAL presence in the urine by impairing proximal tubular reabsorption.

Given the involvement of NGAL in neutrophil function, false-positive increases in NGAL can be induced in neutrophils by various stimuli including inflammation, infections (eg, urinary tract), and neoplasia, which should be considered when positive NGAL signals are seen [53,54].

Clusterin

Clusterin is a 76–80 kDa protein expressed on the dedifferentiated tubular cells after injury and is another promising marker for the detection of acute tubular injury. In the context of kidney injury, clusterin has been suggested to play an antiapoptotic role and to be involved in cell protection, lipid recycling, cell aggregation, and cell attachment [55]. Increased urinary clusterin levels have been seen in a variety of conditions of both proximal and distal tubular injury, but not in those associated with glomerular injury [45,56–58].

Cystatin C

Cystatin C is a low molecular weight (13.3 kDa) basic protein (cysteine protease inhibitor) produced by all nucleated cells at a constant rate and is freely filtered by the kidneys. It is a good candidate as both an index of function as related to GFR as well as a tubular injury indicator. It is not secreted in normal urine and is completely reabsorbed by proximal tubule epithelia [59]. Plasma/serum levels of cystatin C are inversely related to GFR, so that reduced GFR is reflected in increased cystatin C concentrations. Serum concentrations appear to be independent of sex, age, and muscle mass. Cystatin C does not appear in the urine of normal animals but will be increased in the urine in conditions of renal tubular dysfunction [60,61]. The PSTC recently reported that urinary cystatin C can outperform BUN and sCr in detecting early impairment of tubular reabsorption due to glomerular alterations/damage in rat studies [55].

Enzymuria

Enzymes released from damaged renal tubular cells of the proximal and distal tubule have been used as markers of kidney injury in animals for several decades; however, their use in human studies has not been widely accepted. This group of renal injury biomarkers is not generally considered part of next generation or novel renal biomarkers, partly because of the traditional methodology in which most of them are measured (nonimmunoassay-based methods). A variety of enzymes (see Table 17.1) have been utilized for this purpose including alkaline phosphatase (ALP), the lysosomal enzymes N-acetyl-β-glucosaminidase (NAG) and gamma glutamyltransferase (GGT), and the glutathione S-transferases (GSTs) [62]. The appearance of these enzymes in the urine is specific to proximal and distal tubule damage, and they have been shown to be fairly sensitive indicators of nephrotoxicity and injury even preceding increases in sCr [62–64]. These assays are available on most modern clinical chemistry analyzers.

Glomerular Injury Biomarkers

Total Protein, Albumin, and Microglobulins

The glomerular capillaries create a barrier for the passage of proteins any larger than those about the size of albumin (36 Å) into the urine. Depending on charge, smaller proteins (eg, α and β microglobulins) will also pass through the filtration barrier into the tubular fluid ultimately being reabsorbed or broken down by the proximal tubules. For those reasons, the detection of increased concentrations of such proteins in the urine is an indicator of glomerular (albumin or larger proteins) and/or proximal tubular injury (smaller proteins like the microglobulins). In the case of glomerular damage, injury results in large proteins leaking into the urine, which overwhelms the modest ability of the proximal tubule to remove them, whereas injury to the proximal tubule will impair the ability to remove smaller proteins such as $\alpha 1$ or $\beta 2$-microglobulin. They have also been shown to have good sensitivity and specificity in detecting renal injury due to a variety of causes [17,43].

Future Directions

Given the complexity of renal structure and function, the variety of traditional and emerging renal biomarkers in use, and the wide array of new test compounds and associated pathophysiologic observations, it is unlikely that a single biomarker will be the lone answer for the detection of renal injury in toxicology studies in the future. It is more likely that we will continue to use panels of serum and/or urine biomarkers for general assessment, patient monitoring, and investigative nonclinical

and clinical applications for the early detection of renal injury. We anticipate the continued emergence of new biomarkers and those selected for routine use should be ones with a sufficient body of evidence to support their intended use.

CARDIAC AND SKELETAL MUSCLE INJURY BIOMARKERS

Cardiotoxicity can be caused by a variety of xenobiotics and chemical therapeutics including antiarrhythmic agents (eg, β-adrenergic blockers), positive inotropic compounds (eg, digoxin, isoproterenol), anesthetics (eg, isoflurane, propofol), narcotics (eg, cocaine), and antineoplastic agents (eg, doxorubicin, cyclophosphamide). Cardiotoxicity, and the biomarkers used to identify such effects, should be distinguished from cardiovascular, or drug-induced vascular injury (DIVI) biomarkers, which are generally aimed at identifying injury to blood vessels and the vascular system, discussed later in this chapter. Biomarkers used for the identification and characterization of cardiac injury effects can be broadly categorized as those that identify structural or direct cardiac myocyte injury (eg, troponins, fatty acid binding protein) and necrosis, and those that indicate alterations to cardiac function (eg, natriuretic peptides). Although cardiac injury may be detected through a variety of modalities, including electrocardiogram, imaging, and other functional assessments (eg, blood pressure, cardiac output), this discussion will focus on the measurement of biomarkers in blood and other body fluids (serum/plasma), which are more widely used in nonclinical research and toxicology studies.

Biomarkers of Cardiac Structural Injury and Necrosis

The current gold standard for the detection of acute cardiac myocyte injury/necrosis includes the measurement of cardiac troponin I (cTnI) and/or troponin T (cTnT) in serum/plasma (see Table 17.2). Both of these molecules are involved in regulating the excitation and coupling process of the contractile apparatus within the cardiac myocyte, and are released into circulation following cell injury and necrosis. These biomarkers have repeatedly demonstrated their high sensitivity and specificity in detecting acute myocardial injury in a variety of disease and experimental conditions in both humans and animals [65–67]. Elevations in these biomarkers will often precede the first histologic evidence of cardiac injury and correlate well with effects on echocardiography and overall histologic injury scores [68,69]. In healthy animals, cardiac troponins circulate in low, nearly undetectable levels and can increase within hours

TABLE 17.2 Summary of Cardiac and Skeletal Muscle Biomarkers

Leakage Markers	Sources	Interpretation
Cardiac troponin I (cTnI)	Cardiac muscle	Cell injury/necrosis
Cardiac troponin T (cTnT)	Cardiac muscle	Cell injury/necrosis
Heart-type fatty acid binding protein (H-FABP or FABP3)	Cardiac and skeletal muscle	Cell injury/necrosis
Myoglobin	Cardiac and skeletal muscle	Cell injury/necrosis
Myosin light chains (Mlc)	Cardiac and skeletal muscle	Cell injury/necrosis
Creatine kinase (CK)	Cardiac and skeletal muscle, brain, GI tract	Cell injury/necrosis
CK-MM	Cardiac and skeletal muscle	Cell injury/necrosis
CK-MB	Cardiac and skeletal muscle	Cell injury/necrosis
Lactate dehydrogenase (LD)	All muscle types, liver, RBCs	Cell injury/necrosis
Aspartate aminotransferase (AST)	All muscle types, liver, RBCs	Cell injury/necrosis
Skeletal muscle troponin I (sTnI)	Skeletal muscle	Cell injury/necrosis
FUNCTIONAL MARKERS		
Atrial natriuretic peptide (ANP)	Primarily cardiac atria	Atrial wall stretch
Brain natriuretic peptide (BNP, proBNP, NT-proBNP)	Primarily cardiac ventricles	Ventricular wall stretch

following a single cardiac insult [68]. The positive signal is short-lived as clearance of cTn molecules is rapid and occurs within 24–48 following a single insult. Given the sensitivity of many commercial troponin assays, it is generally considered necessary to observe a greater than twofold increase in cTnI values before considering the signal to be biologically/toxicologically significant [70]. As with many of the newer biomarker assays, the lack of standardized methods across industry makes comparison of absolute values between different methods and laboratories problematic. Careful consideration of method and laboratory-specific historical ranges should be made before interpretation of positive signals is determined. Similar troponin molecules also are present in skeletal muscle (skeletal troponin; sTnI) but are antigenically distinct from their cardiac counterparts adding to the specificity of both groups of biomarkers for the detection of cardiac and skeletal muscle injuries, respectively [71]. Although cTnI and cTnT have similar interpretive utility and kinetic characteristics, cTnI assays have been better characterized, are more widely available, and have demonstrated good cross-reactivity and translatability across multiple species. Cardiac troponin I is the most consistently utilized biomarker for detecting myocardial injury in drug safety assessments [66,67].

Heart-type fatty acid-binding proteins (H-FABP or FABP3) have recently been investigated as an early marker for cardiac myocyte injury and associated cell membrane disruption. FABPs are a family of low molecular weight proteins found in multiple tissues including cardiac and skeletal muscle, brain, liver, and small intestine [72]. FABP3 contained in heart muscle is rapidly released into circulation within hours following myocardial injury [73,74]. It has good sensitivity for cardiac injury and has very similar release (within hours) and clearance (≤48 h) kinetics compared to the cTnI; however, it may lack the specificity of the cardiac troponins as significant amounts of FABP3 have been demonstrated in skeletal muscle in rat [75]. Similarly, myosin light chains (Mlc) are a component of the myosin molecule found in cardiac and slow twitch skeletal muscle cells that have been used as indicators of myocardial injury [76]. They have been incorporated into multiplex panels and used in conjunction with other markers to aid in the characterization of myocardial damage.

Myoglobin is found in the cytoplasm of both skeletal and cardiac muscle and is primarily used for the early detection of acute myocardial infarction in humans. However, it lacks specificity for cardiac muscle and occurs in higher concentrations in skeletal muscle precluding its use as an independent marker of cardiac injury [77]. Myoglobin has a short half-life (as short as 20 min in humans) and is used for postcardiac injury monitoring in clinical settings [78].

Historically, a variety of other enzyme biomarkers have been utilized for the detection of cardiac myocyte injury in humans and animals. These include aspartate aminotransferase (AST), lactate dehydrogenase (LD), creatine kinase (CK), and creatine kinase MB isoenzyme (CK-MB), which are no longer recommended for use as cardiac biomarkers due to their low cardiac specificity, inconsistent performance across species, wide tissue distribution, and lack of clinical relevance [77]. However, many of these markers are well suited as biomarkers of skeletal muscle injury, discussed later in this chapter. Additionally, a number of proinflammatory biomarkers (eg, high-sensitivity CRP, TNF-α, and myeloperoxidase) have been used for cardiac injury detection, and occasionally included in cardiac injury biomarker panels; however, these types of endpoints only serve to identify general inflammatory signals and should always be used in conjunction with other more cardiac-specific markers.

Biomarkers of Cardiac Functional Alterations

The natriuretic peptides (see Table 17.2) are a family of related hormones produced in the myocardium that have potent vasoactive and diuretic properties used in the regulation and homeostasis of blood pressure, renal function, and maintenance of cardiac output [79]. Several variants of these peptides exist including ANP (atrial natriuretic peptide), BNP (brain natriuretic peptide), and their N-terminal prohormones (N-terminal proatrial natriuretic peptide (NT-proANP) and N-terminal pro-brain natriuretic peptide (NT-proBNP)), all of which are rapidly released into circulation in response to myocardial wall stretch [80]. BNP is secreted from the ventricles but may also be secreted from the atria in conditions of heart failure [81]. Of this class of peptides, NT-proBNP is the most commonly used biomarker in nonclinical toxicology studies. NT-proBNP has been shown to be a sensitive and specific biomarker in the diagnosis of heart failure in humans and animals and has a positive correlation to ventricular systolic dysfunction [80,82]. BNPs are also elevated in conditions of dilated and hypertrophic cardiomyopathy, diastolic dysfunction, and systemic hypertension, and have been shown to be a good general prognostic indicator of cardiovascular disease states [83–85]. However, natriuretic peptides are also greatly increased in a number of noncardiac conditions related to increased vascular fluid volume and blood pressure including pulmonary embolism, liver cirrhosis, renal disease, and hyperthyroidism [79]. Natriuretic peptides are particularly useful in drug safety assessments when used in conjunction with more specific biomarkers of cardiac structural injury/necrosis, such as cTnI, to provide an overall characterization of both structural and functional effects on the heart.

Biomarkers of Skeletal Muscle Injury

Skeletal muscle toxicity and/or injury is a common finding in nonclinical safety studies following exposure to various chemical compounds (eg, cholinesterase inhibitors, carbofuran) or surgical manipulation in medical device studies. Unlike the extensive research devoted to the development of diagnostic assays for myocardial disease, much less effort has been expended on the development of biomarkers for skeletal muscle injury detection. A number of enzymes (eg, CK, AST, LD) and protein biomarkers (eg, myoglobin) have traditionally been used for this purpose; however, they generally lack the sensitivity and specificity needed to reliably distinguish subtle effects on skeletal muscle from effects on other tissues.

Creatine kinase is a cytosolic enzyme found in a variety of tissues including skeletal and cardiac muscle, brain with lesser amounts in the gastrointestinal tract, uterus, bladder, and kidney [86]. CK is released into circulation following myocyte injury and is rapidly cleared with a half-life of only 2h in dog [39]. It is the most widely used biomarker to detect general muscle injury and has three distinct isoenzymes (CK-MM, CK-BB, and CK-MB), which can be determined through electrophoretic separation. Traditionally CK-MM and CK-MB have been used as markers of skeletal and cardiac muscle injury, respectively; however, the majority of CK activity in both cardiac and skeletal muscle is attributed to CK-MM [77]. There is also a high degree of variability in CK content and isoenzyme proportions between specific muscle locations, muscle types (fast twitch/slow twitch), and between species, particularly in regards to myocardial CK-MB activity [87–89]. CK is a good biomarker for skeletal muscle injury but the CK-MB isoenzyme lacks the specificity and consistency across species to be used alone as a cardiac-specific biomarker.

Lactate dehydrogenase (LD) is an enzyme found in most nucleated and nonnucleated cell types including skeletal and cardiac muscle, liver, and erythrocytes, with highly variable distribution among different tissue types and between species [39,90]. Given its wide tissue distribution, increases in LD activity are not specific to a single organ. LD activity is generally higher in skeletal muscle and liver compared to heart muscle, which supports its use as a marker of skeletal muscle and liver injury [86]. Attempts to use isoenzymes of LD (eg, LD_1, LD_2, etc.) to increase cardiac specificity have been previously performed; however, much like the use of CK isoenzymes, there is considerable variability between specific muscle groups, species, and concentrations within the heart precluding it as a useful cardiac injury biomarker [77].

Aspartate aminotransferase (AST) and alanine aminotransferase (ALT) are both enzymes that have multiorgan tissue distributions that include skeletal muscle and liver. Increased AST activities are generally associated with effects on liver and skeletal muscle, but are also seen with hemolytic conditions [39]. ALT elevations are classically associated with hepatocellular injury; however, cases of significant muscle injury have also been associated with increases in ALT activity [91].

More recently, next-generation biomarkers with improved specificity for skeletal muscle have been discovered and are gaining wider acceptance. The most promising of these markers is skeletal troponin I (sTnI), which has been shown to be a sensitive and specific biomarker for skeletal muscle injury [92]. Skeletal muscle troponin is similar to, but antigenically distinct from its cardiac-specific counterpart cTnI, and has been shown to have the power to distinguish between skeletal and cardiac injury in rats using a variety of cardiac toxins and myotoxins [93]. This biomarker has also been included in several multiplex muscle injury panels aimed at differentiating between cardiac and skeletal muscle injury.

VASCULAR INJURY BIOMARKERS

Drug-induced vascular injury (DIVI) refers to any of a variety of pathologic processes leading to or resulting in injury to blood vessels. It is a significant cause of drug attrition as drug companies seldom proceed into the clinics following identification of a DIVI liability in nonclinical studies. The diagnosis of DIVI in nonclinical animal species generally relies on biomarkers related to the release of endothelial cell (EC) adhesion molecules, EC activation markers, and/or nonspecific acute-phase inflammatory proteins [94]. Although a long list of potential biomarkers can be gathered from a literature search, more recent evidence suggests that the vast majority of markers will not apply equally to all animal species and/or types of injury. This list becomes even shorter when one considers the lack of species-specific assays for all DIVI biomarkers.

The most significant DIVI work in a nonclinical species (rat) to date was performed by the Vascular Injury Working Group (VIWG) of the PSTC. The VIWG aimed to identify candidate biomarkers that would be useful in translating into humans, but also were independent of pathophysiologic mechanism. The latter point being critical as the mechanisms of vascular disease as seen in humans (ie, immune-mediated) appear to be distinctly different than those involved in DIVI in most nonclinical animal species (ie, altered hemodynamics, direct EC toxicity) [95,96]. These differences highlight the challenge in identifying biomarkers that have translatability into man. The VIWG investigated dozens of protein and molecular biomarkers and ultimately identified several candidates that largely fell into one of two general categories: biomarkers of EC activation/injury and biomarkers of inflammation.

Biomarkers of EC injury make up a significant portion of DIVI biomarkers covered in the literature and include the vascular cell adhesion molecules (VCAMs), intracellular adhesion molecules (ICAMs), integrins/selectins, as well as signaling molecules involved in vascular regeneration and repair. Though these families of molecules have many members, only a select few were deemed as useful for characterization of DIVI in the rat by the VIWG. Candidate biomarkers from this group included angiopoietin-2, endothelin-1, E-selectin, thrombospondin-1, and VEGF-α [96]. Following administration of a known vascular toxicant (PDE3i—a phosphodiesterase inhibitor), positive signals in these circulating EC biomarkers were modest (2–5-fold) and tended to be most pronounced at 24–72h postinjury. Notably, most of these biomarkers exhibited increases following injury, while E-selectin showed a decrease from baseline following injury.

The second main category of biomarkers that was found to be helpful in characterizing DIVI by the VIWG were those involved in the inflammatory component. Although these markers are extremely sensitive indicators of inflammation, they lack the specificity to localize injury to the vasculature and require the use of EC-specific markers to be useful in DIVI identification. The markers found to be useful included Timp-1, lipocalin-2, KC/GRO (Cxcl1), α-1 acid glycoprotein 1, and total nitric oxide. These markers tended to give more robust positive signals following PDE3i administration (up to 200-fold) and were observed earlier (as soon as 1–4h) relative to biomarkers of EC activation/injury.

BIOMARKERS OF THE IMMUNE SYSTEM

The immune system is a complex regulatory network of barriers, specialized effector cells, and molecules organized into a defense system that is capable of distinguishing "self" from "nonself." The cells of the immune system include lymphocytes [bone marrow-derived (B-cells), thymus-derived (T-cells), natural killer (NK cells), macrophages/monocytes, neutrophils, eosinophils, basophils, and mast cells. Functionally, the immune system is broadly divided into innate and adaptive immunity based on whether or not the specific protection requires immunologic memory. Innate immunity does not require immunologic memory and includes defensive barriers such as anatomic (skin and mucous membranes), physiologic (temperature and pH), and cellular (phagocytic cells and pathogen-associated molecular patterns)]. The innate immunity mediates its function through an array of soluble (cytokines, chemokines) and cellular (phagocytic and cytolytic) mediators. Acquired immunity requires previous exposure of lymphocytes to the specific antigen, in the context of antigen presenting cells and major histocompatibility complex, which creates immunologic memory for the next encounter of that specific antigen. Any subsequent encounter with the same antigen may elicit humoral (antibody-mediated) or cell-mediated immune response. The details of basic immunology are outside the scope of this chapter. Perhaps the most important point to recognize about safety assessment of the immune system is the complexity and redundancy of the system, which is further complicated by large species differences. Successful nonclinical assessment of immune safety requires a thorough appreciation of these complexities within and across species. For example, recent observation of systemic organ failure during a Phase I clinical trial of anti-CD28 monoclonal antibody, which was not predicted by nonclinical safety assessment, is a reminder of both complexity and species difference within the immune system [97]. Additional information on the details of immunobiology and immunotoxicity can be found in Chapter 22 of this book and elsewhere [98–100].

Xenobiotic-related injury or alteration of the immune system can be organized into five broad categories: immunosuppression, hypersensitivity, immunogenicity, autoimmunity, and adverse immunostimulation [101]. These categories are similar for chemical and biological entities, although molecular weight is a large determinant of immunogenicity. For example, entities with a molecular weight of 1000 Da are not likely to be immunogenic unless their metabolites are attached to endogenous molecules in the form of a haptens.

Biomarker testing of the immune system involves a wide range of strategies including use of cell-based (eg, hematology, immunophenotyping), tissue-based (eg, histopathology, IHC), and protein-based (eg, acute-phase proteins, cytokines, complement) assays. The foundation of immunotoxicity testing involves a tiered approach beginning with the evaluation of standard toxicology endpoints including hematology and clinical chemistry panels, with evaluation of lymphoid tissues for effects on organ weights, and gross and microscopic morphology. As further investigations are warranted, more focused assays such as host resistance, delayed-type hypersensitivity, autoimmunity, and/or macrophage/natural killer cell function are incorporated as needed.

Indicators of Immunosuppression

FDA guidance for immunotoxicity assessment states that all investigational new drugs should be evaluated for the potential to produce immunosuppression. This is usually accomplished by a 28-day daily dosing of the test article through the applicable route(s) of administration in humans. Due to the complexity of the immune system, the markers of immunosuppression are often not one molecule as is common in other systems. Clear suppression of T cell-dependent antibody response (TDAR) may be considered as one marker of immunosuppression but a conclusion of immunosuppression in nonclinical safety assessment

often requires several concordant lines of evidence and uses a weight-of-evidence approach.

Hematology and Clinical Chemistry

Evaluation of the complete blood count (CBC) with differential continues to be a highly effective biomarker in identifying alterations to the immune system for both signals of immunosuppression as well as proinflammatory immune conditions. Lymphoid and/or bone-marrow toxicities are routinely associated with decreases in lymphocyte, neutrophil, and total leukocyte counts ultimately resulting in immunosuppression. Concurrent decreases in platelets and reticulocytes may also be seen. These findings often correlate to decreased organ weights and microscopic cellularity of lymphoid and bone-marrow tissues. The first appearance of mild cytopenias on the hematology panel often precedes decreases in bone-marrow cellularity as seen microscopically on tissue sections.

Stress is common in toxicology studies and causes mild-to-moderate reductions in lymphocytes and eosinophils, often with concurrent increases in neutrophils and/or monocytes. These findings must be distinguished from primary effects on the immune system by careful consideration of other related endpoints (eg, histopathology, organ weights, acute-phase proteins) as specifically suggested in the FDA S8 guidance [102].

Increased Incidence of Tumors

Test article-related increase in the incidence of tumors in 2-year rodent bioassays or other toxicity studies that are not due to genotoxic, hormonal, or other well-understood carcinogenic mechanism need to be further investigated for the likely role of immunosuppression [101]. In cases where further investigation is necessary tumor-host resistance assays with B16F10 melanoma cells or other xenograft models may be the appropriate assay to further evaluate the role of immunosuppression in tumorigenesis.

Increased Incidence of Infections

Treatment-related increase in infections, especially those that involve weakly pathogenic organisms such as *Candida albicans*, are suggestive of immunosuppression. The increased incidence of infection may not be related to alterations in the function and/or number of lymphocytes but the barrier systems of innate immunity. For example, ozone exposure before an aerosol challenge of infectious agents results in treatment-related infections [103]; however, this increase in infection was related to alterations in the innate immune barriers and macrophage phagocytic system. Investigators need to remember that some cases of increased infection may show no effect on TDAR because the test article altered the innate component of the immune system.

Histopathology and Lymphoid Organ Weight

Decreases in spleen and thymic weights in conjunction with correlative histopathology findings may indicate immunosuppression [104]. The associated histopathology findings are usually decreases in lymphocytes within specific compartment(s). Lymphoid organ weight is highly variable within and across species and this variability should be carefully considered while interpreting organ weight data. The variability of median organ weight within thymus of mature Sprague Dawley rats may be up to 70%, while the variability in Beagle dogs may be up to 170% [98]. The weighing of lymph nodes and Peyer's patches is even more variable and the quality of data it generates rarely justifies the effort it requires. The weight of the spleen is also variable across species. For example, the defense spleen has a large amount of lymphocytes and is present in rats, mice, nonhuman primates, and rabbits, while the storage spleen, which may store up to one-third of the circulating blood volume, is seen in dogs [98]. The swine spleen is an intermediate between defense and storage spleen. The methods of euthanasia and exsanguination may affect the spleen weight in several species, but this influence tends to be greater with storage spleen than with defense spleen. In general, spleen and thymus weights are often useful in rodents and should always be collected but their utility in nonrodents is limited and collection of lymphoid organ weights in nonrodents should be addressed case-by-case [105].

To enhance the detection of immunosuppressive effects, the Society of Toxicologic Pathology and the majority of the toxicologic pathology community recommend a descriptive semiquantitative approach to immune system evaluation [104,106,107]. There are nuances to the approaches reported by these authors, but they all emphasize a semiquantitative description of changes in compartments of the lymphoid organs, which derives from the recognition that (1) separate compartments within each lymphoid organ support-specific functions, (2) each compartment should be evaluated for change(s), and (3) descriptive is better than interpretive terminology for characterizing changes that occur in the lymphoid system.

Immune cell phenotyping of lymphoid tissues and/or whole blood may be used to further characterize the nature of identified changes in immune system and their effect(s) on circulating subpopulations of immune cells. Flow cytometry analysis of surface markers of T cells (CD4+ and CD8+), B cells, and NK cells are often utilized as tier I assays in immunotoxicity assessments as recommended by the FDA [102]. Immunophenotyping by flow cytometry is generally not considered to be an adequate standalone test of drug effects on immune function and should be used in context with other immune function

assessments [108]. Immunohistochemistry of the same markers within lymphoid tissues, when feasible, is a necessary adjunct to further integrate changes in cell population with the histopathology findings and hematology observations. Overall an indication of immunosuppression by some of the above indices necessitates immune function studies to further characterize/understand the specific signal.

Immune Function Studies

These studies are designed to investigate functions of components of the immune system when there is reason to be concerned about immunosuppression or occasionally immunostimulation. The principles from FDA guidance indicate that these studies are relevant when (1) the drug is being designed for HIV patients or other immune-compromised population, (2) molecule is structurally similar to known immunosuppressive compounds, (3) pharmacokinetics and/or toxicokinetics indicate that the compounds occurs in immune tissues or cells at relatively high concentrations, and (4) signs suggestive of immunosuppression are seen in clinical trials [101]. In immune function studies, the dose, duration, and route of administration should be consistent with the study in which the original immune effect was observed. The functional studies are divided into tier I and tier II studies based on the ease of incorporating them into standard toxicity studies (STS). Tier I studies are generally easier to incorporate into STS than tier II, which often require separate studies.

Primary Antibody Assays

T-cell dependent antibody response (TDAR) is a tier I assay. It is the most acceptable, general-purpose functional assay because it depends on the appropriate function of antigen-presenting cells, helper T cells, soluble cytokines, and B cells. The TDAR assay evaluates an individual's ability to mount a humoral immune response to a standardized antigenic challenge (eg, KLH, tetanus toxoid, SRBC). Sheep red blood cells (SRBC) were previously used in a plaque assay, but this is increasingly being replaced by Keyhole Limpet Hemocyanin (KLH) and ELISA (enzyme-linked immunosorbent assay) measurement of antigen-specific immunoglobulins. Evaluation of the immune system using a TDAR assay should be performed when assessing compounds with known or potential suppressive or modulatory effects on the immune system [101]. Decreases in antigen-specific antibody levels are indicative of decreased immune function, which is often associated with effects on related endpoints including decreased lymphoid organ weights and microscopic cellularity, decreases in cell counts on the hemogram, and occasional clinical infections.

Natural Killer Cell Activity

Natural killer (NK) cell activity assay is a tier I assay. This assay measures the cytolytic function of NK cells and has been traditionally performed by quantifying test article-related radioactivity in ^{51}Cr-radiolabeled YAC-1 tumor cells. Ideally this assay should also include appropriate immunosuppression and immunostimulation controls. Due to radioactivity concerns, a more-sensitive flow cytometry-based NK cell assay has been developed and is increasingly being used in drug development [109].

Macrophage Function

This is a tier II assay that evaluates the ability of macrophages to phagocytose-labeled antigens. The assay can be performed in vitro with primary peritoneal macrophages isolated from animals that received the test article or in vivo, which involves an antigen challenge to test article-exposed animals and subsequent examination of marker antigen within macrophages in tissues.

Apoptosis and cytokine profiling are tier II assays that help in identifying mechanisms of immunotoxicity or immunosuppression. The measurement and interpretation of circulating cytokines need to consider that xenobiotics induce different cytokines in a variable temporal pattern within and across tissues [6,110]. Therefore the temporal pattern of cytokine induction is just as important for understanding the mechanism as the induced cytokine. Depending on the nature of observed effects (acute vs. chronic) the time points should be chosen to help interpret pathogenesis of the observed findings. At least three time points of cytokine measure will help in elucidating the mechanism in a repeat-dose study. Interpretation of cytokines needs to consider that cytokine quantification does not provide any information about the biological activity/significance of the protein being measured [99].

Host resistance is a tier II assay that may be used to detect the influence of xenobiotics on the host response to bacterial (*Listeria monocytogenes* and *Streptococcus pneumonia*), parasitic (*Plasmodium yoelli*), viral (influenza A2), and tumor (B16F10 melanoma) pathogens. Host-resistance assays are typically standalone studies and can be more challenging to perform as the results are often highly variable, thus a greater number (compared to tier I) of animals may be necessary to achieve statistical significance [99].

Indicators of Adverse Immunostimulation

Some compounds are capable of overstimulating the immune system to produce a range of unintended findings that may include cytokine release, leucocyte infiltration in multiple tissues, complement activation, and chronic inflammation. Vaccines, adjuvants, medical devices, and monoclonal antibody therapeutics may also initiate responses typical of inflammation/immune stimulation

including increases in neutrophils, lymphocytes, acute-phase protein (eg, fibrinogen, CRP), cytokines, and other inflammatory markers. The mechanism of adverse immunostimulation should be investigated/understood in other ways to contextualize potential human risk.

Standard hematology panels can be used to detect increases in leukocytes, neutrophils, and/or lymphocytes that are typical of immune/inflammatory stimulation, either as a primary immunotoxic effect, or secondary to infection or other morbidity. These increases are often associated with bone-marrow hypercellularity, lymphoid organ hyperplasia, extramedullary hematopoiesis in the spleen, and/or other inflammatory lesions. Standard clinical chemistry panels include albumin (negative acute-phase protein) and globulin (positive acute-phase protein), which are both fairly sensitive in the detection of inflammatory and immune signals [39]. There are also a variety of other acute-phase protein assays (eg, C-reactive protein, fibrinogen, serum amyloid A) available on most standard clinical chemistry or coagulation analyzers that are helpful in identifying proinflammatory signals.

Acute-Phase Proteins

Acute-phase proteins (APPs) are circulating blood proteins primarily synthesized in the liver in response to upstream inflammatory signals. APPs serve as excellent biomarkers of immune system perturbation and are used in context with other markers of inflammation to identify subtle inflammatory/immune signals. Acute-phase proteins can either be positive APPs, which increase with inflammation (eg, fibrinogen, C-reactive protein (CRP), serum amyloid A), or negative APP (eg, albumin), which decrease with inflammation. APPs have strong species-specific behaviors and can be classified as either a major or minor APP in any given species (Table 17.3). It is critical to understand which APP is most appropriate for the species in use to avoid mischaracterization of compound liabilities. For example, in the nonhuman primate CRP is major APP, eliciting strong increases in response to inflammatory stimuli while in rodents, the CRP response will be comparatively minor or nonexistent [16]. Most APPs will increase in 24–72 h following an inflammatory stimulus, which should be considered when choosing blood-draw intervals and during data interpretation. Results from these biomarkers should always be interpreted in context with other inflammatory biomarkers (eg, hematology, cytokines, etc.). APP assays are widely available on both automated clinical chemistry analyzers and as single or multiplex ELISA platforms.

Cytokine Evaluation

Cytokines are a heterogeneous collection of peptides that serve as signaling molecules between cells and elicit biological responses, including cell activation, proliferation, growth, differentiation, migration, and apoptosis.

TABLE 17.3 Summary of Major and Minor Positive Acute-Phase Proteins by Species

Species	Major	Minor
Human	C-reactive protein, serum amyloid A	α-1 acid glycoprotein, haptoglobin
Nonhuman primate	C-reactive protein	α2-macroglobulin, serum amyloid A
Rat	α-1 acid glycoprotein, α2-macroglobulin	C-reactive protein, fibrinogen
Mouse	Haptoglobin, serum amyloid A	C-reactive protein, fibrinogen
Dog	C-reactive protein, serum amyloid A	α-1 acid glycoprotein, haptoglobin
Rabbit	Haptoglobin, serum amyloid A	C-reactive protein, fibrinogen
Pig	Haptoglobin, serum amyloid A	α-1 acid glycoprotein

The evaluation of cytokines in immunotoxicity characterization, both in vitro and ex or in vivo, have been in use for some time now for the purposes of hazard identification, mechanistic characterization, as markers of pharmacodynamic activity and/or efficacy, as well as to monitor for adverse drug reactions [111–113]. Blood cytokine measurements are an attractive option due to the ability to perform serial monitoring using readily accessible samples on a multitude of available assay platforms. However, the use of cytokines as biomarkers poses several challenges related to their short half-life and release dynamics, lack of organ specificity, undetectable baseline levels, and lack of standardized methodologies. The overall complexity of the immune system and related cytokine interactions emphasizes the need for focused and deliberate strategies when evaluating these endpoints.

Measurement of serum cytokines may have the most utility in programs or studies that evaluate intended or unintended inflammation and immunomodulation produced by therapeutics. When applying cytokine measurements to nonclinical studies in animals, it is important to take samples at intervals that are physiologically relevant to the specific immunomodulation or immunopathology being induced. Cytokines are released quickly and equally rapid in their clearance, hence serial blood sampling time points should occur at several intervals within the first 24h of dose administration [111]. A standard approach is to sample 2–3 times within 24h of dose administration (eg, 2–6, 12, and 24h postdose) in order to capture the positive cytokine signals, although this will need to be customized to the particular project based on the goals of the study and the known pharmacology of the compound. Ongoing immune/inflammatory stimulation may allow positive signals to be detected at later intervals, although this is more the exception than the rule. Increases in cytokines (2–24h) will usually precede increases in APPs (24–72h). In general, larger multiplex panels including multiple cytokines are used for these purposes. Some of the most common markers evaluated include IL-1, IL-6, TNF-α,

and INF-γ with more advanced panels including MCP-1, VEGF, IL-2, IL-4, IL-8/KC/GRO, IL-10, IL-12, and IL-13.

Although the evaluation of cytokines in animals continues to be common in nonclinical studies, recent examples have demonstrated that in vivo measures of cytokines in animal species are not always predictive of adverse reactions in humans [114]. This sometimes disastrous lack of concordance between nonclinical and human cytokine responses has led to more widespread use of ex and in vivo cytokine release assays (CRAs) in an attempt to bridge the gap between nonclinical species and humans. Although various approaches to CRAs have been published, most often, peripheral blood leukocytes or mononuclear cells (PBMCs) are isolated from blood and incubated with test compounds either in an aqueous solution or solid phase/dry-coat (immobilized on plate) format [112]. Small samples of cell-suspension media are then measured for cytokines at various intervals (eg, 6–72h) following incubation. The notion of performing CRAs in solution or in solid phase or in whole blood versus PBMCs is still under debate with 62% of respondents performing aqueous phase CRAs according to a recent industry survey [112]. It has been argued that whole blood more closely mimics in vivo conditions by involving soluble factors, platelets, and other cells types when compared to PBMCs. In addition, whole-blood CRAs require less technical effort to execute. Soluble or aqueous phase CRAs may use whole-blood or PBMCs and are attractive due to their simplicity but have been criticized for their lack of predictivity, particularly when using TGN1412, when compared to solid-phase CRAs [113].

Indicators of Hypersensitivity

Type I hypersensitivity reactions are usually IgE-mediated, in humans and many nonclinical species, although IgG can also mediate systemic anaphylaxis in guinea pigs, rabbits, rats and mice [98]. Type I hypersensitivity could be systemic (anaphylaxis or urticarial) or respiratory (asthma). The systemic reaction involves the release of one or more vasoactive amines from histamine, kinins, and serotonin. FDA requires that all drugs developed for dosing by inhalation route be evaluated for ability to induce Type I hypersensitivity [101]. Therapeutic proteins may also elicit Type I reactions in monkeys and other nonclinical species [115], but the relevance of such reaction to human risk assessment needs to consider the species source of the protein. The demonstration of drug-specific IgE should be considered a hazard with or without the elevation of Th2 cytokines such IL-4, IL-5, IL-10, and IL-13 [99,101]. The murine local lymph node assay (LLNA) has undergone extensive validation since the first report [116] and has almost replaced other sensitization assays in guinea pigs. It measures lymphocyte proliferation after topical exposure to xenobiotics. A chemical is considered a sensitizer if, at any dose, it induces threefold or greater cell proliferation in local lymph node when compared to concurrent control. For human risk assessment, the comparative thickness of human versus murine skin, which is thinner and more permeable, needs to be considered [117].

Types II and III hypersensitivities are antibody-mediated and tend to cooccur in xenobiotic exposed animals, although Type III is more common in animals dosed with therapeutic proteins [101,115]. They result from IgG and/or IgM mediated antibody-dependent/complement-mediated cytotoxicity or lysis of somatic cells (Type II) or immune complex-related complement-mediated destruction of tissue (Type III). Pathology findings may include one or more of vasculitis, glomerulonephritis, anemia, and thrombocytopenia. Type III hypersensitivity is increasingly being observed in nonclinical safety assessment as the testing of larger molecule biopharmaceuticals increase. Complement-related pathology is thought to arise from failure of the clearance system for soluble immune complexes. In some cases (subclinical) increases in circulating immune complexes and circulating IgM have been reported prior to or concurrent with the drug reaction [115]. The kinetics of IgG/IgM and circulating complement on days preceding the drug reaction may be informative when investigating drug reactions. The investigation of immune complex-mediated pathology requires a weight of evidence approach using some of the following information (1) plasma and/or serum drug and antidrug antibody (ADA) levels; (2) histopathology findings from animals with drug reactions; (3) hematological indices such as erythrocyte numbers and morphology, and platelet numbers; (4) circulating complement component levels, which may not be available due to the manner of death, and is rapid in some cases; and (5) immunohistochemical demonstration of granular deposits of drug, endogenous IgG, IgM, and other complement components [115].

Type IV hypersensitivity is a T-cell mediated delayed type hypersensitivity. Drugs intended for topical use need to be evaluated for their ability to sensitize [101], and the LLNA is increasingly being accepted for the sensitization aspect of Type IV reaction, in addition to Type I testing.

Indicators of Immunogenicity

Molecules above 1000 Da may be immunogenic, thus raising a twofold concern. The first is alteration of pharmacodynamics and loss of efficacy due to binding of the test article to antidrug antibodies (ADA) in circulation, while the second is allergenicity. In general ADA are used to determine the immunogenicity while models of allergenicity testing have not undergone robust validation.

Indicators of Autoimmunity

Xenobiotic-related autoimmunity has been associated with several drugs from different classes. They are related to the formation of hapten for molecules less than 1000 Da and often include a genetic predisposition such as the HLA-DR3 allele in humans [110]. Due to the complex nature of autoimmune diseases there are no generally recognized nonclinical testing approaches. Drugs that cause autoimmune diseases tend to cause hematological disorders such as neutropenia, thrombocytopenia, and anemia. Biotherapeutics are now known to cause unexpected hematological findings and some of these are immune-mediated and not predicted from nonclinical studies. However, nonclinical studies have predicted clinical hematotoxicity for hemophagocytosis (occurs with recombinant cytokines and growth factors) and thrombocytopenia, which is observed with anti-CD40L monoclonal antibodies [118].

In conclusion safety assessment of the immune system requires a weight-of-evidence approach using a variety of modalities to evaluate lymphoid organs and bone marrow with careful understanding of the test article and the immune system of the species in which the test is being conducted. A tiered approach starting with standard toxicology endpoints (eg, hematology, lymphoid organ, and bone-marrow pathology) with the addition of standalone immunotoxicity studies as needed is the current paradigm for characterization of the immune system.

Biomarkers of Toxicity in the Central Nervous System

The central nervous system (CNS) contains a vast array of neuronal cell bodies (nuclei) that have very specific functions. These cell bodies are protected from most xenobiotics by the blood–brain barrier. However, some molecules are designed to cross the blood–brain barrier or do so by nature of their physicochemical properties. There are no routinely used molecular/chemical validated biomarkers to assess xenobiotic-related injury to the nervous system. Functional observation battery (FOB) or other analogous test is required for assessing the effects of test articles on indices of neurobehavioral function such as coordination, motor activity, behavioral changes, sensory/motor reflex responses, and body temperature [119]. The brain and spinal cord are also evaluated histologically as part of most standard nonclinical safety assessment programs. The current neurotoxicity testing paradigm relies heavily on morphological examinations, but the future will probably include additional methods for understanding receptor dynamics as well as cellular and biochemical alterations in the brain [120]. Two methods that might increase the sensitivity of detection and help elucidate mechanisms of CNS toxicity are cerebrospinal fluid (CSF) analysis and molecular imaging.

Cerebrospinal fluid analysis may reveal test article-related changes in CNS alteration through changes in the color and quantity of CSF, number and composition of mononuclear cells in the CSF, and biochemical alterations of CNS [121]. Neurotoxic effects can result in the alteration of neurotransmitters and their metabolites such as dopamine, glutamate, γ-aminobutyric acid, epinephrine, serotonin, homovanillic acid, 5-hydroxyindolacetic acid. For example, homovanillic acid can be measured in the CSF of Collie dogs that develop neurologic signs after Ivermectin exposure [121]. The concentrations of total protein, albumin, C-reactive protein, myelin basic protein, and S-100 can also be indications of toxicant-related alterations in blood–brain barrier and/or CNS. With the continued refinement of metabolomics and spectrometry techniques, CSF analysis might become a better-utilized adjunct for CNS safety assessment.

Recently imaging techniques such as magnetic resonance imaging (MRI), positron-emission tomography (PET), and single photon-emission computed tomography (SPECT) have been used in drug discovery and development. These imaging techniques have been used to (1) detect activated microglia in neuroinflammation by using a radiotracer to target a translocator protein (TP-18), (2) access the quantity and integrity of adhesion molecules (CD62E) and P-glycoptoteins(CD243) in the blood–brain barrier, and (3) CNS glucose metabolism by using [^{18}F]fluorodeoxyglucose uptake [122]. As these imaging technology capabilities improve and reduce in cost, they are likely to provide more comprehensive and specific approaches to assess CNS safety of xenobiotics.

Biomarkers of Toxicity in the Reproductive System

The reproductive system has a complex hormonal regulatory network that ranges from gonadal sex steroid hormones to centrally released luteinizing hormone (LH) and follicle stimulating hormone (FSH). In nonclinical safety assessment there are elaborate toxicity studies designed to assess the effects of xenobiotics on reproduction. However, these studies are expensive, longer term, and tend to occur later in the drug development process. Ideally, noninvasive biomarkers of reproductive toxicity that can be measured in a 28-day repeat-dose toxicity study will be good predictors to provide early warning about reproductive toxicity and help contextualize the morphological findings that occur in the reproductive system during shorter-term studies.

Currently, hormones such as estrogen, progesterone, prolactin, testosterone, LH, and FSH are sometimes used to provide additional context when there is a signal of reproductive effect. However, hormone endpoints can be difficult to assess in large toxicology studies due to the difficulty in controlling variations due to stress, diurnal variation, and menstrual/estrus cycling [123]. For female animals, estrus cycle evaluation provides another index of reproductive health, although the variable length of estrus cycle in different species makes it more useful in those with short cycles (eg, rat) and very difficult in species with longer cycles (eg, dog). For testicular toxicity, histopathology and organ weight of accessory sex organs are currently the most sensitive and reliable ways of detecting test article-related effects [124]. However, there is industry-wide interest in validating the utility of inhibin B or other potential toxicogenomic markers that will translate to human clinical trial scenario [125]. Androgens stimulate sertoli cells to secrete inhibin B, which regulates spermatogenesis in seminiferous tubules. Clinically, serum inhibin B tends to be higher in fertile men than in infertile men [126]. Therefore inhibin B appears to be a good biomarker for testicular toxicity because it can be measured in a nonterminal longitudinal fashion and is translatable.

CONCLUSION

Several routinely and seldom used biomarkers were presented for different tissues and organ systems. A key feature of interpreting data from these biomarkers is to have an appreciation for the heterogeneity of positive biomarker response signals in timing, magnitude, and by species, and to have a good understanding of the analytical performance each individual assay. Such appreciation frequently involves professionals who are trained and experienced in the molecular and comparative physiological foundations of these biomarkers and their clinical relevance. A careful case-by-case and integrative interpretation of data from these biomarkers often provides a better perspective on the potential risk(s) of xenobiotic-related safety issues and informs on the appropriate risk mitigation strategies in drug development.

References

[1] Biomarkers Definition Working Group. Biomarkers and surrogate endpoints: preferred definitions and conceptual frameworks. Clin Pharmacol Ther 2001;69(3):89–95.

[2] Sasseville VG, Mansfield KG, Brees DJ. Safety biomarkers in preclinical development: translational potential. Vet Pathol 2014;51(1):281–91.

[3] Lock EA, Bonventre JV. Biomarkers in translation; past, present and future. Toxicology 2008;245(3):163–6.

[4] Zhu X, Verma S. Targeted therapy in HER2-positive metastatic breast cancer: a review of the literature. Curr Oncol March 2015;22(Suppl. 1):S19–28.

[5] Dean L. Warfarin therapy and the genotypes CYP2C9 and VKORC1. In: Medical genetics summaries. Bethesda (MD): National Center for Biotechnology Information; 2012.

[6] Amuzie CJ, Pestka JJ. Suppression of insulin-like growth factor acid-labile subunit expression – a novel mechanism for deoxynivalenol-induced growth retardation. Toxicol Sci 2010;113(2):412–21.

[7] Lee J, Russ S, Weiner R, Sailstad JM, Bowsher RR, Knuth DW, et al. Method validation and measurement of biomarkers in nonclinical and clinical samples in drug development: a conference report. Pharm Res 2005;22(4):499–511.

[8] Lee J, Devanarayan V, Barrett YC, Weiner R, Allinson J, Fountain S, et al. Fit-for-purpose method development and validation for successful biomarker measurement. Pharm Res 2006;23(2):312–28.

[9] Cummings J, Ward TH, Dive C. Fit-for-purpose biomarker method validation in anticancer drug development. Drug Discov Today 2010;15(19/20).

[10] Policy issues for the development and use of biomarkers in health. 2011. www.Oecd.Org/Sti/Biotechnology.

[11] Lee JW, Pan P, O'Brien P, et al. Development and validation of ligand-binding assays for biomarkers. In: Khan MN, Findlay JWA, editors. Ligand-binding assays: development, validation, and implementation in the drug development arena. Hoboken (NJ): John Wiley and Sons, Inc.; 2010. p. 129–62.

[12] US FDA. Biomarker qualification program. 2012. http://www.fda.gov/Drugs/DevelopmentApprovalProcess/DrugDevelopmentToolsQualificationProgram/ucm284076.htm.

[13] Khan M, Bowsher RR, Cameron M, Devanarayan V, Keller S, King L, et al. Recommendations for adaptation and validation of commercial kits for biomarker quantification in drug development. Bioanalysis 2015;7(2):229–42.

[14] Bioanalytical method validation. U.S. Department of Health and Human Services, Food and Drug Administration, Center for Drug Evaluation and Research (CDER), Center for Veterinary Medicine (CVM); 2013.

[15] Han M, Li Y, Liu M, Cong B. Renal neutrophil gelatinase associated lipocalin expression in lipopolysaccharide-induced acute kidney injury in the rat. BMC Nephrol 2012;13:25.

[16] Cray C, Zaias J, Altman N. Acute phase response in animals: a review. Comp Med 2009;59(6):517–26.

[17] Gautier JC, Gury T, Guffroy M, Khan-Malek R, Hoffman D, Petit S, et al. Normal ranges and variability of novel urinary renal biomarkers in Sprague-Dawley rats: comparison of constitutive values between males and females and across assay platforms. Toxicol Pathol 2014;42:1092–104.

[18] Weiler S, Merz M, Kullak-Ublick GA. Drug-induced liver injury: the dawn of biomarkers. F1000 Prime Rep 2015;7:34.

[19] Boone L, Meyer D, Cusick P, Ennulat D, Provencher Bolliger A, Everds N, et al. Selection and interpretation of clinical pathology indicators of hepatic injury in preclinical studies. Vet Clin Path 2005;34(3):182–8.

[20] Tomlinson L, Boone LI, Ramaiah L, Penraat KA, von Beust BR, Ameri M, et al. Best practices for veterinary toxicologic clinical pathology, with emphasis on the pharmaceutical and biotechnology industries. Vet Clin Pathol 2013;42(3):252–69.

[21] Weingand K, Brown G, Hall R, Davies D, Gossett K, Neptun D, et al. Harmonization of animal clinical pathology testing in toxicity and safety studies. The Joint Scientific Committee for International Harmonization of Clinical Pathology Testing. Fundam Appl Toxicol 1996;29(2):198–201.

[22] Amacher DE. A toxicologist's guide to biomarkers of hepatic response. Hum Exp Toxicol 2002;21:253–62.

[23] Ozer J, Ratner M, Shaw M, Bailey W, Schomaker S. The current state of serum biomarkers of hepatotoxicity. Toxicology 2008;245:194–205.

[24] Amacher DE, Schomaker SJ, Burkhardt JE. The relationship among microsomal enzyme induction, liver weight, and histological change in rat toxicology studies. Food Chem Toxicol 1998;36:831–9.

[25] Amacher DE, Schomaker SJ, Burkhardt JE. The relationship among enzyme induction, liver weight, and histological change in beagle toxicology studies. Food Chem Toxicol 2001;39:817–25.

[26] Ramaiah SK. Preclinical safety assessment: current gaps, challenges, and approaches in identifying translatable biomarkers of drug-induced liver injury. Clin Lab Med 2011;31(1):161–72.

[27] Ozer JS, Chetty R, Kenna G, Koppiker N, Karamjeet P, Li D, et al. Recommendations to qualify biomarker candidates of drug-induced liver injury. Biomarkers Med 2010;4(3):475–83.

[28] Regev A. How to avoid being surprised by hepatotoxicity at the final stages of drug development and approval. Clin Liver Dis 2013;17:749–67.

[29] Blair PC, Thompson MB, Wilson RE, Esber HH, Maronpot RR. Correlation of changes in serum analytes and hepatic histopathology in rats exposed to carbon tetrachloride. J Comp Pathol 1988;98:381–404.

[30] Landi MS, Kissinger JT, Campbell SA, Kenney CA, Jenkins Jr EL. The effects of four types of restraint on serum alanine aminotransferase and aspartate aminotransferase in the Macaca fascicularis. J Am Coll Toxicol 1990;9:517–23.

[31] O'Brien PJ, Slaughter MR, Polley SR, Kramer K. Advantages of glutamate dehydrogenase as a blood biomarker of acute hepatic injury in rats. Lab Anim 2002;36:313–21.

[32] Zollner G, Marschall HU, Wagner M, Trauner M. Role of nuclear receptors in the adaptive response to bile acids and cholestasis: pathogenetic and therapeutic considerations. Mol Pharm 2006;3:231–51.

[33] Meyer DJ, Harvey JW. Hepatobiliary and skeletal muscle enzymes and liver function tests. In: Meyer DJ, Harvey JW, editors. Veterinary laboratory medicine: interpretation and diagnosis. 3rd ed. St. Louis (MO): Saunders; 2004. p. 169–92.

[34] Zucker SD, Qin X, Rouster SD, Yu F, Green RM, Keshavan P, et al. Mechanism of indinavir-induced hyperbilirubinemia. Proc Natl Acad Sci USA 2001;98:12671–6.

[35] Amacher DE, Adler R, Herath A, Townsend RR. Use of proteomic methods to identify serum biomarkers associated with rat liver toxicity or hypertrophy. Clin Chem 2005;51(10):1796–803.

[36] Yang X, Schnackenberg L, Shi Q, Salminen WF. Hepatic toxicity biomarkers. In: Gupta R, editor. Biomarkers in toxicology. Waltham (MA): Elsevier; 2013. p. 241–60.

[37] Schomaker S, Warner R, Bock J, Johnson K, Potter D, Van Winkle J, et al. Assessment of emerging biomarkers of liver injury in human subjects. Toxicol Sci 2013;132(2):276–83.

[38] Schnellman R. Toxic responses of the kidney. In: Casarett, Doulls, editors. Toxicology: the basic science of poisons. 7th ed. New York (NY): McGraw-Hill; 2008. p. 583–608.

[39] Stockham S, Scott M. Enzymes. In: Fundamentals of veterinary clinical pathology. 2nd ed. Ames (IA): Blackwell Publishing; 2008.

[40] Dieterle F, Sistare F, Goodsaid F, Papaluca M, Ozer J, Webb C, et al. Renal biomarker qualification submission: a dialog between the FDA-EMEA and predictive safety testing consortium. Nat Biotechnol 2010b;28:455–62.

[41] Ennulat D, Adler S. Recent successes in the identification, development, and qualification of translational biomarkers: the next generation of kidney injury biomarkers. Toxicol Pathol 2015;43:62–9.

[42] Han W, Bailly V, Abichandani R, Thadhani R, Bonventre J. Kidney injury molecule-1 (KIM-1): a novel biomarker for human renal proximal tubule injury. Kidney Int 2002;62:237–44.

[43] Vlasakova K, Erdos Z, Troth S, McNulty K, Chapeau-Campredon V, Mokrzycki N, et al. Evaluation of the relative performance of 12 urinary biomarkers for renal safety across 22 rat sensitivity and specificity studies. Toxicol Sci 2014;8(1):3–20.

[44] Ichimura T, Bonventre J, Bailly V, Wei H, Hession C, Cate R, et al. Kidney injury molecule-1 (KIM-1), a putative epithelial cell adhesion molecule containing a novel immunoglobulin domain, is up-regulated in renal cells after injury. J Biol Chem 1998;273:4135–42.

[45] Bonventre J, Vaidya V, Schmouder R, Feig P, Dieterle F. Next-generation biomarkers for detecting kidney toxicity. Nat Biotechnol 2010;28(5).

[46] Perez-Rojas J, Blanco J, Cruz C, Trujillo J, Vaidya V, Uribe N, et al. Mineralocorticoid receptor blockade confers renoprotection in preexisting chronic cyclosporine nephrotoxicity. Am J Physiol Renal Physiol 2007;292:F131–9.

[47] Vaidya V, Ramirez V, Ichimura T, Bobadilla N, Bonventre J. Urinary kidney injury molecule-1: a sensitive quantitative biomarker for early detection of kidney tubular injury. Am J Physiol Renal Physiol 2006;290:F517–29.

[48] Liangos O, Perianayagam M, Vaidya V, Han W, Wald R, Tighiouart H, et al. Urinary N-acetyl-beta-(D)-glucosaminidase activity and kidney injury molecule-1 level are associated with adverse outcomes in acute renal failure. J Am Soc Nephrol 2007;18:904–12.

[49] Borregaard N, Sehested M, Nielsen B, Sengelov H, Kjeldsen L. Biosynthesis of granule proteins in normal human bone marrow cells. Gelatinase is a marker of terminal neutrophil differentiation. Blood 1995;85:812–7.

[50] Matthaeus T, Schulze-Lohoff E, Ichimura T, Weber M, Andreucci M. Co-regulation of neutrophil gelatinase-associated lipocalin and matrix metalloproteinase-9 in the postischemic rat kidney. J Am Soc Nephrol 2001;12:787A.

[51] Mishra J, Ma Q, Prada A, Mitsnefes M, Zahedi K, Yang J, et al. Identification of neutrophil gelatinase-associated lipocalin as a novel early urinary biomarker for ischemic renal injury. Am Soc Nephrol 2003;14:2534–43.

[52] Singer E, Marko L, Paragas N, Barasch J, Dragun D, Muller DN, et al. Neutrophil gelatinase-associated lipocalin: pathophysiology and clinical applications. Acta Physiol (Oxf) 2013;207:663–72.

[53] Ohlsson S, Wieslander J, Segelmark M. Increased circulating levels of proteinase 3 in patients with antineutrophilic cytoplasmic autoantibodies-associated systemic vasculitis in remission. Clin Exp Immunol 2003;131:528–35.

[54] Xu S, Pauksen K, Venge P. Serum measurements of human neutrophil lipocalin (HNL) discriminate between acute bacterial and viral infections. Scand J Clin Lab Invest 1995;55:125–31.

[55] Dieterle F, Perentes E, Cordier A, Roth D, Verdes P, Grenet O, et al. Urinary clusterin, cystatin C, β2-microglobulin and total protein as markers to detect drug-induced kidney injury. Nat Biotechnol 2010;28(5):463–8.

[56] Davis J, Goodsaid F, Bral C, Obert L, Mandakas G, Garner C, et al. Quantitative gene expression analysis in a nonhuman primate model of antibiotic-induced nephrotoxicity. Toxicol Appl Pharmacol 2004;200:16–26.

[57] Rosenberg ME, Paller MS. Differential gene expression in the recovery from ischemic renal injury. Kidney Int 1991;39:1156–61.

[58] Witzgall R, Brown D, Schwarz C, Bonventre J. Localization of proliferating cell nuclear antigen, vimentin, c-Fos, and clusterin in the postischemic kidney. Evidence for a heterogenous genetic response among nephron segments, and a large pool of mitotically active and dedifferentiated cells. Clin Invest 1994;93:2175–88.

[59] Filler G, Bokenkamp A, Hofmann W, Le Bricon T, Martinez-Bru C, Grubb A. Cystatin C as a marker of GFR: history, indications, and future research. Clin Biochem 2005;38(1):1–8.

[60] Conti M, Moutereau S, Zater M, Lallali K, Durrbach A, Manivet P, et al. Urinary cystatin C as a specific marker of tubular dysfunction. Clin Chem Lab Med 2006;44:288–91.

[61] Uchida K, Gotoh A. Measurement of cystatin-C and creatinine in urine. Clin Chim Acta 2002;323:121–8.

[62] Clemo F. Urinary enzyme evaluation of nephrotoxicity in the dog. Toxicol Pathol 1998;26(1):29–32.

[63] Emeigh Hart SG. Assessment of renal injury in vivo. Pharmacol Toxicol Methods 2005;52:30–45.

[64] D'Amico G, Bazzi C. Urinary protein and enzyme excretion as markers of tubular damage. Curr Opin Nephrol Hypertens 2003;12:639–43.

[65] Antman E, Bassand J, Klein W, Ohman M, Sendon J, Rydén L, et al. Myocardial infarction redefined—a consensus document of the Joint European Society of Cardiology/American College of Cardiology Committee for the redefinition of myocardial infarction: the Joint European Society of Cardiology/American College of Cardiology Committee. J Am Coll Cardiol 2000;36:959–69.

[66] Apple F, Murakami M, Ler R, Walker D, York M. Analytical characteristics of commercial cardiac troponin I and T immunoassays in serum from rats, dogs, and monkeys with induced acute myocardial injury. Clin Chem 2008;54(12):1982–9.

[67] Bertinchant J, Robert E, Polge A, Marty-Double C, Fabbro-Peray P, Poirey S, et al. Comparison of the diagnostic value of cardiac troponin I and T determinations for detecting early myocardial damage and the relationship with histological findings after isoproterenol-induced cardiac injury in rats. Clin Chim Acta 2000;298(1–2):13–28.

[68] York M, Scudamore C, Brady S, Chen C, Wilson S, Curtis M, et al. Characterization of troponin responses in isoproterenol-induced cardiac injury in the Hanover Wistar rat. Toxicol Pathol 2007;35.

[69] Bertanchant J, Polge A, Juan J, Oliva-Lauraire M, Giuliani I, Marty-Double C, et al. Evaluation of cardiac troponin I and T levels as markers of myocardial damage in doxorubicin-induced cardiomyopathy rats, and their relationship with echocardiographic and histological findings. Clin Chim Acta 2003;329.

[70] Schultze A, Carpenter K, Wians F, Agee S, Minyard J, Lu Q, et al. Longitudinal studies of cardiac troponin-i concentrations in serum from male Sprague Dawley rats: baseline reference ranges and effects of handling and placebo dosing on biological variability. Toxicol Pathol 2009;37:754–60.

[71] Metzger J, Westfall M. Covalent and noncovalent modification of thin filament action. The essential role of troponins in cardiac muscle regulation. Circ Res 2004;94:146–58.

[72] Chmurzyńska A. The multigene family of fatty acid-binding proteins (FABPs): function, structure and polymorphism. J Appl Genet 2006;47(1):39–48.

[73] Clements P, Brady S, York M, Berridge B, Mikaelian I, Nicklaus R, et al. Time course characterization of serum cardiac troponins, heart fatty acid binding protein, and morphologic findings with isoproterenol-induced myocardial injury in the rat. Toxicol Pathol 2010;38.

[74] Ghani F, Wu A, Graff L, Petry C, Armstrong G, Prigent F, et al. Role of heart-type fatty acid-binding protein in early detection of acute myocardial infarction. Clin Chem 2000;46:718–9.

[75] Zhen E, Berna M, Jin Z, Pritt M, Watson D, Ackermann B, et al. Quantification of heart fatty acid–binding protein as a biomarker for drug-induced cardiac and musculoskeletal necroses. Proteomics 2007;1(7):661–71.

[76] Katus H, Yasuda T, Gold H, Leinbach R, Strauss H, Waksmonski C, et al. Diagnosis of acute myocardial infarction by detection of circulating cardiac myosin light chains. Am J Cardiol 1984;54(8):964–97.

[77] Walker D. Serum chemical biomarkers of cardiac injury for nonclinical safety testing. Toxicol Pathol 2006;34.

[78] Ellis A, Little T, Zaki R, Masud A, Klocke F. Patterns of myoglobin release after reperfusion of injured myocardium. Circulation 1985;72:639–47.

[79] Clerico A, Emdin M. Diagnostic accuracy and prognostic relevance of the measurement of cardiac natriuretic peptides: a review. Clin Chem 2004;50:133–50.

[80] Bay M, Kirk V, Parner J, Hassager C, Nielsen H, Krogsgaard K, et al. NT-proBNP: a new diagnostic screening tool to differentiate between patients with normal and reduced left ventricular systolic function. Heart 2003;89(2):150–4.

[81] Yasue H, Yoshimura M, Sumida H, et al. Localization and mechanism of secretion of B-type natriuretic peptide in comparison with those of A-type natriuretic peptide in normal subjects and patients with heart failure. Circulation 1994;90:195–203.

[82] MacDonald K, Kittleson M, Munro C, Kass P. Brain natriuretic peptide concentration in dogs with heart disease and congestive heart failure. J Vet Intern Med 2003;17:172–7.

[83] Mizuno Y, Yoshimura M, Harada E. Plasma levels of A and B-type natriuretic peptides in patients with hypertrophic cardiomyopathy or idiopathic dilated cardiomyopathy. Am J Cardiol 2000;86:1036–40.

[84] Lang C, Prasad N, McAlpine H. Increased plasma levels of brain natriuretic peptide in patients with isolated diastolic dysfunction. Am Heart J 1994;127:1635–6.

[85] Cheung B. Plasma concentration of brain natriuretic peptide is related to diastolic function in hypertension. Clin Exp Pharmacol Physiol 1997;24:966–8.

[86] Cardinet G. Skeletal muscle function. In: Kaneko J, Harvey J, Bruss M, editors. Clinical biochemistry of domestic animals. 5th ed. San Diego (CA): Academic Press; 1997.

[87] Fontanet H, Trask R, Haas R, Strauss A, Abendschein D, Billadello J. Regulation of expression of M, B, and mitochondrial creatine kinase mRNAs in the left ventricle after pressure overload in rats. Circ Res 1991;68:1007–12.

[88] Sharkey S, Murakami M, Smith S, Apple F. Canine myocardial creatine kinase isoenzymes after chronic coronary artery occlusion. Circulation 1991;84:333–40.

[89] Hironaka E, Hongo M, Azegami M, Yanagisawa S, Owa M, Hayama M. Effects of angiotensin-converting enzyme inhibition on changes in left ventricular myocardial creatine kinase system after myocardial infarction: their relation to ventricular remodeling and function. Jpn Heart J 2003;44:537–46.

[90] Chow C, Cross C, Kaneko J. Lactate dehydrogenase activity and isoenzyme pattern in lungs, erythrocytes, and plasma of ozoneexposed rats and monkeys. J Toxicol Environ Health 1977;3:877–84.

[91] Nathwani R, Pais S, Reynolds T, Kaplowitz N. Serum alanine aminotransferase in skeletal muscle diseases. Hepatology 2005;41(2):380–2.

[92] Simpson J, Labugger R, Hesketh G, D'Arsigny C, O'Donnell D, Matsumoto M, et al. Differential detection of skeletal troponin I isoforms in serum of a patient with rhabdomyolysis: markers of muscle injury. Clin Chem 2002;48(7):1112–4.

[93] Tonomuraa Y, Matsushimaa S, Kashiwagi E, Fujisawaa K, Takagi S, Nishimuraa Y, et al. Biomarker panel of cardiac and skeletal muscle troponins, fatty acid binding protein 3 and myosin light chain 3 for the accurate diagnosis of cardiotoxicity and musculoskeletal toxicity in rats. Toxicology 2012;302:179–89.

[94] Weaver J, Snyder R, Knapton A, Herman E, Honchel R, Miller T, et al. Biomarkers in peripheral blood associated with vascular injury in Sprague-Dawley rats treated with the phosphodiesterase IV inhibitors SCH 351591 or SCH 534385. Toxicol Pathol 2008;36:840–9.

[95] Kerns W, Schwartz L, Blanchard K, Burchiel S, Essayan D, Fung E, et al. Drug-induced vascular injury – a quest for biomarkers. Toxicol Appl Pharmacol 2005;203:62–87.

[96] Mikaelian I, Cameron M, Dalmas D, Enerson B, Gonzalez R, Guionaud S, et al. Nonclinical safety biomarkers of drug-induced vascular injury: current status and blueprint for the future. Toxicol Pathol 2014;42:1533–601.

[97] Bhogal N, Combes R. TGN 1412: time to change the paradigm for testing of new pharmaceuticals. Altern Lab Anim 2006;34:225–39.

[98] Haley P. Species differences in structure and function of the immune system. Toxicology 2003;188:49–71.

[99] Kaminski NE, Faubert Kaplan BF, Holsapple MP. Toxic responses of the immune system. In: Klaassen CD, editor. Casarett & Doull's toxicology: the basic science of poisons. 7th ed. New York (NY): McGraw-Hill Companies; 2008. p. 485–555.

[100] House RV, Luster MI, Dean JH, Johnson VJ. Immunotoxicology: the immune system response to toxic insult. In: Hayes AW, Kruger CL, editors. Hayes' principles and methods of toxicology. 6th ed. Boca Raton (FL): CRC Press; 2014. p. 1793–830.

[101] FDA. Guidance for industry: immunotoxicology evaluation of investigational new drugs. Center for Drug Evaluation and Research (CDER), Food and Drug Administration, U.S. Department of Health and Human Services; 2002.

[102] FDA. Guidance for industry: S8 immunotoxicity studies for human pharmaceuticals. US Department of Health and Human Services, Food and Drug Administration, Center for Drug Evaluation and Research (CDER), Center for Biologics Evaluation and Research; 2006.

[103] Coffin DL, Blommer EJ. Acute toxicity of irradiated auto exhaust. Its indication by enhancement of mortality from *Streptococcal pneumonia*. Arch Environ Health 1967;15(1):36–8.

[104] Haley P, Perry R, Ennulat D, Frame S, Johnson C, Lapointe J-M, et al. STP position paper: best practice guideline for the routine pathology evaluation of the immune system. Toxicol Pathol 2005;33:404–7.

[105] Sellers RS, Morton D, Michael B, Roome N, Johnson JK, Yano BL, et al. Society of toxicologic pathology position paper: organ weight recommendations for toxicology studies. Toxicol Pathol 2007;35(5):751–5.

[106] Kuper CF, Harleman JH, Richter-Reichelm HB, Vos JG. Histopathologic approaches to detect changes indicative of immunotoxicity. Toxicol Pathol 2000;28(3):454–66.

[107] Elmore SA. Enhanced histopathology of the immune system: a review and update. Toxicol Pathol 2012;40(2):148–56.

[108] Immunotoxicology Technical Committee, International Life Sciences Institute Health and Environmental Sciences Institute. Application of flow cytometry to immunotoxicity testing: summary of a workshop. Toxicology 2001;163:39–48.

[109] Kim GG, Donnenberg VS, Donnenberg AD, Gooding W, Whiteside TL. A novel multiparametric flow cytometry-based cytotoxicity assay simultaneously immunophenotypes effector cells: comparisons to a 4 h 51Cr-release assay. J Immunol Methods 2007;325(1–2):51–66.

[110] Pestka JJ, Amuzie CJ. Tissue distribution and proinflammatory cytokine gene expression following acute oral exposure to deoxynivalenol: comparison of weanling and adult mice. Food Chem Toxicol 2008;46(8):2826–31.

[111] Tarrant J. Blood cytokines as biomarkers of *in Vivo* toxicity in pre-clinical safety assessment: considerations for their use. Toxicol Sci 2010;117(1):4–16.

[112] Finco D, Grimaldi C, Fort M, Walker M, Kiessling A, Wolf B, et al. Cytokine release assays: current practices and future directions. Cytokine 2014;66(2):143–55.

[113] Vessillier S, Eastwood D, Fox B, Sathish J, Sethu S, Dougall T, et al. Cytokine release assays for the prediction of therapeutic mAb safety in first-in man trials – whole blood cytokine release assay are poorly predictive for TGN1412 cytokine storm. J Immunol Methods 2015;424:43–52.

[114] Eastwood D, Bird C, Dilger P, Hockley J, Findlay L, Poole S, et al. Severity of the TGN1412 trial disaster cytokine storm correlated with IL-2 release. Br J Clin Pharmacol 2013;76(2):299–315.

[115] Rojko JL, Evans MG, Price SA, Han B, Waine G, DeWitte M, et al. Formation, clearance, deposition, pathogenicity, and identification of biopharmaceutical-related immune complexes: review and case studies. Toxicol Pathol 2014;42(4):725–64.

[116] Kimber I, Weisenberger C. A murine local lymph node assay for the identification of contact allergens. Assay development and results of an initial validation study. Arch Toxicol 1989;63(4):274–82.

[117] Gwaltney-Brant S, et al. Immunotoxicity biomarkers.. In: Gupta R, editor. Biomarkers in toxicology. Waltham (MA): Elsevier; 2014. p. 373–83.

[118] Everds N, Tarrant J. Unexpected hematologic effects of biothera-peutics in nonclinical species and in humans. Toxicol Pathol 2013;41(2):280–302.

[119] EMEA. ICH topic S 7 A. Safety pharmacology studies for human pharmaceuticals. European Medicines Agency; 2006. p. 6.

[120] Bolon B, Butt M. Toxicological neuropathology: the next two decades. In: Bolon B, Butt M, editors. Fundamental neuropathology for pathologists and toxicologists. Hoboken (NJ): John Wiley and Sons; 2011. p. 537–40.

[121] Vernau W, Vernau KM, Bolon B. Cerebrospinal fluid analysis in toxicological neuropathology. In: Bolon B, Butt M, editors. Fundamental neuropathology for pathologists and toxicologists. Hoboken (NJ): John Wiley and Sons; 2011. p. 271–81.

[122] Gabrielson K, Fletcher C, Czoty PW, Nader AM, Gluckman T, In vivo imaging applications for the nervous system in animal models. In: Bolon B, Butt M, editors. Fundamental neuropathology for pathologists and toxicologists. Hoboken (NJ): John Wiley and Sons, Inc.; 2011. p. 271–81.

[123] Everds N, Snyder P, Bailey K, Bolon B, Creasy D, Foley G, et al. Interpreting stress responses during routine toxicity studies: a review of the biology, impact, and assessment. Toxicol Pathol 2013;41:560–614.

[124] Creasy DM. Pathogenesis of male reproductive toxicity. Toxicol Pathol 2001;33:404–7.

[125] Sasaki JC, Chapin RE, Hall DG, Breslin W, Moffit J, Saldutti L, et al. Incidence and nature of testicular toxicity findings in pharmaceutical development. Birth Defects Res B 2011;92:511–25.

[126] Myers GM, Lambert-Messerlian GM, Sigman M. Inhibin B reference data for fertile and infertile men in Northeast America. Fertil Steril 2009;92(6):1920–3.

BIOSTATISTICS, REGULATORY TOXICOLOGY, AND ROLE OF STUDY DIRECTORS

18

Biostatistics for Toxicologists

T. Vidmar, L. Freshwater, R. Collins

INTRODUCTION

The objective of this chapter is to develop concepts to aid in the understanding of statistics as applied to toxicology. First, study design concepts will be reviewed from a statistical perspective, followed by some basic statistical concepts, which are presented in a toxicological context. Next, case studies will be presented for data collected for several different examples of typical toxicology studies to illustrate various statistical principles. These case studies will also be used to highlight the differences, from a statistical perspective, between the various types of toxicology studies.

This chapter is not intended to provide cookbook recipes for applying statistical methods to data collected in toxicology studies. As such, formulas and calculations are kept to a minimum unless used to illustrate a concept. Rather, this chapter is intended to provide a basic foundation of statistical principles that will enable the reader to critically appraise the design, conduct, statistical methodology, and interpretation of various toxicology studies in the literature and in a regulatory environment.

The example data used in the case studies to illustrate concepts have been constructed to reflect real data in terms of magnitude and variation.

Study Design

The goal of statistical experimental design is to get as close as possible to the ideal experiment, given the constraints of feasibility, finite resources, inherent variability in animals, and the ability to extend the results beyond

A Comprehensive Guide to Toxicology in Nonclinical Drug Development, Second Edition
http://dx.doi.org/10.1016/B978-0-12-803620-4.00018-9

the current experiment. The ideal experiment will generate data to answer the question it was proposed to answer.

Requirements for a good experiment are listed below (see D.R. Cox [1] for further details):

1. Absence of systematic error. This is a requirement to provide an unbiased estimate of the treatment effect through the comparison of nearly equivalent groups, each receiving differing treatments. Most often, equivalent groups are accomplished through randomization. Randomization is one of the most important concepts when discussing experimental design. Without proper randomization, conclusive evidence can't be derived from an experiment.
2. Precision. If the systematic error is eliminated, then the results obtained in the experiment should differ from the underlying true values by random variation only. To add to precision, the amount of random error should be made as small as possible.
3. Range of validity. As mentioned earlier, can the conclusions from an experiment be applied in a larger context?
4. Simplicity. If the experiment is overly complex, it will be prone to errors and large variability.
5. The calculation of uncertainty. Do the results of the experiment allow the assessment of the uncertainty or error associated with the estimated effects of the treatments applied?

The experimental unit is the smallest division of the experimental material that can receive different treatments. As an example, the experimental unit for data collected from the F0 generation of a developmental and reproductive toxicology (DART) study is the animal receiving the treatment. The experimental unit for the F1 generation is also the animal receiving the treatment, and not the pups from which data are collected. This makes DART experiments unique, and statistical accommodations for this phenomenon will be discussed in the section "Case Study—Developmental and Reproductive Toxicology." Although the number of experimental units to be used in many toxicology experiments is recommended by regulatory agencies, it is instructive to discuss how that number is usually determined. The proper number of experimental units impacts the statistical design principle of precision and avoids wasting precious resources.

The size of the sample must be large enough so that an effect big enough to be of scientific relevance will also be statistically significant. It is just as important that the number of animals not be too large, where an effect of little scientific importance becomes statistically detectable. Sample size is also important for economic reasons. An experiment with too few animals can be a waste of resources, as it does not have the capability to produce useful results, while an oversized experiment consumes more resources than is necessary. Since the experiments in this chapter involve animals, sample size is a pivotal issue for ethical reasons. An undersized experiment exposes the subjects to potentially harmful treatments without advancing knowledge, while an oversized experiment exposes an unnecessary number of animals.

One of the most popular approaches to sample-size determination involves studying the power of a statistical test. The power of a statistical test is its ability to find differences when those differences are real.

The power approach to estimating sample size involves identifying the following elements a priori:

1. Statistical Hypothesis: This is usually the difference between the test-article group and the vehicle group, defined in terms of a statistical parameter (eg, the population mean).
2. Significance Level (α): Based on the statistical outcome, this is the probability of falsely declaring that the test article has an effect.
3. Effect Size (Δ): This should reflect an alternative of scientific interest, usually the size of the treatment effect.
4. Historical Data: This is needed to obtain estimates of other parameters required in order to compute the power function of the test (eg, measures of variability).
5. Desired Power of the Statistical Test: Formulas are available from many statistical reference books once estimates of variability and the size of the treatment effect are obtained.

BASIC STATISTICAL CONCEPTS

Statisticians distinguish descriptive statistics from inferential statistics. The former simply summarize a set of data. Examples include the sample size, arithmetic mean, standard deviation, coefficient of variation, range, and proportion. These statistics are often used in summary tables to "describe" data collected in a study. Calculations for descriptive statistics can be found in any introductory textbook, and statisticians are, for the most part, in agreement as to their computation.

By contrast, the objective of inferential statistics is to utilize information from a controlled study (the sample) to project or draw "inferences" beyond the scope of the study itself. While the objective of descriptive statistics is to summarize the known (collected) information, the objective of inferential statistics is to cast light on the unknown.

Although, in many cases, descriptive statistics adequately address many research questions, regulatory agencies and most journals require statistical confirmation of quantitative experiments. Drawing conclusions from a finite sample (ie, generalizing beyond the scope of the study itself) creates the possibility of errors beyond those of logic. The advantage of applying statistical methodology to toxicological research is that it allows the toxicologist to quantify the probability of making errors or coming to the wrong conclusion. Inferential statistics provides a systematic, objective means by which to quantify the likelihood of observed outcomes and thus to interpret the study results.

Inferential statistics is further broken down into two areas: estimation and hypothesis or "significance" testing.

Estimation

If it were possible to take a precise measurement from every Sprague–Dawley rat in the world, then the average value, for example, would be known exactly without error. This value would no longer be an estimate but rather a characteristic of the population. In practice, a measure from every member of a population is impossible to obtain. Therefore experiments are conducted on a sample from the population of Sprague–Dawley rats, and estimates are made of the characteristics of that population.

When referring to measures in the population, the characteristics are called parameters. These characteristics can be averages, proportions, standard deviations, and so on. When referring to measures of the sample, the numerical characteristics of that sample will be called statistics.

The objective is to use the statistic generated from the sample to make decisions about the population. Clearly, the more precise and accurate the statistic, the better it will be for making decisions about the population.

What actions can be taken to improve the behavior of the statistic, as there is usually only a single chance to run the experiment? The first action is to control bias to improve the accuracy of the estimate. This is usually done through random sampling. Sampling technique matters to avoid bias and to ensure that the sample is representative of the population. For example, if a researcher is interested in estimating the body weight of rats in a TA (test article) group versus a vehicle control group, the best practice is to ensure that the body weights are equivalent in each group before the experiment begins, so no one group is biased as compared to the other.

To control the precision of the estimate, an understanding of the standard error is required. The standard error is a measure of how much the statistic varies from sample to sample. It tells how close the statistic is to the underlying parameter, if bias has been addressed. The formula for the standard error is the standard deviation of the sample divided by the square root of the number of observations: $SE = SD/\sqrt{n}$. As sample size increases, the standard error gets smaller and the estimate of the statistic is more likely to be closer to the value of the parameter. However, as already noted, the size of the sample is determined by several factors, so as to avoid too few as well as too many samples.

Significance Testing

Significance testing (referred to as *hypothesis testing* in most statistical textbooks) involves the use of statistical tests to evaluate the plausibility of a hypothesis, based on collected data. First, the following items are defined: the null hypothesis, the alternative hypothesis, the specific statistical test to be used, and an appropriate significance level. Then, the collected data are utilized to evaluate the plausibility of the null hypothesis. This evaluation is made through a decision rule: it is assumed that the null hypothesis is true unless there is overwhelming evidence in the collected data to suggest otherwise. Overwhelming evidence is defined by the chosen significance level.

In terms of toxicology, significance testing is the use of statistical tests to evaluate the assumption that a TA has no effect.

Null Hypothesis (H_0):	No TA Effect
Alternative hypothesis (H_1):	TA effect

The process of significance testing works much like a court of law in the trial of an individual. The data collected from a toxicology study are akin to the evidence presented in a court trial. At the conclusion of the trial, the jury is instructed to assume that the accused is innocent unless there is overwhelming evidence to the contrary. Likewise, in a toxicology study it is assumed that the TA had no effect unless there is overwhelming evidence in the collected data to suggest otherwise. In significance testing, it is assumed that all observed differences in collected data are due to chance alone until proven otherwise. Understanding the stated assumption is critical to the interpretation of the results of significance testing.

The significance test generates a *p*-value, defined as the probability of the observed results, or more extreme results, if in fact the null hypothesis is true. The *p*-value represents the probability of getting the results in a specific study, or even bigger differences, if the TA truly had no effect.

Statistical significance is defined simply as a numerical difference beyond that which would be expected by chance alone. Note what is missing from this definition:

1. There is no mention of biological relevance, and
2. There is no mention of 0.05.

Rather, statistical significance defines, from a numerical perspective, insufficient versus overwhelming evidence. A small *p*-value, below the predefined level of significance, is considered overwhelming evidence against the hypothesis that the TA has no effect. However, a *p*-value above the predefined level of significance should not be interpreted as confirmation that the TA has no effect. Instead, it suggests there is insufficient evidence in the sample data to refute the assumption that the TA has no effect.

The TA either does or does not have an effect on safety (the true state), and significance testing is a tool used to make inferences about the true state. (One can imagine the "true state" as being the conclusion one would reach if an infinite sample size study could be conducted.) Because the statistical conclusions are based on the limited sample in the study, there is a chance that these conclusions may be wrong relative to the true state. Statisticians refer to these as Type I and Type II errors. More meaningful labels, in terms of their biological relevance, are provided by the terms false positive and false negative. A *false positive* is the result of a statistically significant conclusion when, in fact, the TA does not have any effect. Conversely, a *false negative* is the result of a statistical test that is not significant when, in fact, the TA does have an effect. Because the main objective of toxicology studies is to evaluate the safety of a TA, the possibility of false negatives should be the primary focus in the design, analysis, and interpretation of the study.

At the core of significance testing is the investigation of why all observations are not identical. In a general toxicology study, body weights might be collected on gestation day 20 (GD20) from 40 animals. But the 40 body weights are not identical. Why? In a controlled study, an observed response (one measurement from one animal) is influenced by stimuli that are either controllable or not controllable. Examples of controllable stimuli include breed and supplier of the animals, measuring instrument, time of day of the measurement, the amount of food available to the animal, and location of cage in the room. The list of controllable stimuli that may influence the GD20 body weight of an animal is almost endless, but nearly all of them have one thing in common: they are of little or no interest to the experiment at hand. There is, however, one controllable stimulus that is the primary focus of the study: the TA itself. And that stimulus is controlled by exposing subsets of animals to different dose levels of the TA.

In addition, responses (eg, the GD20 body weights of animals) are influenced by phenomena that cannot be controlled or explained. That is, animals are simply different by nature or by chance. Statisticians refer to these differences caused by nature or chance as *random variation*.

Fig. 18.1 illustrates the GD20 body weights of 40 animals, shown in no particular order on the *x*-axis. From a statistical perspective, the fundamental question is "why don't all 40 values fall on the horizontal line dissecting the data?" This is the total variation in the data. A portion of the total variation is explained if the data are grouped according to the treatment they received. Half of the animals received a zero-dose level (control), and the remaining animals received a single dose of test article. Fig. 18.2 illustrates the general shift downward in body weight of animals receiving test article. The difference in the central tendency of the two groups is the test-article effect, ie, the *between-group variation*. Still, the

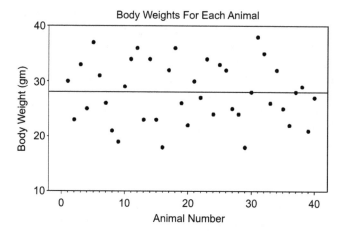

FIGURE 18.1 GD20 body weights for each animal.

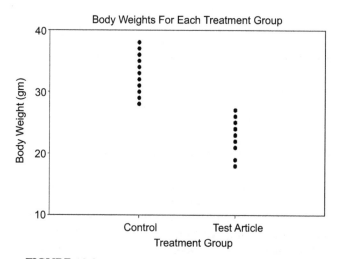

FIGURE 18.2 GD20 body weights at each treatment group.

test-article effect does not entirely explain why all animal body weights are not the same. Even within each of the two groups, where animals received the same dose level, there are differences among the animals. This is the random variation in the data, ie, the *between-animal variation*. Between-animal variation is often referred to as *within-group variation*.

Next, expand the current example to a typical DART study design consisting of 80 female animals distributed equally among four groups, each of which is exposed to a different dose level of TA. Algebraically, we can explain the GD20 body weight of each individual animal as follows:

$$\text{GD20 Body Weight} = \mu + \text{Dose} + e \qquad (18.1)$$

Statisticians refer to μ as the population mean. It is the theoretical mean GD20 body weight of this species in the "true state." But very few animals, if any, have a GD20 body weight exactly equal to μ. (Not all of the values fall on the line.) In our controlled study there are two reasons: (1) subsets of animals received different dose levels of TA (Dose), and (2) animals are simply different (chance or "e").

The statistical model above is that for a one-way analysis of variance (ANOVA). The ANOVA and its different variations will be discussed in greater detail later in this chapter. For now, it is presented simply to illustrate that, at its core, statistics is simply an evaluation of why all values are not the same or, put another way, it is an "analysis of variation" in the data.

The test statistic for a one-way ANOVA is an F-test:

$$F = MS_{Dose}/MS_e \qquad (18.2)$$

where MS_{Dose} is the "mean square" for the dose group and MS_e is the "mean square" for error. For this chapter, the mathematics of the F-test is not important. The calculation can be found in any introductory statistics textbook, and any statistical software package will calculate an ANOVA F-test and its resulting *p*-value. What is important is to see the basic concept of the F-test. MS_{Dose} is a calculated estimate of the variation in the study data that is due to the different dose levels that animals received (between-group). Likewise, MS_e is a calculated estimate of the random variation due to chance (within-group or between-animal variation). Thus the ANOVA F-test is simply a ratio of the variation in the data that is due to the different dose levels of TA relative to the random variation that would be expected simply by chance.

With an understanding of the stimuli that influence measurable responses, the objective of study design and conduct can be defined, in very broad terms, as follows: eliminate or balance controllable sources of variation that are of little or no interest, so that observed differences in a response are attributable solely to the TA or to random variation (chance). In some aspects, this seems obvious. In a rodent study one would never use multiple breeds from multiple suppliers. But other situations are less obvious. Limited resources may present potential sources of variation that should be addressed in the study design. For example, it may not be feasible for a lab to perform all necropsies for a given study on a single day. Rather than performing all control and low-dose necropsies on one day, which might be convenient from a logistical standpoint, followed by mid- and high-dose necropsies the next day, a random sample of equal number from each group should be necropsied on each day. If the day of necropsy has any influence on response, that influence should then be equally distributed across the four dose groups.

Another example is initial body weight. Although it may be argued that initial body weight is a source of random variation, it is a not a source in which we are interested, because the animals have not yet received the TA. We do, however, have at least some control over its influence on responses that are of interest (eg, post-treatment body weight). The study can be designed such that, in general, the initial body weights are equally distributed across the dosage groups. This concept, in which a potential source of variation is incorporated into the study design so as to be balanced across the dosage groups, is referred to as *blocking*.

Recall the definition of statistical significance: a numerical difference beyond what would be expected by chance. At the conclusion of a well-designed study, significance testing can be used to address the question: How much of the observed numerical difference is due to the TA relative to the random variation that would be expected simply by chance? (Recall the F-test statistic in Eq. (18.2) is a ratio of the estimates of variation due to the TA relative to that due to chance.)

Testing Philosophies

The objective of a toxicology study is to answer the simple question "does the TA have an adverse effect?" and the statistical methodology must be customized accordingly. Common designs employed in many toxicology studies lend themselves to two basic statistical testing philosophies: zero-dose comparisons and dose–response trend testing.

Zero-Dose Comparisons

The theory of the zero-dose comparison is that any TA effect will manifest itself as a numerical difference in a parameter derived from a test-article group when compared with the same parameter observed in the zero-dose level control group. As such, the results at each TA dose level are compared, in a pairwise fashion, with that of the control group.

One appeal of the zero-dose comparison approach is that a statistical conclusion is derived for each and every dose level in the study. However, this may also be one of its disadvantages. That is, the zero-dose comparison approach may present statistical conclusions of test article effect at low-dose levels that is not statistically nor scientifically substantiated at higher dose levels.

Dose–Response Trend Testing

The theory of dose–response trend testing is based on the simple concept that "the dose is the poison." The statistical testing philosophy evaluates whether or not increasing doses of a TA elicit increasing effects.

Tukey [2] suggested employing sequential trend testing to identify the level at which there is no statistical significance of trend (NOSTASOT). Adapting Tukey's strategy to a typical toxicology study that includes a zero-dose level Control (C) and three increasing dose levels of TA (low, mid, and high) is illustrated in Fig. 18.3.

The appeal of dose–response trend testing is that it generally reflects the objective of the study design and its scientific evaluation. It is designed to identify the NOSTASOT, which can be considered analogous to the no observable adverse effect level (NOAEL). Also, if the test-article effects truly occur in a dose-related fashion, dose–response trend testing is more powerful than the zero-dose comparison approach. In rare situations one might see a reversal in the trend direction after the initial trend test has been flagged. Once trend direction has been established after the initial comparison the direction cannot be reversed. When these situations occur the trend testing must stop and further evaluation of the differences should occur via alternatives. A criticism of dose–response trend testing is that it may not identify test articles with threshold effects at low-dose levels that do not occur at higher dose levels, ie, the U-shaped or inverted U-shaped response curve. However, these response curves can easily be addressed with a simple modification to Tukey's approach.

The modification will look for a nonmonotonic trend in the treatment means. If the dose–response testing failed to yield a significant effect, then the overall F-test for any treatment effect is examined at $\alpha = 0.1$. If the overall effect is significant, then Dunnett's test [3] is used to compare all TA groups to the control. If the overall treatment effect is not significant, then testing stops. The modified procedure is displayed in Fig. 18.4.

There are several other procedures available to perform testing between the TAs and control. The interested reader is referred to Westfall et al. [4], Hochberg and Tamhane [5], and Hsu [6].

Parametric Versus Nonparametric

Textbooks and courses often present statistical tests in terms of parametric versus nonparametric methods. In statistical terms, *parametric* methods involve the evaluation of parameters from known distributions. In general, as it pertains to toxicology applications, parametric

methods are employed to evaluate the means of data from normal ("bell-shaped") distributions. By contrast, *nonparametric* methods are "distribution-free" and do not rely on specific distributions for their use.

Examples of parametric methods include *t*-tests and the analysis of variance (ANOVA) and its variations (eg, one-way, two-way, repeated measures, and analysis of covariance). One appeal of parametric analyses is that it allows the use of probabilities associated with known distributions. For example, if data come from a normal distribution, then knowledge of that distribution can be used to calculate the probability of observed outcomes. Also, when the conditions necessary for parametric analysis are met, the parametric analysis provides approximately a 5% more powerful statistical test than its nonparametric counterpart.

For large samples, many nonparametric techniques can be viewed as the usual normal theory-based procedures applied to ranks. That is, the data values across all groups are ranked from 1 to N, where 1 is the smallest value and N is the largest. The nonparametric analysis is then based on the ranks rather than the actual data values themselves. One appeal of a nonparametric approach is that it is not unduly influenced by extreme values ("outliers"). For example, a single extremely large value is assigned the rank of N, or one unit more than the next largest value $N-1$. Thus the large value is retained in the analysis, but it does not excessively affect the outcome. For this reason, nonparametric analyses should be presented in summary tables by the median, a rank statistic, rather than the mean, which can be heavily influenced by extreme values in a small sample size.

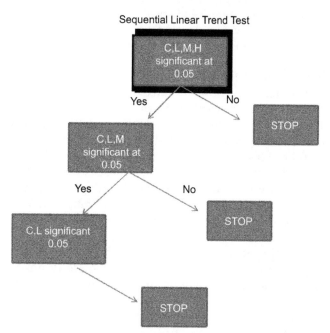

FIGURE 18.3 Sequential linear trend test flow chart.

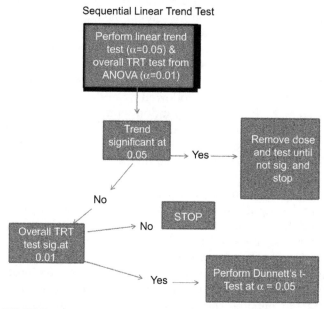

FIGURE 18.4 Sequential linear trend test flow chart with additional path.

Lastly, proponents of nonparametric analyses make the argument that even when the assumptions associated with parametric analysis are met, the loss of power caused by using a nonparametric analysis is marginal. Moreover, the power of a nonparametric approach becomes greater than its parametric counterpart as the deviations from the parametric analysis assumptions become larger.

Table 18.1 lists the names of some normal theory-based procedures and their nonparametric counterparts.

The age-old question confronting most data analysts is: "When should I use parametric analyses and when should I use nonparametric?" Introductory textbooks state that two conditions must be present in order to correctly use parametric analyses: (1) the data must come from a known distribution, which is usually a normal distribution; and (2) the variances among groups must be the same (homogeneity of variance). In practice, these issues are sometimes addressed by applying formal statistical tests to confirm these assumptions. Preliminary statistical tests such as Shapiro–Wilk are used to evaluate normality and Levene's test is often used to examine homogeneity of variance [7].

However, there are several problems with the preliminary formal testing of parametric assumptions. In fact, the usefulness of most preliminary tests is inversely related to where they are most powerful. For example, in small sample sizes, nonparametric analysis may be more appropriate than its parametric counterpart. For small sample sizes, the preliminary tests are less likely to detect deviations from the assumptions. By contrast, preliminary tests for large sample sizes are more likely to detect significant deviations from normality and/or homogeneous variances. But with large, approximately equal sample sizes the parametric analysis of variance is very robust to deviations from the assumptions. That is to say, with larger sample sizes, the loss of power as the result of deviations from the assumptions diminishes. So a situation arises where for large sample sizes the preliminary testing

works well but isn't as critical as in the small sample-size situation. As stated by Box:

> To make preliminary tests on variances is rather like putting to sea in a row boat to find out whether conditions are sufficiently calm for an ocean liner to leave port. *Ref. [8].*

In the toxicology context, our preference is to utilize the knowledge of the vast historical data that is available to determine, a priori, the statistical analysis that should be used for each analysis endpoint. For example, historical body weight data meets the conditions of parametric analysis and should be analyzed accordingly. Similarly, it is known that sperm count data are subject to extreme values and skewed distributions, and a nonparametric approach is more appropriate. Suggestions for analysis methodology for specific toxicology studies are presented in the "Case Studies" section.

Historical data also provide enough information about many toxicology endpoints to select a transformation of the data, achieving the required assumptions for a statistical test. For example, the viability index in a DART study (the percentage of pups that survive at least 4 days) has historically been transformed by use of the Freeman–Tukey arcsine to attain assumptions required by the analysis of variance [9].

Data Characteristics

Data from toxicology studies have various characteristics. Some of the data originate from a continuous distribution. Data can take on any possible value within reasonable limits. An example would be body weight or food consumption. In contrast, some data are from a discrete distribution, and such data can take on only a finite number of values within reasonable limits. An example would be the number of live pups born per litter. Some other data types that require special statistical handling include percentages and incidences. An example of data presented as a percentage would be the percentage of

TABLE 18.1 Commonly Used Parametric and Nonparametric Statistical Tests

Parametric Test	Corresponding Nonparametric Test	Purpose of Test
t-test for independent samples	Mann–Whitney U test; Wilcoxon rank-sum test	Compares two independent samples
Paired t-test	Wilcoxon signed-rank test	Examines a set of differences
Pearson correlation coefficient	Spearman rank correlation coefficient	Assesses the linear association between two variables
One-way analysis of variance (F-test)	Kruskal–Wallis analysis of variance by ranks	Compares three or more groups
Analysis of variance for randomized blocks	Friedman test	Compares groups classified by two different factors

dead or resorbed fetuses per litter. Incidence data examples include endpoints such as necropsy observations. For an individual animal, the value of a particular necropsy observation would be a "yes" or a "no," but for the treatment group, the data would take the form of (# of observations)/(# of animals in the group).

Statistical methods such as least squares and analysis of variance are designed to deal with continuous dependent variables. These can be adapted to deal with count data by using data transformations, such as the square-root transformation, but such methods have drawbacks; they are approximate at best and estimate parameters that are often hard to interpret.

Many biological variables do not meet the assumptions of parametric statistical tests: they may not be normally distributed or the variances (measure of error) may not have exactly the same distribution in each of the treatment groups (homogeneous) or both. In some cases, transforming the data using a mathematical function will make it fit the assumptions better. To transform your data, apply a mathematical function to each observation, and then use these numbers in your statistical test. Popular transformation functions include the logarithm, square root, and the arcsine, which was mentioned in an earlier section. Often and where possible, statistics based on the transformed data are transformed back to the original scale using the inverse transformation. The interested reader is referred to [7] for more details. An example statistical analysis using data transformations is included in the section "Case Study—Endocrine Study."

The Poisson distribution can form the basis for some analyses of count data, and in this case, Poisson regression may be used. This is a special case of the class of generalized linear models, which also contains specific forms of models capable of using the binomial distribution for incidence data (binomial regression, logistic regression). This class also includes the negative binomial distribution, where the assumptions of the Poisson model are violated, in particular when the range of count values is limited or when there is more variability than predicted by the model (a situation called overdispersion) is present. The section "Count Data" as follows is devoted to standard statistical techniques to analyze data that are counts of events or occurrences.

Count Data

As noted, data in toxicology studies are often counts of events. As such they can usually be entered into table form. For the example in Table 18.2 there are two treatment groups: treated with a therapeutic agent and control.

If a researcher was interested in testing the hypothesis that the tumor rate in the treated group is equal to the tumor rate in the control groups, versus the alternative hypothesis that the tumor rate is higher in the treated group, a one-sided test statistic would be used. Assuming that the row totals and column totals are fixed at their observed values, one can then determine how "extreme" the observed table entries are under the assumption that there is no treatment effect. For example, "more extreme" tables would have more animals that had a tumor in the treated group. An example of a more extreme table can be found in Table 18.3.

Note that the treated group now has an additional animal with a tumor. A well-known statistic for evaluating the hypothesis described is Fisher's exact test [7]. Fisher's exact test is well known and included in many software packages. It is used for the situation where the number of entries in the table is "small" since the number of calculations required could be large. The p-value for testing the hypothesis that the tumor rates are equivalent is .0458. The correct conclusion would be that the treated group has a higher tumor rate. The p-value is based on the tables that are as extreme, or more extreme, than what was observed.

TABLE 18.2 Tumors as Events

	Treated	Control	Row Total
Animals with tumor	8	2	10
Animals without tumor	42	48	90
Column total	50	50	

TABLE 18.3 Tumors as Events (More Extreme)

	Treated	Control	Row Total
Animals with tumor	9	1	10
Animals without tumor	41	49	90
Column total	50	50	

When the magnitude of the entries in the cells of the table is "large" a chi-square test would be appropriate. It is constructed as:

$$X^2 = \sum (O_{r,c} - E_{r,c})^2 / E_{r,c} \qquad (18.3)$$

where $O_{r,c}$ is the observed frequency count in population r for level c of the categorical variable, and $E_{r,c}$ is the expected frequency count in population r for level c of the categorical variable. It is used to determine whether frequency counts are distributed identically across different populations; in this case the populations are the animals in the TA groups and those in the vehicle group. The example in Table 18.4 will illustrate the calculation. The data in that table represent the number of litters that had one or more malformations during a DART study.

In the example, $E_{1,1} = (70 \times 50)/140 = 25$ while $O_{1,1} = 30$. The other numbers are calculated in a similar fashion. The X^2 statistic for the example is 3.1111. The p-value is .0778 with 1 degree of freedom. With the traditional cutoff of $p = .05$ a difference is not detected between the rates in the treated group as compared to the control.

Most toxicology studies use more than two groups. The concept of a trend test can be extended to the type of data discussed above. If the first example of tumor counts is extended to four groups: control (0.0 dose), low dose, medium dose, and high dose, one may assess whether tumor rates increase with increasing dose. A statistical test that was developed to test an increasing trend in tumor counts with respect to increasing dose is the Cochran–Armitage test [9]. It is a test that is based on the correlation between the proportions of tumors in each group versus the dose. This concept will be illustrated with an example. In Table 18.5 there are several treatment groups: those animals treated with several doses of a therapeutic agent and control.

Clearly, the proportion of tumors in each group (animals with tumor/animals examined) is increasing with respect to increasing dose. For this example, the Cochran–Armitage statistic has a value of 2.9 with a 1-sided p-value of .002.

CASE STUDIES

Four different case studies will be presented in this section to illustrate statistical concepts that are unique to the various fields of toxicology. These case studies are meant to be an extension to the basic statistical concepts presented thus far.

Case Study—General Toxicology Example

A more complete description of the details needed to completely describe the various general toxicology experiments may be found elsewhere in this book. For the purposes of illustrating statistical concepts, data from a 4-week study consisting of four groups (a vehicle control and three increasing doses of the therapeutic agent) and 10 rats per sex per group will be used. Data typically collected in these experiments include the endpoints: body weight, food consumption, laboratory data (hematology, blood biochemistry, and urinalysis), and organ weights.

The example will use cholesterol (mg/dL) values taken on one day from a hypothetical study consisting of 80 animals evenly distributed between four increasing dose levels of TA and both genders. Usually statistical analyses are performed separately for each sex. For the example we will focus on the males, which will be a total of 40 animals (10 per treatment group and control). Fig. 18.5 shows a visual display of the data, including location [mean (+), median (−)], dispersion (length of the box), and outliers (·).

As already noted, the preferred approach to evaluating dose–response relationships is through a modified

TABLE 18.4 Chi-Square Example

	Treated	Control	Row Total
Litters with malformations	30	20	50
Litters without malformations	40	50	90
Column total	70	70	Total number of litters = 140

TABLE 18.5 Cochran–Armitage Trend Test

	Control (0 Dose)	Dose 1 (Low Dose)	Dose 2 (Medium Dose)	Dose 3 (High Dose)
Animals with tumor	0	1	3	6
Column total (animals examined)	50	50	50	50

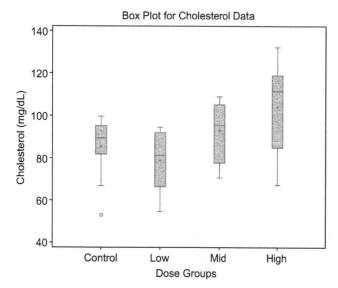

FIGURE 18.5 Box plot for weight data example.

Tukey approach, which is best described as shown in Fig. 18.3.

Primary emphasis is placed on the evaluation of dose-related responses by conducting sequential linear trend tests [2]. Trend tests are first conducted across all dosage groups (control, low, mid, high). If not significant no further trend tests are conducted. If significant, the high dose is considered significant, and a trend test is conducted across control, low, and mid doses. Testing continues until a nonsignificant result occurs.

For evaluation, the cholesterol data can be statistically analyzed with the ANOVA model similar to Eq. (18.1). An annotated summary of the analysis of variance (ANOVA) is given in Table 18.6. Following the dose–response testing strategy in Section "Testing Philosophies", a statistically significant dose response is found when all doses are used ($p=.0045$). When testing for a dose response without the high dose, there is no longer a significant effect ($p=.321$). Testing then stops, and the conclusion that there is a significant trend through the high dose, but there is no significant trend through the mid dose (NOSTASOT).

The example just described provides an evaluation of a snapshot in time; ie, the TA effect on cholesterol. However, rather than a snapshot there is often interest in the effects of TA on a variable such as body weight across the entire course of the experiment where data are collected at 3–4 day intervals during that time period. One way to statistically analyze these data is to perform a one-way ANOVA at each of the individual days of measurement. However, to do so treats the animal body weights on each day of measurement as if they were independent of all other body weight measurements. But this assumption cannot be true, because the measurements are made on the same animal on different days and therefore not independent of one another. It's the same animal at different gestation days.

More efficient use of the multiple measurements taken on the same animal during gestation would be to incorporate them into a single statistical analysis. For example, if body weights are collected on each of 40 animals at six different gestation days (same days for all animals) resulting in 240 body weights the basic question remains the same: "Why aren't all 240 body weights identical?"

Again, each of the 240 body weights can be modeled:

$$\text{Gestation Body Weight} = \mu + \text{Dose} + \text{Time} + \text{Dose} \times \text{Time} + e_B + e_W \qquad (18.4)$$

Why aren't all body weights equal to μ, the theoretical body weight of an animal during gestation? In this case, three reasons can be identified:

1. Groups of animals received different dose levels of TA (Dose);
2. The different days of measurement (Time) have an effect on body (particularly during gestation when we expect these animals to be growing); and
3. The interaction of dose level and time.

There are also two random variations of chance that may influence the individual body weight:

1. Animals are different (designated by e_B for "between-animal" random variation); and
2. Even within the same animal there is a certain amount of random variation associated with multiple measurements (designated by e_W for "within-animal" random variation).

The distinction between within-animal and between-animal variation may be difficult to grasp in the current example. But consider the following example: Yesterday at 8:00 am a technician measured both your and a colleague's blood pressure. Today at 8:00 am the same technician again measured your blood pressure and that of your colleague. We would expect a difference between your blood pressure and your colleague's pressure because people are different. You would also not be surprised if there was a slight difference between your blood pressure yesterday and that of today. The latter is within-subject random variation, while the former is between-subject variation.

From a statistical analysis perspective, the reason within-animal must be distinguished from between-animal variation is that measurements on the same animal are more highly correlated than those between two different animals. That is, within-animal is a different kind of variation and one in which we would expect less variation because of the high correlation.

The statistical model described above is a repeated-measures analysis of variance (RANOVA) [10]. In addition to the two sources of random variation, another key

TABLE 18.6 Annotated ANOVA Summary

Source of Variation	Degrees of Freedom	Sum of Squares	Mean Square Error	F-Value	Prob.[a] > F	Comment
Model	3	3487.224	1162.408	4.42	0.0096	
Error	36	9470.918	263.0811			Estimate of the experimental error
Corrected total	39	12,958.14				
Treatment	3	3487.224	1162.408	4.42	0.0096	Testing for an overall treatment effect
Trend (all doses)	1	2413.311	2413.311	9.17	0.0045	Testing linear trend, using all doses
Trend (C,L,M)	1	267.601	267.601	1.02	0.3199	Testing linear trend, using C,L,M doses

[a]*Probability.*

component of the RANOVA is the interaction term for dose level and time (Dose × Time). Remember, the ultimate objective is to evaluate the effects of the different dose levels of the TA. The Dose×Time interaction term approaches this question by addressing whether or not the evaluation of TA effects depends on which gestation day is being evaluated.

The use of RANOVA in the evaluation of TA effects across time, including the concept of interaction of effects, is explored in greater detail below.

The concepts just discussed are illustrated with an example. Fig. 18.6 and Table 18.7 display average body weights (gm) for each treatment group at each time point, in hours, where data were collected.

For the example, follow the strategy in Fig. 18.7:

- Check to see if the monotonic dose response is the same for each compound across time. The figure depicts that body weight does not increase the same in all treatment groups across time. The statistic verifies this observation ($p < .0001$).
- If so, test for trends across pooled time points. This step is skipped because the trends are not the same across time.
- If the dose response is not the same, then trend testing will be performed for each time point. As an example, testing at Hour 5 is presented. Both the high dose and mid dose are significantly different from control, which agrees with what is observed in the figure. Testing stops at this point.
- Nonmonotonic dose responses will be evaluated whenever no significant linear trends are detected but the treatment and/or treatment by time interaction is significant at the 0.01 level. (This step is not used in this particular example.)

- If the treatment by time interaction is significant, then pairwise comparisons with the control will be conducted for each time point. (This step is not used in this particular example.)
- If only the treatment effect is significant, the comparisons will be conducted across the pooled time points for the overall phase. These nonmonotonic treatment group comparisons will be conducted at the 0.01 significance level. (This step is not used in this particular example.)

The results of the trend-testing scenario may be found in Table 18.8. Note that the construction of the trend test is beyond the scope of this chapter. However, the interested reader is referred to Hoffman et al. [10] for a detailed description of the process.

It is important to note that the analysis of RANOVA described above can sometimes include 24h (or more) of continuously measured data. When this takes place the data are often binned into smaller time intervals for summary and analysis purposes. Care should be taken to establish these bins around periods of interest in a study such as dosing time, light/dark cycles, meals, and known PK characteristics of a TA. This binning is important because without it the small details of what a TA is doing can become buried in an RANOVA analysis that includes too many points in time. The statistical methods described thus far (ANOVA and RANOVA) fall into the category of parametric methods. The term parametric is derived from the fact that these methods evaluate parameters from known distributions. The parametric methods presented here evaluate the population mean (parameter) from the normal distribution. Not all information collected in a general toxicology study presents itself in such a way that means are the most relevant or meaningful descriptors with which to evaluate the effects of a TA.

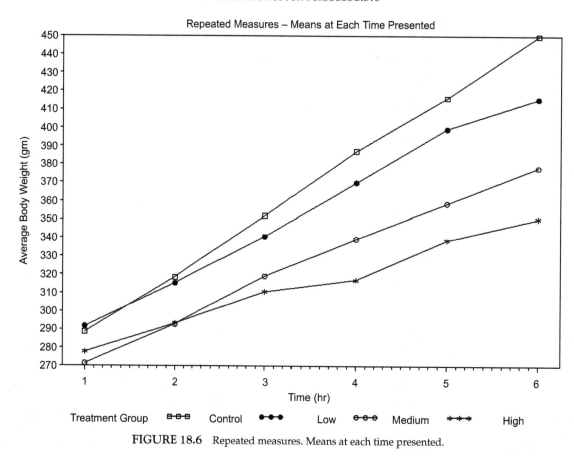

FIGURE 18.6 Repeated measures. Means at each time presented.

TABLE 18.7 Summary Statistics for Repeated Weights

Treatment Group	Statistic	Hour 1	Hour 2	Hour 3	Hour 4	Hour 5	Hour 6
Control	Mean	288.64	318.63	351.98	387.1	416.08	449.83
Control	Standard deviation	11.924	14.652	20.781	22.752	26.791	30.426
Control	n	10	10	10	10	10	10
Low	Mean	291.72	315.32	340.6	369.83	399.11	415.48
Low	Standard deviation	19.361	19.442	24.766	27.958	29.761	29.741
Low	n	10	10	10	10	10	10
Medium	Mean	271.49	292.78	319.04	339.41	358.6	377.95
Medium	Standard deviation	12.369	19.214	24.527	26.399	26.386	24.216
Medium	n	10	10	10	10	10	10
High	Mean	277.76	293.27	310.52	317	338.63	350.32
High	Standard deviation	18.774	20.673	20.29	18.333	19.141	21.8
High	n	10	10	10	10	10	10

Case Study—Developmental and Reproductive Toxicology

What distinguishes DART statistics from other disciplines is the evaluation of data collected from the F1 generation. To understand the unique statistical issues presented by the F1 generation, we must first understand one of the most basic concepts of statistics: the experimental unit. In its simplest terms, the experimental unit (EU) is defined as the smallest entity to which treatment is applied. For the F1 generation, this comes into play in

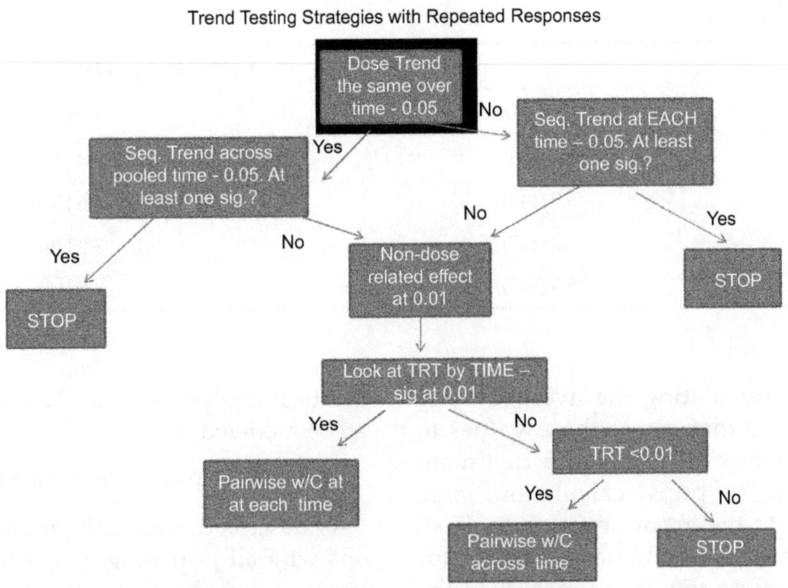

Trend Testing Strategies with Repeated Responses

FIGURE 18.7 Trend testing strategies with repeated measures.

TABLE 18.8 Trend Testing for Repeated Measures

Stage of Testing	Effect	Statistic	p-value
Model	Treatment	(F) 15.72	<.0001
Model	Time (h)	(F) 235.15	<.0001
Model	Treatment by time interaction	(F) 7.21	<.0001
Linearity	Across all times	(F) 19.33	<.0001
At Hour 5	Control versus high dose	(T) −8.63	<.0001
At Hour 5	Control versus mid dose	(T) −5.75	<.0001
At Hour 5	Control versus low dose	(T) −1.7	.0911

terms of exposure to a TA. The F1 generation is exposed to the TA by one or more of the following means:

1. F0: prior to conception (male or female)
2. F0: during gestation (female)

F1: Postnatally

In the first two cases, the fetus/offspring do not receive TA directly; it is received indirectly through the pregnant dam. In such cases, the maternal unit is the smallest entity to which treatment is applied, and thus it is the EU. Equivalently, as being part of the maternal unit, the litter receives treatment as a whole and can therefore be considered the EU for the offspring.

The third case (postnatal treatment) is a little more difficult to understand and, to a certain extent, the best statistical analysis is not always agreed upon among statisticians. An argument can be made that the offspring receive treatment individually and thus should be considered the EU. However, one must consider the definition of "smallest entity." Studies have shown that there

is a much higher correlation between offspring from the same litter than between offspring from different litters [9]. While it is obvious that offspring from different litters represent independent units, the high correlation between offspring from the same litter suggests that they are not independent, at least not in the same sense that offspring from different litters are independent. As such, less random variation is expected in responses from offspring from the same litter than from offspring from different litters. This correlation among siblings is commonly known as the "litter effect." For this reason, it is generally accepted that the litter as a whole presents a single entity (EU) regardless of when treatment is administered, including postnatally. Considering the litter as the EU is important in statistical analysis.

Consider the male pup weights collected on PND 4 prior to culling, as given in Table 18.9.

Means in the first column (n = pups) are calculated by simply averaging across all pups in a treatment group. Means in the second column (n = litters)

TABLE 18.9 Pup Weight Example

	PND 4 Pup Weights (Males)	
Treatment Group	Mean (n = pups)	Mean (n = litters)
C	8.6 (143)	8.8 [20]
L	8.7 (146)	8.6 [20]
M	8.7 (137)	8.8 [19]
H	8.3 (129)	8.5 [18]

are calculated by first calculating the average body weight for each litter and then using those values to calculate the average across all litters of a treatment group. Note that in the "n = pups" calculation, large litters contribute more to the group mean than small litters do (eg, a litter in which n = 16 has greater influence than a litter of n = 9 on the group mean). In the n = litters calculation, all litters contribute equally to the group mean.

The result of ignoring litter as the EU (ie, assuming that all pups are independent of one another) is overstating the sample size (as n = number of pups). Among the consequences of such an oversight is an increased chance of a false-positive conclusion. That is to say, biologically irrelevant TA effects may be identified as statistically significant simply because of the overstated sample size.

In the example above, there were 555 PND 4 pup weights to be analyzed. The basic statistical question remains the same: Why aren't all 555 identical? One stimulus of interest is identified over which the researcher has control (different dose levels of the TA) and two random variations of chance that may influence the individual pup weight on PND 4: (1) the natural variation that occurs between litters (*between litters*), and (2) within the same litter, the natural variation that occurs between pups (*within litter*).

One approach to dealing with the litter effect is through litter-based analysis. In this approach, the litter effect is essentially eliminated by first calculating a mean pup weight per litter and then basing the statistical analysis on the litter means, rather than the individual pup weights. Essentially, this approach eliminates the within-litter random variation because there is only one observation, the average pup weight/litter, representing the litter. (Alternatively, we could randomly choose one pup from each litter to represent the litter.) As a result, there are only two sources of variation remaining (dose and between-litter), and the analysis proceeds with the ANOVA described in the "Case Study—General Toxicology Example" section.

More efficient use of the collected data is to utilize all 555 pup weights and incorporate the litter effect into the statistical analysis model. The individual pup weights can be modeled as:

$$\text{PND 4 male pup weight} = \mu + \text{Dose} + e_L + e_W \quad (18.5)$$

As described above, there are three identifiable reasons why all pup weights are not equal to μ: TA dose effect, between-litter variation (e_L), and within-litter variation (e_W). Although the theory (expected mean squares) behind it is beyond the scope of this chapter, the statistical test for evaluating the TA dose effect is MS_{Dose}/MS_{eL} or the ratio of the estimated variation due to the TA dose effect relative to the random variation between litters.

Consider the data displayed in Table 18.10. For this experiment, dams were treated with either a vehicle control or a low or high dose of drug. Six dams were randomly assigned to each of the three treatments. The weaning weights of the pups (with pup sex not considered) are displayed in the table. There is interest in determining the effect of treatment on weaning weight.

As discussed, EU is the dam or the litter. Therefore each treatment group has six EUs. The statistical analysis could continue using the average value for each litter or using the model described in Eq. (18.4).

Both methods will be illustrated. Fig. 18.8 shows the box plots of the weaning weight for each litter in the control group. The size of each box is representative of the variability within each litter, while the variability between litters is the variability between the "+" symbols in each box. The analysis of litter average values uses the "+" symbols within each treatment group in a one-way analysis of variance.

That analysis yields the results found in Table 18.11. The numerator degrees of freedom is the number of treatment groups −1, while the denominator degrees of freedom is the number of litters −1 times the number of treatment groups (5 times 3 = 15). That number assures us that the EU is indeed the litter. Finally, it can be determined if weaning weights increase or decrease in a dose-related fashion. Fig. 18.9 will illustrate that concept. While both the low and high dose of treatment appears to lower the weaning weight, it is clearly not by a significant amount. The formal statistical test of trend in Table 18.12 confirms the lack of statistical significance.

TABLE 18.10 Weaning Weight of Sprague–Dawley Rats

Treatment Group	Litter 1	Litter 2	Litter 3	Litter 4	Litter 5	Litter 6
Control	49.5	45.2	56.8	43	42.2	53.8
Control	51.5	37.2	59.7	47.7	38.4	47.0
Control	48.6	42.9		45.4	43.9	51.6
Control		45.6				50.8
Low	45.6	40.1	54.1	45.1	40.9	50.0
Low	48.6	40.8	57.4	48.7	36.3	47.8
Low	47.6	41.7		44.7	40.4	46.9
Low		40.5				
Low		40.7				
High	40.6	43.2	53.8	40.0	42.2	46.3
High	44.1	42.5	55.5	45.6	40.6	44.3
High	45.1	41.4		46.8	39.8	46.8
High		39.3			40.2	
High		40.0				

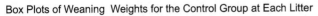

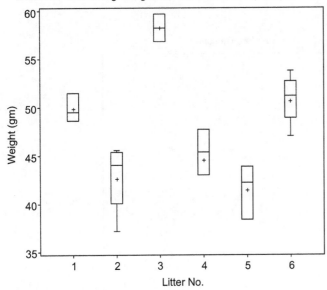

FIGURE 18.8 Box plots of weaning weights for the control group at each litter.

Using the more efficient statistical model in Eq. (18.5), the estimate of the within-litter variability is 5.03, while an estimate of the between-litter variability is 30.8. This agrees with Fig. 18.8 where the size of the boxes appear to be much smaller than the dispersion between the "+" symbols in each box. That analysis provides the results in Table 18.13.

Those results ($p = .6411$) are very similar to the analysis using the average litter values. The result of a test for dose-related trend, noted in Table 18.14, was very similar.

Fig. 18.9 shows that the difference between the vehicle control and the high-dose group is about 3 g. If there is interest in finding a statistical difference at that level many more litters would be required.

Case Study—Carcinogenicity Studies

The objective of long-term carcinogenesis bioassays is to evaluate the carcinogenic potential of a test article when administered over the normal lifetime of a rodent.

Standardized carcinogenicity studies in rodents include at least 50 animals/sex/group in three test article groups and a concurrent control group for 18–24 months (approximately the normal lifespan of a rodent). The high-dose level is generally selected to provide the maximum ability to detect test article-related carcinogenic effects while not causing excess toxicity. The objective of the lower doses is to provide information on the dose–response relationship of the test article. Further details of the study design can be found in "Guidance for Industry" [11]. For detailed discussions of the carcinogenicity study design from a statistical perspective, the reader is referred to Chow and Liu [12], Krewski and Franklin [13], and Gad [14].

A wide range of data is collected in a carcinogenicity study. Methods described earlier in this chapter are appropriate for the statistical analysis of body weight, organ weight, clinical pathology, abnormalities, and most other data collected in a carcinogenicity study. However, the evaluation of mortality and tumor data

TABLE 18.11   ANOVA Results

Test	Numerator D.F.[a]	Denominator D.F.[b]	F-value	Prob.[c] > F
Overall treatment	2	15	0.44	0.6502

[a]*Numerator Degrees of Freedom.*
[b]*Denominator Degrees of Freedom.*
[c]*Probability.*

TABLE 18.12   Trend Test Results

Test	Numerator D.F.[a]	Denominator D.F.[b]	F-value	Prob.[c] > F
Trend	1	15	0.88	0.3643

[a]*Numerator Degrees of Freedom.*
[b]*Denominator Degrees of Freedom.*
[c]*Probability.*

TABLE 18.13   ANOVA Results for Within- and Between-Litter Effects

Test	Numerator D.F.[a]	Denominator D.F.[b]	F-value	Prob.[c] > F
Overall treatment	2	15	0.46	0.6411

[a]*Numerator Degrees of Freedom.*
[b]*Denominator Degrees of Freedom.*
[c]*Probability.*

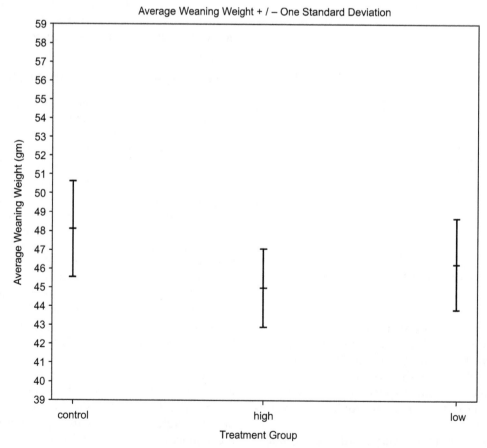

FIGURE 18.9   Average weaning weight.

TABLE 18.14   Trend Test Results for Within- and Between-Litter Effects

Test	Numerator D.F.[a]	Denomination D.F.[b]	F-value	Prob.[c] > F
Trend	1	15	0.90	0.3565

[a]Numerator Degrees of Freedom.
[b]Denominator Degrees of Freedom.
[c]Probability.

present statistical issues that are not only unique within the field of toxicology but, in the case of tumor data, unique to statistical applications in general. For that reason, focus in this section will be directed on the statistical analysis of mortality and tumor data collected from a 2-year rodent study.

Mortality

The reason the analysis of mortality in a 2-year rodent study is unique can be illustrated with two simple examples. The biological relevance of the mortality in two groups, both of which had 60% mortality during the course of a 2-year study, would not be considered negligible if all deaths in one group occurred in the first 50 weeks while all deaths in the second group occurred in the last 20 weeks. Thus statistical methods described earlier for dichotomous responses (dead vs. alive) are inadequate because they don't address the timing of the deaths.

Alternatively, one might consider an analysis of variance to evaluate the time to death. However, not all animals die within the 2-year study and to use any data value for such animals (eg, day of terminal sacrifice or day of terminal sacrifice + 1) introduces the potential for bias in the statistical analysis, particularly in a study design where as many as 50% of the control animals would be expected to be alive after 2 years.

In a standard 2-year carcinogenicity study some animals will die prior to the end of the study while others will remain alive up to the scheduled terminal sacrifice. In addition, a subset of animals may be scheduled for interim sacrifice at specified intervals during the study. Data from animals that live until a scheduled sacrifice are said to be right-censored. A censored observation is one in which the event has not occurred in the allotted time of the study. For these animals the most that can be said, in terms of the analysis endpoint time-to-death, is that they did not die in the allotted time up to their scheduled termination from the study. Statistical methods that take into account the continuous nature of the analysis endpoint, time to spontaneous death, while accounting for censored observations, are known as survival analyses. (Note: because accidental deaths are not considered spontaneous deaths, they are usually considered to be right-censored observations in the survival analysis.)

Although the term "survival" analysis seems appropriate for an evaluation of mortality, it is more specifically

an evaluation of "time-to-an-event." Here, the event is death other than accidental or scheduled termination. Other time-to-an-event endpoints occur in toxicology studies. For example, in a neurobehavioral water maze study the analysis endpoint might be the time it takes an animal to complete the water maze. Here, the analysis endpoint is the time-to-completion of the water maze, and some animals, particularly on their first attempt, may not achieve the event in the allotted time. Another example, discussed later in this section, is the time-to-tumor. These methods are referred to here, and in most toxicology textbooks, as survival analysis methods. Other statistical textbooks may refer to these as failure-time analysis methods.

Two nonparametric tests are commonly employed for survival analysis. These rank tests are censored data generalizations of two nonparametric tests: the log-rank test (also referred to as the generalized Savage test) and the generalized Wilcoxon test. The log-rank test can be thought of as the difference between the number of observed deaths and the number of expected deaths under the null hypothesis of equal survival time distributions. The Wilcoxon test can be thought of as a generalization of the uncensored Wilcoxon test in which the test statistic is the sum of scores assigned to censored and uncensored data individually.

Parametric models are also available but involve complicated distributions and may be difficult for the nonstatistician to implement and interpret. The reader is referred to Krewski and Franklin [13] for further details.

Tumor Data

On the surface, the evaluation of tumor data appears uncomplicated. Naively, one may consider the evaluation of liver adenomas to be a dichotomous response (present vs. not present) and proceed with analysis methods accordingly. However, the standard 2-year carcinogenicity study presents potential confounding factors that may make the simple evaluation of raw proportions of animals with a tumor not only inappropriate but misleading. For example, a rodent that lives for 104 weeks is more likely to develop a tumor than one that lives only 75 weeks, irrespective of exposure to treatment. Simply put, an animal that lives longer is more susceptible to spontaneous tumor development. This becomes relevant to the statistical analysis when a test article has an effect

TABLE 18.15   Example Tumor Incidence Rates

Example		# of Animals With Liver Adenoma/# of Necropsies (%)	
1	Week	Control group	Test-article group
	<80	1/10 [10]	9/40 [23]
	>80	9/40 [23]	1/10 [10]
	Total	10/50 [20]	10/50 [20]
2	<80	1/10 [10]	4/40 [10]
	>80	8/40 [20]	2/10 [20]
	Total	9/50 [18]	6/50 [12]

on the mortality of animals for reasons other than the tumorigenicity itself (competing risks).

Consider the examples presented in Table 18.15. In example 1, 20% of the animals in both the control and test-article group presented with liver adenomas at necropsy over the course of the 2-year study, suggesting no tumorigenic effect. However, breaking the proportions down according to necropsies that were conducted prior to and after week 80 suggests a different interpretation. Of the animals that died early, a larger percentage of test-article animals had the tumor, suggesting that the onset of the tumor may be faster with exposure to the test article.

Example 2 in Table 18.15 illustrates another example of potential bias. In this example, 18% of all control-group animals presented with the liver adenoma compared with only 12% of all test-article group animals, suggesting tumorigenicity was actually decreased by the test article. However, breaking it down according to the interval in which they were observed shows that the percentage of animals with the tumor was identical for test article and control both before and after week 80.

These examples illustrate how the overall incidence rate may present a biased interpretation of the tumorigenic effect in light of the potential for mortality due to competing risks. Therefore the rate of tumor onset, or age-specific rate of tumor incidence, is the most appropriate measure of tumorigenesis (Dinse [15]; McKnight and Crowley [16]; Malani and Van Ryzin [17]). But evaluating tumor onset rates presents another problem. With the exception of tumors that can be detected by palpation in-life (eg, skin and mammary gland tumors), the exact time of onset of a tumor is unknown. Rather, tumors are only detected through necropsy upon death or moribund sacrifice. Consider two animals in which the onset of a nonlethal tumor began at identical times (say, week 70). If one animal dies of a competing cause in week 75, its tumor will be detected earlier than the one that lives until terminal sacrifice at week 104.

To evaluate the rate of tumor onset, Peto et al. [18] proposed a statistical approach that takes into account

the context in which tumors were observed. Tumors that are not directly responsible for an animal's death are classified as incidental. Tumors that are directly responsible for an animal's death are classified as fatal. And tumors that can be detected in-life (eg, skin tumors) are classified as mortality-independent.

Under the assumption that the rate of tumor onset is the most appropriate measure of tumorigenesis, the concept behind the analysis of mortality-independent tumors is the easiest to understand. Only for mortality-independent tumors can the true onset time be defined with at least some degree of accuracy. For these tumors, Peto proposed the onset rate method, a statistical evaluation of the time to (age at) tumor onset. The onset rate method is essentially a variation of the survival analysis described earlier in the evaluation of mortality. In the evaluation of mortality the event of interest was the spontaneous death of an animal. In the onset rate tumor analysis, the event of interest is the detectable occurrence of the tumor itself. Relative to a specific tumor, each animal can be considered censored (death or sacrifice without the tumor) or uncensored (animal has tumor).

The evaluation of fatal tumors utilizes the same statistical concepts as that for mortality-independent tumors. This is sometimes difficult for the nonstatistician to understand. If the same statistical approach is used for a malignant lymphoma as that for a benign adenoma of the mammary gland, then why bother to categorize the tumors in the first place? The reason is that, although the statistical methodology is the same, the "event" in the time-to-event analysis is defined differently in the two approaches. While the onset rate analysis of tumors evaluates the time to "detectable occurrence" of a mortality-independent tumor, the death-rate analysis evaluates the time to "death" of the animal due to the fatal tumor.

The tumor type that presents the most challenge from a statistical perspective is the incidental tumor. Recall that the rate of tumor onset is the most appropriate measure of tumorigenesis. The onset of a mortality-independent tumor can be objectively determined with reasonable accuracy via palpation. The endpoint in the fatal tumor analysis (time of death) is very objective and, while the true onset time of a fatal tumor may be unknown, it is reasonable to assume that, for a given tumor, the time from onset to the animal's death is similar across different animals. That is, we can think of the fatal tumor methodology as an analysis of the onset time "offset" by a constant representing the amount of time it takes that tumor to kill an animal.

But whether or not an animal has an incidental tumor can only be determined when the animal is terminally sacrificed or dies due to competing causes. The time of onset cannot be objectively determined. The Peto et al. [18] solution is the prevalence method, which focuses on age-specific tumor prevalence rates to adjust for intercurrent mortality. Briefly, the study length is divided into fixed intervals and the prevalence rate of the incidental tumors among those animals that were necropsied are compared among groups within each interval. The results are then combined across the multiple intervals to yield an overall test statistic across the length of the study. By comparing animals only within an age-specific fixed interval, the analysis removes, to some degree, the potential bias of age-related tumor development. In other words, animals necropsied within a fixed interval have lived for approximately the same length of time.

The selection of fixed intervals is not as important as one might think. Peto et al. [18] suggested that each interval be:

> not so short that the prevalence of incidental tumors in the autopsies they contain is unstable, nor yet so large that the real prevalence in the first half of one interval could differ markedly from the real prevalence in the second half.

Peto et al. [18] described intervals based on an ad hoc runs procedure. Simpler to employ intervals in 2-year studies are described by the Center for Drug Evaluation and Research [1: 0–50 weeks, 51–80, 81–104, interim sacrifice (if any), and terminal sacrifice] and the National Toxicology Program [1: 0–52 weeks, 53–78, 79–92, 93–104, interim sacrifice (if any), and terminal sacrifice] [11].

One potential problem, noted by pathologists, with the tumor-context approach is that a tumor may be fatal for some animals and incidental for others. (Note that, by definition, a tumor found at the scheduled terminal sacrifice must be incidental since it did not directly cause the animal's death.) The solution is actually quite simple. Statistical methodology allows us to analyze the incidental tumors with the prevalence method and fatal tumors with the death-rate method and then combine to yield a single overall rate for the tumor.

Another issue of concern is the fact that an animal may have multiple occurrences of a specific tumor. For example, one animal may have multiple skin adenomas. Similarly, an animal may have a specific tumor that metastasizes to multiple organs. The solution is that, with respect to a specific tumor, each animal is counted only once in the statistical analysis. If a tumor is mortality-independent, the earliest occurrence would be noted. In the case of a metastatic tumor, only the site of origin would be statistically analyzed. A slight variation of this issue is presented by tumors such as leukemias or systemic tumors that attack the body as a whole rather than organ-specific. These types of tumors are generally grouped under a general, whole-body term such as "hemolymphoreticular neoplasm" or "systemic," or "whole body."

Another concern is the potential for missing true effects by treating each tumor/organ independent of one another. This issue was addressed by McConnell [19] who suggested evaluating relevant combinations. For example, statistical analysis may be conducted for the combination of adenomas and carcinomas in the liver or leiomyosarcomas in both the cervix and uterus. However, any statistical analysis of tumor/organ combinations must adhere to the "each animal counted only once" rule described above.

A statistical issue to which much literature has been devoted over the years is that of adjustments for multiple tests on tumor data. It is not uncommon for a 2-year carcinogenicity protocol to evaluate as many as 40 organs in each animal. Since the statistical analysis is conducted for each tumor type at each organ, the potential for false positives (statistically significant findings that are not real) is a valid concern. Numerous procedures have been proposed for controlling the overall false-positive rates (Lin and Ali [20] and Fairweather et al. [21]).

One common approach is to utilize multiple decision rules (significance levels) based on (1) the type of studies in the overall bioassay, (2) the spontaneous incidence rate of a tumor in historical control data, and (3) the statistical test (trend vs. pairwise comparison with control). For example, the 2001 Draft Guidance for Industry [11] proposes the following significance levels for standard 2-year studies in two species and two sexes: positive trend test—0.005 and 0.025 for common and rare tumors, respectively; pairwise comparisons with control—0.01 and 0.05 for common and rare tumors, respectively. A rare tumor is defined as one with a historical control rate of less than 1% (Haseman [22]). However, the reader should have a full understanding of current guidance relevant to their particular application. The same guidance summarizes alternative significance levels for ICH studies with one 2-year study in one species and one short- or medium-term study in another species.

It has become common practice, particularly since the issuance of the draft guidance [11], for pathologists to evaluate the context of each tumor during the course of a study. However, there are instances of studies where tumor context is not known. Bailer and Portier [25] proposed the poly-k tests, which adjust for intercurrent mortality without relying on tumor context for the statistical analysis. Briefly, the tests adjust the number of animals at risk as follows: an animal that completes the study through scheduled terminal sacrifice contributes $N=1$ to the number of animals at risk. All other animals that died or were moribund sacrificed prior to scheduled terminal sacrifice contribute $N=w(i)$, where $0 < w(i) < 1$. $w(i)$ is calculated for each individual animal (i) and based on how long the animal was in the study (ie, the longer the animal was in the study, the greater $w(i)$ with $w(i)$ approaching $N=1$ if the animal survived the majority of the study).

More information on the analysis of 2-year carcinogenity studies can be found in the following references: Chow and Liu [12], Krewski and Franklin [13], Gad [14], and Guidance for Industry [11].

Case Study—Endocrine Study (Female Pubertal Study)

As stated by the Environmental Protection Agency (EPA) [24], the purpose of the female pubertal assay is to help identify chemicals or mixtures that have the potential to interact with the endocrine system. The assay does this by trying to measure effects on pubertal development and thyroid function in the intact juvenile female rat. The EPA claims that this assay is capable of detecting antithyroid, estrogenic, or antiestrogenic chemicals that alter pubertal development via changes in luteinizing hormone, follicle stimulating hormone, prolactin or growth hormone levels, or via alterations in hypothalamic function.

The EPA has issued a set of standard evaluation procedures (SEPs) [25] that provide guidance for the evaluation of environmental and human health effects data submitted for the Endocrine Disruptor Screening Program (EDSP) Tier 1 battery. There is an individual SEP for each of the 11,890 Guideline Series EDSP Tier 1 assays that comprise the battery, including an SEP for the female pubertal assay. The SEPs provide fairly detailed instructions for the statistical treatment of the data resulting from these assays. However, it is valuable to illustrate these instructions using an example. Several of the procedures suggested for use may not be commonly used and understood by the toxicologist.

Data to be statistically analyzed include the organ weights, organ weight to necropsy body weight ratio (liver, kidneys, pituitary, and adrenal glands), daily body weights (including necropsy body weight), cumulative body weight gain, serum chemistries, hormones, age at vaginal opening, and body weight at vaginal opening. When an animal does not attain vaginal opening, PND 43 (last Study Day + 1) and body weight at necropsy will be used as the age and body weight at vaginal opening, respectively.

Each endpoint will be tested for homogeneity (equality) of variance using Levene's test [26]. If that test is significant at $p = .01$, then a log transform will be applied and Levene's test conducted on the transformed data. Testing at the $(p < .01)$ level is suggested because of the robustness of the analysis of variance to deviations from assumptions [8]. If that test is still significant then the square-root transformation will be applied to the raw data and Levene's test conducted again. If the test is still significant then a nonparametric test, as described below, will be used to analyze the data.

If the variances are homogeneous then an analysis of variance (ANOVA) will be conducted, on the raw or transformed data, as appropriate. The statistical model will contain a factor for treatment group and a blocking factor based on the time of study start. A two-sided Dunnett's test will be conducted, regardless of the outcome of the ANOVA, looking for significant differences in the test-article groups when compared with the vehicle control. If the transformations are unsuccessful in making the variances homogeneous then the nonparametric Kruskal–Wallis test will be used, ignoring the blocking factor, followed by Dunn's test, to compare each of the test-article groups with the vehicle control. Since these are preplanned pairwise comparisons, Dunn's test will be conducted regardless of the outcome of the Kruskal–Wallis test. The tests will be two-sided, at the 0.05 significance level, looking for significant differences from the vehicle control.

In addition, organ weights, age at vaginal opening, and body weight at vaginal opening will be subject to the following analyses if they meet the homogeneity of variance criteria:

1. Analysis of covariance (ANCOVA) with Dunnett's test. The model will be as described above for ANOVA with the exception that initial body weights, usually PND21, will be included as a covariate;
2. Linear trend test using the ANOVA model; and
3. Linear trend test using the ANCOVA model.

To illustrate the methodology, uterine wet-weight data from three treated groups (low, medium, and high doses) and a vehicle control will be used. In each of the groups there are five animals. All the animals started the study and stopped the study on the same days so that a blocking factor to account for different start times was not required.

As stated above, the first step is to examine the variability within each treatment group to ensure that the variability is similar within each group. When this is done using Levene's test it can be observed in Table 18.15 that the p-value is significant $(p < .01)$ for the untransformed data indicating that the variances in each of the treatment groups are significantly different. Fig. 18.10 displays the data distributions for each of the treatment groups.

The algorithm states that the data should be first transformed using the $\log_{10}$ function. As indicated earlier, $\log_{10}$(Wet Uterine Weight + 1) is used to avoid using the transformation on negative values. When Levene's test is applied to the transformed data, Table 18.16 shows that there is no evidence to conclude that the variance in each of the treatment groups is different $(p = .13)$.

The next step is to conduct an analysis of variance on the transformed data followed by Dunnett's test to compare treated groups to the vehicle control. Contrary to popular belief, Dunnett's test can be applied regardless of the outcome in the analysis of variance (Winer [27]).

Table 18.17 summarizes the results for Dunnett's test on the transformed data comparing all treatment groups to vehicle control.

Based on the results in Table 18.16 the conclusion can be made that the medium dose ($p = .0425$) and the high dose ($p = .0125$) are significantly different from the vehicle control. The average values indicate that both of those groups have wet uterine weights that are significantly lower than those in the vehicle control.

As previously stated, endpoints such as organ weights are subject to additional analyses. These include:

1. Analysis of covariance (ANCOVA) with Dunnett's test. The model will be as described above for ANOVA with the exception that PND 21 body weight will be included as a covariate;
2. Linear trend test using the ANOVA model; and
3. Linear trend test using the ANCOVA model.

For consistency, these additional analyses will be performed on the $\log_{10}$ transformed data because as established, the transformation provides equal variances between the treatment groups. The linear trend tests are simple linear contrasts of the treatment group average values.

The results from these additional analyses may be found in Tables 18.17 and 18.18.

In Table 18.18, it can be observed that the high-dose group is significantly different from control ($p = .029$). When the covariate is used in the model, the mid-dose group is no longer significantly different from control. In Table 18.19, the linear trend is statistically significant with and without the covariate. It is clear by observing the average value in both Tables 18.17 and 18.18 that the value of the $\log_{10}$ transformed uterine wet weights decreases in a linear fashion with respect to dose.

DISCUSSION

The statistical design and analysis of toxicology experiments vary depending on the nature and goal of the experiment. Experiments should be designed

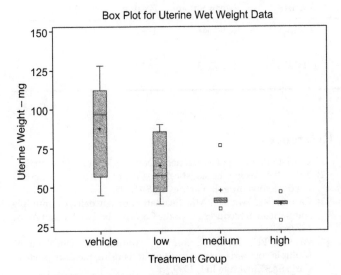

FIGURE 18.10 Box plot for the uterine wet-weight data.

TABLE 18.16 Levene's Test Results

Variable	Transformation	Source of Variability	Degrees of Freedom	Sum of Squares	Mean Square	F-value	p-value
Wet uterine weight	None—raw data	Treatment group	3	1730.5	576.8	6.22	0.0053
Wet uterine weight	None—raw data	Error	16	1483.5	92.7194	–	–
Wet uterine weight	$\log_{10}$	Treatment group	3	0.0714	0.0238	2.2	0.1275
Wet uterine weight	$\log_{10}$	Error	16	0.1729	0.0108	–	–

TABLE 18.17 Analysis Using Transformed Data

Variable	Transformation	Treatment Group	Average Value ($\log_{10}$ Scale)	Dunnett p-value
Wet uterine weight	$\log_{10}$	Vehicle control	1.977259	–
Wet uterine weight	$\log_{10}$	Low dose	1.790734	0.279
Wet uterine weight	$\log_{10}$	Mid dose	1.669898	0.0425
Wet uterine weight	$\log_{10}$	High dose	1.600379	0.0125

TABLE 18.18 Analysis Using Transformed Data

Variable	Transformation	Treatment Group	Adjusted Average Value[a] (log$_{10}$ scale)	Dunnett p-value
Wet uterine weight	Log$_{10}$	Vehicle control	1.961604	–
Wet uterine weight	Log$_{10}$	Low dose	1.778945	.3023
Wet uterine weight	Log$_{10}$	Mid dose	1.685167	.0945
Wet uterine weight	Log$_{10}$	High dose	1.612555	.0291

[a]Adjusted for the initial weight covariate.

TABLE 18.19 Testing for Trend

Variable	Transformation	Test Type	Degrees of Freedom	Sum of Squares	Mean Square	F-value	p-value
Wet uterine weight	Log$_{10}$	Linear trend **without** covariate	1	0.391548	0.391548	11.87	.0033
Wet uterine weight	Log$_{10}$	Linear trend **with** covariate	1	0.287123	0.287123	8.53	.0106

properly, so that valid conclusions can be made without wasting precious resources. Statistical tests should be implemented so as to properly account for the experimental design.

To appreciate the differences between the various experiments, a basic understanding of statistical concepts is required. We can then appreciate the different characteristics of each experimental area that require specialized statistical methods.

Testing for trends evaluates whether or not increasing doses of a therapeutic agent elicit increasing effects. Often trend tests provide a more powerful test in comparison with making multiple tests against the vehicle. Repeated measures procedures are useful when the data are collected from an individual animal over multiple time points. Statistical methods in DART studies may be complicated due to the fact that the litter effect often must be taken into consideration. Long-term carcinogenity studies require statistical methods that handle the tumors appropriately and are able to accommodate the time of death or tumor onset. Specialized studies such as endocrine disrupter experiments have specialized methods for testing distributional assumptions, as suggested by regulatory agencies, which may not be familiar to nonstatisticians. The use of these special cases has been illustrated in case studies.

Finally, this chapter was intended to provide a basic foundation of statistical principles to enable the reader to critically appraise the design, conduct, statistical methodology, and interpretation of toxicology studies in the literature and in a regulatory environment. References have been provided to allow the interested reader to pursue topics in greater detail.

References

[1] Cox DR. Planning of experiments. New York: John Wiley; 1958.
[2] Tukey JW. Testing the statistical certainty of a response to increasing doses of a drug. Biometrics 1985;41:295.
[3] Carmer SG, Swanson MR. Evaluation of ten pairwise multiple comparison procedures by Monte Carlo methods. J Am Stat Assoc 1973;68:314.
[4] Westfall PH, Tobias R, Rom D, Wolfinger R, Hochberg Y. Multiple comparisons and multiple tests using the SAS® system. Cary: SAS® Institute Inc.; 1999.
[5] Hochberg Y, Tamhane AC. Multiple comparison procedures. New York: John Wiley; 1987.
[6] Hsu JC. Multiple comparisons: theory and methods. London: Chapman and Hall; 1996.
[7] Snedecor GW, Cochran WG. Statistical methods. 7th ed. Ames: The Iowa State University Press; 1980.
[8] Box GEP. Nonnormality and tests on variances. Biometrika 1953;40:318.
[9] Selwyn MR. Preclinical safety assessment. Biopharmaceutical statistics for drug development. New York: Marcel Dekker, Inc.; 1988. p. 231.
[10] Hoffman W, Lee C, Chiang A, Guo K, Ness D. Some statistical considerations in nonclinical safety assessment. In: Dmitrienko A, Chuang-Stein C, editors. Pharmaceutical statistics using SAS. Cary: SAS Institute Inc.; 2007. p. 97.
[11] Guidance for Industry. Statistical aspects of the design, analysis, and interpretation of chronic rodent carcinogenicity studies of pharmaceuticals. US Department of Health and Human Services, Food and Drug Administration, Center for Drug Evaluation and Research; May 2001. Draft.
[12] Chow S-C, Liu J-P. Design and analysis of animal studies in pharmaceutical development. New York: Marcel Dekker, Inc.; 1998.
[13] Krewski D, Franklin C. Statistics in toxicology. New York: Gordon and Breach Science Publishers; 1991.
[14] Gad SC. Statistics and experimental design for toxicologists and pharmacologists. Boca Raton: Taylor and Francis; 2006.
[15] Dinse GE. A comparison of tumor incidence analyses applicable in single sacrifice animal experiments. Stat Med 1994;13:689–708.

[16] McKnight B, Crowley J. Tests for differences in tumor incidence based on animal carcinogenesis experiments. J Am Stat Assoc 1984;79:639–48.

[17] Malani HM, Van Ryzin J. Comparison of two treatments in animal carcinogenicity experiments. J Am Stat Assoc 1988;83:1171–7.

[18] Peto R, Pike MC, Day NE, Gray RG, Lee PN, Parish S, et al. Guidelines for simple, sensitive significance tests for carcinogenic effects in long-term animal experiments. Lyon (France): International Agency for Research on Cancer (IARC); 1980. p. 311–426. IARC Monographs on the Evaluation of the Carcinogenic Risk of Chemicals to Humans. Long and short-term screening assays for carcinogens: a critical appraisal, 2, Supplement WHO Publications Center, Albany, New York.

[19] McConnell EE, Solleveld HA, Swenburg JA, Boorman GA. Guidelines for combining neoplasms for evaluation of rodent carcinogenesis studies. J Natl Cancer Inst 1986;76(2):283–9.

[20] Lin KK, Ali MW. Statistical review and evaluation of animal tumorigenicity studies. Statistics in the pharmaceutical industry. In: Buncher CR, Tsay JY, editors. Revised and expanded. 2nd ed. New York: Marcel Dekker, Inc.; 1994.

[21] Fairweather WR, Bhattacharyya PP, Ceuppens PP, Heimann G, Hothorn LA, Kodell RL, et al. Biostatistical methodology in carcinogenicity studies. Drug Inf J 1998;32:401–21.

[22] Haseman JK. A reexamination of false-positive rates for carcinogenesis studies. Fundam Appl Toxicol 1983;3:334–9.

[23] Bailer A, Portier C. Effects of treatment-induced mortality on tests for carcinogenicity in small samples. Biometrics 1988;44:417–31.

[24] Endocrine Disruptor Screening Program Test Guidelines. OPPTS 890.1450: pubertal development and thyroid function in intact juvenile/peripubertal female rats. October 2009.

[25] Pubertal Development and Thyroid Function in Intact Juvenile/Peripubertal Female Rats Assay. Ocspp guideline 890.1450, standard evaluation procedure (SEP), endocrine disruptor screening program. Washington (DC 20460): US Environmental Protection Agency; August 2011.

[26] Levene H. Robust tests for equality of variances. In: Olkin I, editor. Contributions to probability and statistics. Palo Alto, CA: Stanford University Press; 1960.

[27] Winer BJ. Statistical principles in experimental design. 2nd ed. New York: McGraw-Hill; 1971.

CHAPTER

19

Regulatory Toxicology

J.W. Kille

INTRODUCTION

Regulations consist of requirements governments impose on private firms and individuals intended to be for the public good, and include, among others, better and cheaper services and goods, cleaner water and air, safer workplaces and products, and for the pharmaceutical industry and medically ailing public, safer and more effective drugs [1].

The regulation of the nonclinical (preclinical) development of new pharmaceuticals, both small molecule and biologics, has often been prompted by tragic events that caused suffering and even death. It has evolved considerably over the last 100-plus years or so, with the

A Comprehensive Guide to Toxicology in Nonclinical Drug Development, Second Edition
http://dx.doi.org/10.1016/B978-0-12-803620-4.00019-0

499

enactment of laws and defining regulations, and the development of guidelines for the design and implementation of appropriate nonclinical studies (performed under good laboratory practices to ensure the quality of the data) that are intended to establish the safety and effectiveness of a drug before administering it to humans. These studies, primarily in animals, but also in vitro, ex vivo and in silico, are done prior to treatment in man in support of safe exposure for subjects/patients in clinical trials and later for those in the patient populations. These guidelines provide direction for determining what types of studies are most likely to provide the types and quantities of data necessary for regulatory decisions and to minimize the risk of first exposing man to this novel compound in clinical trials. If the drug succeeds in gaining market approval, these nonclinical studies serve as a scientific foundation, which, in concert with the clinical trial data, is intended to provide confidence that the ultimate patient population will derive benefit from treatment that outweighs possible side effects.

This chapter is intended to provide the newer pharmaceutical or biotechnology toxicologist with a background understanding of the events that have prompted the regulation of drug development. Further, it describes how such regulations have been interpreted and shows how they effect changes in the way science is done, so that evermore efficacious and safer drugs are provided to treat patients who need them.

International agreements on the various drug development procedures have been achieved and harmonized guidances have been produced. This chapter reviews the evolution of those international guidances and recent revisions, and their implementation by the toxicologist. Nonclinical toxicology today has a global imprint both in practice and consequence. This chapter assumes that international purpose, primarily from a US (FDA) drug development point of view.

HISTORY OF REGULATIONS: WHY DO WE NEED THEM?

Brief Selective History of Drug Events Leading to Regulations and Toxicology Guideline Development

Why do we even think of toxicology, the study of poisons, in the same context as the development of pharmaceuticals, the activity of producing chemical or biological agents that diagnose, prevent, cure, or mitigate disease? They seem to be totally opposite concepts of what pharmaceutical agents are supposed to do. Nevertheless, the author's early personal experience in the pharmaceutical industry revealed that pharmacological activity and

toxicology go hand in hand, and that if you can't establish toxicity, chances are that a compound may also not be much of a drug, since both require effects on biological function. Yet the other side of that same coin is that the effects of extracts from dangerous animal venoms and various plants have been known from antiquity to the present day to be the source of remedies as well as poisons, and poisons are described along with medical remedies in various medical treatises from ancient Egypt through the Middle Ages and the Age of Enlightenment to modern times. This association between therapeutic and toxic outcomes of a chemical was the basis of the toxicologist's mantra, formulated by Paracelsus (1493–1541) when he stated:

> All substances are poison; there is none that is not a poison. The right dose differentiates a poison and a remedy.

About three centuries later, Orfila (1787–1853), a Spanish physician, was an avid proponent of the experimental pursuit of answers to questions of chemical activity in biological systems. He studied the harmful (as well as therapeutic) effects of chemicals in dogs and developed many assays that advanced the sciences of medicine and toxicology. He believed that analysis of a chemical in a victim's tissue (unheard of in those days) was essential for establishing the relationship between poisonous symptoms and the presence of a chemical in the body [2].

Development of the microscope by Robert Hooke in 1665 and the description of cells and bacteria by van Leeuwenhoek (1667) opened up a completely new world, and, in turn, new theories of biology. As the cellular theory of biological organization was being formulated, toxic responses were beginning to be understood in terms of a chemical reacting with some specific component of the cell. However, therapeutic remedies, for the most part, were still typically based on compounds from natural sources and age-old empirical recipes. While there was certainly some knowledgeable insight into which extracts from what sources would produce desired healthful (or antihealthful in the case of poisons) effects, which continued from ancient times, there wasn't much understanding of how a supposedly therapeutic concoction actually worked at the cellular or chemical stage. Therefore since there wasn't much understanding of a remedy's action, there wasn't much capability to improve upon the therapeutic benefit, except by empirical testing and deductive reasoning (the "practice" of medicine). The concept of asking a question, forming a hypothesis, conducting experiments based on that hypothesis, drawing conclusions, and forming a theory, ie, the scientific method, was taking shape, but was not embraced by all scientists. If we take a look at one example of how scientific advances of that time eventually brought about a giant step in health improvement, we can then ask how such a therapeutic advance, burgeoning with new knowledge and anticipation, could lead to some very serious health consequences prompting government action.

Let's consider how the discovery of the germ theory of disease factored into the earliest recognition of the need for regulatory intervention and guidance. It wasn't until the discovery of the microbial causes of infectious diseases that it was possible to consider how to develop specific chemical or biological measures to counteract the infectious agents. This concept, that specific microorganisms were responsible for specific diseases, was a significant advancement in medicine, and it didn't come about easily.

From Biblical times through the Middle Ages and up to the late 1600s and beyond it was believed that living matter could arise by spontaneous generation. In other words, some life forms arose spontaneously from non-living matter. The practice of science was primarily one of observation, conjecture, perhaps deductive reasoning, and for the most part was usually consistent with the cultural and religious views of the day. For example, it might be observed that if meat was left on the counter to rot, eventually maggots appeared on the meat. People, including scientists, commonly believed that maggots arose spontaneously from the rotten meat. However, the Italian physician Francesco Redi in 1668 went against commonly accepted scientific beliefs and developed the hypothesis that the maggots emerged from eggs that flies had laid on the meat. Not only was his hypothesis contrary to common scientific thought, but he pressed on and sought to prove his hypothesis by experimentation, in those days an uncommon approach to revealing nature's truth.

He tested his hypothesis by placing rotted meat in different flasks, some of which were sealed completely, while others were open to allow the meat to be exposed to air to be sure air was available for spontaneous generation if necessary, and still others were covered with gauze to allow air to enter, but, to prove Redi's point, prevent flies from gaining access to the meat. Thus his experimental scheme included both test and control flasks. When maggots only appeared on meat that was completely exposed and accessible, and not on meat in the completely closed flasks or the ones open but covered with gauze, he clearly demonstrated that the maggots didn't arise spontaneously from the rotting meat itself. Nor did they arise from the combination of air and meat in the gauze-covered flasks, but only arose from the meat in those flasks where eggs had been deposited on the meat by flies. Nevertheless, despite his well-conceived and executed experiments, the belief in spontaneous generation didn't die easily. Even Redi believed that spontaneous generation occurred under certain circumstances. However, despite Redi successfully designing and executing one of the first examples of a modern-day experiment, other scientists of the day performed different experiments that could be interpreted as supportive of spontaneous generation. Whether certain living matter could arise by spontaneous generation proved to be a popular and heated topic of debate for several decades [3].

Over 150 years later a young chemist who had developed an interest and reputation in using science to solve practical problems, found that his scientific skills and insights were sought out to assist in solving problems related to various industrial practices that had economic value. Louis Pasteur was not a licensed physician, the supposed epitome (at least to licensed physicians) of training in the life sciences in the mid-nineteenth century, but he was a trained physicist and chemist and one of the earliest to promote crystallography as important to understanding chemical composition (the subject of his physics thesis) [4]. As an industrial chemist his scientific diligence and his ability to bring together his observations and insights into cohesive deductions lent themselves well to addressing the question of spontaneous generation. This still had not been resolved, even after this expanse of time since Redi's simple but elegant experiments with rotten meat and maggots in the previous century. Disparate views were widespread among different groups of scientists. To make matters worse, the subject of spontaneous generation was one where science, philosophy, and religion all merged, leading to much heat and debate among the proponents of various views. This subject of spontaneous generation had gained such a level of interest and widely divergent followers, even among scientists both for and against, that the French Academy of Sciences sponsored a contest aimed at proving or disproving it. Louis Pasteur was among the contestants. He designed an experiment to disprove spontaneous generation, and show that there were invisible living microorganisms in the air. Furthermore, if these organisms were prevented from entering a flask containing boiled broth, that nothing would spontaneously generate in the broth. New life could not emerge from dead matter, only from other living organisms. To prove this, he heated and bent the neck of a flask containing boiled meat broth into an S shape so that air could enter the neck, but any organisms in the air would settle in the first bend of the S and not gain entry to the broth. Under these circumstances, nothing grew in the broth, as he predicted. However, if he tilted the flask so the broth reached the first bend where his supposed microorganisms from the air would have settled, the broth became contaminated and cloudy from the growth of the microorganisms. This experiment not only won the Academy's prize, the Prix Alhumbert in

1862, it disproved the existence of spontaneous generation and showed that microorganisms are everywhere, even in the air. Furthermore, it demonstrated that new living matter had to have arisen from some other living organism. Nevertheless, it took Pasteur many more experiments to convincingly prove to his peers that if germs are completely excluded, spontaneous generation did not occur.

Pasteur was not only very inquisitive as a basic scientist, but also very adept at deriving valuable insights from his observations, many of which provided practical solutions to industrial problems. His experiments showing that there were organisms in the air led to his being able to solve some vexing problems in the wine industry. He studied various wine diseases and isolated a variety of microorganisms. After some time he determined that each disease was associated with a particular microorganism. Eventually, Pasteur extended his belief to postulate that microorganisms were also the cause of infectious animal and human diseases, and that each particular human disease was caused by a specific microorganism. The result was the germ theory of infectious disease [3].

Pasteur explored this theory by conducting research on animal diseases. At one point, he and the German physician, Robert Koch, independently investigated various aspects of the etiology of the disease anthrax, both of them identifying the causative microorganism, the anthrax bacillus. Koch was able to show that sheep could not only get anthrax from other sheep, but also from the soil. This was because, as Koch was the first to show in 1876, the anthrax bacillus formed spores that can reside in the soil for years [5]. Pasteur, at this time, was also working on anthrax and published several papers. Between them, they clearly explained the etiology of anthrax, and proved that the bacillus was the causative agent, thus firmly establishing the germ theory of disease [6].

Pasteur, like all scientists, built his theories on the previous work of others. He was well aware of the earlier work of Dr. Edward Jenner (1749–1823) who discovered that exposure to similar less virulent viruses could provide immunity against related virulent strains. In the late 1800s, Pasteur followed this line of thinking and discovered not only that different strains had different degrees of virulence and still conferred their immunity, but even that the virulence of a single strain of disease organism varied, producing less virulent forms of the same strain over time. Some forms could also be purposely attenuated such that they became less virulent. Although they were less virulent in producing disease, these forms nevertheless maintained many of their other characteristics. This phenomenon, if true, was ripe for experimentation. After injecting animals with the less virulent attenuated form of anthrax he found that the injected animals were resistant to the fully virulent strain of the disease organism. In the early 1880s he conducted a large experiment in which he inoculated many sheep with attenuated, ie, low virulence, anthrax. Another ("control") group of sheep was not inoculated with anthrax, even the attenuated variety. After 12 days, both groups were injected with a fully virulent strain of anthrax. All of the sheep vaccinated with the attenuated virus survived and remained healthy, while every one of the unvaccinated sheep died [6]. Thus the theory was proved, that a disease was not only the result of an infection with a particular microorganism, but that one could prevent this disease by immunization with a variant form of the microorganism. Here was the cause of the disease, the microorganism itself, being used to prevent the disease. This provided a much refined vision of immunization and, with it, the potential for application to a variety of diseases and the use of a biological agent targeted against a specific organism as a therapeutic. Through the work of Pasteur, Koch, and other prominent scientists of the late nineteenth and early twentieth centuries, medical knowledge of human infectious diseases such as cholera, typhoid, tetanus, and others advanced significantly, and the results of their research showed that vaccination with specific microorganisms had the potential to become an important new means of disease treatment and prevention for humans.

This wasn't the earliest use of a vaccine to prevent disease. It was already known long before the 1600s that people could prevent smallpox if they inoculated themselves by nasally inhaling powdered smallpox scabs as the Chinese had been doing since the mid-1500s. Similar results could be obtained by inoculating with crude tissue or fluid samples from the pustules of mild cases of smallpox, as had been practiced in Turkey and India. Dr. Edward Jenner (mentioned above) heard the common knowledge while growing up in England that milkmaids who got mild cases of cowpox did not get smallpox. Then in 1796 he showed that inoculation with the less virulent, but similar, cowpox provided immunity to the smallpox virus (this was based on clinical responses since actual viruses had not yet been identified). He first tried this on an 8-year-old boy, by injecting him with cowpox, then later with active smallpox, and the boy didn't get the disease. Jenner submitted a paper describing this experiment to the Royal Society in 1797, but they thought this was too revolutionary and wanted more proof. Jenner performed the experiment on several other children, including his own 11-month-old son (!), all with success. He was ridiculed greatly for these experiments, not so much for trying them on his son and other children, but by many, especially clergy, who thought that inoculating someone with material from a diseased animal was repulsive and ungodly. A satirical cartoon about Jenner's work in 1802 depicted a cowpox-inoculated patient sprouting cow's limbs and heads. Nevertheless, the success of these experiments became obvious and vaccination against smallpox became widespread. Jenner called this a "vaccination" after the Latin word *vacca* for cow [7].

So, Pasteur's work wasn't nearly the earliest demonstration that a vaccine made from the disease could immunize others against the same disease. But his research greatly refined and focused the concept of vaccine therapeutics by identifying the specific microorganism (germ) that could be used to develop a vaccine against a specific disease. Out of respect for Jenner's discovery, Pasteur adopted his term, vaccination, for immunization against any disease [8,9].

The advantage of vaccination in conquering these diseases was clinically obvious, and was the medical wonder of the day. However, with little actual experience in developing and using vaccines, there was correspondingly little or no experience in the possible adverse effects of using such therapeutics. Unfortunately, the medical community and the public were soon to become enlightened about the possible downsides of these breakthroughs.

Brief Selective History of Food Events Leading to Regulations and Toxicology Guideline Development

Throughout this same period of the nineteenth and early twentieth centuries when great discoveries were advancing medicine, other events were taking place that also garnered much public attention, such as the automobile, powered flight, and the rapid expansion of the industrial revolution. During this exciting time for science and technology, and even earlier, researchers and authors were demonstrating that there was a darker side to this new lifestyle. Unbeknownst to most consumers, the foods they were eating were often contaminated, purposely or through sloppy practices, with debris, filth, animal waste, toxic chemicals, and other noxious substances, and were otherwise adulterated in ways that made consuming those foods unhealthy.

Of course, there is a long and fascinating history of natural poisons being used deliberately in criminal acts including political assassination and intrigue, and other instances where food has been used as the principal delivery agent for other poisonous substances even to this day. The advantage of putting poison in foods was that until the mid-1800s there was no real test for most poisons. With a little discretion and deceit, killers using poison knew that it was unlikely they would be caught.

Once a test for arsenic was developed in the 1850s, however, one could test for the substance in the tissues of the deceased as evidence that the individual had been poisoned. Tests for the presence of other poisonous substances soon followed.

But what about the adulteration of foods with substances that are not intentionally meant as poisons, but which turn out to be toxic, perhaps deadly? There is literature dating back to the ancient Greeks and Romans documenting the practice by wine merchants of adding noxious herbs to wine to give it a more beautiful color, but also making it a more toxic drink, presaging concerns of modern times about food dyes and other food additives [10]. Food adulteration occurs to this day as it has throughout history.

Adulteration and misbranding of foods and drugs had long been a part of the American cultural scene, but the seriousness of the problem increased by the late 1800s. By this time science had advanced significantly in its ability to detect this sort of fraud, so perhaps the reason things seemed to get worse in the late nineteenth century was simply that there were now scientific means to detect the fraud. In addition, legitimate manufacturers were becoming more concerned that these fraudulent goods would capture a significant portion of their markets. Often the deception was a matter of using less expensive ingredients in order to increase the profit margin. For example, medicines utilizing quinine-containing cinchona bark powder were clinically effective. Also, the medicines were much more profitable, but much less therapeutically effective, if the medically active cinchona powder was cut with just about any other powder source similar to what is done with illegal street drugs today. In the case of foods, high-quality wheat flour could be mixed with alum and clay to increase profits, but provided inferior baked goods [11].

Around the end of the nineteenth century, a chemist in the US Department of Agriculture by the name of Harvey Washington Wiley, following in the footsteps of his predecessor at the Bureau of Chemistry, Peter Collier, became increasingly concerned about the nonfood ingredients that were being added to foods. In particular, certain preservatives were being added that he felt were making people sick. Refrigeration was in its infancy, so food was canned, or kept from perishing by salting or sugaring, smoking, or some other means. Discovery and use of preservatives was obviously very important to the food industry, but there were then no laws limiting what, or how much, could be added to foods, and no requirements that these additives be identified on the label, or that the food products be tested for safety before being put on the market and consumed. Food manufacturers, processors, and packers could do whatever they wanted.

Wiley became very concerned about what food makers were putting into foods and expressed this with great zeal to government officials in an attempt to get them to pass laws against this practice. Congress didn't immediately pass the laws Wiley desired, but they did appropriate $5000 to the Bureau of Chemistry to study chemical preservatives and colors and their effects on digestion and health. He set about to test these preservatives and other chemicals he considered food adulterants to prove they were dangerous. But he decided to test them not in animals, but in people. Defined toxicology animal studies, lab tests, government or public oversight of food safety didn't exist. He formed squads of healthy male employees ("volunteers") who agreed, in the interest of science, to eat meals containing elevated levels of various compounds such as borax (used to preserve meat), formaldehyde (used to keep old milk from souring; preservation was cheaper than pasteurization [12]), copper sulfate (to restore color to canned vegetables) as well as other compounds such as salicylic acid and saccharin. Each squad focused on a single contaminant. They became popularly known as Wiley's "Poison Squads" (Fig. 19.1) and were the subject of frequent newspaper articles.

At one point, one of the squad members, probably in protest as they were getting sicker, wrote up one of their meals containing various servings of borax in the style of a Christmas restaurant menu:

Apple Sauce, Borax,
Soup, Borax,
Turkey, Borax,
Canned Stringed Beans,
Sweet Potatoes,
White Potatoes,
Turnips, Borax,

FIGURE 19.1　Harvey Wiley's Poison Squads. Harvey Wiley, third from right, is photographed with his staff from the Division of Chemistry, US Department of Agriculture, not long after he arrived in Washington in 1883. *Reproduced from* http://www.fda.gov/AboutFDA/WhatWeDo/History/Origin/ucm124403.htm.

Chipped Beef,
Cream Gravy,
Cranberry Sauce,
Celery,
Pickles,
Rice Pudding,
Milk,
Bread and Butter,
Tea, Coffee,
A Little Borax [10].

This got picked up amusingly by journalists, but only served to emphasize Wiley's point that people were getting sick unaware that the causative agents were the dangerous chemicals that manufacturers were putting in their food.

Ever since an alarmist's book was published in England in 1820, it was well known in Britain that food was being adulterated, sometimes with dangerous compounds such as lead, copper, and cyanide-rich laurel leaves simply to improve its appearance or color. This led to the first British law regulating food safety being passed in 1860, but no such law was forthcoming in the United States until the early twentieth century.

None of the men in Wiley's Poison Squads died, but after consuming some of the preservatives, eg, benzoic acid, they lost weight, were nauseous, and several became so sick they had to drop out of the studies, exactly what Wiley figured were possible outcomes of consumers eating those foods. The point of Wiley's studies with his Poison Squads was to raise awareness of the problems of food adulteration, to show that these additives were dangerous, and to build support among lawmakers for national food and drug laws. Despite his aggressive advocacy, Wiley couldn't get Congress to pass substantive laws. A.W. Dunn in an article about Wiley noted [13]:

> He is the victim of his own earnest efforts to enforce the law and to protect the people against those who seek the special privilege of selling fraudulent foods and impure drugs.

But this was now a topic of popular interest, thanks to newspaper and magazine journalists who followed Wiley's experiments closely.

At around the same time, in 1906, Upton Sinclair's book *The Jungle* was published. It described the terrible living and working conditions, and the hopelessness of the workers in the powerful and corrupt Chicago meatpacking industry as well as the filthy food products that were being produced and sold. Sinclair was a socialist and wanted to raise public alarm and indignation about how the powerful capitalist industry exploited poor, often immigrant workers. *The Jungle* succeeded in raising public alarm and outrage, however, not so much for the deplorable plight of the workers as Sinclair had hoped, but rather for the disgusting offal and filthy byproducts being passed off as healthy food for public consumption (Fig. 19.2). Sinclair later commented "I aimed at the public's heart, and by accident I hit it in the stomach" [14].

The Jungle and the common sentiment it raised proved to be the impetus for Congress to act on Wiley's desire for laws protecting the consuming public from adulterated foods. Appropriate legislation was eventually forthcoming. Four years after the Poison Squads began their work, the Pure Food and Drugs Act of 1906 (referred to by some as the "Wiley Act") empowered the Bureau of Chemistry of the Department of Agriculture, of which Wiley was chief, to oversee and enforce the actions specified in the law [10,15].

Misbranding and Deception Not Limited to Foods

The problems associated with adulteration and misbranding with potentially dangerous consequences applied not only to foods. Early drugs were also the focus of those who tried to make their fortunes by passing off altered or misbranded concoctions, or even compilations of mystery ingredients, as actual medicine, called "patent medicines." Although some of these medicines did provide healing effects, the majority made great claims of miraculous health cures for

FIGURE 19.2 Poster for the movie "The Jungle" (1914) based on Upton Sinclair's book of the same title (1906). Upton Sinclair actually appeared at the beginning and end of the movie to give the story credence. *Reproduced from* http://www.fda.gov/AboutFDA/What-WeDo/History/Origin/ucm054819.htm.

these syrups, elixirs, tablets, and powders, but produced none. Very few were ever actually patented. Patent medicines were marketed as such because they included "secret" ingredients and could be purchased over the counter without a doctor's prescription (to this day, we still see outrageous claims for some products available over the counter, or more commonly on the internet, and a significant portion of the public are still willing to believe them). These patent medicines were the stuff of so-called "wonder cures," but were also the cause of tragic events that even included death. As science was advancing, the patent medicine business continued to be perpetrated by charlatans until scientific evidence-based medicines appeared in the late 1800s as a result of the recognition of the germ theory of disease and the application of the scientific method to drug development [16].

Deception and dishonesty with medicines also extended into the biologics used for immunizations since the smallpox antitoxin days. As far back as the first smallpox vaccine in the late 1700s, there were shysters who knowingly peddled ineffective sera as the real drug. However, smallpox, cholera, diphtheria, and others were such devastating and often deadly diseases that the government, wanting to protect the public, realized that people wouldn't bother being vaccinated if they couldn't rely on that drug to provide immunization. In addition, they might have bad effects from the illicit drug even though it had no curative benefit. Most control of misbranded drugs in those days was meted out by individual states, with much inconsistency among them. In the interest of promoting general public health and preventing another smallpox epidemic, the federal government enacted a law to encourage smallpox vaccination. Thus was initiated the Vaccine Act of 1813, the first federal law dealing with consumer protection related to therapeutics [11]. This law didn't actually define any procedures to ensure that the vaccine itself was safe, however, but promoted safety and effectiveness indirectly by formalizing the labeling, handling, and distribution of the vaccine. The smallpox vaccine had to be certified as genuine, and was only to be distributed in person or through the post office by a federal agent appointed by the President. This agent had to swear an oath to provide only genuine vaccine, and was allowed to deliver it only after signing the package with his written name and the written word "vaccination," thus the first label verification of the authenticity of the vaccine contained within. There was much discussion as to whether this was the proper role of the federal government at this point in the nation's development. Politically there was still much sentiment about keeping the influence of the federal government small and not overly powerful in those early days. The Act was repealed in 1822 and regulation of the vaccine was turned over to the states, but the federal government remained the primary authority for imported foods and drugs.

This chain of events set a precedent for situations where the federal government could step in to provide direction as a means of protecting the health of the public, and this led to the subsequent Pure Food and Drugs Act of 1906 (Fig. 19.3). This was not only a result of Harvey Wiley's poison squad experiments on food adulterations, but also of publications on medicines of the day by muckraker/investigative journalists such as Samuel Hopkins Adams. He wrote a series of articles for *Collier's Weekly* in 1905, titled "The Great American Fraud," in which he exposed the outrageous claims made for patent medicines and indicated that many

of these, instead of improving, were actually damaging the health of their users. However, this 1906 Food and Drugs law did not create the Food and Drug Administration (FDA)—that was to come later in 1930. Instead, it empowered the Bureau of Chemistry within the Department of Agriculture (of which Wiley was chief) to inspect meat products, and it prohibited the manufacture, sale, or transportation across state lines of adulterated or misbranded food products and poisonous patent medicines. Furthermore, it required that medicines and liquors had to contain a label specifying their ingredients [12]. Thus the Pure Food and Drugs Act of 1906 was driven both by serious human effects from misbranding, from chemical additives in foods, as well as tragic incidents involving drugs. It was the first of a series of significant consumer protection laws enacted in the twentieth century. Ultimately the Bureau of Chemistry was moved out of the Department of Agriculture, at which point it left behind its insecticide oversight responsibilities and eventually became the Food and Drug Administration.

Thus the seeds of regulatory empowerment for both the food and pharmaceutical industries were planted.

Human Tragedies Spark the Need for Tougher Food and Drug Regulations

Diphtheria Antitoxin

Early in the 1900s the idea of vaccination was still scientifically undeveloped as an avenue of therapeutic intervention. Microbiology and immunology were still somewhat nascent scientific and medical pursuits. Certainly, many of the nuances of the manufacture of vaccines were still to be uncovered and understood, so the degree to which these factors could affect safety and efficacy was not fully appreciated. There were no guidelines or standards for how to produce vaccines of a certain specificity or uniformity from batch to batch. It's not surprising that the potency and quality of vaccines varied widely—so too did their safety.

A diphtheria outbreak, a disease affecting primarily young children, reached epidemic proportions in St. Louis in 1901 and was treated with an antitoxin derived from the serum of horses. The antiserum was produced locally by establishments that had no uniform controls for dealing with any aspect of collecting and storing the sera, no required analysis of the sera for appropriate antibodies, titer, or contaminants, nor apparently even any standards of the health and well-being of the animals that were the sources of the serum. A retired milk-wagon horse named Jim was one of the serum donors. Jim had produced as many as 30 quarts of successful diphtheria antitoxin over a period of 3 years. Unfortunately, Jim

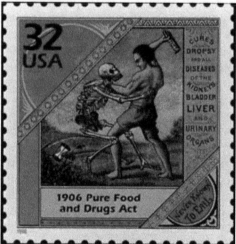

FIGURE 19.3 Pure Food and Drugs Act of 1906. The US Post Office recognized the 1906 Act as a landmark event of the twentieth century when it released a commemorative stamp on February 3, 1998 (first day cover with stamp shown here), the design of which was based on a nineteenth century patent medicine trading card. In the original trading card image shown on the first day cover the hero is Hunt's Remedy, The Great Kidney and Liver Medicine beating Death into submission, causing him to drop his hourglass and scythe. But in the USPS Commemorative stamp version "The Great Kidney and Liver Medicine" is replaced by "1906 Pure Food and Drugs Act," indicating that the real hero was the Pure Food and Drugs Act defending US citizens against unsafe medicines. *Reproduced from* http://www.fda.gov/AboutFDA/WhatWeDo/History/default.htm.

became infected with tetanus and had to be put down, but not before some of his infected antiserum got into the diphtheria vaccination supply chain. There was no vaccine against tetanus yet. Many children were treated with antiserum from Jim, and tragically, thirteen of them died from tetanus in St. Louis. Another nine children died in Camden, NJ likewise as a result of being inoculated with infected antiserum.

Shocked medical and governmental experts and officials discussed how this could possibly have happened. It was realized that without controls, literally anyone with horses and some rudimentary technical abilities to produce the antitoxin and could supply the sera. Without controls and standards this could, and probably would, happen again. Congress responded with legislation requiring biologics regulation, and this was signed into law in 1902 as the Biologics Control Act, also known as the Virus–Toxin Law.

This was the first government control over the manufacture of therapeutic biological products, indeed the first to control any type of therapeutic, as biologics were regulated before small-molecule drugs. It mandated that producers of vaccines, sera, and antitoxins had to be licensed and inspected, and the production processes had to be supervised by a qualified scientist. As noted above, the Pure Food and Drugs Act was subsequently passed in 1906. This Act prohibited adulterated and misbranded foods and drugs in interstate commerce, but in spite of the recent deadly medical experience with diphtheria antitoxin in St. Louis, the new 1906 Act didn't say anything about vaccines [17]. Then, as now, drugs were considered small-molecule pharmaceuticals, whereas biologics were in a different class, even though both were therapeutics. Today, for some therapeutics the line between "drugs" and "biologics" is less distinct.

Diethylene Glycol (Elixir Sulfanilamide)

The Pure Food and Drugs Act of 1906 is often considered the first, if vaccines aren't included, of many US laws enacted to protect the public's health from ineffective or dangerous drugs. The FDA didn't exist at that point, and the provisions of this Act were enforced by the Bureau of Chemistry of the Department of Agriculture. As noted above, the Bureau eventually was to become the FDA in 1930. The 1906 Act was specifically intended to prohibit the manufacture, sale, or transportation of adulterated, misbranded, poisonous, or deleterious foods, liquors, drugs, and medicines, and for other purposes, based primarily on what was claimed and specified on its label [18]. If inaccuracies in the label were identified, the manufacturer could be held criminally responsible. But that law had some deficiencies, among which was that it only required that drugs meet standards of strength and purity, and it didn't require the manufacturer of the drug

to submit information of any kind to the Bureau before putting it on the market. There was also no requirement to prove the drug was effective in producing the cures that were claimed on its label. It was up to the government to prove that the drug's label was false and misleading regarding claims of curative value. The Sherley Amendment in 1912 addressed this and prohibited false therapeutic claims on the label intended to defraud the consumer, in other words false claims of efficacy. However, while this was a step forward, this Amendment didn't completely solve the problem. As it turned out, establishing that the manufacturer knew ahead of time that the product wouldn't deliver the claimed cure, ie, that the claim was false and there was intent to defraud, proved difficult to establish in a court of law. A further shortcoming was that the ingredients of the medicine didn't have to be displayed anywhere on the container. This was clearly a boon to the manufacturer of the "wonder drug" who wanted to keep the formula secret and mysterious. But this led to many serious problems for the unsuspecting sick individual, including death, as described in the caption for Fig. 19.4. It wasn't until the Gould Amendment of 1913 that the manufacturer was required to display the contents plainly and conspicuously on the outside of the package (Fig. 19.4) [19].

FIGURE 19.4 A typical "patent medicine" label of the early 1900s, Mrs. Winslow's Soothing Syrup, was marketed for teething and colicky babies. It very likely lived up to its name and was soothing, and it may have been effective for its claimed use. But its label mentioned nothing about what it contained, especially the morphine, nor did it mention the limits of how much should be administered. Many crying infants died as a result of simply being treated for teething discomfort. Congress enacted the 1912 Sherley Amendment to the Pure Food and Drugs Act of 1906, prohibiting labeling of medicines with false therapeutic claims, and specifically forbidding the presence of 11 dangerous ingredients including alcohol, heroine, morphine and cocaine (Munch and Munch, 1956). But it wasn't until 1913 that the Gould Amendment required that the package contents be plainly and conspicuously marked on the outside of the package. *Reproduced from Munch C, Munch Jr C. Notices of Judgment – Numbers 1001 to 5000, Food Drug Law Journal, p. 28.* http://www.fda.gov/AboutFDA/WhatWeDo/History/Milestones/ucm128305.htm; *January 1956.*

Another glaring omission was the lack of any requirement to provide confirmation, before marketing, that the drug was safe. Once again a tragic event demonstrated clearly that additional controls were needed, and that the Pure Food and Drugs Act needed overhauling. A bill had been introduced in 1933 to make the Act stronger, but there was much political and industry opposition and the bill languished in Congress. In 1937, the S.E. Massengill Co., a medium-size and reasonably well-respected pharmaceutical manufacturer in Tennessee, created a liquid preparation (elixir) of sulfanilamide (a legitimate antibacterial drug). It had already been on the market for a few years in tablet and powder formulations that were successful as a treatment for streptococcal infections, and a liquid formulation (likely intended for sore throats) would fill a marketing niche (Fig. 19.5). The company's chief chemist, Harold Watkins, when trying to make an aqueous solution, found that sulfanilamide was not very soluble in water, but was soluble in diethylene glycol (DEG), a sweet-tasting solvent (a commonly known solvent used in other commercial products including brake fluid and automobile antifreeze). So, with the addition of some raspberry flavoring, the DEG/Elixir Sulfanilamide was ready to go to market. But Watkins didn't test the formulation for safety in animals, nor was he required to do so by the Pure Food and Drugs Act, before distributing it to Massengill's salesmen. It was already known and published in the scientific literature at that time that DEG was toxic, but Watkins was either unaware of this, or economics played a part since DEG was a cheaper ingredient than other solvents available and profit

margins would be improved. As it turned out, DEG was dreadfully toxic to the kidneys. Even though Elixir Sufanilamide was legally marketed, it caused extremely painful deaths by kidney failure of 107 people, many of them children, often within the remarkably short time of 1 to 11 days after ingestion [18]. But since the current Act didn't require the manufacturer to establish the safety of the product before marketing it, getting Elixir Sulfanilamide off the market was difficult. The government, however, was cleverly able to establish that the term "elixir" as then used meant a solution containing alcohol. Since DEG was the solvent in Elixir Sulfanilamide, and it contained no alcohol, this elixir was therefore misbranded and not in compliance with the law. In the wake of these deaths, knowing he was responsible for the decision to use DEG in the elixir, Harold Watkins committed suicide. A positive outcome of this episode was that it drove the passage and enactment of the Federal Food, Drug, and Cosmetic Act (FD&C) of 1938, which superseded the Pure Food and Drugs Act. This latest Act with its amendments was the substantial revision that was needed, and is the basis for the food, drug, and cosmetic laws that are in effect today in the United States. The FD&C Act of 1938 completely overhauled the public health system, and was the first to demand premarket evidence of safety for new drugs. This essentially shifted the burden of proof of safety and efficacy from the FDA to the manufacturer.

Thalidomide

As enforcement of the Act progressed, there were several amendments to address shortcomings of the law as they were discovered. However, it was the Kefauver–Harris Amendments to the FD&C Act in 1962 that had the greatest impact. These amendments came about in response to the thalidomide birth defects tragedy (occurring mostly in Europe, but also in Canada, South America, Australia, and other countries) that had become evident from 1957 through 1961. Several physicians observed that a new drug marketed as a sedative, and given to pregnant women as a treatment for morning sickness, was connected to the birth of babies born without upper and/or lower limbs [20,21]. Before these incidences were firmly associated with thalidomide and all of the distributed drug could be located and recovered, over 10,000 babies were affected worldwide.

The fact that these events essentially didn't occur (minimally by comparison) in the United States is credited to a young FDA employee who had recently moved from an academic research position, Dr. Frances Kelsey. She is credited for insisting on greater scientific rigor and better data from the pharmaceutical sponsor. Some years earlier she had been introduced to the devastating and deadly results of untested toxic pharmaceuticals as a graduate student in the pharmacology department of

FIGURE 19.5 Elixir Sulfanilamide bottles—S.E. Massengill Co., c.1937–1938. *Reproduced from* http://www.fda.gov/AboutFDA/What WeDo/History/ThisWeek/ucm117880.htm?utm_campaign= Google2&utm_source=fdaSearch&utm_medium=website&utm_ term=elixir%20sulfanilamide&utm_content=4.

E.M.K. Geiling at the University of Chicago in 1936. The FDA had asked Dr. Geiling to investigate the then current unusual deaths attributed to Elixir Sulfanilamide. Kelsey worked in the lab on this project, and Geiling's lab ultimately identified diethyleneglycol as the toxic agent. After an early career in university teaching and research in pharmacology, she had been at the FDA for only a month, when, in September 1960, she was given the file of a new drug to review as her first assignment. The William S. Merrell Company had applied to sell a sedative named Kevadon (thalidomide), which had been prescribed in Europe to treat morning sickness in pregnancy (Fig. 19.6).

Dr. Kelsey wasn't satisfied with some of the work in the application and asked Merrell to provide more data regarding its safety before this drug could be approved. In the meantime, she noted a European paper claiming that thalidomide was associated with neurotoxicity. Under the law at the time, the FDA had 60 days to review the data and accept or reject the application. If they didn't make a decision and respond within the 60-day period the drug could be marketed. She wasn't happy with Merrell's response to her questions, considering it as merely anecdotal rather than scientific. She wrote them a letter to this effect, which restarted the 60-day clock. After they once more submitted mostly anecdotal information rather than real data, she again requested more information about this association with

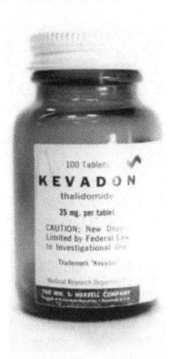

FIGURE 19.6 Bottle of the sedative, thalidomide, brand name Kevadon, which produced as many as 10,000 babies with devastating birth defects, mostly in Europe, in the late 1950s and early 1960s. *Reproduced from* http://www.fda.gov/AboutFDA/WhatWeDo/History/Milestones/ucm128305.htm.

neurotoxicity, much to the consternation of Merrell as the clock was started once again. Thalidomide had been tested on a limited pharmacological basis in mice, which slept restfully in their cages, then awoke with no apparent side effects as would be expected from a good sedative. However, before the company could respond to her satisfaction, two publications came out, one from Germany [20], the other from Australia [21], identifying thalidomide as the likely agent causing malformations in newborn babies, ie, the loss of long bones in the limbs. The physical result was absence or imperfect development of the arms and/or legs, a birth defect known as phocomelia. The German health authorities required the manufacturer to withdraw the drug from the market.

In the United States, Richardson–Merrell had distributed more than 2.5 million thalidomide tablets to over 1000 doctors on an "investigational" basis (it was legal at the time to distribute a new drug for investigational use while its review was pending at the FDA). As a result, 17 babies were born in the United States with thalidomide-related congenital malformations. Nevertheless, this was a much smaller tragedy, thanks to Frances Kelsey. Her determination and insistence on data of sufficient quality, and the FDA's rapid action to get the word out to physicians and recover the outstanding Kevadon, likely saved thousands of American children from being born without limbs or with flipper-like arms and legs.

Before these events with thalidomide, it was widely believed among scientists that the placenta was an impenetrable barrier, protecting the fetus from exposure to harmful chemicals and other agents. Thalidomide proved that that assumption was grossly inaccurate. An article appeared on the front page of the *Washington Post* calling Dr. Kelsey a heroine, and a host of other such articles praised her determination for preventing a great tragedy in America. Senators Kefauver and Harris resurrected a previously unpopular bill, got it passed, and signed by President Kennedy. Dr. Kelsey played a key role in shaping and enforcing these amendments [22]. The amendments strengthened the FDA's control of drug experimentation and, among other things, required premarket demonstration of safety, particularly for the ability to cause birth defects, and, for the first time, of efficacy. Subsequently, tests in a wide variety of animal species have shown that thalidomide is not a particularly potent teratogen in laboratory animals. Although it has been shown to cause a variety of birth defects in at least 17 different species, the limb malformations that characterize the human response of phocomelia have only been observed in rabbits, including the New Zealand White, a common laboratory species, and in primates (except for the prosimian bushbaby, which is not reactive). The mouse and rat embryo are relatively insensitive to thalidomide. The guinea pig is another species in which no birth defects of any kind have been reported from thalidomide treatment [23,24]. Therefore even if thalidomide had been tested in pregnant rats at the time, it's quite likely that effects on fetal development would not have been detected. As a result of these interspecies research findings, and the new requirement that drugs must be proven to be safe (including safe for the embryo/fetus) prior to marketing, studies on fetal development are required in two species, a rodent and nonrodent (usually the rabbit because of its response to thalidomide), in order to cover the possibility that one of those species will be predictive of an effect in humans.

Her regulatory diligence advanced Dr. Kelsey's role in the agency, and she became responsible for directing the surveillance of drug testing at the FDA. She also went on to help write the rules that were to govern clinical trials, which then became the model for much of the industrialized world, and was the first official to oversee them [25]. For her exemplary service to the public she received the President's Award for Distinguished Federal Civilian Service from President Kennedy in 1962. The Kefauver–Harris Amendments strengthened the FD&C Act rules for drug safety and now required manufacturers to prove that their drugs were effective (seemingly an outcome of the overall increased demand and attention to regulations for new drugs, since thalidomide was already well regarded as an effective sedative, and the problem here was its lack of safety) (Fig. 19.7).

Some have complained that one problem with the 1962 Kefauver–Harris Amendments was that they made the FDA too conservative and restrictive of progress. Business claimed that the Amendments created an additional decade of regulatory delay before new drugs could be approved, to the detriment of the public health. For example, one researcher estimated that 10,000 people died unnecessarily each year while beta blockers languished at the FDA, even though they had already been approved in Europe [26]. Nevertheless, it was firmly believed that an episode such as the terrible deformity of thousands of children due to an unsafe drug should never happen again, and must be prevented. Since that time any new molecular entity, large or small, must be proven both safe and effective if it is to be considered a drug for the US market (many countries at that time, if they had regulations at all, only required that the sponsor establish its drug's safety, and not necessarily that it worked to improve the patient's health).

On the 50th anniversary of Dr. Kelsey's regulatory action regarding thalidomide, in 2010 the FDA presented her (then 96 years old) with the inaugural Kelsey Award, named in her honor. Each year this award is presented to an outstanding FDA staff member [27]. After an accomplished career with many accolades, and a long life, Dr.

FIGURE 19.7 **Dr. Frances O. Kelsey receives a pen used by President Kennedy to sign the Kefauver-Harris Amendments to the FD&C Act.** Canadian-born Frances Oldham Kelsey was less than a month on the job at FDA when she was handed her first assignment in September of 1960, to review a submission by the William S. Merrell Company to market in America a sedative already on the market in Europe. That drug, Kevadon (thalidomide), was a very effective sedative, but wasn't tested adequately for adverse effects. Worldwide drug approval practices at the time allowed minimally tested drugs on the market. As a result Kevadon caused thousands of babies in Europe and elsewhere to be born without, or with defective, arms and/or legs (phocomelia). Even before this link with birth defects was known, Dr. Kelsey refused to accept Merrell's application without first seeing more rigorous experimental data, which the company declined to submit. She has since been honored many times over for effectively preventing that major tragedy in the US. *Reproduced from* http://globalnews.ca/news/1470760/canadian-scientist-frances-kelsey-who-spurred-fda-reforms-turns-100/; https://www.flickr.com/photos/fdaphotos/8212346106/in/album-72157624615595535/.

Kelsey passed away in May 2015 at the age of 101. She set a high standard in regulatory toxicology for integrity, scientific quality, and for the appropriate role of government in protecting the public health. Moreover, many will certainly remember her, not only professionally but also personally, as an outstanding role model for women in science.

PREVENTING DRUG DISASTERS FROM RECURRING TODAY: LAWS AND REGULATIONS

Lawmakers, Regulators, and Scientists

Laws are created to address a public need such as those described above. A law addressing the need is written, revised, debated by Congress, and finally passed and affirmed by the signature of the President. The agency of government that is assigned the responsibility of administering the law then proposes regulations that it believes embody its intent. The regulatory agency, such as the FDA, publishes those proposed regulations in the Federal Register and a finite period is opened during which the public may comment on the proposed regulation. After carefully considering these comments, if the FDA determines that the comment has merit, it will modify the proposed regulation and then will publish the final regulation in the Federal Register along with responses from the agency about the comments that were received [28].

Regulations define the actions needed to address the law and provide the enforcing rules of the law. In the case of the FD&C Act of 1938 and its amendments, they completely overhauled the public health system then in place from one of easily accessible patent medicines available over the counter to one that required a physician to prescribe certain medications. In addition, the law authorized the FDA to demand evidence of safety for new drugs, issue standards for foods, and conduct factory inspections.

The ensuing Kefauver–Harris Amendments of 1962 introduced major changes to the Act. They not only strengthened the rules for establishing the safety of drugs, but also required that manufacturers prove that their drugs did what they claimed; ie, that they were actually effective as to their health claims. This requirement, to establish effectiveness, required that a drug company had to do more extensive clinical trials. The earlier Act did not permit a company to ship misbranded drugs (ie, those that could not yet, through lack of evidence, make a health or safety claim) across state lines, which had the effect of limiting shipment of experimental drugs. In order to ship experimental drugs for investigational purposes in humans, the Kefauver–Harris Amendments required a formal exemption from this rule in the form of an investigational new drug (IND) application. This was an attempt to strike a balance between providing evidence of safety before exposing humans and not obstructing progress in drug development. This is a unique requirement, somewhat reminiscent of the earlier new drug application (NDA) requirements in terms of a concession to industry recognizing that the regulatory agency should not place impediments to business progress.

Under those earlier 1906 NDA rules the drug sponsor could market, or at least distribute, the drug while the FDA was reviewing the data that was submitted to establish safety, which was why so many people died in the diethyleneglycol-laced Sulfanilamide Elixir disaster. Even after the extensive changes brought about under the 1938 FD&C Act, drug companies continued to be able to distribute their experimental drug while it was under regulatory review. Furthermore, unless the FDA required additional data within a certain period of time, their NDA was considered as accepted automatically. Fortunately, for many babies born in the United States during the thalidomide episode in the early 1960s, Dr. Kelsey had requested additional data from Merrill,

effectively extending the period during which the company could not distribute the drug to the public.

Under these new rules in the Kefauver–Harris Amendments, an IND application required limited laboratory data to characterize the drug chemically, establish basic safety in in vitro and animal studies, and provide exposure and tolerability information in a small number of healthy human subjects (not patients with the disease) before the rest of the investigational program could continue. If the FDA did not respond within 30 days indicating that their IND data were not acceptable, the sponsor could assume everything was fine and proceed with their program of nonclinical and preliminary clinical investigations, leading to an NDA. This is still the process practiced today.

However, with the Kefauver–Harris Amendments came extended requirements for how clinical studies were to be run, the qualifications of the personnel running the study, and what types of data were necessary to establish safety and effectiveness before marketing approval could be granted. It changed the whole drug approval process from one of premarket notification by the sponsoring pharmaceutical company to one of premarket approval by the agency. Not only that, but the FDA was now also empowered to withdraw NDA approval and take the drug off the market if there was new evidence that it was not safe, or for other reasons such as the discovery that the sponsor withheld critical data, etc.

Additional Food and Drug Regulations

Pharmaceutical regulations have two simultaneous goals:

1. The development and production for market of new and effective therapeutics, and
2. The protection of the patient from unsafe and/or misbranded products.

While patients demand the latter, businesses and sometimes patients alike often complain about the former, feeling that regulations are an impediment to drug development. They maintain that these regulations often keep medical improvements and life-saving drugs from reaching needy patients, since too much time is taken by the FDA to conduct a thorough premarket evaluation. It has been claimed that the 1962 Kefauver–Harris Amendments alone created an additional decade of regulatory delay. These delays were also blamed for greatly increasing the cost of drug development. One economist who compared the pre- and post-1962 drug market estimated (in 1973) that since the acquisition of the FDA's new powers the number of new drugs had been reduced by 60%, so the rate of new drug development was decreasing. Actually, new drugs were getting to market, but while the number of new drugs approximately doubled each year, the pharmaceutical R&D costs grew by a factor of 20 [26].

Pharmaceutical scientists, and medical advisory committees entrusted with the responsibility of ensuring the safety of a new drug, tend to be overly conservative. Furthermore, not all regulatory decisions reflect on the Agency the same way. The FDA makes good decisions when they approve a good drug in a reasonable amount of time that is effective and safe. The Agency can make bad decisions in two ways: approving a drug that turns out to be unsafe, or not approving, ie, taking too long to approve, a good drug. Making bad decisions, especially approving a bad drug, has significantly more impact on the FDA. Retired FDA employee Henry Miller, when interviewed upon his retirement for their historical archives, said [29]:

> This kind of mistake is highly visible and has immediate consequences—the media pounces, the public denounces, and Congress pronounces.

As an example of the response to a bad decision (not drug-related) Miller recalled one incident early in his career where a canner of beets labeled them as "baby beets," Upon inspection of the canning facility, it was noted that the canner was using a small device to scoop out little balls of beets from mature beets and labeling them "baby beets," Not a very serious infraction and not even very fraudulent since they were packed in a glass jar and one could easily tell they were not baby beets. Nevertheless, the FDA seized the product as being mislabeled and took the canner to court. The canner went to his congressman, named Taber, who happened to head up the appropriations committee of which the FDA was a part. Taber was so incensed he said that if the FDA has time to spend on things like this, they have too much money. He cut their funding by 25%, ie, millions of dollars. Miller learned the lesson that seemingly minor regulatory decisions in terms of product quality and marketing can have a major impact on the FDA with serious budgetary consequences, emphasizing the dictum that "...Congress pronounces." Experiences like this can set the tone for being more deliberate in the decision-making process.

During the period following the Kefauver–Harris Amendments of 1962 there was increasingly greater pharmaceutical innovation and, at the same time, increasing regulatory oversight. As noted above, the effect was that the number of NDAs decreased while the time to get them reviewed and approved increased. One of the problems, according to the FDA, was that with the ever-greater number of drugs to review, they just didn't have adequate staff to get the job done more quickly. Yet, Congress would not increase FDA budgets sufficiently to provide enough funds to turn this around.

In an effort to find some way to increase FDA's ability to evaluate and approve more safe drugs in an era of expanding pharmaceutical discovery but limited regulatory resources, the Prescription Drug User Fee Act (PDUFA) was enacted in 1992. This Act authorized FDA to collect fees from companies that produce certain human drugs and biological products whenever they submitted a new drug application, ie, the company would pay to have their drug reviewed. The Act has been renewed (and therefore reconsidered) as part of the Food and Drug Administration Amendments Act (FDAAA) every five years, with the latest at the time of writing being PDUFA IV in 2007. The newest rates for fiscal year 2012 have been published in the Federal Register. The intent of PDUFA was that FDA would be assured of funding, via the sponsors of new drugs, for the additional staff needed to carry out the comprehensive reviews of these new drugs. In exchange, the sponsors would get speedier reviews. This was intended to make new drugs available to patients sooner, something clearly desirable to sponsors and regulators as well as patients [30].

This Act did result in shorter reviewing times. In fact, by 1996, the Center for Drug Evaluation and Research (CDER) approved 53 new molecular entities (NME) in an average of 17.8 months per drug (median 14.3 months). All of these were new records until the present when in 2015 FDA exceeded that record by approving 56 new drugs [31]. Nevertheless, while efforts to streamline the drug-review process were successful, it did not reduce the complexity of the review procedures nor the overall individual drug development times due mainly to increases in clinical development times. This required attention if drug development times were to improve, allowing a greater number of drugs to get to market. Discussions between industry and the FDA as to how to improve the clinical development phase resulted in recommendations to Congress that eventually were included in Congress' reauthorization of PDUFA in 1997 [32]. The renewals of this Act since 1992 attest to its overall success.

Amendments to the original FD&C Act are an expected and ongoing process. As our society progresses, new weaknesses or inadequacies of the law are identified, or new needs arise that the present law doesn't adequately address. In these cases, a new bill will be enacted and amended to the FD&C Act. From 1980 through April 2011, there were 24 significant new Amendments to the FD&C Act, the provisions of which are incorporated into the Act (Table 19.1).

One of the more important Acts amending the FD&C Act was the FDA Modernization Act (FDAMA) of 1997. This followed a series of events in the 1990s where, despite the critical evaluation of the mountains of reports submitted for each drug application, and confirmation of

TABLE 19.1 Significant Amendments to the FD&C Act

Since 1980, listed chronologically; dates shown are when the Public Law was approved. "Summary" indicates link to a summary of the law; other links are to full text. Provisions of these Public Laws are incorporated into the FD&C Act. This is a selected list.

- Infant Formula Act of 1980 (summary) Public Law (PL) 96-359 (October 26, 1980)

- Orphan Drug Act PL 97-414 (January 4, 1983)

- Drug Price Competition and Patent Term Restoration Act of 1984 (summary) PL 98-417 (September 24, 1984)

- Prescription Drug Marketing Act of 1987 PL 100-293 (April 22, 1988)

- Generic Animal Drug and Patent Term Restoration Act of 1988 (summary) PL 100-670 (November 16, 1988)

- Nutrition Labeling and Education Act of 1990 (summary) PL 101-535 (November 8, 1990)

- Safe Medical Devices Act of 1990 (summary) PL 101-629 (November 28, 1990)

- Medical Device Amendments of 1992 (summary) PL 102-300 (June 16, 1992)

- Prescription Drug Amendments of 1992; Prescription Drug User Fee Act of 1992 PL 102-571 (October 29, 1992)

- Animal Medicinal Drug Use Clarification Act (AMDUCA) of 1994 PL 103-396 (October 22, 1994)

- Dietary Supplement Health and Education Act of 1994 PL 103-417 (October 25, 1994)

- FDA Export Reform and Enhancement Act of 1996 PL 104-134 (April 26, 1996)

- Food Quality Protection Act of 1996 PL 104-170 (August 3, 1996)

- Animal Drug Availability Act of 1996 PL 104-250 (October 9, 1996)

- Food and Drug Administration Modernization Act (FDAMA) of 1997 PL 105-115 (November 21, 1997)

- Best Pharmaceuticals for Children Act PL 107-109 (January 4, 2002)

- Medical Device User Fee and Modernization Act (MDUFMA) of 2002 PL 107-250 (October 26, 2002)

- Animal Drug User Fee Act of 2003 PL 108-130 (November 18, 2003)

- Pediatric Research Equity Act of 2003 PL 108-155 (December 3, 2003)

- Minor Use and Minor Species Animal Health Act of 2004 PL 108-282 (August 2, 2004)

- Dietary Supplement and Nonprescription Drug Consumer Protection Act PL 109-462 (December 22, 2006)

- Food and Drug Administration Amendments Act (FDAAA) of 2007 PL 110-85 (September 27, 2007)

- Family Smoking Prevention and Tobacco Control Act (public law 111-31) PL 111-31 (June 22, 2009)

- FDA Food Safety Modernization Act PL 111-353 (January 4, 2011)

http://www.fda.gov/RegulatoryInformation/Legislation/SignificantAmendmentstotheFDCAct/.

safety for its intended use, adverse side effects of some drugs were identified after approval, and several had to be withdrawn from the market. This generated public outcry and demand for FDA reform. Several congressional hearings ensued, and reports from government investigational committees were forthcoming that were very critical of the FDA. In order to address the problems that were identified, the FDAMA was enacted. Many new regulations and updated guidance were necessary to implement the changes in the law the FDAMA mandated. Dr. Jane Henney, then commissioner of the FDA, in testimony before the Senate Committee on Health, Education, Labor and Pensions 2 years later in 1999, claimed that [33]:

> with the tools provided by FDAMA, FDA is becoming a stronger better Agency, one whose actions remain firmly based in science to promote and protect the public health.

She summarized the general outcomes of implementing FDAMA as:

1. Enhancing the public health;
2. Making our regulatory processes more effective and efficient; and
3. Increasing consumer and industry confidence through open, transparent processes and collaboration [33].

What Actions Need To Be Implemented to Address the FD&C Requirements?

While the FD&C Act provided the overall criteria for what was to be done to improve foods and drugs, the FDA was assigned the responsibility for establishing and administering the regulations that would actually interpret and implement the law. As a result, that Agency also acquired the power that comes along with having to interpret those laws. For example, the FDA determines what constitutes "substantial evidence" of safety and efficacy [34].

However, the goals of congressional committees and lawmakers are somewhat different from those of scientists, and the two may not always be compatible. Lawmakers seek to settle human problems by affecting human behavior, preferably based on a foundation of good data. However, their goal is to seek resolution and solve problems regardless of the data available (and sometimes in spite of them). Scientists, on the other hand, seek to explain natural phenomena; they are truth-seekers, and don't necessarily see problem-solving as a prime target [35]. There are some further distinctions, eg, those scientists working within the regulatory agencies conducting safety assessments may view them as hypothesis-based investigations, while the studies suggested by the regulatory agency itself and most of those provided by the sponsor's toxicologists are perhaps less hypothesis-driven and more guideline-based, unless they are seeking to determine mechanisms of toxicity [36].

Because of this slight disparity of goals and viewpoints, health-related laws and regulations, or at least the expectations of the lawmakers, may not always take into account what is possible scientifically. Furthermore, they also may not take into account what advances might take place as science progresses, and this leaves the regulation out of touch with current or future scientific capabilities.

Although it deals with foods rather than drugs, the Delaney Clause is an example of lawmakers' good intentions, but limited understanding of science, in their attempt to solve or head off a potential problem, that of introducing a carcinogen into the food supply during the manufacture of a food product. In the FD&C Act, Congress gave the FDA broad discretionary ability to assess food safety and ensure a safe food supply as they saw fit, but that flexibility was constrained somewhat by a provision known as the Delaney Clause. In this case, there was a series of laws that came about following hearings by Representative James Delaney that addressed pesticide residues (1954), food additives (1958), and color additives (1960) in foods. These laws required the FDA to exert much tighter control over the chemicals that were being added to the food supply. The Delaney provision of the 1958 law prohibited the approval of food additives "found to induce cancer when ingested by man or animals," a commendable goal. There was no consideration, however, of whether a cancer produced in animals was relevant to man, or of the advances in analytical chemistry that would enable chemists to identify a possible carcinogen in ever-smaller amounts, amounts that may not be relevant to human carcinogenicity.

This raised immediate problems with the infinitesimal levels of pesticide residues that were found at that time on fruits and vegetables, as well as certain chemicals already known to be carcinogens that might migrate from packaging to food. Pesticide residues were eventually removed from being considered under the Delaney Clause, and the carcinogenic migrants in packaging were considered safe if extrapolated to have a risk that does not exceed 1 in 1,000,000, and this risk level was then determined to be *de minimus*, ie, essentially zero. Therefore by definition these compounds did not come under the Delaney Clause. Other interpretations, eg, what is considered a "food additive," etc., were devised to exclude other food ingredients from Delaney Clause rule [37]. Thus although the clause within the amended Act had the simple and seemingly appropriate intent of assuring the public that it would not be exposed to carcinogens as the food industry provided new products, it wasn't based on a good understanding of science and didn't allow for future advances in science. In order to abide by the intent of the clause, regulators in the affected agencies devised various ways of interpreting the clause to make it workable for situations present at the time and into the future. In this case, lawmakers misunderstood what science could do, and underestimated what scientists might be capable of doing as the discipline advanced.

Lawmaking, interpreting the laws, and translating those resultant rules and interpretations into actionable directions are not easy exercises for the lawmakers or regulators, nor are they necessarily easy for industry scientists to comply with even under the best of intentions. Therefore once they have determined what types of studies are most likely to produce the evidence needed to prove safety and efficacy, one of the FDA's responsibilities is to communicate its policies and concepts so that industry can satisfactorily address these when developing new pharmaceuticals. The Agency communicates these regulations and interpretations primarily by publishing them in the US Code of Federal Regulations (CFR). The CFR is where those rules and regulations, premarketing requirements, and approval procedures are described that the sponsor should undertake in order to achieve marketing approval. In addition, the FDA supplements these descriptions of the regulations with guidelines that are communicated to industry and the public in general. Of course, today these guidelines are communicated via the internet. The FDA has developed a very comprehensive website that includes not only information on a number of direct Agency topics, but also many links to other important sites, eg, all of the food and drug acts, the Federal Register, Guidelines, other agency and worldwide guidelines, etc. The reader is encouraged to explore their website [34].

TRANSLATING REGULATIONS INTO APPROPRIATE SCIENTIFIC DATA—GUIDELINES

General Steps in Preclinical Drug Development

Since 1938, the FD&C Act has required premarket proof of safety and, since 1962, efficacy. In order to accomplish this, the standard of primary evidence for establishing safety and efficacy is testing the therapeutic agent in humans. However, in order to expose humans for the first time to new chemical entities, there is a distinct need a priori for some understanding of how this chemical affects or alters biological systems. This is the main function of the preclinical program—to ascertain at least a basic understanding of the pharmacologic and toxic effects of the NME in in vitro and in vivo studies before exposing humans. Studies of its pharmacological activity on the molecular target(s) of interest will have been done, and will continue, to establish this molecule as the primary candidate for further development. At this point, limited studies are also done to examine a drug's systemic absorption parameters and metabolism. It is now possible to obtain significantly detailed basic and comparative cross-species information on these basic physiological phenomena from in vitro tissue and/or cell-culture systems. The comparative metabolic profiles between humans and potential toxicology species are determined. At this point, the clearance of the parent molecule and its metabolites are also investigated, as well as their primary routes of elimination. These data aid greatly in selecting the animal species for toxicology studies that are most likely to be predictive of adverse human responses. Cytotoxicity and genotoxicity studies are performed, and acute (ie, single administration) and/or limited multidose general toxicology studies are done in at least two species, a rodent (typically a rat) and a nonrodent (usually a dog, mini-pig, or primate) to establish initial evidence of safety before exposing humans. Currently, it is often advisable (although not required) to perform very limited preliminary studies in pregnant rats and/or rabbits to get an early indication of potential reproductive effects.

There is much to drug development that is more than laboratory science. Table 19.2 provides experienced tips that the pharmaceutical industry toxicologist should consider as a member of a drug development team.

These nonclinical studies will give the sponsor some idea of the range of potential adverse activities of the drug, and, hopefully, provide both the sponsor and the FDA with some evidence that the drug is safe at the intended clinical dose. At this time, the best model other than a human for the complex integration and interaction of biological systems relevant to humans is a living animal. But for all their anatomic, systemic, and functional similarities, animals are not humans. The differences need to be recognized and accounted for in the scientific assessment as well as they possibly can be in order for animal data to be most useful and predictive of human responses. These early investigations provide important information about the compound's effects in complex living systems and help to determine which of several species have the most similar responses to humans. Those selected as most representative become the initial species for the toxicology program (subsequent changes in species may be necessary based on toxicity responses). When this is done satisfactorily, and the data evaluated by scientists with appropriate training, preclinical studies in animals have been useful in predicting most types of human reactions, and have been a critical and necessary element in the safety evaluation of human drugs.

Nevertheless, for both the scientists designing and conducting the studies, and for regulatory reviewers, some consistency in what types of evidence are produced, their extent and their quality are necessary in order for this process to progress optimally. As regulatory toxicology was evolving in the 1960s, there was a need for guidance. Regulatory agencies, industry trade organizations in different countries, and even nongovernment organizations like the World Health Organization (WHO) organized various sets of guidelines to help form common ground on study design and performance [38].

Guidelines and the Need for Harmonization—Origin of ICH

Prior to 1990, regulations for the types of nonclinical studies and types of data that were required to support clinical development of a new drug differed among the various countries of the western world. Primarily involved were those regions where the greatest pharmaceutical innovation and the largest pharmaceutical markets existed, namely North America, the countries of Europe, and Japan. These differences manifested both in the extent and in the types of endpoints each country's regulatory scientists felt were critical for establishing the safety of a compound.

At about the same time, post World War II, the countries of Europe were exploring the political ramifications of joining together as one block to further economic cooperation as the European Union. The seeds of the European Union were actually sown as far back as the 1950s (France and Germany) as the European Coal and Steel Community (ECSC). This was the first supranational organization intended to bind the members economically as one way to promote cooperation in the hope of preventing further war. The Treaty of Paris was signed in 1951 by six countries and provided a common market across Europe for coal and steel. This eventually evolved into the European Economic Community, with broader cooperation both economical and in other areas of mutual interest.

TABLE 19.2   Developing the Drug Preclinical Study Program: Things to Consider as a Toxicologist

See Good Laboratory Practice (GLP) regulations for further details on that aspect of the toxicologist's role – 21 CFR part 58[a]

1. It is imperative that you understand the clinical disease/health indication(s) that will be the target of this program, and which of those indications the company will consider the primary, secondary, etc., indications of importance in terms of the company mission and marketing goals. Drug development is a team activity. You will be a member of a Project Team or Drug Development Team that, besides toxicology, will include pharmacology, chemistry, medical, regulatory, and perhaps marketing and management personnel.

2. Press the clinical development members to narrow the possible clinical indications to one; the one with the greatest health need, with the greatest potential for achieving regulatory approval, and that will require the least cost/effort/time. It may be necessary to remind the team that despite the excitement surrounding the discovery of this new "wonder drug", and the potential for the company's bottom line, a molecule is not a drug until FDA says it's a drug, which requires that it be safe as well as effective. The toxicologist's considered input on the relative toxicity of the different drug candidates can be a defining aspect in the selection of the primary molecule to move forward in development, and is essential for regulatory approval. But never lose sight of the goal, which is to improve human health. So that while the nonclinical toxicology assessment is essential for the approval of a new drug, your ultimate role is in support of safe **human** exposure, and clinical considerations are paramount. Determining the single most important clinical indication will be affected by the primary pharmacodynamic (PD) activity of the drug, and this will guide the proposed clinical regimen for the early trials. Understanding these points will be critical for developing the preclinical toxicology program most appropriate to supporting the anticipated clinical program. Combined with the pharmacology data knowledge of the primary clinical program is necessary for you to determine essential toxicological parameters such as route, dose levels, dose regimen, duration of treatment, etc., and will greatly assist in selecting in vitro systems and whole animal models that will serve as the best surrogates to predict human adverse effects. Try to discourage multiple clinical endpoints, as these will only muddy the drug development and regulatory approval waters (and will probably be discouraged by regulators). If other clinical endpoints are possible and realistic for the best molecular candidate, these should usually be attained by following separate drug development avenues.

3. Since the product label will ultimately be the FDA-approved critical summary of what this drug is, how it works, how the patient will be treated, and what the anticipated side effects might be, use any from a current Physician's Desk Reference as your guide. In fact, have the team develop a prototype label for this drug candidate early on in the discussions (see "What's in a Drug Label"[b]). This team exercise will help identify for everyone the important responsibilities, actions, and results that will be needed from each group, with some idea of their sequence and interrelationship. This can help lead to a more streamlined plan for a successful drug development program for this particular indication with this specific active pharmaceutical ingredient (API). Following this exercise, assist the team leader (not usually the toxicologist) to set up a project management scheme to achieve these endpoints in a manner that will meet the regulatory and marketing target deadlines.

4. Collaborate with pharmacologists on the discovery team and run batteries of tests (keeping in mind the limited amount of API available at this early stage of development, and cost effectiveness of assays selected) to develop a basic understanding of how the API works (eg, 1° and 2° PD, receptor binding, protein binding, comparative in vitro metabolism, PK of API and primary metabolites, GI permeability if an oral drug, cytotoxicity, genotoxicity, safety pharmacology assays, and other test article-specific assays). Some results will provide important sources of basic information, others will be important in selecting the appropriate in vitro systems and the animal toxicology species that will serve as the most predictable human surrogate.

5. Assist the analytical chemist in developing bioanalytical methods capable of identifying the test article in the different in vitro systems and animal species to be used in the toxicology program, and in different matrices (eg, plasma, serum, urine, feces, dosing vehicles, culture medium). Be sure these methods are appropriately validated in order to support GLP studies, because if you cannot unequivocally establish that what you are using in the ensuing tests is the API, the whole program will be worthless!

6. The stability of the test article must be established under the same conditions that will be used during the nonclinical and clinical programs, eg, bulk API, API in formulations, room temperature, refrigeration, freezing, heat, accelerated conditions, light, dark, etc., for durations at least equal to those of the toxicology and clinical studies. Undocumented API stability under the laboratory conditions existing during the course of the toxicology studies may invalidate an otherwise perfect toxicology study, particularly if very little toxicity is evident.

7. Optimize 2–3 route-specific formulations as appropriate for the compound. This work should proceed from an early point in the preclinical program to ensure maximum target tissue exposure in the identified toxicology system or species by the selected route. If the clinical route for some reason is not optimal for the toxicology studies, eg, sufficiently high oral toxicology dosages cannot be achieved in the whole animal, other routes such as intravenous may have to be utilized, with their specific formulations, in order to reach toxicologically relevant circulating or tissue exposure levels.

8. Identify the toxic potential of a candidate as early as possible. If it's going to fail, finding out early will reduce the considerable time and costs of unexpected late clinical stage failure and will open up opportunities for more viable drug candidates for this indication—a decidedly positive and valuable contribution from the toxicology member of the team! However, be advised that not all members of the team may share this positive drug development attitude emanating from your toxicological assessment if it doesn't promote their favorite drug candidate, especially the discovering pharmacologist and perhaps upstream management. In the past, toxicologists have been regarded as the "drug killers", especially by the "drug champions". Now enlightened pharmaceutical companies are including toxicologists on their drug development teams, recognizing that they provide invaluable contributions to the overall drug development goals, and can improve time-to-market for an approvable drug for the clinical indication. Beyond the science, professional care and some political savvy must be developed and nurtured if the toxicologist is to be seen as a valuable team contributor and not merely as a killer of the world's greatest drug breakthrough. Science is a human endeavor.

[a]http://www.accessdata.fda.gov/scripts/cdrh/cfdocs/cfcfrl/CFRSearch.cfm?CFRPart=58.
[b]http://www.fda.gov/drugs/informationondrugs/ucm079846.htm.

The Treaty of Maastricht in 1993 transformed this group into the European Union, which reflected the increased number of member countries as well as the broader scope of integration and cooperation. This is currently a supranational organization with 27[1] member states committed to intergovernmental negotiations to arrive at decisions that work for the common good, the constitutional basis of which was formed in 2009 [39].

With this advancing European political debate and cooperation as a backdrop, it was very apparent, and sometimes disheartening for those trying to develop new drugs in the United States that studies that were done initially to serve the US FDA would not necessarily be acceptable to the regulatory authorities in other world markets if the sponsor decided later to explore markets outside the United States. This was because the study protocol designed for the US FDA wouldn't have included critical elements that were considered essential for review in these other markets. For example, by the 1980s the developmental and reproductive toxicology studies that were expected for regulatory review usually included a fertility study, embryo-fetal development studies in rodents and nonrodents, and a peripostnatal study in order to evaluate the safety of the compound in every aspect of reproduction and embryo/fetal development through a full lifecycle from prefertilization continuing to a fully functional and fertile next generation. However, the standard US protocol for the fertility study (which then required continuing dosing through parturition and lactation) that emerged in 1966 [40] following the thalidomide disaster did not require behavioral testing in the offspring to detect possible drug-related behavior, memory, and functional deficits. In the meantime, it was discovered that widespread industrial discharges of methyl mercury into Minamata Bay in Japan during the late 1950s and early 1960s were responsible for devastating neurobehavioral effects in children and young adults that were exposed in utero due to their mother's contaminated fish-rich diet. While the United States continued to use the 1966 FDA guidelines for pharmaceutical development, the Minamata event caused the reproductive toxicity guidelines for pharmaceuticals to evolve in Japan, the UK, and other countries as scientists recognized that behavioral functional deficits can be just as much of a teratogenic outcome as physical malformations. Their advancing guidelines required that the offspring in the

developmental and reproductive toxicology studies be tested for memory and learning deficits (now included in the prepostnatal 4.1.2 ICH guidelines) [41].

In a US pharmaceutical company, if this intention to include the UK market wasn't made known to the toxicologist early on in the drug development program (meaning that, for the toxicologist, study designs only needed to address US requirements), this particular study when submitted to the UK regulatory authorities, absent behavioral testing of the offspring, was unacceptable in the UK and would have to be repeated to their standards. This, of course, consumed much more resources in animals and capital costs, and since these are lengthy and complex studies, added significant months to more than a year to the critical drug development timelines for international approvals. In addition, this delay to regulatory approval, and thereby a delay in getting the drug on the market, could lose the drug competitive market share that might very well be counted in the millions of dollars.

Therefore while all three major pharmaceutical regions required basically the same questions of safety to be answered, using basically the same toxicology study designs that had first been provided in the US by the FDA guidelines of 1966 and later 1983 (Japan and the EC had developed their similar guidelines), the seemingly slight scientific or technological differences in the protocols between regions were not insignificant in terms of regulatory approval. This resulted in some reports being accepted, but others rejected as inadequate, not just between the US and the UK. Similar differences existed among the general toxicology study protocols of all three regions precluding the use of one set of nonclinical studies to achieve global approval.

Over several years in the 1980s and 1990s, many meetings occurred between the regulatory authorities and industry associations of the three regions to discuss how to resolve these differences and come to agreement or at least consensus on these matters. The main goal was to improve and streamline the drug development process in the three regions: Europe, Japan, and the United States. In these tripartite meetings many important initiatives were proposed, debated, and agreed upon to promote international harmonization of regulatory requirements. Where full unanimity couldn't be achieved, consensus was agreed in principle on the major content, with some limited flexibility allowed for well-specified and documented exceptions that were region-specific (examples of differences in the regional agency positions affecting preclinical study design or duration are presented in the next section).

From these meetings emerged the International Conference on Harmonization of the Technical Requirements for the Registration of Pharmaceuticals for Human Use (ICH), first established in 1990. From these beginnings, the ICH formed the critical center of an ongoing effort by both regulatory and industry trade group representatives

---

1. On June 23, 2016, the United Kingdom voted to leave the European Union, reducing the total number of member states from 28 to 27. The vote on the referendum was close, but had a nearly 72% turnout, the largest since the 1992 general election. The regulatory drug development (as well as many other) ramifications of this outcome are yet to be fully realized. http://www.bbc.com/news/uk-politics-32810887.

from each of the three regions to reduce differences in technical requirements for drug development among regulatory agencies. Representatives of the WHO, the Canadian Health Protection Branch, and the European Free Trade Area attend meetings as observers. The FDA first proposed the implementation of the ICH Safety Working Group Consensus in the US Federal Register in 1992 [42].

As a result of positive experiences emanating from these decisions, the FDA's view on global harmonization is that:

> Such harmonization enhances public health protection and improves government efficiencies by reducing both unwarranted contradictory regulatory requirements and redundant applications of similar requirements by multiple regulatory bodies.

The FDA's goals in participating in international harmonization are:

- To safeguard global public health
- To assure that consumer protection standards and requirements are met
- To facilitate the availability of safe and effective products
- To develop and utilize product standards and other requirements more effectively
- To minimize or eliminate inconsistent standards internationally

The FDA's harmonization efforts are intended to pool regulators' resources in developing standards for public health protection, reduce industry's compliance costs in the global market, and minimize impediments to bringing safe food and safe and effective treatments to consumers and patients around the world [43].

DEVELOPING THE NONCLINICAL TOXICOLOGY PROGRAM

The nonclinical (a term often used interchangeably with "preclinical") toxicity testing of a new drug, whether it be a small-molecule or biotechnological product, is designed to find out some basic safety-related information prior to administration of the drug to humans and during the subsequent clinical trials. The toxicologist wants to know the innate hazard potential of the compound, the target organ(s) of toxicity, at what dose in the most sensitive species is toxicity manifested, what margin of safety is there between the dose that causes no toxicity in the most sensitive animal species and the anticipated clinical dose, if the toxicity is reversible, what to recommend as the safe starting dose for clinical studies, and what, if any, are the premonitory signs indicating a toxic response that would be useful in signaling possible forthcoming adverse events in the clinical trials.

How to find answers to these questions, and what studies are needed, describes the essence of the toxicologist's role in drug development. Two specific pieces

of guidance offer much assistance in this regard: ICH M3(R2) for general advice and more focused advice on small-molecular-weight therapeutics, and ICH S6 for more specific advice on large molecular weight biological therapeutics. For biologics, both should be referenced, as the general drug development guidance appearing in ICH M3(R2) applies also to biologics.

Begin With the Regulatory End Product in Mind

Before considering the scientific approaches to these questions, it's useful for the toxicologist to be familiar with, and keep in mind, the practical regulatory endpoint that has to be achieved once the studies are completed—the study report and data presentation. All the toxicology studies and their data must be assembled with other data on this compound and reported to the regulatory agencies in a way that facilitates their review.

Just as there were initially several different preclinical toxicology programs and study designs in the different regulatory regions prior to harmonization, there were likewise different requirements for how the data and the reports were to be presented to regulatory agencies in Europe, Japan, and the United States. These differed in what should be included in tables, how data should be described and interpreted, how the presentation of the reports should be organized, whether a toxicology overview was necessary and whether a comparison of the animal data with clinical findings was necessary, etc. This reporting format also has now been harmonized so that a single registration dossier containing preclinical studies will be in a format known as the Common Technical Document, or CTD, which will be acceptable for registration in all three regions (see Table 19.3 in the Multidisciplinary section, Guideline M4: Organization of the CTD and Guideline M4S: The CTD – Safety) [44,45]. If properly presented, as this relatively uniform format does (although it wisely provides some flexibility and allows for region-specific information to be presented in Module 1 with uniform presentation of the scientific information in the remaining four Modules), regulatory reviewers in any of the tripartite regions should easily be able to find the desired data and proceed with their review.

It may seem to be putting the cart before the horse mentioning the reporting format before discussing the studies, but if the toxicologist understands generally what is expected in terms of the types of studies and how they are to be presented in the registration documents, this can serve as a guide to organizing the studies for a particular preclinical drug and displaying the data in the proper format from the beginning of the preclinical program, making this process and interaction with the company regulatory affairs (RA) personnel more efficient and productive. Fortunately, there is help at hand, not only in what studies to do to provide the appropriate quality data for regulatory approval (see below), but also help in

TABLE 19.3 ICH Final and Draft Guidelines (Safety, Selected Multidisciplinary)

Category	Title	Type	Date
International Conference on Harmonisation – Safety	S1A The Need for Long-term Rodent Carcinogenicity Studies of Pharmaceuticals (PDF – 100KB)	Final Guidance	03/01/96
	S1B Testing for Carcinogenicity of Pharmaceuticals (PDF – 145KB)	Final Guidance	02/28/98
	S1C(R2) Dose Selection for Carcinogenicity Studies of Pharmaceuticals (PDF – 185KB)	Final Guidance	09/17/08
	S2A Specific Aspects of Regulatory Genotoxicity Tests for Pharmaceuticals (PDF – 123KB)	Final Guidance	04/01/96
	S2B Genotoxicity: A Standard Battery for Genotoxicity Testing of Pharmaceuticals (PDF – 131KB)	Final Guidance	11/21/97
	S2(R1) Genotoxicity Testing and Data Interpretation for Pharmaceuticals Intended for Human Use (PDF – 427KB)	Final Guidance	06/06/12
	S3A Toxicokinetics: The Assessment of Systemic Exposure in Toxicity Studies (PDF – 46KB)	Final Guidance	03/01/95
	S3B Pharmacokinetics: Guidance for Repeated Dose Tissue Distribution Studies (PDF – 14KB)	Final Guidance	03/01/95
	S4A Duration of Chronic Toxicity Testing in Animals (Rodent and Non-rodent Toxicity Testing) (PDF – 21KB)	Final Guidance	06/25/99
	S5A Detection of Toxicity to Reproduction for Medicinal Products S5(R2) Detection of Toxicity to Reproduction for Medicinal Products Toxicity to Male Fertility In November 2005, the ICH incorporated the S5B addendum with S5A and retitled the combined S5 document. The contents of the two guidances were not revised. (PDF – 87KB)	Final Guidance	09/01/94
	S5B Detection of Toxicity to Reproduction for Medicinal Products: S5(R2) Detection of Toxicity to Reproduction for Medicinal Products Toxicity to Male Fertility In November 2005, the ICH incorporated the S5B addendum with S5A and retitled the combined S5 document. The contents of the two guidances were not revised. (PDF – 98KB)	Final Guidance	04/01/96
	S6(R1) Preclinical Safety Evaluation of Biotechnology-Derived Pharmaceuticals (July 2011) with Attachment	Final Guidance	05/17/12
	S7A Safety Pharmacology Studies for Human Pharmaceuticals (PDF – 44KB)	Final Guidance	07/01/01
	S7B Nonclinical Evaluation of the Potential for Delayed Ventricular Repolarization (QT Interval Prolongation) by Human Pharmaceuticals (PDF – 52KB)	Final Guidance	10/19/05
	S8 Immunotoxicity Studies for Human Pharmaceuticals (PDF – 72KB)	Final Guidance	04/12/06
	S9 Nonclinical Evaluation for Anticancer Pharmaceuticals (PDF – 169KB)	Final Guidance	03/05/10
	S10 Photosafety Evaluation of Pharmaceuticals (PDF – 256KB)	Final Guidance	01/26/15
International Conference on Harmonization – Joint Safety/ Efficacy (Multidisciplinary)	M3(R2) Nonclinical Safety Studies for the Conduct of Human Clinical Trials and Marketing Authorization for Pharmaceuticals (PDF – 325KB)	Final Guidance	01/20/10
	M4: Organization of the CTD (PDF – 31KB)	Final Guidance	08/01/01
	M4S: The CTD – Safety (PDF – 60KB)	Final Guidance	08/01/01
	M4S: The CTD – Safety Appendices (PDF – 178KB)	Final Guidance	08/01/01
	M7 Assessment and Control of DNA Reactive (Mutagenic) Impurities in Pharmaceuticals to Limit Potential Carcinogenic Risk (PDF – 260KB)	Final Guidance	06/27/15
	M7(R1) Addendum to ICH M7: Assessment and Control of DNA Reactive (Mutagenic) Impurities in Pharmaceuticals to Limit Potential Carcinogenic Risk; Application of the Principles of the ICH M Guidance to Calculation of Compound-Specific Acceptable Intakes (PDF – 729KB)	Draft Guidance	09/25/15

http://www.fda.gov/Drugs/GuidanceComplianceRegulatoryInformation/Guidances/ucm065006.htm.

IV. BIOSTATISTICS, REGULATORY TOXICOLOGY, AND ROLE OF STUDY DIRECTORS creating the proper end-product, the safety information report that the regulators will use to determine whether the pharmaceutical is worthy of approval. Whether the studies are to be done in-house or externally at a contract research organization (CRO), a summary table of the data for each particular study can be assembled in the format required for the international regulatory dossier, the Common Technical Document (CTD) as the study is being conducted. To aid in this effort, samples of boilerplate data tables acceptable to the agencies for each different type of data and for each study are presented in M4S – Safety Appendices [46]. If the formatted prototypes are set up for the tabulated and written report summaries, they and the reports themselves can be organized and updated in an ongoing manner as the preclinical program progresses and the study reports are completed. The required information will then be organized as required and ready to hand over to RA (who will usually be assembling the full CTD) as soon as they send out the request.

For example, in the Safety portion of the CTD dossier the toxicologist will be mostly involved in preparing portions of Module 2, the Nonclinical Overview (Section 2.4), and the Nonclinical Written and Tabulated Summaries (Section 2.6), and Module 4, Nonclinical Study Reports (Section 4). The tabular summary prototype format can be arranged ahead of time in the correct ICH order by species (eg, mouse, rat, hamster, other rodent, rabbit, dog, nonhuman primate, other nonrodent mammal, and nonmammals), and by route (intended human route, oral, intravenous, intramuscular, intraperitoneal, subcutaneous, inhalation, topical, other), etc., ready for entry of the information. This can facilitate subsequent incorporation of the tabulated and written summaries into the full CTD.

The CTD submission format provides the regulatory reviewer with a relatively straightforward exercise to find the data and reports, in the preferred order, to determine answers to some of their fundamental questions, eg, whether there are sufficient preclinical data, whether the doses for the proposed clinical trials are based on adequate (quality as well as amount) data, and if the preclinical exposures are long enough to support the anticipated exposure duration in the clinical trials. Presenting a complete, well-ordered, and polished document not only will be very much appreciated by the regulatory reviewer (always a wise idea), but is the best opportunity to establish your organization as knowledgeable and professional. You only get one chance to make a good first impression.

ICH Harmonized (and Other) Nonclinical Toxicology Guidelines

In the preclinical toxicology program development of a pharmaceutical should proceed carefully in a stepwise fashion. At present, preclinical assurance of safety is determined first in animals and in other laboratory tests before the drug is administered to normal human subjects (ie, those without the disease indication) to determine human tolerability. As this is proceeding, further animal studies are conducted in a range of doses that exceeds the proposed clinical trial doses and anticipated therapeutic dose, and progresses to multiple doses (if appropriate for the drug, and medical indication) always a step ahead of the next progression in the clinical exposure. In this way one is able to identify and characterize possible toxic effects in animals from single versus multiple doses, dose response, identification of the target organ(s) of toxicity, potential reversibility of a toxic effect, and possible premonitory responses before higher doses and longer exposures are tested in humans.

There are a number of guidances available on many aspects of drug development. Those ICH harmonized guidances that are most useful to the preclinical toxicologist (both finalized and those in draft status) are listed in Table 19.3. Several other guidance documents may also be useful, many of which are not part of the ICH harmonization process, but are unique to the individual agency, eg, FDA-specific, or WHO-specific guidance, and these can be examined online at the appropriate organization's website.

As indicated above, ICH M3(R2), as updated and revised, is the main guidance for small-molecule pharmaceutical drugs indicating the type of preclinical toxicology studies to be done. For biotechnology-derived products, the nonclinical safety studies that should be done are described in ICH S6. However, for biologicals both of these should be considered together because aside from identifying which studies to do, ICH M3(R2) is the one guidance that indicates the critical timing of when these studies, small-molecule or biological, should be done during drug development relative to the timing of certain human clinical trials. For both types of drugs, the timing of the preclinical studies relative to conducting clinical trials is given in Table 19.4.

In addition, ICH M3(R2) discusses many other aspects of preclinical drug development and is a rich source of information and advice. For special situations such as life-threatening diseases with no available treatment, innovative therapeutic modalities such as small interfering RNA and other specific situations that require a more tailored approach to preclinical development, the timing and extent, or even the necessity, of certain preclinical studies may differ from these guidelines and require case-by-case assessment with input from the appropriate FDA reviewing division.

The current in vitro and in vivo toxicology and related studies for the preclinical program generally fall into these categories:

• Safety pharmacology
• Acute toxicity

TABLE 19.4 Duration of Single-Dose and Repeat-Dose
Toxicology Studies to Support Clinical Trials[a]

| Duration of Clinical Trials | Duration of Toxicology Studies | |
	Rodents	Nonrodents
Single dose	2 weeks[b]	2 weeks[b]
Up to 2 weeks	2 weeks	2 weeks
Up to 1 month	1 month	1 month
Up to 3 months	3 months	3 months
Up to 6 months	6 months	6 months
>6 months	6 months	9 months

[a]Check Tables 1 and 2 in ICH M3(R2) for more details of specific situations. Also
see US Food and Drug Administration. ICH: Guidance on the Duration of Chronic
Toxicity Testing in Animals (Rodent and Nonrodent Toxicity Testing); Federal Register;
1999, 64(122):pp. 34259–60.
[b]In the United States, as an alternative to 2-week studies, extended single-dose toxicity
studies can support single-dose human trials. Clinical studies of less than 14 days can
be supported with toxicity studies of the same duration as the proposed clinical study.

- Subacute or subchronic toxicity
- Chronic toxicity
- Genotoxicity
- Carcinogenicity
- Developmental and reproductive toxicity
- Studies in juvenile animals

Studies from all of these or from selected categories may be necessary to include in the preclinical program depending on the clinical indication, the characteristics of the drug, and the duration of the proposed clinical trials. ICH has developed one or more guidelines for each of these categories, and as guideline development is an ongoing process with updates, revisions, and new guidelines added periodically, the current individual ICH guidelines should be consulted for details. In the following, if a more recent revision to the guideline for the activity is available it will be discussed in the study activity section, as this would seem to be more useful to the reader than assembling all the revisions together later. Some study types and their conduct are presented in greater detail elsewhere in this volume, and if so, the appropriate chapter is indicated.

Safety Pharmacology Studies

(See Chapter 7, "Safety Pharmacology")
Safety pharmacology studies are intended to determine whether the test substance in the therapeutic range and above produce effects on physiological functions of vital organ systems (primarily core organs, eg, the cardiovascular, respiratory, and central nervous systems) that may have relevance to human safety (Table 19.3: ICH S7A and S7B). The intent is that these should be conducted before human exposure because if a serious unexpected adverse effect should occur to one or more of these organs

it could be fatal. Of particular concern is the potential for drugs, especially those other than cardiovascular drugs like certain antihistamines, to cause a prolongation of the QT interval of the electrocardiogram (ECG). If heartbeat is altered such that the QT interval is prolonged, there is increased risk of tachyarrhythmia, which very suddenly could be life threatening. Several in vitro approaches are gaining credence for providing useful cardiovascular information such as effects on ion channels, etc.

While functional effects such as the ion-channel assays are important, adverse structural effects can also be critically detrimental. A recent in vitro assay using cardiomyocytes derived from stem cells is claimed to be capable of assessing both structural and functional damage in the same assay, promising to improve predictive capabilities and reduce investigative time and cost [47].

These studies can be added to the conduct of normal general toxicity studies to minimize the use of animals, or they may be performed as standalone studies if a significant toxic response needs to be investigated further.

Acute Toxicity

(See Chapter 5, "Acute, Subacute, and Chronic Toxicity Testing")
Acute toxicity is defined as the toxicity produced by one or more doses administered over a period of 24 h. These studies can be useful for identifying doses causing no adverse effects as well as those causing major life-threatening toxicity. One of the earliest guidances to emerge from the ICH harmonization process was the one on single-dose (acute) toxicity studies. The main intent of the guidance was to confirm that all regulatory regions believed that LD50 studies (the former common practice of administering the drug to fairly large numbers of animals and calculating the dose that caused 50% of them to die) were not necessary, ie, that it was not necessary to intentionally administer doses high enough to kill animals.

Some compounds exhibit very little toxicity (assuming systemic exposure has been confirmed). How high should the range of doses go in these early toxicology studies before they begin to upset normal physiological homeostasis and produce effects that could be mistaken for toxicity? ICH M3(R2) now addresses this question and sets an upper dose limit of 1000 mg/kg for rodents and nonrodents in general toxicity studies if the human dose does not exceed 1 g/day and the exposure ratio, ie, exposure in the preclinical species vs. the clinical exposure, exceeds 10-fold. The upper dose may also be limited if it is not feasible to increase it. This is called the maximum feasible dose (MFD), and applies if it can be shown that physiological mechanisms, eg, absorption for an oral dose, are saturated, or if there are physicochemical limits on the amount of drug that can be presented and sufficient attempts at optimizing formulations have been made.

If the 1000 mg/kg/day dose does not provide a 10-fold exposure margin to the clinical dose, then higher toxicity study doses should be limited by a dose that produces a 10-fold exposure margin or a dose of 2000 mg/kg/day or the MFD, whichever is lower. However, there have been cases where a 10-fold margin is still not achieved at doses of 2000 mg/kg/day. If the MFD has not been reached, then higher dosages may be necessary, or perhaps a different species should be considered. Another approach to determining the limit dose for acute and repeated-dose studies relies on providing a 50-fold margin of exposure (based on group mean area under the blood concentration over time curve, ie, the area under the curve, or AUC) between the exposure in the toxicological species and the clinical systemic exposure.

In addition to the ICH consensus views, the FDA made their own modified acute toxicity guidance (in response to comments received) to provide information that would allow use of single-dose toxicity studies to support single-dose studies in humans. They believed that, although this was not an ICH consensus, it was consistent in general with the ICH position on acute toxicity testing. Therefore this is an FDA-specific modification that only has application in the United States. In these circumstances the acute toxicity study design should be more comprehensive and include pharmacokinetics, clinical pathology, and histology at two points—at an early time in the study and at termination—with the intent of looking for maximum effects and possible recovery [48].

Perhaps the most significant addition to the modified ICH M3(R2) is the possibility of conducting exploratory clinical studies (exploratory INDs in the United States) with minimal toxicology data. These are studies in which, under very prescribed situations, minimal doses of the drug can be administered to humans with limited animal data. The goal is to explore tolerability and (lack of) toxicity in humans during short-term use. They have no diagnostic or therapeutic intent and usually include PK. They require less from the preclinical studies than the normal development plan in order to support the very limited clinical objectives. There is not one approach to conducting a single-dose exploratory study design, but five, and the investigators should choose the most appropriate approach for their purposes. These five approaches include two microdose (≤100 μg) approaches, a single-dose subtherapeutic study, and two repeated-dose exploratory studies. Both repeat-dose studies allow clinical dosing up to 14 days and dose escalation up into the therapeutic range. The ratio between the animal and clinical exposures is determined by the no-observed-adverse-effect-levels (NOAELs) in the rodent and nonrodent studies compared to the clinical dose. For details on each of these five exploratory clinical study designs, see the Exploratory IND section in ICH M3(R2) [49].

Repeat-Dose Toxicity

(See Chapter 5, "Acute, Subacute, and Chronic Toxicity Testing")

Repeat-dose toxicity studies are the backbone of the preclinical drug development program in terms of characterizing the no-observed-effect-levels (NOELs), NOAELs, the maximum-tolerated-dose (MTD), the target organs of toxicity, estimating the human dose, and possible prodromal markers that could be used to monitor onset of adverse responses in man. They also define the multiple dose–response relationship for any observed toxicities and the dose at which they first appear (threshold dose). The possibility of reversal of the adverse effect is also studied. But some questions arise: how many repeat doses are needed to show these effects (duration of the study), and how soon are these data needed in order to be useful in furthering the progress of the clinical trials (timing of the study relative to critical clinical studies)?

Repeat-dose studies can involve durations of 14 days, as well as 1, 3, and 6–9 months. See guidance ICH M3(R2) and S4 for further details on the individual study designs and dose selection. Also see Table 19.4 for the general timing of these individual studies in support of clinical studies of different durations.

Despite the ICH consensus on the conduct of these general toxicity studies, some issues arose during attempts at harmonization with strong, but differing, positions held by certain regions of the tripartite group. Sometimes these different views can have an impact on the individual studies.

Two examples illustrate how such differing regulatory opinions may affect the conduct or timing of repeat-dose studies:

Example 1: Differences remain among the regions on the establishment of reproductive safety prior to admitting men into clinical trials. The Japanese find it necessary to have evidence of the lack of male reproductive toxicity before admitting men into their clinical trials (either a 2-week rat study with testicular histopathology, or a male rat fertility study is required—see Note two in ICH M3(R2)), and the United States and Europe are becoming more sensitive to this, but don't require it at present (see below). The earliest preclinical toxicity study in which histopathology of the testes would normally be conducted is the 14- or 28-day general toxicity study, and current ICH guidelines indicate that histopathology is the most sensitive method to detect effects on spermatogenesis (ICH M3 (R2) and ICH S5 (R2)). Because of the increasing regulatory and reproductive health importance of this parameter, it is a key consideration in these early repeat-dose studies whether to use animals of an age at which the majority have attained puberty.

Current guidelines for these studies call for young adult rats approximately 6 weeks of age when the study is initiated, while dogs should be 4–6 months of age. Rats 6 weeks of age will usually be sexually mature. However, all dogs 4–6 months of age generally will not have attained puberty, therefore making it difficult to achieve a toxicologically meaningful testicular evaluation in the nonrodent species. If the histological evaluation shows no sperm present in the testes or epididymides, is this due to a toxic drug effect or just that the animals weren't mature enough to produce sperm? Male beagles (the most commonly used dog species) attain sexual maturity at 6–12 months of age [50]. While 6 months may be the start of puberty for some dogs, there's quite a bit of variation in the onset of puberty. Accordingly, some veterinary toxico-pathologists specializing in testicular toxicity and effects on spermatogenesis recommend that dogs should be at least 10 months old at the beginning of a study to ensure sexual maturity in a majority of those treated if the reproductive effects are to be evaluated, and this is the practice in several CROs surveyed [51]. Therefore early resolution of this question, ie, in the 28-day repeat-dose general toxicity studies, once again requires consideration of the regulatory region(s) intended for marketing approval, and appropriate animal age selection and study design. If sexually mature animals are used, this study can support men being included in Phase I–II clinical trials with greater assurance of providing necessary reproductive toxicity data in Japan (as well as the other regions), and is an earlier alternative to waiting to conduct a male fertility study.

As an indication of regulatory evolution, the US FDA has recently provided a draft guideline for evaluating the potential for male-mediated developmental risk, ie, to the fetus, in pharmaceuticals [52]. Here, they propose that a potential exists not only for genetic damage to occur during spermatogenesis, but that the presence of the active pharmaceutical ingredient (API) or its metabolites in the seminal fluid or on the surface of the sperm could directly impact the fetus, or be absorbed into the female circulation via the vaginal mucosa. The FDA summarizes their concerns as follows:

> When a trial involves exposure to a potential reproductive or developmental toxicant, issues of risk characterization, informed consent, and contraceptive options are important considerations. Investigators designing clinical studies involving male subjects need to consider the potential for adverse effects on the resulting conceptus with a sexual partner who is or may become pregnant.

This draft guidance is now out for comment, and it is apparent that not all parties agree on the degree of potential risk. For example, the Teratology Society believes, and has officially commented to FDA, that research shows that direct exposure to the embryo/fetus through the vaginal canal is not a plausible route of exposure, and while the drug may be absorbed through the vaginal wall and eventually pass through the placenta, vaginal absorption is usually much lower, by several orders of magnitude, over oral administration [52]. Once all comments are received, the FDA will carefully consider them and adjust the guidance if they determine it's appropriate. Then it will require toxicologists to ascertain regional regulatory differences in the expectations of what nonclinical studies will need to be done to satisfy different regulatory authorities worldwide before men can be admitted into clinical trials for drugs that are potential reproductive toxicants. Since admitting women of childbearing potential into clinical drug trials has required special consideration for years, exposure of men to an experimental molecular entity without regard for reproductive harm to them or their partners has generally been acceptable in the west. That attitude has been long overdue for a significant change, which now seems to be getting attention. Nevertheless, a worldwide uniform guidance may not be forthcoming for some time, or perhaps this will be a case where regional differences get codified (see the next example).

A further indication of the FDA's move to recognize the importance of the reproductive health of male subjects and patients is their new drug label proposed rule (see below) that says the label must now include information under the heading of "Females **and Males** of Reproductive Potential."

Example 2: In other aspects of recent guideline development, the duration of chronic studies was debated among the regulatory regions. Previously, while all three regions could agree that 6 months' duration for the chronic rodent study was sufficient, the duration of the chronic nonrodent study was controversial, with different views among the tripartite regions. Because of their experience with late-emerging toxicities in some compounds, the FDA was convinced that in order to get the most accurate assessment of long-term exposure toxicity, the chronic nonrodent study had to extend to at least 12 months, whereas in Japan and Europe 6 months in rodents and nonrodents were considered sufficient to support long-term clinical trials. In order to get the repeat-dose guideline finalized, the ICH working group agreed to disagree, and the original guideline had an asterisk indicating that for the United States, chronic studies in a nonrodent would extend to 12 months, while Japan and Europe were listed in the table as requiring 6 months. In practice, in order to meet requirements in different regulatory/marketing regions in a timely fashion some sponsors would perform both 6- and 12-month studies simultaneously in dogs (or do a large 12-month dog study with a 6-month pull for necropsy of a portion of the dogs) to speed up their approval timelines for different regions. Both approaches were more expensive and used more animals. In this era of evermore sensitivity to wasteful/unnecessary use of animals (3Rs:

refinement, reduction, replacement), not to mention the monetary cost, this had to be corrected. The tripartite meetings were reconvened on this matter, and old data were reevaluated and new data reviewed. It was finally agreed by consensus that a study duration of 9 months in nonrodents would be acceptable to all three regions for most compounds (with special allowances for certain compounds where durations of 6 months or 12 months might be more appropriate) [53].

Genotoxicity

(See Chapter 6, "Genetic Toxicology")

Genotoxicity tests assess the possibility that adverse genetic effects could occur from exposure to a pharmaceutical. Generally, damage occurs either by effects on the genes, eg, point mutations, deletions, substitutions, or by chromosome damage to the two-stranded chromosome or one of the two strands, or can occur as a result of damage to the spindle mechanism, which would result in an abnormal number of chromosomes in the daughter cells. Assays have been developed to evaluate each of these possible mechanisms, and the battery of tests recommended by the guidelines examines at least two different endpoints, point mutations, and chromosome damage. Compounds that are positive in these tests have the potential to be human carcinogens and/or mutagens. But because more is known about the relationship of chemical exposure and carcinogenesis in humans, and less for heritable diseases, genotoxicity tests have been used mainly to predict carcinogenicity. However, it is possible that a positive result in these assays could suggest a potential for a germ-line mutation, giving rise to a heritable human disease.

Carcinogenicity studies for drugs are usually done in parallel with late-stage clinical trials. Therefore the potential for carcinogenicity is not known at the time humans are first dosed and throughout most of the clinical trials; many people are already exposed before the carcinogenic potential is known. Therefore genotoxicity tests are conducted early in the program to provide some indication of this potential before clinical trials are begun. The initial ICH battery called for a total of three tests: an in vitro Ames bacterial point mutation test, either a mammalian in vitro chromosome aberration test or an in vitro mouse lymphoma thymidine kinase gene mutation test, plus an in vivo rodent bone-marrow chromosome damage test (rodent micronucleus assay). If an in vitro assay were positive, the guideline indicated it should be followed up by another in vivo test in a tissue other than bone marrow (a negative in vitro response now no longer has to be repeated if it was adequately performed). However, the unscheduled DNA synthesis (UDS) test previously performed to satisfy this recommendation rarely, if ever, produced useful information

when used for drugs. For this reason, as well as other concerns that needed to be addressed, and new technologies that have emerged, a new ICH genotoxicity guideline has been prepared [54].

There are several major changes in the new guideline. Among the more significant are:

1. The in vitro micronucleus test is now accepted as an in vitro mammalian assay for chromosomal breakage;
2. A second battery of tests is offered that includes an in vivo test with two endpoints for chromosome damage, the bone-marrow micronucleus, and an assay for DNA-strand breakage in liver cells (eg, comet assay);
3. An encouragement to include genotoxicity endpoints in the repeat-dose general toxicology studies to reduce the total number of animals used.

Interestingly, technology has advanced for systems of automated analysis (eg, image analysis and flow cytometry), and these can now be used to satisfy regulatory assessments for genotoxicity if appropriately validated. For example, the most extensively advanced in terms of validated data is the flow cytometric method for analyzing micronuclei after in vitro or in vivo exposure using anti-CD71, a cell-surface marker for young red blood cells, ie, reticulocytes [55]. This technique can also be employed for analyzing micronuclei in a variety of specialized cell lines via in vitro exposure, which is now acceptable under the new revisions.

Besides chromosome damage evidenced by micronuclei, another genotoxic mechanism, point mutations, can now also be analyzed rapidly using a similar cytometric technique. Mutation in the X-linked Pig-a reporter gene is a very rare event that requires processing a great number of cells in order to be detected. This is well suited to cytometric analysis, which for Pig-a mutations can analyze one to five million cells in 7 min [56–58]. These assays, simply using blood samples, can be accomplished as adjuncts to the general 28-day rat toxicology study, and thereby are good candidates for fulfilling that recommendation of the newly revised genetic toxicity guideline.

Carcinogenicity

(See Chapter 12, "Preclinical Evaluation of Carcinogenicity")

Carcinogenicity is one of the most anxiety-producing side effects of new drug development, and because the disease usually has a long gestation period before manifesting, it requires long-term, usually lifespan, testing in animals to have some idea of the carcinogenic potential of a new pharmaceutical. Also, as stated in the ICH proceedings:

...a carcinogenicity study is one of the most resource-consuming in terms of animals and time. In the interests of decreased animal use and protection, but without prejudicing safety, such studies should only be performed once...

Lifetime carcinogenicity studies are usually required in two species (rat and mouse) by the proposed clinical route or a route that provides the greatest systemic exposure, for any drug that is to be administered chronically, ie, continuously for 6 months or longer, or where the combined total lifespan exposure is at least 6 months.

The FDA does not usually provide guidance on the design of preclinical studies or their conduct other than those presented in the guideline documents. But in the case of carcinogenicity bioassays, review of the study protocol by the Carcinogenicity Assessment Committee (CAC) of the FDA is expected, and they will provide written comments on the appropriateness of the protocol regarding approaches to testing, study type, doses employed, and other design issues. Of course, the sponsor will have reviewed and taken into account the relevant guidances [59–62] before preparing the protocol that is submitted for review. These studies, notably resource intensive, of long duration, and costly, are usually conducted concurrent with the Phase III clinical trials, ie, after clinical usefulness of the drug is confirmed in Phase II. The guideline allows the possibility that sometimes these may be conducted as postmarketing commitments. See the description of the new ICH guideline, S9 (below), for preclinical development of oncology therapeutics, for both small-molecule and biological compounds.

Reproductive and Developmental Toxicity

(See Chapter 9, "Developmental and Reproductive Toxicology")

In the wake of the thalidomide disaster in the late 1950s and early 1960s it became very apparent that drugs intended for use in women of childbearing potential, pregnant or not, must be tested for their potential to cause birth defects prior to being allowed on the market. A three-segment testing paradigm was recommended for evaluating effects on the entire reproductive cycle: Segment I—fertility, Segment II—teratology (birth defects), both in the rat and the rabbit as a nonrodent species, and Segment III—perinatal and postnatal development. However, there was "considerable overlap in methodology" among the three major pharmaceutical regions. In an effort to reduce these differences between the EU, Japan, and the United States, an ICH guideline was developed to describe a series of three studies that basically had the same goal as previously:

to allow detection of immediate and latent effects of exposure, ... through one complete life cycle, i.e. from conception in one generation through conception in the following generation,

but it brought consensus as to how these should be performed. To accomplish this broad undertaking, the lifecycle was divided into six stages:

1. Premating to conception
2. Conception to implantation
3. Implantation to closure of the hard palate (primary organogenesis)
4. Closure of the hard palate to the end of pregnancy (fetal development and growth)
5. Birth to weaning
6. Weaning to sexual maturity.

These are evaluated within the framework of three study designs (differing somewhat from the old Segments I–III) as follows:

4.1.1 Study of Fertility and Early Embryonic Development to Implantation

4.1.2 Study for Effects on Prenatal and Postnatal Development Including Maternal Function

4.1.3 Study for Effects on Embryo-Fetal Development (EFD)

See Chapter 9 in this volume, "Developmental and Reproductive Toxicology," for further details on the design and conduct of these individual studies.

The rat is the primary species used in these studies, with the rabbit serving as a nonrodent for the second species in the embryo-fetal development studies only. ICH S5 (R2) recognizes that other research systems are available that might be appropriate for screening or to elucidate mechanisms, but none currently can cover the full range of incredible maternal/embryo-fetal complexity found in mammalian systems involving a maternal host of homogenetic background, placental interface, and a second potentially exposed organism with heterogenetic background. For that reason, these developmental and reproductive toxicity studies are done now, and will be for the foreseeable future, in living pregnant mammalian animals.

Adult drug toxicokinetic (TK) assessment has likely been conducted in the rat 28-day general toxicology study or earlier, and is not necessary to be done again in pregnant rats (although it may be useful to clarify whether pregnancy affects the PK parameters). The rabbit TK and dose response, however, have usually not been examined previously, and this is advised here as the rabbit often responds differently from the rat to a given drug.

There are possibilities mentioned in the guideline for combining some of these stages in a single rat study, eg, fertility through embryo-fetal development. Other variations and alternative study designs may be used to reduce the time and number of animals if all stages are adequately investigated with sufficient numbers of animals/embryo-fetuses. Be reminded that studying the effects on embryo-fetal development in a nonrodent second species (usually the rabbit, but other qualified nonrodent if the rabbit isn't appropriate) is always expected.

In a recent development for reproductive toxicity testing, the ICH working group evaluated data from several hundred drugs for different indications for the period 1999 to 2006 and found that dose-ranging fetal evaluation studies with visceral/external examinations gave good predictivity for the outcome of the definitive embryo-fetal development studies. They concluded that such dose-ranging studies could be used to support clinical studies of up to 3 months' duration that enrolled only 150 or fewer women of childbearing potential (WOCBP), who must use one or more contraceptive precautions (each of which have less than a 1% failure rate) to prevent pregnancy. The FDA alone presently allows conduct of such clinical studies in WOCBP even without the dose-ranging studies, and will continue to do so because historical evidence indicates to them that the rate of pregnancy in such a small group of women, in trials of this short duration or less, with pregnancy restrictions, is extremely low. In the EU and Japan, however, the new revised guidance of providing dose-ranging embryo-fetal development studies to limited numbers of WOCBP is followed. In all regulatory regions definitive developmental studies are usually required to support inclusion of WOCBP in larger clinical studies, although some exceptions can be made [63–65]. There are also special considerations in the requirement for and/or timing of reproductive toxicity studies for developing oncology therapeutics (ICH S9), biotechnology products (ICH S6(R1)), and vaccines (see ICH M3(R2) and WHO Technical report series 927).

Studies in Juvenile Animals

(See Chapter 11, "Toxicity Studies to Support Clinical Trials in the Pediatric Population")

Many therapeutics marketed in the United States are used in pediatric patients despite a lack of adequate information on safety and/or efficacy in the labeling for a majority of them. Such use assumes that pediatric patients will exhibit similar disease progression and will respond to the drug for a particular indication similarly to adults. However, due to differential organ and physiological development, drug effects in pediatric patients may be different from those known to occur in adults. Some drugs may have no effect in pediatric patients, while others may produce exaggerated effects, or previously unknown adverse events. If the pediatric population is likely to be given the drug, juvenile animal studies may assist in identifying postnatal developmental toxicities that may not be revealed in the general and reproductive toxicity assessments. Such studies may be conducted as standalone studies or as modified study designs, eg, modification of a prepostnatal reproductive study to include animals of similar developmental status as the pediatric

population of concern. They are especially relevant when known target-organ toxicity occurs in tissues that undergo significant postnatal development.

Not all drug indications need to be studied in juveniles, however. The main considerations important in determining the appropriateness and design of juvenile animal studies are:

1. The intended or likely use of the drug in children;
2. The timing of dosing in relation to phases of growth and development in pediatric populations and juvenile animals;
3. The potential differences in pharmacological and toxicological profile between mature and immature systems; and
4. Any established temporal developmental differences in animals relative to pediatric populations.

After considering the points above, and before assuming that juvenile toxicity studies are required for a particular indication/drug, it is advisable that the sponsor confer with the appropriate FDA reviewing division to determine whether juvenile studies will be needed as this is often determined on a case-by-case basis [66].

Oncology Therapeutics

(See Chapter 26, "Preclinical Development of Oncology Drugs")

The development of new cancer therapeutics needs to be very efficient and expeditious because of the life-threatening nature of neoplastic disease. Once again, here is a pressing situation where there are disparate approaches to the preclinical development of these drugs in the EU, Japan, and the United States. Earlier attempts to provide guidance focused mainly on small-molecule drugs and didn't include biological therapeutics. In recognition of the need to develop more comprehensive guidance, ICH has introduced a new guidance, ICH S9, specifically to update, coordinate the various approaches, and address these problems. The scope of the guidance focuses on patients with late-stage or advanced disease, ie, progressive disease for which there are no remaining treatment options, life expectancy is limited, or where the current therapy is ineffective. Therefore although there is still a need for safety evaluation (eg, no mortality or irreversible serious toxicities), there is less concern for side effects as it's critical that the patient derive some pharmacological benefit, which for these types of drugs is usually attained at high doses and side effects are reasonably well tolerated. Establishing preclinical proof of principle and other information that will influence dose selection and identifying investigational biomarkers are minimal but sometimes essential bits of information that will assist in further development. The guidance document doesn't provide specific studies that must be done, but encourages the selection of studies based on sound scientific principles.

The guidance does specify that the core safety pharmacology studies be done, ie, cardiovascular, respiratory, and central nervous system effects, and encourages that these be done in concert with the conduct of normal general toxicology studies. It is also important that pharmacokinetic (PK) information has been obtained. Other main points in ICH S9 are listed below (as revised from Ref. [67]):

- A 1-month toxicology study usually adequate to support phase 1 and 2 (further animal studies will only be conducted on drugs showing clinical promise at this point).
- Limited duration of toxicity study (1 month) supports continued clinical treatment, ie, beyond 1 month, in phases 1 and 2.
- No need for 6/9 month toxicity studies; 3-month toxicology studies are usually adequate to support development.
- Usually no need for separate fertility (histopathology done in general toxicology studies) nor peripostnatal studies.
- Only one embryo-fetal development study is usually needed (can be pilot study) even if that study is positive (likely, since many antineoplastic drugs affect rapidly divide cell populations).
- Need for recovery groups is based on the science of the drug.
- Safety pharmacology assessments can be conducted within the general toxicology studies.
- No need for nonrodent studies for initiation of clinical trials with cytotoxic drugs.
- Main principle to be achieved by initial clinical dose: must have pharmacological effect and be reasonably safe to use (so initial dose not based on NOAEL, but rather on pharmacological effectiveness).
- Initial starting dose based on minimally anticipated biologic effect for protein therapies with immune agonistic properties, but based on toxicity data for antibodies and all other cases.
- Studies to be conducted in late-stage development to conserve resources and reduce animal use [67,68].

Biotechnology: ICH S6(R1) Updates

(See various biotechnology-related chapters.)

Biological therapeutics are a unique class of drugs that present some different properties and, therefore, require different considerations and solutions to those of small-molecule drugs. Nevertheless, the general approaches to preclinical toxicological evaluation described in ICH M3(R2) are still relevant, but must be combined with the exceptions and specific considerations noted in ICH S6 and its addendum, now in the combined designation ICH S6 (R1). Since biologics are usually proteins or other large molecular weight entities, they are likely to be immunogenic in rodents and

will form neutralizing antibodies to the protein drug, particularly in repeat dose studies, that render it ineffective. If it is biologically ineffective, it is also likely to be toxicologically uninformative or any responses noted may be irrelevant to human safety. Nonprimate species may also not have the appropriate molecular target, also rendering the biological drug ineffective. Therefore species specificity is an important criterion to acknowledge and address in the preclinical program. In some cases when there is no relevant species in which to test the biological, it may be possible to create a transgenic animal (rodent) expressing the human target, or produce a homologous protein to the rodent orthologous target. However, if this effort is intended solely for the purpose of generating preclinical data in a second species, this practice is discouraged and is considered unnecessary, except in some cases for hazard identification for medical clarification.

There are several other clarifications and updates due to advances in science that the ICH S6 addendum addresses, eg, those dealing with study design such as dose selection and toxicological response potential after pharmacodynamic saturation of the receptor target, the duration of chronic toxicity studies (6 months in a pharmacologically responsive species with an indication of recovery). Further, although it is expected that human biopharmaceuticals will result in neutralizing, or otherwise antidrug antibodies in test animals, it is now known that measurement of these can be difficult, and, contrary to the original ICH S6, they don't necessarily have to be measured if there is other evidence that is useful in interpreting the findings of the repeat-dose study. The standard carcinogenicity bioassay may also be avoided if there is sufficient other information, eg, from the literature or mechanistic studies, that the biopharmaceutical would not be likely to have carcinogenic potential.

Some of the most difficult to resolve and controversial topics have been the assessment of developmental and reproductive toxicity for biopharmaceuticals, particularly for those that are only biologically active in humans or nonhuman primates. Where the biologic is active in rodents and rabbits, these species should be used in the normal assessments described in ICH S5(R2). However, if it is only active in humans or nonhuman primates, transplacental transfer of macromolecules, ie, embryo-fetal exposure, occurs in primates only toward the latter part of organogenesis, unlike the rodent. An adjustment to the study design that extends the treatment period to ensure fetal exposure is warranted. Such a revised design would cover all ICH developmental stages from embryo-fetal development through peripostnatal development (from ICH S5 stages C through E). Other reproductive parameters should be studied more extensively (perhaps including male and female hormone measurement) in the chronic repeat-dose studies [67,69].

Vaccines

(See Chapter 27, "Preclinical Safety Evaluation of Vaccines")

Nonclinical (preclinical) studies on standard vaccines emphasize characterizing the immune reaction rather than any toxicological endpoints related to the antigen. Vaccines use adjuvants to improve or augment their antigenicity, and toxicology studies are limited to those that would be necessary to affirm the safety of the adjuvant. Currently, aluminum hydroxide and aluminum phosphate (alum) are adjuvants used for standard licensed human vaccines in the United States. Alum binds to proteins, causing them to precipitate, and this elicits an inflammatory response that increases the immunogenicity of the antigen nonspecifically [70]. The potential safety concerns for investigational adjuvants (any other than the aluminum adjuvants) may include injection site reactions, fever, other systemic adverse effects (nausea, headache), immune-mediated events (anaphylaxis, uveitis, or arthritis), systemic chemical toxicity to tissues or organs, teratogenicity, and carcinogenicity. If the sponsor wants to use an adjuvant other than the approved alum, preclinical animal safety studies on the adjuvant/vaccine should be performed, then discussed with FDA's Center for Biologics Evaluation and Research (CBER). The adjuvant–antigen combination, formulated together, is approved as a single product.

New combination vaccines (consisting of two or more live organisms, inactivated organisms, or purified antigens) must be studied for appropriate immunogenicity in an animal model. The response to each of the antigens in the vaccine should be assessed as well as the quality of response, ie, characterization of antibody class, avidity, affinity half-life, or function, eg, examining its ability to neutralize the target agent or toxin.

Protection studies are recommended using an animal model, if available, for new or combination vaccines with a new antigen that has not been previously studied in humans. Protection is demonstrated by challenging with a virulent strain(s) of each organism against which the combination vaccine is intended to protect. Such studies should be performed early in the development cycle, must use scientifically valid procedures, and be robust enough for the results to be statistically valid [71].

Advances in biotechnology have produced novel vaccines that may be, eg, nucleic acid-based (DNA), recombinant fusion protein vaccines, and genetically altered attenuated live vaccines [72]. They may contain novel adjuvants and be administered by unique delivery systems. For the basic toxicity assessment, the relevant animal species and strain, dosing schedule, method of vaccine administration, and timing of evaluation endpoints should be considered in the study design of the single toxicology study. If the vaccine is to be administered to humans via a particular device, the same device should be used in the animal study, if feasible. The toxicity assessment of the vaccine formulation can be done in a standalone toxicity study, but in the interest of reducing the number of animals used, it is advisable to combine toxicity endpoints into studies of safety and activity. Local tolerance should also be assessed.

The safety profile should be characterized in a species that is sensitive to the pathogenic organism or toxin. Toxicity tests in one such relevant species are sufficient for the initiation of clinical trials, but testing in additional species may be necessary to characterize the vaccine product, or to address safety if species or strain-specific differences are noted in pharmacodynamics. The toxicity study should use a dose (determined in pilot studies) that maximizes animal exposure and immune response (eg, producing peak antibody response). The dose that produces the best antibody response (determined from pilot studies) is the single-dose level that is used in the definitive study.

The dosing regime in the toxicology study should mimic that proposed in the human trial, but should be based on the kinetics of the immune response, eg, primary and secondary antibody responses, of the animal species relative to that in human. Accordingly, the timing interval between doses in an animal model may be quite different from what is proposed for the human study in order to mimic the human exposure. The nature of the target and the antibody may determine how many doses are administered. The intended clinical route should be used, but other routes may also be used to understand the toxicity of the product, if necessary. The study design should include a negative control group, and, if appropriate, active control groups (eg, the vaccine formulation without antigen). Additional treatment groups should be used to investigate reversibility at different time points after treatment or for detecting delayed adverse responses.

A broad spectrum of endpoints should be obtained including potential for local inflammatory reactions, effects on draining lymph nodes, systemic toxicity, and on the immune system. Other standard toxicity endpoints should be monitored. The WHO guideline should be reviewed for details of the endpoints recommended. Complete necropsy and histopathology, especially of the immune organs (including Peyer's patches or bronchus-associated lymphoid tissue), and an examination of the site of vaccine administration should be performed. It is important to evaluate local tolerance either in the repeat-dose toxicity study or as a standalone study for all sites that come into contact with the vaccine antigen. Special immunological investigations (eg, immune complexes, humoral or cell-mediated responses) may be necessary.

Developmental toxicity studies are usually not necessary for vaccines indicated for childhood administration. If the target population includes women of childbearing potential, however, developmental toxicology studies should be conducted, perhaps using a variation of the ICH S5(R2) with a combined design that evaluates the embryo, fetal, and newborn development (stages C-E) in a species that mounts an immune response to the vaccine. Confirmation of embryo/fetal exposure should be obtained by measuring induced antibody in cord or fetal blood. Different dosing schemes may be necessary to ensure an immune response is achieved during gestation.

Genotoxicity and carcinogenicity studies are normally not required. Safety pharmacology studies may be desirable if previous data suggest that the vaccine may affect physiological functions. These studies could be combined into the general toxicity studies. As for other types of vaccines, if adjuvants are used with a biotechnology-derived vaccine, their activity and possible toxicity should be considered [72,73].

TRANSLATING NONCLINICAL DATA INTO CLINICALLY USEFUL INFORMATION—DRUG LABELS

One of the most important exercises in drug development is interpreting what the laboratory and animal data mean with regard to the human response. Will this new drug be effective for the target disease? This is primarily the role of the pharmacologist. But before the FDA will accept this new molecular entity as a drug another main question must be addressed: is it safe? This is the main role of the toxicologist, with the assistance of those in other disciplines. In order to accomplish this, the toxicologist must carefully consider all the data at hand that could have a bearing on ultimate toxic effects, not just those data from specific toxicology studies. Then these conclusions must be condensed in a meaningful way to provide useful information to the clinician and the patient and used to format the drug label [74].

One segment of this exercise that has had a difficult time meeting the goal of providing useful clinical information from complex animal data has been that of making sense of the effects on reproduction and embryo/fetal development. We'll use this as an example of the importance of communicating drug risk in the drug label.

Consider the process. Once the reproductive and developmental animal studies are complete and the data are evaluated, the conclusions must be translated into a comprehensive statement that describes the types and degree of potential risk to human fertility, pregnancy, and embryo/fetal development. This is initially the role of the reproductive toxicologist or teratologist who considers the strength of the data (eg, for birth defects, the

incidence of this birth defect in the untreated control animal historical data, how extensively the effect occurs across litters vs. within litters, whether similar effects are present in just rodents or are present across rodent and nonrodent species, etc.) and makes some reference to those determinations in the report conclusions. Other results from techniques such as embryo or tissue culture, while useful, at present can only provide teratogen mechanistic data, not risk assessment. That can come only from a complex whole mammalian system with maternal circulatory/placenta/embryo interfaces and consideration of other pharmacodynamic and toxicologic data in comparison with human data. Ultimately, these study outcomes usually provide the only scientific data available to the clinical researcher who has to try to understand the potential for the drug to adversely effect reproduction and embryo/fetal development before healthy individuals are first exposed in the clinical trials. Almost any clinical trial involving women would likely expose women of childbearing potential to the experimental drug and these subjects could inadvertently get pregnant. The investigating clinician has to be aware of potential fertility and other reproductive problems that might place limitations or concerns on subject recruitment, and could require knowledgeable discussions on these topics for truly informed consent. Likewise for the family physician or Ob&Gyn—these are the only data available to counsel the pregnant patient since it is unethical to test new compounds in women of childbearing potential (except under limited circumstances in the United States—see above) without first having such predictive information.

For many years in the United States, the FDA tried to provide guidance by classifying drugs according to five pregnancy categories, A,B,C,D, and X, based on available information on the potential degree of reproductive and developmental harm. These are described as follows:

A **Controlled studies in humans show no risk** Well-controlled studies in pregnant humans show no risk to the fetus.

B **No evidence of risk in humans** Well-controlled studies in pregnant women show no increased risk of fetal abnormalities, but there are adverse findings in animals; or, there are no adequate human studies, but animal studies show no fetal risk.

C **Risk cannot be ruled out** There are no well-controlled human studies, and studies in pregnant animals are either also nonexistent or show adverse effects. There is a potential risk for fetal harm, but the potential risk to the human fetus cannot be adequately ascertained and the benefits may outweigh the risks.

D **Positive evidence of human risk** Studies in pregnant women or postmarketing data have demonstrated human fetal risk, but the benefits of the drug outweigh the potential risk to the fetus.

X **Contraindicated in pregnancy** Studies in animals or humans, or investigational or postmarketing reports, have demonstrated fetal abnormalities or risk that outweigh any potential benefit to the patient.

Much debate followed for years upon the use of these pregnancy category designations as to how relevant and useful is the information they provide to the clinical situation. Despite good intentions, these categories, other than A or X, do not provide very clear clinical direction. This is especially so when it is apparent from a review of drug labels in the Physician's Desk Reference that most new drugs under investigation ultimately are assigned to pregnancy category C, ie, they either have no reproductive and developmental data or the animal data show some evidence of adverse reproductive or developmental effects, but human data are not available. How is the healthcare professional supposed to meaningfully evaluate the risk of fetal harm for the pregnant patient, or the potential effect on fertility for men or women of childbearing potential?

To improve risk communication generally the FDA undertook to revise the entire drug label, making it more "user friendly." The final rule on content and format of the whole drug label, commonly referred to as the Physician Labeling Rule (PLR), was published in January of 2006 [74], but the sections addressing pregnancy and related areas were purposely left unchanged at that point to allow the FDA time to do more research and to discuss these sensitive matters with the prospective stakeholders. It was determined that because of the confusion noted when interpreting the drug category information it was often difficult for a clinician to determine whether the benefits of the drug outweighed the potential fetal risks identified in the animal studies. A narrative description was deemed to be much preferred over the five-category system.

After a proposed FDA rule dealing with these sections of the drug label was issued in 2008, the final rule known commonly as the Pregnancy, Labeling, and Lactation Rule (PLLR) was published on December 4, 2014, and was effective as of June 30, 2015. It requires:

- The removal of the pregnancy categories A, B, C, D, and X from all human prescription drug and biological product labeling; and
- the old label subsections of "Pregnancy," "Labor and delivery," and "Nursing mothers," to be replaced with "Pregnancy," "Lactation," and "Females and Males of Reproductive Potential."

These revised pregnancy label statements will be a narrative description, following a standardized format, of the scientific information derived from the preclinical studies, and what that information may mean for human pregnancy overall and for the developing fetus. The clinical considerations should be aimed at informing healthcare providers who need to make prescribing decisions and counsel patients. Furthermore, the data underlying the risk summary and clinical considerations should be discussed.

It then describes the order of, and what should be included in, each of these subsections, eg, each of the Pregnancy and Lactation subsections should include "Risk Summary," "Clinical Considerations," and "Data." Under the Pregnancy subsection "Risk Summary" should provide "risk statement(s) that describe for the drug, the risk of adverse developmental outcomes [including a description of the background risk of major birth defects and miscarriage] based on all relevant human data, animal data, and the drug's pharmacology," and these statements must be included even when there are no data or information available because such information should be clearly expressed.

The "Lactation" subsection likewise must have a Risk Summary including a risk–benefit statement (unless breastfeeding is contraindicated), Clinical considerations, and a discussion of the data underlying the Risk and Clinical statements.

If there is no clinical information on whether the drug passes into breast milk (and this is not a normally collected study endpoint in current protocols) the revised label indicates that the animal data should be reviewed. However, at the present time there is no requirement or guidance recommending routinely collecting milk from a lactating animal to determine the passage of a drug into the milk. Reviewing the animal data produced under current guidelines for studies on reproductive effects would, therefore, not be informative. The possibility of the passage of drug into milk would have to be determined in a separate study if the question arose during regulatory review, delaying progress in the drug's development. Since information on a drug's possible effects on lactation, or the presence of the drug in milk have rightly taken on more prominence in the new pregnancy labeling paradigm, there seems to be an implication that this information is regularly at hand, which it is not. There might be data on the drug's octanol/water distribution (partition) coefficient from which some general risk estimate for infant exposure from lactation could be deduced (eg, no risk, or some), but even these ratios are not usually developed in the nonclinical toxicology program. Some regulatory direction on the importance of, and at what point in the program, documenting the presence of drug in milk is desirable. For example, direction on whether it is advisable to collect milk from rats or rabbits routinely as part of the reproduction studies to determine the presence of the test drug in milk would be useful.

THE OPPOSITE END OF THE SPECTRUM—HOMEOPATHY

"Any substance may be considered a homeopathic medicine if it has known 'homeopathic provings' and/or known effects that mimic the symptoms, syndromes, or conditions it is administered to treat, and is manufactured according to the specifications of the Homeopathic Pharmacopoeia of the United States (HPUS). Official homeopathic drugs are those that have been monographed and accepted for inclusion in the HPUS" (http://www.hpus.com). Homeopathic drugs typically contain the lowest concentration of the drug that can mimic (not alleviate) the anticipated symptoms in healthy volunteers, and are therefore suited to consumers who believe in the principle of *similia similibus curentur*—let likes be cured by likes. They are intended for self-limiting conditions since selection of the proper remedy is based on the body's reaction to an illness, presumably with the intent of accelerating the return to health.

While the Physician's Label Rule and the PLLR described above seek to provide clearer communication of efficacy and safety of potent drugs, these drug effects and the potential for scientifically unsupported claims and cures still exist at the other end of the spectrum of drug action, ie, where very little active drug is expected to be present as in homeopathic medications.

Are homeopathic medications drugs or are they in the category of dietary supplements? In many cases, at least in terms of claims for effectiveness, there are many similarities between the two. However, since the category of dietary supplements came along well over a century after the concept of homeopathic medicine, the similarities and distinctions are only relatively recent points of discussion and debate. For the FDA, as long as some agents are promoted as being "intended for use in the diagnosis, cure, mitigation, treatment, or prevention of disease" and are listed in the official US Pharmacopoeia (USP) *or the HPUS*, as are homeopathic medications, they are considered a drug by definition in the FD&C Act of 1938. Dietary supplements, on the other hand, are not allowed to make the claims that identify drugs, and many supplement manufacturers have had to so revise their labels, or be subject to the extensive, and very expensive, safety and efficacy testing required of a New Drug Application (NDA) if they want their product on the market. The homeopathic inclusion in the FD&C Act was due in large part to Senator Royal Copeland of New York, a principal author of the Act who was a physician trained in homeopathy. As such, homeopathic drugs, whether prescription or over-the-counter, have been under the regulatory jurisdiction of FDA since 1938.

Toxicologists who embrace Paracelsus' dictum that the dose makes the poison may not see much cause for concern about adverse side effects from homeopathic medications. However, the FDA does have increasing concern due to the recent growth of the homeopathic industry, the increasing market for these products, and reported adverse effects or the potential for them [75]. While most homeopathic drugs are manufactured and marketed in compliance with existing regulations, the FDA have had to issue warnings in recent years about existing individual products that have exhibited serious problems. For example, Zicam, an "unapproved homeopathic," is indicated for treating colds, but over 130 people reported a loss of a sense of smell, and some have apparently lost their sense of smell permanently.

In another example, Hyland's teething tablets were marketed to alleviate babies' teething pains, reminiscent of Mrs. Winslow's Soothing Syrup in the early 1900s that contained morphine (see Fig. 19.4), except that Hyland's teething tablets, instead of morphine, contain belladonna, a toxic alkaloid (atropine) produced by the deadly nightshade plant. Belladonna has been used medicinally for ages. But it's also long been known and used as a poison because, as we now know, it blocks muscarinic receptors with very serious adverse effects at toxic levels [76]. This is the ingredient that gave deadly nightshade its common name. Is this something that should be used in a medicine intended for babies? Hyland claimed the belladonna to be at homeopathic levels in the teething tablets. FDA's investigation, however, indicated Hyland manufactured the teething tablets under poor manufacturing controls that prevented assurance that nontoxic levels of belladonna were consistently low from batch to batch. There was the potential for batches of the tablets with high levels of belladonna to arrive on store shelves without requiring a prescription for purchase due to their "safe" homeopathic levels. After the FDA made this public announcement of concern they met with Hyland who withdrew the teething tablets from the market, reformulated them (still containing belladonna for redness and inflammation, [77]), and reintroduced them for sale after producing an extensive white paper describing why they should be considered safe. Presumably, the manufacturing control problems have since been addressed to the FDA's satisfaction.

Instances like these raise the FDA's concern about the growing market in homeopathy medications ($2.9 billion in 2007) and the increase in the reporting of adverse reactions to homeopathic agents. In 2012 alone over 10,300 exposure cases related to homoeopathic agents were reported to the National Poison Data System, among which over 8300 cases were for children 5 years of age or and younger, and 697 of the total required treatment at a healthcare facility [78]. These homeopathic drug products can contain all sorts of ingredients not only from plants, but also from healthy or diseased animals, human sources, and minerals and chemicals, whether as active or inactive ingredients. Any of these can cause side effects, drug interactions, or allergic or other adverse effects even at highly diluted concentrations. The FDA announced a public hearing (March 27, 2015) to obtain information and listen to comments on this matter from stakeholders. The Agency provided specific issues to be discussed including not only homeopathic drugs and the FD&C Act, but also the Over-the-Counter Drug Review, the FDA's Compliance Policy Guide, and others including issues that could be raised by stakeholders in writing. There was no indication of a forthcoming report from this hearing, but transcripts should be available under the Freedom of Information Act. From their description of the reasons for the hearing it appears that the FDA is considering taking a more active role in the risk regulation, or at least oversight of homeopathic medications.

ADVANCES IN SCIENCE: IMPACT ON REGULATORY TOXICOLOGY

Some prominent toxicologists in years past have criticized protocol guideline-driven toxicology, claiming that with this approach one could meet all the requirements of the protocol [79]:

> yet fail to identify all possible adverse effects of an agent and the corresponding dose–response relationships. Such studies do not characterize the toxicity of the test agent even though they may establish a "safe" dosage level for the agent.

Furthermore, they claimed that the protocols are designed to provide a yes-no answer to toxicological questions, when most such answers are not so black and white, but are more usually described in shades of gray. These were legitimate criticisms then, and they remain so today. If we had the time and resources we could research further, delve deeper and try to answer the questions that present themselves to basic and applied researchers alike. As an applied industrial scientist himself who made many basic research discoveries, Pasteur, believed [6]:

> There are no such things as pure and applied science. There are only science and the application of science.

For the new pharmaceutical toxicologist fresh out of a research-driven graduate program, or perhaps considering transferring from an academic basic research career to one of applied research, these are serious differences that can impact on career satisfaction. They should be given thoughtful consideration, preferably with an experienced mentor, before embarking on such a career transition.

In line with these concepts, and despite today's much-improved nonclinical toxicity testing program overall, the success rate of predicting human adverse effects or extreme pharmacological responses is woefully low. Only 11% of the number of NMEs that enter clinical development actually become licensed as safe and useful drugs. This lack of success has been laid at the doorstep of inadequate nonclinical testing overall and the poor ability to translate those data into meaningful knowledge about how that drug will work in humans. Unfortunately, putting that 11% success rate into real human terms means that most of the drugs that enter clinical development (in other words, humans are exposed) either are not effective, produce unwanted side effects, or are dangerous to the health and well-being of the clinical trial participants or subsequent patients [80]. Clearly, we must do better.

With greater investigative research in drug development, as suggested by the protocol-driven toxicology critics, we could undoubtedly capture a fuller understanding of the mechanisms of toxicity behind the adverse effects we see, rather than try just to find a safe dose where these effects are not likely to occur in the greatest majority of the population. Perhaps we might even unveil other important toxicities that weren't evident in the protocol-driven studies. If this were the case, and we were able to understand the underlying toxicological mechanism of an adverse side effect, we could perhaps alter the treatment regimen to avoid these effects, or make molecular adjustments through medicinal or combinatorial chemistry that would provide a next generation of the drug with the desired pharmacological activity, but devoid of any side effects.

But research is a costly endeavor, and the cost of more intensive mechanistic and basic toxicologic research before testing in the clinic would certainly prevent many new drug initiatives for existing companies, and would present insurmountable barriers to entry into the drug development business for many basic researchers who dream of starting a company and seeing their discovery become an important drug. At least, that would be true using today's drug development research capabilities.

Admittedly, currently used toxicological testing paradigms are based on antiquated test systems and approaches, which is becoming ever more apparent as science advances. Fortunately, many scientists, both basic research-oriented and applied regulatory toxicology-oriented, recognize that the evaluation of toxicity as it applies to health assessments must undergo a revolution. Advances in combinatorial chemistry, imaging, data mining, the "-omics" such as genomics, transcriptomics, proteomics, metabolomics, etc., may provide just such a revolution. Scientists and regulators saw this coming several years ago and have been meeting and planning how best to incorporate these technologies into a new drug-testing paradigm.

The National Research Council (NRC) (including some of the "protocol-driven toxicology" critics mentioned above) has prepared a vision entitled "Toxicology Testing in the Twenty-first Century: A Vision and A Strategy." It describes how they believe regulatory toxicology should be done in the future by using more timely and more cost-effective methods for toxicity testing and a much reduced reliance on live animals. In their report they see a much expanded use of high- and medium-throughput in vitro screening assays, computational toxicology, and systems biology, along with greater use of emerging technologies such as the "-omics" – genomics, transcriptomics, metabolomics, etc. They anticipate that when fully implemented, this new model for regulatory toxicology will transform the way that toxicity testing is conducted. It will rely much less on measuring apical health endpoints in animals and move toward identification of significant perturbations of toxicity pathways using high- and medium-throughput in vitro assays in human cells and cell components [81].

This vision is essentially shared by forward-looking toxicologists in industry and academia as well as those in the different agencies of government. Although there is much support for these visions, there is also varied criticism from different stakeholders [82]. One point that came out of discussions was that if we are going to focus on molecular targets and biochemical pathways rather than whole animals, it will be critically essential if this process is to advance that we identify the relevant pathways of toxicological concern (RTCPs) [83]. As this "Twenty-first Century Vision" is implemented in some form it will intentionally also transform how regulatory agencies evaluate new chemicals, including drugs and biologics, in terms of what types of data they will expect in support of clinical trials (for the ultimate test model will always be the real or perhaps virtual human—human on a chip?) and from what types of assay systems, many of which have yet to be validated for use in regulatory decision-making. Thus the other critical aspect that must be addressed with regard to this "Twenty-first Century Vision" is the relevant responses for regulation (RRRs) [83]. Other organizations have also been contemplating what the future will bring to drug development with these new technologies. For example, the Institute of Medicine convened a panel of experts in "-omics" and has recently published their set of guidelines on how "-omics" technologies and discoveries can be translated into approvable products for clinical tools [84]. And more recently, the Society of Toxicology conducted the third in a series, a 2-day (November 19–20, 2015) international seminar in Arlington, Virginia entitled "FutureTox III: Transforming Twenty-first Century Science into Risk Assessment and Regulatory Decision-Making" with the objectives of (1) advancing the cornerstones of high-throughput risk assessment, (2) moving in vitro and in silico toxicity testing models forward while minimizing dependence on animal testing, and (3)

identifying the risk assessment and regulatory decision-making challenges that will inevitably result from implementing these new strategies.

The first step in drug discovery, and ultimately the new age of toxicological evaluation, is molecular target identification of the disease that can be modulated by a drug specifically designed for that target and that purpose. The emerging technologies of genomics, proteomics, metabolomics, and other "-omics" are facilitating identification of these targets and the toxicological pathways, especially those in human tissue rather than animal tissue. This can lead to human disease-specific targets that are amenable to modulation by drugs. Adverse effects that occur as a result of these modulations should be identified as perturbations in the relevant toxicological pathways and investigated to provide a basis for safety determinations, as noted above.

Nevertheless, animal experimentation is not over. Such investigation by "-omics" methods in animals or animal tissues can be used to identify appropriate markers of disease onset, as well as prodromic responses of toxicity that could be very important in clinical development if the marker identified in animals is also highly predictive of human disease or adverse effects. The regulatory agencies are not blind to the advances in science and technology and how they may impact on their regulatory responsibilities. In order to improve on this process, government-funded scientific research laboratories have been established to support FDA scientific regulatory activities. For example, the National Center for Toxicological Research (NCTR) is a research arm of the FDA organized to provide leadership and scientific solutions to improve regulatory decision-making. It supports the FDA's public health mission, and does this by using and refining emerging technologies to improve the safety evaluation of the products that FDA regulates. NCTR research aims to define toxicology mechanisms, understand human exposure, and assess human risk of susceptibility to toxins and pathogens. It strives to take a leading role in new technologies that will impact on future products the FDA will have to regulate. They are currently focusing on research areas such as bioinformatics, computational toxicology, and nanotechnology. To advance these capabilities, in 2011 the NCTR partnered with the state of Arkansas to establish a new Center for Regulatory Science [85].

The FDA recognizes that it must not only keep pace with, but more importantly utilize, these new scientific advances in order to accomplish its mission, ie, to protect and promote the health of US citizens. They've formulated several initiatives starting in 2004 with the Critical Path Initiative that started with the publication of a report diagnosing the reasons for the widening gap between scientific discoveries and innovative medical treatments. Acting on the outcomes of this report, they set out to develop corrective measures. Headlining their efforts along these lines, on February 24, 2010, the FDA launched its Advancing Regulatory Science Initiative (ARS), and as part of their goal setting they formed a Strategic Plan for Regulatory Science in 2011 in which they identified eight priority areas for improving ways to develop new tools, standards, and approaches to assess the safety, efficacy, quality, and performance of FDA-regulated products [86].

Moreover, concerned regulatory toxicologists and those from industry and academia are now actively coming together in international workshops to raise awareness, improve regulatory laboratory capabilities, and provide interpretative consensus on the new laboratory and computational methods. In August, 2011, the FDA sponsored the first Global Summit on Regulatory Science Research and Innovation at its NCTR facilities with the aim of training worldwide regulatory agency reviewers and other scientists in the newest technologies [87].

Since that initial event in 2011 annual Global Summits on Regulatory Science (GSRS), each with its own specific regulatory science theme, have convened again at NCTR, in China (2012) and Canada (2014) with the 2015 Summit taking place in Parma, Italy. GSRS2014 provided an effective venue for regulators and researchers to meet, discuss common issues, and develop collaborations to address the challenges posed by the application of genomics to regulatory science, with the ultimate goal of integrating novel technical innovations into regulatory decision-making. At the time of writing over 1200 international scientists have been brought up to date through these meetings [88] with the intent that they will return home and increase their country's regulatory awareness in anticipation of ushering in, and implementing, this new age of toxicological evaluation, risk assessment, and regulatory safety determination.

On a more focused level, one area that has made steady gains over the last 10 years is the Agency's computational abilities. Mitchell Cheeseman, acting director of the FDA's Office of Food Additive Safety (OFAS), says that [36]:

> Today…review scientists [throughout the Agency] have access through research collaboration agreements and cooperative research and development agreements, to every significant commercially available software package for modeling toxicology and metabolism data. …review scientists are also active participants…in the development of these tools for regulatory decision making.

Attendance at any of the toxicology meetings (SOT, ACT, EMS, GTA, Teratology Society, etc.) in recent years has made the toxicologist well aware of the implementation of new technologies to toxicology evaluation of new compounds, including technologies such as toxicity testing based on mode of action (MOA) mediated by nuclear receptor activation. Scientists in the chemical industry tested a compound using transgenic mice and rats ("humanized" mice and rats) that contained human receptors as the targets, and other animals that were null for the receptors. The results showed a lack of tumors in the mice with human nuclear receptors after treatment with the chemical, indicating that the chemical would not induce tumors in humans [89]. This was accomplished with far fewer animals than would be used in a standard toxicological evaluation, and it provided specific information relative to that chemical and its target that probably would not have been attained with other approaches. Even in the extremely complex system of developmental biology, early predictive models evaluating genetic signals for vascular development (cytokines such as vascular endothelial growth factor-A and TGF-beta, chemotactic chemokines) have shown that perturbing these signals can lead to varying degrees of adverse consequences ranging from congenital angiodysplasia to fetal malformations and embryolethality. Disruption of embryonic vascular development can affect development of several different organ systems and may serve as a useful one-step pathway in a high-throughput screening tool for testing a chemical's potential for causing adverse developmental outcomes [90].

Another example of how advancing technological achievements may revolutionize the practice of regulatory toxicology, and perhaps clinical as well as nonclinical evaluation, is a slightly different version of the "humanized mouse" from what was described above. A biotech company has recently received a patent for their immune-depleted mouse model upon which a human immune system is grafted [91]. This allows the mouse to host human tumors without rejection. Such a model system provides a small optimal whole-animal test system in which oncology drugs can be tested directly against a specific human tumor xenograft. The effects of the drug on a specific tumor type, even an individual patient's own tumor, can be investigated. The results from these "mouse avatar" [92] systems may even one day be acceptable as "human" data and be allowed to supplant, or at least supplement, human clinical data in a regulatory evaluation. The high human specificity of test models such as these at the very least provide much reduced margins of error in extrapolating "animal" responses to humans, and thereby will greatly reduce the numbers of animals required to reliably translate the results to treatment of the human disease. While this model appears to have immediate utility in drug discovery, further development may be required before its usefulness in testing toxicological aspects of oncology, or other, drug treatment is fully realized. But these techniques may already provide useful contributions. As has already been discussed, at least for oncology drugs, regulatory reviews today provide broader risk versus benefit leeway for accepting adverse effects from these usually potent drugs. Any reliable human target-specific information is welcome so that people suffering the consequences of cancer and cancer treatment can be offered hope of recovery or at least extended lifespans or improved quality of life.

These new possibilities have generated excitement, not only among pharmaceutical product development and regulatory scientists, but among others as well, eg, those in the animal rights movement who have been pressing for the use of the 3Rs with regard to animal testing, with the hope of eliminating animal testing entirely.

Yet that goal may still be illusory. Some of the earliest pressure to eliminate animal testing in product development has come from Europe. The 2003 amendment to the EU Cosmetics Directive required the end of acute toxicity testing of cosmetics in animals by 2009 and for repeat-dose testing by 2013. Products that used repeat-dose testing in animals were to be banned from the marketplace at that point. However, that has proved to be unrealistic. The Cosmetics Directive was replaced by the Cosmetics Regulation in July 2013 that essentially contained the same provisions, ie, there is still a ban on animal testing in finished products except the ban has been revised to allow whole-animal data from repeat-dose toxicity, reproductive toxicity, and toxicokinetics testing, So, despite great advances, there just doesn't yet seem to be any alternative way in the foreseeable future to predict what effect a foreign molecule could have on the enormous complexity and inter-relationship of all the cells and tissues of the human body in a way that would provide premarketing confidence in the safety of a new pharmaceutical. It seems somewhat naïve to conclude that we are near using computer modeling (which would have to be programmed from biological data) to completely predict the effects of a drug and its toxicological side effects on something as biologically complex as the human body, especially for regulatory decisions regarding safety. This makes the use of the complex whole animal, ie, animal testing, inescapable for at least the near future [93].

Often throughout scientific history, however, a technological advance has revolutionized scientific thought and provided for techniques and discoveries previously believed to be unattainable, even unimaginable, eg, invention of the microscope, or advances in DNA sequencing of the human genome. Several avenues of research are providing cell, tissue, or organ systems that allow in vitro drug testing in human cell-derived systems. For example, the Harvard Wyss Institute is working with pharmaceutical companies to design drug tests that use organs on chips. They have already developed lung, intestine, kidney, and bone marrow on a chip with the goal of producing a battery of organs on chips that can be used to test drugs ultimately for regulatory acceptance and approval. The NIH, FDA and the Defense Advanced Research Projects Agency (DARPA) have partnered to develop human microphysiological systems (MPS) that should provide precise human testing systems that will be more predictive of the human response. Another of their collaborative projects is developing 3D human tissue chips that model the structure and function of human organs, and they already have female reproductive tissue among others. Eventually it is envisioned that different organs on a chip can be integrated into a system that will mimic the drug efficacy and safety functions of the human body [94]. Individual companies have entered this area with exciting in vitro systems that may provide commercial success for significant and practical advances in drug testing. One such advance that appears to have great potential similar to the NIH project is 3D reconstruction of tissues and organs. A San Diego company, Organovo, is developing bioprinting techniques that can form 3D organs. Cells from a research tissue cell line, stem cells, or cancer cells are put into their 3D printer, which can then construct a living tissue amenable to drug testing (Centerforresponsiblescience.com). Recently, the Center for Responsible Science (CRS), a non-partisan, non-profit organization advocating for modern test methods that are more predictive of human responses, have petitioned FDA to update 29 regulations to allow these more human-specific methods for new pharmaceutical regulatory approval testing. Several recent deaths resulted from clinical trials even after the experimental drugs were used in animal studies at multiples of several hundred times over the intended clinical dose, ie, the current nonclinical testing paradigm, and demonstrated to be safe. There is talk of suing FDA to allow use of these new methods now, without further delay. So, in addition to new scientific testing advances, it may take legal action from companies and patient groups to bring these advances to the forefront as important toxicological regulatory tools that can have an impact on the safety of clinical trial subjects (http://www.pharmpro.com/news/2016/03/clinical-trial-deaths-lead-call-amend-fdas-citizen-petition).

HOW MUCH PROGRESS HAVE WE MADE?

Despite the technological advances described above, the practical side of the present-day business of providing safe and effective pharmaceuticals to the patient is constantly being threatened. One would think that in this day and age, more than 75 years after the tragic sulfanilamide episode, that misbranding and adulteration of drugs would have been a thing of the long-distant past, that the manufactured drug of today is consistent from batch to batch, that efficacy should only be altered by the vagaries of individual genetics, and that drugs are as safe for the patient population as they can be. While many advances in science and the legal monitoring and guidance of our drug development programs have produced the safest and most effective pharmaceuticals in history, unfortunately, human nature and its impact on drug efficacy and safety is more difficult to move in consistently positive directions.

Let's consider drug efficacy, what we might think is the easier of the two, safety or efficacy, to assure with greater confidence. Most Americans today have come to assume, without thinking about it, that the drugs in their medicine cabinet or that they receive in the hospital are what was prescribed by their doctor, ie, at least if they came from a reputable pharmacy, and not from the internet. However, fraud and deceit in pharmaceutical manufacturing are still with us, and because of the growth in population worldwide, and growth in technology, this may present even more of a regulatory problem now than previously. As one example, the FDA announced in February 2012 that 19 hospitals and medical centers in the United States unknowingly purchased a counterfeit version of Avastin, an expensive and commonly used anticancer drug. The pharmaceutical industry has evolved, as has industry generally, and manufacturing of many chemical components of pharmaceuticals, or the final drug products themselves, has gone "offshore" and more distant from FDA scrutiny. Current FDA Commissioner Dr. Margaret Hamburg said that thanks to early warnings of problems with substandard Avastin from colleagues in other countries, they were able to move quickly to identify distributors in this country, and that they have the sense that no patients were harmed. (Perhaps not from adverse side effects, but if that fake version was administered, were there those whose cancer outlook worsened because they received ineffective treatment from the dummy drug?) However, because the way the law is currently structured, the FDA doesn't have the authority to seize and destroy these counterfeit drugs. They first have to go to court and get an order allowing them to take action [95].

Vigilance must still be maintained, and the legal authority to act still needs to be updated on a regular basis if the agencies we have put in place to protect us are to do their job effectively, and in a way that doesn't negatively impact legitimate law-abiding pharmaceutical manufacturers. Since our economy has expanded to one that is global, the drugs that we take in this country come from all over the world. A report produced for the US-China Economic and Security Review Commission [96] shows that China is a major producer and exporter of goods regulated by the FDA. Many of these products flaunt compliance with US regulations, not only in pharmaceutical ingredients, but in many product categories. For example, cough syrup and toothpaste have been found in the

recent past to contain diethylene glycol, the poisonous ingredient once added to Elixir Sulfaniliamide almost 80 years ago (1937) that produced many deaths in this country prior to the strengthening of our Pure Food and Drugs Act in 1938. Furthermore, a large portion of US bulk drugs, vitamins, and nutritional supplements (and the majority of over-the-counter drugs) are manufactured in China, which has now surpassed the US as the world's largest manufacturer of these compounds. While the FDA inspects virtually all US pharmaceutical manufacturers, between 2002 and 2006 an average of only 15 of the over 700 Chinese plants that export these products to the United States were inspected by the FDA [97]. FDA is stepping up its overseas manufacturing facility inspections, however.

The FDA recently warned Novartis AG that its generic drugs unit, Sandoz, was in violation of manufacturing practices at two of its Indian plants that make antibiotics and active pharmaceutical ingredients for generics. One of these plants has since been closed and the other has been remediated. Many other foreign firms with manufacturing plants in India (eg, Mylan) have faced serious rebukes following FDA inspections. The result has been that the FDA has banned more than 30 drug-manufacturing plants in India since 2013. This has shaken up the overseas drug-making industry as they try to regain their reputation as a reliable source of cheap generics [98].

Hamburg says:

> Right now 40% of finished drugs Americans take come from other countries, and 80% of the active pharmaceutical ingredients taken here come from other countries. We [the FDA] are responsible for overseeing drugs in 300,000 facilities around the world, coming in from 150 or so different countries. So it's a huge task.

Congress is considering new legislation giving the FDA stronger authority that would stiffen the rules around counterfeit drugs [95]. It seems that human nature being what it is, if the potential for profit is great enough, there will be someone somewhere in the world who is willing to take the risk, who will find the technology, and develop the logistics to beat the system, however dire the health consequences for unaware patients. In these respects, the more things change, ...

CONCLUSIONS

The preclinical development of pharmaceuticals has undergone intensive evolution over the past 50-plus years, in part due to the promulgation of harmonized international guidelines that describe how one should go about designing and conducting studies that produce appropriate and reliable data in support of testing NMEs in humans. Because of the effort put into harmonization of guidelines, various matters of concern, eg, animal welfare, types of studies, study methods, data interpretation, etc., have undergone focused scrutiny and discussion among dedicated regulatory and industry scientists. Consensus on details and application has largely been reached for many important procedures in drug development. In order to put these into practice a preclinical scientific program of study for each individual or class of NME still requires the attention of the toxicologist or toxicologically experienced product development scientist to ensure the appropriate preclinical data (especially reliable safety data) are produced in support of that drug's medical indication and clinical investigatory program. The production of internationally acceptable consensus guidelines has helped to streamline preclinical development and has provided a level of confidence that appropriate data will be produced to answer the questions of the pharmaceutical's, or biologic's, safety and effectiveness, and will be accepted for regulatory review worldwide.

Like all successful evolutionary processes, the preclinical development of pharmaceuticals has not stopped evolving, but change is still happening today and will continue to do so into the future. Yet we are coming upon that future so quickly that scientific advances would seem to be very rapidly outstripping our ability to evaluate and form regulatory consensus on the appropriate ways to perform studies and present data from, eg, toxicogenomics, proteomics, metabolomics, combinatorial methods of evaluation, in vitro cell and tissue cultures, etc. Such new methods and techniques may present many advances in our ability to develop safe drugs more quickly and produce even more effective individualized drugs, as well as significantly reduce the numbers of animals used in this endeavor.

But, technological advances alone are not sufficient for bringing about pharmaceutical improvements to our health. Critical evaluation of these new techniques and types of data must also rapidly advance from a regulatory and drug development standpoint. They must be validated and regulatory consensus formed as to their contribution to the assessment of pharmaceutical safety and effectiveness.

Fortunately, this scientific potential applied to drug development was seen coming years ago as these new approaches and technologies were being discovered and refined. The future regulatory difficulties were foreseen by regulators, industry and basic researchers, and meetings and discussions have been ongoing to try to keep the approval process in sync with the scientific advances. New guidelines are constantly being developed as science progresses. A new era in regulatory toxicology is here. Visions of how toxicology should be done in coming years have been crafted, debated and promoted by expert committees of toxicologists, including those from the regulatory agencies [81]. Future

guidelines will have to be continually developed with some urgency as this new tide of toxicological evaluation comes upon us. As consensus is reached, guidelines are developed and new approaches are incorporated into the regulatory process. Yet, these advanced guidelines must not be allowed to languish as drafts in the hallways of the bureaucratic agencies lest the ultimate tests, those human clinical trials, become less safe for volunteers taking the new panorama of drugs. These advances in toxicological science have the potential to help shorten drug development timelines, improve the bottom line of the sponsoring companies, and hasten the delivery of safe drugs to patients in need. The evolution of this new era of drug evaluation is currently underway and moving steadily forward. Established toxicologists of today are changing their ways and techniques, and adapting to the exciting new scientific horizons before them. It is up to the new generation of toxicologists to embrace these changes whether in academia, industry, or the regulatory agencies, and actively strive to make their own forward-thinking contributions to these twenty-first century visions of drug development.

References

[1] Litan R. Regulation. The Concise Encyclopedia of Economics The Liberty Fund, Inc.; 2008.

[2] Loomis TA, Hayes AW. Loomis's essentials of toxicology. 4th ed. New York, NY: Academic Press; 1996.

[3] Levine R, Evers C. The slow death of spontaneous generation (1668–1859) access excellence. 2009. http://www.accessexcellence.org/RC/AB/BC/Spontaneous_Generation.php.

[4] Barnett B. Louis Pasteur biography and timeline. 2010. http://www.pasteurbrewing.com/biography/biography/history-of-louis-pasteur/78.html.

[5] Koch Edward. On the Anthrax inoculation (1872). 1882. http://www.foundersofscience.net/Anthrax_Inoc.htm.

[6] Ullmann A. Pasteur-koch: distinctive ways of thinking about infectious disease. Microbe, American Society for Microbiology. August 2007. http://www.asm.org/index.php/component/content/article/114-unknown/unknown/4469-pasteur-koch-distinctive-ways-of-thinking-about-infectious-diseases.

[7] Anon. Edward Jenner (1749–1823) from BBC history. 2012. www.bbc.co.uk/history/historic_figures/jenner_edward.shtml.

[8] Scott P. Retrieved March 14, 2012 from University Library, rare books & collections Edward Jenner and the discovery of vaccination. 1996. library.sc.edu/spcoll/nathist/jenner.html.

[9] Stewart AD. The history of the smallpox vaccine. J Infect 2006;52(5):329–34.

[10] Blum D. Death in the Pot. Lapham's quarterly (summer). 2011.

[11] FDA, Swann JP. About FDA. Retrieved 2012, March from FDA's Origin: www.fda.gov/AboutFDA/WhatWeDo/History/Origin/ucm124403.htm; n.d..

[12] Ayers E. What the food law saves us from: adulterations, substitutions, chemical dyes, and other evils. The world's work: a history of our time, vol. XIV. New York, NY: Doubleday, Page & Company; 1907. p. 9316–22. http://books.google.com/books?id=sojNAAAAMAAJ&pg=RA1-PA9316#v=onepage&q&f=false.

[13] Dunn AW. Dr. Wiley and pure food, first article: a twenty-year's fight, the long struggle against 'influence' to enact the law, the harder struggle to enforce it, an amazing story of obstruction. The world's work: a history of our timeGarden City, NY: Doubleday, Page & Company; 1911. p. 14958–65. http://books.google.com/book?id=fHAAAAAAYAAJ&pg=RA1-PA14958#v=onepage&q&f=false.

[14] Sinclair U. The condemned-meat industry. Everybody's Mag 1906;XIV:612–3. A Reply to Mr. M. Cohn Armour', Everybody's Magazine, XIV (pp. 612–613).

[15] Hileman B. Human testing, 'poison squads' tested chemical preservatives. Chem Eng News 2006;84:18.

[16] National Museum of American History. Retrieved March, 2012 from Balm of America: Patent Medicine Collection NMAH. Object Groups; 2009. americanhistory.si.edu/collections/group_detail.cfm?key=1253&gkey=51&page=2.

[17] FDA. The St. Louis Tragedy and Enactment of the 1902 Biologics Control Act. FDA: Science and the Regulation of Biological Products; 2009.

[18] FDA. Promoting Safe and Effective Drugs for 100 Years. FDA Consumer Magazine. 2006.

[19] FDA. Significant Dates in US Food and Drug Law History About FDA. 2010.

[20] Lenz W. Thalidomide and congenital abnormalities. Lancet 1962;1:271–2.

[21] McBride WG. Thalidomide and congenital abnormalities. Lancet 1961;2:1358.

[22] Anon. Dr. Frances Kathleen Oldham kelsey. Celebrating America's women physicians. Washington, DC: National Library of Medicine; 1975.

[23] Schardein JL. Chapter 19, sedatives-hypnotics. In: Schardein JL, editor. Drugs as teratogens. Cleveland, OH: CRC Press; 1976. p. 145–53.

[24] Shepard TH. 2870 thalidomide. In: Shepard TH, editor. Catalog of teratogenic agents. Baltimore, MD: The Johns Hopkins University Press; 2004. p. 388–90.

[25] Bren L. Frances Oldham Kelsey: FDA medical reviewer leaves her mark on history. FDA Consumer Magazine. 2001.

[26] Hooper CL. Pharmaceuticals: economics and regulation. The concise encyclopedia of economics. Liberty Fund, Inc.; 2008. www.econlib.org/library/Enc/PharmaceuticalsEconomicsandRegulation.html.

[27] Harris G. Public's Quiet savior from harmful medicines. New York: New York Times; September 13, 2010.

[28] FDA. How to Comment on Proposed Regulations and Submit Petitions. Regulatory Information. 2009.

[29] Miller DJ. FDA oral history review. History of the US Food and Drug Administration; 1990.

[30] Anon. Fed Regist 2011;76(147):45831–45838.[

[31] Express Scripts: 2015 FDA approvals hit all-time high. http://www.drugstorenews.com/article/express-scripts-01-fda-approvals-hit-all-time-high.

[32] Mathieu M. Chapter 1: an introduction to the US New Drug Approval Process. In: Mathieu M, editor. New drug development: a regulatory overview. 4th ed. Waltham, MA: Parexel International Corporation; 1997.

[33] FDA. Fdama – Statement of Jane E. Henney, M.D. before the Senate Committee on Health, Education, Labor and Pensions. 1999. www.fda.gov/NewsEvents/Testimony.

[34] FDA. Home Page. FDA. US Food and Drug Administration; 2012. www.fda.gov/downloads/Drugs/GuidanceComplianceRegulatoryInformation/Guidance/UCM078749.pdf.

[35] Merrill R. Chapter 34: regulatory toxicology. In: Klaassen CD, editor. Casarett & Doull's toxicology. 6th ed. New York, NY: McGraw-Hill; 2001.

[36] Newsome R. Regulating the safety of food additives. Food Technol 2011;65(11):43–7.

[37] FDA. FDA History – Part III Delaney Clause. FDA Origin & Functions; 2009.

[38] WHO. Guidelines for Evaluation of Drugs for Use in Man. Technical Report Series No. 563. 1975.

[39] Wikipedia. Retrieved 2012 from European Union: http://en.wikipedia.org/wiki/European_Union 2011.

[40] FDA. Guidelines for Reproduction Studies for Safety Evaluation of Drugs for Human Use. Washington, DC: US Food and Drug Administration; 1966.

[41] Holson JF, Nemec MD, Stump DG, Kaufman LE, Lindstrom P, Varsho BJ. Chap. 9, significance, reliability, and interpretation of developmental and reproductive toxicity study findings. In: Hood RD, editor. Developmental and reproductive toxicology – a practical approach. 2nd ed. Boca Raton, FL, US: CRC/Taylor & Francis; 2006.

[42] U.S. Food and Drug Administration. US FDA's proposed implementation of ICH safety working group consensus regarding new drug applications. Fed Regist 1992;57:13105–6.

[43] FDA. Harmonization and Multilateral Relations. International Programs. 2012.

[44] U.S. Food and Drug Administration. M4: Organization of the CTD. Guidance for Industry. 2001.

[45] U.S. Food and Drug Administration. M4S: The CTD – Safety. Guidance for Industry. 2001.

[46] U.S. Food and Drug Administration. M4S: The CTD – Safety Appendices. Guidelines for Industry. 2001.

[47] Clements M, Millar V, Williams A, Kalinka S. Bridging functional and structural cardiotoxicity assays using himkan embryonic stem cell-derived cardiomyocytes for a more comprehensive risk assessment. Toxicol Sci 2015;148(1):241–60.

[48] U.S. Food and Drug Administration. Single dose acute toxicity testing for pharmaceuticals; revised guidance. Fed Regist 1996;61(166):43934–5.

[49] U.S. Food and Drug Administration. M3(R2) nonclinical safety studies for the conduct of human clinical trials and marketing authorization for pharmaceuticals. Guidance. 2008.

[50] Field GJ. Important biological features. Boca Raton, FL: The Laboratory Canine, Taylor & Francis Group; 2007. p. 13.

[51] Creasy D. Commentary on incidence and nature of testicular toxicity findings in pharmaceutical development survey: a Pathologist's perspective. Birth Defects Res Part B: Dev Reprod Toxicol 2011:508–10.

[52] FDA. Assessment of Male-Mediated Developmental Risk for Pharmaceuticals, Guidance for Industry, Draft Guidance Teratology Society, Comments on FDA Draft Guidance for Industry: Assessment of Male-mediated Developmental Risk for Pharmaceuticals. Docket number: FDA-2015-D-2001, July 31, 2015.

[53] U.S. Food and Drug Administration. ICH: guidance on the duration of chronic toxicity testing in animals (rodent and non-rodent toxicity testing). Fed Regist 1999;64(122):34259–60.

[54] ICH. S2(R1): Guidance on Genotoxicity Testing and Data Interpretation for Pharmaceuticals Intended for Human Use., Step 2ICH Harmonized Tripartite Guideline, Step 2. 2008.

[55] Litron Laboratories. Webinar: New ICH S2(R1) Guideline. 2012. http://www.litronlabs.com/ICH_S2(R1www.litronlabs.com/ICH_S2(R1)_guideline.html.

[56] Various authors. EMM special issue, pig-a mutation. Environ Mol Mutagen 2011;52(9).

[57] Dertinger SD. When pigs fly: immunomagnetic separation facilitates rapid determination of Pig-a mutant frequency by flow cytometric analysis. Mutat Res Genet Toxicol Environ Mutagen 2011;721(2):163–70.

[58] Dertinger SD. Editorial: *in vivo* assessment of pig-a gene mutation – recent developments and assay validation. Environ Mol Mutagen 2011;52:681–4.

[59] FDA. Carcinogenicity Study Protocol Submissions. Guidance for Industry. 2002.

[60] ICH. S1C Dose Selection for Carcinogenicity Studies of Pharmaceuticals. Guidance for Industry. 1995.

[61] ICH. S1C(R): Guidance on Dose Selection for Carcinogenicity Studies of Pharmaceuticals: Addendum on a Limit Dose and Related Notes. Guidance for Industry. 1997.

[62] ICH. S1B: Testing for Carcinogenicity of Pharmaceuticals. Guidance for Industry. 1998.

[63] FDA. Reproductive and Developmental Toxicities – Integrating Study Results to Assess Concerns. Guidance for Industry. 2011.

[64] ICH. S5A Detection of Toxicity to Reproduction for Medicinal Products. Guidance for Industry. 1994.

[65] ICH. S5B Detection of Toxicity to Reproduction for Medicinal Products: Addendum on Toxicity to Male Fertility. Guidance for Industry. 1996.

[66] FDA. Nonclinical Safety Evaluation of Pediatric Drug Products. Guidance of Industry. 2006.

[67] Wang T, et al. ICH guidelines: inception, revision, and implications for drug development. Toxicol Sci 2010;118(2):356–67.

[68] ICH. S9 Nonclinical Evaluation for Anticancer Pharmaceuticals. Guidance for Industry. 2010.

[69] EMA. ICH guideline S6(R1) – Preclinical Safety Evaluation of Biotechnologically-derived Pharmaceuticals. Guideline. 2011.

[70] Coico R, Sunshine G. Immunogens and antigens. immunology: a short course. 5th ed. Hoboken, NJ: John Wiley & Sons; 2003. p. 34–5.

[71] FDA. For the Evaluation of Combination Vaccines for Preventable Diseases: Production, Testing and Clinical Studies. Guidance for Industry. 1997.

[72] WHO. Who Technical Report Series (927). 2005. Geneva.

[73] Sutkowski EG. Regulatory considerations in the nonclinical safety assessment of adjuvanted preventive vaccines. In: Schijns VO, editor. Immunopotentiators in modern vaccines. Burlington, Massachusetts: Elsevier Academic Press; 2006. p. 343–58.

[74] Federal Register. Requirements on Content and Format of Labeling for Human Prescription Drug and Biological Products. Published in the Federal Register (71 FR 3922). January 24, 2006.

[75] Johnson SR. FDA considers tougher regulation of homeopathic therapies. 2015. http://www.modernhealthcare.com/article/20150422/NEWS/150429968.

[76] Norton S. Toxic effects of plants, Ch. 27, Casarett & Doull's toxicology, the basic science of poisons. 2001. p. 972.

[77] http://www.drugstore.com/hylands-baby-teething-tablets/qxp371886?catid=183861&aid=337456&aparam=hyland%27s%20teething%20tablets&scinit1=hyland%27s%20teething%20tablets.

[78] Federal Register. Homeopathic Product Regulation: Evaluating the Food and Drug Administration's Regulatory Framework After a Quarter-Century; Public Hearing. March 27, 2015.

[79] Doull J, Bruce M. Origin and scope of toxicology. Chap. 1. In: Klaassen CD, Amdur MO, Doull J, editors. Casarett and Doull's toxicology: the basic science of poisons. New York, NY: Macmillan Publishing Co.; 1986.

[80] Henderson VC, et al. Threats to validity in the design and conduct of preclinical efficacy studies: a systematic review of guidelines for in vivo animal experiments. PLoS Med 2013;10(7):1–4.

[81] National Research Council. Toxicity Testing in the Twenty-first Century: A Vision and A Strategy. 2007.

[82] Andersen M, Krewski D. The vision of toxicity testing in the 21st century: moving from discussion to action. Toxicol Sci 2010;117(1):17–24.

[83] Keller D, et al. Identification and characterization of adverse effects in 21st century toxicology. Toxicol Sci 2012;126(2):291–7.

[84] GenomeWeb staff reporter. Iom Issues Guidelines for Development of 'Omics-based tests'. 2012 (GenomeWeb, Producer) From GenomeWeb http://www.genomeweb.com2012.

[85] Chapelle R. FDA, State of Arkansas sign agreement to advance regulatory science. FDA News Release for August 12, 2011. 2011.

[86] FDA. FDA's Strategic Plan for Regulatory Science. Science and Research, Special Topics, Advancing Regulatory Science. 2011.

[87] NCTR The Global Summit on Regulatory Science, http://www.fda.gov/AboutFDA/CentersOffices/OC/OfficeofScientificandMedicalPrograms/NCTR/WhatWeDo/ucm289679.htm.

[88] Slikker W, Director at NCTR. 2015; personal communication.

[89] Geter DK. Phenobarbitol-like mode of action for liver tumors in CD1 mice and F344 rats exposed to a new developmental compound (X11422208). Society of Toxicology Abstract Planner (Abst. No. 223). 2011.

[90] Knudsen TK. Disruption of embryonic vascular development in predictive toxicology. Birth Defects Res 2011;93(4):312–23.

[91] Williams Stephen J. Immunized mice may revolutionize cancer drug discovery. 2015. http://pharmaceuticalintelligence.com/2015/10/09/humanized-mice-may-revolutionize-cancer-drug-discovery/.

[92] championsoncology.com.

[93] Editorial. Animal tests inescapable. Nature 2008;453:563–4.

[94] http://www.ncats.nih.gov/research/reengineering/tissue-chip/tissue-chip.html.

[95] Hellerman C. FDA commissioner talks counterfeit drugs – CNN. 2012 (2012-03-15T20:53:12Z) CNN.com.

[96] Potential Health & Safety Impacts from Pharmaceuticals and Supplements Containing Chinese-Sourced Raw Ingredients Prepared for U.S. China Economic and Security Review Commission NSD Bio Group, LLC April 2010.

[97] McCormack RA. You Don't know where your drugs come from and neither does the fda; U.S. Imports 90 percent of its antibiotics (and vitamin a) from China. Manuf Technol News May 18, 2010;17(8).

[98] Siddiqui Z. U.S. FDA warns Novartis on manufacturing violations at 2 India plants. October 2015. Reuters, Health.

20

Role of Study Director and Study Monitor in Drug Development Safety Studies

S. Frantz, C. Johnson

INTRODUCTION

Ideally, the roles of study directors and study monitors should complement each other when performing nonclinical studies. The study director focuses on the day-to-day activities while the study monitor serves as a bridge between the study director/laboratory personnel and the sponsor and provides a more global evaluation of the study. This chapter provides both a summary and framework for how the two jobs allow for a harmonized and streamlined approach to study conduct. Ultimately, the goal of both study directors and monitors is to provide the sponsor with a nonclinical study that is acceptable to domestic and international regulatory authorities and allows ongoing clinical development of the drug. With good communication and a collaborative approach between the two parties, this can be achieved and unexpected or adverse findings can be dealt with efficiently.

In the context of conducting nonclinical studies, the study director and study monitor have key, but different responsibilities. (Note: For the purposes of this chapter, it has largely been assumed that the study monitor will be a third-party individual.) In fact, the two roles should complement each other, especially in the eyes of regulatory agencies such as the Food and Drug Administration (FDA) and the European Medicines Agency (EMA).

Effective study director and study monitor communication, particularly at the start of the study, is essential so that all parties can work together to create a scientifically robust study design. Although most interactions between the study director and study monitor will likely focus on addressing scientific questions posed by the sponsor or regulatory authorities, collaboration on all aspects of the study, which occur throughout the in-life and post-in-life phases, are critical to the successful outcome of the study.

This chapter discusses the roles of the study director and study monitor, with a focus on the development of pharmaceutical products. It also illustrates the manner in which these scientists interact to most effectively accomplish the goal of providing a well-conducted, Good Laboratory Practices (GLPs) compliant nonclinical study for regulatory submission. However, its principles also apply to the types of interactions that are important for any non-GLP study. This chapter is not intended to be a comprehensive description of responsibilities, but rather to provide both a summary and framework for how the two jobs allow for a harmonized and streamlined approach to study conduct.

BACKGROUND

In pharmaceutical development, nonclinical toxicology studies are conducted to support clinical trials or marketing. Nonclinical studies are designed to accomplish two main goals:

1. To establish an initial starting dose in humans (based on the early nonclinical studies) and
2. To define the safety of the drug with respect to multiple endpoints (eg, genetic toxicology, reproductive toxicology, pharmacokinetics and metabolism, etc.), and later to establish information to assist in marketing a safe drug.

Safety is only characterized and understood by establishing toxicity. Sponsors who are new to drug development sometimes confuse observations of toxicity as being an indication of a drug's limitations, thinking instead that a "clean" profile is desirable. In fact, the opposite is the case and a successful toxicology study is one that demonstrates a range of effects, including toxic ones.

Only after demonstrating the types of toxicity that a drug produces and the doses and exposures at which these effects occur can clinicians and regulators determine what parameters and exposures need to be monitored in clinical trials. For this reason, toxicology studies are performed at a range of doses that will establish minimal, moderate, and significant toxicity. Ideally, at least one dose will provide evidence of the types of toxicity associated with the drug and at least one dose will produce minimal to no effects. As might be expected, this "ideal" situation is sometimes difficult to achieve, as selecting appropriate doses to produce the desired range of effects is both a science and an art. Consideration of all available information such as pharmacodynamics and mechanism of action, preliminary or short-term toxicology data, and findings from other drugs in the same class is an essential process to selecting the correct doses to achieve success in study performance from both a scientific and regulatory standpoint.

Fig. 20.1 summarizes the types of nonclinical data that are needed at various stages of clinical development. This paradigm is based on a generic new chemical entity (not an oncology agent or biotechnology-derived product) that will be used for a chronic indication in the clinic.

As Fig. 20.1 shows, the types and duration of the nonclinical studies become more comprehensive as the human studies increase in treatment duration and size. In general, the design of these various toxicology studies is well understood by the scientific and regulatory communities. The one drug-specific variable that should be carefully considered for the design of the longer-term repeat-dose studies is the influence of the drug's exposure profile. Exposure differences in these studies should be carefully considered when selecting dose levels,

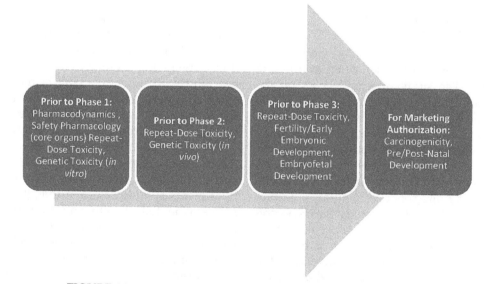

FIGURE 20.1 Progression of nonclinical studies during drug development.

particularly when there may be evidence for saturation of a drug's metabolic and/or elimination pathways that can often lead to accumulation and toxicity outcomes. As described in the 2009 International Conference on Harmonisation (ICH) M3(R2) [2] guidance on the nonclinical studies needed for clinical trials and marketing authorization of human pharmaceuticals, the duration of these repeat-dose studies depends on the duration of the clinical trials. Animals must be treated in the repeat-dose studies for at least as long as volunteers or patients will be treated in the upcoming clinical trial. For Phase I studies, these durations are generally short (ie, 28 days), while the Phase II studies, where efficacy is first studied in patients, are generally longer (ie, 90 days) and the Phase III studies can be longer still (ie, >90 days). The exceptions are oncology agents or biotechnology-derived products where entry into patient populations happens with a reduced nonclinical package. This is detailed in Fig. 20.2, which is adapted from the 2009 ICH M3(R2) guidance and specifies the toxicology study durations during development (ongoing clinical trials).

For ultimate marketing authorization, the following repeat-dose studies are needed (Fig. 20.3).

As a final note, the nonclinical studies conducted on a pharmaceutical need to use the clinical dosing regimen, including route of administration and treatment schedule (ie, once per day, twice per day). If exposure is low via the clinical route, then an alternate route that maximizes systemic exposure may need to be considered. However, any alterations in the dosing route should be discussed with the regulatory authorities prior to initiation of toxicology studies. In addition, it is now expected that toxicokinetic assessments are included in all pivotal toxicology studies. These data are critical during development and for the ultimate submission, as comparisons will be made between exposures at the no adverse effect doses in animals, and exposures in patients at the clinical dose.

With this understanding of the nonclinical data package required at different stages of the drug's development, the roles and responsibilities of study directors and study monitors are discussed below.

STUDY DIRECTORS

Description

A study director is defined as "the individual responsible for the overall conduct of a nonclinical study" according to the Code of Federal Regulations (21 CFR Part 58.3). For any nonclinical study, whether it is compliant with GLPs or not, the performing laboratory (or contract research organization [CRO]) assigns a study director; there is only one study director for a nonclinical study. This individual is responsible for overseeing all elements of study conduct within the testing facility, including, but not limited to: developing the protocol, scheduling the study, obtaining the test article in adequate amounts, ordering animals, meeting with the technicians and staff to review the protocol prior to commencing the study, interacting with the technicians on a regular basis to ensure the study is being conducted to meet the requirements of the protocol, providing updates to the sponsor, informing the sponsor of any findings, working with outside contractors to make sure samples are shipped and received for analysis and that reports are provided, preparing the draft and final study reports, interpreting the data to solidify the conclusions of the study, and reviewing and incorporating comments from the study monitor and/or sponsor. As the single individual accountable for a nonclinical study (often referred to as the "single point of control" for GLP expectations), the study director also becomes responsible for the work of outside contractors that supply critical supportive data for the study.

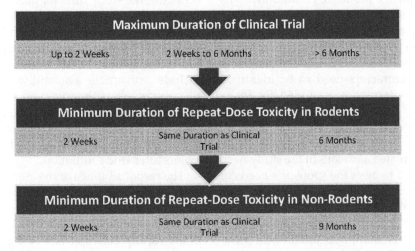

FIGURE 20.2 Duration of repeat-dose toxicity studies during the conduct of clinical trials.

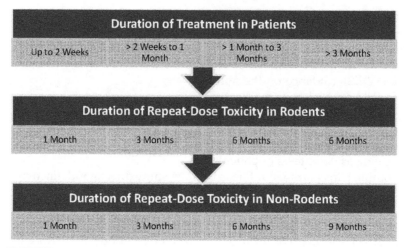

FIGURE 20.3   Duration of repeat-dose toxicity studies for marketing authorization.

Study directors bring a unique perspective to a program based on their experience working with a variety of product types, study designs, animal species, and dosing methods. This experience can be critical in assisting a sponsor in their consideration of the details of the study.

Study Conduct

Once a laboratory has been selected by a sponsor, the first step is to determine who the study director will be. This individual can be assigned by the laboratory or requested by the sponsor. This is followed by the preparation of the protocol. This is a critical process as the protocol describes how the material will be prepared and dosed, what parameters will be assessed, and how often they will be evaluated during the course of the study. Information is shared between the sponsor/study monitor and study director about the type of study needed, as well as the type of product being evaluated and any particular requests from regulatory agencies. For most studies, the general design has been established or is well understood within the scientific community. Any unique features of the study should be discussed early in the protocol development process, so that they can be incorporated and time allotted in case more advanced training or specific procedures need to be followed. In addition, all outside contractors need to be identified and shipping/contact information provided for inclusion in the protocol.

A protocol, once signed, becomes the road map for the study. However, it is not set in stone and protocol amendments must be created as details of the study need to be refined or changed to meet the sponsor's needs or to accommodate unexpected findings. The goal is to have all the details finalized prior to study initiation, but this is not always possible. Still, keeping the number of amendments/changes to a minimum should be a priority so that there is limited opportunity for confusion or missed data collection. Ideally, changes should be made well enough in advance so that the technical staff can incorporate them seamlessly into their study-specific procedures.

After or as the protocol is developed, the more tangible elements of the study start to take place: ordering and receiving animals and obtaining the test article. These ideally need to occur between 2 and 3 weeks prior to initiation of dosing so that there are no delays in the program.

Scheduling

All activities and endpoints assessed in a nonclinical study follow a schedule that is prepared in advance, generally during protocol development, by the laboratory's scheduling group. Although changes to the study schedule are possible and do occur, these can be difficult to incorporate while balancing the timing of the multiple other studies also being performed by the laboratory. Should or when a sponsor requests changes to the study schedule, the study director needs to then work with the scheduling group to integrate all new activities given the availability on the master schedule for the facility. Any changes need to be communicated in an expedited manner to the technical staff. Reasons for rescheduling can include test article availability, ongoing development of supportive methodologies, a scheduling change at an outside contractor, need for expedited review of the data, etc. These changes can either move up or push back a study start or can impact the timing of critical study events after study initiation.

The responsibilities of the study director are manifold and require attention to detail. Although a study schedule provides the framework, the study director and technicians work together to make it happen. Being aware of the various activities and being present for the critical ones is both an expectation of the sponsor and from the

TABLE 20.1 Regulatory Guidance Frequently Asked Questions

The study director is often asked:	• Where do I go to find the applicable regulatory guidance documents?
	• Which guidance do I apply to my study?
	• What role does an anticipated duration of clinical treatment play in study selection?
	• What role does API (active pharmaceutical ingredient) purity play in my study?
	• What part does the sponsor play in those studies conducted at a CRO?

regulatory agencies under GLPs. Furthermore, regular communication on study progress and potential problems is essential. Given the multitude of responsibilities, interactions between study directors and study monitors are key to the successful completion of a study.

Additional Considerations

Throughout this chapter, there are many references to regulatory compliance and the guidance that dictates the standards to which study directors and laboratory staffs are held. However, interpreting the intent behind what is written in specific sections of this guidance is often a subject of great debate. Because of the imprecise and sometimes even vague passages in the regulations, the laboratory conducting a study and its quality assurance unit can find themselves in a difficult situation in attempting to follow their interpretation of the guidance's intent versus the view from the sponsor company. Ultimately, the laboratory must balance protecting itself from receiving a 483 citation, or in extreme situations, an FDA warning letter, which could result from Agency inspections and their subsequent findings with the needs of the sponsor. For these reasons, it is important for a CRO and its management to work together with the sponsor to try to resolve any unclear situations to everyone's mutual satisfaction; this is often easier said than done.

One example of this can occur when the bioanalysis of plasma samples from a toxicokinetics (TK) blood collection in a toxicology study and the subsequent TK data analysis for exposure parameters are conducted by either the sponsor's internal lab staff or by a third-party lab. If the protocol states that the sponsor or third-party lab will conduct both plasma and TK analysis, but the actual TK data analysis is outsourced to yet another party, the protocol has to be amended so that the study director and the lab where the study was conducted are aware of the changes in responsibilities. Should this not happen, a GLP deviation would occur, and this would need to be listed in the final report in order to avoid a 483 citation for the primary (tox) lab. In this particular circumstance, it is better to take a GLP deviation and to cite it in the final report than to risk questions later in an audit of that study by the FDA.

Study directors regularly field the same types of questions from sponsors as they prepare to conduct studies. These questions provide excellent opportunities for the study director to offer guidance that can help ensure the success of the study or studies being conducted. Table 20.1 summarizes some of these typical questions.

The use of appropriate regulatory guidance documents is covered elsewhere in this text (eg, the ICH M3 (R2) guidance) and briefly later in this chapter.

One question that often arises is the purity of the active pharmaceutical ingredient (API) that is used in preclinical studies, particularly in the early development stages (eg, dose ranging and pre-IND toxicity studies) of the program. This is often overlooked and its importance underestimated until it becomes an issue that can lead to an interruption (ie, clinical hold) of a compound's clinical development because an impurity(ies) is/are not qualified first in toxicology studies. Typically, the strategy in early development stages should be to conduct nonclinical studies using the "dirtiest" lots of material (eg, those having the most impurities). This means that careful consideration should be given to the level of purity used in the preclinical studies, starting with smaller, non-GMP qualified lots that tend to be not as pure as the larger kg-scale lots that are manufactured in highly purified, GMP-compliant campaigns for clinical use. It is important to note that these pre-GMP lots of material still need to be characterized and the levels and types of impurities determined. Using the lower purity, smaller quantity lots can avoid the unanticipated situation of potentially exposing clinical subjects to those "impurities not yet tested in nonclinical animal studies," which can lead to being placed on a clinical hold by the Agency. While it is possible to qualify impurities at any stage of development, careful planning will certainly help limit delays in both the cost and timing of the program.

Some additional questions for a sponsor to address to ensure that a high-quality study will be conducted can include the following:

1. Are you providing the CRO with sufficiently detailed outlines so that all important study design aspects will be included in the study(ies) being planned? You can expect that a competent CRO will ask critical questions to make sure that no design features are assumed.

2. Is sufficient information being provided to determine whether a study segment will be conducted at a sponsor's lab or will go to a third-party/subcontract lab? How/when an important study segment that is not done at the CRO is being scheduled will be critical to avoid timing/cost issues, sometimes even when done in the sponsor's lab.
3. Are sponsor expectations for report metrics being communicated clearly to the CRO?
4. How much compound will you "burn through" in preclinical studies and will sufficient API supply become an issue later, in longer-term studies? This is when getting enough API to the CRO on time is critical to avoid timing/cost issues.

These questions and their proactive answers can often make a considerable difference on how smoothly the study will run.

Finally, it must be reiterated that a successful toxicology study is one that demonstrates a range of effects, including toxic ones, and that this is the expectation for both safe and effective drug substances by the FDA and other regulatory agencies around the world. Sponsors in drug companies, particularly in small pharma/biotech firms, need to carefully balance observed toxicities in a given study with the overall program objectives. This means they should prevent the requirement to demonstrate toxicity from becoming a perception of the drug's limitations. The misconception that a "clean" drug profile is desirable can often be a competing objective from boards of directors and funding/venture sources that quickly become nervous at any occurrence of an "unexpected finding." Thus a successful company needs to align funding objectives with safety expectations from reviewing agencies in order to obtain their approval to conduct human clinical trials.

STUDY MONITORS

Description

Perhaps the best way to describe a study monitor is to say that he or she acts as the eyes and ears of the sponsor. Being the point of contact and representative for the sponsor requires an understanding of what is best for both the sponsor and the study. As a result, it is essential to understand the overall goals of the sponsor, not simply for the study, but ultimately for the submission of the data to a regulatory agency. For example, being aware of the corporate objective for timing of a submission is critical when working with the laboratory and the sponsor, as there are times when the target is not feasible given the time required to complete a nonclinical study or studies and coordinate the data for the submission. Alternatively, it is important to understand whether there are particular toxicity flags the sponsor is concerned about. These goals should ideally be understood in advance, particularly if there is a short turnaround between completion of the study and submission to an agency, or if specific findings could terminate a study or program. Also keep in mind that the addition of a recovery period may be important or even critical to the successful outcome of the study, both from the perspective of reversal of effects observed during the dosing period or for the appearance of a delayed effect that takes longer than the dose phase to observe clinically or microscopically. This and any specific requests of a regulatory authority need to be incorporated from the beginning into the study design, as it is oftentimes not possible to make these changes while the in-life phase of a study is under way due to an insufficient number of animals.

Perhaps the most effective assistance a study monitor can provide is to ensure that all parties, laboratory and sponsor, are on the same page with respect to conducting each study. In this way, the number of "surprises" or unrealistic expectations should be minimized.

It is important to note that the "eyes-on" role of a study monitor is not restricted to on-site visits. Rather, monitoring occurs both in person and remotely. In fact, most of the monitoring will likely occur remotely, through e-mails, teleconferences, secure online data sites, and other technologies, since a full-time, on-site individual is generally not a financially feasible option. While available current technologies allow for regular oversight of studies, there are times when a complete understanding of a study can only be obtained by being on site. Decisions about the timing and frequency of such visits should be discussed before the study starts, so that they can be coordinated with the study schedule.

Reasons for Using a Monitor

So why is there a need for a study monitor if the study director actually runs the study? As noted above, the study director is responsible for the day-to-day in-house activities of a study. In comparison, a study monitor provides a different level of input or oversight that is focused less on these details and more on a global or higher level view. There are times when stepping back from the details can provide perspective on the data that is not immediately evident when dealing with the day-to-day activities.

There are several reasons why a sponsor may elect to have a monitor be involved in a study. The first is time. It is a time-consuming effort to regularly be involved with and oversee a nonclinical study. If the sponsor has multiple other obligations and projects that limit their time and availability, then a study monitor can step in and serve this role. The second is experience. Not all sponsors have the expertise in-house to oversee a laboratory and the details of a study. This is particularly true for companies that either do not have a nonclinical group or whose nonclinical group is small and/or includes less-experienced scientists. The third is the decision to have a new or fresh perspective on a study so that it is not affected by previous work on the development program. Although these are just a few reasons, it is likely that all three as well as others could play a role in the decision to select a study monitor.

Selecting a Monitor

Once a decision has been made to include a study monitor in a program, the question becomes how to select the correct individual. This is ultimately a personal preference on the part of the sponsor. Certainly, experience plays a critical role in the decision, but in addition having "good chemistry" (personality and ability to interact with a variety of individuals with a large range of study-specific responsibilities) is key. Recommendations from other colleagues who have worked with study monitors can be extremely valuable.

Because the monitor will serve as the liaison between the lab and the sponsor, observe activities on-site, relay any findings to the sponsor, assist in making decisions during the conduct of the study, and review reports (among other things), a balance of technical expertise and good communication skills is needed. Having a level of sensitivity in how to communicate certain findings is also important, especially when corrections or changes need to be made. A spirit of collaboration and not competition is another useful characteristic in identifying a good study monitor and should not be underestimated or undervalued.

A well-qualified study monitor should have experience with the types of studies that they are being asked to oversee, along with knowledge of the protocol and any relevant regulations. Previous interactions with the laboratory can be very helpful, but are not essential. Being able to assess the overall quality of the laboratory and personnel is important. Although most studies proceed with little to no deviations, mistakes or errors can occur. By working closely with the study director and laboratory staff, the monitor can help to diminish these complications or assist in expediting a resolution on behalf of the sponsor. This rapid and proactive response is facilitated by a good working relationship with the study director.

Whether through an on-site visit or remote communications, confidence needs to be established between the study director and monitor such that there are no delays in understanding how the study is progressing. This becomes particularly important if unexpected findings are obtained or if adjustments need to be made to the design/conduct in the middle of the study. While it is not always possible, a face-to-face visit with the study director at the facility can provide the most effective way to begin or mature this relationship. This can also be particularly effective when the conclusions of the study report are nearing a finalization stage and may need to be discussed.

Finally, a study monitor needs to have experience with regulatory agencies and understand their expectations with respect to what constitutes a well-conducted nonclinical study. This is particularly important should, or when, unexpected events occur during the course of a study (eg, terminating a dose group early in a carcinogenicity study, placing animals on a drug holiday, decreasing a dose). Rapid interactions and agreements to alterations in studies with agency personnel are sometimes required. Here is where experience is critical. These agreements/decisions cannot be facilitated without an understanding of what the regulatory authorities expect and a means to communicate with agency scientists (ie, based on previous interactions). Reviewing guidance documents provides a sense of the agency's perspective/requirements, but only regular and recent interactions will enable a study monitor to make the most appropriate recommendations to the sponsor and study director. The recent interactions are particularly important as feedback and recommendations on the design of studies is generally first communicated in this environment, often months or years before it becomes formally recognized in an official agency document.

Considerations While Monitoring

There are no formal or informal regulations governing or guiding the study monitoring process even though it is an expectation of the regulatory agencies. This allows each monitor to establish his or her own individual processes and procedures for overseeing studies. However, because each monitor may weigh different elements of the study differently, it can be challenging to have a consistent approach to this process. Table 20.2 lists some of the notable things to consider when monitoring.

A final question to consider is when to conduct an on-site monitoring visit: prestudy, during dosing, at necropsy? Any or all of these times will provide useful but different insight into the progress of the study. In addition, the occurrence of unexpected findings is another opportunity to observe and communicate the findings. Under perfect circumstances, the on-site visit is scheduled in advance, but should adverse events occur it is imperative to get on site as quickly as possible. Having said this, the location of the laboratory plays a major role in the extent of on-site monitoring. Some international locations can be difficult to access so this needs to be considered by the sponsor when selecting the CRO.

TABLE 20.2 Study Monitoring Considerations

The degree of monitoring depends on the significance of study.	• For example, a range-finding study likely needs input for dose selection, discussion of observations, and recommendations for dose escalation, which can occur remotely, whereas a pivotal repeat-dose study will likely require an on-site visit and regular interactions with the study director to ensure that the study progresses with a limited number of unexpected events.
Study monitoring is part experience and part intuition.	• There are times when you need to go with your "gut" in regards to making decisions about a study or pursuing explanations for findings.
When observing, the monitor should be present, but not disruptive to the daily activities (eg, dosing, data collection, etc.).	• In other words, it is most helpful to observe without getting in the way of normal study-related procedures.
Questions are good and demonstrate hands-on interactions.	• Questions can be a key source of information taken from the technicians who observe the animals at each dosing or data collection time point.
It is not helpful to monitor the minutia.	• Throughout the course of a study, isolated, aberrant results may occur. Knowing which are important to follow up on and which are not will focus everyone's attention in the right direction.
Be knowledgeable and helpful.	• Know what you know and what you don't know.
Don't offer previews of what the study staff should expect to observe.	• When interacting with technicians, allow them to communicate their observations on the study without biasing them or directing them in a specific manner.

STUDY DIRECTOR CHECKLIST

Before initiating a nonclinical study, several items need to be in place to ensure a high-quality study will be conducted for the sponsor. These most often include, but are not limited to, a study protocol, chemistry considerations, dose formulation and plasma analysis, dose administration, proper selection of the test species, arrival of the test article, or API when dealing with pharmaceutical substances.

It is incumbent upon the study director to explain all of the risks to the sponsor if not all elements of a study are in place prior to starting. Table 20.3 details some of the major responsibilities of the study director, principally as it applies to GLP-compliant studies, but usually applicable for the conduct of non-GLP studies as well.

STUDY MONITOR CHECKLIST

There are four main stages during the lifecycle of a study that a monitor can focus on (Table 20.4; Fig. 20.4).

The activities of the study monitor will intersect with the activities of the study director to a certain extent, but will also be unique in other ways. Table 20.4 provides a list of various tasks to consider in each of the study phases. Although the study monitor may not be involved at all stages, an understanding of each of these elements is extremely helpful.

BRINGING IN EXPERTS

No matter what your level of experience may be, there are times during the performance of a study that

an expert may be needed. It is critical to know when to involve such a specialist and who to contact. These individuals can be a part of the CRO team or an outside consultant or group.

Perhaps the most often utilized expert is a pathologist. Pathology peer review groups or even individual pathologists are often employed to conduct blinded reviews of slides, provide insight into a mechanism, or simply confirm the observations of the study pathologist. Not every study requires such input, but some sponsors as a matter of policy involve a peer review for the more pivotal studies, such as carcinogenicity studies. Other areas for which experts are commonly used include neuropathology, reproductive toxicology, electrocardiography, and ophthalmoscopy.

REGULATIONS

As the drug development process has matured over the years, the regulations that relate to nonclinical studies have expanded. Both the study director and study monitor need to be aware of existing guidelines and how to implement them in order to perform a study that meets both national and international regulatory requirements.

GLPs refer to the principles that govern the conduct of nonclinical studies. These were implemented in the United States (US) by the FDA following investigations into the quality and reliability of certain data submitted to support product registrations. GLPs were officially adopted by the FDA as a final rule in 1978 [1]. In Europe, under the auspices of the Organisation for Economic Co-operation Development (OECD), they were officially adopted in 1981 (c.f. [3]). The OECD GLPs were developed by an expert working group that included

TABLE 20.3 Study Director Checklist

The study director:	• Is responsible for all aspects of the study conduct • Acts as a "single point of control" on all GLP-compliant studies • Is responsible for all study design changes and writing of formal amendments to the study protocol • Assures that all applicable GLPs are followed • Assures that "should read" corrective action is conveyed and documented in a timely manner to all affected study staff • Is available for weekend and holiday study decisions
Additional study director roles:	• Approves the study plan • Assures arrival of the test article • Approves and issues amendments to and acknowledges deviations from the study plan • Visits the study room regularly and documents those visits • Liaises with (and is readily available to) each of the principal investigators on a study • Ensures that all staff are aware of requirements of the study and documents these expectations • Ensures that a final report is prepared

TABLE 20.4 Checklist for Study Monitors

Study Initiation and Setup	Four to eight weeks prior to study start: • Select CRO and ensure that contracts are in place • Schedule study Three weeks prior to study start: • CRO to identify study director • Prepare and review protocol • Identify contractors/principal investigators and inform them of the study schedule • Address test article characterization (eg, identification, stability, etc.) • Discuss dose formulation/preparation • Determine status of analytical/bioanalytical work (eg, dose formulation, plasma/serum analyses, antibody analyses, etc.) Two weeks prior to study start: • Approve protocol (prior to animal receipt) • Work with study director to estimate test article needs and ensure appropriate amounts are shipped to CRO • Ensure that animal order is placed • Confirm that animals have been received in good health One week prior to study start: • Ensure that animals are acclimating • Confirm that prestudy assessments have been conducted • Finalize formulation preparation with pharmacy • Attend study preinitiation meeting
In-Life Activities	• Observe dosing and/or review regular updates from study director • Confirm the collection of critical study parameters (eg, blood samples, formulation samples, in-life assessments) • Regularly discuss study status and findings with study director and sponsor • Visit on-site to observe study-related activities, review study administration and pharmacy books, analyze available data • Address any deviations with study director and sponsor • Review data as they become available • Ensure samples are shipped to outside contractors on a timely basis (this may need to occur at regular intervals during the study)
Postmortem Activities	• Observe necropsy and/or receive update from study director • Review preliminary data • Coordinate any final sample shipments to outside contractors • Alert outside contractors to study timelines • Review reports from outside contractors
Reporting	• Review draft report • Communicate findings/changes with sponsor • Ensure that all principal investigator reports are received by study director

IV. BIOSTATISTICS, REGULATORY TOXICOLOGY, AND ROLE OF STUDY DIRECTORS

FIGURE 20.4 Lifecycle of a nonclinical study.

representatives from 17 countries, including the United States. Since their adoption, revisions or updates to these principles have been published as scientific technology and methodologies have advanced, but the core principles remain the same. In general, nonclinical studies performed by US-based laboratories are in compliance with the FDA GLPs and those performed outside the United States are in compliance with the OECD GLPs. As both sets of GLPs define the same requirements or expectations, they allow global acceptance of nonclinical studies as long as they are performed in compliance with one of these systems. In addition, the United States is a member of the OECD Mutual Acceptance of Data (MAD) programme that further facilitates international acceptance of studies conducted at US CROs.

It is important to clarify that GLPs refer to the processes and procedures that are in place to support the performance of nonclinical studies; they do not describe study designs. Detailed criteria have been outlined for testing facilities and their operating procedures, personnel, equipment, recordkeeping, test and control articles, and other related parameters. Today, it is expected that any pivotal nonclinical study supporting either ongoing clinical trials or a marketing authorization will be performed in compliance with GLPs.

In an effort to harmonize global requirements for nonclinical studies, ICH developed a series of guidelines [2]. The ICH guidance is the most comprehensive and internationally recognized set of documents addressing the nonclinical aspects of pharmaceutical development (see Table 20.5). However, like GLPs, these generally do not outline specific details on study design. Rather, these provide direction on the overall types and timing of nonclinical studies as well as more expanded commentary on these studies. The key guidelines fall under the safety category and address carcinogenicity, genetic toxicity, toxicokinetics, reproductive toxicity, safety pharmacology, immunotoxicology, and photosafety as well as duration of chronic toxicity studies, biotechnology-derived products, and oncology products. The focus is on criteria and/or recommendations for a particular safety endpoint or data interpretation and not generally on study design, although study details are specified for the reproductive toxicity endpoints. By developing the guidance in this way, accommodations for technological advances within the scientific community as well as specific requirements from regional regulatory authorities can be incorporated into the nonclinical studies.

In addition to the ICH guidelines, both FDA and EMA prepare separate supplemental guidance that assists in or describes specific expectations for various nonclinical studies or types of pharmaceutical products. The FDA prepares documents entitled "Guidance for Industry" and EMA prepares documents entitled "Note for Guidance On…" or "Guideline On…." These documents are easily accessible on the websites for each agency. Recent FDA guidance has focused on testicular toxicity and male-mediated developmental effects, enzyme replacement therapy, and endocrine-related toxicities.

There is no singular location where one can find detailed protocols of currently accepted study designs for nonclinical studies to support the development of a pharmaceutical. This is because the details of the studies are constantly evolving based on Agency requests or needs. However, OECD has published a series of guidelines for the testing of chemicals that do outline in detail the design of a wide variety of nonclinical toxicology studies. This is a good starting point for understanding what a regulatory agency will expect. In addition, experienced CROs and scientists are aware of the trends in this area, specifically as they relate to pharmaceuticals, and can provide specific guidance to sponsors with questions.

CONCLUSIONS

The roles of the study director and study monitor are interconnected and effective execution of a nonclinical study thus involves a good working relationship between these two individuals (Fig. 20.5).

There are several things that make this happen. The first is communication. Regular, ongoing, and rapid accessibility of study directors and study monitors can circumvent many potential problems and streamline the overall study performance and outcome. This is further facilitated by initial conversations regarding the purpose of the study so that the end product aligns with the sponsor's objectives and regulatory needs. The second is collaboration. Understanding that both parties are working toward the same goal and are on the same team can alleviate any uncertainties and misunderstandings that may arise. The third is certainty/decisiveness. When decisions need to be made during the course of the study, clear suggestions or proposals are necessary so that the sponsor can, along with the study director and monitor, determine the best path forward.

When study directors and study monitors are in sync, not only do nonclinical studies progress smoothly but any unexpected events are dealt with quickly and in a manner that meets the mutual expectations and requirements of the CRO and the sponsor. Such an environment

TABLE 20.5 ICH Guidelines on the Nonclinical Development of Pharmaceuticals

ICH Guideline Number	Title	Date
S1A	Need for carcinogenicity studies of pharmaceuticals	November 1995
S1B	Testing for carcinogenicity of pharmaceuticals	July 1997
S1C(R2)	Dose selection for carcinogenicity studies of pharmaceuticals	March 2008
S2(R1)	Guidance on genotoxicity testing and data interpretation for pharmaceuticals intended for human use	November 2011
S3A	Note for guidance on toxicokinetics: The assessment of systemic exposure in toxicity studies	October 1994
S3B	Pharmacokinetics: Guidance for Repeated dose Tissue Distribution studies	October 1994
S4	Duration of chronic toxicity testing in animals (Rodent and non Rodent toxicity testing)	September 1998
S5(R2)	Detection of toxicity to Reproduction for Medicinal products & toxicity to male Fertility	November 2005
S6(R1)	Preclinical safety evaluation of biotechnology-derived pharmaceuticals	June 2011
S7A	Safety pharmacology studies for human pharmaceuticals	November 2000
S7B	The nonclinical evaluation of the potential for Delayed Ventricular Repolarization (QT Interval Prolongation) by human pharmaceuticals	May 2005
S8	Immunotoxicity studies for human pharmaceuticals	September 2005
S9	Nonclinical evaluation for Anticancer pharmaceuticals	October 2009
S10	Photosafety testing of pharmaceuticals	November 2013
M3(R2)	Guidance on nonclinical safety studies for the conduct of human clinical trials and marketing authorization for pharmaceuticals	June 2009
M7	Assessment and control of DNA Reactive (Mutagenic) impurities in pharmaceuticals to limit potential Carcinogenic risk	June 2014

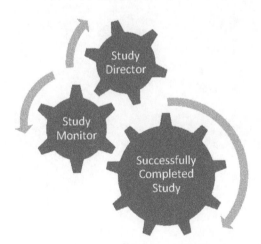

FIGURE 20.5 Collaboration between study directors and study monitors.

creates the ideal setting for accomplishing the ultimate objective of providing reliable nonclinical data to support the clinical development and marketing authorization of pharmaceuticals.

References

[1] Federal Register (FR). Nonclinical laboratory studies. Good Lab Pract Regul 1978;43(247):59986–60025.
[2] International Conference on Harmonization (ICH). Guidance on nonclinical safety studies for the conduct of human clinical trials and marketing authorization for pharmaceuticals. M3(R2). 2009.
[3] Organization for Economic Co-operation and Development. OECD principles on good laboratory practices (as revised in 1997). OECD series on principles of good laboratory Practice and compliance monitoring, number 1. 1998.

SPECIALTY ROUTE OF ADMINISTRATION

21

Infusion Toxicology and Techniques

J.C. Resendez, D. Rehagen

INTRODUCTION

Preclinical study designs for testing investigational drugs have become more complex, often aimed at mimicking clinical protocols. Intravascular administration is the most common infusion route. Long-term intravascular infusion permits the maintenance of a constant, steady state blood-level concentration of a drug and is necessary if that is the intended clinical route of administration. Successful infusion techniques require the integration of numerous technologies, including catheter implantation, protection of externalized equipment, and a method of compound delivery. Having the capability for both tethered and nontethered (ambulatory) models allows the preclinical researcher to select the model that is more appropriate for the physicochemical properties of the test article and duration and frequency of infusion. Infusion systems used today are vastly improved compared to those used in the past for long-term infusion. Development of a successful infusion model requires a system versatile enough to accommodate the activities associated with an IACUC approved and regulatory-compliant study protocol. The ideal infusion system must be adapted to the animal caging, optimize use of space, and allow for standard animal manipulations without interrupting dose administration. Enhancements to animal cages and the infusion systems (ie, harnesses/jackets, catheters, catheter material, swivels, and vascular access ports) have been essential in meeting these requirements.

Novel refinements, adequate planning, proper catheter maintenance, and careful experimental design are crucial to the successful conduct of infusion models in laboratory animals. Improvements to infusion equipment and systems, implantation techniques, and maintenance procedures have made both ambulatory and tethered infusion successful and efficient in various laboratory animal species. This chapter specifically discusses the most common rodent and nonrodent infusion models. Many of the techniques described are similar across species and can be adapted to various preclinical animal models.

PRECLINICAL INFUSION MODELS

The rat (*Rattus norvegicus*) is the usual rodent model used for evaluating the toxicity of various classes of chemicals and for which there is a large historical database. The rat is also the most commonly used animal model for preclinical continuous intravenous infusion [1]. The canine (*Canis familiaris*) has been used as the nonrodent model of choice in experimental research to predict the potential toxicology of new drug entities administered to humans [2]. Because of its extensive use in physiological and surgical research over the past century, a large historical database of anatomic and physiologic endpoints has been amassed about the canine. This vast scientific knowledge has detailed some similarities to humans, with respect to our understanding of anatomy and physiology, making the canine almost exclusively the large animal species for use in general toxicology testing. Coupled with its extensive use in experimental surgical research, the dog is quite advantageous as a model for long-term infusion [3]. In most toxicology studies involving canines, the breed of choice is the beagle mainly because of its availability, size, and temperament [4]. Along with the rat, the rabbit (*Oryctolagus cuniculus*) is a traditional species frequently used

for preclinical developmental and reproductive toxicology (DART) testing associated with small-molecule compounds, many of which are required to be administered via intravenous infusion. The rabbit is the primary second species model for reproductive toxicology testing due in part to a vast historical database, animal availability (sexually mature animals), high fertility rate, low abortion/fetal resorption rate, and large litter size [5]. The nonhuman primate (NHP) is utilized as an alternative nonrodent species to the canine. The growth of the biotechnology industry has resulted in an increased demand for primates in preclinical research, primarily because of the tissue and species specificity of most recombinant proteins [6]. While both the rhesus monkey (*Macaca mulatta*) and the cynomolgus monkey (*Macaca fascicularis*) are the Old World monkey species most commonly used in research, the typically smaller size of the cynomolgus monkey lends itself more adequately to preclinical research in terms of drug volume requirement (mg/kg) and animal handling/restraint/husbandry.

Because of their widespread use in preclinical research, continuous infusion models have been developed for the rat, rabbit, dog, and NHP that allow for preclinical protocols that mimic the intended clinical protocols in man. Although infusion models are not limited to these species alone, for the purpose of this chapter, discussion will be limited to the rat, dog, and NHP as general assumptions regarding infusion techniques, processes, catheter maintenance, and equipment can be extrapolated across multiple species including the mouse, rabbit, and mini-pig.

REGULATORY GUIDELINES

Despite the technically challenging and logistically demanding nature of continuous intravenous infusion studies, regulatory bodies expect these studies to be comparable to general toxicology designs in regard to overall endpoints, data parameters, and animal numbers [6,7]. Similarly, there is no formal regulatory exception afforded to limit the duration of animal infusion studies [7]. As a result, guidelines appropriate for nonclinical safety studies are applicable to infusion studies. Current guidelines state:

> The development of knowledge necessary for the improvement of the health and well-being of humans as well as other animals requires in vivo experimentation with a wide variety of animal species [8].

> Whole animals are essential in research and testing because they best reflect the dynamic interactions between the various cells, tissues, and organs comprising the human body [9].

Additional guidelines include:

- Principles for the utilization and care of vertebrate animals used in testing, research, and training. Federal Register; May 1985;50(97).
- Position statement on the use of animals in research. NIH Guide February 1993;22(8).
- Guidance for industry on nonclinical safety studies for the conduct of human clinical trials and marketing authorization for pharmaceuticals. ICH M3(R2), January 2010.
- Current International Conference on Harmonization (ICH) Harmonized Tripartite Guidelines and generally accepted procedures for the testing of pharmaceutical compounds.
- Preclinical safety evaluation of biotechnology-derived pharmaceuticals. ICH S6 (R1), October 2009.
- US Food and Drug Administration Good Laboratory Practice Regulations, Title 21 of the US Code of Federal Regulations Part 58.
- Organization for Economic Cooperation and Development Principles of Good Laboratory Practice, ENV/MC/CHEM(98)17.
- Guidance for industry, investigators, and reviewers: exploratory IND studies, US FDA Center for Drug Evaluation and Research (CDER), January 2006.

CHOOSING THE APPROPRIATE INFUSION MODEL

In evaluating whether to use a continuous administration (eg, tethered system) or a peripheral percutaneous dosing regimen, the following must be considered:

- Clinical dosing regimen
- Steady-state systemic drug levels required
- Class of drug (eg, anticoagulant)
- Infusate characteristics
- Study duration
- Longer acclimation (to include postsurgery recovery)
- Test article system compatibility
- Frequency of dosing (single vs. multiple)
- Duration of dose administration (minutes vs. hours vs. days)
- Infusion rates and volumes
- Surgical/postsurgical care
- Technical/operational competency

Once the study duration and endpoints have been identified, evaluate the logistics associated with each infusion model. Identify which regimen is more appropriate, understanding its limitations, equipment and material needs, the compound characteristics, study objectives and anticipated test article effects (if known),

practical and regulatory considerations, and overall feasibility [6]. For many study designs, percutaneous IV administration does not allow for extended dosing durations and repeated procedures due to the duration and type of physical restraint required to facilitate the dose. In these cases, chronic vascular implantation is the most appropriate and efficient regimen to consider. Based on the frequency of dose administration, infusion rate and infusion volume, either the tethered or ambulatory (large animal) models of infusion delivery should be considered, both of which involve surgical implantation of IV access devices.

Although most procedures and end parameters included in a typical toxicology study can similarly be included as part of an infusion study, the technical and logistical issues surrounding the use of an indwelling catheter must be considered and planned for [7]. The basic design of an acute, subchronic, and chronic infusion study is usually comparable to standard, traditional dose administration routes; however, there are additional challenges and limitations that must be considered when conducting an infusion study. Infusion studies will require a longer acclimation period allowing for adequate postsurgical recovery. The pre- and postsurgical antibiotic and analgesic regimen must be considered as the potential for possible test-article interactions may exist [7]. Additionally, the physical characteristics of the test material should be known and planned for. Drug-catheter compatibility/suitability studies should be conducted to evaluate any adsorption or leeching of test article formulations with the catheters and/or other components of the infusion system [6,7], along with potential incompatibility between the test article formulations and the solutions (eg, control solution, saline) used to flush the infusion system and maintain catheter patency. Particular attention should be given to vehicle and test article properties such as pH, osmolality, and stability. The stability of the formulated test material may significantly impact the frequency of required formulation preparations. Extremes in pH and osmolality of the infused formulation (discussed further in the section "Challenges/Advantages") may result in local and/or systemic vehicle/test article-related irritation or development of infusion phlebitis [6,7]. As previously mentioned, the infusion rate and volume must be considered when designing infusion studies. Very high infusion rates and/or infusion volumes may result in local irritation and adverse systemic changes that are not test article-related, but rather the result of the infusion procedure. Similarly, long-term infusion studies may result in physiological adaptive changes such as vasodilation and/or pulmonary hypertension and edema associated with large/maximal volumes [6]. Conversely, very low infusion rates can result in loss of catheter patency and compromised catheter function.

INFUSION BEST PRACTICES

Surgical Models

Training

Education and training are critical to ensure that qualified personnel are performing surgery on laboratory animals. Assessment of the surgical skills and knowledge of persons performing animal surgery are difficult due to the vast array of procedures that can be performed. There are, however, basic tenets of surgical technique to which individuals must adhere and demonstrate competence, including a proficiency in proper sterile technique, tissue handling, hemostasis, and closure techniques in addition to perioperative and postoperative care [10]. Personnel performing biomedical research-related animal surgical procedures are responsible for the well-being of the animal and must have adequate training and experience. Individuals should be assessed independently based on experience, background, and training before being allowed to perform surgery [11]. Most research institutions performing experimental surgery have, and conform to, regulations, laws, and standards that require personnel to be trained when performing animal surgery [11]. However, regulations pertaining to surgical training are few, and those that exist lack definition with regard to specifics about surgical training and surgical qualification. The Academy of Surgical Research (ASR) is an international organization that promotes the advancement of professional and academic standards, education, and research in experimental surgery. Through the ASR, a certification program has been established to provide verification of competency in anesthesia, minor surgical procedures, and more complex experimental surgery, with corresponding certification as Surgical Research Anesthetist (SRA), Surgical Research Technician (SRT), and Surgical Research Specialist (SRS), respectively. Recommendations for surgical research guidelines have been described in a publication by the ASR, *Guidelines for Training in Surgical Research with Animals*, (2006), for a laboratory animal surgical training program requiring surgeons to demonstrate proficiency in all facets of the procedures being performed. Other training resources for surgical methods are available through hands-on surgical wet labs sponsored by various organizations including the ASR, the Safety Pharmacology Society (SPS), and the American Association for Laboratory Animal Science (AALAS). Numerous virtual training opportunities are available through webinars and other forms of electronic media. Ultimately, it is incumbent upon the surgeon to demonstrate a working knowledge of the ethical considerations and laws that govern the performance of experimental surgery in animals, and it is the responsibility of an institution to ensure that all personnel performing survival or terminal surgical procedures

on these animals be qualified by experience, education, and training to perform such procedures [11].

Infusion Methodology

For both tethered and untethered (ambulatory) infusion models, the jugular and femoral veins are the two most common sites of catheter implantation for continuous intravenous infusion in laboratory animals. Irrespective of the implantation site, the surgical techniques used for isolating, cannulating, and ligating the target vein are similar. More importantly, established general surgery principles apply to the implantation of intravascular catheters. Asepsis, closure of dead space, hemostasis, minimal tissue trauma, and careful approximation and apposition of the wound/incision are paramount for a successful surgical outcome [10].

As previously discussed, pre- and postsurgical antibiotic and analgesic regimens must be considered as the potential for possible test article interactions could exist [6,7]. This should never preclude the use of antibiotic/analgesic treatment following surgery, but would more specifically identify which drugs are most appropriate (based on the potential for test article interaction) and/or would define an adequate washout period, which could impact the duration of recovery and potentially lengthen the acclimation period. Along with anticipating drug contraindications, the anticipated infusion rate and dosing duration and frequency may dictate the infusion model (ie, tethered/ambulatory vs. peripheral) and the equipment required to accomplish the dose administration. Maximum infusion volumes are dictated by the duration of exposure, the length of the dosing period, chemical characteristics of the formulation, and toxicity of the test material [6]. During the drug delivery portion of an infusion study, recommended flow rates for test article delivery in the rat range from a minimum of 0.4 mL/h to approximately 100 mL/kg/day (~4 mL/kg/hr). In large animals (ie, dogs and NHP), recommended flow rates range from a minimum of 2 mL/h to approximately 100 mL/kg/day (~4 mL/kg/hr). Infusion rates below 0.4 mL/h in the rat and 2 mL/h in large animal species (typical infusion system maintenance rates; keep vein open [KVO] rate) may lead to patency issues such as test article precipitation or clotting and occlusions. Very low infusion rates may lead to insufficient mixing of infusate with intravascular fluids [12]. High infusion rates can lead to fluid overload, resulting in pulmonary edema. However, compensatory responses (such as initial vasodilation and resulting increased renal excretion) enable infusion of much larger volumes over extended infusion durations [6].

Limitations and Advantages of the Infusion Model

As previously mentioned, the jugular and femoral veins are the two most common sites of catheter implantation for continuous intravenous infusion in laboratory animals. Both vessels have advantages and disadvantages. The jugular vein is easy to access and cannulate but because of its proximity (ie, catheter tip) to the heart, the catheter must be carefully positioned as to not lie directly in the left atrium [4], and test articles have less chance to mix with the blood (before entering the heart). The relatively short distance that the catheter is actually in the jugular vein (ie, from the catheter insertion site to the catheter tip) also increases the potential for catheter dislodgment due to head/neck movement. Additionally, cannulation of the jugular vein prevents use of that specific vessel for percutaneous blood-sample collections in the dog/rat, often required for toxicokinetic/pharmacokinetic and clinical pathology evaluations during the study. Blood collection is then limited to the contralateral jugular vein and/or other peripheral vessels. Alternatively, the femoral vein approach provides for more complete systemic distribution of the test article and avoids potential catheter interaction with the heart [4]. Additionally, femoral catheter placement allows for the use of both jugular veins for percutaneous blood-sample collection in the dog/rat. For the purpose of describing surgical cannulation of the vein, use of the femoral vessel will be discussed in subsequent sections of this chapter.

The use of vascular access ports (VAP) as an alternative to externalized catheters has become common in research institutions. With advancements in VAP materials and design, incorporation of access port technology into both tethered and nontethered infusion models is now possible. The use of VAPs has allowed for new research opportunities and refined techniques that have improved the intravenous infusion model as a whole. Because the VAP is not exteriorized, the VAP model provides unique advantages over the traditional externalized catheter technique [13]. Once the blood vessel is cannulated, the catheter is attached to the port body (usually comprised of a small reservoir with an injection septum) that is then positioned subcutaneously. The entire system is therefore completely internalized, which greatly decreases the opportunity for infection and prevents possible catheter dislodgement, thereby improving overall catheter patency over longer durations.

The use of PinPort technology (Instech Laboratories, Inc., Plymouth Meeting, PA) as an alternative to the tethered model or VAP implantation in the rat, allows for fast, aseptic access to externalized catheters for dose administration or blood-sample collection. The PinPort is designed for intermittent, manual access of the surgically implanted catheter via a lightweight port and injector system. Once attached to an externalized catheter, the PinPort provides a closed catheter system that can be quickly and easily accessed using aseptic technique, which decreases the opportunity for systemic infection and allows for improved catheter maintenance

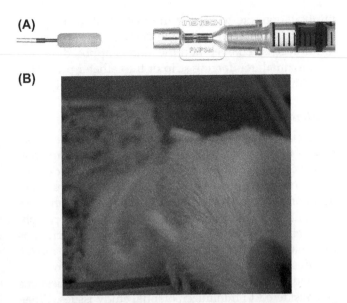

FIGURE 21.1 The PinPort is designed for intermittent, manual access. It consists of a lightweight port (3mm in diameter, 0.1g) and a port injector that is recessed providing complete needle stick protection for personnel (A). Once attached to an externalized catheter, the PinPort provides a closed catheter system that can be quickly and easily accessed using an aseptic technique (B).

procedures, thereby improving system patency over extended periods and repeated use (Fig. 21.1A and B).

Nonsurgical Models

Methods of Restraint and Infusion Techniques

In the rat, the lateral tail veins allow for peripheral vascular access. In the dog and NHP, peripheral limb veins provide the easiest and most appropriate peripheral vascular access. Percutaneous placement of tail-vein catheters (rat) and limb catheters (dogs and NHP) is considered a noninvasive technique that allows short-term access to peripheral vessels through the skin. A standard over-the-needle intravenous catheter (eg, Angiocath) is placed into a peripheral vein and then an injection cap or needle-free valve is attached to close the catheter system. The catheter is then secured to the limb or tail thus allowing percutaneous vascular access to facilitate dose administration.

Another option allows for percutaneous placement of a central, jugular cannula in the dog. A percutaneous indwelling catheter can be introduced into the jugular vein through the skin using a breakaway catheter introducer while the animal is under light sedation [4]. Once the cannula is advanced into the jugular vein, the introducer is removed from the vessel and then "split" away leaving the cannula in place. The cannula is then secured in place to the skin using surface sutures, tape, and overwrap for protection. A variation of this procedure involves making a slight surface incision at the implantation site to expose the vein. Following placement of the catheter using the catheter introducer, the introducer is removed and the skin is apposed around the proximal, reinforcing strip of the catheter providing additional catheter protection and stabilization [4].

Challenges/Advantages

Percutaneous peripheral infusion provides an alternative to the more invasive process of surgical implantation of cannula. Short intermittent infusion study designs (durations usually dictated by the maximum restraint durations allowed by Institutional Animal Care and Use Committees) may allow for the use of temporary peripheral vein catheters. There are, however, considerations that may impact the benefit and utility of this model. The design and logistical planning of the infusion study will require that many scientific and technical questions be considered to minimize potential study issues. When considering a peripheral infusion model over a surgical model, the number of animals and associated technical costs must be addressed. Often, the added logistics involved with animal handling, number of animals, limitations with equipment and workspace, and costs of disposables may in fact justify one model over the other. Scientifically, numerous factors may dictate which model is more appropriate. Characteristics of the test article become very important when considering a percutaneous peripheral dose design. The effects of pH and osmolality are often exacerbated depending on the size of the vessel in relation to the catheter size [7]. When possible, test article and/or vehicle formulations with pH 5.5 to 7.0 and approximately 300 mOsm/L should be used [7]. However, solutions in the pH range of 3.0–9.0, with osmlolality between 100 and 600 mOsm/L, have been found to be tolerated [6]. While a small catheter in a relatively larger vessel (eg, caudal vena cava/jugular vein) allows for almost immediate dilution of the test article into the systemic blood flow, a smaller vessel/catheter size ratio suggests an increased likelihood that test material will come into direct contact with the blood vessel wall before any significant dilution occurs. As a result, the tolerability of extremes in pH and osmolality is influenced by

infusion volume and dose rate. A small infusion volume of very low pH and low osmolality will likely be tolerated; however, increasing the volume of the formulation over a shorter duration (increased rate) will be less tolerated [7]. In this situation, local intolerance associated with vehicles/test articles prone to induce irritation (either by test article properties, extremes in pH or osmolality, associated volume and rate of infusion, etc.), becomes more problematic and often a dose-limiting issue that could result in vascular occlusion or extravasation [6].

INFUSION TECHNIQUES

Surgical Model in the Rat

The surgical infusion model in the rat typically requires that the indwelling vascular catheter be tunneled subcutaneously from the catheterization site to an exteriorization site at the interscapular region. The exteriorized catheter is then connected to an infusion system (eg, jacket/harness, tether, PinPort) to facilitate dose administration using an external infusion pump. Some researchers exteriorize the indwelling catheter at the base of the tail using a tail-cuff. Irrespective of the site of exteriorization, the catheter implantation technique is similar and will be discussed in the following.

Premedication and Anesthesia

To determine the suitability of animals for surgery, a physical examination should be conducted prior to surgery. Only animals determined to be suitable for study should undergo surgical procedures. Rats do not need to be fasted prior to surgery. Prior to surgery, a prophylactic antibiotic such as Baytril should be administered subcutaneously (SC) or intramuscularly (IM) along with an SC dose of an analgesic such as buprenorphine. General anesthesia will be maintained with isoflurane (to effect) delivered in oxygen via a precision vaporizer and rebreathing anesthetic circuit. Lactated Ringer's solution (LRS) will be given subcutaneously (1–5 mL) prior to/during surgery. Other preoperative procedures should be performed as indicated in Table 21.1.

TABLE 21.1 Scheduled Medications and Dosages for Rats

Drug	Interval, Dose, and Route	
	Surgery	Postsurgery
Isoflurane	To effect by inhalation (chamber then facemask)	–
Buprenorphine	0.01 mg/kg SC	
Lidocaine 2%	Topically to vessel for vasospasm as needed	
Lactated Ringer's solution (LRS)	1–5 mL SC	–
Baytril (or other suitable antibiotic)	10 mg/kg SC or IM	10 mg/kg SC or IM

Presurgical Preparation

All surgical procedures should be conducted utilizing routine aseptic techniques and the procedures should be conducted in a dedicated surgical suite. Preoperative preparation should be conducted in a room separate from the operating room [14].

The animals will be prepared for surgery by shaving the area over and adjacent to the surgical sites. The shaved areas should be cleansed with a surgical scrub and solution (eg, iodine, chlorhexidine). Following the final removal of the surgical scrub, an appropriate antiseptic solution should be applied (eg, iodine, alcohol). A sterile ocular lubricant should be applied to the corneal surface of each eye.

Surgical Procedure

Basic tenets of surgical technique have been previously described and should be followed. An incision is made to the inguinal region and the femoral vein is isolated from the surrounding adventitia. A venotomy is made in the vein and a medical-grade catheter is inserted and advanced cranially until the catheter tip is located within the vena cava, documenting the distance the catheter is advanced into the vein. The catheter is secured to the vessel with nonabsorbable suture and then subcutaneously routed to an exteriorization site at the dorsal-thoracic region. The catheter is anchored in place with nonabsorbable suture near the exteriorization site and is then attached to an infusion harness/jacket system or PinPort allowing for infusion administration. All the subcutaneous tissues are closed with absorbable suture. The skin incisions are closed using a subcuticular suture pattern and skin staples, wound clips, and/or tissue glue. Animals are recovered in a warmed recovery cage/area and additional ocular lubricant is applied if necessary.

For study designs requiring extended infusion durations (ie, in excess of 28 days) in rats, utilization of VAPs should be considered. As described previously, the VAP model provides unique advantages over the traditional externalized catheter technique. The implanted catheter is attached to the port body, which is placed into a subcutaneous pocket created at the exteriorization site (positioned to lie behind the jacket/harness system), and is then secured to underlying muscle using an appropriately sized nonabsorbable suture. All the subcutaneous tissue is closed with absorbable suture. The skin incisions are closed using a subcuticular suture pattern and skin staples and/or tissue glue. The entire system is therefore completely internalized, which greatly decreases the opportunity for infection and prevents possible catheter dislodgement, thereby improving overall catheter patency over longer durations.

Maintenance
Recovery Procedures

Baytril (10 mg/kg) may be administered IM or SC the day following surgery. For at least 7–10 days following surgery, animals should be observed for pain and/or discomfort and postoperative complications. Generally, animals should be allowed at least 10–14 days postsurgical recovery to ensure that the prophylactic antibiotics have been eliminated from the animal and that the animal has fully recovered prior to study initiation.

Caging

Applicable National Research Council guidelines [14] should be followed, along with applicable animal welfare regulations. On arrival at the laboratory, the rats should be acclimated for a period of at least 5–7 days. During this period, the animals should be weighed and observed with respect to general health and any signs of disease.

Upon receipt and during the acclimation period prior to surgery, the rats may be initially group housed (single sex, two to three animals/group) in solid-bottomed caging with bedding material. Housing options become more restrictive when conducting continuous infusion studies. The tethered study design and infusion model will not allow for group housing once the animals are cannulated and connected to the tether system, as two tethered rats cannot be kept in the same cage. Physical limitations associated with the equipment (ie, tethers) prevent the rats from being group housed without the potential for tether entanglement and/or infusion system damage. For the initiation of the catheter maintenance period and throughout the treatment period, tethered rats should be individually housed in solid-bottomed cages. To allow for urine collection, wire-mesh bottom inserts can be added to the polyboxes (ie, solid-bottomed cages). Rats implanted with VAPs for discontinuous (intermittent) infusion could be group housed following surgical recovery and throughout the study thereafter, between the periods when the VAPs are accessed for dose administration (and associated animal restraint).

Fluorescent lighting should be provided for approximately 12 h per day. Temperature and humidity should be monitored and recorded daily and maintained to the maximum extent possible between 68°F and 79°F (20–26°C) and 30–70%, respectively. For most rat rooms, 10–15 room air changes per hour is appropriate.

Infusion System Care

The incision and exteriorization site, the jacket/harness fit, and the entire infusion system should be inspected daily for signs of infection (erythema, edema, exudation, etc.), equipment damage, leaking, disconnections, etc. The exteriorization site should be shaved as needed. The entire length of the subcutaneous catheter tract should be observed for possible indications of inflammation, swelling, or infection. A cleansing agent (eg, Novalsan Solution) can be used to clean the incision/exteriorization site as needed. Care should be taken to ensure the site is kept dry for 7–14 days postsurgery. An appropriate antibiotic (eg, gentamicin) may be applied to the incision site(s) for at least 14 days postsurgery and as needed thereafter.

If any portion of the infusion system is disconnected during the maintenance and/or test administration period, any disconnected ends will be aseptically handled and appropriately disinfected (using chlorohexadine, alcohol, etc.) prior to being reconnected.

Once a rat has been jacketed or placed into a harness and attached to the infusion apparatus, the infusion system should be maintained with a solution at physiological pH, such as 0.9% sodium chloride for injection, USP (saline) at a minimum rate of 0.4 mL/h. Animals with VAPs that are not placed on catheter maintenance should be routinely flushed and locked with an adequate volume of catheter lock solution (eg, heparinized saline, taurolidine-citrate-catheter solution [TCS], etc.) to fill the VAP and implanted catheter.

Nonsurgical Model in the Rat

Methods of Restraint and Acclimation

The lateral tail veins provide options for continuous intravenous dose administration, allowing short-term access to peripheral vessels through the skin. Because the peripheral catheter is positioned on the animal's tail, the animal must be restrained during the dose administration to protect the catheter. Typically, rats are mechanically restrained for no more than 1–2 h per dose. Mechanical restraint devices result in minimal stress to the animal while allowing easy and unhindered access to the tail. Short intermittent, peripheral infusions will require appropriate acclimation to the restraint device. Typically, the animals are acclimated to the restraint process for incremental periods up to 1 h in duration. For example, a group of rats scheduled for a 1 h infusion may be acclimated on three separate occasions for incremental durations of 15 min, 30 min, and 1 h during the pretreatment period.

Peripheral Vascular Access

Percutaneous vascular access usually involves a standard over-the-needle intravenous catheter (eg, Angiocath). The catheter is percutaneously placed into a lateral tail vein and then an injection cap or needle-free valve is attached to close the catheter system. The catheter is then secured to the tail with tape, thus allowing vascular access to facilitate dose administration. The area over the catheter site should be cleansed and surgically scrubbed prior to catheter placement.

Caging

Typical percutaneous peripheral infusions use short-term indwelling catheters that are removed following dose administration. As a result, standard rodent housing is appropriate. Additionally, since there is no external equipment associated with the model following dose administration, the rats can easily be group housed and socialized when appropriate.

Infusion System Evaluation and Troubleshooting

During the infusion period, the entire infusion system should be checked for equipment damage, leaking, disconnections, etc. The injection/catheterization site should be continuously monitored for signs of vehicle or test material leakage and/or extravasation. Following removal of the peripheral catheter, the catheterization site should be inspected daily for signs of infection (erythema, edema, exudation, etc.).

Surgical Model in Large Animals

Preparation

Premedication and Anesthesia

To determine the suitability of animals for surgery, a physical examination and an evaluation of clinical pathology parameters should be conducted within 15 days of surgery. Only animals determined to be suitable for study should undergo surgical procedures. Large animal species should be fasted prior to surgery to prevent emesis during the surgical or recovery periods and possible aspiration pneumonia after recovery.

In the dog, a prophylactic antibiotic such as Cefazolin (25 mg/kg) should be administered intravenously before surgery. Canines should be premedicated with an anticholinergic such as atropine (0.05 mg/kg), tranquized with acepromazine (0.1 mg/kg), and anesthetized by intravenous administration of propofol (6 mg/kg to effect). In the NHP, prophylactic Cefazolin should be administered (25 mg/kg) intravenously before surgery. NHPs should be premedicated with atropine (0.04 mg/kg), acepromazine (0.1 mg/kg), and anesthetized by intramuscular administration of ketamine (15–25 mg/kg).

An endotracheal tube will be inserted and general anesthesia will be maintained with isoflurane (0.5–5.0% to effect) delivered in oxygen via a precision vaporizer and rebreathing anesthetic circuit. LRS should be given via a peripheral catheter and infusion pump during surgery. Other preoperative procedures (including analgesic administration) should be performed as suggested in Tables 21.2 and 21.3.

TABLE 21.2 Scheduled Medications and Dosages for Dogs

Drug	Interval, Dose, and Route	
	Surgery	Postsurgery
Acepromazine maleate	0.1 mg/kg SC	–
Atropine sulfate or glycopyrrolate	0.05 mg/kg SC 0.01 mg/kg SC or IM	–
Propofol	6 mg/kg IV to effect	–
Isoflurane	To effect by inhalation	–
Buprenorphine	0.02 mg/kg SC, IM, or IV TID every 6–9 h[b]	
Meloxicam or carprofen	0.2 mg/kg SC SID 4 mg/kg SC or IV	0.1 mg/kg SC SID × 3 days[a] 4 mg/kg SC SID × 3 days or 25–50 mg PO BID × 3 days
Fentanyl patchor tramadol	<10 kg, 25 µg/h transdermal <20 kg, 50 µg/h transdermal >20 kg, 75 µg/h transdermal	Leave in place × 3 days 25–50 mg by mouth (PO) BID every 9–12 h × 3 days[a]
Bupivacaine	2 mg/kg maximum injected into incisions	
Cefazolin	25 mg/kg IV (preoperative)	–
Cefazolin	25 mg/kg SC, IM or IV (postoperative)	–
Cephalexin	–	250–500 mg PO BID every 9–12 h × 7 days
LRS	10–15 mL/kg/hr IV	–

[a]Meloxicam and Tramadol are administered as preferred analgesia.
[b]If Meloxicam and Tramadol are not used then Buprenorphine will be administered postsurgery.

TABLE 21.3 Scheduled Medications and Dosages for Nonhuman Primates

Drug	Interval, Dose, and Route	
	Surgery	Postsurgery
Acepromazine maleate	0.1 mg/kg IM	–
Atropine sulfate	0.04 mg/kg IM	–
Ketamine	15–25 mg/kg IM	–
Isoflurane	To effect by inhalation	–
Buprenorphine	0.02 mg/kg IM TID or every 6–9 h	0.03 mg/kg IM BID every 9–12 h[a] × 3 days
Meloxicam	0.1 mg/kg IM SID	0.1 mg/kg IM SID × 3 days
Bupivacaine	2 mg/kg maximum injected into incisions	
Cefazolin	25 mg/kg IV (preoperative)	–
Cefazolin	25 mg/kg SC, IM or IV (postoperative)	–
Ceftiofur	2.2 mg/kg IM SID	2.2 mg/kg IM SID × 5 days
LRS	10–15 mL/kg/hr IV	–

[a]If Meloxicam is not used, Buprenorphine must be given TID every 6–9 h for 3 days postsurgery.

Presurgical Preparation

All surgical procedures should be conducted utilizing routine aseptic techniques and the procedures should be conducted in a dedicated surgical suite. Preoperative preparation should be conducted in a room separate from the operating room.

The animals are prepared for surgery by shaving the area over and adjacent to the surgical sites. The shaved areas should be cleansed with a surgical scrub and solution (eg, iodine, chlorhexidine). Following the final removal of the surgical scrub, an appropriate antiseptic solution should be applied (eg, iodine, alcohol,

(A)   **(B)**

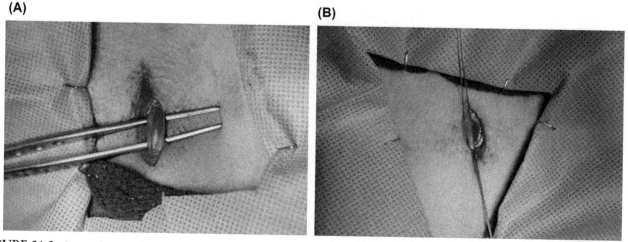

FIGURE 21.2 Femoral vein isolated from surrounding adventitia (A). Nonabsorbable suture used to further isolate the vein and secure the catheter in place (B).

DuraPrep). A sterile ocular lubricant should be applied to the corneal surface of each eye.

Surgical Procedure

Basic tenets of surgical technique have been previously described and should be followed. An incision is made to the inguinal region and the femoral vein is isolated from the surrounding adventitia (Fig. 21.2). A venotomy is made in the vein and a medical grade polyurethane catheter is inserted and advanced cranially (Fig. 21.3) until the catheter tip is located within the vena cava, documenting the distance the catheter is advanced into the vein.

The catheter is secured to the vessel with nonabsorbable suture (Fig. 21.4) and then is subcutaneously routed to an exteriorization site at the dorsal-lateral-thoracic region. The catheter is attached to a vascular access port (eg, AVA LAT Port), placed into a subcutaneous pocket created at the exteriorization site, and is secured to underlying muscle using an appropriately sized nonabsorbable suture.

All the subcutaneous tissue is closed with absorbable suture. The skin incisions are closed using a subcuticular suture pattern and skin staples and/or tissue glue.

Maintenance

Recovery Procedures

Cefazolin (25 mg/kg), or other suitable antibiotic, should be administered IM or IV the afternoon following surgery. Analgesics (eg, Meloxicam) should be administered the afternoon following surgery and for the 3 days immediately following surgery for control of pain. Other postoperative procedures should be performed as suggested in Tables 21.2 and 21.3. For at least 7–10 days following surgery, animals should be observed for pain and/or discomfort and postoperative

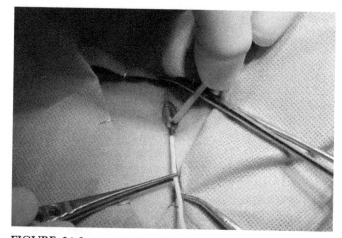

FIGURE 21.3 A medical-grade polyurethane catheter is inserted and advanced cranially until the catheter tip is located within the vena cava.

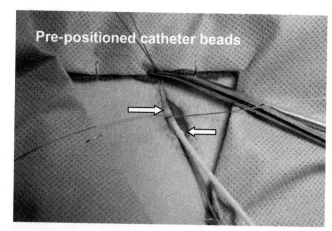

FIGURE 21.4 Catheter is secured to the vessel by ligating the vein around the catheter, distal to a prepositioned catheter bead. The distal portion of the vein is then ligated and the ligating suture is used to further secure the catheter in place by tying it around the catheter, proximal to a second prepositioned catheter bead.

complications. Generally, animals should be allowed at least 10–14 days postsurgical recovery to ensure that the prophylactic antibiotics have been eliminated from the animal and that the animal has fully recovered prior to study initiation.

Caging

Applicable National Research Council guidelines [14] should be followed, along with applicable animal welfare regulations. On arrival at the laboratory, dogs and NHPs should be acclimated for a period of at least 1–2 weeks. During this period, the animals should be weighed weekly and observed with respect to general health and any signs of disease. Ova and parasite evaluation on stool samples should be performed, and if required, appropriate antiparasitic treatment should be administered. If the appropriate vaccinations have not been administered by the supplier the animals should be immunized.

Upon receipt, the animals may be pair-housed (single sex) in double-sized cages during the acclimation period. Housing options become more restrictive when conducting continuous infusion studies. Depending on the study design and infusion model utilized, pair-housing may or may not be appropriate. When using the tethered infusion model, two tethered animals cannot be kept in the same cage. Physical limitations associated with the equipment (ie, tethers) prevent the animals from being pair-housed due to the potential for tether entanglement and/or infusion system damage. For intermittent ambulatory infusion designs (nontethered), the infusion equipment (ie, jackets, catheters, etc.) may be removed following a dosing period, thus allowing same sex pair-housing between test article administrations. However, the animals should be individually housed when protocol functions require individual data collection, eg, food consumption measurement, urine collection. Dogs should be provided the opportunity for exercise unless limited by the tether system used to facilitate a continuous dose administration.

Fluorescent lighting should be provided for approximately 12 h per day. Temperature and humidity should be monitored and recorded daily and maintained to the maximum extent possible between 64°F and 84°F (18–29°C) and 30–70%, respectively. For most animal rooms, 10–15 room air changes per hour is appropriate.

Infusion System Evaluation and Troubleshooting

The incision and exteriorization site (if applicable), the jacket fit, and the entire infusion system should be inspected daily for signs of infection (erythema, edema, exudation, etc.), equipment damage, leaking, disconnections, etc. The exteriorization site should be shaved as needed. The entire length of the subcutaneous catheter tract should be observed and examined for any

possible indications of inflammation, swelling, or infection. A cleansing agent (eg, Nolvasan solution) can be used to clean the incision/exteriorization site as needed. Care should be taken to ensure the site is kept dry for 7–14 days postsurgery. An appropriate antibiotic (eg, gentamicin) should be applied to the incision site(s) for at least 14 days postsurgery and daily following catheter exteriorization.

If any portion of the infusion system is disconnected during the maintenance and/or test administration period, any disconnected ends will be aseptically handled and appropriately disinfected (using chlorohexadine, alcohol, etc.) prior to being reconnected.

Once an animal has been jacketed and attached to the infusion apparatus, the infusion system should be maintained with 0.9% sodium chloride for injection, USP (saline) at a rate of 2–4 mL/h. Animals with VAPs that are not placed on catheter maintenance should be routinely flushed and locked with an adequate volume of catheter lock solution (eg, heparinized saline, TCS, etc.) to fill the VAP and implanted catheter.

Nonsurgical Models

Methods of Restraint and Acclimation

Since many infused test articles are intended for short (typically 0.5–4 h) durations at intermittent frequencies (eg, daily, every other day, weekly, etc.), a surgical procedure may not be appropriate. As previously described, the jugular vein and peripheral limb veins provide options for continuous intravenous dose administration, allowing for short-term percutaneous access to peripheral vessels. Because a peripheral limb catheter is positioned on the animal's forelimb or hind limb, the animal must be restrained during dose administration. A commonly used restraint device used for both canines and NHPs while undergoing infusion procedures is the sling. Typically, dogs and NHPs are restrained in a sling apparatus for no more than 1–2 h per dose. The mobile restraint unit (ie, sling) provides a quick and comfortable way to immobilize the animal with minimal stress, while allowing easy and unhindered access to all four limbs, and provides an efficient and safe working platform for the handler. The frame is usually constructed of lightweight 1′ square tube stainless steel for strength. The frame is mounted on castors which allows for easy movement and transport of the restrained and completely immobilized animal. The sling cover is constructed of robust, washable, canvas-type material. NHPs may also be immobilized in other restraint devices (eg, primate restraint chairs) for no more than 4–6 h per dose.

Most pump manufacturers and vendors are developing infusion pump brackets that allow the infusion pump to be positioned on the sling frame or primate chair next to/near the animal, thus negating the requirement for long infusion extension sets.

Short, intermittent, peripheral infusions will require appropriate acclimation to the restraint device. Typically, the animals are acclimated to the restraint process for incremental periods up to 1–2h in duration. For example, a group of animals scheduled for a 2h infusion may be acclimated on three separate occasions for incremental durations of 30min, 1h, and 2h during the pretreatment period. The acclimation periods expose the animals to the mechanical restraint device and allow technical staff to identify animals that are simply not suited for prolonged restraint. Most dogs and NHPs are typically relaxed and docile during the restraint period. If an animal is overly excited, agitated, or vocalizes during the acclimation periods, it may be a good candidate for replacement/exclusion from the study. These behaviors could be an indication of what to expect during the actual study and therefore pose an increased likelihood for potential problems during dose administration.

Methods of Vascular Access

Percutaneous vascular access usually involves a standard over-the-needle intravenous catheter (eg, Angiocath). The catheter is percutaneously placed into a saphenous or cephalic vein and then an injection cap or needle-free valve is attached to close the catheter system. The catheter is then secured to the limb with tape, thus allowing vascular access to facilitate dose administration. The area over the catheter site should be cleansed and surgically scrubbed prior to catheter placement.

A second peripheral technique is possible for the dog that actually incorporates a percutaneous catheter and a jacketed infusion model. The specific study design usually requires an infusion model that more appropriately mimics a 24-h infusion in man. Of particular importance is the catheter-to-vessel size ratio. A percutaneous peripheral limb placement in the dog better approximates a 1:1–2 catheter-to-vessel size ratio (and more appropriately mimics the catheter-to-vessel size ratio in man). As comparison, a femoral catheter is 5–7 times smaller than the caudal vena cava (1:5–7). A percutaneous catheter is placed (using aseptic technique and sterile bandaging as described earlier) in the cephalic vein distal to the elbow. To facilitate continuous infusion dose administration, the peripheral catheter is attached to an extension set routed underneath a canine jacket and then attached to a tethered/ambulatory infusion system. The animals should be acclimated to wearing a jacket continuously for at least 3 days prior to dose administration. Additionally, the animals should also be acclimated to wearing an Elizabethan collar (E-collar) during the jacket acclimation. Ideally, each animal should be catheterized

the day prior to dose administration. To prevent the animals from accessing/removing the peripherally placed percutaneous catheter, the catheterization site should be bandaged and an E-collar placed on the animal for the duration of the treatment (ie, catheterized period). Note—a standard pillow collar will not prevent the animal from reaching the peripheral cephalic catheter. Thus an E-collar should be used. During the pretreatment period, the venous catheter should be infused continuously at a rate of approximately 2–4mL/h with 0.9% sodium chloride for injection, USP (saline) to maintain catheter patency.

Caging

Typical percutaneous peripheral infusions use short-term indwelling catheters that are removed following dose administration. As a result, standard large animal housing is appropriate. Additionally, since there is no external equipment associated with the model following dose administration, the animals can easily be pair-housed and socialized when appropriate. However, if the peripheral technique incorporating a percutaneous catheter and a jacketed infusion model is employed in the dog, housing limitations are similar to those described in the preceding section.

Infusion System Evaluation and Troubleshooting

During the infusion period, the entire infusion system should be checked for equipment damage, leaking, disconnections, etc. The injection site should be continuously monitored for signs of vehicle or test material extravasation. Following removal of the peripheral catheter, the catheterization site should be inspected daily for signs of infection (erythema, edema, exudation, etc.).

EQUIPMENT

Surgical Models

Surgical Facilities

Regulations require that survival surgery performed in dogs and NHPs occurs in a dedicated surgical facility. Animals should always arrive for surgery via a separate preparation room. Following surgery, animals should leave via a separate recovery room; however, in many facilities, the preparation room also serves as the recovery room [14]. Before each surgery or session of surgeries, the surgical suite should be thoroughly cleaned. Between each animal, the surgical tables, instrument trays, and all work surfaces should be cleaned and disinfected. Separate, sterile surgical packs/instruments will be used for each animal. Each set of instruments should be cleaned, disinfected, and then sterilized prior to subsequent use. Surgeons and surgical support staff should wear single-use, disposable, or autoclavable gowns, hats, masks, and sterile disposable gloves between each animal [14].

Catheters/Vascular Access Ports

The use of VAPs has significantly improved the conduct and success of infusion models and more broadly, infusion programs. The VAP has in many ways revolutionized modern infusion techniques that have resulted in improved catheter patency, reduced incidence of catheter related infection, and has considerably eliminated the potential for catheter dislodgement. As a result, the use of VAPs has allowed for improved research capabilities, refined infusion techniques, and improved animal welfare [13]. Examples of VAPs are shown in Figs. 21.5 and 21.12.

The VAP system is composed of three basic parts: port, septum, and catheter. The port (or port body) allows percutaneous access into a small hollow port reservoir through a compressed silicone septum. To maintain the functional integrity of the VAP, a noncoring Huber point needle must be used to puncture the silicone septum. The noncoring needle allows for repeated VAP access without damaging the silicone rubber. The catheter is implanted into a vessel and connects to the port. The connected port and catheter system make up the typical VAP. The port body is generally designed as either a top-accessed "dome" or a side-accessed lateral port that lies parallel to the skin and muscle. The dome port is accessed perpendicular to the body wall while the lateral port is accessed parallel to the body wall. Although these are the two basic configurations of a VAP, there are numerous iterations of each that differ in size, shape, and port materials ranging from polysulfone plastic to titanium [13].

Similarly, the catheter design and catheter material also come in a variety of options. When selecting an appropriate vascular catheter, one must consider the catheter size (both inner and outer diameters), catheter material and pliability, and intravascular tip shape/

configuration. Catheter materials available include silicone, teflon/PTFE, polyethylene, polyvinyl chloride PVC/tygon, or polyurethane. Most catheters used for VAP systems are either silicone or polyurethane. Each of these materials may offer benefits or have disadvantages. It is often either personal preference of the researcher or suitability/compatibility issues with a specific test formulation that will dictate the catheter material [13].

Maintenance of VAPs has almost exclusively involved "locking" the port and the attached catheter with heparin-containing solutions designed to aid in reducing thrombotic-related occlusions. A nonheparin-containing lock solution—Taurolidine-Citrate Catheter solution (TCS Access Technologies, Skokie, Illinois)—can also be used to maintain VAP and catheter patency in laboratory animals. Extensive evaluation by the author has shown that repeated systemic administration of TCS, often a consequence of port/catheter maintenance, has no effect on clinical pathology parameters. More importantly, the desired anticoagulant properties of TCS did not cause systemic prolongation of prothrombin time or activated partial thromboplastin time (Resendez, unpublished data). These results support the use of TCS as an alternative to heparin-containing lock solutions.

External Infusion Equipment for Rats

The tethered infusion system (Fig. 21.6A–C) generally is comprised of the following components:

- Implanted catheter
- Jacket/harness
- Tether spring
- Swivel
- Extension tubing
- Infusion pump

Traditionally, rodent infusion systems involved a series of catheters and extension sets that were "spliced" together with coupling pins and blunt-end needles. Refinement of the system in recent years has incorporated Luer ends (Fig. 21.7) to virtually all points within the system that required end-to-end connection.

Additionally, a valve-type system has been incorporated into the jacket/harness that allows the animal to be disconnected from the tether (and thus the infusion system) while still maintaining a "closed" vascular system (Fig. 21.8).

This refinement in equipment and technique has provided for a fully modular infusion system that can easily be repaired while still maintaining the integrity and sterility of the implanted catheter (Figs. 21.9–21.11). With the exception of the implanted catheter, all infusion components can be individually changed or replaced with minimal interruption to ongoing treatment/administration. All infusion system components can be provided individually in sterile packaging.

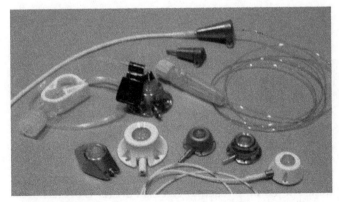

FIGURE 21.5 Typical vascular access ports and catheters.

(A)

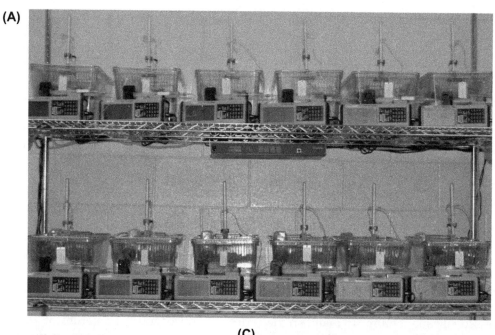

(B)　　　　　　　　　　　　　　　　　**(C)**

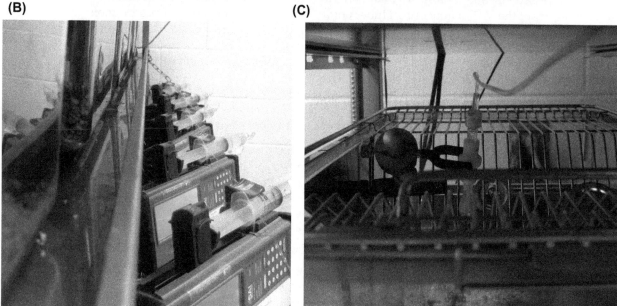

FIGURE 21.6　Rat infusion system (A). Infusion pumps are positioned in front of the animal cage (B). Infusate syringes are attached to the infusion swivel. A spring tether connects the swivel to the animal jacket/harness. The infusion swivel is mounted on the cage top, allowing the tether to rotate freely as the animal moves about the cage (C).

External Infusion Equipment for Large Animals

Recent improvements to the side-accessed lateral port have resulted in a refined approach to long-term infusion studies. Use of the AVA Lateral Vascular Access Port (AVA Biomedical, Winnetka, Illinois) and modifications to caging to support large animal tethered infusion systems have resulted in a refined, standardized infusion program across multiple large animal species. The refinements streamline processes associated with the setup, maintenance, and use of large animal infusion models. With slight modifications, most infusion system components have been standardized across large animal species, thus making the refinements both efficient and cost-effective. Refinements to the large animal infusion model have made it possible for technicians to access most of the infusion system without direct interaction with the animal. This greatly reduces the time necessary for most repairs and/or inspections of the infusion system. The Lateral Vascular Access Port (L-VAP) has been paired with an externalized Cath-in-Cath (CIC) Nylon

FIGURE 21.7 Luer connections on both ends of the swivel allow for quick and secure connections between the extension line and tether and the swivel body.

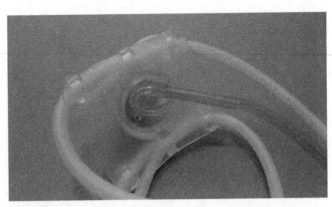

FIGURE 21.10 Infusion harness is equipped with a flexible, coiled adapter pin that facilitates connection of the implanted vascular catheter to the infusion harness.

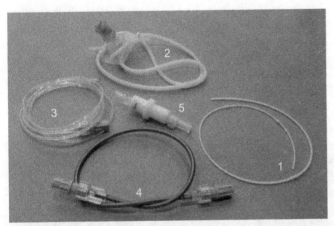

FIGURE 21.8 Typical components of a rat infusion system: vascular catheter (1), infusion harness (2), infusion extension set (3), spring tether (4), and the swivel (5). The infusion harness has a two-way valve incorporated into the harness design that allows quick Luer connection between the harness and the tether and also serves as a valve that closes when the tether is removed, thus maintaining a closed infusion system.

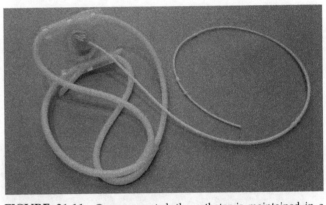

FIGURE 21.11 Once connected, the catheter is maintained in a "closed" and sterile state until the valve on the top side of the harness is accessed.

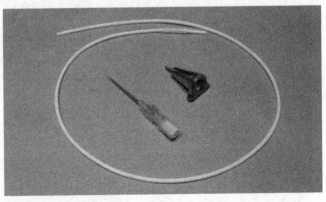

FIGURE 21.12 Lateral Vascular Access Port (L-VAP) and 18G catheter introducer.

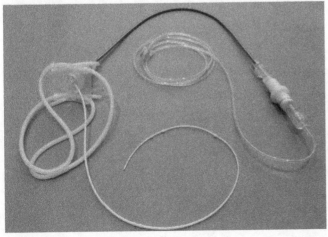

FIGURE 21.9 Fully modular infusion system allows for individual system components to be replaced without compromising the integrity or sterility of the vascular catheter or ongoing infusion.

catheter infusion system (Fig. 21.12) that can accommodate various types of infusions models across multiple laboratory species using a standardized infusion system.

The CIC infusion system has been adopted due to its ease of use and to aid in the potential reduction of infusion system-related infections. When the L-VAP and CIC systems are utilized together, the exteriorization site is reduced in size considerably to that of an 18-gauge needle puncture. When the CIC is not required it can be removed from the L-VAP system, the port can be locked, and it can remain a closed VAP system requiring minimal maintenance.

Prior to the initiation of an infusion, the CIC system is inserted into the L-VAP. This can be accomplished with either a sedated or appropriately restrained animal. The area over the port is aseptically prepared and a sterile drape is placed over the animal leaving only the port area exposed. Sterile gloves and equipment are used to access the port. A needle and inducer are used to advance the catheter through the dermal layer directly cranial to the L-VAP (Fig. 21.13). Using depth marking on the CIC, the nylon catheter is advanced approximately 15–20 cm through the L-VAP into the surgically implanted polyurethane femoral catheter.

The introducer is then removed over the CIC (Fig. 21.14A) and the CIC is left positioned inside the implanted femoral catheter, held securely in place by the L-VAP silicone septum (Fig. 21.14B). Once the CIC is in place and exteriorized, the exteriorization site will be inspected daily for signs of infection. Topical antiseptics and antibiotics may be used to reduce the potential of infection.

An infusion equipment housing system was designed to allow for all the infusion equipment to be externalized outside the animal cage (Fig. 21.15A). The housing system can be utilized on both primate and canine caging. The infusion swivel is mounted to either the top or the bottom of the equipment housing system, which is positioned near the front of the cage door (Fig. 21.15B).

One end of a 3–4-foot tether is attached to the swivel. The other end of the tether is attached to a canine or NHP infusion jacket (Lomir Biomedical, Montreal, Canada). Proper sizing of the jacket to the animal is paramount to ensure proper function of the infusion system and comfort for the animal.

A Tygon extension line is passed through the tether inside the jacket and is then connected to a pin on the rotating end of the swivel. The proximal end of the Tygon extension set has a supplier/vendor attached male Luer connector. The male connector is attached to the female Luer adapter attached to the exteriorized end

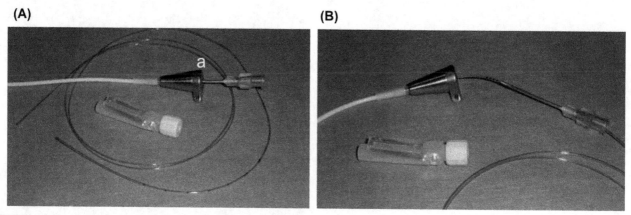

(A)   **(B)**

FIGURE 21.13   L-VAP and CIC infusion system. Catheter introducer is positioned through the port septum (A) into the hollow port reservoir. Once positioned inside the port, the introducer stylet is removed and the CIC catheter is advanced through the introducer (B), through the septum and port body, into the implanted catheter.

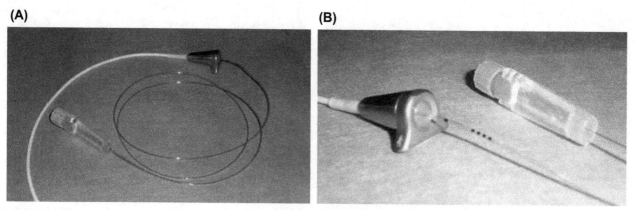

(A)   **(B)**

FIGURE 21.14   Assembled L-VAP and CIC (A) infusion system. Depth markings on the CIC (B) enable determination of the length of the portion of the catheter positioned through the port, into the implanted vascular catheter.

of the CIC Nylon catheter. A second Tygon extension line is attached to the pin on the stationary end of the swivel. This extension line is then attached to the infusion reservoir being used for catheter maintenance or test material administration (Fig. 21.16).

The CIC system can be adapted to various infusion models—both tethered and ambulatory. This model is ideal for intermittent infusions with extended periods of recovery between treatments, thus allowing for the externalized CIC to be removed. The CIC system also allows for adaptation to an untethered, ambulatory infusion model. In this model, the exteriorized end of the CIC Nylon catheter is connected directly to a programmable, battery-operated, ambulatory, infusion pump positioned in a "backpack" infusion jacket (Lomir Biomedical, Montreal, Canada).

(A) (B)

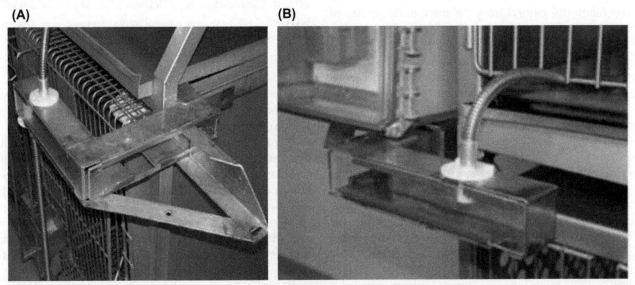

FIGURE 21.15 The stainless-steel arm can be placed on both primate and canine housing. The infusion swivel is mounted to either the top or bottom of the arm (or both), which is located outside and in front of the cage.

(A) (B)

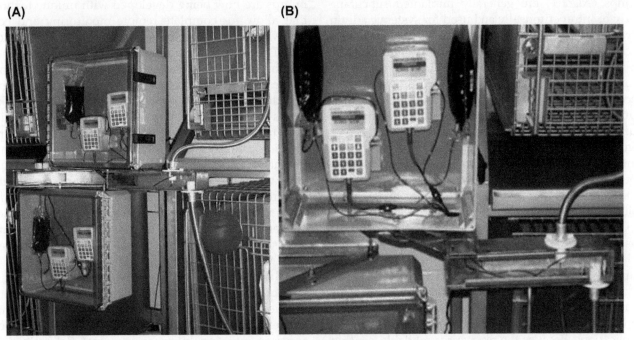

FIGURE 21.16 Infusion pump housing positioned on the stainless-steel arms attached to primate caging. Infusion pumps are positioned inside the pump housing and thus protected from husbandry procedures (eg, room/cage cleaning) and from the animals. Positioned outside the animal cage, the infusion equipment can be manipulated and examined without animal interference or the need to remove the animal from its cage.

In the event the externalized catheter becomes compromised, minor repairs may be made by technical staff without the need for the animal to return to surgery. In most cases, the damaged catheter can simply be removed and a new CIC can be quickly replaced, minimizing the amount of downtime during continuous infusions.

Infusion Pumps

The benefit of designing an infusion program that can be standardized across multiple species is the added flexibility gained from the interchangeability of the various infusion components. Most significant is the infusion pump. Depending on a variety of factors, of which rate and total infusion volume are often the most limiting, the appropriate infusion system can be "assembled" to accommodate almost any study design. Syringe pumps offer an exceptional level of precision and a wide range of flow rates and dosing libraries. They are, however, limited by total infusion volume and the size of the syringe (usually a maximum volume of either 60 or 120 mL). Larger total infusion volumes would require more frequent syringe changes. Ambulatory pumps offer a larger reservoir capacity limited only by the size of IV bag or reservoir connected to the pump. Battery-operated infusion pumps have become compact in size, allowing for true ambulatory administration.

Implantable microinfusion pumps are miniature infusion systems that can be used for administration of small volumes at very slow, controlled infusion rates. Osmotic pumps (ALZET) are generally implanted subcutaneously or intraperitoneally and used for systemic administration in mice and rats. They can also be attached to a catheter for intravascular, intrathecal, intracerebral, or targeted delivery in specific tissues/organs. These pumps operate based on the osmotic pressure difference between different compartment components of the pump. As water enters a semipermeable portion of the pump, it compresses an impermeable internal reservoir containing the test solution, thereby displacing the contents at a controlled rate. The compressed reservoir cannot be refilled, thus continued dosing requires removal of the single-use pump and reimplantation of a new, test solution-filled osmotic pump.

Continued miniaturization of infusion technology has resulted in a programmable, refillable, and implantable infusion pump (iPRECIO). This pump is surgically implanted and accessed much like a VAP. The pump reservoir is filled percutaneously through a resealable septum, and various programmable flow-rate options and infusion modes allow for relatively complex dosing applications. Because the reservoir is refillable, continuous infusions are possible without additional surgeries. While this pump is well suited for rodents, specific microinfusion protocols in large animal species certainly

FIGURE 21.17 Various types of infusion pumps: syringe pumps, peristaltic pumps, micro-piston pumps, etc.

benefit from the miniaturized technology (eg, intrathecal infusions, intracerebralventricular dosing, subcutaneous administrations, etc.).

Most pumps used in the preclinical setting are designed for laboratory use or human clinical dosing and have been used in some variation in clinical medicine for many years (Fig. 21.17). However, these infusion pumps are not designed for the rigorous demands of large-scale GLP preclinical animal studies. It is only recently that manufacturers have targeted the preclinical market with infusion pumps developed specifically for the needs of the preclinical end-user.

Recent advancements in infusion pump technology have led to improved functionality and state-of-the-art communication and connectivity capabilities. Infusion pumps are now being developed with unique features that allow for complete remote monitoring and control while still maintaining Good Laboratory Practices Part 11 compliance. Through the use of wireless and/or Ethernet connectivity, newly designed smart pumps are providing researchers with a level of system integration that, to date, has not been possible. Software platforms are being developed that allow multiple infusion design profiles to be used concurrently, across multiple infusion pumps, with minimal manual "at the pump" interaction. This automation process will reduce human error while still maintaining the necessary user control required to react to study issues. By incorporating this technology into infusion projects and programs, new efficiencies will be realized, new and innovative infusion solutions will emerge, and substantial time and effort will be saved.

All infusion pumps should be bench validated at least quarterly or biannually to confirm that the unit is functioning normally and to confirm accuracy of dose delivery. All pumps are tested at two infusion rates (low accuracy rate and high accuracy rate determined by manufacturer specifications). The pump accuracy must be ±10% of the target volume. If the pump fails the accuracy test, it is returned to the manufacturer for repair.

All infusion pumps should be uniquely identified. All validation and accuracy data should be maintained in the study files.

For intermittent infusion studies, dose accuracy is determined daily during the study. Dose accuracy is calculated as a percentage of the target-dose volume based on pre- and postdose reservoir weights. Most dose-accuracy calculations assume a formulation specific gravity of 1 (unless determined prior to dose administration or defined by the protocol). For continuous infusion dosing, dose accuracy is determined as a function of time and dose delivery. The target volume is calculated based on the actual time of delivery. This value is then factored into the actual dose delivery based on the pre- and postdose reservoir weight as described earlier.

BACKGROUND DATA – RESULTANT PATHOLOGIES

Surgical Models

Complications Associated With the Surgical Process

Implantation of a vascular catheter in laboratory animals has become a relatively standard surgical procedure. However, as with any surgery, there is always the potential for complication during the procedure. Vascular catheters and access ports are foreign bodies. Although rare, there is always the potential for the implant to be rejected. More common but still rare are the occasional localized reactions to sutures. Animal surgery involving implanted materials requires strict attention to aseptic technique and should be performed with a minimalist approach to the procedure. The surgical technique should include gentle tissue handling, effective hemostasis, strict asepsis, accurate tissue apposition, and expeditious performance of the surgical procedure [10]. Complications associated with improper tissue handling can be significant, often requiring correction and use of the contralateral vessel. An incorrectly sized catheter or improper vessel dissection can easily lead to a torn vein. Similarly, improper isolation of the vessel could result in trauma to the adjacent nerve and subsequent limb impairment. It is essential that surgeons understand the appropriate anatomy and aim to leave the animal as normal as possible following the procedure [10].

As alluded to earlier, when planning the surgery, much consideration should be given to the animal size and the size of the catheter to be implanted. While using the smallest outer diameter possible is best practice, study requirements and infusion limitations may require use of slightly larger catheters. Understanding the catheter material being used and how it will react in the vessel, catheter tip configuration and orientation, consequence of vessel ligation, and resultant blood flow are all important aspects of the procedure that should be considered in order to minimize complications.

Issues Associated With Study Design

Appropriately designing an infusion study requires consideration of many technical, scientific, and logistical issues that must be understood in order to successfully initiate and complete the project. Although each project may be unique and have study distinctions dictated by compound characteristics, the number of animals assigned to study and the series of study endpoints and evaluations are frequently dictated by regulatory requirements.

The surgical component of most infusion studies is likely the first challenge. Enough animals must be surgically prepared to ensure that the appropriate number of animals/group is available at study initiation. Potential surgical/postsurgical issues must be considered along with catheter/VAP patency. Additionally, the postsurgery recovery period must be planned for. Adequate recovery should be allowed for incisions to heal and to ensure that postsurgical medications have been eliminated (when considering potential drug interaction with the test compound).

The dosing regimen and infusion volumes must be clearly understood in order to appropriately design the study. Target-dose volume and infusion rates may limit the equipment available (ie, rate outside the functional range of the pumps) for study use. Similarly, the duration and frequency of exposure, the length of the dosing period, chemical characteristics of the dose formulation, and toxicity of the test material will all dictate limitations for infusion volumes.

Larger total dose volumes may require the use of a tethered infusion model while intermittent and shorter duration infusions may be possible using a nonsurgical percutaneous peripheral dose design. These study design decisions will directly impact how operational resources are scheduled and the logistics required to successfully complete the project.

Understanding potential limitations in dose volume may also help in selecting vehicles that provide increased solubility of the test article in order to achieve higher exposure levels during the infusion. Vehicle selection could also influence the types of materials and components used in the infusion system. All infusion reservoirs and infusion lines are available in low- or nonphthalate ester content materials. Diethylhexly-phthalate (DEHP) is a commonly used plasticizer in PVC used to improve pliability. DEHP may be leached from a PVC component into solution depending on the lipid and/or organic content of the infusion solution, duration of solution contact with the material, and temperature. By understanding vehicle characteristics, modifications can be made to the infusion system (eg, using only non-DEHP materials) to minimize the leaching potential [6].

In-Life Changes Associated With the Model

Following surgical implantation of an infusion-dosing catheter, there is no appreciable change in body weight compared to orally treated animals [15,16]. Slight decreases in weight gain during the pretreatment period following surgery are expected and due to the effects of anesthesia and surgical procedure. Clinical findings related to the infusion procedure are primarily due to extended periods of wearing the jacket. Dermal ulcerations, scabbing, and sores in the cervical, axillary, and dorsal thoracic regions are primarily due to an improperly fitted jacket or simple jacket movement over time. Jacket fit should be monitored daily as part of the infusion system checks. Large animal jackets should be changed at least every 2 weeks or as needed if excessive wear or soiling is apparent.

Pathology

Clinical Pathology

Saline infusion in the rat may result in minor effects on hematology parameters (eg, acute-phase increase in fibrinogen), but often clinical pathology values remain within reference ranges [15]. Walker [6] reported mild decreases in red blood cell count, hematocrit, and hemoglobin in NHPs during the initial weeks of a saline infusion, likely the result of frequent blood sample collection and hemodilution effects of the saline treatment. Leucocyte counts generally increase with duration of treatment, suggesting a persistent, chronic inflammatory response with no evidence of effect on platelet counts [6].

Tables 21.4–21.7 show a sample population of historical control clinical pathology data from canines approximately 7–9 months old and a population of surgically altered infusion canines approximately 5–9 months old. All samples were obtained via a percutaneous jugular collection. The surgically altered canines were sampled following surgery pretest (prior to dosing) during the postsurgical recovery period. There are no appreciable changes in clinical pathology parameters in the surgically altered animals compared to the historical controls.

Histopathology

Common Pathological Findings Related to Intravascular Infusion Procedures in Laboratory Animals When test materials are administered to laboratory animals via intravenous infusion, distinguishing between test system-related and test article-related pathological changes can be challenging [17,18]. Even catheterized animals administered physiological saline solution via infusion can exhibit a range of localized and systemic effects.

The use of control groups as well as familiarity with the range of possible background pathological changes in the test system is important in order to accurately interpret potential test article-related findings. Utilization of vehicle and/or saline control groups is necessary for interpretation of study results [16].

As a test model, catheterized animals on intravenous infusion studies undergo multiple procedures that influence the development of lesions. Lesions may be observed either in-life or postmortem. Depending on the model used, lesions can be observed at surgical sites associated with an incision, at the exteriorization site, around VAP, along the catheter tract, or surrounding suture material. Harnesses and jacket systems can be abrasive to the skin, especially if they fit poorly [4,6]. Lesions can be present in the catheterized vessel wall due to focal mechanical trauma at the site of the catheter insertion. Lesions can also be present in the internal lining (endothelium) of the catheterized vessel due to mechanical injury, induction of turbulence in blood flow, and/or the physical properties of the catheter (size, shape, composition) [18]. The volume, rate, and the physical and chemical properties of the infusate may cause localized vascular effects [4,16,19]. And while impeccable care should always be taken to avoid contamination during the surgical placement of the catheter and during catheter maintenance procedures, bacterial infections can be difficult to prevent entirely [19,20]. Bacterial infections may cause severe lesions at the surgery site, along the catheter tract, at the catheter tip, and/or systemically throughout the animal.

In general, tissue responses to catheterization and infusion procedures in laboratory animals appear to be similar regardless of the vessel chosen for the administration (eg, jugular, femoral, cephalic, saphenous veins). And while it is important to consider the various factors that can affect lesion development when interpreting pathology findings in a given infusion study, unless otherwise stated, the range of findings discussed in this section may be observed with any infusion study regardless of study design and species/animal model.

Necropsy Techniques and Tissue Sampling Successful interpretation of pathological findings in infusion studies is only possible when a thorough and consistent necropsy is performed for all animals on study. As always, well-written necropsy procedures, standard operating procedures, and training materials are necessary; however, well-trained and experienced necropsy personnel are critical in order to properly describe and document macroscopic findings and collect tissue samples for microscopic examination. The specific procedures may vary from laboratory to laboratory based on study requirements and previous laboratory experience.

TABLE 21.4 Reference Canine Hematology Parameters

Interval		Males			Females		
		Colony Historical Control	Presurgery	Postsurgery	Colony Historical Control	Presurgery	Postsurgery
Animal age		7–9 months	5–9 months	5–9 months	7–9 months	5–9 months	5–9 months
Leukocyte count (×10³/μL)	Mean	10.84	13.22	11.39	10.66	12.84	11.57
	SD	2.553	2.934	2.191	2.778	2.744	2.702
	N	1073	65	80	1019	65	73
Erythrocyte count (×10⁶/μL)	Mean	6.894	6.716	6.756	6.992	6.874	6.814
	SD	0.5501	0.7317	0.6493	0.5784	0.7132	0.6548
	N	1080	65	81	1028	65	73
Hemoglobin (g/dL)	Mean	15.18	14.65	14.58	15.44	15.17	14.78
	SD	1.192	1.653	1.342	1.273	1.655	1.347
	N	1080	65	81	1031	65	73
Hematocrit (%)	Mean	44.61	43.47	43.56	45.23	45.01	44.32
	SD	3.602	3.962	3.553	3.847	4.055	3.444
	N	1081	65	81	1031	65	73
MCV (fL)	Mean	64.72	64.91	64.63	64.80	65.63	65.19
	SD	2.389	2.608	2.419	2.315	2.578	2.529
	N	1080	65	81	1029	65	73
MCH (pg)	Mean	22.03	21.88	21.60	22.11	22.05	21.71
	SD	0.834	0.670	0.853	0.782	0.684	0.844
	N	1078	64	81	1029	65	73
MCHC (g/dL)	Mean	34.03	33.64	33.45	34.14	33.65	33.32
	SD	0.990	1.055	1.006	1.019	1.072	1.149
	N	1074	65	81	1027	65	73
Platelet count (×10³/μL)	Mean	349.0	391.8	239.5	353.4	384.2	234.8
	SD	74.89	68.83	50.69	79.08	74.14	56.80
	N	1070	65	81	1026	65	72
Absolute Reticulocytes (×10³/μL)	Mean	48.15	–	47.17	42.25	–	36.26
	SD	25.386	–	24.791	23.337	–	18.886
	N	1027	–	77	991	–	73
Reticulocytes (%)	Mean	0.70	–	–	0.60	–	–
	SD	0.359	–	–	0.327	–	–
	N	1027	–	–	990	–	–
Neutrophils (×10³/μL)	Mean	6.961	8.176	7.184	6.809	7.683	7.138
	SD	2.1444	2.4346	1.8591	2.2935	2.0424	2.3466
	N	1075	64	80	1019	65	73
Lymphocytes (×10³/μL)	Mean	2.938	3.800	3.232	2.977	4.038	3.508
	SD	0.8380	0.9659	0.7724	0.7669	1.2374	0.9066
	N	1082	64	81	1028	65	73

Continued

V. SPECIALTY ROUTE OF ADMINISTRATION

TABLE 21.4   Reference Canine Hematology Parameters—cont'd

Interval		Males			Females		
		Colony Historical Control	Presurgery	Postsurgery	Colony Historical Control	Presurgery	Postsurgery
Monocytes ($\times10^3/\mu$L)	**Mean**	**0.622**	**0.811**	**0.555**	**0.557**	**0.720**	**0.525**
	SD	0.2406	0.2748	0.2090	0.2453	0.2690	0.1896
	N	1082	64	81	1028	65	73
Eosinophils ($\times10^3/\mu$L)	**Mean**	**0.220**	**0.256**	**0.340**	**0.209**	**0.240**	**0.283**
	SD	0.1285	0.1282	0.1870	0.1317	0.1354	0.1628
	N	1081	63	81	1029	65	73
Basophils ($\times10^3/\mu$L)	**Mean**	**0.060**	**0.067**	**0.043**	**0.062**	**0.074**	**0.052**
	SD	0.0326	0.0290	0.0198	0.0314	0.0311	0.0185
	N	1083	64	81	1030	65	73
Other cells ($\times10^3/\mu$L)	**Mean**	**0.047**	**0.080**	**0.046**	**0.047**	**0.087**	**0.056**
	SD	0.0323	0.0350	0.0266	0.0315	0.0472	0.0249
	N	1084	63	81	1031	65	73

TABLE 21.5   Reference Canine Clinical Chemistry Parameters

Interval		Males			Females		
		Colony Historical Control	Presurgery	Postsurgery	Colony Historical Control	Presurgery	Postsurgery
Animal age		7–9 months	5–9 months	5–9 months	7–9 months	5–9 months	5–9 months
Sodium (mEq/L)	Mean	147.2	145.7	146.5	147.2	146.0	146.8
	SD	1.97	1.57	1.89	1.91	1.69	1.63
	N	1081	65	75	1026	65	75
Potassium (mEq/L)	Mean	4.75	4.95	4.58	4.68	4.85	4.48
	SD	0.335	0.294	0.245	0.332	0.251	0.241
	N	1082	65	75	1026	64	75
Chloride (mEq/L)	Mean	110.5	109.8	110.4	110.7	110.2	110.7
	SD	2.05	1.43	1.50	2.01	1.88	1.71
	N	1080	65	75	1024	65	75
Calcium (mg/dL)	Mean	10.76	–	10.63	10.77	–	10.64
	SD	0.492	–	0.295	0.502	–	0.292
	N	1079	–	75	1023	–	75
Phosphorus (mg/dL)	Mean	6.10		6.47	5.88	–	6.30
	SD	0.859	–	0.655	0.867	–	0.781
	N	1076	–	75	1022	–	75
Alkaline phosphatase (U/L)	Mean	83.0		89.3	83.4	–	84.5
	SD	24.61	–	24.83	27.11	–	30.16
	N	1077	–	75	1021	–	75

TABLE 21.5 Reference Canine Clinical Chemistry Parameters—cont'd

Interval		Males			Females		
		Colony Historical Control	Presurgery	Postsurgery	Colony Historical Control	Presurgery	Postsurgery
Total bilirubin (mg/dL)	Mean	0.21	–	0.14	0.23	–	0.16
	SD	0.068	–	0.052	0.082	–	0.063
	N	1077	–	75	1023	–	74
Gamma Glutamyltransferase (U/L)	Mean	3.3	–	3.6	3.1	–	3.6
	SD	1.11	–	1.32	0.89	–	1.26
	N	971	–	75	887	–	75
Aspartate aminotransferase (U/L)	Mean	29.1	–	29.8	28.0	–	30.4
	SD	6.82	–	5.07	6.01	–	5.08
	N	1078	–	75	1020	–	75
Alanine aminotransferase (U/L)	Mean	31.0	30.2	24.0	29.5	29.4	24.7
	SD	8.91	8.01	4.59	7.42	6.91	5.77
	N	1087	65	75	1024	65	75
Sorbitol dehydrogenase (U/L)	Mean	7.07	–	5.20	7.49	–	5.34
	SD	2.657	–	1.264	2.803	–	1.324
	N	849	–	18	744	–	18
Creatine kise (U/L)	Mean	211.9	–	223.0	186.2	–	214.3
	SD	86.57	–	56.01	72.93	–	62.30
	N	1086	–	57	203	–	57
Urea nitrogen (mg/dL)	Mean	13.2	12.4	12.8	13.9	12.7	12.3
	SD	2.79	2.44	2.61	2.72	2.11	2.04
	N	1080	65	75	1027	64	75
Creatinine (mg/dL)	Mean	0.61	0.55	0.56	0.60	0.55	0.55
	SD	0.100	0.089	0.110	0.094	0.089	0.088
	N	1083	65	75	1027	65	75
Total protein (g/dL)	Mean	6.03	5.72	5.57	5.88	5.63	5.49
	SD	0.399	0.460	0.312	0.378	0.464	0.287
	N	1082	65	75	1027	65	75
Albumin (g/dL)	Mean	3.11	–	3.05	3.18	–	3.06
	SD	0.251	–	0.202	0.253	–	0.204
	N	1079	–	75	1023	–	75
Globulin (g/dL)	Mean	2.92	–	2.52	2.70	–	2.43
	SD	0.362	–	0.199	0.350	–	0.195
	N	1079	–	75	1020	–	75
Albumin/globulin ratio	Mean	1.08	–	1.21	1.20	–	1.27
	SD	0.174	–	0.113	0.207	–	0.128
	N	1067	–	75	1001	–	75

Continued

V. SPECIALTY ROUTE OF ADMINISTRATION

TABLE 21.5   Reference Canine Clinical Chemistry Parameters—cont'd

		Males			Females		
Interval		Colony Historical Control	Presurgery	Postsurgery	Colony Historical Control	Presurgery	Postsurgery
Triglycerides (mg/dL)	Mean	31.0	–	37.7	31.7	–	37.4
	SD	7.64	–	10.37	7.31	–	9.33
	N	238	–	59	258	–	59
Cholesterol (mg/dL)	Mean	167.8	–	155.2	157.9	–	151.5
	SD	29.69	–	23.04	29.20	–	26.86
	N	1076	–	75	1019	–	75
Glucose (mg/dL)	Mean	92.2	93.1	96.0	91.3	94.1	93.6
	SD	9.10	12.44	9.91	9.19	9.05	8.90
	N	1079	65	75	1027	65	75

TABLE 21.6   Reference Canine Coagulation Parameters

		Males			Females		
Interval		Colony Historical Control	Presurgery	Postsurgery	Colony Historical Control	Presurgery	Postsurgery
Animal age		7–9 months	5–9 months	5–9 months	7–9 months	5–9 months	5–9 months
APTT (sec)	**Mean**	**9.61**	–	**10.89**	**9.81**	–	**11.11**
	SD	0.899	–	0.853	0.978	–	0.795
	N	352	–	52	376	–	52
Prothrombin time (sec)	**Mean**	**7.05**	–	**7.27**	**7.16**	–	**7.27**
	SD	0.383	–	0.437	0.678	–	0.526
	N	349	–	52	376	–	52
Fibrinogen (mg/dL)	**Mean**	**275.9**	–	**181.1**	**248.8**	–	**167.2**
	SD	43.69	–	32.95	50.16	–	20.93
	N	78	–	16	104	–	16

TABLE 21.7   Reference Canine Urinalysis Parameters

		Males			Females		
Interval		Colony Historical Control	Presurgery	Postsurgery	Colony Historical Control	Presurgery	Postsurgery
Animal age		7–9 months	5–9 months	5–9 months	7–9 months	5–9 months	5–9 months
Volume (mL)	**Mean**	**155.66**	–	**122.6**	**130.78**	–	**136.4**
	SD	153.940	–	98.40	120.403	–	235.03
	N	853	–	52	803	–	34
Specific gravity	**Mean**	**1.0199**	–	**1.0375**	**1.0212**	–	**1.0390**
	SD	0.01060	–	0.01648	0.01054	–	0.01873
	N	844	–	52	778	–	34
pH	**Mean**	**7.12**	–	**7.03**	**7.02**	–	**7.16**
	SD	0.690	–	0.614	0.656	–	0.636
	N	853	–	52	796	–	34

The catheterized vessel near the catheter tip along with the surrounding tissues should be collected at necropsy. Some laboratories also collect the entire catheter tract including the vascular insertion point, the subcutaneous catheter tract, the vascular access port, and the exteriorization site [18,19]. For percutaneous administration using temporary catheters, collection of only the infusion site and the surrounding tissues may be necessary. Some laboratories prefer to incise the catheterized vessel lengthwise to identify thrombi and document other macroscopic changes [16], while others may refrain from incising the vessel at necropsy, keeping the vessel and perivascular tissues intact in order to decrease tissue artifacts from handling. Photographic documentation of macroscopic findings may be warranted [16,19]. For toxicity/safety studies, collection of a complete set of tissues from organs throughout the body [6,19], is also recommended, not only for evaluation of systemic toxicity, but also for evaluation of systemic effects of the catheterization and infusion procedures (which most commonly involve the lung, heart, kidneys, and liver). All gross lesions should be collected and evaluated microscopically.

The most important tissue for interpretation of infusion-related pathology is the infusion site consisting of the vessel and perivascular tissues near the catheter tip [16]. The location of the tip of the catheter should be identified and marked, using dye if necessary [16], at necropsy and at tissue trimming. If the catheter tip is palpable in-life, its location should be marked on the skin to help facilitate identification at necropsy, especially if the catheter is removed prior to necropsy. Some labs sample the infusion site longitudinally, in cross section, or using a combination thereof [16]. If cross sections are collected, sections approximately 1 cm proximal to the tip of the catheter (closer to the heart), at the tip of the catheter, and approximately 1 cm distal to the tip of the catheter (farther from the heart) are recommended. For venous catheters, cross sections at the tip of the catheter and proximal to the tip of the catheter will typically capture changes associated with the infusate, while cross sections at the tip of the catheter and distal to the tip of the catheter (along the path of the catheter) will typically demonstrate vascular changes associated with the catheter. A comparison of the vessel in these areas will help differentiate changes associated with catheterization from changes associated with the test material. Consistent and complete collection of the infusion site at necropsy should include a method for identification of tissue orientation, especially if the catheter is removed and it cannot be used for orientation at trimming.

Macroscopic and Microscopic Pathology

External Lesions During the in-life portion of the study and during the necropsy, external lesions can occur in the skin associated with the jacket/harness and at the externalization site. The jacket/harness can be abrasive to the skin, especially if it is not fitted properly, resulting in hair loss, epithelial hyperplasia, abrasions, surface exudation (scabbing), and/or ulceration [4,6,16]. The animal may bite or scratch at the site if it is irritated, leading to further surface trauma [18]. The externalization site can become reddened, swollen, and/or scabbed with inflammation and/or infection [19]. Redness and swelling may also be present macroscopically around the VAP (when used) or along the catheter tract. Acute microscopic lesions may include hemorrhage, edema, and acute inflammation with predominantly neutrophilic infiltrates. With longer periods of catheterization, thick capsules of fibrous tissue and chronic inflammation may form around the VAP or catheter.

The externalization site is a portal of entry through the skin, bypassing the normal defense mechanisms against contamination and infection [16,19]. Even with impeccable sterile catheter-handling techniques, bacteria may gain entry through this site. Medical devices such as the catheter, suture material [19], and VAP can be a favorable environment for the growth and spread of bacteria if contamination occurs during implantation or during a study. Bacteria may form a biofilm on the surfaces of these materials, which can provide protection against the host's natural defenses and antibiotics [20]. Morphological changes at the externalization site or around the VAP and catheter may be severely exacerbated when bacteria are present, including the formation of abscesses [18,19].

Catheterization-related inflammation may cause changes in the draining lymph nodes, which may become enlarged due to reactive hyperplasia, sinus histiocytosis [16], inflammatory cell infiltrates, and/or sinus dilation from fluid drainage. If inflammation is severe or the catheterized vessel becomes occluded, poor venous or lymphatic drainage can lead to dependent edema of the extremities. With jugular catheterization, edema of the face and head is possible [16].

Internal Lesions – Infusion Site Findings Arteries and veins are generally composed of three layers: an inner layer adjacent to the lumen called the tunica intima, a middle layer called the tunica media, and an outer layer called the tunica adventitia. The tunica intima is composed of a flattened, smooth layer of cells, called endothelial cells, which line the lumen. The endothelial cells are supported by subendothelial stroma composed of low numbers of fibrocytes and smooth muscles, elastic fibers, and a small amount of collagen. The tunica media is the thickest layer, primarily composed of smooth muscle and elastic fibers with fewer fibrocytes and collagen. The tunica adventitia blends somewhat with the surrounding tissue and is composed of fibrocytes, collagen, elastic fibers, and nerve fibers. The tunica adventitia of larger vessels also includes the vasa vasorum, which is composed of small vessels and capillaries that provide blood supply to the tunica adventitia and tunica media [19,21].

An intact endothelial layer is critical for normal blood flow through a vein or artery. Biochemical interactions between the endothelium and the blood maintain an environment that inhibits the formation of clots (thrombi). Disruption of the endothelium and exposure of the underlying subendothelial stroma triggers localized release of chemical mediators and cellular responses that lead to thrombus formation and hemostasis [19,22].

Three triggers of thrombosis that can act concurrently, known as Virchow's triad, include endothelial injury, changes in blood flow (hemodynamics), and hypercoagulability [22]. All three of these can be present in a catheterized vessel, leading to the disruption of vascular integrity. At the insertion point, the catheter must breach the vessel wall to gain access to the intravascular space. The presence of the catheter maintains the exposure of subendothelial stroma, which sustains the localized chemical environment conducive to thrombogenesis. The presence of the catheter within the vessel can lead to changes in blood flow, stasis, or turbulence. Furthermore, the catheter wall and tip can cause mechanical damage to the endothelium and vessel wall [16,18]. Starting at the insertion point, thrombi can form along the catheter, resulting in a fibrin sheath around the catheter [16,18,19]. Thrombi may also form at any point along the intravascular portion of the catheter, including its tip. The edge of the catheter tip may abrade the endothelium, but there can also be increased turbulence in the blood flow around the catheter tip [16]. Changes in hemodynamics due to the infusion of fluids can contribute to turbulence at the catheter tip. Hypercoagulability may also contribute to thrombus formation when bacteria are present [22].

Acute thrombi are composed primarily of layers of fibrin, platelets, erythrocytes, and leukocytes. Thrombi can propagate as layers are added, extending in length within the vessel lumen. With chronicity, fibrin thrombi break down (fibrinolysis) or can become organized, undergoing fibrosis and contraction. The fate of thrombi depends on the severity of the thrombus, the degree of vascular damage, and whether the inciting causes persist. A thrombus may resolve completely, restoring normal vessel structure and function. Remodeling may take place, incorporating the thrombus into the vessel wall. Recanalization of the thrombus may lead to the formation of a new lumen or multiple smaller lumina. With complete blockage of the affected vessel, neovascularization may lead to new anastomotic vessels, which bypass the area of thrombosis [22]. If the catheterized vessel is incised at necropsy, larger thrombi may be visualized macroscopically and documented [16].

Catheter-induced acute damage to the vessel wall can cause a loss of endothelium, degeneration, and necrosis of the endothelium, thrombosis, and depending on the severity of the insult, degeneration and necrosis of other layers of the vessel [16]. Microscopically, with acute injury there may be fibrin deposition, hemorrhage, and inflammation within the vessel wall or perivascular tissues [6,16]. Perivascular necrosis can also occur. Acute injury from catheterization can be difficult to distinguish from test article-related vascular toxicity.

Over time, the layers of the vessels have a remarkable ability to adapt to injury and/or regenerate. The endothelium can undergo hypertrophy and hyperplasia, restoring the endothelial cell layer where it was lost [19]. The persistent presence of the catheter frequently induces intimal proliferation, a thickening of the endothelium and subendothelial stroma often associated with the formation of frond-like projections of endothelial-lined stroma into the vessel lumen [16,17,23]. The smooth muscle of the tunica media can undergo regenerative hypertrophy and hyperplasia [19], giving this layer a basophilic appearance. This is generally accompanied by some degree of fibroplasia [6]. Fibroplasia is also a common change in the tunica adventitia and perivascular tissues. Subacute to chronic inflammatory cell infiltrates [6,16], hemosiderin-laden macrophages, and mineralization [19] may be present in any of the layers of the vessel wall. Occasionally, foreign body granulomas are present at the infusion site surrounding hair fragments, keratin, suture material, or other foreign material. Remodeling and incorporation of a chronic thrombus into a vessel wall can obscure the distinctions between the thrombus, tunica intima, and tunica media. With severe damage from catheterization, inflammation and fibrosis may completely obscure or replace the entire vessel wall. Chronic vascular changes can also be exacerbated by test materials.

With prolonged catheterization, acute and chronic changes may be present concurrently. During the necropsy, acute and/or chronic vascular changes may appear as redness and swelling at the insertion point into the vein and in tissues around the tip of the catheter. Consistent documentation of acute and chronic, microscopic and macroscopic vascular changes at the infusion site is necessary in order to distinguish between catheter-induced/infusion-related changes and test article-related vascular damage. Due to the temporary nature of percutaneous catheters, microscopic changes in the vessel wall at the infusion site are generally less severe, more conducive to regeneration, and may lack chronic changes observed with long-term catheterization because of a lack of persistent insult to the vessel wall.

With jugular catheterization, the tip of the catheter may be placed near the heart and occasionally an intracardial catheter placement [6] may occur (intentionally or unintentionally). It is possible to see a range of findings in the right atrium, right ventricle, and heart valves similar to the catheter-induced acute and chronic vascular lesions described previously [23]. For these reasons, alternative catheter placement sites may be preferred in certain species and in certain studies depending on the desired endpoints. For instance, if cardiac toxicity is a concern, catheter-induced lesions in the heart may confound electrocardiographic [6] and histopathological data.

Bacterial contamination of the infusion site can also exacerbate acute and chronic vascular changes in catheterized animals, often resulting in severe morphological changes. Bacteria may gain entry during surgical placement of the catheter or from the spread of infection along the catheter line [19]. Contamination may also occur through the lumen of the catheter during infusion or from flushing the catheter during maintenance procedures. However, even with the most stringent surgical and maintenance techniques, some catheterized animals will manage to pull catheters out or chew the catheter, which will contaminate an otherwise sterile line, often leading to complications. With bacterial colonization, increased severity of thrombosis, acute inflammation, and degeneration/necrosis are the most common findings at the infusion site; however, with prolonged infection, chronic-active changes and abscess formation can also occur.

Internal Lesions – Systemic Findings Catheterized animals on infusion studies can develop systemic lesions, which are often sequelae to the morphological changes described previously. Systemic lesions are generally associated with thromboembolism, bacterial infection, inflammation, and/or stress. On rare occasions, foreign body granulomas may develop in tissues such as the lung surrounding hair or keratin fragments, which are considered to be due to embolization during surgery, during catheter placement, or perhaps during other injection procedures [19,24].

Fibrin thrombi are often friable and portions may break off in the bloodstream resulting in embolism. Embolization may occur spontaneously, but vigorous flushing of the catheter may also dislodge fragments of thrombi. Emboli generally pass freely through the right atrium and right ventricle, lodging in the first capillary bed encountered in the lungs [16]. Affected lungs may have red foci in multiple lobes due to hemorrhage and necrosis within the alveoli and pulmonary parenchyma [6]. Occasionally, emboli may pass through the lung and occlude a vessel in another organ. Red foci of hemorrhage and foci of necrosis (acute infarcts) may be present in the heart, kidneys, or other tissues [6,18]. Chronic infarcts characterized by areas of tissue loss, chronic inflammation, and fibrosis may appear as shrunken, tan, scars at necropsy.

With bacterial infection of the infusion site, bacteria-laden thrombi can develop and embolization of bacteria can occur [19]. The heart valves are particularly susceptible to infection in bacteremic animals and may develop vegetative endocarditis [18]. Affected heart valves become thickened due to inflammation, edema, and proliferation of the endothelium or subendocardial stroma. Fibrin and thrombi generally form on the surface of affected valves, which may fragment, further predisposing the animal to systemic thromboembolism [22]. Foci of inflammation, hemorrhage, necrosis, or abscessation may occur in any tissue associated with bacteremia; however, these lesions may be more common when heart valves are also affected. Highly vascularized tissues such as the adrenal gland and pituitary gland, or other capillary beds such as the meninges [19] and choroid plexus of the brain [6], the synovium of joints, or the eye [6] can be particularly sensitive to systemic infections. In addition to infarction and other focal inflammatory lesions, the kidneys can develop glomerulitis from the deposition of bacteria, fibrin, or other inflammatory mediators within the capillaries of the glomerular tufts [16,19]. The lung may develop multifocal to diffuse interstitial inflammation. Body cavities such as the abdominal cavity, thoracic cavity, and pericardium can also become infected and develop peritonitis, pleuritis, and pericarditis, respectively.

In addition to changes described earlier, septicemia may cause a systemic drop in blood pressure due to widespread vasodilation. Leukocytosis and disseminated intravascular coagulation can also occur, resulting in hematology changes and lengthening of clotting times [22]. Organs that filter pathogens from the blood may exhibit microscopic changes including Kupffer cell hypertrophy and hyperplasia in the liver; generalized neutrophilic infiltration, leukocytosis, or reticuloendothelial hyperplasia in the red pulp of the spleen; or lymphoid hyperplasia in the white pulp of the spleen.

Bacterial infections of the catheter and infusion site, along with secondary systemic changes, can be more common with immunomodulatory compounds and with compounds that induce immunosuppression such as chemotherapeutic drugs and steroids. It is important to be familiar with the range of findings that can be associated with bacterial infections in catheterized animals because dose-related increases in bacterial infections and associated morphologic changes may be present. Distinguishing dose-related secondary findings from direct test article-related findings can be difficult.

Erythrocytes can be damaged by passing through areas with thrombi or through areas of turbulence. Erythrophagocytosis and hemosiderin may be present in tissues such as the liver and spleen as damaged erythrocytes are removed from the circulating blood [16]. Localized inflammation, systemic inflammation, and/

or decreases in red cell numbers can trigger bone marrow hyperplasia and extramedullary hematopoiesis in tissues such as the liver and spleen.

Interpretation of macroscopic splenic enlargement can be difficult in the dog. In most species, the spleen may become enlarged due to septic shock, leukocytosis secondary to inflammation, lymphoid hyperplasia, extramedullary hematopoiesis, and/or erythrophagocytosis [4,16,18]. However, in dogs, barbiturate euthanasia solutions typically cause marked splenic congestion and enlargement [6]. The degree of splenic enlargement due to barbiturate administration can vary from animal to animal; therefore histopathology is necessary to accurately interpret splenic enlargement in the dog.

With stress, adrenal enlargement due to cortical vacuolation and/or hypertrophy may be present [4,16,18]. The thymus is particularly susceptible to stress and may decrease in size due to lymphocyte apoptosis, markedly decreasing the numbers of lymphocytes within the thymic cortex and medulla. Lymphoid depletion due to stress can be difficult to differentiate from physiological thymic involution. Infusion studies using dogs and monkeys frequently have a low number of animals in each group. By chance, spontaneous changes such as physiological thymic involution can be more common in animals treated with test article, artifactually creating dose-related distribution of findings. On these occasions, historical control data should be utilized if available. Interpretation of stress-related pathological changes can be difficult and should utilize all of the available information from hematology results and other examined tissues such as the infusion site, the adrenal glands, and any other lesions in the animal.

Organ Weight Changes As might be expected from the macroscopic and microscopic findings described previously, organ weight changes may also be present in catheterized animals on infusion studies. Spleen weights may be increased associated with leukocytosis, extramedullary hematopoiesis [16], erythrophagocytosis, or septic shock. However, as discussed previously, spleen size and weight changes can be difficult to interpret in dogs euthanized with barbiturates. Associated with stress, adrenal gland weights may be increased due to cortical vacuolation and/or hypertrophy [16], and thymus weights may be decreased due to lymphoid depletion. However, lymphoid depletion and low thymus weights may also occur associated with physiological involution. Lung weights may be increased due to hemorrhage or inflammation.

Species Differences As discussed previously, the range of tissue responses to catheterization and infusion procedures are generally similar between the various species of animal models [18]; however, a few notable exceptions exist. For instance, the diameter of the catheter relative to the diameter of the vessel lumen can affect the severity and rate of lesion development. Ideally, the catheter should occupy a relatively low percentage of the lumen, which is possible to achieve with the jugular vein, caudal vena cava, or femoral vein in larger species such as the dog and monkey. However, in rodents, even when small catheters are placed in the largest vessels, the catheters occupy a significant portion of the lumen. This predisposes rodents to increased catheter-related trauma and hemodynamic effects near the catheter tip. Therefore catheterized rodents tend to develop more extensive vascular changes at the infusion site more quickly than larger species.

Lilbert and Mowat [25] reported that:

> endothelial hyperplasia…and intimal thickening at the injection site…and interstitial pneumonitis in the lungs…[are] all seen at a higher incidence in dogs than in primates.

However, it was also noted that the apparent species difference in pulmonary involvement was potentially associated with the route of catheterization utilized. The reviewed data included femoral-catheterized monkeys and jugular-catheterized dogs, and therefore it was suggested that:

> The larger diameter of the jugular vein in the dog with its greater turbulence of blood flow possibly predisposes to fragmentation and dispersal of thrombi [25].

Species-specific systemic lesions can also occur. It has been shown that rats infused with large volumes of isotonic saline can develop periarterial interstitial infiltrates of eosinophils in the lungs, potentially due to large volumes or high rates of fluid administration. While low numbers of eosinophils may be present around pulmonary vessels in naïve controls, a dose-related increase in severity of eosinophilic infiltration was observed in saline-treated animals. Rats receiving infusions of isotonic saline can also develop pulmonary arterial endothelial hypertrophy and hyperplasia as well as pulmonary arterial medial thickening [24].

CONCLUDING REMARKS

Successfully conducting an infusion study in laboratory animals requires specific attention to study design and operational planning while understanding the limitations of not only the infusion model(s), but also the limitations and experiences of the laboratory. Various factors will influence the selection of an appropriate infusion model or system and having the flexibility to adapt a model to the unique challenges that often arise because of the complexity of these studies can greatly maximize a successful outcome. Infusion studies are quite involved and similarly require the involvement of a collaborative group of talented individuals. From study design and model selection to daily operational planning and accurate data collection, all aspects of a project require acute attention to detail. This chapter presented general guidelines and best practices to follow. Various infusion models, both tethered and nontethered, were discussed, and the advantages and disadvantages of each presented.

With the advent of remote infusion pump monitoring and control, more aspects of routine study processes will become automated. Improved wireless technologies are allowing multiple (and different) pumps to communicate with a single automation platform. This will ultimately allow the standardization of operational process across projects and, more importantly, between functional groups. Infusion pumps are becoming more compact with added features and technology, all of which will soon revolutionize how infusion studies are conducted. With continued emphasis on the basic principles of infusion techniques and technology, strict adherence to the basic tenets of surgery and asepsis, and proper study design/conduct/data collection, the outcome of an infusion study will be valuable.

References

[1] Healing G, Smith D. Handbook of pre-clinical continuous intravenous infusion. New York: Taylor & Francis; 2000.

[2] Guidance for industry, investigators, and reviewers: exploratory IND studies. US F.D.A. Center for Drug Evaluation and Research (CDER); 2006.

[3] Haggerty G, Thomassen S, Chengelis C. The dog. In: Gad S, Chengelis C, editors. Animal models in toxicology. New York: Marcel Dekker; 1992. p. 567–674.

[4] Gleason TR, Chengelis CP. The ambulatory model in dog multidose infusion toxicity studies. In: Healing G, Smith D, editors. Handbook of pre-clinical continuous intravenous infusion. New York: Taylor & Francis; 2000. p. 148–60.

[5] Chellman GJ, Bussiere JL, Makori N, Martin PL, Ooshima Y, Weinbauer GF. Developmental and reproductive toxicology studies in nonhuman primates. Birth Defects Res B 2009;86:446–62.

[6] Walker MD. Multidose infusion toxicity studies in the large primate. In: Healing G, Smith D, editors. Handbook of pre-clinical continuous intravenous infusion. New York: Taylor & Francis; 2000. p. 181–209.

[7] Washer GR. Nonclinical safety evaluation by intravenous infusion – technical and design considerations. Regulatory and Safety Evaluation Specialty Section – Newsletter of the Society of Toxicology; Fall 2001.

[8] Principles for the utilization and care of vertebrate animals used in testing, research, and training. Fed Regist 1985;50(97).

[9] Position statement on the use of animals in research. NIH Guide 1993;22(8).

[10] Mendenhall V, Cornell S, Scalaro MA. Surgical preparation and infusion of the large primate. In: Healing G, Smith D, editors. Handbook of pre-clinical continuous intravenous infusion. New York: Taylor & Francis; 2000. p. 163–80.

[11] Guidelines for training in surgical research with animals. J Invest Surg 1996;22(3):218–25.

[12] Blacklock JB, Wright DC, Dedrick RL, Blasberg RG, Lutz RJ, Doppman JL, et al. Drug streaming during intra-arterial chemotherapy. J Neurosurg 1986;64(2):284–91.

[13] Swindle M, Nolan T, Jacobson A, Wolf P, Dalton M, Smith A. Vascular access port (VAP) usage in large animal species. Contemp Top 2005;44(3):7–17.

[14] Institute of Laboratory Animal Resources Commission on Life Sciences National Research Council. Guide for the care and use of laboratory animals. Washington (DC): The National Academies Press; 2011.

[15] Healing G. Multidose infusion toxicity studies in the rat. In: Healing G, Smith D, editors. Handbook of pre-clinical continuous intravenous infusion. New York: Taylor & Francis; 2000. p. 31–42.

[16] Pickersgill N, Burnett R. The non-ambulatory model in dog multidose infusion toxicity studies. In: Healing G, Smith D, editors. Handbook of pre-clinical continuous intravenous infusion. New York: Taylor & Francis; 2000. p. 135–47.

[17] Lilbert J, Burnett R. Main vascular changes seen in the saline controls of continuous infusion studies in the cynomolgus monkey over an eight-year period. Toxicol Pathol 2003;31:273–80.

[18] Weber K, Mowat V, Hartmann E, Razinger T, Chevalier H, Blumbach K, et al. Pathology in continuous infusion studies in rodents and non-rodents and ITO (Infusion Technology Organisation)-recommended protocol for tissue sampling and terminology for procedure-related lesions. J Toxicol Pathol 2011;24:113–24.

[19] Evans JG, Kerry PJ. Common pathological findings in continuous infusion studies. In: Healing G, Smith D, editors. Handbook of pre-clinical continuous intravenous infusion. New York: Taylor & Francis; 2000. p. 253–64.

[20] Percival SL, Kite P. Intravascular catheters and biofilm control. J Vasc Access 2007;8(2):69–80.

[21] Plendl J. Cardiovascular system. In: Eurell JA, Frappier BL, editors. Dellmann's textbook of veterinary histology. Ames (IA): Blackwell Publishing; 2006. p. 117–33.

[22] Mitchell RN. Hemodynamic disorders, thromboembolic disease, and shock. In: Kumar V, Abbas AK, Fausto N, Aster JC, editors. Robbins and Cotran pathologic basis of disease. Philadelphia (PA): Saunders Elsevier; 2010. p. 111–34.

[23] Mesfin GM, Higgins MG, Brown WP, Rosnick D. Cardiovascular complications of chronic catheterization of the jugular vein in the dog. Vet Pathol 1988;25:492–502.

[24] Morton D, Safron JA, Glosson J, Rice DW, Wilson DM, White RD. Histologic lesions associated with intravenous infusions of large volumes of isotonic saline solution in rats for 30 days. Toxicol Pathol 1997;25:390–4.

[25] Lilbert J, Mowat V. Common vascular changes in the jugular vein of saline controls in continuous infusion studies in the beagle dog. Toxicol Pathol 2004;32:694–700.

22

Photosafety Assessment

D.B. Learn, P.D. Forbes, C.P. Sambuco

INTRODUCTION

Photosafety testing is an important component in preclinical drug development, but in this field the evaluation timing, accepted methodologies, expectations of the regulatory agencies, and interpretation of results are not widely familiar. The aim of this chapter is to help the reader understand the historical and regulatory context of photosafety testing and to develop a rational photosafety program.

The information presented in this chapter is a review of primary sources (ie, scientific and clinical literature), regulatory and guidance documents, and the experience of the authors in performing preclinical photosafety evaluations. Common methodologies used for regulatory photosafety submissions are included here.

REGULATORY STATUS

Since the first edition of this book was published, the International Conference on Harmonization of Technical Requirements for Registration of Pharmaceuticals for Human Use (ICH) S10 guidance on *Photosafety Evaluation of Pharmaceuticals* was released as Step 4 in November 2013 [55]. Even though the ICH S10 has been accepted, an understanding of the regulatory history of photosafety testing that led to this guidance is instructive in understanding its content.

Efforts to establish a regulatory framework for photosafety testing began in the 1990s in both Europe and United States. A draft proposal for a new OECD guideline called "Acute Dermal Photoirritation Screening Test" (TGP951) was issued in 1995 [84]. This draft defined in general terms the use of the rabbit or guinea

A Comprehensive Guide to Toxicology in Nonclinical Drug Development, Second Edition
http://dx.doi.org/10.1016/B978-0-12-803620-4.00022-0

pig as preferred species for in vivo phototoxicity evaluations. However, after the comment period, no further work was reported with this draft guideline.

Issuance of the European Agency for the Evaluation of Medicinal Products (EMA) Note for Guidance on Photosafety Testing [31], followed by the US Food and Drug Administration (FDA) Guidance for Industry, Photosafety Testing [123], provided a formal framework under which a photosafety program for pharmaceuticals should be conducted. Both guidances recommended photosafety testing for chemicals with spectrophotometric absorption between 290 and 700 nm (the ultraviolet and visible portion of the solar spectrum that reaches the Earth's surface), and the test material topically or locally applied to the skin or reaches the eyes or skin following systemic administration. The FDA document recommended that materials known to affect the condition of the skin or eyes be evaluated. But the documents differed in several areas.

The EMA guidance included the evaluation of biotechnology-derived pharmaceuticals along with new chemical entities. Less background information was provided, light sources/irradiation conditions were discussed in brief, and the use of in vitro assays, especially the 3T3 assay, were emphasized. Preclinical photoallergy testing using the guinea pig model was recognized as useful, but the guidance mentioned that the UV-local lymph node assay and the mouse ear-swelling test were under development, and while they could become valuable in the future, their validity was not proven. In vitro photogenotoxicity assays, specifically photoclastogenicity assays, were recognized as having potential for evaluation of photocarcinogenic potential, while recognizing that experience with these models and in vivo photogenotoxicity assays was limited. Photocarcinogenesis testing using the established (internationally standardized) mouse model was deemphasized, with a suggestion that in vitro mechanistic studies, including photogenotoxicity, might yet prove useful. For compounds with a positive in vitro phototoxicity/photogenotoxicity signals, the use of warning statements for human use were proposed as an adequate option and further testing was not required.

Drugs such as immunosuppressants could be presumed to enhance photocarcinogenesis without testing using photocarcinogenesis models. Materials that may affect the skin and, as demonstrated with the mouse model, affect photocarcinogenesis, would be better evaluated in humans by evaluating changes in sensitivity to ultraviolet radiation (UVR). A single simplified flowchart was provided to guide photosafety assessment. This testing was proposed to be done independently, rather than sequentially.

The FDA guidance provided substantial background with references, a rationale for photosafety evaluation, noted the ability of topically administered materials to affect phototoxic responses by affecting skin structure, and provided general considerations to follow while designing a testing strategy. There was no mention of evaluation of biotechnology-derived (eg, peptides, oligonucleotides) materials. A decision tree-based approach was provided for:

1. Phototoxicity testing
2. Evaluation of the reformulation of an approved topical product
3. Evaluation of photocarcinogenesis of either materials that were potentially direct phototoxins or those that could indirectly affect a potential photocarcinogenic response (eg, immunosuppressants)

The use of in vitro assays was not emphasized and no UVR source or irradiation conditions were specified. Preclinical photoallergy assays were deemed not useful in predicting human photoallergens and their inclusion in regulatory submissions was discouraged.

Issuance of the FDA and EMA photosafety provided some structure to the approach to photosafety evaluation. Industry began to generate data and, along with regulatory groups, began to assess the data to determine how well the guidance-recommended approaches were addressing photosafety concerns. These reviews soon revealed shortcomings in both documents and raised concerns about the utility of the recommended approaches to testing and the utility of some of the generated data.

In November 2007, the Drug Information Association (DIA) workshop on photosafety evaluation of drugs brought key stakeholders from industry, regulatory bodies, and academia together to discuss basic photochemistry and physics related to preclinical and clinical evaluation of phototoxicology, and regulatory photosafety assessment and risk assessment were also reviewed. The organizers recognized the OECD in vitro 3T3 NRU phototoxicity, No. 432 [69] as the only validated assay for phototoxicity and, while not formally validated at that time, the UV-local lymph node assay as validated in distinct test facilities. The lack of validated assays for other in vitro or in vivo photosafety testing was recognized, and indeed, the lack of real standards on how to perform those assays, the varying endpoints used and ways to interpret the data generated, and overall lack of clarity and consistency in the performance of the assays. These disparities were compounded by the lack of consistency between both documents.

The EMA adopted the concept paper on the Need for Revision of the Note for Guidance on Photosafety Testing [32]. The problem statement recognized the substantial shortcomings of the current guideline recommendations and recognized that new data and developments in the field allowed for better-designed guidance. Recognized deficiencies included:

- The criteria used for determining whether photosafety testing were nonspecific and caused the testing of many pharmaceuticals that may not have been necessary.

- The parallel approach to testing, where multiple endpoints were addressed simultaneously, was recognized as not allowing testing to be stopped, leading, in theory, to testing for photoallergy and/or photogenotoxicity, even after a negative response in the in vitro phototoxicity test was obtained.
- Oversensitivity (the 3T3 assay) and "pseudoeffects" (photogenotoxicity) were recognized as serious problems.
- The timing of testing in the drug development cycle was not addressed.

The document recommended that the current guideline be revised to address these shortcomings, based on the experience of the testing performed over the previous years and new developments in the field.

The EMA issued *Questions and Answers on the Note for Guidance on Photosafety Testing* (2011) [33], clarifying approaches to photosafety testing and the criteria for testing.

- Question 1 centered around refining the criteria for triggering photosafety testing (absorption in the 290–700 nm range) and the presence of compounds in target tissues. The molar extinction coefficient (MEC), based on the publication of Henry et al. [51], indicated that an MEC of <1000 L/mol cm is an acceptable threshold below which photosafety evaluations would not be warranted. This applies also to the criterion listed in the OECD 432 3T3 guidance for triggering testing with this assay. Regarding a specific concentration threshold in target tissues below which photoadverse reactions were unlikely and therefore no testing was required, there are no data that delineate such a general threshold for new compounds. Therefore assessment of relevance of very low levels of exposure in either skin or eyes has to be made on a case-by-case basis.
- Question 2 centered around the use of a tiered rather than a parallel approach to testing, specifically if a compound was negative in one or more relevant phototoxicity assays, was it necessary to do further testing for photogenotoxicity or photoallergy? In short, a tiered approach is acceptable, and further testing, once a negative result is obtained, is normally not necessary. Phototoxic compounds should be evaluated for photoallergy only if they are administered by the topical route.
- Question 3 centered around the recommendation in the concept paper to not perform photogenotoxicity assays on compounds that were found to be phototoxic. As reported by Lynch et al. [74], for regulatory use the in vitro photoclastogenicity assays (chromosomal aberration or micronucleus test) were substantially oversensitive and demonstrated

pseudoclastogenicity. Therefore these assays are not recommended for regulatory photogenotoxicity testing. Photogenotoxicity screens were initially considered as an approach to predict possible photocarcinogenic potential, but photogenotoxicity data demonstrated that those data and their correlation to clinically relevant enhancement of UVR-mediated skin cancer is unclear in most cases and cannot be used for evaluation of potential photocarcinogenic potential. Evaluation of potential photocarcinogenic risk was to be based on clinical phototoxicity risk or potential for risk from chemically related compounds and the extent of human exposure.

- Question 4 centered on the 3T3 PT NRU assay's perceived high incidence of positive responses and its perceived poor predictivity of phototoxicity in vivo [73] and if the assay could be replaced by a well-conducted animal study or clinical trial. In short, while recognizing the shortcomings of the 3T3 assay, replacement is not a viable alternative. The assay has a good negativity history (no false negatives) and, based on a tiered approach, a negative response (see Question 2) is generally accepted as sufficient evidence of lack of phototoxic potential and remains the only fully validated photosafety assay. The European Union directive on the protection of animals for scientific purposes [24] states that replacement of a validated in vitro assay with an animal test evaluating the same endpoint is generally not acceptable, thus making a strong case for use of the 3T3 assay. A straight approach with clinical trials is acceptable in place of performing the 3T3 assay, providing the assay is sufficiently sensitive to detect photoadverse effects in humans, but there is no need to perform a 3T3 assay if the in vivo animal or human studies demonstrate a negative response. A positive 3T3 assay followed by a preclinical study or a clinical trial is acceptable to determine phototoxic potential in an in vivo system. A negative in vivo response will always transcend a positive in vitro response, and a human negative response will transcend a positive preclinical response.
- Question 5 centered on the timing of evaluation of photosafety during drug development. As noted in ICH M3(R2) IV (14) (2009) [57], when an identified potential risk for phototoxicity exists, experimental evaluation should be performed before exposure of large numbers of people (Phase III).
- Question 6 addressed the need for photosafety testing of peptides/proteins. These compounds will show absorption past 290 nm, as the aromatic amino acids act as chromophores. This does not denote a photosafety concern and in general is not a criterion for photosafety testing.

The previously mentioned considerations were included in some form in the ICH S10 *Photosafety Evaluation of Pharmaceuticals*, which, after the standard development milestones, the Step 4 version was issued in November 2013. Step 5 was adopted by the EU in December 2013 [55], the Japanese MHLW in May 2014 [57], and the US FDA version on March 26, 2015 [56].

The intent of the guidance is to "recommend international standards for photosafety assessment, and to harmonize such assessments that support human clinical trials and marketing authorizations for pharmaceuticals," including new pharmaceutical actives, new excipients, dermal formulations (including dermal patches), and photodynamic agents. The guidance provides the most comprehensive recommendations for photosafety evaluation issued to date, incorporating the most relevant parts of the preceding guidance, literature, and other published recommendations.

The guidance is available in its entirety elsewhere. General topics are summarized here, and as applicable, sections are referenced in the relevant parts of this chapter, and referenced by the FDA section numbers, with the Step 4 sections included in parentheses.

Areas specifically excluded from general phototoxicity evaluation include photodynamic therapy agents, where the intent of the molecule is to induce phototoxicity. However, an understanding of the toxicokinetics and tissue distribution of these agents is necessary to allow management of unintentional light (and thus phototoxic) responses and to provide acceptable risk management in patients. Also, because of their inherent absorptive characteristics in the specified spectrum without evidence of photochemistry, peptides, proteins, antibody drug conjugates, or oligonucleotides do not, in general, require photosafety evaluation. Finally, the guidance does not apply to components of marketed products, unless the reformulation or other change in this final form is a reason for concern. The FDA Step 5 version includes Endnote 5, not included in other Step 5 versions, indicating that a clinical trial of dermal products, including the active pharmaceutical ingredient and all excipients "…can be warranted in support of product approval."

The guidance indicates in I.D. (1.4) that for a chemical to elicit phototoxicity, the following criteria are critical:

- Absorbs in the range of natural sunlight (290–700 nm)
- Generates a reactive species following absorption of UVR or visible light
- Distributes sufficiently to light exposed tissues (eg, skin or eye)

In addition, a molar absorption characteristic of greater than 1000 L/mol cm at any wavelength between 290 and 700 nm is recognized as a cutoff for sufficient photoreactivity to have phototoxic potential and should be considered when evaluating compounds for photosafety evaluation.

Tissue distribution and pharmacodynamics are discussed in II.B (2.2). Obviously, the test material has to distribute to light-exposed tissues. The complex nature of plasma/tissue pharmacodynamics along with the light/test material photochemistry precludes a general rule for minimal test material exposure to trigger or preclude photosafety testing. In specific cases where distribution is very low or with other unique characteristics, photosafety testing may not be warranted. Tissue binding, especially to melanin-containing tissues, can increase local test material concentrations, but there is no overall evidence that this can enhance phototoxicity. Metabolites, in general, do not warrant separate evaluation, as known metabolic pathways do not typically result in substantial changes to chromophores as compared with the parent compound. Compounds that are immunosuppressive or may change heme metabolism are recognized to enhance light sensitivity, including photocarcinogenesis or photosensitivity, respectively, in clinical experience and preclinical studies, and a photosafety strategy should take these specific compounds in mind during safety evaluation.

The ICH S10 III.E and V.B.2 (3.5 and 5.2.2) indicates that preclinical photoallergy assessment of topical formulations is generally not recommended because of the lack of concordance between preclinical and clinical results. Should evaluation of photoallergy be required, an evaluation in a clinical setting using the to-be-marketed formulation is appropriate.

As outlined in this chapter, the conditions of the evaluations and the test systems used should be considered carefully to address the photosafety concerns and have high specificity and sensitivity. A negative in vitro result, typically the neutral red 3T3 assay, precludes further photosafety evaluation. A negative preclinical in vivo result will negate a positive in vitro result, as will a negative clinical result overrule a positive preclinical in vivo result. The design of the clinical photosafety study is determined on a case-by-case basis.

The guidance for industry S9, *Nonclinical Evaluation for Anticancer Pharmaceuticals* II.I (2.9) (2009) [58] addresses photosafety testing for drugs in this class. Initial assessment of phototoxic potential should be conducted before Phase I, based on photochemical properties and information on the class of compound. If a potential risk to humans is identified, appropriate protection of patients during outpatient trials should be undertaken. If the risk cannot be adequately evaluated on the basis of existing nonclinical data or clinical experience, an evaluation consistent with the recommendations of the ICH M3 [57] should be provided before marketing (see the following). One practical concern that has arisen from this last statement is the assumption that photosafety testing can be deferred until after first-in-man exposure. One consequence of this delay is the necessity to include sun protection in the clinical protocol. As these compounds are tested in patients who often have a terminal disease and most likely have already endured multiple therapies, their quality of life is of great interest to them. Sun-exposure protection requirements that will further restrict their life activities may not be well received. In addition, if phototoxic potential of a compound is not determined and protection is not included in the clinical protocol, there is real risk of an adverse phototoxic response to sun exposure.

Phototoxicity testing is also addressed in ICH M3(R2) (2009) [57]. The appropriateness or timing of photosafety testing should be influenced by photochemical properties of the molecule, information on the phototoxicity of chemically related compounds, tissue distribution, and clinical or nonclinical findings indicative of phototoxicity. If potential for phototoxicity exists, human subjects should be protected during clinical trials. In addition, nonclinical evaluation of drug distribution to the skin and eyes should be undertaken to further define potential human risk and the need for further testing. Then, if appropriate, an evaluation (nonclinical, in vitro or in vivo, or clinical) of phototoxic potential should be undertaken before exposure to large numbers of patients (Phase III). Instead of this stepwise approach, direct assessment in a clinical or nonclinical study may be undertaken. If negative, no further testing is required.

If the results of the phototoxicity evaluation indicate potential for photocarcinogenic risk, the guidance states that the risk can usually be adequately managed in patients with protective measures such as warning statements in informed consents during clinical trials and in product information for marketing. Note 6 of this guidance elaborates on photocarcinogenesis and the use of the rodent model for evaluation of photocarcinogenicity. Despite the acceptance of the rodent model by the Commission Internationale de l'Eclairage [17] and previous extensive regulatory use, the assay, with no further scientific rationale, was considered not useful or recommended for pharmaceutical development. The guidance indicates that, should an appropriate (and undefined) assay become available, "the study should usually be completed before marketing and the results should be considered in the human risk assessment."

Chemical Evaluation. While outside of the evaluation of preclinical drug development, Regulation (EC) No. 1907/2006 of the European Parliament and of the Council [96], or the REACH regulations, include the evaluation of photosafety, and specifically references the use of the 3T3 assay as the first evaluation. The Commission Regulation (EU) No. 283/2013 agrichemical regulation [18] also mentions the use of the 3T3 assay in the data requirement Section [19]. What is not addressed in either document is how to proceed should chemicals be positive.

PHOTOSAFETY EVALUATION STRATEGY

A photosafety strategy should be developed and utilized during the drug development process. Regardless of the final form, the basis of this strategy must take into account the ICH S10. The most relevant section of the guidance for this strategy is V. (5), "Assessment Strategies" gives an effective overview of the strategies that

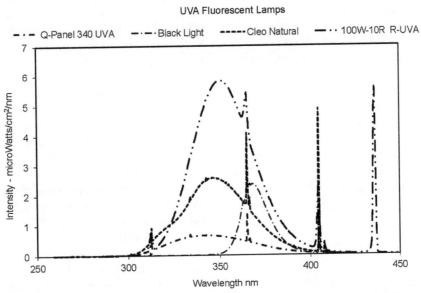

FIGURE 22.1 The spectral distribution and emission peaks of UVA 'type' fluorescent lamps differ widely, and a concise description of these spectral characteristics must be described in any publication and taken into account when designing studies and comparing results across studies.

can be employed. Starting with physical chemistry, candidate compounds with absorbance in the relevant portions of the spectrum should be flagged for evaluation at a place in the candidate selection process that reflects the company's overall development strategy and philosophy. Non-GLP reactive oxygen species (ROS) and 3T3 assays can be used for early evaluations and candidate selection. A robust historical control database with both known and internal compounds, including how these results translate into in vivo responses, is critical to allow valid interpretation of these results and the assays for predicting promising candidates. Chemical modification to remove phototoxic potential while retaining therapeutic activity is most effectively addressed early in the development process before substantial time and resources have been expended on a candidate. As compounds advance through the general toxicity studies, photosafety evaluations should be performed before first-in-man exposure to relieve the clinical protocol of any sun protection measures and prevent unintended adverse clinical responses. Questions regarding photosafety can be expected during the Investigational New Drug (IND, US FDA) or Clinical Trial Application (CTA; EU) process. In the United States, questions may arise during the pre-IND meeting. While the work may not be required for these discussions, a plan should be in place to address it.

The photosafety strategy should reflect the intended use of the drug and risk/benefit. A drug intended for orthopedic wound decontamination may not require testing before first-in-man use, while a systemic drug with substantial spectral absorption and distribution to and long half-life in sun-exposed tissues should be evaluated to ensure human subject safety during clinical trials. Regardless, be certain that the strategy will withstand the arguments that may be made against it.

An integrated photosafety testing strategy, encompassing both in vitro and in vivo aspects of preclinical photosafety evaluations, has been published [107]. The strategy starts with spectral absorption determination, followed by the 3T3 assay, and, when appropriate, inclusion of a modified murine photolocal lymph node assay with multiple dose levels. The strategy allows, with high probability, the identification of compounds that may be phototoxic in humans and also correlate with the magnitude of phototoxicity identified in vitro. An extensive in-house historical control database provides confidence in the strategy and results of the overall evaluation of each compound.

LIGHT DOSIMETRY

To ensure a consistent response to light exposure, a defined amount (dose) of light of a known spectral configuration (quality) is required; the application of that light is constrained by the limits of both physics and physiology. Phototoxicology incorporates, in essence, a search for interactive effects involving defined optical radiation and defined chemical material. In practice, phototoxicity is said to be in evidence when a defined biological response is greater in the presence of the test agent than from exposure to the radiation alone. Defining and delivering the desired energy (as light) is as important as defining and quantifying a chemical agent or other test material.

Understanding the definitions and applications of the terminology used to describe a spectrum, including that part of the solar optical spectrum called "ultraviolet radiation" and "visible light" is essential. Many publications address these definitions and measurements of light. Some are well illustrated [50,68,109,110], are particularly easy to read and understand [93], or are directly relevant to testing [43,112]. Others are exhaustively detailed, and well suited to those working in the field of optical physics [64] or risk assessment [76]. These radiometric qualities and units are officially recognized [114].

Radiometry is the measurement of radiant (electromagnetic) energy, including "optical radiation" with wavelengths between 10^1 and 10^6 nanometers (nm). The optical radiation spectrum is composed of the ultraviolet, the visible, and the infrared regions. Of the many standard units and quantities used in radiometry, the principal concern is power per unit area, defined as irradiance (expressed in some form of watts $(W)/m^2$), or with the time integral of power per unit area, using terms such as fluence or dose, expressed as $W\text{-sec}/m^2$ or joule $(J)/m^2$, because $1\,W$ of power for a duration of $1\,s$ is defined as $1\,J$.

Photometry is limited to the visible spectrum as defined by the response of the eye. Typical photometric units include lumens, lux, and candelas, and, with the exceptions of ocular phototoxicity and photodynamic agent photosafety evaluations, are rarely used in photosafety evaluations. Note the major difference in the application of the biologically oriented radiometric approaches. The visual (retinal) function (and thus photometric terminology) is principally concerned with "intensity," whereas the cutaneous function (and thus cutaneous radiometric terminology) is principally concerned with exposure integrated over time or "dose."

Radiometry can be performed using both radiometers and spectroradiometers. Radiometers provide estimates of irradiance in W/m^2. Within the design of detector or filter types, specific radiometers make their estimates over narrow or broad wavebands within the optical spectrum. Radiometers may be engineered to use a specified weighting function, in which case their read-out will provide an estimate of irradiance in terms associated with that weighting function (eg, erythema). In contrast, spectroradiometers provide estimates of irradiance over relatively narrow wave bands, and thus the output can be stated in terms of $W/m^2/nm$. While integrating the irradiance over time (calculating a fluence/dose), or applying a weighting function to the output data (providing a biologically effective energy) may be a subsequent activity, they are not inherent in the conduct of a spectroradiometric assessment.

Cutaneous radiometry is a generic subset of radiometry, and its purview is a specific organ—the skin. Cutaneous radiometry is like general radiometry except that dosimitry is usually weighted by the spectral response for a specific biological endpoint of the skin. That spectral response is often described as a "weighting function" or an "action spectrum." Clinical cutaneous radiometry uses the skin as a comparison detector, while physical cutaneous radiometry uses either optical radiation detectors constructed to mimic the spectral response of the skin, or spectroradiometry coupled with appropriate calculations to do the skin response weighting. Understanding the terms is critical to properly interpreting published work and when translation of experimental exposure conditions to human relevance is required.

The arcane terminology of clinical cutaneous (weighted) radiometry has included MED (minimal erythema dose), SBU (sunburn unit), RBU (Robertson–Berger unit), and the Finsen unit (Table 22.1). The only commonly used term is MED, and this term is less common in current work. The CIE promulgated a standard that introduced a new dose unit of biologically effective UVR, the "standard erythema dose unit" or SED [16]. This CIE standard makes the following distinctions.

- MED: A subjective measure based on the reddening of the skin; it depends on many variables, eg, individual sensitivity to UVR, radiometric characteristics of the source, skin pigmentation, anatomic site, elapsed time between irradiation, and observing the reddening (typical value: 24h), etc. The dose of UVR to produce erythema in lightly pigmented individuals ranges from about 150 to about $300 (J/m^2)_e$. The term MED should now be reserved solely for describing the sensitivity of an individual, rather than as a term connoting an exact physical dimension.

- SED: A standardized measure of erythemogenic UV radiation, one SED unit is equivalent to an erythemal effective radiant exposure of $100 J/m^2$. The same standard defines "erythemal effective" in terms of a specified weighting function:

"The erythemal effective irradiance (Eer) from a UVR source is obtained by weighting the spectral irradiance of the radiation at wavelength × nm by the effectiveness of radiation of this wavelength to cause a minimal erythema and summing over all wavelengths present in the source spectrum." The standard presents a formula that assigns a weight to each nanometer of wavelength from 250 to 400.

In several published studies and from historical precedent, the delivered UVR was quantified in terms of RBU, an instrumental description of biologically effective radiation [125]. In brief, 400 RBU would be equivalent to one instrumental MED, or 1 MED_i. One MED_i is nominally equivalent to two SED units. While now rarely used for other purposes, RBU has been the UVR dose unit of choice for photocarcinogenesis studies, which in large part reflects the historic development of the assay, as described in that section of this chapter.

TABLE 22.1 Summary of Broad Band UVR "Dose" Effectiveness Terms

Term[a]	UVR Quantity	Comment
Standard erythema dose (SED)[b]	$100 (J/m^2)_e$[c]	Approximates 0.5 MED_i
Minimal erythema dose (MED, instrumental) (MED_i)	$200 (J/m^2)_e$[d]	Analogous to standard instrumental photometric quantities
Minimal erythema dose (MED, observational)	Individually determined	Any measured quantity that produces the defined erythema response in skin
Robertson–Berger unit (RBU)[e]	$0.5 (J/m^2)_e$	400 RBU ≈ $200 (J/m^2)_e$ ≈ 1.0 MED_i[f]
Sunburn unit (SU)[g]	$200 (J/m^2)_e$	1 SU ≈ 1 MED_i ≈ 2.0^3 Finsen-seconds

[a]For additional information on definitions and sources of the listed terms, see Ref. [125].
[b]CIE [16].
[c]The subscript e (for effective) indicates that the determined values are multiplied by the specified weighting function.
[d]$200 (J/m^2)_e$ represents the dose of radiation from a polychromatic source needed to produce a threshold erythema equivalent to that from $200 J/m^2$ of UVR at wavelength 296.5 nm. Instrumental equivalence is based on the use of a defined weighting function such as the CIE action spectrum for erythema [16]. For derivation of instrumental MED, see Ref. [48].
[e]Robertson [97].
[f]≈ (Approximations): The Green and Miller [48], Robertson [97], and Berger et al. [5] calculations were based on erythema weighting functions in use before the adoption of the CIE standard erythema action spectrum [16].
[g]Berger et al. [5].

At the Second International Congress of the Comité International de la Lumière in Copenhagen, Coblentz [14] made several seminal statements about derivation of radiometric terms. The chief reasons for adopting homogeneous radiation of wavelength 297 nm as a standard for erythemal and radiometric comparison are this emission line appears to coincide closely with the wavelength of maximum erythemic susceptibility, it is reproducible and easily obtainable in sufficient intensity, and it is easily evaluated in absolute measure by direct comparison with a standard of radiation. Coblentz also reported that it required a minimum of $200\,J/m^2$ of 297 nm radiation to produce an MED.

The use of MED as an estimate of cutaneous sensitivity to a variety of UVR-emitting light sources has been done for at least 75 years. Considering the inherent limitations (eg, differences in light sources, radiometers, spectroradiometers, skin types, evaluation techniques, etc.), the fact that reported data for MED at 297 nm vary between 140 and $650\,J/m^2$ is not at all surprising. The higher numbers are associated with the earliest papers, and reported MED values have tended to decrease with the advent of improved instrumentation. By comparison, published values for the analogous threshold response to UVR exposure of mouse skin (edema) are all of more recent and are associated with much less variability [125].

In this context, MED is used not as an absolute value of energy, but rather to describe the amount of UVR required to elicit a particular type of skin response in a particular individual from a specific source. This use of "MED" is more properly assigned to the term "observational MED," or "MED_O." Under other circumstances or conditions, the MED for the same individual (or other individuals) might be a very different quantity, even for UVR of the same spectrum. The value of the MED_O is operational; it is a threshold response that can be produced rapidly and is fairly reproducible by single doses of radiation of tolerable duration and intensity, and can be readily recognized. No other cutaneous photobiological response exhibits this emphasis as an experimental endpoint, either in preclinical or clinical work, thus assuring its perpetuation as an observational endpoint for cutaneous phototoxicity.

The concept of MED was probably most intensely scrutinized during the era of the US Department of Transportation's Climatic Impact Assessment Program (CIAP), dealing with concerns related to potential reductions in stratospheric ozone and consequent increases in terrestrial UVR. Recognizing the need for physical dose units related to biological responses, several investigators utilized a strategy based on analogies to vision-weighted measures, described earlier by Luckiesh [72]. Green and Miller [48] state that:

The problem is similar to that of defining units of illuminance in which the light energy in W/m^2 is weighted by a factor based on the spectral sensitivity of the human eye. Thus, one watt of light energy at 555 nm (green) is given more weight than is one watt in either the blue or red end of the spectrum in establishing the number of lumens per watt.

The authors developed a concept of the MED as an analog of the lumen. In brief, they adopted an absolute value for the minimum erythema dose at 296.5 nm as $200\,J/m^2$. Then, using the best available description of an erythemal weighting function (action spectrum), they offer the unit $1\,MED = 200\,(J/m^2)_e$, where the term $(J/m^2)_e$ represents the dose of 296.5 nm UV radiation, or radiation from a polychromatic source, needed to yield the same biologic response (erythema). The authors' choice of $200\,J/m^2$ was probably influenced by the work of Robertson [97]. The great value of this definition and function of MED is best appreciated by considering the analogy to the lumen: each provides an index with a defined radiometric equivalent, removing the variability of the individual biologic response from the equation. Erythemal effectiveness weighting of radiometric units was also explicit in the expression erythema effective energy, or EEE, a term used by a number of investigators [81] with the same intended meaning as the subscript "e" in Green's "$(J/m^2)_e$" (1975).

In the 1960s, Robertson had developed and used a unique dosimeter for monitoring environmental UVR (1975). His data were essential to the development of the worldwide UVR monitoring network associated with the Climatic Impact Assessment Program (CIAP) [97]. The "Robertson meter" utilized a phosphor/photocell system that provided an estimate of sunburn effectiveness. Robertson offered the "sunburn unit," or SU (400 counts on the meter's readout), as an instrumental or electronic equivalent to the observational MED of dermatologists. Robertson noted that the erythemal response to a 400-count exposure (eg, in sunlight) was similar to that of $200\,J/m^2$ of 296.7 nm UV radiation. As described previously, this influenced the proposal to define the "instrumental MED" as $200\,(J/m^2)_e$, and the incorporation of 400 "Robertson-Berger Units" as equivalent to the SU in Berger's broadband radiometer [6]. According to Robertson, $200\,J/m^2$ of 296.7 nm UVR would also be equivalent to 2×10^3 E-viton-sec per cm^2 or 2×10^3 Finsen-sec (Table 22.1).

These important efforts in quantifying doses and associated biological responses, coupled with the adoption of a reference action spectrum for erythema [125] and with advances in dosimetric instrumentation, have contributed to the development of risk estimates and other tools for decision making. Urbach and Forbes provide examples of comparing instrumental and erythemal responses as predictors of photocarcinogenesis response in hairless mice, and the development of action spectra for photocarcinogenesis [17]. These advances were possible only with the advent of the radiometric and rapid computational tools unavailable to earlier researchers.

The MED thus has the appearance of a simple observation and the history of a profound concept. Its definition has evolved along both parallel and divergent paths. In some hands it serves as a rather crude sensitivity estimate, and in others as the analog of a defined radiometric term, dependent on sophisticated instrumentation. This ambiguity is less of an issue today since the photobiology community now prefers "instrumental MED" in favor of the "standard erythema dose" unit, as proposed in the CIE Standard [16].

There is no perfect radiometric (instrumental) match, of course, for the spectrum of human skin response to UVR, or that of a laboratory test model, be it in vitro or in vivo. Just as photometers are engineering attempts at a reasonable approximation of the human visual spectral characteristics, radiometers (at least those that display output based on a skin response such as erythema) are an engineering attempt at a reasonable approximation of the human erythema response. The degree to which the engineering efforts are successful (in terms of stability, operating conditions, comparisons with spectroradiometers, etc.) has been the subject of many publications [5,20–23,53,82,83,99,126].

The only way to avoid this biological response bias is to use radiometers and detectors that read only as absolute power (without any biological weighting) and calculate the biological response with the test model used in that assay. But even then the detector, by virtue of its response characteristics, may not reflect the absolute power in a specific section of the UVR spectrum. The response of a detector may not be "flat" across the portion of the spectrum of interest (eg, UVA). And the absolute measurement is also dependent on the power distribution of the source across this portion of the spectrum, and the measured intensity and related biological response may not be the same for a different source. To accomplish this, spectroradiometric measurement with integration under the curve of the region of interest is required to describe the delivered energy in absolute terms. These data can then be used to "force" a meter and detector combination, for a specific source, to read in absolute units, or provide a correction factor to the readings. This conversion is only applicable to this combination of meter, detector, and source. Any change in these components will require the process to be performed again.

LIGHT SOURCES

A central requirement for photosafety evaluation is a proper light source. Here we focus on UVR (290–400 nm), as this portion of the spectrum drives the vast majority of the photosafety assessment studies. However, applications for visible light (eg, photodynamic therapy) or the emerging field of near infrared fluorescence for tumor detection require evaluation and thus understanding of those portions of the spectrum.

ICH S10 III.A (3.1) addresses irradiation sources and conditions and recognizes the variability of natural sunlight based on time of day, season, and geographical location. In addition, the variability sensitivity of humans to UVR exposure further complicates the choice of light exposure conditions. An emphasis on the UVA portion of the spectrum with doses ranging from 5 to $20 \, \text{J/cm}^2$ is recommended. This dose range is relevant to environmental exposure. If UVB is included in the experimental source, it cannot limit the UVA exposure. UVB poorly penetrates the skin and is primarily limited to the epidermis, while UVA penetrates to the dermis and thus the dermal blood supply. Based on this differential anatomic exposure, UVA is considered more relevant for systemically administered compounds, while UVB is considered more relevant for topically administered compounds.

Light is the second test material in these studies, and the characteristics of the light source must be characterized, not unlike the characteristics of a test article. The spectral intensity evaluation can be considered the source certificate of analysis and the determination of the amount of light the formulation analysis of that delivered dose, both of which are critical in ensuring that the elicited responses can be interpreted. Regardless of the system used, a firm understanding of the spectral output is essential. Commercially supplied units and lamps are normally supplied with spectral data. However, systems should be verified by spectroradiometric evaluation and, if the system is used for regulated work, a certificate (similar to a certificate of analysis for a test material) be issued to satisfy Good Laboratory Practices requirements.

A thorough understanding of a laboratory model's response to the light source is also critical to the evaluation of any phototoxic response. The emission spectrum of the source can also affect a biological response, eg, immunosuppression [66] and has to be recognized when developing an assay system and especially when trying to compare results across study designs. The choice of an inappropriate source, based on the mismatch of the test material's absorption spectrum and the emission spectrum of the lamp, can result in adverse clinical phototoxicity responses. An evaluated circumstance where vemurafenib-induced clinical phototoxicity resulted from use of the incorrect lamp in preclinical phototoxicity evaluations was recently published [10] and serves as a real-world example of the critical importance of matching lamps to spectral absorbance.

For the majority of the work performed for preclinical use, relatively few sources are employed, eg, commonly commercially available fluorescent, metal halide, or xenon arc lamps. To be of benefit, photobiology and phototoxicology publications include useful information on the light source used and either those references or their predecessors include the spectra of the sources (eg, Ref. [45]). The ICH S10 and OECD 432 guidance also reference spectral distribution and UVA dose recommendations.

Fluorescent lamps are commonly used for photosafety testing, as they are readily available, their spectral distribution is known, they are relatively easy to use, and they are economical. The output from fluorescent lamps will decrease with use (but the spectral profile does not change) and intensity of the lamps must be monitored to compensate for this reduction. Filtration with simple material can be used to modify their spectral output to meet specific needs. When using any filter material, a spectral evaluation through the filter must be performed to determine the resultant spectrum. Window glass [69] and polyester film [1] removes wavelengths below 320nm and allows the use of the UVA portion of lamps emitting shorter wavelengths. Cellulose triacetate (eg, Kodacel TA401/407) removes short wavelength (below 290nm) UVR [1,66] and allows the use of UVB lamps emitting outside the 290–700nm range. Kodacel and polyester film will "solarize" with increasing opacity over time and act as a neutral density filter, affecting the emitted power, but solarization of these materials has no effect on the spectral distribution [1].

No individual fluorescent lamp provides a continuous spectrum across the ultraviolet and visible portions of the spectrum, mimicking sunlight. This discontinuity can be partially addressed by using lamps with different spectral distributions, including visible light lamps [3]. If different types of lamps are used, they should be mounted in a single fixture and used simultaneously rather than sequentially.

Different manufacturers may use different descriptions of the same fluorescent lamp type, but when the peak absorbance and spectral distribution emitted by a set number of phosphors used are very similar substitution among lamps produced by various manufacturers is acceptable. The fluorescent lamps commonly used for photosafety evaluations include those labeled as UVA lamps (Fig. 22.1), which may or may not include some UVB, and those labeled as UVB lamp (Fig. 22.2), which also include some UVA. The spectral shapes or emission spectra of these lamps are not identical and the designation "UVA lamp" is, at best, generic. Each lamp may be unique in the absolute power that is emitted, and the power (and thus dose during a given exposure period) may differ for each lamp and configuration. UVB lamps customarily include emission into the UVC portion of the spectrum that can be removed by Kodacel filtration and the UVB from either UVB or UVA lamps can be removed with plate-glass filtration. The narrowband TL01 lamp (peak emission ~311nm), used primarily for human phototherapy, can be used for evaluation of drugs specific for use in combination with this lamp.

Lamps for recreational tanning can also be used, and if required, filtered with plate glass to remove UVB from the spectrum (Fig. 22.3). Tanning bed canopies have the advantages of commercial availability, large size (nominal 72inch lamps) and thus irradiance area, multiple

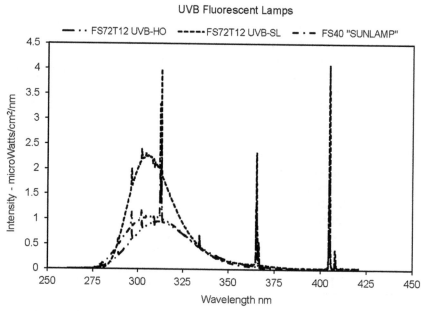

FIGURE 22.2   The spectral distribution and emission peaks of UVB or 'sunlamp' type fluorescent lamps differ less than the UVA lamps, but the low wavelength spectral differences can have profound differences in biological responses. Note that these lamps do not contain any appreciable visible light and thus are not true sunlamps.

lamps, and reflectors that maximize power output. These features are important when many animals are exposed at one time, or for the exposure of large animals (eg, pigs). Certain lamps are only available in this size and connector configuration, but as required for custom configurations, the fixtures can be retrofitted with different lamp-end connectors and, as necessary, ballasts, to accommodate any lamp type.

If visible light is required, a "daylight" fluorescent lamp that provides the spectral distribution close to that of visible sunlight is the best choice (eg, Fig. 22.4). For applications where visible light is either the activating wavelength or protection from the activating wavelengths is required (eg, photodynamic drugs), the use of specific filter material may be required. Suppliers such as Rosco (http://www.rosco.com) provide a wide

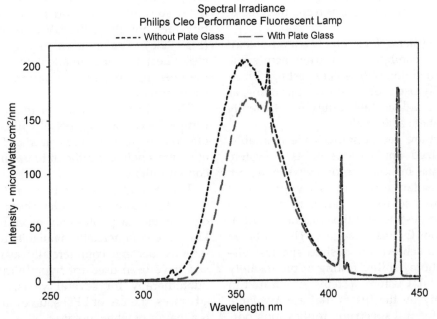

FIGURE 22.3 Recreational tanning lamps have a relatively broad spectral distribution and can be used to mimic either full spectrum UVR (UVA and UVB) or be filtered with plate glass to remove the UVB portion of the spectrum.

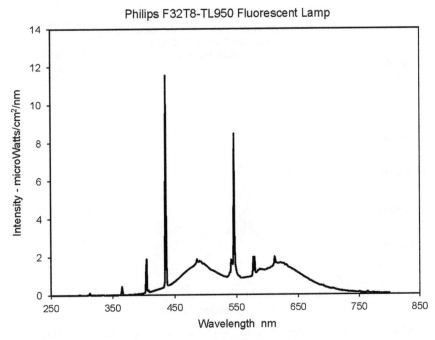

FIGURE 22.4 One example of a 'daylight' fluorescent lamp spectral distribution.

selection of filter material that, with a full spectrum fluorescent lamp or other full spectrum source, can be precisely matched to the required spectral characteristics to either activate or protect the test system from the activating spectrum. Fluorescent lamp units designed specifically for use with a photosensitizer that emit the required wavelengths should be used when available. Surgical lamps can be used, and should be for evaluation the safety of materials used during surgery or materials distributed to internal organs and activated by visible light (eg, photodynamic drugs), as recommended in ICH S10 II.C (2.3).

Mercury halide systems (eg, http://www.honleuv.com/sol) provide a contiguous spectrum across the range to be evaluated for photosafety testing. These units are customarily used for in vitro applications, as their small output area limit their utility for efficiently exposing large numbers of animals.

Long- and short-arc xenon sources are available, either for customized applications or as a system (eg, http://www.atlas-mts.com, http://www.newport.com, http://www.solarlights.com). They provide a continuous spectrum across the range to be evaluated for photosafety testing and the spectral distribution is available from the manufacturer. The units are normally filtered to achieve the desired spectral distribution (eg, for photostability testing or photosafety testing requirements). Custom systems are limited in spectral output only by the filters that are available for use. Filtration for full spectrum applications normally consist of a long-pass optical glass filter such as a Schott WG 320 (http://www.us.schott.com) that cuts off at ~290 nm and passes the remaining UVR and

visible light. The spectral cutoff is affected by the thickness of any specific filter, with increasing thickness increasing the cutoff wavelength, as demonstrated by increasing the thickness from 1 to 4 mm (Fig. 22.5), that, while removing some short wavelength UVB, allows for increased UVA exposure without the risk of inducing responses from the exposure alone and to meet increased UVA doses as recommended by the ICH S10 (5–20 J/cm²). For the 3T3 assay, the xenon arc lamp equipped with the 1 mm WG 320 filter along with the tissue culture plate lid attenuates some of the UVB but does not affect the UVA portion of the spectrum (Fig. 22.6). The melt of any glass-based filter can also affect the fine detail of the cutoff, emphasizing the need for spectral evaluation to clearly define the transmission data.

The industrial division of many photographic filter companies can supply specialty filters with differing cutoffs to meet specific study needs. However, these filters are often small and difficult to use in standard exposure configurations.

The emerging technology of light-emitting diode (LED) light sources provides another potential technology for use in photosafety assessment. UVR-emitting LEDs are commercially available, and LED units have recently become commercially available for psoriasis and have been used for hyperbilirubinemia of infancy phototherapy for several years. As this technology advances, the use of LED sources in photosafety testing is a matter of when, not if.

The emerging use of eximer lamps to take advantage of the germicidal efficiency of very shortwave UVC may also trigger future photosafety evaluations [12].

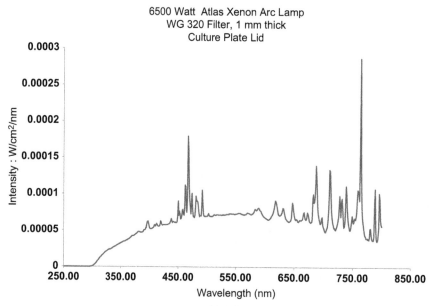

FIGURE 22.5   Spectral distribution of the 6500 W long arc xenon lamp equipped with a 1 mm thick WG 320 filter and including filtration through the culture plate lid used for the 3T3 assay. This configuration includes some UVB along with the full UVA spectrum.

SPECTRAL ABSORPTION

Absorption of photons using a chemical is required to initiate the photochemical events that may (or may not) elicit a phototoxic response. The first step in evaluation of phototoxic potential is whether the chemical absorbs light in the spectral distribution (290–700 nm). The OECD Test Guidance 101 [85] provides one methodology for evaluating the spectral absorption under several solubility conditions. Physical chemistry laboratories that perform these assays on a routine basis have detailed methodologies and standard operating procedures and can provide these data to the drug development team when evaluation of potential phototoxic potential first enters the development process. The discovery team can use this absorption profile as one criterion for candidate selection, but it should not be the primary limiting factor at this stage in development.

The method recommends the use of a recording double-beam spectrophotometer to ensure reproducibility and sensitivity. Solutions should result in at least one absorbance maximum in the range of 0.5–1.5 units, and all chemical forms (acidic, basic, or neutral) of the material in an aqueous medium should be measured. If aqueous media are not appropriate, a suitable organic solvent (methanol is recommended) must be used. Calculation of the molar absorption coefficient is also addressed, as is reporting of the results.

As defined in ICH S10 I.4 (1.4), absorption in the range of 290–700 nm is one and perhaps the primary trigger for phototoxicity testing, since without absorption of photons, there is no photochemistry and thus phototoxicity. However, what level of absorption is correlated with a phototoxic response in vivo, and thus what trigger should be used for further testing, is a matter of debate. The OECD 432 guidance indicates that a level less than 10 L/mol cm is unlikely to be photoreactive. This very low absorption level led to considerable discussion, which, based on a review of known human phototoxins and their absorption profiles [13,73], resulted in the recommended revision of this cutoff to 1000 L/mol cm as reflected in ICH S10 V.A.1 (5.1.1) and Endnote 4.

Bauer et al. [2] reviewed 76 compounds across a wide range of chemical classes and correlated their MEC in methanol to their known photoirritancy factor (PIF) derived from the 3T3 neutral red Uptake Phototoxicity Test. For those compounds classified as formally positive (PIF > 5) as per the OECD 432, the lowest MEC in methanol was 1700 L/mol cm, and the majority were much higher, up to 40,000 L/mol cm. This survey verified that the MEC cutoff of 1000 L/mol cm is a reasonable and pragmatic cutoff for evaluation of photosafety.

ICH S10 Endnote 3 also indicates that if the chemical characteristics of a test material result in "significant differences are seen between measurements obtained in methanol versus pH-adjusted conditions, the MEC threshold of 1000 L/mol cm cannot be used to obviate further photosafety assessment."

REACTIVE OXYGEN SPECIES ASSAY

Early stages of drug development include physicochemical evaluations of candidate compounds, including the absorption spectrum and molar extinction

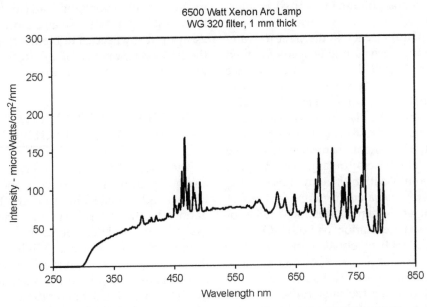

FIGURE 22.6 Spectral distribution of the 6500 W long arc xenon lamp equipped with a 4 mm thick WG 320 filter used for in vivo phototoxicity assays. The configuration attenuates the UVB and allows delivery of at least 10 J/cm² of UVA without eliciting a skin response from the irradiation alone.

coefficient. While these two endpoints provide some information as to the potential phototoxicity of a compound, it does not address its photochemical potential and thus phototoxic potential. Evaluation of ROS after irradiation of the compound in a suitable solvent can provide that information. Kleinman et al. [63] provides a good review of chemical photoreactivity and its relationship to phototoxicity, and demonstrates that, while absorption of light is critical to phototoxicity reactions, the resulting generation of singlet oxygen or superoxide, or the lack thereof, is crucial for actual elicitation of phototoxicity.

Onoue et al. [90] demonstrated a method for irradiation of compounds under standard conditions, which provides information on ROS generation and also allows for high-throughput compound screening. The assay detects ROS generated by Type I reactions (eg, superoxide) and Type II reactions (eg, singlet oxygen), both involved in phototoxic reactions. A series of drugs and chemicals with known phototoxic profiles were evaluated to demonstrate the sensitivity and selectivity of this assay. The compounds were dissolved in a phosphate buffer and placed in a quartz 96 multiwell plate. For determination of generated superoxide, the compounds were irradiated in the presence of nitroblue tetrazolium (NBT) and the reduction of NBT determined by the increase in absorbance at 560 nm. For determination of generated singlet oxygen, the bleaching of p-nitrosodimethyanaline (RNO) at 440 nm was used. Irradiation was performed under controlled temperature of 25°C, as this temperature was found to generate the most similar levels of both ROS, as measured by percent of control.

To clearly define the system's response and variables that may affect the response, quinine was used as a test compound. Precision of the assay was evaluated with three concentrations of quinine across the same day and different days. This approach is highly recommended for any laboratory employing the assay, as confidence in the assay's precision and reproducibility is vital to the data generated for unknown materials. The uniformity of the response across the plate was evaluated, and the center of the plate provided the most homogeneous exposure, presumably from slight changes in irradiance at the edges of the plate. Several organic solvents that may be used in the solubilization of compounds in the phosphate buffer were evaluated to define any effect on superoxide or singlet oxygen production. Methanol and ethanol suppressed generation of both ROS, but dimethyl sulfoxide (DMSO) potentiated the response, isopropanol had no effect on either ROS, and acetonitrile suppressed generation of superoxide. These results point to the necessity of using the same buffer/solvent system across the entire assay, and performing preliminary work with quinine to define any such effect.

The evaluation of 33 known phototoxins and six nonphototoxic compounds at a fixed concentration of 200 µM demonstrated high concordance with the generation of one or both ROS and phototoxic potential. Some nonphototoxic compounds (eg, erythromycin) did not show strong UVR absorption, while others, such as benzocaine, did show strong absorption but little ROS generation. In contrast, reported clinical phototoxins such as ibuprofen showed little UVR absorption. These results all indicate that, at least for the compounds evaluated, generation of ROS and UVR absorption are closely but not exclusively linked to phototoxic potential. The use of the assay continues to be evaluated as an early predictor of phototoxic potential [66].

Onoue et al. [91] also published the results of an assay based on derivatives of ROS using N,N-diethyl-p-phenylenediamine as the indicator for alkoxy and peroxy radicals. This assay system also demonstrated good concordance with the 3T3 assay and a photocleavage assay, with the added benefit of reducing runtime because of the short (1 min) exposure time required to generate the ROS derivative signal, allowing for even faster screening. Subsequent work [92] has demonstrated intra- and interlaboratory validation.

The assay is referenced in ICH S10, III.B. (3.2) as a possible indicator of phototoxic potential, with several qualifying comments. The data suggest that the assay has high sensitivity for predicting direct in vivo phototoxins but has low specificity and generates a high percentage of false-positive results. Results, provided that the 200 µM concentration is achieved, "would indicate a very low probability of phototoxicity," and a positive result at any concentration "would only be a flag for follow-up assessment." While the assay may have utility in early development and lead candidate selection, until there is a larger database and more experience with the assay (and any needed refinement), eg, as was done with the 3T3 assay, the use of the ROS assay for regulatory purposes will remain unclear.

IN VITRO 3T3 NEUTRAL RED UPTAKE PHOTOTOXICITY TEST

The single phototoxicity assay to be validated for use and accepted by a regulatory agency is the in vitro 3T3 neutral red Uptake Phototoxicity Test (3T3 NRU). As defined by the OECD Test Guideline 432 (2004) [87], the assay can be used to evaluate the phototoxic potential of a chemical when exposed to light. The work validating the guidance serves as an excellent source of information on the assay, and subsequent references provide further information on the details of the assay and interpretation of the data [9,94,115,116]. The assay is also discussed in ICH S10 III.3 (3.3).

The assay is based on the ability of cells to take up the vital neutral red dye after exposure to the solubilized chemical without and with UVR exposure. The assay requires the solubilization of the chemical, already identified as absorbing between 290 and 700 nm, in an aqueous medium (eg, Dulbecco's Phosphate Buffered Saline or Earle's Balanced Salt Solution). Serum or protein is not included in the medium. The guidance-recommended maximum concentration is 1000 μg/mL (see the following). The osmolarity should be no greater than 10 milliosmolar and the pH of the final formulations should remain in the range of 6.5–7.8; again, with the reduced concentration this is very rarely a concern. A preliminary evaluation is first conducted to establish the solubility of the test material. This can be evaluated either in the medium alone or, if the solubility is very limited, the material can first be dissolved in a suitable organic solvent such as DMSO with subsequent dilution in the aqueous medium, keeping the final DMSO concentration at 1–3% of total. In practice, the use of DMSO with the final solution of 1% DMSO is the default medium used. From this maximum dilution, a geometric range of eight dilutions in 0.5 (customary progression) or 0.33 log increments is made in the medium. In the standard assay six replicates of these test material dilutions are evaluated per plate.

The permanent fibroblast cell line Balb/c 3T3, clone 31 was used for the validation work and is recommended for use in the assay. Two plates per test material are seeded with 3T3 cells (recommended 1×10^4 cells/well) and are allowed to establish with an overnight incubation. The culture medium is washed off and the cells exposed to the test material formulations for 1h in the incubator. The plates are removed from the incubator and allowed to equilibrate to the temperature used for the exposure. One plate then remains in the dark, while the other plate is exposed to a UVA dose of 5 J/cm^2. The test material formulations are then removed, the cells washed twice with the aqueous medium, and cell-culture medium added. The cells are then incubated overnight. After this incubation, the cells are evaluated by light microscopy for morphological changes, then washed with aqueous medium, a solution of neutral red in cell-culture medium is then added, and the cells incubated again for 3h. After this incubation, the neutral red medium is removed, the cells are washed and a solution of water, and ethanol and acetic acid is added to lyse the cells and release the accumulated neutral red. After shaking for approximately 10 min, the optical density of each well is measured at 540 nm with a microplate spectrophotometer.

Customarily, a range-finding assay is performed and, based on the results, two definitive assays are performed to further refine the results. Smaller dilution increments of the test material are used (eg, one-quarter log in the definitive assays), based on the range-finding assay

solubility and IC$_{50}$ data. These assays are performed as described previously.

The absorption data are evaluated, most commonly using the Phototox software developed specifically for this purpose [94], to calculate the PIF and the mean photo effect (MPE). The criteria for determination of phototoxic potential, based on ICH S10, Endnote 4, was revised for pharmaceuticals to a PIF value of >5, and/or an MPE value of >0.15, with elimination of the probable phototoxic PIF and MPE endpoints. The data are evaluated by fitting the set of dose-response values using an appropriate continuous dose-response curve model. The use of a bootstrap procedure is recommended to assess the variability of the data on the fitted curve.

If cytotoxicity IC$_{50}$ is not achieved but phototoxicity IC$_{50}$ is achieved, a formal PIF cannot be calculated, but it is apparent that phototoxicity has occurred. In this case, a ">PIF" is calculated and the highest testable test article concentration (−UVR) is used for calculation. Since the ">PIF" is not an exact numerical value, no biostatistical procedure can be applied to determine the optimum cutoff of toxicity. Consequently, the classification rule is, if only a ">PIF" can be obtained, then any value >1 predicts phototoxic potential. In this instance, the MPE is also valuable for assessing phototoxic potential (see the following).

If both IC$_{50}$ (−UVR) and IC$_{50}$ (+UVR) cannot be calculated (the test article does not show cytotoxicity without or with UVR exposure), this indicates a lack of phototoxic potential. In this case, a formal PIF = *1 is used to characterize and report this result.

In addition, the MPE is calculated by the Phototox software [94]. This calculation is based on the comparison of the complete concentration response curve for both cytotoxicity and phototoxicity, and not just the IC$_{50}$ value, as is the PIF. This measure of phototoxicity is most useful when phototoxicity is present, but cytotoxicity IC$_{50}$ has not been achieved, and as per ICH S10 Endnote 4, when the PIF value is between 2 and 5.

In addition, each definitive assay should contain a positive control article to ensure that the response of the cells to a cytotoxin and phototoxin are consistent with historical data. Chlorpromazine is the most-used positive control, as it gives both responses (recommended IC$_{50}$ ranges for phototoxicity of 0.1–2.0 μg/mL and cytotoxicity of 7.0–90.0 μg/mL and a PIF > 6 in each assay). Other compounds, most commonly promethazine, can also be used. The optical density of the solvent/control wells in each assay should remain above 0.400 and the survival of the cells in these wells, based the optical density, only exposed to UVR should remain above 80%. The responses from each assay should be compared with the laboratory historical control data for all endpoints to ensure that the assay is consistent across replicates.

Each laboratory should internally validate the assay using some or all of the positive and negative compounds used during the validation work [115,116] to ensure that the assay is performing nominally before evaluating test materials.

The UVR source to be used for these assays is not defined. What is defined is that the UVA dose of $5 J/cm^2$ should be delivered in a time frame that minimizes the duration of time that the cells are outside of the incubator. The OECD 432 guidance (2004) illustrates one spectral distribution that was used during the validation work, which included UVB. The sensitivity of the cells to UVB has been accepted as being too great to allow the use of this portion of the spectrum to evaluate phototoxicity. The conventional wisdom is that the toxicity of UVB alone to the cells prevents its use. As a result, the assay has been criticized, and not used, for evaluation of chemicals that absorb exclusively or primarily in the UVB portion of the spectrum (290–320 nm). However, the 3T3 cells are not exquisitely sensitive to UVB and it can be included in the spectrum [108]. In this instance, with the $5 J/cm^2$ UVA dose through the plate cover, a UVB dose of $19–22 mJ/cm^2$ was delivered, and with the plate cover off a dose of $32–35 mJ/cm^2$ was delivered, with no effect on the survival and OD_{540} criteria that would invalidate the assay. Thus so long as these criteria with a source including UVB are within specification and sufficient historical data exist to demonstrate the appropriate functioning of the positive control article, the assay can be used to evaluate chemicals that absorb in the UVB region of the spectrum.

One limitation is that the assay is not appropriate for topically applied products. In addition, the chemical must dissolve in the biologically acceptable medium at an acceptable concentration. The acceptable concentration is best determined by the experience of the testing facility. If these issues cannot be resolved, alternative methods must be used to evaluate the phototoxic potential of the chemical.

The assay can be modified to serve as a screening tool in the discovery phase of drug development. For instance, instead of using the six replicates of each formulation, two can be used to increase the number of evaluations per culture plate and allow for a high throughput of chemicals in this development phase. For a single point evaluation and rough screen, the highest achievable concentration, in duplicate, can also be evaluated to provide a simple yes/no answer for phototoxic potential. In both instances and other iterations of a screening approach, the cell survival and positive control criteria still apply to ensure a valid assay [108].

For Good Laboratory Practices (GLP)-compliant studies, analysis of the dosing formulations can be problematic, based primarily on the low concentrations used, and from a practical point of view, the formulations are often in a medium that will only be used in very few if any other assays. The development and validation of such assays, especially in a GLP environment, can be many times the cost of the actual assay. Analysis of the DMSO stock solutions used to prepare the dosing solutions can be done, as this matrix is often used across multiple in vitro assays, and while it does not completely remove the GLP issue of lack of formulation analysis, it provides some assurance, that, along with a careful review of the formulation data, the formulations were properly prepared.

As the use of the 3T3 assay became widespread, accumulated knowledge and experience soon demonstrated some shortcomings. Review of available data [10,66] revealed that a large number (~47%) of chemicals that were positive in the assay, while the actual number that were positive in in vivo studies was closer to 10%. This disparity triggered a serious reevaluation of the 3T3 assay as it is currently practiced, and the recommendations reflected in ICH S10, III.C, V.A.1, and 2 (3.3, 5.1, and 2) and Endnotes 1 and 4. The reevaluation resulted in reduction of the highest concentration evaluated to $100 \mu g/mL$, increase the molar extinction cutoff to $1000 L/mol cm$, and remove the probable phototoxicity PIF and MPE criteria. However, these criteria remain in the OECD 432 and are presumably still applicable to evaluation of nonpharmaceuticals, including consumer care, cosmetics, and chemicals.

RECONSTRUCTED SKIN EPIDERMIS SYSTEMS

While the 3T3 assay provides a fast and simple answer to phototoxic potential, the system has mechanistic limitations, specifically the need for solubilization of the test material, concentration limitations caused by that solubilization requirement, and the inability to evaluate test materials in topical formulations. The use of reconstructed epidermal skin systems allows for evaluation of finished formulations and materials that cannot, by virtue of chemical incompatibility, pH values, or complex formulations, be evaluated in the 3T3 assay, and as described in ICH S10, III.C, and V.B.2 (3.3 and 5.3.2). This system uses skin epithelial cells in a three-dimensional structure, with a stratum corneum and a differentiated cell layer more analogous to normal human skin. It allows direct administration to the surface to mimic topical administration, and also administration to the medium underlying the system to mimic systemic administration.

Commercial suppliers of these systems provide large amounts of technical and background information for their systems. This information, along with methods for the determination of cell damage, is available on supplier websites. The general structure of the constructs is similar across suppliers. Human keratinocytes, seeded on a collagen matrix that serves as a dermal substitute, are cultured on an underlying culture medium layer with the keratinocyte layer exposed to the air, allowing the keratinocytes to develop into a multilayer, differentiated, human epidermis construct. At an optimum development time for the differentiated structure to be developed, the constructs are shipped to the customer for use. After arrival, the systems are stabilized, usually by overnight incubation.

The system is transferred to a 12-well plate containing a suitably balanced salt solution with calcium and magnesium cations for use. A duplicate set of plates is used, one for cytotoxicity and the other for phototoxicity evaluation. For topical administration, a known volume of the test material formulation is administered to the surface of the appropriate system and then, after a period of incubation, the excess is removed and the construct then irradiated. For a systemic administration approach, the test material formulation is added to the underlying balanced salt solution. One plate is then irradiated, normally with $5\,J/cm^2$ of UVA without or with UVB, and the systems are rinsed and then incubated overnight with fresh culture medium.

For evaluation of phototoxic or cytotoxic damage, the culture medium can be evaluated for inflammatory molecules such as interleukin 1α, cell viability by the conversion of the yellow tetrazolium MTT, genetic damage markers, and/or histopathology. Comparisons versus the cytotoxicity (dark) plate results are calculated to determine phototoxic potential. As with any model, the response of the system to the UVR source, to known phototoxins such as chlorpromazine, and the methods for evaluation of UVR-induced damage must be well defined and understood. The appropriate historical control data should be available for use in interpreting study results.

The assay has undergone some validation effort [71] and evaluation in a tiered testing strategy [70]. While acceptable for cosmetic and over-the-counter drug testing and exploratory evaluations, the use of these systems for pharmaceutical regulatory submission is unclear. ICH S10, III.C (3.3) includes the caveats that the assay's sensitivity may be less than for human skin (minimal effective concentration higher than for humans) and understanding sensitivity comparison is important. The relative low number of topical pharmaceutical drugs is also a practical limiting factor in the routine use of this assay for regulatory submission.

of a material to be converted into a photochemical carcinogen when activated with either ultraviolet or visible radiation, with one goal of this work to replace the photocarcinogenesis bioassay with an in vitro assay. The recommended methodologies were defined by an international working group [47], and the use of a photoclastogenicity assay (chromosomal aberration or micronucleus test in mammalian cells) was recommended. The guidance did recognize the very limited experience with these models for photogenotoxicity testing.

Review of photogenotoxicity data generated by the industry revealed serious concerns with the use of this assay, namely the lack of specificity of the results. The utility of photogenotoxicity assays for regulatory purposes was formally questioned in the concept paper on the need for revision of the *Notes for Guidance on Photosafety Testing* [33] and led to a review of available data [74]. The potential for pseudoclastogenicity by four compounds that did not absorb in the 290–700 nm range in the Chinese hamster ovary cell assay, along with one that did absorb, was a phototoxin and cytotoxic, but was not a known genotoxin. Two of the compounds that did not absorb (cyclohexamide and disulfoton) demonstrated photoclastogenicity but not clastogenicity. The phototoxic compound (tetracycline) was also photoclastogenic but not clastogenic. The other two nonabsorbers (aminotriazole and propantheline) were not clastogenic without or with UVR exposure. These "pseudophotoclastogenic" results confirmed the findings for zinc oxide and cast further doubt on the value of the in vitro photoclastogenicity assay and its use for regulatory photosafety testing purposes.

Based on this report and information shared in the industry and within the regulatory agencies, in vitro photogenotoxicity testing was formally "no longer recommended" with the issuance of the questions and answers in the *Notes for Guidance of Photosafety Testing* [33], further clarified in ICH S10, I.D (1.2) [55] and Endnote 2 and reviewed by Mueller and Gocke [80]. The authors concluded that photogenotoxicity, while obviously of human safety relevance, is complex and subject to many modifiers, especially in in vitro mammalian cell culture. Thus current assays are not suitable for a general testing framework within testing guidelines for cosmetics and pharmaceuticals and, in comparison with UVR exposure alone, is considered a comparatively minor human safety risk.

IN VITRO PHOTOGENOTOXICITY

The EMA Note for Guidance on Photosafety Testing [31], Section 3.6, indicated that the purpose of the photogenotoxicity testing was to assess the potential

GENERAL IN VIVO TECHNIQUES

While in vivo models and endpoints can vary, each study should be approached with firm knowledge of the test material to be used, the possible clinical use, and possible nonphoto-related toxicity. Many technical considerations carry across all study types and models and these principles are noted throughout the ICH S10 and are included here.

The number of oral/IV administrations used should ensure that a stable concentration of the test material is achieved in the target tissue. For dermal administrations, as noted in ICH S10 III.3 and V.2 (3.3 and 5.2), in general the clinical formulation should be tested, and the intended clinical conditions of administration should be used to the extent possible. Normally a single administration is used, but multiple administrations may be necessary, based on the characteristics of the test material and the intended clinical use [ICH S10 III.D (3.4)]. Exposure after dermal administrations should be based on specific properties of the formulation evaluated [ICH S10 III.E (3.5)]. For oral or intravenous administration, multiple administrations are recommended to ensure the presence of the test material in the target tissues at a steady state level. The number of administrations can vary, based on the absorption, distribution, metabolism, and elimination characteristics of the test material in those tissues, and the ultimate decision for doses used is based on these data.

When defined sites are to be exposed to UVR, an opaque mask with one or more exposure sites removed is applied to the animal. This technique allows comparison of the exposure site with surrounding skin and identification of subtle changes that may not be apparent if the entire animal is irradiated or primary irritation from topical administration is induced. This is especially important if more than one test material concentration is topically administered to a single animal, eg, the pig, but also simplifies exposure site evaluation when a single site is used, eg, the mouse.

Test materials can be administered to the ear (pinna), normally in the mouse. Formulations are administered to both sides of the ear and approximately 60 min after administration, the ears wiped to remove any test material. The mice are then exposed to UVR and ear thickness measurements performed immediately after exposure to identify materials that cause an immediate response (eg, photodynamic materials and anthracene), along with 24 and 48 h after exposure.

For dermal administration, the amount of test material administered to the site should remain localized to the administration site. Multiple applications can be made a short time apart to administer the proper volume if a single administration would run off the administration site. The amount of test material on the skin after the solvent evaporates or the formulation is absorbed should not form an obvious and visible layer that could interfere with irradiation. The interval between application and irradiation should be justified based on the specific properties of the formulation to be tested, ICH S10

III.D (3.4), and the administered material is not removed before irradiation to mimic the conditions of clinical use. Vehicle groups, or if the model used is sufficiently large, sites, must be included to evaluate any vehicle effect. Comparison of the exposed skin to which the vehicle formulation has been administered is critical to determine whether a response is caused by the test material in the vehicle (phototoxicity) or the vehicle alone (irritation). While simple vehicles of known minimal irritancy potential (eg, methanol) can be used, in most instances the clinical vehicle formulation is used, and its response on the skin must be defined for the model used, either as part of the phototoxicity study or in a separate arm of the study. Dermal administrations can lead to ingestion of the administered test materials from grooming, resulting in systemic exposure. Systemic exposure can be controlled either by using restraint devices such as Elizabethan collars, dressings, and/or restrictive caging. The use of any dressings may affect absorption of the applied material and lead to unintended general toxicity or irritation, and should be controlled in the study design. In general, assessment of systemic drug exposure is not required in dermal phototoxicity studies, since systemic exposure is normally not a concern and such work is normally performed as part of other toxicity studies.

With oral or intravenous administration, vehicle-induced enhancement of phototoxic response is very unlikely. However, vehicle groups serve as confirmation that UVR exposure alone does not cause a response and allow for comparison of any skin reactions in the groups administered the test material. If the response of the model to UVR is well characterized, a group not administered any formulation is not necessary, and historical control data can be used to document the model's response to UVR. Doses should be chosen using good general practices and doses used in other toxicology studies. The top dose can, to meet other dose-selection criteria, induce a minor general toxicity effect, normally noted by a reduction in body weight gain, with at least two lower doses chosen in logical (eg, half-log) intervals. The maximum tolerated dose information is usually known from previous general toxicity work performed with the test material and can serve as a starting point for dose selection. If no general toxicity information exists for the chosen model, a tolerance study should be performed to ensure that mortality or significant morbidity does not occur in the phototoxicity study. Overt toxicity should be avoided, as the additional stress of irradiation and, in some cases, the agents used to immobilize the animal for that irradiation, can potentiate the toxicity and cause unacceptable morbidity or death. The time of irradiation should coincide with the T_{max} of the test material in the plasma or, if the information is known, the skin (or other target organ with oral or IV administration) and ensure that the conditions are maximized to elicit a response. If this information is not known, a preliminary toxico-kinetic study to define this exposure is necessary. If this information is known, blood samples for test material analysis can be taken from a satellite group of animals to confirm dose-dependent exposure across groups at the time of irradiation. There is no need to perform a complete time course in this assay if the exposure profile is known, as the single time point at irradiation confirms test material exposure.

When exposure methods are used that require the animal to be sedated, most commonly accepted veterinary anesthesia agents are acceptable. If adverse interactions between the test material and anesthesia used is known or suspected, this should be evaluated with a tolerance phase to ensure that no adverse interactions, usually noted as death during UVR exposure, occur. This is critical for oral or IV administrations, but not usually necessary for topically administered materials. The commonly used agents (eg, chloral hydrate, ketamine/xylazine mixtures) have no known effect on phototoxic responses, but effects of restraint under sedation must be defined before doses are used on study. Pigs can be sedated with a combination of an injectable agent for initiation and an inhalation agent for maintenance of sedation during exposure. Knowledgeable veterinary support is essential for choosing appropriate agents and minimizing adverse effects from sedation.

Unless there is a scientific reason to include both genders, only one gender is customarily included in phototoxicity studies. Both genders are included only where exposure to the test material is substantially different between the genders or there are other gender-dependent reasons (eg, toxicity) to include both. Skin sensitivities of any model should be experimentally established, and where possible this sensitivity with known phototoxins also established. For instance, in Long–Evans rats, females have greater skin sensitivity to UVR responses than males [67], but the eyes of the genders in this species show no discernable differences in responses [59].

As noted in ICH S10 III. D. (3.4), single or repeated UVR exposures can be used and may result in visible damage based on repeated insults. In practice, a single exposure after one or more administrations is the norm, with multiple exposures only employed because of specific characteristics of the test material being evaluated. Where only one UVR exposure is performed, mice and rats are customarily lightly sedated and restrained to ensure consistent exposure of the skin and, when applicable, the eyes. Exposure of free-moving animals can also be done, depending on the requirements of the study. If free-moving animals are exposed, their movement should be constrained with caging to control, to the extent possible, variability in exposure from their

movements. The UVR dose required to cause a biological response must be determined under these circumstances. For chronic exposures, issues with variable exposure at any one exposure session may not be of concern, as the variations tend to equilibrate over the many exposures, but must be understood and taken into account when evaluating the results.

The inclusion of a positive control article group in each study, regardless of the route of administration, is dependent on the comfort of the laboratory with the techniques used, the chosen model and their historical control data for that model and technique. If historical control data are used to confirm the validity of the study design, data should be generated on a regular basis. These data should be collated and audited and when necessary included in reports that do not include a positive control group.

EVALUATION OF IN VIVO PHOTOTOXIC RESPONSES

The decision to declare a positive phototoxic response from the results of an assay requires the evaluation of all the data, historical controls, and the familiarity of the scientist making the decision with the test, test system, and test material class. Responses in the test material groups should be compared against the positive control responses used either in this assay, or if sufficient experience exists, comparison against historical control data. Use of a series of concentrations will allow for determination of a no observed effect or no adverse effect level. While clear-cut responses are easy to interpret, subtle responses, for instance, either in duration or intensity, may require additional testing to clearly define phototoxic potential.

For all animal models, following UVR exposure, evaluations of the skin responses are customarily performed at least once on the day of UVR exposure, and then 24 and 48 h after exposure. Early observations are critical (eg, 1 and 4 h after exposure), since some materials, such as anthracene, fluoroquinolones, and acridine [36], show early responses that, depending on the dose used, may not be obvious at a later time point but are indicative of phototoxicity. Later evaluation times (72–96 h) may reveal other phototoxic responses, such as flaking, and should be considered, based on the experience of the laboratory, with known phototoxins of various classes and the class of test material being evaluated. More than one evaluation per day may also prove useful for capturing subtle responses that may appear and then fade in a short period of time. The use of masks or other coverings that limit the exposure to a defined site also helps in discrimination of changes in the irradiated site, in comparison with the surrounding unirradiated skin.

The skin sites are evaluated using a Draize-type scale [25], documenting erythema, edema, and flaking responses at each evaluation time using a scale of 0–4. For all endpoints, skin responses of 3 or greater should result in early euthanasia of that animal, as the required endpoint has been achieved and further evaluation is not required. Documented training of technical staff in evaluating these skin responses in each model used and experience of these personnel with evaluating positive controls and different classes of phototoxins are critical in ensuring these responses are consistently graded across studies, especially for subtle changes or responses that may not follow the classical patterns.

Hyperpigmentation or hypopigmentation can be evaluated using standard color cards such as the Munsell type to match the shades of brown/black, or be quantitatively determined using a handheld spectrophotometer measuring in the known color spaces (l*, a*, b*). Comparison against the normal skin adjacent to the treated sites serves as good means to discriminate subtle differences that may be difficult to discriminate.

Visible evaluation of skin reactions is the traditional preclinical and clinical endpoints for phototoxic evaluations, and in general, histopathological evaluation of the skin is not required. Caution should be taken in using histopathology in regulated studies, as subvisual responses identified microscopically may prove difficult to interpret from a risk assessment perspective. If histopathological evaluation of the skin is required/requested for confirmation of the observed response or to evaluate mechanisms of phototoxicity, temporal evaluation is necessary to determine changes over time. The skin's repair capacity is rapid enough that, provided the phototoxic damage is not severe, histopathological evidence of this damage may be unclear if evaluation is performed at the end of the evaluation (48–72 h). Subtle changes may be present from the irradiation alone, and, especially for topically applied materials, the vehicle may also have microscopic effects that are not visually apparent. A robust historical control data set is necessary to put UVR exposure and topical vehicle observations in context, especially if similar findings are present in the test material groups. Biomarkers, such as DNA damage, apoptosis, mismatch repair, and other molecular endpoints can be used, especially in instances where some correlation with potential photocarcinogenic effects is desired [19].

If mouse ear swelling is used as a response endpoint, ear thickness is normally evaluated using a calibrated spring micrometer [37,45,100]. Quantitative data and comparisons of vehicle and test material groups allow more precise evaluation of a response than clinical observations may provide. Measurement of ear thickness at the outer edge is made, with two measurements per ear performed in different locations. Measurements can be made throughout the observation period to provide information on the temporal changes in the response. Measurements either longer or shorter than this time frame can be used, but all should be confirmed against a known set of phototoxins and concentrations to ensure that early or late effects are not missed, and when a temporal response determination is required. If the response (edema) is excessive, compressibility of the ear can be a concern and experience of the testing facility and expertise of the technical staff can help in understanding which measurement of the ear is most representative of the response (eg, initial contact versus stable measurement). Alternatively, for terminal evaluations, punch biopsy sections can be removed and weighed in pairs [107] to provide another semiquantitative measure of inflammation that avoids the compressibility issue.

Skinfold thickness measurement on the dorsum of animals, normally mice, can also be used for evaluating responses, and provides a quantitative data set for comparison of effects, and can also provide a temporal data set to evaluate response over time [3,66].

Preclinical ocular phototoxicity evaluation is an area of controversy. ICH S10 I. C, III. C (1.3, 3.3), and Endnote 1 all mention ocular phototoxicity evaluation in some form. With the exception of Endnote 1, the evaluation of ocular phototoxicity is not emphasized. Endnote 1 indicates that except for compounds absorbing above 400 nm, retinal phototoxicity is of low concern in adults, while in children some UVR transmission to the retina is possible. However, the anterior compartment and the lens are exposed to various degrees of UVA and UVB, and the guidance is silent on the evaluation of these tissues for xenobiotic-related phototoxicity. In addition, except for 8-methoxpsoralen, chlorpromazine, promethazine, and systemically administered photodynamic drugs, human xenobiotic-induced phototoxicity is extremely rare, even when current experience and practice in this laboratory is, from an abundance of caution, to evaluate ocular phototoxicity in the Long–Evans rat model, as described in the following. One integrated preclinical safety testing strategy includes retinal histopathology only for those compounds >400 nm [107], as noted in the ICH S10. The relevance and overall utility of ocular phototoxicity evaluation requires review of the current data and experience, and ultimately clarification at the regulatory level.

Observations of ocular phototoxicity are best performed by a veterinary ophthalmologist with experience in phototoxicity endpoints. Both the anterior and posterior compartments of the eye should be evaluated by slit-lamp examination and indirect ophthalmoscopy, respectively. Evaluation before study assignment is necessary to exclude any animal with defects in eye structures. Some findings, such as corneal dystrophy in Long–Evans rats and hyaloid remnant in relatively young animals, are considered normal, and these animals can be used on study. As appropriate, fluorescein staining can be used to visualize subtle surface corneal changes. Phototoxic damage to the corneal epithelium can result in corneal scarring or, in severe cases, ulceration. Swelling of the corneal stroma will result in corneal edema, or corneal opacity without this edema, can both be indications of phototoxicity. Cataract formation may also occur in some instances of acute phototoxic responses, and is more probable with chronic exposure to UVR, either without or with administration of test material. Retinal changes in preclinical phototoxicity studies are rarely observed, in part because UVR does not reach the retina in any toxicologically relevant quantity [62,113], and visible light-induced compounds are typically only observed with photodynamic agents or laser applications. Areas of small retinal degeneration or retinopathy may be present in the eyes of animals that are sedated and restrained during UVR exposure from the focusing of the light on the inferior area of the retina by the lens during exposure. As this will also be evident in the group administered the vehicle formulation, the historical control data will help to determine if this finding is (or is not) a phototoxic response to the test material. The clinical appearance of this lesion is also important, as a sharply defined border indicates a light-induced insult, while a softer border, suggesting an active inflammatory process, may indicate phototoxicity. These lesions can also be evaluated by histopathological evaluation, but will require careful positioning of the eye during embedding with serial sectioning to ensure the lesion is captured.

Histopathological evaluation of the eyes is critical, as phototoxic damage may occur that cannot be visualized by the ophthalmologist [59]. Histopathological evidence of ocular phototoxicity (and the lack thereof) normally reflects the findings of the ophthalmic evaluations, but occasionally damage not apparent by ophthalmological evaluation is revealed by microscopic evaluation. Damage due to UVR exposure alone (photic) or procedural changes must be differentiated from test material-induced phototoxicity [79]. In general, the severity of the response is a key determinant in this differentiation. In the cornea, degenerative epithelial changes and changes consistent with inflammatory responses are common, and may be associated with extension of inflammation into the anterior chamber and iris. Damage to the lenticular epithelium and lens fibers can result in early cataract formation. As discussed previously, focal retinopathy is commonly found in both vehicle control and treated rats; these are considered to be indicative of photic, rather than phototoxic, injury. Little, if any, photic damage is seen in the ciliary body, vitreous chamber, choroid, sclera, and optic nerve. If intravitreal administration was performed, mechanical damage by the injection may be present, and should also be, to some degree, in the unexposed but injected eyes at a similar incidence. The totality of the histopathological changes in the eye, along with ophthalmological and the cutaneous observations, are critical in evaluating the phototoxic potential of a test material and assessing its overall phototoxic risk.

THE MOUSE

The mouse is possibly the most commonly used in vivo model for photosafety testing, with established procedures for acute phototoxicity, photocarcinogenesis, photogenotoxicity, and photoallergy evaluations. Haired strains present the complicating factor of hair removal for topical administration, exposure, and evaluations for skin responses, but may be desired because the assay was defined in a haired model. Hair removal by clipping followed, if necessary, by chemical depilation is recommended and any variables from the procedures can be addressed with good technique that minimizes skin irritation. Hairless strains, such as the Crl:SKH1-hr albino hairless mouse, have been extensively used for evaluation of both acute phototoxicity and photocarcinogenesis (eg, Refs. [15,36,100]). The lack of hair removes the complications noted previously when the dorsal skin is the exposure target, and their response to acute UVR has been demonstrated to be similar to that of human skin [15].

For acute phototoxicity evaluations, the dorsal skin is a convenient target, especially using the hairless mouse. A mark is tattooed on the dorsum to define the UVR exposure site and simplify comparison of the site with the surrounding skin for identification of subtle responses, or with dermal administration, any unexpected primary irritation. After administration, the mice are sedated with chloral hydrate administered by the intraperitoneal route, and then restrained with laboratory tape to ensure a controlled UVR exposure. A mask with a circular hole is then placed just behind the tattoo site and the remainder of the mouse is shielded with aluminum foil. Evaluation of the skin reactions is as described in that section of this chapter. The ear can also be the target for the phototoxicity reaction [45,100] and this method allows for quantitative evaluation of the response by measuring the change in ear thickness (edema) in response to the phototoxic insult. This method is applicable for both topical and oral/intravenous administration of test materials. UVR-induced skinfold thickness of the back [66] and biomarkers [19] can also be evaluated with whole-mouse exposure.

The hairless mouse can be used to evaluate the ability of a test material to affect the skin's response to UVR using a variant of the minimal erythema dose-evaluation method. The mice are administered the test material, either topically or orally/intravenously, and at the appropriate time after administration, a series of sites on the dorsum are exposed to a stepwise increased series of UVR exposures. Using a study design similar to clinical sunscreen testing based on the US FDA sunscreen testing method (US FDA 21 CFR part 352; Sambuco and Forbes [100]), a series of six exposures, normally in a 1.4-fold step increase and covering a range that begins below the UVR dose that will induce a response on the skin (instrumental minimal erythema dose, MED_i) and ranges higher than the minimal dose. This series allows the evaluation of the potential increase or reduction in UVR response from the test material. The responses in the skin sites are evaluated at 24 and 48h after exposure and an observational minimal erythema dose (MED_o) calculated and compared with the MED_o of mice administered either the vehicle or no formulation.

The mouse has also been used for evaluation of photoallergy, with ear swelling as the photoallergic endpoint [45,46]. As with the guinea pig, the contact irritation and phototoxic potential for the topically administered test materials should be determined before the photoallergy evaluation, and the study design must allow for distinction between photoallergy and contact hypersensitivity. The mice are pretreated for 3 days with cyclophosphamide and, after pretreatment, induction performed by administering the test material to the clipped dorsum and the mice then irradiated with primarily UVA but some UVB. Seven days after induction, baseline ear measurements are performed, the test material administered to the ears, the ears wiped approximately 60 min after administration, and the mice are then irradiated. Ear thickness is determined 24h after exposure. This method demonstrates photoallergic responses to both strong and weak photoallergens. However, as noted in the ICH S10, the utility of preclinical photoallergy evaluations is questionable, and not recommended for safety evaluation.

The murine local lymph node assay [88] for contact sensitization can be modified to evaluate photoallergy [106,121]. The recommended methodologies in the guidance are the basis of the assay, with the addition of UVR exposure on the days of formulation administration. The required vehicle controls, the response to UVR exposure alone, responses to known photoallergens, and the possible contact allergenic potential of the test materials must be evaluated to ensure that the results truly represent a photoallergic response.

THE GUINEA PIG

The guinea pig was an early model for photosafety testing (eg, Refs. [65,105]) and the classic model for contact hypersensitivity, easing its early acceptance as a model for photosafety testing [84]. Their relatively large size,

allowing multiple administration sites per animal, minimizes the total number of animals used. One drawback is the difficulty with oral and intravenous administration, limiting their practical use to dermal administration. If haired guinea pigs are used, they should be closely clipped to remove hair from the administration/exposure area, followed by shaving or depilation to remove any hair stubble. Again, careful technique and experience are essential to minimize any adverse effects from these manipulations and confounding any results obtained from experimental procedures. Alternatively, the hairless guinea pig can be used, eliminating this potentially complicating manipulation and minimizing worker exposure to allergens released by the clipping. Evaluations of the microstructure of the skin [117] and their response to contact and photocontact allergens [77] are similar to haired strains.

For phototoxicity evaluation, a group of animals for evaluation of the topical irritation of all the evaluated formulations (without UVR exposure) should be used. At least one other group of animals serves as the irradiation group and is administered the same formulation as the irritation group. Ideally, the irritation potential of the formulations [89] is evaluated first, and as necessary concentrations can be revised to minimize or eliminate the confounding effects of the irritation from evaluation of the phototoxic response. Formulations are administered to sites defined either by indelible marker or tattoo sites at an administration volume that minimizes run-off. If desired, administrations can also be done using Hill Top Chambers and occlusion to enhance delivery into the skin. The animals are then placed in a restrainer that minimizes their movement but allows free exposure, usually with a stainless steel-wire grid cover. At a set time after administration (normally 30–60 min) the animals are exposed to a suberythematous UVR dose. During exposure, the eyes of the animals should be protected by placing opaque material over that portion of the restrainer. After exposure, the administration sites can be wiped to remove any remaining formulations, and animals are then returned to their home cages. Evaluation of skin responses is performed as noted in that section of this chapter.

The guinea pig is the classic model for photoallergy evaluation. While the procedures are described here, as noted for the mouse, the utility of preclinical photoallergy evaluations is questionable, and not recommended for safety evaluation. Multiple publications (eg, Refs. [44,65,77,78]) have outlined procedures for this evaluation, with variations in induction methods, use of adjuvants, mechanical or chemical irritation during the induction phase, numbers of animals per group, etc., to ensure identification of both strong and weak photosensitizers. A common theme is that all are based on a contact hypersensitivity model, eg, the Buehler method [86]. To ensure that a correct conclusion is made from the photoallergy evaluation, preliminary determination of the primary irritancy and phototoxicity potential of the formulations should be evaluated before the initiation of the photoallergy assay. If either of these two endpoints cannot be eliminated, doses that will not affect evaluation of a photoallergy response should be chosen. In addition, preliminary or concurrent evaluation of contact hypersensitivity should be performed using the same methods for induction and challenge with the exception of UVR exposure unless data are available that show there is no contact hypersensitivity potential of the test material.

The hair is removed from haired strains with clippers and the site depilated as necessary for all administrations and irradiations. The nuchal area is used for induction, with a single set of four injections of Freund's complete antigen defining the corners of the induction site on the first day. The skin is then tape stripped to enhance penetration of the test material. The test material is administered using a Hill Top Chamber occluded with dental dam and affixed in place with a suitable dressing for approximately 2h. After administration, the nuchal site is wiped and the guinea pig exposed to a suberythemogenic dose of UVR, primarily UVA without or with some UVB. Shielding is used only to expose the nuchal area during irradiation. Induction is performed three times per week for 2weeks as described earlier (the adjuvant injections are only performed on the first day), then the animals are rested for 2weeks. Challenge is done using the dorsum of the back, using the vehicle and at least two concentrations of the test material administered with Hill Top Chambers as per the induction but without tape stripping. After removal of the Hill Top Chambers, the administration sites are wiped and the animals exposed to a suberythemogenic dose of UVR. The administered skin sites are evaluated as previously described. Rechallenge of the photoallergy group is performed when unclear or equivocal responses occur from the challenge.

A group administered a positive control article such as 3,3′,4′,5-tetrachlorosalicylanide (TCSA) dissolved in acetone should be included in the assay to verify the conditions of the study will induce a photoallergic response. TCSA is also a contact sensitizer, allowing the same material to be used to evaluate the contact hypersensitivity potential of the test material in the study. TCSA-inducted photoallergy is distinguished from contact hypersensitivity based on the severity of the cutaneous responses. Other positive controls, such as musk ambrette or 6-methylcumarin, can also be used.

THE RAT

The literature does not recognize the rat as a common model for photosafety testing, but it is used regularly for phototoxicity evaluations by Charles River Laboratories. The Long–Evans rat is used, rather than an albino strain, based on the potential for melanin binding of test materials to affect phototoxicity (eg, Ref. [49]) and ICH S10 Section II.B, and that in this model both skin and eyes are evaluated. The pigmentation pattern on the rats allows for exposure of both pigmented and nonpigmented skin sites on the dorsum, and if melanin binding of the test material affects the phototoxic response, any response should be greater in the darkly pigmented site. In addition, the pigmented tissues in the eye also allow evaluation of these tissues for melanin interaction and phototoxicity [59] and the ability of the pigmented eye to recover from light exposure is much better than the eyes of albino animals [79].

Rats are chosen for study based on the pigmentation pattern on the back and lack of adverse eye signs after ophthalmological evaluation along with the usual clinical condition criteria. The backs of the rats are closely clipped at the time of randomization to the study and then after the final administration on the day of irradiation. The UVR exposure sites in the lightly and darkly pigmented skin are marked with a tattoo spot. Formulations are administered to the rats, and at the appropriate time after the final administration, the rats are lightly sedated with a mixture of ketamine and xylazine can also be used. Both of these compounds have been associated with adverse eye findings [119,120] and if used, careful comparisons with vehicle group findings are important to differentiate between test material and sedation materials. After sedation, the rats are restrained and a mask with a 1.3cm round hole taped immediately caudal to the individual tattooed skin sites. The remainder of the clipped skin and the tail and feet are covered with aluminum foil to isolate the UVR exposure to these skin sites. The eyes are held open with tape to ensure consistent exposure, and a sterile ophthalmologic lubricating solution is applied before, during, and after irradiation to minimize the desiccation that may occur during the exposure. The solution used is evaluated for UVR transmission to ensure that no absorption is present that could affect the exposure. After exposure, the skin sites and eyes are evaluated as described elsewhere.

The rat can also be used for evaluation of topical ocular instillation of test materials. The use of the rat also obviates the societal sensitivity of using the rabbit for ocular administration toxicity studies. The formulations can be administered, normally with a precision pipetting instrument to mimic clinical use and ensure steady state levels of test material in the eye tissues. Before the final administration and UVR exposure, an additional ophthalmological evaluation is performed to identify any effects of the administration(s). For UVR exposure, the rats are sedated and the final administration performed so some test material is present on the surface of the eye. The ophthalmic lubricating solution is used after the final administration to prevent corneal desiccation during exposure. The eyes are exposed to UVR and evaluated as discussed.

THE RABBIT

The rabbit has been proposed as a standard model for dermal phototoxicity [2], but the number of references to its use in the literature is low and requests for work for regulated studies, based on the authors' experience, are rare. Where the rabbit has had significant utility is in the evaluation of ocular phototoxicity [118]. The development of drugs administered directly to the interior of the eye (eg, intravitreal administration) raises the question of evaluation of potential phototoxicity from these drugs. The use of the rabbit for general and specialty toxicity testing by the intraocular route is well recognized. Adaptation of the rabbit for phototoxicity testing of intraocular administration of drugs is technically straightforward for laboratories experienced in intravitreal administrations. Typically, a mydriatic agent is administered to the eyes of the rabbit before initiation of anesthesia using an inhalation agent and then again shortly before the injection occurs to ensure full dilation of the pupil. The eye is then flushed with a preparatory solution and topical anesthetic is then administered to the eye. The eyelids are held open with an eyelid speculum and the intravitreal administration is then performed. After administration, the condition of the vitreal chamber and surrounding tissues are evaluated by indirect ophthalmoscopy to ensure proper placement of the injection and to evaluate the condition of the interior of the eye. The rabbit is then allowed to recover from anesthesia and cared for as appropriate for rabbits so manipulated.

The characteristics of the distribution of the drug in the intravitreal space (depot at the retina versus diffusion throughout the space) will determine the time between administration and exposure. At the appropriate time after administration, the rabbit is again anesthetized with an inhalation anesthetic or sedated with an injectable agent. The rabbit is placed in the exposure field, the eyelids are held apart by an eyelid speculum or taped open, and the exposure performed, delivering a dose of UVR that is not sufficient to induce an unacceptable response in the eye, primarily the anterior segment. The exposure field can be set up, or the rabbit positioned, to expose only one eye, with the other serving as the unirradiated control to determine any general toxic effect from the administration, versus phototoxicity. Care should be taken to ensure that any exposed skin not covered with fur is shielded from the light source during irradiation. During the exposure, a lubricating ophthalmic solution is periodically administered to the eye to ensure that the surface of the cornea does not dry out, which can lead to corneal epithelial changes, including corneal scarring, and if severe, ulceration.

The rabbit, upon recovery, should have its eyes evaluated at least daily for general external observations, including the conjunctiva, for signs of general irritation, and if warranted, including indirect ophthalmoscopy and slit-lamp evaluations. Typically, 3 days after irradiation, full evaluation of the anterior and posterior segments of the eyes is performed. The rabbit is then euthanized and the eyes enucleated and processed for histopathological evaluation for phototoxic damage.

THE PIG

The pig is a well-documented model for dermal toxicology studies [8,75]. The suitability of the pig has long been recognized for evaluation of phototoxicity, pigmentation responses, and tanning enhancement [101,104]. As with all models, handling of the pigs for either dermal, oral, or parenteral administration, UVR exposure and sample collection at relevant toxicologic endpoints are crucial for successful studies, along with appropriate UVR exposure. The size of the pigs and the specific considerations required for their handling and exposures warrant special considerations unique to this model. However, the pig provides benefits, not only in the closer anatomic relevance of the skin to humans (eg, Ref. [75]), but also a large body surface area for administration and nonterminal skin sample collections.

The use of the pig follows the same general scheme for dermal administration and UVR exposure using other species. The skin area is prepared by clipping the hair and marking the exposure sites either with indelible marker or tattoo. Suitable sedation and restraint is used to position the pig under the UVR source. Threshold UVR doses for elicitation of the endpoint to be used in the assay (erythema and/or tanning) are established to ensure that the UVR dose alone will not induce a response. The formulations are administered to the defined skin sites, without or with masking of the surrounding skin, and the skin sites are exposed to the UVR source. The reactions are evaluated as noted elsewhere. The pig also allows in-life sampling for histopathology.

Leigh et al. [69] documented good practices for the use of the pig for phototoxicity testing. Both Hanford miniature and Yucatan swine were evaluated and compared for erythema and tanning responses from UVR exposure. The positive control article 8-methoxypsoralen (8-MOP) was also evaluated in both species. Histopathological evaluation of the exposed sites demonstrated microscopic evidence of the UVR-induced damage and the enhancement of this damage by the inclusion of 8-MOP. Of particular interest in this publication is the great care taken to characterize the lamp system, and use of the observational minimal erythema dose compared with the instrumental minimal erythema dose.

The pig can also be used for the evaluation of visceral phototoxicity, especially for photodynamic agents. Surgical expertise along with controlled exposure to surgical lighting can be used to evaluate the time after administration of such agents where insufficient test material is present to cause an adverse response on the surface of the exposed thoracic or abdominal organs. Clinical observations, clinical pathology, and body weight effects, along with organ weights and histopathological evaluations, can be used to assess any potential phototoxic effects.

While the pig has the cited benefits for evaluation of phototoxic responses, the limitations of large size, relatively high cost, and large amount of test article required, as compared with the more common species (rats, mice), and from the authors' experience, limited requests for the model for regulatory use, limit the practical use of the model in standard phototoxicity testing. As a reflection of the relative lack of their use, a recent review article [75] detailing the use of the mini-pig as a model for dermal toxicity did not mention their use in phototoxicology studies. However, as noted by Jacobs [60], the pig has been used for phototoxicity evaluations in new drug applications submitted to the FDA, and the published literature may not truly reflect the extent of their current use in photosafety testing.

Photocarcinogenesis

As indicated previously, regulators recommended testing for the modification of photocarcinogenesis for select drugs and chemicals for over 3 decades, and 50 to 60 such studies have been conducted. More recently, regulatory interest in such studies has waned. Even in the first guidance on photosafety testing promulgated by the EMA [31] there was an undertone of skepticism about the clinical relevance and value of the photocarcinogenesis assay. The lack of formal validation (which is a self-fulfilling prophecy, as based on lack of resource commitment and resistance to in vivo model use, no such model will be validated) and perceived lack of mechanistic understanding of the albino hairless mouse model were noted as a concern. Furthermore, the perceived lack of established human "photocarcinogens" was considered problematic. While these concerns can be challenged scientifically, the important fact is that the EMA rarely, if ever, recommends the conduct of photocarcinogenesis studies as part of the toxicology package for drug development.

The FDA photosafety guidance document [123] had a more favorable outlook on the photocarcinogenesis animal model and nearly all of the conducted studies were driven by FDA recommendations. This guidance recognized that mouse and human skin share many of the same responses to sunlight and drugs. Despite the once favorable view of this assay by the FDA, this document listed alternatives to address the potential of a drug to enhance photocarcinogenesis including labeling (ie, description of the test findings in the package insert) without the need to conduct a study, the use of biomarker assays that would translate these markers with photocarcinogenic risk assessment, and in vitro assays. Even when drugs have been found to enhance photocarcinogenesis in the animal assay, labeling is the standard approach employed by drug developers.

Reflecting the EMA stance, ICH M3(R2) Endnote 6 includes the following statements:

> Testing for photocarcinogenicity in rodents using currently available models (eg, hairless rodents) is not considered useful in support of pharmaceutical development and generally is not recommended. If the phototoxicity assessment suggests a potential photocarcinogenic risk and an appropriate assay becomes available, the study should usually be completed before marketing and the results should be considered in the human risk assessment.

This note is also the only reference to photocarcinogenesis in the ICH S10 I.4 (1.4). While the first sentence is unequivocal, and the second is incomprehensible, it has ended the use of the photocarcinogenesis assay for safety assessment of pharmaceuticals.

The standard protocol for photocarcinogenesis safety testing has been exhaustively described [35,39–41,102,103]. While the model was designed to evaluate direct or indirect effects of small molecule test materials on photocarcinogenesis, the model can also be used to evaluate biologicals, specifically their effect on immune function and tumor surveillance [11]. And, while outside the scope of this chapter, the assay has been used to evaluate sunscreen safety [42] and the use of the assay for registration of new sunscreen agents in consumer care applications cannot be ruled out.

P.G. Unna [124] was the first to determine that repeated sunlight exposure among sailors resulted in "seaman's skin" that included histopathological lesions described as a precancerous condition. Additional early observers recognized that sunlight was an important causative agent in human skin cancer [4,26,54,111]. Within a few years, laboratory studies involving the use of animal models started to appear in the literature supporting the theory that sunlight exposure caused skin cancer. Findlay [34] reported the induction of skin tumors in mice using a mercury arc source. Similar early laboratory investigations in mice [52] and rats [98] demonstrated that animal models could be used to demonstrate UVR-induced skin tumors. These early studies were hampered by the normal hairiness of the models.

Skin tumors tended to arise either in skin with less dense hair growth (eg, ears, noses, tails, and paws) or in skin subjected to artificial depilation, and histopathological evaluation of these tumors often revealed that they were primarily sarcomas or papillomas and occasionally carcinomas [7]. Since the basic skin tumors produced in man by sunlight exposure are epidermal in origin, what was needed was an animal model that developed primarily UVR-induced carcinomas and that allowed for relatively easy light exposure to the skin. Winkelmann et al. [127] reported the production of squamous cell carcinomas on the backs of hairless mice with UVR exposure. The hairless mouse proved to be an excellent model for evaluation of UVR-induced epidermal carcinogenesis [27] and enabled researchers interested in the mechanisms of carcinogenesis to study qualitative and quantitative aspects of skin tumor development.

In the 1960s, investigations were conducted in hairless mice to evaluate the modification of UVR-induced skin tumor production by chemical entities. Initially, these investigations were limited to known chemical carcinogens (eg, coal tar and 7,12-dimethylbenz(a)anthracene) and tumor promoters (eg, croton oil and 12-O-tetradecanoyl-phorobol-13-acetate). Not surprisingly, topical administration of these kinds of chemicals or compounds often enhanced photocarcinogenesis [28,29]. These studies were useful in eliciting some mechanistic aspects of tumorigenesis, but the findings were not considered serious clinical problems because it was unlikely that people would be subjected to the appropriate combinations of sunlight and chemical, with the possible exception of industrial users (eg, oilfield workers and roofers). This lack of scientific and regulatory concern was about to change.

Epstein conducted a relatively small and simple experiment in which one group of hairless mice was topically administered a 0.3% retinoic acid cream and exposed to UVR and another group received the vehicle (cream base) plus UVR [30]. For at least some time during this study, skin tumors occurred earlier and were more prevalent in mice topically administered the retinoic acid cream, as compared with the control mice. If this finding had clinical relevance, it could be very important because retinoids, including retinoic acid (all-trans retinoic acid), were being extensively used clinically, and their usage was anticipated to continue and grow. Forbes et al. [38] undertook a series of studies involving UVR and retinoic acid and reported that topical application of retinoic acid to the skin of albino hairless mice significantly enhanced the carcinogenic effectiveness of simulated sunlight. Based on the work on retinoids and some other drugs and chemicals, the regulatory agencies became concerned about the possible clinical relevance of these experimental findings. For the next 3 decades, regulators often recommended the conduct of studies to evaluate the potential of products to modify UVR-induced skin tumor development.

The study design consists of five to eight groups of albino hairless mice (Crl:SKH1-*hr*), 36 per group per sex, with the standard study consisting of six groups. Mice are individually housed in stainless-steel cages especially designed to allow for UVR exposure of free-moving mice. The route of administration reflects the proposed clinical route, and is customarily topical, oral, or subcutaneous. Formulation administration and UVR exposure are conducted for 40 consecutive weeks. On Monday, Wednesday, and Friday of each week, formulations are administered before UVR exposure; on Tuesday and Thursday, formulations are administered after UVR exposure. The alternating regimen of formulation administration and UVR exposure addresses the possible interactive effect(s) of photolability on a test article (ie, the alternating regimen allows for detection of modification of photocarcinogenesis with test articles which are activated, deactivated, or unmodified by UVR).

Two groups in each study are only exposed to UVR and represent calibration groups and provide a bracket of responses for the UVR response and allow the comparison of the responses of the test material groups against these groups. In the standard design, one of the calibration groups and the groups administered any formulation receive a UVR dose of approximately 600 Robertson–Berger units (RBU) per week and the other calibration group receives 1200 RBU per week. For evaluation of sunscreens, the UVR dose used for the high-dose calibration group (1200 RBU per week) is used for the groups administered the formulations. 6500W xenon long arc, water-cooled burner filtered with a 1mm Schott WG 320 doped glass filter, is the UVR source (Fig. 22.5). Each rack is monitored by a customized radiometry system, which records both intensity and UVR dose in RBU, the historical engineering unit used for this assay, as described in the dosimetry section of this chapter.

Clinical observations, including evaluation of nontumor skin responses, are performed at least weekly and body weights are recorded weekly. Skin tumor data are recorded weekly using a specially designed computer system that captures the anatomical position, size, and fate of each tumor. Mice are removed from the study when specified tumor size criteria are achieved. At the end of 52weeks, all surviving mice are euthanized. Necropsies are performed on all mice. No histopathological evaluation of the tumors is performed.

Clinical observations, nontumor skin reactions, body weight data, and necropsy observations are analyzed and reported according to common toxicology procedures. Skin tumor data are evaluated with a computer program designed to tabulate, plot, and statistically analyze the data (ie, the RoeLee system, P.N. Lee Statistics, and Computing Ltd, Sutton, United Kingdom). Separate calculations are performed for each of the following size-based acceptance criteria:

all observed tumors
tumors at least 1 mm in maximum planar diameter
tumors at least 2 mm in maximum planar diameter
tumors at least 4 mm in maximum planar diameter

In reporting results, the following descriptive parameters are used.

1. "Median Onset" or "Unbiased Median Week to Tumor": The time at which one-half of the members of the groups have acquired one or more qualifying tumors.
2. "Mortality-free Prevalence": The proportion of mice in a group exhibiting one or more qualifying tumors, as a function of time, and adjusted for the effects of competing mortality. This descriptor is the complementary probability to the Kaplan–Meier "probability of survival without a tumor" and is derived from calculations of the Kaplan–Meier type [61].
3. "Tumor Yield": The number of tumors present, divided by the number of surviving mice (ie, average number of tumors per mouse).
4. Tumor Potency Factor: The UVR calibration groups provide a dynamic range of the skin tumor response, permitting accurate interpolation and reasonable extrapolation for data from the groups also receiving the formulations. Deviations from a "zero-effect" level in tumor response can be expressed in terms of a "tumor potency factor" (ie, expressed as the mathematic equivalent of changing the UVR dose by a specified fraction).

Peto analyses determine whether differences in time to tumor between treatment groups are statistically significant [95]. If significant reductions in time to tumor are found between the groups administered formulations and the UVR calibration group exposed to the equivalent dose of simulated sunlight, formulation administration can be said to enhance photocarcinogenesis. Calculation of the tumor potency factor can provide an estimate of the magnitude of the modification of photocarcinogenesis.

References

[1] Adamse P, Brintz SJ. Spectral quality of two fluorescent sources during long-term use. Photochem Photobiol 1992;56:641–4.
[2] Bauer D, Averett LA, De Smedt A, Kleinman MH, Muster W, Petterson BA, Robles C. Standardized UV-vis spectra as a foundation for a threshold-based, integrated photosafety evaluation. Regul Toxicol Pharmacol 2014;68:70–5.
[3] Beasley DG, Beard J, Stanfield JW, Roberts LK. Evaluation of an economical sunlamp that emits a near solar UV power spectrum for conducting photoimmunological and sunscreen immune protection studies. Photochem Photobiol 1996;64:303–9.
[4] Bellini A. Della'influenza degli agenti fisici e piu particolaramente della luce nella etiologia dell epithelioma cutaneo. Gior Ital di Mal Ven e Pelle 1909;50:732.
[5] Berger D, Robertson DF, Davies RE, Urbach F. Field measurements of biologically effective UV radiation. Appendix D. In: Nachtwey DS, editor. Impacts of climatic change on the biosphere (CIAP monograph 5, Part 1-Ultraviolet radiation effects, Chapters 1 through 3). 1975. DOT document available through the National Technical Information Service, Springfield, VA 2215, pp 2–235 through 2–264.
[6] Berger DS. The sunburning ultraviolet meter: design and performance. Photochem Photobiol 1976;24:587–93.
[7] Blum HF. Sunlight and cancer of the skin. J Natl Cancer Inst 1940;1:397–421.
[8] Bode G, Clausing P, Gervais F, Loegsted J, Luft J, Nogues V, Sims J. The utility of the minipig as an animal model in regulatory toxicology. J Pharmacol Toxicol Methods 2010;62:196–220.
[9] Borenfreund E, Puerner JA. Toxicity determined in vitro by morphological alterations and neutral red absorption. Toxicol Lett 1985;24:119–24.
[10] Boudon SM, Plappert-Heibig U, Odermatt A, Bauer D. Characterization of vemurafenib phototoxicity in a mouse model. Toxicol Sci 2013. http://dx.doi.org/10.1093/toxsci/kft237.
[11] Bracken W, Learn D, Blaich G, Veldman T. Subcutaneous Administration Study to determine the influence of an antimouse IL-12/IL-23p40 antibody on photocarcinogenesis in hairless mice. Poster presented at the 50th Annual Meeting of the Society of Toxicology, 2011.
[12] Buonanno M, Randers-Pehrson G, Bigelow AW, Trivedi S, Lowy FD, Spotnitz HM, Hammer SM, Brenner DJ. 207-nm UV light – a promising tool for safe low-cost reduction of surgical site infections. I: In vitro studies. PLoS One 2013;8(10):e76968. http://dx.doi.org/10.1371/journal.pone.0076968.
[13] Ceridono M, Siviglia E, Bauer D, Barroso J, Alepée N, Corvi R, De Smedt A, Fellows MD, Gibbs NK, Heisler E, Jacobs A, Jirova D, Jones D, Kandárová H, Kasper P, Akunda JK, Krul C, Learn D, Liebsch M, Lynch AM, Muster W, Nakamura K, Nash JF, Pfannenbecker U, Phillips G, Robles C, Rogiers V, Van de Water F, Wändel Liminoga U, Vohr H, Wattrelos O, Woods J, Zuang V, Kreysa J, Wilcox P. The 3T3 neutral red uptake phototoxicity test: practical experience and implications for phototoxicity testing – the report of an ECVAM-EFPIA workshop. Regul Toxicol Pharmacol 2012;63:480–8.
[14] Coblentz WW. Erythemal and radiometric comparisons of the ultraviolet emitted by various sources as a basis for specification of the unit dosage intensity. In: Proceedings of the Second International Congress of the Comité Internationale de la Lumière. 1932. p. 322–44.
[15] Cole CA, Davies RE, Forbes PD, D'Alosio LC. Comparison of action spectra for cutaneous responses to ultraviolet radiation: man and albino hairless mouse. Photochem Photobiol 1983;37:623–31.
[16] Commission Internationale de l'Eclairage. Erythema reference action spectrum and standard erythema dose. Publication CIE S 007/e, Vienna, Austria. 1997.
[17] Commission Internationale de l'Eclairage. Standardized protocols for photocarcinogenesis safety testing. Publication 138/3 TC-6–34. Vienna, Austria. 2000.
[18] Commission Regulation (EU) No 283/2013 of 1 March 2013 setting out the data requirements for active substances, in accordance with Regulation (EC) No 1107/2009 of the European Parliament and of the Council concerning the placing of plant protection products on the market. 2013. http://eur-lex.europa.eu/legal-content/EN/TXT/PDF.
[19] Coston T, Learn D, Sambuco C, Forbes D, Johannsen S, Guenther C. A 13-week nonclinical study in hairless mice to characterize the biomarker responses of high doses of ultraviolet radiation (UVR) and 8-methoxypsoralen (8-MOP). Int J Toxicol 2012;31:114.

[20] Di Menno I, Moriconi ML, Di Menno M, Casale GR, Siani AM. Spectral ultraviolet measurements by a multichannel monitor and a brewer spectroradiometer: a field study. Radiat Prot Dosim 2002;102:259–63.

[21] di Sarra A, Disterhoft P, DeLuisi J. On the importance of spectral responsivity of Robertson-Berger-type ultraviolet radiometers for long-term observations. Photochem Photobiol 2002;76:64–72.

[22] Diffey BL. The calculation of the spectral distribution of natural ultraviolet radiation under clear day condition. Phys Med Biol 1977;22:309–16.

[23] Diffey BL. Solar ultraviolet radiation effects on biological systems. Rev Phys Med Biol 1991;36:299–328.

[24] Directive 2010/63/EU of the European Parliament and of the Council of 22 September 2010 on the protection of animals used in for scientific purposes. Off J Eur Union October 20, 2010;L 276:33–79.

[25] Draize JH, Woodard G, Calvery HO. Methods for the study of irritation and toxicity of substances applied topically to the skin and mucous membranes. J Pharmacol Exp Ther 1944;82:377–90.

[26] Dubreuilh W. Des hyperkeratoses circonscrites. Ann de dermat 1896;7:1158.

[27] Epstein JH, Fukuyama K, Dobson RL. Ultraviolet light carcinogenesis. In: Urbach F, editor. The biologic effects of ultraviolet radiation. London: Pergamon Press; 1969. p. 551–68.

[28] Epstein JH. Comparison of the carcinogenic and cocarcinogenic effects of ultraviolet light on hairless mice. J Natl Cancer Inst 1965;34:741–5.

[29] Epstein JH. Chemicals and photocarcinogenesis. Australas J Dermatol 1977;18:57.

[30] Epstein JH. Effects of retinoids on ultraviolet-induced carcinogenesis. J Invest Dermatol 1981;77:144–6.

[31] European Agency for the Evaluation of Medicinal Products. Note for guidance on photosafety testing. Committee for Proprietary Medicinal Products. CPMP/SWP/398/01; June 27, 2002.

[32] European Agency for the Evaluation of Medicinal Products. Concept paper on the need for revision of the note for guidance on photosafety testing. CPMP/SWP/398/01. January 24, 2008.

[33] European Medicines Agency. Questions and answers on the 'Note for guidance of photosafety testing'. Committee for Proprietary Medicinal Products. EMA/CHMP/SWP/336670/2010; March 17, 2011.

[34] Findlay GM. Ultra-violet light and skin cancer. Lancet 1928;215:1070.

[35] Forbes PD, Sambuco CP. Assays for photocarcinogenesis: relevance of animal models. Int J Toxicol 1998;17:577–88.

[36] Forbes PD, Davies RE, Urbach F. Phototoxicity and photocarcinogenesis: comparative effects of anthracene and 8-methoxypsoralen in the skin of mice. Food Chem Toxicol 1976;14:303–6.

[37] Forbes PD, Urbach F, Davies RE. Phototoxicity testing of fragrance materials. Food Cosmet Toxicol 1977;15:55–60.

[38] Forbes PD, Urbach F, Davies RE. Enhancement of experimental photocarcinogenesis by topical retinoic acid. Cancer Lett 1979;7:85–90.

[39] Forbes PD, Davies RE, Sambuco CP. Drug products and photocarcinogenesis. In: Riklis E, editor. Photobiology: the science and its applications. New York: Plenum Press; 1991. p. 663–9.

[40] Forbes PD, Sambuco CP, Davies RE. Photocarcinogenesis safety testing. J Am Coll Toxicol 1993;12:417–24.

[41] Forbes PD, Beer JZ, Black HS, Cesarini J-P, Cole CP, Davies RE, Davitt JM, deGruijl F, Epstein J, Foutanier A, Green A, Koval T, Ley RD, Mascotto R, Morison W, Osterberg R, Sliney D, Urbach F, van der Leun J, Young AR. Standardized protocols for photocarcinogenesis safety testing. Front Biosci 2003;8:d848–854.

[42] Fourtanier A, Labat-Robert J, Kern P, Berrebi C, Gracia AM, Boyer B. *In vivo* evaluation of photoprotection against chronic ultraviolet-A irradiation by a new sunscreen Mexoryl® SX*. Photochem Photobiol 1992;55:549–60.

[43] Gasparro FP, Brown DB. Photobiology 102: UV sources and dosimetry – the proper use and measurement of UVR as a reagent. J Invest Dermatol 2000;114:613–5.

[44] Gerberick GF, Ryan CA. Contact photoallergy testing of sunscreens in guinea pigs. Contact Dermatitis 1989;20:251–9.

[45] Gerberick GF, Ryan CA. Use of UVA and UVB to induce and elicit contact photoallergy in the mouse. Photodermatol Photoimmunol Photomed 1990;7:13–9.

[46] Gerberick GF, Ryan CA. A predictive mouse ear-swelling model for investigating topical photoallergy. Food Chem Toxic 1990;28:361–8.

[47] Gocke E, Müller L, Guzzie PJ, Brendler-Schwaab S, Bulera S, Chignel CF, Henderson LM, Jacobs A, Murli H, Snyder RD, Tanaka N. Considerations on photochemical genotoxicity: report of the international workshop on genotoxicity test procedures working group. Environ Mol Mutagen 2000;35:173–84.

[48] Green AES, Miller JH. Measures of biologically effective radiation in the 280–340 nm region. In: Nachtwey DS, editor. Impacts of climatic change on the biosphere (CIAP monograph 5, Part 1-ultraviolet radiation effects, Chapters 1 through 3)1975. DOT document available through the National Technical Information Service, Springfield, VA 2215, pp. 2–60 through 2–78.

[49] Hamanaka H, Mizutani H, Asahig K, Shimizu M. Melanocyte melanin augments sparfloxacin-induced phototoxicity. J Dermatol Sci 1999;21:27–33.

[50] Hardcastle III HK. The making of reference solar spectral power distribution. SunSpots, Atlas Material Testing Product and Technology News Summer 2001;31(65):4–8.

[51] Henry B, Foti C, Alsante K. Can light absorption and photostability data be used to assess the photosafety risks in patients for a new drug molecule? J Photochem Photobiol B 2009;96:57–62.

[52] Herlitz CW, Jundell I, Wahlgren F. Durch Ultraviolettbestrahlung erzeugte maligne Neubildungen bei weissen. Acta Paediat 1931;10:321.

[53] Herman JR, McKenzie RL, Diaz SB, Kerr JB, Seckmeyer G. Surface ultraviolet radiation. In: Scientific assessment of ozone depletion 1998: Chapter 9, World Meteorological Organization. 1999. Global Ozone Research and Monitoring Project – Report No. 37, UNEP, P.O. Box 30552, Nairobi, Kenya.

[54] Hyde JN. On the influence of light on the production of skin cancer. Am J Med Sci 1906;132:1.

[55] ICH Harmonised Tripartite Guideline. Photosafety evaluation of pharmaceuticals. S10. Step 4. November 13, 2013.

[56] ICH Harmonised Tripartite Guideline. Photosafety evaluation of pharmaceuticals. S10. Step 5, vol. 80, No. 17. United States Federal Register; March 26, 2015. p. 4282–3. Docket No. FDA/2013/D/0068.

[57] ICH Harmonised Tripartite Guideline. Guidance on nonclinical safety studies for the conduct of human clinical trials and marketing authorization for pharmaceuticals M3(R2). Note for guidance on nonclinical safety studies for the conduct of human clinical trials and marketing authorization for pharmaceuticals. Step 5, vol. 75, No 13. United States Federal Register; January 21, 2010. p. 3471. Docket No. FDA/2008/D/0470.

[58] ICH Harmonized Tripartate Guideline. Nonclinical evaluation for anticancer pharmaceuticals. S9. Step 5, vol. 75, No.44. Federal Register; March 08, 2010. p. 10487. Docket No. FDA/2009/D/0006.

[59] Jackman SM, Coston TS, Baker JF, Rubin LF, Learn DB, Hoberman AM. Cutaneous, ophthalmologic and histopathologic phototoxicity historical control data in the Long-Evans rat. Int J Toxicol 2011;30:101.

[60] Jacobs A. Use of nontraditional animals for evaluation of pharmaceutical products. Expert Opin Drug Metab Toxicol 2006;2:345–9.

[61] Kaplan EL, Meir P. Nonparametric estimation from incomplete observations. J Am Stat Assoc 1958;53:457–81.

[62] Kinsey VE. Spectral transmission of the eye to ultraviolet radiation. Arch Ophthalmol 1948;39:508–13.

[63] Klienman MH, Smith MD, Kurali E, Kleinpeter S, Jiang K, Zhang Y, Kennedy-Gabb SA, Lynch AM, Geddes CD. An evaluation of chemical photoreactivity and the relationship to phototoxicity. Regul Toxicol Pharmacol 2010;58:224–32.

[64] Kostkowski HJ. Reliable spectroradiometry. Spectroradiometry Consulting; 1997. P.O. Box 2747, La Plata, Maryland, 20646–2747, ISBN:0-9657713-0-X.

[65] Lambert LA, Wamer WG, Kornhauser A. Animal models for phototoxicity testing. Toxicol Methods 1996;6:99–114.

[66] Learn DB, Beasley DG, Giddens LD, Beard J, Stanfield JW, Roberts LK. Minimum doses of ultraviolet radiation required to induce murine skin edema and immunosuppression are different and depend on the ultraviolet emission spectrum of the source. Photochem Photobiol 1995;62:1066–75.

[67] Learn D, Dougherty M, Jackman S, Arocena M, Hoberman A. Relative sensitivity of preclinical phototoxicity test systems to UVR exposure and the effect of phototoxins on this response. Int J Toxicol 2013;32:73.

[68] Lee F, Van Teylingen C. Xenon arc lamp. SunSpots, Atlas Material Testing Product and Technology News Fall 2000;30(63):9–10.

[69] Leigh H, Forbes PD, Lawson C, Kim DY, White D, Brown LD, Wehmeier DR, Lui J, Bouchard GF. Miniature swing model of phototoxicity testing. Photodermatol Photoimmunol Photomed 2012;28(34):41.

[70] Lelievre D, Justine P, Christiaens F, Bonaventure N, Coutet J, Marrot L, Tinous-Tessonneaud E, Cotovio J. The EpiSkin phototoxicity assay (EPA): development of an *in vitro* tiered strategy to predict phototoxic potential. Toxicol In Vitro 2007;21:977–95.

[71] Liebsch M, True D, Barrabas C, Speilmann T, Gerberick GF, Cruse L, Diembeck W, Pfannenbecker U, Spicker J, Holzhütter HG, Brantom T, Aspin P, Sothee J. Prevalidation of the EpiDerm phototoxicity test. In: Clark D, Liasansky S, Macmillan R, editors. Alternatives to animal testing II: Proceedings of the second international scientific conference organized by the European Cosmetic Industry. Brussels (Belgium); Newbury (UK): CPL Press; 1999. p. 160–6.

[72] Luckiesh M. Applications of germicidal, erythemal and infrared energy. New York (NY, USA): D. Van Nostrand Co., Inc.; 1946.

[73] Lynch AM, Wilcox P. Review of the performance of the 3T3 NRU in vitro phototoxicity assay in the pharmaceutical industry. Exp Toxicol Pathol 2011;63:209–14.

[74] Lynch AM, Robinson SA, Wilcox P, Smith MD, Kleinman M, Jiang K, Rees RW. Cyclohexamide and disulfoton are positive in the photoclastogenicity assay but do not absorb UV irradiation: another example of pseudophotoclastogenicity? Mutagenesis 2008;23:111–8.

[75] Makin A, Mortensen JT, Brock WJ. Dermal toxicity studies. Skin architecture, metabolism, penetration and toxicological and pharmacological methods. In: McAnaulty PA, Dylan AD, Makin A, Mortensen JT, Brock WJ, Ganderup N-C, Hastings KL, editors. The Minipig in Biomedical Research. Boca Raton; London; New York: CRC Press; 2012. p. 185–209.

[76] Matthes R, Sliney D, editors. Measurements of optical radiation hazards. A reference book based on presentations given by health and safety experts on optical radiation hazards. International Commission on Non-ionizing Radiation Protection; 1998.

[77] Miyauchi H, Horio T. A new animal model for contact dermatitis: the hairless guinea pig. J Dermatol 1992;19:140–5.

[78] Morikawa F, Nakayama Y, Fukuda M, Hamano M, Yokoyama Y, Nagura T, Ishihara M, Toda K. Techniques for evaluation of phototoxicity and photoallergy in laboratory animals and man. In: Fitzpatrick TB, editor. Sunlight and man. Normal and abnormal photobiologic responses. Tokyo: University of Tokyo Press; 1974. p. 529–57.

[79] Mudry MCV, Kronenberg S, Komatso S, Aguirre G. Blinded by the light: retinal phototoxicity in the context of safety studies. Toxicol Pathol 2013;41:813–25.

[80] Müller L, Gocke E. The rise and fall of photomutagenesis. Mutat Res 2013;752:67–71.

[81] Nachtwey DS. General aspects of dosimetry. In: Nachtwey DS, editor. Impacts of climatic change on the biosphere (CIAP monograph 5, Part 1-Ultraviolet radiation effects, Chapters 1 through 3). 1975. DOT document available through the National Technical Information Service, Springfield, VA 2215, pp. ss2–49 through 2–60.

[82] NASA Panel for Data Evaluation. Chemical kinetics and photochemical data for use in atmospheric studies. JPL Publications 02-25. Evaluation Number 14. February 1, 2003.

[83] NASA. Surface ultraviolet radiation levels have increased from 1979 to 1992. Dow Jones Publications Library; January 08, 1996.

[84] OECD Guideline for Testing of Chemicals. Draft proposal of a new guideline. Acute dermal photoirritation screening test. TGP951. February 1995.

[85] OECD Guideline for the Testing of Chemicals. UV-VIS Absorption Spectra (Spectrophotometric Method) No.101. 1981.

[86] OECD Guideline for the Testing of Chemicals. Skin Sensitization. No. 406. 1992.

[87] OECD Guideline for the Testing of Chemicals. In Vitro 3T3 NRU Phototoxicity Test. No. 432. 2004.

[88] OECD Guideline for the Testing of Chemicals. Skin Sensitization: Local Lymph Node Assay. No. 429. 2010.

[89] OECD Guidelines for the Testing of Chemicals. Acute Dermal Irritation/Corrosion. No. 404. 2002.

[90] Onoue S, Igarashi N, Yamada S, Tsuda Y. High throughput reactive oxygen species (ROS) assay: an enabling technology for screening of phototoxic potential of pharmaceutical agents. J Pharm Biomed Anal 2008;46:187–93.

[91] Onoue S, Ochi M, Gandy G, Seto S, Igarashi N, Tamauchi Y, Yamada S. High-throughput screening system for identifying phototoxic potential of drug candidates based on derivatives of reactive oxygen species. Pharm Res 2010;27:1610–9.

[92] Onoue S, Hosoi K, Wakuri S, Iwase Y, Yamamoto T, Matsuoka N, Nakamura K, Toda T, Takagi H, Osaki N, Matusmoto Y, Kawakami S, Seto Y, Kato M, Yamata S, Ohno Y, Kojima H. Establishment and intra-/inter-laboratory validation of a standard protocol of reactive oxygen species assay for chemical photosafety evaluation. J Appl Toxicol 2012. http://dx.doi.org/10.1002/jat2776.

[93] Palmer J. Radiometry and photometry FAQ; Research Professor; Optical Sciences Center. Tucson (AZ): University of Arizona; www.optics.arizona.edu/Palmer.

[94] Peters B, Holzhütter HG. In vitro phototoxicity testing: development and validation of a new concentration response analysis software and biostatistical analyses related to the use of various prediction models. ATLA 2002;30:415–32.

[95] Peto R, Pike MC, Day NE, Gray RG, Lee PN, Parish S, Peto J, Richards S, Wahrendorf J. Guidelines for simple, sensitive significance tests for carcinogenic effects in long-term animal experiments. IARC Monogr 1980;(Suppl. 2):311–426. Long-term and short-term screening assays for carcinogenesis: A critical appraisal. Annex.

[96] Regulation (EC) No 1907/2006 of the European Parliament and of the Council of 18 December 2006 concerning the Registration, Evaluation, Authorisation and Restriction of Chemicals (REACH), establishing a European Chemicals Agency, amending Directive 1999/45/EC and repealing Council Regulation (EEC) No 793/93 and Commission Regulation (EC) No 1488/94 as well as Council Directive 76/769/EEC and Commission Directives 91/155/EEC, 93/67/EEC, 93/105/EC and 2000/21/EC. 2006.

[97] Robertson DF. The sunburn unit for comparison of erythemal effectiveness. In: Nachtwey DS, editor. Impacts of climatic change on the biosphere (CIAP Monograph 5, Part 1-Ultraviolet radiation effects, Chapters 1 through 3). 1975. DOT document available through the National Technical Information Service, Springfield, VA Appendix B, pp 2–202 through 2–212.

[98] Roffo AH. Cancer y sol. Bol Inst de med exper para estud y trat d cancer 1933;10:417.

[99] Ronto GY, Berces A, Grof P, Fekete A, Kerekgyarto T, Gaspar S, Stick C. Monitoring of environmental UV radiation by biological dosimeters. Adv Space Res 2001;26:2021–8.

[100] Sambuco CP, Forbes PD. Quantitative assessment of phototoxicity in the skin of hairless mice. Food Chem Toxic 1984;22: 233–6.

[101] Sambuco CP, Cole CA, Forbes PD, Urbach F. Photobiologic effects of cosmetic tanning enhancers in miniature pigs. In: Fitzpatrick TB, Forlot P, Mathak MA, Urbach F, editors. Psoralens: Past, present and future of photochemoprotection and other biological activities. Paris: John Libbey Eurotext; 1989. p. 300–405.

[102] Sambuco CP, Davies RE, Forbes PD, Hoberman AM. Photocarcinogenesis and consumer product testing: technical aspects. Toxicol Methods 1991:75–83.

[103] Sambuco CP, Forbes PD, Davies RE, Learn DB, D'Alosio LC, Arocena M, Hoberman AM. Photocarcinogenesis: measuring the reproducibility of a biologic response to ultraviolet radiation exposure in mice. Front Biosci 2003;8:a26–33.

[104] Sambuco CP. Miniature swine as an animal model in photodermatology: factors influencing sunburn cell formation. Photodermatology 1985;2:144–50.

[105] Sams WM, Epstein JH. The experimental production of drug phototoxicity in guinea pigs. J Invest Dermatol 1967;48:89–94.

[106] Scholes EW, Basketter DA, Lovell WW, Sarll AE, Pendlington RU. The identification of photoallergic potential in the local lymph node assay. Photodermatol Photoimmunol Photomed 1991;8:249–54.

[107] Schümann J, Boudon S, Ulrich P, Loll N, Garcia D, Schaffner R, Streich J, Kittel B, Bauer D. Integrated preclinical photosafety testing strategy for systemically applied pharmaceuticals. Toxicol Sci 2014. http://dx.doi.org/10.1093./toxsci/kfu026.

[108] Schwartz M, Learn DB, Arocena M, Brower A, Brennan M, Hoberman AM. The in vitro neutral red update phototoxicity test: historical control data demonstrate reproducibility with multiple test substances and different irradiation conditions. Int J Toxicol 2012;31:101.

[109] Scott KP. Light: its relevance, characterization, and measurement in weathering tests. SunSpots, Atlas Material Testing Product and Technology News Spring 2003;33(69):5–22.

[110] Severon B. Environmental testing – solar radiation simulation test. SunSpots, Atlas Material Testing Product and Technology News Winter 2002;32(67):7–11.

[111] Shield M. A remarkable case of multiple growths of the skin caused by exposure to the sun. Lancet 1899;1:22.

[112] Sliney DH. Measuring and quantifying ultraviolet radiation exposures. In: Marzulli FN, Maibach HL, editors. Dermatotoxicology. 5th ed. Washington (DC): Taylor and Francis; 1996. p. 177–88.

[113] Sliney DH. How light reaches the eye and its components. Int J Toxicol 2002;21:501–9.

[114] Sliney DH. Radiometric quantities and units used in photobiology and photochemistry: Recommendations of the Commission Internationale de l'Eclairage (International Commission on Illumination). Photochem Photobiol 2007;83:425–32.

[115] Spielmann H, Balls M, Brand M, Döring B, Holzhütter H-G, Kalweit S, Klecak G, Eplattenier HL, Liebsch M, Lovell WW, Mauer T, Pfanenbecker U, Potthast JM, de Silva O, Steiling W, Willshaw A. EEC/COLIPA project on in vitro phototoxicity testing: first results obtained with a BALB/C 3T3 cell phototoxicity assay. Toxicol In Vitro 1994;8:793–6.

[116] Spielmann H, Balls M, Dupuis J, Pape WJ, Pechovitch G, de Silva O, Holzhütter H-G, Clothier R, Desolle P, Gerberick F, Liebsch M, Lovell WW, Mauer T, Pfannenbecker U, Potthast JM, Csato M, Dladowski D, Steiling W, Brantom P. The international EU/COLIPA in vitro phototoxicity validation study: results of phase II (blind trial). Part 1: The 3T3 NRU phototoxicity test. Toxicol In Vitro 1998;12:305–27.

[117] Suiki H, el Gammal C, Kudoh K, Kligman AM. Hairless guinea pig skin: anatomical basis for studies in cutaneous biology. Eur J Dermatol 2000;10:357–84.

[118] Thackaberry EA, Farman C, Bantsheev V, Schuetz C, Baker JF, Brown MH, Learn DB. Intravitreal administration of known phototoxicants in the rabbit fails to produce phototoxicity: implications for phototoxicity testing of intravitreally administered small molecule therapeutics. Cutan Ocul Toxicol November 06, 2014. http://dx.doi.org/10.3109/15569527.2014.961070.

[119] Tita B, Leone MG, Casini ML, Corubolo C, Bordi F, Guidolin D, Fumagalli E, Romanelli L, Mattioli F, Feher J, Saso L. Corneal toxicity of xylazine with clonidine, in combination with ketamine, in the rat. Ophthalmic Res 2001;33:345–52.

[120] Turner PV, Albassam MA. Susceptibility of rats to corneal lesions after injectable anesthesia. Comp Med 2005;55:175–82.

[121] Ulrich P, Streich J, Suter W. Intra-laboratory validation of alternative endpoints in the murine local lymph node assay for the identification of contact allergic potential: primary ear skin irritation and ear-draining lymph node hyperplasia induced by topical chemicals. Regul Toxicol 2001;74:733–44.

[122] United Stated Department of Health and Human Services, Food and Drug Administration. Final monograph Title 21 Food and Drugs, Chapter 1, Subchapter D, Drugs for human use, Part 352, Sunscreen drug products for over-the-counter use, Subpart D. Testing procedures, subparts 352.71 and 352.72.

[123] United States Department of Health and Human Services, Food and Drug Administration, (CDER). The guidance on photosafety testing, vol. 68, No. 88. United States Federal Register; 2003. p. 24487. FR Doc. 03–11216, Docket No. 99D–5435.

[124] Unna PG. Die Histopathologie der Hautkrankheitin. Berlin: Hirschwald; 1894.

[125] Urbach F, Forbes PD. The historical basis of the MED as a measure of skin sensitivity to ultraviolet radiation. In: Hönigsmann H, editor. Landmarks in photobiology. Proceedings of the 12th International Congress on Photobiology. Milan: OEMF; 1998. p. 303–7.

[126] Wengraitis S, Benedetta D, Sliney DH. Intercomparison of effective erythemal irradiance measurements from two types of broad-band instruments during June 1995. Photochem Photobiol 1998;68:179–82.

[127] Winkelmann RK, Baldes EJ, Zollman PE. Squamous cell tumors induced in hairless mice with ultraviolet light. J Invest Dermatol 1960;34:131–8.

NONCLINICAL DEVELOPMENT OF MONOCLONAL ANTIBODIES, STEM CELLS, ONCOGENIC AND NON-ONCOGENIC DRUGS, OLIGONUCLEOTIDES, AND VACCINES

23

Preclinical Development of Monoclonal Antibodies

K.B. Meyer-Tamaki

INTRODUCTION

The use of mAbs as therapeutics has provided patients with targeted and effective medicines to treat numerous diseases. Currently 31 mAbs are approved by the US FDA, and five of these mAbs, infliximab (Remicade), rituximab (Rituxan), trastuzumab (Herceptin), bevacizumab (Avastin), and adalimumab (Humira), generated sales of over $4 billion in 2008, and global sales for the entire sector surpassed $30 billion in sales that year [2].

As knowledge and experience in the field of mAbs has grown, the biopharmaceutical industry has greatly accelerated its pursuit of therapeutic mAb products. Presently over 250 mAbs are in various stages of clinical development [3]. Of the product candidates in the pipelines of 27 biotechnology companies, about 88%

(114 out of 130) are in early Phases I and II clinical development. More than half (55%) are intended for the treatment of cancer, while 32% target immunological and inflammatory disorders, and 13% are in development for treating infectious diseases, cardiovascular indications, and other illnesses. There has been a relatively high success rate (23%) for mAb development, with notable success in immunological and inflammatory indication pursuits (24%) and cancer indications (14%) [3]. In contrast, the overall success rates for new chemical entities (NCEs) as a whole and for NCEs for oncology are reported to be 11% and 5%, respectively [4]. The current FDA-approved mAbs are summarized in Table 23.1.

As this field has evolved and matured, so has the practice of nonclinical safety evaluation supporting their clinical development. The nonclinical development of mAbs is distinct from that of small-molecule therapeutics, with a greater focus on selecting the appropriate species for testing, species that show pharmacological activity with the therapeutic mAb. Guidance documents from international and national regulatory authorities have set the stage for the philosophy and principles behind nonclinical safety evaluation, emphasizing that a case-by-case approach is necessary for mAb development. This case-by-case approach takes into account the disciplines of pharmacology, pharmacokinetics, and toxicology. Following a brief introduction to antibody history, structure, and function, this chapter will summarize the general principles and practice of nonclinical safety evaluation of therapeutic mAbs.

HISTORY OF ANTIBODY THERAPEUTICS: THE DISCOVERY OF SERUM THERAPY

The concept of using antibodies to treat disease originated in the late 1800s, during the great expansion of knowledge in the field of bacteriology, when the utility of serum antitoxins to target infectious agents was beginning to be elucidated. In 1882, Robert Koch assembled a team of researchers in Berlin, including Paul Ehrlich, Emil von Behring, Erich Wernicke, and Shibasaburo Kitasato. All would make significant contributions to the early stages of antibody-based therapy (reviewed in Refs. [2,5]). Berlin was the center of bacteriology in Germany, similar to France under the guidance of Louis Pasteur.

In 1901, Behring was awarded the first Nobel Prize for his work on serum therapy and its uses to treat diphtheria. This work, conducted with Kitasato, was based on observations of immunity to diphtheria and tetanus infection in rats. They discovered that

substances in the blood, referred to as antitoxins, were able to neutralize toxins produced by these infectious organisms. Antitoxin produced in one animal was capable of protecting another animal from infection, and could cure an animal actually showing symptoms of diphtheria [6,7]. Similar observations were made with anthrax infection in rats, demonstrating the breadth of the principle.

In 1892, prior to the availability of antidiphtheria serum therapy, approximately 50,000 children died of diphtheria in Germany, and lethality exceeded 50% [2,6]. Behring and Ehrlich worked together to conduct experiments that generated a high-quality, standardized antidiphtheria serum in dairy cattle. Their collaboration with the pharmaceutical manufacturer Farbwerke Hoechst provided seven pediatric wards in Berlin hospitals with a vast amount (75,225 vials) of standardized serum [6]. Roux followed Behring's methods to produce antidiphtheria serum in Paris, and this decreased mortality in Paris from 52% to 25% [8]. Behring used the funds from his Nobel Prize to seed a new company in 1904, which still exists today as Novartis (Chiron) Behring, a vaccine manufacturer, still located on Emil von Behring Strasse in Marburg, Germany [6].

In 1908, Ehrlich was awarded the Nobel Prize in Physiology and Medicine for his work that set the foundation for the concept of a magic bullet for treating disease. Ehrlich demonstrated that the toxin-antitoxin reaction was a chemical reaction, accelerated by heat and diminished by cold. He extended this concept to chemical substances, hypothesizing that chemicals, like antitoxins, must have certain affinities for pathogenic organisms. Chemicals thus could serve as magic bullets, heading straight to the organisms at which they were aimed [9]. His work with arsenical compounds targeting treating syphilis supported this concept. Today, with the advent of mAbs, the specificity of the magic bullet concept has been realized.

Serum therapy was not without its challenges, and patients developed fevers, chills, anaphylaxis, and serum sickness, characterized by malaise, rash, fever, and arthralgias (reviewed in Ref. [10]). Techniques to purify the serum improved, but foreign polyclonal Abs continued to induce significant immune responses in humans. With the discovery and development of antibiotics in the early 1900s, the focus on serum therapy diminished.

ANTIBODY STRUCTURE AND FUNCTION

Antibodies are heavy (~150 kDa) globular plasma proteins that belong to the immunoglobulin superfamily and function to identify and neutralize foreign

TABLE 23.1 Summary of FDA-Approved Therapeutic Monoclonal Antibodies

Product Trade Name (Generic Name)	Target Description	mAb Isotype	Indication	AntiDrug Antibodies[a]	Date Approved
THERAPEUTIC AGENTS					
Cyramza (ramucirumab)	Human vascular endothelial growth factor receptor 2 antagonist	IgG1	Gastric cancer, as a single agent, or in combination with paclitaxel, is indicated for the treatment of patients with advanced or metastatic, gastric, or gastroesophageal junction adenocarcinoma, with disease progression on or after prior fluoropyrimidine or platinum-containing chemotherapy Nonsmall cell lung cancer, in combination with docetaxel, is indicated for the treatment of patients with metastatic nonsmall cell lung cancer with disease progression on or after platinum-based chemotherapy; patients with EGFR or ALK genomic tumor aberrations should have disease progression on FDA-approved therapy prior to receiving Cyramza Colorectal cancer, in combination with FOLFIRI, is indicated for treatment of patients with metastatic colorectal cancer with disease progression on or after prior therapy with bevacizumab, oxaliplatin and a fluoropyrimidine	Yes	2014
Sylvant (siltuximab)	Human IL-6	Human-mouse chimeric IgG1	Treatment of patients with multicentric Castleman's disease who are human HIV negative and human Herpes Virus-8 negative	Yes	2014
Entyvio (vedolizumab)	α4β7 integrin	IgG1	Adult patients with moderately to severe ulcerative colitis or Crohn's disease who have had an inadequate response with, lost response to or were intolerant to a TNF blocker or immunomodulator, or had an inadequate response to or demonstrated dependence on corticosteroids	Yes	2014
Keytruda (pembrolizumab)	Human programmed cell death receptor (PD-1)	IgG4	Treatment of patients with unresectable or metastatic melanoma and disease progression following ipilimumab and, if BRAF V600 mutation positive, a BRAF inhibitor	No	2014
Blincyto (blinatumomab)	Bispecific CD-19-directed CD3 T-cell engager	2 scFvs	Treatment of Philadelphia chromosome-negative relapsed or refractory B-cell precursor acute lymphoblastic leukemia (ALL)	Yes	2014
Opdivo (nivolumab)	Human programmed cell death receptor (PD-1)	IgG4	Treatment of patients with unresectable or metastatic melanoma and disease progression following ipilimumab and, if BRAF V600 mutation positive, a BRAF inhibitor	Yes	2014
Kadcyla (ado-transtuzumab emtansine)	HER-2 receptor and microtubule inhibitor conjugate	IgG1	Treatment of patients with HER-2 positive metastatic breast cancer who previously received treatment of trastuzumab and a taxane, separately or in combination	Yes	2013
Simponi Aria (golimumab)	Human TNFα	IgG1	Treatment of adult patients with moderately to severely active rheumatoid arthritis in combination with methotrexate	Yes	2013
Gazyva (obinutuzumab)	Human CD20	IgG1	Treatment of patients with previously untreated chronic lymphocytic leukemia, in combination with chlorambucil	Yes	2013
Perjeta (pertuzumab)	HER2/neu receptor	IgG1	In combination with trastuzumab and docetaxel, treatment of patients with HER2-positive metastatic breast cancer who have not received prior antiHER2 therapy or chemotherapy for metastatic disease, or as neoadjuvant treatment with HER2-positive, locally advanced, inflammatory or early state breast cancer	Yes	2012

Continued

TABLE 23.1 Summary of FDA-Approved Therapeutic Monoclonal Antibodies—cont'd

Product Trade Name (Generic Name)	Target Description	mAb Isotype	Indication	AntiDrug Antibodies[a]	Date Approved
Raxibacumab	PA component of *Bacillus anthracis*	IgG1	Treatment of adult and pediatric patients with inhalational anthrax in combination with appropriate antibacterial drugs, and for prophylaxis or inhalational anthrax when alternative therapies are not available or not appropriate	No	2012
Adcetris (brentuximab)	CD30-directed antibody—monomethyl auristatin E (MMAE; drug (microtubule disrupting) conjugate	IgG1	Treatment of patients with Hodgkin's lymphoma after failure of autologous stem cell transplant or after failure of at least two prior multiagent chemotherapy regimens in patients who are not ASCT candidates, and patients with systemic anaplastic large cell lymphoma after failure of at least one prior multiagent chemotherapy regimen	Yes	2012
Benlysta (belimumab)	Human mAb to B-lymphocyte stimulator (BLyS)- specific inhibitor	IgG1	Treatment of adult patients with active, autoantibody-positive, systemic lupus erythematous who are receiving standard therapy	Yes	2011
Yervoy (ipilimumab)	Human mAb to cytotoxic T-lymphocyte antigen 4 (CTLA-4) blocking antibody	IgG1	Treatment of unresectable or metastatic melanoma	Yes	2011
Actemra (tocilizumab)	Human mAb to IL-6 receptor	IgG1 k	Treatment of adult patients with moderate to severe active RA who have inadequate response to one or more TNF antagonist therapies; patients 2 years of age or older with active sJIA	Yes	2010
Prolia (denosumab)	Human mAb to RANKL (receptor activator of nuclear factor kappa-B ligand)	IgG2	Treatment of postmenopausal women with osteoporosis at high risk for fracture	Yes	2010
Simponi (golimumab)	Human mAb to TNF alpha	IgG1k	Treatment of severely active rheumatoid arthritis; active psoriatic arthritis; active ankylosing spondylitis; +/−MTX	Yes	2009
Ilaris (canakinumab)	Human mAb to IL-1β	IgG1 k	Treatment of cryopyrin-associated periodic syndromes (CAPS), in adults and children 4 years and older including familial cold auto inflammatory syndrome (FCAS) and Muckle–Wells syndrome (MWS)	Yes	2009
Stelara (ustekinumab)	Human mAb to p40 protein subunit used by both IL-12 and IL-23	IgG1k	Treatment of adult patients with moderate to severe plaque psoriasis who are candidates for phototherapy or systemic therapy	Yes	2009
Arzerra (ofatumumab)	Human mAb to CD20	IgG1 k	Treatment of patients with chronic lymphocytic leukemia (CLL) refractory to fludarabind and alemtuzumab	None detected	2009
Arcalyst (rilonacept)	Fusion protein of human Fc and ligand binding domains of IL-1 receptor component and IL-1 receptor accessory protein	IgG1 Fc	Treatment of Cryopyrin-associated periodic syndromes (CAPS), including familial cold autoinflammatory syndrome (FCAS) and Muckle–Wells syndrome (MWS)	Yes	2008
Cimzia (certolizumab pegol)	Humanized Fab′ fragment to human TNF-alpha conjugated to PEG	Fab′ fragment	Treatment of moderate to severely active Crohn's and rheumatoid arthritis	Yes	2008
Soliris (eculizumab)	Humanized mAb to complement protein C5	IgG2/4	Treatment of paroxysmal nocturnal hemoglobinuria to reduce hemolysis	Yes	2007

Continued

Name	Description	Isotype	Indication	Approved	Year
Lucentis (ranibizumab)	Humanized mAb fragment to human VEGF-A	IgG1 Fab'	Treatment of wet age-related macular degeneration and macular edema following retinal vein occlusion (intravitreal injections)	Yes	2006
Vectibix (panitumumab)	Human mAb to epidermal growth factor receptor (EGFR)	IgG2	Treatment of EGFR-expressing metastatic colorectal carcinoma with disease progression on or following chemotherapy. Approval based on progression-free survival; no data demonstrate improvement in disease-related symptoms or increased survival	Yes	2006
Orencia (abatacept)	Fusion protein of human IgG1 Fc and human T-lymphocyte associated antigen 4 (CTLA-4)	IgG1 Fc fused to CTLA-4	Treatment of moderate to severe active RA; juvenile idiopathic arthritis	Yes	2005
Avastin (bevacizumab)	Humanized mAb to human VEGF	IgG1 k	Treatment of metastatic cancer of the colon or rectum; nonsquamous small cell lung cancer; metastatic breast cancer; glioblastoma; renal cell carcinoma	Yes	2004
Erbitux (cetuximab)	Chimeric human/murine mAb to epidermal growth factor receptor	IgG1 k	Treatment of EGFR expressing metastatic colorectal cancer; advanced squamous cell carcinoma of the head and neck	Yes	2004
Tysabri (natalizumab)	Humanized mAb against α4 family of integrins (on all leukocytes except neutrophils)	IgG4	Treatment of relapsing forms of multiple sclerosis; treatment of Crohn's disease	Yes	2004
Amevive (alefacept)	Human fusion protein of and CD2 binding portion of human leukocyte function antigen 3 (LFA-3)	IgG1 Fc fused to CD2	Treatment of moderate to severe plaque psoriasis	Yes	2003
Bexxar (tositumomab)	mAb to CD20 covalently linked to I-131	Murine IgG2a	Radioimmuno-therapeutic agent for patients with CD20 positive follicular non-Hodgkin's lymphoma	Yes	2003
Xolair (omalizumab)	Humanized mAb to IgE	IgG1	For patients with moderate to severe persistent asthma who have a positive skin test or reactivity to a perennial aeroallergen	Yes	2003
Humira (adalimumab)	Human mAb to TNFα	IgG1	Treatment of moderate to severe active RA; juvenile idiopathic arthritis; psoriatic arthritis; ankylosing spondylitis; Crohn's disease; plaque psoriasis	Yes	2002
Zevalin (ibritumomab tiuxetan)	Chimeric murine mAb to CD20, covalently bound to linker-chelator tiuxetan to chelate Indium-111 and Yttrium-90; administered with rituxamab	IgG1	For treatment of relapsed or refractory B-cell non-Hodgkin's lymphoma; previously untreated follicular NHL	Yes	2002
Campath (alemtuzumab)	Humanized mAb to CD52	IgG1	Treatment of B-cell CLL patients (treatment with alkylating agents and failed fludaribine)	Yes	2001
Mylotarg (gemtuzumab ozogamicin)	Humanized mAb targeting CD33 (adhesion protein on cell surface of leukemic blasts and immature myelomono-cytic cells) and conjugated with cytotoxin antibiotic calicheamicin	IgG4	Treatment of CD33 positive acute myeloid leukemia in relapse (60 years or older)	Yes	2000

TABLE 23.1 Summary of FDA-Approved Therapeutic Monoclonal Antibodies—cont'd

Product Trade Name (Generic Name)	Target Description	mAb Isotype	Indication	AntiDrug Antibodies[a]	Date Approved
Enbrel (etanercept)	Fusion protein of human and human ligand-binding domain of TNF receptor	IgG1 Fc fused to TNF R	Treatment of moderate to severe active RA, JIA, psoriatic A, anklyosing spondylitis	Yes	1998
Herceptin (trastuzumab)	Humanized mAb to human epidermal growth factor receptor 2 (HER2)	IgG1	Metastatic breast cancer and metastatic gastric or gastroesophageal junction adenocarcinoma overexpressing HER2	Yes	1998
Remicade (infliximab)	Chimeric (murine variable and human constant regions) mAb to human TNFα	IgG1k	Treatment of moderate to severe active or fistulizing Crohn's disease; ulcerative colitis; RA; ankylosing spondylitis, psoriatic arthritis, plaque psoriasis	Yes	1998
Simulect (basaliximab)	Chimeric (human/-murine) mAb to IL-2Rα (CD25)	IgG1k	For prophylaxis of acute organ rejection in renal transplant recipients	Yes	1998
Synagis (palivizumab)	Humanized mAb to respiratory syncytial virus (RSV)	IgG1	Prevention of serious lower respiratory tract disease caused by RSV in pediatric patients at high risk for RSV disease (infants)	Yes	1998
Rituxan (rituximab)	Chimeric human/murine mAb to CD20 antigen on human B cells	IgG1 k	For treatment of relapsed or refractory CD20 positive B-cell non-Hodgkin's lymphoma	Yes	1997
Zenapax (daclizumab)	Humanized mAb to alpha subunit of IL-2 receptor on T cells	IgG1	For prophylaxis of acute organ rejection in renal transplant recipients (adults and pediatrics)	Yes	1997
Reopro (abciximab)	Fab fragment of chimeric human/murine mAb 7E3 inhibiting platelet aggregation	Murine IgG2a	As adjunct to percutaneous transluminal coronary angioplasty intervention for the prevention of cardiac ischemic complications	Yes	1993

[a]As noted in labeling or regulatory documents.

substances such as viruses and bacteria. There are five classes, or isotypes, of antibodies in humans and other placental mammals. These differ in their heavy chain sequences including alpha (α), gamma (γ), delta (δ), epsiolon (ε), and mu (μ) found in IgA, IgG, IgD, IgE, and IgM antibodies, respectively (for a review see Ref. [11]). The most prevalent isotype is IgG, which constitutes about 85% of serum immunoglobulins, with an average concentration of 11–14 g/L in normal adults. Because of its role in humoral protection, the IgG isotype and its derivatives are the primary focus of therapeutic development [12].

An antibody is shaped like the letter Y, and is composed of two identical heavy and two identical light chains connected by disulfide bonds (Fig. 23.1). Each heavy chain can pair with one of two light chains, either kappa (κ) or lambda (λ). The majority of antibodies are monomers, composed of two heavy and two light chains, but IgA can exist as a dimer and IgM as a pentamer. Antibody size, evaluated by biophysical analysis, is estimated to be about 12 nm long, with three rod-shaped arms each about 3.5 nm in diameter. They are intermediate in size between albumin and mammalian hemoglobin [13].

Antibody structure, elucidated using X-ray crystallography, has been shown to comprise folds of repeated ~110 amino-acid segments (Fig. 23.2), or domains, that form compact functional units (see Ref. [11]). The domains can be further grouped into Fab and Fc regions. Fab stands for fragment-antibody binding; the tips of the Fab bind to the target antigen, and this region is composed of heavy and light chain, variable, and constant regions. This region includes the CH1 heavy-chain domain and the C light-chain domain.

The antigen-binding site is comprised of the Fab variable regions of light and heavy chains. Six linear polypeptide segments called complementarity determining regions (CDR) loops form the antigen recognition site. Three of these CDR loops come from the light chain and three from the heavy chain. The enormous diversity of antigen binding is derived from these six CDR loops, which are hypervariable in sequence [14,15].

The Fc region (standing for fragment-crystallizable) is the most easily crystallized. It is composed of two heavy-chain regions in most antibody isotypes, and three regions in IgM and IgE. The Fc region is responsible for effector functions, such as antibody-dependent cellular cytotoxicity (ADCC) and complement-dependent cytotoxicity (CDC). This region binds to a specific class of Fc cellular receptors and other immune molecules, such as complement proteins, which leads to the generation of the appropriate immune response to a specific antigen.

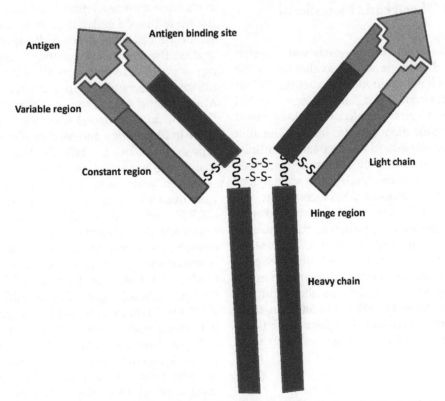

FIGURE 23.1 **The basic structure of an antibody is composed of two heavy chains and two light chains held together by disulfide bonds.** The antigen-binding section consists of the variable regions from both heavy and light chains.

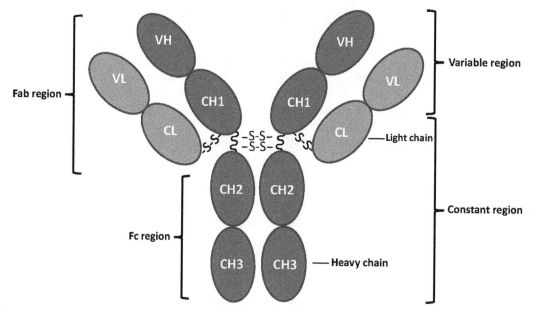

FIGURE 23.2 **Antibody structure has been shown to fold into ~100 amino domains that form compact functional units referred to the Fab and Fc regions.** For the IgG molecule, the heavy chain is made up of one variable and three constant domains, and the light chain is composed of one variable and one constant domain.

This interaction with the Fc receptor results in different physiological effects including recognition of opsonized particles, lysis of cells, degranulation of mast cells, basophils, and eosinophils [16,17].

The Evolution of Therapeutic Monoclonal Antibodies

Over 70 years passed between the early use of serum therapy for treating diphtheria and the availability of the first licensed monoclonal antibody therapeutic. In this time, a greater understanding of immunology coupled with key discoveries in cell and molecular biology paved the way for generating monospecific mAbs. The first mAbs were of mouse origin, and their repeated administration to patients resulted in robust immune responses generating antidrug antibodies (ADA) and subsequent loss of efficacy. With advances in DNA technology, animal sequences in the mAb were gradually replaced with human sequences, gradually producing fully human mAbs, for use as therapeutics as well as laboratory reagents (Fig. 23.3). This evolution in mAb structure generally reduced the immune response to the foreign mAb, although even fully human mAbs can elicit immune responses (however, these are often milder than their mouse or chimeric mAb cousins). This next section will briefly describe the evolution of mouse mAbs to fully human mAbs.

Mouse mAbs

A great paradigm change in the field of antibody technology came when mAbs could be produced to bind to a desired target. In 1975, Köhler and Milstein published their seminal paper describing the hybridoma methodology and the capability of producing unlimited quantities of mAbs of predefined specificity [18]. They fused mouse myeloma cells with B lymphocytes from a mouse immunized with a specific antigen (sheep red blood cells), thus generating hybrid immortal mouse cells that produced a specific mAb directed against the immunizing antigen. Hybridoma technology was not patented, thus allowing many scientists to utilize the technology and to produce mAbs. Köhler, Milstein, and Jerne (whose plaque assay was used in the hybridoma process) were awarded the 1984 Nobel Prize in Physiology and Medicine for this discovery [5]. However, a major limitation of this technology was the inability to produce human mAbs.

Eleven years later, the first approved mAb derived from this technology was muromonab-CD3 (Orthoclone OKT-3), indicated for the inhibition of transplanted organ rejection. This mouse IgG_2 mAb targets the membrane surface protein CD3 on human T lymphocytes, essential for T-lymphocyte function. Muromonab-CD3 binds to CD3, initially leading to T-lymphocyte activation and subsequently inducing inhibition and apoptosis of the T lymphocyte. Normal T-lymphocyte function is restored within 1 week of administration. Use of this mAb has been associated with anaphylactoid and anaphylactic reactions as well as cytokine release syndrome. Subjects treated with muromonab developed neutralizing antidrug antibodies to the murine mAb during or following the 2nd week of therapy [19]. Newer mAbs targeting human CD3 such as otelixizumab (chimeric

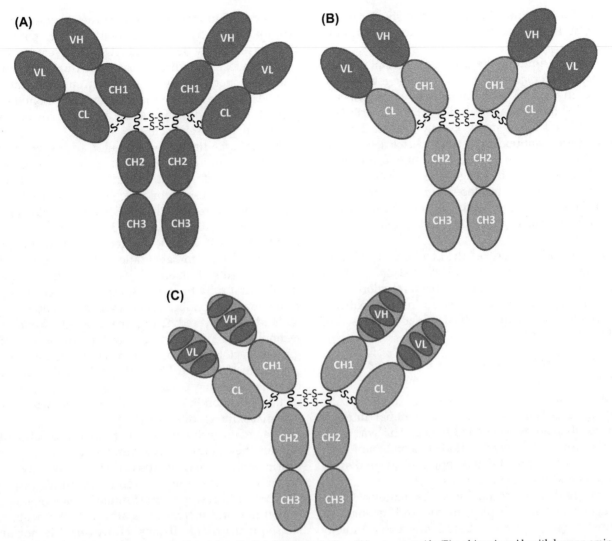

FIGURE 23.3   The different forms of monoclonal antibodies (mAb), including (A) a mouse mAb; (B) a chimeric mAb with human amino acid regions (light gray) replacing the mouse regions (dark gray); (C) a humanized mAb (light gray) with mouse regions (dark gray) remaining only in the complementarity determining region responsible for binding.

mAb) and visilizumab (humanized mAb) are currently in development [20].

The main drawback of administering therapeutic mouse mAbs to humans was that the mouse-protein sequences were recognized as foreign, often resulting in a robust immune response, including the generation of human antimouse antibodies, increased clearance of the mAb, and injection site and hypersensitivity reactions.

Chimeric and Humanized mAbs

Experience with recombinant DNA technology, along with an increased understanding of mAb structure and function, led the way to the production of less immunogenic alternatives. Murine immunoglobulin VH and VL chains were fused with human immunoglobulin constant regions [21,22], generating chimeric mAbs. These proteins contain about one-third murine sequences (2VH

and 2VL subunits) and two-thirds human sequences, including the human Fc region, and are produced using cell-culture technology.

The first chimeric mAb to be produced was abciximab (ReoPro), which was made in immunoglobulin form, then cleaved to a Fab fragment, and marketed as a mAb fragment. The first chimeric IgG to be produced was rituximab (Rituxan), still a strongly selling product, with >$3 billion in sales annually [5]. Antidrug antibodies have been reported following treatment with rituximab. However, since the drug targets and depletes B lymphocytes, the potential producers of ADA, it is not a good representation of the ADA response found with chimeric mAbs. A better example is infliximab, which is also an immunosuppressant. Data for this drug show that up to 51% of psoriasis patients in the Phase III study developed ADA, following IV administration at 3 mg/kg every 8 weeks for 1 year [23]. The development of ADA with infliximab has resulted in shorter dosing intervals and increases in dose level to maintain efficacy [24].

Due to the immune response in patients, efforts were made to replace the mouse-variable-region DNA sequences in the CDR with human sequences. This process is called humanization, and was first described by Winter and colleagues in 1986. They grafted the CDR from a murine antibody into its most closely related human framework, then made the amino-acid changes required to stabilize the engineered constructs [25]. Queen and colleagues developed a detailed process for CDR grafting, which formed the basis for humanization of many mAbs currently on the market and in clinical trials [26–28].

In 1997, the FDA approved the first humanized mAb, which was daclizumab, an anti-CD25 (IL-2 alpha subunit indicated for the treatment of transplant rejection). Anti-drug antibodies (14%) were detected in adult patients, but a reduction in clinical efficacy was not observed [23,29].

Fully Human mAbs Using Phage Display or Transgenic Mice

The ultimate goal was to make fully human mAbs, which were anticipated to elicit a minimal immune response when administered to humans. This was made possible with the further evolution of recombinant DNA techniques leading to the generation of phage-display techniques and transgenic animals.

In phage-display technology, filamentous bacteriophages naturally display minor and major coat proteins on their surface. Using molecular biology techniques these proteins can be engineered to display repertoires of antibody fragments fused to the minor coat protein [30–33]. To obtain the genes that code for the antibody fragments displayed by the phage, the light- and heavy-chain variable (V) gene repertoires are harvested from a population of lymphocytes, or assembled in vitro, and cloned, yielding surface expression on the phage. These phage-displayed antibodies can be selected by binding to a target protein/antigen and then used to infect bacteria that will then secrete the target-specific single-chain antibody fragment. Human antibody fragments have thus been isolated with specificities against both foreign and self-antigens, including haptens, carbohydrates, secreted and cell surface proteins, viral coat proteins, and intracellular antigens from the lumen of the endoplasmic reticulum. The DNA from the selected phage is then reformatted into a full-length mAb and expressed in mammalian cells. The first phage-display-derived, fully human mAb on the market was adalimumab (Humira, 2002), an IgG1 mAb that targets human TNF alpha, indicated for the treatment of moderate-to-severe rheumatoid arthritis. Approximately 5% of rheumatoid arthritis patients in the Phase 3 study developed ADA that were neutralizing when tested in vitro at least once during treatment. Patients concomitantly treated with methotrexate had a lower ADA response than patients on monotherapy (1% vs. 12%), and there was no apparent correlation of ADA with adverse effects.

At the same time, the generation of transgenic mice capable of producing fully human mAbs was taking place. The ability to introduce genes, hundreds of kb in size, into mouse embryonic stem cells provided the opportunity to replace the mouse immunoglobulin loci with human antibody genes [34]. These mice can be immunized with specific antigens and their B cells can then be selected for generation of hybridoma, which will yield fully human mAbs of predefined specificity. The first fully human mAb to be derived using this technology was panitumumab (Vectabix), a human IgG2 antibody discovered using the Abgenix XenoMouse technology (2006) and targeting the human epidermal growth factor receptor. Antidrug antibodies (~4.6%) were detected in the Phase III study, with about 1.6% of patients testing positive for neutralizing antibodies. Antidrug antibodies were not correlated with altered pharmacokinetics or toxicity.

The main advantage of humanized and fully human therapeutic mAbs compared with the earlier murine and chimeric mAbs is that there is a lower risk of patients developing a robust immune response, which would result in injection-site reactions, hypersensitivity, and increased clearance of the drug, with subsequent loss of efficacy. However, it is not unexpected that ADA will be generated by human/humanized mAbs, especially with chronic administration. In clinical trials, ADA are routinely measured to understand their overall incidence and the magnitude of a response. The incidences cannot truly be compared between mAbs as the bioanalytical assays measuring the drug differ between products, with different limits of sensitivity among the assays.

As assessed by evaluation of the immunology sections in the package inserts of the FDA-approved human/humanized mAbs (Table 23.1), there are ADA responses seen in the trials supporting registration of all approved mAbs except of atumumab, which targets CD20 on B lymphocytes, and pembrolizumab, which targets the human programmed cell-death receptor (PD-1). The absence of detectable ADA for these mAbs may be related to the true lack of ADA, low sensitivity of the assay, and/or assay interference in the presence of high circulating levels of mAb.

The half-life of mAbs generally increases with the degree of humanization. The half-life of a murine mAbs is about 1.5 days, of chimeric mAbs, about 10 days, of humanized mAbs, about 12–20 days, and of fully human mAbs, about 15–20 days [35]. The shorter half-life of murine mAbs is attributed to the lack of binding to Fc neonatal receptor (FcRn), which has been demonstrated to be responsible for protection of IgG against systemic elimination by recycling the receptor-bound mAb back into the systemic circulation [36–38].

Next-Generation Antibody Therapeutics

Once humanized and fully human mAbs, with reduced risk of immunogenicity [39], were created, effort was then directed at engineering both the antigen binding domains (affinity maturation, stability) and altering the effector functions (ADCC, clearance rate, CDC) [40,41]. Much antibody engineering effort has also gone into designing mAb-drug conjugates (ADCs) for cancer therapy and other creative ways to enhance the utility of mAb therapeutics, such as bispecific antibodies with unique CDR regions, each arm with a unique target [42–44].

mAb-drug conjugates are biopharmaceutical molecules consisting of a small molecule covalently linked to a monoclonal antibody moiety via a stable cleavage or noncleavable linker. The first two FDA-approved ADCs are humanized mAbs conjugated to antimicrotubule cytotoxic agents. Adcetris (brentuximab vedotin) is composed of a chimeric anti-CD30 mAb conjugated by a protease-cleavable linker to four molecules of monomethylauristatin E (MMAE) and indicated for relapsed/refractory Hodgkin lymphoma and anaplastic large-cell lymphoma [45,46]. Kadcyla (ado-trastuzumab emtansine) is comprised of a trastuzumab antibody linked to a tubulin polymerization inhibitor, mertansine, [45,47] for treatment of human estrogen receptor (HER)-positive metastatic breast cancer. Currently, the vast majority of the 29 ADCs in clinical trials use either auristatins or maytansinoids as drug payload [45]. Nonclinical safety evaluation of these hybrid molecules, consisting of a mAb, linker, and small molecule, offers new challenges and is based on a case-by-case scientific approach [48].

The first FDA-approved bispecific antibody was Blincyto (blinatumomab), with one arm engineered to bind CD19 and the other to CD3, and classified as a bispecific T-cell engager (BiTE) molecule for treatment of B-cell lymphoma. This bispecific design brings two cells in close proximity and thus activates T cells to destroy the CD19-positive tumor cell [49,50]. Blincyto is composed of two single-chain variable regions (targeting either CD3 or CD19) that heterodimerize noncovalently to form the active diabody antibody fragment [49]. There are currently over 30 bispecific antibodies in clinical development [44].

These next-generation antibodies, including antibody–drug conjugates, bispecific antibodies, and antibody fragments will bring many novel therapeutic applications into the clinic.

NOMENCLATURE OF MONOCLONAL ANTIBODIES

Therapeutic mAb candidates and products are given generic, or nonproprietary, names based on their class of drug and intended target. This naming scheme is used for both the WHO International Nonproprietery Names (INN) and the US Adopted Names (USAN) for pharmaceuticals (July 2011). In general, word stems are used to identify classes of drugs, and all mAb names end with the stem -mab. Unlike most pharmaceuticals, mAb-antibody nomenclature uses different preceding word parts depending on structure and function, which are called substems. The nomenclature system is summarized in Table 23.2. For example, the name infliximab describes a chimeric mAb therapeutic that targets the immune system.

PRECLINICAL DEVELOPMENT OF MONOCLONAL ANTIBODIES

The preclinical development of mAbs encompasses several important fields of study including ADME (absorption/metabolism/distribution/elimination), pharmacology, pharmacokinetics (PK), tissue cross-reactivity (TCR), toxicology/nonclinical safety evaluation, and bioanalytical development. This section will discuss the roles of these disciplines in the development of mAb therapeutics.

The nonclinical safety evaluation process differs for small- and large-molecule therapeutics, due to the inherent differences in their characteristics, which are summarized in Table 23.3.

The Fate of Monoclonal Antibodies in the Body

The fate of a therapeutic mAb following administration is governed by several key factors including its route of administration, dose, distribution, elimination, and Fc neonatal receptor (FcRn) interaction. Additionally, the size of the target-receptor population, degree of receptor downregulation or shedding, and generation of ADA also play roles in the fate of mAb [36,37,51].

For practical reasons, new mAb development programs often utilize IV administration for initial clinical

TABLE 23.2 Nomenclature of Monoclonal Antibodies

Prefix	Target Subsystem			Source Substem		
	Old	New	Meaning	Substem	Meaning	Stem
Variable-	-anibi-	–	Angiogenesis (inhibitor)	-a-	Rat	-mab
	-ba(c)-	-b(a)-	Bacterium	-e-	Hamster	
	-ci(r)-	-c(i)-	Circulatory system	-i-	Primate	
	-fung-	-f(u)-	Fungus	-o-	Mouse	
	-ki(n)-	-k(i)-	Interleukin	-u-	Human	
	-les-	–	Inflammatory lesion	-xi-	Chimeric (human/-foreign)	
	-li(m)-	-l(i)-	Immune system	-zu-	Humanized	
	-mul-	–	Musculoskeletal system	-Xizu-[a]	Chimeric/-humanized hybrid	
	-neu(u)(r)-	-n(e)-[a]	Nervous system	-axo-	Rat/mouse hybrid	
	-os-	-s(o)-	Bone			
	-toxa-	-tox(a)-	Toxin			
	-co(l)-	-t(u)-	Colon tumor			
	-go(t)-	-t(u)-	Testicular tumor			
	-go(v)-	-t(u)-	Ovarian tumor			
	-ma(r)-	-t(u)-	Mammary tumor			
	-me(l)-	-t(u)-	Melanoma			
	-pr(o)-	-t(u)-	Prostate tumor			
	-tu(m)-	-t(u)-	Miscellaneous tumor			
	-vi(r)-	-v(i)-	Virus			

[a]Under discussion.

TABLE 23.3 Differences in Characteristics Between Small-Molecule and Biologic Therapeutics

Characteristic	Small Molecule	Biologic
Molecular weight	<1000 Da	>1000 Da (mAb ~150,000 Da)
Production	Chemically synthesized	Cell culture, recombinant DNA technology
Route	Generally oral	Generally IV, SC, IM
Metabolism	Generally liver and kidney; pathways well characterized	Catabolized and degraded into amino acids; biotransformation not occurring
Metabolites	Potentially toxic	Typically not toxic
Genotoxicity	Potentially genotoxic – needs testing	Typically not genotoxic – testing not needed
Species limitations	Generally no; 2 species	Potentially yes, 1 species acceptable
Immunogenicity	Generally no; exception hapten protein compounds	Frequent
Food effects	Potential concern	Generally no
Half-life	Shorter	Longer
Drug:drug interaction	Potential concern	Generally no

testing. Development of an IV formulation is often less challenging than developing the more concentrated formulation necessary for SQ or IM administration, and enables a faster launch into the clinical development program. The advantages of IV administration include rapid achievement of high serum concentrations, full systemic availability, and the ability to administer high doses if needed. During the Phase I study, effort is focused on developing a stable, more concentrated formulation that can be administered by SC administration in later clinical studies. The limitation of the IV route is primarily inconvenience, as trained personnel and hospitalization are necessary for drug administration.

Following IV administration, mAbs are initially confined to the circulating vasculature, with initial plasma concentrations consistent with a volume of distribution of ~45–50 mL/kg, approximately equal to the plasma volume. The distribution of mAbs outside the vasculature depends on the rate and extent of mAb extravasation within tissue [37], with a distributional volume of about 0.1 L/kg, approximately equal to the volume of extracellular fluid [12].

Following SC and IM administration, mAbs enter the systemic circulation by absorption into the lymphatic vessels, which tends to be slow due to the low flow rate of lymph [35]. As lymph fluid drains slowly into the vasculature, the absorption of mAbs from the injection site can continue for hours. In general, mAbs administered via extravascular routes exhibit high bioavailability (about 50%) [52,53], with maximal plasma concentrations achieved 1–8 days after SC or IM administration [54–56]. The major shortcoming of these routes is that volumes greater than 2.5 or 5 mL (via SC and IM injection, respectively) cannot be administered due to practical limitations such as mAb solubility (~100 mg/mL) and discomfort at the site of administration [37].

In contrast to small-molecule therapeutics, mAbs are not administered orally. Their oral bioavailability is minimal, due to degradation and poor absorption of mAbs from the gastrointestinal tract. For example, when low-birth-weight human infants were given purified IgG (100–800 mg/kg/day for 5 days) or an IgG-IgA formulation (600 mg/day for 28 days), there was no increase in serum IgG concentrations [57], demonstrating poor oral bioavailability. The therapeutic utility of orally administered mAbs may be limited to local exposure in the gastrointestinal tract for treatment of gastrointestinal infections.

The metabolism/elimination of mAbs is primarily governed by normal protein catabolism, interaction with the FcRn, target-mediated elimination, and immunogenicity [58]. The metabolic products of mAb catabolism are generally not considered to be a safety risk [12]. mAbs are taken up into cells by processes such as endocytosis/pinocytosis, carrier-mediated or membrane receptor-mediated transport, where they eventually undergo degradation (for a review see Refs. [37,59,60]). Enzymes involved in catabolism are ubiquitous in the body and break down the mAbs into its amino-acid constituents. The receptors involved in uptake can include receptors specific for mAbs, such as members of the Fcγ receptor family or the FcRn receptor, and the membrane-bound therapeutic target receptor. It is the interaction with the FcRn (also known as the Brambell receptor) that plays a major role in the fate and recycling of mAbs (Fig. 23.4).

The mAb is taken up into the endosome, and as the pH of the endosome decreases from 7.4 to 6.0, the affinity of the FcRn for the Fc region of the mAb increases. The contents of the endosome are later sorted into two different endosome vesicles, with one containing the FcRn-mAb complexes and the other containing free mAb. The endosome containing the complexes then fuses with the cell membrane, thus releasing the mAb back into circulation [60]. The free mAb remaining in the endosome is eventually catabolized into smaller peptides in the lysosome.

The FcRn was first discovered in rats, where it was found to transport IgG from the mother's milk across the epithelium of the newborn's gut into its bloodstream [61]. A similar protein, with a comparable function and also a role in recycling IgG to the cell's surface, was later found in humans. Transgenic mice lacking FcRn have been shown to have a 10–15 times faster elimination of IgG than wildtype mice [62,63]. Other immunoglobulin isotypes do not bind the FcRn and, as expected, have shorter half-lives than IgGs. The FcRn structure differs in specificity between species, with the human/humanized mAbs showing poor binding affinity to mouse FcRn receptors. Due to these species differences in FcRn, care should be taken when interpreting PK data following administration of human/humanized mAbs to mice, and should be complemented by binding studies with human FcRn [64].

High levels of circulating mAb or IgG can saturate the FcRn recycling pathway, which can lead to increased clearance of the mAb. Endogenous IgG levels and standard therapeutic dose levels of mAbs administered in the clinic (~0.5–10 mg/kg) are not expected to saturate the FcRn pathway [12]. Higher mAb levels used in toxicology studies can have the potential to saturate the pathway and enhance clearance.

With regard to circulation to the kidney, the majority of mAbs transported into the urinary space of the glomerulus is reabsorbed in proximal tubules and reenters the systemic circulation [37]. Lower-molecule-weight

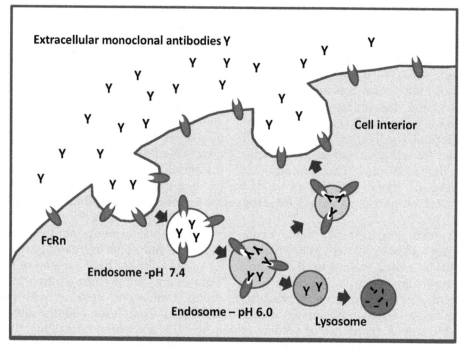

FIGURE 23.4 FcRn-mediated uptake and recycling of monoclonal antibodies (mAbs). Extracellular mAbs are taken into the cell via pinocytosis into endosomes. As the endosome pH decreases (6.0), the mAb binds with the FcRn. The contents of the endosome are sorted upon fusion with lysosomes. Any unbound mAb is released into the lysosome and degraded by proteases. Bound mAb remains in the endosome, and upon fusion with the plasma membrane as well as exposure to higher pH (7.4), is released into the plasma.

fragments (Fab) are filtered by the glomerulus and are subsequently reabsorbed and catabolized by proximal tubule cells. The excretion of intact mAb is a minor component of the overall elimination process, and very little is excreted in the urine or bile.

Therapeutic mAbs, even human/humanized mAbs, can induce an immune response in humans, with the development of an ADA response. This can lead to enhanced clearance of the ADA-bound drug, with a subsequent loss of efficacy depending on the magnitude of the response. The type of immunogenicity that plays a role in mAb clearance will be discussed further in a later section.

Pharmacokinetics, Toxicokinetics, and Pharmacodynamics of Monoclonal Antibody Therapeutics

Pharmacokinetics (PK)/toxicokinetics (TK) and pharmacodynamics (PD) together play an integral role in drug development. Pharmacokinetics evaluation provides information on the exposure profile of a drug in the body over a given period of time following administration, employing multiple blood samplings through the duration of study. These exposure measurements can be used to compare and extrapolate drug exposure across species, to determine the levels of drug required for therapeutic efficacy as well as

toxicity, to facilitate selection of an initial safe starting dose for clinical studies, and to estimate safety margins.

Toxicokinetics is the term used to evaluate the relationship between the PK profile and any safety-related findings in a toxicology study. TK is defined as:

> The generation of pharmacokinetic data, either as an integral component in the conduct of nonclinical toxicity studies or in specially designed supportive studies, in order to assess exposure ICH S3A [65]

For toxicology studies, the sampling times are more sparse than found in the PK studies, with blood samples typically taken predose, midway (depending on the duration of the study), and at the end of the study. In rodent toxicology studies, a separate group of animals are often designated as TK animals as to allow multiple sampling times. These data may be helpful in the interpretation of toxicology findings and determining their relevance to potential clinical safety issues.

The International Conference on Harmonization (ICH) S3A guidance document [65] provides a good summary of the goals and objectives of TK evaluation, including describing the levels of systemic exposure achieved in animals, the dose–response relationship and the time course of effects in the toxicology study, and understanding how exposure in toxicology studies is related to adverse findings. In addition, TK data play a role in assessing the relevance of these findings to clinical safety, supporting the selection of relevant species and treatment regimens in toxicology studies, and facilitating design of the subsequent toxicology studies.

Pharmacodynamics is defined as the desirable and undesirable pharmacological effects of a drug on the body. Integration of PK/TK exposure data in animal studies with PD data on pharmacological or toxicological findings defines the exposure–response relationship (PK/PD), which allows a continuous description of the effect of the drug over time. Understanding the PK/PD relationship is important to anticipate the pharmacological or toxicological behavior of these agents, and is critical for the development of appropriate dose regimens and the planning of future studies. In addition, determining whether a mAb exhibits linear or nonlinear clearance, and whether the clearance is stable or changes over time, is necessary for the determination of safe and effective dosing regimens [12].

An elegant example of defining the PK/PD relationship of a therapeutic mAb was described by Bauer and colleagues [66] for an anti-CD11a mAb, efalizumab (Raptiva), in subjects with psoriasis. CD11a is a subunit of LFA-1, a cell-surface molecule involved in T-cell-mediated immune responses. Blocking the function of CD11a leads to a reduction of T-cell trafficking and has been shown to be effective treatment for psoriasis (although no longer on the market due to safety issues). The humanized IgG1 mAb binds only to chimpanzee and human CD11a, thus the PK/PD evaluations were conducted in the chimpanzee to predict the PK/PD relationship in humans.

Following IV infusion to chimpanzees, efalizumab caused a rapid reduction in the number of CD11a cells detected on the surface of circulating T cells until a new steady-state level of ~20% compared to predose numbers was achieved (Fig. 23.5). CD11a expression remained suppressed until drug levels approached 3 μg/mL and then recovered to predose levels about 7–10 days later.

To build the PK/PD model, data on the binding affinity for human and chimpanzee CD11a, number of CD11a target molecules on the surface of T cells, amount of drug needed to saturate the CD11a target molecules, and plasma drug levels over time were used. Two models were developed for predicting the PK profile in humans and for selecting the doses for a study in subjects with psoriasis. One model was based on Michaelis–Menton clearance designed to represent the clearance of efalizumab based on binding to CD11a receptors, which was a saturable process due to the limited number of receptors on the T cells. The other

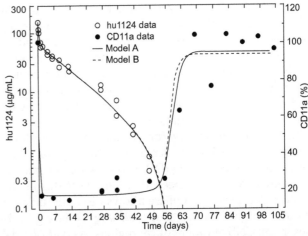

FIGURE 23.5 Michaelis–Menten (Model A) or dynamic receptor-mediated (Model B) clearance of plasma hu1124 and downregulation of CD11a in a nonhuman primate. One animal received 8 mg/kg hu1124 intravenously. The figure shows the hu1124 concentration in μg/mL (*symbols*), and the predicted concentration of hu1124 as a function of time based on the ADAPT-II log-maximum likelihood analyses (*lines*) of Models A or B. Also, percentages of predose CD11a expression (*symbols*), and the predicted %CD11a based on the analyses (*lines*) are shown (Bauer et al. [66]).

model, a dynamic receptor-mediated clearance model, represents clearance of efalizumab based on interaction with a dynamically changing CD11a receptor population. Both models predicted the response seen in the clinical studies, showing that efalizumab clearance accelerates after plasma concentration drops to a level that is subsaturating for CD11a binding (<10 ug/mL). This PK/PD model was further modified for use during the clinical evaluation of efalizumab, and proved to be a valuable tool for predicting the therapeutic response in patients.

The PK/PD evaluation has become an essential tool for enhancing the decision-making process in drug development.

Tissue Cross-Reactivity Studies

Tissue cross-reactivity studies are used to assess the tissue-binding profile of mAbs, evaluating patterns of on-target (CDR-mediated) and off-target (non-CDR-mediated) staining of therapeutic mAbs to tissue cryosections. Tissue cross-reactivity staining can reveal potential targets related to efficacy or toxicity, as well as provide novel information regarding potential sites of expression of the target epitope or related off-target cross-reactive epitopes [67].

Tissue cross-reactivity studies use immunohistochemical staining methods to determine the binding profile of a mAb on a panel of cryosections from normal, healthy tissues. The recommended list from the FDA comprises about 33 different tissues, mounted on glass slides. The test-article mAb can be used unlabeled or can be labeled using biotin or other reagents, and is applied to the tissue sections and incubated for a predetermined amount of time. There are a series of incubation steps that result in either a fluorescent or chromagenic signal originating from the location of the binding mAb. A board-certified pathologist typically conducts the slide evaluation.

Tissue cross-reactivity can be added to the development plan during the screening phase, prior to the investigational new drug (IND) submission, or later on a case-by-case basis if needed. Using TCR during the screening and selection phase allows discontinuation of any mAb candidate that shows off-target binding to tissues in the CNS or other critical regions. As part of a risk mitigation plan, omitting these mAbs from development will likely save headaches later.

Tissue cross-reactivity can be used to address specific questions asked during development. It can be used to characterize the protein-expression profile of the target ligand as well as its receptor. Tissue cross-reactivity methodology is also available, which can distinguish endogenous antibodies from the human/humanized therapeutic mAb in a tissue section, facilitating understanding of whether the therapeutic mAb or endogenous antibodies are present at a site of inflammation or other site of interest.

The FDA and other international regulatory authorities strongly recommend TCR studies as part of the IND application, and additional studies may be helpful during the course of development. Prior to the ICH S6(R1), TCR studies were recommended to facilitate species selection, and the mAb candidate was tested on full panels of tissues from several species and humans. The new guidance states that immunohistochemical examination of potential binding of mAbs to its target epitope should not be used for selecting relevant species for safety evaluation. TCR studies in toxicology species are considered to have limited value and are not generally recommended.

The presence of positive staining does not equal toxicity, and conversely the absence of positive staining does not necessarily ensure safety. Rather, the data reveal potential sites where the mAb may bind after administration. Membrane staining is more important than cytoplasmic staining for preclinical development, since the potential negative consequences of binding in the cytoplasm is minimal since the mAb cannot access the interior of the cell. The mAb gains access to the cytoplasm only in tissues that are prepared as cryosections. Guidance ICH S6(R1) states that "Binding to areas not typically accessible to biopharmaceuticals in vivo (ie, cytoplasm) might not be relevant." Thus it is possible to focus only on the membrane staining patterns of human tissues for risk-assessment purposes.

The interpretation of therapeutic mAb staining is critical and should always be done in the context of published literature, knowledge of histological and physiological processes, the potential for in vivo distribution, and common sense [67].

Nonclinical Safety Evaluation

Designing the nonclinical safety evaluation program for a therapeutic mAb candidate should be based on a case-by-case, science-driven assessment, taking into account the characteristics of the mAb, the biology of the disease, the consequences of target-molecule inhibition, modulation or activation, and the degree of similarity of the biology of the toxicology species and humans. There are key philosophies in designing nonclinical programs to support first-in-human (FIH) studies, which will be discussed later in this section. Three important regulatory documents are available to provide overall guidance to nonclinical safety evaluation programs for mAbs, and these will also be summarized in this section. They are:

- Guidance for Industry – ICH S6 Preclinical Safety Evaluation of Biotechnology-Derived Pharmaceuticals (1997)
- Draft Addendum to ICH S6: Preclinical Safety Evaluation of Biotechnology-Derived Pharmaceuticals S6(R1) (2009)
- M3(R2) Guidance on Nonclinical Safety Studies for the Conduct of Human Clinical Trials and Marketing Authorization for Pharmaceuticals (2008)

These ICH guidance documents represent the current thinking of the United States, EU, and Japanese regulatory authorities on the nonclinical safety evaluation of mAbs, and the timing of studies to support clinical development. There are many other ICH and national guidance documents that address specific types of toxicology evaluation; however, these three documents provide a good overall picture of the philosophy and thinking of the regulatory authorities, and are a good place to start when designing nonclinical safety evaluation plans.

The goals of nonclinical safety evaluation are to characterize the potential toxicity profile of a new drug, to extrapolate the specific risk of adverse effects to humans, and to provide guidance during clinical development. The toxicology studies can facilitate identification of potential target organs of toxicity and determine whether such toxicity is reversible. These studies also aid in selection of an initial safe dose and subsequent dose-escalation schemes in humans, and identify safety parameters for clinical monitoring of potentially adverse effects (described in more detail in ICH S6(R1) and ICH M3 and reviewed by Refs. [68,69]).

The more that is known about the intended use of the drug in the clinical program, the better the nonclinical safety plan can be designed to support the clinical studies. The plan should parallel to the greatest extent feasible any plans for anticipated clinical use with respect to dose, concentration, route of administration, dosing schedule, and duration. The range of doses selected for study should include at least one dose that is equivalent to and one dose that is a multiple of the highest anticipated clinical dose. Although limited at the start of clinical development, the nonclinical safety studies should be sufficient to characterize any potential toxic effects that might occur under the conditions of the supported clinical trial.

Timing of the nonclinical studies for mAbs is generally similar to the timing expected for small-molecule drug candidates, as summarized in the ICH M3 guidance document.

Animal Care and Use

Nonclinical safety evaluation studies, including toxicology and pharmacokinetics studies, use research animals to characterize the toxicology profile of therapeutic mAbs, as well as small-molecule drugs. These animal studies provide the foundation for ensuring the safety of new drugs intended for human as well as veterinary patients. Great effort has been made over the years to improve and ensure the humane care and use of laboratory animals. The testing laboratories must comply with all applicable laws, regulations, and policies governing the care and use of laboratory animals in accordance with the regulations of the USDA Animal Welfare Act (ie, 9 CFR, Parts 1, 2, and 3) and/or Public Health Service Policy (PHS 2002). Testing laboratories follow the Guide for the Care and Use of Laboratory Animals (2011) [70], which:

> Promotes the humane care and use of laboratory animals by providing information that will enhance animal well-being, the quality of research, and the advancement of scientific knowledge that is relevant to both humans and animals.

All protocols must be reviewed and approved by the testing facility's Institutional Animal Care and Use Committee (IACUC) prior to initiation of a study, and it is recommended to conduct nonclinical safety testing in laboratories that are Association for Assessment and Accreditation of Laboratory Animal Care International (AAALAC International) accredited, where the animal care and use programs have been vetted by veterinarians. Most sponsoring companies and the testing facilities adhere to the 3Rs and make efforts to "reduce, replace, and refine" the use of laboratory animals, and incorporate the industry standards on group sizes for toxicology testing using various species. Ensuring that laboratory animals are treated according to high ethical and scientific standards is paramount in nonclinical safety evaluation testing.

Good Laboratory Practice

The conduct of nonclinical safety studies, especially those utilized for the extrapolation of risk from animals to humans, must conform to the good laboratory practice (GLP) standards (21 CFR Part 58). Good laboratory practice applies to nonclinical studies conducted for the assessment of the safety or efficacy of chemicals (including pharmaceuticals) to humans, animals, and the environment. An internationally recognized definition of GLP can be found on the website for the Medicines and Healthcare Products Regulatory Agency – UK, which defines GLP as:

> Good Laboratory Practice (GLP) embodies a set of principles that provides a framework within which laboratory studies are planned, performed, monitored, recorded, reported and archived. These studies are undertaken to generate data by which the hazards and risks to users, consumers and third parties, including the environment, can be assessed for pharmaceuticals (only preclinical studies), agrochemicals, cosmetics, food additives, feed additives and contaminants, novel foods, biocides, detergents etc.… GLP helps assure regulatory authorities that the data submitted are a true reflection of the results obtained during the study and can therefore be relied upon when making risk/safety assessments.

Conforming to GLP standards in nonclinical safety evaluation studies ensures the uniformity, consistency, reliability, reproducibility, quality, and integrity of the data used for human risk assessment.

Species Selection for Nonclinical Testing

Due to the inherent specificity of mAbs directed to human targets, it is of foremost importance to select animal species for nonclinical safety evaluation that are pharmacologically responsive to the mAb. As one of the primary goals of the nonclinical safety testing is to extrapolate risk from animal data to humans, using animal species that respond in a similar manner to humans will enhance the robustness of the risk assessment process.

Species selection is typically based on information from two major categories, (1) the biology of the target in humans and animals, and (2) information about the activity of the therapeutic mAb in vitro and in pharmacology studies. Early in the research stage of a project, the biology of the target in healthy and disease states in both humans and animals is evaluated, and much effort is focused on understanding the consequences of inhibition and/or activation of the target. Studies from the literature describing the effects of removing the gene of interest (for both ligand and receptor) in cells or mice are also valuable, as this information can be used to gain a sense of the types of safety issues that may be related to inhibiting or activating a particular target and its associated biological pathway. Gene-homology data from the target expressed in human and animals is also typically evaluated, although species selection is not only made on the basis of homology, as even a single amino-acid change at the binding site of a target can have profound effects on the binding affinity of a mAb. Gene-homology data can be useful in understanding differences in mAb-binding affinity and activity between species.

The binding and functional activities of the therapeutic mAb are characterized in both human and animal species to facilitate species selection. The binding affinity of the mAb to its human and animal species target is typically measured using surface plasmon-resonance techniques. To understand pharmacological similarities or differences between the human and animal species, mAb activity can be characterized in cell lines or primary cell-culture experiments, and the data from these evaluations are most relevant when both ligand and receptor pair are used from the same species. If cells expressing the desired target are not available, transfected cells expressing either human or animal target can be used. In addition, the distribution of expression of the target (and corresponding receptor or ligand) should also be understood in both human and animal species.

The next step is to test the effectiveness of the therapeutic mAb in pharmacology studies in healthy animals and/or disease models. Such studies may be designed to determine receptor occupancy, receptor saturation, and/or pharmacological effects and to assist in the selection of an appropriate animal species for further in vivo pharmacology and toxicology studies. Here the differences in binding affinity and/or functional activity should be taken into account in the design of animal studies, with the goal of having equivalent saturation of receptors in vivo. These studies are the first to administer the therapeutic mAb to animals, and valuable information regarding tolerability and the dose–response relationship can be obtained. Although there are no hard and fast rules about the limits of the differences between binding affinity and functional activity between human and toxicology species, staying within a 10-fold range is a conservative goal.

Two species, generally a rodent and nonrodent, are required. However, due to the specificity of mAbs for their human-target molecules, the therapeutic mAb may not show binding or functional activity with the rodent-target molecule. This situation is quite different than that involving NCEs, which are active in most species and rely heavily on metabolic-profile evaluation for species selection.

If the rodent and nonrodent species show adequate cross-reactivity with the therapeutic mAb candidate, development of the mAb will be easier, especially during the later stages where potential reproductive toxicity is assessed. One recommended strategy is to have a design goal so that the mAb selected for development cross-reacts with both rodent and nonrodent species.

There are alternative pathways to choose based on species cross-reactivity, as reviewed in ICH S6(R1). If only one species is available, then a justification needs to be presented as to why one species is sufficient. In the case where there is no relevant species because the mAb does not interact with the target in any species, then homologous molecules, transgenic animals, and/or animal models of disease can be considered. These options each have their challenges.

For homologous molecules, the same standards for manufacturing the clinical candidate will be needed, and the sponsor will need to justify its relevance, and show that it functions in the same manner as the clinical candidate. Homologous murine mAbs were used to support the development of efalizumab (Raptiva; only cross-reactive in chimpanzee), canakinumab (Ilaris; no cross-reactivity to rodents), tocilizumab (Actemra; no cross-reactivity to rodents), and ustekinumab (Stelara; no cross-reactivity to rodents).

For the transgenic animal model, the main challenge may be the lack of historical data to help interpret any toxicological findings. Is the model understood well enough to be able to distinguish whether a histopathological finding is a rare background event or is test-article-mediated?

The ICH S6(R1) guidance document also covers mAbs and related products directed at foreign targets (eg, bacteria, viruses, toxins) where no endogenous target exists in normal, healthy animals, or humans. Here the recommendation is to evaluate the toxicity profile in an animal model of disease. This option comes with its own set of challenges, including the ability to ascertain which pathological features are related to the disease, and which may be related to toxicity of the mAb. Effort will be needed to understand the natural history of the disease in animals and humans and justify how the animal disease mirrors the human disease. The relevance of a toxicological finding in the disease model to human disease would need to be evaluated.

Another option for the case in which there is no appropriate animal species due to lack of pharmacological activity would be to consider a microdosing study in humans, where anticipated subpharmacological doses are administered in the first-in-study (FIH) study, and these levels are then carefully escalated. Details about this type of clinical testing can be found in ICH S6(R1).

NONCLINICAL SAFETY EVALUATION/TOXICOLOGY PLANS TO SUPPORT THE FIRST-IN-HUMAN STUDY

For a mAb, the nonclinical safety evaluation program to support the FIH clinical study is often composed of non-GLP proof-of-concept studies, PK studies, dose range-finding/tolerability studies, and GLP TCR- and

GLP IND-enabling toxicology studies. The aim is to obtain as much information as possible from the toxicology studies to help inform the design and potential risks of the FIH study.

Prior to initiating the nonclinical safety program, all available internal (eg, binding, functional activity, pharmacology) data plus literature information (eg, class effects, gene knock-out data) should be reviewed to determine whether there is any anticipated toxicity based on the mechanism of action of the mAb. Biomarkers of pharmacological activity or clinical effectiveness as well as biomarkers of toxicity should be included in the design of the toxicology study, if possible. These markers will allow analysis of their relationship with systemic drug levels, thus facilitating dose selection and safety margin determination. These biomarkers may also play a valuable role in clinical development.

One of the first items to address is species selection, and whether one or two species will be needed for testing. These choices will need to be justified to the regulatory agencies. The optimum situation is to have cross-reactivity in both rodent and nonrodent species. The nonhuman primate (NHP) is often used for safety testing of mAbs because of the close species similarities among NHP and human therapeutic target molecules. Historical data from the NHP are plentiful, due to the number of therapeutic mAbs tested in this species. Dogs, rabbits, and pigs, used extensively in small-molecule nonclinical safety studies, have not been broadly tested with mAbs, but are possible alternatives.

If ample rodent pharmacology studies have been conducted with the mAb and some safety information is available from these studies, selecting doses and designing a non-GLP dose-range-finding study in the rodent is rather straightforward. If the mAb cross-reacts with the nonrodent species, it is prudent to conduct a small proof-of-concept (POC), PK, and/or dose-range-finding/tolerability study in this species to ensure pharmacological activity in vivo as well as acquire a sense of the tolerability of the mAb before embarking on the large and expensive GLP toxicology studies.

The test article should be given by the same route as planned in the Phase I trial, which is usually IV administration, with options of infusion or slow-push bolus injection. Initially information on the stability and solubility of the mAb is sparse and the early formulations will not contain the optimal concentration to be used in later studies. Thus to expedite clinical development, the IV formulation is used initially, and during Phase I clinical studies, a more concentrated SC formulation is developed and tested in later toxicology and clinical studies.

Single-dose toxicology studies are not typically conducted with mAb therapeutics, mainly because the only findings are often related to exaggerated pharmacological responses. Thus with POC and/or PK data in hand, one can proceed directly to a range-finding multiple-dose toxicology study administering the therapeutic mAb IV once weekly for 4 weeks (days 1, 8, 15, 22, and 29) to support most FIH indications (should be determined on a case-by-case basis). The design supports clinical administration of a single mAb dose as well as up to 5 weekly IV doses. The GLP multiple-dose toxicology study is designed on the basis of the results of the range-finding study.

For the design of the GLP repeat-dose toxicology study supporting the FIH study, a vehicle control group and three dose levels of the therapeutic mAb are tested; however, in some cases, two dose levels of therapeutic mAb may be sufficient and for others more than three may be needed. If the PD marker can be estimated with great certainty, then it might be possible to reduce the therapeutic mAb groups to two. If there is a steep dose–response curve based on an expected exaggerated pharmacological effect, more doses may be needed.

The standard endpoints used in toxicology studies of small molecules are also used to test mAbs, including detailed clinical observation, body weight, food consumption, clinical chemistry, hematology, urinalysis, ophthalmology, and macroscopic and microscopic pathology. For studies in NHP, safety pharmacology measurements such as ECG, blood pressure, and CNS assessments are incorporated into the toxicology study to reduce the number of animals needed. If findings in these evaluations show a cause for concern, then additional standalone pharmacology studies may be appropriate.

Based on the mechanism of action of the therapeutic mAb, specific pharmacodynamic endpoints can be incorporated into the design of the toxicology study. For example, denosumab (Prolia), an inhibitor of receptor activator of nuclear factor kappa-B ligand (RANKL), a protein essential for osteoclast formation, function, and survival, showed rapid reduction in serum levels of C-telopeptide, a marker of osteoclast function in cynomolgus monkeys [71], demonstrating the anticipated pharmacological activity of the mAb. Bevacizumab (Avastin), which inhibits vascular endothelial growth factor (VEGF) activity, was shown in repeat-dose IV toxicity studies to cause a dose-related increase in the incidence of physeal dysplasia in the bone-growth plates in young-adult cynomolgus monkeys, thus this type of histopathological finding can be used as a marker for antiangiogenic pharmacological activity in toxicology studies [72].

If the mechanism of action of the therapeutic mAb is immunomodulation, additional endpoints can be incorporated into the study design, such as fluorescence-activated cell sorting analysis to evaluate lymphocyte subpopulations, or immunization with neoantigens (eg, tetanus toxoid, KLH) to assess the T-cell-dependent antibody response (TDAR).

Pharmacokinetics/toxicokinetics sampling should be included. Due to the longer half-lives of mAbs compared to small-molecule therapeutics, the PK sampling times differ considerably. For PK/TK evaluations for nonclinical and clinical studies, analytical methods need to be developed and validated (for GLP studies) to measure the amount of mAb in serum. These methods may be developed on platforms such as enzyme-linked immunosorbant assay or meso scale discovery.

As human/humanized therapeutic mAbs are regarded as foreign to the animal species tested, an ADA response is anticipated, and an ADA assessment should be included in the study. Typically, predose and end-of-study samples are collected during the study. Although the regulations state that ADA testing may not be needed when pharmacodynamic activity is evident in toxicology studies (ICH S6(R1)), it is prudent to collect the ADA samples during the study and then decide if analysis is warranted or not. Immunogenicity will be discussed further in the following sections.

To select the dose levels for the IND-enabling toxicology study, the first step is to estimate a dose or dose range where clinical efficacy would be expected, which is referred to as the pharmacologically active dose (PAD). This estimation can be based on information collected from in vitro binding assays, receptor occupancy data, cell-culture activity, and PK/PD studies. Physiological-based PK/PD modeling data can also be very useful. The PAD dose/dose range will be used to select the low dose for the toxicology study. Optimally, it would be helpful to have pharmacological activity in the low-dose group for the toxicology study, but at a level low enough not to yield any exaggerated pharmacological or adverse effects.

In practice, selection of a high dose for toxicology studies of mAbs is done on a case-by-case basis. This is a very different process than that for small-molecule therapeutics, where the high dose is related to a maximum tolerated dose (MTD). mAbs are expected to show evidence of exaggerated pharmacodynamic activity but not frank toxicity, as seen with small-molecule therapeutics (although there is always the exception!). The high dose is often selected taking several considerations into account, including the maximal feasible dose (MFD), which is related to the test-article concentration and volume that can be administered to animals, saturation level of target or receptors, and/or an appropriate pharmacologically active dose that has shown signs of exaggerated pharmacology in POC, PK and/or range-finding studies. High-dose selection should have a sound scientific basis related to the activity of the mAb.

The no-observed-adverse-effect level (NOAEL) dose will be determined from the GLP toxicology study, and will play an important role in dose selection for the FIH clinical study.

DOSE SELECTION FOR THE FIH STUDY

The safety of human subjects is the primary concern when selecting a dose for initial clinical studies. Due to the long half-life and subsequent residence time in the body (~5 half-lives) of mAb therapeutics, subjects with the disease of interest rather than healthy volunteers are typically enrolled in the FIH study. The challenge is to select an FIH dose that is initially too low to produce clinical benefit, but will with escalation arrive at one that could potentially provide benefit to the diseased subject. The process for determining the FIH dose for adult subjects in clinical trials is discussed in regulatory guidance documents and reviewed in the literature [73–75]. Two important regulatory documents that provide guidance on selecting the FIH dose are summarized in this section:

- FDA Guidance for Industry: Estimating the Maximum Safe Starting Dose in Initial Clinical Trials for Therapeutics in Adult Healthy Volunteers, July 2005
- EMEA/CHMP Draft Guideline on Requirements for First-in-Man Clinical Trials for Potential High-Risk Medicinal Products, March 22, 2007

A case-by-case evaluation is needed to make an FIH dose recommendation for mAb therapeutics. Special considerations need to be taken into account for mAbs with activation of biological processes as their mode of action [74], and for mAbs targeting certain cytokines, chemokines, or other low-level systemically expressed targets where the PAD is expected to be in the microgram/kg range or there is no measureable pharmacodynamic activity.

The first step in FIH dose selection is to determine the maximum recommended starting dose (MSRD), a process that takes into consideration all the available in vitro and in vivo pharmacological, pharmacodynamic, pharmacokinetic, physiological, and toxicological data. The MSRD is calculated from the NOAEL, and needs to be compared with the PAD and the minimal-anticipated-biological-effective-level (MABEL).

The NOAEL is a generally accepted benchmark for safety and is the traditional method used to select FIH doses. For mAbs, it is derived from the GLP repeat-dose toxicity study(ies) designed to support the FIH clinical study. It can be derived from significant findings in toxicological studies, including signs of overt toxicity (eg, clinical signs, macroscopic or microscopic lesions), surrogate markers of toxicity (eg, serum liver enzymes, elevations in serum levels of cellular proteins), or exaggerated pharmacological effects [76,77].

Based on FDA (2005) guidance:

> As a general rule, an adverse effect observed in nonclinical toxicology studies used to define the NOAEL for the purpose of dose-setting should be based on an effect that would be unacceptable if produced by the initial dose of a therapeutic in Phase I clinical trials conducted in healthy volunteers.

If several species were used in the IND-enabling toxicology studies, the most sensitive species should be used to calculate the MSRD.

Once the NOAEL has been determined, it can be converted to a human-equivalent dose (HED) using appropriate scaling factors, if needed. For small-molecule therapeutics, the NOAEL dose is converted to the HED using body-surface area correction factors ($BW^{2/3}$). This conversion is not necessary for mAb therapeutics that show a robust correlation between dose (mg/kg) and plasma drug levels (C_{max} and AUC). According to the FDA guidance (2005), proteins with a molecular weight above 100,000 Da should be normalized to mg/kg for HED calculation. Thus if the NOAEL dose in animals for a mAb is 10 mg/kg, the HED is also 10 mg/kg.

The next step in calculating the MSRD is to apply a safety factor to the HED to increase assurance that the first dose in subjects will not cause adverse effects. A safety factor of 10 is generally used, based on uncertainties in extrapolating from animal data to studies in humans. These uncertainties may include differences in sensitivity to pharmacological activity of the mAb, differences in target affinities or receptor distribution, differences in ADME profiles between animal and human, difficulties in detecting certain types of toxicity in animal studies such as headache or myalgia, and unexpected toxicities.

A factor greater than 10 can be used if there is evidence that this may be necessary. Causes for concern that would support raising the safety factor include a steep dose–response curve, severe toxicities, toxicity without premonitory signs, nonmonitorable toxicity, variable bioavailability, irreversible toxicity, unexplained mortality, large variability in dose or plasma drug levels, nonlinear PK, inadequate dose–response data, novel therapeutic targets, and/or animal models with limited utility [76,77].

Thus to calculate the MSRD, the HED is divided by an appropriate safety factor, typically using a value of 10, but can be increased or decreased based on available data. For a mAb with an HED of 10 mg/kg and using a safety factor of 10, the MSRD would be 1 mg/kg.

Once the MSRD has been determined, it is advisable to compare it to the PAD. This is especially important for mAb therapeutics that may not show any toxicity in the repeat-dose studies, thus resulting in high NOAEL values based on the highest dose tested (~100 mg/kg). For such a case, the NOAEL is 100 mg/kg, the HED is 100 mg/kg, and the MSRD would be 10 mg/kg (using a safety factor of 10), which would be considered a high mAb dose. The PAD, derived from in vitro and/ or in vivo pharmacology models, for such a case may be a more sensitive indicator of biological activity and/or potential toxicity than the NOAEL, and thus may support lowering the MSRD.

The second method for FIH dose calculation is the MABEL in humans. This method is an extension of the concepts behind the PAD, and is directed toward potential high-risk medicinal products, which are defined as products where there are concerns that serious adverse effects may occur in the FIH study. The EMEA guidance document (2007) was produced after the tragedy involving the TeGenero monoclonal antibody TGN1412, where the FIH dose caused a cytokine storm following administration to healthy volunteers [78]. The premise here is that potentially high-risk medicinal products may need a more conservative approach to dose selection, as the ability of nonclinical studies to predict safety issues in humans may be reduced if the nature of the target is more specific to humans.

The EMEA guidance (2007) notes that some new drugs should be considered high risk due to concerns arising from particular knowledge, or uncertainties in their mode of action, nature of target, or relevance of animal models. The MABEL dose calculation is a special precaution to minimize the risk of adverse effects. With respect to mode of action, increased risk is associated with the novelty of the target, and the extent of knowledge of its mode of action. A compound with a pleiotropic mechanism that leads to various physiological effects, or one that bypasses normal physiological control mechanisms (eg, CD28 agonists), would be considered high risk. The nature of the target may impact on the risk inherent in FIH dosing, thus the biology of the target, and downstream effects in human species, and the biology and PD effects in both normal and diseased states needs consideration. The relevance of the animal models in predicting the risk to humans needs evaluation. If the available animal models are of limited relevance to predict PD and toxic effects, then the product should be considered high risk.

To calculate the MABEL, all relevant in vitro and in vivo pharmacological, PK/PD, and toxicity data need to be taken into account and integrated into a PK/PD modeling approach. A safety factor is then applied, defaulting to 10. This can be increased or decreased on a case-by-case basis, by considering available data. As with the PAD, the MABEL dose may be a more sensitive method for determining potential toxicity than the NOAEL. When the methods (NOAEL, PAD, MABEL) give different estimates of the FIH dose, the lowest value should be used.

REPEAT-DOSE TOXICOLOGY STUDIES BEYOND FIH

Once the Phase I study is under way, many other nonclinical development activities are necessary, all governed by the clinical development plan and timing of clinical studies. As development of a mAb therapeutic starts with the Phase I study, safety and signs of biological activity and/or clinical efficacy support the investment in further nonclinical studies, and with an acceptable safety profile in the nonclinical studies,

TABLE 23.4 ICH Recommended Duration of Repeat-Dose Toxicity Studies to Support the Conduct of Clinical Trials

Maximum Duration of Clinical Trial	Recommended Minimum Duration of Repeat-Dose Toxicity Studies to Support Clinical Trials	
	Rodents	Nonrodents
Up to 2 weeks	2 weeks	2 weeks
Between 2 weeks and 6 months	Same as clinical trial	Same as clinical trial
>6 months	6 months	9 months (6 months for mAbs is acceptable)

TABLE 23.5 ICH Recommended Duration of Repeated-Dose Toxicity Studies to Support Marketing

Duration of Indicated Treatment	Rodent	Nonrodent
Up to 2 weeks	1 month	1 month
>2 weeks to 1 month	3 months	3 months
>1 month to 3 months	6 months	6 months
>3 months	6 months	9 months (6 months for mAbs is acceptable)

further investment in clinical development follows. This careful, step-wise approach balances risk and investment related to nonclinical and clinical studies.

The ICH M3 and S6(R1) provide guidance regarding the timing of nonclinical studies needed to support clinical activity (Tables 23.4 and 23.5). Table 23.4 summarizes the duration of repeat-dose toxicity studies for small- and large-molecule therapeutics needed to enable similar durations in clinical testing. In general, clinical studies of certain durations should be supported by repeat-dose toxicology studies of at least an equivalent duration. For mAb therapeutics, 6-month rodent and/or nonrodent (based on species cross-reactivity) studies will generally support clinical studies of greater than 9-month duration.

Table 23.5 summarizes the recommended duration of repeat-dose toxicity studies needed to support the marketing authorization for small- and large-molecule therapeutics. For chronic use of mAbs, 6-month repeat-dose studies are adequate for marketing authorization (ICH S6(R1)).

The need to continue using two species beyond the IND-enabling studies is determined on a case-by-case basis, by considering the pharmacology/toxicology profile. If the toxicological findings from the 1-month studies are similar in both species, then longer-term studies in one species are usually considered sufficient, and the rodent species should be used, unless there is a reason for using the nonrodent species (ICH S6(R1)).

The dosing schedule in the animal studies generally varies between once 1 week and once 1 month, based on the half-life of the mAb, the duration of pharmacodynamic effect, and any clinical indications. It uses the route of administration to be used in the clinic.

The initial nonclinical studies generally include recovery periods. These are periods of time after dosing has stopped, to assess recovery from toxicity or PD effects, with the objective of assessing animals after the recovery period to evaluate the reversibility of any effects, but not delayed toxicity. Demonstration of complete recovery from these effects is generally not necessary. The regulatory guidance documents (ICH S6(R1)) note that the addition of a recovery period is not appropriate if the goal is just to assess immunogenicity (low levels of drug at the end of a recovery period allow improved detection of ADA). The decision regarding whether or not to include recovery groups in the subchronic and chronic toxicity studies will need to be made on a case-by-case basis, determined by the pharmacodynamic and toxicity parameters as well as recovery observed in the 1-month studies.

IMMUNOGENICITY OF MONOCLONAL ANTIBODIES

The evolution in antibody engineering has ultimately led to the production of fully human mAbs that are significantly less immunogenic than the early mouse mAbs. For example, the immune response to the murine mAb, muromonab, resulted in its clearance from the circulation after about 2 weeks of treatment [19], whereas human therapeutic mAbs, such as denosumab, can be successfully administered on a chronic basis to postmenopausal patients with osteoporosis.

The assessment of the immunogenicity of mAbs is typically included in nonclinical safety evaluation studies, and is standard practice in clinical studies, but the objectives of assessing the presence of ADA in these studies are somewhat different. The purpose of the former is to gain a thorough understanding of levels of systemic exposure to the mAb over the duration of the study and to aid in interpretation of the study. In a robust immune response, the ADA can bind to the mAb therapeutic, resulting in increased clearance of the drug. Alternatively, the ADA interferes with the binding of the mAb to its therapeutic target, thus possibly masking pharmacological or toxicological effects, making it challenging to assess the safety of the mAb. If no toxicity or PD activity is observed, then it is important to have data showing a lack of neutralizing antibodies as well as PK data showing drug presence, since these data can support the argument that exposure was adequately assessed in the toxicology study [79]. For this reason, at the onset of a toxicology program, ADA samples should be collected from animals for possible future analysis.

For clinical studies, the objective of ADA assessment is to evaluate clearance of the drug, possible immunotoxicity, and to determine whether the presence of ADA leads to a reduction in efficacy of the therapeutic mAb.

Testing for ADA generally follows a tiered approach (reviewed by the FDA Immunogenicity Testing Draft Guidance, 2009; [80]), including a screening assay, a confirmatory assay (where the unlabeled mAb therapeutic is used to compete with ADA binding), and a titer assay. Characterization of ADA-neutralizing activity is needed on a case-by-case basis for toxicology studies, mainly to aid in the interpretation of the study, if needed, and is expected to be conducted for clinical studies. The bioanalytical field continues to develop new methods to measure and characterize ADA.

The immune response to human or humanized mAbs is expected to be greater in animals than in humans, due to the differences in the mAb protein structure between the different species. Thus any immunogenicity in animals is expected to overestimate the immune response anticipated in humans. For this reason, immunogenicity data from animal studies is not used to predict the immune response to a mAb therapeutic in humans (for a review see Refs. [79,81,82]).

The generation of ADA may have little or no impact on the PK/PD and/or toxicity of a therapeutic mAb; however, in some cases, circulating ADA-mAb complexes may lead to hypersensitivity reactions (eg, Type III reactions, according to Coombs and Gell classification), or deposition of ADA-mAb complexes in the kidney, possibly leading to glomerular nephritis. The potential pathogenic properties of ADA-mAb complexes are incompletely understood, but have been found to depend on a ratio of the concentrations of ADA to therapeutic mAb, as well as the overall amount of antibody in the circulation [83,84].

IMMUNOTOXICITY

The evaluation of potential immunotoxicity in new therapeutic mAbs is critical, especially since a large number of the mAbs marketed intentionally target the immune system. The ICH S8 (Guidance for Industry – S8 Immunotoxicity Studies for Human Pharmaceuticals, [85]) provides regulatory guidance on nonclinical testing approaches to identify potentially immunotoxic drugs, and a weight-of-evidence approach to decision-making for immunotoxicity testing. As per ICH S8, immunotoxicity is defined as unintended immunosuppression or enhancement.

The potential for immunotoxicity is assessed in a tiered manner, starting with general toxicology studies.

Signs of immunotoxicity can be ascertained by gross pathology and organ-weight assessment, histopathological evaluation of the spleen, lymph nodes, and bone marrow as well as assessment of clinical pathology parameters (hematology and clinical chemistry). Findings indicating immunotoxicity can be further investigated in studies designed to address specific questions.

If immunomodulation of the immune system is anticipated from the mechanism of action of a mAb, special evaluations such as T-cell-dependent antibody response (TDAR) and/or immunophenotyping, using immunohistochemistry or flow cytometry methods, can be incorporated into the toxicology studies. With immunophenotyping, the lymphocyte subpopulations (absolute values and percentages) can be examined.

Other immune function assays available include natural killer cell activity assays, macrophage/neutrophil function assays, and cell-mediated immunity/delayed-type hypersensitivity (DTH) assays. Host-resistance assays, which can evaluate a wide range of pathogens (eg, *Listeria monocytogenes, Streptococcus pneumonia*), are also available, if warranted [86]. In vitro studies are typically conducted to assess the potential for ADCC and CDC.

As many of the marketed mAbs targeting the human immune system are pharmacologically active only in nonhuman primates, this species has been used extensively in the assessment of immunotoxicity risk [87]. Several reviews on immunotoxicity testing of immunomodulatory biological therapeutics are available [88,89].

For mAbs where immunosuppression or immunostimulation is anticipated from their mechanism of action, special attention is needed to understand the biological consequences of inhibiting or activating pathways involving the immune system, both in the toxicology species and in humans, in order to assess risk. The TeGenero case is a very unfortunate example in which rodent and NHP toxicology data did not predict the activity of an immunomodulatory superagonist anti-CD28 mAb in humans [78]. This mAb, referred to as TGN1412, was administered as a single dose to six healthy volunteers (0.1 mg/kg dose), and a cytokine-release syndrome or "cytokine storm" occurred, involving multiorgan failure. All patients were transferred to intensive care, where at least four suffered multiple organ dysfunction. Retrospective analysis of the FIH dose has implied that a careful analysis of all the available in vitro and in vivo immunological and pharmacological data [90] would have dictated the selection of a lower FIH dose. This tragedy has resulted in renewed awareness of the need to assess all data associated with a new mAb therapeutic, plus others with similar mechanism of action, when extrapolating risk from animals to humans [91]. A new EMEA Guideline to assist with the process of FIH dose selection has also been published [92–94].

REPRODUCTIVE AND DEVELOPMENTAL TOXICITY EVALUATION

Evaluation of the potential of a new drug to cause harm to the fertility, reproductive, and/or developmental processes in animals is critical to the progression of clinical development. Although the general concepts for testing are the same in the ICH countries (the US, EU, and Japan), the timing of when the data are needed to support the different stages of clinical development varies among the countries. Regulatory guidance documents recommended for these reproductive system assessments for mAbs are listed in the following, and their content will be summarized in this section:

- ICH Harmonised Tripartite Guideline – Detection of Toxicity to Reproduction for Medicinal Products & Toxicity to Male Fertility, S5(R2), 2005
- ICH S6(R1)

Although mAbs and small-molecule therapeutics undergo similar nonclinical testing to determine their potential toxicity to the reproductive system, mAbs generally are associated with lower risk. Small-molecule therapeutics are capable of easily crossing cell membranes and gaining access to the interior of the cell. This enables travel across the placenta and access to the developing embryo/fetus, as well as postnatal access to offspring through maternal milk. For mAbs, transport across placenta is generally via the FcRn, allowing access to the embryo/fetus at times that are largely dependent on the expression profile of the maternal FcRn. mAbs have been found in fetal serum and also maternal milk.

Small-molecule therapeutics are also metabolized, which can produce metabolites with greater toxicity than the parent molecule, thus supporting the necessity of testing reproductive system toxicity in two species, due to the variability in metabolism between species. For mAbs, metabolism results in degradation into amino acids, which do not present the same risk as small-molecule metabolites.

The nonclinical safety assessment is:

> Expected to cover all stages of development from conception to sexual maturity, and to allow detection of immediate and latent effects of exposure by following the animals through one complete life cycle (ie, from conception in one generation through conception in the following generation). (ICH S5(R2))

Traditionally, toxicology evaluation studies assessing reproduction have been divided into three parts: Segment I (male and female fertility and early embryonic development), Segment II [embryo-fetal development (EFD)], and Segment III (pre-/postnatal development). Segment I generally covers premating through implantation, Segment II studies cover implantation through the end of pregnancy, and Segment III studies cover closure of the hard palate to weaning and sexual maturity of the F1 pups.

For a new mAb therapeutic, only pharmacologically active species should be used in the evaluation of potential toxicity to the reproductive system. This is where the challenge arises, since traditional rodent and rabbit species may not demonstrate cross-reactivity with the mAb, so the sponsor may need to use NHP or other nontraditional species, and employ creative approaches to safety evaluation of the reproductive system.

Due to issues with cross-reactivity, the NHP has become a more common species for reproductive toxicity assessment, and the traditional Segment I–III studies have been modified in design to facilitate its use and to reduce the number of animals studied. The term enhanced pre-/postnatal development study (ePPD) has emerged for NHP studies and combines fertility, EFD, and postnatal evaluations. Several reviews are available on reproductive toxicity testing with NHP [95,96].

Traditional study designs can be modified based on an understanding of species specificity, the nature of the product, mechanism of action, immunogenicity, and/or PK behavior and embryo-fetal exposure. Once again, a case-by-case science-based assessment will be needed to design these studies. This is especially the case for NHP studies, since they are more complex in nature than the traditional rodent and rabbit studies.

Fertility

For mAb therapeutics, ICH S6(R1) states that for products where rodents are a relevant species, an assessment of fertility can be made in this species, and the fertility studies for small-molecule and biologic therapeutics in rodents are similar in nature.

For female and male fertility assessment in rodents, during the premating period, females are administered the therapeutic mAb 2 weeks prior to dosing and males administered mAb 4 weeks prior to mating. Treatment continues throughout mating at least through implantation for females and study termination for males. The assessments include a general macroscopic evaluation at necropsy, preservation of tissues with any findings as well as the reproductive organs for possible future evaluation, numerical assessment of corpora lutea and implantation sites in the uterus, and counting of live and dead conceptus. Sperm analysis can be done to assess potential effects on spermatogenesis.

Based on ICH S6(R1), when the NHP is the only pharmacologically relevant species, the potential effects on male and female fertility can be assessed by standard histopathological evaluation and assessment of menstrual cyclicity in the repeat-dose toxicity studies of at least 3 months' duration using sexually mature NHPs. If there is a specific cause for concern, specialized assessments such as sperm count, sperm morphology/motility, testicular volume, and male or female reproductive hormone levels should be evaluated in the repeat-dose toxicity study.

If there is cause for concern regarding potential effects on conception/implantation based on the pharmacological activity of a mAb, this can be investigated experimentally by using a homologous product or transgenic model to assess potential effects on conception or implantation.

When considering timing to support clinical studies, according to ICH M3(R1) men and women can be enrolled in Phases I and II clinical studies before male and female fertility studies have taken place, since evaluation of the male and female reproductive organs has been performed in the repeat-dose toxicity studies. Nonclinical male and female fertility studies should be completed prior to the initiation of Phase III clinical trials, or other large-scale or long-duration studies.

Embryo-Fetal Development

Study designs for small-molecule and mAb therapeutics are similar for EFD studies using rodents and rabbits, with dosing occurring during the period of major organogenesis. The situation is more challenging if there is no species cross-reactivity with the rodent or rabbit, if NHP are used, or if other models need to be developed.

If NHP or other novel models are used, it is important to understand the reproductive biology of the species being tested, the course of development of specific systems of interest (eg, immunological system development), the pharmacological and possible toxicological endpoints to build into the study design for evaluation, PK sampling to understand maternal exposure, and if possible, PK sampling of the offspring. For the NHP, assessment of pregnancy outcome at natural delivery is typically performed, evaluating offspring viability, survival, external malfunction, skeletal effects, and visceral morphology at necropsy.

Based on ICH S6(R1), one species can be sufficient for EFD evaluation if more than one relevant species exists, provided there is a scientific rationale supporting species selection. For other mAbs such as natalizumab (Tysabri; developed prior to ICH S6(R1)), only the guinea pig and NHP showed pharmacological activity with the mAb and were used in the reproductive toxicity assessment. The guinea pig, a nontraditional species for EFD studies, was evaluated for feasibility and then used for assessment of potential toxicity to embryo-fetal development [97] as well as fertility [98].

For products that are only pharmacologically active in NHP, one well-designed study that includes dosing from day 20 of gestation to birth can be considered (ICH S6(R1)). This is referred to as an enhanced pre-/postnatal development (ePPND) study. It evaluates all the stages in traditional EFD (Segment II) and pre-/postnatal (Segment III) studies, but uses fewer animals, since the parameters from the two studies are combined into one. It is also possible to evaluate potential effects on EFD and postnatal development using alternative study designs or a homologous product in rodents.

For efalizumab (Raptiva), which showed species cross-reactivity only in the chimpanzee and human, a homologous mAb was developed that cross-reacted with the mouse, and the mouse model was used for EFD and fertility assessment [99].

There is room for flexibility and creativity in the designs of these studies based on the characteristics of the mAb, intended pharmacological activity, potential toxicity, and duration of intended effect, as long as the study design is based on a science-driven rationale.

In the United States, assessment of EFD should be conducted prior to enrolment of women of childbearing potential (WOCBP) using precautions to prevent pregnancy in Phase III studies. In the EU and Japan, definitive nonclinical EFD toxicity studies should be completed before exposure of WOCBP.

Reproductive toxicology studies might not be warranted when the weight of evidence (eg, mechanism of action, phenotypic data from KO mice, class effects) suggests that there will be an adverse effect on pregnancy outcome, and these data possibly could provide adequate information to communicate risk.

Pre-/Postnatal Development Studies

The objective of pre-/postnatal development studies is to assess the potential toxicity of a new drug to development occurring during the period preceding birth, the neonatal stage, and development and sexual function of the F1 pups. Female animals are exposed to the mAb from implantation to the end of lactation. Species selection will be dependent on mAb pharmacological activity. The traditional species is the rodent (rat). If the NHP is the only species available for testing, consideration should be given to combining the endpoints with those in the EFD, if possible (see ePPND study previously mentioned).

For maternal animals, endpoints typically include clinical observations, body weights, food consumption, duration of pregnancy and parturition, number of implantations, and any abnormalities. For the offspring, observations include viability of offspring at birth, body weight at birth, pre- and postweaning survival and growth/body weight, maturation, and fertility. Physical development, sensory functions, and reflexes and behavior are also evaluated.

In the United States, EU and Japan, the pre-/postnatal development study should be conducted prior to marketing authorization.

CARCINOGENICITY

Based on ICH S1A, carcinogenicity assessment is anticipated to support clinical development and marketing authorization of small-molecule therapeutics intended for treating chronic (greater than 6 months of continuous treatment duration) diseases, and traditionally encompasses 2-year carcinogenicity bioassays in both mice and rats [100]. In some instances, a 6-month transgenic mouse study may be substituted for the 2-year mouse study, based on the mechanism of action of the drug and associated scientific rationale. For mAb therapeutics, which are not metabolized to reactive metabolites, cannot access the cell interior, and do not come in contact or cause damage to DNA, the genotoxic potential is considered to be low, thus supporting the rationale for not conducting the standard battery of genotoxicity tests. For these reasons as well as issues where the mAb is not pharmacologically active in rodent species, or is active but generates a robust immunogenicity response resulting in mAb clearance from the systemic circulation, the traditional rodent carcinogenicity bioassays are not conducted. However, there is a theoretical concern that immunomodulatory mAb therapeutics may affect normal immune surveillance mechanisms and result in increase in the incidence or proliferation rate, or a specific type of neoplasm or group of neoplasms.

Regulatory guidance documents that should be reviewed on this subject include ICH S6(R1) and S1A (Guideline on the Need for Carcinogenicity Studies of Pharmaceuticals). The ICH S1A is most relevant for small-molecule carcinogenicity evaluation, but does recognize the challenges for evaluating mAbs as well as other biological therapeutics. Thus an assessment of the necessity for evaluating potential tumorigenicity risk should be conducted on a case-by-case basis, taking into account the intended clinical population and treatment duration [100].

To determine whether additional studies are needed to assess tumorigenicity risk, a weight-of-evidence assessment is recommended, taking into account data from the published literature (information on transgenic animals, knock-out models, human genetic disease, drug class effects, target biology) as well as data on the mAb from in vitro studies, chronic toxicology studies, and clinical data.

If the weight of evidence suggests a concern about carcinogenic/tumorigenic potential, additional nonclinical studies could be conducted that may mitigate this concern. In some cases, the available data can be considered sufficient to address carcinogenic potential and inform clinical risk without warranting additional nonclinical studies. For example, immunomodulators and growth factors pose a potential carcinogenic risk that can be evaluated by postmarketing clinical surveillance

more effectively than further clinical studies (FDA ICH S6(R1)). Vahle and colleagues [101] reviewed past and current practices regarding carcinogenicity assessments of biological therapeutics and provided recommendations for carcinogenicity assessments. Of the 21 mAbs reviewed, none were tested in 2-year rodent bioassays. One (mouse homolog; efalizumab) was tested in the p53(+/+) transgenic model, and showed a negative response; one (mouse homolog; infliximab) was tested in a 6-month repeat-dose study with negative tumorigenicity results; and one (natalizumab) was tested in in vitro proliferation assays and in a tumor xenograft model, with negative results for proliferation and tumor growth rate/metastasis, respectively.

For assessing the carcinogenicity risk of a mAb therapeutic, rodent 2-year bioassays or short-term tumorigenicity studies with rodent homologs are generally of limited value and generally are not recommended by regulatory authorities.

DRUG INTERACTIONS

As mAbs are not metabolized by cytochrome (CYP) 450 enzymes, they have not been expected to play an important role in drug–drug interactions in the clinic, and have not historically been evaluated for such effects. Recently, however, it has been shown that therapeutic proteins, including mAbs, may impact the disposition of drugs metabolized by CYP 450 (Ref. [102], reviewed by Ref. [103]). mAbs and other therapeutic proteins that target pathways reducing inflammation and/or infection have been shown to affect CYP 450 enzyme expression, likely resulting from changes in transcription factor activity for CYP enzyme expression or changes in CYP enzyme activity due to altered immune status [103,104].

This is an evolving area of study, and mAbs-targeting cytokines, interferons, and growth factors may need to undergo assessment. In vitro studies investigating CYP 450 inhibition and/or induction may be relevant on a case-by-case basis, and further evaluation in the clinical studies may be warranted.

PARTNERSHIP IN MAB DEVELOPMENT

Advancing a new mAb therapeutic from the benchtop to the clinic requires the concerted efforts of many people in numerous different fields of study and expertise, and successful development is based on good communication and partnerships between the sponsoring company, regulatory agencies, as well as the contract research organizations involved in many nonclinical and clinical studies, with the ultimate goal of providing safe and effective new medicines for patients.

SUMMARY

The use of antibodies for disease treatment has come a long way since the early days of serum therapy for patients with diphtheria, with the origin of Ehrlich's concept of medicines serving as magic bullets to target disease. Together with the growing fields of molecular biology and antibody engineering, humanized and fully human therapeutic mAbs with less risk of immunogenicity are available for treatment of serious diseases. The understanding and practice of nonclinical safety evaluation of mAbs has advanced together with this growth in technology and remains a case-by-case, science-driven assessment.

References

[1] Ecker DM, Jones SD, Levine HL. The therapeutic monoclonal antibody network. mAbs 2015;7(1):9–14.

[2] Yamada T. Therapeutic monoclonal antibodies. Keio J Med 2011:37–46.

[3] www.bio.org New report shows monoclonal antibody development times are lengthening. 2011.

[4] Reichert J, Rosensweig C, Faden L, Dewitz M. Monoclonal antibodies successes in the clinic. Nat Biotechnol 2005;23(9):1073–8.

[5] Strohl W. Therapeutic monoclonal antibodies: past, present, and future, in therapeutic monoclonal antibodies. In: An A, editor. From the bench to the clinic. Hoboken: John Wiley & Sons; 2009. p. 3–50.

[6] Winau F, Winau R. Emil von Behring and serum therapy. Microbes Infect 2002;4:185–8.

[7] nobelprize.org.Behring. Emil von Behring biography. 2011. nobelprize.org.

[8] Llewelyn M, Hawkins R, Russell S. Discovery of antibodies. Br Med J 1992;305:1269–72.

[9] nobelprize.org.Erhlich. Paul Ehrlich – biography. 2011.

[10] Casadevall A, Scharff M. Serum therapy revisited: animal models of infection and development of passive antibody therapy. Antimicrob Agents Chemother 1994;38(8):1695–702.

[11] Alberts B, Bray D, Lewis J, Raff M, Roberts K, Watson J. In: Robertson R, editor. Molecular biology of the cell. Second edition. The immune system. New York: Garland Publishing, Inc.; 1989. p. 1002–57. [chapter 18].

[12] Mould D, Green B. Pharmacokinetics and pharmacodynamics of monoclonal antibodies: concepts and lessons from drug development. BioDrugs 2010;24(1):23–39.

[13] Allansmith M, de Ramus A, Maurice D. The dynamics of IgG in the cornea. Assoc Res Vis Ophthal, Inc 1979;18(9):947–55.

[14] Kabat E, Wu T. Attempts to locate complementarity-determining residues in the variable positions of light and heavy chains. Ann NY Acad Sci 1971;190:382–93.

[15] Wu T, Kabat E. An analysis of the sequences of the variable regions of Bence Jones proteins and myeloma light chains and their implications for antibody complementarity. J Exp Med 1970;132(2):211–50.

[16] Heyman B. Complement and Fc-receptors in regulation of the antibody response. Immunol Lett 1996;54(2–3):195–9.

[17] Woof J, Burton D. Human antibody-Fc receptor interactions illuminated by crystal structures. Nat Rev Immunol 2004;4(2):89–99.

[18] Kohler G, Milstein C. Continuous cultures of fused cells secreting antibody of predefined specificity. Nature 1975;256:495–7.

[19] Orthoclone package labeling.

[20] Wikipedia. Muromonab-CD3. 2012.

[21] Morrison S, Johnson M, Herzenberry L, Oi V. Chimeric human antibody molecules: mouse antigen-binding domains with human constant region domains. Proc Natl Acad Sci 1984;81:6851–5.

[22] Boulianne G, Hozumi N, Shulman M. Production of functional chimaeric mouse/human antibody. Nature 1984;312:643–6.

[23] Remicade package labeling, Remicade – Centocor, Inc.

[24] Ogale S, Hitraya E, Henk H. Patterns of biological agent utilization among patients with rheumatoid arthritis: a retrospective cohort study. Musculoskelet Disord 2011;12:204–14.

[25] Jones P, Dear P, Foote J, Neuberger M, Winter G. Replacing the complementarity-determining region in a human antibody with those from a mouse. Nature 1986;321:522–5.

[26] Queen C, Schneider W, Selick H, Payne P, Landofi N, Duncan J, et al. A humanized antibody that binds to the interleukin 2 receptor. Proc Natl Acad Sci 1989;86:10029–33.

[27] Co M, Queen C. Humanized antibodies for therapy. Nature 1991;351:501–2.

[28] Ostberg L, Queen C. Human and humanized monoclonal antibodies: preclinical studies and clinical experience. Biochem Soc Trans 1995;23:1038–43.

[29] Zenapax package labeling, Zenapax – Hoffman – La Roche.

[30] McCafferty J, Griffiths A, Winter G, Chiswell D. Phage antibodies: filamentous phase displaying antibody variable domains. Nature 1990;348(6301):552–4.

[31] Marks J, Hoogenboom H, Bonnert T, McCafferty J, Griffiths A, Winter G. By-passing immunization. Human antibodies from V-gene libraries displayed on phage. J Mol Biol 1991;222(3):581–97.

[32] Winter G, Griffiths A, Hawkins R, Hoogenboom H. Making antibodies by phage display technology. Ann Rev Immunol 1994;12:433–55.

[33] Carmen S, Jermutus L. Concepts in antibody phage display. Brief Funct Genomic Proteomic 2002;1(2):189–203.

[34] Jakobovits A, Moore A, Green L, Vergara G, Maynard-Curie C, Austin H, et al. Germ-line transmission and expression of a human-derived yeast artificial chromosome. Nature 1993;362:255–8.

[35] Ternant D, Paintaud G. Pharmacokinetics and concentration-effect relationships of therapeutic monoclonal antibodies and fusion proteins. Expert Opin Biol Ther 2005;5(Suppl. 1):S37–47.

[36] Tabrizi M, Roskos L. Preclinical and clinical safety of monoclonal antibodies. Drug Discov Today 2006;12(13/14):540–7.

[37] Lobo E, Hansen R, Balthasar J. Antibody pharmacokinetics and pharmacodynamics. J Pharm Sci 2004;93(11):2645–68.

[38] Tabrizi M, Roskos L. Preclinical and clinical safety of monoclonal antibodies. Drug Discov Today 2007;12(13/14):540–7.

[39] Presta L. Engineering of therapeutic antibodies to minimize immunogenicity and optimize function. Adv Drug Deliv Rev 2006;58:640–56.

[40] Presta L. Molecular engineering and design of therapeutic antibodies. Curr Opin Immunol 2008;20(4):460–70.

[41] Petkova S. Enhanced half-life of genetically engineered human IgG1 antibodies in a humanized FcRn mouse model: potential application in humorally mediated autoimmune disease. Int Immunol 2006;18(12):1759–69.

[42] Shalaby M, Shepard H, Presta L, Rodrigues M, Beverley P, Feldmann M, et al. Development of humanized bispecific antibodies reactive with cytotoxic lymphocytes and tumor cells overexpressing the HER2 protooncogene. J Exp Med 1992; 175:217–25.

[43] Moore P, Zhang W, Rainey G, Burke S, Li H, Huang L, et al. Application of dual affinity retargeting molecules to achieve optimal redirected T-cell killing of B-cell lymphoma. Blood 2011;117(17):4542–51.

[44] Spiess C, Zhai Q, Carter PJ. Alternative molecular formats and therapeutic applications for bispecific antibodies. Mol Immunol 2015;67:95–106.

[45] Klute K, Nackos E, Tasaki S, Nguyen DP, Bander NH, Tagawa ST. Microtubule inhibitor-based antibody-drug conjugates for cancer therapy. OncoTargets Ther 2014;7:2227–36.

[46] Bouchard H, Viskov C, Garcia-Echeverria C. Antibody-drug conjugates – a new wave of cancer drugs. Bioorg Med Chem Lett 2014;24:5357–63.

[47] Barok M, Joensuu H, Isola J. Trastuzumab emtansine: mechanisms of action and drug resistance. Breast Cancer Res 2014;16:209–20.

[48] Hinrichs MJ, Dixit R. Antibody drug conjugates: nonclinical safety evaluation considerations. AAPS J 2015;17(5):1055–64.

[49] Wu J, Zhang M, Liu D. Blinatumomab: a bispecific T cell engager (BiTE) antibody against CD19/CD3 for refractory acute lymphoid leukemia. J Hematol Oncol 2015;8:104–10.

[50] Suresh T, Lee LX, Joshi J, Barta SK. New antibody approaches to lymphoma therapy. J Hematol Oncol 2014;7:58–69.

[51] Kuus-Reichel K, Grauer L, Karavodin L, Knott C, Krusemeier M, Kay N. Will immunogenicity limit the use, efficacy, and future development of monoclonal antibodies? Clin Diagn Lab Immunol 1994;1(4):365–72.

[52] Scheinfeld N. Adalimumab (HUMIRA): a review. J Drugs Dematol 2003;2(4):375–7.

[53] Tang L, Persky A, Hochhaus G, Balthasar J, Meibohm B. Pharmacokinetic aspects of biotechnology products. J Pharm Sci 2004;93(3):2184–204.

[54] Lin Y, Nguyen C, Mendoza J, Escandon E, Fei D, Meng Y, et al. Preclinical pharmacokinetics, interspecies scaling, and tissue distribution of a humanized monoclonal antibody against vascular endothelial growth factor. J Pharmacol Exp Ther 1999;288:371–8.

[55] Korth-Bradley J, Rubin A, Hanna R, Simcoe D, Lebsack M. The pharmacokinetics of etanercept in healthy volunteers. Ann Pharmacother 2000;34:161–4.

[56] Davis C, Hepburn T, Urbanski J, Kwok D, Hart T, Herzyk D, et al. Preclinical pharmacokinetic evaluation of the respiratory syncytial virus-specific reshaped human monoclonal antibody RSHZ19. Drug Metab Dispos 1995;23:1028–36.

[57] Blum P, Phelps D, Ank B, Krantman H, Steihm E. Survival of oral human immune serum globulin in the gastrointestinal tract of low birth weight infants. Pediatr Res 1981;15:1256–60.

[58] Mahmood I, Green M. Drug interaction studies of therapeutic proteins or monoclonal antibodies. J Clin Pharmacol 2007;47(12):1540–54.

[59] Baumann A. Early development of therapeutic biologics: pharmacokinetics. Curr Drug Metab 2006;7(1):15–21.

[60] Leslie R. Macrophage interactions with antibodies and soluble immune complexes. Immunobiology 1982;161(3–4):322–33.

[61] Jones E, Waldmann T. The mechanism of intestinal uptake and transcellular transport of IgG in the neonatal rat. J Clin Invest 1972;51:2916–27.

[62] Ghetie V, Hubbard J, Kim J, Tsen M, Lee Y, Ward E. Abnormally short half-lives of IgG in beta 2-microglobulin-deficient mice. Eur J Immunol 1996;26(3):690–6.

[63] Israel E, Wilsker D, Hayes K, Schoenfeld D, Simister N. Increased clearance of IgG in mice that lack beta-2 microglobulin: possible protective role of FcRn. Immunology 1996;89(4):573–8.

[64] Ober R, Radu C, Ghetie V, Ward E. Differences in promiscuity for antibody-FcRn interactions across species: implications for therapeutic antibodies. Int Immunol 2001;13(12):1551–9.

[65] ICH. S3A toxicokinetics: the assessment of systemic exposure in toxicity studies. 1995.

[66] Bauer R, Dedrick R, White M, Murray M, Garovoy M. Population pharmacokinetics and pharmacodynamics of the anti CD11a antibody hu1124 in human subjects with psoriasis. J Pharmacokinet Biopharm 1999;27(4):397–420.

[67] Hall W, Price-Schiavi S, Wicks J, Rojko J. Tissue cross-reactivity studies for monoclonal antibodies: predictive value and use for selection of relevant animal species for toxicity testing. In: Cavagnaro J, editor. Preclinical safety evaluation of biopharmaceuticals. Hoboken: John Wiley & Sons, Inc.; 2008. p. 207–40.

[68] Cavagnaro J. The principles of ICH S6 and the case-by-case approach. In: Cavagnaro J, editor. Preclinical safety evaluation of biopharmaceuticals. Hoboken: John Wiley & Sons; 2008. p. 45–66.

[69] Serabian M, Pilaro A. Safety assessment of biotechnology-derived pharmaceuticals: ICH and beyond. Toxicol Pathol 1999;27(1):27–31.

[70] Committee for the Update of the Guide for the Care and Use of Laboratory Animals. I.f.L.A.R., division on earth and life sciences, guide for the care and use of laboratory animals. 8th ed. Washington: The National Academies Press; 2011. p. 220.

[71] Ominsky M, Stlouch B, Schroeder J, Pyrah I, Stolina M, Smith S, et al. Denosumab, a fully human RANKL antibody, reduced bone turnover markers and increased trabecular and cortical bone mass, density, and strength in ovariectomized cynomolgus monkeys. Bone 2011;49(2):162–73.

[72] Ryan A, Eppler D, Hagler K, Bruner R, Thomford P, Hall R, et al. Preclinical safety evaluation of rhuMAbVEGF, an anti-angiogenic humanized monoclonal antibody. Toxicol Pathol 1999;27(1):78–86.

[73] Visich J, Ponce R. Science and judgment in establishing a safe starting dose for first-in-human trials of biopharmaceuticals. In: Cavagnaro J, editor. Preclinical safety evaluation of biopharmaceuticals. Hoboken: John Wiley & Sons, Inc.; 2008. p. 971–84.

[74] Lowe P, Tanninbaum S, Wu K, Lloyd P, Sims J. On setting the first dose in man: quantitating biotherapeutic drug-target binding through pharmacokinetic and pharmacodynamic models. Basic Clin Pharmacol Toxicol 2009;106:195–209.

[75] Tibbitts J, Cavagnaro J, Haller C, Marafino B, Andrews P, Sullivan J. Practical approaches to dose selection for first-in-human clinical trials with novel biopharmaceuticals. Regul Toxicol Pharmacol 2010;58:243–51.

[76] US FDA. Guidance for industry: estimating the maximum safe starting dose in initial clinical trials for therapeutics in adult healthy volunteers. 2005.

[77] Dorato M, Englehardt J. The no-observed-adverse-effect-level in drug safety evaluations: use, issues and definition(s). Regul Toxicol Pharmacol 2005;42:265–74.

[78] Suntharalingam G, Perry M, Ward S, Brett S, Castello-Cortes A, Brunner M, et al. Cytokine storm in a phase 1 trial of the antiCD28 monoclonal antibody TGN1412. N Engl J Med 2006;355:1–11.

[79] Ponce R, Abad L, Amaravadi L, Gelzleichter T, Gore E, Green J, et al. Immunogenicity of biologically-derived therapeutics: assessment and interpretation of nonclinical safety studies. Regul Toxicol Pharmacol 2009;54:164–82.

[80] Koren E, Smith H, Shores E, Shankar G, Finco-Kent D, Rup B, et al. Recommendations on risk-based strategies for detection and characterization of antibodies against biotechnology products. J Immunol Methods 2008;333:1–9.

[81] Shankar G, Shores E, Wagner C, Mire-Sluis A. Scientific and regulatory considerations on the immunogenicity of biologics. Trends Biotechnol 2006;24(6):274–80.

[82] Bugelski P, Treacy G. Predictive power of preclinical studies in animals for the immunogenicity of recombinant therapeutic proteins in humans. Curr Opin Mol Ther 2004;6(1):10–6.

[83] Steensgaard J, Johansen A. Biochemical aspects of immune complex formation and immune complex diseases. Allergy 1980;35:457–72.

[84] Shmagel K, Chereschnev V. Molecular bases of immune complex pathology. Biochemistry 2009;74(5):469–79.

[85] ICH. S8 immunotoxicity studies for human pharmaceuticals. 2006.

[86] Burleson F, Burleson G. Host resistance assays including bacterial challenge models. Methods Mol Biol 2010;598:97–108.

[87] Haggarty H. Immunotoxicity testing in nonrodent species. J Immunotoxicol 2007;4:165–9.

[88] Gribble E, Sivakumar P, Ponce R, Hughes S. Toxicity as a result of immunostimulation by biologics. Expert Opin Drug Metab Toxicol 2007;3(2):209–34.

[89] Brennan F, Morton L, Spindeldreher S, Kiessling A, Allenspach R, Hey A, et al. Safety and immunotoxicity assessment of immunomodulatory monoclonal antibodies. mAbs 2010;2(3):233–55.

[90] Horvath C, Milton M. The TeGenero Incident and the Duff Report conclusions: a series of unfortunate events or an avoidable event? Toxicol Pathol 2009;37:372–83.

[91] Milton M, Horvath C. The EMEA guideline on first-in-human clinical trials and its impact on pharmaceutical development. Toxicol Pathol 2009;37:363–71.

[92] EMA. Guideline on strategies to identify and mitigate risks for first-in-human clinical trials with investigational medicinal products. 2007.

[93] EMA. Guideline on requirements for first-in-man clinical trials for potential high-risk medicinal products. 2007.

[94] EMA, EMEA. Workshop on the guideline for first-in-man clinical trials for potential high-risk medicinal products. 2007.

[95] Faqi A. A critical evaluation of developmental and reproductive toxicology in nonhuman primates. Syst Biol Reprod Med 2012;58:23–32.

[96] Chellman G, Bussiere J, Makori N, Martin P, Ooshima Y, Weinbauer G. Developmental and reproductive toxicology studies in nonhuman primates. Birth Defects Res B Dev Reprod Toxicol 2009;86(6):446–62.

[97] Wehner N, Shopp G, Rocca M, Clarke J. Effects of natalizumab, an alpha4 integrin inhibitor, on the development of Hartley guinea pigs. Birth Defects Res B Dev Reprod Toxicol 2009;86(2):98–107.

[98] Wehner N, Skov M, Shopp G, Rocca M, Clarke J. Effects of natalizumab, an alpha4 integrin inhibitor, on fertility in male and female guinea pigs. Birth Defects Res B Dev Reprod Toxicol 2009;86(2):108–16.

[99] Raptiva package labeling, Raptiva – Genentech.

[100] ICH. S1A the need for long-term rodent carcinogenicity studies for pharmaceuticals. 1996.

[101] Vahle J, Finch G, Heidel S, Hovland Jr DH, Ivens I, Parker S, et al. Carcinogenicity assessments for biotechnology-derived pharmaceuticals: a review of approved molecules and best practice recommendations. Toxicol Pathol 2010;38:522–53.

[102] Zidek Z, Anzenbacher P, Kmonickova E. Current status and challenges of cytokine pharmacology. Br J Pharmacol 2009;157:342–61.

[103] Lee J, Zhang L, Men A, Kenna L, Huang S. CYP-mediated therapeutic protein-drug interactions – clinical findings, proposed mechanisms and regulatory implications. Clin Pharmacokinet 2010;49(5):295–310.

[104] Aitken A, Morgan E. Gene-specific effects of inflammatory cytokines on cytochrome P450 2C, 2B6 and 3A4 mRNA levels in human hepatocytes. Drug Metab Dispos 2007;35(9):1687–93.

Nonclinical Safety Assessment of Cell-Based Therapies

C.J. Amuzie, A. Faqi

INTRODUCTION

The annotation of the human genome and the subsequent increase in the understanding of the molecular basis of various diseases has led to an expansion of biotherapeutics (medicines that contain gene, protein, carbohydrate, and/or whole-cell moieties) in recent years. This expansion of therapeutic options notwithstanding, significant unmet medical needs remain, especially with respect to degenerative diseases in the aging population. The need to expand therapeutic options in tissues that have limited regenerative capacity (eg, retina, brain, heart) and tissues that require extensive regeneration to be functional (eg, hematopoietic system) has necessitated innovations in cell-based therapy (CT) generation

and delivery. Cell-based therapies are predominately generated from stem cells, which are characterized by their immense capacity for renewal and ability to generate fully differentiated cells of several lineages from many tissue sources [1]. The regenerative reserve of stem cells makes them the core ingredient for CT and the frontier for regenerative medicine with inherent promise and challenges. The promise of CT stems from the fact that scientists are better positioned, now than at any previous time, to create therapeutic and/or regenerative solutions for debilitating and often terminal disease such as Parkinson's, Alzheimer's, ischemic diseases and their myocardial/nervous consequences, degenerative retinal diseases, etc. The challenge associated with CT, especially in nonclinical development and safety assessment,

A Comprehensive Guide to Toxicology in Nonclinical Drug Development, Second Edition
http://dx.doi.org/10.1016/B978-0-12-803620-4.00024-4

stems from the fact that regulators, pharmaceutical and biotech companies, and academic institutions do not have the long history of collective experience that is found in other segments of therapeutic material research such as synthetic small molecules. This limited regulatory experience is complicated by the fact that cell reactivity and proliferation are relatively more context-dependent for CT than small molecules because CT, like other living things, are constantly being modified by their environment (other cells, excipients, temperature, growth factors, etc.). In addition to the contextual nature of CT-host tissue interaction, CT biological responses often do not fit the kind of generalizations in reactivity that are associated with functional groups of different chemical therapeutic classes. Therefore the nonclinical program for a CT for a particular disease has to be contextually designed and contextually implemented within the confines of that specific disease in the most relevant nonclinical species for the most relevant dose(s) and duration(s). In this chapter, general considerations for nonclinical CT development have been outlined, based on existing regulatory guidelines, peer-reviewed scientific literature, and the authors' experiences in functional CT safety assessment and observations of the patterns of regulatory agency requests. In the United States, sponsors are encouraged to present a well-considered individualized nonclinical CT program proposal with the Center for Biologics Evaluation and Research (CBER) at the US FDA in a pre–pre-IND interaction [2]. The CBER evaluates the proposal and makes suggestions early in the program to ensure that the studies in the nonclinical program are sufficient to generate the data that is needed to assess human safety. Under this paradigm, a proposal for the use of minimally altered and commonly used autologous (derived from the patient) CT may not require a broad nonclinical program, while cells that are intended for site/function other than their original site/function (nonhomologous use) will require appropriate testing for safety and efficacy [3].

CT SOURCES

The source of a CT is a determinant of its safety profile and may be characterized in a few different ways. The cell source could be characterized with respect to the donor's relationship with the intended patient as allogeneic (another individual from the same species), syngeneic (from a genetically identical individual such as an identical twin), autologous (from the same patient's cells), and xenogeneic (from a different species), mostly applicable in nonclinical testing. Cell-based therapies sources may also be classified with respect to tissue sources into four broad categories that are based on developmental stage of the tissues from which they were

obtained: (i) embryonic stem cells; (ii) fetal tissues which include amniotic fluid; (iii) perinatal stem cells, which includes placental tissues and umbilical cord blood; and (iv) adult stem cells, which includes hematopoietic, neural, cardiac, mesenchymal, and integumentary sources. A large fraction of the CT in current clinical trial is mesenchymal-derived stem cells. Mesenchymal-derived stem cells can further differentiate into osteogenic, chondrogenic, and adipogenic lineages [4]. Mesenchymal CT may be immune-modulatory and can be programmed to suppress or enhance immune response as part of cancer therapy [5]. The hematopoietic- and neural-derived stem cells are also used in current research in regenerative medicine.

Fetal tissues, predominately in the form of umbilical cord blood, are used to regenerate tissues, especially in cases of hematopoietic malignancy. The advantage of fetal CT is that cord blood from an individual may be stored at birth and used in an autologous fashion for a disease in the same individual during their adult life. Cord blood has pluripotent potential and may be programmed to other cell lineages. Embryonic stem cells, derived from the zygote or morula, can differentiate into all three germ layers, endoderm, ectoderm, and mesoderm, and as such are considered totipotent [6]. The totipotency of embryonic stem cells also makes them prone to increased teratoma (neoplasm) formation, which may be a challenge for safety as discussed in the following. In recent years, the policy debate surrounding the generation and use of human embryonic stem cells has become cumbersome for scientific applications that rely on embryonic sources of CT [7], in spite of the development of an embryo-safe single-cell biopsy technique [6]. Due to the debate surrounding the use of fetal and/or embryonic stem cells in some countries, the global innovation in cellular reprogramming and the use of adult cells/tissues for generating pluripotent stem cells has expanded.

A relatively recent breakthrough in stem-cell research is the discovery that specialized adult cells can be "reprogrammed" into cells that behave like embryonic stem cells, called induced-pluripotent stem cells (iPSCs). The discovery of iPSCs has increased the possibility that CT could be made from a patient's adult skin in order to treat their disease and reduce the risk of immune rejection. For example, adult skin fibroblasts can be programmed to become iPSC by activation of a combination of genes, while ova from adult females can be reprogrammed to become pluripotent stem cell through an asexual process called parthenogenesis [8].

Cell-based therapies products may also be characterized with regard to their stage of differentiation as stem-cell CT or functionally differentiated CT. The biological activity of induced pluripotent stem cells may mimic stem cell-derived CT and/or functionally differentiated cell-derived CT.

CT CHARACTERIZATION

The biological activity and safety profile of CT are influenced by the donor, tissue source, manipulation, and the stage of CT differentiation when introduced into the patient [2]. A successful CT needs to be consistent in biological character, safe, and effective for the intended patient population and must be comparable throughout in vitro, preclinical, and clinical development [9]. Heterogeneity in the cell-culture system may lead to variable nutrient, oxygenation, and/or growth factor states within the culture, thereby creating different CT microenvironments, cell populations, and/or biological activities [9]. Due to the potential for different CT microenvironment, CT culture systems are rigorously monitored for balance of nutrient input, waste removal, and perfusion rate. The US FDA expects CT to be characterized by four major quality attributes: (a) identity, (b) purity, (c) safety, and (d) potency [5]. Identity criterion seeks to establish or verify the presence of bioactive cellular components and parameters of CT manufacturing control. Purity is to ensure the absence of contaminant and unintended components such as cellular and chemical contaminants. The safety component of characterization demonstrates the absence of other biological material (contaminating bacteria, fungi, protozoa, viruses) while potency shows that the CT has biological properties that are therapeutically relevant for the intended indication. Pluripotent stem cells are subject to genetic instability, thus in vitro characterization should attempt to define acceptable levels of genetic stability for the specific CT and the intended use. Differentiation propensity, surface marker and transcription factor expressions, and in vitro proliferative potential are characteristics that need to be well understood and monitored throughout a CT program. A robust characterization profile that addresses cell identity, expansion, kinetics, growth curve, viability, storage condition, and proliferation plateau is expected in the nonclinical program.

REGULATORY FRAMEWORK FOR NONCLINICAL ASSESSMENT OF CT

In the United States, products derived from stem cells are regulated as biologics, and are deemed to be a subclass of somatic cellular therapies. Scientific advice regarding these products is provided by the Cellular, Tissue, and Gene Therapies Advisory Committee (CTG-TAC), under the auspices of the FDA's Office of Cellular, Tissue, and Gene Therapies (OCTGT).

Cell-based therapies in the EU is regulated under the advanced therapy medicinal products (ATMP) regulatory framework, which is aimed at making novel CT accessible to patients across the EU, while ensuring a high level of health protection for the patients. Under the ATMP regulatory framework, the Committee on Advanced Therapies (CAT) assesses the quality, safety, and efficacy of CT, and draft opinions on the specific CT application are submitted to the European FDA equivalent, the EMEA, to be ultimately considered by its Committee for Medicinal Products for Human Use (CHMP).

Early experience with CT treatment in humans highlighted significant risk to some patients. For example, there were multifocal tumors in the brain and spinal cord of a boy that received intracerebellar and intrathecal fetal allogeneic neural stem cells for ataxia telangiectasia [10]. The salient points in this case report were that (a) tumor was characterized by molecular and cytogenetic techniques to arise from nonhost tissue and (b) tumor diagnosis was made 4 years after the first CT treatment in the patient. This event also illustrates that the nature of the safety issues posed by CT can be different from those typically associated with other types of pharmaceuticals. Regulatory authorities around the world are familiar with cases like the highlighted example and have designed their regulatory frameworks to stem these unique safety concerns.

The FDA's regulatory framework focuses on three general areas: (i) requiring an appropriate demonstration of safety and effectiveness for cells and tissues that present greater risks due to their processing or their use, (ii) establishing manufacturing practices that minimize the risk of contamination, and (iii) limiting the risk of transmission of communicable disease from donors to recipients [11]. Based on these regulatory concerns, clinical use of stem cells is not permitted until (a) efficacy and safety of the procedure is established; (b) origin, safety, and composition of the product is adequately defined and labeled; and (c) conditions for storage and use are given in detail [12].

PRECLINICAL STUDY OBJECTIVES

The objective of preclinical studies for a CT are to address the biological plausibility of the CT for the intended indication, determine biologically active doses of CT and identify potential starting dose levels in clinical trials. Preclinical studies also address the feasibility and safety of proposed route of administration and the identification of physiologic parameters that will inform patient eligibility and clinical monitoring [2]. In addition to these, any potential CT risk to caregivers and health-care professionals may be addressed. The biological plausibility and feasibility of the intended program needs to be adequately considered and any unreasonable restriction to innovation placed on the specific CT by the current guidance may be raised early in a pre–pre-IND conversation with the regulators. The current FDA guidance for CT testing states that "when possible…product that will be administered to the patient population should be used in the definitive preclinical studies" [2]. It is important to underscore "when possible" because the guideline requirement for formulation consistency may not always be scientifically justifiable, so the guidance acknowledges that in certain circumstances a well-characterized analogous product may be a suitable preclinical alternative for the clinical grade CT. For example, intravenous injection of xenogeneic CT has an increased potential for adverse event due to immune response in test species that may not be relevant for humans; as such, programs involving safety assessment of human CT in laboratory animal species may consider generating an analogous CT, derived from their chosen preclinical species, for the nonclinical program. The concept of analogous product may also be applicable to biological components of vehicles or formulations. For example, a human CT that includes human albumin in its formulation may be tested in the preclinical program in its original form, regardless of what nonclinical species was chosen. However, the ultimate decision needs to consider that human (xenogeneic) albumin is highly immunogenic in preclinical species, even when chemical immunosuppression was used (Fig. 24.1). The strong lymphofollicular response to xenogeneic albumin formulations has been observed in the cardiovascular system of swine and sheep (CJA). A thoughtful view to the expectation for a consistent formulation across all phases of a CT program in all species should consider the robust immune response that may be generated, and what it

might mean for the preclinical data. When xenogeneic proteins are ultimately used in CT formulation, additional control groups may be necessary to separate CT effects on disease and/or safety from formulation-specific effects. Due to the challenges posed by the xenogeneic components of CT formulation, the current CT development trend is moving toward xeno-free or serum-free formulation [9]. It is important that all issues around CT formulation, activity, and safety are adequately considered and addressed in pre–pre-IND meetings and preclinical study design.

PRECLINICAL STUDY DESIGN

A successful preclinical CT program will address the safety and efficacy of the CT in nonclinical species while thoroughly and adequately addressing safety issues that are unique to the CT and/or its specific indication. Common issues to consider in preclinical study design for CT are (i) there is a complex change and interaction of cells over time in response to their environment, (ii) cells might migrate in vivo, and (iii) xenotransplantation might elicit immune rejection in preclinical species. In addition to these, the specific human disease pathogenesis needs to be modeled in a way that closely mimics the proposed clinical application and the survival of CT products in the proposed species. A detailed discussion on the pathogenesis of the indicated human disease and how available scientific data support the selection of the proposed animal model is a useful inclusion in the preclinical document.

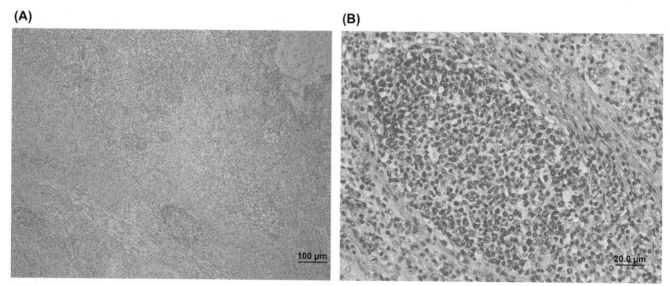

(A)　　　　　　　　　　　　　　　　　　　　　**(B)**

FIGURE 24.1　(A) robust lymphofollicular response to human albumin effacing the normal myocardium (top right) of swine and (B) higher magnification of (A) showing large lymphocytes with moderate cytoplasm in the center, surrounded by smaller lymphocytes. The lymphoid response in the myocardium resembles a lymphoid follicle. This animal was also treated with an immune-suppressant.

Animal Models

One major decision in the early preclinical program will relate to whether an animal model of disease will be used, alone or in conjunction with healthy animals, and whether the preclinical program will be performed in more than one species. Biological response to the CT needs to be demonstrated in any chosen preclinical species. The factors to consider in choosing species are comparable anatomy and physiology to humans, immune tolerance to the proposed CT, and feasibility of the planned clinical delivery procedure [2]. Data from well-designed in vitro and proof-of-concept studies (discussed in the following) are often used to determine the most relevant species for the preclinical program. A tiered approach is often useful for selecting the appropriate animal model when peer-reviewed literature and sponsors' experience does not provide enough certainty regarding the choice of species. In a tiered approach, proof-of-concept studies are often useful for the generation of additional data to support species selection.

Proof-of-Concept Studies

Proof-of-concept studies (POC) are designed to explore the details of a potential benefit associated with a CT while generating additional pathophysiological data that will help in selecting the most appropriate species. Proof-of-concept studies should address issues around pharmacologically effective dose range (minimum to optimum dose), feasibility of proposed route of administration, confirmation that CT reaches the target anatomic site/tissue, explore/determine an optimal time of CT relative to onset of disease, and explore an appropriate dosing schedule. Data from POC studies can also inform a discussion on the mechanism of action for the CT. Proof-of-concept studies can help address a number of clinical outcomes such as survival, organ function recovery, or improvement of behavior. In vitro POC studies can explore growth factor or neurotransmitter secretion, while in vivo POC studies in animal models of disease help to characterize morphologic and functional/behavioral changes. A POC study might also explore two animal models for the same human disease in order to identify potential comparative pathophysiological nuances that will inform the clinical program.

A POC study for Parkinson's disease (PD) was recently reported [13] and highlighted, in exhaustive detail, the complex biology that may be considered in a POC study. We have included a discussion of animal models of PD to highlight the complex decision-making process involved in selecting animal models of disease.

Animal Models of Disease in CT

Parkinson's disease is a neurodegenerative disorder of aging characterized by the degeneration of dopaminergic neurons in the substantial nigra, thus leading to the initiation of both motor symptoms and nonmotor symptoms. The disease affects about 1% of the population above 60 years and 3–5% of the population above the age of 85 [14]. An ideal model of PD should exhibit pathological and clinical characteristics of PD, to include dopaminergic and nondopaminergic systems, central and peripheral nervous systems, as well as motor and nonmotor symptoms. In addition, the model should manifest age-dependent onset and progressive nature of PD [15]. However, none of the current preclinical models displays all of these PD features.

Currently, preclinical models of PD range from acute pharmacological models (reserpine- or haloperidol-treated rats that display one or more PD signs) to models that exhibit destruction of the dopaminergic nigrostriatal pathway, such as 6-hydroxydopamine (6-OHDA) rat and 1-methyl-4-phenyl-1,2,3,6-tetrahydropyridine (MPTP) mouse models [16]. A variety of other chemical (rotenone and paraquat) and genetic models exist for PD. Some genetic alteration models include those with mutations similar to those found in familial cases of PD (eg, α-synuclein, DJ-1, PINK1, Parkin), while other alterations selectively disrupt nigrostriatal neurons (MitoPark, Pitx3, Nurr1) [17,18]. The most utilized toxin-based animal model of PD is the 6-OHDA and 1-methyl-4-phenyl-1,2,3,6-tetrahydropyridine (MPTP). The rodent 6-OHDA and primate MPTP are better preclinical models for PD and have been used for POC studies in cell-engraftment programs [13,19] and will be presented in further detail.

6-Hydroxydopamine

The catecholaminergic molecule 6-OHDA is formed endogenously in PD patients [20], and is thought to be involved in the PD pathogenesis [21]. 6-hydroxydopamine does not effectively cross the blood–brain barrier; it requires intracerebral infusion in rats to induce massive destruction of nigrostriatal dopaminergic neurons [22]. The magnitude of the lesion depends on the amount of 6-OHDA injected, the site of injection, and the animal species used. The 6-OHDA is frequently used as a unilateral model, which allows each animal to serve as its own control, with a lesioned and nonlesioned hemisphere. The 6-OHDA PD model is a low-cost, relatively low complexity, reproducible, and versatile option [8]. The main pathological characteristic of PD predominantly displayed by the 6-OHDA model is degeneration of the nigrostriatal tract. When the lesion is induced animals may be treated with the proposed CT and monitored for behavioral and neurotransmitter differences, relative to the animals that are not receiving CT.

1-Methyl-4-phenyl-1,2,3,6-tetrahydropyridine

The MPTP is another widely used model of PD and was identified when clinicians noted that certain people who abused meperidine were showing severe symptoms similar to PD [23]. It was later discovered that these patients had self-administered synthetic meperidine that was contaminated with MPTP [24]. 1-methyl-4-phenyl-1,2,3,6-tetrahydropyridine appears to specifically target neurons that are involved in PD, and mitochondrial dysfunction has been identified as a potential pathogenesis mechanism for neuronal death [15]. The MPTP model has been developed in various mammalian, but the MPTP-monkey models are widely used in preclinical testing because they reproduce most of the clinical and pathological hallmarks of PD [25]. In monkeys, MPTP is administered via intracarotid artery or via systemic (IV or SC) routes or a combination of intracarotid artery and systemic injections. The characteristics of the syndrome may depend on the route of administration and dosing [26]. Gonzalez et al. [13] demonstrated the successful engraftment of human parthenogenetic stem cell-derived neural stem cells in the substantia nigra and other locations that are most relevant for PD in both rodent OHDA and primate MPTP models, and showed biological activity of their CT in both species as evidenced by the elevation of dopamine levels over controls. In addition, they extensively characterized the CT with regard to molecular marker expression in vitro and in vivo in both models. Well-designed POC studies provide a lot of information on efficacy and safety for the definitive preclinical study, patient eligibility, and clinical monitoring.

There are several other animal models of disease such as those for acute myocardial infarction, retinal diseases, multiple sclerosis, etc., that may be used in a CT program. Understanding the unique features of each model of disease is critical in deciding the translational value of these models. For PD and other disease models, it may be difficult to recapitulate the pathological and clinical features in a single model system, thus combination studies of different models may provide insight into PD or other disease of choice.

Animal Species

Species choice is most influenced by the consideration of the critical features of the intended therapeutic indication for a specific CT. Other considerations in species selection are the feasibility CT delivery, CT efficacy, CT toxicity, and tumorigenicity modeling in the chosen species. Preclinical studies also have to consider the human-equivalent dose, which is a common reason for considering larger species over rodents. The anatomy and function of the particular organ system in which disease is localized or CT will be delivered needs to be considered. For example, many cardiovascular CT programs include swine models because of the similarity of their cardiovascular anatomy and function to that of humans. In addition to the factors listed earlier, other relevant considerations for species selection are whether to use healthy or diseased animals or immune-competent and immune-compromised animals. Immune-compromised animals are relevant for studies that are seeking to address long-term survival of engrafted CT. Since CT in development are often human-origin (xenogeneic) to the preclinical host species, some form of immune suppression/compromise is necessary for CT engraftment and survival. Immune suppression/compromise needs to be incorporated in the preclinical species selection.

Immune-Compromised or Immune-Suppressed CT Models

Nude rats and mice have deficient T cells and are generally hairless, hence the nickname. T-cell alteration in nude rats and mice is achieved by alteration in the *Foxn*1 gene in these species, resulting in the absence of thymus tissue, T-lymphocytes, and inefficient cytotoxic immunity. Some immune-compromised rodent models for preclinical studies of CT contain critical changes in T- and/or B-cell functions such as those related to immunoglobulin formation (recombination activating genes-*RAG*1 and *RAG*2) and cytokine receptor function (*IL2R*$^{\gamma null}$). Other genetic functions that may be altered in immune-compromised animals are those related to the enzymes involved in gene-rearrangement aspects of immune function such as nonhomologous end joining (protein kinase, DNA-activated, catalytic polypeptide-Prkdc/scid mice). The highlighted genetic alterations make engraftment of xenogenic CT easier in these rodent models, making them the preferred models for CT tumorigenicity testing. In addition to genetic alterations, drugs such as cyclosporine may be used in immune-competent animals during preclinical CT programs. It needs to be emphasized that immunosuppressive drugs like cyclosporine can alter the health of animals that are being used for the preclinical program, especially when the preclinical species are not "specific-pathogen free." For example, animals with latent viral infections may become recrudescent when dosed with cyclosporine for CT testing as illustrated in Fig. 24.2.

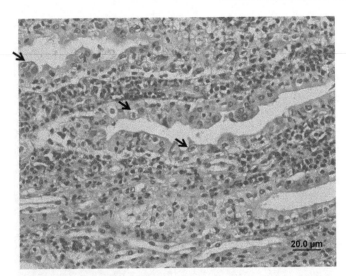

FIGURE 24.2 Large eosinophilic intranuclear inclusions (*arrows*) within marginated chromatin in epithelial cells, surrounded by mixed inflammatory infiltrates in the renal papilla of a domestic Yorkshire pig that was treated with an immune-suppressive dose of cyclosporine.

CONSIDERATIONS FOR DOSE AND ROUTE OF ADMINISTRATION IN CT TESTING

Dose selection in nonclinical safety assessment of CT should focus on a dose range, in the preclinical species, that spans from the minimum dose required for the desired biological/therapeutic activity to the maximum feasible dose [3]. Such dose range will highlight the margin of safety (difference between the toxic and therapeutic CT doses) and inform human dose equivalence for clinical trials. Discussions on human equivalent dose (HED) are commonly raised with the regulatory agency during the pre–pre-IND meetings. The traditional paradigm for determining HED in small molecule or other biotherapeutics may not be useful for a specific CT program. Depending on route of delivery, and disease indication, 20% of the safe CT dose in a nonhuman primate might be considered a safe starting human dose. However, investigators in consultation with regulators may find scientifically valid reason(s) to use higher or lower than 20% of the primate dose as HED. Unique issues relating to HED for a specific CT are deliberated in a pre–pre-IND or investigated in a POC study to provide the justification for the safety of the proposed HED.

Cell-based therapy is occasionally introduced through less common routes of administration like subretinal, intrathecal, intravitreal, and intratracheal. Any unique biology related to CT route of delivery needs to be understood in a preclinical program, preferably in a POC study. For example, efforts to deliver CT through the upper airway may be hindered by a robust particulate disposal/degradation system that is present in the lung of many species. The airway particulate disposal system has been observed to engulf CT in the lung. Cell-based therapy programs that are exploring therapeutic options within airways might explore methods of suppressing or overcoming the pulmonary phagocytic system in a POC study.

FATE OF CT POSTADMINISTRATION (BIODISTRIBUTION)

Depending on the route of administration CT may be distributed locally (the majority of CT are delivered into the central nervous or ocular system) or systemic (intravenous administration). A determination of the sites where CT were delivered or engrafted in the short and long term of a study are necessary to ensure that adequate assessment of safety for all relevant organs/organ systems was performed. The distribution of cells might also help to further elucidate the propensity of investigational cells to accumulate at the targeted site of action [3].

There are two broad categories of tools to track human cells in nonclinical species. They involve (a) using polymerase chain reaction (PCR) to detect a specific human sequence and/or (b) using a form of immunolabeling (immunohistochemistry, immunofluorescence, flow cytometry) to track the injected cells. Polymerase chain reaction is generally more sensitive and has a higher throughput than most immune-labeling assays. We recommend PCR as a first screen of all relevant tissues and time points for biodistribution in a preclinical study, and immune-labeling should be reserved for contextual characterization of the administration site and any PCR-positive tissues.

It is important to ensure that PCR and the immune-labeling system used for biodistribution study is specific for humans and to ensure no cross-reactivity in all species that will be used in the nonclinical phase. Primers against *Alu* (an abundant transposable element in the human genome) may be used to detect human cells. Alternatively, human- or other species-specific primer may be used to detect other abundantly expressed genes such as beta globin [27]. The interpretation of PCR-positive tissues in CT study needs to be done in context and should rigorously exclude collection artifacts. We have observed PCR-positive tissues adjacent to sites of engraftment in a "dose-dependent" manner. In such cases, a careful histopathological examination followed by evaluation of immune-labeled slides of the PCR-positive tissue will reveal the absence of engraftment. Additional investigation might reveal that the contamination of adjacent tissues occurred at necropsy when tissues were being dissected. Due to the sensitivity of PCR and nature of necropsy, it will be difficult to consistently avoid any contamination tissues that are within close to

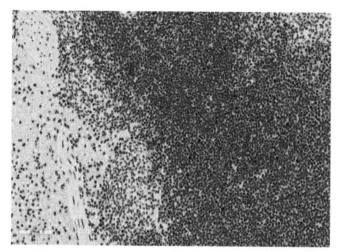

FIGURE 24.3   Spleen of a pig with robust positive nuclear labeling with HuNu antibody, a reagent that was supposed to be human-specific. Note that lymphocytes and smooth muscle cells all show positive nuclear labeling.

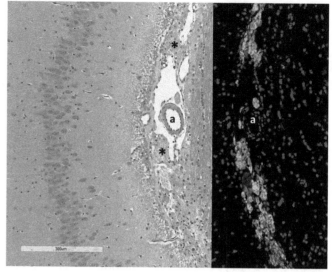

FIGURE 24.4   Hematoxylin and Eosin photomicrograph (left) indicating tissue nests of allogeneic tissue (*) that surround a small artery (a) in the brain. Immunolabeling of a serial section from the same tissue (right) highlights the tissue engraftment around the same artery to a greater extent.

the site of engraftment. Therefore it is the duty of the study director and all scientists on study to ensure that positive PCR results are verified and are strongly corroborated by immune-labeling or other technique.

Immunolabeling is very useful to help verify/contextualize true and aberrant PCR-positive results. Different nuclear (eg, HuNu), cytoplasmic (eg, STEM121 and HuMito), and membrane (eg, HLA) cell markers are available for immuno-histochemical/immuno-fluorescent labeling of engrafted tissues in preclinical species. One point to emphasize, especially for preclinical programs that involve nonrodent species, is that the chosen immune-labeling marker might cross-react with nonhuman host species tissues, although they are marketed as "human-specific." In our experience, some cell markers that are supposed to be human-specific cross-react with swine tissues (Fig. 24.3). It is important for each program to validate the preferred human cell marker(s) for all the species that are relevant to the program very early in the program. Failure to validate markers can create significant problems and delays in execution of the preclinical phase of a program as the program moves across species.

Immunolabeling can also be a valuable adjunct to routine hematoxylin and eosin (H&E) staining for identifying engrafted tissues. The staining properties of engrafted tissues and sampling variability necessitate the careful use of both H&E and immune-labeled slides to identify engrafted CT in preclinical studies. Fig. 24.4 illustrates the utility of immunofluorescence, especially cytoplasmic markers, for engrafted cell detection. The engrafted tissue may not be apparent to the study pathologist during routine evaluation, but the combined evaluation of immune-labeled tissue slides and H&E increases the sampling and the chance of identifying or recognizing a small graft.

SAFETY CONCERNS ASSOCIATED WITH CT

Safety concerns associated with CT depend on the (in vitro and in vivo) cell properties and the host response [28], which may be related to the route of administration and formulation properties. The safety concerns may be discussed under three broad categories, route-related, immunogenicity-related, and proliferation-related concerns, some of which are highlighted in Fig. 24.5. These safety concerns are usually more significant for CT that is being developed for nonhomologous use [3]. Current nonclinical assessment methods and guidelines are more robust for route- and proliferation-related safety concerns than immunogenicity concerns.

Route-Related Safety Concerns

Cell-based therapies delivered through an intravenous system present a different set of safety challenges at the higher cell doses (often greater than 1 million cells per bolus for rats). At high doses, intravascular delivery of CT is associated with thromboemboli in the cardiopulmonary (heart and lung) compartment. The thromboemboli is often present in the right ventricular chamber of the heart and is associated with cellular emboli within the small vessels of the lungs. The pathogenesis of this occurrence reflects the 100% venous return of blood mixed with injected cells that return to the right ventricle. To our knowledge, the thromboemboli has not been observed in the kidney or left ventricle, suggesting that the small vessels of the lung may be acting as a CT trap,

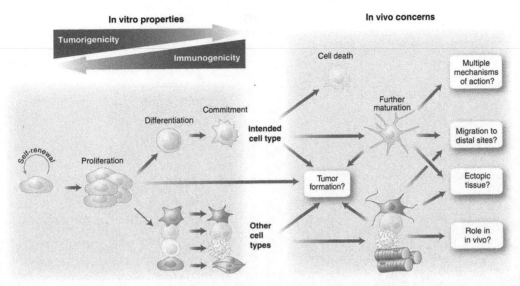

FIGURE 24.5 Indicates the safety concerns for CT that are based on in vitro (self-renewal, proliferation, and differentiation) and in vivo (maturation and tumor formation) properties. With increasing maturation/differentiation and in vivo adaptation (engraftment) of CT, there is decreasing risk for tumorigenicity and an increasing risk for immunogenicity, especially for allogenic CT. *With permission from Fink Jr DW. FDA regulation of cell-based products. Science 2009;324:1662–4.*

filtering out the circulating CT that was received from the right ventricle. These cardiopulmonary CT depositions are often associated with clinical signs of pulmonary compromise such as rapid, shallow, or labored breathing. The thromboembolism phenomenon may be observed with both xenogeneic and allogeneic cells in rodents, and has been reported in pigs that were given intravenous stem cells [29], but may be mitigated by adjusting the delivery rate of the intravenous infusion cells [30]. Other route-related safety concerns are relatively site-specific, compared to thromboembolism. For example, there may be site-specific injury in the brain and eye when CTs are injected in these locations. These site-specific injuries are often procedure-related, inflammatory in nature, and may not cause extensive dysfunction in these tissues when appropriate surgical techniques are utilized. Preclinical program designs need to consider the potential for route and/or site-specific issues and explore their safety implications in pre–pre-IND meetings and/or POC studies.

Immunogenicity-Related Safety Concerns

The use of allogeneic CT is challenging because of the cytotoxicity of immune cells such as cytotoxic T cells and natural killer cells to foreign cells. Another immune-related concern is that CT, on maturation in human patients, will be altered by molecules and receptors in the innate and adaptive immune system [31]. Currently, we are not aware of any reliable nonclinical models (in vitro or in vivo) to adequately assess the potential immunogenicity of CT. Sponsors need to discuss any immunogenicity concerns with the regulators, who might have

access to relevant data that will inform immunogenicity experiments for the specific CT and/or indication.

Proliferation-Related Safety Concerns

Proliferation-related safety concerns are usually explored in immune-suppressed or immune-deficient laboratory animal species as described earlier. Tumorigenicity studies are initiated when POC or earlier studies have indicated capacity for cell survival and engraftment in the preclinical host. The extent of concern and design for safety studies that investigate tumorigenicity risk often contextualizes the therapeutic indication, patient population, and intrinsic CT properties. A rigorous and cost-effective combination of PCR, immunolabeling, and H&E evaluation are necessary for a thorough evaluation of engraftment/proliferation. Furthermore, thorough sampling of the administration/engraftment site is often necessary for adequate assessment. Some pathologists recommend the collection of serial tissue segments at 1-mm intervals [6], using tissue matrices for cost-effective evaluation of the entire tissue. We agree with this recommendation as a general guideline for the sampling of tissues, with a slight nuance for suspected engraftment/proliferation sites. The examination of the potential engraftment sites at 1-mm interval may not be sufficient to capture proliferative changes around the engraftment sites within the brain and retina. First, the extensive tissue sampling strategy is most relevant for administration sites, recognized target tissues, and PCr-positive tissues. The specific sampling technique needs to consider the specific proliferation risk and employ a tissue-specific strategy for the CT. For example, the teratoma in Fig. 24.6 was

(A)

(B)

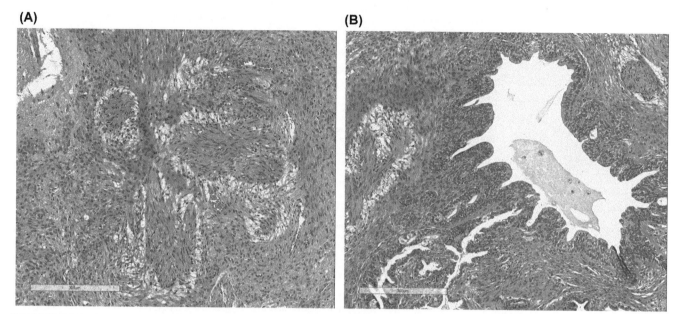

FIGURE 24.6 (A) shows proliferation of smooth muscles and vacuolated cells in the brain of a rat, consistent with mesodermal origin, while (B) shows the same mesodermal differentiation in (A) and tall columnar epithelium, which is consistent with endodermal differentiation. The step section in (B), 60 μm separated from (A), was necessary to diagnose teratoma.

not identified macroscopically and was confined within a tissue slice of less than 0.5 mm. In addition to thorough sampling, step sectioning of odd findings (about 5 steps that are 20 μm apart) might give the pathologist a more diagnostic sample. Fig. 24.6B highlights a teratoma in the brain of a rat, and was only 60 μm removed from Fig. 24.6A, which is not diagnostic for teratoma. CT-related teratomas pose a potential human risk that is not well understood and characterized, but it should be noted that the frequency of teratomas in immune-compromised rodents increase with the dose of undifferentiated cells, approximately 1 million diploid pluripotent cells per mouse [32]. A proper risk assessment for teratomas that were observed in nonclinical species might include additional biomarkers, and should include the perspective of expert physicians who are very familiar with teratoma prognostication in humans. Scientists performing risk assessment in nonclinical settings should be aware that tumors that arise from cultured pluripotent stem cells are more consistent with benign (Type 1) teratoma of humans and that large benign spontaneous human teratomas are generally cured by surgical resection alone [32]. To our knowledge, besides teratomas CT-related tumors are rare in nonclinical settings. Some immune-suppressed rodents have increased incidence of lymphomas, which should be reflected in the concurrent study controls. Lymphoma and any other background or aging-related conditions in the chosen test species need to be considered in safety data interpretation. Experienced veterinary pathologists are invaluable for considering CT-related tumors in the test species.

The second aspect of CT-related proliferative concern deals with uncontrolled division of mature engrafted cells as was reported in a patient that received neural stem cells [10]. The nonclinical strategy to deal with this concern involves the assessment of the proliferative capacity of engrafted tissues by molecular markers such as proliferating cell nuclear antigen (PCNA) and Ki-67. Ki-67 is generally preferred because its detection is less sensitive to formalin-related effects. The use of PCNA in proliferation assessment needs to consider that PCNA level in tissues may be reflecting biological processes that are unrelated to proliferation per se, such as apoptosis and DNA repair [33]. The kinetics of proliferation index is an underemphasized but important aspect of CT-proliferation risk assessment. Stem cells are expected to have a high proliferation capacity at the beginning of engraftment and decrease with maturity/differentiation. Therefore the proliferation index at a single time point in a tumorigenicity study is difficult to interpret. We have used three time points that cover 30–100% (3, 6, and 9-month for a 9-month study) of the preclinical study duration to study proliferation kinetics. We recommend this strategy, although a carefully considered two time point-assessment strategy might be equally relevant. The assessment of proliferation index over multiple time points allows the safety assessor to evaluate whether proliferation rate is increasing, decreasing, or steady over the specified time and gives a better perspective of risk than a single time point.

The location of the engrafted tissue/tumor or the microenvironment influences the histology [32]. We have observed that within the central nervous system, CT engrafted around the meninges generally tend to have higher proliferative indices than those engrafted within the neuropil. This observation is relevant for the comparison of CT-proliferation indices across animals and across tissues within an animal. Therefore assessment of CT-proliferation index should be contextualized to include the kinetics of proliferation and segregated to include the location of the graft, whenever feasible. The final nonclinical document should integrate all CT-related findings and be presented to reflect the level of thoughtfulness and rigor that went into the implementation of the nonclinical program.

Overall a nonclinical CT program needs to justify the basis for human testing by providing robust efficacy and safety data for the specific CT and clinical indication using the most appropriate in vitro and in vivo models that were reasonably justified for the appropriate regulatory agency in a pre–pre-IND meeting. The inclusion of all relevant safety endpoints in the pivotal study/studies, and presentation of an integrated and properly contextualized nonclinical data report to the regulatory agency, is the sponsor's responsibility and almost always precedes human CT testing.

References

[1] Gonzalez MA, Bernad A. Characteristics of adult stem cells. Adv Exp Med Biol 2012;741:103–20.

[2] United States Department of Health and Human Services. CBER, FDA. Guidance for industry: preclinical assessment of investigational cellular and gene therapy products. 2013. http://www.fda.gov/BiologicsBloodVaccines/GuidanceComplianceRegulatoryInformation/Guidances/default.htm.

[3] Frey-Vasconcells J, Whittlesey KJ, Baum E, Feigal G. Translation of stem cell research: points to consider in designing preclinical animal studies. Stem Cells Transl Med 2012;1:353–8.

[4] Goldring CEP, Duffy PA, Benvenisty N, Andrews PW, Ben-David U, Eakins R, et al. Assessing the safety of stem cell therapeutics. Cell Stem Cell 2011;8:618–28.

[5] Basu J, Assaf BT, Bertram TA, Rao M. Preclinical biosafety evaluation of cell-based therapies: emerging global paradigms. Toxicol Pathol 2015;43:115–25.

[6] Baker JFM, Assaf BT. Preclinical study design for evaluation of stem cell–derived cellular therapy products: a pathologist's perspective. Toxicol Pathol 2015;43:126–31.

[7] Doeppner TR, Hermann DM. Stem cell-based treatments against stroke: observations from human proof-of-concept studies and considerations regarding clinical applicability. Front Cell Neurosci 2014;8(357):1–6.

[8] Joers VL, Emborg ME. Preclinical assessment of stem cell therapies for neurological diseases. ILAR J 2009;5(1):24–41.

[9] Campbell A, Brieva T, Raviv L, Rowley J, Niss K, Brandwein H, et al. Concise review: process development considerations for cell therapy. Stem Cells Transl Med 2015;4:1155–63.

[10] Amariglio N, Hirshberg A, Scheithauer BW, Cohen Y, Loewenthal R, Trakhtenbrot L, et al. Donor-derived brain tumor following neural stem cell transplantation in an ataxia telangiectasia patient. PLoS Med 2009;6(2):221–30.

[11] US Food and Drug Administration. Guidance for industry. Current good tissue practice (CGTP) and additional requirements for manufacturers of human cells, tissues, and cellular and tissue-based products (HCT/Ps). 2011. http://www.fda.gov/downloads/BiologicsBloodVaccines/GuidanceComplianceRegulatoryInformation/Guidances/Tissue/UCM285223.pdf.

[12] George B. Regulations and guidelines governing stem cell based products: clinical considerations. Perspect Clin Res 2011; 2(3):94–9.

[13] Gonzalez R, Garitaonandia I, Carin A, Poustovoitov M, Abramihina T, Noskov A, et al. Proof of concept studies exploring the safety and functional activity of human parthenogenetic-derived neural stem cells for the treatment of Parkinson's disease. Cell Transplant 2015;24:681–90.

[14] de Rijk MC, Launer LJ, Berger K, Breteler MM, Dartigues JF, Baldereschi M, et al. Prevalence of Parkinson's disease in Europe: a collaborative study of population-based cohorts. Neurol Dis Elder Res Group Neurol 2000;54(11 Suppl. 5):S21–3.

[15] Tieu KA. A guide to neurotoxic animal models of Parkinson's disease. Cold Spring Harb Perspect Med 2011;1(1):a009316.

[16] Duty S, Jenner P. Animal models of Parkinson's disease: a source of novel treatments and clues to the cause of the disease. Br J Pharmacol 2011;164(4):1357–91.

[17] Blesa J, Phani S, Jackson-Lewis V, Przedborski S. Classic and new animal models of Parkinson's disease. J Biomed Biotech 2012:1–10.

[18] Gubellini P, Kachidian P. Animal models of Parkinson's disease: an updated overview. Rev Neurol (Paris) 2015;171(11):750–61.

[19] Roy NS, Cleren C, Singh SK, Yang L, Beal MF, Goldman SA. Functional engraftment of human ES cell-derived dopaminergic neurons enriched by coculture with telomerase-immortalized midbrain astrocytes. Nat Med 2006;12:1259–68.

[20] Glinka Y, Gassen M, Youdim MB. Mechanism of 6-hydroxydopamine neurotoxicity. J Neural Transm Suppl 1997;50:55–66.

[21] Soto-Otero R, Méndez-Alvarez E, Hermida-Ameijeiras A, Muñoz-Patiño AM, Labandeira-Garcia JL. Autoxidation and neurotoxicity of 6-hydroxydopamine in the presence of some antioxidants: potential implication in relation to the pathogenesis of Parkinson's disease. J Neurochem 2000;74(4):1605–12.

[22] Simola N, Morelli M, Carta AR. The 6-hydroxydopamine model of Parkinson's disease. Neurotox Res 2007;11(3–4):151–67.

[23] Davis GC, Williams AC, Markey SP, Ebert MH, Caine ED, Reichert CM, et al. Chronic parkinsonism secondary to intravenous injection of meperidine analogs. Psychiatry Res 1979;1:249–54.

[24] Langston JW, Ballard P, Irwin I. Chronic parkinsonism in humans due to a product of meperidine-analog synthesis. Science 1983;219:979–80.

[25] Porras G, Li Q, Bezard E. Modeling Parkinson's disease in primates: the MPTP model. Cold Spring Harbor Perspect Med 2012;2(3):a009308. http://dx.doi.org/10.1101/cshperspect.a009308.

[26] Emborg ME. Nonhuman primate models of Parkinson's disease. ILAR J 2007;48(4):339–55.

[27] Stacey GN, Byrne E, Hawkins JR. DNA profiling and characterization of animal cell lines. Methods Mol Biol 2014;1104:57–73.

[28] Fink Jr DW. FDA regulation of cell-based products. Science 2009;324:1662–3.

[29] Kobayashi E, Hishikawa S, Teratani T, Lefor AT. The pig as a model for translational research: overview of porcine animal models at Jichi Medical University. Transplant Res 2012;1(8): 1–9.

[30] Lynch JL, Bhatia R, Brosnan K, Lilova K, Sachs C, Newcombe DL. Mitigation of infusion reactions for cell-based therapies. Toxicol Suppl Tox Sci 2015;188.

[31] Preynat-Seauve O, de Rham C, Tirefort D, Ferrari-Lacraz S, Krause K, Villard J. Neural progenitors derived from human embryonic stem cells are targeted by allogeneic T and natural killer cells. J Cell Mol Med 2009;13(9b):3556–69.

[32] Cunningham JJ, Ulbright TM, Pera MF, Looijenga LHJ. Lessons from human teratomas to guide development of safe stem cell therapies. Nat Biotech 2013;30(9):849–57.

[33] Wood CE, Hukkanen RR, Sura R, Jacobson-Kram D, Nolte T, Odin M, et al. Scientific and regulatory Policy Committee (SRPC) Review: interpretation and use of cell proliferation data in cancer risk assessment. Toxicol Pathol 2015;43:760–75.

CHAPTER

25

Preclinical Development of Nononcogenic Drugs (Small and Large Molecules)

J.B. Colerangle

INTRODUCTION

Preclinical/nonclinical development of new molecular entities (NMEs) is a stepwise process that involves evaluation of both safety and efficacy in animals prior to human exposure. Preclinical development generally includes efficacy, pharmacology, and toxicology studies to determine the dose, route, and frequency required for subsequent studies. It is necessary to demonstrate using one or more animal models of disease that the initial pharmacology or efficacy studies show that treatment with the NME has the desired therapeutic effect. Efficacy studies also help identify the best NME that should be pursued for further development. Several studies are conducted to address the absorption, distribution, metabolism, and excretion (ADME) characteristics of the NMEs. Bioavailability studies are generally conducted in vivo with NMEs intended to be administered by nonintravenously. Data from bioavailability studies provide information on the amount of NME that is absorbed by the body as defined by quantity in plasma. Pharmacokinetics (PK) studies provide information on the maximum attainable plasma concentration (C_{max}), the time after dose administration to C_{max} (t_{max}), the mean residence time in the plasma, clearance, and other information used to characterize the body's effect on the NME.

Dose range-finding and toxicity studies such as single- and multiple-dose studies are initially conducted to determine the maximum tolerated dose (MTD), to identify observable signs of toxicity, and to provide a rationale for selecting dose levels in subsequent definitive studies. As per regulatory requirements, definitive studies should be conducted in at least two animal species, one rodent (rat or mouse) and one nonrodent (rabbit, dog, nonhuman primate, or other suitable species). Initial toxicity, bioavailability, and PK studies should also include one or more rodent and nonrodent species, including the species to be used in the definitive toxicity studies.

Definitive animal toxicity studies establish the safety characteristics, including the no observable adverse effect level (NOAEL), of the NME. With very few exceptions, these studies are conducted under regulatory guidelines such as the FDA's good laboratory practices (GLP). The highest dose levels tested in the definitive animal toxicity studies are almost always based on the MTD determined from the range-finding studies. By the time an NME reaches definitive animal safety testing, a human trials clinician is included in the drug development team to provide study details on the proposed first in human (FIH) clinical trial. In general, the route and frequency of drug administration to be used in initial human trials must be the same or similar to that used in the definitive animal toxicity studies.

To account for differences between humans and laboratory animal species, a safety margin is established based on the NOAEL in the "most sensitive" of the tested species. Toxicology studies are commonly conducted in rats and dogs, although other large animal species may be appropriate for specific products or therapeutic applications. For example, rabbits are frequently the species of choice for safety testing of vaccines. Preliminary toxicity studies are often performed as part of the lead compound-selection process. For investigational new drug (IND)-directed safety studies, two complete GLP-compliant safety studies are generally required. The route of administration in these studies must be the same as the proposed clinical route. If the proposed route is oral, the drug is administered by gavage to rats and by gavage or capsule to dogs. The duration of administration and dose regimen must, at a minimum, conform to the proposed clinical protocol. For example, if 14 days of continuous drug administration is proposed for the Phase I clinical trial, then animal toxicity studies of at least 14–28 days are typically required to support a clinical study of this length. Although usually occurring after Phase I dosing, longer term animal studies (eg, 90 days and longer) will be needed to support later stage human clinical trials.

The frequency of dosing in the animal studies should also mimic the clinical dosing schedule. Pivotal safety studies are performed, with the drug being manufactured under good manufacturing practice (GMP) conditions whenever possible, although the FDA does not state this requirement. In the event that a drug is not manufactured under GMP conditions, the investigator is required to demonstrate that the clinical drug is essentially the same as that used in animal safety studies. If significant differences are observed between GMP materials scheduled for the clinic and the materials used in a pivotal preclinical safety studies, the regulating agency may deem the safety study invalid and request that bioequivalence studies be conducted or the pivotal study be repeated using the correct materials. One strategy used by some investigators to preemptively qualify some of the possible manufacturing impurities, such as enantiomers or side reactions, that may be present in batch production is to utilize a batch in the animal studies that contains at least 95% purity of the drug and up to 5% impurities. Because most repeat-dose toxicity studies of therapeutics reveal some adverse effects at higher dose levels, group assignment also includes a recovery group to evaluate whether the adverse effects are transient or irreversible after repeat dosing. For dose-level selection, allometric body surface area scaling may be used to convert from many preclinical species to human dose levels, with additional multiples added to account for interspecies differences and potential safety factors.

In addition to the pivotal safety studies, required ancillary studies specified in ICH guidelines complete most regulatory packages. Safety pharmacology studies are required regulatory elements outlined in ICH guideline S7A [1]. Standard procedures are established for the safety pharmacology core battery, which includes assessments for the central nervous system, cardiovascular system, and respiratory system. Genetic toxicology studies, outlined in ICH guidelines S2A [2], are required for most small molecules. The FDA requires submission of data from three genetic toxicology assays for most IND applications: gene mutation in bacteria, including four strains of *Salmonella typhimurium* and one strain of *Escherichia coli* (Ames test); an in vitro mammalian cell assay (either evaluation of chromosomal damage in Chinese hamster ovary cells or the mouse lymphoma mutagenesis assay); and in vivo chromosomal damage in rat or mouse hematopoietic cells (such as the rodent bone-marrow micronucleus assay). If the candidate drug may have immunosuppressive effects identified in earlier toxicity or safety studies, ICH guideline S8 [3] provides an overview of follow-up programs. Other studies that are frequently required in later stage drug submissions (after Phase I clinical studies) include carcinogenicity and reproductive toxicology studies.

PRECLINICAL DEVELOPMENT OF SMALL MOLECULES

Preclinical studies are a critical part of the drug development process. Their main purpose is to characterize the adverse effects associated with an NME with respect to target organs, relationship to exposure, dose dependency, and the potential reversibility of the adverse effects. Different types of preclinical studies are conducted for small and large molecules. The data generated from these studies allow the allometric estimation of a safe starting dose of the NME for clinical trials in humans and to identify parameters for clinical monitoring of potential adverse effects.

Preclinical studies are often divided into two areas: pharmacology and toxicology. Together, pharmacology and toxicology studies are designed to provide an integrated overview of a drug's effects in various animal species. Pharmacology studies are generally conducted first because insights gained from them, particularly those pertaining to adverse effects, can influence the direction of later toxicological testing. Preclinical studies represent only part of a drug's nonclinical development. The comprehensive nonclinical testing program needed to support marketing approval involves years of work and several different types of study. Generally, both in vitro and in vivo tests are conducted. Typically, in drug development the preclinical safety evaluation is performed in two animal species. The most commonly used species are murine and canine (mainly for small

molecules), although primates are also used (typically for large molecules). The choice of species is based on the animal that will give the best correlation to human trials. Differences in the gut, enzyme activity, circulatory system, or other considerations make certain animal models more appropriate based on the dosage form, site of activity, or noxious metabolites. For example, canines may not be good models for solid oral dosage forms because the characteristic carnivore intestine is underdeveloped compared to the omnivores, and gastric emptying rates are increased. Also, rodents are not good models for antibiotic drugs because the resulting alteration to their intestinal flora causes significant adverse effects. Depending on a drug's functional groups, it may be metabolized in similar or different ways between species, which will affect both efficacy and toxicity. In addition, some species are used for similarity in specific organs or organ system physiology (swine for dermatological and coronary stent studies, dogs for gastric studies, etc.).

Pharmacology Studies

Pharmacology Screening

The pharmacological study of a new drug proceeds in phases. The initial pharmacological screening phase is part of the discovery process. This involves testing the NME using in vitro and in vivo assays to determine whether the NME has any pharmacological activity. Several NMEs may be subjected to these screenings and those demonstrating significant pharmacological effect would be selected as "lead candidates" for further testing.

Pharmacodynamics

Following the selection of a lead drug candidate, more pharmacology testing is conducted to generate a complete qualitative and quantitative pharmacological profile of the lead drug candidate. The tests conducted are mainly pharmacodynamic studies to demonstrate the action of the lead drug candidate on various receptors or physiological systems in animals.

Safety Pharmacology

Safety pharmacology studies are used to explore the drug's potential effects on vital functions. The cardiovascular, respiratory, and central nervous systems are usually considered the vital organ systems that should be studied in the safety pharmacology core battery [1]. Effects of the drug candidate on the cardiovascular, respiratory, and central nervous systems and the parameters to be evaluated are indicated in Table 25.1.

Cardiovascular System

In vivo, in vitro, and/or ex vivo methods may be used to evaluate the effects of the drug candidate on the cardiovascular system. Methods to assess repolarization and conductance abnormalities should be considered. Heart rate, blood pressure, and electrocardiogram should be evaluated.

Central Nervous System

Effects of the drug candidate on the central nervous system should be assessed. Behavioral changes, sensory/motor reflex responses, motor activity, coordination, and body temperature should be evaluated. The functional observational battery (FOB) [4], modified Irwin's test [5], and other tests [6] can be used to evaluate the effects of the drug.

Respiratory System

Appropriate assessment of the effects of the drug candidate on the respiratory system should be carried out. Respiratory rate as well as other measures of respiratory function (eg, hemoglobin O_2 saturation, tidal volume [7]) should be evaluated.

It is possible that the safety pharmacology core battery may not address all the potential adverse effects of the drug candidate. Adverse effects may be suspected based on the drug class. Additional safety concerns may arise from in vitro or in vivo studies, clinical trials, or from the safety pharmacology core battery. When these potential adverse effects raise concern for human safety, they should be followed up with supplemental safety pharmacology studies to provide a greater depth of understanding. The supplemental safety pharmacology studies are meant to evaluate potential adverse pharmacodynamic effects on organ system functions not addressed by the core battery or repeated-dose toxicity studies when there is a cause for concern. A list of studies to supplement the safety pharmacology core battery is provided in Table 25.2.

Safety pharmacology studies may not be needed for locally applied agents (eg, dermal or ocular) where the pharmacology of the test substance is well characterized and where systemic exposure or distribution to other

TABLE 25.1 Safety Pharmacology Core Battery

Vital Organs	Methods	Parameters to Be Evaluated
Cardiovascular system	In vivo, in vitro and/or ex vivo	Heart rate, blood pressure, electrocardiogram, repolarization, and conductance abnormalities.
Central nervous system	In vivo	Behavioral changes, sensory/motor reflex responses, motor activity, coordination, and body temperature should be evaluated. The functional observational battery (FOB) [2], modified Irwin's test [3], and other tests [4] can be used to evaluate the effects of the drug.
Respiratory system	In vivo	Respiratory rate as well as other measures of respiratory function (eg, hemoglobin O_2 saturation, tidal volume) [5] should be evaluated.

TABLE 25.2 Supplemental Safety Pharmacology Studies

Vital Organs	Methods	Parameters to Be Evaluated
Cardiovascular system	In vivo, in vitro and/or ex vivo	Cardiac output, ventricular contractility, vascular resistance, the effects of endogenous and/or exogenous substances on the cardiovascular responses.
Central nervous system	In vivo/in vitro	Behavioral pharmacology, learning and memory, ligand-specific binding, neurochemistry, visual, auditory, and/or electrophysiology examinations.
Respiratory system	In vivo/in vitro/ ex vivo	Airway resistance, compliance, pulmonary arterial pressure, blood gases, blood pH.
Gastrointestinal system	In vivo/in vitro/ ex vivo	Gastrointestinal injury potential, bile secretion, gastric secretion, transit time in vivo, ileal contraction in vitro, gastric pH measurement, and pooling may be considered.
Renal/urinary system	In vivo/in vitro/ ex vivo	Urinary volume, specific gravity, osmolality, pH, fluid/electrolyte balance, proteins, cytology, and blood chemistry determinations such as blood urea nitrogen, creatinine, and plasma proteins may be considered.
Autonomic nervous system	In vivo/in vitro/ ex vivo	Binding to receptors relevant for the autonomic nervous system, functional responses to agonists or antagonists in vivo or in vitro, direct stimulation of autonomic nerves and measurement of cardiovascular responses, baroreflex testing, and heart rate variability may be considered.
Other organ systems	In vivo/in vitro/ ex vivo	Effects of the drug candidate on organ systems not investigated elsewhere should be assessed when there is a concern for human safety. For example, dependency potential or skeletal muscle, immune, and endocrine functions can be investigated.

organs or tissues is demonstrated to be low. Similarly, safety pharmacology studies prior to the first administration in humans may not be needed for cytotoxic agents for treatment of end-stage cancer patients. However, for cytotoxic agents with novel mechanisms of action, there may be value in conducting safety pharmacology studies [1].

The effects of a drug candidate on the vital functions listed in the safety pharmacology core battery should be investigated prior to first in humans dosing. If there is a cause for concern not addressed by the safety pharmacology core battery, supplemental studies should be conducted. Toxicology studies adequately designed and conducted to address safety pharmacology endpoints can reduce or eliminate the need for separate safety pharmacology studies.

PHARMACOKINETICS AND TOXICOKINETICS

To obtain information on the extent and duration of systemic exposure to a drug candidate, pharmacokinetic testing should be conducted. Pharmacokinetic testing is a pharmacology component of the preclinical development plan. These studies are generally performed both in vitro and in vivo in multiple species using both radiolabeled and unlabeled drugs. Toxicokinetics is defined as the generation of pharmacokinetic data, either as an integral component in the conduct of preclinical toxicity studies or in specially designed supportive studies, in order to assess systemic exposure. These data may be used in the interpretation of toxicology findings and their relevance to clinical safety issues. Toxicokinetic measurements are normally integrated within the toxicity studies. Various components of the total preclinical pharmacokinetics and metabolism program may contribute to the interpretation of toxicology findings. However, the toxicokinetic data focus on the kinetics of a new therapeutic agent under the conditions of the toxicity studies themselves.

Pharmacokinetic studies are generally designed to yield information about a drug candidate's ADME.

Absorption

Preclinical studies to characterize absorption of the drug candidate generally involve serial determinations of the drug concentration in blood and urine after dosing to determine the extent and rate of absorption (eg, following oral administration). Studies using the intravenous route should be conducted to serve as a reference. Typically the pharmacokinetic parameters of the drug assessed include plasma area under the curve (AUC), maximum plasma concentration (C_{max}), and plasma concentration at a specified time (C_{time}) after administration of a given dose of the drug. Bioavailability, which is defined as the amount of the drug that reaches the systemic circulation, is dependent on the extent of absorption and the extent of the drug's metabolism prior to entering systemic circulation.

Distribution

To generate information on the extent and time course of tissue accumulation and elimination of the drug and/or its metabolites, distribution studies should be conducted. The organs and tissues to which the drug is distributed can be assessed by sacrificing the study animals at specified times after dosing, and measuring the concentration of the drug and/or its metabolites in selected tissues. Typically only single-dose studies of distribution are conducted. However, repeat-dose distribution studies should be considered under the following circumstances:

1. When single-dose tissue distribution studies suggest that the apparent half-life of the drug (and/or metabolites) in organs or tissues significantly exceeds the apparent half-life of the elimination phase in plasma and is also more than twice the dosing interval in the toxicity studies.
2. When steady-state levels of the drug/metabolite in the circulation, determined in repeated-dose pharmacokinetic or toxicokinetic studies, are markedly higher than those predicted from single-dose kinetic studies.
3. When histopathological changes, critical for the safety evaluation of the drug, are observed that would not be predicted from short-term toxicity studies, single-dose tissue distribution studies, and pharmacological studies, repeated-dose tissue distribution studies may help in the interpretation of these findings. The target (ie, the site of the lesions) should be the focus of such studies.
4. When the drug is being developed for site-specific targeted delivery, repeated-dose tissue distribution studies may be appropriate.

Another parameter that is useful in assessing a drug's distribution is the volume of distribution. The volume of distribution relates the amount of the drug in the body to the concentration of the drug in blood or plasma. For drugs that are extensively bound to plasma proteins but with limited binding to tissue components, the volume of distribution will approach the plasma volume [8–10].

Metabolism

To get a complete understanding of a drug's safety and efficacy, it is necessary to assess and quantify the drug's metabolic profile in the animal species that would be used for the toxicology studies. It should be noted that species differences in toxicity may be related to differences in metabolism of the drug. The metabolic profile of a drug is best assessed by determining the concentration of the drug and its major metabolite(s) in plasma, feces, bile, urine, and other tissues over a period of time following administration.

Drugs undergo biotransformation via Phase 1 and Phase 2 metabolic pathways when they enter the body. Due to the nature of the chemical reactions involved, metabolites formed from Phase 1 reactions are more likely to be chemically or pharmacologically active and, therefore, more likely to need safety evaluation. An active metabolite may bind to the therapeutic target receptors or other receptors, interact with other targets (eg, enzymes, proteins), and cause unintended effects. This is a particularly important problem when such a metabolite is formed in humans and not in animals, but such occurrences are rare. A more common situation is the formation of a metabolite at disproportionately higher levels in humans than in the animal species used in safety testing of the parent drug. This disproportionality arises due to the typical qualitative and/or quantitative differences in metabolic profiles between humans and animals. If at least one animal test species forms this drug metabolite at adequate exposure levels (approximately equal to or greater than human exposure), as determined during toxicology testing of the parent drug, it can be assumed that the metabolite's contribution to the overall toxicity assessment has been established [11,12].

Metabolites that form chemically reactive intermediates can be difficult to detect and measure because of their short half-lives. However, they can form stable products (eg, glutathione conjugates) that can be measured and, therefore, may eliminate the need for further evaluation. Phase 2 conjugation reactions generally render a compound more water soluble and pharmacologically inactive, thereby eliminating the need for further evaluation. However, if the conjugate forms a toxic compound such as acylglucuronide, additional safety assessment may be needed [13]. A metabolite that is pharmacologically inactive at the target receptor should not be assumed to be nontoxic. It should be tested in nonclinical toxicity studies.

Preclinical evaluation of drug safety usually consists of standard animal toxicology studies that include assessment of drug exposure, primarily parent drug plasma concentration. Plasma concentration and systemic exposure of the drug in the test animal species are compared with systemic exposure in humans to determine the potential risks suggested by preclinical findings and guide monitoring in clinical trials. This testing strategy is usually sufficient when the metabolic profile in humans is similar to that in at least one of the test animal species used in preclinical studies. However, both quantitative and qualitative differences in metabolic profiles may occur across species and there are cases where

clinically relevant metabolites have not been identified or adequately evaluated during preclinical safety studies. This situation arises if the metabolite is formed only in humans and is absent in the test animal species or if the metabolite is present at disproportionately higher levels in humans than in the animal species used in the standard toxicity testing with the parent drug.

Preclinical characterization of a human metabolite(s) is only warranted when that metabolite(s) is observed at exposures greater than 10% of total drug-related exposure and at significantly greater levels in humans than the maximum exposure seen in the toxicity studies. Such studies should be conducted to support Phase III clinical trials. For drugs for which the daily administered dose is <10 mg, greater fractions of the drug-related material might be more appropriate triggers for testing. Some metabolites are not of toxicological concern (eg, most glutathione conjugates) and do not warrant testing. The preclinical characterization of metabolites with an identified cause for concern (eg, a unique human metabolite) should be considered on a case-by-case basis [12]. The choice of a level of greater than 10% for characterization of drug metabolites is consistent with FDA and Environmental Protection Agency guidance [14,15]. A metabolite identified in animals that is not present in humans may suggest that toxicity observed in that animal species, attributed to the metabolite, may not be relevant to humans. Conversely, a drug metabolite identified during clinical development that is not present in test animal species or is present at much lower levels in animals than in humans may suggest the need for further studies in animals to determine the potential toxicity of the metabolite. In such cases, two approaches can be considered to assess the drug metabolite. The first approach is to identify an animal species routinely used in toxicity studies that forms the metabolite at adequate exposure levels (equivalent to or greater than the human exposure), and then investigate the drug's toxicity in that species. The second approach, if a relevant animal species that forms the metabolite cannot be identified, is to synthesize the drug metabolite and directly administer it to the animal for further safety evaluation. In this approach, analytical methods that are capable of identifying and measuring the metabolite in nonclinical toxicity studies should be developed [14–17].

The difficulties associated with synthesizing a specific metabolite as well as the inherent complexities that accompany its direct administration are acknowledged. Direct dosing of a metabolite to animals may lead to subsequent metabolism that may not reflect the clinical situation and thus may complicate the toxicity evaluation. Moreover, new and different toxicities may arise from administration of the metabolite that were not observed with the parent drug. However, notwithstanding these possible complications, identification and evaluation of the potential toxicity of the drug metabolite is considered important to ensure clinical safety, and the decision to conduct direct safety testing of a metabolite should be based on a comprehensive evaluation of the data on the parent drug and any information available for the metabolite [11].

Toxicokinetics is an integral part of the preclinical testing program. It enhances the value of the toxicological data generated, both in terms of understanding the toxicity tests and in comparison with clinical data as part of the assessment of risk and safety in humans. Due to its integration into toxicity testing and its bridging character between preclinical and clinical studies, the focus is primarily on the interpretation of toxicity tests and not on characterizing the basic pharmacokinetic parameters of the substance studied. As the development of a pharmaceutical product is a dynamic process that involves continuous feedback between preclinical and clinical studies, no rigid detailed procedures for the application of toxicokinetics are recommended. It may not be necessary for toxicokinetic data to be collected in all studies, and scientific judgment should dictate when such data may be useful. The need for toxicokinetic data and the extent of exposure assessment in individual toxicity studies should be decided in a flexible step-by-step approach using a case-by-case decision-making process to provide sufficient information for a risk and safety assessment [9].

According to ICH S3A [8], in vitro metabolic and plasma protein-binding data for animals and humans and systemic exposure data in the species to be used for repeated-dose toxicity studies generally should be evaluated before initiating human clinical trials. Additional information on PK (eg, absorption, distribution, metabolism, and excretion) in test species and in vitro biochemical information relevant to potential drug interactions should be available before exposing large numbers of human subjects or treating for long duration (generally before Phase III of clinical development). These data can be used to compare human and animal metabolites and for determining whether any additional testing is warranted.

Elimination

Elimination or clearance of a drug is a measure of the test animal's ability to eliminate the drug after its administration. The rate at which a drug is eliminated from the body depends on the concentration of the drug. Generally, clearance (CL) is defined as the quotient of the rate of elimination and concentration.

$$CL = \text{Rate of elimination}/C$$

Generally, rapid and complete elimination of drugs are associated with decreased toxic potential.

TOXICITY STUDIES

In vivo animal toxicology studies and in vitro studies are conducted to determine a drug's short- and long-term functional and morphologic adverse effects. The nature of a drug, its intended use, and the extent of its proposed study in clinical trials determine the appropriate toxicity-testing program. A toxicity-testing program may consist of some or all of the studies listed in Table 25.3.

Acute (Single-Dose) Toxicity Studies

Acute toxicity studies are conducted to determine the short-term adverse effects of a drug when administered in a single dose, or in multiple doses during a period of 24h in two mammalian species (one nonrodent). Acute toxicity studies provide information on:

- The potential for acute toxicity in humans;
- An estimate of safe acute doses for humans;
- The potential target organs of toxicity;
- Time course of drug-induced clinical observations;
- The appropriate dosage for multiple-dose toxicity studies; and
- Species differences in toxicity.

Historically, acute toxicity information has been obtained from single-dose toxicity studies in two mammalian species using both the clinical and a parenteral route of administration. However, such information can be obtained from appropriately conducted dose-escalation studies or short-duration dose-ranging studies

TABLE 25.3 Types of Toxicity Studies

Types of Studies
Acute toxicity studies
Subacute toxicity studies
Subchronic toxicity studies
Chronic toxicity studies
Reproductive toxicity studies • Segment 1: Fertility and general reproductive performance studies • Segment 2: Teratology/embryo-fetal/fetal toxicity studies • Segment 3: Perinatal and postnatal development studies
Genotoxicity studies • Bacterial reverse mutation test (Ames test) in vitro • In vitro cytogenetic test for chromosomal damage • An in vivo test for genotoxicity
Carcinogenicity studies
Special toxicity studies • Immunotoxicity • Photosafety testing • Nonclinical abuse liability

that define an MTD in the general toxicity test species [12,18,19]. Acute toxicity studies can be limited to the clinical route only and such data can be obtained from non-GLP studies if clinical administration is supported by appropriate GLP repeated-dose toxicity studies. Lethality should not be an intended endpoint in studies assessing acute toxicity [12].

Information on the acute toxicity of drugs could predict the consequences of human overdose situations and should be available to support Phase III. An earlier assessment of acute toxicity could be important for therapeutic indications for which patient populations are at higher risk for overdosing (eg, depression, pain, and dementia) in outpatient clinical trials [12].

Repeated-Dose Toxicity Studies

Repeated-dose toxicity studies consist of subacute toxicity studies, subchronic toxicity studies, and chronic toxicity studies conducted in two animal species (one nonrodent). These studies are conducted to evaluate a drug's potential adverse effects over a longer period. The duration of the repeated-dose toxicity studies at any point in preclinical development should in principle be equal to or exceed the duration of the human clinical trials up to the maximum recommended duration of the repeated-dose toxicity studies (Table 25.4). The test compound, usually an NME, is administered daily for a specified duration. The target organs of toxicity should be clearly identified and the reversibility of the toxic effects should be determined. The highest dose used in these studies is selected to deliberately induce toxicity. The lowest dose is selected to identify a NOAEL. When possible, the NOAEL dose should provide an adequate multiple of the projected maximum clinical dose. Subacute and subchronic toxicity studies are also used to determine dose levels for carcinogenicity studies, such as the MTD. The MTD, which is usually used as the highest dose for a carcinogenicity study, is a dose just high enough to elicit signs of minimal toxicity without significant alteration of the animal's normal lifespan due to effects other than carcinogenicity.

TABLE 25.4 Recommended Duration of Repeated-Dose Toxicity Studies to Support Marketing

Duration of Clinical Treatment	Rodent	Nonrodent
Up to 2 weeks	1 month	1 month
>2 weeks to 1 month	3 months	3 months
>1 month to 3 months	6 months	6 months
>3 months	6 months	9 months

Adopted from ICH M3(R2).

Subacute Toxicity Studies

Subacute toxicity studies are conducted to evaluate a new drug's potential adverse effects following a treatment period of 2–4 weeks' duration. Subacute toxicity studies are conducted as range-finding studies in order to choose dosage levels to be used in subsequent subchronic and chronic toxicity studies. In addition, subacute toxicity studies may support initial clinical trials where the duration of treatment may be up to 4 weeks. These studies are designed to assess the progression and regression of drug-induced lesions but are generally of insufficient duration to identify all secondary effects that may arise during long-term clinical use or during chronic toxicity and carcinogenicity testing.

Subchronic Toxicity Studies

Subchronic toxicity studies are generally 1–3 months (90 days) in duration. Upon evaluation of an NME's potential subchronic toxic effects, the study may be used to support clinical trials whose duration may be up to 3 months (Table 25.4).

Chronic Toxicity Studies

Chronic toxicity studies are generally 6 months to 1 year in duration. These studies are designed to determine:

- The potential target organs of toxicity;
- The reversibility of toxicities observed;
- The NOAEL; and
- The potential clinical risk in relation to the anticipated clinical dose following long-term treatment.

With regards to chronic toxicity testing, the ICH S4A guidance [20] recommends 6-month chronic toxicity studies in rodents and 9-month chronic toxicity studies in nonrodents. While the FDA considers 9-month studies in nonrodents acceptable for most drug development programs, shorter studies may be equally acceptable in some circumstances and longer studies may be more appropriate in others, as follows:

1. Six-month studies may be acceptable for indications of chronic conditions associated with short-term, intermittent drug exposure, such as bacterial infections, migraine, erectile dysfunction, and herpes.
2. Six-month studies may be acceptable for drugs intended for indications for life-threatening diseases for which substantial long-term human clinical data are available, such as cancer chemotherapy in advanced disease or in adjuvant use.

3. Twelve-month studies may be more appropriate for chronically used drugs to be approved on the basis of short-term clinical trials employing efficacy surrogate markers where safety data from humans are limited to short-term exposure, such as some acquired immunodeficiency syndrome (AIDS) therapies.

4. Twelve-month studies may be more appropriate for NMEs acting at new molecular targets where postmarketing experience is not available for the pharmacological class. Thus the therapeutic is the first in a pharmacological class for which there is limited human or animal experience on its long-term toxic potential.

Chronic toxicity studies should be initiated when Phase II clinical trials demonstrate the efficacy of an NME. These studies could be conducted concurrently with Phase III clinical trials and should be used to support the safety of long-term clinical trials and marketing approval.

Genotoxicity Studies

Genotoxicity studies include in vitro and in vivo tests designed to detect compounds that induce genetic damage directly or indirectly by various mechanisms. These tests enable hazard identification with respect to DNA damage and its fixation. Fixation of damage to DNA in the form of gene mutations, larger-scale chromosomal damage, recombination, and numerical chromosome changes is generally essential for heritable effects and in the multistep process of malignancy, a complex process in which genetic changes may play only a part. NMEs that are positive in tests that detect such kinds of damage have the potential to be human carcinogens and/or mutagens. Preclinical drug development and registration of NMEs requires a comprehensive assessment of their genotoxic potential. Since no single test is capable of detecting all relevant genotoxic agents, the usual approach is to carry out a battery of in vitro and in vivo tests for genotoxicity, which complement each other [21].

ICH S2B [21] recommends the following standard test battery:

1. A test for gene mutation in bacteria (Ames test).
2. An in vitro test with cytogenetic evaluation of chromosomal damage with mammalian cells *or* an in vitro mouse lymphoma TK assay.
3. An in vivo test for chromosomal damage using rodent hematopoietic cells.

For NMEs that test negative, the completion of the standard test battery will usually provide a sufficient level of safety to demonstrate the absence of genotoxic potential. For NMEs that test positive in the standard test battery, depending on their therapeutic use, more extensive testing may be needed [2].

A gene mutation assay is generally considered sufficient to support all single-dose clinical development trials. To support repeated-dose clinical development trials, an additional assessment capable of detecting chromosomal damage in a mammalian system(s) should be completed [21]. The complete battery of genotoxicity tests should be completed before initiation of Phase II trials [21].

Carcinogenicity Studies

Carcinogenicity studies for drugs are not required until registration and, in certain cases, as postapproval commitment or not at all. Carcinogenicity studies are typically conducted using mice and rats. The study duration is generally 2 years. Ideally, the route of administration selected for carcinogenicity studies should be the intended clinical route. Carcinogenicity studies should be performed for any NME whose expected clinical use will be continuous for at least 6 months [22]. Certain classes of compounds may not be used continuously over a minimum of 6 months but may be expected to be used repeatedly in an intermittent manner. It is difficult to determine and to justify scientifically what time represents a clinically relevant treatment period for frequent use with regard to carcinogenic potential, especially for discontinuous treatment periods. For NMEs that will be used frequently in an intermittent manner in the treatment of chronic or recurrent conditions, carcinogenicity studies are generally needed. Pharmaceuticals administered infrequently or for short duration of exposure (eg, anesthetics and radiolabeled imaging agents) do not need carcinogenicity studies unless there is cause for concern [22].

Carcinogenicity studies should be recommended for NMEs if there is concern about their carcinogenic potential. Factors to consider may include:

1. Previous demonstration of carcinogenic potential in the product class that is considered relevant to humans;
2. Structure–activity relationship suggesting carcinogenic risk;
3. Evidence of preneoplastic lesions in repeated-dose toxicity studies;
4. Long-term tissue retention of parent compound or metabolite(s) resulting in local tissue reactions or other pathophysiological responses; and
5. Genotoxicity: Unequivocally genotoxic compounds, in the absence of other data, are presumed to be *trans*-species carcinogens, implying a hazard to humans.

Such NMEs need not be subjected to long-term carcinogenicity studies. However, if such a drug is intended to be administered chronically to humans, a chronic toxicity study (up to 1 year) may be necessary to detect early tumorigenic effects [22]. NMEs that show equivocal or inconclusive results from in vitro tests and limited in vivo bioassays should be considered for carcinogenicity studies.

When carcinogenicity studies are required they usually should be completed before application for marketing approval. However, completed rodent carcinogenicity studies are not needed in advance of the conduct of large-scale clinical trials unless there is special concern for the patient population. For NMEs developed to treat certain serious diseases, carcinogenicity testing need not be conducted before market approval, although these studies should be conducted postapproval. This speeds the availability of pharmaceuticals for life-threatening or severely debilitating diseases, especially where no satisfactory alternative therapy exists. In instances where the life expectancy of the target population is short (ie, less than 2–3 years), no long-term carcinogenicity studies may be required.

Reproduction Toxicity Studies

Reproductive toxicology is the study of the occurrence, causes, manifestations, and sequelae of adverse effects of exogenous agents on reproduction [23]. The FDA requires reproductive toxicity testing for any NME to be used in women of childbearing potential, regardless of whether the target population is pregnant women. Reproductive toxicity studies have generally been conducted in a three-segment testing protocol:

- **Fertility and general reproductive performance** (Segment I)—involves study of both male and female rat;
- **Teratology or embryo-fetal toxicity studies** (Segment II)—conducted in rat and rabbit; and
- **Perinatal and postnatal development** (Segment III)—conducted in the rat to evaluate drug effects during the last trimester of pregnancy and the period of lactation.

As per ICH S5B [24], reproductive toxicity studies should be conducted as is appropriate for the population that is to be exposed to the NME.

Men can be included in Phase I and II trials before the conduct of the male fertility study, since an evaluation of the male reproductive organs is performed in the repeated-dose toxicity studies. An assessment of male and female fertility by thorough standard histopathological examination of the testis and ovary in a repeated-dose toxicity study (generally rodent) of at least 2-week duration is considered to be as sensitive as fertility studies for detecting toxic effects on male and female reproductive organs [24–26]. A male fertility study [24] should be completed before the initiation of large scale or long duration clinical trials (eg, Phase III trials).

According to ICH M3(R2) guidance [12], there is a high level of concern for the unintentional exposure of an embryo or fetus before information is available concerning the potential benefits versus potential risks. Therefore for women of childbearing potential (WOCBP) it is important to characterize and minimize the risk of unintentional exposure of the embryo or fetus when including WOCBP in clinical trials. Characterization and minimization of the risk of unintentional exposure of the embryo or fetus can be achieved in two ways:

1. Conduct reproductive toxicity studies to characterize the inherent risk of an NME and take appropriate precautions during exposure of WOCBP in clinical trials.
2. Limit the risk by taking precautions to prevent pregnancy during clinical trials. Precautions to prevent pregnancy include pregnancy testing, use of highly effective birth control methods, and study entry only after a confirmed menstrual period.

Women not of childbearing potential (ie, permanently sterilized, postmenopausal) can be included in clinical trials without reproductive toxicity studies if the relevant repeated-dose toxicity studies (which include an evaluation of the female reproductive organs) have been conducted [12]. All female reproduction toxicity studies [24] and the standard battery of genotoxicity tests [21] should be completed before inclusion, in any clinical trial, of WOCBP not using highly effective birth control or whose pregnancy status is unknown. Before the inclusion of pregnant women in clinical trials, all female reproduction toxicity studies [24] and the standard battery of genotoxicity tests [21] should be conducted. In addition, safety data from previous human exposure should be evaluated.

It should be noted that where appropriate preliminary reproduction toxicity data are available from two species, and where necessary precautions are used to prevent pregnancy in clinical trials, inclusion of WOCBP (up to 150) receiving investigational treatment for a relatively short duration (up to 3 months) can occur before conducting definitive reproduction toxicity studies. This is based on the very low rate of pregnancy in controlled clinical trials of this size and duration, and the ability of adequately designed preliminary studies to detect most developmental toxicity findings that could raise concern for enrolment of WOCBP in clinical trials [12].

In the European Union (EU) and Japan, definitive nonclinical developmental toxicity studies should be completed before exposure of WOCBP to an NME. In the United States, assessment of embryo-fetal development can be deferred until before Phase III for WOCBP when precautions to prevent pregnancy in clinical trials are used. In all ICH regions, WOCBP can be included in repeated-dose Phases I and II trials before conduct of the female fertility study, since an evaluation of the female reproductive organs is performed in the repeated-dose toxicity studies [12]. Preclinical studies that specifically address female fertility [24] should be completed to support inclusion of WOCBP in large-scale or long-duration clinical trials (eg, Phase III trials). In all ICH regions, the pre- and postnatal developmental study would be required for marketing approval.

Before the inclusion of pregnant women in clinical trials, all female reproduction toxicity studies [24] and the standard battery of genotoxicity tests [21] should be conducted.

SAFETY EVALUATION OF IMPURITIES AND DEGRADANTS IN NEW DRUG PRODUCTS

Additional preclinical studies, such as studies to qualify impurities and degradants in drug substance/product, are outlined in ICH Q3A and Q3B [27,28]. Specific studies needed to qualify an impurity or degradant are generally not warranted before Phase III unless there are changes that result in a significant new impurity profile (eg, a new degradant formed by interactions between the components of the formulation, a new synthetic pathway). If a new degradant is formed by interactions between the components of the formulation, appropriate qualification studies should be conducted to support Phase II or later stages of development [12].

Any degradation product observed in stability studies conducted at the recommended storage condition should be identified when present at a level greater than the identification thresholds given in Table 25.5. When identification of a degradation product is infeasible, a summary of the laboratory studies demonstrating the unsuccessful efforts to identify it should be included in the registration application [28].

Degradation products present at a level less than or equal to the identification threshold generally would not need to be identified. However, analytical procedures should be developed for those degradation products that are suspected to be unusually potent, producing toxic or significant pharmacological effects at levels less than or equal to the identification threshold. In unusual circumstances, technical factors (eg, manufacturing capability, a low drug substance-to-excipient ratio, or the use of excipients that are crude products of animal or plant origin) can be considered part of the justification for selection of alternative thresholds based on manufacturing experience with the proposed commercial process [28].

Any degradation product at a level greater than the reporting threshold (see Table 25.5), and total degradation products observed in the relevant batches of the new drug product, should be reported. All degradation products at a level greater than the reporting threshold should be summed and reported as total degradation products.

If a degradation product is greater than the identification threshold and safety data for this degradation product or its structural class precludes human exposure at the concentration present, then the concentration of the degradant should be reduced to a safe level. Alternatively, if the structure of the degradant cannot be identified then it may be safe to reduce the level of the degradant to less than or equal to the identification threshold. Lower thresholds can be appropriate if the degradation product is unusually toxic. Where the structure of the degradant cannot be identified, and its concentration cannot be reduced to less than or equal to the identification threshold, the sponsor should consider the target patient population and duration of use of the drug product and consider the appropriate safety evaluation of the drug product containing the degradant or impurity. Generally the preclinical studies conducted

TABLE 25.5 Thresholds for Degradation Products in New Drug Products

REPORTING THRESHOLDS	
Maximum daily dose[a]	Threshold[b,c]
≤1g	0.1%
>1g	0.05%

IDENTIFICATION THRESHOLDS	
Maximum daily dose[a]	Threshold[b,c]
<1mg	1.0% or 5 µg TDI, whichever is lower
1–10mg	0.5% or 20 µg TDI, whichever is lower
>10mg–2g	0.2% or 2mg TDI, whichever is lower
>2g	0.10%

QUALIFICATION THRESHOLDS	
Maximum daily dose[a]	Threshold[b,c]
<10mg	1.0% or 50 µg TDI, whichever is lower
10–100mg	0.5% or 200 µg TDI, whichever is lower
>100mg–2g	0.2% or 3mg TDI, whichever is lower
>2g	0.15%

[a]The amount of drug substance administered per day.
[b]Thresholds for degradation products are expressed either as a percentage of the drug substance or as total daily intake (TDI) of the degradation product. Lower thresholds can be appropriate if the degradation product is unusually toxic.
[c]Higher thresholds should be scientifically justified.
Adopted from Guidance for industry Q3B(R2). Impurities in new drug products. 2006.

to evaluate the safety of degradants and/or impurities include:

- Genotoxicity studies: If considered desirable, a minimum screen (eg, genotoxic potential) should be conducted. A study to detect point mutations and one to detect chromosomal aberrations, both in vitro, are considered an appropriate minimum screen [28].
- General toxicology studies: If general toxicity studies are desirable, one or more studies should be designed to allow comparison of unqualified to qualified material. The study duration should be based on available relevant information and performed in the

species most likely to maximize the potential to detect the toxicity of a degradation product. On a case-by-case basis, single-dose studies can be appropriate, especially for single-dose drugs. In general, a minimum duration of 14 days and a maximum duration of 90 days would be considered appropriate [28].
- Other toxicity endpoints as appropriate should be considered for evaluation.

A decision tree for identification and qualification of a degradation product and the steps necessary to characterize the safety of the degradation product are provided in Fig. 25.1.

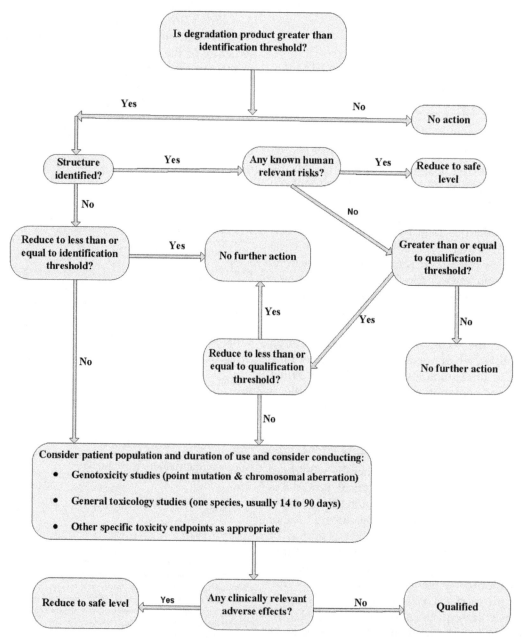

FIGURE 25.1 Decision tree for identification and qualification of a degradation product. *Adopted from Guidance for industry Q3B(R2). Impurities in new drug products. 2006.*

CONSIDERATIONS FOR THE CONDUCT OF JUVENILE ANIMAL TOXICITY STUDIES

The decision to conduct or not to conduct juvenile animal toxicity studies to evaluate the safety of an NME is driven by whether pediatric populations would be included in clinical trials and what safety data from previous adult human experience is available. When pediatric patients are included in clinical trials, safety data from previous adult human experience would usually represent the most relevant information and should generally be available before initiation of pediatric clinical trials [12]. The extent and appropriateness of adult human data should be determined on a case-by-case basis. For pediatric-specific indications, extensive adult experience might not be available before pediatric exposures.

Before initiation of trials in pediatric populations, results from repeated-dose toxicity studies of appropriate duration in adult animals (Table 25.6), the core safety pharmacology package, and the standard battery of genotoxicity tests should be available. Reproductive toxicity studies relevant to the age and gender of the pediatric patient populations under study can also be important to provide information on direct toxic or developmental risks (eg, fertility and prepostnatal developmental studies). Embryo-fetal developmental studies are not critical to support clinical studies for males or prepubescent females.

Consideration should be given to the conduct of any juvenile animal toxicity studies only when previous animal data and human safety data, including effects from other drugs of the pharmacological class, are judged to be insufficient to support pediatric studies. If a study is warranted, one relevant species, preferably rodent, is generally considered adequate. A study in a nonrodent species can be appropriate when scientifically justified. Generally, juvenile animal toxicity studies are not considered important for short-term PK studies (eg, one to three doses) in pediatric populations [12].

TABLE 25.6 Recommended Duration of Repeated-Dose Toxicity Studies to Support the Conduct of Clinical Trials

Maximum Duration of Clinical Trial	Recommended Maximum Duration of Repeated-Dose Toxicity Studies to Support Clinical Trials	
	Rodents	Nonrodents
Up to 2 weeks	2 weeks	2 weeks
Between 2 weeks and 6 months	Same as clinical trial	Same as clinical trial
>6 months	6 months	9 months

Adopted from ICH M3(R2).

When an assessment of juvenile animal toxicity study is recommended to support long-term clinical trials in pediatric populations, the nonclinical studies should be completed before the initiation of the trials. Where a pediatric population is the primary population and previous animal studies (toxicology or pharmacology) have identified potential developmental concerns for target organs, long-term juvenile animal toxicity testing may be appropriate in some of these cases. A chronic study initiated in the appropriate age and species with the relevant endpoints to address the developmental concern (eg, 12 months' duration in dog or 6 months' in rodent) can be appropriate. A 12-month study can cover the full development period in the dog. These studies could be designed and adapted to replace the corresponding standard chronic study and a separate juvenile animal study in some circumstances.

The need for carcinogenicity testing should be addressed before long-term exposure in pediatric clinical trials. Unless there is a significant cause for concern (eg, evidence of genotoxicity in multiple tests, or concern for procarcinogenic risk based on mechanistic considerations or findings from general toxicity studies), carcinogenicity studies are not recommended to support the conduct of pediatric clinical trials [12].

SPECIAL TOXICOLOGY STUDIES

Immunotoxicity Studies

All NMEs under development as human pharmaceuticals should be evaluated for their potential to produce immunotoxicity using standard toxicity studies and additional immunotoxicity studies as appropriate, based on a weight-of-evidence review, including immune-related signals from standard toxicity studies [3]. If additional immunotoxicity studies are required, these should be completed before exposure of a large population of patients (eg, Phase III).

Photosafety Testing

Photosafety testing has become a necessary component of preclinical drug development. Drug-induced phototoxic skin reactions as well as phototoxic ocular damage are increasingly recognized to be important by regulatory agencies and the pharmaceutical industry. The appropriateness or timing of photosafety testing in relation to human exposure should be influenced by:

1. The photochemical properties of the NME;
2. The phototoxic potential of structurally related compounds;
3. Distribution to eyes and skin; and
4. Nonclinical findings suggestive of phototoxicity.

The decision to conduct an initial assessment of phototoxic potential of an NME should be based on the photochemical properties and pharmacological/chemical class of the NME. If assessment of all the available data and the proposed clinical plan indicates a potential for significant human phototoxicity risk, appropriate protective measures should be taken during clinical studies. In addition, a subsequent evaluation of the preclinical drug distribution to skin and eye should be completed to acquire further information on human risk and the need for additional testing. If appropriate, an experimental evaluation (preclinical: in vitro or in vivo, or clinical) of phototoxic potential should be undertaken before exposure of large numbers of subjects (eg, Phase III). If a potential photocarcinogenic risk is perceived based on the phototoxicity assessment, the risk should be adequately managed in patients by protective measures including a warning statement in the informed consent for clinical trials and in product information for marketing [12].

Preclinical Drug Abuse Liability Assessment

An assessment of abuse potential may be needed for new drugs, including NMEs. For drugs that produce central nervous system activity, regardless of therapeutic indication, it should be considered whether or not an evaluation of abuse liability is warranted. Preclinical studies should support the design of clinical evaluations of abuse potential, classification/scheduling by regulatory agencies, and product information. There are regional guidance documents on the conduct of preclinical abuse liability assessment that can be helpful in designing specific abuse liability packages.

Approaches and Methods for Abuse Potential Assessments

A variety of approaches that can be used to assess the abuse potential of a drug product are discussed in the Guidance on Assessment of Abuse Potential of Drugs [29–31].

Preclinical Screening

Preclinical screening of new drugs with abuse potential using in vitro receptor binding studies are important because they are very useful in interpreting the results of other animal and human studies, as well as in the planning of future investigations. In vitro binding studies should be conducted to determine the pharmacological site of action of the drug and active metabolites in the brain (eg, receptor, transporter, ion-gated channel system). Drugs with novel mechanisms of action may be associated with previously unrecognized abuse potential in humans. Although a drug may have a single high-affinity site, it is important that direct and indirect

actions and effects of the drug on other neurotransmitter systems associated with abuse potential be evaluated. Some neurotransmitter systems of interest include the following:

- Dopamine
- Norepinephrine
- Serotonin
- Gamma-aminobutyric acid (GABA)
- Acetylcholine
- Opioid
- N-methyl-D-aspartate (NMDA)
- Cannabinoid

Preclinical data collected early in the drug development process can be useful in identification of early indicators of abuse potential. These early indicators would typically be available before first human dose and include the PK/PD profile to identify the duration of action, similarity of chemical structure to known drugs of abuse, receptor-binding profile, and behavioral/clinical signs from in vivo preclinical studies. When no abuse potential is apparent from these early studies, extensive testing in preclinical abuse liability models might not be warranted. Generally, if the active substance shows signals associated with known abuse liability patterns or the active substance has a novel mechanism of action on the central nervous system, further preclinical studies are recommended to support large clinical trials (eg, Phase III) [12].

The preclinical abuse liability evaluations should be conducted in rodents if the metabolite profile and the target for drug activity in rodent are similar to that of humans. Where there is clear evidence that nonhuman primates would be predictive of human abuse liability and the rodent model is inadequate, they should be considered. Three types of study are often conducted to evaluate the potential for abuse liability. They include:

- Drug discrimination;
- Self-administration of the compound; and
- An assessment of withdrawal [29–31].

Studies of drug discrimination and self-administration are generally conducted standalone. Assessments of withdrawal can sometimes be incorporated in the design of the reversibility arm of a repeated-dose toxicity study. A maximum dose that produces a plasma concentration several-fold higher than that obtained at the therapeutic clinical dose is considered appropriate for these preclinical abuse assessments.

It is recommended that sponsors consult with the Agency early in the development of NMEs to determine the need for, and optimal timing of, animal abuse potential studies. The consultation is most useful before the end of Phase II of the development to facilitate planning of late stage clinical trials. Usually any necessary animal abuse potential studies conducted early in development will provide the sponsor with more information for consideration in the overall development of the drug. However, during Phase I, because a drug's clinically effective dose may not be known, animal abuse potential studies may not evaluate the appropriate doses. Animal studies that do not use an appropriate dose may not be useful for assessing abuse potential or in the design of human abuse potential studies later in development [29]. A maximum dose that produces a plasma concentration several-fold higher than the therapeutic clinical dose is considered appropriate for these preclinical abuse assessments [12].

Local Tolerance Studies

When necessary, local tolerance studies should be conducted for NMEs in animals using routes relevant to the proposed clinical administration prior to human exposure. It is preferable to evaluate local tolerance by the intended therapeutic route. To cut down on the number of animals used in toxicology experiments, local tolerance studies should not be conducted as standalone studies, but they should be part of the general toxicity studies.

For parenteral drugs, evaluation of local tolerance at unintended injection sites should be conducted before exposure of large numbers of patients (eg, Phase III clinical trials) [12]. While such studies are generally not recommended in the United States, Japan and the EU recommend single-dose paravenous administration for the IV route [12]. If a novel intravenous vehicle is to be used, then local tolerance of the vehicle should be assessed [12].

A summary of the preclinical regulatory requirements for the development of pharmaceuticals (small molecules) is provided in Fig. 25.2.

PRECLINICAL DEVELOPMENT OF BIOTECHNOLOGY-DERIVED PHARMACEUTICALS (LARGE MOLECULES)

Biotechnology-derived pharmaceuticals, or biopharmaceuticals, or biologics, represent a class of complex, high-molecular weight products, such as monoclonal antibodies, recombinant proteins, and nucleic acids. Conventional safety evaluation programs used for small molecules are generally not appropriate for biopharmaceuticals. Therefore the preclinical "package" for each biopharmaceutical needs to be individually designed. The main differences between small molecules and biopharmaceuticals are listed in Table 25.7.

Pharmaceutical and biotechnology companies have in recent years made significant investments in the research and development of products derived from biotechnology processes. This has been facilitated by advances in recombinant DNA technology and driven by the possibility of producing novel therapeutic strategies to treat, or cure, conditions such as cancer and genetic diseases.

The objectives of the preclinical safety evaluation program for biopharmaceuticals are similar to those for conventional small molecules: to recognize potential toxicities, to identify appropriate parameters for clinical monitoring, and to determine the human dosage. However, significant differences exist in study designs. First, the route and frequency of dosing in animal studies more closely parallels the proposed treatment regimen for humans, and second, toxicology studies are mostly carried out in biologically and pharmacologically relevant (responsive) animal species. A relevant species is one in which the test material is pharmacologically active, due to expression of the appropriate epitope (for mAbs) or receptor (for proteins) or the promoter sequence (for gene therapies). The use of a relevant species allows for the evaluation of toxicity that results from the pharmacological action of the drug. In some instances, nonrelevant species may be used (eg, when no relevant species is available or when one is assessing toxicity that results from contaminants).

PRECLINICAL SAFETY TESTING OF BIOTECHNOLOGY-DERIVED PHARMACEUTICALS

The objectives of preclinical safety testing are to characterize the pharmacological and toxicological effects of the new biological entity prior to initiation of human studies and throughout clinical development. Both in vitro and in vivo studies contribute to this characterization. Biopharmaceuticals that are structurally and pharmacologically comparable to a product for which there is significant clinical experience may need less extensive toxicity testing.

Preclinical safety testing should consider:

- Selection of the relevant animal species;
- Age;
- Physiological state;
- The manner of delivery, including dose, route of administration, and treatment regimen; and
- Stability of the test material under the conditions of use.

To the extent possible, toxicity studies should be conducted in compliance with GLP [32]. For biopharmaceuticals, it is recognized that some studies that use specialized test systems may not be able to comply fully with GLP. Areas of noncompliance should be identified and their significance evaluated relative to the overall safety assessment. In some cases, lack of full GLP compliance does not necessarily mean that the data from these studies cannot be used to support clinical trials and marketing authorizations [33]. Differences in the preclinical development package for biopharmaceutical and pharmaceuticals are given in Table 25.8.

Pharmacodynamics (Biological Activity)

The pharmacological activity of a biopharmaceutical is evaluated using in vitro and/or in vivo assays. These assays include in vitro binding assays to demonstrate the affinity of the biopharmaceutical for the target and in vivo studies to establish the potential biological activity in appropriate animal models. These studies provide information on the mechanism of the product and its

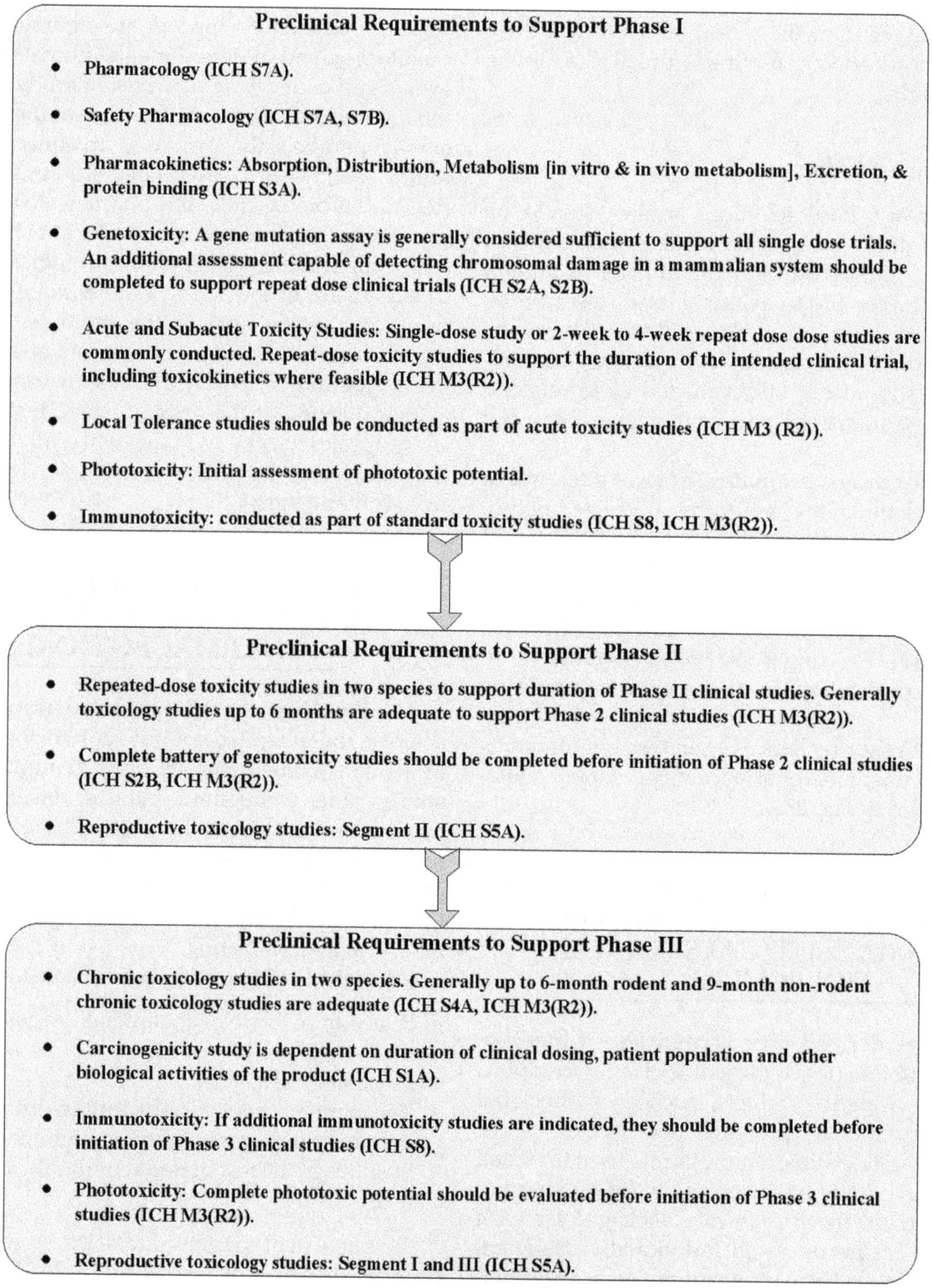

Preclinical Requirements to Support Phase I

- Pharmacology (ICH S7A).

- Safety Pharmacology (ICH S7A, S7B).

- Pharmacokinetics: Absorption, Distribution, Metabolism [in vitro & in vivo metabolism], Excretion, & protein binding (ICH S3A).

- Genetoxicity: A gene mutation assay is generally considered sufficient to support all single dose trials. An additional assessment capable of detecting chromosomal damage in a mammalian system should be completed to support repeat dose clinical trials (ICH S2A, S2B).

- Acute and Subacute Toxicity Studies: Single-dose study or 2-week to 4-week repeat dose dose studies are commonly conducted. Repeat-dose toxicity studies to support the duration of the intended clinical trial, including toxicokinetics where feasible (ICH M3(R2)).

- Local Tolerance studies should be conducted as part of acute toxicity studies (ICH M3 (R2)).

- Phototoxicity: Initial assessment of phototoxic potential.

- Immunotoxicity: conducted as part of standard toxicity studies (ICH S8, ICH M3(R2)).

Preclinical Requirements to Support Phase II

- Repeated-dose toxicity studies in two species to support duration of Phase II clinical studies. Generally toxicology studies up to 6 months are adequate to support Phase 2 clinical studies (ICH M3(R2)).

- Complete battery of genotoxicity studies should be completed before initiation of Phase 2 clinical studies (ICH S2B, ICH M3(R2)).

- Reproductive toxicology studies: Segment II (ICH S5A).

Preclinical Requirements to Support Phase III

- Chronic toxicology studies in two species. Generally up to 6-month rodent and 9-month non-rodent chronic toxicology studies are adequate (ICH S4A, ICH M3(R2)).

- Carcinogenicity study is dependent on duration of clinical dosing, patient population and other biological activities of the product (ICH S1A).

- Immunotoxicity: If additional immunotoxicity studies are indicated, they should be completed before initiation of Phase 3 clinical studies (ICH S8).

- Phototoxicity: Complete phototoxic potential should be evaluated before initiation of Phase 3 clinical studies (ICH M3(R2)).

- Reproductive toxicology studies: Segment I and III (ICH S5A).

FIGURE 25.2   Summary of preclinical regulatory requirements for development of pharmaceuticals (small molecules).

potential for clinically relevant activity. Because biopharmaceutical products are selected based on their high specificity for their receptors, general screening studies evaluating effects produced by the binding of the product to targets unrelated to the therapeutic target are not routinely conducted.

Safety Pharmacology Studies

For most small molecule drugs, the preclinical studies include a core battery of safety pharmacology studies to evaluate the effects of an NME on specific physiological

functions, such as the respiratory, cardiovascular, and central nervous systems [1]. The objectives of safety pharmacology studies are to identify potential undesirable pharmacodynamic effects of a drug that may be clinically relevant. Because biopharmaceuticals are generally highly targeted, these safety pharmacology studies are usually not required as standalone studies. Instead, the preclinical toxicology studies should be designed to address the objectives for traditional safety pharmacology studies.

Pharmacokinetics and Toxicokinetics

Pharmacokinetic (PK) and/or toxicokinetic (TK) studies are conducted to understand the relationship between systemic exposure to a drug and its therapeutic action and toxicity. Absorption of the drug, its distribution, metabolism, and excretion affect the extent of systemic exposure. The key parameters for characterizing systemic exposure include area under the plasma concentration–time curve (AUC) and the maximum concentration (C_{max}). Once these key pharmacokinetic parameters are determined, other parameters such as plasma clearance (CL), half-life, and volume of distribution (V_d) are calculated. It is generally recommended that PK parameters be included in general toxicology as they are essential for accurate interpretation of toxicity data.

Biopharmaceuticals, unlike small molecule drugs, are not metabolized by the cytochrome P_{450} enzyme system. They are catabolized into small peptides and individual

TABLE 25.7 Differences Between Biopharmaceuticals and Pharmaceuticals

Biopharmaceuticals (Biologics)	Pharmaceuticals (Small Molecules)
Produced in living cells	Chemically synthesized
High molecular weight	Low molecular weight
Target specific	Less target specific
Safety evaluation in relevant and nonrelevant species	Generally active in many species
Potentially immunogenic	Generally no immunogenic potential
Undergoes proteolytic degradation	Undergoes metabolism
Toxicity due to exaggerated pharmacology	Toxicity from parent drug or metabolite

TABLE 25.8 Differences in Preclinical Development Package for Biopharmaceuticals (Biologics) and Pharmaceuticals (Small Molecules)

	Pharmaceuticals	Biopharmaceuticals
General toxicology	• Up to 6 months: rodent • Up to 9–12 months: nonrodent [ICH M3 (R2)] • 2 Animal species required	• Generally up to 6 months: rodent and nonrodent (ICH S6) • Generally have only 1 relevant species
Tissue cross reactivity	• Not required	• Required for mAbs and mAb derivatives
Safety pharmacology	• Core battery of safety pharmacology studies required—standalone studies: rodent and nonrodent	• Safety pharmacology studies not required as standalone studies. Some endpoints may be incorporated into general toxicology studies
Metabolic profiling	• Required	• Generally not required
Genotoxicity testing	• Standard battery required	• Generally not required
Local tolerance	• Required	• Required—incorporated into general toxicology studies
Phototoxicity testing	• Required for drugs that absorb light in the 290–700 nm range	• Generally not required
Immunogenicity	• Not required	• Required—as an endpoint in toxicology studies
Reproductive toxicology	• Required in 2 species: rat and rabbit	• May be required in 1 species only
Carcinogenicity testing	• Required in 2 species: generally rat and mouse	• Determined on case-by-case basis
Absorption, metabolism, distribution, and excretion (ADME)	• Required	• Limited

amino acids that may then be excreted or reused for protein synthesis. Therefore classical biotransformation studies as performed for small-molecule drugs are generally not warranted for biopharmaceuticals. In contrast, administration of a radiolabeled biopharmaceutical in tissue distribution studies may provide insight into its localization. This may help identify organ systems at risk from the radiolabeled moiety. Tissue concentrations of radioactivity and/or autoradiography data using radiolabeled proteins may be difficult to interpret due to rapid in vivo metabolism or unstable radiolabeled linkage. Therefore caution should be exercised in the interpretation of studies using radioactive tracers incorporated into specific amino acids because of recycling of amino acids into nondrug related proteins/peptides.

Pharmacokinetic studies should, whenever possible, utilize drug preparations that are representative of those intended for toxicity testing and clinical use, and employ a route of administration that is relevant to the anticipated clinical studies. Patterns of absorption may be influenced by formulation, concentration, site of administration, immunogenicity, and/or volume. Alterations in the pharmacokinetic profile due to immune-mediated clearance mechanisms may affect the kinetic profiles and the interpretation of the toxicity data. Whenever possible, systemic exposure should be monitored during the toxicity studies. Pharmacokinetic sampling should be sufficient to describe the profile for a minimum of three to five half-lives.

Routinely, pharmacokinetic parameters are calculated following administration of the biopharmaceutical to healthy animals of a relevant species. Consideration should be given to the use of an animal model of the disease of interest as they may not only reflect the pharmacodynamic properties and clinical outcome, but may also provide a more clinically representative pharmacokinetic profile. Assessment of pharmacokinetic profile in a nonrelevant species is not encouraged. This is usually of little value since the mechanisms of elimination of the biopharmaceutical from circulation (binding to target and internalization) may be low or absent.

Some information on absorption, disposition, and clearance in relevant animal models should be available prior to clinical studies in order to predict margins of safety based on exposure and dose [33].

Toxicology Assessment

Prior to entry of a biopharmaceutical into humans, preclinical toxicology testing should be performed in animals. To identify potential toxicity endpoints to be monitored in clinical trials and to determine the human starting dose, it is essential that the preclinical studies are properly designed. In general, preclinical safety evaluation of biopharmaceuticals should be performed in at least one pharmacologically relevant animal species. If the biopharmaceutical is pharmacologically active in two species following up to 28-day studies, then the two species should be considered for toxicity testing. Should toxicity be similar in both species after the 28-day study, then longer-term studies in only one species may be justified. Similarly, if the biological activity of the biopharmaceutical is well understood in one species and it is pharmacologically active in only one species, studies in a second species with a homologous product are not recommended. The toxicology studies should be designed to answer questions regarding what risks are acceptable to patients and to predict what expected toxicities may occur following exposure of humans.

The overall goal of the preclinical safety testing for biopharmaceuticals is to define the toxicological properties of the drug in question and to provide information for product development. The main objectives of the preclinical safety evaluation are:

- Identification of target organs of toxicity and to determine whether the toxicity is reversible following treatment;
- Identification of a safe starting dose for human Phase I clinical trials and subsequent dose escalation schemes;
- Provide information on safety parameters to be monitored in clinical trials; and
- Provide safety data to support claims on the product label [34].

Selection of a Relevant Animal Species

A successful preclinical safety evaluation of a biopharmaceutical begins with toxicity testing in the most relevant animal species [34]. A relevant species is one in which the biopharmaceutical is pharmacologically active, due to the expression of the target antigen or epitope or orthologous drug receptor and whose tissue cross-reactivity profile should be similar to humans [35–37]. Using immunochemical or functional assays, a relevant animal species that expresses the desired epitope and demonstrates a tissue cross-reactivity profile similar to human tissues can be identified [37]. Species cross-reactivity studies involve an immunohistochemical survey of tissues from a variety of species using commercially available multispecies tissue microarrays [37]. Alternatively, evaluation of biopharmaceutical binding to cells from these animals by flow-activated cell sorting (FACS) is typically more sensitive than immunohistochemical analysis of tissue sections [36]. DNA and amino acid sequences of the target antigen should be compared across species; the homology between species should be determined [36].

In addition, the distribution, function, and structure of the antigen should be comparable between the relevant animal species and humans to allow evaluation of toxicity arising from antibody binding of the target antigen, which is referred to as on-target toxicity [33,38]. Furthermore, strong similarities in target antigen tissue distribution in the animal species and humans make it more likely that target organs of toxicity identified in animals will predict potential toxicities in humans. A lack of similarity in antigen tissue distribution between the animal species and humans does not entirely preclude use of the animal species for toxicity studies, but these differences must be taken into consideration in human risk assessment. Justification for the relevance of the species selected for toxicity testing should be included in the regulatory submission. If only one species is used for safety evaluation, a summary of experiments that demonstrate the absence of additional relevant species is warranted.

In the event that a relevant animal species cannot be identified, two acceptable options are available. The first option is the use of transgenic animals engineered to express the human target antigen [39]. The success of using this type of animal model for safety evaluation relies on the extent to which the pharmacodynamics resulting from the antibody–antigen interaction are similar to those expected in humans. The second option is the development of a surrogate antibody to the human therapeutic antibody that cross-reacts with the homologous antigen in animals suitable for toxicity testing [35,40,41]; however, the safety evaluation in this case will not be performed on the therapeutic antibody to be administered to humans. An inherent risk of this approach stems from the fact that no two antibodies are exactly alike. Not only does this approach add significant cost to product development, but in addition, many parameters including the production process, presence of impurities, pharmacokinetics, binding affinity, and mechanism of action may differ between the surrogate and therapeutic antibodies [35]. Indeed, studies of surrogate antibodies have been successfully performed for the evaluation of reproductive and developmental toxicity and licensure of mAb products such as infliximab and efalizumab [35,42]. When neither of these options is available, evaluation of the off-target toxicities of the antibody including functional effects on the major physiological systems may still be warranted. In addition, in vitro systems using human cells that express target antigen could in some cases be used to determine on-target toxicity and to determine the effective biologic dose of the therapeutic antibody. However, these types of studies present a challenge to predicting their relevance to human risk assessment, although more information on the pharmacology of the antibody intended for clinical use allows better assessment of these alternative approaches [43].

Toxicology Studies

Single-Dose Toxicity Studies

While single-dose toxicity studies may generate useful data to describe the relationship between dose and systemic and/or local toxicity, these studies are currently skipped to a great extent by sponsors. The data generated from these studies can be used to select doses for repeated-dose toxicity studies. Information on dose–response relationships may be obtained through the conduct of a single-dose toxicity study or as a component of pharmacology or animal model efficacy studies. The incorporation of safety pharmacology parameters in the design of these studies is recommended.

Repeated-Dose Toxicity Studies

Two relevant species are generally recommended for safety evaluation programs. However, in certain justified cases one relevant species may suffice. For example, if only one relevant species can be identified or when the biological activity of the biopharmaceutical is well understood, the use of only one species may be justified. Even where two species may be necessary to characterize toxicity in short-term studies, it may be possible to justify the use of only one species for subsequent long-term toxicity studies if the toxicity profile in the two species is similar in short-term studies. The route and dosing regimen should mimic the intended clinical use or exposure. When feasible, these studies should include toxicokinetics.

The duration of repeated-dose studies should be based on the intended duration of clinical exposure and disease indication. For most biotechnology-derived pharmaceuticals, the duration of toxicology studies has generally been 1–3 months. For biopharmaceuticals intended for short-term use (eg, ≤7 days) and for acute life-threatening diseases, repeated-dose studies up to 2 weeks' duration have been considered adequate to support clinical studies as well as marketing authorization. For biopharmaceuticals intended for chronic indications, the duration of long-term toxicity studies should be scientifically justified. Studies of 6 months' duration have generally been accepted by regulatory agencies. However, in some cases, shorter or longer durations may adequately support marketing authorization. A recovery period should generally be included in study designs to determine the reversal or potential worsening of pharmacological/toxicological effects, and/or potential delayed toxic effects. If a biopharmaceutical is noted to induce prolonged pharmacological/toxicological effects, the recovery animals should be monitored until reversibility is demonstrated.

An important factor that affects the duration of preclinical toxicity studies is the development of antidrug antibodies to the biopharmaceuticals. The presence of these antibodies may result in alteration of the pharmacological activity, the pharmacokinetic profile, and/or the toxicity observed. Therefore peripheral blood samples should be obtained for measurement of both total and neutralizing antibodies against biopharmaceuticals for all repeated-dose toxicity studies to support clinical investigation of biopharmaceuticals. In general, blood samples should be collected from the test animals prior to study initiation, once during the dosing period, at scheduled necropsy following the final dose, and from the surviving animals at the end of the treatment-free recovery period. The presence of antidrug antibodies is not enough to justify the early termination or modification of a preclinical toxicity study unless the antibodies confound the interpretation of toxicity, and pharmacokinetic or pharmacodynamic activities of the biopharmaceutical.

Dose selection for biopharmaceuticals for toxicology testing should be based on preliminary activity data generated from in vitro and in vivo studies, and doses that demonstrated biological activity in pharmacology models. The doses should take into consideration the projected clinical equivalent dose. The studies should be designed to identify a NOAEL and include a dose that is overtly toxic. Generally the highest dose tested in toxicology studies should provide at least 10-fold exposure multiple over the anticipated highest clinical dose.

The route of administration of toxicology studies should mimic that intended for clinical use. The intravenous or subcutaneous routes of administration are commonly used. Oral administration of biopharmaceuticals is unlikely due to the rapid degradation by gastrointestinal proteases and peptidases.

Immunogenicity

Many biopharmaceuticals intended for humans are immunogenic in animals. Therefore it is important to measure antibodies associated with administration of these types of products when conducting repeated-dose toxicity studies to aid in the interpretation of these studies. ICH S6 [33] recommends that antibody responses should be characterized (eg, titer, number of responding animals, neutralizing or nonneutralizing) and their appearance should be correlated with any pharmacological and/or toxicological changes. The guidance further recommends that the effects of antibody formation on pharmacokinetic/pharmacodynamic parameters, incidence and/or severity of adverse effects, complement activation, or the emergence of new toxic effects should be considered when interpreting the data. Attention should also be paid to the evaluation of possible pathological changes related to immune complex formation and deposition [33].

Unless the antidrug antibodies (ADA) neutralize the pharmacological and/or toxicological effects of the biopharmaceutical in a large proportion of the animals, the presence of antidrug antibodies should not be the sole criterion for the early termination of a preclinical toxicology study or modification of the duration of the study. If interpretation of the data from the toxicology study is not compromised by these issues, then no special significance should be ascribed to the antibody response. Generally, the immune response to biopharmaceuticals in animals is just as variable as that observed in humans.

It should be noted that the induction of antibody formation in animals is not predictive of potential for antibody formation in humans. Humans may develop serum antibodies against a humanized biopharmaceutical without any impact on the pharmacodynamics of the biopharmaceutical. Routine evaluation of recombinant biopharmaceuticals for anaphylaxis in guinea pigs is of little value as the test results are generally positive and not predictive of reactions in humans. In addition, the occurrence of severe anaphylactic responses to recombinant proteins is rare in humans.

Antidrug antibodies (ADA) may exert toxicity not directly attributable to the biopharmaceutical. They can cause immune-complex diseases due to deposition of the ADA:product complexes in the vasculature with subsequent activation of inflammatory pathways. The ADA may also cross-react with endogenous proteins in test animals and neutralize or alter their biological function. The altered function of endogenous proteins may manifest as toxicity.

Immunotoxicity Studies

Immunotoxicity studies are generally conducted to determine the adverse effects of biotherapeutics on the immune system [44,45]. Identification of such effects is warranted as part of their initial safety evaluation. Many biotherapeutics stimulate or suppress the immune system. Others, such as monoclonal antibodies (mAbs) directed against growth factors, may indirectly interfere with immune cell function; for example, antibodies directed against the insulin-like growth factor (IGF-1) receptor will inhibit IGF-1 effects on T-cell maturation in the thymus [46]. Stimulation and expansion of immune cells leading to an autoimmune disease, immune suppression resulting in decreased host resistance to infectious agents, or tumor cells are considered as the main adverse events affecting the immune system. In standard toxicity studies, evaluation of total leukocyte counts, absolute differential leukocyte counts, lymphoid tissues at necropsy, and histopathology of the spleen and thymus may indicate toxicity to the immune response. Changes in immune parameters may also result from stress due to doses near or at the maximum tolerated dose, and these effects are most likely mediated by increased corticosterone or cortisol release. The following stress-related immune changes are commonly observed: increases in circulating neutrophils, decreases in circulating lymphocytes, decreases in thymus weight, decreases in thymic cortical cellularity and associated histopathologic changes, changes in spleen and lymph node cellularity, and increases in adrenal gland weight. Clinical observations, such as decreased body weight gain and activity, may suggest that the changes to lymphoid tissue and hematology parameters are a result of stress rather than to a direct immunotoxic effect. However, compelling evidence of stress is necessary in order to discount the immunotoxic effects of the antibody. An initial evaluation of a biotherapeutic's potential adverse effects on the immune system may be obtained from repeated-dose toxicity studies by measuring hematological and serum chemistry changes and obtaining lymphoid organ weights in conjunction with gross evaluation of size and structure and microscopic evaluation of cellular changes within these organs. If evidence of immunotoxicity is uncovered in the initial toxicity studies, then specific endpoints should be included in subsequent general toxicity studies or in additional specific immunotoxicity studies. Immunophenotyping, which is the identification and/or enumeration of leukocyte subsets with specific antibodies, is one of the easier endpoints to incorporate into standard toxicity studies. This assay is usually conducted by FACS or immunohistochemistry (IHC). Since immunophenotyping is not a functional assay, other parameters such as the T cell-dependent antibody response are measured to assess mAb immunotoxicity. Functional assays are described in the ICH S8 guidance for immunotoxicity studies for human pharmaceuticals [3].

As with general toxicology studies, it is important to utilize pharmacologically relevant animal species for immunotoxicity testing biopharmaceuticals. It should be noted that marked differences in the immune system across different species may limit the feasibility of testing and/or the interpretation and relevance of the data generated [47]. Although lymphocyte subset analyses can be easily performed in the mouse, human, and some nonhuman primates, specific phenotypic markers of interest may not be expressed identically by all species. Moreover, the currently available markers for lymphocyte subset analysis have not been demonstrated to be good predictors of immunotoxicity [48]. In some cases, even the pharmacologically relevant animal species may not accurately predict the human immune response. It is therefore necessary to be cautious when interpreting and extrapolating immune function data. The results should

be reconciled against clinical findings or with in vitro studies using human leukocytes to validate that the findings in animals are predictive of immune response in humans.

Developmental and Reproductive Toxicity Studies

The need for reproductive toxicology studies for biopharmaceuticals is dependent on the indication, the patient population for which it is intended, and the characteristics of the product. Because of the inherent nature of biopharmaceuticals with regards to issues related to species specificity, immunogenicity, biological activity, and/or long eliminating half-life, the study design and dosing schedule could be challenging. It is therefore recommended that consultation with the appropriate division of Center for Drug Evaluation and Research (CDER) is sought to discuss the need for and design of suitable reproductive toxicology studies.

Reproductive toxicology studies are designed to identify the effects of the biopharmaceutical on mammalian reproduction and include exposure of mature adults, as well as all stages of development from conception to sexual maturity [49]. The studies should address the effects of the biopharmaceutical on fertility and early embryonic development; prenatal and postnatal development, including maternal function; and embryo-fetal development [33,49,50]. Concerns regarding potential developmental immunotoxicity, which may apply particularly to certain biopharmaceuticals (eg, monoclonal antibodies) with prolonged immunological effects, could be addressed in a study design modified to assess immune function of the neonate [33]. Repeated-dose toxicity studies performed during the earlier phases of clinical development offer information regarding potential effects on reproduction, particularly on male fertility. Developmental and reproductive toxicity (DART) studies should be completed for registration. The EU and Japanese regulatory agencies require these studies to be completed before Phase III. The clinical indication and intended recipient population dictate the required reproductive and developmental toxicity studies. These studies should be conducted if the biopharmaceutical is intended for repeat or chronic administration to women of childbearing potential.

For biopharmaceuticals, it is recommended that reproductive toxicology studies should be conducted in pharmacologically relevant animal species. If the biopharmaceutical is active in the commonly used species, then the studies should be conducted in compliance with guidance provided in ICH M3(R2) [12] and ICH S6 [33].

In many instances, the nonhuman primate is the only relevant species for conducting reproductive toxicology studies. The use of monkeys is not without challenges and limitations. These challenges and limitations include:

- The availability of sexually mature animals is limited;
- Nonhuman primates are markedly heterogeneous compared to in bred laboratory animals;
- Nonhuman primates produce one offspring per pregnancy;
- Spontaneous abortions occur at high rates; and
- Gestation periods are approximately 5–7 times longer relative to those of rats and rabbits.

It is recommended that "embryo-fetal development" study be conducted when necessary to assess risks to the conceptus with nonhuman primate [23]. Effects on male and female fertility may be sufficiently addressed by incorporating appropriate endpoints in the nonhuman primate repeated-dose toxicology studies. However, if tissue cross-reactivity studies reveal binding of the biopharmaceutical to reproductive organs and/or repeated-dose toxicology studies reveal concerns, "fertility to early embryonic development" studies should be considered in nonhuman primates. Due to the lengthy maturation and small number of offspring, complete "prenatal and postnatal development" studies cannot be expected in nonhuman primates. If the biopharmaceutical is an immune modulator and immune assessments of the offspring are desirable, relevant endpoints can be included in a modified "embryo-fetal development" study. When no relevant animal species is available, transgenic mice or analogous proteins should be considered.

Genotoxicity Studies

The standard battery of genetic toxicology tests recommended by the ICH S2B guidance [21] for pharmaceuticals are designed to detect substances that interact with DNA to induce mutations, chromosome aberrations, and/or DNA damage. Because biopharmaceuticals are not able to pass through the cellular and nuclear membranes of intact cells due to their large size and interact with DNA or other chromosomal material, the range and type of genotoxicity studies routinely conducted for pharmaceuticals are not applicable to biopharmaceuticals and therefore are not needed.

Carcinogenicity Studies

Although standard carcinogenic bioassays are not required for biopharmaceuticals, additional mechanistic studies may be needed to fully evaluate the risk of carcinogenic potential of the compound based on the intended patient population, duration of treatment, and biological activity [33]. The need for a product-specific assessment of the carcinogenic potential for biopharmaceuticals should be determined with regard to the intended clinical population and treatment duration [22]. When an

assessment is warranted, the sponsor should design a strategy to address the issue. Standard carcinogenicity bioassays are inappropriate for biopharmaceutical products (eg, antibodies), and as a result, currently marketed antibodies have not been evaluated for carcinogenicity. However, assessment of carcinogenic potential should be considered if a potential for this risk exists. If a risk is identified, the ability of the biopharmaceutical to stimulate growth of normal or malignant cells expressing the antigen should be determined. Studies in relevant animal models and in vitro cellular proliferation should be evaluated in long-term repeated-dose toxicity studies in order to address carcinogenicity of the antibody.

The strategy to assess the potential for carcinogenicity could be based on a review of relevant data from a variety of sources. The data sources can include published data (eg, information from transgenic, knock-out or animal disease models, human genetic diseases), information on class effects, detailed information on target biology, in vitro data, data from chronic toxicity studies, and clinical data. The product-specific assessment of carcinogenic potential is used to communicate risk and provide input to the risk management plan along with labeling proposals, clinical monitoring, postmarketing surveillance, or a combination of these approaches [51]. In some cases, the available information can be considered sufficient to address carcinogenic potential and provide information on clinical risk without warranting additional preclinical studies. For example, immunomodulators and growth factors pose a potential carcinogenic risk that can best be evaluated by postmarketing clinical surveillance rather than further preclinical studies.

The mechanism of action of some biopharmaceuticals may raise concerns regarding potential for tumor induction or tumor promotion. Rodent bioassays are not warranted if data from in vitro or chronic toxicity studies support the concern regarding the carcinogenic potential. When in vitro and chronic toxicity studies do not support this theoretical risk but the sponsor prefers not to have this risk communicated in the label, the sponsor can propose additional studies to mitigate the concern. Where there is inadequate knowledge about a biopharmaceutical's characteristics and mechanism of action in relation to carcinogenic potential, a more extensive assessment may be required. The sponsor should consider the inclusion of additional endpoints in toxicity studies. If the weight of evidence from the assessment (eg, in vitro and chronic toxicity studies) of a biopharmaceutical's carcinogenic potential does not suggest a carcinogenic potential, a rodent bioassay is not recommended. If the weight of evidence suggests a concern for carcinogenic potential, then the label should reflect the concern or the sponsor can propose additional preclinical studies to mitigate the concern. Rodent bioassays or short-term carcinogenicity studies with homologous products are generally of limited value to assess carcinogenic potential of the clinical candidate [51].

Local Tolerance Studies

Local tolerance should be studied in a relevant animal species using the formulation intended for marketing, the same dosing regimen, and routes relevant to the proposed clinical administration. In certain justified cases, the testing of representative formulations may be acceptable. The evaluation of local tolerance should be performed prior to human exposure. The assessment of local tolerance may be part of other toxicity studies. In some cases, the potential adverse effects of the biopharmaceutical can be evaluated in single- or repeated-dose toxicity studies, thus obviating the need for separate local tolerance studies.

Local irritation may be caused by:

- T-lymphocyte activation associated pathology;
- Immune complex deposition;
- Hypersensitivity reaction to or irritation from formulation components; and
- Mechanical injury caused by injection needles.

A histological evaluation of the injection sites is generally recommended during toxicology studies. Caution should be exercised when interpreting the results of local tolerance studies since repeated injection of human proteins into animals may cause severe local intolerance that will not occur in human.

Comparability Studies

Changes in the manufacturing process of biopharmaceuticals occur frequently during clinical development as well as after approval. The product used in the preclinical studies is not required to be "identical" to that used in clinical trials but it has to be "comparable."

Comparability assessments are used to demonstrate that pre- and postchange products are either "comparable" or "not comparable." The assessments consist of physicochemical characterization and in vitro functional comparison of the pre- and postchange products [52–54]. These series of assessments are conducted to determine if the manufacturing changes will impact the identity, safety, purity, or efficacy of the product.

Pre- and postchange products are said to be "comparable":

- If the physicochemical properties, biological activity, and immunochemical properties are highly similar; and
- When physicochemical differences are detected but have no adverse impact on safety and efficacy of the product [52].

If the products are deemed "not comparable," the preclinical pharmacology and toxicology studies conducted with the product manufactured prior to the process change needs to be assessed to determine if it can be used to support further clinical trials and/or marketing applications with the postchange product.

Generally, comparison of in vitro quality attributes of the pre- and postchange products is enough to determine whether the products are comparable. However, when the quality data are not adequate to ensure product comparability, bridging studies in an appropriate animal model may be considered as a replacement for human clinical data. Since many manufacturing changes result in alterations in properties of the active moiety known to affect product exposure in vivo, bridging pharmacokinetic studies are most often required. In the pharmacokinetic studies, direct comparison of pharmacokinetic parameters of the pre- and postchange products is performed in a pharmacologically relevant animal species. The animal species chosen should have a PK profile for the prechange product that is similar to that of humans, if that data were acquired in a clinical trial for comparison.

There may be cases where additional animal studies that evaluate pharmacodynamic properties and/or toxicity may be necessary to establish comparability. The need for additional animal studies is dictated by the safety profile of the prechange product, the magnitude of the manufacturing changes, and any identified differences in product purity, structure, or in vitro activity. Sponsors are encouraged to discuss plans for animal bridging studies with the regulatory agencies to ensure the appropriate studies are conducted to adequately assess comparability.

A summary of the preclinical regulatory requirements for the development of biopharmaceuticals (large molecules) is provided in Fig. 25.3.

Preclinical Requirements to Support Phase I

- Studies to support pharmacological rationale and relevant species selection (ICH S6).

- In vitro assays to determine receptor occupancy, receptor affinity and/or pharmacological effects in human and other species.

- Immunohistochemistry to show any unintentional reactivity and/or cytotoxicity towards human tissues that are distinct from the intended target.

- Single-dose study or 2-week study (ICH S6) (single-dose range-finding and 4-week repeated dose with weekly dosing commonly carried out).

- Repeated-dose toxicity studies to support the duration of the intended clinical trial, including toxicokinetics where feasible (ICH S6/ICH M3(R2)).

- Absorption and distribution studies (ICH S6).

- Immunogenicity: characterization of antibody responses for repeated-dose clinical trials (ICH S6).

- Local tolerance using intended clinical formulation (ICH S6) (incorporated into general toxicology studies).

- Safety pharmacology studies (ICH S7A): generally not required as standalone studies, but endpoints may be incorporated into general toxicology studies.

Preclinical Requirements to Support Phase II

- Repeated-dose toxicity studies in a relevant species to support duration of Phase II clinical studies. Generally 1 to 3 months toxicology studies in a relevant animal species are adequate (ICH S6).

- Reproductive toxicology studies (ICH S5A) (Segment II, case-by-case basis).

Preclinical Requirements to Support Phase III

- Chronic toxicology studies in a relevant species. Generally up to 6 months' rodent and non-rodent chronic toxicology studies are adequate (ICH S6). 9 months' non-rodent chronic toxicity studies, and for some biologicals, even up to 12 months' chronic toxicity studies are recommended (ICH M3(R2)).

- Carcinogenicity study is dependent on duration of clinical dosing, patient population and other biological activities of the product (ICH S6).

- Reproductive toxicology studies (ICH S5A) (Segment I and III).

FIGURE 25.3   Summary of preclinical regulatory requirements for development of biopharmaceuticals (large molecules).

References

[1] ICS S7A. Safety pharmacology studies for human pharmaceuticals. 2001.

[2] ICH S2A. Specific aspects of regulatory genotoxicity tests for pharmaceuticals. 1996.

[3] ICH S8. Immunotoxicity studies for human pharmaceuticals. 2005.

[4] Mattsson JL, Spencer PJ, Albee RR. A performance standard for clinical and functional observational battery examinations of rats. J Am Coll Toxicol 1996;15:239.

[5] Irwin S. Comprehensive observational assessment: 1a. A systematic, quantitative procedure for assessing the behavioral and physiologic state of the mouse. Psychopharmacologia (Berlin) 1968;13:222–57.

[6] Haggerty GC. Strategies for and experience with neurotoxicity testing of new pharmaceuticals. J Am Coll Toxicol 1991;10:677–87.

[7] Murphy DJ. Safety pharmacology of the respiratory system: techniques and study design. Drug Dev Res 1994;32:237–46.

[8] ICH S3A. Toxicokinetics: the assessment of systemic exposure in toxicity studies. 1995.

[9] New Drug Development. A regulatory overview. Mark Mathieu. 5th ed. Waltham (MA): Paraxel International Corporation; 1999.

[10] ICH-S3B. Pharmacokinetics: guidance for repeated dose tissue distribution studies. 1995.

[11] Guidance for Industry. Safety testing of drug metabolites. US Department of Health and Human Services, Food and Drug Administration, Center for Drug Evaluation and Research (CDER); 2008.

[12] ICH M3(R2). Nonclinical safety studies for the conduct of human clinical trials and marketing authorization for pharmaceuticals. 2010.

[13] Faed EM. Properties of acyl glucuronides. Implications for studies of the pharmacokinetics and metabolism of acidic drugs. Drug Metab Rev 1984;15:1213–49.

[14] US Environmental Protection Agency. Health effects test guidelines, OPPTS 870.7485, metabolism and pharmacokinetics. 1998.

[15] US Food and Drug Administration. Guideline for metabolism studies and for selection of residues for toxicological testing. Center for Veterinary Medicine; 2002.

[16] Baillie TA, Cayen MN, Fouda H, Gerson RJ, Green JD, Grossman SD, et al. Drug metabolites in safety testing. Toxicol Appl Pharmacol 2002;182:188–96.

[17] Hastings KL, El-Hage J, Jacobs A, Leighton J, Morse D, Osterberg R. Drug metabolites in safety testing. Toxicol Appl Pharmacol 2003;190(1):91–2.

[18] National Center for the Replacement, Refinement and Reduction of Animals in Research. Challenging requirements for acute toxicity studies: workshop report. 2007.

[19] Robinson S, Delongeas JL, Donald E, Dreher D, Festag M, Kervyn S, et al. A European pharmaceutical company initiative challenging the regulatory requirement for acute toxicity studies in pharmaceutical drug development. Regul Toxicol Pharmacol 2008;50:345–52.

[20] ICH S4A. Duration of chronic toxicity testing in animals (rodent and non-rodent toxicity testing). 1999.

[21] ICH S2B. Genotoxicity: a standard battery for genotoxicity testing of pharmaceuticals. 1998.

[22] ICH S1A. The need for long-term rodent carcinogenicity studies of pharmaceuticals. 1996.

[23] Johnson EM. Perspectives on reproductive and developmental toxicity. Toxicol Ind Health 1986;2(4):453–82.

[24] ICH S5B. Reproductive toxicology: detection of toxicity to reproduction for medicinal products. 1997.

[25] Sakai T, Takahashi M, Mitsumori K, Yasuhara K, Kawashima K, Mayahara H, et al. Collaborative work to evaluate toxicity on male reproductive organs by 2-week repeated-dose toxicity studies in rats. Overview of the studies. J Toxicol Sci 2000;25:1–21.

[26] Sanbuissho A, Yoshida M, Hisada S, Sagami F, Kudo S, Kumazawa T, et al. Collaborative work on evaluation of ovarian toxicity by repeated-dose and fertility studies in female rats. J Toxicol Sci 2009;34(Suppl. 1):1–22.

[27] ICH Q3A(R2). Impurities in new drug substances. 2006.

[28] ICH Q3B(R2). Impurities in new drug products. 2006.

[29] Draft Guidance for Industry. Assessment of abuse potential for drugs. 2010.

[30] Draft Guidelines for Research Involving the Abuse Liability Assessment of New Drugs. FDA, Center for Drug Evaluation and Research, Division of Anesthetic, Critical Care and Addiction Drugs Products. 1997.

[31] Guideline on the nonclinical investigation of the dependence potential of medicinal products. EMEA/CHMP/Safety Working Party/94227; March 23, 2006.

[32] CFR58. Good laboratory practice for nonclinical laboratory studies. 2004.

[33] ICH S6. Preclinical safety evaluation of biotechnology-derived pharmaceuticals. 1997.

[34] Cavagnaro JA. The principles of ICH S6 and the case-by-case approach. In: Cavagnaro JA, editor. Preclinical safety evaluation of biopharmaceuticals. Hoboken (NJ): Wiley; 2008. p. 45–65.

[35] Chapman K, Pullen N, Graham M, Ragan I. Preclinical safety testing of monoclonal antibodies: the significance of species relevance. Nat Rev Drug Discov 2007;6:120–6.

[36] Subramanyam M, Mertsching E. Selection of relevant species. In: Cavagnaro JA, editor. Preclinical safety evaluation of biopharmaceuticals. Hoboken (NJ): Wiley; 2008. p. 181–205.

[37] Hall WC, Price-Schiavi SA, Wicks J, Rojko JL. Tissue cross-reactivity studies for monoclonal antibodies: predictive value and use for selection of relevant animal species for toxicity testing. In: Cavagnaro JA, editor. Preclinical safety evaluation of biopharmaceuticals. Hoboken (NJ): Wiley; 2008. p. 207–40.

[38] Green MD, Hartsough M. The role of pharmacokinetics and pharmacodynamics in selecting a relevant species. In: Cavagnaro JA, editor. Preclinical safety evaluation of biopharmaceuticals. Hoboken (NJ): Wiley; 2008. p. 277–91.

[39] Podolin PL, Webb EF, Reddy M, Truneh A, Griswold DE. Inhibition of contact sensitivity in human CD4$^+$ transgenic mice by human CD4-specific monoclonal antibodies: CD4$^+$ T-cell depletion is not required. Immunology 2000;99:287–95.

[40] Yocum DE, Solinger AM, Tesser J, Gluck O, Cornett M, O'Sullivan F, et al. Clinical and immunologic effects of a PRIMATIZED antiCD4 monoclonal antibody in active rheumatoid arthritis: results of a phase I, single dose, dose escalating trial. J Rheumatol 1998;25:1257–62.

[41] Sharma A, Davis CB, Tobia LA, Kwok D, Tucci MG, Gore ER, et al. Comparative pharmacodynamics of keliximab and clenoliximab in transgenic mice bearing human CD4. J Pharmacol Exp Ther 2000;293:33–41.

[42] Clarke J, Leach W, Pippig S, Joshi A, Wu B, House R, et al. Evaluation of a surrogate antibody for preclinical safety testing of an antiCD11a monoclonal antibody. Regul Toxicol Pharmacol 2004;40:219–26.

[43] Lynch CM, Hart BW, Grewal IS. Practical considerations for nonclinical safety evaluation of therapeutic monoclonal antibodies. mAbs 2009;1(1):2–11.

[44] Cavagnaro J. Immunotoxicity assessment of biotechnology products: a regulatory point of view. Toxicology 1995;105:1–6.

[45] Brennan FR, Shaw L, Wing MG, Robinson C. Preclinical safety testing of biotechnology-derived pharmaceuticals. Mol Biotechnol 2004;27:59–74.

[46] Timsit J, Savino W, Safieh B, Chanson P, Gagnerault MC, Bach JF, et al. Growth hormone and insulin-like growth factor-1 stimulate hormonal function and proliferation of thymic epithelial cells. J Clin Endocrinol Metab 1992;75:183–8.

[47] Haley PJ. Species differences in the structure and function of the immune system. Toxicology 2003;188:49–71.

[48] FDA Guidance for Industry. Immunotoxicology evaluation of investigational new drugs. 2002.

[49] ICH S5(R2). Detection of toxicity to reproduction for medicinal products & toxicity to male fertility. 2000.

[50] Horvath C. Comparison of preclinical development programs for small molecules (drug/pharmaceuticals) and large molecules (biologics/biopharmaceuticals): studies, timing, materials and cost. In: Cavagnaro JA, editor. Preclinical safety evaluation of biopharmaceuticals. Hoboken (NJ): Wiley; 2008. p. 125–60.

[51] Addendum to ICH S6. Preclinical safety evaluation of biotechnology-derived pharmaceuticals S6(R1). 2009.

[52] FDA guidance concerning demonstration of comparability of human biological products, including therapeutic biotechnology-derived products; April 1996.

[53] ICH Q5E. Comparability of biotechnology/biological products subject to changes in their manufacturing process. 2005.

[54] Points to consider in the manufacture and testing of monoclonal antibody products for human use. US Department of Health and Human Services, Food and Drug Administration, Center for Biologics Evaluation and Research. 1997.

Preclinical Development of Oncology Drugs

H.H. Oh, S. Surapaneni, J.Y. Hui

OUTLINE

INTRODUCTION

Much progress has been made in understanding the molecular and cellular biology of cancer in recent decades, and in combination with new diagnostic and imaging technologies, this has resulted in improved therapy for the treatment of cancer. Development of anticancer therapeutics is regarded as a high priority for pharmaceutical companies because of the high unmet medical need. The American Cancer Society estimated that about 1,596,670 new cancer cases were expected

to be diagnosed in the United States and about 571,950 Americans were expected to die of cancer in 2011 [1]. The number of new cancer cases per year is predicted to triple by the year 2030. These daunting figures show that oncology drug development needs to follow an unconventional paradigm to enable new therapeutic treatments to rapidly reach those who have no other options.

Historically, the success rate for developing anticancer therapy has been less than desirable, and much lower than drugs in other therapeutic classes [2,3]. Due to the high failure rate, each drug that successfully reaches the market

A Comprehensive Guide to Toxicology in Nonclinical Drug Development, Second Edition
http://dx.doi.org/10.1016/B978-0-12-803620-4.00026-8

also has to bear the research and development costs of those that failed. Paul et al. [2] estimated that the total capitalized cost of an average new molecular entity developed by a typical pharmaceutical company is about $1.8 billion, over a total development time of 13.5 years. A recent analysis showed that the attrition rate for the new molecularly targeted oncology agents is slightly lower than historical data including the cytotoxic agents. According to a Pharmaceutical Research and Manufacturers of America publication, at the end of 2010 there were more than 800 anticancer agents in active clinical development. This number represents a 143% rise in the number of oncology drugs being developed in the last decade alone [4]. As oncology therapy has become a main focus for pharmaceutical companies, a thorough understanding of the process, criteria, and issues with its development is essential. This chapter provides an overview of the major classes of anticancer therapeutics and the preclinical aspects of their development.

CYTOTOXIC VERSUS TARGETED DRUGS

Cytotoxic drugs are a unique therapeutic class that has been widely used in antineoplastic chemotherapy. These drugs belong to a variety of chemical and chemotherapeutic classes. These drugs are cytotoxic by design and cause serious dose-limiting adverse effects at therapeutic doses, which are attributed to their poor selectivity of targets that are common to both cancer and normal cells with high turnover rates [5]. As a result, most antineoplastic dosing strategies focus on minimizing cytotoxicity rather than optimizing efficacy. The common toxicities associated with cytotoxic drugs include hemato-lymphotoxicity, gastrointestinal toxicity, hepatotoxicity, cardiotoxicity, respiratory toxicity, nephrotoxicity, and neurotoxicity [5]. In general, rats and dogs are better predictors of the human toxicity of cytotoxic drugs [6]. The main issues in chemotherapy using cytotoxic drugs include a durable antineoplastic efficacy, a reduction of toxicities, and prevention of drug resistance [7].

Cytotoxicity caused by cytotoxic agents is attributed, but not limited, to the following mechanisms:

1. Disruption of DNA through interference with purine and pyrimidine biosynthesis (pentostatin and N-(phosphonacetyl)-L-aspartic acid), inhibition of dihydrofolate reductase (methotrexate), inhibition of DNA biosynthesis (cytarabine), intercalation of double-stranded DNA (anthracyclines and anthracenediones), DNA scission and fragmentation (bleomycin), inhibition of DNA topoisomerases (camptothecin, anthracyclines, anthracenediones, anthrapyrazole, and etoposide), and formation of DNA adducts (cyclophosphamide, melphalan, chlorambucil, hexamethylmelamine, busulfan, dacarbazine, mitomycin C, and cisplatin);

2. Disruption of RNA (inhibition of RNA biosynthesis by anthracyclines and anthracenediones), nucleoprotein (inhibition of nucleoprotein synthesis by L-asparagenase), and microtubule (antitubulin, colchicine, dolastatin, taxol, tritylcysteine, vinblastine, and vincristine);

3. Modulation of mitochondrial permeability transition pores, thus affecting energy transfer pathways in neoplastic cells, which have a higher mitochondrial membrane potential, resulting in cytotoxicity (staurosporine, poly (ADP-ribose) polymerase, 6-aminonicotinamide, 6-methyl-mercaptopurine riboside, and N-(phosphonacetyl)-L-aspartic acid).

Nontargeted cytotoxic drugs have been identified by phenotypic screening of natural products or chemical libraries using in vitro cytotoxicity assays against established cancer-cell lines. This is followed by in vivo assessment of toxicity (tolerability) and efficacy without any knowledge of the target. Thus nontargeted cytotoxic drugs cause serious dose-limiting toxic effects at therapeutic doses due to their lack, or poor selectivity, of targets.

Over the past decade, new, less toxic, molecularly targeted drugs have emerged that target molecular pathways that underline the carcinogenic process and maintain the cancer phenotype [8]. Targeted drugs include biopharmaceuticals (eg, monoclonal antibodies, antibody fragments, and fusion proteins) and highly specific small molecules, and are designed to selectively inhibit specific targets, often in signaling pathways that are abnormal in malignant cells compared with normal cells, thereby minimizing off-target toxicities. The paradigm of molecular targeting in the treatment of cancer is based on the premise that most cancers are associated with one or more genetic abnormalities that result in increased production or activation of some molecules (eg, oncogenes) and/or decreased production or inactivation of some molecules (eg, tumor suppressor genes) [9].

Molecular-targeted agents include, but are not limited to, tyrosine kinase inhibitors, mammalian target of rapamycin (mTOR) inhibitors, farnesyl transferase inhibitors, signal transduction inhibitors, cell cycle inhibitors, antiangiogenic agents, matrix metalloproteinase inhibitors, proteosome inhibitors, and agents that inhibit DNA repair. For example, trastuzumab (Herceptin) is a monoclonal antibody that targets Her-2/Neu, an oncogenic receptor tyrosine kinase in certain forms of breast cancer. Gleevec (Glivec, imatinib mesylate) is a small-molecule tyrosine kinase inhibitor that acts at Bcr-Abl and c-kit for the treatment of chronic myelogenous leukemia (CML) and gastrointestinal stromal tumors (GISTs). Along with Gleevec, other small-molecule kinase inhibitors including erlotinib, sorafenib, sunitinib, nilotinib, lapatinib, and dasatinib have each provided new treatment options for cancer patients. Most recently, a highly selective V600E B-Raf kinase inhibitor, Vemurafenib, has received accelerated approval from FDA for the treatment of refractory metastatic melanoma based on its strong Phase I and II clinical data [10]. Vemurafenib is an oral, small-molecule kinase inhibitor indicated for the treatment of patients with unresectable or metastatic melanoma with B-Raf V600E mutation as detected by an FDA-approved diagnostic test. Vemurafenib is not recommended for use in melanoma patients who lack the B-Raf V600E mutation. As such, Vemurafenib is an excellent example of a highly selective, molecularly targeted drug and personalized therapy in oncology drug development.

The emergence of molecularly targeted drugs in oncology has not only improved the care of cancer patients, but has also changed the daily practice of clinical oncologists. Molecularly targeted drugs often differ from traditional cytotoxic drugs in their administration schedules and routes, their toxicity profiles, and/or the assessment of their efficacy. It is remarkable that molecularly targeted drugs have provided some benefits to previously untreatable cancers; however, these drugs have their own new problems. Nonclinical and clinical studies have shown that treatment with kinase inhibitors (trastuzumab, imatinib, sorafenib, sunitinib, lapatinib, nilotinib, and dasatinib) is associated with cardiovascular toxicity [11–13]. This suggests that such drugs can produce not only significant improvements in efficacy with better selectivity but also unexpected toxicities [13,14]. From the efficacy point of view, selective inhibition of an enzymatic target can have unexpected consequences [15]. These include the rapid development of resistance, which is more likely if a single molecular target is inhibited selectively. This was demonstrated by Gleevec (imatinib), which in many cases becomes ineffective after prolonged treatment [16]. This makes sense, because the progression of a normal cell to a cancer cell has been shown to involve dozens of genetic mutations, and therefore, targeting just a few gene products may be ineffective [17,18]. Furthermore, recent data show that up to 12 different pathways can be involved in a single cancer type [17,18], which means that other pathways can be upregulated to compensate when one pathway is blocked.

An alternative strategy to overcome the limited antitumor activity observed when molecular targeted drugs are administered alone is combining these drugs together or with cytotoxic drugs [19,20]. For example, bevacizumab, a monoclonal antibody that blocks the binding of vascular endothelial growth factor to its receptors, when used in combination with carboplatin and paclitaxel, produced a significant increase in median survival of small-cell lung cancer patients, although the treatment-related deaths were also increased [21].

In spite of these problems, the targeted approach for oncology drug development is still promising delivery of safer and more effective medication. This is based on several premises:

1. Increased knowledge of cancer biology will identify critical targets and their inhibitors at a more rapid pace;
2. New techniques will allow more rapid progression from target identification to clinical candidates;
3. Detailed knowledge of the target in the context of specific malignancies will produce predictive pharmacodynamic biomarkers and companion diagnostic tests that will enable more precise prescribing of drugs (personalized medicine); and
4. Understanding the target in detail will uncover the mechanisms of drug resistance and point to how they can be overcome [22].

CANCER IMMUNOTHERAPY

Immunotherapy is a rapidly advancing field of cancer treatment. These therapies increase the strength of the immune responses against tumors by stimulating specific immune activities or counteracting signals produced by cancer cells that suppress immune responses. Treatment approaches include immune checkpoint inhibitors, therapeutic antibodies, immune cell therapy, immune system modulators, and cancer treatment vaccines [23].

IMMUNE CHECKPOINT INHIBITORS

Checkpoint proteins normally keep immune responses in check by preventing overly intense responses that might damage normal and abnormal cells. Tumor cells often take advantage of these checkpoints to avoid detection and killing by the immune system. Blocking the activity of these immune checkpoint proteins releases the "brakes" on the immune system to increase its ability to destroy cancer cells. The first checkpoint inhibitor that received regulatory approval is ipilimumab (Yervoy), which blocks the activity of cytotoxic T lymphocyte-associated antigen 4 (CTLA-4). CTLA-4 has been shown to be aberrantly upregulated and present on the surface of T cells in certain cancers, dampening T-cell activation in response to tumor cells; ipilimumab binds to CTLA-4 and prevents it from sending its inhibitory signal [24]. Two other more recently approved checkpoint inhibitors, nivolumab (Opdivo) and pembrolizumab (Keytruda), work in a similar way, but target a different checkpoint protein on activated T cells known as PD-1, which has also been found to be upregulated in certain tumors [25].

THERAPEUTIC ANTIBODIES

Tumor-specific monoclonal antibody drugs have been developed to elicit a direct or indirect immune response that leads to killing of cancer cells. These drugs can induce cancer-cell death by multiple mechanisms, and a good example is rituximab (Rituxan), which targets the CD20 protein on the surface of B lymphocytes and has become a mainstay in the treatment of some B-cell malignancies. When CD20-expressing cells become coated with rituximab, the drug kills the cell by inducing apoptosis, as well as by antibody-dependent cell-mediated cytotoxicity and complement-dependent cytotoxicity [23].

Antibody-drug conjugates (ADCs) represent a new wave of cancer drugs that have recently gained regulatory approvals [26]. Antibody-drug conjugates are created by covalent linking of a cytotoxic agent (payload) to antibodies or fragments of antibodies directed to antigens differentially overexpressed in tumor cells. These drugs are expected to selectively deliver toxic drugs to tumor cells with minimized systemic toxicity. A number of ADCs have gained regulatory approval for treatment of various types of cancers, and these include ado-trastuzumab emtansine (Kadcyla), brentuximab vedotin (Adcetris), and ibritumomab tiuxetan (Zevalin).

IMMUNE-CELL THERAPY

Progress is being made with immunotherapy such as chimeric antigen receptor T-cell therapy. In this treatment approach, a patient's T cells are collected from the blood and genetically modified to express a protein known as a chimeric antigen receptor. The modified cells are then grown in the laboratory to produce large populations of these cells, which are then infused into the patient. Chimeric antigen receptors are modified forms of a protein called T-cell receptor, which is expressed on the surface of T cells and allow the modified T cells to attach to specific proteins on the surface of cancer cells and activates killing of these cells [27].

OTHER IMMUNOTHERAPIES

Immune system modulators, such as cytokines, are proteins that normally help modulate immune activity to enhance the body's immune response against cancer. These are nonspecific cancer immunotherapies because they don't target specific cancer cells. Interleukins and interferons are two types of cytokines used to treat patients with cancer. The use of vaccines is another approach to treat cancer. These vaccines can be produced from the patient's own tumor cells or from substances produced by tumor cells. Sipuleucel-T (Provenge) is the only vaccine currently approved in the United States for cancer treatment.

PHARMACOLOGY EVALUATION

Overview

The direction of the oncology drug development has changed from nonspecific cytotoxic drugs to less toxic, highly selective molecularly targeted drugs that target cancer-specific genetic abnormalities or protein expression. In turn, the classical model of screening cytotoxic drugs across the National Cancer Institute (NCI) 60 panel without a clear mechanism-based rationale is being replaced with more strategic drug discovery practices focused on the selection of models based on target expression or genetic alterations in pathways. Predicting, from preclinical studies, whether a potential new anticancer drug will have a therapeutic benefit in patients remains a challenge, and there is no perfect in vitro or in vivo preclinical animal model. However, scientific efforts to develop better predictive pharmacology models for various tumor types are continuing to improve the translation of drug efficacy to patient care.

Prior to Phase I clinical studies, a preliminary characterization of the mechanism of action and schedule dependency, as well as antitumor activity of the drug, should be made. Selection of an appropriate animal model is essential during the drug discovery process and should be based on the target and mechanism of action. However, it is not necessary for the drug to be studied using the same tumor types intended for clinical evaluation [28]. The objectives of preclinical pharmacology studies are to:

1. Provide nonclinical proof of principle;
2. Guide schedules and dose-escalation schemes;
3. Provide information for selection of test species;
4. Aid in start dose selection and selection of investigational biomarkers;
5. If relevant, justify drug combinations; and
6. Understand pharmacokinetic–pharmacodynamic relationships.

The key factors that should be considered during preclinical testing in order to minimize false-positive conclusions or the risks of false-negative results are the selection of a proper tumor model targeting the relevant mechanism, development of a good experimental design, and selection of a proper treatment plan and endpoints.

In Vitro Models

The development of anticancer agents usually starts with in vitro testing. The low cost and high speed of in vitro assessments allow rapid screening of large numbers of discovery compounds. Later in development, in vitro studies can be used to model the optimal features of drug candidates and to link mechanisms of action with potentially valuable biomarkers for non-clinical and clinical evaluations [29,30]. Thus there is no question that in vitro testing is essential, but it does not adequately model many features of cancer, and is insufficient to predict efficacy in cancer patients.

In Vitro National Cancer Institute Screening Model

Historically, the NCI screening system has been based on a panel of 60 different human tumor-cell lines of diverse histologies derived from seven types of cancer (brain, colon, leukemia, lung, melanoma, ovarian, and renal), including drug-resistant cell lines [31]. Each compound is tested over a 5-log concentration range in a 2-day assay to generate 60 dose–response curves. Three endpoints are calculated to determine compound activity and whether it should be considered for further evaluation: the GI_{50} (concentration required to inhibit growth of that cell line by 50%), TGI (minimum concentration that causes total growth inhibition), and LC_{50} (concentration required to kill 50% of cells). These data generate a characteristic profile, called the mean graph, of sensitivity/resistance of all cell lines to the compound. Compounds with similar mechanisms of action tend to have similar mean graphs. A computer program is used to detect compounds that produce strikingly different mean graphs, which often have a unique mechanism of action. Bortezomib, a proteosome inhibitor, is an example of a success achieved by using this screening paradigm.

Since the early 1990s, data on the expression of molecular characteristics within the 60-cell lines panel have been accumulated and a program to characterize molecular targets within this panel has been initiated [32]. Accumulated data over the years have led to a better understanding and collection of molecular target information, including kinases, phosphatases, genes associated with cell cycle control, apoptosis, DNA repair, signal transduction, oncogenes, and drug-metabolizing reductase enzymes. Microarray data on the expression of thousands of genes have also become available, and together with mean graph data, these can be used to identify possible correlations. In 1999, an in vitro prescreen was introduced by NCI whereby compounds were screened only in three highly sensitive cell lines: MCF-7 (breast carcinoma), NCI-H460 (lung carcinoma), and SF-268 (glioma). The rationale for introducing this prescreen was the observation that 85% of the compounds screened in the past had shown no evidence of antiproliferative activity, and the three-line prescreen was shown to efficiently remove many inactive compounds from unnecessary and costly full-scale evaluation in the 60-line panel.

Cell-culture systems usually employ an artificial environment of high serum, growth factors, nutrients, and oxygen, and are most often grown in monolayers. These conditions are different from those of tumors in patients, and it is also difficult to model host–tumor interactions in tissue culture. This has led to the development of three-dimensional cell culture and coculture systems to better mimic the structural and functional properties of normal and tumor tissues and to bridge the gap between cell-based assays and animal studies [29].

The above-described NCI screening program is technically simple, relatively rapid, cost-effective, reproducible, and provides valuable data indicative of mechanistic activity and target interaction. Even though this program is not without false-negative and positive results, the original intention was to produce a high-throughput in vitro screen that would be sufficiently discriminatory to ensure that only a relatively small number of compounds would be selected for further evaluation in human tumor xenograft models. However, when the number of potential compounds arising from this in vitro screening program exceeded the capacity of the xenograft assay, the in vivo hollow fiber assay was developed in an attempt to prioritize compounds for secondary screening.

Hollow-Fiber Assay

The in vivo hollow-fiber assay (HFA) was developed at the NCI to help bridge the gap between the in vitro cell-based assays and human xenograft models in immune-deficient mice [33]. The goal was to develop an assay to help predict those compounds found active in the 60-cell line panel that would be active in subsequent xenograft models, thus reducing the time and cost of conducting animal studies. The HFA is a short-term, in vivo assay in which tumor cells are grown in biocompatible hollow fibers for 24–48h in vitro, followed by in vivo implantation at both intraperitoneal (IP) and subcutaneous sites in nude mice. These fibers have pores small enough to retain the cancer cells, but large enough to permit entry of potential drugs with molecular weights of <500 kDa, including peptides and large proteins. It has been found that the greater the response in the HFA, the greater the likelihood that a compound will be active in xenograft models. For compounds tested in both assays, there was a good correlation of activities, suggesting that a xenograft-positive compound was unlikely to be missed by testing in the HFA. This prediction was better with the fibers implanted IP.

The HFA has been more recently used to investigate the pharmacodynamics of anticancer agents in vivo [34,35]. Pharmacodynamic endpoints include protein/gene/mRNA expression, assessment of DNA damage (comet assay), cell-cycle perturbation, and cell death, including apoptosis. This is a valuable tool for studying drug–target interaction in vivo and helps selection of compounds at an early stage of development.

Assay Development for Molecularly Targeted Therapies

Molecularly targeted agents, unlike cytotoxic agents, target specific cell-signaling events, which play critical roles in growth of cancer cells. With an acceptable toxicity profile, these therapies could be used on a prolonged basis with the goal of turning cancer into a chronic disease. The success of a new, targeted therapy depends on the identification of a key regulator of cancer-cell growth, survival, proliferation, or metastasis. The approaches that have been used in target identification include genomic (DNA), transcriptomic (gene expression at the RNA level), proteomic (protein expression), metabolomic (metabolite profiling), and clinical (associated disease correlation) techniques. A typical approach to identifying inhibitors of molecular targets includes a primary biochemical assay with a recombinant protein or engineered mammalian cells followed by cell-based in vitro assays [36]. A key part of developing targeted therapies is the measurement of target inhibition at a point as close to the target as possible, thus development of targeted inhibition assays for use in all phases of drug development is vital for success. These assays need to have the required selectivity and specificity to be useful preclinically and clinically. Cell-based efficacy models that measure the effects of a drug on a biological endpoint, such as growth or apoptosis, can be used to further validate a target. However, assay results should be interpreted carefully, because off-target effects often obscure the targeted effects.

In Vivo Models

The most common step following in vitro assays is an efficacy assessment in a rodent tumor model. The ideal preclinical animal model is selective, predictive, and reproducible. Such models are lacking in oncology, in contrast with other therapeutic areas such as infectious diseases or inflammation, where a variety of model systems are predictive of clinical success. Once immunologically compromised mice capable of supporting human tumor growth became widely available in the early 1980s, human tumor xenograft models were developed, and now are the most commonly used models in the current preclinical efficacy studies. Unfortunately, the predictive value of preclinical rodent-based tumor models has been poor, as many drugs fail in the clinic, despite demonstrating antitumor efficacy in preclinical animal models. However, it is important to note that many clinically approved drugs have demonstrated antitumor activity in a variety of preclinical models [37–39]. Although controversy exists regarding the optimal animal model

for assessing the antitumor activity of candidate drugs, human tumor xenografts are ideal systems for modeling biomarker responses in target tumor tissues and safety liabilities in the host as the molecularly targeted therapies continue to grow in the oncology drug discovery process.

Various mouse models are reviewed and discussed by Teicher [40] and Firestone [41]. They are divided into immunocompromised models and immunocompetent models. Autochthonous models (syngeneic tumor models) are those in which a tumor of mouse origin is transplanted into a mouse, whereas xenograft models involve the transplantation of a tumor from a heterologous species (eg, human) into a mouse. Transgenic models are generated by genetically altering the mouse genome to increase tumor occurrence.

The advantages of syngeneic tumor models include relatively low cost, reproducibility, growth in immunocompetent hosts, availability of a wide variety of tumor types, generally nonimmunogenicity, a long history of use and therefore a strong baseline of drug response data, readily available hosts, and studies that are easy to conduct with statistically meaningful numbers of mice per group. Their disadvantages are that the tumor cells are rodent, and therefore express mouse or rat homologues of the desired targets, and they tend to grow quickly. As for antibody therapeutics, the homology between the human and mouse targets can become a serious limiting factor for syngeneic models.

The most commonly used immunocompromised models are subcutaneous and orthotopic xenografts using either human cancer-cell lines or fresh human patient-derived tumors. The availability of athymic mice (*nu/nu*) and immunodeficient mouse strains with other genetic lesions (severe combined immunodeficiency) has enabled the development of these models, which are provided to test many oncology drugs including cytotoxic agents. In the case of molecularly targeted drugs, the pharmacological activity can be evaluated by using human cancer-cell lines that harbor known genetic lesions or genetically engineered cell lines that can be implanted subcutaneously in immunocompromised mice. This model can evaluate the impact of drug candidates on tumor growth, pharmacodynamic target modulation, and downstream signaling. Thus the subcutaneous xenograft model can be the most appropriate tool for drugs that target signaling pathways. Further, combinations of specific targeted drugs can also be tested in human cancer-cell line xenografts to inhibit multiple pathways that may be aberrantly regulated in the same tumor.

However, this traditional subcutaneous xenograft model has many limitations, as listed in Table 26.1. Its major limitations are the lack of an appropriate tumor microenvironment (stromal components and immune

TABLE 26.1 Advantages and Disadvantages of Human Subcutaneous Xenograft Mouse Models

Advantages	Disadvantages
• Technical simplicity • Many different human tumor-cell lines transplantable • Suitable for high-throughput screening • Allows for evaluation of therapeutic index (PK/PD relationship) • Good correlation with drugs active in human lung, colon, breast, and melanoma cancers • Well established (current NCI method of choice) • Several decades of experience	• Different biological behavior • Lack of appropriate microenvironment (tumor–stromal interaction, host immune cells) • Lack of heterogeneity • Metastases are rare • Survival is not an ideal endpoint • Shorter doubling times than original tumor growth in human • Less necrosis and better blood supply • Death from bulk of tumor masses • High infection risks • Difficult to model for brain tumor • Not suitable for host-directed therapies (antiangiogenesis and immunomodulators) • Incompatible mouse versus human signaling

cells) and the absence of spontaneous metastases to clinically relevant sites. To address these concerns, the orthotopic xenograft model has been developed. The orthotopic model can implant tumor-cell lines directly into the anatomical location of origin, putting tumor–stromal interactions into the appropriate microenvironment and giving the advantage of frequently developing metastatic disease. This more closely mimics the disease observed in patients. However, it remains uncertain whether orthotopic xenografts are more suitable than subcutaneous xenografts in predicting therapeutic benefit.

Instead of human cancer-cell lines, fresh human-patient-derived tumors can be implanted into immunocompromised mice. These grafts, implanted subcutaneously or orthotopically, preserve the histological phenotype of the donor and seem to offer a more clinically relevant tumor model with stromal involvement.

The selection of appropriate preclinical model should be based on the biology of the pathway that is being abnormally regulated and the mechanism of action of the therapeutic drug. In general, if the drug target is an oncogene, a subcutaneous xenograft of a human-cell line or primary patient isolate with a known genetic lesion would be the right model to characterize the pharmacokinetics-pharmacodynamics (PK-PD) relationship and evaluate antitumor activity. If the drug target is a pathway that is implicated in cell migration or invasion, an orthotopic xenograft model would be appropriate, because this model better mimics the metastatic disease observed in patients. The study of tumor initiating cells may also best be evaluated in xenografts of fresh human-patient-derived isolates that maintain the heterogeneity and architecture of the original patient tumor.

Mouse xenograft models engrafted with human materials have limitations including the compromised immune system, differences in species specificity of proteins, and an inability to capture early events in tumorigenesis. The development of genetically engineered immunocompetent mouse models has addressed these limitations. Genetically engineered immunocompetent mouse models (transgenic, knock-out, and knock-in) have been recently developed as the involvement of multiple genetic lesions is discovered during the human carcinogenesis. These models have enabled the study of spontaneous tumor initiation in a competent host strain. The major issue of the transgenic model is that tumorigenesis is initiated following introduction of a mutation or gene deletion in all cells of the body. Thus the development of tissue-specific, conditional, knock-out or knock-in models has offered a more relevant disease model in which a tissue-specific oncogene mutation or loss of a tumor suppressor gene can be studied in a mature animal. An additional benefit of the genetically engineered mouse model is that allografted, subcutaneously implanted tumors arising from genetically engineered mouse models may allow the investigation of resistance mutations in genetically altered pathways. The advantages in studying tumorigenesis in the immunocompetent host are the abilities to evaluate the role of the tumor microenvironment on tumor initiation, maintenance, and progression and to examine a complex interaction between the host immune system and the tumor that is involved early in cancer prevention and later in progression. The disadvantages of transgenic mouse models include the fact that breeding and maintaining a colony large enough to generate sufficient numbers of mice at the same age and gender is costly, tumors arise at variable stages in different animals and nodules, the stroma is rodent, the tumors are difficult to follow, the endpoint is frequently survival, and statistics are difficult. The most current transgenic models are probably more useful for studying the biology of hyperproliferative and malignant cells than for drug discovery.

Selecting the appropriate preclinical pharmacology model is essential during the in vivo evaluation of novel therapeutics. The currently available models have both advantages and disadvantages. Making the right choice requires knowledge of the biological features of the model, an understanding of the area under the pharmacologic plasma concentration-time curve, which produces the desired target effect, and an understanding of the pharmacodynamic action of the drug in the tumor.

TRANSLATIONAL MEDICINE

Biomarkers

Oncology drug development has a higher failure rate than that for drugs of other diseases [3]. One primary reason for this is believed to be the lack of rigorous and predictive animal models that reflect the right human cancer types. The development of a new animal model is usually not attractive to the pharmaceutical industry, because it has to be developed at the time of drug discovery before any promising clinical candidate is identified and will require a large investment. On the other hand, the strategies traditionally used for developing standard cytotoxic chemotherapy may not be appropriate for molecularly targeted agents. Conventional dose determination, based on maximum tolerability and efficacy obtained from objective tumor response, may not be suitable for targeted agents, since many of them have a wide therapeutic index and inhibit tumor growth without demonstrable cytotoxicity. As such, the utilization of biomarkers in early clinical trials (Phase I and II) is appealing to potentially serve as surrogates for drug efficacy and toxicity and to evaluate the effects of drug on molecular targets. Thus there has been increasing interest in the use of biomarkers to aid the evaluation of new oncology drugs in early clinical trials [42].

The main reasons for the growing interest for cancer biomarkers are:

1. To correlate clinical data with target modulation, and
2. Advances in technologies have enabled measurement of specific tumor targets (such as special imaging studies and immunohistochemistry studies to measure receptor expression or phosphorylation of the downstream substrate as pharmacodynamic biomarkers).

Biomarkers may play several roles in the progression of a drug from research to personalized medicine. In particular, they can be used to understand the mechanism of action of a drug, to monitor the modulation of the intended target, to assess efficacy and safety, to adapt dosing, schedule, and escalation, to select patients, and to correlate to clinical outcome.

The different phases of drug development in oncology involve different categories of biomarkers. They are divided into four categories (prognostic, predictive, pharmacodynamic/mode of action (PD/MoA), and safety biomarkers), each being well defined and described by Marrer and Dieterle [43].

Prognostic biomarkers predict the course of disease and are associated with clinical outcome, independent of any treatment. Clinical staging, tumor grading, and classification are well-known examples of prognostic biomarkers. They are usually based on molecular readouts involving new technologies such as genetics, genomics, and proteomics (DNA, RNA, and protein levels). Two examples are based on mRNA profiles, and are used primarily in breast cancer to make a decision regarding the use of adjuvant chemotherapy in patients with early-stage breast cancer. The first test is a DNA microarray-based diagnostic kit (called MammaPrint, Agendia, Amsterdam, The Netherlands) that measures the gene-expression levels of 70 genes in breast cancer-tumor biopsies and aims to determine the probability of early-stage breast-cancer recurrence 5–10 years after treatment. The second test is a 21-gene panel assay that has been associated with chemotherapy response on the basis of RT-PCR (PCR after reverse transcription of RNA) (called Oncotype DX assay, Genomics Health, Inc., Redwood City, CA, USA) and has been validated in women with lymph-node negative, estrogen receptor-expressing breast cancer. These assays aim to optimize risk classification and prediction of recurrence, thereby improving the selection of patients for adjuvant therapy.

Predictive biomarkers are the most successfully applied biomarkers in oncology drug development to date and help to identify those patients most likely to respond and/or least likely to show adverse events in the context of a specific treatment. Their application is also known as "personalized medicine" because predictive biomarkers help in selecting the right drug for the right patient. The Her2/neu diagnostic test is used for choice of treatment with trastuzumab (Herceptin) as a first-line therapy in combination with paclitaxel chemotherapy for the treatment of Her2-positive metastatic breast cancer. The overexpression of Her2 is assessed either by immunohistochemistry, which measures Her2 protein level or by fluorescence in situ hybridization, which measures the Her2 gene copy number. Patients with pml-rara translocation-related leukemia respond to all-*trans* retinoic acids, whereas Philadelphia chromosome-related leukemia patients respond to Gleevec (imatinib) [44].

The best example of genetic diagnostic testing, which specifically directs targeted therapy, is the detection of bcr-abl translocations in patients with CML. Bcr-abl translocation between chromosome 22 and 9 (Philadelphia chromosome) indicates imatinib mesylate as therapy, which inhibits the proliferation of bcr-abl expressing hematopoietic cells [45]. Likewise, most GISTs express constitutively activated mutant isoforms of c-kit protein. Thus the detection of the c-kit protein in tissue biopsies supports the diagnosis of GISTs, and is used to decide on the eligibility of patients to imatinib therapy for the treatment of c-kit-positive unresectable and/or meta-static malignant GISTs [46]. Activating mutations in the B-Raf oncogene are linked to 65% of malignant mela-noma and other malignancies. In particular, the V600E B-Raf missense mutation has been reported in >80% of B-Raf alleles associated with constitutive activation of B-Raf kinase. A highly selective inhibitor of V600E B-Raf kinase (Vemurafenib) in combination with an in vitro diagnostic test has recently been approved by the FDA. V600E mutation-positive patients should receive great benefit from Vemurafenib treatment.

Another example is epidermal growth factor recep-tor (EGFR) pharmDX (DakoCytomation, Carpinteria, CA, USA), an assay used to identify colorectal cancer patients eligible for treatment with cetuximab (Erbitux). This was a test required by the FDA. EGFR is also a pre-dictive biomarker for treatment of head and neck can-cer with cetuximab, for pancreatic cancer and NSCLC treated with erlotinib (Tarceva), and for NSCLC treated with gefitinib (Iressa).

PD/MoA biomarkers are most likely to be used in research or early development to verify that a drug reaches and inhibits its target, to examine its mecha-nism of action, to measure PK and PD correlations, and to optimize dose and schedule. Thus these markers are closely related to the therapeutic targets to be inhibited. PD markers can be used to collect quantitative infor-mation on exposure, kinetics of target inhibition, and percentage of target inhibition. Qualitative information obtained by PD markers includes:

1. The activity achieved on the intended molecular target (eg, inhibition of kinase substrate and phosphorylation of downstream substrate) and/or the modulation of signaling pathways;
2. Identifying whether the desired biological effects (eg, apoptosis, invasion, and angiogenesis) occur; and
3. Measuring clinical outcome (eg, tumor regression, time to regression, overall survival, etc.).

One example is the kinase activity of bcr-abl as the PD biomarker in tumor cells of imatinib-treated CML patients. This demonstrated that the same doses inhibit the target and produce a clinical response without inducing adverse effects. Many kinase inhibitors inhibit the phosphorylation of substrates of the signaling path-ways. mTOR inhibition by RAD001 can be monitored by determining the level of the phosphorylated form of the ribosomal protein S6. Similarly, phospho-EGFR can be used as a PD biomarker to monitor the efficacy of gefinitib (Iressa) treatment. Furthermore, PD biomark-ers can also become safety biomarkers, in which the observed adverse events are directly related to the tar-get inhibition. One example is bortezomib (Velcade), a 20s proteosome inhibitor. In a Phase I trial, it has been demonstrated that the percentage of inhibition of the 20s

proteasome in whole blood can be directly correlated with toxicity and dosing. Adverse events (neuropathy, fatigue, and diarrhea) were observed with 70% of inhibi-tion of the 20s proteasome activity, which corresponds to a dose of 3–3.5 mg given on day 1 and on day 4 every other week [47].

Safety biomarkers are identified based on toxicities observed in animal toxicology studies and can help in monitoring and managing potential on- and off-target adverse effects of drugs.

Recommended validated testing markers exist for predicting metabolism and exposure, such as genotyp-ing of CYP450s (CYP2C9 and CYP2D6) for susceptibil-ity of toxicity assessments by tamoxifen [48] and genetic polymorphisms of uridine diphosphate (UDP)-glucuro-nosyltransferase 1A1 (UGT1A1) and its potential associa-tion with hyperbilirubinemia during nilotinib treatment [49]. It is also well known that treatment of cytotoxic drugs (cisplatin or methotrexate) induces kidney tox-icity. In addition to urinary albumin and total protein, serum creatinine and blood urea nitrogen in peripheral clinical tests, new sensitive renal safety biomarkers (eg, kidney injury marker 1, urinary clusterin, urinary trefoil factor 3, urinary cystatin C, β_2-microglobulin) have been recently identified, characterized, and qualified. These can be used for the early identification of acute, drug-induced kidney injury [50].

Cytotoxic and targeted drugs used to treat cancer, including classical chemotherapeutic agents, mono-clonal antibodies that target tyrosine kinase receptors, small-molecule tyrosine kinase inhibitors, and even antiangiogenic drugs and hemoprevention agents such as cyclooxygenase-2 inhibitors, all affect the cardio-vascular system. Combination therapy often amplifies cardiotoxicity, and radiotherapy can also cause heart problems, particularly when combined with chemo-therapy [51]. The most frequently used and effective approaches to monitoring cardiac function and its impairment are:

1. Assessment of left ventricular ejection fraction by either echocardiography or multigated acquisition scan, a noninvasive technique; and
2. Electrophysiological measurement of QT/QTc duration, assessed by electrocardiogram, for predicting risk of a potentially fatal arrhythmia called torsades de pointes [51,52].

Drug-induced liver injury has been extensively discussed both at the industry and regulatory levels. In oncology, drug-induced hepatotoxicity has been reported for chemotherapy drugs (cyclophospha-mide, chlorambucil, platinum agents, procarbazine, and dacarbazine), antitumor antibiotics (doxorubicin and bleomycin), microtubule-targeting drugs (vinca alkaloids and taxanes), topoisomerase inhibitors (topotecan, irinotecan, and etoposide), and targeted drugs (bevacizumab, gefitinib, imatinib, and bortezomib). Hepatotoxicity may be identified in nonclinical studies and easily monitored in clinical trials using serum samples by standard clinical chemistry assessment. Typical clinical chemistry markers include alanine aminotransferase, aspartate aminotransferase, alkaline phosphatase, total bilirubin, gamma glutamyltransferase, glutamate dehydrogenase, sorbitol dehydrogenase, lactate dehydrogenase, total bile acid, unconjugated bilirubin, 5′-nucleotidase, and ornithine carbamyltransferase (OCT) [53].

The use of biomarkers from drug discovery to clinical proof of concept is extremely helpful, especially in oncology drug development, as the new trend in oncology is focusing on targeted therapies. In terms of efficacy, cancers will progress during the treatment rather than regress, if the wrong drug is given. In terms of safety, these patients will be placed at high risk due to the side effects of wrong treatment. Thus choice of the right drug, in combination with monitoring specific biomarkers, will guide the choice of treatment, dosing, schedule, and escalation, and will minimize adverse effects and therefore increase overall survival.

Focusing on peripherally accessible biomarkers (such as genetic alterations in the circulating tumor cells or changes of the serum proteins) is highly desirable. An invasive procedure is needed to evaluate biomarkers in biopsied tumor tissue, which is less desirable for patients.

PHARMACOKINETIC AND PHARMACODYNAMIC MODELING

Pharmacokinetics (PK) is the study of a drug and/ or its metabolite kinetics in the body, from which drug concentration-time profiles are generated. Pharmacodynamics (PD) measures how the body responds to the presence of drug, eg, changes in biomarker levels or tumor-growth inhibition, from which dose–effect relationships are generated. Pharmacodynamics is the relationship between drug concentrations and pharmacological effects. Both the PK and the PD of drugs can be described using mathematical and statistical functions. The dose–exposure–effect relationship, one in which "exposure" can be the area under the concentration curve or the maximal concentration C_{max} and "effect" may be modulation of biomarker, tumor growth inhibition, etc., an index of efficacy, or a measure of safety.

As described above, understanding the modulation of biomarkers and related exposure–effect relationships in preclinical settings is very important for developing models with predictive value. Translating PK-PD from laboratory animals to humans is often accomplished through an understanding and extrapolation of preclinical models to the clinical setting. The purpose of a well-developed PK-PD model is to:

1. Enable dose selection and optimization,
2. Facilitate prediction and monitoring of response,
3. Provide understanding of mechanism of action, and
4. Act as an early surrogate for efficacy or safety.

PK-PD modeling will relate plasma concentration or exposure data to effects at the target site (eg, inhibition of phosphorylated biomarker in tumors or tumor volume or growth rate). PK-PD models are broadly classified as direct or indirect. Direct PK-PD models are employed when there is a good relationship between concentration data and the corresponding PD effect, without a delay in response. The simplest of these models uses the Hills equation, where the response is related to maximal effect, concentration of drug at 50% of maximal effect, and a response factor. Other direct models are also used, and the reader is referred to an excellent review of this area [54,55]. Some anticancer drugs may affect biochemical pathways (eg, phosphorylation of an enzyme) with relaxation times that are very short in comparison with drug clearance times. In such cases, the PD biomarker may reflect an inhibited reaction and therefore may track closely with the drug concentration or exposure. The anticancer thymidylate synthase inhibitor Thymitaq (AG337) enters and exits cells very rapidly, and its inhibitory effects on thymidylate synthase are immediate. The Phase I clinical trial used circulating deoxyuridine as a measure of thymidylate synthase inhibition, and the kinetics of the system are such that this plasma biomarker tracks a direct PK-PD relationship [56].

However, the pharmacokinetics of anticancer drugs is complex and involves a series of biological processes with several levels of processes and feedback mechanisms. These complex processes may not be adequately captured in direct response models, and hence require indirect PK-PD models. Examples of indirect PD models are anticancer drugs that cause cell-cycle perturbations, either by cell-cycle arrest or inducing apoptosis. The effect of the drug lags the drug concentrations, and may be observed after a few hours following drug clearance. For example, many targeted anticancer agents inhibit tyrosine kinases, and phosphorylated proteins have become an important source of biomarkers in tumors [57]. Biomarkers have been developed for c-Met kinases, mitogen-activated protein kinase kinase (MEK), and PI-3 kinases [58–60]. PK-PD modeling was developed to relate the extent of inhibition of phosphorylation pathways to tumor response in mice, and to suggest clinical dosing based on preclinical data, including identification of optimal combinations of targeted agents [57].

TOXICOLOGY EVALUATION

The objectives of the preclinical toxicology evaluation of oncology drugs are to:

1. Identify an appropriately safe starting dose for the initial clinical trial;
2. Characterize target organ toxicities, exposure-toxic response relationship, and reversibility; and
3. Assist in identifying an appropriate dose escalation scheme for the clinical trials.

Ideally, the objectives can be accomplished in an optimized program to enable prompt introduction of novel anticancer agents into patients without compromising their safety. In this section, the following topics are discussed:

1. Key information in the ICH S9 guidance (International Conference on Harmonization of Technical Requirements for Registration of Pharmaceuticals for Human Use, "Nonclinical Evaluation for Anticancer Pharmaceuticals");
2. Investigational New Drug Application (IND) and New Drug Application (NDA)-enabling toxicology programs; and
3. First-in-human dose selection.

ICH S9

The usual time and cost requirements needed to develop therapeutic drugs are very high and marketing approval rates are very low. The average time to develop a new drug (10–15 years) largely exceeds the time over which they are given to patients with nonresponsive late stages of cancers and short life expectancies (from a number of months to 2 years). New and effective anticancer drugs need to be provided more expeditiously to patients with late stages of cancer and short life expectancies. To expedite the development of new oncology drugs, ICH S9 guidance [28] was established with inputs from European, Japanese, and US working groups. This guidance applies to both small molecules and biopharmaceuticals, and is devoted only to drugs intended to treat patients with advanced cancers and limited therapeutic options. Its goals are to facilitate and accelerate the development of oncology drugs and to protect patients from unnecessary adverse effects, while avoiding unnecessary use of animals, in accordance with the 3R (reduce/refine/replace) principles. It is important to note that the development of pharmaceuticals intended for the treatment of nonterminal diseases (ie, cancer prevention, treatment of symptoms or side effects of chemotherapies, studies in healthy volunteers, vaccines, or cellular or gene therapy) should follow ICH M3(R2) guidance [61]. Good laboratory practice (GLP)-compliant studies with the same route of administration and formulation and similar or approximate dosing schedule should be conducted for evaluations.

Nonclinical Pharmacology: Preliminary characterization of the mechanism(s) of action and schedule dependencies as well as the antitumor activity of the drug should be made in appropriate models, although it is not necessary to study in the same tumor types intended for clinical evaluation. Pharmacology studies can provide nonclinical proof of principle, guide schedules and dose-escalation schemes, provide information for selection of test species, aid in start-dose selection and selection of investigational biomarkers, justify combinations with other oncology drugs, and aid in understanding the secondary pharmacodynamic effects (safety).

Safety Pharmacology: An assessment of oncology drugs on vital organ functions (cardiovascular, respiratory, and central nervous systems) can be included in general toxicology studies. In cases where specific concerns have been identified that could put patients at significant additional risks in clinical trials, appropriate safety pharmacology studies are recommended (ICH S7A and S7B) [62,63]. In the absence of a specific risk, dedicated studies are not needed to support clinical trials or for market approval.

Pharmacokinetics (PK): The evaluation of limited PK parameters (eg, peak plasma/serum levels (C_{max}), area under the curve (AUC), and half-life) in general toxicology studies can facilitate dose selection, schedule, and escalation during Phase I studies. Information on absorption, distribution, metabolism, and excretion of the drug in animals can be generated in parallel with clinical development. Details on this evaluation are described in the "Drug Metabolism and Pharmacokinetics" section.

General Toxicology: Initial nonclinical evaluations for oncology drugs are conducted to identify the pharmacologic properties of a pharmaceutical, to establish a safe initial dose level for the first human exposure, and to understand its toxicological profile (eg, identification of target organs, exposure–response relationship, and reversibility). These data are used to inform the clinicians of the potential of a drug for particular toxicities and to guide the dose-escalation scheme in clinical trials.

For the oncology drugs intended to treat patients with advanced cancers, the determination of no-observed-adverse-effect level (NOAEL) or no-observed-effect level (NOEL) in toxicology studies is not necessary to support first-in human clinical trials. This is commonly acknowledged based on the facts that the pharmacologically active dose for oncology drugs usually carries a substantial risk of toxicity and the evaluation of oncology drugs requires a balancing of risk and benefit for patients. The reversibility of serious adverse effects should be addressed in the pivotal studies, although the demonstration of complete recovery is not considered essential. Toxicokinetic evaluation is important to correlate the toxicity and exposure.

For small molecules, the general toxicology testing species are rodent and nonrodent. In the case of genotoxic drugs targeting rapidly dividing cells, a repeat-dose toxicity study in one rodent species is considered sufficient, provided the rodent is a relevant species. For biopharmaceuticals, a toxicology study should be conducted in the pharmacologically active species, where most cases are nonhuman primates (ICH S6(R1)) [64].

Conduct of pivotal toxicology studies using the intended clinical route of administration and formulation and an approximation of its clinical schedule is important. Examples of duration and schedule for toxicology studies to support various initial clinical trials are presented in Table 26.2. The nonclinical data to support Phase I and the clinical Phase I data would normally be sufficient for moving to Phase II and into second or first-line therapy in patients with advanced cancers. The results from 3-month repeat-dose studies should be available prior to initiating Phase III and for marketing.

Reproductive Toxicology: Embryo-fetal toxicity studies of anticancer drugs should be available when the marketing application is submitted, but are not needed to support clinical trials for the treatment of patients with advanced cancer. These studies are not considered essential for the purpose of marketing applications for drugs that are genotoxic and target rapidly dividing cells (eg, crypt cells, bone marrow) or belong to a class that has been known to cause developmental toxicity. For small molecules, embryo-fetal toxicity studies are conducted in two species (ICH S5(R2)) [65], but a confirmatory study in a second species is usually not warranted in cases where embryo-fetal lethality or teratogenicity was seen in the studies with two species.

TABLE 26.2　Examples of Treatment Schedules for Anticancer Pharmaceuticals to Support Initial Clinical Trials

Clinical Schedule	Nonclinical Treatment Schedule
Once every 3–4 weeks	Single dose
Daily for 5 days every 3 weeks	Daily for 5 days
Daily for 5–7 days, alternating weeks	Daily for 5–7 days, alternating weeks (two dose cycles)
Once a week for 3 weeks, 1 week off	Once a week for 3 weeks
Two or three times a week	Two or three times a week for 4 weeks
Daily	Daily for 4 weeks
Weekly	Once a week for 4–5 doses

Adapted from ICH S9. March 2010. Nonclinical Evaluation for Anticancer Pharmaceuticals.

For biopharmaceuticals, an assessment in one pharmacologically relevant species is usually sufficient. Alternatively, literature assessment, assessment of placental transfer, the direct or indirect effects, or any other factors may be used if scientifically justified. Fertility and early embryonic development study and a pre- and postnatal development toxicity study are not necessary to support clinical trials or marketing. Information (eg, effect on reproductive organs) from general toxicology studies can be used for the assessment of fertility impairment.

Genotoxicity and Carcinogencity: Genotoxicity studies are not essential to support clinical trials, but should be available to support marketing. If in vitro assays are positive, an in vivo assay is not warranted. Carcinogenicity studies are not needed to support marketing.

Immunotoxicity: The standard assessment parameters of general toxicology studies are considered sufficient to evaluate immunotoxic potential and support marketing. For immunomodulatory anticancer drugs, additional endpoints (eg, immunophenotyping) can be included in the general toxicology studies.

Photosafety: An initial assessment of phototoxic potential should be conducted prior to Phase I for drugs that demonstrated photochemical properties. If initial assessment showed potential risk, adequate protective measures should be guided to patients who participate in the clinical trials. If photosafety cannot be adequately evaluated on the basis of nonclinical and clinical data, a photosafety study should be provided prior to marketing.

Combination: One of the most common strategies in oncology research is a combination approach as more drugs with novel mechanisms of action are being developed and cancer is a complex disease. This is based on the hypothesis that two separate drug targets will have a synergistic effect on tumor growth and survival. Typical combinations would be two approved drugs, or one approved drug and one investigative drug (one having Phase I clinical data). In general, toxicology studies investigating the safety of combinations of drugs intended to treat patients with advanced cancer are not warranted, provided that the toxicity profile of each individual drug is well characterized in toxicology studies. If the combination is between an approved drug and an investigational drug, which is in an early stage of development (ie, no human-toxicity profile characterized), a pharmacology study to support the rationale for the combination should be provided. This study should include evidence of increased pharmacologic activity in the absence of a substantial increase in toxicity on the basis of limited safety endpoints (eg, mortality, clinical signs, and body weight).

Pediatric Population: The general paradigm for investigating oncology drugs in pediatric patients is first to define a relatively safe dose in adult populations and then to assess some fraction of that dose in initial pediatric clinical studies. Studies in juvenile animals are usually not conducted to support inclusion of pediatric populations for the treatment of cancer. Conduct of such studies is considered only when human safety data and previous animal studies are considered insufficient for a safety evaluation in the intended pediatric patients. Design of juvenile toxicity studies, such as species, duration of treatment, parameters to evaluate, recovery period, should be carefully considered, and when possible, inputs from regulatory authorities should be sought.

Conjugated Products: Conjugated products are drugs covalently bound to carrier molecules, such as proteins, lipids, or sugars. The main concern of conjugated products is the safety of the unconjugated material, including the linker used. Thus stability of the conjugate in the test animals and human plasma and toxicokinetic evaluations of the conjugated and unconjugated compounds should be provided.

Liposomal Products: The safety assessment of liposomal products includes a complete toxicological evaluation of the final liposomal product and a limited evaluation of the unencapsulated drug and carrier liposomes (eg, a single arm in a toxicology study). Toxicokinetics of both the liposomal product and the free compound after administration of the liposomal product is desired.

Metabolites: For metabolites that have been identified in humans but not in animal studies, a separate toxicity evaluation is generally not warranted.

Impurities: In general, the impurity and residual solvent specifications for anticancer drugs should be set according to ICH Q3A, Q3B, and Q3C guidance [66,67]. When a reduction in impurity level is not feasible and it is necessary to exceed the limits set forth in this guidance, a justification should be provided in the marketing application. The justification should take into consideration intended patient populations, therapeutic areas, and duration of treatment. If information is available, a comparison of pharmacologic and toxicity profiles, such as general toxicity, genotoxicity, and carcinogenicity, between the parent and the impurity, should be made. For genotoxic impurities, approaches have been used to set limits based on increases in lifetime risk of cancer. These limits may not be appropriate to use for anticancer therapeutics, especially those intended for patients with advanced disease and limited therapeutic options. Qualification of impurities can also be based on levels tested in nonclinical studies relative to levels in clinical dose. If an impurity is found as human metabolite, it is also considered qualified.

Investigational New Drug Application and New Drug Application-Enabling Toxicology Program

An investigational new drug (IND) application must be filed prior to initiating clinical trials. The preclinical testing program for IND application depends on both the intended use of the drug and the population of patients being treated in the initial, limited, clinical trials. The proposed therapeutic indication, the outcome of early clinical development, the nature of toxicities seen in animals and in patients, and the projected duration of clinical treatment all determine the package of preclinical studies necessary to support an NDA. The toxicology programs to enable the IND and NDA of most oncology drugs are summarized in Table 26.3.

Oncology drugs are classified into two groups: those for advanced and life-threatening cancers and those for nonlife-threatening cancers. The preclinical program for oncology drugs treating advanced late stages of cancers differs from that for drugs used chronically (chemopreventive drugs, hormonal drugs, immunomodulators), drugs treating early stages of cancers, or drugs intended to enhance the efficacy or diminish the toxicity of currently used anticancer therapies. In situations where potential benefits outweigh the risk of drug-related adverse effects (such as advanced and life-threatening cancers), greater toxicity risks can be acceptable and the required toxicology program can be minimal.

Similar general considerations exist for preclinical toxicology studies in oncology and nononcology drugs. The choice of species for toxicology studies with small molecules are in general the rodent (rat) and nonrodent (dog or nonhuman primate), but should be justified on the basis of exposure, metabolism, and pharmacological activity. For biopharmaceuticals, toxicology studies should be conducted in the pharmacologically active species, which in most cases is the nonhuman primate. To obtain the best possible information to use in humans, pivotal toxicology studies should be conducted using schedules and durations (see Table 26.2: examples of duration and schedule for toxicology studies to support various initial clinical trials), formulations, and routes comparable to those intended in clinical studies, as well as in accordance with GLP. They should include parameters to assess at least, but not only, clinical signs, body weight, food consumption, clinical pathology, gross pathology, and histopathology. Toxicity should be assessed in relation to toxicokinetics and pharmacodynamics, if possible for the safety of first-time use of drug in humans. The pharmacodynamic data are helpful for calculating initial doses in humans that have a greater likelihood of activity without serious adverse effects and can contribute to optimal dose escalation in early clinical trials.

The preclinical toxicology program of drugs intended to treat advanced and life-threatening cancers follows ICH S9. As described in ICH S9, the IND-enabling toxicology program for drugs intended to treat advanced cancers is minimal and includes repeat-dose general toxicology studies in two species (rodent and nonrodent).

TABLE 26.3 IND- and NDA-Enabling Toxicology Program

Stage	Advanced Life-Threatening Cancers	Nonlife-Threatening Cancers
IND	• General toxicology in rodent and nonrodent[a] • Phototoxicants: initial assessment of phototoxic potential • Conjugated products: stability in the test animals and human plasma and toxicokinetic evaluations of the conjugated and unconjugated compounds • Liposomal products include limited evaluation of the unencapsulated drug and carrier liposomes in the general toxicology studies; toxicokinetic evaluations of the final liposomal products and free drugs	• General toxicology in rodent and nonrodent[b] • Genetic toxicology core battery[c] • Safety pharmacology core battery[d]
NDA	• 13-week (3 months) general toxicology in rodent and nonrodent • Genetic toxicology core battery • Reproductive and developmental toxicology (only Segment II in rodent and nonrodent)[f] • Phototoxicants: photosafety study if the photosafety can not be adequately evaluated based on nonclinical and clinical data	• Subchronic and chronic general toxicology in rodent and nonrodent[e] • Reproductive and developmental toxicology (Segments I, II, and III) • Carcinogenicity studies in two rodents[g] • Other studies (immunotoxicology, combination, and juvenile toxicology studies) • Special toxicity studies if deemed necessary based on specific drug-induced toxicity (eg, cardiotoxicity study)

[a]*Duration and schedule for toxicology studies to support various initial clinical trials (see examples in Table 26.2); for biopharmaceuticals, the drug should be tested in pharmacologically active species. Safety pharmacology and immunotoxicity endpoints (clinical signs, behavior, and cardiovascular parameters) can be evaluated as part of general toxicology studies.*
[b]*In general, 28-day toxicology studies usually suffice for initial Phase I clinical trial.*
[c]*In vitro Ames and chromosome aberration assays and in vivo micronucleus assay.*
[d]*Assessment of vital functions in cardiovascular, central nervous, and pulmonary systems.*
[e]*In general, the dosing regimen (schedule, route, and formulation) in the toxicology study should mimic the clinical trials. Chronic toxicology studies are conducted with equivalent duration to labeled use up to 6 months in rodent and 9 months in nonrodent (small molecule) or 6 months in relevant species (biopharmaceuticals).*
[f]*Information (eg, effect on reproductive organs) from general toxicology studies can be used for the assessment of fertility impairment.*
[g]*Carcinogenicity studies are generally waived for biopharmaceuticals if pharmacologically active species is only nonhuman primates.*

For genotoxic small molecules, a repeat-dose toxicity study in one rodent species is considered sufficient, provided the rodent is a relevant species. In support of the continued development of drugs, the results from 13-week (3 months) repeat-dose toxicology studies should be available prior to initiating Phase III studies, and the general toxicology studies of 3 months' duration are considered sufficient for NDA submission. An initial assessment of phototoxic potential should be conducted prior to Phase I for drugs that demonstrated photochemical properties. If the initial assessment showed a potential risk, adequate protective measures should be provided to patients who participate in the clinical trials. If the photosafety cannot be adequately evaluated based on nonclinical and clinical data, a photosafety study should be provided with NDA submission. For conjugated products, the main concern is the safety of the unconjugated material, including the linker used. Thus the stability of the conjugate should be evaluated in the test animals and human plasma. Toxicokinetic evaluations of both conjugated and unconjugated compounds should be included in the general toxicology studies. The safety assessment of the liposomal product should include a standard toxicological evaluation of the final liposomal product and a limited evaluation of the unencapsulated drug and carrier liposomes (ie, additional arms in a toxicology study). Toxicokinetics of both the liposomal product and the free compound after

administration of the liposomal product is highly recommended in the general toxicology studies. Standalone safety pharmacology studies or assessment of potential immunotoxicity are not needed and can be incorporated as part of the general toxicology studies. Genetic toxicology and reproductive and developmental toxicology studies are not essential for IND submission or to support clinical trials; however, genetic toxicology core battery and embryo-fetal developmental toxicology studies in rodent and nonrodent (Segment II) should be provided with NDA submission. For biopharmaceuticals, an assessment of embryo-fetal developmental toxicity in one pharmacologically relevant species is usually sufficient. Alternatively, literature assessment, assessment of placental transfer, the direct or indirect effects, or any other factors may be used if scientifically justified. A fertility and early embryonic development study (Segment I) and a pre- and postnatal development toxicity study (Segment III) are not necessary to support clinical trials or marketing. Evaluation of the effect(s) of the drug on reproductive organs as performed in the general toxicology studies is sufficient for the assessment of fertility impairment. Carcinogenicity studies are not needed to support marketing of either small molecules or biopharmaceuticals.

The preclinical toxicology program of chronically administered drugs intended to treat nonlife-threatening cancers (eg, chemopreventives, adjuvant therapy, hormonal drugs, and immunomodulators) is well described in an article published by DeGeorge et al. [68] and in general follows the ICH M3(R2) guidance. In these cases, the acceptable risks are much smaller than those in life-threatening cancers, and preclinical toxicology evaluation should be more extensive, as when developing nononcology drugs.

The IND-enabling toxicology program includes repeat-dose general toxicology studies in two species (rodent and nonrodent), genetic toxicology core battery studies, and safety pharmacology core battery studies. Identification of the NOAEL in the general toxicology studies is important to support the selection of the starting dose in Phase I clinical trial. Additional studies for the NDA filing of these drugs include subchronic and chronic general toxicology studies in two species, reproductive and developmental toxicology studies (Segments I, II, and III), carcinogenicity studies, and other special toxicity studies as deemed necessary depending on drug-specific toxicity or target patient population (eg, pediatric population).

For adjuvant therapy drugs, the toxicology studies depend on the prior human experiences with drugs, the anticipated risks and benefits for the intended patients, and the expected mechanism of action. There is usually a package of preclinical data and substantial clinical experience with these drugs by the time they are considered for adjuvant therapy in patients who have had their primary tumor removed or controlled. For NDA filing, additional, long-term, chronic toxicology studies should be conducted for drugs of which there is limited long-term clinical experience, and which are intended for chronic treatment of patients in whom the risk of recurrence of cancer is relatively low. Hormonal drugs are usually not directly cytotoxic, but may act as antiestrogens, progestins, antiprogestins, androgens, antiandrogens, aromatase inhibitors, or gonadotropin-releasing hormone agonists. The safety assessment should focus on long-term effects on organ systems, reproductive function, fertility, and teratogenicity, and potential induction of reproductive tract malignancy and abnormalities. Immunomodulators modulate the body's immune response to cancer cells at concentrations significantly lower than those, which cause severe toxicities in animals. Thus the assessment of surrogate biomarker activity is very important and useful when selecting a starting dose in a clinical trial. General toxicology studies that combine a measurement of the appropriate immunological response including surrogate biomarker in addition to standard toxicity assessment are useful because these drugs have sometimes exhibited bell-shaped dose–response curves for desired activities. In some cases, standalone immunotoxicology studies should be conducted.

First-in-Human Dose Selection

One of the primary objectives of preclinical toxicology studies is to estimate a safe starting dose for Phase I trials in humans. This determination is quite different for oncology drugs compared to nononcology drugs. The typical calculation (the NOAEL determined in the most sensitive species, with an additional default safety factor of 10) is not applied due to the general acceptance of greater risk, based on the risk–benefit ratio for oncology drugs indicated for advanced and/or refractory cancers. Some limited core safety data from toxicology studies is required to support initial clinical trials so that drug development can proceed efficiently for the unmet need.

The starting dose for clinical trials of small-molecule oncology drugs is generally chosen as one-tenth (a safety factor of 10) of the dose that causes severe toxicity (not necessarily death) in 10% of rodents (STD_{10}) on a body-surface area basis (mg/m^2), provided that this starting dose does not cause serious irreversible toxicity in a nonrodent species [68]. If irreversible toxicities are produced at the proposed starting dose in nonrodents (usually dogs) or if the nonrodent is known to be the most sensitive species or appropriate animal model, then the starting dose would be one-sixth (a safety factor of six) of the highest nonseverely toxic dose (HNSTD) in nonrodents that does not cause severe life-threatening, irreversible toxicity. Severe toxicities include but are not limited to deaths, encephalopathy, seizures, paralysis, irreversible ataxia, irreversible cardiac damages, etc. For small molecules, STD_{10} and HNSTD are converted to the body-surface area based mg/m^2, as this method provides the most accurate dose–toxicity relationships (FDA Guidance, 2005). Unlike nononcology drugs, the safety factors used for starting-dose estimation in oncology drugs are usually not altered to reflect special cases, such as steep dose-toxic response curves, or in the case that a drug has a novel mechanism of action when the dose is estimated based on either STD_{10} or HNSTD. Instead, a small increment of dose escalation is recommended in clinical studies.

For oncology biopharmaceuticals (monoclonal antibodies, antibody fragments, and fusion proteins), the test species for toxicology studies is usually limited to nonhuman primates, because biopharmaceuticals are not pharmacologically active in most standard toxicology testing species (mice, rats, and dogs). In general, the toxicities associated with biopharmaceuticals are the effects of target-mediated exaggerated pharmacology. As many biopharmaceuticals have high molecular weights (>100 kDa) and are administered intravenously (ie, they are largely confined to the vascular space), human doses are scaled on a body-weight basis (mg/kg), not body surface area [69]. A safety factor of 10 is usually applied to the NOAEL determined in the toxicology study in the pharmacologically relevant species. There may be adjustments for differences of target affinity in human versus monkey or pharmacologically relevant species. Additional safety considerations for biopharmaceuticals are uncertainty factors such as long half-lives of drugs and potential immunogenicity (antidrug antibodies).

If no animal species are available for toxicity testing of biopharmaceuticals, a minimal anticipated biological effect level (MABEL) approach is taken instead of the NOAEL approach [70]. The MABEL is the anticipated dose level leading to a minimal biological effect in humans. MABEL calculations should utilize all in vitro and in vivo information from PK/PD studies, including in vitro target binding and receptor occupancy data in target human and animal cells, in vitro concentration–response curves in human cells, and in vivo dose-exposure data in relevant animals. A safety factor may be applied to the MABEL if deemed necessary based on types of toxicities; however, selection of too low a starting dose, which does not provide benefit to the patients with advanced cancers, is discouraged. The main goal of the MABEL approach in oncology drug development is to determine the lowest dose level that is anticipated to produce a pharmacological response based on binding affinity and predicted PK and PD data.

The first-in-human dose selection for nonlife-threatening oncology drugs (eg, chemopreventives, adjuvant therapy, hormonal drugs, and immunomodulators) follows the algorithm recommended by the FDA for nononcology drugs. This is because the level of acceptable risks to patients with nonlife-threatening cancer is much lower than that for those with life-threatening cancer. Thus the NOAEL is important to support the selection of the starting dose in Phase I clinical trials. A default safety factor of 10 is applied to the NOAEL determined in the most sensitive species tested in toxicology studies. Additional safety factors may be considered if there is a steep dose-toxic response curve, severe toxicities such as central nervous system (CNS) disruptions, or toxicities that are not easily monitored clinically.

DRUG METABOLISM AND PHARMACOKINETICS

Drug metabolism and pharmacokinetics (DMPK) plays an important part in drug discovery and development within oncology programs. Metabolism and PK studies are conducted to evaluate a series of compounds early in the program to select a candidate with optimal properties for further development. Detailed PK/absorption, distribution, metabolism, and excretion (ADME) studies are then conducted to characterize the bioavailability, metabolic properties, distribution, and excretion and elimination of the drug. These studies provide information to assess safety and provide data for registration. Fig. 26.1 shows the various DMPK studies conducted at different stages of drug development. The list is a general outline, and the precise

timing of these studies depends not only on the drug and its properties but also the intended therapeutic benefit and target population. There are a number of regulatory guidance documents issued by regulatory authorities (FDA, EMEA, etc.), and these guidelines are expected to be adhered to during in vitro and in vivo metabolism studies. In addition, DMPK function provides bioanalytical support for safety (toxicology and first-in-human) and efficacy (proof of concept or pivotal clinical) studies. The method development, validation, and sample analysis are expected to be conducted according to the guidelines issued by regulatory agencies worldwide and any sample analysis conducted under GLP guidelines is expected to meet the standards set out under the relevant guidelines.

Pharmacokinetics

Pharmacokinetic/toxicokinetic data aid the interpretation of efficacy and safety information. Evaluation of pharmacokinetic or toxicokinetic information facilitates dose selection, schedule, and escalation during Phase I studies. Analysis of samples and method validation in regulated toxicology studies needs to be conducted as per GLP guidelines [71,72]. Although bioanalytical methods are validated to ensure that they function and perform as intended, the actual study or "incurred" samples from animals and human subjects may differ in composition and could potentially differ in their behavior compared to standard or quality-control samples. This has resulted in a recommendation to analyze a fraction of study samples for reproducibility. The current regulatory expectations are such that many companies routinely conduct incurred sample reanalysis to ensure the reproducibility and quality of study sample data. A detailed discussion of regulatory requirements is not within the scope of this chapter, but the reader is referred to recent reviews in this area [73–75]. The bioanalytical methods used in toxicology studies should describe the species, detection and quantitation limits, accuracy and precision (inter- and intrarun), and stability at intended collection, processing, and storage conditions.

Absorption

Single-dose pharmacokinetic studies are conducted in rodent (rats and mice) and nonrodent (dog or monkey) species to assess absorption (extent and rate of absorption), bioavailability (%F), dose proportionality, and kinetic parameters (C_{max}, AUC, and $t_{1/2}$). One criterion for species selection is the metabolic similarity between the animal species and humans based on in vitro metabolism studies. Metabolites generated in humans should be produced in at least one of the species used for toxicology studies. The route of administration should be based on

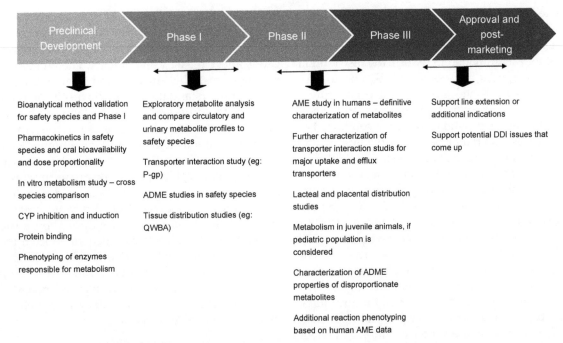

FIGURE 26.1 DMPK studies conducted at various stages of drug development.

the intended route of delivery in humans. Although many drugs are delivered orally, single-dose intravenous pharmacokinetic studies are also conducted to characterize the absolute bioavailability, clearance, and volume of distribution of molecule for better understanding of oral kinetics. The exposure data should be generated across a dose range to assess dose proportionality. Any nonlinearity in pharmacokinetics (sub- or superdose proportionality) should be assessed and should aid in dose selection for safety studies. Typically, absorption and exposure assessment is done in male and female animals to evaluate any gender differences. This information should be taken into consideration when selecting doses for toxicology studies. It is important that the pharmacokinetic studies employ dose volumes and acceptable formulations used in toxicology studies so that the data obtained in pharmacokinetic studies can be used for carrying out safety studies. The pharmacokinetic analysis typically employs noncompartmental methods and describes PK information such as C_{max}, T_{max}, AUC, CL, $V_{s.s}$, $t_{1/2}$, and %F.

Distribution

Following absorption, the drug and its metabolites partitions in and out of various cells and tissues. Drug distribution into tissues requires cell-membrane permeation, which in turn depends on the physico-chemical properties of the compound (log P, pKa, molecular weight, protein binding, etc.) [76]. However, there are specialized barriers such as the blood–brain barrier that express transporter proteins (eg, P-glycoprotein) to prevent or minimize access to tissue.

Plasma-Protein Binding: Plasma-protein binding dictates the rate and extent of the distribution of the drug in the body. It is generally believed that the free drug is considered pharmacologically and toxicologically relevant [76,77]. The fraction of free drug dictates its distribution, clearance, and half-life; therefore understanding the extent of protein binding across species is an important consideration for determining efficacy and safety. Marked species differences in protein binding should be taken into consideration when explaining the effects observed in pharmacology or toxicology studies. Protein binding should be determined over the range of concentrations observed in efficacy and safety studies in various species, and any saturation in protein binding needs to be identified. Disease conditions and age may alter the levels of plasma proteins, thereby influencing the free drug concentrations, clearance, and distribution [78]; therefore the plasma-protein binding in disease populations may be important to assess, particularly for very highly protein-bound drugs.

In addition to plasma-protein binding, blood-to-plasma partitioning is important for drugs that distribute into blood cells and bind to cellular components [79]. In cases where blood to plasma partitioning is much greater than one, the plasma pharmacokinetic profile may not adequately reflect the true pharmacokinetics of the drug. Therefore it is important to understand the blood portioning of compounds early on so the pharmacokinetics can be assessed in the relevant matrix (plasma or blood).

Tissue Distribution: Tissue-distribution studies are critical for understanding the distribution of drug and its metabolites into tissues and any potential for accumulation. The studies need to determine the distribution of drug-related material (parent and metabolites), the potential for accumulation in tissues, the distribution into tissues with special barriers (eg, CNS), and to provide dosimetry analysis and guidance for conducting a radiolabeled human absorption, metabolism, and excretion study. Typically, distribution studies are conducted as single-dose studies with radiolabeled compounds (eg, ^{14}C or ^3H) via the intended route of administration [80]. Following administration, the tissues of interest are analyzed over a period of time for radioactivity (up to 1–2 weeks).

Alternatively, quantitative whole-body autoradiography is used for the determination of tissue distribution, because of its ease and comprehensive nature [80]. This technique is versatile and allows the measurement of concentrations in virtually all tissues. The sections are also available for any further investigations if questions arise later in drug development. However, this technique is more suitable for small animals and any studies with large animals may have to use a more traditional method. Caution should be exercised in data interpretation, as the concentrations obtained from these studies are based on total radioactivity and not that of the parent compound. Data should be combined with other pharmacokinetic information before making any inferences.

In addition to tissue-distribution studies, drug distribution into milk and placenta is assessed during development to understand the potential exposure and risk for breastfeeding infants and fetus, respectively. These studies are carried out much later in the drug development as a part of the registration package (NDA/MAA), and are typically conducted in species used for reproductive and developmental toxicology species. For chronically administered drugs intended to treat nonlife-threatening cancers (eg, chemopreventives, adjuvant therapy, hormonal drugs, and immunomodulators), both FDA and EMEA guidance on reproductive and developmental toxicity make statements that imply that the distribution of drug and/or its metabolites into milk and placenta (fetus) should be evaluated [81,82]. For example, the EMEA draft guidance ("Guideline on Risk Assessment of Medicinal Products on Human Reproduction and Lactation," 2006) states that "information about the excretion into milk of the active substance and/or metabolites should be available." Similarly, ICH guidance (ICH S3A) refers to the need for assessment of exposure in newborns, dams, or fetuses and states secretion in milk may be assessed to define its role in the exposure to newborns.

Metabolism

Most drugs are biotransformed to metabolites before being excreted in urine, bile, and feces. In drug discovery, compounds are characterized and optimized for their metabolic properties, resulting in a compound with desired PK properties. The metabolism and excretion of a drug and the rate and route of its metabolism can significantly affect its safety and efficacy. Therefore a number of metabolism studies (in vitro and in vivo) are conducted to fully understand the metabolic profile of a compound in order to address potential metabolism-based issues, such as reactive metabolites of safety concern, potential drug–drug interactions due to cytochrome P450 (CYP) induction or inhibition, pharmacokinetic variability due to polymorphism, effect of organ impairment (eg, hepatic, renal), and potential active metabolites influencing PK-PD understanding and intellectual property rights. These studies take place throughout drug development, and the information generated from them constitutes an integral part of IND and NDA filings.

In Vitro Metabolism Studies: In vitro drug metabolism studies are conducted to identify potential safety and efficacy issues related to drug or metabolites. The main goals of these studies are:

1. To characterize comparative metabolic profiles in rodent, nonrodent species, and humans in order to identify and select relevant species for safety assessment;
2. To identify any potential for causing drug–drug interactions due to inhibition or induction of enzymes;
3. To identify the enzymes responsible and to determine any genetic polymorphisms that may influence the pharmacokinetics, pharmacodynamics, and safety of the drug; and
4. To generate any potential reactive or genotoxic metabolite structural alerts that require further assessment in safety studies.

Liver subcellular fractions such as microsomes or S9 and hepatocytes are predominantly used for in vitro metabolism studies. Regulatory agencies have issued guidance regarding the conduct of in vitro metabolism and drug–drug interaction studies during development [83–86]. Guidance documents outline the various model systems, acceptable probe substances, and experimental considerations (choice of concentrations and time course). The choice of test system should be justified based on metabolic pathways of drug, and the test needs to be shown functioning with use of proper positive controls. The guidance document states that in vitro studies should be conducted at concentrations similar to those seen in vivo. This is particularly important if a metabolic pathway is saturable. Depending on the concentration used, the metabolic rate and relative abundance of metabolites may be different. The guidance emphasizes that the in vitro studies should be confirmed with in vivo studies and may not replace them. They should be used as guidance and be confirmed with in vivo data.

In Vivo Metabolism (ADME) Studies: Biodisposition or in vivo ADME studies provide important information regarding the absorption of the drug, the distribution of drug-related material into target tissues, important metabolic pathways, and the eventual excretion of the drug-related material from the body [87]. The information generated from these studies is helpful in understanding the outcomes of the safety studies and efficacy of pharmacology studies [87]. Therefore in vivo metabolism studies with radiolabeled tracers have become a crucial component of the drug development package for regulatory submissions.

Typically, in vivo drug metabolism and disposition studies are conducted with a radiolabel (^{14}C or ^{3}H) to provide quantitative information on the rate and extent of metabolism, routes of excretion for parent compound and its metabolites, and circulating metabolites. The nonclinical ADME studies are conducted rodents (rat or mouse) and nonrodents (dog or monkey) and the choice is based on the species used in toxicology studies. The selection of dose, the route of administration, and formulations should mimic the safety studies. These studies are typically single-dose studies with sample collection up to a week, but longer duration of sample collection may be needed if the drug has a long half-life. Plasma, urine, and fecal samples are collected during the study to analyze for radioactivity and for metabolite profiling. Tissue samples may be collected and banked to address any specific safety concerns. Metabolic profiles of plasma, urine, and fecal samples are generated by a combination of techniques (eg, HPLC-radioactivity detection, LC fractionation followed by scintillation counting, and LC-MS coupled to radioactivity detection). These studies will assess the extent of absorption, important metabolic pathways, role of the kidney or liver in elimination, and whether any metabolites formed have safety or efficacy concerns. These data allow identification of major circulatory metabolites, the calculation of exposure to metabolites, and measure the half-life of metabolites that could potentially result in accumulation on repeat administration. In addition, it provides information about metabolites that would enable comparison between toxicology species and humans.

Metabolites in Safety Testing (MIST): One of the most debated guidance on metabolism was issued by the FDA in 2005 and related to metabolites in safety testing [88]. This draft guidance made recommendations on when to identify and characterize metabolites. Following extensive discussion at scientific meetings, workshops, and in the literature, the FDA issued a final guidance in 2008 [89], which stated that the disproportionate metabolites, present at >10% of the parent or total drug-related material, need to be considered for safety assessment. The guidance recommends conducting drug metabolite-profiling and identification early in development, so that any metabolites of safety concern (disproportionate or unique human metabolites) are addressed before exposing large numbers of patients in pivotal clinical studies. The guidance states that coverage of disproportionate metabolites observed in humans must be demonstrated in at least one of the species used for toxicology studies. This has led to conducting radiolabeled mass balance studies in humans prior to the initiation of Phase III studies. For any disproportionate metabolites observed in humans but not present in either of the safety test species, further testing by directly dosing the metabolite in general toxicity studies needs to be considered.

Drug–Drug Interaction Studies

CYP Inhibition: Metabolism is the major route of clearance for most drugs and approximately 75% of the drugs metabolized by this family of enzymes [90]. The major CYP enzymes involved in drug metabolism are CYP3A4, CYP2D6, CYP2C9, CYP2C19, CYP1A2, CYP2E1, CYP2B6, and CYP2A6. Inhibition of these enzymes can result in altered clearance and pharmacokinetics of drugs, leading to adverse effects. This is particularly important for elderly patients, who often take several drugs (polypharmacy) for various ailments. Typically these studies are conducted prior to IND filing and provide useful information regarding the exclusion/inclusion criteria for clinical protocols when the drug is coadministered with other drugs in the clinical setting.

CYP Induction: Induction of drug metabolism enzymes refers to a process where the activity of an enzyme increases on repeated administration of a compound, through increased expression and synthesis, or by stabilization of that enzyme. Most drug-metabolizing enzymes and drug transporters are inducible to a varying degree. There are three principal nuclear receptors, namely pregnane X receptor (PXR), the constitutive androstane receptor (CAR), and the aryl hydrocarbon receptor (AhR), which regulate the induction of CYP enzymes [91]. Interaction between a drug and these nuclear receptors leads to a series of molecular events resulting in increased mRNA expression and synthesis of the enzyme. Increased enzyme levels then increase the clearance and reduce the exposure of drugs that are metabolized by the induced enzyme(s) and/or transporters. Enzyme induction leads to reduced pharmacodynamic activity due to lowered exposures, although there is potential for manifestation of toxicity due to increased levels of metabolite(s) that are of safety concern.

Regulatory agencies have issued guidance for the assessment of the induction potential of a drug, and it is expected that this information is available prior to conducting large trials or at the time of filing the NDA [83–86]. The FDA guidance outlines experimental conditions, use of positive controls and probe substrates, test-article concentrations, etc. The positive control inducers should produce at least two-fold induction at the recommended concentrations. Following treatment, the enzymatic activity of CYP3A, CYP2B6, and CYP1A2 should be evaluated using recommended probe substrates. Although enzymatic activity determination is most reliable, other means of induction evaluation such as immunoquantitation of enzymes, mRNA determination, and reporter gene assays are also acceptable. However, a recent survey by PHARMA recommends enzymatic as well as mRNA determination [92]. If a drug produces a change that is >40% of the positive control then it is considered as an inducer and further evaluation in the clinic is warranted.

Transporter-Interaction Studies: Transporters are expressed at key physiological barriers to limit the distribution of drugs or facilitate excretion, and they can be major determinants for absorption, distribution, and disposition. Transporters are broadly classified into solute transporters (SLC) or ATP-binding cassette (ABC) transporters. Modulation of transporter function can result in drug–drug interactions (eg, statins, digoxin, and cephalosporin antibiotics) [93,94].

Transporter-based drug interactions have been recognized by regulatory agencies worldwide. For example, FDA draft guidance issued in 2006 lists some of the major human transporters and known substrates, inhibitors, and inducers. Of all the drug transporters, P-glycoprotein (P-gp) is the best studied. P-gp is expressed at the intestinal barrier, and it may limit drug absorption. It is also expressed in the kidney and liver, where it plays a critical role in the excretion of drugs and their metabolites. P-gp also plays a critical role in limiting distribution of drugs into the CNS and fetus due to its expression at the relevant barriers [94]. Any interference with P-gp function can change the levels of drugs in circulation and tissues and may compromise their safety and efficacy. Therefore studies should be conducted to determine whether a drug candidate is a substrate or inhibitor of P-gp. This can be accomplished with Caco-2 cells or other engineered cell lines that overexpress P-gp. Irrespective of the test system used, the experiment should include known substrates and inhibitors to demonstrate the suitability of test systems. Bidirectional transport measurements are preferred and net flux should be calculated for interpretation of results. If the compound has a net flux ratio of >2 then it is considered a substrate and further evaluation should be carried out. If the test compound has an efflux ratio <2 then it is not a P-gp substrate and further studies are not needed.

Depending on the maximal concentrations observed in plasma and at the intestinal barrier, and the solubility of drug, a range of concentrations (eg, 1, 10, and 100 times the predicted concentrations) should be considered during evaluation. The drug should be tested for its inhibition, irrespective of whether or not it is a substrate. Again, a wide range of concentrations should be used to generate inhibitory data (IC_{50} or Ki). The draft guidance provides a list of acceptable probe substrates and positive control inhibitors. If the test compound has $I/IC_{50} > 0.1$ then it is an inhibitor of P-gp and an in vivo interaction study should be conducted with digoxin as a probe. If the ratio is <0.1 then the test compound is a weak inhibitor and an in vivo interaction study is not needed. The potential for P-gp induction is also discussed in the guidance document and it is recommended that if the drug is shown not to induce CYP3A in vivo, then no further test of P-gp induction in vivo is necessary. However, if the in vivo CYP3A induction test is positive, then an additional study of the investigation drug's effect on a P-gp probe substrate is recommended.

The EMEA provides similar guidance but includes other transporters such as organic anion transporters (OAT), organic anion transporting polypeptide (OATP), organic cation transporters (OCT), and efflux transporters (breast cancer research protein (BCRP) and bile-salt exporting pump (BSEP)). In a recent white paper, the International Transporter Consortium (ITC), consisting of experts from industry, academia, and regulatory agencies, recommended that interactions be assessed using in vitro methods for seven specific transporters, and this recommendation was subsequently endorsed by the FDA Pharmaceutical Science and Clinical Pharmacology Advisory Committee [94].

Identification of Enzymes Responsible for Metabolism: It has been reported that 75% of marketed drugs are primarily metabolized by the CYP system. Although many CYP enzymes have overlapping substrate specificity, in most cases a single isoform seems to contribute to the majority of the metabolism. Therefore the goal is to determine whether the drug is metabolized by a single or multiple enzymes and whether a polymorphic enzyme is involved. Recent FDA guidance addresses reaction phenotyping in detail, and states that if human in vivo data indicate that CYP enzymes contribute >25% of a drug's clearance, studies should be done to identify drug-metabolizing CYP enzymes [84]. The guidance provides detailed information regarding experimental test systems and conditions, concentrations to be used, and acceptable techniques to use for identification and confirmation.

Excretion

Absorption, distribution, metabolism, and excretion studies provide important information regarding metabolism and excretion of compounds into urine and feces. The purpose of these studies is not only to understand the metabolism, but also how both parent and metabolites are eliminated. The information generated from these studies is useful in determining whether the kidney or liver is an important organ in elimination, and whether there is any safety concern in hepatic or renally impaired populations. In addition, the excretion data also shed light on the role of transporters. For example, if the renal excretion of parent or metabolite is greater than the glomerular filtration then it is likely that active secretion may be occurring, and further studies need to be conducted to evaluate any potential issues. Excretion studies are conducted early in development in intact and bile-duct-cannulated rodent and nonrodents to understand the excretion of the drug and its metabolites. These studies indicate whether the drug is excreted intact or metabolized, show the relative contribution of liver and kidney in excretion, and compare the species in excretory profiles of parent and metabolites. These studies are typically not included as part of the IND, but are conducted later in development and are required for NDA filing.

OTHER CONSIDERATIONS: CHANGES IN ROUTE OR FORMULATION

If a clinical trial is proposed using an oral route for a drug that has already been investigated by intravenous administration, additional toxicology studies are recommended to address whether there is enhanced liver toxicity, gastrointestinal toxicity, or altered metabolism. In addition to the IND package for intravenous administration, an oral repeat-dose toxicology study with bioavailable data or an oral efficacy animal study with assessment of gastrointestinal and liver toxicity can be conducted with the same schedule and route of drug administration proposed in clinical trials.

When intravenous administration is proposed for a drug that was investigated using oral administration, the main safety concern is the much greater systemic exposure and resulting toxicity that may be encountered. No additional toxicology studies need to be conducted as long as the clinical exposure after intravenous administration is adequately covered by exposures in animals and humans after oral administration. In case of change in drug formulation, a bioavailability study comparing old and new formulations should be conducted in an appropriate species.

References

[1] American Cancer Society. Cancer Facts and Figures. www.cancer.org/Research/CancerFactsFigures/index.

[2] Paul SM, Mytelka DS, Dunwiddie CT, Persinger CC, Munos BH, Lindborg SR, et al. How to improve R&D productivity: the pharmaceutical industry's grand challenge. Nat Rev Drug Discov 2010;9:203–14.

[3] Kola I, Landis J. Can the pharmaceutical industry reduce attrition rates? Nat Rev Drug Discov 2004;3:711–5.

[4] Arrondeau J, Gan HK, Razak ARA, Paoletti X, Le Tourneau C. Development of anticancer drugs. Discov Med 2010;10:355–62.

[5] Colombo P, Gunnarsson K, Iatropoulos M, Brughera M. Toxicological testing of cytotoxic drugs (review). Int J Oncol 2001;19:1021–8.

[6] Smith AC, Rubenstein I, Koutsoukos A, Christian M, Grieshaber CK, Tomaszewski JE, et al. Evaluation of preclinical toxicity models for Phase I clinical trials of anticancer drugs: the NCI experience (1983–1992). Proc Am Assoc Cancer Res 1994;35:2741–9.

[7] Gibbs JB. Mechanism-based target identification and drug discovery in cancer research. Science 2000;287:1969–73.

[8] Workman P. Genomics and the second golden era of cancer drug development. Mol Biosyst 2005;1:17–26.

[9] Rosa DD, Ismael G, Lago LD, Awada A. Molecular-targeted thepapies: lessons from years of clinical development. Cancer Treat Rev 2008;34:61–80.

[10] Flaherty K, Puzanov I, Sosman J, Kim K, Ribas A, McArthur G, et al. Phase I study of PLX4032: proof of concept for V600E BRAF mutation as a therapeutic target in human cancer. J Clin Oncol 2009;27(Suppl.). Abstract 9000.

[11] Kerkelä R, Grazette L, Yacobi R, Iliescu C, Patten R, Beahm C, et al. Cardiotoxicity of the cancer therapeutic agent imatinib mesylate. Nat Med 2006;12:908–16.

[12] Force T, Krause DS, Van Etten RA. Molecular mechanisms of cardiotoxicity of tyrosine kinase inhibition. Nat Rev Cancer 2007;7:332–44.

[13] Rosenfeldt H, Kropp T, Benson K, Ricci MS, McGuinn WD, Verbois SL. Regulatory aspects of oncology drug safety evaluation: past practice, current issues, and the challenge of new drugs. Toxicol Appl Pharmacol 2010;243:125–33.

[14] Maziasz T, Kadambi VJ, Silverman L, Fedyk E, Alden CL. Predictive toxicology approached for small molecule oncology drugs. Toxicol Pathol 2010;38:148–64.

[15] Annenante G, Reid RC, Fairlie DP. 'Clean' or 'dirty' – just how selective drugs need to be? Aust J Chem 2008;61:654–60.

[16] Jones D, Thomas D, Yin CC. Kinase domain point mutations in Philadelphia chromosome-positive acute lymphoblastic leukemia emerge after therapy with BCR-ABL kinase inhibitors. Cancer 2008;113:985–94.

[17] Jones S, Zhang X, Parsons DW. Core signaling pathways in human pancreatic cancers revealed by global genomic analysis. Science 2008;321:1801–6.

[18] Parsons DW, Jones S, Zhang X. An integrated genomic analysis of human glioblastoma multiforms. Science 2008;321:1807–12.

[19] Blagosklonny MV. Analysis of FDA approved anticancer drugs reveals the future of cancer therapy. Cell Cycle 2004;3:1035–42.

[20] Hambley TW. Is anticancer drug development heading in the right direction? Cancer Res 2009;69:1259–61.

[21] Sandler A, Gray R, Perry MC. Paclitaxel-carboplatin alone or with bevacizumab for nonsmall cell lung cancer. N Engl J Med 2006;355:2542–50.

[22] Hait WN. Targeted cancer therapeutics. Cancer Res 2009;69:1263–7.

[23] National Cancer Institute. Immunotherapy: using the immune system to treat cancer. http://www.cancer.gov/research/areas/treatment/immunotherapy-using-immune-system [accessed 21.01.16].

[24] Pardoll DM. The blockade of immune checkpoints in cancer immunotherapy. Nat Rev Cancer 2012;12(4):252–64.

[25] Postow MA, Callahan MK, Wolchok JD. Immune checkpoint blockade in cancer therapy. J Clin Oncol 2015;33(17):1974–82.

[26] Bouchard H, Viskov C, Garcia-Echeverria C. Antibody-drug conjugates – a new wave of cancer drugs. Bioorg Med Chem Lett 2014;24:5357–63.

[27] Gill S, June CH. Going viral: chimeric antigen receptor T-cell therapy for hematological malignancies. Immunol Rev 2014;263:68–89.

[28] ICH S9. Nonclinical evaluation for anticancer pharmaceuticals. March 2010.

[29] Damia G, D'Incalci M. Contemporary preclinical development of anticancer agents – what are the optimal preclinical models? Eur J Cancer 2009;45:2768–81.

[30] Suggitt M, Bibby MC. 50 years of preclinical anticancer drug screening: empirical to target-driven approaches. Clin Cancer Res 2005;11:971–81.

[31] Boyd MR, Paull KD. Some practical considerations and applications of the National Cancer Institute in vitro anticancer drug discovery screen. Drug Dev Res 1995;34:91–109.

[32] Holbeck SL. Update on NCI in vitro drug screen utilities. Eur J Cancer 2004;40:785–93.

[33] Decker S, Hollingshead M, Bonomi CA, Carter JP, Sausville EA. The hollow fiber model in cancer drug screening: the NCI experience. Eur J Cancer 2004;40:821–6.

[34] Suggitt M, Cooper PA, Shnyder SD, Bibby MC. The hollow fiber model – facilitating anticancer preclinical pharmacodynamics and improving animal welfare. Int J Oncol 2006;29:1493–9.

[35] Temmink OH, Prins HJ, van Gelderop E, Peters GJ. The hollow fiber assay as a model for in vivo pharmacodynamics of fluoropyrimidines in colon cancer cells. Br J Cancer 2007;96:61–6.

[36] Perry WL, Weitzman A. The development of molecularly targeted anticancer therapies: an Eli Lilly and company perspective. Drugs Pipeline 2005;3:199–238.

[37] Johnson JI, Decker S, Zaharevitz D. Relationships between drug activity in NCI preclinical in vitro and in vivo models and early clinical trials. Br J Cancer 2001;84:1424–31.

[38] Voskoglou-Nomikos T, Pater JL, Seymour L. Clinical predictive value of the in vitro cell line, human xenograft, and mouse allograft preclinical cancer models. Clin Cancer Res 2003;9:4227–39.

[39] Kerbel RS. Human tumor xenografts as predictive preclinical models for anticancer drug activity in humans. Cancer Biol Ther 2003;2(4 Suppl.):S134–9.

[40] Teicher BA. Tumor models for efficacy determination. Mol Cancer Ther 2006;5:2435–43.

[41] Firestone B. The challenge of selecting the 'right' in vivo oncology pharmacology model. Curr Opin Pharmacol 2010;10:391–6.

[42] Kelloff GJ, Bast Jr RC, Coffey DS. Biomarkers, surrogate end points, and the acceleration of drug development for cancer prevention and treatment: an update prologue. Clin Cancer Res 2004;10:3881–4.

[43] Marrer E, Dieterle F. Biomarkers in oncology drug development: rescuers or troublemakers? Expert Opin Drug Metab Toxicol 2008;4:1391–402.

[44] Haferlach T, Bacher U, Kern W. Diagnostic pathways in acute leukemias: a proposal for a multimodal approach. Ann Hematol 2007;86:311–27.

[45] Druker BJ. Imatinib as a paradigm of targeted therapies. Adv Cancer Res 2004;91:1–30.

[46] Heinrich MC, Corless CL, Demetri GD. Kinase mutations and imatinib response in patients with metastatic gastrointestinal stromal tumors. J Clin Oncol 2003;21:4342–9.

[47] Hamilton AL, Eder JP, Pavlick AC. Proteosome inhibition with bortezomib (PS-341): a phase I study with pharmacodynamic ent points using a day 1 and day 4 schedule in a 14-day cycle. J Clin Oncol 2005;23:6107–16.

[48] De Leon J, Susce MT, Murray-Carmichael E. The AmpliChip CYP450 genotyping test: integrating a new clinical tool. Mol Diagn Ther 2006;10:135–51.

[49] Singer JB, Shou Y, Giles F. UGT1A1 promoter polymorphism increases risk of nilotinib-induced hyperbilirubinemia. Leukemia 2007;21:2311–5.

[50] EMEA. Committee for medicinal products for human use: final conclusions on the pilot joint EMEA/FDA VXDS experience on qualification of nephrotoxicity biomarkers. January 2009.

[51] Albini A, Pennesi G, Donatelli F, Cammarota R, De Flora S, Noonan DM. Cardiotoxicity of anticancer drugs: the need for cardio-oncology and cardio-oncological prevention. J Natl Cancer Inst 2010;102:14–25.

[52] Fingert H, Varterasian M. Safety biomarkers and the clinical development of oncology therapeutics: considerations for cardiovascular safety and risk management. AAPS J 2006;8:E89–94.

[53] EMEA. European Medicines Agency, reflection paper on nonclinical evaluation of drug-induced liver injury (DILI), EMEA/CHMP/SWP/150115/2006. June 24, 2010.

[54] Sharma A, Jusko W. Characterization of four basic models of indirect pharmacodynamic responses. J Pharmacokinet Biopharm 1996;24:611–35.

[55] Jackson RC. Computer techniques in preclinical and clinical drug development. Boca Raton, Florida: CRC Press; 1996. p. 105–11.

[56] Rafi I, Taylor GA, Calvete JA, et al. Clinical pharmacokinetic and pharmacodynamic studies with the nonclassical antifolate thymidylate synthase inhibitor 3,4-dihydro-2-amino-6-methyl-4-oxo-5-(4-pyridylthio)-quinazolone dihydrochloride (AG337) given by 24-hour continuous intravenous infusion. Clin Cancer Res 1995;1:1275–84.

[57] Iadevaia S, Morales FC, Mills GB, Ram PT. Identification of optimal drug combinations targeting cellular networks: integrating phospho-proteomics and computational network analysis. Cancer Res 2010;70:6704–14.

[58] Yamazaki S, Skaptason J, Romero D, et al. Pharmacokinetic/pharmacodynamic modelling of biomarker response and tumor growth inhibition to an orally available cMet kinase inhibitor in human tumor xenograft mouse models. Drug Metab Dispos 2008;36:1267–74.

[59] Lee L, Niu H, Rueger R, et al. The safety, tolerability, pharmacokinetics and pharmacodynamics of single oral doses of CH4987655 in healthy volunteers: target suppression using a biomarker. Clin Cancer Res 2009;15:7368–74.

[60] Salphati L, Wong H, Belvin M, et al. Pharmacokinetic-pharmacodynamic modelling of tumor growth inhibition and biomarker modulation by the novel phosphoinositol 3-kinase inhibitor GDC-0941. Drug Metab Dispos 2010;38:1436–42.

[61] ICH M3(R2). Guidance on nonclinical safety studies for the conduct of human clinical trials and marketing authorization for pharmaceuticals current step 4 version. June 11, 2009.

[62] ICH S7A. Safety pharmacology studies for human pharmaceuticals. November 2000.

[63] ICH S7B. The non-clinical evaluation of the potential for delayed ventricular repolarization (QT interval prolongation) by human pharmaceuticals. May 2005.

[64] ICH S6 (R1). Preclinical safety evaluation of biotechnology-derived pharmaceuticals. June 2001.

[65] ICH S5(R2). Detection of toxicity to reproduction for medical products & toxicity to male fertility. November 2005.

[66] ICH Q3A(R2). Impurities in new drug substances. October 2006.

[67] ICH Q3B(R2). Impurities in new drug products. June 2006.

[68] DeGeorge JJ, Ahn C-H, Andrews PA, Brower ME, Giorgio DW, Goheer MA, et al. Regulatory considerations for preclinical development of anticancer drugs. Cancer Chemother Pharmacol 1998;41:173–85.

[69] Food and Drug Administration Guidance for Industry. Estimating the maximum safe starting dose in initial clinical trials for therapeutics for adult healthy volunteers. 2005.

[70] European Medicines Agency. Guideline on strategies to identify and mitigate risks for first-in-human clinical trials with investigational medicinal products. 2007.

[71] Guidance for Industry. Bioanalytical method validation. US Department of Health and Human Services, Food and Drug Administration (FDA), Center for Drug Evaluation and Research (CDER) and Center for Veterinary Medicine (CVM); May 2001.

[72] ICH Q2A – text on validation of analytical procedures and ICH Q2B – validation of analytical procedures – methodology.

[73] Viswanathan CT, Bansal S, DeSilva B, et al. Quantitative bioanalytical method validation and implementation: best practices for chromatographic and ligand binding assays. AAPS J 2007;9(1):E30–42.

[74] Bansal S, DeStefano A. Key elements of bioanalytical method validation for small molecules. AAPS J 2007;9(1):E109–14.

[75] Rocci ML, Devanarayanan V, et al. Confirmatory reanalysis of incurred bioanalytical samples. AAPS J 2007;9(1):E336–43.

[76] Schmidt S, Gonzalez D, Derendorf H. Significance of protein binding in pharmacokinetics and pharmacodynamics. J Pharm Sci 2009;99:1107–22.

[77] MacKichan JJ. Influence of protein binding and use of unbound (free) drug concentration. In: Evans WE, Schentag JJ, Jusko WJ, editors. Applied pharmacokinetics: principles of therapeutic drug monitoring. 3rd ed. Vancouver, Wash: 5-1-5-48 Applied Therapeutics, Inc.; 1992.

[78] Rolan PE. Plasma protein binding displacement interactions – why are they still regarded as clinically important? Br J Clin Pharmacol 1994;37:125–8.

[79] Rowland M, Tozer TN. Clinical pharmacokinetics: Concepts and applications. 3rd ed. Philadelphia, Pa: Williams &Wilkins; 1995. p. 137–55.

[80] Marathe PH, Shyu WC, Humphreys WG. The use of radiolabeled compounds for ADME studies in discovery and exploratory development. Curr Pharm Des 2004;10:2991–3008.

[81] FDA Guidance for Industry. Clinical lactation studies – study design, data analysis, and recommendations for labeling. 2005.

[82] FDA Reviewer Guidance. Integration of study results to assess concerns about human reproductive and developmental toxicities. 2001.

[83] FDA guidance for industry. Drug metabolism/drug interaction studies in the drug development process: studies in vitro. 1997.

[84] FDA draft guidance. Drug interaction studies – study design, data analysis, and Implications for dosing and labeling. 2006.

[85] Health Canada. Drug-drug interactions: studies in vitro and in vivo. 2000.

[86] EMEA guidance. Guideline on the investigation of drug interactions (draft). 2010.

[87] Campbell DB. Are we doing too many animal biodisposition investigations before Phase I studies in man? A re-evaluation of the timing and extent of ADME studies. Eur J Drug Metab Pharmacokinet 1994;19:283–93.

[88] FDA guidance (draft) for industry: safety testing of drug metabolites. Center for Drug Evaluation and Research. Food and Drug Administration.

[89] US Food and Drug Administration (FDA). Guidance for industry: Safety testing of drug metabolites. Washington, DC. 2008.

[90] Williams J, Bauman JN, Cai H, Conlon K, Hansel S, Hurst S, et al. In vitro ADME phenotyping in drug discovery: current challenges and future solutions. Curr Opin Drug Discov Dev 2005;8:78–88.

[91] Lin JH. CYP induction-mediated drug interactions: in vitro assessment and clinical implications. Pharm Res 2006;23(6):1089–116.

[92] Chu V, Einolf HJ, Evers R, Kumar G, Moore D, Ripp S, et al. In vitro and in vivo induction of cytochrome P450: a survey of the current practices and recommendations. A Pharm Res Manuf Am Perspect 2007;37(7):1339–54.

[93] Xia CQ, Milton MN, Gan LS. Evaluation of drug-transporter interactions using in vitro and in vivo models. Curr Drug Metab May 2007;8(4):341–63.

[94] Giacomini KM, Huang SM, Tweedie DJ, Benet LZ, Brouwer KLR, Chu X, et al. Membrane transporters in drug development. Nat Rev Drug Discov 2010;9(3):215–36.

27

Preclinical Toxicology of Vaccines[1]

M.D. Green, N.H. Al-Humadi

INTRODUCTION TO VACCINES/ ADJUVANTS FOR THE PREVENTION OF INFECTIOUS DISEASES

Vaccines are biological preparations that augment immunity to targeted diseases. These biological preparations stimulate the recipient's immune system to recognize targeted aspects of infectious organisms as foreign and generate host mechanisms to control or eliminate them. Additionally, they evoke mechanisms to form an immunological memory of the antigen(s), which provides efficacy against future infections by the same or similar organisms.

Vaccines are created from inactivated or attenuated organisms, or are derived from purified or recombinant subcomponents of these organisms. They provide antigens that may be incorporated into vaccines composed of peptides, proteins, and polysaccharides. They may also be indirectly introduced to the host immune system through recombinant DNA plasmids or chimeric virus vectors. Inactivated vaccines are killed through the use of heat or chemicals, whereas attenuated vaccines contain live, less virulent organisms. Often these vaccines are derived from live viruses that have been cultured under conditions that disable their pathogenic

[1] Disclaimer: The findings and conclusions in this chapter have not been formally disseminated by the Food and Drug Administration and should not be construed to represent any Agency determination or policy.

2017, Published by Elsevier Inc.

properties. Attenuated vaccines often produce a durable immunological response and thus are preferred for many classes of infectious agents. Subcomponents of microorganisms may also be used as antigens in vaccines. For example, toxoid vaccines are made from inactivated toxic components and offer protection from the effects of the infection. Additionally, fragments or subunits of an attenuated or inactivated microorganism can also be used as the basis of an antigenic response to a vaccine. Subcomponents may also be used for other purposes. For example, poorly immunogenic components of microorganisms can be improved by their conjugation to proteins that typically are toxins. This approach is often used in conjunction with polysaccharides, which form the outer coat of some infectious bacteria such as *Haemophilus influenzae* type B vaccine. Immunization with DNA plasmids and virus vectors involves vaccines that encode an antigen protein that are subsequently expressed within cells of the recipient following administration of the vaccine.

Monovalent vaccines are designed to provoke an immune response to a single antigen or microorganism. Multivalent or polyvalent vaccines are meant to evoke immune responses to several antigens or microorganisms; however, when various antigens are combined, both synergistic and inhibitory interactions are potential outcomes in terms of the immunological response.

The process of vaccination introduces an external substance to the host immune system, which induces or increases responses to specific antigens with sufficient vigor to provide levels of immunity to prevent the onset of disease and protect the host against the future risk of infectious disease. Responses to vaccines follow a complex and coordinated set of physiological and immune-based reactions that are tightly controlled and involve different cell types and biochemical intermediates.

Both antibody and cell-mediated responses may occur following immunization with various vaccine antigens, and are significantly influenced by the type of adjuvant used in the vaccine product. Host responses to the antigens within vaccines encompass adaptive humoral and cell-mediated immune responses and innate immune responses. Antigen-presenting cells (APCs), B cells, and T cells are initially involved. Vaccine proteins and peptides as presented by APCs interact directly with T-cell receptors that recognize the specific amino-acid sequence in association with class I or class II major histocompatibility complex (MHC) receptors, and humoral antibody production is mediated by B cells. Humoral responses include both neutralizing and nonneutralizing antibodies that involve complement-dependent and independent mechanisms and may involve T-cell dependent interactions with helper T cells and CD8+ dependent lytic and soluble-factor activities.

Vaccine-induced effectors of immunity are typically antibodies produced by B lymphocytes. Other potential effectors of immunity, such as cytotoxic CD8+ T lymphocytes, are also involved. The activities of these effectors are mediated by regulatory T-cells (Treg), which maintain immune tolerance but represent only 5–10% of the peripheral CD4 T-cell population. These cells serve to inhibit immune responses that are potentially harmful by inhibiting or increasing Th1 or Th2 activity. Treg activity is believed to play a role in controlling autoimmune diseases that could possibly arise from wayward responses to the antigen contained in vaccines through antigen-spread response. An interaction between vaccine antigens and adjuvants with Treg is likely but remains unclear and requires further research [1]. Both the generation and maintenance of B and CD8+ T cells are governed by the activity of CD4+ T helper lymphocytes, and these cells are frequently subdivided into T-helper 1 (Th1) and T-helper 2 (Th2) subtypes.

Antigens can be recognized by an antibody or T-cell receptor; however, not all antigens evoke a sufficient immune response by themselves to make them suitable vaccine components. To overcome the limitations of weak antigens, various changes are sometimes made to the vaccines. These may take the form of conjugations to the antigen itself and/or enhancement of the immune response by the inclusion of additional vaccine components such as adjuvants. For example, the ability to elicit an immune response to the antigenic components of *Streptococcus pneumoniae* in a heptavalent and triskaivalent vaccine was increased by conjugation to proteins such as diphtheria proteins. Additionally, the response to various antigens is affected by various factors, such as dose and concentration of the antigen, quantity and nature of the adjuvant, time between inoculations, and route of exposure.

Following the inoculation with a vaccine, primary and secondary immune responses occur. The schedule between injections of the vaccine can be an important determinant of the immune response, and may vary among different vaccines. After the initial primary exposure and immune response, subsequent or secondary exposures are mediated by specific populations of cells, namely short- and long-lived antibody secreting plasma cells and memory B cells.

SPECIAL TOPICS

Adjuvants

To evoke effective immune responses to a vaccine, a variety of adjuvants (chemical and biological additives) may be used [2] (Table 27.1).

TABLE 27.1 Adjuvants and Their Impact on Vaccination

Adjuvant	Effect
Alum	Denature protein
Oil (mineral)	Antigen depot formation
DEAE dextran	B-cell mitogen activation
Cholera/enterotoxin	Mucosal stimulation
Cytokines	Increase cellular immunity response
CpG	Activate CMI

Edelman [3] and Griffin [2] classified adjuvants into two groups:

1. Substances that increase the immune response to the antigen, and
2. Immunogenic proteins that modify T-cell activities.

To enhance uptake by antigen-presenting phagocytic cells, protein antigens will be denatured and precipitated by alum adjuvant [4]. When an antigen depot is created, for example by an oil-based adjuvant, slow release of the antigen occurs over a period of weeks and evokes strong immune reactions [5]. B-cell stimulation may also produce enhanced antibody responses and may be achieved by using DEAE dextran [6] or bacterial toxins [7]. Adjuvants may target innate responses that are necessary to activate specific pathways of acquired immunity [2]. Increased activity of Th1 cells, resulting in enhanced cell-mediated immunity (CMI) through selective activation of innate immunity, mediated by toll-like cell surface receptors could be caused by microbial CpG adjuvant [8].

Aluminum Adjuvants (Salts)

Aluminum-based adjuvants are well established and the most widely used, although the basis of their action remains unclear. It has been postulated that aluminum-based vaccines may function in various ways including the creation of a depot that maintains presentation of the antigen, stimulation of APCs, formation of particulate antigens from otherwise soluble antigens that increases the immunological response, and pharmacological effects mediated through the inflammasome NALP3 [9–13].

In spite of the fact that alum-based vaccines are generally well tolerated, these adjuvants may produce granulomas after subcutaneous or intradermal injections, adverse effects that are not associated with the intramuscular route of injection [14].

A number of vaccines in current use contain aluminum adjuvants [15]. Although they have less adjuvant activity than more recently developed adjuvants, their extensive human experience makes them useful and a frequent choice for vaccine candidates. The commonly used aluminum adjuvants are available in a variety of forms, such as aluminum phosphate ($AlPO_4$), aluminum hydroxide ($Al(OH)_3$), and potassium aluminum sulfate ($KAl(SO_4)_2$). The term alum specifically refers to potassium aluminum sulfate, although it may be used in a broader context to refer to other aluminum salts. The elemental aluminum content of licensed US vaccines is limited to 0.85 mg per individual dose of vaccine [15]. Aluminum salts may remain at the site of injection for long periods of time [16] and some portion of the aluminum salt is internalized by dendritic cells [17]. Nevertheless, they do undergo biodistribution and excretion over an extended period of time [18].

Despite aluminum salts having an extensive record of experience and safety, they are not ideal adjuvants. A significant problem is a potential lack of consistency in the adsorption of antigens, as different lots and brands of the same type of aluminum salt can demonstrate an inconsistent adsorptive capacity [19]. Furthermore, a potential exists for the exchange of protein antigens adsorbed to aluminum salts for interstitial proteins after injection [20–22].

The variation in adsorptive capacity and in situ interactions is likely due to the number of chemical forces binding the antigens to the aluminum adjuvants. This binding can involve a variety of factors including electrostatic bonding, hydrophobic interactions, van der Waals forces, and hydrogen bonding, and the strength of these depend on the charge on the aluminum salt and protein antigen, the physical structure of the aluminum salt, and the pH and buffer used [16,23–27].

Typically, aluminum salts induce local redness and swelling at the injection site [28], but these toxicities are readily tolerated. Local inflammation after the intramuscular injection of aluminum salts is thought to occur as the material migrates into the subcutaneous space following the needle track created on injection of the vaccine [3]. Additionally, nodules that may occur after repeated injections of these adjuvants are associated with the subcutaneous route of injection [29].

However, reports of adverse clinical findings regarding the aluminum containing adjuvant $Al(OH)_3$ producing macrophagic myofasiitis (MMF). Beginning in 1993, an increasing number of cases were reported of unusual infiltrations of skeletal-muscle connective-tissue structures by nonepithelioid histiocytic cells [30]. Patients tended to exhibit chronic myalgia in their affected limbs, and a cluster of findings presented a more coherent picture that associated MMF with aluminum salts. These cases exhibited some common characteristics:

1. The site of macrophage infiltration was focal and typically restricted to the site of injection.
2. Muscle damage was almost always absent.

3. The infiltrates of macrophages formed well-delineated sheets of histocytes.

These findings led to the conclusion that MMF is the result of long-term persistence of aluminum hydroxide at the site of injection of the vaccine [31]. The underlying causes of this human toxicity remain unclear and may be related to impaired elimination of aluminum or genetic dispositions to inflammatory disease. With respect to the latter, Authier et al. [32] examined whether differences in Th1- or Th2-biased immunity could influence the expression of MMF in a rodent animal model. These authors found that Lewis rats with a Th1-biased immune response differed in their reaction to aluminum hydroxide adjuvanted vaccine from Sprague–Dawley rats, which have a more balanced Th1/Th2 immune response. Lewis rats demonstrated significantly smaller MMF lesions than Sprague–Dawley rats. In another study, monkeys given diphtheria–tetanus vaccines containing aluminum adjuvants were found to have varying degrees of macrophage aggregation at the site of injection, although no evidence of either behavioral or muscular weakness was evident [33]. A WHO meeting on the issue of MMF highlighted the need for more research on this topic [34].

Newer, recombinant or synthetic antigens for vaccines are generally less immunogenic than older live, killed, or attenuated whole organism-based vaccines. This has resulted in the development of more powerful adjuvants to compensate for the potentially diminished immune response. Nevertheless, alum remains the major adjuvant used in vaccines used to immunize humans. Alum has the propensity to induce effective levels of antibodies mediated by Th2 responses, but has little capacity to stimulate cellular responses mediated by Th1 mechanisms. The latter is an important aspect of immunity for some newer efforts in the development of vaccines [35]. Additionally novel adjuvants address the need to develop more powerful antibody responses in human populations with insufficient responses to vaccines using alum, such as the newborn, elderly, and immunocompromised individuals. They also reduce the amount of administered antigen (antigen sparing). Although a number of recently developed adjuvants clearly demonstrate the potential for increased immunogenicity, concerns about their safety remain [36–41]. Adjuvants may be classified in various ways reflecting various properties (see Table 27.1).

TOXICITIES ASSOCIATED WITH VACCINES

Vaccines typically produce various adverse clinical effects, such as inflammation and pain at the site of injection, malaise, fatigue, and slight febrile responses. These may have their counterparts expressed in toxicity studies, such as infiltration of inflammatory cells at the site of administration, decreased food consumption, loss of body weight, or elevation in body temperature. These adverse effects reflect the activation of various components of the immune system, and will vary with the specific nature of the vaccine antigen and/or adjuvant. Similar to naturally occurring infections, the administration of a vaccine results in the activation of cells regulating immunity and the resultant inflammation is accompanied by the release of various proinflammatory cytokines and frequently evokes an acute-phase response. For example, van der Beek et al. [42] reported that after the administration of an attenuated yellow fever vaccine to healthy human subjects IL-6, C-reactive protein (CRP), and fibrinogen were found to be elevated in blood samples. Other similar studies have revealed increases in the blood levels of various cytokines and acute-phase reactants involved in immune and inflammatory responses. Reinhardt et al. [43] observed increases in β2-microglobulin after administration of a yellow fever vaccine and, additionally, Hacker et al. [44] found increases in plasma levels of tumor necrosis factor (TNF) after administration of this same vaccine.

The expression of these inflammatory cytokines and their entry into the bloodstream contributes to the expression of systemic manifestations of toxicity, like fever or malaise, which are sometimes observed after the administration of vaccines in clinical populations. In addition, other physiological effects are not well characterized and require further investigations to determine their impact on overall safety. For example, Liuba et al. [45] reported decreases in flow-mediated dilatation responses indicative of altered arterial endothelial function when measured at the brachial artery in 8 human subjects, which persisted for 2 weeks following the administration of an inactivated trivalent, split influenza vaccine. Changes in the arterial response to hyperemia were accompanied by small increases in CRP and fibrinogen levels, which were considered to be indicative of a systemic inflammatory response to the vaccine. Dilatory responses to sublingual glyceryl trinitrate and carotid intima-media thickness as measured by external ultrasound were not altered. Similarly, Hingorani et al. [46], in a small number of human subjects, found that after the administration of an attenuated capsular polysaccharide vaccine of *Salmonella typhi*, significant dysregulation of arterial endothelial function occurred in both resistance and conduit blood vessels that was accompanied by a systemic inflammatory response characterized by elevations in white blood cell count and serum levels of IL-6 and IL-1 receptor antagonist. Beyond influences on cardiovascular physiology, changes in underlying cytokine levels were reported to be factors in alterations of negative mood affect following administration of the *S. typhi* vaccine [47,48], which may be linked to the direct influence of the inflammatory actions of vaccines on malaise, lethargy, and impaired cognitive ability sometimes observed in clinical populations.

Rarely, more serious adverse events are associated with the administration of vaccines. In many instances, it has not been possible to demonstrate a definite link between the vaccine and serious, significant toxicities.

Given the small amount of material administered in vaccines, direct local or systemic toxicity is extremely rare. More commonly, toxicities associated with vaccines arise from various factors involved in the inflammatory events that are an intrinsic part of the response to the administered antigen and/or adjuvant. Additionally, vaccines may contain excipients and preservatives, including antibiotics, that may be linked to these toxicities.[2] These additional components serve various purposes. For example, some chemicals are added during production to prevent bacterial growth or remain from the manufacturing process (extraneous proteins like egg proteins in influenza vaccines or formalin, which is found in trace amounts in several vaccine products).

Vaccines are frequently given by intramuscular injection. In addition to the toxicities caused by the vaccine components, the trauma caused by the injection introduces histological changes at the site of injection that must be considered relative to the picture of any inflammation caused by the vaccine. Thuillez et al. [49] summarized the findings of seven studies that were conducted using rats, mice, and rabbits and single or repeated injections of saline. Mice were injected in the right and left gluteus-medium muscle; rats in the left and right gluteus medium or left and right quadriceps femoris muscle, and rabbits in the dorsolumbar muscle. Mice were given 0.05 mL, while rats were given 0.2 mL and rabbits 0.5–1 mL. The authors reported that at 2 days after intramuscular injection, the lesions consisted of mainly infiltrations of inflammatory cells consisting of neutrophils or heterophils, lymphocytes and macrophages, hemorrhage, myofiber degeneration, and/or muscle necrosis. By day 10 following injection, the site contained reduced numbers of inflammatory cells along with histological evidence of healing including regeneration of myofibers and fibrosis. These findings are consistent with local, minimal trauma.

Intramuscular injections of vaccines that include alum show a similar histological picture. Verdier et al. [33] investigated the local histological effects of two aluminum-containing vaccines in monkeys after a single intramuscular injection at 3, 6, or 12 months. In these investigations, two groups of monkeys were immunized with either diphtheria–tetanus vaccine adjuvanted with aluminum hydroxide or aluminum phosphate. At 3 months, aggregations of macrophages accompanied by lymphocytic infiltrations were found at the site of injection and one monkey given aluminum hydroxide was found to have a cyst-like structure lined with macrophages and fibrocytes. Later, histological examination revealed a minimal number of lymphocytes with or without focal fibrosis in the animals given aluminum phosphate, which greatly diminished in 1 year. In monkeys given the vaccine containing aluminum hydroxide, aggregates of macrophages were evident in three of four animals and remained at 1 year.

Additionally, isolated examples of toxicities or enhanced disease in association with vaccination are known or suspected. In some aspects, these cases appear to mimic the course of increased disease severity, or adverse events due to natural infections. The most well-established examples of increased disease severity occur with respiratory syncytial, dengue, and measles virus infections. Children immunized with formalin-inactivated respiratory syncytial virus (FI)-RSV or RSV G vaccines were infected with RSV. This infection was associated with enhanced disease and pulmonary eosinophilia that was believed to be due to an exaggerated memory Th2 response [50–56]. Animal models of respiratory syncytial virus infection have suggested various mechanisms as a causal role, including sensitizing antibodies to untoward sites, unfavorable T-cell responses, or overexuberant immune responses involving cytokines or interleukins [57].

Another serious potential toxicity infrequently associated with vaccines is autoimmune disease. In this regard, three different mechanisms may be at work, namely molecular mimicry, epitope spreading, and autoimmune dysregulation. The incidence of autoimmune-induced disease is low, and in many cases cannot be reliably associated with the administration of vaccines. Although no unequivocal associations are known, various possible pathogenic mechanisms exist. Molecular mimicry is the result of an immune response to shared epitopes between antigens of the host and antigenic components of the vaccine. To assess this potential toxicity, protein sequences may be screened in computer base searches of amino-acid structures between antigenic protein components and known protein structures. Another possible mechanism for the autoimmune phenomenon is epitope spreading. Three different types of this are believed possible: shared identical amino-acid sequences between peptides and/or proteins, homologous but nonidentical amino-acid sequences, and epitopes on dissimilar chemical structures such between DNA and peptides or carbohydrates and peptides.

[2] http://www.cdc.gov/vaccines/pubs/pinkbook/downloads/appendices/B/excipient-table-1.pdf.

http://www.cdc.gov/vaccines/pubs/pinkbook/downloads/appendices/B/excipient-table-2.pdf.

Although the immune response to the unintended antigen may be indirect and of lower affinity or avidity, it could theoretically be of sufficient strength to provoke antibody-mediated cytotoxicity by activating complement or cell-mediated signals. Molecular mimicry of T cells differs from that mediated by antibodies. Mimicry for T cells is a type of immune degeneracy in which T cells recognize and respond to untoward antigens. T cells may exhibit epitope spreading as a response, which is not directed at the original epitope, but as recognition of epitopes in target-tissue proteins expressed in the inflammatory process caused by the vaccine. Additionally, other theoretical mechanisms exist. These include activation by superantigens of a large fraction of T-cell populations and induction of inflammatory cytokines and costimulatory molecules. However, there is currently a lack of in vivo evidence that molecular mimicry is associated with vaccines, although it remains an issue of concern.

TOXICOLOGY STUDIES FOR VACCINES (ADJUVANTS)

Types of Study and Their Endpoints

FDA regulations for preclinical toxicology studies of vaccines require the components (eg, antigens and adjuvants) to also be tested for any adverse effects. These studies should follow good laboratory practice (GLP)[3] guidelines as described in the Code of Federal Regulation (CFR) 21 [58]. In general, there are five types of toxicology study:

1. Single and/or repeat dose
2. Reproductive and developmental
3. Mutagenicity
4. Carcinogenicity
5. Safety pharmacology (normally included in the repeat-dose toxicity study if needed)

Single- and/or Repeat-Dose Toxicology Studies

Developing a new vaccine requires preclinical testing for any adverse effects (local or systemic) of the test article. Depending on the stage of vaccine development, single and/or multiple dose, dose response, and/or time response studies should be conducted.

---

[3]GLP system means the organizational structure, responsibilities, procedures, processes, and resources for implementing quality management in the conduct of nonclinical laboratory studies [58]. Part 58 in these regulations includes the specific GLP requirements for both in vivo and in vitro studies. Parts 11 and 809 of CFR 21 explain the GLP requirements for handling the toxicology study records and the requirements for diagnostic products for human use, respectively.

Species selection for any study should be based on the desired clinical immune response(s). For example, C57BL/6 mice are used to replicate Th1 cellular immune responses [59]. An alternative animal model is the rabbit, which is used to reproduce humoral immune responses. Other selection criteria, such as anatomical and physiological relevance to humans, may be considered. For studying intracutaneous or topical vaccines, the minipig is considered a good model [59]. The baboon was used to investigate a novel adjuvant for intranasal immunization because of its physiological and pharmacological similarities with humans [60]. For more specific investigations, such as RSV vaccine, hamsters [61] are sometimes used. Animal models for vaccine preclinical toxicology studies will be discussed in more detail later in this chapter.

Different vaccines and/or adjuvants may require different approaches for immunogenicity testing. Enhancing IgA responses might be more appropriate for mucosal vaccines development [62–64]. T-cell-mediated responses may play a key role in the vaccines' immunogenicity just as or more important than the humoral response (see "Introduction" section).

Preclinical toxicology studies should be carefully designed to include not only the relevant species, but also an appropriate number of animals (eg, 5 rabbits or 10 mice/sex/group for both main and recovery groups), route of administration of the test article (normally the same as the intended clinical route), dose level (same as the intended clinical dose), and number of doses ($N+1$, where N = number of clinical dose(s)). If the number of doses is not $N+1$, then the number employed should be justified. The number of animals in each group should be adequate to ensure reliable statistical analysis of the data can be performed, with sufficient statistical power to evaluate potential differences [65].

The study design should include all treatment groups and should include testing of the vehicle, adjuvant(s), and the antigen. Table 27.2 is an example of simple experimental design.

Test and Control Article Characterization (21 CFR Part 58.105 [58])

Identity, strength, purity, and composition should be determined for each batch of test article. Methods of synthesis, fabrication, or derivation of the test and control articles should be documented. Marketed products should be characterized by their labeling.

Stability of Test and Control Articles (21 CFR Part 58.105 [58])

Stability of the test and control articles should be determined before study initiation or concomitantly according to an approved standard operating procedure,

TABLE 27.2 Example of Experimental Design

Group Number	Identity of Group	Total Dose Volume (mL)	Dose Concentration (μg/mL)	Number of Animals/ Sex	Number of Animals Euthanized/Sex			
					Core Study Animals		Recovery Animals	
					Day	Day	Day	Day
1	Vehicle	0.5	Same as clinical	5 rabbits				
2	Adjuvant(s) + vehicle	0.5	Same as clinical	5 rabbits				
3	Antigen + vehicle	0.5	Same as clinical	5 rabbits				
4	Antigen + adjuvant(s) + vehicle	0.5	Same as clinical	5 rabbits				

which provide for periodic analysis of each batch. Stability of the test article ensures delivery of consistent concentrations of the active materials. This, in turn, ensures the consistency in the immune responses in nonclinical/clinical studies.

A preclinical study protocol should be written following the instructions in 21 CFR part 58.120 [58]. The preclinical laboratory study should be conducted in accordance with the protocol. All protocol amendments and deviations should be included in the final report. The details for reporting of nonclinical laboratory study results are included in 21 CFR part 58.185 [58]. All toxicology studies should be included in the package of the investigational new drug (IND) application.

Toxicology studies normally include the following endpoints:

Cage-side and clinical observations: Mortality, morbidity, general health, and any signs of toxicity should be monitored on a daily basis. Evaluation of skin and fur, eye and mucus membranes, respiratory, circulatory, autonomic and central nervous systems, somatomotor and behavior, should be recorded on a daily basis, or once weekly. Most of the time there are no, minimal, or mild changes in the animals' health due to vaccine treatment. Changes (if any) in animals' health due to test-article treatment could be serious and require immediate attention, or in rare cases require termination of the animal. Including recovery groups in the study will help to determine whether these changes are recoverable over time or not.

Food consumption and body weight: Changes in food consumption and body weight could be an indication of an adverse effect of the test article. Physiological events that are triggered as responses to the ingestion of food are important episodic signals [65]. Initially the brain detects, via sensory input, the amount of food ingested and its nutrient content. Specialized chemo- and mechano-receptors that monitor physiological activity are located in the gastrointestinal tract. They pass information to the brain mainly via the vagus nerve [66]. This afferent information constitutes one class of "satiety signal" and forms part of the preabsorptive control of appetite.

Appetite is controlled by chemicals released by gastric stimuli or by food processing in the gastrointestinal tract [67]. Changes in food consumption might be caused by many of these chemicals (which are peptide neurotransmitters) [68]. The release of cholecystokinin (CCK) (a hormone believed to mediate meal termination) is triggered by food consumption. This in turn activates CCK-A receptors in the pyloric region of the stomach [69]. The vagus nerve transmits this signal to the nucleus tractus solitarius in the brain stem. This signal is relayed to the hypothalamic region where integration with other signals occurs. Peptides such as enterostatin [70], neurotensin, and glucagon-like-peptide represent other potential peripheral satiety signals [71]. Any adverse effect of the test article on these chemicals will affect appetite/food consumption. Any changes in food consumption will in turn affect the body weight.

Body temperature: Body temperature and the immune system are closely related to each other during infections. Signals to the brain that control body temperature are sent during infections to elevate the temperature of the entire body, and this causes fever. No real infection exists during vaccination but the immune system may perceive one. The body learns how to fight off a real infection during vaccination. Body temperature should be measured at 6, 24, 48, and 72 h after each dose.

Injection-site evaluation: Draize scoring could be used for injection-site evaluation. It should include evaluation of edema, erythema, and eschar formation. The site of injection should be evaluated predosing, and at 24, 48, and 72 h post dosing. Inflammatory skin reactions should be graded according to the Draize (or modified) scales [72].

Ophthalmologic examination: Eyes are normally examined predosing and during the week prior to scheduled necropsy. The exam could include observation of the internal and external structures of the eye, such as the cornea, lens, and other transplant media (aqueous and vitreous humor), fundus including blood vascular, and optic disc.

The ophthalmologic examination could be (eg, uveitis[4]) indicative of inflammation in the eyes as reported in some vaccines.

Clinical chemistry: Blood samples for clinical chemistry evaluations could be collected in lithium heparin tubes for plasma. Clinical chemistry tests are used to diagnose disease, to monitor disease progression or response to therapy or toxin exposure, and to screen for the presence of underlying disease in apparently healthy animals. A wide variety of clinical chemistry tests are used for this purpose. The results of the following parameters are included in the clinical chemistry testing [73]:

1. Electrolyte balance (calcium, chloride, phosphorus, potassium, and sodium). Changes in free water and changes in electrolytes themselves (rate of intake, excretion/loss, and translocation within the body) affect the electrolyte levels in blood. As electrolytes are essential to the proper functioning of cells, the body maintains electrolyte concentrations within narrow limits.

2. Carbohydrate metabolism (glucose (principal source of energy for mammalian cells)). Sources of glucose include digestion of dietary carbohydrates, break down of glycogen in the liver (glycogenolysis), and production of glucose from amino-acid precursors in the liver (gluconeogenesis). Hormones (eg, insulin, glucagon, catecholamine, growth hormone, and corticosteroids) affect blood glucose concentration by facilitating its entry into or removal from the circulation. Changes in blood glucose levels due to test-article treatment could be an indication of an adverse event through the above-mentioned pathways.

3. Liver function (alanine animotransferase (ALT), aspartate aminotransferase (AST), sorbitol dehydrogenase (SDH), glutamate dehydrogenase (GLDH), total bile acids, alkaline phosphate (ALP), gamma-glutamyl transferase (GGT), and total bilirubin). Injury to liver parenchymal cells can be detected by measuring the hepatocellular leakage enzymes (ALT, AST, SDH, and GLDH). Enzyme leakage from cells through damaged cell membranes is indicated by the increased serum activity of these enzymes. Cholestasis, which implies impairment of bile flow, is diagnosed by the changes in ALP and GGT levels. Cholestasis

will result in elevations of bilirubin in blood if it is severe. The main value of these enzymes is their greater sensitivity for this abnormality as compared to serum bilirubin levels alone. Gamma-glutamyl transferase is more specific than alkaline phosphatase for this purpose.

4. Muscle enzymes (AST (used also as liver injury marker, see above), creatine kinase, and lactate dehydrogenase). Creatine kinase, present in high concentration in the cytoplasm of myocytes, is the most widely used enzyme for evaluation of neuromuscular disease and is a "leakage" enzyme. This enzyme functions by making ATP available for contraction in muscles. This is done by the phosphorylation of ADP from creatine phosphate by catalyzing the reversible phosphorylation of creatine by ATP to form phosphocreatine+ADP. Phosphocreatine is the major storage form of high-energy phosphate in muscle. Lactate dehydrogenase is an enzyme that catalyzes the conversion of lactate to pyruvate. It is not tissue-specific, being found in a variety of tissues, including liver, heart, and skeletal muscle. Lactate dehydrogenase levels could be elevated by exercise, liver disease, muscle disease, and neoplasia.

5. Kidney function (creatine and blood urea nitrogen). Urea and creatinine tests are normally used as indicators of glomerular filtration rate (GFR). Ammonia, generated by catabolism of amino acids derived either from digestion of proteins in the intestines or from endogenous tissue proteins, is used by hepatocytes to synthesize urea. Urea is excreted by the kidney and intestine and in saliva and sweat. Plasma urea nitrogen concentrations depend on hepatic urea production and renal tubular flow rate. Increases in protein catabolism and digestion and decreases in GFR cause an increase in urea nitrogen levels. Plasma urea nitrogen levels are decreased when protein intake is decreased, protein anabolism, increase in excretion, and decrease in production (eg, liver disease). Muscle metabolism results in the production of creatinine. An energy-storing molecule in muscle called phosphocreatine undergoes spontaneous cyclization to form creatine and inorganic phosphorous. Creatinine is the result of creatine decomposition.

6. Proteins (total protein, albumin, globulin, and A:G ratio). Total protein and albumin are the measured parameters, and globulins and A:G ratio are calculated from them. Quantitative values for the above major proteins are the test results. However, there are many different types of proteins within the globulin fraction besides immune globulins, such as those associated with the acute-phase response, and this measurement does not provide information

---

[4] The middle layer of the eye is called uvea, which provides most of the blood supply to the retina. Uveitis is swelling and irritation of the uvea and could be caused by autoimmune disorders such as rheumatoid arthritis or ankylosing spondylitis, infection, or exposure to toxins. [Pubmed health (http://www.ncbi.nlm.nih.gov/pubmedhealth/PMH0002000/).]

on these fractions. Both quantitative and qualitative data for the different fractions that comprise total protein could be obtained by electrophoresis. Electrophoresis can be used on serum, urine, or body-cavity fluid samples (eg, cerebrospinal fluid).

7. Lipids (triglycerides, cholesterol). In serum, triglycerides are incorporated into lipoproteins that are composed of a coat of phospholipid, cholesterol, and proteins (apolipoproteins) enclosing a hydrophobic center of cholesterol esters and triglycerides. The most commonly occurring steroid is cholesterol. Cholesterol is a precursor of cholesterol esters, bile acids, and steroid hormones. It is derived from dietary sources and synthesized in vivo from acetyl-CoA in the liver (main site) and other tissues (intestines, adrenal glands, and reproductive organs).

Hematology: Blood samples for hematology evaluation could be collected in tubes containing EDTA (ethylenediaminetetraacetate). Blood samples for fibrinogen, prothrombin time, and activated partial-thromboplastin time could be collected in tubes containing sodium citrate.

The following parameters are included in hematology testing [74]:

(a) Red blood cells (hematocrit, hemoglobin, mean corp. Hb, mean corp. Hb. Conc., mean corp. volume, total erythrocyte count, and reticulocytes). Hematocrit (HCT) is calculated as the product of the mean cell volume (MCV) and the red blood cell (RBC) count. Packed cell volume (PCV) is a directly measured value obtained from centrifuging blood in a microhematocrit tube in a microhematocrit centrifuge. Hemoglobin concentration (Hb) is reported as grams of hemoglobin per deciliter of blood (g/dL). Hemoglobin concentration of whole blood normally is about one third of the HCT (ie, the MCHC is 33%) because red cells are approximately 33% hemoglobin. The MCV, expressed in femtoliters (fL; 10^{-15} L), indicates the volume of the "average" red cell in a sample. Mean cell hemoglobin (MCH) represents the absolute amount of hemoglobin in the average red cell in a sample and its units are picograms (pg) per cell. The MCH is calculated from the Hb and the RBC values using the following equation: MCH (pg) = (Hb × 10) ÷ RBC. The MCHC is the mean cell hemoglobin concentration, expressed in g/dL. It is calculated from the Hb and the PCV using mean corpuscular hemoglobin concentration (MCHC) = (Hb ÷ PCV) × 100. The term "hypochromic" is used for red cell populations with values below the reference interval. This can occur in a strongly regenerative anemia, where an increased population of reticulocytes with low Hb content "pulls" the average value

down. Low MCHC can also occur in iron deficiency anemia, where microcytic, hypochromic red cells are produced because of the lack of iron to support hemoglobin synthesis.

Reticulocytes, which are released in increased numbers into the blood from bone marrow as a response to anemia, are young, anucleate erythrocytes. Hemolysis (destruction) or loss (hemorrhage) of erythrocytes, in most species, is the cause of anemia. To determine whether the bone marrow is responding to an anemia (given sufficient time) by increasing red blood cell production, identification of immature anucleate red blood cells is required. This is termed a regenerative response. Detecting immature erythrocytes by virtue of the presence of RNA in the form of ribosomes and rough endoplasmic reticulum in their cytoplasm is required to evaluate the bone marrow response. The more immature the cell, the more RNA it contains. In contrast, mature red blood cells, which are no longer synthesizing hemoglobin, contain very small amounts or no RNA.

(b) White blood cells [(WBCs) basophils, eosinophils, lymphocyte, macrophage/monocyte, neutrophil, leukocytes, and large unstained cells]. The WBC (thousands/μL), total number of leukocytes, is a count of nuclei or total nucleated cell count. If nucleated red blood cells (nRBCs) are circulating in blood, they will be included in the nucleated cell count. The WBC, in this case, represents the leukocyte count only after it has been corrected for the nucleated red cells (nRBCs). The correction is made as follows: corrected WBC = nucleated cell count × (100 ÷ [nRBC + 100]).

(c) Clotting parameter (mean platelet volume, fibrinogen, prothrombin time, and activated partial-thromboplastin time). Platelets play a fundamental role in hemostasis (formation of blood clots) and are a natural source of growth factors. A subjective estimation of platelet numbers could be made during examination of the stained blood film by plate smear. The size and number of platelet clumps is included in this estimation. Fibrinogen *(factor I)* [75] is synthesized by the liver and is soluble plasma glycoprotein that is converted by thrombin into fibrin during blood coagulation. To form a clot, fibrin is then cross-linked by factor XIII. It has been shown, in recent research, that fibrin plays a key role in the inflammatory response and development of rheumatoid arthritis. Prothrombin time is a blood test that measures the time it takes for plasma to clot, to check for bleeding problems, or to check whether medicine to prevent blood clots is working. Activated partial-thromboplastin time is used to detect abnormalities in blood clotting [76] and to monitor the effectiveness of heparin treatment.

Urinalysis: Urinalysis is the physical, chemical, and microscopic examination of urine. It involves a number of tests to detect and measure various compounds that pass through the urine. There is an array of tests performed on urine and one of the most common methods of medical diagnosis [77]. Urine samples will be tested for the following:

1. Physical color and appearance: What does the urine look like to the naked eye? Is it clear or cloudy?
2. Is it pale or dark yellow or another color?
3. The urine-specific gravity test reveals how concentrated or dilute the urine is.
4. Microscopic appearance: The urine sample is examined under a microscope to look at cells, urine crystals, mucus, and other substances in the sample and to identify any bacteria or other germs that might be present.
5. Chemistry: A special stick ("dipstick") tests for various substances in the urine. The stick contains little pads of chemicals that change color when they come in contact with the substances of interest.

Bone-marrow smears: A bone-marrow sample is usually collected from the posterior iliac crest. Reasons to do a bone marrow biopsy include anemia of unknown cause, leukopenia, leukocytosis with immature granulocytes and/or blasts in the blood, and occurrence of unusual cells in blood (dwarf megakaryocytes, thrombocytopenia, and marked thrombocytosis).

C-reactive protein: C-reactive protein (CRP) is the primary acute-phase reactant in rabbits, monkeys, and humans. For these species, assays for CRP measurement are commercially available. When adequately sampled, CRP is indicative of a systemic inflammatory response that could be an indicator of potential toxicity [216]. This is particularly true when evidence of other toxicities, such as weight loss, are also found. Acute-phase reactants are a nonspecific inflammatory response and are not specifically associated with a particular type, variety, or class of injury (eg, liver or renal harm). When CRP is measured in rabbits or monkeys, there is no need to run serum electrophoresis analysis because adequate information on acute-phase reactions will be generated from the CRP data.

C-reactive protein is not the primary acute-phase reactant in rodents (rat or mouse); however, α1-acidic glycoprotein and α2-macrogobulin are responsive, inflammatory markers. Hence, although there is no need to measure CRP when rodents are proposed for use in a study, the equivalent, responsive acute-phase reactants should be measured. Alternatively, rodent acute-phase reactants may be measured by plasma electrophoresis since they occur in a fractionated part of the different globulins.

Creatine kinase (also known as creatine phosphokinase or phospho-creatine kinase): This is an enzyme expressed by various tissues and cell types. An inflammatory response to intramuscular injection of the vaccine might cause some minimal muscle degeneration, which may be reflected in creatine kinase levels. This inflammatory response is considered part of the expected mechanism of toxicity due to the means of vaccine administration.

Clinically, creatine kinase is assayed in blood tests as a marker of myocardial infarction (heart attack), rhabdomyolysis (severe muscle breakdown), muscular dystrophy, the autoimmune myositides, and in acute renal failure.

Antibody analysis (serology): It is critical to measure the immune responses for any vaccine and/or adjuvant and this is recommended in the WHO guideline [64]. The homeostatic condition in which the body maintains protection from infectious disease is called immunity. Immunity allows an individual to distinguish foreign material from "self" and neutralize and/or eliminate the foreign matter through a series of delicately balanced, complex, multicellular, and physiological mechanisms [78]. Promoting the cellular and/or the humoral immune responses are the primary purpose of vaccine developments. Serology data help in demonstrating the exposure to the vaccine, confirms the relevance of the animal model for evaluating the potential toxicity of the vaccine, and might allow the correlation between a toxic effect and the immune response induced [79]. ELISA (enzyme-linked immunosorbent assay) and other methods are used to measure specific antibody responses (humoral arm of the immune response). In the meantime, assays measuring cytokine-secreting antigen-specific T lymphocytes such as γ-interferon ELIspot [80] are used to evaluate the cellular arm of the immune response.

Necropsy: Animals are normally euthanized at different time points, depending on the study design and the expected responses to the test article under investigation. Terminal animals are usually necropsied a few days (eg, 2–7 days) after the last treatment, which helps in investigating the early effects after vaccination. Recovery animals are normally used to detect any delayed toxicity and/or to determine whether any earlier detected effects (if any) have resolved over time. Normally the number of animals in both terminal and recovery groups per sex are the same.

Histopathological evaluation: Gross examinations should be conducted on all major organs, and microscopic evaluation should be conducted on a complete list of tissues [64]. The site of vaccine injection (quadriceps and skin over the quadriceps for intramuscular (IM) injection) should be examined carefully. Brain, kidneys, liver, and reproductive organs are considered pivotal, and should be evaluated for any adverse changes. Immune organs such as spleen, thymus, and draining lymph nodes are evaluated for any changes that might indicate a positive and/or negative response. The seriousness of the histopathological findings in some cases depends on other findings (eg, clinical pathology results). For example, vacuolation in the liver can be a normal finding, or may be indicative of toxicity. Vacuolation when accompanied by increases in clinical chemistry parameters such as liver enzymes (which in themselves would be of concern) is considered an indication of toxicity. However, vacuolation is considered an adaptive response when it occurs without other accompanying changes. For instance, metabolic activation could lead to vacuolation in many cell types, and would not be accompanied by other changes indicative of frank toxicity.

Unless they are severe, the intended immunological and inflammatory responses to the vaccine are not considered adverse effects. In repeat-dose studies, inflammation at the site of injection, hyperplasia and hypertrophy of lymph nodes draining the injection site, increase in spleen weight, and clinical pathology changes (eg, increases in white blood cells, increases in serum globulin, and decreases in serum albumin) are considered the intended immunological and inflammatory responses.

Reproductive and Developmental Toxicology Studies

Reproductive and developmental toxicology studies should be included in the IND package if the vaccine under study is intended to be administered to women of childbearing potential. This is also the case if the vaccine is specifically designed for maternal immunization to prevent infectious disease in the neonate by the passive transfer of antibodies (eg, the vaccine against group B streptococcus, which can be life threatening during the neonatal period) [81]. There are exceptions, as certain vaccines may automatically be contraindicated for pregnant women or to those planning to become pregnant [82]. For example, the smallpox vaccine is contraindicated for women who are pregnant, and women who plan to become pregnant within 4 weeks of vaccination. In addition, pregnant women are advised to avoid close contact with persons recently vaccinated, as in the case of rubella [83].

Studying the potential effects of the vaccine on fertility, fetal development, and postnatal development of the offspring is critical [84]. Sexual organs and their functions, endocrine regulation, fertilization, transport of the fertilized ovum, implantation, and development could all be affected by toxic effects of the vaccine [85]. Abnormal development of the fertilized egg through the embryo, fetus, and the offspring all the way to maturity, due to test-vaccine exposure, is a subset of reproductive toxicology called developmental toxicology. Developmental studies include the studies of the prenatal (embryonic and fetal) and postnatal (development following birth until the end differentiation of organs is achieved) events.

Choice of species depends on vaccine immunogenicity, and on the relative rate and timing of the placental transfer of antibodies. For example, in rats and mice, 90% of antibodies are transferred (postnatally) in milk. However, the majority of antibody transfer in rabbits occurs across placenta (prenatal).

Reproductive studies should be designed following ICH S5(R2) guidelines [86]. One species is required for this kind of study. Animals should be immunized a few weeks before mating and boosted immediately prior to mating (Fig. 27.1). One subset of pregnant females (20/group) should be submitted to cesarean section and fetal examination on gestation day (GD) 18 for mice and on GD 20 for rats. Another subset (20/group) should be allowed to litter, and the postnatal development (PND) of the pups should be followed up to weaning (rodent – PND 21). To assess the potential for long-lasting, permanent changes, the study could be extended to include assessment of the immune system (developmental immunotoxicity testing) in the offspring at 6–8 weeks.

Serum antibody levels should be determined as follows:

- F0 females: At predose, end of gestation and lactation periods.
- F1 fetus: Cord blood.
- F1 pup: Postnatal day 21.

Additional assessments can be conducted. Histochemical analysis for antibody deposition could be conducted if the vaccine induced adverse effects. Neurological assessments and immunological endpoints could be also included.

CBER guidelines[5,6] indicate that subjects may be included in clinical trials without developmental toxicity studies, provided appropriate precautions are taken to avoid vaccination during pregnancy. Developmental toxicity study reports can then be supplied with the biologics license application submission. Depending on the available toxicology information from the preclinical and the clinical studies, test articles are assigned different pregnancy categories. The FDA has assigned the following pregnancy categories.[7] Pregnancy and lactation labeling

---

[5] http://www.fda.gov/BiologicsBloodVaccines/Guidance ComplianceRegulatoryInformation/Guidances/Vaccines/ ucm076611.htm.
[6] http://www.fda.gov/OHRMS/DOCKETS/98fr/992079gd.pdf.
[7] http://www.scribd.com/doc/2278291/FDA-Pregnancy-Categories.

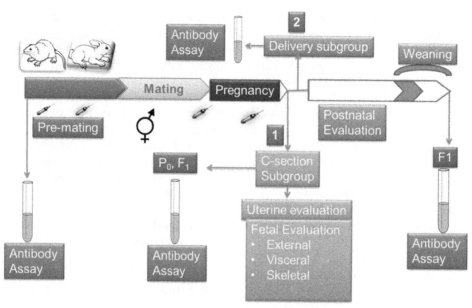

FIGURE 27.1   Schematic representation of Development Toxicology Study Design for vaccines. *Figure courtesy of Ali S. Faqi from MPI Research.*

rules published on December 4, 2014 are to replace the pregnancy categories below. The new rules are to:

1. Amend the physician labeling rule.
2. All prescription drugs approved on or after June 30, 2001 must revise content and format of the pregnancy and nursing mothers (lactation) subsections of labeling (pregnancy letter categories are replaced with an integrated risk summary).
3. All prescription drugs are required to remove pregnancy letter categories.
4. Staggered implementation over 3–5 years.

The required labeling elements are:

1. Pregnancy exposure registry
2. Risk summary that includes:
   a. Risk statement based on human data (if available)
   b. Risk statement based on animal data (summary of the available animal data, a statement if studies do not meet current standards, or a statement for no data existence)
   c. Risk statement based on pharmacology (statement regarding the mechanism of action (MOA) and potential associated risks when the drug has a well-understood MOA)
   d. Background risk information in general population (background risk for major birth defects and miscarriage in the US general population)
   e. Background risk information in disease population (background risk for major birth defects and miscarriage in the US diseased population)

Previously, the FDA had assigned the following pregnancy categories,[7] which are no longer applicable:

Category A

Adequate and well-controlled studies have failed to demonstrate a risk to the fetus in the first trimester of pregnancy (and there is no evidence of risk in later trimesters) in women.

Category B

Animal reproduction studies have failed to demonstrate a risk to the fetus and there are no adequate and well-controlled studies in pregnant women.

Category C

Animal reproduction studies have shown an adverse effect on the fetus and there are no adequate and well-controlled studies in humans, but potential benefits may warrant use of the drug in pregnant women despite potential risks.

Category D

There is positive evidence of human fetal risk based on adverse reaction data from investigational or marketing experience or studies in humans, but potential benefits may warrant use of the drug in pregnant women despite potential risks.

Category X

Studies in animals or humans have demonstrated fetal abnormalities and/or there is positive evidence of human fetal risk based on adverse reaction data from investigational or marketing experience, and the risks involved in use of the drug in pregnant women clearly outweigh potential benefits.

Mutagenicity Studies

Generally, mutagenicity studies are not required for vaccines (WHO guidelines on nonclinical evaluation of vaccine [64] and European Medicines Evaluation Agency (EMEA) [63]). Genotoxicity studies might not be relevant for adjuvant of biological origin [87]. The potential for gene mutation, chromosome aberrations, and primary DNA damage might be needed for synthetic adjuvants, because they are considered to be new chemical entities [88].

Carcinogenicity Studies

Generally, carcinogenicity studies are not required for vaccines (WHO guidelines on nonclinical evaluation of vaccine [64] and EMEA [63]). This is because of the low dose and the low usage of the adjuvants, meaning that the risk of tumor induction is very small, according to EMEA guidelines [89].

Safety Pharmacology Studies

These studies are performed to evaluate the adverse effects of the test article on physiological functions such as those of the cardiovascular system, respiratory system, and central nervous system [90]. Central nervous system studies include the evaluation of motor activity, behavioral changes, coordination, sensory/motor reflex responses, and body temperature. Cardiovascular system evaluation includes blood pressure, heart rate, and electrocardiogram measurements. In vivo, in vitro, and/or ex vivo evaluations, including methods for repolarization and conductance abnormalities, should also be considered. Respiratory rate, tidal volume, or hemoglobin oxygen saturation should be measured as part of the respiratory system evaluation. For vaccines, separate safety pharmacology studies are not performed [91]. These studies, which evaluate body temperature, electrocardiogram, and the central nervous system, could be included in the repeat-dose toxicity study if needed [64]. For more details about the safety pharmacology studies, refer to "Guidance for Industry S7A. Safety Pharmacology Studies for Human Pharmaceuticals" [90].

Other Toxicity Studies

For certain types of vaccine, specialized toxicity studies are needed. For new, live attenuated virus vaccines that have either a theoretical or an established potential for reversion of attenuation [92] or neurotropic activity [64], virulence and neurovirulence studies are needed. Polio and yellow fever vaccines fall into this category. This is based on the detailed knowledge of their neurotropic behavior. A neurovirulence test for a polio vaccine is part of routine batch-release procedures, and for yellow fever vaccine is designed to allow quantitative assessment of the effects of the virus by examination of specific areas following directed inoculation.

Vaccines with good safety records, such as measles, mumps, and varicella viruses, do not require reevaluation by neurovirulence tests when there are minimal changes to seed lots or to manufacture [92].

Since the early 1990s, a new approach to vaccination has been actively developed. These novel approaches include the direct introduction of plasmid DNA containing the gene encoding the antigen against which an immune response is sought by incorporating antigens into appropriate host tissues and the in situ production of the target antigen(s). The advantages of this approach over traditional approaches are that it stimulates both B- and T-cell responses, the vaccine has improved stability, the absence of any infectious agents, and the relative ease of large-scale manufacture [93]. Vaccines are generally used as biological medicinal products for the prophylaxis of infectious disease, but DNA vaccines are also being developed for therapeutic use (eg, against infectious disease or other diseases such as cancer). Using genes from a variety of infectious agents, including influenza virus, hepatitis B virus, human immunodeficiency virus, rabies virus, lymphocytic choriomeningitis virus, West Nile virus, malaria, and *mycoplasma*, many scientific publications [93] explore the potential of DNA vaccination and immune responses in animals. For nucleic acid and viral vector-based vaccines, biodistribution studies are necessary to determine the tissue distribution following administration and the potential for the vector to integrate into the host genome [93,94]. The design of nonclinical safety tests should take into consideration the use of the DNA vaccine and the risk/benefit situation. In addition to following GLP requirements for preclinical toxicology studies (see above), DNA studies should also evaluate any local inflammatory response (eg, myositis), organ-specific autoimmunity, immunopathology, and other relevant parameters. In particular, where the encoded antigen is a self-antigen, or may show self-antigen mimicry, a wider range of studies (including autoantibodies) may be necessary to address the specific concerns [93].

ANIMAL MODELS FOR VACCINE RESEARCH

Pasteur investigated anthrax, *Pasteurella multocida*, and rabies pathogenesis in animal models [95]. He confirmed that different species could be infected by certain pathogens. He also confirmed that an old culture of *P. multocida* (chicken cholera) kept in the laboratory without passage could protect chickens against virulent *P. multocida* challenge [95]. The concept of vaccinating dogs against rabies was also discovered by Pasteur [96]. Other examples of animal usage in vaccine research include the use of virus-like particles (VLPs) for immunization against papillomavirus [97]. To control the disease caused by bovine, canine, and rabbit papillomavirus, recombinant papillomavirus VLPs was used [98,99]. This provided the basis for subsequent licensure of a bivalent and quadrivalent human papillomavirus (HPV) vaccine to prevent cervical cancer [100,101]. It has been confirmed through the development of this vaccine that studies in animals remain relevant to the control of infectious diseases in humans. Animal models in human vaccine development have different applications, such as:

1. Route of infection, transmission of disease, and analysis of disease pathogenesis
2. Host immune responses to natural infection and vaccination characterization
3. Onset and duration of vaccine-induced immunity assessment
4. Mucosal versus systemic immunity induction
5. Novel strategies for vaccine delivery and formulation development.
6. Clinical symptoms and disease transmission following infection reduction
7. Novel vaccination concepts (such as in utero or maternal immunization) development

Vaccine parameters requiring the consideration of animal models are [102]:

1. Vaccine safety
2. Duration and onset of immunity
3. Mucosal, maternal, and neonatal vaccination
4. Novel vaccine technologies
5. Vaccination of the elderly
6. Therapeutic vaccines for noninfectious diseases

Whether the study is intended to study toxicology or measure the efficacy of a new vaccine, selecting the right animal model is critical. For instance, a limited number of hosts including nonhuman primates, germ-free or barrier raised piglets, germ-free dogs and cats will be colonized by *Helicobacter pylori*. Investigators prefer working with small animals to larger animals. For example, the ferret has been successfully used to investigate gastritis and antimicrobial agents and *Helicobacter felis* mice have been used as an animal model for the study of *H. pylori* [103].

The ability to reproduce aspects relevant to human physiology is the hallmark of an appropriate animal model and its utility for vaccine development [59]. Humans or animals are ultimately the target population for the vaccine. Good models should share the same physiological characteristics (ie, humans and pigs share the same physiology of the skin), or at least reflect them as closely as possible. Ethical use of animals in human vaccine research requires the selection of those

that match the human disease as closely as possible. The overall number of animals used for biomedical research will be reduced according to this criterion.

Anatomical, physiological, and immune system differences between species influence their relative responses. As part of the effort to find and develop new vaccines or adjuvants, animal models are typically used to discriminate between various antigens and their combination with different adjuvants. These animal models are useful because they possess the biological complexity of the immune system that may be predictive of humans and potential adverse effects. Although models such as transgenic animals exist, which possess enhanced qualities to represent various aspects pertinent to modeling the human immune system, these are not commonly used for toxicity assessment at this time. Strain- and antigen-dependent immunological responses will occur in both rats and mice [104]. These differences exist for both humoral and cell-mediated immunity [104].

For the host, criteria to consider when choosing animal models for vaccine development are similarities in:

1. Immune organ development
2. Transport of antibodies across the mucosal surfaces (surface IgA)
3. Route of transmission
4. Duration of immune memory
5. Pattern of pathogenesis
6. Receptors
7. The immune response ontogeny
8. Lifespan and duration of neonatal, adolescent, and adult period
9. Physiology (ie, skin) for specific delivery
10. Access to mucosal and systemic immune compartments
11. Transfer of passive immunity via the placenta, colostrum, and milk.

The pathogen criteria are similarities in:

1. Replication and spread of the pathogen
2. Virulence and pathogenesis
3. Route of entry of the pathogen in animal model
4. Genetic and antigenic characteristics.

To elucidate aspects of immune physiology in vivo, the mouse is an excellent animal model [2]. Although frequently used, it does have limitations in the study of the etiology of infection and disease pathogenesis. Murine models are suitable to study acute extracellular bacterial infections, but they are of limited value for the study of intracellular viral, bacterial, or parasitic infections [2]. The value of mice and rats as models to study most intracellular infections is limited because of the complex and unique etiology of intracellular infections and the narrow host range of infectivity of individual pathogens [2]. Exceptions to this general concept are a small number of specific intracellular murine infections, like the one involving lymphocytic choriomeningitic virus infection [105], which has yielded unique insights into the understanding of protective immunity and intracellular infection.

Primates, guinea pigs, rabbits, cats, and ferrets have been used selectively as relevant models to study vaccination. In earlier studies on tuberculosis [106] (Tb) and more recently for simian immunodeficiency virus (SIV) studies [107] as a model for Tb and HIV in humans, primate models have been used. As an experimental infection model to evaluate human tuberculosis vaccines, guinea pigs have been used [108]. Guinea pigs are inordinately susceptible to tuberculosis following infection with *Mycobacterium tuberculosis* or *M. bovis*. While potentially useful when studying pathogenesis, this may limit the value of the guinea pig as a model to study Tb protective immunity. Because they produce tubercles and granulomatous disease (similar to that found in domestic livestock and humans), guinea pigs have been used extensively in tuberculosis research.

Orme et al. [109] reported the advantages and disadvantages of a range of animal models of tuberculosis as shown in Table 27.3.

Influenza Vaccines and the Selection of the Appropriate Animal Model

Because human influenza virus isolates replicate in both the upper and lower respiratory tracts with clinical signs of disease at reasonable virus doses in ferrets, they were used in studies to support the safety of live influenza vaccines [110]. However, because antigen-specific CD8+ T cells can easily be measured in the lymph nodes, circulation, and lungs of the mouse, this animal model is suitable to generate data to support the potential immunogenicity of a novel vaccine targeting the induction of these effector cells [110].

Mice, Cotton Rats and Guinea Pigs

To understand the mechanisms of the immune protection and the contributions of IgA, IgG, CD4+, and CD8+ T cells to immunity, mice were used on regular basis [111]. Mice have been used to evaluate the pathogenesis of avian influenza viruses and the 2009H1N1 virus and to examine the protective activity of vaccines against these strains [112–115]. As in any animal model, the above-mentioned advantages of using mice in influenza studies are offset by their disadvantages. One of these is that the mice are not a natural host of the influenza virus. Thus to determine vaccine effectiveness, studies are usually performed with virus strains that have been adapted to replicate in mice [116]. Alternatively, large inocula are administered directly to the lower respiratory tract to induce disease.

Prior to using this model for testing novel vaccines, differences between mouse and human innate and adaptive immunologic interactions should be considered [117]. For RSV infection, the BALB/c mouse was used because it mimics human respiratory disease [50,54].

Cotton rats have also been used for studies of immunity and viral pathogenesis [118]. Clinical signs of infection are evident after intranasal inoculation with reasonable virus doses in this model [119]. In addition, in this model, respiratory rate as a measure of influenza virus-induced disease is helpful in providing a relevant endpoint to evaluate disease in live animals over an extended period of time [120]. The cotton rat was also a good model for evaluating the impact of the early innate response on immunity [121].

Mice and cotton rats are not good models for evaluating the spread of infection between animals, because influenza viruses are not transmissible between them.

TABLE 27.3 Advantages and Disadvantages of Animal Models of Tuberculosis

Species	Advantages	Disadvantages
Mouse	Inexpensive Extensive immunological database Inbred strains show considerable range of resistance or susceptibility to aerosol infection importance and role of T-cell subsets consistent with observations in humans	Delayed type hypersensitivity response is poor Hard to measure convincingly Takes months to develop necrotic pathology in lungs Small window of protection in vaccine studies (1.0–1.25 log)
Guinea pig	Progression of disease very similar to humans Large window of protection in vaccine studies (2–3 log)	Expensive; requires large aerosol chamber and extensive P3 facilities Limited immunological reagents
Rabbit	Models "extremes" of disease such as liquefied cavities and miliary disease Quick; develops severe disease in 6–8 weeks	Expensive; requires extensive P3 facilities Animal husbandry issues (eg, sheds bacteria in urine) Limited immunological reagents
Monkey	Similarity to humans Probably required for regulatory approval before widespread human testing	Expensive Requires extensive P3 facilities Aggressive (can bite) Might carry pathogenic viruses General public opposes use

The guinea pig is a good model to be used in such studies [122,123] because this animal model supports influenza virus replication in its upper and lower respiratory tracts [124]. In addition, the guinea pig provides a means of comparing the effectiveness of influenza vaccines by showing the differences in protection after immunization with inactivated and live, attenuated vaccines [125]. However, because a correlation between this endpoint in an animal model and infection or disease rate in humans has not been demonstrated, the real value of determining the impact of vaccination on virus transmission in guinea pigs is questionable [110].

Ferrets

Ferrets have been used for influenza virus studies since 1933. In experiments, these animals showed sign of disease following inoculation with filtered nasal secretions from an individual with respiratory symptoms [126]. Human H5N1 are highly pathogenic in ferrets, inducing sneezing, coughing, fever, weight loss, diarrhea, and neurological signs [110]. Not only could the virus replicate in the nasal turbinates and lungs, H5N1 can spread to the brain, spleen, and intestine in these animals [127]. Therefore ferrets are commonly used to evaluate the immunogenicity and effectiveness of pandemic influenza vaccines. For the advantages and disadvantage of this animal model when studying the influenza virus, Eichelberger and Green [110] should be consulted.

Pigs and Cats

There was renewed interest in the pig as a model for studies of influenza viruses after the emergence of the pandemic swine-origin H1N1 strain in 2009 [128]. Nasal discharge, cough, fever, labored breathing, and weight loss have been reported in pigs as the cause of certain swine strains, which made this animal a useful model for studies of immunity and pathogenesis [129–131]. For study of the 2009H1N1 pandemic virus (A/California/04/09), specific-pathogen-free miniature pigs were used [132]. This model was particularly attractive because of the availability of a number of reagents enabling studies of immune correlates of protection [133]. Highly pathogenic avian viruses did not cause severe clinical signs of disease in pigs [134]. However, highly pathogenic H5N1 viruses did cause disease and death in cats [135,136]. Thus cats were considered a good model to test protection against disease and death due to highly pathogenic avian-origin strains. H1N1 virus causes a moderate level of disease in cats when infected intratracheally, replicating primarily in the lungs but can also be isolated from other organs [137]. Pigs and cats are not extensively used for studies of pathogenesis, immunity, or transmission of human influenza and therefore are not currently used routinely to support human vaccine studies [110].

Monkeys

Cynomolgus, rhesus, and pigtailed macaques have been used for influenza virus infection [138–140]. The cynomolgus macaque has been designated as a good model for the study of the H1N1 virus of 1918. This type of monkey showed an atypical innate immune response correlating with lethal disease [141]. It has also been used to evaluate the effectiveness of a recombinant modified vaccinia Ankara virus expressing HA against highly pathogenic H5N1 infections [142].

In general, to study influenza [143] and distemper [144] infections, ferrets have been used.

The Selection of Animal Models for Other Vaccines

Because the immunological cells cannot be transferred between histoincompatible outbred individuals, the use of the outbred animals is limited. Cats are used to study feline immunodeficiency virus (FIV), which is the analog of HIV infection in humans [145], whereas rabbits have been used to study immunity to a variety of toxinogenic bacterial infections, which require neutralizing antibodies as the main pathway for protection [146].

Guinea pigs were the first model to be used for *Leishmania enrietti* infection. T-cell responses to parasite antigens develop within 2 weeks of infection, and the lesions heal within ~10 weeks in guinea pigs [147]. Infection of inbred mice with *Leishmania* species pathogenic for humans superseded the *L. enriettii* guinea pig model [148]. The spectrum of disease manifestations observed in human leishmaniasis can be mimicked in the laboratory by infection of different inbred strains of mice with *L. major*. Including a range of susceptibility states depending on the strain of mouse used, the mouse model reproduces many aspects of human disease. Upon infection, BALB/c mice develop large skin ulcers, which expand and metastasize, leading to death. However, C57BL/6 and CBA/N mice are resistant; they develop small lesions that cure in 10–12 weeks, and are resistant to reinfection. Intermediate susceptibility was reported in most other strains of mice [149]. Both susceptible and resistant mice produce Th2 cytokines during the period of active lesion development [150,151]. The difference between susceptible and resistant mice is that the latter are able to switch to a Th1 profile and control the disease [152,153].

The golden hamster was one of the early animal models for the study of visceral leishmaniasis. Visceral disease and death is the result of infection with *L. donovani* in this model. The aspects of the human disease mimicked in the hamsters are anemia, hyperglobulinemia, and cachexia, making it a useful tool for the characterization of molecules and mechanisms involved in pathogenesis [154]. Recently, the hamster has been used primarily as a source of *L. donovani* amastigotes, which seem to be the required lifecycle stage for infecting mice, the currently preferred model animal for visceral leishmaniasis. Inbred strains of mice display marked differences in susceptibility to infection with *L. donovani* [155]. The best animal model for visceral leishmaniasis is the dog, in which relevant immunological studies and vaccine development can be performed [156,157].

Other than humans, the only species susceptible to HIV-1 infection are the great apes, of which the chimpanzee has been used to study this virus. Limitations include scarcity of animals, cost, limited viral replication, and absence of disease when infected with patient isolates. The Asian macaque monkey has been used as a good model for SIV studies. The SIV-infected macaque has been used as a model for assessing HIV-1 vaccine strategies, because it develops an AIDS-like disease. Limitations include differences from HIV-1 in viral sequence and envelope epitopes. Recently, chimeric viruses have been constructed in the laboratory that express HIV-1 envelopes on an SIV backbone [158–160]. These constructed viruses are called simian/human immunodeficiency viruses (SHIVs). In macaques, the in vivo passage of these chimeric viruses resulted in SHIV induction of CD4+ lymphocyte loss, and death as a result of opportunistic infections [161].

Because genital disease in guinea pigs closely resembles that of humans [162], it has been used to test potential vaccines [163,164] and antiviral chemotherapies [165] for genital herpes. McClements et al. [166] reported that immunization with DNA-encoding herpes simplex virus type 2 full length glycoprotein D (HSV-2 gD) or a truncated form of HSV-2 g-induced immune responses in mice and protected them from lethal challenge with HSV-2. They also showed that a combination of these two DNAs protected guinea pigs from primary genital disease. McClements et al. [166] also found that protective immunity could be induced by low doses of DNA in the mouse model with only a single immunization. Additionally, other investigators demonstrated protective immunity in the mouse [167–169] and guinea pig [170], HSV-infection models were induced by multiple immunizations with higher doses of gD DNA or gB DNA. Provost et al. [171] reported that both the marmoset and the chimpanzee are useful models for hepatitis A virus behavior in man.

To select the right animal model for any vaccine development, safety and efficacy should be taken (equally) into consideration. A safe vaccine without good efficacy will be of no use and vice versa.

A good understanding of responses to vaccination in both neonates and the elderly is also required because they are at increased risk of contracting infectious disease. Studies in the mouse model have suggested that vaccine responses may be compromised in these age groups. The development of the murine immune system may not provide an appropriate model for evaluating immune responses in these two age groups. To evaluate vaccine immune responses in the neonate, and to address questions regarding possible interactions between vaccines and maternal antibodies, large-animal models may be much more appropriate [172–174]. However, other than mice, there have been very few investigations of vaccine responses in geriatric animals [175,176]. For the screening of adjuvants, the horse could provide geriatric populations [177].

An appropriate animal model is also needed for the development of mucosal vaccines. Disease protection against a wide variety of pathogens that invade through mucosal surfaces could be achieved by mucosal vaccination. Difficulties associated with efficient vaccine delivery and weak immune responses following mucosal immunization made the induction of protective immune responses at mucosal surfaces an elusive goal. Thus for the evaluation of mucosal vaccine-delivery technologies, effective and safe mucosal adjuvants, and the characterization of mucosal immune responses, an appropriate animal model is required. In mice, intranasal vaccination may be associated with inhalation and ingestion of vaccine antigens. This makes it difficult to discriminate between intranasal, oral, and intrapulmonary vaccination. However, larger animals like the pig or the cow can be used for the controlled delivery of vaccines to the nasal passages [178,179]. The nasal passages of these animals more closely resemble that of humans than do those of the mouse. Surgical models have also been useful for screening a variety of mucosal vaccine delivery technologies and potential mucosal adjuvants [180,181].

It is critical, when choosing an animal model, to ensure that the selected model simulates as closely as possible the events occurring in humans. The greater the similarity in patterns of pathogenesis between the two, the more likely it is that relevant correlates of immune-mediated protection will emanate from the model. The same route of exposure should be used. If the respiratory tract is the pathogens' route of entrance, then the aerosol challenge to expose the pathogen to the defenses of the upper respiratory tract should be used. Intratracheal challenge would not be considered appropriate, because it circumvents the various barriers of the upper respiratory tract. A similar pathogen dose to that which would occur naturally should be used. Use of excessive pathogen challenge, or an unnatural route of infection, might overcome the adaptive immune response. The structure, function, and development of the respiratory tract in the animal model should resemble that of humans when choosing a model for respiratory infections.

Because of the above-mentioned reasons, animal models will continue to play a critical role in human-vaccine development, especially in the preclinical discovery phase. Thus it is critical to choose the most appropriate models and not restrict investigations to the least expensive and most convenient animal models. This will help make optimal use of animals and more rapidly bring safe and effective vaccines to the market.

ROUTES OF VACCINE ADMINISTRATION

Selection of an appropriate route for vaccine administration is a critical component of a successful immunization. Vaccines are normally administered by injection, either intravenous (IV), intramuscular (IM), or subcutaneous (SC) administration [182]. There are advantages and disadvantages for these routes of administrations. Vaccines could also be administered orally or intranasally, and these routes also have advantages and disadvantages, which will be discussed later in this section.

Intramuscular (IM) Vaccine Administration: The needle used to administer the vaccine to the muscle should be long enough to reach deep into the muscle. It should be inserted at a 90 degree angle to the skin with a quick thrust. It is not necessary to aspirate when using this route. A minimum of 1-inch separation is necessary when using multiple injections in the same extremity. The following vaccines should be administered by the intramuscular (IM) route: diphtheria–tetanus (DT, Td) with pertussis (DTaP, Tdap); Haemophilus influenzae type b (Hib); hepatitis A (HepA); hepatitis B (HepB); human papillomavirus (HPV); inactivated influenza (TIV); quadrivalent meningococcal conjugate (MCV4); and pneumococcal conjugate (PCV). Inactivated polio (IPV) and pneumococcal polysaccharide (PPSV23) could be administered either by IM or SC routes.

Subcutaneous (SC) Vaccine Administration: Subcutaneous tissue should be pinched up to prevent injection into muscle. The needle should be inserted at a 45 degree angle to the skin. It is not necessary to aspirate when using this route. A minimum of 1-inch separation is necessary when using multiple injections in the same extremity. The following vaccines should be administered by the SC route: measles, mumps, and rubella (MMR), varicella (VAR), meningococcal polysaccharide (MPSV4), and zoster (shingles (ZOS)).

To optimize the immunogenicity of the vaccine and minimize adverse reactions at the injection sites, most vaccines should be given via the intramuscular route into the deltoid or the anterolateral aspect of the thigh. Vaccine failure might be the result of injecting a vaccine into the layer of subcutaneous fat, where poor vascularity might result in slow mobilization and processing of antigen [183]. This might be the case in hepatitis B [184], rabies, and influenza vaccines [185]. Subcutaneous injection of hepatitis B vaccine leads to significant lower seroconversion rates and more rapid decay of antibody response when compared to intramuscular administration [183].

To initiate an immune response, the appropriate cells, eg, phagocytic or antigen-presenting cells, should be involved [186]. The layers of fat do not contain these cells, and when deposited in fat, the antigen may take longer to reach the circulation, potentially leading to a delay in processing by macrophages and eventual presentation to the T and B cells of the immune response. Antigens may also be denatured by enzymes if they remain in fat for hours or days. Thicker skin folds are associated with a lowered antibody response to vaccines [183,184].

Because adipose tissue has much poorer drainage channels than muscle, it retains injected material for longer periods, and is therefore more susceptible to its adverse effects [187]. Thus subcutaneous injections can cause abscesses and granulomas [183,187,188]. Because of its abundant blood supply, muscle tissue is probably spared the harmful effects of substances injected into it [187]. The antigen is adsorbed to an aluminum salt adjuvant in hepatitis A, hepatitis B, and diphtheria, tetanus, and pertussis vaccines, hence the intramuscular route is strongly preferred. Superficial administration of these vaccines may lead to an increased incidence of local reactions, such as irritation, inflammation, granuloma formation, or necrosis [184,189,190].

How deep a substance is injected is determined by the injection technique and needle size. A wide variation exists in thickness of the deltoid fat pad, with women having significantly more subcutaneous fat than men [183]. The use of longer needles might cause the patient more discomfort, but, because skeletal muscle has a poorer supply of pain fibers than skin and subcutaneous tissue, discomfort might be less [191]. Needle gauge is another important factor in vaccine administration [192], as the vaccine is dissipated over a wider area when using a wider bore needle. This reduces the risk of localized redness and swelling [193].

Intranasal Vaccines

Alternative routes of administration have been used to improve the protective immune responses at the very places in the body that certain viruses and bacteria are likely to target. Intranasal vaccines can induce protective immunity in the respiratory tract where the viruses attack.[8] By either slowing the rate of uptake of the antigens (eg, intranasal vaccines are taken into the body more slowly than injectable vaccines, thus reducing the risk of allergic reaction) or by administering the vaccine viruses to an area of the body that they do not typically grow in (thus reducing the disease-causing effects of some of the

[8] http://www.sciencedaily.com/releases/2011/04/110411194821.htm.

strains of live vaccine viruses), the side effects of the vaccine will be reduced. Intranasal administration is easy and acceptable to both humans and animals.

Avirulent intranasal vaccines could be given via the nostrils using special applicators. The cells lining the upper respiratory tract (nasal passages, throat, trachea) would then be coated by the vaccine and the virus would subsequently replicate in these cells. These viruses (and/or bacteria) will be attacked by the immune cells present in the respiratory tract, inducing a protective immune response that tends to remain within or near the respiratory tract.

If an animal received an intranasal vaccine, the lining of its respiratory tract would be coated with protective antibodies. Hundreds of memory cells, primed to recognize the antigens contained on the invading respiratory viruses, will be included in the regional, respiratory-system lymph nodes [194]. When the invading viruses and bacteria reach the respiratory tract, these antibodies and memory cells would react and eliminate them. This response is much more rapid than that produced by an injectable vaccine. This is because the resultant immune defenses are located in the same region as the invading pathogens. The invading viruses will not get the opportunity to damage many cells in this case. Moreover, clinical signs of disease should not occur or, if they do, they should be very mild.

There are advantages and disadvantages for intranasal vaccination [195]. The advantages are:

1. Improved patient compliance [196].
2. Improved penetration of (lipophilic) low molecular weight drugs through the nasal mucosa [197].
3. Due to large absorption surface and high vascularization, rapid absorption and fast onset of action is expected.
4. Avoidance of the gastrointestinal tract environmental conditions (chemical and enzymatic degradation of drugs) and the hepatic first-pass metabolism.
5. Direct delivery of vaccine to the lymphatic tissue [198].
6. Induction of a secretory immune response at distant mucosal site [198].
7. Because the uptake of viral antigen into the body is slower in intranasal vaccination, allergic reactions are less likely to happen.

The disadvantages are:

1. Mild upper respiratory tract infection could be induced. This is characterized by watery nasal and ocular discharge, sneezing, and even coughing. However, this is usually self limiting and very mild.
2. They are generally only effective against respiratory pathogens.
3. Intranasal vaccines needed every year.

4. Severe liver damage and even death of the animal could be caused by an accidental injection of the intranasal *Bordetella* vaccines [194].
5. Penetration to the brain through the olfactory region may be caused by nasally administered substances, including toxins and attenuated microorganisms.[9] For some vaccines and drugs targeting neurological diseases, such direct nose-to-brain transport may be advantageous but raises concerns about potential adverse effects when the brain is not the target organ.[8]

Alternative Routes

Few other noninjectable routes exist beside intranasal application. Orally and intraperitoneally administered vaccines (given into the abdominal cavity) have been investigated or approved for human use. These routes are used to improve the response of the gastrointestinal immune system to diseases like parvovirus and coronavirus. Polio vaccine, rotavirus, adeno, or typhoid are examples of orally administered vaccines. Dermal patches, sprays (vaccines applied to the skin surface), and transdermal vaccines (aerosolized vaccine particles that are forced at high pressure through the skin using special instruments, thus avoiding the need for needles) have been developed. DNA plasmid vaccines are typically administered by the IM or ID route and may be given by electroporation that propels DNA-coated gold particles into various tissues [199].

Vaccine Injection Versus Intranasal Administration (Live Attenuated Vaccines Versus Killed Vaccines) [200–202]

Killed (or subunit) vaccines do not replicate and stay in one spot for the immune system to "kill." Without virus replication, the immune system does not become exposed to the massive amounts of antigen generated by live viruses. Inefficient humoral immunity (fewer memory B cells and smaller amounts of antibody that don't last in the body as long) and cell-mediated immunity (not as many memory T cells waiting to target the next wild-type virus that comes along) will be developed. Humoral and cell-mediated immunity can be improved by:

1. Adding large quantities of killed virus or bacterial matter into each inactivated vaccine. The amount of antigen available for the immune system to recognize will be increased this way. However, this will increase the risk of allergic and local inflammatory injection site reactions.

[9] http://www.optinose.no/assets/documents/20030129173426_Nasal_delivery_of_vaccines.pdf.

2. Adding adjuvants to the vaccine designed to increase the effectiveness of the immune response. However, some adjuvants might increase the risk of allergic reactions, anaphylaxis, and injection site reactions. Most require a minimum of two doses to achieve the desired effect (risk of vaccine reaction with the second dose). They must be given by injection (not available by other routes of administration).

Live vaccines are more amplified and promote longer lasting humoral and cell-mediated immune responses, resulting in longer lasting, more rapidly induced immune protection. Because it replicates in the body, only a small amount of viral material needs to be injected. Less viral material means a reduced risk of allergic and injection site reactions. No adjuvant is required in this kind of vaccine, hence the risks of allergic and injection site reactions are reduced. Other than injection, live vaccines can be given by other routes (eg, intranasal). Thus live vaccines can potentially be tailored to induce immunity in the areas of the body where it will be most effective (eg, immunity in respiratory system to protect against respiratory viruses). The drawbacks of live vaccines are:

1. It must be stored carefully, or its potency may be lost.
2. Immunocompromised or pregnant animals/humans might get the disease.
3. Severe complications might be caused by certain live vaccines (eg, live rabies vaccines can cause fatal neurological disease in some dogs and cats).
4. Poorly produced vaccines may contain virulent organisms that could produce severe disease.
5. Some live vaccines can cause severe illness if given by the wrong route (eg, injectable cat flu vaccine viruses that accidentally get inhaled by a cat will produce marked signs of cat flu, and intranasal *Bordetella* vaccine viruses can cause liver damage and death if injected).

PRODUCT CHARACTERIZATION

In addition to toxicity studies, in vivo and in vitro assays play a significant role in assessing critical safety characteristics of vaccines. Testing encompasses assessments for identity, purity, safety, and efficacy in terms of antigenicity and potency. Generally, these types of study are aimed at detecting undesirable contaminants or impurities, characterizing the vaccine product, and ensuring conformation to specified manufacturing standards. Unlike toxicity studies, which explore the potential for unanticipated risk, or further refine the understanding of adverse effects, product characterization studies emphasize, quantify, and examine aspects that are associated with the properties of vaccines such as potency and are important to the consistent and safe manufacture of

vaccines. In some respects, these studies may be considered to be focused toxicity studies that have restricted or narrow endpoints that include survival or clinical signs. Among the most important are tests for potency, general safety (21CFR610.11), neurovirulence (IABS Scientific Workshop on Neurovirulence Tests for Live Vaccines, WHO, 2005), tumorigenicity (Meeting Report, WHO Study Group on Cell Substrates for Production of Biologicals, WHO, 2007; European Pharmacopoeia Section 5.2.3), and pyrogenicity (21CFR610.13). The degree and nature of these tests depend on the immunological mechanisms involved in the action of the vaccine or the nature of potential unwanted constituents.

Vaccine potency tests typically measure the level of protection, either against a direct challenge using known quantities of infectious organisms, or more indirectly through exposure to serum containing neutralizing antibodies following incubation with a toxin. Determination of potency is generally made through a series of dilutions that are compared to standard references.

Unlike typical immunization protocols that utilize a prime and boost strategy of successive injections spaced over time, immunogenicity testing for product characterization is often limited to a single injection, because the initial response is believed to better discriminate the amount and quality of an immunogen.

The infrequent serious toxicities that have been associated with vaccines are often linked to the manufacturing process. Some early lots of the polio or "Salk" vaccine were not completely inactivated. This allowed contamination by live polioviruses and resulted in the paralysis of over 200 individuals [203,204]. Additionally, contamination of commercial vaccines, such as poliovirus, adenovirus [205,206], and yellow fever [204,207–210], during the 1940 and 1950s, demonstrated the potential for harm.

Among the different types of product characterization studies with toxicity-related endpoints are the following:

1. Insertional mutagenesis of DNA vaccines
2. Attenuation
3. Untoward immunization—hypersensitivity, autoimmunity, breaking immune tolerance

PEDIATRIC DRUG DEVELOPMENT (PRECLINICAL SAFETY EVALUATIONS)

Pediatric evaluations are required as part of new drug and biologics licensing applications in the United States and every marketing authorization application in Europe, unless a waiver has been granted [211]. It is advisable to acquire the approval of regulatory agencies (FDA and EMA) for any pediatric development plans before starting any pediatric clinical trials.

For juvenile toxicity studies (if pharmacological activity has been demonstrated), one species is acceptable [212–214]. The rat is the recommended species (if relevant), because it has developmental systems that can be easily monitored [211]. Other animal models could be used after careful consideration of its organ-system development relative to that of humans. Because species selection is limited by target specificity, the nonhuman primate (NHP) is the only suitable species for toxicity assessment [211]. The core requirement for preclinical testing of biopharmaceuticals is to establish pharmacological relevance in the test species [215]. Morford et al. [211] reported the advantages and disadvantages of species (NHP, rodents, dogs, and mini-pigs) for juvenile toxicity testing with biopharmaceuticals.

A number of documents developed by various regulatory agencies can provide supplementary information concerning various aspects of the topics discussed in this chapter:

1. WHO Guideline on Nonclinical Evaluation of Vaccines,
   a. Annex 1, WHO Technical Report Series No. 927, 2005. This provides a good overall summary of both manufacturing and toxicity testing paradigms for vaccine products. Various sections cover a wide number of topics including toxicity study design, assessments as well as adjuvants and potency tests.
   b. Annex 2, WHO Technical Report Series No. 987, 2014. This is an updated and more extensive guidance on the nonclinical and preclinical testing of adjuvants and adjuvanted vaccines. Due to the increased usage of novel adjuvants to enhance the immune responses of vaccines, this guidance should allow manufacturers and regulators to proceed in an efficient manner toward development and licensure of adjuvanted vaccines.
   c. Note for Guidance on Preclinical Pharmacological and Toxicological Testing of Vaccines, CPMP, EMEA, CPMP/465/95, 1997. This briefly describes a broader range of subjects in the nonclinical testing of vaccines.
   d. Workshop on Nonclinical Safety Evaluation of Preventative Vaccines Recent Advances and Regulatory Considerations. The Society of Toxicology, Contemporary Concepts in Toxicology Section, US Department of Health and Human Services, Office of Women's Health, FDA, 2002. This is a transcript of a meeting between members of the FDA and various representatives from industry. Various perspectives and approaches to toxicity testing of vaccines are discussed.
   e. Characterization and Qualification of Cell Substrates and Other Biological Materials Used in the Production of Viral Vaccines for Infectious Disease Indications. CBER, FDA, US Department of Health and Human Services, 2010. This describes different product characterization studies including tumorigenicity and in vivo tests for adventitious agents.
   f. Guidance for Industry: Considerations for Plasmid DNA Vaccines for Infectious Disease Indications. CBER, FDA, US Department of Health and Human Services, 2007. This contains a section on biodistribution as well as nonclinical tests for immunogenicity and safety regarding plasmid DNA vaccines.
   g. Guidance for Industry: Consideration for Developmental Toxicity Studies for Preventive and Therapeutic Vaccines for Infectious Disease Indications. CBER, FDA, US Department of Health and Human Services, 2006. This provides information on timing and study design for nonclinical toxicity studies that target developmental and reproductive endpoints.

References

[1] Burdin N, Guy B, Moingeon P. Immunological foundations to the quest for new vaccine adjuvants. BioDrugs 2004;18:79–93.

[2] Griffin JF. A strategic approach to vaccine development: animal models, monitoring vaccine efficacy, formulation and delivery. Adv Drug Deliv Rev 2002;54:851–61.

[3] Edelman R. Vaccine adjuvants. Rev Infect Dis 1980;2:370–83.

[4] Shirodkar S, Hutchinson RL, Perry DL, White JL, Hem SL. Aluminum compounds used as adjuvants in vaccines. Pharm Res 1990;7:1282–8.

[5] Audibert FM, Lise LD. Adjuvants: current status, clinical perspectives and future prospects. Immunol Today 1993;14:281–4.

[6] Joo I, Emod J. Adjuvant effect of DEAE-dextran on cholera vaccines. Vaccine 1988;6:233–7.

[7] Lycke N, Tsuji T, Holmgren J. The adjuvant effect of *Vibrio cholerae* and *Escherichia coli* heat-labile enterotoxins is linked to their ADP-ribosyltransferase activity. Eur J Immunol 1992;22: 2277–81.

[8] Krieg AM. The role of CpG motifs in innate immunity. Curr Opin Immunol 2000;12:35–43.

[9] De GE, Tritto E, Rappuoli R. Alum adjuvanticity: unraveling a century old mystery. Eur J Immunol 2008;38:2068–71.

[10] Eisenbarth SC, Colegio OR, O'Connor W, Sutterwala FS, Flavell RA. Crucial role for the Nalp3 inflammasome in the immunostimulatory properties of aluminium adjuvants. Nature 2008;453:1122–6.

[11] Franchi L, Nunez G. The Nlrp3 inflammasome is critical for aluminium hydroxide-mediated IL-1beta secretion but dispensable for adjuvant activity. Eur J Immunol 2008;38:2085–9.

[12] Kool M, Soullie T, van Nimwegen M, Willart MA, Muskens F, Jung S, et al. Alum adjuvant boosts adaptive immunity by inducing uric acid and activating inflammatory dendritic cells. J Exp Med 2008;205:869–82.

[13] Li H, Willingham SB, Ting JP, Re F. Cutting edge: inflammasome activation by alum and alum's adjuvant effect are mediated by NLRP3. J Immunol 2008;181:17–21.

[14] Butler NR, Voyce MA, Burland WL, Hilton ML. Advantages of aluminium hydroxide adsorbed combined diphtheria, tetanus, and pertussis vaccines for the immunization of infants. Br Med J 1969;1:663–6.

[15] Baylor NW, Egan W, Richman P. Aluminum salts in vaccines – US perspective. Vaccine 2002;20(Suppl. 3):S18–23.

[16] Gupta RK. Aluminum compounds as vaccine adjuvants. Adv Drug Deliv Rev 1998;32:155–72.

[17] Morefield GL, Sokolovska A, Jiang D, HogenEsch H, Robinson JP, Hem SL. Role of aluminum-containing adjuvants in antigen internalization by dendritic cells in vitro. Vaccine 2005;23:1588–95.

[18] Hem SL. Elimination of aluminum adjuvants. Vaccine 2002;20(Suppl. 3):S40–3.

[19] Wassef NM, Alving CR, Richards RL. Liposomes as carriers for vaccines. Immunomethods 1994;4:217–22.

[20] Heimlich JM, Regnier FE, White JL, Hem SL. The in vitro displacement of adsorbed model antigens from aluminium-containing adjuvants by interstitial proteins. Vaccine 1999; 17:2873–81.

[21] Iyer S, HogenEsch H, Hem SL. Relationship between the degree of antigen adsorption to aluminum hydroxide adjuvant in interstitial fluid and antibody production. Vaccine 2003;21:1219–23.

[22] Seeber SJ, White JL, Hem SL. Solubilization of aluminum-containing adjuvants by constituents of interstitial fluid. J Parenter Sci Technol 1991;45:156–9.

[23] Callahan PM, Shorter AL, Hem SL. The importance of surface charge in the optimization of antigen-adjuvant interactions. Pharm Res 1991;8:851–8.

[24] Feldkamp JR, Shah DN, Meyer SL, White JL, Hem SL. Effect of adsorbed carbonate on surface charge characteristics and physical properties of aluminum hydroxide gel. J Pharm Sci 1981;70:638–40.

[25] Rinella Jr JV, White JL, Hem SL. Treatment of aluminium hydroxide adjuvant to optimize the adsorption of basic proteins. Vaccine 1996;14:298–300.

[26] Seeber SJ, White JL, Hem SL. Predicting the adsorption of proteins by aluminium-containing adjuvants. Vaccine 1991;9:201–3.

[27] Wittayanukulluk A, Jiang D, Regnier FE, Hem SL. Effect of microenvironment pH of aluminum hydroxide adjuvant on the chemical stability of adsorbed antigen. Vaccine 2004;22:1172–6.

[28] Jefferson T, Rudin M, Di PC. Adverse events after immunisation with aluminium-containing DTP vaccines: systematic review of the evidence. Lancet Infect Dis 2004;4:84–90.

[29] Frost L, Johansen P, Pedersen S, Veien N, Ostergaard PA, Nielsen MH. Persistent subcutaneous nodules in children hyposensitized with aluminium-containing allergen extracts. Allergy 1985;40:368–72.

[30] Gherardi RK, Coquet M, Cherin P, Authier FJ, Laforet P, Belec L, et al. Macrophagic myofasciitis: an emerging entity. Groupe d'Etudes et Recherche sur les Maladies Musculaires Acquises et Dysimmunitaires (GERMMAD) de l'Association Francaise contre les Myopathies (AFM). Lancet 1998;352:347–52.

[31] Gherardi RK, Coquet M, Cherin P, Belec L, Moretto P, Dreyfus PA, et al. Macrophagic myofasciitis lesions assess long-term persistence of vaccine-derived aluminium hydroxide in muscle. Brain 2001;124:1821–31.

[32] Authier FJ, Sauvat S, Christov C, Chariot P, Raisbeck G, Poron MF, et al. AlOH3-adjuvanted vaccine-induced macrophagic myofasciitis in rats is influenced by the genetic background. Neuromuscul Disord 2006;16:347–52.

[33] Verdier F, Burnett R, Michelet-Habchi C, Moretto P, Fievet-Groyne F, Sauzeat E. Aluminium assay and evaluation of the local reaction at several time points after intramuscular administration of aluminium containing vaccines in the Cynomolgus monkey. Vaccine 2005;23:1359–67.

[34] Vaccine safety. Macrophagic myofascitis and aluminum-containing vaccines. Wkly Epidemiol Rev 1999;74:338–40.

[35] Lindblad EB. Aluminum adjuvants. In: Stewart-Tull DES, editor. The theory and practical application of adjuvants. Chichester: John Wiley & Sons Ltd; 1995. p. 21–35.

[36] Allison AC, Byars NE. Immunological adjuvants: desirable properties and side-effects. Mol Immunol 1991;28:279–84.

[37] Edelman R. An update on vaccine adjuvants in clinical trial. AIDS Res Hum Retroviruses 1992;8:1409–11.

[38] Vogel FR. Adjuvants in perspective. Dev Biol Stand 1998;92:241–8.

[39] Warren HS, Vogel FR, Chedid LA. Current status of immunological adjuvants. Annu Rev Immunol 1986;4:369–88.

[40] Warren HS, Chedid LA. Future prospects for vaccine adjuvants. Crit Rev Immunol 1988;8:83–101.

[41] Waters RV, Terrell TG, Jones GH. Uveitis induction in the rabbit by muramyl dipeptides. Infect Immun 1986;51:816–25.

[42] van der Beek MT, Visser LG, de Maat MP. Yellow fever vaccination as a model to study the response to stimulation of the inflammation system. Vascul Pharmacol 2002;39:117–21.

[43] Reinhardt B, Jaspert R, Niedrig M, Kostner C, L'age-Stehr J. Development of viremia and humoral and cellular parameters of immune activation after vaccination with yellow fever virus strain 17D: a model of human flavivirus infection. J Med Virol 1998;56:159–67.

[44] Hacker UT, Jelinek T, Erhardt S, Eigler A, Hartmann G, Nothdurft HD, et al. In vivo synthesis of tumor necrosis factor-alpha in healthy humans after live yellow fever vaccination. J Infect Dis 1998;177:774–8.

[45] Liuba P, Aburawi EH, Pesonen E, Andersson S, Truedsson L, Yla-Herttuala S, et al. Residual adverse changes in arterial endothelial function and LDL oxidation after a mild systemic inflammation induced by influenza vaccination. Ann Med 2007;39:392–9.

[46] Hingorani AD, Cross J, Kharbanda RK, Mullen MJ, Bhagat K, Taylor M, et al. Acute systemic inflammation impairs endothelium-dependent dilatation in humans. Circulation 2000;102:994–9.

[47] Strike PC, Wardle J, Steptoe A. Mild acute inflammatory stimulation induces transient negative mood. J Psychosom Res 2004;57:189–94.

[48] Wright CE, Strike PC, Brydon L, Steptoe A. Acute inflammation and negative mood: mediation by cytokine activation. Brain Behav Immun 2005;19:345–50.

[49] Thuilliez C, Dorso L, Howroyd P, Gould S, Chanut F, Burnett R. Histopathological lesions following intramuscular administration of saline in laboratory rodents and rabbits. Exp Toxicol Pathol 2009;61:13–21.

[50] Castilow EM, Olson MR, Varga SM. Understanding respiratory syncytial virus (RSV) vaccine-enhanced disease. Immunol Res 2007;39:225–39.

[51] Chin J, Magoffin RL, Shearer LA, Schieble JH, Lennette EH. Field evaluation of a respiratory syncytial virus vaccine and a trivalent parainfluenza virus vaccine in a pediatric population. Am J Epidemiol 1969;89:449–63.

[52] Fulginiti VA, Eller JJ, Sieber OF, Joyner JW, Minamitani M, Meiklejohn G. Respiratory virus immunization. I. A field trial of two inactivated respiratory virus vaccines; an aqueous trivalent parainfluenza virus vaccine and an alum-precipitated respiratory syncytial virus vaccine. Am J Epidemiol 1969;89:435–48.

[53] Graham BS. Biological challenges and technological opportunities for respiratory syncytial virus vaccine development. Immunol Rev 2011;239:149–66.

[54] Johnson TR, Teng MN, Collins PL, Graham BS. Respiratory syncytial virus (RSV) G glycoprotein is not necessary for vaccine-enhanced disease induced by immunization with formalin-inactivated RSV. J Virol 2004;78:6024–32.

[55] Kapikian AZ, Mitchell RH, Chanock RM, Shvedoff RA, Stewart CE. An epidemiologic study of altered clinical reactivity to respiratory syncytial (RS) virus infection in children previously vaccinated with an inactivated RS virus vaccine. Am J Epidemiol 1969;89:405–21.

[56] Kim HW, Canchola JG, Brandt CD, Pyles G, Chanock RM, Jensen K, et al. Respiratory syncytial virus disease in infants despite prior administration of antigenic inactivated vaccine. Am J Epidemiol 1969;89:422–34.

[57] Openshaw PJ, Culley FJ, Olszewska W. Immunopathogenesis of vaccine-enhanced RSV disease. Vaccine 2001;20(Suppl. 1): S27–31.

[58] Good Laboratory Practice Regulations. Code of federal regulations, title 21, part 58 (21 CFR 58), http://www.accessdata.fda.gov/scripts/cdrh/cfdocs/cfcfr/cfrsearch.cfm?cfrpart=58&showfr=1.

[59] Gerdts V, Littel-van den Hurk SD, Griebel PJ, Babiuk LA. Use of animal models in the development of human vaccines. Future Microbiol 2007;2:667–75.

[60] Glueck R. Preclinical and clinical investigation of the safety of a novel adjuvant for intranasal immunization. Vaccine 2001; 20(Suppl. 1):S42–4.

[61] Tang RS, Spaete RR, Thompson MW, MacPhail M, Guzzetta JM, Ryan PC, et al. Development of a PIV-vectored RSV vaccine: preclinical evaluation of safety, toxicity, and enhanced disease and initial clinical testing in healthy adults. Vaccine 2008;26:6373–82.

[62] Brennan FR, Dougan G. Nonclinical safety evaluation of novel vaccines and adjuvants: new products, new strategies. Vaccine 2005;23:3210–22.

[63] EMEACPMP/SWP/465/95. Note for guidance on preclinical pharmacological and toxicological testing of vaccines. 1997. http://www.ema.europa.eu/docs/en_GB/document_library/Scientific_guideline/2009/10/WC500004004.pdf.

[64] WHO. WHO guidelines on nonclinical evaluation of vaccines. 2003. http://www.who.int/biologicals/publications/nonclinical_evaluation_vaccines_nov_2003.pdf.

[65] [a] Blundell JE. The control of appetite: basic concepts and practical implications. Schweiz Med Wochenschr 1999;129:182–8.
[b] Dell RB, Holleran S, Ramakrishnan R. Sample size determination. ILAR J 2002;43(4):207–13.

[66] Mei N. Intestinal chemosensitivity. Physiol Rev 1985;65:211–37.

[67] Read NW. Role of gastrointestinal factors in hunger and satiety in man. Proc Nutr Soc 1992;51:7–11.

[68] Smith GP, Gibbs J. Peripheral physiological determinants of eating and body weight. In: Brownell KD, Fairburn CG, editors. Eating disorders and obesity: a comprehensive handbook. New York: Guildford Publications; 1995. p. 8–12.

[69] Dourish CT. Multiple serotonin receptors: opportunities for new treatments for obesity? Obes Res 1995;3(Suppl. 4):449S–62S.

[70] Erlanson-Albertsson C, Larson A. The activation peptide of pancreatic procolipase decreases food intake in rats. Regul Pept 1988;22:325–31.

[71] Levine AS, Billington CJ. Peptides in regulation of energy metabolism and body weight. In: Bouchard C, Bray GA, editors. Regulation of body weight: biological and behavioral mechanisms. Chichester: John Wiley and Sons; 1996. p. 179–91.

[72] Draize JH, Woodard G, Calvery HO. Methods for the study of irritation and toxicity of substances applied topically to the skin and mucous membranes. J Pharmacol Exp Ther 1944;82:377–90.

[73] French TW, Blue JT, Stokol T. eClinPath the on-line textbook. Cornell University, College of Veterinary Medicine; 2011. http://ahdc.vet.cornell.edu/clinpath/modules/chem/chempanl.htm.

[74] French TW, Blue JT, Stokol T. eClinPath the on-line textbook. Cornell University, College of Veterinary Medicine; 2011. http://ahdc.vet.cornell.edu/clinpath/modules/index.htm.

[75] Wikipedia. Wikipedia-1. 2011. http://en.wikipedia.org/wiki/fibrinogen2011.

[76] MedlinePlus Medical Encyclopedia. Partial thromboplastin time (PTT). 2011. http://www.nlm.nih.gov/medlineplus/ency/article/003653.htm2011.

[77] Simerville JA, Maxted WC, Pahira JJ. Urinalysis: a comprehensive review. Am Fam Physician 2005;71:1153–62.

[78] Klaassen C, Doull'S. Toxicology. McGraw-Hill; 2001. p. 419–70.

[79] Wolf JJ, Kaplanski CV, Lebron JA. Nonclinical safety assessment of vaccines and adjuvants. In: Davies G, editor. Vaccine adjuvants. LLC: Springer Science + Business Media; 2010. p. 29–40.

[80] Casimiro DR, Tang A, Perry HC, Long RS, Chen M, Heidecker GJ, et al. Vaccine-induced immune responses in rodents and nonhuman primates by use of a humanized human immunodeficiency virus type 1 *pol* gene. J Virol 2002; 76:185–94.

[81] Gruber MF. Maternal immunization: US FDA regulatory considerations. Vaccine 2003;21:3487–91.

[82] Gould S, Oomen R. Nonclinical predictive strategies. In: Xu JJ, Urban L, editors. Predictive toxicology in drug safety. Vaccine Toxicology Cambridge University Press; 2010. p. 344–70.

[83] Amstey MS, Gall SA. Smallpox vaccine and pregnancy. Obstet Gynecol 2002;100:1356.

[84] CBER FDA. Guidance for industry: considerations for developmental toxicity studies for preventive and therapeutic vaccines for infectious disease indications. 2006. http://www.fda.gov/BiologicsBloodVaccines/GuidanceComplianceRegulatoryInformation/Guidances/Vaccines/ucm074827.htm2006.

[85] Luttrell WE, Jederberg WW, Still KR. Toxicology principles for the industrial hygienist. Fairfax, VA: American Industrial Hygiene Association; 2008.

[86] Detection of toxicity to reproduction for medicinal products and toxicity to male fertility. S5(R2), http://www.ich.org/fileadmin/Public_Web_Site/ICH_Products/Guidelines/Safety/S5_R2/Step4/S5_R2__Guideline.pdf1993.

[87] ICH S6 (R1). ICH guideline S6 (R1) – preclinical safety evaluation of biotechnology-derived pharmaceuticals. 2011. http://www.ema.europa.eu/docs/en_GB/document_library/Scientific_guideline/2009/09/WC500002828.pdf2011.

[88] ICH S2B. Genotoxicity: a standard battery for geno-toxicity testing of pharmaceuticals. ICH. 1997. http://www.fda.gov/downloads/Drugs/GuidanceComplianceRegulatoryInformation/Guidances/ucm074929.pdf1997.

[89] EMEA/CHMP/VEG/134716/2004. Guideline on adjuvants in vaccines for human use. 2005. http://www.ema.europa.eu/docs/en_GB/document_library/Scientific_guideline/2009/09/WC500003809.pdf2005.

[90] ICH S7. In: International Conference on Harmonization, G.S., editor. Safety pharmacology studies for human pharmaceuticals. 2000. http://www.ich.org/fileadmin/Public_Web_Site/ICH_Products/Guidelines/Safety/S7A/Step4/S7A_Guideline.pdf.

[91] Gruber MF. Nonclinical safety assessment of vaccines. MD. Bethesda: CBER Counter Terrorism Workshop; 2003.

[92] IABs. IABs scientific workshop on neurovirulence tests for live virus vaccines. January 31–February 1, 2005, Geneva. Biologicals 2006;34:233–6.

[93] WHO. Guidelines for assuring the quality and nonclinical safety evaluation of DNA vaccines. Switzerland, Geneva. 2005. http://www.who.int/biologicals/publications/trs/areas/vaccines/dna/Annex%201_DNA%20vaccines.pdf2005.

[94] CBER/FDA. Guidance for industry: considerations for plasmid DNA vaccines for infectious disease indications. CBER/FDA. 2007. http://www.fda.gov/biologicsbloodvaccines/guidancecomplianceregulatoryinformation/guidances/vaccines/ucm074770.htm.

[95] Pasteur L. Del' attenuation du virus du cholera des poules. C R Acad Sci 1880;91:673–80.

[96] Pasteur L. Methode pour prevenir la rage apres morsure. C R Acad Sci 1885;51:765–73.

[97] Adams M, Jasani B, Fiander A. Human papilloma virus (HPV) prophylactic vaccination: challenges for public health and implications for screening. Vaccine 2007;25:3007–13.

[98] Kirnbauer R, Chandrachud LM, O'Neil BW, Wagner ER, Grindlay GJ, Armstrong A, et al. Virus-like particles of bovine papillomavirus type 4 in prophylactic and therapeutic immunization. Virology 1996;219:37–44.

[99] Suzich JA, Ghim SJ, Palmer-Hill FJ, White WI, Tamura JK, Bell JA, et al. Systemic immunization with papillomavirus L1 protein completely prevents the development of viral mucosal papillomas. Proc Natl Acad Sci USA 1995;92:11553–7.

[100] Hampl M. Prevention of human papilloma virus-induced preneoplasia and cancer by prophylactic HPV vaccines. Minerva Med 2007;98:121–30.

[101] Reisinger KS, Block SL, Lazcano-Ponce E, Samakoses R, Esser MT, Erick J, et al. Safety and persistent immunogenicity of a quadrivalent human papillomavirus types 6, 11, 16, 18 L1 virus-like particle vaccine in preadolescents and adolescents: a randomized controlled trial. Pediatr Infect Dis J 2007;26:201–9.

[102] Schmidt CS, Morrow WJ, Sheikh NA. Smart adjuvants. Expert Rev Vaccines 2007;6:391–400.

[103] Lee A. Animal models and vaccine development. Baillieres Clin Gastroenterol 1995;9:615–32.

[104] Schunk MK, Macallum GE. Applications and optimization of immunization procedures. ILAR J 2005;46:241–57.

[105] Zinkernagel RM, Doherty PC. Restriction of in vitro T-cell-mediated cytotoxicity in lymphocytic choriomeningitis within a syngeneic or semiallogeneic system. Nature 1974;248:701–2.

[106] Muscoplat CC, Thoen CO, McLaughlin RM, Thoenig JR, Chen AW, Johnson DW. Comparison of lymphocyte stimulation and tuberculin skin reactivity in Mycobacterium bovis-infected Macaca mulatta. Am J Vet Res 1975;36:699–701.

[107] Hirsch VM, Lifson JD. Simian immunodeficiency virus infection of monkeys as a model system for the study of AIDS pathogenesis, treatment, and prevention. Adv Pharmacol 2000;49:437–77.

[108] Smith D, Harding G, Chan J, Edwards M, Hank J, Muller D, et al. Potency of 10 BCG vaccines as evaluated by their influence on the bacillemic phase of experimental airborne tuberculosis in guinea-pigs. J Biol Stand 1979;7:179–97.

[109] Orme IM, McMurray DN, Belisle JT. Tuberculosis vaccine development: recent progress. Trends Microbiol 2001;9:115–8.

[110] Eichelberger MC, Green MD. Animal models to assess the toxicity, immunogenicity and effectiveness of candidate influenza vaccines. Expert Opin Drug Metab Toxicol 2011;7(9):1117–27.

[111] Peiris JS, Hui KP, Yen HL. Host response to influenza virus: protection versus immunopathology. Curr Opin Immunol 2010;22:475–81.

[112] Belser JA, Wadford DA, Pappas C, Gustin KM, Maines TR, Pearce MB, et al. Pathogenesis of pandemic influenza A (H1N1) and triple-reassortant swine influenza A (H1) viruses in mice. J Virol 2010;84:4194–203.

[113] Bodewes R, Rimmelzwaan GF, Osterhaus AD. Animal models for the preclinical evaluation of candidate influenza vaccines. Expert Rev Vaccines 2010;9:59–72.

[114] Kistner O, Crowe BA, Wodal W, Kerschbaum A, Savidis-Dacho H, Sabarth N, et al. A whole virus pandemic influenza H1N1 vaccine is highly immunogenic and protective in active immunization and passive protection mouse models. PLoS One 2010;5:e9349.

[115] Zhou B, Li Y, Belser JA, Pearce MB, Schmolke M, Subba AX, et al. NS-based live attenuated H1N1 pandemic vaccines protect mice and ferrets. Vaccine 2010;28:8015–25.

[116] Narasaraju T, Sim MK, Ng HH, Phoon MC, Shanker N, Lal SK, et al. Adaptation of human influenza H3N2 virus in a mouse pneumonitis model: insights into viral virulence, tissue tropism and host pathogenesis. Microbes Infect 2009;11:2–11.

[117] Mestas J, Hughes CC. Of mice and not men: differences between mouse and human immunology. J Immunol 2004;172:2731–8.

[118] Eichelberger MC. The cotton rat as a model to study influenza pathogenesis and immunity. Viral Immunol 2007;20:243–9.

[119] Ottolini MG, Blanco JC, Eichelberger MC, Porter DD, Pletneva L, Richardson JY, et al. The cotton rat provides a useful small-animal model for the study of influenza virus pathogenesis. J Gen Virol 2005;86:2823–30.

[120] Eichelberger MC, Prince GA, Ottolini MG. Influenza-induced tachypnea is prevented in immune cotton rats, but cannot be treated with an anti-inflammatory steroid or a neuraminidase inhibitor. Virology 2004;322:300–7.

[121] Stertz S, Dittmann J, Blanco JC, Pletneva LM, Haller O, Kochs G. The antiviral potential of interferon-induced cotton rat Mx proteins against orthomyxovirus (influenza), rhabdovirus, and bunyavirus. J Interferon Cytokine Res 2007;27:847–55.

[122] Lowen AC, Mubareka S, Tumpey TM, Garcia-Sastre A, Palese P. The guinea pig as a transmission model for human influenza viruses. Proc Natl Acad Sci USA 2006;103:9988–92.

[123] Sun Y, Bi Y, Pu J, Hu Y, Wang J, Gao H, et al. Guinea pig model for evaluating the potential public health risk of swine and avian influenza viruses. PLoS One 2010;5:e15537.

[124] Phair JP, Kauffman CA, Jennings R, Potter CW. Influenza virus infection of the guinea pig: immune response and resistance. Med Microbiol Immunol 1979;165:241–54.

[125] Lowen AC, Steel J, Mubareka S, Carnero E, Garcia-Sastre A, Palese P. Blocking interhost transmission of influenza virus by vaccination in the guinea pig model. J Virol 2009;83:2803–18.

[126] Smith W, Andrewes CH, Laidlaw PP. A virus obtained from influenza patients. Lancet 1933;ii:66–8.

[127] Govorkova EA, Rehg JE, Krauss S, Yen HL, Guan Y, Peiris M, et al. Lethality to ferrets of H5N1 influenza viruses isolated from humans and poultry in 2004. J Virol 2005;79:2191–8.

[128] CDC. The 2009 H1N1 pandemic: summary highlights. CDC; 2010. http://www.cdc.gov/h1n1flu/cdcresponse.htm2010.

[129] Khatri M, Dwivedi V, Krakowka S, Manickam C, Ali A, Wang L, et al. Swine influenza H1N1 virus induces acute inflammatory immune responses in pig lungs: a potential animal model for human H1N1 influenza virus. J Virol 2010;84:11210–8.

[130] Van RK, Labarque G, De CS, Pensaert M. Efficacy of vaccination of pigs with different H1N1 swine influenza viruses using a recent challenge strain and different parameters of protection. Vaccine 2001;19:4479–86.

[131] Van RK, Van GS, Pensaert M. Correlations between lung proinflammatory cytokine levels, virus replication, and disease after swine influenza virus challenge of vaccination-immune pigs. Viral Immunol 2002;15:583–94.

[132] Itoh Y, Shinya K, Kiso M, Watanabe T, Sakoda Y, Hatta M, et al. In vitro and in vivo characterization of new swine-origin H1N1 influenza viruses. Nature 2009;460:1021–5.

[133] Haverson K, Saalmuller A, Alvarez B, Alonso F, Bailey M, Bianchi AT, et al. Overview of the third international workshop on swine leukocyte differentiation antigens. Vet Immunol Immunopathol 2001;80:5–23.

[134] Maines TR, Jayaraman A, Belser JA, Wadford DA, Pappas C, Zeng H, et al. Transmission and pathogenesis of swine-origin 2009 A(H1N1) influenza viruses in ferrets and mice. Science 2009;325:484–7.

[135] Kuiken T, Rimmelzwaan G, van Riel D, van Amerongen G, Baars M, Fouchier R, et al. Avian H5N1 influenza in cats. Science 2004;306:241.

[136] Rimmelzwaan GF, van Riel D, Baars M, Bestebroer TM, van Amerongen G, Fouchier RA, et al. Influenza A virus (H5N1) infection in cats causes systemic disease with potential novel routes of virus spread within and between hosts. Am J Pathol 2006;168:176–83.

[137] van den Brand JM, Stittelaar KJ, van Amerongen G, van de Bildt MW, Leijten LM, Kuiken T, et al. Experimental pandemic (H1N1) 2009 virus infection of cats. Emerg Infect Dis 2010;16:1745–7.

[138] Baskin CR, Garcia-Sastre A, Tumpey TM, Bielefeldt-Ohmann H, Carter VS, Nistal-Villan E, et al. Integration of clinical data, pathology, and cDNA microarrays in influenza virus-infected pigtailed macaques (Macaca nemestrina). J Virol 2004;78:10420–32.

[139] Rimmelzwaan GF, Baars M, van Beek R, van Amerongen G, Lovgren-Bengtsson K, Claas EC, et al. Induction of protective immunity against influenza virus in a macaque model: comparison of conventional and iscom vaccines. J Gen Virol 1997;78(Pt 4):757–65.

[140] Villinger F, Miller R, Mori K, Mayne AE, Bostik P, Sundstrom JB, et al. IL-15 is superior to IL-2 in the generation of long-lived antigen specific memory CD4 and CD8 T-cells in rhesus macaques. Vaccine 2004;22:3510–21.

[141] Kobasa D, Takada A, Shinya K, Hatta M, Halfmann P, Theriault S, et al. Enhanced virulence of influenza A viruses with the haemagglutinin of the 1918 pandemic virus. Nature 2004;431:703–7.

[142] Kreijtz JH, Suezer Y, de Mutsert G, van den Brand JM, van Amerongen G, Schnierle BS, et al. Recombinant modified vaccinia virus Ankara expressing the hemagglutinin gene confers protection against homologous and heterologous H5N1 influenza virus infections in macaques. J Infect Dis 2009;199:405–13.

[143] Haff RF, Schriver PW, Engle CG, Stewart RC. Pathogenesis of influenza in ferrets. I. Tissue and blood manifestations of disease. J Immunol 1966;96:659–67.

[144] Ryland LM, Gorham JR. The ferret and its diseases. J Am Vet Med Assoc 1978;173:1154–8.

[145] Hartmann K. Feline immunodeficiency virus infection: an overview. Vet J 1998;155:123–37.

[146] Frerichs GN, Gray AK. The relation between the rabbit potency test and the response of sheep to sheep clostridial vaccines. Res Vet Sci 1975;18:70–5.

[147] Mauel J, Behin R, Louis J. Leishmania enriettii: immune induction of macrophage activation in an experimental model of immunoprophylaxis in the mouse. Exp Parasitol 1981;52:331–45.

[148] Handman E. Leishmaniasis: current status of vaccine development. Clin Microbiol Rev 2001;14:229–43.

[149] Preston PM, Dumonde DC. Experimental cutaneous leishmaniasis. V. Protective immunity in subclinical and self-healing infection in the mouse. Clin Exp Immunol 1976;23:126–38.

[150] Morris L, Troutt AB, Handman E, Kelso A. Changes in the precursor frequencies of IL-4 and IFN-gamma secreting CD4+ cells correlate with resolution of lesions in murine cutaneous leishmaniasis. J Immunol 1992;149:2715–21.

[151] Morris L, Troutt AB, McLeod KS, Kelso A, Handman E, Aebischer T. Interleukin-4 but not gamma interferon production correlates with the severity of murine cutaneous leishmaniasis. Infect Immun 1993;61:3459–65.

[152] Heinzel FP, Sadick MD, Mutha SS, Locksley RM. Production of interferon gamma, interleukin 2, interleukin 4, and interleukin 10 by CD4+ lymphocytes in vivo during healing and progressive murine leishmaniasis. Proc Natl Acad Sci USA 1991;88:7011–5.

[153] Solbach W, Laskay T. The host response to Leishmania infection. Adv Immunol 2000;74:275–317.

[154] Hommel M, Jaffe CL, Travi B, Milon G. Experimental models for leishmaniasis and for testing anti-leishmanial vaccines. Ann Trop Med Parasitol 1995;89(Suppl. 1):55–73.

[155] Bradley DJ. Letter: genetic control of natural resistance to Leishmania donovani. Nature 1974;250:353–4.

[156] Mendonca SC, De Luca PM, Mayrink W, Restom TG, Conceicao-Silva F, et al. Characterization of human T lymphocyte-mediated immune responses induced by a vaccine against American tegumentary leishmaniasis. Am J Trop Med Hyg 1995;53:195–201.

[157] Moody DB, Ulrichs T, Muhlecker W, Young DC, Gurcha SS, Grant E, et al. CD1c-mediated T-cell recognition of isoprenoid glycolipids in Mycobacterium tuberculosis infection. Nature 2000;404:884–8.

[158] Igarashi T, Shibata R, Hasebe F, Ami Y, Shinohara K, Komatsu T, et al. Persistent infection with SIVmac chimeric virus having tat, rev, vpu, env and nef of HIV type 1 in macaque monkeys. AIDS Res Hum Retroviruses 1994;10:1021–9.

[159] Li J, Lord CI, Haseltine W, Letvin NL, Sodroski J. Infection of cynomolgus monkeys with a chimeric HIV-1/SIVmac virus that expresses the HIV-1 envelope glycoproteins. J Acquir Immune Defic Syndr 1992;5:639–46.

[160] Luciw PA, Pratt-Lowe E, Shaw KE, Levy JA, Cheng-Mayer C. Persistent infection of rhesus macaques with T-cell-line-tropic and macrophage-tropic clones of simian/human immunodeficiency viruses (SHIV). Proc Natl Acad Sci USA 1995;92:7490–4.

[161] Reimann KA, Li JT, Veazey R, Halloran M, Park IW, Karlsson GB, et al. A chimeric simian/human immunodeficiency virus expressing a primary patient human immunodeficiency virus type 1 isolate env causes an AIDS-like disease after in vivo passage in rhesus monkeys. J Virol 1996;70:6922–8.

[162] Stanberry LR, Kern ER, Richards JT, Abbott TM, Overall Jr JC. Genital herpes in guinea pigs: pathogenesis of the primary infection and description of recurrent disease. J Infect Dis 1982;146:397–404.

[163] Stanberry LR, Bernstein DI, Burke RL, Pachl C, Myers MG. Vaccination with recombinant herpes simplex virus glycoproteins: protection against initial and recurrent genital herpes. J Infect Dis 1987;155:914–20.

[164] Stanberry LR, Myers MG, Stephanopoulos DE, Burke RL. Preinfection prophylaxis with herpes simplex virus glycoprotein immunogens: factors influencing efficacy. J Gen Virol 1989;70(Pt 12):3177–85.

[165] Bravo FJ, Stanberry LR, Kier AB, Vogt PE, Kern ER. Evaluation of HPMPC therapy for primary and recurrent genital herpes in mice and guinea pigs. Antiviral Res 1993;21:59–72.

[166] McClements WL, Armstrong ME, Keys RD, Liu MA. Immunization with DNA vaccines encoding glycoprotein D or glycoprotein B, alone or in combination, induces protective immunity in animal models of herpes simplex virus-2 disease. Proc Natl Acad Sci USA 1996;93:11414–20.

[167] Kriesel JD, Spruance SL, Daynes RA, Araneo BA. Nucleic acid vaccine encoding gD2 protects mice from herpes simplex virus type 2 disease. J Infect Dis 1996;173:536–41.

[168] Manickan E, Rouse RJ, Yu Z, Wire WS, Rouse BT. Genetic immunization against herpes simplex virus. Protection is mediated by CD4+ T lymphocytes. J Immunol 1995;155:259–65.

[169] Manickan E, Yu Z, Rouse RJ, Wire WS, Rouse BT. Induction of protective immunity against herpes simplex virus with DNA encoding the immediate early protein ICP 27. Viral Immunol 1995;8:53–61.

[170] Bourne N, Stanberry LR, Bernstein DI, Lew D. DNA immunization against experimental genital herpes simplex virus infection. J Infect Dis 1996;173:800–7.

[171] Provost PJ, Bishop RP, Gerety RJ, Hilleman MR, McAleer WJ, Scolnick EM, et al. New findings in live, attenuated hepatitis A vaccine development. J Med Virol 1986;20:165–75.

[172] Gerdts V, Snider M, Brownlie R, Babiuk LA, Griebel PJ. Oral DNA vaccination in utero induces mucosal immunity and immune memory in the neonate. J Immunol 2002;168:1877–85.

VI. NONCLINICAL DEVELOPMENT

[173] Mutwiri G, Bateman C, Baca-Estrada ME, Snider M, Griebel P. Induction of immune responses in newborn lambs following enteric immunization with a human adenovirus vaccine vector. Vaccine 2000;19:1284–93.

[174] van Drunen Littel-van Den Hurk, Braun RP, Lewis PJ, Karvonen BC, Babiuk LA, Griebel PJ. Immunization of neonates with DNA encoding a bovine herpesvirus glycoprotein is effective in the presence of maternal antibodies. Viral Immunol 1999;12:67–77.

[175] Joseph A, Itskovitz-Cooper N, Samira S, Flasterstein O, Eliyahu H, Simberg D, et al. A new intranasal influenza vaccine based on a novel polycationic lipid-ceramide carbamoyl-spermine (CCS) I. Immunogenicity and efficacy studies in mice. Vaccine 2006;24:3990–4006.

[176] Tang Y, Akbulut H, Maynard J, Petersen L, Fang X, Zhang WW, et al. Vector prime/protein boost vaccine that overcomes defects acquired during aging and cancer. J Immunol 2006;177:5697–707.

[177] Arora S, Sharma S, Goel SK, Singh US. Effect of different adjuvants in equines for the production of equine rabies immunoglobulin. Natl Med J India 2005;18:289–92.

[178] Alcon V, Baca-Estrada M, Vega-Lopez M, Willson P, Babiuk LA, Kumar P, et al. Mucosal delivery of bacterial antigens and CpG oligonucleotides formulated in biphasic lipid vesicles in pigs. AAPS J 2005;7:E566–71.

[179] Reddy PS, Idamakanti N, Pyne C, Zakhartchouk AN, Godson DL, Papp Z, et al. The immunogenicity and efficacy of replication-defective and replication-competent bovine adenovirus-3 expressing bovine herpesvirus-1 glycoprotein gD in cattle. Vet Immunol Immunopathol 2000;76:257–68.

[180] Gerdts V, Uwiera RR, Mutwiri GK, Wilson DJ, Bowersock T, Kidane A, et al. Multiple intestinal 'loops' provide an *in vivo* model to analyse multiple mucosal immune responses. J Immunol Methods 2001;256:19–33.

[181] Mutwiri G, Bowersock T, Kidane A, Sanchez M, Gerdts V, Babiuk LA, et al. Induction of mucosal immune responses following enteric immunization with antigen delivered in alginate microspheres. Vet Immunol Immunopathol 2002;87:269–76.

[182] Institute for Safe Medication Practices. ISMP's list of error-prone abbreviations, symbols, and dose designations. 2011. http://www.ismp.org/Tools/errorproneabbreviations.pdf2011.

[183] Poland GA, Borrud A, Jacobson RM, McDermott K, Wollan PC, Brakke D, et al. Determination of deltoid fat pad thickness. Implications for needle length in adult immunization. JAMA 1997;277:1709–11.

[184] Shaw Jr FE, Guess HA, Roets JM, Mohr FE, Coleman PJ, Mandel EJ, et al. Effect of anatomic injection site, age and smoking on the immune response to hepatitis B vaccination. Vaccine 1989;7:425–30.

[185] Groswasser J, Kahn A, Bouche B, Hanquinet S, Perlmuter N, Hessel L. Needle length and injection technique for efficient intramuscular vaccine delivery in infants and children evaluated through an ultrasonographic determination of subcutaneous and muscle layer thickness. Pediatrics 1997;100:400–3.

[186] Zuckerman JN. The importance of injecting vaccines into muscle. Different patients need different needle sizes. BMJ 2000;321:1237–8.

[187] Michaels L, Poole RW. Injection granuloma of the buttock. Can Med Assoc J 1970;102:626–8.

[188] Haramati N, Lorans R, Lutwin M, Kaleya RN. Injection granulomas. Intramuscle or intrafat? Arch Fam Med 1994;3:146–8.

[189] American Academy of Pediatrics. Report of the committee on infectious diseases. Washington: AAP; 2015.

[190] Ipp MM, Gold R, Goldbach M, Maresky DC, Saunders N, Greenberg S, et al. Adverse reactions to diphtheria, tetanus, pertussis-polio vaccination at 18 months of age: effect of injection site and needle length. Pediatrics 1989;83:679–82.

[191] Greenblatt DJ, Koch-Weser J. Intramuscular injection of drugs. N Engl J Med 1976;295:542–6.

[192] Salisbury DM, Begg NT. Immunisation against infectious diseases. London: HMSO; 1996.

[193] Mayon-White R, Moreton J. Immunizing children. London: Radcliffe; 1998. p. 28.

[194] Neutra MR, Kozlowski PA. Mucosal vaccines: the promise and the challenge. Nat Rev Immunol 2006;6:148–58.

[195] Jadhav KR, Gambhire MN, Shaikh IM, Kadam VJ, Pisal SS. Nasal drug delivery systme-factore affecting and applications. Curr Drug Ther 2007;2:27–38.

[196] Johansson CJ, Olsson P, Bende M, Carlsson T, Gunnarsson PO. Absolute bioavailability of nicotine applied to different nasal regions. Eur J Clin Pharmacol 1991;41:585–8.

[197] Striebel HW, Pommerening J, Rieger A. Intranasal fentanyl titration for postoperative pain management in an unselected population. Anaesthesia 1993;48:753–7.

[198] Davis SS. Nasal vaccines. Adv Drug Deliv Rev 2001;51:21–42.

[199] Partidos CD. Delivering vaccines into the skin without needles and syringes. Expert Rev Vaccines 2003;2:753–61.

[200] NIAID.NIH, http://www.niaid.nih.gov/topics/vaccines/understanding/pages/typesvaccines.aspx2011; 2011.

[201] The College of Physicians of Philadelphia. History of vaccine. 2011. http://www.historyofvaccines.org/content/articles/different-types-vaccines2011.

[202] Wikipedia. Wikipedia-2. 2011. http://en.wikipedia.org/wiki/Vaccine2011.

[203] Nathanson N, Langmuir AD. The Cutter incident. Poliomyelitis following formaldehyde-inactivated poliovirus vaccination in the United States during the Spring of 1955. II. Relationship of poliomyelitis to Cutter vaccine. 1963. Am J Epidemiol 1995;142:109–40.

[204] Parish H. A history of immunization. Edinburgh: E.S. Livingston, Ltd; 1965.

[205] Brown F, Lewis AM. Simian virus 40 (SV40): a possible human polyomavirus, symposium proceedings. Dev Biol Stand 1998;94:1–406.

[206] Strickler HD, Rosenberg PS, Devesa SS, Hertel J, Fraumeni Jr JF, Goedert JJ. Contamination of poliovirus vaccines with simian virus 40 (1955–1963) and subsequent cancer rates. JAMA 1998;279:292–5.

[207] Meyer KF, Sawyer WA, Eaton MD, Bauer JH, Putnam P, Schwentker FF. Jaundice in Army personnel in the western region of the United States and its relation to vaccination against yellow fever. Parts II, III and IV. Am J Hyp 1944;40:35–107.

[208] Norman JE, Beebe GW, Hoofnagle JH, Seeff LB. Mortality follow-up of the 1942 epidemic of hepatitis B in the US Army. Hepatology 1993;18:790–7.

[209] Sawyer WA, Meyer KF, Eaton MD, Bauer JH, Putnam P, Schwentker FF. Jaundice in Army personnel in the western region of the United States and its relation to vaccination against yellow fever. Part Am J Hyp 1944;39:337–40.

[210] Seeff LB, Beebe GW, Hoofnagle JH, Norman JE, Buskell-Bales Z, Waggoner JG, et al. A serologic follow-up of the 1942 epidemic of post-vaccination hepatitis in the United States Army. N Engl J Med 1987;316:965–70.

[211] Morford LL, Bowman CJ, Blanset DL, Bogh IB, Chellman GJ, Halpern WG, et al. Preclinical safety evaluations supporting pediatric drug development with biopharmaceuticals: strategy, challenges, current practices. Birth Defects Res B Dev Reprod Toxicol 2011;92(4):359–80.

[212] EMA. European medicines agency (EMA), committee for human medicinal products (CHMP), guideline on the need for nonclinical testing in juvenile animals of pharmaceuticals for paediatric indications. 2008. http://www.ema.europa.eu/docs/en_GB/document_library/Scientific_guideline/2009/09/WC500003305.pdf2008.

[213] FDA. In: FDA, editor. Non clinical safety evaluation of pediatric drug products. United States Food and Drug Administration; 2006. http://www.fda.gov/ohrms/dockets/98fr/03d-0001-gdl002.pdf2006.

[214] ICH. In: International Conference on Harmonization M3(R2) guidance on nonclinical safety studies for the conduct of human clinical trials and marketing authorization for pharmaceuticals. 2009. http://www.fda.gov/RegulatoryInformation/Guidances/ucm129520.htm2009.

[215] ICH. Preclinical safety evaluation of biotechnology-derived pharmaceuticals. 1997. ICHS6 http://www.fda.gov/downloads/regulatoryinformation/guidances/ucm129171.pdf1997.

[216] Green MD. Acute phase responses to novel, investigational vaccines in toxicology studies: the relationship between C-reactive protein and other acute phase proteins. Int J Toxicol September 2015;34(5):379–83.

Overview of the Nonclinical Development Strategies and Class-Effects of Oligonucleotide-Based Therapeutics

H.S. Younis, M. Templin, L.O. Whiteley, D. Kornbrust, T.W. Kim, S.P. Henry

INTRODUCTION

Oligonucleotide-based therapeutics (ONTs) have been investigated over the last 20–30 years for the treatment of human disease, and their promise as a new drug modality is now being realized. In the last decade, the interest and investment in ONTs has been reinvigorated, given the discovery of RNA interference (RNAi) as an endogenous mechanism to regulate target mRNAs. In addition to the obvious and rational premise that ONTs can modulate mRNA transcripts by antisense mechanisms, other important mechanisms have been described that do not involve mRNA degradation. Of the two ONTs [mipomersen (Kynamro) and pegaptanib (Macugen)], that are currently commercially available for clinical use, pegaptanib works by an aptameric mechanism (binding to proteins). Approval of pegaptanib and mipomersen were granted in the

United States in 2004. However, the first approved ONT was fomivirsen (Vitravene), which was administered by intraocular injection into the vitreous, targeting mRNA transcripts associated with cytomegalovirus infection in patients with HIV [1]. Much progress has been made in the understanding of the pharmacological mechanism(s), pharmacokinetics, and clinical safety of ONTs since the discovery and approval of fomivirsen in 1998. There have been approximately 45 investigational new drug applications of modalities defined as ONTs. Moreover, over 20 clinical studies are reported to be active in the United States that utilize an ONT (Clintrials.gov).

Significant improvements in the manufacture of ONTs, such as reduced cost of goods, has made this modality commercially viable in treating human disease, accompanying small-molecule and protein therapeutics. The objective of this chapter is to provide an overview of the key chemical and mechanistic classes of ONTs, to describe the general strategies used in developing the nonclinical safety program for this relatively new class of therapeutics, and to provide a general characterization of class- and chemistry-dependent toxicity observed in species used for nonclinical safety assessment.

REVIEW OF PHARMACOLOGICAL CLASSES OF ONTs

Synthetic oligonucleotides may be utilized to capitalize on one or more mechanisms of pharmacology (Fig. 28.1). The pharmacological mechanism(s) most utilized for clinical application involve the targeting of specific RNA transcripts for cleavage and subsequent degradation. This pharmacological mechanism is referred to as an antisense mechanism of action, and may be achieved utilizing two different intracellular pathways for mRNA cleavage: Ribonuclease H (RNase H) or RNAi via a multiprotein complex known as RISC (RNA-induced silencing complex). In either case, efficacy is achieved as the copy number of target mRNAs is reduced, which leads to subsequent reduction in the level of the translated target protein. In contrast, an aptameric mechanism of action for ONTs involves the direct binding to and modulation of a target protein. The aptameric mechanism has an obvious advantage over the antisense mechanism in terms of potential onset of action, since it directly modulates the ultimate target of interest (ie, protein), which affords potential for agonist properties. However, the pharmacological stoichiometry of directly targeting a protein may not be as efficient as targeting the message (mRNA). Other mechanisms that have been described include modulation of pre-mRNA splicing,

inhibition of mRNA translation, exon skipping, and modulation of microRNA (miRNA), but, to date, there is limited clinical experience with these approaches. The following provides a brief overview of the antisense and aptameric mechanisms, since most ONTs in clinical development have been designed to employ one of these mechanisms.

Antisense Mechanism of Action Mediated by RNase H

RNase H enzymes are ubiquitously expressed and hydrolyze RNA in an RNA/DNA duplex [2]. The function and endogenous substrates of RNase H enzymes have yet to be determined; however, they are believed to play a role in repair processes in cases where RNA/DNA duplexes are generated during DNA replication [3]. The exquisite specificity by which RNase H recognizes RNA:DNA duplexes afforded the discovery and utility of this mechanism to perform antisense pharmacology, as first described by Zamecnik and Stephenson [4] targeting the Rous sarcoma virus 35S RNA. In this approach, a synthetic DNA-like oligonucleotide with a complementary (ie, antisense) sequence to the RNA target binds via Watson–Crick base-pairing principles. The RNA/DNA duplex may be engaged by RNase H and subsequently results in the cleavage of the mRNA strand, while the DNA-like oligonucleotide (antisense oligonucleotide (ASO)) is released and available to bind to subsequent target RNAs. The subsequent processing and fate of the cleaved RNA strands is not well understood. Nonetheless, RNase H-mediated cleavage leads to up to ≥90% reduction of full-length mRNAs, which subsequently results in reduced protein levels.

Although the precise sequence specificity for cleavage by RNase H has yet to be determined, the biochemical properties of RNase H-mediated recognition and cleavage are well described [3]. The specific RNase H that is responsible for antisense-mediated cleavage of target RNAs is reported to be RNase H1 for the ASO class of ONTs [5]. Moreover, RNase H1 has been localized to the nucleus and cytoplasm and may be active in both compartments [2]. Therefore synthetic DNA-like ASOs may be designed to either intronic or exonic regions of pre-mRNAs and exonic regions of processed mRNAs (Fig. 28.1).

There currently exist more than 25 ASOs in clinical development, in multiple therapeutic areas, for the treatment of cardiovascular, metabolic, ocular, and oncogenic diseases, among others. The most advance molecules have demonstrated proof of mechanism (ie, target modulation) and therapeutic efficacy. For example, mipomersen (IONIS Pharmaceuticals), designed to target the Apob mRNA, has demonstrated significant reductions in Apob protein that translate

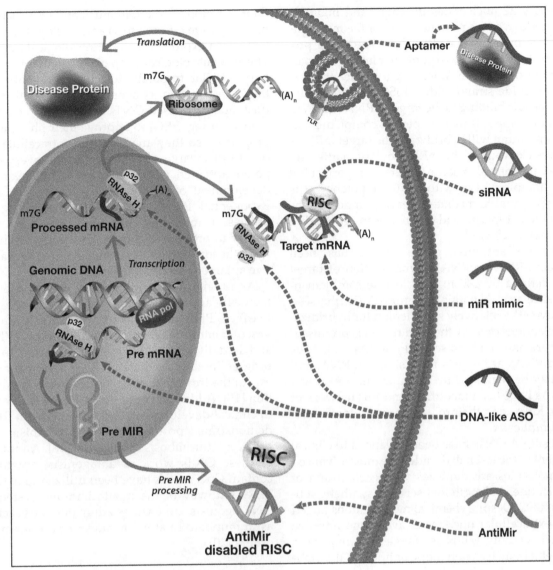

FIGURE 28.1 Pathways of pharmacological action for oligonucleotide-based therapeutics.

to marked reductions in LDL in patients with familial hypercholesterolemia [6]. Mipomersen was filed for regulatory approval in 2011 and approved in the United States as the first systemically acting antisense ONT. Additional drugs have demonstrated positive Phase II proof of mechanism and/or efficacy for the treatment of metabolic disease (IONIS 113715, IONIS Pharmaceuticals [8]), and thrombosis (IONIS FXIrx, IONIS Pharmacetuticals [9]).

Antisense Mechanism of Action Mediated by RNA Interference

An endogenous antisense pathway to regulate mRNA was first described in plants [10]. A decade later,

this process was termed RNA interference (RNAi) in a hallmark paper by Fire et al. [11] that described the use of double-stranded RNAs to function as gene silencers in mammalian systems. The molecular biology and processing of RNAi is well conserved throughout evolution and has been well studied in multiple organisms. Comprehensive reviews of RNAi are available elsewhere [12–14]. In brief, this regulatory pathway involves the formation of noncoding RNA (pri-miRNA) via RNA polymerase II. The pri-miRNAs are substrates for the endonuclease Drosha in the nucleus leading to the formation of shorter pre-miRNAs that get actively exported to the cytoplasm. These exported pre-miRNAs are processed by Dicer in the cytoplasm, creating double-stranded small interfering (si)RNAs that are approximately 22 nucleotides in length and maintain two nucleotide overhangs in the 3' end of the molecule. The siRNA is then associated with an argonaute protein within the RISC [15]. Argonaute cleaves the passenger strand of the siRNA, leaving a single-stranded antisense or guide strand within RISC that allows for sequence specific binding to the target mRNAs via Watson–Crick principles. If there is perfect complementarity, the guide strand will hybridize to the target mRNAs and triggers cleavage of the mRNA by argonaute proteins. Cleavage may also occur if there is imperfect but sufficient homology, but with reduced potency. The presence of argonaute-mediated cleavage appears to be limited to the cytoplasm and has not been reported in the nucleus (Fig. 28.1).

The mature antisense guide strand has been termed micro-RNA (miRNA). Hybridization of target mRNA is defined by a 2- to 8-nucleotide complementary sequence stretch within the miRNA (ie, the seed region). Given the relatively short length for hybridization (8 nucleotides or less), the seed region is promiscuous in nature and binds to several mRNAs [16]. Thus multiple mRNAs are targets for a single miRNA, and mRNAs may be regulated by multiple miRNAs. Over 100 miRNAs have been identified, and this network of noncoding RNAs and their role in transcriptional regulation is complicated.

Several siRNA ONTs have been advanced to clinical development in the last half decade. The most advanced of these molecules are duplexes with each strand of 20–22 nucleotides in length that serve as synthetic substrates for RISC. Despite chemical modifications aimed to reduce extracellular nuclease cleavage and improve intracellular activity, siRNAs frequently require a delivery vehicle such as polymeric or liposomal formulations for systemic delivery and efficacy. However, the most advanced siRNAs in the clinic are unformulated ONTs for local delivery. For example, intravitreal injection or inhalation routes of delivery have been used for the treatment of ocular disease or respiratory simian virus, in the eye or lung, respectively [15]. Significant progress in the development of novel formulations for systemic delivery of siRNA ONTs has recently afforded the use of such molecules for systemic applications [17]. To date, there are over 15 siRNA ONTs in clinical development for the treatment of ocular disease, cancer, kidney disorders, and antiviral or cardiovascular indications [15].

Pharmacology Mediated by Aptamer Interactions With Proteins

The complex three-dimensional structure afforded by an oligonucleotide sequence can be used to selectively and specifically bind to proteins to modulate their function. These oligonucleotide physicochemical properties are referred to as aptameric interactions, and have been exploited for pharmacological intervention. The pharmacological properties of aptamer ONTs are fairly similar to small-molecule therapeutics, in that they can function as agonists or antagonists. In contrast, aptamer-based ONTs are typically conjugated to a polymer (eg, PEG) to improve their pharmacokinetic properties, so they are devoid of intracellular activity due to their large size/mass. The discovery of highly potent aptamers was accelerated and pioneered by the development of Systematic Evolution of Ligands by Exponential Enrichment (SELEX) technology, which utilizes a reiterative high-throughput nucleic acid library to produce highly potent (target-binding affinity in the low nanomolar to picomolar range) and selective aptamer-based ONTs [18].

As previously mentioned, the first and only commercially approved aptamer is Macugen (pegaptanib, EyeTech/Pfizer Inc.). Macugen selectively scavenges a vascular endothelial growth factor protein (VEGF-165) and is delivered by intravitreal injection to prevent progression and mediate reversal of retinal angiogenesis in the treatment of age-related macular degeneration [19]. Additional aptamer ONTs [8] have advanced to clinical development, and one of which, REG1, has demonstrated positive proof of mechanism and efficacy for a thrombosis application [18]. Although most of these ONTs work as antagonists, aptamers that contain CpG motifs have been utilized to activate the TLR9 pathway of the innate immune system. These ONT agonists are used as adjuvants for vaccines and as immunomodulators in cancer or autoimmune disorders [20].

Overview of Common Chemical Structure Activity Relationships and Pharmacokinetic Properties

In general, DNA- or RNA-based ONTs that contain no chemical modifications (ie, native) have poor drug-like properties. For example, DNA or RNA are excellent substrates for nucleases, which are ubiquitously present in extracellular and intracellular milieu. In addition, ONTs with a natural phosphodiester backbone possess little or no potential for binding to blood proteins (eg, albumin), which results in very rapid elimination from the blood compartment by glomerular filtration. Collectively, this leads to extensive and rapid degradation and excretion of synthetic unmodified DNA or RNA, and results in very short half-lives (<5 min) in plasma. This severely impairs their distribution and/or residence in target tissues [21]. Therefore chemical modifications are required to impart drug-like properties to DNA and/or RNA, especially those intended for systemic delivery.

A breakthrough in the chemical design of ONTs was the incorporation of the phosphorothioate (PS) moiety that involves the replacement of one of the unbridged oxygen atoms of the phosphate backbone with sulfur. The addition of PS into the backbone of an ONT confers increased resistance to nuclease-mediated cleavage and degradation [22]. Phosphorothioate modifications also render the molecules to be more polyanionic, thus increasing their affinity to plasma proteins and ultimately increasing the plasma half-life. The full-length PS modification of the backbone led to the advancement of several ASOs into clinical development. This chemistry is referred to as the "first generation" of ASOs, and has provided validation of the antisense mechanism in animals and humans. Further improvements were made to the PS first-generation chemistry with the addition of a wide variety of other chemical modifications that conferred increased stability and/or more desirable pharmacokinetics. Many of these modifications were imparted to the ribose moiety of the individual nucleotides. One particularly effective modification of this type is the introduction of a 2′-O-methoxyethyl (MOE) moiety on the ribose. The addition of MOE to an ONT that contains a PS backbone improves hybridization binding affinity to mRNA targets and further confers protection against nuclease-mediated degradation, relative to first-generation PS ASOs [23,24]. The "second-generation" MOE chemistry is often placed on the outermost nucleotides (1–5) at the 5′ and 3′ ends (ie, "wings"), while the innermost nucleotides (referred to as the "gap") remain as unmodified DNA [25,26]. This configuration enables efficient antisense activity through RNase H to bind and cleave the target mRNA through the DNA "gap," since the MOE chemistry placed in the "gap" of an ONT hinders the engagement of RNase H to the resulting oligonucleotide:mRNA duplex. More recently, ribose modifications that incorporate bicyclic configurations such as cET or LNA chemistries confer greater hybridization affinity than that of MOE ASOs. The utility of these chemistries appears to translate to 5- to 10-fold greater in vivo potency in animals [27,28].

siRNA and aptamer ONTs also selectively incorporate chemical modifications such as PS and/or 2′-O-methyl to reduce susceptibility to nucleases. Other chemistries employed in antisense inhibitors include the morpholino class of ONTs, where the ribose/phosphate backbone of an oligonucleotide is replaced by a neutral hexamer. In general, the morpholino class of ONTs has similar hybridization affinity, and these molecules have reduced bioavailability following systemic delivery when compared to MOE-containing ASOs [29]. The morpholino chemistry does not support RNase H or RNAi antisense mechanisms [30], so, to date, their application has been limited as modulators of pre-mRNA splicing and translational arrest [31]. A comprehensive review of the chemical structure–activity relationships for such chemical modifications, among others, is given elsewhere [32].

The physical–chemical properties of ONTs define their in vivo pharmacokinetic properties. In contrast to small- and large-molecule drugs, ONTs within a chemical class demonstrate similar pharmacokinetics, which are predictable across several nonclinical species and humans [33]. The translation of nonclinical pharmacokinetics from rodents, dogs, and nonhuman primates to humans is most consistently based on mg/kg dosing for RNA- and DNA-like ONTs. In general, the oral bioavailability of ONT is typically very low (>1% for naked and 5–15% for formulated ONTs, respectively) due to their large size (6000–15,000 MW), structure and hydrophilic nature. Thus parenteral routes of delivery are required for efficient exposure to target disease tissues. The ASO class of ONTs is often formulated in a simple aqueous buffer for intravenous infusion or subcutaneous injection. Systemically delivered siRNA ONTs are typically administered by intravenous infusion, particularly since most of them are prepared as liposomal or other nanoparticle formulations. The utility of chemical modifications that confer improved pharmacokinetic properties for ASOs are more limited for siRNAs, since some do not support RISC loading and activity with a modified guide strand [34]. Therefore the siRNA class of ONTs requires more complex formulation relative to the ASO class because of their greater susceptibility to metabolism by nucleases. Thus the delivery formulation is the dominant factor in the pharmacokinetics of formulated ONTs such as siRNA.

As described above, first- and second-generation ASO ONTs have much improved drug-like pharmacokinetic properties, compared to native DNA. The improved binding of PS and MOE ASOs to plasma proteins allows for systemic distribution to key organs, such as the liver, kidney, spleen, lymphoid tissues, adipose, and bone, among others. Although the plasma half-life of such ASOs is shorter than that of many small molecules (<1 h), the half-life in tissues such as the liver and kidney is relatively long (eg, 14–30 days for an MOE ASO). Thus once therapeutic concentrations are reached in tissue the frequency of maintenance therapy may range from once weekly to once monthly. Similarly, the potential for relatively prolonged pharmacodynamic effects of siRNA ONTs coupled with long tissue half-life may also allow weekly to monthly dosing regimens for these therapeutics. The loading and maintenance dosing intervals for ONTs also depend on the amount of mRNA target reduction and protein required for the desired therapeutic response, as well as the turnover of the target mRNA and protein.

GENERAL STRATEGY FOR TOXICOLOGY TESTING OF ONTs

A fundamental objective for nonclinical toxicity evaluation is to understand the potential adverse effects of the ONT candidate to support clinical development. In addition to the common considerations of the design of general toxicology studies, eg, selection of relevant rodent and nonrodent species, route of delivery, and dose levels/exposure profile, special consideration for ONTs include the assessment of exaggerated pharmacology and potential use of surrogate molecules specific to the selected toxicology species. Genetic toxicology, safety pharmacology, immunotoxicology, reproductive toxicology, and carcinogenicity studies may also be required for ONTs, as appropriate for the indication(s) being pursued.

Regulatory Considerations

The design of a toxicology program often starts with consideration of the regulatory guidelines for the class of the drug candidate being pursued. At present, there are no guidelines specific to ONTs, so the toxicologist must consider guidelines that are in effect for other classes of drugs. For example, ICH guidelines for safety assessment, eg, ICH M3 "Guidance on Nonclinical Safety Studies for the Conduct of Human Clinical Trials and Marketing Authorization for Pharmaceuticals," provide a framework for a staged-development toxicology program for an ONT. However, it is the responsibility of the toxicologist to determine what portions of the guidelines are appropriate and relevant for each program, given the diverse chemical and pharmacological spectrum for ONT drug candidates, as previously discussed. Moreover, conjugation or formulation of ONTs with polymers (eg, polyethylene glycol), lipids (eg, cholesterol or fatty acids), proteins, or other unique chemical structures employed to improve delivery to the intended organs and tissues and also contributes to their diversity.

In general, the regulatory experience for ONTs has aligned most closely with that of small molecules. Oligonucleotide-based therapeutics are, almost exclusively, produced by chemical synthesis, and the chemistry and manufacturing processes are familiar to regulatory chemists that work with small molecules; moreover, toxicology testing strategies are often tightly linked with the chemistry and manufacturing for a novel drug candidate. However, other features of ONTs may be more akin to biologics, eg, antibodies or therapeutic proteins, given that both modalities afford high specificity for a single target and may have limitations with regard to cross-species activity

in nonclinical species. As such, the regulation of ONTs may be approached as a small-molecule paradigm with additional considerations applied to biologics.

Selection of Species and Study Design of General Toxicity Studies

Mice and rats have been employed as the rodent species for the toxicity testing of ONTs, and the basis for selection appears to be company- and program-dependent. The mouse has commonly been used in the evaluation of pharmacology, particularly for those subclasses of ONTs that target mRNA levels or function, eg, ASO or siRNA. However, data essential to the toxicology evaluation can be readily obtained in rat, and thus, species selection is program-specific. Furthermore, for those ONTs targeting mRNA expression, relevant pharmacological activity is dependent on the degree of sequence homology between the ONT and the target mRNA across species. The level of homology between rodents and humans, or rodents and nonhuman primates (NHPs), is often poor. Therefore a rodent-active surrogate may need to be identified to enable pharmacology studies in a rodent species. The rodent surrogate ONT can then be used to address the potential adverse effects of exaggerated pharmacological activity by inclusion in the toxicity study for the human-active ONT as a separate treatment group.

The primary nonrodent species for safety assessment of ONTs has been the NHP, typically a macaque species such as the cynomolgus monkey. For those programs targeting mRNA, the phylogenic closeness to humans often results in a high degree or complete sequence homology to a target mRNA between NHPs and humans. This has allowed for assessment of exaggerated pharmacology in the general toxicity study of the clinical candidate in NHPs. However, it should be noted that even single base mismatches can significantly reduce or eliminate activity for those ONTs that rely on hybridization for mechanism of action, and even 100% homology does not guarantee activity in animal species. Thus some demonstration of pharmacological activity (either in vitro or in vivo) in the species chosen for the nonclinical program may be warranted.

The use of a surrogate raises several issues, including, but not limited to, synthesis of a sufficient quantity to support the toxicity study, increased cost of such a study, and other concerns relating to the relevance and/or risk of generating toxicity data with a sequence that is not the clinical candidate. Therefore the toxicologist should approach the use of a surrogate with careful consideration. For some programs, it may be appropriate to select lead candidates, in part based on robust cross-species activity, thereby obviating the need for a surrogate. There is currently no general agreement or regulatory guidance as to whether exaggerated pharmacology should be addressed in one or two species; nonetheless, there have not been any reported examples of dose-limiting toxicity due to exaggerated pharmacological activity for an ONT. Thus exaggerated pharmacology should be sufficiently addressed in at least one pharmacologically responsive species. The NHP may be the preferred species, assuming complete or sufficient sequence homology for pharmacology to occur. However, an alternative species (eg, rodent) in which there is an available and appropriate surrogate, or sequence homology that has translated into demonstrable pharmacology, can and should also be considered, especially when assessing the role of target modulation in reproductive or carcinogenicity studies.

In the early days of ONT development, the high cost of manufacturing favored use of NHP due to their lower body weight relative to the dog (~2.4 vs. ~8–10 kg). It was soon recognized that PS ASOs induced a number of effects such as complement activation in NHPs, which raised concern about their clinical safety [35]. These observations are reviewed in subsequent sections and are considered nonspecific class effects. Of note, these observations have set a strong preference for using NHP for ONTs, as a whole. The pharmacokinetic properties and sensitivity to proinflammatory effects in NHPs, for the most part, appear also to appropriately reflect the response in humans. Furthermore, the focus on the use of NHPs for toxicity testing has been the subject of regulatory-based review articles [36,37] that reinforce the expectation to employ an NHP species for nearly all ONT programs. To some extent, it was assumed that the similarity of NHPs to humans implied a high degree of relevance about the findings to human safety, although this relationship remains a topic for continuing evaluation.

Alternative nonrodent species, such as dog, rabbit, and mini-pig, have been used for specific indications or routes of administration, such as dermal applications (mini-pig and rabbit) or intraocular injection (rabbit and dog). Thus based on the specific properties of the drug candidate, a species other than NHP may be relevant and/or more practical for general toxicity evaluation, assuming ample documentation of pharmacological activity for the selected nonrodent species. However, as noted above, even if the ONT has robust cross-species activity to assess general toxicology and exaggerated pharmacology, some testing in NHPs may be expected by regulatory authorities based on the potential for complement activation. It should be recognized that complement activation does not occur in rodents and has not been well documented in other nonrodent species. Thus one approach to address this is to independently investigate the potential for complement activation in NHPs, eg, as part of a dose-escalation safety pharmacology study. Nevertheless, while the NHP is a species that is sensitive for this effect, the overall objective of the toxicology program should be a broad-reaching evaluation, and bias toward a specific endpoint may not be warranted. If the NHP is not selected as a species for evaluation, it is prudent to review the rationale for the plan with regulatory agencies.

As with all toxicology studies, characterization of a no-effect level (NOEL) or no-adverse-effect level (NOAEL) is a desirable outcome in order to determine the margin of safety relative to the intended clinical starting dose level and the intended clinical dose range. As the NOAELs become defined, the most appropriate means of scaling doses of ONTs from animals to humans is a topic of debate. Since the pharmacokinetic properties of several ONT subclasses have been reported to be similar across species, including humans [38–40], standard allometric scaling of converting body weight-based doses (ie, mg/kg) to calculate a human-equivalent dose (HED) may be more applicable than body surface area (ie, mg/m^2). This subject has been raised, in part, by the US FDA in the "Guidance for Industry – Estimating the Maximum Safe Starting Dose in Initial Clinical Trials for Therapeutics in Adult Healthy Volunteers" (July 2005), which outlined circumstances where the dose in mg/kg may be appropriate for scaling animal NOAELs to an HED. For the MOE ASO class of ONTs, scaling of animal exposure to humans was determined to be most predictive using body weight-based dosing from the monkey or mouse based on evaluation of up to nine molecules where preclinical and clinical pharmacokinetics data were available [41]. Given the complexity and importance of this subject, early consideration of the doses to be evaluated and the intended cross-species comparisons is warranted, and discussions with regulatory agencies on the most appropriate determination of an HED should be considered.

In regard to metabolism, natural nucleotides are considered to be readily processed by various scavenging pathways and are unlikely to form reactive intermediates or disrupt natural nucleotide pools and recycling pathways [42,43]. Certain chemical modifications, such as PS, 2′-O-methyl, and MOE chemistry, have been investigated for their potential to generate toxic metabolites. The results suggest that toxic metabolites are not produced from these chemical modifications. While this may justify minimal characterization of metabolism for some ONTs, novel or less well-characterized chemistries may necessitate more extensive investigation of metabolism, and the ultimate fate of the ONT should be evaluated in the nonclinical program.

The above points for consideration are fundamental to a toxicology program across multiple classes of drug candidates and not just for ONTs. Hence, proper safety assessment of an ONT should include general assessments common for toxicology studies, along with specific types of endpoints to evaluate potential toxicities that have been observed for the various ONT subclasses, as will be reviewed in subsequent sections. Monitoring for such effects is important in the nonclinical program for existing (eg, PS, MOE, LNA, etc.) and novel chemistries, and possibly for other pharmacological subclasses of ONTs. Nevertheless, each sequence, chemical modification, and delivery formulation has its own spectrum of effects, and the toxicology program should be tailored to characterize potential toxicity of the candidate ONT on an individual basis.

Safety Pharmacology, Genetic and Special Toxicity Studies

Safety Pharmacology Assessment

Assessment of safety pharmacology is typically required for ONTs, and may be evaluated in dedicated studies or as part of the general toxicity studies using standard study designs. The class of ONTs most studied has been the DNA-like ASO molecules (first- and second-generation chemistry). In general, there have been no reported direct effects on respiratory, neurological, or cardiovascular function [44]. However, cardiovascular effects that are secondary to complement activation have been observed with PS ASOs (described in subsequent sections). For cardiovascular risk assessment, the in vitro hERG assay has also been performed for several (>10) ASO molecules, and no clinically relevant inhibition of this ion channel has been observed (ie, IC50 values are typically >100 μM). Therefore the hERG assay is not performed for ASOs, rather a cardiovascular assessment in NHPs, or other relevant species, may be more appropriate [45]. In addition to the telemetry-enabled cardiovascular endpoints for evaluation in NHPs, it is possible to include a basic evaluation of respiratory function (eg, respiration rate and blood gas measurements), as well as a basic evaluation of neurological function to evaluate possible effects on these organ systems and satisfy regulatory requirements. The intensity of such evaluations in a single study with tele-metered animals must be tempered by the objective of minimizing handling stress, as this may confound the blood pressure and heart rate measurements. However, if properly designed, this type of study may serve as a relatively broad safety pharmacology evaluation to support clinical trials.

A conventional strategy of conducting separate neurotoxicity and respiratory function studies in rodents may be conducted. Evaluation of >10 ASOs (PS and MOE chemistries) in such studies has not identified class-dependent effects on neurobehavioral or respiratory function, or on cardiovascular parameters (excluding changes observed secondary to complement activation) [45]. Renal function/urinary system effects are not routinely investigated in dedicated studies, and can usually be sufficiently addressed by routine serum chemistry and urinalysis in the repeat-dose general toxicity studies, which may be supplemented with specialized parameters that reflect renal function.

Immunotoxicology Testing

Immunotoxicology studies are not commonly evaluated for most ONT programs. However, special endpoints to assess the immune system may be considered for the subclass of ONTs that are designed to have a direct action on the immune system (eg, CpG immunostimulatory ONTs). However, it is well recognized that many ONTs have the potential to interact with the innate immune system to produce low grade proinflammation, and this is discussed in the section on class effects. Proinflammation is most prominent in rodents and typically includes lymphoid hyperplasia in the spleen and lymph nodes and mononuclear cell infiltration in tissues. These manifestations of proinflammation are identified in the standard histopathology evaluation so no specialized tests are warranted. In addition, because of the species differences in the proinflammatory response, ie, the reduced responses in NHPs relative to rodents, these effects in rodents are generally not regarded as toxicities that are directly relevant for human safety assessment.

Genetic Toxicity Testing

The basis of pharmacological activity for most ONTs is an interaction with mRNA, based on Watson–Crick base pairing, and little, if any, effects on the genome (ie, DNA) are anticipated. For other subclasses of ONTs, such as aptamers, there is no intended interaction with nucleic acids. Therefore ONTs are distinct from gene therapy since they do not incorporate into the genome, and no relevant interactions with DNA have been observed. In addition, the nuclease-mediated metabolism of ONTs is unlikely to generate reactive intermediates that can directly damage DNA or RNA. The EMA has published a position paper on genetic toxicity testing of ONTs, ie, the "CHMP SWP Reflection Paper on the Assessment of the Genotoxic Potential of Antisense Oligodeoxynucleotides" that concluded:

phosphorothioate nucleotides (as potential degradation products/metabolites from the PS oligodeoxynucleotides) are unlikely to pose a genotoxic hazard via incorporation into newly synthesized DNA.

While this generally supports the view that such testing may not be warranted for PS ASOs, this specific position is not likely to be universal across ONTs. The US FDA has yet to comment on their position regarding genetic toxicity testing of ONTs.

PS ASOs have been the most extensively studied class for genetic toxicity, and the results to date have been negative. Nevertheless, genetic toxicity testing must be considered in the nonclinical program, and will likely be required for the foreseeable future. For ONTs that contain well-studied chemistries that have been negative for genetic toxicity, a possible strategy may be to only perform in vivo genetic toxicity testing, rather than the full standard battery. However, that approach should be negotiated with regulatory agencies prior to submission of the nonclinical data package. Oligonucleotide-based therapeutics that contain novel chemistries and/or structures should be considered as unknowns with respect to their potential to cause genetic toxicity, and the standard battery of tests (eg, bacterial mutagenicity assay (Ames test); in vitro chromosomal aberration test with Chinese hamster ovary cells or human lymphocytes; and in vivo micronucleus assay in mouse or rat) should be performed.

The timing of the genetic toxicity studies is at the discretion of the toxicologist and depends on the status of the program. One approach for the micronucleus assay is incorporation into a repeat-dose toxicity study in mice or rats. For this, consideration must be given to the recommendations for testing a maximum tolerated dose. Furthermore, it is not uncommon to conduct this test with an animal-active surrogate, either as part of the general toxicity study or in a dedicated micronucleus study (along with the human active candidate). Although positive responses are unlikely, in the event that this does occur, it would be expected to expand the battery with other tests (eg, a mouse lymphoma assay), as is done with other drug candidates, to enable a weight of the evidence approach to judging whether the specific ONT has true genotoxic potential.

Reproductive Toxicity and Carcinogenicity Testing

Reproductive toxicity and carcinogenicity studies are best approached on a case-by-case basis. The objectives and design of reproductive toxicity studies for ONTs are not different from small-molecules drugs. It is important to mention that little, if any, exposure to reproductive or fetal tissue has been observed for ONTs such as DNA-like ASOs [46], and studies have been uniformly negative for this subclass [47,48]. When appropriate and the need has been determined, the timing of conducting these studies relative to the clinical program is dependent on the level of concern and the intended patient population. A full evaluation may require a species-specific surrogate if the ONT candidate is not active in the species being used for evaluation of reproductive toxicity. This comes with the caveats already discussed for the use of species-specific surrogates. Key considerations and study design characteristics in the conduct of fertility and embryo/fetal development studies for ONTs and strategies for testing pharmacology-dependent effects are the subject of a recent white paper article [49].

The appropriateness of carcinogenicity studies is also dependent on the intended use in patients and generally conforms to the considerations for other types of drug candidates, such as small molecules.

DISCOVERY TOXICOLOGY OF ONTs

The drug discovery process for ONTs may be considered more efficient relative to small-molecule therapeutics with regard to the identification of the lead human clinical drug candidate. This is especially true for the antisense class of ONTs (ASO and siRNA) since the target receptor (ie, mRNA) of interest is often well annotated given the advances in sequencing of the human transcriptome and relevant animal species (rodents and NHPs). Thus the in silico design of thousands of ONT molecules may be achieved in a few days for any given mRNA target. Since the chemical synthesis of most classes of ONTs is well established, hundreds to thousands of molecules may be produced in milligram quantities using automated methods for in vitro pharmacology screening in several weeks. Thus 10 to 100 ONT drugs are often discovered with picomolar to low micromolar IC50s to human mRNA targets in vitro within weeks to months of target sanction. As mentioned previously, classes of ONTs advanced to human testing, to date, have been negative in the standard genetic toxicity and safety pharmacology studies. Thus in vitro screening for genetic toxicity or hERG in the discovery phase is unproductive for this class of ONTs. However, in vitro screening of ASO or siRNA type ONTs for proinflammatory effects in human whole blood or a peripheral blood mononuclear cell fraction has been described to be beneficial in selecting molecules devoid of proinflammatory properties in humans [50]. In this regard, avoiding known sequence motifs (eg, CpG motifs and G-quartets) that would contribute to certain inflammatory effects is also important in selecting the most well-tolerated compound. As a whole, the toxicity-testing cascade for these ONTs (typically <50 to 100 drug candidates) primarily involves sequential in vivo toleration assessment in rodents and NHPs, since standard in vitro assays of toxicity are not typically predictive or relevant for ONTs. Although the potential for hybridization to off-target mRNA transcripts is considered early in the in silico design and selection of ONTs for in vitro pharmacology screening, a more thorough evaluation of the relevance of off-target hits should be considered at this later stage of drug discovery. Strategies for consideration in evaluating off-target hits and in vivo toleration screening are reviewed by Lindow et al. [51] and briefly discussed below.

Homology/Hybridization-Dependent Off-Target Effects

Like small-molecule therapeutics, the assessment of off-target effects should be incorporated into the evaluation and selection of ONTs during early stages of candidate selection. Since ASO and siRNA ONTs bind to their mRNA targets via Watson–Crick base-pairing, in silico methods can be reliably used to identify unintended off-targets based on their homologies in humans and nonclinical species. The assessment of homology-dependent off-target effects for single-stranded ASO and double-stranded siRNA ONTs should include an understanding of the molecular mechanism of how these molecules inhibit mRNA translation, the temporal expression and tissue distribution of the homologous off-target RNA during embryo/fetal development, the tissue distribution and concentration of the ONT, the relative inhibitory potency between the intended (on-) target and off-target, and the potential for the biology of the off-target to elicit an adverse effect [4,11,12,52]. While efforts should be made to minimize off-target homologies, it is unlikely and not necessary that a sequence be designed that is completely free of some degree of homology to unintended targets. However, sequences with perfect homology to unintended targets should be avoided. To date, homology to unintended targets has not been recognized as a development-limiting issue during the nonclinical or clinical development of ONTs. Nevertheless, this area should be given careful consideration during early and late drug development activities.

In general, some level of in silico assessment of off-target homology should be conducted during the early selection process at about the same time that in vitro screening of on-target potency is being performed. Once potent on-target ASO or siRNA sequences are identified in vitro, the degree of off-target homology should be factored into the selection of the lead drug candidates for further in vivo and in vitro characterization. No single database can be recommended as the source for searching for homology between ONT and off-target mRNA sequences; hence, a robust approach is to use multiple databases. When choosing

the in silico search algorithm one should not use heuristics that will inappropriately miss potential homology off-target hits (eg, using BLAST with too long of a word-size setting). The algorithms and methods available for in silico prediction are also under continuous development, and care should be taken to identify and use the current best practices. The way the search is conducted also plays a significant role in its utility. Complete homology with a sequence that lies within the exon for a ubiquitously expressed gene would be of the highest concern, but this circumstance is rare. Screening for a lesser degree of homology is common practice, but there are no general rules or guidance about the degree of homology that renders a candidate of concern or of no concern, ie, setting a stringent set point (eg, >90% homology) of where to draw the line on the number of mismatches.

The mechanism of action of ONTs also plays an important factor in the relevance of off-target homology. The specific number and location of mismatches that RNase H can tolerate and still result in RNA degradation for the ASO class of ONTs is not fully known [2,32]. Nonetheless, it is influenced by the nucleotide chemistry, the length of the ONT, and the intracellular concentration. For siRNAs, mRNA inhibition may be mediated by either a transcriptional repression miRNA-like effect on mRNAs with as few as 7 nucleotide matches to the seed-region of the siRNA (nucleotide 2–8 from the 5′-end of the antisense strand) or when there is complete homology of the siRNA sequence by direct cleavage of the mRNA at position 9–10 of the antisense guide strand [16,53]. Thus the number of perfect nucleotide matches required to elicit an off-target effect may be dependent on the pharmacological mechanism. Consequently, in silico searches and hits should be defined based on the most recent understanding of mismatch tolerance for each mechanism, as well as the effects of the position of the mismatch(es). The exact locations of the off-target "hits" (ie, homologous sequences) resulting from the genome search is critical information in determining the potential implications of those hits, as a large percentage may lie within introns, gene spacer regions, or other areas that are not transcribed. For siRNA ONTs, homologies that fall within introns of a premRNA may not be relevant since siRNA activity appears to be limited to the cytoplasm.

Once potential off-target matches are identified in silico, it is important to assess the propensity of the ONT to modulate those off-targets and potential for producing adverse effects. The first step in this assessment is an understanding of the cellular distribution of the off-target relative to the on-target activity of the ONT. If there is little or no distribution of the ONT to the cells expressing the off-target, then concern for adverse effects is minimized. If there is the potential for the drug to distribute to a cell type expressing the off-target, then an in vitro assessment of the relative potency of the inhibition of on- vs. off-target inhibition should be performed. This assessment should preferably be done in a cell (primary or cell-line) that expresses the intended mRNA target and the off-target to determine if an appropriate therapeutic index exists. In addition to this in vitro work, a literature review should be conducted to understand the biology of the off-target and physiological effects that its reduction may elicit. Additional considerations include the temporal expression of the potential off-target gene (eg, neonatal, juvenile, adult), the potential for short- or long-term inhibition, the expected phenotype of the off-target event, should it occur, and the risk vs. benefit of modulating the off-target. In addition to assessing the potential for off-target homology in humans, an assessment of off-target homology should also be made in the species that will be used for the nonclinical safety evaluation. The ideal situation is when the human off-target homology also exists in at least one of the nonclinical species that are used in the regulatory toxicology studies. In the event that the homology to an off-target is only present in humans, a risk assessment should be conducted, and the identification of a biomarker that assesses off-target modulation should be considered.

The utility of using microarrays for an initial assessment of off-target effects in cells and/or tissues is questionable [54–56]. The interpretation of these microarray experiments is confounded by the need to differentiate primary modulation effects from secondary effects that may be related to downstream pathways of the on-target or off-target, or secondary effects related to nonhybridization-dependent protein interactions that may also modulate mRNA levels. The best way to evaluate the potential for homology-dependent off-target effects is to do a thorough in silico assessment of potential targets, evaluate their potential relevance in in vitro systems and potential for in vivo adverse pathophysiology of the off-target, followed by traditional toxicology studies in two species. Similar to small molecules, any strategy for off-target assessment will not eliminate all potential adverse effects in humans, which is why clinical trials are performed initially in a small number of individuals and conducted with gradual dose escalation and careful monitoring.

In Vivo Screening-Toleration Studies in Animals

The conduct of single- or repeat-dose toleration and/or dose range-finding studies, typically ≤14 days in duration, prior to selection of a clinical candidate molecule, is often performed for most classes of drugs, including ONTs. This allows selection of a drug candidate with the most favorable safety profile based on a limited set of toxicity endpoints, and guides the selection of doses for regulatory toxicity studies in animals. Such studies are performed for most classes of ONTs at a single high dose with repeat dosing for 4–12 weeks, most commonly in mice, rats, and/or NHPs. The rationale for the longer duration of treatment for ONTs is that 6–12 weeks of treatment is typically required to achieve steady-state levels in target tissues, when effects due to drug accumulation and proinflammation manifest. The top dose for ONT molecules is usually limited based on nonspecific effects for each class of ONTs, which will be reviewed in the following section. For example, doses ≥50–100 mg/kg in rodents of PS and MOE ASOs produce dose-limiting tissue exposure, and 3–6 weeks of treatment is required to profile the scope of proinflammatory effects. In NHPs, doses that produce marked complement activation and subsequent acute hemodynamic effects should be avoided. The extent of complement activation at such doses limits the assessment of the general safety profile of these molecules in the subchronic setting and, hence, is not a useful strategy for candidate differentiation. Therefore utilizing doses below those that produce marked complement activation (eg, ≤20–40 mg/kg by subcutaneous injection) would be appropriate in screening/candidate selection studies.

Likewise, the top doses of formulated siRNAs are often limited in rodents and NHPs due to toxicity associated with the formulation constituents rather than the siRNAs [57,58]. Doses above 10–20 mg/kg of formulated ONT, with the dose based on the amount of siRNA present, can produce dose-limiting toxicity in NHPs and rodents. However, the dose–response varies widely among formulations, and is highly dependent on the excipients (eg, cationic, neutral, or anionic lipids), as well as the ratio of the excipients to the siRNA content. In contrast, doses of nonformulated siRNAs are generally well tolerated in rodents and NHPs at doses >100 mg/kg, in part, due to their faster rate of clearance as well as lower potential for interaction with proteins in blood.

NONSPECIFIC CLASS EFFECTS OF ONTs

The similarity in physicochemical and pharmacokinetic properties (eg, length, solubility, charge-to-mass ratio, hydrophilicity, tissue distribution, metabolism, and protein binding, among others) of ONTs within each chemical class leads to qualitatively similar toxicological properties from one sequence to the next. However, it is important to mention that significant differences within and between chemical classes exist even with relatively minor chemical differences. For example, the presence of a 2′-hydrogen vs. a 2′-hydroxyl that distinguishes DNA from RNA can greatly impact the mechanism of antisense activity, as well as the type and nature of potential nonspecific effects. The most well-described nonspecific class effects have also been compiled based on ONTs that have survived the discovery screening process and advanced to clinical development. Thus the range of toxicities that may be observed for ONTs, as a whole, may extend beyond the class effects described herein. Therefore it is important that the toxicity profile for each ONT candidate be thoroughly evaluated with special consideration of class effects, given the ever-expanding variety and complexity of ONTs.

Most of the findings observed in toxicology studies for the ASO class are due to interaction of the ONT with proteins or its accumulation within cells, rather than sequence-dependent effects. Although MOE ASOs (20 nucleotides in length) have the most extensive nonclinical and clinical experience, most of the class effects were initially described for the first generation PS ASO chemistry [59]. It is now realized that the improvement in the toxicological profile for MOE ASOs relative to PS ASOs is attributed, in large part, to the relatively lower nonspecific protein binding of the MOE chemistry [60].

Effects related to interaction between ASOs and proteins can occur either in plasma or in tissue [46]. The acute and transient alterations in clotting time and activation of the alternative complement pathway are examples of class effects that are associated with reversible binding of the ONT to specific plasma proteins. PS ASO-mediated alterations in clotting time and activation of the alternative complement pathway have been well characterized with regard to mechanism and their dose–response, time course, and plasma ONT concentration relationships [60]. These effects are correlated with peak plasma concentrations, occur within hours of dose administration, and reverse rapidly as the ONT is cleared from the circulation. The mechanism for these effects is the same for all ASOs; however, differences in chemical and sequence composition will potentially affect the degree to which these nonspecific class effects are observed. Thus it is important that all ONTs be assessed for these endpoints.

Inhibition of Clotting Time

The elevations of clotting time for PS and MOE ASOs are specific for the intrinsic clotting pathway, affecting activated partial thromboplastin time (APTT) but not PT [61–63]. Specific mechanistic studies with PS ASOs have identified noncovalent and reversible interactions between the ONT and components of the intrinsic tenase complex. Again, the elevations in APTT are largely independent of sequence, occur in rodent and nonrodent species, and return to predose levels as the ONT is cleared from plasma [62,63]. Although the transient prolongation of APTT has not proven to be a significant safety concern,

toxicology studies in NHPs are still designed to evaluate the effects on clotting time immediately post dose [46]. Determining the plasma kinetics that coincide with the peak effects on clotting times is important to document.

The PS content of an ONT contributes greatly to its protein binding properties, so shorter ONTs with reduced PS content are predicted to have less nonspecific protein binding. Indeed, reducing the length of a fully modified PS ASO was found to directly correlate with decreased inhibition of APTT (Fig. 28.2). Thus modest decreases in the length of ASOs can decrease this class effect. Antisense oligonucleotides that contain more potent 2'-modification on the ribose backbone, eg, LNA or cEt, are typically of reduced length (<20 nucleotides) so there is the opportunity for such ONTs to have reduced interaction with the intrinsic tenase complex. ONTs that do not have PS backbone linkages, eg, siRNAs and morpholinos, are less likely to affect clotting times due to their potential for reduced plasma protein binding and more rapid clearance from the circulation. However, the absence of PS linkages does not exclude the potential interaction with clotting proteins. For example, aptameric ONTs have been designed and selected to specifically interact with thrombin and inhibit its function [64]. Aptamers intended for this activity have specific consensus sequences that are composed largely of guanosine and thymidine residue and have been shown to interact specifically with either anion Exosite I or Exosite II. While these specific ONTs function through a different mechanism than ASOs, it is evident that sequence-specific interactions can exist. Therefore it is important to evaluate clotting time parameters as part of the nonclinical toxicology studies given the potential for sequence-dependent and sequence-independent effects.

Consideration should also be given to chemical modification or formulations that are designed to prolong the residence time of ONTs in circulation. For example, pegylated aptamer ONTs, including the thrombin-binding aptamers, have increased residence time in plasma. Although formulations that encapsulate ONTs are predicted to prevent direct contact between the ONT and clotting factors, charged surfaces common to liposomal- and nanoparticle-based formulations can serve as a contact point for binding to the coagulation proteins. So, in this case, the pharmacokinetic profile should be fully evaluated to coincide with that of the clotting sampling time points to capture the peak ONT plasma concentrations and the duration of effect.

Complement Activation

The activation of the alternative pathway of complement in NHPs is another common class effect of PS ASOs that is due to ONTs reversibly binding to complement Factor H [65]. The mechanism and secondary changes

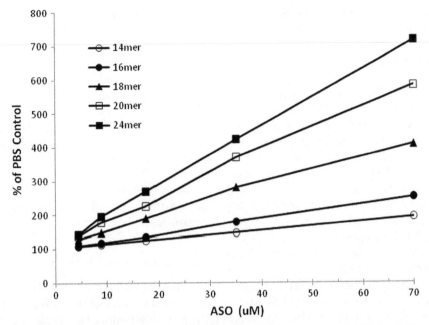

FIGURE 28.2 The relationship between oligonucleotide length and clotting time. Rat plasma was incubated with various lengths of an MOE ASO (14–24 nucleotides) at several concentrations (4–70 μM) for 0.5 h at room temperature, at which point APTT was measured using an ACL 1000 (IL Instrumentation, Beckman Coulter, Fullerton, CA). Data expressed as percent increase of the PBS control treatment.

associated with PS ASO-mediated complement activation in NHPs have been well studied, and are reviewed elsewhere [60]. The effect on the complement cascade appears selective to NHPs, and either does not occur in other laboratory animals (eg, rodent) or is much less potent (eg, dogs). This is different than the effects on clotting time, which occurs across multiple rodent and nonrodent species. Nonetheless, this is an important class effect to document in NHP studies in order to define the dose-concentration-effect relationship and to provide the most appropriate interpretation of the full study results. In NHP toxicology studies, complement activation is determined by measuring complement split products (eg, C5a, Bb) or total complement proteins (eg, CH50, C3). The clearance rate varies considerably among the potential options so measuring the plasma kinetics of the ONT and the complement proteins is important to accurately capture the changes. The C5a split product, for example, is cleared from plasma very quickly, so only samples collected at or very near the peak of activation are meaningful. The Bb split product is a preferred marker as it has slower systemic clearance and is selective for the alternative pathway. Although Bb tends to be a more robust measure than C5a, it is still important to collect plasma samples near the time of peak activation. The complement parent proteins or functional measures of the complement system (eg, CH50) are decreased upon activation. Such decreases can be used to monitor complement activation, but tend to be less sensitive than measuring the increases in split products. The kinetics of the parent proteins are different in that they take

2–3 days to return to normal levels (vs. 24 h for Bb) as this is dependent on the production of new protein.

ONT-mediated complement activation in NHPs is an important evaluation endpoint because it has been associated with a number of secondary effects that are manifested in the toxicology data. Complement activation, for example, has been shown to be the source of acute hemodynamic changes in NHPs treated with PS ASOs following bolus intravenous injection [66]. More recently, as a number of development programs have progressed to chronic toxicology studies, it has also been recognized that repeated complement activation, which occurs after each dose, may result in secondary effects (ISIS Pharmaceuticals, unpublished observations). During chronic complement activation there is a tendency for basal levels of the activation split products to increase and for total complement C3 levels to decrease over time. These can then lead to secondary inflammatory changes and impair the function of the complement system. The activation of the alternative pathway of complement by ONTs has not been observed in clinical trials, and there are data to suggest that humans are less sensitive to alternative pathway activation [60]. Nonetheless, clinical dose regimens typically avoid attaining plasma concentrations that produce complement activation in NHPs [65,67].

The activation of complement is a common effect for PS ASOs, but the degree of activation can vary between sequences within a chemical subclass. Since the activation is attributed to interaction between the ONT and plasma proteins of the complement cascade, the magnitude of complement activation is correlated with the degree of nonspecific protein binding, similar to that of clotting time inhibition. Chemical modifications that affect the degree of protein binding will influence complement activation. For example, the overall potency for complement activation by MOE ASOs appears lower than that observed for PS ASOs [60]. There is also a direct correlation with ONT length, since progressively shorter ONTs produce less complement activation (Fig. 28.3). Again, this is attributed to the lower degree of protein binding imparted either by the MOE substituent or the shorter ASO length [68]. This was observed in vivo as NHPs treated with an MOE ASO of 12-nucleotides in length produced no complement activation [69].

As discussed with the clotting time effects, the chemical class of ONTs that does not possess PS modifications may not activate complement. In most cases, ONTs that do not contain PS will have reduced potential for plasma protein binding, and thus are rapidly cleared from circulation. However, as other chemical modifications are incorporated, such as pegylation in the case of aptamers, the residence time in plasma is prolonged, which increases the potential interaction between the ONT and complement proteins. An ONT in a fully encapsulated liposomal or nanoparticle formulation is less likely to interact directly with the complement proteins. However, composition of the liposome or nanoparticle, the charge of each component, and overall particle charge can play a role in the potential for complement activation. For example, charged liposomes may interact with

the complement proteins and produce activation; most often this involves the classical pathway but the alternative pathway may also be activated in certain species, including humans [70,71]. In this scenario, the mechanism for activation will be different from that of a PS ASO, and thus the assessment should include both alternative and classical pathways. The blood and tissue kinetics will also be distinct for each formulation and the sampling strategy should again be designed to assess both the peak concentration and the duration of exposure. Thus ONTs that are absent of the PS chemical modification or those administered in liposomal or nanoparticle formulations should still be evaluated for complement activation.

Proinflammatory Effects

Whereas the clotting time and complement effects are attributed to interaction with plasma proteins, the class-based inflammatory effects are attributed to interactions between ONTs and cellular proteins. While manifested in multiple organs in rodents, the proinflammatory findings generally reflect a single process. For example, the inflammatory effects for MOE ASOs are associated with release of inflammatory chemokines following activation of monocytes or dendritic cells in target organs and in skin at the subcutaneous injection sites. These effects are especially prominent in rodent species and less evident in NHPs. The scope and magnitude of the inflammatory effects of ONTs can vary dramatically between chemical

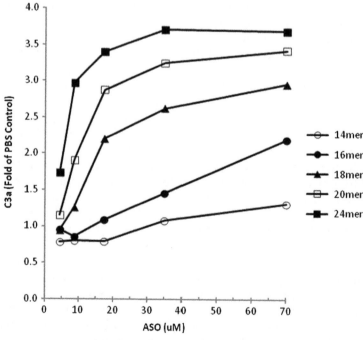

FIGURE 28.3   The relationship between oligonucleotide length and complement activation. NHP serum was incubated with various lengths of an MOE ASO (14–24 nucleotides) at several concentrations (4–70 μM) for 0.5 h at 37°C, at which point the complement split product C3a was measured by ELISA Data expressed as a fold increase of the PBS control treatment.

classes and sequences. Nonetheless, these proinflammatory effects are relatively subtle when compared to those produced by the immunostimulatory ONTs that contain CpG motifs. Such immunostimulatory ONTs produce elevated inflammatory cytokines as part of their pharmacological action.

Dose-dependent thrombocytopenia is another characteristic effect of the PS ASO class of compounds in mice and rats, and is occasionally seen to a lesser extent in NHPs [60]. The mechanism for this change is not well understood at this point, but it has been shown to be reversible. Although decreases in platelet count are not typically seen in clinical studies, platelet count should be closely monitored because it can be a useful screening endpoint when selecting the clinical candidate.

Tissue and Cellular Accumulation

The long tissue residence time of some ONT chemical classes is related to accumulation of the ONT in certain tissues and cell types. The uptake and accumulation of ASOs into the kidney, liver, and macrophages typically produces histological changes in the renal tubular epithelium, Kupffer cells, and resident macrophages in other tissues, respectively. Histological changes include the presence of basophilic granules (due to staining of ONT molecules in cells by hematoxylin), cellular hypertrophy (considered an adaptive change), and degenerative and/or regenerative findings at high doses. The degenerative/regenerative findings are very similar across MOE ASOs and across species, and are only associated with functional changes when present at very high doses, or result from dose regimens that result in excessive accumulation [46]. In fact, the correlation between tissue drug concentrations and the effects resulting from ONT accumulation are similar for ASOs of different sequence and chemistry. While the ASO class of ONTs has a long half-life in tissues, steady-state tissue concentrations are achievable and predictable. The lack of continued tissue accumulation over chronic periods of treatment results in little to no progression of the histological or functional changes once the steady-state concentration is achieved.

Translation of Key Preclinical Safety Findings to Humans

An important aspect of toxicity evaluation in animal models is to understand the relative species sensitivity of the class effects compared to the human response. The transient effects on APTT observed in all species, including humans, can be managed with prolonged intravenous infusion or subcutaneous injection to minimize peak plasma concentrations [67,72,73]; but no clinical sequelae have been associated with APTT prolongation even when present. Complement activation is easily and routinely monitored in clinical trials by measuring the same complement activation split products examined in NHPs (eg, C3a, C5a, and/or Bb). To date, there has been no treatment associated alternative complement pathway activation associated with subcutaneous injection or short intravenous infusion [67,73,74] in humans for MOE ASOs at the doses examined. This, in part, is due to the fact that plasma levels in human trials remain below the threshold levels required for activation in NHPs. With regard to the proinflammatory effects, it has been shown that rodents appear to be the most sensitive species for such effects. Assessing these effects in NHPs has been complicated by the fact that the higher doses studied were associated with activation of the alternative complement pathway, which can also contribute to the development of inflammatory effects. Thus it is difficult to ascribe the changes in NHPs either to complement activation or to the direct inflammatory effects of ASOs [66,75]. In clinical trials, injection-site reactions and flu-like symptoms have been indicative of local and systemic inflammation.

The safety and toxicology evaluation of ONTs continues to progress. The experience gained with MOE ASOs suggest that this class of inhibitors appears to have a tolerability profile sufficient to support safe testing in many different types of therapeutic indications. Over the years a thorough understanding of the dose, time course, and mechanistic basis for most target organ toxicities has been established for the ASO class of ONTs. This knowledge along with the relative consistency of the toxicological properties from one sequence to another contributes to the safe and effective application of these ONT inhibitors in clinical trials. As the field of ONTs continues to evolve with other types of ONTs, including siRNAs and more potent bicyclic modified ASOs, the balance between efficacy and tolerability will require further fine-tuning.

Safety Implications for Formulated ONTs

A means for efficient and effective tissue distribution and cell uptake is often required for some classes of ONTs, such as double-stranded siRNAs. In-depth reviews of the potential toxicity of multiple formulation modalities used for delivery of ONTs are available elsewhere [58,76,77]. The toxicology studies required to characterize the delivery components would also be expected to follow established regulatory guidelines. Novel components or unprecedented combinations of components may require further testing. The context for evaluation must also be considered, ie, testing an individual component may reveal a toxicity profile very different from a profile obtained when the component is included within a liposomal or nanoparticle structure. This can be approached by evaluation of particles alone in the absence of an ONT, so-called empty liposomes or empty nanoparticles, or by including a nonactive (control) ONT as the cargo. With the former approach one should consider the similarity between the formulated ONT and the empty formulation with regard to size, charge, distribution, etc., to provide confidence that the evaluation will provide relevant information for safety assessment of the ONT candidate intended for humans. For the latter approach, the considerations are similar to that described for use of a surrogate, such as manufacture of a sufficient quantity and quality to support the toxicity study, increased program and study cost, and the relevance and/or risk of generating toxicity data with an ONT that is not the actual development candidate.

EXPANDING PROSPECTS FOR ONTs

The regulation of messenger RNAs and the role of noncoding RNAs in this process is an active area of research. As the biology of noncoding RNAs becomes unraveled it is anticipated that greater opportunities will surface on how modulation of such factors may benefit human health. For example, our limited understanding of miRNAs has already revealed endocrine, cardiovascular, and oncogenic diseases where modulation of these regulators of coding RNAs may have therapeutic benefit [78–80]. Indeed, the pharmaceutical industry is now pursuing miRNAs as therapeutic targets, and strategies include replenishment (MIR mimic ONTs) or inhibitors (anti-MIRs) of miRNAs (Fig. 28.1). In contrast to the antisense approaches described herein where single mRNAs are targeted, modulation of a single miRNA leads to the regulation of several coding RNAs. Therefore assessment of potential toxicities associated with miRNA ONTs as it relates to exaggerated pharmacology becomes a bigger challenge [81]. Nonetheless, the understanding gained from work with the ASO and siRNA class of ONTs will provide good foundation for the clinical development of miRNA ONTs.

Another important area of potential growth for ONTs is in modulation of gene splicing. A number of genetic diseases exist where defects in splicing produces inactive or insufficient protein. For example, in Duchenne muscular dystrophy mutations or deletion of exons of the dystrophin gene leads to premature processing of the dystrophin transcript and nonfunctional dystrophin protein. Oligonucleotide-based therapeutics designed to hybridize in proximity to mutated exons have been shown to promote exon skipping to allow reading of the rest of the transcript to produce a more functional dystrophin protein [82,83]. There exist numerous other disorders where deficits in gene splicing are the cause of disease, and the utility of ONTs for such applications is promising.

References

[1] Grillone LR, Lanz R. Fomivirsen. Drugs Today 2001;37(4):245–55.

[2] Crooke ST. Molecular mechanisms of action of antisense drugs. Biochim Biophys Acta 1999;1489(1):31–44.

[3] Cerritelli SM, Crouch RJ. Ribonuclease H: the enzymes in eukaryotes. FEBS J 2009;276(6):1494–505.

[4] Zamecnik PC, Stephenson ML. Inhibition of Rous sarcoma virus replication and cell transformation by a specific oligodeoxynucleotide. Proc Natl Acad Sci 1978;75(1):280–4.

[5] Wu H, Lima WF, Zhang H, Fan A, Sun H, Crooke ST. Determination of the role of the human RNase H1 in the pharmacology of DNA-like antisense drugs. J Biol Chem 2004;279(17):17181–9.

[6] Bell DA, Hooper AJ, Burnett JR. Mipomersen, an antisense apolipoprotein B synthesis inhibitor. Expert Opin Investig Drugs 2011;20(2):265–72.

[7] Deleted in review.

[8] Brandt TA, Crooke ST, Ackermann EJ, Xia S, Morgan ES, Liu Q, et al. Isis 113715, a novel PTP-1B antisense inhibitor, improves glycemic control and dyslipidemia and increases adiponectin levels in T2DM subjects uncontrolled on stable sulfonylurea therapy. Diabetes 2010;59(Suppl. 1):A84.

[9] Liu Q, Bethune C, Dessouki E, Grundy J, Monia BP, Bhanot S. ISIS-FXIRx, a novel and specific antisense inhibitor of factor XI, caused significant reduction in FXI antigen and activity and increased aPTT without causing bleeding in healthy volunteers. Blood 2011;118:209 (ASH Annual Meeting Abstracts).

[10] Ecker JR, Davis RW. Inhibition of gene expression in plant cells by expression of antisense RNA. Proc Natl Acad Sci 1986;83(15):5372–6.

[11] Fire A, Xu S, Montgomery MK, Kostas SA, Driver SE, Mello CC. Potent and specific genetic interference by double-stranded RNA in Caenorhabditis elegans. Nature 1998;391(6669):806–11.

[12] Grimm D. Small silencing RNAs: state-of-the-art. Adv Drug Deliv Rev 2009;61(9):672–703.

[13] Rácz Z, Kaucsár T, Hamar P. The huge world of small RNAs: regulating networks of microRNAs. Acta Physiol Hung 2011;98(3):243–51.

[14] Melnyk CW, Molnar A, Baulcombe DC. Intercellular and systemic movement of RNA silencing signals. EMBO J 2011;30(17):3553–63.

[15] Davidson BL, McCray PB. Current prospects for RNA interference-based therapies. Nat Rev Genet 2011;12(5):329–40.

[16] Jackson AL, Burchard J, Schelter J, Chau BN, Cleary M, Lim L, et al. Widespread siRNA "off-target" transcript silencing mediated by seed region sequence complementarity. RNA 2006;12:1179–87.

[17] Shim MS, Kwon YJ. Efficient and targeted delivery of siRNA in vivo. FEBS J 2010;277(23):4814–27.

[18] Esposito CL, Catuogno S, de Franciscis V, Cerchia L. New insight into clinical development of nucleic acid aptamers. Discov Med 2011;11(61):487–96.

[19] Apte RS. Pegaptanib sodium for the treatment of age-related macular degeneration. Expert Opin Pharmacother 2008;9(3):499–508.

[20] Vollmer J, Krieg AM. Immunotherapeutic applications of CpG oligodeoxynucleotide TLR9 agonists. Adv Drug Deliv Rev 2009;61(3):195–204.

[21] Levin AA, Yu RY, Geary RS. Basic principles of the pharmacokinetics of antisense oligonucleotide drugs. In: Crooke ST, editor. Antisense drug technology: principles, strategies and applications. Boca Raton: Taylor and Francis; 2008. p. 183–216.

[22] Eckstein F. Phosphorothioate oligodeoxynucleotides: what is their origin and what is unique about them? Antisense Nucleic Acid Drug Dev 2000;10:117–21.

[23] Martin P. New access to 2′-O-alkylated ribonucleosides and properties of 2′-O-alkylated oligoribonucleotides. Helv Chim Acta 1995;78:486–504.

[24] Teplova M, Minasov G, Tereshko V, Inamati G, Cook PD, Manoharan M, et al. Crystal structure and improved antisense properties of 2'-O-(2-methoxyethyl)-RNA. Nat Struct Biol 1999;6:535–9.

[25] Monia BP, Lesnik EA, Gonzalez C, Lima WF, McGee D, Guinosso CJ, et al. Evaluation of 2'-modified oligonucleotides containing 2'-deoxy gaps as antisense inhibitors of gene expression. J Biol Chem 1993;268:14514–22.

[26] Altmann KH, Martin P, Dean NM, Monia BP. Second generation antisense oligonucleotides – inhibition of pkc-alpha and c-raf kinase expression by chimeric oligonucleotides incorporating 6'-substituted carbocyclic nucleosides and 2'-O-ethylene glycol substituted ribonucleosides. Nucleosides Nucleotides 1997;16:917–26.

[27] Seth PP, Siwkowski A, Allerson CR, Vasquez G, Lee S, Prakash TP, et al. Short antisense oligonucleotides with novel 2'-4' conformationally restricted nucleoside analogues show improved potency without increased toxicity in animals. J Med Chem 2009;52:10–3.

[28] Straarup EM, Fisker N, Hedtjarn M, Lindholm MW, Rosenbohm C, Aarup V, et al. Short locked nucleic acid antisense oligonucleotides potently reduce apolipoprotein B mRNA and serum cholesterol in mice and non-human primates. Nucleic Acids Res 2010;38(20):7100–11.

[29] Amantana A, Iversen PL. Pharmacokinetics and biodistribution of phosphorodiamidate morpholino antisense oligomers. Curr Opin Pharmacol 2005;5:550–5.

[30] Stein D, Foster E, Huang SB, Weller D, Summerton JA. Specificity comparison of four antisense types: morpholino, 2'-O-methyl RNA, DNA, and phosphorothioate DNA. Antisense Nucleic Acid Drug Dev 1997;7:151–7.

[31] Arora V, Devi GR, Iversen PL. Neutrally charged phosphorodiamidate morpholino antisense oligomers: uptake, efficacy and pharmacokinetics. Curr Pharm Biotechnol 2004;5:431–9.

[32] Swayze EE, Bhat B. The medicinal chemistry of oligonucleotides. In: Crooke ST, editor. Antisense drug technology: principles, strategies, applications. Boca Raton: Taylor and Francis; 2008. p. 143–82.

[33] Geary RS, Yu RZ, Siwkowski A, Levin AA. Pharmacokinetic/pharmacodynamic properties of phosphorothioate 2'-O-(2-methoxyethyl)-modified antisense oligonucleotides in animals and man. In: Crooke ST, editor. Antisense drug technology: principles, strategies and applications. Boca Raton: Taylor and Francis; 2008. p. 305–26.

[34] Haringsma HJ, Li JJ, Soriano F, Kenski DM, Flanagan WM, Willingham AT. mRNA knockdown by single strand RNA is improved by chemical modifications. Nucleic Acids Res January 16, 2012:1–12.

[35] Henry SP, Monteith D, Kombrust DJ, Levin AA. Effects of intravenous infusion of phosphorothioate oligonucleotides on coagulation, complement activation and hemodynamics. Nucleosides Nucleotides 1997;16(7–9):1673–6.

[36] Black LE, Degeorge JJ, Cavagnaro JA, Jordan A, Ahn CH. Regulatory considerations for evaluating the pharmacology and toxicology of antisense drugs. Antisense Res Dev 1993;3(4):399–404.

[37] Black LE, Farrelly JG, Cavagnaro JA, Ahn CH, DeGeorge JJ, Taylor AS, et al. Regulatory considerations for oligonucleotide drugs: updated recommendations for pharmacology and toxicology studies. Antisense Res Dev 1994;4(4):299–301.

[38] Geary RS, Leeds JM, Henry SP, Monteith DK, Levin AA. Antisense oligonucleotide inhibitors for the treatment of cancer: 1. Pharmacokinetic properties of phosphorothioate oligodeoxynucleotides. Anticancer Drug Des 1997;12(5):383–93.

[39] Yu RZ, Geary RS, Leeds JM, Watanabe T, Moore M, Fitchett J, et al. Comparison of pharmacokinetics and tissue disposition of an antisense phosphorothioate oligonucleotide targeting human Ha-ras mRNA in mouse and monkey. J Pharm Sci 2001;90(2):182–93.

[40] Geary RS, Yu RZ, Levin AA. Pharmacokinetics of phosphorothioate antisense oligodeoxynucleotides. Curr Opin Investig Drugs 2001;2(4):562–73.

[41] Yu RZ, Grundy JS, Henry SP, Kim TW, Norris DA, Burkey J, et al. Predictive dose-based estimation of systemic exposure multiples in mouse and monkey relative to human for antisense oligonucleotides with 2'-O-(2-methoxyethyl) modifications. Mol Ther Nucleic Acids January 20, 2015;4:e218.

[42] Gaus HJ, Owens SR, Winniman M, Cooper S, Cummins LL. Online HPLC electrospray mass spectrometry of phosphorothioate oligonucleotide metabolites. Anal Chem 1997;69(3):313–9.

[43] Griffey RH, Greig MJ, Gaus HJ, Liu K, Monteith D, Winniman M, et al. Characterization of oligonucleotide metabolism in vivo via liquid chromatography/electrospray tandem mass spectrometry with a quadrupole ion trap mass spectrometer. J Mass Spectrom 1997;32(3):305–13.

[44] Berman CL, Cannon K, Cui Y, Kornbrust DJ, Lagrutta A, Sun SZ, et al. Recommendations for safety pharmacology evaluations of oligonucleotide-based therapeutics. Nucleic Acid Ther 2014;24(4):291–301.

[45] Kim TW, Kim KS, Seo JW, Park SY, Henry SP. Antisense oligonucleotides on neurobehavior, respiratory, and cardiovascular function, and hERG channel current studies. J Pharmacol Toxicol Methods 2014;69(1):49–60.

[46] Henry SP, Kim TW, Kramer-Strickland K, Zanardi TA, Fey RA, Levin AA. Toxicological properties of 2'-O-methoxyethyl chimeric antisense inhibitors in animals and man. In: Crooke ST, editor. Antisense drug technology: principles, strategies and applications. Boca Raton: Taylor and Francis; 2008. p. 327–63.

[47] Henry SP, Denny KH, Templin MV, Yu RZ, Levin AA. Effects of an antisense oligonucleotide inhibitor of human ICAM-1 on fetal development in rabbits. Birth Defects Res B Dev Reprod Toxicol 2004;71(6):368–73.

[48] Henry SP, Denny KH, Templin MV, Yu RZ, Levin AA. Effects of human and murine antisense oligonucleotide inhibitors of ICAM-1 on reproductive performance, fetal development, and post-natal development in mice. Birth Defects Res B Dev Reprod Toxicol 2004;71(6):359–67.

[49] Cavagnaro J, Berman C, Kornbrust D, White T, Campion S, Henry S. Considerations for assessment of reproductive and developmental toxicity of oligonucleotide-based therapeutics. Nucleic Acid Ther 2014;24(5):313–25.

[50] Gantier MP, Tong S, Behlke MA, Irving AT, Lappas M, Nilsson UW, et al. Rational design of immunostimulatory siRNAs. Mol Ther 2010;18(4):785–95.

[51] Lindow M, Vornlocher HP, Riley D, Kornbrust D, Whiteley LO, Kamens J, et al. Assessing unintended hybridization induced biological effects of oligonucleotides. [Submitted for publication] Nat Biotechnol Oct 2012;30(10):920–3.

[52] Bilanges B, Stokoe D. Direct comparison of the specificity of gene silencing using antisense oligonucleotides and RNAi. Biochem J 2005;388(Pt 2):573–83.

[53] Khan AA, Betel D, Miller ML, Sander C, Leslie CS, Marks DS. Transfection of small RNAs globally perturbs gene regulation by endogenous microRNAs. Nat Biotechnol 2009;27:549–55.

[54] Cho YS, Kim MK, Cheadle C, Neary C, Becker KG, Cho-Chung YS. Antisense DNAs as multisite genomic modulators identified by DNA microarray. Proc Natl Acad Sci 2001;98:9819–23.

[55] Fisher AA, Ye D, Sergueev DS, Fisher MH, Shaw BR, Juliano RL. Evaluating the specificity of antisense oligonucleotide conjugates. A DNA array analysis. J Biol Chem 2002;277:22980–4.

[56] Jackson AL, Bartz SR, Schelter J, Kobayashi SV, Burchard J, Mao M, et al. Expression profiling reveals off-target gene regulation by RNAi. Nat Biotechnol 2003;21:635–7.

[57] Ma Z, Li J, He F, Wilson A, Pitt B, Li S. Cationic lipids enhance siRNA-mediated interferon response in mice. Biochem Biophys Res Commun 2005;330(3):755–9.

[58] Zhang S, Zhao B, Jiang H, Wang B, Ma B. Cationic lipids and polymers mediated vectors for delivery of siRNA. J Control Release 2007;123(1):1–10.

VI. NONCLINICAL DEVELOPMENT

[59] Levin AA, Henry SP, Monteith D, Templin MV. Toxicity of antisense oligonucleotides. In: Crooke ST, editor. Antisense drug technology principles, strategies, and applications. New York: Marcel Dekker; 2001. p. 201–67.

[60] Henry SP, Geary RS, Yu R, Levin AA. Drug properties of second-generation antisense oligonucleotides: how do they measure up to their predecessors? Curr Opin Investig Drugs 2001;2(10):1444–9.

[61] Henry SP, Novotny W, Leeds J, Auletta C, Kornbrust DJ. Inhibition of coagulation by a phosphorothioate oligonucleotide. Antisense Nucleic Acid Drug Dev 1997;7:503–10.

[62] Sheehan JP, Lan HC. Phosphorothioate oligonucleotides inhibit the intrinsic tenase complex. Blood 1998;92(5):1617–25.

[63] Sheehan JP, Thao PM. Phosphorothioate oligonucleotides inhibit the intrinsic tenase complex by an allosteric mechanism. Biochemistry 2001;40(16):4980–9.

[64] Jeter ML, Ly LV, Fortenberry YM, Whinna HC, White RR, Rusconi CP, et al. RNA aptamer to thrombin binds anion-underbinding exosite-2 and alters protease inhibition by heparin-binding serpins. FEBS Lett 2004;568(1–3):10–4.

[65] Henry SP, Giclas PC, Leeds J, Pangburn M, Auletta C, Levin AA, et al. Activation of the alternative pathway of complement by a phosphorothioate oligonucleotide: potential mechanism of action. J Pharmacol Exp Ther 1997;281(2):810–6.

[66] Henry SP, Beattie G, Yeh G, Chappel A, Giclas P, Mortari A, et al. Complement activation is responsible for acute toxicities in rhesus monkeys treated with a phosphorothioate oligodeoxynucleotide. Int Immunopharmacol 2002;2(12):1657–66.

[67] Sewell KL, Geary RS, Baker BF, Glover JM, Mant TG, Yu RZ, et al. Phase I trial of ISIS 104838, a 2′-methoxyethyl modified antisense oligonucleotide targeting tumor necrosis factor–alpha. J Pharmacol Exp Ther 2002;303(3):1334–43.

[68] Watanabe TA, Geary RS, Levin AA. Plasma protein binding of an antisense oligonucleotide targeting human ICAM-1 (ISIS 2302). Oligonucleotides 2006;16(2):169–80.

[69] Zanardi TA, Han SC, Jeong EJ, Rime S, Yu RZ, Chakravarty K, et al. Pharmacodynamics and subchronic toxicity in mice and monkeys of ISIS 388626, a second-generation antisense oligonucleotide that targets human sodium glucose cotransporter 2. J Pharmacol Exp Ther 2012;343(2):489–96.

[70] Devine DV, Wong K, Serrano K, Chonn A, Cullis PR. Liposome-complement interactions in rat serum: implications for liposome survival studies. Biochim Biophys Acta 1994;1191(1):43–51.

[71] Moghimi SM, Hamad I. Liposome-mediated triggering of complement cascade. J Liposome Res 2008;18(3):195–209.

[72] Yacyshyn BR, Chey WY, Goff J, Salzberg B, Baerg R, Buchman AL, et al. Double blind, placebo controlled trial of the remission inducing and steroid sparing properties of an ICAM-1 antisense oligodeoxynucleotide, alicaforsen (ISIS 2302), in active steroid dependent Crohn's disease. Gut 2002;51(1):30–6.

[73] Kastelein JJ, Wedel MK, Baker BF, Su J, Bradley JD, Yu RZ, et al. Potent reduction of apolipoprotein B and low-density lipoprotein cholesterol by short-term administration of an antisense inhibitor of apolipoprotein B. Circulation 2006;114(16):1729–35.

[74] Chi KN, Siu LL, Hirte H, Hotte SJ, Knox J, Kollmansberger C, et al. A phase I study of OGX-011, a 2′-methoxyethyl phosphorothioate antisense to clusterin, in combination with docetaxel in patients with advanced cancer. Clin Cancer Res 2008;14(3):833–9.

[75] Frank MM, Fries LF. The role of complement in inflammation and phagocytosis. Immunol Today 1991;12(9):322–6.

[76] Whitehead KA, Langer R, Anderson DG. Knocking down barriers: advances in siRNA delivery. Nat Rev Drug Discov 2009;8(2):129–38.

[77] Ozpolat B, Sood AK, Lopez-Berestein GJ. Nanomedicine based approaches for the delivery of siRNA in cancer. J Intern Med 2010;267(1):44–53.

[78] Esteller M. Noncoding RNAs in human disease. Nat Rev Genet 2011;12(12):861–74.

[79] Fichtlscherer S, Zeiher AM, Dimmeler S. Circulating microRNAs: biomarkers or mediators of cardiovascular diseases? Arterioscler Thromb Vasc Biol 2011;31(11):2383–90.

[80] Zalts H, Shomron N. The impact of microRNAs on endocrinology. Pediatr Endocrinol Rev 2011;8(4):354–62.

[81] van Rooij E, Purcell AL, Levin AA. Developing microRNA therapeutics. Circ Res 2012;110:483–95.

[82] Moulton HM, Wu B, Jearawiriyapaisarn N, Sazani P, Lu QL, Kole R. Peptide-morpholino conjugate: a promising therapeutic for Duchenne muscular dystrophy. Ann NY Acad Sci 2009;1175:55–60.

[83] van Deutekom JC, Janson AA, Ginjaar IB, Frankhuizen WS, Aartsma-Rus A, Bremmer-Bout M, et al. Local dystrophin restoration with antisense oligonucleotide PRO051. N Engl J Med 2007;357(26):2677–86.

SAFETY EVALUATION OF OCULAR DRUGS, BOTANICAL PRODUCTS, AND MEDICINAL DEVICES

Safety Evaluation of Ocular Drugs

M. Ferrell Ramos, M. Attar, M.E. Stern, J.A. Brassard, A.S. Kim,
S. Matsumoto, C. Vangyi

OUTLINE

A Comprehensive Guide to Toxicology in Nonclinical Drug Development, Second Edition
http://dx.doi.org/10.1016/B978-0-12-803620-4.00029-3

INTRODUCTION

Twenty-three drugs for ophthalmic use have been approved by the U.S. Food and Drug Administration (FDA) since 2001 (Table 29.1). Of these:

1. Approximately 75% are small molecules.
2. 50% are new medical entities (including biologics).
3. 40% are for chronic conditions.

Topical ocular (eye drops) is the most common administration route, followed by intravitreal (IVT) injection. Systemic (eg, oral for Valcyte) or other administration routes (eg, intranasal for Astepro) can also be used for treating ocular conditions but are less common.

Administration by topical drops effectively delivers drugs to the anterior segments of the eye and is commonly used to treat conditions targeted to those tissues. Targeted drug delivery to other parts of the eye can be accomplished by injectables or implants. For example, IVT injection of drugs to the posterior segment of the eye has been successfully used to treat neovascular (wet) age-related macular degeneration (AMD) (eg, Macugen, Lucentis, and Eylea) and macular edema following branch retinal vein occlusion or central retinal vein occlusion (eg, Ozurdex and Lucentis).

Ocular drug development requires both systemic and local characterization, and challenges remain despite recent advances made in the field of ocular drug development. The current regulatory guidance documents on nonclinical pharmacokinetic and toxicology studies generally applied to systemic agents are also applicable to ocular drugs. However, the regulatory expectations for ocular safety are not well defined [1,2]. This poses challenges in developing nonclinical safety strategies for ocular drugs, especially those that are new molecular or biologic entities or that employ novel drug delivery methods. This chapter presents important considerations for nonclinical testing in ocular drug development with an emphasis on interspecies ocular structure and function.

PHARMACOKINETICS AND DRUG DISPOSITION IN THE EYE

A foundational understanding of drug pharmacokinetics and disposition following the desired route of administration is an important component of any ocular safety program. The pharmacokinetic processes of absorption, distribution, metabolism, and elimination determine the concentration of drug delivered to the site of pharmacodynamic and/or toxicodynamic action. Characterization of ocular pharmacokinetics is an integral component of the nonclinical safety assessment of ocular drugs. Drug exposure in ocular tissues and the systemic compartment are key parameters in developing an understanding of the relationship between dose level, dose regimen, dose route, and the time course of toxicological findings. These data are then used to help interpret toxicology findings relative to their implications for clinical safety and use.

Unique challenges exist with respect to the design of ocular pharmacokinetic studies, including inherent variability associated with nonserial sampling of ocular tissues, as well as the bioanalytical methods used to measure drug concentrations in multiple matrices (ie, ocular tissues and the systemic compartment) with sensitive lower limits of detection. This section presents a discussion of pharmacokinetic strategies in the nonclinical safety evaluation of drugs with general principles that apply to both small and large molecules. With the emergence of large molecule biologic drugs to treat ocular disease, a section dedicated to the immunologic considerations associated with large molecule drug development is included.

Ocular Pharmacokinetic Profiling

Topical Ophthalmic

Topical ophthalmic eye drops, particularly when formulated with small molecules, are commonly used to treat diseases of the anterior segment of the eye. Drug formulation is administered as a drop on the ocular

TABLE 29.1 FDA Approved Drugs for Ophthalmology (2001–2015)[a]

Approval Year	Drug	Active Ingredient	Indication	Administration Route	Chemical Type[b]
2001	Lumigan	Bimatoprost	Reduction of intraocular pressure	Topical ocular	1
	Travatan	Travoprost	Reduction of intraocular pressure	Topical ocular	1
	Valcyte	Valganciclovir HCl	Cytomegalovirus retinitis	Oral	2
2002	Restasis	Cyclosporine	Low tear production	Topical ocular	3
2004	Macugen	Pegaptanib sodium	AMD	Intravitreal injection	1
2006	Lucentis	Ranibizumab	AMD	Intravitreal injection	1
2007	AzaSite	Azithromycin	Bacterial conjunctivitis	Topical ocular	3
2008	Akten	Lidocaine HCl	Anesthesia[c]	Topical ocular	4
	Astepro	Azelastine HCl	Allergic rhinitis	Intranasal	–
	Durezol	Difluprednate	Pain, inflammation[d]	Topical ocular	1
2009	Acuvail	Ketorolac tromethamine	Pain, inflammation[e]	Topical ocular	4
	Bepreve	Bepotastine besilate	Itching[f]	Topical ocular	1
	Besivance	Besifloxacin	Bacterial conjunctivitis	Topical ocular	1
	Ozurdex	Dexamethasone	Macular edema[g]	Intravitreal injection	3
	Zirgan	Ganciclovir	Herpetic keratitis	Topical ocular	3
2010	Zymaxid	Gatifloxacin	Bacterial conjunctivitis	Topical ocular	4
2011	Eylea	Aflibercept	AMD	Intravitreal injection	1
2012	Zioptan	Tafluprost	Reduction of intraocular pressure	Topical ocular	1
2012	Lucentis	Ranibizumab	DME	IVT	5
2012	Jetrea	Ocriplasmin	Symptomatic vitreomacular adhesion	IVT	1
2012	Cystaran	Cysteamine hydrochloride	Corneal cysteine crystal accumulation due to cystinosis	Topical ocular	3
2014	Oralair	Sweet vernal, orchard, perennial rye, timothy, and Kentucky blue grass mixed pollens allergen extract	Grass pollen-induced allergic rhinitis with or without conjunctivitis	Tablet for sublingual use	3
2014	Omidria	Phenylephrine and ketorolac	For used during eye surgery to prevent intraoperative miosis and reduce postoperative pain	Irrigation solution	3
2014	Hetlioz	Tasimelteon	Non-24-h sleep-wake disorder in the totally blind	Capsule for oral use	1

AMD, Neovascular (wet) age-related macular degeneration; *DME*, Diabetic macular edema; *IVT*, intravitreal.

[a]*http://www.centerwatch.com/drug-information/fda-approvals/drug-areas.aspx?AreaID = 13; http://www.accessdata.fda.gov/scripts/cder/drugsatfda/index.cfm.*

[b]*1 = New molecular or biologic entity; 2 = New ester, new salt, or other noncovalent derivative; 3 = New formulation, new dosage form, or new combination; 4 = New manufacturer; 5 = new indication; – = Not specified.*

[c]*During ophthalmic procedures.*

[d]*Associated with ocular surgery.*

[e]*Following cataract surgery.*

[f]*Associated with allergic conjunctivitis.*

[g]*Following branch retinal vein occlusion or central retinal vein occlusion.*

VII. SAFETY EVALUATION OF OCULAR DRUGS, BOTANICAL PRODUCTS, AND MEDICINAL DEVICES

surface, of which the majority of drug is lost to precorneal drainage and absorption at the nasolacrimal duct, where drug can then become systemically available. The small fraction of drug that is ocularly absorbed most often follows the route across the corneal epithelium. Differences in thickness and cellular structure of the cornea across species (Table 29.2) can contribute to differences in rates of absorption and bioavailability in the anterior chamber and distribution to intraocular tissues. The conjunctival–scleral route is an alternate path for the penetration of drugs into intraocular tissues and is shown to be important in the absorption of compounds such as gentamicin, prostaglandins, and timolol maleate [3–7]. Drugs absorbed through the latter route are typically hydrophilic and have large molecular weights or poor corneal permeability. Elucidating the primary routes of absorption and distribution to various ocular tissues in comparison with other compounds is an important component in building an understanding of the activity of ophthalmic drugs, as demonstrated by Pamulapati and Schoenwald in describing and rank ordering the pharmacokinetic (PK)/pharmacodynamic (PD) properties of the novel antiglaucoma agent tetrahydroquinoline analog [8,9].

TABLE 29.2 Ocular Dynamics of Various Species

	Rat[a]	Rabbit[b]	Dog[c]	Monkey[d]	Human[e]
Corneal thickness (mm)	0.17	0.40	0.585–0.670	0.44	0.52
Anterior chamber volume (mL)	0.015	0.25–0.3	0.4–0.77	0.072–0.220	0.1–0.25
Aqueous flow rate (mL/min)	0.64	3–4.7	4–6	1–2	2–3
Vitreous volume (mL)	<0.02	1.4–1.7	3.2	1.5–4.0	3.9–5
Retina	Macular area (superior band shaped)	Visual streak (horizontal band ventral to ONH)	Area centralis (temporal to ONH); tapetum	Macula with fovea (temporal to ONH)	Macular with fovea (temporal to ONH)
Retinal Vascular Pattern & supply	Holangiotic posterior ciliary arteries	Merangiotic posterior ciliary arteries	Holangiotic short posterior ciliary arteries	Holangiotic central retinal artery	Holangiotic central retinal artery
ONH	Small circular, mild myelination	Physiological pit, horizontal band of myelin "medullary rays"	Triangular, variable myelination	Vertically oval, mild myelination	Vertically oval, mild myelination
Body weight (kg)	0.25–0.3	2–3	10–12	2–3	60

ONH, Optic nerve head.

[a]Leeds JM, Henry SP, Bistner S, Scherrill S, Williams K, Levin AA. Pharmacokinetics of an antisense oligonucleotide injected intravitreally in monkeys. Drug Metab Dispos 1998;26:670–5.

[b]Leeds JM, Henry SP, Truong L, Zutshi A, Levin AA, Kornbrust D. Pharmacokinetics of a potential human cytomegalovirus therapeutic, a phosphorothioate oligonucleotide, after intravitreal injection in the rabbit. Drug Metab Dispos 1997;25:921–6; Worakul N, Robinson JR. Ocular pharmacokinetics/pharmacodynamics. Eur J Pharm Biopharm 1997;44:71–83.

[c]Cawrse MA, Ward DA, Hendrix DVH. Effects of topical application of 2% solution of dorzolamide on intraocular pressure and aqueous humor flow rate in clinically normal dogs. Am J Vet Res 2001;62:859–63; Ward DA, Cawrse MA, Hendrix DVH. Fluorophotometric determination of aqueous humor flow rate in clinically normal dogs. Am J Vet Res 2001;62:853–8.

[d]Bill A, Hellsing K. Production and drainage of aqueous humor in the cynomolgus monkey. Invest Ophthalmol 1965;4:920–6; Greenbaum S, Lee PY, Howard-Williams J, Podos SM. The optically determined corneal and anterior chamber volumes of the cynomolgus. Curr Eye Res 1985;4:187–90; Johnson SB, Passmore JA, Brubaker RF. The fluorescein distribution volume of the anterior chamber. Invest Opthalmol Vis Sci 1977;16:633–36; Pearson PA, Jaffe GJ, Martin DF, Cordahi GJ, Grossniklaus H, Schmeisser ET, Ashton P. Evaluation of a delivery system providing long-term release of cyclosporine. Arch Ophthalmol 1996;114:311–17.

[e]Leeds JM, Henry SP, Bistner S, Scherrill S, Williams K, Levin AA. Pharmacokinetics of an antisense oligonucleotide injected intravitreally in monkeys. Drug Metab Dispos 1998;26:670–5; Worakul N, Robinson JR. Ocular pharmacokinetics/pharmacodynamics. Eur J Pharm Biopharm 1997;44:71–83.

Subconjunctival

Drug administration in the subconjunctival space allows for sustained delivery from a localized drug depot. It is generally accepted that a drug injected into the subconjunctival space can distribute by the transscleral route into intraocular tissues, or is cleared via conjunctival blood and/or lymphatic flow. For example, a subconjunctival dose of prednisolone to rabbits distributes to the precorneal area (1.7%), corneal epithelium (0.1%), and into the aqueous and vitreous humors (0.2%) to a small extent, while the remaining dose is absorbed systemically [10]. Similarly, following subconjunctival administration of gadolinium-labeled diethylenetriaminopentaacetic acid and gadolinium labeled albumin in rabbits, the major clearance pathway for both is via the systemic blood circulation, while lymphatic clearance interestingly was not as significant [11]. In addition, larger injection volumes allowed for longer retention times of the drug depot and prolonged drug delivery. Subconjunctival drug administration tends to be less efficient at delivering drugs to the posterior segment of the eye. Bevacizumab (Avastin) administered in the subconjunctival space in rabbits distributes to the iris–ciliary body and choroid–retina, but to a lesser extent than following IVT administration [12].

With subconjunctivally injected drugs, conjunctiva-associated lymphoid tissue [13] and direct drainage into draining lymph nodes is a consideration as both a drug absorption-limiting barrier in addition to a potential pathway for drug action. Importantly, drugs that elicit a therapeutic effect by acting on dendritic cells may do so either directly at the ocular surface or may do this in the draining lymph nodes [14,15].

Intravitreal and Intracameral

Direct administration into the posterior or anterior chamber bypasses classic ocular barriers to drug penetration, and allows a soluble drug to bathe the target tissue, typically either the retina or iris–ciliary body, respectively. The pharmacokinetics of drugs administered into the vitreous or anterior chamber are significantly influenced by the rate of dissolution from the drug formulation. Following IVT administration, a drug can be eliminated via two pathways:

1. The anterior, through the aqueous humor.
2. The posterior, across the retinal surface.

It is well established that the rate of vitreal elimination is inversely proportional to a drug's molecular weight [16–18]. Clearance of drugs from the anterior chamber is generally thought to be via aqueous humor turnover. Therefore, important considerations in designing nonclinical ocular toxicity studies with respect to adequate drug exposure include:

1. Differences in vitreous and aqueous volumes across species that influence rate of dissolution.
2. Differences in vitreous and aqueous humor turnover that can influence clearance.

Drug Metabolism and Transporters

Enzyme systems that exist in systemic tissues have been identified in the various tissues of the eye (Table 29.3). The majority of published work has focused on enzyme systems that are active at the ocular surface. While some overlap of specific enzymes characterized at the ocular surface and back of the eye exists, different enzyme systems and different enzyme isoforms are expressed in the different ocular tissues. These differences likely arise from the unique functions served by each tissue. The observation of regional and gender-specific gene expression patterns in drug metabolizing enzymes in rat ocular tissues supports the notion that these enzymes play selective roles to maintain normal ocular function [19]. In general, ocular metabolizing enzymes and drug transporters do not pose a significant barrier to drug bioavailability in the eye after local administration. Rather these enzyme systems play a role in maintaining normal physiology in the eye and may

TABLE 29.3 Drug Metabolizing Enzymes Characterized in Ocular Tissues

Enzyme
Oxidoreductase
Aldose reductase
Aldehyde oxidase
Ketone reductase
Cyclooxygenase
Monoamine oxidase
Cytochrome P450
Hydrolytic
Aminopeptidase
Acetylcholinesterase
Butyrylcholinestesase
Carboxylesterase
Phosphatase
Aryl sulfatase
N-acetyl-β-glucosaminidase
β-glucuronidase
Conjugating
Arylamine acetyltransferase
Glutathione S-transferase

be involved in disease processes. The one exception are hydrolytic enzymes such as esterases, which have been used to enhance delivery of active moiety by employing a prodrug strategy hydrolyzed [20–24]. Further reading on this subject is recommended in previously published reviews [25,26].

Melanin Binding

Melanins are a group of natural pigments found in humans and animals. In the eye, melanin is present in the uveal tract and the pigmented epithelial layer of the retina. Melanin is thought to play a protective role through absorbing most of the visible light that penetrates the lens and through binding free radicals [27–29]. In general, basic lipophillic drugs are known to bind melanin. The toxicological consequences of this binding are controversial; it has been proposed that drugs may elicit toxic effects either through accumulation in tissues through melanin binding and prolonged exposure or through binding melanin and interfering with its protective role. Alternatively, melanin–drug complexes may sequester a drug, making it unavailable to elicit toxic effects. Systemically administered drugs that are known to bind to melanin (eg, phenothiazines) and accumulate in the pigmented ocular tissues of animals are also known to elicit ocular toxicity such as retinopathy [30]. It has been proposed that the binding of a drug by melanin involves a "charge transfer" reaction in which the transfer of an electron from the drug to melanin acts as an "electron trap" and thus firmly binds the drug. In the presence of increasing concentrations of chlorpromazine, a drug known to bind melanin, ultraviolet irradiation of bovine retinal epithelial cells inhibits cell growth and elicits cell lysis [31]. However, Leblanc [28] reported that melanin binding was not predictive of drug-induced ocular toxicity, following an extensive review of the literature that included classic examples of drugs both known to bind melanin and being associated with retinal toxicity, specifically, chloroquine and phenothiazines. Furthermore, the authors argued that the albino rabbit, a commonly used nonclinical toxicity model, adequately predicts the absence of toxicity that also occurs in pigmented tissues with the same drug based on review of data in pigmented animals versus albino rabbits.

Study Considerations

A pharmacokinetic study design that reduces inherent study variability, in which each animal and tissue is sampled at each timepoint in a serial manner to generate a concentration–time profile, is generally not applicable to ocular pharmacokinetic studies. Serial sampling of solid ocular tissues for pharmacokinetic

measurements is impractical, and therefore ocular pharmacokinetic study designs must rely on nonserial sampling schemes where a different animal is sampled at each timepoint to characterize the drug concentration–time profile in ocular tissues. Statistical methods have been developed to analyze data sets generated from these studies [32].

To develop a comprehensive understanding of drug absorption, distribution, and metabolism following ocular administration, selective and sensitive bioanalytical methods must be developed. This can be challenging, as each ocular tissue represents a distinct biological matrix for which the conditions for reliable and reproducible sample collection, handling, storage, extraction, and quantitative analytical methods must be qualified. With this in mind, bioanalytical methods for ocular tissues are generally not validated for Good Laboratory Practice (GLP) analyses, and generally these studies are conducted under non-GLP conditions.

PHARMACOKINETIC CONSIDERATIONS FOR LARGE MOLECULES

Determination of Free Drug and Target-Bound Drug Complex

Similar to small molecules, there is value to characterizing drug levels of large molecules in ocular tissues and the systemic compartment. The preclinical programs for both Lucentis and Eylea included characterizing drug levels in the eye and serum [33,34] (FDA SBA Lucentis; FDA SBA Eylea). During the development of Eylea, both free and vascular endothelial growth factor (VEGF)-bound drug levels were determined. The discussion that follows describes the value of characterizing both analytes.

A more comprehensive characterization of total drug levels, free drug, and VEGF-bound drug in both the eye and the systemic compartment was achieved, which allows for better interpretation of drug effect findings. It was revealed in the vitreous, the major analytical species was free Eylea, thereby indicating free drug was available to partition into the retina and choroid, the sites of action, to elicit the desired pharmacological effect. Whereas in the systemic compartment, free drug was only available immediately after dosing; and in the long-term, the VEGF–Eylea complex (biologically active form) was the major circulating species. The fact that VEGF–Eylea is the major systemically circulating species in long-term safety studies is an important piece of information when interpreting toxicity data, as it indicates that free drug was not available to elicit undesirable effects through binding systemic endogenous VEGF.

TABLE 29.4 Comparison of Bioanalytical Considerations for Small and Large Molecules

Consideration	Large Molecule	Small Molecule
Assay development in ocular tissues and the systemic compartment	Needed	Needed
Assay development across animal species	Needed	Needed
Assay for free drug	Needed	Needed
Assay for target-bound drug	Valuable when feasible (can be requested by regulators)	Generally not required
Assay for antibodies	Required	Not required
Assay to determine nature of the antibody	Required	Not required
Common types of assays	Immunoassays	Liquid chromatography tandem mass spectrometry

Bioanalytical Assay Development

Similar to small molecules, bioanalytical assays must be developed for ocular matrices and the systemic compartment. However, the overall bioanalytical method development is more complex for protein therapeutics (see Table 29.4).

Regulatory Considerations in Ocular Safety Assessment

Development of ocular drugs may involve new medical entities (eg, Xalatan and Eylea; Tables 29.1 and 29.5) but can also include reformulation of systemic drugs for local use (eg, AzaSite, Ozurdex, and Restasis; Table 29.1). Regulatory considerations for ocular drug development can be derived from information available on approved drugs (Table 29.5), coupled with available regulatory guidance documents and presentation for nonclinical pharmacokinetic and toxicology studies.

TABLE 29.5 Nonclinical Programs: Examples of FDA Approved Ocular Drugs[a]

	Xalatan	Travatan	Lumigan	Lucentis	Eylea
NDA/BLA (approval year)	NDA 020597 (1996)	NDA 021257 (2001)	NDA 021275 (2001)	BLA 125156 (2006)	BLA 125387 (2011)
Active ingredient	Latanoprost	Travoprost	Bimatoprost	Ranibizumab	Aflibercept
Dosage form/route	Solution/topical ocular (TO)			Solution/intravitreal injection	
Indication	Reduction of elevated intraocular pressure in patients with open angle glaucoma or ocular hypertension			Neovascular (wet) age-related macular degeneration	
Pharmacokinetics[b]	Rats (PO, IV, TO), rabbits (IV, TO), dogs (IV), monkeys (PO, IV, TO)	Rats (IV, SC), rabbits (IV, TO), dogs (IV, TO)	Mice (IV, PO), rats (IV, PO), rabbits (TO), monkeys (IV, PO, TO)	Rabbits (IV, IVT), monkeys (IVT)	Rats (IV, SC), rabbits (IVT), monkeys (IV, IVT, SC)
Repeat-dose ocular toxicity[c]	1Y: rabbits, monkeys (TO)	6M: rabbits (TO); 1Y: Monkeys (TO)	6M: rabbits (TO); 1Y: monkeys (TO)	26W: monkeys (IVT)	8M: monkeys (IVT)
Repeat-dose systemic toxicity[c]	13W: mice (PO), rats (PO, IV), dogs (IV)	13W: mice, rats (IV); 6M: rats (SC)	1Y: rats (PO); 17W: monkeys (IV)	–	13W: rats (SC); 6M: monkeys (IV)
Genotoxicity	√	√	√	–	–
Carcinogenicity	Mice, rats (PO)	Mice, rats (SC)	Mice, rats (PO)	–	–
DART	Rats, rabbits (IV)	Mouse, rats (IV, SC)	Mouse, rats (PO)	–	Rabbits, monkeys (IV)
Safety pharmacology	√ (IV)	√ (IV, SC)	√ (IV)	√ (IVT)[d]	√ (IV)

DART, Developmental and reproductive toxicity; *IV*, Intravenous; *IVT*, Intravitreal injection; *M*, Month; *PO*, Oral; *SC*, Subcutaneous; *TO*, Topical Ocular; *W*, Week; *Y*, Year; √, Evaluation included in the program; –, No studies were conducted.

[a]*www.fda.gov; www.pharmapendium.com; product inserts.*
[b]*Absorption, distribution, metabolism, and/or elimination.*
[c]*Studies with the longest treatment duration; ocular toxicity studies included evaluation of systemic tissues.*
[d]*Safety pharmacology endpoints were incorporated into repeat-dose toxicity studies.*

VII. SAFETY EVALUATION OF OCULAR DRUGS, BOTANICAL PRODUCTS, AND MEDICINAL DEVICES

Nonclinical pharmacokinetic studies using the same ocular route as that intended for humans are expected to be conducted in order to characterize ocular distribution and melanin binding as well as systemic bioavailability [35] (see "Pharmacokinetics and Drug Disposition in the Eye" earlier in the chapter). For repeat-dose toxicity studies, the International Conference on Harmonization of Technical Requirements for Registration of Pharmaceuticals for Human Use [36] recommends one rodent and one nonrodent species. For ocular drugs, two nonrodent species are acceptable for ocular toxicity studies using the same ocular route of administration as that intended for humans; evaluation of animals with pigmented eyes should be conducted with melanin-binding compounds [35]. Systemic tissues are evaluated in addition to ocular effects in these studies but usually at much lower systemic drug exposure levels than those achievable using a systemic administration route. One species may be acceptable when evaluating biologics for which only one relevant species exists [37], and for those drugs with known ocular toxicity profiles [35]. Treatment duration of up to 6months in the first species and up to 9months in the second species are recommended depending on the intended clinical usage [36].

Ocular toxicity studies should be conducted using the same vehicle formulation that will be used in the clinical formulation, and the drug concentrations and dosing frequency should be at least as high as, and preferably exceed, those intended for clinical use [35]. If the vehicle formulation composition and/or excipient concentrations change during the course of nonclinical testing, either bridging nonclinical studies evaluating the clinical formulation, or justification for not testing the clinical formulation in nonclinical studies, is warranted. Especially when any changes made to the formulation result in a longer ocular drug exposure, additional studies may be expected.

Systemic characterization of ocular drugs mirrors that of systemic drugs, including administration routes (eg, oral and IV) and evaluation parameters. The decision to evaluate one or two species (one rodent and one nonrodent) depends on multiple factors [35]:

1. New medical entities (two species).
2. Known toxicity profiles (one species).
3. Low toxicity potential (one or two species).
4. Low systemic exposure following ocular administration (one species).
5. Biologics with one relevant species (one species).

For drugs with low toxicity potential, two species may be expected for short-term studies and one species for longer-term studies. Systemic target tissues may only be identified using a systemic administration route(s), as toxicity can be evaluated at an exaggerated systemic drug exposure level above those achievable via the intended clinical ocular administration route. A margin of exposure is usually derived from systemic route studies using a more sensitive species and by comparing the level of systemic drug exposure at a no observed adverse effect level to that observed clinically. A margin of exposure at least between 50 and 100 is not uncommon.

Additional types of studies evaluating genotoxicity, carcinogenicity, reproductive and development toxicity, and safety pharmacology that are expected in the evaluation of systemic drugs are also expected for ocular drugs unless there is a justification for not conducting them. When assessed, a systemic route of administration is typically used for studies conducted in vivo.

PRACTICAL CONSIDERATIONS IN ASSESSING OCULAR SAFETY

Study Objective

The stage in drug development determines the objective and type of toxicology study. Pivotal repeat-dose studies are expected to be conducted under GLP regulations, and regulatory guidelines determine the study duration for an Investigational New Drug (IND) or a New Drug Application (NDA) [38,39]. In early development, non-GLP screening studies are used to determine the dose range of ocular tolerability of various formulations. Ocular tolerability studies are often less than one week in duration and may include only in-life endpoints, such as clinical observations of ocular irritation, slit lamp biomicroscopy, intraocular pressure (IOP), and ophthalmoscopy without histopathology evaluation (see the section "Standard Ocular Examination Procedures" later in the chapter). Many dose treatment groups may be evaluated in a tolerability study, and the animals (usually rabbits) may be reused after an appropriate washout period. An ocular toxicity will typically have a smaller number of groups (five to six animals per group) and will include in-life endpoints, as well as ocular tissue histopathology. In vitro tolerability studies may be used to screen out highly irritating or cytotoxic compounds [40,41] or ocular vehicle formulations.

Test Formulation

The vehicle formulation of ophthalmic drugs should cause little or no irritation, so as not to interfere with interpretation of the drug's effect and to provide clinical acceptability. This imposes formulation requirements beyond maintenance of drug solubility and stability. The concentration of surfactants, excipients, or preservatives may be a compromise between their physicochemical or antimicrobial functions and potential cytotoxic effects on the corneal epithelium. The cornea is covered by a nonkeratinized stratified epithelium that forms a permeability barrier and is highly innervated, while the conjunctiva is a mucus membrane that may respond to injury with hyperemia or inflammatory cell infiltrates (see "Structure and Function of the Eye" later in the chapter). Ocular drugs must be formulated to be within a pH range that is nonirritating (pH 4.3–8.4) [42,43] and noncorrosive (pH 2–11.5) [44] and with a nonirritating osmolarity (<500 mOsm) [45]. Even greater restrictions are placed on intracameral and IVT formulations because of the sensitivity of the exposed tissues (endothelium, iris–ciliary body, lens, and retina), the small chamber volumes, and slow fluid circulation of the aqueous and vitreous. Topical ocular solutions should be sterile or preserved to prevent bacterial growth that could result in ocular infection. Intraocular injections have stringent requirements for sterility and low pyrogenicity to prevent endophthalmitis.

Test Species

The choice of nonclinical species is determined by ocular dimensions, pharmacokinetics properties, target tissues, background ocular lesions, and limited regulatory guidelines (see "Structure and Function of the Eye" later in the chapter, "Pharmacokinetics and Drug Disposition in the Eye" earlier in the chapter, and "Regulatory Considerations in Ocular Safety Assessment" earlier in the chapter). Rabbits, beagle dogs, and cynomolgus monkeys are the most common species used for ocular toxicity studies because their large eyes are favorable for ocular dosing (especially IVT) and ocular examination. Additional practical factors include the ease of handling rabbits and dogs, whose eyes can be dosed and examined without anesthesia. There is emerging interest in the use of mini-pigs because their eyes lack a tapetum, have holangiotic retinal vasculature, and have a cone to rod ratio similar to that in humans [46]. Although the rabbit is the species most frequently used to test for ocular irritation of eye drops, it may not always be the most sensitive species depending on the nature of the irritant chemical [47,48]. Conjunctival hyperemia may be produced by manipulation of the eyelids of albino rabbits, and variable conjunctival hyperemia may occur as a background finding in beagle dogs. Ocular exposure may be exaggerated by the relatively low blink rate of rabbits (0.05–0.3 blink/min) and dogs (1–2 blinks/min) compared to primates (4–22 blinks/min) [49–51]. Both rabbits and dogs have a nictitating membrane (third eyelid) that may affect topical drug exposure. Dogs and cats have a tapetum lucidum that may bind the drug [52] and change its bioavailability. Some regulatory agencies may request an ocular toxicity study in a pigmented species.

However, drug binding to melanin in the uveal tract and retinal pigment epithelium may not be predictive of ocular toxicity in pigmented species [28]. On the other hand, some drugs (eg, IVT or subcutaneous gentamicin) cause greater retinal toxicity in albino compared to pigmented rabbits, likely due to binding of drug to melanin, resulting in decreased retinal exposure in pigmented strains [53,54]. Test results may be affected by the condition of the animal; eg, stress affects IOP, and depth of anesthesia affects electroretinography (ERG). The avoidance of animal stress and discomfort is very important, and animal welfare is safeguarded by adherence to the guidelines of the Association for Research on Vision and Ophthalmology (www.arvo.org).

Route of Administration

The dose and administration route will depend on expected target tissue toxicity (see "Structure and Function of the Eye" later in the chapter) as well as tissue exposure (see "Pharmacokinetics and Drug Disposition in the Eye" earlier in the chapter). The volume of a topically instilled dose will affect drug exposure (see "Pharmacokinetics and Drug Disposition in the Eye" earlier in the chapter). The typical clinical drop volume is 30–40 μL, and this volume is often used in nonclinical studies that often dispense the formulation with the intended clinical dropper bottle. However, the average normal human tear volume is 6.2 μL and the human palpebral fissure can retain maximally 25 μL with the excess overflowing the lid or draining through the nasolacrimal duct [55]. For ocular dosing of rabbits in the Draize test [44], the standard test volume is 100 μL, even though a portion of this volume will overflow out of the eye when the rabbit blinks. A topical low-dose test volume of 10 μL has been recommended, as this accounts for the smaller size of a rabbit eye relative to the human eye and may provide better correlation to human eye irritation [56]. Given the limitation in maximum dose volume, the nonclinical frequency of topical instillations may exaggerate the clinical dosing frequency, eg, nonclinical TID or QID compared to clinical BID, in order to provide a higher exposure multiple when it is difficult to increase the maximum drug concentration for physicochemical reasons. For IVT administration in rabbits, an injection volume of ≤50 μL is recommended because a larger volume will cause an IOP spike or may require the removal of an equivalent volume of vitreous humor. The controls for ocular dosing could be untreated eyes (possibly the untreated contralateral eye), eyes given vehicle (or placebo implant), or sham injected eyes.

Other modes of ocular drug delivery provide advantages of localized exposure of the target tissue and/or prolonged duration of exposure [1,57–60]. Drug delivery systems include nanoparticles (diameter <1 μm), microspheres (diameter 1–1000 μm), liposomes, rod-shaped pellets (mm size), reservoir implants, and tissue plugs. The sites of implantation include the anterior chamber, vitreous humor, sclera, conjunctiva, and choroid. Some implant materials, such as those made from polylactic acid or polylacticglycolic acid, are biodegradable. The potential physical and chemical adverse effects of the implant material itself must be evaluated as the implant degrades or changes size over time.

Study Endpoints

Parameters measured in an ocular study typically include viability, clinical observations, gross ocular observations, ophthalmic examinations, IOP, body weight, food consumption, toxicokinetics, clinical pathology, and anatomic pathology (macroscopic and microscopic evaluation of ocular and systemic tissues). The procedures used to evaluate ocular toxicity are described in more detail in "Toxicokinetics and Exposure Assessment," "Techniques for In-Life Ocular Evaluation," and "Histopathology" later in the chapter.

Toxicokinetics and Exposure Assessment

A drug can, and does, become available in the systemic compartment following ocular administration, although exposure is generally very low, and sensitive bioanalytical methods are necessary to characterize this. Systemic drug exposure measured in early human studies following ophthalmic administration can be compared to that measured in systemic toxicity studies to establish margins of safety. The lower limit of quantitation (LLOQ) is the lowest concentration of the standard curve that can be measured with acceptable accuracy and precision as described in the 2001 FDA Guidance for Industry: Bioanalytical Method Validation. Characterizing the drug concentration versus time profile is dependent on the LLOQ of the bioanalytical method. However, the drug may be available systemically at levels below the LLOQ, which can truncate the measurement of AUC and half-life, and thus poses a challenge in calculating safety margins. Fig. 29.13 illustrates how the LLOQ can artificially alter the magnitude of a safety margin calculated from the same data set when comparing drug exposure in a nonclinical species versus the human. Practical considerations when establishing the LLOQ in bioanalytical methods used to support nonclinical development include limitation of animal blood sample volume relative to human, analyte stability in nonclinical species, and early development timelines and cost, which together contribute to what is deemed feasible. Ultimately, methods must be developed that take into account the potency of the drug at eliciting both pharmacological and toxicological effects in addition to practical considerations. Although systemic levels are very low after ophthalmic administration, and are typically designed to be well below biologically active levels, reports do exist that describe systemic side effects of drugs reflecting mechanism-based or exaggerated pharmacology [61].

TECHNIQUES FOR IN-LIFE OCULAR EVALUATION

Standard Ocular Examination Procedures

The standard procedures for ocular toxicity evaluation used during the in-life phase include clinical observations of ocular irritation, ophthalmic examinations (slit lamp biomicroscopy including fluorescein staining, pupillary reflex, and ophthalmoscopy), and measurement of IOP (tonometry). Additional details for these standard ocular examinations can be found in several reviews [38,39,62–64]. Conscious rodents, rabbits, dogs, and cats may be examined using manual restraint. Ocular examination in nonhuman primates is carried out following sedation. Tonometry may be conducted on conscious nonhuman primates acclimated to a tube restraint device, which eliminates confounding effects of anesthetics on IOP.

Examination of the cornea and conjunctiva may be carried out by gross examination with or without magnification, or by using a slit lamp biomicroscope, which can be used to visualize the corneal cross-section including stromal opacities or deposits. The evaluation of ocular irritation has a long history, beginning with the Draize test [44]. The use of rabbits for ocular irritation testing far outnumbers the use of other species for historical and practical reasons. Based on an extensive comparison of nonclinical findings with reported human effects, the rabbit ocular irritation test predicts human results 85% of the time, overpredicts 10%, and underpredicts 5% [39]. The classical Draize scale is appropriate for evaluation of accidental exposure to moderately or severely irritating and corrosive test articles, as this scale gives a higher weight to findings such as corneal opacity [39,44]. The modified Hackett–McDonald grading scale is more appropriate for evaluating the milder effects of topical ophthalmic agents, as it has finer gradations for corneal and conjunctival findings [65]. Contemporary formulations designed for repeated topical ocular instillation rarely cause severe damage resulting in corneal opacity; however, such formulations may cause mild to moderate ocular irritation characterized by conjunctival hyperemia or corneal fluorescein staining. In nonclinical ocular toxicity studies, corneal staining is a useful indicator of corneal damage that is often found to have a histopathological correlate. Corneal epithelial defects may be visualized as patterns of fluorescence after topical application of a dilute sodium fluorescein solution to the tear film. A slit lamp biomicroscope using a blue filter (400–500 nm) for illumination reveals fluorescein fluorescence, which is often improved by viewing through a yellow filter (Kodak Wratten 12). Although in widespread use, the cellular basis of corneal fluorescein staining is not well understood [66,67]. The observation of corneal punctate staining may be due to pooling of dye in small depressions in the ocular surface, uptake of dye by damaged epithelial cells, or dye penetration of the epithelial barrier past damaged tight junctions [66,67].

Ophthalmic examination of the anterior chamber, iris, lens, and anterior vitreous using a slit lamp biomicroscope and a direct or indirect ophthalmoscope are preferably performed by a veterinary ophthalmologist, certified by the American College of Veterinary Ophthalmology. Cells or protein (flare) in the anterior chamber may be visualized with a slit lamp. Nonclinical grading scales are based upon clinical grading scales provided by the Standard Uveitis Nomenclature Working Group [68]. In the case of inflammation caused by an innate response to endotoxin, anterior chamber cells and flare can appear within hours [69]. Pupillary response to light, iris inflammation, and synechiae (adhesions of iris to the lens) may also be detected with a slit lamp. Following anterior chamber evaluation, a mydriatic drug is instilled to dilate the iris to improve visualization of the fundus. A pigmented iris may be more resistant to dilation because of binding of the mydriatic to melanin [70]. Rabbits may be resistant to iris dilation by atropine due to the presence of atropine esterase activity in this species [38], and tropicamide is an alternative mydriatic. The size and position of lens opacities can be detected with a slit lamp or direct ophthalmoscope. However, punctate lens opacities visualized by ophthalmoscopy are often difficult to confirm by histopathology due to the complexity of capturing the section containing the lesion on a glass slide. Inflammatory cells or keratin precipitates on the anterior lens capsule, and cells in the anterior vitreous may be also detected with this procedure. A direct or indirect ophthalmoscope is used by a trained ophthalmologist to visualize the ocular fundus (posterior vitreous, retina, choroid, and optic nerve head).

IOP measured by tonometry may be used to detect damage to aqueous humor production by the ciliary body, obstruction of the aqueous outflow pathways in the trabecular meshwork and Schlemm's canal, and anterior uveitis. Applanation tonometers require a topical anesthetic, while rebound tonometers do not. Tonometry should be carried out at the same time of the day because of diurnal variation in IOP. It should be noted that the normal physiological sleep patterns of nonclinical species are affected by laboratory light cycles and lab personnel activity [69,71,72]. Care should be taken to acclimate the animal to the tonometry procedure

and to reduce environmental disruptions because IOP is affected by blood pressure and stress response. Implanted IOP sensors with telemetry have been used to continuously measure IOP in rabbits in order to record diurnal variation and minimize effects of animal handling [71,73].

Nonclinical ocular examinations must take into account species-specific differences in the anatomy of the eye, including presence of a nictitating membrane in rabbits, dogs, and cats; varying number and position of lacrimal glands; the presence or absence of a Harderian gland; occurrence of epiphora in rabbits and chromodacryorrhea in rats; differing absolute and relative volumes of anterior chamber, lens, and vitreous; the presence of a tapetum lucidum in dogs and cats; and differences in retinal vasculature (see "Structure and Function of the Eye" later in the chapter) [62–64,70]. Ocular lesions may be present due to genetic defects occurring in certain strains. For example, a background incidence of corneal dystrophy in Dutch belted rabbits is present even in current commercial laboratory stocks [74]. The present day use of specific pathogen-free laboratory animal stocks has eliminated almost all confounding effects of ocular infectious agents [70].

Specialized Ocular Examination Techniques

Nonclinical ocular toxicity evaluation has been greatly advanced by new technology for in vivo ophthalmic examination. Specialized techniques may be utilized to examine a specific ocular structure or function, when warranted by the drug effect. Many of these in vivo techniques can serve as biomarkers for translation to the clinic. This section provides a broad overview of these techniques, indicating their application to ocular tissues or function, and citing reviews which give details on physical principles, instrumentation, and procedures. The usefulness of various ocular examination techniques for studying ocular structure and function is summarized in Table 29.6.

Specular microscopy produces en-face images of the corneal endothelium and is used to measure the number, density, and shape of corneal endothelial cells of rabbits, dogs, and nonhuman primates [75,76]. The significance of endothelial cell shape and density for evaluating endothelial barrier function and damage is described in the section "Structure and Function of the Eye" later in the chapter. Instruments are available that do or do not make contact with the cornea; however, the animals must still be anesthetized because immobility of the eye is required for imaging.

Ultrasound pachymetry is used to measure corneal thickness, which reflects the ability of the epithelial and endothelial barriers to maintain corneal hydration. Conventional ultrasound instruments operate at frequencies

TABLE 29.6　Ocular Examination Techniques

Ocular Structure or Property	Technique
Cornea	Gross ocular examination, slit lamp biomicroscopy, high-frequency ultrasound imaging, in vivo confocal microscopy (IVCM), optical coherence tomography (OCT), Scheimpflug photography
Corneal thickness	Ultrasound pachymetry, optical coherence tomography (OCT), optical low coherence reflectometer, Scheimpflug photography
Corneal endothelial cells	Specular microscopy
Corneal permeability	Fluorophotometry
Tear film	In vivo confocal microscopy (IVCM)
Tear secretion, tear flow	Schirmer tear test, fluorophotometry
Conjunctiva	Gross ocular examination, slit lamp biomicroscopy
Conjunctival goblet cells, inflammatory cells	Conjunctival impression cytology
Anterior chamber	Slit lamp biomicroscopy, high frequency ultrasound imaging, optical coherence tomography (OCT)
Anterior chamber flare	Slit lamp biomicroscopy, laser flare photometer
Intraocular pressure	Tonometry
Aqueous fluid dynamics	Fluorophotometry
Iris	Slit lamp biomicroscopy, optical coherence tomography (OCT)
Blood–aqueous barrier	Fluorophotometry
Lens	Slit lamp biomicroscopy, direct/indirect ophthalmoscopy
Vitreous	Indirect ophthalmoscopy
Vitreous fluid dynamics	Fluorophotometry
Retina, fundus	Direct/indirect ophthalmoscopy, confocal scanning laser ophthalmoscopy (SLO), optical coherence tomography (OCT)
Blood–retinal barrier	Fluorophotometry, fluorescein angiography (FA)
Retinal blood flow, oximetric state	Laser Doppler flowmetry
Retinal function	Electroretinography (ERG), multifocal ERG (mfERG), visual evoked potential (VEP)
Visual acuity	Visual evoked potential (VEP), optomotor reflex

of 10–20 MHz, have a resolution of millimeters, contact the eye, and can image the entire eye even through the eyelid or a cataract. Measurements of corneal thickness in rabbits show that there is good correlation between ultrasound pachymetry and confocal microscopy [77]. High-resolution ultrasound has a resolution of 20–80 μm and can be used to visualize anterior chamber and lens, thickness of cornea, sclera iris, angle, ciliary cleft, and trabecular meshwork in larger species, such as dogs [78] or primates.

High-frequency ultrasound imaging (50–70 mHz) provides wide-field, high-resolution images of the cornea and has been used to continuously measure cornea stromal thickness over 10 mm diameter in humans [79]. An eyecup water bath is required. Ultrasound can also be used to examine anterior uveitis to visualize cells and flare, keratic precipitates, synechiae, iris–ciliary body edema, and vitreous exudates [80].

In vivo confocal microscopy (IVCM) produces high-resolution images of the total cornea, including epithelial, stromal, Bowman's, and endothelial layers [75,77,81–83]. Two types of instrument, tandem scanning and slit scanning confocal microscopes, detect light at the focal plane and reject out-of-focus light. Using an objective lens in contact with the surface of the eye, the focal point is scanned in three planes (X, Y, and Z axes) to reconstruct the entire image of the specimen with current resolution capabilities of 9 μm in the Z-axis, 0.5–1.0 μm for the X-Y axis, and 1500 μm total depth range. Video images and three-dimensional reconstruction of the cornea are possible. Individual cells of the epithelium, stroma [77], endothelium, and in addition, corneal nerve fibers, inflammatory cells, and the tear film may be visualized. These techniques have been successfully used with rabbit, cat, dog, rat, mouse, and sheep [75,77,82,83].

Confocal scanning laser ophthalmoscopy (SLO) [84] scans the retina with a point of light moving in a raster pattern and detects the reflected light in a confocal process that allows the reconstruction of a three-dimensional image of the retina. SLO has been used for fundus imaging and dynamic retinal angiography in dogs, monkeys, and mini-pigs [85,86], and has been applied to small rodent retinal models including gerbils and hamsters [86]. SLO has been used for quantitative measurements of fundus autofluorescence of lipofuscin in retinal pigment epithelium (RPE) as a measure of retinal degeneration in humans [87].

Optical coherence tomography (OCT) is the most powerful recent technique for ophthalmology examination. Over 7000 publications relating to OCT and application in the eye were found in a PubMed search between 1991 and 2011. Spectral-domain (or Fourier-domain) OCT and time-domain OCT instruments are available. Commercial OCT instruments are predominantly the former type and can provide cross-sectional or three-dimensional images of the eye with depth resolution of 4–6 μm and a transverse resolution of 15–20 μm [88–91]. For comparison, the peripapillary retinal nerve fiber layer thickness ranges from approximately 60–130 μm depending on location. The noninvasive nature, safe intensity of light exposure, and user-friendly instrumentation facilitate nonclinical and clinical correlations and study of lesion progression or resolution over time in one individual. All segments of the eye from the cornea to the retina may be imaged, although some instruments require optional lenses and other instruments are specialized for the front or back of the eye [92]. Some instruments combine OCT with SLO [84] or OCT with laser Doppler flowmetry. Advances such as the use of adaptive optics [88,93–95] or polarized light detection [96] have increased the cellular resolution and tissue-specific contrast capabilities of OCT. Cell layers in the retina may be distinguished by OCT due to their different densities and light backscattering properties. Retinal OCT images closely reflect the layer-specific architecture and can be used to quantitatively evaluate anatomic structure, thickness, and structural integrity. Macular edema, retinal detachment and atrophy, epiretinal membrane formation, and neoplastic growths are a few of the features that may be monitored in the clinic by OCT. Retinal structure and thickness have been measured by OCT in rodents, rabbits, cats, dogs, pigs, and monkeys [89] and is particularly useful in discovery phases of development. OCT is also used to examine the cornea. Practical applications in humans include measurements to assess changes of corneal thickness due to disease (eg, dry eye), following chronic use of antiglaucoma drugs [97], and with contact lens wear

[98]. Uveitis-associated corneal edema, opacification, and endothelial keratic precipitates are readily detected by OCT, as are inflammatory cells within the anterior chamber [99]. OCT may be employed in nonclinical studies to assess potential changes in corneal thickness with a resolution of 1.3 μm and is sensitive enough to discriminate changes in the corneal epithelium [100].

Scheimpflug photography is based on an optical principle that provides sufficient depth of focus to image the anterior segment of the eye from the cornea surface to the posterior lens capsule with minimal distortion [101]. Commercial instruments can perform ocular biometry, including corneal thickness measurement, but excel at cross-sectional densitometry or light scattering of cornea and lens to detect toxic effects or cataracts in humans, mice, rats, rabbits, dogs, cats, and monkeys [62,64,101].

The optical low coherence reflectometer is mounted on a regular slit lamp, does not contact the corneal surface, and is used to measure central corneal thickness in rats, mice, and rabbits [102].

Laser flare photometry provides a quantitative measurement of anterior chamber flare. It can be significantly more sensitive in assessing uveitis compared to aqueous cell density determined by slit lamp [103,104].

The quality of the tear film affects the health and visual acuity of the ocular surface [105,106]. The rate of tear secretion is measured by the Schirmer test, which uses a strip of filter paper placed in the lid margin and the wetted length (measured in millimeters) over a fixed time. The stability of the tear film is measured in terms of tear breakup time [105] using interferometry. These tests measure different tear properties and are not correlated [105,106]. The surface dynamics and topography of the tear film may be studied by ocular surface wavefront aberrations [107–109]. This method has been applied to awake cats using a Shack–Hartmann wavefront sensor [110].

Conjunctival impression cytology uses filter paper to obtain an imprint of the conjunctival surface, which may be examined microscopically for goblet cell density and signs of ocular surface inflammation [111]. Immunochemistry may be used to detect specific cell types by immunohistochemistry (IHC) or flow cytometry [111,112].

Fluorophotometry is used to investigate the permeability barriers of various ocular compartments by measurement of the relative fluorescence of fluorescein dye at locations in the eye from the tear film to the choroid [64]. After topical instillation of fluorescein, fluorophotometry has been used to measure variations in corneal permeability [113] and effects of tear volume and tear secretion in normal and dry eye patients [114]. Fluorophotometry is used to investigate the integrity of the blood–aqueous and blood–retinal barriers, as well as fluid dynamics in the aqueous humor and vitreous humor following IV injection of dye [64,115]. This technique also has been used in rabbits to determine the transscleral delivery of fluorescein or fluoresceinated dextrans to the retina, choroid, and vitreous following subconjunctival injection [116].

Fluorescein angiography (FA) is used to determine the morphology and permeability of retinal vessels following IV injection of dye and fundus photography [63,117]. FA is particularly suited for monitoring vascular diseases of the retina such as neovascularization, which occurs with age-related macular degeneration, and diabetic retinopathy. In nonclinical development, FA is frequently used to assess therapeutic efficacy in animal models of retinal neovascularization and vascular leak. The optic disc, choroid, macula, and RPE are also visualized by FA. Indocyanine green has been used as an alternative to fluorescein because its fluorescence is not masked by pigments in the RPE. In addition to in vivo studies, isolated perfused eyes may be used to study retinal vascular response, and this has been carried out with cat, monkey, dog, pig, guinea pig, and rat eyes [63,117,118].

Laser Doppler flowmetry uses an infrared laser to detect the motion of red blood cells in the retina [62,119]. Scanning laser ophthalmoscopy may also be used to measure retinal blood flow [119]. A Retinal Function Imager based on multispectral imaging at high frequency (50–100 Hz) measures retinal blood flow velocity, oximetric state, metabolic responses to photic activation, and capillary perfusion mapping [120]. High-resolution magnetic resonance imaging [121] using microcrystalline iron oxide nanocolloid has been used to measure retinal blood volumes in rats [121].

Retinal function is measured by ERG and visual evoked potential (VEP) [62–64]. ERG and VEP are used to detect drug effects on photoreceptor (PR) response, bipolar cells, retinal neurons, and phototransduction, as well as glaucomatous damage to nerve fiber layer, retinitis pigmentosa, diabetic retinopathy, and optic neuritis [122]. Evaluation of ERG has become a regulatory expectation for ocular toxicity studies [35]. Full-field or "flash" ERG is most commonly used in nonclinical studies. In full-field ERG, a corneal electrode measures the retinal electrical response to a flash of light as a negative deflection (a-wave) followed by a positive b-wave in a dark-adapted eye. The a-wave is generated by the PR in response to closure of the sodium and potassium channels in the outer segment. The positive b-wave is produced by the summation of cellular response, primarily by the bipolar cells of the inner nuclear layer, which either depolarize or hyperpolarize to the diminished glutamate release from the PR, and secondarily by depolarization of Müller cells. However, action potentials generated by the retinal ganglion cells (RGCs), the cells that transduce the visual signal, are not recorded by ERG. Thus an ERG response does not reflect visual perception, and may occur concurrently with blindness. The VEP is an electrical recording derived from the visual cortex response to retinal stimulation by a light flash or contrast-reversing pattern and is used as a surrogate for visual acuity. Normal VEP recordings are an indicator that the visual pathway from the RGC to the visual cortex is intact [123].

The extrapolation of visual function results from animals to humans must take into account similarities and differences in neural structure [124]. The applications and limitations of ERG in animal models have been discussed [125], and recommendations for toxicological screening in animal models have been proposed [126]. Although the standard clinical ERG protocol is often used for nonclinical studies, a case has been made for its modification for nocturnal versus diurnal species due to different rod and cone densities [126], and specific ERG procedures for rabbits [127] and dogs [128] have been presented. Full-field ERG is useful for detecting functional deficits in a relatively large area of the retina, but is insensitive to small, localized damage to the retina. Multifocal ERG (mfERG) [47] may be used to detect localized retinal changes [63]. For example, localized retinal separation made by subretinal injection of balanced salt solution (100 μL) in monkeys caused transient suppression of mfERG responses in the injected region, correlating physically to diminished inner segment/outer segments shown by OCT in the region of injection [129].

Optomotor reflex can measure the effect of drugs on the visual acuity of conscious, unrestrained nonclinical species, offering an alternative to ERG as a visual function measurement [130]. The optomotor reflex consists of stereotypical head-tracking movements that are elicited in all visual animals by exposure to vertical grating patterns. The animal, eg, a rat, is placed in a chamber surrounded by four computer monitors displaying vertical grating patterns. The grating is rotated (starting at 2 rpm) to elicit head tracking movements in the same direction as the motion of the grating. A video camera above the chamber allows the observer to determine whether the animal does or does not make head tracking movements. The frequency of the grating rotation is increased in steps until there is no head tracking movement, indicating the threshold of visual resolution.

Histopathology

The complex nature of the ocular tissues requires careful attention to enucleation and processing techniques. The following sections describe techniques to minimize the introduction of artifacts which can confound histological interpretation to even the experienced pathologist. Because the retina rapidly undergoes autolysis, the eyes should be enucleated immediately upon euthanasia and placed in the appropriate fixative.

Tissue Collection

The animal should be euthanized using an approved method and positioned to allow easy access to the eye. To enucleate, the eyelids should be grasped with forceps and the skin incised around the eye socket using a scalpel. The deep ocular muscles should be sectioned to the optic nerve by cutting close to the orbital bone, leaving several millimeters of optic nerve attached to the ocular globe. Gentle traction should be used during enucleation to avoid retinal detachment and corneal and optic nerve artifacts. The entire globe with lids, conjunctiva, and segment of optic nerve attached should be removed and rinsed with normal saline or an appropriate buffer solution. The extraocular tissues attached to the globe should be removed (with the exception of bulbar conjunctiva, which should remain attached to the globe) in order to see landmarks and to more easily trim the globe, but should also be retained for histological evaluation. These tissues consist of the eyelids, extraocular muscles, and lacrimal gland in all animals, the Harderian gland in rabbits and rodents, and the nictitating membrane in dog, rabbit, rat, and mouse. When handling the globes, avoid compression, which can cause artifact retinal detachment, and touching the cornea, which can cause mechanical corneal epithelial desquamation. To facilitate orientation during processing, each globe should be marked to designate the 12-o'clock (dorsal midsagittal) position and any site of injection using indelible dye, tattoo ink, or suture. It is best not to incise the globes prior to the initial fixation as the globe will collapse, causing distortion of the internal structures. Place right and left eyes in individual, appropriately marked jars so that, during histopathologic evaluation, unilateral clinical correlations can be matched to the correct eye.

Preservation

Fixation: Common fixatives for the eye include neutral buffered formalin (NBF), Bouin's, and Davidson's [131]. Each fixative creates its own set of artifacts, and the choice of fixative will depend on the specific ocular structure that is investigated. The recommended fixations according to structure of interest are given in Table 29.7.

Trimming and Embedding

Ocular Globe

For the treated eye, make parasagittal cuts tangential to the temporal and nasal aspects of the cornea at the limbus. The marking dye may be reapplied to the sclera at the clock position of the injection site as needed. The temporal aspect should be oriented in the down position in the cassette for processing. The temporal aspect is similarly oriented for embedding of the eye as well. The

TABLE 29.7 Common Fixatives for Ocular Tissues

Ocular Structure of Interest	Appropriate Fixative	Comments
Cornea, anterior chamber, lens	NBF	Not good for general fixation of eye due to high incidence of artifactual retinal detachment.
Retina	Davidson's	Fast-acting fixation. Excellent preservation of retina with minimal artifactual detachment. Fixation artifacts of the cornea, lens, optic nerve are common. Leave in fixative for 10–24 h. Transfer to 70% ethanol for 24 h before trimming. Process from 2nd station (70–80% ethanol).
General	Davidson's	See above.

bulbar conjunctiva should remain attached to the eye, and oriented such that it is captured in section, with the epithelium present.

Extraocular Tissues

The upper eyelid, nictitating membrane, lacrimal gland(s), and Harderian gland can be embedded for cross-sectioning together. The lower eyelid, extraocular muscles, and optic nerve can be embedded together with cross-sectioning of the eyelid and optic nerve, and longitudinal sectioning of the muscles.

Sectioning

For Standard (Sagittal) Ocular Sectioning

The block should be faced into until the optic disc is present. Sections should be captured in the vertical plane for all species other than primates, and those retained for histopathology should contain the optic disc, lens, and pupil. For primates, sections should be made in the horizontal plane through the optic disc and macula to capture the fovea. Slow, complete turns (avoid rocking) of the microtome are required to prevent the lens from shattering.

Special sectioning techniques may be required if there is an injection site present that needs to be evaluated. These may be best captured by trimming and separate embedding; communication with the histologists is key to avoid loss of these important sites during processing.

For Extraocular Tissues Sectioning

Tissues should be oriented properly in the cassettes such that eyelid epidermis and conjunctival surfaces are present, both sides of the nictitating membrane are present, and the optic nerve is present in cross-section.

EXAMPLES OF ADVERSE EFFECTS IN THE EYE

The following examples illustrate effects of drug treatment or toxins on ocular tissues.

Ocular Surface

Toxicity to the cornea may be shown by epithelial damage, a breakdown in epithelial barrier function that may lead to corneal edema, a change in thickness, or increased corneal opacity. Corneal damage may cause the release of inflammatory cytokines leading to conjunctival hyperemia or corneal neovascularization. Conjunctival swelling and discharge may be acute responses to topical irritants, while a decrease in goblet cell density or tear volume production may be chronic sequelae.

The many nonclinical ocular toxicity studies carried out with benzalkonium chloride [132] are informative about the mechanism of and methods used to study ocular irritation. The motivation for these studies is the predominant use of BAK (0.005–0.02%) as a preservative in commercial topical ophthalmic products, many of which have been used daily for many years. Ocular irritants with surfactant properties similar to BAK cause desquamation or cell death of the corneal epithelium, disruption of the corneal barrier function, and resulting conjunctival hyperemia, inflammation, changes in corneal epithelial thickness, increased endothelial permeability, goblet cell loss, decreased mucin, and stromal disorganization [133–135]. Agents delivered into the anterior chamber (intracameral) may be toxic to corneal endothelial cells that are crucial to maintenance of the hydration state of the cornea. Endothelial cells of the cornea do not proliferate, so cytotoxicity results in a decreased cell density and altered cell shape detectable with specular microscopy. Corneal swelling and haze may be observed as a consequence of increased permeability, which can be measured as increased central corneal thickness, such as that observed with intracameral injection of gentamicin [136], besifloxacin, azithromycin, or ciprofloxacin antibiotics [137].

The transparency of the cornea allows ready visualization of potential drug deposits in the stroma that may be less apparent in other tissues, such as those that occur with oral chlorpromazine, an antipsychotic [138], and by phosphate buffer, which causes calcium deposits secondary to alkali burn [139].

Ocular accessory tissues such as the meibomian or lacrimal glands may also be affected by drugs or toxicants, in particular inflammation, with potential to progress to atrophy. The topical antiviral Cidofovir may cause allergic inflammation and narrowing of the lacrimal canal [140]. Oral toxaphene, a chlorinated pesticide, has been associated with inflammation and enlargement and impaction of the meibomian glands [141].

Anterior Chamber

Corticosteriods used for the treatment of anterior segment inflammation are commonly associated with elevated IOP, whether administered topical, subconjunctival, or intracameral. The mechanism is not understood; however, studies in rabbits suggest a role for increased blood flow resistance in the ophthalmic artery [142], or accumulation of acid mucopolysaccharides in Schlemm's canal and the trabecular meshwork [143]. Nonclinical models to screen new corticosteroids for this adverse effect are needed, but are still not well established. For example, topical dexamethasone phosphate (1%, BID, TID, 2–3 weeks) in cats [144,145], topical prednisolone acetate (0.5%, TID, 4 weeks) in sheep [146], subconjunctival betamethasone in rabbits [147], and subconjunctival dexamethasone in mice [148] have been shown to cause an IOP increase, but the results have not been consistently reproduced. Structural modification of corticosteroids has led to compounds that retain potent antiinflammatory efficacy with lower propensity to elevate IOP in sensitive individuals [149].

Lens

Lens cell proliferation and crystalline structure are essential for transparency, so both cell-cycle inhibitors and oxidizing agents may cause lens opacities. Cataracts have been attributed to agents that cause lens epithelial cell-cycle arrest: intraperitoneal (IP) injection of Myleran, an alkylating agent, in rats [150], or acetaminophen analgesic plus 3-methylcholanthrene (CYP inducer) in mice [151]; separation of lens fibers (IVT Diquat herbicide in rabbits [152]); and presumptive inhibition of cell membrane synthesis (cholesterol synthesis inhibitors in dogs or mice [153]). Drugs may form deposits in several tissues, and the deposits will be especially apparent in the transparent lens. Yellow discoloration of the lens was caused by oral Rifabutin, an RNA polymerase inhibitor, antibiotic in rabbits [154].

Fundus

Retinal diseases, such as macular degeneration and diabetic retinopathy, are important targets of drug development, which has made IVT injection of drugs more common. The complex structure and function of the retina makes it very susceptible to toxic injury. Fortunately, many in vivo imaging techniques that are highly correlated with histopathology are available to examine the retina; however, there are many instances that illustrate histopathology as the most sensitive endpoint.

Methanol effects on retina structure and function provide an illustration of the methods used to detect retinal toxicity. Formaldehyde, a metabolite of methanol, is thought to be the source of retinal toxicity [155]. Optic disc hyperemia, peripapillary nerve fiber layer swelling, retinal edema, and visual impairment are manifestations of methanol toxicity common to all species and readily observed clinically by ophthalmoscopy, fluorescein angiography, and OCT [156]. Functional endpoints may have some species variation, however. For example, depressed ERG b-wave amplitudes occur in rats [157,158], but not monkeys [159], with methanol toxicity, although monkeys do show reduced oscillatory potentials.

The use of sodium iodate as an intravenous antiinfection agent in the 1920s resulted in cases of human blindness. This chemical is a strong oxidizing agent that is primarily toxic to the RPE, and subsequently has been used as a model agent for producing specific retinotoxicity. Sodium iodate administered IV to rats produces visual acuity loss at 2h postdose measured by optomotor reflex and associated with vacuolation and degeneration of RPE, rods, and cones observed by histopathology, IHC, and TEM [130]. PR inner and outer segment destruction following IV administration of iodoacetate in rabbits is readily detected by both OCT and histopathology [160].

Antibiotics are given by IVT injection to treat severe intraocular infection, and so their potential for retinal toxicity has been assessed. IVT administration of gentamicin to rabbits results in the diffuse disruption of nerve fiber layer and inner plexiform layer of retina, the latter correlating with the elimination of ERG b-wave (although the a-wave remains intact). More severe damage occurs in albino rabbits than in pigmented rabbits [53,54], likely due to melanin binding of gentamicin, preventing it from reaching the retina. ERG changes that may include decreased a- and b-wave amplitude and oscillatory potential may be a harbinger of anatomical changes to the retina, particularly of the photoreceptors, such as seen with enrofloxin, a fluoroquinolone antibiotic [161]; IVT daptomycin antibiotic [162]; and IVT cefuroxime antibiotic [163]. These examples demonstrate the high sensitivity of retinal cells to some antibiotics, which may limit the choices for intraocular use against strains of bacteria. On the other hand, no structural changes are caused by IVT piperacillin/tazobactam (ureidopenicillin/β-lactamase inhibitor), despite decreased b-wave amplitude and increased implicit time [164].

The highly effective therapy of IVT ranibizumab (Lucentis) for age-related macular degeneration has led to many studies of other agents blocking vascular endothelial growth factor activity in the eye (see "Structure

and Function of the Eye" later in the chapter) [165]. As an example, the anti-VEGF full-length antibody, bevacizumab (Avastin) [166], was shown to be as effective as ranibizumab in the clinic, where its lower cost is resulting in increased off-label use. Nonclinical studies have been conflicting with respect to potential functional or anatomical effects induced by bevacizumab administration. In primates, transient, decreased scotopic ERG a- and b-wave amplitudes and prolonged implicit times, but no anatomical changes, were caused by IVT bevacizumab [167], contrasting to other reports of PR damage, reduction of choriocapillaris endothelial fenestrations, and increased leukocytes in choriocapillaris [168]. In rabbits, ERG and VEP remain unchanged [166], although PR and RPE degeneration [165] and retinal cell apoptosis have been reported [169]. The ongoing interpretation of these studies is important for assessing their clinical significance regarding the safety of bevacizumab, and more generally for understanding the advantages and disadvantages of the nonclinical models for the study of anti-VEGF agents.

Translation of Nonclinical Findings

When comparing nonclinical findings with adverse ocular effects of drugs in humans as described in the literature [170–176], the overall trend demonstrates translation of nonclinical results to humans. Lack of correlation may be due to species-specific pharmacology, effects that require chronic use over many years, or low incidence of findings that may only appear in large populations. Examples of comparisons between clinical and nonclinical ocular responses to drugs follow.

Chloroquine is an antimalarial that is known to cause retinopathy [170,173]. The analog, hydroxychloroquine, is less toxic and more widely used. Chloroquine is a cationic amphiphilic drug that may accumulate in association with increased phospholipids within lysosomes [177]. Patients who had taken oral chloroquine or hydroxychloroquine for at least 5 years had a pigmentary change of the macula with sparing of the foveal center (bull's-eye maculopathy) that may be accompanied by central visual loss, visual field defects, color vision deficiency, and other symptoms [178,179]. In later stages of the disease, there is atrophy of the RPE and neurosensory retina. OCT demonstrates peripapillary retinal nerve-fiber layer thinning and selective thinning of perifoveal inner retinal layers [178,179], while OCT, fundus photography, and fluorescein angiography collectively show outer retina disruption in macula, and loss of perifoveal PR inner segment/outer segment junction in patients [180]. Although full-field ERG may be normal, mfERG showed severe dysfunction in the parafoveal and perifoveal areas with normal function in the fovea [181]. For comparison, monkeys given intramuscular chloroquine for 4years showed no ophthalmologic change and no retinal function change by ERG, but drug was bound to pigmented tissues (choroid/RPE, ciliary body/iris) and there was long-term degeneration of RGC, PR, and later RPE and choroid [182]. In studies conducted in pigmented rats given IP chloroquine for 7days by osmotic pump [183] and pigmented mice given IP chloroquine [184], cytoplasmic bodies were reported in several cell types, including RGC, PR, and RPE. The mechanism of retinal toxicity is hypothesized to be drug accumulation in lysosomes causing lysosomal acidification, which leads to cytotoxicity.

Amiodarone is an antiarrhythmic agent taken orally for recurrent ventricular tachycardia or fibrillation [170,173]. An ocular side effect reported in up to 40% of patients is the appearance of colored rings around lights with daily dosing for 1–2years [185]. Amiodarone is also a cationic amphiphilic drug that can induce phospholipidosis [177]. Corneal epithelial opacities resembling "cat's whiskers" occur in 70–100% of patients and lens opacities in 50–60% of patients. Six beagle dogs were given daily oral amiodarone for 11weeks, and slit lamp and indirect ophthalmoscopy exam found corneal deposits in both eyes of only one dog, confirmed by histopathology [186]. Possible reasons for the low incidence in dogs were insufficient duration of dosing and lack of sunlight exposure, which is believed to exacerbate corneal deposits of amiodarone in humans.

Sildenafil [187] is an inhibitor of phosphodiesterase-5 (PDE-5) that is used to treat erectile dysfunction. A less common side effect is change in color perception toward a blue tint along with increased perception of brightness [170]. In dogs given IV sildenafil, there was a dose-related reduction in the a-wave amplitude and increases in a- and b-wave implicit times, though the effects were transient and reversible [187]. The cause of the changes in retinal function may be that sildenafil not only inhibits PDE-5 but also is a weak inhibitor of PDE-6, which is involved in cGMP-mediated phototransduction in rod and cone PR.

Ethambutol is a bacteriostatic agent that is used to treat tuberculosis and has been associated with optic neuropathy in 2–6% of patients [173]. Patients treated with ethambutol may have ERG abnormalities: double a-wave, indistinct oscillatory potentials, and abnormal flicker and multifocal responses [188]. Decreased retinal nerve fiber layer thickness can be detected by OCT after clinical treatment with oral ethambutol [189]. Rats given subcutaneous ethambutol had normal ERG, but abnormal VEP [190]. When rats were given oral ethambutol, there was selective loss of RGC detected by retrograde labeling of retina whole mounts [191]. The mechanism of ethambutol retinotoxicity is not completely understood, but may involve chelation and depletion of zinc and/or copper in RGC mitochondria, which exacerbates RGC

death in patients with a pathogenic mitochondrial mutation [192].

Vigabatrin is an irreversible inhibitor of γ-aminobutyric acid (GABA) transaminase that is used as an oral anticonvulsant to treat epilepsy. This drug has been associated with bilateral constriction of the visual field [193]. Fundus examination by ophthalmoscopy was not sufficient to diagnose the vigabatrin-induced visual field loss, but OCT and SLO showed very high correlation with decreased retinal nerve fiber layer thickness [193]. A clinical full-field ERG study showed abnormal 30-Hz flicker cone b-wave response without any significant effect on rod function [194]. Rabbits given oral vigabatrin also show reduced cone b-wave amplitude (light adapted) and normal rod function (dark adapted) by ERG [195]. Histopathology of retinas from rabbits given vigabatrin shows abnormal glial cells and inner plexiform layer with damaged Müller cells. A possible mechanism is that vigabatrin causes an increase the modulatory neurotransmitter, GABA, in Müller cells of the peripheral retina, leading to an impairment of their contribution to the b-wave amplitude [195].

OCULAR IMMUNOLOGY: SPECIAL CONSIDERATIONS FOR BIOLOGIC THERAPEUTICS AND UNDERSTANDING PRECLINICAL FINDINGS

Ocular Immunology

The eye, in general, and the ocular surface in particular, has a system of immune responses that have evolved to protect the eye and vision from invading pathogens as well as environmental stresses. As with the immune system from a systemic perspective, recognition of "self" is a key aspect so that these tissues are not adversely affected by anomalous activation of prolonged inflammation.

The most basic portion of the immune protection is the presence of epithelial barriers that restrict movement of pathogens, proteins, and other environmental irritants to the interior structures of the eye. This is in the form of zonular occludens surrounding the surface epithelium of the conjunctiva and cornea. This barrier is constantly refreshed and reformed as senescent surface epithelial cells are sloughed and replaced by the underlying epithelial cells.

Upon detection of a pathogenic challenge, an innate response is initiated which is immediate yet nonspecific. This is done through signaling by pattern receptors on ocular surface immune cells. An immediate secretion of a several inflammatory cytokines from trafficking "immunovigilant" T-cells and tissue-based γδ T-cells which secrete IL-17, IFN-γ, IL-2, and several other cytokines and chemokines is designed to rapidly eliminate offending pathogens.

The initiation of the innate immune response also serves as the initiating process of a more specific and potent immune response targeted at the offending antigen. This is known as an "adaptive immune" response. It has been known for many years that the conjunctiva contained a population of dendritic cells that express MHCII even in the normal eye. These Langerhans cells were known to respond quickly to antigens and initiate an adaptive response. In 2010, Hamrah et al. [196,197] found that there were populations of immature dendritic cells on the corneal surface that could rapidly activate in the presence of an immune challenge. These cells could mature while processing ocular surface antigens. They utilize CCR7 to migrate, via the ocular surface lymphatics, to the draining lymph nodes. Upon arrival at the cervical (draining) lymph nodes, these dendritic cells present the processed antigen to a population of naïve T-cells, thus directing their development into primed and targeted TH1/TH17 cells. This is known as the afferent branch of the adaptive immune response. The efferent branch consists of the migration of the primed and targeted T-helper cells back to the tissues of the ocular surface, where they initiate a more specific attack on the offending pathogen. The chronicity of this response resides in the constant presence of antigen on the surface tissues. It is for this reason that antigenicity of topically dosed therapies needs to be evaluated.

In contrast to the corneal surface, the intraocular environment is not normally subject to immune surveillance, and exists as a site of immune privilege similar to the brain. In the healthy eye, regulatory T cells (Tregs) predominate and the cellular and cytokine milieu minimize inflammatory responses that are potentially tissue destructive [198,199]. Anterior chamber-associated immune deviation (ACAID) is predicated on the presence of an intact blood–ocular barrier (BOB) [200], maintained through tight junctions of the iris vasculature and pigmented epithelium of the iris and ciliary body. The BOB is maintained by RPE tight junctions in the posterior segment, and immune privilege is referred to as vitreous chamber-associated immune deviation.

Immune privilege (more contemporarily called deviation) does not imply that an immune response is not generated, but rather that it occurs in a manner that limits cytotoxic or delayed hypersensitivity responses. The administration of therapeutic proteins to the eye can generate both innate and adaptive immune responses and can result in the loss of ocular immune deviation. Soluble proteins may exit the eye and enter the systemic vasculature either through Schlemm's canal or the posterior vasculature [201], with subsequent presentation in lymphoid organs, resulting in a humoral response [202]. APCs bearing ocular antigens are also directly transported by the vasculature to the spleen [203]. If immune deviation remains intact, non-complement-fixing antibodies and CD8+ T cells may develop, but a proinflammatory outcome is thwarted by Tregs [203]. However, in diseased eyes, the blood–ocular barrier is often compromised, and antigenic introduction may result in a proinflammatory outcome with the generation of TH1/TH17 cells. Similarly, biologics optimized for human delivery can elicit an adaptive response when delivered to the eye of an animal in preclinical development. There can be marked individual variation in both humoral (ie, ADA production) and inflammatory responses observed within and across dose groups in a safety study.

Immungenicity Considerations

Considerations outlined in ICH Guideline *Preclinical Safety Evaluation of Biotechnology-Derived Pharmaceuticals* S6(R1) are relevant to ocular drug development. This section describes considerations in line with this ICH guideline and focuses on unique considerations to ocular drug development. In addition, EMA draft *Guideline on Immunogenicity Assessment of Biotechnology-Derived Therapeutic Proteins* should be consulted.[1]

Ther FDA, in its *Guidance for Industry: Immunogenicity Assessment of Therapeutic Protein Products*, defines immunogenicity as "the propensity of the therapeutic protein product to generate immune responses to itself and to related proteins or to induce immunologically related adverse clinical events." While immunogenic responses in animals may not translate to human, these data are important to aid in the interpretation of nonclinical toxicology, pharmacokinetic, and pharmacodynamics findings. Moreover, these data can begin to elucidate the consequences of an antibody response if it is associated with a biological effect such as toxicity.

General Considerations

Consistent with other biologics [204], the preclinical safety assessment of an ocularly administered therapeutic protein should consider the following when characterizing the preclinical safety profile:

1. Determination of antidrug antibodies over the course of a study, with inclusion of late blood collection time points.
2. Determination of antidrug antibodies in correlation with the systemic exposure (toxicokinetics).
3. Careful interpretation of the toxicokinetic profile and pharmacodynamic effect in case of immune-mediated clearance or immune-mediated sustained exposure.

---

[1] European Medicines Agency Guideline on Immunogenicity assessment of biotechnology-derived therapeutic proteins (draft; September 24, 2015).

Ocular Route of Administration and Caution Regarding Dose Response

The route of administration influences the tendency of a therapeutic protein to elicit an immunogenic response. The ocular route of administration, particularly the IVT route, is thought to tend to elicit immunogenicity in line with intradermal, subcutaneous, and inhalational routes of administration that are associated with increased immunogenicity as compared to intramuscular and intravenous routes. Additionally, the ocular IVT route likely achieves lower drug levels that can be sporadic, but these sporadic levels can be sustained for a long period of time, which may also contribute to the propensity to elicit an immunogenic response. This is a consideration for a bolus intravitreal dose and may become more of a focus with current efforts to develop sustained-release drug formulations. For example, it is known for biologics that a lower dose administered intermittently may be more immunogenic than a larger dose administered without interruption. This lower dose would be analogous to ocular dosing, which typically achieves high drug levels at the site of administration and low drug levels systemically. For this reason, toxicity findings must be interpreted with caution, in particular when an immunogenic response may contribute to the finding. Conventional thinking that as dose increases, the severity and/or incidence of a toxicity increases in many instances, is not applicable to ocular therapeutic drugs that elicit an immunogenic response.

Species Selection

Rodents

Ocular drug development programs typically utilize the rabbit animal model. This is due to the large size of the eye and anatomic and physiological similarities to humans. In addition, there is a large body of literature data describing nonclinical ocular findings in rabbits. Indeed both Lucentis and Eylea utilized the rabbit as part of their nonclinical program to support the approval and registration of these drug products (FDA websites[2] SBA Lucentis,[1] and SBA Eylea[3]). However, the rabbit model poses a challenge in the development of biologics due to its high propensity to elicit an immunogenic response. In fact, it is for this reason that rabbits are a commonly used animal model to raise antibodies. Thus, data generated in rabbits, either immunogenicity or potential consequences of immunogenicity, must be interpreted with caution with respect to translation to humans. Moreover, the use of rabbits in chronic studies may not be relevant, in particular

if an immunogenic response alters drug exposure. In the Summary Basis of Approval for Eylea, it was reported that enhanced clearance in pregnant rabbits of the drug indicated limited use of this animal model in chronic studies.

Other rodent models such as mice and rats may be considered for systemic safety studies; however, the propensity for an immunogenic response may invalidate these models. Eylea could not be studied in rats or mice for repeat-dose systemic safety studies due to an antibody response associated with nephropathy and enhanced clearance that precluded long-term dosing [34].

Nonrodents

Dogs and monkeys, like rabbits, are attractive animal models for ocular drug development due to the size and anatomic and physiological similarities to human eyes. Although the use of monkeys should be judicious, they are often needed in preclinical development if their biochemistry and physiology is the only model representative of and thus predictive for humans. Development programs for Lucentis and Eylea used cynomologus monkeys as the animal model for pivotal safety studies. Similar to other biologics, the considerations for immunogenicity in nonhuman primates are consistent for ocular drug development.

Translation of Immunogenicity From Animals to Humans

Translation of immunogenicity data collected during preclinical development to human is challenging with ocular therapeutics as with other biologics. The immunogenicity measured for a biologic, in particular a humanized protein, that is administered to animals must be interpreted with caution. The nature, incidence, and frequency that is observed in preclinical species has limited predictive value to humans. With that said, the predictive value of animal models depends on both the type of animal model and what is being predicted [205]. Table 29.8 compares the immunogenicity data generated in humans and animals for Lucentis and Eylea as described in the Summary Basis of FDA Approval Documents. Our understanding of how best to use animal data to predict human immunogenic response is evolving for protein therapeutics in general, and considering the limited number of ocular biologic therapeutics, this is certainly an area where industry will continue to build a knowledge base.

OCULAR IMMUNOPATHOLOGY

Innate Immune Responses

Needle insertion into the intracameral space or vitreous can cause protein extravasation into the anterior chamber, assessed in vivo as flare using a slit lamp or

---

[2] http://www.accessdata.fda.gov/drugsatfda_docs/ nda/2006/125156s0000_LucentisTOC.cfm.

[3] http://www.accessdata.fda.gov/drugsatfda_docs/ nda/2011/125387s0000TOC.cfm.

TABLE 29.8   Cross-Species Comparison of Immunogenicity for Lucentis and Eylea

Drug		Immunogenic Response			
	Human	**Monkey**	**Rabbit**	**Rat**	**Mouse**
Lucentis	The pretreatment incidence of immunoreactivity to Lucentis in serum was 0–5% across treatment groups. After monthly dosing with Lucentis for 6–24 months, antibodies to Lucentis in serum were detected in approximately 1–9% of patients. The clinical significance of immunoreactivity to Lucentis is unclear at this time. Among neovascular AMD patients with the highest levels of immunoreactivity, some were noted to have iritis or vitritis. Intraocular inflammation was not observed in patients with DME and DR at baseline, or RVO patients with the highest levels of immunoreactivity.	Antidrug antibodies detected in vitreous and serum after intravitreal dosing.	Antitrug antibodies detected in vitreous and serum after intravitreal dosing.		
Eylea	In wet AMD, RVO, and DME studies, the pretreatment incidence of immunoreactivity to Eylea was approximately 1–3% across treatment groups. After dosing with EYLEA for 24–100 weeks, antibodies to EYLEA were detected in a similar percentage range of patients. There were no differences in efficacy or safety between patients with or without immunoreactivity.	ADA detected in monkeys, but did not in all studies/animals correlate with changes in either bound of free drug.	ADA detected in pregnant rabbits. Drug cleared faster.	ADA detected with nephropathy.	ADA detected with nephropathy.

FDA SBA Lucentis; FDA SBA Eylea.

laser flare photometer. Flare correlates on histology as a pale eosinophilic matrix (resembling edema in other tissues) of low cellularity residing in the anterior chamber. Flare rapidly resolves within hours, assuming administration of a physiologically compatible, nonpyrogenic solution. Otherwise, flare may be accompanied by an infiltrate of white blood cells. An acute, minimal reaction is associated with an influx of polymorphonuclear cells (PMNs). Anterior chamber cells can be assessed using a slit lamp biomicroscope. An acute, innate inflammatory response associated with an influx of predominantly PMNs and extravasation of plasma of higher protein content into the anterior chamber can occur with administration of solutions that are not physiologically optimal. Red blood cells are observed if hemorrhage occurs. Vascular inflammation can occur in the ciliary processes, ciliary body, and iris. Vascular congestion within the iris can be observed on ophthalmic examination, particularly in albino animals. Vascular congestion has been ascribed as "iritis" clinically, but should be avoided in pathology, which does not generally correlate with ophthalmic findings. Although acute inflammation in the ocular space is predominantly neutrophilic, variable numbers of lymphocytes and macrophages may also be present. Accumulation of cells at the surface of the cornea endothelium and anterior margins of the iris is common, although cells may be dispersed throughout the anterior chamber, or form aggregates. Hypopyon, observed clinically as a fluctuant, white mass in the ventral margins of the anterior chamber, can be observed in severe inflammation, or with inflammation that elicits a granulomatous reaction. Protein deposits or cellular debris (keratotic precipitates) may be observed on the cornea endothelium on ophthalmoscopy. These are generally difficult to detect on histology unless careful sectioning has been planned with advance knowledge of their presence and precise location. Inflammation can extend throughout the entire uveal tract, resulting in inflammation in the choroid or vitreous.

During drug development, innate inflammatory reactions are often associated with the administration of solutions that contain pyrogenic factors, in particular endotoxin. Endotoxin is a component of the outer cell wall, lipopolysaccharide, of gram-negative bacteria such as *Escherichia coli*, and is a frequent contaminant of medical solutions, surgical instruments, and devices. Residual endotoxin and other host cell proteins occur in biologics that are produced in bacterial expression systems, such as *E. coli*, and thus may be present in formulations used in preclinical development that have not been manufactured as stridently required for Good Manufacturing Practice (GMP). Inflammation resulting from endotoxin contamination can be detected on ophthalmic examination ≥0.1 IU/eye [206]. Endotoxin causes an acute influx of protein and PMNs into the anterior chamber and vitreous, and is generally dose-dependent in severity. Leukocytes transit the uveal tissues at the ciliary body, processes, and the pars plana. Inflammation generally resolves in the aqueous within a few days, but may persist in the vitreous as mononuclear infiltrates at the peripheral margins, primarily posterior to the ciliary processes, at the retinal surface, and behind the lens. Histologically, inflammation in the vitreous can be observed as low as 0.01 EU/eye [206]. Most often, inflammation from endotoxin uncomplicated by other factors resolves gradually within the vitreous and is generally uneventful, although cells may persist for weeks in the vitreous due to slow fluid dynamics. Inflammation of increased severity may extend into the superficial retina, and occasionally be associated with cell loss and necrosis of the inner layers of the retina. In preclinical development, persistence of infiltrates—often consisting of degenerate macrophages—demonstrates slow recovery, and may be present despite a lapse of 2 months or more from time of last drug administration. Responses may vary drastically between species, and rabbits may be exquisitely sensitive to endotoxin compared to other species. A spectrum of responses can occur within a given dose group during a safety study, indicating the importance of individual host factors such as genetic variation, immune status, and concurrent morbidity.

Adaptive Immune Responses

Humoral responses are generally detected 10–14 days or longer following administration of a biologic in the eye when they occur, similar to systemic delivery. Histological findings (infiltrates of lymphocytes and macrophages) may correlate with antibody production and detection in the eye or serum and are generally assumed to be immune-mediated. In the eye, an adaptive response of minor consequence is observed as minimal to mild perivascular infiltrates of lymphocytes around retinal and optic nerve vessels; on fundic imaging they are observed as white/off-white expansions of the normal vasculature pattern, colloquially termed frosted branch angiitis. These generally occur as small cuffs, two to four cell layers thick, with minimal impact to the adjacent tissue. Similar cuffs are also observed at the injection site, and within the ciliary body and choroid, although these must be differentiated from background changes, particularly in nonhuman primates. Such infiltrates generally resolve without incidence, have no functional impact, and within the retina, seem to rarely result in cellular loss beyond isolated cells in the inner nuclear layer. Infiltrates of lymphocytes and macrophages are frequently observed within the body of the vitreous, at the peripheral margins of the vitreous body, and at the surface of the optic disc. On occasion, perivascular lymphocytic infiltrates may only be observed at the optic disc, or within the optic nerve. Drugs injected into the vitreous exit via the trabecular meshwork anteriorly, or through the posterior blood–retinal barrier [201]. Drug clearance may also occur via vasculature in the optic nerve. Significant inflammation in the optic nerve (clinically referred

to as optic neuritis) includes vascular damage, influx of neutrophils, tissue necrosis, and hemorrhage.

Vitreous inflammation is slow to resolve and when global, can have a significant impact to visual function, preventing repeat dosing on a safety study. Matrix changes to the vitreous can create generalized opacities that obscure the visual pathway. For these reasons, dosing through hypersensitivity responses with the intent of inducing tolerance is not possible in the eye, although it can be a successful strategy employed systemically. More often, overt inflammation in the eye resolves with physical bystander damage to sensitive neural tissues, which does not recover, but resolves with loss of structure (retinal or optic nerve atrophy), or scarring. Infiltrates of lymphocytes occur in the retina, choroid, optic nerve, and vitreous, and may be associated with extensive retinal necrosis. Immune complex disease, the formation of antigen–antibody complexes that deposit in tissues and subsequently activate compliment (Type III hypersensitivity), may provoke an inflammatory reaction primarily around blood vessels (vascular inflammation) within the retina and optic nerve. Vascular cuffs composed of WBC infiltrates are larger than described earlier, and contain lymphocytes, neutrophils, and macrophages. Vascular congestion, accumulation of intravascular WBCs and extravasation, endothelial cell activation, and fibrinous changes within the vascular wall may be observed. Fundic imaging may be obscured due to inflammation and vascular leak.

It is important to distinguish inflammation resulting from immune-mediated causes and that resulting from possible pharmacological causes, particularly vascular inflammation. The former may not be clinically relevant in humans, but the later may curtail further drug development. There is a certain level of tolerance from regulatory agencies to histological findings for an expected adaptive immune response [207]. Detection of immune complexes on tissue sections with vascular lesions by IHC can mitigate otherwise negative findings. The reader is referred to recent excellent reviews for further details on the immunohistochemical detection of immune complexes in drug development [208–210]. Definitive evidence for immunogenicity can be lacking, as for example, antigen–antibody complexes that have been cleared from tissue prior to necropsy. In these cases, a "weight of evidence" approach must be applied. Correlating exposure data, systemic ADA, and ADA in ocular fluids or tissues may bolster a case for immune complex disease [211].

Inflammatory Outcomes Associated With Devices and Implants

Cytokines within the TGFβ family, and particularly TGFβ-2 [200,203,212], have key roles in modulating inflammation and maintaining an environment that is antiinflammatory. However, TGFβ is also elaborated under inflammatory conditions, and conversely, activation of untargeted soluble TGFβ has been implicated in ocular fibrotic disease [203]. Inflammation in the eye causes a local upregulation of TGFβ-2 production, which can modulate the immune outcome. TGFβ-2 in concert with other cytokines (PDGF, HGF, MCP-1) are participants in tissue repair processes, and regulate the proliferation, migration, and transdifferentiation of cells (including ocular cells) to assume a fibroblastic, membranous phenotype [213–215]. These processes have been implicated in spontaneous diseases of the eye that result in formation of subretinal membranes that occur in age-related macular degeneration.

The formation of epiretinal membranes (ERM) and vitreous membranes are manifestations of ocular cell plasticity that can occur with administration of devices or implants used as sustained drug-delivery strategies. ERMs are composed of linear proliferations of ocular cells on the inner surface of the retina, while vitreous membranes are composed of collagenous matrix and fusiform cells oriented in linear arrays within the vitreous. The predominant cell types have been identified using specific cell markers by IHC as hyalocytes, glial cells, Müller cells, RPE, and astrocytes [216–218]. Both types of membranes have morphological resemblance to fibrous tissue reactions involved in systemic wound healing, and tend to have a myofibroblastic phenotype that has been shown to contract when exposed to TGFβ-2 [213,214,218]. Secretion of extracellular matrix and subsequent membrane formation in the eye recapitulates systemic events in wound healing, and can be an undesirable outcome associated with inflammatory events occurring with delivery of biological therapeutics and devices to the eye.

Vitreous membranes often appear to originate in the vicinity of the ciliary process and pars plana in proximity to the site of injection. Inwardly protruding plugs of fibrous connective tissue at the injection often co-mingle with vitreous membranes, which in turn tend to co-mingle with cells that transfix the lens (zonule fibrils), as well as those of the superficial retina (glial, astrocytes, Müller cells) and vitreous (hyalocytes). Vitreous membranes have a tendency to tether to fixed structures such as the retina, lens, and optic nerve, and because they are contractile, place tension on those structures. Contraction can result in lens displacement, retinal detachment, and prolapse of the optic nerve.

Devices, or solutions that aggregate and form gels on administration, tend to gravitate to the ventral aspect of the vitreous. Prolonged retinal contact is associated with ERM formation, which can result in displacement or detachment of the underlying retina. Membranes may develop in absence of any significant inflammatory response.

Devices with biophysical or chemical properties that are less than optimal can also elicit an innate inflammatory response. This can be associated with formation of a provisional matrix over the device (viewed as an eosinophilic matrix on histology), derived from the initial leakage of serum and protein in the eye, which then serves as a substrate for attachment of WBCs and compliment factors [219]. The release of cytokines from WBCs promotes cellular recruitment and membrane formation, which appears to isolate the device within the ocular space.

Recruitment of WBCs to these sites can be associated with "frustrated phagocytosis," characterized by macrophage breakdown and release of lysosomal contents (proteolytic enzymes of low pH), in proximity to sensitive ocular tissues and the generation of free radicals causing further necrosis. Frustrated phagocytosis can occur on devices exceeding the size limitation of a macrophage to engulf it (~10 um). Devices ≥10 um may also elicit a foreign body or granulomatous reaction, the accumulation and fusion of macrophages (multinucleated giant cells) around the device.

Smaller delivery devices may be innocuous, or also stimulate a granulomatous response. Microspheres have a tendency to aggregate at the periphery of the vitreous gel and cause retinal compression at points of contact. Microspheres sometimes migrate into problematic places, including the stroma of the iris, the trabecular meshwork, retina, subretinal space, choroid, and optic nerve.

Delivery devices below 5–10 um, including nanoparticles, may be susceptible to phagocytosis and elimination through macrophages or hyalocytes. Because of the acidic and enzymatic nature of the internal lysosomal environment, potential impact to drug pharmacometrics should be considered.

STRUCTURE AND FUNCTION OF THE EYE

As a three-dimensional object, the ocular globe is an irregular oblong spheroid. The clear cornea constitutes the anterior part and covers ~1/6 of the surface area. The remaining is composed of an opaque scleral shell. The globe is slightly compressed, so that the greatest vertical diameter is slightly less than the greatest horizontal diameter in the rat, dog, and primate. In the rabbit, the compression is anterioposterior [220]. The relative size of the cornea varies among animal species, generally being larger in nocturnal and crepuscular animals and smaller in diurnal animals. Thus the percent of cornea as compared to the volume of the globe is larger in the mouse, rat, and rabbit than in the dog and nonhuman primate. Internally, the eye is divided into anterior and posterior segments (Fig. 29.1). The anterior segment consists of the

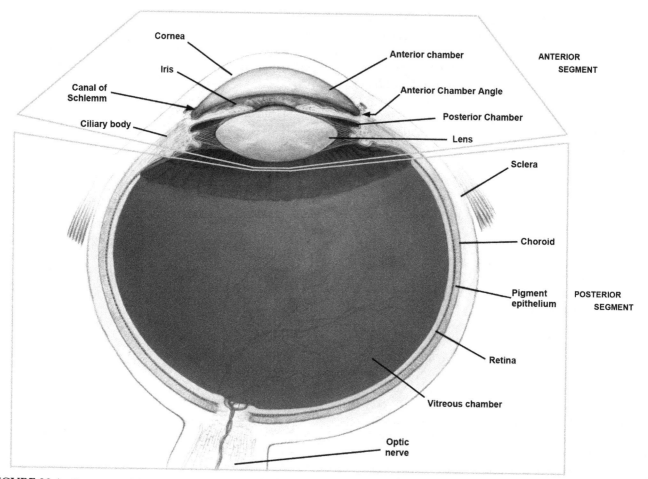

FIGURE 29.1 Structures of the eye. The eye can be divided into two segments: anterior and posterior. The anterior segment consists of the lens and all structures anterior to it, and is divided into two chambers: anterior chamber and posterior chamber. The anterior chamber is delimited by the anterior surface of the iris and the posterior surface of the cornea. The posterior chamber is contained by the posterior surface of the iris and the anterior capsule of the lens. Aqueous is formed in the posterior chamber and circulates through the pupil to the anterior chamber. The posterior segment is bound anteriorly by the posterior lens capsule and peripherally by the sclera.

aqueous humor and structures in front of the vitreous humor: cornea, iris, ciliary body, and lens. The posterior segment consists of the vitreous humor and structures behind the lens: vitreous, optic nerve, retina, and retinal pigment cells (RPEs). Salient anatomical considerations of the eye for common nonclinical species as compared to the human are presented in Table 29.2.

Ocular Blood Supply and Drainage

Blood flow to the eye is high relative to its small tissue mass, which is indicative of the high metabolic demands of the ocular tissues. The ocular blood supply is derived from the ophthalmic artery (internal and/or external), the first branch off the internal carotid artery (humans, primates), or from a branch off the internal maxillary artery supplied by the external carotid (most domestic species) [221]. Branches off the ophthalmic artery include the central retinal artery (CRA), the short and long posterior ciliary arteries (PCAs), and the anterior ciliary arteries

(ACAs). Circulation to the iris and ciliary body are via the ACAs, the long PCA, and anastomotic connections from the anterior choroid vasculature. The ACAs travel with the extraocular muscles and pierce the sclera near the limbus to join the major arterial circle of the iris. The long PCAs (usually two) pierce the sclera near the posterior pole, and then travel anteriorly between the sclera and choroid to also join the major arterial circle of the iris. The major arterial circle of the iris gives off branches to both the iris and ciliary body. The superficial ciliary branch supplies the rectus muscles via the ACAs, and continues forward to form the episcleral arterial circle, a ring of connected vessels that encircles the globe posterior to the limbus and superficial to the intraocular circle. The CRA and the short PCA provide blood supply to the retina. The CRA travels in or beside the optic nerve as it passes through the sclera, then branches to supply the layers of the inner retina. There are marked species differences in the inner retinal vascularization. These differences are described in the section on the posterior segment, below. The vascular supply of the optic nerve is complex and best described in relationship to the lamina cribosa sclerae, the mesh-like portion of the sclera, which is perforated for the passage of the optic nerve. The portion of the optic nerve that is pre-lamina cribosa (inside the eye relative to the lamina cribosa) is supplied by collaterals from the choroid and retina circulations. The lamina cribosa zone is supplied by branches from the short PCA and pial arteries. The post laminar zone is supplied by the pial arteries. Venous drainage is via the central retinal vein and pial veins [78,222] (Fig. 29.2).

Anterior Segment

There are two fluid-filled chambers:

1. Anterior chamber, between the endothelial surface of the posterior cornea and the anterior surface of the iris.
2. Posterior chamber, between the posterior surface of the iris and the front face of the vitreous.

These chambers contain aqueous humor, a clear fluid secreted by the ciliary processes in the posterior segment, which provides nutrients to the surrounding structures. The anterior chamber size corresponds to the cornea size; animals with large corneas have large anterior chambers filled with greater volumes of aqueous humor.

Cornea

The cornea is the anterior transparent part of the eye's tough fibrous exterior and is shaped to be a powerful lens that refracts light toward the visual axis of the eye. The corneal diameter is not round and the vertical dimension is shorter than the horizontal in most species. Of the standard laboratory animal species, the cornea surface area is greatest in rabbits and smallest in nonhuman primates. Moving from anterior to posterior, the cornea is composed of five layers: epithelium, epithelial basement membrane with or without an obvious Bowman's layer, corneal stroma, Descemet's membrane, and endothelium (Fig. 29.1). The anterior surface of the cornea is covered with nonkeratinizing squamous epithelium that is continuous with the bulbar conjunctiva at the limbus. The corneal epithelium makes up approximately 10% of the total corneal thickness, ranges from 5 to 20 cells thick depending on species, is normally nonpigmented, and is arranged in three distinct layers:

1. Superficial layer of two to four layers of nonkeratinizing squamous cells with flattened or absent nuclei.
2. Middle layer of three or four layers of polyhedral cells known as wing cells.
3. Deep single layer of columnar cells known as basal cells (Fig. 29.3).

The basal cells are anchored to a basement membrane consisting of collagens IV, VI, and VII, laminin, and fibronectin [78,223]. Corneal epithelial turnover or renewal is continual. Current literature suggests that corneal epithelial renewal has up to five components:

1. Transient amplifying cells generated from stem cells at the limbus entering into the cornea.
2. Proliferation of the basal epithelium.
3. Differentiation of daughter cells into wing cells while moving toward the surface (vertical movement).
4. Horizontal movement of wing cells and superficial cells toward the central cornea.
5. Desquamation of surface cells into the tear film.

The corneal epithelium is completely replaced every 4–8 days in this manner. Corneal epithelial cells synthesize two major tissue-restricted keratins, K3 and K12, which can be used as biomarkers to distinguish this population of cells from the adjacent conjunctival epithelial cells [224].

The earliest and most common corneal epithelial manifestation of toxic injury is focal superficial desquamation. Keratitis, keratoconjunctivitis, erosions, and ulcerations may follow. With chronic injury, adaptive changes of epithelial hyperplasia, metaplasia, or dysplasia may occur; but keratinization is a rare event. If the epithelial basement membrane is injured, it is regenerated by the basal epithelial cells to its previous, normal state; however, it can be synthesized in excess or in an altered form. Edema can be seen with epithelial hypoxia and trauma, and may be intracellular, extracellular, or both. With intercellular edema, if the fluid separates the epithelium from the basement membrane, blister-like bullae form. Numerous systemically administered drugs can accumulate in the epithelium, including amiodarone, chlorpromazine, indomethacin (rarely), tilorone, chloroquine, naproxen, perhexiline, suramin, the thioxanthines, and tamoxifen. These drugs enter the cytoplasmic lysosomes and combine with bipolar lipids to form lipid–drug lamellar complexes that are refractory to enzymatic digestion. The severity of these lipid–drug deposits is directly proportional to the total drug dose, and when the drug is withdrawn, the deposits gradually disappear [225]. Corneal vascularization occurs with more serious or extensive injury, persistent hypoxia, and chronic inflammation [226,227].

In only a few species (pinnipeds, cetaceans, and most primates), the corneal epithelial basal cell membrane is separated from the corneal stroma by a distinct acellular condensation of fibrillar matrix known as Bowman's layer [228]. This layer is a mat consisting of randomly woven small collagen types I, III, V, and VII fibrils, and a fine subepithelial nerve plexus [228]. A rudimentary Bowman's layer has been reported in mice, rats, and rabbits, but not in dogs [229–232]. Bowman's layer plays a role in epithelial–stromal communications; breakage or disruption of

(A)

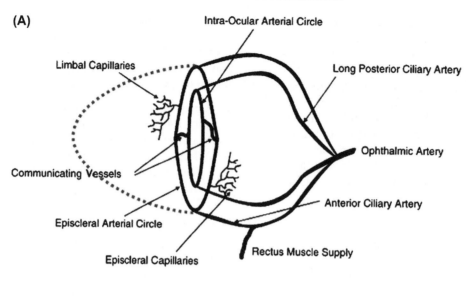

(B)

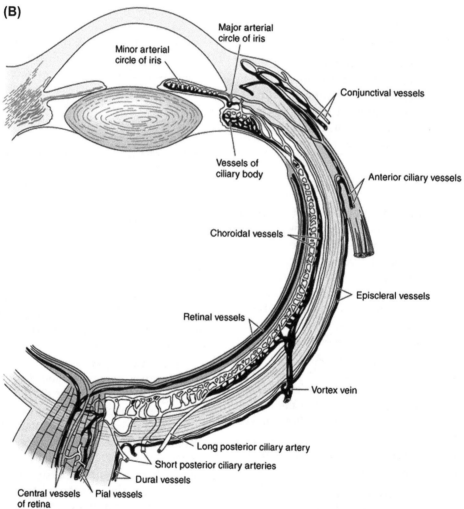

FIGURE 29.2 (A) Simplified schematic diagram of the ocular blood supply. *(From Papas E. The Limbal Vasculature. Cont Lens Anterior Eye 2003;26:71. With permission from Elsevier.)* (B) Vascular supply to the eye. All arterial branches originate with the ophthalmic artery. The first intraorbital branch of the ophthalmic artery is the central retinal artery, which enters the optic nerve behind the globe. The short posterior ciliary arteries supply the choroid and parts of the optic nerve. The two long posterior ciliary arteries supply the ciliary body and anastomose with each other and with the anterior ciliary arteries to form the major arterial circle of the iris. The anterior ciliary arteries are derived from the muscular branches to the rectus muscles. They supply the anterior sclera, episclera, limbus, and conjunctiva as well as contributing to the major arterial circle of the iris. *(From Riordan-Eva P. Anatomy & Embryology of the Eye. In: Riordan-Eva P, Cunningham ET, Vaughan and Asbury's General Ophthalmology. 18th ed. New York: McGraw-Hill; 2011 [chapter 1]. With permission.)*

CROSS-SECTIONAL VIEW OF THE CORNEAL EPITHELIAL CELL LAYER

(A)

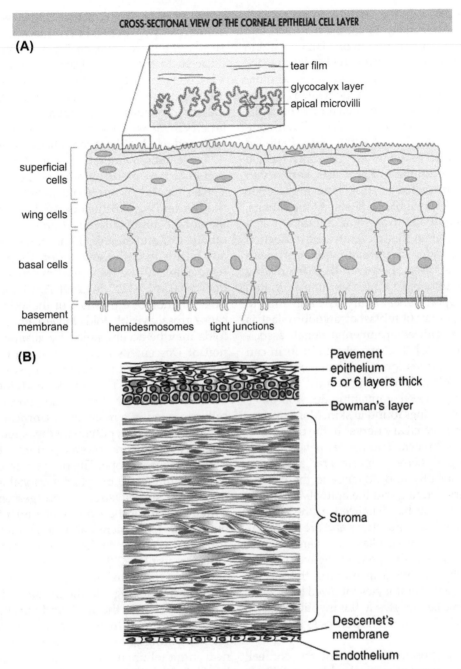

tear film
glycocalyx layer
apical microvilli

superficial cells

wing cells

basal cells

basement membrane

hemidesmosomes   tight junctions

(B)

Pavement epithelium 5 or 6 layers thick

Bowman's layer

Stroma

Descemet's membrane

Endothelium

FIGURE 29.3 (A) Cross-sectional view of the corneal epithelium. The superficial cells form an average of two to three layers of flat, polygonal cells. The cell membrane is arranged in extensive apical microvilli and microplicae, which are covered by a glycocalyceal layer. These features increase the surface area of contact and adherence to the mucinous undercoat of the tear film. Laterally, superficial cells are joined by barrier tight-junctional complexes to restrict entry of tears into the intercellular spaces. Beneath the superficial cell layer are the suprabasal or wing cells. This layer is about two to three cells deep and consists of cells that are less flat than the overlying superficial cells, but possess similar tight, lateral, intercellular junctions. Beneath the wing cells are the basal cells. The basal cell layer is composed of a single-cell layer of columnar epithelium. *(From Farjo A, McDermott M, Soong H. Corneal Anatomy, Physiology, and Wound Healing. In: Yanoff M, Duker J. Ophthalmology. 3rd ed. Philadelphia, Mosby (Elsevier); 2009 [chapter 4.1]. With permission.)*

the membrane alters epithelial–stromal interactions and may result in subepithelial fibrosis [233]. When corneal epithelial injury extends to Bowman's layer in primates, resulting in its damage or destruction, it does not regenerate [234]. Instead, fibroblastic cells thought to be derived from keratocytes migrate immediately beneath the epithelium and form disorganized connective tissue to fill

the defect, thus creating a permanent scar [235] that may be observed as opacities. These cells are replaced by mitosis of neighboring cells and, if there is no further injury, there is no further keratocyte response.

Most of the remaining cornea consists of stroma composed of small-diameter collagen fibers (primarily type I, with some type III, V, and VI) organized into flat sheets (lamellae) separated by proteoglycan matrix [52]. The lamellae run orthogonally to each other such that the fibrils are seen in cross-section in one lamella and in longitudinal section in an adjacent lamella. Within each lamella, the collagen fibers run parallel to one another and to the corneal surface. This arrangement, as well as continuous slow turnover of the collagen, is essential for maintaining corneal transparency. The cellular component of the stroma consists of keratocytes, flattened dendriform fibroblastic cells that are generally located between the lamellae. Similar to fibroblasts, keratocytes have an extensive intracellular cytoskeleton and secrete procollagens that self-assemble to fibers. At the limbus, fibers run circumferentially to form an annulus of collagen fibers that maintain the curvature and refraction of the cornea. Keratocytes are normally quiescent, with a turnover rate of 2–3 years; however, they are readily stimulated to either undergo apoptosis or transition into repair phenotypes upon corneal injury. The transition to a repair phenotype, either fibroblast or myofibroblast, is dependent on the specific environmental signals associated with the injury [236]. The myofibroblast form can be identified by its expression of alpha-smooth muscle actin (α-SMA) [235,237,238]. The corneal stroma is densely innervated [223,239], containing 300–400 times the number of nerve endings found in skin. Most are sensory nerves derived from ciliary nerves of the trigeminal ganglion ophthalmic branch. The nerves penetrate the cornea through the peripheral stroma in a radial pattern, shed their myelin sheaths, and advance to the epithelium to become nerve endings on the epithelial surface. Unmyelinated nerves can be visualized in the corneal stroma of H&E-stained ocular sections and are occasionally mistaken for collapsed capillaries. When the corneal stroma is injured, as with a penetrating wound that disrupts the epithelial basement membrane, there is an initial apoptosis of some keratocytes followed by activation of the remaining keratocytes to the myofibroblastic phenotype [234,236,237]. Stromal responses to injury are detailed further below.

Located along the posterior border of the corneal stroma is Descemet's membrane, the highly specialized collagenous basement membrane of corneal endothelial cells. It is dense in appearance, and stains pale eosinophilic with H&E staining and positive with Periodic Acid Schiff (PAS) staining. The anterior (stromal) side of Descemet's membrane is produced before birth. This part of Descemet's membrane looks smooth and homogeneous by light microscopy, and has a banded appearance ultrastructurally. The posterior (chamber) side is produced postnatally and throughout the remainder of life. This part of Descemet's membrane appears more granular by light microscopy and is unbanded ultrastructurally. Thus, Descemet's membrane continues to expand with age due to accumulation of the unbanded layers on the

posterior side. The collagen types within Descemet's membrane vary depending on location. Adjacent to the stroma there are collagen types IV, VI, and VIII, while adjacent to the endothelium are collagen types V and VI. Collagen VIII is found only in the peripheral Descemet's membrane at its termination. In all, Descemet's membrane consists of collagen types I, III, IV, V, VI, XII, and XVIII, as well as many noncollagenous components arranged in a highly ordered hexagonal array [240–242].

Descemet's membrane terminates within the limbal region at the anterior border of the iridocorneal angle. The termination is referred to as Schwalbe's line or anterior border ring of Schwalbe. In the primate, Descemet's membrane termination is rather abrupt. In the dog, rabbit, rat, and mouse, Descemet's membrane gradually blends in with the anterior iris pillars or pectinate ligaments and the trabecular meshwork within the iridocorneal angle [223,243,244]. Any condition that causes inflammation of the cornea or the anterior chamber can cause grossly visible folds in Descemet's membrane. The folds may be accompanied by stromal edema. Separation of Descemet's membrane can provide the trigger for proliferation of the underlying stromal tissue at the wound site [233]. The corneal endothelium makes up the innermost layer of the cornea, consisting of flattened cells arranged in a monolayer. Corneal endothelial cells are uniform in size, polygonal (hexagonal) in shape, and arranged in a distinct mosaic pattern when viewed with a specular microscope. The primary roles for the corneal endothelium are to maintain a critical level of dehydration for the stroma (stromal deturgescence) and to act as a final barrier for the anterior chamber while remaining permeable to nutrients and other molecules from the aqueous humor since the corneal layers do not have a vascular supply [223].

Corneal endothelial regeneration capacity varies with species and age. In the primate, there is no regenerative capacity in the adult and minimal, if any, capacity in the young. In the dog, regenerative capacity is seen in young animals. In the rabbit and rat, the corneal endothelium has regenerative capacity throughout life [245–250]. The regenerative capacity of the mouse corneal endothelium remains unknown [251]. Specular microscopy is used to analyze endothelial cell layer changes through cell density (cells/mm^2), cell area (μm^2/cell), and pleomorphism (% of 3, 4, 5, 6, 7, or 8-sided cells); it is a more sensitive method for detecting endothelial cell loss than histology. Age-related increases in the size of corneal endothelial cells, coupled with age-related decreases in endothelial cell densities, have been observed by specular microscopy in the human [252], macaque [253], dog [254], rabbit [255], rat [256], and mouse [257], suggesting that, regardless of proliferative capacity, endothelial proliferation does not keep pace with cell loss in most mammalian species. When the corneal endothelial cells are stressed by damage or disease, they may secrete banded Descemet's membrane to form a posterior banded layer. This layer of abnormal Descemet's membrane has also been termed a posterior collagenous layer and it is distinct from the unbanded collagen accumulations associated with age. Spontaneous accumulation of a posterior collagenous layer is seen in aging mice [258]. Histologically, endothelial injury and loss are difficult to assess aside from noting increases in nuclear and/or cell size with cell hypertrophy and decreases in endothelial cell nuclei numbers and attenuation of endothelial cell bodies with cell loss.

There are numerous spontaneous and background findings in the cornea, many of which are species-specific. Corneal opacity is common in mice and rats, and is often due to mineralization of the subepithelial basement membrane and anterior stroma. This change, which is also referred to as corneal dystrophy, has been described in numerous mouse strains, including Swiss, BALB/C, C2H, DBA/2, and C57BL/6 [259–261]. In rats, mineralization of the epithelial basement membrane or anterior stroma has been described in Sprague–Dawley, F344, and Wistar rats [262–264]. In rabbits, corneal dystrophy refers to an epithelial change with or without a basement membrane change. In Dutch belted rabbits, the epithelium is thin and disorganized, basal cells are small and hyperchromatic, and there are focal detachments from the basement membrane [74]. In NZW rabbits, corneal dystrophy is characterized by a thickened, elevated epithelium interspersed with areas of abnormally thin epithelium; the basal epithelial cells and basement membrane are normal [265]. In dogs, corneal dystrophy has not been described in purpose-bred beagles; however, corneal opacity due to large accumulations of neutral lipids within stromal keratocytes and smaller accumulations between stromal collagen bundles have been reported in older beagles without hyperlipidema [266].

The normal cornea is devoid of both blood and lymphatic vessels in all layers, and avascularity is actively maintained under inflammatory and other angiogenic conditions. This condition is known as corneal angiogenic privilege [267], and is considered to be a component of the phenomenon known as immune privilege. Corneal immune privilege describes the phenomenon in which allografts placed into the cornea experience prolonged survival rates compared with other recipient sites. This is partly dependent on angiogenic privilege [267]. In addition, corneal endothelium provides a somewhat impenetrable barrier between the anterior chamber and the corneal stroma, and corneal endothelial cells reportedly secrete molecules that suppress inflammation and lymphocyte activation and inhibit complement activation. As such, corneal manifestations of toxic injury tend to be subtle with a limited number of responses to

injury. Otherwise, there could be damage to the tissues and cells responsible for vision.

For the purpose of describing corneal responses to injury, toxic or otherwise, Waring and Rodrigues [268] proposed dividing the cornea into four zones:

1. Epithelium.
2. Subepithelial zone (epithelial basement membrane, Bowman's layer, superficial stroma).
3. Stroma.
4. Endothelium and Descemet's membrane.

Waring and Rodrigues also divided all possible corneal pathologic responses to injury into six categories:

1. Defects and their repair (partial or complete loss of corneal tissue from any cause).
2. Fibrosis and vascularization (collagen and other components of the extracellular matrix assembled in an irregular structure or new blood vessel formation create a corneal opacity).
3. Edema and cysts (accumulation of fluid in stroma, displacing regular structural elements and resulting in corneal opacity).
4. Inflammation and immune responses (leukocyte migration, immune complex deposition with stromal melting).
5. Deposits (accumulation of abnormal types or amounts of material, including lipid, pigment, drug (rare), abnormal substance (as in dystrophies).
6. Proliferation (epithelial or stromal).

Wilson et al. [237] followed up with a cascade of events to encompass corneal healing that are initiated rapidly, regardless of the type of injury (Fig. 29.4).

At its periphery, the clear cornea transitions to opaque conjunctiva and sclera anteriorly and to the iridocorneal angle (the primary structure of the aqueous humor outflow system) posteriorly. This zone of transition, known as the limbus, maintains nourishment of the peripheral cornea through its vasculature, and contains the pathways for aqueous outflow [269]. The limbus is not a distinct anatomical site and it is important for the pathologist to know that the boundary lines are defined differently by various medical disciplines. The pathologist's limbus is the triangular segment between the vertical line from the termination of Bowman's layer to the termination of Descemet's membrane (Schwalbe's line) on the corneal side, and a vertical line perpendicular to the surface above the scleral spur (a wedge-shaped protrusion of sclera into the angle space that is the point of insertion for the longitudinal bundle of the ciliary muscle [270]) (in the primate) or where the trabecular meshwork inserts into the sclera (in the dog, rabbit, rat, and mouse). The histologist's limbus is the transition from corneal epithelium to conjunctival epithelium and from the regular corneal stromal lamellae to the irregular

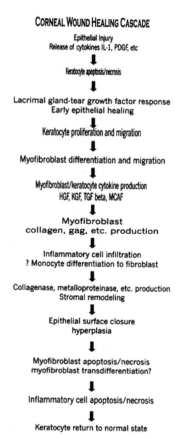

CORNEAL WOUND HEALING CASCADE

Epithelial Injury
Release of cytokines IL-1, PDGF, etc

↓

Keratocyte apoptosis/necrosis

↓

Lacrimal gland-tear growth factor response
Early epithelial healing

↓

Keratocyte proliferation and migration

↓

Myofibroblast differentiation and migration

↓

Myofibroblast/keratocyte cytokine production
HGF, KGF, TGF beta, MCAF

↓

Myofibroblast
collagen, gag, etc. production

↓

Inflammatory cell infiltration
? Monocyte differentiation to fibroblast

↓

Collagenase, metalloproteinase, etc. production
Stromal remodeling

↓

Epithelial surface closure
hyperplasia

↓

Myofibroblast apoptosis/necrosis
myofibroblast transdifferentiation?

↓

Inflammatory cell apoptosis/necrosis

↓

Keratocyte return to normal state

FIGURE 29.4 Simplified schematic diagram of some events that occur in the corneal wound healing response following corneal epithelial injury or surgery involving the cornea. Note that not all events are included and that many of the events can occur simultaneously. *(From Wilson S, Mohan R, Mohan R, Ambrosio R, Hong J, Lee J. The Corneal Wound Healing Response: Cytokine-Mediated Interaction of the Epithelium, Stroma, and Inflammatory Cells. Prog Retin Eye Res 2001;20(5):625. With permission from Elsevier.)*

scleral stromal lamellae. The anterior aspect of the histology limbus is easier to discern: it is the abrupt transition of the relatively thicker corneal epithelium to the thinner bulbar conjunctival epithelium. The transition from corneal stroma to scleral stroma is less distinct; the interface appears oblique relative to the epithelial surface. The clinician's limbus is the transition from clear cornea to opaque sclera and is referred to as the corneolimbal junction. This is also known as the surgical limbus, or the blue or gray zone—based on its blue-gray appearance when viewed externally after the conjunctiva has been reflected from the limbus.

As mentioned, the limbus is a transition zone: corneal epithelium transitions to conjunctival epithelium, Bowman's layer transitions to conjunctival lamina propria, corneal stroma transitions to sclera stroma (or substantia propria), Descemet's membrane transitions to trabecular stroma, and corneal endothelium transitions to fibroblastic trabecular cells. The limbus is also the site where corneal epithelial stem cells reside (in the basal layer of the limbal epithelium) [224,269,271,272]. By the same token, the internal limbal border zone between corneal endothelium and iridocorneal angle appears to contain specialized secretory cells (Schwalbe's line cells) that, when activated, migrate and repopulate the trabecular meshwork after trabecular injury [269,271,273].

Compared to the corneal epithelium, which is normally nonpigmented, the limbal conjunctiva contains pigmented cells scattered in all but the superficial squamous layer of the conjunctiva. Also, while the corneal epithelium is normally free of leukocytes, lymphocytes may be interspersed within the conjunctival basal cell layer and lamina propria. The limbal stroma is arranged loosely and contains blood vessels and lymphatics as compared to the highly organized avascular corneal stroma. The limbal arterial supply originates from the episcleral arterial and intraocular arterial circles, rings of connected vessels that encircle the globe posterior to the limbus. Two types of arterioles arise from the arterial circle. The first are terminal vessels that pass anteriorly and form the peripheral corneal or limbal arcades. The network of capillaries results from the repeated division and recombination of vessels within the arcades. Bowman's layer marks the anterior extent of the capillaries; most loop around and return posteriorly, though some terminate abruptly within the peripheral cornea, forming so-called straight or spike vessels. The capillaries at the peripheral corneal stroma do not extend beyond the limbus. Vascular drainage is by venules that reverse over the same direction. The limbal vasculature supplies the peripheral cornea, conjunctiva, episclera, limbal sclera, and peripheral uvea. The avascular peripheral cornea relies on the limbal vasculature and aqueous humor to meet its metabolic needs [269,274]. At one time, ocular lymphatics were believed to be limited to the bulbar conjunctiva. Recent development and use of multiple lymphatic endothelial markers (ie, podoplanin (Pdpn), VEGFR-3, lymphatic vessel endothelial hyaluronic acid receptor-1 (LYVE-1), Prox-1) and chemokine ligands associated with collecting lymphatics (CCL 19, CCL21) have allowed for lymphatics to be identified in tissue sections with greater certainty [275–277]. IHC experiments on ocular tissues using these markers have provided further evidence toward the absence of lymphatic vessels in the anterior eye segment; however, LYVE-1 expression by many dendritic cells of the trabecular meshwork and cells within the iris, and Pdpn expression by all trabecular cells and/or surface cells throughout the aqueous outflow track, including the limbus, Schlemm's canal, anterior ciliary muscle tips and the iris root, does occur. These findings suggest that the aqueous humor outflow tissues share some characteristics with lymphatic vessels and may have surrogate lymphatic functions [276]. The conjunctival–limbal distribution of lymphatics appears to be uneven, at least in the mouse, where the nasal-side polarized distribution of both blood and lymph vessels has been characterized [278].

In a highly vascularized tissue like the limbus, it makes sense that the earliest response to limbal injury is vasodilation with increased blood flow, increased vascular permeability, and leakage of proteins and fluid (plasma) into the surrounding tissues, resulting in edema. With progressively severe injury, other blood components (immunoglobulins, neutrophilic polymorphonuclear leukocytes, macrophages, lymphocytes, erythrocytes) escape into the extravascular spaces. Limbus vasculature is also responsive to corneal injury, and can progress to peripheral corneal neovascularization. Limited lymphangiogenesis into injured cornea has been demonstrated as well, although the relative importance of lymphatic vessels versus blood vessels in vascularized corneas is not clear [279–281].

Conjunctiva

The conjunctiva is a mucous membrane that extends from the limbo-corneal junction of the globe to the mucocutanous junction of the eyelid, covering the exposed surface of the ocular globe and lining the inner surface of the eyelids. It consists of stratified nonkeratinizing epithelium resting on fibrovascular connective tissue (substantia propria), and varies in both thickness and appearance, depending on its location. The conjunctiva is divided into three regions:

1. A bulbar portion that covers the noncorneal anterior surface of ocular globe.
2. A tarsal or palpebral portion that lines the inner surface of the eyelids.
3. A fornix portion, where the palpebral conjunctiva reflects onto the surface of the globe and forms a loose pocket called the conjunctival cul-de-sac, which permits independent movement of the eye and eyelids.

Conjunctival epithelium is stratified polyhedral to columnar in the primate, dog, rabbit, and mouse. In the rat, it is stratified squamous and similar to corneal epithelium. The conjunctiva differs from other stratified epithelium in that goblet cells are interspersed between conjunctival epithelial cells. The goblet cells secrete mucus that lubricates the eyeball and contributes some components in tear production. In the primate, dog, rabbit, and mouse, goblet cells are distributed randomly throughout the epithelium. In the rat, goblet cells are aggregated into clusters that are largely composed of columnar cells with occasional tuft cells having thick apical microvilli. The highest density of goblet cells is found in the fornix and bulbar regions. Conjunctival stem cells are uniformly distributed in these two regions as well. Closer to the cornea, dendritic Langerhans cells become

more prominent and goblet cells disappear. The bulbar conjunctival epithelium is thin and translucent with the underlying blood vessels readily visible. In the primate, dog, and rabbit, scattered conjunctival associated lymphoid tissue (CALT) is present in the bulbar conjunctiva. CALT increases from birth to puberty, and then declines with age. Rabbits have M-cells in the overlying follicle-associated epithelium. In the mouse and rat, CALT is absent and mononuclear leukocytes are rarely found in the epithelial layers [282,283]. The superficial conjunctival substantia propria (or stroma) is a loose connective tissue that normally contains light mononuclear cell infiltrates and lymphoid aggregates, but not lymphoid follicles. The deeper layer of the substantia propria is more dense and fibrous, and contains blood vessels, lymphatics, and nerves. The blood vessels within this deeper layer arise from the anterior ciliary arteries and drain in the episcleral venous plexus. The accompanying lymphatics drain into the episcleral plexus and through to the submandibular and preauricular lymph node systems.

Acute conjunctival responses to injury include increased dilation and prominence of vasculature followed by leakiness with development of stromal edema in the substantia propria. If the injury progresses, there are inflammatory cell infiltrates ranging from neutrophilic and mixed to mononuclear, lymphoid, or granulomatous, depending on the stimulus. In those species with CALT, there is lymphoid follicle formation with mound-like elevation of the overlying conjunctiva. Goblet cell density is typically increased. If goblet cell density is decreased, the conjunctival epithelium undergoes squamous metaplasia with keratinization.

Iridocorneal Angle

The iridocorneal angle (ICA) is located at the periphery of the anterior chamber and is the outflow apparatus for aqueous humor, which is produced in the posterior chamber by ciliary processes. Aqueous flows into the anterior chamber through the pupil, and exits the eye through a series of continuous outflow channels that make up the ICA. The ICA resides in the limbus, formed by the base of the iris and the corneal-scleral tunic. The ICA extends into the anterior ciliary body forming a recession, the ciliary cleft or cilioscleral sinus, where the TM is located. The TM is composed of crisscrossing cords or sheets of collagen and elastin that appear to be anterior tendinous extensions of ciliary body musculature. The TM surface is covered by a unique population of endothelial-like trabecular cells that are continuous with the endothelium of the cornea and the downstream collecting duct [221]. These three endothelial cell populations have similarities (ie, phagocytic capabilities [284,285]), and differences (ie, different growth patterns in primary cultures [286]), and may represent three distinct endothelial cell types. The TM is subdivided into three distinct layers (in order of aqueous flow): uveoscleral, or uveal meshwork; corneoscleral meshwork; and juxtacanalicular, or cribriform meshwork (JCM). The corresponding intratrabecular spaces become progressively smaller, resulting in increased aqueous outflow resistance as aqueous flows through the TM, and out the JCM.

There are structural differences in the ICA between mammalian species that are related to the role and limitations of visual (lens) accommodation in lower species, rather than to the physiology of aqueous humor dynamics [243] (Fig. 29.5). The primate has the greatest capacity for lens accommodation amongst mammals and has an ICA characterized as "anthropoid" that is well developed, with a large, muscular ciliary body and extensive TM. The dog, a carnivore, represents an intermediate step along an ascending evolutionary scale in the mechanism of accommodation. The ICA type, characterized as carnivore, has a smaller, less muscular ciliary body and slightly less complex meshwork. The rabbit, rat, and mouse represent the lowest level of lens accommodation, characterized as herbivore, and have a small, minimally muscled ciliary body and minimal TM. Unique aspects of each species are detailed next. As there is little agreement on the anatomical names of many structures, synonyms are provided, starting with those for ICA: anterior chamber angle, corneoiridociliary angle, filtration angle, iris angle, and outflow angle. The three ICA types are shown schematically in Fig. 29.5.

In the primate ICA, the anterior ciliary body is a large, pyramidal, muscular structure that forms a strong baseplate for the attachment to the iridal root [243]. Because of the large ciliary body, the primate ICA space is small and consists solely of TM [243] that fills the sclera sulcus (a small indentation in the peripheral limbus) with four or more laminae of trabeculae that continues internally with another four to eight (or more) laminae. The internal trabeculae have tendinous endings with the ciliary muscle posteriorly, and fuse with peripheral cornea anteriorly at Schwalbe's line. This area, referred to as the corneoscleral TM, occupies the sclera sulcus and extends from the anterior ciliary body to the peripheral cornea. Synonyms for this meshwork are angular meshwork, sclera trabeculae, and scleral meshwork. The filtering portion of the anterior angle opening begins with iris pillars (synonym: pectinate ligaments), which are seen in all mammals, and traditionally have been subdivided into two types: primary pectinate ligaments and accessory pectinate ligaments. Primary iris pillars/pectinate ligaments form an anterior comb-like row arising from the anterior base of the iris and ciliary base and extending to the termination of Descemet's membrane in the limbal cornea. Accessory iris pillars/pectinate ligaments are

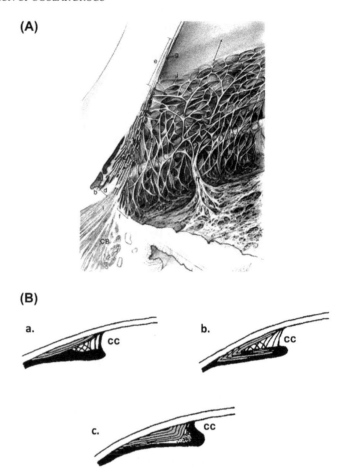

FIGURE 29.5 (A) Schematic illustration of the anterior iridociliary angle of the primate eye, showing the aqueous humor outflow pathways (arrows). The trabecular meshwork can be subdivided into uveal (closer to the chamber) and corneoscleral (closer to Schlemm's canal) expanded between ciliary muscle (4) and scleral spur (3) posteriorly, and cornea anteriorly. The cribriform or subendothelial region (punctated) is between the meshwork and Schlemm's canal. (A = anterior, nonfiltering; B = filtering portion of the meshwork.) Aqueous humor conventionally leaves the eye through the filtering portion of the meshwork into Schlemm's canal (1) and collector channels (2), and nonconventionally leaves through the ciliary muscle and sclera (C). *(From Lutjen-Drecoll E. Functional Morphology of the Trabecular Meshwork in Primate Eyes. Prog Retin Eye Res 1998;18(1):91. With permission from Elsevier.)* (B) Schematic diagrams of three basic iridocorneal angle configurations, including ciliary body musculature. (a) Herbivore (mouse, rat, rabbit). (b) Carnivore (dog). (c) Anthropoid (nonhuman primate). (CC, ciliary cleft.) Ciliary body musculature is in gray. *(With permission from author.)*

typically smaller, and more posteriorly located strands that also extend from the iris base to Descemet's membrane. The iris pillars/pectinate ligaments are covered by variably pigmented trabecular cells [287–289].

In the dog ICA, the anterior ciliary body is smaller and bifurcates into two leaves (outer and inner), creating a cleft that allows extension of the ICA into the ciliary body [243]. Terms for this cleft include ciliary cleft, ciliary sinus, ciliary canal, and cilioscleral sinus. The TM within the ciliary cleft is referred to as uveal meshwork (synonyms:

ciliary meshwork and reticular meshwork). The outer ciliary leaf, which lies next to the sclera, extends to corneoscleral TM. The inner leaf ends near the base of the iris and forms tendinous connections with the inner uveal trabeculae. The scleral sulcus is very shallow in the dog, and so the corneoscleral TM is sometimes referred to as uveoscleral meshwork. Uveal trabeculae are slender and widely spaced, and meridional in orientation. Iris pillars/pectinate ligaments are often prominent in the dog.

In the rabbit ICA, the ciliary body birfurcates into two leaves to form a ciliary cleft that is deeper than in the dog. Of the two leaves, one is a connective tissue baseplate that extends from the iris root to the ora ciliaris retinae; the other is a smooth muscle layer pressed against the sclera and extending toward the ora. There is an uveoscleral mesh that is separated from the ciliary cleft by broad spaces. In the rat and mouse, the ciliary body bifurcates to form a small ciliary cleft. The ciliary body is weakly developed with minimal smooth muscle in the outer ciliary leaflet.

In the primate, dog, and rabbit, the anterior opening of the ICA is covered by a peripheral extremity of Descemet's membrane called the operculum. In turn, the operculum covers the anterior portion of the corneoscleral TM to a varying extent. The operculum is often vestigial in the primate. The dense composite membrane of the operculum distinguishes it from the TM. The operculum is a nonfiltering portion of the trabecular mesh, as it has no direct contact with the Schlemm's canal or angular aqueous plexus [273,290]. The cells lining the operculum are called Schwalbe's line cells, and are considered a subpopulation of the trabecular cells. These cells are secretory and may function as stem cells for the trabecular mesh. Schwalbe's line cells have been described in the macaque and dog. Little is known of these cells other than they secrete neuron enolase and hyaluron synthase, and may function as stem cells for the TM [271,273]. They are considered to be a subpopulation of trabecular cells. Fibrous strands from the corneoscleral TM may insert into the inner surface of the operculum.

TM response to injury appears to be limited. When damage is minimal, as by transient elevation in IOP or by laser trabeculoplasty, and adequate scaffolding remains, TM cell migration and proliferation is possible and there is reorganization of the trabeculae. Activation of TM cells appears to be a universal response regardless of the injury or irritating stimuli, which can range through surgery, laser, phagocytic particle insult, and noxious agents. TM cell activation has been associated particularly with a heightened metabolic state needed for the phagocytosis of debris entering the meshwork. In addition to migration and proliferation, activated TM cells are capable of forming distinct spindle shapes, expressing α-SMA, synthesizing new basement membrane and other collagens, and establishing phagocytosis [291–295].

Aqueous Humor Outflow

Aqueous humor exits the JCM and continues with the juxtacanalicular connective tissue (JCT), Schlemm's canal or aqueous angle plexus, and the aqueous veins [296–299]. The JCT is adjacent to Schlemm's canal and follows the last trabecular ligament and extends to the inner wall of Schlemm's canal. Schlemm's canal includes its inner wall endothelium through which the aqueous humor must pass, the canal lumen, and the collector channel ostia by which the canal connects to the aqueous veins that carry the aqueous humor to the episcleral veins on the surface of the eye [300]. There is a modest difference in the JCT between the primate and the dog, rabbit, rat, and mouse. While it is dense and filled with extracellular material in the primate, it opens with little extracellular material in the remaining species [301].

Another species difference is seen in the drainage vessels. The dog and rabbit do not have a single Schlemm's canal. Instead, they have a complex of angular draining vessels [223,302]. The topography and the structural and ultrastructural morphology of the angular drainage vessels are fairly similar between Schlemm's canal and the angular draining vessels, with the plexiform nature of the angular drainage vessels being the only significant difference. Schlemm's canal most likely represents an evolutionary adaptation for the small, more compact TM that is present in an angle that is bordered by a larger and more highly developed ciliary body musculature in primates [286,296,303]. Collection and removal of aqueous humor along the outer angle into Schlemm's canal or angular aqueous plexus is referred to as conventional outflow. There are also unconventional outflow routes, the most prominent being the uveoscleral route, where aqueous humor moves through the ciliary body and into supraciliary and suprachoroidal spaces along the outer choroid. Of the different ancillary routes, uveoscleral outflow has been shown to be the most prominent in nonhuman primates, having accounted for as much as 30–65% of the total amount of aqueous humor to leave the eye. In rabbits it accounted for 13%, 15% in dogs, 3% in cats, and 4–14% in humans [304–306].

Ciliary Body

The ciliary body is responsible for aqueous humor production and outflow, secretion of hyaluronic acid into the vitreous, and lens accommodation. It is also a critical component of the blood–aqueous barrier. The ciliary body is divided into an anterior pars plicata and posterior pars plana. The pars plicata is a ring of 70–100 ciliary processes with intervening valleys [307]. The processes increase the area for aqueous humor production; the number of processes is directly related to the relative size of the anterior chamber. The lenticular zonules (zonular ligaments that suspend the lens) anchored on the epithelial apical basement membrane of the processes, connecting the ciliary body to the lens. The main mass of the ciliary body is smooth muscle in mammals. The relative tone of smooth muscle within the ciliary body controls the visual accommodation of the lens; thus the relative amount of smooth muscle present in the ciliary body is reflective of visual acuity. The ciliary muscle is robust in primates, and accommodation is far more effective in these species than in most other mammals. In those animals with poor lens accommodation (dog, rabbit, rat, and mouse), the ciliary muscle is poorly developed. The ciliary muscle also plays a role in aqueous filtration in primates by regulating the tension of the trabecular meshwork at the level of Schlemm's canal.

The ciliary processes vary in appearance among species. In dogs, the processes are thin with rounded tips that serve as attachment sites for the lenticular zonules. There are secondary folds present that originate near the pars plana. Each ciliary process has a central core of stroma and blood vessels covered by a dual epithelial layer, an inner nonpigmented cuboidal layer and an outer, pigmented cuboidal layer. The nonpigmented layer is confluent with the sensory retina at the ora serrata and the posterior pigmented epithelium of the iris. The pigmented ciliary epithelium is a continuation of the retinal pigmented epithelium. The ciliary epithelium plays an important role in the establishment and maintenance of ACAID. Activated T cells are converted to regulatory T (Treg) cells through contact-dependent mechanisms with the epithelial cells of the iris and ciliary body [198,308]. Immune cells reacting to antigens in the globe are programmed as they traverse the ciliary epithelium to hone to the spleen upon exiting the eye. In the spleen, they differentiate as T-regulatory (Treg) cells or suppressor T-cells that promote immune tolerance rather than immunoreactivity.

Ciliary body blood vessels are derived from the two long posterior ciliary arteries and anterior ciliary arteries. There are numerous anatomic variations to this scheme. The ciliary processes of primate, dog and rabbit have well-developed capillary beds for extensive aqueous production while the rat and mouse have underdeveloped capillary beds (Fig. 29.12A,B).

Iris

The iris is the highly vascularized, anterior portion of the uveal tract, dividing the anterior compartment into anterior (space between the cornea and anterior surface of the iris) and posterior (space between the posterior surface of the iris, lens, and anterior face of the vitreous) chambers. The chambers are connected by the pupillary space, formed within the inner marginal rim of the iris. Both chambers contain aqueous humor, which is secreted by the ciliary epithelium into the posterior chamber, and flows through the pupil into the anterior chamber. The iris forms a circumferential diaphragm in front of the lens that modulates light penetration by contraction of myoepithelial cells (sympathetic innervation) or smooth muscle fibers (parasympathetic innervation) that permit dilation (mydriasis), and constriction (miosis) of the pupil, respectively. The sphincter muscle consists of circumferentially arranged smooth muscle fibers that encircle the margin of the pupil. The posterior dilator muscle is comprised of radially arranged smooth muscle fibers posterior to the sphincter muscle in the iris stroma. The pupil size and shape varies between species and state of contraction; being round in the primate, dog, and rodent; vertically oval in the rabbit; and slit-like in the cat.

The anterior surface has no epithelial lining, but is lined by a discontinuous layer of stromal cells. Aqueous diffuses freely between the anterior chamber and the iris stroma, comprised of fibroblasts, collagen, nerve fibers, smooth muscle, melanocytes, and blood vessels. The posterior surface of the iris is lined by simple, cuboidal pigmented epithelium (posterior pigmented epithelium), which is in direct contact with the posterior chamber. Tight junctions between these cells create a barrier between the posterior chamber and iris stroma. Iris color is mainly due to type and density of melanin pigment rather than the total number of melanocytes present. Cats have pheomelanin, a light-colored pigment that consists of long and thin filaments compared to the round granules contained in typical melanocytes. Additional factors that determine iris color include the amount and quality of stromal pigment, and backscatter of incident light from stromal collagen fibers, the latter giving the blue irides of albino rodents and rabbits their appearance [309]. Pigmentation of the iris is important, as it serves to limit light transmission through the pupil, reducing incident light that may interfere with visual perception in bright light conditions. It also has a protective role to the retina; individuals with blue irises may be at increased risk of developing macular degeneration [310].

The major arterial circle of the iris is supplied by anastomoses of the anterior ciliary arteries and the long posterior arteries [274,311]. Blood vessels residing in the iris stroma tend to be relatively thick, so that blood flow is constant regardless of pupil constriction or dilation [312]. The blood–aqueous barrier of the anterior segment is composed of tight junctions between endothelial cells of the iridal vessels, and tight junctions between epithelial cells of the posterior iris, ciliary body (which contains fenestrated capillaries), and ciliary processes. This is an important component of ACAID (previously discussed).

The term "iritis" is a misnomer as it is used clinically, because it denotes congestion of the vessels of the iris irrespective of the presence or, more commonly, a lack of inflammation. Vascular congestion may be difficult to discern in pigmented eyes, but is readily apparent in albino species such as the NZW rabbit, accounting in part for it popular use in nonclinical studies. Congestion is often accompanied by vessel dilation; however, in general, both iritis and dilation are limited to clinical diagnoses, as both conditions are susceptible to alterations postmortem and following fixation such that neither can be reliably diagnosed on histology.

Anterior uveal inflammation is associated with compromise of either or both barriers. Compromise of endothelial cell tight junctions results in the accumulation of protein, which is diagnosed as flare on ophthalmoscopy, and white blood cells in the anterior chamber. The degree of flare present generally correlates with the extent of breakdown of the blood–aqueous barrier [313]. Transient flare may be observed with the simple passing of a needle through the uvea. Persistent flare associated with cellular influx may occur with the injection of irritating or proinflammatory compounds. Compromise of the epithelial barrier results in an inflammatory exudate into the anterior chamber associated with the ciliary processes. The types of cells present in the aqueous reflect the cause of inflammation, and microscopic examination of aqueous fluid aspirates is useful in diagnosis. Inflammation of any cause may be associated with dispersion of pigment into the stroma, or pigment and/or pigmented cells into the aqueous. Synechiae, the adherence of the iris to the cornea or lens (anterior and posterior synechiae, respectively), is a potential sequelae to anterior uveitis. Anterior synechiae can potentially block outflow of the aqueous humor through the filtration angle, causing increased IOP. Pigment found on the anterior lens capsule suggests prior occurrence of posterior synechiae. Synechiae may be detected on examination by topical instillation of a mydriatic agent; dilation is associated with distortion of the pupil. Spontaneous synechiae may be observed in SD rats [260].

The iris stroma contains resident macrophages and dendritic cells that, contrary to systemic antigen-presenting cells (APCs), modulate inflammatory reactions in the anterior segment in response to the introduction of antigens, thus conferring immune privilege to internal ocular tissues [203]. These cells are capable of antigen engulfment; however, as APCs they are relatively poor at stimulating the T-cell response necessary to elicit delayed hypersensitivity reactions or complement-fixing antibodies. In some cases they are thought to diminish the T-cell response. This anterior chamber-associated immune deviation (ACAID) in part accounts for survival of corneal grafts and suppression of autoimmune uveitis. Immunosuppressive factors present in the aqueous, and cell receptors on the surface of the iris, promote a microenvironment within the anterior chamber that aids in minimizing inflammation and thus collateral damage to delicate ocular tissues, and spares the visual axis in the presence of inflammation or infection [314,315]. Although therapeutic strategies to capitalize on ACAID in the treatment of inflammatory eye disease and grafts are in development, the potential role in minimizing unfavorable reactions to other intraocular therapies (ie, monoclonal antibodies) is uncertain.

Persistent pupillary membranes are remnant vascular strands of the developing iris that fail to undergo postnatal atrophy; they may be free-floating, bridge the iris, or extend from the iris to the cornea where they are associated with corneal opacification. They may be observed in beagle dogs and rats, and individuals with this finding should be excluded from ocular studies.

Lens

The crystalline lens is located behind the iris, in the posterior chamber of the anterior segment. This transparent, avascular, flexible structure refracts light onto the retina while also changing the refractive index to allow for sharp focusing on objects at various distances.

The lens shape is biconvex in the primate, dog, and rabbit and round in the rat and mouse. In the biconvex lens, the posterior surface is the most steeply curved in both the unaccommodated and maximally accommodated configurations relative to the anterior surface. The lens increases in sagittal thickness throughout life and both surfaces (in the unaccommodated state) steepen with age. The round lens of the rat and mouse is proportionately larger than the biconvex lens of the primate, dog, and rabbit; it occupies about 75% of the ocular space.

The lens capsule encases the cellular elements of the lens. This capsule is a highly elastic thickened PAS positive basement membrane secreted by a monolayer of epithelial cells lining the membrane within the lens. Except at the equator, where differentiation and elongation occur (described below), lens epithelial cells appear cuboidal in section, and roughly hexagonal in flat mount (the "orange peel" effect seen with the slit lamp). Neighboring cells have interdigitations with each other associated with junctional specializations (desmosomes and gap junctions), which hold the cells tightly together. These lateral interdigitated membranes are involved in enzyme production and with the active transport systems such as the sodium ion pump. The bulk of the lens consists of lens fibers, which are vastly elongated lens epithelial cells that have lost their nuclei and many of their organelles as they mature and migrate to the lens interior. Since they are no longer cells and are of great length they are called lens fibers.

Epithelial cells have many roles in addition to lens fiber production, including synthesis of crystallins and membrane proteins, transport through active pumps of ions and water, and secretion of capsular precursors. Because lens epithelial cells lack nerve and blood supplies, junctional specializations are critical for the transport of ions and metabolites between cells, and for the mechanical stability required of a flexible, yet transparent tissue. Throughout life, the lens increases in size and weight as the epithelial cells continue to divide and develop into new lens fibers that extend anteriorly under the epithelium and posteriorly under the lens capsule toward an ever-expanding suture. The oldest or primary lens fibers remain in the center of the lens, forming the embryonic nucleus of the lens. Subsequent populations of lens fibers form in layers like an onion around the primary fibers. The newest lens fibers are found in the outermost layer in the superficial cortex; these fibers comprise the region known as the lens bow due to the arrangement of the cell nuclei. Lens fibers are tightly joined by a network of junctional structures and membrane modifications with little intracellular space.

The lens is suspended radially from the ciliary body by the zonular fibers arising from the ciliary epithelium and attaching on either side of its equator. The ciliary body encircles the lens and is roughly triangular in cross-section. It forms a separated ring roughly concentric with the lens, being attached anteriorly at the sclera, and posteriorly at the ora serrata. When the muscle within this ciliary body contracts, the body swells radially and reduces the ciliary annulus, which via the zonules, allows the elastic lens to take up its preferred accommodated (and more spherical) state. Tension is returned to the lens zonule system by relaxation of the ciliary muscle, causing the lens to flatten ready for distance focusing.

In the primate, dog, and rabbit, the lens curvature is flexible and can be adjusted in a process called accommodation to fine-tune the focus depending upon an object's distance. The primate lens has the greatest capacity for accommodation. In fact, the entire eye has evolved to the highest level amongst mammals, having attained true photopic vision with the development of the fovea. Primate ocular structures are optimized toward visual acuity: smallest cornea, anterior chamber and anterior chamber angle, and the largest ciliary musculature. In addition, the highly rostral placement of the orbits in the primate allows for binocularity. In comparison, the dog and rabbit have limited capacity for accommodation and visual acuity. As for the rat and mouse, they have no capacity for visual accommodation; however, the round lens is able to provide a greater range of focus when the pupil is constricted.

LEC are capable of proliferation and transformation to α-smooth muscle actin positive myofibroblasts when stimulated by injury, and the transformed cells are capable of producing type I and type III collagen and glycosaminoglycans. Both traumatic tears and surgical sections into the lens capsule are repaired by this wound-healing response. After maturation of the fibrous tissue, the superficial LEC form a new lens capsule. Most wounds to the lens result in the formation of cataracts, although small wounds may result only in small focal opacities. Cataracts consist of insoluble aggregates of crystallin proteins that obstruct the passage of light. The detailed molecular mechanisms of cataract formation, particularly the mature-onset type, are not known; however, oxidative stress is hypothesized to be an underlying mechanism due to the presence of extensive oxidative damage to proteins, lipids, and DNA.

There are postmortem and fixation artifacts that may be confused with cataracts or other pathological change: splitting of the cortical tissue and separation of capsule from cortex are the most common artifacts. Granular material typically occupies the artifactual space.

Back of the Eye and Posterior Segment

Blood flow to the choroid and choriocapillaris, the bed of capillaries that abuts Bruch's membrane (basement membrane of the posterior segment), are supplied by the posterior ciliary arteries (temporal and nasal). Blood from the choriocapillaris support the metabolic demands of the outer portion of the retina, extending to the inner nuclear layer. The external choroid contains a few large arteries, but is otherwise a venous plexus that drains (with vessels serving other parts of the eye) into vortex veins, which in turn drain into the superior and inferior orbital veins. Midsized anastomosing vessels, supported by pigmented reticular connective tissue, are distributed between the vessels of the outer choroid and the choriocapillaris. Specialized pigmented macrophages, melanocytes, are distributed in this layer and have a role in absorption of excess radiation. Conversely, most domestic species have a layer of reflective tissue, the tapetum lucidum, interspersed between the choriocapillaris and the midsize vessels. In the dog, the tapetum is a multilayered complex of polyhedral cells (iridocytes) that contain light-reflective crystals composed of zinc cysteine (Fig. 29.6) [221]. Conventional thought is that the tapetum reflects light that has passed through the retina back to the photoreceptors to increase stimulation, enhancing vision under scotopic conditions. The organelle and chemical composition of these cells varies across species and may have implications with respect to drug-binding characteristics. A tapetum is not present in the primate, rabbit, or rodent.

Although ocular blood circulation has commonality across mammalian species, there are distinct differences that occur in retinal design that reflect functional adaptation to environmental demands. In most mammals, the blood distribution to the retina is holangiotic (the rabbit,

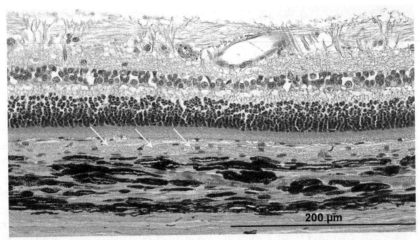

FIGURE 29.6 Cellular tapetum of the dog. The tapetum of the dog consists of a multilayered complex of polyhedral cells that reside interspersed between the choriocapillaris and the choroid in the dorsal posterior retina (*white arrows*). Paraffin-embedded section, H&E, 400×.

a notable exception, is merangiotic). In the holangiotic retina, the inner 2/3 of the retina is supplied by arteries limited to the nerve fiber layer; branching superficial capillaries supply the ganglion cell and nerve fiber layer, while deeper capillaries penetrate the retina to the inner nuclear layer. Blood flow to the retina is derived from the CRA, branching off the ophthalmic artery in humans and nonhuman primates [316], species that have a macula with a fovea, a cone-exclusive region of the retina designed for acute photopic vision. The CRA emerges from the optic nerve head to form superior and inferior branches. The temporal branches supply the macula, arching and creating a 0.4-mm capillary-free zone around a depression known as the fovea [317]. This design optimizes light transmission while minimizing scatter to the cone-rich photoreceptors of this region that permits vision acuity.

In species that lack a macula, the retinal blood supply is derived from the posterior ciliary arteries branching off the external ophthalmic artery. Although the vascular pattern is divergent across species, in general the vessels form a radial pattern originating from the posterior ciliary artery at the optic disc. In dogs and pigs, the retina contains a region of increased ganglion cell and cone-rich density that is lateral and slightly dorsal to the optic disc, referred to as the area centralis. The area centralis is relatively devoid of blood vessels, and a fovea of sorts is present that is the source of visual acuity. Rodents display weak propensities for centralized cone concentrations in any portion of the retina.

The retina of the rabbit is merangiotic; the arteries are derived similarly from the posterior ciliary arteries; however, the retina is avascular. Vessels lie internal to the retina in close opposition to the internal limiting laminae through glial cell attachments, and within invaginations of the neural fiber layer [318]. Blood vessel loops extend from the optic disc in the ventral and lateral planes the extent of the medullary rays, the myelinated axons of the ganglion cells that course on top of the retina before exiting the globe through the optic nerve. Rabbits possess an extended region comparable to the area centralis known as the visual streak, a horizontal band in the posterior retina inferior to the optic disc (positioned in the dorsal posterior pole). In this region, ganglion cells and photoreceptors occur in higher density than that of the peripheral or dorsal retina.

Despite the extensive vascular supply to the eye, exposure to the intraocular tissues from systemically administered drugs is limited by the blood–ocular barrier, conceptually similar to the blood–brain barrier. Tight junctions (zonulae occludens) of the retinal endothelium provide a barrier to macromolecule diffusion from blood vessels that is additionally supported by a discontinuous layer of surrounding cells with smooth-muscle characteristics—pericytes—and by basement membrane of Müller cells and astrocytes. Capillaries of the choriocapillaris do not possess tight junctions; rather, the endothelium is fenestrated, allowing for leakage of macromolecules into the extracellular space of the choroid that are used to support the metabolic needs of the outer retina. However, RPE (peripheral-lining, nonsensory, epithelial support cells to the retina) tight junctions prevent leakage into the retina of the healthy eye, and create osmotic pressure that assists in drawing fluid out of the retina through cellular mechanisms. Leakage of blood constituents into the retina or subretinal space may occur with the loss of pericytes in diseases such as diabetic retinopathy, or in degenerative RPE disease that occur with aging (ie, macular degeneration), promoting neovascularization. The eye may be rendered vulnerable to systemic drug exposure with compromise of the blood–ocular barrier such as occurs with systemic vascular diseases, particularly those that may have ocular components in their pathologies. The integrity of the vasculature system can be evaluated through FA coupled with timed photography focused to capture perfusion of either the anterior or posterior segments (see "Specialized Ocular Examination Techniques" earlier in the chapter).

A basement membrane complex resides between the choriocapillaris and the RPE known as Bruch's membrane, an exterior lining of the RPE, extending anterior to the ora serrata, and penetrated posteriorly by the optic nerve. The basement membranes of the choriocapillaris and RPE form the outer and inner layers, respectively, of Bruch's membrane. In humans, nonhuman primates, and most diurnal species including pigs, Bruch's membrane is a pentalaminar structure consisting of a middle layer of elastin sandwiched between two layers of collagen that is covered by the inner and outer basement membranes. Ultrastructural analysis suggests that Bruch's membrane is also pentalaminar in rabbits, guinea pigs, and rats [319]. In dogs, Bruch's membrane appears trilaminar, with the inner and outer membranes separated by a single layer of collagen [221]. Bruch's membrane aids in the support of the internal structures of the eye, and selectively filters the passage of macromolecules between the retina and choriocapillaris. In humans, Bruch's membrane is subject to a variety of senescent changes representing a significant cause of age-related visual defects, including age-related macular degeneration (AMD).

Ocular Functional Neuroanatomy

Retinal Pigment Epithelium

The RPE is a single layer of nonsensory cuboidal epithelial cells that underlie and isolate the retina. It is a morphologically heterogeneous population, as smaller cells are found in the macula and area centralis/visual streak (regions of greatest visual acuity, and typically subject to higher light exposure) while larger cells predominate peripherally. The apical processes of the RPE interdigitate with the outer segments of photoreceptors forming cylindrical (rods) or leaf-like (cones) shape sheaths [320]. The close association between the outer segments and the apical processes enables active and efficient turnover of the discs as they are shed from the photoreceptors [321]. Phagocytosis, degradation, and membrane turnover of phospholipids derived from the shed discs occurs in RPE lysosomes. The accumulation of inclusion bodies containing photoreceptor outer segment (POS) membranes can be observed in aging RPE, and are associated with RPE degeneration that can lead to blindness. These contain autofluorescent pigments, and appear as abnormal changes in color, or as AF spots when viewed with appropriate filters, on fundic examination. Similar lesions occur spontaneously in Dutch belted rabbits, associated with RPE degeneration and necrosis (Fig. 29.7A). Drusen, subretinal deposits associated with macular degeneration, are rarely observed in species other than humans. Hard drusen may be infrequently observed in some species (Fig. 29.7B).

The interface between RPE processes and photoreceptor segments, the interphotoreceptor matrix (IPM), is a complex containing hyaluronan, proteoglycans, glycosaminoglycans, matrix metalloproteases, and growth and immunosuppressive factors secreted by RPE [322]. The IPM has roles in mediating retinal adhesion and facilitates the supportive function the RPE has to the retina. Transport binding proteins, that move proteins between RPE and photoreceptors can be found in the IPM. Interphotoreceptor retinal binding protein, a protein secreted

(A)

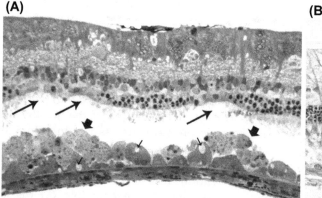

(B)

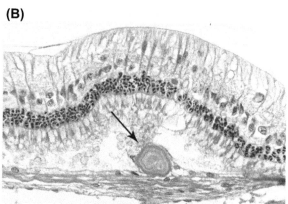

FIGURE 29.7 (A) Spontaneous degeneration of RPE with retinal detachment in a rabbit. Degenerated and detached RPE are present in the subretinal space (*thick arrows*), corresponding to regions of photoreceptor loss in the segments and outer nuclear layer (*thin arrows*). The remaining RPE are hypertrophied and lack cellular detail. Enlarged vacuoles/inclusions (whose contents were lost during processing) are occasionally observed in the RPE. Plastic-embedded section, Richardson's stain, 200×. (B) Hard drusen in an NZW rabbit. A concentric lamellar mass is located in the subretinal space. Paraffin-embedded section, H&E, 400×. *(This image adapted from Ramos M, Reilly MC, Bolon B. Toxicological Pathology of the Retina and Optic Nerve. Fundamental Neuropathology for Pathologists and Toxicologists: Principles and Techniques. In: Bolon B, Butt MT. New Jersey: John Wiley & Sons, Inc.; 2011. p. 385–412.)*

by both photoreceptors and RPE, transports retinoid between RPE and photoreceptors as part of the vitamin A cycle [323]. Other factors within the IPM help to prevent vascular proliferation in the surrounding tissues. Although the metabolic demands of the outer retina are supplied by the fenestrated choriocapillaris, tight junctions between RPE cells create a syncytium that prevents leakage of fluid and molecules into the subretinal space. Transcellular movement of glucose, retinol, amino acids, and other nutrients to the retina, and of ions and metabolic waste back to the choriocapillaris, is regulated by a series of receptors, ion channels and exchangers, and organelles. These have a polar distribution in RPE that account for the regulated movement of ions through the cell, creating RPE membrane potentials that can be measured by ERG. Successive hyperpolarization of the RPE apical and basal membranes returns potassium to, and removes sodium from, the subretinal space subsequent to diminished sodium (influx) and potassium (efflux) currents that occur in the outer and inner segments respectively of the photoreceptors due to a light stimulus [322]. The movement of ions by the RPE creates an ionic gradient in the IPM that maintains photoreceptor excitability, permitting the electrical transmission of the light stimulus by the photoreceptor. Ionic flux also stabilizes IPM pH, and contributes to the passive removal of water from the retina, an end-product of metabolic activity. While this activity is critical to prevent fluid from accumulating in the subretinal space, it also creates hydrostatic pressure that contributes to retinal–RPE adhesion. RPE hyperpolarization is recorded as the C-wave in the ERG, providing a functional evaluation of RPE integrity. However, technical challenges in animals limit the conventional use of the c-wave in nonclinical drug development.

Melanosomes, elliptical-shaped granules of melanin pigment found in the apical and midportion cytoplasm of the RPE, are present in most mammalian species. Melanosomes of rodents (and in general nocturnal species) tend to be comparatively rounder, and fewer in number, commensurate with the low-light conditions of their visual needs. The RPE of albino species (Spraque-Dawley rats and NZW rabbits) lack melanin granules. RPE cells overlying the tapetum lack melanin pigment to facilitate the transfer of light to light-reflective tapetal cells, and back to the photoreceptors, enhancing visual perception in low-light conditions. Melanin, however, absorbs scattered light, enhancing object discrimination by the photoreceptors under bright light. Melanosomes are present at higher density in RPE of the central retina compared to those peripheral. By absorbing excess radiation, melanin reduces the potential for photo-oxidative damage by dissipating the energy of light photons, and simultaneously acts as a free-radical scavenger through its electron-exchange properties [324]. However,

melanin also generates free radicals, which can be cytotoxic, and may gradually become pro-oxidant through senescence and the formation of conjugates. As melanin content declines with age, an associated accumulation of lipofuscin in RPE due to incomplete digestion of the POS occurs. Lipofuscin may form conjugates with melanin (melanolipofuscin), impairing light absorption, and reducing the antioxidant capacity of RPE. The brown pigmentation observed on fundic examination is related primarily to the distribution of the melanin in the RPE. Altered pigmentary patterns are associated with visual impairment and may show classic changes in some retinal diseases or to the administration of certain drugs. Some pharmacological agents, particularly substances with cationic properties (amines and metals) [324], bind to melanin, and induce pigmentary changes that can be monitored by fundic examination in vivo (see "Standard Ocular Examination Procedures" earlier in the chapter). Alternatively, melanin may unintentionally sequester the drug from the intended target; prolong exposure to sensitive ocular tissues if binding is reversible; enhance free-radical release from melanin pigments; and cause retinal toxicity through RPE impairment (see "Melanin Binding" earlier in the chapter). Affected regions of the retina are not typically uniform, but may be regionally isolated, or more commonly multifocal. Fundic photography should be used to guide sectioning of the eye to ensure relevant histological examination of eyes with regional lesions.

RPE have a critical role in the visual cycle of vitamin A and the generation of the analog 11-cis-retinaldehyde, which upon interaction with opsin in the photoreceptors, forms the visual pigments (rhodopsin in rods) that are essential to vision. RPE are equipped with a number of receptors, and membrane and cytoplasmic proteins that enable the uptake and intracellular transport of vitamin A from the blood, from the IPM following light bleaching reduction (all-trans-retinol) and release from photoreceptors, or through phagocytosis of shed outer segments. Multiple enzymes service a number of metabolic pathways that allow conversion to analogs for storage or other cellular functions, or to the active analog for vision. Aging and photooxidative stress can disrupt the balance of vitamin A cycling between the RPE-IPM-photoreceptor and lead to degeneration of the retina. Analogs toxic to the RPE have a role in the formation of lipofuscin fluorophores associated with AMD.

During processing for histology, the retina is vulnerable to artifactual separation from the RPE, particularly in the rabbit, presumably due in part to the lack of retinal vessels in this species. True separation is associated with RPE "tombstoning" (Fig. 29.8), POS fragmentation, collection of cells, debris, or fluid beneath the retina, and in longstanding separation, by retinal atrophy. It is important to bear in mind that RPE produce and secrete a milieu of growth

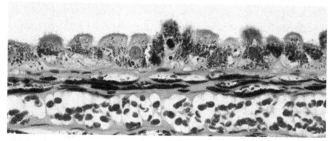

FIGURE 29.8 Hypertrophy of the retinal pigmented epithelium (RPE) in a dog. Note the swollen ("tombstone") appearance of the cells with apical melanosome dispersion. Apical localization of melanosomes may also occur with artifactual separation. Paraffin-embedded section, H&E, 400 ×. (*This image adapted from Ramos M, Reilly MC, Bolon B. Toxicological Pathology of the Retina and Optic Nerve. Fundamental Neuropathology for Pathologists and Toxicologists: Principles and Techniques. In: Bolon B, Butt MT. New Jersey: John Wiley & Sons, Inc.; 2011. p. 385–412.*)

factors and cytokines that normally contribute to retinal homeostasis that conversely may have adverse consequences. RPE likely have roles in the formation of epiretinal membranes (EPM) and in neovascularization observed in AMD through secretion of VEGF and other growth factors.

Sensory and Neuronal Retina

The eye is a specialized extension of the central nervous system designed for photoreception and the conversion of light energy into graded electrical signals that allow visual perception. The photosensitive retina lies internal to the RPE in the posterior compartment extending from the optic nerve head, and terminating at the ora serrata (primates, including humans) or ora ciliaris (most other species) posterior to the ciliary body. A continuation of nonsensory epithelium, the pars plana, lies anterior to the ora serrata as a single (most species) or double layer (primates and humans) to merge with the lining epithelium of the ciliary body and apparatus. The retina is a highly organized, multilayered complex of photosensitive neurons along with integrating and transmission neurons that initially process the visual stimulus [125]. There are marked morphological differences in the retina across species; however, the circuitry and function of the retina is remarkably conserved. The photosensitive retina (described below) is classically viewed as nine distinct histological layers (Fig. 29.9A). These can also be discriminated on in vivo imaging using newer-generation OCT (see "Specialized Ocular Examination Techniques" earlier in the chapter) that—although lacking in cellular detail—approaches that obtained in histology (Fig. 29.9B). OCT images coupled with fundic imaging are useful aids to guide sectioning of the eye for histological examination.

Photoreceptor Segments

Photoreceptors are bipolar cells oriented perpendicularly within the retina. The perikarya and nuclei of the photoreceptor reside in the outer nuclear layer with axons radiating inward, while the dendrite forms the inner and outer segments. The outer segments are composed of stacked membranous discs containing the photosensitive pigments used in the visual cycle. Rods contain rhodopsin, used in low light (scotopic) conditions and motion detection, while cones, which provide visual acuity, contain one of three opsins with sensitivity to red, green, or blue light (long, medium, and short wavelength, respectively). Opsins collectively permit visual detection within the spectral range of red through violet. For mammalian species, only primates are known to have all three types of cones [325].

Rods are the predominant photoreceptor in all mammalian retinas (95% in humans [326]). Rod discs are cylindrical and ensheathed by the apical processes of the RPE. Discs are continuously shed and phagocytized by RPE, which recycle the vitamin A analogs crucial to the conversion of light to an electrical transduction impulse. Discs are continuously replaced from the inner segment, where the mitochondria and Golgi reside, which is connected by a thin dendritic process to the outer segment. Cone discs taper in the outer segment to form a cone-like shape, the widest part continuous with the inner segment of the dendrite. RPE processes form leaf-like sheaths that surround cone discs. Mechanisms of cone disc shedding are less clear than those known for rods. Production of discs and opsin proteins is continuous, as is the synthesis of associated transport proteins and enzymes that are consumed and recycled by RPE phagocytosis.

Although rods predominate in all species, the respective numbers of cones and rods and the spatial arrangement within the retina have considerable species variation. The fovea, a depression within an avascular zone of the central retina (macula), of humans and most nonhuman primates, is cone exclusive. The fovea is devoid of other cells with the exception of Müller cells. The distribution of red, green, and blue cones in the primate eye appears to be random, with the exception of the fovea, where blue cones are absent [326]. Cone pedicles are densely packed and interconnected by gap junctions of fine processes that mediate electrical coupling, particularly between red and green sensitive cones, reducing noise while simultaneously reinforcing the light signal between neighboring cones [326]. In humans and nonhuman primates, cell axons are radially arranged around the macula. This design permits maximal visual acuity under bright light (photopic) conditions. Rods, which function under scotopic conditions, progressively dominate in the peripheral regions of the retina. Although rods can respond to a single photon, signals are pooled to improve sensitivity in dim light [326].

The regional concentration of cones in the retinas of other species and relative proportion to rods likely reflects behavioral accommodations for visual needs pertinent to the environmental niche occupied. Most mammals are dichromatic; however, they may possess hybrid cones

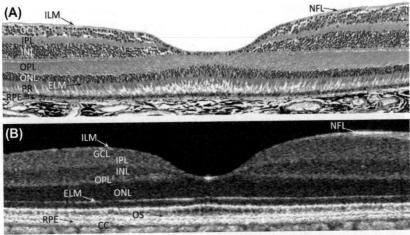

FIGURE 29.9 **Normal retina from an adult nonhuman primate near the fovea centralis (the central depressed region).** (A) The photosensitive retina has nine layers. *PR*, photoreceptors (rods and cones); *ELM*, external limiting membrane; *ONL*, outer nuclear layer (photoreceptor cell bodies); *OPL*, outer plexiform layer; *INL*, inner nuclear layer (amacrine, bipolar, and horizontal neurons as well as Müller [glial] cells); *IPL*, inner plexiform layer; *GCL*, ganglion cell layer; *NFL*, neural (optic) fiber layer; *ILM*, inner limiting membrane. Retinal pigmented epithelium (RPE), nonsensory support cells to the retina. Paraffin-embedded section, H&E, 100×. (B). Optical coherence tomography (OCT) image of the same eye. Retinal layers are visualized as alternating light and dark bands, based on differential light reflectivity from structures with different densities. Retinal layers are labeled as in A. (*OS*, outer segments of *PR*; *Ch*, choriod.) In vivo image acquired using a spectral domain OCT (SDOCT) instrument *(Bioptigen, Inc., Research Triangle Park, NC)*. Axial resolution = 5 μm. *(This image adapted from Ramos M, Reilly MC, Bolon B. Toxicological Pathology of the Retina and Optic Nerve. Fundamental Neuropathology for Pathologists and Toxicologists: Principles and Techniques. In: Bolon B, Butt MT. New Jersey: John Wiley & Sons, Inc.; 2011. p. 385–412.)*

with divergent spectral sensitivity that likely similarly reflects their behavioral needs (see Peichl for review [327]). Rabbits have a wide horizontal plane of vision (the visual streak) suited for assessing predator encroachment. The visual streak is a linear horizontal band (three to two mm wide) centered ~3 mm ventral to the optic disc, parallel and below the ventral margin of the medullary ray [328]. The retina is thicker in the ventral streak, which contains a higher density of photoreceptors and inner nuclear cells for sensory processing, and ganglion cells for signal transduction. Cones are sparsely confined to this region and are predominantly a red/green hybrid. Although the proportion of rods is overall greater, the combination of cones and rods in this region makes the rabbit eye suitable for crepuscular activities. Blue cones predominate in the ventral retina below the visual streak [329].

The carnivore retina concentrates cones and ganglion cells in an oval zone arranged in a horizontal plane dorsolateral to the optic disc [330]. Dogs' retinas are predominated by hybrid red/green cones and fewer blue cones [330]. Rodents may have blue, blue/green, or green/red hybrid cones, and have regional distribution patterns that vary by species [327]. Some mice have a preponderance of blue cones in the ventral retina [329]. Retinas of nocturnal rodents contain few cones; diurnal rodents have a relatively high concentration of cones (30–40%) [331,332] and may be a better model to study photoreceptor pathologies.

External Limiting Membrane

The external limiting membrane is a dense junctional zone between Müller cells and photoreceptors. Müller cells are the primary support glial cell of the retina with processes that extend between the external and internal limiting membranes.

Outer Nuclear Layer

Photoreceptors are bipolar cells oriented perpendicularly within the retina. The perikaryon and nucleus of the photoreceptor cell reside in the outer nuclear layer. The nuclei of rod cells, which have a dendrite process bridging the inner segment to the nucleus, are distributed throughout the layer, while nuclei of the cones form a row immediately inner to the external limiting membrane. The axons radiate inward to form synapses in the outer plexiform layer with the dendrites of second-order neurons.

Outer Plexiform Layer

The outer plexiform layer contains the synapses between the axon terminals of the photoreceptor cells and interneurons of the inner nuclear layer. Bipolar cells may have synaptic relationships with multiple receptors; in turn, they transfer the visual signal to ganglion cells through synapses formed in the inner plexiform layer. Horizontal cells form connections between groups of rods and cones through lateral synapses.

Inner Nuclear Layer

Perikarya and nuclei of bipolar cells, horizontal cells, amacrine cells, and Müller cells reside in the inner nuclear layer. The first three are second-order neurons responsible for the initial processing of the visual stimulus. Horizontal cells are located externally and modify signals through negative feedback between photoreceptor cells and bipolar cells, which aids in image resolution [326]. Bipolar cells are typed to rods or cones, and function vertically to modulate brightness and color information. Several types of cone bipolar cells have been identified through special staining; however, only one rod bipolar cell has been described. Cone bipolar cells carry the vision impulse to the ganglion cells' third-order neurons. Amacrine cells are located on the inner aspect of the inner nuclear layer and modify the signal input to the ganglion cells. Specialized amacrine cells are interposed between rod bipolar and ganglion cells [325]. Cell bodies of interplexiform cells, the function of which is yet to be entirely elucidated, are distributed amongst the amacrine cells, with their processes extending to both inner and outer plexiform layers. Müller cells are specialized glial cells that are the primary structural and metabolic support cell of the retina. Müller cells are high in glycogen, which serves as an important source of retinal nourishment. Müller cell processes extend from the external to the internal limiting membrane (forming a basement membrane) and completely surround the somata of photoreceptors and ganglion cells. Healthy Müller cells express glial fibrillary acidic protein (GFAP), which is limited to the inner aspect of the cell process near the inner limiting membrane. An early indication of metabolic stress is associated with a change in Müller GFAP expression, where it can be throughout the length of the cell. Cystoid spaces observed within the inner and outer plexiform layers of the aged retina are actually formed within the Müller cell cytoplasm. Peripheral cysts located at the ora ciliaris are a common finding in older primates and dogs. In species that have a retinal vasculature, Müller cells have a close spatial relationship to vessel pericytes that contribute to the maintenance of the blood–retinal barrier. Rabbits have an unusually large glial cell (25 µm+) that may be found in the inner nuclear layer or residing in the inner or outer plexiform layers. The significance of these cells is currently unknown.

Inner Plexiform Layer

Synapses between bipolar, amacrine, and interplexiform cells integrate and refine the signals from the photoreceptors in the inner plexiform layer. Amacrine cells form lateral connections while interplexiform cells feed back to the outer plexiform layer [326]. Axons from these cells in turn synapse with dendrites from the ganglion cells.

Ganglion Cell Layer

Ganglion cells are third-order neurons that collect integrated signals from the interneurons of the inner nuclear layer. Axons from the ganglion cells transmit impulses and collectively exit the eye as the optic nerve. Astrocytes and displaced amacrine cells also reside in the ganglion cell layer.

Nerve Fiber Layer

The summation of the visual stimulus is transmitted as a nerve impulse by retinal ganglion cells. Ganglion cell axons reside in the nerve fiber layer to converge at the optic disc to form the optic nerve. The vision impulse traverses the optic nerve to reach the brain. Fibers are interspersed with astrocytes and other retinal glial cells in the nerve fiber layer. In those species with a retinal vasculature, the nerve fiber layer also contains the blood supply emanating from the CRA.

Internal Limiting Lamina (Membrane)

The internal limiting lamina is a thin, transparent basement membrane secreted by the basal foot process of the Müller cell (retinal glia). The inner limiting lamina (ILL) seaparates the retina from the vitreous body, and provides important sources of attachment for the vitreous collagen fibrils. The ILL ceases at the rim of the optic disc, which is instead covered by a basal lamina, thought to be derived from astrocytes in the disc [333].

Retinal response to injury is not unlike that which occurs in the brain. Glial cell proliferation is a common reactive response. Overt cell necrosis may be generalized or limited to a select population. Evidence of retinal injury at times may be subtle, and may be limited to apoptosis followed by cellular drop-out. Because the density of the nuclear layers varies by location within the retina, it is critical to have good communication with the technical staff processing the tissues to ensure consistency in sectioning and proper interpretation. Acute cell drop-out can be observed as displaced pyknotic nuclei in the vitreous–retina interface, the plexiform, or PR segment layers. Reduced nuclear density, plexiform rarefaction, retinal thinning and atrophy are observed in chronic conditions. Cell loss also occurs with senescence, and thus it is important to use aged-matched controls throughout the course of a study to ensure proper interpretation of cellular changes. Recent advances in IHC have increased our ability to differentiate retinal cells, and when coupled with retinal mapping this is useful in discerning subtle cellular toxicity. IHC may also be employed to identify rod and cone pathways (including differentiating opsins), discriminate structural components and define cellular relationships, and for the histological detection of enzymes, neurotransmitters, and receptors. Confocal and multispectral microscopy have improved histological resolution and enabled 3-D constructs contributing to advancements in our understanding of retinal circuitry. Because rabbits are commonly used to produce antibodies used in research, IHC remains a challenge in this species.

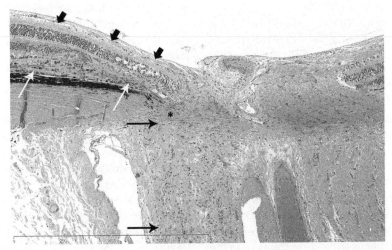

FIGURE 29.10 **Optic atrophy in a cynomolgus monkey.** Axons are decreased in the temporal side of the optic nerve (*thin black arrows*) and nerve fiber layer (*short black arrows*) associated with a paucity of ganglion cells. The lamina cribosa (*) is compressed. A focus of epiretinal membranes in the subretinal space (*white arrows*) suggests trauma as an etiology; unlike spontaneous atrophy, this case was unilateral. Paraffin-embedded section, H&E, 100×.

Optic Nerve

Axons from the retinal ganglion cells converge at the optic disc (also referred to as the optic nerve head) in the posterior segment of the eye, passing through a sieve-like region of the choroid and sclera known as the area cribrosa, to form the optic nerve. Axons are arranged into bundles by surrounding fibrous astrocytes and collagenous tissue, which form trabeculae containing vascular channels in the area cribrosa. In some species (ie, dog, rabbit), the optic disc is myelinated by oligodendrocytes; in other species, myelination commences at the outer margins of the area cribrosa (primates, pigs) [334]. The optic nerve is surrounded by extensions of the meningeal sheaths of the central nervous system, most intimately with the pia mater, which also sends septae into the nerve [221]. The position of the optic nerve head shows some species variation. In the rabbit, it is positioned in the dorsal posterior pole. In dogs and primates, it tends to be more equatorial. Nonhuman primates should be screened for the occurrence of spontaneous bilateral optic atrophy, which has been reported in rhesus [335] and cynomolgus macaques [336] by fundic examination and OCT. Decreased ganglion cells and axons in the temporal nerve fiber layer of the retina with corresponding atrophy of optic nerve fascicles are observed on histology (Fig. 29.10). Optic neuritis (inflammation of the optic nerve head) can be observed with the IVT administration of biologics that induce an immune response. Infiltrates of lymphocytes and perivascular cuffing with or without focal areas of necrosis may be seen.

Sclera

The posterior compartment of the eye is ensheathed in an outer spherical tunic of dense fibroelastic connective tissue known as the sclera, which is arranged in bundles that course parallel to the ocular surface. The sclera begins at the limbus, transitioning from regular corneal lamellae to irregular lamellae of the sclera, which branch and interweave. The sclera is penetrated posteriorly by the optic nerve and merges with the surrounding dura mater. The sclera has roles in protecting the eye from injury, maintaining ocular shape and IOP during movement of the eye, and aiding visual acuity by reducing backscatter from light. Tenon's capsule, a dense membrane of collagen bundles, courses over the sclera to the optic nerve. Tenon's capsule is attached at the limbus, and merges with the perimysium of the ocular muscles; this arrangement allows it to function as a sort of pulley for the ocular muscles [337]. The sclera has a rich nerve supply, but lacks a specific vascular bed (although it is penetrated by the ocular blood supply), rendering the eye vulnerable to particularly painful and prolonged inflammation. Systemic connective tissue disease often has a sceral component. Immune reactions culminating with sclera necrosis are not uncommon sequelae to inflammatory events or bystander transudation due to sluggish removal and cell turnover in the sclera [337].

Vitreous

The vitreous is a translucent, spherical, extracellular gel-like matrix occupying the vitreous cavity in the posterior compartment of the eye. More than 95% of the vitreous weight is water [338]. The balance is composed of structural elements of heterotypic fibrils of collagens type II, V/XI, and IX, hyaluronan, fibronectin, and other proteoglycans organized into a delicate scaffold that gives the vitreous spherical integrity while ensuring translucency, which is dependent on the spatial arrangement of these components.

Sourcing for vitreous collagen appears controversial, and has been variably ascribed to synthesis within the ciliary body, hyalocytes, and retinal Müller cells [338–340]. Collagen molecules assemble into highly organized, long, thin fibrils of copolymers; heterotype collagen V/XI forms a central core that is surrounded by a cross-linked, staggered array of type II collagen [338]. Type IX collagen, a chondroitin sulfate proteoglycan, is interspersed between, and cross-linked, to the fibrils, and has a role in spacing and distribution of fibrils within the vitreous. The maintenance of the spatial configuration between fibrils imparts an essential function to the vitreous that facilitates light transmission, reduces scatter, and promotes translucency [341]. Arrays of hyaluronan, a hydrophilic glycoprotein, and other glycoproteins are interspersed between the fibrils providing stability to the scaffold [342,343]. Hyaluronan attracts counter ions that contribute to spacing, and water, which gives dimension to the vitreous [339].

There are species and age-related differences in the relative composition of the structural components of the vitreous. Vitreous structural differences across species are related to differences in hyaluronan concentration, the primary component of liquid portion of the vitreous, located within the medullary (core) vitreous. Structurally, the concentration of hyaluronan relative to collagen is low in the rabbit, dog, cat, and rodent compared to that of humans and nonhuman primates, and thus they have a predominantly gel vitreous throughout life [344]. Among laboratory animals, the vitreous of the rhesus monkey (*Macaca mulatta*) has the most similarities to that of the human, with respect to collagen and hyaluronan content, structural characteristics, and aging [344]. In these species, aging of the vitreous is associated with a loss of collagen IX, collapse of the collagen network, and subsequent close apposition of collagen bundles, resulting in the formation of liquid pools in a process known as vitreous liquefaction [338].

Despite species differences, differential distribution of collagen and proteoglycans within the vitreous results in two basic zones of varying densities, the cortical (peripheral) vitreous and medullary (core) vitreous. The bulk of the vitreous is formed by the medullary vitreous, a cell-free mixture of collagens and hyaluronic acid existing either in a gel or a liquid state depending on the species, age, and condition of the eye. Within the medullary vitreous, the collagen fibrils generally course in an anterior posterior direction. Anteriorly, these fibrils blend with those of the basal vitreous and posteriorly they insert into the vitreous cortex.

The cortical vitreous is relatively more condensed and fibrillar compared to the medullary vitreous. The highest concentration of collagen fibers occurs in the vitreous base of the cortex, which circumferentially straddles the ora serrata. The fibers of the vitreous base are arranged perpendicular to the surface of the retina. Interdigitations of short collagen fibrils with the basement membrane of the ciliary epithelium, and neuroglia of the peripheral retina anchor the vitreous base anterior and posterior to the ora serrata, respectively [345–347].

The anterior vitreous cortex extends anterior from the vitreous base to adhere to the posterior lens capsule by the annular ligament of Weiger [348]. Posterior zonule fibers that originate from the ciliary body have been shown to anchor the anterior vitreous cortex [347]. The posterior vitreous extends posteriorly from the vitreous base to the rim of the optic disc, which is not covered by vitreous [345]. Cloquet's canal, the remnant of the hyaloid artery of the embryonic (primary) vitreous, courses centrally through the vitreous from the opening of the ligament of Weiger, to a funnel-shape opening over the optic disc (the area devoid of vitreous), known as the area of Martegiani. Central sheaths of low-density fibrils parallel Cloquet's canal, which likely creates the appearance that the vitreous is composed of the undulating sac-like cisternae that have been described following fixation and dye injection. Studies using these techniques demonstrate similarity between human, nonhuman primate, and rabbit vitreous structure [349,350]. The periphery of vitreous cortex is composed of parallel sheaths of collagen fibrils that course circumferentially along the inner limiting laminae of the retina to insert at the posterior cortex at relatively high density. Tight adhesions are formed between the vitreous fibers and the internal limiting membrane (ILM) and glia surrounding the optic disc, macula (primates), and medullary ray (rabbit). Adhesions at the posterior pole are strongest surrounding the macula and optic disc, and at contact points with the vasculature. Traction on the vitreous thus renders these areas vulnerable to detachment and hemorrhage, and potentially can stimulate neovascularization. With aging, these adhesions weaken, and separation between the retina and vitreous, known as posterior vitreous detachment (PVD), may occur completely without pathological consequence.

The mechanism of adhesion between the remainder of the retina and the vitreous has not been definitely defined. Molecular components of the ECM (chondroitin sulfate glycosaminoglycans, fibronectin, opticin, laminin) residing within the vitreoretinal interface are currently thought to provide a biomechanical adhesion between the retina and the remainder of the posterior vitreous [333,345].

The various components of the eye, including the vitreous, undergoes rate-differential fixation. The attachments between the vitreous and retina can place traction on various parts of the retina that histologically translate as retinal folds or rosettes. This artifact is particularly common in albino rabbits, and must be differentiated from pathological degeneration.

Physiologically, the vitreous has roles in embryonic development and growth of the eye, protection from trauma, maintaining translucency, restricting cell migration and macromolecule diffusion, and providing metabolic support to the lens [348]. The vitreous contains a number of molecules that regulate or inhibit angiogenesis, including opticin, pigment epithelium derived growth factor (PEDF), leucine-rich alpha-2 glycoprotein (LRG1), and thrombospondins. Opticin, a glycoprotein distributed throughout the vitreous, but particularly in association with the ILM of the retina, is an important inhibitor of angiogenesis, preventing endothelial cell adhesion to collagen fibrils [338]. Thrombospondins 1 and 2 inhibit the proliferation and migration of endothelial cells [203,338].

The vitreous contains a small population of monocytic cells with phagocytic activity known as hyalocytes that reside in the cortical vitreous, mainly abutting the inner surface of the retina, concentrating in the anterior vitreous base, near the ciliary processes, and surrounding the optic disc [333,340]. Halocytes are 10–15 μm diameter, have a lobulated nucleus, contain lysosomes and phagosomes, and express F4/80, a marker common to tissue macrophages, although they do not express CD68 [351]. Hyalocytes express other cell surface antigens characteristic of monocyte/macrophage leukocyte lineage including CD45 (leukocyte common antigen), CD64 (Fc receptor I), CD11a (leukocyte-function antigen-1), histocompatibility complex (MHC) class II antigens [215], and receptors for complement and IgG have been identified on halocytes suggesting a role in inflammation of the eye [352]. Experimental evidence suggests that hyalocytes in the vitreous have a role in conferring immune deviation and modulating inflammation that occurs with delayed hypersensitivity to antigens [215,352]. In noninflamed eyes, this has been coined vitreous cavity-associated immune deviation, and is similar to ACAID. Hyalocytes have been shown to secrete TGF-β, an inhibitor of RPE, endothelial, and fibroblast proliferation, and thus are hypothesized to have a role in the prevention of pathological membrane formation at the retinal surface [353]. However, current literature also suggests that hyalocytes play a crucial role in the formation and contraction of proliferative membranes that form in diseased eyes, such as proliferative diabetic retinopathy and proliferative vitreoretinopathy (PVR), in response to overexpressed growth factors [215]. Hyalocytes have also been postulated to have a role in the synthesis of hyaluronon and other glycoproteins, and to release enzymes [341].

Fibroblasts are also found in the vitreous, localized at the base near the ciliary processes and over the optic disc. These are postulated to have a role in collagen synthesis under pathological conditions [348]. The abnormal proliferation of cells of fibroblastic morphology into or behind the vitreous can be associated with the formation of fibrotic vitreous strands (Fig. 29.11A). Structural changes to the vitreous can occur secondary to inflammation. Gel contraction associated with liquid extraction, increased insoluble material, and changes to the collagen matrix have been demonstrated in models of intraocular inflammation [354]. The influx of inflammatory cells, release of proteolytic enzymes, and generation of free radicals are postulated to produce cross-linkages between vitreous collagen fibers. This can be observed on ophthalmology as condensations, which may impair vision by impeding light transmission. These may correlate on histopathology as relatively acellular eosinophilic strands.

In humans, the vitreous is susceptible to natural biochemical changes with age that result in progressive liquidity, concurrent with loss of gel volume, and collagen aggregation. These changes can produce pockets of liquid (lacunae) most often observed clinically in the posterior vitreous. As adhesions between the vitreous and the retina weaken, fluid can leak into the vitreous–retina interface, resulting in collapse of the vitreous, traction, and PVD. Anomalous PVD develop when there are persistent adhesions, and tractions result in retinal tearing or detachments, or lead to schisms in the vitreous that result in remnants attached to the retina that cause additional macula pathologies. The aged rhesus monkey may be a model for this [344].

Traction placed on the retina due to vitreous collapse can induce glial cell proliferation at the surface of the inner retina, producing epiretinal membranes (ERM). Membranes may also occur in response to trauma at the retinal surface due to the elaboration of growth factors, platelet derived growth factor (PDGF) and transforming growth factor beta (TGFβ). Activated macrophages, hemorrhage (activated platelets), and RPE may be sources for growth factors involved in membrane formation. Membranes composed primarily of Möller cells and astrocytes are weakly contractile [355] and may have relatively benign effects structurally if there is no impact to the macula (Fig. 29.11B). However, they are strongly adherent to the retina, and may serve as transducers of contraction by other cells on the underlying retina, ie, motile RPE, which migrate through a series of extension and retraction of adherent lamellipodia [356,357].

PVR represents an insidious cycle of cellular proliferation and collagen production that results in membrane formation on either side of the retina. PVR are readily induced in laser models of choridal neovascularization (Fig. 29.12). IHC evaluation has shown that membranes may be comprised of retinal glial cells, halocytes, activated macrophages, fibroblasts, and RPE [358]. RPE subject to trauma (ie, retinal detachment) may transform and assume a fibroblastic profile capable of producing collagen and fibronectin under TGFβ stimulation [341,357]. Fibronectin is an adhesion molecule that provides tight

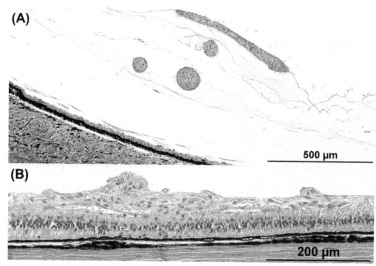

FIGURE 29.11   Primate eyes containing pathological membranes in the posterior segment; note the similarity in cellular phenotype. (A) Vitreous membranes. Several concentric and linear masses of cells are present in the vitreous near the ciliary body. Paraffin-embedded section, H&E, 100×. (B) Epiretinal membranes. Nodular and linear arrays of cells are located on the inner surface of the retina, associated with disruption of the nuclear and plexiform layers and atrophy. Paraffin-embedded section, H&E, 200×.

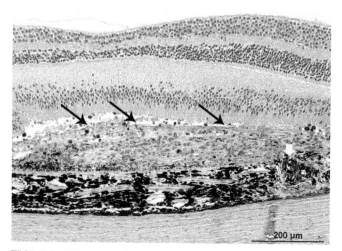

FIGURE 29.12   Subretinal neovascularization in primate laser model of CNV. Regional disruption in Burch's membrane (*white arrowhead*) has resulted in a multilayered membrane of cells and blood vessels residing in the subretinal space of the macula with subsequent retinal separation (*black arrows*). Paraffin-embedded section, H&E, 200×.

contact points between cellular and collagen constituents and thus has a crucial role in wound contraction both systemically and in the eye. Fibronectin may be introduced with serum leakage due to breakdown of the blood–ocular barrier, or be elaborated from activated macrophages during ocular inflammation. Because they contain contractile elements, contraction of the membranes may themselves cause retinal traction and eventual detachment that may impact visual function.

The introduction of drug formulations or implants into the vitreous may elicit changes in the vitreous that promote degeneration or create conditions that promote epiretinal membrane formation. In some cases these are

species-specific, and thus animal models may be poor predictors of the clinical experience. Mechanisms behind species differences are poorly understood, as are differences in biochemical composition of the vitreous across species. In nonclinical toxicology programs it is important to design studies that are best predictive of the target population. The vitreous serves as a reservoir for drugs delivered by IVT administration, and influences movement of drug particles in the eye. Drugs administered into the aged eye that has degenerative changes in the vitreous, or in one in which the vitreous was removed (vitrectomy), may have a different PK/PD profile than that of a younger patient [359]. The use of biomarkers is relatively nascent in ocular drug development, but will likely acquire a role of increasing importance as resources are devoted to the identification of reliable indicators of disease progression, drug toxicity, or therapeutic efficacy that permit repeated sampling (ie, vitreous or aqueous humor) reducing animal usage, and ensuring the use of relevant animal models.

INTEGRATED ASSESSMENT OF OCULAR TOXICITY

The complexity of ocular anatomy requires unique considerations for the potential tissue-specific pharmacokinetics. Ocular pharmacokinetic assessments pose challenges in the study design due to the inherent variability associated with nonserial sampling and the technical hurdles associated with developing sensitive bioanalytical methods in multiple matrices. Drug absorption and disposition at the pharmacodynamic and toxicodynamic site(s) of action are important data in the interpretation of toxicological findings when evaluating clinical relevance.

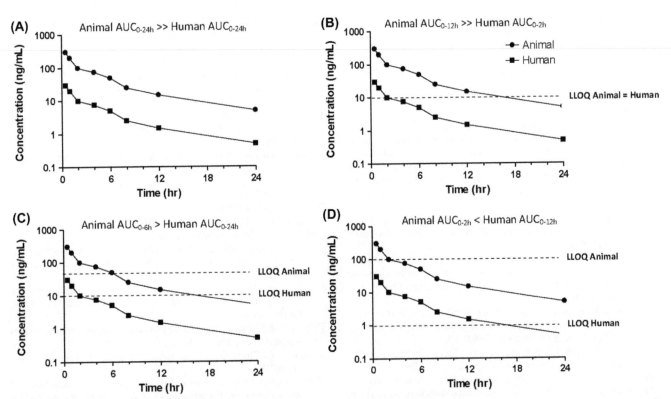

FIGURE 29.13 Illustration of the role lower limit of quantitation (LLOQ) of bioanalytical methods in animals and humans can play in altering the apparent safety margins. In each panel the same data set for systemic exposure in animals and humans is presented; however, depending on the differential between LLOQs, the extent or existence of an adequate apparent safety margin can change depending on the last quantifiable timepoint in the determination of AUC.

Histopathology examination is the basis for detecting structural changes of the eye. A goal of in vivo ophthalmic examination is to provide a correlate of histopathology changes that may be used sequentially during the life of the animal to show progression or regression of lesions. As such, the ophthalmology endpoints may serve as biomarkers for translation to the clinic. Techniques such as OCT, SLO, and IVCM can now give images of all segments of the eye in vivo, and with improvements such as adaptive optics the resolution approaches that obtained by light microscopy. Ophthalmological and histological methods have inherent strengths and weaknesses. Ophthalmology examination is wide field and excels at detection of diffuse or scattered changes: punctate corneal staining, cells or flare in anterior chamber or vitreous, and pinpoint lens opacities. Histopathology provides high cellular resolution of all tissues with a relatively limited and selected sampling area, so this method has difficulty detecting low-density and scattered changes. To enhance the capture of ophthalmic findings histologically, it is useful to have detailed observations and images available at the time of trimming and sectioning, with good communication between the ophthalmologist, pathologist, and histology technicians. Histopathology can also detect retinal and RPE changes when the fundus is obscured to optical detection due to miosis or

inflammation. Functional measurements such as corneal barrier permeability, IOP, pupillary reflex, ERG, and optomotor reflex complement the findings of histopathological changes. A decrease in full-field ERG response is almost always accompanied by histopathology findings in the retina. However, there are examples where functional deficits do not have a histological correlation.

An integrated analysis is necessary for the development and registration of ocular therapeutics. The increased demand for eye care in emerging markets and due to the aging demographic of the developed world, combined with the availability of advanced tools for ocular evaluation, offer opportunities to positively impact the field of ophthalmology.

References

[1] Short BG. Safety evaluation of ocular drug delivery formulations: techniques and practical considerations. Toxicol Pathol 2008;36:49–62.

[2] Huml RA, Rich C, Chance K. Key challenges to US topical ocular drug development. 2009. p. 47–52.

[3] Lee DY, Schoenwald RD, Barfknecht CF. Biopharmaceutical explanation for the topical activity of 6-hydroxyethoxy-2-benzothiazolesulfonamide in the rabbit eye. J Ocul Pharmacol 1992;8:247–65.

[4] Doane MG, Jensen AD, Dohlman CH. Penetration routes of topically applied eye medications. Am J Ophthalmol 1978;85:383–6.

[5] Bloomfield SE, et al. Soluble gentamicin ophthalmic inserts as a drug delivery system. Arch Ophthalmol 1978;96:885–7.

[6] Bito LZ, Nichols RR, Baroody RA. A comparison of the miotic and inflammatory effects of biologically active polypeptides and prostaglandin E2 on the rabbit eye. Exp Eye Res 1982;34:325–37.

[7] Ahmed I, Patton TF. Importance of the noncorneal absorption route in topical ophthalmic drug delivery. Invest Ophthalmol Vis Sci 1985;26:584–7.

[8] Pamulapati CR, Schoenwald RD. Ocular pharmacokinetics of a novel tetrahydroquinoline analog in rabbit: compartmental analysis and PK-PD evaluation. J Pharmacol Sci 2012;101:414–23.

[9] Pamulapati CR, Schoenwald RD. Ocular pharmacokinetics of a novel tetrahydroquinoline analog in rabbit: absorption, disposition, and non-compartmental analysis. J Pharm Sci 2011;100:5315–23.

[10] Tsuji A, Tamai I, Sasaki K. Intraocular penetration kinetics of prednisolone after subconjunctival injection in rabbits. Ophthalmic Res 1988;20:31–43.

[11] Kim SH, Csaky KG, Wang NS, Lutz RJ. Drug elimination kinetics following subconjunctival injection using dynamic contrast-enhanced magnetic resonance imaging. Pharm Res 2008;25:512–20.

[12] Nomoto H, et al. Pharmacokinetics of bevacizumab after topical, subconjunctival, and intravitreal administration in rabbits. Invest Ophthalmol Vis Sci 2009;50:4807–13.

[13] Knop N, Knop E. Conjunctiva-associated lymphoid tissue in the human eye. Invest Ophthalmol Vis Sci 2000;41:1270–9.

[14] Schaumburg CS, et al. Ocular surface APCs are necessary for autoreactive T cell-mediated experimental autoimmune lacrimal keratoconjunctivitis. J Immunol 2011;187:3653–62.

[15] Yamagami S, Dana MR, Tsuru T. Draining lymph nodes play an essential role in alloimmunity generated in response to high-risk corneal transplantation. Cornea 2002;21:405–9.

[16] Maurice DM. In: Leopold IH, Burns RP, editors. Symposium on ocular therapy. John Wiley and Sons; 1976. p. 59–72.

[17] Maurice D. Review: practical issues in intravitreal drug delivery. J Ocul Pharmacol Ther 2001;17:393–401.

[18] Araie M, Maurice DM. The loss of fluorescein, fluorescein glucuronide and fluorescein isothiocyanate dextran from the vitreous by the anterior and retinal pathways. Exp Eye Res 1991;52:27–39.

[19] Nakamura K, Fujiki T, Tamura HO. Age, gender and region-specific differences in drug metabolising enzymes in rat ocular tissues. Exp Eye Res 2005;81:710–5.

[20] Lee VH, Iimoto DS, Takemoto KA. Subcellular distribution of esterases in the bovine eye. Curr Eye Res 1982;2:869–76.

[21] Lee VH, Morimoto KW, Stratford Jr RE. Esterase distribution in the rabbit cornea and its implications in ocular drug bioavailability. Biopharm Drug Dispos 1982;3:291–300.

[22] Essner E, Gorrin GM, Griewski RA. Localization of lysosomal enzymes in retinal pigment epithelium of rats with inherited retinal dystrophy. Invest Ophthalmol Vis Sci 1978;17:278–88.

[23] Stampfli HF, Quon CY. Polymorphic metabolism of flestolol and other ester containing compounds by a carboxylesterase in New Zealand white rabbit blood and cornea. Res Commun Mol Pathol Pharmacol 1995;88:87–97.

[24] Lee VH, Urrea PT, Smith RE, Schanzlin DJ. Ocular drug bioavailability from topically applied liposomes. Surv Ophthalmol 1985;29:335–48.

[25] Attar M, Shen J, Ling KH, Tang-Liu D. Ophthalmic drug delivery considerations at the cellular level: drug-metabolising enzymes and transporters. Expert Opin Drug Deliv 2005;2:891–908.

[26] Vadlaptla RK, Vadlapudi AD, Pal D, Mitra AK. Role of membrane transporters and metabolizing enzymes in ocular drug delivery. Curr Drug Metab 2014;15:680–93.

[27] Sarna T. Properties and function of the ocular melanin – a photobiophysical view. J Photochem Photobiol B 1992;12:215–58.

[28] Leblanc B, Jezequel S, Davies T, Hanton G, Taradach C. Binding of drugs to eye melanin is not predictive of ocular toxicity. Regul Toxicol Pharmacol 1998;28:124–32.

[29] Koneru PB, Lien EJ, Koda RT. Oculotoxicities of systemically administered drugs. J Ocul Pharmacol 1986;2:385–404.

[30] Mason CG. Ocular accumulation and toxicity of certain systemically administered drugs. J Toxicol Environ Health 1977;2:977–95.

[31] Persad S, Menon IA, Basu PK, Carre F. Phototoxicity of chlorpromazine on retinal pigment epithelial cells. Curr Eye Res 1988;7:1–9.

[32] Tang-Liu DD, Burke PJ. The effect of azone on ocular levobunolol absorption: calculating the area under the curve and its standard error using tissue sampling compartments. Pharmacol Res 1988;5:238–41.

[33] Genentech I. 2006.

[34] Regeneron Pharmaceuticals I. 2011.

[35] Chambers WA. Int Soc Ocul Toxicol 2008.

[36] ICH-M3(R2), editor. The International Conference on harmonisation of technical requirements for registration of pharmaceuticals for human use. 2010.

[37] ICH-S6(R1), editor. The International Conference on harmonisation of technical requirements for registration of pharmaceuticals for human use. 2011.

[38] Kuiper B, et al. Ophthalmologic examination in systemic toxicity studies: an overview. Lab Anim 1997;31:177–83.

[39] Gad SC, Chengelis CP. In: Acute toxicology testing. Academic Press; 1997. p. 57–84.

[40] Lehmann DM, Richardson ME. Impact of assay selection and study design on the outcome of cytotoxicity testing of medical devices: the case of multi-purpose vision care solutions. Toxicol Vitro 2010;24:1306–13.

[41] Khoh-Reiter S, Jessen BA. Evaluation of the cytotoxic effects of ophthalmic solutions containing benzalkonium chloride on corneal epithelium using an organotypic 3-D model. BMC Ophthalmol 2009;9:5. http://dx.doi.org/10.1186/1471-2415-9-5.

[42] Worth AP, Cronin MTD. The use of pH measurements to predict the potential of chemicals to cause acute dermal and ocular toxicity. Toxicology 2001;169:119–31.

[43] Motolko M, Breslin CW. The effect of pH and osmolarity on the ability to tolerate artificial tears. Am J Ophthalmol 1981;91:781–4.

[44] Wilhelmus KR. The Draize eye test. Surv Ophthalmol 2001;45:493–515.

[45] Liu H, et al. A link between tear instability and hyperosmolarity in dry eye. Invest Ophthalmol Vis Sci 2009;50:3671–9.

[46] Lalonde MR, Chauhan BC, Tremblay F. Retinal ganglion cell activity from the multifocal electroretinogram in pig: optic nerve section, anaesthesia and intravitreal tetrodotoxin. J Physiol 2006;570:325–38.

[47] Buehler EV, Newmann EA. A comparison of eye irritation in monkeys and rabbits. Toxicol Appl Pharmacol 1964;6:701–10.

[48] Bito LZ. Species differences in the responses of the eye to irritation and trauma: a hypothesis of divergence in ocular defense mechanisms, and the choice of experimental animals for eye research. Exp Eye Res 1984;39:807–29.

[49] Toshida H, Nguyen DH, Beuerman RW, Murakami A. Evaluation of novel dry eye model: preganglionic parasympathetic denervation in rabbit. Invest Ophthalmol Vis Sci 2007;48:4468–75.

[50] Stevens JR, Livermore Jr A. Eye blinking and rapid eye movement: pulsed photic stimulation of the brain. Exp Neurol 1978;60:541–56.

[51] Maurice D. The effect of the low blink rate in rabbits on topical drug penetration. J Ocul Pharmacol Ther 1995;11:297–304.

[52] Dillberger JE, Peiffer RL, Dykstra MJ, O'Mara M, Patel DK. The experimental antipsychotic agent 1192U90 targets tapetum lucidum in canine eyes. Toxicol Pathol 1996;24:595–601.

[53] Zemel E, Loewenstein A, Lei B, Lazar M, Perlman I. Ocular pigmentation protects the rabbit retina from gentamicin-induced toxicity. Invest Ophthalmol Vis Sci 1995;36:1875–84.

[54] Loewenstein A, Zemel E, Vered Y, Lazar M, Perlman I. Retinal toxicity of gentamicin after subconjunctival injection performed adjacent to thinned sclera. Ophthalmology 2001;108:759–64.

[55] Mishima S, Gasset A, Klyce J, Baum JL. Determination of tear volume and tear flow. Invest Ophthalmol 1966;5:264–76.

[56] Lambert LA, et al. The use of low-volume dosing in the eye irritation test. Food Chem Toxicol 1993;31:99–103.

[57] Weiner AL, Gilger BC. Advancements in ocular drug delivery. Vet Ophthalmol 2010;13:392–406.

[58] Shah SS, et al. Drug delivery to the posterior segment of the eye for pharmacologic therapy. Expert Rev Ophthalmol 2010;5:75–93.

[59] Lee SS, Hughes P, Ross AD, Robinson MR. Biodegradable implants for sustained drug release in the eye. Pharm Res 2010;27:2043–53.

[60] Kompella UB, Kadam RS, Lee VH. Recent advances in ophthalmic drug delivery. Ther Deliv 2010;1:435–56.

[61] Micieli JA, Micieli A, Smith AF. Identifying systemic safety signals following intravitreal bevacizumab: systematic review of the literature and the Canadian Adverse Drug Reaction Database. Can J Ophthalmol 2010;45:231–8.

[62] Somps CJ, et al. A current practice for predicting ocular toxicity of systemically delivered drugs. Cutan Ocul Toxicol 2009;28:1–18.

[63] Penha FM, et al. Retinal and ocular toxicity in ocular application of drugs and chemicals – Part I: animal models and toxicity assays. Ophthalmic Res 2010;44:82–104.

[64] Peiffer RL, et al. Contemporary methods in ocular toxicology. Toxicol Methods 2000;10:17–39.

[65] Hackett RB, McDonald TO. In: Marzulli FN, Maibach HI, editors. Dermatotoxicology. Taylor & Francis; 1996. p. 557–67.

[66] Ward KW. Superficial punctate fluorescein staining of the ocular surface. Optom Vis Sci 2008;58:8–16.

[67] Morgan PB, Maldonado-Codina C. Corneal staining: do we really understand what we are seeing? Cont Lens Anterior Eye 2009;32:48–54.

[68] Jabs DA. Standardization of uveitis nomenclature for reporting clinical data. Results of the first international workshop. Am J Ophthalmol 2005;140:509–16.

[69] Del Sole MJ, et al. Characterization of uveitis induced by use of a single intravitreal injection of bacterial lipopolysaccharide in cats. Am J Vet Res 2008;69:1487–95.

[70] Kern TJ. Rabbit and rodent ophthalmology. Semin Avian Exot Pet Med 1997;6:138–45.

[71] Akaishi T, Shida N, Shimazaki A, Hara H, Kuwayama Y. Continuous monitoring of circadian variations in intraocular pressure by telemetry system throughout a 12-week treatment with timolol maleate in rabbits. J Ocul Pharmacol Ther 2005;21:436–44.

[72] Aihara M, Lindsey JD, Weinreb RN. Twenty-four-hour pattern of mouse intraocular pressure. Exp Eye Res 2003;77:681–6.

[73] Todani A, et al. Intraocular pressure measurement by radio wave telemetry. Invest Ophthalmol Vis Sci 2011;52:9573–80.

[74] Moore CP, Dubielzig R, Glaza SM. Anterior corneal dystrophy of American Dutch Belted rabbits: biomicroscopic and histopathologic findings. Vet Pathol 1987;24:28–33.

[75] Cavanagh HD, El-Agha MS, Petroll WM, Jester JV. Specular microscopy, confocal microscopy, and ultrasound biomicroscopy: diagnostic tools of the past quarter century. Cornea 2000;19:712–22.

[76] Miller JM, et al. Corneal endothelial cell density measurements using noncontact specular microscopy in rabbits, dogs and monkeys. Invest Ophthalmol Vis Sci 2008;49:2819.

[77] Twa MD, Giese MJ. Assessment of corneal thickness and keratocyte density in a rabbit model of laser in situ keratomileusis using scanning laser confocal microscopy. Am J Ophthalmol 2011;152:941–53.

[78] Bentley E, Miller PE, Diehl KA. Evaluation of intra- and interobserver reliability and image reproducibility to assess usefulness of high-resolution ultrasonography for measurement of anterior segment structures of canine eyes. Am J Vet Res 2005;66:1775–9.

[79] Reinstein DZ, Archer TJ, Gobbe M, Silverman RH, Coleman DJ. Stromal thickness in the normal cornea: three-dimensional display with artemis very high-frequency digital ultrasound. J Refract Surg 2009;25:776–86.

[80] Peizeng Y, et al. Longitudinal study of anterior segment inflammation by ultrasound biomicroscopy in patients with acute anterior uveitis. Acta Ophthalmol 2009;87:211–5.

[81] Jalbert I, Stapleton F, Papas E, Sweeney DF, Coroneo M. In vivo confocal microscopy of the human cornea. Br J Ophthalmol 2003;87:225–36.

[82] Li HF, et al. Epithelial and corneal thickness measurements by in vivo confocal microscopy through focusing (CMTF). Curr Eye Res 1997;16:214–21.

[83] Reichard M, et al. Comparative in vivo confocal microscopical study of the cornea anatomy of different laboratory animals. Curr Eye Res 2010;35:1072–80.

[84] Podoleanu AG. Combining SLO and OCT technology. Bull Belg Soc Ophthalmol 2006:133–51.

[85] Rosolen SG, Saint-Macary G, Gautier V, LeGargasson JF. Ocular fundus images with confocal scanning laser ophthalmoscopy in the dog, monkey and minipig. Vet Ophthalmol 2001;4:42–5.

[86] Huber G, et al. Novel rodent models for macular research. PLoS One 2010;5:e13403. http://dx.doi.org/10.1371/journal.pone.0013403.

[87] Delori F, et al. Quantitative measurements of autofluorescence with the scanning laser ophthalmoscope. Invest Ophthalmol Vis Sci 2011;52:9379–90.

[88] Drexler W, Fujimoto JG. State-of-the-art retinal optical coherence tomography. Prog Retin Eye Res 2008;27:45–88.

[89] Gabriele ML, et al. Optical coherence tomography: history, current status, and laboratory work. Invest Ophthalmol Vis Sci 2011;52:2425–36.

[90] Geitzenauer W, Hitzenberger CK, Schmidt-Erfurth UM. Retinal optical coherence tomography: past, present and future perspectives. Br J Ophthalmol 2011;95:171–7.

[91] Kiernan DF, Mieler WF, Hariprasad SM. Spectral-domain optical coherence tomography: a comparison of modern high-resolution retinal imaging systems. Am J Ophthalmol 2010;149:18–31.

[92] Jancevski M, Foster CS. Anterior segment optical coherence tomography. Semin Ophthalmol 2010;25:317–23.

[93] Fernandez EJ, et al. Ultrahigh resolution optical coherence tomography and pancorrection for cellular imaging of the living human retina. Opt Express 2008;16:11083–94.

[94] Godara P, Dubis AM, Roorda A, Duncan JL, Carroll J. Adaptive optics retinal imaging: emerging clinical applications. Optom Vis Sci 2010;87:930–41.

[95] Williams DR. Imaging single cells in the living retina. Vis Res 2011;51:1379–96.

[96] Pircher M, Hitzenberger CK, Schmidt-Erfurth U. Polarization sensitive optical coherence tomography in the human eye. Prog Retin Eye Res 2011;30:431–51.

[97] Francoz M, Karamoko I, Baudouin C, Labbe A. Ocular surface epithelial thickness evaluation with spectral-domain optical coherence tomography. Invest Ophthalmol Vis Sci 2011;52:9116–23.

[98] Haque S, Jones L, Simpson T. Thickness mapping of the cornea and epithelium using optical coherence tomography. Optom Vis Sci 2008;85:E963–76.

[99] Agarwal A, Ashokkumar D, Jacob S, Agarwal A, Saravanan Y. High-speed optical coherence tomography for imaging anterior chamber inflammatory reaction in uveitis: clinical correlation and grading. Am J Ophthalmol 2009;147:413–6.

[100] Reiser BJ, et al. In vitro measurement of rabbit corneal epithelial thickness using ultrahigh resolution optical coherence tomography. Vet Ophthalmol 2005;8:85–8.

[101] Wegener A, Laser-junga H. Photography of the anterior eye segment according to Scheimpflug's principle: options and limitations – a review. Clin Exp Ophthalmol 2009;37:144–54.

[102] Schulz D, Iliev ME, Frueh BE, Goldblum D. In vivo pachymetry in normal eyes of rats, mice and rabbits with the optical low coherence reflectometer. Vis Res 2003;43:723–8.

[103] Bernasconi O, Papadia M, Herbort CP. Sensitivity of laser flare photometry compared to slit-lamp cell evaluation in monitoring anterior chamber inflammation in uveitis. Int Ophthalmol 2010;30:495–500.

[104] Ladas JG, Wheeler NC, Morhun PJ, Rimmer SO, Holland GN. Laser flare-cell photometry: methodology and clinical applications. Surv Ophthalmol 2005;50:27–47.

[105] Kallarackal GU, et al. A comparative study to assess the clinical use of Fluorescein Meniscus Time (FMT) with Tear Break up Time (TBUT) and Schirmer's tests (ST) in the diagnosis of dry eyes. Eye 2002;16:594–600.

[106] Wang J, Palakuru JR, Aquavella JV. Correlations among upper and lower tear menisci, noninvasive tear break-up time, and the Schirmer test. Am J Ophthalmol 2008;145:795–800.

[107] Charman WN. Wavefront technology: past, present and future. Cont Lens Anterior Eye 2005;28:75–92.

[108] Koh S, et al. Simultaneous measurement of tear film dynamics using wavefront sensor and optical coherence tomography. Invest Ophthalmol Vis Sci 2010;51:3441–8.

[109] Zhu M, Collins MJ, skander DR. Dynamics of ocular surface topography. Eye 2007;21:624–32.

[110] Huxlin KR, Yoon G, Nagy L, Porter J, Williams D. Monochromatic ocular wavefront aberrations in the awake-behaving cat. Vis Res 2004;44:2159–69.

[111] Calonge M, et al. Impression cytology of the ocular surface: a review. Exp Eye Res 2004;78:457–72.

[112] Brignole-Baudouin F, Ott AC, Warnet JM, Baudouin C. Flow cytometry in conjunctival impression cytology: a new tool for exploring ocular surface pathologies. Exp Eye Res 2004;78:473–81.

[113] Joshi A, Maurice D, Paugh JR. A new method for determining corneal epithelial barrier to fluorescein in humans. Invest Ophthalmol Vis Sci 1996;37:1008–16.

[114] Eter N, Gobbels M. A new technique for tear film fluorophotometry. Br J Ophthalmol 2002;86:616–9.

[115] Raines MF. Vitreous fluorophotometry: a review. J R Soc Med 1988;81:403–6.

[116] Berezovsky DE, Patel SR, McCarey BE, Edelhauser HF. In vivo ocular fluorophotometry: delivery of fluoresceinated dextrans via transscleral diffusion in rabbits. Invest Ophthalmol Vis Sci 2011;52:7038–45.

[117] Hayreh SS. Recent advances in fluorescein fundus angiography. Br J Ophthalmol 1974;58:391–412.

[118] Yu DY, Su EN, Cringle SJ, Yu PK. Isolated preparations of ocular vasculature and their applications in ophthalmic research. Prog Retin Eye Res 2003;22:135–69.

[119] Pournaras CJ, Rungger-Brändle E, Riva CE, Hardarson SH, Stefansson E. Regulation of retinal blood flow in health and disease. Prog Retin Eye Res 2008;27:284–330.

[120] Izhaky D, Nelson DA, Burgansky-Eliash Z, Grinvald A. Functional imaging using the retinal function imager: direct imaging of blood velocity, achieving fluorescein angiography-like images without any contrast agent, qualitative oximetry, and functional metabolic signals. Jpn J Ophthalmol 2009;53:345–51.

[121] Nair G, et al. MRI reveals differential regulation of retinal and choroidal blood volumes in rat retina. Neuroimage 2011;54:1063–9.

[122] Brigell M, Dong CJ, Rosolen S, Tzekov R. An overview of drug development with special emphasis on the role of visual electrophysiological testing. Doc Ophthalmol 2005;110:3–13.

[123] Perlman I. Testing retinal toxicity of drugs in animal models using electrophysiological and morphological techniques. Doc Ophthalmol 2009;118:3–28.

[124] Geller AM. Homology of assessment of visual function in human and animal models. Environ Toxicol Pharmacol 2005;19:485–90.

[125] Rosolen SG, Kolomiets B, Varela O, Picaud S. Retinal electrophysiology for toxicology studies: applications and limits of ERG in animals and ex vivo recordings. Exp Toxicol Pathol 2008;60:17–32.

[126] Rosolen SG, Rigaudiere F, Le Gargasson JF, Brigell MG. Recommendations for a toxicological screening ERG procedure in laboratory animals. Doc Ophthalmol 2005;110:57–66.

[127] Gjörloff K, Andréasson S, Ehinger B. Standardized full-field electroretinography in rabbits. Doc Ophthalmol 2004;109:163–8.

[128] Narfstrom K, et al. Guidelines for clinical electroretinography in the dog. Doc Ophthalmol 2002;105:83–92.

[129] Nork TM, et al. Functional and anatomic consequences of subretinal dosing in the cynomolgus macaque. Arch Ophthalmol 2012;130:65–75.

[130] Redfern WS, et al. Evaluation of a convenient method of assessing rodent visual function in safety pharmacology studies: effects of sodium iodate on visual acuity and retinal morphology in albino and pigmented rats and mice. J Pharmacol Toxicol Methods 2011;63:102–14.

[131] Latendresse JR, Warbritton AR, Jonassen H, Creasy DM. Fixation of testes and eyes using a modified Davidson's fluid: comparison with Bouin's fluid and conventional Davidson's fluid. Toxicologic Pathol 2002;30:524–33.

[132] Liang H, Brignole-Baudouin F, Pauly A, Riancho L, Baudouin C. Polyquad-preserved travoprost/timolol, benzalkonium chloride (BAK)-preserved travoprost/timolol, and latanoprost/timolol in fixed combinations: a rabbit ocular surface study. Adv Ther 2011;28:311–25.

[133] Chen W, et al. Corneal alternations induced by topical application of benzalkonium chloride in rabbit. PLoS One 2011;6:e26103.

[134] Denoyer A, et al. Very-high-frequency ultrasound corneal imaging as a new tool for early diagnosis of ocular surface toxicity in rabbits treated with a preserved glaucoma drug. Ophthalmic Res 2008;40:298–308.

[135] Kovoor TA, et al. Evaluation of the corneal effects of topical ophthalmic fluoroquinolones using in vivo confocal microscopy. Eye Cont Lens 2004;30:90–4.

[136] Kobayakawa S, Hiratsuka Y, Watabe Y, Murakami A, Tochikubo T. Comparison of the influence of intracameral gentamicin, gatifloxacin, and moxifloxacin on the corneal endothelium in a rabbit model. Jpn J Ophthalmol 2010;54:481–5.

[137] Ness PJ, et al. An anterior chamber toxicity study evaluating besivance, azasite, and ciprofloxacin. Am J Ophthalmol 2010;150:498–504.

[138] Barron CN, Rubin LF, Steelman RL. Chlorpromazine and the eye of the dog. IV. Reversibility of ocular lesions. Exp Mol Pathol 1972;16:163–8.

[139] Schrage NF, Schlomacher B, Aschenbernner W, Langefeld S. Phosphate buffer in alkali eye burns as an inducer of experimental corneal calcification. Burns 2001;27:459–64.

[140] Inoue H, Sonoda KH, Ishikawa M, Kadonosono K, Uchio E. Clinical evaluation of local ocular toxicity in candidate anti-adenoviral agents. In vivo Ophthalmol 2009;223:233–8.

[141] Bryce F, et al. Effects elicited by toxaphene in the cynomolgus monkey (Macaca fascicularis): a pilot study. Food Chem Toxicol 2001;39:1243–51.

[142] Galassi F, et al. A topical nitric oxide-releasing dexamethasone derivative: effects on intraocular pressure and ocular haemodynamics in a rabbit glaucoma model. Br J Ophthalmol 2006;90:1414–9.

[143] Ticho U, Lahav M, Berkowitz S, Yoffe P. Ocular changes in rabbits with corticosteroid-induced ocular hypertension. Br J Ophthalmol 1979;63:646–50.

[144] Bhattacherjee P, Paterson CA, Spellman JM, Graff G, Yanni JM. Pharmacological validation of a feline model of steroid-induced ocular hypertension. Arch Ophthalmol 1999;117:361–4.

[145] Zhan GL, Miranda OC, Bito LZ. Steroid glaucoma: corticosteroid-induced ocular hypertension in cats. Exp Eye Res 1992;54:211–8.

[146] Gerometta R, Podos SM, Danias J, Candia OA. Steroid-induced ocular hypertension in normal sheep. Invest Ophthalmol Vis Sci 2009;50:669–73.

[147] Melena J, Santafe J, Segarra J. The effect of topical diltiazem on the intraocular pressure in betamethasone-induced ocular hypertensive rabbits. J Pharmacol Exp Ther 1998;284:278–82.

[148] Whitlock NA, Mcknight B, Corcoran KN, Rodriguez LA, Rice DS. Increased intraocular pressure in mice treated with dexamethasone. Invest Ophthalmol Vis Sci 2010;51:6496–503.

[149] McGhee CNJ, Dean S, Danesh-Meyer H. Locally administered ocular corticosteroids benefits and risks. Drug Saf 2002;25:33–55.

[150] Grimes P, VonSallman L, Frichette A. Influence of Myleran on cell proliferation in the lens epithelium. Invest Ophthalmol 1964;3:566–76.

[151] Lubek BM, Basu PK, Wells PG. Metabolic evidence for the involvement of enzymatic bioactivation in the cataractogenicity of acetaminophen in genetically susceptible (C57BL/6) and resistant (DBA/2) murine strains. Toxicol Appl Pharmacol 1988;94:487–95.

[152] Bhuyan KC, Bhuyan DK, Chiu W, Malik S, Fridovich I. Desferal-Mn(III) in the therapy of diquat-induced cataract in rabbit. Arch Biochem Biophys 1991;288:525–32.

[153] Pyrah IT, et al. Toxicologic lesions associated with two related inhibitors of oxidosqualene cyclase in the dog and mouse. Toxicol Pathol 2001;29:174–9.

[154] Myers AC, et al. Rifabutin accumulates in the lens and reduces retinal function in the rabbit eye. Retina 2009;29:106–11.

[155] Hayasaka Y, Hayasaka S, Nagaki Y. Ocular changes after intravitreal injection of methanol, formaldehyde, or formate in rabbits. Pharmacol Toxicol 2001;89:74–8.

[156] Fujihara M, Kikuchi M, Kurimoto Y. Methanol-induced retinal toxicity patient examined by optical coherence tomography. Jpn J Ophthalmol 2006;50:239–41.

[157] Garner CD, Lee EW. Evaluation of methanol-induced retinotoxicity using oscillatory potential analysis. Toxicology 1994;93:113–24.

[158] Seme MT, Summerfelt P, Henry MM, Neitz J, Eells JT. Formate-induced inhibition of photoreceptor function in methanol intoxication. J Pharmacol Exp Ther 1999;289:361–70.

[159] Blomstrand R, Ingemansson SO. Studies on the effect of 4-methylpyrazole on methanol poisoning using the monkey as an animal model: with particular reference to the ocular toxicity. Drug Alcohol Depend 1984;13:343–55.

[160] Yamauchi Y, et al. Correlation between high-resolution optical coherence tomography (OCT) images and histopathology in an iodoacetic acid-induced model of retinal degeneration in rabbits. Br J Ophthalmol 2011;95:1157–60.

[161] Messias A, et al. Retinal safety of a new fluoroquinolone, pradofloxacin, in cats: assessment with electroretinography. Doc Ophthalmol 2008;116:177–91.

[162] Comer GM, et al. Intravitreal daptomycin: a safety and efficacy study. Retina 2011;31:1199–206.

[163] Shahar J, Zemel E, Perlman I, Loewenstein A. Physiological and toxicological effects of cefuroxime on the albino rabbit retina. Invest Ophthalmol Vis Sci 2012;53:906–14.

[164] Ozkiris A, Evereklioglu C, Kontas O, Oner AO, Erkilic K. Determination of nontoxic concentrations of piperacillin/tazobactam for intravitreal application an electroretinographic, histopathologic and morphometric analysis. Ophthalmic Res 2004;36:139–44.

[165] Kocak N, et al. The effects of intravitreally injected bevacizumab on the retina and retina pigment epithelium: experimental in vivo electron microscopic study in intact versus vitrectomized eyes. Cent Eur J Med 2010;5:745–51.

[166] Shahar J, et al. Electrophysiologic and retinal penetration studies following intravitreal injection of bevacizumab (Avastin). Retina 2006;26:262–9.

[167] Sakurai K, et al. Effect of intravitreal injection of high-dose bevacizumab in monkey eyes. Invest Ophthalmol Vis Sci 2009;50:4905–16.

[168] Peters S, et al. Ultrastructural findings in the primate eye after intravitreal injection of bevacizumab. Am J Ophthalmol 2007;143:995–1002.

[169] Inan UU, et al. Preclinical safety evaluation of intravitreal injection of full-length humanized vascular endothelial growth factor antibody in rabbit eyes. Invest Ophthalmol Vis Sci 2007;48:1773–81.

[170] Fraunfelder FW. Ocular adverse drug reactions. Expert Opin Drug Saf 2003;2:411–20.

[171] Fraunfelder FW. Corneal toxicity from topical ocular and systemic medications. Cornea 2006;25:1133–8.

[172] Hollander DA, Aldave AJ. Drug-induced corneal complications. Curr Opin Ophthalmol 2004;15:541–8.

[173] Li J, Tripathi RC, Tripathi BJ. Drug-induced ocular disorders. Drug Saf 2008;31:127–41.

[174] Pflugfelder SC. Tear dysfunction and the cornea: LXVIII Edward Jackson Memorial Lecture. Am J Ophthalmol 2011;152:900–9.

[175] Tripathi RC, Tripathi BJ, Haggerty C. Drug-induced glaucomas: mechanism and management. Drug Saf 2003;26:749–67.

[176] Wilson FM. Adverse external ocular effects of topical ophthalmic therapy: an epidemiologic, laboratory, and clinical study. Trans Am Ophthalmol Soc 1983;81:854–965.

[177] Reasor MJ, Kacew S. Drug-induced phospholipidosis: are there functional consequences? Exp Biol Med 2001;226:825–30.

[178] Pasadhika S, Fishman GA. Effects of chronic exposure to hydroxychloroquine or chloroquine on inner retinal structures. Eye 2010;24:340–6.

[179] Pasadhika S, Fishman GA, Choi D, Shahidi M. Selective thinning of the perifoveal inner retina as an early sign of hydroxychloroquine retinal toxicity. Eye 2010;24:756–63.

[180] Chen E, et al. Spectral domain optical coherence tomography as an effective screening test for hydroxychloroquine retinopathy (the 'flying saucer' sign). Clin Ophthalmol 2010;4:1151–8.

[181] Kellner U, Kraus H, Foerster MH. Multifocal ERG in chloroquine retinopathy: regional variance of retinal dysfunction. Graefe's Archive Clin Exp Ophthalmol 2000;238:94–7.

[182] Rosenthal AR, Kolb H, Bergsma D, Huxsoll D, Hopkins JL. Chloroquine retinopathy in the rhesus monkey. Invest Ophthalmol Vis Sci 1978;17:1158–75.

[183] Mahon GJ, et al. Chloroquine causes lysosomal dysfunction in neural retina and RPE: implications for retinopathy. Curr Eye Res 2004;28:277–84.

[184] Gaynes BI, Torczynski E, Varro Z, Grostern R, Perlman J. Retinal toxicity of chloroquine hydrochloride administered by intraperitoneal injection. J Appl Toxicol 2008;28:895–900.

[185] Mantyjarvi M, Tuppurainen K, Ikaheimo K. Ocular side effects of amiodarone. Surv Ophthalmol 1998;42:360–6.

[186] Bicer S, Fuller GA, Wilkie DA, Yamaguchi M, Hamlin RL. Amiodarone-induced keratopathy in healthy dogs. Vet Ophthalmol 2002;5:35–8.

[187] Laties AM, Zrenner E. Viagra (sildenafil citrate) and ophthalmology. Prog Retin Eye Res 2002;21:485–506.

[188] Vistamehr S, Walsh TJ, Adelman RA. Ethambutol neuroretinopathy. Semin Ophthalmol 2007;22:141–6.

[189] Menon V, Jain D, Saxena R, Sood R. Prospective evaluation of visual function for early detection of ethambutol toxicity. Br J Ophthalmol 2009;93:1251–4.

VII. SAFETY EVALUATION OF OCULAR DRUGS, BOTANICAL PRODUCTS, AND MEDICINAL DEVICES

[190] Sato S, Sugimoto S, Chiba S. Effects of sodium iodate, iodoacetic acid and ethambutol on electroretinogram and visual evoked potential in rats. J Toxicol Sci 1984;9:389–99.

[191] Heng JE, et al. Ethambutol is toxic to retinal ganglion cells via an excitotoxic pathway. Invest Ophthalmol Vis Sci 1999;40:190–6.

[192] Yu-Wai-Man P, Griffiths PG, Chinnery PF. Mitochondrial optic neuropathies – disease mechanisms and therapeutic strategies. Prog Retin Eye Res 2011;30:81–114.

[193] Wild JM, Robson CR, Jones AL, Cunliffe IA, Smith PEM. Detecting vigabatrin toxicity by imaging of the retinal nerve fiber layer. Invest Ophthalmol Vis Sci 2006;47:917–24.

[194] Ponjavic V, Andréasson S. Multifocal ERG and full-field ERG in patients on long-term vigabatrin medication. Doc Ophthalmol 2001;102:63–72.

[195] Ponjavic V, Granse L, Kjellstrom S, Andreasson S, Bruun A. Alterations in electroretinograms and retinal morphology in rabbits treated with vigabatrin. Doc Ophthalmol 2004;108:125–33.

[196] Hamrah P, Dana R. In: Dartt DA, Dana R, L'Amore P, Niederkorn JY, editors. Immunology, inflammation and diseases of the eye. Elsevier, Ltd; 2010. p. 50–7.

[197] Hamrah P, et al. Visualization of corneal antigen-presenting cell migration by multi-photon intravital microscopy. Invest Ophthalmol Vis Sci 2010;51:3436.

[198] Niederkorn JY. Regulatory T cells and the eye. Chem Immunol Allergy 2007;92:131–9. http://dx.doi.org/10.1159/000099263.

[199] Streilein JW, Cousins S, Williamson JS. Ocular molecules and cells that regulate immune responses in situ. Int Ophthalmol 1990;14:317–25.

[200] Streilein JW. Anterior chamber associated immune deviation: the privilege of immunity in the eye. Surv Ophthalmol 1990;35:67–73.

[201] Lin P, Menda S, de Juan EJ. In: Sebag J, editor. Vitreous: in health and medicine. Springer Science-Business Media; 2014. p. 509–21.

[202] Rocha G, Baines MG, Deschenes J. The immunology of the eye and its systemic interactions. Crit Rev Immunol 1992;12:81–100.

[203] Masli S, Vega JL. In: Cristina Cuturi M, Anegon I, editors. Suppression and regulation of immune responses. Methods in molecular biology, vol. 677. Springer Science + Business Media; 2011. p. 449–58.

[204] Marascheillo C. The relevance of immunogenicity in preclinical development. J Bioanalysis Biomed 2014;6:1–4. http://dx.doi.org/10.4172/1948-593X.1000099.

[205] Brinks V, Jiskoot W, Schellekens H. Immunogenicity of therapeutic proteins: the use of animal models. Pharm Res 2011;28:2379–85.

[206] Streit T, et al. Determination of a no observable effect level (NOEL) for endotoxin following a single intravitreal administration to male Dutch belted rabbits. Presented at ARVO Annual Meeting; 2015.

[207] Ponce R, et al. Immunogenicity of biologically-derived therapeutics: assessment and interpretation of nonclinical safety studies. Regul Toxicol Pharmacol 2009;54:164–82. http://dx.doi.org/10.1016/j.yrtph.2009.03.012.

[208] Leach MW, et al. Immunogenicity/hypersensitivity of biologics. Toxicol Pathol 2014;42:293–300. http://dx.doi.org/10.1177/0192623313510987.

[209] Rojko JL, et al. Formation, clearance, deposition, pathogenicity, and identification of biopharmaceutical-related immune complexes: review and case studies. Toxicol Pathol 2014;42:725–64. http://dx.doi.org/10.1177/0192623314526475.

[210] Frazier KS, et al. Scientific and regulatory policy committee points-to-consider paper*: drug-induced vascular injury associated with nonsmall molecule therapeutics in preclinical development: Part I. Biotherap Toxicol Pathol 2015. http://dx.doi.org/10.1177/0192623315570340.

[211] Leach MW. Regulatory forum opinion piece: differences between protein-based biologic products (biotherapeutics) and chemical entities (small molecules) of relevance to the toxicologic pathologist. Toxicol Pathol 2013;41:128–36. http://dx.doi.org/10.1177/0192623312451371.

[212] Caspi RR. A look at autoimmunity and inflammation in the eye. J Clin Invest 2010;120:3073–83. http://dx.doi.org/10.1172/jci42440.

[213] Mehta S, Zhang L, Grossniklaus HE. In: Sebag J, editor. Vitreous: in health and disease. Springer Science + Business Media; 2014. p. 395–405.

[214] Kohno RI, et al. Possible contribution of hyalocytes to idiopathic epiretinal membrane formation and its contraction. Br J Ophthalmol 2009;93:1020–6. http://dx.doi.org/10.1136/bjo.2008.155069.

[215] Kita T, Sakamoto T, Ishibashi T. In: Sebag J, editor. Vitreous: In health and disease. Springer Science + Business Media; 2014. p. 151–64.

[216] Joshi M, Agrawal S, Christoforidis JB. Inflammatory mechanisms of idiopathic epiretinal membrane formation. Mediators Inflamm 2013;2013:192582. http://dx.doi.org/10.1155/2013/192582.

[217] Schumann RG, et al. Immunocytochemical and ultrastructural evidence of glial cells and hyalocytes in internal limiting membrane specimens of idiopathic macular holes. Invest Ophthalmol Vis Sci 2011;52:7822–34. http://dx.doi.org/10.1167/iovs.11-7514.

[218] Zhao F, et al. Epiretinal cell proliferation in macular pucker and vitreomacular traction syndrome: analysis of flat-mounted internal limiting membrane specimens. Retina 2013;33:77–88. http://dx.doi.org/10.1097/IAE.0b013e3182602087.

[219] Anderson JM. In: Wright JC, Burgess DJ, editors. Advances in delivery science and technology. Controlled Release Society; 2012. p. 25–55. [chapter 3].

[220] Davis FA. The anatomy and histology of the eye and orbit of the rabbit. Trans Am Ophthalmol Soc 1929;27:400–41.

[221] Samuelson DA. In: Gelatt KN, editor. Veterinary ophthalmology. Blackwell Publishing; 2007. p. 37–148.

[222] Kiel JW. In: Granger DN, Granger JP, editors. Integrated systems physiology: From molecule to function. Morgan & Claypool Life Sciences; 2011. p. 1–81.

[223] Nishida T, Saika S. In: Krachmer JH, Mannis MJ, Holland EJ, editors. Cornea. Elsevier Mosby; 2005. p. 3–24. [chapter 1].

[224] Sun TT, Lavker RM. Corneal epithelial stem cells: past, present, and future. J Invest Dermatol Symp Proc 2004;9:202–7.

[225] Waring GO, Bouchard CS. In: Krachmer JH, Mannis MJ, Holland EJ, editors. Cornea. Mosby; 2011. p. 47–79.

[226] Beebe DC. Maintaining transparency: a review of the developmental physiology and pathophysiology of two avascular tissues. Semin Cell Dev Biol 2008;19:125–33.

[227] Basu PK. Toxic effects of drugs on the corneal epithelium: a review. Cutan Ocul Toxicol 1983;2:205–27.

[228] Wilson SE, Hong J-W. Bowman's layer structure and function: critical or dispensable to corneal function? a hypothesis. Cornea J Cornea External Dis 2000;19:417–20.

[229] Oda Y, Fukuda S. Electron microscopic studies on the animals cornea. J Electron Microsc 1962;11:179–84.

[230] Merindano Ma D, Costa J, Canals M, Potau JM, Ruano D. A comparative study of Bowman's layer in some mammals: relationships with other constituent corneal structures. Eur J Anat 2002;6:133–9.

[231] Labbe A, et al. Comparative anatomy of laboratory animal corneas with a new-generation high-resolution in vivo confocal microscope. Curr Eye Res 2006:501–9.

[232] Hayashi S, Osawa T, Tohyama K. Comparative observations on corneas, with special reference to Bowman's layer and Descemet's membrane in mammals and amphibians. J Morphol 2002;254:247–58.

VII. SAFETY EVALUATION OF OCULAR DRUGS, BOTANICAL PRODUCTS, AND MEDICINAL DEVICES

[233] Obata H, Tsuru T. Corneal wound healing from the perspective of keratoplasty specimens with special reference to the function of the Bowman layer and Descemet membrane. Cornea 2007;26:S82–9.

[234] Wilson SE, Kim WJ. Keratocyte apoptosis: implications on corneal wound healing, tissue organization, and disease. Invest Ophthalmol Vis Sci 1998;39:220–1.

[235] Wilson SE, Netto M, Ambrósio J. Corneal cells: Chatty in development, homeostasis, wound healing, and disease. Am J Ophthalmol 2003;136:530–6.

[236] West-Mays JA, Dwivedi DJ. The keratocyte: corneal stromal cell with variable repair phenotypes. Int J Biochem Cell Biol 2006;38:1625–31.

[237] Wilson SE, et al. The corneal wound healing response: cytokine-mediated interaction of the epithelium, stroma, and inflammatory cells. Prog Retin Eye Res 2001;20:625–37.

[238] Tomasek JJ, Gabbiani G, Hinz B, Chaponnier C, Brown RA. Myofibroblasts and mechano-regulation of connective tissue remodelling. Nat Rev Mol Cell Biol 2002;3.

[239] Muller LJ, Marfurt CF, Kruse F, Tervo TMT. Corneal nerves: structure, contents and function. Exp Eye Res 2003;76:521–42.

[240] Tamura Y, Konomi H, Sawada H, Takashima S, Nakajima A. Tissue distribution of type VIII collagen in human adult and fetal eyes. Invest Ophthalmol Vis Sci 1991;32:2636–44.

[241] Schlotzer-Schrehardt U, et al. Characterization of extracellular matrix components in the limbal epithelial stem cell compartment. Exp Eye Res 2007;85:845–60.

[242] Levy SG, Moss J, Sawada H, Dopping-Hepenstal PJC, McCartney ACE. The composition of wide-spaced collagen in normal and diseased Descemet's membrane. Curr Eye Res 1996;15:45–52.

[243] Samuelson DA. A reevaluation of the comparative anatomy of the Eutherian iridocorneal angle and associated ciliary body musculature. Vet Comp Ophthalmol 1996;6:153–72.

[244] Eagle R. In: Eye pathology: an Atlas and text. Wolters Kluwer/Lippincott Williams & Wilkins; 2011. p. 1–13.

[245] Van Horn DL, Hyndiuk RA. Endothelial wound repair in primate cornea. Exp Eye Res 1975;21:113–24.

[246] Staatz WD, Van Horn DL. The effects of aging and inflammation on corneal endothelial wound healing in rabbits. Invest Ophthalmol Vis Sci 1980;19:983–6.

[247] Schwartzkopff J, Bredow L, Mahlenbrey S, Boehringer D, Reinhard T. Regeneration of corneal endothelium following complete endothelial cell loss in rat keratoplasty. Mol Vis 2010;16:2368–75.

[248] Matsuda M, et al. Cellular migration and morphology in corneal endothelial wound repair. Invest Ophthalmol Vis Sci 1985;26:443–9.

[249] Befanis PJ, Peiffer J, Brown D. Endothelial repair of the canine cornea. Am J Vet Res 1981;42:590–5.

[250] Bahn CF, Glassman RM, MacCallum DK. Postnatal development of corneal endothelium. Invest Ophthalmol Vis Sci 1986;27:44–51.

[251] Smith R, Sundberg J, John S. In: Smith R, editor. Systematic evaluation of the mouse eye. CRC Press; 2001. p. 3–23.

[252] Laing RA, Sandstrom MM, Berrospi AR, Leibowitz HM. Changes in the corneal endothelium as a function of age. Exp Eye Res 1976;22:587–94.

[253] Baroody RA, Bito LZ, DeRousseau CJ, Kaufman PL. Ocular development and aging. 1. Corneal endothelial changes in cats and in free-ranging and caged rhesus monkeys. Exp Eye Res 1987;45:607–22.

[254] Gwin RM, Lerner I, Warren JK, Gum G. Decrease in canine corneal endothelial cell density and increase in corneal thickness as functions of age. Invest Ophthalmol Vis Sci 1982;22:267–71.

[255] Doughty MJ. The cornea and corneal endothelium in the aged rabbit. Optom Vis Sci 1994;71:809–18.

[256] Fitch KL, Nadakavukaren MJ, Richardson A. Age-related changes in the corneal endothelium of the rat. Exp Gerontol 1982;17:179–83.

[257] Fitch KL, Nadakavukaren MJ. Age-related changes in the corneal endothelium of the mouse. Exp Gerontol 1986;21:31–5.

[258] Jun AS, Chakravarti S, Edelhauser HF, Kimos M. Aging changes of mouse corneal endothelium and Descemet's membrane. Exp Eye Res 2006;83:890–6.

[259] Van Winkle TJ, Balk MW. Spontaneous corneal opacities in laboratory mice. Lab Anim Sci 1986;36:248–55.

[260] Taradach C, Greaves P. Spontaneous eye lesions in laboratory animals: incidence in relation to age. Crit Rev Toxicol 1984;12:121–47.

[261] Hubert MF, Gerin G, Durand-Cavagna G. Spontaneous ophthalmic lesions in young Swiss mice. Lab Anim Sci 1999;49:232–40.

[262] Losco PE, Troup CM. Corneal dystrophy in Fischer 344 rats. Lab Anim Sci 1988;38:702–10.

[263] Bruner RH, et al. Spontaneous corneal dystrophy and generalized basement membrane changes in Fischer-344 rats. Toxicol Pathol 1993;20:357–66.

[264] Bellhorn RW, Korte GE, Abrutyn D. Spontaneous corneal degeneration in the rat. Lab Anim Sci 1988;38:46–50.

[265] Port CD, Dodd DC. Two cases of corneal epithelial dystrophy in rabbits. Lab Anim Sci 1983;33:587–8.

[266] Roth AM, Ekins MB, Waring III GO. Oval corneal opacities in beagles. III. Histochemical demonstration of stromal lipids without hyperlipidemia. Invest Ophthalmol Vis Sci 1981;21:95–106.

[267] Streilein JW. Ocular immune privilege: therapeutic opportunities from an experiment of nature. Nat Rev Immunol 2003;3:879–89.

[268] Waring III GO, Rodrigues MM. Patterns of pathologic response in the cornea. Surv Ophthalmol 1987;31:262–6.

[269] Van Buskirk EM. The anatomy of the limbus. Eye 1989;3:101–8.

[270] Gong H, Tripathi RC, Tripathi BJ. Morphology of the aqueous outflow pathway. Microsc Res Tech 1996;33:336–67.

[271] Raviola G. Schwalbe line's cells: a new cell type in the trabecular meshwork of Macaca mulatta. Invest Ophthalmol Vis Sci 1982;22:45–56.

[272] Pellegrini G, et al. Location and clonal analysis of stem cells and their differentiated progeny in the human ocular surface. J Cell Biol 1999;145:769–82.

[273] Samuelson D, Plummer C, Lewis P, Gelatt K. Schwalbe line's cell in the normal and glaucomatous dog. Vet Ophthalmol 2001;4:47–53.

[274] Papas EB. The limbal vasculature. Cont Lens Anterior Eye 2003;26:71–6.

[275] Nakao S, Hafezi-Moghadam A, Ishibashi T. Lymphatics and lymphangiogenesis in the eye. J Ophthalmol 2012:1–11. http://dx.doi.org/10.1155/2012/783163.

[276] Birke K, Lütjen-Drecoll E, Kerjaschki D, Birke MT. Expression of podoplanin and other lymphatic markers in the human anterior eye segment. Invest Ophthalmol Vis Sci 2010;51:344–54.

[277] Baluk P, McDonald DM. Markers for microscopic imaging of lymphangiogenesis and angiogenesis. Ann New York Acad Sci 2008;1131:1–12.

[278] Ecoiffier T, Yuen D, Chen L. Differential distribution of blood and lymphatic vessels in the murine cornea. Invest Ophthalmol Vis Sci 2010;51:2436–40.

[279] Smolin G. Cellular response to inflammation at the limbus. Eye 1989;3:161–71.

[280] Cursiefen C, Chen L, Dana MR, Streilein JW. Corneal lymphangiogenesis: evidence, mechanisms, and implications for corneal transplant immunology. Cornea 2003;22:273–81.

[281] Collin HB. Limbal vascular response prior to corneal vascularization. Exp Eye Res 1973;16:443–55.

[282] Setzer PY, Nichols BA, Dawson CR. Unusual structure of rat conjunctival epithelium. Light and electron microscopy. Invest Ophthalmol Vis Sci 1987;28:531–7.

[283] Cain C, Phillips TE. Developmental changes in conjunctiva-associated lymphoid tissue of the rabbit. Invest Ophthalmol Vis Sci 2008;49:644–9.

[284] Llobet A, Gasull X, Gual A. Understanding trabecular meshwork physiology: a key to the control of intraocular pressure? News Physiol Sci 2003;18:205–9.

[285] Alvarado JA, Betanzos A, Franse-Carman L, Chen J, Gonzaóülez-Mariscal L. Endothelia of Schlemm's canal and trabecular meshwork: distinct molecular, functional, and anatomic features. Am J Physiol Cell Physiol 2004;286:C621–34.

[286] Tripathi RC, Tripathi BJ. Human trabecular endothelium, corneal endothelium, keratocytes, and scleral fibroblasts in primary cell culture. A comparative study of growth characteristics, morphology, and phagocytic activity by light and scanning electron microscopy. Exp Eye Res 1982;35:611–24.

[287] Samuelson DA, Gelatt KN. Aqueous outflow in the beagle. II. Postnatal morphologic development of the iridocorneal angle: corneoscleral trabecular mesh work and angular aqueous plexus. Curr Eye Res 1984;3:795–808.

[288] Samuelson DA, Gelatt KN. Aqueous outflow in the beagle. I. Postnatal morphologic development of the iridocorneal angle: pectinate ligament and uveal trabecular meshwork. Curr Eye Res 1984;3:783–94.

[289] Bergmanson JPG. The anatomy of the rabbit aqueous outflow pathway. Acta Ophthalmol 1985;63:493–501.

[290] Rohen JW, Van Der Zypen E. The phagocytic activity of the trabecular meshwork endothelium – an electron-microscopic study of the vervet (Cercopithecus aethiops). Albrecht von Graefe's Archive Clin Exp Ophthalmol 1968;175:143–60.

[291] Sherwood ME, Richardson TM. Phagocytosis by trabecular meshwork cells: sequence of events in cats and monkeys. Exp Eye Res 1988;46:881–95.

[292] Rohen JW, Lütjen-Drecoll E, Barany E. The relation between the ciliary muscle and the trabecular meshwork and its importance for the effect of miotics on aqueous outflow resistance – a study in two contrasting monkey species, Macaca irus and Cercopithecus aethiops. Albrecht von Graefes Arch Klin Exp Ophthalmol 1967;172:23–47.

[293] Lütjen-Drecoll E, Barany EH. Functional and electron microscopic changes in the trabecular meshwork remaining after trabeculectomy in cynomolgus monkeys. Invest Ophthalmol 1974;13:511–24.

[294] Lütjen-Drecoll E. Electron microscopic studies on reactive changes of the trabecular meshwork in human eyes after microsurgery. Albrecht von Graefe's Arch Clin Exp Ophthalmol 1972;183:267–85.

[295] Grierson I, Unger W, Webster L, Hogg P. Repair in the rabbit outflow system. Eye 2000;14:492–502.

[296] Tripathi RC, Tripathi BJ. The mechanism of aqueous outflow in lower mammals. Exp Eye Res 1972;14:73–9.

[297] Tripathi RC. Ultrastructure of the exit pathway of the aqueous in lower mammals: (A preliminary report on the 'angular aqueous plexus'). Exp Eye Res 1971;12:311–4.

[298] Ruskell GL. Aqueous drainage paths in the rabbit. A neoprene latex cast study. Arch Ophthalmol 1961;66:861–70.

[299] Reme C, Urner U, Aeberhard B. The occurrence of cell death during the remodelling of the chamber angle recess in the developing rat eye. Graefe's Archive Clin Exp Ophthalmol 1983;221:113–21.

[300] Johnson M, Johnson DH, Kamm RD, DeKater AW, Epstein DL. The filtration characteristics of the aqueous outflow system. Exp Eye Res 1990;50:407–18.

[301] Johnson M, Erickson K. In: Albert DM, Miller JW, Azar DT, Blodi BA, editors. Albert & Jakobiec principles & practices of ophthalmology. WB Saunders Co; 2008.

[302] Van Buskirk EM. The canine eye: the vessels of aqueous drainage. Invest Ophthalmol Vis Sci 1979;18:223–30.

[303] Fowlks WL, Havener VR. Aqueous flow into the perivascular space of the rabbit ciliary body. Invest Ophthalmol 1964;3:372–83.

[304] Nilsson SFE. The uveoscleral outflow routes. Eye 1997:149–54.

[305] Barrie KP, Gum GG, Samuelson DA, Gelatt KN. Morphologic studies of uveoscleral outflow in normotensive and glaucomatous beagles with fluorescein-labeled dextran. Am J Vet Res 1985;46:89–97.

[306] Barrie KP, Gum GG, Samuelson DA, Gelatt KN. Quantitation of uveoscleral outflow in normotensive and glaucomatous beagles by 3H-labeled dextran. Am J Vet Res 1985;46:84–8.

[307] Prince JH, Ruskell GL. The use of domestic animals for experimental ophthalmology. Am J Ophthalmol 1960;49:1202–7.

[308] Mochizuki M, Sugita S, Kamoi K. Immunological homeostasis of the eye. Prog Retin Eye Res 2013;33:10–27. http://dx.doi.org/10.1016/j.preteyeres.2012.10.002.

[309] Wilkerson CL, et al. Melanocytes and iris color. Light microscopic findings. Arch Ophthalmol 1996;114:437–42.

[310] Chakravarthy U, et al. Clinical risk factors for age-related macular degeneration: a systematic review and meta-analysis. BMC Ophthalmol 2010;10:31.

[311] Riordan-Eva P. In: Riordan-Eva P, Cunningham ET, editors. Vaughan and Asbury's general ophthalmology. 2011. [chapter 1].

[312] Barskey D. In: Tasman W, Jaeger EA, editors. Duane's ophthalomology. Lippincott Williams & Wilkens; 2006. p. 1–11.

[313] Murray PH. In: Albert DA, Miller JW, editors. Albert & Jakobiec's principles and practice of ophthalmology. Saunders Elsevier; 2008. p. 1137–50.

[314] Taylor AW, Kaplan HJ. Ocular immune privilege in the year 2010: ocular immune privilege and uveitis. Ocul Immunol Inflamm 2010;18:488–92.

[315] Taylor AW. Ocular immune privilege. Eye 2009;23:1885–9.

[316] Harris A, Bingaman D, Ciulla TA, Martin B. In: Ryan SJ, editor. Retina. Elsevier Mosby; 2006. p. 83–102.

[317] Hayreh SS. In: Besharse J, Bok D, editors. The retina and its disorders. Academic Press; 2011. p. 653–60.

[318] Tripathi B, Ashton N. Vaso-glial connections in the rabbit retina. Br J Ophthalmol 1971;55:1–11.

[319] Nakaizumi Y. The ultrastructure of Bruch's membrane. I. Human, monkey, rabbit, guinea pig, and rat eyes. Arch Ophthalmol 1964;72:380–7.

[320] Marmor MF. In: Marmor MF, Wolfensberger TW, editors. The retinal pigment epithelium. Oxford University Press; 1988. p. 23–40.

[321] Besharse JC, Defoe DM. In: Massey SC, Wolfensberger TW, editors. The retinal pigment epithelium. Oxford University Press; 1998. p. 152.

[322] Strauss O. The retinal pigment epithelium in visual function. Physiol Rev 2005;85:845–81.

[323] Chader GJ, Pepperberg DR, Crouch R, Wiggert B. In: Massey SC, Wolfensberger TW, editors. Retinal pigment epithelium, vol. 135–151. Oxford University Press; 1988.

[324] Boulton M. In: Marmor MF, Wolfensberger TW, editors. Retinal pigment epithelium. Oxford University Press; 1988. p. 68–85.

[325] Boycott B, Wassle H. Parallel processing in the mammalian retina: the Proctor Lecture. Invest Ophthalmol Vis Sci 1999;40:1313–27.

[326] Massey SC. In: Ryan SJ, editor. Retina. Elsevier Mosby; 2006. p. 43–82.

[327] Peichl L. Diversity of mammalian photoreceptor properties: adaptations to habitat and lifestyle? Anatom Rec Part A 2005;287A:1001–12.

[328] Prince JH, McConnell DG. In: Prince JH, editor. The rabbit in eye research. Charles C Thomas; 1964. p. 385–448.

[329] Juliusson B, et al. Complementary cone fields of the rabbit retina. Invest Ophthalmol Vis Sci 1994;35:811–8.

[330] Mowat FM, et al. Topographical characterization of cone photoreceptors and the area centralis of the canine retina. Mol Vis 2008;14:2518–27.

[331] Saidi T, Mbarek S, Chaouacha-Chekir RB, Hicks D. Diurnal rodents as animal models of human central vision: characterisation of the retina of the sand rat Psammomys obsesus. Graefe's Archive Clin Exp Ophthalmol 2011;249:1029–37.

[332] Bobu C, Bobu C, Lahmam M, Vuillez P, Ouarour A, Hicks D, et al. Photoreceptor organisation and phenotypic characterization in retinas of two diurnal rodent species: potential use as experimental animal models for human vision research. Vis Res 2008;48:424–32.

[333] Halfter W, Sebag J, Cunningham Jr ET. In: Sebag J, editor. Vitreous: in health and disease. Springer Science+Business Media; 2014. p. 165–91.

[334] Ramos M, Reilly CM, Bolon B. In: Bolon B, Butt MT, editors. Fundamental Neuropathology for pathologists and toxicologists: principles and techniques. John Wiley & Sons, Inc; 2011. p. 385–412.

[335] Fortune B, Wang L, Bui BV, Burgoyne CF, Cioffi GA. Idiopathic bilateral optic atrophy in the rhesus macaque. Invest Ophthalmol Vis Sci 2005;46:3943–56.

[336] Dubielzig RR, Leedle R, Nork TM, Ver Hoeve JN, Christian BJ. Bilateral optic atrophy: a background finding in cynomolgus macaques used in toxicologic research. Invest Ophthalmol Vis Sci 2009;50:5344.

[337] Watson PG, Young RD. Scleral structure, organisation and disease. A review. Exp Eye Res 2004;78:609–23.

[338] Bishop PN. In: Sebag J, editor. Vitreous: in health and disease. Springer Science+Business Media; 2014. p. 3–20.

[339] Crafoord S, Ghosh F, Sebag J. In: Sebag J, editor. Vitreous: in health and disease. Springer Science+Business Media; 2014. p. 81–92.

[340] Kingston ZS, Provis JM, Madigan MC. In: Sebag J, editor. Vitreous: in health and disease. Springer Science+Business Media; 2014. p. 95–108.

[341] Sebag J. The vitreous, structure, function, and pathobiology. Springer-Verlag; 1989.

[342] Scott JE. The chemical morphology of the vitreous. Eye 1992;6:553–5.

[343] Balazs EA, Toth LZ, Eckle EA, Mitchell AP. Studies on the structure of the vitreous body. XII. Cytological and histochemical studies on the cortical tissue layer. Exp Eye Res 1964;3:57–71.

[344] Denlinger JL, Balazs EA. In: Sebag J, editor. Vitreous: in health and disease. Springer Science+Business Media; 2014. p. 13–20.

[345] Tozer K, Johnson MW, Sebag J. In: Sebag J, editor. Vitreous: in health and disease. Springer Science+Business Media; 2014. p. 131–50.

[346] Hogan MJ, Feeny L. The ultrastructure of the retinal blood vessels. I. The large vessels. J Ultrastruct Res 1963;39:10–28.

[347] Bernal A, Parel JM, Manns F. Evidence for posterior zonular fiber attachment on the anterior hyaloid membrane. Invest Ophthalmol Vis Sci 2006;47:4708–13.

[348] Sebag J. Anatomy and pathology of the vitreo-retinal interface. Eye 1992;6:541–52.

[349] Worst JG, Los LI. Comparative anatomy of the vitreous body in rhesus monkeys and man. Doc Ophthalmol 1992;82:169–78.

[350] Los LI. The rabbit as an animal model for post-natal vitreous matrix differentiation and degeneration. Eye 2008;22:1223–32.

[351] Lazarus HS, Hageman GS. In situ characterization of the human hyalocyte. Arch Ophthalomol 1994;112:1356–62.

[352] Sakamoto T, Ishibashi T. Hyalocytes: essential cells of the vitreous cavity in vitreoretinal pathophysiology? Retina 2011;331:222–8.

[353] Lazarus HS, et al. Hyalocytes synthesize and secrete inhibitors of retinal pigment epithelial cell proliferation. Arch Ophthalmol 1996;114:731–6.

[354] Hikichi T, Ueno N, Chakrabarti B, Trempe CL, Yoshida A. Evidence of cross-link formation of vitreous collagen during experimental ocular inflammation. Graefe's Archive Clin Exp Ophthalmol 1996;234:47–54.

[355] Gilbert C, Hiscott P, Unger W, Grierson I, McLeod D. Inflammation and the formation of epiretinal membranes. Eye 1988;2 Suppl.:S140–56.

[356] Hiscott PS, Unger WG, Grierson I, McLeod D. The role of inflammation in the development of epiretinal membranes. Curr Eye Res 1988;7:877–92.

[357] Allamby D, Foreman D, Carrington L, McLeod D, Boulton M. Cell attachment to, and contraction of, the retina. Invest Ophthalmol Vis Sci 1997;38:2064–72.

[358] Nork TM, Wallow IH, Sramek SJ, Stevens TS, De VG. Immunocytochemical study of an eye with proliferative vitreoretinopathy and retinal tacks. Retina 1990;10:78–85.

[359] Wilson CG, Tan LE, Mains J. In: Kompella UB, Edelhauser HF, editors. Drug product development for the back of the eye AAPS advances in the pharmaceutical sciences series 2. American Association of Pharmaceutical Scientists; 2011. p. 125–58.

30

Nonclinical Safety Assessment of Botanical Products

A.S. Faqi, J.S. Yan

INTRODUCTION OF BOTANICAL PRODUCTS

Herbs or plants have a long history of use in medicine and have been used by all cultures or ethnic groups throughout history. They have been used throughout history to improve human health; their use is similar to the way modern pharmaceuticals are used today. It is the oldest form of therapy practiced by mankind and continues to serve as the basis for many pharmaceuticals used today. Plants have always been a common source of

medicine either in the form of traditional preparations or as pure active principles.

Many botanical medicines contain curative principal active substances, which have proven to be valuable as primary or supplemental therapies when carefully applied. Traditional healers have learned which species of plants may help alleviate certain ailments and have passed their knowledge from generation to generation through oral history: the individual medicinal plants, the plant part to be used, and methods of preparation and administration. Most therapeutics of botanical

A Comprehensive Guide to Toxicology in Nonclinical Drug Development, Second Edition
http://dx.doi.org/10.1016/B978-0-12-803620-4.00030-X

813

origin derive from medicinal plants that have been cultivated for increased yields of bioactive components. The domestication of agricultural crops resulting in the enhanced content of some bioactive compounds and diminished content of others has resulted in the change of the phytochemical composition of many plants [1].

In 1897, Arthur Eichengrün and Felix Hoffmann, working at Friedrich Bayer, developed the first synthetic drug, aspirin, a stable form of the drug that was easier and more pleasant to take. This was followed by the development of penicillin in 1928 by Alexander Fleming, adding microbes as an important source of novel drugs [1]. It was the beginning of the pharmaceutical revolution, opening a chapter for evidence-based drug discovery. Indeed in the 20th century, the pharmaceutical industry intensified its drug discovery effort and began replacing natural extracts with synthetic molecules that do not contain plant products [2]. Medicinal plant drug discovery continues to provide new and important leads against various pharmacological targets including cancer, HIV/AIDS, Alzheimer's, malaria, and pain [3]. Approximately 75% of the new chemical entities reported between 1981 and mid-2006 resulted from studies of natural products [4].

Herbal products are classified as drugs if they are intended for diagnosis, mitigation, therapeutic, or prophylactic use. If the intended use of a botanical product is to affect the structure or function of the human body, it may be regulated either as dietary supplement or as a drug, depending on the circumstances.

The objective of this chapter is to discuss the regulations of dietary supplement, dietary supplement claims, and nonclinical safety testing of botanical drugs. Botanicals used for food are regulated as food and are beyond the scope of this chapter.

DIETARY SUPPLEMENTS

Dietary supplement use is increasingly common in the Western world. Many American adults use vitamins, minerals, botanicals, and other dietary supplements on a regular basis, and nearly one in five people in the U.S. population report using an herb for treatment of health conditions and/or health promotion [5]. Dietary supplements may be grouped into three major categories based on dietary function or origin: (1) substances with established nutritional function, such as vitamins, minerals, amino acids, and fatty acids; (2) botanical products, their concentrates and extracts; and (3) other substances with a wide variety of origins and physiologic roles (eg, pyruvate, steroid hormone precursors, and chondroitin sulfate) [6].

Botanical dietary supplements with a long history of safe human use may not require the same level of

toxicity testing as synthetic pharmaceutical drugs or botanical drugs aimed to cure, prevent, and treat diseases. In the United States, herbal products are regulated both at the state and federal level, with distinct pathways dependent upon intended utility. The establishment of a dedicated review team in the FDA's Center for Drug Evaluation and Research (CDER) greatly facilitated the transformation from dietary supplement to botanical drug [7]. In 1994 the Dietary Supplement Health and Education Act (DSHEA) was issued, allowing marketing of dietary supplements such as botanicals without any submission to the FDA, but making the manufacturer responsible for ensuring the safety of the products and placing the burden of proof on the FDA for enforcement [8]. Similar legislation was also adapted in Europe.

The DSHEA defines a dietary supplement as a product (other than tobacco) that is intended to supplement the diet; contains one or more dietary ingredients (including vitamins, minerals, herbs, or other botanicals, amino acids, and other substances) or their constituents; is intended to be taken by mouth as a pill, capsule, tablet, or liquid; and is labeled on the front panel as being a dietary supplement [9].

Dietary supplements used for oral ingestion may be lawfully marketed with a statement that (1) claims a benefit related to a classical nutrient deficiency disease, (2) describes how the product is intended to affect the structure or function of the human body (but not a disease), (3) characterizes the documented mechanisms of action, and (4) describes general well-being due to consumption of the product [8]. Indeed it is not mandatory to register the product unless the dietary supplement contains a new ingredient. In contrast, a botanical drug that claims to cure, prevent, or treat human disease is classified as a drug product and is subject to FDA regulation [10]. Under the DSHEA, the FDA may take action if a product poses a direct health threat, but only after adverse health effects have already occurred. The DSHEA was passed by the congress with the intent of striking a balance between providing consumers access to safe dietary supplements and help maintain or improve their health. In addition, it gives the FDA authority to regulate and take action against manufacturers of supplements or supplement ingredients that present safety problems or are presented with false or misleading claims, or are adulterated or misbranded [11]. The dietary supplement legislation in the United States lacks an enhanced oversight to increase the safety of these products for the American consumer [12].

The primary problem with the DSHEA is that it severely limits the FDA's ability to ban unsafe dietary supplements because it forces the FDA to regulate dietary supplements reactively instead of proactively [13]. It is difficult to determine the quality, safety, and efficacy of a dietary supplement product from its label because of the lack of requirements for quality, safety, and efficacy assessments. Labels may be incorrect intentionally or inadvertently. However, in March 2003 the FDA published a proposed rule that was intended to ensure that manufacturing practices would result in an unadulterated dietary supplement and that dietary supplements are accurately labeled and must comply with food Good Manufacturing Practices [9].

A bill [14] to improve the safety of dietary supplements was introduced by Senator Dick Durbin of Illinois in 2011. This bill will involve amending the Federal Food, Drug, and Cosmetic Act to require manufacturers of dietary supplements to register dietary supplement products with the FDA and to amend labeling requirements with respect to dietary supplements. The legislation directs the FDA to establish a definition for "conventional foods," which would clarify which products are food and should be regulated as such and which products are meant to aid health and should be regulated as dietary supplements [15]. However, critics warn that the supplement bill could be seen as an FDA power grab.

Food and dietary supplement labels in the United States fall into three categories of claims: (1) health claims, (2) nutrient content claims, and (3) structure/function claims. According to the FDA, a "health claim" by definition has two essential components: (1) a substance (whether a food, food component, or dietary ingredient) and (2) a disease or health-related condition. A statement lacking either one of these components does not meet the regulatory definition of a health claim in the United States. The FDA is mandated to regulate health claims on food labels by the Nutrition Labeling and Education Act of 1990. This ACT permits the use of health claims based on scientific evidence and agreement among experts to support the claim [16].

The FDA Modernization Act of 1997 (FDAMA) expanded procedures under which the FDA can authorize health claims and nutrient content claims without reducing the statutory standard [17].

Health claims are authorized in the United States by the FDA only after a systematic review of scientific evidence [18]. However, under FDAMA, a new health claim can be authorized by submitting a notification to FDA of a claim based on an "authoritative statement" from certain scientific bodies of the U.S. Government or the National Academy of Sciences [18]. Health claims are directed to the general population or designated subgroups (eg, elderly persons) and are intended to assist the consumer in maintaining healthful dietary practices. Therefore, only studies conducted in "healthy populations" are considered.

In Europe, Regulation no. 1924/2006 [19], which was approved by the European Parliament and the Council

on December 20, 2006, is used to regulate supplements on nutrition and health claims made on foods. It defines "health claim" as "any claim that states, suggests, or implies that a relationship exists between a food category, a food or one of its constituents and health." To ensure a high level of protection for consumers and to facilitate their choice, the regulations call for products put on the market to be safe and adequately labeled.

Health claims are only authorized in the community following scientific assessment of the highest standard performed by the European Food Safety Authority (EFSA) taking into account the availability of scientific data, and by weight of evidence [19]. Moreover, health claims other than those referring to the reduction of disease risk, based on generally accepted scientific data, undergo a different type of assessment and authorization. The opinion of EFSA should be taken into account in the authorization procedure to ensure that health claims are truthful, clear, reliable, and useful to the consumer [19].

BOTANICAL DRUG PRODUCTS

Until recently, plants were an essential source for the discovery of novel pharmacologically active compounds, with many blockbuster drugs being derived directly or indirectly from plants [4]. The FDA defines a "botanical drug" as any product containing ingredients of vegetable matter or its constituents as a finished product. According to the FDA's CDER Botanical Review Team (BRT), a botanical drug product is intended for use in the diagnosis, cure, mitigation, treatment, or prevention of disease in humans. A botanical drug (1) consists of vegetable materials, which may include plant materials, algae, macroscopic fungi, or combinations thereof; (2) may be available as (but not limited to) a solution (eg, tea), powder, tablet, capsule, elixir, topical, or injection; (and 3) often has unique features, for example, complex mixtures, lack of a distinct active ingredient, and substantial prior human use.

There are some key issues inherent to the botanical products that complicate their development as a drug. Wu et al. [10] highlighted these issues in their manuscript entitled "Regulatory Science: A Special Update from the United States Food and Drug Administration." Preclinical issues and status of investigation of botanical drug products states that botanical products contain potentially multiple active components, but usually the active constituents are not always identified, isolated, or chemically defined and generally lack a well-characterized full spectrum of biological activity. Nevertheless, standardization of botanical therapeutics can only be achieved when the active compounds are identified and biological activity is confirmed, thus ensuring a consistent product [20]. Botanical products derived from the same species may have significant variability in their ingredients that influences their strength/potency and impurities due to variations in geographic locations, harvest time, and part of plants used. It is difficult to quantify the principle active ingredients due to the lack of authoritative reference standards. It is important to keep in mind that chemical standardization is important, but its utility is limited when the starting material is not well characterized. Many botanical products have been prepared for a long time as traditional medicine using preparative methods that are difficult to standardize. In addition, harvesting, processing, and formulating methods may dramatically affect the quality and consistency of the final product by altering the desired marker components or by increasing the possibility of unwanted contaminants [21]. Availabilities of validated methods are necessary tools to ensure quality control in manufacturing and storage of the botanical products for maintaining optimal efficacy and safety of the product. The quality of botanical products is a big challenge for scientists involved in the research on botanical products as the inherent nature of these products is that they are, generally, extracts of plants rather than chemically pure compounds [22]. Also, lack of unified regulatory framework among the western nations is another major issue hindering the marketing of botanical products.

Despite these challenges, approval of the first botanical prescription drug, Veregen (sinecatechins) ointment shows they can be successfully met [23]. A botanical drug's special features require consideration and adjustment during the FDA review process. In June 2004, the FDA's CDER issued Guidance for Industry, Botanical Drug Products Guidance to take into consideration these features and to facilitate development of new therapies from botanical sources [24]. The Botanical Guidance applies to only botanical products intended to be developed and used as drugs. To date, one botanical product [25] that fulfills the Botanical Guidance definition of a botanical drug product has been approved for marketing as a prescription drug in the United States on October 31, 2006, which is made from the extract of green tea leaves for topical use of warts on the outside of the genitals and around the outside of the anus [25]. Botanical drugs are clinically evaluated for safety and efficacy just as regular drugs, but the drug development process (Fig. 30.1) can be expedited because of the history of safe human use [1]. Pharmaceutical and biotech companies or researchers intending to market a botanical drug product are required to follow the IND and NDA regulatory processes described under Section 21 of the U.S. Code of Federal Regulations [11].

In Europe, effort has been made to harmonize medicinal use of herbal substances through draw and delivery of the so-called Traditional Herbal Medicinal Product

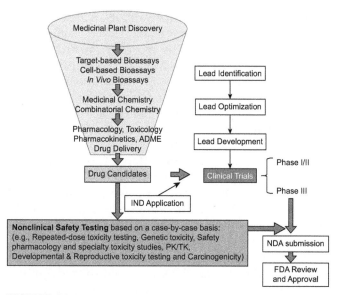

FIGURE 30.1 Botanical drug discovery and development process. *Modified from Balunas MJ, Kinghorn AD. Drug discovery from medicinal plants. Life Sci 2005;78(5):431–41.*

Directive (THMPD) 2004/24/EC, which became effective in April 2011. The objective was to protect public health as well as guaranteeing the free movement of herbal products within the European Union (EU) [26].

Directive 2004/24/EC on traditional herbal medicinal products states that the product may be categorized as a traditional herbal medicinal product provided time-related criteria are met (ie, 30 years of use). Under 2004/24/EC, the Committee for Herbal Medicinal Products within the European Agency for Evaluation, composed of experts in the field of herbal medicinal products, will be responsible in carrying out tasks concerning the simplified registration and authorization of medicinal products. The committee is also tasked to establish community herbal monographs relevant for the registration as well the authorization of medicinal products. The simplified registration is acceptable only where the herbal medicinal product may rely on sufficiently long medicinal use in the community [27].

The community herbal monographs include a scientific opinion of the Committee for Herbal Medicinal Products on safety and efficacy data concerning a herbal substance and information on what are adequate herbal preparations intended for medicinal use. The set of information included in the monograph contains clinical (indication, posology, etc.) and safety (warnings, recommendations, and contraindications) issues.

Herbal medicinal products can be commercialized as medicinal products if they have a "well-established use" based on the existence of sufficient of body of evidence to show clinical efficacy in specific therapeutic indications. On the contrary, botanical products for which proof of clinical efficacy does not exist or is poor or not sufficiently convincing can be registered as traditional medicinal products only if the use in specific therapeutic indications (not requiring medical supervision) is plausible according to their traditional long-standing utilization and if they present an acceptable safety level.

In Australia, products derived from medicinal plants are regulated as drugs under the Therapeutics Goods Act 1989 to ensure their quality, safety, efficacy, and timely availability, and must be manufactured under the same code of Good Manufacturing Practice as other therapeutics [28]. The Therapeutic Goods Administration (TGA) is responsible for executing the relevant provisions, which divide the regulatory process into a two-tiered system based on risks classified as low and higher risk [29].

CHEMISTRY, MANUFACTURING, AND CONTROLS INFORMATION FOR BOTANICAL DRUGS

Botanical drug products have specific issues including, but not limited to, lack of a defined chemical structure, lack of identification of active constituents, lack of well-characterized biological activities, and product preparation made of complex mixtures; therefore the chemistry, manufacturing, and controls (CMC) documentation for botanical drugs will not often include the active ingredients at least during the IND stage. The most significant element of the IND application for botanical products is the CMC information.

According to the FDA guidance document [24], it would not be critical for a sponsor of a botanical drug to identify the active constituents, although the FDA recommends this to be done and provided if feasible in an NDA submission. The sponsor must ensure the botanical drug's identity, purity, quality, strength, potency, and consistency. In this regard, the FDA may rely on a combination of tests and controls to ensure the identity, purity, quality, strength, potency, and constituency of botanical drugs. These tests may include (1) multiple sets for drug substance and drug product (eg, spectroscopic and/or chromatographic fingerprints, chemical assay of characteristic markers, and biological assay); (2) raw material and process controls (eg, strict quality controls for botanical raw materials and adequate in-process controls); and (3) process validation, especially for the drug substance.

QUALITY CONTROL FOR BOTANICAL PRODUCTS

Quality control plays a crucial role in the process of rendering the traditional medicinal plants into modern evidence-based therapies [30]. Purity and quality of botanical products is an essential component of safety. However, development of vigorous quality control metrics

is a great challenge for plant extracts containing tens to hundreds of characteristic phytochemicals [31]. The environment in which the plants are grown can considerably alter phytochemical profiles and the efficacy of the botanical end-product [32]. It is mandatory to standardize the composition of the total extracts and make them free of any potential contaminations. Identification and selection of the correct plant species is the key step in assuring efficacy, quality, and safety of the botanical products. The strict quality control measures for each plant raw material need to be assessed. These may include genus/species identification by genotypic, phenotypic, and chemical tests; growth conditions; processing methods; shipping and storage; and characterization of adulteration from other plant species. In addition, records should be maintained for the source of the plant, locations, conditions of cultivation, and exposure to possible chemical treatments such as pesticides [20].

The World Health Organization (WHO) has developed the Guidelines on Good Agricultural and Collection Practices (GACP). The objectives of these guidelines are to improve the quality, safety, and efficacy of finished herbal products; guide the formulation of national and/or regional GACP guidelines and GACP monographs for medicinal plants and related standard operating procedures; and encourage and support the sustainable cultivation and collection of medicinal plants of good quality [33].

According to the FDA guideline [24], the quality control tests performed on each batch of the drug substance should contain the analytical procedures used and the available test results. The test should minimally include:

1. Appearance.
2. Chemical assay (ie, assay) for active constituents or characteristic markers.
3. Biological assay, if available.
4. Strength by dry weight (equivalent to botanical raw material).
5. Heavy metals.
6. Microbial limits.
7. Animal safety test, if applicable.
8. A description of the container/closure in which the botanical drug substance is to be stored and/or shipped.
9. Stability data on the drug substance.
10. The container label and recommended storage conditions.

Likewise, the FDA guidance document [24] recommends the quality control tests for the Botanical Drug Product to contain:

1. Appearance.
2. Chemical identification by spectroscopic and/or chromatographic fingerprints.

3. Biological assay, if available.
4. Strength by dry weight (of drug substance).
5. Microbial limits.
6. A description of the container/closure in which the drug product is to be packaged.
7. Stability data on the drug product.

Botanical formulations manufactured under standardized manufacturing protocols can yield highly consistent batches of products if rigorous quality controls using analytically sensitive chemoprofiling and comprehensive chemical and biological fingerprinting are employed [20]. Chemoprofiling using high performance liquid chromatography, high performance thin layer chromatography, and gas chromatography have wide applicability in quality control of herbal products [34]. There are also varieties of molecular techniques, including restriction fragment length polymorphism, random amplification of polymorphic DNA, and DNA sequencing, that can be used to authenticate plant material and detect adulterant plant species [35,36]. Other molecular techniques that provide a comprehensive and cost-effective quality control metric of the biological activities of botanical drugs include a genome-wide biological response fingerprinting (BioReF) approach intended to define a set of marker genes that characterize the signature pattern for a specific botanical formulation [30]. Nevertheless, a systematic approach must be taken to cover a wide range of investigations including but not limited to mechanistic studies, potential herb–drug interactions, pharmacokinetics, and bioavailability that will help in the optimization of herbal formulations in the preclinical stage of development before they can be considered for clinical trials [37].

SAFETY PACKAGE FOR INVESTIGATIONAL NEW DRUG (IND) AND NEW DRUG APPLICATION (NDA) OF BOTANICAL DRUGS

The regulatory path to marketing botanical drugs is no more complicated than the path for any other drugs (Fig. 30.2). However, given the wide availability of previous human experiences and nonclinical study data of these products, the FDA guidance document [24] provides a unique approach to reducing requirements for animal toxicology studies prior to the initial Phase I/II studies. Under the FDA guidance document [24], initial clinical trials involve a limited number of patients and shorter duration of treatment. However, to support large Phase III clinical studies and NDA, the botanical drugs will be treated like any other new drug under development.

The requirements of the safety package to support the initial Phase I/II clinical studies are mainly based on the safety concerns, legal availability in the United States,

and the preparation methods of the botanical products. It is essential that sponsors compile all available information and discuss it, along with the design of the proposed preclinical and clinical trials, with the appropriate division of the FDA in a pre-IND meeting. In this meeting, the sponsor should also request that representatives of the BRT attend the meeting [38]. Information to be provided in an IND for a botanical drug [24] is provided in Fig. 30.3.

BOTANICAL PRODUCTS WITHOUT SAFETY CONCERNS

Further nonclinical safety testing will not be necessary for all botanical products with no safety concern that have been marketed in the United States as dietary supplements and are prepared according to a traditional methodology. The following information should be sufficient to support the initial clinical trials (Phase I/II) [24]:

1. Provide data including previous human experience and available animal toxicity data regarding the clinical formulation and the individual botanical ingredients within the formulation of the botanical drug for the proposed use.
2. A database search should be conducted, if available, to identify information relevant to the safety and effectiveness of the following:
   a. The final formulation of the intended commercial botanical drug product, the individual botanical ingredients, and the known chemical constituents of the botanical ingredients.
3. An integrated summary of available data from human and toxicological databases (eg, Medline, Toxline, and other databases) must be submitted for review. The sponsor should address, as appropriate for the proposed study, the following safety information concerning the botanical drug product using the information gathered from the literature:
   a. General toxicity and mutagenic, carcinogenic, or teratogenic potential of any botanical ingredient in the product and relationship of dosage and duration to toxic responses.

Additional information should be provided to assist the FDA in determining the safety of the product for use in initial Phase I/II clinical studies for a botanical product that is not lawfully marketed in the United States, regardless of whether it has been previously marketed in other countries and used in humans according to methodologies without safety concerns. The information should include (1) data supporting safe human use, (2) the annual sales volume, (3) an estimate of the size of the exposure population, and (4) available data on the degree of adverse effects [24]. Once the information is provided, the FDA will then determine on a case-by-case basis the

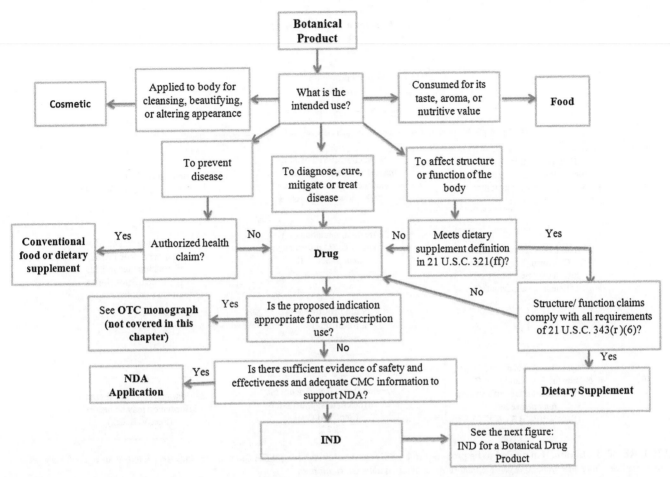

FIGURE 30.2 Regulatory approaches for marketing botanical drug products. *FDA Guidance for Industry. Botanical drug products guidance. 2004. Available from: http://www.fda.gov/RegulatoryInformation/Guidances/default.htm.*

nature of nonclinical toxicology study or studies needed to support the initial clinical studies based on the indications; proposed dose, duration, and length of the study; and available data supporting safe human experience.

For a botanical drug product that is not prepared according to a traditional methodology, a full detailed description of the extent of variation from the traditional formulation, preparation, or processing should be provided. The FDA will then determine the requirement of nonclinical package on a case-by-case basis, depending on the indications, extent of safe human experience, and safety concerns about the new formulation, preparation, or processing methodology used [24].

to help establish safe doses and monitoring potential toxicities in humans [24]. All the nonclinical toxicity studies should be conducted according to 21 CFR 312.23(a) (8) [39]. The FDA encourages sponsors to seek input from CDER review divisions to ensure that appropriate information is submitted and the clinical plan is well designed and presented. According to the FDA guidance document [24], the FDA can place an IND for initial studies on hold if it finds that the IND application does not contain sufficient information required. The sponsors are advised to consult with CDER's guidance for industry on the content and format of IND applications for Phase 1 studies of drugs including well-characterized, biotechnology-derived products [40] for possible grounds of a clinical hold.

BOTANICAL DRUGS WITH SAFETY CONCERNS

A botanical drug is considered to have safety concerns when there is evidence that it causes serious and/or possible life-threatening adverse effects. Nonclinical safety evaluation to characterize the toxicities may be appropriate

SAFETY PACKAGE TO SUPPORT PHASE III CLINICAL STUDIES AND NDA OF BOTANICAL DRUGS

A botanical drug product submitted for marketing approval as a drug will be treated like any other new

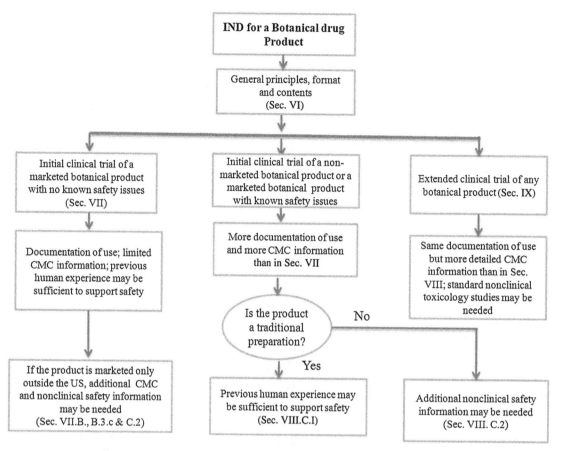

FIGURE 30.3 Information needed to be provided in an IND for a botanical drug. *FDA Guidance for Industry. Botanical drug products guidance. 2004. Available from: http://www.fda.gov/RegulatoryInformation/Guidances/default.htm.*

chemical entity (NCE) under development. The regulatory approaches for marketing botanical drug products are provided in Figure [24].

The nonclinical pharmacology and toxicology studies generally would be needed before later phases of clinical development and approval for marketing a botanical drug [24]. For botanical drugs indicated for chronic therapy, previous human experience may be insufficient to demonstrate the safety of a botanical drug product. However, safety data from previous clinical trials conducted in foreign countries will be considered in determining the need for nonclinical safety studies. In addition to the systematic toxicological evaluations from standard toxicology studies in animals, available knowledge on the general toxicity, teratogenicity, mutagenicity, and carcinogenicity potential of the final botanical drug product should be supplemented to support safety for expanded clinical studies or to support marketing approval of a botanical drug product. Depending on the availability and quality of the existing data, the chronic animal toxicity studies may be waived if previous human experience or animal toxicity studies could support a longer term clinical trial. This is because botanical drugs have been used historically or are readily available in the

current dietary supplement market; therefore "previous human experience" as defined under federal regulations is designed to play an important role in providing equivalent safety evidence in support of initial Phase I/II clinical trials, in addition to existing animal data for nonclinical support [41].

The safety data will be evaluated on a case-by-case basis, with complete or bridging studies requested.

GENERAL TOXICITY STUDIES

Acute toxicology studies: As stated earlier, many botanical drug products should have sufficient previous human experience and are often granted a waiver for toxicology studies before an initial clinical trial. Therefore, a single-dose acute toxicity study is not necessary for botanical drugs being developed under IND.

Repeat-dose toxicity studies: Similar to NCE, repeat-dose toxicity studies of a botanical drug should usually be evaluated in two mammalian species (a rodent and a nonrodent) using sufficiently high doses to produce a toxic effect or by using a maximum feasible dose. The drug should be tested using the same route of administration as proposed for clinical use if possible. The durations of the repeat-dose toxicity studies should depend on the indication and the length of the proposed clinical trial and should be at least equal to that of the clinical trial (usually a minimum of 2 weeks) in accordance with the ICH Guidance M3 (R2) Nonclinical Safety Studies for the Conduct of Human Clinical Trials for Pharmaceuticals [42]. The duration of the repeated-dose toxicities study should not exceed 6 months in rodents and 9 months in nonrodent species. In the nonclinical safety study, the same drug substance should be used as in clinical trials [24].

GENETIC TOXICITY

Genetic toxicity testing on botanical drugs is required by law. However, it must also be noted that contingent on previous human experience, in the United States, botanical new drugs are entitled to a waiver for preclinical pharmacology/toxicology studies, including genotoxicity testing, in support of an initial clinical trial under IND.

A standard of battery of genotoxicity tests should be completed to assess genotoxic potential and fulfill final NDA requirements when an herbal IND advances to Phase III clinical trials [41]. The standard battery for genotoxicity consist of (1) a test for gene mutation in bacteria, (2) an in vitro test with cytogenetic evaluation of chromosomal damage with mammalian cells or an in vitro mouse lymphoma TK assay, and (3) an in vivo test for chromosomal damage using rodent hematopoietic cells.

If one of the three tests shows positive findings, alternative assays may be requested to determine whether those herbals intended for non-life-threatening conditions should be allowed to be studied in Phase III clinical trials. Healthy volunteers may be tested in an initial Phase I/II clinical trial on the botanical drug. As the FDA's objective is to avoid exposing patients to genotoxic compounds unnecessarily in clinical trials, it has conducted a survey on genotoxicity data in botanical INDs submitted to CDER [41] with the intention of evaluating, under the current regulatory environment, the status and trend of botanical IND submissions that provide genotoxicity information during clinical development. The survey covered INDs of botanical drug across all therapeutic categories in the period from 2001 to 2008. The results of this survey demonstrated that there is a significant awareness of the impact of genotoxicity in the overall safety evaluation of the botanical drug products. The authors concluded that sponsors of botanical drug INDs may have increasingly recognized the importance of genotoxicity information and have prioritized the inclusion of genotoxicity testing in their strategic drug development programs. Considering that genotoxicity studies are comparably cost-effective and highly

reproducible, it is highly recommended that information on the potential of a botanical drug to produce genetic toxicity be obtained as early as possible, preferably before the initiation of human clinical trials.

PHARMACOKINETICS AND TOXICOKINETICS

In the botanical guidance document, the preclinical requirements of pharmacokinetics or toxicokinetics have not been extensively addressed. Botanical products often consist of more than one chemical constituent and the active constituents are often unknown; therefore, standard pharmacokinetic measurements to demonstrate systemic exposure to a product in animals and/or humans may be difficult to obtain. However, when feasible, sponsors are encouraged to monitor the blood levels of known active constituents, representative markers, or major chemical constituents in a botanical drug product [24,41]. The monitoring of these representative markers or/and chemical constituents in a botanical drug can provide valuable information regarding systemic exposure. The general principle of the study designs and performance should follow ICH S3A, "Toxicokinetics: The Assessment of Systemic Exposure in Toxicity Studies" [43] and ICH S3B, "Pharmacokinetics: Guidance for Repeated Dose Tissue Distribution Studies" [44]. It is important to note that a better understanding of the pharmacokinetics and bioavailability of botanical drugs can aid in dose selections and interpretation of safety data.

SAFETY PHARMACOLOGY STUDIES AND SPECIAL TOXICITY STUDIES

Safety pharmacology studies described in ICH S7A and/or S7B should be performed to support expanded clinical studies or to support marketing approval of a botanical drug product [45,46]. The core battery of safety pharmacology studies includes the assessment of effects on cardiovascular, central nervous, and respiratory systems, and should generally be conducted before expanded Phase III clinical studies. When warranted, supplemental and follow-up safety pharmacology studies can be conducted during later clinical development.

If unique toxicities to certain organs and/or systems are evident or in some of the special indications, the in vitro or/and in vivo special toxicity studies should be conducted to provide the further explanation of the mechanism of toxic actions and address the special safety concerns [24]. Refer to Chapter 7 for further details for the study designs and conduct.

DEVELOPMENTAL AND REPRODUCTIVE TOXICITY STUDIES

Developmental and reproductive toxicity (DART) studies are needed to support clinical trials and the filing of an NDA of botanical drug products to provide information on the potential toxicity during the different stages of reproductive and developmental processes. In general, the assessment procedures for developmental and reproductive toxicology should follow those described in the ICH Guidance M3 (R2) [42] and ICH S5 (R2) [47], including assessment of potential safety concerns of fertility or early embryonic development to implantation, teratology in both a rodent species and a mammalian nonrodent species, and effects on pre- and postnatal development as well as maternal function. However, the requirements of these studies may be modified depending on the indication and patient population exposed to the botanical drug products. Refer to the DART Chapter 9 for further details for the study designs and conduct.

CARCINOGENICITY STUDIES

Carcinogenicity studies may be needed to support marketing approval for some botanical drug products. This depends on the chronic use of the drug or botanical drugs with specific cause for concern. However, the need and the timing relative to clinical development of conducting carcinogenicity studies can be impacted by the toxicity profile of the botanical drug, indications, and durations of the intended use in humans. Carcinogenicity information is generally not needed for NDA filing if the duration of treatment is short (eg, <2 weeks in certain antibiotic therapies). For any botanical drug product intended for intermittent subchronic or chronic use (>3 months or 6 months), two carcinogenicity studies should be performed. But under certain circumstances, the second study may be waived on a case-by-case basis. Draft protocols for carcinogenicity studies should be submitted to the appropriate review division and the CDER Carcinogenicity Assessment Committee for review and concurrence prior to the initiation of such studies to ensure the acceptability of dose selection and study design [24]. Carcinogenicity studies should be assessed based on the ICH guidance S1B, "Testing for Carcinogenicity of Pharmaceuticals" [48]. Refer to Chapter 12 for further details for the study designs and conduct.

CONCLUDING REMARKS

In the United States, herbal products are regulated both at the state and federal level, with distinct pathways depending upon intended use. The regulation of herbal products depends on whether they are considered as a drug or dietary supplement. The DSHEA allows marketing of dietary supplements such as botanicals without any submission to the FDA, but making the manufacturer responsible for ensuring the safety of the products and placing the burden of proof on the FDA for enforcement. In contrast, the regulatory pathway to marketing botanical drugs is no more complicated than the path for any other drugs. Due to wide availability of previous human experiences and nonclinical study data of products, the FDA guidance document [24] emphasizes that botanical new drugs are entitled to a waiver for preclinical pharmacology/toxicology studies in support of an initial clinical trial under IND. Consequently, the FDA will determine the requirement of a nonclinical package on a case-by-case basis, depending on the indications, extent of safe human experience, and safety concerns. However, to support large Phase III clinical studies and NDAs, the botanical drugs will be treated like any other new drug under development.

Acknowledgment

We would like to thank Ms. Lisa Heimsath for her technical assistance.

References

[1] Schmidt B, Ribnicky DM, Poulev A, Logendra S, Cefalu WT, Raskin I. A natural history of botanical therapeutics. Metabolism 2008;57(Suppl. 1):S3–9.

[2] Raskin I, Ribnicky DM, Komarnytsky S, Ilic N, Poulev A, Borisjuk N, et al. Plants and human health in the twenty-first century. Trends Biotechnol 2012;20(12):522–31.

[3] Balunas MJ, Kinghorn AD. Drug discovery from medicinal plants. Life Sci 2005;78(5):431–41.

[4] Newman DJ, Cragg GM, Snader KM. The influence of natural products upon drug discovery. Nat Prod Rep 2000;17:215–34.

[5] Gardiner P, Graham R, Legedza AT, Ahn AC, Eisenberg DM, Phillips RS. Factors associated with herbal therapy use by adults in the United States. Altern Ther Health Med 2007;13(2):22–9.

[6] Hathcock J. Dietary supplements: how they are used and regulated. J Nutr 2001;131:1114S–7S.

[7] Liu Y, Wang M-W. Botanical drugs: challenges and opportunities: contribution to Linnaeus Memorial Symposium 2007. Life Sci 2007;82:445–9.

[8] www.cfsan.fda.gov/~dms/lab-qhc.html.

[9] Rapaka RS, Coates PM. Dietary supplements and related products: a brief summary. Life Sci March 27, 2006;78(18):2026–32.

[10] Wu K-M, DeGeorge JG, Atrakchi A, Barry E, Bigger A, Chen C, et al. Regulatory science: a special update from the United States Food and Drug Administration, preclinical issues and status of investigation of botanical drug products in the United States. Toxicol Lett 2000;111:199–202.

[11] Frankos VH, Street DA, O'Neill RK. FDA regulation of dietary supplements and requirements regarding adverse event reporting. Clin Pharmacol Ther 2010;87(2):239–44.

[12] Morrow JD. Why the United States still needs improved dietary supplement regulation and oversight. Clin Pharmacol Ther 2008;83(3):391–3.

[13] Nowak RE. DSHEA'S failure: why a proactive approach to dietary supplement regulation is needed to effectively protect consumers. University of Illinois law review, vol. 2010. 2010. 1045.

[14] http://www.govtrack.us/congress/bill.xpd?bill=s112-1310.

[15] http://www.packagingdigest.com/article/518677-Durbin_introduces_Dietary_Supplement_Labeling_Act_to_protect_consumers.php.

[16] Nutrition Labeling and Education Act. 1990. Pub L 101–535, US Code title 104, section 2353.

[17] US Food and Drug Administration. FDA Modernization Act of 1997 (FDAMA) claims, http://www.fda.gov/food/labeling nutrition/labelclaims/fdamodernizationactfdamaclaims/default.htm.

[18] US Food and Drug Administration. Qualified health claims, http://www.fda.gov/food/labelingnutrition/labelclaims/qualifiedhealthclaims/.

[19] Regulation (EC) No 1924/2006 of the European Parliament and of the Council of 20 December 2006 on nutrition and health claims made on foods. Off J Eur Union 2006;L404:9–25.

[20] Ribnicky DM, Poulev A, Schmidt B, Cefalu WT, Raskin I. Evaluation of botanicals for improving human health. Am J Clin Nutr 2008;87(2):472S–5S.

[21] Khan IA. Issues related to botanicals. Life Sci March 27, 2006; 78(18):2033–8.

[22] Coates PM, Meyers CM. The National Institutes of Health investment in research on botanicals. Fitoterapia 2011;82(1):11–3.

[23] Chen ST, Dou J, Temple R, Agarwal R, Wu K-M, Walker S. New therapies from old medicines (commentary). Nat Biotechnol 2008;26:1077–83.

[24] FDA Guidance for Industry. Botanical drug products guidance. 2004. Available from: http://www.fda.gov/RegulatoryInformation/Guidances/default.htm.

[25] Veregen® Ointment NDA No: 021–902 Approval Date: 10/31/2006. Available at: http://www.fda.gov/cder/foi/nda/2006/021902s000TOC.html.

[26] Miroddi M, Mannucci C, Mancari F, Navarra M, Calapai G. Research and development for botanical products in medicinals and food supplements market. Evidence-Based Complementary Altern Med 2013;2013(2013). Article ID 649720, 6 pages.

[27] Directive 2004/24/EEC of the European parliament and of the council of 31 March 2004 amending, as regards traditional herbal medicinal products, directive 2001/83/EC on community code relating to medicinal products for human use. Off J Eur Communities 2004;L136:85–90.

[28] Australian Government Department of Health and Ageing. Therapeutic goods administration J. The regulation of complementary medicines in Australia: an overview, Symonston, Australia. 2006.

[29] Bensoussan A, Lewith GT. Complementary medicine research in Australia: a strategy for the future. Med J Aust 2004;181:331–3.

[30] Rong J, Tilton R, Shen J, Ng KM, Liu C, Tam PK, et al. Genome-wide biological response fingerprinting (BioReF) of the Chinese botanical formulation ISF-1 enables the selection of multiple marker genes as a potential metric for quality control. J Ethnopharmacol August 15, 2007;113(1):35–44.

[31] van Breemen RB, Fong H, Farnsworth NR. The role of quality assurance and standardization in the safety of botanical dietary supplements. Chem Res Toxicol 2007;20(4):577–82.

[32] Poulev A, O'Neal JM, Logendra S, et al. Elicitation, a new window into plant chemodiversity and phytochemical drug discovery. J Med Chem 2003;46:2542–7.

[33] WHO. WHO guidelines on good agricultural and collection practices (GACP) for medicinal plants. Geneva: World Health Organization; 2003. p. 1–72.

[34] Warude D, Patwardhan B. Botanicals: quality and regulatory issues. J Sci Ind Res 2005;64:83–92.

[35] He K, Pauli GF, Zheng B, Wang H, Bai N, Peng T, et al. *Cimicifuga* species identification by a high performance liquid chromatography-photodiode array/mass spectrometric/evaporative light scattering detection for quality control of black cohosh products. J Chromatogr A 2006;1112(1–2):241–54.

[36] Mattoli L, Cangi F, Maidecchi A, Ghiara C, Ragazzi E, Tubaro M, et al. Metabolomic fingerprinting of plant extracts. J Mass Spectrom 2006;41(12):1534–45.

[37] Poojari RJ, Patil AG, Gota VS. Development of botanical principles for clinical use in cancer: where are we lacking? J Postgrad Med 2012;58(1):63–7.

[38] Kumar M, Jethwani H. Developing traditional Chinese medicines as botanical drugs for the US market. 2009. http://www.amarexcro.com/articles/docs/RAPS_Focus_ChineseMeds_BotDrugs_Aug2009.pdf.

[39] FDA 21 CFR 312. Investigational new drug application. 1987. Available from: http://www.accessdata.fda.gov/scripts/cdrh/cfdocs/cfCFR/CFRSearch.cfm?fr=312.23.

[40] ICH. Harmonized tripartite guideline. Male fertility studies in reproductive toxicology. In: D'Arcy PF, Harron DWG, editors. Proceedings of the Third International Conference on Harmonization. 1995. p. 245–52. IFPMA, 1996, Greystone Books, Ltd. Antrim, N. Ireland.

[41] Wu KM, Dou J, Ghantous H, Chen S, Bigger A, Birnkrant D. Current regulatory perspectives on genotoxicity testing for botanical drug product development in the U.S.A. Regul Toxicol Pharmacol 2010;56:1–3.

[42] ICH M3 (R2). Nonclinical safety studies for the conduct of human clinical trials for pharmaceuticals. 2009. Available at: http://www.ich.org/products/guidelines/safety/article/safety-guidelines.html.

[43] ICH S3A Guidance Document. Note for guidance on toxicokinetics: the assessment of systemic exposure in toxicity studies. 1994. Available at: http://www.ich.org/products/guidelines/safety/article/safety-guidelines.html.

[44] ICH S3B Guidance Document. Pharmacokinetics: repeated dose tissue distribution studies. 1994. Available at: http://www.ich.org/products/guidelines/safety/article/safety-guidelines.html.

[45] ICH S7A Guidance Document. Safety pharmacology studies for human pharmaceuticals. 2000. Available at: http://www.ich.org/products/guidelines/safety/article/safety-guidelines.html.

[46] ICH S5B (R2) Guidance Document. Detection of toxicity to reproduction for medicinal products: addendum on toxicity to male fertility. 2005. Available at: http://www.ich.org/products/guidelines/safety/article/safety-guidelines.html.

[47] Guidance Document ICH. S7B. The non-clinical evaluation of the potential for delayed ventricular repolarization (QT interval prolongation) by human pharmaceuticals. 2005. Available at: http://www.ich.org/products/guidelines/safety/article/safety-guidelines.html.

[48] Guidance Document ICH. S1B Testing for carcinogenicity of pharmaceuticals. 1997. Available at: http://www.ich.org/products/guidelines/safety/article/safety-guidelines.html.

31

Biocompatibility Evaluation of Medical Devices

N.S. Goud

INTRODUCTION

What are medical devices? According to section 201(h) of the Federal Food Drug & Cosmetic (FD&C) Act, "medical devices are defined as an instrument, apparatus, implement, machine, contrivance, implant, in vitro reagent, or other similar or related article, including a component part, or accessory, that is:

- Recognized in the official National Formulary, or the US Pharmacopoeia, or any supplement to them;
- Intended for use in the diagnosis of disease or other conditions, or in the cure, mitigation, treatment, or prevention of disease, in man or other animals, or;
- Intended to affect the structure or any function of the body of man or other animals, and which does not achieve any of its primary intended purposes through chemical action within or on the body of man or other animals and which is not dependent upon being metabolized for the achievement of any of its primary intended purposes."

There is a clear distinction between drugs and medical devices. It is well known that drugs achieve their intended use through chemical action or by being metabolized in the body. In contrast, medical devices are not

supposed to degrade. However, with the advent of combination products (medical devices containing drugs or bioabsorbable materials), the classic definition of medical device is getting blurred and a revised definition is required. Medical devices, similar to drugs, are also subject to pre- and postmarketing regulatory controls by the FDA and other regulatory bodies.

Benefits: Medical devices provide immense clinical benefit to patients. They improve quality of life by relieving the pain and suffering associated with various clinical conditions such as helping patients who have difficulty passing urine (urology catheters), patients with irregular heart beat (implantable pacemakers), seriously ill and geriatric patients who cannot eat (percutaneous endoscopic gastrostomy (PEG) feeding tubes), etc.

Examples of Medical Devices: Medical devices are currently available for almost every organ in the body. Some common examples are:

- Catheters (vascular and urology)
- Brain Implants (for epilepsy and Parkinson's disease)
- Contact lenses
- Condoms and other contraceptives
- Dental devices (plastic/metal-based dentures, dental cement, and filling material resins)

A Comprehensive Guide to Toxicology in Nonclinical Drug Development, Second Edition
http://dx.doi.org/10.1016/B978-0-12-803620-4.00031-1

- Diabetes test strips
- Hemodialysis membranes
- Hearing aids and cochlear implants
- Neurovascular coils
- Orthopedic implants (hip and knee replacement devices)

Classification of Medical Devices: The FDA classifies medical devices into three broad categories based on the intended clinical use as well as the controls needed to provide reasonable assurance of safety and effectiveness. These classes also correspond to the potential risk to patient, with class I devices being low-risk and class III devices with highest risk potential.

Class I: Dental floss and adhesive bandages to cover wounds.

Class II: Urology drainage catheters and intravenous infusion catheters.

Class III: Heart stents, Hip implants, and Neurovascular coils.

Combination Products: In recent years there has been a surge of new combination products consisting of devices combined with drugs, pharmaceutical agents, or biologics. Two such examples in this category are as follows:

Orthopedic Implants: Devices are first coated with collagen matrix-containing bioactive materials such as antibiotics, drugs, growth factors, or a combination thereof. These bioactive compounds are intended to provide an infection-free implant site or to help augment integration of the implant into the patient's body.

Cardiovascular Stents: Drug-eluting stents fall under the combination products category. The device is usually a metallic stent coated with or without a polymer matrix containing a drug. The most common drugs in this device family are Paclitaxel and Everolimus/Sirolimus. Patients implanted with bare-metal stents usually develop scar tissue at the implantation site in the artery. Drug-coated stents inhibit cell growth, thus preventing scar-tissue formation or restenosis.

When do medical devices have to be tested? Biocompatibility testing of a medical device is required or at least evaluated when:

- A new device is developed
- There is a manufacturing process change
- A new material is introduced to the existing device
- There is a change of the vendor/material supplier
- A change in the sterilization method or cycle occurs
- The presence of a foreign material or unknown chemical is used in the device
- There is a change in the shape or geometry of the existing device
- A new clinical intended use of an existing device is determined

- A change (or revision) of an existing biocompatibility standard, update of EU technical file, or design dossier occurs
- There is a change in the shelf-life or shipping/storage condition
- A report of an adverse event in patient—postmarket surveillance is noted
- There is a change in the inner packaging material
- Anomalies during production or manufacturing floor occur

EVALUATION OF THE BIOLOGICAL EFFECTS OF MEDICAL DEVICES

In today's global economy, medical devices are often assembled/manufactured in one country but marketed in other countries. Similarly the raw materials used are sourced across many continents. Therefore in order to have consistency in evaluating the toxicity and biocompatibility of medical devices, a set of established test procedures with well-defined pass/fail criteria are essential. These methods are described in a series of ISO (International Standards Organization) 10993 standards (Parts 1–23) on Biological Evaluation of Medical Devices (Table 31.1). This and other excellent resources provide detailed descriptions of biocompatibility test methods and can be obtained from the respective organizations as follows:

- ANSI/AAMI/. ISO 10993–1: 2009/(R) – Biological Evaluation of Medical Devices – Part 1: Evaluation and Testing within a Risk Management Process 2013 (http://webstore.ansi.org/)
- ASTM Test Methods for Medical Devices (http://www.astm.org/Standards/medical-device-and-implant-standards.html)
- US Pharmacopeia – Biocompatibility of Medical Devices (http://www.usp.org/usp-nf)
- FDA Guidance: Use of International Standard ISO 10993-1, "Biological evaluation of medical devices – Part 1: Evaluation and testing within a risk management process." Guidance for Industry and Food and Drug Administration Staff. Document issued on: June 16, 2016. http://www.fda.gov/downloads/medicaldevices/deviceregulationandguidance/guidancedocuments/ucm348890.pdf.
- Japanese Regulations for Evaluating the Biological Safety of Medical Devices 2012 (http://www.pmda.go.jp/english/)

Regulatory Approvals: In the United States, medical devices need FDA approval before being used in patients. These approvals generally fall under three broad categories: IDE (Investigational Device

TABLE 31.1 ISO 10993 Standards – Biocompatibility

ISO 10993	Standards Biological Evaluation of Medical Devices
ISO 10993-1	Evaluation and testing within a risk management process
ISO 10993-2	Animal welfare requirements
ISO 10993-3	Tests for genotoxicity, carcinogenicity end reproductive toxicity
ISO 10993-4	Selection of tests for interactions with blood
ISO 10993-5	Tests for in vitro cytotoxicity
ISO 10993-6	Tests for local effects after implantation
ISO 10993-7	Ethylene oxide sterilization residuals
ISO 10993-9	Identification and quantification of potential degradation products
ISO 10993-10	Tests for irritation and skin sensitization
ISO 10993-11	Tests for systemic toxicity
ISO 10993-12	Sample preparation and reference materials
ISO 10993-13	Identification of degradation products from polymeric medical devices
ISO 10993-14	Identification and quantification of degradation products from ceramics
ISO 10993-15	Identification and quantification of degradation products from metals
ISO 10993-16	Toxicokinetics of degradation products
ISO 10993-17	Establishment of allowable limits for leachable substances
ISO 10993-18	Chemical characterization of materials
ISO 10993-19 (TS)	Physico-chemical and morphological characterization of materials
ISO 10993-20 (TS)	Immunotoxicology testing of medical devices
ISO 10993-22 (TR)	Guidance on nanomaterials
ISO 10993-33 (TR)	Guidance on genotoxicity tests http://www.iso.org, http://www.aami.org/

Exemption), PMA (Pre-Market Approval), or 510 (k). For marketing products in the European Union, there are many private agencies, called notified bodies which are listed on the European Commission's website (http://ec.europa.eu/growth/tools-databases/nando/index.cfm?fuseaction=directive.notifiedbody&dir_id=13). For regulatory approval by the US FDA, the biocompatibility testing has to be conducted under GLP (good laboratory practice) conditions. The notified bodies in Europe accept testing conducted at laboratories accredited by ISO 17025 (General Requirements for the Competence of Testing and Calibration Laboratories; https://www.iso.org/obp/ui/#iso:std:iso-iec:17025:ed-2:v1:en).

Biocompatibility Testing—Dosing/Extraction of the Test Article: Traditionally, when patients are treated with pharmaceuticals and drugs, these products are absorbed, metabolized, and distributed in the body. In contrast, medical devices are generally intended not to degrade. Devices provide comfort to patients and perform the

intended function without losing their structural integrity (with the exception of bioabsorbable materials). But how can we assess patient risk and toxicity of potential leachables from device materials? This can be achieved by:

1. Direct exposure/implant of the device into in vitro or in vivo test systems
2. Collecting an extract of the device and applying that extract to cells in the in vitro condition or injecting into animals in the in vivo condition

Extraction Ratios: Since medical devices come in various shapes and forms, the extraction conditions need to be uniformly applicable to all devices irrespective of whether testing is conducted in a North American or European or Asian lab. Extraction ratios are inversely proportional to the thickness of the device material. Care should be taken to ensure the test samples used for dosing/extraction are representative of

TABLE 31.2   Guidelines on Test-Article Extraction

	Device thickness	Extraction ratio (surface area/volume)	Catheter, tubing, sheet, or any molded item
	<0.5 mm	6 cm²/mL	
	0.5–1.0 mm	3 cm²/mL	
	>1.0	1.25 cm²/mL	
		Extraction ratio (mass/volume)	Irregularly shaped solid devices (foam, pellets, powder)
		0.2 g/mL	
		Extraction ratio (mass/volume)	Porous membranes (low-density material)
		0.1 g/mL	

Adapted from ISO 10993-12.

the patient-contacting portion of the device. Table 31.2 provides a summary of extraction regimens for different types of medical devices. Generally extraction ratios based on surface area/volume are preferred for evaluating the biocompatibility, but if the surface area of a device is not available, then weight can be used.

Extraction Solvents: Test-article extractions are carried out using various polar and nonpolar solvents:

- Polar solvents: water, saline, or cell-culture media without serum
- Nonpolar solvents: cotton-seed oil (CSO), sesame oil, or dimethyl sulfoxide (DMSO)
- Additional extraction solvents: mixtures of ethanol/water, ethanol/saline, or cell-culture media with serum

For the in vivo studies, the polar extracts are generally injected intravenously (IV) and nonpolar solutions are injected intraperitoneally (IP) or subcutaneously (SC). For in vitro studies, any polar solutions described above can be used. DMSO is used under the nonpolar category.

Extraction Temperature: After selecting the appropriate dimensions of the test article, samples of the device are cut, placed in the appropriate solvent, and extracted at various temperatures and time points as described below.

- 37°C for 72 h
- 50°C for 72 h
- 70°C for 24 h
- 121°C for 1 h

It is recommended that the solvents and glassware used in sample preparation/extraction are sterilized appropriately. The choice of temperature and the type of solvent have to be justified for the specific device material. Investigators may wish to discuss extraction methods with relevant regulatory agencies before initiating biocompatibility testing.

For biocompatibility testing, devices have to be fully packaged and sterilized similar to commercially marketed products. In some cases, devices such as colonic implants are sold as nonsterile. However, those devices still have to be treated with an appropriate sterilizing agent to prevent failure of the biocompatibility assays due to any residual microbial contamination.

Sterilization of Test Article: Medical devices may be sterilized with E-beam, gamma radiation, ethylene oxide (EO) gas, dry heat, or steam before being sold for use in patients. A small proportion of devices containing animal tissues and biologics are sterilized chemically using hydrogen peroxide, glutaraldehyde or chlorine dioxide etc. By far the great majority of medical devices are sterilized with EO.

Biocompatibility testing is done on devices treated with the same sterilizing agent/same cycle as the commercially marketed product. If the sterilizing agent used on a particular device is EO, then the residuals should be monitored on the device surface. Ethylene oxide is a flammable gas with a sweetish odor that dissolves easily in water and most organic solvents. It is considered to be toxic due to its nature as an alkylating agent. Ethylene oxide at high doses is known to be genotoxic [1,2], found to induce irritation [3], and can

TABLE 31.3 Allowable Limits for EO Residues on Medical Devices

Device Category	EO Residue
Limited contact duration (<24 h)	4 mg
Prolonged contact duration (24 h–30 d)	60 mg/30 d
Permanent contact duration (>30 d)	2.5 g/lifetime
Tolerable contact limits (TCL)	10 μg/cm²
Intraocular lens	0.5 μg/lens/d
Blood cell separator (apheresis)	10 mg
Cardiopulmonary bypass devices	20 mg
Blood purification devices (hemodialysers)	4.6 mg

Adapted from ISO 10993-7.

also affect the reproductive system [4]. Therefore the sterilization method for each device has to be validated to ensure the levels of EO residuals on the device are within the allowable limits described in Table 31.3.

Biocompatibility Test Methods: The biocompatibility evaluation of a device depends primarily on the following factors:

- Patient contacting duration
- Type of tissue contact
- Chemical nature of device materials
- Potential toxicity of materials and its leachable profile
- Availability of preexisting data on the device materials

The most commonly used test systems in biocompatibility evaluation are described in Table 31.4, which can be used to develop a test strategy. The nature and type of tests to be conducted may vary depending on the specific recommendations of the regulatory body of the country in which the device is going to be marketed. If a medical device includes an implant and delivery catheter it is always recommended to test these components separately as they have different chemical compositions and to avoid potentially diluting the chemical composition of test extracts.

CYTOTOXICITY

Cytotoxicity is the first biocompatibility assay to be performed before initiating the detailed in vivo testing in laboratory animals. To minimize unnecessary use of test animals ISO 10993-2 recommends testing of medical-device materials in vitro before commencing testing in animals. This in vitro assay is easy to perform and results can be obtained within 2–3 days. The most widely used cell lines in this assay are L929, 3T3, or V79. There are a number of in vitro cytotoxicity methods available for testing of medical devices (ISO 10993-5) as described in Table 31.5.

Why should we test a device for cytotoxicity? History provides a valuable lesson for ignoring biocompatibility testing and in particular in vitro cytotoxicity. This example dates back to when there were no formal regulations for testing a device for its biological effects. In the early 1980s a group of male patients who underwent open-heart surgery developed urethral strictures (scar tissue around urethra, blocking the flow of urine). Further investigations revealed that all these patients were implanted with urology catheters made of latex. Later, latex was found to be cytotoxic on uroepithelial cells [5].

Which type of cytotoxicity assay is appropriate for my device? The answer to this question depends on the clinical intended use of the device. For example, surface-contacting devices can be tested using "direct contact cytotoxicity" or "agar diffusion (also known as agar overlay) assay." For implantable devices in tissue, bone, or blood, the biological hazard of potentially toxic leachables can be assessed by the addition of test extracts to cell cultures for MEM Elution, CFU, NRU, or MTT assays.

MEM Elution Cytotoxicity Assay: In this assay, extraction of the device is usually carried out in tissue-culture media with serum at 37±1°C for 24±2 h. These extraction conditions are appropriate for this assay, as longer time periods or higher temperatures may affect the stability and chemical composition of MEM media. However, devices can also be extracted in saline or DMSO and then diluted in culture media with serum.

Cell cultures are incubated with test-article extracts at 37°C in a humidified CO_2 incubator for 2 days. The negative control can be high-density polyethylene (HDPE), and positive controls can be cadmium chloride, PVC (polyvinyl chloride) stabilized Organo-tin (PVC-Sn). Triplicate cultures are preferred in each group. At the end of 24 and 48 h, cytotoxicity is recorded based on the morphology of cells and area of growth inhibition. If 70% or more of the cell layers contain rounded (instead of the normal spindle shaped) or lysed cells, then the assay is classified as "fail."

TABLE 31.4 Biocompatibility Test Matrix

| Device Categories | | Biological Effects | | | | | | | | | | |
Body Contact	Contact Duration	Cytotoxicity	Irritation	Sensitization	Acute Systemic Toxicity	Subchronic Toxicity	Genotoxicity	Implantation	Hemocompatibility	Chronic Toxicity	Carcinogenicity	Reproductive Toxicity
Surface devices — Skin	A	X	X	X								
	B	X	X	X								
	C	X	X	X								
Mucous membrane	A	X	X	X								
	B	X	X	X	O	O		O				
	C	X	X	X	O	X	X	O		O		
Breached or compromised surface	A	X	X	X	O							
	B	X	X	X	O	O	O					
	C	X	X	X	O	X	X	O		O		
Externally communicating devices — Blood path indirect	A	X	X	X	X				X			
	B	X	X	X	X				X			
	C	X	X	X	X	X	X	O	X	O	O	
Tissue/bone and dentin	A	X	X	X	O							
	B	X	X	X	X	X	X	X				
	C	X	X	X	X	X	X	X		O	O	
Circulating blood	A	X	X	X	X	O	O		X			
	B	X	X	X	X	X	X	X	X			
	C	X	X	X	X	X	X	X	X	O	O	
Implant devices — Tissue/bone	A	X	X	X	O	X	X	X				
	B	X	X	X	X	X	X	X				
	C	X	X	X	X	X	X	X		O	O	
Blood	A	X	X	X	X	X	X	X	X			
	B	X	X	X	X	X	X	X	X			
	C	X	X	X	X	X	X	X	X	O	O	

A, limited (<24h); B, prolonged (24h–30d); C, permanent(>30d); O, additional tests may be required by US FDA; X, tests to be considered per ISO 10993-1
From ISO 10993-1 and FDA-G95.

TABLE 31.5 Types of In Vitro Cytotoxicity Assays

Qualitative Assays	Quantitative Assays
MEM elution assay	Neutral red uptake (NRU) assay
Direct contact test	Colony-forming unit (CFU) assay
Agar diffusion assay	MTT assay

Direct Contact Assay: Here, pieces of test article (1 × 1 cm) are placed directly on the near-confluent cell cultures. Alternatively filter paper disks (10 mm) are saturated with test-article extract and placed directly on cell cultures. The negative control cultures will have HDPE (1 × 1 cm). The positive control could be latex rubber (1 × 1 cm) or filter paper disks saturated with aqueous phenol (0.45%). It is preferable to have triplicate cultures in each group. At the end of 24 h, test article and media are removed. The cultures are stained either with neutral red (0.01%) or trypan blue (0.01%) and incubated for an additional hour. The plates are scored visually based on the extent of the zone of inhibition of cytotoxicity. A test is considered to have failed if the area of the zone of cytotoxicity is extended beyond the test specimen by 1.0 cm or more.

Agar Diffusion Assay: In this assay, near-confluent L929 cell cultures in a petri dish are overlaid with 1% molten agar. Strips of test and control articles are placed on the agar surface. If the device contains any potentially toxic materials they are thought to leach out and travel through the agar, reaching cell layers at the bottom. Cultures are incubated at 37°C in a humidified CO_2 incubator for 24 h. The cytotoxicity of the device is evaluated per the criteria for MEM elution assay.

NRU Assay: Balb/c 3T3 cells are exposed to a range of diluted test and control extracts for a period of 24 h in a 96-well microtiter plate. Cells are then washed with phosphate buffered saline and neutral red stain is added to each well for 3 h. Cells are lysed with ethanol/acetic acid mixture and microtiter plates are read at 540 nm. Viable cells absorb neutral red dye, and cytotoxicity is expressed in terms of IC_{50} (the concentration required to cause a 50% reduction of dye uptake). The recommended positive controls are zinc dibutyl dithiocarbamate (ZDBC) and zinc diethyl dithiocarbamate (ZDEC), which can be obtained from Hatano Research laboratory, Japan. The NRU assay may not be sensitive for all materials, because nanoparticle-based carbon is known to cause artifacts by interacting with neutral red [6], compromising the end results.

CFU Assay

Log-phase cells are cultured in six-well tissue-culture plates. Test and control device extracts are added in different concentrations along with positive controls - ZDBC and ZDEC. Compared to other cytotoxicity assays, very few cells (approximately 50 per well) are cultured per plate; otherwise, the higher cell densities result in numerous overlapping colonies, making it difficult to count them. Plates are incubated for 6–9 days, fixed with methanol, and colonies are stained with Giemsa solution. If the plating efficiency for the highest concentration of the test sample is less than 70% of the negative control group, the device is considered potentially cytotoxic.

MTT Assay

This assay measures the metabolic activity of the cells as an endpoint to assess cell survival. The mitochondria of live cells pick up the yellow tetrazolium salt (4, 5-dimethyl-thiazol-2-yl)-2, 5-diphenyltetrazolium bromide (MTT) and reduce it to a purple water-insoluble formazan compound. The amount of formazan dye produced is directly proportional to the number of metabolically active cells.

In brief, L929 cells in a 96-well plate are treated with test-article extracts for 24 h in a humidified incubator at 37°C. Positive controls for the MTT assay can be ZDBC or triton X-100. After removing the test and control articles, cultures are stained with MTT dye for another 2 h. The cells are then fixed in ethanol and UV-vis absorbance is read at 570 nm. Comparisons between the spectra of treated and untreated cells give a relative estimation of cytotoxicity.

Although the MTT method is fast and provides quantitative results, it does have certain limitations because it measures metabolic activity, not necessarily viability. Doxorubicin, a known cytotoxic agent, has been shown to exhibit increased viability by MTT assay in lymphocyte cultures [7].

Examples of Cytotoxicity in Medical Devices: Elastic materials used in certain orthodontic procedures were found to be cytotoxic (due to the presence of latex) in NRU assay using L-929 cells [8]. Similarly, acrylic resin denture materials were found to be cytotoxic due to the leaching of formaldehyde and methyl-methacrylate monomers [9]. Therefore it is recommended that such resin materials be prerinsed (in hot water to let the toxic chemicals leach out) before using in the clinic to minimize adverse reactions in patients.

IRRITATION

Irritation can be induced by the physical action of rubbing/friction of the device with the patient's outer skin or in inner body tissues at the site of implantation. Irritation can also result from the action of chemicals present in the device or personal hygiene products (nickel, silver, zinc, and perfumes) or chemical residues (acids, bases, adhesives, glues, or fat dissolving solvents) used in the manufacturing processes [10]. It is a nonspecific inflammatory response due to single or repeated exposure or injury from a foreign substance. Symptoms of irritation include rash, redness (erythema), pain, and swelling (edema) and can be manifested within a few minutes of exposure or the symptoms may develop within 24–48h after exposure. There are several irritation assays available to cover different regions of the body. The most common assays include:

- Intracutaneous reactivity test
- Primary skin Irritation
- Special irritation assays: bladder, ocular, oral mucosa, vaginal, penile, or rectal
- In vitro irritation assays

Intracutaneous Reactivity Test: This method is the preferred choice to test the irritation potential for all implantable devices contacting tissue, bone, or blood. In this assay, test-article extracts (polar and nonpolar) are injected into rabbits by intracutaneous injection. The control group receives only vehicle solvent. A total of three animals (of either sex) are used per extract. Each animal receive 0.2mL of test-article extract at five sites on one side of the dorsal midline. An equal amount of vehicle controls are injected at five sites on the other side of the dorsal midline. The injection sites are examined for signs of skin reaction at 24 ± 2, 48 ± 2, and 72 ± 2h after treatment. The intensity of skin reactions are given scores from 0 to 4, with 0 showing no symptoms and 4 exhibiting severe erythema (skin reddening like beet root) or severe edema (swelling of more than 1mm and extending beyond exposure area). The total score for each animal is divided by 15 (3 scoring time points $\times$ 5 injection sites). Add the scores of control or treated groups and divide by the number of replicate samples (generally 3) to get the mean irritation score. Subtract the vehicle control scores from the test scores. The test is considered as passed (nonirritant) if the score is 1 or less.

Primary Skin Irritation: This assay is ideal for surface (skin)-contacting devices such as bandages, surface-contacting electrodes, or probes used in clinical procedures such as MRI or ultrasound. The test article—molded solid material, gel, liquid, or powder (0.5g or 0.5mL)—is applied directly to the shaved skin of the rabbit as a patch. It is held firmly to the back of the animal using a nonocclusive dressing or gauze with a hypoallergenic tape for a period of 4h. After the patch is removed, the location of the test/control article is marked on the skin with permanent ink. Responses are scored at 24, 48 and 72h after patch removal and graded as described above for intracutaneous irritation. The sensitivity of this model needs to be demonstrated at least once every 3–6months with a known detergent chemical such as sodium lauryl sulfate (SLS).

Special Irritation Tests: Irritation assays have been developed for several mucosal-lined organs where medical devices are used. Examples of devices that fall under this category include male and female contraceptives, douching materials, contact lenses, rectal implants, enema kits, etc. Animals (mostly rabbits) are treated with medical devices (or its extracts) for defined periods, and the irritation response is determined by histopathological analysis of the tissues involved. Detailed experimental procedures for such irritation assays are described in ISO 10993-10.

Vaginal, Bladder, or Rectal Irritation: A minimum of three test and control rabbits are used. Animals are exposed to the test-article extract or vehicle controls (about 1mL each) every day for a minimum of 5 consecutive days. About 24h after the last dose, animals are euthanized and macroscopic evaluation is performed for signs of irritation, erythema, edema or injury to the epithelial layers of the tissues involve. Then vagina, bladder, or rectal tissues are dissected and examined histologically for epithelial cell degeneration, metaplasia, and leukocyte infiltration and for signs of edema compared to controls.

In Vitro Skin Irritation Models: Recently there has been more focus on developing alternative in vitro models for screening chemicals for irritation, mainly to reduce pain and suffering in animal species. Research in this area is being funded and/or coordinated by private industry and government agencies including the Interagency Coordinating Committee on the Validation of Alternative Methods (ICCVAM) and the European Centre for the Validation of Alternative Methods (ECVAM). Currently several multilayered (3D) cultures of human skin cells that provide a barrier function like the surface of normal skin are available commercially. If an irritant chemical enters the skin, it may cause cytotoxicity in the underlying cells. Alternatively if the chemical is weak in its cytotoxic response, it may activate the keratinocytes in the skin to release inflammatory cytokines.

In the EpiDerm model, cell cultures are treated with test sample for a minimum of 15min. If the test article is solid, it can be applied directly or is grounded to powder before application. After treatment, cells are washed and incubated in fresh medium for another 40h so the cells can recover from the toxic insult. Cytotoxicity is determined using the MTT assay. To increase the sensitivity of the assay, secretion of cytokine IL-1α can also be measured. It should be noted that the in vitro irritation skin models have not been validated for medical devices with traditional polar/nonpolar solvent extraction systems.

Example of Irritation: A device extract may show positive irritation response not because of the presence of any toxic chemical but due to the acidic or alkaline nature of the extract. As per the ISO 10993-10 (2010), if the pH of the extract is ≤2 or ≥11.5, the device should not be tested in any of the irritation assays to avoid causing undue pain or suffering to the animals. Alternatively, the nonpolar solvent CSO (used in device extraction) by itself induces slight irritation. Therefore each lot should be prescreened for background irritation response before the start of the study.

Sometimes, excess residual solvent in the finished product can also result in irritation. For example, chitosan films used in wound dressings and its animal irritation response. Chitosan AA (prepared by acetic acid) was shown to be significantly more irritating than Chitosan LA (prepared by lactic acid) in rabbits [11]. This differing irritant potential of the device may be due to residual solvents, since lactic acid is known to be more biodegradable than acetic acid.

Sensitization: Sensitization is also known as allergic-contact dermatitis (a type IV hypersensitivity reaction) generated after exposure to an allergen. However, sensitization reactions typically manifest only after repeated exposure and not with single exposure. Sensitization assays are recommended for all implantable tissue/bone or blood-contacting devices. The phenomenon of sensitization induced by medical devices is measured by two main assays in experimental animals.

Guinea Pig Maximization Assay: This assay was originally developed by Dr. Bertil Magnusson of the University of Gothenburg, Sweden and Dr. Albert Kligman of the University of Pennsylvania in the United States [12]. Their method is still widely used for determining allergic dermatitis or skin-sensitizing potential of environmental chemicals, pharmaceuticals and drugs, and medical devices.

The study, which takes about a month, is conducted in two phases. For the Induction I step, test-article extracts are mixed with Freund's adjuvant (heat-killed tuberculosis bacteria plus mineral oil) and injected by intradermal injection to a group of 10 guinea pigs (about five animals per sex/extract). Vehicle controls are injected into five animals of either sex. A week later for the Induction II phase, animals are topically treated with surfactant sodium lauryl sulfate (SLS) followed by application of test article extracts. Two weeks after the topical induction phase, the animals are challenged

with filter paper disks saturated with test-article extracts wrapped around the trunks of the animals with occlusive dressing. Animals are examined for symptoms of erythema and edema at 24 and 48h after removal of the dressings. Guinea pigs showing no signs of erythema or edema will get a score of "0," animals with discrete and patchy erythema will have a score of 1, animals with moderate and confluent erythema will get a score of 2, and those exhibiting intense erythema or edema will get a score of 3. The positive controls—dinitro chlorobenezene (DNCB), hexyl cinnamaldehyde, formaldehyde, or benzocaine mixed with Freund's adjuvant—needs to be tested concurrently or at least once every 3months. A test article is considered as a sensitizer if the test group exhibits grades of 1 or higher and the control group score is less than 1.

Buehler Assay: Edwin Buehler developed this assay originally intended for cosmetics and consumer products while working at Hill Top Research Labs in Cincinnati, OH [13]. As a rule, all surface-contacting devices are tested by Buehler assay. Since such devices are not implantable, there is no need to inject them intradermally and no need for mixing the test article with adjuvant.

Examples of Sensitization: Several well-known metallic compounds in their pure form are known to induce allergic contact dermatitis. Their degree of sensitivity when tested in guinea pigs was potassium dichromate > nickel sulfate > zirconium chloride [14]. However, it should be noted that metallic alloys of cobalt, chromium, titanium, etc., are widely used in the medical-device industry and are considered safe unless they leach out free metallic ions into the patient's body. Nickel sensitivity was more pronounced in females than in males in experimental animals [15]. Therefore medical devices should be tested in both male and female animals to assess their sensitization potential before being used in patients. Allergic-contact dermatitis is common with many wound dressing/wound healing products (such as lotions, topical creams, and ointments) used in the clinic [16].

TABLE 31.6 Systemic Toxicity

Treatment Duration	Acute	Subacute/Subchronic	Chronic
	1–5	14–28	6, 8, or 12months
OBSERVATION/PARAMETERS			
Body weight	+	+	+
Clinical observations	+	+	+
Gross pathology		+	+
Histopathology		+	+
Hematology		+	+
Serum/clinical chemistry		+	+

SYSTEMIC TOXICITY

There are three types of systemic toxicity assays commonly performed in the medical-device industry (Table 31.6). The type of assay to be conducted depends on the clinical use, contact duration of the device, and toxicity potential of the device materials.

Acute Systemic Toxicity: This is the preliminary in vivo test recommended for any implantable device. Generally mice are employed in this assay but rats can also be used. A minimum of five animals of either sex (unless the clinical use of the device is specific for a particular sex) is used per group. Animals are injected with a polar (by IV route) and nonpolar extract (by IP route) of the device. The control group is given polar/non-polar solvents alone. Animals are examined for body weight, changes in skin or fur, eyes, mucous membranes, abnormal respiration, and adverse symptoms such as prostration, convulsions, or death. Animals are observed immediately, 24, 48, and 72 h after injection. A test is considered a failure and the device is classified as toxic if two or more animals die or show adverse clinical symptoms or show loss of body weight of 10% or more. If any animal shows abnormal clinical symptoms and one test animal shows gross signs of toxicity or dies, then the test can be repeated with 10 test and 10 control animals. Depending on the extent of test article-induced toxicity, additional hematology and histopathology parameters can be added to the study design.

Examples of Acute Systemic Toxicity: One of the ingredients of contact lenses is the methacrylate monomer. The amount of methacrylic acid in contact lenses is estimated is about 6 ppm. To assess acute systemic toxicity, methacrylic acid was dissolved in sesame oil and mice were injected IP at doses of 0.6, 6.0, 60, or 600 ppm. The results showed no abnormal clinical symptoms at 2, 8, 24, 48, or 72 h in any of the treated groups [17].

Subacute Toxicity: The duration of this test can be 14 daily consecutive injections of test-article extracts by IP or IV route in rodents. Alternatively the test article can be implanted in the animals for up to 28 days and the animal tissues analyzed for any systemic toxicity parameters.

Examples of Subacute Toxicity: Bioabsorbable polymers are being increasingly used for sustained drug delivery so the drug exerts its effects at the localized tissues, thus sparing the systemic toxicity. In a subacute toxicity study, rats were implanted with bioabsorbable polyester anhydride ricinoleic acid (RA) by subcutaneous (SC), intramuscular (IM), and intracranial (IC) methods. There was no evidence of systemic toxicity or polymer-induced lesions in any of the treated animals. At some of the implantation sites in the SC or IM groups, there was evidence of typical foreign body reaction to biomaterial, which was followed by tissue repair. In some IC-treated animals, there was mild but transient inflammation of glial cells at days 14 and 21. Overall the

study showed that the bioabsorbable polymer is biocompatible and nontoxic [18].

Chronic Toxicity: This test is required for all long-term implants (tissue, bone or blood contacting devices) known to contain any potentially toxic chemicals. The study design for chronic toxicity in rodents should contain the following features:

- Duration of study can range from 6 to 12 months
- Number of animals in each group: 10–15 per sex/group
- An appropriate negative/reference control group
- Route of test-article administration that matches the clinical use of the device
- Test-article extract can be injected or a representative portion of the device can be implanted in the animal, complying with both systemic toxicity (ISO 10993-11) and implantation (ISO 10993-6).
- If the device is coated with a drug/pharmaceutical or contain any toxic chemical, the dose selected should provide sufficient margin of human safety.

The test parameters to be evaluated include daily/weekly body weights, clinical signs, hematology, serum chemistry, organ histology, etc. In the case of implanted test article, collect specimens during necropsy for evaluation of local tissue effects at the implantation sites by histopathology. This will help reduce the time and cost to conduct a separate implantation test.

Examples of Chronic Systemic Toxicity: Bone loss occurs due to bone fractures, development of bone tumors, or osteoporosis. One of the treatment options is to inject the bioactive bone-inducing material (BBIM) such as collagen scaffolds. To evaluate the potential toxicity, in a 6-month chronic systemic toxicity study, groups of rats were implanted subcutaneously on either side of the spinal column with BBIM blocks (each $0.5 \times 0.5 \times 0.5$ cm). The control group was sham operated. At termination, various organs such as liver, spleen, kidney, adrenal gland, heart, thymus, testis, and brain were explanted. The wet-organ weights and histopathology data did not show significant differences compared to the control group. The blood collected from these animals was analyzed for routine hematological parameters such as white, red blood cell, and platelet counts, mean corpuscular volume, hematocrit, and prothrombin time. Similarly the clinical chemistry parameters include alanine aminotransferase, glucose, urea, bilirubin, triglycerides, etc. The results showed no significant differences between the treated and control groups, indicating that the bone-bioactive material is nontoxic, biocompatible, and safe for human use [19].

Material-Mediated Rabbit Pyrogen Assay: A pyrogen is a substance that when introduced into a patient's bloodstream produces fever. Pyrogens derived from the cell walls of gram-negative bacteria are called endotoxins, which are usually detected during routine microbiological testing of medical devices using the LAL (limulus amoebocyte lysate) test. The rabbit pyrogen assay can detect both endotoxin- and nonendotoxin-related pyrogens, whereas the LAL test is specific only to endotoxins. Some substances produced by gram-positive bacteria are difficult to detect in the LAL test and are not reactive in the rabbit pyrogen test yet cause fever, inflammation, and aseptic peritonitis in patients. These nonendotoxin pyrogens are known as peptidoglycans and can be detected by the silkworm larvae plasma test; their adverse responses in patients is known to be mediated by IL-6 and TNF-α [20].

Examples of Material-Mediated Pyrogens: Fever is a normal adaptive physiological response by the brain to pyrogenic stimuli. A common material-mediated nonendotoxin pyrogen include 2-, 4-dinitrophenol injected at a dose of 20 mg/kg induced pyrogenic response in male rabbits [21]. Similarly, interferon (10^{-2} to 10^{-6} μg) or its inducer polyriboinosinic acid–polyribocytidylic acid (poly I: C) at 0.012–12 μg produced a dose-dependent pyrogenic response in rabbits [22].

GENOTOXICITY

Before initiating genotoxicity testing, there should be a proper investigation to assess the genotoxic risk of the device and its materials, based on a literature review. Then a detailed chemical characterization, identification of degradation products/metabolites, any data on predicate device, exposure route, patient population, and whether the chemical exposure is limited to localized tissues or systemic exposure should be noted. If there is insufficient data for identifying hazards or estimation of risks to patients, then proceed with genotoxicity testing.

As per ISO 10993-3 (2014), the following scheme of genotoxicity testing is recommended:

- Initial Ames bacterial reverse mutagenicity test;
- In vitro chromosomal aberration test and/or an in vitro gene mutation assay (such as mouse lymphoma);
- If either of the in vitro assays fails, then the root cause of the failed test has to be ascertained. If it is determined that the device contains any toxic leachables with a genotoxicity risk to patients, then an in vivo mammalian genotoxicity assay (mouse bone-marrow chromosomal aberration test or a mouse micronucleus assay) is recommended.

Methodology: The procedures for conducting the various in vitro and in vivo mutagenicity assays can be based on the appropriate Organization for Economic Cooperation and Development (OECD) guidelines with some exceptions on test-article preparation. Methods for

sample preparation or test-article extract need to comply with the ISO 10992-12 guideline. Only the patient-contacting portion of the device needs to be tested.

Examples of Genotoxicity: Acrylamide used in the manufacture of some polymeric materials when analyzed in the Ames assay was found to be genotoxic in two (TA 98 and TA 100) out of the four bacterial tester strains. In the in vivo assay, acrylamide induced a significant increase of micronucleated erythrocytes in mice treated with high lethal doses (near LD_{50}) but not at lower doses [23].

Carcinogenicity: This test is recommended only after determining that the device contains carcinogenic chemicals, they are bioavailable, and adequate carcinogenic risk to the patient has been established. Due attention has to be given to determine if the device or its extract is mutagenic in the in vitro or in vivo genotoxicity assays. While most carcinogenic agents are known to be mutagens not all mutagens are carcinogens [24]. There is an excellent prescreening test for potential carcinogenic agents in the in vitro cell transformation assay using Balb/c 3T3 cells or Syrian hamster ovary cells. Furthermore, instead of the conventional 2-year rodent carcinogenesis assay, using transgenic mice (rasH2 or p53) can provide more precise information on the genetic pathways involved and the carcinogenic potential of a chemical can be obtained more quickly in about 6 months [25].

Example of Carcinogenesis: Vanadium is present in many medical devices including in implantable battery systems. Rats treated with 7, 12-dimethylbenz (α) anthracene (DMBA) developed mammary tumors at a high frequency. But animals treated with DMBA and supplemented with vanadium in drinking water developed significantly fewer tumors than groups treated with DMBA alone [26]. The exact mechanism of this chemopreventive effect is not clear, but it is known that vanadium inhibits formation of DNA single-strand breaks and chromosomal aberrations in mammary epithelial cells.

Reproductive/Developmental Toxicity: If a device contains any chemical/physical/biologic agents that are deemed to be potentially toxic to reproductive system or developing embryo/fetus, or come into direct contact with reproductive organs including gonads or its leachables have the potential to reach these organs, then it has to be tested for reproductive toxicity. OECD 421 provides an excellent resource on test methodology for assessing reproductive toxicity. Other useful references include OECD 414 (for prenatal development), OECD 415 (one-generation toxicity), and OECD 416 (two-generation toxicity).

Examples of Reproductive/Developmental Toxicity: Diethylhexyl phthalate (DEHP) is added to plastics to make them more soft and flexible. Therefore there is risk of phthalates from medical devices (such as infusion sets and feeding tubes) leaching into patients. In rats, the main target organ for DEHP is testis. Immature young animals are known to be more susceptible to testicular toxicity of

DEHP than older mature animals. Diethylhexyl phthalate was found to induce atrophy of seminiferous tubules and reduction in seminal vesicle and prostate weight in 4-week-old but not in 15-week-old rats [27]. In another study, neonatal rats were treated intravenously or orally with DEHP at 60, 300, or 600 mg/kg/day from day 3 to day 21. There were no adverse effects in the low-dose (60 mg/kg) group. But in the high-dose (300 or 600 mg/kg) group there was a decrease in testis weight as evidenced by partial depletion of germinal epithelium. However, as these neonatally treated animals matured by day 90, the germinal epithelium repopulated with no effects on sperm count, sperm morphology, or motility, indicating the repair mechanism in all dose groups [28]. Further, even though high-dose phthalates are known to cause testicular toxicity in rodents, there is no such proof of any adverse events in humans.

Hemocompatibility: All devices contacting blood (directly/indirectly) need to be evaluated for their hemocompatibility. The type of testing depends on the contact duration with the patient and the presence of any potentially toxic chemicals in the device or its extracts. Hemocompatibility tests are also recommended when there is a change in manufacturing process, sterilization of the device, changes to the geometry or chemical composition of an existing device, etc. The various tests to be considered for blood contacting devices are described in Table 31.7.

Hemolysis: This is the most widely used and sensitive hemocompatibility assay. The thin erythrocyte membranes are easily damaged when they come into contact with surfaces of medical devices, shear stress, pH changes, or entry of metallic ions/toxic chemicals. The hemolysis test is usually performed using the ASTM F-756 method. In this assay, fresh rabbit blood is diluted to a hemoglobin concentration of 10 mg/mL. Blood is incubated with the device samples (direct contact) or with device extract (indirect method) for 3 h at room temperature with vortexing. Negative control is generally high-density polyethylene (HDPE) and positive control can be plastisol, water, BUNA rubber, or Genapol X-080. After incubation with test-article, negative or positive controls, the blood samples are centrifuged and supernatant is collected. The cell-free supernatants are incubated with Drabkin's reagent for 15 min to measure absorbance at

540 nm. Free hemoglobin in the sample is estimated using a standard curve. The percent hemolysis and hemolytic index are calculated as described in ASTM F-756 or in the current ISO 10993-4.

A sample is considered to have passed if the hemolytic index is 5 or less. Samples with hemolytic index of >5 are considered to fail, or in other words are hemolytic.

Example of Hemolysis: Devices leaching copper may show a positive hemolytic response in rabbit blood. A dose of 30 μM Cu (II) was found to cause hemolysis but addition of normal serum proteins (albumin or ceruloplasmin) increased the duration of the induction period and decreased the overall rate of hemolysis of red blood cells [29]. This particular study shows the limitation of in vitro assays as the hemolysis observed in rabbit blood may not occur in an in vivo situation in humans. Specifically it is well known that in normal physiological situation in humans both albumin and ceruloplasmin effectively bind the copper ions and transport them to liver for storage.

Complement Activation: The complement system is part of the innate immune mechanism that protects the body against infections and it participates in many host immune responses. Complement proteins present in blood are activated by the direct (classical) or indirect (alternate) pathways that can be measured in the serum by the levels of C3a and sC5b-9 fragments. To measure complement activation, device materials are incubated with normal human serum for 60 min. The serum is then added to microtiter plates and the complement proteins are assessed using an ELISA method with HRP-labeled antibodies by measuring absorbance at 450 nm. Generally cobra venom factor is used as positive control. The amount of complement proteins are quantified (μg/mL) and expressed as percent positive controls. Fresh human plasma not exposed to any material will serve as negative control. Further details on this assay can be found in ASTM F2382-04.

Examples of Complement Activation: Dialysis membranes are known to activate complement fragments. In a clinical study, cellulose acetate membrane elevated C3a protein to as high as 3500–4000 ng/mL

TABLE 31.7   Tests for Effects on Blood

Device Examples	Hemolysis	Complement Activation	Coagulation	Hematology and Platelets	Thrombosis
Blood storage and blood-collection devices	x		x	x	
Hemodialysis, and hemofiltration equipment	x	x	x	x	x
Catheters and guide wires	x		x	x	x
Stents, heart valves, vena cava filters, and endovascular grafts	x	x		x	x

within 15 min of dialysis but the levels dropped to baseline levels of 1500 ng/mL by 4 h. In contrast the polymethylmethacrylate membranes showed no such activation of C3a proteins [30].

Coagulation: When a tissue in the body is injured, it begins to bleed, initiating a sequence of events called the coagulation cascade and ultimately leading to the formation of blood clots. Generally coagulation is measured by PTT (partial thromboplastin time), which evaluates the intrinsic coagulation system. In this test, a test article is incubated with human blood plasma for 15 min at 37°C, then a fixed amount of calcium chloride and rabbit brain cephalin (source of phospholipid) is added to the reaction mixture. The clot formation is measured using a cascade coagulation analyzer. The time required for clot formation is expressed as percentage of negative control. Human plasma generally clots in about 300 s. Black rubber serves as a positive control, and HDPE as reference control.

Examples of Coagulation: Hemostatic agents are applied topically to control bleeding during surgical operations. In an effort to test the biocompatibility of a new dihydroxyacetone material, researchers conducted a series of hemocompatibility tests. Rat blood was mixed with a new derivative of dihydroxyacetone and assayed for PTT. The results showed that dihydroxyacetone did not affect the inherent coagulation cascade, as the PTT values in the test-article treated group were similar to negative controls. However, in a rat partial hepatectomy model, when dihydroxyacetone was topically applied on the injured liver, there was a statistically significant decrease in blood loss compared to the control group. This shows the effectiveness of dihydroxyacetone compound as topical hemostatic agent [31].

Hematology and Platelets: Interaction of medical devices with blood can affect various hematological parameters, which can be measured by counting the number of erythrocytes, lymphocytes, monocytes, and platelets using electronic cell counters. Similarly device materials are known to cause platelet activation and degranulation events.

Examples of Hematology and Platelet Activation: At a hospital in a Canadian province, a group of patients treated with e-beam sterilized dialyzer showed significant thrombocytopenia. However, the platelet counts recovered when dialysis was performed using non-e-beam sterilized membrane. Therefore, it is essential to select an appropriate sterilizing agent for the device to prevent future adverse events in the patients [32].

There was increased expression of P-Selectin molecules (measured by ELISA) on platelet surfaces after incubation (37°C for 1 h) with polysulfone membranes. In the same study, there was increased adhesion of neutrophils to the membrane, which may be due to the production of reactive oxygen species [33].

Thrombosis: A thrombus (blood clot) contains a mixture of red cells, aggregated platelets, fibrin, and other cellular elements. It can occur in vivo or ex vivo in flowing whole blood due to activation of platelets and the coagulation system. The most widely used method to detect thrombogenic potential of a device is the canine model conducted in the presence or absence of an anticoagulant such as heparin. The method is also referred to as AVI (anticoagulated venous implant) or NAVI (nonanticoagulated venous implant). Briefly two to three adult animals of either sex are anesthetized and the medical device (typically in the form of a catheter) is inserted into the femoral (or jugular) veins for 4 h. The test article is implanted in the left vein and a reference/predicate or a competitor's product is inserted in the right vessel of the same animal. At the end of treatment period, the blood vessels are explanted and the device is examined for thrombus formation under light microscopy and scored as described in Table 31.8.

This method is not without pitfalls as it is more subjective in nature and sometimes gives false-positive responses. Thus some investigators prefer gravimetric analysis of the observed thrombus and vessel patency [34]. Apart from the 4 h canine model, devices such as heart stents (bare metal and coated) can also be implanted in porcine coronary arteries for several weeks/months to study formation of thrombus, fibrin, and neointimal area by various histomorphology and histopathological methods [35]. A number of in vitro blood-loop models

TABLE 31.8 Assessment of Thrombosis

Thrombus Formation	Score
None (a small clot at point of insertion)	0
Minimal (thrombus covering <25% of device surface)	1
Moderate (thrombus covering up to 50% of device surface)	2
Severe (thrombus covering up to 75% of device surface)	3
Extensive (thrombus covering 100% of device surface)	4

are also available to measure thrombosis of medical devices [36–38].

Examples of Thrombosis: To study the biocompatibility and safety of biodegradable magnesium alloy stents were implanted in the coronary and femoral arteries of dogs. Animals were euthanized on 1, 3, 7, 14, 21, and 28 days. The results showed the stent was fully absorbed and not visible by day 7. There was only mild hyperplasia two weeks after implantation, with no obvious inflammatory response and no evidence of thrombosis [39].

Implantation: This test needs to be considered for devices that are implanted in tissue/bone or blood for prolonged and permanent durations. It can be subcutaneous or intramuscular implantation in a mouse, rat, or rabbit model. However, the implantation test can also be performed in other species such as in dog, sheep, goat, or porcine models with documented justification of the method to simulate clinical use of the device. The duration of implantation needs to be proportional to the clinical use of the device and lifespan of the animal species. For example, it can range from 4 to 8 weeks, 3, 6, or 12 months. Generally three rabbits/group and at least 10 control and 10 test samples are evaluated for each implantation period. The number of implant sites can be a maximum of six in rabbits (3 control and 3 treated) but in higher species of dog and sheep due to their large body size there is a scope of 12 implant sites (6 each for control or test specimens). The specimens should be 10 mm in diameter, with a thickness ranging from 0.3 to 1.0 mm. At the termination of each study, animals are euthanized, device samples extracted, and surrounding tissues dissected, processed, and stained for routine histopathological examination. Tissue samples from both control and treated sites need to be examined for inflammation (infiltration of polymorphs, lymphocytes, and macrophages), neovascularization, fibrosis and necrosis, etc. Monitoring of local tissue effects at the site of implantation should also include any evidence of material degradation and formation of fibrous capsule due to toxic leachables.

Examples of Implantation: There are many advantages of clinical treatment with specific localized tissue implantation rather than systemic administration. For example, eye lesions such as uveitis require treatment with drug cyclosporine. But systemic administration of cyclosporine induces many toxic effects and immunosuppression. Therefore microspheres of biodegradable polymer PLGA (polylactic and glycolic acid) coated with cyclosporine after intraocular implantation in rabbits not only yielded sustained release of the drug in the affected eye providing therapeutic benefit but at the same time caused less toxicity as evidenced by the decreased severity of inflammation, leucocyte infiltration, and protein levels in the eye [40,41].

CHEMICAL CHARACTERIZATION AND RISK ASSESSMENT

Medical devices are made with a variety of materials including plastics, resins, adhesives, metals, ceramics and hydrophilic coatings for ease of insertion in the body, and adverse effects depend on toxic leachables coming out of the device. Hence the scientific community is placing more emphasis on chemical characterization of device materials and is focusing on determining the leachable profile of chemicals in order to determine any patient risk. The new ISO 10993-1 (2013) recommends performing chemical characterization of a medical device to identify any potential toxicological risk before venturing into full-scale in vitro and in vivo biocompatibility testing.

The chemical composition can be ascertained from the supplier/vendor provided material data sheets. If needed leachables from a device can be identified by various methods such as FTIR (Fourier transform infrared spectroscopy), ICP (inductively coupled plasma), GC–MS (gas chromatography–mass spectrometry), LC–MS (liquid chromatography–mass spectrometry), EDS (energy-dispersive spectrometry) etc. Once the chemical nature of the device material is identified the approximate quantity of the leachables from the device extract need to be determined. The biological hazards of the chemical in question can be obtained from literature. ISO 10993-17 (2009) provides guidance on establishing tolerable intake (TI) and tolerable exposure (TE) levels using health-based endpoints such as NOAEL.

$$TI = NOAEL \div MF$$

where MF (modifying factor) is the product of two or more uncertainty factors (UF) to account for differences in species, route of administration (oral/IV or SC), quality/relevance of experimental data, etc.

$$TE = TI \times BW$$

where BW is 70 kg for an adult.

Margin of safety (MoS) is determined by calculating the ratio of TE to the worst-case clinical exposure. This assumes 100% of the chemical entity will leach out and be available systemically.

$$MoS = TE \div Exposure_{worst\text{-}case\ clinical}$$

A MoS value greater than 1 is determined to be toxicologically insignificant.

Cardiovascular stents are increasingly being coated with drugs (Paclitaxel or Everolimus) to prevent restenosis and intimal hyperplasia in the treated blood vessels [42]. Long-term indwelling catheters and other implantable devices are being coated with antimicrobials (Rifampicin or Miconazole) to eliminate the growth of harmful microorganisms (*Candida albicans* and *S. aureus*) and to prevent biofilm formation [43] on device surfaces. Although the amount of drug coated on the device is relatively small compared to the high doses used in clinic for cancer treatment, to prevent infections or organ rejection, adequate test methods need to be incorporated in the study plan to identify the kinetics, degradation profiles, and potential toxicity of these chemicals.

Since some devices such as orthopedic implants or vascular stents contain metals there is a risk of metallic ions leaching out from such devices into patients' body fluids and tissues. There is a new FDA guidance describing the permissible daily exposure (PDE) levels of elements such as platinum, chromium, titanium, etc., which is useful in assessing the toxicological risk of devices containing metallic components [44].

Many chemical solvents (eg, tetrahydrofuran, dimethylformamide) are utilized during manufacturing of medical devices. However, most of these solvents evaporate during routine heating and drying processes, but the final residual level of these solvents needs to be analyzed in a fully processed, packaged, and sterilized device. There is a good reference available documenting the PDE values of various solvents, which is useful in toxicological risk assessment [45].

Medical devices, in particular delivery catheters and their components, contain colorants. They do not have any physiological function except to aid the physician during the clinical procedure. The FDA recently published a list of color additives used in medical devices that are exempt from certification (21 CFR 73, Subpart D) or subject to certification (21 CFR 74, Subpart D) and their purity requirements [46]. Care should be taken to ensure the level of impurities of toxic chemicals such as lead, arsenic, or aniline present in a vendor's formulation matches the requirement set by the FDA. A recent webinar by the FDA provides in-depth guidelines on the use of colorants in medical devices for different patient-contact durations [47]. Lastly, when there is inadequate toxicity information on leachables, the patient safety of those chemicals can be assessed by the concept of TTC (threshold of toxicological concern) applicable to medical devices [48].

References

[1] Generoso WM, Cain KT, Krishna M, et al. Heritable translocation and dominant lethal mutation induction with ethylene oxide in mice. Mutat Res 1980;73:133–42.

[2] Zong BZ, Gu ZW, Whong WZ, Wallace WE, Ong TM. Comparative study of micronucleus assay and chromosomal aberration analysis in V79 cells exposed to ethylene oxide. Teratog Carcinog Mutagen 1991;11:227–33.

[3] Anand VP, Cogdill CP, Klausner KA, Lister L, Barbolt T, Page BF, et al. Reevaluation of ethylene oxide hemolysis and irritation potential. J Biomed Mater Res A 2003;15:648–54.

[4] Snellings WM, Maronpot RR, Zelenak JP, et al. Teratology study in Fischer 344 rats exposed to ethylene oxide by inhalation. Toxicol Appl Pharmacol 1982;64:476–81.

[5] Pariente JL, Bordenave L, Jacob F, Bareille R, Baquey C, Le Guillou M. Cytotoxicity assessment of latex urinary catheters on cultured human urothelial cells. Eur Urol 2000;38:640–3.

[6] Monteiro-Riviere NA, Inman AO, Zhang LW. Limitations and relative utility of screening assays to assess engineered nanoparticle toxicity in a human cell line. Toxicol Appl Pharmacol 2009;234:222–35.

[7] Jaszczyszyn A, Gasiorowski K. Limitations of the MTT assay in cell viability testing. Adv Clin Exp Med 2008;17:525–9.

[8] dos Santos RL, Pithon MM, Martins FO, Romanos MT, de Oliveira Ruellas AC. Evaluation of the cytotoxicity of latex and nonlatex orthodontic separating elastics. Orthod Craniofac Res 2010;13:28–33.

[9] Tsuchiya H, Hoshino Y, Tajima K, Takagi N. Leaching and cytotoxicity of formaldehyde and methyl methacrylate from acrylic resin denture base materials. J Prosthet Dent 1994;7:618–24.

[10] Ljubojević S, Lipozencić J, Celić D, Turcić P. Genital contact allergy. Acta Dermatovenerol 2009;17:285–8.

[11] Peh K, Khan T, Ch'ng H. Mechanical, bioadhesive strength and biological evaluations of chitosan films for wound dressing. J Pharm Pharm Sci 2000;3:303–11.

[12] Magnusson B, Kligman AM. The identification of contact allergens by animal assay. The guinea pig maximization test. J Invest Dermatol 1969;52:268–76.

[13] Buehler EV. Delayed contact hypersensitivity in the guinea pig. Arch Dermatol 1965;91:171–7.

[14] Ikarashi Y, Momma J, Tsuchiya T, Nakamura A. Evaluation of skin sensitization potential of nickel, chromium, titanium and zirconium salts using guinea-pigs and mice. Biomaterials 1996;17:2103–8.

[15] Van Hoogstaten IM, de Groot J, Boden D, von Blomberg BM, Kraal G, Scheper RJ. Development of a concomitant nickel and chromium sensitization model in the guinea pigs. Int Arch Allergy Immunol 1992;87:258–66.

[16] Alavi A, Sibbald RG, Ladizinski B, Saraiya A, Lee KC, Skotnicki-Grant S, et al. Wound-related allergic/irritant contact dermatitis. Adv Skin Wound Care 2016;29:278–86.

[17] Marcus R, Hunt C, Windhorst R, Jose J, Mandell RB. Acute systemic toxicological tests of soft contact lens extractives. Am J Optom Physiol Opt 1980;57:360–2.

[18] Vaisman B, Motiei M, Nyska A, Domb AJ. Biocompatibility and safety evaluation of a ricinoleic acid-based poly (ester-anhydride) copolymer after implantation in rats. J Biomed Mater Res A 2010;92:419–31.

[19] Han Q, Zhang B, Chen B, Dai J, Xu J, Wang C, et al. Evaluation of a bioactive bone-inducing material consisting of collagen scaffolds and collagen-binding bone morphogenetic protein 2. J Biomed Mater Res A 2014;102:3093–101.

[20] Martis L, Patel M, Giertych J, Mongoven J, Taminne M, Perrier MA, et al. Aseptic peritonitis due to peptidoglycan contamination of pharmacopoeia standard dialysis solution. Lancet 2005;365:588–94.

[21] Itami T, Ema M, Kanch S. Antipyretic mechanism of Indomethacin in rabbits. J Pharmacobiodyn 1986;9:271–5.

[22] Won SJ, Lin MT. Pyrogenicity of interferon and its inducer in rabbits. Am J Physiol 1988;254:R499–507.

[23] Yang HJ, Lee SH, Jin Y, Choi JH, Han CH, Lee MH. Genotoxicity and toxicological effects of acrylamide on reproductive system in male rats. J Vet Sci 2005;6:103–9.

[24] Reddy JK, Scarpelli DG, Subbarao V, Lalwani ND. Chemical carcinogens without mutagenic activity: peroxisome proliferators as a prototype. Toxicol Pathol 1983;11:172–80.

[25] Pritchard JB, French JE, Davis BJ, Haseman JK. The role of transgenic mouse models in carcinogen identification. Environ Health Perspect 2003;111:444–54.

[26] Ray RS, Basu M, Ghosh B, Samanta K, Vanadium CM. A versatile biochemical effector in chemical rat mammary carcinogenesis. Nutr Cancer 2005;51:184–96.

[27] Gray TJ, Gangolli SD. Aspects of the testicular toxicity of phthalate esters. Environ Health Perspect 1986;65:229–635.

[28] Cammack JN, White RD, Gordon D, Gass J, Hecker L, Conine D, et al. Evaluation of reproductive development following intravenous and oral exposure to DEHP in male neonatal rats. Int J Toxicol 2003;22:159–74.

[29] Caffrey Jr JM, Smith HA, Schmitz JC, Merchant A, Frieden E. Hemolysis of rabbit erythrocytes in the presence of copper ions. Inhibition by albumin and ceruloplasmin. Biol Trace Elem Res 1990;25:11–9.

[30] Hakim RM, Fearon DT, Lazarus JM. Biocompatibility of dialysis membranes: effects of chronic complement activation. Kidney Int 1984;26:194–200.

[31] Henderson PW, Kadouch DJ, Singh SP, Zawaneh PN, Weiser J, Yazdi S, et al. A rapidly resorbable hemostatic biomaterial based on dihydroxyacetone. J Biomed Mater Res A 2010;93:776–82.

[32] Kiaii M, Djurdjev O, Farah M, Levin A, Jung B, MacRae J. Use of electron-beam sterilized hemodialysis membranes and risk of thrombocytopenia. JAMA 2011;306:1679–87.

[33] Itoh S, Susuki C, Tsuji T. Platelet activation through interaction with hemodialysis membrane induces neutrophils to produce reactive oxygen species. J Biomed Mater Res A 2006;77:294–303.

[34] Wolf MF, Anderson JM. Practical approach to blood compatibility assessments: general considerations and standards. In: Boutrand J-P, editor. Biocompatibility and performance of medical devices. Woodhead Publishing Ltd; 2012. p. 159–96.

[35] Eppihimer MJ, Sushkova N, Grimsby JL, Efimova N, Kai W, Larson S, et al. Impact of stent surface on thrombogenicity and vascular healing: a comparative analysis of metallic and polymeric surfaces. Circ Cardiovasc Interv 2013;6:370–7.

[36] Sinn S, Scheuermann T, Deichelbohrer S, Ziemer G, Wendel HP. A novel in vitro model for preclinical testing of the hemocompatibility of intravascular stents according to ISO 10993-4. J Mater Sci Mater Med 2011;22:1521–8.

[37] McClung WG, Babcock DE, Brash JL. Fibrinolytic properties of lysine-derivatized polyethylene in contact with flowing whole blood (Chandler loop model). J Biomed Mater Res A 2007;81:644–51.

[38] Grove K, Deline S, Schatz T, Howard S, Smith M. Thrombogenicity testing for blood-contacting medical devices in an in vitro ovine blood-loop. J Med Devices 2016;10:1–3.

[39] Yue Y, Wang L, Yang N, Huang J, Lei L, Ye H, et al. Effectiveness of biodegradable magnesium alloy stents in coronary artery and femoral artery. J Interv Cardiol 2015;28:358–64.

[40] He Y, Wang JC, Liu YL, Ma ZZ, Zhu XA, Zhang Q. Therapeutic and toxicological evaluations of cyclosporine a microspheres as a treatment vehicle for uveitis in rabbits. J Ocul Pharmacol Ther 2006;22:121–31.

[41] He Y, Wang JC, Liu YL, Ma ZZ, Zhu XA, Zhang Q. Cyclosporine-loaded microspheres for treatment of uveitis: in vitro characterization and in vivo pharmacokinetic study. Invest Ophthalmol Vis Sci 2006;47:3983–8.

[42] Chitkara K, Pujara K. Drug-eluting stents in acute coronary syndrome: is there a risk of stent thrombosis with second-generation stents? Eur J Cardiovasc Med 2010;1:20–4.

[43] Yücel N, Lefering R, Maegele M, Max M, Rossaint R, Koch A, et al. Reduced colonization and infection with miconazole-rifampicin modified central venous catheters: a randomized controlled clinical trial. J Antimicrob Chemother 2004;54:1109–15.

[44] ICH. Q3D elemental impurities. Guidance for Industry; 2015. http://www.fda.gov/downloads/drugs/guidancecompliance-regulatoryinformation/guidances/ucm371025.pdf.

[45] European Medicine Agency. ICH guideline Q3C (R5) on impurities: guideline for residual solvents. 2015. http://www.ema.europa.eu/docs/en_GB/document_library/Scientific_guideline/2011/03/WC500104258.pdf.

[46] FDA. Color additives listed for use in medical devices (from the code of federal regulations). September 16, 2016. http://www.ecfr.gov/cgi-bin/text-idx?SID=79a76b1d7e7a98ae9459d88005ab7058&mc=true&node=pt21.1.73&rgn=div5#sp21.1.73.d/InMedicalDevices/ucm130030.htm.

[47] FDA. Color additives and the medical device review. February 12, 2016. http://www.fda.gov/downloads/MedicalDevices/NewsEvents/WorkshopsConferences/UCM486081.pdf.

[48] Brown R. Practical application of the TTC approach for compounds released from device materials. November 16, 2015. http://www.toxicology.org/groups/ss/MDCPSS/docs/MDCPSS_Webinar_111615_Brown.pdf.

PREDICTIVE TOXICOLOGY, TOXICOMETABOLOMICS, TOXICOGENOMICS, AND IMAGING

32

Application of Evolving Computational and Biological Platforms for Chemical Safety Assessment

R.S. Settivari, J.C. Rowlands, D.M. Wilson, S.M. Arnold, P.J. Spencer

INTRODUCTION

Evaluating the toxicity of a new drug or pesticide is no small task. Regulatory agencies around the world require a comprehensive array of standardized toxicity tests, which form the basis for decisions about whether or not to allow commercialization of the new compound, as well as how much human or environmental exposure can be allowed to define conditions of safe use. For example, a new drug or pesticide candidate typically is subjected to well over 100 different tests to evaluate safety, including a core battery consisting of toxicology studies in mammalian species, particularly rats and mice. Industrial chemicals are also subject to similar requirements for toxicity

A Comprehensive Guide to Toxicology in Nonclinical Drug Development, Second Edition
http://dx.doi.org/10.1016/B978-0-12-803620-4.00032-3

testing, although these requirements typically are tiered based on exposure considerations, anticipated toxicity based on structurally similar molecules, and the results of early-stage tests [1]. A significant example of such regulation is the European Union's REACH program, which requires that chemicals produced in excess of 100 metric tons per year be subject to a suite of toxicity tests similar to that required of pesticides. Testing requirements for moderate-tonnage production volume chemicals are scaled down accordingly, but still are quite substantial.

The toxicity testing methods employed for these evaluations are specified in great detail in various regulatory agency testing guidelines. The testing protocols are rooted in general study designs that were established several decades ago, fresh on the heels of several widely known tragedies such as the Minamata Bay methylmercury poisonings and the thalidomide disaster. These tests were designed with the principal aim of preventing such tragedies from occurring in the future. Whole animal models were employed as the best surrogates available at the time to represent human physiology and disease, and several design features were included to maximize detection of potential effects, such as the use of very high dose levels and large numbers of animals. The endpoints were descriptive in nature, often involving a comprehensive assessment of organ system effects that relied heavily on histopathological evaluations, but a mechanistic understanding of the observed effects was frequently lacking. Over time, the tests were incrementally refined, mainly through the addition of more and more end toxicity points, including functional assessments (eg, neurobehavior) as well as toxicokinetics. Some of the tests, such as the developmental neurotoxicity study and multigeneration study, have evolved into proverbial "Cadillacs," ie, "fully loaded" test systems that are extremely comprehensive, generating thousands of data points collected at a variety of life stages.

It should come as no surprise, then, that conventional toxicology testing packages often cost millions of dollars and usually take several years just to test a single chemical [2]. They also use large numbers of animals, particularly in the areas of reproductive and developmental toxicity due to the large numbers of offspring. For example, the two-generation reproductive toxicity study uses well over 3000 animals just to test one chemical [2]. To provide some perspective on the magnitude of the toxicity testing enterprise, estimated costs and animal usage for the REACH program have been as high as 9 billion Euro and 54 million vertebrates, respectively [3]. This huge investment in money, time, and animals is of course intended to protect people and the environment from the potential adverse effects of drugs, pesticides, and industrial chemicals. Indeed, the

conventional tests are incredibly comprehensive and are generally considered the gold standard by which regulatory decisions are made. The incredible longevity of this testing system and its role in preventing overt toxicological disasters like thalidomide is a tribute to its original designers, and a strong testament that it was well fit for its original purpose.

NEW NEEDS OF THE 21ST CENTURY REQUIRE NEW APPROACHES

When one looks across the entire range of chemical agents, it is clear that conventional toxicology has been (appropriately) focused on a relatively small subset of chemicals considered to warrant the most thorough of evaluations: namely new drugs, pesticides, and high production volume chemicals. In fact, good toxicology data are available for essentially all new drugs and pesticides and the majority of high production volume chemicals. Nonetheless, there are thousands more chemicals that have been synthesized at one time or another, some of which have never made it out of the research lab in which they were first synthesized, but many others of which are, or have been, in commerce with some potential for human exposure. Often these lower production volume chemicals are evaluated based on the toxicity of structurally similar molecules, as well as physical–chemical properties, etc., but they typically are not subject to the complete battery of animal tests. One should also not forget the thousands of naturally occurring compounds present in the environment, many of which have significant biological activity, but usually have little to no toxicity data available.

In recent years, interest in obtaining more and/or better toxicity data on these chemicals has increased greatly. On the commercial level, the focus has been on incorporating safety assessment earlier into the drug or new chemical development process so as to increase the chances of developing products that are both safe and efficacious. From an environmental chemicals perspective, there has been much discussion about a "toxics information gap" [4] due to untested chemicals. Just how big of a problem this gap represents is debatable, as often the number of chemicals in commerce is greatly overestimated and the number of chemicals evaluated greatly underestimated. That said, it is worth examining the issue of untested chemicals to see if there are opportunities to improve the quantity and quality of data on these chemicals.

Theoretically, one way to address these concerns would simply be to increase testing capacity. However, the amount that testing capacity would need to increase is quite significant and it is difficult to see how this could be achieved in any practical manner. Furthermore, increasing conventional toxicology capacity runs counter to society's increasing concerns over animal testing. In fact, regulations such as those promulgated in the Seventh Amendment to the European Union Cosmetics Directive have placed an outright ban on animal testing for certain products, and pressure in this direction is only likely to increase.

Even if these realities were not an issue, would conventional toxicology as currently practiced be the right solution for assessing large numbers of low-level exposure chemicals and new R&D chemicals? The answer is clearly no. The costs and time involved in conventional toxicology testing are all too great to meet such needs. Let us take, for example, the new drug or pesticide development process. Here the need is to conduct a preliminary evaluation of newly synthesized candidates from which one or two need to be selected for further development in a process called lead optimization. The amounts of chemical are often none to extremely small, the chemicals have never been tested in animals, and one can only make estimations about potential toxicity based on chemical structure, physical–chemical properties, and intended target, to the extent that it is known. Another common example is the evaluation of a class of structurally related industrial chemicals for which there are good data on some compounds in the class, but few data on the others. There are thousands of chemicals like this which fall within a general chemical class and which are regulated by a process of "read across" in which the members of the group are assumed to act similarly and thus do not warrant their own separate package of conventional toxicity data. Finally, we have real-life cases like the 2009 Gulf Oil spill, which involved a mixture of compounds released into the environment, and a general public and government agencies demanding answers very quickly in order to drive clean up strategy and obtain an initial assessment of environmental damage. Conventional toxicology was simply not designed with these purposes in mind.

In addition to these issues, many in the toxicology community have been reassessing some of the fundamental precepts of conventional toxicology and looking for ways to improve upon them. One of these fundamental assumptions is the relevance of animal test results to human risk. This assumption is increasingly being scrutinized based on examples in which laboratory animal results conflict with human epidemiological data, as well as other cases in which molecular mechanisms of action in animals were shown not to be relevant to humans. We also have many cases of discordance between test species, such as differences between the rat and mouse cancer bioassays, or the rat and rabbit developmental toxicity studies, and these have led to questions about the ability of these species to predict human toxicity.

Another conventional practice being questioned is the use of extremely high doses in animals to assess human risk, even when human exposures are orders of magnitude lower than the doses tested in animals. What we've found in recent years is that the toxicity seen at high doses often involves mechanisms unique to these high-dose exposures and are not relevant to lower-dose exposures. Lengthy investigational studies are required to elucidate these mechanisms, often only to show even more convincingly that the original high-dose effect is not relevant for normal human exposures.

A NEW APPROACH: PREDICTIVE TOXICOLOGY

These new drivers for change in toxicology have been occurring during a time of rapid advancement in science and technology, and this convergence of new needs and new technology is leading to transformational proposals for fundamentally different approaches to drug and chemical safety assessment, often referred to in a broad sense as Toxicity Testing in the 21st Century (TT21C), or more specifically as predictive toxicology. These new paradigms differ from conventional toxicology in some fundamental ways (Table 32.1). Whereas conventional toxicology is an empirical science, which relies on *observation* of adverse effects after they have occurred, predictive toxicology is more prospective as it attempts to *predict* toxicity based on knowledge of underlying biological and chemical properties and molecular initiating events. In predictive toxicology, animal testing is largely replaced with a combination of cheminformatics and human cells-based in vitro tests, which enhance human relevance. The focus also is on early molecular and cellular events (eg, receptor binding, altered cell signaling) leading to toxicity rather than final outcomes (eg, increased tumors, infertility, liver pathology). These in vitro systems also make it practical to evaluate many more dose levels than the typical three dose levels used in conventional toxicity testing, thus enabling a more robust understanding of dose–response. In addition, the limitations of conventional testing in terms of speed and throughput are not an issue with predictive toxicology, as many assays can be scaled for high throughput using robotics, which also can greatly lower unit costs. Once a high-throughput screening system is set up, it is possible for hundreds of assays to be run, on hundreds or thousands of chemicals, in a relatively short period of time (Table 32.1).

TABLE 32.1   Comparison of Conventional and Predictive Toxicology

Characteristic	Conventional Toxicology	Predictive Toxicology
Test systems	Mammalian whole-animal models	Human cells in vitro, lower organisms
Endpoints	Descriptive, apical	Mechanistic
Information content	Relatively low	High
Dose levels	Typically only three, often very high	Many dose levels possible, broad range of doses
Turnaround time	Months to years	Hours to days
Throughput (no. of chemicals)	Low	High
Expense (per chemical)	High	Low

Perhaps one the greatest challenges facing predictive toxicology is the need to integrate highly reductionist data into meaningful biological and toxicological knowledge. In conventional toxicology, the animal model itself is the highly integrated biological system. We know that the animal model provides complex physiological systems that are networked via the nervous, endocrine, and other regulatory control systems, and it also provides critical determinants of toxicity such as pharmacokinetics. Predictive toxicology lies at the other end of the spectrum, in that mechanistic data are derived from separate, highly focused assays that in isolation are often of little value. To overcome this problem, predictive toxicology relies on systems biology, bioinformatics, and advanced statistical tools to provide integration. Systems biology has been defined by Hyman [5] as:

the approach of collecting quantitative biological information at one level of complexity, and using it to build models that describe the next level of complexity.

This integrative capability not only requires sophisticated computational tools, but also detailed knowledge of normal biological pathways for which our understanding is growing rapidly. It also requires an unprecedented level of collaboration between biologists, computational scientists, and mathematicians.

Recent History

Many of the pioneers of predictive toxicology came from the pharmaceutical industry, driven by the desire to reduce late-stage drug failures due to toxicity. Many pharmaceutical companies now have significant in-house Discovery Toxicology units that essentially practice predictive toxicology, supplemented by a potpourri of relatively small contract research organizations that offer biological screening services. Regulatory agencies such as the U.S. Environmental Protection Administration (EPA) also have been eager to capitalize on the promise of predictive toxicology,

and in 2005 created a new National Center for Computational Toxicology (NCCT) for this purpose. This was followed a few years later by formation of the Tox21 partnership, which includes the EPA, the National Institute for Environmental Health Safety–National Toxicology Program's High-Throughput Screening Program, the National Institutes of Health (NIH) National Human Genome Research Institute, the NIH Chemical Genomics Center (NCGC), and the U.S. Food and Drug Administration. The global reach of this movement became evident in 2010 with the addition to this partnership of the European Union Joint Research Center's Institute for Consumer Protection.

These government programs are now generating several million data points per year on industrial chemicals, crop protection compounds, and pharmaceuticals. For example, the EPA NCCT's ToxCast high-throughput screening program has screened nearly 2000 chemicals in more than 700 high-throughput screening assays (http://www.epa.gov/ncct/toxcast). The National Toxicology Program of the National Institute of Environmental Health Sciences is currently testing a library of more than 8100 chemicals, each in approximately 70 assays at 15 concentrations per chemical [6]. As these data rapidly amass, the toxicology and risk-assessment communities are actively exploring new ways to model by using high-end computational tools and network models for efficient safety characterization and for prioritizing chemicals for more comprehensive testing [7,8]. In parallel, increasing efforts are underway for exposure assessment (eg, the ExpoCast program) to complement hazard-based characterization for developing risk-based chemical prioritization [9–11]. The ExpoCast program implements multiple simple to complex high-throughput computational models to predict chemical exposures. When the ToxCast data were complemented with ExpoCast values, a chemical prioritization outcome very different from that based on hazard information alone emerged. This analysis suggests that human exposures to about 90% of the ToxCast chemicals fall several orders of magnitude below the lowest concentration eliciting an in vitro test system response [10,11].

Overall, predictive toxicology holds great promise for overcoming some of conventional toxicology's weaknesses, but to date, few if any of these promises have been proven or realized. No system is ever perfect, and it is likely that some combination of predictive and conventional approaches will coexist for some years until a new paradigm becomes solidified. The authors firmly believe that the journey toward a new paradigm is a journey well worth taking, but is one that needs to be taken with eyes and mind wide open. Toward that end, we review here the major predictive toxicology biological assay platforms that are currently available. We begin with the more complex, whole-organism models and proceed in decreasing order of biological complexity to single-cell-type culture systems. The chapter will close with a discussion of various scenarios and strategies for the use of these platforms.

CHEMINFORMATICS AND BIOLOGICAL PROFILING PLATFORMS

Cheminformatics

Cheminformatics uses in silico approaches to assess and predict potential biological properties of compounds in relation to chemical structure. Such approaches can often be implemented quickly in high-throughput mode using free or licensed software and desktop computers. Prediction models include those broadly grouped according to either mammalian, environmental, metabolic, or physicochemical properties, including specific quantum-chemical attributes that may distinguish inherent reactivity. Currently, in silico approaches can be segregated into at least five major bins: (1) quantitative structure activity relationship models (QSAR; http://www.qsardb.org/), (2) automated decision trees [12–15], (3) structural filters using two-dimensional chemical scaffolds associated with a toxic endpoint, (4) structural read-across using expert knowledge to query apical toxicity databases, and (5) profiling of compounds using an electronic toolbox that groups compounds according to possible chemical reactivity mechanism or activity relative to apical toxicity endpoints [16]. Whereas some of these tools were trained on or directly assess potential activity for an apical toxicity endpoint, others are directed towards various molecular targets whose relation to toxicity are complex and necessitate integrating ADME/PK and tissue-specific responses. Cheminformatics is rapidly evolving to include statistical models that can access, integrate, and derive mathematical predictive algorithms across large, complex data streams including in vitro

high-throughput screening (HTS) data. QSAR DB is a repository of available QSAR models and datasets for discovery, exploring, and citing (http://www.qsardb.org/). Gleeson et al. [17] provided a comprehensive review of the challenges involved in modeling toxicity data in silico. There are several detailed reviews for in silico tools and models for genotoxicity and cancer as well as developmental and reproductive toxicity [18,19].

Application of cheminformatics to predict toxicity is a growing science for which there is much interest because of the speed and lack of requirement of test material for in silico screening. This technology could be used early in product development for ranking candidate R&D compounds, prioritization for further studies [eg, screening associated with the Endocrine Disruptor Screening Program (EDSP)], and for compounds currently on the market. There are applications for read-across to data-rich compounds, and for using select QSARs for screening for sensitive endpoints when exposures to newly identified impurities or metabolites might occur but only at trace levels. Historically, models that predict acute toxicity to aquatic species are generally agreed upon by the scientific community to be successful as long as the test compound is within the domain of the compounds used to develop the model. The same is true for some models that predict endpoints considered to be driven by chemical reactivity between electrophiles and nucleophiles and for which large training sets were available to train the models, such as skin sensitization and mutagenicity. The general consensus among scientific experts is that current global QSAR models are not able to predict local ocular or dermal irritant effects or complex toxicity endpoints such as neurotoxicity, repeat-dose toxicity, developmental and reproductive toxicity, or cancer. This may be due to an overall lack of detailed knowledge on the specific interactions of most compounds with their toxicologically relevant targets, and the hypothesis that many of these targets are proteins and the realization that even subtle structural variations can manifest markedly different interactions.

Recently, there has been heightened attention to the importance of mechanistic considerations for in silico analysis, the critical role of mechanistic data in improving QSAR approaches and integrative statistical approaches combining cheminformatics and bioinformatics [20]. Mechanistic understanding can make a significant impact on the reliability and scientific confidence of an in silico assessment and its application in a risk-assessment framework, especially considering potential route and target specificity and human relevancy.

In summary, advances with in silico computational toxicology tools and methods offer promise for screening, prioritization, and risk assessment. Currently, no single off-the-shelf QSAR tool has been vetted to allow global computational assessments for broad apical toxicity end-points. The tools are most advanced for environmental and ecological endpoints as well as those dominated by chemical reactivity such as genotoxicity and skin sensitization. Available tools require at least a moderate level of expertise in chemistry and toxicology to direct and interpret expert systems and chemical grouping tools that could be used for predicting toxicity endpoints and filling data gaps using read-across approaches. There is a need for publicly available high-quality curated data and a realization that much of the mechanistic data needed for refined models will likely be generated in the future using robotized in vitro high-throughput screening.

Model Organisms

The term "model organism" refers to simple lower organisms used as surrogates to provide insight into the complex cellular and molecular processes of higher vertebrates, including humans [21,22]. Over the past century, a handful of these organisms, such as the bacterium *Escherichia coli*, baker's yeast *Saccharomyces cerevisiae*, the nematode *Caenorhabditis elegans*, the fruit fly *Drosophila melanogaster*, and the zebrafish *Danio rerio*, have played significant roles in advancing our understanding of the biological and biomedical sciences. The major advantage of model organisms is their retention of whole-organism complexity [23], yet at the same time, their convenience and high throughput similar to that of in vitro models. Furthermore, the revolutionary upsurge of molecular biology and biotechnology techniques in the past decade has led to a deep understanding of the cellular and molecular mechanisms in these models. Zebrafish and *C. elegans* embryos have emerged as preferred models for toxicological profiling. Herein we provide a brief description of the general biology of zebrafish and *C. elegans*, their utility in toxicity assessment, and some of limitations associated with these models for toxicity screening.

Zebrafish Embryo
General Description

The zebrafish is a small freshwater fish endemic to tropical to subtropical zones. While adult zebrafish have been used for some types of research, the zebrafish embryo has drawn the most attention for biomedical research and toxicity testing [24]. Its advantages include its small size, ease of maintenance, low cost, short reproductive cycle, and large brood size (100–200 eggs per breeding pair) [24]. They also develop quite rapidly, with all the anlagen of the brain, eyes, and heart formed by 24 h postfertilization, and by 96 h postfertilization, most of the internal organs including the cardiovascular system and the hepatic, renal, and gastric systems are fully developed (Fig. 32.1; Table 32.2) [25,26]. Moreover, its genome is

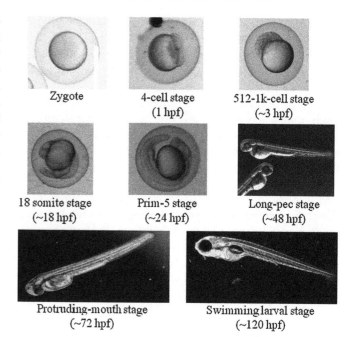

FIGURE 32.1 Overview of zebrafish development depicting early embryonic through 5-day larval stages. Following fertilization, zebrafish embryo undergoes rapid development. Within the first 3 days postfertilization, the embryo undergoes complete organogenesis (including formation of compartmentalized brain, ears, eyes, and all internal organs). Swimming and feeding behavior begins by day 5 postfertilization. *hpf*, Hours postfertilization.

completely sequenced, and in general, a strong conservation (around 70% homology) exists between zebrafish and humans at the gene and protein level. The zebrafish model also is amenable to the generation of transgenic mutants, and specific gene knock-down models for a wide range of physiological and pathological conditions [27]. Under European legislation (EU Directive 2010/63/EU), zebrafish embryos up to 120 h postfertilization are not typically counted as experimental animals as they live off their yolk and do not yet feed independently [23,28].

A particular advantage for use in toxicology is the ability to assess effects on multiple endpoints, ranging from developmental and acute toxicity to complex behavioral, physiological, and genomic parameters in the context of an intact, relatively complex organism [23]. This inherent flexibility can offer economies of scale that otherwise would not be possible in settings that require assessment of a wide variety of endpoints. The transparent nature of the embryos allows the ready visualization of effects on internal organs, including the brain, liver, cardiovascular system, etc. Finally, mechanistic endpoints such as cell-cycle inhibition, apoptotic cell death, and angiogenesis can be easily visualized under phase contrast or fluorescence microscopy (using fluorescent dyes or generation of transgenic strains expressing tissue specific GFP) without having to undergo laborious immunohistochemical staining procedures (Fig. 32.2) [25,29].

TABLE 32.2 Zebrafish Embryo Developmental Stages

Time Postfertilization (h)	Embryo/Larva Stage	Characterization[a]
0	Zygote period	One-cell stage
0.75	Cleavage period	Two-cell stage
1		Four-cell stage
1.25		Eight-cell stage
1.5		Sixteen-cell stage
2	Blastula period	Initiation of blastula stage
3		Blastodisc containing approximately 256 blastomers
4		Flat interface between blastoderm and yolk
5.25	Gastrula period	Interface between periblast and blastoderm become curved
8		75% of epibolic movement
10		Blastopore is nearly closed, completion of epibolic movement
10.5	Segmentation	First somite furrow
12		Development of somites, segmented tail
20		Muscular twitches, well-extended tail
22		Side-to-side flexures, formation of otoliths
24	Pharyngula period	Spontaneous movements, tail detached from yolk, early pigmentation
30		Pigmented retina, reduced spontaneous movement, circulation in aortic arch
36		Tail pigmentation, strong circulation, irregularly beating heart
72–96	Hatching period	Regular heartbeat, begin tapering of yolk extension, dorsal and ventral pigmentation stripes meet at tail, segmental blood vessels, foregut development

[a]At 26 ± 1°C.

Modified from Nagel R. DarT: the embryo test with the Zebrafish Danio rerio – *a general model in ecotoxicology and toxicology. ALTEX 2002;19(Suppl. 1):38–48.*

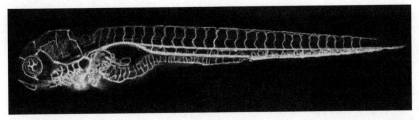

FIGURE 32.2   The zebrafish vascular system. Confocal image of the vascular system of a 4.5-day-old zebrafish larva labeled by injection of fluorescent microspheres. The transparency of zebrafish larvae enables utilization of high-resolution optical imaging methods to visualize the entire vasculature in detail. *Courtesy of Sumio Isogai and Brant Weinstein, NICHD, NIH.*

Use in Toxicity Assessment

For many years, the adult fish acute lethality test has been routinely required for regulatory evaluation of chemicals (eg, OECD testing protocol 203; 1992). In this test, salmonid fish species and/or fathead minnows are exposed to the test chemical for up to 96h and the concentration resulting in 50% lethality (LC50) is

calculated. Recently, the zebrafish embryo test (ZET) has been explored as an alternative test for acute toxicity to adult fish [23,30]. In the ZET, fertilized eggs are placed individually in 24- or 96-well plates and exposed for up to 5days and then evaluated under a dissecting microscope for morphological characteristics. Lammer et al. [31] tested the effects of 143 chemicals on lethality and developmental toxicity in the ZET and observed a high correlation between adult fish and zebrafish embryos, suggesting that zebrafish embryos are excellent surrogates for acute toxicity tests in adult fish. Recently, Vaughan and van Egmond [32] demonstrated that the LC50 data for 15 surfactants (cationic and anionic) was comparable between the 48-h embryo and adult zebrafish tests. From this study, the authors concluded that the 48-h zebrafish assay can be utilized to predict surfactant-mediated acute fish toxicity. In 2002, German authorities began using the zebrafish embryo model to evaluate acute toxicity of whole-effluent discharges, and by 2005 the zebrafish embryo test became mandatory for this purpose and jurisdiction (DIN, 2001; ISO, 2007). OECD has developed a draft fish embryo toxicity assay test guideline (OECD TG 203) which is currently under review.

Zebrafish have also been used to examine neurotoxicity development and progression [33]. The neuroanatomy of zebrafish is similar to that of vertebrates, with a central nervous system composed of fore-, mid-, and hind-brain and spinal cord. A number of behavioral endpoints, consisting of swimming activity, turning rate, sensorimotor responses, phototaxis, exploratory behavior and stress response, learning and memory have been developed to evaluate neurotoxicity [33,34]. The majority of these behavioral endpoints can be evaluated on zebrafish as early as 3 to 4 days postfertilization, except for learning and memory endpoints, which require more advanced stages of development [33].

The zebrafish model has also been used for chemical-mediated neurodegeneration studies. Neurotoxicants that decrease catecholamine levels in humans and rodents (6-hydroxy dopamine, MPTP) exert similar

effects in zebrafish [35]. As in mammals, reduction in catecholamine levels alter locomotion pattern in zebrafish (swimming pattern and reduced speed) as well suggesting conservation of these molecular mechanisms across species [35]. Transgenic zebrafish expressing a fluorescent protein in specific neuronal subpopulations are in use especially in screening purposes. Targeted zebrafish screens have been used to identify novel compounds that suppress the effects of L-hydroxyglutaric acid neurotoxicity and MPTP-induced neurotoxicity [26,36].

Cardiac and vascular toxicity are other commonly tested endpoints in zebrafish. Cardiotoxic agents generally appear to exert similar effects both in zebrafish and humans. For instance, 20 of 23 chemicals causing bradycardia in humans were cardiotoxic in zebrafish [37]. Similarly, known antiangiogenic chemicals (total 18 chemicals) in mice exhibited comparable effects in zebrafish [25]. Embryos treated at one day postfertilization with angiogenic inhibitors (SU5416 and TNP470) or stimulant (VEGF) exhibited similar vascular phenotypes (development of dorsal aorta and axial vein) as those observed in mammalian models [38]. Similarly to vertebrate models, thalidomide induced morphological changes in major blood vessels and depleted vascular endothelial growth factor receptor (neurophillin-1 and flk-1) in zebrafish [39]. As in higher mammals, point mutations in the *gridlock/hey2* gene disrupt aortic blood flow.

The zebrafish embryo model has also been used for developmental toxicity screening (Table 32.3). Recently, Brannen et al. [40] studied the teratogenic effects of 31 compounds using dechorionated zebrafish embryos. The authors determined the ratio of no-observed-adverse-effect-level (NOAEL) to the 25% lethal concentration (LC25), as a metric to differentiate between teratogens

TABLE 32.3   Summary of Commonly Used Alternative Models to Assess Developmental Toxicity

Parameter	Micromass	EST	WEC	Caenorhabditis elegans	Zebrafish
Duration of study (d)	5	10	2	2–3	3–5
Developmental process assessed	Differentiation into chondrocytes	Differentiation into cardiomyocytes	Embryo organogenesis	Complete organogenesis	Complete organogeneis
Endpoints measured	Alcian blue staining cartilage	No. of beating cardiomyocytes	Growth, morphology, organ malformations	Growth, morphology, expression of developmentally conserved genes	Growth, morphology, organ malformations, expression of developmentally conserved genes
Technical difficulty	Low	Moderate	High	Low	Low
Vertebrate animal use	Yes	No	Yes	No	No
Xenobiotic biotransformation	Limited	Limited	Limited	Moderate	Limited to moderate
Throughput	Low	Low to moderate	Low	Moderate to high	Low to moderate

EST, embryonic stem cell test; *WEC*, whole-embryo culture.

and nonteratogens. In this study, the zebrafish developmental test exhibited 87% concordance with in vivo mammalian data. Selderslaghs et al. [41] developed a teratogenic index as the ratio of LC50 to EC50 for teratogenicity. They correctly predicted all tested teratogens (4) and nonteratogens (2). Hermsen et al. [42] (tested 11 chemicals) and Hill et al. [43] (tested 85 chemicals) found 64% and 89% concordance between zebrafish embryo toxicity studies and in vivo mammalian data. Recently, Padilla et al. [44] screened 309 ToxCast Phase I chemicals in a zebrafish embryo (6–8h postfertilization) developmental assay with key endpoints consisting of lethality, nonhatching, and malformation. When compared to rat and rabbit in vivo test guideline study results, concordance was only 55% [45]. However, these results may have been affected by the criteria for a positive in vivo study, which included a wide range of general developmental endpoints (eg, decreased fetal body weight) in addition to teratogenicity.

Clearly these studies show variable levels of predictivity for the zebrafish embryo assay. As with most models, predictivity can be quite good for certain classes of chemicals, but very poor for others. Similarly, the zebrafish embryo is more likely to be a good predictor of certain endpoints (eg, teratogenicity) than other developmental endpoints (eg, fetal body weight) that have a strong maternal influence in pregnant mammals. Therefore, it is important to establish the validity of the zebrafish (or any other model) for the particular purpose at hand, via the use of well-characterized reference chemicals.

It is possible to enhance the utility of the ZET, as well as other alternative models, via incorporation of high information content methods such as toxicogenomics. For example, Yang et al. [46] correctly classified environmental toxicants, teratogens and antiepileptic drugs based on toxicogenomic profiles in zebrafish embryos. Using gene expression profiling, Lim [47] demonstrated that arsenic generates hepatic damage in zebrafish similar to that in mammals. At least conceptually, toxicogenomics signatures can bring an additional level of specificity to toxicity evaluations.

Limitations

One of the most significant limitations in the use of the zebrafish embryo for toxicity evaluations regards differences in bioavailability relative to mammalian models. Although chemicals soluble in water or DMSO freely diffuse into zebrafish embryos, hydrophobic chemicals are poorly absorbed. This poor bioavailability may be due to the chorion, which has often been speculated to function as an embryo-specific barrier for penetration of chemical agents [48,49]. To circumvent this problem, the chorion can be disrupted either enzymatically (2mg/L pronase) or mechanically to facilitate uptake of chemicals into the embryo [48,50]. Others have microinjected chemicals

directly into the perivitelline space of the embryo [48]. However, all of these approaches pose technical limitations as well as nonphysiological testing conditions. Another limitation of the zebrafish is that the hepatic detoxification mechanisms are not well developed during the early embryonic stages [51]. Finally, the husbandry requirements to maintain a healthy fish colony should not be underestimated, as the fish need to be fed 2–3 times a day to support high production of eggs, and vigilant maintenance of water quality is necessary to support a healthy colony.

Caenorhabditis elegans

General Description

C. elegans is a free-living, soil-dwelling nematode that has been extensively used as a model for genetic studies, and more recently is finding application in toxicology. Many essential biochemical pathways and stress responses observed in humans are well conserved in *C. elegans*. Apoptosis and RNA interference are some of the best examples of highly conserved mechanisms in *C. elegans*. In fact, *C. elegans* was the model that led to the discovery of these pathways, for which Sydney Brenner et al. (2002) and Andrew Fire and Craig Mello (2006) were awarded Nobel Prizes. *C. elegans* was also the first multicellular eukaryotic organism whose genome was successfully sequenced, leading to the finding that *C. elegans* has orthologs for 60–80% of human genes [52].

C. elegans is easy to maintain under laboratory conditions, very inexpensive, transparent, small in size (1mm in length), has a short generation time (3.5days), produces large numbers of offspring (300–350), and can be cultivated in a small amount of laboratory space (~10,000 worms/Petri dish) (Fig. 32.3). Wild-type *C. elegans* consists of 959cells whose cell lineage has been completely mapped. The nervous system in *C. elegans* is particularly interesting in that approximately one-third of the total number of cells (302) are neurons, and the nervous system is completely mapped at the ultrastructural level [53]. Because of their transparent nature, some of the physiological or pathological processes such as apoptosis can be visualized (highly reflective, button-like appearance) in unstained living worms under Nomarski differential interference contrast optics [54]. Also, transgenic strains expressing fluorescent markers (GFP, YFP, RFP, CFP) tagged to specific gene promoters or protein sequences facilitate the study of key regulatory processes, such as apoptosis [55]. Gene knockdown methodologies are quite simple and rapid in *C. elegans*. Remarkably, genetic alterations can be accomplished simply by feeding the worms gene-specific dsRNA that are expressed in *Escherichia coli* [56,57].

Because the genetics of *C. elegans* is so well characterized, it is possible to identify genes and pathways that contribute to the phenotype using a genetic suppressor screen (gene targets that reverse the phenotype).

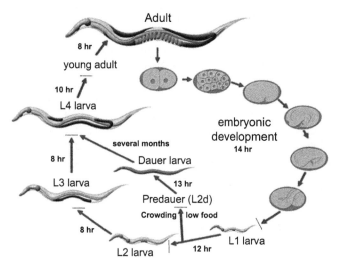

FIGURE 32.3 **The life-cycle of** *Caenorhabditis elegans*. *C. elegans* is a rapidly growing nematode; its entire development from egg to adult takes only 3–4 days under favorable conditions. Following embryogenesis, *C. elegans* progress through four larval stages (L1 to L4) before becoming an adult. In response to harsh environmental conditions, such as food shortage, crowding, or high temperatures, *C. elegans* can enter into a physiologically specialized state called dauer stage to survive during adverse environmental conditions, and possesses long-term survival. As the favorable conditions return, the dauer stage larva progress to L4 and continue to exhibit a regular life-cycle. *Reproduced with permission from Zeynep Altun and Chris Crocker, Wormatlas.*

Alternatively, if the toxic properties of a set of chemicals are predicted following in silico approaches, the set of chemicals can be tested in mutant strains that are hypo- or hyperresistant to the phenotype. If the mutants for the given phenotype are not available, almost any gene in the whole genome can be silenced using the RNA interference method (through simple feeding mechanisms). Results from such studies would enable confirmation of in silico approaches, with much less expense and effort.

Like the zebrafish model, *C. elegans* offers many of the practical advantages of in vitro systems (eg, assays conducted in 96-well plates), yet an infinitely greater degree of biological complexity and physiology relative to systems such as cell lines. This feature enables one to study effects on functional endpoints such as feeding, reproduction, lifespan, locomotion [58,59], and even learning and behavior. These endpoints have been engineered for medium to high throughput evaluations via automated imaging methods for absorbance, fluorescence, or morphometric measurements [60,61] as well as flow-cytometric and microfluidic sorting [62,63].

Use in Toxicity Assessment

Some of the earliest examples demonstrating the use of *C. elegans* in toxicology came from studies on heavy metals. Williams and Dusenbery [64] tested eight different metal salts in *C. elegans* and observed that the LD50 values in *C. elegans* were comparable to the acute LD50

values in rodents. Tatara et al. [65] showed that rodent acute toxicity for the heavy metals Ca, Cu, Cd, Hg, Mg, Mn, Ni, Pb, and Zn could be predicted based on 24h LC50 values using *C. elegans*.

Considering the fact that the nervous system in *C. elegans* is simple and well characterized, this model is increasingly being used to evaluate neurotoxicants [66]. Cole et al. [58] demonstrated a high correlation between LD50 values for 15 organophosphate pesticides in *C. elegans* compared to LD50 values in rats and mice. Williams and Dusenbery [59] developed a neurobehavioral toxicity test using *C. elegans* movement behavior, based on which the authors correctly predicted the neurotoxic effects of the tested six chemicals. Similarly, Melstrom and Williams [67] observed acetylcholinesterase inhibition and reduced movement following exposure to carbamates, which is consistent with observations in rodent models. They also observed a high correlation with the rank order of toxicity of carbamates between *C. elegans* and rodent models.

Recently, Freedman's group at NIEHS developed a high-throughput screen to quantify chemical effects on reproductive efficiency, feeding, and growth using Complex Object Parametric Analyzer and Sorter (COPAS) Biosort, a fluorescence-activated worm sorter that can accurately dispense *C. elegans* at specific developmental stages in a 96-well format [68]. Using the Biosort technology, the authors observed concentration-dependent decreases in reproduction efficiency in *C. elegans* exposed to a diverse array of metals, pesticides, mutagens, and drugs. The same group performed a high-throughput screen to test ToxCast Phase I chemicals (mainly pesticides) and Phase II chemicals (chemically diverse failed drugs, food additives, industrial chemicals), in which *C. elegans* at first larval stage (L1) were incubated with the test chemical at seven concentrations at 48h, following which growth and development and population distribution were analyzed using COPAS Biosort. A chemical was defined as positive (active), if it inhibited development at or below 200 μM for Phase I chemicals and at or below 100 μM for Phase II chemicals. Sixty-four percent of the Phase I chemicals and 57% of the Phase II chemicals were classified as active [68]. However, to date, no analyses have been published to determine whether these results bear any correlation to in vivo toxicity data. Such a robust validation exercise will be necessary in order to determine the predictive capability of the *C. elegans* model. In addition, more research to refine criteria for active vs. inactive is needed in order to enhance the discriminating power of the assay [68].

Limitations

Although *C. elegans* is widely agreed as one of the best models for genetic studies, it clearly is just beginning to emerge as a model for toxicity testing. One key consideration for its use in toxicity testing and data interpretation is its thick outer cuticle, which forms a barrier to certain hydrophilic chemicals. Therefore, it is generally necessary to expose the worms to higher doses to achieve intracellular concentrations comparable to mammalian models. In fact, this is the likely reason for the relatively high concentrations (100 or 200 μM) used as the cut-off for classification as "inactive" in the ToxCast screening studies [69]. To partially circumvent this limitation, a number of C. elegans strains have been developed with mutations that increase permeability of the outer cuticle. Other key considerations for using this model relate to species-specific metabolism and pharmacokinetics. For example, in mammals, the genotoxic promutagen aflatoxin B1 is activated by CYP1, CYP2, and CYP3 family members, whereas exclusively CYP1 family members activate the promutagen benzo[a]pyrene (BaP). However, C. elegans lack CYP1 enzymes; therefore worms can metabolically activate aflatoxin B1, but not BaP [70,71].

Mammalian Whole-Embryo and Organotypic Cultures

The zebrafish and C. elegans platforms reviewed in the previous sections are advantaged by their high level of biological complexity, but disadvantaged by their phylogenetic distance from humans. The mammalian whole-embryo and organotypic culture platforms do not have that problem. These models all involve the explantation of tissues from mammalian species and maintenance of those tissues in short-term culture.

Whole-Embryo Culture

General Description

The whole-embryo culture (WEC) model has been a workhorse in teratology screening and mechanism of action investigations for five decades [72], and is considered the most complete alternative for in vitro teratogenesis screening (Table 32.3) [73]. In this assay, postimplantation rodent or rabbit embryos in early organogenesis (gestation day 9–12 for rats and rabbits; gestation day 8–11 for mouse) are excised from the uterus, dissected free of decidual tissue, and are cultured with intact yolk sac in a roller bottle apparatus containing culture media composed mainly of blood serum for up to 48h [74,75]. During this period, the embryos undergo very rapid growth and morphological changes such as somitogenesis, neural tube closure, limb bud formation, and craniofacial development. Developmental abnormalities are quantified using morphological scoring systems as a guide, while embryo growth is evaluated by measuring yolk sac diameter and head length, and by counting the number of somite pairs [76,77]. Although the stages of embryogenesis only cover a small portion

of the total gestational period, WEC is conducted during an extremely active and impactful period of embryogenesis. The availability of rat, mouse, and rabbit WEC models can be exploited to study mechanisms responsible for species-specific responses to chemical and drug exposure, which are fairly common in developmental toxicity testing [72]. Another powerful application of WEC is to assess the toxicity of a chemical's metabolites. Because the embryos have generally low xenobiotic metabolizing activity, embryos can be directly exposed to individual metabolites without them being metabolized further.

Use in Toxicity Assessment

Studies to validate the ability of WEC to predict teratogenicity have been going on for over three decades. In 1985, Schmid [78] tested 39 chemicals (18 known teratogens and 21 nonteratogens) at three to five concentrations each using rat WEC and reported that WEC correctly identified all the tested teratogens and most of the nonteratogenic compounds. In a subsequent study, Cicurel and Schmid tested 27 chemicals, with WEC correctly identifying all 17 known teratogenic compounds and 8 of the 10 nonteratogens [79]. WEC has since become one of the three alternative approaches validated by ECVAM (European Center for the Validation of Alternative Methods) for the identification of teratogenic agents. As part of their validation study, ECVAM analyzed a set of 20 reference compounds that already had high quality human and laboratory animal data [80]. The WEC assay correctly predicted 80% of the ECVAM validation chemical set. The assay exhibited 100% predictivity and precision for strong embryotoxic test chemicals, whereas for the nonembryotoxic and weakly embryotoxic compounds, the predictivity was only 70% and 65%, respectively.

Comparison of the benchmark dose for the same set of chemicals revealed a high reproducibility for the assay in three out of four participating laboratories [81]. WEC was also included in another European alternatives project called ReProTect. As part of this project, Schenk et al. [82] conducted a ring trial in which 10 chemicals were evaluated for teratogenic potential using a battery of complementary in vitro tests including WEC. WEC correctly predicted teratogenic potential for six chemicals (four positives, two negatives), but falsely predicted three chemicals (one false positive, two false negatives), whereas one chemical exhibited ambiguous results in vivo and in vitro [82]. These findings indicate that WEC is useful for predicting strong developmental toxicants, but is less reliable for predicting weak teratogens.

Limitations

The limited metabolic capabilities of WEC are considered one of the model's major limitations for use in predictive toxicology, as chemicals such as cyclophosphamide, which require metabolic activation, are falsely predicted as negative [83]. Although several groups have tried to add metabolic enzyme preparations to circumvent the problem, it is difficult to obtain a similar metabolic profile as obtained in vivo. Another potential limitation is that it requires excellent microdissection skills as well as a sound understanding of embryo morphology and developmental biology. Its labor-intensive nature greatly limits throughput. The method also is not animal-free, as pregnant females are needed to supply embryos.

Organ and Tissue Slices

General Description

Organ slices have been used for decades in biochemical studies, where organs such as liver are excised from animals, sliced in cold oxygenated buffers, and incubated for short periods of time. Early methods were limited by arduous tissue-preparation work and more importantly, irregular slice thicknesses. The introduction of precision-cut liver slicing has enormously improved the uniformity of slice thicknesses, leading to more repeatable results (Table 32.4). Similar to in vivo conditions, the tissue slices possess all the cells of the tissue with intact cell–matrix interactions and therefore are considered as a bridge between in vivo and cell culture systems [84,85]. Precision-cut tissue slices can also be prepared from a variety of other organs, most notably lungs, kidneys, heart, prostate, and intestine.

Use in Toxicity Assessment

Precision-cut liver slices are commonly used to evaluate chemical-induced alterations in the expression of cytochrome P450 enzymes, stress proteins, and peroxisomal enzymes [84,85], to predict metabolite profiles [84–86], and to study mechanisms of tissue injury [84]. Precision-cut liver slices have been reported to metabolize many of the tested chemicals similar to in vivo hepatic tissue; moreover, the chemicals generate lesions at sites of liver slice similar to that of liver tissue in vivo [84,87]. For instance, metabolism and biotransformation rates of caffeine were very comparable between hepatic liver slices and hepatic tissue or in vitro microsomal preparations [87]. Similarly, toxicities associated with paracetamol, aflatoxin B1, endotoxin, cocaine, paraquat, dimethylnitrosamine, etc., were comparable between liver slices and in vivo [88–90]. Furthermore, halogenated hydrocarbon-mediated lipid peroxidation, and DNA damage, were comparable between liver sections and in vivo [91,92].

Similar to hepatic slices, kidney slices have been used to study renal responses to a variety of endogenous

TABLE 32.4 Advantages and Limitations of Some In Vitro Liver Models Used Most Widely in Toxicology Studies

	Advantages	Limitations
Liver slices	Tissue architecture partly preserved.	Availability of healthy human liver slices.
	Functions close to in vivo liver.	Rapid phenotypic changes.
	Possesses better metabolic capabilities.	Biological variability. Difficult procedure.
	Morphological studies possible.	Cryopreservation needs further optimization.
		Low throughput.
		Short viability.
Primary hepatocytes	Strong resemblance to in vivo liver.	Availability.
	Interspecies comparison of toxicants possible.	Difficult procedure. Short viability.
	Well established and characterized.	Biological variability.
	Cryopreservation possible.	Time-dependent loss of liver-specific functions.
HepG2 cells	Most frequently used and well characterized for toxicity studies.	Low metabolizing enzyme expression, relative to in vivo.
	Express variety of liver-specific metabolic functions.	Culture media composition impact type of CYP isoforms expression.
	Reproducible and consistent data.	Transformed cells.
HepaRG cells	Majority of liver-specific enzymes expressed.	Transformed cells.
	Reproducible and consistent data.	Originate from single donor.
	Cell proliferation and differentiation.	

and exogenous toxicants, such as chloroform, cisplatin, acetaminophen, mercury, and cadmium, to name a few [93,94]. Precision-cut slices from lung tissue have been used to evaluate mechanisms associated with endotoxin-mediated mitogenesis, bleomycin-mediated pulmonary fibrosis, paraquat-induced lung toxicity, ozone-mediated fibrosis, etc. [95–98]. The PCLS were part of the European Union project Sens-it-iv, which involved 28 partners from European countries. The overall objective of Sens-it-iv project was to develop alternative testing strategies that can replace animal testing for safety assessment of chemical-mediated dermal and respiratory sensitizers. Heart slices have been employed successfully to demonstrate toxic effects of antineoplastic agents on myocardial tissue [85]. Also, precision-cut prostate slices reproduced the toxic properties of cadmium ranging from cell proliferation at lower concentrations to complete cellular necrosis at higher concentrations [99].

Limitations

A major limitation of tissue slices is that they remain viable only for about 24h for most tissues (up to 96h for liver) under optimal incubation conditions [86]. In fact, from the moment they are explanted, their expression of metabolizing enzymes decreases [100], making their use a race against time. Maintenance of optimal tissue slice thickness (12–14cell layers deep) is very critical for toxicity testing. Tissue slices less than 12cell layers thick have reduced viability, while slices with more than 14 layers exhibit oxygen and nutrient deprivation of the inner layers [101]. This, and the generally labor intensive nature of this method, greatly limits the throughput of organ slices.

Isolated Tissues to Evaluate Eye Irritation Potentials

General Description

Several organotypic models also are available for assessing eye irritation potential. These include the Hen's Egg Test-Chorioallantoic Membrane (HET-CAM) assay, the Isolated Rabbit or Chicken Eye models (IRE and ICE, respectively), and the Isolated Bovine Corneal Opacity and Permeability (BCOP) assay. In the HET-CAM assay, chemicals are directly applied onto the CAM of the hen's egg for 5min. The chemical is scored for irritancy based on its ability to damage vasculature or membrane and the time taken for the injury to occur. The IRE and ICE assays utilize isolated rabbit or chicken eyes, where the enucleated eyes are exposed to test chemicals and the effects on corneas (corneal swelling, corneal opacity, and epithelial integrity) are quantified to identify chemicals with eye irritation potential. In the BCOP assay, changes in corneal opacity and permeability are quantified with an opacitometer and a visible light spectrophotometer, based on which the chemicals are evaluated for their eye irritation potential [102].

Use in Toxicity Assessment

Of the models described above, only the BCOP and ICE assay have been accepted internationally as a replacement for the traditional in vivo Draize test for detecting ocular corrosives and nonirritants. As a result, these are becoming widely used for regulatory testing. However, the others may still be quite useful as screens for nonregulatory purposes. The BCOP assay exhibited reproducible results across 12 laboratories (52 test chemicals) and the correlation between the BCOP and Draize assays was 73%, with 8% false positives and 8% false negatives [102]. The BCOP is one of the three assays in the U.S. EPA-proposed tiered approach for characterizing ocular irritation potential of antimicrobial products intended for clearing purposes (EPA, 2015). The ICE test in three separate studies exhibited relatively high accuracy (72–97%), with sensitivity (50–100%), specificity (75–100%), false positives (0–25%), and false negatives (0–50%) compared to the Draize test [103,104]. Like other assays, the predictivity of the assays appears to be highly dependent on the chemical class evaluated.

Limitations

The eye irritation models share most of the same general limitations of any organ culture system. In addition, all of the methods require access to either a slaughterhouse (eg, BCOP) or other source of animal tissues. With respect to performance, the BCOP assays underestimate the irritation potential of mild irritants. In addition, both BCOP and ICE assays suffer from high false-positive rates for alcohols and ketones, and high false-negative rates for solid materials (ICCVAM test method evaluation report, 2006). None of these assays has been approved as a complete replacement of the Draize test to predict the entire range of GHS classifications.

Primary Cultures

Like organ cultures, primary cultures are isolated directly from tissues. However, the tissues are processed further in order to establish cultures of individual cells. Intact embryonic/adult organs are collected and dissociated into single-cell suspensions either by enzymatic digestion or mechanical force. Primary cultures maintain many of the biochemical and physiological characteristics as those of the original tissue. Although primary cultures can be obtained from almost any organ, hepatic primary cultures are among the most commonly used primary cultures for toxicology investigation [105].

Primary Hepatocytes

General Description

As liver is the major xenobiotic metabolizing site in the human body, primary cultures obtained from liver are particularly useful for xenobiotic metabolism studies

(Table 32.4) [106]. Fresh primary human and animal hepatocytes express various drug metabolizing enzymes at comparable levels to those found in vivo. The availability of human and animal primary hepatocyte cultures enables comparative studies for estimating the metabolism of a compound in humans and to determine the relevance of an animal test species for modeling toxicity in humans [107,108].

The most commonly used method to isolate hepatocytes is collagenase digestion [109,110], which involves perfusion of the liver with buffer containing collagenase to disrupt intercellular adhesion. The isolated hepatocytes are dispersed in medium containing 5% fetal calf serum and washed by low-speed centrifugation. The cells are then cultured on collagen (type I)-coated or Matrigel plates in culture medium for several days to weeks, during which they retain morphology and some function but do not replicate [110]. Unfortunately, some of the hepatocyte-specific characteristics are lost during isolation procedures (eg, decreases in CYP and other enzyme activities) and their further maintenance of liver-specific functions strongly depends on culture conditions [111]. Not surprisingly, one of the active areas of research in primary cell culture is development of optimal growth conditions and matrix composition so as to improve cell survival and maintain hepatocyte-specific characteristics. For instance, hepatocytes grown in collagen sandwich cultures in the presence of dexamethasone exhibit characteristic morphology and gene and protein expression similar to in vivo for several weeks [112,113]. Similarly, Tuschl and Mueller [114] demonstrated that primary rat hepatocytes cultured in collagen sandwich with serum-free medium adopt their characteristic polygonal shape, clear cytoplasm, and bile canaliculi-like structures, and maintain CYP expression longer compared to the cells grown on collagen monolayers with serum-containing medium. Further understanding in this area would enable utilization of primary hepatocyte cultures for studying longer-term toxicant exposure effects and thereby better characterize drug/chemical-induced toxicities in vitro.

Use in Toxicity Assessment

In addition to studying xenobiotic metabolism, primary hepatocyte cultures are also used to determine compound- and species-specific kinetic parameters, inhibition and induction effects, and to screen for drug interaction effects on metabolizing enzymes [115–117]. Primary hepatic cultures can be used to screen for or investigate mechanisms of toxicant-induced liver damage. For example, Story et al. [117] analyzed 34 structurally and functionally diverse chemicals for hepatotoxic response in rat primary hepatic cultures. A good correlation was observed between in vitro and in vivo hepatotoxicity, where all the chemicals tested positive in vivo

were also toxic in primary hepatic cultures. Using rat primary hepatic cultures, Tyson et al. [118] evaluated 33 chemicals with known diverse hepatotoxic potency in vivo. They found that 31 out of 33 chemicals were toxic to primary hepatic cultures as well. Primary hepatocyte cultures also have been used in an "unscheduled DNA synthesis (UDS) assay" to study genotoxic agents of a wide variety of structural classes [119,120]. The genotoxic action of carcinogens on primary hepatocytes is detected by evaluating unscheduled incorporation of radiolabeled thymidine into DNA (as a measure of DNA repair process) by autoradiography or liquid scintillation counting, but the latter approach can lead to severe artifacts [120,121].

Limitations

Primary cultures are less homogeneous relative to cell lines, and as previously mentioned, liver-specific specialized characteristics depend on the culture conditions, which in turn can lead to difficulties with reproducibility. Also, the rate of decline in metabolic activity varies across species, which makes it difficult to draw confident interpretations across species, especially in longer-term cultures [119,122]. Moreover, the availability of freshly prepared primary human hepatocytes is a limitation. Human primary hepatocytes exhibit interindividual variations in drug-metabolizing enzyme profile [123], making it critical to test at least two different cell populations [124]. Throughput is greater than liver slices, but still much less than that of cell lines and other platforms to be described subsequently.

Three-Dimensional Cultures
General Description

The majority of the in vitro cell-based assays to date have been conducted using two-dimensional (2D) monolayers grown on plastic dishes. However, under in vivo conditions, mammalian cells are connected to their adjacent cells through extracellular matrix (ECM) proteins (such as collagen, elastin, and laminin integrins), which also provide mechanical support and mediate communication among cells [125]. In three-dimensional (3D) cultures, cells are embedded in structures that mimic in vivo ECM. The 3D cultures present a gradient for nutrients and gases, which causes cells at different levels from the surface to differ in their physiology, gene expression pattern, cell proliferation, and response to chemicals [126]. In short, cells grown in 3D cultures possess physiology and gene expression more similar to in vivo conditions.

Recently, the Hamner Institute for Health Sciences initiated research using 3D assays for in vitro toxicity testing with the goal of generating "better human tissue surrogates" for chemical testing. Along the same lines, a team of development biologists led by Kenneth

Yamada at the National Institute of Dental and Cranio-facial Research at Maryland showed that fibroblasts and collagen-secreting cells grow and develop more quickly in 3D cultures and attain the characteristic in vivo-like asymmetric pattern [127]. Hepatocytes that are grown on collagen-based 3D cultures retain their natural cuboidal morphology, maintain hepatic functions longer with greater viability (1–2 months for 3D compared to 1 week for 2D cultures), and express higher levels of Phase I, II, and III drug metabolizing genes under both basal and induced conditions [128,129]. The 3D cultures have also been utilized in cancer research to better understand tumor microenvironment [130]. In their landmark paper, Bissell's group used 3D cultures to demonstrate the causal role of integrin misregulation in human epithelial breast cell malignancies [125]. Friedl's group, initially using 3D cultures, showed that cancerous cells during metastasis change to an amoeba-like form and spread to other regions of tissue; they demonstrated a similar cell-shape pattern with in vivo mouse models, suggesting similarities between the two model systems [131].

One of the active areas of research related to 3D culture is the identification of optimal culture conditions of diverse cell lines, with a major emphasis on determining appropriate matrix conditions that can recapitulate ECM in vivo. Some of the current commonly used matrixes include:

1. Simple collagen gels or ECM obtained from the relevant tissue.
2. Commercially available Matrigel (which consists of laminin, collagen and other structural proteins, enzymes, and growth factors obtained from mouse tumors).
3. Silk fibroin conjugate sponges [132].

Although the ECM extracted from the relevant tissues is preferred, batch variability, cost, and animal usage issues are driving the exploration and development of synthetic matrixes such as synthetic polymers, poly(lactide-co-glycolide), and amino acid nanoscale structures for consistent results.

Use in Toxicity Assessment

To date, the most common use of 3D models in predictive toxicology is for the assessment of ocular (EpiOcular) and dermal irritation (EpiDerm and EPISKIN). The epidermis in these models exhibits similarity to human tissue in terms of morphology, lipid composition, and other ocular- and dermal-specific biochemical markers [133]. In these assays, test material is applied directly to the cell surface to mimic human topical exposure, and then mitochondrial activity is determined as an indicator of cell viability using the MTT (a tetrazolium salt) assay. These 3D models underwent an ECVAM-validated process, and have demonstrated overall accuracy of around

85% compared to respective in vivo Draize tests [134]. Based on these findings, the ECVAM Scientific Advisory Committee approved these assays as alternatives to in vivo testing for distinguishing between irritants and nonirritants [135]. The EpiDerm models are also evaluated for determining phototoxicity as well as for drug and xenobiotic transportation across skin [133].

Limitations

Due to the nature of tissue isolation, most of the cultures possess nonuniform dimensions, creating problems with evaluating cells in different regions within the three-dimensional construct [126]. Confocal imaging is one of the common approaches to circumvent the problem. However, this approach is slow and technically challenging [126]. One other challenge associated with 3D cultures is that multiple cell layers may impede oxygen and nutrient supply to the core of cell culture, leading to starvation of the cells as well as metabolite accumulation, resulting in cell necrosis [136]. The EpiDerm and EPISKIN models are available only as relatively expensive proprietary kits, with narrow windows around their shipping and use.

Cell-Line Models

As defined in the report of the Terminology Committee of the Tissue Culture Association, a cell line is derived from a primary culture by further dissociating and transferring cells into new vessels (called passaging or subculturing) [137]. Through repeated subculturing, a single cell type derived from one of the multiple lineages of the original primary culture is established. Most cell lines eventually acquire the ability to proliferate indefinitely either through random mutation or deliberate modification, and are referred to as "immortalized." Alternatively, cell lines can be developed by transfecting normal cells with a viral oncogene (eg, SV40 virus large T antigen) to generate genetically stable cell lines. Cell lines have also been developed by chemically mutating normal cells and isolating immortalized cells.

Hundreds of cell lines are available, many from repositories such as the American Type Culture Collection or the German Collection of Microorganisms and Cell Cultures, which ensure high-quality, well-characterized cells that are shipped frozen to investigators around the world. Cell lines have a decided advantage over organ cultures and primary cultures in that frozen cells can be held in long-term storage and reestablished quickly when needed; they are amenable to high-throughput scale-up; the cells are homogeneous, which enhances reproducibility; and they can be maintained at low cost in any conventional cell-culture facility. Perhaps most important is the availability of human cell lines, which of course is the species in whom we are trying to predict toxicity in the first place. This presents the opportunity to directly probe human cellular and molecular responses and at the same time circumvents issues associated with the use of animals. Only human cell lines obtained using ethical and rigorously controlled procedures should be used.

A major limitation of cell lines is the lack of interaction with other cell types [73]. As the cell lines have undergone a number of transformations, it is very likely that they are quite different from the original tissue as well. Also, some of the cell lines have very limited metabolic capacity. To circumvent this limitation, metabolizing systems can be added, such as:

1. Organ-specific S9 microsomal fraction.
2. Preincubation of the test material with primary hepatocytes culture.
3. Co-culture of the target cells with hepatocytes [105].

Another major limitation of cell lines is that they are not normal cells. Therefore, they can be genetically unstable, especially cancer cells, and may not express, or may overexpress, important transcription cofactors that regulate gene transcription. In addition, cell lines are often not metabolically competent or have significantly reduced or enhanced metabolic enzyme activities. Other common hurdles for in vitro assays such as chemical solubility, rate of hydrolysis, chemical reactivity with serum and culture dishes, etc., can reduce their utility for predicting effects in normal cells.

In predictive toxicology, batteries of different cell lines are generally employed, with some cell lines being used to evaluate effects of chemicals on basal functions (common to all cell types) and others used to evaluate specialized cell functions or specific toxicities [105]. Endpoints of basal function include viability as measured using vital dyes such as Trypan blue or neutral red, and biochemical and metabolic functions such as cytosolic enzyme release, cell growth, O_2 consumption, or ATP levels. Assessment of specialized cell functions of course requires selection of a cell line that retains the specific cell function of interest (eg, glycogen metabolism by hepatocyte cultures, keratin production by keratinocytes, phagocytosis by macrophages). Like all of the other platforms, cell lines are compatible with imaging and omics methodologies, which can be used to probe more deeply into cellular and molecular mechanisms of toxicity [136]. Here we highlight just a few of the cell lines that are commonly used in predictive toxicology.

Hepatic Cell Lines

General Description

Hepatic cell lines are obtained either from tumors (eg, HepG2, Hep3B, PLC/PRFs Huh7, HBG) or by transfecting normal hepatocytes with SV40 virus large T antigen to generate genetically stable cell lines such as Fa2N-4

[100,138]. The human HepG2 cell line is one of the most commonly used hepatic cell lines, which was isolated by Aden et al. [139] from a primary hepatoblastoma. The cell morphology resembles liver parenchymal cells and they synthesize and secrete several proteins that are characteristic of normal human cells [140,141]. HepG2 cells also express various drug-metabolizing enzymes, including many cytochrome P450s and transporters; however, the expression levels of the majority of nuclear transporters and xenobiotic metabolic enzymes are more than 50-fold lower than hepatocytes in vivo (Table 32.4) [100] or in primary culture [100,142–144]. These differences in the expression pattern of Phase I and II enzymes could result in an under- or overestimation of toxicity for certain chemicals.

In the last few years a new human hepatoma cell line, HepaRG, was derived from a liver tumor of a female patient suffering from hepatocarcinoma. HepaRG cells, when seeded at low density (2×10^4 cells/cm^2), acquire characteristic features of hepatic progenitor cells, and are able to actively divide and reach confluency within a week. At confluency, the cells are able to differentiate into a population comprised of about 50% hepatocytes and 50% biliary epithelial cells [145]. HepaRG cells express high levels of CYPs (including CYP 1A2, 2B6, 2C9, 2E1, and 3A4), nuclear receptors (PXR, CAR, AhR, and PPARα), Phase II enzymes (including GSTs, thioredoxin, and UGT), and various multidrug-resistance-associated proteins (including ABC transporters, organic anion and cation transporting polypeptides, and bile salt export pump) [141,143,146]. In fact, HepaRG is the first hepatoma cell line identified so far to express high levels of CAR [147]. Functional activities of various CYPs and phase II enzymes are relatively stable for up to four weeks after achievement of confluency [124], HepaRG cells cultured for longer periods of time exhibit other hepatocyte-specific functions including lactate production, albumin secretion, and elimination of galactose and sorbitol at levels are comparable to primary hepatic cultures [124]. Unlike other hepatic cell lines, HepaRG exhibit only limited chromosomal rearrangement, which is the probable explanation for the similarity between these cells and primary human hepatic cultures [141,148].

Use in Toxicity Assessment

HepG2 cells have been widely used to evaluate toxic effects of a wide variety of chemicals and drugs [149,150]. The HepG2 cell line has also been used in genotoxicity testing, as these cells express metabolizing enzymes required for activation of DNA-reactive carcinogens [140,150]. Consistent with in vivo liver, HepG2 cells exhibit enhanced DNA damage and apoptosis following exposure to the hepatotoxicant aflatoxin B1 [151]. Furthermore, genotoxic potencies of different members of PAHs and HAAs observed in HepG2 cells correlate with their carcinogenic activities in rodents [140]. Diverse classes of environmental carcinogens such as nitrosamines, aromatic and heterocyclic amines, polycyclic aromatic hydrocarbons, and azo dyes (Disperse Red 1, Disperse Orange 1, and Disperse Red 13) are identified as genotoxic using HepG2 cells [152,153]. Genotoxicity assays in HepG2 cells can also differentiate between structurally related carcinogens and noncarcinogens (pyrene, 4-AAF).

Consistent with the observation that HepaRG cells exhibit higher expression of drug-metabolizing enzymes, chemicals such as aflatoxin B1 and acetaminophen that undergo bioactivation in vivo exhibit greater cytotoxicity in HepaRG compared to HepG2 cells. Aflatoxin B1 has an IC50 at $5\,\mu M$ in HepaRG cells. However, the IC50 for the mycotoxin in HepG2 cells is greater than $100\,\mu M$ [143]. Similarly, the HepaRG cell-based in vitro micronucleus assay correctly predicted the genotoxic potential of known human promutagens, direct-acting mutagens, and nonmutagens [154].

Limitations

As mentioned, HepG2 cells have limited metabolic capability and the lower expression of nuclear receptors relative to in vivo or primary cultures. HepaRG cells circumvent these limitations, but they are expensive and originate from a single donor. Therefore phenotypic changes as a consequence of altered karyotype polymorphism of specific genes are a possibility. For example, glutathione transferase A1 is not induced following phenobarbital treatment in HepaRG cells [100]; similarly, the expression of CYP2E1 is a limiting factor in these cells [155].

Cell Lines Used in Mutagenicity Testing

General Description

An assessment for gene mutations is one of the very first tests to be conducted on a new molecule, and mammalian cell culture systems (along with bacterial systems) are generally used for this initial screening. Some of the commonly used mammalian cell-based models are the L5178YTK$^{+/-}$ mouse lymphoma assay, hypoxanthine guanine phosphoribosyl transferase (HPRT) assay in Chinese hamster ovary (CHO) cells, and unscheduled DNA synthesis assay in hepatocytes (described earlier).

In normal cells, thymidine is one of the four principal deoxyribonucleotides in DNA. The enzyme thymidine kinase (TK) phosphorylates thymidine to form thymidine monophosphate (TMP), which is used in normal DNA replication. However, when thymidine is replaced by certain pyrimidine analogs such as trifluorothymidine (TFT), the cells cannot replicate, and die. Thymidine kinase-deficient cells that lack TK activity are therefore resistant to the cytotoxic effects of the pyrimidine analogs. In the mouse lymphoma assay, L5178Y cells are incubated with the test material and TFT in the presence or absence of S9 fraction. Under these growth conditions, only cells that have undergone forward mutation at the TK locus (caused by base pair changes, frame-shift, and small deletions) can survive [156,157]. The mutagenicity of the test chemical is quantified by an increase in the number of mutant cells and colonies. Based on the size of the colony, the chemical can be further predicted to cause gene or chromosomal mutations. The mutated cells in the large colonies grow at comparable rates of that of parent cells and possess intragenic mutations as well as total deletion of the TK+ alleles, whereas the mutated cells in small colonies (less than 0.6 mm in diameter) grow slower than normal cells and exhibit a variety of genetic damage ranging from intragenic mutations to chromosomal rearrangements and deletions [158,159]. Therefore the MLA is able to identify a broad spectrum of chemically mediated gene and chromosomal mutations.

Another commonly used mammalian cell-based mutation assay to screen for chemicals mutagens is the HPRT assay. In mammalian cells, purine nucleotides are primarily synthesized de novo and the HPRT pathway is a salvage pathway in the biosynthesis of these nucleotides. The V79 CHO cells that are used in the assay express only one copy of the HPRT gene. Replacement of purine with an analogs such as 6-thioguanine (6-TG) is cytotoxic to the cell, and only cells that lack HPRT activity survive and form colonies. In this assay, cells are exposed to the test chemical and 6-TG in the presence or absence of S9 fraction. Cells are then plated for colony growth, and after several days, colony numbers and colony size are recorded. The cells that form colonies are assumed to have undergone mutation caused by the chemical agent. As described above, human or rodent hepatocytes can also be used to evaluate chemical-mediated DNA damage by quantifying unscheduled DNA synthesis.

Use in Toxicity Assessment

In 1997, a USEPA-appointed expert panel reviewed and evaluated all the literature on MLA published between 1976 and 1993. The database included 602 chemicals, of which 343 were rated as positive, 44 as negative, 18 as equivocal, 54 inappropriate for evaluation, and 142 as inadequately tested. Comparison of a subset of 130 (120 positive and 10 negative) MLA-tested chemicals with NTP's rodent carcinogenesis bioassay results revealed 94% accuracy for the positive (7 false positives) and 100% accuracy for the negative chemicals. However, the overall specificity for the assay was about 59%, as only 10 of the 17 noncarcinogens were correctly predicted as negative for mutagenesis. Based on the evaluation, the panel concluded that the MLA is a well-characterized and sensitive assay to predict most classes of chemicals for their mutagenic and carcinogenic properties [160]. Moreover, the assay is able to detect a broad spectrum of genetic damage including both gene and chromosomal mutations.

Similar to the evaluation of MLA, the USEPA Gene-Tox Phase III program evaluated the performance of the CHO/HPRT assay using published information from 1979 to 1986 on 121 chemicals (belonging to 25 chemical classes) [81]. Among the evaluated chemicals, 87 chemicals were identified as positive, 3 were negative, and 31 chemicals had inconclusive data (the chemicals were not tested both in the presence and absence of activation). Mutagenicity results on 49 of 121 chemicals were compared with in vivo carcinogenicity data. The chemicals evaluated included 43 in vivo carcinogens, of which 40 were predicted positive in the CHO/HPRT assay. Only one noncarcinogen in the group of 49 chemicals was correctly predicted as negative in CHO/HPRT assay as well. Based on these findings, the Gene-Tox review concluded that CHO/HPRT assay can predict genotoxic carcinogens representing a large variety of chemical classes; however, determining the specificity of the assay was not possible, as only one noncarcinogen was compared between CHO/HPRT and in vivo results. Following the USEPA evaluation, 9 noncarcinogens were evaluated using CHO/HPRT assay, of which 7 were correctly predicted as negative, one was predicted as positive, and results for the other chemical were unclear [161]. The CHO/HPRT assay was also successfully used to identify chlorohydroxyfuranone mixtures-mediated chromosomal damage as well as N-ethyl-N-nitrosourea-mediated point mutations [162,163].

Limitations

The mouse lymphoma assay has the potential of high false-positive rate and therefore this assay cannot be used as a standalone assay for human use of drug and chemicals [164]. As HPRT is an X-linked gene, this assay is not efficient in detecting chromosomal recombination and nondisjunction events.

Cell Lines for the Assessment of Skin Sensitization Potential

General Description

Skin sensitization is a key endpoint for safety assessment, especially for chemicals in cosmetic and personal care products [165]. It is an immune reaction to exogenous reactive haptens or prohaptens, which react with skin proteins and render them immunogenic [166]. The whole process can be broadly divided into sensitization and elicitation phases. In the sensitization phase, the chemical agent reacts with skin proteins, and dendritic cells process the modified proteins and present the antigen to naive T-cells in the local lymph nodes, leading to expansion of antigen-specific T-cell clones. On subsequent exposure to the same sensitizer, a specific T-cell mediated immune response can be elicited (elicitation phase) [167]. Historically, skin sensitization has been assessed using animal tests, such as the guinea pig tests (maximization rest, and the Buehler test, which evaluate elicitation phase) and the mouse local lymph node assay (LLNA) (which evaluates the sensitization phase at the draining lymph nodes) [168,169]. Currently, several regulatory agencies consider the LLNA as the preferred assay for predicting skin-sensitizing chemicals.

In recent years, considerable progress has been made in the development of nonanimal in vitro methods, mostly targeting the sensitization phase of the immune reaction. Several of the more successful assays have focused on characterizing a specific key event in the skin sensitization pathway, which includes quantifying chemical–peptide reactivity (as measured by the direct peptide reactivity assay, or DPRA); intracellular stress proteins (Nrf2-dependent proteins; KeratinoSens assay or LuSens assays); cell-surface markers (CD86 and CD54; human-Cell Line Activation Test; h-CLAT); and specific chemokines (IL-8 and IL-18) as predictive markers for skin-sensitizing chemicals [167,170–173].

Use in Toxicity Assessment

The DPRA and KeratinoSens have been validated and approved by ECVAM for identifying dermal sensitizers (Fig. 32.4). Similarly, the h-CLAT assay is in advanced stages of the ECVAM validation process. Each of these alternative methods provided overall accuracy of 80–85% compared to in vivo models, depending on the validation chemical set and conducting laboratory. Interestingly, the results from alternative test methods match more closely to human sensitization results than to the in vivo animal models. However, as the skin sensitization is a complex immune process, no single in vitro assay is expected to reliably replicate the complete biological responses that occur in vivo [174,175]. Therefore, current research is focused towards developing integrated testing strategies consisting of data from in silico in chemico and in vitro methods and using various statistical approaches such as the Bayesian Network model, principal component analysis, partial least squares, and generalized linear models [176,177].

Limitations

The KeratinoSens assay cannot recognize the skin sensitizers that react with lysine residues instead of cysteines (eg, trimellitic anhydrides) due to the fact that the endogenous protein sensor relies on Keap1, which is activated only through cysteine residues. Similarly, the majority of the existing cell-based assays are limited by the lack of ability to determine potency of the test material and their utility to identify formulations/

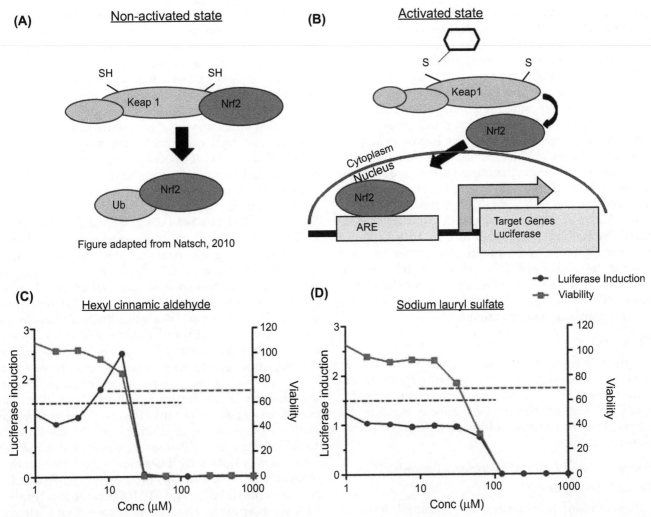

FIGURE 32.4 **The KeratinoSens assay can detect chemicals with skin sensitization potential.** Skin sensitizers in general are electrophiles, which react with nucleophilic sites on endogenous proteins. Under nonstress conditions, Keap1 sequesters Nrf2 in the cytoplasm, which targets it for proteolytic degradation (A). However, electrophilic chemicals (sensitizers) are able to covalently modify cysteine residues in Keap1, leading to Nrf2 release, its nuclear translocation, and subsequent binding to antioxidant response element (ARE) in the promoter regions of target genes (B). The KeratinoSens assay determines sensitizer-mediated Nrf2-ARE pathway activation in transgenic human keratinocyte (HaCaT) cells that stably express the luciferase gene, and has been used as a tool to identify chemicals with skin sensitization potential. In the KeratinoSens assay, a chemical is considered a sensitizer (C) if the luciferase induction is more than 1.5-fold and cell viability is greater than 70% at concentrations below 1 mM. If any of the three parameters are not met, then the chemical is considered a nonsensitizer (D).

mixtures that have skin sensitization potential are not well characterized.

Cell Lines Used to Predict Eye Irritation

General Description

In addition to the previously described organ-based methods (eg, ICE and BCOP) for predicting eye irritation potential, cell-culture techniques that assess cytotoxicity in corneal as well as noncorneal cell lines are also available as predictors of eye irritation potential. These cell line approaches are based on the fact that eye irritation is often driven by general properties such as cytotoxicity and/or altered membrane permeability. Some of the cell lines used for eye irritation tests include SIRC cells

derived from rabbit cornea, HeLa cells, HepG2 cells, Hp2 cells, NCTC L929 cells and BALB/c 3T3 cells from mouse fibroblasts, and V79 cells from Chinese hamster tissue. Cytotoxicity is determined by staining with fluorescein diacetate/ethidium bromide, uridine uptake inhibition assay, estimation of intracellular ATP levels, quantification of alkaline phosphatase release, inhibition of cell protein synthesis, neutral red absorption, estimation of changes in cell morphology, colony formation of the surviving cells, etc.

Use in Toxicity Assessment

Among the most promising alternative cell-line methods for eye irritation is the neutral red release (NRR) cytotoxicity test in 3T3 cells. In 1988, ZEBET conducted an interlaboratory study (12 toxicology laboratories) of 32 diverse chemicals in the NRR assay. Although results from both alternative methods correlated sufficiently well with the results obtained from the Draize test, the neutral red cytotoxicity assay exhibited better intra- and inter-laboratory reproducibility than the HET-CAM assay. The neutral red assay exhibited 16% false-positive and 16% false-negative results [178]. Itagaki et al. [179] studied eye irritation potential of three cationic surface-active agents, five anionic surfactants, and two nonionic agents and two amphoterics using the Draize test and HeLa S3 cells and SIRC cells. They quantified the cyto-toxicity of the cell cultures using the crystal violet stain-ing (CVS) method in a 96-well format. They observed high correlation between the in vivo Draize test and either of the cell lines (85.5% or 86.3% for HeLa or SIRC cells, respectively), based on which they concluded that either cell line provided high prediction scores for the tested eye irritants and nonirritants.

Limitations

Although many alternative approaches have been proposed for predicting chemicals with eye irritation, so far there is no one assay that can accurately predict across all chemical classes. Furthermore, none of the validated in vitro assays address reversibility, which is often a critical issue.

Embryonic and Induced Pluripotent Stem Cells

General Description

Stem cells are self-renewing progenitor cells found in all multicellular organisms and are pluripotent [180,181]. Stem cells in mammals can be obtained from the inner cell mass of blastocysts (embryonic stem cells, or ESCs) or from adult tissues (bone marrow, blood, adipose tis-sue, etc.). In addition, recent advances have enabled iso-lation induced pluripotent stem cells (iPS cells), which are generated from nonpluripotent cells through forced expression of stem-cell-specific genes (eg, Oct3/4, Sox2. C-Myc, and Klf4) and proteins [182,183]. The iPSCs pos-sess a normal karyotype, and express telomerase activ-ity, cell-surface markers, and genes that are characteristic of human ESCs.

Stem cells are increasingly being explored for use as in vitro model systems for predicting chemical- and drug-induced toxicity. Indeed, both ESCs and iPSCs can be directed to differentiate into a variety of adult cell lin-eages such as hepatocytes, cardiocytes, osteocytes, neu-rons, dermal cells, etc., which could be further used for the in vitro testing of respective target organ toxicities [184]. Advances in the development of iPSCs could play an important role as a source for both embryonic as well as differentiated cell types (ie, for testing hepatic, cardiac, or neurotoxicities, etc.). This application would be much more valuable when utilized for iPSCs of human origin, as it would circumvent ethical concerns associated with ESCs as well as limitations associated with interspecies extrapolations. These applications qualify both ESCs and iPSCs to be considered as excellent platforms, as the stem cells could be used as a source for multiple predic-tive toxicity endpoints.

Another application of stem cell technology that has already advanced quite far is the mouse embryonic stem cell test (EST) for potential teratogenicity screen-ing. The ESCs mimic early in vivo embryonic devel-opment processes, which is an important factor for testing embryo toxicity and organogenesis [185,186]. The mouse EST has been developed and validated by ECVAM as a nonanimal alternative screen for chemi-cals with teratogenic potential [187,188]. This assay exploits the fact that D3 mouse ESCs differentiate into beating cardiomyocytes, and that chemicals with teratogenic potential often inhibit this differentiation process [189,190]. The D3 mouse ESC cell line forms embryoid bodies (EB) in the absence of cytokine leu-kemia inhibiting factor (LIF), which, after 10 days in culture, differentiate spontaneously into cardiomyo-cytes. The test requires morphological analysis of beat-ing cardiomyocyte clusters in differentiated EBs, and evaluation of concentration of the test material at which cardiac differentiation is inhibited by 50% (ID50) after 10 days of exposure. Cytototoxicity potential of the test material is evaluated by determining the concentration of test material that inhibits proliferation by 50% in D3 and 3T3 cells (D3 IC50 and 3T3 ID50, respectively) after 10 days of exposure. The chemicals are scored as strong, weak, and nontoxic to embryo based on a biostatistical prediction model built using ID50, D3 IC50, and 3T3 ID50 values [80,184,191].

Use in Toxicity Assessment

As part of an ECVAM validation exercise, four labora-tories tested 20 compounds preclassified as non-, weak, or strong developmental toxicants [80,187]. Using a pre-defined algorithm, the EST correctly predicted 78% of the tested chemicals. Paquette et al. [188] further modi-fied ECVAM's EST protocol by altering the source of stem cells and media that allowed the assay to produce contracting cardiomyocytes greater than 95% of the time. Using their modified approach, the authors tested a total of 63 chemicals that included 15 ECVAM-tested, 19 Pfizer Pharmaceutical, and 29 commercially avail-able compounds. They observed overall accuracy of 75% (90%, 71%, and 60% for low-, moderate-, and strong teratogens), which was similar to the initial ECVAM study.

Several recent studies suggested that ESTs work best when used in combination with other teratoge-nicity assays, ie, when used as part of an integrated test strategy. For instance, in a European project called ReProTect, 10 chemicals were tested for teratogenic potential using a battery of three complementary in vitro tests (EST, WEC, ReProGlo assay) performed in parallel [82]. The integrated testing strategy correctly classified seven chemicals (five positive and two negative teratogens), with one false positive and one false negative and one chemical yielding ambiguous results [82]. In an attempt to improve predictivity, investigators are exploring additional differentiation endpoints such as nervous tissue, bone, cartilage, and epithelial markers, as this would ensure detecting teratogens that affect diverse lineages [192–194]. For example, the EC50 of thalidomide is about 30-fold lower when ES cells are triggered to differentiate into bone tissue along with cardiomyocytes rather than just cardiac differentiation. Similarly, valproic acid has been recognized to be at least 10-fold more active when ES cells were allowed to differentiate down a neuronal lineage [194]. Others have used various biochemical and molecular biology techniques including microarrays, quantitative PCR, reporter constructs, immunohistochemistry, and fluorescent-activated cell sorting (FACS) to improve the EST model [195–199].

Limitations

Presently, the use of human embryonic stem cells in research or toxicity testing is limited by the large number of ethical concerns. The EST model is further limited by the lack of metabolic competence and insufficient understanding of lineage specification and markers. Furthermore, adult stem cells have limitations with regard to their differentiation into other cell types, and they are far less stable and homogeneous. Similarly, iPSCs are heterogeneous, and it is challenging to consistently and efficiently generate human iPSCs for medium- to high-throughput assays. Although gene expression patterns of iPSCs are similar to those of ESCs, they are not identical [200,201].

Furthermore, the EST is laborious and time-consuming (takes about 10 days). Inclusion of S9 mix to compensate for lack of metabolic capability of stem cells was not successful, as the mix appears to be toxic to D3 mouse ESCs [184]. The assay is not capable of identifying teratogenic chemicals with mechanisms of action beyond the initial embryo differentiation processes. Although the chemicals are scored based on morphology, the assay does not provide information anywhere near the level of morphological information characteristic of WEC [184]. With respect to iPSCs, the use of viral transduction of recombinant DNA to generate iPSCs from adult somatic cells may lead to integration of foreign genome into the genome of iPSCs lines or their differentiated cells, which may contribute to discrepancies, especially when exposed to toxicants [184].

SCENARIOS FOR THE APPLICATION OF PREDICTIVE TOXICOLOGY

Now that we have described the basic characteristics, strengths, and weaknesses of various technology platforms, we next address their strategic application. Unlike regulatory testing, which follows globally standardized testing protocols and test requirements, predictive toxicology is not dictated by any government regulations but instead the testing approach is designed by the users to meet their own purposes. Some of the major uses of predictive toxicology center on the evaluation of new chemical entities, such as newly discovered compounds in early stages of the drug or crop protection molecule development process. In more recent years there have been efforts to apply predictive approaches to obtain more data on data-poor chemicals already in the environment and to prioritize these for further evaluation in more conventional tests. Finally, as described at the start of this chapter, the entire field of toxicology is moving toward more predictive approaches, as envisioned in the 2007 NRC report and exemplified by new programs such as EPA ToxCast, Tox21, and EPA NexGen risk assessment. Here we describe these general examples and discuss some important considerations for choosing biological platforms to meet the needs of each.

Use in the Selection and Evaluation of New Chemical Analogs

Predictive Toxicology has its early roots in the drug development process. Although the desire to screen out new drug candidates with excessive toxicity had been attempted for decades, predictive approaches became possible only when drug discovery began to evolve from an empirical, trial-and-error process to a more targeted drug design process built around a deepening understanding of the cellular and molecular pathways controlling normal biology as well as disease states. This same knowledge of biological pathways has now enabled investigators to make predictions about the negative consequences of altering these targets. As a result, many pharmaceutical companies began to move from broad, effects-based toxicity screening programs to very targeted, hypothesis-driven early-stage toxicity evaluations. In this scenario, assays are customized around a specific therapeutic target area rather than using a one-size-fits-all approach. The biological assays also feed into structure–activity models to further guide the drug development process.

In concept, similar approaches can also be applied in the design and early-stage evaluation of new pesticides. However, one key difference from the pharmaceutical situation is that modern pesticides are designed to hit targets that are unique to an insect, fungus, or other plant pathogen, but which are not present in humans. This generally precludes a targeted approach for the prediction of potential toxicity in humans. Instead, a general, effects-based approach is in most cases more effective as a tool for the selection of candidate molecules, at least at this time.

Applications for predictive toxicology also are beginning to arise for the assessment of industrial and consumer product chemicals. The major societal emphasis on sustainability has spurred new product innovation to support sustainable solutions, such as materials for solar and wind energy, clean water, lighter vehicles, etc. The related Green Chemistry movement is driving additional research and development to find less hazardous replacements for many existing chemicals. While this concept sounds simple enough on the surface, in actual practice it is quite challenging, as a successful substitute chemical must still retain a set of desired functional properties (eg, chelant, surfactant, emulsifier) but without the attendant toxicity. However, these functional properties are what often drive toxicity. Also, the desire to find a substitute is typically triggered by a specific adverse effect as identified in animal toxicity studies (eg, teratogenicity). While a predictive toxicity program can be designed to screen for the absence of the specific toxic effect, alteration of the molecule could result in entirely new types of effects, making the new chemical even more hazardous than the original one!

Use in Evaluating Existing Chemicals

Predictive toxicology is not only confined to new chemicals, but is poised to become an important tool to address the so-called "toxics information gap" [5] on chemicals that are already in commerce and/or in the environment. As mentioned earlier in the chapter, many of these "untested" compounds are lower production volume chemicals that have been evaluated based on extrapolation from structurally related compounds that have robust toxicity data (known as "read-across"), rather than direct testing of each of these compounds in animals. Many of the chemicals in these read-across categories are simple derivatives (eg, salts, esters, amines of the core compound), with the derivative commonly being readily metabolized to the core compound. Therefore, testing each of these derivatives in a full battery of animal tests is not warranted. The European Union's REACH program allows registrants to propose waiving animal testing by using the toxicity data from a data-rich compound within the class as a surrogate for the untested compounds. The assumption is that the chemicals within the read-across category act similarly, and are no more toxic than the data-rich reference compound. One approach to strengthening read-across justifications and reducing uncertainty

is to consider the use of read-across in the context of the broader 21st-century toxicity testing paradigm (eg, the U.S. EPA's ToxCast and the Tox21 programs). For example, when forming a category of substances, currently available in silico tools may assist in the identification of analogs and in vitro screening assays (such as cytotoxicity, protein reactivity, oral bioavailability, and receptor-binding assays) may provide similarity among category members at the biological or toxicological level [202–204]. These assays allow initial assessment of the overall toxicological profile of a group of substances without the need for extensive animal test methods. In addition, the data from these assays can be used in conjunction with traditional toxicology studies to assess whether category members follow an adverse outcome pathway for a particular endpoint, thereby providing a mechanistic basis for the use of read-across. Furthermore, the use of toxicogenomics or metabolomics provides a means to conduct global analysis of the biologic activity (large number of mechanisms) of structurally related chemicals and thus may serve to refine the structure activity relationship (SAR)-based predictions and the use of read-across. Toxicogenomic approaches have a history of use in the characterization of MoA for industrial and environmental chemicals using in vitro cultures, and therefore may support for the grouping of substances without resorting to extensive in vivo studies [205]. Another possibility for using these tools to reduce the uncertainty associated with read-across is to build them into an integrated testing strategy and to make use of Bayesian network approaches [206]. Using such an approach enables the quantification of uncertainty from heterogeneous input sources, assessment of relationships between them, and creation of a testing strategy that targets the reduction of uncertainty.

Although promising, not all geographical regulatory frameworks are currently receptive to the read-across-based chemical categorization approach. For example, China's current new substance regulation does not permit the use of read-across unless exceptional circumstances prevent testing of the substance being registered. However, as the chemical regulations within China continue to evolve, the use of alternative approaches, including read-across, may become acceptable in future regulatory frameworks. The read-across frameworks are difficult to apply to substances with multiple constituents or variable compositions. Furthermore, it is challenging at this stage to address uncertainty associated with negative read-across [207]. Despite these challenges, the rapid advancements in 21st-century toxicity approaches present a great promise to support the grouping of substances into categories and further support the use of read-across approaches to significantly reduce the need for new animal-based toxicological studies.

Other approaches to improving the assessment of data-poor chemicals already in commerce include exposure assessment to complement hazard characterization for risk-based prioritization of chemicals. By understanding the potential human exposures to chemicals, this information can be compared with the concentrations needed to produce activities in vitro to determine a margin of exposure (MOE) as the primary metric for safety assessment. To this end, the U.S. EPA, the Hamner Institutes, and others are collaborating to develop an MOE approach that relates in vitro based bioactivity concentrations to external exposure [11,208–210]. Using chemical-specific high-throughput data (in vitro hepatic clearance and plasma protein binding), simple pharmacokinetic models are built for each chemical based upon in vitro to in vivo extrapolation (IVIVE). Oral steady-state exposure concentrations are then calculated that are equivalent to the activity concentrations determined in the in vitro bioactivity assays. These values can then be compared to estimated exposure concentrations (either calculated or biomonitoring data) for the general population for determination of an MOE. While the results of these high-throughput tools have large uncertainty ranges, they can be used as conservative approaches for regulatory decisions such as testing prioritization, emergency response assessments, and safety assessments. Such frameworks have been developed and are gaining acceptance as useful regulatory approaches in screening chemicals for prioritization for further conventional testing, such as the EPA's Endocrine Disruptor Screening Program, and are under consideration for situations where risk assessments are required for chemicals with little or no toxicity information, such as for environmental clean-up or accidental spills. Thomas et al. [9] developed a detailed MOE-based framework that could even serve as the basis for new product registrations. This tiered approach proposes to use in vitro assays such as the EPA ToxCast assays to screen chemicals first to determine whether a specific mode of action (MOA) is indicated, and then use the in vitro derived point of departure (POD) to extrapolate a human equivalent exposure to compare with human exposure information and derive the MOE. For chemicals that do not appear to possess a specific MOA, the second tier proposes to conduct short-term animal studies and utilize the transcriptional response from tissues to derive a transcriptional POD as the basis for determining the MOE. For chemicals where the MOE is not considered sufficiently protective, a third tier is proposed to use conventional animal testing to determine the MOE. Even while the remaining challenges for in vitro-based hazard assessments are solved, Thomas et al. [9] provides a path for current application of alternative in vitro approaches for determining important regulatory decisions and conducting safety assessments (Fig. 32.5).

Use in Value-Chain Decisions

One of the more interesting and beneficial applications of predictive toxicity is for product safety assurance of products already on the market. Even if a chemical is determined safe for its intended use and is already used in commercially available products, there is always the possibility that consumers may become concerned about potential health effects that are believed to not have been properly assessed during the regulatory review. Predictive toxicology started out as tools to assist in the research and development of new chemicals to help identify the most promising sustainable candidates for commercialization and assist in the development of intelligent conventional testing plans for regulatory approvals. Many of these approaches are now being accepted as alternative tests for regulatory approvals, and this trend will continue to accelerate (Fig. 32.6). Using these predictive toxicology tools, it is now possible to assess an additional measure of assurance of the safety of these products. For example, if concerns about endocrine disruption arise over some chemical ingredient, it is relatively easy to assess that chemical for endocrine activity by computer modeling and testing with in vitro assays. Even if some activity is observed for an ingredient, when combined with exposure information, the risk from use of the product can be put into context through an MOE determination. Moreover, product formulations in toto can be tested for possible unwarranted effects. More sophisticated molecular approaches will soon be available that will provide even more confidence in the safety of product ingredients and formulations.

Future Paradigms for Safety Assessment

The ultimate application of predictive approaches is to use them to replace conventional animal toxicity tests as the basis for human safety assessment. Such a vision was articulated in a landmark report of the U.S. National Research Council entitled "Toxicity Testing in the Twenty-First Century: A Vision and a Strategy" (NRC, 2007). More recently, the Councils of Canadian Academies (CCA, 2012) addressed this new vision as well. Both reports expressed a strong desire to move away from apical, descriptive endpoints in animals exposed to high doses of test chemicals, toward more predictive, mechanism-based assessment strategies that focus on human cells and molecular events at concentrations relevant to human exposures. Both reports also emphasized that any new paradigm should not simply involve a replacement of animal tests with human cell cultures, but requires a fundamental change in objectives and approach. For example, it should be clear from the information in this chapter that biological assay platforms have some inherent limitations that effectively preclude

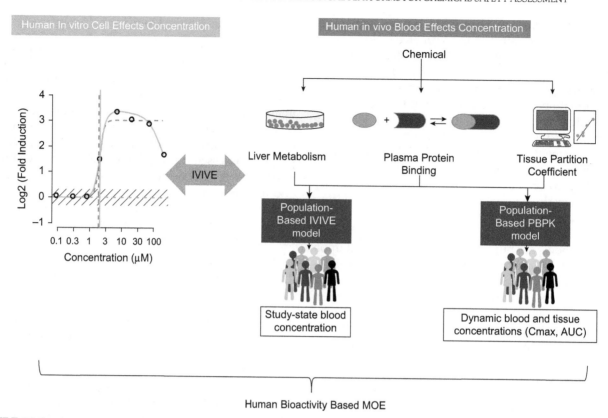

FIGURE 32.5 **Margin of exposure (MOE) safety assessments.** Bioactivities measured in alternative approaches combined with human exposure determined through in vitro to in vivo extrapolations (IVIVE) or human biomonitoring studies can be used for regulatory decisions such as testing prioritization, emergency response assessments, and safety assessments.

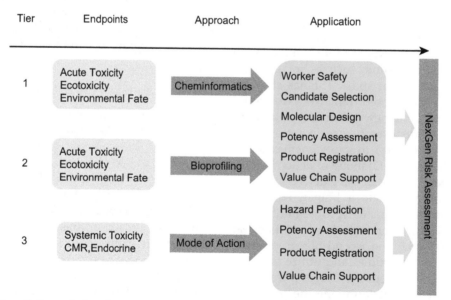

FIGURE 32.6 **Use of predictive toxicology in value chain.** Predictive toxicology can be applied throughout the value chain for new and existing chemicals and the products that they go into. They are useful tools to assist in the research and development of new chemicals and can be used as alternative tests for regulatory approvals, and utilized to provide additional assessments and increased assurance for their safe use. *CMR*, carcinogenic, mutagenic, reproductive toxicants.

any given in vitro assay from predicting specific adverse outcomes.

Some newly proposed schemes recognize these limitations and therefore call for a shift from predicting specific adverse effects to identifying concentrations that cause significant perturbations of key biological control pathways. The premise is that a sufficient assessment of key biological pathways can be made using a battery of assays that cover a broad range of the major biological pathways in order to identify what one proposal refers to as the "biological pathway altering dose" [210]. Another proposal is emerging that compares test concentrations that show alteration of biological pathways to estimated blood concentrations reflective of human exposure in order to calculate a "region of safety" [210,211]. A detailed discussion of these approaches is beyond the scope of this chapter, but these examples illustrate the need to rethink basic premises of safety assessment in order to convert the current system to one that is more predictive and, hopefully, greatly improved.

CONCLUSIONS

In this chapter we have outlined how the demands upon 21st-century toxicology differ from those of the preceding century, we have reviewed many of the biological tools currently available, and have presented several different scenarios by which these tools might be applied to meet these new demands. Specific strategies for applying these tools in a strategic manner are just starting to emerge and will undoubtedly evolve considerably over the coming years.

As this journey unfolds, it is critical that the tools do not become the end game, but that the specific problems at hand drive the selection of the tools. One example regards the needs around throughput and speed of evaluation. In almost all cases, 21st-century safety assessment is demanding faster evaluation, but this is not necessarily the case for throughput. When evaluating potential substitutes for an existing industrial chemical, often the number of candidates is relatively small due to the need for the chemical to perform a highly specific function or to fall within a very narrow range of physical–chemical properties. Similarly, the range and nature of endpoints may vary across different scenarios, and this in turn may warrant more functional or effects-based assay platforms versus more reductionist assays that target highly specific cellular and molecular control points. The more reductionist the assays, the greater the need to incorporate a systems biology approach that uses bioinformatics and advanced statistical methods (along with expert-driven judgment) in order to integrate individual data points into meaningful information. We also must not assume that more data always lead to better information. To achieve the latter, the limits of predictive toxicology assays must always be considered, as one would with any assay. Finally, the importance of linking biological assay findings to human exposure concentration via tools collectively referred to as quantitative in vitro–in vivo extrapolation (QIVIVE) cannot be underestimated.

Acknowledgments

The authors are grateful to Dr. Matt LeBaron of the Dow Chemical Company for critical review of this manuscript.

Dr. Edward W. Carney (1959–2015) has long been a diplomat for the 3Rs of animal use—reduce, refine, and replace—at the Dow Chemical Company. For many years, Ed fostered integrated study designs to consolidate multiple endpoints into a single study to reduce animal use. He was an advocate of the kinetically derived maximum dose (KMD) as a way to refine animal dosing and ensure that resulting data were relevant for risk assessment. In recent years, he crafted a vision to markedly reduce the number of animals used in toxicity testing by using 21st-century toxicology tools for a more strategic approach to product safety assessments. Toward this goal, Ed launched Dow's Predictive Toxicology Platform. This program was developed through Ed's ingenuity, intelligence, and ability to effectively interact with scientists from regulatory agencies, research organizations, industry partners, and nongovernmental organizations. Dow's new program is a testament to Ed's forward-thinking passion for effecting scientific change. As we at Dow move forward to implement his vision, we hope that our accomplishments will be a legacy that would make Ed proud.

References

[1] Becker RA, Plunkett LM, Borzelleca JF, Kaplan AM. Tiered toxicity testing: evaluation of toxicity-based decision triggers for human health hazard characterization. Food Chem Toxicol 2007;45(12):2454–69.

[2] Bus JS, Becker RA. Toxicity testing in the 21st century: a view from the chemical industry. Toxicol Sci 2009;112(2):297–302.

[3] Rovida C, Hartung T. Re-evaluation of animal numbers and costs for in vivo tests to accomplish REACH legislation requirements for chemicals – a report by the transatlantic think tank for toxicology (t(4)). ALTEX 2009;26(3):187–208.

[4] Locke PA, Myers Jr DB. A replacement-first approach to toxicity testing is necessary to successfully reauthorize TSCA. ALTEX 2011;28(4):266–72.

[5] Hyman AA. Whither systems biology. Philos Trans R Soc Lond Ser B Biol Sci 2011;366(1584):3635–7.

[6] Tice RR, Austin CP, Kavlock RJ, Bucher JR. Improving the human hazard characterization of chemicals: a Tox21 update. Environ Health Perspect 2013;121(7):756–65.

[7] Judson R, Richard A, Dix DJ, Houck K, Martin M, Kavlock R, et al. The toxicity data landscape for environmental chemicals. Environ Health Perspect 2009;117(5):685–95.

[8] Rusyn I, Gatti DM, Wiltshire T, Kleeberger SR, Threadgill DW. Toxicogenetics: population-based testing of drug and chemical safety in mouse models. Pharmacogenomics 2010;11(8):1127–36.

[9] Thomas RS, Philbert MA, Auerbach SS, Wetmore BA, Devito MJ, Cote I, et al. Incorporating new technologies into toxicity testing and risk assessment: moving from 21st century vision to a data-driven framework. Toxicol Sci 2013;136(1):4–18.

[10] Wambaugh JF, Setzer RW, Reif DM, Gangwal S, Mitchell-Blackwood J, Arnot JA, et al. High-throughput models for exposure-based chemical prioritization in the ExpoCast project. Environ Sci Technol 2013;47(15):8479–88.

[11] Wetmore BA, Wambaugh JF, Allen B, Ferguson SS, Sochaski MA, Setzer RW, et al. Incorporating high-throughput exposure predictions with dosimetry-adjusted in vitro bioactivity to inform chemical toxicity testing. Toxicol Sci 2015;148(1):121–36.

[12] Patlewicz G, Jeliazkova N, Safford RJ, Worth AP, Aleksiev B. An evaluation of the implementation of the Cramer classification scheme in the Toxtree software. SAR QSAR Environ Res 2008;19(5–6):495–524.

[13] Munro IC, Ford RA, Kennepohl E, Sprenger JG. Correlation of structural class with no-observed-effect levels: a proposal for establishing a threshold of concern. Food Chem Toxicol 1996;34(9):829–67.

[14] Wu S, Fisher J, Naciff J, Laufersweiler M, Lester C, Daston G, et al. Framework for identifying chemicals with structural features associated with the potential to act as developmental or reproductive toxicants. Chem Res Toxicol 2013;26(12):1840–61.

[15] Grindon C, Combes R, Cronin MT, Roberts DW, Garrod JF. Integrated decision-tree testing strategies for developmental and reproductive toxicity with respect to the requirements of the EU REACH legislation. Altern Lab Anim 2008;36(Suppl. 1):123–38.

[16] http://www.oecd.org/chemicalsafety/risk-assessment/theo-ecdqsartoolbox.htm TOQT.

[17] Gleeson MP, Modi S, Bender A, Robinson RL, Kirchmair J, Promkatkaew M, et al. The challenges involved in modeling toxicity data in silico: a review. Curr Pharm Des 2012;18(9):1266–91.

[18] Serafimova R, Gatnik MF, Worth A. Review of QSAR models and software tools for predicting genotoxicity and carcinogenicity, https://eurl-ecvamjrceceuropaeu/laboratoriesresearch/predictive_toxicology/doc/EUR_24427_ENpdf.

[19] Piparo EL, Worth A. Review of QSAR models and software tools for predicting developmental and reproductive toxicity, http://publicationsjrceceuropaeu/repository/handle/JRC59820.

[20] ENV/JM/MONO. Fundamental and Guiding Principles for (Q) SAR analysis of chemical carcinogens with mechanistic considerations. Series on Testing and Assessment No. 229. 2015.

[21] Strange K. Model organisms: comparative physiology or just physiology? Am J Physiol Cell Physiol 2000;279(6):C2050–1.

[22] Fields S, Johnston M. Cell biology. Whither model organism research? Science 2005;307(5717):1885–6.

[23] Strahle U, Scholz S, Geisler R, Greiner P, Hollert H, Rastegar S, et al. Zebrafish embryos as an alternative to animal experiments – a commentary on the definition of the onset of protected life stages in animal welfare regulations. Reprod Toxicol 2011;33.

[24] Zhong H, Lin S. Chemical screening with zebrafish embryos. Methods Mol Biol 2011;716:193–205.

[25] Parng C, Seng WL, Semino C, McGrath P. Zebrafish: a preclinical model for drug screening. Assay Drug Dev Technol 2002;1(1 Pt 1):41–8.

[26] Parng C, Ton C, Lin YX, Roy NM, McGrath P. A zebrafish assay for identifying neuroprotectants in vivo. Neurotoxicol Teratol 2006;28(4):509–16.

[27] Sumanas S, Larson JD. Morpholino phosphorodiamidate oligonucleotides in zebrafish: a recipe for functional genomics? Brief Funct Genomic Proteomic 2002;1(3):239–56.

[28] Hermsen SA, Pronk TE, van den Brandhof EJ, van der Ven LT, Piersma AH. Chemical class-specific gene expression changes in the zebrafish embryo after exposure to glycol ether alkoxy acids and 1,2,4-triazole antifungals. Reprod Toxicol 2011;32(2):245–52.

[29] Peterson RT, Shaw SY, Peterson TA, Milan DJ, Zhong TP, Schreiber SL, et al. Chemical suppression of a genetic mutation in a zebrafish model of aortic coarctation. Nat Biotechnol 2004;22(5):595–9.

[30] Braunbeck T, Boettcher M, Hollert H, Kosmehl T, Lammer E, Leist E, et al. Towards an alternative for the acute fish LC(50) test in chemical assessment: the fish embryo toxicity test goes multispecies – an update. ALTEX 2005;22(2):87–102.

[31] Lammer E, Carr GJ, Wendler K, Rawlings JM, Belanger SE, Braunbeck T. Is the fish embryo toxicity test (FET) with the zebrafish (Danio rerio) a potential alternative for the fish acute toxicity test? Comp Biochem Physiol Toxicol Pharmacol 2009;149(2):196–209.

[32] Vaughan M, van Egmond R. The use of the zebrafish (Danio rerio) embryo for the acute toxicity testing of surfactants, as a possible alternative to the acute fish test. Altern Lab Anim 2010;38(3):231–8.

[33] Tierney KB. Behavioural assessments of neurotoxic effects and neurodegeneration in zebrafish. Biochim Biophys Acta 2011;1812(3):381–9.

[34] Beauvais SL, Jones SB, Parris JT, Brewer SK, Little EE. Cholinergic and behavioral neurotoxicity of carbaryl and cadmium to larval rainbow trout (Oncorhynchus mykiss). Ecotoxicol Environ Saf 2001;49(1):84–90.

[35] Anichtchik OV, Kaslin J, Peitsaro N, Scheinin M, Panula P. Neurochemical and behavioural changes in zebrafish Danio rerio after systemic administration of 6-hydroxydopamine and 1-methyl-4-phenyl-1,2,3,6-tetrahydropyridine. J Neurochem 2004;88(2):443–53.

[36] McKinley ET, Baranowski TC, Blavo DO, Cato C, Doan TN, Rubinstein AL. Neuroprotection of MPTP-induced toxicity in zebrafish dopaminergic neurons. Brain Res Mol Brain Res 2005;141(2):128–37.

[37] Milan DJ, Peterson TA, Ruskin JN, Peterson RT, MacRae CA. Drugs that induce repolarization abnormalities cause bradycardia in zebrafish. Circulation 2003;107(10):1355–8.

[38] Serbedzija GN, Flynn E, Willett CE. Zebrafish angiogenesis: a new model for drug screening. Angiogenesis 1999;3(4):353–9.

[39] Yabu T, Tomimoto H, Taguchi Y, Yamaoka S, Igarashi Y, Okazaki T. Thalidomide-induced antiangiogenic action is mediated by ceramide through depletion of VEGF receptors, and is antagonized by sphingosine-1-phosphate. Blood 2005;106(1):125–34.

[40] Brannen KC, Panzica-Kelly JM, Danberry TL, Augustine-Rauch KA. Development of a zebrafish embryo teratogenicity assay and quantitative prediction model. Birth Defects Res B Dev Reprod Toxicol 2010;89(1):66–77.

[41] Selderslaghs IW, Van Rompay AR, De Coen W, Witters HE. Development of a screening assay to identify teratogenic and embryotoxic chemicals using the zebrafish embryo. Reprod Toxicol 2009;28(3):308–20.

[42] Hermsen SA, van den Brandhof EJ, van der Ven LT, Piersma AH. Relative embryotoxicity of two classes of chemicals in a modified zebrafish embryotoxicity test and comparison with their in vivo potencies. Toxicol In Vitro 2011;25(3):745–53.

[43] Hill AJJM, Dodd A, Diekmann H. A review of developmental toxicity screening using zebrafish larvae. Int J Toxicol 2011;30:105–12.

[44] Padilla S, Corum D, Padnos B, Hunter DL, Beam A, Houck KA, et al. Zebrafish developmental screening of the ToxCast Phase I chemical library. Reprod Toxicol 2011;33.

[45] Sipes NS, Padilla S, Knudsen TB. Zebrafish: as an integrative model for twenty-first century toxicity testing. Birth Defects Res C Embryo Today 2011;93(3):256–67.

[46] Yang L, Kemadjou JR, Zinsmeister C, Bauer M, Legradi J, Muller F, et al. Transcriptional profiling reveals barcode-like toxicogenomic responses in the zebrafish embryo. Genome Biol 2007;8(10):R227.

[47] Lim IK. TIS21 (/BTG2/PC3) as a link between ageing and cancer: cell cycle regulator and endogenous cell death molecule. J Cancer Res Clin Oncol 2006;132(7):417–26.

[48] Mizell M, Romig ES. The aquatic vertebrate embryo as a sentinel for toxins: zebrafish embryo dechorionation and perivitelline space microinjection. Int J Dev Biol 1997;41(2):411–23.

[49] Schirmer K, Tanneberger K, Kramer NI, Volker D, Scholz S, Hafner C, et al. Developing a list of reference chemicals for testing alternatives to whole fish toxicity tests. Aquat Toxicol 2008;90(2):128–37.

[50] Kim DH, Hwang CN, Sun Y, Lee SH, Kim B, Nelson BJ. Mechanical analysis of chorion softening in prehatching stages of zebrafish embryos. IEEE Trans Nanobiosci 2006;5(2):89–94.

[51] Alderton W, Berghmans S, Butler P, Chassaing H, Fleming A, Golder Z, et al. Accumulation and metabolism of drugs

and CYP probe substrates in zebrafish larvae. Xenobiotica 2010;40(8):547–57.

[52] Kaletta T, Hengartner MO. Finding function in novel targets: *C. elegans* as a model organism. Nat Rev Drug Discov 2006;5(5):387–98.

[53] White JG, Southgate E, Thomson JN, Brenner S. The structure of the ventral nerve cord of *Caenorhabditis elegans*. Philos Trans R Soc Lond Ser B, Biol Sci 1976;275(938):327–48.

[54] Sulston JE, Schierenberg E, White JG, Thomson JN. The embryonic cell lineage of the nematode *Caenorhabditis elegans*. Dev Biol 1983;100(1):64–119.

[55] Lu N, Yu X, He X, Zhou Z. Detecting apoptotic cells and monitoring their clearance in the nematode *Caenorhabditis elegans*. Methods Mol Biol 2009;559:357–70.

[56] Timmons L, Fire A. Specific interference by ingested dsRNA. Nature 1998;395(6705):854.

[57] Boutros M, Ahringer J. The art and design of genetic screens: RNA interference. Nat Rev Genet 2008;9(7):554–66.

[58] Cole RD, Anderson GL, Williams PL. The nematode *Caenorhabditis elegans* as a model of organophosphate-induced mammalian neurotoxicity. Toxicol Appl Pharmacol 2004;194(3):248–56.

[59] Williams PL, Dusenbery DB. A promising indicator of neurobehavioral toxicity using the nematode *Caenorhabditis elegans* and computer tracking. Toxicol Ind Health 1990;6(3–4):425–40.

[60] Tsibidis GD, Tavernarakis N. Nemo: a computational tool for analyzing nematode locomotion. BMC Neurosci 2007;8:86.

[61] Simonetta SH, Golombek DA. An automated tracking system for *Caenorhabditis elegans* locomotor behavior and circadian studies application. J Neurosci Methods 2007;161(2):273–80.

[62] Pulak R. Techniques for analysis, sorting, and dispensing of *C. elegans* on the COPAS flow-sorting system. Methods Mol Biol 2006;351:275–86.

[63] Rohde CB, Zeng F, Gonzalez-Rubio R, Angel M, Yanik MF. Microfluidic system for on-chip high-throughput whole-animal sorting and screening at subcellular resolution. Proc Natl Acad Sci USA 2007;104(35):13891–5.

[64] Williams PL, Dusenbery DB. Using the nematode *Caenorhabditis elegans* to predict mammalian acute lethality to metallic salts. Toxicol Ind Health 1988;4(4):469–78.

[65] Tatara CP, Newman MC, McCloskey JT, Williams PL. Predicting relative metal toxicity with ion characteristics: *Caenorhabditis elegans* LC50. Aquat Toxicol 1997;39:279–90.

[66] Settivari R, Levora J, Nass R. The divalent metal transporter homologues SMF-1/2 mediate dopamine neuron sensitivity in *Caenorhabditis elegans* models of manganism and parkinson disease. J Biol Chem 2009;284(51):35758–68.

[67] Melstrom PC, Williams PL. Reversible AChE inhibitors in *C. elegans* vs. rats, mice. Biochem Biophys Res Commun 2007;357(1):200–5.

[68] Boyd WA, Smith MV, Kissling GE, Freedman JH. Medium- and high-throughput screening of neurotoxicants using *C. elegans*. Neurotoxicol Teratol 2010;32(1):68–73.

[69] Boyd WA, McBride SJ, Rice JR, Snyder DW, Freedman JH. A high-throughput method for assessing chemical toxicity using a *Caenorhabditis elegans* reproduction assay. Toxicol Appl Pharmacol 2010;245(2):153–9.

[70] Leung MC, Goldstone JV, Boyd WA, Freedman JH, Meyer JN. *Caenorhabditis elegans* generates biologically relevant levels of genotoxic metabolites from aflatoxin B1 but not benzo[a]pyrene in vivo. Toxicol Sci 2010;118(2):444–53.

[71] Goldstone JV, Goldstone HM, Morrison AM, Tarrant A, Kern SE, Woodin BR, et al. Cytochrome P450 1 genes in early deuterostomes (tunicates and sea urchins) and vertebrates (chicken and frog): origin and diversification of the CYP1 gene family. Mol Biol Evol 2007;24(12):2619–31.

[72] Ellis-Hutchings RG, Carney EW. Whole embryo culture: a "New" technique that enabled decades of mechanistic discoveries. Birth Defects Res B Dev Reprod Toxicol 2010;89(4):304–12.

[73] Piersma AH. Validation of alternative methods for developmental toxicity testing. Toxicol Lett 2004;149(1–3):147–53.

[74] New DA. Whole-embryo culture and the study of mammalian embryos during organogenesis. Biol Rev Camb Philos Soc 1978;53(1):81–122.

[75] Sadler TW, Warner CW. Use of whole embryo culture for evaluating toxicity and teratogenicity. Pharmacol Rev 1984;36(2 Suppl.):145S–50S.

[76] Van Maele-Fabry G, Gofflot F, Picard JJ. Whole embryo culture of presomitic mouse embryos. Toxicol In Vitro 1995;9(5):671–5.

[77] Carney EW, Tornesi B, Keller C, Findlay HA, Nowland WS, Marshall VA, et al. Refinement of a morphological scoring system for postimplantation rabbit conceptuses. Birth Defects Res B Dev Reprod Toxicol 2007;80(3):213–22.

[78] Schmid BP. Xenobiotic influences on embryonic differentiation, growth and morphology in vitro. Xenobiotica 1985;15(8–9):719–26.

[79] Cicurel L, Schmid BP. Post-implantation embryo culture: validation with selected compounds for teratogenicity testing. Xenobiotica 1988;18(6):617–24.

[80] Genschow E, Spielmann H, Scholz G, Seiler A, Brown N, Piersma A, et al. The ECVAM international validation study on in vitro embryotoxicity tests: results of the definitive phase and evaluation of prediction models. European Centre for the Validation of Alternative Methods. Altern Lab Anim 2002;30(2):151–76.

[81] Li AP, Gupta RS, Heflich RH, Wassom JS. A review and analysis of the Chinese hamster ovary/hypoxanthine guanine phosphoribosyl transferase assay to determine the mutagenicity of chemical agents. A report of phase III of the U.S. Environmental Protection Agency Gene-Tox Program. Mutat Res 1988;196(1):17–36.

[82] Schenk B, Weimer M, Bremer S, van der Burg B, Cortvrindt R, Freyberger A, et al. The ReProTect feasibility study, a novel comprehensive in vitro approach to detect reproductive toxicants. Reprod Toxicol 2010;30:200–18.

[83] Fantel AG, Greenaway JC, Juchau MR, Shepard TH. Teratogenic bioactivation of cyclophosphamide in vitro. Life Sci 1979;25(1):67–72.

[84] Gandolfi AJ, Wijeweera J, Brendel K. Use of precision-cut liver slices as an in vitro tool for evaluating liver function. Toxicol Pathol 1996;24(1):58–61.

[85] Parrish AR, Gandolfi AJ, Brendel K. Precision-cut tissue slices: applications in pharmacology and toxicology. Life Sci 1995;57(21):1887–901.

[86] de Graaf IA, Olinga P, de Jager MH, Merema MT, de Kanter R, van de Kerkhof EG, et al. Preparation and incubation of precision-cut liver and intestinal slices for application in drug metabolism and toxicity studies. Nat Protoc 2010;5(9):1540–51.

[87] Berthou F, Ratanasavanh D, Riche C, Picart D, Voirin T, Guillouzo A. Comparison of caffeine metabolism by slices, microsomes and hepatocyte cultures from adult human liver. Xenobiotica 1989;19(4):401–17.

[88] Mourelle M, McLean AE. Electron transport and protection of liver slices in the late stage of paracetamol injury of the liver. Br J Pharmacol 1989;98(Suppl.). 825P.

[89] Boelsterli UA, Goldlin C. Biomechanisms of cocaine-induced hepatocyte injury mediated by the formation of reactive metabolites. Arch Toxicol 1991;65(5):351–60.

[90] Togashi H, Shinzawa H, Wakabayashi H, Nakamura T, Yong H, Yamada N, et al. Superoxide is involved in the pathogenesis of paraquat-induced injury in cultured rat liver slices. Hepatology 1991;14(4 Pt 1):707–14.

[91] Fraga CG, Leibovitz BE, Tappel AL. Halogenated compounds as inducers of lipid peroxidation in tissue slices. Free Radic Biol Med 1987;3(2):119–23.

[92] Fraga CG, Zamora R, Tappel AL. Damage to protein synthesis concurrent with lipid peroxidation in rat liver slices: effect of halogenated compounds, peroxides, and vitamin E1. Arch Biochem Biophys 1989;270(1):84–91.

[93] Smith JH, Hook JB. Mechanism of chloroform nephrotoxicity. II. In vitro evidence for renal metabolism of chloroform in mice. Toxicol Appl Pharmacol 1983;70(3):480–5.

[94] Suzuki CA, Cherian MG. Renal glutathione depletion and nephrotoxicity of cadmium-metallothionein in rats. Toxicol Appl Pharmacol 1989;98(3):544–52.

[95] Hass MA, Massaro D. Mitogenic response of rat lung to endotoxin exposure. Biochem Pharmacol 1987;36(22):3841–6.

[96] Giri SN, Younker WR, Schiedt MJ. Effects of bleomycin on 14C-proline uptake, its incorporation into proteins and hydroxylation in collagenous proteins of hamster lung slices. J Appl Toxicol 1985;5(2):89–93.

[97] Karl PI, Friedman PA. Competition between paraquat and putrescine for accumulation by rat lung slices. Toxicology 1983;26(3–4):317–23.

[98] Wright ES, Kehrer JP, White DM, Smiler KL. Effects of chronic exposure to ozone on collagen in rat lung. Toxicol Appl Pharmacol 1988;92(3):445–52.

[99] Parrish AR, Sallam K, Nyman DW, Orozco J, Cress AE, Dalkin BL, et al. Culturing precision-cut human prostate slices as an in vitro model of prostate pathobiology. Cell Biol Toxicol 2002;18(3):205–19.

[100] Guguen-Guillouzo C, Guillouzo A. General review on in vitro hepatocyte models and their applications. Methods Mol Biol 2010;640:1–40.

[101] Catania JM, Pershing AM, Gandolfi AJ. Precision-cut tissue chips as an in vitro toxicology system. Toxicol In Vitro 2007; 21(5):956–61.

[102] Gautheron P, Giroux J, Cottin M, Audegond L, Morilla A, Mayordomo-Blanco L, et al. Interlaboratory assessment of the bovine corneal opacity and permeability (BCOP) assay. Toxicol In Vitro 1994;8(3):381–92.

[103] Prinsen MK. The chicken enucleated eye test (CEET): a practical (pre)screen for the assessment of eye irritation/corrosion potential of test materials. Food Chem Toxicol 1996;34(3):291–6.

[104] Prinsen MK, Koeter HB. Justification of the enucleated eye test with eyes of slaughterhouse animals as an alternative to the Draize eye irritation test with rabbits. Food Chem Toxicol 1993;31(1):69–76.

[105] Ekwall B, Silano V, Paganuzzi-Stammati A, Zucco F. In: Bourdeau P, et al., editor. Toxicity tests with mammalian cell cultures. John Wiley & Sons Ltd; 1990.

[106] Turpeinen M, Ghiciuc C, Opritoui M, Tursas L, Pelkonen O, Pasanen M. Predictive value of animal models for human cytochrome P450 (CYP)-mediated metabolism: a comparative study in vitro. Xenobiotica 2007;37(12):1367–77.

[107] Dahlin DC, Miwa GT, Lu AY, Nelson SD. N-acetyl-p-benzoquinone imine: a cytochrome P-450-mediated oxidation product of acetaminophen. Proc Natl Acad Sci USA 1984;81(5):1327–31.

[108] Holme JA, Dahlin DC, Nelson SD, Dybing E. Cytotoxic effects of N-acetyl-p-benzoquinone imine, a common arylating intermediate of paracetamol and N-hydroxyparacetamol. Biochem Pharmacol 1984;33(3):401–6.

[109] Quistorff B, Romert P. High zone-selectivity of cell permeabilization following digitonin-pulse perfusion of rat liver. A reinterpretation of the microcirculatory zones. Histochemistry 1989;92(6):487–98.

[110] Lecluyse EL, Alexandre E. Isolation and culture of primary hepatocytes from resected human liver tissue. Methods Mol Biol 2010;640:57–82.

[111] Reid LM, Jefferson DM. Culturing hepatocytes and other differentiated cells. Hepatology 1984;4(3):548–59.

[112] Dunn JC, Tompkins RG, Yarmush ML. Long-term in vitro function of adult hepatocytes in a collagen sandwich configuration. Biotechnol Prog 1991;7(3):237–45.

[113] Sidhu JS, Liu F, Omiecinski CJ. Phenobarbital responsiveness as a uniquely sensitive indicator of hepatocyte differentiation status: requirement of dexamethasone and extracellular matrix in establishing the functional integrity of cultured primary rat hepatocytes. Exp Cell Res 2004;292(2):252–64.

[114] Tuschl G, Mueller SO. Effects of cell culture conditions on primary rat hepatocytes-cell morphology and differential gene expression. Toxicology 2006;218(2–3):205–15.

[115] Begue JM, Le Bigot JF, Guguen-Guillouzo C, Kiechel JR, Guillouzo A. Cultured human adult hepatocytes: a new model for drug metabolism studies. Biochem Pharmacol 1983;32(10):1643–6.

[116] Pichard L, Fabre I, Fabre G, Domergue J, Saint Aubert B, Mourad G, et al. Cyclosporin A drug interactions. Screening for inducers and inhibitors of cytochrome P-450 (cyclosporin A oxidase) in primary cultures of human hepatocytes and in liver microsomes. Drug Metab Dispos 1990;18(5):595–606.

[117] Story DL, Gee SJ, Tyson CA, Gould DH. Response of isolated hepatocytes to organic and inorganic cytotoxins. J Toxicol Environ Health 1983;11(4–6):483–501.

[118] Tyson CA, Mitoma C, Kalivoda J. Evaluation of hepatocytes isolated by a nonperfusion technique in a prescreen for cytotoxicity. J Toxicol Environ Health 1980;6(1):197–205.

[119] Guillouzo A. Liver cell models in in vitro toxicology. Environ Health Perspect 1998;106(Suppl. 2):511–32.

[120] Williams GM. Detection of chemical carcinogens by unscheduled DNA synthesis in rat liver primary cell cultures. Cancer Res 1977;37(6):1845–51.

[121] Yager Jr JD, Miller Jr JA. DNA repair in primary cultures of rat hepatocytes. Cancer Res 1978;38(12):4385–94.

[122] Le Bigot JF, Begue JM, Kiechel JR, Guillouzo A. Species differences in metabolism of ketotifen in rat, rabbit and man: demonstration of similar pathways in vivo and in cultured hepatocytes. Life Sci 1987;40(9):883–90.

[123] Cicurel L, Schmid BP. Postimplantation embryo culture for the assessment of the teratogenic potential and potency of compounds. Experientia 1988;44(10):833–40.

[124] Lubberstedt M, Muller-Vieira U, Mayer M, Biemel KM, Knospel F, Knobeloch D, et al. HepaRG human hepatic cell line utility as a surrogate for primary human hepatocytes in drug metabolism assessment in vitro. J Pharmacol Toxicol Methods 2011;63(1):59–68.

[125] Weaver VM, Petersen OW, Wang F, Larabell CA, Briand P, Damsky C, et al. Reversion of the malignant phenotype of human breast cells in three-dimensional culture and in vivo by integrin blocking antibodies. J Cell Biol 1997;137(1):231–45.

[126] Derda R, Tang SK, Laromaine A, Mosadegh B, Hong E, Mwangi M, et al. Multizone paper platform for 3D cell cultures. PLoS One 2011;6(5):e18940.

[127] Cukierman E, Pankov R, Stevens DR, Yamada KM. Taking cell-matrix adhesions to the third dimension. Science 2001; 294(5547):1708–12.

[128] Schutte M, Fox B, Baradez MO, Devonshire A, Minguez J, Bokhari M, et al. Rat primary hepatocytes show enhanced performance and sensitivity to acetaminophen during three-dimensional culture on a polystyrene scaffold designed for routine use. Assay Drug Dev Tech 2011;9(5):475–86.

[129] Nakamura K, Mizutani R, Sanbe A, Enosawa S, Kasahara M, Nakagawa A, et al. Evaluation of drug toxicity with hepatocytes cultured in a micro-space cell culture system. J Biosci Bioeng 2011;111(1):78–84.

VIII. PREDICTIVE TOXICOLOGY, TOXICOMETABOLOMICS, TOXICOGENOMICS, AND IMAGING

[130] Kim JB, Stein R, O'Hare MJ. Three-dimensional in vitro tissue culture models of breast cancer – a review. Breast Cancer Res Treat 2004;85(3):281–91.

[131] Wolf K, Mazo I, Leung H, Engelke K, von Andrian UH, Deryugina EI, et al. Compensation mechanism in tumor cell migration: mesenchymal-amoeboid transition after blocking of pericellular proteolysis. J Cell Biol 2003;160(2):267–77.

[132] Gotoh Y, Ishizuka Y, Matsuura T, Niimi S. Spheroid formation and expression of liver-specific functions of human hepatocellular carcinoma-derived FLC-4 cells cultured in lactose-silk fibroin conjugate sponges. Biomacromolecules 2011;12(5):1532–9.

[133] Netzlaff F, Lehr CM, Wertz PW, Schaefer UF. The human epidermis models EpiSkin, SkinEthic and EpiDerm: an evaluation of morphology and their suitability for testing phototoxicity, irritancy, corrosivity, and substance transport. Eur J Pharm Biopharm 2005;60(2):167–78.

[134] Liebsch M, Traue D, Barrabs C, Spielmann H, Uphill P, Wilkins S, et al. The ECVAM prevalidation study on the use of EpiDerm for skin corrosivity testing. ATLA 2000;28:371–401.

[135] Balls M, Hellsten E, ECVAM. Statement on the scientific validity of EpiDerm human skin model for skin corrosivity testing. Altern Lab Anim 2000;28:365–6.

[136] van Vliet E. Current standing and future prospects for the technologies proposed to transform toxicity testing in the 21st century. ALTEX 2011;28(1):17–44.

[137] Fedoroff S. Proposed usage of animal tissue culture terms. In Vitro 1966;2:155–9.

[138] Mills PC, Siebert GA, Roberts MS. A model to study intestinal and hepatic metabolism of propranolol in the dog. J Vet Pharmacol Ther 2004;27(1):45–8.

[139] Aden DP, Fogel A, Plotkin S, Damjanov I, Knowles BB. Controlled synthesis of HBsAg in a differentiated human liver carcinoma-derived cell line. Nature 1979;282(5739):615–6.

[140] Knasmuller S, Parzefall W, Sanyal R, Ecker S, Schwab C, Uhl M, et al. Use of metabolically competent human hepatoma cells for the detection of mutagens and antimutagens. Mutat Res 1998;402(1–2):185–202.

[141] Jennen DG, Magkoufopoulou C, Ketelslegers HB, van Herwijnen MH, Kleinjans JC, van Delft JH. Comparison of HepG2 and HepaRG by whole-genome gene expression analysis for the purpose of chemical hazard identification. Toxicol Sci 2010;115(1):66–79.

[142] Ogino M, Nagata K, Yamazoe Y. Selective suppressions of human CYP3A forms, CYP3A5 and CYP3A7, by troglitazone in HepG2 cells. Drug Metab Pharmacokinet 2002;17(1):42–6.

[143] Aninat C, Piton A, Glaise D, Le Charpentier T, Langouet S, Morel F, et al. Expression of cytochromes P450, conjugating enzymes and nuclear receptors in human hepatoma HepaRG cells. Drug Metab Dispos 2006;34(1):75–83.

[144] Guillouzo A, Corlu A, Aninat C, Glaise D, Morel F, Guguen-Guillouzo C. The human hepatoma HepaRG cells: a highly differentiated model for studies of liver metabolism and toxicity of xenobiotics. Chem Biol Interact 2007;168(1):66–73.

[145] Parent R, Marion MJ, Furio L, Trepo C, Petit MA. Origin and characterization of a human bipotent liver progenitor cell line. Gastroenterology 2004;126(4):1147–56.

[146] Le Vee M, Jigorel E, Glaise D, Gripon P, Guguen-Guillouzo C, Fardel O. Functional expression of sinusoidal and canalicular hepatic drug transporters in the differentiated human hepatoma HepaRG cell line. Eur J Pharm Sci 2006;28(1–2):109–17.

[147] Zelko I, Negishi M. Phenobarbital-elicited activation of nuclear receptor CAR in induction of cytochrome P450 genes. Biochem Biophys Res Commun 2000;277(1):1–6.

[148] Kanebratt KP, Andersson TB. Evaluation of HepaRG cells as an in vitro model for human drug metabolism studies. Drug Metab Dispos 2008;36(7):1444–52.

[149] Wang DP, Stroup D, Marrapodi M, Crestani M, Galli G, Chiang JY. Transcriptional regulation of the human cholesterol 7 alpha-hydroxylase gene (CYP7A) in HepG2 cells. J Lipid Res 1996;37(9):1831–41.

[150] Majer BJ, Mersch-Sundermann V, Darroudi F, Laky B, de Wit K, Knasmuller S. Genotoxic effects of dietary and lifestyle related carcinogens in human derived hepatoma (HepG2, Hep3B) cells. Mutat Res 2004;551(1–2):153–66.

[151] Costa S, Utan A, Speroni E, Cervellati R, Piva G, Prandini A, et al. Carnosic acid from rosemary extracts: a potential chemoprotective agent against aflatoxin B1. An in vitro study. J Appl Toxicol 2007;27(2):152–9.

[152] Babich H, Sardana MK, Borenfreund E. Acute cytotoxicities of polynuclear aromatic hydrocarbons determined in vitro with the human liver tumor cell line, HepG2. Cell Biol Toxicol 1988;4(3):295–309.

[153] Sanyal R, Darroudi F, Parzefall W, Nagao M, Knasmuller S. Inhibition of the genotoxic effects of heterocyclic amines in human derived hepatoma cells by dietary bioantimutagens. Mutagenesis 1997;12(4):297–303.

[154] Le Hegarat L, Dumont J, Josse R, Huet S, Lanceleur R, Mourot A, et al. Assessment of the genotoxic potential of indirect chemical mutagens in HepaRG cells by the comet and the cytokinesis-block micronucleus assays. Mutagenesis 2010;25(6):555–60.

[155] Laurent V, Fraix A, Montier T, Cammas-Marion S, Ribault C, Benvegnu T, et al. Highly efficient gene transfer into hepatocyte-like HepaRG cells: new means for drug metabolism and toxicity studies. Biotechnol J 2010;5(3):314–20.

[156] Clive D, Spector JF. Laboratory procedure for assessing specific locus mutations at the TK locus in cultured L5178Y mouse lymphoma cells. Mutat Res 1975;31(1):17–29.

[157] Oberly TJ, Yount DL, Garriott ML. A comparison of the soft agar and microtitre methodologies for the L5178Y tk± mouse lymphoma assay. Mutat Res 1997;388(1):59–66.

[158] Hozier J, Sawyer J, Clive D, Moore M. Cytogenetic distinction between the TK+ and TK− chromosomes in the L5178Y TK+/− 3.7.2C mouse-lymphoma cell line. Mutat Res 1982;105(6):451–6.

[159] Applegate M, Juhn G, Liechty M, Moore M, Hozier J. Use of DNA purified in situ from cells embedded in agarose plugs for the molecular analysis of tk−/− mutants recovered in the L5178Y tk+/− 3.7.2C mutagen assay system. Mutat Res 1990;245(1):55–9.

[160] Mitchell AD, Auletta AE, Clive D, Kirby PE, Moore MM, Myhr BC. The L5178Y/tk+/− mouse lymphoma specific gene and chromosomal mutation assay a phase III report of the U.S. Environmental Protection Agency Gene-Tox Program. Mutat Res 1997;394(1–3):177–303.

[161] Li AP, Aaron CS, Auletta AE, Dearfield KL, Riddle JC, Slesinski RS, et al. An evaluation of the roles of mammalian cell mutation assays in the testing of chemical genotoxicity. Regul Toxicol Pharmacol 1991;14(1):24–40.

[162] Chen T, Harrington-Brock K, Moore MM. Mutant frequency and mutational spectra in the Tk and Hprt genes of N-ethyl-N-nitrosourea-treated mouse lymphoma cellsdagger. Environ Mol Mutagen 2002;39(4):296–305.

[163] Maki-Paakkanen J, Komulainen H, Kronberg L. Bacterial and mammalian-cell genotoxicity of mixtures of chlorohydroxyfuranones, by-products of water chlorination. Environ Mol Mutagen 2004;43(4):217–25.

[164] Caldwell J. Perspective on the usefulness of the mouse lymphoma assay as an indicator of a genotoxic carcinogen: ten compounds which are positive in the mouse lymphoma assay but are not genotoxic carcinogens. Teratog Carcinog Mutagen 1993;13(4):185–90.

VIII. PREDICTIVE TOXICOLOGY, TOXICOMETABOLOMICS, TOXICOGENOMICS, AND IMAGING

[165] Lalko JF, Kimber I, Dearman RJ, Gerberick GF, Sarlo K, Api AM. Chemical reactivity measurements: potential for characterization of respiratory chemical allergens. Toxicol In Vitro 2011;25(2):433–45.

[166] Karlberg AT, Bergstrom MA, Borje A, Luthman K, Nilsson JL. Allergic contact dermatitis–formation, structural requirements, and reactivity of skin sensitizers. Chem Res Toxicol 2008;21(1):53–69.

[167] Andreas N, Caroline B, Leslie F, Frank G, Kimberly N, Allison H, et al. The intra- and inter-laboratory reproducibility and predictivity of the KeratinoSens assay to predict skin sensitizers in vitro: results of a ring-study in five laboratories. Toxicol In Vitro 2011;25(3):733–44.

[168] Kimber I, Basketter DA. The murine local lymph node assay: a commentary on collaborative studies and new directions. Food Chem Toxicol 1992;30(2):165–9.

[169] Magnusson B, Kligman AM. The identification of contact allergens by animal assay. The guinea pig maximization test. J Invest Dermatol 1969;52(3):268–76.

[170] Aeby P, Ashikaga T, Bessou-Touya S, Schepky A, Gerberick F, Kern P, et al. Identifying and characterizing chemical skin sensitizers without animal testing: Colipa's research and method development program. Toxicol In Vitro 2010;24(6):1465–73.

[171] Corsini E, Mitjans M, Galbiati V, Lucchi L, Galli CL, Marinovich M. Use of IL-18 production in a human keratinocyte cell line to discriminate contact sensitizers from irritants and low molecular weight respiratory allergens. Toxicol In Vitro 2009;23(5):789–96.

[172] Ashikaga T, Yoshida Y, Hirota M, Yoneyama K, Itagaki H, Sakaguchi H, et al. Development of an in vitro skin sensitization test using human cell lines: the human Cell Line Activation Test (h-CLAT). I. Optimization of the h-CLAT protocol. Toxicol In Vitro 2006;20(5):767–73.

[173] Galbiati V, Carne A, Mitjans M, Galli CL, Marinovich M, Corsini E. Isoeugenol destabilizes IL-8 mRNA expression in THP-1 cells through induction of the negative regulator of mRNA stability tristetraprolin. Arch Toxicol 2011;86.

[174] Jowsey IR, Basketter DA, Westmoreland C, Kimber I. A future approach to measuring relative skin sensitising potency: a proposal. J Appl Toxicol 2006;26(4):341–50.

[175] Gerberick GF, Vassallo JD, Bailey RE, Chaney JG, Morrall SW, Lepoittevin JP. Development of a peptide reactivity assay for screening contact allergens. Toxicol Sci 2004;81(2):332–43.

[176] Jaworska JS, Natsch A, Ryan C, Strickland J, Ashikaga T, Miyazawa M. Bayesian integrated testing strategy (ITS) for skin sensitization potency assessment: a decision support system for quantitative weight of evidence and adaptive testing strategy. Arch Toxicol 2015;89(12):2355–83.

[177] Rovida C, Alepee N, Api AM, Basketter DA, Bois FY, Caloni F, et al. Integrated testing strategies (its) for safety assessment. ALTEX 2015;32(1):25–40.

[178] Spielmann H, Gerner I, Kalweit S, Moog R, Wirnsberger T, Krauser K, et al. Interlaboratory assessment of alternatives to the Draize eye irritation test in Germany. Toxicol In Vitro 1991;5(5–6):539–42.

[179] Itagaki H, Hagino S, Kato S, Kobayashi T, Umeda M. An in vitro alternative to the Draize eye-irritation test: evaluation of the crystal violet staining method. Toxicol In Vitro 1991;5(2):139–43.

[180] Avery S, Inniss K, Moore H. The regulation of self-renewal in human embryonic stem cells. Stem Cell Dev 2006;15(5):729–40.

[181] Laustriat D, Gide J, Peschanski M. Human pluripotent stem cells in drug discovery and predictive toxicology. Biochem Soc Trans 2010;38(4):1051–7.

[182] Takahashi K, Yamanaka S. Induction of pluripotent stem cells from mouse embryonic and adult fibroblast cultures by defined factors. Cell 2006;126(4):663–76.

[183] Jaenisch R, Young R. Stem cells, the molecular circuitry of pluripotency and nuclear reprogramming. Cell 2008;132(4):567–82.

[184] Estevan C, Romero AC, Pamies D, Vilanova E, Sogorb MA. In: Kallos MS, editor. Embryonic stem cells in toxicological studies. InTech; 2011.

[185] Trosko JE, Chang CC. Factors to consider in the use of stem cells for pharmaceutic drug development and for chemical safety assessment. Toxicology 2010;270(1):18–34.

[186] Miki T, Ring A, Gerlach J. Hepatic differentiation of human embryonic stem cells is promoted by three-dimensional dynamic perfusion culture conditions. Tissue Eng Part C Methods 2011;17(5):557–68.

[187] Genschow E, Spielmann H, Scholz G, Pohl I, Seiler A, Clemann N, et al. Validation of the embryonic stem cell test in the international ECVAM validation study on three in vitro embryotoxicity tests. Altern Lab Anim 2004;32(3):209–44.

[188] Paquette JA, Kumpf SW, Streck RD, Thomson JJ, Chapin RE, Stedman DB. Assessment of the embryonic stem cell test and application and use in the pharmaceutical industry. Birth Defects Res B Dev Reprod Toxicol 2008;83(2):104–11.

[189] Seiler AE, Buesen R, Visan A, Spielmann H. Use of murine embryonic stem cells in embryotoxicity assays: the embryonic stem cell test. Methods Mol Biol 2006;329:371–95.

[190] Spielmann H, Pohl I, Doring B, Liebsch M, Moldenhauer F. The embryonic stem cell test (EST), an in vitro embryotoxicity test using two permanent mouse cell lines: 3T3 fibroblasts and embryonic stem cells. In Vitro Toxicol 1997;10:119–27.

[191] Genschow E, Scholz G, Brown N, Piersma A, Brady M, Clemann N, et al. Development of prediction models for three in vitro embryotoxicity tests in an ECVAM validation study. In Vitro Mol Toxicol 2000;13(1):51–66.

[192] Augustine-Rauch K, Zhang CX, Panzica-Kelly JM. In vitro developmental toxicology assays: a review of the state of the science of rodent and zebrafish whole embryo culture and embryonic stem cell assays. Birth Defects Res C Embryo Today 2010;90(2):87–98.

[193] Spielmann H, Seiler A, Bremer S, Hareng L, Hartung T, Ahr H, et al. The practical application of three validated in vitro embryotoxicity tests. The report and recommendations of an ECVAM/ZEBET workshop (ECVAM workshop 57). Altern Lab Anim 2006;34(5):527–38.

[194] Marx-Stoelting P, Adriaens E, Ahr HJ, Bremer S, Garthoff B, Gelbke HP, et al. A review of the implementation of the embryonic stem cell test (EST). The report and recommendations of an ECVAM/ReProTect workshop. Altern Lab Anim 2009;37(3):313–28.

[195] Bigot K, de Lange J, Archer G, Clothier R, Bremer S. The relative semi-quantification of mRNA expression as a useful toxicological endpoint for the identification of embryotoxic/teratogenic substances. Toxicol In Vitro 1999;13(4–5):619–23.

[196] Pennings JL, van Dartel DA, Pronk TE, Hendriksen PJ, Piersma AH. Identification by gene coregulation mapping of novel genes involved in embryonic stem cell differentiation. Stem Cell Dev 2011;20(1):115–26.

[197] van Dartel DA, Pennings JL, Robinson JF, Kleinjans JC, Piersma AH. Discriminating classes of developmental toxicants using gene expression profiling in the embryonic stem cell test. Toxicol Lett 2011;201(2):143–51.

[198] Paparella M, Kolossov E, Fleischmann BK, Hescheler J, Bremer S. The use of quantitative image analysis in the assessment of in vitro embryotoxicity endpoints based on a novel embryonic stem cell clone with endoderm-related GFP expression. Toxicol In Vitro 2002;16(5):589–97.

[199] Buesen R, Visan A, Genschow E, Slawik B, Spielmann H, Seiler A. Trends in improving the embryonic stem cell test (EST): an overview. ALTEX 2004;21(1):15–22.

[200] Amabile G, Meissner A. Induced pluripotent stem cells: current progress and potential for regenerative medicine. Trends Mol Med 2009;15(2):59–68.

[201] Chin MH, Mason MJ, Xie W, Volinia S, Singer M, Peterson C, et al. Induced pluripotent stem cells and embryonic stem cells are distinguished by gene expression signatures. Cell Stem Cell 2009;5(1):111–23.

[202] Wu S, Blackburn K, Amburgey J, Jaworska J, Federle T. A framework for using structural, reactivity, metabolic and physicochemical similarity to evaluate the suitability of analogs for SAR-based toxicological assessments. Regul Toxicol Pharmacol 2010;56(1):67–81.

[203] Ball N, Bartels M, Budinsky R, Klapacz J, Hays S, Kirman C, et al. The challenge of using read-across within the EU REACH regulatory framework; how much uncertainty is too much? Dipropylene glycol methyl ether acetate, an exemplary case study. Regul Toxicol Pharmacol 2014;68(2):212–21.

[204] Patlewicz G, Ball N, Boogaard PJ, Becker RA, Hubesch B. Building scientific confidence in the development and evaluation of read-across. Regul Toxicol Pharmacol 2015;72(1):117–33.

[205] Lamb J, Crawford ED, Peck D, Modell JW, Blat IC, Wrobel MJ, et al. The connectivity map: using gene-expression signatures to connect small molecules, genes, and disease. Science 2006;313(5795):1929–35.

[206] Jaworska J, Dancik Y, Kern P, Gerberick F, Natsch A. Bayesian integrated testing strategy to assess skin sensitization potency: from theory to practice. J Appl Toxicol 2013;33(11):1353–64.

[207] Patlewicz G, Ball N, Becker RA, Booth ED, Cronin MT, Kroese D, et al. Read-across approaches–misconceptions, promises and challenges ahead. ALTEX 2014;31(4):387–96.

[208] Isaacs KK, Glen WG, Egeghy P, Goldsmith MR, Smith L, Vallero D, et al. SHEDS-HT: an integrated probabilistic exposure model for prioritizing exposures to chemicals with near-field and dietary sources. Environ Sci Technol 2014;48(21):12750–9.

[209] Wambaugh JF, Wang A, Dionisio KL, Frame A, Egeghy P, Judson R, et al. High throughput heuristics for prioritizing human exposure to environmental chemicals. Environ Sci Technol 2014;48(21):12760–7.

[210] Rotroff DM, Wetmore BA, Dix DJ, Ferguson SS, Clewell HJ, Houck KA, et al. Incorporating human dosimetry and exposure into high-throughput in vitro toxicity screening. Toxicol Sci 2010;117(2):348–58.

[211] Wetmore BA, Wambaugh JF, Ferguson SS, Sochaski MA, Rotroff DM, Freeman K, et al. Integration of dosimetry, exposure, and high-throughput screening data in chemical toxicity assessment. Toxicol Sci 2012;125(1):157–74.

[212] Nagel R. DarT: the embryo test with the Zebrafish *Danio rerio*– a general model in ecotoxicology and toxicology. ALTEX 2002;19(Suppl. 1):38–48.

33

Toxicometabolomics: Technology and Applications

M.V. Milburn, J.A. Ryals, L. Guo

INTRODUCTION TO BIOMARKER DISCOVERY AND VALIDATION IN TOXICOLOGY

Many "omics" technologies have now become the primary way of discovering new biomarkers, and validation of these biomarkers is a relatively new and evolving concept. Whether it's genomics (profiling RNA and DNA), proteomics (profiling proteins), metabolomics (profiling biochemicals or metabolites), or some other discovery technology, the process starts with an idea of the type of biomarkers that are needed for a condition/disease/or health risk. For example, kidney dysfunction is a well-studied condition that can lead to a number of health problems, including kidney failure. A number of simple fasting blood and urine biomarkers do exist for kidney function and have their utilities. Creatinine is cleared slowly from the blood through the kidneys and

is continuously produced from creatine in the muscle [1]. An increase or decrease in serum creatinine (SCr) is commonly used as an assessment of kidney function, since it measures how well the metabolite is cleared from the blood into the urine. Other biomarkers of kidney function include blood urea levels (BUN), albumin in urine, and total protein in urine. Several alternative biomarkers have also been proposed in the literature, including urinary kidney injury molecule-1 (KIM-1), neutrophil gelatinase-associated lipocalin (NGAL), osterponein, and others [2]. However, new and more predictive biomarkers of kidney function are needed to better assess those patients that are at risk of developing more serious kidney dysfunction. By the time many of these current biomarkers (both metabolites and proteins) are detectable, kidney impairment is usually fairly advanced and it can be too late to reverse the loss of kidney function [3]. Also, unlike liver injury, which may be able to heal itself over time, kidney injury is often permanent and effects patients for the rest of their lives.

There are other modalities of treatment, including holidays from chemotherapy, alternative dosages, and alternative treatments that can be applied if a patient is suspected of potential kidney injury. Currently, most oncologists are guided by globular filtration rate and other kidney function indicators to decide whether/when to change a course of treatment. Earlier and more predictive biomarkers of kidney function or injury would help guide oncologists in making this choice, leading to therapy regimens with deceased risk of kidney injury, lower incidences of permanent loss of kidney function, and improved chemotherapy effectiveness.

If earlier and more predictive kidney injury biomarkers are needed, then the next step is a biomarker discovery and feasibility study to better understand whether it is possible to identify new biomarkers (Fig. 33.1). Clinical biomarker discovery studies usually involve identifying appropriate study populations that can distinguish individuals with the treatment effects (cases) from the nontreatment effected individuals (case controls) [4–6]. For example, in the case of *cis*-platinum

induced kidney injury one would choose a clinical population group that had received treatment. Once a study population is identified, the next question is what type of samples should be acquired and whether they are present in sufficient amounts with the necessary *meta*-data to perform a discovery study. These types of decisions are usually best addressed from a clinical utility standpoint. The types of samples required are sometimes limited to what is available—obviously in the case of kidney injury it would be advantageous to use kidney tissue samples, but obtaining them would be highly invasive. Most convenient sample types are based on either urine or blood. Once the type of sample has been decided the next question to address is how many samples are required in each group—kidney injury versus no injury, for example.

Another important consideration is the power of the study required for the metabolomics technology that is employed [5,7,8], which will determine the number of cases and controls required in the study. The number of samples usually depends on two main factors: biological variability in the groups (age, sex, gender, etc.), and the process variability of the technology employed (number

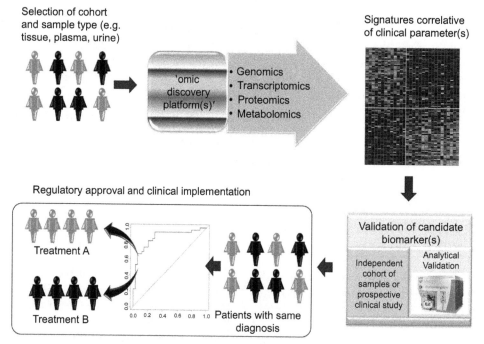

FIGURE 33.1 Process flow using "omics" technologies for biomarker discovery and validation. The initial work begins with decisions on the types of samples to be analyzed, number of subjects and samples required for the biomarker discovery study, and the relevant case and case controls that will be used. Many of these decisions are based on the types of technologies employed on the samples. Other decisions are based more on the clinical aspects of how the ultimate biomarker or diagnostic test will be used and its clinical utility. After the samples are received the discovery technology can be employed and analyzed. The analysis of "omics" technologies is beyond the scope of this chapter, but can involve complex multivariate analysis and methods to control for false discovery. Ultimately the aim of the discovery study is to develop a shorter list of candidate biomarkers that can be further validated with independent assays and hopefully independent cohorts of samples. Rarely is the discovery technology itself employed on an individual basis, although some technologies are moving in this direction. In most cases, the biomarker assay to validate is a more specific quantitation of the analyte under strict clinical protocols. Ultimately these assays will be further validated in the clinic to decide on their clinical usefulness and utility. In some cases this will also involve FDA approval of the assay or at a minimum certification to run the assay in a centralized laboratory.

of analytes being measured and the average precision of each analyte being analyzed) [9].

As with many initial toxicometabolomic discovery studies, the outcome of a biomarker feasibility study can often be mixed, in spite of being well-designed and sufficiently powered. Unfortunately, these types of studies can be complicated by the unforeseen impacts of age, gender, or other confounding effects (eg, diet, medications, lifestyle, etc.), making the analysis challenging [10–12]. How well the samples have been handled and curated in the sample bank can also have a profound effect on the discovery study. Unfortunately many questions and issues related to sample handling and storage are only now being addressed, which means this is clearly an area for improvement for the future [13]. In fact, many current metabolomics studies are focused on addressing some of the issues arising from the fact that biochemicals are often more stable in long-term analysis than are RNA or proteins. In addition, when a very large number of measurements [eg, 1 million single nucleotide polymorphisms (SNPs)] are made on only a small number of subjects per group (eg, 50 individuals per group) the probability of separating the groups by chance alone is enormous and often leads to "false" discovery [9]. As a result, more than one feasibility study may be required to produce findings and justify the investment in the resources required for biomarker validation.

Once it seems reasonable that the sample type for the biomarkers is suitable (blood, urine, etc.) and a sufficient number of samples are available, then larger, well-powered clinical studies are warranted. In most cases, these studies will contain enough subjects not only to discover biomarkers but to do so on an independent test set of subjects, ie, subjects who haven't been used as part of the discovery analysis. This analysis of independent samples is a key step in these multivariate analyses in which the potential for false discovery exists [6,14,15]. Another important consideration in biomarker discovery and validation is how demographically relevant the subjects are in the discovery population are to those in whom the test will be applied. For instance, using only European populations for the discovery and development of the biomarkers may be a concern if the test will also be employed in Japan.

As outlined at the bottom of Fig. 33.1, analytical assay development and biomarker validation should have significantly less risk associated with developing the biomarker but can be equally time-consuming. Sufficient numbers of samples from the test population are still necessary to analytically validate the methods. In addition, the assay throughput requirements for the assay setting (eg, hospital, point-of-care, central laboratory) often become important and require specific formats for the biomarker measurement that usually differ from the

discovery technology methods and assays. As an example, gene chips are often used for the discovery analysis of genetic biomarkers but to satisfy the throughput, cost, and quantitation requirements, other methods, such as PCR-based assays, have been developed [16]. One of the major advantages of metabolomics or biochemical profiling is the ease of moving from a profiling technology to a specific clinical assay given the number of clinical platform technologies currently available for small molecules [17,18].

In summary, biomarker discovery and validation require proper and appropriate number of samples to be assessed with a discovery technology. Secondly, once candidate biomarkers have been discovered and tentatively identified, they need to be validated using cohorts of subjects who are independent of those used in the discovery analysis (Fig. 33.1). Unfortunately, this type of approach has not always yielded overwhelming success [11,19–22]. Over 150,000 papers have been written about these technologies in the last 15 years, but fewer than 100 biomarkers have been validated for routine clinical practice, and even fewer are embraced by physicians today. The primary issues are whether the underlying technologies themselves can work, whether the biomarkers actually exist, or whether the diseases and complications are too complicated. Metabolomics, or biochemical profiling, is one technology that has grown very rapidly in its use as a discovery tool, and has often been validated in follow-up clinical studies [4,11,14,15,23–26]. In the next section we explore why this technology might be better suited for routine biomarker discovery and validation.

ADVANTAGES OF METABOLOMICS IN BIOMARKER DISCOVERY

The word "metabolomics" (or "metabonomics") first appeared in journal articles in 1999–2000 [27,28]. Only a few papers were published on metabolomics that year, but by 2009 that number rose to over 1300 [29]. In fact, metabolomics publications are now one of the most rapidly growing areas in scientific publication. Although analytical chemists and biochemists have been identifying small molecules in biological samples for many years, as a robust, nontargeted discovery tool, the technology is new and rapidly evolving. In addition to the increasing number of publications in the last few years, several significant biomarker reports using metabolomics that include supporting validation data for these discoveries have been published [6,14,15,26].

The major challenge for metabolomics has been to develop a technology that can extract, identify, and quantitate the entire spectrum of small molecules (MW < 1500 Da) in any biological sample [30]. While this is clearly a significant goal, the number of small molecules that exist in biological samples is hotly debated. Some databases of metabolites list as many as 5000–6000 metabolites in the human metabolome [31]. However, deeper analysis reveals that several 1000 molecules can be simply grouped as different combinations of complex lipids or small peptides [32,33]. Many of these lipid and peptide species are derived from the degradation and nonenzymatic oxidation of macromolecules. Their biological relevance has not been well demonstrated. From a primary metabolism standpoint, there are probably fewer than 3000 significant human metabolites. Importantly, in any one sample matrix (eg, blood, urine, tissue, etc.) there will always be many fewer metabolites than the total number synthesized in the entire organism.

Most importantly, this number (less than 3000) is much smaller than the other "omics" technologies such as genomics or proteomics and may represent a significant advantage for metabolomics in biomarker discovery (Fig. 33.2). A smaller number of total possible measurements for any individual allows the application of more robust statistical testing methodologies and results in fewer false discoveries [34], two factors that have plagued other biomarker discovery technologies. This simple mathematical effect, called false discovery, is often overlooked but represents a severe limitation in the general profiling of genes and proteins. These technologies can also be limited by the number of samples that can be tested in a reasonable amount of time.

The underlying math is actually quite simple to explain. As the total number of observations per individual subject increases, the likelihood of separating groups of individuals purely by chance goes up significantly. For instance, in a study of two groups of 100 subjects, the likelihood of separating them by random measurements is significantly higher if measuring 100,000 variables per individual than if measuring 1000 variables per individual. The false discovery problem is much less significant in metabolomics than any other "omic" technology, simply because the total number of unique biochemicals is so much smaller than the 35,000 or so genes, or the >100,000 different proteins [9] (Fig. 33.2).

Based on the analysis of small molecules, metabolomics analysis and interpretation is based on our depth of understanding in biochemistry. Biochemistry is a relatively mature, more highly developed field of science than molecular biology and proteomics [35]. This provides a significant advantage in the interpretation of metabolomics experiments. While the newer genomic/proteomic technologies have received the vast majority of attention in recent years, it is noteworthy that many of the Nobel Prizes in Medicine before the 1960s were awarded in biochemistry.

Today, we routinely depend on metabolite-based disease diagnosis. For instance, high glucose in urine was one of the earliest tests for diabetes, and cholesterol is used to measure the risk of heart disease. Metabolic panels of fatty acids, bile acids, sugars, creatine, creatinine, urea, etc., are routinely used clinically to assess organ function or risk of many diseases, as well as for disease diagnosis. Clearly, the field of metabolomics is well positioned to take advantage of this repository of biochemical pathway knowledge.

Another important advantage of metabolomics, especially for developing tests that rely on more noninvasive samples, is that essentially any type of sample can be analyzed. Metabolites can be routinely measured in urine, feces, sweat, saliva, blood, tissue, etc., most of which can often be challenging sources for obtaining genetic or protein information. A number of papers have been published recently describing the use of metabolomics assessment of more creative sample types for disease monitoring [14,29,36,37].

The development of metabolomics as a tool to leverage this body of knowledge has not been straightforward. Most laboratories have focused on targeted metabolomic analysis, specializing in the measurement of 20–100 different metabolites, which, most often, are within a common class of compounds [5,38,39]. For example, a number of companies and academic labs have developed methods for detecting lipid compounds [40,41]. Although lipids represent a smaller set of the total biologically relevant metabolites, these data have proven useful for biomarker discovery efforts [42].

Other groups have focused on methods to truly investigate all of the small molecules in a sample, which is called global metabolomics. "Global" or "unbiased" metabolomics has been plagued by difficulties stemming from the diverse physical properties of small molecules. These properties can vary greatly, with significant differences in solubility, and molecular weights ranging from 20 to >1000 Da. It is therefore difficult to develop a single chromatography method to separate all of the compounds and even more difficult to analyze individual compounds without chromatographic separation. Further complications arise if studies are expected to be completed with a reasonable turnaround time. Currently these methods are being developed by coupling multiple analytical chromatography platforms to small-molecule detection equipment, primarily mass spectrometry, to allow general profiling of the small molecules in a biological sample. This approach allows for comprehensive biochemical profiling, combining many new and advancing technologies. In addition, many of these methods have mandated the development of new software methods and technology to analyze the vast amount of data that is generated. As this new technology develops and its use in biomarker detection studies increases, it is rapidly becoming clear that metabolomics will likely represent a high-impact technology in

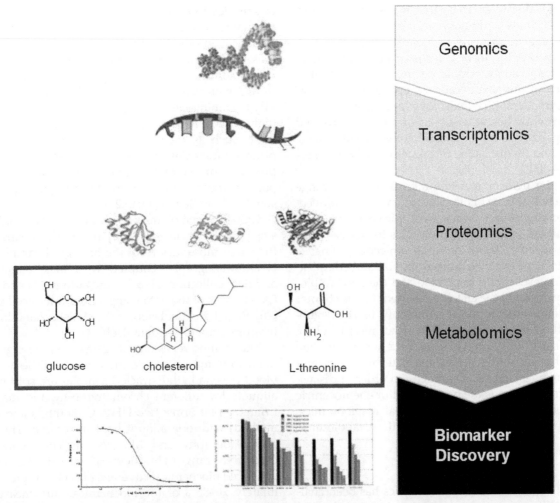

FIGURE 33.2 Progression of genes to metabolites and how each step comprises the "omics" technologies. With a little over 30,000 genes and over 100,000 possible transcripts and proteins, metabolites represent a far smaller total number (<3000) than these other two technologies. The consequence of this far smaller number is that for any discovery study metabolomics is likely to be fraught with far fewer false discovery effects than these other technologies. In addition, nearly any type of sample will contain biochemicals (sweat, saliva, urine, feces, etc.) compared to the other "omics" technologies. Perhaps the most striking difference is how closely the measurements of metabolites reflect the current phenotype of the test subject as compared to genomics and proteomics, and this is likely why the results can be much more practical for solving metabolism and mechanism problems.

various healthcare-related fields such as the diagnosis of disease, identification of drug targets, evaluation of the effects of drugs, and selection of patients most likely to respond to drug therapy (ie, personalized medicine).

Many practical applications of global metabolomics can reveal detailed information about phenotypic mechanisms for cells, animals, and humans. While genetics can play an important part in predisposing an individual to a drug's side effects or to a disease, the biochemistry of an individual is likely a more informative measurement of an individual's current state and condition. This strong relationship between phenotype and biochemical profiling was made even clearer by a recent, comprehensive, genome-wide association study using global metabolomics [23]. Combining genetic predisposition

with environmental and health status measurements, as can be achieved with metabolomics, will likely be an ever-increasing discovery tool for new biomarkers.

TOXICOMETABOLOMIC PLATFORM TECHNOLOGIES

There has been renewed interest in understanding metabolism and biochemistry in healthcare. Much of this is driven by discoveries that numerous oncogenes and tumor suppressors exert their function through alterations of metabolism [35,43]. The other driver has been the growing impact of understanding toxicological findings through biochemistry or metabolomics. Over 1000 papers were published in 2009 that used metabolomics in toxicological studies, compared to just two research papers in 2000 [44]. Although metabolomics still trails behind toxicogenomics and toxicoproteomics, it is closing the gap rapidly. In fact, *Nature* said in December 2009 that metabolomics would be one of the most influential fields in the next decade, as opined by scientists and policymakers [7]. Toxicology and metabolomics has only recently been the subject of intense study and is now regarded as an important method of mechanistic insight and identification of toxicological biomarkers [10,25,29,44,45].

Within the field of metabolomics there are a range of approaches and technologies that can be employed. Some technologies rely on spectroscopic small molecule signals without isolating the molecules to analyze individual or specific classes of small molecules. What is common to all of these methods is the size and complexity of the dataset that is generated and the need to biochemically interpret the effects measured. In this chapter we investigate four types of commonly used metabolomic method in more depth. This is not meant to be a complete list, but it should give the reader an up-to-date view of the prevailing metabolomic technologies and their advantages and disadvantages. In order of discussion, the four methods are nontargeted or chemocentric global metabolomics, ion-centric global metabolomics, targeted metabolomics, and finally NMR metabolomics.

Chemocentric Global Metabolomics

"Global" or "unbiased" metabolomics has been challenged by difficulties stemming from the diverse physical properties of small molecules. Unlike fingerprinting technologies (discussed later), chemocentric global metabolomics attempt to assign as many measured peaks as possible and to identify and quantitate all the small molecules in the sample. The chemical properties can vary greatly between the different physicochemical classes of small molecule. Differences in solubility and molecular weights affect how small molecules can be measured and solublilized. A single chromatographic method to separate all of the compounds is impossible, and it is even more difficult to analyze individual compounds without chromatographic separation. Further complications arise if studies are expected to be completed within a reasonable time. Methods that can only analyze a few samples per day would simply be impractical from a discovery technology and statistical standpoint.

These challenges are currently being addressed through the development of very advanced software and multisystem approaches, which run in tandem with the best separation and detection instrumentation [30,46]. This approach allows a comprehensive biochemical profiling approach to be applied and the ability to mechanize the method to enable hundreds if not thousands of samples to be profiled. As of this writing, this new technology can routinely detect over 500 individual biochemicals in blood samples and over 800 in urine samples [25,47] and is the most comprehensive published metabolomics method. As this technology develops and its use in biomarker detection studies increases, it is rapidly becoming clear that metabolomics will represent a high-impact technology in various healthcare-related fields such as the diagnosis of disease, identification of drug targets, evaluation of the effects of drugs, food products, or external chemical agents, and selection of patients most likely to respond to drug therapy (ie, personalized medicine) [14,15,25].

Global metabolomics operates in essentially four steps, as shown in Fig. 33.3 [30]. Step 1 is extraction of the small molecules from the biological sample. Step 2 is chromatography coupled with mass spectrometry and data collection. Step 3 is the automated and manual QC analysis of the data using visual-interfaced software [46]. Step 4, the final step, is the statistical and biological interpretation of the data itself.

The method relies on extracting a wide range of very polar to nonpolar compounds from as little as $50\,\mu L$ of blood plasma [30]. Extracted samples are split into four aliquots for different chromatography and mass spectrometry platforms: two UHPLC methods and one GC method, with one aliquot held in reserve. These three chromatography and MS systems complement each other in the range of biochemicals measured and provide enhanced biochemical coverage of each sample. Approximately 70–80% of the biochemicals are measured on more than one platform with 30–40% measured on all three platforms. For compounds observed on multiple platforms, the platform with the best analytical characteristics (eg, fewest interfering peaks or highest signal to noise) is generally used for analysis of that compound. In general, the GC method provides better separation of molecules that tend to be more difficult to separate using a typical reverse phase LC method (eg, carbohydrates).

After the raw data have been acquired, a suite of software packages automatically integrates each ion across its retention time, and then uses that information, which may include additional MS/MS fragmentation information and retention times, to identify the compound [46]. After a compound is identified in a sample, one of its characteristic and higher abundance ions is used to determine relative concentration of that compound in each sample. Day-to-day instrument variation can be corrected by simple scaling of multiday means, but this requires the samples to be randomized across the run days. This approach assures that the compound will be represented only once in the subsequent statistical analysis, thus significantly decreasing the possibility of aberrant differences in samples. When the software has finished analyzing the samples, all of the data are loaded

Global Metabolomics Platform Technology

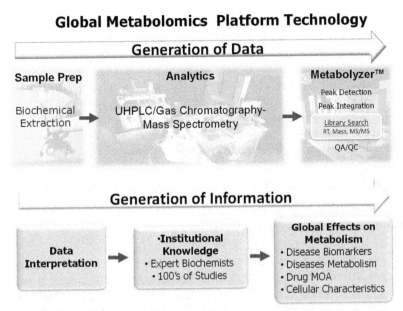

FIGURE 33.3 The top half of the figure depicts the four steps of a global metabolomics method being applied to a biological sample. The first three steps, biochemical extraction, multiple chromatography, and mass spectrometry analysis, are then followed by an unbiased global informatics method to reduce the raw machine data to the biochemicals in the sample and the relative concentration of each biochemical in each sample. The bottom half of the analysis involves the data interpretation and statistical analysis that leads to the metabolic understanding available with this method.

into a visual user interface that allows the scientist to curate the data for QC purposes and visually inspect how well each compound was identified and verify that only those compounds with the highest degree of confidence are included in the final data set. A variety of statistical approaches can be applied to the final data set at that point, including ANOVA, *t*-tests, random forest, PCA, etc. The goal of this statistical treatment is to identify the biochemicals that best represent the most significant changes in concentration between the groups in the study. One advantage of biochemistry is that a number compounds in a particular biochemical pathway may be significantly altered, giving an even higher degree of confidence to the importance of that biochemical change. In this respect, it is important to point out that most statistical treatments assume independent variables when, in fact, we know that certain biochemicals are related to the same or similar pathways. Metabolomic labs are developing large databases of these types of biochemical changes as well as those that result from toxicity, drug mechanism, disease, etc. This knowledge will enhance the technology's ability to provide a biological interpretation for each study it performs.

In summary, the chemocentric global metabolomics method described here is the most comprehensive published metabolomic method, with over 40 scientific papers currently published that describe it. Many of the case studies further reviewed in this chapter are taken directly from publications primarily using this method to perform global metabolomics analysis. As this technology

continues to advance it is not unrealistic to expect new types of metabolomic bench-top instruments to be developed and routinely used in laboratories, exploiting the software and methods developed to enable this chemocentric global metabolomics technology.

Ion-Centric Global Metabolomics

A standard method of processing metabolomic data for analysis that has met with limited success has been to only focus on the individual ion features of the compounds or "fingerprinting methods." This type of method doesn't depend on the clustering of peak information to individual compounds but simply performs statistical analysis of peak data. Ion features, defined here as a chromatographic peak in retention time for a molecule with an m/z value and an associated ion-intensity measurement. These "fingerprints" can contain thousands of individual data points that are usually not associated with the molecule of origin. The statistically significant ion features can then be used to prioritize which peaks to use for analysis as well as potential metabolite identification. These types of data sets are often input into multivariate statistical tools, such as principal component analysis (PCA). The advantages of this method are that it requires limited technology to perform, little data annotation or quality control (QC), and can be rapidly applied. This type of fingerprinting technology has been routinely employed in toxicology, and many findings have been published [48–50].

Although this method avoids many of the complexities involved in the more comprehensive chemocentric method described earlier, it also has some very significant disadvantages. First, the approach is very convoluted, with different ions all belonging to the same compound being statistically analyzed together, which greatly enhances the potential for false discovery, or separation of experimental groups purely by chance. Most biochemicals detected in traditional GC- or LC-MS-based analysis produce several different ions and each contributes to the massive size and complexity of a metabolomic data set. Second, although in principle it seems straightforward to go from ion information to a specific molecule this can often be a very challenging if not an impossible task. Many of these published studies simply show separation of groups without any mechanistic or biological context to the results.

Targeted Metabolomics

The wide diversity of molecular physical properties makes a comprehensive method such as the chemocentric global metabolomics method difficult to employ without significant investment in the technology. A useful metabolomics method that has met with success has been the implementation of multiple reaction monitoring (MRM) methods using tandem quadruple mass spectrometry (TQMS), which monitors both the specific precursor ions and ion products of specific metabolites or biochemicals. It is a relatively standard method used today for much of the analytical work performed by mass spectrometry and can be adapted to measure upward of 100–200 metabolites in many samples with relatively good quantitation. Some labs seem to employ this method without the use of standards, which is not good analytical practice, since it relies on the MS/MS spectra and correct identification of the precursor ion. The detection of this product ion is therefore diagnostic information of the compound identification. It is also a sensitive technique, since the resulting ion is specific to that compound, and there is little background interference from other ions. Many reviews and textbooks have been written on tandem mass spectrometry and a few recent ones are listed here [4,51,52].

To use this type of method properly, most groups establish automated flow injection analysis of a library of authentic compounds. This allows a large data set of MS and MS/MS spectra to be generated and made available for analysis. You can then apply the same methods to the samples and potentially generate 100–200 compound measurements for each sample [53–56]. The limitations of this method are primarily time of analysis and you can only find what you have standards for ahead of

time. There are only so many ions that can be prosecuted in a reasonable time for each sample, and this becomes a bigger problem as the study size increases. Although instruments have faster and faster scan speeds, it still takes time to perform an MRM for each ion of a molecule. Secondly, and this is perhaps a bigger issue in that the only compounds identified will be those for which the investigator has a standard that will be included in the analysis. Global metabolomics methods in general offer both the advantage of targeted methods and the enhanced ability to measure metabolites of new and/or of novel origin.

NMR Metabolomics

Perhaps the earliest studies in the field of toxicology using metabolomics were performed using NMR analysis [50,57–60]. NMR can easily be applied to samples such as urine and even can be used with little or no manipulation of the sample itself (see Fig. 33.4). Unfortunately, because of the limited number of compounds that can be identified and measured with NMR, it has largely been superseded by mass spectrometry. Although there will continue to be uses for NMR in metabolomics, in toxicometabolomics its use does seem to have leveled off. Although in principle NMR can be used for quantitative as well as qualitative analysis, there are unfortunately few good examples of using quantitative NMR and most applications rely on relative differences. Primarily, because of the sensitivity issues with NMR, it will likely have more limited uses in the field of metabolomics.

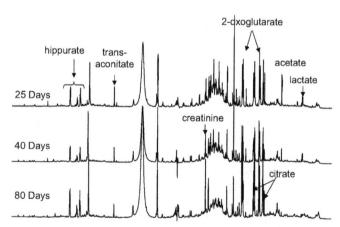

FIGURE 33.4 Graphical NMR spectrum of a metabolomics study. Overlaid representative NMR spectra displayed at different time points from rat urine. *Figure was reproduced from Schnackenberg et al. BMC Bioinformatics 2007;8(Suppl. 7):S3.* Creative Commons Attribution License (http://creativecommons.org/licenses/by/2.0), which permits unrestricted use, distribution, and reproduction in any medium, provided the original work is properly cited.

TOXICOMETABOLOMIC APPLICATIONS

Nontargeted global metabolomic profiling can be a powerful tool for assessing the drug efficacy and side effects in preclinical and clinical studies. The biochemical compositions of matrices such as plasma, urine, and tissue provide a comprehensive understanding of both cellular metabolism and organ functions. Through the measurement of individual metabolites, one can truly investigate the phenotype or actual processes occurring. These may not be reflected in the proteins or genes being expressed at any one time. A typical toxicological experimental setup consists of drug-treatment and vehicle-control groups and may have multiple doses and time points. Statistical and biochemical analysis of the metabolite profiles in the study subjects can identify drug-induced changes and generate efficacy and toxicology biomarkers for clinical management.

Beyond the ability to detect changes in metabolites, the ultimate success of any metabolomic analysis relies on biochemical interpretation. The ability to understand the data in a biochemical context can yield insight into the mechanism and biological function involved in any experimental condition. For example, with this approach it is possible to understand defects in a target enzyme, receptor, or signaling system through analysis of the precursors and products of these proteins or biochemical pathways. In this context, biochemical reactions operate as a network of changes rather than a linear set of reactions. The biochemical approach to data interpretation has the potential to yield highly relevant hypotheses that can be directly tested. Another very powerful outcome is that the technology can make use of more than 100 years' worth of detailed biochemical experience. When metabolomic data are viewed in their biochemical context, their interpretation is often immediate, likely to be highly relevant, and, in hindsight, often obvious.

It has also been demonstrated recently that the genetic contribution to the metabolome is quite significant, or put another way, the penetrance of an individual's genetics is quite strong in their measured biochemical levels, even in blood [23]. Although the identification of certain alleles can be indicative of disease, or dysfunction in an enzyme, other alleles have appeared to have no function of consequence. However, a recent large-scale metabolomics analysis clearly revealed that certain enzyme alleles can significantly affect the metabolite levels even in blood and can do so based on an increase or decrease in copy number of that allele. In fact, novel functional information on enzymes of unknown function has been obtained from this global metabolomics analysis and the association of metabolite levels with genes. The implications of this recent study are that biochemical measurements might be an ideal way to segregate populations based on their genetic differences and individual

responses to drugs. This is further discussed in the last case study presented.

Fenofibrate

Fenofibrate has been widely used to treat patients with atherogenic dyslipidemia. It is a second-line treatment to lower cholesterol and low-density lipoprotein (LDL). It also increases high-density lipoprotein (HDL) as well as reduces triglyceride levels. The mechanism of fibrate action is known to be mediated through binding of the fibric-acid derivative to peroxisome proliferator-activated receptor alpha (PPARa), a transcriptional factor that plays key regulatory roles in fatty-acid and cholesterol metabolism. In addition to the therapeutic effects, fenofibrate and other PPARa agonists have been shown to cause significant peroxisome proliferation, lipolysis, and increased synthesis of apolipoprotein A1 and AII.

In rodents, fenofibrate is known to induce hepatomegaly and well as promote tumors. The precise mechanism of liver tumor formation induced by the PPARa agonists in rodents is not well understood. A range of experimental evidence suggests that multiple factors could be involved, including oxidative stress and altered cell-proliferation processes. In humans, the clinical use of fenofibrate has been generally regarded as safe, and it has been used in the clinic for over 40 years [61]. However, the toxicological risk of fenofibrate and PPAR agonists in general remains a concern [62,63].

To better understand the drug mechanisms and effects of fenofibrate in rodents, a global metabolomics study was undertaken using groups of six rats, each treated with either fenofibrate (300/mg/kg/day) or vehicle control. Blood plasma and urine was collected at two time points (day 2 and day 14) and the animals were sacrificed for pathological examination. Both the relative weights of the liver and kidneys increased significantly at this dose by day 14 and showed signs of hepatic necrosis and hypertrophy.

The metabolomics study was performed using 100 μL of both urine and blood plasma and the samples were prepared for analysis as previously described. The global metabolomics analysis yielded over 500 biochemical concentrations in blood and 900 biochemical measurements in urine. This study represents one of the most comprehensive metabolomic studies undertaken to date, in terms of the breadth of biochemicals measured within blood or urine. A simple Welch's T-test was used to identify metabolites that showed altered levels between drug treatment and control groups.

Fenofibrate clearly had dramatic effects on cellular metabolism, especially energy homeostasis. Indeed, as Fig. 33.5A shows, all of the measured intermediates in the citric-acid cycle were significantly decreased compared to vehicle control at day 14, and even trended

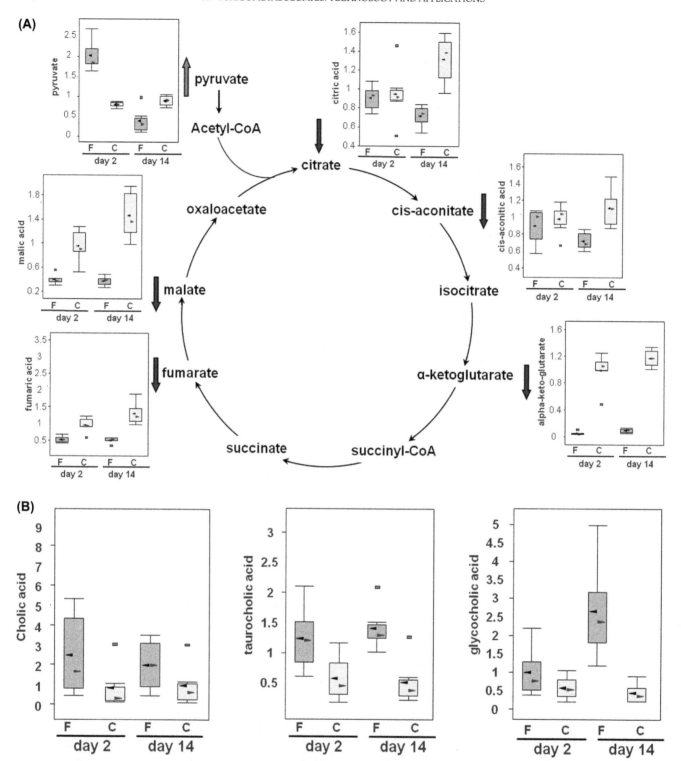

FIGURE 33.5 Alterations of TCA cycle metabolites by fenofibrate treatment. (A) The levels of pyruvate, citrate, aconitate, α-ketoglutarate, fumarate, and malate in the urine of the control rats (C, *open bars*) and the fenofibrate-treated rats (F, *gray bars*) at day 2 and day 14 are shown with *box plots* (median-scaled values are represented on the *y*-axis so that all graphs are comparable). Note the very significant difference between all six control animals to drug treated in the urine, particularly α-ketoglutarate, malate, and fumate. (B) The levels of cholic acid, taurocholic acid, and glycocholic acid in the plasma of the control rats (C, *open bars*) and the fenofibrate-treated rats (F, *gray bars*) at day 2 and day 14. All fenofibrate-treated animals are elevated in these bile acids, indicating potential liver function issues early and increasing with time of dosing.

lower in the first 2 days of drug treatment. This was a very pronounced and not previously reported effect of fenofibrate drug action, which suggests that the animals are obtaining energy from an alternative source of metabolism to maintain homeostasis. Another dramatic effect was observed with an increase in fatty-acid oxidation across all the clinically relevant changes typically observed in this mitochondrial function. However, this is a previously well-known effect of the PPARa agonist, and one of the primary therapeutic effects of the drug is increased fatty-acid metabolism and lipolysis. In fact, blood plasma levels of fatty acids showed a noticeable and significant drop, while other metabolites such as 3-hydroxy butyrate, a byproduct of fatty-acid oxidation, were very significantly increased with drug treatment. Overall, a simple energy metabolism effect and conclusion can be drawn from the fenofibrate treatment from these results. The animals appear to maintain an overall homeostatic energy level while shifting their source of energy from the citric-acid cycle to fatty-acid oxidation as a result of PPARa activation. One of the implications of this study is that perhaps a decrease in carbohydrate in the diet, coupled with fatty-acid oxidation from fenofibrate treatment, could increase weight loss and help weight management.

Another significant alteration observed in this study was a change in tryptophan metabolism. Tryptophan is normally metabolized to serotonin, but under oxidative stress, infection, or other metabolic stresses on the organism, it is rapidly broken down in the kynurenine pathways. In this study, significant lowering of blood levels of serotonin and an increase in the kynurenine pathway suggest stress on the animals as a result of fenofibrate treatment. In fact, levels of quinolinate in this study actually increased 12-fold, and it is worth noting that quinolinate itself is a strong inducer of reactive-oxygen species. Along with other elevated oxidative stress markers observed in this study, it can be concluded that oxidative stress plays a significant role in the toxicological consequences of fenofibrate treatment.

Perhaps the most significant effects of fenofibrate treatment observed in this study were the alterations in liver function, and significant changes in the liver itself. Although pathology also suggested significant effects on the liver, as it doubled in weight, a number of specific liver metabolism changes were observed in this study. For instance, cholesterol initially showed a significant decrease at day 2 but then later significantly increased at day 14 relative to the vehicle control. One might postulate that cholesterol would be lower as a result of increase fatty-acid oxidation but the increase at day 14 suggests effects on the liver's ability to properly handle the cholesterol in the bloodstream. One of the major functions of the liver is to capture and metabolize dietary cholesterol

in circulation. The increase in the cholesterol level of fenofibrate-treated subjects at the later time point could be due to decreased liver function.

The significant increase in many of the bile acids supports this conclusion. The plasma levels of three bile acids (glycocholic acid, taurocholic acid, and cholic acid) increased significantly following fenofibrate treatment at both time points (see Fig. 33.5B). Bile acids are used to emulsify foods in the digestive tract, and although they are synthesized in the liver from cholesterol, they are stored in the gall bladder before secretion into the intestine. However, 95% of bile is recirculated back to the liver, specifically absorbed by the liver, and reused for digestion. This ability to recirculate bile acids can be compromised if liver function is affected, and thus bile acids can increase in the blood when the liver is under stress. Fasting serum bile-acid levels have been widely used as indicators to examine liver function, and are considered more sensitive than most traditional liver enzyme assays [64].

Overall, significant metabolome changes were observed with this global metabolomics analysis at both time points, in both the plasma and urine of fenofibrate-treated rats. The changes in metabolites were the result of the on-target (pharmacological activities) and off-target (toxic) effects of fenofibrate. Numerous potential biomarkers could be suggested and further investigated as a result of this study. Energy metabolism was significantly shifted by fenofibrate toward fatty-acid oxidation while glycolysis and amino-acid metabolism were decreased. The changes in various toxicological markers suggest that oxidative stress and liver malfunction were among the consequences of fenofibrate treatment.

Ethylene-Glycol Monomethyl Ether

Ethylene-glycol monomethyl ether (EGME) is an industrial solvent used in cellulose and semiconductor manufacturing. It is also used in quick drying paints, wood stains, and varnishes. It is known to cause adverse effects in humans and other mammalian species, especially to organs with high metabolic rates and rapidly dividing cells, such as the testes. A concentration-dependent decrease in testes weight has been observed in male rabbits exposed to increasing doses of EGME. In toxicology studies, EGME is often used as a gold standard for inducing testicular toxicity. Although many animal toxicology studies have been published regarding EGME, very little is known about the underlying molecular mechanism of its toxicity.

In order to gain a more complete mechanistic understanding of EGME-induced toxicity, a chemocentric global metabolomic analysis was carried out in rats [25]. In this study, EGME was administered to male rats at 30 and 100 mg/kg/day for 14 days by gavage. At days

1, 4, and 14, serum, urine, liver tissues, and testis tissues were collected for metabolomic analysis. All of the samples were prepared and analyzed as previously reported. The goal of the study dosing regimen was to induce testicular toxicity as specifically as possible without introducing other organ toxicities and it appears that the study met this objective. Histopathological examination showed testicular toxicity at day 14 in the 100 mg/kg/day group only, with no toxic effects on the liver or kidney observed.

Nearly 1900 metabolites across the four matrices were profiled using LC-MS/MS and GC–MS as previously reported. To date, this is the most comprehensive metabolomic toxicology study undertaken in terms of the number of metabolites analyzed. Statistical analysis of the data revealed that the most significant metabolic perturbations manifested from the early time points by EGME were on choline metabolism and branched-chain amino-acid catabolism (see Fig. 33.6). Choline is metabolized through a series of demethylation steps to produce betaine, dimethylglycine, sarcosine, and glycine. Interestingly, two of the metabolites in this pathway were very significantly increased in urine samples—namely, dimethylglycine and sarcosine. The significant accumulation of urinary dimethylglycine and sarcosine by EGME strongly suggested that the enzymes converting the two metabolites, dimethylglycine dehydrogenase (DMEGH) and sarcosine dehydrogenase (SDH), were inhibited by EGME.

In addition, the catabolism of isoleucine and leucine generates acetyl-CoA, succinyl-CoA, and acetoacetate, which further incorporate into the TCA cycle for energy production. When the enzymes in these catabolic pathways are impaired, their substrates may accumulate. The accumulation of 2-methylbutyroylcarnitine and 2-methylbutyrylglycine in the isoleucine catabolic pathway suggests that branched chain acyl-CoA dehydrogenase was inhibited. Consistent with this theory, 3-hydroxy-2-ethylpropionate, ethylmalonate, butyrylglycine, and butyrylcarnitine were found to be increased. Similarly, increases of isovalerylglycine and hydroxyisovaleroylcarnitine in the leucine catabolic pathway suggested isovaleryl-CoA dehydrogenase was inhibited by the EGME treatment.

Mapping these altered metabolites to their respective biochemical pathways found that all the disrupted steps were catalyzed by enzymes in the primary flavoprotein dehydrogenase family with electron transfer flavoprotein (ETF) as a cofactor, suggesting that EGME produces toxicity via inhibition of the flavoprotein dehydrogenase-catalyzed reactions. Taken together, the enzymes at the inhibited steps in both the choline oxidation and BCAA catabolism were all found to be primary flavoprotein dehydrogenases with flavin adenine dinucleotide (FAD) as the prosthetic factor.

The conclusion that EGME inhibits primary flavoprotein dehydrogenase reactions is supported by published studies on genetic disorders of acyl-CoA dehydrogenases in humans. In patients with multiple acyl-CoA dehydrogenase deficiency (MADD), acyl-CoA dehydrogenase reactions are impaired. The urinary and serum profiles of MADD patients are found to share remarkable similarities with the ones observed in this rat study. Although this is not direct evidence of the mechanism of EGME toxicity, it strongly supports the mechanistic underpinning proposed by this global metabolomics study.

Indoxyl Sulfate

A potent nicotinic acid receptor (NAR) agonist, SCH 900424, was investigated for toxicity in the routine development of the compound [65]. The resulting toxicity study demonstrated acute renal failure (ARF) and a global metabolomics study was undertaken to better understand the molecular underpinnings of the observed toxicity. In addition, it was hoped that earlier and predictive biomarkers of ARF could aid in the detection of this toxicity in mice. The metabolomics study revealed that 3-indoxyl sulfate (3IS) was the most sensitive marker of SCH 900424-induced renal toxicity (see Fig. 33.7). An LC-MS assay for the quantitative determination of 3-indoxyl sulfate (3IS) in mouse matrices was also developed.

As previously reported, a number of early metabolic changes were observed in both the blood plasma and urine of the metabolomics study that suggested acute renal failure. For instance, blood glucose and a number of amino acids significantly and dose-dependently decreased in blood. Concurrently, these same metabolites increased in urine in a dose-dependent manner, suggesting uremia, aminoaciduria, and glycosuria. Many of the classic biomarkers of renal damage, such as urea and creatinine also were significantly altered.

However, the most pronounced metabolic change in blood plasma was in 3-indoxyl sulfate (3IS) levels, which increased markedly in murine plasma (see Fig. 33.7). 3-indoxyl sulfate and indoxyl itself are known renal toxins that when elevated in the blood can induce significant renal toxicity. 3IS in blood and urine originates from the metabolism of tryptophan by intestinal bacteria. Intestinal bacteria metabolize L-tryptophan to indole, which is absorbed into the blood and metabolized in liver to indoxyl sulfate. It is well known that the accumulation of 3IS in blood promotes the progression of chronic renal failure (CRF). The levels of 3IS were significantly higher and increased faster than any other metabolite measured as a result of drug treatment and immediately suggested a possible mechanism of drug-induced renal failure as well as suggesting a potential biomarker to monitor such an effect.

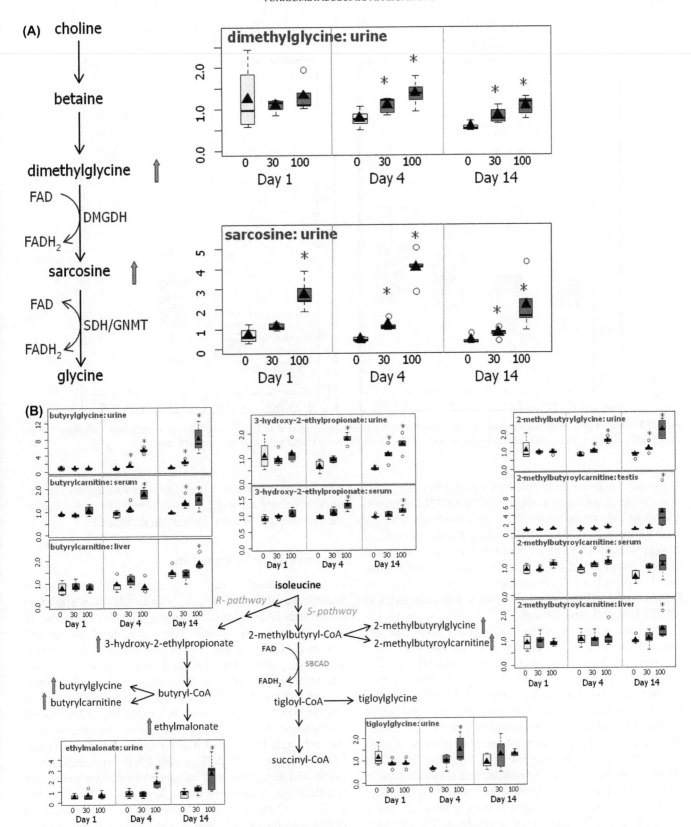

FIGURE 33.6 (A) Isoleucine metabolism effects by EGME treatment. (B) Choline metabolism effects demonstrated by EGME treatment. *Asterisk* denotes statistically significant to the control group.

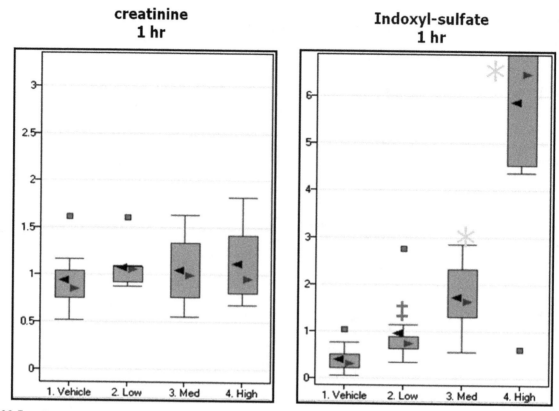

FIGURE 33.7　Effect on the standard kidney function biomarker creatinine compared to 3-indoxyl-sulfate upon treatment with drug. 3IS has significantly higher acceleration of effects than creatinine and is likely an earlier and more potent biomarker of toxicity.

In order to more mechanistically prove the role of 3IS in acute renal failure as a result of SCH 900424 treatment, and negative control experiment was performed in the analysis as well. SCH 900765 is a closely related chemical analog to SCH 900424 that does not produce acute renal failure. Blood plasma levels of the negative control also failed to reproduce the significant increase in 3IS levels, further supporting the role of this metabolite in SCH 900424-induced renal failure.

The basic conclusions from this study were that 3IS was identified as a top plasma marker, and was more sensitive in predicting renal failure induced by SCH 900424 than creatinine or urea. 3IS is synthesized by conversion of tryptophan in the intestinal microbiome, and this host/parasite relationship could be a very important mechanism in the development of this particular chemically induced toxicity. The gut bacteria have also been reported to produce drug-induced toxicities for other types of drugs and toxicity effects, and this area clearly warrants further study. As expected, a negative control for the renal toxicity using a closely related chemical analog failed to reproduce the increase of 3IS, supporting the theory that this metabolite plays a role in toxicity development. Therefore this global metabolomics study suggested that 3IS shows promise as a potential plasma marker of renal toxicities during drug-mediated

acute renal failure in mice. Further studies with other renal toxicants are required to confirm 3IS as a potential plasma marker of renal toxicity in general.

Cigarette-Smoke Exposure

A metabolomics study was performed to investigate the biochemical profiles of human alveolar epithelial carcinoma (A549) cells following in vitro exposure to mainstream whole smoke (WS), wet total particulate matter (WTPM), or gas/vapor phase (GVP) [66]. In this study, cell pellets were analyzed for perturbations in biochemical profiles along with an examination of biochemical and physiological effects on the cells. Some of the largest effects resulted from WS exposure, with altered glutathione (GSH) levels, enhanced polyamine and pantothenate levels, and likely increased beta oxidation of fatty acids. Both WTPM and GVP exposures likely decreased glycolysis and increased oxidative stress and cell damage. Alterations in the Krebs cycle and the urea cycle were unique to WTPM exposure, while induction of hexosamines and alterations in lipid metabolism were unique to GVP exposure.

Glutathione, glutamine, and pantothenate showed the most significant changes following cigarette smoke exposure in A549 cells overall. Many of the reported effects of cigarette exposure had previously been observed and published, but the global metabolomic approach offers the advantage of observing changes in hundreds of biochemicals in a single experiment, and offers the possibility of new discoveries. This approach may thus be used as a screening tool to evaluate conventional and novel tobacco products offering the potential to reduce the risks of smoking.

Pentamethylchromanol

Pentamethyl-6-chromanol (PMCol) is a chromanol-type compound related to vitamin E that has been investigated as an anticancer agent and reported in a number of studies [67]. However, in longer-term dosing studies, PMCol has been shown to have a number of toxicological effects, on the liver in particular [68]. A metabolomics study was performed to determine the mechanisms of toxicity and to identify sensitive early markers of hepatic and renal injury [69]. Metabolomic evaluations of liver tissue revealed time- and dose-dependent changes. In particular, PMCol was observed to induce depletion of total glutathione and its conjugates, as well to decrease methionine and cysteine, which are intermediates in glutathione synthesis.

Glutathione is the major reducing agent in the liver, and is critical in preventing liver injury during chemical onslaught. In addition to depleting liver glutathione, PMCol appeared to compromise hepatic function as evidenced by alterations in sulfur and polyamine metabolism. Depletion of glutathione ultimately yields an adaptive metabolic response with the consumption of hepatic dietary antioxidants and increased methionine to cysteine conversion. Based on the global biochemical changes associated with PMCol-induced liver damage and dysfunction, it was suggested that glutathione depletion results from the inhibition of cysteine synthesis, depletion of liver glutathione, and modification of other drug metabolism pathways.

The Future of "Omics" Technologies in Toxicity Studies

Understanding the role of genetic predisposition to toxicity has been a major objective since the sequencing of the human genome. We know that individual genetics or SNPs can lead to wide differences in the way in which drugs are metabolized, and these variations are currently being exploited in developing a range of individualized dosages that decrease the risk of drug-induced toxicities. The major causes of attrition of new drugs in the clinic in 2000 were lack of efficacy and safety, both accounting for approximately 30% of all drug failures. Most of the FDA-approved companion diagnostics are for liver enzymes involved in drug metabolism that can greatly influence

the individual pharmacokinetics and pharmacodynamics of a drug. The expectations of toxicogenomics and the role it will play in improving drug attrition and individualized medicine have been very high, but the impact of this technology is still very recent and largely unproven.

Recently it has been shown that the genetic penetrance of individuals to their blood concentrations of metabolites is very high and in fact the number of alleles per individual can in a pseudo dose response way strongly influence the concentrations of highly associated biochemicals. A comprehensive, genome-wide association study was performed, measuring levels of over 250 biochemical in blood samples and looking at associations with over 2500 individuals having approximately 600,000 genotyped SNPs. This study identified over 37 independent loci that reach genome-wide significance in the analysis, with 23 of these describing new associations and the others further validating some that had been previously demonstrated. Many other potentially strong associations were identified, including well over 100 that were slightly lower than this rigid genome-wide significance. In addition, most of these associations, approximately 30, had a sentinel SNP mapped to a protein that was biochemically linked to the associating metabolite, strongly validating the results and technology used in the analysis.

As an example, N-acetylation is an important mechanism for detoxifying nephrotoxic medications and environmental toxins. A reduction in the ability to detoxify such substances could lead to impaired kidney function. A key enzyme N-acetyltransferase 8 (NAT8) locus was highly associated with N-acetylornithine, and previously this enzyme had also been associated with kidney function. In this study it was verified that the levels of N-acetylornithine were associated with glomerular filtration rate. Thus through the measurement of a metabolite in blood, one could potentially segregate the genetic population on the basis of a predisposition to improved kidney function, which could enhance acceptance of certain drugs.

This result is counterintuitive to most scientists, who see that levels of biochemicals in blood are strongly associated with time of day, diet, and other external influences. In fact, this study demonstrates that there is significant penetrance of genetic information into even blood biochemical levels, and this has a potentially profound effect on how we think about the discovery of new biomarkers for toxicity in the future.

CONCLUDING REMARKS AND FUTURE DIRECTIONS

To address the high rate of clinical product failure due to unanticipated toxicities, even after drug approval, in the future the preclinical toxicologist will need to rely on a variety of technologies to improve the risk assessments of new drugs. In contrast to many previous technologies, toxicometabolomics offers a number of simple advantages that should enable significant progress in the future. One of the biggest advantages of profiling biochemicals is that it is an ideal way of understanding metabolism and phenotype, and in many drug studies alterations of metabolism in the liver, kidney, testes, and other organs can have a profound, measurable, biochemical effect. Understanding the mechanisms of toxicity in these systems will provide a wealth of potential new biomarkers. Metabolomics is probably the most closely related profiling technology to understanding phenotypes unlike other "omic" technologies.

As mentioned in this chapter, one of the most exciting developments in metabolomics that has the potential for a big impact in toxicology is the new understanding of how genetically penetrant individual genetics are to metabolite levels in the blood. Profiling biochemicals in blood is relatively straightforward and is less fraught with issues of false discovery. Routine metabolomics could become the discovery method of choice, not just for metabolism discoveries based on lifestyle and diet, but also for segregating biomarkers of population genetic differences in drug response and toxicity. The largest challenge to this growing technology is the early phase of the technology itself with few groups having developed fully validated global metabolomics methods, and many groups having very limited exposure to using and understanding the data. Hopefully, as the importance of metabolomic studies becomes realized, it will spawn a renaissance of biochemical learning that will inspire a new breed of scientists that are just as versed in their biochemistry as they are in molecular biology and genetics.

References

[1] Morgan DB, Payne RB. Laboratory test for kidney function – urea or creatinine. Lancet 1979;2:1014.

[2] Bonventre JV, Vaidya VS, Schmouder R, Feig P, Dieterle F. Next-generation biomarkers for detecting kidney toxicity. Nat Biotechnol 2010;28:436–40.

[3] Murray PT. Diagnosis of kidney damage using novel acute kidney injury biomarkers: assessment of kidney function alone is insufficient. Crit Care 2011;15:170.

[4] Smith RD. Mass spectrometry in biomarker applications: from untargeted discovery to targeted verification, and implications for platform convergence and clinical application. Clin Chem 2011;58:528–38.

[5] Blow N. Metabolomics: biochemistry's new look. Nature 2008;455:697–700.

[6] Sreekumar A, Poisson LM, Rajendiran TM, Khan AP, Cao Q, Yu J, et al. Metabolomic profiles delineate potential role for sarcosine in prostate cancer progression. Nature 2009;457:910–4.

[7] 2020 visions. Nature 2010;463:26–32.

[8] Bramer SL, Kallungal BA. Clinical considerations in study designs that use cotinine as a biomarker. Biomarkers 2003;8:187–203.

[9] Benjamini Y, Hochberg Y. Controlling the false discovery rate: a practical and powerful approach to multiple testing. J R Stat Soc Ser B 1995;57:289–300.

[10] Bren L. Metabolomics: working toward personalized medicine. FDA Consum 2005;39:28–33.

[11] Sigdel TK, Sarwal MM. Recent advances in biomarker discovery in solid organ transplant by proteomics. Expert Rev Proteomics 2011;8:705–15.

[12] Christin C, Bischoff R, Horvatovich P. Data processing pipelines for comprehensive profiling of proteomics samples by label-free LC-MS for biomarker discovery. Talanta 2011;83:1209–24.

[13] Kugler KG, Hackl WO, Mueller LA, Fiegl H, Graber A, Pfeiffer RM. The impact of sample storage time on estimates of association in biomarker discovery studies. J Clin Bioinforma 2011;1:1–9.

[14] Barnes VM, Teles R, Trivedi HM, Devizio W, Xu T, Lee DP, et al. Assessment of the effects of dentifrice on periodontal disease biomarkers in gingival crevicular fluid. J Periodontol 2010;81:1273–9.

[15] Zhang Y, Dai Y, Wen J, Zhang W, Grenz A, Sun H, et al. Detrimental effects of adenosine signaling in sickle cell disease. Nat Med 2011;17:79–86.

[16] Xie Z, Thompson A, Kashleva H, Dongari-Bagtzoglou A. A quantitative real-time RT-PCR assay for mature C. albicans biofilms. BMC Microbiol 2011;11:93.

[17] Murray R. Innovation in analytical chemistry. Anal Chem 2011;83:6431.

[18] Enke CG. Analytical chemistry, a great success despite the unfortunate divisions in academic departments. Talanta 2011;85:2247–8.

[19] Du J, Yang SY, Lin XL, Shang WL, Zhang W, Huo SF, et al. Biomarker discovery and identification from nonsmall cell lung cancer sera. Front Biosci 2011;3:1–10.

[20] Bosques CJ, Raguram S, Sasisekharan R. The sweet side of biomarker discovery. Nat Biotechnol 2006;24:1100–1.

[21] Latterich M, Schnitzer JE. Streamlining biomarker discovery. Nat Biotechnol 2011;29:600–2.

[22] Proceedings of the Biomarker Discovery by Mass Spectrometry Symposium, Amsterdam, The Netherlands. J Chromatogr B Analyt Technol Biomed Life Sci 2007;847:1–69.

[23] Suhre K, Shin SY, Petersen AK, Mohney RP, Meredith D, Wagele B, et al. Human metabolic individuality in biomedical and pharmaceutical research. Nature 2011;477:54–60.

[24] Wetmore DR, Joseloff E, Pilewski J, Lee DP, Lawton KA, Mitchell MW, et al. Metabolomic profiling reveals biochemical pathways and biomarkers associated with pathogenesis in cystic fibrosis cells. J Biol Chem 2010;285:30516–22.

[25] Takei M, Ando Y, Saitoh W, Tanimoto T, Kiyosawa N, Manabe S, et al. Ethylene glycol monomethyl ether-induced toxicity is mediated through the inhibition of flavoprotein dehydrogenase enzyme family. Toxicol Sci 2010;118:643–52.

[26] Suhre K, Meisinger C, Doring A, Altmaier E, Belcredi P, Gieger C, et al. Metabolic footprint of diabetes: a multiplatform metabolomics study in an epidemiological setting. PLoS One 2010;5:e13953.

[27] Thomas GH. Metabolomics breaks the silence. Trends Microbiol 2001;9:158.

[28] Nicholson JK, Lindon JC, Holmes E. 'Metabonomics': understanding the metabolic responses of living systems to pathophysiological stimuli via multivariate statistical analysis of biological NMR spectroscopic data. Xenobiotica 1999;29:1181–9.

[29] Boudonck KJ, Rose DJ, Karoly ED, Lee DP, Lawton KA, Lapinskas PJ. Metabolomics for early detection of drug-induced kidney injury: review of the current status. Bioanalysis 2009;1:1645–63.

[30] Evans AM, DeHaven CD, Barrett T, Mitchell M, Milgram E. Integrated, nontargeted ultrahigh performance liquid chromatography/electrospray ionization tandem mass spectrometry platform for the identification and relative quantification of the small-molecule complement of biological systems. Anal Chem 2009;81:6656–67.

[31] Psychogios N, Hau DD, Peng J, Guo AC, Mandal R, Bouatra S, et al. The human serum metabolome. PLoS One 2011;6:e16957.

[32] Kopka J, Schauer N, Krueger S, Birkemeyer C, Usadel B, Bergmuller E, et al. The Golm metabolome database. Bioinformatics 2005;21:1635–8. GMD@CSB.DB.

[33] Wishart DS, Tzur D, Knox C, Eisner R, Guo AC, Young N, et al. HMDB: the human metabolome database. Nucleic Acids Res 2007;35:D521–6.

[34] Lage-Castellanos A, Martinez-Montes E, Hernandez-Cabrera JA, Galan L. False discovery rate and permutation test: an evaluation in ERP data analysis. Stat Med 2010;29:63–74.

[35] Warburg O. Annual review of biochemistry. Prefatory chapter. Annu Rev Biochem 1964;33:1–14.

[36] Kutyshenko VP, Molchanov M, Beskaravayny P, Uversky VN, Timchenko MA. Analyzing and mapping sweat metabolomics by high-resolution NMR spectroscopy. PLoS One 2011;6:e28824.

[37] Barnes VM, Ciancio SG, Shibly O, Xu T, Devizio W, Trivedi HM, et al. Metabolomics reveals elevated macromolecular degradation in periodontal disease. J Dent Res 2011;90:1293–7.

[38] D'Alessandro A, Federica G, Palini S, Bulletti C, Zolla L. A mass spectrometry-based targeted metabolomics strategy of human blastocoele fluid: a promising tool in fertility research. Mol Biosyst 2011;8:953–8.

[39] Albinsky D, Sawada Y, Kuwahara A, Nagano M, Hirai A, Saito K, et al. Widely targeted metabolomics and coexpression analysis as tools to identify genes involved in the side-chain elongation steps of aliphatic glucosinolate biosynthesis. Amino Acids 2010;39:1067–75.

[40] Giovane A, Balestrieri A, Napoli C. New insights into cardiovascular and lipid metabolomics. J Cell Biochem 2008;105:648–54.

[41] Morris M, Watkins SM. Focused metabolomic profiling in the drug development process: advances from lipid profiling. Curr Opin Chem Biol 2005;9:407–12.

[42] German JB, Gillies LA, Smilowitz JT, Zivkovic AM, Watkins SM. Lipidomics and lipid profiling in metabolomics. Curr Opin Lipidol 2007;18:66–71.

[43] Vander Heiden MG. Targeting cancer metabolism: a therapeutic window opens. Nat Rev Drug Discov 2011;10:671–84.

[44] Robertson DG, Watkins PB, Reily MD. Metabolomics in toxicology: preclinical and clinical applications. Toxicol Sci 2011;120(Suppl. 1):S146–70.

[45] Kim KB, Yang JY, Kwack SJ, Park KL, Kim HS, Ryu do H, et al. Toxicometabolomics of urinary biomarkers for human gastric cancer in a mouse model. J Toxicol Environ Health A 2010;73:1420–30.

[46] Dehaven CD, Evans AM, Dai H, Lawton KA. Organization of GC/MS and LC/MS metabolomics data into chemical libraries. J Cheminform 2010;2:9.

[47] Ohta T, Masutomi N, Tsutsui N, Sakairi T, Mitchell M, Milburn MV, et al. Untargeted metabolomic profiling as an evaluative tool of fenofibrate-induced toxicology in Fischer 344 male rats. Toxicol Pathol 2009;37:521–35.

[48] Wang J, Reijmers T, Chen L, Van Der Heijden R, Wang M, Peng S, et al. Systems toxicology study of doxorubicin on rats using ultra performance liquid chromatography coupled with mass spectrometry based metabolomics. Metabolomics 2009;5:407–18.

[49] Dieterle F, Ross A, Schlotterbeck G, Senn H. Metabolite projection analysis for fast identification of metabolites in metabonomics. Application in an amiodarone study. Anal Chem 2006;78:3551–61.

[50] Beckonert O, Keun HC, Ebbels TM, Bundy J, Holmes E, Lindon JC, et al. Metabolic profiling, metabolomic and metabonomic procedures for NMR spectroscopy of urine, plasma, serum and tissue extracts. Nat Protoc 2007;2:2692–703.

[51] van den Ouweland JM, Kema IP. The role of liquid chromatography-tandem mass spectrometry in the clinical laboratory. J Chromatogr B Analyt Technol Biomed Life Sci 2012;1:883–4.

[52] Hsu KF, Chien KY, Chang-Chien GP, Lin SF, Hsu PH, Hsu MC. Liquid chromatography-tandem mass spectrometry screening method for the simultaneous detection of stimulants and diuretics in urine. J Anal Toxicol 2011;35:665–74.

[53] Janeckova H, Hron K, Wojtowicz P, Hlidkova E, Baresova A, Friedecky D, et al. Targeted metabolomic analysis of plasma samples for the diagnosis of inherited metabolic disorders. J Chromatogr A 2012;1226:11–7.

[54] Wang Z, Tang WH, Cho L, Brennan DM, Hazen SL. Targeted metabolomic evaluation of arginine methylation and cardiovascular risks: potential mechanisms beyond nitric oxide synthase inhibition. Arterioscler Thromb Vasc Biol 2009;29:1383–91.

[55] Zivkovic AM, Wiest MM, Nguyen U, Nording ML, Watkins SM, German JB. Assessing individual metabolic responsiveness to a lipid challenge using a targeted metabolomic approach. Metabolomics 2009;5:209–18.

[56] Kusano M, Fukushima A, Redestig H, Saito K. Metabolomic approaches toward understanding nitrogen metabolism in plants. J Exp Bot 2011;62:1439–53.

[57] Bailey NJ, Oven M, Holmes E, Nicholson JK, Zenk MH. Metabolomic analysis of the consequences of cadmium exposure in *Silene cucubalus* cell cultures via ^{1}H NMR spectroscopy and chemometrics. Phytochemistry 2003;62:851–8.

[58] Aranibar N, Ott KH, Roongta V, Mueller L. Metabolomic analysis using optimized NMR and statistical methods. Anal Biochem 2006;355:62–70.

[59] Lindon JC, Nicholson JK, Holmes E, Antti H, Bollard ME, Keun H, et al. Contemporary issues in toxicology the role of metabonomics in toxicology and its evaluation by the COMET project. Toxicol Appl Pharmacol 2003;187:137–46.

[60] Lindon JC, Keun HC, Ebbels TM, Pearce JM, Holmes E, Nicholson JK. The Consortium for Metabonomic Toxicology (COMET): aims, activities and achievements. Pharmacogenomics 2005;6:691–9.

[61] Shepherd J. The fibrates in clinical practice: focus on micronised fenofibrate. Atherosclerosis 1994;110(Suppl.):S55–63.

[62] Castillero E, Nieto-Bona MP, Fernandez-Galaz C, Martin AI, Lopez-Menduina M, Granado M, et al. Fenofibrate, a PPAR{alpha} agonist, decreases atrogenes and myostatin expression and improves arthritis-induced skeletal muscle atrophy. Am J Physiol Endocrinol Metab 2011;300:E790–9.

[63] Zhao X, Li LY. PPAR-alpha agonist fenofibrate induces renal CYP enzymes and reduces blood pressure and glomerular hypertrophy in Zucker diabetic fatty rats. Am J Nephrol 2008;28:598–606.

[64] Suchy FJ. Urinary bile acids: a noninvasive measure of liver function and bile acid metabolism? J Pediatr Gastroenterol Nutr 1984;3:649–51.

[65] Zgoda-Pols JR, Chowdhury S, Wirth M, Milburn MV, Alexander DC, Alton KB. Metabolomics analysis reveals elevation of 3-indoxyl sulfate in plasma and brain during chemically-induced acute kidney injury in mice: investigation of nicotinic acid receptor agonists. Toxicol Appl Pharmacol 2011;255:48–56.

[66] Vulimiri SV, Misra M, Hamm JT, Mitchell M, Berger A. Effects of mainstream cigarette smoke on the global metabolome of human lung epithelial cells. Chem Res Toxicol 2009;22:492–503.

[67] Gorman GS, Coward L, Kerstner-Wood C, Freeman L, Hebert CD, Kapetanovic IM. In-vitro and in-vivo metabolic studies of the candidate chemopreventative pentamethylchromanol using liquid chromatography/tandem mass spectrometry. J Pharm Pharmacol 2009;61:1309–18.

[68] Lindeblad M, Kapetanovic IM, Kabirov KK, Detrisac CJ, Dinger N, Mankovskaya I, et al. Assessment of oral toxicity and safety of pentamethylchromanol (PMCol), a potential chemopreventative agent, in rats and dogs. Toxicology 2010;273:19–28.

[69] Parman T, Bunin DI, Ng HH, McDunn JE, Wulff JE, Wang A, et al. Toxicogenomics and metabolomics of pentamethylchromanol (PMCol)-induced hepatotoxicity. Toxicol Sci 2011;124:487–501.

VIII. PREDICTIVE TOXICOLOGY, TOXICOMETABOLOMICS, TOXICOGENOMICS, AND IMAGING

34

Toxicogenomics in Preclinical Development

T.C. Fuchs[a], G.L. Truisi[a], P.G. Hewitt

[a] Authors contributed equally to this chapter.

A Comprehensive Guide to Toxicology in Nonclinical Drug Development, Second Edition
http://dx.doi.org/10.1016/B978-0-12-803620-4.00034-7

INTRODUCTION

The Human Genome Project, started in 1990 and finalized in 2003, was initialized to identify all the genes in human DNA and to discover the sequences of the entire genome. Therefore, this approach was the first important step in the overall understanding of the regulatory mechanisms of the genome and the basis of much subsequent research. Additionally, this project had a great impact on the development of new technologies and testing strategies of several branches of biology. Progress in automated instrumentation, information transfer, computational efficacy, and data storage were driven by the need of biological research for higher-throughput measurements. Since then the sequences of 173 eukaryotic genomes have been completed and reported, and 2385 are in assembly or the sequencing is still in progress [1]. However, still today the function of ~30,000 human genes, the role of noncoding regions, repeats in the genome, and the role of single base changes within the genome, so-called single nucleotide polymorphisms (SNPs), are not yet completely understood.

This paradigm shift has also had a fundamental effect on the field of toxicology, which has been revolutionized by this new way of research. Analysis of the adverse effects of compounds on the DNA, RNA, or protein level in different cell types, tissues, organisms, genders, and life stages or disease progressions, and not only on a single gene or protein but on a global basis, has enormous potential to improve our understanding and discovery of the mechanism of toxicity of a compound.

TOXICOGENOMICS

In traditional toxicology the focus is on the phenotypic changes observed or measured after exposure of an organism to chemical, physical, or biological agents. Such changes can include reversible alterations, chronic damage, and even lethality. In toxicology, whole-animal studies normally include acute (single-dose) studies to assess the tolerability of a given compound and repeated-dose studies (multiple doses) including assessment of endpoints like body and organ weight alterations, clinical signs, and chemical and histopathological responses. In addition to animal studies, in silico (computational simulations) and in vitro (ex vivo organ or cell culture models) approaches are also used in modern toxicology for specific questions. Further approaches used in pharmaceutical safety assessment, and which are related to toxicology, include pharmacovigilance data and epidemiological studies to examine the relationship between a drug and adverse effects observed in humans after market release of a drug.

In order to increase the power of traditional and regulated toxicological safety assessment, novel technologies are used to increase the number of endpoints for in vivo and in vitro testing and to get more sensitive, specific, and reliable information and data out of each study. One of these novel approaches is the field of toxicogenomics.

The term "toxicogenomics" is a combination of the word "toxicology", which describes the science of compound-induced adverse/toxic effects on living systems or the environment, and the word "genomics," which is a hyponym for the genetic discipline focused on studying the whole genome of an organism. Thus, toxicogenomics deals with the discovery and understanding of the influence of toxins on the regulation of genes and their involvement in a potential outcome. The focus of toxicogenomics is formally, but not limited, to the study of messenger RNA (mRNA).

Toxicogenomics is often described as a toxicological subdiscipline of pharmacogenomics, which is defined as the study of interindividual variations in whole-genome or candidate gene single-nucleotide polymorphism maps, haplotype markers, and alterations in gene expression that might correlate with drug responses [2,3]. Toxicogenomics was mentioned for the first time in the literature in 1999 by Nuwaysir [4]. However, the term toxicogenomics is still not universally used or even accepted, and others have offered alternative terms such as chemogenomics to describe essentially the same area [5]. In this chapter, the term toxicogenomics will be used, unless otherwise mentioned, to describe the global study of the transcriptome. The disciplines of proteomics and metabolomics, which are often included in toxicogenomics, will be briefly described in a separate chapter within this book.

Since the one-gene-one-polypeptide hypothesis was revised, which states that each gene controls the production, function, and specificity of a particular protein, the whole picture of gene expression and regulation has become more complex. Fig. 34.1 gives an overview of the increasing number of regulatory activities influencing the regulation of genes. Toxicogenomics in general deals with all of these individual steps, including pre- and posttranscriptional regulation, as well as epigenetic factors. For example, the regulation of transcription can be regulated by several transcription factors and cofactors, formally proteins activating or inhibiting specific genes via transcription factor-binding sites. It is also known that alternative splicing can lead to several mRNA species from one single gene, leading to independent proteins. In the human genome approximately 95% of all genes, including those with multiple exons, can be alternatively spliced [6]. Additionally regulation of gene expression depends on epigenetic factors influencing the condition of the DNA.

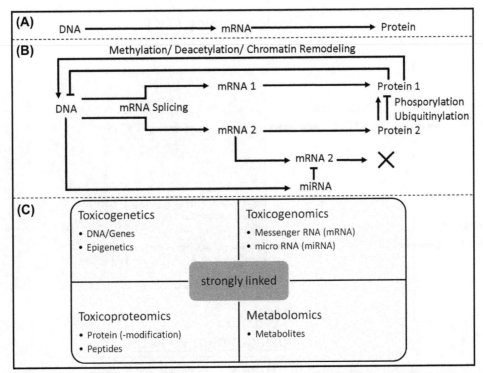

FIGURE 34.1 An overview of the increasing complexity of gene regulation from (A) the one-gene-one-polypeptide-hypothesis to (B) a simplified picture of the state-of-the-art understanding of gene expression regulation. The individual molecular classes are investigated by (C) Toxicogenetics, -genomics, -proteomics, and metabolomics.

Examples of such changes might be DNA methylation, chromatin remodeling, or histone deacetylation, which can serve to suppress gene expression without altering the sequence of the silenced genes. Changes of the DNA methylation or histone deacetylation status can be influenced by endogenous or exogenous causes and therefore can deliver information about a potential impact of a compound on the gene expression. Small noncoding RNA (ncRNA) species like microRNAs (miRNA) or small interfering RNA (siRNA) can also be used to get a better understanding of the underlying regulation and mechanism of action of a drug candidate.

The Principle of Compound-Induced Alteration in Gene Expression

The high sensitivity of analyzing transcript alterations is based on the fact that changes at the mRNA level appear before changes on the protein or the functional level can be observed. Therefore, toxicogenomics can deliver additional information to the standard toxicokinetic (TK) and toxicodynamic (TD) approaches (see Fig. 34.2).

Traditional toxicological measurements provide functional or structural alterations, but mark the end of a cascade of events happening in the target tissue/organ. However, the toxicological outcome strongly depends on the dose used and the time of treatment. A lack of

significant pathological changes and/or functional properties can appear by using too low doses, too short treatment periods, or even specific treatment patterns, including periods without treatment. In these cases alterations at the cellular/molecular level can already be in progress and therefore can be observed by toxicogenomic approaches (see Fig. 34.3). However, changes in this phase of treatment include adaptive alteration of a xenobiotic stressor, as cells attempt to maintain the homeostatic property of the stressed target tissue. If a second threshold is exceeded, real toxicological gene expression changes appear, potentially leading to additional toxic effects.

TOXICOGENOMICS APPROACHES

The underlying theory is that many mechanisms evoked by a toxicant are initiated on the DNA/RNA level. In the following the different approaches that evolved over time and advanced into highly sophisticated systems are explained.

Genomic Approaches

This section describes the importance and applied technologies of genome sequencing, genotyping, and epigenetic approaches in toxicology.

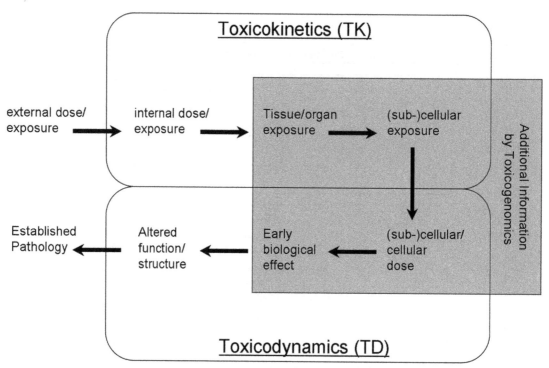

FIGURE 34.2 Toxicokinetics describes the uptake, cellular internalization, metabolism, and excretion of a drug. Toxicodynamics describes what organ, tissue, or cellular changes are induced by a drug or their metabolites. Toxicogenomics can help to get further information on the variability in exposure and susceptibility on a cellular or subcellular level.

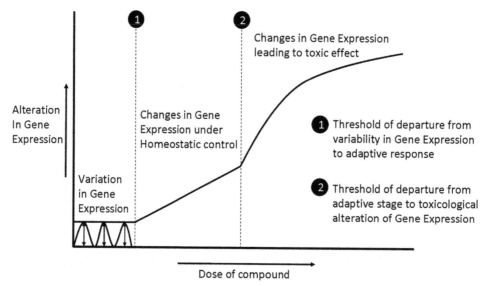

FIGURE 34.3 The regulation and expression of genes under physiological conditions show a variability that can lead to slightly higher or lower expression of some transcripts over time or between animals. The foundation of toxicogenomics assessment is, that depending on an increasing dose of a potential toxic compound, gene transcription leads to a change from the norm. This alteration takes place by exceeding a limit value of biological impact caused by the compound. This impact is still under homeostatic control, until a second threshold of departure is crossed, ultimately leading to toxic effects.

Genome Sequencing—The Next Generation

The sequencing of an organism's genome describes the process of determining the base-pair order of the DNA. In 1977 Sanger et al. [7] described a new method for detecting the DNA nucleotide sequence. Sanger sequencing was the method of choice for almost two decades and is considered as "first-generation" sequencing. Continuous innovations in technologies have led to the revolution and improvement over the time- and cost-consuming traditional sequencing methods.

"Next-generation" sequencing (NGS) technology has the potential to take over the field of toxicogenomics—and potentially replace microarray technology. An important aspect when introducing a new technology is the proof of its benefit over the current "gold standard" procedure, including liability and robustness, prior to its adoption. Generally, gene expression profiling using microarray methodologies has a number of shortcomings, including potentially low sensitivity, specificity, and a relatively low dynamic range that might affect its accuracy. By contrast, NGS provides sample measurements with high sensitivity, accuracy, and a wide dynamic range, ie, detecting genes with extremely low expression levels [8]. Furthermore, NGS enables an unbiased approach by sequencing and counting every existing RNA transcript instead of measuring a predefined set of annotated genes. The FDA perceives NGS as one key technology (together with microarrays) in pharmaco- and toxicogenomics, and launched the third phase of the MicroArray Quality Control project MAQC-III (see "Toxicogenomics in preclinical toxicology" for MAQC-I and –II), which is also known as Sequencing Quality Control (SEQC) in December 2008. Within the MAQC-III project three NGS platforms, Illumina HiSeq, Life Technologies SOLiD, and Roche 454, were assessed according to their technical performance by generating benchmark datasets, including reference samples. Additionally, NGS was compared to microarray technology and bioinformatics strategies in RNA and DNA analyses and were evaluated with respect to their advantages and limitations [9].

Overall, global transcriptome analysis using NGS appears to be a suitable approach during drug discovery and development phases, aiming to gain valuable mechanistic information on the adverse effects of drug candidates and holding the potential to discover novel and innovative, safety-relevant biomarkers.

Genotyping

A polymorphism is a DNA region that varies between individuals. When only single bases are different it is referred to as single nucleotide polymorphism (SNP). Most SNPs do not have any impact on the resulting phenotype and appear therefore less relevant for toxicological investigation. At the same time there are many SNPs that account for a large number of inter- and intraspecies differences—for example, the cytochrome P450 (CYP) enzymes.

The CYP family plays an important role in Phase I drug-metabolizing reactions of endo- and exogenous molecules. Many CYP enzymes known to be involved in xenobiotic metabolism belong to the CYP families 1 to 3 and show a high degree of polymorphism, in contrast to CYPs of the families 4 to 51, which are mainly involved in endogenous metabolism and biosynthesis

and show a low degree of polymorphism [10]. More importantly, different polymorphic forms translate into various phenotypes with respect to the particular enzyme, namely poor metabolizer showing no activity, intermediate metabolizer having a decreased activity, extensive metabolizer with an increased activity, and ultrarapid metabolizer, which carry two or more active gene copies resulting in extremely high activity of a certain enzyme.

The identification of SNPs is commonly achieved through genotyping, but today various methods are available and the choice depends on the number of SNPs and the amount of DNA available. In principle, for genome-wide assessments the Affymetrix systems (GeneChip Mapping, SNP Array, and Axiom Arrays) and Illumina's HumanCore, HumanOmni, or Infinium BeadChip systems are preferred, whereas for a smaller number of SNPs the TaqMan real-time polymerase chain reaction (PCR) technology is favored. By means of genotyping analysis such phenotypes can be identified, thus providing a useful toxicogenomic parameter that may help to understand varying responses in patients to an identical drug candidate. However, preclinical assessment of genotype-dependent responses is more difficult, since the standard species used in toxicology studies do not show as many polymorphisms as humans do. Overall, genotyping is a step toward personalized medicine, whereby identification of the genotype in a large population represents a great challenge.

Epigenetics

The environment interacts with the genome of a living being every single day, resulting in adaptation of the genome over time, which constitutes the epigenome. In principle the epigenome introduces another dimension of complexity to the genome, since inheritable changes do not occur on the base-pair level, ie, the genotype (DNA sequence) remains identical. DNA methylation, histone modifications, and micro-RNAs (miRNA) represent key mechanisms leading to epigenetic changes.

Generally, physiological DNA methylation refers to the addition of a methyl group to the 5′ position of cytosine (C), typically taking place only at cytosines located next to guanine (G), so-called CpG (Cytosine-phosphatidyl-Guanine) dinucleotide sites (or CpG islands). It plays an important role during (1) proofreading after the DNA-replication process, (2) detection of foreign DNA, and (3) differentiation between active and inactive areas of the DNA sequence. Physiological examples where DNA methylation is required include X-chromosome inactivation during mammalian development and genomic imprinting.

In recent years epigenetics has emerged as an important aspect in oncology, where it is used to explain the differences between the normal and diseased state of a tissue [11]. In the field of toxicology epigenetic alterations may act as early biomarkers for genotoxic and nongenotoxic carcinogens [12]. Furthermore, the gene regulation of influx and efflux transporters, Phase I and II drug-metabolizing enzymes, and transcription factors are known to be epigenetically encoded. Comprehensive reviews were published by Klaassen et al. [13], Duarte [14], and Tang et al. [15]. Interestingly, epigenomic analyses allow the determination of tissue-specific gene regulations and interindividual variations, thus bearing the potential to elucidate differential toxicity responses to compound treatment. The possibility to connect the toxicity of metals to epigenetic alteration in the form of DNA methylation changes (by nickel, lead, chromium, and arsenic) and specific histone modifications (nickel, chromium, copper, arsenic, and cadmium) [16] is the first indication and additional confidence that this field will probably prove to be significant in drug development in the near future.

In terms of sample preparation a distinction can be made between three major approaches: (1) identification of C to T transition induced by bisulfite, (2) utilization of methylation-sensitive restriction enzymes cleaving genomic DNA, and (3) immunoprecipitation with antibodies or proteins that bind methylated cytosines. Subsequently, microarray- and sequencing-based analyses allow for genome-wide DNA methylation profiling [17].

Transcriptomic Approaches

The transcriptome reflects the entirety of RNA molecules in a cell, including messenger RNA (mRNA), ribosomal RNA (rRNA), and noncoding RNA, such as transfer RNA (tRNA), micro-RNA (miRNA), and small interfering RNA (siRNA). Commonly, transcriptomics has frequently been referred to as gene expression profiling, and is defined as the analysis of mRNA expression levels in a defined cell population or biological system at a defined point in time. Based on the leading paradigm that a cellular response (phenotype) is initiated on the gene level, transcriptional variations are a promising tool to understand biological affects either in terms of endogenous cellular development, diseases, or reactions to xenobiotics.

There exist many approaches to examine changes within the transcriptome, ranging from highly sensitive real-time PCR (RT-PCR) and sophisticated gene expression microarrays to the already discussed next-generation sequencing technologies (known as RNA Seq). Here, whole genome and customized transcriptome approaches will be addressed, focusing on the respective scope and their pros and cons.

Whole-Transcriptome Analysis

Whole-genome technologies allow the simultaneous analysis of thousands of genes in a single experiment, thus enabling examination of the entire transcriptome in one experiment. More importantly, the measurement of genome-wide changes allows a global and therefore comprehensive investigation of underlying mechanisms of action an unphysiological influencing compound may have. Transcriptomics can be considered as meaningful, because the response of a biological system is not restricted to a small subset of predefined transcripts.

Today, the microarray technology is recognized as a common and well-established technology that is applied to generate large datasets, at favorable costs. What is of greater importance today is the proper interpretation of the biological response on a gene expression level to adverse compound exposure, ie, a profound biostatistical and toxicological knowledge is essential.

However, there are obvious limitations related to genome-wide microarray technologies. For example, the expression profile is restricted to those transcripts that are included in the annotated gene list, ie, only mRNA molecules. Other important molecules potentially having an impact on the gene expression profile, such as noncoding RNAs, are not included. Furthermore, the possibility exists that substances exert their adverse effect by directly affecting proteins or organelles in the cell, hence causing damage without changing gene expression significantly. In principal gene expression changes are often secondary effects after toxic insults. Lastly, protein inhibition by the compound itself or induced (de-) phosphorylation cannot be measured with transcriptomics. By contrast, NGS is an unbiased approach that simply sequences the available RNA, with the potential to overcome some of these deficiencies described.

Overall, global gene expression profiling technologies are a powerful tool, which help not only to understand adverse processes but also to discover new predictive biomarkers and extrapolate to putative in vivo mechanisms from either in vivo samples or in vitro test systems.

Customized Transcript Approaches

There are many different technologies available from which one can choose to perform transcriptome analysis of a predefined number of genes. These include the classical northern blot analysis to characterize single transcripts, while quantitative real-time PCR (qRT–PCR), branched DNA, or customized microarray platforms are typical examples and commonly used for multiple gene expression analysis. Generally, these techniques have high sensitivity and specificity. Subsets of important or predictive genes (potential biomarkers) discovered by global-expression profiling are often verified using these customized transcript technologies.

A clear disadvantage of customized gene expression analysis is the limited number of transcripts that are analyzed simultaneously. This limitation may result in a biased biological interpretation if expression changes are solely evaluated using a small, potentially wrong, group of genes. Additionally, the experiment performance of northern blotting using radioactively labeled probes is a further deficit as sample quantity is relatively high.

TOXICOGENOMICS TECHNOLOGIES

In the following two sections high- and low-throughput technologies are addressed.

High-Throughput Technologies/Whole-Genome Profiling

With the implementation of genome-wide expression analysis technologies, which allow the investigation of all transcripts at the same time, extremely complex systems have become accessible. Meanwhile a number of different technology providers is available. In principle, the general process, ie, sample preparation, hybridization, and the read-out methodology, is very similar across the various platforms. Here, the general process of microarray processing is presented.

RNA Isolation

Nearly all transcriptomic techniques begin with the isolation of total RNA from a cell population or tissue, thus it is essential to isolate high-quality RNA. Gene expression data can only be as good as the starting material they are derived from.

Many different commercial kits are available for the isolation of total RNA or mRNA, adjusted to any type of cells or tissue source. These kits are easy to use and help to minimize the source of error when working with such sensitive molecules as RNA. Several approaches utilize the "single-step" method of total RNA isolation by acid guanidinium thiocyanate-phenol-chloroform extraction, described in 1987 by Chomczynski and Sacchi [18]. Guanidinium thiocyanate lyses the cells and inactivates RNA digesting enzymes in one step. Generally, this method is based on the fact that after a centrifugation step three phases emerge, where total RNA (situated in the upper aqueous phase) gets separated from DNA (situated in the mid interphase) and proteins (situated in the bottom organic phase). After recovering the aqueous phase, RNA is precipitated either with 2-propanol or ethanol, washed, and dissolved in nuclease-free water or appropriate buffer.

For applications that require mRNA a further purification step has to be performed. Here, a major difference between mRNAs and residual RNA molecules is exploited, namely the poly(A) tail at the mRNA's 3′ end. Commonly spin columns are used that bind the poly(A) tail of mRNA molecules, hence removing non-polyadenylated RNA and other contaminants. In a last step mRNA can be eluted from the column, washed, and dissolved as for total RNA. Subsequently, concentration and quality of the total RNA or mRNA are measured.

cDNA Synthesis

cDNA synthesis includes a two-step (first- and second-strand synthesis) conversion of the cleaned up RNA to more stable copy DNA (cDNA). For this purpose the specialized enzyme reverse transcriptase is utilized, which converts single-stranded RNA (ssRNA) into DNA.

For microarray sample preparation the first-strand synthesis begins by reverse transcription with an oligo(dT) primer, which anneals efficiently to the poly(A) tails of the mRNA. It is exactly this step that also allows the application of total RNA, since only those RNA molecules containing the poly(A) tail will be further processed, ie, the mRNA. The starting material for the second-strand synthesis is mRNA–cDNA hybrid molecules. Before the DNA polymerase can synthesize the second strand of the cDNA, RNase H is added to the mRNA–cDNA hybrid transcripts. RNase H digests only the ss mRNA at unspecific sites, thus creating short mRNA fragments that remain bound to the ss cDNA and are utilized by the DNA polymerase as primers for the second-strand synthesis. The resulting material, which will be further processed, is double-stranded cDNA (ds cDNA).

Labeling

Prior to hybridization to the respective probes on the microarray it is important to label the newly synthesized ds cDNA transcripts, thus making them detectable (visible), which is achieved by using specific fluorophores. Generally, there are two approaches to the labeling: (1) by directly introducing the label during cDNA synthesis or (2) by indirectly labeling a previously incorporated intermediate deoxyribonucleotide triphosphates (dNTPs) (postsynthesis).

The direct method can be achieved by enzymatically (RNA or DNA polymerase) introducing fluorescein-labeled dNTPs/NTPs. Another possibility is the so-called "nick translation DNA labeling," which labels the already created cDNA. First, "nicks" are introduced by random digestion with DNase. Following this the DNA polymerase reinserts the removed nucleotides by using dNTPs labeled with biotin, fluorescein, for example. Generally, this method can be problematic because labeled nucleotides are incorporated by the enzymes, with lower efficiency than their unlabeled counterparts.

In the indirect method this shortcoming is circumvented due to the fact that modifications are introduced to the already synthesized transcripts. Here during first-strand synthesis dTTPs are substituted by amino allyl-dUTPs/UTPs, which introduces primary aliphatic amino groups that have the ability to bind to fluorescent dye molecules having activated N-hydroxysuccinimide, eg, Cyanine3 (Cy3) or Cy5.

A very efficient approach used by the Illumina system [19] is the introduction of biotin-labeled dNTPs during in vitro transcription (IVT). Here the ds cDNA serves as a template for IVT with RNA polymerase, creating biotinylated cRNA. The staining with streptavidin-Cy3 results in a tight biotin-streptavidin bond and is performed during the washing procedure.

Hybridization

For the hybridization of the labeled cDNA/cRNA different microarrays require different sample preparations, eg, denaturation of microarray probes and/or samples, rehydration of microarrays, etc.

A predefined amount of sample is usually given onto an array and then allowed to incubate for a specified period of time, usually between 18 and 23h at 42–50°C [20]. The use of a defined incubation time and temperature are essential for hybridization of the transcripts to the corresponding probes situated on the microarray. Furthermore, one has to make sure that the arrays do not dry out during the hybridization process, since this will result in highly fluorescent artifacts. Generally, it is considered advisable to apply identical settings to samples of one experiment, which have to be processed at different time points.

Washing

The posthybridization washing method is known to affect the equilibrium adsorption isotherm of microarray probes in a sequence-dependent manner [21]. At this stage unbound and unspecific (thus loosely) bound transcripts are removed by a thorough multistep washing procedure. Different protocols are recommended by different manufacturers. Usually microarrays are washed in a series of buffers varying in detergent concentration and salt composition. Prior to image acquisition the washing represents a very important step because inaccurate elimination of falsely paired probes will result in false-positive data for the corresponding gene or reduction of the dynamic range due to high background signals.

Image-Data Acquisition

For the image acquisition of fluorescent dyes, special laser-scanning confocal microscope systems are routinely applied, where the image acquisition is based on simple fluorescence measurements. When two-dye systems are applied the array will be scanned at the respective two wavelengths, thus resulting in two images plus an overlay image that allows examination of differentially expressed genes.

In the end the imaging software generates the raw data from a microarray experiment by converting obtained fluorescence signals into numerical values that will be processed in the data-analysis approach (see the "Data Analysis—Biostatistical Analysis of Genomic Data" section).

Low-Throughput Technologies/Single-Gene Detection

There is not always the need to screen the whole genome for gene expression. The analysis of single genes or low numbers of genes is appealing with respect to the wide dynamic range, high sensitivity, and specificity that most low-throughput technologies hold. Often such technologies are applied for verification and evaluation purposes of high-throughput approaches. Furthermore, when a subset of biomarkers has been identified, future analysis can be performed on a low-throughput scale.

Northern Blot

Gene expression monitoring during differentiation, or treated versus untreated condition, as well as discovery of alternatively spliced transcripts are counted among the main applications of this technology.

This molecular biology technique starts with the isolation of total RNA from cells or tissue of interest followed by its purification in order to obtain mRNA. First, the intact mRNA molecules are separated according to size via electrophoresis on an agarose gel. In order to make the RNA accessible for detection, the transcripts are blotted (transferred) to a positively charged nylon membrane and immobilized by UV light or heat. After addition of the labeled antisense probe that hybridizes to the complementary sequence, the specific target can be visualized on the membrane. The membrane is washed thoroughly prior to evaluation using an appropriate detection method, which depends on the label used. Here, radioactive isotopes, enzymes, or fluorescence probes have been reported. With suitable detectors, commercially available software tools, and dilution series of the target sequence the detected RNA in the sample can be quantified accurately. Overall, this method is extremely sensitive, which is a main advantage of this procedure, but it is no longer routinely used in preclinical drug development.

Quantitative Real-Time PCR (TaqMan/SYBR)

Based on the traditional PCR, real-time PCR uses fluorescent reporter molecules that target DNA, thus allowing quantification of the specific transcript during its amplification by measurement of the fluorescent signal.

The method utilizes cDNA generated from total RNA (using a random primer) or mRNA (using an oligo(dT) primer) as starting material, as well as the basic PCR-mix, which consists of forward and reverse primers, dNTPs, and thermostable DNA polymerase. The fluorescent label added to the PCR mix is excited by a light source in the real-time PCR instrument, while a camera captures the emitted signal. In the course of continuous amplification, the fluorescent signal increases as the DNA is being synthesized. This process is visualized in a real-time PCR graph that can be sectioned into three phases (exponential, linear, and plateau), whereas the focus for data interpretation relies on the exponential phase during which all the reaction components are in abundance and the PCR product doubles every cycle, thus providing the most accurate data for quantification. Values calculated from this phase include the threshold line (level of detection) and the cycle threshold (Ct) value (cycle at which the sample reaches the threshold line).

There are various types of fluorescence detection available. The two most widely used techniques are (1) TaqMan probe and (2) SYBR green dye. In the so-called "TaqMan system" the addition of a TaqMan probe to the PCR mix is required. The TaqMan probe is an oligonucleotide with a minimum length of 20–30 nucleotides to guarantee sufficient specificity and targets a predefined sequence in the DNA of interest. This oligonucleotide contains a fluorescent reporter dye (at the 5′ end) and a quencher (at the 3′ end), hence when the probe is intact there is no fluorescence because the quencher is in close proximity to the reporter dye and thus quenches the emitted light of the reporter dye (FRET). As DNA polymerase progresses it cleaves the TaqMan probe bound in the midregion of the target DNA, thus separating the reporter dye from its quencher and is then able to fluoresce. This fluorescence is measured during real-time PCR.

SYBR green dye binds nonspecifically to dsDNA, resulting in a fluorescent signal due to the fact that the SYBR green dsDNA-complex fluoresces. Notably, the resulting fluorescence is proportional to the amount of dsDNA. When working with the SYBR green system a DNA melting-curve analysis has to be run in parallel to make sure the correct transcript has been amplified.

In this field the TaqMan Array Micro Fluidic Cards, which allows the simultaneous analysis of up to 384 genes per sample, enable a higher throughput than older technologies. Here, probe and primers for a respective gene are present as lyophilisates in a multiwell format and gene selection can be customized [22].

A further advancement are the TaqMan OpenArray Real-Time PCR Plates, where 3072 reactions can be performed on one plate. The preparation workflow is simple, and sample and master mix are merged and loaded onto a PCR plate preloaded with a customized or preselected set of TaqMan gene expression assays. This new system enables the performance of real-time PCR in a higher-throughput manner [23].

Branched DNA

Instead of amplifying the target sequence to yield high sensitivity, this method relies on the signal amplification of the branched DNA (bDNA) probe [24] that binds to a specific nucleotide sequence [25].

The bDNA assay is also known as the sandwich nucleic-acid hybridization method, because the sequence of interest is captured in between target-specific oligonucleotides. The first-generation of bDNA assays were viral quantification assays, developed for the detection of viral loads (HIV-1 and HCV) in humans [26,27]. Currently, the application is widespread, ranging from microarray validation and biomarker discovery to predictive toxicology, when applied to screening compounds in early preclinical phases.

A clear advantage of the bDNA assay is the fact that no RNA/DNA isolation, purification, or amplification is required prior to assay performance, ie, any sample can be utilized (cultured cells, fresh, frozen, or formalin-fixed, paraffin-embedded (FFPE) tissue, whole blood, viruses, bacteria, plants, but also purified RNA and DNA). The used tissue has to be lysed in order to make the target sequence (RNA or DNA) accessible for analysis. The target-specific designed probe-set oligonucleotides include the "capture extender" and the "label extender". The two-part capture extender binds with one part to the target sequence and with the other one to the capture probes, which are immobilized on beads or on the bottom of a multiwell plate. At the same time the two-part label extender hybridizes with one segment to the opposite side of the target, leaving the other free for the preamplifier oligonucleotide. The target nucleotide sequence is captured between the capture and label extenders (forming a "sandwich"). Subsequently, the signal "tree" for amplification can be constructed. This is achieved by hybridization of the preamplifier to the label extender, then the amplifier to the preamplifier, and finally the label probe to the amplifier.

Diagrammatically this results in:

Immobilized Capture Probe – Capture Extender – Target Sequence – Label Extender – Preamplifier – Amplifier – Label Probe (see Fig. 34.4).

The label probe is usually alkaline phosphatase (AP)-labeled oligonucleotide, which after addition of a corresponding substrate, creates a chemiluminescence signal that is proportional to the amount of target sequence in the sample.

The QuantiGene assays from Affymetrix enable a customized probe set design for this application and the multiplexing of up to 36 target RNAs [28] and 33 target DNAs [29].

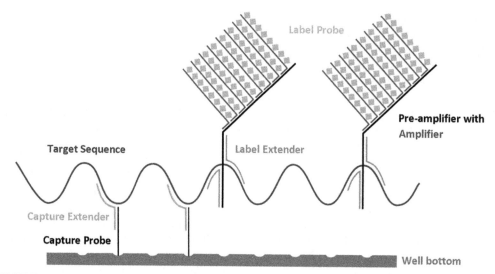

FIGURE 34.4　Illustration of branched DNA assay where capture probes are immobilized on the well bottom.

DATA ANALYSIS—BIOSTATISTICAL ANALYSIS OF GENOMIC DATA

For analyzing the enormous amount of data produced by novel genomic technologies, specialized computational analyses are needed to extract reliable results and to identify biological relevant information. Bioinformatics itself is a branch of computational biology focused on the analysis of numerical biological data, as well as data management, collection, and storage. Therefore advanced computational techniques are applied, including elements that are essential to all genomic technologies. It is important to note that the analysis and interpretation of genomics data is only possible in a reliable way by bioinformatic techniques. However, this is not covered here.

Analysis of microarray experiments focused on the detection of thousands of transcripts can be formally divided into the four categories: (1) class discovery, (2) class comparison, (3) class prediction, and (4) mechanistic analysis. It is essential to take these strategies into account prior to starting the analysis and even before planning the actual experiment because of the different goals of these approaches. In the following these analyzing strategies are described in more detail.

Each of these methods of analysis can help address different questions and be used for hypothesis testing. The toxicogenomics technology, in combination with a suitable analyzing model, has already proven in recent years that it can provide additional information about chemical–gene/protein interactions, chemical–toxicity, and gene–toxicity relationships. Depending on the scientific or regulatory question these information can be analyzed and evaluated from different perspectives. Subsequently, toxicogenomics data can be integrated with functional and pathway data to aid in the development of hypotheses about the mode of action (MoA) of a test compound. Consequently, a subset of altered genes can indicate what kind of chemical is used or which toxic alterations can be observed. A chemical, on the other hand, can be grouped to a class of substances based on the genetic-alteration profile. It is also possible that the magnitude of gene expression changes can give further information on the exposure of a specific target organ. Therefore, depending on the question concerning a chemical, toxicity (eg, mechanism, target organ, etc.), or the involvement of specific genes can be addressed. Another important benefit of toxicogenomics data is that hypothesis testing can also be based on already available data. With the progress in toxicological knowledge as well as bioinformatic technologies novel hypotheses can be tested on already existing data without performing new animal studies, for example. A schematic overview of possible interactions of parameters that can be analyzed is provided in Fig. 34.5.

Class Discovery

The first step in analyzing toxicogenomics data is focused on class discovery. It is a general and unbiased look at the data for identifying simple group classes in the data. The aim of this analysis is the grouping of similar effects of the gene expression pattern to discover similarities and differences of the individual treatment or pathology groups. The simplest example is the comparison of treated versus control groups. If the treatment leads to an alteration in gene expression it is expected that these class discovery statistical methods will cluster the control replicates together and the treatment groups separately. With this analyzing strategy several factors can be taken into account. Different compounds, doses, time points, developmental stages, or even targeted cell types can be displayed and studied. Class discovery is an unsupervised method, and has the benefit that the sample classification is not used as input. The class

discovery groups samples together based on their similarity in expression pattern, independent of the group.

The three most widely used mathematical approaches are the principal component analysis (PCA) [30], k-means clustering [35] and hierarchical clustering [36] methods. Some additional methods are given in Table 34.1 [31–34,37–53]. In general all these algorithms use specific parameters and rules to determine similarities in the expression pattern as a value of a relationship of these groups. Fig. 34.6 gives an example of such a class discovery approach by using PCA.

These algorithms can also be used to group genes within one or even more groups showing similar effects. Consequently, class discovery of treatments with several compounds can be used to confirm or refute a hypothesis based on gene clusters and therefore deliver more information, for example, on the mode of action associated with the response of a group of compounds.

The individual clusters these methods create do not necessarily have any biological relevance. Determining whether a grouping is meaningful requires further analysis and the (toxicological) expertise of the user. By handling toxicogenomics data the critical observation and assessment of the results is of essential importance. Consequently, for this type of analysis a robust and highly standardized procedure from sample collection processing up to running of the microarrays is

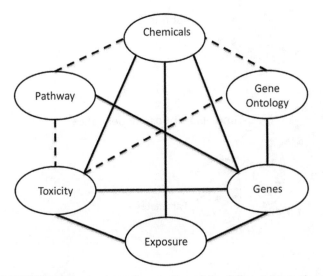

FIGURE 34.5 A schematic overview of the different interactions and relationships of chemicals, genes and gene ontology, exposure, toxicity, and pathway is displayed. The interaction and relationships can be understood in both directions. *Solid lines* indicate direct relationships and *broken lines* indicate derived information.

TABLE 34.1 Overview of Mathematical Algorithms and Their Usability in Different Analyzing Strategies for Gene Expression Data

	Mathematic Algorithm	References
Class discovery	Principal component analysis (PCA)	Raychaudhuri et al. [30]
	Self-organizing maps (SOM)	Toronen et al. [31], Tamayo et al. [32], Wang et al. [33]
	Self-organizing trees	Herrero et al. [34]
	k-means clustering	Soukas et al. [35]
	Hierarchical clustering	Wen et al. [36], Eisen et al. [37]
	Relevance networks	Butte and Kohane [38]
	Force-directed layouts	Kim et al. [39]
Class comparison	t-test	Baggerly et al. [40]
	Analysis of variance (ANOVA)	Long et al. [41]
	Significance analysis of microarrays	Tusher et al. [42]
Prediction/classification model	Support vector machines	Brown et al. [43], Ramaswamy et al. [44]
	k-nearest neighbors	Theilhaber et al. [45]
	Weighted voting	Golub et al. [46]
	Artificial neural networks	Bloom et al. [47], Ellis et al. [48]
	Discriminant analysis	Nguyen and Rocke [49], Orr and Scherf [50], Antoniadis et al. [51], Le et al. [52]
	Classification and regression trees	Boulesteix et al. [53]

Software tools for mechanistic and network analysis were not included because they are not limited to an individual algorithm, but the analysis is formally based on data- and text-mining.

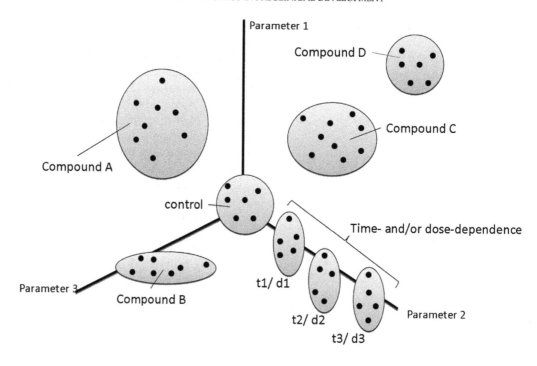

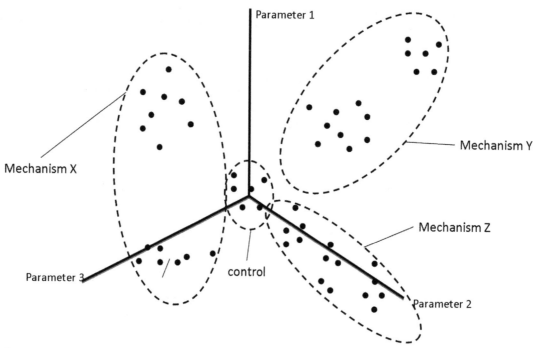

FIGURE 34.6 A principal component analysis (PCA) is given as an example of an unsupervised class discovery. Individual gene expression profiles from different studies or using different time points, doses, or even compounds were clustered depending on their similarity. The PCA therefore enables discrimination of the specific factor mentioned above, if they have an impact on the similarity of the profiles. The reduced components, evaluated by the PCA, are shown in a three-dimensional graph.

of crucial importance to generate reliable data because of the high sensitivity of this analysis [54–57]. Otherwise, clusters reflecting variation in the processing steps and not the biological or pathological changes can occur.

Comparison of Groups and Classes

The class-comparison experiment is the standard approach to analyzing gene expression data. Gene expression profiles and individual genes of different phenotypic groups can be compared. The simplest case is again the comparison of treated and control groups, with the aim of discovering genes and gene profiles that best discriminate these two groups. At this point the gene expression pattern of the control group is expected to reflect the normal, physiological pattern. Therefore, the study design, including culture conditions (for in vitro approaches), administration, diet, time, and many other factors are of crucial importance. Because of the high resolution of these technologies, even minor changes in the environment or study can have a strong impact on the gene expression pattern.

Every departure from the normal physiological pattern can be assumed to be caused by the compound treatment and therefore classified as pathologically relevant. Notably, biological variability is also present in the gene expression pattern (see Fig. 34.3). A wide variety of statistical tools can be used and the easiest and most common statistical tests are the t-test (two-group comparison) and the analysis of variance (multiple-group comparison). These methods assign a p-value to genes based on their ability to distinguish the studied groups. Normally a significance level is assumed to be 0.05 or 0.01. A common problem in the case of genomics data that occurs with this statistical approach is multiple testing. In a microarray with 20,000 genes, applying a 95% confidence limit on gene selection ($p \leq .05$) will lead, by chance, to 500 genes being significantly "altered." More stringent gene selection, by using a smaller p-value threshold, can minimize but not eliminate this problem. On the other hand, the "MicroArray Quality Control" (MAQC) project, which compared several microarray technologies for their reproducibility, led to the conclusion that less stringent p-value cut-offs combined with fold-change (FC) ranking (eg, a ratio of treated vs. control group) deliver more reliable results by enhanced reproducibility and balanced sensitivity and specificity [58]. Several other statistical tests can be used or combined to identify altered, treatment-dependent genes. For example, a combination of the p-value and the q-value by Benjamini and Hochberg [59] can be used to minimize misclassification by only taking the p-value into account. The q-value is a measure of the false discovery rate, and is a control statistic used to correct in a list of rejected hypotheses the expected proportion of incorrect rejected null hypotheses. Consequently, one must keep in mind that the values of statistical methods are there only to prioritize genes from the whole dataset based on cut-off values defined by the user.

Mechanistic and Network Analysis

The overall aim of this type of analysis is to deliver a deeper impact on the underlying mechanism of action/toxicity. Initially, other strategies such as class prediction (see below) can deliver information about the response

a compound can induce. However, for a more detailed understanding further analysis is needed. To achieve this shift from class prediction to a mechanistic understanding, additional work on translating toxicogenomic-based hypotheses into valid functional-linked findings has to be performed. It is clear that the measurement of global gene expression profiles delivers de facto information about the effect of a compound on the genome and the transcriptome, but it cannot give final information about the phenotype resulting from these molecular changes. Therefore, additional validation experiments have to be performed, focused on proteins, metabolites, and physiological parameters to discover the true mechanism.

Bioinformatics tools are key to develop a suitable hypothesis. The integration of information related to the altered transcripts, such as gene ontology (GO) terms, related functions, cellular processes and localization, pathway analysis, dose–response curves, and structure–activity relationships (SAR) can facilitate interpretation and therefore lead to robust and scientifically anchored hypotheses. Multitudes of software are available to facilitate this analysis. The best-known and most frequently used tools free of charge include GOMiner [60], EASE [61], and MAPPFinder [62]. In addition, many commercial software tools are available, such as GeneGo's MetaCore (plus ToxHunter [63], and Ingenuity Pathway Analyser (IPA)) [64]. Because of the growing importance and the wider dissemination of toxicogenomics, especially in the pharmaceutical and chemical industries, toxicology-focused analysis modules have now been included in the tools and databases. The Comparative Toxicogenomics Database (CTD) [65] is a publicly available database that provides curated information about chemical–gene/protein-disease interactions and relationships. These data can be used for functional and pathway analysis to aid in development of hypotheses [66]. Because there is no harmonized and universally accepted standard for analyzing gene expression profiles the analysis strongly depends on the scientific background and the creativity of the user. Because of this lack in standardization novel approaches are being developed to identify gene-interaction networks. These models, like Bayesian networks [67–71], (probabilistic) Boolean networks [69,72–75], or centrality analysis [76,77] deal with individual objects, in this case genes, transcripts, or proteins, as "edges" and "nodes" in a graph to represent their interactions. Specific rules for characterizing each edge represent the strength of the interaction and therefore the particular response. However, all these models only deliver descriptive data, meaning that additional work is still necessary to convert the results into predictive, biological hypotheses.

Toxicogenomic data are also valuable even when not used in a "systems biology" approach. One long-term aim of toxicogenomics is to achieve this systematic understanding of biological responses and the relationship to an upcoming insult and the development of a future pathological phenotype. It is likely that the development of novel technologies and bioinformatics models will significantly extend our ability to model complex systems, and therefore toxicogenomics research will continue to benefit from these advanced systems biology approaches.

Toxicological Prediction Models

Class-prediction analysis deals with the prediction of a specific biological response or a toxicological outcome based on gene expression profiles associated with compound exposure. The assumption of this approach is based on the fact that comparable effects/pathologies caused by different compounds show similar effects on the gene expression level. The foundation that allows the building of a prediction model is the need for a database of gene expression data, achieved using known and well-characterized compound-induced pathologies. Genes can be identified by computational algorithms to find the ideal set that can discriminate between different phenotypes or pathologies. In this case the ideal gene set is defined by a minimized misclassification rate, ie, a minimum false-positive and minimum false-negative classification (see Fig. 34.7). For this gene ranking a multitude of mathematical models are available and include analysis of variance (ANOVA) [78], support vector machine weight (SVM) [79], and the recursive feature elimination (RFE) [80]. Table 34.1 gives an overview of the

statistical/bioinformatics approaches that can be used for different analyzing strategies. For further information see the pertinent literature.

The genes identified by these methods are formally used to develop mathematical rules that enable the assignment of a compound to a specific pathology (phenotype class) based only on the gene expression profile. It is important to note that the genes identified by this approach are not necessarily linked to the toxicological mechanism or the phenotype in a biological context. These genes are identified using the test set in a first approach and require an independent dataset (ie, new gene expression profiles) for a cross-validation approach. This is needed to evaluate the misclassification rate of the genes and to calculate the sensitivity, specificity, and predictivity of the model.

Many algorithms have been used for this purpose such as artificial neural networks [47,48], discriminant analysis [49–52], classification and regression trees [53], support vector machines [43,44], and k-nearest neighbors [45]. In principal all these algorithms work in a similar manner, by using an original dataset (the training set) to develop a rule based on the gene expression data. For an unknown compound, this rule can be used to identify the class of the compound without any further information. Fig. 34.8 gives an overview of the general workflow of building a prediction model.

Beside this computational approach, genes identified by mechanistic analysis can also be used to build a prediction model. This approach has the benefit that the genes are selected based on a hypotheses or validated mechanism, which gives a more robust and understandable rational to the resulting classification. Examples of prediction/classification models used in toxicology to predict drug-induced geno-, hepato-, nephro-, and cardiotoxicity will be given in the "Nephrotoxicity" section.

Identification and Qualification of Novel Identified Biomarkers

The identification of safety-related biomarkers, or bioindicators, is not a defined, mathematical-statistical process and is not limited to a specific class of molecules. In general, a biomarker, as defined by the National Institutes of Health (NIH) Initiative on Biomarkers and Surrogate Endpoints, is "a characteristic that is objectively measured and evaluated as an indicator of normal biologic processes, pathogenic process, or pharmacologic responses to a therapeutic intervention" [81].

There are some fundamental characteristics a good safety biomarker must have, which should be independent of the molecular class, the technology used, or the

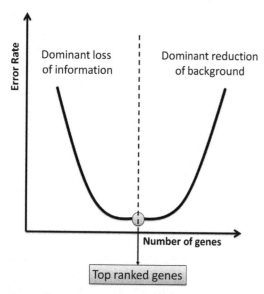

FIGURE 34.7 To get the most suitable genes for discriminating between toxic and nontoxic compounds, the previously ranked genes are used for classification of substances with known toxicological endpoints. By using different algorithms to test the genes the ideal gene set can be identified by the lowest misclassification (error) rate.

matrix used for detection. The following list of characteristics was adapted from [82]:

- Indicative after active observable damage or real predictive (biomarkers should appear prior to histopathological changes);
- Highly sensitive in correlation with the area and severity of damage;
- Specific for an organ, tissue, or special kind of injury/mechanism;
- Independent of age, gender, and other external factors (eg, diet, exercise);
- Ideally it should be accessible in body fluids like urine or blood (if this is not possible a peripheral tissue is also acceptable for potential translational usability);
- It should bridge across species and be translational to humans; and
- The mechanism of biomarker induction/release should be known.

Within the pharmaceutical industry, as well as in chemical and cosmetic companies, there is great demand for specific and sensitive biomarkers that predict adverse effects earlier and that can bridge across discovery, over preclinical phases through to humans in clinical trials.

Toxicogenomics technologies have been used by several institutions and consortia over the past 10 years, with a specific focus on the discovery of novel biomarkers. There is a widespread expectation (hope) that biomarker discovery can be enhanced by the use of toxicogenomics and that these novel predictive biomarkers can lead to safer drugs and a reduction of costs in pharmaceutical drug development.

Each gene expression profile measured from a toxicological sample gives a cumulative response of complex intra- and intercellular interactions within the tissue, organ, and/or the whole organism. This determined response is also a combination of pharmacological and toxicological effects of the drug/chemical (see Fig. 34.9). On one hand, the altered transcripts can be correlated to a specific toxicological mechanism. This type of transcript can be identified from network analysis and be used as a mechanistic biomarker. For example, genotoxic observations, where many distinct pathways and key transcripts that are already known, are of special interest. On the other hand, the transcriptional biomarkers can be linked to the toxicological/pathological phenotype. A general example of this is the upregulation of pro-inflammatory molecules in organ inflammation, in response to excessive necrosis. Transcriptional biomarkers can also be

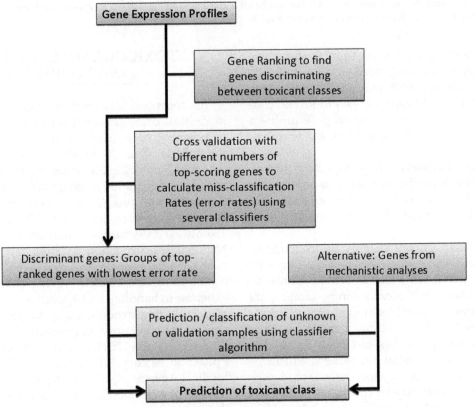

FIGURE 34.8 A general workflow of building a genomics-based prediction model. In the first step a list of ranked genes is evaluated, used for the cross-validation with compounds inducing well-described pathologies. Out of this approach the top-scoring genes can be selected by the lowest misclassification rate. By building a novel prediction model these genes in combination with the underlying computer-based rules are tested with a test set of gene expression data to evaluate the predictivity of the classifier.

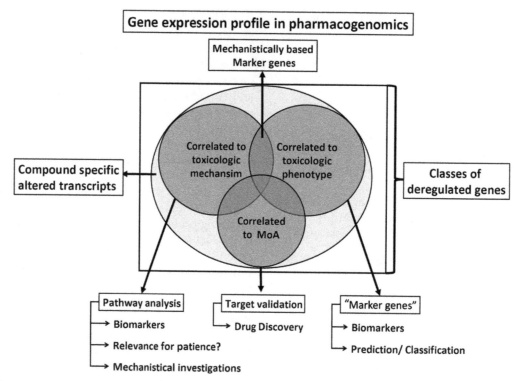

FIGURE 34.9 Three major subclasses of altered transcripts are displayed. One can discriminated between gene responses linked to the toxicological mechanism, the toxicological phenotype, and the "mode of action" (MoA) of a drug. The subdivision is not as stringent, thus overlaps between these rational defined classes exist. The most promising transcripts, to serve as marker genes, are both based on the toxicological mechanism and the phenotype. However, each individual subclass can be used and analyzed for different purposes like, biomarker or drug discovery, mechanistical investigation, or the building of a classification model.

identified by showing gene expression changes specific to the MoA of the drug used. For example, the "glitazones" or "fibrates," both peroxisome–proliferator–activating receptor (PPAR) agonists, lead in several cases to comparable endpoints, including adipose proliferation, fluid accumulation, edema, anemia, and lymphoid depletion.

For all of these biomarkers it is important that the expected interactions can be correlated to an endpoint (molecular, physiological, or morphological) and subsequently proven to be reproducible across multiple studies and sites.

One major disadvantage of this toxicogenomics approach to biomarker discovery is that the target tissue needs to be extracted, which is invasive. This has greater consequences in clinical settings, limiting the usefulness of transcriptional biomarkers. One exception to this is of course blood-based transcriptional biomarkers. Toxicogenomics approaches can easily be used to generate first hints of potential biomarkers, which can then be used as the basis of targeted analysis to identify the related proteins, that may be measured in different body fluids. One example of a toxicogenomic-based biomarker discovery approach leading to the qualification of protein biomarkers is described in the "Nephrotoxicity" section.

TOXICOGENOMICS IN DRUG DEVELOPMENT

Toxicogenomics is used in preclinical trials in pharmaceutical drug development to study adverse effects of potential new drugs, their metabolites, or even of the vehicle. The US Food and Drug Administration (US FDA) published a white paper in 2004 that proposed the integration of genomics technologies into the developmental process at several stages. This process was encouraged by the report "Toxicity Testing in the Twenty-First Century: A Vision and a Strategy" from the National Research Council (NRC) in 2007. On the European side, the Innovation Task Force (ITF) was founded by the European Medical Agency (EMA) to offer their expertise in handling and application of omics technologies, including genomics, and to provide information concerning regulatory requirements [83].

Generally, the US FDA, EMA, the US Environmental Protection Agency (EPA), and the Pharmaceutical and Medical Agency (PMDA) in Japan are open to the submission of genomics data on a voluntary basis. However, they currently preclude basing regulatory decision-making on genomics data alone. Currently, the US FDA and EMA are considering using submissions data for populating relevant comparative databases, including traditional toxicological data. The Critical Path Initiative (CPI), which was launched by the US FDA in March 2004, follows the mission to facilitate drug development [84]. As stated in the CPI's "Challenges and Opportunities Report" "proteomic and toxicogenomics approaches may ultimately provide sensitive and predictive safety assessment techniques" [85]. Thus, toxicogenomics is seen as a key possibility to improve scientific processes during preclinical drug development.

The FDA has also invested in several MicroArray Quality Control (MAQC) projects: (1) MAQC-I, which addressed the reliability of microarray technology as well as the standardization of laboratory techniques and data analysis methods [86]; (2) MAQC-II, which assessed the opportunities and limitations of microarray-derived predictive models, including development and validation strategies [87]; and (3) MAQC-III, which benchmarked RNA-seq data for the assessment of RNA-sequencing technologies and data analysis methods [88].

It is of major interest to generate as much reliable data as possible to build a complete picture of the mechanism and the risk a novel drug candidate presents. Therefore, improved risk assessment is an essential aim of using toxicogenomic technologies. The potential to enhance understanding of the underlying mechanism, the dose–response relationships, exposure quantification, cross-species extrapolations, and the basis of individual susceptibilities to particular compounds are some of the new opportunities attributable to toxicogenomic studies.

However, even if these technologies have strong potential to affect decision-making, they are no yet ready to replace existing testing systems in regulatory toxicology and risk assessment.

EXAMPLES FOR THE USE OF TOXICOGENOMICS IN PRECLINICAL TOXICOLOGY

During preclinical drug discovery the application of toxicogenomics to study adverse effects on function and structure of an organism's genome in response to xenobiotics has become common practice. Today, toxicogenomics is not limited to in vivo, ie, using animals, but has also been successfully applied to established in vitro systems. Although it is important to stress that most toxicogenomics outcomes resulting from in vitro experiments cannot be seen as a solid evidence for the in vivo situation [89]. In general, in vitro models have been mainly applied to the identification of distinct gene expression signatures, which are suggestive of a general pathophysiologic manifestation [90]. Despite the fact that in vitro systems are often criticized for lack of predictive value a lot of data derives from these kinds of studies (including cell lines, primary cell cultures, and organ cultures) [91]. This is probably due to the numerous advantages that in vitro studies possess. In vivo studies are time- and cost-consuming, and a relatively large amount of test compound is needed, making the in vivo approach inappropriate for the evaluation of the high number of drug candidates in the earlier phases of drug discovery. By contrast, in vitro systems are time- and cost-effective and only small quantities of substance are required. Additionally, most in vitro experiments examine cells isolated from the whole-organ system, potentially easing the complicated interpretation of data. The implementation of in vitro systems also contributes to the "Three Rs" principal proposed by Russell and Burch [92].

When working with in vitro systems it is important to keep in mind that adverse effects often occur in distinct organs, thus making the choice of the applied in vitro system essential for the correct outcome [93]. Additionally, interindividual differences should be expected once human material (eg, primary human hepatocytes) is utilized in experiments, because of the high genetic variability among donors [94].

Nonetheless, there are still issues to be addressed in order to move these technologies forward. First, data storage requirements, especially since the utilization of microarrays for global gene expression analysis and NGS generate huge amounts of complex data. Second, evaluation of toxicogenomics data, for this step a standardized procedure is needed, because different bioinformatics approaches may very likely affect the result of differentially expressed genes and thus, the interpretation of the data—the used data analysis method represents a crucial detail when mechanisms of actions are being analyzed. Third, building of data repositories, by making these repositories open to the public, since shared experiences facilitate the use of toxicogenomics data and hence improve our understanding of biological relationships and toxicities. There are several data repositories publicly available, namely NCBI's Gene Expression Omnibus (GEO) and EMBL-EBI's ArrayExpress, although neither is tailored specifically for toxicological issues. The more useful databases that focus on toxicological concerns are the manually curated Comparative Toxicogenomics Database (CTD) [95] and the TG GATEs (Genomics-Assisted Toxicity Evaluation System) of the Japanese National Institute of Biomedial Innovation (NIBIO) [96]. Databases consisting of gene expression profiles with well-known toxic and nontoxic compounds would allow the rapid screening of uncharacterized compounds, ie, using these databases as prediction models, with several examples being published over the past few years [97–101].

Genotoxicity

The genotoxic potential of a pharmaceutical has become an indispensable piece of information for regulatory authorities all over the world. If the toxicological data reveals a compound's hazard in respect to DNA damage, ie, genotoxicity, this drug will be unlikely to advance further in any medical indications other than oncology. Standard genotoxicity testing for new chemical entities consists of in vivo and/or in vitro experiments that are covered by the current International Conference on Harmonisation (ICH) guideline S2(R1) [102]. Overall, the general term genotoxicity covers a variety of underlying mechanisms. In principle, DNA damage and its fixation can occur on the level of the nucleotides (gene mutations), the chromosomes (structural or numerical changes), and the nucleus (micronucleus formation due to clastogenicity or aneugenicity). However, the recommended standard test battery still fails to detect some genotoxic carcinogens in both in vitro and in vivo assays, often due to inappropriate metabolism and toxicokinetic properties of the used systems [93].

In this context toxicogenomics has already proven to be a useful tool for the detection of genotoxicity in vivo and in vitro. Le Fevre et al. [103] conducted in vitro experiments and identified 28 marker genes by which a discrimination between genotoxic and nongenotoxic anticancer drugs was feasible. A general and recurring finding in the literature is the identification of genes and pathways that are commonly deregulated by genotoxic carcinogens and agents [104–107], hence allowing a gene expression profiling (modeling) approach to classify novel compounds according to their mechanism of action [108–110]. Notably, a cross-validation study performed by the Carcinogenicity Working Group of CPI's Predictive Safety Testing Consortium (PSTC) demonstrated the robustness of gene expression data by comparing gene signatures built at two different sites, even using different microarray platforms [111].

Organotoxicity

Hepatotoxicity

During clinical phases a high percentage of new molecules fail due to unacceptable liver toxicity, which is still the leading cause of drug failures and market withdrawals [112]. As the main drug-metabolizing organ, the liver is the first tissue to encounter most xenobiotics and their metabolic products in high concentrations. The principal cell type in terms of quantity and endogenous metabolizing capacity are hepatocytes, which account for 80% of the liver volume, hence making this organ extremely homogenous. This homogenicity is quite an important aspect when it comes to toxicogenomic approaches, because it guarantees that gene expression derives from a relatively consistent tissue composite and data interpretation is therefore simplified.

Several research groups have shown that short-term rodent experiments during preclinic development deliver gene expression profiles useful to identify adverse changes in the liver prior to their detection with classical toxicological methods (eg, histopathology) [113–115].

Roth et al. [100] reported on the cessation of the development program for a compound series due to early prediction of liver toxicity, which was revealed by means of gene expression analysis. Their tentative conclusion was that considering in vivo hepatotoxicity prediction (eg, in short-term rodent experiments), including mechanistic information deriving from relevant in vitro experiments, indicated potential human relevance.

In vitro approaches are continuously in focus for their potential to refine, reduce, or even replace in vivo experiments during earlier phases of the drug development process. Numerous successes have been reported. For example, a preliminary pilot study using long-term primary rat hepatocytes and gene expression analysis, where a computer-based discrimination model allowed the classification of hepatotoxicants with a low misclassification rate of 7.5% [99].

Many attempts have been reported to prove the value of in vitro experiments using hepatic cell lines including toxicogenomics [89], primary hepatocytes [89,116,117], or liver slices [89,118,119].

The FDA's CPI considers drug-induced liver injury (DILI) a crucial area where knowledge has to be provided in order to bring forward compound classification according to its toxicity and biomarker identification. With regard to this aspect, the Liver Toxicity Knowledge Database (LTKB) project was funded, which basically aims to collate and release a benchmark dataset. This drug list can be used to assess a drug's DILI potential and to support the evaluation of existing and development of novel biomarkers found by toxicogenomics technologies [120]. A further initiative in the field of DILI, launched in February 2012, is the MIP-DILI (Mechanism-based Integrated systems for the Prediction of Drug-Induced Liver Injury) project. Here, the aim is the development of a nonclinical testing strategy, which reveals drug candidates holding reduced potential to cause DILI in humans [121].

Nephrotoxicity

The kidney is one of the major target organs routinely assessed in preclinical toxicity studies. The routine assessment of renal injury is, besides histopathological observation, the measurement of the two blood analytes, serum creatinine, and blood urea nitrogen (BUN). These two parameters are also the gold standard in clinical trials to monitor dialyzed patients. However, it is well known that these functional parameters lack any specificity because several nonrenal-related causes can alter their blood level, such as shock, dehydration, or congestive heart failure. In addition, the sensitivity of these markers is relatively low, and acute kidney injury (AKI), for example, cannot normally be recognized by these parameters.

In the last few decades several initiatives and consortia have addressed this lack of specificity and sensitivity of serum creatinine and BUN. The first project addressing nephrotoxicity by using toxicogenomics approaches was the ILSI/HESI-Nephrotoxicity Working Group of the HESI Application of Genomics to Mechanism-Based Risk Assessment Technical Committee founded in 1999. The aim of the project group was to identify renal-specific biomarkers on the transcriptional and protein level by microarray analysis. Therefore, gene expression data were generated from three rat toxicity studies with three well-described model compounds (gentamicin, cisplatin, and puromycin) and in addition compared with traditional histopathology and clinical–chemical parameters [122–124]. Many altered transcripts in relation to drug-induced nephrotoxicity were identified, including Havcr1, Clu, Spp1, and Lcn2. Subsequently, continued work by the PSTC finally led to the first qualification process of novel identified biomarkers. The project members, consisting of world-leading pharmaceutical companies and public institutions under the roof of the US FDA, aimed to validate novel nephrotoxicity biomarkers and methods to enhance the usefulness of routine preclinical safety testing.

The nephrotoxicity working group investigated eight nephrotoxic compounds as well as two hepatotoxic compounds that served as negative controls. As a result 23 potential urinary protein biomarkers (some of them were also deregulated on gene expression level) and many transcriptional biomarkers were validated. After the qualification process that followed 7 out of the 23 urinary biomarkers were qualified by the FDA, EMA, and PMDA for their use in acute rat toxicity studies up to 14 days [125].

Many other projects, like Innomed/PredTox [126] and the Toxicogenomics Project in Japan (TG-GATE [96]), focused on the systematic identification and validation of transcriptional biomarkers with slightly different scientific approaches. The latter was a 5-year collaboration project started in 2002 with the National Institute of Health Science and 17 Japanese pharmaceutical companies, which only focused on toxicogenomics (transcriptomics) technologies, with the aim to elucidate the interrelationship between gene expression changes and toxicants and to build a publicly available database and prediction models. Approximately 150 chemicals were used to generate gene expression profiles from rats (in vivo; kidney and liver) and rat/human primary hepatocytes. Out of these data computer-based

prediction models have been built, including the prediction of nephrotoxicity [127].

Cardiotoxicity

Cardiovascular disease represents the major cause of death in high-income countries [128], while cardiotoxicity is one of the most common reasons for delays in regulatory approval and why drugs are withdrawn from the market. The preclinical assessment of drug-induced cardiotoxicity includes mainly in vivo models, ex vivo systems, and in vitro approaches. Typical gold-standard ex vivo models include Langendorff-perfused explanted hearts, preparations of papillary muscles, and Purkinje fibers, all of which are time-consuming and of low throughput. The QT interval, representing the de- and repolarization time of both ventricles, is a readout parameter assessed during preclinical drug discovery. Overall, QT-interval prolongation is a risk factor linked to tachycardia and potentially to the life-threatening Torsade de Pointes [129]. There are various methods used to examine adverse effects on the physiological QT interval, eg, direct in vivo monitoring of the interval (derivable from ECG), ex vivo experimentation on isolated Purkinje fibers in order to examine the cardiac action potential duration, and hERG expressing cell lines to determine any compromising or inhibitory effect on this specific (and important) potassium ion channel.

The implementation of toxicogenomics in this field of organotoxicity does not appear to be as prominent as for the other target organs described previously. However, gene expression analysis was reported to be applied to prioritize compounds prior to the performance of time- and cost-consuming experiments [130].

Mori Y et al. [131] conducted microarray analysis on cardiac tissues from rats treated with prototypical cardiotoxicants, and was able to reveal potential genomic biomarkers. The application of a high-throughput quantitative real-time PCR (Taqman chemistry) in an in vivo experiment using 56 marker genes selected from literature data allowed the detection of early gene expression changes that could be used to predict organ-specific adverse responses, including cardiotoxicity [132]. In this example, adverse effects on the heart were revealed for the antiinflammatory drug sulfasalazine and the chemotherapeutic substance doxorubicin. Doxorubicin is well known for its cardiotoxicity and effected gene expression alterations in a dose-dependent manner. Doxorubicin-induced cardiomyopathy was also analyzed by Shuai et al. [133] who described how Metallothionein protects against cardiotoxicity by applying gene expression analysis. Furthermore, a toxicogenomics approach unveiled specific genes alterations that were involved in the development of cardiac dysfunction [134]. Nishimura et al. [135] built a multigene model based on eight genes identified as genomic biomarker candidates for cardiotoxicity in rats. Their multigene model proved to be more predictive for cardiotoxicity compared to traditional approaches. Overall, the application of toxicogenomics in the field of cardiotoxicology appears to show some potential to predict a toxic insult when there is still no pathological readout.

Idiosyncrasy

Idiosyncratic toxicity can be described as an unpredictable characteristic adverse reaction of an individual and is a major issue in all phases of clinical drug development. Idiosyncratic drug toxicities usually occur in only a small proportion of individuals who are exposed to therapeutic doses of a pharmaceutical, hence appearing not until a vast number of patients have been exposed to the compound (ie, in Phase III or postmarketing). The latter being the reason idiosyncratic drug reactions are the most frequent cause for postmarketing (black box) warnings and withdrawals. It has been estimated that over 10% of acute liver failures are due to idiosyncratic hepatotoxicity. Notably, in the majority of cases routine animal toxicity investigations during preclinical safety assessment failed to uncover such risks. As a general rule an idiosyncratic reaction is not related to the pharmaceutical target of the drug and even though the underlying mechanisms are not fully understood there is a general consensus that genetic and environmental factors account for these adverse reactions [136].

The application of toxicogenomics in this field seems difficult, and has limited utility. Certainly, gene expression analysis allows the exploration of genetic factors, but the functional interaction among individuals and the study of environmental factors is not possible with this technology alone. There are various hypotheses describing underlying mechanisms that lead to idiosyncratic drug reactions, eg, the "Hapten Hypothesis" [137,138], the "Danger Hypothesis" [139], and the "Pharmacological Interaction Hypothesis" [140].

Leone et al. [141] were able to detect reactive metabolite formation and oxidative stress occurrence by gene expression analysis along with the assessment of hepatic covalent binding. A different approach was undertaken by Shaw et al. [142] who utilized cotreated mice with trovafloxacin or levofloxacin with lipopolysaccharide, the latter to render the animal more sensitive to known idiosyncratic hepatotoxic compounds. In fact this group was able to identify altered expression of gene clusters prior to the onset of liver injury, notably only in those animals treated with the antibiotic trovafloxacin, which caused idiosyncratic hepatotoxicity in humans.

Generally, the evaluation of in vivo transcriptomics changes caused by drugs with an idiosyncratic risk versus those without such a risk holds the potential to better understand the underlying mechanisms leading to adverse events. Thus, assessment of a patient's genotype might help to determine if a person is at risk of an idiosyncratic drug reaction [143].

SPECIFIC APPLICATIONS OF TOXICOGENOMICS

Initial expectations of this newly evolved technology, especially transcriptomics, was certainly excessively optimistic. Nonetheless, there has been significant progress in its implementation in traditional drug-safety assessment.

Mechanistic Information

Knowledge about how a compound exerts its pharmacological and toxicological effect, and how to distinguish between these two, is of considerable importance. There are many difficulties to consider with the elucidation of relevant mechanistic information, eg, the determination of time and doses at which changes are meaningful, since both variables have an impact on the validity of the drug response [144]. Furthermore, the fact that for a given time point there might be more than one relevant mode of action (on-target and off-target effects) and depending on the applied experimental design only weak conclusions might be drawn. Toxicogenomics allows a global and therefore unbiased approach, potentially strengthening the mechanistic conclusions. It has to be kept in mind that the gene expression profile also resembles only a snapshot in time.

A promising strategy is the use of transcript profiles, which based on the identification of common mechanisms, help to classify substances according to their specific toxicity. The generation of databases containing expression profiles or gene expression signature sets is an often addressed strategy. Genes identified by mechanistic analysis can also be used to build a prediction model(s). In order to obtain a valuable prediction tool it is important to generate these signatures within the database on an extensive training set of reference compounds [145]. Overall, knowledge of the molecular/toxicological mechanisms of a compound is of valuable benefit throughout preclinical development and toxicogenomics facilitates the discovery of such information.

Risk Assessment

The mechanistic understanding of a new drug's toxic liability has become more important for the risk-assessment process [144]. Toxicogenomics in isolation is generally insufficient for a comprehensive risk assessment, but working together with pathologists and toxicologists these changes in gene expression can be put in a meaningful context [146].

Variability in Susceptibility

A large variety of responses to treatments is to be expected as patients are not all identical. This becomes clear especially when looking at underlying genotypes leading to corresponding phenotypes. A well-studied example is the metabolic capacity, which varies between individuals and can be ascribed to inherited genomes and/or frequently occurring SNPs. The different metabolic phenotypes can be classified as poor, intermediate, extensive, and ultrarapid. For most drugs this knowledge is essential since the parent compound will accumulate in poor metabolizers, potentially leading to detrimental toxicities. In contrast, in extensive or ultrarapid metabolizers the plasma-level concentration of the drug will probably not reach therapeutically relevant levels because the compound is metabolized and excreted too quickly after uptake. As previously described in the "Genotyping" section these genotypic variations can be identified by different technologies, thus giving the opportunity to understand potential individual differences in metabolic activity prior to a patient receiving a drug.

Infants are also very susceptible to differing genotypes/phenotypes. During clinical phases the drug is applied to healthy volunteers (Phase I), selected patients (Phase II), and finally a large group of patients (Phase III), usually employing only adults. Furthermore, some diseases affecting children do not have adult counterparts [147]. The application of toxicogenomics in this area can highlight understanding of the genetic background, which helps to improve drug treatment in children. Importantly, gene expression signatures of a pediatric disease can be specific to an assigned point in time, whereas it has to be taken into account that the process of human development changes in a rapid manner. A major shortcoming in this area is the accessibility of high-quality biological material at corresponding phases of development for gene expression analysis [147].

Cross-Species Extrapolation

One of the most basic and essential issues pharmaceutical industries consistently face in preclinical phases is the question of whether the assessed safety profile reflects the risk to exposed human. In general, extrapolation from one species to another is a major obstacle for drug development, and is also the reason regulatory guidelines specify the use of at least two different species, usually rat (rodents) and dog (nonrodents) in toxicological studies.

Therefore, it makes sense that conserved orthologous genes between humans and the test-animal species build confidence in extrapolating results. This is also true for conserved pathways and networks as well as individual genes [148].

STUDY DESIGN OF TOXICOGENOMICS APPROACHES IN PRECLINICAL TOXICOLOGY

In pharmaceutical toxicological studies, strict guidelines dictate routine methods to be used. The animal species and strains are used to match the scientific questions in the most appropriated way. However, toxicogenomics methods do not necessarily have the same requirements as these traditional toxicology methods. Therefore, it is of crucial importance to plan and design a toxicogenomics approach that will give optimum data quality and meaning. Fig. 34.10 gives an overview of the individual steps of planning a toxicogenomics approach and important points to address while analyzing the data. The first important step is to choose the right model and to define the experimental approach. It can make a difference if the evaluation of the gene expression pattern is included in a routine toxicology study with multiple endpoints or if it is an experiment especially designed and performed for gene expression analysis. Independent of the model used or the experimental setup, group sizes have to be defined depending of the expected outcome. For example, if a toxicological outcome can be influenced by interindividual variations or certain important genes are expected to increase only slightly, a higher number of replicates maybe required. Consequently, it is important to plan a matched control for each treatment condition because a small change in the experimental setup can have a strong impact on the gene expression. One key parameter is the planning of sample collection and preparation. Because RNAs are normally very susceptible to degradation by RNase, heat, and shear forces, steps have to be taken to protect RNAs against degradation. In addition, samples collected for routine methods normally cannot be used for toxicogenomics approaches. Blood samples collected in ethylenediaminetetraacetic acid (EDTA) columns, for example, cannot be used for gene expression analysis because of a decrease in RNA yield and significant changes of the gene expression pattern [149]. Formalin-fixed tissue can also not usually be used (at least using standard gene expression techniques) because of covalent cross-links formed between formalin and intracellular molecules (see the section Formalin-Fixed, Paraffin-Embedded Tissue). Generally, microarrays are the best choice for almost all toxicogenomics approaches, but they still have the disadvantage that they generate hypotheses-driven results. This disadvantage is being overcome by using sequencing technologies.

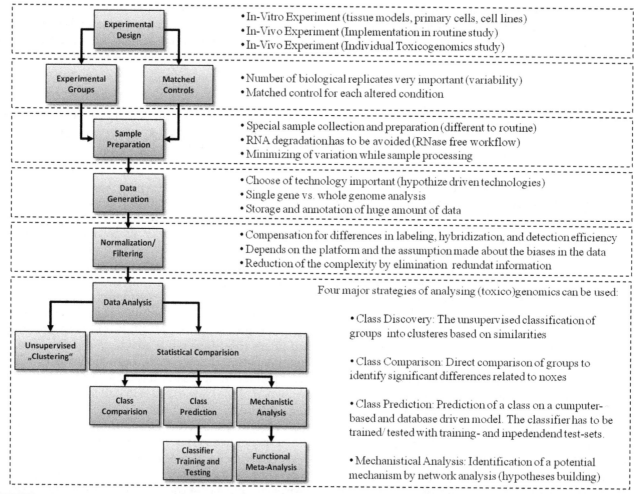

FIGURE 34.10 An overview of a scientific toxicogenomics approach in preclinical drug development. The study design, from the experimental test system (in vivo, in vitro), the grouping (number of replicates, definition of control groups) to sample collection/preparation (choice of biological matrix and additionally needed reagents/devices), and data generation (hypothesis driven/amount of data/information needed) is shown. The major focus is on the data analysis because of the complexity of toxicogenomics data generated. Statistical analysis needs to be planned from the beginning to avoid strong impacts of external sources or the study design.

Since no gene/transcript specific probe is used, the generated gene expression data does not reflect the expected transcripts only but all information available. The consequence of these new technologies is a significant increase in complexity in data analysis and storage requirements. By using real-time PCR-based methods or by designing customized arrays, this disadvantage can also be circumvented. As a consequence the number of transcripts that can be studied in parallel is more limited. However, since the MAQC Project, it is clear that different platforms deliver reliable and comparable results, giving confidence in each technology chosen. For the analysis several bioinformatics software tools (open-source/commercial) are available and described elsewhere. There are fundamental differences regarding functionality, usability, cycles for updates, statistical normalization, and connect databases. However, in the end it is a question of preferences and historically experience to determine which software to use.

FUTURE PERSPECTIVES

MicroRNA

The field of microRNA (miRNA) research is a rapidly expanding area in all bioscience-related fields, including toxicology. miRNAs are small, ~22-nucleotide long, noncoding regulatory nucleic acids with a central role in regulation of gene expression, by posttranscriptional silencing or degradation of mRNA species. The study of miRNAs in oncology is a well-established methodology, but in toxicology the first approaches only began in the last few years. It is well known that miRNAs are involved in many processes of vertebrate development but also in upcoming and established diseases [150]. To date, several miRNAs have been described to show altered expression patterns for specific compound-induced toxicities. For example, the miRNA let-7C seems to be involved in hepatocyte proliferation in mice after treatment with Wy14643, a peroxisome proliferator-activated receptor alpha (PPARα) agonist [151]. The miRNAs miR-298, -370, -192, and -122 were shown to be involved in acetaminophen-induced hepatotoxicity [152,153]. In hexahydro-1,2,3-trinitro-1,2,3-triazine-induced neurotoxicity miRNA-206, -30, and -195 seem to play a role by targeting the brain-derived neurotrophic factors [154]. For cisplatin-induced nephrotoxicity miRNA-34a was shown to be induced via p53-driven apoptosis [155].

Beside the important role in regulation of gene expression, miRNAs have some additional benefits. One of the most notable advantages is the high stability compared to other RNA-species. This stability makes it possible to isolate circulating miRNAs from plasma. Even urine-derived miRNAs can be used to assess specific organ injuries (eg, those shown by Yang and colleagues [156]). In this approach urinary miRNA profiles were derived from rats treated with acetaminophen (hepatotoxicant), carbon tetrachloride (hepatotoxicant), and penicillin (nonhepatotoxicant). Several significantly altered miRNAs were identified and were dependent on the liver insult.

However, beside the potential benefits of miRNA, the role they play in toxicological processes is not yet understood. Since a single miRNA can interact with numerous mRNA species and several different miRNA can interact often in combination, the regulatory network is very complex [157]. To discover these networks combinations of toxicogenomic technologies have to be used to get a clearer picture of the interactions. Because miRNAs regulate protein expression, a combination of mRNA and miRNA evaluation could potentially be a better predictor of drug toxicity. For the well-studied chemical benzo[a]pyrene, a comprehensive data integration of mRNA–miRNA–circRNA has already shown novel insights into mechanisms of benzo[a]pyrene-induced carcinogenicity [158].

Next-Generation Sequencing

The possibility of determining the whole genome, including DNA (gDNA, mDNA) and RNA species (mRNA, miRNA, rRNA), copy number variation (CNV), single nucleotide polymorphisms (SNPs) as well as different posttranslational modifications such as methylation or phosphorylation will aid in the acceleration of toxicogenomic research in the future and be able to cover a wide range of relevant biological processes using a single platform [159]. This holistic approach is the key benefit of next-generation sequencing (NGS) technology. Integration of the information from different molecular levels and therefore from different levels in the response cascade can negate the inherent disadvantages of traditional toxicogenomics approaches. The hope is that this will enhance both the specificity and selectivity of the

model system and ultimately lead to a better understanding of the biological context.

There are still some major disadvantages of this technology that have to be solved before NGS will be accepted for routine use in toxicology. One major hurdle is still the high cost of NGS (compared to the costs of real-time PCR and microarrays), and as a consequence limits the number of samples that can be assessed by this technology. This has a greater impact on toxicological studies where many samples are usually generated (multiple time points, multiple doses, etc.). The second challenge lies in the complexity and the enormous volume of data and information generated by these methods. On one hand, this makes it necessary to establish new systems and routines of data storage and handling, and on the other hand, requires the development of new algorithms, visualization tools, and data analysis software to enable a more sophisticated view of toxicological mechanism.

Formalin-Fixed, Paraffin-Embedded Tissue

In pharmaceutical and chemical toxicological safety departments a huge number of tissue samples have been collected and stored. In routine toxicology animal studies, organs and tissues are collected, fixed in formalin to avoid autolysis, and placed in paraffin blocks to enable long-term storage. For histopathological observation, the organs need to be stabilized to allow slices to be cut, enabling the microscopic evaluation of potential toxicologically relevant changes. These tissue blocks can be stored in the company archives for several decades. However, from a toxicogenomics perspective, the fixation step leads to excessive cross-links between cellular membranes, proteins, and nucleic acids, which on one hand is essential to preserve the tissue, but on the other hand makes the whole tissue more or less useless for routine toxicogenomics approaches. Because of a significant decrease in the RNA yield and quality, novel strategies have to be used to isolate and process the RNA from FFPE tissues. Currently there are several providers offering methods and technologies to assess gene expression profiles from FFPE tissue. So far, these technologies have been used primarily for clinical samples, where fresh (or frozen) tissues are not easily accessible. The most critical determining factor for usable RNA (and proteins) extracted from FFPE tissues is the time in formalin. Here, again shorter fixation times are usually ensured due to the need for immediate diagnosis. In routine toxicology studies, the fixation time can vary within and between studies, which can lead to a decrease in comparability or to the total failure of RNA extraction. Therefore, the most important issue for any potential use of FFPE tissues is a revision of the standard operation procedures and workflows used in toxicology labs, whereby the time a tissue is kept in formalin before embedding is kept to less than 1 week. The major benefit of using FFPE tissue revolves around the ability to perform retrospective evaluation of "old" samples. Samples from very old studies (reported to be up to 15–20 years old) could be used for the detection of novel biomarkers for an enhanced safety profile of a drug. In addition, they could be used for mechanistic analysis, if findings in later toxicological or even clinical studies suggest a potential unexpected toxicological problem. In general, all types of toxicogenomic analysis can be performed with FFPE tissue, negating the need for expensive tissue collection and storage procedures.

CONCLUSION

In the field of toxicology profound knowledge of the compound-induced adverse reactions on the molecular level is crucial. The discipline of toxicogenomics offers the opportunity to study gene expression changes in response to a toxic insult. Here we presented an overview of the importance of toxicogenomics in the context of preclinical drug development during which an expensive safety profile of a new drug candidate is assessed. Finally the core statements of this chapter can be summarized as follows:

- Global gene expression profiling is essential for the identification of novel, target-organ specific biomarkers.
- Toxicogenomics is now well established and used on a case-by-case basis, as with other standard techniques.
- A wide range of technologies allow various strategies to perform genomic analyses on a genome-wide, customized/preselected set or single-gene level.
- Global gene expression analyses are still mostly based on mRNA (transcript) analysis using microarray platforms.
- The overall aim of toxicogenomics is the systematic understanding of biological responses to a toxicant prior to their pathological manifestation.
- Toxicogenomics can be used for the generation of hypotheses for a specific toxicological outcome. However, in-depth understanding of mechanisms will always involve further downstream assays.
- Interpretation of toxicogenomic data is critical, and will need the combination of both bioinformatics experts as well as toxicological expert knowledge.
- Current obstacles in the area of genome-wide methodologies such as data storage and analysis are being solved by advances in storage media and biostatistics software tools, respectively.

- Organ-specific toxicities can be addressed by toxicogenomics.
- Use of genomics technologies is helping to reveal idiosyncratic toxicities, a problematic and prominent aspect during clinical development phases
- Generally, toxicogenomics helps to estimate/understand: (1) mechanistic information, (2) risk assessment, (3) variability in susceptibility, and (4) cross-species extrapolation.
- Future trends expanding the field of toxicogenomics include:
  - Toxicogenomics in drug development will probably be more focused on smaller subsets of genes and/or proteins.
  - The study of miRNAs, which was implemented in toxicology only recently, and holds great potential to reveal specific compound-induced toxicities by analysis of alterations in miRNA-expression patterns.
  - Next-generation sequencing is probably the most promising technology, because it allows a more holistic and therefore unbiased opportunity for data interpretation.
  - Feasibility to analyze the gene expression of archived FFPE tissues presents a possibility to gain valuable information of already conducted studies and to use this knowledge in a retrospective manner.

References

[1] Genome Online Database, https://gold.jgi.doe.gov.
[2] Lesko LJ, Woodcock J. Translation of pharmacogenomics and pharmacogenetics: a regulatory perspective. Nat Rev Drug Discov 2004;3:763–9.
[3] Lesko LJ, Salerno RA, Spear BB, Anderson DC, Anderson T, Brazell C, et al. Pharmacogenetics and pharmacogenomics in drug development and regulatory decision making: report of the first FDA-PWG-PhRMA-DruSafe Workshop. J Clin Pharmacol 2003;43:342–58.
[4] Nuwaysir EF, Bittner M, Trent J, Barrett JC, Afshari CA. Microarrays and toxicology: the advent of toxicogenomics. Mol Carcinog 1999;24:153–9.
[5] Fielden MR, Pearson C, Brennan R, Kolaja KL. Preclinical drug safety analysis by chemogenomic profiling in the liver. Am J Pharmacogenomics 2005;5:161–71.
[6] Pan Q, Shai O, Lee LJ, Frey BJ, Blencowe BJ. Deep surveying of alternative splicing complexity in the human transcriptome by high-throughput sequencing. Nat Genet 2008;40:1413–5.
[7] Sanger F, Nicklen S, Coulson AR. DNA sequencing with chain-terminating inhibitors. Proc Natl Acad Sci USA 1977;74:5463–7.
[8] Su Z, Li Z, Chen T, Li QZ, Fang H, Ding D, et al. Comparing next-generation sequencing and microarray technologies in a toxicological study of the effects of aristolochic acid on rat kidneys. Chem Res Toxicol 2011;24:1486–93.
[9] FDA's MicroArray Quality Control (MAQC), http://www.fda.gov/ScienceResearch/BioinformaticsTools/MicroarrayQualityControlProject/.
[10] Johansson I, Ingelman-Sundberg M. Genetic polymorphism and toxicology–with emphasis on cytochrome p450. Toxicol Sci 2011;120:1–13.

[11] Esteller M. Epigenetics in cancer. N Engl J Med 2008;358:1148–59.

[12] Koturbash I, Beland FA, Pogribny IP. Role of epigenetic events in chemical carcinogenesis–a justification for incorporating epigenetic evaluations in cancer risk assessment. Toxicol Mech Methods 2011;21:289–97.

[13] Klaassen CD, Lu H, Cui JY. Epigenetic regulation of drug processing genes. Toxicol Mech Methods 2011;21:312–24.

[14] Duarte JD. Epigenetics primer: why the clinician should care about epigenetics. Pharmacotherapy 2013;33:1362–8.

[15] Tang J, Xiong Y, Zhou HH, Chen XP. DNA methylation and personalized medicine. J Clin Pharm Ther 2014;39:621–7.

[16] Fragou D, Fragou A, Kouidou S, Njau S, Kovatsi L. Epigenetic mechanisms in metal toxicity. Toxicol Mech Methods 2011;21:343–52.

[17] Bibikova M, Fan JB. Genome-wide DNA methylation profiling. Wiley Interdiscip Rev Syst Biol Med 2010;2:210–23.

[18] Chomczynski P, Sacchi N. Single-step method of RNA isolation by acid guanidinium thiocyanate-phenol-chloroform extraction. Anal Biochem 1987;162:156–9.

[19] Illumina® TotalPrep™-96 RNA Amplification Kit, https://www.thermofisher.com/order/catalog/product/4393543.

[20] Banerjee M, Giri AK. Toxicogenomics: an overview with special reference to genetic and genomic approaches to the identification of toxic effects. In: General, applied and systems toxicology. John Wiley & Sons, Ltd; 2009.

[21] Binder H, Krohn K, Burden CJ. Washing scaling of GeneChip microarray expression. BMC Bioinformatics 2010;11:291.

[22] Applied Biosystems TaqMan® Array micro fluidic cards, http://www3.appliedbiosystems.com/cms/groups/mcb_support/documents/generaldocuments/cms_062836.pdf.

[23] TaqMan® OpenArray® Real-Time PCR Plates. https://www.thermofisher.com/de/de/home/life-science/pcr/real-time-pcr/real-time-pcr-assays/taqman-gene-expression/taqman-openarray-real-time-pcr-plates.html.

[24] Horn T, Chang CA, Urdea MS. Chemical synthesis and characterization of branched oligodeoxyribonucleotides (bDNA) for use as signal amplifiers in nucleic acid quantification assays. Nucleic Acids Res 1997;25:4842–9.

[25] Tsongalis GJ. Branched DNA technology in molecular diagnostics. Am J Clin Pathol 2006;126:448–53.

[26] Pachl C, Todd JA, Kern DG, Sheridan PJ, Fong SJ, Stempien M, et al. Rapid and precise quantification of HIV-1 RNA in plasma using a branched DNA signal amplification assay. J Acquir Immune Defic Syndr Hum Retrovirol 1995;8:446–54.

[27] Alter HJ, Sanchez-Pescador R, Urdea MS, Wilber JC, Lagier RJ, Di Bisceglie AM, et al. Evaluation of branched DNA signal amplification for the detection of hepatitis C virus RNA. J Viral Hepat 1995;2:121–32.

[28] QuantiGene® Plex 2.0 Assay – multiplex gene expression analysis, https://www.ebioscience.com/application/gene-expression.htm.

[29] QuantiGene® Plex DNA Assay – multiplex copy number analysis, https://www.ebioscience.com/application/gene-expression.htm.

[30] Raychaudhuri S, Stuart JM, Altman RB. Principal components analysis to summarize microarray experiments: application to sporulation time series. Pac Symp Biocomput 2000:455–66.

[31] Toronen P, Kolehmainen M, Wong G, Castren E. Analysis of gene expression data using self-organizing maps. FEBS Lett 1999;451:142–6.

[32] Tamayo P, Slonim D, Mesirov J, Zhu Q, Kitareewan S, Dmitrovsky E, et al. Interpreting patterns of gene expression with self-organizing maps: methods and application to hematopoietic differentiation. Proc Natl Acad Sci USA 1999;96:2907–12.

[33] Wang J, Delabie J, Aasheim H, Smeland E, Myklebost O. Clustering of the SOM easily reveals distinct gene expression patterns: results of a reanalysis of lymphoma study. BMC Bioinformatics 2002;3:36.

[34] Herrero J, Valencia A, Dopazo J. A hierarchical unsupervised growing neural network for clustering gene expression patterns. Bioinformatics 2001;17:126–36.

[35] Soukas A, Cohen P, Socci ND, Friedman JM. Leptin-specific patterns of gene expression in white adipose tissue. Genes Dev 2000;14:963–80.

[36] Wen X, Fuhrman S, Michaels GS, Carr DB, Smith S, Barker JL, et al. Large-scale temporal gene expression mapping of central nervous system development. Proc Natl Acad Sci USA 1998;95:334–9.

[37] Eisen MB, Spellman PT, Brown PO, Botstein D. Cluster analysis and display of genome-wide expression patterns. Proc Natl Acad Sci USA 1998;95:14863–8.

[38] Butte AJ, Kohane IS. Unsupervised knowledge discovery in medical databases using relevance networks. Proc AMIA Symp 1999:711–5.

[39] Kim SK, Lund J, Kiraly M, Duke K, Jiang M, Stuart JM, et al. A gene expression map for Caenorhabditis elegans. Science 2001;293:2087–92.

[40] Baggerly KA, Coombes KR, Hess KR, Stivers DN, Abruzzo LV, Zhang W. Identifying differentially expressed genes in cDNA microarray experiments. J Comput Biol 2001;8:639–59.

[41] Long AD, Mangalam HJ, Chan BY, Tolleri L, Hatfield GW, Baldi P. Improved statistical inference from DNA microarray data using analysis of variance and a Bayesian statistical framework. Analysis of global gene expression in Escherichia coli K12. J Biol Chem 2001;276:19937–44.

[42] Tusher VG, Tibshirani R, Chu G. Significance analysis of microarrays applied to the ionizing radiation response. Proc Natl Acad Sci USA 2001;98:5116–21.

[43] Brown MP, Grundy WN, Lin D, Cristianini N, Sugnet CW, Furey TS, et al. Knowledge-based analysis of microarray gene expression data by using support vector machines. Proc Natl Acad Sci USA 2000;97:262–7.

[44] Ramaswamy S, Tamayo P, Rifkin R, Mukherjee S, Yeang CH, Angelo M, et al. Multiclass cancer diagnosis using tumor gene expression signatures. Proc Natl Acad Sci USA 2001;98:15149–54.

[45] Theilhaber J, Connolly T, Roman-Roman S, Bushnell S, Jackson A, Call K, et al. Finding genes in the C2C12 osteogenic pathway by k-nearest-neighbor classification of expression data. Genome Res 2002;12:165–76.

[46] Golub TR, Slonim DK, Tamayo P, Huard C, Gaasenbeek M, Mesirov JP, et al. Molecular classification of cancer: class discovery and class prediction by gene expression monitoring. Science 1999;286:531–7.

[47] Bloom G, Yang IV, Boulware D, Kwong KY, Coppola D, Eschrich S, et al. Multiplatform, multisite, microarray-based human tumor classification. Am J Pathol 2004;164:9–16.

[48] Ellis M, Davis N, Coop A, Liu M, Schumaker L, Lee RY, et al. Development and validation of a method for using breast core needle biopsies for gene expression microarray analyses. Clin Cancer Res 2002;8:1155–66.

[49] Nguyen DV, Rocke DM. Tumor classification by partial least squares using microarray gene expression data. Bioinformatics 2002;18:39–50.

[50] Orr MS, Scherf U. Large-scale gene expression analysis in molecular target discovery. Leukemia 2002;16:473–7.

[51] Antoniadis A, Lambert-Lacroix S, Leblanc F. Effective dimension reduction methods for tumor classification using gene expression data. Bioinformatics 2003;19:563–70.

[52] Le QT, Sutphin PD, Raychaudhuri S, Yu SC, Terris DJ, Lin HS, et al. Identification of osteopontin as a prognostic plasma marker for head and neck squamous cell carcinomas. Clin Cancer Res 2003;9:59–67.

[53] Boulesteix AL, Tutz G, Strimmer K. A CART-based approach to discover emerging patterns in microarray data. Bioinformatics 2003;19:2465–72.

[54] Bammler T, Beyer RP, Bhattacharya S, Boorman GA, Boyles A, Bradford BU, et al. Standardizing global gene expression analysis between laboratories and across platforms. Nat Methods 2005;2:351–6.

[55] Dobbin KK, Beer DG, Meyerson M, Yeatman TJ, Gerald WL, Jacobson JW, et al. Interlaboratory comparability study of cancer gene expression analysis using oligonucleotide microarrays. Clin Cancer Res 2005;11:565–72.

[56] Irizarry RA, Warren D, Spencer F, Kim IF, Biswal S, Frank BC, et al. Multiple-laboratory comparison of microarray platforms. Nat Methods 2005;2:345–50.

[57] Larkin JE, Frank BC, Gavras H, Sultana R, Quackenbush J. Independence and reproducibility across microarray platforms. Nat Methods 2005;2:337–44.

[58] Shi L, Jones WD, Jensen RV, Harris SC, Perkins RG, Goodsaid FM, et al. The balance of reproducibility, sensitivity, and specificity of lists of differentially expressed genes in microarray studies. BMC Bioinformatics 2008;9(Suppl. 9):S10.

[59] Benjamini Y, Hochberg Y. Controlling the false discovery rate: a practical and powerful approach to multiple testing. J R Stat Soc Ser B 1995;57:289–300.

[60] Zeeberg BR, Feng W, Wang G, Wang MD, Fojo AT, Sunshine M, et al. GoMiner: a resource for biological interpretation of genomic and proteomic data. Genome Biol 2003;4:R28.

[61] Hosack DA, Dennis Jr G, Sherman BT, Lane HC, Lempicki RA. Identifying biological themes within lists of genes with EASE. Genome Biol 2003;4:R70.

[62] Doniger SW, Salomonis N, Dahlquist KD, Vranizan K, Lawlor SC, Conklin BR. MAPPFinder: using Gene Ontology and GenMAPP to create a global gene-expression profile from microarray data. Genome Biol 2003;4:R7.

[63] MetaCore™ toxicity analysis, http://lsresearch.thomsonreuters.com/pages/solutions/1/metacore.

[64] Ingenuity® pathway analyser, http://www.ingenuity.com/products.

[65] Comparative Toxicogenomics Database, www.ctdbase.org.

[66] Davis AP, Grondin CJ, LennonHopkins K, Saraceni-Richards C, Sciaky D, King BL, et al. The Comparative Toxicogenomics Database's 10th year anniversary: update 2015. Nucleic Acids Res 2014:D914–20.

[67] Friedman N, Linial M, Nachman I, Pe'er D. Using Bayesian networks to analyze expression data. J Comput Biol 2000;7:601–20.

[68] Imoto S, Kim S, Goto T, Miyano S, Aburatani S, Tashiro K, et al. Bayesian network and nonparametric heteroscedastic regression for nonlinear modeling of genetic network. J Bioinform Comput Biol 2003;1:231–52.

[69] Savoie CJ, Aburatani S, Watanabe S, Eguchi Y, Muta S, Imoto S, et al. Use of gene networks from full genome microarray libraries to identify functionally relevant drug-affected genes and gene regulation cascades. DNA Res 2003;10:19–25.

[70] Tamada Y, Kim S, Bannai H, Imoto S, Tashiro K, Kuhara S, et al. Estimating gene networks from gene expression data by combining Bayesian network model with promoter element detection. Bioinformatics 2003;19(Suppl. 2):ii227–236.

[71] Zou M, Conzen SD. A new dynamic Bayesian network (DBN) approach for identifying gene regulatory networks from time course microarray data. Bioinformatics 2005;21:71–9.

[72] Akutsu T, Miyano S, Kuhara S. Algorithms for identifying Boolean networks and related biological networks based on matrix multiplication and fingerprint function. J Comput Biol 2000;7:331–43.

[73] Soinov LA. Supervised classification for gene network reconstruction. Biochem Soc Trans 2003;(Pt 6):1497–502.

[74] Datta A, Choudhary A, Bittner ML, Dougherty ER. External control in Markovian genetic regulatory networks: the imperfect information case. Bioinformatics 2004;20:924–30.

[75] Hashimoto RF, Kim S, Shmulevich I, Zhang W, Bittner ML, Dougherty ER. Growing genetic regulatory networks from seed genes. Bioinformatics 2004;20:1241–7.

[76] Junker BH, Koschutzki D, Schreiber F. Exploration of biological network centralities with CentiBiN. BMC Bioinformatics 2006;7:219.

[77] Koschutzki D, Schreiber F. Centrality analysis methods for biological networks and their application to gene regulatory networks. Gene Regul Syst Bio 2008;2:193–201.

[78] Bushel PR, Hamadeh HK, Bennett L, Green J, Ableson A, Misener S, et al. Computational selection of distinct class- and subclass-specific gene expression signatures. J Biomed Inform 2002;35:160–70.

[79] Mundra P, Rajapakse J, Chetty M, Ngom A, Ahmad S. Support vector based t-score for gene ranking pattern recognition in bioinformatics, vol. 5265. Heidelberg: Springer Berlin; 2008. p. 144–53.

[80] Furlanello C, Serafini M, Merler S, Jurman G. Entropy-based gene ranking without selection bias for the predictive classification of microarray data. BMC Bioinformatics 2003;4:54.

[81] Atkinson AJ, Colburn WA, DeGruttola VG, DeMets DL, Downing GJ, Hoth DF, et al. Biomarkers and surrogate endpoints: preferred definitions and conceptual framework. Clin Pharmacol Ther 2001;69:89–95.

[82] Robinson S, Pool R, Giffin R, Forum on Drug Discovery, Development, and Translation, Institute of Medicine. Chapter 7: Qualifying biomarkers. Emerging safety science: workshop summary. Washington (DC): The National Academies Press; 2008.

[83] EMA. Innovation task force. 2009. http://www.ema.europa.eu/ema/index.jsp?curl=pages/regulation/general/general_content_000334.jsp.

[84] Critical path initiative, http://www.fda.gov/ScienceResearch/SpecialTopics/CriticalPathInitiative/ucm076689.htm.

[85] Innovation or stagnation: challenge and opportunity on the critical path to new medical products. U.S. Department of Health and Human Services. Food and Drug Administration; March 2004. http://www.fda.gov/downloads/ScienceResearch/SpecialTopics/CriticalPathInitiative/CriticalPathOpportunitiesReports/ucm113411.pdf.

[86] Shi L, Reid LH, Jones WD, Shippy R, Warrington JA, Baker SC, et al. The MicroArray Quality Control (MAQC) project shows inter- and intraplatform reproducibility of gene expression measurements. Nat Biotechnol 2006;24:1151–61.

[87] FDA's MicroArray Quality Control (MAQC), http://www.fda.gov/ScienceResearch/BioinformaticsTools/MicroarrayQualityControlProject/default.htm#MAQC-I.

[88] SEQC/MAQC-III Consortium. A comprehensive assessment of RNA-seq accuracy, reproducibility and information content by the Sequencing Quality Control Consortium. Nat Biotechnol 2014;32:903–14.

[89] Boess F, Kamber M, Romer S, Gasser R, Muller D, Albertini S, et al. Gene expression in two hepatic cell lines, cultured primary hepatocytes, and liver slices compared to the in vivo liver gene expression in rats: possible implications for toxicogenomics use of in vitro systems. Toxicol Sci 2003;73:386–402.

[90] Heinloth AN, Irwin RD, Boorman GA, Nettesheim P, Fannin RD, Sieber SO, et al. Gene expression profiling of rat livers reveals indicators of potential adverse effects. Toxicol Sci 2004;80:193–202.

[91] Pettit S, des Etages SA, Mylecraine L, Snyder R, Fostel J, Dunn 2nd RT, et al. Current and future applications of toxicogenomics: results summary of a survey from the HESI Genomics State of Science Subcommittee. Environ Health Perspect 2010;118:992–7.

[92] 3R-INFO-BULLETIN 7-March 1996. The three R's of Russel & Burch. 1959. http://www.forschung3r.ch/de/publications/bu7.html.

VIII. PREDICTIVE TOXICOLOGY, TOXICOMETABOLOMICS, TOXICOGENOMICS, AND IMAGING

[93] Ku WW, Bigger A, Brambilla G, Glatt H, Gocke E, Guzzie PJ, et al. Strategy for genotoxicity testing–metabolic considerations. Mutat Res 2007;627:59–77.

[94] Josse R, Dumont J, Fautrel A, Robin MA, Guillouzo A. Identification of early target genes of aflatoxin B1 in human hepatocytes, inter-individual variability and comparison with other genotoxic compounds. Toxicol Appl Pharmacol 2012;258:176–87.

[95] CTD, http://ctdbase.org/.

[96] TG-GATE, http://toxico.nibiohn.go.jp/english/.

[97] Dai X, He YD, Dai H, Lum PY, Roberts CJ, Waring JF, et al. Development of an approach for ab initio estimation of compound-induced liver injury based on global gene transcriptional profiles. Genome Inform 2006;17:77–88.

[98] Zidek N, Hellmann J, Kramer PJ, Hewitt PG. Acute hepatotoxicity: a predictive model based on focused illumina microarrays. Toxicol Sci 2007;99:289–302.

[99] Hrach J, Mueller SO, Hewitt P. Development of an in vitro liver toxicity prediction model based on longer term primary rat hepatocyte culture. Toxicol Lett 2011;206:189–96.

[100] Roth A, Boess F, Landes C, Steiner G, Freichel C, Plancher JM, et al. Gene expression-based in vivo and in vitro prediction of liver toxicity allows compound selection at an early stage of drug development. J Biochem Mol Toxicol 2011;25:183–94.

[101] Roemer M, Eichner J, Metzger U, Templin MF, Plummer S, Ellinger-Ziegelbauer H, et al. Cross-platform toxicogenomics for the prediction of nongenotoxic hepatocarcinogenesis in rat. PLoS One 2014;9:e97640.

[102] ICH Harmonised Tripartite Guideline, Guidance on Genotoxicity Testing and Data Interpretation for pharmaceuticals intended for human use, S2(R1), current step 4 version dated 9 November 2011. http://www.ich.org/fileadmin/Public_Web_Site/ICH_Products/Guidelines/Safety/S2_R1/Step4/S2R1_Step4.pdf.

[103] Le Fevre AC, Boitier E, Marchandeau JP, Sarasin A, Thybaud V. Characterization of DNA reactive and nonDNA reactive anticancer drugs by gene expression profiling. Mutat Res 2007;619:16–29.

[104] Ellinger-Ziegelbauer H, Stuart B, Wahle B, Bomann W, Ahr HJ. Characteristic expression profiles induced by genotoxic carcinogens in rat liver. Toxicol Sci 2004;77:19–34.

[105] Dickinson DA, Warnes GR, Quievryn G, Messer J, Zhitkovich A, Rubitski E, et al. Differentiation of DNA reactive and nonreactive genotoxic mechanisms using gene expression profile analysis. Mutat Res 2004;549:29–41.

[106] Amundson SA, Do KT, Vinikoor L, Koch-Paiz CA, Bittner ML, Trent JM, et al. Stress-specific signatures: expression profiling of p53 wild-type and -null human cells. Oncogene 2005;24:4572–9.

[107] Ellinger-Ziegelbauer H, Stuart B, Wahle B, Bomann W, Ahr HJ. Comparison of the expression profiles induced by genotoxic and nongenotoxic carcinogens in rat liver. Mutat Res 2005;575:61–84.

[108] van Delft JH, van Agen E, van Breda SG, Herwijnen MH, Staal YC, Kleinjans JC. Comparison of supervised clustering methods to discriminate genotoxic from nongenotoxic carcinogens by gene expression profiling. Mutat Res 2005;575:17–33.

[109] Ellinger-Ziegelbauer H, Gmuender H, Bandenburg A, Ahr HJ. Prediction of a carcinogenic potential of rat hepatocarcinogens using toxicogenomics analysis of short-term in vivo studies. Mutat Res 2008;637:23–39.

[110] Boehme K, Dietz Y, Hewitt P, Mueller SO. Genomic profiling uncovers a molecular pattern for toxicological characterization of mutagens and promutagens in vitro. Toxicol Sci 2011;122:185–97.

[111] Fielden MR, Nie A, McMillian M, Elangbam CS, Trela BA, Yang Y, et al. Interlaboratory evaluation of genomic signatures for predicting carcinogenicity in the rat. Toxicol Sci 2008;103:28–34.

[112] CPI – NCTR Project Summaries, http://www.fda.gov/downloads/ScienceResearch/SpecialTopics/CriticalPathInitiative/UCM249262.pdf.

[113] Heijne WH, Jonker D, Stierum RH, van Ommen B, Groten JP. Toxicogenomic analysis of gene expression changes in rat liver after a 28-day oral benzene exposure. Mutat Res 2005;575:85–101.

[114] Minami K, Saito T, Narahara M, Tomita H, Kato H, Sugiyama H, et al. Relationship between hepatic gene expression profiles and hepatotoxicity in five typical hepatotoxicant-administered rats. Toxicol Sci 2005;87:296–305.

[115] Uehara T, Kiyosawa N, Hirode M, Omura K, Shimizu T, Ono A, et al. Gene expression profiling of methapyrilene-induced hepatotoxicity in rat. J Toxicol Sci 2008;33:37–50.

[116] Kienhuis AS, van de Poll MC, Dejong CH, Gottschalk R, van Herwijnen M, Boorsma A, et al. A toxicogenomics-based parallelogram approach to evaluate the relevance of coumarin-induced responses in primary human hepatocytes in vitro for humans in vivo. Toxicol In Vitro 2009;23:1163–9.

[117] Black MB, Budinsky RA, Dombkowski A, Lecluyse EL, Ferguson SS, Thomas RS, et al. Cross-species comparisons of transcriptomic alterations in human and rat primary hepatocytes exposed to 2,3,7,8-tetrachlorodibenzo-p-dioxin. Toxicol Sci 2012;127:199–215.

[118] Elferink MG, Olinga P, Draaisma AL, Merema MT, Bauerschmidt S, Polman J, et al. Microarray analysis in rat liver slices correctly predicts in vivo hepatotoxicity. Toxicol Appl Pharmacol 2008;229:300–9.

[119] Elferink MG, Olinga P, van Leeuwen EM, Bauerschmidt S, Polman J, Schoonen WG, et al. Gene expression analysis of precision-cut human liver slices indicates stable expression of ADME-Tox related genes. Toxicol Appl Pharmacol 2011;253:57–69.

[120] Chen M, Vijay V, Shi Q, Liu Z, Fang H, Tong W. FDA-approved drug labeling for the study of drug-induced liver injury. Drug Discov Today 2011;16:697–703.

[121] MIP-DILI, http://www.mip-dili.eu/index.php?page=home.

[122] Amin RP, Vickers AE, Sistare F, Thompson KL, Roman RJ, Lawton M, et al. Identification of putative gene based markers of renal toxicity. Environ Health Perspect 2004;112:465–79.

[123] Kramer JA, Pettit SD, Amin RP, Bertram TA, Car B, Cunningham M, et al. Overview on the application of transcription profiling using selected nephrotoxicants for toxicology assessment. Environ Health Perspect 2004;112:460–4.

[124] Thompson KL, Afshari CA, Amin RP, Bertram TA, Car B, Cunningham M, et al. Identification of platform-independent gene expression markers of cisplatin nephrotoxicity. Environ Health Perspect 2004;112:488–94.

[125] Fuchs TC, Hewitt P. Preclinical perspective of urinary biomarkers for the detection of nephrotoxicity: what we know and what we need to know. Biomark Med 2011;5:763–79.

[126] Suter L, Schroeder S, Meyer K, Gautier JC, Amberg A, Wendt M, et al. EU framework 6 project: predictive toxicology (PredTox)–overview and outcome. Toxicol Appl Pharmacol 2011;252:73–84.

[127] Kondo C, Minowa Y, Uehara T, Okuno Y, Nakatsu N, Ono A, et al. Identification of genomic biomarkers for concurrent diagnosis of drug-induced renal tubular injury using a large-scale toxicogenomics database. Toxicology 2009;265:15–26.

[128] WHO: media centre, http://www.who.int/mediacentre/factsheets/fs310/en/index.html.

[129] Redfern WS, Carlsson L, Davis AS, Lynch WG, MacKenzie I, Palethorpe S, et al. Relationships between preclinical cardiac electrophysiology, clinical QT interval prolongation and torsade de pointes for a broad range of drugs: evidence for a provisional safety margin in drug development. Cardiovasc Res 2003;58:32–45.

[130] Hirakawa B, Jessen BA, Illanes O, de Peyster A, McDermott T, Stevens GJ. Toxicogenomic analysis of cardiotoxicity in rats. Genomics Insights 2008;1:3–13.

[131] Mori Y, Kondo C, Tonomura Y, Torii M, Uehara T. Identification of potential genomic biomarkers for early detection of chemically induced cardiotoxicity in rats. Toxicology 2010;271:36–44.

[132] Fabian G, Farago N, Feher LZ, Nagy LI, Kulin S, Kitajka K, et al. High-density real-time PCR-based in vivo toxicogenomic screen to predict organ-specific toxicity. Int J Mol Sci 2011;12:6116–34.

[133] Shuai Y, Guo J, Dong Y, Zhong W, Xiao P, Zhou T, et al. Global gene expression profiles of MT knockout and wild-type mice in the condition of doxorubicin-induced cardiomyopathy. Toxicol Lett 2011;200:77–87.

[134] Richard C, Ghibu S, Delemasure-Chalumeau S, Guilland JC, Des Rosiers C, Zeller M, et al. Oxidative stress and myocardial gene alterations associated with Doxorubicin-induced cardiotoxicity in rats persist for 2 months after treatment cessation. J Pharmacol Exp Ther 2011;339:807–14.

[135] Nishimura Y, Morikawa Y, Kondo C, Tonomura Y, Fukushima R, Torii M, et al. Genomic biomarkers for cardiotoxicity in rats as a sensitive tool in preclinical studies. J Appl Toxicol 2013;33:1120–30.

[136] Kaplowitz N. Idiosyncratic drug hepatotoxicity. Nat Rev Drug Discov 2005;4:489–99.

[137] Landsteiner K, Jacobs J. Studies on the sensitization of animals with simple chemical compounds. J Exp Med 1935;61:643–56.

[138] Parker CW, Deweck AL, Kern M, Eisen HN. The preparation and some properties of penicillanic acid derivatives relevant to penicillin hypersensitivity. J Exp Med 1962;115:803–19.

[139] Matzinger P. Tolerance, danger, and the extended family. Annu Rev Immunol 1994;12:991–1045.

[140] Pichler WJ. Pharmacological interaction of drugs with antigen-specific immune receptors: the p-i concept. Curr Opin Allergy Clin Immunol 2002;2:301–5.

[141] Leone AM, Kao LM, McMillian MK, Nie AY, Parker JB, Kelley MF, et al. Evaluation of felbamate and other antiepileptic drug toxicity potential based on hepatic protein covalent binding and gene expression. Chem Res Toxicol 2007;20:600–8.

[142] Shaw PJ, Ditewig AC, Waring JF, Liguori MJ, Blomme EA, Ganey PE, et al. Coexposure of mice to trovafloxacin and lipopolysaccharide, a model of idiosyncratic hepatotoxicity, results in a unique gene expression profile and interferon gamma-dependent liver injury. Toxicol Sci 2009;107:270–80.

[143] Uetrecht J. Idiosyncratic drug reactions: past, present, and future. Chem Res Toxicol 2008;21:84–92.

[144] Lord PG. Progress in applying genomics in drug development. Toxicol Lett 2004;149:371–5.

[145] Searfoss GH, Ryan TP, Jolly RA. The role of transcriptome analysis in preclinical toxicology. Curr Mol Med 2005;5:53–64.

[146] Irwin RD, Boorman GA, Cunningham ML, Heinloth AN, Malarkey DE, Paules RS. Application of toxicogenomics to toxicology: basic concepts in the analysis of microarray data. Toxicol Pathol 2004;32(Suppl. 1):72–83.

[147] Leeder JS. Translating pharmacogenetics and pharmacogenomics into drug development for clinical pediatrics and beyond. Drug Discov Today 2004;9:567–73.

[148] National Research Council. Application of toxicogenomics to cross-species extrapolation: A Report of a Workshop. Washington (DC): The National Academies Press; 2005.

[149] Rainen L, Oelmueller U, Jurgensen S, Wyrich R, Ballas C, Schram J, et al. Stabilization of mRNA expression in whole blood samples. Clin Chem 2002;48:1883–90.

[150] Kloosterman WP, Plasterk RH. The diverse functions of microRNAs in animal development and disease. Dev Cell 2006;11:441–50.

[151] Shah YM, Morimura K, Yang Q, Tanabe T, Takagi M, Gonzalez FJ. Peroxisome proliferator-activated receptor alpha regulates a microRNA-mediated signaling cascade responsible for hepatocellular proliferation. Mol Cell Biol 2007;27:4238–47.

[152] Fukushima T, Hamada Y, Yamada H, Horii I. Changes of microRNA expression in rat liver treated by acetaminophen or carbon tetrachloride–regulating role of micro-RNA for RNA expression. J Toxicol Sci 2007;32:401–9.

[153] Wang K, Zhang S, Marzolf B, Troisch P, Brightman A, Hu Z, et al. Circulating microRNAs, potential biomarkers for drug-induced liver injury. Proc Natl Acad Sci USA 2009;106:4402–7.

[154] Zhang B, Pan X. RDX induces aberrant expression of microRNAs in mouse brain and liver. Environ Health Perspect 2009;117:231–40.

[155] Bhatt K, Zhou L, Mi QS, Huang S, She JX, Dong Z. MicroRNA-34a is induced via p53 during cisplatin nephrotoxicity and contributes to cell survival. Mol Med 2010;16:409–16.

[156] Yang X, Greenhaw J, Shi Q, Su Z, Qian F, Davis K, et al. Identification of urinary microRNA profiles in rats that may diagnose hepatotoxicity. Toxicol Sci 2012;125:335–44.

[157] Lema C, Cunningham MJ. MicroRNAs and their implications in toxicological research. Toxicol Lett 2010;198:100–5.

[158] Caiment F, Gaj S, Claessen S, Kleinjans J. High-throughput data integration of RNA-miRNA-circRNA reveals novel insights into mechanisms of benzo[a]pyrene-induced carcinogenicity. Nucleic Acids Res 2015;43:2525–34.

[159] Lister R, Pelizzola M, Dowen RH, Hawkins RD, Hon G, Tonti-Filippini J, et al. Human DNA methylomes at base resolution show widespread epigenomic differences. Nature 2009;462:315–22.

35

Use of Imaging for Preclinical Evaluation

Z.J. Wang, T.-T.A. Chang, R. Slauter

MOLECULAR IMAGING TECHNOLOGY AND DRUG DEVELOPMENT

Drug development is a lengthy, high-risk, and costly process, which usually spans 10–15 years, following the established paradigms [1]. Drug companies currently have hundreds of thousands of potential drug compounds; however, using traditional discovery and development methods, less than 1 in every 10,000 will eventually enter the market as an FDA-approved treatment. The most recent techniques available for real-time molecular imaging (MI) of the disposition of drugs in the body provide a unique, early opportunity to identify which drugs will fail in the later stages of drug development, thereby improving the quality of

the molecules ultimately selected to move forward. This cutting-edge research area is so important that a separate chapter is dedicated to discovery imaging technologies in this book.

Molecular imaging technology is the visualization, characterization, and measurement of biological processes at the molecular and cellular levels in humans and other living systems. In the past decade, it has been increasingly recognized as an important preclinical and clinical research tool that can be used to speed up the long-term engagement of the drug development process [2]. This emerging field focuses on using noninvasive techniques to visualize anatomic structures and physiological activity, in both animal models in preclinical research and patients in clinical practice. Modern imaging assessments provide information about tissues by penetrating the living body via physical phenomena (see Fig. 35.1), such as magnetic field/radiofrequency (magnetic resonance imaging/MRI), X-rays (computed tomography/CT), high-frequency sound waves (ultrasound/US), optical (bioluminescence/fluorescence), gamma rays (single-photon emission computed tomography/SPECT), and annihilation twin photons from beta emission (positron-emission tomography/PET). These imaging techniques have been reengineered for use with small animals by pushing the resolution and sensitivity of each modality to its physical limit (see Fig. 35.1). The higher resolution and extreme sensitivity make imaging technology highly translational in the preclinical drug development process.

Noninvasive imaging technology can provide evidence of the in vivo biodistribution of imaging probes, confirm on-target biological activity, illustrate disease mechanisms, and validate the efficacy of drug treatment. Maximizing the collection of in vivo biological information during the preclinical phases of drug development can be highly valuable during the lead selection/optimization of promising drug candidates. The use of MI in these stages can provide critical information that was previously unavailable, or only available indirectly through the interpretation of long-term preclinical studies. The use of MI in preclinical drug development, when balanced with well-established and accepted practices, can significantly reduce both time and expense in the development of both small molecules and biologics. Several excellent review articles have been published on the general role of MI on the process of both translational and clinical drug development research [3,4]. In this chapter, we will explore the role of MI in preclinical drug discovery and novel solutions to improve the efficiency of the drug development process.

MULTIMODALITY IMAGING TECHNIQUES

Magnetic resonance imaging, SPECT, PET, CT, ultrasound, and optical imaging all generate sectional images that can be reconstructed into two-dimensional (2D) or three-dimensional (3D) images. For preclinical evaluations, the imaging technique must have a spatial resolution that is adequate for small animals, and enough sensitivity to detect biochemical events. Each technique has certain advantages and limitations; platform selection is dependent upon which techniques can provide the greatest complementary information toward answering a particular preclinical question. Using a combination of techniques on the same animal, such as PET/CT, SPECT/CT, and PET/MRI coregistration, can provide temporal pathophysiological information such as development of structural changes, progression, and resolution during disease treatment.

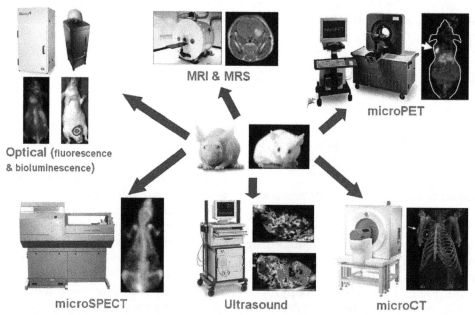

FIGURE 35.1 Multimodality imaging instrumentations. The modern MI equipment includes magnetic field/radiofrequency (magnetic resonance imaging/MRI), X-ray (computed tomography/CT), high-frequency sound waves (ultrasound/US), optical (bioluminescence/fluorescence), gamma rays (single-photon emission computed tomography/SPECT), and annihilation twin photons from beta emission (positron-emission tomography/PET). *Images are provided by MIPS, Stanford University.*

IMAGING PROBES AND BIOMARKERS

Molecular imaging probes are agents used to visualize, characterize, and measure biological processes in living systems. MI instrumentation, including MRI, CT, US, optical, SPECT, and PET, are tools that enable the visualization and quantification in space and over time of signals from MI probes. In preclinical research, diagnostic probes are administered in trace amounts and typically do not induce any physiological response or significant pharmaceutical effect in living systems.

Hundreds of MI probes, including radiolabeled small molecules and various biological macromolecules, have been developed and tested in preclinical research, and some are used in routine clinical practice [5]. A radiotracer can be defined as a specific radiolabeled molecule that monitors the in vivo behavior of a functional molecule, and can be used to provide biological information in a living system. The synthesis of a radiotracer generally includes radiolabeling of test article, purification of final product, testing specific activity, and analysis of in vivo stability. Commercially available MI probes and customized radiotracers for PET or SPECT imaging can be used to detect such things as cerebral blood flow, myocardial perfusion, glucose metabolism, infection, bone lesion, kidney function, apoptosis, angiogenesis, thyroid dysfunction, tumor detection, gene expression, neuroreceptor binding, and cell-trafficking processes [6].

FUNCTIONAL MOLECULAR IMAGING TECHNIQUES

The radiotracer approach used for PET and SPECT functional imaging is especially valuable in the early stages of drug discovery, where researchers can directly label a drug lead to determine its fate in the body. If the drug candidate does not distribute to its intended physiological target, as desired, it can be excluded from further development at an early stage. In addition, PET and SPECT imaging experiments can reveal molecular changes in tissues brought about by the drug. This is an extremely important capability, in view of the fact that changes on the molecular level occur long before becoming visible in any anatomic imaging. Such approaches allow the rank ordering of development candidates based on relevant physiological processes very early in development.

In vivo imaging techniques such as PET and SPECT provide a means of performing pharmacokinetic (PK) and pharmacodynamic (PD) studies in animal models without sacrificing the animal. With the introduction of dynamic and static imaging techniques, it is now possible to obtain high-resolution PET and SPECT images of "motion-frozen" time-points in PK and PD studies and to be able to quantify the amount of drug in the target organs of interest.

SINGLE-PHOTON EMISSION COMPUTED TOMOGRAPHY

Single-photon emission computed tomography (SPECT) cameras image individual high-energy photons, gamma rays, resulting from radionuclide decay. The technique requires injection of a gamma-emitting radioisotope into the subject. Radioisotopes can be bound to a test article (ligand) to enable the evaluation of its chemical binding properties. The radioisotope–ligand combination will bind to a place of interest in the body of the subject, and this can be detected by the gamma ray detectors, thus producing an image by computed tomography. For example, an imaging agent with affinity for areas of growing bone can be utilized to evaluate potential impact of a test article on the process of ossification (see Fig. 35.2).

The single-photon emissions radiate from the source in all directions with equal probability. Because of this, an aperture composed of highly attenuating material is required to identify the path of origin of each emission prior to being able to create an image with a gamma camera. In preclinical SPECT imaging, the most recently developed multipinhole collimator technology achieves submillimeter resolution in small animals.

Single-photon emission computed tomography can be used to complement any gamma imaging studies, such as in vivo biodistribution, tumor imaging, infection localization, bone growth, and cardiac gated imaging [7]. Single-photon emission computed tomography imaging on small animals offers high image resolution and sensitivity that can translate into human SPECT imaging in clinical practice. It also can provide both qualitative and quantitative measurements of physiological processes. The isotopes used for SPECT scan (ie, ^{123}I, ^{125}I, ^{99m}Tc, ^{111}In) are readily available and relatively inexpensive, with longer half-lives than those commonly used in PET imaging. The extended half-life of these isotopes translates to longer scan times and/or scanning periods without the need for secondary isotope administration. This means that smaller quantities of isotope are needed, as well as lower numbers of subjects—ie, more data are obtained, using fewer animals over a longer investigational period. Single-photon emission computed tomography imaging/isotopes also provide the ability to simultaneously image multiple radiopharmaceuticals of different energies (ie, ^{99m}Tc and ^{125}I). MicroSPECT functional imaging is able to coregister with a high-quality

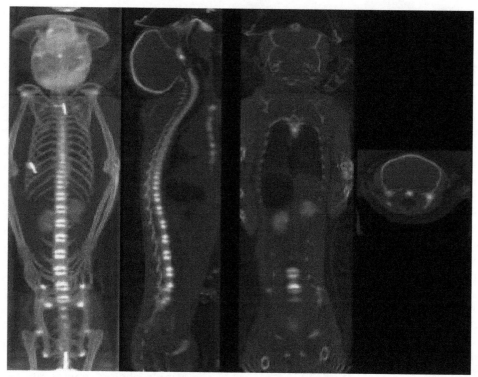

FIGURE 35.2   SPECT/CT images of NHP. This collection of images demonstrates SPECT/CT imaging of a nonhuman primate model (*Simia sciureus*, squirrel monkey). Isotope/Imaging parameters: 3 mCi of ^{99m}Tc-MDP; dose administration 75 min prior to SPECT scan initiation; SPECT scan duration of 56 min; CT scan duration of 25 min. *The image reconstruction and imaging data analysis are provided by MPI Research Inc. and inviCRO LLC.*

CT imaging framework for anatomical imaging comparison (see Fig. 35.3).

One disadvantage of SPECT imaging is the infrastructure and instrumentation cost, as well as the need for radioactive material handling and knowledgeable investigators to ensure that study designs will provide an adequate data set to meet their objectives. Although the molecular sensitivity of SPECT is almost one order of magnitude lower than that of PET, it continues to be widely used in both clinical practice and preclinical research, due to its advantages of lower cost, dual-labeled compounds, and relatively long half-life radionuclides, which allow lengthier monitoring periods of in vivo biological processes.

POSITRON-EMISSION TOMOGRAPHY

In positron-emission tomography (PET) imaging, a compound (a natural biological molecule or a small-molecule drug) labeled with a positron-emitting radioisotope is injected into the subject in nonpharmacological trace quantities. A positron ejected by a radionuclide combines with an electron in adjacent tissue to emit a pair of photons (511 keV) resulting from annihilation of a positron–electron pair. The PET scanner uses the annihilation coincidence detection (ACD)

method to obtain projection images of the location and amount of the radiolabeled compound in the living subject [8]. PET imaging technology can be used for drug distribution [9], organ perfusion, cell trafficking [10], tumor targeting, tumor metabolism/proliferation, tumor angiogenesis (see Fig. 35.4), tumor hypoxia, tumor apoptosis, tumor volume, anticancer therapeutic response [11], bone growth/healing, and disease mechanism studies in CNS and autoimmune disease animal models [12,13].

The advantages of this technique include high molecular sensitivity (nanomolar) with unlimited depth penetration. Its disadvantages include radiation safety and relatively high cost. Positron-emission tomography functional imaging is often combined with either microCT or animal MRI for better identification of functional change in deep tissue against anatomical structure in a living subject.

MICRO X-RAY COMPUTED TOMOGRAPHY

Computed tomography is an application of X-ray imaging that provides a 3D anatomical image [14]. In CT, X-rays are emitted from a source that rotates around the subject in the center of the CT scanner. A detector opposite

(A)   **(B)**   **(C)**

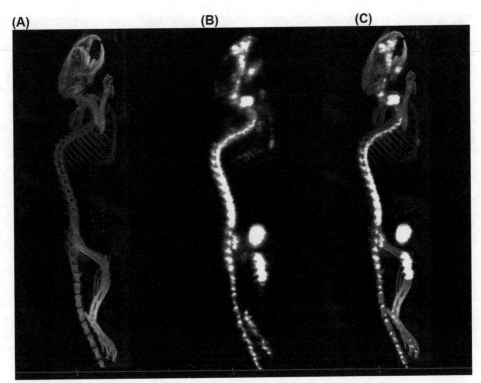

FIGURE 35.3   MicroSPECT/CT imaging of mouse injected with ⁹⁹ᵐTc-MDP for monitoring osteoblastic activity. (A) MicroCT image offers good anatomical information. (B) MicroSPECT image offers functional or physiological information. In this case ⁹⁹ᵐTc-MDP was used to visualize osteoblastic activity. (C) MicroCT/SPECT fused imaging can offer additional insights by providing anatomical locality to sometimes cryptic physiological data. *Images are provided by Small Animal Imaging Facility at Van Andel Research Institute.*

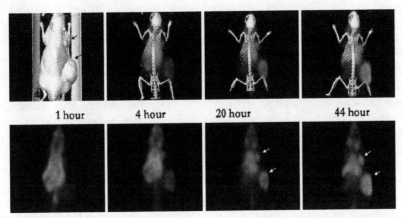

FIGURE 35.4   PET/CT images of tumor angiogenesis. This figure shows microPET/CT fused images acquired at 1, 4, 20, and 44 h postinjection of 200 μCi/40 μg ⁶⁴Cu-bevacizumab in an MIAPaCa-2 pancreatic xenograft tumor model. The top-left subfigure contains either surface-rendering image performed using Amira *(Mercury Computer System Inc.)* to show relative tumor location *(arrows)*. The dynamic imaging data show whole-body distribution of ⁶⁴Cu-bevacizumab in tumor animal model in which the tumor sites are pointed to by *arrows*. *Images are provided by MPI Research, Van Andel Research Institute and UTHSCSA.*

the X-ray source senses X-rays that are not absorbed by the tissue; this absorption is inversely related to the density of the tissue structures. The X-ray absorption profile is then used to reconstruct high-resolution (roughly 6–50 μm with no depth limit) tomographic anatomical images. MicroCT can be used for bone studies (eg, osteoporosis, see Fig. 35.5), vascular studies, lung studies, and fetal skeletal evaluations for developmental toxicology (DART, see Fig. 35.6). The use of contrast media enables soft-tissue segmentation and some functional imaging, for example, in kidney function studies (see Fig. 35.7). The disadvantages of microCT include low soft-tissue contrast, use of radiation, and limited molecular applications. MicroCT is able to provide a high-quality anatomical framework for functional imaging techniques, particularly in PET and SPECT imaging analysis.

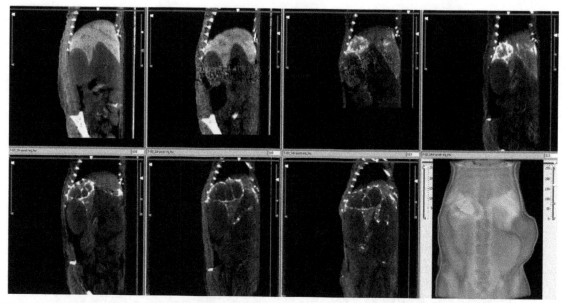

FIGURE 35.5 Typical whole-mouse microCT images of tumor model. The images were reconstructed from a tomographic data set as 2D sagittal slices (black and white) showing bone structure and abdominal soft tissues. The microCT surface image (orange (gray in print versions)) is also shown for appreciation of the tumor size on the surface of the flank position. *Images are provided by Small Animal Imaging Facility at Van Andel Research Institute.*

In our preclinical imaging facility, a high-resolution X-ray microCT scanner (microCAT II, Siemens Preclinical Solutions) is used for fetal skeletal evaluation. For all imaging studies (mouse, rat, and rabbit), the microfocus X-ray source is configured with an anode current of 500 mA and a voltage of 80 kVp. The X-ray detector has a pixel size of 34 mm, and a detector bin factor of two was used during the scan, providing an effective pixel size of 68 mm. For each scan, 360 projections are acquired over 360 degree. The exposure time for each projection is kept at 500 ms, and because of the high-resolution imaging, the total scan time is about 10 min per fetus. Given the divergent cone-beam geometry of the system, there is a built-in system magnification, allowing images to be reconstructed on a 50 mm isotropic voxel grid. A high-speed cone-beam reconstruction (modified Feldkamp) system is used to reconstruct the image volumes in parallel with the scan. Images are then reconstructed and viewed in Amira (version 3.1, Mercury Computer Systems) (see Fig. 35.7).

MAGNETIC RESONANCE IMAGING/ MAGNETIC RESONANCE MICROSCOPY

Magnetic resonance imaging (MRI) utilizes nuclear magnetic resonance (NMR), in which the signal is derived primarily from the hydrogen nuclei (protons) within water molecules. The technique uses a powerful magnetic field to align the magnetic fields with the nuclei of atoms in the organism, and then a pulse of radio frequency radiation is applied to alter the alignment of

this magnetization. The scanner then detects the rotating magnetic field to produce an image of the scanned area [15]. Unlike radiography or CT, no ionizing radiation is used. Intravenous contrast agents are used to enhance the signal and/or help delineate vessels or tumors. Magnetic resonance imaging is most useful for imaging soft tissues, especially those with little density contrast, such as the liver or brain, and is most frequently used to provide anatomical images and delineate lesions such as tumors or areas of necrosis in living animal models (see Fig. 35.8).

Magnetic resonance microscopy (MRM) is magnetic resonance imaging with resolutions of better than 100 μm³. Advantages of this technique include high resolution (roughly 10–100 μm with no limit of depth) and high soft-tissue contrast; disadvantages include limited molecular applications and long scanning times [16]. Functional information can be gathered using a related technique known as magnetic resonance spectroscopy (MRS) [17], which provides information either on particular endogenous biochemical (metabolites) since a specific pattern of metabolites can be associated with certain diseases and tumors, or on the concentration and distribution of magnetic nuclear isotope-labeled drugs in tissues.

OPTICAL IMAGING

Varieties of optical imaging techniques have been developed for biomedical applications. They include various microscopy methods such as confocal

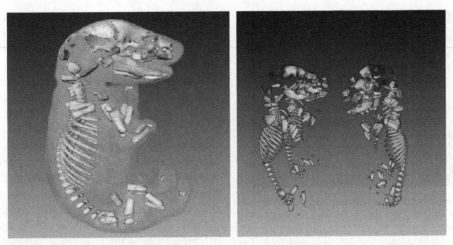

FIGURE 35.6 **CT imaging of developmental and reproductive toxicology (DART).** The images were reconstructed from a tomographic data set as 360 projection showing bone structural development with CT scan duration of 10 min for fetus. *Image reconstruction provided by MPI Research Inc.*

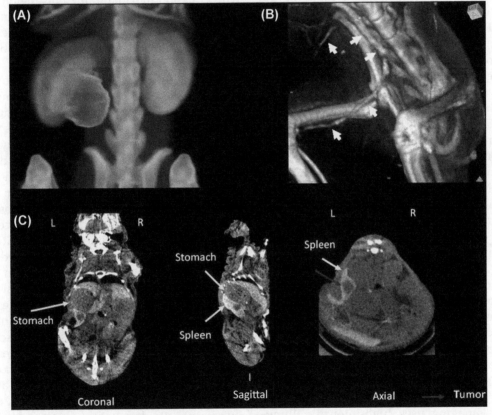

FIGURE 35.7 **Computed tomography images of kidney function.** (A) Image of a kidney cyst transgenic mouse model after 3D reconstruction. A cyst in the right kidney has been clearly revealed through microCT images of a mouse injected with contrast agent. (B) Image of vascular structure (*arrows*) in a healthy mouse after 3D reconstruction. Vascular structure can be identified by microCT images when mice are injected with appropriate contrast agent. (C) Images of a pancreatic tumor liver metastasis orthotopic mouse model. Mice with appropriate contrast agent scanned by microCT can be used to identify the tumors or pathological lesions. The contrast of liver lobes and spleen was increased by injecting liver CT contrast agent into mouse. The dark area pointed by *blue arrows* (gray in print versions) in the spleen is a metastatic tumor. *Images are provided by Small Animal Imaging Facility at Van Andel Research Institute.*

microscopy, two-photon microscopy, and coherent anti-Stokes-Raman scattering (CARS) microscopy for in vitro and ex vivo applications. These techniques are combined with a number of methods for in vivo applications such as microscopic imaging, bioluminescence imaging, fluorescence imaging, diffused optical tomography, and optical coherence tomography to name just a few. Over the last 10 years, the various modes of optical imaging have

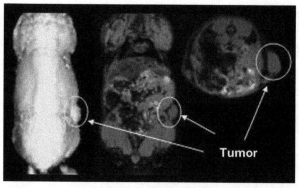

FIGURE 35.8   MRI imaging of xenograft pancreatic cancer mouse model. MRI scan was performed in a xenograft mouse tumor model with a tumor size (~250 mm³) at day 16 after tumor implantation with UKPAN-1 cancer cells. The image demonstrates the tumor located at the right flank. *Images are provided by UTHSCSA (unpublished results).*

grown in popularity and sophistication. Today optical imaging has a wide variety of applications in genomics, proteomics, cell biology, and drug discovery and development. It has emerged as a real-time, sensitive, and noninvasive modality for the visualization, localization, and measurement of bioactive molecules and molecular processes in vivo.

Even though optical imaging still cannot compete with PET, SPECT, MRI, and CT in clinical applications today, its advantages (ie, convenience, sensitivity, cost effectiveness, and nonradioactive material safety) have made it very popular among the traditional imaging modalities for MI in preclinical studies. Optical imaging of receptors, enzymes, gene expression, in vitro live cells, and tumors cells in vivo has deepened our understanding of disease progression and therapeutic response at the molecular, cell, tissue, and whole-animal levels.

In vivo optical imaging includes fluorescence and bioluminescence imaging. Both techniques are highly sensitive (picomolar) at limited depths of a few millimeters, quick and easy to perform (with a high-throughput capability), and in general do not require costly instrumentation [18]. This latter attribute makes it particularly suited to the drug development and validation process.

Fluorescence imaging uses high-intensity illumination at a certain wavelength to excite fluorescent molecules in a sample. When a molecule absorbs photons of the appropriate wavelength, its electrons are excited to a higher energy level. As these excited electrons "relax" back to the ground state, vibrational energy is lost and, as a result, the emission spectrum is shifted to longer wavelengths. Fluorescence imaging causes excitation of certain fluorophores in a living system by using external light and then detects fluorescence emission with a sensitive charge-coupled device (CCD) camera. The fluorophores can be

endogenous molecules (such as collagen or hemoglobin); exogenous fluorescent molecules such as green fluorescent protein (GFP); or small synthetic optical contrast agents (see Fig. 35.9).

One great limitation of in vivo fluorescence imaging is from light attenuation and scattering by adjacent living tissues. Light in the near infrared (NIR) range (650–900 nm) instead of visible light can improve the light penetration. It can also minimize the autofluorescence of some endogenous molecules, such as hemoglobin, water, and lipids. In a whole-mouse illumination experiment, photon counts in the NIR range (670 nm) are about four orders of magnitude higher than those in the green light range (530 nm) under similar conditions. Near-infrared fluorescence imaging has provided an effective solution for improving the imaging depth along with sensitivity and specificity [19]. Therefore fluorophores with emission maxima in the NIR region are important for successful in vivo optical imaging and future clinical applications. Commercially available fluorophores, with well-defined excitation and emission spectra, can be used to "stain" specific structures or molecules in a specimen. Judicious choice of fluorophores allows the identification of multiple targets as long as emission spectra can be cleanly separated and distinguished from autofluorescence.

Bioluminescence imaging (BLI) is typically based on the ATP- and O_2-dependent enzymatic conversion of exogenous luciferin to oxyluciferin by luciferase within living cells [20]. The reaction can produce photons with a broad red and far-red emission spectrum that can be detected by a highly sensitive CCD camera at 10–12 min after intraperitoneal injection of luciferin. Bioluminescence imaging has allowed quantitative measurements of tumor burden, treatment response, immune cell trafficking, and detection of gene transfer.

In bioluminescence imaging, an enzyme that is capable of generating light in the presence of a substrate (ie, D-luciferin) is used as a reporter to assess the transcriptional activity in cells that are transfected with a genetic construct containing the enzyme's gene under the control of a promoter of interest [20]. The enzymes can also be used to detect the level of cellular ATP (cell viability or kinase activity assays) or to detect other enzyme activity (ie, caspase, cytochrome P450). Thus the externally detected light is an indicator of biological/molecular processes. The imaging process involves anesthesia of the subject, injection of the respective substrate, and placement of the subject in a dark chamber with a thermoelectrically cooled CCD camera that is extremely sensitive to even weak luminescence sources. The light emitted can then be semiquantitatively analyzed. Disadvantages of optical imaging include low depth penetration and limited clinical translation.

Confocal imaging involves serially scanning the specimen to create computer-generated optical sections down

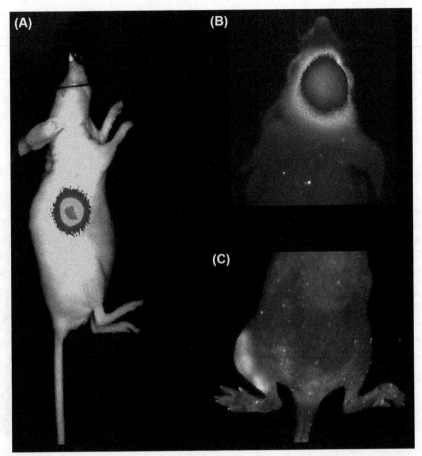

FIGURE 35.9   In vivo optical imaging images. (A) Bioluminescence imaging (BLI) of a mouse glioblastoma xenograft model. (B) Fluorescence image of a mouse glioblastoma orthotopic model. (C) Fluorescence image of a mouse osteosarcoma orthotopic model. Tumor cells express GFP. *Images are provided by Small Animal Imaging Facility at Van Andel Research Institute.*

to 250-nm thickness using visible light [21]. These optical sections may be stacked to provide a 3D digital reconstruction of the specimen. In confocal microscopy, image data is confined to a defined plane through the specimen. It avoids interference from light emanating from above and below this plane. Signal-to-noise ratios are dramatically better than other microscopy techniques. Confocal imaging is most frequently associated with fluorescence techniques. It can be used with both fixed and live specimens. Fluorescence confocal imaging is particularly important in live-cell imaging, where multiple probes can be identified at high resolution. Dynamic events in cells can be imaged with the help of time-lapse imaging and can be viewed in 3D. Spinning disk and swept field confocal systems are ideal for the imaging of high-speed intracellular events such as calcium ion flux dynamics.

ULTRASONOGRAPHY

The principles of ultrasound imaging are based on the basic physical interaction of sound waves with living tissues of various densities. Ultimately the results of these interactions are displayed as an image. Doppler-based modes can also be utilized to evaluate fluid dynamics, primarily velocity, of the circulatory system or within specific organs. Ultrasonography can be used to evaluate both structural and functional endpoints of multiple target organs within various species, including small and large animals. This technique has become a key tool in research projects due to its noninvasive nature as well as the ability of the newest incarnations of the technology to provide greater imaging resolution in very specific settings. Contrast agents, such as microbubbles, can be functionalized with specific molecules, such as monoclonal antibody, thus improving image quality [22]. Microultrasound is a useful tool for volume measurement. It is more precise and accurate than conventional methods that use calipers for measurement (see Fig. 35.10).

Ultrasonography is practiced in various formats such as brightness mode (B-mode), motion mode (M-mode), Doppler (including both Color Flow and spectral Doppler), and contrast-enhanced imaging. One of its distinct advantages is simply the many applications that can be practiced in preclinical development. Subjects can be imaged at several time points within a given study, and

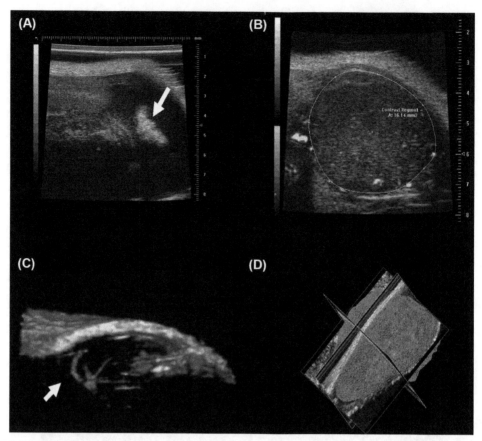

FIGURE 35.10 **Microultrasound images.** (A) B-mode image of pancreatic tumor in transgenic mouse model. B-mode is used to reveal the anatomical structure. A pancreatic tumor (*arrow*) is identified by micro ultrasound. (B) Image of a mice xenograft tumor injected nontargeted microbubbles. Microbubbles are the most commonly used contrast agent for ultrasound imaging. Nontargeted microbubbles can be used in evaluating microperfusion within a region of interest (ROI). Custom designed targeted microbubbles can be used to measure the expression of specific molecular markers. (C) 3D Power Doppler image of mouse lower hind limb. Power Doppler mode is used to measure the perfusion or the percentage of vascularity within a region of interest in ultrasound imaging. The branch-like structure where the *arrow points* is the primary vessel of the lower limb. (D) Image of a mouse xenograft tumor after 3D reconstruction. *Images are provided by Small Animal Imaging Facility at Van Andel Research Institute.*

multiple targets can be evaluated. A disadvantage is the lack of high-resolution capabilities, as well as the need for an experienced imaging expert to obtain acceptable images for analysis. Poor image capture will ultimately lead to unsatisfactory datasets. Ultrasonography represents a noninvasive imaging solution that can be utilized to provide quantitative structural and functional datasets. Investigators have many options available to match the imaging format to the specific needs of their research projects.

APPLICATIONS OF PRECLINICAL IMAGING

Molecular Imaging as an ADME Platform in Drug Development

Over 80% of investigational new drugs fail during development because of unsatisfactory absorption,

distribution, metabolism, and excretion (ADME) characteristics. Tools that help to predict these responses early in development present an advantage as they avoid wasting valuable resources on compounds that will fail. A multitude of noninvasive, high-resolution, imaging technologies are used regularly in the study of ADME processes during drug discovery and development. In this section, we will overview PET and SPECT and other techniques, emphasizing the importance of these technologies in ADME studies.

Traditional preclinical studies on ADME are currently conducted by introducing a radiolabeled drug candidate into animals, usually rodents, and then sacrificing a certain number of the animals at times following dosing that represent each step in the ADME process. The animals are then either necropsied or sectioned, examined, and the radioactivity is quantitated by scintillation counters, or by using quantitative whole-body autoradiography (QWBA), respectively, to determine the locations where the

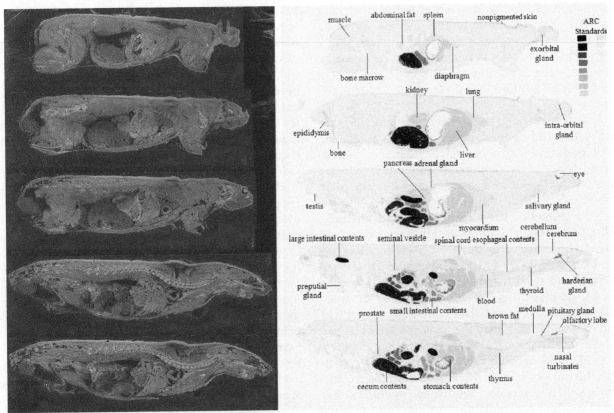

FIGURE 35.11 Quantitative whole-body autoradiography (QWBA) images of tissue distribution of ^{14}C radiolabeled test article in rat. Five levels of section specimen are collected per animal to obtain necessary tissues, organs, and biological fluids. The freeze-dry sections are exposed to phosphor imaging screen for 4 days to capture scintillation light signals, which are converted into digital images to imaging data analysis of drug distribution in tissue and organs. *The image is provided by MPI Research Inc.*

drug is distributed, and how it was excreted (see Fig. 35.11) at high resolution and in a timely fashion. This traditional approach to ADME is a labor-intensive process that requires several groups of animals, with four to six animals per group and 5 to 10 groups, to avoid random variations in the data.

Positron emission tomography, SPECT, fluoroscopy, high-resolution ultrasound, optical, and other imaging techniques offer numerous benefits in ADME studies. Positron emission tomography and SPECT/CT imaging enables the measurement of rapid kinetic processes in real-time and can therefore generate a more accurate picture of the ADME profile. Many of these imaging technologies allow the use of mice as animal models, thereby reducing costs. The continued survival and analysis of the same subject animal model through the entire imaging process also minimizes variability and ensures accuracy of data.

By attaching relatively short-lived medical isotopes such as SPECT and PET tracers to potential drugs, researchers can follow a prospective drug candidate through live animals to define ADME characteristics in real-time. This means that fewer animals are needed to see how drugs work. In addition, in vivo imaging provides biodistribution information in real-time, compared to the extensive postmortem evaluation procedures required for more traditional approaches. No longer do many animals have to be serially sacrificed for statistics, as in the traditional method, hence dynamic MI is faster, with higher temporal resolution and it also saves animals.

In preclinical imaging studies, animals can be imaged with the same radioisotopes as used in the clinic for humans, but at dose levels adapted to the smaller subjects. As a result, successful preclinical studies in animals quickly translate to clinical studies on humans [23]. Provided that small-animal imagers are indeed able to image small subjects with the same utility as humans in the clinic, the ability to use the same tracers in human clinical trials as those used in preclinical animal testing can result in significant efficiency improvement and time and cost savings when translated into humans in clinical trials.

Positron emission tomography and SPECT imaging have important roles to play in both the preclinical stages as well as the human clinical research, leading up to submission of a prospective drug to the FDA for marketing approval. In vivo MI permits earlier determination of whether a given group of drug candidates will work or not in animal models. By using imaging to look at responses earlier in animals, safety can be further ensured and resources can be saved by abandoning drugs that do not translate to the human model in favor of those that do by early "go/no go" decisions.

In a drug-screening study using imaging [9], for example, the author used microPET to evaluate the tumor-targeting ability of biological molecules, including three types of single-domain antibodies (sdAbs): sdAb itself (EG2, ~16 kDa, one antigen binding site), pentabody (V2C-EG2, ~126 kDa, five antigen binding sites), and chimeric HCAb (cHCAb named EG2-hFc, ~80 kDa, two antigen binding sites) that were designed to target epidermal growth factor receptor. Respectively, EG2, V2C-EG2, and EG2-hFc were all labeled with 64Cu and used for imaging a human pancreatic carcinoma model, MIA PaCa-2, established in nude mouse for each construct. The combined microPET/CT images suggested that the majority of EG2 and V2C-EG2 localized in the kidneys 1h after injection (Fig. 35.12A and B). Both proteins were barely detectable in the tumor at 1 and 4h. In contrast, microPET/CT images of the mouse administered with EG2-hFc revealed gradual accumulation in tumor and gradual reduction in other organs for the observed period (up to 44h). No obvious kidney uptake was noticed (Fig. 35.12C). In addition, good tumor/muscle contrast was observed after 20h, and the contour of the tumor in the PET image matched the true tumor shape. While EG2 and V2C-EG2 localized mainly in the kidneys after i.v. injection, EG2-hFc exhibited substantial tumor accumulation. The outstanding tumor imaging of 64Cu-EG2-hFc is largely attributed to its long serum half-life, which is comparable to that of IgGs. The moderate size (~80 kDa) and intact human Fc make HCAbs a unique antibody format that may outperform whole IgGs as an excellent imaging and/or a potential therapeutic reagent.

On the other hand, microscopic imaging is also increasingly being recognized as a valuable tool in ADME testing, and can be employed in both in vitro and in vivo preclinical studies. Microscope images can reveal several pieces of information regarding the cellular response to drug compounds in one experiment. This might include the simultaneous acquisition of data on drug-receptor binding and any morphological effects of drug treatment. The ability to use several, protein-specific fluorescent probes in one experiment is a key enabling technique in high content imaging. Fluorescence microscopic imaging allows molecules beyond the resolution limit of the light microscope to be visualized [24]. Fluorescence microscopy is a key technique in clinical diagnosis as well as in research settings. Confocal fluorescence microscopy, in particular, has become an essential tool central to the study of structural and molecular dynamics in living cells. Time-lapse imaging can be used to monitor downstream drug effects and, ultimately, excretion from the cell. Once images have been digitally captured, it is also possible to examine the data retrospectively in response to new questions about the drug compound. Microscopy images have the advantage of being easily machine-readable by the appropriate image analysis software. This makes microscopy amenable to medium-to high-throughput analysis. Motorized and computer controlled microscopes are essential for automated image capture and for incorporation into medium-to-high-throughput environments.

It is ideal to have an imaging agent that selectively targets the specific organ or pathophysiological lesions for the best imaging contrast and diagnostic accuracy in vivo. Nevertheless, most of the dyes themselves are not target-specific. The in vivo performance of an imaging probe can be complicated by its interactions with many biomolecules, membranes, and related cellular permeability or tissue penetration as well as pharmacokinetic processes including ADME. Therefore it has been challenging to discover and develop an optimal imaging agent for in vivo, namely targeted, imaging.

Imaging in Oncology

Cancer drug discovery is a relatively long process. Many imaging techniques have been routinely used in the drug discovery process to directly monitor the drug in blood and tumor tissues to evaluate the effects of drug treatment in the context of tumor. Molecular imaging has become increasingly popular recently, as it can be used to monitor the changes at the molecular level in vivo, and it can help in evaluating treatment efficacy much earlier than traditional clinical endpoints. For example, 18F-fluoro-2-deoxy-D-glucose positron emission tomography (18FDG-PET) imaging is one of the most powerful MI techniques so far available for clinical use to detect staging, monitor, and evaluate the prognosis of cancer [25]. In both preclinical research and clinical practice, 18FDG could offer adequate contrast and tumor detection in several cancers, such as lung, colon, breast cancer, and lymphoma. However, the diagnostic imaging result is not satisfactory in other cancers, such as renal, head and neck, prostate, and pancreatic cancer because of various biological reasons [26].

New imaging probes are needed for early tumor detection in both preclinical and clinical research. Among them, 3'-deoxy-3'-[18F]fluorothymidine (FLT) is the most extensively investigated tracer for imaging cell proliferation and cancer progression. Most recently, one tumor imaging study aims at verifying the capability of 64Cu (a positron emitter, half-life, 12.7h) labeled bevacizumab,

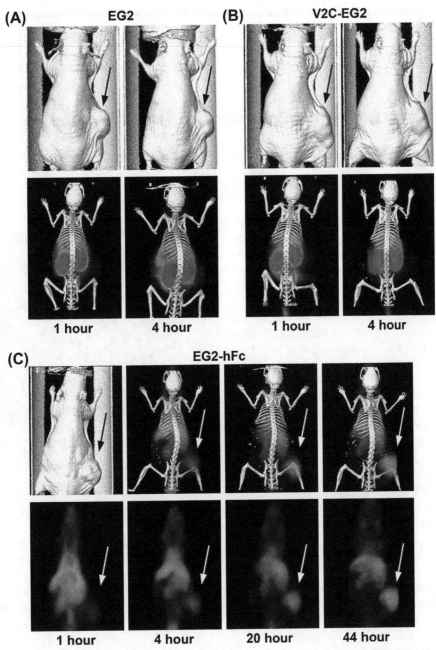

(A) EG2

1 hour   4 hour

(B) V2C-EG2

1 hour   4 hour

(C) EG2-hFc

1 hour   4 hour   20 hour   44 hour

FIGURE 35.12   **Fused microPET/CT images of human pancreatic carcinoma model MIA PaCa-2. Mice bearing established tumors were i.v. injected with 64Cu-DOTAEG2.** (A) 64Cu-DOTA-V2C-EG2 and (B) 64Cu-DOTA-EG2-hFc. (C) For EG2 and V2C-EG2, the mice were imaged at 1, 4, and 20 h postinjection (20 h data not shown). For EG2-hFc, the mouse was imaged at 1, 4, 20, and 44 h postinjection. The top row in each subfigure contains either surface rendering images performed using Amira (Mercury Computer System Inc.) to show relative tumor location (*arrows*) (A–C at 1 h) or fused microPET/CT images (C at 4, 20, and 44 h). The bottom row in each subfigure contains either fused microPET/CT images (A and B) or microPET images (C). *Images are adapted from Bell A, Wang Z, Arbabi M, Chang TA, Durocher Y, Jaramillo M, et al. Differential tumor targeting ability of three sdAb-based antibodies. Cancer Lett 2009;289:81–90.*

an anticancer therapeutic antibody-targeted tumor angiogenesis, in detecting different types of tumors [27]. In an early stage of tumor model and comparing with the gold standard ^{18}FDG. The project used a different strategy from ^{18}FDG to accurately detect tumors at earlier stages, and effectively decrease the nontumor related hot spots in the background of the ^{18}FDG-PET image

(see Fig. 35.4). Preliminary results illustrate that ^{64}Cu-bevacizumab could be used as a new tumor detection probe that may outperform ^{18}FDG probes in preclinical imaging studies.

Imaging techniques can also be used to evaluate the efficacy and therapeutic response of more than one anticancer drug candidate in the same tumor model, thus

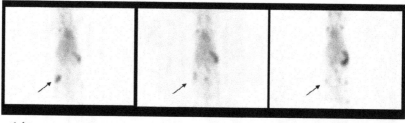

4 days post treatment   8 days post treatment   15 days post treatment

FIGURE 35.13   MicroPET images of cell therapy and tumor ablation. ^{64}Cu-labeled-Thy1.2 antibody specifically detects the tumors (*arrow*), major lymph nodes, and spleens in DUC18/CMS5 tumor mouse model. Two-dimensional images are shown to represent an experimental mouse in the 4 days, 8 days, and 15 days posttreatment with adoptively transferred tumor-specific T cells. *Black arrows* were used to indicate tumors for the purpose of presentation. *Images are provided by MPI Research Inc. and Washington University Medical School.*

minimizing subject-to-subject variability and reducing the number of animals required compared to more traditional methods. An imaging study has been used as a powerful way of tracking adoptively transferred T-cells and studying their in vivo distribution and therapeutic effect in DUC18/CMS5 tumor model by microPET imaging [11]. In the efficacy study, the anti-Thy1.2 antibodies were conjugated to 1,4,7,10-tetraazacyclododecane-tetraacetic acid (DOTA) and radiolabeled with [64]Cu. These were administered to three groups of BALB-Thy1.1 mice on days 4, 7, or 14 post-DUC18 T-cell transfer. The imaging probe successfully detected the transferred cells in tumor tissue and imaged the size and shape of the tumors in the same living subject for therapeutic evaluation. Information obtained from such studies could aid in designing protocols that would enhance the efficacy of tumor-specific T cells (see Fig. 35.13). This cutting-edge imaging technology helps us further understand the trafficking behavior of adoptively transferred tumor-specific T cells. Additionally, studies are more efficient, as they use many fewer animals, since the same animal can be repeatedly imaged on different days posttreatment, when the tumor is growing or ablated due to treatment.

Optical imaging techniques can also be used in combination, either simultaneously or sequentially, to provide information from cancer cells and tumor tissues in living animal models. Both fluorescence and bioluminescence imaging techniques have found wide applications for in vivo optical imaging in mouse tumor models (see Fig. 35.9). These approaches enable the collection of convenient, sensitive, frequent visualization, and measurement of tumor biomarkers in a real-time and noninvasive way.

Imaging CNS Disease

Neurodegenerative diseases, such as Alzheimer's disease (AD) and Parkinson's disease (PD), are becoming increasingly urgent public health concerns, particularly among aging populations. Positron emission tomography and SPECT imaging of brain functions helps to

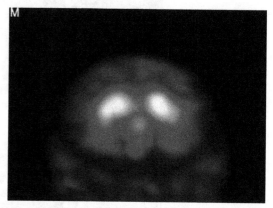

FIGURE 35.14 Functional brain imaging with 2.5 mCi of ^{123}I labeled dopamine transporter probe at 3 h postinjection time point in a normal rat imaged by a NanoSPECT/CT scanner. *Image provided by MPI Research Inc. and inviCRO LLC.*

illustrate the mechanisms and progress of AD and PD at the cellular and molecular level.

Parkinson's disease (PD) is associated with nigral degeneration and striatal dopamine deficiency and is not known to occur in any species other than humans. One of the most widely used animal models for this disease is the toxicity induced in the nigrostriatal pathway of C57BL6 mice following the administration of 1-methyl-4-1, 2, 3, 6-tetrahydropyridine (MPTP). ^{18}F-FDG PET imaging reveals reduced lentiform nucleus glucose metabolism in the MPTP-induced PD animal model. Noninvasive functional imaging of dopaminergic change in the striatum was produced by using PET to visualize and quantify the uptake of ^{18}F-dopamine in the brain of a PD animal model [28]. Demonstrating striatal dopamine terminal dysfunction with PET supports the diagnosis and rationalizes the use of dopaminergic medications. Positron emission tomography imaging can detect changes in striatal dopamine levels after ^{18}F-dopamine administration and relate these functional changes to motor responses.

Single-photon emission computed tomography imaging is also frequently used to detect loss of nigrostriatal cells in Parkinsonism by comparison with brain imaging of normal animal models (see Fig. 35.14). For example, ^{123}I-β-CIT

(^{123}I-2β-carbomethoxy-3β-(4-iodophenyl)-tropane) studies have shown a significant increase in striatal-to-nonspecific β-CIT binding ratios after treatment with selective serotonin reuptake inhibitors [29].

In AD, the severity of cognitive dysfunction is correlated with loss of cholinergic synaptic elements in the cortex and subcortical brain areas. The neurobiological processes support the use of metabolic imaging techniques, particularly ^{18}FDG-PET imaging, in the study of AD as brain perfusion imaging. Amyloid imaging has been used in studies seeking to elucidate the natural history of AD and early detection of it [30]. In recent years, the Food and Drug Administration (FDA) has approved three amyloid plaque-imaging agents, [^{18}F]Florbetapir in 2012, [^{18}F]Flutemetamol in 2013, and [^{18}F] Florbetaben in 2014, to detect cognitive decline in the diagnosis of AD [31]. These new tracers can also be used in preclinical imaging to evaluate efficacy of anti-AD drug candidates on AD animal models [32].

Imaging Autoimmune Diseases

Autoimmune diseases are a heterogeneous class of diseases characterized by chronic inflammation of the target organ and often requiring lifelong treatment. One of the most important progresses in the study of autoimmune diseases is the development of modern MI techniques by the production of a specific radiopharmaceutical probe that contributes to the identification of immune processes responsible for various autoimmune diseases, such as rheumatoid arthritis (RA), age-related muscular degeneration (AMD), Type 1 diabetes mellitus (IDD), and Crohn's disease. An example is the study of the initiation and progression mechanism of RA in a mouse model by using dynamic PET imaging techniques (see Fig. 35.15) [12]. These imaging studies used a novel detection system for determining the localization patterns of glucose-6-phosphate isomerase (GPI) IgG in the joints of normal healthy mice, using rodent-scale PET (microPET). The microPET R4 scanner permits dynamic noninvasive high-resolution imaging of radiolabeled GPI-specific IgG in mice at multiple time points. The results illustrated that anti-GPI IgG rapidly localized within minutes to distal joints of the front and rear limbs and remained there for at least 24h [13]. These kinetic data were consistent with a mechanism of direct antibody recognition of GPI in the joints, which triggered RA in the animal model. The imaging results provided a visual link between the infection and autoimmune disease at the molecular and cellular level. Image analysis illustrated that the immune complexes, FcRIII receptor, TNF (tumor necrosis factor), neutrophils, and mast cells are all involved in an essential initial stage of the joint localization of autoantibody, and provided a conceptual framework for the design and interpretation of therapeutic interventions of antibody-mediated types of rheumatoid arthritis. Molecular imaging technology will be crucial for the development of more potent drugs for the treatment of RA and other autoimmune diseases.

Imaging Cardiac Disease

Imaging-based approaches to the noninvasive evaluation of myocardial function are playing an increasingly important role in preclinical imaging research and clinical practice. Several imaging probes are available for evaluating the relative distribution of myocardial blood flow based on SPECT imaging or for measuring regional blood flow in quantitative units (mL/min/g) based on PET imaging. For example, ^{99m}Tc-MIBI is a good myocardial blood flow perfusion imaging agent. ^{201}Tl in the form of thallous chloride behaves like a K$^+$ analog and is

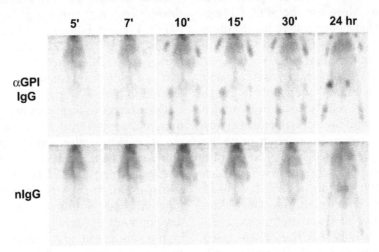

FIGURE 35.15 Initiation of rheumatoid arthritis with a rapid localization of ^{64}Cu-anti-GPI IgG to the distal joints shown by dynamic PET imaging. *Images are adopted from Wipke BT, Wang Z, Kim J, McCarthy JT, Allen PM. Dynamic visualization of the rapid initiation of a joint-specific autoimmune response through positron emission tomography. Nat Immunol 2002;3:366–72.*

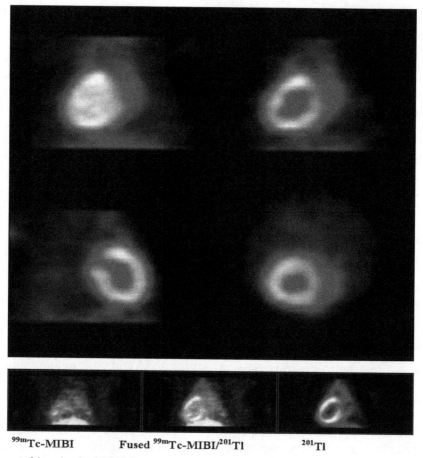

| ^{99m}Tc-MIBI | Fused ^{99m}Tc-MIBI/²⁰¹Tl | ²⁰¹Tl |

FIGURE 35.16 **Cardiac gated imaging by SPECT.** Rat was injected with 1.5 mCi ^{99m}Tc-MIBI and 2.5 mCi ^{201}Tl with a simultaneous imaging of multiple radiolabeled compounds using different isotopes for fused myocardial perfusion imaging. *The image reconstruction and imaging data analysis are provided by MPI Research Inc. and inviCRO LLC.*

rapidly extracted by myocardial cells. Following intravenous administration, ^{201}Tl is rapidly cleared from the circulation and presents mostly in the coronary arteries, thus serving as an excellent probe on myocardial perfusion imaging, which can be fused and compared with ^{99m}Tc-MIBI (see Fig. 35.16). More specific SPECT imaging probes can efficiently detect congestive heart failure (^{123}I-MIBG), cardiac neuroreceptors (^{99m}Tc-Tetrofosmin), and vulnerable plaque (^{111}In-nanoparticle).

In the use of a combination of bioluminescent cells and fluorescent probes, Weissleder et al. were able to image the beating of heart cells at a cellular level in live mice (see Fig. 35.17). Combined with the intravital microscopy and multiphoton imaging, the authors demonstrate the in vivo optical sectioning and dual-channel time-lapse fluorescence imaging of cardiac ischemia [33] The near-infrared fluorescence (NIRF) imaging has also been used for imaging of plaques in coronary arteries. Weissleder and colleagues developed an NIRF catheter for intravascular imaging of protease activity [34]. The catheter used for the study was of clinical grade and allowed for efficient visualization of plaques in a rabbit model using a commercially available NIRF agent called Prosense. This study allows for the theranostic use of NIRF imaging of plaques in high-risk patients, thus potentially reducing incidences of acute coronary syndrome with interventional pharmaceutical or mechanical interventions.

Additionally, PET radiotracers are rapidly being developed for imaging myocardial metabolism (^{18}FDG), heart failure (^{11}C-HED), atherosclerosis [35], thrombosis (^{64}Cu-DOTA-P280 peptide), angiogenesis (^{18}F-glucoRGD), apoptosis (^{64}Cu-DOTA-Annexin V), and cell trafficking for stem-cell therapy in myocardial infarction [36].

Positron emission tomography and SPECT imaging are most effective if motion artifacts can be filtered out. This is typically performed by using physiological monitoring equipment to introduce "gating" tags to the raw acquisition data, indicating the start of the cardiac and respiratory cycles to study visualized myocardial functions and dysfunctions in cardiac diseases. Current development of highly targeted imaging reporters and high-resolution imaging systems (MRI, SPECT, PET, CT, optical, and ultrasound) position MI to contribute critically to diagnostic cardiac disease, drug discovery, and efficacy evaluation.

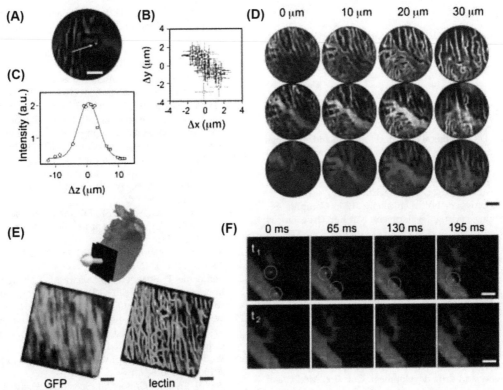

FIGURE 35.17 Image the beating of heart cells at a cellular level in live mice. (A) A stabilized image of a fluorescein isothiocyanate (FITC)-labeled bead (diameter: 5 μm), trapped within a microvessel, used to determine the overall stabilized imaging resolution. Red (dark gray in print versions): lectin-stained capillaries; blue (darker gray in print versions): Angiosense-680 (blood pool imaging agent); yellow (gray in print versions): the FITC-labeled bead. Scale bar, 50 μm. (B) The planar position coordinates of the trapped bead are plotted at different time points to allow acquisition of consecutive unprocessed images. Error bars correspond to error in position determination. A resolution of 4 μm was achieved with hardware stabilization. Gating improved the resolution to 2 μm. (C) Characterization of the axial resolution achieved using the gating modality in combination with the motion compensation stabilizer. Here, the axial position of the bead within the imaging time gating window was determined at different depths. (D) In vivo optical sectioning of the myocardium. Top row, lectin. Middle row, Angiosense-680. Bottom row, fusion of top and middle row images. Images were taken at different depths in 10 μm increments, using a 20× MicroProbe objective. Scale bar, 50 μm. (E) Optical sectioning along the indicated direction (*yellow arrow* (lightest gray in print versions)) allowed three-dimensional reconstructions in a GFP-expressing mouse. Green (gray in print versions): GFP-expressing myocytes. Orange (lighter gray in print versions): lectin. Scale bars, 50 μm. (F) Time-lapse (65 ms step) fluorescence imaging allowed tracking of cells in vivo in the beating heart (Green (black in print versions): Rhodamine 6G-stained leukocytes; red (gray in print versions): vessels stained with Angiosense-680). Top row, the *blue circle* highlights a leukocyte rolling along the inner surface of the vessel, whereas the leukocyte in the *green circle* is in the lumen of the vessel and is therefore traveling faster. Bottom row shows a leukocyte initiating rolling. *Shadows* within the vessels represent red blood cells. *Reprinted with permission from Macmillan Publishers Ltd. Nature Commun;3:1054–62, copyright (2013).*

REMARKS AND FUTURE DIRECTIONS

The various modalities of MI are quickly demonstrating their value to many investigators in both preclinical and clinical research [37]. Multiple imaging agents and platforms, designed to take advantage of the basic physical elements of each, can be used to provide insights into the mechanisms of action and basic biological function of targets under development, whether they are small molecules or biological macromolecules. Care should be taken when selecting the appropriate imaging solution for each target. Likewise, special consideration should be given to the potential impact on the native function of test articles when imaging requirements include the binding of a radioisotope to the test article. By understanding the strengths and limitations of each imaging platform, one

can use them together, an approach known as a multimodal imaging process, to maximize the understanding of concurrent morphological and functional changes in a living body.

Recent studies have shown that MI can provide insight into whole-body drug behavior. Although currently underused, MI could therefore become relevant as a tool to guide rational drug development and treatment. Progress in tracer development and imaging platforms will enhance the potential of MI in this setting [38]. The incorporation and use of MI solutions are becoming better understood in preclinical drug development and the corresponding clinical trials. The application of the appropriate imaging platforms can prove invaluable information, with respect to both time and expense, in drug discovery and drug development process.

Acknowledgments

This work is supported by MPI Research Inc., Van Andel Research Institute and inviCRO LLC.

References

[1] Drews J. Drug discovery: a historical perspective. Science 2000;287:1960–4.

[2] Rogge MC, Taft DR. Preclinical drug development. 2nd ed. Drugs and pharmaceutical sciences, vol. 187. New York: Informa Healthcare; 2010.

[3] Rudin M, Weissleder R. Molecular imaging in drug discovery and development. Nat Rev Drug Discov 2003;2:123–31.

[4] Willmann JK, Bruggen NV, Dinkelborg LM, Gambhir SS. Molecular imaging in drug development. Nat Rev Drug Discov 2008;7:591–607.

[5] Agent category and method detection in Molecular Imaging and Contrast Agent Database (MICAD) at: http://www.ncbi.nlm.nih.gov/books/NBK5330/.

[6] Cai W, Chen X. Multimodality agents. In: Weissleder R, Ross BD, Rehemtulla A, Gambhir SS, editor. Molecular imaging: principals and practice. Shelton (CT): PMPH-USA; 2010. p. 445–70. [chapter 29].

[7] Wernick MN, Aarsvold JN. Emission tomography: the fundamentals of SPECT and PET. San Diego (CA): Elsevier; 2004. p. 270–92.

[8] Wang J, Maurer L. Positron emission tomography: applications in drug discovery and drug development. Curr Top Med Chem 2005;5:1053–75.

[9] Bell A, Wang Z, Arbabi M, Chang TA, Durocher Y, Jaramillo M, et al. Differential tumor targeting ability of three sdAb-based antibodies. Cancer Lett 2009;289:81–90.

[10] Ojeda S, Wang Z, Mares C, Chang T, Li Q, Morris E, et al. Rapid dissemination of *Francisella tularensis* and the effect of route of infection. BMC Microbiol 2008;8:215–28.

[11] Matsui K, Wang Z, McCarthy TJ, Allen PM, Reichert DE. Quantitation and visualization of tumor-specific T cells in the secondary lymphoid organs during and after tumor elimination. Nucl Med Biol 2004;31:1021–31.

[12] Wipke BT, Wang Z, Kim J, McCarthy JT, Allen PM. Dynamic visualization of the rapid initiation of a joint-specific autoimmune response through positron emission tomography. Nat Immunol 2002;3:366–72.

[13] Wipke BT, Wang Z, Nagengast WB, Reichert DE, Allen PM. Staging the initiation autoantibody-induced arthritis: a critical role for immune complexes. J Immunol 2004;172:7694–702.

[14] Paulus MJ, Gleason SS, Kennel SJ, Hunsicker PR, Johnson DK. High resolution X-ray computed tomography: an emerging tool for small animal cancer research. Neoplasia 2000;2:62–70.

[15] Seemann MD. Whole-body PET/MRI: the future in oncological imaging. Technol Cancer Res Treat 2005;4:577–82.

[16] Beckmann N. *In vivo* MR techniques in drug discovery and development. New York: Taylor & Francis; 2006. p. 566–9.

[17] Gillies RJ, Morse DL. *In vivo* magnetic resonance spectroscopy in cancer. Annu Rev Biomed Eng 2005;7:287–326.

[18] Negrin RS, Contag CH. *In vivo* imaging using bioluminescence: a tool for probing graft-versus-host disease. Nat Rev Immunol 2006;6:484–90.

[19] Frangioni JV. *In vivo* near-infrared fluorescence imaging. Curr Opin Chem Biol 2003;7(5):626–34.

[20] Badr CE, Tannous BA. Bioluminescence imaging: progress and applications. Trends Biotechnol 2011;29(12):624–33.

[21] Majlof L, Forsgren PO. Confocal microscopy: important considerations for accurate imaging. Methods Cell Biol 2002;70:149–64.

[22] Lindner JR. Molecular imaging with contrast ultrasound and targeted microbubbles. J Nucl Cardiol 2004;11:215–21.

[23] US FDA. Guidance for industry, investigators, and reviewers. Exploratory IND studies radiation-emitting products and medical imaging. 2006. Available at: http://www.fda.gov/cder/guidance/7086fnl.pdf.

[24] Giepmans BNG, Adams SR, Ellisman MH, Tsien RY. The fluorescent toolbox for assessing protein location and function. Science 2006;312:217–24.

[25] Reske SN, Kotzerke J. FDG–PET for clinical use. Eur J Nucl Med 2001;28(11):1707–23.

[26] Belhocine T, Spaepen K, Dusart M, Castaigne C, Muylle K, Bourgeois P, et al. ^{18}FDG PET in oncology: the best and the worst (review). Int J Oncol 2006;28:1249–61.

[27] Wang Z, Chang TT, Lane M, Xiao JH, Rogers T. A new PET imaging agent for preclinical evaluation of tumor angiogenesis. Next Gener Pharm Eur 2008;6:17–8.

[28] Brooks DJ. Imaging approaches to Parkinson disease. J Nucl Med 2010;51(4):596–609.

[29] Booij J, Tissingh G, Boer GJ, Speelman JD, Stoof JC, Janssen AG, et al. [123I]FP-CIT SPECT shows a pronounced decline of striatal dopamine transporter labelling in early and advanced Parkinson's disease. J Neurol Neurosurg Psychiatry 1997;62(2):133–40.

[30] Choi SR, Schneider JA, Bennett DA, Beach TG, Bedell BJ, Zehntner SP, et al. Correlation of amyloid PET ligand florbetapir F-18 binding with Aβ aggregation and neuritic plaque deposition in postmortem brain tissue. Alzheimer Dis Assoc Disord 2012;26(1):8–16.

[31] Sabri O, et al. Florbetaben PET imaging to detect amyloid beta plaques in Alzheimer disease: phase 3 study. Alzheimers Demen 2015;11:964–74.

[32] Dubois B, et al. Advancing research diagnostic criteria for Alzheimer's disease: the IWG-2 criteria. Lancet 2014;13:614–29.

[33] Lee S, et al. Real-time in vivo imaging of the beating mouse heart at microscopic resolution. Nat Commun 2012;3:1054–62.

[34] Zhu BH, Jaffer FA, Ntziachristos V, Weissleder R. Development of a near infrared fluorescence catheter: operating characteristics and feasibility for atherosclerotic plaque detection. J Phys D Appl Phys 2005;38:2701–7.

[35] Herrero P, Weinheimer CJ, Dence C, Oellerich WF, Gropler RJ. Quantification of myocardial glucose utilization by PET and 1-carbon-11-glucose. J Nucl Cardiol 2002;9:5–14.

[36] Wu JC, Bengel FM, Gambhir SS. Cardiovascular molecular imaging. Radiology 2007;244:337–55.

[37] Wang Z, Lane M, Haller S. Molecular imaging in preclinical research and drug development. Int Pharm Ind 2011;3:38–42.

[38] Vries EG, Jong S, Gietema JA. Molecular imaging as a tool for drug development and trial design. J Clin Oncol 2015;33(24):2585–7.

Index

'Note: Page numbers followed by "f" indicate figures and "t" indicate tables.'

World Health Organization (WHO),
178–179, 266, 293–294, 515,
528, 817
WS. *See* Whole smoke (WS)
WTPM. *See* Wet total particulate matter
(WTPM)
WU rat. *See* Wistar Unilever rat (WU rat)

X

Xenobiotic(s), 40–41, 349
xenobiotic-metabolizing enzymes, 54–56
xenobiotic-related injury, 462

Y

Yeast DEL assay, 145

Z

ZDBC. *See* Zinc dibutyl dithiocarbamate
(ZDBC)
Zebrafish
embryo, 848–851
alternative models to assessing
developmental toxicity, 850t
limitations, 851
model, 850–851

use in toxicity assessment, 849–851
vascular system, 849f
zebrafish development, 848f, 849t
morphological score system, 240
Zebrafish embryotoxicity test (ZET),
238–239, 849–850
Zelnorm. *See* Tegaserod
Zero-dose comparisons, 479
"Zero-effect" level, 611
ZET. *See* Zebrafish embryotoxicity test (ZET)
Zinc dibutyl dithiocarbamate (ZDBC), 831
Zinc fixatives, 409–410
Zoster shingles (ZOS), 726

CPSIA information can be obtained
at www.ICGtesting.com
Printed in the USA
BVHW06*1425020718
520366BV00004B/7/P